CAMBRIDGE
DICTIONARY *of*

AMERICAN
ENGLISH

CAMBRIDGE
UNIVERSITY PRESS

PUBLISHED BY THE PRESS SYNDICATE OF THE UNIVERSITY OF CAMBRIDGE
The Pitt Building, Trumpington Street, Cambridge, United Kingdom

CAMBRIDGE UNIVERSITY PRESS

The Edinburgh Building, Cambridge CB2 2RU, UK
http://www.cup.cam.ac.uk

40 West 20th Street, New York, NY 10011-4211, USA
http://www.cup.org

10 Stamford Road, Oakleigh, Melbourne 3166, Australia

Ruiz de Alarcón 13, 28014 Madrid, Spain

Printed in the United States of America

Library of Congress Cataloging-in-Publication data

Cambridge dictionary of American English.
    p. cm.
  Edited by Sidney I. Landau.
  ISBN 0-521-47761-1 (paperback). — ISBN 0-521-77974-X (paperback with CD-ROM)
  1. English language—Dictionaries. 2. English language—United
States Dictionaries. 3. Americanisms Dictionaries. I. Landau,
Sidney I.
PE1628.C22 1999
423—dc21
                                                                99-33397
                                                                CIP

ISBN 0 521 47761 1 paperback
ISBN 0 521 77974 X paperback with CD-ROM

Cambridge Dictionary of American English

Editor in Chief
Sidney I. Landau

Managing Editor
Paul Heacock

Senior Editor
Cynthia A. Barnhart

Editors
Beth Boda, M.A.
John K. Bollard, Ph.D.
Carol-June Cassidy
Orin Hargraves
Ramona R. Michaelis, M.A.
Susan Norton
Susan Schwartz

Pronunciations
John K. Bollard, Ph.D.

Language Portraits
Sharon Goldstein, M.A.
Walter Havighurst
John K. Bollard, Ph. D.
Jean Z. Heacock, M.A.

Illustrations editor
Donna M. T. Cr. Farina, Ph.D.

Illustrators
Corinne Burrows
Ray Burrows
Peter Ambush
Daisy De Puthod

Systems development manager
Andrew Harley

Software support
Robert M. Fleischman
Automated Document Systems, Inc.

Type composition
Stephen F. Perkins
dataformat.com

Special consultants
Marianne Celce-Murcia, Ph.D.
  (Language Portraits)
Terence Odlin, Ph.D.
  (Grammar)
T. K. Pratt, Ph.D.
  (Canadian English)

ESL/EFL consultants
Erika Konrad, Dept. of English, Northern
  Arizona University, Flagstaff, AZ, USA
Donald Occhiuzzo, Director of Alumni,
  Binational Center, Sao Paulo, Brazil
Robert Quirk, Instituto AngloMexicano de
  Cultura, A.C., San Rafael, Mexico
Herbert W. Seliger, Director, English
  Language Institute, Queens College,
  C.U.N.Y., Flushing, NY, USA
Takashi Shimaoka, Professor of Phonetics
  and English Teaching, Ibaraki Christian
  College, Tokyo, Japan
Avril Taylor, Coordinator, English Language
  Studies, Mohawk College, Hamilton,
  Ontario, Canada
Frank Tedesco, Dept. of English, Sejong
  University, Seoul, Korea
Gayle E. Yondorf, Executive Director, Instituto
  Mexicano Norteamericano de Relaciones
  Culturales de Saltillo, A.C., Mexico
Instituto Cultural Peruano Norteamericano,
  Lima, Peru

ESL focus groups arranged by
Gerard Dalgish, ESL Director, Baruch College,
  New York, NY, USA
Leona Marsh, School of Education, New York
  University, New York, NY, USA

Administrative assistants
Debbie Ausch
Jennifer Steenshorne

Cambridge International Corpus
Ann Fiddes, corpus coordinator
Donna M. T. Cr. Farina, Ph.D., corpus
  acquisitions editor
Jean Hudson, Ph.D., consultant
Robert Fairchild, software

Based on the *Cambridge International Dictionary of English*, Paul Procter, Editor in Chief.

Contents

Language Portraits

Preface

The ancient Romans said that in matters of language, usage is more powerful than Caesar. Their language was Latin, but this saying applies to English at the end of the 20th century as well. There is no central authority that decides what is and is not correct; it is all those who speak and write English, either as their first language or as a language they have learned later in life, who determine the ways in which the language grows and changes.

This dictionary describes the ways American English is used now—what words mean, how they are pronounced, their usual grammatical behavior, and typical contexts in which they appear. It was written using the Cambridge International Corpus, a computerized collection that includes some 100 million words of written and spoken American English taken from recent books, magazines, newspapers, radio and television broadcasts, and even telephone conversations. This resource provides substantial evidence of how words are used, which allows dictionary writers to describe the language accurately and to give examples that are based on genuine, present-day writing and speech.

The *Cambridge Dictionary of American English* has a number of features that make it a very user-friendly dictionary: GUIDEWORDS help you find the meaning of a word you are looking for; LANGUAGE PORTRAITS explain the complexities of English, from "Addresses" to "Zero"; IDIOMS and COMPOUNDS are defined within the entry for their first important word; the IDIOMS INDEX helps you find an idiom even if you only can remember part of it; USAGE LABELS tell you when a word is appropriate, and when it is not; USAGE NOTES give additional information about a word; and FULL COVERAGE of the words and phrases that students of American English will want to look up.

Every effort has been made to make this book the most accurate, realistic, up-to-date, and helpful tool of its kind. Like many types of tools, it will become even more useful as you become more familiar with it. The following pages explain the various features of *CDAE* and how to make the dictionary work for you. We hope this book will help you to master the challenging language known as English, so that your usage will help influence the ways in which it changes and grows during the 21st century.

Paul Heacock
Managing Editor
June 1999

Finding Your Way Around the Dictionary

The following examples are designed to help you find information in the *Cambridge Dictionary of American English*.

A typical entry:

HEADWORD and DEFINITION

> **speak** FORMAL TALK /spiːk/ *v* [I] *past simple* **spoke** /spouk/, *past part* **spoken** /'spoʊ·kən/ to give a formal talk • *Will you be speaking at the conference?* ○ *Ted will speak about careers in education.* • USAGE: The related noun is SPEECH FORMAL TALK.

different PARTS OF SPEECH with meanings related to the headword

> **speaker** /'spiː·kər/ *n* [C] a person who gives a speech at a public event • *There will be three speakers at the graduation ceremony.* ○ *She's not a good public speaker.* • A speaker is also the person who controls the way in which business is done in an organization which makes laws, such as the US House of Representatives: *the Speaker of the House* • See also **speaker** at SPEAK KNOW A LANGUAGE; SPEAKER.
>
> **speaking** /'spiː·kɪŋ/ *n* [U] • *She looks on public speaking as an opportunity to share information.* ○ *He has several speaking engagements* (= occasions when he will give a talk) *next month.*

headword and SECOND MEANING

> **speak** SUGGEST /spiːk/ *v* [I/T] *past simple* **spoke** /spouk/, *past part* **spoken** /'spoʊ·kən/ to show or express (something) without using words • *The incident spoke of shady financial dealings between the partners.* [I always + adv/prep] ○ *Her face spoke volumes* (= showed clearly what she thought). [T]

PHRASAL VERBS formed with the headword

> □ **speak for** /'--/ *v prep* [T] to express the opinions or wishes of (someone) • *I can't speak for the others.* • People say **speak for yourself** when they want to make it clear that they do not agree with what you said: *"None of us like the hotel." "Speak for yourself—I think it's OK."*
>
> □ **speak out** /'--/ *v adv* [I] to say, esp. publicly, what you think about something such as a law or an official plan or action • *He spoke out against the school's admissions policy.*
>
> □ **speak up** TALK LOUD /'--/ *v adv* [I] to speak louder • *Speak up! We can't hear you in the back.*
>
> □ **speak up** EXPRESS OPINION /'--/ *v adv* [I] to express your opinion about something or someone • *If you disagree, please speak up.* ○ *He spoke up for me when I was in trouble.*

Different kinds of entry:

some ABBREVIATION entries have a definition, cross-reference to the full form, and an example sentence

other ABBREVIATION entries are only a cross-reference to the full form

many VARIANT forms are entered as headwords and cross-referenced to the appropriate full form

ESL *n* [U] *abbreviation for* **English as a second language,** see at ENGLISH • *Luisa teaches ESL in California.*

esp. *adv abbreviation for* ESPECIALLY

fries /fraɪz/ *pl n* FRENCH FRIES

Parts of an entry:

the HEADWORD appears in dark type at the beginning of an entry

the GUIDEWORD in a box helps you to find the meaning you are looking for when a headword has more than one meaning

VARIANT SPELLINGS for both singular and plural forms of a word are given after the preferred form

the PRONUNCIATION is given after the headword and guideword. For more information about pronunciations, see page xvii

ten /ten/ *number* 10 • *The twins are ten.* ○ *a ten-seat minivan* • Ten can also mean ten o'clock. • LP NUMBERS
   tenth /tenθ/ *adj, adv* [not gradable], *n* [C] • *My sister spoke tenth, right after me.* ○ *It was the tenth of May.* [C] • A tenth is one of ten equal parts of something. [C]

family PARENTS AND CHILDREN /'fæm·ə·li, 'fæm·li/ *n* [C/U] a social group of parents, children, and sometimes grandparents, uncles, aunts, and other relatives • *Her family moved here when she was eleven.* [C] ○ *Many people cope with the demands of both career and family.* [U] ○ *She wants to get married and have a family* (= have children). [C] • Your **family name** is your **last name**. See at LAST FINAL.
family BIOLOGICAL TYPE /'fæm·ə·li, 'fæm·li/ *n* [C] *specialized* a large group of related types of animals or plants • *The lion is a member of the cat family.*

chili (pepper), **chile** /'tʃɪl·i/ *n* [C/U] *pl* **chilies** or **chiles** any of several types of red PEPPER (= type of vegetable) that are used to make foods spicy • Chili is also a spicy dish made with beans, chilies, and usually meat.

special PARTICULAR /'speʃ·əl/ *adj* [not gradable] having a particular purpose • *Kevin goes to a special school for the blind.* ○ *She's a special correspondent for the National Public Radio.* • **Special education**/**special ed** is education for children with physical or mental problems, who need to be taught in a different way.

if an entry is a VERB with INFLECTED FORMS or variant spellings of inflected forms that are not regular, these are provided

do FOR QUESTIONS / NEGATIVES /duː/ *v aux* he/she/it **does** /dʌz, dəz/, *past simple* **did** /dɪd/, *past part* **done** /dʌn/ used with another verb to form questions and negative sentences • *Where do you work?* ○ *Why don't we have lunch together on Friday?* ○ *"Didn't you know Sophie was coming?" "Of course I did."* ○ *Don't talk about that.* • USAGE: The negative contractions are doesn't, didn't, and don't. • LP AUXILIARY VERBS

knit MAKE CLOTHES /nɪt/ *v* [I/T] **knitting**, *past* **knitted** or **knit** to make (cloth or clothing) by connecting YARN (= fiber threads) into rows with two long needles, or to do this with a machine • *She's knitting a scarf for her daughter.* [T]

VARIANT FORMS in British and Canadian English follow the pronunciation

specialty /ˈspeʃ·əl·ti/, *Br* **speciality** /ˌspeʃ·iːˈæl·ət̬·i/ *n* [C] the subject of one's study or work, or a particular skill • *Her specialty is heart surgery.* ○ *The company's specialty is high-performance cars.*

the DEFINITION is the most common or main meaning for a word

donor /ˈdoʊ·nər/ *n* [C] a person who gives money or something else of value to an organization • *A large gift from an anonymous donor will allow us to continue our work.* • A donor is also someone who gives some of their blood or who agrees to give an organ or part of their body to help someone else.

SENTENCE DEFINITIONS provide additional meanings for a headword and are given immediately after examples in which the first definition is used

friend /frend/ *n* [C] a person you know well and like a lot, but who is usually not a member of your family • *I dreamed my school friends were being chased by a whale.* ○ *Today I got a call from a friend of mine.* ○ *Chloë was her best friend.* ○ *I moved to California, made friends* (= became friends with people), *and started dating.* • Friend can also be used when you are speaking to someone: *Well, friends, I think it's time to go.* • A person or organization that is a friend to/of a group or organization helps and supports them: *He was no friend to slavery.* ○ *The Senator was a friend of business interests.* • If you have **friends in high places**, you know important people whom you can ask for support and help in getting what you want.

IDIOMS follow after the example and sentence definitions

hit ARRIVE AT /hɪt/ *v* [T] **hitting**, *past* **hit** *infml* to arrive at (a place, position, or state) • *The company's profits hit an all-time high last year.* • If you **hit the ceiling/roof**, you become extremely angry: *Dad will hit the roof when he finds out I dented a fender of the car.* • If you **hit the deck**, you lie down quickly and suddenly so that you are hidden from view or sheltered from something dangerous.

common COMPOUNDS, formed from the
headword and one or more other words, are
entered and defined after the idioms in an
entry

time. • If someone goes **head over heels,**
their body rolls forward, esp. when falling: *She
tripped on the curb, and went head over heels
into the bushes.* • If someone is **head over
heels in love,** they love another person very
much: *Laura fell head over heels in love with
Chris.* • A **headache** is a pain you feel inside
your head. • A **headache** is also something
that causes you difficulty or worry: *Finding a
babysitter for New Year's Eve is going to be a
real headache.* • A **headband** is a narrow strip
of material worn around the head, usually to
keep the hair back from the face. • A **head
count** is the exact number of people in a place
that you discover by counting, or the act of

RUNON ENTRIES are usually different parts
of speech from the main entry and follow
immediately after it

aim |INTEND| /eɪm/ *v* [I] to plan for a specific pur-
pose; intend • *The measures are aimed at preserving family life.* ° *This book is not aimed at
the serious reader.*

aim /eɪm/ *n* [C] a result that your plans or actions are intended to achieve • *The commission's aim was to convince workers of their extreme importance in ship production.*

aimless /'eɪm·ləs/ *adj* without having any
clear purpose or specific reason • *aimless violence*

aimlessly /'eɪm·lə·sli/ *adv*

aimlessness /'eɪm·lə·snəs/ *n* [U]

PHRASAL VERBS are marked by a small box
and follow after all other entries for a word

Forms derived from a phrasal verb follow
immediately after it

count |OPINION| /kɑʊnt/ *n* [C usually pl] a state-
ment of belief in a discussion or argument •
I think you're wrong on all counts.

□ **count down** /'-'-/ *v adv* [I] to count backward
to zero • *She counts down the top 10 music videos every week.*

countdown /'kɑʊnt·dɑʊn/ *n* [C] an act of
counting backward to zero, esp. before sending a spacecraft into space, or a period leading
to an important event • *The countdown to
Tuesday's primary elections has begun.*

□ **count** *obj* **in** /'-'-/ *v adv* [T] *infml* to include
(someone) in an activity or plan • *"We're go-
ing to the ballgame—want to come?" "Sure,
count me in."*

Special helps for the user:

USAGE LABELS, following the part of
speech, give special information about the
use of a word. For more information, see
pages xiv–xv.

esophagus /ɪ'sɑf·ə·gəs/ *n* [C] *specialized* the
tube in the body that carries food from the
mouth to the stomach

tempest /'tem·pəst/ *n* [C] *literary* a violent
storm • A **tempest in a teapot** is something
of no importance that causes a great deal of
excitement: *It seemed like an innocent remark,
but it set off a tempest in a teapot.*

USAGE LABELS also warn the user about when a word can be used, or if it should not be used at all

piss /pɪs/ v [I/T] *rude slang* to urinate
piss /pɪs/ n [C/U] *rude slang* urine, or the act of urinating
▫**piss away** *obj*, **piss** *obj* **away** /'--'-/ v adv [M] *rude slang* to waste (something) • *They pissed away the money Grandma left them.*
▫**piss off** *obj*, **piss** *obj* **off** /'-'-/ v adv [M] *rude slang* to anger or annoy (someone) • *It pisses me off when she doesn't call.*
pissed (off) /'pɪst ('ɔːf)/ *adj* [not gradable] *rude slang* • *I get pissed off when people do stupid things.*

▫**chill out** /'-'-/ v adv [I] *slang* to relax instead of worrying or feeling anxious • *If anything major happens we're going to find out, so let's chill out and just do what we need to do.*

USAGE notes mark special information provided as guidance for the user

Eskimo /'es·kə,moʊ/, **Inuit** n [C] pl **Eskimos** a member of a group of people who live in the cold northern areas of North America, Russia, and Greenland • USAGE: In Canada and Greenland, the preferred name is Inuit.

When a related part of speech is very different in form from the headword, a USAGE label directs the user to the correct form

speak FORMAL TALK /spiːk/ v [I] *past simple* **spoke** /spoʊk/, *past part* **spoken** /'spoʊ·kən/ to give a formal talk • *Will you be speaking at the conference?* ○ *Ted will speak about careers in education.* • USAGE: The related noun is SPEECH FORMAL TALK.

Every reference to a picture is marked by the symbol PIC

sole BOTTOM PART OF FOOT /soʊl/ n [C] the bottom part of a foot which touches the ground when you stand or walk, or the front part of the bottom of a shoe • *shoes with leather/rubber soles* • PIC FOOT

Every reference to a Language Portrait is marked by the symbol LP

the ENOUGH /ðiː, ðə/ *definite article* enough • *He hasn't got the experience for this kind of work.* • LP ARTICLES, DETERMINERS

Grammar Codes

Grammar codes are used in the dictionary to give additional information about how words with different parts of speech can be used. These codes are given at the beginning of most entries to show the grammatical pattern or patterns covered in the entry. If more than one pattern is possible, each example is coded to show which pattern is being shown.

Noun codes

C	**countable noun** Shows that the noun can be used in both singular and plural forms.	**apple** **ripple** **gesture**
C usually pl	Shows that the noun is countable, but is more commonly used in a plural form.	**prop** THEATER/MOVIES **misgiving** **lace** CORD
C usually sing	Shows that the noun is countable, but is more commonly used in a singular form.	**instant** **mess** DISORDER **understanding**
U	**uncountable noun** Shows that the noun can only be used in a singular form, and cannot be used with the indefinite articles *a* or *an*.	**brightness** **carpentry** **dynamite**
C/U	Shows that the noun has both countable and uncountable uses.	**discovery** *Many discoveries are made by accident.* [C] • *The discovery of gold changed history.* [U] **September** *You should come in September.* [U] • *Did they visit last September?* [C]
pl or pl n	Shows that the noun is always plural, and takes the plural form of a verb.	*a city's* **finances** • *the* **guts** *of a machine* • *your* **insides** (= stomach)

LP ARTICLES, PLURALS OF NOUNS

Verb codes

I	**intransitive verb** Shows that the verb does not have a direct object in the sentence identifying the person or thing being acted on.	**skid** **dive** MOVE DOWN **drop by**
T	**transitive verb** Shows that the verb has a direct object in the sentence identifying the person or thing being acted on.	**trick** **create** **miss** NOT FIND
I always + adv/prep	Shows that the verb is intransitive and must be followed immediately by an adverb or preposition.	**climb** MOVE **look** SEARCH **stretch** SPREAD OVER AREA
T always + adv/prep	Shows that the verb is transitive and that the object of the verb must be followed by an adverb or preposition.	**strap** **smear** SPREAD **word**
always + adv/prep	Used with verbs that can be transitive, intransitive, or both, but which always must be followed by an adverb or preposition.	**swirl** **hold** KEEP IN PLACE **live** SPEND LIFE
M	Shows that a phrasal verb (= verb + adverb/preposition) takes an object, but the object can come before or after the adverb/preposition. The two positions of the object are shown at the beginning of the entry.	**call out** *obj* SHOUT, **call** *obj* **out** **carry out** *obj*, **carry** *obj* **out** **take** *obj* **up with** *obj*, **take up** *obj* **with** *obj*

| I/T | Shows that a verb can be used in both intransitive and transitive patterns. | **change** *I changed jobs last year.* [T] • *Things seem to change quickly.* [I]
fool *She tries to fool people.* [T] • *I was only fooling.* [I] |

| I/M | Shows that a verb can be used in both intransitive and transitive patterns, but when it is transitive it is always followed by an adverb or preposition, and its object can come before or after the adverb or preposition. The two positions of the object are usually shown in parentheses at the beginning of the entry. | **back up** (*obj*) DRIVE BACKWARD, **back** (*obj*) **up**
shut off (*obj*) STOP, **shut** (*obj*) **off** |

| T/M | Shows that a verb is transitive, but that sometimes it is followed by an adverb or preposition and the object can come before or after the adverb or preposition. | **brush** *She brushed her hair.* [T] • *He brushed the crumbs off his coat.* [M]
heat *It costs a lot to heat the house.* [T] • *I'll heat up some soup.* [M] |

| L | **linking verb**
Shows that the verb is used to connect the subject of the sentence to its characteristics, which are usually described by an adjective or noun. | **look** SEEM
fall CHANGE STATE
get BECOME |

LP) AUXILIARY VERBS, CONTRACTIONS OF VERBS, DO: VERBS MEANING "PERFORM", *GET, HAVE,* AND OTHER VERBS USED TO MEAN "CAUSE," THE -ING FORM OF VERBS, LINKING VERBS, VERBS WITH TWO OBJECTS, PHRASAL VERBS, TENSES, TRANSITIVE AND INTRANSITIVE VERBS

Adjectives

| only after n | Shows that an adjective is only used after a noun. | the president-elect • McLaughlin Glass, **Incorporated** |

LP) ADJECTIVES

Complements

These codes show that a verb, adjective, or noun is used in combination with particular types of words or phrases. If a verb can be either transitive or followed by a *that* clause or *wh-* word, the headword is followed by (*obj*).

| + *that* clause | Shows that a verb, adjective, or noun can be followed immediately by a clause beginning with *that*. | **agree** *Most people agree that it's a good idea.*
convince *I'm convinced that she is lying.* |

| + (*that*) clause | Shows that the verb, adjective, or noun is immediately followed by a clause which can begin with the word *that* but does not have to. | **admit** *She admits that she made a mistake* or *She admits she made a mistake.*
unlikely *It's unlikely that we will ever know* or *It's unlikely we will ever know.* |

| + *to* infininitive | Shows that a verb, adjective, or noun is followed immediately by a *to* infinitive. | **able** *I wasn't able to afford that new apartment.*
deserve *We deserve to know what happened.* |

| + *wh-* word | Shows that a verb, adjective, or noun is followed immediately by *who, what, why, when, where, how,* or *whether.* | **see** *I'll see how I feel tomorrow.*
surprised *You'd be surprised how quickly the time passes.* |

Usage Labels

Most words in the English language can be used in any context. Some words will not be appropriate or will seem strange when used in a particular context. Labels in the dictionary serve as a guide to help you decide whether or not a term would be suitable. These tables list the labels used in this dictionary, describe them, and give examples of them.

Words used in some places

Br	British English term	**fortnight** (= two weeks) • **tyre** (= tire WHEEL))
Cdn	Canadian English term	**loonie** (= a Canadian dollar coin)
regional	terms used only in parts of the US	**submarine** (= sandwich) • **soda** and **pop** (= soft drink)

Words used among some groups

law	terms used by lawyers, judges, and people involved in legal matters	**burden of proof** (= responsibility for proving that something is true in a court of law)
literary	terms used in literature and similar writing	**wretch** (= someone who is suffering) • **slumber** (= sleep)
medical	terms used by doctors, nurses, and people talking about medical care	**c-section** (= an operation that allows a baby to be born) • **hypothermia** (= a dangerous condition where the body temperature is too low)
specialized	terms used in science, university studies, and particular types of work	**alkali** (= a substance that has a particular chemical behavior) • **effluent** (= liquid waste that is sent out from factories)
trademark	a product name that is owned by a company	**Band-Aid** (= a thin strip used to cover small cuts) • **Xerox** (= a copy made on a photocopier)

Words from the past

dated	terms used more often before the 1970s	**coed** (= a female student in a college) • **domestic** (= person paid to do work in a house)
old use	terms used before the 20th century	**alas** (used to express sadness or regret) • **hither** (= to or toward this place)

Shortened forms and special symbols

abbreviation	a shortened form of a word or phrase, usually taken from the first letter of each word in a phrase	**ESL** (= English as a second language) • **PTA** (=Parent Teacher Association) • **UFO** (=unidentified flying object)
contraction	a combination of two words that leaves out one or more letters	**don't** (= do not) • **I'd** (= I would) • **she'll** (= she will)
short form	a word taken from the first or last part of a longer word	**sub** (= submarine) • **burger** (= hamburger)
symbol	something that represents a word	× (= multiplication sign) • # (= pound sign)

Words used only for women or only for men

female	terms applied only to females	**she** (= the female being spoken about) • **policewoman** (= female member of the police force)
male	terms applied only to males	**he** (= the male being spoken about) • **policeman** (= male member of the police force)

Words that express an attitude

approving	terms that show a good opinion of someone or something	**discerning** (= able to make careful judgments) • **spunk** (= brave determination and confidence)
disapproving	terms that show a bad opinion of someone or something	**cowardice** (= fear and avoidance of danger or pain) • **riffraff** (= people with a bad reputation)
a child's word for	terms that are suitable for use to or by children	**boo-boo** (= a small injury) • **icky** (= disgusting)
fig.	**figurative** terms that are not used with their basic meaning but to suggest part of that meaning	**bathe** (= cover) *(fig.) The afternoon sun bathed the city in pink and gold* • **absorb** (= take in a liquid) *(fig.) The country absorbed millions of immigrants over the years.*
humorous	terms that are used to show an amused attitude toward something	**fiend** (= an evil or cruel person)) *What fiend would design such ugly clothes?* • **jalopy** (= an old car in bad condition)

Words that are suitable for some people or in some situations

fml	**formal** terms used in specialized written English or in formal speech, but not in ordinary written or spoken English	**absolve** (= to officially remove guilt) • **laud** (= to praise) • **propensity** (= a tendency to behave in a particular way)
slightly fml	**slightly formal** terms used mostly in written English that show the writer is educated, but that are also used in newspapers	**affix** (= to attach, add, or join) • **perspiration** (= salty liquid excreted through the skin) • **warrant** (= to make something necessary)
infml	**informal** terms that can be used in speaking and writing to friends, but not in writing for school or work	**broke** (= without money) • **pick-me-up** (= something that makes you feel better) • **snap** (= something that can be done without any difficulty)
not standard	terms that are not considered to be correct in most writing or speech	**alright** (= all right) • **irregardless** (= regardless) • **like** (= used in conversation to emphasize what follows)
slang	very informal terms used among friends, by people of the same age group, or by people who share a partcular interest	**blow away** (= to please or surprise someone greatly) • **dweeb** (= an awkward person) • **hot** (= sexually attractive)
rude slang	terms that are considered to be in bad taste, and should usually be avoided	**bitch** (= a woman you do not like) • **piss off** (= to anger or annoy)
taboo slang	words having to do with sex and race that should be avoided completely	**fuck** (= to have sex with someone)

Qualifiers for other labels

esp. (especially)	a term that is particularly used this way or in this variety of English, but may be used in others	**grey** *esp. Br and Cdn for* gray
often	a term that is frequently used this way, but may be used in other ways	**sentiment** EMOTION *often disapproving*
usually	a term that is almost always used in a particular way, although it can be used in other ways as well	**imperial** *usually disapproving* (= relating to a country that rules other countries)

Parts of speech and other labels

label	function	examples
adj (adjective)	describes a noun or pronoun	*wonderful* · *pretty*
adv (adverb)	describes or gives more information about a verb, adjective, other adverb, or phrase	*always* · *amazingly*
combining form	added to other words to change their meaning	**micro-** · **mid-**
comparative	shows more of a quality, amount, or degree described by an adjective or adverb	**faster** · **better**
conjunction	connects words, phrases, and clauses in a sentence	**and** · **but** · **because**
definite article **(the)**	identifies a noun as a particular thing	**the** ocean · **the** baby · **the** balloon
exclamation	expresses a sudden reaction	**Wow!** · **Ugh!** · **Ouch!**
indefinite article **(a, an)**	identifies a noun as a general thing	**a** book · **a** cup · **an** insect
noun	names a person, place, or thing	**doctor** · **party** · **flower**
number	names a number	**one** · **hundred**
past part/ past participle	shows past action and makes perfect tenses	**dug** · **sung** · **walked**
past simple	shows action that happened before this time	**worked** · **bought**
phrasal auxiliary	shows that the action of a verb happened in the past or will happen in the future	**used to** · **going to**
pl (plural)	shows there is more than one of something	**boxes** · **trees**
prep (preposition)	connects nouns or phrases to other words, especially to verbs	**in** · **until**
present participle	shows continuous action	**running** · **being** · **buying**
present simple	shows action happening now	**writes** · **runs** · **laughs**
pronoun	used instead of a noun or noun phrase	**she** · **it** · **them** · **you**
superlative	shows the greatest quality, amount, or degree described by an adjective or adverb	**most** · **greatest** · **best**
v (verb)	shows action, condition, or experience	**feel** · **wreck** · **bark**
v adv (phrasal verb)	shows that a verb + adverb combine to create a specific meaning	**get around** · **look back**
v adv prep (phrasal verb)	shows that a verb + adverb + preposition combine to create a specific meaning	**move in on** · **take up with**
v aux (auxiliary verb)	gives additional grammatical information not given by the main verb in a sentence	**can** · **have** · **must** · **would**
v prep (phrasal verb)	shows that a verb + preposition combine to create a specific meaning	**go for** · **laugh at** · **care for**

Pronunciation Symbols

The lists below show how the symbols of the *International Phonetic Alphabet* are used in this dictionary to indicate the pronunciation of an entry word. Next to each symbol are one or two English words in which a particular sound occurs.

As is the case with any dictionary, the pronunciation system used in the *Cambridge Dictionary of American English* provides a guide to pronunciation to help the user who does not know how a word is pronounced, but does not impose a "correct" pronunciation. In the US, pronunciation often varies from one region to another, just as pronunciations vary from person to person. The goal for any speaker is to be understood, and the pronunciations in this dictionary are designed to help the student of English reach that point.

Vowel Symbols

æ	bat, hand
ɑ	hot, barn
ɑː	aunt, tomato (*variant pronunciations*)
ɑ̃	genre (*variant pronunciation*)
ɑɪ	bite, sky
ɑʊ	house, now
e	bet, head
eɪ	late, play
ɪ	fit, bid
iː	feet, please
i	*either* /iː/ *or* /ɪ/
ɔː	saw, dog
ɔ̃ː	salon (*variant pronunciation*)
ɔɪ	boy, join
oʊ	go, boat
ʊ	put, good
uː	rude, boot
ʌ	cut, love
ʌ̃	Huh
ɝ	bird, fur (*used only before* /r/ *in stressed syllables*)
ə	sitter, alone

Other Symbols

ˈ	Stress mark placed before a syllable with the heaviest stress, as before the first syllable of **business** /ˈbɪz·nəs/
ˌ	Stress mark placed before a syllable with lighter stress, as before the last syllable of **businesslike** /ˈbɪz·nəs‚lɑɪk/
·	The raised dot separates syllables.
-	The hyphen shows that only part of a variant pronunciation is given. It also represents a syllable in showing stress patterns for phrasal verbs.

Consonant Symbols

b	bid, job
d	do, lady
dʒ	jump, bridge
f	foot, safe
g	go, dog
h	home, behind
hw	which, where (*Many people say* /w/ *instead of* /hw/.)
j	yes, onion
k	kiss, come
l	look, pool
ᵊl	little, metal (*Used in a syllable with no vowel sound.*)
m	many, some
ᵊm	hm (*Used in a syllable with no vowel sound.*)
n	need, open
ᵊn	hidden, cotton (*Used in a syllable with no vowel sound.*)
ŋ	sing, sink
p	pen, hope
r	road, card
s	see, recent
ʃ	shoe, nation
t	team, meet
t̬	meeting, latter
θ	think, both
ð	this, father
tʃ	choose, rich
v	visit, save
w	watch, away
x	Chanukah (*variant pronunciation*)
z	zoo, these
ʒ	beige, measure

A, a

A ⃞LETTER , **a** /eɪ/ *n* [C] *pl* **A's** or **a's** the first letter of the English alphabet

A ⃞MUSICAL NOTE /eɪ/ *n* [C/U] *pl* **A's** or **As** the sixth note in the **major scale** (= series of notes) that begins on the note C, or a set of notes based on this note

A ⃞MARK /eɪ/ *n* [C] *pl* **A's** or **As** a mark that means excellent, given to something of the highest quality, esp. school work • *The teacher gave me an A for my essay.*

a ⃞GENERAL THING /ə, eɪ/, **an** *indefinite article* used before nouns to refer generally to someone or something that has not been mentioned before • *This is a very mild cheese.* ○ *Can I have a banana, please?* ○ *There was a sudden loud noise.* ○ *Is he a friend of yours?* ○ *My birthday is on a Friday this year.* • You can also use "a" before some words expressing an amount: *a few days* ○ *a great number* ○ *a lot of money* • ⃞LP ARTICLES, DETERMINERS

a ⃞PARTICULAR THING /ə, eɪ/, **an** *indefinite article* used before nouns to refer to someone or something specific that has not been mentioned before • *I'd love a Pepsi.* • "A" can be used to mean a work created by someone: *Experts think that the painting may be a Picasso.* • "A" can also be used to mean any person or thing of a specific type: *A cheetah can run faster than a lion.* ○ *She wants to be a doctor when she grows up.* • "A" in front of a name means you are referring to a particular person: *Do you know a Julio Perez?* • ⃞LP ARTICLES, DETERMINERS

a ⃞ONE /ə, eɪ/, **an** *indefinite article* one • *a hundred/million/dozen* ○ *a quarter of an hour* • ⃞LP ARTICLES, DETERMINERS

a ⃞EACH OR EVERY /ə/ *prep* in or for each or every; PER • *Take one tablet three times a day.* ○ *These shoes cost $30 a pair.*

abacus /'æb·ə·kəs, ə'bæk·əs/ *n* [C] a frame that holds thin metal rods with balls that slide on them, used for counting, adding, and subtracting

abandon /ə'bæn·dən/ *v* [T] to leave behind or run away from (someone or something), or to give up (something) • *Air attacks forced the villagers to abandon their homes.* ○ *The weather was so bad, we abandoned our plans for a picnic.*

abandoned /ə'bæn·dənd/ *adj* • *Shelters are full of abandoned pets.* ○ *The fire started in an abandoned warehouse.*

abandonment /ə'bæn·dən·mənt/ *n* [U] • *Child abandonment is a serious problem.*

abate /ə'beɪt/ *v* [I/T] to become less strong, or to make (something) less strong • *Our desire for consumer goods has not abated.* [I]

abbey /'æb·i/ *n* [C] a building for MONKS (= religious men) or NUNS (= religious women) to live in

abbreviation /ə,briː·viː'eɪ·ʃən/ *n* [C] a shortened form esp. of a word or phrase • *UN is the abbreviation for the United Nations.* ○ *I.e. is an abbreviation of a Latin phrase that means "that is."* • ⃞LP PERIOD

abbreviate /ə'briː·viː,eɪt/ *v* [T] to shorten (a word or words), or to make (something) shorter • *We had to abbreviate the names of the states.*

abbreviated /ə'briː·viː,eɪt·əd/ *adj* [not gradable] • *An abbreviated version was published last year.*

ABC's /,eɪ·biː'siːz/ *pl n infml* the alphabet • The ABC's of something is basic information about it: *I need a book that covers the ABC's of gardening.*

abdicate /'æb·də,keɪt/ *v* [I/T] to give up (something, esp. a position) formally, or to fail to take responsibility for something • *King Edward VIII abdicated the British throne in 1936.* [T]

abdication /,æb·də'keɪ·ʃən/ *n* [C/U] • *I think it's an abdication of your responsibility if you don't vote.* [U]

abdomen /'æb·də·mən/ *n* [C] the part of the body that contains the stomach, bowels, and other organs in a person or animal

abdominal /æb'dɑm·ən·ªl, əb-/ *adj* [not gradable] • *This virus causes terrible abdominal pain.*

abduct /æb'dʌkt, əb-/ *v* [T] to take (a person) away by force • *Kidnappers abducted the child from the playground.*

abduction /æb'dʌk·ʃən, əb-/ *n* [C/U] • *The abduction took place in front of several helpless witnesses.* [C]

aberration /,æb·ə'reɪ·ʃən/ *n* [C] a change from what is typical or usual, esp. a temporary change • *The drop in our school's test scores was dismissed as an aberration.*

abet /ə'bet/ *v* [T] **-tt-** to help or encourage (a person or thing) to do something, esp. something wrong or illegal • *Shady lawyers abetted the company's officers in stealing the funds.*

abhor /əb'hɔːr/ *v* [T] **-rr-** to hate (something or someone) • *His opponent abhors the death penalty.*

abhorrent /əb'hɔːr·ənt, -'hɑr-/ *adj* • *His attitude of superiority is abhorrent.*

abhorrence /əb'hɔːr·əns, -'hɑr-/ *n* [U] • *She has an abhorrence of violence.*

abide /ə'bɑɪd/ *v* [T] • If you **can't abide** something or someone, you do not accept them: *He can't abide laziness.*

▢ **abide by** /-'-,-/ *v prep* [T] to accept or obey (an agreement, decision, rule, etc.) • *Competitors must abide by the judges' decision.*

abiding /ə'baɪd·ɪŋ/ *adj* lasting for a long time • *Muir had an abiding interest in dogs. .*

ability /ə'bɪl·ət̬·i/ *n* [C/U] the mental or physical power or skill needed to do something • *Someone with that kind of ability will do well.* [U] ○ *Her teammates respect her abilities.* [C] • USAGE: The related adjective is ABLE.

abject /'æb·dʒekt/ *adj* hopeless or extreme • *They live in abject poverty.* ○ *My experiment was an abject failure.*

ablaze /ə'bleɪz/ *adj* [not gradable] burning or very bright • *Fire spread quickly until the whole building was ablaze.* ○ *The ballroom was ablaze with lights.*

able HAVING WHAT IS NEEDED /'eɪ·bəl/ *adj* [+ to infinitive] having what is needed to do something, esp. the physical or mental power, skill, time, money, or opportunity • *I lost my job and wasn't able to afford my old apartment.* ○ *We won't be able to keep up this kind of effort much longer.* • USAGE: The related noun is ABILITY.

able SKILLFUL /'eɪ·bəl/ *adj* good at what you do • *He is an able student.* • USAGE: The related noun is ABILITY.

ably /'eɪ·bli/ *adv* • *He does his job very ably.*

abnormal /æb'nɔːr·məl, əb-/ *adj* not usual or average • *We had an abnormal amount of snow.* ○ *He has an abnormal heartbeat.*

abnormality /ˌæb·nɔːr'mæl·ət̬·i, -nər-/ *n* [C/U] • *No abnormalities showed up in the blood tests.* [C]

abnormally /æb'nɔːr·mə·li, əb-/ *adv* • *It was abnormally hot this summer.*

aboard /ə'bɔːrd, -'boʊrd/ *adv* [not gradable], *prep* on or onto a ship, aircraft, bus, or train • *We finally went aboard the plane three hours later.*

abode /ə'boʊd/ *n* [C/U] *literary* the place where someone lives • *He was a wanderer with no permanent abode.* [C]

abolish /ə'bɑl·ɪʃ/ *v* [T] to put an end to (something, such as an organization or custom) • *Massachusetts voters abolished rent control.*

abolition /ˌæb·ə'lɪʃ·ən/ *n* [U] the official ending of an activity or custom • *In the US, abolition also means the official end to SLAVERY, which took place in 1863.*

abolitionist /ˌæb·ə'lɪʃ·ə·nəst/ *n* [C] a person who supports an end to something, esp. (in the past) someone who wanted to end SLAVERY in the US

abominable /ə'bɑm·ə·nə·bəl/ *adj* very bad or unpleasant • *The abominable working conditions made many workers sick.*

aboriginal /ˌæb·ə'rɪdʒ·ən·əl/ *adj* having lived or existed in a place since the earliest known time • *The exhibit was of aboriginal plants of this area.*

Aborigine /ˌæb·ə'rɪdʒ·ə·ni/ *n* [C] a member of any of the groups of people who first lived in Australia

abort STOP /ə'bɔːrt/ *v* [T] to stop (something) before it has begun or to cause (something) to

fail before it is complete • *Engineers aborted the test flight at the last minute.*

abortive /ə'bɔːrt̬·ɪv/ *adj* [not gradable] • *An abortive uprising led to his exile.*

abort END PREGNANCY /ə'bɔːrt/ *v* [I/T] to end a pregnancy esp. by an operation before the baby is ready to be born • *Should a woman who was raped be allowed to abort the fetus?* [T]

abortion /ə'bɔːr·ʃən/ *n* [C/U] • *Abortion clinics have been under attack by protesters.* [U]

abound /ə'baʊnd/ *v* [I] to exist in large numbers • *The streams and rivers abound in fish.*

about CONNECTED WITH /ə'baʊt/ *prep* on the subject of; connected with • *"What's that book about?" "It's about the Civil War."* ○ *I don't know what all the fuss is about.* ○ *There's something about her attitude that worries me.*

about APPROXIMATELY /ə'baʊt/ *adv* [not gradable] a little more or less than a specific number; approximately • *He's about six feet tall.* ○ *It happened about two months ago.* ○ *I've had just about enough of your complaining* (= I don't want to hear any more). • If you say that something **is/was about it**, you mean nothing more is/was involved : *We talked about the election—that was about it.* • (*infml*) If you say that it's **about time** someone did something, you mean that they should have done it long ago: *It's about time (that) she got a job.*

about IN THIS PLACE /ə'baʊt/, **around** *adv* [not gradable], *prep, adj* [not gradable] positioned or moving in or near a place • *Reporters stood about, waiting for more news.*

about INTENDING /ə'baʊt/ *adj* [+ to infinitive; not gradable] almost ready to do something, or intending to do something soon • *He looked as if he was about to burst into tears.* ○ *I'm not about to apologize to him.*

about–face /ə'baʊt'feɪs/ *n* [C usually sing] a complete change of direction, opinion, or way of acting • *About-face is also an order given to soldiers to tell them to turn around and face the other way.*

above /ə'bʌv/ *adv, prep* higher than, more than, or at a level greater than • *The helicopter was hovering above the building.* ○ *Temperatures here rarely rise above freezing in winter.* ○ *Our wages are above average.* ○ *I could hardly hear him above the blare of the music.* • In writing, **above** can mean as stated higher up on this page or on a previous page: *Refer to the diagram shown above.* • To be **above** doing something is to consider yourself too important or too moral to do it: *He's not above lying to protect himself.* • **Above all** means most importantly: *Above all, don't forget to call when you arrive there.*

above /ə'bʌv/ *pl n* those mentioned earlier • *All of the above are to be included.*

aboveboard /ə'bʌv,bɔːrd, -,boʊrd/ *adj* easily seen, honest, not trying to deceive • *The discussions were completely open and aboveboard.*

abrasive ROUGH /ə'breɪ·sɪv, -zɪv/ *adj* having a

rough surface that will rub off a thin layer of another surface • *The paint comes off with an abrasive steel-wool pad.*

abrasive [UNPLEASANT] /ə'breɪ·sɪv, -zɪv/ *adj* rude and unkind • *His abrasive style puts people off.*

abreast /ə'brest/ *adv* next to another person and facing in the same direction • *We were running two abreast around the track.* • If you keep abreast of a subject, you stay informed about new developments in it: *Staying abreast of new software releases takes lots of time.*

abridge /ə'brɪdʒ/ *v* [T] to make (something written, such as a book, speech, or article) shorter

abridged /ə'brɪdʒd/ *adj* • *They listened to an abridged version on tape.*

abroad /ə'brɔːd/ *adv* [not gradable] in or to a foreign country or countries • *They used to go abroad every summer.*

abrupt [SUDDEN] /ə'brʌpt/ *adj* sudden and not expected, often with unpleasant results • *There was an abrupt change in her mood.* ○ *We came to an abrupt curve in the road.*

abruptly /ə'brʌp·tli/ *adv* • *They abruptly left the party.*

abrupt [NOT FRIENDLY] /ə'brʌpt/ *adj* not friendly or polite; showing little interest in talking to other people • *His abrupt manner makes me uncomfortable.*

abscess /'æb·ses/ *n* [C] a painful, swollen area in the body that contains PUS (= a thick, yellow liquid)

abscond /əb'skɑnd, æb-/ *v* [I] to escape and hide somewhere, esp. because you have stolen something • *They absconded with $100,000 of the company's money.*

absence /'æb·səns/ *n* [C/U] the state of not being somewhere, or a period in which you are not somewhere • *She has had repeated absences from school this year.* [C] • An absence can also be a lack of existence: *He drew attention to the absence of any solid evidence against the defendant.* [U]

absent /'æb·sənt/ *adj* [not gradable] • *If Callie is absent from school, she should bring a note from home.* • If you are **absent-minded**, you forget things, or do not give your attention to what is happening because you are thinking of other things.

absently /'æb·sənt·li/ *adv* • *He stared out the window, absently rubbing his cheek.*

absentee /ˌæb·sən'tiː/ *n* [C] someone who is absent • An **absentee ballot** is a piece of paper that voters can write their vote on and send in by mail if they cannot vote in person at an election.

absolute [WITHOUT LIMIT] /'æb·sə,luːt, ˌæb·sə 'luːt/ *adj* [not gradable] without limit, very great, or to the largest degree possible • *She demanded absolute silence.* ○ *The day was an absolute (= complete) disaster.* • [LP] VERY, COMPLETELY, AND OTHER INTENSIFIERS

absolute [CERTAIN] /'æb·sə,luːt, ˌæb·sə'luːt/ *adj* [not gradable] certain; not to be doubted • *Health insurance is an absolute necessity.*

absolutely /'æb·sə,luːt·li, ˌæb·sə'luːt·li/ *adv* [not gradable] completely; beyond any doubt • *You are absolutely right.* ○ *Are you absolutely sure that you locked the front door?* • Absolutely is also used in conversation to show emphasis in agreeing to something: *"Can you lend me $10 till tomorrow?" "Absolutely, it's no problem."* • If you say absolutely not, you are showing emphasis in not agreeing to something: *"You mean you won't sign this?" "No, absolutely not."* • [LP] VERY, COMPLETELY, AND OTHER INTENSIFIERS

absolve /əb'zɑlv, -'zɔːlv/ *v* [T] *fml* to officially remove guilt or responsibility from (someone) for something wrong they have done or might have done • *He was absolved of all wrongdoing.*

absorb [SUCK IN] /əb'zɔːrb, -'sɔːrb/ *v* [T] (of a substance or object) to take in (a liquid, gas, or chemical) and make a part of itself • *The black clay soil around here doesn't absorb water very well.* ○ *(fig.) The country has absorbed millions of immigrants over the years.*

absorbent /əb'zɔːr·bənt, -'sɔːr-/ *adj* able to take in liquids esp. through the surface • *absorbent paper towels*

absorb [TAKE ATTENTION] /əb'zɔːrb, -'sɔːrb/ *v* [T] to completely take the attention of (someone) • *She was absorbed in listening to music.* • To absorb knowledge, ideas, or information is to understand them completely and store them in your memory: *It was difficult to absorb so much information.*

absorption [TAKING IN] /əb'zɔːrp·ʃən, -'sɔːrp-/ *n* [U] the process by which a substance or object takes in a liquid, gas, or chemical and makes it a part of itself

absorption [ATTENTION] /əb'zɔːrp·ʃən, -'sɔːrp-/ *n* [U] the condition of giving your complete attention to something

abstain /æb'steɪn, əb-/ *v* [I] to not do something you could do, esp. something pleasurable or unhealthy • *You've got to abstain from alcohol completely.* • If you abstain from voting, you do not vote although you are permitted to vote.

abstinence /'æb·stə·nəns/ *n* [U] the act of not doing something, esp. something pleasurable

abstract /æb'strækt, 'æb·strækt/ *adj* existing as an idea, feeling, or quality, not as a material object • *"Humanity" is an abstract idea.* • If a statement, argument, or discussion is abstract, it is general and not based on particular examples. • A painting, drawing, or SCULPTURE is described as abstract if it tries to represent the qualities of objects or people but does not show their outer appearance: *abstract art*

absurd /əb'sɜrd, -'zɜrd/ *adj* ridiculous or completely unreasonable • *It is absurd for the* *council to cut taxes without proposing another way to raise money.* [+ *to* infinitive]

absurdity /əb'sɜrd·ət̬·i, -'zɜrd-/ *n* [C/U]

abundant /ə'bʌn·dənt/ *adj* more than enough; a lot • *It is a region with abundant natural resources.*

abundance /ə'bʌn·dəns/ *n* [U] • *We all seem to have an abundance of those plastic grocery bags.*

abundantly /ə'bʌn·dənt·li/ *adv* [not gradable] very • *The solution to the problem seemed abundantly clear.*

abuse /ə'bjuːs/ *n* [C/U] bad or cruel treatment of a person or animal, or the use of something in an unsuitable or wrong way • *child abuse* [U] ○ *sexual abuse* [U]

abuse /ə'bjuːz/ *v* [T] to treat (a person or animal) badly or cruelly, or to use (something) wrongly • *He was always welcome but he never abused the privilege by visiting us too often.*

abuser /ə'bjuː·zər/ *n* [C]

abusive /ə'bjuː·sɪv, -zɪv/ *adj* treating someone badly or cruelly, esp. physically • *He was a very strict parent, but never abusive.*

abysmal /ə'bɪz·məl/ *adj* very bad • *This experiment could help a lot of people, or it could be an abysmal failure.*

academic [SCHOOL RELATED] /ˌæk·ə'dem·ɪk/ *adj* relating to schools, esp. colleges and universities, or connected with studying and thinking, not with practical skills

academic /ˌæk·ə'dem·ɪk/ *n* [C] a person who teaches in a college or university

academic [NOT IMPORTANT] /ˌæk·ə'dem·ɪk/ *adj* theoretical and not having any practical importance • *Which diamond ring you like more is purely academic, because I can't afford either one.*

academy /ə'kæd·ə·mi/ *n* [C] a school that teaches a particular subject or trains people for a particular job, or an organization that supports art, literature, or science • *a military/police academy* • (*trademark*) An **Academy Award** (also **Oscar**) is one of a set of prizes given each year by a US film organization to recognize the best movie and the people involved in the best movies.

accelerate /ɪk'sel·ə‚reɪt, æk-/ *v* [I/T] to move more quickly, or to make (something) happen faster or sooner • *He stepped on the gas and accelerated rapidly to pass a car.* [I]

acceleration /ɪk‚sel·ə'reɪ·ʃən, æk-/ *n* [U] • *The car has good acceleration.*

accelerator /ɪk'sel·ə‚reɪt̬·ər, æk-/ *n* [C] a PEDAL (= part worked with the foot) in a car that makes the car go faster when pressed

accent [WAY OF PRONOUNCING] /'æk·sent/ *n* [C] the way in which people in a particular area or country pronounce words • *She spoke with a slight southern accent.* • An **accent** (**mark**) is a mark written or printed over a letter to show how to pronounce it.

accent [EMPHASIS] /'æk·sent/ *n* [C] a special em-phasis given to a syllable in a word or to a word in a sentence • *In "government," the accent is on the first syllable.*

accent /'æk·sent, æk'sent/ *v* [T] • *In Spanish, you usually accent the next-to-last syllable.*

accentuate /ɪk'sen·tʃə‚weɪt, æk-/ *v* [T] to emphasize (a particular feature of something) or to make (something) more noticeable • *The short black dress accentuated her slenderness.*

accept /ɪk'sept, æk-/ *v* [T] to agree to take (something), or to consider (something) as satisfactory, reasonable, or true • *She accepted the job offer.* ○ *He was accused of accepting bribes.* ○ *Do you accept credit cards?* ○ *He refuses to accept the fact that he could be wrong.* • If you accept an offer or an invitation, you say yes to it: *We accepted an invitation to visit China.* • To accept is also to allow (someone) to become a member of an organization or group: *He was accepted by three colleges.* • To accept is also to consider (someone) as now belonging to your group as an equal: *She never felt accepted by the other girls in her sorority.*

acceptable /ɪk'sep·tə·bəl, æk-/ *adj* satisfactory; good enough • *An offer that is acceptable to the union leaders might still be voted down by the union members.* • If behavior is acceptable, it is considered to be within the range of behavior that is permitted and is not disapproved: *In those days, it was not acceptable for women to wear short skirts.*

acceptance /ɪk'sep·təns, æk-/ *n* [U] • *Congress opposed the president's acceptance of the international trade agreement.* • Acceptance of an offer or an invitation means that you say yes to it: *The White House indicated its acceptance of the offer to visit Russia.* • Acceptance of a person is the act of agreeing to that person's becoming a member of an organization or group, or to that person's belonging to your group as an equal.

access /'æk·ses/ *n* [U] the method or way of approaching a place or person, or the right to use or look at something • *Without an official pass, the guards will deny you access to* (= will not let you enter) *the courthouse.* • Access to something can also mean the opportunity or ability to use it: *Many of the families do not have access to health care.*

access /'æk·ses/ *v* [T] • *People now can access information from the Internet as never before.*

accessible /ɪk'ses·ə·bəl, æk-/ *adj* • *The island is accessible only by ferry.* ○ *By using more illustrations, he made the magazine more accessible to the public* (= easier to understand).

accessory [EXTRA] /ɪk'ses·ə·ri, æk-/ *n* [C usually pl] something extra that improves or completes the thing it is added to • *We sell plants, seeds, fertilizer, and gardening accessories, such as tools and gloves.*

accessory [CRIMINAL] /ɪk'ses·ə·ri, æk-/ *n* [C] *law* someone who helps another person to commit a crime but does not take part in it

accident INJURY /'æk·səd·ənt, -sə,dent/ n [C] an event not intended by anyone but which has the result of injuring someone or damaging something • *He was killed in an automobile accident at the age of 21.* • An accident-prone person seems to have accidents frequently in which they injure themselves.

accident EVENT NOT PLANNED /'æk·səd·ənt, -sə,dent/ n [C] something that happens unexpectedly and unintentionally • *It's no accident that* (= There are reasons that explain why) *she was chosen to be a member of the most powerful committee in Congress.* • *She hit me with her hand, apparently* by accident (= without intending to).

accidental /,æk·sə'dent·ᵊl/ adj • *The fire began shortly after 1:30 a.m. and appears to have been accidental.*

accidentally /,æk·sə'dent·ᵊl·i/ adv

acclaim PRAISE /ə'kleɪm/ n [U] enthusiastic approval and praise • *Despite critical acclaim, the TV show always ran third in the ratings.*

acclaim /ə'kleɪm/ v [T] • *The orchestra was widely acclaimed as one of the best in the nation.*

acclaim ELECT /ə'kleɪm/ v [T] *Cdn* to elect (someone) without opposition • *Marion was acclaimed president of the club.*

acclamation /,æk·lə'meɪ·ʃən/ n [U] loud and enthusiastic praise or approval • *(Cdn)* If someone is elected by acclamation, they are elected without opposition.

acclimate /'æk·lə,meɪt/ v [I/T] to change to suit different conditions of life, or (of conditions) to cause (someone) to change to suit them • *Apparently the zoo animals had become acclimated to the crowd noise and were no longer startled by it.* [I]

accommodate FIND A PLACE FOR /ə'kɑm·ə,deɪt/ v [T] to provide with a place to live or to be put • *The new dormitory will be able to accommodate an additional 200 students.*

accommodations /ə,kɑm·ə'deɪ·ʃənz/ pl n, **accommodation** /ə,kɑm·ə'deɪ·ʃən/ n [U] a place to stay, esp. a hotel room • *Tour operators are advertising accommodations as low as $79 per night in first-class hotels.*

accommodate SUIT /ə'kɑm·ə,deɪt/ v [T] to give what is needed to (someone) • *We certainly try to accommodate students with disabilities.*

accommodating /ə'kɑm·ə,deɪt·ɪŋ/ adj • *The airline could not have been more accommodating* (= willing to help) *in getting me on a connecting flight.*

accompany /ə'kʌm·pə·ni/ v [T] to go with (someone) or to exist at the same time as (something) • *Students cannot leave the building during class hours unless they are accompanied by an adult.* • In music, to accompany is to play an instrument in support of (someone) who is playing an instrument or singing.

accompaniment /ə'kʌm·pə·ni·mənt/ n [C/U] something done in support of something else, esp. (in music) the playing of an instrument in support of someone else who is playing an instrument or singing

accomplice /ə'kɑm·pləs, -kʌm-/ n [C] a person who helps someone else to commit a crime or do something morally wrong • *The gunmen and two accomplices made away with over $25,000 in cash.*

accomplish /ə'kɑm·plɪʃ, -'kʌm-/ v [T] to do or finish (something) successfully; achieve (something) • *On retiring from the Congress, he said he had accomplished everything he set out to do.*

accomplished /ə'kɑm·plɪʃt, -'kʌm-/ adj • *She's an accomplished* (= skilled) *violinist.*

accomplishment /ə'kɑm·plɪʃ·mənt, -'kʌm-/ n [C/U] • *There's a feeling of accomplishment* (= achievement) *from having a job and all that goes with it.* [U]

accord AGREEMENT /ə'kɔːrd/ n [C/U] a formal agreement, or the condition of agreeing • *Both parties signed an accord last week in Geneva that may finally bring an end to the bloody conflict.* [C]

accord with /ə'kɔːrd,wɪð, -,wɪθ/ v prep [T] • *This statement does not altogether accord with* (= agree with) *the facts.*

accordance /ə'kɔːrd·ᵊns/ n • If you do something in accordance with a rule, you follow or obey that rule: *In accordance with school rules, the teacher asked him to remove his hat when inside the building.*

accord GIVE /ə'kɔːrd/ v [T] *fml* to give officially (something desirable) • *Reporters asked why the United States did not accord full recognition to the Lithuanian government.*

accordingly /ə'kɔːrd·ɪŋ·li/ adv in a way that suits the situation • *Surveys suggest that these shows are not what most people want to watch. Accordingly* (= Therefore), *one network is now scheduling a made-for-TV movie every Sunday night.*

according to AS STATED BY /ə'kɔːrd·ɪŋ·tə, -,tʊ, -,tuː/ prep as stated by • *According to my mother, even one drink is too many when you are going to drive.*

according to FOLLOWING /ə'kɔːrd·ɪŋ·tə, -,tʊ, -,tuː/ prep in a way that agrees with; by • *The teacher sorted the exams according to grade, with the A's on top and the F's on the bottom.*

accordion /ə'kɔːrd·iː·ən/ n [C/U] a musical instrument with a row of keys and a folding central part that is pushed closed between the hands to force air through thin metal pieces and produce notes when the keys are pressed, or this type of instrument generally

accost /ə'kɔːst, ə'kɑst/ v [T] to approach or stop and speak to (someone, esp. someone you do not know) in a threatening way • *The woman was accosted on the doorstep by a young man who made a crude sexual overture.*

account FINANCIAL SERVICE /ə'kaʊnt/ n [C]

money kept in a bank or other organization that you can add to or take back • *I have about $800 in my checking account.* • An account is also an arrangement with a store or a company that allows you to buy things and pay for them later: *Our company has accounts with all the major wholesalers.*

accountant /ə'kɑʊnt·ᵊnt/ *n* [C] someone who keeps or examines the records of money received, paid, and owed by a company or person • *a tax accountant*

account REPORT /ə'kɑʊnt/ *n* [C] a written or spoken description of an event • *Her account of the incident was contradicted by others.* ○ *By his own account* (= according to his own statement)*, he had been married and divorced three times.*

account REASON /ə'kɑʊnt/ *n* • Something that is done **on account of** something else is done for that reason: *She claimed that she was denied admission to the school on account of her race.* • **On** my **account** means just for me: *Don't cook on my account, I'm perfectly happy with a sandwich.*

□ **account for** EXPLAIN /-'--/ *v prep* [T] to explain the reason for (something) • *There was a fishy flavor to the milk that I could not account for.*

□ **account for** BE /-'--/ *v prep* [L] to form the total of; to be • *In Florida, senior citizens account for more than 25 percent of the population.*

accountable /ə'kɑʊnt·ə·bəl/ *adj* responsible for and having to explain your actions • *He knew he would be held accountable for any flaws in the programming.*

accreditation /ə,kred·ə'teɪ·ʃən, -əṭ'eɪ·ʃən/ *n* [U] official approval or acceptance, esp. in order to maintain satisfactory standards • *The hospital was threatened with the loss of accreditation if it did not improve the quality of its care.*

accredited /ə'kred·əṭ·əd/ *adj* [not gradable] • *Only accredited journalists are admitted to White House press conferences.*

accrue /ə'kruː/ *v* [I/T] to increase over a period of time, or to get (an amount of something) gradually over time • *Interest on this savings account accrues at the rate of 4 percent.* [I]

accumulate /ə'kjuː·mjə,leɪt/ *v* [I/T] to collect or increase gradually, esp. over a period of time • *We've accumulated a lot of junk over the years.* [T] ○ *He accumulated a fortune in the music business.* [T]

accumulation /ə,kjuː·mjə'leɪ·ʃən/ *n* [C/U] • *the accumulation of wealth* [U]

accurate CORRECT /'æk·jə·rət/ *adj* correct and without any mistakes • *The radio will give you the accurate time.* ○ *We need accurate information before we can develop a plan of action.*

accurately /'æk·jə·rət·li/ *adv* • *Can anyone accurately predict future climate change?*

accuracy /'æk·jə·rə·si/ *n* [U] • *He challenged the accuracy of the research results.*

accurate EXACT /'æk·jə·rət/ *adj* (of an object)

exactly aimed and moving on an intended path • *Good golfers usually make accurate approach shots from the tee.*

accuracy /'æk·jə·rə·si/ *n* [U] • *The predawn raid was executed with pinpoint accuracy.*

accusative /ə'kjuː·zəṭ·ɪv/ *adj* [not gradable] specialized (in grammar) having or relating to the CASE (= form) of a noun, pronoun, or adjective used to show that a word is the **direct object** *of a verb*

accuse /ə'kjuːz/ *v* [T] to say to or about (someone) that they are responsible for a crime or for having done something wrong • *He was accused of failing to pay his taxes.* ○ *She accused me of lying.*

accusation /,æk·jə'zeɪ·ʃən/ *n* [C] • *He denied the accusation, saying he was innocent.*

accused /ə'kjuːzd/ *n* [C] *pl* **accused** *law* a person or people who may be guilty of a crime and who are being judged in a court of law

accustom /ə'kʌs·təm/ *v* [T] to make (someone, esp. yourself) familiar with new conditions • *It takes awhile to accustom yourself to working at night.*

accustomed /ə'kʌs·təmd/ *adj* • *She's accustomed to waking at 6 a.m.*

ace PLAYING CARD /eɪs/ *n* [C] one of the four playing cards with a single mark or spot, which have the highest or lowest value in many card games

ace SKILLED PERSON /eɪs/ *n* [C] *infml* a person who is unusually good at doing something skillful • *Yankee ace David Cone will pitch tonight's game.*

ace TENNIS /eɪs/ *n* [C] (in tennis) a SERVE (= hit of the ball that starts play) that is so strong and fast the other player cannot return the ball

ache /eɪk/ *n* [C] a continuous pain that is unpleasant but not usually strong • *She has a fever, muscle aches, and a cough.* • Ache is often used in combination: *earache/headache/toothache*

ache /eɪk/ *v* • *They did pushups until their arms ached.* [I] ○ *(fig.) Her heart ached* (= She felt very sorry) *for the people who had lost their loved ones in the plane crash.* [I]

achieve /ə'tʃiːv/ *v* [T] to do or obtain (something) that you wanted after planning and working to make it happen • *She achieved her objective of qualifying for the US Olympic team.* ○ *I am hopeful that we can achieve peace eventually, but it is not going to be easy.*

achievable /ə'tʃiː·və·bəl/ *adj* [not gradable] • *Increasing sales by 5 percent is an achievable goal.*

achievement /ə'tʃiːv·mənt/ *n* something that you did or got after planning and working to make it happen, and that therefore gives you a feeling of satisfaction, or the act of working to make this happen • *a scientific achievement* [C] ○ *For an actor, winning an Oscar is one of the greatest achievements you can hope for.* [C]

• An **achievement test** is a test of a student's knowledge of a subject, which can be compared with the performance of other students taking the same test. Compare **intelligence test** at INTELLIGENCE THINKING ABILITY.

Achilles heel /ə,kɪl·iːz'hiːl/ *n* [C usually sing] a weak point in a person or system that can result in its failure

acid /'æs·əd/ *n* [C/U] any of various chemical substances that can produce salts and usually have a sour taste, some of which are able to damage whatever they touch • *Acids in the stomach aid digestion.* [C] ○ *Sulfuric acid is highly corrosive and dangerous.* [U] • (*slang*) Acid is also LSD (= an illegal drug that makes people see things that do not exist). [U] • **Acid rain** is rain containing harmful chemicals as a result of burning substances such as coal and oil. • The **acid test** is the true test of the value of something: *It looks good on paper, but will it sell? That's the acid test.*

acid /'æs·əd/ *adj* sour in taste • *The salad dressing has an acid taste.* • (*fig.*) An acid comment/remark is something said or written in strong criticism.

acknowledge /ɪk'nɑl·ɪdʒ, æk-/ *v* [T] to accept the truth or recognize the existence of (something) • *The president acknowledged his mistake in not vetoing the tax bill.* ○ *He's acknowledged as a leader in the Latino community.* ○ (*fml*) *Please acknowledge receipt of this letter* (= tell us when you receive it).

acknowledgment, acknowledgement /ɪk'nɑl·ɪdʒ·mənt, æk-/ *n* [C/U] • *Her resignation was an acknowledgment of defeat.* [C] ○ *I applied for a grant and just received an acknowledgment* (= letter saying that my letter was received). [C]

acme /'æk·mi/ *n* [U] the highest point of perfection or achievement • *Chaplin's "City Lights" marked the acme of his filmmaking career.*

acne /'æk·ni/ *n* [U] a disease of the skin in which small red spots appear, usually on the face and neck, esp. in young people

acorn /'eɪ·kɔːrn, -kərn/ *n* [C] the fruit of the OAK tree, consisting of an oval nut growing inside a cuplike outer part

acoustic /ə'kuː·stɪk/ *adj* [not gradable] relating to sound or hearing • *Scientists have developed a tiny acoustic device to improve hearing aids.* • An acoustic musical instrument is one that is not made louder by electrical equipment. • Acoustic also means designed to control sound so that you can hear only the sounds you want to hear: *acoustic tile*

acoustics /ə'kuː·stɪks/ *pl n* the way in which the structural characteristics of a place relate to how well sound can be heard in it • *The acoustics in the recital hall are very good.*

acquaint obj **with** obj /ə'kweɪnt,wɪð, -,wɪθ/ *v* prep [T] *fml* to give (someone) information about (something) • *The museum offers work-*

shops to acquaint children with the world of radio.

acquaintance /ə'kweɪnt·ᵊns/ *n* [C/U] a person whom you know but do not know well and who is therefore not exactly a friend • Acquaintance is also knowledge about something: *The young have little acquaintance with real-life tragedy.* [U]

acquainted /ə'kweɪnt·əd/ *adj* knowing or being familiar with someone or something • *"Do you know Megan?" "No, we're not acquainted."* ○ *We got acquainted when they gave us a ride home last night.*

acquiesce /,æk·wiː'es/ *v* [I] to accept or agree to something, often without really wanting to • *The bank acquiesced to an extension of the loan.*

acquiescence /,æk·wiː'es·əns/ *n* [U] • *Only a man with the stature of Mandela could have won the acquiescence of South African whites to black-majority rule.*

acquire /ə'kwaɪr/ *v* [T] to obtain or begin to have (something) • *His family acquired the property in 1985.* ○ *She acquired her love of the outdoors as a child.* • An **acquired taste** is something, such as a food or an experience, that you may not like at first but may begin to like after you have tried it over a period of time.

acquisition /,æk·wə'zɪʃ·ən/ *n* [C/U] the act of obtaining or beginning to have something, or something obtained • *The museum has made several recent acquisitions.* [C] ○ *The acquisition of a new language requires a commitment of time and effort.* [U]

acquit DECIDE NOT GUILTY /ə'kwɪt/ *v* [T] **-tt-** to decide officially in a court of law that (someone) is not guilty of a particular crime • *She was acquitted.* ○ *The jury acquitted him.* • USAGE: The opposite of acquit is CONVICT.

acquittal /ə'kwɪt̬·ᵊl/ *n* [C/U] • *He hoped for an acquittal.* [C]

acquit PERFORM /ə'kwɪt/ *v* [T] **-tt-** *fml* to cause (yourself) to perform or behave in the stated way • *She acquitted herself well, finishing second.*

acre /'eɪ·kər/ *n* [C] a unit for measuring area, equal to 43,560 square feet or 4047 square meters • *They bought half an acre of land to build their house on.*

acreage /'eɪ·kə·rɪdʒ/ *n* [U] • *Forest covers half the acreage.*

acrid /'æk·rəd/ *adj* (of a smell or taste) strong, bitter, and unpleasant, causing a burning feeling • *The electrical fire sent thick clouds of acrid smoke through the office.*

acrimonious /,æk·rə'moʊ·niː·əs/ *adj* angry and including strongly critical accusations • *After an acrimonious debate, the proposal was adopted.*

acrimony /'æk·rə,moʊ·ni/ *n* [U] • *The acrimony of a legal battle destroyed their friendship.*

acrobat /'æk·rə,bæt/ *n* [C] a person who

entertains people by carrying out difficult and skillful physical actions, such as walking on a wire high above the ground • *a circus acrobat*
acrobatic /ˌæk·rə'bæt̬·ɪk/ *adj* (of an action) involving a lot of skill and energy in controlling the movement of your body to do something difficult • *Karate is a very acrobatic martial art.*

acronym /'æk·rə,nɪm/ *n* [C] a word created from the first letters of each word in a series of words • *AIDS is the acronym for acquired immune deficiency syndrome.*

across /ə'krɔːs/ *adv* [not gradable], *prep* from one side to the other side of (something), or at the other side of (something) • *We walked across the bridge.* ○ *She was sitting across the aisle.* ○ *He opened a store across the street from the theater.* ○ *Over 300,000 refugees fled across the Turkish border.* • If something is happening across the country, it is happening in all parts of the country. • Something that is done **across the board** has an effect on everyone or everything of a particular type: *The mayor threatened across-the-board spending cuts.*

acrylic /ə'krɪl·ɪk/ *adj* [not gradable] of or made from a type of acid or a RESIN (= chemically produced sticky substance) which is used in making plastic, cloth, and paint • *acrylic paint* ○ *They used acrylic yarn for the sweaters.*
acrylic /ə'krɪl·ɪk/ *n* [C usually pl] • *He paints with acrylics.*

act DO SOMETHING /ækt/ *v* [I] to do something for a particular purpose or in a particular way • *The president acted quickly to bring federal aid to areas damaged by flooding.* [+ to infinitive] ○ *She acted responsibly.* ○ *He acted as if he'd never seen me before.* ○ *She acted as* (= performed in the position of) *a tour guide for the group.* • To **act** your **age** is to behave in a way suitable for someone as old as your are: *Stop being silly and act your age!* • If you **act on** what someone has told you, you do what they suggest: *He gave me good advice, but I didn't act on it.* • If a person, esp. a child, **acts up**, they behave badly: *Tiffany started acting up.* • If a machine or something that has an effect on your body **acts up**, it performs badly or becomes active in a bad way: *My allergies started to act up.*
act /ækt/ *n* [C] • *an act of bravery/love/madness* ○ *a selfish/senseless/thoughtless act* ○ *an criminal/illegal/terrorist act* • An **act of God** is an unusual natural event, such as a flood or earthquake, that could not have been reasonably expected to happen. • An **act of war** is an event that could begin a war.

acting /'æk·tɪŋ/ *adj* [not gradable] • *Ms. Lopez-Smith will be the acting treasurer* (= temporarily perform those duties).

act PERFORM /ækt/ *v* [I/T] to take (the part of a character) in a theatrical performance; play (a part) in a movie or play • *He acts the part of a*

small-town lawyer. [T] ○ *She has acted in lots of television sitcoms.* [I] • If someone **acts out** something, their behavior expresses their emotions, often in ways that they are not aware of: *Fighting was this boy's way of acting out his frustrations.*

act /ækt/ *n* [C] one of a set of short performances that are parts of a show, or the person or group who performs one of these parts • *a circus act* ○ *(fig.) His story is just an act* (= is pretended and not sincere). • An act is also one of the main parts of a play or opera: *The play is presented in three acts.*

actor /'æk·tər/, *female* **actress** /'æk·trəs/ *n* [C] a person who plays the part of a character in a movie or play • *The play has a cast of six actors.*

act LAW /ækt/ *n* [C] *law* a law made by Congress or another legislative group • *an act of Congress*

action SOMETHING DONE /'æk·ʃən/ *n* [C/U] the process of doing something, or something done, esp. for a particular purpose • *Quick action in calling the fire department saved many lives.* [U] ○ *It was a reckless action which he later came to regret.* [C] ○ *Action to prevent the spread of AIDS is high on the government's agenda.* [+ to infinitive] ○ *Financial advisers urged the city to take action* (= do something) *to deal with the fiscal crisis.* [U] • Action is also fighting in a war: *Her younger son was killed in action.* [U] • In an action film/movie, there is usually a lot of violence and many exciting things happen. • *It was an* **action-packed** *movie* (= full of exciting events). • **Actions speak louder than words** means that what you do is more important and shows your intentions and feelings more clearly than what you say.

action MOVEMENT /'æk·ʃən/ *n* [C/U] the way something moves or works, or the effect it has on something else • *The heart's action in regulating blood flow is critically important.* [C]

action LEGAL PROCESS /'æk·ʃən/ *n* [C/U] *law* a process introduced by a person or group in a court of law to correct what they claim is a wrong by which they have been hurt • *She brought an action against the hospital for negligence.* [C]

activate /'æk·tə,veɪt/ *v* [T] to cause (something) to start working • *Something activated the car alarm.* • In sports, to activate is to bring a player back to the regular team, usually after they have had an injury which has healed.

activation /ˌæk·tə'veɪ·ʃən/ *n* [U]

active DOING SOMETHING /'æk·tɪv/ *adj* doing something as you usually do, or being able to do something physically or mentally • *He was still an active runner at 55.* ○ *She's active in her church* (= involved in its work). ○ *She intends to remain politically active.* ○ *His National Guard unit was put on active duty* (= made part of the regular fighting force). • An active VOL-CANO is one that might begin to throw out hot gases, liquid, or rocks at any time.

actively /ˈæk·tɪv·li/ *adv* • *He isn't actively involved in the day-to-day management of the business anymore.*

activity /ækˈtɪv·ət̬·i/ *n* [C/U] the doing of something, or something that you are doing, have done, or could do • *There were lots of activities for children at the museum.* [C] ◦ *Her favorite activity is visiting antique shops.* [C] ◦ *He denied that he was engaged in criminal activity.* [U]

active GRAMMAR /ˈæk·tɪv/ *adj* [not gradable] *specialized* (in grammar) describing a verb or sentence in which the subject is the person or thing that does what is stated • *In "Alex gave me a gift," the verb "give" is active, and in "I was given a gift by Alex," "give" is passive.* • Compare PASSIVE GRAMMAR.

activism /ˈæk·təˌvɪz·əm/ *n* [U] the use of direct and public methods to try to bring about esp. social and political changes that you and others want • *political/social activism*

activist /ˈæk·tə·vəst/ *n* [C] • *a civil-rights activist*

actor /ˈæk·tər/, *female* **actress** /ˈæk·trəs/ *n* [C] • See at ACT PERFORM.

actual /ˈæk·tʃə·wəl, -ʃə·wəl/ *adj* [not gradable] real; existing in fact • *We expected 50 people, but the actual number was a lot higher.*

actually /ˈæk·tʃə·wə·li, -ʃə·wə·li/ *adv* [not gradable] used to say that something is true, esp. when the true situation may not be known • *We actually had a hard time moving the sofa.* • Actually is often used when you want to emphasize that something is surprising or unusual: *She actually expected me to pay for her dinner.*

acumen /əˈkjuː·mən, ˈæk·jə·mən/ *n* [U] the ability to make correct judgments • *Mr. Estavez has a real business acumen.*

acupuncture /ˈæk·jəˌpʌŋ·tʃər/ *n* [U] a treatment for pain and illness that originated in China, and in which special needles are put into the skin at particular positions

acute EXTREME /əˈkjuːt/ *adj* very serious, extreme, or severe • *The area has an acute water shortage.* • In medicine, acute describes severe conditions, illnesses, or injuries that need immediate, specialized care: *Not all hospitals can provide acute care.*

acute ACCURATE /əˈkjuːt/ *adj* (esp. of thinking, feeling, or seeing) aware of or able to see small differences between things, or understanding well or being accurate in judging something • *He has very acute hearing.*

acutely /əˈkjuːt·li/ *adv* • *I was acutely aware of their problems.*

acute ANGLE /əˈkjuːt/ *adj* (of an angle) less than 90° • Compare OBTUSE ANGLE.

ad /æd/ *n* [C] *short form of* advertisement, see at ADVERTISE

A.D. *abbreviation for* anno Domini (= in the year of God), used to show that a year is after the year in which Jesus was thought to have been born • *the 12th century A.D.* ◦ *The Roman empire ended in A.D. 476.* • USAGE: A.D. usually appears before the year and after a century. • Compare B.C..

adage /ˈæd·ɪdʒ/ *n* [C] a wise saying or PROVERB • *He remembered the old adage, "Look before you leap."*

adamant /ˈæd·ə·mənt/ *adj* unwilling to be persuaded to change an opinion or decision • *She was adamant about becoming a dancer.*

adamantly /ˈæd·ə·mənt·li/ *adv* • *The mayor adamantly refused to consider a tax increase.*

Adam's apple /ˌæd·əmˈzæp·əl/ *n* [C] the front part of the neck that sticks out, esp. in a man, and moves up and down when you speak or swallow

adapt /əˈdæpt/ *v* [I/T] to adjust to different conditions or uses, or to change to meet different situations • *I adapted this recipe from one in an old cookbook.* [T]

adaptable /əˈdæp·tə·bəl/ *adj* able or willing to change • *He's pretty adaptable, and change doesn't bother him.*

adaptation /ˌæd·əpˈteɪ·ʃən, -ˌæp-/ *n* [C/U] • *The movie was an adaptation of a novel.* [C]

add /æd/ *v* [I/T] to put (something) with something else to increase the number or amount or to make it more important • *Beat the butter and sugar together, and then add the eggs.* [T] ◦ *"Thanks for all your help!" he added as he was leaving.* [T] ◦ *We've added on a couple of rooms to the house.* [M] ◦ *Factors beyond their control added to their success.* [I] • To add means to calculate the total of a group of numbers: *If you add three and four you get seven.* [T] • If something fails to **add up**, it is not reasonable: *His story just doesn't add up.* • If two or more things **add up to** something, they amount to something else: *Great food and good prices add up to a real bargain in dining.* • To **add fuel to the fire** or **add insult to injury** means to make a bad situation worse: *The President said he wouldn't add fuel to the fire by commenting without knowing all the facts.* ◦ *I was late and, to add insult to injury, forgot my keys.*

added /ˈæd·əd/ *adj* [not gradable] • *He had the added disadvantage of being the only man present.*

addiction /əˈdɪk·ʃən/ *n* [C/U] the need or strong desire to do or to have something, or a very strong liking for something • *His addiction began with prescription drugs.* [U] ◦ *I have an addiction to mystery stories.* [C]

addict /ˈæd·ɪkt/ *n* [C] a person who is unable to stop doing or using something • *Addicts don't care how they get hold of drugs.*

addicted /əˈdɪk·təd/ *adj* • *She was addicted to TV.*

addictive /ə'dɪk·tɪv/ *adj* • *Video games can be addictive.*

addition /ə'dɪʃ·ən/ *n* [C/U] the joining of something to something else to make it larger or more important • *Harold is the newest addition to our staff.* [C] • Addition is calculating the total of a group of numbers: *We learn addition and subtraction in first and second grade.*

additional /ə'dɪʃ·ən·ᵊl/ *adj* [not gradable] • *There's no additional charge for children under twelve.*

additive /'æd·ət̬·ɪv/ *n* [C] something added to a substance, esp. food, to improve it or to preserve it • *Additives keep certain foods fresh.* ○ *This paint has an additive that keeps mold from growing on it.*

address PLACE /ə'dres, 'æd·res/ *n* [C] the specific place where a person, business, or other organization can be found and where mail or telephone calls or electronic communications can be received • *What is your street address now?* ○ *I need your home and your business address.* ○ *I've changed my e-mail address, so let me give you the new one.*

address /ə'dres/ *v* [T] • *I addressed envelopes all morning.*

ADDRESSES

Numbers in addresses are spoken in different ways depending on how large the numbers are.
Series of two numbers are usually said as ordinary numbers.

49 ("forty-nine") *Grand Avenue* • *apartment 22E* ("twenty-two E")

Series of three numbers are generally said without using the word hundred, unless they end in 00.

310 ("three ten") *Elm Street* • *645* ("six forty-five") *Dakota Drive* • *room 409* ("four o nine") • *200* ("two hundred") *Main Street*

Notice that if the middle number is 0, it is said as "o."
Series of four numbers are often grouped into twos, unless the number ends with 00.

5260 ("fifty-two sixty") *Washington Street* • *4102* ("forty-one o two") *Cedar Drive* • *room 1900* ("nineteen hundred")

address SPEAK TO /ə'dres/ *v* [T] to speak or write to (someone), or to direct information to (someone) • *The First Lady addressed the meeting briefly.* ○ *He likes to be addressed as "Father Paul."*

address /ə'dres, 'æd·res/ *n* [C] a formal speech • *The graduation address was very dull.*

address DEAL WITH /ə'dres/ *v* [T] to give attention to or to deal with (a matter or problem) • *We'll address that question at the next meeting.*

adept /ə'dept/ *adj* skilled • *He's adept at making people feel at ease.*

adequate /'æd·ɪ·kwət/ *adj* enough or satisfactory for a particular purpose • *He didn't have adequate time to prepare for the exam.*

adequately /'æd·ɪ·kwət·li/ *adv* • *Were you adequately paid, or do you need more money?*

adhere /əd'hɪr, æd-/ *v* [I] to stick or be attached firmly to a surface • *Glue won't adhere to any surface that's wet.*

adhesive /əd'hi:·sɪv, æd-, -zɪv/ *adj* • *The pages were held together with adhesive tape.*

adhesive /əd'hi:·sɪv, æd-, -zɪv/ *n* [C/U] glue • *Use a water-resistant adhesive.* [C]

□ **adhere to** /-'--/ *v prep* [T] to continue to obey, believe in, or support (something, esp. a custom or belief) • *College coaches have to adhere to the rules about recruiting high school students.*

adherence /əd'hɪr·əns, æd-/ *n* [U] • *He insists upon adherence to every rule, no matter how silly.*

adherent /əd'hɪr·ənt, æd-/ *n* [C] • *She has been an adherent of home schooling for years.*

ad hoc /æd'hak, -'houk/ *adj, adv* for a particular purpose or need, esp. for an immediate need • *The ad hoc committee will meet next week.* ○ *Unfortunately, we deal with problems ad hoc.*

adjacent /ə'dʒeɪ·sənt/ *adj* [not gradable] very near, or with nothing in between • *They work in adjacent buildings.*

adjective /'ædʒ·ɪk·tɪv/ *n* [C] specialized (in grammar) a word that describes a noun or pronoun • *"Big," "purple," "quick," "obvious," and "silvery" are adjectives.*

adjectival /ˌædʒ·ɪk'taɪ·vəl/ *adj* [not gradable] • *an adjectival phrase*

adjoining /ə'dʒɔɪ·nɪŋ/ *adj* [not gradable] with nothing in between, or touching • *We had adjoining rooms in the hotel.*

adjourn /ə'dʒɜrn/ *v* [I/T] to rest or pause during (esp. a meeting or trial) • *They adjourned the meeting until after lunch.* [T]

adjournment /ə'dʒɜrn·mənt/ *n* [C/U] • *There was a two-day adjournment in the trial.* [C]

adjudicate /ə'dʒuː·də̯ˌkeɪt/ *v* [T] to act as a judge of (an argument) • *He has adjudicated many labor disputes.*

adjunct /'ædʒ·ʌŋt/ *n* [C] something added or connected to something larger or more important • *Canada's economy is not an adjunct to the US's but rather is expanding on its own.* • An **adjunct (professor)** is a temporary teacher at a college or university.

adjust /ə'dʒʌst/ *v* [I/T] to change (something) slightly to make it fit, work better, or be more suitable • *Adjust the angle of your monitor so you can easily read it.* [T] ○ *You need time to adjust to a new situation.* [I]

adjustable /ə'dʒʌs·tə·bəl/ *adj* • *The height of the steering wheel is adjustable.*

adjustment /ə'dʒʌst·mənt/ *n* [C/U] • *Only a few adjustments were needed to make her dress fit perfectly.* [C]

ad-lib /'æd'lɪb/ *v* [I/T] **-bb-** to do something

ADJECTIVES
Most adjectives can go in two different places in a sentence:
- **Before nouns,** as in *a funny story.* This is called the ATTRIBUTIVE position.
- **After verbs,** especially linking verbs like *be* and *seem,* as in *Don't laugh—it isn't funny.*

Some adjectives can also go:
- **After nouns,** as in *There was no money* **available.**

adjectives used only before a noun
These adjectives often:
- **add emphasis**
  The man's a **complete** *fool.* • *The current situation is a* **real** *mess.* • *I felt like a* **perfect** *fool when I forgot her name.*
  [LP] **Very, completely, and other intensifiers** at VERY
- **limit the noun**
  in **certain** *circumstances* • *the* **only** *solution* • *on the* **same** *day*
- **refer to a relationship with the present**
  my **old** *house* (= the one I used to have) • *his* **future** *wife* • *the* **late** *Mr. Lucas* (= he is no longer living)
- **refer to a place or position**
  an **outdoor** *concert* • **underwater** *photography* • *the* **front** *row* • *the* **eastern** *part of the state* • *the* **top/bottom** *drawer of the dresser*

adjectives used only after verbs
These adjectives often:
- **begin with a-**
  She's **asleep/awake.** • *They're so* **alike.** • *I think he's still* **alive.**
- **describe health or feelings**
  I'm all **right/fine** • *I bet she's* **sorry** *now.* • *Mom was* **upset.**

adjectives used only after a noun
A small number of adjectives are used only after a noun. These adjectives often:
- **are used with measurements or numbers**
  The pool was 20 feet **long** *and 12 feet* **wide.**
- **are used in certain fixed expressions, usually after titles**
  She works for TPC **Incorporated.** • *The President-***elect** *is giving an interview.*

---

without preparation or planning • *She had lost her notes, so she ad-libbed for ten minutes.* [I]
ad–lib /'æd'lɪb/ *adj, adv* • *I did not want to give an ad-lib speech.*
administer MANAGE /əd'mɪn·ə·stər/ *v* [T] to manage or control (the operation of something); govern • *The British administered Hong Kong for 99 years.*
administer GIVE /əd'mɪn·ə·stər/ *v* [T] to be responsible for giving (something) to someone • *Two proctors administered the exam.* ○ *She administers medicines to patients.*
administration /əd,mɪn·ə'streɪ·ʃən/ *n* [C/U] the management or control of an organization • *He's studying business administration.* [U] An administration in the US is the period when a President is in office: *The Clinton administration has been full of surprises.* [C]
administrative /əd'mɪn·ə,streɪt·ɪv/ *adj* • *You will do mainly administrative work.* • An **administrative assistant** is a person whose job is to help someone in charge.
administrator /əd'mɪn·ə,streɪt·ər/ *n* [C] • *She works as a school administrator.*

admiral /'æd·mə·rəl/ *n* [C] a naval officer of the highest rank
admire /əd'mɑɪr/ *v* [T] to respect and approve of (someone or something) • *I admire that music more than any other.*
admirable /'æd·mə·rə·bəl/ *adj* • *The police did an admirable job of calming down the crowd.*
admirably /'æd·mə·rə·bli/ *adv* • *I think she coped admirably with a very difficult situation.*
admiration /,æd·mə'reɪ·ʃən/ *n* [U] • *My admiration for her grows daily.*
admirer /əd'mɑɪr·ər/ *n* [C] • *Many admirers waited in the rain just to see their hero.*
admissible /əd'mɪs·ə·bəl/ *adj law* able to be considered in a court of law • *The judge ruled that this new evidence was admissible.*
admission PERMISSION TO ENTER /əd'mɪʃ·ən/ *n* [C/U] permission to study at a school or college, or permission to enter a theater or other building • *How many students will gain admission to Yale?* [U] ○ *The club refuses admission to those under 18.* [U] • Admission is also the price paid to enter a place: *Museum admission is $5.* [C]
admissions /əd'mɪʃ·ənz/ *pl n* the people allowed into a college, hospital, or other place,

or the process of allowing people in • *The city opened admissions to anyone who lived there.* ○ *He's been director of admissions at Boston University.*

admission STATEMENT /əd'mɪʃ·ən/ *n* [C/U] a statement accepting the truth about something • *There was no admission of guilt from anyone.* [U]

admit (*obj*) ACCEPT /əd'mɪt/ *v* -tt- to recognize or accept (something) as true • *He admitted his guilt.* [T] ○ *She admitted (that) she had made a mistake.* [+ (*that*) clause]

admit ALLOW IN /əd'mɪt/ *v* [T] -tt- to allow (someone or something) to enter • *Each ticket admits one member and a guest.*

admittance /əd'mɪt·ᵊns/ *n* [U] • *He was refused admittance to the club.*

admonish /əd'mɑn·ɪʃ, æd-/ *v* [T] to express disapproval of (actions or behavior), esp. in a kindly way, or to tell (someone) to do something • *His mother admonished him for eating too quickly.*

admonition /ˌæd·mə'nɪʃ·ən/, **admonishment** /əd'mɑn·ɪʃ·mənt/ *n* [C] • *As I left I heard my husband's admonition—"Don't be late."*

ado /ə'duː/ *n* [U] delay or unnecessary activity • *Without further ado, I shall introduce tonight's speaker.*

adobe /ə'doʊ·bi/ *n* [U] a mixture of wet earth and grass made into bricks and dried in the sun, used to build houses • *Adobe houses were common in the Southwest.*

adobe house

adolescent /ˌæd·ᵊl'es·ənt/ *adj* (of a young person) between childhood and adulthood • *The two adolescent boys made their mother very tired.* • If you describe an adult as adolescent, you mean that they are silly and childish.

adolescent /ˌæd·ᵊl'es·ənt/ *n* [C] • *I teach in a middle school, because I like young adolescents.*

adolescence /ˌæd·ᵊl'es·əns/ *n* [C/U] • *He had an unhappy adolescence.* [C]

adopt TAKE CHILD /ə'dɑpt/ *v* [I/T] to take (another person's child) legally into your own family to raise as your own child • *They adopted Raphael last September.* [T] • Compare FOSTER TAKE CARE OF.

adoption /ə'dɑp·ʃən/ *n* [C/U] • *The agency handles about a hundred adoptions a year.* [C]

adoptive /ə'dɑp·tɪv/ *adj* [not gradable] • *Her adoptive parents were farmers.*

adopt START /ə'dɑpt/ *v* [T] to accept or begin to use (something) • *The new law means companies will adopt energy-saving measures.* • If an organization adopts a rule, it votes to accept it: *The motion to increase fees was adopted.*

adoption /ə'dɑp·ʃən/ *n* [U] • *The adoption of a different insurance company caused a lot of confusion.*

adore /ə'dɔːr, ə'doʊr/ *v* [T] to love and respect (someone) very much, or to like (something) very much • *Both girls adored their father.* ○ *I adore those shoes!*

adorable /ə'dɔːr·ə·bəl, -'doʊr-/ *adj* (of a person or animal) charming, attractive, and easily loved • *He was an absolutely adorable child.*

adoration /ˌæd·ə'reɪ·ʃən/ *n* [U] • *His adoration of his wife is obvious.*

adorn /ə'dɔːrn/ *v* [T] to make (something) more attractive by putting something on it • *The bride's hair was adorned with fresh flowers.*

adornment /ə'dɔːrn·mənt/ *n* [C/U] • *Her only adornment was a ruby necklace.* [C]

adrenaline /ə'dren·ᵊl·ən/ *n* [U] a HORMONE (= chemical substance) produced by the body when a person is frightened, angry, or excited, which makes the heart beat faster and prepares the body to react to danger

adrift /ə'drɪft/ *adj, adv* (of a boat) not fastened and moving with the sea and wind, or (*fig.*) not controlled and living without a clear purpose or direction • (*fig.*) *Hopeful actors from small towns are often adrift in New York.*

adroit /ə'drɔɪt/ *adj* very skillful and quick in the way you think or move • *She became adroit at dealing with difficult people.*

adroitly /ə'drɔɪt·li/ *adv* • *He adroitly slid the money into his pocket.*

adulation /ˌædʒ·ə'leɪ·ʃən/ *n* [U] too much admiration or praise for someone • *He couldn't deal with the adulation of his fans.*

adult /ə'dʌlt, 'æd·ʌlt/ *adj* (of a person or an animal) grown to full size and strength • *She spent most of her adult life in prison.* • Adult also means suitable for grown people and not childish: *It's a kids' show, but they sneak in some adult humor,* • Adult movies, magazines, shows, and books usually provide sexual entertainment and are intended for adults only.

adult /ə'dʌlt, 'æd·ʌlt/ *n* [C] • *We invited only adults to the wedding.*

adulthood /ə'dʌlt·ˌhʊd/ *n* [U] • *When she reached adulthood, she moved away.*

adulterate /ə'dʌl·təˌreɪt/ *v* [T] to make (something, esp. drink or food) weaker or of worse quality by adding something else to it • *The wine was adulterated with water.*

adultery /ə'dʌl·tə·ri, -tri/ *n* [U] sex between a married person and someone who is not their wife or husband • *Adultery causes many divorces.*

adulterous /ə'dʌl·tə·rəs, -trəs/ *adj* • *How many stories are based on an adulterous relationship?*

advance MOVE FORWARD /əd'væns/ *v* [I/T] to go or move (something) forward, or to develop or improve (something) • *Research has advanced our understanding of the virus.* [T] ○ *Tonight's winner advances to the semifinals.* [I]

advance /əd'væns/ *n* [C/U] • *Technological advances have changed TV news.* [C] ○ *The ar-*

my's *advance was halted.* [U] ∘ (*fig.*) *She rejected his unwelcome advances* (= attempts to make her sexually interested in him). [C]

advanced /əd'vænst/ *adj* highly developed or difficult • *Are you taking any advanced courses?*

advancement /əd'væn·smənt/ *n* [U] • *They did nothing for the advancement of women.*

advance HAPPENING EARLY /əd'væns/ *adj* happening before an event • *We got no advance warning of the changes.*

advance /əd'væns/ *n* [C] money paid before something happens • *Most authors get an advance on royalties they'll earn later.* • **In advance** means before something happens: *If you're coming to the party, please let me know in advance.*

advantage /əd'vænt·ɪdʒ/ *n* [C/U] a condition giving a greater chance of success • *His long arms give him a big advantage over other boxers.* [C] ∘ *She sees no advantage in being a freshman.* [U] • If something is **to** your **advantage**, it helps you: *Celebrities use their fame to their advantage.*

advantageous /ˌæd,væn'teɪ·dʒəs, -vən-/ *adj* • *The agreement is advantageous to both sides.*

advent /'æd·vent/ *n* [U] the beginning of an event, the invention of something, or the arrival of a person • *Transportation was transformed by the advent of the internal combustion engine.* • For Christians, Advent is the period of four weeks before Christmas.

adventure /əd'ven·tʃər/ *n* [C/U] an unusual, exciting, and possibly dangerous activity, trip, or experience, or the excitement produced by such activities • *She had some exciting adventures in Peru.* [C] ∘ *Henry is looking for thrills and adventure.* [U]

adventurer /əd'ven·tʃə·rər/ *n* [C] someone who enjoys and looks for dangerous and exciting experiences • *An intrepid adventurer, he loves exploring the wilderness.*

adventurous /əd'ven·tʃə·rəs/, **adventursome** /əd'ven·tʃər·səm/ *adj* • *I'm pretty adventurous in cooking* (= willing to try new and unusual things).

adverb /'æd·vɜrb/ *n* [C] *specialized* (in grammar) a word that describes or gives more information about another word, esp. a verb, adjective, or other adverb, or about a phrase • *In the sentences, "She smiled cheerfully" and "He waited right outside the door," "cheerfully" and "right" are adverbs.*

adverbial /æd'vɜr·biː·əl/ *adj* [not gradable] • *an adverbial phrase*

adversary /'æd·vər,ser·i/ *n* [C] an enemy • *He saw her as his main adversary within the company.*

adversarial /ˌæd·vər'ser·iː·əl/ *adj* involving opposition or disagreement • *Lawyers enjoy being adversarial.*

adverse /æd'vɜrs, 'æd·vɜrs/ *adj* going against

something, or harmful • *Her policies may have adverse effects on the economy.*

adversity /æd'vɜr·sət̬·i/ *n* [C/U] a difficult or unlucky situation or event • *She's cheerful in the face of adversity.* [U]

advertise /'æd·vər,taɪz/ *v* [I/T] to make (something) known generally or in public, esp. in order to sell it • *He advertises his business on the Internet.* [T] ∘ *I'm going to advertise for* (= put a notice in the newspaper asking for) *someone to clean my house.* [I]

advertisement /ˌæd·vər'taɪz·mənt, əd'vərt̬·əz·mənt/, *short form* **ad** *n* [C] a paid notice that tells people about a product or service • *I saw an advertisement for the job in yesterday's paper.*

advertiser /'æd·vər,taɪ·zər/ *n* [C] • *Car companies are major TV advertisers.*

advertising /'æd·vər,taɪ·zɪŋ/ *n* [U] • *an advertising campaign* ∘ *She works in advertising.*

advice /əd'vaɪs/ *n* [U] an opinion that someone offers you about what you should do or how you should act in a particular situation • *She gave me some good advice.* ∘ *I think I'll take your advice and go home.*

advise /əd'vaɪz/ *v* [I/T] to give advice to (someone), or to suggest (something) • *I advised him to stay home.* [T] ∘ *Parental supervision is advised.* [T] ∘ *I wouldn't advise you to walk there alone.* [T] ∘ *I'd advise against staying.* [I] ∘ *Experts advised the president* (= gave information and suggested action). [T]

advisable /əd'vaɪ·zə·bəl/ *adj* • *It's not advisable to contradict him.*

adviser, **advisor** /əd'vaɪ·zər/ *n* [C] • *She's the chief economic adviser to the president.*

advisory /əd'vaɪ·zə·ri/ *adj* • *She serves on the newspaper's advisory board.*

advocate /'æd·və,keɪt/ *v* [T] to speak in support of (esp. an idea or course of action) • *They advocate a woman-centered approach to family planning.*

advocate /'æd·və·kət/ *n* [C] • *She's a strong advocate of women's rights.*

advocacy /'æd·və·kə·si/ *n* [U] • *His advocacy of school prayer may have cost him the election.*

aerial BROADCASTING /'er·iː·əl, 'ær-/ *n* an ANTENNA BROADCASTING

aerial IN AIR /'er·iː·əl, 'ær-/ *adj* [not gradable] of, from, or in the air • *Aerial photographs are used in making these maps.*

aerobics /er'oʊ·bɪks, ær-/ *n* [U] energetic physical exercises that make the heart, lungs, and muscles stronger and increase the amount of oxygen in the blood • *I do aerobics and weight training at the gym.*

aerobic /er'oʊ·bɪk, ær-/ *adj* [not gradable] • *aerobic exercise*

aerodynamics /ˌer·oʊ·daɪ'næm·ɪks, ˌær-/ *n* [U] the science that studies the movement of gases and the way solid bodies, such as aircraft, move through them

ADVERBS

Important types of adverbs

Used to describe how, where, when, how often, or for how long something happens

How?	*The dog barked* **excitedly**. • *She was driving too* **fast**.
Where?	*Come* **outside**. • *They built a factory* **nearby**.
When?	*It's going to rain* **soon**. • *I haven't read the newspaper* **yet**.
How often?	*You're* **always** *complaining*. • *We* **usually** *eat out on Sunday*.
How long?	*The bridge is* **temporarily** *closed for repairs*. • *I won't stand here* **forever**.

Used to change the strength of a verb, adjective, or adverb

verb	*The car* **almost** *crashed*. • *The medicine helped him* **enormously**.
adjective	*It's* **really** *cold*. • *The situation is* **extraordinarily** *complex*.
adverb	*We'll finish* **pretty** *soon*. • *He talks* **unbelievably** *fast*.

LP) **Very, completely and other intensifiers**

Used to give information about the attitude of the speaker or writer.

Adverbs like these typically modify the entire clause or sentence and are sometimes called sentence adverbs.

Surprisingly, *all the children came on time* • **Unfortunately** *I disagree with you*. • *It's* **obviously** *too expensive*. • **Hopefully** (= I hope that) *I'll be back before nine*. (Some people consider this use of *hopefully* to be incorrect, although it is very common in speech.)

Used to show how certain the speaker or writer is of something

Maybe *the team will win*. • *The doctor said it was* **probably** *nothing serious*. • *Have you* **definitely** *decided to quit your job?*

Used to describe the point of view from which something is considered

The movie was **commercially** *successful in spite of the bad reviews*. • *He was careful to use* **politically** *correct language that wouldn't offend anyone*.

Used to limit reference to a particular case or add emphasis

I bought this **especially** *for you*. • *You can* **only** *get there by car*. • **Even** *Joanna thought the movie was funny*.

Used to show a connection between sentences or clauses

Lara's plan seemed good. Her boss didn't like it **though**. • *Let me finish this, and* **then** *I can help you*. • *I don't know* **why** *John left*.

Used before a preposition or adverb.

A few adverbs can be used immediately before another adverb or a prepositional phrase. They often mean "exactly" or "completely."

It broke **right** *down the middle*. (used with a prepositional phrase) • *Go* **right** *ahead*. (used with an adverb)

Other adverbs like this are **all**, **bang**, **full**, and **smack**.

Order of adverbs

When a sentence has more than one adverb at the end, the normal order answers the questions "how," "where," and "when"?

	HOW	WHERE	WHEN
The girls were playing	**quietly**	**outside**.	
We'll have to go		**back**	**soon**.

---

aerodynamic /ˌer·ou·daɪˈnæm·ɪk, ˌær-/ *adj* • *The car's design is splendidly aerodynamic.*

aeroplane /ˈer·ə‚pleɪn, ˈær-/ *n* [C] *Br for* **airplane**, see at AIR |FLIGHT|

aerosol /ˈer·ə‚sɔːl, ˈær-, -‚sɑl/ *n* [C] a container in which liquids are kept under pressure and forced out in a SPRAY (= mass of small drops) • *The gasses used in aerosols were damaging the atmosphere.*

aerospace /ˈer·ou‚speɪs, ær-/ *adj* [not gradable] producing or operating aircraft or spacecraft • *the aerospace industry*

aesthetic, esthetic /esˈθeţ·ɪk/ *adj* relating to the enjoyment or study of beauty, or (of an object or work of art) showing great beauty • *Those buildings have little aesthetic appeal.*

aesthetics, esthetics /esˈθeţ·ɪks/ *n* [U] the formal study of the principles of art and beauty

aesthetically, esthetically /es'θeṭ·ɪ·kli/ adv • I like objects to be both functional and aesthetically pleasing.

afar /ə'fɑr/ adv [not gradable] literary from or at a great distance • He watched the proceedings from afar.

affable /'æf·ə·bəl/ adj friendly, kind, relaxed, and easy to talk to • It's hard not to like such an affable fellow.

affair SITUATION /ə'fer, ə'fær/ n [C] a situation or subject that is being dealt with or considered; a matter • The meeting was addressed by an expert in South American affairs. ○ What I do in my spare time is my own affair (= a private matter). • Affairs of state are government matters.

affair RELATIONSHIP /ə'fer, ə'fær/ n [C] a sexual relationship, esp. a secret one • She's had many love affairs.

affair EVENT /ə'fer, ə'fær/ n [C] an event • Their wedding was a pretty boring affair.

affect INFLUENCE /ə'fekt/ v [T] to have an influence on (someone or something) • The disease only affects cattle. ○ I was deeply affected by the film. • Compare EFFECT RESULT.

affect PRETEND /ə'fekt/ v [T] to pretend to be or have (something) • Since joining the band he's affected a ridiculous southern accent.

affected /ə'fek·təd/ adj artificial and not sincere • He has a very affected style of writing.

affectation /ˌæf·ek'teɪ·ʃən/ n [C/U] speech or behavior that is not natural or sincere and is used to produce a certain effect • She has many annoying little affectations. [C]

affection /ə'fek·ʃən/ n [C/U] a feeling of liking someone or something • Pets should be treated with affection. [U] ○ Harriet felt great affection for him. [U]

affectionate /ə'fek·ʃə·nət/ adj • an affectionate child

affectionately /ə'fek·ʃə·nət·li/ adv • He was affectionately known as "Bobo".

affidavit /ˌæf·ə'deɪ·vət/ n [C] law a written statement that someone makes after they have sworn to tell the truth which might be used in a court of law

affiliate /ə'fɪl·iː·ˌeɪt/ v [I/T] to become or cause (a person or group) to become part of or form a close relationship with esp. a larger group or organization • I'm not affiliated with any political party. [T] ○ The two schools will affiliate next year. [I]

affiliate /ə'fɪl·iː·ət, -ˌeɪt/ n [C] one part of a larger group or organization • The show is broadcast on most of the network's affiliates.

affiliation /əˌfɪl·iː'eɪ·ʃən/ n [C/U] • The group has affiliations with several organizations abroad. [C]

affinity /ə'fɪn·əṭ·i/ n [C/U] a close similarity between two things, or an attraction or sympathy for someone or something, esp. because of shared characteristics • Many people really feel an affinity for/with dolphins. [C]

affirm (obj) /ə'fɜrm/ v to state (something) as true, or to state your support for (an idea, opinion, etc.) • Boyer affirmed her plans to become a nun. [T] ○ These stories affirmed that the world is strange. [+ that clause]

affirmation /ˌæf·ər'meɪ·ʃən/ n [C/U] • We're looking for affirmation of the city's goal. [U]

affirmative /ə'fɜr·məṭ·ɪv/ adj positive, or showing agreement • There should be an affirmative role for government in social problems. • If a government or an organization takes **affirmative action**, it tries to improve the educational and employment opportunities of women, people who are not white, or other groups that have often been treated unfairly. • Compare NEGATIVE NO.

affirmative /ə'fɜr·məṭ·ɪv/ n [C/U] • He replied in the affirmative (= He said yes). [U]

affirmative /ə'fɜr·məṭ·ɪv/ adv used to mean yes in an answer to a question, esp. in a military context • "Can you hear me?" "Affirmative."

affirmatively /ə'fɜr·məṭ·ɪv·li/ adv • She answered affirmatively.

affix /ə'fɪks, æ-/ v [T] slightly fml to attach, add, or join (one thing) to another • The sticker must be affixed to your windshield.

afflict /ə'flɪkt/ v [T] to make (someone or something) suffer physically or mentally • He was afflicted with severe asthma.

affliction /ə'flɪk·ʃən/ n [C] • Illiteracy is a serious affliction.

affluent /'æf·luː·ənt, ə'fluː-/ adj having a lot of money or possessions; rich • We live in an affluent neighborhood.

affluence /'æf·luː·əns, ə'fluː-/ n [U] • She makes a display of affluence.

afford /ə'fɔːrd, ə'foʊrd/ v [I/T] to have enough money or time to buy, keep, or do (something) • I don't know how he can afford a new car. [T] ○ Can you afford to take any time off work? [I]

affordable /ə'fɔːrd·ə·bəl, ə'foʊrd-/ adj not expensive • Affordable housing isn't enough—we also need job opportunities.

affront /ə'frʌnt/ n [C] a remark or action intended to insult or upset someone • Such statements are an affront to people of conscience.

afloat /ə'floʊt/ adj floating on or in water • They couldn't keep the ferry afloat. ○ (fig.) Loan programs are aimed at keeping small businesses afloat (= operating).

afoot /ə'fʊt/ adj [not gradable] happening, or being planned or prepared • Big changes are afoot at Lake Utah.

afraid FEARFUL /ə'freɪd/ adj feeling fear, or feeling anxiety about the possible results of a particular situation • She was afraid, but never thought of quitting. ○ I've always been afraid of heights. ○ Dad's afraid I'll end up like my cousin. ○ He's not afraid of losing.

afraid REGRET /ə'freɪd/ adj [not gradable] feeling regret, esp. because something is not the way you think it should be • *A lot of those stores will cheat you, I'm afraid.*

afresh /ə'freʃ/ *adv* [not gradable] *esp. literary* again, esp. from a new beginning • *She tore up the letter and started afresh.*

African /'æf·rɪ·kən/ *n* [C], *adj* (a person) of or from Africa • An **African-American** (also **Afro-American**) is an American who has at least some family members in the past who were from Africa. See note at BLACK DARK SKIN. • The **African Methodist Episcopal Church** (*abbreviation* **AME Church**) is a Christian religious group that is one of the Protestant churches. Its members are mostly African-Americans.

aft /æft/ *adj, adv* [not gradable] in or toward the back part of a boat • *The aft gun crew opened fire.*

after FOLLOWING /'æf·tər/ *prep* following in time, place, or order • *What do you want to do after breakfast?* ○ *I expect to return to work after the baby comes.* ○ *Repeat these words after me.* ○ *I'll see you the day after tomorrow.* ○ *It's ten minutes after four.* ○ *Week after week* (= For many weeks)*, he's been too busy to help.* • An **aftereffect** is a result of a condition or event: *Headaches are an aftereffect of this sort of accident.* • An **afterlife** is the life that some people believe begins after death, esp. in heaven.

after /'æf·tər/ *conjunction* • *The house was empty for three months after they moved out.*

after /'æf·tər/ *adv* [not gradable] • *Hilary drove up and Nick arrived soon after.*

after BECAUSE /'æf·tər/ *prep* as a result of; because • *After what she did to me, I'll never trust her again.* ○ *She's named after her aunt* (= given the same name in her honor).

after DESPITE /'æf·tər/ *prep* despite • *Even after everything that's happened here, his behavior seems odd.* • *The rain stopped and the game went ahead* **after all** (= despite problems or doubts). • *"Of course I love her—***after all** (= the fact is), *she's my sister."*

after WANTING /'æf·tər/ *prep* wanting to find or have • *The police are after him.* ○ *He's after Jane's job.*

aftermath /'æf·tər,mæθ/ *n* [U] the period following an event, such as an accident or war, and the effects caused by the event • *We all worked together in the aftermath of the earthquake.*

afternoon /,æf·tər'nuːn/ *n* [C/U] the period that starts at about twelve o'clock or after the meal in the middle of the day and ends at about six o'clock or when the sun goes down • *She works three afternoons a week at the library.* [C] ○ *My baby usually sleeps in the afternoon.* [U] ○ *I spoke to her yesterday afternoon.* [U] • (**Good**) **afternoon** is also a greeting: *Afternoon, Mr. Hopkins.* LP GREETINGS

aftershock /'æf·tər,ʃɑk/ *n* [C] a sudden movement of the earth's surface that often follows an **earthquake** and is less violent than the first main movement • (*fig.*) *The aftershocks* (=

powerful emotional effects) *of the massacre are still being felt.*

aftertaste /'æf·tər,teɪst/ *n* [C usually sing] the flavor that a food or drink leaves in your mouth when you have swallowed it • *Some vinegars have a sweet aftertaste.*

afterthought /'æf·tər,θɔːt/ *n* [C usually sing] an idea or plan that was not originally intended • *Pine included the song almost as an afterthought on his last album.*

afterward /'æf·tər·wərd/, **afterwards** /'æf·tər·wərdz/ *adv* [not gradable] after the time mentioned; later • *We had a swim and afterward we lay on the beach for a while.*

again /ə'gen, ə'geɪn/ *adv* [not gradable] once more, or as before • *Could you spell your name again please?* ○ *Get some rest and you'll soon be well again.* ○ *Don't be late again* (= another time). • *I've told you* **again and again** (= many times) *that I don't know anything about it.*

against IN OPPOSITION /ə'genst, ə'geɪnst/ *prep* in opposition to; opposed to • *I know you'd like to get a more expensive car, but I'm against it.* ○ *It's against the law to throw your trash there* (= It's illegal). ○ *She voted against the tax increase.* ○ *He warned them against repeating* (= not to repeat) *the mistakes of the former administration.* • Against also means in competition with: *He would have to run against O'Toole for county treasurer.* • To go against something means to go in the opposite direction to it: *swimming against the current* • If something is **against** your **better judgment**, you think it would be wiser not to do it: *Even though it was against his better judgment, he gave John the job.* • If you do something **against** your **will**, you do it because you are forced to: *She was searched against her will.*

against DIRECTED AT /ə'genst, ə'geɪnst/ *prep* (of something negative) directed at or toward • *Among the charges leveled against them were bribery and tax evasion.* ○ *We are trying to find ways to combat violence against children.*

against TOUCHING /ə'genst, ə'geɪnst/ *prep* next to and touching or being supported by (something) • *It would save space if we put the bed against the wall.* ○ *Her hair brushed against him as she passed.*

age TIME SPENT ALIVE /eɪdʒ/ *n* the length of time someone has been alive or something has existed • *At age 24 he won a starring role in his first movie.* [C] ○ *She was 74 years of age when she wrote her first novel.* [U] ○ *The program is aimed at viewers in the 18-to-30 age group.*

age /eɪdʒ/ *v* [I/T] (of a person) to become or appear old, or to cause (someone) to appear old • *She's aged a lot since the last time we met.* [I] • To age food or drink is to give it time to become ripe or develop a full flavor: *The brandy is aged in oak casks for ten years.* [T]

aged /eɪdʒd/ *adj* [not gradable] • *They have one daughter, aged three* (= three years old).

ageless /'eɪdʒ·ləs/ *adj* never seeming to get or look older • *ageless beauty*

age PERIOD /eɪdʒ/ *n* [C] a particular period in time • *the modern/nuclear/Victorian age* • *It's an* **age-old** *story of love and betrayal* (= a very old story).

ages /'eɪ·dʒəz/ *pl n* a very long time • *It's been ages since I've seen you.*

aged /'eɪ·dʒəd/ *adj* old • *an aged man*

aged /'eɪ·dʒəd/ *pl n* old people • *The apartment was built to meet the needs of the aged.*

ageism /'eɪˌdʒɪz·əm/ *n* [U] unfair treatment of people who are becoming old or who are old • *At 56, no one would hire her, and she felt she was a victim of ageism.*

agenda /ə'dʒen·də/ *n* [C] a list of matters to be discussed at a meeting • *Among the items on the agenda were next year's budget and raising the membership dues.* • An agenda can also refer to any matters that have to be dealt with: *Finding a job is at the top of my agenda.* • (*esp. disapproving*) An agenda is also a particular program of action, often one that is not directly expressed: *She has a political agenda.*

agent REPRESENTATIVE /'eɪ·dʒənt/ *n* [C] a person who acts for or represents another • *a travel agent* ○ *He is the agent for several of the highest paid players in baseball.* • An agent is also someone who works secretly for a government or other organization: *a secret agent* ○ *an undercover agent*

agency /'eɪ·dʒən·si/ *n* [C] a business acting for or representing a person, an organization, or another business • *an advertising/employment agency* ○ *a real estate agency* • An agency is also a government organization: *federal agencies* ○ *the Central Intelligence Agency or CIA*

agent CAUSE /'eɪ·dʒənt/ *n* [C] a person or thing that produces a particular effect or change • *a cleaning agent*

aggravate MAKE WORSE /'æg·rə,veɪt/ *v* [T] to make (something bad) worse • *Road repair work has aggravated the problem of traffic congestion.*

aggravate ANNOY /'æg·rə,veɪt/ *v* [T] *infml* to make (someone) feel very annoyed and upset • *It really aggravates me when the car won't start, after all the money we put into it.*

aggravating /'æg·rə,veɪt̬·ɪŋ/ *adj infml* • *It's so aggravating to have an injury like that, when you can't lift anything or bend down and tie your shoelaces.*

aggravation /ˌæg·rə'veɪ·ʃən/ *n* [U] *infml* • *I won't bother returning it—it isn't worth the aggravation.*

aggregate /'æg·rɪ·gət/ *adj* [not gradable] formed by adding together several amounts or things; total • *The seven companies made an aggregate profit of $10.2 million.*

aggregate /'æg·rɪ·gət/ *n* [C] • *The family owned over 2 million shares in the aggregate.*

aggression /ə'greʃ·ən/ *n* [U] actions or behavior that is threatening or that uses force against others, often ignoring their rights or physically attacking them • *We regard the presence of troops on our border as an act of aggression.*

aggressive /ə'gres·ɪv/ *adj* • *Jack was a large, aggressive child given to outbursts of temper.*

aggressor /ə'gres·ər/ *n* [C] a person, group, or country that starts an argument, fight, or war by attacking first • *He claimed that he was just defending himself, and that the other guy was the aggressor.*

aggressive /ə'gres·ɪv/ *adj* using strong, forceful methods esp. to sell or persuade • *The organization mounted an aggressive campaign against drunk driving.* ○ *You have to be aggressive if you want to succeed in this business.*

aggressively /ə'gres·ɪv·li/ *adv* • *The company is aggressively pursuing new business opportunities.*

aggrieved /ə'griːvd/ *adj* unhappy, hurt, and angry because of unfair treatment • *Our hearts go out to the aggrieved families of the innocent victims.*

aghast /ə'gæst/ *adj* [not gradable] shocked or surprised in an unpleasant way • *Her husband was aghast when she danced with other men.*

agile /'ædʒ·əl, -aɪl/ *adj* able to move about quickly and easily • *Years of ballet and modern dance had made her strong and agile.* ○ (*fig.*) *He has an agile mind* (= He can think quickly).

agility /ə'dʒɪl·ət̬·i/ *n* [U] • *A top-rated football player, he combines speed and agility.* ○ (*fig.*) *Her voice has the lightness and agility that Handel's music demands.*

agitate ARGUE /'ædʒ·ə,teɪt/ *v* [I] to argue energetically, esp. in public, in order to achieve a particular type of change • *He continued to agitate for Polish independence.*

agitator /'ædʒ·ə,teɪt̬·ər/ *n* [C] • *They blamed the strike on political agitators.*

agitate MAKE ANXIOUS /'ædʒ·ə,teɪt/ *v* [T] to make (someone) feel excited and anxious because of worry or fear that is difficult to control • *Any mention of his son agitated him.*

agitated /'ædʒ·ə,teɪt̬·əd/ *adj* • *Gordon became visibly agitated when asked about the minimum wage issue.* ○ *Many times the private hospitals transfer their terribly aggressive, agitated patients to us because they cannot handle them.*

agitation /ˌædʒ·ə'teɪ·ʃən/ *n* [U] • *He arrived home in a state of agitation.*

aglow /ə'gloʊ/ *adj* bright; shining • *His eyes were aglow with pleasure.*

agnostic /æg'nɑs·tɪk/ *n* [C] someone who believes that it is impossible to know whether or not God exists

ago /ə'goʊ/ *adv* [only after n; not gradable] back in the past; back in time from the present • *That was a few years ago.* ○ *Your mother* *called about an hour ago.* ∘ *Some time ago I read a book about that.* ∘ *Are you still seeing Vivian? No, we stopped seeing each other a long time ago.*

agonize /ˈæg·ə,naɪz/ *v* [I] to spend time anxiously trying to make a decision • *She agonized for days over whether she should take the job.*

agonizing /ˈæg·ə,naɪ·zɪŋ/ *adj* • *After years of agonizing debate, French-speaking Quebeckers rejected separation from the rest of Canada.*

agony /ˈæg·ə·ni/ *n* [C/U] extreme physical or mental pain or suffering, or a period of such suffering • *They put her on painkillers, but they didn't do enough, and she was in agony.* [U]

agree /əˈgriː/ *v* to have the same opinion, or to accept a suggestion or idea • *I agree with you.* [I] ∘ *We all agree on that point.* [I] ∘ *In settling the dispute, he agreed to pay $60,000 in damages.* [+ *to* infinitive] ∘ *Most economists agree that it would be unwise to cut taxes right now.* [+ *that* clause] ∘ *Both sides agreed to the terms of the peace treaty.* [I] ∘ *I agree with letting children learn at their own pace.* [I] • *If two sets of information agree, they are generally the same: Since their stories did not agree at all, he knew one of them was lying.* [I]

agreeable /əˈgriː·ə·bəl/ *adj* acceptable or satisfactory • *We prefer to reach a solution agreeable to all interested parties.* • *If someone is agreeable to doing something, they are willing to do it: We can close the deal tomorrow if your client is agreeable.*

agreement /əˈgriː·mənt/ *n* [C/U] the condition of having the same opinion, or a decision or arrangement between two or more people or groups to do something or to obey the same rules • *a new trade agreement* [C] ∘ *Both sides were in agreement on the basic terms, but many details still had to be worked out.* [U] ∘ *Leaders of both countries signed an agreement to exchange diplomats.* [C] ∘ *Let us help you to reach agreement.* [U]

□**agree with** /-ˈ--/ *v prep* [T] to cause (someone) to feel healthy and happy • *You both look great—marriage must agree with you.* ∘ *The fish dinner on our flight did not agree with me* (= made me feel sick).

agreeable /əˈgriː·ə·bəl/ *adj* pleasant; pleasing • *She has an agreeable personality.*

agreeably /əˈgriː·ə·bli/ *adv* [not gradable] with enjoyment or pleasure • *They were agreeably surprised to see that he'd come after all.*

agriculture /ˈæg·rə,kʌl·tʃər/ *n* [U] the practice or work of farming • *Agriculture and tourism are both important to the region's economy.*

agricultural /ˌæg·rəˈkʌl·tʃə·rəl/ *adj* • *Chicago was an important shipping point for agricultural products and livestock.*

aground /əˈgraʊnd/ *adv* [not gradable] (of a ship in water) touching the ground below the

water, causing the ship to become stuck • *The tanker ran aground and leaked 11 million gallons of crude oil.*

ah /ɑ/ *exclamation* used to show a sudden feeling, such as one of surprise, pleasure, or understanding • *Ah, so that's what the problem was!*

aha /ɑˈhɑ, əˈhɑ/ *exclamation* used to express pleasure at suddenly understanding or learning the truth about something • *Aha! So they were secretly married over a year ago!*

ahead IN FRONT /əˈhed/ *adv* [not gradable] (directly) in front • *She only had a few things in her shopping cart, so I told her she could go ahead of me in the checkout line.* • Ahead also means further along in development or achievement: *Sophie is way ahead of the rest of her class.*

ahead IN THE FUTURE /əˈhed/ *adv* in or into the future • *We have a lot of hard work ahead of us.* ∘ *You have to plan ahead when you're thinking of going to graduate school.* • We had a date for lunch, and I said I'd call her **ahead of time** (= in advance) *to decide where.*

ahold /əˈhoʊld/ *n* • If you **get ahold of** someone, you communicate with them: *I'm trying to get ahold of some of these people for our meeting tomorrow.*

aid /eɪd/ *n* [C/U] help or support, or something that provides it • *He gets around with the aid of a cane.* [U] ∘ *She went to the aid of a man trapped in his car.* [U] ∘ *A good dictionary can be a useful aid to understanding a new language.* [C] • Aid is often used to refer to help given in the form of food, money, medical supplies, etc., to a country or group of people that is in need or because of an emergency: *foreign aid* [U] ∘ *Aid for the flood victims was on the way.* [U]

aid /eɪd/ *v* [T] • *The project is designed to aid the homeless.* ∘ *He was aided in his research by his knowledge of Greek.*

aide /eɪd/ *n* [C] a person whose job is to help someone important, such as a member of a government or a military officer of high rank • *The senator asked an aide to distribute copies of his speech.*

AIDS /eɪdz/ *n* [U] *abbreviation for* acquired immune deficiency syndrome (= serious disease caused by a virus that destroys the body's natural protection from infection and can result in death)

ail /eɪl/ *v* [I/T] to feel or cause (someone) to feel ill, unhealthy, or weak • *I don't know what's ailing her.* [T]

ailing /ˈeɪ·lɪŋ/ *adj* [not gradable] unhealthy or weak, and not getting any better • *The plan was supposed to give a boost to our ailing economy.*

ailment /ˈeɪl·mənt/ *n* [C] an illness or health problem • *He was an alcoholic and was plagued by a variety of ailments.*

aim POINT /eɪm/ *v* [I/T] to point or direct (a

weapon or other object) toward someone or something • *I turned and saw a big man aiming a camera at me.* [T] • To aim something is also to direct it toward someone whom you want to influence or toward achieving something: *These ads are aimed at young people.* [T]

aim /eɪm/ *n* [U] the act of pointing a weapon toward something • *She raised her gun, took aim, and fired.*

aim INTEND /eɪm/ *v* [I] to plan for a specific purpose; intend • *The measures are aimed at preserving family life.* ○ *This book is not aimed at the serious reader.*

aim /eɪm/ *n* [C] a result that your plans or actions are intended to achieve • *The commission's aim was to convince workers of their extreme importance in ship production.*

aimless /'eɪm·ləs/ *adj* without having any clear purpose or specific reason • *aimless violence*

aimlessly /'eɪm·lə·sli/ *adv*

aimlessness /'eɪm·lə·snəs/ *n* [U]

ain't *not standard* /eɪnt/ *contraction of* **am not, is not, are not, has not,** or **have not** • *"Is Terry here?" "No, he ain't coming in today."*

air GAS /er, ær/ *n* [U] the mixture of gases that surrounds the earth and that we breathe • *Let's go outside for some fresh air.* • An **air bag** is a bag in a vehicle that very quickly fills with air if the vehicle is involved in an accident, in order to protect the driver or a passenger from injury. • **Air conditioning** is a system for keeping the air cool inside a building, vehicle, etc., with a special machine called an **air conditioner**. ○ *The restaurant is* **air-conditioned** (= equipped with an air conditioner to keep the air cool). • **Air pressure** is the force that air produces when it presses against any surface. • If a container is **airtight**, it is completely closed so that no air can get in or out: *Put the cookies in an airtight jar to keep them fresh.*

airless /'er·ləs, 'ær-/ *adj* (of an inside space) having little or no air from outside, and having no movement of air • *My hotel room was small, airless, and uncomfortable.*

air SPACE ABOVE /er, ær/ *n* [U] the space above, esp. high above, the ground • *Keith kicked the football high in the air.*

air FLIGHT /er, ær/ *n* [U] flight above the ground, esp. in an aircraft • *air travel* ○ *You can get there by train, but it's faster by air.* • An **air base** is a place for the storage, operation, and care of military aircraft. • Something that is **airborne** is in the air, or carried by air or wind or by an aircraft: *The plane was not yet airborne when the engine failed.* • An **airfare** is the price of a trip by aircraft. • An **air force** is the part of a country's military forces using aircraft in fighting a war. • An **airline** is a business that operates regular services for carrying passengers or goods by aircraft. • An **airliner** is a large passenger aircraft. • **Airmail** is a system of sending letters and pack-

ages by aircraft. • An **airplane** is a vehicle powered by engines and having wings on its sides that can fly above the ground. • An **airport** is a place where aircraft regularly take off and land, with buildings for passengers to wait in and equipment for controlling flights. • An **air raid** is an attack by enemy aircraft, usually dropping bombs.

air BROADCAST /er, ær/ *v* [I/T] to broadcast (something) on radio or television • *The game will be aired at 9 p.m. tomorrow.* [T]

air /er, ær/ *n* [U] • If a program or a person is on/off the air, they are/are not broadcasting on radio or television: *His show is on the air from 8 to 8:30 every Tuesday night.* • **Airtime** is the amount of time that someone or something has on television or radio: *The candidates complained that they weren't given enough airtime to debate the issues.* • **Airwaves** are the radio waves used for broadcasting radio and television programs, or more generally, radio or television broadcasting: *The president took to the television airwaves to explain the reasons for going to war.*

airing /'er·ɪŋ, 'ær-/ *n* [C] • *The third airing of the miniseries will begin next week.*

air MAKE KNOWN /er, ær/ *v* [T] to make (your opinions, complaints, etc.) known to other people • *The meeting gave us a chance to air our complaints.*

air MANNER /er, ær/ *n* [C] a manner or appearance • *She had an air of confidence.*

air CLEAN /er, ær/ *v* [I/T] to let air esp. from the outside come in (a room or other inside space) to make it smell cleaner, or to put (something) outside in the air to make it smell cleaner • *Let's open some windows and air out this place.* [M]

aircraft /'er·kræft, 'ær-/ *n* [C] *pl* **aircraft** any vehicle made to fly • An **aircraft carrier** is a large ship with a long, flat surface where military aircraft can take off and land.

airlift /'er·lɪft, 'ær-/ *n* [C] an operation organized to move supplies or people by aircraft to or from a place, esp. in a difficult or dangerous situation • *The airlift moved thousands of refugees away from the fighting.*

airlift /'er·lɪft, 'ær-/ *v* [T] • *They airlifted food and supplies to people stranded on the snow-covered mountains.*

airsick /'er·sɪk, 'ær-/ *adj* having the feeling that you will vomit because of the movement of an aircraft you are traveling in

airy /'er·i, 'ær·i/ *adj* spacious and light • *The new offices are bright and airy.*

aisle /aɪl/ *n* [C] a long, narrow space between rows of seats in an aircraft, theater, church, etc., or between the rows of shelves in a store

ajar /ə'dʒɑr/ *adj* (of a door) almost closed; slightly open • *I left the door ajar so that I could hear the baby.*

aka /ˌeɪˌkeɪ'eɪ/ *abbreviation for* also known as (= having as another name) • *James Brown,* *aka "the Godfather of Soul", is one of my musical heroes.*

akin /ə'kɪn/ *adj* having some of the same qualities; similar • *They speak a language akin to French.*

à la carte /ˌæl·ə'kɑrt, ˌɑl-/ *adj, adv* [not gradable] (of food in a restaurant) as separate dishes with different prices, rather than as a fixed, complete meal at a total price • *You get more choices if you order à la carte.*

alacrity /ə'læk·rət̬·i/ *n* [U] speed and eagerness • *He invited us all to have a drink, and we agreed with alacrity.*

à la mode /ˌæl·ə'moʊd, ˌɑl-/ *adj* served with ice cream • *pie à la mode*

alarm ANXIETY /ə'lɑrm/ *n* [U] sudden anxiety and fear, esp. that something very bad or dangerous might happen • *Nicholas detected a note of alarm in her voice.*

alarm /ə'lɑrm/ *v* [T] • *They are particularly alarmed by the growing threat of AIDS to minorities and children.*

alarming /ə'lɑr·mɪŋ/ *adj* • *A new report shows an alarming rise in the use of alcohol by teenagers.*

alarmist /ə'lɑr·məst/ *n* [C] a person who communicates anxiety and fear, esp. unnecessarily • *Some in the insurance industry consider Weiss an alarmist, but others think his predictions are accurate.*

alarm WARNING /ə'lɑrm/ *n* [C] a warning signal such as a loud noise or flashing light that gets your immediate attention, or a device that produces such a signal • *Firefighters said the tragedy could have been avoided if the house had had smoke alarms.* • An **alarm clock** is a clock with a device that you can set to make a noise at a particular time, esp. to wake you from sleep.

alas /ə'læs/ *exclamation old use* used to express sadness or regret • *Alas! What are we to do now?*

albino /æl'bɑɪ·noʊ/ *n* [C] *pl* **albinos** a person or animal having a condition that causes their skin and hair to appear white or very pale

album RECORDING /'æl·bəm/ *n* [C] a recording of several pieces of music • *Her new album includes two hit singles.*

album BOOK /'æl·bəm/ *n* [C] a book with pages for keeping photographs or other paper objects that you have collected and may want to look at in the future

alcohol /'æl·kə,hɔːl/ *n* [U] a liquid that is produced in making wine, beer, and LIQUOR and that can cause changes in behavior in people who drink it, and that is also used as a SOLVENT (= substance that dissolves another) and in fuel and medicines • *Most wines contain about 12% alcohol.*

alcoholic /ˌæl·kə'hɔː·lɪk, -'hɑl·ɪk/ *adj* • *This vodka has a high alcoholic content.*

alcoholic /ˌæl·kə'hɔː·lɪk, -'hɑl·ɪk/ *n* [C] a person who is unable to give up the habit of drinking too much alcohol

alcoholism /'æl·kə,hɔː,lɪz·əm, -,hɑl,ɪz-/ *n* [U] the condition of being unable to stop drinking too much alcohol, often causing you to be unable to live and work in society • *Alcoholism cost me my job.*

alcove /'æl·koʊv/, **recess** *n* [C] a small space in a room, formed by one part of a wall being farther back than the parts on each side

alderman /'ɔːl·dər·mən/ *n* [C] *pl* **-men** /'ɔːl·dər·mən, -,men/ an elected member of some city governments

ale /eɪl/ *n* [C] a type of beer, esp. one that is darker and more bitter than other beers

alert /ə'lɜrt/ *adj* quick to see, understand, and act in a particular situation • *When you're driving, you must stay alert.* ○ *We had to be alert to any danger signs in the economy.*

alert /ə'lɜrt/ *n* [C/U] a warning to people to get ready to deal with something dangerous • *The police were on the alert for* (= watching carefully for) *any sign of trouble.* [U]

alert /ə'lɜrt/ *v* [T] • *The auto company mailed letters to owners of that model car, alerting them of safety risks.*

algae /'æl·dʒiː/ *pl n* very simple plants that grow in or near water and do not have ordinary leaves or roots

algebra /'æl·dʒə·brə/ *n* [U] a part of mathematics in which signs and letters represent numbers

alias /'eɪ·liː·əs/ *n* [C], *adv* a false name that someone uses in order to keep their real name secret • *He admitted that the name Rupert Sharp was an alias.* ○ *Paul Sopworth, alias* (= also known as) *Rupert Sharp, went to prison today.*

alibi /'æl·ə,bɑɪ/ *n* [C] proof that someone who is thought to have committed a crime could not have done it, esp. the fact or claim that they were in another place at the time it happened • *An alibi is also an excuse for something: You're late again—what's your alibi this time?*

alien /'eɪ·liː·ən/ *n* [C] a person who lives in a country but is not a CITIZEN (= member of a country with specific rights) • *An alien is also a creature from a different planet.*

alien /'eɪ·liː·ən/ *adj* coming from a different country, race, or group; foreign • *alien customs*

alienate /'eɪ·liː·ə,neɪt/ *v* [T] to cause (someone, or esp. a group of people) to stop supporting someone or to stop feeling welcome • *All these changes to the newspaper have alienated its old readers.*

alienation /ˌeɪ·liː·ə'neɪ·ʃən/ *n* [U] • *The alienation of young adults has lowered the number of people who vote.*

alight GET OUT /ə'lɑɪt/ *v* [I] to get out of a vehicle • *He helped her alight from the train.*

alight TO LAND /ə'lɑɪt/ *v* [I] (of something flying) to come down and land • *The butterfly alighted on a flower.*

align /ə'laɪn/ v [T] to put (two or more things) into a straight line • *You need to align the numbers properly in a column.* ○ *(fig.) Business leaders are aligned with* (= agree with) *the president on this issue.*

alignment /ə'laɪn·mənt/ n [C/U] • *You hear that noise because the wheels are out of alignment.* [U]

alike SIMILAR /ə'laɪk/ adj similar; like each other • *You and your father don't look very much alike.*

alike EQUALLY /ə'laɪk/ adv [only after n; not gradable] equally; both • *She received hundreds of letters of support from friends and strangers alike.*

alimony /'æl·ə,moʊ·ni/ n [U] a regular amount of money that a court of law orders a person to pay to his or her partner after a DIVORCE (= marriage that has legally ended) or a legal separation

alive /ə'laɪv/ adj [not gradable] living; having life; not dead • *I survived the accident with minor injuries, and I was happy to be alive.* • Alive can also mean active and energetic or exciting: *The club really comes alive on weekends.* • *Traditional jazz is still* **alive and well/kicking** (= active) *in New Orleans.*

alkali /'æl·kə,laɪ/ n [C] pl **alkalis** or **alkalies** specialized a substance that has the opposite effect or chemical behavior of an acid

alkaline /'æl·kə,laɪn/ adj • *alkaline soil*

all EVERY ONE /ɔːl/ adj every one of, or the complete number of • *All four of her children are under six.* ○ *Not all my friends approved of what I did.* • If a person is **on all fours**, they have both knees and hands on the ground: *Shirelle was on all fours, looking for her contact lens.* • **All manner of** something means a great variety of types of it: *He's survived all manner of difficulties.* • **All of** means only: *His book has sold all of 200 copies.* • People say **of** all **people/things/places** to mean especially: *I thought that you, of all people, would believe me* • LP AMOUNTS, DETERMINERS

all /ɔːl/ pronoun • *All of her kids have been in jail.* • All also means the one thing: *Speed is all that matters.* ○ *All I need is a hot shower.* • *There were 550 people there* **all told** (= in total).

all COMPLETELY /ɔːl/ adv [not gradable] completely or wholly • *This coat is all wool.* ○ *Is the milk all gone?* ○ *Did you drink it all?* ○ *Don't get all upset.* • All is also used after a number to mean that both teams or players in a game have equal points: *The score at halftime was 10 all.* • **All at once** and **all of a sudden** mean quickly and without warning: *All at once we heard a loud noise.* • *Do you think he's been cheating us* **all along** (= from the beginning)? • If something is **all over** a place, it is everywhere in that place: *Soon the news was all over town.* • When something is **all over**, it's completely finished: *I used to have a thriving business and a happy marriage, but that's all over*

now. • If something is **all the same to** you, it is not important to you which of several things is chosen: *We could eat at home or go out—it's all the same to me.* • *She made me feel as if she had* **all the time in the world** (= an unlimited amount of time). • **All too** means more than is desirable: *The week passed all too quickly and it was time to go back home.* • For this sauce, fresh basil is the **all-important** ingredient (= the most or very important one). • If something is **all-inclusive**, it includes everything related to it: *an all-inclusive vacation package* • An **all-star** team is one that is full of excellent players.

all /ɔːl/ adj [not gradable] • *I've been trying all day to contact you.*

Allah /'æl·ə, 'ɑl·ə, ɑ'lɑ/ n [U] the Islamic name for God

all-American /,ɔː·lə'mer·ɪ·kən, -'mær-/ adj having or showing the values that are typical of Americans, or made up completely of the best American things or people • *He made the all-American team in his last two years of college.*

all-American, **All-American** /,ɔː·lə'mer·ɪ·kən, -'mær-/ n [C] • *He was a great athlete, and an academic all-American as well.*

all-around /'ɔːl·lə,raʊnd/, **all-round** /'ɔːl·raʊnd/ adj [not gradable] having a good variety of skills or abilities • *Gretzky was an all-around great hockey player.*

allay /æ'leɪ, ə-/ v [T] to make (a negative emotion) less strong or (a problem) less difficult • *I was nervous, but seeing her allayed my fears.*

allege /ə'ledʒ/ v [T] (esp. in legal matters) to state that (something bad) is a fact without giving proof • *It was alleged that Johnson had struck Mr. Rahim on the head.*

alleged /ə'ledʒd/ adj [not gradable] • *It took years for the alleged criminals to prove their innocence.*

allegedly /ə'ledʒ·əd·li/ adv [not gradable] • *She allegedly murdered her husband.*

allegation /,æl·ə'geɪ·ʃən/ n [C] (esp. in legal matters) a statement, made without giving proof, that someone has done something wrong or illegal • *The allegations of corruption were not true.*

allegiance /ə'liː·dʒəns/ n [C/U] loyalty and support for a leader, country, group, or belief • *To become a citizen, you must swear allegiance to the United States.* [U]

allegory /'æl·ə,gɔːr·i, -,goʊr·i/ n [C/U] a story, play, poem, picture, or other work in which the characters and events represent particular qualities or ideas, related to morality, religion, or politics

allegorical /,æl·ə'gɔːr·ɪ·kəl, -'gɑr-/ adj • *Apples represent people in this allegorical contest between wilderness and civilization.*

allergy /'æl·ər·dʒi/ n [C] a condition that makes a person become ill or develop skin or breathing problems because they have eaten certain foods or come in contact with certain substances • *Your rash is caused by an allergy to peanuts.*

allergic /ə'lɜr·dʒɪk/ *adj* • *I'm allergic to cats.*

alleviate /ə'liː·viː,eɪt/ *v* [T] to make (esp. pain or problems) less severe • *The drugs did nothing to alleviate her discomfort.*

alley /'æl·i/, **alleyway** /'æl·iː,weɪ/ *n* [C] a narrow road or path between buildings, esp. between the backs of buildings • *I ran down the alley and up the back stairs.*

alliance /ə'laɪ·əns/ *n* See at ALLY

allied /'æl·aɪd, ə'laɪd/ *adj* See at ALLY

alligator /'æl·ə,geɪt·ər/, *short form* **gator** *n* [C] a large, hard-skinned REPTILE (= type of animal) with a long nose that is shorter and slightly wider than that of a CROCODILE and which lives in and near rivers and lakes in the parts of the US and China

allocate /'æl·ə,keɪt/ *v* [T] to give (something) as a share of a total amount • *State funds will not be allocated to the program next year.*

allocation /,æl·ə'keɪ·ʃən/ *n* [C/U] the act or process of giving out parts of a whole, or a part given out in this way • *The allocation of space in this office is unusual.* [U]

allot /ə'lɑt/ *v* [T] -tt- to give (esp. a share of something available) for a particular purpose • *The board allotted $5000 to the recreation center.*

allotted /ə'lɑt·əd/ *adj* [not gradable] • *Use only the allotted time.*

allotment /ə'lɑt·mənt/ *n* [C/U] • *There are huge differences in the allotment of highway funds around the state.* [U]

allow PERMIT /ə'laʊ/ *v* [T] to let (someone) do something or let (something) happen; permit • *You're not allowed to talk during the exam.* ○ *Are you allowed in the building on weekends?* ○ *How could anyone allow a child to be abused?*

allowable /ə'laʊ·ə·bəl/ *adj* • *Our well water has nitrates above the allowable level.*

allow MAKE AVAILABLE /ə'laʊ/ *v* [T] to make (esp. time or space) available for something • *He didn't allow enough time to finish the test.* ○ *Be sure to allow room in your bags for the souvenirs you'll want to bring home.*

allowance /ə'laʊ·əns/ *n* [C] the amount of something available or needed for a particular purpose • *What is the recommended daily allowance of vitamin A?* • An allowance is also money given by parents to a child every week that the child can spend.

□**allow for** /-'--/ *v prep* [T] to take (something) into consideration; plan for (something) • *Does your insurance allow for home nursing care?*

alloy /'æl,ɔɪ, ə'lɔɪ/ *n* [C] a metal that is made by mixing together two or more metals, or a metal and another substance • *Brass is an alloy of copper and zinc.*

all right SATISFACTORY , *not standard* **alright** /ɔːl'raɪt/ *adj*, *adv* [not gradable] (in a way that

is) satisfactory or reasonably good • *The movie was all right—not great, though.* ○ *Are you managing all right in your new job?* • (*slang*) **All right** can be used to express praise or happiness over what has been said or done: *"Did you hear I won that writing contest?" "All right!"*

all right SAFE , *not standard* **alright** /ɔːl'raɪt/ *adj*, *adv* [not gradable] safe, well, or not harmed • *She was really sick for a while but she's all right now.*

all right AGREED, *not standard* **alright** /ɔːl 'raɪt, ɔːl'raɪt/ *exclamation*, *adj* [not gradable] used to show that something is agreed, understood, or acceptable • *I'd rather not go to Jane's party if that's all right with you.* • You can answer **It's/That's all right** to someone who has just thanked you for something or just said they are sorry for something they have done, as a way of showing that the matter is not important to you.

all right CERTAINLY , *not standard* **alright** /ɔːl 'raɪt/ *adv* [not gradable] *infml* certainly or without any doubt • *"Are you sure he was the guy who hit you?" "It was him all right."*

allude to /ə'luːd·tə, -tʊ, -,tuː/ *v prep* [T] to refer to (someone or something) in a brief or indirect way • *He alluded to problems with the new computers.*

allure /ə'lʊr/ *n* [U] attraction, charm, or excitement • *The allure of the stage drew him back to acting.*

alluring /ə'lʊr·ɪŋ/ *adj* • *There's something alluring about motorcycles.*

allusion /ə'luː·ʒən/ *n* [C] a brief or indirect reference • *He made some allusion to the years they lived apart.*

ally /'æl·aɪ, ə'laɪ/ *n* [C] a country that has agreed to give help and support to another, esp. during a war, or a person who helps and supports someone else • *North Korea is one of China's closest allies.*

ally /ə'laɪ, 'æl·aɪ/ *v* [T always + adv/prep] • *I refused to ally myself with that mob.*

alliance /ə'laɪ·əns/ *n* [C/U] a group of countries, political parties, or people who work together because of shared interests or aims, or the act of forming such a group • *Switzerland does not belong to any military alliance.* [C] ○ *Alliance against our common enemy is our only hope for survival.* [U]

allied /'æl·aɪd, ə'laɪd/ *adj* connected, esp. by having many things in common • *Allied forces invaded the capital.* ○ *It takes a lot of enthusiasm allied with a love of children to make a good teacher.*

alma mater /,æl·mə'mɑt·ər, ,ɑl-/ *n* [C usually sing] the school, college, or university where you studied, or the official song of a school, college, or university • *Former students are asked to donate money to their alma mater.*

almanac /'ɔːl·mə,næk, 'æl-/ *n* [C] a book published every year that contains facts and information, esp. tables showing the days, weeks, and months, important holidays, and times when the sun and moon rise, or a book containing facts and information about a particular subject • *a baseball almanac*

almighty /ɔːlˈmɑɪṭ·i/ *adj* [not gradable] having the power to do everything • *the Almighty Creator* • Almighty also means very strong and powerful: *the almighty dollar*

Almighty /ɔːlˈmɑɪṭ·i/ *n* [U] God • *We prayed to the Almighty for mercy.*

almond /ˈɔː·mənd, ˈɔːl-; ˈɑm·ənd, ˈɑl·mənd/ *n* [C] an edible, oval nut with a hard shell, or the tree that it grows on

almost /ˈɔːl·moʊst, ɔːlˈmoʊst/ *adv* [not gradable] nearly but not quite • *It'll cost almost as much to repair your computer as to buy a new one.* ○ *We were bitten by mosquitoes almost every night.*

alms /ɑmz, ɑlmz/ *pl n old use* clothing, food, or money that is given to poor people

aloft /əˈlɔːft/ *adv* [not gradable] in the air or in a higher position • *Her kite remained aloft for hours.*

alone WITHOUT PEOPLE /əˈloʊn/ *adj, adv* without other people • *She decided to climb the mountain alone.* ○ *We're alone together at last, my darling.* • Compare LONELY.

alone ONLY /əˈloʊn/ *adj* [not gradable] without any others, or only • *I based my decision on her recommendation alone.* • LP WORDS WITH THE MEANING "ONE" at ONE SINGLE

along BESIDE /əˈlɔːŋ/ *prep* in the same direction as, or beside • *We walked along the canal path.* • Along also means at a particular point or continuing to go on: *My office is the third door along the hallway on the left.* • *My sister works in publishing, and I'm hoping to do something* **along the same lines** (= similar). • *I've been here for thirty years, and I've picked up a lot of experience* **along the way** (= during this time).

along FORWARD /əˈlɔːŋ/ *adv* [not gradable] toward a direction or goal; forward • *You wait ages for a bus, then three come along all at once.* ○ *How far along are you with your homework?*

along WITH OTHERS /əˈlɔːŋ/ *adv* [not gradable] with the person or persons already mentioned • *Why don't you take him along?* • **Along with** means in addition to: *Now we've got hospital bills along with our usual expenses.*

alongside /əˈlɔːŋˌsɑɪd/ *prep, adv* [not gradable] beside, or together with • *They put out cookies alongside the cake.*

aloof /əˈluːf/ *adj, adv* (of a person) not taking part in things, esp. in a way that seems unfriendly • *Is she aloof and arrogant or just shy?* ○ *When they argued, I remained aloof.*

aloud /əˈlɑʊd/ *adv* [not gradable] in a voice loud enough to be heard • *I wondered aloud whether it would be worth the wait.*

alphabet /ˈæl·fəˌbet/ *n* [C] a set of letters arranged in a fixed order that is used for writing a language • *the Cyrillic/Hebrew alphabet*

alphabetical /ˌæl·fəˈbeṭ·ɪ·kəl/ *adj* [not gradable] • *The names are in alphabetical order.*

alphabetically /ˌæl·fəˈbeṭ·ɪ·kli/ *adv* [not gradable] • *Recipes are arranged alphabetically by type of food.*

alpine /ˈæl·pɑɪn/ *adj* relating to high, mountainous areas, esp. the Alps (= the highest mountains in Europe) • *Alpine skiing* ○ *an alpine meadow*

already /ɔːlˈred·i/ *adv* [not gradable] earlier than the time expected, in a short time, or before the present time • *Are you buying Christmas cards already? It's only September!* ○ *I've already seen that movie.* • Already can also mean now: *It's bad enough already—don't make it any worse.*

alright /ɔːlˈrɑɪt, ˈɔːl·rɑɪt/ *adj, adv* [not gradable], *exclamation not standard* ALL RIGHT

also /ˈɔːl·soʊ/ *adv* [not gradable] in addition • *She's a photographer and also writes books.* • Also can also mean similarly: *That's funny, I'm also on a diet.*

altar /ˈɔːl·tər/ *n* [C] a type of table used in religious ceremonies • An **altar boy** is a boy who helps a priest in worship services.

alter /ˈɔːl·tər/ *v* [I/T] to change (a characteristic), often slightly, or to cause this to happen • *The coat was too long, so I took it back to the store to have it altered.* [T]

alteration /ˌɔːl·təˈreɪ·ʃən/ *n* [C/U] • *I had to make some alterations in my research paper.* [C]

altercation /ˌɔːl·tərˈkeɪ·ʃən/ *n* [C] a loud argument or disagreement • *Phil got into an altercation with his partner.*

alternate /ˈɔːl·tərˌneɪt/ *v* [I/T] to cause (two things) to happen or exist one after the other repeatedly • *The children alternated between being excited and being tired.* [I] ○ *I like to alternate physical and intellectual activities.* [T]

alternate /ˈɔːl·tər·nət/ *adj* [not gradable] (of sets of two) every second, or every other • *I visit my father on alternate weekends.*

alternate /ˈɔːl·tər·nət/ *n* [C] one that can take the place of another • *David was too sick to attend, so Janet served as his alternate.*

alternately /ˈɔːl·tər·nət·li/ *adv* in a manner in which two things each replace the other • *The movie is alternately depressing and amusing.*

alternative /ɔːlˈtɜr·nəṭ·ɪv/ *n* [C] something that is different, esp. from what is usual; a choice • *You can make it look good by comparing it to a crummy alternative.* ○ *I have no alternative but to ask you to leave.*

alternative /ɔːlˈtɜr·nəṭ·ɪv/ *adj* [not gradable] • *People stay because they don't have alternative opportunities.* • Alternative medicine is a wide range of treatments for medical conditions that people use instead of, or with, Western medicine.

alternatively /ɔːlˈtɜr·nəṭ·ɪv·li/ *adv* [not gradable] • *We could go to the Mexican restaurant,* *or alternatively* (= instead of that), *we could try that new Italian place.*

although /ɔːlˈðoʊ/ *conjunction* despite the fact that, or despite being • *He decided to go, although I begged him not to.*

altitude /ˈæl·təˌtuːd/ *n* [C] height above sea level • *The city of Denver is situated at an altitude of almost exactly one mile.*

alto /ˈæl·toʊ/ *n* [C] *pl* **altos** a woman's or boy's singing voice in the range lower than a SO-PRANO, or a singer or musical instrument with this range

altogether /ˌɔːl·təˈɡeð·ər/ *adv* [not gradable] completely or in total • *The train slowed down and then stopped altogether.* ○ *He was altogether exhausted.* ○ *Altogether, she gave away some $60 million in her lifetime.*

altruism /ˈæl·truˌɪz·əm/ *n* [U] the attitude of caring about the good of others, leading to acts that help them although you do not gain anything by doing them • *Nobody believes those people are donating money to the president's party purely out of altruism.*

altruistic /ˌæl·truˈɪs·tɪk/ *adj* • *altruistic motives*

aluminum /əˈluː·mə·nəm/, *Br* **aluminium** /ˌæl·jʊˈmɪn·iː·əm/ *n* [U] a light, silver-colored metal used esp. for making containers, cooking equipment, and aircraft parts

alumni /əˈlʌmˌnɑɪ/ *pl n* men and women who have completed their studies esp. at a college or university • *a reunion of Yale alumni of the class of 1990* ○ *Vassar alumni* • USAGE: Alumni can be used to refer to men only, and in that case alumnae is used to refer to women only, but more often alumni is used to refer to either or both sexes where both attend the same school. The singular forms are alumnus for a man, and alumna for a woman.

always /ˈɔːl·wiːz, -weɪz/ *adv* [not gradable] every time, all the time, or forever • *He always enjoyed having wine with dinner.* ○ *You always try to do your best.* ○ *I'll always remember her.* ○ *She's always* (= very often) *late.* • Always is sometimes used after can or could to suggest another possibility: *If you don't like what's on TV, you can always change the channel.*

Alzheimer's (disease) /ˈɔːlts·hɑɪ·mərz (dɪˌziːz)/ *n* [U] a disease that results in the gradual loss of memory, speech, movement, and the ability to think clearly, and that is common esp. among older people

am BE /æm, əm, m/ *v* (used with I) BE • *I am 48 years old.* ○ *I am getting ready now.*

AM RADIO /ˈeɪˈem/ *n* [U] *abbreviation for* one of two main types of radio waves used to broadcast in the US • *Most of the talk radio programs can be found on AM stations.* • Compare FM.

a.m., A.M. /ˈeɪˈem/ *adv* [not gradable] used when referring to a time between twelve o'clock at night and twelve o'clock in the middle of the day; past the middle of the night, or in the morning • *We fly out of New York late in*

the evening and arrive in London at 7 a.m. the next morning. • Compare P.M. LP TIME

amalgamate /əˈmæl·ɡəˌmeɪt/ *v* [I/T] (of separate organizations or groups) to join together or unite, or to cause (separate organizations or groups) to join together • *The two towns amalgamated to combine their police and fire protection.* [I]

amass /əˈmæs/ *v* [T] to gather a large amount of (something, esp. money) by collecting it over a period of time • *By the time he was 40, he had amassed a fortune.*

amateur /ˈæm·əˌtɜr, -əˌtʃʊr, -ət·ər/ *adj* taking part in an activity for pleasure and not as a job, or (of an activity) done for pleasure and not as a job • *He was an amateur archaeologist.* • Compare **professional** at PROFESSION.

amateur /ˈæm·əˌtɜr, -əˌtʃʊr, -ət·ər/ *n* [C] • *The sailing competition is for wealthy amateurs.* • An amateur is also someone who lacks skill in what they do: *Some of the people who show up at practice shooting ranges are real amateurs.* • Compare **professional** at PROFESSION.

amateurish /ˌæm·əˈtɜr·ɪʃ, -ˈtʃʊr·ɪʃ/ *adj* performed without much skill • *The movie drags along, made even worse by amateurish acting.*

amaze /əˈmeɪz/ *v* [T] to cause (someone) to be extremely surprised • *The prices they're getting for vegetables just amaze me.* ○ *I'm amazed at how well your little girl can read.*

amazement /əˈmeɪz·mənt/ *n* [U] • *Much to my amazement, she liked the idea.*

amazing /əˈmeɪ·zɪŋ/ *adj* • *It's pretty amazing how much top athletes get paid.*

ambassador /æmˈbæs·əd·ər/ *n* [C] an official who represents their own country in a foreign country • *the US ambassador to Sweden*

ambidextrous /ˌæm·bɪˈdek·strəs/ *adj* able to use both your right and left hand equally well

ambience, ambiance /ˈæm·biː·əns, ˌɑm·biːˈɑs/ *n* [U] the character of a place or the quality it seems to have • *The city's ambience, particularly on the waterfront, is changing quickly.*

ambiguous /æmˈbɪɡ·jə·wəs/ *adj* having or expressing more than one possible meaning, sometimes intentionally • *The movie's ending is ambiguous.*

ambiguity /ˌæm·bəˈɡjuː·ət̬·i/ *n* [C/U] • *This is a first step toward clarifying things, but there are still many ambiguities.* [C]

ambition /æmˈbɪʃ·ən/ *n* [C/U] a strong desire for success, achievement, power, or wealth • *His presidential ambitions were frustrated in the 1980s.* [C] ○ *No one ever accused him of lacking ambition.* [U]

ambitious /æmˈbɪʃ·əs/ *adj* • *Even as a young man he was ambitious and self-assured.* • If you describe an activity as ambitious, you mean that it involves a lot of effort or expense: *It was an ambitious project to restore the public parks.*

ambivalent /æmˈbɪv·ə·lənt/ *adj* having two opposing feelings at the same time, or being uncertain about how you feel • *My wife is a devout church-goer, but I have ambivalent feelings about religion.*

ambivalence /æmˈbɪv·ə·ləns/ *n* [U]

amble /ˈæm·bəl/ *v* [I always + adv/prep] to walk in a slow and relaxed way • *The couple ambled along, arm in arm.*

ambulance /ˈæm·bjə·ləns, -ˌlæns/ *n* [C] a vehicle specially equipped to take injured or sick people to the hospital

ambulatory /ˈæm·bjə·ləˌtɔːr·i, -ˌtoʊr·i/ *adj* (of people being treated for an injury or illness) able to walk, and, when treated in a hospital, usually not staying for the night in a bed • *We will soon be opening two new ambulatory care facilities.*

ambush /ˈæm·bʊʃ/ *n* [C] a sudden and surprising attack on a person or group by one or more people who have been hiding and waiting for them • *Seven commandos were killed in an ambush.*

ambush /ˈæm·bʊʃ/ *v* [T] • *The Air Cavalry was ambushed and suffered big losses.*

AME Church /ˌeɪˌemˈiː/ *n* [U] *abbreviation for* **African Methodist Episcopal Church**, see at AFRICAN

amen /ɑˈmen, eɪ-/ *exclamation, n* [C] (said or sung at the end of some prayers or religious songs) it is so • *You can say amen to show that you agree strongly with something that someone has just said: "I wouldn't bring up children again for all the world." "Amen."*

amenable /əˈmiː·nə·bəl, -ˈmen·ə-/ *adj* willing to accept or be influenced by a suggestion • *He was amenable to suggestion, and really worked hard to improve himself.*

amend /əˈmend/ *v* [T] to change the words of (esp. a law or a legal document) • *The terms of the contract were amended in later years.*

amendment /əˈmend·mənt/ *n* [C] • *The president opposes a constitutional amendment that would ban abortions.*

amenity /əˈmen·əʈ·i, əˈmiː·nəʈ·i/ *n* [C usually pl] something intended to make life more pleasant or comfortable for people • *Straus established employee amenities such as restrooms, medical care, and a lunchroom.*

American /əˈmer·ə·kən, əˈmær-/ *n* [C], *adj* (a person) of or coming from the United States, or of or coming from North America or South America • **American English** is the English language as it is spoken and written in the US. ⏩ BRITISH ENGLISH AND AMERICAN ENGLISH PRONUNCIATION • An **American Indian** (also **Native American**) is someone who has a member of their family who belonged to one of the groups of people that originally lived in North America before the Europeans arrived.

Americanize /əˈmer·ə·kəˌnɑɪz, əˈmær-/ *v* [T] to make (someone or something) more typical of Americans in appearance, customs, or language • *In the 1890s, Jewish immigrants into* the U.S.A. *organized a night school to help them become Americanized.*

amiable /ˈeɪ·miː·ə·bəl/ *adj* pleasant and friendly • *He was amiable and charming, and he possessed an ability to make people feel comfortable in his presence.*

amicable /ˈæm·ɪ·kə·bəl/ *adj* friendly in attitude, or (of decisions or agreements) achieved with friendly attitudes and without unpleasant argument • *Wagner predicted the whole issue would be resolved in an amicable manner.*

amicably /ˈæm·ɪ·kə·bli/ *adv* • *They stayed together almost a year and parted amicably.*

amid /əˈmɪd/, **amidst** /əˈmɪdst, əˈmɪtst/ *prep* in the middle of or surrounded by; among • *Pope John Paul arrived in New Delhi amid tight security to begin a 10-day tour of India.*

amiss /əˈmɪs/ *adj* not right; not suitable or as expected • *He suspected something was amiss.*

ammonia /əˈmoʊn·jə/ *n* [U] a gas or liquid with a strong smell, having various industrial uses such as in cleaning

ammunition /ˌæm·jəˈnɪʃ·ən/, *infml* **ammo** /ˈæm·oʊ/ *n* [U] objects such as bullets and bombs, used to injure and kill people or animals and to destroy things • *(fig.) The president's endorsement of the crime bill has deprived his opponents of ammunition (= something that could have been used to attack him with) to paint him as soft on crime.*

amnesia /æmˈniː·ʒə/ *n* [U] *medical* loss of the ability to remember

amnesty /ˈæm·nə·sti/ *n* [C/U] a decision by a government to forgive people who have committed particular illegal acts or crimes, and not to punish them • *The government declared a general amnesty for its political prisoners and freed over 200 men and women.* [C]

among /əˈmʌŋ/, **amongst** /əˈmʌŋst/ *prep* in the middle of or surrounded by • *She felt lonely among all these strange people.* • *Among also means as part of a group or in the group of people or things named: They discussed it among themselves.* ○ *Among the problems we have to deal with, improving education is probably the most difficult.*

amoral /eɪˈmɔːr·əl, -ˈmɑr-/ *adj* [not gradable] without moral principles • *A thief and a swindler, his approach to life was thoroughly amoral.*

amorous /ˈæm·ə·rəs/ *adj* *literary* of or expressing sexual desire • *amorous adventures*

amorphous /əˈmɔːr·fəs, eɪ-/ *adj* having no fixed form or shape; not clear or not determined • *Plans for a 40-acre shopping center section remain so amorphous that the project has been shelved.*

amount /əˈmɑʊnt/ *n* [C] the degree to which something is a lot or a little; how much something is • *She's made a tremendous amount of progress since the accident.* ○ *He liked to carry a large amount of money around with him.*

amount to /əˈmɑʊnt·tə, -ˌtuː/ *v prep* [T] to add

WORDS THAT DESCRIBE AMOUNTS

Words like *some, little,* and *few* describe how much of something is being referred to. Different words are used depending on the type of amount. Some words are used only with singular countable nouns, some with plural countable nouns, and some with uncountable nouns.

Words that refer to total amounts: <u>every</u>, <u>all</u>, <u>each</u>, <u>both</u>

• for three or more things

Every is used with a singular [C] noun to refer to all the members of a group.

Every *child needs affection.* • *I worked* **every** *day last week.*

All is used with plural [C] nouns and with [U] nouns to refer to every member of a group or to everything of a particular kind.

All *children should receive an education.* • **All** *meat is rich in protein.*

All is also used with some singular [C] nouns to refer to the whole of a period of time.

I worked **all** *day.*

• for two or more things

Each is used with singular [C] nouns to refer to the members of a group individually.

He had a cup of coffee in **each** *hand.* • *I checked* **each** *page carefully.*

• for two things

Both is used with plural [C] nouns.

She held onto the rope with **both** *hands.*

Words that refer to amounts that are not exact: <u>some</u>, <u>any</u>

Some is used with plural [C] nouns, with [U] nouns in positive statements, and in questions to which the answer will probably be "yes."

We had **some** *problems.* • *I bought* **some** *bread.* • *Would you like* **some** *coffee?*

Any is used with plural [C] nouns and with [U] nouns in negative statements, in questions, and in statement to refer to one of something when it is not important which one.

I don't think we have **any** *candy left.* • *Do you have* **any** *suggestions?* • **Any** *drink will do as long as it's cold.*

Words that refer to a large amount: <u>many</u>, <u>much</u>, <u>a lot of</u>, <u>lots of</u>, <u>most</u>

Many is used with plural [C] nouns to refer to a large number of something.

Many *tourists visit the park.* • *There aren't* **many** *tickets left.*

Much is used with [U] nouns to refer to a large amount. It is used especially in negative statements, in questions, and after the words *so, too,* and *as.*

I don't have **much** *cash on me.* • *Will it take* **much** *time?* • *There's too* **much** *furniture in this room.*

A lot of and, informally, **lots of** are used with plural [C] nouns to refer to a large number, or with [U] nouns to refer to a large amount.

He asked **a lot of** *questions.* • *I have* **a lot of** *work to do.* • *I can fit* **lots of** *stuff in this bag.*

Most is used with plural [C] nouns and with [U] nouns for a number or amount of something that is larger than any other.

Most *trains arrive on time.* • **Most** *gold is used to make jewelry.*

Words that refer to a small amount: <u>few</u>, <u>little</u>, <u>a few</u>, <u>a little</u>, <u>several</u>

Few and **a few** are used with plural [C] nouns. **Little** and **a little** are used with [U] nouns. **Few** and **little** are used in negative statements to mean "not many" or "not much."

Few *people realized who she was.* • *We've had very* **little** *snow this year.*

A few and **a little** are used in positive statements to mean "some."

We invited **a few** *friends over.* • *Drink* **a little** *water.*

Several is used with plural [C] nouns to refer to an approximate number that is more than two but is not large.

He made several attempts to call.

Words that compare amounts: more/most, fewer/fewest, less/least

More and **most** are used with plural [C] nouns to refer to a larger number, or with [U] nouns to refer to a larger amount.

I scored the most points on the team this year. • *Ken has more luggage than me.*

More can also refer to an additional number or amount without comparing.

Would you like more cake?

Fewer and **fewest** are used with plural [C] nouns to refer to a smaller number of something.

They're offering fewer flight to Boston than they used to.

Less and **least** are used with [U] nouns to refer to a smaller amount.

I had less money than I needed.

A word that refers to the amount that is needed: enough
Enough is used with plural [C] nouns and with [U] nouns.

Do we have enough chairs? • *There wasn't enough time to finish.*

A word that refers to a negative amount: no
No is used with singular [C] nouns, plural [C] nouns, and [U] nouns.

I had no chance to explain. • *He left no instructions.* • *There's no ice left.*

---

up to, be in total, be equal to, or be the same as • *Federal and state costs for building and operating prisons amounted to $25 billion.* • To **amount to** something is to become successful or important: *He's lazy, and he'll never amount to anything.*

amp /æmp/, *specialized* **ampere** /'æm·pɪr/ *n* [C] a unit of measurement of the strength of an electrical current

amphetamine /æm'feṭ·ə,miːn, -mɪn/ *n* [C] a drug that is used as a STIMULANT (= a substance to make the mind or body more active) and is often used illegally

amphibian /æm'fɪb·iː·ən/ *n* [C] a type of animal that lives both on land and in water • *Frogs and turtles are amphibians.*

amphibious /æm'fɪb·iː·əs/ *adj* [not gradable] able to live or operate on land and in water • *Amphibious military vehicles were used to land troops on the beach.*

amphitheater, **amphitheatre** /'æm·fə,θiː·əṭ·ər, 'æm·pə-/ *n* [C] a circular or oval area around which rows of seats are arranged on a steep slope, esp. for watching the performance of plays and musical entertainment outside

ample /'æm·pəl/ *adj* enough, or more than enough, or (esp. of body size) large • *There will be ample opportunity for everyone here to speak.*

amply /'æm·pli/ *adv* • *The research was amply funded.*

amplify /'æm·plə,fɑɪ/ *v* [T] to increase the strength of (a sound); make louder • *Electric guitars are amplified through loudspeakers.* • To amplify is also to add to the information

given in (something): *This study amplifies earlier research.*

amplification /,æm·plə·fə'keɪ·ʃən/ *n* [C/U] • *sound amplification* [U]

amplifier /'æm·plə,fɑɪ·ər/ *n* [C] an electronic device that strengthens the electric signal used to carry sound

amputate /'æm·pjə,teɪt/ *v* [I/T] to cut off (esp. part of the body) • *Doctors had to amputate his leg below the knee.* [T]

amputation /,æm·pjə'teɪ·ʃən/ *n* [C/U] • *Frostbite led to the amputation of three fingers.* [U]

Amtrak /'æm·træk/ *n* [U] the US national passenger railroad system

amuse ENTERTAIN /ə'mjuːz/ *v* [T] to keep the attention of (someone) by entertaining them • *It's a relief when your child can amuse herself for a whole hour.*

amusement /ə'mjuːz·mənt/ *n* [C/U] • *For the children's amusement, Elizabeth helped them put on a play.* [U] • An **amusement park** is place where people can go to enjoy games, rides, and other activities.

amuse MAKE LAUGH /ə'mjuːz/ *v* [T] to make (someone) smile or laugh • *His subtle humor amused me.* ○ *Her ability to hack into computer systems did not amuse her superiors.*

amusing /ə'mjuː·zɪŋ/ *adj* • *One amusing story after another kept the audience laughing.*

amusement /ə'mjuːz·mənt/ *n* [C/U] • *We watched the clown with great amusement.* [U]

an /æn, ən/ *indefinite article* (used when the word following begins with a vowel sound) A • *an apple* ○ *an honest man* • LP ARTICLES, DETERMINERS

anachronism /ə'næk·rə,nız·əm/ *n* [C] someone or something placed in the wrong historical period, or something that is not modern and belongs to the past rather than the present • *For a historical drama, the movie was filled with anachronisms.* ○ *Is the man who opens a door for a woman an anachronism or a gentleman?*
anachronistic /ə,næk·rə'nıs·tık/ *adj* • *He uses only e-mail, never anachronistic regular mail.*

anagram /'æn·ə,græm/ *n* [C] a word or phrase made by using the letters of another word or phrase in a different order • *"Amen" is an anagram of "mean."*

anal /'eın·əl/ *adj* • See at ANUS.

analgesic /,æn·əl'dʒiː·zık, -sık/ *adj* tending to reduce or prevent pain • *Did you know that the caffeine in coffee has analgesic qualities?*

analogy /ə'næl·ə·dʒi/ *n* [C/U] a comparison of the features or qualities of two things to show their similarities • *In arguing against welfare, he used the analogy of feeding a wolf and making it dependent.* [C]
analogous /ə'næl·ə·gəs/ *adj* • *Forcing him to retire is analogous to murdering him.*

analysis /ə'næl·ə·səs/ *n* [C/U] *pl* **analyses** /ə'næl·ə,siːz/ the process of studying or examining something in an organized way to learn more about it, or a particular study or examination of something • *Chemical analysis of the woman's dress revealed traces of blood.* [C] • Analysis is also a short form of PSYCHO-ANALYSIS.

analyze /'æn·əl,aız/ *v* [T] to study (something) in a systematic and careful way • *In the article, several experienced diplomats analyzed the president's foreign policy.*

analyst /'æn·əl·əst/ *n* [C] • *She is a financial analyst* (= someone who studies financial investments). • Analyst is also a short form of **psychoanalyst**. See at PSYCHOANALYSIS.

analytical /,æn·əl'ıt·ı·kəl/, **analytic** /,æn·əl'ıt·ık/ *adj* involving the careful, systematic study of something • *An analytical approach to the problem had surprising results.*

anarchy /'æn·ər·ki, -,ɑr·ki/ *n* [U] a lack of organization and control in a society or group, esp. because either there is no government or it has no power • *Civil war has led to anarchy.* ○ *The crowd was restless and verging on anarchy.*
anarchist /'æn·ər·kəst, 'æn,ɑr-/ *n* [C] • *Belief in freedom doesn't make you an anarchist.*

anathema /ə'næθ·ə·mə/ *n* [U] something that is considered completely wrong and offensive • *The idea of higher taxes is anathema to most conservatives.*

anatomy /ə'næt̬·ə·mi/ *n* [U] the scientific study of the structure of animals or plants, or of a particular type of animal or plant • *You have to know something about anatomy if you want to draw the human body well.* ○ *(fig.) he*

was studying the anatomy of long-term relationships (= their structure).
anatomical /,æn·ə'tɑm·ı·kəl/ *adj* [not gradable] • *anatomical drawings*

ancestor /'æn,ses·tər, -səs-/ *n* [C] any member of your family from long ago, for example, the grandparents of your grandparents • *He returned to Ireland, where his mother's ancestors lived.*

ancestry /'æn,ses·tri/ *n* [C usually sing] • *She was of Spanish and French ancestry.*

anchor HEAVY WEIGHT /'æŋ·kər/ *n* [C] a heavy metal object attached to a boat by a rope or chain that, when dropped into the water and resting on the bottom, keeps the boat from moving • *We dropped the anchor and took out our fishing rods.* • An anchor is also someone or something that gives support when needed: *She's looking for a spiritual anchor.*
anchor /'æŋ·kər/ *v* [I/T] • *We anchored our sailboat near the shore.* [T]

anchor NEWS PERSON /'æŋ·kər/, **anchorman** (*pl* **anchormen**) /'æŋ·kər,mæn/, **anchorwoman** (*pl* **anchorwomen**) /'æŋ·kər,wʊm·ən/ *n* [C] a person who reports the news and manages the program • *The mayor grants frequent interviews to local news anchors.*
anchor /'æŋ·kər/ *v* [T] • *He anchored the morning news for many years.*

anchovy /'æn,tʃoʊ·vi, æn'tʃoʊ-/ *n* [C] *pl* **anchovy** or **anchovies** a small fish which is usually preserved in oil with salt, giving it a strong, salty taste

ancient /'eın·tʃənt/ *adj* of or from a very long time ago • *Archaeologists study the remains of ancient civilizations.* • *(infml)* Something that is ancient is very old or not modern: *This computer is ancient—I've got to get a new one.*

and ALSO /ænd, ənd/ *conjunction* (used to join two words, phrases, or parts of sentences) in addition to; also • *boys and girls* ○ *We were tired and hungry.* • And can be used when you add numbers: *Three and two are five.* • **And so on** or **and so forth** means together with other things: *Kids need to learn how to treat people, deal with things, and so on and so forth.*

and THEN /ænd, ənd/ *conjunction* (used to join two parts of a sentence, one part happening after or because of the other part) after that; then • *I met Jonathan, and we went out for a cup of coffee.*

and TO /ænd, ənd/ *conjunction* *infml* (used after some verbs) to, or in order to • *Let's try and get tickets for the hockey game tonight.*

and VERY /ænd, ənd/ *conjunction* (used to join two words, esp. two that are the same, to make their meaning stronger) • *The sound grew louder and louder.*

and/or /'æn'dɔːr/ *conjunction* (used to refer to both things or either one of the two mentioned) either "and" or "or" • *If the game is* *canceled, you will get a refund and/or new tickets.*

android /'æn·drɔɪd/ *n* [C] a ROBOT (= computerized mechanical device) that looks like a person • *He acted just like a clever android, avoiding any expression of affection.*

anecdote /'æn·ɪkˌdoʊt/ *n* [C] a short, often amusing story about an event, usually involving a particular person • *He told some funny anecdotes about famous people.*

anecdotal /ˌæn·ɪkˈdoʊt·əl/ *adj* [not gradable] based on reports or things someone saw rather than on proven facts • *There is only anecdotal evidence that the medicine works.*

anemia /əˈniː·miː·ə/ *n* [U] having too few red blood cells, causing a lack of energy

anemic /əˈniː·mɪk/ *adj* • *I was anemic for a while after my operation.* ○ *(fig.) First-quarter sales were anemic* (= weak).

anesthesia /ˌæn·əsˈθiː·ʒə/ *n* [U] the condition of not feeling pain, esp. by use of special drugs • *The procedure is performed under general anesthesia.*

anesthetic /ˌæn·əsˈθet̬·ɪk/ *n* [C] a drug that makes the body unable to feel pain • *With a local anesthetic, a patient is awake during surgery.*

anesthetist /əˈnes·θət̬·əst/ *n* [C] medical a medical specialist who gives ANESTHESIA, esp. during an operation

anesthetize /əˈnes·θəˌtaɪz/ *v* [T] • *The vet anesthetized my dog to take x-rays.*

anew /əˈnuː/ *adv* [not gradable] once more; again • *After a short time, their old arguments simply began anew.*

angel /'eɪn·dʒəl/ *n* [C] a heavenly servant of God, often represented in art as a human with wings • *An angel is also someone who is very good or kind: You're an angel to bring me this coffee.* • **Angel food cake** is a light cake made without egg YOLKS or fat.

angelic /ænˈdʒel·ɪk/ *adj* belonging to an angel, or pretty or kind like an angel • *an angelic face* ○ *The shepherds heard an angelic voice.*

anger /'æŋ·gər/ *n* [U] a feeling of fierce annoyance because of something unfair or hurtful that has happened • *When my father saw the plumber's bill, he erupted in anger.*

anger /'æŋ·gər/ *v* [T] • *His constant complaining only angered her.*

angry /'æŋ·gri/ *adj* • *The poor guy lost his temper when his angry girlfriend gave him a sock in the jaw.*

angrily /'æŋ·grə·li/ *adv* • *He angrily slammed the door.*

angle MEASUREMENT /'æŋ·gəl/ *n* [C] the space measured in degrees between two lines or surfaces from the point where they meet • *The angles of a square are 90 degrees.* • PIC RIGHT DIRECTION

angle VIEW /'æŋ·gəl/ *n* [C] a position from which something is seen, or a way of seeing something • *The photographer kept moving around to find the best angle for the picture.* ○ *Look at this from another angle.* • If something is **at an angle**, it is not straight: *The picture hung at an angle, which drove me crazy.*

angle /'æŋ·gəl/ *v* [I/T] to turn, or to move (something) so that it is not in a straight line or in the center • *The path angles to the left.* [I] ○ *We angled the light to take the picture.* [T]

▫**angle for** /'---/ *v prep* [T] to try to get or achieve (something), esp. without saying what your goal is • *The way he hangs around, he must be angling for a job.*

anglicize /'æŋ·gləˌsaɪz/ *v* [T] to change (a word or name) to make it sound or look like English • *Many immigrants anglicized their names to make life easier.*

angling /'æŋ·glɪŋ/ *n* [U] the sport of trying to catch fish with a rod, LINE (= string), and hook

angler /'æŋ·glər/ *n* [C] • *Anglers line the stream, fishing for salmon.*

Anglo /'æŋ·gloʊ/ *n* [C] *pl* **Anglos** an American who is white and not from a Latin American country • *The students are Anglos, Latinos, and Native Americans.*

Anglo- /ˌæŋ·gloʊ/ *combining form* ENGLISH or BRITISH • **Anglo-American** means British and American: *There is a new Anglo-American trade agreement.* • An **Anglo-Canadian** (also **English Canadian**) is a Canadian citizen whose first language is English.

angora /æŋˈgɔːr·ə, æn-, -ˈgoʊr·ə/ *n* [U] a soft wool made from the long hair of a type of goat or rabbit

angrily /'æŋ·grə·li/ *adv* • See at ANGER.

angry /'æŋ·gri/ *adj* • See at ANGER.

angst /ɑŋst, æŋst/ *n* [U] a feeling of extreme anxiety and unhappiness • *The boy's mysterious disappearance has caused angst and guilt for the family.*

anguish /'æŋ·gwɪʃ/ *n* [U] extreme pain or suffering • *Somehow we deal with the anguish of serious illness.*

anguished /'æŋ·gwɪʃt/ *adj* • *The anguished song at the end was beautiful.*

angular /'æŋ·gjə·lər/ *adj* thin and bony • *She was tall and angular.*

animal LIVING THING /'æn·ə·məl/ *n* [C] a living thing that can move and eat and react to the world through its SENSES, esp. of sight and hearing • *Mammals, insects, reptiles, and birds are all animals.* • In ordinary use, animal means all living beings except humans: *A lion is a wild animal, and a dog is a domestic animal.* ○ *Tests of the drug were done on laboratory animals.* • You may say that someone is an animal because their behavior is violent or lacks control: *I wouldn't go out with that animal if you paid me to!* • An animal is also a person who likes something or does something more than most people do: *a party animal* ○ *He's the most political animal on the city council.* • **Animal rights** is the idea that animals should not be treated cruelly by people.

animal PHYSICAL /'æn·ə·məl/ *adj* [not gradable] relating to physical needs or desires, such as to eat or reproduce • *Animal instincts apply to all animals, including humans.*

animate /'æn·ə,meɪt/ *v* [T] to cause (someone or something) to be more active or full of life • *He knows exactly what to say to animate a crowd.*

animated /'æn·ə,meɪt̬·əd/ *adj* full of interest and energy • *We had a very animated discussion.* • An animated movie or CARTOON, is made up of a series of slightly different drawings of people, animals, and objects that make them appear to move.

animation /,æn·ə'meɪ·ʃən/ *n* [U] energy and enthusiasm • *Her voice was full of animation.* • Animation is also the process by which an ANIMATED movie, esp. a CARTOON, is made from drawings done by hand or by a computer.

animosity /,æn·ə'mɑs·ət̬·i/ *n* [C/U] a violent dislike that influences behavior, or an example of such behavior • *The animosity between them finally led to a fist fight.* [C]

ankle /'æŋ·kəl/ *n* [C] the joint connecting the foot to the leg, or the thin part of the leg just above the foot • PIC FOOT

anklet /'æŋ·klət/ *n* [C] a short sock that reaches to the ANKLE

annals /'æn·əlz/ *pl n* the record of an activity or organization, arranged year by year, or a history that covers a long period of time • *This period was one of the darkest in the annals of US history.*

annex TAKE /ə'neks, 'æn·eks/ *v* [T] to take possession of (an area of land or a country) and add it to a larger area, usually by force • *The United States annexed parts of Texas and New Mexico, which belonged to Mexico.*

annexation /,æn,ek'seɪ·ʃən, ,æn·ək-/ *n* [C/U] • *the annexation of Latvia by the Soviet Union* [U]

annex ADDED BUILDING /'æn·eks, -ɪks/ *n* [C] an addition to a building, or another building, used with an existing building • *The old warehouse became an annex of the main store.*

annihilate /ə'nɑɪ·ə,leɪt/ *v* [T] to destroy completely, leaving nothing • *They ran for their lives, knowing the enemy planned to annihilate them.*

annihilation /ə,nɑɪ·ə'leɪ·ʃən/ *n* [U] • *The annihilation of smallpox is a triumph of medicine.*

anniversary /,æn·ə'vɜr·sə·ri/ *n* [C] a day in a previous year on which something important happened • *To celebrate our wedding anniversary, we gave a big party.*

announce /ə'nɑʊns/ *v* [T] to state officially or make known publicly • *She announced her resignation last Monday.*

announcement /ə'nɑʊn·smənt/ *n* [C] • *Wedding announcements were mailed a week after their marriage.*

announcer /ə'nɑʊn·sər/ *n* [C] someone who speaks on radio or television broadcasts or at a sports event • *He was the announcer for the Mamaroneck Tigers baseball team.*

annoy /ə'nɔɪ/ *v* [T] to make (someone) slightly angry or upset • *I know you're doing this only to annoy me.*

annoyed /ə'nɔɪd/ *adj* • *He gave me an annoyed look and left without speaking.*

annoying /ə'nɔɪ·ɪŋ/ *adj* • *It's annoying to have to explain this a second time.*

annoyingly /ə'nɔɪ·ɪŋ·li/ *adv* • *Ads annoyingly interrupted the TV movie.*

annoyance /ə'nɔɪ·əns/ *n* [C/U] • *As soon as he saw me, a look of annoyance crossed his face.* [U]

annual ONE YEAR /'æn·jə·wəl/ *adj* [not gradable] of or for a period of one year • *an annual salary* ○ *annual rainfall* ○ *Our annual costs have risen steadily.*

annual /'æn·jə·wəl/ *n* [C] a publication appearing once a year • *the "Sports Illustrated" swimsuit annual*

annual PLANT /'æn·jə·wəl/ *n* [C] a plant that grows, produces seeds, and dies within one year • Compare BIENNIAL; PERENNIAL PLANT.

annuity /ə'nu:·ət̬·i/ *n* [C] *specialized* an amount of money paid to someone every year, usually until their death, or the INSURANCE agreement or investment that provides money that is paid this way • *A small annuity lets her travel.*

annul /ə'nʌl/ *v* [T] **-ll-** *law* to announce officially (a law, marriage, or other contract) as no longer existing • *The marriage was finally annulled.*

annulment /ə'nʌl·mənt/ *n* [C] *law* • *You will need a court hearing to get an annulment.*

anoint /ə'nɔɪnt/ *v* [T] to make (someone) holy in a religious ceremony, by putting holy water or oil on them • *The archbishop was anointed in a ceremony at the cathedral.*

anomaly /ə'nɑm·ə·li/ *n* [C] something that is unusual enough to be noticeable or seem strange • *The government does computer checks of tax returns to find anomalies that might indicate fraud.*

Anon. *n abbreviation for* ANONYMOUS (= a writer whose name is not known)

anonymous /ə'nɑn·ə·məs/ *adj* [not gradable] (made or done by someone) with a name that is not known or not made public • *an anonymous donor* ○ *an anonymous gift*

anonymously /ə'nɑn·ə·mə·sli/ *adv* • *The donation was made anonymously.*

anonymity /,æn·ə'nɪm·ət̬·i/ *n* [U] • *For witnesses who may be afraid to speak out, the police have guaranteed anonymity* (= their names will not be told to others).

anorexia (nervosa) /,æn·ə'rek·si:·ə (nɜr 'voʊ·sə)/ *n* [U] *medical* an illness often resulting in dangerous weight loss, in which a person, usually a girl or woman, refuses to eat

enough over a long period of time • Compare
BULIMIA (NERVOSA).

anorexic /ˌæn·ə'rek·sɪk/ *adj*

another ADDITIONAL /ə'nʌð·ər, æ-/ *adj, pronoun* one more (person or thing) or an additional (amount) • *We have two tickets and need another (one).* ○ *Summer will be here in another three months* (= three months in the future). ○ *We have room in the car for another if we all sit close together.* • LP DETERMINERS

another DIFFERENT /ə'nʌð·ər, æ-/ *adj, pronoun* a different (person or thing) • *Do you want to exchange this dress for another (one), or do you want your money back?* ○ *It's raining today, so we'll have to have the picnic another day.* • LP DETERMINERS

answer REACTION /'æn·sər/ *n* [C] something said or written in reaction to a question or statement • *If you are asking me if I want to go into business with you, the answer is no.* ○ *I called several times, but there was no answer.* • An answer is also a reaction to a question asked as part of a test: *I think I got most of the answers right on the exam.*

answer /'æn·sər/ *v* [I/T] • *I knocked on your door last night, but no one answered.* [I] ○ *"I don't know," he answered.* ○ *She answered that she couldn't arrive before nine o'clock.* [+ that clause] ○ *She refused to answer questions on whether she would run for the Senate.* [T] • An **answering machine** is a device connected to a telephone that answers calls automatically and records messages from callers. LP TELEPHONE

answer SOLUTION /'æn·sər/ *n* [C] a solution to a problem • *There is no easy answer to the problem.*

◻**answer for** /'---/ *v prep* [T] to be responsible for having done (something bad) • *The slaveholders of the South had much to answer for.*

◻**answer to** /'---/ *v prep* [T] to take orders from and explain your actions to (someone) • *The great thing about having your own business is that you don't have to answer to anyone.*

ant /ænt/ *n* [C] a small insect that lives in large and highly organized social groups

antacid /ænt'æs·əd/ *n* [C/U] a medicine you can take to reduce or prevent the uncomfortable feeling of having too much acid in the stomach

antagonism /æn'tæg·ə,nɪz·əm/ *n* [C/U] strong dislike or opposition, or a particular example of it • *Immigrants are encountering increasing antagonism from the community.* [U]

antagonist /æn'tæg·ə·nəst/ *n* [C] a person who opposes or disagrees with another

antagonistic /æn,tæg·ə'nɪs·tɪk/ *adj* expressing strong dislike or opposition • *He's extremely antagonistic toward critics.* ○ *Recent rulings have been antagonistic to single-sex education.*

antagonize /æn'tæg·ə,naɪz/ *v* [T] • *If you pub-*

lish this book, you may antagonize a lot of people.

Antarctic /ænt'ɑrk·tɪk, -'ɑrt̬·ɪk/ *n* [U] the very cold area around the South Pole that includes Antarctica and the surrounding seas • Compare ARCTIC.

ante /'ænt̬·i/ *n* [C usually sing] an amount of money that each person must risk in order to be part of a game of GAMBLING (= risking money in the hope of winning more) • *If you* **raise/up the ante**, you increase the risk involved in a deal, esp. by asking for or offering more money in a business deal: *He bought more stock and raised the ante to $24 per share.*

◻**ante up** *(obj)*, **ante** *(obj)* **up** /'ænt̬·iː'ʌp/ *v adv* [I/M] *infml* to produce (an amount of money or of something else) in order to be a part of a game or operation • *The two new baseball teams each had to ante up a huge entry fee to the major leagues.* [M]

antecedent /ˌænt̬·ə'siːd·ᵊnt/ *n* [C usually pl] something existing or happening before, esp. as the cause of an event or situation • *The book dealt with the historical antecedents of the Civil War.* • *(specialized)* In grammar, an antecedent is a word or phrase that a pronoun refers to: *In the sentence, "Joe threw the ball to Wendy, and Wendy threw it back," "the ball" is the antecedent of "it."*

antelope /'ænt̬·ᵊl,oup/ *n* [C] a large animal that looks like a deer, with wide branching horns

antenna INSECT /æn'ten·ə/ *n* [C] *pl* **antennae** /æn'ten·iː/ either of the two long, delicate, wirelike parts which are attached to the head of an insect, and which it uses to feel its way • *(fig.) Her political antennae helped her answer questions without offending anyone.*

antenna BROADCASTING /æn'ten·ə/ *n* [C] *pl* **antennas** a structure made of metal rods or wires, often positioned on top of a building or vehicle, that receives or sends radio or television signals

anthem /'æn·θəm/ *n* [C] a song that has special importance for a particular group of people or country, often sung on special occasions

anthology /æn'θɑl·ə·dʒi/ *n* [C] a collection of stories, poems, etc., by different writers

anthropology /ˌæn·θrə'pɑl·ə·dʒi/ *n* [U] the study of the human race, its culture and society, and its physical development

anthropological /ˌæn·θrə·pə'lɑdʒ·ɪ·kəl/ *adj*
anthropologist /ˌæn·θrə'pɑl·ə·dʒəst/ *n* [C] a person who is an expert in anthropology

anti– /ˌænt̬·i, ˌæn,taɪ/ *combining form* opposed to or against • *antiabortion* • Compare PRO-SUPPORT.

antibiotic /ˌænt̬·i·baɪ'ɑt̬·ɪk, ˌæn,taɪ-/ *n* [C] a medicine or chemical that can destroy harmful bacteria in the body or limit their growth • *I'm taking an antibiotic for a throat infection.*

antibody /'ænt̬·i,bɑd·i/ *n* [C] *specialized* a PROTEIN (= type of chemical) produced in the blood that fights diseases by attacking and killing harmful bacteria • *Antibodies found in breast milk protect babies against infection.*

anticipate *(obj)* /æn'tɪs·ə,peɪt/ *v* to imagine or expect that (something) will happen, sometimes taking action in preparation for it • *No job cuts are anticipated under the new ownership.* [T] ○ *I don't anticipate (that) we'll solve all our problems with one meeting.* [+ *(that)* clause] ○ *We anticipate criticism but plan to go ahead anyway.* [T] ○ *At this stage we can't anticipate what will happen.* [+ *wh-* word]

anticipation /æn,tɪs·ə'peɪ·ʃən/ *n* [U] • *A number of industrial companies are raising prices in anticipation of future inflation.* • Anticipation is also a feeling of excitement about something that is going to happen in the near future: *Skiers look forward to the first snow of winter with eager anticipation.*

anticlimactic /,ænt·i·klɑɪ'mæk·tɪk, ,æn,tɑɪ-/ *adj* [not gradable] causing disappointment because something is less exciting than expected or not as interesting as something that happened earlier • *The announcement of his resignation was anticlimactic, as we all knew he could no longer stay in the job.*

antics /'ænt·ɪks/ *pl n* amusing, silly, or strange behavior • *The antics of the clowns amused the children.*

antidepressant /,ænt·i·dɪ'pres·ənt, ,æn,tɑɪ-/ *n* [C] a type of drug that is used to reduce feelings of being unhappy and hopeless

antidote /'ænt·ɪ,doʊt/ *n* [C] a chemical, esp. a drug, that acts against the bad effects of a poison to limit the harm it can do • *an antidote for snake venom* • *(fig.)* An antidote is also a way of preventing or acting against something bad: *Exercise can be an antidote to depression.*

antifreeze /'ænt·i,friːz/ *n* [U] a liquid that lowers the temperature at which water freezes, and that is added to the water in car engines in winter to keep it from freezing

antihistamine /,ænt·i'hɪs·tə,miːn, ,æn,tɑɪ-, -mən/ *n* [C] a drug taken to limit the bad effect of the body's reaction to some substances • *I took an antihistamine for my runny nose.*

antipathy /æn'tɪp·ə·θi/ *n* [U] strong dislike or opposition • *His letters show a deep and intense antipathy toward workers.*

antiperspirant /,ænt·i'pɜr·spə·rənt, ,æn,tɑɪ-/ *n* [C] a substance that is put on the skin, esp. under the arms, in order to prevent or reduce PERSPIRATION (= the excretion of liquid through the skin)

antiquated /'ænt·ɪ,kweɪṱ·əd/ *adj* old-fashioned or unsuitable for modern society • *antiquated ideas/technology*

antique /æn'tiːk/ *n* [C] something made in an earlier period and valued because it is old, rare, or of high quality • *He sold antiques for a while.*

antique /æn'tiːk/ *adj* • *an antique dealer/show*

antiquity /æn'tɪk·wəṱ·i/ *n* [C/U] the distant past, esp. before the MIDDLE AGES (= before the sixth century), or something of great age • *We spent some time in the museum looking at Roman antiquities.* [C]

anti–Semitism /,ænt·i'sem·ə,tɪz·əm, ,æn,tɑɪ-/ *n* [U] hate or strong dislike of Jews, or actions that express hate or dislike of Jews • *Nazi anti-Semitism forced him to emigrate to the U.S.A.*

anti–Semitic /,ænt·i·sə'mɪṱ·ɪk, ,æn,tɑɪ-/ *adj* • *anti-Semitic literature*

anti–Semite /,ænt·i'sem,ɑɪt, ,æn,tɑɪ-/ *n* [C] a person who hates or strongly dislikes Jews • *He denied that he was an anti-Semite.*

antiseptic /,ænt·ɪ'sep·tɪk/ *n* [C] a chemical used to prevent infection from an injury, esp. by killing bacteria

antiseptic /,ænt·ɪ'sep·tɪk/ *adj* • *an antiseptic ointment*

antisocial /,ænt·ɪ'soʊ·ʃəl, ,æn,tɑɪ-/ *adj* harmful to society • *Some critics argued that movies caused antisocial behavior.* • Antisocial also means not wanting to spend time with or be friendly with other people: *If you don't hang out with your friends, they'll consider you weird and antisocial.*

antithesis /æn'tɪθ·ə·səs/ *n* [C/U] *pl* **antitheses** /æn'tɪθ·ə,siːz/ the exact opposite, or opposition • *Violence is the very antithesis of government by consent.* [C]

antlers /'ænt·lər/ *pl n* the pair of horns that grow from the head of the male of some animals, such as deer, and that look like branches

antonym /'ænt·ə,nɪm/ *n* [C] *specialized* a word or phrase whose meaning is the opposite of another word or phrase • Compare SYNONYM.

antsy /'ænt·si/ *adj slang* anxious and excited in an unpleasant way; extremely nervous • *I'm as antsy as I was before my first class.*

anus /'eɪ·nəs/ *n* [C] the opening at the end of the INTESTINES (= tube in the body in which food is digested) through which solid excrement leaves the body

anal /'eɪn·əl/ *adj* [not gradable] • *anal warts*

anxiety /æŋ'zɑɪ·əṱ·i/ *n* [C/U] an uncomfortable feeling of worry about something that is happening or might happen, or a cause of this • *For many children, every new school year causes anxiety.* [U] ○ *Don't you have any fears or anxieties about middle age?* [C]

anxious /'æŋ·ʃəs/ *adj* • *They exchanged anxious glances in the doctor's office.*

anxiously /'æŋ·ʃə·sli/ *adv* • *We waited anxiously by the phone.*

anxious /'æŋ·ʃəs/ *adj* wanting very much for something to happen; eager • *I've been anxious to meet you.* [+ *to* infinitive] ○ *It was getting late, and I was anxious to get home.* [+ *to* infinitive]

any SOME /'en·i/ *adj, pronoun* (used in negative statements and questions) some, or even the smallest amount (of) • *We didn't have any* *idea what the airfare would be.* ○ *There was hardly any snow this winter.* ○ *Is there any hope that he will recover?* ○ *Are any of the concerts on a Saturday night?* • LP AMOUNTS, DETERMINERS

any NOT IMPORTANT WHICH /'en·i/ *adj, pronoun* one of or each of, or a stated amount of (something that is more than one or has a number of parts), without saying which particular part is meant • *You can have any three items of clothing you like for $30.* ○ *Any advice that you can give me would be greatly appreciated.* ○ *They should be here any minute* (= soon). ○ *Any way you look at it, the investment was a bad idea.* ○ *I saw some beautiful cars at the auto show, any of which I'd like to have.* • *I don't think they liked my idea—at any rate* (= more exactly), *they weren't enthusiastic.* • *You should be able to catch a bus, but in any case* (= whatever happens) *you can always take a taxi home.* • LP DETERMINERS

any AT ALL /'en·i/ *adv* [not gradable] at all or in the least • *I can't say any more.* ○ *He wasn't any smarter than I was.* ○ *If she comes any later, we'll miss the show.* • LP DETERMINERS

anybody /'en·i:,bɑd·i, -bəd·i/ *pronoun* ANYONE • *Does anybody have change for a $10 bill?*

anyhow /'en·i:,hɑu/ *adv* [not gradable] *infml* ANYWAY • *Anyhow, I didn't ask you to come here to talk about your business.*

anymore /,en·i:'mɔːr, -'mour/, **any more** *adv* [not gradable] (used esp. in negative statements) any longer • *I don't know who to trust anymore.* ○ *She doesn't work here anymore.* • Anymore also means now or from now on, often even in positive statements: *We never go out—all we do anymore is watch TV.* ○ *I'm scared to be alone anymore.*

anyone /'en·i:·wən, -,wʌn/, **anybody** /'en·i: ,bɑd·i, -bəd·i/ *pronoun* any person whatever, or (esp. in negative statements and questions) a person, but without saying which person • *Hello, is anyone home?* ○ *If anyone calls, tell them I'm out of the office.* ○ *We didn't know anyone when we first moved here, but now we have lots of friends.* ○ *I can't think of anyone with more imagination than Maggie.*

anyplace /'en·i:,pleɪs/ *adv* [not gradable] ANYWHERE • *There wasn't anyplace to pull off the road if your car broke down.*

anything /'en·i:,θɪŋ/ *pronoun* any event, act, or object whatever, or (esp. in negative statements or questions) something • *Is there anything I can do to help?* ○ *I didn't know anything about computers till I started this job.* ○ *I don't want to say anything to upset her.* ○ *(infml) It was a fantastic party—I wouldn't have missed it for anything* (= for any reason). • *She was* **anything but** *friendly* (= not friendly at all) *the last time I saw her.* • *The pictures on cereal boxes don't look* **anything like** (= are not at all similar to) *the actual stuff you eat.*

anytime /'en·i:,tɑɪm/ *adv* [not gradable] at any time or at a time, but without saying which time • *Come to see me anytime.* ○ *I'm not planning on leaving anytime soon.* ○ *Joe and his family ought to be here anytime now* (= soon).

anyway /'en·i:,weɪ/, *infml* **anyhow** *adv* [not gradable] not considering other facts or conditions; considered independently, without being influenced by other things • *Of course I don't mind taking you home—I'm going that way anyway.* ○ *The economy was slowing down anyway, so there was no need to worry about inflation.* • In conversation, anyway is often used to support or clarify a previous statement: *So, you're right, there are very few black quarterbacks in football, or at least that are starting anyway.* • In conversation, anyway is often used to change the subject, return to an earlier subject, or get to the most interesting point, and is also used to take up time so that you can decide what to say next: *So anyway, what are you going to do tonight?* ○ *Anyway, in the end we just agreed to stop seeing each other.*

anywhere /'en·i:,wer, -,wær/, **anyplace** *adv* [not gradable] in, to, or at any place whatever or (esp. in negative statements and questions) a place, but without saying which place • *I can't find my scarf anywhere.* ○ *There are plants in this desert that you won't find anywhere else.* ○ *There are no reserved seats—just sit anywhere you like.* • Anywhere also means within the range of or approximately: *The turkey can weigh anywhere from ten to twenty pounds.*

apart /ə'pɑrt/ *adv* separated by a distance • *Stand with your feet wide apart and bend from the waist.* ○ *How far apart should I put my stereo speakers?* ○ *We both travel a lot, but when we're apart we keep in touch by phone.* ○ *(fig.) The strike continued, and both sides remained very far apart.* • *(esp. of a machine) Apart can also mean separated into its parts: He had to take the hot-water pump apart to repair it.* • Apart can also mean separated in time: *Our two kids were born just eighteen months apart.* • **Apart from** (= except for) *the low salary, it's not a bad job.*

apartheid /ə'pɑr,tɑɪt, -,teɪt/ *n* [U] (in the past) a political system in South Africa that legally separated people of different races

apartment /ə'pɑrt·mənt/ *(abbreviation* **apt.**, *esp. Br* **flat**) *n* [C] a set of rooms for living in, usually including a kitchen and bathroom, and one or more bedrooms • *They lived in a six-room apartment on the eighth floor.* • An **apartment building/house** is a building designed mainly for apartments.

apathy /'æp·ə·θi/ *n* [U] lack of interest, or the attitude of not caring resulting from it • *There is a growing sense of apathy among teens and a feeling that there are no opportunities, he said.*

apathetic /,æp·ə'θeṭ·ɪk/ *adj* • *apathetic voters*

ape ANIMAL /eɪp/ n [C] a mammal that has long arms and no tail or a short tail and that is related to monkeys • *Chimpanzees, gorillas, and orangutans are all apes.*

ape COPY /eɪp/ v [T] *often disapproving* to copy (something or someone) • *Because of snob appeal, high-priced American clothing stores ape British usage and call suspenders "braces."*

aperture /ˈæp·ɚˌtʃʊr, -tʃɚ/ n [C] a small and often narrow opening, esp. one that allows light into a camera

apex /ˈeɪ·peks/ n [C usually sing] the highest point or top of something • *the apex of a pyramid* ○ *He reached the apex of his career during that period.*

aphorism /ˈæf·əˌrɪz·əm/ n [C] a short saying that is intended to express a general truth

aphrodisiac /ˌæf·rəˈdiːˌziːˌæk, -ˈdɪzˌiː-/ n [C] something, esp. a drug or food, that is believed to increase sexual desire in people

apiece /əˈpiːs/ adv [not gradable] each • *In good condition, dolls from this period sell for $500 apiece.*

apocalypse /əˈpɑk·əˌlɪps/ n [U] an event resulting in great destruction and violent change • *In the Bible, the Apocalypse is the total destruction of the world.*

apolitical /ˌeɪ·pəˈlɪt̬·ɪ·kəl/ adj not interested in or connected with politics • *The appointment of judges, they said, should be apolitical.*

apologetic /əˌpɑl·əˈdʒet̬·ɪk/ adj expressing regret about having caused someone inconvenience or unhappiness • *He was apologetic for not returning my call.*

apologetically /əˌpɑl·əˈdʒet̬·ɪ·kli/ adv

apologize /əˈpɑl·əˌdʒɑɪz/ v [I] to tell someone that you are sorry for something that has caused them inconvenience or unhappiness • *She apologized for her husband's rudeness.* ○ *If I offended you, I apologize.* ○ *He said he had nothing to apologize for.*

apology /əˈpɑl·ə·dʒi/ n [C] an act of saying that you are sorry • *I have an apology to make to you—I opened your letter by mistake.* ○ *He owes me an apology* (= He should say he is sorry). ○ *My apologies* (= I am sorry) *for not writing you sooner.*

apostle /əˈpɑs·əl/ n [C] any of the twelve men whom Jesus Christ chose to teach other people about Christianity, or someone who strongly supports a particular belief or political movement

apostrophe /əˈpɑs·trə·fi/ n [C] a mark (') used in writing to show that a letter or a number has been omitted, or before or after s to show possession • LP CONTRACTIONS OF VERBS, THE POSSESSIVE FORM

appall /əˈpɔːl/ v [T] to cause (someone) to be extremely upset or shocked • *I was appalled by the underwear ads of the young men.*

appalling /əˈpɔː·lɪŋ/ adj • *Prisoners were kept in the most appalling conditions, in filthy rooms with one open toilet.*

apparatus EQUIPMENT /ˌæp·əˈræt̬·əs, -ˈreɪt̬-/ n [C/U] pl **apparatuses** or **apparatus** a set of equipment, tools, or a machine that is used for a particular purpose • *The garage had an apparatus to lift cars up.* [C]

apparatus SYSTEM /ˌæp·əˈræt̬·əs, -ˈreɪt̬-/ n [C] pl **apparatuses** or **apparatus** a system or method by which an organization is operated or maintained • *the UN's military peacekeeping apparatus*

apparel /əˈpær·əl/ n [U] clothes, esp. of a special type • *children's/women's apparel* ○ *riding/sports apparel*

apparent /əˈpær·ənt, -ˈper-/ adj able to be seen or understood • *It was becoming increasingly apparent that he could no longer look after himself.* [+ *that* clause] • Apparent also means seeming to be true: *The apparent cause of death was drowning, but further tests were needed.*

apparently /əˈpær·ənt·li, -ˈper-/ adv according to what seems to be true or what is likely, based on what you know • *The computer trouble was apparently caused by a programming error.*

apparition /ˌæp·əˈrɪʃ·ən/ n [C] something you believe, imagine, or dream you see, esp. the spirit of a dead person

---

APOSTROPHE [']

An apostrophe is used:

to show the possessive form of nouns

Use **s** for most singular nouns and indefinite pronouns:

the girl's toy • my sister-in-law's opinion • Luis's bicycle • someone's hat

and for irregular plural nouns not ending in **s**:

the children's library • these bacteria's effects

Use the apostrophe alone for plural nouns ending in **s**:

the boys' team • the Rocky Mountains' crest

Sometimes the apostrophe alone is also used for singular nouns ending in **s** or **z**:

Liz' son Adam • Socrates' trial

to show that letters or numbers have been left out

We'll (= We will) *see you later. • They're* (= They are) *waiting outside. • If you can't* (= cannot) *beat 'em* (= them), *join 'em. • rock 'n' roll* (= rock and roll) *music • 'Night* (= Good night), *Dad. • the great storm of '88* (= 1988)

to form the plurals of letters, abbreviations, and numbers

Her u's and n's look the same to me. • I got 91's on the math and history tests and two B's as final grades. • Some of the teachers have Ph.D.'s.

LP **Contractions of Verbs**

appeal ATTRACT /ə'piːl/ *v* [I] to be interesting or attractive • *Such music managed to appeal to the tastes of both young and old.*

appeal /ə'piːl/ *n* [U] • *Eating out has lost much of its appeal, since I can't drink any wine.*

appealing /ə'piː·lɪŋ/ *adj* • *The package describing European tours certainly made them seem appealing.*

appeal ARGUE /ə'piːl/ *v* [I/T] to request formally that a decision, esp. a legal or official one, be changed • *The verdict was appealed to a higher court.* [T]

appeal /ə'piːl/ *n* [C/U] • *The decision was reversed on appeal.* [U]

appeal REQUEST /ə'piːl/ *v* [I] to make a serious or formal request for help, esp. in an emergency • *Blood supplies are running low, and the Red Cross is appealing for blood donations.*

appeal /ə'piːl/ *n* [C] • *Many charities issued an appeal for contributions to help victims of the earthquake.*

appear BE PRESENT /ə'pɪr/ *v* [I] to become noticeable or to be present • *At this point the ferry boat suddenly appeared.* ○ *Her picture appeared on the front page of the newspaper.* ○ *We have to appear in court next week.* • To appear is also to be made available: *The interview with the president will appear next Sunday.*

appearance /ə'pɪr·əns/ *n* [C] • *It was his first television appearance.* • *I didn't really want to go to the party but I thought I should* **put in/ make an appearance** (= be present, if only for a short time).

appear SEEM /ə'pɪr/ *v* to seem • *The governor appeared confident of victory on the eve of the election.* [L] ○ *It appears (that) she had asked someone to drive her home from the party.* [+ (that) clause] ○ *There appears to be some mistake.* [+ to infinitive]

appearance /ə'pɪr·əns/ *n* [U] the way a person or thing looks or seems to other people • *More attention is paid to her appearance than to her skating.*

appearances /ə'pɪr·ən·səz/ *pl n* what things look like or seem to be rather than what they actually are • *He was a far more complicated man than outward appearances suggested.*

appear PERFORM /ə'pɪr/ *v* [I always + adv/ prep] to perform publicly in a play, movie, dance, or other similar event • *He is currently appearing in two movies.*

appearance /ə'pɪr·əns/ *n* [C] • *Her only screen appearances were in two made-for-television movies.*

appease /ə'piːz/ *v* [T] (in arguments or war) to prevent further disagreement by giving to (the other side) something that they have demanded • *They questioned whether, in his desire to appease the conservatives in his own party, the president was selling out to them.*

appeasement /ə'piːz·mənt/ *n* [U] • *a policy of appeasement*

append /ə'pend/ *v* [T] *fml* to add (something)

to the end of a piece of writing • *Several footnotes were appended to the text.*

appendage /ə'pen·dɪdʒ/ *n* [C] a smaller or less important part that is attached to something • *The organism has small, leaflike appendages.*

appendicitis /ə,pen·də'saɪt̬·əs/ *n* [U] a painful and serious infection of the APPENDIX, which often results in the appendix being removed by an operation

appendix BODY PART /ə'pen·dɪks/ *n* [C] *pl* **appendixes** /ə'pen·dɪk·səz/ or **appendices** /ə'pen·də,siːz/ a small, curved part attached to the INTESTINES (= tube in the body in which food is digested) which has no known use

appendix BOOK PART /ə'pen·dɪks/ *n* [C] *pl* **appendices** /ə'pen·də,siːz/ or **appendixes** /ə'pen·dɪk·səz/ a separate part at the end of a book or report that gives additional information • *The appendix lists all the Olympic champions.*

appetite /'æp·ə,taɪt/ *n* [C] a desire or need for something, esp. food • *a good/healthy appetite* ○ *an appetite for adventure*

appetizing /'æp·ə,taɪ·zɪŋ/ *adj* interesting or attractive, esp. because you think it will be good to eat • *an appetizing dessert*

appetizer /'æp·ə,taɪ·zər/ *n* [C] a small amount of food eaten before a meal or as the first part of it

applaud CLAP /ə'plɔːd/ *v* [I/T] to show your enjoyment or approval of (esp. a performance or speech) by clapping your hands repeatedly

applaud PRAISE /ə'plɔːd/ *v* [T] to say that you admire and agree with (a person's action or decision) • *We applaud the family's decision to protect the privacy of their child.*

applause /ə'plɔːz/ *n* [U] the action or sound made by a number of people clapping their hands repeatedly to show their enjoyment or approval, esp. of a performance or speech

apple /'æp·əl/ *n* [C/U] a round, edible fruit having a red, green, or yellow skin, or the tree on which it grows • **Applesauce** is a sweet food made from cooked apples.

appliance /ə'plaɪ·əns/ *n* [C] a device, machine, or piece of equipment, esp. an electrical one that is used in the home, such as a REFRIGERATOR or washing machine • *electrical/ home/household/kitchen appliances*

apply REQUEST /ə'plaɪ/ *v* [I] to request something, usually officially, esp. by writing or by sending in a form • *to apply for a job/loan* ○ *She applied for admission to law school.*

application /,æp·lə'keɪ·ʃən/ *n* [C/U] • *a letter of application* [U] ○ *I've sent off applications for four different jobs.* [C]

applicant /'æp·lɪ·kənt/ *n* [C] a person who formally requests something, such as a job or admission to a college or university

apply HAVE TO DO WITH /ə'plaɪ/ *v* [I] (esp. of rules or laws) to have to do with someone or something; relate • *The same rules apply to everybody.*

applicable /'æp·lɪ·kə·bəl, ə'plɪk·ə-/ *adj* • *This law is only applicable to nonprofit organizations.*

apply PUT ON /ə'plaɪ/ *v* [T] to spread or rub (cream, paint, etc.) on a surface • *She applied the lotion gently to her sunburned arms.*

application /ˌæp·lə'keɪ·ʃən/ *n* [C] • *Allow two hours between applications of the paint to let it dry.*

apply USE /ə'plaɪ/ *v* [T] to make use of (something) for a particular purpose • *As a translator, he was able to apply his knowledge of foreign languages.* ○ *The driver failed to apply his brakes in time.* • If you apply yourself to something, you work hard at it.

applied /ə'plaɪd/ *adj* (of a subject of study) having a practical use rather than being only theoretical • *applied mathematics*

application /ˌæp·lə'keɪ·ʃən/ *n* [C] a particular use • *An application is a computer program that is designed for a particular purpose.*

appoint /ə'pɔɪnt/ *v* [T] to choose (someone) officially for a job or responsibility • *Commissioner Curtis was appointed by President Bush.*

appointment /ə'pɔɪnt·mənt/ *n* [C/U] • *There were questions about Lynch's appointment to a federal post.*

appointment /ə'pɔɪnt·mənt/ *n* [C/U] a formal arrangement to meet or visit someone at a particular time and place • *I have a doctor's appointment tomorrow.* [C] • **By appointment** means with an appointment: *The museum is open by appointment only.*

apportion /ə'pɔːr·ʃən, -'poʊr-/ *v* [T] to give or share (something) among several people or things • *How should medical care be funded and apportioned?*

appraise /ə'preɪz/ *v* [T] to judge the quality, success, or needs of (someone or something) • *Social workers appraise the needs of each family.* • Appraise also means to judge the worth of something: *A professional appraised my jewelry.*

appraisal /ə'preɪ·zəl/ *n* [C/U] • *I was pleased with the appraisal of my work.*

appreciable /ə'priː·ʃə·bəl, ə'prɪʃ·ə-/ *adj* (esp. of amounts or changes) large enough to be noticed or to have an effect • *My little donation will not make an appreciable difference.*

appreciate (obj) VALUE /ə'priː·ʃiː,eɪt, ə'prɪʃ·iː-/ *v* to be aware of (something), or to understand that (something) is valuable • *I appreciate that this is a difficult decision for you.* [+ *that* clause] • To appreciate something also means to be grateful for something: *I appreciated your help very much.* [T]

appreciation /ə,priː·ʃiː'eɪ·ʃən, ə,prɪʃ·iː-/ *n* [U] • *"I'd just like a little appreciation," she sobbed.*

appreciative /ə'priː·ʃət·ɪv, ə'prɪʃ·ət-/ *adj* • *An appreciative audience wildly applauded the performance.*

appreciatively /ə'priː·ʃət·ɪv·li, ə'prɪʃ·ət-/ *adv* • *She smiled appreciatively at him.*

appreciate INCREASE /ə'priː·ʃiː,eɪt, ə'prɪʃ·iː-/ *v* [I/T] to increase in value • *Our house appreciated by 20% in two years.* [I]

appreciation /ə,priː·ʃiː'eɪ·ʃən, ə,prɪʃ·iː-/ *n* [U] • *New funds are generated by the appreciation of our assets.*

apprehend /ˌæp·rɪ'hend/ *v* [T] to catch (a person) and put them under police control; to ARREST • *Last night police apprehended the suspect.*

apprehension /ˌæp·rɪ'hen·tʃən/ *n* [U] • *There's an $8000 reward for the apprehension of the perpetrators.*

apprehension /ˌæp·rɪ'hen·tʃən/ *n* [U] anxiety about the future; fear of something unpleasant happening • *I felt great apprehension over my first day at work.*

apprehensive /ˌæp·rɪ'hen·sɪv/ *adj* • *We're all apprehensive about tomorrow's meeting.*

apprehensively /ˌæp·rɪ'hen·sɪv·li/ *adv* • *They looked apprehensively around the room.*

apprentice /ə'prent·əs/ *n* [C] someone who works for an expert to learn a particular skill or job • *He worked for two years as a plumber's apprentice*

apprentice /ə'prent·əs/ *v* [I/T] • *I apprenticed with my father, who was a stonemason.* [I]

apprise /ə'praɪz/ *v* [T] *slightly fml* to tell or inform (someone) about something • *The parents were apprised of their son's injuries.*

approach COME NEAR /ə'proʊtʃ/ *v* [I/T] to come nearer to (something or someone) • *We could see the train approaching from the distance.* [I] • If you approach someone, you meet or communicate directly with them: *We approached the bank about a loan.* [T]

approach /ə'proʊtʃ/ *n* [C/U] • *The approach of winter sends many birds flying south.* [U]

approachable /ə'proʊ·tʃə·bəl/ *adj* easy to talk to; friendly • *Malcolm is always very approachable—talk it over with him.*

approach DEAL WITH /ə'proʊtʃ/ *v* [T] to deal with (something) • *We should approach this problem logically.*

approach /ə'proʊtʃ/ *n* [C] • *We need to adopt a different approach to the problem.*

approbation /ˌæp·rə'beɪ·ʃən/ *n* [U] *fml* approval or agreement, often given by an official group; praise • *Kids need their fathers' approbation.*

appropriate CORRECT /ə'proʊ·priː·ət/ *adj* correct or right for a particular situation or occasion • *Punishment should be appropriate to the crime.* ○ *I don't have any appropriate clothes.*

appropriately /ə'proʊ·priː·ət·li/ *adv* • *Those kids aren't appropriately dressed for the cold.*

appropriateness /ə'proʊ·priː·ət·nəs/ *n* [U] • *I wonder about the appropriateness of borrowing money from my brother.*

appropriate TAKE /ə'proʊ·priː,eɪt/ *v* [T] to take and use for a purpose • *The state appro-*

priated funds for more clinics. • Appropriate also means to steal: *He lost his job after he appropriated some of the company's money.*

appropriation /ə,proʊ·priː'eɪ·ʃən/ *n* [C] • *The city council approved an appropriation of $10,000 to plant trees.*

approve AGREE WITH /ə'pruːv/ *v* [I] to have a good opinion of someone or something • *I wish my mother approved of my friends.*

approval /ə'pruː·vəl/ *n* [U] • *She craves the approval of her classmates.*

approve PERMIT /ə'pruːv/ *v* [T] to accept or allow (something) officially • *Finally the court approved the sale of the property.*

approval /ə'pruː·vəl/ *n* [U] • *You'll need your parents' approval to take this field trip.*

approximate /ə'prɑk·sə·mət/ *adj* almost exact • *Can you tell me the approximate value of this watch?*

approximate /ə'prɑk·sə,meɪt/ *v* [T] to come near in quality, amount, value, or character • *The painting only approximated the mountain landscape.*

approximately /ə'prɑk·sə·mət·li/ *adv* • *The job will take approximately three weeks to do.*

approximation /ə,prɑk·sə'meɪ·ʃən/ *n* [C] • *I only have an approximation of the size of the room.*

apricot /'æp·rə,kɑt, 'eɪ·prə-/ *n* [C] a small orange fruit

April /'eɪ·prəl/ (*abbreviation* **Apr.**) *n* [C/U] the fourth month of the year, after March and before May • **April Fools' Day** is April 1, a day when people deceive others for amusement and then say, "April fool."

apron /'eɪ·prən/ *n* [C] a piece of clothing worn over the front of other clothes to keep them clean when doing a dirty or messy job, esp. cooking

apt CORRECT /æpt/ *adj* correct or right for a particular situation • *Chris's apt comments summed up our opinions.*

aptly /'æp·tli/ *adv* • *He was very tall and was aptly called "Stretch."*

apt LIKELY /æpt/ *adj* [+ *to* infinitive] likely • *This old roof is apt to leak when it rains.*

apt. APARTMENT *n* [C] *abbreviation for* APARTMENT

aptitude /'æp·tə,tuːd/ *n* [C/U] natural ability or skill • *My son has no aptitude for sports.* [U] • An **aptitude test** measures your ability to succeed at something.

aqua /'æk·wə, 'ɑk-/, **aquamarine** /,æk·wə·mə'riːn, ,ɑk-/ *adj* [not gradable], *n* [U] (of) the color or that is a mixture of blue and green • *an aqua sea* ○ *You look good in aqua.* [U]

aquarium /ə'kwer·iː·əm, ə'kwær-/ *n* [C] a glass container or pool in which small fish and other water animals and plants are kept, or a building, usually open to the public, in which many different fish and other water animals live and can be studied

Aquarius /ə'kwer·iː·əs, ə'kwær-/ *n* [C/U] the eleventh sign of the ZODIAC, covering the period January 20 to February 18 and represented by a person carrying water, or a person born during this period

aquatic /ə'kwæt̬·ɪk/ *adj* [not gradable] living in, happening in, or connected with water • *Waterskiing is my favorite aquatic sport.*

aqueduct /'æk·wə,dʌkt/ *n* [C] a structure like a bridge for carrying water across land in pipes or an open channel

Arab /'ær·əb/ *n* [C], *adj* a person whose language is Arabic, an important language of the Middle East, or who comes from an Arabic-speaking country, esp. in the Middle East • *A number of Arab states are unhappy about the agreement.*

Arabic numeral /,ær·ə·bɪk'nuː·mə·rəl/ *n* [C] one of the symbols (1, 2, 3, etc.) used by many people to write numbers • Compare ROMAN NUMERAL.

arable /'ær·ə·bəl/ *adj* (of land) used for or right for growing crops • *The country is rich in arable land.*

arbiter /'ɑr·bət̬·ər/ *n* [C] a person who acts as a judge in an argument or of a subject of interest • *Certain magazines are arbiters of fashion.* • An arbiter is also an **arbitrator**. See at ARBITRATE.

arbitrary /'ɑr·bə,trer·i/ *adj* based on a desire or idea or chance rather than reason • *Her outfit was an arbitrary choice but was just perfect.*

arbitrarily /,ɑr·bə'trer·ə·li/ *adv* • *We didn't think much about it, just arbitrarily decided to go to Italy.*

arbitrariness /,ɑr·bə'trer·iː·nəs/ *n* [U] disapproving • *The arbitrariness of human nature infuriates me.*

arbitrate /'ɑr·bə,treɪt/ *v* [I/T] to make a formal judgment to decide an argument • *A referee was hired to arbitrate the dispute.* [T]

arbitration /,ɑr·bə'treɪ·ʃən/ *n* [U] the formal process of having an outside person, chosen by both sides to a disagreement, end the disagreement • *Both labor and management have agreed to arbitration.*

arbitrator /'ɑr·bə,treɪt̬·ər/, **arbiter** *n* [C] • *The independent arbitrator has the approval of both sides in the dispute.*

arc /ɑrk/ *n* [C] a part of a circle, or the shape of a curved line • *The ball rose in a high arc and landed beyond the fence.*

arcade /ɑr'keɪd/ *n* [C] an area where there are many electronic or other coin-operated games for the public • *video-game arcades* ○ *a carnival arcade* • An arcade is also a covered area between buildings, esp. one with arches and columns where there are shops.

arch /ɑrtʃ/ *n* [C] a structure consisting of a curved top on two supports which holds the weight of something above it, or something decorative that has this shape • *Two rows of arches support the roof of the church.* • The arch of your foot is the higher, curved part on the bottom.

arch /ɑrtʃ/ v [I/T] • *Cats often arch their backs when they stretch.* [T]

arched /ɑrtʃt/ adj • *Arched bookcases filled each end of the room.*

archaeology, **archeology** /ˌɑr·kiːˈɑl·ə·dʒi/ n [U] the study of ancient cultures through examination of their buildings, tools, and other objects

archaeological, **archeological** /ˌɑr·kiː·əˈlɑdʒ·ɪ·kəl/ adj [not gradable] • *I always wanted to go on an archaeological dig.*

archaeologist, **archeologist** /ˌɑr·kiːˈɑl·ə·dʒəst/ n [C] • *A marine archaeologist has uncovered the wreck of the sunken ship.*

archaic /ɑrˈkeɪ·ɪk/ adj of or belonging to the distant past; from an ancient period in history • *Some people like to show off by using archaic words.*

archbishop /ɑrtʃˈbɪʃ·əp, ˈɑrtʃˌbɪʃ-/ n [C] a BISHOP (= an important priest) of the highest rank, in charge of the churches and other bishops in a large area

archdiocese /ɑrtʃˈdɑɪ·ə·səs, -ˌsiːz/ n [C] the area of which an ARCHBISHOP is in charge

archer /ˈɑr·tʃər/ n [C] a person who shoots with a BOW (= long stick held bent by a string tied to the ends) and arrow, usually for sport

archery /ˈɑr·tʃə·ri/ n [U] the skill or sport of shooting arrows

archipelago /ˌɑr·kəˈpel·əˌɡoʊ, ˌɑr·tʃə-/ n [C] pl **archipelagoes** or **archipelagos** a group of islands, or an area of sea where there are many islands • *The Hawaiian archipelago is made up of a number of large islands and some extremely small ones.*

architect /ˈɑr·kəˌtekt/ n [C] a person who designs new buildings and is responsible for how they are built • *(fig.) President Roosevelt was the architect of the New Deal during the Great Depression.*

architecture /ˈɑr·kəˌtek·tʃər/ n [U] the skill and science of designing and putting buildings together, or the style of a building • *He studied architecture with Gropius.* ○ *This church is a fine example of late Gothic architecture.*

architectural /ˌɑr·kəˈtek·tʃə·rəl/ adj [not gradable] • *Framed architectural drawings hung on the walls of his office.*

archive /ˈɑr·kɑɪv/ n [C], **archives** pl n the historical records of a place, organization, or family, or the place where these are kept • *The author's manuscripts are in the college archives.*

archival /ɑrˈkɑɪ·vəl/ adj [not gradable] • *I'm doing some archival research on my family's history.*

Arctic /ˈɑrk·tɪk, ˈɑrt·ɪk/ n [U] the large and extremely cold area around the North Pole • *The Arctic is not a barren wasteland.* • Compare ANTARCTIC.

arctic /ˈɑrk·tɪk, ˈɑrt·ɪk/ adj extremely cold •

Arctic air stung New England with freezing temperatures.

ardent /ˈɑrd·ᵊnt/ adj showing strong feelings; eager • *They were ardent pacifists.*

ardor /ˈɑrd·ər/ n [U] a strong emotion, esp. love and sexual desire for someone or excitement and enthusiasm for something • *His ardor for her cooled after only a few weeks.* ○ *Her ardor for basketball impressed me.*

arduous /ˈɑr·dʒə·wəs/ adj difficult and tiring, or needing a great deal of effort • *In those days, a trip to the West was an arduous journey.*

are /ɑr, ər, r/ present simple of BE, used with you/we/they • *Are you hungry?* ○ *They are late.*

area PLACE /ˈer·iː·ə, ˈær-/ n [C] a part of the earth's surface of land and water, or a particular part of a country, city, town, etc. • *an industrial/suburban/mountainous area* • An area is also a particular part of anything that takes space: *This area of the brain is called the cerebral cortex.* • An **area code** is a set of three numbers that you have to use before the main number when you want to telephone someone outside of your local area. LP TELEPHONE

area MEASURE /ˈer·iː·ə, ˈær-/ n [C/U] the measure of a flat space or surface • *You get the area of a rectangle by multiplying its length by its width.* [C]

area SUBJECT /ˈer·iː·ə, ˈær-/ n [C] a particular subject or activity • *His area of expertise includes learning disorders.*

arena /əˈriː·nə/ n [C] a central, level area for the performance of sports or entertainment, having raised seats around it from which people can see the activities, or a building containing the seats and performance area • *a sports arena* • An arena is also a particular activity, esp. one that involves competition and gets a lot of public attention: *She entered the political arena as a young woman.*

aren't /ɑrnt, ˈɑr·ənt/ contraction of **are not** • *They aren't here yet.* • **Aren't I** is used in questions for am I not: *Aren't I crazy to do this?*

argue DISAGREE /ˈɑr·ɡjuː/ v [I] to disagree esp. strongly and sometimes angrily in talking or discussing something • *They argued about money.* ○ *I can't argue with you about that* (= I agree with you).

argument /ˈɑr·ɡjə·mənt/ n [C] • *I had an argument with my boss.*

argue GIVE REASONS /ˈɑr·ɡjuː/ v [I/T] to give the reasons for your opinion about the truth of something or to explain why you believe something should be done • *They argued for/against a tax cut.* [I] • *(law)* To argue is also to represent the case of someone in a court of law.

arguable /ˈɑr·ɡjə·wə·bəl/ adj [not gradable] possible to give reasons for and against; DEBATABLE • *It's arguable that another route would be just as bad.*

arguably /'ɑr·gjə·wə·bli/ *adv* [not gradable] • *She was, arguably, the best female basketball player of all time.*

argument /'ɑr·gjə·mənt/ *n* [C] • *A good argument can be made for providing health insurance for all children.* • (*law*) An argument is a lawyer's representation of a case in a court of law.

argumentative /,ɑr·gjə'ment·əţ·ɪv/ *adj* quick to disagree and argue • *Don't be so argumentative.*

aria /'ɑr·iː·ə/ *n* [C] a song sung by one person in an opera or in some other types of music

arid /'ær·əd/ *adj* (of land or weather) having little rain; very dry • *an arid region*

Aries /'er·iːz, 'er·iː,iːz, 'ær-/ *n* [C/U] the first sign of the ZODIAC, covering the period March 21 to April 19 and represented by a RAM, or a person born during this period

arise HAPPEN /ə'rɑɪz/ *v* [I] *past simple* **arose** /ə'roʊz/, *past part* **arisen** /ə'rɪz·ən/ to come into existence or begin to be noticed; happen • *Problems arise when kids leave school.* ○ *When the opportunity arose, he decided to take it.*

arise GET UP /ə'rɑɪz/ *v* [I] *past simple* **arose** /ə'roʊz/, *past part* **arisen** /ə'rɪz·ən/ *esp. literary* to get up, esp. from bed after sleeping • *We arose early on Christmas morning.*

aristocracy /,ær·ə'stɑk·rə·si/ *n* [C] a class of people of high social rank

aristocrat /ə'rɪs·tə,kræt, 'ær·ə·stə-/ *n* [C] • *a prep-school-educated American aristocrat*

aristocratic /ə,rɪs·tə'kræţ·ɪk, ,ær·ə·stə-/ *adj* • *His aristocratic manner alienated many voters.*

arithmetic /ə'rɪθ·mə,tɪk/ *n* [U] the process of making calculations such as adding, multiplying, and dividing by using numbers, or the study of this

arm BODY PART /ɑrm/ *n* [C] either of the two long parts of the upper body that are joined to the shoulders and have hands at the end • *She put her arm around his waist.* 0 ○ *He held her in his arms* (= with his arms around her). • The arm of a piece of clothing or furniture is

a part of it that you put your arm in or on: *the arm of a jacket/chair* • An arm of an organization is a part of it with particular responsibilities: *the publishing arm of the church* • **Arm in arm** means with your arm resting on another person's: *We walked arm in arm through the park.* • *He held the snake* at **arm's length** (= as far away from his body as possible). • An **armchair** is a comfortable chair with two resting places for the arms. • An **armpit** is the hollow place under your arm where your arm joins your upper body.

armful /'ɑrm·fʊl/ *n* [C] the amount that a person can carry in one or both arms • *an armful of groceries*

arm PROVIDE WEAPONS /ɑrm/ *v* [T] to provide (yourself or others) with a weapon or weapons • *He armed himself with a baseball bat before going outside.*

armed /ɑrmd/ *adj* [not gradable] using or carrying weapons • *armed guards* ○ *armed robbery* • If you are armed with something, you know or have access to something that can be useful to you: *Kids should be armed with the facts about the disease.* • The **armed forces** are a country's military forces, usually an army, navy, and air force.

arms /ɑrmz/ *pl n* weapons and explosives used in fighting wars • *He believes in the right to own and bear arms.* • **Arms control** is the international effort to limit the number and types of weapons that countries are allowed to have. • An **arms race** is a situation in which two or more countries are increasing the number and strength of their weapons because each wants to be stronger than any other.

armadillo /,ɑr·mə'dɪl·oʊ/ *n* [C] *pl* **armadillos** a small animal found in South America, Central America, and in the southern US which has a body covered by hard, bony strips that allow it to curl into a ball to protect itself when attacked

armament /'ɑr·mə·mənt/ *n* [C/U] the weapons, explosives, and other equipment used in fighting a war • *The US is a leading seller of armaments.* [C]

armistice /'ɑr·mə·stəs/ *n* [C] an agreement between two countries or groups at war to stop fighting for a period of time, esp. to talk about possible peace

armor /'ɑr·mər/ *n* [U] strong protective covering, esp. for the body • *samurai armor* • Armor is also military vehicles that are covered in strong metal.

armored /'ɑr·mərd/ *adj* covered with special protective metal • *an armored personnel carrier* • An armed military division has vehicles covered with armor. • An **armored car** is a small truck that is covered with protective metal and that is used esp. to move large amounts of money from one place to another.

armory /'ɑr·mə·ri/ *n* [C] a place where weapons and other military equipment are

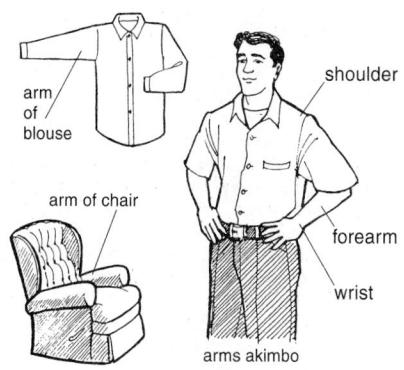

arm of blouse
shoulder
arm of chair
forearm
wrist
arms akimbo

arms

stored • An **armory** is also a large building where members of local military units meet to train and where other events are sometimes held.

arms /ɑrmz/ *pl n* • See at ARM PROVIDE WEAPONS.

army /'ɑr·mi/ *n* [C] a military force, usually belonging to a country, that has the training and equipment to fight on land • *She decided to join the army.* • An **army** is also any large group: *An army of homeless men slept in the streets.*

aroma /ə'rou·mə/ *n* [C] a strong, usually pleasant smell • *the aroma of coffee and frying eggs*

aromatic /ˌær·ə'mæt̬·ɪk/ *adj* • *an aromatic pine forest*

arose /ə'rouz/ *past simple of* ARISE

around IN THIS DIRECTION /ə'raʊnd/ *prep, adv* [not gradable] in a position or direction surrounding, along the outside of, or from one part of to another • *We sat around the table.* ◦ *Go around to the back of the house and come in through the kitchen.* ◦ *We drove around town for a while, looking for a place to park.* ◦ *She turned around* (= so that she was facing in the opposite direction) *and waved goodbye.* ◦ (*fig.*) *He built his story around the theme of spiritual loneliness.* • *The skater twirled* **around and around** (= in a circle). • **Around the clock** (also **round the clock**) means continual or continually: *They're working around the clock to get it done.* • If a place is **around the corner**, it is very close, on the street that crosses the one you are on: *There's a deli around the corner.*

around HERE / NEAR /ə'raʊnd/ *adv, adj* positioned or moving in or near a place • *I used to live around here.* ◦ *Will you guys be around next week?*

around TO ALL PARTS /ə'raʊnd/ *prep, adv* [not gradable] in or to many parts of or all directions • *Car phones are common all around the country.* ◦ *People came from miles around.*

around APPROXIMATELY /ə'raʊnd/ *adv* about; approximately • *Around 40 people showed up.* ◦ *He arrived in Kansas City around 1984.*

arouse /ə'raʊz/ *v* [T] to cause someone to have (a particular feeling) • *He works hard to arouse his students' curiosity.* • A person who is (sexually) aroused feels sexual excitement.

arraign /ə'reɪn/ *v* [T] *law* to formally accuse (someone) of a particular crime in a court of law and ask them to state whether they are guilty or not • *He was arraigned on a robbery charge.*

arraignment /ə'reɪn·mənt/ *n* [C] *law* • *They pleaded not guilty at their arraignment.*

arrange PLAN /ə'reɪndʒ/ *v* [I/T] to plan or make preparations for (something) or for something to happen • *He arranged a meeting between the two leaders.* ◦ *My friends arranged to eat with me.* [+ *to* infinitive] ◦ *Shelly arranged for the publication of her the-*

sis. [I] • An **arranged marriage** is one in which the parents choose the person their son or daughter will marry.

arrangement /ə'reɪndʒ·mənt/ *n* [C] a plan or preparation for something, esp. for something to happen in a particular way • *She had an arrangement to work at home two days a week.* ◦ *Since the hotel was full, we had to make other arrangements.*

arrange PUT IN POSITION /ə'reɪndʒ/ *v* [T] to put (something) in a particular order • *We arranged the chairs in a circle.* ◦ *Books should be arranged alphabetically by author.*

arrangement /ə'reɪndʒ·mənt/ *n* [C] • *a flower arrangement*

arrange WRITE MUSIC /ə'reɪndʒ/ *v* [T] to write (the parts of a piece of music) so that it can be played by a particular instrument or instruments

arrangement /ə'reɪndʒ·mənt/ *n* [C] • *an arrangement for trumpet and cello*

arranger /ə'reɪn·dʒər/ *n* [C] • *Ellington was a composer, arranger, and pianist.*

array /ə'reɪ/ *n* [C] a large group of things or people, esp. when shown or positioned in an attractive way • *The airport shops offer a wide array of merchandise.*

array /ə'reɪ/ *v* [T] • *A battery of cameras was arrayed before them.*

arrest CATCH /ə'rest/ *v* [T] (of the police) to use lawful authority to catch (someone) and take them to a place where they may be accused of a crime • *Three women were arrested on prostitution charges.*

arrest /ə'rest/ *n* [C/U] • *FBI agents made the arrest.* [C] ◦ *He was placed under arrest by federal marshals.* [U]

arrest STOP /ə'rest/ *v* [T] to stop or slow (an activity) • *Antibiotics arrest the development of harmful bacteria.*

arresting /ə'res·tɪŋ/ *adj* • If something is arresting, it causes you to stop and notice it: *The house has an arresting view of the river.*

arrive /ə'raɪv/ *v* [I] to come to a place, esp. after traveling • *What time is their plane scheduled to arrive?* • If someone or something arrives, it appears: *Sausages suddenly arrived on our table.* • (*infml*) If someone has arrived, they have become successful. *When they sent a limo for us, I knew we'd arrived.*

arrival /ə'raɪ·vəl/ *n* [C/U] the act of someone or something that reaches a place or comes into existence, or a person or thing that reaches a place • *The arrival of the railroad changed the western US.* [U] ◦ *The arrival of the new year was greeted with joy.* [U] ◦ *There were so many refugees that tents were needed to house new arrivals.* [C]

□ **arrive at** /-'--/ *v prep* [T] to come to a decision about (something) after much consideration • *How did he arrive at this estimate?*

arrogant /'ær·ə·gənt/ *adj* unpleasantly proud and behaving as if you are better or more important than other people • *I never met a more conceited and arrogant young man.*

arrogantly /ˈær·ə·gənt·li/ *adv* • *Lapham arrogantly claimed the land was his.*

arrogance /ˈær·ə·gəns/ *n* [U] *I was disgusted by his arrogance.*

arrow /ˈær·oʊ/ *n* [C] a long, thin stick, pointed at one end, that can be used in hunting or as a weapon when shot from a BOW • An arrow is also a sign (↑) consisting of a straight line with an upside down V shape at one end, which points in a particular direction. • PIC BOW

arroyo /əˈrɔɪ·ə, -ˌoʊ/ *n* [C] (in the southwestern US) a narrow channel in the ground that is usually dry but becomes a stream after heavy rain

arsenal /ˈɑr·sən·əl/ *n* [C] a building or place where weapons and military equipment are made or stored, or a collection of weapons • *Both countries sought to modernize their nuclear arsenals.*

arsenic /ˈɑr·snɪk, ˈɑr·sə·nɪk/ *n* [U] a very poisonous substance, used to kill RATS (= animals like mice, but larger) and harmful insects

arson /ˈɑr·sən/ *n* [U] the crime of intentionally starting a fire in order to damage or destroy something, esp. a building

arsonist /ˈɑr·sə·nəst/ *n* [C] • *He was a convicted arsonist and murderer.*

art /ɑrt/ *n* [U] the making or doing of something whose purpose is to bring pleasure to people through their enjoyment of what is beautiful and interesting, or things often made for this purpose, such as paintings, drawings, or SCULPTURES • *ancient/modern art* ○ *American/French/Japanese art* ○ *an art museum/gallery* • An art is also a skill or ability: *He never learned the art of saying "Thank you."* • An **artwork** is an object made by an artist, esp. a picture or statue. • Artwork is also the drawings and photographs that are used in books, newspapers, and magazines.

artist /ˈɑrt̬·əst/ *n* [C] a person who paints, draws, or makes SCULPTURES • An artist is also someone who performs as an actor, musician, dancer, singer, etc.

artistic /ɑrˈtɪs·tɪk/ *adj* • *These were the years of his finest artistic creativity.* • An artistic person has skill or ability in painting, dancing, singing, etc.

artistically /ɑrˈtɪs·tɪ·kli/ *adv* • *It was her most artistically impressive performance to date.*

artistry /ˈɑrt̬·ə·stri/ *n* [U] the special skills possessed by someone who has the ability to make art • *No American composer has topped the sheer artistry, elegance, and wit of Cole Porter.*

arts /ɑrts/ *pl n* the making, showing, or performance of painting, acting, dancing, music, etc. • *fine/decorative/performing arts* • **Arts and crafts** are the skills of making objects, such as decorations, furniture, and POTTERY (= objects made from clay), by hand.

arty /ˈɑrt̬·i/, **artsy** /ˈɑrt·si/ *adj infml disapproving* trying to be like artists or dress and live in the style typical of artists, esp. while lacking any real understanding of art or the work of artists • *an arty crowd*

artery TUBE /ˈɑrt̬·ə·ri/ *n* [C] one of the larger tubes that carry blood from the heart to other parts of the body • *a coronary artery* • Compare VEIN TUBE.

artery ROAD /ˈɑrt̬·ə·ri/ *n* [C] an important road, river, or other transportation route

artesian well /ɑrˈtiː·ʒənˈwel/ *n* [C] a WELL (= deep hole in the ground) in which the water is forced to the surface by natural pressure

artful /ˈɑrt·fəl/ *adj* intelligent and skillful, esp. in persuading, sometimes without being completely honest • *His politics was an artful blend of high-minded patriotism and malicious gossip about his opponents.*

artfully /ˈɑrt·fə·li/ *adv* • *The machinery is artfully concealed in a polished cabinet.*

arthritis /ɑrˈθraɪt̬·əs/ *n* [U] a disease in which a person's joints become swollen, and in which there is some loss in the ability to move them without pain

arthritic /ɑrˈθrɪt̬·ɪk/ *adj* • *an arthritic knee*

artichoke /ˈɑrt̬·ə,tʃoʊk/ *n* [C] a tall plant with a rounded edible top that is enclosed by thick, pointed leaves

article PIECE OF WRITING /ˈɑrt̬·ɪ·kəl/ *n* [C] a piece of writing on a particular subject in a newspaper or magazine • *an article on Chinese art*

article OBJECT /ˈɑrt̬·ɪ·kəl/ *n* [C] a particular thing or item • *The police want a description of each missing article.*

article SMALL WORD /ˈɑrt̬·ɪ·kəl/ *n* [C] *specialized* (in grammar) any of the English words "a," "an," and "the," or words in other languages that are used in a similar way as these • See **definite article** at DEFINITE; **indefinite article** at INDEFINITE.

articulate /ɑrˈtɪk·jə·lət/ *adj* expressing or able to express things easily and clearly • *The First Lady was an intelligent and articulate spokeswoman for a lot of causes.*

articulate /ɑrˈtɪk·jə,leɪt/ *v* [T] to explain in words, esp. to express (something) clearly • *She has not yet articulated her vision of why she wants to be governor.*

artifact /ˈɑrt̬·ɪ,fækt/ *n* [C] an object made by a person, such as a tool, esp. one that is of historical interest • *The museum has artifacts dating back to prehistoric times.*

artificial PRODUCED /ˌɑrt̬·əˈfɪʃ·əl/ *adj* made by people, often as a copy of something natural • *artificial flowers* ○ *artificial grass* ○ *an artificial leg* • **Artificial intelligence** is the use of computers programs that have some of the qualities of the human mind, such as the ability to understand language, recognize pictures, and learn from experience. • **Artificial respiration** is the act of forcing air in and out

DEFINITE AND INDEFINITE ARTICLES: *THE, A,* AND *AN*

The, a, and **an** are most often used before nouns to refer to people, things, or ideas. Generally, no article is used before the names of particular people or singular places.

South America • Main Street • Everest • Lake Ontario • President Bush • Stanford University • Dr. Lyons.

Plural place names and some names of geographical areas take **the.**

We flew from **the** *United States to* **the** *Caribbean. •* *We're going skiing in* **the** *Rockies. • They crossed* **the** *Sahara Desert.*

a / an

USED TO REFER TO A PARTICULAR ITEM THAT IS NOT YET KNOWN TO THE SPEAKER, THE LISTENER, OR BOTH

The indefinite article is used to introduce a single item for the first time.

Is that noise **an** *ambulance or* **a** *police car? • Do you have* **a** *pen I could use?*

USED TO STATE WHAT TYPE OF THING SOMETHING IS

A and **an** are used to say what group a particular person or thing belongs to.

She's **an** *economist. • This is* **a** *wonderful surprise!*

USED TO MEAN "ONE" OR "EACH"

The indefinite article is preferred to *one* when talking about a single thing or person.

The thieves took **a** *painting and four silver candlesticks. • They're only going to stay for* **a** *day or two.*

It is also commonly used with words for quantities ending in 00 and with *dozen.*

a *hundred,* **a** *thousand,* **a** *million*

One is used for emphasis or in order to contrast with other numbers.

Give me **one** *good reason why I should! • Last year we sold three thousand copies, but we sold only* **one** *thousand this year.*

A and **an** are used with units and some other words to mean "each."

It costs $12.95 **a** *yard* (= for each yard). *• He reads three books* **a** *week.*

the

USED TO REFER TO ONE OR MORE PARTICULAR ITEMS THAT ARE KNOWN

The is used when something introduced earlier is referred to again.

They served a piece of meat and some potatoes. **The** *meat was revolting, but I managed to eat* **the** *potatoes.*

The is also used when it is very clear what is being referred to, even if it has not been mentioned before.

The *moon looks beautiful tonight. •* **The** *phone's ringing. • What's* **the** *date? • Can I use* **the** *bathroom?*

LP Numbers

USED TO MAKE GENERAL OR INDEFINITE PHRASES THAT REFER TO PARTICULAR ITEMS

In the examples below, the nouns in the sentences on the left refer generally to a group of items, or to particular items that are not known or specified. In the sentences on the right, the noun phrases refer to particular things. The definite article is then required.

Normally I like music.	*Normally I like* **the** *music you like.*
Managers often complain.	**The** *managers in our office often complain.*
A man called.	**The** *man you met yesterday called.*

no article

USED TO MAKE GENERAL STATEMENTS

A noun that has no plural is labeled [U]. In general statements using [U] nouns, no article is used.

History is my favorite subject. • Life is too short to worry about money. • Classical music will never be as popular as pop music.

Usually with [C] nouns the plural is used without an article in general statements.

Elephants can't jump. • Do you like strawberries?

It is also possible to make general statements using a definite or indefinite article before a [C] noun.
An injured lion (= any injured lion) *is **an** extremely dangerous animal.* • *Does **the** computer* (= Do computers in general) *really save time and money?* • ***The** Italians and **the** Turks are very different, I think.*

Some general rules
Example sentences in the dictionary show how particular nouns are used with **a**, **an**, and **the**, or with no article. The following table gives approximate rules for some common types of nouns.

LP **Determiners**

a or an	the	no article		
✓		✓	days, months, holidays	*Come on Monday.* • *I was born on* a *Friday.* • *I'm going home for Thanksgiving.*
		✓	languages	*I'm trying to learn Japanese.*
✓		✓	nationalities ending in -s	(*the*) *Mexicans*
	✓		nationalities (other endings)	**the** *French*
		✓	meals	*I don't usually eat breakfast.*
✓	✓	✓	musical instruments	*I play drums.* • *She's learning* **the** *piano.* • *He bought* a *guitar.*
✓			job names	*She's* a *dancer.*
		✓	professions	*He wants to go into teaching.*
		✓	sports and games	*Do you play chess?*
	✓		titles used alone	**the** *Pope* • **the** *president*
		✓	years	*Tyler was born in 1985.*
	✓		years in groups	*He grew up during* **the** *1950s.*

of the lungs of a person who has stopped breathing on their own, esp. by blowing into the mouth.

artificially /ˌɑrt̬·ə'fɪʃ·ə·li/ *adv* • *Those oranges have been artificially colored.*

artificiality /ˌɑrt̬·ə,fɪʃ·iː'æl·ət̬·i/ *n* [U]

artificial NOT SINCERE /ˌɑrt̬·ə'fɪʃ·əl/ *adj* not sincere; not truly intended • *an artificial smile*

artillery /ɑr'tɪl·ə·ri/ *n* [U] large guns that are moved on wheels or metal tracks, or the part of an army that uses these • *He served as an artillery officer in Vietnam.*

artisan /'ɑrt̬·ə·zən, -sən/ *n* [C] a person who does skilled work with his or her hands • *You will learn how eighteenth-century artisans did their work.*

artist /'ɑrt̬·əst/ *n* [C] • See at ART.

artistic /ɑr'tɪs·tɪk/ *adj* • See at ART.

artistically /ɑr'tɪs·tɪ·kli/ *adv* • See at ART.

artistry /'ɑrt̬·ə·stri/ *n* [U] • See at ART.

arts /ɑrts/ *pl n* • See at ART.

arty /'ɑrt̬·i/ *adj* • See at ART.

arugula /ə'ruː·gə·lə, -gjə-/ *n* [U] a green, leafy plant that is eaten in salads

as COMPARISON /æz, əz/ *adv* [not gradable], *prep*, *conjunction* used in expressions that compare two things, persons, groups, or qualities • *This jacket costs twice as much as that one.* ○ *They live in the same town as my parents.* ○ *She'll soon be as tall as her mother.* • If some-

thing is **as American as apple pie**, it is considered typical of the United States or of the people of the United States. • If you say **as far as** someone **is concerned**, you mean in order to satisfy that person's wants or needs: *There's no reason to wait, as far as I'm concerned.* • *You can have a dog **as long as** (= if) you promise to take care of it.* • *He's **as old as the hills** (= very old).* • *The box is made of plastic, **as opposed to** wood* (= rather than wood). • *We'll come **as soon as** we can* (= in the shortest possible time). • *They advertised the new movie on television, and in newspapers **as well*** (= also). • *We have a responsibility to our community **as well as** (= and also) to our families.*

as BEING /æz, əz/ *prep* appearing to be, or being • *He went to the Halloween party dressed as a banana.* ○ *As a child, Miriam had lived in India.* ○ *The news came as no surprise.* • **As a (general) rule** (= Usually), *we don't allow children in here.* • **As a matter of fact** adds emphasis to what you are saying, or to show that it is not what others might have thought: *"Are you new around here?" "As a matter of fact, I've lived here for ten years."* • **As such** means in the exact meaning of the word or phrase: *There weren't many vegetarian dishes as such, although there were several different kinds of cheese.* • If you say something happens **as usual**, you mean that it most often happens in this way and is to be expected: *As usual, she was wearing jeans.*

as ⌐BECAUSE⌐ /æz, əz/ *conjunction* because • *As it was getting late, I decided to stop at a motel.*

as ⌐WHEN⌐ /æz, əz/ *conjunction* while; during the time that • *As I was getting out of the car, my heel caught on something and I fell.* • **As of** (= Starting) *next month, all the prices will go up.*

as ⌐ALTHOUGH⌐ /æz, əz/ *conjunction* although • *Angry as he was, he had to smile.*

as ⌐THE SAME WAY⌐ /æz, əz/ *conjunction* in the way that; like • *Do exactly as I say.* ○ *As is often the case with children, Aimee was completely better by the time the doctor arrived.* ○ *Just as I thought, Derrick was to blame.* ○ *Use your coat as a blanket.* • You use **as follows** to introduce a list of items, often in a particular order: *The finishers were as follows—Smith, Mitchell, Glowser, and Bryce.* • **As if/as though** means in a way that suggests what the real situation is: *She acts as though she wasn't warned.* • **As if** can also be used to emphasize a negative: *As if I didn't have enough problems* (= I have too many problems even now)*!* • If you buy something **as is**, you accept it in its present condition: *All merchandise is sold as is—no refunds, no exchanges.* • **As it is** can mean already: *No, I'm not buying you children anything else today—I've spent far too much money as it is.* • **As for** means to change the subject to: *As for the money, we'll talk about that later.* • *There is no problem* **as regards** (= about) *the financial arrangements.* • **As to** means about: *I can't answer questions as to how long the concert will last.*

asap /ˌeɪˌesˌeɪˈpiː, ˈæsˌæp/ *abbreviation for* as soon as possible

asbestos /æsˈbesˌtəs, æz-/ *n* [U] a soft, gray-white material that does not burn and was used in buildings as a protection against fire, and as a form of INSULATION (= way of stopping heat from escaping) • *Inhaling asbestos fibers can make you sick.*

ascend /əˈsend/ *v* [I/T] to move up or climb (something) • *They slowly ascended the steep path up the mountain.* [T] ○ *A long flight of steps ascends* (= leads up) *to the door of the church.* [I]

ascent /əˈsent/ *n* [C] • *She made a successful ascent* (= climb) *of Mt. McKinley last year.* [C]

ascertain *(obj)* /ˌæsˌərˈteɪn/ *v* to discover (a fact); to make certain • *The fire department has been unable to ascertain the cause of the fire.* [T]

ascetic /əˈset̪ˌɪk/ *adj* avoiding physical pleasures and living a simple life, often for religious reasons

ASCII, ascii /ˈæsˌkiː/ *n* [U] *abbreviation for* American Standard Code for Information Interchange (= a way of storing text or information on a computer) • *All the files are in ASCII.*

ascribe *obj* **to** *obj* /əˈskraɪbˌtə, -tʊ, -ˌtuː/ *v prep* [T] to consider (something) to be caused, created, or owned by (someone or something) • *To what do you ascribe the enormous success of*

your latest book? ○ *People like to ascribe human feelings to animals* (= believe animals have human feelings).

ash ⌐POWDER⌐ /æʃ/ *n* [C/U] the soft, gray or black, powdery substance left after something has burned • *cigarette ash* [U] ○ *volcanic ash* [U] ○ *We cleaned the ashes out of the fireplace.* [C] • An **ashtray** is a small dish or container in which smokers leave ashes and cigarette ends.

ashes /ˈæʃˌəz/ *pl n* the ash left after a dead body has been CREMATED (= burned in a special way) • *My grandmother's ashes were scattered over this lake.*

ash ⌐TREE⌐ /æʃ/ *n* [C/U] a tree that has a smooth gray BARK (= strong outer covering), or the hard wood of this tree

ashamed /əˈʃeɪmd/ *adj* feeling bad because you are aware that others know that you or someone connected with you has done something wrong or embarrassing • *Pedro was never ashamed to admit his mistakes.* [+ to infinitive] ○ *I felt deeply ashamed for my father's impoliteness.* ○ *You have nothing to be ashamed of.* ○ *She was ashamed to ask her brother for money.* [+ to infinitive]

ashen /ˈæʃˌən/ *adj* (of a person's face) looking pale and gray from illness, shock, or fear

ashore /əˈʃɔːr, əˈʃoʊr/ *adv* [not gradable] toward or onto land from an area of water, or on land after coming from an area of water • *Julie jumped off the boat and swam ashore.*

Asian /ˈeɪˌʒən, -ˌʃən/ *n* [C], *adj* (a person) of or coming from Asia

aside /əˈsaɪd/ *adv* [not gradable] on or to one side • *I pushed aside the curtain and looked out the window.* ○ *I took her aside* (= out of hearing distance of other people) *to tell her to behave herself.* ○ *The governor wants to set aside* (= keep separate and not spend) *$50 million for emergencies.* • *I don't watch any television,* **aside from** (= except for) *the news.*

asinine /ˈæsˌəˌnaɪn/ *adj* foolish or stupid • *an asinine comment*

ask ⌐QUESTION OR REQUEST⌐ /æsk/ *v* [I/T] to state (a question to someone), or to request (something) from (someone) • *Can I ask you a question?* [T] ○ *If you are asking me if I was foolish, yes, I was foolish.* [T] ○ *We kept asking why he had done it.* [+ wh- word] ○ *He asked how much the necklace cost.* [+ wh- word] ○ *He asked for more time to repay the loan.* [I] ○ *You should ask your lawyer for advice.* [T] ○ *I'd like to ask your advice on a financial matter.* [T] ○ *I asked to see my accountant.* [+ to infinitive] ○ *"How much time do we have left?" he asked.* ○ *Our neighbors are selling their house, but I don't know how much they're asking for it* (= how much they want for it). [I] • If you are **asking for trouble**, you behave in a manner that is likely to cause problems for you: *Drinking before driving is asking for trouble.*

ask ⌐INVITE⌐ /æsk/ *v* [T] to invite (someone) to go

somewhere • *"Are you going to Michelle's party?" "No, I haven't been asked." ○ Megan's asked us over for dinner next Friday.* • To **ask** someone **out** is to invite them to go with you somewhere socially, esp. when there is the possibility of romantic interest: *He was recently divorced, and had not asked a woman out for over seventeen years.*

askew /ə'skju:/ *adj, adv* not straight or level • *His shirt was wrinkled and his tie was askew.*

asleep /ə'sli:p/ *adj* [not gradable] sleeping or not awake • *I fell asleep* (= began to sleep) *while watching television.* ○ *I didn't hear the phone—I was fast/sound asleep* (= sleeping and not easily awakened). • If your arm or leg is asleep, you have no feeling there because the flow of blood to that part has been reduced by being in the same position for too long.

asparagus /ə'spær·ə·gəs/ *n* [U] a plant with green or white stems that are cooked and eaten as a vegetable

aspect /'æs·pekt/ *n* [C] a particular feature of or way of thinking about something, esp. something complicated • *There's another aspect of the cost of caring for old parents at home that I'd like to mention.* ○ *He knows every aspect of the criminal justice system.* ○ *A farmer has to handle various aspects of the business.*

asphalt /'æs·fɔːlt/ *n* [U] a black substance mixed with small stones, sand, etc., that forms a hard surface when it dries and is commonly used as a surface for roads

asphyxiate /æs'fɪk·si:,eɪt/ *v* [I/T] to be unable to breathe, usually resulting in death, or to cause (someone) to be unable to breathe; SUFFOCATE • *The men were asphyxiated by smoke.* [T]

asphyxiation /æs,fɪk·si:'eɪ·ʃən/ *n* [U]

aspire to /ə'spaɪr·tə, -tʊ, -,tuː/ *v prep* [T] to have a strong hope to do or have (something) • *Rebecca worked as a waitress but aspired to be a dancer.*

aspiration /,æs·pə'reɪ·ʃən/ *n* [C] a strong hope or wish for achievement or success • *He has political aspirations, and hopes to run for Congress some day.*

aspiring /ə'spaɪ·rɪŋ/ *adj* [not gradable] wishing to become (the stated thing) • *Marcus is an aspiring actor.*

aspirin /'æs·prən, -pə·rən/ *n* [C/U] *pl* **aspirin** or **aspirins** a drug taken to reduce pain, fever, and swelling

ass ANIMAL /æs/ *n* [C] a DONKEY (= animal like a small horse)

ass PERSON /æs/ *n* [C] a person who does or says stupid things • *a pompous ass*

ass BUTTOCKS /æs/ *n* [C] *rude slang* the part of your body that you sit on; your buttocks • If someone tells you to get your ass somewhere, they want you to go there quickly: *Get your ass out of here before I call the cops!*

assail /ə'seɪl/ *v* [T] to criticize (something or someone) strongly, or to cause (someone) to ex-

perience unpleasant thoughts or feelings • *Many parents assailed the proposal to lengthen the school day.* ○ *After the decision to quit his job, he was assailed by doubts.*

assailant /ə'seɪ·lənt/ *n* [C] someone who attacks another • *He fought off the assailant while his wife ran to call the police.*

assassinate /ə'sæs·ə,neɪt/ *v* [T] to murder (a famous or important person) for political reasons or in exchange for money • *President Kennedy was assassinated in Dallas, Texas in 1963.*

assassin /ə'sæs·ən/ *n* [C] a person who murders a famous or important person for political reasons or in exchange for money

assassination /ə,sæs·ə'neɪ·ʃən/ *n* [C/U] • *the assassination of John Lennon*

assault /ə'sɔːlt/ *v* [T] to make a sudden, violent attack on (someone) • *A man grabbed the girl from behind and sexually assaulted her in the utility room.*

assault /ə'sɔːlt/ *n* [C/U] • *University officials are concerned about a series of assaults on teachers and students near the campus.* [C]

assemble /ə'sem·bəl/ *v* [I/T] to bring or come together in a single group or place, or to put together the parts of (something) • *When the fire alarm rings, everyone is supposed to leave the building and assemble in the schoolyard.* [I] ○ *Workers were earning $20 an hour assembling cars.* [T]

assembly GATHERING /ə'sem·bli/ *n* [C/U] a group of people, esp. one gathered together regularly for a particular purpose • In the US, an assembly is one of the two parts of the government in many states that makes laws: *The state assembly will vote on a death penalty bill next week.* [C] • An assembly in a school is a gathering of several classes for a group activity that is usually educational. [C]

assemblyman (*pl* **-men**) /ə'sem·bli:·mən/, **assemblywoman** (*pl* **-women**) /ə'sem·bli:,wʊm·ən/ *n* [C] a member of an official law-making body in some states

assembly JOINING /ə'sem·bli/ *n* [C/U] the process of putting together the parts of a machine or structure, or the thing produced by this process • An **assembly line** is an arrangement of machines and workers in a factory, in which each has a particular job to complete before the next job is started by another machine or worker.

assent /ə'sent/ *n* [U] *slightly fml* agreement to an idea, plan, or request, esp. after serious consideration • *He gave a nod of assent, and we knew we had a deal at last.*

assent /ə'sent/ *v* [I] *slightly fml* • *At long last, the general assented to a halt in the bombing.*

assert /ə'sɜrt/ *v* [T] to state (an opinion) or claim (a right) forcefully • *It is nonsense to assert that smoking does not damage people's health.* [+ *that* clause] • To assert is also to behave in a way that shows (power, authority, or control): *Several members of Congress called upon the president to assert leadership.* • If you assert yourself, you act forcefully in a way that expresses your confidence: *You have to learn to speak up and assert yourself at meetings, or you'll never get anywhere.*

assertion /əˈsɜr·ʃən/ *n* [C] • *Critics say the company forces workers to drive recklessly, an assertion the company denies.*

assertive /əˈsɜrt·ɪv/ *adj* behaving confidently and able to say in a direct way what you want or believe • *If you really want the promotion, you'll have to be more assertive.*

assess JUDGE /əˈses/ *v* [T] to form a judgment about (esp. a situation or a person's qualities) • *A college is going to assess a student's ability based on grades.* • To assess is also to judge the cost or value of (something): *Government officials assessed the flood damage in the millions of dollars.*

assessment /əˈses·mənt/ *n* [C] • *This is an interesting assessment of Mark Twain's importance in American literature.*

assess ASK FOR MONEY /əˈses/ *v* [T] to charge (someone) an amount of money as a special payment • *In order to complete the new clubhouse, all members will be assessed an additional $200 a year.*

assessment /əˈses·mənt/ *n* [C] • *Co-op owners had to pay an assessment to cover the cost of the roof repair.*

asset /ˈæs·et, -ət/ *n* [C usually pl] something having value, such as a possession or property, that is owned by a person, business, or organization • An asset is also any positive feature that gives you an advantage: *Her knowledge of Spanish and French is a real asset in her work.* • Compare LIABILITY.

asshole /ˈæs·hoʊl/ *n* [C] *taboo slang* a person you do not like • *What an asshole he is!*

assign /əˈsaɪn/ *v* [T] to give to someone (a job or responsibility), or to decide on (a person) for a particular job or responsibility • *We assigned Alberto the task of watching the children.* • If someone is assigned to a place, they are sent there to do a job: *Judith was assigned to the office in Washington, D.C.* • If you assign (things) to people, you give them out in an orderly way: *We're assigning seats on a first-come, first-serve basis.*

assignment /əˈsaɪn·mənt/ *n* [C/U] a particular job or responsibility given to you • *The homework assignment was to read Chapter 2 in our history book.* [C] • *The two journalists met while on assignment* (= doing a job) *in Colombia.*

assimilate /əˈsɪm·əˌleɪt/ *v* [I/T] to take in and make a part of your basic knowledge (something learned from others), so that you can use it as your own • *We hoped the students would assimilate the information contained in the lecture.* [T] • If people are or become assimilated in a society, they become similar to others by learning and using the customs and culture of

the new society: *The Indians who did not live on reservations had by then been assimilated into the white society.* [T]

assimilation /əˌsɪm·əˈleɪ·ʃən/ *n* [U] the process of becoming similar to others by taking in and using their customs and culture • *The assimilation of immigrants into American culture has been a constant feature of US history.*

assist /əˈsɪst/ *v* [I/T] to take action to help (someone) or support (something) • *The company said it would assist workers in finding new jobs.* [T] ○ *No one knew where my grandfather was, and many came to assist in the search.* [I]

assistance /əˈsɪs·təns/ *n* [U] • *With some financial assistance, we'll be able to start our own business.*

assistant /əˈsɪs·tənt/ *n* [C] a person who helps someone else to do a job or who holds a less important position in an organization • *an assistant coach/professor* ○ *My assistant will show you around the factory.*

associate SPEND TIME /əˈsoʊ·siːˌeɪt, -ʃiː-/ *v* [I always + adv/prep] to spend time with someone or have some connection with someone or something • *I don't want you associating with that wild crowd any more.*

associate /əˈsoʊ·siːˌət, -ˈʃiː-/ *n* [C] someone who is connected to another person as a business partner or companion • *Claire invited several business associates to dinner.* • An associate is also a person who has a position in a job or type of work that is just below the top position: *an associate director/professor* • An **associate degree** is the level of achievement recognized for a student by a **community college** on successful completion of two years of study.

association /əˌsoʊ·siːˈeɪ·ʃən, -ʃiː-/ *n* [C] a group of people united in an organization because of their common interests • *The AARP, the American Association of Retired Persons, is a huge organization with millions of members.*

associate CONNECT MENTALLY /əˈsoʊ·siːˌeɪt, -ʃiː-/ *v* [T] to think about (something) as being connected to something else • *He always associated that perfume with Lila.*

association /əˌsoʊ·siːˈeɪ·ʃən, -ʃiː-/ *n* [C/U] • *French bread has pleasant associations for me because I enjoyed my trip to France so much.* [C]

assorted /əˈsɔːrt·əd/ *adj* consisting of various types mixed together • *a box of assorted chocolates*

assortment /əˈsɔːrt·mənt/ *n* [C] a mixture or combination of different types • *"That's Dancing!" contains an assortment of musical numbers from famous Hollywood films.*

assume ACCEPT /əˈsuːm/ *v* [T] to accept (something) as true without question or proof • *We can't assume (that) he's innocent simply because he says he is.* [+ *(that)* clause] ○ *I assumed* *(that) nobody was home because the car wasn't in the driveway.* [+ *(that)* clause]

assuming (that) /ə'suː·mɪŋ (ðət, ðæt)/ *conjunction* accepting (something) as true; if • *My plans include you, she said, assuming I could discover a way to interest you.*

assume PRETEND /ə'suːm/ *v* [T] to pretend to be (someone you are not), or to express (a feeling) falsely • *During the investigation, two detectives assumed the identities of antique dealers.* ○ *Jim assumed a look of indifference.*

assume TAKE CONTROL /ə'suːm/ *v* [T] to take (control) or claim (authority), sometimes without the right to do so • *The terrorists assumed control of the plane and forced it to land in the desert.*

assumption ACCEPTANCE /ə'sʌmp·ʃən/ *n* [C] an acceptance of something as true without question or proof • *The plan was based on the assumption that the schedule could be substantially speeded up by adding more people.* [+ *that* clause]

assumption CONTROL /ə'sʌmp·ʃən/ *n* [U] the act of taking control or claiming authority • *Given the chaotic situation, many in the country welcomed the army's assumption of power.*

assure PROMISE /ə'ʃʊr/ *v* [T] to promise or tell something to (someone) confidently or firmly, or to cause (someone) to feel certain by removing doubt • *She assured him (that) the check was in the mail.* ○ *The governor assured the voters (that) taxes would not be raised.*

assurance /ə'ʃʊr·əns/ *n* [C/U] • *He gave me his assurance that he would give us an answer by the end of the week.* [C] • Assurance is also a feeling of confidence in your abilities: *She answered all the questions put to her with assurance and poise.* [U]

assure MAKE CERTAIN /ə'ʃʊr/ *v* [T] to cause (something) to be certain • *Her future was assured when her performance drew rave reviews from all the critics.*

assuredly /ə'ʃʊr·əd·li/ *adv* • *These problems might not be solved by money alone, but they will assuredly (= certainly) not be solved without it.*

asterisk /'æs·tə,rɪsk/ *n* [C] a symbol (*) shaped like a star that is used to refer readers to a note at the bottom of a page of text

asthma /'æz·mə/ *n* [U] a chest disease in which breathing can become difficult, often caused by an ALLERGIC reaction

astonish /ə'stɑn·ɪʃ/ *v* [T] to surprise (someone) very much • *We were astonished at how much she had aged.* ○ *It was astonishing to see the size of the crowds for the Pope.*

astonishment /ə'stɑn·ɪʃ·mənt/ *n* [U] • *To the astonishment of her colleagues, she turned down the award.*

astound /ə'staʊnd/ *v* [T] to surprise (someone) so much that it shocks them, esp. with news of something that is completely unexpected • *Considering how badly they're paid*

and what little support they get, the dedication of these teachers astounds me.

astray /ə'streɪ/ *adv* away from the correct path or way of doing something • *The climate of sexual permissiveness, he said, has caused a lot of our children to go astray.*

astride /ə'straɪd/ *adv, prep* with one leg on either side (of something) • *He sat astride a horse.*

astrology /ə'strɑl·ə·dʒi/ *n* [U] the ancient practice of studying the movements and positions of the sun, moon, planets, and stars in the belief that they influence human behavior

astronaut /'æs·trə,nɔːt, -,nɑt/ *n* [C] a person who is trained for traveling in spacecraft

astronomical /,æs·trə'nɑm·ɪ·kəl/ *adj* extremely large • *The costs were astronomical.*

astronomy /ə'strɑn·ə·mi/ *n* [U] the scientific study of the universe as a whole and of objects that exist naturally in space, such as the stars

astronomical /,æs·trə'nɑm·ɪ·kəl/ *adj* [not gradable] connected with ASTRONOMY • *astronomical observations*

astronomer /ə'strɑn·ə·mər/ *n* [C]

astute /ə'stuːt/ *adj* quick to see how to use a situation to your advantage • *He was politically astute, and was soon appointed to a number of powerful committees in Congress.*

asylum PROTECTION /ə'saɪ·ləm/ *n* [U] protection or safety, or a protected and safe place, given esp. to someone who has left a country or place for political reasons • *The refugees have asked the US government for political asylum.*

asylum HOSPITAL /ə'saɪ·ləm/ *n* [C] dated a mental hospital, or any other INSTITUTION giving shelter and other help to poor or suffering people • *He was committed to an insane asylum in 1899.*

at PLACE / TIME /æt, ət/ *prep* used to show a particular place or a particular time • *I'll meet you at the theater at 7:45 tonight.* ○ *Call me at work.* ○ *There's someone at the door* (= outside the door). ○ *I wasn't here to meet you because I was in Detroit at the time* (= then).

at DIRECTION /æt, ət/ *prep* in the direction of • *They waved at us as we drove by.* ○ *She aimed at the target, but missed.*

at CAUSE /æt, ət/ *prep* used to show the cause of something, esp. a feeling • *I was so happy at the news.*

at CONDITION /æt, ət/ *prep* used to show a state, condition, or continuous activity • *The country was at peace/war.* ○ *I love watching the children at play.* ○ *She was hard at work* (= working hard).

at AMOUNT /æt, ət/ *prep* used to show a price, temperature, rate, speed, etc. • *They're selling these coats at 30% off this week.*

at JUDGMENT /æt, ət/ *prep* used to show the activity in which someone's ability is being judged • *I'm really not very good at math.* ○

Sheila is really terrible at getting to places on time.

at THE MOST /æt, ət/ *prep* used before a superlative • *I'm afraid we can only pay you $12 an hour at (the) most.* ○ *At best you'll get to speak to some assistant—you'll never reach anyone important.*

at all /æt'ɔːl, ət'ɔːl, ə'tɔːl/ *adv* (used to make negatives and questions stronger) in any way or of any type • *I haven't been at all well recently.* ○ *He's had no food at all.* ○ *I'm not at all worried about it.*

ate /eɪt, *not standard* et/ *past simple of* EAT

atheist /'eɪ·θiː·əst/ *n* [C] someone who believes that God does not exist

atheistic /ˌeɪ·θiː'ɪs·tɪk/ *adj*

atheism /'eɪ·θiː‚ɪz·əm/ *n* [U] the belief that God does not exist

athlete /'æθˌliːt, *not standard* 'æθ·ə‚liːt/ *n* [C] a person who is trained or skilled in a sport and esp. one who regularly competes with others in organized events • *a professional athlete* • **Athlete's foot** is a disease in which the skin between the toes cracks and feels uncomfortable.

athletic /æθ'let·ɪk/ *adj* • *an athletic competition*

athletics /æθ'let·ɪks/ *n* [U] sports and games • *Girls who participate in high school athletics are three times more likely to graduate than those who don't.* • (*esp. Br*) Athletics is another way of saying **track and field**. See at TRACK SPORTS .

atlas /'æt·ləs/ *n* [C] a book containing maps • *a road atlas*

ATM *n* [C] *abbreviation for* automated/automatic teller machine (= a machine from which you can get money) • An **ATM machine** is a **cash machine**. See at CASH.

atmosphere AIR /'æt·məˌsfɪr/ *n* [C usually sing] the mixture of gases that surrounds some planets, such as the earth; the air

atmosphere CHARACTER /'æt·məsˌfɪr/ *n* [U] the character or mood of a place or situation • *The club provided a relaxed and friendly atmosphere for its members.*

atom /'æt·əm/ *n* [C] the smallest unit of any chemical element, consisting of a positive NUCLEUS surrounded by negative ELECTRONS. Atoms can combine to form a MOLECULE.

atomic /ə'tɑm·ɪk/ *adj* • *atomic energy/scientists* • (*dated*) An **atomic bomb** (also **atom bomb**) is a bomb that uses the explosive power that results from dividing the atom.

atone /ə'toʊn/ *v* [I] to do something that shows you are sorry for something bad that you did or for something that you failed to do • *He gave large sums of money to charities in an effort to atone for his sins.*

atop /ə'tɑp/ *prep* on or at the top of • *She and Harry toyed with the idea of living in a penthouse atop the building.*

atrocious /ə'troʊ·ʃəs/ *adj* of very bad quality • *His Russian was atrocious, but he communi-*

cated. • An action that is atrocious is extremely cruel: *Bombing innocent people is an atrocious act of barbarism.*

atrocity /ə'trɑs·ət·i/ *n* an extremely cruel act, or the committing of such acts • *They are accused of committing hundreds of wartime atrocities against the civilian population.* [C]

attach /ə'tætʃ/ *v* [T] to fasten or fix (something) in position, esp. in relation to something else • *You attach this device to your windshield, and it sends a signal that opens the garage door.* • To attach a particular quality to something is to consider it to have that quality: *If you attach a negative label to a group, you can then treat all the members of that group badly.*

attached /ə'tætʃt/ *adj* feeling close to emotionally, or loving • *She really gets attached to her cats.*

attachment /ə'tætʃ·mənt/ *n* [C/U] a strong feeling of being emotionally close to someone or something • *She had a special attachment to these students.* [C] • An attachment is an extra piece of equipment that can be added to a machine: *computer attachments* [C]

attaché /ˌæt·ə'ʃeɪ, ˌæˌtæ-/ *n* [C] a person who works in an EMBASSY (= group representing their country in a foreign country) and has a particular area of responsibility in which they have special knowledge • *a military attaché*

attaché case /ˌæˌtæ'ʃeɪˌkeɪs, ˌæt·ə-/ *n* [C] a hard-sided, rectangular container used esp. for carrying business papers; a type of BRIEFCASE

attaché case

attack HURT /ə'tæk/ *v* [I/T] to try to hurt or defeat (someone or something) using violence • *Two campers were attacked by a bear last night.* [T] ○ *Soldiers waited for the order to attack.* [I] • If a disease or a chemical attacks something, it damages it: *AIDS attacks the body's immune system.* [T]

attack /ə'tæk/ *n* [C/U] • *a missile attack* [C] ○ *The city was under attack from artillery.* [U] • An attack is also a sudden, short period of illness, or a sudden feeling that you cannot control: *an asthma attack* [C] ○ *How do you let your kids go without having anxiety attacks?* [C]

attacker /ə'tæk·ər/ *n* [C] • *The victim never saw her attackers.*

attack CRITICIZE /ə'tæk/ *v* [T] to criticize (someone or something) strongly • *Critics have attacked her ideas as antidemocratic.* ○ *In TV ads, he attacked his opponent's record.*

attack /ə'tæk/ *n* [C/U] • *The more he speaks out, the more he comes under attack.* [U] • If someone is **on the attack**, they are acting in a strong, determined way to defeat someone or something.

attain /ə'teɪn/ *v* [T] to achieve (something difficult to do or obtain) • *You need financial security in order to attain emotional well-being.*

attainable /ə'teɪ·nə·bəl/ *adj* • *You need to set goals that are clear and attainable.*

attainment /ə'teɪn·mənt/ *n* [C/U]*fml* • *Abiola pledged his life to the attainment of justice.* [U]

attempt /ə'temt/ *v* to try to make or do (something) • *The team's quarterback attempted only 12 passes during the entire game.* [T] ○ *Don't attempt to do these tricks at home.* [+ to infinitive]

attempt /ə'temt/ *n* [C] • *The pilot made several attempts to regain control of the aircraft.* [+ to infinitive] • An attempt on someone's life is an act of trying to kill them: *a failed attempt on the president's life*

attend /ə'tend/ *v* [I/T] to be at (an event) or go to (a place) • *She attends classes on Tuesdays.* [T] ○ *You don't have to attend if you don't want to.* [I]

attendance /ə'ten·dəns/ *n* [U] • *Attendance at rehearsals is required.* • Attendance is also the number of people present: *Annual attendance at the museum is nearly 100,000.*

□**attend to** /-'--/ *v prep* [T] to deal with (something or someone) • *Her company helps employees attend to elderly relatives.*

attention NOTICE /ə'ten·tʃən/ *n* [U] the act of directing the mind to listen, see, or understand; notice • *In order to learn anything, you have to pay attention.* ○ *It's hard to command the attention of 23 eight year olds.* ○ *Let me finish this, then I'll give you my undivided attention.* • An **attention span** is the period during which you can stay interested or listen carefully to something.

attention WAY OF STANDING /ə'ten·tʃən/ *exclamation, n* [U] (in the armed forces) an order to stand straight and not move, with your feet together, arms by your sides, and head facing to the front, or this way of standing • *Each cadet stood at attention for inspection.*

attention CARE /ə'ten·tʃən/ *n* [U] time or effort that you are willing to give to help someone or something because you care about them • *It's an old house, and needs a lot of attention.*

attentive /ə'tent·ɪv/ *adj* listening or watching carefully • *an attentive audience*

attentively /ə'tent·ɪv·li/ *adv* • *The children listened attentively to the story.*

attest /ə'test/ *v* (of a person) to state with authority that something is true, or (of a situation or event) to show that something is likely to be true • *As one who worked there for years, I can attest that applications are carefully reviewed.* [+ that clause] ○ *Her wealth was attested to by her fur coat and designer shoes.* [I]

attic /'æṭ·ɪk/ *n* [C] a space in a house just under the roof, often used for storing things

attire /ə'taɪr/ *n* [U] clothes, esp. of a particular type • *business/formal attire*

attired /ə'taɪrd/ *adj* [not gradable] • *She was tastefully attired in a simple black dress.*

attitude /'æṭ·ə,tuːd/ *n* [C/U] the way you feel about something or someone, or a particular feeling or opinion • *Start each day with a positive attitude.* [U] ○ *People's attitudes toward religion and the family are set very early in life.* [C] • (*infml*) If you say that someone has an attitude, you mean that you find them unwilling to be helpful or polite. [C]

attorney /ə'tɜr·ni/ *n* [C] a LAWYER • *a defense attorney*

Attorney General /ə,tɜr·ni'dʒen·rəl/ *n* [C] *pl* **Attorneys General** /ə,tɜr·niz'dʒen·rəl/ the most important legal officer in a state or in the US

attract /ə'trækt/ *v* [T] to cause (something) to come toward something else, or to cause (a person or animal) to become interested in someone or something • *An open flame attracts moths.* ○ *The tennis championship will attract a lot of tourists to the city.* ○ *This movie is going to attract a lot of attention.* • If someone is attracted to someone else or is attracted by them, they like them or are interested in them physically or sexually.

attraction /ə'træk·ʃən/ *n* [C/U] a quality or force of someone or something that tends to pull others toward them or create interest in them • *The company's excellent employee benefits package is a major attraction.* [C] ○ *She held little physical attraction for him.* [U] • An attraction is also something that makes people want to go to a place: *Florida has numerous tourist attractions.* [C]

attractive /ə'træk·tɪv/ *adj* causing interest or pleasure • *They made me a very attractive job offer.* ○ *She has two attractive and personable daughters.* ○ *One of the less attractive features of California is the threat of earthquakes.*

attractively /ə'træk·tɪv·li/ *adv* • *She likes to be attractively dressed.*

attribute /'æ·trə,bjuːt/ *n* [C] a quality or feature of a person or thing, esp. one that is an important part of its nature • *Self-confidence is a rare attribute in a 17 year old.* ○ *She has the physical attributes to become a championship swimmer.*

attribute *obj* **to** (*obj*) /ə'trɪb·jət, -,juːt/ *v prep* [T] to say or think that (something) is the result or work of (something or someone else) • *He attributed the project's success to a sophisticated computer program.* ○ *Most experts have attributed the etching to Dürer.*

attributable /ə'trɪb·jəṭ·ə·bəl/ *adj* • *Her death was attributable to natural causes.*

attribution /,æ·trə'bjuː·ʃən/ *n* [U] • *He borrowed from other people's writing without attribution.*

attributive /ə'trɪb·jəṭ·ɪv/ *adj* [not gradable] *specialized* (in grammar) of an adjective, noun, pronoun, or phrase placed before the noun it describes • *an attributive noun* ○ *In "a* *young woman," "young" is an adjective in the attributive position.* • LP ADJECTIVES

attrition /ə'trɪʃ·ən/ n [U] *slightly fml* a gradual reduction or weakening of something, esp. a reduction in the number of people who work for an organization that is achieved by not replacing those who leave • *Most of the job losses will come through attrition.*

attuned to /ə'tuːnd·tə, -tʊ, -,tuː/ *adj* especially able to understand or deal with • *People in New York seem attuned to fashion.*

atypical /eɪ'tɪp·ɪ·kəl/ *adj* not typical; different from most others of its type • *This game is very atypical of how we played this year.*

auburn /'ɔː·bərn/ *adj* [not gradable], *n* [U] (of) a red-brown color • *auburn hair* ○ *Browns in the picture were highlighted with auburn.* [U]

auction /'ɔːk·ʃən/ *n* [C/U] a usually public sale of goods or property, where people make higher and higher BIDS (= offers of money) for each item, until there are no higher BIDS and it is sold for the most money offered • *an auction of early American furniture* [C] ○ *bulls sold at auction* [U]

auction /'ɔːk·ʃən/ *v* [T] • *They finally auctioned (off) the house for $20,000.* [T/M]

auctioneer /,ɔːk·ʃə'nɪr/ *n* [C] a person in charge of an auction

audacious /ɔː'deɪ·ʃəs/ *adj* showing an unusual willingness to take risks • *Such audacious crimes attract a lot of attention.*

audacity /ɔː'dæs·ət·i/ *n* [U] unusually strong and esp. rude confidence in yourself • *Our mayor has the audacity to claim credit for improvements he had nothing to do with.* [+ to infinitive]

audible /'ɔːd·ə·bəl/ *adj* loud enough to be heard • *Her voice was barely audible above the roar of the engines.*

audibly /'ɔːd·ə·bli/ *adv* • *He sighed audibly.*

audience /'ɔːd·iː·əns, 'ɑd-/ *n* [C] the people, considered as a group, who watch or listen to a performance, movie, public event, etc., either together in one place or separately • *a live/television audience* ○ *The magazine is trying to reach a younger audience.* • An audience is also a formal meeting that you have with an important person: *an audience with the pope*

audio /'ɔːd·iː·,oʊ/ *adj* [not gradable] of or involving sound and the recording and broadcasting of sound • *We lost the audio portion of the TV broadcast.* • An **audiocassette** is a CASSETTE on which music is recorded. • An **audiotape** (*short form* **tape**) is a thin, magnetic strip, usually made of plastic, on which sound is recorded. • Something that is **audiovisual** (*abbreviation* **AV**) involves both seeing and hearing: *The audiovisual presentation included slides of the birds and tapes of their songs.* • Compare VIDEO.

audit EXAMINATION /'ɔːd·ət/ *n* [C] an official examination of records • *The agency is subject to regular financial audits.*

audit /'ɔːd·ət/ *v* [T] • *We hired accountants to audit the company's books.*

auditor /'ɔːd·ət·ər/ *n* [C] a person trained to make an official examination of financial records

audit BE AT CLASS /'ɔːd·ət/ *v* [T] to go regularly to (a class) without being formally involved in it • *I audited some of her seminars.*

audition /ɔː'dɪʃ·ən/ *n* [C] a short performance given by an actor, dancer, musician, or other performer that tests whether their skills are suitable for a particular event or group • *The boys' choir held rigorous auditions before each new member was admitted.*

audition /ɔː'dɪʃ·ən/ *v* [I/T] to give, watch, or listen to a short performance that tests whether a performer's skills are suitable for a particular event or group • *You'll have to audition for the role.* [I] ○ *They auditioned 125 dancers before choosing ten.* [T]

auditorium /,ɔːd·ə'tɔːr·iː·əm, -'toʊr-/ *n* [C] a large room with rows of seats and often a stage which is used for performances and for public events or meetings, or a building containing such a room • *a school/municipal auditorium*

auditory /'ɔːd·ə,tɔːr·i, -,toʊr·i/ *adj* [not gradable] *specialized* of or involving hearing • *The stroke impaired her auditory function but not her vision.*

augment /ɔːg'ment/ *v* [T] to make (something) larger or fuller by adding something to it • *He augmented his income by taking a second job.*

august IMPORTANT /ɔː'ɡʌst/ *adj* *slightly fml* having great importance and respect in society • *We toured the august chambers of the Supreme Court.*

August MONTH /'ɔː·ɡəst/ (*abbreviation* **Aug.**) *n* [C/U] the eighth month of the year, after July and before September

aunt /ænt, ɑːnt, ɑnt/ *n* [C] the sister of someone's mother or father, or the wife of someone's uncle • *We stopped off to visit my aunt and uncle in Boston.* • PIC FAMILY TREE LP TITLES AND FORMS OF ADDRESS

au pair /oʊ'per, -'pær/ *n* [C] *pl* **au pairs** a foreign person, usually a young woman, who lives with a family and looks after their children or cleans the house in return for meals, a room, and a small payment

aura /'ɔːr·ə/ *n* [C] a feeling or character that a person or place seems to have • *The hotel had an aura of fading glamor about it.*

aural /'ɔːr·əl/ *adj* [not gradable] relating to hearing • *She doesn't speak English well, but her aural comprehension is good.*

auspices /'ɔː·spə·səz, -,siːz/ *pl n* approval, support, and control • *Relief volunteers worked under the auspices of the Red Cross.*

auspicious /ɔː'spɪʃ·əs/ *adj* suggesting a positive and successful future • *Winning her first* *seven cases was an auspicious beginning for the young lawyer.*

austere /ɔːˈstɪr/ *adj* plain and without decoration, comforts, or anything extra • *Nuns lead an austere life.* ○ *She depicts the austere beauty of the desert.* • An austere person does not seem friendly.

austerity /ɔːˈster·ət·i, -ˈstɪr-/ *n* [U] • *The warriors led a life of austerity.* • Austerity is also a bad economic condition that does not allow luxuries: *Military spending continues even in periods of austerity.*

authentic /ɔːˈθent·ɪk/ *adj* being what it is claimed to be; GENUINE • *an authentic Goya drawing* ○ *How can we be sure the signature is authentic?* ○ *Sylvia's serves authentic soul food.*

authenticity /ˌɔː·θenˈtɪs·ət·i, -θən-/ *n* [U] • *Officials questioned the authenticity of his claim.*

author /ˈɔː·θər/ *n* [C] a writer of a book, article, etc., or a person whose main job is writing books • *a talented young author* ○ *He is the author of seven books.*

author /ˈɔː·θər/ *v* [T] • *Murphy authored the new legislation.*

authorship /ˈɔː·θərˌʃɪp/ *n* [U] the origin of a written work • *No one would admit authorship of the memo.*

authoritarian /ɔːˌθɔːr·əˈter·iː·ən, -ˌθɑr-/ *adj* demanding total obedience to those in positions of authority • *an authoritarian ruler/parent*

authority /əˈθɔːr·ət·i, əˈθɑr-/ *n* [C/U] the power to control or demand obedience from others • *The police have no legal authority in these disputes.* [U] ○ *We have to find someone in authority* (= a position of power). [U] • An authority is someone with official responsibility for a particular area of activity: *government/church authorities* [C] • The authorities are the police or other government officials: *No attacks were reported to the authorities.* • An authority on a subject is an expert on it: *an authority on immigration law* [C]

authoritative /əˈθɔːr·əˌteɪt̬·ɪv, əˈθɑr-/ *adj* having the power of special knowledge, or (of a person) showing the confidence of having special knowledge • *an authoritative manner* ○ *Her opinion on the subject was considered authoritative.*

authoritatively /əˈθɔːr·əˌteɪt̬·ɪv·li, əˈθɑr-/ *adv* • *He spoke authoritatively about police work.*

authorize /ˈɔː·θəˌraɪz/ *v* [T] to give official permission for (something) to happen, or to give (someone) official permission to do something • *The board authorized a new contract.*

authorization /ˌɔː·θə·rəˈzeɪ·ʃən/ *n* [C/U] • *I can't issue a check without authorization.* [U]

autism /ˈɔː·tɪz·əm/ *n* [U] *medical* an illness that starts in early childhood, in which behavior is unusually centered on the self and social skills, language development, and communication with others are all severely limited

autistic /ɔːˈtɪs·tɪk/ *adj* • *She works with autistic children.*

auto /ˈɔːt̬·oʊ, ˈɑt̬-/ *n* [C] *pl* **autos** short form of AUTOMOBILE • *auto makers/manufacturers* ○ *the auto industry*

autobiography /ˌɔːt̬·ə·baɪˈɑg·rə·fi/ *n* [C/U] the story of a person's life as written by that person, or the area of literature relating to books that describe such stories • *The book was a mixture of family history and autobiography.* [U] • Compare BIOGRAPHY.

autobiographical /ˌɔːt̬·ə·baɪ·əˈgræf·ɪ·kəl/ *adj* describing the writer or based on the writer's life • *an autobiographical novel*

autocracy /ɔːˈtɑk·rə·si/ *n* [C/U] government by a single person or small group that has unlimited power or authority, or a country or society that has this form of government

autocratic /ˌɔːt̬·əˈkræt̬·ɪk/ *adj* • *an autocratic regime*

autograph /ˈɔːt̬·əˌgræf/ *n* [C] a signature, esp. of a famous person • *He thought I was a famous actor and asked for my autograph.*

autograph /ˈɔːt̬·əˌgræf/ *v* [T] to write your signature on (something), often for someone else to keep

automated /ˈɔːt̬·əˌmeɪt̬/ *adj* (esp. of a process in business or industry) made to operate by machines or computers in order to reduce the work done by humans • An **automated teller machine** (*abbreviation* **ATM**) is a **cash machine**. See at CASH.

automation /ˌɔːt̬·əˈmeɪ·ʃən/ *n* [U] • *factory automation*

automatic INDEPENDENT /ˌɔːt̬·əˈmæt̬·ɪk/ *adj* able to operate independently of human control • *An automatic pistol or rifle can fire repeatedly with one pull of the trigger.* • An **automatic teller machine** (*abbreviation* **ATM**) is a **cash machine**. See at CASH.

automatically /ˌɔːt̬·əˈmæt̬·ɪ·kli/ *adv* • *The camera focuses automatically.*

automatic NOT CONSCIOUS /ˌɔːt̬·əˈmæt̬·ɪk/ *adj* (of an action) done without thinking about it • *Soon enough, taking her pill every morning became automatic.*

automatic CERTAIN /ˌɔːt̬·əˈmæt̬·ɪk/ *adj* happening according to rules that are certain to be followed, and therefore not needing a decision • *Citizenship is automatic for children born in the US.* ○ *People on Social Security get automatic cost-of-living increases each year.*

automatically /ˌɔːt̬·əˈmæt̬·ɪ·kli/ *adv* • *You get a pay increase automatically after six months.*

automobile /ˈɔːt̬·ə·moʊˌbiːl, ˌɔːt̬·ə·moʊˈbiːl/, short form **auto** *n* [C] a car • *the automobile industry* • PIC CAR

automotive /ˌɔːt̬·əˈmoʊt̬·ɪv/ *adj* [not gradable] relating to road vehicles • *automotive equipment/fuels/supplies*

autonomy /ɔːˈtɑn·ə·mi/ *n* [U] the right of a group of people to govern itself or to organize its own activities • *As a minority ethnic group, they have been fighting for autonomy for years.*

autonomous /ɔːˈtɑn·ə·məs/ *adj* • *the autonomous Palestinian authorities*

autopsy /ˈɔːˌtɑp·si, ˈɔːtˌ·əp-/ *n* [C] the act of cutting open and examining a dead body in order to discover the cause of death • *Police said they were awaiting the results of an autopsy.*

autumn /ˈɔːtˌ·əm/ *n* [C/U] the season of the year between summer and winter, lasting from September to December north of the equator and from March to June south of the equator; fall

auxiliary /ɔːgˈzɪl·jə·ri/ *adj* giving help or support, esp. to a more important person or thing • *The hospital has an auxiliary power supply in case of a power failure.* • (*specialized*) In grammar, an **auxiliary verb** gives grammatical information, for example about tense, that is not given by the main verb of a sentence:

"*Has*" is an auxiliary verb in the sentence "*She has finished her book.*"

AV *adj abbreviation for* **audiovisual**, see at AUDIO

avail *obj* **of** /əˈveɪl·əv, -ˌʌv, -ˌɑv/ *v prep* [T] *fml* • If you avail yourself of something, you use it for your benefit: *Voters should avail themselves of all the tools available to get information about the candidates.*

available /əˈveɪ·lə·bəl/ *adj* able to be obtained, used, or reached • *Her new book is available in bookstores all across America.*

availability /əˌveɪ·lə·ˈbɪl·ət·i/ *n* [U] • *I'll check on the availability of tickets.*

avalanche /ˈæv·əˌlæntʃ/ *n* [C] a large amount of ice, snow, mud, or rock falling suddenly and quickly down the side of a mountain • (*fig.*) An avalanche is also the sudden arrival of too many things: *We received an avalanche of complaints.*

avant–garde /ˌɑv·ɑntˈgɑrd, ˌæv·ɔːˈgɑrd/ *n* [U]

AUXILIARY VERBS

Auxiliary verbs are marked [v aux] in the dictionary.

Be, do, have, and **will** are the auxiliary verbs that give information about the tense of the main verb. ⓛⓟ TENSES **Be** is also used to form the passive: *The book* **was** *printed in Singapore.*

Can, could, may, might, shall, should, will, would, must, and **ought** are the auxiliary verbs that give other information about the main verb, for example about whether an action is necessary or possible. They are also used for making suggestions, offers, and requests.

important uses of auxiliary verbs

- **to ask questions**

  Did *she go to the concert?* • **Can** *your friend ski?* • *Where* **do** *you work?*

- **to make negatives**

  It **doesn't** *matter.* • *You* **shouldn't** *worry so much.*

- **to avoid repeating the main verb:**

  Jamie had forgotten all about it. I **had,** *too.* • *I'm sure he earns more than I* **do.** • *I didn't like the movie, but Marta* **did.** • *I'll return it as soon as I* **can.** • *"You'll forget to pick up the tickets." "No, I* **won't.**" • *"Can/Could I ask a question?" "Yes, of course you* **can.**"

- **to add emphasis or stress a difference** (in speaking, the auxiliary verb is given heavy stress):

  But I **do** *believe you.* • *I disagree—I think we* **should** *invite him.*

Notice that in all these cases, if there is no other auxiliary, a form of **do** can be used unless the main verb is **be:** *"Was it very difficult?" "No, it* **wasn't.**"

grammar of auxiliary verbs

Do is used when making questions and negatives if there is no other auxiliary verb. It is not used if another auxiliary verb is present.

- **negatives**

auxiliary verb	*She has been to Russia.*	*She* **hasn't** *been to Russia.*
modal auxiliary	*We should go now.*	*We* **shouldn't** *go now.*
ordinary verb	*You play tennis.*	*You* **don't** *play tennis.*

- **ordinary question forms**

auxiliary verb	*She has been to Russia.*	**Has** *she been to Russia?*
		Where **has** *she been?*
modal auxiliary	*We should go now.*	**Should** *we go now?*
		What **should** *we do?*
ordinary verb	*You play tennis.*	**Do** *you play tennis?*
		Where **do** *you play tennis?*

- **question tags**

auxiliary verb	*She has been to Russia.*	*She has been to Russia,* **hasn't** *she?*
	She hasn't been to Russia.	*She hasn't been to Russia,* **has** *she?*
modal auxiliary	*We should go now.*	*We should go now,* **shouldn't** *we?*
	We shouldn't go now.	*We shouldn't go now,* **should** *we?*
ordinary verb	*You play tennis.*	*You play tennis,* **don't** *you?*
	You don't play tennis.	*You don't play tennis,* **do** *you?*

contractions of auxiliary verbs

These are often used in everyday speech and informal writing (ⓁⓅ Contractions of verbs).

- **in statements**

  I'm, he's, she'd, we'll

- **in negatives and questions**

  they can't, he isn't, it's not, aren't you?

special grammar of auxiliary verbs

Special grammar rules apply to auxiliary verbs.

- **They are usually followed by an infinitive without to**

  You should tell him. • *I thought the rain would never stop.*
  But **ought** takes a *to* infinitive: *You ought* **to** *tell him.*

- **They each have only one form**

  the third person singular does not take *-s*: *He* **can** *fly a plane.*
  there is no past participle or *-ing* form
  there is no *to* infinitive

- **They do not show tense the way other verbs do**
  There is an exception for *will*, which is one way to indicate future time. Notice that the same auxiliary can be used with different time references

  I **could** *see a faint light in the distance.* (past) • *If we miss this train, we* **could/can** *always catch the next one.* (future)

- **Could, might, should,** and **would** look like past forms, but are more often used for particular meanings of verbs.

  You **could** *take the dog for a walk.* (present meaning) • *The phone is ringing—it* **might/must** *be Jim calling.* (present meaning) • *You* **should** *be ashamed of yourself.* (present meaning)

- Auxiliaries that do not have a matching past form may need to be replaced with different auxiliaries to express the past tense.

  Everyone entering the building **must** *show identification.* (present tense) / *Everyone entering the building* **had to** *show identification.* (past tense)

auxiliaries can be used to show past time

- **Could** is used as the past simple of **can** in various meanings.

  By the time he was ten, he **could** *speak three languages.* • *I* **couldn't** *understand a thing she said.* • **Could** *women votes in those days?*

- **Would** is used in negative sentences as the past simple of **will** to express intentions.

  She **wouldn't** *say why she was angry.* • *I tried to explain, but no one* **would** *listen.* • *The car* **wouldn't** *start this morning.*

- **Would** is also used to show that something in the past always or often happened.

  He **would** *always smile at us.*

- In indirect speech, **could, might, should,** and **would** are often used as past forms.

  "It **may** *be dangerous," he said.* / *He said it* **might** *be dangerous.* • *I think everything* **will** *work out fine.* / *I thought everything* **would** *work out fine.*

- **Must,** which has no matching past tense form, is also sometimes used in reporting indirect speech.

  "You **must** *get more exercise."* / *She said I* **must** *get more exercise.*

the painters, writers, musicians, and other artists whose ideas, styles, and methods are highly original or modern in the period in which they live

avant-garde /ˌɑv‚ɑntˈɡɑrd, ˌævˌɔːˈɡɑrd/ *adj* • *avant-garde art*

avarice /ˈæv‧ə‧rəs/ *n* [U] an extremely strong desire to obtain or keep wealth

avaricious /ˌæv‧əˈrɪʃ‧əs/ *adj* • *avaricious land speculators*

Ave. /æv/ *n abbreviation for* AVENUE STREET • *Our new address is 1366 Columbus Ave.*

avenge /əˈvendʒ/ *v* [T] to get satisfaction by harming or punishing the person responsible for (something bad done to you or your family or friends) • *In the second half of the movie, she seeks to avenge her husband's death.*

avenue STREET /ˈæv‧ə‚nuː/ *n* [C] a street, often a wide one, in a city or town • *Michigan Avenue in Chicago is famous for its elegant stores.* • LP) ADDRESSES

avenue POSSIBILITY /ˈæv‧ə‚nuː/ *n* [C] a method or way of doing something; a possibility • *China and the United States are exploring avenues of military cooperation.* ○ *Only two avenues are open to us—accept his offer or file a lawsuit.*

average USUAL STANDARD /ˈæv‧rɪdʒ, -ə‧rɪdʒ/ *n* [U] a standard or level that is considered to be typical or usual • *The quality of her work is well above average.* • **On average** (= usually), *a person's income is highest when they are in their mid-50s.*

average /ˈæv‧rɪdʒ, -ə‧rɪdʒ/ *adj* [not gradable] • *Janeen was of average height but had great jumping ability.* ○ *"Was the movie good?" "It wasn't great, just average."*

average AMOUNT /ˈæv‧rɪdʒ, -ə‧rɪdʒ/ *n* [C] the result obtained by adding two or more amounts together and dividing the total by the number of amounts, or by another total • *I'm 35 and my brothers are 32 and 26, so the average of our ages is 31.* ○ *In his third season on the team, he raised his batting average to .270.* ○ *Interest rates rose on average to 10.05% in January.*

average /ˈæv‧rɪdʒ, -ə‧rɪdʒ/ *adj* [not gradable] • *The average sales price for a house around here is about $150,000.*

average /ˈæv‧rɪdʒ, -ə‧rɪdʒ/ *v* [I/T] • *Trainees average* (= earn an average of) *$20,000 a year.* [T] ○ *My grades vary from year to year, but they average* (out) *3.2, or a little better than a B.* [I/T]

▫**average out** /'--'-, '---'-/ *v adv* [I] to become equal or similar over a period of time • *The highs and lows of life tend to average out.*

averse /əˈvɜrs/ *adj* strongly disliking or opposed to • *Few politicians are averse to appearing on television.*

aversion /əˈvɜr‧ʒən, -ʃən/ *n* [C] a feeling of strong dislike or unwillingness to do something • *I felt an instant aversion to his parents.* ○ *She has a deep aversion to getting up early.*

avert PREVENT /əˈvɜrt/ *v* [T] to prevent (something bad) from happening; avoid • *The last-minute agreement averted renewed fighting.*

avert TURN AWAY /əˈvɜrt/ *v* [T] to turn away (your eyes or thoughts) • *When the bloody pictures were shown of the crime scene, several people averted their eyes.*

aviation /ˌeɪ‧viːˈeɪ‧ʃən/ *n* [U] the activity of flying aircraft, or of designing, producing, and maintaining them

aviator /ˈeɪ‧viː‚eɪt‧ər/ *n* [C] *dated* • *Charles Lindbergh was the first aviator to fly nonstop across the Atlantic Ocean.*

avid /ˈæv‧əd/ *adj* extremely eager or interested • *Knowles is an avid runner and cross-country skier.*

avidly /ˈæv‧əd‧li/ *adv* • *We listened avidly to the news from our secret radios.*

avocado /ˌɑv‧əˈkɑd‧oʊ, ˌæv-/ *n* [C] *pl* **avocados** a fruit with thick green or black skin, a large round seed at the center, and oily green or yellow flesh, which is often eaten as a vegetable in salads

avoid /əˈvɔɪd/ *v* [T] to stay away from (someone or something), or prevent (something) from happening, or not allow yourself to do (something) • *Do you think Robert is avoiding me? I haven't seen him for a month.* ○ *I try to avoid going shopping on Saturdays because the stores are so crowded.* ○ *If you want to lose weight, avoid eating between meals.*

avoidance /əˈvɔɪd‧ʰns/ *n* [U] • *The avoidance of injury is more important than winning a game.*

avowed /əˈvaʊd/ *adj* stated or admitted • *an avowed drug addict*

avowedly /əˈvaʊ‧əd‧li/ *adv* • *an avowedly old-fashioned teacher*

await /əˈweɪt/ *v* [T] to wait for or be in the future of (someone or something) • *The two men are awaiting trial, scheduled to begin next month.* ○ *There are no jobs awaiting those farmers.*

awake /əˈweɪk/ *adj* not sleeping; in the state of consciousness • *If I drink coffee late in the day, I can't sleep and stay awake all night.*

awake /əˈweɪk/ *v* [I/T] *past simple* **awoke** /ə'woʊk/ *or* **awaked**, *past part* **awoken** /əˈwoʊ‧kən/ to stop sleeping, or to cause (someone) to stop sleeping • *I awoke at 7, as usual.* [I]

awaken /əˈweɪ‧kən/ *v* [I/T] to stop sleeping, or to cause (someone) to stop sleeping • *The family was awakened by a noise.* [T] • *(fig.)* If interest is awakened, it is made more active: *His television series awakened popular interest in American architecture.* [T]

award /əˈwɔrd/ *v* [T] to give (something valuable, such as money or a prize) following an official decision • *Her poodle was awarded first prize in the dog show.* ○ *Their company was awarded a contract worth $40 million by the federal government.*

award /əˈwɔrd/ *n* [C] • *Marion Jones won the*

Jesse Owens award as the outstanding athlete of the year.

aware /ə'wer, ə'wær/ *adj* knowing that something exists, or having knowledge or experience of a particular thing • *We were just not aware (that) garbage would be a problem, that we ever would need to recycle.* [+ (*that*) clause] ○ *Are you aware of any reason why you cannot act fairly as a juror in this trial?*

awareness /ə'wer·nəs, ə'wær-/ *n* [U] • *Public awareness of AIDS has helped to limit the spread of the disease.*

away SOMEWHERE ELSE /ə'weɪ/ *adj, adv* [not gradable] somewhere else, or to or in a different place, position, or situation • *Barbara is away on vacation until the end of the week.* ○ *The Jeffersons went away for the weekend, but they'll be back on Monday.*

away DISTANT /ə'weɪ/ *adv* [not gradable] at a distance (from this place) • *How far away is the station?*

away IN THE FUTURE /ə'weɪ/ *adv* [not gradable] in the future; from now • *The wedding is still six months away.*

away INTO PLACE /ə'weɪ/ *adv* [not gradable] in or into the usual or a suitable place, esp. one that is enclosed • *Put the groceries away before you go out again.*

away GRADUALLY /ə'weɪ/ *adv* [not gradable] gradually until mostly or completely gone • *The music faded away.*

away CONTINUOUSLY /ə'weɪ/ *adv* [not gradable] continuously or repeatedly, or busily • *Chris has been working away on the car all day.*

awe /ɔː/ *n* [U] a feeling of great respect, usually mixed with fear or surprise • *I was too much in awe of him to address him directly.* • If something is awe-inspiring, it causes you to admire or respect it greatly: *Niagara Falls is an awe-inspiring sight.*

awe /ɔː/ *v* [T] **awing** • *The school kids were awed when Doug Flutie, the football star, entered the room.*

awesome /'ɔː·səm/ *adj* causing feelings of great admiration, respect, or fear • *an awesome achievement* ○ (*slang*) *Your new haircut is awesome* (= extremely good).

awful BAD /'ɔː·fəl/ *adj* very bad, unpleasant, or of low quality • *The weather was awful the whole time—cold and wet.* ○ *Fox TV has canceled the truly awful sitcom "Monty" after a short tryout.*

awful VERY GREAT /'ɔː·fəl/ *adj* • **An awful lot** is a very great amount: *I don't know an awful lot about art, but I'm learning.*

awfully /'ɔː·fliː, -fə·liː/, *infml* **awful** /'ɔː·fəl/ *adv* very or extremely • *Your fever is awfully high—I think we'd better call a doctor.* ○ *I'm awfully sorry, but there are no rooms in the hotel available right now.* ○ *We were awfully pleased when our daughter was named the best student in her class.* • LP VERY, COMPLETELY, AND OTHER INTENSIFIERS

awhile /ə'hwɑɪl, ə'wɑɪl/ *adv* [not gradable] for a short time • *I'd like to rest awhile before we continue.*

awkward DIFFICULT /'ɔː·kwərd/ *adj* difficult to use, do, or deal with • *The computer came in a big box that was awkward to carry.*

awkward ANXIOUS /'ɔː·kwərd/ *adj* causing inconvenience, anxiety, or embarrassment • *It was an awkward situation, because the restaurant was too expensive for us but we didn't want to just get up and walk out.* • If someone feels awkward, they feel embarrassed or nervous: *We were the first to arrive at the party and felt a little awkward.*

awkwardly /'ɔː·kwər·dliː/ *adv* • *The publication of the article was awkwardly timed for the government.*

awkwardness /'ɔː·kwərd·nəs/ *n* [U] • *His awkwardness with girls disappeared once he got to college.*

awkward LACKING GRACE /'ɔː·kwərd/ *adj* lacking grace or skill when moving • *He's too awkward—he'll never be a good dancer.*

awkwardly /'ɔː·kwər·dliː/ *adv* • *He sat awkwardly on the floor.*

awning /'ɔː·nɪŋ/ *n* [C] a piece of material supported by a frame and used to protect part of a building from the sun or rain

awoke /ə'woʊk/ *past simple of* AWAKE

awoken /ə'woʊ·kən/ *past participle of* AWAKE

AWOL /'eɪ·wɔːl; ˌeɪˌdʌb·əl·juˌoʊ'el/ *adj* [not gradable] *abbreviation for* (esp. of soldiers) absent without LEAVE (= permission) • *The corporal went AWOL, and we haven't seen him since.*

awry /ə'rɑɪ/ *adj, adv* not in the intended manner, or out of position, or wrong • *There are too many people involved, and something is bound to go awry.*

ax TOOL, **axe** /æks/ *n* [C] a tool consisting of a heavy iron or steel blade at the end of a long wooden handle, used for cutting wood

ax STOP /æks/ *v* [T] to order (someone) suddenly to give up their job, or to stop or reduce (something) suddenly • *The company has already axed 14 people, and many more may lose their jobs.* ○ *Yesterday the airline axed three of its daily flights to Chicago.*

ax, **axe** /æks/ *n* [C usually sing] • **The ax** is the order to give up your job or to stop or prevent something from happening: *Three staff members got the ax yesterday.* ○ *If the budget is cut, educational programs will get the ax.* ○ *Everyone is scared to death wondering where the ax will fall next.*

axiom /'æk·siː·əm/ *n* [C] a statement or principle that is generally accepted to be true

axiomatic /ˌæk·siː·ə'mæt̬·ɪk/ *adj* obvious and not needing proof

axis /'æk·səs/ *n* [C] *pl* **axes** /'æk·siːz/ a real or imaginary straight line that goes through the center of a spinning object, such as the earth, or a line that divides a shape into two equal halves • An axis is also a line on a GRAPH used to show the position of a point. • The **Axis Powers** in World War II were Germany, Italy, and Japan.

axle /ˈæk·səl/ n [C] a bar connected to the center of a circular object such as a wheel that allows or causes it to turn, esp. one connecting two wheels of a vehicle

aye /ɑɪ/ adv [not gradable], n [C] (used esp. in voting) yes, or a vote that means yes and supports a suggestion or plan of action • *All those who support this proposal say aye.* ○ *The ayes have it, 20 to 12, and the motion is carried.*

B, b

B LETTER , **b** /biː/ *n* [C] *pl* **B's** or **Bs** or **b's** or **bs**
the second letter of the English alphabet

B MUSICAL NOTE /biː/ *n* [C/U] *pl* **B's** or **Bs** the seventh note in the **major scale** (= series of notes) that begins on the note C, or a set of notes based on this note

B MARK /biː/ *n* [C] *pl* **B's** or **Bs** a mark that means very good, given to something of satisfactory quality, esp. school work • *Mrs. Madden gave me a B on my essay for English.*

B.A., A.B. *n* [C] *abbreviation for* Bachelor of Arts (= a first college degree in the arts or **social sciences**) • LP EDUCATION IN THE US

babble /ˈbæb·əl/ *v* [I/T] to speak quickly, in a confused, excited, or foolish way • *She was babbling on about a robbery.* [I]

babble /ˈbæb·əl/ *n* [U] • *The baby's babble would soon turn into language.* • Babble also means a low, continuous sound: *It was hard to talk over the babble of voices in the room.*

babe /beɪb/ *n* [C] a small baby, or (*infml*) an affectionate way of addressing a wife, husband, or lover • (*slang*) A babe is an attractive woman or girl. This use is considered offensive.

baboon /bæˈbuːn/ *n* [C] a PRIMATE (= animal that is most like humans) found in Africa and southern Asia that has a long nose, short tail, and is related to monkeys

baby /ˈbeɪ·bi/ *n* [C] a very young child • *Sandra had a baby on May 29th.* ○ *My younger brother is the baby of the family.* • Baby can be used to refer to anything young or smaller than usual: *baby corn/lima beans* • (*disapproving*) Baby can also mean someone who is behaving childishly. *She complained like a baby about her boyfriend.* • Baby is an affectionate way of addressing a wife, husband, or lover. • (*infml*) A baby can also be a project or job someone has a special interest in or responsibility for: *The new computer system is really Phil's baby.* • A **baby boom** is a large increase in the number of babies born in a particular place during a particular time. • A **baby boomer** is a person who was born during a baby boom in the US between 1947 and 1961. • A **baby carriage** is a vehicle that a baby lies or sits in, that has four wheels and a handle for pushing.

baby /ˈbeɪ·bi/ *v* [T] • *Some parents baby their children too much.* ○ *I like to be babied when I'm sick.*

babyish /ˈbeɪ·bi·ɪʃ/ *adj disapproving* • *Aren't those toys a bit babyish for him?*

baby–sit /ˈbeɪ·biːˌsɪt/, **sit** *v* [I/T] **-tt-** to take care of (a baby or child), esp. as a job • *I'm going to baby-sit on Tuesday night.* [I]

baby–sitter /ˈbeɪ·biːˌsɪt̬·ər/, **sitter** *n* [C] • *Our baby-sitter is from the local college.*

bachelor /ˈbætʃ·ə·lər/ *n* [C] a man who is not married • *He remained a confirmed bachelor until he was 60.* • A **bachelor party** is for males only that is given for someone about to be married.

bachelor's (degree) /ˈbætʃ·ə·lərz (dɪˈgriː)/ *n* [C] a first degree at a college or university; B.A. or B.S.

back RETURN /bæk/ *adv* [not gradable] in, at, or toward a previous place or condition or an earlier time • *When you're done, please put back my scissors.* ○ *She just came back from vacation yesterday.* ○ *He looked back to see if he was being followed.* ○ *I heard from them back in January.* • Back can also mean in return or in reply: *Can I call you back in a few minutes?* • If you get **back to basics**, you return to the simple, most important things: *In her latest album, she has gone back to basics, using acoustic instruments with wonderful results.* • If someone goes **back to the drawing board** or **back to square one** they start over: *With the peace accord in shreds, we must head back to the drawing board.*

back /bæk/ *adj* [not gradable] • *She went out shopping earlier, but I think she's back.*

back FARTHER AWAY /bæk/ *adv* [not gradable] farther away; to a farther place • *We can push the table back and have more room.* ○ *Stand back!* ○ *She lay back in the chair and napped.* ○ *Marsha always wears her hair pulled back from her face.* • If something moves **back and forth**, it moves first in one direction and then in the opposite one: *She swayed back and forth to the music.*

back /bæk/ *v* [I/T] to move backward • *I backed the car into a big rock.* [T] ○ *He backed away from the guy.* [I]

back FARTHEST PART /bæk/ *n* [U] the part of something that is farthest from the front • *I found my tennis racket at the back of the closet.* ○ *We sat in the back of the bus.* • The back of your hand is the side opposite the PALM that has hair growing on it. • **In back of** means behind: *They sat in back of us on the plane.* • If something is **in/at the back of** your **mind**, you have thought about it from time to time: *In the back of my mind I guess I always thought I would be a ballplayer.* • **Backstage** means behind the stage of a theater: *We went backstage after the show to meet the actors.* • A **backyard** is the area behind a house, or more generally, an area near the place you live: *Residents don't want a nuclear power plant in their backyard.*

back /bæk/ *adj* [not gradable] • *She left the house by the back door.* • Anything on **the back burner** is not of great importance and can be taken care of later: *Their complaints have definitely been pushed to the back burner.* • A **back road** is a small road without much traffic, away from a main road. • A **backseat** is the seat behind the driver of a car. • A **backseat** is also a position of less importance: *Nelson will never take a backseat to anyone.* • A **backseat driver** is a person who gives unwanted advice or criticism, esp. to the driver.

back [SUPPORT] /bæk/ *v* [T] to give support to (someone or something) with money or words • *The board refuses to back our plan.*

backing /'bæk·ɪŋ/ *n* [U] • *If I go ahead with this project, can I count on your backing?*

backer /'bæk·ər/ *n* [C] • *We'll need financial backers to do this.*

back [BODY PART] /bæk/ *n* [C] the part of your body opposite the front, from your neck to the top of your legs • *He lay on his back, staring at the ceiling.* ○ *She didn't want to talk and turned her back to him.* • The back of a seat is the part your back leans against. • A **backache** is a pain in your back. • Your **backbone** is your SPINE. See also BACKBONE [IMPORTANT PART] and BACKBONE [CHARACTER]. • **Back-to-back** means with backs touching or toward each other: *We stood back-to-back to see who was taller.* See also BACK-TO-BACK. • [PIC] SMALL OF THE BACK

□**back down** /'-'-/, **back off** *v adv* [I] to move away from someone, or to stop supporting a position • *Since the gunmen had a hostage, he ordered his officers to back off.* ○ *Officials planned to open a drug treatment camp, but backed down after residents opposed the decision.*

□**back out** /'-'-/ *v adv* [I] to refuse to do something you earlier had agreed to do • *You said you'd come—you can't back out now!*

□**back up** *(obj)* [DRIVE BACKWARD], **back** *(obj)* **up** /'-'-/ *v adv* [I/M] to drive (a car) backward • *It was hard to back up in such a narrow driveway.* [I]

□**back up** *(obj)* [BE UNABLE TO MOVE], **back** *(obj)* **up** /'-'-/ *v* [I/M] to stop traffic or something liquid from moving, causing it to collect in one place • *The sink backed up.* [I] ○ *The accident backed traffic up for miles.* [M]

□**back up** *obj* [PROVIDE SUPPORT], **back** *obj* **up** /'-'-/ *v adv* [M] to provide support or help to (someone) • *The last witness backed up what other people had said happened.*

backup /'bæk·ʌp/ *n* [U] • *a backup generator* ○ *They didn't realize when they hired him that he had a backup band.* ○ *We want to have the factual backup to make our case.*

□**back up** *obj* [MAKE EXTRA COPY], **back** *obj* **up** /'-'-/ *v adv* [M] to make a copy of information in a computer that is stored separately • *We back up our files every day on a disk.*

backup /'bæk·ʌp/ *n* [C] • *Backup disks help a lot when your computer crashes.*

backbiting /'bæk,baɪt̬·ɪŋ/ *n* [U] unpleasant or unkind remarks made about a person who is not present • *There's a lot of backbiting and disarray among key officials.*

backboard /'bæk·bɔːrd, -bourd/ *n* [C] (in BASKETBALL) a board behind the metal ring that you have to throw the ball through to score • *He missed, and the ball bounced off the backboard.* • [PIC] DUNK

backbone [IMPORTANT PART] /'bæk·boun/ *n* [U] the part of something that provides strength and support • *Newcomers are now the backbone of this team.* • See also **backbone** at BACK [BODY PART].

backbone [CHARACTER] /'bæk·boun/ *n* [U] strength of character or bravery • *The delegates had enough backbone to reject the proposal.* • See also **backbone** at BACK [BODY PART].

backbreaking /'bæk,breɪ·kɪŋ/ *adj* very tiring or needing a lot of physical energy • *Digging a trench is backbreaking work.*

backfire [HAVE BAD RESULT] /'bæk·faɪr/ *v* [I] (of a plan) to have the opposite result from the one you intended • *Some hotel owners worry that the idea of attracting more visitors may backfire and make the place less attractive.*

backfire [MAKE NOISE] /'bæk·faɪr/ *v* [I] (of an engine) to make a loud noise because the fuel burned too soon

backgammon /'bæk,gæm·ən/ *n* [U] a game for two players in which the winner is the first to move their pieces around a special board

background [THINGS BEHIND] /'bæk·graund/ *n* [C/U] things that appear to be farther away or behind what is nearer or in front, esp. in a picture • *He photographed the models against different backgrounds.* [C] ○ *With so much noise in the background, I couldn't hear what she was saying.* [U] ○ *The city's skyline was our background.* [C] • A background can also be whatever is happening around you but not involving you directly: *Worry was always part of the background.*

background [EXPERIENCE] /'bæk·graund/ *n* [C] the things that have made you into the person you are, esp. family, experience, and education • *The school has students from many different backgrounds.* • An event's background is facts or history that help to explain how or why it happened: *To understand the war, we need to consider its historical and political background.*

backhand /'bæk·hænd/ *n* [C] (in sports such as tennis) a way of hitting the ball in which the back of the hand holding the RACKET is turned in the direction you want to hit the ball • *He has a fabulous backhand.* • Compare FOREHAND. [PIC] FOREHAND

backhanded /'bæk'hæn·dəd/ *adj* (of something said) not clear and usually meaning the opposite of what it seems to mean • *Her backhanded compliments annoyed everyone.*

backlash /'bæk·læʃ/ *n* [C] a strong, negative reaction to something, esp. to change • *The mayor foresaw no political backlash against his proposal.*

backlog /'bæk·lɔːg, -lɑg/ *n* [C usually sing] a

large number of things waiting to be done • *I have a huge backlog of work on my desk.*

backpack /'bæk·pæk/, *short form* **pack** *n* [C] a bag carried on the back, usually of cloth with many pockets and straps that go over your shoulders, used to carry things

backpack

backpack /'bæk·pæk/ *v* [I] to walk long distances, carrying your things in a backpack • *We backpacked through the Colorado Rockies last summer.*

backpacker /'bæk·pæk·ər/ *n* [C] • *A string of backpackers passed us on the trail.*

backside /'bæk·sɑɪd/ *n* [C] *infml* the part of the body you sit on; your buttocks

backslide /'bæk·slɑɪd/ *v* [I] *past* **backslid** /'bæk·slɪd/ to return to old, esp. bad, habits • *I stop drinking for a while, then I find myself backsliding.*

back-to-back /,bæk·tə'bæk/ *adv, adj* one following after another • *The soccer team won back-to-back victories last weekend.* • See also **back-to-back** at BACK BODY PART.

backtrack /'bæk·træk/ *v* [I] to go back the same way you came, or to consider information again • *We need to backtrack a bit and examine the history of this problem.* • If you backtrack from something you previously said or agreed to do, you begin to stop supporting it: *The government backtracked on plans that would have increased taxes.*

backup /'bæk·ʌp/ *n* [C/U] • See at BACK UP PROVIDE SUPPORT, BACK UP MAKE EXTRA COPY.

backward TOWARD THE BACK /'bæk·wərd/, **backwards** /'bæk·wərdz/ *adv* [not gradable] toward the direction that is opposite to the one in which you are facing or opposite to the usual direction • *He took a step backward.* ○ *He began counting backward: "Ten, nine, eight . . ."* ○ *She was skating around the rink, backward and forward.* • Compare FORWARD LEADING.

backward /'bæk·wərd/ *adj* [not gradable] • *He did a terrific backward somersault.*

backward NOT MODERN /'bæk·wərd/ *adj* not modern or economically developed • *The state needs to reform its backward election laws.* • Compare FORWARD.

backwardness /'bæk·wərd·nəs/ *n* [U] • *The country must first overcome its backwardness and poverty.*

backwater /'bæk,wɔːt̬·ər, -,wɑt̬-/ *n* [C] a place that does not seem knowledgeable of the world and its ways • *Miami transformed from a cultural backwater to a culinary trendsetter.*

backwoods /'bæk·wʊdz/ *pl n* a place that is off by itself, not near to transportation or a larger town • *I grew up in the backwoods of North Carolina.*

bacon /'beɪ·kən/ *n* [U] salted or smoked meat from the back or sides of a pig, usually eaten sliced and fried

bacteria /bæk'tɪr·iː·ə/ *pl n* very small organisms that are found everywhere and are the cause of many diseases • *Antibiotics usually cure illnesses caused by bacteria.*

bacterial /bæk'tɪr·iː·əl/ *adj* [not gradable] • *My sore throat came from a bacterial infection.*

bad UNPLEASANT /bæd/ *adj* **worse** /wɜrs/, **worst** /wɜrst/ not good; disappointing or unpleasant, or causing difficulties or harm • *We heard the bad news about Dorothy's illness.* ○ *Flights were delayed because of bad weather.* ○ *Too much salt is bad for you* (= has a harmful effect on your health). • Bad can also mean serious or severe: *a bad accident/storm* • **Not (too) bad** is a way of saying that things are satisfactory: *"How are you?" "Not too bad, all things considered."* • **Bad breath** is breath that smells unpleasant. • A person who is **bad-tempered** becomes annoyed or angry very easily.

badly /'bæd·li/, *not standard* **bad** *adv* **worse** /wɜrs/, **worst** /wɜrst/ in an extreme way; seriously or severely • *His face was badly bruised and swollen after the accident.* ○ *He took the news of his sister's death badly.* • See also BADLY.

bad LOW QUALITY /bæd/ *adj* **worse** /wɜrs/, **worst** /wɜrst/ of very low quality; not acceptable • *bad manners* ○ *We thought the hotel was bad and the food was terrible.* ○ *That was one of the worst movies I've ever seen.*

badly /'bæd·li/, *not standard* **bad** *adv* [not gradable] **worse** /wɜrs/, **worst** /wɜrst/ • *Her husband treated her badly, and finally she left him.* • See also BADLY.

bad EVIL /bæd/ *adj* **worse** /wɜrs/, **worst** /wɜrst/ (of people or actions) evil or morally unacceptable • *He's a bad person.* ○ *Cheating on your wife is a really bad thing to do.*

bad UNHEALTHY /bæd/ *adj* **worse** /wɜrs/, **worst** /wɜrst/ (of a person) sick or not well, or (of an illness) serious or severe • *a bad back/heart* ○ *a bad cough* ○ *bad health* ○ *He's in really bad shape.* ○ *He's got bad arthritis and can hardly walk.*

bade /bæd, beɪd/ *past simple of* BID TELL

badge /bædʒ/ *n* [C] a small piece of metal worn to show your membership in a group or your authority within an organization such as the police

badger ANIMAL /'bædʒ·ər/ *n* [C] an animal that digs holes in the ground, where it lives, and comes out at night to feed

badger ASK /'bædʒ·ər/ *v* [T] to annoy (someone) by telling them repeatedly to do something or by questioning them repeatedly • *He badgered officials at the American Embassy to help.*

badlands /'bæd·lændz/ *pl n* a dry area without plants and with large rocks that the weather has worn into strange shapes

badly /ˈbæd·li/, *not standard* **bad** /bæd/ *adv* [not gradable] much or very much • *The UN sent 90 tons of badly needed food.* ○ *Texas wants very badly to be considered tops in the school system.* • See also **badly** at BAD UNPLEASANT, BAD LOW QUALITY. LP VERY, COMPLETELY, AND OTHER INTENSIFIERS

badminton /ˈbæd·mɪnt·ən/ *n* [U] a sport in which two or four people hit a SHUTTLECOCK (= small, very light object with feathers) over a high net

bad–mouth /ˈbæd·maʊθ, -maʊð/ *v* [T] *esp. disapproving* to make criticisms about (someone or something) • *Why are you always bad-mouthing the medical profession?*

baffle /ˈbæf·əl/ *v* [T] to cause (someone) to be unable to understand or explain something • *Even his friends were baffled by his behavior.*

baffling /ˈbæf·lɪŋ/ *adj* • *a baffling murder case*

bag SIMPLE CONTAINER /bæg/ *n* [C] a simple container of paper or light plastic that is open at the top, used esp. to hold things you have bought • *a grocery/shopping bag* • **Bags under the eyes** are dark circles, sometimes with loose or swollen skin, under the eyes. • If something is **in the bag**, success or victory is certain: *When the score reached 12 to 2 we knew the game was in the bag.*

bag /bæg/ *v* [T] **-gg-** to put (items) in a bag • *I'll bag your groceries for you.*

bag STRONG CONTAINER /bæg/ *n* [C] a strong container of leather, stiff plastic, or cloth material for carrying clothes or other objects, esp. when you are traveling • *You can leave your bags in the hotel room, and I'll send someone up for them later.* • A bag is also a woman's POCKETBOOK: *I carry a large shoulder bag.*

bag KILL /bæg/ *v* [T] **-gg-** to hunt and kill (an animal or bird) • *Only 15 percent of last year's hunters actually bagged a deer.*

bagel /ˈbeɪ·gəl/ *n* [C] a soft, chewy, circular piece of bread with a hole in the center

baggage BAGS /ˈbæg·ɪdʒ/ *n* [U] the bags that you take with you when you travel; LUGGAGE • *How many pieces of baggage do you have?*

baggage FEELINGS /ˈbæg·ɪdʒ/ *n* [U] the beliefs and feelings that you have which influence how you think and behave • *Everybody brings their own baggage to viewing a work of art.*

baggy /ˈbæg·i/ *adj* (of clothes) hanging loosely because of being too big or having been stretched • *a baggy sweater*

bagpipes /ˈbæg·paɪps/ *pl n* a musical instrument played by blowing air into a bag and forcing it out through pipes, used esp. in Scotland

bail MONEY /beɪl/ *n* [U] a sum of money given to a law court by a person accused of a crime so that they can be released until their trial, at which time the money will be returned to them • *The judge set bail at $100,000.*

bail REMOVE WATER /beɪl/ *v* [I/T] to remove (water) from a boat by using a container • *I'd float around for hours fishing and bailing out the water leaking in.* [T]

□ **bail out** *obj* HELP, **bail** *obj* **out** /ˈbeɪlˈaʊt/ *v adv* [M] to help (someone in difficulty) esp. by giving or lending them money • *When the savings and loan companies began to fail, they asked the government to bail them out.*

bailout /ˈbeɪlaʊt/ *n* [C] • *The government mounted a massive bailout of troubled savings and loan institutions.*

□ **bail out** JUMP /ˈbeɪlˈaʊt/ *v adv* [I] to jump out of an aircraft with a PARACHUTE, esp. because the aircraft is about to have an accident • *The pilot barely had time to bail out.* • (*fig.*) To bail out is also to stop doing or being involved in something: *The TV show triggered a number of protests, and some of the sponsors bailed out.*

bailiff /ˈbeɪ·ləf/ *n* [C] an official who is responsible for prisoners who are appearing in court

bait FOOD /beɪt/ *n* [U] a small amount of food used to attract and catch a fish or animal • *The fishermen bought some worms to use as bait.* • (*fig.*) Bait is also anything used to persuade someone to do something: *Lawyers making the investment offering will find out today whether someone is ready to take the bait.*

bait /beɪt/ *v* [T] • *You can bait the mousetrap with a piece of cheese.*

bait MAKE ANGRY /beɪt/ *v* [T] to intentionally make (someone) angry by saying or doing things to annoy them • *She enjoys baiting her brother by teasing him about his girlfriend.*

bake /beɪk/ *v* [I/T] to cook inside an OVEN • *to bake a cake/bread/cookies* [T] • PIC COOKING METHODS

baker /ˈbeɪ·kər/ *n* [C] a person whose job is to make bread and cakes for sale

bakery /ˈbeɪ·kə·ri/ *n* [C] a place where bread, cakes, and pastries are made or sold

balance POSITION /ˈbæl·əns/ *n* [U] the condition of someone or something in which its weight is equally divided so that it can stay in one position or be under control while moving • *He jumped off the porch and lost his balance when he landed on the grass, falling to the ground.* ○ *We're teaching Sue how to ride a bike, but she's still having trouble keeping her balance.*

balance /ˈbæl·əns/ *v* [I/T] • *He balanced the book on top of his coffee cup.* [T]

balance OPPOSING FORCES /ˈbæl·əns/ *n* [U] a situation in which two opposing forces have or are given the same power • *He works toward a balance between extremes.* ○ *As a journalist, you try to strike a balance between serious reporting and the temptation to say clever things.* • If a BUDGET (= financial plan) is **in balance**, no more money will be spent than is taken in during a particular period: *We want to cut the budget to get it in balance by the year 2002.* • **On balance** means after considering the power or influence of both sides of a question: *The job offer had some advantages, but on balance he thought he was better off where he was.* • A country's **balance of payments** or **balance of trade** is the difference between the money from EXPORTS (= goods and services sold to other countries) and the cost of IMPORTS (= goods and services bought from other countries). • A **balance of power** is a situation in which no country is powerful enough to control the others.

balance /'bæl·əns/ *v* [T] to put (opposing forces) into a position in which neither controls the other • *I had to balance the children's needs against my own.* • *The government is required to* **balance the budget** (= not spend more money than it receives).

balanced /'bæl·ənst/ *adj* • *The news program prided itself on its balanced reporting* (= one that considered all sides). • A **balanced budget** is a financial plan in which the amount of money spent is not greater than the amount received. • A **balanced diet** is a combination of the correct types and amounts of food.

balance AMOUNT /'bæl·əns/ *n* [C usually sing] the amount of money you have in a bank account or an amount of money owed • *a bank balance* • A balance is also the amount of something that you have left after you have spent or used up the rest: *We'll go over your homework for the first half hour and use the balance of the class period to prepare for the exam.* • A **balance sheet** is a record of the value of things a company owns and of its debts for a particular period, usually a year.

balcony /'bæl·kə·ni/ *n* [C] a narrow floor that is attached to the outside wall of a building above the ground, usually with sides or bars, or an area of seats at an upper level in a theater • *Our hotel room has a balcony that looks out over the pool.*

bald WITHOUT HAIR /bɔːld/ *adj* [-er/-est only] without hair on the head, or without much hair

balding /'bɔːl·dɪŋ/ *adj* [not gradable] beginning to lose the hair on your head • *He was plump and balding but very attractive to women.*

baldness /'bɔːld·nəs/ *n* [U]

bald PLAIN /bɔːld/ *adj* basic and with no unnecessary words; not detailed • *She just left a bald statement of resignation without any explanation.*

bale /beɪl/ *n* [C] a large amount of something such as HAY (= dry grass), paper, wool, or cloth that has been tied tightly together

balk /bɔːk/ *v* [I] to be unwilling to do something or let something happen • *I balked at the prospect of spending four hours on a train with him.*

ball ROUND OBJECT /bɔːl/ *n* [C] a round object that can roll and usually bounce and that is used in many games in which it is thrown, hit,

or kicked • *a golf/soccer/tennis ball* • The ball of the foot is the curved part where the big toe joins the foot. • To **get/start the ball rolling** is to begin something or get it going: *We have to get the ball rolling on this project soon.* • To be **on the ball** is to be aware of all developments and to be quick to react to them: *We need someone who's really on the ball.* • A **ballgame** is a baseball game or a similar game. • A **ballgame** is also a set of conditions that control how something can be done: *Working for a large corporation was one thing, but now that we're in business for ourselves, it's a whole new ballgame.* • A **ballpark** is a large structure enclosing a field on which games, esp. baseball games, are played. • The **ballpark** is also an acceptable range in the amount or number of something when you do not know or cannot agree on an exact amount or number: *I'd sell the house for $150,000, but his offer isn't even in the ballpark.* ○ *A ballpark figure of $3,000 would be realistic.*

ball DANCE /bɔːl/ *n* [C] a large, formal occasion where people dance • *(infml)* A ball is also any very enjoyable experience: *"How was your weekend?" "We had a ball!"* • A **ballroom** is a large room that is used for dancing or other activities.

ballad /'bæl·əd/ *n* [C] a song or poem that tells a story, or a slow love song

ballerina /ˌbæl·əˈriː·nə/ *n* [C] a female BALLET dancer

ballet /bæl'eɪ/ *n* [C/U] a type of dancing in which controlled movements of the body are designed to express the beauty of physical motion, often while telling a story, or a piece of music for such dancing

ballistic missile /bəˈlɪs·tɪkˈmɪs·əl/ *n* [C] a MISSILE (= flying weapon) that is powered as it rises, but then falls freely

ballistics /bəˈlɪs·tɪks/ *n* [U] the study of objects that are shot or thrown through the air, such as a bullet from a gun

balloon /bəˈluːn/ *n* [C] a small, thin, rubber bag that you can fill with air or another gas until it is round in shape, often used for decoration at parties or as a child's toy • A balloon is also a very large, round container filled with a gas that can rise in the air and carry people riding under it in an attached box.

balloon /bəˈluːn/ *v* [I] to become larger, esp. quickly • *The rumors soon ballooned into* (= quickly became) *a full-grown scandal.*

ballot /'bæl·ət/ *n* [C/U] a piece of paper on which you write a secret vote • The ballot is also a system or occasion of secret voting: *Issues need to be considered in open debate or put on the ballot.* [U]

ballpoint (pen) /'bɔːl·pɔɪnt ('pen)/ *n* [C] a pen with a small, metal ball at the end that rolls ink out when you press the ball against paper to write

balls /bɔːlz/ *pl n rude slang* TESTICLES • *(slang)*

Balls can also mean bravery: *It takes balls to go off into the woods alone for two weeks.*

balm /bɑm, bɑlm/ *n* [C/U] an oily substance rubbed into the skin and used esp. to treat injuries or reduce pain

balmy /ˈbɑm·i, ˈbɑl·mi/ *adj* (of weather) pleasantly warm • *a balmy night*

baloney NONSENSE /bəˈloʊ·ni/ *n* [U] *infml* nonsense • *That's a lot of baloney!*

baloney FOOD /bəˈloʊ·ni/ *n* [U] BOLOGNA

bamboo /bæmˈbuː/ *n* [C/U] a tall grass that grows in hotter regions and that has hard, hollow stems, or the stems of this plant

ban /bæn/ *v* [T] **-nn-** to forbid (someone) from doing something or (something) from being done • *The new regulations ban smoking from all work sites.*

ban /bæn/ *n* [C] • *The president supported a ban on assault weapons.*

banal /bəˈnæl, -nɑl; ˈbeɪn·ᵊl/ *adj* too often used in the past and therefore not interesting • *He just sat there making banal remarks all evening.*

banana /bəˈnæn·ə/ *n* [C/U] a long, curved fruit with a usually yellow skin and soft, sweet flesh inside

bananas /bəˈnæn·əz/ *adj* [not gradable] *infml* a state of great excitement because of pleasure, anger, or another emotion • *She'll go bananas when you tell her the news.*

band MUSICIANS /bænd/ *n* [C] a group of musicians who play music together, esp. popular music • *a jazz/rock band* ○ *a marching/military band* • A **bandleader** is a person who leads a large group of musicians while they play, and who often plays an instrument at the same time.

band GROUP /bænd/ *n* [C] a group of people who have joined together for a special purpose, or a group of animals • *a band of outlaws*

band together /ˈ--ˈ--/ *v adv* [I] to join together as a group, often for a specific purpose • *The workers banded together to demand better working conditions.*

band STRIP /bænd/ *n* [C] a thin, flat strip of a material put around something to fasten or strengthen it, or a strip of color, light, etc., that is different from its surrounding area • *The silver band from his wristwatch left a green ring over his wrist.*

bandage /ˈbæn·dɪdʒ/ *n* [C] a strip of cloth that is used to cover an injury on someone's body to protect it

bandage /ˈbæn·dɪdʒ/ *v* [T] • *They bandaged his wounds.*

Band–Aid /ˈbæn·deɪd/ *n* [C] *trademark* a thin piece of cloth on a strip which sticks to the skin and is used to cover small cuts • A **Band-Aid** is also a temporary solution to a problem that is unlikely to be successful: *It was a Band-Aid solution for a major, long-term problem.*

bandanna, **bandana** /bænˈdæn·ə/ *n* [C] a large, brightly colored HANDKERCHIEF that is worn around your neck or head

bandit /ˈbæn·dət/ *n* [C] an armed thief, esp. (in older use) one who attacks people while they are traveling • *Bandits attacked the travelers just outside of town.*

bandwagon /ˈbænˌdwæg·ən/ *n* [C usually sing] an activity or idea that has become very popular • To **get/jump on the bandwagon** is to join an activity or change an opinion to one that has become very popular so that you can share in its success: *After a couple of politicians won elections by promising to cut taxes, most of the others jumped on the bandwagon.*

bandy *obj* **about** /ˈbæn·diːˈˈaʊt/ *v adv* [T] to talk about (something) without careful consideration • *Wild guesses of the value of the painting were being bandied about.*

bane /beɪn/ *n* [U] something that is particularly effective in causing you trouble or worry • *Instead of doing his homework, my son is always playing computer games—they're the bane of my existence these days.*

bang /bæŋ/ *v* [I/T] to make or cause (something) to make a sudden loud, usually short noise, esp. by hitting two things together • *He banged his head on the open cupboard door.* [T] • To bang out something is to do something quickly: *I sat down at the piano and banged out a tune.* [M]

bang /bæŋ/ *n* [C] • *She ran out of the room and slammed the door with a bang.* • **Bang for the buck** means value in return for your money: *They're very careful when they spend money, and they're going to insist on getting the most bang for their buck.*

▫**bang up** *obj*, **bang** *obj* **up** /ˈ-ˈ-/ *v adv* [M] to damage or injure (someone or something) by hitting • *He banged up the car backing out of the garage.*

bangs /bæŋz/ *pl n* the hair, usually cut straight across the front of the face above the eyes

bang–up /ˈbæŋ·ʌp/ *adj* [not gradable] *infml* very good; excellent • *She did a bang-up job.*

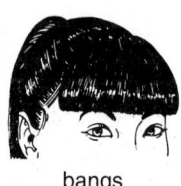
bangs

banish /ˈbæn·ɪʃ/ *v* [T] to send (someone) away and forbid them to come back • *Adam and Eve were banished from the Garden of Eden.* • To banish is also to get rid of: *Their goal is to banish war forever.*

banister /ˈbæn·ə·stər/ *n* [C] a row of wooden or metal poles at the side of stairs and the bar attached to them on top

banjo /ˈbæn·dʒoʊ/ *n* [C] *pl* **banjos** or **banjoes** a musical instrument with four or five strings and a body like a drum that is played by pulling at the strings with the fingers or a small piece of plastic

bank ORGANIZATION /bæŋk/ *n* [C] an organization that holds money belonging to others, investing and lending it to get more money, or the building in which the organization is situated • A bank of blood or human organs is a place that stores these things for later medical use: *a blood bank* • In a CASINO, the bank is money that is used to pay the players who win. • A **bank account** is an arrangement with a bank in which the bank holds your money, which you can remove when you want.

bank /bæŋk/ *v* [I/T] • *I bank at First National because it's near where I work.* [I always + adv/prep]

banker /'bæŋ·kər/ *n* [C] a person who has an important position in a bank

banking /'bæŋ·kɪŋ/ *n* [U] the business of operating a bank • *a career in international banking*

bank RAISED GROUND /bæŋk/ *n* [C] sloping raised land, esp. along the sides of a river or lake, or a mass of something that has been piled together and has sloping sides • *We walked along the river bank.* • A bank of clouds is a group of clouds that look as if they are piled together. • A bank is also a row of similar objects: *The gambling casinos have banks of slot machines.*

bank TURN /bæŋk/ *v* [I] (of an aircraft) to fly with one wing higher than the other when turning • *We banked to make a left turn as we approached the airport.*

▫ **bank on** (obj) /'-,-/ *v prep* to expect (something) or depend on (something) happening • *You can bank on my support.* [T]

bankrupt /'bæŋ·krəpt/ *adj.* without enough money to pay your debts • *If I don't find a job, I'll be bankrupt in two months.* • (law) When a company or person is bankrupt, a court of law gives control of the finances to someone who will arrange to pay as much as possible of what is owed.

bankrupt /'bæŋ·krəpt/ *v* [T] • *The senator said the president's plan would bankrupt the country.*

bankruptcy /'bæŋ·krəp·si/ *n* [C/U] the inability to pay your debts, or a particular example of this, involving the sale of your property or some other arrangement to pay as much as possible of the money you owe • *If sales don't improve, we'll have to declare bankruptcy within a year.* [U]

banner /'bæn·ər/ *n* [C] a strip of material showing a name, such as of a sports team, or a message, which is often put in a place where it can be seen by many people • *The museum had a huge banner over its front entrance advertising its current show.* • A **banner year** is an unusually good year: *This is clearly not a banner year for Canadian poetry.*

banquet /'bæŋ·kwət/ *n* [C] a large formal meal for many people, often followed by speeches in honor of someone • *Christopher Reeve will receive the award at the organization's annual banquet.*

banquette /bæŋ'ket, bæn-/ *n* [C] a long seat covered with cloth or similar material and situated against a wall, esp. with tables and chairs facing it in a restaurant • *She sat on the banquette because she likes to look at everyone in the restaurant.*

banter /'bænt·ər/ *n* [U] conversation that is not serious and is often playful • *That kind of banter isn't appropriate at work.*

baptism /'bæp,tɪz·əm, *Southern also* 'bæb-/ *n* [C] a ceremony in which a person has water poured on their head or is briefly covered completely by water, and is named and recognized as a Christian • *We're hoping to be able to get to Pasadena for the baptism of our grandson.*

baptize /bæp'taɪz, *Southern also* bæb'taɪz/ *v* [T] • *She was baptized a Catholic at age 20.*

Baptist /'bæp·təst, *Southern also* 'bæb-/ *n* [C], *adj* [not gradable] (a member of) a Christian religious group that is one of the Protestant churches • *the Baptist church* ○ *a Baptist minister*

bar POLE /bɑr/ *n* [C] a strong pole, esp. one made of metal, used as a support, to force something to move, or to block an opening • *He stuck his hand through the bars of the cage* • A bar is also any of various small objects having a rectangular shape: *a granola bar* • A **bar code** is a small rectangle of black lines of different widths printed on an outside surface of an object that is sold, and which contains information that can be read by a computer, such as the price of the item.

bar /bɑr/ *v* [T] **-rr-** to put a strong pole or poles across (an opening) • *We barred the windows as protection against burglars.*

bar PREVENT /bɑr/ *v* [T] **-rr-** to prevent (someone) from doing something or going somewhere • *Protesters tried to break into the building, but the police barred their way.*

bar DRINKING PLACE /bɑr/ *n* [C] a place, sometimes within a restaurant, where alcoholic drinks are served, or a long, high table in such a place along which people stand or sit while drinking • *He used to just sit in a bar and listen to jazz.* ○ *She sat at the bar and chatted with the bartender.*

bar MUSIC /bɑr/, **measure** *n* [C] one of the small equal parts into which a piece of music is divided, containing a fixed number of beats • *He played four bars of music.* • A bar is also one of the vertical lines that divide a piece of music into equal parts.

bar LAWYERS /bɑr/ *n* [U] all lawyers considered as a group • *She passed the Massachusetts bar exam on her first try.*

bar EXCEPT /bɑr/ *prep* except for • *He's the greatest pitcher of all time, bar none* (= no one else is better).

barring /'bɑr·ɪŋ/ *prep* • *We were assured that, barring unexpected developments, we would get the contract.*

barb SHARP END /bɑrb/ *n* [C] the sharp part of

a fish hook or arrow that makes it difficult to remove from something caught on it

barbed /barbd/ *adj* • **Barbed wire** is a type of strong wire with sharp points on it, used to prevent people or animals from entering or leaving a place.

barb CRUEL REMARK /barb/ *n* [C] an intelligent but critical remark that is intended to hurt • *Some of Weaver's sharpest barbs were aimed at his boss.*

barbed /barbd/ *adj* • *a barbed comment*

barbarian /bar'ber·i·ən, -'bær-/ *n* [C] a person who has no experience of the habits and culture of modern life, and whose behavior you therefore consider strange or offensive • *They thought I was some kind of barbarian because I didn't know how to use a computer.*

barbarous /'bar·bə·rəs/ *adj* characteristic of people who have no experience of the habits and culture of modern life, and whose behavior you therefore consider strange or offensive • *His manners were barbarous—he ate everything with his fingers.* • Barbarous also means BARBARIC.

barbaric /bar'bær·ɪk/, **barbarous** /'bar·bə·rəs/ *adj* extremely cruel • *In my opinion, spanking a child is barbaric.*

barbecue /'bar·bɪ,kju:/ (*abbreviation* **BBQ**) *n* [C] a metal frame on which food is cooked outside over a fire or hot coals, or a meal prepared using such a frame and usually eaten outside • *I like catfish cooked on a barbecue.* ○ *Our neighbors invited all of us to a backyard barbecue.*

barbecue /'bar·bɪ,kju:/ *v* [T] • *During the summer we barbecue all the time.*

barber /'bar·bər/ *n* [C] a person whose job is cutting hair, esp. of men and boys • *I was sitting in the **barber shop** (= place where esp. men and boys get their hair cut) when I heard the news.*

barbiturate /bar'bɪtʃ·ə·rət/ *n* [C] a strong drug that makes people calm or helps them sleep

bare /ber, bær/ *adj* [*-er/-est* only] without any clothes or not covered by anything • *The hot sand burned my bare feet.* ○ *Inside, the floors were bare and there was very little furniture.* • Bare also means the least possible or only this much of something: *They had nothing beyond the bare necessities (of life)* (= the most basic things you need).

bare /ber, bær/ *v* [T] to show (something that is usually covered) • *The dog bared its teeth and growled.*

bareback /'ber·bæk, 'bær-/ *adj, adv* [not gradable] without a SADDLE (= leather seat) on the back of a horse that someone is riding • *a bareback rider*

barefoot /'ber·fʊt, 'bær-/, **barefooted** /'ber·fʊt·əd, 'bær-/ *adj, adv* [not gradable] not wearing any shoes or socks • *A young barefoot girl led him away.*

bareheaded /'ber'hed·əd, 'bær-/ *adj, adv* [not gradable] without any covering on your head • *Some of the men wore hats, and some were bareheaded.*

barely /'ber·li, 'bær-/ *adv* [not gradable] by the smallest amount; only just • *There was barely enough room for the two of them.* ○ *Their marriage lasted barely three years.*

barf /barf/ *v* [I] *slang* to vomit

bargain AGREEMENT /'bar·gən/ *n* [C] an agreement between two people or groups in which each promises to do something in exchange for something else • *He failed to carry out his side of the bargain.*

bargaining /'bar·gə·nɪŋ/ *n* [U] • *Harriman pressed for tougher bargaining by the American side.* • A **bargaining chip** is something that one side can use to persuade the other side to reach an agreement: *Union leaders used the threat of a strike during the busy season as a bargaining chip.*

bargain LOW PRICE /'bar·gən/ *n* [C] something sold for a price that is lower than usual or lower than its value • *We got tickets to the show at half-price, a real bargain.* • *Farmers bought up the land at **bargain-basement** (= extremely low) prices.*

bargain /'bar·gən/ *v* [I] to try to reach agreement with someone in order to get a lower price • *You can usually bargain with antique dealers.*

□**bargain on** /'--,-/ *v prep* [T] to expect (something to happen) • *We hadn't bargained on an entire week of rain.*

barge BOAT /bardʒ/ *n* [C] a long boat with a flat bottom, used for carrying heavy loads

barge HURRY /bardʒ/ *v* [I always + adv/prep] to force your way rudely or carelessly and quickly • *You ought to knock instead of just barging into my bedroom.*

baritone /'bær·ə,toʊn/ *n* [C] a man's singing voice in the range lower than a TENOR, or a singer or musical instrument with this range

bark DOG /bark/ *v* [I/T] to make the loud, short noise that a dog and some other animals make • When a human barks something, they shout it suddenly and strongly: *The lieutenant barked (out) a command.* [T/M] • If you say that someone's **bark is worse than** their **bite**, you mean that although they sound frightening, their behavior will not be so severe: *The boss seems mean, but his bark is worse than his bite.* • If you are **barking up the wrong tree**, you are trying to do something in a way that will not work: *They want more treatment for drug addicts because putting addicts in jail is barking up the wrong tree.*

bark /bark/ *n* [C] • *The dog gave two loud barks.*

bark TREE /bark/ *n* [U] the hard, outer covering of a tree

barley /'bar·li/ *n* [U] a tall grasslike plant, or

the grain obtained from this plant and used for food and for making some alcoholic drinks

bar mitzvah /bɑrˈmɪts·və/ *n* [C] (in the Jewish religion) a ceremony held when a boy reaches the age of 13 and has the responsibilities of an adult man

barn /bɑrn/ *n* [C] a large building on a farm in which HAY (= dried grass) and grain and often farm animals are kept • A **barnyard** is the area around a barn, often fenced so that animals cannot get away.

barnacle /ˈbɑr·nɪ·kəl/ *n* [C] a small sea creature with a shell that fastens itself tightly and in large numbers to rocks and the bottoms of boats

barnstorm /ˈbɑrn·stɔːrm/ *v* [I/T] to travel to (many places) briefly in order to give a performance or to make a political appearance • *He barnstormed (through) the West.* [I/T]

barometer /bəˈrɑm·əţ·ər/ *n* [C] a device that measures air pressure which shows when the weather is likely to change

baroque /bəˈroʊk, -ˈrɑk, -ˈrɔːk/ *adj* relating to the highly decorated style in buildings, art, and music that was popular in Europe in the 17th century and the early part of the 18th century • *baroque architecture*

barracks /ˈbær·əks/ *n* [C] *pl* **barracks** a building or group of buildings where soldiers live • *The 15 tents were normally used as barracks for Marines.*

barrage /bəˈrɑʒ, -ˈrɑdʒ/ *n* [C usually sing] a continuous firing of large guns, esp. to protect soldiers advancing on an enemy • *an artillery barrage* • A barrage is also a great number of complaints, criticisms, or questions suddenly directed at someone: *Morris fired off a barrage of questions about Halperin's politics.*

barrel CONTAINER /ˈbær·əl/ *n* [C] a large wooden container with a flat top and bottom and curving sides that are wider in the middle • A barrel is also a unit of measurement of volume equal to 31.5 gallons (119 liters) or, of oil, equal to 42 gallons (159 liters).

barrel MOVE FAST /ˈbær·əl/ *v* [I always + adv/prep] to travel or move very fast • *We were barreling along at 80 miles an hour.*

barrel GUN PART /ˈbær·əl/ *n* [C] the long part of a gun that is shaped like a tube

barren /ˈbær·ən/ *adj* (of land) not producing or unable to produce plants • *The landscape was barren, with not a tree or shrub in sight.* • (*old use*) If a woman is barren, she is unable to have a baby.

barrette

barrette /bəˈret, bɑ-/ *n* [C] a fastener, often decorative, that women and girls use to hold their hair in place

barricade /ˈbær·əˌkeɪd/ *n* [C] a large object or objects that are used to stop people from going where they want to go

barricade /ˈbær·əˌkeɪd/ *v* [T] to block anyone from reaching (a place) • *The protesting students barricaded the streets leading to the university.*

barrier /ˈbær·iː·ər/ *n* [C] anything used or acting to block someone from going somewhere or from doing something, or to block something from happening • *The Secret Service erected concrete barriers around the White House.* ○ *Jackie Robinson was the African-American who succeeded in breaking major league baseball's color barrier* (= use of race to block something from happening).

barring /ˈbɑr·ɪŋ/ *prep* • See at BAR EXCEPT.

barrio /ˈbɑr·iːˌoʊ, ˈbær-/ *n* [C] *pl* **barrios** in the US, a part of a city where mainly Spanish-speaking people live

bartender /ˈbɑrˌten·dər/ *n* [C] someone who makes and serves drinks in a bar

barter /ˈbɑrţ·ər/ *v* [I/T] to exchange (goods) for other things rather than for money • *In the marketplace, you can barter for souvenirs by offering jeans and lipstick.* [I]

base BOTTOM /beɪs/ *n* [C] the bottom of an object; the part on which it rests • *This lamp has a heavy base so it won't tip over.*

base MAIN PLACE /beɪs/ *n* [C] the place from which a business operates or a person works • *We have an office in San Diego, but Washington is still our base.* • A base is also a place from which the military operates that provides weapons storage and housing: *The military has bases all over the US.*

base /beɪs/ *v* [T always + adv/prep] • *Where is your company based?*

base LARGEST PART /beɪs/ *n* [C usually sing] the main part of something, or the people or activities that form the main part of something • *The sauce has an olive oil base.* ○ *Tourism remains the city's economic base.* ○ *He'll need a wide base of regional support to win the election.*

base BASEBALL /beɪs/ *n* [C] (in the game of baseball) one of the four corners of a square, all of which a player must touch in order to score • *He reached first base on a single.* • A **base hit** (also **hit**) is a play in which a player hits the ball and successfully reaches the first base.

□**base** *obj* **on** *obj* /ˈ-ˌ-/ *v adv* [T] to use (information) to support or prove (an opinion or belief) • *We based our decision on the facts in the report.* • If you base a story, painting, or other work on something else, you use the other thing as the main idea for creating the story: *The book is based on the life of abolitionist John Brown.*

baseball /ˈbeɪs·bɔːl/ *n* [C/U] a game with two teams of nine players in which a ball, thrown by a PITCHER, is hit by a player with a BAT (= special stick) who then tries to run around four BASES before visor being stopped by the other team • *Austin never played baseball like the other kids.* [U] • A baseball is the ball used in this game.

baseball cap

[C] • A **baseball cap** is a hat with a flat piece sticking out on the front as protection from the sun, originally worn by baseball players. • PIC SWING

baseless /'beɪ·sləs/ *adj* without supporting facts • *Investigation showed these were baseless accusations.*

basement /'beɪ·smənt/ *n* [C] a part of a building that is below the level of the first floor • *The hardware department is in the basement.*

bases /'beɪ·siːz/ *pl of* BASIS

bash HIT /bæʃ/ *v* [T] *infml* to attack (someone or something) with an object • *He bashed his arm against a shelf.* • If you bash someone with words, you criticize them severely: *Some of these countries have been bashing the United States.*

bashing /'bæʃ·ɪŋ/ *n* [U] • *The more things I do to get this union on the right track, the more of a bashing I take.*

bash PARTY /bæʃ/ *n* [C] *infml* a large, energetic party • *He had a big bash, including live music, for his 18th birthday.*

bashful /'bæʃ·fəl/ *adj* easily embarrassed and uncomfortable; shy • *She gave a bashful smile when she was introduced.*

basic /'beɪ·sɪk/ *adj* most important or central to something • *In physics we study basic principles of force and motion.* ○ *We help with basic needs like food and shelter.*

basics /'beɪ·sɪks/ *pl n* the central and most important principles of something • *Pablo has promised to teach me the basics of sailing.*

basically /'beɪ·sɪ·kli/ *adv* [not gradable] • *The two cars are basically the same.*

basil /'bæz·əl, 'beɪ·zəl/ *n* [U] an herb with a strong smell that is used to flavor foods in cooking

basin /'beɪ·sən/ *n* [C] a large, open bowl, or the amount such a container will hold • *I left the napkins soaking in a basin.* • The basin of a river or body of water is the land that surrounds it and the streams that flow into it. • A basin is also a sheltered area of water deep enough for boats, or an area of land that is lower than all the surrounding land.

basis /'beɪ·səs/ *n* [C] *pl* **bases** /'beɪ·siːz/ the most important facts or principles or ideas that support something • *There is no basis for their statements.* • A basis is also a way or method of doing something: *Mostly people work on a parttime basis.*

bask /bæsk/ *v* [I always + adv/prep] to lie or sit and enjoy warmth • *On top of the wall, a cat basked happily in the sun.* ○ *(fig.) Marina basked in the crowd's admiration (= enjoyed it).*

basket CONTAINER /'bæs·kət/ *n* [C] a container like a rounded box, often with a handle, which is used for carrying or storing things and made of woven strips of dried grass or other material, or the amount such a container holds • *a wicker basket* ○ *a wastepaper basket* ○ *a basket of flowers*

basket GOAL /'bæs·kət/ *n* [C] (in the game of BASKETBALL) an open net hanging from a metal ring which players must throw the ball through to score, or a successful throw through the ring • *She made three baskets in a row.*

basketball /'bæs·kət,bɔːl/ *n* [C/U] a game played by two teams of five players who score points by throwing the ball through a net that hangs from a metal ring, or the ball used in this game • *We played basketball all the time.* [U] • PIC DUNK

basket case /'bæs·kət,keɪs/ *n* [C usually sing] *infml* someone who is made very anxious by the demands and pressures of something, esp. work • *I was a basket case by the end of the day.*

bas mitzvah /bɑs'mɪts·və/ *n* [C] BAR MITZVAH

bass MUSICAL RANGE /beɪs/ *n* [C/U] the lowest range of a voice or musical instrument, or a singer or musical instrument with this range • *The qualities of his voice make you forget he is a bass.* [C] • *(infml)* A bass or **bass fiddle** is a DOUBLE BASS.

bass FISH /bæs/ *n* [C/U] *pl* **bass** any of several related fishes found in rivers or the sea, used for food • *striped bass* [C]

bassoon /bə'suːn/ *n* [C/U] a tube-shaped musical instrument that produces low notes and is played by blowing through two REEDS (= thin pieces of wood) and pressing keys on its front to produce notes, or this type of instrument generally; a WOODWIND

bastard /'bæs·tərd/ *n* [C] *rude slang* an extremely unpleasant person, esp. a man • *You stupid little bastard!*

baste /beɪst/ *v* [T] to put (fat or meat juices) on food, esp. meat, while it cooks • *We basted the turkey every twenty minutes.*

bat STICK /bæt/ *n* [C] a specially shaped stick of wood or metal, used for hitting the ball esp. in baseball • *I hear the crack of a bat and the voices of children.* • If you are **at bat**, it is your turn to try to hit the ball in a baseball game. • PIC SWING

bat /bæt/ *v* [I/T] **-tt-** • *He batted the ball high into the air.* [T] • If you bat at something, you hit it lightly: *She batted at the air, trying to shoo the bugs.* [I]

batter /'bæt̬·ər/ *n* [C] (in baseball) the player whose turn it is to hit the ball • See also BATTER. • PIC SWING

bat ANIMAL /bæt/ *n* [C] a small, flying animal with big ears and wings of skin • *(infml)* Someone who has **bats in the belfry** is silly or crazy. See also BATTY.

bat MOVE EYE /bæt/ v [T] **-tt-** to open and close (your eyes) quickly several times, esp. to attract attention or admiration • *She smiled and batted her eyes.* • If you do not **bat an eye** or **eyelid** you show no sign of surprise or shock when something unexpected happens: *Gail didn't bat an eye when Mark said he had wrecked the car.*

batch /bætʃ/ n [C] people or things dealt with as a group or at the same time • *Mom just made a fresh batch of cookies.* ○ *I've got a whole batch of applications to read through.*

bath /bæθ/ n [C] the activity of washing yourself or another person or an animal in a large container filled with warm water • *I gave the dog a bath.* • When describing homes, a bath can also mean a BATHROOM: *a three bedroom, two-bath apartment* • A **bath mat** is a cloth put on the floor to stand on after a bath or a piece of rubber on the bottom of a bath or SHOWER to keep someone from sliding and falling. • A **bath towel** is a large TOWEL (= piece of cloth) for drying off after a bath or SHOWER. • A **bathtub** (also **tub**) is a container large enough for a person to sit in to take a bath. • PIC BATHROOM

bathe WASH /beɪð/ v [I/T] to wash someone, usually with soap and water in a **bathtub** • *I had to change the kids' diapers and feed them and bathe them.* [T]

bathe COVER /beɪð/ v [T] to cover with a liquid, esp. as a treatment for pain or injury • *I bathed my foot in warm salt water.* ○ *(fig.) The afternoon sun bathed the city in pink and gold.*

bathing suit /ˈbeɪ·ðɪŋˌsuːt/ n [C] a **swimsuit**, see at SWIM

bathrobe /ˈbæθ·roʊb/, **robe** n [C] a piece of clothing rather like a loose-fitting coat, worn to cover up after a bath, or before getting dressed

bathroom /ˈbæθ·ruːm, -rʊm/ n [C] a room with a toilet and a place to wash your hands, and often a **bathtub** and a SHOWER (= device

that sprays water on a person's body) • *Our bathroom is the warmest room in the house.*

batik /bəˈtiːk, bæ-/ n [U] a way of printing patterns on cloth by covering the design with wax and coloring the cloth that does not have wax on it with DYE

bat mitzvah /bɑtˈmɪts·və, bɑs-/, **bas mitzvah** n [C] (in the Jewish religion) a ceremony performed when a girl reaches 12 to 14 years of age and is old enough to take on the responsibilities and duties of an adult

baton /bəˈtɑn/ n [C] any of various specially designed sticks used in races, to lead a group of musicians, or thrown in the air by people who are marching • *She twirls a baton as the parade passes by.* ○ *He waves his fork like a conductor's baton.*

battalion /bəˈtæl·jən/ n [C] a large military unit under a single leader, consisting of three or more COMPANIES

batter HIT /ˈbæt̬·ər/ v [I/T] to hit (a person) again and again, over a long period of time, or to hit (something) forcefully over and over again • *Her first husband battered her.* [T] ○ *Thunderstorms were battering Kansas again on Sunday.* [T] • See also **batter** at BAT STICK.

battered /ˈbæt̬·ərd/ adj • *The group set up a home for battered women.*

battering /ˈbæt̬·ə·rɪŋ/ n [C/U] • *Battering is the major cause of injury to women.* [U] • A **battering ram** is a long, heavy pole, used to break down doors.

battery /ˈbæt̬·ə·ri/ n [U] the crime of attacking someone by beating them

batter FOOD /ˈbæt̬·ər/ n [U] any liquid mixture containing milk, eggs, and flour, as used to make cake, PANCAKES, or other similar food, or to cover food before frying it • See also **batter** at BAT STICK.

battery ELECTRICAL DEVICE /ˈbæt̬·ə·ri/ n [C] a device that produces electricity to provide power for radios, cars, toys, etc. • *What size battery do you need for the alarm clock?*

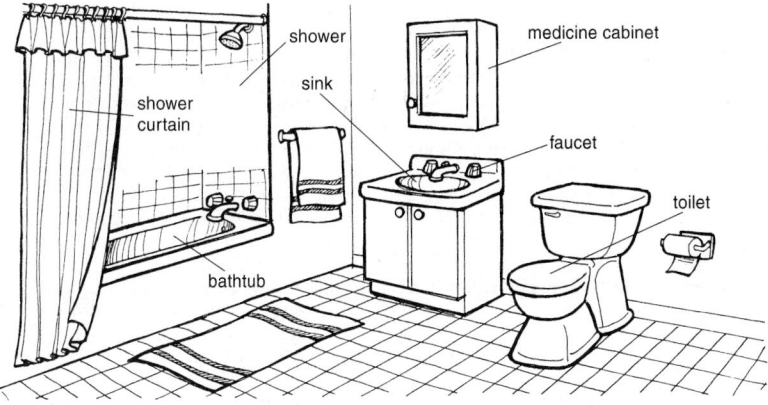

shower

sink

medicine cabinet

shower curtain

faucet

toilet

bathtub

bathroom

battery LARGE NUMBER /'bæt̬·ə·ri/ *n* [C] a number of things of a similar type • *You have to pass a whole battery of tests to get into that school.*

battle /'bæt̬·əl/ *n* [C/U] a fight between armed forces, or an argument between two groups • *The battle between street gangs went on for years.* [C] ∘ *Her brother was killed in battle.* [U] ∘ *They're in a battle with their publisher over electronic rights.* [C] • A battle can also be an serious effort to change a situation: *Doctors Without Borders is a group that wages battles against hunger and disease.* [C] • A **battle of wits** is when people use their intelligence to defeat each other. • A **battlefield** is a place where a battle is being fought or was fought: *We visited the Civil War battlefield at Gettysburg.*

battle /'bæt̬·əl/ *v* [I/T] • *Congress is battling with the White House over funding.* [I] ∘ *Long Horse died battling the Sioux in 1875.* [T] ∘ *I thought we had the game under control, but they really battled back.* [I]

battleground /'bæt̬·əl,ɡraʊnd/ *n* [C] an area of strong disagreement • *Science classrooms have become a battleground over teaching evolution.* • A battleground is also a **battlefield**. See at BATTLE.

batty /'bæt̬·i/ *adj infml disapproving* foolish or crazy

bawdy /'bɔːd·i/ *adj* [-er/-est only] containing humorous remarks about sex • *He sang clever, bawdy songs.*

bawl /bɔːl/ *v* [I] to cry or shout loudly • *He started bawling when the dog snatched his toy.* • *Even though I didn't do it, I got* **bawled out** (= loudly criticized).

bay SHELTERED WATER /beɪ/ *n* [C] an area of water sheltered by land on three sides • *We went sailing in Cape Cod Bay.*

bay SPACE /beɪ/ *n* [C] a partly enclosed space • *A truck in the loading bay is blocking my car.* • If you keep something **at bay**, you keep it away: *Reed insulated the room to keep noise at bay.*

bay CALL /beɪ/ *v* [I] (of dogs and similar animals) to make a loud, long, deep cry

bay leaf /'beɪ·liːf/ *n* [C] *pl* **bay leaves** /'beɪ·liːvz/ the leaves of an evergreen tree, which are dried and used in cooking to add flavor

bayonet /'beɪ·ə·nət, ˌbeɪ·ə'net/ *n* [C] a long, sharp blade attached to a gun

bayonet /'beɪ·ə·nət, ˌbeɪ·ə'net/ *v* [T] **-t-** or **-tt-** • *In training, we learned to bayonet a straw dummy.*

bayou /'baɪ·uː, -oʊ/ *n* [C] (in the southern US) an area of slowly moving or still water connected to a river or lake

bazaar /bə'zɑr/ *n* [C] an open market where people sell things, or any group of small shops or people selling goods • A bazaar is also an event where people sell things to raise money for an organization, such as a church or hospital: *St. Luke's is having its springtime bazaar next Saturday.*

BB gun /'biː·biːˌɡʌn/ *n* [C] an air gun that shoots small, round balls • *The boy saved his allowance to buy a BB gun.*

BBQ *n* [C] *abbreviation for* BARBECUE

BBS *n* [C] *abbreviation for* bulletin board system (= a computer system allowing users to exchange messages and information)

B.C. *abbreviation for* before Christ, used to show that a year or century comes before the year in which Jesus is thought to have been born • *Caesar was assassinated in 44 B.C.* • Compare A.D..

be RELATIONSHIP /biː/ *v* I **am** /æm/ you/we/they **are** /ɑr/ he/she/it **is** /ɪz/, **being** /'biː·ɪŋ/, *past simple* I/he/she/it **was** /wʌz/ you/we/they **were** /wɜr/, *past part* **been** /bɪn/ used to connect two things or a thing with something that it has as a quality or condition • *It is cold today.* [L] ∘ *My name is Andy.* [L] ∘ *She is a doctor.* [L] ∘ *How old are you?* [L] ∘ *These books are* (= cost) *$12.99 each.* [L] ∘ *Please be patient.* [L] • Be is also used to show the position of a person or thing in space or time: *The food was on the table.* [I always + adv/prep] ∘ *Tony is in trouble again.* [I always + adv/prep] • LP CONTRACTIONS OF VERBS, LINKING VERBS

be EXIST /biː/ *v* [L] I **am** /æm/ you/we/they **are** /ɑr/ he/she/it **is** /ɪz/, **being** /'biː·ɪŋ/, *past simple* I/he/she/it **was** /wʌz/ you/we/they **were** /wɜr/, *past part* **been** /bɪn/ to exist • *She apologized for the way things are around here.* ∘ *There was no sound.* • LP LINKING VERBS

be CONTINUE /biː/ *v aux* I **am** /æm/ you/we/they **are** /ɑr/ he/she/it **is** /ɪz/, **being** /'biː·ɪŋ/, *past simple* I/he/she/it **was** /wʌz/ you/we/they **were** /wɜr/, *past part* **been** /bɪn/ used with the present participle of other verbs to describe actions that are or were continuing • *You are being very selfish.* ∘ *She was studying to be a lawyer.* ∘ *It is raining.* ∘ *I'll be coming back* (= I plan to come back). • LP AUXILIARY VERBS

be PASSIVE /biː/ *v aux* I **am** /æm/ you/we/they **are** /ɑr/ he/she/it **is** /ɪz/, **being** /'biː·ɪŋ/, *past simple* I/he/she/it **was** /wʌz/ you/we/they **were** /wɜr/, *past part* **been** /bɪn/ used with the past participle of other verbs to form the passive • *He was asked to wait.* ∘ *Please be seated.* ∘ *The World Trade Center was built in the early 1970s.* • LP AUXILIARY VERBS

be POSSIBLE CONDITION /biː/ *v aux past simple* I/he/she/it **were** /wər/ used to show the possibility of a condition or of something happening in the future • *If I were afraid of you, why would I be here?* ∘ *If you were allowed to have one wish, what would it be?* • USAGE: In grammar, this form of be is called the SUBJUNCTIVE. • LP AUXILIARY VERBS

be FUTURE /biː/ *v aux* I **am** /æm/ you/we/they **are** /ɑr/ he/she/it **is** /ɪz/, *past simple* I/he/she/it **was** /wʌz/ you/we/they **were** /wɜr/ *slightly fml* used to say what will happen • *The president is to decide this issue very soon.* [+ *to* infinitive] • LP AUXILIARY VERBS

be ALLOW /biː/ *v aux* I **am** /æm/ you/we/they **are** /ɑr/ he/she/it **is** /ɪz/, *past simple* I/he/she/it **was** /wʌz/ you/we/they **were** /wɜr/ *slightly fml* used to tell someone they must or should do something • *Their mother said they were to play nearby.* [+ *to* infinitive] • LP AUXILIARY VERBS

beach /biːtʃ/ *n* [C] a flat, sloping area of sand or small stones beside the sea or a lake • *Let's go to the beach.* • A **beach ball** is a large, light, brightly colored ball filled with air that people play with esp. on a beach.

beacon /ˈbiːkən/ *n* [C] a light, esp. on a hill or near the sea, that acts as a signal or warning • *(fig.) They considered America a beacon of liberty for the world.*

bead /biːd/ *n* [C] a small, often round piece of plastic, wood, glass, or other material with a hole through it, which is put on a string to make jewelry such as a NECKLACE • *She fingered the beads of her rosary.* ○ *(fig.) Beads of sweat formed on his forehead as he worked in the sun.*

beady /ˈbiːdi/ *adj* (of eyes) small and shiny, esp. like a bird's eyes • *Her beady eyes stared from behind thick glasses.*

beak /biːk/ *n* [C] the hard, pointed part of a bird's mouth

beam LIGHT /biːm/ *n* [C] a line of light coming from the sun or a bright light, esp. as seen against a darker background • *a beam of sunlight* ○ *A laser beam scans the disc's surface.*

beam /biːm/ *v* [I/T] • *The sun beamed down on the ballfield.* [I] ○ *Detroit stations are beamed* (= broadcast) *to Canadian communities.* [T]

beam WOOD /biːm/ *n* [C] a long, thick piece of wood, metal, or concrete, esp. one used to support weight in a building or other structure

beam SMILE /biːm/ *v* [I] to smile with obvious pleasure • *His face beamed as if he'd won a gold medal at the Olympics.*

bean /biːn/ *n* [C] a seed, or the POD (= seed container) of various plants, eaten as a vegetable • *string beans* • A **beanbag** is a large cloth bag filled with dried beans or some similar filling that is used for sitting on, or a small bag of the same type used as a children's toy. • **Bean curd** is TOFU. • **Bean sprouts** are beans that have started to grow and which are eaten as vegetables.

bear ANIMAL /ber, bær/ *n* [C] a large, strong mammal with thick fur that lives esp. in colder parts of the world • *a black/grizzly/polar bear* • A **bear hug** is the action of putting your arms around someone and holding them against you tightly.

bear CARRY /ber, bær/ *v* [T] *past simple* **bore** /bɔːr, boʊr/, *past part* **borne** /bɔːrn, boʊrn/ to carry or bring (something) • *Fans bearing banners ringed the stadium.* ○ *He firmly believes in the right to bear arms.*

bearer /ˈber·ər, ˈbær·ər/ *n* [C] • *Stretcher bearers carried the injured across the lawn.*

bear SUPPORT /ber, bær/ *v* [T] *past simple* **bore** /bɔːr, boʊr/, *past part* **borne** /bɔːrn, boʊrn/ to hold or support (something) • *The bridge has to be strengthened to bear heavier loads.*

bear ACCEPT /ber, bær/ *v* *past simple* **bore** /bɔːr, boʊr/, *past part* **borne** /bɔːrn, boʊrn/ to accept (something painful or unpleasant) with determination and strength • *Since you will bear most of the responsibility, you should get the rewards.* [T] ○ *He could not bear to see her suffering.* [+ *to* infinitive]

bear HAVE /ber, bær/ *v* [T] *past simple* **bore** /bɔːr, boʊr/, *past part* **borne** /bɔːrn, boʊrn/ to have as a quality or characteristic • *My life bore little resemblance to what I'd hoped for.*

bear PRODUCE /ber, bær/ *v* [T] *past simple* **bore** /bɔːr, boʊr/, *past part* **born** /bɔːrn, boʊrn/ or **borne** /bɔːrn, boʊrn/ (of mammals) to give birth to (young), or (of a tree or plant) to give or produce (fruit or flowers) • *She bore three children in five years.* • To **bear fruit** is to be successful esp. after a lot of work or effort: *Some of their research is now bearing fruit.* • USAGE: When talking about mammals, use the past participle spelling "born" to talk about a person or animal's birth, and the spelling "borne" to talk about a mother giving birth to a child: *She had borne four boys.*

bear TRAVEL /ber, bær/ *v* [I always + adv/prep] *past simple* **bore** /bɔːr, boʊr/, *past part* **borne** /bɔːrn, boʊrn/ to travel or move in the stated direction • *After you pass the light, bear left until you come to a church.*

bearings /ˈber·ɪŋz, ˈbær·ɪŋz/ *pl n* an understanding of directions and positions that helps you know where you are • *It's sometimes hard to get your bearings in the dark.* • See also BEARING CONNECTION, BEARING BODY POSITION.

□ **bear down** INCREASE EFFORT /ˈ-ˈ-/ *v adv* [I] to put more effort into doing something • *I knew I had to bear down hard in order to hit the ball.*

□ **bear down** PUSH /ˈ-ˈ-/ *v adv* [I] to push or press down on something • *The midwife told her it was time to bear down and push that baby out.*

□ **bear down on** /ˈ-ˈ-ˌ-/ *v adv prep* [T] to move toward (someone or something) in a way that threatens them • *He leaped away from the car bearing down on him.*

□ **bear out** *obj*, **bear** *obj* **out** /ˈ-ˈ-/ *v adv* [M] to support the truth of (something) • *The facts don't bear out your fears.*

□ **bear up** /ˈ-ˈ-/ *v adv* [I] to show bravery despite

difficulties • *How is Carmine bearing up since his wife died?*

▫**bear with** /'-'-/ *v prep* [T] to be patient with (someone) • *Just bear with me while I finish downloading this file.*

beard /bɪrd/ *n* [C] hair that grows on the lower part of a man's face, sometimes including the hair that grows above the lips

bearing CONNECTION /'ber·ɪŋ, 'bær-/ *n* [U] connection to or influence on a result • *The fact that he was ordered to stand trial has no bearing on whether he'll be found guilty.* • See also **bearings** at BEAR TRAVEL.

bearing BODY POSITION /'ber·ɪŋ, 'bær-/ *n* [U] the particular way you find it natural to hold your body or the way you appear to other people • *He had an erect, military bearing.* • See also **bearings** at BEAR TRAVEL.

bear market /'ber'mɑr·kət, 'bær-/ *n* [U] a time when investments in the financial markets are generally falling in value • Compare BULL MARKET.

beast /biːst/ *n* [C] a wild animal • *A* **beast of burden** is an animal used to perform work.

beat HIT /biːt/ *v* [I/T] *past simple* **beat**, *past part* **beaten** /'biːt·ən/ *or* **beat** to hit against (someone or something) repeatedly • *He was severely beaten and left unconscious on the street.* [T] ○ *The children were beating on the table.* [I] • If you beat a liquid food, you mix it with a fast circular motion: *Beat in the egg yolks.* [M] • If you **beat around the bush**, you avoid talking about what is important: *Quit beating around the bush and say what's on your mind.* • (*slang*) If a person says **beat it**, they are telling you to leave immediately.

beater /'biːt̬·ər/ *n* [C] • *He was accused of being a wife beater.* • A beater is also a device used for mixing foods.

beating /'biːt̬·ɪŋ/ *n* [C] • *He suffered head injuries in the beating.* ○ (*fig.*) *When tourists are killed, the city's image takes a beating* (= is damaged).

beat DEFEAT /biːt/ *v* [T] *past simple* **beat**, *past part* **beaten** /'biːt̬·ən/ *or* **beat** to defeat (a competitor), or to do or be better than (someone or something) • *In football, the Giants beat the 49ers, 17-3.* ○ *Most people think that the governor will beat his opponent.* ○ *The room wasn't much, but it beat driving to a hotel 20 miles away.* • To beat something that is going to happen is to take action that will prevent it from having an effect on you: *I leave work early to beat the traffic.* • (*slang*) (**It**) **beats me** means I don't know or cannot understand: *"Any idea who won the pennant last year?" "Beats me."*

beat (*obj*) MAKE SOUND /biːt/ *v* *past simple* **beat**, *past part* **beaten** /'biːt̬·ən/ *or* **beat** to make (a rhythmic sound or movement), or to hit (something) in rhythm to make such a sound • *I was so nervous I could feel my heart beating.* [I] ○ *He steadily beat the drum.* [T]

beat /biːt/ *n* [C usually sing] • *We clapped in time to the beat.*

beat AREA /biːt/ *n* [C usually sing] an area for which someone, esp. a police officer, has responsibility as part of their job • *People are comforted to see cops on the beat.*

beat TIRED /biːt/ *adj infml* extremely tired • *I'm beat—I'm going to bed.*

▫**beat down** /'-'-/ *v adv* [I] (of rain) to strongly come down, or (of sun) to shine powerfully • *We lay in bed listening to the rain beat down on the metal roof.*

▫**beat out** *obj*, **beat** *obj* **out** /'-'-/ *v adv* [M] to defeat or finish before (a competitor) • *Chicago beat out Washington for the last playoff spot.*

▫**beat** *obj* **to** *obj* /'--, '-'-/ *v prep* [T] to do (something) before (someone else) • *I wanted to call with the news, but Steve beat me to it.*

▫**beat up** *obj*, **beat** *obj* **up** /'-'-/ *v adv* [M] to hurt (someone) badly by hitting them repeatedly • *He claims the police beat him up after they arrested him.*

beat-up /'biːt̬'ʌp/ *adj* damaged and in bad condition • *He drove an old, beat-up station wagon.*

▫**beat up on** /'-'-,-/ *v adv prep* [T] *infml* to attack (someone) unfairly • *She didn't like being beat up on by the press.*

beautician /bjuː'tɪʃ·ən/ *n* [C] someone who works in a **beauty parlor** cutting and styling hair and improving people's appearance

beautiful /'bjuːt̬·ɪ·fəl/ *adj* having an attractive quality that gives pleasure to those who experience it or think about it • *I thought she was the most beautiful woman I'd ever seen.* ○ *The scenery around here is beautiful.* ○ *We heard beautiful music every night.* ○ *It was a beautiful plan.*

beautifully /'bjuːt̬·ɪ·fli, -fə·li/ *adv* • *She sings beautifully.*

beauty /'bjuːt̬·i/ *n* [C/U] an attractive quality that gives pleasure to those who experience it or think about it, or a person who has this attractive quality • *The Grand Canyon's natural beauty attracts tourists from all over.* [U] ○ *At 37 she was known as a great beauty.* [C] • Beauty can also mean an attractive appearance: *Women's magazines feature articles about diets and beauty tips.* [U] • **The beauty of** something is a quality of something that makes it good, easy, or worth doing: *One of the beauties of soccer is that you don't have to be big to play the game.* • A **beauty contest/ pageant** is a competition in which women are judged according to how physically attractive they are. • A **beauty parlor** (also **beauty salon** or **beauty shop**) is a place where women go to have their hair cut and styled and their appearance improved.

beaver /'biː·vər/ *n* [C] a small mammal that lives in water esp. in rivers and lakes, and has smooth fur, sharp teeth, and a wide, flat tail

bebop /'bi:·bɑp/ n [U] BOP MUSIC

because /bɪˈkɔːz, -ˈkʌz/ conjunction for the reason that • *"Why did you throw it?" "Because Carlos told me to."* ○ *We can't go to Julia's party because we're going away that weekend.* • **Because of** means as a result of: *The flight was delayed because of bad weather.*

beck /bek/ n [U] • If you are **at** someone's **beck and call**, you are ready to act any time they ask you to do something: *Most people like their police department to be at their beck and call.*

beckon /'bek·ən/ v [I/T] to move your hand or head in a way that tells (someone) to come nearer • *Fargis beckoned to the waiter.* [I]

become BE /bɪˈkʌm/ v [L] past simple **became** /bɪˈkeɪm/, past part **become** to start to be • *He became a US citizen in 1955.* ○ *The days are becoming shorter.* ○ *It's becoming obvious that Dorothy doesn't like me.* • LP LINKING VERBS

become SUIT /bɪˈkʌm/ v [T] past simple **became** /bɪˈkeɪm/, past part **become** to cause (someone) to look attractive, or to be suitable for (someone) • *That color really becomes you.*

becoming /bɪˈkʌm·ɪŋ/ adj • *a becoming* (= attractive) *dress*

□ **become of** /-'--/ v prep [T] • **What/Whatever became of** means what happened to: *What could have become of my car keys?* ○ *Whatever became of Jennie O'Hearn?*

bed FURNITURE /bed/ n [C] a large piece of furniture with a flat surface that a person can lie on to sleep or rest • *He felt sick and decided to stay in bed that day.* ○ *He sat down on the bed and took off his shoes.* ○ *Some mornings it's really hard to get out of bed.* • She found her husband **in bed with** (= having sex with) *another woman.* • A **bed-and-breakfast** is a small hotel or private house that rents rooms and provides a morning meal. • (*infml*) **Bedclothes** are BEDDING. • A **bedpan** is a container serving as a toilet for people who are too ill to get out of bed. • If a person is **bedridden**, they are not able to leave their bed because of illness or injury. • A **bedroom** is a room with a bed or beds for sleeping. • A **bedspread** is a decorative cover put on a bed over the sheets and BLANKETS (= covers to keep you warm). • **Bedtime** is the time that you usually go to bed at night: *Come on, Joey, it's past your bedtime.*

bed BOTTOM OF THE SEA /bed/ n [C] the bottom of a river, lake, or sea

bed AREA OF GROUND /bed/ n [C] an area of ground used for planting flowers • *a flower bed* • A **bed of roses** is an easy existence without troubles: *Life is no bed of roses, you know.*

bedding /'bed·ɪŋ/, *infml* **bedclothes** n [U] the sheets, BLANKETS (= covers to keep you warm), and other covers that you put on a bed • *The new recruits at the army base were lined up to pick up their bedding.*

bedlam /'bed·ləm/ n [U] complete disorder and confusion • *In the bedlam of shouting, screaming, running people, some ran toward the stage.*

bedraggled /bɪˈdræg·əld/ adj (of a person or their appearance) messy, dirty, and often wet • *We picked up four bedraggled sailors who had weathered the storm in a lifeboat.*

bedrock /'bed·rɑk/ n [U] the hard, solid area of rock in the ground that supports the earth above it • (*fig.*) *The minister said that the family is the bedrock of* (= the solid base of) *society.*

bedside /'bed·saɪd/ n [U] the place next to a bed • *She sat by his bedside, holding his hand.*

bedside /'bed·saɪd/ adj [not gradable] • **Bedside manner** is the way a doctor behaves toward people being treated to make them feel comfortable: *He's a good surgeon but he has an awful bedside manner.*

bee /biː/ n [C] a flying insect that has a yellow and black body and is able to sting • A **beehive** is a boxlike container where bees are kept so that their HONEY (= the sweet substance they produce) can be collected. • PIC BUMBLEBEE

beech /biːtʃ/ n [C/U] a tree with a smooth, gray trunk, or the wood of this tree

beef MEAT /biːf/ n [U] the flesh of cattle eaten as meat • *a roast beef sandwich*

beefy /'biː·fi/ adj (of a person, esp. a man) large, heavy, and powerful looking • *a big, beefy football player*

beef up obj, **beef** obj **up** /'-'-/ v adv [M] to make (something) stronger or more effective, esp. by adding more support • *They're beefing up security at the airports to discourage terrorism.*

beef COMPLAIN /biːf/ v [I] slang to complain • *Stop beefing about having to work late—you're not the only one.*

beef /biːf/ n [C] slang • *My beef is, how come I'm not making as much as you?*

been /bɪn/ past participle of BE • Been is also used to mean visited or traveled: *"Have you ever been to Africa?" "No, I've never been there, but I'd love to go."*

beep /biːp/ v [I/T] to make a high, brief, mechanical sound or series of sounds, or cause (a device) to make such a sound • *The computer started beeping, so I knew something was wrong.* [I]

beep /biːp/ n [C] • *The recording told me to leave a message after the beep.*

beeper /'biː·pər/ n [C] a small electronic device that you carry or wear that makes a noise or shows a message to tell you that someone wants you to telephone them; a PAGER

beer /bɪr/ n [C/U] a slightly bitter, alcoholic drink made from grain, or a serving of this drink in a glass or other container

beet /biːt/ n [C/U] the small, round, dark red root of a plant, which is cooked and eaten as a vegetable

beetle /'biːt̬·əl/ *n* [C] any of various insects with a hard, shell-like back

befall /bɪ'fɔːl/ *v* [T] *past simple* **befell** /bɪ'fel/, *past part* **befallen** /bɪ'fɔː·lən/ (esp. of something bad) to happen to (someone) • *He was promised that no harm would befall him if he released his hostages unharmed.*

befit /bɪ'fɪt/ *v* [T] **-tt-** to be suitable or right for • *As befits its rural mountain setting, the nine-room inn serves up a huge country breakfast.*

before EARLIER /bɪ'fɔːr, -'four/ *prep, adv* [not gradable], *conjunction* at or during a time earlier than (the thing mentioned) • *I left early because I wanted to arrive home before dark.* ○ *Before making up your mind, think about all your options.* ○ *It was another half hour before* (= until) *the ambulance finally arrived.* ○ *Less than a week before, he'd been paroled from prison.* • The day/night/week **before last** is two days/nights/weeks ago: *Today is Monday so the day before last was Saturday.* • *He should be getting back in shape* **before long** (= soon). • *We'll be there* **before you know it** (= very soon).

before IN FRONT /bɪ'fɔːr, -'four/ *prep* in front of • *It took courage to stand before a courtroom full of people.*

beforehand /bɪ'fɔːr,hænd, -'four-/ *adv* [not gradable] earlier (than a particular time); in advance • *She had phoned beforehand to let me know she was coming.*

befriend /bɪ'frend/ *v* [T] to be friendly to (esp. someone who needs help) • *While at college, he had befriended a young student from China.*

befuddled /bɪ'fʌd·əld/ *adj* confused and unable to think clearly • *The movie depicts all government officials as stupid and befuddled.*

beg /beg/ *v* [I/T] **-gg-** to ask for money, or to ask (someone) to do something in an urgent way • *There are a lot of homeless people begging on the streets these days.* [I] ○ *My girlfriend begged me to quit smoking.* [T] • If a dog begs, it sits with its front legs in the air as if to ask for something. [I] • To **beg off** is to ask to be excused from something that you are expected to do: *I had to beg off from the meeting because I had too much work to do.* • **(I) beg your pardon** is a polite way of asking someone to repeat what they just said. • **(I) beg your pardon** is a polite expression you can use to ask people to move out of your way or to excuse you for touching them when you did not intend to.

beggar /'beg·ər/ *n* [C] a poor person who lives by asking others for money or food • **Beggars can't be choosers** means that if you want something and you cannot or will not pay for it, you will have to take whatever you can get.

begin /bɪ'gɪn/ *v* [I/T] **beginning**, *past simple* **began** /bɪ'gæn/, *past part* **begun** /bɪ'gʌn/ to do or be the first part of something that continues; start • *He begins his new job on Monday.* [T] ○ *The movie begins at seven.* [I] ○ *I began by* explaining why I had come. [I] • *We had an awful time! To begin with* (= first), *George got sick the day we arrived.*

beginner /bɪ'gɪn·ər/ *n* [C] a person who is just learning how to do an activity • *a karate class for beginners* • **Beginner's luck** is unexpected early success.

beginning /bɪ'gɪn·ɪŋ/ *n* [C/U] • *She arrived late on her first day of work—it was not a good beginning.* [C] ○ *He sat down and read the story from beginning to end.* [U]

begonia /bɪ'goun·jə/ *n* [C] any of a variety of plants with brightly colored flowers and decorative leaves

begrudge /bɪ'grʌdʒ/ *v* [T] to allow or give unwillingly • *He's worked every weekend for the last three months, so you can't begrudge him a little time off now.*

beguile /bɪ'gaɪl/ *v* [T] *esp. literary* to charm, attract, or interest, sometimes in order to deceive • *I had to show I was not beguiled by his good looks.*

beguiling /bɪ'gaɪ·lɪŋ/ *adj* • *a beguiling smile*

begun /bɪ'gʌn/ *past participle of* BEGIN

behalf /bɪ'hæf/ *n* [U] • If something is done **in/on behalf of** someone or **in/on** someone's **behalf**, it is done for that person's benefit or support, or because you are representing the interests of that person: *I'd like to say on behalf of the whole group that we wish you well in your new job.*

behave /bɪ'heɪv/ *v* [I/T] to act in a particular way, or to act in a way that is considered correct • *The judge will instruct the jury on how it is to behave.* [I]

behavior /bɪ'heɪ·vjər/ *n* [C/U] a particular way of acting • *Many people complained about the behavior of some fans who were drunk, loud, and threatening to those around them.* [U] ○ *They engaged in high-risk behaviors such as drug use and unprotected sex.* [C]

behead /bɪ'hed/ *v* [T] to cut off the head of (a person)

behest /bɪ'hest/ *n* [U] *fml* a request • *Congress adopted the budget resolution at the behest of the president.*

behind IN BACK OF /bɪ'haɪnd/ *prep, adv* [not gradable] in or to the back (of) • *The sun came out from behind the clouds.* ○ *He opened the door and went in, pulling it shut behind him.* ○ *A police car pulled up behind us.* ○ *I realized I'd left my umbrella behind* (= in the place I had left). • Behind can also mean responsible for or causing: *What was the motive behind the bombing?* • To be **behind** someone is to support them in what they intend to do: *Her family was solidly behind her.* • *What do they say about me* **behind** *my* **back** (= when I am not present)? • If someone is **behind bars**, they are in prison. • Something said or done **behind closed doors** is meant to be a secret: *a meeting held behind closed doors.* • Something that is **behind-the-scenes** is unknown to the public: *behind-the-scenes negotiations*

behind BODY PART /bɪˈhaɪnd/ *n* [C] *infml* the part of the body on which a person sits; the buttocks

behold /bɪˈhoʊld/ *v* [T] *past* **beheld** /bɪˈheld/ *literary* to see or look at • *He looked up and beheld the stranger sitting across the table, smiling a secret smile.*

beholden /bɪˈhoʊl·dən/ *adj* feeling you have a duty to someone because they have done something for you • *They do not benefit from state subsidies and therefore are not beholden to the government.*

beige /beɪʒ/ *adj* [not gradable], *n* [U] (of) a pale, creamy, brown color

being BE /ˈbiː·ɪŋ/ *present participle of* BE

being PERSON /ˈbiː·ɪŋ/ *n* [C/U] a person or thing that exists, or the state of existing • *human/living/supernatural beings* [C] ○ *The group came into being* (= began to exist) *to help relatives of the terminally ill.* [U]

belabor /bɪˈleɪ·bər/ *v* [T] to explain (something) more than necessary • *I don't want to belabor the point, but I still don't think you understand.*

belated /bɪˈleɪt̬·əd/ *adj* coming later than expected • *He did make a belated attempt to apologize.*

belatedly /bɪˈleɪt̬·əd·li/ *adv*

belch /beltʃ/ *v* [I/T] to have air from the stomach come out in a noisy way through the mouth • *If something is belched or belched out, it comes out in quick, violent bursts: The chimney was belching (out) thick smoke.* [I/T]

beleaguered /bɪˈliː·gərd/ *adj* having so many difficulties that you feel as if you are being attacked from every direction • *As a candidate, she had promised tax relief for the beleaguered middle class.*

belie /bɪˈlaɪ/ *v* [T] **belying**, *past* **belied** *slightly fml* to represent (something) falsely or to hide (something) behind something very different • *His gruff manner belied a gentle personality.*

belief /bɪˈliːf/ *n* [C/U] the feeling of being certain that something exists or is true • *religious beliefs* [C] ○ *He made no secret of his belief that she was guilty.* [C] ○ *She often wrote of her strong belief in God.* [U]

believe /bɪˈliːv/ *v* [I/T] to think that something is true or correct • *One juror said he didn't believe the policeman's testimony.* [T] ○ *She believed (that) abortion should be legal.* [+ (that) clause] • *If you believe in something, you feel that it is right: I believe in giving a person a second chance.* [I always + adv/prep] • *To believe in something is also to be certain that it exists: Do you believe in God?* [I always + adv/prep] • *If you say* **believe it or not,** *you mean that something you are about to say is surprising but true: Believe it or not, they got married after knowing each other only a week.*

• *If you say* **believe me,** *you want to emphasize something you are about to say or have just said: Believe me, I was scared!*

believable /bɪˈliː·və·bəl/ *adj* belonging to a type that seems real; realistic • *a believable character/plot/story*

believer /bɪˈliː·vər/ *n* [C] a person who feels certain about the existence of God or the truth of a religion or religious ideas • A believer is also someone who has a strong opinion that something is right or good: *I'm a believer in the public's right to know.*

belittle /bɪˈlɪt̬·əl/ *v* [T] to make (an action or a person) seem unimportant • *He belittled the opinions of the women in his family.*

bell /bel/ *n* [C] a hollow, cup-shaped, metal object that makes a ringing sound when a part hanging inside swings against its sides, or when it is hit by any hard object • *The church bells were ringing.* • A bell is also a **doorbell.** See at DOOR.

bellhop /ˈbel·hɑp/ *n* [C] a person in a hotel employed to carry bags for customers and perform other services

belligerent /bəˈlɪdʒ·ə·rənt/ *adj* eager to fight or argue • *She was so belligerent that I gave up trying to explain.*

belligerence /bəˈlɪdʒ·ə·rəns/ *n* [U]

bellow /ˈbel·oʊ/ *v* [I/T] to shout in a loud voice • *"I don't believe this!" the old man bellowed.*

bellwether /ˈbel·weð·ər/ *n* [C] something that shows what the general future of changes or developments will probably be • *In Massachusetts, a bellwether state for the region, more people are buying and building houses.*

belly /ˈbel·i/ *n* [C] *infml* the stomach, or, more generally, the front part of a person's body below the waist and above the legs • *Pregnancy had begun to make her belly swell.* • (*infml*) A **belly button** is a NAVEL.

belong /bɪˈlɔːŋ/ *v* [I] to be in the right place, or (of a person) to feel that you are in the right place • *Your shoes belong in the closet, not in the middle of the room.* ○ *Tom, it's great to see you on TV—you belong here.* ○ *That kind of person belongs in* (= should be in) *jail.* • To **belong to** means to be the property of (someone) or to be a member of (a group): *Does this book belong to you or to Sarah?* ○ *We belong to the same church.*

belongings /bɪˈlɔːŋ·ɪŋz/ *pl n* the things that a person owns, esp. those that can be taken with them • *Fleeing the flood waters, families here packed their belongings and headed to higher land.*

beloved /bɪˈlʌv·əd, -ˈlʌvd/ *adj* loved very much • *His beloved wife died last year, and he is still grieving.*

below /bɪˈloʊ/ *adv* [not gradable], *prep* in a lower position (than); under • *The author's name was printed below the title.* ○ *The hemline of the skirt comes to just below the knee.* ○

There's a basement below the first floor. • Below also means less in number or value: *It's been below freezing every day this week.* ○ *It's for young kids below the age of six.*

belt STRIP /belt/ *n* [C] a strip of leather or other material worn around the waist • *a black leather belt* • A belt is also a continuous strip of material that moves as part of a machine. • A **beltway** is a main road that goes around the edge of a city.

belt HIT /belt/ *v* [T] *infml* to hit (someone or something) hard • *He belted the ball out of the park for a home run.*

belt AREA /belt/ *n* [C] an area that is known for a particular characteristic • *Vacationers flock to the sun belt* (= warm, dry regions) *this time of year.*

□ **belt out** *obj*, **belt** *obj* **out** /'-'-/ *v adv* [M] *infml* to sing loudly and with enthusiasm • *The four of us belted out Christmas carols.*

belying /bɪ'laɪ·ɪŋ/ *present participle of* BELIE

bemused /bɪ'mjuːzd/ *adj* slightly confused; not knowing what to do or how to understand something • *He was looking from one face to the other with an air of bemused disbelief.*

bench /bentʃ/ *n* [C] a long seat for two or more people, often of wood and usually used outside • *a park bench* • The bench is a court of law, or the place where a judge or judges sit in court: *Face the bench when you are talking, Mr. Smith.*

bench

benchmark /'bentʃ·mɑrk/ *n* [C] a standard for measuring or judging other things of the same type • *Her performances set a new benchmark for classical pianists.*

bend /bend/ *v* [I/T] *past* **bent** /bent/ to change the position of your body or a part of your body so that it is no longer straight but curved or forming an angle • *She dropped her umbrella and bent down to pick it up.* [I always + adv/prep] ○ *Bend your knees and keep your back straight when lifting heavy objects.* [T] • To **bend over backwards** is to try very hard to be fair or to be helpful: *Mann insisted that he bent over backwards to be objective in presenting the story.* • To **bend the rules** is to break the rules in a way that you consider unimportant or not harmful: *You've got know when to bend the rules a little.* • See also BENT.

bend /bend/ *n* [C] a curved path or an angle • *a bend in the road*

beneath /bɪ'niːθ/ *prep* in or to a lower position than; under • *Jerry hid the letter beneath a pile of papers.* ○ *The cool grass felt good beneath their feet.*

benediction /ˌben·ə'dɪk·ʃən/ *n* [C] a prayer asking for God's help and protection

benefactor /'ben·əˌfæk·tər/ *n* [C] someone who gives money to help an organization, society, or person

beneficial /ˌben·ə'fɪʃ·əl/ *adj* tending to help; having a good effect • *Moderate exercise is really beneficial.*

beneficiary /ˌben·ə'fɪʃ·iːˌer·i, -'fɪʃ·ə·ri/ *n* [C] a person or group who receives money or other benefits as a result of something else • *Among major beneficiaries of the new tax law will be giant telecommunications companies.*

benefit /'ben·ə,fɪt/ *n* [C/U] a helpful or good effect • *It was a giveaway to the rich, he said, and not something that's a benefit to most Americans.* [C] ○ *She wanted her money to be used for the benefit of* (= to help) *poor children.* [U] • A benefit is also a helpful service given to an employee in addition to their pay or to someone else who needs help: *health/medical benefits* [C] ○ *I'm collecting unemployment benefits.* [C]

benefit /'ben·ə,fɪt/ *v* [I/T] • *I have benefited greatly from her wisdom.* [I]

benevolent /bə'nev·ə·lənt/ *adj* kind and helpful • *I grew up happily under the benevolent influence of my Uncle Walt.*

benevolence /bə'nev·ə·ləns/ *n* [U]

benign /bɪ'naɪn/ *adj* pleasant and kind; not harmful or severe • *a benign smile* ○ *His humor was benign, never cruel or hurtful.* • *(medical)* (of a disease or tissue growing because of a disease) not likely to result in death: *a benign tumor* Compare MALIGNANT.

bent BEND /bent/ *past simple and past participle of* BEND

bent TENDENCY /bent/ *n* [U] *fml* a natural tendency • *the philosophical bent of his mind*

bent DETERMINED /bent/ *adj* • If you are **bent on** doing something, you are determined to do it: *He was bent on quitting even though he was making a lot of money.*

bequeath /bɪ'kwiːθ, -'kwiːð/ *v* [T] to give (esp. money or property) to others after your death • *Her father bequeathed the business to her.*

bequest /bɪ'kwest/ *n* [C] the money or property that someone, after their death, gives to someone else • *Her will included large bequests to charity.*

berate /bɪ'reɪt/ *v* [T] to criticize (someone) in an angry manner • *His mother berated him for making a mess.*

bereaved /bɪ'riːvd/ *adj* [not gradable] having lost a close relative or friend because they have died

bereaved /bɪ'riːvd/ *pl n* the people who are sad because someone close to them has died

bereft /bɪ'reft/ *adj* having to do without something or someone and suffering from the loss • *During the years when he was drinking too much, he was bereft of new ideas.*

beret /bə'reɪ/ *n* [C] a round, flat hat made of soft material

berry /'ber·i/ *n* [C] any of various small, round fruits that grow on plants and trees

berserk /bər'zɜrk, -'sɜrk/ *adj* not in control and violent • *A drug addict had gone berserk and had torn out the plumbing in his hotel room.*

berth /bɜrθ/ *n* [C] a bed in a boat or train, or a place for a ship or boat to stay in a port

beset /bɪ'set/ *adj* hurt or troubled by something bad • *These were neighborhoods beset by drug-related violence.*

beside /bɪ'saɪd/ *prep* at the side of; next to • *Come and sit here beside me.* • *The exact cost is* beside the point (= not important)—*what's important is that we get the job done.* • *If you are* beside yourself, *you are extremely upset: He was beside himself when he realized he'd lost his wallet.*

besides /bɪ'saɪdz/ *adv* [not gradable], *prep* in addition to; also • *Do you play any other sports besides golf?* ○ *He won't mind if you're late—besides, it's not your fault.*

besiege /bɪ'siːdʒ/ *v* [T] to surround (a place), esp. with an army, to prevent people or supplies from getting in or out • *(fig.) After the controversial show, the television network was besieged with complaints.* • *If a person is* besieged, *they are surrounded: Mick Jagger was besieged by fans at the airport.*

best HIGHEST QUALITY /best/ *adj, adv, superlative of* GOOD *or* WELL; of the highest quality, to the greatest degree, in the most effective way, or being the most suitable or pleasing • *He's one of our best students.* ○ *Which of the songs did you like best?* ○ *She was my best friend at school.* • *Someone's* best bet *is the action most likely to be successful: If you want to get to the theater on time, your best bet is to get a cab.* • *The* best man *at a marriage ceremony is the male friend or relative of the* BRIDEGROOM *who stands with him.* • *Best wishes* is a polite way of finishing a letter to someone.

best EXCELLENCE /best/ *n* [U] the most excellent in a group of things or people • *As an athlete, Jim Thorpe is one of the best of all time.* ○ *I like all of Hitchcock's films, but I think "Notorious" is the best.* • *At* best *means even if the best possible result should happen: If he drops the course now, at best he'll get an incomplete, and he could fail.* • *To* do *your* level/very best *is to make the greatest effort possible: We did our level best to give our kids a good education.*

best DEFEAT /best/ *v* [T] to defeat (someone) in a fight or competition • *In chess, I was bested by my 13-year-old niece.*

bestial /'bes·tʃəl, 'biːs-/ *adj* fierce and cruel, and without any human feelings • *bestial attacks on defenseless people*

bestow /bɪ'stoʊ/ *v* [T] *fml* to give (something) as an honor or present • *The country's highest medal was bestowed upon him for heroism.*

best-seller /'best'sel·ər/ *n* [C] a new book that has sold a great number of copies

bet /bet/ *v* [I/T] **betting**, *past* **bet** to risk (a sum of money) on the unknown result of an event in the hope of winning more money than you have risked • *He goes to the track and bets on horses.* [I] ○ *I'll bet you $5 that the Yankees do not win the pennant this year.* [T] • *If you* bet (someone) *that something is true or will happen, you think it is likely: I bet (you) she missed the bus.* [T] • *If you say* don't bet on it/I wouldn't bet on it, *you mean that you think what someone has just said is unlikely to be true or to happen: "Do you think I'll get my money back?" "I wouldn't bet on it."*

bet /bet/ *n* [C] • *He placed bets on the first two races.* • *A* bet *is also a guess or opinion: My bet is that the senator will decide not to run again.* • *A* bet *is also a chance or opportunity: Putting your savings in a high-interest account is a good bet/your best bet.*

betray BE NOT LOYAL /bɪ'treɪ/ *v* [T] to be not loyal to your country or a person who believes you are loyal to them, often by doing something that hurts them • *Some lawmakers say they feel betrayed by the president.*

betrayal /bɪ'treɪ·əl/ *n* [C/U] • *I felt a sense of betrayal when my friends refused to lend me money.* [U]

betray SHOW /bɪ'treɪ/ *v* [T] to show (esp. a feeling) without intending to • *She could not help betraying her sympathy for us.*

better HIGHER STANDARD /'bet̬·ər/ *adj* [not gradable], *comparative of* GOOD; of a higher standard, or more suitable, pleasing, or effective than other things or people • *He sat near the front to get a better view.* ○ *Relations between the two countries have never been better.* ○ *She is much better at tennis than I am.* ○ *The longer you keep this wine, the better it tastes.* • *Better can also be used as the comparative to form adjectives beginning with good: She's good-looking, and her brother is even better-looking.* • *Better late than never* means that it is better for someone to arrive or do something late than not to arrive or do it at all. • *Better safe than sorry* means it is wise to be careful and protect yourself against risk rather than be careless. • *It's too bad you failed your driving test, but* better luck next time (= I hope you will succeed when you try again). • *The* better part *of something is most of it: We waited on line for the better part of an hour.*

better GREATER DEGREE /'bet̬·ər/ *adv* [not gradable], *comparative of* WELL; to a greater degree, or in a more suitable, pleasing, or satisfactory way • *The next time he took the test, he was better prepared.* ○ *I like this jacket much better than the brown one.* ○ *She knows her way around the college better than I do.* ○ *She did* much better (= She was more successful) *in the second part of the exam.* • *If you are or get better after an illness or injury, you are healthy and no longer ill.* • *Give her a call, or* better still/even better, *go see her* (= this would be more satisfactory). • *To be* better off *is to be in a more satisfactory or more successful situ-*

ation than you were before: *I know you're unhappy that the relationship ended, but you're better off without him.*

better IMPROVE /'beṭ·ər/ *v* [T] *slightly fml* to improve (a situation, condition, or person) • *The organization was established to better conditions for the disabled.*

better /'beṭ·ər/ *n* [U] used in comparisons to show that a condition is improved • *The cleaner the glass is, the better you can see.*

between SPACE /bɪ'twiːn/, **in between** /ˌɪn·bɪ 'twiːn/ *prep, adv* [not gradable] in or into the space that separates two places, people, or objects • *We live halfway between Toronto and Montreal.* ○ *She squeezed in between the parked cars.* • If something is between two amounts, it is greater than the first amount but smaller than the second: *She weighs between 55 and 60 pounds.*

between TIME /bɪ'twiːn/, **in between** /ˌɪn·bɪ 'twiːn/ *prep, adv* in the period of time that separates two different times or events • *There's a ten-minute break between classes.* ○ *You should arrive between 8 and 8:30.* ○ *In between sobs, he managed to tell them what had happened.*

between AMONG /bɪ'twiːn/ *prep* shared by or involving two or more people or things • *The money was divided equally between her three children.* ○ *Trade between the two countries has increased sharply.* ○ *There is a great deal of similarity between Caroline and her mother.* ○ *Between the three of us, we were able to afford a nice graduation gift.* ○ *You'll have to choose between dinner and a movie.* ○ *Next week's game will be between the two finalists.* • **Between you and me** means that what you are about to say should be kept secret: *Just between you and me, I think she made the whole thing up.*

between CONNECTING /bɪ'twiːn/ *prep* connecting two or more places, things, or people • *There is regular train service between New York and Philadelphia.* ○ *The survey shows a link between asthma and air pollution.*

between SEPARATING /bɪ'twiːn/ *prep* separating two places or things • *The wall between East and West Berlin came down in 1989.* ○ *What's the difference between this $100 watch and the $500 one (= In what way are they different)?*

beverage /'bev·rɪdʒ/ *n* [C] a drink of any type • *alcoholic/nonalcoholic beverages* ○ *What's your favorite beverage?*

bevy /'bev·i/ *n* [C] a large group • *a bevy of lawyers*

beware /bɪ'wer, -'wær/ *v* [I/T] to be very careful about (something or someone) • *In grassy areas, beware of ticks.* [I] • USAGE: Beware is only used in the present tense in commands and warnings.

bewildered /bɪ'wɪl·dərd/ *adj* confused and uncertain • *He sat up in bed, bewildered, unsure of where he was.*

bewildering /bɪ'wɪl·də·rɪŋ/ *adj* • *Buying a car can be a bit bewildering.*

bewilderment /bɪ'wɪl·dər·mənt/ *n* [U] • *Parents expressed bewilderment and anger at the meeting.*

bewitched /bɪ'wɪtʃt/ *adj* extremely attracted, or completely controlled • *Once kids step inside a circus tent, they're bewitched.*

bewitching /bɪ'wɪtʃ·ɪŋ/ *adj* • *a bewitching actress*

beyond FARTHER AWAY /biː'ɑnd/ *prep, adv* [not gradable] farther away in the distance than something • *Beyond the river was a small town.* ○ *From the top of the hill we could see our house and the woods beyond.*

beyond OUTSIDE A LIMIT /biː'ɑnd/ *prep, adv* [not gradable] outside or after a stated limit • *Few people live beyond the age of a hundred.* ○ *Beyond a certain level of tiredness, it is impossible to work productively.* ○ *Tonight's performance has been cancelled due to circumstances beyond our control.* • Beyond also means more than: *I've got nothing to tell you beyond what I said earlier.* ○ *My job goes beyond teaching facts—my aim is to get children to think for themselves.* • Beyond also means at a point where something could not be: *She has changed beyond recognition.* ○ *The car was damaged beyond repair.* • *(infml) How they can live in such chaos is* **beyond me** (= I don't understand it). • *Suddenly she was rich* **beyond** *her* **wildest dreams** (= richer than she had ever thought possible).

biannual /baɪ'æn·jə·wəl/ *adj* [not gradable] happening twice a year • *a biannual report/meeting* • Compare BIENNIAL.

bias /'baɪ·əs/ *n* [C/U] an unfair personal opinion that influences your judgment • *They vowed to fight racial bias in the school.* [U] ○ *Does news coverage reflect a reporter's bias?* [C usually sing]

bias /'baɪ·əs/ *v* [T] **-s-** or **-ss-** • *The judge withheld the information on the grounds that it would bias the jury.*

biased /'baɪ·əst/ *adj* showing an unreasonable preference or dislike based on personal opinion • *The newspapers gave a biased report of the meeting.*

bib /bɪb/ *n* [C] a cover made of cloth or plastic that is worn by young children when eating to prevent their clothes from getting dirty

Bible /'baɪ·bəl/ *n* [C/U] the holy writings of the Christian religion consisting of the **Old Testament** and the **New Testament**, or the holy writings of the Jewish religion consisting of the TORAH and other writings, or a book containing either of these sets of writings • *Her parents gave her a Bible when she was young.* [C] • A bible is also a book that gives important advice and information about a particular subject: *Vogue magazine became the bible of fashionable women.* [C]

biblical /ˈbɪb·lɪ·kəl/ *adj* [not gradable] in or relating to the Bible • *Isaac is a biblical name.*

bibliography /ˌbɪb·liːˈɑg·rə·fi/ *n* [C] a list of the books and articles that have been used by someone when writing a book or article

bicentennial /ˌbɑɪˌsenˈten·iː·əl, -sən-/, **bicentenary** /ˌbɑɪˌsenˈten·ə·ri, -sən-/ *n* [C] the day or year that is 200 years after a particular event, esp. an important one; a 200th ANNIVERSARY • *The university marked its bicentennial with a weeklong celebration.*

biceps /ˈbɑɪ·seps/ *n* [C] *pl* **biceps** the large muscle at the front of the upper arm • *He flexed his biceps.*

bicker /ˈbɪk·ər/ *v* [I] *disapproving* to argue about unimportant matters • *We bickered over his leaving the toilet seat up.*

bicycle /ˈbɑɪ·sɪk·əl/, **bike** *n* [C] a vehicle with two wheels and a seat for a rider whose feet push PEDALS around in circles to make the wheels turn • *He rides his bicycle to school.* • A **bicycle helmet** is a hard hat that you wear while riding a bicycle.

bicycle /ˈbɑɪ·sɪk·əl/ *v* [I] • *I saw you bicycling through town yesterday.*

bid OFFER /bɪd/ *v* [I/T] **bidding**, *past* **bid** to offer (a particular amount of money) for something when competing against other people to buy it • *A collector bid $500,000 for the portrait.* [T] • If people bid for/on a job, they offer to do it for a particular amount of money. [I] • If someone bids to do something, they compete with others to do it: *Paris is bidding to host the next Olympics.* [I]

bid /bɪd/ *n* [C] an offer of a particular amount of money for something that is for sale • *The minimum bid for these dolls is $75.* • A bid is also an offer to do a job for a particular price: *His bid to build the garage was too high.* • A bid for something is an attempt to achieve or obtain it: *Her bid for reelection was unsuccessful.*

bidder /ˈbɪd·ər/ *n* [C] a person who offers money for goods or property when competing with other people to buy it, or someone who offers to do a job for a particular price

bid TELL /bɪd/ *v* [T] **bidding**, *past simple* **bid** or **bade** /bæd, beɪd/, *past part* **bidden** /ˈbɪd·ən/ or **bid** *literary* to give (a greeting) to someone, or to ask (someone) to do something • *He bade us farewell.*

bidding /ˈbɪd·ɪŋ/ *n* [U] *slightly fml* a request or an order • *At my grandmother's bidding, I wore my best dress.*

bide /bɑɪd/ *v* • If you **bide your time**, you wait patiently for a good opportunity to do something: *He's just biding his time until a permanent job opens up.*

biennial /bɑɪˈen·iː·əl/ *adj* [not gradable] happening once every two years • *a biennial exhibit* • Compare BIANNUAL.

biennial /bɑɪˈen·iː·əl/ *n* [C] a plant that lives for two years, producing seeds and flowers in its second year • Compare ANNUAL PLANT; PERENNIAL PLANT.

bifocals /ˈbɑɪˌfoʊ·kəlz/ *pl n* glasses with an upper part for looking at things far away and a lower part for reading or looking at things that are near

bifocal /bɑɪˈfoʊ·kəl, ˈbɑɪˌfoʊ-/ *adj* [not gradable] • *bifocal lenses*

big LARGE /bɪg/ *adj* [-*er*/-*est* only] **-gg-** large in size or amount • *a big ant/man/building/city* ○ *Do you have these shoes in a bigger size?* ○ *He tried to impress his friends by using big words.* ○ *She got a big raise.* ○ *I had a great big slice of chocolate cake.* ○ *This is the region's biggest bicycle race.* • Big can also to a large degree: *a big spender/eater* • (*infml*) Big can also mean older: *a big sister/brother* • (*infml*) Big can also be used to add emphasis: *You're a big bully!* • (*infml*) If someone is **big on** something, they like it very much: *I'm not very big on classical music.* • (*infml*) New York City is sometimes known as **the Big Apple**. • The **big bang theory** is the belief that the universe

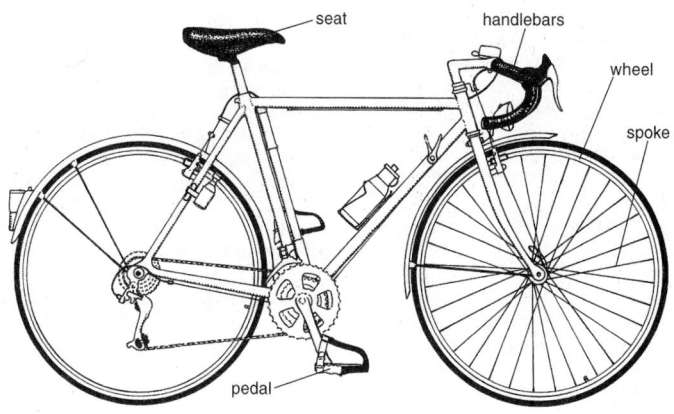

bicycle

originated as the result of a large explosion of a single mass of matter. • The **Big Dipper** is a group of seven bright stars that can be seen in the northern part of the world. • If someone is **bighearted**, they are kind and generous.

biggie /'bɪg·i/ n [C] *infml* something that is large • *We got a new client, and it's a biggie.*

big IMPORTANT /bɪg/ adj [-er/-est only] -**gg**- important, because of being powerful, influential, or having a serious effect • *He had a big decision to make about his future.* ○ *There's a big difference between starting up a business and just talking about it.* ○ *The big story in the news this week is the blizzard in the Midwest.* ○ *We just bought a house, so today's a big day for us.* • (*infml*) If a product or activity is big, it is extremely popular: *Those toys are very big in Japan.* • (*infml*) A **big deal** is something important: *Going to college is still a big deal.* ○ *I'd like to work out today, but if I can't it's **no big deal** (= not important).* • (*infml*) **Big deal** also means you do not think that what someone has said or done is important or special: *"I ran five miles this morning." "Big deal! I ran ten."* • **Big Brother** is a government, ruler, or person in authority that tries to control people's behavior and thoughts. • **Big business** means powerful, influential businesses and financial organizations considered as a group. • (*infml*) A **big gun/big shot/big wheel/bigwig** is a person who has an important or powerful position: *He's a big shot in the computer business.* • (*infml*) The **big leagues** is the top level of a particular sport, business, or activity: *the big leagues of horse racing* • (*infml*) A **big name** is a famous or important person: *She's a big name in local politics.* • (*infml*) The **big time** is the state of being famous or successful: *You've really hit the big time now.* • LP VERY, COMPLETELY, AND OTHER INTENSIFIERS

biggie /'bɪg·i/ n [C] *infml* something that is very important or successful • *Finger food is a biggie with the kids.*

bigamy /'bɪg·ə·mi/ n [U] the crime of marrying a person while already legally married to someone else

bigot /'bɪg·ət/ n [C] a person who has strong beliefs and refuses to consider seriously any other belief that is different, or a person who dislikes people of other races or religions • *Some of the townsmen are bigots who call the Indians terrible names.*

bigoted /'bɪg·ət·əd/ adj • *He was removed from the committee for making bigoted remarks.*

bigotry /'bɪg·ə·tri/ n [U] • *racial/religious bigotry*

bigwig /'bɪg·wɪg/ n [C] *infml* an important or powerful person • *The network television bigwigs loved the show.*

bike /baɪk/ n [C] a bicycle • A bike is also a

motorbike or **motorcycle**, see at MOTOR ENGINE. • PIC BICYCLE

bike /baɪk/ v [I] • *She got in the habit of biking to work when the weather was good.*

biker /'baɪ·kər/ n [C] someone who rides a **motorcycle** or bicycle

bikini /bə'kiː·ni/ n [C] a two-piece **swimsuit** for women or a one-piece swimsuit for men that covers very little of the body

bilateral /baɪ'læt̬·ə·rəl/ adj [not gradable] involving two groups or countries • *The countries signed a bilateral agreement to help prevent drug smuggling.*

bile /baɪl/ n [U] a bitter, yellow liquid produced by the LIVER (= organ in the body) that helps to break down fats so that you can digest them • Bile is also a strong feeling of anger and bitterness.

bilingual /baɪ'lɪŋ·gwəl, -gjə·wəl/ adj [not gradable] able to speak or using two languages • *Kate is bilingual.* ○ *a bilingual dictionary* • Compare MONOLINGUAL.

bill REQUEST FOR PAYMENT /bɪl/ n [C] a list of expenses to be paid, or the total amount of costs or expenses • *We still have doctors' bills to pay.* • A bill is also a CHECK REQUEST FOR PAYMENT.

bill /bɪl/ v [T] to send (someone) a statement of what they owe • *Some places will bill you, but at others you have to pay right away.*

bill MONEY /bɪl/ n [C] a piece of paper money • *He pulled out a thick wad of bills and gave me $20.*

bill LAW /bɪl/ n [C] a formal statement of a planned new law that is discussed by a government or legislature before being voted on • *After a bill is passed by both houses of Congress, it becomes law when the president signs it.* • The **Bill of Rights** is a statement of the rights of US citizens, as added to the country's CONSTITUTION.

bill BIRD /bɪl/ n [C] the beak of a bird

billboard /'bɪl·bɔːrd, -boʊrd/ n [C] a very large board on which advertisements are shown, esp. at the side of a road

billfold /'bɪl·foʊld/ n [C] a small, folding case or WALLET for carrying money

billiards /'bɪl·jərdz/ n [U] a game played by two or more people on a table covered in green cloth in which a CUE (= long pole) is used to hit a ball against other balls to send them into the holes along the edge of the table

billion /'bɪl·jən/ number 1,000,000,000 • *Congress cut spending by $255 billion.* • LP NUMBERS

billionaire /ˌbɪl·jə'ner, -'nær/ n [C] someone who has more than a BILLION dollars (= $1,000,000,000) in property, possessions, or savings

billow /'bɪl·oʊ/ v [I] to spread over a large area, or (esp. of items made of cloth) to become filled with air and appear to be larger • *The building is draped in blue plastic sheeting that flaps and billows like a sail.*

billow /ˈbɪl·oʊ/ *n* [C usually pl] a large wave or any large, swelling mass • *billows of smoke*

bimbo /ˈbɪm·boʊ/ *n* [C] *pl* **bimbos** *slang* a young woman considered attractive but stupid • USAGE: This word is offensive.

bimonthly /baɪˈmʌnθ·li/ *adj, adv* [not gradable] happening or appearing every two months • *a bimonthly report* • Bimonthly is sometimes used to mean twice a month.

bin /bɪn/ *n* [C] a large storage container • *a compost/storage bin* • (*Br*) A bin is also a **trash bin**. See at TRASH.

bind TIE /baɪnd/ *v* [T] *past* **bound** /baʊnd/ to tie (someone) so that they cannot move freely, or to wrap (an object) or fasten together (objects) with cord or something similar • *They bound his arms and his legs and tied him to a bedpost.* • (*fig.*) To bind someone is also to force them to keep a promise: *This contract binds the state to use this land as a park, said Judge Harry Smith.* • To bind a book is to fasten one edge of the pages together inside a cover to make a book.

binder /ˈbaɪn·dər/ *n* [C] a stiff cover that can hold loose papers, often having a part that fastens them • *a three-ring binder*

binding /ˈbaɪn·dɪŋ/ *n* [C] • The binding of a book is the type of cover it has: *a cloth binding*

bind UNPLEASANT SITUATION /baɪnd/ *n* [U] a difficult situation in which none of the choices available are good • *If you lose a lot of your customers, you'll soon get in a financial bind.*

binding /ˈbaɪn·dɪŋ/ *adj law* (esp. of an agreement) not to be avoided or broken • *Both sides agreed to submit the dispute to binding arbitration* (= to a decision they would have to obey).

binge /bɪndʒ/ *n* [C] an occasion when an activity is done in an extreme way, esp. eating, drinking, or spending money • *They went on a buying binge in the mall.* • To go on a binge is to drink a lot of alcohol in a short time. ○ *Half the men students and 39% of the women practice binge drinking—four or five drinks at a time.*

binge /bɪndʒ/ *v* [I] **binging** or **bingeing** to eat or drink in a way that is extreme and not controlled • *I tend to binge on ice cream when I'm lonely.*

bingo /ˈbɪŋ·goʊ/ *n* [U] a game of chance often played for prizes in which people are given cards and cover each number on their cards as it is called, winning if they are the first to cover a whole line of numbers on any card • *Mother loved to play bingo at her church.*

binoculars /bəˈnɑk·jə·lərz, baɪ-/ *pl n* a device for making distant objects appear nearer and larger, and consisting of two attached tubes that you hold up to your eyes to look through • *a pair of binoculars*

biochemistry /ˌbaɪ·oʊˈkem·ə·stri/ *n* [U] the scientific study of the chemistry of living things, such as animals, plants, and body organs

biochemical /ˌbaɪ·oʊˈkem·ɪ·kəl/ *adj*

biodegradable /ˌbaɪ·oʊ·dɪˈɡreɪd·ə·bəl/ *adj* (of a substance) able to decay naturally and without harming the environment

biography /baɪˈɑɡ·rə·fi/ *n* [C/U] the story of the life of a person written by someone else, or the area of literature relating to books that describe such stories • *He wrote a biography of Lincoln.* [C] • Compare AUTOBIOGRAPHY.

biographer /baɪˈɑɡ·rə·fər/ *n* [C] someone who writes about the life of a particular person or of various people

biology /baɪˈɑl·ə·dʒi/ *n* [U] the scientific study of the natural processes of living things

biological /ˌbaɪ·əˈlɑdʒ·ɪ·kəl/ *adj* connected with the natural processes of living things • *the biological sciences* • Biological also means being related to a child because of having been one of the two parents who caused the child to be born: *The biological father/mother/parents gave up the baby for adoption.* • **Biological warfare** (also **germ warfare**) and **biological weapons** involve the use of living matter such as bacteria to seriously harm and kill people and animals and damage crops.

biologist /baɪˈɑl·ə·dʒəst/ *n* [C] a scientist who studies the natural processes of living things

biopsy /ˈbaɪˌɑp·si/ *n* [C] the removal of a small amount of cells from a living body in order to examine them to learn if they show signs of a disease

biotechnology /ˌbaɪ·oʊ·tekˈnɑl·ə·dʒi/ *n* [U] the use of living things, esp. cells and bacteria, in industrial processes

bipartisan /baɪˈpɑrṭ·ə·zən, -sən/ *adj* [not gradable] involving or having the support of both sides, esp. of political parties • *a bipartisan agreement*

birch /bɜrtʃ/ *n* [C] a tree with a smooth, often white BARK (= outer covering), or the wood of this tree

bird /bɜrd/ *n* [C] a creature with feathers and wings, usually able to fly • *a flock of birds* • Bird is often used in combination to describe a particular type of bird: *a bluebird/hummingbird/mockingbird* • To have a **bird's eye view** is to look at something from a very high

bird

place so that you see a large area below you: *From the top of this building, you can get a bird's eye view of the city.* • **The birds and the bees** means the basic facts about sex: *She's only six, but she knows about the birds and the bees.* • A **bird of prey** is a bird, such as a HAWK or an EAGLE, that kills and eats small birds and animals. • **Birdseed** is seed for feeding birds.

birth /bɜrθ/ *n* [C/U] the occasion when a baby comes out of its mother's body • *He remembered the birth of their first child.* [C] ○ *Their son weighed eight pounds at birth.* [U] • Birth also refers to your family origin: *She was Swedish by birth.* [U] • When a woman gives birth, one or more babies come out of her body: *She gave birth to twins.* [U] • A **birth certificate** is an official document recording the fact of a baby's birth and including such information as the name of the baby and of the parents, the time and place of birth, and often the baby's weight. • **Birth control** means the various methods or devices that allow people to have sex without having children as a result. • A **birth control pill** (also **the pill**) is a pill taken by a woman that prevents her from becoming pregnant if she has sex. • A **birthday** is the day that is an exact year or number of years after a person was born: *Today is my mother's 49th birthday.* • A **birthmark** is a brown or red mark that may be a part of a person's skin from the time they are born. • A **birthrate** is a measure of how many children are born during a period of time in a particular place: *Officials expressed concern over Quebec's declining birthrate.*

birthright /'bɜrθ·raɪt/ *n* [C/U] something that is received or owned esp. because of where you were born or your family or social situation, without having to be worked for or bought • *She argued that career women pose a real threat to men who see the better paid, more powerful jobs as their birthright.* [U]

biscuit /'bɪs·kət/ *n* [C] a small, soft, raised bread • *homemade biscuits* • A biscuit is also a type of hard cracker: *dog biscuits*

bisect /'baɪ·sekt, baɪ'sekt/ *v* [T] to divide into two usually equal parts • *The new road would bisect a designated historic district.*

bisexual /baɪ'sek·ʃə·wəl/ *adj* [not gradable] attracted sexually to both men and women

bisexual /baɪ'sek·ʃə·wəl/ *n* [C] a person who is bisexual

bishop /'bɪʃ·əp/ *n* [C] a priest of high rank who is in charge of the priests of lower rank in a particular area • In the game of CHESS, a bishop is a piece that can move only in a diagonal way along squares of the same color.

bison /'baɪ·sən/ *n* [C] *pl* **bison** a large, wild animal, similar to a cow but having a larger head and hairy shoulders, found esp. in North America • *Large herds of bison, popularly known as buffalo, used to live on the plains of western North America.*

bit PIECE /bɪt/ *n* [C] a small piece or a small amount of something • *little bits of paper* ○ *We need every bit of evidence we can find.* ○ *We showed a little bit on videotape.* ○ *Could you talk a bit* (= for a short period) *about your wartime experiences?* • A bit or a little bit can mean slightly or to some degree: *We found the dinner a little bit of a disappointment.*

bit HORSE /bɪt/ *n* [C] a piece of metal put in a horse's mouth to allow the person riding it to control its movements • If someone is **chafing/champing/chomping at the bit,** they are very eager to do something.

bit COMPUTER /bɪt/ *n* [C] the smallest unit of information in a computer, represented by either 0 or 1

bit TOOL /bɪt/ *n* [C] the part of a tool used for cutting or DRILLING (= making holes)

bit BITE /bɪt/ *past simple and past participle of* BITE

bitch ANIMAL /bɪtʃ/ *n* [C] a female dog

bitch COMPLAIN /bɪtʃ/ *v* [I] *slang* to complain • *Don't start that bitching and moaning again about what I pay you.*

bitch /bɪtʃ/ *n* [C usually sing] *slang* something that is very difficult or annoying • *Painting the trim around all the windows was a bitch.*

bitch WOMAN /bɪtʃ/ *n* [C] *rude slang* a woman you do not like or who in your opinion is not kind or pleasant to other people • *She can be a real bitch sometimes.* • USAGE: When used to address a woman, this word is intended as an insult and is very offensive.

bitchy /'bɪtʃ·i/ *adj slang* • *That was a bitchy remark.*

bite USE TEETH /baɪt/ *v* [I/T] *past* **bit** /bɪt/, *past part* **bitten** /'bɪt·ən/ to use your teeth to cut into (something) • *He bit (into) the apple.* [I/T] ○ *You have to teach your children not to bite (other kids).* [I/T] • If an insect bites, it breaks the surface of the skin of a person and leaves a sore place: *We can't eat outside tonight—the mosquitoes are biting.* [I] • If fish bite, they take a fishing hook in their mouths: *We were on the lake all day but the fish just weren't biting.* [I] • To **bite** someone's **head off** is to speak to them in anger when there is no reason to: *I only asked if I could help—you don't have to bite my head off!* • To **bite off more than you can chew** is to try to do something that is too difficult for you. • To **bite the bullet** is to force yourself to perform an unpleasant or difficult action or to be brave in a difficult situation: *Someone has got to bite the bullet and tell the American people that taxes have to be raised.* • To **bite the dust** is to die or to stop working: *I think our car just bit the dust.* • If you **bite** your **tongue,** you stop yourself from saying something: *I wanted to tell him that he was a liar, but I bit my tongue and said nothing.*

bite /baɪt/ *n* [C] the act of using your teeth to cut and tear something, or the piece torn away

• *He took a few bites of the chicken and drank some water.* • **A bite (to eat)** is some food: *You'll feel better once you've had a bite to eat.* • A bite is also a sore place on the surface of your skin made by an insect: *mosquito bites* • In fishing, a bite is a fish taking a hook in its mouth.

bite HAVE AN EFFECT /baɪt/ *v* [I] *past* **bit** /bɪt/, *past part* **bitten** /'bɪt·ᵊn/ to have an effect that is often unpleasant or severe • *When the recession began to bite, people spent less on eating out in restaurants.*

bite /baɪt/ *n* [C usually sing] • *The tax bite with a 13 percent flat tax would be a lot worse.*

biting /'baɪt·ɪŋ/ *adj* severe and unpleasant; strong enough to hurt • *A cold, biting wind blew in from the north.* • If you describe a remark as biting, you mean that it was strongly critical, often accurate, and likely to hurt someone's feelings: *He delivered a biting attack on political favoritism.*

bitter TASTE /'bɪt̬·ər/ *adj* having a slightly stinging, strong taste, not salty or sweet • *The coffee was bitter.*

bitter ANGRY /'bɪt̬·ər/ *adj* showing or causing deep anger and pain • *Losing the election was a bitter disappointment.* • **To** or **until the bitter end** means to the completion of something difficult that will likely have a bad ending: *The president fought for his plan to the bitter end.*

bitterly /'bɪt̬·ər·li/ *adv* [not gradable] • *When he couldn't have the bike, my son was bitterly disappointed.* • LP VERY, COMPLETELY, AND OTHER INTENSIFIERS

bitterness /'bɪt̬·ər·nəs/ *n* [U] • *She has no bitterness about the past.*

bitter COLD /'bɪt̬·ər·nəs/ *adj, adv* extremely cold • *A bitter wind kept everyone indoors.*

bitterly /'bɪt̬·ər·li/ *adv* • *a bitterly cold day*

bittersweet /'bɪt̬·ər,swiːt/ *adj* containing a mixture of sadness and happiness • *The bittersweet end to the movie is just right.* • **Bittersweet chocolate** tastes both bitter and sweet.

biweekly /baɪ'wiː·kli, 'baɪ,wiː-/ *adj, adv* [not gradable] happening or appearing every two weeks • *The magazine is published biweekly.*

bizarre /bɪ'zɑr/ *adj* strange and unusual • *That party was too bizarre for me!*

blab /blæb/ *v* [I/T] **-bb-** *infml* to talk too much or speak without thinking • *She just blabs to anyone who will listen.* [T]

blabbermouth /'blæb·ər,maʊθ/ *n* [C] *infml* a person who talks too much

black COLOR /blæk/ *adj* [-*er/-est* only], *n* [U] (of) the darkest color there is, like night • *He was dressed all in black.* • To be **in the black** is to have money or to earn more money than you spend: *This year our business is in the black.* Compare **in the red** at RED. • To be **black-and-blue** is to have a dark mark on your skin from an injury: *The fall left her leg all black-and-blue.* • A **black-and-white** photograph or movie has no colors except black, white, and

gray: *(fig.) The press has been presenting the conflict in black-and-white terms* (= being much clearer than it is). • If something is in **black and white**, it is written: *I had to believe it, because it was there in black and white.* • If someone is a **black belt**, they have reached the highest level of JUDO or KARATE (= methods of fighting): *She announced, "Bill's a black belt and could kill you with one blow."* • A **blackboard** is a chalkboard. See at CHALK. • **Black coffee** is coffee without milk or cream. • If you have a **black eye**, the skin around your eye has become dark from being injured or hit: *(fig.) The controversy gave him a political black eye.* • **Blacktop** is the material used on the surface of most roads.

blacken /'blæk·ən/ *v* [T] to make (something) black • *For miles around, trees were blackened by the fire.*

blackness /'blæk·nəs/ *n* [U] • *In such complete blackness, we couldn't see a thing.*

black DARK SKIN /blæk/ *adj* [-*er/-est* only] of or belonging to a group of people having skin that is brown, or being related to an **African-American** • *As a black woman, I am proud of my African-American heritage.* • **Black English** is a variety of American English spoken esp. by some groups of black people in North America. • USAGE: Although African-American is the word preferred by many, black (or Black) is also widely used and is not offensive: *Black leaders disagreed over how to respond.* As a noun, African-American is now more commonly used, but when describing historical events, black is still often used.

black SAD OR BAD /blæk/ *adj* without hope, very bad, or sad • *The blackest time of all was when his eyes failed.* • **Black magic** is the use of magic for evil purposes: *Things were going so badly, I though I must be black magic.* • A **black sheep** is someone who is thought of as an embarrassment to a group, esp. a family, because they are different or have gotten into trouble: *She had different interests, and we stupidly thought of her as a black sheep.*

▫ **black out** *obj* LOSE LIGHTS, **black** *obj* **out** /'-'-/ *v adv* [M] to have a failure in the supply of electricity, causing a loss of lights • *The power failure blacked out all of northern Illinois.* • If you black out something, you prevent it from being seen: *On my copy, they blacked all the names out so I couldn't read them.*

blackout /'blæk·aʊt/ *n* [C] • *A blackout ended the game early.*

▫ **black out** LOSE CONSCIOUSNESS /'-'-/ *v adv* [I] to lose consciousness • *I blacked out right after the accident.*

black hole /'blæk'hoʊl/ *n* [C] *specialized* a region in space where the force of GRAVITY is so strong that nothing, not even light, can escape from it

blackjack /'blæk·dʒæk/ *n* [U] a type of card game played for money

blacklist /'blæk·lɪst/ v [T] to put (someone's name) on a list of people who are considered not acceptable, which keeps them from getting jobs, going certain places, or doing particular things • *The industry blacklisted him for exposing its corruption.*
blacklist /'blæk·lɪst/ n [C] • *The blacklist destroyed his career.*

blackmail /'blæk·meɪl/ n [U] the act of threatening to harm someone or their reputation unless they do as you say, or a payment made to someone who has threatened to harm you or your reputation if you failed to pay them • *Reckless behavior made him an easy target for blackmail.*
blackmail /'blæk·meɪl/ v [T] • *The guy who blackmailed my father went to jail.*

black market /'blæk'mɑr·kət/ n [C/U] an illegal trade in goods or money • *You can sell dollars on the black market.* [U]

blackness /'blæk·nəs/ n [U] See at BLACK COLOR

blacksmith /'blæk·smɪθ/ n [C] a person who makes **horseshoes** (= U-shaped metal objects attached to a horse's feet) and other things from iron

bladder /'blæd·ər/ n [C] an organ inside the body that stores urine until it can be excreted

blade /bleɪd/ n [C] the thin, flat cutting part of a tool or weapon • *The blade on this knife isn't very sharp.* • A blade is also a thin, flat leaf of grass: *The boy made a whistle from a blade of grass.*

blah /blɑ/ adj infml boring or ordinary • *I thought the show was blah.* • **Blah, blah, blah** is used to represent something said over and over: *The critics always say, "There's no melody, the words are stupid, blah, blah, blah."*

blame /bleɪm/ v [T] to make (someone or something) responsible for something • *You can't blame the government for all your troubles.* • If you say that you can't or don't blame someone for doing or thinking something, you mean that they were acting reasonably: *I can't blame her for not wanting the surgery.*
blame /bleɪm/ n [U] • *He put the blame on everyone but himself.*

blameless /'bleɪm·ləs/ adj • *In this situation, no one is completely blameless.*

blanch BECOME PALE /blæntʃ/ v [I] to become pale, esp. from being surprised • *When he realized who was on the phone, he blanched.*

blanch BOIL /blæntʃ/ v [T] to boil (food, esp. vegetables) for a short time • *Blanch the peaches before peeling them.*

bland /blænd/ adj [-er/-est only] lacking a strong or particular flavor; not interesting • *This sauce has a sharp taste and isn't bland at all.*

blank /blæŋk/ adj having no printing, writing, or images • *I needed a blank form to fill in.* ◦ *The computer screen suddenly went blank.* • A blank expression on someone's face shows no

emotion. • A **blank check** is the authority and the ability to do whatever you decide is necessary: *I was given a blank check to set up my own lab.*

blank /blæŋk/ n [C] a form that has spaces to write in, or a space on a form • *Just fill out the order blank and fax it to me.* • A **blank (cartridge)** is a container filled with explosive powder but without a bullet, and fired from a gun to make a loud noise.

blankly /'blæŋ·kli/ adv without expression • *She stared blankly out of the window.*

blank out obj, **blank** obj **out** /'blæŋk'aʊt/ v adv [T] to forget (something) • *I've blanked out everything about the accident.*

blanket COVER /'blæŋ·kət/ n [C] a cloth cover used to keep warm, esp. on a bed • (fig.) *Congress was nearly buried under a blanket of criticism.*
blanket /'blæŋ·kət/ v [T] to cover • *All week, smog has blanketed much of this hot, baked countryside.*

blanket UNLIMITED /'blæŋ·kət/ adj [not gradable] without a limit • *You have blanket authority to hire anyone you want.*

blare /bler, blær/ v [I] to make a very loud noise • *Music blared from a radio.*
blare /bler, blær/ n [U] • *The siren's blare was deafening.*

blasé /blɑ'zeɪ/ adj bored or not very interested • *How could she be so blasé about her victory?*

blasphemous /'blæs·fə·məs/ adj (of speech or writing) showing lack of respect to God or to a religion • *Some people believe such art is blasphemous.*

blasphemy /'blæs·fə·mi/ n [U] • *It is hard to believe that today a writer can be condemned for blasphemy.*

blast EXPLOSION /blæst/ n [C] an explosion, or something sudden and violent • *a shotgun blast* ◦ *One blast of wind blew out a couple of windows.* ◦ *The symphony begins with a trumpet blast.*
blast /blæst/ v [I/T] to break apart or destroy by using explosives • *To make the tunnel, engineers will have to blast through solid rock.* [I]

blast CRITICIZE /blæst/ v [T] to criticize strongly • *The mayor blasted the press for not printing the facts.*

blast ENJOYMENT /blæst/ n [C usually sing] slang an exciting and enjoyable experience • *The party was a blast.*

◻ **blast off** /'·'-/ v adv [I] (esp. of a spacecraft) to take off • *The space shuttle blasted off on schedule.*
blastoff /'blæs,tɔːf/ n [C/U] • *Blastoff is scheduled for eight tonight.* [U]

blatant /'bleɪt·ənt/ adj (of an action) obvious or intentional, and done without worry about what others think • *His behavior showed a blatant lack of respect.*

blatantly /ˈbleɪt·ənt·li/ *adv* • *It was a blatantly unfair decision.*

blaze BURN /bleɪz/ *v* [I] to burn brightly and strongly • *The fires blazed for days.* • If someone's eyes blaze, they seem to shine brightly: *Her eyes blazed with anger.*

blaze /bleɪz/ *n* [C] • *Three fire companies fought the blaze.* • A blaze is also a bright show of something: *Times Square is a blaze of lights.*

blazing /ˈbleɪ·zɪŋ/ *adj* • *They worked all day in the blazing sun.*

blaze SHOW THE WAY /bleɪz/ *v* [T] to make (a new path or way) by marking it so that others can follow • *It took the Cherokee two years to blaze a trail between Texas and Kansas.* ○ (*fig.*) *Science blazed the trail that opened up space exploration.*

blazer /ˈbleɪ·zər/ *n* [C] a type of jacket of one color, usually with metal buttons • *He wore a navy blue blazer and gray pants.*

bleach /bliːtʃ/ *n* [U] a liquid or powder used to clean or make something whiter or lighter in color

bleach /bliːtʃ/ *v* [T] • *Her hair was bleached by the sun.*

bleachers /ˈbliː·tʃərz/ *pl n* (in a building or structure for viewing sports) seats that are usually not covered and often farthest from the action

bleak /bliːk/ *adj* [-er/-est only] (esp. of a place or the weather) cold and not welcoming • *It was a bleak, unpleasant day in December.* • Bleak also means hopeless: *With no job, the future looked bleak.*

bleary /ˈblɪr·i/ *adj* (of eyes) tired, red, or watery • *After studying all night, his eyes were bleary.*

bleat /bliːt/ *v* [I] to produce the sound made by a sheep or goat • *The brass section bleated like goats with bad colds.*

bleat /bliːt/ *n* [C] • *We could hear the bleat of sheep in the meadow.*

bleed /bliːd/ *v* [I/T] *past* **bled** /bled/ to lose blood • *Before help could reach him, the man bled to death.* [I] ○ (*fig.*) *Because of the taxes, our state is bleeding jobs* (= they are rapidly leaving). [T] • (*disapproving*) A **bleeding heart** is someone who is too sympathetic about people in need: *He is not a typical bleeding heart, which makes his support for child care so important.*

blemish /ˈblem·ɪʃ/ *n* [C] a mark or fault that spoils the appearance of someone or something • *Makeup can cover up your skin blemishes.* • A blemish can also be a mistake or fault: *Only one blemish spoiled her school record.*

blend /blend/ *v* [I/T] to mix together or combine • *The president's daughter hopes to blend in with the other students.* [I]

blend /blend/ *n* [C] • *His books are a blend of journalism and history.*

blender /ˈblen·dər/ *n* [C] an electric machine that cuts or crushes foods into small pieces or liquids, used esp. in cooking

bless /bles/ *v* [T] to ask for God's help and protection for (someone or something), or to call or make (someone or something) holy • *May God bless you all.* [T] • If you are **blessed with** something, you have been given something special: *I was blessed with good health.* • When a person says **bless** your **heart** or **bless you**, they show their sympathy or affection: *My dad, bless his heart, is 92 today.* ○ *My niece sent me the sweetest card, bless her.* • **(God) bless you!** is said to someone who has just sneezed.

blessed /ˈbles·əd/ *adj* holy • *The mother of Jesus is sometimes referred to as the Blessed Mother.* • Blessed also means bringing happiness or comfort: *She found the routine of a regular job a blessed relief.*

blessing /ˈbles·ɪŋ/ *n* [C] a prayer asking for God's help, or a prayer of thanks for God's help • *Before we eat, Sam will say the blessing.* • A blessing can mean something that is very good or lucky: *It was a blessing that nobody was hurt in the accident.* • A blessing also means the approval to do something: *My parents finally gave their blessing to my marriage.* • A **blessing in disguise** is something that seems bad or unlucky at first but causes something good to happen later: *Being laid off was a blessing in disguise—within a month I got a much better job.*

blew /bluː/ *past simple of* BLOW

blight /blaɪt/ *n* [C/U] something that spoils or destroys or causes decay • *The city stopped urban blight by rebuilding neighborhoods.* [U] • (*specialized*) A blight is also any of various deadly diseases in plants.

blight /blaɪt/ *v* [T] • *Poverty and disease blighted their lives.*

blimp /blɪmp/ *n* [C] an aircraft without wings, consisting of a very large bag that is filled with gas and has a structure attached to the bottom in which people ride, which moves and turns under power provided by engines

blind NOT SEEING /blaɪnd/ *adj* [-er/-est only] not able to see • *He began to go blind a year ago.* ○ (*fig.*) *She is completely blind to his faults.* • A **blind alley** is something that leads you nowhere or is of no use: *All our work has only led us up a blind alley.* • A **blind date** is a social meeting arranged between two people who have never met before, or refers to one of the people involved. • A **blind spot** is an area you cannot see outside your car when driving. • A person's **blind spot** is also a subject or area in which their ability to understand is weak or lacking: *He was a great scientist, but he had his blind spots.*

blind /blaɪnd/ *v* [T] to make (someone) unable to see • *The sun blinded me for a moment.* ○ (*fig.*) *We cannot let feelings blind us to the facts.*

blindness /ˈblaɪn·nəs/ *n* [U]

blind NOT THINKING /blɑɪnd/ *adj* [not gradable] not able to be influenced by thought or reason • *He declared that the verdict was the result of blind prejudice.*

blind WINDOW COVER /blɑɪnd/ *n* [C] a cover for a window, esp. a VENETIAN BLIND

blindfold /'blɑɪnd·foʊld/ *n* [C] a strip of cloth that covers someone's eyes to keep them from seeing

blindfold /'blɑɪnd·foʊld/ *v* [T] • *She was blindfolded and taken somewhere in the back of a van.*

blink CLOSE EYES /blɪŋk/ *v* [I/T] to close and open (the eyes) quickly, once or several times • *He stared at us without blinking.* [I] • *If a light blinks, it flashes off and on.* [I]

blink FAULTY /blɪŋk/ *n* [U] • If something is **on the blink**, it is not working right: *The coffee machine is on the blink again.*

blip /blɪp/ *n* [C] an unexpected and unusual condition that is usually temporary • *The drop in sales last month was just a blip, nothing to worry about.* • A blip is also a small spot of light that appears on a RADAR screen and shows where a physical object is.

bliss /blɪs/ *n* [U] complete happiness • *Two weeks lying on a beach is my idea of absolute bliss.*

blister /'blɪs·tər/ *n* [C] a painful swelling on the skin, often filled with a watery liquid, caused by a burn or by rubbing against something • *I got blisters from my new shoes.* • A blister is also a raised place on a painted surface.

blister /'blɪs·tər/ *v* [I/T] • *Grace's feet were blistered and numb with cold.* [T]

blistering /'blɪs·tə·rɪŋ/ *adj* very strong and severe • *The vice president launched a blistering attack on Senate Republicans.*

blithe /blɑɪð, blɑɪθ/ *adj* [-er/-est only] satisfied and without worry • *I am upset by the author's blithe indifference toward facts.*

blithely /'blɑɪð·li, 'blɑɪθ-/ *adv* • *Without reading the contract, she blithely agreed to sign it.*

blitz /blɪts/ *n* [C] a sudden and violent military attack, usually with bombs dropped from aircraft • A blitz is also a big and determined effort to do something, esp. in business: *That computer needs an advertising blitz to sell it.*

blizzard /'blɪz·ərd/ *n* [C] a severe snow storm with strong winds • *We didn't get out for three days after the blizzard was over.*

bloated /'bloʊt̬·əd/ *adj* swollen from containing too much air, liquid, or food • *I feel bloated from having too much to eat.*

blob /blɑb/ *n* [C] a large, round drop, usually of something sticky or thick • *a blob of glue/paint*

bloc /blɑk/ *n* [C] a group of countries or people that have similar goals and work together to achieve them • *a powerful voting bloc*

block LUMP /blɑk/ *n* [C] a solid, straight-sided lump of hard material • *The warehouse stores building material, including cement blocks.* •

A block is also a child's toy, usually a set of pieces of wood that can be arranged to make towers, walls, etc.

block GROUP /blɑk/ *n* [C] a group of things considered together, or an amount of something • *a block of tickets/seats* ∘ *a block of time*

block AREA OF A CITY /blɑk/ *n* [C] the buildings next to each other between crossing streets, or the distance from one street to the next in a city or town • *There's a good deli on this block.* • A block is also an area enclosed by four streets that form a rectangle in a city or town: *The new building will take up an entire city block.*

block PREVENT /blɑk/ *v* [T] to prevent movement through or past (something), or to prevent (something) from happening or succeeding • *A fallen tree blocked the road.* ∘ *A large man in front of me blocked my view.* ∘ *Earl scored 28 points and blocked five shots.* ∘ *Congress blocked US aid to the government because of its segregation and human rights policies.*

□ **block out** PLAN /'-,-/ *v adv* [T] to arrange to have time or space for (something) by planning in advance • *She blocked out time each day to work on her book.*

□ **block out** *obj* STOP RECEIVING , **block** *obj* **out** /'-'-/ *v adv* [M] to prevent (the ability to receive or remember something) • *Instinctively I blocked out all memory of being raped.* ∘ *The electronic device allows television viewers to block out violent programs.*

blockade /blɑ'keɪd/ *n* [C] the act of using force or the threat of force to stop the movement of people or goods into or out of a country or area, or the people or objects used to prevent such movement • *The blockade consisted of a dozen ships surrounding the port.*

blockade /blɑ'keɪd/ *v* [T] • *The army blockaded roads leading into the city.*

blockbuster /'blɑk,bʌs·tər/ *n* [C] *infml* a book or movie that is very successful • *We all felt the movie was a potential blockbuster.*

bloke /bloʊk/ *n* [C] *Br infml* a man

blond, *esp. female* **blonde** /blɑnd/ *adj* [-er/-est only] (esp. of hair) pale yellow or golden

blond, *esp. female* **blonde** /blɑnd/ *n* [C] • *Do you think she's a natural blonde, or is her hair bleached?*

blood LIQUID /blʌd/ *n* [U] the red liquid that is sent around the body by the heart and that is necessary for life • *He lost a lot of blood in the accident.* • A **blood bank** is a place where blood given by people is collected and stored. • A **bloodbath** refers to the killing of a great number of people. • A **blood group** or **blood type** is any of several types of blood that a person can have: *Hospitals have to be very careful to match the blood type of the donor to the blood type of the person getting the blood.* • **Blood pressure** is a measure of the pressure at which the blood is sent by the heart through the body: *I take medicine for my high blood pressure.* • A **bloodstain** is a mark made by

blow

blood: *The police found bloodstains on the seat of the car.* • The **bloodstream** is the flow of blood through the body: *Most medicines reach the body through the bloodstream.* • A **blood test** is an examination of the chemicals in a person's blood to find out whether they have any diseases or lack any important substances, or whether they have taken drugs or alcohol. • **Bloodthirsty** means eager to see or take part in violence and killing: *bloodthirsty terrorists* • A **blood vessel** is any of the tubes through which blood flows in the body.

bloody /'blʌd·i/ *adj* showing blood or losing blood • *a bloody knife* ○ *His cousin hit him and he had a bloody nose.* • Bloody also means with much loss of life and many serious injuries: *The Civil War was a very bloody war.*

bloodless /'blʌd·ləs/ *adj* happening without the use of violence • *The rebel soldiers seized power in a bloodless coup.*

blood RELATIONSHIP /blʌd/ *n* [U] a person's relationship to a family or a nation by birth rather than by marriage • *They are related by blood.* ○ *She has Russian blood in her veins.*

blood /blʌd/ *adj* [not gradable] related by birth • *blood relatives* ○ *a blood brother*

bloodcurdling /'blʌd,kɜrd·əl·ɪŋ/ *adj* causing a feeling of extreme fear • *a bloodcurdling story*

bloodhound /'blʌd·haʊnd/ *n* [C] a type of dog with an unusually good ability to smell something, sometimes used for hunting animals or finding people

bloodshed /'blʌd·ʃed/ *n* [U] a great amount of killing and injury • *The government must find a way to restore order and end the bloodshed.*

bloodshot /'blʌd·ʃɑt/ *adj* (of the eyes) with the white part showing red or pink • *Hay fever gives me a runny nose and bloodshot eyes.*

bloom /bluːm/ *v* [I] (of a plant or tree) to produce flowers, or (of a flower) to open or be open • *Alta loved watching her flowers bloom in the spring.* ○ *(fig.) Their interest suddenly bloomed when they knew they would make money out of the deal.*

bloom /bluːm/ *n* [C/U] a flower, or the condition of having flowers • *Roses in bloom are a beautiful sight.* [U]

blooper /'bluː·pər/ *n* [C] a mistake, often amusing, made by a person in public

blossom /'blɑs·əm/ *v* [I] (of a tree or plant) to produce flowers that develop into fruit • *The cherry tree is beginning to blossom.* ○ *(fig.) She is blossoming into a very attractive woman.*

blossom /'blɑs·əm/ *n* [C/U] • *The tree was covered with white blossoms.* [C] ○ *The scent of apple blossom filled the air.* [U]

blot MARK WITH INK /blɑt/ *v* [T] **-tt-** to spoil (a letter, drawing, etc.) with scattered drops of ink

blot /blɑt/ *n* [C] • *Ink blots covered the page.* • A blot is also a fault that spoils the appearance

or reputation of someone or something: *This arrest is a blot on his reputation.*

blot DRY /blɑt/ *v* [T] **-tt-** to dry (something) by using an absorbent tissue or cloth to pick up a liquid • *I've spilled some coffee—can you bring me some paper towels to blot it up?*

□ **blot out** *obj*, **blot** *obj* **out** /'-'-/ *v adv* [M] to cause (something) to disappear, or to remove (something unpleasant) from your thoughts • *A dark cloud blotted out the sun.* ○ *He blots out the painful memories by keeping very busy.*

blotch /blɑtʃ/ *n* [C] an unwanted mark on a surface that is different from the surrounding area • *There were red blotches on her face and neck.*

blouse /blaʊs, blaʊz/ *n* [C] a shirt for a woman or girl • *a sleeveless blouse*

blow MAKE AIR CURRENT /bloʊ/ *v* [I/T] *past simple* **blew** /bluː/, *past part* **blown** /bloʊn/ to make a current of air, or to move (something) or be moved with a current of air • *The wind blew over a garbage can* (= pushed it down on its side). [M] ○ *We brought in the birthday cake and watched Lisa blow out the candles.* [M] • To blow up something is to push air inside it to make it larger: *We blew 12 balloons up for Charles' party.* [M] • If you blow your nose, you force air through it to push out something that is blocking it, so that you can breathe better. • To **blow the whistle on** someone or something is to bring it to the attention of other people in order to stop something bad from happening: *The company stopped using certain chemicals only after some workers blew the whistle on it.*

blow DESTROY /bloʊ/ *v* [I/T] *past simple* **blew** /bluː/, *past part* **blown** /bloʊn/ to destroy (something) in an explosion, esp. by a bomb, or to be destroyed in this way • *The bomb blew a huge hole in the ground.* [T] ○ *The explosion from the gas leak blew all the windows out.* [M] • *(infml)* To blow a sum of money is to spend it, esp. a lot of it in a foolish or wasteful way: *I blew my first paycheck on a night out with my friends.* [T] • *(infml)* If you **blow it** or **blow your chance**, you lose an opportunity to do something by doing or saying the wrong thing: *I guess I blew it when I criticized the way the company had been run.* • *(slang)* If something **blows** your **mind**, you find it very exciting and unusual: *The concert was so good, it blew my mind.* • *(infml)* To **blow** your **stack/top** is to become extremely angry: *My father will blow his top when he sees the scratches on the car.*

blow HIT /bloʊ/ *n* [C] a hard hit with the hand or a weapon • *A sharp blow on the chest sent him spinning to the floor.* • A blow is also an unexpected, harmful event: *Her death at twenty was a terrible blow to her parents.* • If people come to blows, they physically fight: *The brothers almost came to blows over sharing the car.* • If you give a **blow-by-blow** account/

description of something, you describe every detail and action: *We had to sit through a blow-by-blow account of how they missed their flight to Las Vegas.*

▫**blow away** obj PLEASE GREATLY , **blow** obj **away** /'--'-/ v adv [M] slang to please or surprise (someone) greatly • *Winning first prize and a full scholarship blew her away.*

▫**blow away** obj DEFEAT , **blow** obj **away** /'--'-/ v adv [M] infml to defeat completely • *We just got blown away yesterday, losing 12 to 0.* • *(slang)* To blow (someone) away is also to kill them by shooting.

▫**blow off** obj, **blow** obj **off** /'-'-/ v adv [M] slang to decide not to do something you are expected to do or have agreed to do • *"Aren't you going to the meeting?" "No, I'm going to blow it off."*

▫**blow over** /'-'--/ v [I] to pass by or to end • *The storm blew over and missed our area.* ○ *We hope that this crisis will soon blow over.*

▫**blow up** obj INCREASE SIZE , **blow** obj **up** /'-'-/ v adv [M] to increase the size of (something) • *Could you blow this picture up to 8 by 10?*

blowup /'bloʊ·ʌp/ n [C] • *We need a blowup of this picture.*

▫**blow up** BECOME ANGRY /'-'-/ v adv [I] infml to become suddenly very angry • *He may blow up when he finds out how much I spent.*

blow–dry /'bloʊ·draɪ/ v [T] to dry (hair) with a small electric device that blows out hot air • *I'll be ready as soon as I blow-dry my hair.*

blow job /'bloʊ·dʒab/ n [C] taboo slang a sexual activity in which a man's penis is excited by the touch of someone's mouth

blowout AIR BURST /'bloʊ·aʊt/ n [C] a sudden bursting and release of air from a tire on a moving vehicle • *He narrowly averted crashing into another car after the blowout.*

blowout SPORTS VICTORY /'bloʊ·aʊt/ n [C] a sports competition in which one side wins by a very large amount • *If the game is a blowout, fans start to leave before it's over.*

blowtorch /'bloʊ·tɔːrtʃ/ n [C] a tool that produces a very hot flame, used to heat metal or remove paint from a surface

blubber FAT /'blʌb·ər/ n [U] the layer of fat under the skin of sea mammals such as WHALES which keeps them warm • *Some of the larger whales are insulated by a two-foot layer of blubber.* ○ *(fig.) I'm on a diet, trying to lose some of this blubber around the middle.*

blubber CRY /'blʌb·ər/ v [I] **-bb-** to cry in a noisy and childish way

bludgeon /'blʌdʒ·ən/ v [T] to hit (someone) hard and repeatedly with a heavy weapon • *He was bludgeoned to death.*

blue COLOR /bluː/ adj [-er/-est only], n [C/U] (of) the color of the sky on a clear, bright day • *She has blue eyes.* • A **blueberry** is the dark blue fruit of a common North American bush: *blueberry pie* • **Blue cheese** is a cheese with a strong flavor that has some blue spots within

it. • **Blue-collar** means relating to people who do physical work rather than mental work, and who usually do not work in an office: *blue-collar workers.* Compare **white-collar** at WHITE COLOR . • A **bluejay** is a common North American bird that is mainly blue and has a growth of feathers on the top of its head. • **Blue jeans** are pants made of blue DENIM (= strong, cotton cloth), usually worn on informal occasions. • A **blueprint** is a photographic copy of a plan for a building or machine, with white lines on a blue background. • A **blueprint** for doing something is a complete plan that explains how to do it: *The report provided a blueprint for relieving the county's crowded jail facilities.* • **Blue-ribbon** means expert: *Critics asked the president to appoint a blue-ribbon commission to investigate police practices.*

blue SAD /bluː/ adj [-er/-est only] sad; unhappy • *I don't know what's wrong—I just feel blue.*

blues /bluːz/ n [U] a type of music originating among African-American musicians in the southern US, in which the singer often sings about his or her difficult life and bad luck in love • **The blues** are a mood of sadness: *She's got a bad case of the blues.*

blue–chip /ˌbluː'tʃɪp/ adj [not gradable] specialized (of a company) considered to be a safe investment for your money because it is well-established and has performed well in the past • **Blue-chip** also means of top quality: *Even a profitable team like the Cowboys can't keep all their blue-chip players.*

bluegrass /'bluː·græs/ n [U] a type of COUNTRY music from the southern US played on instruments with strings such as guitars, BANJOS, and VIOLINS

blue law /'bluː·lɔː/ n [C] a law that prevents or limits particular activities on Sundays, such as opening stores or selling alcoholic drinks

bluff PRETEND /blʌf/ v to try to trick (someone) into wrongly believing that you intend to act in a particular way, or into believing that you possess powers that you do not have, esp. in order to get an advantage over them • *The landlord claimed to have the right to raise his rent, but we believed he was bluffing and refused to pay it.* [I]

bluff /blʌf/ n [C] • *The threat to go on strike was no bluff, the union leaders insisted.*

bluff CLIFF /blʌf/ n [C] (used in many names of places) a cliff or steep slope, often above a river • *Council Bluffs, Iowa*

blunder /'blʌn·dər/ n [C] a big mistake, especially one resulting from a lack of care or thought • *His failure to respond immediately to the accusations was a major political blunder.*

blunder /'blʌn·dər/ v [I] • *He feared he had blundered.*

blunt DIRECT IN SPEECH /blʌnt/ adj saying what

you think without trying to be polite or caring about other people's feelings • *blunt criticism* ○ *Blunt and outspoken, he often quarreled with fellow officials.*

blunt NOT SHARP /blʌnt/ *adj* [-er/-est only] not having a sharp edge or point • *The victim was struck on the head with a blunt instrument, possibly a baseball bat.*

blunt /blʌnt/ *v* [T] to make (something) less strongly felt • *Eating between meals will blunt your appetite.*

blur /blɜr/ *n* [U] something whose shape is not clear • A blur is also something that you cannot remember clearly: *It all happened so long ago that it's just a blur to me now.*

blur /blɜr/ *v* [I/T] **-rr-** • *These deals are blurring the distinction between local and long-distance telephone service.* [T]

blurry /ˈblɜr·i, ˈblʌ·ri/ *adj* • *The exhibit consisted of blurry, blown-up, black-and-white photographs.*

blurb /blɜrb/ *n* [C] a brief description of something, often intended to make it seem attractive when offered for sale • *The blurb on the back of the book says that "it will touch your heart."*

blurt out *obj*, **blurt** *obj* **out** /ˈblɜrt̬ˈɑʊt/ *v* [M] to say (something) suddenly, and without thinking of the results • *At one point, Goetz blurted out, "The subways down there are terrible."*

blush REDDEN /blʌʃ/ *v* [I] to become redder or darker in the face, usually from embarrassment • *He blushed at the thought of what he'd done.*

blush MAKEUP /blʌʃ/ *n* [U] a substance, often a powder, put on the face to add a slightly red color

bluster /ˈblʌs·tər/ *n* [U] talk intended to seem important or threatening but which is not taken seriously and has little effect • *For all his bluster about his military adventures, McLaughlin was enormously likable.*

blustery /ˈblʌs·tə·ri/ *adj* (of the weather) stormy and windy • *a cold and blustery night*

B.O. *n* [U] *abbreviation for* **body odor**, see at BODY PHYSICAL STRUCTURE

boa (constrictor) /ˈboʊ·ə (kənˌstrɪkˈtər)/ *n* [C] a large, strong snake, found in South and Central America, that kills animals and birds by wrapping itself around them and crushing them to death

boar /bɔr, boʊr/ *n* [C] a male pig kept for breeding on a farm, or a type of wild pig

board WOOD /bɔrd/ *n* [C] a long, thin, flat piece of cut wood or other hard material • *The floor boards of the old house squeaked as he walked across them.* • A board is also a flat piece of wood or other hard material that is made to be used for a particular purpose: *an ironing board* ○ *a cheese board* • A **board game** is any game in which pieces are moved in particular ways on a board marked with a

pattern: *All our old board games like Monopoly were gathering dust in a closet.* • A board can be a **chalkboard**. See at CHALK. • A **boardwalk** is a path usually built of wooden boards near the sea, often raised above the back part of a beach.

board up *obj*, **board** *obj* **up** /ˈbɔrdˈʌp, ˈboʊrd-/ *v adv* [M] to cover (esp. a front or window) with thin, flat pieces of cut wood, to protect it or keep people out • *The vacant store had been boarded up for several years.*

board PEOPLE /bɔrd, boʊrd/ *n* [C] the group of people who are responsible for controlling the operation of a public or private organization • *a community/school board* ○ *She sits on the board of several large companies.*

board MEALS /bɔrd, boʊrd/ *n* [U] meals provided when you are staying somewhere

board /bɔrd, boʊrd/ *v* [T] to arrange for (an animal) to be temporarily taken care of and fed at a place other than its home • *We board our dogs at the kennel when we go away.* [T]

boarder /ˈbɔrd·ər, ˈboʊrd-/ *n* [C] someone who pays for a place to sleep and meals in someone else's house

board GET ON /bɔrd, boʊrd/ *v* [I/T] to get onto or allow people to get onto (an aircraft, train, or ship) • *Flight 701 to Los Angeles is now boarding at gate 14A.* [I] • A **boarding pass** is a card that a passenger must have to be allowed to enter an aircraft or ship.

board /bɔrd, boʊrd/ *n* • **On board** means on or in an aircraft, train, or ship: *All passengers should be on board at this time.*

boarding house /ˈbɔrd·ɪŋˌhɑʊs, ˈboʊrd-/ *n* [C] *pl* **boarding houses** /ˈbɔrd·ɪŋˌhɑʊ·zəz, ˈboʊrd-, -səz/ a private house that a person pays to stay in and receive meals

boarding school /ˈbɔrd·ɪŋˌskuːl, ˈboʊrd-/ *n* [C] a school equipped with rooms where its students live instead of living in their own homes

boast SPEAK PROUDLY /boʊst/ *v* to speak too proudly or show too much satisfaction about something or someone connected with you • *They are always boasting about how smart their children are.* [I] ○ *She boasted that she had never had an accident.* [+ *that* clause]

boast /boʊst/ *n* [C] • *It was his proud boast that he had run over 20 marathons.*

boastful /ˈboʊst·fəl/ *adj* having a tendency to praise yourself and what you have done

boast POSSESS /boʊst/ *v* [T] to have or possess (something to be proud of) • *New Orleans boasts great music and excellent restaurants.*

boat /boʊt/ *n* [C] a vehicle for traveling on water, esp. one that is not very large • *a fishing boat* • **Boat people** are people who have left their country by boat, usually in the hope of finding safety in another place.

bob MOVE /bɑb/ *v* [I] **-bb-** to move up and down quickly and gently • *Empty cans and bottles bobbed in the water of the harbor.*

bob HAIRSTYLE /bɑb/ *n* [C] a hairstyle that is short at the front while the other hair is cut to neck length all around the head • *She wears her hair in a bob.*

bobby pin /'bɑb·iː‚pɪn/ *n* [C] a U-shaped pin tightly bent so that the two sides touch, used esp. to keep hair in a desired way

bobcat /'bɑb·kæt/ *n* [C] a wild animal of North America of the cat family, having brown hair, pointed ears, and a short tail

bode /boʊd/ *v* [I] to be a sign of something (good or bad) for the future • *This does not bode well for the future of the peace process.*

bodega /boʊ'deɪ·ɡə/ *n* [C] (in a neighborhood with a lot of Spanish-speaking people) a small store that sells food and other items for the house • *Would you run down to the bodega and pick up a quart of milk and some kitty litter?*

bodice /'bɑd·əs/ *n* [C] the upper part of a woman's dress

body PHYSICAL STRUCTURE /'bɑd·i/ *n* [C] the whole physical structure that is a person or animal • *A good diet and plenty of exercise will help you keep your body healthy.* • Sometimes body can refer to the main, physical part of a person or animal but not include the head, or not include the head and the arms and legs. • A body is also a dead person: *They recovered a rifle near the place where they found the woman's body.* • A **bodyguard** is a person paid to protect another person from danger, esp. from physical danger. • **Body language** is the movements or positions by which you show other people your feelings without using words: *Their body language said that they were really enjoying each other's company.* • **Body odor** (*abbreviation* **B.O.**) is the unpleasant smell of a person's body that is caused by SWEAT (= liquid you excrete through your skin).

bodily /'bɑd·ᵊl·i/ *adv, adj* [not gradable] relating to a person's physical structure • *He picked her up bodily.*

body MAIN PART /'bɑd·i/ *n* [U] the main part of something such as a book, a large building, or a vehicle • *Most scientists will be less interested in the body of the article than in the detailed notes at the end.*

body GROUP OF PEOPLE /'bɑd·i/ *n* [C] a group of people who have joined together for a particular reason • *Congress is a legislative body created to consider and pass laws.*

body AMOUNT /'bɑd·i/ *n* [C] an amount of something • *There is a growing body of evidence to support their innocence.* • A body of water is a large area of water, such as a lake.

bog /bɑɡ, bɔːɡ/ *n* [C] an area of soft, wet earth

▫**bog down** *obj*, **bog** *obj* **down** /'bɑɡ'dɑʊn, 'bɔːɡ-/ *v adv* [M] to cause (someone or something) to stop from moving on or progressing • *Let's not get bogged down with individual complaints—we're here to discuss general guidelines on how to proceed.*

bogey /'bʊɡ·i, 'boʊ·ɡi, 'buː·ɡi/, **boogeyman** /'bʊɡ·iː‚mæn, 'buː·ɡi-/ *n* [C] something feared, esp. when the fear is not based on reason • *Too many economists are scared by the bogey of inflation, he says.*

boggle /'bɑɡ·əl/ *v* [I/T] to have difficulty imagining or accepting something as true or possible, or to give (the mind) such difficulty • *It boggles the mind to think about how much money was wasted.* [T]

bogus /'boʊ·ɡəs/ *adj* (of something) not what it appears or claims to be; false but made to look real • *He was arrested and charged with carrying a bogus passport.*

bohemian /boʊ'hiː·miː·ən/ *n* [C] a person who lives in a very informal style that is different from the way most people live

bohemian /boʊ'hiː·miː·ən/ *adj* • *She belonged to a West Coast group of bohemian writers and intellectuals.*

boil HEAT /bɔɪl/ *v* [I/T] (of a liquid) to start to turn into a gas because of being heated, or to cause (a liquid) to turn into a gas in this way • *The water is boiling.* [I] ◦ *We'd better boil this water before we drink it.* [T] • If you say that a container has boiled, the liquid in it has started to turn into a gas: *The pot's beginning to boil.* [I] • If food boils, or you boil food, it is cooked by being put in water that is heated until the water is in the process of turning into a gas: *I boiled some potatoes for dinner.* [T] • If a liquid boils over, it rises up as it starts to turn into a gas and flows over the edge of a container. [I] • PIC COOKING METHODS

boil /bɔɪl/ *n* [U] • If you bring something to a boil, or let something come to a boil, you heat it until it starts to turn into a gas: *Bring the water to a boil, then add the pasta.*

boiler /'bɔɪ·lər/ *n* [C] a device that heats water esp. to provide heating and hot water in a house

boiling /'bɔɪ·lɪŋ/ *adj* [not gradable] • *a pot of boiling water* • Boiling can also mean extremely angry: *He was boiling with rage.* • The **boiling point** of a liquid is the temperature at which it becomes a gas: *The boiling point of water is 212°F or 100°C.* Compare **freezing point** at FREEZE

boil SWELLING /bɔɪl/ *n* [C] a painful, red swelling on the skin that is filled with PUS (= a yellow liquid from an infection)

▫**boil down**, **boil** *obj* **down** /'-'-/ *v adv* [M] to reduce (information), usually so that it contains only its most important part • *The boss wants me to boil down the ten-page sales report to one page.*

▫**boil down to** /-'--/ *v adv prep* [T] to result from (something) basically • *What it all boils down to is a lack of communication.*

boisterous /'bɔɪ·stə·rəs/ *adj* noisy and not controlled • *The audience burst into boisterous laughter.*

bold BRAVE /boʊld/ *adj* [-*er*/-*est* only] not fearful of doing something risky or brave • *He is a qualified politician with bold ideas.* • Bold can also mean not shy, and almost rude: *She was friendly without being bold.* • USAGE: The opposite of bold is TIMID.

boldly /'bool·dli/ *adv* • *He dealt boldly with the problem and hoped he was right.*

bold NOTICEABLE /boold/ *adj* [-*er*/-*est* only] likely to attract your attention; showy • *The costumes were in beautiful, bold colors.*

bologna /bə'lou·ni/, **baloney** *n* [U] a cooked, smoked SAUSAGE (= mixed meat in a tube shape) that is sliced and eaten cold • *Lunch was a bologna sandwich and cold soda.*

bolster SUPPORT /'bool·stər/ *v* [T] to support (something), or make (something) stronger • *The UN is sending more troops to bolster the peacekeepers.*

bolster OBJECT ON BED /'bool·stər/ *n* [C] a long PILLOW (= cloth bag filled with material), usually shaped like a tube

bolt LOCK /boolt/ *n* [C] a small metal bar that slides across a door or window to lock it • *I fastened the door with a bolt.* • (*specialized*) A bolt is also a part of a gun that you slide back when getting ready to fire.

bolt /boolt/ *v* [T] • *Be sure to bolt the door when you go to bed!*

bolt SCREW /boolt/ *n* [C] a metal screw without a point, used to fasten things together, often with a NUT (= small piece of metal that attaches to it) • PIC NUT

bolt /boolt/ *v* [T always + adv/prep] • *He sat on a wooden bench bolted to the floor.*

bolt LIGHTNING /boolt/ *n* [C] a flash of lightning, esp. followed by thunder • *Did a bolt of lightning set fire to the barn?* • If something is **a bolt from the blue** or **a bolt out of the blue**, it happens suddenly or unexpectedly: *The resignation of the chairman came like a bolt from the blue.*

bolt MOVE SUDDENLY /boolt/ *v* [I/T] to move suddenly and quickly • *At the first whiff of smoke, the horse bolted from the barn.* [I] ∘ *He bolted down some breakfast.* [M]

bolt ROLL /boolt/ *n* [C] a roll of cloth or paper, esp. WALLPAPER

bolt STRAIGHT /boolt/ *adv* [not gradable] • **Bolt upright** means vertical and straight: *She suddenly awoke and sat bolt upright in bed.*

bomb WEAPON /bam/ *n* [C] a weapon that explodes • *Was there any warning before the bomb went off?*

bomb /bam/ *v* [T] to explode (bombs), or to drop (bombs) from aircraft • *They bombed enemy airfields.*

bomber /'bam·ər/ *n* [C] a person who makes or explodes bombs • *The bomber sent packages that exploded when opened.* • A bomber is also an aircraft designed to carry and drop bombs.

bomb FAIL /bam/ *v* [I] *infml* to fail completely • *A lot of students bombed on that last exam.*

bomb /bam/ *n* [C] *infml* • *The last play was a bomb.*

bombard /bam'bard, bəm-/ *v* [T] to attack (a place) with continuous shooting or bombs • (*fig.*) *I was bombarded with phone calls and faxes.*

bombardment /bam'bard·mənt, bəm-/ *n* [U] • *The long bombardment destroyed the city.*

bombed /bamd/ *adj* [not gradable] *slang* very drunk, or strongly feeling the effects of a drug

bombshell /'bam·ʃel/ *n* [C usually sing] a shocking piece of news • *He dropped a bombshell when he announced he would resign.*

bona fide /'bou·nə,faɪd, 'ban·ə-, -,faɪd·i/ *adj* [not gradable] real or true; not false • *This is my first bona fide job.*

bonanza /bə'næn·zə/ *n* [C] something that suddenly produces large profits or great opportunities • *The improved economy was a bonanza for local stores.*

bond CONNECTION /band/ *n* [C] a close and lasting relationship between people • *The bond between parents and children is usually very strong.*

bond /band/ *v* [T] • *The puppy and his master bonded quickly.*

bonding /'ban·dɪŋ/ *n* [U] • *Much of the bonding between mother and child takes place in those early weeks.*

bond GLUE /band/ *v* [I/T] to stick something together, esp. using glue • *The pieces will bond in less than a minute.* [I]

bond DOCUMENT /band/ *n* [C] an official document that states you will be paid a certain amount of money because you have lent money to a government or company • *The county issued $4 million in bonds for road construction.*

bondage /'ban·dɪdʒ/ *n* [C] the state of one person being owned by another person, as a piece of property • *Most runaway slaves preferred death to hopeless bondage,*

bone /boun/ *n* [C] any of the hard pieces that form the SKELETON (= frame) of a human or animal body • *She had broken a bone in her foot.* • **A bone of contention** is something that two sides cannot agree about: *Turning in weapons is the last bone of contention.* • If something is **bone-chilling**, it is extremely cold: *The air at that altitude was bone-chilling.* • **Bone marrow** or MARROW is the soft fatty tissue in the center of bones: *A bone marrow transplant can be risky.*

bony /'bou·ni/ *adj* very thin, so that bones can be seen, or (of fish) having a lot of bones in it • *She had a long, bony face.*

bone /boun/ *v* [T] to remove the bones from (fish or meat)

boneless /'boun·ləs/, **boned** /bound/ *adj* [not gradable] (of meat or fish) without any bones • *boneless breast of chicken*

□**bone up** /'bou'nʌp/ *v adv* [I] *infml* to study a

subject as much as you can in a short period of time • *She boned up on her Spanish before going to Mexico.*

bonfire /'bɑn·faɪr/ *n* [C] a large fire that is made outside • *We built a bonfire on the beach.*

bongo (drum) /'bɑŋ·goʊ (ˌdrʌm)/ *n* [C usually pl] *pl* **bongos** or **bongoes** one of a pair of small drums that are played with the hands

bonkers /'bɑŋ·kərz, 'bɔːŋ-/ *adj* [not gradable] *slang* very enthusiastic; crazy • *Kids really went bonkers over that video game.*

bonnet /'bɑn·ət/ *n* [C] a hat for a baby that covers the head and ties under the CHIN, or a woman's hat

bonus /'boʊ·nəs/ *n* [C] an extra amount of money given to someone as a reward for work or as encouragement • *The salary was $40,000, plus a bonus.* • A bonus is also any result that is an unexpected benefit: *After the heart transplant, every day is a bonus for me.*

bony /'boʊ·ni/ *adj* • See at BONE.

boo DISAPPROVE /buː/ *v* [I/T] he/she/it **boos**, **booing**, *past* **booed** to call out the word "boo" to express disapproval • *They booed him off the stage.* [T]

boo /buː/ *n* [C] *pl* **boos** • *Students showed their dislike with a chorus of boos.*

boo SURPRISE /buː/ *exclamation* used to surprise or frighten another person, and usually said loudly • *He snuck up behind me and said, "Boo!"*

boob /buːb/ *n* [C usually pl] *rude slang* a woman's breast

boo–boo /'buː·buː/ *n* [C] *pl* **boo-boos** *infml* (used esp. as a child's word by adults) a mistake, or a small cut or injury • *I did a boo-boo! I spilled coffee!*

boob tube /'buːb·tuːb/ *n* [C] *infml* television

booby prize /'buː·bi·ˌpraɪz/ *n* [C] a prize given as a joke to the person who loses a game or competition

booby trap /'buː·bi·ˌtræp/ *n* [C] a hidden weapon that explodes when moved or touched

booby–trap /'buː·bi·ˌtræp/ *v* [T] **-pp-** • *Don't open the door—it may be booby-trapped.*

boogeyman (*pl* **-men**) /'bʊg·iːˌmæn, 'buː·giː-/ *n* [C] a BOGEY

book TEXT /bʊk/ *n* [C] an object consisting of a number of pages of text or pictures fastened together along one edge and fixed inside two covers • *The artist's sketch books filled several shelves.* • A book is also a number of similar items fastened together inside a cover: *a book of matches/stamps* • A **bookcase** is a piece of furniture with shelves to hold books. • A **bookshelf** is a shelf for books or a shelf in a bookcase. • A **bookend** is one of a pair of objects used to keep a row of books standing up. • A **bookmark** is anything placed between the pages of a book to show where a person stopped reading. • A **bookstore** is a store that sells books. • (*infml*) A **bookworm** is someone who likes to read books. • See also BOOKS.

bookish /'bʊk·ɪʃ/ *adj* enjoying books more than other things • *He's pleasant but a shy, bookish type.*

book ARRANGE /bʊk/ *v* [I/T] to arrange to have (the use of a seat, room, etc.) at a particular time in the future • *Our travel agent booked us on a flight to Paris.* [T] • If someone books a performer, they arrange a performance: *They booked the Rolling Stones for two concerts in New York.* [T]

book ACCUSE /bʊk/ *v* [T] to officially accuse (someone) of a crime • *Detectives booked him for resisting arrest.*

bookie /'bʊk·i/, **bookmaker** /'bʊkˌmeɪ·kər/ *n* [C] a person whose business is accepting and paying out money risked on a particular result of something, esp. horse races

bookkeeping /'bʊkˌkiː·pɪŋ/ *n* [U] the job or activity of keeping a record of money spent or received by a business or other organization

bookkeeper /'bʊkˌkiː·pər/ *n* [C] • *A good bookkeeper does careful work.*

booklet /'bʊk·lət/ *n* [C] a small book, usually with a paper cover; a PAMPHLET

books /bʊks/ *pl n* written records of money that has been spent or received by a company

boom PERIOD OF GROWTH /buːm/ *n* [C] a period of sudden economic growth • *Somehow farmers have survived the booms and busts of the past 50 years.* • A **boom town** is a small town that grows quickly as a result of a sudden increase in local economic activity.

boom /buːm/ *v* [I] • *At that time, Alaska was booming.*

boom MAKE A DEEP SOUND /buːm/ *v* [I/T] to make a deep, loud sound • *A voice boomed through the microphone.* [I]

boom /buːm/ *n* [C] • *What you heard was the boom of a rocket.* • (*slang*) A **boom box** is a radio and TAPE or CD player able to produce a loud sound, which you can carry with you.

boom POLE /buːm/ *n* [C] a long, movable pole that holds the bottom edge of a sail and is attached to the MAST of a boat • In television and movie making, a boom is a long, movable pole that has a MICROPHONE (= device that records sound) or camera on one end.

boomerang /'buː·məˌræŋ/ *n* [C] a curved stick that, when thrown, comes back toward the person who threw it

boon /buːn/ *n* [C] something good or very helpful • *Spring rains are a boon to local farmers.*

boondocks /'buːnˌdɑks/, **boonies** /'buː·niːz/ *pl n infml* an area far from any city or town, with few people and little to do for entertainment • *He edits a little paper in the boondocks.*

boondoggle /'buːnˌdɑg·əl, -ˌdɔː·gəl/ *n* [C] a wasteful and expensive program, esp. one using public money • *Voters say they are fed up with such boondoggles.*

boor /bʊr/ *n* [C] a person who behaves rudely

boorish /'bʊr·ɪʃ/ *adj* • *I'm sick of your drunken, boorish behavior.*

boost MAKE BETTER /buːst/ *v* [T] to improve or increase (something) • *We took various steps to try to boost sales.*

boost /buːst/ *n* [C usually sing] • *The president's approval rating got a boost following his speech.*

booster /ˈbuː·stər/ *n* [C] • *Winning this game was a great morale booster for the team.* • A booster is also someone who is an enthusiastic supporter of something.

boost LIFT /buːst/ *v* [T always + adv/prep] to lift someone or something by pushing from below • *She boosted the little boy up to see over the fence.*

boost /buːst/ *n* [C] • *I need a boost to get over the wall.*

booster /ˈbuː·stər/ *n* [C] *specialized* the first stage of a ROCKET (= object sent into space) that pushes it off the ground

boot SHOE /buːt/ *n* [C] a type of shoe that covers the foot and the lower leg • *work boots* ○ *cowboy boots* • If someone **gets the boot** or is **given the boot**, they are forced to leave: *They tried to get into the locker room, but the coach gave them the boot.* • **To boot** means also or in addition: *She gets motion sickness, and she's afraid of flying to boot.* • **Boot camp** is a place where new members of the US military receive their first training. • **Boot camp** is also a prison for esp. younger people where they receive training to change their behavior.

boot /buːt/ *v* [T] to kick (something) • *She booted me in the butt.*

boot MAKE READY /buːt/ *v* [I/T] *specialized* to cause (a computer or a computer program) to become ready for use • *Before you can do anything, you have to boot up.* [I]

boot STORAGE SPACE /buːt/ *n* [C] *Br for* TRUNK STORAGE SPACE

bootee, bootie /ˈbuː·t̬·i/ *n* [C] a warm, soft sock for a baby

booth /buːθ/ *n* [C] *pl* **booths** /buːðz, buːθs/ a small structure just big enough for one person to use • *There was a line of people waiting for the phone booth.* • A booth is also a partly enclosed area in a restaurant where people sit on long seats on opposite sides of a table. • A booth can also be a small, partly open structure for showing and selling things at a FAIR or market: *If we get separated, let's meet at the information booth.*

bootleg /ˈbuːt·leg/ *adj* [not gradable] made illegally or copied • *Bootleg tapes are easy to get hold of on the street.*

bootleg /ˈbuːt·leg/ *v* [I/T] **-gg-** • *They bootleg software, depriving big companies of income.* [T]

bootlegger /ˈbuːt·leg·ər/ *n* [C] • *The trial was livened up by the testimony of a bootlegger.*

booty /ˈbuː·t̬·i/ *n* [U] anything valuable that is stolen, by an army or by thieves • *The thieves quarreled over the booty like dogs with a bone.*

booze /buːz/ *n* [U] *infml* alcoholic drink • *Did you bring any booze?*

bop HIT /bɑp/ *v* [T] **-pp-** *infml* to hit (something) lightly, not hard • *I just bop the puppy with a bit of newspaper when he pees where he shouldn't.*

bop /bɑp/ *n* [C] • *I got a bop on the head.*

bop MUSIC /bɑp/, **bebop** /ˈbiː·bɑp/ *n* [U] a type of jazz from the 1940s that has complicated rhythms and is often played fast

border DIVISION /ˈbɔːrd·ər/, **borderline** *n* [C] the line that divides one country from another • *The Rio Grande forms part of the US border.*

border /ˈbɔːrd·ər/ *v* [I/T] • *Guatemala borders Mexico.* [T] ○ *Wisconsin borders on Illinois.* [I]

border EDGE /ˈbɔːrd·ər/ *n* [C] a strip that goes around or along the edge of something, or the edge itself • *The card has a pretty design around the border.*

border /ˈbɔːrd·ər/ *v* [T] • *The road borders the coast for several miles.*

□**border on** /ˈ--ˌ-/ *v adv* [T] to be almost like (esp. a quality) • *The things we'd do for candy bordered on the extraordinary.*

borderline /ˈbɔːrd·ərˌlaɪn/ *adj* between two very different conditions, with the possibility of being unacceptable • *My blood pressure was borderline, and the doctor said I should lose weight.*

bore FAIL TO INTEREST /bɔːr, boʊr/ *v* [T] to make (someone) lose interest • *Am I boring you?*

bore /bɔːr, boʊr/ *n* [C] someone or something that is not interesting • *All he talks about is money—he's such a bore.*

bored /bɔːrd, boʊrd/ *adj* • *He was getting bored doing the same thing every day.* • *(infml) I pretended to listen, but I was bored stiff/to tears/to death* (= completely bored).

boring /ˈbɔːr·ɪŋ, ˈboʊr·ɪŋ/ *adj* • *The car ride was really boring.*

boredom /ˈbɔːrd·əm, ˈboʊrd-/ *n* [U] • *She varies her workouts to avoid boredom.*

bore MAKE A HOLE /bɔːr, boʊr/ *v* [I/T] to make a hole in (something) using a tool • *Workmen bored through the rock.* [I]

bore BEAR /bɔːr, boʊr/ *past simple of* BEAR

born BEGAN TO EXIST /bɔːrn/ *adj* [not gradable], *past participle of* BEAR; having come into existence by birth • *He was born in 1950.* • A **born-again Christian** is someone who has accepted a particular type of EVANGELICAL Christianity, esp. after a deep religious experience.

born NATURAL /bɔːrn/ *adj* [not gradable] having a natural ability or tendency • *It was obvious that Rachel was a born leader.* ○ *Stephen was born to ride motorcycles.* [+ *to* infinitive]

borne /bɔːrn, boʊrn/ *past participle of* BEAR

borough /ˈbɜr·oʊ, ˈbʌ·roʊ/ *n* [C] one of the five divisions of New York City or, in some states, a town or part of a town • In Alaska, a borough is a political division similar to a COUNTY in other states.

borrow /'bar·ou, 'bɔːr-/ v [I/T] to take (something) from someone with the intention of giving it back after using it • *Could I borrow your bike until next week?* [T] ○ *(fig.) We constantly borrow words from other cultures.* [T] • If someone or something is **on borrowed time**, they are living or working longer than expected: *We're on borrowed time with that hot-water heater.* • USAGE: Compare LEND.

borrower /'bar·ə·wər, 'bɔːr-/ n [C] • *The rate charged to borrowers is 9.7%.*

borrowing /'bar·ə·wɪŋ, 'bɔːr-/ n [C/U] • *Jefferson opposed government borrowing.* [U]

bosom /'buz·əm/ n [C usually sing] a woman's breasts or the front of a person's chest, esp. when thought of as the center of human feelings • The bosom of a group is the middle of it: *He felt safe in the bosom of his family.* • A **bosom buddy** is a friend that you are very close to.

boss /bɔːs, bas/ n [C] the person who is in charge of an organization or a department and who tells others what to do • *I'll ask my boss if I can take the afternoon off.*

boss (around) obj, **boss** obj **(around)** /'bɔːs (ə 'raund), 'bas/ v [T/M] infml to tell (someone) what to do, esp. if that is not your job • *I wish he'd stop bossing me around.* [M]

bossy /'bɔː·si, 'bas·i/ adj disapproving • *"Move over," she said in a bossy tone.*

botany /'bɑt·ᵊn·i/ n [U] the scientific study of plants

botanical /bə'tæn·ɪ·kəl/, **botanic** /bə'tæn·ɪk/ adj [not gradable] • *a botanical garden* ○ *botanical specimens*

botanist /'bɑt·ᵊn·əst/ n [C] a scientist who studies plants

botch /bɑtʃ/ v [T] to spoil (something) by doing it badly • *He thinks the police botched the investigation.*

both /bouθ/ pronoun, adj [not gradable] used to refer to two people or things together • *Would you like milk or sugar or both in your coffee?* ○ *If both parents work, who will care for the kids?* ○ *Are both of us invited, or just you?* ○ *Keep both hands on the steering wheel.* • LP AMOUNTS, DETERMINERS

bother MAKE AN EFFORT /'bɑð·ər/ v [I] to make an effort to do something, esp. something inconvenient • *You won't get any credit for doing it, so why bother?* ○ *Don't bother doing the laundry.* ○ *He didn't even bother to say goodbye.* [+ to infinitive] • If you **cannot be bothered** to do something, you are unwilling to make the effort needed to achieve it: *I asked him to clean his room, but he just couldn't be bothered.*

bother /'bɑð·ər/ n [U] • *I'm not sure gardening is worth the bother.*

bother ANNOY /'bɑð·ər/ v [I/T] to annoy, worry, or cause problems for (someone) • *The heat was beginning to bother him, so he sat down.* [T] ○ *Does it bother you if your children aren't interested?* [T]

bother /'bɑð·ər/ n [U] • *That dog has never been a bother to anyone.*

bothersome /'bɑð·ər·səm/ adj causing annoyance or trouble • *Bothersome family obligations keep interfering with my plans.*

bottle /'bɑt̬·ᵊl/ n [C] a container for liquids, usually made of glass or plastic, with a narrow neck • *a bottle of perfume* • A **bottle cap/bottle top** is a circular piece of metal or plastic used to close a bottle.

bottle /'bɑt̬·ᵊl/ v [T] to put (liquid) into bottles • *The wine was bottled in California.*

□**bottle up** obj, **bottle** obj **up** /'--'-/ v adv [M] to refuse to talk about (something that angers or worries you) • *Feelings that had been bottled up for years came flooding out.*

bottleneck /'bɑt̬·ᵊl,nek/ n [C] a section of road where traffic moves slowly • *Traffic is causing a bottleneck on I-75.* • A bottleneck is also any delay: *Bureaucratic bottlenecks delayed the project's start.*

bottom LOWEST PART /'bɑt̬·əm/ n [C usually sing] the lowest part of something • *He stood at the bottom of the stairs and called up to me.* • A bottom is the lower part of an item of clothing that consists of two parts: *a bikini bottom* ○ *pajama bottoms* • The bottom is also the least important position: *The manager of the hotel started at the bottom 30 years ago.* • The **bottom of the barrel** is the worst of a group of things or people: *None of these dresses are pretty, but this one is the bottom of the barrel.* • The **bottom line** in the finances of a company or organization is the total profit or loss: *How will the rise in interest rates affect our bottom line?* • The **bottom line** is also the final result or the most important consideration of a situation, activity, or discussion: *The bottom line is that they lost the game.* • USAGE: The opposite of bottom is TOP HIGHEST PART.

bottomless /'bɑt̬·əm·ləs/ adj [not gradable] seemingly without a bottom, limit, or end • *Could the pond really be bottomless?* ○ *I wish I had a bottomless source of ideas.*

bottom BODY PART /'bɑt̬·əm/ n [C] the buttocks

□**bottom out** /'bɑt̬·ə'maut/ v adv [I] to reach the lowest point in a changing situation and be about to improve • *The housing market has bottomed out in this part of the country.*

bough /bau/ n [C] a large branch of a tree

bought /bɔːt/ past simple and past participle of BUY

boulder /'boul·dər/ n [C] a large, rounded rock that has been smoothed by the action of the weather or water

boulevard /'bul·ə,vard, 'buː·lə-/ n [C] a wide street in a town or city, usually with trees on each side or along the center • *Billy owned a pizza place on the boulevard.*

bounce JUMP /bauns/ v [I/T] to move up or away after hitting a surface, or to cause (something) to move this way • *The basketball bounced off the rim of the basket.* [I] ∘ *She bounced the baby on her knee.* [T] ∘ *(fig.) Tom bounced into the room* (= walked in a happy, energetic way). [I] • If you **bounce back** from an unpleasant experience or an illness, you soon return to your usual state or activities: *I bounced back pretty quickly after my operation.*

bounce /baʊns/ *n* [C/U] • *In tennis you must hit the ball before its second bounce.* [C]

bouncing /ˈbaʊn·sɪŋ/ *adj* [not gradable] (of babies) happy and healthy • *a bouncing baby girl*

bouncy /ˈbaʊn·si/ *adj* • *Hard ground makes balls more bouncy.* ∘ *(fig.) He's always bouncy* (= happy and energetic) *in the morning.*

bounce NOT PAY /baʊns/ *v* [I/T] *infml* (of a check) to not be paid or accepted by a bank because of a lack of money in the account, or to pay with a check for which there is not enough money in the account • *He's bounced checks before, but never on this account.* [T]

bouncer /ˈbaʊn·sər/ *n* [C] *infml* a strong man paid to stand outside a bar, party, etc., and either stop people from coming in or force them to leave if they cause trouble • *a nightclub bouncer*

bound TIE /baʊnd/ *past simple and past participle of* BIND TIE

bound CERTAIN /baʊnd/ *adj* [not gradable] certain or extremely likely to happen • *You're bound to feel nervous about your interview.* [+ to infinitive] • *They are* **bound and determined** *to build their own house* (= seriously intending to do this).

bound TIED /baʊnd/ *adj* [not gradable] tied tightly or fastened • *Police found the girl in the bedroom, bound and gagged.*

bound FORCED /baʊnd/ *adj* having a moral or legal duty to do something • *She is not legally bound to pay the debts, but she has agreed to do it anyway.*

bound LIMIT /baʊnd/ *v* [T] to mark or form the limits of • *The town is bounded on one side by a river.*

boundless /ˈbaʊn·dləs/ *adj* seemingly endless or unlimited • *boundless energy*

bounds /baʊnz/ *pl n* limits of an activity or behavior • *His desire for political power apparently knows no bounds.*

boundary /ˈbaʊn·dri, -də·ri/ *n* [C] an edge or limit of something • *You can camp anywhere inside the boundaries of the park.* ∘ *Your work is limited only by the boundaries of your imagination.*

bound DIRECTION /baʊnd/ *adj* [not gradable] traveling in the direction of • *She was on a plane bound for Fairbanks.* ∘ *(fig.) These two young musicians are bound for success.*

bound JUMP /baʊnd/ *v* [I always + adv/prep] to move quickly with large, jumping movements • *A deer bounded across the road.*

bound /baʊnd/ *n* [C] • *With one bound the dog was over the fence.*

bounty REWARD /ˈbaʊnt·i/ *n* [C] a sum of money paid as a reward • *City officials offered a bounty for his capture.*

bounty LARGE AMOUNT /ˈbaʊnt·i/ *n* [C/U] a large amount of something, esp. food • *I was amazed by the bounty of our garden.* [C]

bountiful /ˈbaʊnt·ɪ·fəl/ *adj* (of a person) generous, or (of a thing) large in amount • *This field produced a bountiful supply of corn.*

bouquet FLOWERS /boʊˈkeɪ, buː-/ *n* [C] a group of flowers that have been attractively arranged so that they can be given as a present or carried on a formal occasion

bouquet SMELL /boʊˈkeɪ/ *n* [U] the smell of something, esp. wine • *a fruity bouquet*

bourbon /ˈbɜr·bən/ *n* [C/U] a type of WHISKEY (= strong alcoholic drink)

bourgeois /ˈbʊrʒ·wɑ, bʊrˈʒwɑ/ *adj esp. disapproving* belonging to or typical of the **middle class** (= a social group between the rich and the poor), esp. in supporting established customs and values or in having a strong interest in money and possessions • *She's become very bourgeois since she left college.*

bourgeoisie /ˌbʊrʒ·wɑˈziː/ *n* [U] *esp. disapproving* • *Hirsch's art is meant to shock the bourgeoisie.*

bout BRIEF PERIOD /baʊt/ *n* [C] a brief period of illness or involvement in an activity • *She had bouts of fever as a child.*

bout SPORTS /baʊt/ *n* [C] a boxing or WRESTLING match

boutique /buːˈtiːk/ *n* [C] a small store that sells fashionable clothes, shoes, jewelry, etc.

bovine /ˈboʊ·vɑɪn/ *adj* connected with cows, or like a cow because of being slow or stupid

bow BEND /baʊ/ *v* [I/T] to bend (the head or body) forward, esp. as a way of showing someone respect or expressing thanks to people who have been watching you perform • *We knelt and bowed our heads in prayer.* [T]

bow /baʊ/ *n* [C] • *The troupe's artistic director took a bow with his dancers at the final curtain last night.*

bow INSTRUMENT /boʊ/ *n* [C] a long, thin piece of wood with many hairs stretched between its ends, used to play musical instruments that have strings • *a violin bow*

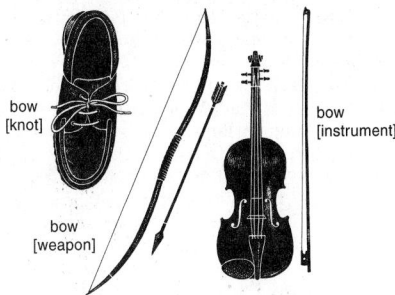

bow
[knot]

bow
[instrument]

bow
[weapon]

bow WEAPON /boʊ/ *n* [C] a weapon for shooting arrows, often used for sport, made of a long, narrow piece of wood bent into a curve by a string that is stretched tightly between its two ends

bow SHIP PART /baʊ/ *n* [C] the front part of a ship • Compare STERN SHIP PART.

bow KNOT /boʊ/ *n* [C] a knot with two curved parts and two loose ends, which is used as a decoration or to tie shoes • A **bow tie** is a special type of TIE (= strip of cloth put around a collar) that is knotted like a bow.

bow tie

□ **bow down** /baʊ ˈdaʊn·tə, -tʊ, -,tuː/ *v adv prep* [T] to obey completely • *He expects me to bow down to him, but I won't do it.*

□ **bow out** /ˈbaʊ·aʊt/ *v adv* [I] to give up something, or to decide not to do something you were considering doing • *He said he was bowing out of the race for senator.*

□ **bow to** /ˈbaʊ·tə, -tʊ, -,tuː/ *v prep* [T] to accept (something) unwillingly • *The company president finally bowed to pressure and resigned.*

bowels /ˈbaʊ·əlz, baʊlz/, **bowel** /ˈbaʊ·əl, baʊl/ *pl n* a long tube through which food travels while it is being digested after leaving the stomach; INTESTINES • (*fig.*) The bowels of something are the deepest parts of it: *Immigrants were generally confined to the bowels of the ship.* • A **bowel movement** is the excretion of solid waste from the body.

bowl DISH /boʊl/ *n* [C] a round container that is open at the top and is used esp. to hold liquids or other food, or the food it contains • *a salad/soup bowl* ○ *She eats a bowl of cereal every morning.* • A bowl is also the curved, inside part of something: *a toilet bowl* • A bowl is also a large, circular building used esp. for sports, or a special football game played in it after the regular season has ended: *the Rose Bowl*

bowl ROLL /boʊl/ *v* [I/T] to roll (a ball) along a smooth surface during a game, especially in the game of BOWLING. • *It's your turn to bowl.* [I] ○ *She bowled a strike.* [T]

bowling /ˈboʊ·lɪŋ/, **tenpins** *n* [U] a game in which you stand at one end of a long smooth surface and roll a heavy ball along it to try to knock down a group of ten wooden objects arranged in a triangle at the other end • A **bowling alley** is a long, smooth, narrow track along which you roll a ball during the game of bowling, or a building where this game is played. • A **bowling ball** is a heavy ball, usually with three holes that you put your fingers in to lift the ball and roll it in the game of bowling.

□ **bowl** *obj* **over** /ˈ-ˈ--/ *v adv* [T] to surprise and please (someone) greatly • *She was bowled over when her employer offered his entire staff to help her move to her new apartment.*

box CONTAINER /baks/ *n* [C] a container with stiff sides, shaped like a rectangle, or the contents of such a container • *a cardboard/cereal box* ○ *a box of chocolates* (= the container and its contents) • A box is also a small space on a form marked by lines in the shape of a square: *If you want to receive electronic updates, put a check in the box.* • A box is sometimes a small enclosed place: *the jury box* • A **box office** is a place in a theater where tickets are sold.

box /baks/ *v* [T] to put (something) in a box • *Someone from the nursing home must have boxed up his clothes.* [M] ○ (*fig.*) *My car was boxed in* (= blocked) *by two other cars, and I couldn't get out.* [M] • To **box** someone **in** is to limit their choices in a difficult situation: *Reagan appears to have boxed himself in, committed to military action or looking weak and foolish if he does nothing.*

box FIGHT /baks/ *v* [I/T] • See at BOXING.

boxcar /ˈbak·skar/ *n* [C] a railroad car with sliding doors and a roof, which is used to carry freight

boxer /ˈbak·sər/ *n* [C] a type of dog of medium size with short, light brown hair and a flat nose

boxer shorts /ˈbak·sər ˈʃɔːrts/ *pl n* loosely fitting men's underwear that covers the area between the waist and the tops of the legs

boxing /ˈbak·sɪŋ/ *n* [U] a sport in which two competitors fight by hitting each other with their closed hands • **Boxing gloves** are a pair of large, thick, hand coverings that are worn for protection in the sport of boxing. • A **boxing ring** is a square area surrounded by ropes, within which fighters compete in the sport of boxing.

box /baks/ *v* [I/T] to fight (someone) or be active in the sport of boxing • *I'd like to box him, and there's a chance that we will box again in Germany.* [I/T]

boxer /ˈbak·sər/ *n* [C] • *an amateur boxer*

boy /bɔɪ/ *n* [C] a male child or, more generally, a male of any age • *Some boys were playing basketball in the schoolyard.* • Boy sometimes means son: *We have two children—a boy and a girl.* • **(Oh) boy!** is an exclamation that is used to express excitement or to say something with emphasis: *Boy, that was good!* • The **Boy Scouts** is an organization for boys that encourages them to take part in activities outside and to become responsible and independent. A **Boy Scout** is a member of this organization.

boyhood /ˈbɔɪ·hʊd/ *n* [U] • *Much of his boyhood* (= the time when he was a boy) *was spent in Europe.*

boyish /ˈbɔɪ·ɪʃ/ *adj* like a boy • *She found his boyish good looks very attractive.*

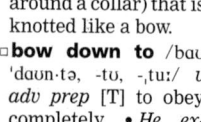

boycott /'bɔɪ·kɑt/ v [T] to refuse to buy (a product) or take part in (an activity) as a way of expressing strong disapproval • *The union called on its members to boycott the meeting.*
boycott /'bɔɪ·kɑt/ n [C] • *She organized an economic boycott of the company's products.*
boyfriend /'bɔɪ·frend/ n [C] a man or boy with whom a person is having a romantic or sexual relationship • Compare GIRLFRIEND.
bozo /'bou·zou/ n [C] pl **bozos** slang a foolish or careless person • *Some bozo on a motorcycle almost ran me over just now.*
bra /brɑ/, **brassiere** n [C] a piece of woman's underwear that supports the breasts
brace PREPARE /breɪs/ v [T] to prepare (yourself) physically or mentally for something unpleasant • *The weather forecasters told us to brace ourselves for a heavy storm.*
brace SUPPORT /breɪs/ n [C] something that supports, fastens, or strengthens • *He was recently fitted with a brace for his bad back.*
brace /breɪs/ v [T] • *She braced herself against the dresser.*
braces /'breɪ·səz/ pl n a set of wires attached to a person's teeth to move them gradually in order to straighten them • (*esp. Br*) Braces are also SUSPENDERS.
bracelet /'breɪ·slət/ n [C] a piece of jewelry that is worn around the wrist or arm • *a silver bracelet*
bracket SYMBOL /'bræk·ət/ n [C usually pl] either of a pair of marks [], or the information inside them, used in a piece of writing to show that what is inside these marks should be considered as separate from the main part • LP PARENTHESES
bracket /'bræk·ət/ v [T] to enclose (something) in brackets • *Deleted text is bracketed.*
bracket GROUP /'bræk·ət/ n [C] a set group with fixed upper and lower limits • *Most college students are in the 18 to 22 age bracket.* ○ *Her new job puts her in a higher income/tax bracket.*
bracket /'bræk·ət/ v [T] to consider (something) as similar to or connected to something else • *The mayor likes to bracket having more cops with the lower crime rate.*

bracket

bracket SUPPORT /'bræk·ət/ n [C] a metal or wood piece, usually L-shaped, whose vertical part is fastened to a wall and whose horizontal part is used to support something, such as a shelf
brackish /'bræk·ɪʃ/ adj (of water) slightly

salty • *As a river approaches the sea, its water becomes brackish.*
brag /bræg/ v [I] **-gg-** to speak with pride, often with too much pride, about something you have done or something you possess • *He bragged about robbing people when he was a boy.* ○ *The government has been bragging about the good economy.*
braid HAIR /breɪd/ v [I/T] to join three or more lengths of (hair or other material) by putting them over each other in a special pattern • *My sister taught me how to braid (my hair).* [I/T]
braid /breɪd/ n [C] • *Andrea wears her hair in braids.*
braid CLOTH /breɪd/ n [U] a thin strip of cloth or twisted threads used as decoration esp. in uniforms • *gold braid*

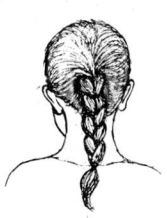

braid

Braille /breɪl/ n [U] a system of printing for blind people in which each letter is represented as a raised pattern that can be read by touching it with the fingers
brain /breɪn/ n [C] the organ inside the head that controls thought, memory, feelings, and physical activity • *a brain tumor* ○ *brain surgery* ○ *They found fractured ribs, other bone injuries, and brain damage.* • (*infml*) A brain is also a very intelligent person: *We've got the best brains in the country working on this problem.* • A **brain drain** is the loss of many highly skilled and educated people from one country to another country, usually because the pay and living conditions are better.
brainless /'breɪn·ləs/ adj stupid or thoughtless • *That was a brainless thing to do!*
brains /breɪnz/ pl n intelligence • *An individual who has brains and foresight can make a lot of money in this business.*
brains /breɪnz/ n [U] the most intelligent person in a group or the one who plans what a group will do • *He was the brains behind the biggest art theft in recent times.*
brainy /'breɪ·ni/ adj infml intelligent • *Sarah was beautiful and brainy.*
brainchild /'breɪn·tʃaɪld/ n [U] something originally invented or thought of by someone • *The encyclopedia was the brainchild of historian John C. McCormick.*
brainstorm SUGGEST IDEAS /'breɪn·stɔːrm/ v [I/T] to suggest a lot of ideas for (a future activity) very quickly before considering some of them more carefully • *They brainstormed and mapped plans for dealing with problems like affordable housing and the budget shortfall.* [I]
brainstorming /'breɪn,stɔːr·mɪŋ/ n [U] • *We need to do some brainstorming before we get down to detailed planning.*
brainstorm NEW IDEA /'breɪn·stɔːrm/ n [C]

infml a sudden, new idea that you are enthusiastic about • *They got this brainstorm that they could make a living by buying and selling antiques.*

brainwash /'breɪn·wɑʃ, -wɔːʃ/ v [T] to make (someone) believe only what you want them to believe by continually telling them that it is true and preventing any other information from reaching them • *A California woman charged that her teenage daughter was brainwashed and held against her will by the religious group.*

brake /breɪk/ n [C] a device that slows or stops the movement of a vehicle • *anti-lock brakes* ○ *He saw a deer crossing the road and hit/ slammed on the brakes* (= stopped as quickly as possible).

brake /breɪk/ v [I] • *When it's icy, you have to brake gently.*

bramble /'bræm·bəl/ n [C/U] a bush with THORNS (= sharp pointed growths)

bran /bræn/ n [U] the outer covering of grain that is separated when making white flour and is valued as a food for its FIBER • *We had bran muffins for breakfast.*

branch TREE PART /bræntʃ/ n [C] one of the parts of a tree that grows out from the main trunk and has leaves, flowers, or fruit on it • *After the storm, the ground was covered with twigs and branches.* ○ (*fig.*) *This branch of the river* (= lesser part that joins the main flow) *eventually empties into the Atlantic Ocean.*

branch /bræntʃ/ v [I] • (*fig.*) *We drove down a narrow track that branched off from the main road* (= started from it and went in a different direction).

branch PART /bræntʃ/ n [C] a part of something larger • *A branch is one of the offices or groups that form part of a large business organization: a local branch of the bank* ○ *Pediatrics is a branch of medicine* (= a subject that is part of a larger subject).

□ **branch out** /'-'-/ v adv [I] to do something that is related to what you have done in the past but takes you in a new direction • *The clothing manufacturer recently branched out into children's wear.*

brand PRODUCT /brænd/ n [C] a type of product made by a particular company • *This isn't my usual brand of deodorant.* • A **brand name** is the special name a company gives to its products or services: *All the car makers spend heavily to promote their brand names.*

brand JUDGE /brænd/ v [T] to consider or refer to (someone) as being or having done something bad • *They called Nixon "Tricky Dick" and branded him as a man without moral convictions.*

brand MARK /brænd/ v [T] to burn a mark on the skin of (esp. a cow) to show that you own it

brandish /'bræn·dɪʃ/ v [T] to wave (something) in the air in a threatening or excited way • *He brandished a gun and told everyone not to move.*

brand–new /'bræn'nuː/ adj [not gradable] completely new, esp. not used before • *It's a brand-new recipe, and I've never tried it before.*

brandy /'bræn·di/ n [C/U] a strong alcoholic drink, usually made from wine and sometimes flavored with fruit

brash /bræʃ/ adj [-er/-est only] having a lot of energy and the confidence to succeed, and not having much respect for others or worrying about their feelings • *His lawyer was brash, arrogant, and egocentric, but he usually won his cases.* • In fashion, brash can mean energetic and full of new ideas: *a designer known for his brash and innovative style*

brass METAL /bræs/ n [U] a bright yellow metal made from COPPER and ZINC • *brass lamps* ○ *brass door handles*

brass MUSICAL INSTRUMENTS /bræs/ adj [not gradable] (of a musical instrument) made of a metal tube bent into a particular shape and played by blowing • *The trumpet and the trombone are brass instruments.* ○ *He plays in the brass section of the orchestra.* • PIC) TROMBONE, TRUMPET

brass OFFICERS /bræs/ n [U] high-ranking officers in an organization, esp. the military • *The Pentagon brass went along with the plan but they were not happy about it.*

brassiere /brə'zɪr/ n [C] BRA

brassy /'bræs·i/ adj having complete confidence in yourself, sometimes in a way that shows a lack of respect • *She was a fearless journalist, bold and brassy and never afraid to ask the toughest questions.* ○ *The show's musical numbers are big, brassy* (= loud and showy), *and spectacular.*

brat /bræt/ n [C] *infml* a child who behaves badly or one you do not like • *My nephew is a little spoiled brat.*

bravado /brə'vɑd·oʊ/ n [U] a show of bravery, esp. when unnecessary and dangerous, to make people admire you

brave WITHOUT FEAR /breɪv/ adj [-er/-est only] showing no fear of dangerous or difficult things • *She liked to read stories of brave pioneer women who had crossed the country in covered wagons.* ○ *Of the three organizations criticized, only one was brave enough to face the press.*

brave /breɪv/ v [T] • *He braved the anger/ wrath of his father by quitting law school and becoming an artist.*

bravely /'breɪv·li/ adv • *"The pain isn't so bad," she said bravely.*

bravery /'breɪ·və·ri/ n [U] • *They were awarded medals for bravery.*

brave FIGHTER /breɪv/ n [C] *dated* a male Native American Indian WARRIOR (= fighter) • USAGE: This word is offensive when used to or about an American Indian by someone who is not an American Indian.

bravo /ˈbrɑv·oʊ, brɑˈvoʊ/ *exclamation* an expression used to show pleasure and admiration when someone, esp. a performer, has done something well

brawl /brɔ:l/ *n* [C] a physical fight involving a group of people, esp. in a public place • *A barroom brawl left the place a mess.*

brawn /brɔːn/ *n* [U] physical strength and big muscles • *It is a school where brains are respected much more than brawn.*

brawny /ˈbrɔː·ni/ *adj* • *He grabbed me with his brawny arms.*

bray /breɪ/ *v* [I] to make the loud sound that a DONKEY makes

brazen /ˈbreɪ·zən/ *adj* (of something bad) done without trying to hide it • *a brazen robbery in the downtown area*

breach BREAK /briːtʃ/ *n* [C] an act of breaking a rule, law, custom, or practice • *In a breach of security, unauthorized people were able to board the plane.*

breach OPENING /briːtʃ/ *n* [C] an opening in a wall or fence or in a line of military defense
breach /briːtʃ/ *v* [T] • *The river breached the dams.*

bread /bred/ *n* [C/U] a basic food made from flour, water, and YEAST mixed together and baked • *a slice/loaf of bread* [U] • (*slang*) Bread is also money. [U] • *Photography is my* **bread and butter** (= how I earn money to live on). • **Bread-and-butter** ideas or problems are the basic things that directly relate to most people: *Health and education are the sort of bread-and-butter issues that people vote on.*

breaded /ˈbred·əd/ *adj* [not gradable] (of food) covered with bits of dry bread before being cooked • *breaded chicken breasts*

breadth /bretθ, bredθ/ *n* [U] the distance from one side of an object to the opposite side, esp. when it is shorter than the distance between the object's other two sides • *The length of this box is twice its breadth.* • Breadth is also the range or areas of knowledge or ability that someone has: *The breadth of his knowledge of history was impressive.*

breadwinner /ˈbred·wɪn·ər/ *n* [C] the person in a family who works to provide the money that the family needs to live on • *She's always been the breadwinner for her family.*

break DAMAGE /breɪk/ *v* [I/T] *past simple* **broke** /broʊk/, *past part* **broken** /ˈbroʊ·kən/ to separate (something) suddenly or violently into two or more pieces, or to stop working by being damaged • *I broke a glass in the kitchen and have to vacuum it up.* [T] ◦ *Our toaster broke, so we have to get a new one.* [I] ◦ *The police broke the door down to get into the apartment.* [M] • If you break a part of your body, you damage a bone which cracks or separates into pieces: *The top women's downhill skier broke her leg in a freak collision.* [T] • If you break (a bill of a particular amount of money), you exchange it for smaller bills whose to-

tal equals the amount of your bill: *Can you break a \$50 bill for me?* [T] • *It* **breaks** *my* **heart** (= makes me sad) *to see him so unhappy.* • To **break** a game **open** is to score a lot of points so that your team is very likely to win: *In hockey, the Flyers broke the game open with five goals in the second period.* • To **break the ice** is to begin an activity to make people feel more comfortable: *Let's break the ice by having everyone give their name and say a few words about their job.* • The **breaking point** is the stage at which your control over yourself or over a situation is lost: *We've been working 18 hours a day and we are all at the breaking point.*

break /breɪk/ *n* [C] • *A break in a water main caused a whole section of the city to flood.* • A break in a bone is a place where it has cracked or separated into pieces.

break SEPARATE /breɪk/ *v* [I/T] *past simple* **broke** /broʊk/, *past part* **broken** /ˈbroʊ·kən/ to escape or separate from (something or someone) suddenly • *The dog broke free and ran into traffic.* [I always + adv/prep] ◦ *The handle on the teapot just broke off.* [I always + adv/prep]

break INTERRUPT /breɪk/ *v* [I/T] *past simple* **broke** /broʊk/, *past part* **broken** /ˈbroʊ·kən/ to interrupt or to stop (something) for a brief period • *Let's continue for another ten minutes and then break for lunch.* [I]

break /breɪk/ *n* [C] an interruption, esp. in a regular activity, or a short period of rest when food or drink is sometimes eaten • *a lunch/coffee break* ◦ *a break in the heat wave* • A break is also a time away from work or school, or a vacation: *I went skiing in the mountains during spring break* (= period in early spring when school classes temporarily stop).

break END /breɪk/ *v* [I/T] *past simple* **broke** /broʊk/, *past part* **broken** /ˈbroʊ·kən/ to end or change (something), or to stop • *Cheryl found the habit of drinking a lot of coffee hard to break.* [I] ◦ *She broke the record for the 5000 meters* (= she did better than the record). [T] ◦ *They worked hard to break the deadlock in the negotiations.* [T] • To **break even** is to earn enough money to pay for expenses, without any profit: *We'd have to sell 2000 copies of the book to break even.*

break NOT OBEY /breɪk/ *v* [T] *past simple* **broke** /broʊk/, *past part* **broken** /ˈbroʊ·kən/ to fail to obey or follow (a law, rule, or promise) • *He didn't know he was breaking the law.* ◦ *My daughter got sick and I had to break my appointment.*

break MAKE KNOWN /breɪk/ *v* [I/T] *past simple* **broke** /broʊk/, *past part* **broken** /ˈbroʊ·kən/ to become known or cause (something) to be known, esp. to the public • *The newspaper reporters who broke the story won the Pulitzer prize.* [T] ◦ *People wept when the news broke that the plant was closing for good.* [I]

break /breɪk/ n [U] • *We set out at the break of day* (= as the sun was rising).

break OPPORTUNITY /breɪk/ n [C] an opportunity for improving a situation, esp. one that happens unexpectedly • *Getting that first job was a lucky break.*

break MOVE /breɪk/ v [I] (of a wave moving toward land) to suddenly change from a rising curl of water, sometimes showing white, to a spreading layer that flattens out on reaching land

□**break down** STOP WORKING /'-'-/ v adv [I] to stop working or not be successful • *Our car broke down on the thruway.*

breakdown /'breɪk·daʊn/ n [C] • *There was evidently a breakdown in communication leading to the false report.*

□**break down** BECOME UPSET /'-'-/ v adv [I] to become very upset • *The victim's mother broke down and cried at the jury verdict.*

breakdown /'breɪk·daʊn/ n [C] the condition of suffering from extreme anxiety that prevents you from living and working as you usually do

□**break down** obj DIVIDE, **break** obj **down** /'-'-/ v adv [M] to divide (something) into smaller parts • *It's easier to handle the job if you break it down into several specific assignments.*

breakdown /'breɪk·daʊn/ n [C] • *We need a breakdown of the crime statistics into violent and nonviolent crimes.*

□**break in** obj TRAIN , **break** obj **in** /'-'-/ v adv [M] to train (a person) to do a new job, to train (an animal) to behave in an obedient way, or to use (something) to make it not as new and more comfortable • *We will have to break in three new staff members.* ○ *I'm still breaking in this new pair of running shoes.*

□**break in** ENTER ILLEGALLY /'-'-/ v adv [I] to enter a building illegally, usually by damaging a door or window, esp. for the purpose of stealing something • *Thieves broke into our office downtown and stole the computers.*

break-in /'breɪ·kɪn/ n [C] • *After the break-in, we installed a new security system.*

□**break into** BEGIN TO DO /'-,--/ v adv [T] to begin suddenly to do (something) • *He broke into a run, and we couldn't catch him.*

□**break into** USE FORCE /'-,--/ v adv [T] to force your way into (something) • *He's had his apartment broken into twice.*

□**break off** obj, **break** obj **off** /'-'-/ v prep [M] to end a relationship • *The governments broke off diplomatic relations.* ○ *She returned the ring and they broke off their engagement.*

□**break out** BEGIN /'-'-/ v adv [I/T] to begin • *A fight almost broke out.* [I] ○ *Let's break out* (= open) *another bottle of wine.* [T]

□**break out** ESCAPE /'-'-/ v adv [I] to escape from a place or a situation • *Two inmates broke out of prison and are still at large.*

□**break out** SKIN CONDITION /'-'-/ v adv [I] to suddenly begin to have a RASH (= spots on the skin) • *Detergents make my hands break out.* ○ *I hate it when I break out in hives.*

□**break through** /'-'-/ v adv [I/T] to force a way through (something) • *High waves broke through the barrier beach.* [T]

□**break up** (obj) DIVIDE , **break** (obj) **up** /'-'-/ v adv [I/M] to divide (something) into smaller pieces or separate parts • *The company has been totally broken up.* [T] ○ *The ship broke up on the reef.* [I] ○ *We're breaking up our trip by stopping for a few days in Singapore.* [M]

breakup /'breɪ·kʌp/ n [U] • *The breakup of the oil tanker caused severe damage to animal and plant life.*

□**break up** (obj) END , **break** (obj) **up** /'-'-/ v adv [I/M] to end or cause to end • *The meeting didn't break up until about two a.m.* [I]

□**break up** (obj) END A RELATIONSHIP , **break** (obj) **up** /'-'-/ v adv [I/M] to end a personal or business relationship • *Their marriage broke up after six months.* [I]

breakup /'breɪ·kʌp/ n [C] • *the breakup of a marriage/business partnership*

□**break** obj **up** MAKE LAUGH /'-'-/ v adv [T] *infml* to cause (someone) to laugh a lot • *That show really broke me up.*

breakfast /'brek·fəst/ n [C/U] a meal eaten in the morning as the first meal of the day • *We had bacon and scrambled eggs for breakfast.* [U]

breakneck /'breɪk·nek/ adj carelessly fast and dangerous • *They were cycling along at breakneck speed.*

breakthrough /'breɪk·θruː/ n [C] an important discovery or development that helps to solve a problem • *The Polaroid camera was a technological breakthrough.*

breast OF A WOMAN /brest/ n [C] either of the two soft, rounded parts of a woman's chest that can produce milk after she has a baby • *If a woman* **breast-feeds** *a baby, she feeds it with milk from her breasts.*

breast OF A BIRD /brest/ n [C/U] the front part of a bird's body • *Would you prefer breast of chicken or a drumstick?* [U]

breaststroke /'bres·stroʊk/ n [U] a way of swimming in which both arms are moved together forward from your chest under the water and then pulled back toward either side

breath /breθ/ n [C/U] the air that you take into and let out of your lungs • *She drew/took a deep breath.* [C usually sing] ○ *He seemed a little out of breath* (= to be breathing too fast). [U] ○ *As he jumped in the pool, he held his breath* (= delayed releasing the air in his lungs). [C usually sing] • A **breath test** is a test in which the police ask a driver to blow into a special device to show whether they have drunk too much alcohol to be allowed to drive.

breathe /briːð/ v [I/T] to take (air) into the lungs and let it out again • *He was so choked up with emotion that it was hard to breathe.* [I] ○ *It was great to be outside again and breathe the fresh air.* [T] • To **breathe easier** is to be able to relax esp. after a difficult or dangerous event: *Our little boat found it rough going, and once we got back near the shore we all breathed a little easier.* • To **breathe life into** something is to bring new ideas and energy to it: *The new chef has breathed life into this once-great French restaurant.*

breathing /'briː·ðɪŋ/ *n* [U] • *Dora was asleep, and I listened to the sound of her deep breathing.*

breather /'briː·ðər/ *n* [C] a brief rest after a period of work • *Let's take a breather before we finish loading the truck.*

breathless /'breθ·ləs/ *adj* breathing too fast, and therefore unable to get enough air into your lungs to be comfortable • *She was breathless with excitement.*

breathtaking /'breθ,teɪ·kɪŋ/ *adj* extremely good, beautiful, or exciting • *The violin solo was breathtaking.*

breathtakingly /'breθ,teɪ·kɪŋ·li/ *adv* [not gradable] • *breathtakingly beautiful scenery*

breeches, britches /'brɪtʃ·əz/ *pl n* pants • *She pulled on her riding breeches and got into her boots.*

breed /briːd/ *n* [C] a particular type of animal or plant • *the different breeds of dogs* • A breed is also a type of person or thing: *Authentic blues singers are a dying breed* (= there are not many of them left).

breed *(obj)* /briːd/ *v* [I/T] *past* **bred** /bred/ to keep (animals or plants) for the purpose of producing young animals or plants, often for chosen qualities, or (of animals) to have sex and reproduce • *He bred hogs and cows and sold the meat and dairy products.* [T]

breeding /'briːd·ɪŋ/ *n* [U] • *(dated)* A person who has good breeding has been trained in their childhood to be polite and behave correctly. • A **breeding ground** is a place or condition that produces or causes a lot of something, esp. something bad: *Poverty is a breeding ground for crime.*

breeze WIND /briːz/ *n* [C] a light wind • *He sat in the sun, enjoying the gentle sea breeze.*

breezy /'briː·zi/ *adj* • *It was a sunny, breezy day, just right for sailing.*

breeze WALK /briːz/ *v* [I always + adv/prep] *infml* to walk somewhere quickly and confidently • *Twenty minutes into the lecture she just breezed in and took a seat in the front row.*

breezy /'briː·zi/ *adj* [-er/-est only] *infml* quick, informal, and confident • *She revolutionized fashion reporting with her breezy style.*

breeze SOMETHING EASY /briːz/ *n* [C usually sing] *infml* something that is easy to do • *The entrance exam turned out to be a breeze.*

breeze /briːz/ *v* [I always + adv/prep] *infml* to achieve something easily • *She breezed to victories in the 100 and 200 meters.* ○ *He breezed through four years of Latin.*

brethren /'breð·rən/ *pl n fml* (used as a form of address to members of an organization or religious group) brothers

brevity /'brev·əṭ·i/ *n* [U] the use of few words • *The essays were written with admirable brevity.* • Brevity can also mean a short time: *the brevity of life*

brew /bruː/ *v* [I/T] (of tea or coffee) to become stronger in taste in the container in which it is made, or to make (a hot drink or beer) • *This beer was brewed using traditional methods.* [T] • If something bad is brewing, it is about to start: *I felt that trouble was brewing.* [I]

brew /bruː/ *n* [C] beer or another drink made by brewing

brewery /'bruː·ə·ri/ *n* [C] a company that makes beer or a place where beer is made

bribe /braɪb/ *n* [C] the act of giving someone money or something else of value, often illegally, to persuade them to do something you want • *Congressmen have been accused of accepting bribes to pass bills favoring particular companies.*

bribe /braɪb/ *v* [T] • *He was accused of bribing a building inspector.*

bribery /'braɪ·bə·ri/ *n* [U] • *Charges of bribery and official corruption were made.*

bric–a–brac /'brɪk·ə,bræk/ *n* [U] small, decorative objects of various types and of no great value

brick /brɪk/ *n* [C] a rectangular block of hard material used for building walls and houses • A **brick wall** is something that prevents you from doing something that you want very much to do: *In their campaign to keep the football team from moving to another city, city officials found themselves up against a brick wall.* • A **bricklayer** is a person whose job is building walls or buildings using bricks.

bride /braɪd/ *n* [C] a woman who is about to get married or just got married • *The bride and groom wrote their own wedding vows.*

bridal /'braɪd·əl/ *adj* [not gradable] of a woman about to be married, or of a wedding • *a bridal gown*

bridegroom /'braɪd·gruːm, -grʊm/ *n* [C] a GROOM MAN

bridesmaid /'braɪdz·meɪd/ *n* [C] a girl or woman, usually not married, who takes part in a wedding and helps the woman who is getting married

bridge LARGE STRUCTURE /brɪdʒ/ *n* [C] a structure that is built over a river, road, or railroad to allow people and vehicles to cross from one side to the other • *We drove across the bridge from Brooklyn to Manhattan.* • PIC SUSPENSION BRIDGE

bridge /brɪdʒ/ *v* [T] • *The shopping complex bridges a highway.* • If a difference is bridged, it is made smaller: *Swing music bridged the gap between popular and classical music.*

bridge NOSE /brɪdʒ/ *n* [C usually sing] the top part of the nose, between the eyes, or the piece on a pair of glasses that is supported by the

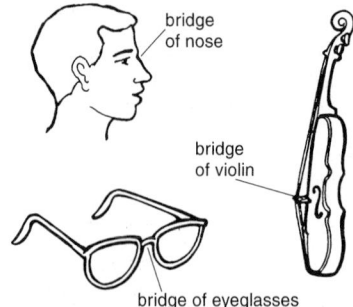

bridge
of nose

bridge
of violin

bridge of eyeglasses

top part of the nose • *He rubbed the bridge of his nose.*

bridge MUSICAL INSTRUMENT /brɪdʒ/ *n* [C] a small piece of wood on a musical instrument, such as a guitar or VIOLIN, over which strings are stretched

bridge TEETH /brɪdʒ/, **bridgework** /'brɪdʒ·wɜrk/ *n* [C] a piece of material that keeps artificial teeth in place by being fastened to the natural teeth

bridge PART OF A SHIP /brɪdʒ/ *n* [C] the raised part of a ship on which the CAPTAIN and other officers stand and from where they control the movement of the ship

bridge GAME /brɪdʒ/ *n* [U] a card game for four players who form two partnerships and try to win the cards they say they will win

bridle LEATHER STRAPS /'braɪd·əl/ *n* [C] a set of leather straps that are put around a horse's head to allow its rider to control it

bridle SHOW ANGER /'braɪd·əl/ *v* [I] to show annoyance or anger • *Homeowners bridled at the new regulations.*

brief SHORT IN TIME /briːf/ *adj* [-er/-est only] lasting only a short time or containing few words • *Rory had a brief career as an actor.*

briefly /'briː·fli/ *adv* for a short time or using few words • *We chatted briefly about the weather.*

brief GIVE INSTRUCTIONS /briːf/ *v* [T] to give (someone) instructions or information about what they should do or say • *We were briefed on what the plans.* • Compare DEBRIEF.

briefing /'briː·fɪŋ/ *n* [C] information that is given to someone just before they do something, or a meeting where information is given • *He discussed the report at a White House briefing on Tuesday.*

briefcase /'briːf·keɪs/ *n* [C] a usually flat, rectangular container, used esp. for carrying business papers • PIC ATTACHÉ CASE

briefs /briːfs/ *pl n* underwear worn by men and women which covers the area between the waist and the tops of the legs

brigade /brɪ'ɡeɪd/ *n* [C] one of the groups into which an army is divided, consisting of two or more BATTALIONS, or a group of people who are organized to perform a particular job • *A*

brigade of volunteers campaigned for his election.*

bright LIGHT /braɪt/ *adj* [-er/-est only] full of light, or shining • *the bright lights of downtown*

brighten /'braɪt·ən/ *v* [I/T] • *The lights dimmed, then brightened.* [I] ○ *Betty painted the room white to brighten it up.* [M]

brights /braɪts/ *pl n* a car's **headlights** (= the powerful lights at the front) when they are on full power

brightly /'braɪt·li/ *adv* • *a brightly lit room*

brightness /'braɪt·nəs/ *n* [U] • *The brightness of the summer day made him blink.*

bright COLOR /braɪt/ *adj* [-er/-est only] strong in color • *a bright green hat*

brightly /'braɪt·li/ *adv* • *brightly colored dresses*

bright INTELLIGENT /braɪt/ *adj* [-er/-est only] (of a person) intelligent and quick to learn • *He's a bright, well-organized guy.* ○ *She was full of bright ideas.*

bright HAPPY /braɪt/ *adj* full of hope or happiness • *He has a bright future ahead of him.*
• The **bright side** of a bad situation is its good characteristics: *Look on the bright side—you can do what you like without him.*

brighten /'braɪt·ən/ *v* [I/T] • *Her presence brightens my days.* [T] ○ *Anna's face brightened at the thought of Christmas.* [I]

brightly /'braɪt·li/ *adv* • *"I'm leaving," Consuela said brightly.*

brilliant INTELLIGENT /'brɪl·jənt/ *adj* extremely intelligent or highly skilled • *a brilliant plan* ○ *Armstrong was one of the most brilliant musicians in jazz.*

brilliantly /'brɪl·jənt·li/ *adv* • *Randy runs his company brilliantly.*

brilliance /'brɪl·jəns/ *n* [U] • *Few people want to hear about your child's brilliance.*

brilliant SHINING /'brɪl·jənt/ *adj* full of light, shining, or bright in color • *The sky was a brilliant blue.*

brilliance /'brɪl·jəns/ *n* [U] • *the sun's brilliance*

brim TOP /brɪm/ *n* [C] the very top edge of a container • *He filled his cup to the brim.*

brim /brɪm/ *v* [I] **-mm-** to fill or be full to the top • *Her eyes brimmed with tears.* ○ *(fig.) She's brimming with confidence.*

brim PART OF HAT /brɪm/ *n* [C usually sing] the bottom part of a hat that sticks out • *He pulled the brim of his hat down over his eyes.* • Compare CROWN TOP PART.

brine /braɪn/ *n* [U] water with salt in it

bring TAKE /brɪŋ/ *v* [T] *past* **brought** /brɔːt/ to take or carry (someone or something) to a place or a person, or in the direction of the person speaking • *Bring me that knife/Bring that knife to me.* ○ *I brought my daughter to the office.* ○ *Next time you come, bring your boyfriend along.* [M] ○ *It started raining, so I*

brittle

brought in the laundry. [M] ○ *This broadcast was brought to you* (= paid for) *by Burger King.*

bring CAUSE /brɪŋ/ *v* [T] *past* **brought** /brɔːt/ to cause, result in, or produce (a state) • *The rain brought some relief from this heat.* ○ *The explosion brought the building crashing to the ground.* ○ *What brings you here?* ○ *Prosecutors brought charges against the program's director.* ○ *Funding cuts brought an end to the project.* ○ *Wicks brought her to the attention of a movie producer.* • *Her research has* **brought to light** *new information about Jefferson's early life* (= caused it to be known). • *That music* **brings to mind** *our first date* (= makes me remember it).

bring FORCE /brɪŋ/ *v* [T] *past* **brought** /brɔːt/ to make (yourself) do something that you do not want to do • *I couldn't bring myself to disappoint her.*

□ **bring about** *obj*, **bring** *obj* **about** /'--'-/ *v adv* [M] to cause (something) to happen • *Harold's working to bring about changes in the industry.*

□ **bring** *obj* **around** PERSUADE /'--'-/ *v adv* [T] to persuade (someone) to have the same opinion as you have • *She tried to bring them around to accepting a settlement.*

□ **bring** *obj* **around** MAKE CONSCIOUS /'--'-/ *v adv* [T] to make (someone) become conscious again after being unconscious • *Medics tried to bring him around.*

□ **bring back** *obj* DO AGAIN, **bring** *obj* **back** /'-'-/ *v adv* [M] to cause (something) to come into use or popularity again • *He's planning to bring back disco music.*

□ **bring back** *obj* THINK OF AGAIN, **bring** *obj* **back** /'-'-/ *v adv* [M] to cause (something) to be thought of • *That music always brings back happy memories.*

□ **bring down** *obj* MAKE POWERLESS, **bring** *obj* **down** /'-'-/ *v adv* [M] to cause (someone) to lose power • *An economic crisis could bring down the government.*

□ **bring down** *obj* MAKE LESS, **bring** *obj* **down** /'-'-/ *v adv* [M] to cause (something) to become less • *Drugs can bring your blood pressure down.*

□ **bring forth** /'-'-/ *v adv* [T] to cause (something) to happen or be seen or known • *Maddie brought forth a new line of clothes.*

□ **bring forward** *obj*, **bring** *obj* **forward** /'-'--/ *v adv* [M] to make (something) known • *Several accusations have been brought forward.*

□ **bring in** *obj*, **bring** *obj* **in** /'-'-, '--/ *v prep* [M] to earn (money) • *She brings in about $600 a week.*

□ **bring off** *obj*, **bring** *obj* **off** /'-'-/ *v adv* [M] to succeed in doing (something difficult) • *Terry brought off the presentation without a hitch.*

□ **bring on** *obj*, **bring** *obj* **on** /'-'-, '--/ *v prep* [M] to cause (esp. something bad) to happen • *I think the loud music brought my headache on.*

□ **bring out** *obj* PRODUCE A QUALITY, **bring** *obj* **out** /'-'-/ [M] to produce (a particular quality) • *Sometimes a crisis brings out the best in people.* ○ *The right lighting can bring out the beauty in a room.*

□ **bring out** *obj* PRODUCE FOR SALE, **bring** *obj* **out** /'-'-/ [M] to produce (something) for people to buy • *They're bringing out a more powerful laptop computer in the fall.*

□ **bring up** *obj* RAISE A CHILD, **bring** *obj* **up** /'-'-/ *v adv* [M] to care for (a child) until it is an adult • *An aunt brought him up.* ○ *He was brought up on jazz* (= experienced it a lot as a child).

□ **bring up** *obj* TALK ABOUT, **bring** *obj* **up** /'-'-/ *v adv* [M] to talk about (something) • *I hate to bring up business at lunch.*

brink /brɪŋk/ *n* [U] the edge of a cliff or other high area, or the point at which something good or bad will happen • *War brought the region to the brink of famine.*

briquette, **briquet** /brɪˈket/ *n* [C] a small block made from coal dust or CHARCOAL, used as fuel in a fire

brisk /brɪsk/ *adj* [-er/-est only] quick, energetic, and active • *I took a brisk walk.* ○ *Business has been brisk lately.* ○ *A brisk* (= cold but pleasant) *wind blew across the field.*

briskly /'brɪs·kli/ *adv* • *She moved briskly toward the car.*

bristle /'brɪs·əl/ *n* [C/U] a short, stiff hair • *The old brush had lost most of its bristles.* [C usually pl]

bristle /'brɪs·əl/ *v* [I] (of hairs) to stand up because of fear or anger, or (of people) to show anger • *The cat's fur bristled.* ○ *She bristles at injustice.*

bristly /'brɪs·li/ *adj* • *a bristly chin*

britches /'brɪtʃ·əz/ *pl n* BREECHES

British /'brɪt̬·ɪʃ/ *adj* of or coming from the United Kingdom of Great Britain and Northern Ireland • **British English** is the English language as it spoken and written in England.

British /'brɪt̬·ɪʃ/ *pl n* people from Great Britain

Briton /'brɪt̬·ən/ *n* [C] a person from Great Britain

brittle /'brɪt̬·əl/ *adj* delicate and easily broken • *As you get older your bones become increasingly brittle.*

AMERICAN ENGLISH AND BRITISH ENGLISH PRONUNCIATIONS

Differences in the sounds

Some vowels and consonants are usually pronounced differently in British and American English, as shown in the following chart.

CONTINUED)

	American English	*British English*
go	/goʊ/	/gəʊ/
caught	/kɔːt, kɑt/	/kɔːt/
cot	/kɑt/	/kɒt/
cloth	/klɔːθ/	/klɒθ/
foreign	/ˈfɔːrən, ˈfɑrən/	/ˈfɒrən/
duty	/ˈduːti̬/	/ˈdjuːti/
farther	/ˈfɑrðər/	/ˈfɑːðə/

*Some American speakers also drop the /r/ sound before another consonant and at the end of a word.

/æ/ and /ɑː/: A number of words with the vowel /æ/ in American English have the vowel /ɑː/ in British English, as in **class**: American /klæs/, British /klɑːs/. This difference is found in such words as *advantage, answer, ask, banana, basket, bath, brass, broadcast, cast, caste, chance, chant, circumstance, command, craft, dance, demand, disaster, draft, enchant, epitaph, example, grasp, last, master, pass, past, path, plant, raft, rascal, slant, staff, task, trance,* and *vast.*

Stress: In many words of more than three syllables, American speakers have secondary stress (= stress that is not as strong as the main stress of a word) and British speakers have no stress, as in:

secretary	American /ˈsekrəˌteri/	British /ˈsekrətri/
dictionary	American /ˈdɪkʃəˌneri/	British /ˈdɪkʃənəri/.

Similar differences can be heard in such words as *category, ceremony, commentary, contemporary, explanatory, sedentary, transitory,* and *visionary.*

Other differences between American and British ways of saying some words are listed below.

	American English	*British English*
accent	/ˈæksent/	/ˈæksənt/
comrade	/ˈkamræd/	/ˈkɒmreɪd/
controversy	/ˈkantrəˌvɜrsi/	/ˈkɒntrəvɜːsi, kənˈtrɒvəsi/
derby	/ˈdɜrbi/	/ˈdɑːbi/
figure	/ˈfɪgjər/	/ˈfɪgjə/
garage	/gəˈraʒ, gəˈradʒ/	/ˈgæraːʒ, ˈgærɪdʒ/
herb	/ɜrb/	/hɜːb/
laboratory	/ˈlæbrəˌtɔːri, -ˌtoʊri /	/ləˈbɒrətri/
lieutenant	/luːˈtenənt/	/lefˈtenənt/
missile	/ˈmɪsəl/	/ˈmɪsaɪl/
patriot	/ˈpeɪtriːət, -ˌɑt/	/ˈpætriːət/
privacy	/ˈpraɪvəsi/	/ˈprɪvəsi/
schedule	/ˈskedʒuːl, -əl/	/ˈʃedjuːl, ˈskedjuːl/
solder	/ˈsadər/	/ˈsoʊldə/
tomato	/təˈmeɪtoʊ, -maːt̬-/	/təˈmaːtəʊ/
z	/ziː/	/zed/
zebra	/ˈziːbrə/	/ˈzebrə/
zenith	/ˈziːnəθ/	/ˈzenɪθ/

broach /broʊtʃ/ *v* [T] to begin a discussion of (something difficult) • *How do you broach the topic of death?*

broad WIDE /brɔːd/ *adj* [*-er/-est* only] very wide • *He flashed a broad grin at us.* • If something happens **in broad daylight**, it happens when everyone can see it: *He was attacked in broad daylight.* • If you are **broad-minded**, you accept behavior or beliefs that are different from your own.

broaden /ˈbrɔːd·ən/ *v* [I/T] to become wider, or to cause (something) to be wider • *They are broadening the road to speed up the flow of traffic.* [T]

broad GENERAL /brɔːd/ *adj* including many types of things; general • *The magazine covers a broad range of subjects.* ◦ *He explained it in very broad terms.*

broaden /ˈbrɔːd·ən/ *v* [T] to increase the range of (something) • *Going to college will broaden your interests.*

broadly /ˈbrɔːd·li/ *adv* • *Broadly speaking, don't you think women are better drivers than men?*

broad WOMAN /brɔːd/ *n* [C] rude slang a woman • *I hate that broad.*

broadcast /ˈbrɔːd·kæst/ *v past* **broadcast** or

broadcasted to send out sound or pictures that are carried over distances using radio waves • *The game will be broadcast live on ESPN.* [T] ○ (*fig. infml*) Please don't broadcast (= tell everyone) that I'm having an operation. [T]

broadcast /'brɔːd·kæst/ *n* [C] • *a television broadcast*

broadcaster /'brɔːd,kæs·tər/ *n* [C] a person who presents discussions or information on radio or television, or the owner of a radio or television station

broadcasting /'brɔːd,kæs·tɪŋ/ *n* [U] • *He's looking for a job in broadcasting.*

broadside ATTACK /'brɔːd·saɪd/ *n* [C] a strong written or spoken attack • *Republicans launched another broadside at the president.*

broadside /'brɔːd·saɪd/ *adv* [not gradable] on or from the side • *Her car was struck broadside by a truck.*

Broadway /'brɔːd·weɪ/ *n* [U] a street in the entertainment section of New York City where there are many theaters, or the theater in this area • *a Broadway play/musical* ○ *Tyler hopes to be on Broadway one day* (= performing there).

brocade /broʊ'keɪd/ *n* [U] heavy, decorative cloth with a raised design often of gold or silver threads

broccoli /'brɑk·li/ *n* [U] a vegetable with a thick, green stem and a green, treelike top

brochure /broʊ'ʃʊr/ *n* [C] a type of small magazine that contains pictures and information on a product or a company • *travel brochures*

brogue /broʊg/ *n* [C usually sing] an Irish or Scottish way of speaking English • *She spoke with a soft brogue.*

broil /brɔɪl/ *v* [T] to cook (something) with the heat coming from directly above or below it • *Broil the steak for five minutes.*

broiler /'brɔɪ·lər/ *n* [C] a part of a stove in which food can be cooked directly under or over the heat • A broiler is also a young chicken.

broke BREAK /broʊk/ *past simple of* BREAK

broke POOR /broʊk/ *adj infml* without money • *I can't go to the movies—I'm flat broke.* ○ *Is Social Security going broke* (= changing to a condition in which it has no money)*?*

broken BREAK /'broʊ·kən/ *past participle of* BREAK

broken DAMAGED /'broʊ·kən/ *adj* [not gradable] damaged, or no longer able to work • *My camera is broken.* • If something is **broken-down**, it is in bad condition or does not work: *a broken-down car* • *When he left she was* **broken-hearted** (= extremely unhappy).

broken INTERRUPTED /'broʊ·kən/ *adj* interrupted or not continuous • *a broken line* ○ *He spoke very broken English.*

broken ENDED /'broʊ·kən/ *adj* [not gradable] destroyed or ended • *a broken engagement* ○

She comes from a broken home (= the parents no longer live together).

broken NOT KEPT /'broʊ·kən/ *adj* [not gradable] (of a law, rule, or promise) disobeyed or not kept • *a broken promise*

broker /'broʊ·kər/ *n* [C] a person who acts for or represents another in the buying and selling of shares in companies or protection against risk, or who arranges for the lending of money • *I told my broker to sell the stock.*

broker /'broʊ·kər/ *v* [T] • *He brokered a deal to buy the company.*

bronchitis /brɑŋ'kaɪt̬·əs/ *n* [U] an illness in which the air passages between the WINDPIPE (= tube in the throat) and the lungs become infected and swollen, resulting in coughing and difficulty in breathing

bronco /'brɑŋ·koʊ/ *n* [C] *pl* **broncos** a wild horse of the western US

bronze /brɑnz/ *n* [C/U] hard, bright brown metal made of COPPER and TIN, or a statue made of this metal • A **bronze medal** is a disk-shaped prize made of bronze or that is bronze in color and which is given to a person or team that is third in a competition. Compare **gold medal** at GOLD METAL; **silver medal** at SILVER METAL.

bronzed /brɑnzd/ *adj* covered in bronze, or brown esp. from having been in the sun • *bronzed baby shoes* ○ *bronzed skin*

brooch /broʊtʃ, bruːtʃ/ *n* [C] a small piece of jewelry with a pin at the back that is fastened to a woman's clothing

brood GROUP /bruːd/ *n* [C] a group of young birds all born at the same time, or (*infml*) a person's children • (*infml*) *I moved in with Annie and her brood.*

brood THINK /bruːd/ *v* [I] to think silently for a long time about things that make you sad, worried, or angry • *He brooded over the insult.*

brooding /'bruːd·ɪŋ/ *adj* • *Her films have a brooding atmosphere.*

brook STREAM /brʊk/ *n* [C] a small stream • *A brook runs past the house.*

brook ALLOW /brʊk/ *v* [T] to allow or accept (esp. difference of opinion or intention) • *She won't brook any criticism of her work.*

broom /bruːm, brʊm/ *n* [C] a brush with a long handle, used for cleaning the floor • *I use that broom to sweep the kitchen floor.* • A **broomstick** is a long handle of a broom, or an old-fashioned type of broom flown on by WITCHES in children's stories.

broth /brɔːθ/ *n* [U] *pl* **broths** /brɔːθs, brɔːðz/ a thin soup, often with vegetables or rice in it, usually made with the liquid in which meat bones have been boiled

brothel /'brɑθ·əl, 'brɔː·θəl/ *n* [C] a place where men go and pay to have sex with PROSTITUTES

brother MALE PERSON /'brʌð·ər/ *n* [C] a male who has the same parents as another person •

an older/younger brother • A brother is also a member of the same race, church, religious group, or organization: *a fraternity brother* • Brother may be used by a man to address another man: *Hey, brother, can you spare a quarter?* • PIC FAMILY TREE

brother-in-law /'brʌð·ə·rən,lɔɪ/ *n* [C] *pl* **brothers-in-law** /'brʌð·ər·zən,lɔɪ/ the husband of someone's sister, or the brother of their wife or husband, or the husband of the sister of their wife or husband • PIC FAMILY TREE

brotherly /'brʌð·ər·li/ *adj* like or characteristic of a brother • *brotherly advice*

brother EXCLAMATION /'brʌð·ər, 'brʌ'ðɚr/ *exclamation* used to express annoyance or surprise • *Oh, brother, are we in a mess now!*

brotherhood /'brʌð·ər,hʊd/ *n* [U] a feeling of shared interests and support among men, or more generally, among all humans • A brotherhood is also the membership of an organization of men, or the organization itself.

brought /brɔɪt/ *past simple and past participle of* BRING

brouhaha /'bruː,ha:,ha:/ *n* [U] a situation that causes upset, anger, or confusion • *There was a big brouhaha when the town council decided to close the park.*

brow /braʊ/ *n* [C] the FOREHEAD (= the face above the eyes) • *He wiped the sweat from his brow.* • A brow is also an **eyebrow**. See at EYE.

browbeat /'braʊ·biːt/ *v* [T] *past simple* **browbeat**, *past part* **browbeaten** /'braʊ,biːt·ən/ to ask (someone) or demand continually that they do something until they do it • *He objected that McDonald was browbeating the witness.*

brown /braʊn/ *adj* [-*er/-est* only], *n* [C/U] (of) the color of chocolate or earth • *a brown suit*
brown /braʊn/ *v* [T] • *First brown the meat and then cook it slowly.*

brownie /'braʊ·ni/ *n* [C] a small, square, chocolate cake, often containing nuts

Brownies /'braʊ·niːz/ *pl n* [U] the level of the **Girl Scouts** for girls 6 to 8 years old
Brownie /'braʊ·ni/ *n* [C] a member of the Brownies • (*humorous*) **Brownie points** are approval for something helpful you have done: *I earned some Brownie points for washing the car.*

brownstone /'braʊn·stoʊn/ *n* [C] a city house with its front built of a red-brown stone

browse /braʊz/ *v* [I/T] to look at or through (something) to see what is there • *I browsed in a bookstore until she showed up.* [I] ◦ *You can browse the library's computerized card catalog.* [T]

browser /'braʊ·zər/ *n* [C] a special type of computer program that lets you use the INTERNET

bruise /bruːz/ *n* [C] a place on a person's skin that is darker from bleeding under the skin,

usually from an injury • *My little boy fell off his bike and has a bad bruise on his shoulder.*
bruise /bruːz/ *v* [T] • *He crashed into a table and bruised his shin.*

brunch /brʌntʃ/ *n* [C] a meal sometimes eaten in the late morning that combines breakfast and lunch

brunette /bruː'net/ *n* [C] a white woman or girl with dark hair

brunt /brʌnt/ *n* • To **bear/carry/get the brunt** of something, esp. something unpleasant, is to suffer the main force of it: *He claimed that the middle class would bear the brunt of the tax increase.*

brush TOOL /brʌʃ/ *n* [C] any of various utensils consisting of hairs or fibers arranged in rows or grouped together, attached to a handle, and used for smoothing the hair, cleaning things, painting, etc. • *I need a better brush for my hair.* • Brush is often used as a combining form: *hairbrush* ◦ *toothbrush* ◦ *paintbrush*

brush

brush /brʌʃ/ *v* [T/M] to remove (something) using your hand or a brush, or to use a brush to improve the appearance of (something) • *She brushed her hair.* [T] ◦ *She brushed a strand of hair from her face.* [T] ◦ *The child fell off her bike, brushed herself off and got right back on.* [T] ◦ *He brushed the crumbs off his coat and got up.* [M] • To brush your teeth is to clean them using a small brush and **toothpaste.** [T]

brush TOUCH /brʌʃ/ *v* [I/T] to touch (something) lightly • *She brushed my arm with hers.* [T] ◦ *The cat brushed against my leg.* [I]
brush /brʌʃ/ *n* [C usually sing] • *He felt the brush of her hand on his.* • A brush with something or someone is a close and usually unpleasant meeting: *He had a few brushes with the authorities over smoking marijuana.*

brush BUSHES /brʌʃ/ *n* [U] low, dense bushes that grow on open land • *The river banks were covered with brush.*

▫ **brush aside** *obj*, **brush** *obj* **aside** /'--'-/ *v adv* [M] to refuse to consider (an opinion or request) as having any value or importance • *Duke brushed aside suggestions that his campaign was finished.*

□**brush off** *obj*, **brush** *obj* **off** /'-'-/ *v adv* [M] to refuse to listen to (someone), usually to end a discussion • *The committee chairman brushed her off when she tried to raise the issue.*

brushoff /'brʌʃ·ɔːf/ *n* [U] • *She called to complain but got the brushoff from the store manager.*

□**brush up on** /'-'-ˌ-/ *v adv prep* [T] to improve your knowledge of (something already learned but partly forgotten) • *You'd better brush up on your French before going to Paris.*

brusque /brʌsk/ *adj* quick and direct in manner or speech, and often not polite • *As the president's chief of staff, he offended many with his brusque manner.*

Brussels sprouts /ˌbrʌs·əl'sprɑʊts/ *pl n* a green vegetable like very small CABBAGES

brutal /'bruːt̬·ºl/ *adj* cruel and violent • *There were reports from the area of brutal beatings and murders.* • (*fig.*) Brutal can also mean unpleasant or difficult: *The weather was brutal—hot and humid.* • Brutal can also mean plain and direct, without worrying about anyone's feelings: *She spoke with brutal honesty about his behavior.*

brutally /'bruːt̬·ºl·i/ *adv* • *He was brutally beaten, his scalp laid open to the skull, and thrown in a cell without windows.*

brutality /bruː'tæl·ət̬·i/ *n* [C/U] an act or behavior that is cruel and violent • *He said that police brutality and bad discipline had led up to the riot.* [U]

brutalize /'bruːt̬·ºlˌɑɪz/ *v* [T] to act cruelly and violently toward (someone) • *His lawyer said Murphy had been brutalized by the cops.*

brute /bruːt/ *n* [C] a person who is offensive and rude, and often violent • *He's a brute who doesn't hesitate to batter Beth when she is slow doing what he wants.* • A brute is also a large, strong animal. • If something is done with **brute force**, it is done with a great amount of force: *They had to use brute force to knock down the door.*

B.S. *n* [C] *abbreviation for* Bachelor of Science (= a first college degree in a science) • LP ED-UCATION IN THE US

bubble /'bʌb·əl/ *n* [C] a ball of air in a liquid or on its surface, or in the air • *When water begins to boil, small bubbles form around the edge of the pot.* • **Bubble gum** is **chewing gum** that you can blow into the shape of a ball. See at CHEW.

bubble /'bʌb·əl/ *v* [I] • *The water in the pot began to bubble.* ○ (*fig.*) We were bubbling with excitement as we watched the Olympic flame being lit.

bubbly /'bʌb·li/ *adj* filled with bubbles • Bubbly also means very energetic and pleasant: *a bubbly personality*

□**bubble up** /'--'-/ *v adv* [I] to rise to the surface or become obvious • *She laughs, a tin-kling musical child's laugh, bubbling up out of her.* ○ *Racism keeps bubbling up.*

buck MONEY /bʌk/ *n* [C] *infml* a DOLLAR • *It cost me ten bucks.*

buck ANIMAL /bʌk/ *n* [C] a male deer • Compare DOE.

buck JUMP /bʌk/ *v* [I] (esp. of a horse) to jump into the air with the head down and the back arched • *The horse bucked every time he got in the saddle.*

buck OPPOSE /bʌk/ *v* [T] to oppose or refuse to go along with (something) • *As a designer, she bucked the trend and succeeded with her own original ideas.*

bucket /'bʌk·ət/ *n* [C] a container with an open top and a handle, or the amount such a container will hold • *a bucket of water*

buckets /'bʌk·əts/ *pl n infml* a great amount; a lot • *The rain came down in buckets.*

buckle FASTENER /'bʌk·əl/ *n* [C] a fastener for a belt • *a silver buckle*

buckle /'bʌk·əl/ *v* [I/T] • *Please buckle your seat belts.* [T]

buckle BEND /'bʌk·əl/ *v* [I/T] to bend or become uneven, often as a result of force, heat, or weakness • *After eight hours of hiking, our knees were beginning to buckle.* [I] • If someone buckles or buckles under, they give in to something, such as pressure or opposition: *The judge threatened her with jail, but she refused to buckle and would not say where she got the information.* [I]

□**buckle down** /'--'-/ *v adv* [I] to start working hard • *He'll have to buckle down if he expects to pass that course.*

□**buckle up** /'--'-/ *v adv* [I] to fasten your **seat belt** (= belt attached to a seat) • *I hope a lot more people will make it a habit to buckle up as soon as they get in their cars.*

bud /bʌd/ *n* [C] the part of a plant that develops into a flower or leaf

bud /bʌd/ *v* [I] **-dd-** • *In early spring the trees begin to bud.*

budding /'bʌd·ɪŋ/ *adj* growing or developing • *The high school jazz group included a number of budding musicians.*

Buddhism /'buːd,ɪz·əm, 'bʊd-/ *n* [U] a religion that originally comes from India and teaches that improvement of the spirit will bring an end to personal confusion and suffering

Buddhist /'buːd·əst, 'bʊd-/ *n* [C], *adj* [not gradable] (a follower) of or belonging to Buddhism • *Buddhist monasteries*

buddy /'bʌd·i/ *n* [C] *infml* a close friend • *We were great buddies and did many things together.*

budge /bʌdʒ/ *v* [I/T] to move or cause (someone or something) to move • *The demonstrators would not budge from the governor's office.* [I] ○ *We tried to open a window but couldn't budge any of them.* [T]

budget FINANCIAL PLAN /'bʌdʒ·ət/ *n* [C] a financial plan that lists expected expenses and income during a particular period • *Congress voted more funds for the defense budget.* • A balanced budget is a financial plan in which expenses are no greater than income.

budget /'bʌdʒ·ət/ *v* [I/T] to plan to spend (money) for a particular purpose • *They budgeted $6000 for property taxes this year.* [T] • To budget is also to plan how to use something of which you have a limited supply: *You will have to learn how to budget your time to get all your work done.* [T]

budget CHEAP /'bʌdʒ·ət/ *adj* [not gradable] low in price; cheap • *Budget airlines have forced major airlines to lower some of their prices.*

buff MAKE SHINE /bʌf/ *v* [T] to rub (a surface) with a soft material to make it shine • *First you apply the wax to the floor, let it dry, and then buff it.*

buff PERSON /bʌf/ *n* [C] *infml* a person who is very interested in a subject and knows a lot about it • *a history/movie buff*

buff NAKED /bʌf/ *n* [U] *infml* • If someone is **in the buff**, they have no clothes on: *He always slept in the buff.*

buffalo /'bʌf·ə,loʊ/ *n* [C] *pl* **buffaloes** or **buffalo** any of various large animals of the cattle family found in Africa, Asia, and North America • *The huge herds of buffalo on the Great Plains of the west were hunted almost to extinction.*

buffer /'bʌf·ər/ *n* [C] something that helps protect from harm • *Some people buy stocks as a buffer against inflation.* [C] • A **buffer zone** is an area between two other areas created to avoid threatening situations or to protect something: *There is a buffer zone between the wildlife sanctuary and the area where people live.*

buffet MEAL /bə'feɪ, bu:'feɪ/ *n* [C] a meal where people serve themselves food that is arranged on a table • *Will it be a buffet or a sit-down meal?*

buffet HIT /'bʌf·ət/ *v* [T] to hit (something or someone) repeatedly and, usually, hard • *Many fierce storms had buffeted the coast before, but this one was worse than usual.*

buffoon /bə'fuːn/ *n* [C] a person who does silly things, sometimes intentionally, that make other people laugh • *He was not the buffoon that people said he was.*

bug INSECT /bʌg/ *n* [C] an insect • *Some tiny white bugs had eaten the leaves of my house plants.* • A bug is also a small organism that causes an illness: *The flu bug is going around, and almost everyone is sick.*

buggy /'bʌg·i/ *adj* full of annoying bugs • *It's too buggy to eat outside this time of year.*

bug FAULT /bʌg/ *n* [C] a mistake or problem in the way something works • *He said they had*

eliminated all the bugs in the software, and we hoped this was true.

bug DEVICE /bʌg/ *n* [C] a small device that is easily hidden, used to record people's conversations without their knowledge

bug /bʌg/ *v* [T] **-gg-** • *She suspected that her phone had been bugged.*

bug ANNOY /bʌg/ *v* [T] **-gg-** *infml* to annoy, esp. repeatedly • *My lawyer is bugging me for stuff I just don't have.*

bug ENTHUSIASM /bʌg/ *n* [U] *infml* a strong enthusiasm for something • *When I was about 17, I was bitten by the acting bug and began to try out for parts.*

□ **bug out** /'-'-/ *v adv* [I] *slang* to leave suddenly, esp. to avoid something • *When we heard them begin to argue, we bugged out.*

bugle /'bjuː·gəl/ *n* [C] a small BRASS musical instrument, used esp. in the military, played by blowing into it

build MAKE /bɪld/ *v* [I/T] *past* **built** /bɪlt/ to make (a structure or something else) by putting materials together in a particular way • *Without a plan, you can't build a house.* [T] ○ *Some owls had built a nest in the chimney.* [T] ○ *We decided to build on high ground, above the river.* [I]

builder /'bɪl·dər/ *n* [C] • *There's a lot of pressure on real estate brokers and home builders to hold down costs.*

build DEVELOP /bɪld/ *v* [T] *past* **built** /bɪlt/ to develop (something) • *They were able to build a family business.* ○ *She was building a reputation as a designer.*

build BODY /bɪld/ *n* [C] the particular form of someone's body • *He was short, with a muscular build.*

□ **build in** /'-'-, -'-/ *v prep* [T] to include (something) in something being created • *You must build in some way to cancel this contract if things don't work out.* ○ *Software developers built in a privacy system.*

built-in /'bɪl·tɪn/ *adj* [not gradable] • *With this software, safeguards are built-in.*

□ **build** *obj* **into** *obj* /'-,-·-/ *v prep* [T] to include (something) when (something) is first created • *We have built new safety systems into the software design.*

□ **build up** *obj* INCREASE , **build** *obj* **up** /'-'-/ *v adv* [M] to cause (something) to increase or become greater • *She does exercises daily to build up her strength.* ○ *We tried to build his confidence up.*

buildup /'bɪl·dʌp/ *n* [C] • *The buildup of troops on the border was a worry.*

□ **build up** *obj* PRAISE , **build** *obj* **up** /'-'-/ *v adv* [M] to praise (someone or something), esp. to increase their popularity • *The ads built up the show, but it wasn't really that good.*

buildup /'bɪl·dʌp/ *n* [C] • *The circus always gets a big buildup when it comes to town.*

building /'bɪl·dɪŋ/ *n* [C/U] a structure with

walls and a roof, such as a house or factory, to give protection to people, animals, or things • *an apartment/office building* [C] ○ *Many buildings were badly damaged or destroyed by the earthquake.* [C] • Building is also the activity or business of putting together structures with walls and a roof. [U]

built BUILD /bɪlt/ *past simple and past participle of* BUILD • A structure that is **built-in** is made to be a permanent part of something: *Built-in bookcases lined the walls of the library.*

built BODY TYPE /bɪlt/ *adj* (of someone's body) having a particular body type, or (slang) being very attractive • *He was built like an athlete.*

bulb LIGHT /bʌlb/ *n* [C] a **light bulb**, see at LIGHT ENERGY • *The bulb burned out in the kitchen.*

bulb PLANT /bʌlb/ *n* [C] a ball-like root from which some plants grow • *Lilies and tulips grow from bulbs.*

bulge /bʌldʒ/ *v* [I] to stick out or be swollen • *The girl's cheek bulged with a wad of gum.* • If you say that someone's eyes bulge, you mean that their eyes are opened wide esp. because they are frightened, surprised, or excited.

bulge /bʌldʒ/ *n* [C] • *The bulge in his pocket showed where he kept his wallet.*

bulimia (nervosa) /bjuːˈliː·miː·ə (nərˈvoʊ·sə), -ˈlɪm·i:·ə/ *n* [U] *medical* a condition in which a person eats extremely large amounts of food in a short time and then vomits intentionally • *Bulimia is really an eating disorder, and it affects mostly females.* • Compare ANOREXIA (NERVOSA).

bulk /bʌlk/ *n* [U] something very large, or a large amount, not divided into smaller parts • *Tankers carry bulk shipments of oil.* • The bulk of something is the larger part of it: *He gave the bulk of his paintings to the museum.* • **In bulk** means in large amounts: *The relief organization buys food in bulk.*

bulky /ˈbʌl·ki/ *adj* • *She carried a very bulky package on the bus.*

bull ANIMAL /bʊl/ *n* [C] the male of various animals, such as cattle • *Our herd has two bulls and twenty cows.* • A **bullfight** is a traditional public entertainment in many Spanish-speaking countries where a person fights a bull, sometimes killing it with a long knife. A **bullfighter** is the person who fights the bull.

bull NONSENSE /bʊl/ *n* [U] *infml* nonsense or a lie; BULLSHIT • *Don't give me that bull about not getting my message.*

bulldog /ˈbʊl·dɔːg/ *n* [C] a type of dog that looks fierce, with a strong body, short legs, a flat nose, and a large, square face

bulldozer /ˈbʊl·doʊ·zər/ *n* [C] a heavy vehicle with a large blade in front used for moving and flattening the ground

bulldoze /ˈbʊl·doʊz/ *v* [T] • *Several homes will have to be bulldozed to make room for the highway expansion.*

bullet /ˈbʊl·ət/ *n* [C] a small, metal object that is fired from a gun • Something that is **bulletproof** prevents bullets from going through it: *The limo has bulletproof glass.*

bulletin /ˈbʊl·ət·ən, -ə·tən/ *n* [C] a short piece of news on television or radio, or a short report or news item released by an organization • *The museum publishes a monthly bulletin about coming events.* • A **bulletin board** is a board on a wall for putting up notices. • A **bulletin board system** (*abbreviation* BBS) is also a computer system that allows users to leave messages and see information.

bullhorn /ˈbʊl·hɔːrn/ *n* [C] an electric-powered, cone-shaped device that makes your voice louder when you speak into it

bullion /ˈbʊl·jən/ *n* [U] pure gold or silver formed into bars • *A shipment of gold bullion was stolen.*

bullish /ˈbʊl·ɪʃ/ *adj* (of markets and investments) with prices rising, or (of people) expecting good things, esp. of business • *She's bullish on high-tech companies.*

bull market /ˈbʊlˈmɑr·kət/ *n* [U] a period when financial investments are rising in value • Compare BEAR MARKET.

bullpen /ˈbʊl·pen/ *n* [C] (in baseball) a place near the playing area where PITCHERS can throw the ball to get ready to play in the game

bull's-eye /ˈbʊl·zaɪ/ *n* [C] the center inside a number of circles that you want to hit when shooting or playing particular games, or the shot or throw that hits this inner circle

bullshit /ˈbʊl·ʃɪt/ *n* [U], *exclamation rude slang* a lie or nonsense

bullshit /ˈbʊl·ʃɪt/ *v* [I/T] **-tt-** *rude slang* to tell lies to (someone), esp. with the intention of persuading them of something • *He bullshits all the time about how great he is.* [I]

bully /ˈbʊl·i/ *v* [T] to threaten to hurt (someone), often frightening them into doing something you want them to do • *He managed to bully her into giving her his car.*

bully /ˈbʊl·i/ *n* [C] • *Teachers usually know who the bullies are in a class.*

bum PERSON /bʌm/ *n* [C] *disapproving* a person who gets money by asking other people for it • (*infml*) A bum is also someone who treats other people badly: *What a bum—he left his wife when she was eight months pregnant!*

bum /bʌm/ *v* [T] **-mm-** to ask someone for (esp. money, food, or cigarettes) with no intention of paying for them • *Could I bum a cigarette from somebody?*

bum USELESS /bʌm/ *adj slang* useless or not to be trusted to perform well • *He's got a bum knee from playing football.* • (*slang*) A **bum rap** is a false or unfair accusation: *It's a bum rap to say we didn't try to win.* • (*slang*) A **bum**

steer is bad advice: *Someone gave us a bum steer to a hotel that was awful.*

bumblebee /ˈbʌm·bəlˌbiː/ *n* [C] a large, hairy bee

bumbling /ˈbʌm·blɪŋ/ *adj* confused, esp. in the way someone moves or speaks • *The players look like bumbling idiots on the field.*

bumblebee

bummer /ˈbʌm·ər/ *n* [C] *slang* a situation or event that is unpleasant or disappointing • *Waiting all day at the airport is a real bummer.*

bump RAISED AREA /bʌmp/ *n* [C] a raised area on a surface • *The mosquito bites left bumps on her face.*

bumpy /ˈbʌm·pi/ *adj* rough or uneven • *We drove along bumpy dirt roads for hours.*

bump HIT /bʌmp/ *v* [I/T] to hit against (something or someone), esp. by accident • *The child fell and bumped his head.* [T]

bump PUSH AWAY /bʌmp/ *v* [T] to move (someone or something) out of their place, esp. in order to take their place • *I knew if they got someone more qualified, I'd be bumped.*

□ **bump into** /ˌ-ˈ--/ *v prep* [T] to meet (someone) unexpectedly • *We bumped into Kayla in a shop.*

□ **bump off** *obj*, **bump** *obj* **off** /ˈ-ˈ-/ *v adv* [M] *slang* to kill (a person) • *They say the mob bumped him off.*

bumper VEHICLE PART /ˈbʌm·pər/ *n* [C] a bar at the front and back of the body of a motor vehicle that keeps it from being damaged when hit • *If traffic is **bumper to bumper**, there is almost no space from one car to the next.* • A **bumper sticker** is a small sign on a car bumper that expresses an opinion or tells a joke. • PIC CAR

bumper-to-bumper traffic

bumper LARGE /ˈbʌm·pər/ *adj* [not gradable] unusually large • *Farmers expect a bumper corn crop this year.*

bun BREAD /bʌn/ *n* [C] a small, round piece of bread, used for a sandwich, or a small, round, sweet bread • *Buy some hamburger buns for supper.* • PIC HAMBURGER

bun KNOT /bʌn/ *n* [C] hair arranged into a round knot at the back of the head

bunch /bʌntʃ/ *n* [C] a number of things of the same type fastened or closely grouped together, or any particular group of things or people • *We ate a whole bunch of grapes.* ○ *They're a nice bunch of people.* ○ (*infml*) *I've got a bunch of things to do.*

bunch /bʌntʃ/ *v* [I/T] to pull together or gath-

er into a unit • *Beth sat in bed with pillows bunched behind her, reading.* [I]

bundle GROUP /ˈbʌn·dəl/ *n* [C] a number of things that are fastened or held together • *He carried bundles of newspapers to the garage.* • (*infml*) A bundle is also a large amount of money: *When they sold their house, they made a bundle.* • If you are **a bundle of nerves**, you are extremely nervous: *Since the robbery, I've been a bundle of nerves.*

bundle /ˈbʌn·dəl/ *v* [T] • *We're supposed to bundle magazines before throwing them away.* [I/T] • To **bundle up** means to wear enough to keep very warm: *You'd better bundle up because it's below freezing outdoors.*

bundle MOVE QUICKLY /ˈbʌn·dəl/ *v* [always + adv/prep] to cause (someone) to move quickly • *We bundled into the car.* [I] ○ *Every morning I bundled the children off to school.* [T]

bungalow /ˈbʌŋ·gəˌloʊ/ *n* [C] a small house all on one level

bungle /ˈbʌŋ·gəl/ *v* [T] to do (something) badly, or spoil (something) • *The police bungled the investigation.*

bunion /ˈbʌn·jən/ *n* [C] a painful swelling on the main joint of the big toe

bunk BED /bʌŋk/ *n* [C] either of two beds arranged one above the other • *I had the lower bunk, and my older brother had the upper bunk.*

bunk NONSENSE /bʌŋk/ *n* [U] *infml* complete nonsense, or something that is meant to deceive • *Most doctors think his theories are bunk.*

bunks

bunker /ˈbʌŋ·kər/ *n* [C] an underground shelter used as protection from bombs

bunny (rabbit) /ˈbʌn·i (ˈræb·ət)/ *n* [C] a child's word for a rabbit

buns /bʌnz/ *pl n slang* the buttocks

buoy OBJECT IN WATER /ˈbuː·i, bɔɪ/ *n* [C] an object that floats on the water to show ships where it is safe to go

buoyancy /ˈbɔɪ·ən·si, ˈbuː·jən-/ *n* [U] the ability to float • *We tested different materials for buoyancy.*

buoy FEEL HAPPY /ˈbuː·i, bɔɪ/ *v* [T] to encourage or make (someone) feel better • *I was really buoyed by the nice comments on my work.*

buoyant /ˈbɔɪ·ənt, ˈbuː·jənt/ *adj* • *It was her wedding day, and she was in a buoyant mood.*

burden /ˈbɜrd·ən/ *n* [C] a duty or responsibility that is hard to bear • *I don't want to be a burden on my children.* • (*law*) The **burden of proof** is the responsibility for proving that something is true.

burden /ˈbɜrd·ən/ *v* [T] • *He was burdened with debts.*

bureau DEPARTMENT /ˈbjʊr·oʊ/ *n* [C] a department of government, or a division that performs a particular job • *You've got to go the Bureau of Motor Vehicles to renew your driver's license.*

bureau FURNITURE /ˈbjʊr·oʊ/ *n* [C] **a chest of drawers,** see at CHEST BOX

bureaucracy /bjʊˈrɑk·rə·si/ *n* [C/U] the officials, employees, and people who run government departments and offices, or similar officers and employees who manage the details of operating a large business • *The city's bureaucracy is almost unmanageable.* [C] • (*disapproving*) Bureaucracy is also official rules that make it difficult to do things: *The president wants to add more bureaucracy to our daily lives.* [U]

bureaucrat /ˈbjʊr·ə,kræt/ *n* [C] a member of a bureaucracy • *School administrators, she said, who are the on-the-spot bureaucrats, should make these decisions rather than Washington bureaucrats.*

bureaucratic /ˌbjʊr·əˈkræt̬·ɪk/ *adj* • *Bureaucratic bungling is the most likely explanation for things going wrong.*

burgeoning /ˈbɜr·dʒə·nɪŋ/ *adj* growing or developing quickly • *A burgeoning tourist industry lifted the state's economy.*

burger /ˈbɜr·gər/ *n* [C] *short form of* HAMBURGER • PIC HAMBURGER

burglar /ˈbɜr·glər/ *n* [C] a person who forces their way illegally into a building to steal things

burglarize /ˈbɜr·glə,rɑɪz/, *infml* **burgle** /ˈbɜr·gəl/ *v* [T] • *The doctor's office was burglarized and drugs were taken, according to police.*

burglary /ˈbɜr·glə·ri/ *n* [C/U] • *He committed more than dozen burglaries in the last year.* [C]

burial /ˈber·i:·əl/ *n* [C/U] the act of putting a dead body into the ground, or the ceremony performed when this is done • *We went back to Minnesota for my uncle's burial.* [C] • A **burial ground** is an area of land where bodies are buried. • USAGE: The related verb is BURY.

burlap /ˈbɜr·læp/ *n* [U] a type of strong, rough cloth, used to make bags and as a covering for something • *a burlap bag* ○ *Large plants are wrapped in burlap to protect them from ice.*

burly /ˈbɜr·li/ *adj* (of a person) large and strong • *Two burly men pushed the car to the side of the road.*

burn BE IN FLAMES /bɜrn/ *v* [I/T] *past* **burned** /bɜrnd, bɜrnt/ or **burnt** /bɜrnt/ to produce flames and heat • *A fire still burned in the fireplace.* [I] • If something burns a fuel, it uses that fuel to produce energy: *Some new fuels burn more efficiently than gasoline.* [I] ○ *Running is a good way to burn off calories.* [M]

burner /ˈbɜr·nər/ *n* [C] anything that produces controlled flames for cooking, or heat for a building

burning /ˈbɜr·nɪŋ/ *adj* [not gradable] hot, or flaming • *Fire engines surrounded the burning house.* • (*fig.*) Burning also means of extreme interest or importance: *Building the new school is a burning local issue.* ○ *You have to have a burning desire to win.* • See also BURNING.

burn HURT BY FIRE /bɜrn/ *v* [T] *past* **burned** /bɜrnd, bɜrnt/ or **burnt** /bɜrnt/ to hurt, damage, or destroy (something) by fire or extreme heat • *She burned her hand on the hot iron.* ○ *People still burn trash although it's illegal.* • (*infml*) If you are burned by an activity, you are hurt emotionally or financially because of it: *He got burned in an investment and lost a lot of money.* • If something is **burned to a crisp,** it is blackened and dried out: *The toast was burned to a crisp.*

burn /bɜrn/ *n* [C] • *One worker had severe burns on his face and hands.*

□**burn down** (*obj*), **burn** (*obj*) **down** /-ˈ-/ *v adv* [I/M] to destroy (something) with fire, to or be destroyed in this way • *They weren't injured, but their house burned down.* [I]

□**burn out** (*obj*) DAMAGE FROM HEAT , **burn** (*obj*) **out** /-ˈ-/ *v adv* [I/M] to stop (something) from working because of damage from heat • *When we lost power, many refrigerators and air conditioners burned out.* [I]

□**burn out** (*obj*) LOSE ENERGY , **burn** (*obj*) **out** /-ˈ-/ *v adv* [I/M] to cause (someone) to lose most of their energy and enthusiasm for their work because of having worked too hard for too long, or from stress • *They asked her to slow down because they don't want her to burn out.* [I]

burnout /ˈbɜr·nɑʊt/ *n* [U] • *He had a severe case of burnout from overwork.*

□**burn up** *obj* DESTROY , **burn** *obj* **up** /-ˈ-/ *v adv* [M] to destroy (something) with fire • *A huge fire burned up the church.*

□**burn up** *obj* ANGER , **burn** *obj* **up** /-ˈ-/ *v adv* [M] to make (someone) angry • *I was really burned up by her comment.*

burnt /bɜrnt/ *past simple and past participle of* BURN

burp /bɜrp/ *v* [I/T] to force air from the stomach to come out through the mouth with a noise; BELCH • If you burp a baby, you help it to get rid of air in its stomach by gently rubbing or gently hitting its back. [T]

burp /bɜrp/ *n* [C] • *The baby gave a contented burp.*

burrito /bəˈriːt̬·oʊ/ *n* [C] *pl* **burritos** a type of food originally from Mexico that is made by folding a TORTILLA (= thin, round piece of bread) and putting esp. meat or beans inside it

burrow /ˈbɜr·oʊ, ˈbʌ·roʊ/ *n* [C] a hole dug in the ground that an animal, such as a rabbit, lives in

burrow /'bɜr·oʊ, 'bʌ·roʊ/ v [I always + adv/ prep] • *Moles burrowed under our lawn.*

bursar /'bɜr·sər/ n [C] the person in a university or school who is responsible for its finances

burst /bɜrst/ v [I/T] *past* **burst** to break open or apart suddenly, or to cause (something) to break open or apart • *Fireworks burst across the night sky.* [I] ○ *I thought I might have burst a blood vessel.* [T] • (*fig.*) If a person is bursting, they are extremely eager or enthusiastic: *I was bursting with excitement.* [I] • If something is **bursting at the seams**, it is extremely full: *When everyone comes home, the house is bursting at the seams.*

burst /bɜrst/ n [C] a sudden, brief increase in something, or a short appearance of something • *With a burst of speed, the horse won easily.*

□ **burst in/into** /'-'-; '-'--/ v adv [T] to enter (a place) suddenly or unexpectedly • *He burst into the room and shouted orders at us.*

□ **burst into** /'-,--/ v adv [T] to begin to produce (something) • *I burst into tears.* ○ *The car burst into flames.*

□ **burst out** /'-,-/ v adv [T] to begin to do (something) • *She burst out sobbing.* ○ *Everyone burst out laughing.*

bury /'ber·i/ v [T] to put (a dead body) into the ground • *My father is buried in Kentucky.* • To bury something is also to put it into the ground: *Squirrels bury nuts and dig them up later to eat them.* • To bury something is also to hide it by covering it: *She buried her face in her hands.* ○ *The article was buried in the middle of the newspaper.* • If two people **bury the hatchet**, they agree to end the disagreement that has divided them. • USAGE: The related noun is BURIAL.

bus VEHICLE /bʌs/ n [C] a large motor vehicle with seats for many people • *The tour bus was the easiest way to see the area.*

bus /bʌs/ v [T] to take (people) to a place in a bus • *The governor bused supporters to the capital for his inauguration.*

bus SERVE /bʌs/ v [T] to move dishes to and from (tables) in a restaurant as a job • *I started out busing tables.*

busboy /'bʌs·bɔɪ/ n [C] a person who helps in a restaurant, esp. by carrying dishes, passing out bread, and filling water glasses

bush PLANT /bʊʃ/ n [C] a low plant with many small branches • *The smell of lilac bushes in bloom reminds me of home.* ○ *The meadow was covered with small bushes and grass.*

bush AREA OF LAND /bʊʃ/ n [U] (esp. in Australia and Africa) an area of land covered with bushes and trees that has never been cultivated and where few people live • *If you live in the bush, a small plane is the best means of transportation.*

bushed /bʊʃt/ adj infml very tired • *I mowed the lawn this morning, and now I'm bushed.*

bushel /'bʊʃ·əl/ n [C] a unit of measurement of volume of dry products equal to 32 quarts, or approximately 35.2 liters

bushy /'bʊʃ·i/ adj (of hair or fur) thick or full • *A lot of his face was hidden behind a bushy moustache.*

busily /'bɪz·ə·li/ adv • See at BUSY.

business BUYING AND SELLING /'bɪz·nəs, -nəz/ n [C/U] the activity of buying and selling goods and services, or a particular company that does this, or work in general rather than pleasure • *He runs a dry cleaning business.* [C] ○ *I'm in Baltimore on business.* [U] ○ *Our firm does a lot of business with overseas customers.* [U] ○ *She's going into business* (= starting a business) *as a management consultant.* [U] • Business is also the degree of success of a company or of your work: ○ *How's business?* [U] ○ *Business has been good.* [U] • *Once we get the computer installed we'll* **be in business** (= able to start doing what we planned). • **Business as usual** means that things are continuing in their usual way: *Today is a legal holiday, but it's business as usual around here.*

businessman (*pl* **-men**) /'bɪz·nəs·mən, -nəz-, -,mæn/, **businesswoman** (*pl* **-women**) /'bɪz·nəs ,wʊm·ən, -nəz-/ n [C] a person who works in business, esp. if they have a high position in a company

business A MATTER /'bɪz·nəs, -nəz/ n [U] a matter or a situation • *I have some business to settle with Mr. Redford.* ○ *Preparing your taxes can be a tricky business.*

business THINGS YOU DO /'bɪz·nəs, -nəz/ n [U] the things that you do or the matters that relate only to you • *What she does after work is her own business.* ○ *When I asked him what he was doing, he told me it was none of my business* (= it did not involve me).

businesslike /'bɪz·nəs,lɑɪk, -nəz-/ adj happening in a way that is practical and effective and is not personal, or typical of business • *We hope the meeting can be conducted in a businesslike way, without a lot of emotional statements.*

bust BREAK /bʌst/ v [I/T] infml to burst or break (something) • *He busted out laughing.* [I always + adv/prep] ○ *The cops had to bust the door down.* [M] • (*slang*) If a person is busted, they are caught by the police and accused of a crime, such as selling or using an illegal drug. [T] • (*rude slang*) If you **bust your ass**, you try very hard to do something: *I busted my ass to get an A in that course.*

bust /bʌst/ n [C] slang an occasion when people are caught by the police and accused of a crime, esp. selling or using an illegal drug • *a drug bust*

bust STATUE /bʌst/ n [C] a statue of the upper

part of a person's body • *a bust of George Washington*

bust BREASTS /bʌst/ *n* [C] a woman's breasts, or the measurement around a woman's body at the level of her breasts

bustle /'bʌs·əl/ *v* [I] to do things in a hurried and busy way • *Thomas bustled around the apartment, getting everything ready.*

bustle /'bʌs·əl/ *n* [U] busy activity • *the bustle of the downtown business district*

busy /'bɪz·i/ *adj* [-*er*/-*est* only] (of a person) actively involved in doing something or having a lot of things to do, or (of a time or place) when or where a lot of things are happening • *a busy street* ○ *the busy summer months* ○ *I've been so busy lately that I haven't had time to have any social life.* ○ *Getting the house ready for her relatives kept her busy the whole day.* • If a telephone is busy, it is being used by someone else: *Her line is still busy.* ○ *I keep getting a* **busy signal** (= repeating sound that means that the telephone is being used by someone else). LP TELEPHONE

busy /'bɪz·i/ *v* • If you **busy** your**self** doing something, you spend time doing it, esp. in order to avoid doing or thinking about something else: *The kids were busying themselves with pocket video games.*

busily /'bɪz·ə·li/ *adv*

busybody /'bɪz·iː,bɑd·i/ *n* [C] *disapproving* a person who is interested in things that do not involve them, esp. other people's private matters

but DIFFERENCE /bʌt, bət/ *conjunction* used to express a difference or to introduce an added statement • *You can take Route 14 to get there, but it may take you a little longer.* ○ *We enjoyed our vacation a lot, but it was expensive.*

buts /bʌts/ *pl n* an excuse or an argument against something • *No buts about it—you're going to school today.*

but EXCEPT /bʌt, bət/ *prep* except • *Nobody but John was willing to talk to her.* ○ *This car has been nothing but trouble—it's always breaking down!*

butcher /'bʊtʃ·ər/ *n* [C] a person whose job is to kill animals for meat or who prepares and sells meat in a store • A butcher is also a murderer, esp. of a lot of people.

butcher /'bʊtʃ·ər/ *v* [T] to kill animals and prepare them to be sold as meat • To butcher is also to kill people in a cruel way.

butler /'bʌt·lər/ *n* [C] the most important male servant in a house • *The British butler was brilliantly played by Anthony Hopkins.*

butt THICK END /bʌt/ *n* [C] the thick end of something, esp. a RIFLE (= type of gun)

butt CIGARETTE /bʌt/ *n* [C] the part of a cigarette that is left after smoking • *an ashtray full of cigarette butts*

butt BOTTOM /bʌt/ *n* [C] *slang* a person's bot-

tom • *She told him to get off his butt and do something useful.*

butt HIT /bʌt/ *v* [I/T] to hit (the head) hard against something, or to have (the heads of two people or animals) hit against each other • *(fig.) She often butted heads with school officials in disagreements over her teaching methods.* [T]

butt PERSON /bʌt/ *n* [C usually sing] a person who is joked about or laughed at • *He was fed up with being the butt of their jokes.*

□**butt in** /'-'-/ *v adv* [I] *infml* to interrupt • *Sorry to butt in on you like this, but there's an important call.*

□**butt out** /'-'-/ *v adv* [I] *slang* to be not involved with something • *This is none of your business, so just butt out!*

butter /'bʌt·ər/ *n* [U] a pale yellow, fatty solid made from cream that is spread on bread or used in cooking

□**butter up** *obj*, **butter** *obj* **up** /'bʌt·ər'ʌp/ *v adv* [M] to please (someone) esp. by praising them in order to get them to agree to something • *Gina was trying to butter up the boss before asking for a day off.*

buttercup /'bʌt·ər,kʌp/ *n* [C] a small, yellow wild flower

butterfly /'bʌt·ər,flɑɪ/ *n* [C] a type of flying insect with four large, often brightly colored wings • If you have **butterflies in** your **stomach**, you are feeling very nervous or frightened about something.

buttermilk /'bʌt·ər,mɪlk/ *n* [U] the liquid that is left after taking the fat from milk or cream to make butter

butterscotch /'bʌt·ər,skɑtʃ/ *n* [C/U] a hard, yellow-brown candy made by boiling butter, brown sugar, and water together, or a flavoring that tastes like this candy

buttock /'bʌt·ək/ *n* [C usually pl] either of the two fleshy parts of the body below the back that support the body when sitting

button CLOTHING FASTENER /'bʌt·ᵊn/ *n* [C] a small, usually circular object that is sewn on a shirt, coat, or other piece of clothing, and is used to fasten it • A button is also a small, usually circular sign that may be worn on the clothes: *When you pay the admission fee at the museum, they give you a button to wear to show you've paid.* • A **buttonhole** is a narrow hole that a button is pushed through to fasten a shirt, coat, etc.

button /'bʌt·ᵊn/ *v* [T] • *He buttoned his shirt.* • A **button-down** shirt is one with a collar that has the pointed ends fastened to the shirt by buttons.

button OBJECT YOU PRESS /'bʌt·ᵊn/ *n* [C] a small object that you press to operate a device or a machine • *The button on the left starts the tape recorder and the one on the right stops it.*

buttonhole /'bʌt.ʰn̩ˌhoʊl/ v [T] to stop (someone) and make them listen to you • *They took out newspaper ads and buttonholed politicians to lobby for the change.*

buttress /'bʌ·trəs/ v [T] to give support to or strengthen (something) • *He looked for things that would buttress the prosecution case and win a conviction.*

buttress /'bʌ·trəs/ n [C] *specialized* a structure made of stone or brick that sticks out from and supports a wall of a building

buxom /'bʌk·səm/ adj (of a woman) having large breasts

buy PAY FOR /baɪ/ v [T] *past* **bought** /bɔːt/ to obtain (something) by paying money for it • *She was saving to buy a car.* ○ *He bought some flowers for his girlfriend.* ○ *They bought into a software company* (= bought a part of it in order to have some control over it). • If you buy someone off, you get their help, esp. in a matter that may not be legal, by giving them money. [M] • To buy up something is to buy large amounts of it, or all that is available: *He bought up all the land in the surrounding area.* [M] • *He tried to* **buy time** (= be allowed more time) *by saying he hadn't been well.*

buy /baɪ/ n [C] an occasion in which you pay less for something than what it is worth, and are therefore pleased • *The rug turned out to be quite a buy.*

buyer /'baɪ·ər/ n [C] a person who pays money for something, or a person whose job is to decide what goods will be brought into a store for sale • *He's still looking for a buyer for his house.*

buy BELIEVE /baɪ/ v [T] *past* **bought** /bɔːt/ *infml* to believe that something is true • *She'll never buy that story about having to take care of your sick grandmother.*

□ **buy out** /'-'-/ v adv [M] (of a person) to give (someone) money so that you own the part of a business that previously belonged to them • *She bought out her partner and now she owns the whole company.*

buyout /'baɪ·aʊt/ n [C] • *The law firm was active in management buyouts, mergers, and acquisitions.*

buzz MAKE SOUND /bʌz/ v [I/T] to make a continuous, low sound such as the sound some insects make, or to move quickly while making this sound • *Something was buzzing around me as I tried to sleep.* [I] • To buzz someone is to call them by using a device that makes a low, continuous sound: *All were expected to run, literally, into McLaughlin's office whenever he buzzed them.* [T]

buzz /bʌz/ n [C usually sing] • *the buzz of conversation* • *(infml)* A buzz is also a telephone call: *I'll give you a buzz early next week.*

buzzer /'bʌz·ər/ n [C] a device that makes a low, continuous sound

buzz BE FILLED WITH /bʌz/ v [I] to be filled with excitement, activity, or sounds • *The place was buzzing with excitement.*

buzzard /'bʌz·ərd/ n [C] a large North American bird that eats the flesh of dead animals; a VULTURE

buzz word /'bʌz·wɜrd/ n [C] a word or expression that is very often used, esp. in public discussions, because it represents opinions that are popular • *"Listening to the people" was the buzz word among politicians.*

by CAUSE /baɪ/ prep used to show the person or thing that causes something to happen or to exist • *The car was driven by a short, bald man.* ○ *I'm reading some short stories by Chekhov.* ○ *I took her umbrella by mistake.* • A **byline** is a line giving a writer's name at the top of a newspaper or magazine article.

by METHOD /baɪ/ prep used to show how something is done • *They thought about flying to Boston but decided to go by car.* ○ *She did the repair work by herself* (= without help). ○ *Do you want to be paid in cash or by check?* ○ *He learned English by listening to the radio.* • **By and large** means speaking generally: *By and large, you're better off making reservations well in advance.*

by ACCORDING TO /baɪ/ prep according to • *By my watch, it's 2 o'clock.* ○ *The students were listed by name.*

by NOT LATER THAN /baɪ/ prep not later than; at or before • *She promised to be back by 10 p.m.*

by MEASUREMENT /baɪ/ prep used to show measurements or amounts • *Their wages increased by 12%.* ○ *The room measures 15 feet by 20 feet.*

by DURING /baɪ/ prep during • *We traveled by night and rested by day.*

by NEAR /baɪ/ prep, adv [not gradable] near, beside, or (in distance or time) past • *A small child stood quietly by her side.* ○ *Claire waved as she drove by.* ○ *As time went by, she became more attached to him.*

bye /baɪ/ exclamation short form of GOODBYE

bye-bye /'baɪ'baɪ/ exclamation GOODBYE

bygone /'baɪ·gɔːn/ adj [not gradable] belonging to or happening in a past time • *The empty factories are relics of a bygone era.*

bypass /'baɪ·pæs/ v [T] to avoid (something) by going around it • *Take the highway that bypasses Richmond to avoid heavy traffic.* ○ *(fig.)* Posting news on the Internet bypasses traditional news sources such as radio and TV.

bypass /'baɪ·pæs/ n [C] a road built around a city to take traffic around the edge of it rather than through it • A **bypass (operation)** is a medical operation in which the path of a person's blood esp. in the heart is changed to improve the flow of blood.

by-product, **byproduct** /'baɪˌprɑd·əkt, -ˌʌkt/ n [C] something that is produced as a result of making something else, or something un-expected that happens as a result of something else • *The deep depression he fell into was a by-product of his disease.*

bystander /'baɪˌstæn·dər/ *n* [C] a person who is standing near and watching something that is happening but is not involved in it • *Many innocent bystanders were injured by the explosion.*

byte /baɪt/ *n* [C] *specialized* a unit of computer information, consisting of a group of usually eight BITS

byword /'baɪ·wɜrd/ *n* [C] a name of a person or thing that is closely connected with a particular quality • *In Hollywood's golden era, "Betty" was a byword for glamour.*

C, c

C LETTER , **c** /siː/ *n* [C] *pl* **C's** or **Cs** or **c's** or **cs** the third letter of the English alphabet

C MUSICAL NOTE /siː/ *n* [C/U] *pl* **C's** or **Cs** the first note in the **major scale** (= series of notes) that begins on the note C, or a set of notes based on this note

C MARK /siː/ *n* [C] *pl* **C's** or **Cs** a mark given for an exam, a course, or a piece of work which shows that your work is average or acceptable and not particularly good or bad • *Rachel got a C on her French exam.*

C NUMBER , **c** /siː, 'hʌn·drəd/ *number* the ROMAN NUMERAL for the number 100

C TEMPERATURE /siː/ *n abbreviation for* CELSIUS • *The temperature today reached 25°C.*

cab VEHICLE /kæb/ *n* [C] a TAXI (= car with a driver whom you pay to take you where you want to go) • A **cabdriver** (also *infml* **cabbie**) is a person whose job is driving a TAXI.

cab PART OF VEHICLE /kæb/ *n* [C] the separate part at the front of some vehicles in which the driver sits • *the cab of a truck*

cabaret /ˌkæb·ə'reɪ/ *n* [C/U] a restaurant or bar that provides esp. musical entertainment • *In Paris, we visited several cabarets.* [C]

cabbage /'kæb·ɪdʒ/ *n* [C/U] a large, round vegetable that is green or red and can be eaten cooked or raw • *We had corned beef and cabbage.* [U]

cabin ROOM /'kæb·ən/ *n* [C] a separate space in an aircraft for passengers or for the people operating it, or a room on a ship equipped with beds for sleeping • *They gave us seats in the first-class cabin of the plane.*

cabin HOUSE /'kæb·ən/ *n* [C] a small, simple house • *We stayed in a cabin in the mountains for two weeks.* • **Cabin fever** is a condition in which a person feels anxious or bored because they have spent too much time in the house, esp. in winter.

cabinet FURNITURE /'kæb·ə·nət/ *n* [C] a piece of furniture with shelves or drawers that is used for storing useful things or showing decorative things • *a medicine cabinet* • A filing cabinet is a set of large drawers in which papers can be stored.

cabinet GOVERNMENT /'kæb·ə·nət/ *n* [C] a small group of people within a government who advise the highest leader, such as the president or **prime minister** • *In the US, the Secretary of Defense is a member of the president's Cabinet.*

cable WIRE /'keɪ·bəl/ *n* [C/U] (a length of) wire, esp. twisted into thick, strong rope or used to carry electricity • *They dug up the road in order to lay phone cables.* [C] • A **cable car** is a vehicle that is attached to a cable which pulls it up steep slopes. • **Cable television** (also ca-ble TV) is a system of sending television pictures and sound along cables.

cable MESSAGE /'keɪ·bəl/ *n* [C] (in the past) a message sent by electric signal
cable /'keɪ·bəl/ *v* [I/T]

cache /kæʃ/ *n* [C] a secret or hidden store of things, or the place where they are kept • *Authorities believe the robber was after a hidden cache of $2,500 kept in a box under the counter.*

cachet /kæ'ʃeɪ/ *n* [U] a quality of someone or something that makes it especially attractive or admirable • *the cachet of the Ivy League schools*

cackle /'kæk·əl/ *v* [I] to make the loud sound of a chicken, or (of a person) to laugh or talk in a loud, high voice • *The hens cackled in alarm.*
cackle /'kæk·əl/ *n* [C] • *He burst into cackles of laughter.*

cactus /'kæk·təs/ *n* [C] *pl* **cactuses** or **cacti** /'kæk·taɪ/ any of a type of plant that grows in the desert, having thick stems for storing water and usually SPINES (= sharp points)

cacti

cadaver /kə'dæv·ər/ *n* [C] *medical* a dead human body, esp. one used by medical students for study

caddie, **caddy** /'kæd·i/ *n* [C] a person who carries the equipment for someone while they are playing golf

cadence /'keɪd·ᵊns/ *n* [C] a regular rise and fall of sound, esp. of the human voice • *I listened to the cadence of her deep breathing in sleep.*

cadet /kə'det/ *n* [C] a student who is training to be a military or police officer

cadre /'kɑd·ri, 'kæd-, -reɪ/ *n* [C] a small group of trained people who form the basic unit of a military, political, or business organization • *I was part of the cadre for a new armored division.*

café, **cafe** /kæ'feɪ/ *n* [C] a small restaurant where simple meals and usually alcoholic drinks are served, esp. where music is sometimes performed • *We had a glass of wine in a sidewalk café.* • A **café car** on a train is a CAR (= one of the connected but separate sections) where food and drinks can be bought.

cafeteria /ˌkæf·əˈtɪr·iː·ə/ n [C] a restaurant where people choose what they want from the foods and drinks that are offered in a serving area and carry the items to a table after paying for them

caffeine /kæˈfiːn/ n [U] a chemical found in coffee and tea that is a STIMULANT (= something that tends to make you more active)

cage /keɪdʒ/ n [C] a structure shaped like a box but with bars or wires as its sides, for keeping pets or for housing animals • *The lab was stocked with wire cages for mice.*

cagey /ˈkeɪ·dʒi/ adj **cagier, cagiest** not wanting to say plainly what you think or intend to do • *He was pretty cagey about his money.*

cajole /kəˈdʒoʊl/ v [T] to try to persuade (someone) to do something by saying things that please them or that make them feel important • *She is constantly cajoling her countrymen to adopt modern ideas and methods.*

Cajun /ˈkeɪ·dʒən/ n [C], adj [not gradable] (a person) belonging to a group of French-speaking people living in southern Louisiana in the US

cake FOOD /keɪk/ n [C/U] a sweet food made from flour, eggs, fat, and sugar mixed together and baked • *a chocolate cake* [C]

cake SHAPE /keɪk/ n [C] a small, flat object made by pressing together a soft substance • *a cake of soap*

caked /keɪkt/ v [T] (of a surface) covered with a thick layer of something • *I looked at my fingers, now caked with dirt.*

calamity /kəˈlæm·ət̬·i/ n [C] an event that causes much suffering to many people • *The factory closings were a calamity for the whole city.*

calcium /ˈkæl·siː·əm/ n [U] a chemical element present in teeth, bones, and CHALK (= type of soft, white rock)

calculate (obj) /ˈkæl·kjəˌleɪt/ v to judge the amount or value of (something) by using information and esp. numbers • *We tried to calculate how fast he was moving when the car crashed.* [+ wh- word] ○ *I calculated the total cost to be over $9000.* [T] ○ *Lieutenant Chilton calculated that six men had been lost.* [+ that clause]

calculation /ˌkæl·kjəˈleɪ·ʃən/ n [C/U] • *The original calculations ignored weather conditions.* [C]

calculator /ˈkæl·kjəˌleɪt̬·ər/ n [C] an electronic device used for doing mathematical processes such as adding, subtracting, dividing, and multiplying numbers

calculated /ˈkæl·kjəˌleɪt̬·əd/ adj planned or arranged in order to produce a particular effect • *The movie is calculated to appeal to young girls.*

calculating /ˈkæl·kjəˌleɪt̬·ɪŋ/ adj using other people or situations as a way to get something you want, esp. in a selfish or secret way • *The letter reveals a very calculating young man who had always sought a career in politics.*

calculus /ˈkæl·kjə·ləs/ n [U] specialized the mathematical study of continually changing values

calendar /ˈkæl·ən·dər/ n [C] a printed table showing the arrangement of the days, weeks, and months of the year • A calendar is also a list of meetings or things you have to do at particular times: *My calendar is pretty crowded over the next few weeks.* • A calendar is also a system for deciding the beginning and end of years, their total length, and the parts into which they are divided: *The Gregorian calendar is used today in most parts of the world.*

calf ANIMAL /kæf/ n [C] pl **calves** /kævz/ a young cow, or the young of various other large mammals, including ELEPHANTS and WHALES

calf LEG /kæf/ n [C] pl **calves** /kævz/ the curved, fleshy part of the back of the human leg between the knee and the foot

caliber QUALITY /ˈkæl·ə·bər/ n [U] the degree of quality or excellence of something or someone • *It's not easy to recruit high caliber personnel.*

caliber MEASUREMENT /ˈkæl·ə·bər/ n [C] the width of the inside of a pipe, esp. of the long, cylindrical part of a gun, or the width of a bullet • *a .22-caliber rifle*

calibrate /ˈkæl·əˌbreɪt/ v [T] specialized to make, adjust, or check the settings used to make measurements with (a tool or measuring device) • *Our radar was calibrated for 100,000 yards.*

calico /ˈkæl·ɪˌkoʊ/ n [U] a cotton cloth with a printed pattern

calisthenics /ˌkæl·əsˈθen·ɪks/ pl n physical exercises usually done repeatedly to keep your muscles in good condition and improve the way you look or feel • *The class began with 20 minutes of calisthenics.*

call NAME /kɔːl/ v [T] to give (someone or something) a name, or to know or address (someone) by a particular name • *They can't decide whether to call their new baby Carol or Alice.* ○ *His name is Anthony, but everyone calls him Tony.* • To **call** someone **names** is to use rude or insulting words to describe someone: *He says I'm a liar, but I don't want to waste time calling people names.*

call TELEPHONE /kɔːl/ v [I/T] to telephone (someone) • *I called (you) last night and left a message while you were out.* [I/T] ○ *Jenny called me (up) and invited us over for the weekend.* [T/M] • If you **call** someone **collect**, you telephone someone who agrees to pay for the cost of speaking to you. • LP TELEPHONE

call /kɔːl/ n [C] • *Did I get any (phone) calls while I was out?* ○ *You have a call from your wife.* • A **call-in** is a television or radio program in which members of the public can telephone the program to express their opinions or ask questions, and the resulting conversation is broadcast.

caller /'kɔː·lər/ n [C] a person who telephones someone else

call SAY /kɔːl/ v [I/T] to say (something) in a loud voice, esp. in order to get someone's attention • *Answer "Here!" when I call your name, the teacher said.* [T] • If you **call the roll**, you read aloud the names of all the people on a list to make certain that they are present: *The teacher calls the roll at the start of each day.*

call /kɔːl/ n [C] • *Muslims listen for the call to prayer given from the tower of a mosque.*

call ASK TO COME /kɔːl/ v [I/T] to ask (someone) to come to you • *I ran to Jonathan as soon as I heard him call.* [I] ○ *You'd better call an ambulance.* [T] ○ *Susan, would you call in the next patient, please?* [M]

call /kɔːl/ n [C] a visit that someone makes esp. as part of their job • *The locksmith is out on a call right now.* • People who work in medicine and other important activities are sometimes said to be **on call** if they are available to make visits or to speak to someone on the telephone at any time: *Dr. Menendez is on call for the next 24 hours.*

call CONSIDER /kɔːl/ v [T] to consider (someone or something) to be (something) • *I wouldn't call him a friend—he's just someone I met.* ○ *The umpire called him safe on a close play.* • If you **call it a day**, you are stopping work for that day: *We've planted hundreds of flowers—let's call it a day.* • If you **call it quits**, you agree to stop what you are doing: *Let's call it quits for today and get together first thing tomorrow.*

call /kɔːl/ n [C] a decision • *I really don't know what to do—it's your call.*

call ASK FOR /kɔːl/ v [T] to ask for or demand (something), or to decide officially to have (a particular event) • *The mayor called a meeting of local organizations to discuss budget priorities.* • To **call a halt** to something is to stop it: *The Red Cross had to call a halt to its work because the situation was getting too dangerous.* • In sports, to **call time** is to ask that the action and timing of the game temporarily stop.

call /kɔːl/ n [C/U] a reason or cause • *There's no call for you to get so angry—I was just kidding.* [U] • (*usually humorous*) A **call of nature** refers to the need to use a toilet.

□ **call back** *(obj)*, **call** *(obj)* **back** /'-'-/ v adv [I/M] to telephone (someone) who has telephoned you, often to answer a message they have left, or to telephone again • *He called her three times but she never called the guy back.* [M] ○ *If I'm not there at noon, call back later.* [I]

□ **call for** COME TO GET /'--/ v prep [T] to go to a place in order to meet (someone) and travel with them to another place • *He'll call for you at 7 and bring you to the restaurant.*

□ **call for** SUGGEST STRONGLY /'--/ v prep [T] to suggest strongly that something should happen or is necessary • *Many minority leaders called for the immediate resignation of the police commissioner.* ○ *Talking that way to your parents just wasn't called for* (= was extreme and not necessary).

□ **call forth** /'-'-/ v adv [T] *fml* to cause (something) to exist • *The American Civil War continues to call forth controversy.*

□ **call off** *obj*, **call** *obj* **off** /'-'-/ v adv [M] to decide that (a planned event) will not happen • *Union leaders called the strike off at the last minute.* • To call off is also to order (esp. a dog) to stop attacking someone or something.

□ **call on** ASK TO DO /'-,-/ v prep [T] to ask (someone) to do something • *She called on Americans to be more tolerant of each other.* • To call on is also to ask (someone) to speak, esp. in a public meeting or a class of students: *The teacher called on me, and I didn't know the answer.*

□ **call on** VISIT /'-,-/ v prep [T] to come to see (someone); visit • *She went to the hospital to call on a sick friend.*

□ **call out** *obj* SHOUT , **call** *obj* **out** /'-'-/ v adv [M] to speak loudly • *Speak up—call the names out so we can all hear.*

□ **call out** *obj* MAKE ACTIVE , **call** *obj* **out** /'-'-/ v adv [M] to officially order that (a military unit) become ready for action • *The governor called out the National Guard to stop looting.*

□ **call up** *obj*, **call** *obj* **up** /'-'-/ v adv [M] to order (someone) to join the armed forces • *He was called up at the beginning of the war.*

calligraphy /kə'lɪg·rə·fi/ n [U] the art of producing beautiful writing, often created with a special pen or brush

calling /'kɔː·lɪŋ/ n [C] *fml* an activity that is a person's most important job, esp. one in which they have an unusually strong interest and ability • *He felt the calling to become a priest.*

callous /'kæl·əs/ adj without sympathy or feeling for other people • *As callous as it may sound, trying to help some students is a waste of time.*

callus /'kæl·əs/ n [C] an area of hard, thickened skin, esp. on the feet or hands • *He had thick calluses on the soles of his feet.*

callused, **calloused** /'kæl·əst/ adj • *He stood looking down at the dark, callused palms of his hands.*

calm /kɑm, kɑlm/ adj [-er/-est only] peaceful, quiet, or relaxed; without hurried movement, anxiety, or noise • *The pilot said we'd have to make an emergency landing, and the flight attendants tried to keep us calm.* • If weather is described as calm, it is not windy, and if the sea is described as calm, it is still or has only small waves: *Our ship arrived at the Mississippi delta on a calm, clear night.*

calm /kɑm, kɑlm/ *n* [U] • *There is a ceasefire in the fighting, but the calm may be short-lived.*

calm /kɑm, kɑlm/ *v* [I/T] • *He tried his best to calm her (down).* [T] ○ *I needed some time to calm down.* [I]

calmly /'kɑm·li, 'kɑlm-/ *adv* • *He calmly made both free throws to win the game.*

calmness /'kɑm·nəs, 'kɑlm-/ *n* [U] • *The calmness and professionalism of the crew gave us confidence.*

calorie FOOD /'kæl·ə·ri/ *n* [C] a unit used in measuring the amount of energy food provides when eaten and digested • *The typical US daily menu contains 3000 calories and should contain 2300.*

calorie HEAT /'kæl·ə·ri/ *n* [C] *specialized* a unit equal to the amount of heat needed to increase the temperature of one gram of water by one degree CELSIUS

calves /kævz/ *pl of* CALF

calypso /kə'lɪp·soʊ/ *n* [C/U] *pl* **calypsos** or **calypsoes** a type of popular West Indian song whose words are often invented as the song is sung

camaraderie /ˌkɑm·ə'rɑd·ə·ri/ *n* [U] a friendly feeling toward people with whom you share an experience or with whom you work • *For me mountain climbing is less about physical effort than about cooperation and camaraderie.*

camcorder /'kæm,kɔːrd·ər/ *n* [C] a type of camera that records and plays images and sound on VIDEOTAPE and is small enough to hold in one hand

came /keɪm/ *past simple of* COME

camel /'kæm·əl/ *n* [C] a large animal of desert areas that has a long neck and a back with either one or two HUMPS (= large raised parts)

cameo JEWELRY /'kæm·iː,oʊ/ *n* [C] *pl* **cameos** a piece of usually oval jewelry on which the shape of a head or another shape is represented against a background of a noticeably different color

cameo PERFORMANCE /'kæm·iː,oʊ/ *n* [C] *pl* **cameos** a brief but noticeable part, esp. in a movie, television program, or theatrical performance, usually by someone who is famous • *The former vice president makes a cameo appearance in the movie.*

camera /'kæm·rə/ *n* [C] a device for taking photographs, making films, or recording images on VIDEOTAPE • A **cameraman** or **camerawoman** is a man or woman who operates a camera, esp. as their regular job, in making movies or television programs.

camisole /'kæm·ə,soʊl/ *n* [C] a piece of women's underwear for the top half of the body with thin straps that go over the shoulders

camomile /'kæm·ə,maɪl, -,miːl/ *n* CHAMOMILE

camouflage /'kæm·ə,flɑʒ, -,flɑdʒ/ *n* [U] a condition in which the appearance of someone or something when placed against a background makes them difficult or impossible to see • *The leafhopper is a little green insect that uses*

camouflage to blend in with the colors of the leaves. • In military use, camouflage is an appearance created to hide soldiers and equipment on the ground, esp. from being seen by enemy aircraft, by making them look like their surroundings.

camouflage /'kæm·ə,flɑʒ, -,flɑdʒ/ *v* [T] • *The guns are dug in and camouflaged.*

camp TENTS / BUILDINGS /kæmp/ *n* [C/U] a place where people stay in tents or other temporary structures • *We set up camp for the night near a stream.* [U] • A camp is also a place in the countryside organized for people, esp. children, to visit or live for a while to enjoy nature: *We sent our son away to (a) summer camp.* [C/U] • A camp is also a place where people, esp. military people, are trained, where military prisoners are kept, or where people have to live temporarily. [C] • A **campfire** is a fire outside that is made and used esp. by people who are staying in tents. • A **campground** (also **campsite**) is an area where people on vacation can bring tents and stay in them.

camp

camp /kæmp/ *v* [I] to set up a tent or other temporary structure to give you shelter outside while you sleep or rest • *We camped in a valley between the two mountains.* ○ *We used to go camping out west when I was a child.* • To **camp out** is to stay and sleep in an outside area for one or more days and nights, usually in a tent: *I've done a lot of canoeing in that park, but never have camped out over night.*

camper /'kæm·pər/ *n* [C] • *In the summer several thousand campers use this park every day.* • A camper is also a large vehicle in which you can sleep and eat, sometimes built as one unit with a car and sometimes as a unit that can be separated. PIC RECREATIONAL VEHICLE

camping /'kæm·pɪŋ/ *n* [U] • *In 1993, camping was the fifth most popular American vacation activity.*

camp GROUP /kæmp/ *n* [C] a group of people who share an opinion, esp. a political one • *Voters in the governor's camp will believe whatever he says about the state budget.*

campaign /kæm'peɪn/ *n* [C] a plan consisting

of a number of activities directed toward the achievement of an aim • *He ran the governor's campaign for reelection.* ○ *In October 1942, General George Patton launched his famous military campaign in north Africa.*

campaign /kæm'peɪn/ *v* [I] to try to achieve something, such as the election of someone to a political office, by taking part in a number of planned activities • *She campaigned for a law that would force the town to clean up the lake.*

camper /'kæm·pər/ *n* • See at CAMP TENTS/ BUILDINGS.

camphor /'kæm·fər/ *n* [U] a white substance with a strong smell which is used in medicine and to keep MOTHS (= flying insects) away from clothes that are stored

camping /'kæm·pɪŋ/ *n* • See at CAMP TENTS/ BUILDINGS.

campus /'kæm·pəs/ *n* [C/U] the grounds, sometimes including the buildings, of a university, college, or school • *Surrounded by lovely trees, the Dartmouth campus is big and beautiful.* [C] ○ *Freshmen at many universities are not allowed to live off campus (= in houses not on university property).* [U]

campy /'kæmp·i/ *adj* [-*er*/-*est* only] (of behavior, appearance, or an activity) amusing because it is obviously intended to be strange or shocking and seems to be ridiculing itself • *The movie is a mixed bag of campy humor, wild-eyed fantasy, and high-tech special effects.*

can CONTAINER /kæn/ *n* [C] a metal container, esp. a closed, cylindrical container in which food and drink are packaged • *a gas/watering can* ○ *The vending machine has soda in cans.* • A can can also be the amount of food or drink that a can holds: *I had a can of soup for lunch.* • A **can opener** is a device for opening metal cans, esp. cans of food.

can /kæn/ *v* [T] **-nn-** to preserve food by putting it into a can • *They can all kinds of fruit.* • (*slang*) If you get canned, you are dismissed from your job: *No, I'm not on vacation—I got canned last week.*

canned /kænd/ *adj* [not gradable] • *We keep a lot of canned food on hand.* • (*fig.*) Canned music is recorded music, esp. played in public places: *Canned music annoys me.*

can ABLE /kæn, kən/ *v aux* he/she/it **can**, *past simple* **could** /kʊd, kəd/ to be able to • *She can speak four languages.* ○ *We're doing the best we can, but we won't make our deadline.* • LP AUXILIARY VERBS

can PERMIT /kæn, kən/ *v aux* he/she/it **can**, *past simple* **could** /kʊd, kəd/ to be allowed or to have permission • *You can park on the street.* ○ *You can do it by yourself.* • Can is also used informally to request something: *Can you help me lift this box?* ○ *Can I have a tissue, please?* • USAGE: *Can* is the word usually used in standard spoken English when asking for permission. It is acceptable in most forms of written

English, although in very formal writing, such as official instructions, *may* is usually used instead: *Persons under 14 unaccompanied by an adult may not enter.* • LP AUXILIARY VERBS

can BE POSSIBLE /kæn, kən/ *v aux past simple* **could** /kʊd, kəd/ used to express possibility in the present • *You can get stamps at the post office.* • LP AUXILIARY VERBS

can OFFER /kæn, kən/ *v aux past simple* **could** /kʊd, kəd/ used in polite offers of help or by someone who provides service, as in a store • *Can I help you with those bags?* • LP AUXILIARY VERBS

Canadian /kə'neɪd·iː·ən/ *n* [C], *adj* (a person) of or coming from Canada • **Canadian English** is the English language as it is spoken and written in Canada. • **Canadian whisky** is a strong alcoholic drink made from cereal grain.

canal /kə'næl/ *n* [C] a channel of water artificially made for boats to travel through or to carry water from one area to another • *Today, the canal is still used by ships.*

canary /kə'ner·i/ *n* [C] a small, yellow bird, popular as a pet in a cage

cancel /'kæn·səl/ *v* [I/T] **-l-** or **-ll-** to decide that (something arranged in advance) will not happen, or to state that you do not wish to receive (something) • *We were supposed to meet for dinner but Elise had to cancel at the last minute.* [I] • If a stamp or check is canceled, it is marked to show it has been used: *He collects cancelled stamps.* [T] PIC POSTMARK

cancellation /ˌkæn·sə'leɪ·ʃən/ *n* [C/U] • *All the tickets were sold, so we waited to see if there were any cancellations.* [C]

□ **cancel out** *obj*, **cancel** *obj* **out** /'--'-/ *v adv* [M] to take away the effect of one thing by doing another thing which has exactly the opposite effect • *It was as if his compliment canceled out all the bad things he had said about her.*

cancer DISEASE /'kæn·sər/ *n* [C/U] a disease in which cells in the body grow without control, or a serious medical condition caused by this disease • *He died from cancer of the stomach.* [U] • Compare CARCINOMA.

cancerous /'kæn·sə·rəs/ *adj* • *Surgeons removed a cancerous growth from her breast.*

Cancer SIGN /'kæn·sər/ *n* [C/U] the fourth sign of the ZODIAC, covering the period June 22 to July 22 and represented by a CRAB, or a person born during this period

candid /'kæn·dəd/ *adj* truthful and honest • *We had a candid discussion about her poor job performance.*

candidate /'kæn·də,deɪt, -dəd·ət/ *n* [C] a person who is competing to get a job or elected to a position • *There are three candidates running for sheriff.*

candidacy /'kæn·dəd·ə·si/ *n* [U] • *She announced her candidacy for governor on the weekend.*

candle /'kæn·dəl/ *n* [C] a piece of wax shaped

like a stick with a WICK (= string) in the middle that burns slowly, giving off light • A **candlestick** is a base that holds a candle: *The silver candlesticks gleamed on the table.*

candor /ˈkæn·dər/ n [U] the quality of being honest, sincere, and kind in dealing with other people • *"We want to help but really don't know how,"* she said with surprising candor.

candy /ˈkæn·di/ n [C/U] a small piece of sweet food made from sugar with chocolate, fruit, nuts, or flavorings added • *We dove into the beautiful box of chocolate candy as if we were starving.* [U] • A **candy bar** is candy shaped like a thin brick: *When I need a sugar fix, I get a couple of candy bars.* • A **candy cane** is flavored hard candy shaped like a CANE (= walking stick) and hung on the Christmas tree.

cane /keɪn/ n [C/U] the long, hollow stems of particular plants such as BAMBOO • *Chair seats are often woven out of cane.* [U] • A cane is also a walking stick with a curved handle, used to help someone walk. [C]

canine /ˈkeɪ·naɪn/ adj of or like a dog • *This vet specializes in canines.*

canister /ˈkæn·ə·stər/ n [C] a container with a cover, used for storing foods or objects • *I bought brightly colored canisters to hold sugar and flour.*

cannabis /ˈkæn·ə·bəs/ n [U] the HEMP plant, whose leaves and flowers are used to make MARIJUANA and HASHISH • *Police seized two thousand cannabis plants.*

cannibal /ˈkæn·ə·bəl/ n [C] a person who eats human flesh, or an animal which eats the flesh of its own type of animal

cannon /ˈkæn·ən/ n [C] pl **cannons** or **cannon** a large, powerful gun fixed onto a ship or onto a structure on land

cannot /kəˈnɑt, ˈkæn·ɑt/, contraction **can't** /kænt, kɑːnt/ v aux can not; to be unable or not allowed to • *I cannot imagine what will happen next.*

canny /ˈkæn·i/ adj clever and careful • *He is a canny investor.*

canoe /kəˈnuː/ n [C] a small, light, narrow boat, pointed at both ends and moved by a person using a PADDLE (= a stick with a wide, flat end)

canoe

canoe /kəˈnuː/ v [I always + adv/prep] **canoeing**, past **canoed** • *They canoed across the lake.*

canon /ˈkæn·ən/ n [C] a principle or law, or a set of these, esp. in a Christian church • *The canon for lawyers has clear restrictions.*

canopy /ˈkæn·ə·pi/ n [C/U] a cover like a roof for shelter or decoration, or the branches and leaves that spread out at the tops of trees in the woods • *Many animals live in the forest canopy.* [U]

can't /kænt, kɑːnt/ contraction of CANNOT • *Speak up! I can't hear you.*

cantaloupe /ˈkænt·əlˌoʊp/ n [C] a round MELON (= fruit) with yellow or green skin and sweet, orange flesh • *Cantaloupes from Texas are extremely good this year.*

cantankerous /kænˈtæŋ·kə·rəs/ adj annoyed and tending to argue and complain • *By dinner, we were all tired and cantankerous.*

canteen RESTAURANT /kænˈtiːn/ n [C] a small store or restaurant esp. in a factory or school where food and meals are sold

canteen CONTAINER /kænˈtiːn/ n [C] a small container for carrying something to drink, esp. water

canter /ˈkænt·ər/ v [I] (of a horse) to move in a way that is like a slow GALLOP

cantor /ˈkænt·ər/ n [C] an official of a Jewish SYNAGOGUE who sings and leads prayers

canvas /ˈkæn·vəs/ n [C/U] strong, rough cloth made from cotton or other fibers, used for making tents, sails, strong bags, or work clothes • Canvas is also the cloth artists paint on, or a painting itself: *Two valuable canvases hung in the room.*

canvass /ˈkæn·vəs/ v [I/T] to go to (each house in an area) to find out how many people live there or what their opinions are, or to get support • *Candidates canvassed the city's neighborhoods for votes.* [T]

canyon /ˈkæn·jən/ n [C] a deep valley with steep sides and usually a river flowing along the bottom

cap HAT /kæp/ n [C] a soft, light hat, esp. one with a curved part sticking out at the front • *a painter's cap* ○ *My uncle must have a hundred baseball caps to choose from.* • PIC BASEBALL CAP

cap LIMIT /kæp/ v [T] -pp- to put a limit on (expenses or amounts charged) • *Our mortgage is capped for five years.*

cap /kæp/ n [C] • *The state has put a cap on the budget.*

cap COVER /kæp/ n [C] a small lid or cover • *a pen cap* ○ *I can't get the cap off this bottle.* • A cap is also a CROWN (= cover for a tooth).

cap /kæp/ v [T] -pp- • *From my window, I could see mountains capped with snow.* • **To cap** something **off** means to finish or end it: *To cap off a really bad week, I lost my wallet.*

cap EXPLOSIVE /kæp/ n [C] a small amount of explosive powder on a paper roll, used esp. in toy guns to make a loud noise

capable /ˈkeɪ·pə·bəl/ adj having the skill or

ability or strength to do something • *She's a very capable lawyer.*

capability /ˌkeɪ·pəˈbɪl·əţ·i/ n [C/U] • *Automation gives us the capability to do certain jobs quickly and well.* [U]

capacity ⟨AMOUNT⟩ /kəˈpæs·əţ·i/ n the amount that can be held or produced by something • *The stadium has a seating capacity of 50,000.* [C]

capacity ⟨ABILITY⟩ /kəˈpæs·əţ·i/ n [C] the ability to do something in particular • *He has an enormous capacity for work.*

capacity ⟨POSITION⟩ /kəˈpæs·əţ·i/ n [C] a particular position or job; a ROLE • *She was speaking in her capacity as a judge.*

cape ⟨LAND⟩ /keɪp/ n [C] a very large piece of land that sticks out into the sea • *Cape Cod*

cape ⟨COAT⟩ /keɪp/ n [C] a loose, sleeveless coat which is fastened at the neck and hangs from the shoulders

caper ⟨ACTIVITY⟩ /ˈkeɪ·pər/ n [C] a robbery or other illegal activity • *a bank caper* • A caper is also an action that is amusing but wrong: *In this latest caper, Bell was caught using a doctored bat.*

caper ⟨FOOD⟩ /ˈkeɪ·pər/ n [C usually pl] a small, dark green flower BUD prepared for use as a flavoring for food

capillary /ˈkæp·əˌler·i/ n [C] *specialized* the smallest of the tubes that carry blood around the body

capital (letter) /ˈkæp·əţ·əl/ (ˈleţ·ər)/ n [C] a form of a letter used to begin sentences and proper names • *THIS SENTENCE IS PRINTED IN CAPITALS/CAPITAL LETTERS.* • Compare SMALL ⟨LETTER SIZE⟩.

capital /ˈkæp·əţ·əl/ *adj* [not gradable] • *Do you write "Calvin" with a capital "C"?*

capitalize /ˈkæp·əţ·əlˌaɪz/ v [T] • *The names of streets are always capitalized.* • See also CAPITALIZE ON.

capitalization /ˌkæp·əţ·əl·əˈzeɪ·ʃən/ n [U] • *Rules of capitalization vary from language to language.*

capital ⟨CITY⟩ /ˈkæp·əţ·əl/ n [C] a city which is the center of government for a country or other political area

capital ⟨MONEY⟩ /ˈkæp·əţ·əl/ n [U] wealth, esp. money used to produce more wealth through investment or a new business • *She invested well, and can live on the interest without touching the capital.* • **Capital gains** are profits made by selling esp. shares of a company or buildings and land.

capital ⟨DEATH⟩ /ˈkæp·əţ·əl/ *adj* [not gradable] (of a crime) punishable by death • *a capital offense* • **Capital punishment** (also the **death penalty**) is punishment by death.

capitalism /ˈkæp·əţ·əlˌɪz·əm/ n [U] an economic system based on private ownership of property and business, with the goal of making the greatest possible profits for the owners • Compare COMMUNISM; SOCIALISM.

capitalist /ˈkæp·əţ·əl·əst/, **capitalistic** /ˌkæp·əţ·əlˈɪs·tɪk/ *adj* • *The US has a capitalist economy.*

capitalist /ˈkæp·əţ·əl·əst/ n [C] • *Anyone can be a capitalist.*

capitalize on /ˈkæp·əţ·əlˌɑɪˌzɔːn, -ˌzɑn/ v *prep* [T] to use (something) to your own advantage • *She capitalized on her experience to get a better paying job.* • See also **capitalize** at CAPITAL (LETTER).

Capitol /ˈkæp·əţ·əl/ n [C usually sing] the building in which the US Congress meets • **Capitol Hill** (also **the Hill**) is the hill on which the Capitol stands, or the legislative part of the US government, which meets there: *The president will go to Capitol Hill to meet with lawmakers.*

Capitol

capitulate /kəˈpɪtʃ·əˌleɪt/ v [I] to accept defeat, or to give up or give in • *I capitulated and let my daughter go with her friends.*

capitulation /kəˌpɪtʃ·əˈleɪ·ʃən/ n [C/U] • *This was not a capitulation but an agreement.* [C]

cappuccino /ˌkæp·əˈtʃiː·noʊ/ n [C/U] pl **cappuccinos** strong coffee mixed with hot milk, or a cup of this coffee • *Do you prefer espresso or cappuccino?* [U]

capricious /kəˈprɪʃ·əs, -ˈpriː·ʃəs/ *adj* likely to change, or reacting to a sudden desire or new idea • *We have had very capricious weather lately.*

Capricorn /ˈkæp·rəˌkɔːrn/ n [C/U] the tenth sign of the ZODIAC, covering the period December 22 to January 19 and represented by a goat, or a person born during this period

capsize /ˈkæpˌsɑɪz/ v [I/T] to turn over or cause (a boat or ship) to turn over in the water • *A passenger ferry capsized in rough seas Sunday morning.* [I]

capsule ⟨MEDICINE⟩ /ˈkæp·səl, -suːl/ n [C] a measured amount of medicine in a very small, rounded, soft container which is swallowed

capsule ⟨SPACECRAFT⟩ /ˈkæp·səl, -suːl/ n [C] the part of an old-fashioned spacecraft where people lived and in which they returned to earth • *the Apollo 11 capsule*

captain /ˈkæp·tən/ n [C] a naval officer of high rank, above a COMMANDER, or a military officer of middle rank, above a LIEUTENANT • A captain is the person in charge of a ship or aircraft. • A captain is also an officer in a police

---

CAPITAL LETTERS

Capitals are generally used for the first letters of names and other words that have a special importance. A capital letter is used at the beginning of:

a sentence, or a word or phrase that stands alone

The stores are closed today. • *Perhaps.* • *Yes.*

a direct quotation

She whispered, "Can you hear me?" He answered, "Of course."

But if a quoted sentence is interrupted in the middle, the second part begins with a small letter.

"When the pie is done," he said, "let it cool on a table."

If a quotation is part of the structure of a sentence, it begins with a small letter.

She said she was "very pleased" to be invited.

proper nouns, that is, names of particular persons, places, or things

These include names of cities, countries, nationalities, and organizations, as well as the names of the days and months and times in history.

Maria R. Gonzales • *133 Elm Street* • *the United States* • *the South* • *the Red Sea* • *Central Park*
BUT *traveling south* • *a red tie* • *a walk in the park*

two Germans and a Mexican • *the US Army* • *the National Basketball Association* • *She won an Oscar* • *First National Bank*

on June 10 • *next Tuesday* • *during the Middle Ages*

adjectives based on names or proper pronouns

the Canadian dollar • *Shakespearean drama* • *an African-American woman*

But when these words have an independent meaning, they are usually spelled with a small letter.

a china cup • *a grilled frankfurter* • *a glass of scotch*

people's titles

Mr. Bernstein • *Ms. Lee* • *Dr. Silva* • *President Clinton* • *Good morning, Doctor.*
BUT: *She's a doctor,* AND USUALLY: *He was elected president.*

words for members of a family when they are used as a title before a name, or used alone instead of a name

Uncle Fred and Cousin Ashley
BUT *She is visiting her uncle and her cousin.*

words for religions and their adjectives

the history of Judaism • *She's a Catholic.* • *Islamic law*

The word **God** is capitalized when it means the single creator of the universe.

Do you believe in God?

BUT **god** is written with all small letters when it refers to one of several gods.

The ancient Greeks had many gods.

the first word and all the important words in the titles of books, movies, television programs, etc.

I'm reading A Modern Guide to the Ancient World. • *Have you seen* The Godfather?

---

or fire department. • A captain is also the leader of a sports team.

captain /ˈkæp·tən/ *v* [T] • *She captains the women's rowing team.*

caption /ˈkæp·ʃən/ *n* [C] brief text over or under a picture in a book, magazine, or newspaper that describes the picture or explains what the people in it are doing or saying

captivate /ˈkæp·təˌveɪt/ *v* [T] to hold the attention of (someone) by being extremely interesting, exciting, charming, or attractive • *Her singing captivated audiences everywhere.*

captive /ˈkæp·tɪv/ *n* [C] a prisoner, esp. a person held by the enemy during a war

captive /ˈkæp·tɪv/ *adj, adv* • *Several diplomats were held captive by the terrorists.* • *When selling to people in their homes, you've got a* **captive audience** (= people who cannot leave).

captivity /kæpˈtɪv·ət̬·i/ *n* [U] • *Most animals bred in captivity would probably not survive in the wild.*

capture POSSESS /ˈkæp·tʃər, -ʃər/ *v* [T] to take (someone) as a prisoner, or to take (something) into your possession, esp. by force • *The soldiers were captured and imprisoned.* • If something **captures** your **attention**, it interests you: *Television captured the public's attention.*

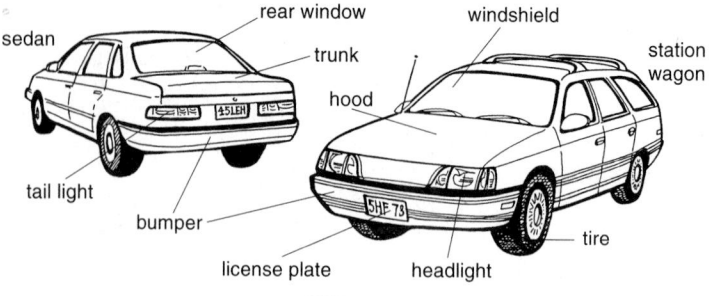

sedan · rear window · trunk · windshield · station wagon · hood · tail light · bumper · license plate · headlight · tire

cars

capture /ˈkæp·tʃər, -ʃər/ *n* [U] • *They were shown on TV soon after their capture.*

capture RECORD /ˈkæp·tʃər, -ʃər/ *v* [T] to record (sound or images), or to express (a feeling) • *She captured the incident on video.* ○ *Those songs capture the romantic mood of the movie.*

car /kɑr/, **automobile** *n* [C] a road vehicle with an engine, usually four wheels, and seating for between one and five people • *a car accident* ○ *She goes to work by car.* • A car is also one part of a train: *a dining/passenger/freight car* • A **carport** is a shelter for cars that has a roof and one or more open sides, and which can be built against the side of a house. • A **car seat** is a seat for a small child that can be attached to a seat in a car.

carport

carafe /kəˈræf, -ˈrɑf/ *n* [C] an open glass container for serving wine or water, esp. in a restaurant, or the amount it contains

caramel /ˈkɑr·məl; ˈkær·ə·məl, -ˌmel/ *n* [C/U] cooked sugar used to give flavor and a brown color to food, or a chewy candy made from cooked sugar, butter, and milk

carat /ˈkær·ət/ *n* [C] a unit for measuring the weight of jewels • *The diamonds had a combined weight of 5.87 carats.* • Compare KARAT.

caravan /ˈkær·əˌvæn/ *n* [C] a group of people with vehicles or animals who travel together for safety through a dangerous area, esp. across a desert on CAMELS

carbohydrate /ˌkɑr·bəˈhɑɪˌdreɪt/ *n* [C/U] a substance such as sugar or STARCH that provides the body with energy, or a food containing such a substance • *Bread and rice are high in carbohydrates.* [C]

carbon /ˈkɑr·bən/ *n* [U] a chemical element that is contained in all animals and plants, is an important part of other substances such as coal and oil, and exists in its pure form as DIAMONDS and GRAPHITE • A **carbon copy** is an exact copy of something: *(fig.) The girl is a carbon copy of her mother* (= they are very simi-

lar). • **Carbon dioxide** is the gas produced when animal or vegetable matter is burned, or when animals breathe out. • **Carbon monoxide** is the poisonous gas produced when carbon is partly burned, esp. in car fuel.

carbonated /ˈkɑr·bəˌneɪt·əd/ *adj* (of a drink) bubbly because it contains **carbon dioxide** • *carbonated drinks/water*

carburetor /ˈkɑr·bəˌreɪt·ər, -bjə-/ *n* [C] the part of an engine that mixes fuel and air, producing the gas that is burned to provide the power needed to operate a vehicle or machine

carcass /ˈkɑr·kəs/ *n* [C] the body of a dead animal • *The carcass of a deer lay near the road.*

carcinogen /kɑrˈsɪn·ə·dʒən/ *n* [C] *medical* a substance that can cause CANCER (= a serious illness that causes tissues and cells to grow too quickly)

carcinogenic /ˌkɑr·sə·nəˈdʒen·ɪk/ *adj medical* (of a substance) able or likely to cause CANCER

carcinoma /ˌkɑr·səˈnoʊ·mə/ *n* [C] *medical* a lump of tissue that forms on or inside the body; a TUMOR

card INFORMATION /kɑrd/ *n* [C] a small, rectangular piece of stiff paper or plastic with information on it that shows who you are or allows you to do something • *a library/membership/business card* ○ *I used my credit/debit/charge card to pay for the groceries.*

card /kɑrd/ *v* [T] *infml* to ask (someone) to show you a document that shows how old they are • *She looks really young—she's always carded when she goes into bars.*

card GAME /kɑrd/, **playing card** *n* [C] one of a set of 52 small, rectangular pieces of stiff paper, each with a number or letter and one of four symbols printed on it, used in games • *a deck of cards* • If **the cards are stacked against** you, you are not likely to succeed, esp. because you are not being given a fair chance. • If you **lay/put** your **cards on the table**, you are honest and don't hide what you are thinking or doing. • A **card table** is a light table with folding legs used for playing cards. • PIC SUITS

cards /kɑrdz/ *n* [U] any game played with cards, such as POKER or BRIDGE • *Let's play cards.*

card GREETING /kɑrd/ *n* [C] a rectangular piece

of stiff paper, folded in half, usually with a picture on the front and often a message printed inside, sent on a special occasion • *a birthday/ Christmas/get-well card* • A card is also a POSTCARD.

cardboard /'kɑrd·bɔːrd, -boʊrd/ *n* [U] very thick, stiff paper, usually pale brown in color, used esp. for making boxes • *She packed the books in a cardboard box.*

cardiac /'kɑrd·iˌæk/ *adj* [not gradable] *medical* of the heart or heart disease • *cardiac surgery* • **Cardiac arrest** is a condition in which the heart stops beating.

cardigan /'kɑrd·ɪ·gən/ *n* [C] a SWEATER (= piece of clothing that covers the upper part of the body and the arms) that fastens at the front with buttons and is usually worn over other clothes

cardinal PRIEST /'kɑrd·ən·əl/ *n* [C] a priest of high rank in the Roman Catholic Church

cardinal IMPORTANT /'kɑrd·ən·əl/ *adj* of great importance; main • *Finding food was a cardinal concern.*

cardinal BIRD /'kɑrd·ən·əl/ *n* [C] a North American bird, the male of which has bright red feathers and a black face

cardinal (number) /'kɑrd·ən·əl ('nʌm·bər)/ *n* [C] a number like 1, 2, 3 that represents amount, rather than position in a list • Compare ORDINAL (NUMBER). LP NUMBERS

cardiology /ˌkɑrd·iːˈɑl·ə·dʒi/ *n* [U] *medical* the study and treatment of medical conditions of the heart

cardiologist /ˌkɑrd·iːˈɑl·ə·dʒəst/ *n* [C] *medical* a doctor who specializes in treating medical conditions of the heart

care HELP /ker, kær/ *n* [U] the process of providing for the needs of someone or something • *The quality of care at this hospital is very good.* ○ *Trees on city property don't get any care.* • If a letter is sent **(in) care of** (abbreviation **c/o**) someone, it is mailed to you at someone else's address: You can write me in care of my grandmother. • A **caregiver** (also **caretaker**) is a person who gives care to children or ill people.

care ATTENTION /ker, kær/ *n* [U] serious attention, esp. to the details of a situation or a piece of work • *She painted the window frames with great care.*

careful /'ker·fəl, 'kær-/ *adj* giving attention to something in order to avoid esp. an accident or problem • *Norman is a careful driver.* ○ *Give my suggestion careful consideration.* ○ *He's in a really bad mood so be careful what you say to him.* [+ wh- word] ○ *Be careful where you put that hot pan.* [+ wh- word] ○ *Be careful to look both ways when you cross the street.* [+ to infinitive]

carefully /'ker·fə·li, 'kær-/ *adv* with great attention, esp. to detail or safety • *She carefully embroidered the pillow.* ○ *Drive carefully—it's raining.*

careless /'ker·ləs, 'kær-/ *adj* not using enough care • *Careless drivers cause accidents.* ○ *My son's schoolwork is often careless and sloppy.*

carelessly /'ker·lə·sli, 'kær-/ *adv* • *She carelessly left her purse on the train.*

carelessness /'ker·lə·snəs, 'kær-/ *n* [U] • *Carelessness leads to shoddy work.*

care WORRY /ker, kær/ *v* to be interested in something, or to be anxious or upset about something • *Don't you care about what happens to the children?* [I] ○ *I really don't care if we go or not* (= It doesn't matter to me). [I] ○ *I don't care how much it costs, just buy it.* [+ wh- word]

care /ker, kær/ *n* [C/U] • *She seemed weighed down by all her cares.* [C] • If someone doesn't have **a care in the world**, they have no worries: *Jamahl skipped down the street, seemingly without a care in the world.*

care WANT /ker, kær/ *v* [I] *fml* (used in polite offers and suggestions) to want something • *Would you care to join us for dinner?* [+ to infinitive]

□ **care for** PROVIDE FOR /'--, '-ˌ-/ *v prep* [T] to provide (a person or animal) with what they need and to protect them, esp. because they are young or ill • *Bob and his sister take turns caring for their elderly mother.*

□ **care for** LIKE /'--, '-ˌ-/ *v prep* [T] to like (something or someone) • *I don't care for seafood.*

careen /kəˈriːn/ *v* [I] to go forward, esp. quickly, while moving from side to side • *The car skidded and careened wildly across several lanes of traffic.*

career JOB /kəˈrɪr/ *n* [C] a job for which you are trained and in which it is possible to advance during your working life, so that you get greater responsibility and earn more money • *He's hoping for a career in social work.* ○ *She left college to pursue an acting career.*

career /kəˈrɪr/ *adj* [not gradable] done as a job all your life • *a career politician* ○ *career criminals*

career MOVE /kəˈrɪr/ *v* [I always + adv/prep] (esp. of a vehicle) to move fast and without control • *The bus careered down a slope and hit a telephone pole.*

carefree /'ker·friː, 'kær-/ *adj* having no worries, problems, or anxieties; happy • *Anna has a carefree summer ahead of her.*

careful /'ker·fəl, 'kær-/ *adj* • See at CARE ATTENTION.

carefully /'ker·fə·li, 'kær-/ *adv* • See at CARE ATTENTION.

careless /'ker·ləs, 'kær-/ *adj* • See at CARE ATTENTION.

carelessly /'ker·lə·sli, 'kær-/ *adv* • See at CARE ATTENTION.

carelessness /'ker·lə·snəs, 'kær-/ *n* • See at CARE ATTENTION

caress /kəˈres/ *n* [C] a gentle loving touch or kiss • *a mother's soft caress*

caress /kəˈres/ *v* [I/T] • *I caressed her face.* [T]

caretaker /'ker,teɪ·kər, 'kær-/ *n* [C] a person employed to take care of a large building or property, doing cleaning, repairs, gardening, or other jobs • *The building's caretaker reported the fire.* • A caretaker government is one that is in power for a short period of time until a new one is chosen. • A caretaker is also a **caregiver**. See at CARE HELP.

cargo /'kɑr,goʊ/ *n* [C/U] *pl* **cargoes** or **cargos** goods carried by a ship, aircraft, or other vehicle • *The department inspects cargo coming into Hawaii.* [U]

Caribbean /,kær·ə'biː·ən, kə'rɪb·iː·ən/ *n* [U], *adj* (relating to) the sea that is east of Central America and north of South America, or the islands in it and the countries that border this sea • **Caribbean English** is the variety of English, influenced strongly by European languages and CREOLE, spoken in many parts of the Caribbean region.

caribou /'kær·ə,buː/ *n* [C] *pl* **caribous** or **caribou** a large deer with long, branchlike horns that lives in North America

caricature /'kær·ɪ·kə,tʃʊr, -tʃər/ *n* [C/U] a drawing or a written or spoken description of someone that makes part of their appearance or character more noticeable than it really is, and which can make them look ridiculous, or the skill of doing this • *I saw a wonderful caricature of the president in the newspaper.* [C]

caricature /'kær·ɪ·kə,tʃʊr, -tʃər/ *v* [T] to show or describe a person in a way that makes them look ridiculous • *It's so easy to caricature politicians.*

carjacking /'kɑr,dʒæk·ɪŋ/ *n* [C/U] an act of stealing a car while someone is in it

carnage /'kɑr·nɪdʒ/ *n* [U] the violent killing of large numbers of people, esp. in war • *The Battle of Gettysburg was a scene of dreadful carnage.*

carnal /'kɑrn·ᵊl/ *adj slightly fml* relating to the physical feelings and desires of the body; sexual • *carnal desires/pleasure* • **Carnal knowledge** is INTERCOURSE.

carnation /kɑr'neɪ·ʃən/ *n* [C] a small flower that has a sweet smell and is usually white, pink, or red

carnival /'kɑr·nə·vəl/ *n* [C/U] a place of outside entertainment where there are machines you can ride on and games that can be played for prizes • *There's a carnival in Payson Park this weekend.* [C] • A carnival is also a time of public enjoyment and entertainment when people wear unusual clothes, dance, and eat and drink, usually in the streets of a city. [C/U]

carnivore /'kɑr·nə,vɔːr, -,voʊr/ *n* [C] an animal that eats meat

carnivorous /kɑr'nɪv·ə·rəs/ *adj* [not gradable] • *Lions and tigers are carnivorous.*

carol /'kær·əl/ *n* [C] a **Christmas carol**, see at CHRISTMAS

carol /'kær·əl/ *v* [I] **-l-** or **-ll-** to sing carols, esp. by going from house to house • *We went caroling in the neighborhood.*

carouse /kə'raʊz/ *v* [I] to enjoy yourself by drinking alcohol and speaking and laughing loudly in a group of people • *They were up carousing till dawn.*

carousel AMUSEMENT /,kær·ə'sel/ *n* [C] a MERRY-GO-ROUND

carousel MOVING STRIP /,kær·ə'sel/ *n* [C] a continuous moving strip at an airport, from which passengers pick up their bags at the end of a trip

carp COMPLAIN /kɑrp/ *v* [I] to complain about unimportant matters • *However much people carp about junk mail, many of them read it.*

carp FISH /kɑrp/ *n* [C] *pl* **carp** or **carps** a large, edible fish that lives in lakes and rivers

carpenter /'kɑr·pən·tər/ *n* [C] a person whose job is making and repairing wooden objects and structures

carpentry /'kɑr·pən·tri/ *n* [U] the skill or trade of a carpenter, or the work done by a carpenter • *That staircase is a beautiful piece of carpentry.*

carpet /'kɑr·pət/ *n* [C/U] thick, woven material for covering floors, or a piece of this material

carpet /'kɑr·pət/ *v* [T] to cover (a floor surface) with a carpet

car pool /'kɑr·puːl/ *n* [C] an arrangement in which a group of people take turns driving each other or their children to and from work or school

car–pool /'kɑr·puːl/ *v* [I] • *It's easier to car-pool, but you can't choose when to leave.*

carriage VEHICLE /'kær·ɪdʒ/ *n* [C] a vehicle with four wheels pulled by a horse or horses • A carriage is also a **baby carriage**. See at BABY.

carriage POSITION /'kær·ɪdʒ/ *n* [U] *fml* the way in which a person holds their body when standing or moving around • *She had great stage presence and perfect carriage.*

carrot VEGETABLE /'kær·ət/ *n* [C] a long, pointed, orange root, eaten as vegetable, either raw or cooked

carrot REWARD /'kær·ət/ *n* [C] something that is offered to someone in order to encourage them to do something • *If they finished the construction ahead of schedule, they were offered the carrot of a bonus.*

carry TRANSPORT /'kær·i/ *v* [T] to transport or take from one place to another • *The plane carried 116 passengers and a crew of seven.* ○ *Would you like me to carry your bag for you?* ○ *Underground cables carry electricity to all parts of the city.* • All **carry-on** luggage (= bags that you take into an aircraft with you) *must be stored under the seat in front of you or in one of the overhead compartments.*

carrier /'kær·iː·ər/ *n* [C] a person or thing that carries or delivers something • *She's got a job as a letter carrier.*

carry HAVE WITH YOU /'kær·i/ *v* [T] to have (something) with you, esp. during your usual activities • *I carry my wallet in my back pocket.* ○ *I don't carry a lot of cash.*

carry SPREAD /'kær·i/ *v* [T] to take (something) from one person or thing and give it to another person or thing; to spread • *The Europeans who first settled in North America carried new diseases, which eventually were passed to the Indians.*

carrier /'kær·iː·ər/ *n* [C] *medical* a person who can give a disease to other people but may not show any signs of having the disease

carry HAVE /'kær·i/ *v* [T] to have (something) as a part, quality, or result • *All our rental cars carry collision insurance.* ○ *I'm sorry, we don't carry shoes* (= we do not sell shoes). ○ *His argument carries a lot of conviction* (= is supported by strong belief). • If someone's opinion **carries weight**, it is considered seriously and influences other people.

carry SUPPORT WEIGHT /'kær·i/ *v* [T] to support (the weight of something) • *The weight of the roof is carried by steel beams.*

carry KEEP IN OPERATION /'kær·i/ *v* [T] to support, keep in operation, or make a success • *We cannot afford to carry people who don't do their share of the work.* • If we want the presentation done well, Barbara's the person to **carry the ball** (= take responsibility for the success of it).

carry WIN /'kær·i/ *v* [T] to win the support, agreement, or sympathy of (a group of people) • *Gore is expected to carry* (= get the most votes) in) *the midwestern states.*

carry APPROVE /'kær·i/ *v* [T] to give approval to (something suggested), esp. by voting • *With 21 votes for, and 8 opposed, the motion is carried.*

carry COMMUNICATE /'kær·i/ *v* [T] to include (a particular item of news, information, etc.) in something printed, broadcast, or sent electronically • *Newspapers and radio and TV stations throughout Missouri carried the story.*

carry REACH /'kær·i/ *v* [I] (esp. of sounds) to be able to reach or travel a particular distance • *The actors' voices carried all the way to the back of the theater.*

carry MOVE NUMBER /'kær·i/ *v* [T] to put (a number) into another column when doing addition

carry MOVE BODY /'kær·i/ *v* [T] to move and hold (your body) in a particular way • *You can tell she's a dancer by the way she carries herself.*

carry MUSIC /'kær·i/ *v* [T] • To **carry a tune** is to make the correct musical sounds of a tune: *My brother is tone deaf and can't even carry a tune.*

□ **carry** *obj* **away** /'---'-/ *v adv* [T] to cause (someone) to become very excited and to lose control • *I got carried away and spent too much money.*

□ **carry off** *obj* SUCCEED , **carry** *obj* **off** /'---'-/ *v*

adv [M] to succeed in doing or achieving (esp. something difficult) • *I wouldn't dare wear anything that outrageous, but Michelle carried it off wonderfully.*

□ **carry off** *obj* REMOVE , **carry** *obj* **off** /'---'-/ *v adv* to remove (something) • *Thieves broke the store window and carried off jewelry worth many thousands of dollars.*

□ **carry on** CONTINUE /'---'-/ *v adv* [I/T] to continue to do or be involved with (something) • *Dianne is carrying on the family tradition by becoming a lawyer.* [T] ○ *You've got to carry on as though nothing happened.* [I] ○ *It's hard to carry on a business and take care of a small child at the same time.* [T]

□ **carry on** BEHAVE /'---'-/ *v adv* [I] to behave in an excited or anxious way that is not controlled • *The kids have been carrying on all day.*

□ **carry out** *obj*, **carry** *obj* **out** /'---'-/ *v adv* [M] to perform or complete (a job or activity); to fulfill • *I was elected to carry out a program, the governor said, and I have every intention of carrying it out.*

□ **carry over** *(obj)*, **carry** *(obj)* **over** /'---'--/ *v adv* [I/M] to move to or to come from (a place or time) • *I try not to let my problems at work carry over into my private life.* [I] ○ *She couldn't pay all of her credit-card debt and carried over part of it to the next month.* [M]

□ **carry** *obj* **through** *(obj)* HELP /'---'-/ *v adv* [T] to help in a difficult situation • *Many animals store food in the fall to carry them through the winter.*

□ **carry through** *obj* COMPLETE , **carry** *obj* **through** /'---'-/ *v adv* [M] to bring to a successful end; to complete • *We are determined to carry our plans through to completion.*

carryout /'kær·iː‚ɑʊt/ *n* [C] a TAKEOUT • *They shared lunch from a McDonald's carryout.*

carsick /'kɑr·sɪk/ *adj* (of a passenger in a car) feeling like you want to vomit because of the movement of the car

carsickness /'kɑr‚sɪk·nəs/ *n* [U]

cart /kɑrt/ *n* [C] a vehicle with either two or four wheels that is pushed by a person, or pulled by an animal, esp. a horse, and is used for carrying goods • A cart is also a **shopping cart**. See at SHOP BUY THINGS.

□ **cart away** /'kɑrt̬·ə'weɪ/, **cart off** /'kɑrt̬'ɔːf/ *v adv* [M] to take (something or someone) somewhere, esp. using a lot of effort • *We cleaned out the garage and carted tons of stuff away.* ○ *He was carted off to jail.*

cartel /kɑr'tel/ *n* [C] a group of similar independent companies or countries who join together to control prices and limit competition

cartilage /'kɑrt̬·əl·ɪdʒ/ *n* [U] a strong, elastic type of tissue found in humans in the joints and other places such as the nose, throat, and ears

cartography /kɑr'tɑg·rə·fi/ *n* [U] the science or art of making or drawing maps

carton /'kɑrt·ᵊn/ *n* [C] a box made from cardboard for storing goods, or a container made from cardboard or plastic in which esp. milk or fruit juice is sold

cartoon DRAWING /kɑr'tuːn/ *n* [C] a drawing, esp. in a newspaper or magazine, that tells a joke or makes an amusing political criticism

cartoonist /kɑr'tuː·nəst/ *n* [C] • *a popular political cartoonist*

cartoon MOVIE /kɑr'tuːn/, **animated cartoon** *n* [C] a movie made using characters and images that are invented and drawn

cartridge /'kɑr·trɪdʒ/ *n* [C] a container that is used in a larger piece of equipment, and which can be replaced with another similar part • *a video game cartridge* • A cartridge is also a tube containing an explosive substance and often a bullet for use in a gun: *This rifle only holds one cartridge at a time.*

cartwheel /'kɑrt·hwiːl, -wiːl/ *n* [C] a fast, skillful movement in which you stretch out your arms and throw yourself sideways and upside down onto one, then both, hands with your legs straight and pointing up, before landing on your feet again

carve /kɑrv/ *v* [I/T] to make (something) by cutting into esp. wood or stone, or to cut into the surface of (esp. stone or wood) • *This totem pole is carved from a single tree trunk.* [T] • To carve a large piece of cooked meat is to cut thin pieces from it: *Would you like me to carve (the turkey)?* [I/T]

carving /'kɑr·vɪŋ/ *n* [C/U] a decorative object made from esp. wood or stone, or the art of making patterns in or objects from these materials

□ **carve out** /'-'-/ *v adv* [T] to create or obtain (esp. a reputation, rank, or job) by skillful activities • *She carved out a reputation for herself as a high-powered lawyer.*

□ **carve up** *obj*, **carve** *obj* **up** /'-'-/ *v adv* [M] to divide (esp. land or a business) into parts • *The new owner carved up the company and sold off several divisions.*

cascade /kæs'keɪd/ *n* [C] a short, steep **waterfall** (= place where a river falls to a lower level), often one of a series • (*fig.*) *A cascade of golden hair fell down her back* (= Her hair seemed to flow down her back).

cascade /kæs'keɪd/ *v* [I always + adv/prep] to fall quickly and in large amounts; to flow • *The blast shattered windows, sending pieces of glass cascading to the pavement.*

case SITUATION /keɪs/ *n* [C] a particular situation or example of something • *We don't normally accept credits from courses taken at another university, but we'll make an exception in your case.* ○ *It was a case of not knowing what to say.* ○ *She said I refused to answer the question, but that is not the case* (= that is not accurate). ○ *In the case of teenage girls who want to have abortions, parents have to give their consent.* • **In case** means if something else should happen: *I don't expect much traffic, but in case there is, I think we should leave early.* • **In case of** means if something should happen, esp. something unusual or unexpected: *In case of fire, go immediately to the nearest emergency exit.*

case PROBLEM /keɪs/ *n* [C] an item or particular matter that is being dealt with as a problem to be solved, or a person considered in this way • *There were many reported cases of child abuse.* ○ *He is a sad case—out of work and living in the streets.* • A **case study** is a detailed examination of a particular process or situation over a period of time: *She published a series of case studies on how schools used computers in language learning.*

case ARGUMENT /keɪs/ *n* [C] arguments, facts, and reasons in support of or against something • *He presented the case against cutting the military budget.* • (*law*) In a court of law, a case is a matter to be decided by a judge or JURY (= group of people): *She claimed the city's negligence caused her accident, but she lost the case.*

case CONTAINER /keɪs/ *n* [C] a container used for protecting or storing things • *Two cases of liquor were delivered.*

case GRAMMAR /keɪs/ *n* [C] *specialized* (in grammar) the form a noun, pronoun, or adjective takes depending on its relationship to other words in a sentence • *The possessive case of a noun is usually formed with the ending -'s.*

cash /kæʃ/ *n* [U] money in the form of bills and coins • *Are you going to pay by credit card or cash?* • In a business, **cash flow** is the rate at which money comes in and is spent. • A **cash machine** (also **ATM machine**, *Br* **cashpoint**) is a machine from which you can take money out of your bank account by using a special card. • A **cash register** is a machine in a store or other business that records sales and into which money is put.

cash /kæʃ/ *v* [T] to get cash in exchange for (esp. a check) • *Can I cash a traveler's check here?* • To **cash in on** something is to use an opportunity to do something to your own advantage, esp. a financial advantage: *The law prohibits criminals from cashing in on their crimes by selling their stories to publishers.*

cashew /'kæʃ·uː, kə'ʃuː/ *n* [C] a small, edible nut

cashier /kæ'ʃɪr/ *n* [C] a person whose job is to receive and pay out money in a store, bank, restaurant, etc.

cashmere /'kæʒ·mɪr, 'kæʃ-/ *n* [U] a type of very soft woolen material that is made from the hair of goats from Kashmir • *a fine cashmere sweater*

casing /'keɪ·sɪŋ/ *n* [C] a container or cover that goes around something to hold it together or protect it • *A metal casing enclosed the three-inch thick cable.*

casino /kə'siː·noʊ/ *n* [C] *pl* **casinos** a building or business in which people GAMBLE (= risk losing money in the hope of winning more) by playing games of cards and other games, esp. **slot machines**

cask /kæsk/ *n* [C] a strong, round, wooden container used for storing liquid

casket /'kæs·kət/ *n* [C] a COFFIN

casserole /'kæs·ə,roʊl/ *n* [C] a dish made by cooking meat, vegetables, or other foods inside a heavy container at low heat, or the heavy, deep container with a lid used in cooking such dishes

cassette /kə'set/ *n* [C] a flat, rectangular device containing a very long strip of magnetic material that is used to record sound or pictures; an **audiocassette** or **videocassette** • *He listens to cassettes, CDs, even vinyl records.* ◦ *Insert the cassette and press play.* • People sometimes say cassette when they are talking about a **cassette player**, which is a machine that plays cassettes, or a **cassette recorder** which is a machine that can both play from and record onto cassettes.

cast CAUSE TO APPEAR /kæst/ *v* [T] *past* **cast** to cause (something) to appear, as if by throwing something • *People complained about the shadows cast by the new skyscraper.* ◦ *(fig.) A new scientific study may cast some light on (= help to explain) why women live longer than men.* • In the sport of fishing, if you cast something, such as a line or a net, you throw it far into the water: *We watched the trout fishermen casting their lines.* • To **cast doubt on** something is to cause uncertainty about it: *New evidence has cast doubt on the guilty verdict.*

cast CHOOSE ACTORS /kæst/ *v* [T] *past* **cast** to choose actors to play particular parts in (a play, movie, or show), or to choose (an actor) for a part • *They are casting the show in New York right now.* ◦ *She was always cast as a sexy but dumb blonde.*

cast /kæst/ *n* [C] all the actors in a movie, play, or show

cast SHAPE /kæst/ *v* [T] *past* **cast** to make (an object) by pouring liquid, such as melted metal, into a shaped container to become hard • *The bronze statue is being cast next week.*

cast /kæst/ *n* [C] an object made in a particular shape by pouring a liquid substance into a container having that shape and letting the liquid harden • **Cast iron** is a type of iron that is made into shapes by being poured into containers when melted: *a cast-iron frying pan*

cast PROTECTIVE COVERING /kæst/ *n* [C] a hard, protec-

cast

tive covering used to keep a broken bone in the correct position until it heals

cast VOTE /kæst/ *v* [T] *past* **cast** to give (a vote) • *Altogether, 358 votes were cast.*

□ **cast off** /'-'-/ *v adv* [I] (of a ship) to leave • *The ship was scheduled to cast off at 8 p.m.*

castaway /'kæs·tə,weɪ/ *n* [C] a person who has escaped from a ship that has sunk and managed to get to an island or country where there are few or no other people

caste /kæst/ *n* [C/U] a system of dividing Hindu society into classes, or any of these classes • Caste can also refer generally to a system in any society that divides people into classes: *the South's caste system* [U]

caster /'kæs·tər/ *n* [C] a small wheel, usually one of a set, that is fixed to the bottom, usually of the leg, of a piece of furniture so that it can be moved easily

castigate /'kæs·tə,geɪt/ *v* [T] to criticize (someone or something) severely • *Health inspectors castigated the kitchen staff for not keeping the place clean.*

castle /'kæs·əl/ *n* [C] a large building with strong walls, built in the past by a king or other important person for protection against attack • A castle is also a ROOK.

castoff /'kæs·tɔːf/ *n* [C] something, esp. a piece of clothing, that you no longer want and give away • *His family was poor, and he always wore castoffs.*

castrate /'kæs·treɪt/ *v* [T] to remove the TESTICLES (= sex organs that produce sperm) of (a male human or animal)

casual NOT SERIOUS /'kæʒ·ə·wəl/ *adj* not serious or careful in attitude; only partly interested • *a casual glance at a magazine* ◦ *Even to the casual observer, the forgery was obvious.*

casual INFORMAL /'kæʒ·ə·wəl/ *adj* not formal; relaxed in style or manner • *We have a small office and I am very casual and wear slacks and sports shirts and things like that.*

casually /'kæʒ·ə·wə·li/ *adv* • *We were told to dress casually for the walking tour.*

casual TEMPORARY /'kæʒ·ə·wəl/ *adj* not regular or frequent; temporary or done sometimes • *He was a casual user of marijuana, but never used hard drugs.* • Casual also means slight: *He was only a casual acquaintance—I didn't know him well.*

casual NOT PLANNED /'kæʒ·ə·wəl/ *adj* not intended or planned • *a casual remark* ◦ *casual conversation*

casualty /'kæʒ·wəl·ti, 'kæʒ·əl·ti/ *n* [C] a person hurt or killed in a war or other event, or something harmed or destroyed by an event • *Every war has civilian casualties.* ◦ *New team uniforms were a casualty of the budget cuts.*

cat ANIMAL /kæt/ *n* [C] a small, furry animal with four legs and a tail, often kept as a pet, or any of a group of related animals that are wild, and some of which are large and fierce, such as the lion

CAT EXAMINATION /kæt/ *n* [U] *abbreviation for* computerized axial tomography (= a way of taking computerized pictures of structures inside the body), useful in finding out what is wrong with someone • A **CAT scan** is a computerized picture of structures inside the body.

cataclysm /'kæt̬·ə‚klɪz·əm/ *n* [C] an extremely destructive event or violent change • *the cataclysm of a world war*

cataclysmic /‚kæt̬·ə'klɪz·mɪk/ *adj*

catalog, catalogue /'kæt̬·əl‚ɔːg, -‚ɑg/ *n* [C] a listing, sometimes with explanations or pictures, of items offered for sale, of items that are available for use, or of objects described for a scientific purpose • *The company's spring catalog is filled with pictures of beautifully made clothing for girls.* ○ *Students can search the library's on-line catalog and order books.* ○ (*fig.*) *I have a whole catalog of things that need to be done.*

catalog, catalogue /'kæt̬·əl‚ɔːg, -‚ɑg/ *v* [T] • *Scientists were cataloging the plants of their regions.*

catalyst /'kæt̬·əl·əst/ *n* [C] a condition, event, or person that is the cause of an important change • (*specialized*) A catalyst is also a substance that causes or speeds a chemical reaction without itself being changed.

catapult /'kæt̬·ə‚pʌlt, -‚pʊlt/ *v* [T always + adv/prep] to become famous or important very suddenly, in the process moving beyond others who had been more famous or important than you • *The album of hit songs catapulted her almost overnight into national stardom.* • To catapult (something or someone) is to throw them forward with great force or speed.

cataract EYE CONDITION /'kæt̬·ə‚rækt/ *n* [C] an area of the eye that changes to become unclear, causing a person not to see well, or this condition of the eye

cataract FALLING WATER /'kæt̬·ə‚rækt/ *n* [C] a place in a river where the water falls to a lower level

catastrophe /kə'tæs·trə·fi/ *n* [C] a sudden event that causes great suffering or destruction • *Losing his job was a financial catastrophe for his family.* ○ *A chemical plant leak could cause an environmental catastrophe.*

catastrophic /‚kæt̬·ə'strɑf·ɪk/ *adj* • *Continued rain will cause catastrophic flooding.*

catch TAKE HOLD /kætʃ, ketʃ/ *v* [I/T] *past* **caught** /kɔːt/ to take or get hold of (a moving object) or to hold (someone) to prevent them from getting away esp. when they have done something wrong • *She tossed him the car keys and yelled, "Catch!"* [I] ○ *He sneaked into the fairgrounds without paying and hoped nobody would catch him.* [T] • To **catch** someone's **eye** is to cause them to notice something or someone: *I was looking for a gift for my husband and walked around the store, hoping some-*

thing would catch my eye. • To **catch** your **breath** is to wait and rest for a moment when you have been very active, so that you can begin to breathe more slowly: *Don't try to talk, just sit down and catch your breath.* • If you **catch** someone **off guard**, you surprise them by doing something that is not expected: *The news really caught her off guard.* • If you get **caught up in** something you become involved in it: *He got caught up in some kind of illegal business.*

catch /kætʃ, ketʃ/ *n* [C/U] the act of taking hold of something that is thrown or comes through the air • *The ball was hit well, but the centerfielder made a leaping, one-handed catch to end the game.* [C] • Catch is also the activity of throwing and receiving a ball with another person: *My kids are always begging me to play catch.* [U]

catcher /'kætʃ·ər, 'ketʃ-/ *n* [C] (in baseball) a player who catches the ball when it is thrown to the player who is hitting for the opposing team

catch DISCOVER /kætʃ, ketʃ/ *v* [T] *past* **caught** /kɔːt/ to find or discover (something, esp. something unusual or bad) • *If the disease is caught in time, most patients get well quickly.* ○ *I hope I catch all the mistakes in my term paper.* • If you **catch sight of** or **catch a glimpse of** something, you see it only for a moment: *I caught sight of someone with red hair and knew it was you.* • If you say that you **wouldn't be caught dead** doing something, you mean that you dislike even the thought of doing it: *It's so crowded with teenagers, I wouldn't be caught dead going there.*

catch SEE /kætʃ, ketʃ/ *v* [T] *past* **caught** /kɔːt/ to see or hear (something or someone), or to understand • *I'm sorry, I didn't quite catch what you said.*

catch TRAVEL /kætʃ, ketʃ/ *v* [T] *past* **caught** /kɔːt/ to travel or be able to travel on (a train, bus, aircraft, etc.) • *He always caught the 6:05 train out of Grand Central.*

catch BECOME INFECTED /kætʃ, ketʃ/ *v* [T] *past* **caught** /kɔːt/ to get (an illness) • *I caught a cold.*

catching /'kætʃ·ɪŋ, 'ketʃ-/ *adj* (of an illness) able to be given to someone else • *I've got a rash, but I don't think it's catching.*

catch SPREAD /kætʃ, ketʃ/ *v past* **caught** /kɔːt/ • To **catch fire** is to start burning: *Once the curtains caught fire, they knew the whole house would soon be ablaze.*

catch PROBLEM /kætʃ, ketʃ/ *n* [C] *infml* a hidden problem or disadvantage • *That sales price sounds too good to be true—there must be a catch to it somewhere.* • A **catch-22** is a situation in which there are only two possibilities, and you cannot do either because each depends on having done the other first.

catch DEVICE /kætʃ, ketʃ/ *n* [C] a small device with a movable part that is used to fasten something • *The catch on the bracelet is broken.*

□ **catch on** BECOME POPULAR /ˈ-ˈ-/ *v adv* [I] to become fashionable or popular • *It was amazing how quickly the Internet has caught on.*

□ **catch on** UNDERSTAND /ˈ-ˈ-/ *v adv* [I] to understand • *We were teasing Jim, but he was slow to catch on that we were joking.*

□ **catch up** /ˈ-ˈ-/ *v adv* [I] to reach (someone or something) by moving faster than they are • *She is really fast, and I couldn't catch up with her.* ○ (fig.) *We're a young, growing company, and we're trying to catch up to the competition.*

catch–up /ˈkætʃ·ʌp, ˈketʃ-/ *n* [U] • (fig.) *Having started his fund-raising late, he had to play catch-up if he wanted to get enough money for his political campaign.*

catch up on /ˈkætʃ'ʌp·ɔːn, -ɑn/ *v adv prep* [T] to need to do (something that you have not been able to do) and want to continue to do • *I have to catch up on my reading.*

catchy /ˈkætʃ·i, ˈketʃ·i/ *adj* (esp. of a tune or song) pleasing and easy to remember • *a catchy melody*

catechism /ˈkæt̬·ə,kɪz·əm/ *n* [C] a set of questions and answers used to teach basic facts about a Christian religion, esp. in the Roman Catholic Church

categorical /ˌkæt̬·ə'ɡɔːr·ɪ·kəl, -'ɡɑr-/ *adj* without doubt or possibility of not being true; certain • *The president issued a categorical denial.*

category /ˈkæt̬·ə,ɡɔːr·i, -,ɡoʊr·i/ *n* [C] a grouping of people or things by type in any systematic arrangement • *The light trucks weigh less than 5,000 pounds and are in a category that includes minivans, pickups, and sport utility vehicles.*

categorize /ˈkæt̬·ə·ɡə,rɑɪz/ *v* [T] • *The books are categorized by subject.*

cater /ˈkeɪt̬·ər/ *v* [I/T] to provide food and drinks for an occasion or event • *Who catered your party?* [T]

caterer /ˈkeɪt̬·ə·rər/ *n* [C] • *an experienced caterer*

□ **cater to** /ˈ---/ *v prep* [T] to provide what (someone or something) needs or wants • *Our magazines cater to professionals such as lawyers and physicians.*

caterpillar /ˈkæt̬·ə,pɪl·ər, ˈkæt̬·ər-/ *n* [C] a small animal with a narrow body and many legs, and which feeds on the leaves of plants and later develops into a BUTTERFLY or MOTH (= flying insect)

catfish /ˈkæt·fɪʃ/ *n* [C] an edible fish with a flat head and stiff growths like hairs around its mouth, found in rivers and lakes

catharsis /kə'θɑr·səs/ *n* [C/U] *pl* **catharses** /kə'θɑr,siːz/ the experience of expressing strong emotions that previously were blocked • *It's the director's hope that Germans who see his movie will go through a catharsis similar to his own.* [C]

cathartic /kə'θɑrt̬·ɪk/ *adj* • *a cathartic experience*

cathedral /kə'θiː·drəl/ *n* [C] a large and important church, esp. one that is the center of a large area

catheter /ˈkæθ·ət̬·ər/ *n* [C] *specialized* a thin tube put into the body temporarily to help remove a liquid or to put in medicine • *a urinary catheter*

Catholic /ˈkæθ·lɪk, -ə·lɪk/ *n* [C], *adj* [not gradable] ROMAN CATHOLIC

Catholicism /kə'θɑl·ə,sɪz·əm/ *n* [U] **Roman Catholicism**, see at ROMAN CATHOLIC

catnap /ˈkæt·næp/ *n* [C] a short sleep, esp. during the day

catsup /ˈketʃ·əp, ˈkæt̬·ʃəp/ *n* [U] KETCHUP

cattle /ˈkæt̬·əl/ *pl n* large farm animals kept for their milk or meat; cows and BULLS • *beef/ dairy cattle*

catty /ˈkæt̬·i/ *adj* (of words, esp. speech) intended to hurt someone; unkind • *catty remarks*

catwalk /ˈkæt·wɔːk/ *n* [C] a narrow structure built beside a bridge or building or above a stage, used for walking or performing work • *A catwalk is also a long, narrow stage used in a fashion show by* MODELS (= people employed to show how new clothes look when they are worn).

Caucasian /kɔː'keɪ·ʒən/ *n* [C] a white person

caucus /ˈkɔː·kəs/ *n* [C] a meeting of the people who run a political party to plan activities and to decide which people the party will support in an election • *A caucus is also a group of people within a larger organization, esp. Congress, who have similar interests: the Congressional Black Caucus*

caught /kɔːt/ *past simple and past participle of* CATCH

cauliflower /ˈkɑl·ɪ,flɑʊ·ər, ˈkɔː·lɪ-, -,flɑʊr/ *n* [C/U] a firm, round, white vegetable that is eaten cooked or raw

cause REASON /kɔːz/ *n* [C/U] something without which something else would not happen • *The investigation will determine the cause of the airplane accident.* [C] ○ *She studied the causes of human behavior.* [C] • Cause is also reason for doing or feeling something: *He had just cause to feel disturbed by these events.* [U] ○ *There is no cause for alarm.* [U]

cause /kɔːz/ *v* [T] • *The wind and rain caused several accidents.*

cause PRINCIPLE /kɔːz/ *n* [C] an idea or principle strongly supported by some people • *He devoted himself to charitable causes and gave away millions of dollars.*

causeway /ˈkɔːz·weɪ/ *n* [C] a raised road, esp. across water

caustic /ˈkɔː·stɪk/ *adj* strongly critical • *a caustic remark* • (*specialized*) (of chemicals) Caustic means able to burn through things.

caution /ˈkɔː·ʃən/ *n* [C] a warning • *It's a good*

time to invest, he said, but a word of caution is in order.

caution /'kɔː·ʃən/ *v* [I/T] to warn (someone) about a possible problem or danger • *They cautioned her not to walk through the park at night.* [T] ○ *Experts caution against reading too much into the decline of stock market prices.* [I always + adv/prep]

cautious /'kɔː·ʃəs/ *adj* not acting quickly in order to avoid risks; careful • *Most doctors are cautious about advising you to have surgery.* ○ *Auto companies are taking a cautious approach toward introducing electric cars.*

caution /'kɔː·ʃən/ *n* [U] careful attention • *Use caution when approaching the railroad crossing.*

cautiously /'kɔː·ʃə·sli/ *adv* • *She was in the habit of driving cautiously.*

cavalier /ˌkæv·ə'lɪr/ *adj* not serious or caring enough about matters that other people are serious about • *a cavalier attitude toward public health concerns*

cavalry /'kæv·əl·ri/ *n* [C] a group of soldiers in an army who fight from protective vehicles, or (esp. in the past) a group in an army who fought while riding on horses

cave /keɪv/ *n* [C] a large hole in the side of a hill, cliff, or mountain, or underground • *It was very dark and cold inside the cave.*

□ **cave in** FALL IN /'keɪ'vɪn/ *v adv* [I] (of a structure) to fall in suddenly, esp. because of a lack of support • *The building's roof caved in under the weight of the snow.*

□ **cave in** AGREE TO /'keɪ'vɪn/ *v adv* [I] to agree to demands that you originally opposed because you have become tired or fearful • *She accused the university of caving in to political pressures.*

caveman (*pl* **-men**) /'keɪv·mæn/, **cavewoman** (*pl* **-women**) /'keɪv·wʊm·ən/ *n* [C] a person who lived in a cave early in human history

cavern /'kæv·ərn/ *n* [C] a large cave

cavernous /'kæv·ər·nəs/ *adj* (of a space) very large • *the cavernous Los Angeles Coliseum*

caviar /'kæv·iː,ɑr, 'kɑv-/ *n* [U] the eggs of various large fish, salted and eaten as a delicacy

cavity /'kæv·ət̬·i/ *n* [C] a hole in a surface or a hollow inside something • *the abdominal/chest cavity* • A cavity is also a hollow place in a tooth caused by decay.

cavort /kə'vɔːrt/ *v* [I] to move about freely or wildly, having a noisy good time • *A group of teenagers were cavorting in the park.*

CD *n* [C] *abbreviation for* compact disc (= small, plastic disk with a metallic surface on which information or sound is recorded) • *I bought a new CD player.* • A **CD-ROM** is a CD that contains information that can be read on a computer but not changed.

cease /siːs/ *v* [I/T] to stop (an action or condition) • *Clapp had to cease publication because of lack of money.* [T] ○ *It was hard to accept that one day he would simply cease to exist.* [+

to infinitive] • A **ceasefire** is an agreement, esp. between two armies, to stop fighting.

ceaseless /'siː·sləs/ *adj* [not gradable] continuing without ever stopping • *Peres vowed to wage a ceaseless war on terrorism.*

ceaselessly /'siː·slə·sli/ *adv* [not gradable] • *He campaigned ceaselessly against the death penalty.*

cedar /'siːd·ər/ *n* [C/U] a tall, wide, evergreen tree, or its wood, which has a sweet smell • *a cedar chest* [U]

cede /siːd/ *v* [T] *fml* to give (control or possession of something, esp. land) to someone else, often unwillingly or because forced to do so • *New Orleans was ceded to Spain in 1763.*

ceiling /'siː·lɪŋ/ *n* [C] the upper surface of a room that you see when you look above you • *The kitchen ceiling needs painting.* • A ceiling is also an upper limit put on something that varies: *There is a 10% ceiling on rent increases.*

celebrate /'sel·ə,breɪt/ *v* [I/T] to recognize (an important occasion) by taking part in an activity that makes it special • *Children's Day has been celebrated in Japan for hundreds of years.* [T]

celebration /ˌsel·ə'breɪ·ʃən/ *n* [C/U] • *a Fourth of July celebration* [C]

celebrated /'sel·ə,breɪt̬·əd/ *adj* famous for some special quality or ability • *Kelley was the most celebrated clown of his era.*

celebrity /sə'leb·rət̬·i/ *n* [C] someone who is famous, esp. in the entertainment business • *Hollywood celebrities turned up at Laguna Beach.*

celery /'sel·ə·ri/ *n* [U] a vegetable with long, green stems that can be eaten raw or cooked

celestial /sə'les·tʃəl/ *adj* of or from the sky above us • *The moon is a celestial body.*

celibate /'sel·ə·bət/ *adj* [not gradable] not having sex, esp. because of religious principles

celibacy /'sel·ə·bə·si/ *n* [U] • *Celibacy is highly respected in Hindu society.*

cell ORGANISM /sel/ *n* [C] the smallest basic unit of a plant or animal • *skins cells* • USAGE: The related adjective is CELLULAR.

cell ROOM /sel/ *n* [C] a small room, esp. in a prison

cellar /'sel·ər/ *n* [C] a room under the ground floor of a building, esp. a house, that is usually used for storage

cello (*pl* **cellos**) /'tʃel·oʊ/ *n* [C/U] a large, wooden musical instrument with four strings which a player rests on the floor, holding it between the legs while sitting, and plays with a BOW (= stick with hairs fixed to it), or this type of instrument generally • PIC BOW

cellist /'tʃel·əst/ *n* [C] • *a cellist with the Chicago Symphony*

cellophane /'sel·ə,feɪn/ *n* [U] a thin, transparent material used for covering food and other items

cellular /'sel·jə·lər/ *adj* [not gradable] having

to do with the cells of an organism • *cellular biology*

cellular phone /'sel·jə·lər'foun/, **cell phone** /'sel·foun/ *n* [C] a telephone that can be used anywhere you go because it operates with radio signals

celluloid /'sel·jə,lɔɪd/ *n* [U] a type of plastic used in the past to make many items, esp. film for movies

cellulose /'sel·jə,lous, -,louz/ *n* [U] the main substance in the cell walls of plants, which is used in making paper, artificial fibers, and plastics

Celsius /'sel·si:·əs/, **centigrade**, *abbreviation* **C** *n* [U] a scale for measuring temperature in which water freezes at 0° and boils at 100° • Compare FAHRENHEIT.

cement /sɪ'ment/ *n* [U] a gray powder that is mixed with water, sand, and other substances, becomes very hard when dry, and is used in making concrete • Cement also means concrete: *There weren't any chairs, so she sat on the cement.*

cement /sɪ'ment/ *v* [T] to attach firmly, or to cover with cement • *The dentist cemented the tooth back in place.* • If you cement an agreement or relationship, you make it unlikely to change: *She cemented the sale with a down payment.*

cemetery /'sem·ə,ter·i/ *n* [C] an area of ground in which dead bodies are buried

censor /'sen·sər/ *v* [T] to remove parts of (something to be read, seen, or heard) because it is offensive or considered morally wrong, or because it is secret • *She opposes efforts to censor the Internet.*

censor /'sen·sər/ *n* [C] a person whose job is to read books or watch movies or television programs in order to remove anything offensive from them

censorship /'sen·sər,ʃɪp/ *n* [U] • *Censorship was imposed on state-run television and radio.*

censure /'sen·tʃər/ *n* [U] strong criticism or disapproval, esp. when it is the official judgment of an organization

censure /'sen·tʃər/ *v* [T] • *The Senate rarely censures its members.*

census /'sen·səs/ *n* [C] a count for official purposes, esp. one to count the number of people living in a country and to obtain information such as age, sex, race, etc.

cent /sent/ *n* [C] a unit of money worth ¹/₁₀₀ of a dollar • *The newspaper costs 50 cents.*

centennial /sen'ten·i:·əl/, **centenary** /sen'ten·ə·ri, 'sent·ᵊn,er·i/ *n* [C] the day or year that is 100 years after a particular event, esp. an important one; the 100th ANNIVERSARY • *The sculpture commemorates Wyoming's centennial.*

center MIDDLE /'sent·ər/ *n* [C] the middle point or part • *She stood in the center of the stage.* • In politics, the center is a set of opinions that are not extreme. • In some sports, esp. football

and BASKETBALL, a center on a team is a player whose position is between other players or in the center. • *He likes being* **the center of attention** (= the person everyone notices).

center /'sent·ər/ *v* [T] to put (something) in the center • *The headings should be centered on the page.* • If someone's life, work, or thoughts **center around/on** something, it is their main interest: *Women's lives should not necessarily be centered around men.*

center PLACE /'sent·ər/ *n* [C] a building or set of buildings having a particular purpose, or a place connected with a particular activity • *a shopping center* ○ *the Kennedy Center for the Performing Arts* ○ *New York is a center for the arts.*

centerpiece /'sent·ər,pi:s/ *n* [C usually sing] the most important part of something • *The centerpiece of most environmental studies is conservation.*

centigrade /'sen·tə,greɪd/ *n* [U] CELSIUS

centimeter /'sent·ə,mi:t·ər/ (*abbreviation* **cm**) *n* [C] a unit of measurement of length equal to 0.01 meter or 0.39 inch

centipede /'sent·ə,pi:d/ *n* [C] a small animal like a WORM with a long, thin body and many legs

central NEAR THE MIDDLE /'sen·trəl/ *adj* in, at, from, or near the center • *He grew up in central Illinois.*

centrally /'sen·trə·li/ *adv* near the center • *We want a hotel that's centrally located.*

central IMPORTANT /'sen·trəl/ *adj* main or important • *American novels often take money as their central concern.*

central CONTROLLED /'sen·trəl/ *adj* (of something having separate parts) controlled from a single place or by a single organization • *A central computer tracks reservations.*

centralize /'sen·trə,laɪz/ *v* [T] to bring (separate parts) together so that they are organized or controlled from one place • *The law centralized control over the banking industry.*

century /'sen·tʃə·ri/ *n* [C] a period of 100 years • *Her medical career spanned half a century.* • A century is also one of the periods of 100 years counted from the year of the birth of Jesus: *the fourth century B.C.* (= the period 400 years to 300 years before the birth of Jesus) ○ *His music was influential in the 19th and 20th centuries.*

CEO *n* [C] *abbreviation for* **chief executive officer**, see at CHIEF PERSON IN CHARGE

ceramics /sə'ræm·ɪks/ *n* [C/U] objects produced by shaping pieces of clay that are then hardened by baking, or the skill of making such objects

ceramic /sə'ræm·ɪk/ *adj* [not gradable] • *ceramic kitchen tiles*

cereal FOOD /'sɪr·i:·əl/ *n* [C/U] a food made from grain that is eaten esp. for breakfast • *Do you want cereal or eggs?* [U]

cereal GRASS /'sɪr·i:·əl/ *n* [C/U] a type of grass

that is cultivated to produce grain • *Wheat, rice, and corn are cereals.* [C]

cerebral /sə'ri:·brəl, 'ser·ə-/ *adj* relating to the brain, esp. the front part of the brain • **Cerebral palsy** is a physical condition involving permanent tightening of the muscles that is caused by damage to the brain during or before birth.

ceremony /'ser·ə‚mou·ni/ *n* [C/U] a set of acts, often traditional or religious, performed at a formal occasion esp. to recognize an important event, or the performing of such acts • *a graduation/wedding ceremony* [C] ○ *She was buried without ceremony.* [U]

ceremonial /‚ser·ə'mou·ni:·əl/ *adj* • *The queen's role is largely ceremonial.*

certain KNOWING TO BE TRUE /'sɜrt·ᵊn/ *adj* knowing that something is true or will happen and having no cause to feel that it may not be true or may not happen; having no doubt • *"I think Emily is going to pick up Judy." "Are you certain?"* ○ *One thing is certain—supporters of the bill are not giving up.* ○ *I'm certain (that) he'll be there.* [+ (*that*) clause] ○ *I'm not certain how much it will cost.* [+ *wh*- word] ○ *When you report a robbery, make certain a police report is filled out* (= check that this happens).

certainly /'sɜrt·ᵊn·li/ *adv* • *I value his opinion, and I'll certainly miss him.* ○ *I certainly don't spend it watching TV in the evenings.* • When said in answer to a question asking for help, **certainly** means yes: *"Can you give me a hand?" "Certainly."*

certain PARTICULAR /'sɜrt·ᵊn/ *adj* particular but not named or described • *Parents expect their kids to leave home at a certain point.*

certain /'sɜrt·ᵊn/ *pronoun* • *Certain of these antiwar groups are actually anti-American.*

certain LIMITED /'sɜrt·ᵊn/ *adj* [not gradable] some but not exactly stated; limited • *She enjoys sports to a certain extent.* ○ *There's a certain amount of exaggeration in all ads.*

certainty SURE KNOWLEDGE /'sɜrt·ᵊn·ti/ *n* [U] the sure knowledge that something is true • *Can you say with absolute certainty that this is the man you saw?*

certainty CERTAIN EVENT /'sɜrt·ᵊn·ti/ *n* [C] something that has no possibility of any other result; something that you know will happen in a particular way • *There are few certainties in life.*

certificate /sər'tɪf·ɪ·kət/ *n* [C] an official document that gives information • *a birth/death/marriage certificate*

certify /'sɜrt̬·ə‚fɑɪ/ *v* [T] *fml* to state (something) officially, esp. that (something) is true or correct or that (someone) has been trained to a particular standard • *Inspectors must certify that the building is safe.* • A **certified check** is a check that a bank has already paid for. • **Certified mail** is mail for which proof of delivery is obtained.

certified /'sɜrt̬·ə‚fɑɪd/ *adj* [not gradable] having a document that proves you have successfully completed a course of training • *a certified teacher* ○ *She is certified to practice medicine.* [+ *to* infinitive] • A **certified public accountant** (*abbreviation* **CPA**) is a person who has completed the training and passed a state exam to become an accountant.

cervix /'sɜr·vɪks/ *n* [C] *medical* the narrow, lower part of a woman's uterus that leads into the vagina

cervical /'sɜr·vɪ·kəl/ *adj* [not gradable] *medical* • *cervical cancer*

cesarean (section), caesarean /sɪ'zær·i:·ən/ ('sek·ʃən‚, -'zer-/ (*abbreviation* **C–section**) *n* [C] *medical* an operation in which a pregnant woman's stomach and uterus are cut to allow a baby to be born

cessation /ses'eɪ·ʃən/ *n* [C/U] *slightly fml* the ending of a condition or the stopping of an activity • *a cessation of violence* [C usually sing]

cesspool /'ses·pɪt/ *n* [C] a large, underground hole or container that is used for collecting and storing human waste and dirty water • (*fig.*) *State government here is a cesspool of corruption.*

chafe RUB /tʃeɪf/ *v* [I/T] to make or become damaged or sore by rubbing • *That bracelet chafed my wrist.* [T]

chafe BE ANNOYED /tʃeɪf/ *v* [I always + adv/prep] to be or become annoyed or lose patience • *Some students chafed at the increased security presence.*

chagrin /ʃə'grɪn/ *n* [U] disappointment or annoyance, esp. when caused by a failure or mistake • *We grow lots of squash, much to my children's chagrin.*

chagrined /ʃə'grɪnd/ *adj* • *She was chagrined to discover her mistake.*

chain CONNECTED RINGS /tʃeɪn/ *n* [C] a length of metal rings that are connected together and used for fastening or supporting, and in machinery • *She looped the chain around her bike and locked it to the fence.* • A chain is also a length of connected rings worn as jewelry: *Mary wore a silver chain around her neck.* • A **chain-link fence** is a strong, metal fence made with chainlike connections. • A **chain saw** is a cutting tool that is powered by a motor and has a continuous chain with sharp points along its outer edge that cut as the chain moves.

chain saw

chain /tʃeɪn/ *v* [T] • *We don't like to keep the dog chained (up) all the time.* [T/M]

chain RELATED THINGS /tʃeɪn/ *n* [C] a set of connected or related things • *a mountain chain* ○ *a chain of supermarkets* ○ *That set in motion a chain of events that changed her life forever.* • A **chain of command** is the way people with authority in an organization, esp. in the military, are ranked, from the person with the most authority to the next one below, and so on. • A **chain reaction** is a set of related events in which each event causes the next one: *The accident caused a chain reaction in which seven trucks piled up on the bridge.* • A person who **chain-smokes** or is a **chain-smoker** smokes almost continuously, often lighting one cigarette from the end of the previous one.

chair FURNITURE /tʃer, tʃær/ *n* [C] a movable seat for a person that has a part for their back to rest against, usually four legs, and sometimes two side parts for their arms • *(infml)* **The chair** is the **electric chair**. See at ELECTRIC.

chair BE IN CHARGE /tʃer, tʃær/ *v* [T] to be the person in charge of (a meeting) • *Would you chair tomorrow's meeting?*

chair /tʃer, tʃær/ *n* [C] a CHAIRPERSON

chairmanship /'tʃer·mən,ʃɪp, 'tʃær-/ *n* [C usually sing] the state or period during which a particular person is a CHAIRPERSON • *the chairmanship of the Alabama Republican Committee*

chairperson (*pl* **-people**) /'tʃer,pɜr·sən, 'tʃær-/, **chairman** (*pl* **-men**) /'tʃer·mən, 'tʃær-/, **chairwoman** (*pl* **-women**) /'tʃer,wʊm·ən, 'tʃær-/ *n* [C] a person in charge of a meeting, organization, or department • *All the members of the committee take turns acting as chairperson.* • USAGE: Although chairman can refer to a person of either sex, chairperson or chair is often preferred to avoid giving the idea the person is necessarily male.

chalet /ʃæ'leɪ, 'ʃæl·eɪ/ *n* [C] a small, wooden house found in mountainous areas and used esp. by people on vacation

chalk /tʃɔːk/ *n* [C/U] a type of soft, white rock, or a similar substance, esp. in the shape of a stick and sometimes colored, used for writing or drawing • A **chalkboard** (also **blackboard**) is a dark surface on a wall or frame on which you write with chalk.

▫**chalk up** /'-'-/ *v adv* [T] to have or record (something good or bad) • *The team chalked up its first regular-season victory by beating Miami.* ○ *Most of the largest banks in the country chalked up large losses on foreign loans.*

▫**chalk** *obj* **up to** *obj*, **chalk up** *obj* **to** *obj* /'-'--/ *v adv prep* [T] to consider (something) as being caused by (something else) • *He was clearly lying, and now he's trying to chalk it up to a poor memory.*

challenge DIFFICULT JOB /'tʃæl·əndʒ/ *n* [C/U] something needing great mental or physical effort in order to be done successfully, or the situation of facing this kind of effort • *It's a*

challenge being in a marriage when both partners have high-pressure jobs. [C] ○ *No matter how long you write, poetry remains a challenge.* [C] ○ *Germany faces broad challenges in the coming years.* [C]

challenge /'tʃæl·əndʒ/ *v* [T] • *It's easy enough to crank out college graduates, but a good education should really challenge them.*

challenged /'tʃæl·əndʒd/ *adj* having a physical or mental condition that makes ordinary activities more difficult than they are for other people; handicapped • Compare **handicapped** at HANDICAP PHYSICAL CONDITION.

challenging /'tʃæl·ən·dʒɪŋ/ *adj* • *For a reporter, covering the White House is a challenging assignment.*

challenge ASK TO COMPETE /'tʃæl·əndʒ/ *v* [T] to invite (someone) to take part in a competition • *The other candidates challenged the president to take part in a debate.*

challenge /'tʃæl·əndʒ/ *n* [C] something that competes with you or is a threat • *The governor barely survived a challenge from an unknown opponent in the primary.*

challenger /'tʃæl·ən·dʒər/ *n* [C] someone who tries to win a competition and achieve a position, esp. in politics or sports, against someone who has won it and now has that position • *An aide to Buchanan said the conservative challenger for the presidency would hold a press conference tomorrow.*

challenge EXPRESSION OF DOUBT /'tʃæl·əndʒ/ *n* [C/U] a questioning or expression of doubt about the truth, legality, or purpose of something, or the right of a person to have or do something • *Because of the way this research was done, its findings are open to challenge.* [U] ○ *The president is clearly anticipating a new challenge to his authority.* [C]

challenge /'tʃæl·əndʒ/ *v* [T] • *The convicted terrorist challenged the authority of the court.*

chamber ROOM /'tʃeɪm·bər/ *n* [C] a room or space used for a particular purpose • *He was executed in the gas chamber* (= room filled with poison gas) *at San Quentin prison.* ○ *the Nazi gas chambers*

chambers /'tʃeɪm·bərz/ *pl n* a judge's private office, where the judge may have legal discussions with lawyers

chamber LEGISLATURE /'tʃeɪm·bər/ *n* [C] a group of people who are part or all of a legislature, or an official place where they meet • *Most states have two chambers, a senate and a house of representatives, modeled after the US Congress.* • A **chamber of commerce** is an organization consisting of people who work together to improve business in their city or local area.

chamber SPACE /'tʃeɪm·bər/ *n* [C] an enclosed space • *The human heart has two chambers.*

chamber music /'tʃeɪm·bər,mjuː·zɪk/ *n* [U] music written for a small group of performers

chameleon /kə'miːl·ʃ·ən/ n [C] a LIZARD (= type of creature) that changes its skin color to match its surroundings so that it cannot be seen, or (fig.) a person who changes their opinions or behavior to please others • (fig.) Opponents called him a political chameleon for shifting his position on a range of issues.

chamomile, **camomile** /'kæm·ə,maɪl, -,miːl/ n [U] a plant whose white and yellow flowers are used to make an herbal tea

champagne /ʃæm'peɪn/ n [U] a pale yellow or pink, bubbly wine made in France, or a similar wine from somewhere else • The newlyweds were toasted with champagne.

champion WINNER /'tʃæm·piː·ən/, short form **champ** /'tʃæmp/ n [C] someone or something, esp. a person or animal, that has beaten all other competitors in a competition • a tennis champion

championship /'tʃæm·piː·ən,ʃɪp/ n [C] the position of being the best in a particular sport or competition, or the competition that decides who is the best • She has held the championship for the past three years.

champion SUPPORT /'tʃæm·piː·ən/ n [C] a person who enthusiastically supports, defends, or fights for a belief or principle • a champion of free speech

champion /'tʃæm·piː·ən/ v [T] • He championed protection of the wilderness.

chance LUCK /tʃæns/ n [U] the happening of something in a way that no one could have known, so that it seems to have no cause • Four years ago we met by chance in Paris. ○ Do you by any chance know when the last bus leaves tonight?

chance /tʃæns/ v [I] to happen or find something in a way that is not planned or expected • I chanced upon some old love letters in a drawer.

chance LIKELIHOOD /tʃæns/ n [U] a level of possibility that something will happen; likelihood • I've applied to seven different universities, and there's a good chance I'll get into two of them. • "Do you think I could pass for a 21-year-old?" "**Not a chance** (= There is no possibility of that)!"

chances /'tʃæn·səz/ pl n • Chances are, they'll be late as usual. ○ What are the chances of getting a ticket to the concert tonight?

chance OPPORTUNITY /tʃæns/ n [C] an occasion that allows something to be done; an opportunity • If you get a chance, come over and see me. ○ You had many chances to back out of the deal, and you didn't do it. ○ She'd been a substitute on the team, and she wanted a chance to play every day.

chance RISK /tʃæns/ n [C] a possibility that something bad will happen; a risk • There's a chance of injury in almost any sport. ○ You don't get anywhere in life without taking chances.

chance /tʃæns/ v [T] to do (something) although it is risky • It's a very popular restaurant, and we may not get a table, but let's chance it.

chancy /'tʃæn·si/ adj risky • The show's financing was chancy, and that made us all nervous.

chancellor /'tʃæn·sə·lər/ n [C] a person in a position of the highest or high rank, esp. in a government or university • Helmut Kohl became the first chancellor of a united Germany in 1990.

chandelier /,ʃæn·də'lɪr/ n [C] a decorative light that hangs from the ceiling and has several parts like branches for holding **light bulbs** or, esp. in the past, candles • A gorgeous crystal chandelier hung in the dining room.

change BECOME DIFFERENT /tʃeɪndʒ/ v [I/T] to make or become different, or to do, use, or get one thing in place of another thing, esp. of a similar type • I've changed jobs twice in the past ten years. [T] ○ I changed my hair style—do you like it? [T] ○ Attitudes about sex changed a lot in the 1960s. [I] ○ It's surprising how fast kids change during their teen years. [I] • To change (over) from one thing to something else is to stop doing or using one thing and to start doing or using another: We just changed from oil heat to gas. [I] • Something is said to **change hands** if it goes from one owner to another: That restaurant isn't as good since it changed hands. • If you **change** your **mind**, you form an opinion or make a decision about something that is not the same as the one you first had: At first I thought she was unfriendly, but I've changed my mind.

change /tʃeɪndʒ/ n [C/U] • Let me know if you have any change of plans. [U] ○ We decided we needed a change, so we went to Florida for a couple of weeks. [C] • **A change** often refers to something unusual or new that is better than what existed before, or more pleasant: Rhodes felt calm and at ease with the world, for a change. ○ Why don't we eat on the porch for a change? ○ Can't you stop talking, for a change? • A **changeover** is a replacement of one system or method by another: The changeover to the new accounting system created a lot of problems.

changeable /'tʃeɪn·dʒə·bəl/ adj changing often • The weather is very changeable this time of year.

changed /tʃeɪndʒd/ adj [not gradable] • A person can be described as a changed man/woman if their behavior and character have become different to an unusual degree: After 15 years in prison, he was a changed man.

change CLOTHES / BEDS /tʃeɪndʒ/ v [I/T] to remove one set of clothes and put a different set on yourself or someone else, such as a baby, or to remove dirty sheets from a bed and put clean ones on it • I'll just change into (= put on) something a little dressier. [I] ○ Could you change the baby/the baby's diaper (= put on a clean one)? [T] ∘ *I changed the sheets/the bed* (= the sheets on the bed) *in the guest room.* [T]

change /tʃeɪndʒ/ *n* [C] a set of clothes that is additional to the clothes that you are wearing • *Bring a change of clothes with you in case we stay overnight.*

change MONEY /tʃeɪndʒ/ *v* [T] to get or give (money) in exchange for money, either because you want it in smaller units, or because you want the same value in foreign money • *Can you change a $100 bill for me?* ∘ *I had to change some American money into pesetas before I arrived in Spain.*

change /tʃeɪndʒ/ *n* [U] the difference in money, returned to the buyer, between what is paid for something and the lesser amount that it costs • *It costs $17 and you gave me $20, so here's your $3 change.* • Change also refers to smaller units of money whose total value is equal to that of a larger unit: *I need change for a $50 bill because I want to take a taxi.* ∘ *Do you have change for/of a dollar?* • Change can refer to coins rather than bills: *Bring a lot of change for using the public telephones.*

change TRANSPORT /tʃeɪndʒ/ *v* [I/T] to get off (an aircraft, train, bus, etc.) and catch another in order to continue a trip • *I had to change planes twice to get there.* [T] ∘ *Change at Hartford for the train to Springfield.* [I]

change /tʃeɪndʒ/ *n* [C] • *You used to have to make a change in Chicago, but now you can fly direct.*

channel TELEVISION STATION /'tʃæn·əl/ *n* [C] a television station • *She switched to another channel to watch the news.* • (*slang*) **Channel-surfing** is the practice of changing frequently from one channel to another, using a **remote control** (= device for operating something from a distance).

channel PASSAGE /'tʃæn·əl/ *n* [C] a passage for water or other liquids to flow along, or a part of a river or other area of water that is deep and wide enough to provide a route for ships to travel along • A channel is also a narrow part of the sea between a continent and an island: *the English Channel*

channel DIRECT /'tʃæn·əl/ *v* [T] to direct (something) into a particular place or situation • *A lot of money has been channeled into AIDS research.*

channel /'tʃæn·əl/ *n* [C] a way of giving, directing, or communicating something • *We've established a regular distribution channel for these products.*

chant /tʃænt/ *v* [I/T] to sing (a religious prayer or song) to a simple tune, or to repeat or sing (a word or phrase) continuously • *We sat for hours listening to the monks chanting.* [I]

chant /tʃænt/ *n* [C] • *I bought an album of Gregorian chants.*

Chanukah /'hɑn·ə·kə, 'xɑn-/ *n* [U] HANUKKAH

chaos /'keɪ·ɑs/ *n* [U] a state of disorder and confusion • *Repairs to the major highway this summer will bring chaos to commuters.*

chaotic /keɪ'ɑt̬·ɪk/ *adj* • *The house is a little chaotic right now—we're in the middle of repainting.*

chapel /'tʃæp·əl/ *n* [C] a small church or an enclosed place in a large church for worship by a small group, or a room in a building set apart for worship

chaperon, chaperone /'ʃæp·ə,roʊn/ *n* [C] an older person who is present at a social event to encourage correct behavior • *Several teachers acted as chaperons for the school dance.*

chaplain /'tʃæp·lən/ *n* [C] an official who is responsible for the religious needs of an organization • *a military/police chaplain*

chapped /tʃæpt/ *adj* (of skin) sore, rough, and cracked, esp. when caused by cold weather • *chapped lips*

chaps /tʃæps, ʃæps/ *pl n* protective leather clothing worn over pants by COWBOYS when riding a horse

chapter BOOK PART /'tʃæp·tər/ *n* [C] any of the separate parts into which a book or other piece of text is divided, usually numbered or given a title • (*law*) **Chapter 11** is a legal process in the US by which a company, when it owes money that it cannot pay, can stay in business while it organizes itself in a new way and agrees to pay some debts over a period of time.

chapter PERIOD /'tʃæp·tər/ *n* [C] a period that is part of a larger amount of time during which something happens • *The prohibition era, when alcoholic drinks could not be legally sold, was an interesting chapter in American history.*

chapter SOCIETY /'tʃæp·tər/ *n* [C] a local division of a larger organization • *The local chapter of the League of Women Voters meets at the library.*

character QUALITY /'kær·ɪk·tər/ *n* [C/U] the particular combination of things about a person or place, esp. things you cannot see, that make that person or place different from others • *The idea was to modernize the house without changing its homey character.* [C] • Character is often used in a positive way to mean qualities that are interesting and unusual: *It's a theater with a lot of character.* [U]

characteristic /ˌkær·ɪk·tə'rɪs·tɪk/ *adj* typical of a person or thing • *The creamy richness is characteristic of cheese from this region.*

characteristic /ˌkær·ɪk·tə'rɪs·tɪk/ *n* [C] something that is typical or noticeable about someone or something that makes that person or thing different from others • *Curly hair is one of my family characteristics.* ∘ *Aggressiveness, independence, and ambitiousness were long regarded as undesirable characteristics in a woman.*

characteristically /ˌkær·ɪk·tə'rɪs·tɪ·kli/ *adv* •

She gave a characteristically brilliant performance.

characterize /'kær·ɪk·tə,rɑɪz/ *v* [T] to have as a main characteristic or quality • *The current system is characterized by obsolete technology.* • To characterize something also means to describe it by stating its main qualities: *She characterized the novel as wordy in places but very funny.*

characterization /,kær·ɪk·tə·rə'zeɪ·ʃən/ *n* [C] a description of the most typical or important characteristics of someone or something • *I don't agree with your characterization of my home town as a boring place to live.*

character REPRESENTATION /'kær·ɪk·tər/ *n* [C] a person represented in a movie, play, or story • *The story revolves around three main characters.* • A character is also a person, esp. with reference to a particular quality that they have: *There were one or two suspicious-looking characters hanging around.*

character MARK /'kær·ɪk·tər/ *n* [C] a letter, number, or other mark or sign used in writing or printing, or the space one of these takes • *This computer screen is 66 characters wide.*

charade /ʃə'reɪd/ *n* [C] an act or event that is obviously false, although represented as true • *From the beginning we knew who would get the job—the interviews were just a charade.*

charades /ʃə'reɪdz/ *pl n* a team game in which each member tries to communicate to others of his or her team a particular word or phrase while remaining silent and using only actions to represent the sounds or meanings

charcoal /'tʃɑr·koʊl/ *n* [U] a hard, black substance similar to coal that can be used as fuel or, in the form of sticks, as something to draw with • **Charcoal gray** is a dark gray color: *a charcoal gray suit*

charge ASK FOR MONEY /tʃɑrdʒ/ *v* [I/T] to ask for (a price) for something • *I think they charge too much for football tickets.* [T] • LP PRICE

charge /tʃɑrdʒ/ *n* [C] • *There's no charge for children under six.*

charge OWE /tʃɑrdʒ/ *v* [T] to buy (something) and agree to pay for it later • *I didn't have any cash, so I charged the food.*

charge /tʃɑrdʒ/ *n* [C] • *You have a lot of charges on your bill.* • A **charge account** allows a customer to buy things and pay for them after being billed at a later time. • A **charge card** is **credit card**. See at CREDIT PAYMENT LATER.

charge ACCUSE /tʃɑrdʒ/ *v* [T] to accuse (someone) of something, esp. to officially accuse (someone) of a crime • *He was charged with resisting arrest.*

charge /tʃɑrdʒ/ *n* [C] • *They face civil and criminal charges.*

charge MOVE FORWARD /tʃɑrdʒ/ *v* [I/T] to move forward quickly, esp. to attack • *When the batter was hit with the pitch, he dropped his bat and charged the pitcher.* [T]

charge CONTROL /tʃɑrdʒ/ *n* [U] responsibility for the control of something or the care of someone • *Marilyn agreed to take charge of fundraising.* • To be **in charge** is to be the person responsible: *Who's in charge here?*

charge /tʃɑrdʒ/ *v* [T] • *The troopers were charged with guarding the governor.*

charge STORE ENERGY /tʃɑrdʒ/ *v* [I/T] to put electrical energy into a storage device such as a BATTERY • *It takes several hours for my laptop's batteries to charge.* [I]

charge /tʃɑrdʒ/ *n* [C/U] the amount of electricity that an electrical device stores or carries • (*specialized*) A positive or negative electrical charge is a basic characteristic of matter: *A proton has positive charge and an electron has negative charge.* [U]

charged /tʃɑrdʒd/ *adj* • *They study electrically charged particles.* • If an event is charged, people at it are behaving excitedly: *The meeting was emotionally charged.* • Someone who is **charged up** is too excited: *He was so charged up, he couldn't sleep.*

charge INSTRUCT /tʃɑrdʒ/ *v* [T] law to instruct (the people deciding a legal case) what the law is in a particular case • *The judge charged the jury before deliberations began.*

charge EXPLOSIVE /tʃɑrdʒ/ *n* [C] the amount of explosive to be fired at one time

chariot /'tʃær·iː·ət/ *n* [C] a two-wheeled vehicle pulled by a horse, used in ancient times by the military and in racing

charisma /kə'rɪz·mə/ *n* [U] the ability to attract the attention and admiration of others, and to be seen as a leader • *To be a great leader, a person has to have some charisma.*

charismatic /,kær·əz'mæt̬·ɪk/ *adj* • *He was the charismatic leader his people had hoped for.*

charitable /'tʃær·ət̬·ə·bəl/ *adj* tending to be kind rather than critical • *The public is not in a charitable mood toward politicians these days.*

charitably /'tʃær·ət̬·ə·bli/ *adv* • *She was charitably described as "handsome."*

charity /'tʃær·ət̬·i/ *n* [C/U] the giving of money, food, or help to those who need it, or an organization that does this • *She does a lot of work for charity.* [U] ○ *We donate to a number of charities.* [C] • Charity is also the belief that you should help people: *He visits homeless shelters out of charity.* [U]

charitable /'tʃær·ət̬·ə·bəl/ *adj* • *She was involved in many charitable organizations.*

charlatan /'ʃɑr·lət̬·ən, -lə·tən/ *n* [C] a person who pretends to have skills or knowledge that they do not have

charley horse /'tʃɑr·liː,hɔːrs/ *n* [C] *pl* **charley horses** a CRAMP (= a sudden, painful tightening of a muscle), esp. in the leg

charm ATTRACTION /tʃɑrm/ *n* [C/U] a special quality of a person or thing that makes them attractive • *I never could resist the charms of the city.* [C]

charm /tʃɑrm/ v [T] • *Charlie charms everyone.*

charming /'tʃɑr·mɪŋ/ adj • *He was thoughtful and charming.*

charm LUCKY OBJECT /tʃɑrm/ n [C] an object or saying that is believed to bring good luck • *Many people carry good luck charms.*

charmed /tʃɑrmd/ adj • A **charmed life** is a lucky life, one without any serious worries or problems: *Horrors such as war seemed to be little more than backdrops to his charmed life.*

charred /tʃɑrd/ adj burned and blackened from fire • *The house was just a pile of charred wreckage.*

chart /tʃɑrt/ n [C] a way of presenting information, usually by putting it into vertical rows and boxes on a sheet of paper, so that different parts of it can be easily compared • *The nurse studied the patient's temperature chart.*

chart /tʃɑrt/ v [T] to record (changes in something or the progress of something) • *The magazine charts current trends in fashion.* • If someone charts a series of actions, they plan them: *The president plans to chart a new economic policy.*

charter DOCUMENT /'tʃɑrt·ər/ n [C] a formal statement, esp. by a government or ruler, of the rights of a group organized for some purpose • *The United Nations charter sets forth goals we all admire.* • A person who is a **charter member** of an organization helped start the organization or became a member when it began. • A **charter school** is a school that is paid for with public money but is organized by a private group for a special purpose and admits only students who meet its standards: *They formed a charter school for girls who are good at math and science.*

charter RENT /'tʃɑrt·ər/ v [T] to rent (a vehicle) for a special use • *He wanted to charter an airplane.*

charter /'tʃɑrt·ər/ n [C] • *Charters with low fares have attracted new airline passengers.*

chase FOLLOW /tʃeɪs/ v [I/T] to hurry after (someone or something) intending to catch them • *The dog chased squirrels in the park.* [T] ○ *(fig.) Everett is always chasing women* (= trying to make them become sexually or romantically interested in him). [T]

chase /tʃeɪs/ n [C] • *The dog got tired and gave up the chase.*

chase MAKE LEAVE /tʃeɪs/ v [T] to act in a threatening way in order to make (a person or animal) leave • *She's always chasing rabbits out of her garden, but they keep coming back.*

chasm /'kæz·əm/ n [C] a deep opening in earth or rock • *The little bridge over that deep chasm looked very unsafe.*

chassis /'tʃæs·i, 'ʃæs·i/ n [C] pl **chassis** /'tʃæs·iz, 'ʃæs·iz/ the frame of a vehicle, including the wheels and engine, which supports the upper, covering part

chaste /tʃeɪst/ adj not having or involving sex, except sexual behavior that is considered moral • *The main character lives a chaste, uneventful life.*

chastity /'tʃæs·tət·i/ n [U] the state of not having sexual relationships or never having had sex

chasten /'tʃeɪ·sən/ v [T] to make (someone) aware that they have failed or done something wrong • *The Celtics, after giving up a lead in the fourth quarter and losing the game, were a pretty chastened bunch afterwards.*

chastise /tʃæs'taɪz, 'tʃæs·taɪz/ v [T] to punish or criticize (someone) strongly • *Economists like to chastise the public for not saving.*

chat /tʃæt/ v [I] -tt- to talk to someone in a friendly informal way • *We stopped to chat with the neighbors.*

chat /tʃæt/ n [C] • *Sometimes Don would just stop by for a chat.*

chatty /'tʃæt̬·i/ adj • *I sat next to a friendly, chatty woman.*

chateau /ʃæ'tou/ n [C] pl **chateaus** /ʃæ'touz/ or **chateaux** /ʃæ'tou, -'touz/ a large house, esp. in France, or a castle in France

chatter /'tʃæt̬·ər/ v [I] to talk continuously and usually for no serious purpose • *The boys and girls kept chattering during the movie.* • If your teeth chatter, you are so cold or frightened that you can't stop your upper and lower teeth from hitting against each other. • An animal or a machine that chatters makes a sound like fast, continuous talking: *Birds chattered in the trees.* ○ *The printer was chattering away on the desk.*

chatter /'tʃæt̬·ər/ n [U] • *The air was full of the chatter of birds.* • A **chatterbox** is someone who talks continuously: *Our three-year-old is a real chatterbox.*

chauffeur /'ʃou·fər, ʃou'fɜr/ n [C] a person employed to drive a private car belonging to someone else

chauffeur /'ʃou·fər, ʃou'fɜr/ v [T] • *I was chauffeured around town by my uncle.*

chauvinism /'ʃou·və,nɪz·əm/ n [U] the strong and unreasonable belief that your own country, sex, or racial group is the best or most important • *The president appealed to national pride and chauvinism.*

chauvinist /'ʃou·və·nəst/ n [C] • *Her husband was an impossible chauvinist, always downplaying the importance of women.*

cheap LOW IN COST /tʃiːp/ adj [-er/-est only] costing little money or less than is usual or expected • *After World War II, the US had cheap labor, cheap energy, cheap raw materials, cheap housing, cheap food, and cheap transportation.* • If a place that sells goods or services is cheap, it charges low prices: *a cheap department store* • Goods that are cheap are low in price but of poor quality: *He smokes cheap, smelly cigars.* • *(disapproving)* Someone who is cheap is unwilling to spend money: *The boss* *is cheap—he'll never buy a new truck if he can squeeze a few more miles out of the old one.* • A **cheapskate** is someone unwilling to give or spend any money: *That cheapskate won't even pay for a postage stamp.*

cheaply /'tʃiː·pli/ *adv* • *You can buy paper goods more cheaply if you buy in quantity.*

cheapness /'tʃiːp·nəs/ *n* [U] • *They chose to build here because of the cheapness and lack of problems the site offered.*

cheap OF BAD CHARACTER /tʃiːp/ *adj* [-er/-est only] having or showing bad moral character, esp. in sexual behavior • *She played cheap women in several movies in the 50s.* • A **cheap shot** is an unfair, negative remark made by someone to achieve an advantage over someone else: *Making fun of his name was a cheap shot.* • In sports, esp. boxing, football, and HOCKEY, a **cheap shot** is a physical play that is unnecessarily violent against a player who was not prepared for it.

cheapen /'tʃiː·pən/ *v* [T] to make (someone) feel as if they have a bad character or judgment and do not deserve respect • *She felt cheapened by his remarks.*

cheat /tʃiːt/ *v* [I/T] to act in a way that is dishonest, or to make (someone) believe something that is not true in order to get something for yourself • *The insurance companies were found to be cheating consumers.* [T] ○ *They got cheated out of their money.* [T] • To **cheat on** the person you are married to or have a romantic relationship with is to have a sexual relationship with someone else: *He cheated on his wife.*

cheat /tʃiːt/ *n* [C] • *He is a liar and a cheat.*

check EXAMINE /tʃek/ *v* [I/T] to look at or give your attention to (something) to get information, often to help you decide if something is correct, safe, or suitable • *Check to see what the weather is like outside.* [+ *to* infinitive] ○ *I brought the car to the garage to have the brakes checked.* [T] ○ *We checked our records for any information about him.* [T] ○ *We have a claim for lost luggage, and we are checking into it.* [I] ○ *The doctors checked his heart and said it was fine.* [T] ○ *Before you hand in your papers, check your spelling.* [T] ○ *You have to check out the nursing home before putting your mother in it.* [M]

check /tʃek/ *n* [C] • *The FBI did a thorough background check on him* (= looked into his past experience and relationships).

check STOP /tʃek/ *v* [T] to stop (someone) from doing or saying something, or to prevent (something) from increasing or continuing • *He started to interrupt but checked himself and said nothing.* ○ *The campaign about safe sex is designed to check the spread of AIDS.*

check /tʃek/ *n* • If something is **in check**, it is being controlled within reasonable limits: *We've got to find ways of keeping our expenses in check.*

check MONEY /tʃek/ *n* [C] a printed form, used instead of money, to make payments from your bank account • *I've got to cash my pay check.* ○ *She wrote me a check for $120.* • A **checkbook** is a number of checks attached at one end so that you can keep them together and remove one easily when you need it, and which usually includes a place to write information about each check you write. • A **checking account** is a bank account from which money can be taken by the customer using a check.

check LEAVE /tʃek/ *v* [T] to leave (your outer clothing or property) temporarily in the care of someone else, usually as a convenience • *Let's check our coats before going through the galleries.* ○ *Passengers on this flight will be allowed one carry-on bag, and will have to check any additional bags.*

check /tʃek/ *n* [C] the ticket or small object that you are given and that you use to get back your coat or other personal possessions left in the care of someone else for a short period • *I thought I put the coat check in my pocket.*

check PATTERN /tʃek/ *n* [C] a pattern made of different colored squares, or one of these squares • *The shirt has a pattern of blue and yellow checks.*

checkered /'tʃek·ərd/ *adj* having a pattern of different colored squares • *a red and white checkered tablecloth*

check MARK /tʃek/ *n* [C] a sign (√), often placed next to an item esp. in a list to show that it has been looked at or that it is correct • *Put a check next to the names of the people who have already paid for their tickets.* • A **checklist** is a list of things that you must remember to do or consider doing: *We went over the checklist of things we had to do before leaving for South Africa.*

check /tʃek/ *v* [T] • *Check the box corresponding to the correct answer to each question.*

check REQUEST FOR PAYMENT /tʃek/ *n* [C] a request for payment of money owed to a restaurant, or the piece of paper on which it is written • *Waiter, may I have the check, please?*

□ **check in** /'-'-/ *v adv* [I] to report your arrival, esp. at an airport or hotel, so that you can be given the service you are paying for • *Be sure to check in at least an hour before your flight.*

□ **check off** *obj*, **check** *obj* **off** /'-'-/ *v adv* [M] to mark (names or items on a list) as correct or as having been dealt with • *He checked off their names on the list as they got on the bus.*

□ **check out** /'-'-/ *v adv* [I] to leave a hotel after paying for your room and services • *The Gardners checked out early this morning to catch a plane to Toronto.*

checkout /'tʃek·aʊt/ *n* [U] • *The checkout time at this motel is noon.*

□ **check out** *obj* PAY FOR, **check** *obj* **out** /'-'-/ *v adv* [M] to take (the goods you have bought), esp. in a large food store, to an area where you pay for them • *I was checking out my groceries when I remembered that I hadn't gotten any milk.*

checkout (counter) /ˈtʃek·aʊt/ *n* [C] • *She had to wait in line at the checkout.* ○ *They'll weigh your vegetables at the checkout counter.*

□ **check out** (obj) DECIDE IF TRUE , **check** (obj) **out** /ˈ-ˈ-/ *v adv* [I/M] (of information) to seem to be true because it agrees with other information, or to discover whether (information) agrees with other information and is therefore likely to be true • *Her statement checks out with most of the eye-witness reports.* [I] ○ *The police commissioner sent a deputy to Florida to check out the latest tip in the murder investigation.* [M]

□ **check up on** /ˈ-ˈ-,-/ *v adv prep* [T] to find out (what someone is doing) in order to make certain that they are behaving correctly or legally • *Dad is always checking up on me to make sure I'm doing my homework.*

checkers /ˈtʃek·ərz/ *pl n* a game played by two people on a square board, in which each player has twelve circular pieces that are all moved in the same way

checkup /ˈtʃek·ʌp/ *n* [C] a medical examination to test your general state of health • *You should have an annual medical checkup.*

cheddar /ˈtʃed·ər/ *n* [U] a hard cheese that is yellow or white in color

cheek BODY PART /tʃiːk/ *n* [C] either side of your face below the eyes, where except at the top the skin has no bone behind it and is therefore soft • *She welcomed me with a kiss on the cheek.* • (*infml*) A cheek is also a BUTTOCK. • A **cheekbone** is either of the two bones at the sides of your face at the top of your cheeks, just below your eye.

cheek RUDE BEHAVIOR /tʃiːk/ *n* [U] rudeness or lack of respect • *First he messed up my work and then he had the cheek to accuse me of being disorganized.* [+ *to* infinitive]

cheer /tʃɪr/ *v* [I/T] to give a shout of approval or encouragement for (someone) • *I was one of the people who jumped up and cheered after that speech.* [I]

cheer /tʃɪr/ *n* [C] • *He demanded the resignation of the police chief, touching off loud applause and cheers in the audience.*

cheers /tʃɪrz/ *exclamation* a friendly expression spoken by people just before they start to drink a usually alcoholic drink

□ **cheer up** (obj), **cheer** (obj) **up** /ˈ-ˈ-/ *v adv* [I/M] to feel encouraged and happier, or to cause (someone) to feel this way • *She plays music to cheer her husband up.* [M] ○ *Cheer up! Things aren't really that bad.* [I]

cheerful /ˈtʃɪr·fəl/ *adj* happy and positive in feeling or attitude • *a cheerful face/spirit* ○ *He was a cheerful man with a kind word for everybody.* • If a thing or place is cheerful, it is pleasant and friendly and is likely to make you feel positive and happy: *The guest bedroom was bright, airy, and cheerful, overlooking the garden.*

cheerfully /ˈtʃɪr·fə·li/ *adv* • *Jonas cheerfully agreed to sleep on the sofa.*

cheerfulness /ˈtʃɪr·fəl·nəs/ *n* [U]

cheery /ˈtʃɪr·i/ *adj* expressing happiness, or making you feel happier • *She always gave us a cheery greeting.*

cheerleader /ˈtʃɪr,liːd·ər/ *n* [C] a young person who leads a crowd at a sports event in shouting encouragement and supporting a team

cheers /tʃɪrz/ *exclamation* • See at CHEER.

cheese /tʃiːz/ *n* [C/U] a type of solid food made from milk, used with many other foods and eaten plain, esp. with crackers • *American/Swiss cheese* [U] ○ *I'd like a pizza with extra cheese, please.* [U]

cheeseburger /ˈtʃiːz,bɜr·gər/ *n* [C] a HAMBURGER with a slice of melted cheese on it

cheesecake /ˈtʃiːz·keɪk/ *n* [C/U] a cake made from a sweet pastry base covered with a mixture of soft cheese, eggs, sugar, and sometimes fruit • *I like strawberry cheesecake.* [U]

cheesy /ˈtʃiːz·i/ *adj* cheap or of low quality • *The tourist shops had nothing but cheesy souvenirs.*

cheetah /ˈtʃiːt·ə/ *n* [C] a large, wild cat that has yellow-brown fur and black spots and that lives in Africa and south Asia, and is known for its speed

chef /ʃef/ *n* [C] a skilled and trained cook who works in a restaurant, esp. the most important cook

chemical /ˈkem·ɪ·kəl/ *n* [C] any basic substance that is used in or produced by a reaction involving changes to atoms or MOLECULES • *His business manufactured farm chemicals.*

chemical /ˈkem·ɪ·kəl/ *adj* • *the chemical industry* ○ *a chemical plant producing plastics and rubber* • **Chemical weapons** are substances such as poisonous gases, rather than explosives, which can be used to kill or injure people.

chemically /ˈkem·ɪ·kli/ *adv* • *chemically treated paper*

chemistry /ˈkem·ə·stri/ *n* [U] the basic characteristics of substances and the different ways in which they react or combine with other substances, or the scientific study of such substances and the way they act with other substances • *a chemistry department/laboratory* • (*infml*) Chemistry is also understanding and attraction between two people: *We dated for a while, but the chemistry just wasn't right and eventually we stopped seeing each other.*

chemist /ˈkem·əst/ *n* [C] a scientist who works with chemicals or studies their reactions • (*Br*) A chemist is a **drugstore**. See at DRUG MEDICINE.

chemotherapy /ˌkiː·moʊˈθer·ə·pi/ *n* [U] the

treatment of diseases, esp. CANCER, using chemicals

cheque /tʃek/ n [C] Cdn and Br for CHECK MONEY

cherish /'tʃer·ɪʃ/ v [T] to keep (hopes, memories, or ideas) in your mind because they are important to you and bring you pleasure • We cherish the many memories we have of our dear mother.

cherished /'tʃer·ɪʃt/ adj bringing the pleasure of love or caring about someone or something that is important to you • Her most cherished possession is a 1926 letter from F. Scott Fitzgerald.

cherry /'tʃer·i/ n [C] a small, round, soft, red or black fruit with a single, hard seed in the middle, or the tree on which the fruit grows

chess /tʃes/ n [U] a game played by two people on a square board, in which each player has 16 pieces that can be moved on the board in different ways

chest BODY PART /tʃest/ n [C] the upper front part of the body of humans and some animals, between the stomach and the neck, enclosing the heart and lungs • He folded his arms across his chest.

chest BOX /tʃest/ n [C] a large, strong box, usually made of wood, which is used for storing valuable goods or possessions or for moving possessions from one place to another • A **chest of drawers** (also **bureau**) is a piece of furniture with drawers in which you keep things such as clothes.

chesterfield /'tʃes·tər,fiːld/ n [C] Cdn a SOFA

chestnut /'tʃes·nʌt/ n [C/U] a large, shiny, red-brown nut, or the tree on which the nuts grow • Chestnut is also a deep red-brown color. [U]

chew /tʃuː/ v [I/T] to crush (food) into smaller, softer pieces with the teeth so that it is easier to swallow • The steak was tough and hard to chew. [I] • To **chew the fat** is to talk about ordinary things of no special importance: We were just sitting around chewing the fat. • **Chewing gum** is a soft, usually sweet, sticky substance that you chew to get its flavor, but which you do not swallow: Would you like a stick/piece of chewing gum?

chewy /'tʃuː·i/ adj (of food) needing to be crushed a lot with the teeth before it is swallowed • We enjoyed the fine, chewy, thick-crusted bread.

chic /ʃiːk/ adj stylish and fashionable • There's an increasing demand for the more chic, higher-quality merchandise.

chicanery /ʃɪ'keɪ·nə·ri/ n [U] dishonest but attractive talk or behavior that is used to deceive people • The investigation has revealed political chicanery and corruption at the highest levels.

Chicano male (pl **Chicanos**) /ʃɪ'kɑn·oʊ, tʃɪ-/, female **Chicana** (pl **Chicanas**) /ʃɪ'kɑn·ə, tʃɪ-/ n [C] a person living in the US who was born in Mexico or whose parents came from Mexico

chick BIRD /tʃɪk/ n [C] a baby bird, esp. a young chicken

chick WOMAN /tʃɪk/ n [C] slang a young woman • USAGE: This word is considered offensive by many women.

chicken BIRD /'tʃɪk·ən/ n [C/U] a type of bird kept on a farm for its eggs or its meat, or the meat of this bird which is cooked and eaten • **Chicken wire** is netting made of metal wire, often used as a simple fence to enclose small animals or to keep wild animals out. • USAGE: A male chicken is called a rooster or a cock, and a female chicken is called a hen.

chicken COWARD /'tʃɪk·ən/ n [C] infml disapproving a person who is too frightened to do something risky

chicken /'tʃɪk·ən/ adj infml disapproving • Why don't you jump? Are you chicken?

chicken out /,tʃɪk·ə'naʊt/ v adv [I] infml to decide not to do (something) because you are too frightened • We were going to go bungee jumping, but Sandra chickened out at the last minute.

chickenfeed /'tʃɪk·ən,fiːd/ n [U] slang an amount of money that is so small in comparison with other amounts that it is unimportant and can be ignored • They lost $200,000 on this deal, but that's chickenfeed for a company that big.

chickenpox /'tʃɪk·ən,pɑks/ n [U] an infectious disease that causes a slight fever and red spots on the skin

chickpea /'tʃɪk·piː/, **garbanzo (bean)** n [C] a hard, pale brown, round seed which can be cooked and eaten • Chickpeas are used to make hummus and falafel.

chicory /'tʃɪk·ə·ri/ n [U] a plant with blue flowers, often grown for its edible roots and leaves

chide /tʃaɪd/ v [T] to speak (to someone) severely because they have behaved badly • She chided him for his bad manners.

chief MOST IMPORTANT /tʃiːf/ adj [not gradable] most important • Their chief objection to the appointment was that she had no judicial experience.

chiefly /'tʃiː·fli/ adv • Today John-Philip Sousa is known chiefly for his music played by marching bands all over the US.

chief PERSON IN CHARGE /tʃiːf/ n [C] the person in charge of a group or organization, or the ruler of a TRIBE (= a group of families) • the chief of police

chief /tʃiːf/ adj [not gradable] highest in position or power • the chief economist/engineer/nurse ∘ He is chairman and chief executive of the company. • In the US, the **Chief Executive** is the US president. • A **chief executive officer** (also abbreviation **CEO**) of a company is usually the most powerful person in the company, with the most important responsibilities. • A **chief justice** is the judge of a court of law holding the highest position: *The Chief Justice of the United States presides over the US Supreme Court.*

chieftain /'tʃiːf·tən/ *n* [C] the leader of a TRIBE (= a group of families)

child /tʃaɪld/ *n* [C] *pl* **children** /'tʃɪl·drən/ a person from the time of birth until he or she is fully grown, or a son or daughter of any age • *Jan has a three-year-old child and two school-age children.* ○ *Now in their 60s, Jerome and Sally have two grown children* (= adult sons or daughters). • **Child's play** is something that is very easy to do: *For her, computer programming is mere child's play.* • **Child abuse** is severe physical or emotional damage done to a child, including sexual harm. • **Childbearing** means relating to the ability to have babies: *women of childbearing age* • **Childbirth** is the act of giving birth to a baby. • **Child care** is care for children provided by a person or organization while the parents are at work or are absent for another reason. LP EDUCATION IN THE US • A bottle or container that is **childproof** is one that is difficult for children to open in order to prevent them from using something dangerous. • **Child support** is money paid by a parent for the living expenses of their child when they are no longer living with the child.

childhood /'tʃaɪld·hʊd/ *n* [C/U] the time when a person is a child • *She spent most of her childhood on a farm in Texas.* [C]

childish /'tʃaɪl·dɪʃ/ *adj* like or typical of a child, or intended for children • *a childish body* ○ *The pictures made the magazine look childish.* • When you describe the behavior of an adult or an older child as childish, you mean they are behaving in a foolish way that is typical of a young child's behavior.

childishly /'tʃaɪl·dɪʃ·li/ *adv*

childishness /'tʃaɪl·dɪʃ·nəs/ *n* [U] behavior typical of a child

childless /'tʃaɪl·dləs/ *adj* [not gradable] without children • *a childless couple*

childlike /'tʃaɪl·dlaɪk/ *adj* • *childlike enthusiasm/innocence*

children /'tʃɪl·drən/ *pl of* child

chili (pepper), chile /'tʃɪl·i/ *n* [C/U] *pl* **chilies** or **chiles** any of several types of red PEPPER (= type of vegetable) that are used to make foods spicy • Chili is also a spicy dish made with beans, chilies, and usually meat. [U]

chill /tʃɪl/ *v* [I/T] to make or become cold but not freeze • *Allow the pudding to chill.* [I] • *Chill the pudding before serving.* [T] • *Walking home in the snow, we got* **chilled to the bone** (= extremely cold).

chill /tʃɪl/ *n* [C] a cold feeling • *The sun was bright, but there was a chill in the air.* • A chill is also a feeling of cold in your body that makes you shake slightly: *She came home with a headache and chills.* ○ *(fig.) His words sent a*

chill down her spine (= made her suddenly very fearful).

chilly /'tʃɪl·i/ *adj* • *a chilly morning* ○ *(fig.) Their relationship was decidedly chilly* (= unfriendly) *after the argument.*

chilling /'tʃɪl·ɪŋ/ *adj* • *a chilling wind* • Chilling also means frightening: *Chilling reports of civilian concentration camps appeared two years ago.*

□ **chill out** /'-'-/ *v adv* [I] *slang* to relax instead of worrying or feeling anxious • *If anything major happens we're going to find out, so let's chill out and just do what we need to do.*

chime /tʃaɪm/ *v* [I/T] (of bells) to make a clear ringing sound • *The church bells began to chime.* [I]

chime /tʃaɪm/ *n* [C] a ringing sound

□ **chime in** /'-'-/ *v adv* [I] to speak in a conversation, esp. by interrupting • *Everyone at the table began to chime in with their opinions.*

chimney /'tʃɪm·ni/ *n* [C] a hollow structure that allows the smoke from a fire inside a building, esp. from a fireplace, to escape to the air outside

chimpanzee /ˌtʃɪm·pænˈziː/, *short form* **chimp** /tʃɪmp/ *n* [C] an African APE (= animal related to monkeys) with black or brown fur

chin /tʃɪn/ *n* [C] the part of a person's face below their mouth

china /'tʃaɪ·nə/ *n* [U] high quality clay that is shaped and then heated to make it permanently hard, or objects made from this such as cups and plates

Chinatown /'tʃaɪ·nəˌtɑʊn/ *n* [C/U] an area of a city outside China where many Chinese people live and where there are a lot of Chinese restaurants and shops

chink CRACK /tʃɪŋk/ *n* [C] a narrow crack or opening • *Weeds were growing from a chink in the sidewalk.*

chink SOUND /tʃɪŋk/ *n* [U] a light ringing sound • *the chink of glass against glass*

chinos /'tʃiː·noʊz/ *pl n* cotton pants, often of a pale color

chintz /tʃɪnts/ *n* [U] cotton cloth, usually printed with flowery patterns, that has a slightly shiny appearance • *chintz curtains*

chintzy /'tʃɪn·si/ *adj slang* (of things) cheap and poorly made, or (of people) not willing to spend money • *He never tipped enough—he was too chintzy.*

chip PIECE /tʃɪp/ *n* [C] a small piece that has broken off a larger object, or the mark left on an object where a small piece has broken off • *Paint was peeling from the ceiling, and chips littered the floor.* • Someone who is **a chip off the old block** is similar in character to their father or mother. • Someone who has **a chip on** their **shoulder** seems angry all the time because they feel they have been treated unfairly.

chip /tʃɪp/ *v* [T] **-pp-** • *My little boy fell off his* bicycle and chipped a tooth. ○ This plate is chipped.

chip COMPUTER PART /tʃɪp/ n [C] a very small piece of SILICON used in a computer and containing electronic systems and devices that can perform particular operations

chip PLASTIC COIN /tʃɪp/ n [C] a small plastic disk used to represent a particular amount of money in GAMBLING

□ **chip in** (obj) /'-'-/ v adv to give (some money), esp. when several people are giving money to pay for something together • They each chipped in $50 to take their parents out to dinner. [T]

chipmunk /'tʃɪp·mʌŋk/ n [C] a small, furry, North American animal with dark strips along its back

chipper /'tʃɪp·ər/ adj happy and energetic • You seem mighty chipper this morning.

chips /tʃɪps/ pl n **potato chips**, see at POTATO • (Cdn and Br) Chips are FRENCH FRIES.

chiropractor /'kaɪ·rə,præk·tər/ n [C] a medical person trained to treat pain and injury esp. by pressing the muscles of a person's back to adjust the positions of the bones

chiropractic /,kaɪ·rə'præk·tɪk/ n [U] the system of treatment used by a chiropractor

chirp /tʃɜrp/ v [I] (esp. of a bird) to make a short high sound or sounds

chisel /'tʃɪz·əl/ n [C] a tool with a long, metal blade that has a sharp edge for cutting esp. wood or stone

chisel /'tʃɪz·əl/ v [T] to cut with a chisel

chiseled /'tʃɪz·əld/ adj approving clearly marked with firm lines • a face with finely chiseled features

chit /tʃɪt/ n [C] a note giving information or showing a sum of money that is owed or has been paid • When our flight was delayed, they gave us a chit to get a free meal.

chitchat, chit-chat /'tʃɪt·tʃæt/ n [U] informal conversation about unimportant matters

chivalrous /'ʃɪv·əl·rəs/ adj (of men) very polite, honorable, and kind toward women

chivalry /'ʃɪv·əl·ri/ n [U] very polite and honorable behavior, esp. such behavior shown by men toward women

chives /tʃaɪvz/ pl n a plant with long, thin leaves, or the leaves when cut into small pieces and used in cooking to give a flavor similar to onions

chlorine /'klɔːr·iːn, 'kloʊr-/ n [U] a poisonous gas, one of the chemical elements, used esp. to purify water

chlorinate /'klɔːr·ə,neɪt, 'kloʊr-/ v [T] to add chlorine to (water) in order to kill organisms that might cause infection

chlorophyll /'klɔːr·ə,fɪl, 'kloʊr-/ n [U] the green substance in plants that allows them to use the energy from the sun

chock–full /'tʃɑk·fʊl, 'tʃʌk-/ adj [not gradable] very full • The place was chock-full of people.

chocolate /'tʃɑk·lət, 'tʃɔːk-/ n [C/U] a food made from COCOA and often sugar, usually brown and eaten as candy or used in other food such as cakes • chocolate ice cream [U] ○ a box of chocolates (= candies made of chocolate) [C]

choice ACT /tʃɔɪs/ n [C/U] an act of choosing; a decision • a difficult/easy choice [C] ○ When you're trying to cut the budget deficit, you've got to make tough choices. [C]

choice POSSIBILITY /tʃɔɪs/ n [C/U] the right to choose, or the possibility of choosing • Well, I still think people have a choice. [C] ○ Given a choice between lying and making everyone hate you, what would you do? [C] ○ I asked if I could have a choice which science course to take. [C] ○ We have no choice but to drive to the airport (= That is the only thing we can do). [U]

choice VARIETY /tʃɔɪs/ n [C] a range of different things you can choose • A wide choice of colors is available in this size. [C]

choice PERSON / THING /tʃɔɪs/ n [C] a person or thing that has been chosen or that can be chosen • She would be my first choice for the job.

choice EXCELLENT /tʃɔɪs/ adj [-er/-est] only] of high quality • a choice cut of meat

choir /kwaɪr/ n [C] a group of people who sing together, esp. for a church or school

choke STOP BREATHING /tʃoʊk/ v [I/T] to be unable to breathe because the air passage inside the throat is blocked, or to cause (someone) to be unable to breathe • He was eating a piece of steak when he began to choke and turn red. [I] • If a person chokes someone else, they put their hands around the other person's neck and press hard to stop them from breathing. [T] ○ (fig.) The narrow streets were choked (= blocked) with traffic. [T] • PIC HEIMLICH MANEUVER

choke FAIL /tʃoʊk/ v [I] infml to be unable to do something, esp. win a competition, because you are aware of its importance and worried about not doing well • He always ran well in practice, but at major meets he usually choked and finished last.

□ **choke off** /'-'-/ v adv to stop the movement or progress of (something) • He told his staff to stop discussing the scandal in the hope of choking off damaging publicity.

□ **choke** obj **up** /'-'-/ v adv [T] to show strong emotion while speaking, so that continuing to speak becomes difficult • During his farewell talk the coach got all choked up and started to cry.

choker /'tʃoʊ·kər/ n [C] a piece of jewelry that fits very closely around the neck • a pearl choker

cholera /'kɑl·ə·rə/ n [U] a serious infection of the bowels caused by bacteria esp. in water, causing severe DIARRHEA and sometimes death

cholesterol /kə'les·tə,rɔːl/ n [U] a fatty substance that is found in the body tissue and blood of all animals, and which is thought to be part of the cause of heart disease if there is too much of it

chomp /tʃamp, tʃɔːmp/, **champ** v [I/T] to bite on (something) and make a chewing movement with your teeth • *He chomped on his cigar butt.* [I]

choose /tʃuːz/ v [I/T] *past simple* **chose** /tʃoʊz/, *past part* **chosen** /'tʃoʊ·zən/ to think about (which one) of several things is the one you want, and take the action to get it • *Parents can choose the schools that they want their kids to go to.* [T] ○ *He supports a woman's right to choose (abortion).* [I/T] ○ *On this issue, Congress chose to fight the president.* [+ to infinitive] ○ *There was not much to choose between them* (= They are similar). [I] ○ *You can choose what you like and we'll send it to you.* [+ wh-word]

choosy /'tʃuː·zi/ adj difficult to please because of being very exact about what you like • *He's choosy about what kind of wine he will drink.*

chop CUT /tʃap/ v [T] **-pp-** to cut (something) into pieces with a sharp tool, such as an AX • *Cal went out to chop some wood for the fireplace.* • To chop something off is to separate it from what it was part of by cutting: *Chop the ends off the carrots.* • If you chop up something, you cut it into small pieces: *She chopped up some celery for the salad.*

chop MEAT /tʃap/ n [C] a small piece of meat with a bone still in it • *a lamb/pork/veal chop*

chopper /'tʃap·ər/ n [C] a HELICOPTER

choppy /'tʃap·i/ adj (of the sea or other area of water) with lots of small waves caused by a strong wind

chopstick /'tʃap·stɪk/ n [C usually pl] either of a pair of thin, narrow sticks used for eating food

choral /'kɔːr·əl, koʊr-/ adj • See at CHORUS SINGING GROUP.

chord /kɔːrd/ n [C] three or more musical notes played at the same time

chore /tʃɔːr, tʃoʊr/ n [C] a job or piece of work that needs to be done regularly • *By the time he'd finished all the household chores it was mid-afternoon.* • A chore is also something that is difficult and unpleasant: *It was a real chore trying to give our dog a bath.*

choreography /ˌkɔːr·iː'ɑg·rə·fi, ˌkoʊr-/ n [U] the movements used by dancers esp. in performing BALLET, or the art of planning such movements

choreographer /ˌkɔːr·iː'ɑg·rə·fər, ˌkoʊr-/ n [C]

chortle /'tʃɔːrt̬·əl/ v [I] to laugh with pleasure and satisfaction

chorus SONG PART /'kɔːr·əs, 'koʊr-/ n [C] a part of a song that is repeated, usually after each VERSE (= the set of lines that are new in each part of the song) • *I'll sing the verses but I'd like all of you to join in the chorus.*

chorus SINGING GROUP /'kɔːr·əs, 'koʊr-/ n [C] a group of people who are trained to sing together • *He sings with the Los Angeles Gay Men's Chorus.* • A chorus is also a musical part intended to be sung by a chorus or a CHOIR.

choral /'kɔːr·əl, 'koʊr-/ adj relating to music intended to be sung by a chorus or a CHOIR • *choral music*

chorus THEATER GROUP /'kɔːr·əs, 'koʊr-/ n [C] a group of performers who, as a team, have a supporting position singing or dancing in a show • *She was a member of the chorus before she took over the lead role.*

chorus GROUP ACTION /'kɔːr·əs, 'koʊr-/ n • A chorus of something is an action by a large group of people at the same time: *In recent weeks, a chorus of criticism has been directed at Congressional leaders.*

chose /tʃoʊz/ *past simple of* CHOOSE

chosen /'tʃoʊ·zən/ *past participle of* CHOOSE

chow /tʃaʊ/ n [U] *slang* food, esp. when prepared for a meal

chowder /'tʃaʊd·ər/ n [U] a type of thick soup made with milk, vegetables, and often fish or other sea creatures • *clam/corn chowder*

Christ /kraɪst/ n [U] JESUS (CHRIST)

christen /'krɪs·ən/ v [T] to call (a person, esp. a baby) a Christian through the ceremony of BAPTISM and by naming them • *The parents christened their second child Maria.* • If a ship is christened, it is officially given its name: *The First Lady christened the ship, "USS Arizona".* • If you christen something new, you use it for the first time: *I'm going to christen my new golf clubs this week.*

christening /'krɪs·ə·nɪŋ/ n [C] • *We celebrated the christening of my boss's new baby in grand style.*

Christian /'krɪs·tʃən, 'krɪʃ-/ n [C], adj [not gradable] (a person) following or belonging to a religion based on the worship of one God and the teachings of Jesus Christ as described in the Bible • *The Roman Catholic church is the largest of the Christian churches.* • If you describe a person or their actions as Christian, you mean that they act according to Christian principles of goodness and kindness toward others: *It wasn't very Christian of you to make him walk home in this rain.* • The **Christian era** is the period of time from the year when Jesus Christ was thought to be born to the present. • A **Christian name** is a name someone is given at BAPTISM (= a ceremony at which a person is named as a Christian). • A **Christian name** is also a person's **first name**; see at FIRST. • **Christian Science** is a Christian religion whose members believe illness can be cured by belief and a true understanding of the teachings of Jesus Christ, and by following those teachings.

Christianity /ˌkrɪs·tʃiː'æn·əț·i, ˌkrɪʃ-/ n [U] the Christian faith, a religion based on the belief in one God and on the teachings of JESUS CHRIST, as set forth in the BIBLE

Christmas /ˈkrɪs·məs/ *n* [C/U] December 25th, a day celebrated each year to honor the birth of Jesus, or the period of time just before and after December 25th • *People usually visit their families at Christmas.* [U] ○ *I hope you have a very Merry Christmas!* [U] • A **Christmas card** is a decorated card expressing good wishes and sent to someone at Christmas. • A **Christmas carol** is a song of joy or praise sung at Christmas. • **Christmas Day** is December 25th: *We always spend Christmas Day with our whole family.* • **Christmas Eve** is December 24th, the day before Christmas. • **Christmastime** is the Christmas season, or the period from about December 24th to January 1st or January 6th . • A **Christmas tree** is a real or artificial evergreen tree that is set up inside the house and decorated with lights and colored balls, or a living tree outside, usually decorated with lights during the Christmas season.

chrome /kroʊm/ *n* [U] CHROMIUM • *The car has bright chrome trim.*

chromium /ˈkroʊ·miː·əm/ *n* [U] a hard, bluegray, metallic element used in combination with metals or put on a material to form a shiny covering

chromosome /ˈkroʊ·mə,zoʊm, -,soʊm/ *n* [C] any of the structures shaped like rods that are found in living cells and contain the GENES (= chemical patterns) which control what an animal or plant is like • *The X and Y chromosomes determine the sex of a human being.*

chronic /ˈkrɑn·ɪk/ *adj* (esp. of a disease or something bad) continuing for a long time • *Mr. George is resigning because of chronic heart disease.* ○ *There is a chronic shortage of teachers.* • **Chronic Fatigue Syndrome** is a group of illnesses that causes people to be extremely tired.

chronically /ˈkrɑn·ɪ·kli/ *adv* • *The hospital provides care to chronically ill patients for as long as they need it.*

chronicle /ˈkrɑn·ɪ·kəl/ *n* [C] a record of events in the order in which they happened • *This book is the most eloquent chronicle of an empire's downfall that I have seen.* ○ (*infml*) *The diary, although a personal story, is really a chronicle of an important period of history.*

chronicle /ˈkrɑn·ɪ·kəl/ *v* [T] to make (a record) or tell (the history) of something • *His one-man show chronicles the life of Mark Twain.*

chronology /krəˈnɑl·ə·dʒi/ *n* [C] a list or explanation of events in the order in which they happened • *He gave a detailed chronology of the events of the past three days.*

chronological /,krɑn·əˈlɑdʒ·ɪ·kəl/ *adj* • *Give me the dates in chronological order.*

chronologically /,krɑn·əˈlɑdʒ·ɪ·kli/ *adv* • *Please name the presidents chronologically.*

chrysalis /ˈkrɪs·ə·ləs/ *n* [C] an insect at the stage of development when it is like a worm inside a hard, protective cover, before it becomes a MOTH or BUTTERFLY

chrysanthemum /krəˈsæn·θə·məm/, *short form* **mum** *n* [C] any of several types of garden plants that flower in the fall, including some that produce many small flowers and others that have very large, brightly colored flowers

chubby /ˈtʃʌb·i/ *adj* (esp. of children) softly rounded in a pleasant and attractive way • *The perfect baby has, we are told, chubby little fingers and toes, chubby legs, and chubby cheeks, but the perfect teenager has not one thing that is chubby.*

chuck THROW /tʃʌk/ *v* [T] to throw (something) carelessly • *Chuck me the keys.* • If you **chuck** something **out**, you put it in the garbage: *Mom told me to chuck out my favorite old T-shirt.*

chuck END /tʃʌk/ *v* [T] *infml* to end, give up, or leave (something) • *Last summer, he chucked his ten-year career as a stockbroker.* ○ *How can you chuck an old friendship like that?* • If people in charge of a place **chuck** you **out**, they force you to leave: *He says he's been chucked out of some of the best bars in Miami.*

chuckle /ˈtʃʌk·əl/ *v* [I] to laugh quietly or softly • *She was chuckling as she read the letter.*

chuckle /ˈtʃʌk·əl/ *n* [C] • *I always get a chuckle out of the Doonesbury comic strip.*

chug MAKE SOUND /tʃʌg/ *v* [I always + adv/prep] **-gg-** to make the sound of an engine or motor, or to move making this sound • *The train chugged up the hill.* • To chug also means to move steadily, like a little train: *Yeah, my life is chugging right along, thanks.*

chug /tʃʌg/ *n* [C] • *We heard the chug of the boat's engine in the distance.*

chug DRINK /tʃʌg/, **chug-a-lug** /ˈtʃʌg·ə,lʌg/ *v* **-gg-** *slang* to swallow (a drink) completely without stopping to breathe • *He chugs a tequila and Coke from a paper cup.* [T]

chum /tʃʌm/ *n* [C] *infml* a friend • *Some of our college chums are a little wild.*

chummy /ˈtʃʌm·i/ *adj infml* • *She tells the two of them to look chummy for the picture.*

chump /tʃʌmp/ *n* [C] *infml* a foolish or stupid person • *What a chump he was to quit his job.*

chunk /tʃʌŋk/ *n* [C] a thick piece or lump • *A large chunk of plaster crashed down from the ceiling.* • (*infml*) A chunk is a large part of something: *Her books must be read in chunks to follow the plot.*

chunky /ˈtʃʌŋ·ki/ *adj* • *She wears chunky earrings and rings and a baggy sweater.* • Chunky foods have pieces or lumps mixed into a smooth base: *I love chunky peanut butter!* • A person who is chunky is strong and built solidly: *She's a chunky woman with a powerful personality.*

church BUILDING /tʃɜrtʃ/ *n* [C] a building for Christian religious activities • *We came to a church and went inside to sit and enjoy the quiet.* • A **churchyard** is a garden or grassy area around a church, often where people are buried.

church ORGANIZATION /tʃɜrtʃ/ n [C/U] a Christian religious organization • *He went on a trip with some of his friends from church.* [U] • Church is also a group of people meeting for a religious gathering: *I'll see you after church.* [U] • A church is also one of the major divisions within Christianity: *The Episcopal and Roman Catholic churches have many similarities.* [C] • Church can also mean organized religion generally: *The separation of church and state is an important feature of the US Constitution.* [U] • **Churchgoers** are people who go to church regularly. • A member of the **Church of Jesus Christ of Latter-day Saints** is a MORMON.

churlish /'tʃɜr·lɪʃ/ adj rude, unfriendly, and unpleasant • *They invited me to dinner and I thought it would be churlish to refuse.* [+ to infinitive]

churlishly /'tʃɜr·lɪʃ·li/ adv • *I churlishly told him to go bother someone else.*

churn /tʃɜrn/ v [I/T] to move violently • *The water was churning and the boat was rocking.* [I] ○ *The fish churned up the water when we threw them some food.* [M] ○ (*fig.*) *Seeing the car ahead flip over churned his stomach.* [T] • To churn butter means to beat cream into butter using a special container. [T] • If you **churn** something **out**, you produce it automatically, without much thought, and in large amounts: *Hollywood studios have been churning out some bad movies the past several years.*

churn /tʃɜrn/ n [C] a container in which cream is made into butter

chute SLIDE /ʃuːt/ n [C] a narrow, steep slide for objects or people to go down • *The garbage chute empties into a big bin.* ○ *We had to use the emergency chute to get out of the plane.*

chute CLOTH DEVICE /ʃuːt/ n [C] short form of PARACHUTE

chutney /'tʃʌt·ni/ n [C/U] a sauce containing small pieces of fruit, spices, sugar, and vinegar, eaten with cold meats and other foods to add flavor • *Mango chutney is absolutely my favorite.* [C]

chutzpah /'hʊt·spə, 'xʊt-/ n [U] behavior that is extremely confident and often rude, with no respect for the opinions or abilities of anyone else • *The movie was made with a little money and a lot of chutzpah.* ○ *I wonder who had the chutzpah to disagree with him?*

CIA n [U] abbreviation for Central Intelligence Agency (= the US government organization that collects secrets about other countries and determines the importance of that information) • *We do not know what role the CIA played.*

ciao /tʃaʊ/ exclamation infml hello or goodbye • *He greeted me with his usual all-purpose "Ciao, baby!"*

cicada /sə'keɪd·ə, -'kɑd·ə/ n [C] pl **cicadas** a large insect with transparent wings which it rubs together to produce a high, continuous sound esp. when the weather is hot • *Cicadas buzzing in the maple trees is the sound of hot summer.*

cider /'saɪd·ər/ n [U] apple juice made from crushed apples, used as a drink or to make vinegar

cigar /sɪ'gɑr/ n [C] a tight roll of dried tobacco leaves that people smoke • *Cuban cigars are supposed to be the world's best.*

cigarette /ˌsɪg·ə'ret/ n [C] a small tube of thin paper filled with pieces of cut tobacco, which people smoke • *He smokes two packs of cigarettes a day.* • A **cigarette butt** is the part of the cigarette that is left after smoking: *After the party, every ashtray was full of cigarette butts.*

cinch SOMETHING EASY /sɪntʃ/ n [C] infml something that is very easy or certain to be done or happen • *Training a puppy is a cinch if you bribe him with treats.*

cinch STRAP /sɪntʃ/ n [C] a strap that goes around esp. a horse to hold the SADDLE (= the seat put on an animal for a rider) in place

cinch /sɪntʃ/ v [T] • *My guide cinched the llama's saddle tight enough to stay in place.*

Cinco de Mayo /ˌsɪn·koʊ·deɪ'maɪ·oʊ, -də-/ n [C/U] May 5th, a Mexican holiday celebrating a victory by Mexicans over an invading French army • *Cinco de Mayo events this year include cookouts, parades, beauty contests, and dances.* [U]

cinder /'sɪn·dər/ n [C] a small piece of partly burned coal or wood • *Get rid of the cinders before you build a new fire.* • A **cinder block** is a hollow block made of concrete mixed with cinders that is used esp. in building walls.

Cinderella /ˌsɪn·də'rel·ə/ n [C] someone or something that is unexpectedly successful, esp. after being ignored or not helped • *She's a regular Cinderella, going from nothing to marrying the governor's son.*

cinema /'sɪn·ə·mə/ n [C/U] movies, or the art or business of making movies • *Her lectures on the cinema were very interesting.* [U] • (*esp. Cdn and Br*) A cinema is also a movie theater: We'd already been to the local cinema twice that week. [C]

cinematic /ˌsɪn·ə'mæt̬·ɪk/ adj • *The cinematic effects in this film are utterly remarkable.*

cinematography /ˌsɪn·ə·mə'tɑg·rə·fi/ n [U] the art and methods of photography used in making a movie • *The cinematography is what makes this film as wonderful as it really is.*

cinnamon /'sɪn·ə·mən/ n [U] a spice, made from the BARK (= outer covering) of a tropical tree, usually available in the form of powder or a rolled piece of bark • *The smell of cinnamon makes me hungry for cookies.* • Cinnamon is also a red-brown color: *The dress is available in cinnamon and green.* • A **cinnamon roll** or **cinnamon bun** is a round, sweet bread flavored with cinnamon: *Robert had stuffed half a cinnamon bun in his mouth and couldn't say a word.*

cipher [SECRET WRITING] /'saɪ·fər/ *n* [C] a system of writing that most people cannot understand, so that the message is secret; a CODE • *We spent a lot of time figuring out the enemy's cipher.*

cipher [NOTHING] /'saɪ·fər/ *n* [C] a zero, or a person or thing that has no value or importance • *In the hands of a lesser actor, the role could have easily been a cipher.*

circa /'sɜr·kə, 'kɪr·kə/ (*abbreviation* **c**, **ca**) *prep fml* (used before a year) about or approximately • *The Greek philosopher Socrates was born circa 470 BC.*

circle [SHAPE] /'sɜr·kəl/ *n* [C] a continuous curved line which is always the same distance away from a fixed central point, or the area enclosed by such a line • *Colored paper was cut into circles, squares, and triangles.* ○ *A circle of chairs had been arranged in the center of the room.* • If you go **in circles**, you do a lot or are very busy without achieving anything: *We just keep going in circles, talking without deciding anything.*

circle /'sɜr·kəl/ *v* [I/T] • *A hawk circled high overhead, looking for food.* [I] ○ *I circled the block to find a parking space.* [T] • (*fig.*) If you circle around a subject, you talk about things related to it, often to avoid talking about the subject itself: *He circled around the idea of paying authors more for their books.* [I] • If a group or organization **circles the wagons**, it stops communicating with others in order to protect its members: *The company has circled the wagons as a defense against further public criticism.*

circle [GROUP] /'sɜr·kəl/ *n* [C] a group of people who are connected by family, work, or society, or who share an interest • *There's a small circle of people who sell and exhibit their work at the same shows.* ○ *The mayor's inner circle met with him throughout the crisis to give advice.*

circuit [CLOSED SYSTEM] /'sɜr·kət/ *n* [C] a closed system esp. of wires through which electricity can flow • *Big electronic circuits can carry huge amounts of data.* • A circuit is also a system that allows people to communicate with each other: *Holiday phone calls always overload the circuits.* • A **circuit board** is a small board on which circuits are attached or printed: *The remote-controlled firing device was connected to the bomb through a circuit board.* • A **circuit breaker** is a safety device that stops the flow of current to an electrical system: *I cut off all the circuit breakers in the house, but I could still hear a humming sound.* ○ Compare FUSE [SAFETY DEVICE].

circuitry /'sɜr·kə·tri/ *n* [U] • *The circuitry in this computer is protected from power surges.*

circuit [CIRCLE] /'sɜr·kət/ *n* [C] something shaped like a circle, esp. a route, path, or

sports track that starts and ends in the same place • *She has ridden on tough racing circuits such as the New York and Florida tracks.* • A circuit can be a path or route in the shape of a circle: *Fish swam continuously, making the endless circuit of the tank.*

circuit [SERIES] /'sɜr·kət/ *n* [C] a regular series of events that happen in different places • *She has won a number of tournaments on this year's tennis circuit.*

circuit [LEGAL AREA] /'sɜr·kət/ *n* [C] an area under the authority of a particular court • A **circuit court** is one that tries cases in different places within the area under its authority: *Mr. Blackford was acquitted in the circuit court.* • A federal **Circuit Court of Appeals** is a court in one of eleven areas in the US in which lawyers can argue that a decision made in a lower court be changed: *The 4th U.S. Circuit Court of Appeals refused to rule on that case.* • A **circuit judge** is a judge who decides cases that are brought to a circuit court: *The Circuit Judge issued a temporary restraining order.*

circuitous /sər'kjuː·ət·əs/ *adj* not straight or direct; ROUNDABOUT • *We took a circuitous route home.*

circuitously /sər'kjuː·ət·ə·sli/ *adv* • *The train tracks wound circuitously through the canyons.*

circular [ROUND] /'sɜr·kjə·lər/ *adj* in the shape of a circle; round • *One man built a circular barn for his cows.* ○ *The circular area is used for parking.* • A circular argument or discussion is one which keeps returning to the same points and does not advance to any new points or to agreement.

circular [PRINTED PAPER] /'sɜr·kjə·lər/ *n* [C] a letter or notice given to a large number of people • *The discount chain advertises sales with circulars.*

circulate /'sɜr·kjə·leɪt/ *v* to move around or through • *Hot water circulates through the pipes.* [I] ○ *They're circulating a petition calling for tighter controls on gun ownership.* [T]

circulation /ˌsɜr·kjə'leɪ·ʃən/ *n* [C/U] movement, esp. of blood inside the body or air or water in a space or system • *Your doctor can tell something about your circulation by taking your blood pressure.* [U] • A magazine or newspaper's circulation is the number of people who read it: *The Chronicle has a daily circulation of 505,000.* [C] • If something is in circulation, it is available: *Are the new dollar coins in circulation yet?* [U] ○ (*fig. infml*) *I hear Betty broke up with Ben and is back in circulation.* [U] • If something is out of circulation, it is not available: *The company takes its movies out of circulation, then shows them again.* [U] ○ (*fig. infml*) *She's been out of circulation since her accident.* [U]

circumcise /'sɜr·kəm,saɪz/ *v* [T] to cut off the FORESKIN of a boy's penis for medical, cultural, or religious reasons • *Some girls are al-*

so circumcised by removing parts of their sex organs for cultural or religious purposes.

circumcision /ˌsɜr·kəmˈsɪʒ·ən/ *n* [C/U] • *Religious circumcisions are part of a ceremony.* [C]

circumference /sərˈkəm·fə·rəns/ *n* [C/U] the distance around a circle, the distance around the widest part of a round object, or a line enclosing a circular space • *Draw a circle 5 inches in circumference.* [U] • The circumference of an area of any size or shape is its complete outside edge: *We walked the circumference of the field so we wouldn't interrupt the game.* [C]

circumstance /ˈsɜr·kəmˌstæns/ *n* [C/U] an event or condition connected with what is happening or has happened • *The circumstances of the theft of the painting were not known.* [C] ○ *The circumstances surrounding his disappearance are under investigation.* [C]

circumstantial /ˌsɜr·kəmˈstæn·tʃəl/ *adj* relating to the circumstances in which something happened, but not to the thing itself • *The report said most of the data was circumstantial, so no conclusions could be drawn from it.* ○ *The judge reminded the jury that circumstantial evidence is information that may be important but is not proof of guilt.*

circumvent /ˌsɜr·kəmˈvent/ *v* [T] to avoid (something) by going around it • *Young people still want to circumvent their parents' control.*

circus /ˈsɜr·kəs/ *n* [C] a group of traveling entertainers including ACROBATS, CLOWNS, and trained animals, or a performance by such a group, often in a tent • *He quit school in the eighth grade to join the circus.* ○ *We saw the circus set up in a tent in the middle of the city.* • A circus is also something noisy and confused: *The media circus covering the trial took over the courthouse steps.*

cirrhosis /səˈrou·səs/ *n* [U] *medical* a serious disease of the LIVER (= an organ in the body) that can result in death • *Alcoholics often die from cirrhosis of the liver.*

cistern /ˈsɪs·tərn/ *n* [C] a large container for storing water, esp. one kept on the roof of a large building to catch rain

cite MENTION /saɪt/ *v* [T] to mention (something) as proof for a theory or as a reason why something has happened, or to speak or write (words taken from a written work) • *He cited a study of the devices as proof that the company knew they were dangerous.* ○ *Scientists cite this experiment as their main support for this theory.* • To cite someone else's words when speaking or writing is to use them: *If you cite too many writers, readers will wonder if you have any ideas of your own.* • In law, if a person or organization is cited, they are named in a legal action: *The mine operator was cited with 33 violations of federal safety standards.*

citation /saɪˈteɪ·ʃən/ *n* [C/U] • *Citation of her mother's wisdom did not change her ways.* [U] ○ *She checked all the citations from other writ-*

ers *I used in my book.* [C] • *(law)* A citation is an official notice from a court of law: *The court could issue a citation against her for disclosing information.* [C] ○ *County police say that no citations have been issued since the law went into effect.* [C]

cite PRAISE /saɪt/ *v* [T] to praise (someone) publicly for something they have done • *He was cited for bravery.*

citation /saɪˈteɪ·ʃən/ *n* [C] • *The four soldiers are to receive citations from the president.*

citizen /ˈsɪt·ə·zən/ *n* [C] a person who was born in a particular country and has certain rights or has been given certain rights because of having lived there • *Nabokov was a Russian, then had British citizenship, and then became an American citizen.* ○ *A large part of our job is to educate citizens about their rights.* ○ *Old people have been treated like second-class citizens.* • A citizen is also a person who lives in a particular place: *My sister is now a New Hampshire citizen.*

citizenry /ˈsɪt·ə·zən·ri/ *n* [U] the group of people who live in a particular country or place • *An angry citizenry organized resistance to the harsh new laws.*

citizenship /ˈsɪt·ə·zənˌʃɪp/ *n* [U] the state of having the rights of a person born in a particular country • *He was granted Canadian citizenship last year.* ○ *Harold holds dual citizenship in New Zealand and the US.* • Citizenship is also carrying out the duties and responsibilities of a member of a particular society: *Good citizenship requires that you do all the things a citizen is supposed to do, such as pay taxes, serve on juries, and vote.*

citrus /ˈsɪt·trəs/ *n* [C] *pl* **citrus** or **citruses** any of a group of plants that produce juicy, acidic fruits • *Oranges, lemons, limes, and grapefruit are types of citrus fruit.*

city /ˈsɪt·i/ *n* [C] a place where many people live, with many houses, stores, businesses, etc., and which is bigger than a town • *Canadians have built big, pleasant, and livable cities.* ○ *When their team won the World Series, the whole city celebrated.* ○ *Wellington is the capital city of New Zealand.* • A **city council** is the legislature of a city. • A **city hall** is a building used by the mayor and the city government, and where usually the city offices are: *Protesters hurled eggs during a ceremony in front of city hall.* • **City hall** also means the government of a city: *There are a lot of problems at city hall.*

citywide /ˈsɪt·iːˌwɑɪd/ *adj, adv* [not gradable] including all of a city and affecting all of its residents • *In a series of hearings held citywide, residents complained more about the schools than about crime.*

civic /ˈsɪv·ɪk/ *adj* [not gradable] of a town or city or the people who live in it • *A group of prominent civic leaders have been among the school system's harshest critics.* • A **civic**

association is an organization that tries to improve a city or town: *She was a member of the Mamaroneck Civic Association.*

civics /'sɪv·ɪks/ *n* [U] the study of the rights and duties of citizens

civic /'sɪv·ɪk/ *adj* [not gradable] • *Civic responsibility includes voting and serving on juries.*

civil ORDINARY /'sɪv·əl/ *adj* of or relating to the ordinary people of a country, rather than members of religious organizations or the military • *These helicopters are for rescue and other civil use.* ○ *We were married in a civil ceremony at City Hall, not in a church.* • Civil also refers to the legal system governing personal and business matters: *civil court* ○ Compare CRIMINAL. • **Civil disobedience** is the refusal to obey certain laws or pay taxes as a peaceful way for citizens to express disapproval of particular government actions and to press for change: *Campaigns of civil disobedience forced an end to segregation.* • **Civil engineering** is the planning and building of public roads, bridges, and buildings. Someone who does this is a **civil engineer.** • **Civil liberties** are the basic rights of citizens: *The right of free speech is one of our most important civil liberties.* • **Civil rights** are the rights of each person in a society, including equality under the law and in employment and the right to vote: *In the 1960s, civil rights were extended by law to include all Americans.* • The **civil service** consists of all government departments that are not part of the military. • A **civil servant** is a person who works in the civil service. • A **civil war** is a war fought between groups of people living in the same country.

civilian /sə'vɪl·jən/ *n* [C] a person who is not a member of the police, the armed forces, or a fire department • *The bomb killed three civilians.*

civilian /sə'vɪl·jən/ *adj* [not gradable] • *A civilian group reviews complaints about police activity.*

civil POLITE /'sɪv·əl/ *adj* polite and formal • *We were civil to each other, but we were both still angry.*

civilize /'sɪv·ə,lɑɪz/ *v* [T] to make (a society) more highly developed • *Preachers arrived to civilize violent frontier towns.*

civilization /,sɪv·ə·lə'zeɪ·ʃən, -lɑɪ-/ *n* [C/U] a highly developed culture, including its social organization, government, laws, and arts, or the culture of a social group or country at a particular time • *Widespread use of the Internet may change modern civilization.* [U] ○ *The Inca civilization flourished for a long time.* [C]

civilized /'sɪv·ə,lɑɪzd/ *adj* (of a country) having a highly developed society • *We believe today that civilized society is based on the rule of law.* • Civilized also means pleasant, comfortable, well-educated, or orderly: *civilized behavior* ○ *a civilized vacation*

clack /klæk/ *n* [C usually sing] a short, metallic sound made when two hard objects hit

clack /klæk/ *v* [I] • *Her shoes clacked on the tile floor.*

clad /klæd/ *adj* [not gradable] *esp. literary* (of people) dressed, or (of things) covered • *A stranger appeared, clad in white.*

claim SAY /kleɪm/ *v* [T] to state that (something) is true or is a fact • *Ervin claims (that) he is bankrupt.* [+ *(that)* clause]

claim /kleɪm/ *n* [C] • *They say it works, but there is no evidence to support those claims.* • A **claim to fame** is a reason why someone or something is famous: *This little town's claim to fame is that a president was born here.*

claim REQUEST /kleɪm/ *v* [T] to demand (something of value) because you believe it belongs to you or you have a right to it • *If no one claims the money, I can keep it.* • If a storm, crime, or other violence claims someone's life, the person was killed suddenly as a result of that event: *The earthquake claimed hundreds of lives.*

claim /kleɪm/ *n* [C] a written request to an organization to pay you a sum of money which you believe they owe you • *After the storm, dozens of claims were filed to collect crop insurance.* • A claim is also a statement saying that you have a right to something: *Lawyers tried to establish their claim to refugee status.*

clam /klæm/ *n* [C] a type of sea creature with a hard shell in two parts, or its soft body that can be eaten raw or cooked

clam up /'klæm'ʌp/ *v adv* [I] *infml* to refuse to talk or answer • *He just clammed up when I walked in.*

clamber /'klæm·bər, -ər/ *v* [I always + adv/prep] to climb somewhere with difficulty, often needing to use both hands and feet • *The baby clambered up the stairs.*

clammy /'klæm·i/ *adj* slightly wet and cool, in an unpleasant way • *Her forehead was hot, but her hands were clammy.*

clamor /'klæm·ər/ *v* [I] to make a loud complaint or demand • *The audience clamored for an encore.*

clamor /'klæm·ər/ *n* [U] • *The clamor for freedom in recent years has been strong.* • Clamor is also loud noise, esp. made by people's voices: *The clamor of their voices rose.*

clamp /klæmp/ *n* [C] a device used to hold two things tightly together • *A small clamp at the bottom edge holds it in place.*

clamp /klæmp/ *v* [T always + adv/prep] to use a device to hold (two things) tightly together • *Clamp the pieces together while the glue dries.* [M] • If you clamp something, you hold it firmly so that it does not move: *He clamped his fingers around her wrist.* • If you

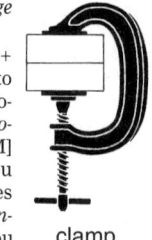

clamp

classic

clamp down on something, you act to stop or limit it: *Stores use electronic devices to clamp down on theft.*

clan /klæn/ *n* [C] *infml* a family, esp. a large group of relatives • *Is the whole clan gathering at your house for Thanksgiving?*

clandestine /klæn'des·tən/ *adj* (esp. of something illegal or not acceptable) planned or done in secret • *a clandestine meeting*

clandestinely /klæn'des·tən·li/ *adv* • *Activists were forced to work clandestinely.*

clang /klæŋ/ *v* [I/T] to make a loud, ringing sound like metal being hit, or to cause (something) to make such a sound, esp. by hitting it • *On Sunday mornings, church bells clang in the distance.* [I]

clang /klæŋ/ *n* [C usually sing] • *The door rolled shut with a clang.*

clank /klæŋk/ *v* [I/T] to make a short, loud sound like that of metal objects hitting each other, or to cause (something) to make such a sound • *Ray's van clanked down the driveway.* [I]

clank /klæŋk/ *n* [C usually sing] • *the clank of silverware on plates*

clap PUT HANDS TOGETHER /klæp/ *v* [I/T] -pp- to make a short, loud noise by hitting your hands together • *She clapped her hands to call the dog in.* [T] • People will clap at the end of a speech or a performance to show that they are pleased: *Everyone was clapping and cheering.* [I]

clap /klæp/ *n* [C] • *There were a few claps, and then embarrassing silence.* • A clap of thunder is the sudden, loud noise of thunder.

clap HIT LIGHTLY /klæp/ *v* [T always + adv/prep] -pp- to hit (someone) lightly on the shoulder or back in a friendly way to express pleasure • *The governor clapped him on the back and congratulated him.*

clapboard /'klæb·ərd; 'klæp·bɔːrd, -boʊrd/ *n* [U] a narrow board used to cover the outside walls of a building by laying one board over part of the one already attached below it • PIC OVERLAP

clapper /'klæp·ər/ *n* [C] a piece of metal hanging inside a bell which makes the bell ring by hitting its sides

clarify /'klær·ə,fɑɪ/ *v* [T] to make (something) clearer or easier to understand • *I hope this analysis will clarify the debate.* ○ *Talking it through with you has helped me to clarify my own thinking about the problem.*

clarification /,klær·ə·fə'keɪ·ʃən/ *n* [C/U] • *Two of your points deserve further clarification.* [U]

clarinet /,klær·ə'net/ *n* [C/U] a tube-shaped musical instrument that is played by blowing through a single REED (= thin piece of wood) and pressing keys on its front to produce notes, or this type of instrument generally; a WOODWIND

clarinetist, clarinettist /,klær·ə'net·əst/ *n* [C] • *He's a respected jazz clarinetist.*

clarity /'klær·ət·i/ *n* [U] the quality of being clear and easy to understand, see, or hear • *He conveys information with great clarity.* ○ *The story is filmed with razor-sharp clarity.* ○ *The sound was loud, but it lacked clarity.*

clash FIGHT /klæʃ/ *v* [I] to fight or disagree • *The army clashed with rebels near the capital.* ○ *The president and Congress clashed again over the budget.*

clash /klæʃ/ *n* [C] • *a clash of interests/personalities* ○ *Violent clashes between rioters and police occurred on Friday.*

clash NOT MATCH /klæʃ/ *v* [I] (of colors or styles) to look ugly or wrong together • *I do not think that red clashes with orange.*

clash SOUND /klæʃ/ *n* [C] a loud sound like that made when metal objects hit

clash /klæʃ/ *v* [I/T] • *From the kitchen you could hear dishes clashing as they were stacked.* [I]

clasp /klæsp/ *v* [T] to hold (someone or something) firmly in your hands or arms • *He clasped the vase, afraid he would drop it.*

clasp /klæsp/ *n* [C] • *She had a firm clasp on her daughter's hand.* • A clasp is a small metal device used to fasten a belt, a bag, or a piece of jewelry.

class TEACHING GROUP /klæs/ *n* [C] a group of students who are taught together at school, or a short period in which a particular subject is taught • *She got in trouble for talking in class.* • The class of a particular year is the group of students who will complete their studies that year: *The class of 2003 is very large.* • A **classroom** is a room where groups of students are taught. • **Classwork** is work you do in class.

class ECONOMIC GROUP /klæs/ *n* [C/U] a group of people within a society who have the same economic and social position • *Most of us think of ourselves as middle class.* [U] • (*law*) A **class-action lawsuit** is a legal action for the benefit of a large group of people claiming to have suffered a similar injury.

class RANK /klæs/ *n* [C] the ranking of goods and services or people's skills according to what they provide or how good they are • *Whenever I fly, I go business class.* ○ *She's a first-class teacher.* • Someone or something **in a class by itself** is excellent or the best of its kind: *Her singing is in a class by itself.*

class /klæs/ *v* [T] to rank • *I would class her with the best American violinists.*

class STYLE /klæs/ *n* [U] the quality of being stylish or fashionable • *She dresses with a lot of class.*

classy /'klæs·i/ *adj* • *He drives a very classy car.*

class BIOLOGY /klæs/ *n* [C] a group of plants or animals with similar biological structure

classic HIGH QUALITY /'klæs·ɪk/ *adj* having a high quality or setting the standard against which other things are judged • *Have you ever read Fielding's classic novel "Tom Jones"?*

classic /ˈklæs·ɪk/ *n* [C] a well-known piece of writing, musical recording, or film which is of high quality and lasting value • *Chaplin's films are regarded as American classics.*

classic TRADITIONAL /ˈklæs·ɪk/ *adj* traditional in design or style • *She wore a classic blue suit and a straw hat.*

classic TYPICAL /ˈklæs·ɪk/ *adj* having all the characteristics or qualities that are typical of something • *The building is a classic example of poor design.*

classical ANCIENT /ˈklæs·ɪ·kəl/ *adj* belonging to or relating to the culture of ancient Rome and Greece • *classical architecture/languages* • USAGE: The related noun is CLASSICS.

classical TRADITIONAL /ˈklæs·ɪ·kəl/ *adj* traditional in style or form, or using methods developed over a long period of time • *classical ballet* • **Classical music** is a form of music developed from a European tradition: *My wife likes classical music but I prefer jazz.*

classics /ˈklæs·ɪks/ *pl n* the study of ancient Greek and Roman culture, esp. their languages and literature • USAGE: The related adjective is CLASSICAL ANCIENT.

classified /ˈklæs·ə·faɪd/ *adj* (of information) officially secret • *These documents contain classified material.*

classified (ad) /ˈklæs·ə·faɪd (ˈæd)/, **want ad** *n* [C] a small advertisement in a newspaper or magazine offering or requesting a job, furniture, cars, houses, etc.

classify /ˈklæs·ə·faɪ/ *v* [T] to divide (things) into groups according to type • *We classify our books by subject.* ○ *Biologists classify animals and plants into groups.*

classification /ˌklæs·ə·fəˈkeɪ·ʃən/ *n* [C/U] • *a system of classification* [U] ○ *Hotels are listed in four classifications from economy to deluxe.* [C]

classmate /ˈklæs·meɪt/ *n* [C] someone who is in the same class as you in school • *Trish is taller than most of her classmates.*

clatter /ˈklæt̬·ər/ *v* [I/T] to make loud noises, or to hit (hard objects) against each other • *Don't clatter the pots and pans—you'll wake the baby up.* [T]

clatter /ˈklæt̬·ər/ *n* [U] • *She could hear the clatter of horses' hooves trotting down the road.*

clause GRAMMAR /klɔːz/ *n* [C] *specialized* (in grammar) a group of words that includes a subject and a verb but usually forms only part of a sentence • *"If I go to town" is a clause not a sentence.* • LP COMMA

clause LEGAL STATEMENT /klɔːz/ *n* [C] *law* a part of a written legal document • *He had a clause in his movie contract that let him work in the theater.*

claustrophobia /ˌklɔː·strəˈfoʊ·biː·ə/ *n* [U] an extreme fear of being in an enclosed or crowded space

claustrophobic /ˌklɔː·strəˈfoʊ·bɪk/ *adj* • *I feel claustrophobic in an elevator.*

claw /klɔː/ *n* [C] one of the sharp, curved nails at the end of each of the toes of some animals and birds • *Our cat likes to sharpen her claws on the legs of the dining table.* • A claw is also the curved, movable part at the end of the leg of some insects and sea animals, such as CRABS and LOBSTERS: *Watch out—the lobster's claws pinch.* PIC LOBSTER

claw /klɔː/ *v* [I/T] to cut (esp. flesh) with claws • *Nora's cat attacked him and began clawing his back.* [T] • If someone claws their way somewhere, they use a lot of effort to achieve something: *The team trailed, 24-13, after one quarter but clawed to 26-18 by halftime.* [I]

clay /kleɪ/ *n* [U] thick, heavy earth that is soft when wet, and hard when dry or baked • *Clay is used for making bricks and pots.*

clean NOT DIRTY /kliːn/ *adj* [-er/-est only] free of dirt or other unwanted parts or pieces • *Make sure you wear a clean shirt.* ○ *Hospital rooms have to be kept clean.* • Clean also means free from harmful substances, or pure: *clean air/water*

clean /kliːn/ *v* [I/T] to remove dirt or other unwanted parts or pieces from (something), or to make (something) neat and orderly • *Saturday morning is our time to clean the house.* [T] ○ *You should clean a wound immediately to avoid infection.* [T] ○ *I wish I could find the time to clean out these closets* (= throw away things that are not needed). [M] ○ *We quit work 15 minutes early to give ourselves time to clean up* (= wash ourselves to get rid of dirt). [I always + adv/prep] ○ *I have to clean (things) up* (= make things neat) *before the guests arrive.* [I/M]

cleaner /ˈkliː·nər/ *n* [C] a business that cleans clothes by using chemicals • A cleaner is also a person whose job is cleaning: *a window cleaner* • A cleaner is also a product that removes dirt: *a household cleaner*

cleanliness /ˈklen·liː·nəs/ *n* [U] the habit or state of keeping yourself or your environment free from dirt • *Her job involved checking the cleanliness of restaurants.*

clean HONEST /kliːn/ *adj* [-er/-est only] honest or fair; not breaking rules or laws • *"Let's make it a clean fight," said the referee.* ○ *Before his conviction for fraud, he had a clean record* (= he had not been involved in crime previously). ○ (*slang*) *They searched him for weapons, but he was clean* (= he was not carrying a weapon). • Clean also means moral, and esp. not about sex: *clean living* ○ *a clean joke*

clean COMPLETE /kliːn/ *adj* [-er/-est only] complete • *It's better for both of us if we make a clean break and stop seeing each other.* • A person who is **clean-cut** looks neat and attractive in a traditional way: *Whitmore fits the profile of a conservative, clean-cut, competent guy.* • A man who is **clean-shaven** cuts off all the hair on the lower part of his face. • A **clean sweep** is a complete change or complete victory: *Kenyan runners made it a clean sweep by taking the top five places in the race.*

clean /kli:n/ *adv* [not gradable] *infml* • *The bullet went clean through his shoulder and out the other side.*

clean NOT USED /kli:n/ *adj* [*-er/-est* only] new and not used • *a clean sheet of paper* • *The previous negotiations did not go anywhere, and we intend to start with a* **clean slate** (= not considering past events at all) *on the new round of negotiations.*

□**clean out** *obj*, **clean** *obj* **out** /ˈ-ˈ-/ *v adv* [M] *infml* to take or steal all the money or goods of (someone) • *Buying our new house just about cleaned us out.*

□**clean up** *obj* REMOVE EVILS , **clean** *obj* **up** /ˈ-ˈ-/ *v adv* [M] to remove illegal or dishonest activity from (a place) • *We need a mayor who is tough enough to clean up this town.*

□**clean up** WIN MONEY /ˈ-ˈ-/ *v adv* [I] *infml* to win a lot of money • *We cleaned up at the gambling casino last night.*

cleanse /klenz/ *v* [T] to remove all the dirt or harmful substances from (something) • *Thoroughly cleanse the wound and the area around it.*

cleanser /ˈklen·zər/ *n* [C/U] a substance used for cleaning • *kitchen cleansers* [C]

cleanup /ˈkli:·nʌp/ *n* [U] the process of removing a dirty or dangerous substance, esp. when it has been left in the environment as a result of an accident • *The cleanup after the oil spill cost over $10,000,000.*

clear UNDERSTANDABLE /klɪr/ *adj* [*-er/-est* only] easy to understand, or easy to see or hear • *I left clear instructions that no one was to come in my office.* ○ *He spoke in a clear voice.* ○ *It wasn't clear what he meant.* • *(humorous) The computer manual was* **(as) clear as mud** (= very difficult to understand).

clearly /ˈklɪr·li/ *adv* • *I think this report clearly shows why we have to act now.*

clear CERTAIN /klɪr/ *adj* [*-er/-est* only] certain or obvious; not in any doubt • *It's clear now that it was a mistake to have raised prices last spring.* [+ *that* clause] ○ *It isn't clear how long the strike will continue.* [+ *wh-* word] • *It was a* **clear-cut** *case of fraud* (= There are no doubts about it).

clearly /ˈklɪr·li/ *adv* certainly; obviously; without a doubt • *The accident was clearly the truck driver's fault.*

clear NOT CONFUSED /klɪr/ *adj* [*-er/-est* only] free from confusion; able to think quickly and well • *Mary is good at making decisions because she's a very clear thinker.* ○ *I'm not having wine because I have to be* **clearheaded** (= able to think clearly) *for a meeting this afternoon.*

clear BE NOT GUILTY /klɪr/ *v* [T] to show (some-

one) to be not guilty • *He was cleared of all charges, and the judge said he was free to go.*

clear /klɪr/ *adj* [*-er/-est* only] free from guilt • *My conscience is clear—I did what I could to help her.* • If someone is **in the clear**, they are not guilty of a crime, or were not involved in doing something bad.

clear GET RID OF /klɪr/ *v* [T] to remove or get rid of (something) or remove something blocking (the way), or to move people away from (a place) • *It took several hours to clear the road after the accident.* ○ *After the bomb threat, police cleared the area until it was searched.* ○ *Just let me clear the dishes off the table and put them in the sink.* [M] • *She* **cleared** *her* **throat** *before she began to speak* (= gave a small cough to remove anything that made speaking difficult). • To **clear the way** is to lead to something desired by removing something that was blocking it: *The test results could clear the way for wider approval of the drug.*

clear /klɪr/ *adj* [*-er/-est* only] not blocked or filled; open or available • *We have a clear view of the ocean from our hotel window.* ○ *The only time the doctor has clear today is 3:30—can you make it then?*

clearance /ˈklɪr·əns/ *n* [U] • If goods are reduced for clearance, they are offered for sale at a lower than usual price so that people will buy them and there will be space for new goods: *a clearance sale* • See also **clearance** at CLEAR NOT TOUCH, CLEAR GIVE PERMISSION .

clearing /ˈklɪr·ɪŋ/ *n* [C] an area in a woods or forest from which trees and bushes have been removed

clear SEEING THROUGH /klɪr/ *adj* [*-er/-est* only] easy to see through; not cloudy or foggy • *clear water* ○ *a clear day* ○ *(fig.) I have clear memories of* (= I can remember well) *visiting my grandfather's farm when I was a child.* • If a person's skin is clear, it has no marks or spots on it: *a clear complexion*

clear /klɪr/ *v* [I] • *The children stirred the mud at the bottom of the pond, then watched the water slowly clear.* • *We had a pretty fierce argument, but I guess it helped* **clear the air** (= get rid of the bad feelings) *between us.*

clear NOT TOUCH /klɪr/ *v* [I/T] to pass near (something) without touching it • *With the high-jump bar at 6 feet 2 inches, she cleared easily.* [I]

clear /klɪr/ *adv* [not gradable] • *Stand clear of the doors, please.* ○ *(fig.) His parents warned him to keep/stay clear of* (= avoid) *trouble.*

clearance /ˈklɪr·əns/ *n* [U] the amount of space available for an object to pass through an opening without touching anything, or for two objects to pass each other without touching • *The sign on the overpass says that its clearance is 12 feet, and our truck is 10 feet high, so we should have 2 feet of clearance when we*

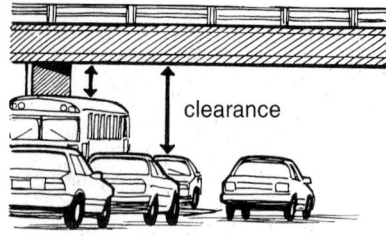

clearance

go under it. • See also **clearance** at CLEAR GET RID OF, CLEAR GIVE PERMISSION.

clear GIVE PERMISSION /klɪr/ v [T] to give official permission for (something), or to satisfy the official conditions of (something) • *Our plane has been cleared for takeoff, so will the flight attendants please be seated.* ○ *I'm still waiting for my paycheck to clear* (= be officially approved and processed) *so I can pay my bills.*

clearance /'klɪr·əns/ n [U] • *You can't visit military headquarters until you get security clearance.* • See also **clearance** at CLEAR GET RID OF, CLEAR NOT TOUCH.

□ **clear out** /'-'-/ v adv [I] to leave a building or other place, esp. without much warning • *Her landlord gave her a week to clear out of her apartment.*

□ **clear up** obj REMOVE DOUBT, **clear** obj **up** /'-'-/ v [M] to remove (doubts, confusion, or wrong ideas) • *I want to clear up any misconceptions you might still have.*

□ **clear up** GET BETTER /'-'-/ v adv [I] (of an illness or bad weather) to go away, changing into a better condition • *If my cold doesn't clear up, it will ruin my vacation.* ○ *Let's hope the weather clears up.*

cleat /kliːt/ n [C usually pl] one of the small, hard pieces on the bottom of special shoes worn in some sports because they catch in the ground and keep you from falling

cleavage /'kliː·vɪdʒ/ n [C/U] the space between a woman's breasts that can be seen when her clothing does not cover the top part of them

cleaver /'kliː·vər/ n [C] a knife with a large, square blade, used esp. for cutting meat

clef /klef/ n [C] a sign put at the beginning of a line of music to show how high or low the notes are

cleft /kleft/ n [C] an opening or crack, esp. in a rock or the ground

cleft /kleft/ adj • *He was strikingly handsome, with dark, wavy hair, a cleft chin* (= with a deep vertical line), *and penetrating blue eyes.* • A **cleft palate** is a condition in which a person is born with an opening in the roof of the mouth.

clemency /'klem·ən·si/ n [U] forgiveness for a crime by someone in authority, esp. by reducing a punishment • *The governor refused to grant him clemency, and he was executed at 9 a.m. yesterday.*

clench /klentʃ/ v [T] to hold (something) tightly, or press together (your lips or your hands) in anger or determination • *He clenched his fist and waved it at the crowd.*

clergy /'klɜr·dʒi/ pl n the religious leaders whose job is serving the needs of their religion and its followers; priests, ministers, rabbis, etc.

clergyman /'klɜr·dʒiː·mən/ n [C] **-men** /'klɜr·dʒiː·mən/ a religious leader whose job is serving the needs of their religion and its followers

cleric /'kler·ɪk/ n [C] a religious leader; a member of the CLERGY • *The committee was composed of Jewish, Catholic, Protestant, and Muslim clerics.*

clerical /'kler·ɪ·kəl/ adj relating to the type of work usually done in an office, or to the work of a CLERK

clerk /klɜrk/ n [C] a person who works in an office, dealing with records or performing general office duties • A clerk is also a person who deals with customers in a store or hotel: *The sales clerk helped me find a sweater in my size.*

clever /'klev·ər/ adj having or showing a quick intelligence in doing something or in persuading people to do something • *It was certainly a clever ad and got a lot of attention.*

cleverly /'klev·ər·li/ adv • *Did you notice how she cleverly avoided answering most of my questions?*

cliché /kliː'ʃeɪ/ n [C] an idea or expression that has been used too often and is often considered a sign of bad writing or old-fashioned thinking • *The story is shamelessly corny, and grownups will groan at its clichés.*

click SOUND /klɪk/ n [C] a short, metallic sound • *You'll know your seat belt is fastened properly when you hear a click.*

click /klɪk/ v [I/T] • *As the door clicked shut behind her, she realized she'd forgotten her key.* [I]

click BECOME FRIENDLY /klɪk/ v [I] infml to become friendly or be successful • *Liz and I really clicked, from the first time we met.* ○ *The show never really clicked.*

click BECOME CLEAR /klɪk/ v [I] infml to be understood or become clear suddenly • *Something clicked, and I remembered where I'd seen her before.*

client /'klaɪ·ənt/ n [C] a person who receives services, esp. from a lawyer or other person who gives advice • *He's a sports agent and has a lot of basketball players as clients.*

clientele /ˌklaɪ·ən'tel, ˌkliː-/ n [C] all the customers of a business when they are considered as a group

cliff /klɪf/ n [C] a high area of rock with a steep side, often on a coast

cliffhanger /'klɪf,hæŋ·ər/ n [C] a story or situation, often dangerous or of great importance, where two opposite results are possible and you do not know what the result will be until the last moment • *The polls are too close to call, and it looks like this election is going to be a real cliffhanger.*

climactic /klaɪˈmæk·tɪk/ *adj* being the most important or exciting point in a story or situation • *She was marvelous in the climactic sleepwalking scene in Macbeth.* • USAGE: The related noun is CLIMAX.

climate WEATHER /ˈklaɪ·mət/ *n* [C/U] the general weather conditions usually found in a particular place • *My parents like the warm, dry climate of Arizona.* [C]

climate ATTITUDE /ˈklaɪ·mət/ *n* [C] a general attitude, opinion, or feeling • *There's never been a climate of trust between labor and management in this industry.*

climax /ˈklaɪ·mæks/ *n* [C] the most important or exciting part in the development of a story or situation, which usually happens near the end • *The movie reaches its climax when George takes her out on a boat to kill her but decides he can't go through with it.* • A climax is also the moment of greatest pleasure and excitement in sexual activity. • USAGE: The related adjective is CLIMACTIC.

climax /ˈklaɪ·mæks/ *v* [I] to reach the greatest point or level of activity • *There had been a sharp rise in anti-Semitic incidents that climaxed with the attack on the Rome synagogue by terrorists.*

climb RISE /klaɪm/ *v* [I/T] to go up, or go up (something) or to the top of (something) • *We climbed to the top of the hill, where we had a great view.* [I] ○ *She climbed the stairs to the third floor.* [T] ○ *The plane is still climbing and will level off at 33,000 feet.* [I] ○ *(fig.) As he climbed the corporate ladder* (= moved into better and better positions in business), *his salary increased dramatically.* [I] • To climb is also to increase: *The cost of goods is climbing.* [I]

climb /klaɪm/ *n* [C] an act of going up • *It was a long, difficult climb to the top of the hill.*

climber /ˈklaɪ·mər/ *n* [C] a person who climbs mountains as a sport

climb MOVE /klaɪm/ *v* [I always + adv/prep] to move in a way that uses your arms and legs and often involves careful control over your body • *He climbed down from the ladder to get some more paint.*

clinch /klɪntʃ/ *v* [T] to succeed in making (an agreement) certain, esp. after a long period of discussion • *The deal was clinched when they agreed to share the shipping costs.*

clincher /ˈklɪn·tʃər/ *n* [C] *infml* a final item to be considered that makes a decision firm after you have been tending toward it, or anything that finally decides a matter • *The minivan was big enough for eight people and when we heard the price—that was the clincher!*

cling /klɪŋ/ *v* [I] *past* **clung** /klʌŋ/ to hold tightly or to stick; to refuse to stop holding • *They clung together in terror.* ○ *We were soaking wet and our clothes clung to us.* ○ *(fig.) She clings to*

the hope that her husband will come back to her.

clinic BUILDING /ˈklɪn·ɪk/ *n* [C] a building or part of a hospital where people go for medical care or advice • *Prenatal clinics provide care for pregnant women.*

clinic INSTRUCTION /ˈklɪn·ɪk/ *n* [C] instruction to a group of people in a particular subject, activity, or sport • *a summer baseball clinic for boys*

clinical /ˈklɪn·ɪ·kəl/ *adj* [not gradable] (of medical work or teaching) relating to the examination and treatment of sick people • *Clinical tests have so far failed to show the cause of her illness.* • Clinical also means considering a situation without showing or feeling any emotion: *He viewed the misery of the poor with clinical detachment.*

clink /klɪŋk/ *v* [I/T] to make a short, ringing sound like that of pieces of glass or metal knocking together

clink /klɪŋk/ *n* [C/U] • *the clink of coins* [U]

clip FASTENER /klɪp/ *n* [C] a usually metal or plastic object used for fastening things together or holding them in position • *Her long hair was held back with a hair clip.* • A **clipboard** is a board with a clip at the top that holds sheets of paper in position and provides a surface for writing on. • Clip-on means attached with a clip: *clip-on earrings*

clip /klɪp/ *v* [always + adv/prep] **-pp-** to fasten with a clip • *He had a beeper clipped to his belt.* [T]

clip CUT /klɪp/ *v* [T] **-pp-** to cut (a piece) from something larger or whole • *She clipped the coupons out of the newspaper.* ○ *He had his beard clipped.*

clip /klɪp/ *n* [C] a small piece of something • A clip is a short part of a film or VIDEO shown alone: *a news clip*

clippers /ˈklɪp·ərz/ *pl n* any of various tools used for clipping esp. nails, hair, wire, or plants

clip SPEED /klɪp/ *n* [U] *infml* a rate of speed • *I drove home at a good clip.*

clip GUN PART /klɪp/ *n* [C] a container holding bullets and that is put into a gun

clique /kliːk, klɪk/ *n* [C] a small group of people who spend time together and do not want other people to join the group

clitoris /ˈklɪṭ·ə·rəs/ *n* [C] a small, fleshy organ above the vagina that gives a woman pleasure when it is sexually excited

cloak PIECE OF CLOTHING /kloʊk/ *n* [C] a loose outer piece of clothing without sleeves that fastens at the neck and hangs from the shoulders • A **cloakroom** is a room in a public building where coats, bags, and hats can be left while their owners are in the building.

cloak HIDE /kloʊk/ *v* [T] to cover or hide (something) • *The deal was cloaked in secrecy.*

cloak /kloʊk/ *n* [C usually sing] • A **cloak-**

and-dagger activity is one involving mystery and secrecy: *a cloak-and-dagger spy mission*

clobber HIT /ˈklɑb·ər/ *v* [T] *infml* to hit hard • *Austin clobbered another kid at recess.*

clobber DEFEAT /ˈklɑb·ər/ *v* [T] to defeat completely • *The party has been clobbered by a string of humiliating political losses.*

clock /klɑk/ *n* [C] a device for measuring and showing time, often placed on a surface or attached to a wall • *an alarm clock* ○ *The clock is about ten minutes fast/slow* (= it shows a later/earlier time than it should). ○ *Cleveland tied the game with five seconds on the clock* (= still available). • A **clock radio** is a radio that shows the time and can be set so the radio automatically begins to play at a time you choose. • **Clockwork** is machinery with springs and wheels that makes older types of clocks, toys, and other devices work.

clock /klɑk/ *v* [T] to use (an amount of time), esp. as measured by a clock • *She clocked the fastest time in practice runs for the women's downhill skiing event.*

clockwise /ˈklɑk·wɑɪz/ *adj, adv* [not gradable] (moving around) in the same direction as the pointers of a clock or watch • Compare COUNTERCLOCKWISE.

clod LUMP /klɑd/ *n* [C] a lump of dirt

clod PERSON /klɑd/ *n* [C] *infml* a stupid or awkward person

clog BLOCK /klɑg, klɔːg/ *v* [I/T] **-gg-** to become blocked or filled so that movement or activity is slowed or stopped, or to cause this to happen • *During rush hour, downtown streets are clogged with commuters.* [T] ○ *Too much cholesterol clogs up your arteries.* [M]

clog SHOE /klɑg, klɔːg/ *n* [C] a shoe with a thick, often wooden bottom and a top that covers the front of the foot, but not the heel

clog

cloister /ˈklɔɪ·stər/ *n* [C] a covered passage around esp. a square open space within a religious building, or the space such a passage goes around

clone /kloʊn/ *n* [C] a cell or organism that has the exact same chemical patterns in its cells as the original from which it was artificially produced • A clone is also a computer that is very similar to one made by a large company.

clone /kloʊn/ *v* [T] • *The debate continues over whether it is ethically right to clone a human embryo.*

close NEAR /kloʊs/ *adj, adv* [-er/-est only] near in position, time, or condition • *The store was close by, so they decided to walk.* ○ *It's close to 7 o'clock—we'd better leave now.* ○ *The child moved closer to his mother.* ○ *She was very close to death for awhile.* • A **close call** or **close shave** is something bad that almost happened: *We nearly had an accident driving over here—it was really a close call.* • A **closeup** is an image taken from very near so that the subject appears large.

closely /ˈkloʊ·sli/ *adv* • *We had to huddle more closely together.*

close CONNECTED /kloʊs/ *adj* [-er/-est only] connected or involved in strong relationship with someone • *Charmaine is my closest friend.* ○ *Joyce and I used to be close, but now we seldom see each other.* • If a group of people such as a family is **close-knit**, they share a strong, caring relationship.

closely /ˈkloʊ·sli/ *adv* [not gradable] • *We worked together closely for years.* ○ *The city and the air force base have been closely linked since 1943.*

close SIMILAR /kloʊs/ *adj* [-er/-est only] similar; of the same type • *Your computer is pretty close to the one I have.* • If a game or competition is close, both sides have almost the same score.

close CAREFUL /kloʊs/ *adj* [-er/-est only] giving your full attention to something so that you notice its details • *I wasn't the one driving, so I wasn't paying close attention to the route we took.*

closely /ˈkloʊ·sli/ *adv* [not gradable] • *We watched her closely to make sure her fever did not go up again.* ○ *Economists closely follow auto sales.*

close WARM /kloʊs/ *adj* [not gradable] very warm, with no movement of air • *It was uncomfortably close in the gym.*

close MAKE NOT OPEN /kloʊz/ *v* [I/T] to change from being open to not being open, or to cause this to happen • *Come in and close the door.* [T] ○ *Because of an accident, police closed* (= blocked) *two lanes of the expressway.* [T] ○ *Grace closed her eyes to think.* [T]

closed /kloʊzd/ *adj* [not gradable] • If a society or economy is closed, it does not allow free exchanges or trade with other societies or countries. • **Closed circuit** television is a system that sends television signals from various places within or around a store or building to a limited number of screens, as a way to prevent stealing or other illegal activities. • A **closed shop** is a place of work where you have to belong to a particular **labor union** (= organization of workers).

close END / STOP /kloʊz/ *v* [I/T] to end or stop operating, or to cause this to happen • *Authorities closed the aging nuclear plant.* [T] ○ *After a run of three months, the show closes on Saturday.* [I] • (esp. of a business) To close is also to temporarily stop being available to customers: *The store closes at 9 tonight.* [I]

close /kloʊz/ *n* [C usually sing] • *The ski season has come to a close.*

closed /kloʊzd/ *adj* [not gradable] temporarily not open for business • *The race track is closed on Tuesday.*

close COMPLETE /kloʊz/ *v* [I/T] to make (esp. a business arrangement) complete • *The manu-*

facturer is closing a deal to sell its boating division. [T]

closing /ˈkloʊ·zɪŋ/ *n* [C] • *The closing for the house was set for April.*

▫ **close down** (*obj*), **close** (*obj*) **down** /ˈ-ˈ-/ *v adv* [I/M] to end the operation of (esp. a place of business) • *He said he would close down before he would force all hands to join the union.* [I]

▫ **close in** /ˈ-ˈ-/ *v adv* [I] to move toward someone or something gradually and from all angles • *It felt as though the walls of the room were closing in on her.*

▫ **close off** *obj*, **close** *obj* **off** /ˈ-ˈ-/ *v adv* [M] to stop people or vehicles from going to (a place) • *They closed Pennsylvania Avenue off to vehicles.*

closed /kloʊzd/ *adj* • See at CLOSE MAKE NOT OPEN, CLOSE END/STOP.

closet /ˈklɑz·ət/ *n* [C] a small room or space in a wall where you can store things such as clothes, sheets, etc., often having a door so that it can be closed • *a clothes/linen closet*

closet /ˈklɑz·ət/ *adj* kept secret from others • *a closet liberal* ○ *a closet homosexual*

closet /ˈklɑz·ət/ *v* [T always + adv/prep] to arrange to meet privately with someone where you will not be interrupted • *The president and his advisers closeted themselves with the congressional leadership.*

closure STOP OPERATING /ˈkloʊ·ʒər/ *n* [C] the act of stopping operations of a business, school, hospital, etc. • *A storm forced the closure of many schools and businesses.*

closure SATISFACTION /ˈkloʊ·ʒər/ *n* [U] the satisfying feeling that something bad or shocking has finally ended • *Only the recovery of the bodies of the victims of the crash would bring closure to their families.*

clot /klɑt/ *n* [C] a lump, esp. a lump of thickened blood • *Heart attacks occur when a blood clot blocks vessels to the heart.*

clot /klɑt/ *v* [I/T] to become thicker and more solid, or to cause (a liquid) to do this • *My hair was all clotted with dust and blood.* [T]

cloth /klɔːθ/ *n* [C/U] material made by weaving cotton, wool, or other fibers, or a piece of such material • *cloth diapers* [U] ○ *cloth napkins* [U] ○ *a cloth coat* [U] ○ *He used a damp cloth to clean the windshield.* [C]

clothe /kloʊð/ *v* [T] to provide or cover (someone) with things to wear • *They have eight kids to feed and clothe.* ○ *Lynn stretched out fully clothed on the bed.*

clothes /kloʊðz, kloʊz/ *pl n* coverings for a person's body; the things you wear to keep you warm, to be comfortable, or for the way they make you look • *I've got all these clothes that I never wear.* • A **clothesline** is a length of rope from which wet clothes are hung, usually outside, to dry. PIC LINES • A **clothespin** is a small plastic or wood object that is used to fasten clothes to a rope while they dry.

clothing /ˈkloʊ·ðɪŋ/ *n* [U] coverings to wear; clothes • *The warmer it gets the less clothing I wear.*

cloud /klaʊd/ *n* [C/U] a white or gray mass of very small drops of water or ice that float in the sky • *Those dark clouds look like we're going to get some rain.* [C] • A cloud is also a mass of something, such as dust or smoke, that moves together: *The distant cloud of dust in the valley announced the approach of a car.* [C] • A cloud is also something which causes sadness or fear: *After the diagnosis of cancer, she lived under a cloud.* [C] • A **cloudburst** is a heavy fall of rain that begins and ends suddenly.

cloud /klaʊd/ *v* [T] • *Smoke clouded the sky.* [T] • If something clouds a situation or feeling, it makes it less clear: *The fact that Jack was an old friend clouded her judgment.* • If it is **clouding over/up**, clouds are filling the sky.

cloudless /ˈklaʊd·ləs/ *adj* [not gradable] (of the sky) without clouds

cloudy /ˈklaʊd·i/ *adj* full of clouds • *a cloudy day*

clout POWER /klaʊt/ *n* [U] power and influence over other people or events • *The small firms banded together so they would have more clout in Washington.*

clout HIT /klaʊt/ *v* [T] *infml* to hit (someone) heavily with the hand or an object

clove PLANT PART /kloʊv/ *n* [C] a section of the ball-like root of a GARLIC plant

clove SPICE /kloʊv/ *n* [C/U] a spice that is the dried flower of a tree

clover /ˈkloʊ·vər/ *n* [C/U] a small plant with three round, green leaves that are joined together

cloverleaf /ˈkloʊ·vər,liːf/ *n* [C] *pl* **cloverleafs** or **cloverleaves** /ˈkloʊ·vər,liːvz/ a connection between two roads consisting of four smaller, curved roads which allows vehicles to move from one road to the other without crossing the flow of traffic

cloverleaf

clown /klaʊn/ *n* [C] an entertainer who wears silly clothes and makes people laugh by performing tricks without speech • (*infml*) A clown is also someone who behaves in a foolish or stupid way: *The people running this school are a bunch of clowns.*

clown /klaʊn/ *v* [I] to act silly • *Stop clowning around and get serious!*

club GROUP /klʌb/ *n* [C] an organization of

people with a common purpose or interest who meet regularly and share activities • *My book club meets the first Tuesday of every month to discuss a new book we've all read.* • A club is also a team: *a major league baseball club*

club GOLF STICK /klʌb/ *n* [C] a long, thin stick with a wide part at the bottom, used to hit the ball in the game of golf

club WEAPON /klʌb/ *n* [C] a heavy stick used as a weapon

club /klʌb/ *v* [T] **-bb-** • *She was clubbed to death with a weight-lifting bar.*

clubs /klʌbz/ *pl n* one of the four SUITS (= groups) of playing cards, the symbol for which is a black sign with three circular parts and a stem • PIC SUITS

club soda /klʌb'soʊd·ə/ *n* [C/U] bubbly water that is sometimes mixed with alcoholic drinks

cluck /klʌk/ *v* [I/T] to make a sound like a chicken

clue /kluː/ *n* [C] information that helps you to find the answer to a problem, question, or mystery • *For five months, Russell remained a fugitive, leaving no clues as to his whereabouts.*

□ **clue** *obj* **in** /'kluːˈɪn/ *v adv* [T] *infml* to give (someone) information that is necessary or new • *Trev will clue me in on developments.*

clump GROUP /klʌmp/ *n* [C] a group, esp. of plants • *Small clumps of hardy grass had sprung up between the rocks.*

clump /klʌmp/ *v* [I/T] to gather in a group, or to cause this to happen • *In our office, the desks are clumped together with partitions around them.* [T]

clump WALK /klʌmp/ *v* [I always + adv/prep] to walk in a noisy way with heavy steps • *He clumped up the steps.*

clumsy /'klʌm·zi/ *adj* awkward in movement or manner • *I'm so clumsy—I keep dropping things.* • Clumsy also means done in an awkward or embarrassing way: *He subsequently wrote a letter to the magazine in an admittedly clumsy try at explaining his viewpoint.* • Something that is clumsy is too big or complicated to be dealt with easily: *She would be at the mercy of a clumsy bureaucracy.*

clung /klʌŋ/ *past simple and past participle of* CLING

clunk /klʌŋk/ *v* [T] to make the sound of heavy objects hitting together, or to cause this sound to be made • *She emptied the change out of her purse and clunked it into her piggy bank.*

clunk /klʌŋk/ *n* [C] • *We heard a loud clunk as the ferry hit the side of the dock.*

cluster /'klʌs·tər/ *v* [I] to form or gather together • *All his grandchildren clustered around him.*

cluster /'klʌs·tər/ *n* [C] a group of similar things growing or held together, or a group of people or things that are close together • *dense clusters of delicate pink blossoms* ○ *This section*

of town contains a large cluster of Jewish dwellings and businesses.

clutch HOLD /klʌtʃ/ *v* [I/T] to hold or try to hold (something) tightly, often because of a state of fear or anxiety • *The preschooler clutched his mother tightly.* [T]

clutches /'klʌtʃ·əz/ *pl n* control or power over someone, esp. in a way that harms them • *Both boys fell into the clutches of* (= were controlled by) *a drug dealer.*

clutch VEHICLE PART /klʌtʃ/ *n* [C usually sing] a device in a car or other vehicle that you press with your foot in order to change GEARS (= set of wheels that control power)

clutch PERFORMING WELL /klʌtʃ/ *adj* able to do something when it is especially needed • *Moose, always reliable under pressure, was a tremendous clutch hitter.*

clutch /klʌtʃ/ *n* [U] • *Rhoda always comes through in the clutch* (= You can depend on her to do what is needed).

clutter /'klʌt·ər/ *n* [U] a condition of disorder, or a lot of objects that are in a state of disorder • *The basement work area is filled with creative clutter.*

clutter /'klʌt·ər/ *v* [T] • *The family room was cluttered with toys.*

cm *n* [C] *pl* **cm** *abbreviation for* CENTIMETER

c'mon *not standard* /kəˈmɔːn, -ˈmɑn/ *contraction of* (spelled the way it is often spoken) COME ON HURRY • *C'mon in, the door's open.*

co– /koʊ/ *combining form* together; with • *They were named co-winners of the Big Sky player of the week honor.*

c/o *abbreviation for* (used in written addresses) care of • *You can write me c/o Roberta Moody, at 12 Townsend Place, Newark, New Jersey.*

coach TEACHER /koʊtʃ/ *n* [C] (esp. in sports) a person who is responsible for managing and training a person or a team • *a basketball coach* • A coach is also an expert who trains someone learning or improving a skill, esp. one related to performing: *an acting coach*

coach /koʊtʃ/ *v* [I/T] • *He coached the Giants until 1997.* [I/T]

coach PART OF VEHICLE /koʊtʃ/ *n* [C/U] the less expensive sections of an aircraft that most people sit in • *We were in coach on the flight to Seattle.* [U] • A coach is also one of the separate parts of a train. [C] • A coach is also a kind of old-fashioned vehicle pulled by one or more horses. [C] • (*Br*) A coach is a BUS.

coagulate /koʊˈæɡ·jəˌleɪt/ *v* [I/T] (of a liquid) to become or cause to become thicker so that it will not flow • *When making cheese, enzymes are added to make the milk coagulate.* [I]

coal /koʊl/ *n* [C/U] a hard, black substance that is dug from the earth in lumps and used as a fuel, or a single piece of this substance • *Some of those schools still use coal for their heating.* [U] • A **coal mine** is the deep hole or connected passages under the ground from which coal is removed.

coalition /ˌkou·əˈlɪʃ·ən/ n [C] a group formed of different organizations or people who agree to act together, usually temporarily, to achieve something • *a governing coalition* ○ *the National Coalition on Black Voter Participation*

coarse ROUGH /kɔːrs, koʊrs/ adj [-er/-est only] rough and not smooth or soft • *coarse hair* ○ *coarse linen shirts*

coarsely /ˈkɔːr·sli, ˈkoʊr-/ adv • *Our recipe calls for coarsely chopped pistachios.*

coarse RUDE /kɔːrs, koʊrs/ adj [-er/-est only] rude or offensive in manner or speech • *Now and then coarse laughter broke out.*

coarseness /ˈkɔːr·snəs, ˈkoʊr-/ n [U] • *He was shocked by the coarseness of his guest.*

coast LAND /koʊst/ n [C] the land next to or close to the sea • *We lived on the southeast coast of Florida.* • If you say **the coast is clear**, you mean that someone can safely do something without being seen or noticed: *The boss has left for lunch, so the coast is clear—we can talk freely at last.* • In North America, if you travel **coast to coast**, you travel from near the Atlantic Ocean to near the Pacific Ocean, or from near the Pacific to near the Atlantic: *The first nonstop, coast-to-coast flight occurred in 1923.* • The **Coast Guard** is a part of the US military forces that is responsible for guarding the land next to the sea, seeing that boats and ships follow US laws, and helping people in emergencies. • The **coastline** of a country or other place is the shape of its land next to the sea, esp. when seen from the air or as shown on a map.

coastal /ˈkoʊ·stəl/ adj [not gradable] near the coast • *coastal waters* ○ *coastal communities*

coast MOVE EASILY /koʊst/ v [I] (of a vehicle) to continue moving from its own forward force, without the addition of any power • *He coasted to a stop.* • To coast is also to advance without effort: *She coasted through her senior year of high school.*

coaster /ˈkoʊ·stər/ n [C] a small, flat piece of material, often decorative, that you put a glass or cup on in order to protect the surface of furniture

coat CLOTHING /koʊt/ n [C] any of various types of outer clothing that are worn over other clothes, usually open in the front, and are often used for warmth • *She put on her heavy winter coat.* • When you say a man is wearing a coat and tie, the coat is a jacket or part of a SUIT. • Coat is often used as a combining form: *a raincoat* • A **coat hanger** is a HANGER.

coat ANIMAL /koʊt/ n [C] the natural hair, wool, or fur of an animal • *The dog's coat is shiny and clean.*

coat LAYER /koʊt/ n [C] a layer of a substance • *There were about six coats of paint over the brick.*

coat /koʊt/ v [T] • *Everything was coated with a fine layer of dust.*

coating /ˈkoʊt̬·ɪŋ/ n [C] a COAT LAYER • *Use a baking pan with a nonstick coating.*

coax /koʊks/ v [T] to try to persuade (someone) to do something by asking or encouraging them gently or patiently • *He'll talk if you coax him.*

cobbled /ˈkɑb·əld/ adj [not gradable] surfaced with a layer of stones • *cobbled streets*

cobra /ˈkoʊ·brə/ n [C] a poisonous snake from Africa or southern Asia that can make itself look bigger by spreading the skin at the back of its head

cobweb /ˈkɑb·web/ n [C usually pl] a structure of thin, sticky threads made by a SPIDER (= insectlike creature), esp. when they are covered with dust • *Cobwebs hung down from the rafters.*

Coca-Cola /ˌkoʊ·kəˈkoʊ·lə/, **Coke** n [C/U] *trademark* a sweet, bubbly, brown drink that does not contain alcohol, or a glass of this drink

cocaine /koʊˈkeɪn/, *slang* **coke** n [U] a dangerous drug taken illegally for pleasure, often as a powder breathed through the nose

cock BIRD /kɑk/ n [C] a ROOSTER (= an adult male chicken)

cock TURN /kɑk/ v [T] to turn a (part of the body) in a particular direction • *He cocked his head to one side.*

cock PREPARE GUN /kɑk/ v [T] to prepare (a gun) so that it is ready for firing • *They stood guard on the roof, rifles cocked.*

cock PENIS /kɑk/ n [C] *taboo slang* a penis • *(taboo slang)* A **cocksucker** is a person, esp. a male person, you do not like. This word is offensive.

cock–a–doodle–do /ˌkɑk·ə¸duːd·əlˈduː/ *exclamation* a child's word for the sound made by a ROOSTER (= type of bird)

cockamamie /ˌkɑk·əˈmeɪ·mi/ adj *slang* ridiculous or crazy • *He had some cockamamie idea for turning food into food for people.*

cockeyed SLOPING /ˈkɑkˈɑɪd/ adj, adv not level but set at an angle • *That picture looks cockeyed—it tilts to the left.*

cockeyed RIDICULOUS /ˈkɑkˈɑɪd/ adj completely unreasonable; ridiculous • *The movie is based on a cockeyed premise.*

cockpit /ˈkɑk·pɪt/ n [C] the enclosed space where the PILOT sits in an aircraft, or where the driver sits in a racing car

cockroach /ˈkɑk·roʊtʃ/, *short form* **roach** n [C] a flat brown or black insect sometimes found in a house

cocksure /ˈkɑkˈʃʊr, *Southern often* -ˈʃoʊr/ adj [not gradable] *disapproving* too confident • *a strong, cocksure young man*

cocktail DRINK /ˈkɑk·teɪl/ n [C] a drink, esp. an alcoholic one, made by mixing two or more drinks together • *Would you like a cocktail?* • A cocktail is also a mixture of different things: *I take a cocktail of AIDS drugs.* • A **cocktail dress** is a stylish dress suitable for an evening party. • A **cocktail lounge** is a bar or a room in a restaurant or hotel where you can be served alcoholic drinks. • A **cocktail party** is a party, usually in the late afternoon or early evening, at which alcoholic drinks are served.

cocktail FOOD /'kɑk·teɪl/ n [C/U] a small dish of particular foods sometimes eaten at the beginning of a meal • *I'd like the shrimp cocktail, please.* [C]

cocky /'kɑk·i/ adj too confident • *Hugh is knowledgeable but not cocky.*

cocoa /'koʊ·koʊ/ n [U] a dark brown powder made from the crushed beans of a tree, used to make chocolate and give the taste of chocolate to food and drink • Cocoa is also a drink made from cocoa powder that is sweetened and mixed with hot water or milk.

coconut /'koʊ·kə,nʌt/ n [C/U] a large, nutlike fruit with a hard, brown shell and firm, white, edible flesh, or the white flesh of this fruit, sometimes used in cooking

cocoon /kə'kuːn/ n [C] the silky covering that encloses and protects CATERPILLARS (= a type of insect) during a stage in their lives before they develop into adults • (*fig.*) A cocoon is also a safe, quiet place: *the warm, safe cocoon of childhood*

cod FISH /kɑd/ n [C/U] *pl* **cod** a large sea fish that can be eaten

C.O.D. adv [not gradable] *abbreviation for* cash on delivery, or collect on delivery (= payment will be made when goods are delivered) • *Can I have that shipped C.O.D.?*

coddle /'kɑd·əl/ v [T] to protect (someone or something) too much • *Americans don't support coddling criminals.*

code SPECIAL LANGUAGE /koʊd/ n [C/U] a system for representing information with signs or symbols that are not ordinary language, or the signs or symbols themselves • *Andrew writes computer code.* [U] ◦ *Callers punch in four-digit access codes for various topics.* [C] • A **code word** is a word or sign with a special meaning, or a word used to keep something secret: *He uses "multiculturalism" as a code word for his political agenda.*

code /koʊd/ v [T] • *Many areas of the brain code and store information.*

coded /'koʊd·əd/ adj [not gradable] • *Electronically coded cards are issued to food-stamp recipients.*

code RULES /koʊd/ n [C] rules for the way people should behave, or a set of written rules or laws that tell people what to do • *Faculty members are expected to follow the school's honor code.* ◦ *Is there a dress code where you work?* ◦ *Fire codes prohibit locking classroom doors.*

codeine /'koʊ·diːn/ n [U] a drug made from OPIUM which is used in medicine to block pain

coed /'koʊ·ed/ adj [not gradable] for male and female students together • *a coed private school* ◦ *a coed bathroom*

coed /'koʊ·ed/ n [C] *dated* a female student in a college or university that has both male and female students

coefficient /ˌkoʊ·ɪ'fɪʃ·ənt/ n [C] *specialized* (in mathematics) a number or symbol that is written in front of and multiplies another number or symbol • *In 2x, 2 is the coefficient of x.*

coerce /koʊ'ɜrs/ v [T] to persuade (someone) forcefully to do something that they may not want to do • *I don't think anybody should be coerced into praying.*

coercion /koʊ'ɜr·ʒən/ n [U] • *They used threats and coercion to keep the others in line.*

coercive /koʊ'ɜr·sɪv/ adj • *coercive threats/ governments*

coexist /ˌkoʊ·ɪg'zɪst/ v [I] to live or exist together, esp. peacefully, at the same time or in the same place • *There's little hope that Bosnia's ethnic groups can again coexist.*

coexistence /ˌkoʊ·ɪg'zɪs·təns/ n [U] • *Peaceful coexistence is our only real hope.*

coffee /'kɔː·fi, 'kɑf·i/ n [C/U] a dark brown, slightly bitter drink that is usually served hot, esp. in the morning and at the end of meals, or the beans from which this drink is made • *Would you like some more coffee?* [U] • A **coffee break** is a short rest from work in the morning or afternoon. • A **coffeehouse** is a small, informal restaurant where people can buy drinks and small meals and where there is sometimes entertainment. • A **coffeemaker** is a machine that makes coffee. • A **coffee pot** is a container for making or serving coffee. • A **coffee shop** is an informal and usually cheap restaurant where drinks and simple meals are served. • A **coffee table** is a low table usually placed in front of a SOFA (= long, soft seat) for holding drinks, magazines, and other small objects.

coffers /'kɔː·fərz, 'kɑf·ərz/ *pl n* the financial accounts of a government or an organization • *Tourism brought $200 million into local government coffers.*

coffin /'kɔː·fən, 'kɑf·ən/ n [C] a long box in which a dead person is buried or CREMATED (= burnt) • *Genny stared into the open coffin.*

cog /kɑg/ n [C] a toothlike part around the edge of a wheel in a machine that fits between those on a similar wheel, causing both wheels to move • A person who is a **cog in a machine** has a small but active job in a large organization, along with many others: *He's a pretty important cog in our machine.*

cogent /'koʊ·dʒənt/ adj (esp. of an argument or opinion) persuasive and well expressed • *He makes a cogent argument for improving early childhood education.*

cogency /'koʊ·dʒən·si/ n [U] *slightly fml* • *Her writing combines fluency with cogency.*

cognac /'koʊn·jæk, 'kɑn-/ n [C/U] BRANDY (= strong alcoholic drink) of high quality, esp.

one made in western France, or a glass of this drink

cohabitation /ˌkoʊˌhæb·ə'teɪ·ʃən/ *n* [U] *fml* (esp. of a man and woman who are not married) the act of living together • *There's more cohabitation, which means their divorce rates are lower.*

coherent /koʊ'hɪr·ənt/ *adj* having its parts related in a reasonable or understandable way • *The president has not presented a coherent plan for dealing with it.* • Coherent also means expressing yourself clearly: *I should warn you, she's not always coherent.*

coherence /koʊ'hɪr·əns/ *n* [U] • *Is there a larger vision, a coherence behind any of this?*

cohesion /koʊ'hi:·ʒən/ *n* [U] (of objects) the state of sticking together, or (of people) being in close agreement and working well together • *The team just seems to lack cohesion.*

cohesive /koʊ'hi:·sɪv, -zɪv/ *adj* • *We were not a very cohesive family.*

coil /kɔɪl/ *n* [C] a length of rope or wire curled to form a series of circles, one above the other • *Rob raised the heavy coil of rope to his shoulder.* • A coil is also anything having the shape of a series of circles, one above the other: *A coil of smoke rose from the chimney.*

coil /kɔɪl/ *v* [I/T] • *She coiled my hair, clipping curls with bobby pins.* [T]

coin MONEY /kɔɪn/ *n* [C] a small, flat, round piece of metal used as money, with a number showing its value and often a decorative picture • *Let's flip a coin to see who goes first?* ○ *He fished about in his pockets, taking out a handful of coins.*

coin INVENT /kɔɪn/ *v* [T] to invent or be the first to use (a new word or expression) • *Kraft coined the term "middle America" in the 1960s.*

coincide /ˌkoʊ·ən'saɪd/ *v* [I] to come together in position or happen at or near the same time • *Power failures coincided with the hottest weather.*

coincidence /koʊ'ɪn·səd·ʰns, -sə،dens/ *n* [C/U] an occasion when two or more things happen at the same time, esp. in a way that is unexpected or unlikely, or the unlikely fact of such things happening at the same time • *Was our meeting here a coincidence?* [C] ○ *By coincidence, both teams happen to be coached by men.* [U]

coincidental /koʊ·ɪn·sə'dent·ʰl/ *adj* [not gradable] • *Resemblances between their stories are purely coincidental.*

coincidentally /koʊ·ɪn·sə'dent·ʰl·i/ *adv* [not gradable] • *Mo shut his eyes and swung, the ball and the bat coincidentally arriving at the same place at the same time.*

Coke DRINK /koʊk/ *n* [C/U] *trademark* COCA-COLA

coke DRUG /koʊk/ *n* [U] *slang* COCAINE

coke FUEL /koʊk/ *n* [U] a solid substance obtained from coal and used as a fuel

cola /'koʊ·lə/ *n* [C/U] a sweet, bubbly, brown drink that does not contain alcohol

colander /'kɑl·ən·dər, 'kʌl-/ *n* [C] a bowl with many holes in it, used for washing food or for removing water from food that has been cooked

colander

cold LOW TEMPERATURE /koʊld/ *adj* [-er/-est only] having a low temperature, esp. when compared to the temperature of the human body, and not hot or warm • *cold weather* ○ *I forgot my gloves and my hands are getting cold.* • A person might be said to **get/have cold feet** when they experience a loss of confidence and sometimes unwillingness before doing something risky or difficult. • To go **cold turkey** is to suddenly and completely stop a habit that has made you dependent on it, such as taking a drug or smoking: *Six years ago, she went cold turkey on a four-pack-a-day smoking habit.* • The temperature of **cold-blooded** animals, such as snakes and fish, varies according to the temperature around them. Compare **warm-blooded** at WARM HIGH TEMPERATURE. • **Cold cuts** are thin, flat slices of cold meat. • A **cold snap** is a short period of very cold weather.

cold /koʊld/ *n* [U] • The cold is cold temperature or cold weather: *Don't stand out there in the cold—come in here and get warm.*

cold UNFRIENDLY /koʊld/ *adj* [-er/-est only] not showing or influenced by affection, kindness, or feeling; not friendly • *a cold greeting/reception* • *He was killed in cold blood* (= with extreme cruelty). • If someone is a **cold-blooded** criminal/killer they commit crimes, esp. murder, cruelly and without seeming to feel any emotion. • **Cold-hearted** means not caring about other people: *She said that the city's decision to close the homeless shelter was cold-hearted.* • A **cold war** is a continuing and dangerous state of unfriendliness existing between countries which is expressed not through fighting but in political ways, often including threats of war.

coldly /'koʊld·li/ *adv* • *"Please don't come here again," he said coldly.*

cold ILLNESS /koʊld/ *n* [C] a common infection, esp. in the nose and throat, which often causes you to sneeze and cough, to feel tired, and sometimes to have pain in the muscles • *I'm afraid I'm catching a cold.* • A **cold sore** is a painful, red swelling on esp. the lips or nose which is caused by a viral infection.

coleslaw /'koʊl·slɔ/ *n* [U] thinly cut raw vegetables, esp. CABBAGE leaves, covered in a thick, creamy sauce and eaten cold

colic /'kɑl·ɪk/ *n* [U] a severe but not continuous pain in the bottom part of the stomach or bowels, esp. of babies

collaborate WORK WITH /kə'læb·ə,reɪt/ v [I] to work together or with someone else for a special purpose • *Rodgers and Hammerstein collaborated on a number of successful musicals for the Broadway stage.*

collaboration /kə,læb·ə'reɪ·ʃən/ n [C/U]

collaborate SUPPORT AN ENEMY /kə'læb·ə,reɪt/ v [I] to help an enemy of your own country, esp. one which has taken control of your country • *The Soviet government accused them of collaborating with Nazis in World War II.*

collage /kə'lɑʒ, kɔ:-/ n [C/U] a picture that includes various materials or objects glued to a surface, or the art of making such a picture

collapse FALL /kə'læps/ v [I/T] to fall down suddenly, or to cause to fall down • *He was killed when a piece of the wall collapsed on top of him.* [I]

collapse /kə'læps/ n [U] • *Toward the end of the race he was near collapse.*

collapse FAIL /kə'læps/ v [I] to be unable to continue or to remain in operation; fail • *Talks between management and unions collapsed today.*

collapse /kə'læps/ n [C/U] • *the collapse of the Soviet empire* [U]

collar NECK /'kɑl·ər/ n [C] the part of a piece of clothing that goes around the neck • A collar is also a narrow piece made of leather or other strong material that is put around the neck of an animal, esp. a dog or cat kept as a pet. • A **collarbone** is a bone between the shoulder and the base of the neck on each side of the body.

collar CATCH /'kɑl·ər/ v [T] *infml* to catch and hold (someone) so that they can't escape • (*fig.*) *We decided to skip the meeting but she collared us in the hotel lobby.*

collate /kə'leɪt, 'kɑl·eɪt, 'koʊ·leɪt/ v [I/T] to collect and arrange in correct order (the sheets of a document) • *Will the new photocopier collate the pages?* [T]

collateral /kə'læt̬·ə·rəl/ n [U] *specialized* valuable property owned by someone who wants to borrow money, which they agree will become the property of the lender if the debt is not paid back • *She put up her house as collateral for the loan.*

colleague /'kɑl·iːg/ n [C] one of a group of people who work together • *He always got along well with his colleagues in the university.*

collect GATHER /kə'lekt/ v [I/T] to come or bring together from a variety of places or over a period of time • *A crowd of people soon collected at the scene of the accident.* [I] ○ *Information about employment is collected from every state.* [T] • People sometimes collect one particular type of object as a hobby: *I've got three kids who collect football cards.* [T]

collection /kə'lek·ʃən/ n [C] • *We're taking*

(*up*) *a collection for his retirement gift* (= getting money from people who want to give it).

collector /kə'lek·tər/ n [C] someone who collects certain things as a job or as a hobby • *An avid art collector, he owned at least a dozen Picassos.*

collectible /kə'lek·tə·bəl/ n [C] an item that some people want to collect as a hobby

collect RECEIVE /kə'lekt/ v [I/T] to receive (esp. money) that you are owed or have earned • *You can begin to collect benefits under Social Security at age 62.* [T]

collect TELEPHONE /kə'lekt/ adj, adv [not gradable] (of a telephone call or the act of calling) done in a way that will be paid for by the person receiving it • *a collect call* ○ *You can call me collect.* • LP TELEPHONE

collective /kə'lek·tɪv/ adj of or shared by every member of a group of people • *It was a collective decision/effort.* • **Collective bargaining** is the system in which employees deal with their employers as a group and to try to agree on matters such as pay and working conditions.

college /'kɑl·ɪdʒ/ n [C] a place of higher education usually for people who have finished twelve years of schooling and where they can obtain more advanced knowledge and get a degree to recognize this • A college is also one of the separate parts into which some universities are divided: *She graduated from the university's College of Business Management.*

collegiate /kə'liː·dʒət/ adj of or belonging to a college or its students • *collegiate activities/sports*

collide /kə'lɑɪd/ v [I always + adv/prep] (esp. of moving objects) to hit something violently • *He went off the road to avoid colliding with another car.*

collision /kə'lɪʒ·ən/ n [C] the violent coming together of two or more moving objects, such as vehicles • *The collision involved a pickup truck and a car.* • If two people or organizations are **on a collision course**, they have very different aims or opinions and are likely to disagree strongly: *The city council is on a collision course with the mayor.*

collie /'kɑl·i/ n [C] any of several types of dogs with long hair, originally bred for controlling sheep

colloquial /kə'loʊ·kwiː·əl/ adj (of words and expressions) informal and conversational, and more suitable for use in speech than in writing

collusion /kə'luː·ʒən/ n [U] agreement, esp. in secret for an illegal or dishonest reason • *The companies were accused of acting in collusion to fix prices.*

cologne /kə'loʊn/ n [U] a type of PERFUME (= liquid having a pleasant smell that is put on the body)

colon MARK /'koʊ·lən/ n [C] a mark (:) used in

COLON [:]

Colons are found most often in formal writing and on lists, forms, and documents. A colon is used:

to direct attention, like a pointing finger, to what follows

The speaker continued: "Today we are gathered. . . ." • Dear Mr. Ziemacki: • Memo to:

to introduce a list

She had three brothers: Michael, Brandon, and Tony.

If the items following the colon are long or contain commas, they are separated from each other by semicolons.

In case of a fire: sound the alarm; close all windows, including those in the hallways; and leave the building.

to introduce an independent part of a sentence that explains or illustrates the main part

We have made a difficult decision: the company will close.

to separate parts or numbers, as of a two-part title, a ratio, or a time of day

My textbook is called Statistics: An Introduction. *• a ratio of 3:2* (spoken as "three to two") *• 2:45 p.m.* (spoken as "two forty-five p.m.")

writing esp. to introduce a list of things or a sentence or phrase taken from somewhere else

colon BODY PART /'koʊ·lən/ n [C] the lower and larger part of the bowels through which food travels while it is being digested

colonel /'kɜrn·əl/ n [C] a military officer of high rank, above a MAJOR

colonnade /ˌkɑl·ə'neɪd/ n [C] a row of columns separated from each other by an equal distance

colony /'kɑl·ə·ni/ n [C] a country or area controlled politically by a more powerful country • A colony is also a group of people with a shared interest or job who live together: *an artists' colony* • A colony is also a group of animals, insects, or plants of the same type that live together: *an ant colony*

colonial /kə'loʊ·niː·əl/ adj • *the former colonial rulers of South Africa*

colonist /'kɑl·ə·nəst/ n [C] a person living in a country or area controlled politically by a more powerful country • *He arrived in Maryland with the first American colonists in 1634.*

colonize /'kɑl·ə,nɑɪz/ v [T] • *Peru was colonized by the Spanish in the 16th century.*

color APPEARANCE /'kʌl·ər/ n [C/U] the appearance that something has as a result of reflecting light • *The dress comes in blue, green, red, and other colors.* [C] ○ *Some of the pictures in the book are in color, and some are in black and white.* [U] • A color is also a substance, such

as a paint or DYE, which you add to something to make it have the appearance of a particular color. [C/U] • If a person is **colorblind**, they have something wrong with their eyes and are unable to see the difference between particular colors, esp. red and green. See also **colorblind** at COLOR SKIN.

color /'kʌl·ər/ adj [not gradable] showing things in all their colors, not just black and white • *color photos* ○ *a color TV*

color /'kʌl·ər/ v [I/T] to change the color of (something) by using paint or a DYE • *So he gives the boy books to read, and he buys him paints to color with.* [I always + adv/prep] • *(fig.)* If something or someone colors your thoughts or opinions, it influences them, often in a negative way: *His attitude toward marriage was colored by his unhappy childhood and his parents' divorce.* [T]

colored /'kʌl·ərd/ adj • *I saw an unusual, beautifully colored fish.*

colorful /'kʌl·ər·fəl/ adj having a bright color or a lot of different colors • *a colorful blue and yellow dress* • See also COLORFUL.

coloring /'kʌl·ə·rɪŋ/ n [C] a substance added to food or drink to change its color artificially • *The label says that no preservatives or artificial colorings were added to this cake.*

colorless /'kʌl·ər·ləs/ adj [not gradable] containing no color • *Carbon monoxide is a colorless, odorless, poisonous gas.* • See also COLORLESS.

color SKIN /'kʌl·ər/ n [U] the natural color of a person's skin, esp. when used to decide which race they belong to • Many people with dark skin describe themselves as people of color: *He says the courts are not doing enough to protect the rights of people of color.* • Color can mean a healthy appearance of the skin: *She'd been ill for a while, but when I saw her last Friday, she had good color.* • If someone or an organization is **colorblind**, skin color or race does not influence them when judging people or deciding whether to give them jobs. See also **colorblind** at COLOR APPEARANCE.

colored /'kʌl·ərd/ adj [not gradable] dated having dark skin • USAGE: In the US, colored was used esp. of people whose family originally came from Africa. This word is now offensive.

coloring /'kʌl·ə·rɪŋ/ n [U] the combined effect of the colors of a person's skin and hair • *He claimed that when people don't get enough protein in their food, their coloring isn't so good.*

colorful /'kʌl·ər·fəl/ adj having a lot of variety and therefore interesting • *colorful language* ○ *He had a colorful past and could tell some amusing stories.* • See also **colorful** at COLOR APPEARANCE.

colorless /'kʌl·ər·ləs/ adj having no unusual qualities and therefore not interesting • *He plays the part of a shy, colorless, average man.* • See also **colorless** at COLOR APPEARANCE.

colors /ˈkʌl·ərz/ *pl n* the official flag of a country, ship, or military group

colossus /kəˈlɑs·əs/ *n* [C] *pl* **colossi** /kəˈlɑs·ˌaɪ/ a very large statue, or (fig.) someone or something that is very great in size or importance • *a marble colossus from the sixth century B.C.* ○ *(fig.) He talked about the emerging colossus of the Internet.*

colossal /kəˈlɑs·əl/ *adj* [not gradable] (esp. of something bad) very great • *The whole business has been a colossal failure/mistake.* ○ *It was a colossal waste of time.*

colt /koʊlt/ *n* [C] a young, male horse • Compare FILLY.

column BUILDING /ˈkɑl·əm/ *n* [C] a tall, vertical post used as a support for the roof of a building or for decoration • A column is also anything or any set of things having a long, narrow shape: *a column of soldiers* ○ *a column of smoke*

column PRINTING /ˈkɑl·əm/ *n* [C] one of several vertical blocks of print into which a page of a newspaper or magazine is divided • *The article filled two columns.* • A column is also a piece of writing in a newspaper or magazine that is written by the same person and appears regularly, usually on a particular subject: *a column on sports* • A column is also any vertical block of words or numbers: *a column of figures*

columnist /ˈkɑl·əm·nəst/ *n* [C] someone who writes a regular article for a newspaper or magazine

com /kəm/ *n* [U] used at the end of US INTERNET addresses to show that the address belongs to an organization established to make a profit • *harold@dataformat.com*

coma /ˈkoʊ·mə/ *n* [C] a state of being unconscious, in which a person cannot be waked, usually caused by illness or injury • *He had a high fever and fell into a coma.*

comatose /ˈkoʊ·mə.toʊs, ˈkɑm·ə-/ *adj medical* (of a person) unconscious and not able to be awakened, usually because of illness or injury • *The traffic accident left him comatose with massive brain damage.*

comb HAIR TOOL /koʊm/ *n* [C] a strip of plastic, wood, or metal with a row of long, narrow parts along one side, which is used to arrange or hold the hair • *Combs have been used from ancient times by women to hold and fix their hair.*

comb /koʊm/ *v* [T] • *She combed her hair and put on some lipstick.*

comb SEARCH /koʊm/ *v* [T] to search (a place or an area) very carefully • *The police combed the surrounding woods for evidence.*

combat /ˈkɑm·bæt/ *n* [U] fighting during a time of war • *a combat jacket/zone/casualty* ○ *No one knew how many troops had died in combat.* • Combat is also a fight between two people or things: *The film explores the combat between good and evil.*

combat /kəmˈbæt, ˈkɑm·bæt/ *v* [T] to try to stop (something unpleasant or harmful) from happening or increasing • *We must try to combat poverty and illiteracy.*

combatant /kəmˈbæt·ənt, ˈkɑm·bət·ənt/ *n* [C] a person who fights in a war

combative /kəmˈbæt·ɪv/ *adj* • *When you are in a combative mood, you are not pleasant company.*

combine /kəmˈbaɪn/ *v* [I/T] to unite or to join together to make a single thing or group • *None of us has much money so let's combine what we've got.* [T] ○ *The two countries combined against their common enemy.* [I] • If you combine two activities, you do both at the same time: *She manages to successfully combine motherhood and a career.* [T]

combine /ˈkɑm·baɪn/ *n* [C] a group of people or organizations acting together • *Over the years they established a large media combine.*

combination /ˌkɑm·bəˈneɪ·ʃən/ *n* [C/U] a mixture obtained when two or more things are combined • *Green is a combination of blue and yellow.* [C] ○ *A combination of tiredness and boredom made me doze off in class.* [C] • **In combination** means together: *We'll be working in combination with other departments on this project.*

combo /ˈkɑm·boʊ/ *n* [C] *pl* **combos** a small group of musicians who play together, esp. jazz musicians

combustion /kəmˈbʌs·tʃən/ *n* [U] the process of burning • *Fuel combustion produces energy to run machines.*

combustible /kəmˈbʌs·tə·bəl/ *adj* • *Gasoline is a highly combustible substance.*

come APPROACH /kʌm/ *v* [I] *past simple* **came** /keɪm/, *past part* **come** to move or travel toward the speaker or with the speaker • *Will you come here, please?* ○ *Did you come here by car?* ○ *Come on in! The water's great.* ○ *Are you coming over to my house tonight?* ○ *Is he coming to the movies with us?* ○ *The man is coming to fix the dryer this afternoon.* ○ *He came rushing over when I fell.* • To **come forward** is to offer to give help: *Nobody has come forward yet with any information relating to the girl's death.* • If something **comes to** your **attention**, you have seen it or learned about it: *It has come to my attention that several people have been arriving late for work.*

coming /ˈkʌm·ɪŋ/ *adj* • *We look forward to even greater success in the coming year.*

come MOVE TO LISTENER /kʌm/ *v* [I] *past simple* **came** /keɪm/, *past part* **come** to move or travel in the direction of the person being spoken to • *I thought I'd come and see your new house.* ○ *I've come to read the gas meter.*

come ARRIVE /kʌm/ *v* [I] *past simple* **came** /keɪm/, *past part* **come** to get to a particular place • *Has the mail come yet?* ○ *Spring came early this year—look at all the flowers!* • When something comes in it is received: *Reports are* *just coming in of the fire.* • The sea or TIDE **comes in** when the water reaches farther up onto the beach or coast. Compare **go out** at GO LEAVE. • If someone **comes to** your **rescue**, they help you out of a bad situation: *I was about to drop a huge tray of dishes when Hugh came to my rescue.* • If something has **come a long way**, it has improved greatly: *In the past 20 years, information technology has come a long way.* • If something will **come in handy**, it will be useful: *This money will come in handy.*

come ORIGINATE /kʌm/ *v* [I always + adv/prep] *past simple* **came** /keɪm/, *past part* **come** to be or start from a particular place; to originate • *She comes from Italy.* ○ *Does that quotation come from Shakespeare?*

come EXIST /kʌm/ *v* [I always + adv/prep] *past simple* **came** /keɪm/, *past part* **come** to exist or be obtainable • *The dress comes in three sizes— small, medium, and large.* ○ *This cuddly doll comes with her own blanket and bottle.*

come HAPPEN /kʌm/ *v* [I] *past simple* **came** /keɪm/, *past part* **come** to happen • *Your birthday only comes around once a year.* ○ *How did you two come to be friends?* [+ *to* infinitive] • To **come to an end** is to reach the end of something: *I'm enjoying my English class, but it's about to come to an end.* • If something you desire **comes true**, it happens: *I'd always dreamed of owning my own home and now my dream has come true.*

come ORDER /kʌm/ *v* [I always + adv/prep] *past simple* **came** /keɪm/, *past part* **come** to be in a particular relation to others in an order • *April comes before May.* ○ *In your cookbook you'll see that pies come under the heading "Desserts."* • If something comes under an official organization, that organization is responsible for it: *Snow removal comes under the highway department.* • If something **comes before** other things, it is more important: *His job always came before the family.*

come CHANGE /kʌm/ *v past simple* **came** /keɪm/, *past part* **come** to change or be in a different position or condition • *The stitching on my briefcase is coming apart.* [I always + adv/ prep] ○ *A wire had come loose at the back.* [L] *He pulled the knob and it came off in his hand.* [I always + adv/prep] ○ *I couldn't stand him at first, but I've come to like him.* [+ *to* infinitive] • If you come under something, you are suddenly caused to experience or suffer it: *Our troops have come under heavy bombardment.* [I always + adv/prep] • To **come of age** means to reach the age when you are legally an adult: *We used to come of age at 21, now it's 18 unless you want to buy a drink, when it's the old 21 again.* • If a situation **comes to a head**, it reaches a point where some strong action has to be taken: *Things finally came to a head when she failed to show up at school.* • She has really **come up in the world** (= risen in rank or

importance) *since she went into business for herself.*

come SEX /kʌm/ *v* [I] *past simple* **came** /keɪm/, *past part* **come** *slang* to have an ORGASM

☐ **come across** FIND /ˌ--ˈ-, ˈ--ˌ-/ *v prep* [T] to find (something or someone) by chance • *He came across some old love letters.*

☐ **come across** SEEM /ˌ--ˈ-/ *v prep* [I] to give other people a certain feeling or opinion • *He comes across as a bit of a bore.*

☐ **come along** /ˈ--ˈ-/ *v adv* [I] to advance or improve • *How's your English coming along?*

☐ **come around** CHANGE YOUR MIND /ˈ--ˈ-/ *v adv* [I] to change your opinion of something • *He'll come around to my point of view eventually.*

☐ **come around** BECOME CONSCIOUS /ˈ--ˈ-/ *v adv* [I] to become conscious again after an accident or medical operation • *She hasn't come around yet.*

☐ **come at** /ˈ-ˌ-, ˈ-ˈ-/ *v prep* [T] to move quickly toward (someone) to attack them • *He came at me with a knife.*

☐ **come back** /ˈ-ˈ-/ *v adv* [I] to return • *Come back and see us again sometime.* • If something comes back to you, you remember it: *As soon as she entered the school, childhood memories came rushing back.*

comeback /ˈkʌm·bæk/ *n* [C] a return to an earlier position or condition • *After being away from boxing for three years, he tried to make a comeback.*

☐ **come between** /ˈ--ˈ-/ *v prep* [T] to cause problems between (two people) or interrupt (two people) • *Don't let one little quarrel come between you!*

☐ **come by** /ˈ-ˈ-/ *v prep* [T] to obtain (something) • *A good boss is not so easy to come by.* ○ *I'd like to know how she came by that black eye.*

☐ **come down** /ˈ-ˈ-/ *v adv* [I] to become lower in position or value • *I am not going to buy any more coffee until the price comes down.* • *(fig.)* If you come down from a feeling of excitement or from the effects of a drug, you start to feel ordinary again. • If you **come down in the world**, you lose your social position or your financial situation gets worse.

comedown /ˈkʌm·daʊn/ *n* [U] • *I liked most of the book, but the ending was a real comedown.*

☐ **come down on** /ˌ-ˈ-ˌ-/ *v adv prep* [T] to punish or blame (someone) for something • *They're coming down heavily on people for not paying their taxes.*

☐ **come down to** /ˌ-ˈ-ˌ-/ *v adv prep* [T] to have (a particular thing) as the most important matter • *It all comes down to money in the end.*

☐ **come down with** /ˌ-ˈ--ˈ/ *v adv prep* [T] to catch or show signs of (an illness) • *I feel like I'm coming down with a cold.*

☐ **come in for** /ˌ-ˈ--ˈ/ *v adv prep* [T] to receive (blame or criticism) • *The mayor came in for a lot of criticism of his remarks.*

☐ **come into** /ˌ-ˈ--ˈ/ *v prep* [T] to enter a place or a new position or state • *The new safety regu-*

lations **come into effect** at the beginning of the month. ○ *As we drove over the hill, the ocean came into view.* • If someone **comes into money** or **property**, they receive it as a result of the death of a relative: *She came into a fortune when her father died.*

□ **come off** `SUCCEED` /ˈ-ˈ-/ *v adv* [I] to happen as planned or to succeed • *I thought the party came off really well.*

□ **come off** `END UP` /ˈ-ˌ-/ *v adv* [I always + adv/prep] to end up in a particular position • *The little dog actually came off better, with only a few scratches.*

□ **come off** `COMPLETE` /ˌ-ˈ-/ *v adv* [T] to be finished with or removed from (something) • *Marcia comes off maternity leave in March.* • People say **come off it** to get them to stop doing something: *Come off it, Pete—that's not fair.*

□ **come on** `HURRY` /kəˈmɔːn, -ˈmɑn; kʌmˈɔːn, -ˈɑn/, *not standard* **c'mon** *v adv* [I] to move or act quickly or more quickly • *Come on—we're going to be late if you don't hurry!* • You can also say **come on** to express annoyance or lack of belief: *Oh, come on! You don't expect me to give up my bed for him?*

□ **come on** `FIND` /ˌ-ˌ-/ *v prep* [T] COME UPON

□ **come on** `MAKE INTEREST KNOWN` /ˈ-ˈ-, ˈ-ˌ-/ *v adv* [I] *slang* to make your sexual interest known to someone • *It was obvious that she was coming on to him at the party.* • If a person **comes on strong**, they are either strongly attracted sexually to someone, or they deal with them severely: *You came on too strong—she didn't do that on purpose.*

come–on /ˈkəmˌɔːn, -ˌɑn/ *n* [C] *infml* something that makes your sexual interest known to someone, or something that someone who is selling a product uses to interest a customer • *Offering cash back on a purchase is one of the oldest come-ons in the world.*

□ **come on** `START TO DEVELOP` /ˈ-ˈ-/ *v adv* [I] to start to develop gradually, as an illness or a mood • *He felt one of his headaches coming on.*

□ **come out** `BECOME KNOWN` /ˈ-ˈ-/ *v adv* [I] to become known or be made public • *When the facts came out, there was public outrage.* • People are said to **come out** when after a period of secrecy they say publicly that they are homosexual. • When a book, magazine, or newspaper **comes out**, it begins to be sold to the public: *Her latest book is coming out in July.* • If someone **comes out of** their **shell**, they become more comfortable and friendly with people: *What made Dan come out of his shell?*

□ **come out** `APPEAR` /ˈ-ˈ-/ *v adv* [I] to move into full view • *Later in the afternoon, it stopped raining and the sun came out.*

□ **come out** `GIVE OPINION` /ˌ-ˈ-/ *v adv* [I always + adv/prep] to express an opinion in public • *The candidate came out in favor of lower taxes.*

□ **come out** `FINISH` /ˌ-ˈ-/ *v adv* [I always + adv/

prep] to be in a particular condition when finished • *Your painting came out really well.*

□ **come out** `MAKE A PICTURE` /ˈ-ˈ-/ *v adv* [I] to produce a picture on film • *My camera broke and none of the skiing photographs came out.*

□ **come out with** /ˌ-ˈ--/ *v adv prep* [T] to say (something) unexpectedly or suddenly • *You come out with some strange comments sometimes!*

□ **come over** /ˌ-ˈ--/ *v prep* [T] to influence (someone) suddenly to behave in a particular way • *I'm sorry! That was a stupid thing to say—I don't know what came over me.*

□ **come through** /ˈ-ˈ-/ *v adv* [T] to continue to live after (an accident or a dangerous situation) • *It was a miracle that he came through that car crash alive.*

□ **come to** `REACH` /ˈ--/ *v prep* [T] to reach (a particular point) • *His hair comes down to his shoulders.* ○ *We haven't come to a decision on the matter yet.* • If you **come to terms with** something, you learn to understand and accept it: *He's trying to come to terms with his wife's death.* • If something **comes to light**, it becomes known: *Fresh evidence has recently come to light.* • If something **comes to rest**, it stops: *The car hit the curb and came to rest in a ditch.* • If you **come to** your **senses**, you begin to use good judgment: *It's time she came to her senses and got a better job.*

□ **come to** `BECOME CONSCIOUS` /ˈ-ˈ-/ *v adv* [I] to become conscious again after an accident or medical operation • *She sat by the child's bedside until he came to.*

□ **come up** `BE MENTIONED` /ˈ-ˈ-/ *v adv* [I] to be mentioned or talked about in conversation • *What points came up at the meeting?*

□ **come up** `HAPPEN` /ˈ-ˈ-/ *v adv* [I] to happen, usually unexpectedly • *I've got to go—something's just come up at home and I'm needed there.*

□ **come up with** /ˌ-ˈ--/ *v adv prep* [T] to suggest or think of (an idea or plan) • *Reublinger came up with a great idea for the ad campaign.*

□ **come upon** /ˈ--ˌ-/, **come on** /ˈ-ˌ-/ *v prep* *literary* to find or meet (someone or something), esp. unexpectedly • *She came upon an odd little man in the forest.*

comedy /ˈkɑm·əd·i/ *n* [C/U] a movie, play, or book that is intentionally amusing either in its characters or its action • *A lot of Shakespeare's plays are comedies.* [C] • Comedy is also the amusing part of a situation: *When John forgot his lines in the middle of the speech it provided some good comedy.* [U]

comedian /kəˈmiːd·i·ən/, **comic** /ˈkɑm·ɪk/, *female* **comedienne** /kə،miːd·iˈen/ *n* [C] a person whose job is to make people laugh by telling jokes and amusing stories or by copying the behavior or speech of famous people • *a stand-up comedian*

comet /ˈkɑm·ət/ *n* [C] a body of icy rock that travels around the sun and that, as it nears the sun, develops a long tail of particles that can be seen

comeuppance /kʌmˈʌp·əns/ n [U] a punishment or some bad luck that is considered to be fair and deserved punishment for something bad that someone has done • *She'll get her comeuppance, don't worry.*

comfort /ˈkʌm·fərt/ n [C/U] the pleasant and satisfying feeling of being physically or mentally free from pain and suffering, or something that provides this feeling • *He's a great comfort to his mother.* [C] ○ *I have to take an exam, too, if it's any comfort to you.* [U]

comfort /ˈkʌm·fərt/ v [T] • *I tried to comfort him, but it was no use.*

comfortable /ˈkʌm·fərt·ə·bəl, ˈkʌmf·tər·bəl/, *infml* **comfy** /ˈkʌm·fi/ adj producing a feeling of physical relaxation esp. because of shape, softness, or materials • *a comfortable bed/car/dress* ○ *Are you comfortable or is it too hot?* • Comfortable also means relaxed: *I'm not comfortable speaking in front of an audience.* • Comfortable also means having enough money for a good standard of living: *They're not rich but I think they're quite comfortable.* • In a competition, if you have a comfortable lead over the other competitors you are winning easily.

comfortably /ˈkʌm·fərt·ə·bli, ˈkʌmf·tər·bli/ adv • *They were comfortably settled in on the sofa.* ○ *After three periods, the Knicks comfortably led the Pacers.*

comforter /ˈkʌm·fərt·ər/ n [C] a thick cover for a bed filled with feathers or other material for extra warmth

comic AMUSING /ˈkɑm·ɪk/ adj making you want to laugh; amusing • *a comic actor/performance/writer*

comical /ˈkɑm·ɪ·kəl/ adj • *Tell me the truth— do I look comical* (= strange or foolish) *in this hat?*

comic MAGAZINE /ˈkɑm·ɪk/, **comic book** /ˈkɑm·ɪk ˌbʊk/ n [C] a magazine, esp. for children, that contains a set of stories told in pictures with a small amount of writing • A **comic strip** is a short series of amusing drawings with a small amount of writing that is usually published in a newspaper.

comic PERSON /ˈkɑm·ɪk/ n [C] a **comedian**, see at COMEDY

comings and goings /ˈkʌm·ɪŋ·zənˈɡoʊ·ɪŋz/ pl n movement or activity • *With so many comings and goings in this office I just can't seem to concentrate.*

comma /ˈkɑm·ə/ n [C] a mark (,) used in writing to separate parts of a sentence showing a slight pause, or to separate the various single items in a list • LP PERIOD

command (obj) ORDER /kəˈmænd/ v to give (someone) an order or orders with authority • *The police commanded the driver to stop the car.* [T] ○ *The captain commanded that the troops prepare to move forward.* [+ that clause]

COMMA [,]

The comma represents a short pause in speech or a small change in the direction of thought. Its main purpose is to separate parts of a sentence so that the meaning of the sentence is clear. It also makes reading and understanding easier. Commas are used:

to separate words or groups of words in a series

Two Cokes, three glasses of soda water, and an orange juice, please. • *The boat ride was a beautiful, relaxing, completely enjoyable experience.*

The comma is often left out before *and*.

The sick man ate well, got plenty of rest and slowly gained his strength.

before and after phrases that add extra information or information that is needed to understand the rest of the sentence

Lake Superior, the largest of the Great lakes, is about 350 miles long. • *Old castles, which are often poorly insulated, have a special atmosphere about them.*

to separate words or phrases that introduce, interrupt, describe, or comment on the main part of the sentence

When the war ended, Andy returned home and went to college. • *This book, once you've done with it, can be returned to any branch of the library.*

before a conjunction—and, but, or—that connects full clauses and between very short clauses that are not connected by a conjunction

She did not play at her best, but she still won the tennis match. • *I rang the bell, I shouted, I rang the bell again.*

to separate quoted speech from the words identifying the speaker

"I can manage," she insisted. • *"Still," he said thoughtfully, "we have one last chance."*

to separate long numbers into groups of three, beginning at the right

The population in 1990 was 8,560,000 • *$13,500*

But years, page numbers, addresses, and some other long numbers are written without commas:

the year 1789 • *p. 1624* • *1600 Pennsylvania Ave* • *account no. 053-6043751*

command /kəˈmænd/ n [C/U] an order, or the authority to give orders • *"When I give the command, fire!" the officer shouted.* [C] ○ *General MacArthur took command of* (= took military control over) *United Nation forces in Korea.* [U] • In computing, a command is an instruction to a computer to perform a specific action. [C]

commanding /kəˈmæn·dɪŋ/ adj having a position of authority or control • *Her command-*

ing officer said her performance was excellent.
• A **commanding** voice or manner is one that seems to have authority and therefore gets your attention.

command KNOWLEDGE /kə'mænd/ *n* [U] a good knowledge of something and the ability to use it • *The study of physics requires a command of mathematics.*

command RECEIVE /kə'mænd/ *v* [T] to deserve and receive because of special qualities or actions • *She commands one of the highest salaries in Hollywood.*

commandant /'kɑm·ən,dænt, -,dɑnt/ *n* [C] an officer who is in charge of a military unit or school • *the commandant of West Point*

commandeer /,kɑm·ən'dɪr/ *v* [T] to take possession or control of (private property), esp. by force • *Three men were arrested for commandeering a woman's car at gunpoint.*

commander /kə'mæn·dər/ *n* [C] a naval officer of middle rank, above LIEUTENANT • A **commander in chief** is in charge of all the armed forces of a country or of all the forces fighting in a particular area or operation: *The president of the United States is also commander in chief.*

Commandment /kə'mænd·mənt/ *n* [C] any of the ten important rules of behavior that the Bible says were given by God to Moses

commando /kə'mæn·doʊ/ *n* [C] *pl* **commandos** a small group of soldiers trained to make quick and often dangerous attacks inside enemy areas, or a member of such a group • *a team of commandos*

commemorate /kə'mem·ə,reɪt/ *v* [T] to show honor to the memory of (an important person or event) in a special way • *The ceremonies commemorated the 20th anniversary of the end of the Vietnam War.*

commemorative /kə'mem·ə·rət̬·ɪv/ *adj* • *The Elvis Presley commemorative stamp was eagerly bought by collectors.*

commence /kə'mens/ *v* [I/T] to begin (something) • *He commenced speaking before all the guests had arrived.* [T]

commencement /kə'men·smənt/ *n* [C] • A **commencement** is a ceremony at which students formally receive their DIPLOMAS (= documents to show they have successfully completed their studies).

commend /kə'mend/ *v* [T] to formally praise or mention with approval (someone or something) • *Lamos should be commended for creating important opportunities for minority actors.*

commendable /kə'men·də·bəl/ *adj* • *The reporter did a commendable job under difficult circumstances.*

commendation /,kɑm·ən'deɪ·ʃən/ *n* [C/U] • A **commendation** is a formal statement of praise for someone who has done something admirable. [C]

commensurate /kə'men·sə·rət/ *adj* suitable in amount or quality compared to something else; matching in degree • *The agency's workload has increased without any commensurate increase in staff.*

comment /'kɑm·ent/ *v* [I] to express an opinion • *The lawyer won't comment publicly on the case.*

comment /'kɑm·ent/ *n* [C/U] an opinion or remark • *One of his comments had to do with the state taxes.* [C] ○ *The reporter couldn't reach any government officials for comment* (= to ask for their opinions). [U]

commentary /'kɑm·ən,ter·i/ *n* [C/U] a series of remarks describing an event, esp. on radio or television, or a set of written notes explaining or expressing an opinion on a text or subject • *the television commentary on the Olympic Games* [C]

commentator /'kɑm·ən,teɪt̬·ər/ *n* [C] a person on radio or television who describes and discusses news events, sports, books, or other subjects

commerce /'kɑm·ɜrs/ *n* [U] the buying and selling of goods and services, esp. in large amounts • *Congress has the power to regulate commerce between the states.*

commercial /kə'mɜr·ʃəl/ *adj* intended to make money, or relating to a business intended to make money • *The movie was a commercial success* (= it made money), *but the critics hated it.*

commercially /kə'mɜr·ʃə·li/ *adv*

commercialism /kə'mɜr·ʃə,lɪz·əm/ *n* [U] the methods used to advertise and sell goods and services, esp. (disapproving) such methods used only and obviously for profit

commercialize /kə'mɜr·ʃə,lɑɪz/ *v* [T] • *Many universities are trying to commercialize their research* (= make use of it for profit).

commercialization /kə,mɜr·ʃə·lə'zeɪ·ʃən/ *n* [U]

commercial /kə'mɜr·ʃəl/ *n* [C] a paid advertisement on radio or television • *We all ran to get something to eat during the commercials.*

commie /'kɑm·i/ *n* [C] *dated, disapproving slang for* COMMUNIST

commiserate /kə'mɪz·ə,reɪt/ *v* [I] to feel or express sympathy for someone's suffering or unhappiness • *She called to commiserate over his loss.*

commiseration /kə,mɪz·ə'reɪ·ʃən/ *n* [U]

commission GROUP /kə'mɪʃ·ən/ *n* [C] a group of people who have been formally chosen and given the authority to get information about a problem or to perform other special duties • *Congress appointed a commission to study immigration policy.*

commission WORK REQUEST /kə'mɪʃ·ən/ *n* [C] a formal request to do a special piece of work for payment • *She received a commission to paint the governor's portrait.*

commission /kə'mɪʃ·ən/ *v* [T] to choose (someone) to do a piece of work, or to have (a piece of work) done • *The newspaper commissioned a series of articles on the fashion industry.*

commission MILITARY /kə'mɪʃ·ən/ *n* [C] the official authority to be an officer in the armed forces • *She received her commission as a lieutenant in the US Army.*

commission /kə'mɪʃ·ən/ *v* [T] • *He was commissioned a captain in the navy last June.*

commission CRIME /kə'mɪʃ·ən/ *n* [U] the act of doing something that is illegal or considered wrong • *the commission of a crime*

commission PAYMENT /kə'mɪʃ·ən/ *n* [C/U] a system of payment based on a percentage of the value of sales or other business done, or a payment to someone working under such a system • *As a real estate agent, her commission is between 4% and 6% on every sale.* [C]

commissioner /kə'mɪʃ·ə·nər/ *n* [C] an official in charge of a government department or other organization • *the police commissioner*

commit CRIME /kə'mɪt/ *v* [T] **-tt-** to do (something illegal or considered wrong) • *Critics have charged that some rap music lyrics encourage people to commit crimes.* • A person who **commits suicide** kills himself or herself.

commit PROMISE /kə'mɪt/ *v* [I/T] **-tt-** to promise to give (yourself, your money, your time, etc.) to support something • *They wouldn't commit (to giving) enough time or money to the project.* [I/T] • If you do not commit yourself about something, you refuse to express an opinion about it: *Neither candidate would commit himself on the issue of abortion.* [T]

commitment /kə'mɪt·mənt/ *n* [C/U] • *Try the product for two weeks with no commitment to buy.* [C]

commit SEND FOR TREATMENT /kə'mɪt/ *v* [T] **-tt-** *fml* to cause (someone) to stay (in a mental hospital or drug-treatment center) • *He was once committed to a state mental hospital.*

committee /kə'mɪt·i/ *n* [C] a group of people chosen from a larger group to act on or consider matters of a particular kind • *She sits on the city's finance committee.*

commodity /kə'mad·əṭ·i/ *n* [C] anything that can be bought and sold • *The goal is to raise the productivity of basic food commodities such as grains.*

common USUAL /'kam·ən/ *adj* found frequently in many places or among many people • *Money worries are a common problem for people raising children.* • The **common cold** is a slight illness caught by a lot of people that causes a cough and sore throat and makes breathing through the nose difficult. • **Common knowledge** is something that is known to many people but often not made known officially: *It was common knowledge that several doctors at that hospital were incompetent.* • **Common law** is a legal system that has developed over a period of time from customs and court decisions. • **Common sense** is the basic

ability to use practical knowledge to live in a reasonable and safe way.

commonly /'kam·ən·li/ *adv* • *"The" is the most commonly used word in English.*

common SHARED /'kam·ən/ *adj* [not gradable] belonging to or shared by two or more people or things • *Guilt and forgiveness are themes common to all of her works.* • **In common** means sharing the same interests or having similar characteristics: *I didn't think Larry and Patricia had anything in common.* • A **common denominator** is a fact or quality that is shared: *The one common denominator of this group is that they have all been mistreated by the police at one time or another.* • **Common ground** is an area of shared interests or opinions held by two or more people or groups: *When I found out he was also going to Alaska, we were on common ground.* • (*specialized*) In grammar, a **common noun** is the name for all of the people, places, or things that are of the same type: *The words "teacher," "river," and "table" are common nouns.* Compare **proper noun** at PROPER SUITABLE.

common LAND /'kam·ən/ *n* [C] an area of grassy land that is open for everyone to use, usually near the center of a town or city • *The Boston Common is the oldest park in the US.*

commonplace /'kam·ən,pleɪs/ *adj* happening or seen frequently and so not considered special or unusual • *Unfortunately, crimes like those have become commonplace.*

Commons /'kam·ənz/ *n* [U] *Cdn infml* the **House of Commons**, see at HOUSE POLITICS

commonwealth /'kam·ən,welθ/ *n* [C] a country or state that is governed by its people or their elected representatives

commotion /kə'moʊ·ʃən/ *n* [C/U] a sudden, brief period of noise, confusion, or excited movement • *There was a commotion outside the embassy.* [C]

communal /kə'mjuːn·əl, 'kam·jən·əl/ *adj* belonging to or used by all members of a group • *The neighborhood council organized voluntary communal patrols.*

commune /'kam·juːn/ *n* [C] a small group of families or single people who live and work together and share possessions and responsibilities, or (in some countries) the smallest unit of local government

communicate /kə'mjuː·nə,keɪt/ *v* [I/T] to give (messages or information) to others through speech, writing, body movements, or signals • *She said we should communicate our requests in writing rather than over the telephone.* [T] • If two people communicate (with each other), they are able to understand each other and have a satisfactory relationship: *The play deals with the inability of people to communicate with the people they love.* [I]

communicable /kə'mjuː·nɪ·kə·bəl/ *adj* able to be given to others • *communicable diseases such as AIDS*

communication /kə,mjuː·nə'keɪ·ʃən/ n [C/U] the process by which messages or information is sent from one place or person to another, or the message itself • *E-mail is an increasingly important means of business communication.* [U] • Communication is also the exchange of information and the expression of feeling that can result in understanding: *There was very little communication between the two brothers.* [U]

communications /kə,mjuː·nə'keɪ·ʃənz/ pl n the various systems used for sending (esp. electronic) information, such as radio, television, telephone, and computer networks • *They have made heavy investments in the communications industry.* • Communications are also the exchanges of information and expressions of feeling that can result in understanding: *A breakdown in communications between labor and management led to the strike.*

communion /kə'mjuːn·jən/ n [C] a Christian ceremony based on Jesus's last meal with his friends

communism /'kɑm·jə,nɪz·əm/ n [U] an economic system based on public ownership of property and control of the methods of production, and in which no person profits from the work of others • Compare CAPITALISM; SOCIALISM.

communist /'kɑm·jə·nəst/ adj [not gradable] • *the Communist party*

communist /'kɑm·jə·nəst/ n [C] a person who believes in or belongs to a party that supports communism

community /kə'mjuː·nəṭ·i/ n all the people who live in a particular area, or a group of people who are considered as a unit because of their shared interests, background, or nationality • *the scientific community* [C] ○ *Bus fares were raised despite the protests of the community.* [C] ○ *There's a real sense of community* (= caring and friendly feeling) *in this neighborhood.* [U] • The community is sometimes used to mean society in general: *She believed that the greatest goal in life was to serve the community.* [U] • A **community college** (also **junior college**) is a local two-year college at which students can learn a skill or prepare to enter a university. ⓛⓟ EDUCATION IN THE US • **Community service** is work that people do without payment to help other people, and which people may sometimes be ordered to do as punishment for crimes that are not too serious. *The judge ordered him to pay a fine and perform 100 hours of community service.*

commute TRAVEL /kə'mjuːt/ v [I] to travel regularly a distance between work and home • *She commutes to the city by car every day.*

commute /kə'mjuːt/ n [C] • *The commute is not too bad—just over an hour.*

commuter /kə'mjuːṭ·ər/ n [C] • *The 5:30 train is always packed with commuters.*

commute CHANGE /kə'mjuːt/ v [T] to change (a punishment into another that is less severe) • *The governor commuted his sentence from death to life imprisonment.*

compact CLOSE TOGETHER /kəm'pækt, kɑm-; 'kɑm·pækt/ adj closely or neatly put together • *The newer cameras have a flatter, more compact design.* • A **compact disc** is a CD.

compact /kəm'pækt, kɑm-; 'kɑm·pækt/ v [T] to press (something) tightly and solidly together • *The morning traffic had compacted the snow until it was a sheet of ice.*

compactor /kəm'pæk·tər, 'kɑm,pæk-/ n [C] a device that crushes garbage into a smaller and denser form

compact AGREEMENT /'kɑm·pækt/ n [C] an agreement between two or more people, organizations, or countries • *The parties to the settlement made a compact not to reveal any details.*

compact CAR /'kɑm·pækt/ n [C] a small car • *Compacts are easier to park than full-size cars and save on gas.*

compact CASE /'kɑm·pækt/ n [C] a small, flat case that usually contains face powder and a mirror

companion /kəm'pæn·jən/ n [C] someone with whom you share an activity, or a person or animal you spend a lot of time with • *He is a pleasant traveling companion because he never complains.* • A companion is also someone who has lived with you for a long time as a friend or lover: *He is survived by his longtime companion, Daniel James.*

companionable /kəm'pæn·jə·nə·bəl/ adj friendly and pleasant to be with

companionship /kəm'pæn·jən,ʃɪp/ n [U] the enjoyment of being with someone • *Besides sharing the cost of my apartment, he provides companionship.*

company BUSINESS /'kʌm·pə·ni/ n [C] an organization that produces or sells goods or services in order to make a profit • *He owns part of a company that manufactures software for personal computers.*

company OTHER PEOPLE /'kʌm·pə·ni/ n [U] the presence of someone who is with you, or the person or people who are with you • *It was a long trip and I was grateful for his company.* ○ *I traveled to Chicago in the company of two teachers* (= with them). ○ *We're having company* (= guests) *for dinner tonight.*

company GROUP /'kʌm·pə·ni/ n [C] a group of people who work or perform together • *She's spending the summer as part of a touring theatrical company.* • A company is also a military unit consisting of a large group of soldiers, usually with a CAPTAIN in charge of them.

comparative /kəm'pær·əṭ·ɪv/ n [C] specialized (in grammar) the form of an adjective or adverb that shows the thing or action described has more of the quality than some oth-

COMPARING

higher and lower degree

If you want to use an adjective or adverb to say that a quality is of a higher degree, you can usually add **-er** to the end of it or qualify it with **more**.

Your hair is **longer** *now than it was last year.* • *This chair is much* **more comfortable** *than the other one.* • *She works* **harder** *than her brother.* • *The situation became* **more and more serious.**

To say that a quality is of a lower degree, you can usually add -er to the end of a negative adjective or adverb, or qualify it with **less**.

Your hair is **shorter** *now than it was last year.* • *This chair is much* **less comfortable** *than the other one.* • *The situation became* **less and less bearable.**

This is called the COMPARATIVE. Notice that *than* follows the adjective or adverb when you are comparing something to something else that is mentioned.

highest and lowest degree

If you want to say that something is of the highest degree, you add **-est** to the end of the adjective or adverb or qualify it with **most**.

This is the **longest** *letter I've ever written.* • *He is one of the* **most successful** *young actors in Hollywood.* • *Hurricanes occur* **most frequently** *in August and September.*

If you want to say that something is of the lowest degree, you add **-est** to the end of the adjective or adverb, or qualify it with **least**.

This is the **shortest** *letter I've ever written.* • *He is one of the* **least successful** *writers I know.* • *Which painting did you like (the)* **least**? • *Hurricanes occur* **least frequently** *in April.*

This is called the SUPERLATIVE. Notice that *the* (or a possessive) is required when the superlative is used before a noun or when a phrase describing the group that is the basis for comparison follows.

Our biggest <u>problem</u> *right now is lack of cash.* • *He's* **the youngest** <u>of four boys</u>.

which comparative and superlative forms to use: adjectives

One-syllable adjectives usually form the comparative and superlative with **-er** and **-est**.

small, smaller, smallest; hot, hotter, hottest.

But *real, right,* and *wrong* only take **more** and **most**.

Most two-syllable adjectives can take **more/less** and **most/least**. Some can take -er and -est, including the following:

- **adjectives ending in -*y* and -*ow***
  angry, busy, dirty, early, easy, friendly, funny, happy, lazy, lucky, noisy, pretty, wealthy, narrow, shallow
- **adjectives ending in -*le***
  able, gentle, noble, simple, subtle
- **adjectives ending in -*er* and -*ure***
  clever, mature, obscure
- **a number of other adjectives**
  common, cruel, handsome, pleasant, polite, quiet, remote, stupid

Adjectives of three or more syllables generally form the comparative and superlative only with **more/less** and **most/least**

interesting, more/less interesting, most/least interesting.

But some adjectives with the prefix *un-* can also take **-er** and **-est**.

unhappy, unclear

A few adjectives have **irregular** comparative and superlative forms.

good, better, best
bad, worse, worst
far, farther or further, farthest or furthest
well, better, best

Note that the adjective **well**, meaning "healthy," is not used in the superlative.

which comparative and superlative forms to use: adverbs

Most adverbs use **more** (or **less**) and **most** (or **least**) to form the comparative and superlative.

often, more/less often, most/least often
efficiently, more/less efficiently, most/least efficiently

(CONTINUED)

Some one- and two-syllable adverbs can form the comparative and superlative with **-er** and **-est**.

close, deep, early, fast, hard, high, late, long, loud, low, near, slow, soon, straight, tight, wide

A few adverbs have **irregular** comparative and superlative forms.

well, better, best
badly, worse, worst
far, farther or further, farthest or furthest

how to add -er and -est

In most cases, just put **-er** or **-est** on the end of the adjective or adverb.

tough, tougher, toughest
fast, faster, fastest.

But notice the following adjectives and adverbs:

ending in a single consonant (other than *w* or *y*) with the vowel before it spelled with a single letter: Double the consonant before adding **-er** or **-est**.

big, bigger, biggest

ending in -y: Change *y* to *i* before adding **-er** or **-est**.

happy, happier, happiest
early, earlier, earliest

But a few adjectives ending in -*y* do not change *y* to *i*.

shy, shyer, shyest
sly, slyer, slyest
dry, drier or dryer, driest or dryest

ending in -e: Drop the *e* before adding **-er** or **-est**.

late, later, latest blue, bluer, bluest

When the dictionary shows **[-er/-est only]**, this means the word forms its comparative and superlative only by adding these endings, not with *more* and *most*.

adjectives and adverbs that are not used to compare

Most adjectives and adverbs are gradable and can be used in comparative and superlative forms or with words such as *very* and *extremely* (LP Very, completely). But adjectives and adverbs labeled **[not gradable]** in the dictionary cannot be used in these ways, usually because the quality they refer to is either present or not. For examples, you could not say "my most Asian friend" or "a very wooden spoon."

adjectives and adverbs that describe an extreme limit

absolute/absolutely
utter/utterly
total/totally
dead

adjectives and adverbs that restrict the word they modify to a particular state of being

only
same
identical/identically
main/mainly

adjectives formed from nouns by adding -ic, -al, or -ar, and related adverbs ending in -ly

electronic/electronically
mathematical/mathematically
polar
solar

Some adjectives and adverbs with these endings can be gradable in some meanings.

democratic/democratically

ers of the same type • *"Faster" is the comparative of "fast."* ○ *"Better" is the comparative of "good."* • Compare SUPERLATIVE GRAMMAR.

comparative /kəm'pær·əţ·ɪv/ *adj* [not gradable]

compare EXAMINE DIFFERENCES /kəm'per, -'pær/ *v* [T] to examine or look for the differences be-

tween (persons or things) • *This store's prices are high compared to what some other stores charge.* • To **compare notes** is to exchange information and opinions: *We met at the coffee shop to compare notes on the new professor.*

comparative /kəm'pær·əţ·ɪv/ *adj* [not gradable] considering the differences between one thing and another • *We wanted to study the comparative effectiveness of the two drugs.*

comparatively /kəmˈpær·ət·ɪv·li/ *adv* • *The job was comparatively well paid, as factory jobs go.*

compare CONSIDER SIMILARITIES /kəmˈper, -ˈpær/ *v* [I/T] to consider or suggest that (something) is similar or equal to (something else) • *Instant coffee doesn't compare with freshly ground coffee* (= fresh coffee is much better). [I]

comparable /ˈkɑm·pə·rə·bəl/ *adj* • *The candidates have comparable* (= similar) *educational backgrounds.*

comparison DIFFERENCE /kəmˈpær·ə·sən/ *n* [C/U] an examination of the differences between persons or things • *We kept a copy of an earlier letter for comparison.* [U] ○ *Though over six feet tall, he was small by comparison with* (= compared to) *his teammates on the basketball team.* [U]

comparison SIMILARITY /kəmˈpær·ə·sən/ *n* [C/U] the act of showing that something is similar or equal to something else • *She drew a comparison* (= showed the similarities) *between the Roosevelt and Kennedy administrations.* [C]

compartment /kəmˈpɑrt·mənt/ *n* [C] any of the enclosed parts into which a space, a vehicle, or an object used for storing things is divided • *She folded her coat and put it in the overhead luggage compartment.*

compass DIRECTION /ˈkʌm·pəs/ *n* [C] a device for finding direction with a pointer that turns freely and always points north

compass DRAWING /ˈkʌm·pəs/ *n* [C], **compasses** /ˈkʌm·pə·səz/ *pl n* a device in the shape of an upside down V whose two pointed, movable parts can be used to draw circles or measure distances on maps

compassion /kəmˈpæʃ·ən/ *n* [U] a strong feeling of sympathy and sadness for other people's suffering or bad luck and a desire to help

compassionate /kəmˈpæʃ·ə·nət/ *adj* • *a compassionate man*

compatible /kəmˈpæt·ə·bəl/ *adj* able to exist or work with something else, or (of a person) able to live or work with someone else • *The computer software isn't compatible with your operating system.* ○ *Levine said he is lucky he and his roommate are compatible.* • Compatible also means being suitable or right for: *Their blood types are not compatible, so we cannot use his blood.*

compatriot /kəmˈpeɪ·triː·ət/ *n* [C] a person who comes from your own country • *This writer and several of her Russian compatriots now live in New York.* • A compatriot is also a friend or someone you work with: *After work, I went to a bar with some of my office compatriots.*

compel /kəmˈpel/ *v* [T] **-ll-** to force (someone) to do something • *At school, we were compelled to wear uniforms, which I hated.*

compelling /kəmˈpel·ɪŋ/ *adj* forceful and persuasive • *a compelling argument* • A performance, painting, or other work of art is compelling when it has unusual power to hold your attention: *His account of his life is one of the most compelling books about the brutality of slavery.*

compendium /kəmˈpen·diː·əm/ *n* [C] *pl* **compendiums** or **compendia** /kəmˈpen·diː·ə/ a short but complete account of a particular subject, esp. in the form of a book • *She put together a compendium of early American furniture.*

compensate PAY MONEY /ˈkɑm·pən·seɪt/ *v* [T] to pay (someone) money in exchange for work done, for something lost or damaged, or for some inconvenience • *Our company tries to keep salaries low, and they compensate employees more with bonuses.*

compensation /ˌkɑm·pənˈseɪ·ʃən, -ˌpen-/ *n* [U] • *The chief executive's compensation package was worth $350,000.* ○ *He applied for unemployment/workers' compensation* (= money paid to you by a government, usually temporarily, when you do not have a job).

compensate EXCHANGE /ˈkɑm·pən·seɪt/ *v* [I] to take the place of something useful or needed with something else of similar value • *When you have a disability, you learn to compensate by doing other things well.*

compete /kəmˈpiːt/ *v* [I] to do an activity with others and try to do better than they do • *Two TV stations are competing for the top spot in the state of Iowa.* • To compete is also to be part of a sports activity in which you are trying to win: *He will compete in track this spring and play football next fall.*

competent /ˈkɑm·pət·ənt/ *adj* having the skills or knowledge to do something well enough to meet a basic standard • *All we want is someone competent to manage the staff.* [+ to infinitive] • *(law)* having enough mental ability for a particular purpose: *The judge decided that he was competent to stand trial.* [+ to infinitive]

competence /ˈkɑm·pət·əns/ *n* [U] • *He reached a reasonable level of competence in English.*

competition /ˌkɑm·pəˈtɪʃ·ən/ *n* [C/U] an activity done by a number of people or organizations, each of which is trying to do better than all of the others • *Competition for the job was fierce.* [U] ○ *Traditional booksellers face stiff competition from companies selling via the Internet.* [U] • The competition is the people or organizations you are trying to do better than: *In this business, we always have to be aware of the competition.* [U] • Competition is also the activity of a sport in which each of the people or teams is trying to win, or a particular event at which this activity happens: *Few of the players on the team were experienced* *in international competition.* [U] ○ *The figure-skating competition will be held in the main arena.* [C]

competitor /kəm'peṭ·əṭ·ər/ *n* [C] • *He's a tough competitor and will probably do well in business.*

competitive /kəm'peṭ·əṭ·ɪv/ *adj* • *a competitive person* ○ *We will be facing weaker teams, which should give us a competitive advantage/ edge.* • Competitive also means able to compete at the same level: *If we have to lower our prices to remain competitive, we will.*

compile /kəm'pɑɪl/ *v* [T] to collect (information) from a variety of places and arrange it in a book, report, or list • *We're compiling some facts and figures for an article on the Russian economy.*

compilation /ˌkɑm·pə'leɪ·ʃən/ *n* [C/U] • *The compilation of all his speeches took several months.* [U] • A compilation is also a book, report, etc., that is a collection of separate things: *a compilation of modern poetry* [C]

complacency /kəm'pleɪ·sən·si/ *n* [U] *esp. disapproving* a feeling of calm satisfaction with your own abilities or situation that prevents you from trying harder • *We're finally making a profit, but there is no reason for complacency.*

complacent /kəm'pleɪ·sənt/ *adj esp. disapproving* • *a complacent attitude*

complain /kəm'pleɪn/ *v* [I] to say that something is wrong or not good enough • *Bill and Nancy are always complaining about their neighbor, whose dog frightens their kids.* ○ *She complained that she had too much work to do.* [+ *that* clause] • If you complain of a physical condition, you describe something that hurts or makes you feel ill: *She complained of aching knees from her arthritis.*

complaint /kəm'pleɪnt/ *n* [C/U] a statement that something is wrong or not good enough, the act of complaining, or the thing you are complaining about • *a letter of complaint* [U] ○ *Her only complaint is that she sometimes didn't get enough heat in her apartment.* [C] • *(law)* A complaint is also a formal statement to a government authority that you have a legal cause to complain about the way you are been treated: *He filed a complaint with the commission, charging discrimination based on his disability.* [C]

complement /'kɑm·plə,ment/ *v* [T] to help make (something or someone) more complete or effective • *She used photographs to complement the text of the news story.*

complement /'kɑm·plə·mənt/ *n* [C] • *He sees rail travel as a complement to road travel, not as a replacement.* • A complement is a number of people or things that makes something complete: *We had a full complement of reporters and photographers along.* • *(specialized)* In grammar, a complement is a part of a word or phrase that completes the PREDICATE (= the part of a sentence that gives informa-

tion about the subject), as "nothing" in "They told him nothing."

complete WHOLE /kəm'pliːt/ *adj* containing all the parts or pieces; whole • *a complete set of dishes* ○ *the complete works of Dickens* ○ *We wanted a complete record of what everyone said.*

complete /kəm'pliːt/ *v* [T] • *She needed one more course to complete the requirements for a teaching degree.*

complete FINISH /kəm'pliːt/ *v* [T] to finish doing (something) • *John has completed 15 marathons.* ○ *She completed three years of college, and then took a year off.*

complete /kəm'pliːt/ *adj* • *The painting is nearly complete.*

completion /kəm'pliː·ʃən/ *n* [U] • *He was the architect who supervised the completion of the cathedral.*

complete VERY GREAT /kəm'pliːt/ *adj* very great, without limit, or to the largest degree possible • *The trip began in complete confusion.* ○ *She gave me a look of complete indifference.* ○ *Toby and Alfredo are complete opposites.*

completely /kəm'pliːt·li/ *adv* • *To be completely honest, I was too scared to say anything.* • LP VERY, COMPLETELY, AND OTHER INTENSIFIERS

complex HAVING MANY PARTS /kəm'pleks, 'kɑm·pleks/ *adj* having many parts related to each other in ways that may be difficult to understand • *a complex surgical procedure* ○ *The question of who is legally responsible is a complex issue.*

complexity /kəm'plek·səṭ·i/ *n* [C/U] • *You must understand the variety and complexity of tasks assigned to the police.* [U]

complex BUILDING /'kɑm·pleks/ *n* [C] a group of buildings that are related, or a large building having different parts • *an apartment complex for elderly people*

complex ATTITUDES /'kɑm·pleks/ *n* [C] a group of attitudes and feelings that influence a person's behavior, often in a negative way • *an inferiority complex*

complexion /kəm'plek·ʃən/ *n* [C] the color or appearance of the skin of a person's face • *a dark/light complexion*

compliance /kəm'plɑɪ·əns/ *n* [U] • See at COMPLY.

complicate /'kɑm·plə,keɪt/ *v* [T] to make (something) more difficult to deal with or do • *The rescue operation was complicated by bad weather.* ○ *His recovery was complicated by his generally poor condition.*

complicated /'kɑm·plə,keɪṭ·əd/ *adj* having many parts that are organized in a way that may be difficult to understand • *a complicated machine/process* ○ *He gave me directions, but they were so complicated I got lost.*

complication /ˌkɑm·plə'keɪ·ʃən/ *n* [C] something that makes a situation more difficult • *This complication had not been foreseen.* •

(*medical*) A complication is a problem that develops from an existing illness, making treatment more difficult: *He died from complications of diabetes.*

complicity /kəm'plɪs·əṭ·i/ *n* [U] *fml* involvement with others in a crime or in another activity that is wrong

compliment /'kɑm·plə·mənt/ *n* [C] a remark or action that expresses approval, admiration, or respect • *She paid him a high compliment by saying she read all his books.* ○ *He was surprised by her remark, but decided to take it as a compliment.*

compliment /'kɑm·plə,ment/ *v* [T] • *I complimented Robert on his great cooking.*

complimentary /,kɑm·plə'ment·ə·ri/ *adj* • *Everybody was complimentary about the hotel service.* • If something is complimentary, it is given to you without charge: *As theater employees, we get complimentary tickets.*

comply /kəm'plaɪ/ *v* [I] *fml* to obey an order, rule, or request • *Comosa says he will comply with the judge's ruling.*

compliance /kəm'plaɪ·əns/ *n* [U] *fml* • *The company said that it had always acted in compliance with environmental laws.*

component /kəm'poʊ·nənt/ *n* [C] one of the parts of a system, process, or machine • *Fair pay for child-care providers is a vital component of welfare reform.*

compose COMBINATION /kəm'poʊz/ *v* [T] to produce or create (music, poems, or a piece of writing) • *The opera was composed in 1931 but wasn't performed until 1940.*

composer /kəm'poʊ·zər/ *n* [C] a person who writes music

compose FORM /kəm'poʊz/ *v* [T] to form or make up (something) • *The metropolitan area is composed of New York City and parts of New Jersey and Connecticut.*

composite /kɑm'pɑz·ət, kəm-/ *adj* made of various parts or substances • *a composite material* ○ *a composite sketch of a man wanted for questioning*

composition WRITING /,kɑm·pə'zɪʃ·ən/ *n* [C/U] something that a person has created or written, esp. a text or a piece of music, or the act of creating or writing something • *a composition for piano and flute* [C] ○ *In school we had to write a composition* (= short piece of writing) *on our favorite TV programs.* [C]

composition MIXTURE /,kɑm·pə'zɪʃ·ən/ *n* [U] the mixture of things or people that are combined to form something • *The composition of the city's population has changed dramatically in the past 20 years.*

compost /'kɑm·poʊst/ *n* [U] decaying material of plants, unwanted food, etc., added to dirt to improve the growth of new plants

composure /kəm'poʊ·ʒər/ *n* [U] the quality of being calm and not emotional • *You may feel nervous but don't lose your composure in front of the camera.*

compound COMBINATION /'kɑm·paʊnd/ *n* [C] a mixture of two or more different parts or elements • *His jokes have been described as a compound of fears, anxieties, and insecurities.* • (*specialized*) A compound is a chemical substance that combines two or more elements. • (*specialized*) In grammar, a compound or **compound word** is a word consisting of two or more words: *"Black eye" and "teaspoon" are compounds.*

compound WORSEN /kɑm'paʊnd, 'kɑm·paʊnd/ *v* [T] to make (something) worse by increasing or adding to it • *Lack of rain compounded the problems farmers are having.*

compound AREA /'kɑm·paʊnd/ *n* [C] a fenced or enclosed area that contains buildings • *We left the compound early to find and photograph wild animals.*

comprehend /,kɑm·prə'hend/ *v* [T] to understand (something), esp. completely • *If you don't comprehend something, don't be afraid to seem dumb, just speak out.*

comprehensible /,kɑm·prə'hen·sə·bəl/ *adj* • *The directions were written in clear, comprehensible English.*

comprehension /,kɑm·prə'hen·tʃən/ *n* [U] the ability to understand something, esp. completely • *Some religious truths, he said, are clearly beyond our comprehension.*

comprehensive /,kɑm·prə'hen·sɪv/ *adj* including everything that is necessary; complete • *They put forward comprehensive legislation to revise the rules for financing political campaigns.*

compress PRESS /kəm'pres/ *v* [T] to press (something) into a smaller space • *Firmly compress the dirt in the pot to hold the plant upright.* • To compress also means to shorten (something) so that it takes less time: *Four years of normal mortgage business is being compressed into two months.*

compression /kəm'preʃ·ən/ *n* [U] • *data compression*

compress CLOTH /'kɑm·pres/ *n* [C] a thick, soft piece of cloth that is pressed to a part of a person's body esp. to help a healing process • *Apply warm compresses to the infected area.*

comprise /kəm'praɪz/ *v* [L] to consist of or to be made up of • *The Pacific Rim comprises countries bordering the Pacific, including the US, Canada, Japan, China, and the Koreas.* ○ *The ninth district is comprised of* (= consists of) *15 cities and towns, including Boston.*

compromise AGREEMENT /'kɑm·prə,maɪz/ *n* [C] an agreement between two sides who have different opinions, in which each side gives up something they had wanted • *Under the compromise, car manufacturers must use cleaner fuel but have more time to do it.*

compromise /'kɑm·prə,maɪz/ *v* [I] • *Republicans were refusing to compromise on health-care legislation.*

compromise LOWER STANDARDS /'kɑm·prə

,maɪz/ *v* [T] to lower or weaken (standards) • *His opponents charged that the deal would compromise conservative principles.*

compromising /ˈkɑm·prəˌmaɪ·zɪŋ/ *adj* tending to lower respect for someone; embarrassing • *He discovered compromising letters that reveal her past relationship with Morris.*

comp time /ˈkɑmp·taɪm/ *n* [U] extra time put in by a worker that can be exchanged for an equal amount of time to be used as vacation days, with no loss in pay

comptroller /kənˈtroʊ·lər, ˈkɑmˌtroʊ-/ *n* [C] a **controller**, see at CONTROL

compulsion /kəmˈpʌl·ʃən/ *n* [U] a force that makes you do something • *Management felt no compulsion to provide housing for families.*

compulsive /kəmˈpʌl·sɪv/ *adj* having or characterized by a very strong or uncontrollable desire, esp. to do something repeatedly • *Compulsive gambling is on the increase.*

compulsion /kəmˈpʌl·ʃən/ *n* [C] • *an arsonist's compulsion to set fires*

compulsively /kəmˈpʌl·sɪv·li/ *adv* • *He is compulsively neat.*

compulsory /kəmˈpʌl·sə·ri/ *adj* (of something) that must be done; necessary by law or a rule • *Chapel attendance at this school is compulsory.*

compunction /kəmˈpʌŋ·ʃən/ *n* [U] a feeling of guilt or anxiety about something you have done or might do • *I would have no compunction about quitting.*

compute /kəmˈpjuːt/ *v* [T] to calculate (something) using mathematics or a calculator

computation /ˌkɑm·pjəˈteɪ·ʃən/ *n* [C/U] • *the computation of population by county* [U]

computer /kəmˈpjuːţ·ər/ *n* [C] an electronic device that can store large amounts of information and be given sets of instructions to organize and change it very quickly • *a desktop/personal computer* ○ *a computer program* ○ *computer hardware/software*

computerize /kəmˈpjuːţ·əˌraɪz/ *v* [T] to use computers to operate or store (something) • *Our law firm is in the process of computerizing our old files.*

computerization /kəmˌpjuːţ·ə·rəˈzeɪ·ʃən/ *n* [U]

comrade /ˈkɑm·ræd/ *n* [C] a friend or trusted companion, esp. one with whom you been involved in difficult or dangerous activities, or another soldier in a soldier's group • *Many of his comrades were killed in the battle.*

con /kɑn/ *v* [T] **-nn-** *infml* to deceive (someone) by using a trick, or to cheat (someone) of money • *I know when I'm being conned.*

con /kɑn/ *n* [C] • A **con game** is a plan to trick people: *Integration was not just a liberal con game.* • A **con man** (also **con artist**) is a person who uses tricks to cheat people, esp. to get their money or possessions.

concave /kɑnˈkeɪv, kɑn-/ *adj* curved inward • *a concave lens* • Compare CONVEX.

conceal /kənˈsiːl/ *v* [T] to prevent (something) from being seen or known about; to hide (something) • *It's so easy to conceal a handgun.* ○ *He made no attempt to conceal his satisfaction.*

concede /kənˈsiːd/ *v* to admit that something is true, or to allow (something) • *Officials concede (that) the plan isn't the best one.* [+ *(that)* clause] • If you concede in a competition, you admit that you have lost: *She conceded (the election) yesterday.* [I/T]

conceit /kənˈsiːt/ *n* [U] the habit or attitude of thinking yourself better than others, even when there is no reason to think so

conceited /kənˈsiːţ·əd/ *adj* • *He's a great musician, and not conceited at all.*

conceive *(obj)* IMAGINE /kənˈsiːv/ *v* to bring (a thought or idea) into being; imagine • *When they talk about billions of dollars, I can't even conceive of that much money.* [I always + adv/prep] ○ *It's hard to conceive what the world will be like a hundred years from now.* [+ *wh-* word]

conceivable /kənˈsiː·və·bəl/ *adj* possible to imagine or think of • *Books on every conceivable subject lined one wall.* ○ *It's conceivable (that) none of the proposals will be accepted.* [+ *(that)* clause]

conceivably /kənˈsiː·və·bli/ *adv* [not gradable] • *We could conceivably finish ahead of schedule.*

conceive BECOME PREGNANT /kənˈsiːv/ *v* [I/T] *fml* to become pregnant, or to cause (a baby) to begin to form

concentrate GIVE ATTENTION /ˈkɑn·sənˌtreɪt/ *v* [I/T] to direct a lot of attention and thought to an activity or subject, or to direct (effort) toward achieving a result • *In her later years, she concentrated on her writing and teaching.* [I always + adv/prep] ○ *The police are concentrating their search in the area where the child was last seen.* [T]

concentration /ˌkɑn·sənˈtreɪ·ʃən/ *n* [U] • *He had a look of intense concentration on his face.*

concentrate COME TOGETHER /ˈkɑn·sənˌtreɪt/ *v* [I/T] to bring or come together in a large number or amount in one particular area • *Most of the country's population is concentrated in the cities.* [T]

concentration /ˌkɑn·sənˈtreɪ·ʃən/ *n* a large amount of something in the same place • *There's a heavy concentration of poor and elderly in the district.* [C] • A **concentration camp** is a prison where, esp. during a war, people who are considered enemies are forced to stay.

concentrate LIQUID /ˈkɑn·sənˌtreɪt/ *n* [U] liquid from which some of the water has been removed • *orange juice made from concentrate*

concentric /kənˈsen·trɪk/ *adj* (of circles and rings) being one inside another and having the same center

concept /ˈkɑn·sept/ *n* [C] a principle or idea •

He introduced the concept of selling books via the Internet.

conception IDEA /kən'sep·ʃən/ *n* [C/U] an idea or a particular way you understand or think about something, or a basic understanding of a situation or principle • *Most children have no conception of time.* [U]

conception BABY /kən'sep·ʃən/ *n* [U] the process in which a baby starts to form in the uterus from the coming together of a sperm and an egg

concern WORRY /kən'sɜrn/ *v* [T] to trouble (someone) with feelings of anxiety; worry • *The loss didn't bother him, but his team's confidence concerns him.*

concern /kən'sɜrn/ *n* [C/U] a worried feeling, or a state of anxiety • *Parents expressed a lot of concerns about the changes in school policies.* [C]

concerned /kən'sɜrnd/ *adj* • *Sarah is very concerned about your safety.*

concern INVOLVE /kən'sɜrn/ *v* [T] to involve (someone or something); have to do with • *This is an issue that should concern everyone.* • If a story concerns a particular subject, it tells a story about that subject: *The movie concerns a young woman who falls in love with an older man.*

concern /kən'sɜrn/ *n* [U] a matter of importance esp. because it involves you • *Issues of good and evil are not our primary concern here.* ○ *What you do is no concern of mine* (= I do not care).

concerned /kən'sɜrnd/ *adj* [not gradable] involved or involving • *They say that free trade will benefit all concerned.* ○ *Her job is only concerned with costs and fees.*

concerning /kən'sɜr·nɪŋ/ *prep* about • *If you have any information concerning the incident, please contact the police.*

concern BUSINESS /kən'sɜrn/ *n* [C] *slightly fml* a company • *He heads a large concern in the midwest.*

concert /'kɑn·sɜrt, -sərt/ *n* [C] a performance of music by one or more musicians or singers

concerted /kən'sɜrt̬·əd/ *adj* (of an attempt to do something) determined and serious, or done together with others • *I really made a concerted effort to get involved in community affairs.*

concerto /kən'tʃɛrt̬·oʊ/ *n* [C] *pl* **concertos** a piece of music usually written for one instrument and an ORCHESTRA (= a large combined group of musicians) • *a violin/piano concerto*

concession SOMETHING GIVEN UP /kən'seʃ·ən/ *n* [C/U] something allowed or given up, often in order to end a disagreement, or the act of allowing or giving up something • *Both sides involved in the talks made concessions.* [C] • Concession can also be the act of admitting defeat: *a concession speech* [U]

concession SALES PLACE /kən'seʃ·ən/ *n* [C]

permission to sell something, esp. in part of a store owned by someone else, or a business that sells something • *A lot of movie theater profits come from their candy concessions.*

conciliatory /kən'sɪl·i·ə,tɔːr·i, -,toʊr·i/ *adj* intended to show someone who is angry or upset with you that you care about their feelings or understand their opinions • *Fitzwater struck a conciliatory tone, saying he didn't think anybody was to blame.*

conciliation /kən,sɪl·i·'eɪ·ʃən/ *n* [U] • *Conciliation, not confrontation, is the key to ending the conflict.*

concise /kən'saɪs/ *adj* expressing what needs to be said without unnecessary words; short and clear • *She wrote up a concise summary of the day's events.*

conclude END /kən'kluːd/ *v* [I/T] to cause (something) to end, or to end • *She concluded her remarks by thanking her supporters.* [T] ○ *I'd like to conclude with a song by Tim Buckley.* [I] • If you conclude a business deal or official agreement, you agree on it: *Sadat was intent on concluding a peace agreement.* [T]

conclusion /kən'kluː·ʒən/ *n* [C] the last part of something • *The novel's conclusion is disappointing.* • A speaker or writer says **in conclusion** to show that they are coming to an end, and want to make one final statement.

conclude (obj) JUDGE /kən'kluːd/ *v* to judge after some consideration • *We concluded that we could not afford to buy a new car.* [+ *that* clause] ○ *The judges concluded the same thing I did.* [T]

conclusion /kən'kluː·ʒən/ *n* [C] a decision made after a lot of consideration • *Dr. Gille couldn't reach any conclusions based on the symptoms I described.* ○ *We came to the conclusion that someone was not telling the truth.* [+ *that* clause]

conclusive /kən'kluː·sɪv, -zɪv/ *adj* (of facts, proof, or arguments) ending any doubt or uncertainty about a situation • *There's no conclusive evidence that power lines are a health risk.*

conclusively /kən'kluː·sɪv·li/ *adv* without any doubt • *Polls conclusively show public support for the bill.*

concoct /kən'kɑkt/ *v* [T] to invent (a story or excuse), esp. to deceive others • *She had concocted an elaborate story about a carjacker.* • To concoct is also to make something new from different things: *He concocted a tasty stew from the leftovers.*

concoction /kən'kɑk·ʃən/ *n* [C] something put together from different things, esp. something to eat or drink • *She drinks this herbal concoction.*

concourse /'kɑn·kɔːrs, 'kɑŋ-, -koʊrs/ *n* [C] a large space or room in a public building such as an airport or train station, which people gather in or pass through

concrete HARD MATERIAL /'kɑn·kriːt, kɑn'kriːt/ *n* [U] a very hard building material made by mixing together CEMENT (= powdered substance), sand, small stones, and water • *concrete steps*

concrete CERTAIN /'kɑn·kriːt, kɑn'kriːt/ *adj* based on sure facts or existing things rather than guesses or theories • *Police have no concrete evidence linking him to the crime.* ◦ *We have not yet received a concrete proposal.*

concur /kən'kɜr/ *v* [I] **-rr-** *slightly fml* to agree or have the same opinion as someone else • *He said the mayor should not be reelected, and the voters concurred.*

concurrent /kən'kɜr·ənt, -'kʌ·rənt/ *adj* happening at the same time • *He's serving two concurrent 10-year sentences.*

concurrently /kən'kɜr·ənt·li, -'kʌ·rənt-/ *adv* • *He dealt with several issues concurrently.*

concussion /kən'kʌʃ·ən/ *n* [U] a usually temporary injury to the brain caused by a fall or hit on the head or by violent shaking

condemn CRITICIZE /kən'dem/ *v* [T] to criticize (something or someone) strongly, usually for moral reasons • *The movie was condemned for glorifying violence.*

condemnation /ˌkɑn·dəm'neɪ·ʃən, -ˌdem-/ *n* [U] • *The bombing brought swift condemnation from world leaders.*

condemn PUNISH /kən'dem/ *v* [T] to punish (someone) severely because they have committed a crime, or to force (someone) to suffer • *He was condemned to death for murder.* ◦ *Illness condemned her to spend her remaining days in a home.*

condemn CALL NOT SAFE /kən'dem/ *v* [T] to decide officially say that (a building) is not safe for people to use

condense MAKE SHORTER /kən'dens/ *v* [T] to make (a text) shorter by using fewer words to express the same idea • *Condense the report to a single page.*

condense MAKE WATER APPEAR /kən'dens/ *v* [I/T] to make (water in the air) appear on a surface • *Humidity condensed on the bathroom walls.* [I]

condensation /ˌkɑn·dən'seɪ·ʃən, -ˌden-/ *n* [U] the drops of water that appear on cold surfaces such as windows as a result of hot air or steam becoming cool

condensed /kən'denst/ *adj* with water removed • *condensed soup* • **Condensed milk** is thick, sweet milk from which water has been removed and to which sugar has been added.

condescend /ˌkɑn·dɪ'send/ *v* [I] to treat (someone) in a way which shows that you consider yourself to be better or more intelligent • *Dorrance never condescends to the women he coaches.* • (*often disapproving*) If someone **condescends to** do something, they agree to do it although it is not good enough for their social position: He would occasionally condescend to applaud.

condescending /ˌkɑn·dɪ'sen·dɪŋ/ *adj* showing that you consider yourself better or more in-

telligent • *His condescending attitude offended his teammates.*

condescension /ˌkɑn·dɪ'sen·tʃən/ *n* [U] • *Some directors treat actors with condescension.*

condiment /'kɑn·də·mənt/ *n* [C] a substance such as a spice that you add to food to improve its taste

condition STATE /kən'dɪʃ·ən/ *n* the particular state that something or someone is in • *We spent a lot of money to get the house in good condition.* [U] ◦ *She was hospitalized in fair condition after the accident.* [U] ◦ *He's in no condition to drive* (= He should not drive). [+ to infinitive] • A condition can also be a state of not operating correctly: *a heart condition* [C]

conditions /kən'dɪʃ·ənz/ *pl n* all the particular things that influence someone's living or working environment • *Working conditions here are primitive.* ◦ *Riis devoted his life to improving conditions in urban slums.*

condition AGREED LIMITATION /kən'dɪʃ·ən/ *n* [C] something that must exist before something else can happen • *Certain conditions must be met before the aid will be provided.* ◦ *He spoke on condition that he not be identified.*

conditional /kən'dɪʃ·ən·əl/ *adj* • *The sales is conditional on approval from government regulators.*

conditional /kən'dɪʃ·ən·əl/ *adj* [not gradable] *specialized* (in grammar) relating to a sentence, often starting with "if" or "unless," in which one half expresses something which is dependent on the other half

conditioner /kən'dɪʃ·ə·nər/ *n* [U] a thick liquid that people put on their hair after washing it to improve its appearance

condolence /kən'doʊ·ləns/ *n* [C/U] an expression of sympathy esp. for the family of a person who has recently died, or the sympathy expressed • *a letter of condolence* [U] ◦ *The mayor offered his condolences.* [C]

condom /'kɑn·dəm/ *n* [C] a thin, rubber covering that a man can wear on his penis during sex to prevent a woman from becoming pregnant or to protect against the spread of infectious diseases

condominium /ˌkɑn·də'mɪn·iː·əm/, *short form* **condo** /'kɑn·doʊ/ *n* [C] an apartment in a building in which each apartment is owned separately by the people living in it, or a building having such apartments

condone /kən'doʊn/ *v* [T] *disapproving* to ignore or accept as harmless (behavior that some people consider wrong) • *How can you condone violence?*

conducive /kən'duː·sɪv/ *adj* providing the right conditions for something to happen or exist • *Our mild climate is conducive to outdoor entertaining.*

conduct DIRECT /kən'dʌkt/ *v* [T] to organize and direct (a particular activity) • *The experiments were conducted by leading scientists.*

conduct MUSIC /kən'dʌkt/ v [I/T] to direct the performance of (musicians or a piece of music) • *The orchestra was conducted by Thomas.* [T]

conductor /kən'dʌk·tər/ n [C] • *He's the conductor of the Toronto Symphony.*

conduct BEHAVE /kən'dʌkt/ v [T] to cause (yourself) to behave in a particular or controlled manner • *I won't tell them how to conduct their lives.*

conduct /'kɑn·dʌkt/ n [U] behavior • *His conduct at the cemetery was inappropriate.*

conduct ALLOW THROUGH /kən'dʌkt/ v [T] to allow (electricity or heat) to go through • *Copper conducts electricity.*

conductor /kən'dʌk·tər/ n [C] • *Metal is a good conductor of heat.*

conductor /kən'dʌk·tər/ n [C] a person who is in charge on a train or other public vehicle and also sells or checks tickets

cone /koʊn/ n [C] a solid shape with a round base that narrows to a point at the top, or any of various objects shaped like this, some of which are hollow and open at the end • *ice cream in a waffle cone* ○ *Roll the paper into a cone.* • A cone is also the hard, oval fruit of an evergreen tree.

conical /'kɑn·ɪ·kəl/ adj shaped like a cone

Confederacy /kən'fed·ə·rə·si/ n [C/U] the eleven southern states that fought against the north in the US Civil War • *A confederacy is also a* CONFEDERATION. [C]

Confederate /kən'fed·ə·rət/ adj • *Confederate soldiers*

confederate /kən'fed·ə·rət/ n [C] a soldier or supporter of the Confederacy

confederation /kən,fed·ə'reɪ·ʃən/, **confederacy** /kən'fed·ə·rə·si/ n [C/U] a group of countries, organizations, or people who have joined together for economic or political reasons • *a union confederation* [C] • *(Cdn)* Confederation is the joining of regions that had been British to create the independent country of Canada. [U]

confer TALK /kən'fɜr/ v [I] **-rr-** to talk together and exchange ideas, often with the intention of reaching a decision about something • *I need to confer with my lawyer.*

confer GIVE /kən'fɜr/ v [T] **-rr-** to give (an honor, official title, or ability) to someone • *The US Constitution confers certain powers on the president.*

conference /'kɑn·fə·rəns/ n [C/U] a large, formal meeting at which there are groups of talks on a particular subject, or a small, private meeting for discussion of a particular matter • *She spoke at an AIDS conference in Geneva.* [C]

confess /kən'fes/ v [I/T] to admit that you have done something wrong, or to admit unwillingly that something is true • *I've got something to confess—I ate the pie.* [T] ○ *He confessed to the crime.* [I] • In some Christian religions, esp. the Roman Catholic Church, a person confesses by telling God or a priest about the things they have done wrong so that guilt or responsibility can be removed. [I/T]

confession /kən'feʃ·ən/ n [C/U] • *He made a confession to the police.* [C] ○ *I've got a confession—I lost the book you lent me.* [C] • Confession is the activity of formally telling a priest about the things you have done wrong so that guilt or responsibility can be removed. [C/U]

confetti /kən'feṭ·i/ n [U] small bits of colored paper that you throw when celebrating • *At midnight, we all cheered and threw confetti.*

confidant /'kɑn·fə,dænt, -,dɑnt/ n [C] a person with whom you can share your feelings and secrets • *Her brother is her closest confidant.*

confide /kən'faɪd/ v to tell something secret or personal to someone whom you trust not to tell anyone else • *As sisters, they have always confided in each other.* [I] ○ *She confided that most of her clients were actors.* [+ that clause]

confidence SURE FEELING /'kɑn·fəd·əns, -fə,dens/ n [U] a feeling of having little doubt about yourself and your abilities, or a feeling of trust in someone or something • *He has a sense of confidence, even arrogance, about what he does.* ○ *Consumers' confidence in the economy is strong.* ○ *Her colleagues lost confidence in her.*

confident /'kɑn·fəd·ənt, -fə,dent/ adj • *a confident smile* ○ *I'm confident we'll succeed.*

confidently /'kɑn·fəd·ənt·li, -fə,dent·li/ adv • *North confidently predicted victory.*

confidence SECRET /'kɑn·fəd·əns, -fə,dens/ n [C/U] a secret, or a feeling of trust that a secret will be kept • *They exchanged confidences like old friends.* [C] ○ *I'm telling you this in confidence.* [U]

confidential /,kɑn·fə'den·tʃəl/ adj • *confidential reports/memos* ○ *All applications are strictly confidential.*

confidentiality /,kɑn·fə,den·tʃi:'æl·əṭ·i/ n [U] • *Tests will be handled with absolute confidentiality.*

configuration /kən,fɪg·jə'reɪ·ʃən/ n [C] the particular arrangement of the parts of something or of a group of things • *The two-lane configuration of the road leads to congestion.*

confine /kən'faɪn/ v [T] to keep (someone or something) within limits • *Prisoners are confined to their cells.* ○ *Harris does not confine her stage work to Broadway.* • If something is confined to a particular group of people, it exists only among them: *Cancer is not confined to old people.*

confinement /kən'faɪn·mənt/ n [U] • *The prisoner was kept in solitary confinement.*

confined /kən'faɪnd/ adj • *You can't keep kids in a confined space for long.*

confines /'kɑn·faɪnz, kən'faɪnz/ pl n the limits or borders of something • *He feels safe within the confines of his home.*

confirm *(obj)* MAKE PLANS /kən'fɜrm/ v to

make (an arrangement, meeting, etc.) certain or fixed • *The hotel has confirmed our reservation.* [T] ○ *Seventy people have confirmed that they will attend the conference.* [+ *that* clause]

confirmation /ˌkɑn·fər'meɪ·ʃən/ *n* [C/U] • *He'd heard rumors of the sale, but had no confirmation of it yet.* [U]

confirm APPROVE /kən'fɜrm/ *v* [T] to approve (someone or something) officially by formal agreement • *His appointment has not been confirmed by the Senate.*

confirmation /ˌkɑn·fər'meɪ·ʃən/ *n* [U] • *confirmation hearings*

confirm (obj) PROVE TRUE /kən'fɜrm/ *v* to prove or state the truth of (something that was previously not completely certain) • *Health officials confirmed that there's a flu epidemic underway.* [+ *that* clause]

confirmation /ˌkɑn·fər·meɪ·ʃən/ *n* [U] • *There was no immediate confirmation of the attack.*

confirm RELIGION /kən'fɜrm/ *v* [T] to accept (someone) formally into the membership of certain Christian churches

confirmation /ˌkɑn·fər'meɪ·ʃən/ *n* [C/U] a ceremony at which someone is accepted into membership in a church

confirmed /kən'fɜrmd/ *adj* firmly fixed in a particular habit or way of life and unlikely to change • *a confirmed bachelor*

confiscate /'kɑn·fə,skeɪt/ *v* [T] to officially take (private property) away from someone, usually by legal authority • *Government agents confiscated the guns.*

confiscation /ˌkɑn·fə'skeɪ·ʃən/ *n* [C/U] • *The law allows for confiscation of vehicles used in crimes.* [U]

conflict /'kɑn·flɪkt/ *n* [C/U] an active disagreement, as between opposing opinions or needs • *Conflicts between parents and children become more frequent when the children become teenagers.* [C] ○ *Science sometimes comes into conflict with religion.* [U] • Conflict can also mean war: *If armed conflict occurs, everyone will suffer.* [U] • A **conflict of interest** is a situation in which someone's private, esp. financial, interests are opposed to their responsibilities to other people: *Council members should avoid any potential conflict of interest.*

conflict /kən'flɪkt/ *v* [I] • *We received reports that conflict with each other.*

conflicting /kən'flɪk·tɪŋ/ *adj* • *There are many conflicting studies of breast cancer.*

conform /kən'fɔːrm/ *v* [I] to behave according to a group's usual standards and expectations, or to operate according to a rule • *Barton refused to conform to the usual woman's role.* ○ *Wood-burning stoves must conform to the fire code.*

conformity /kən'fɔːr·məṱ·i/ *n* [U] • *He felt suffocated by the conformity of suburban life.*

confound /kən'faʊnd, kɑn-/ *v* [T] to confuse (someone) by being difficult to explain or deal

with • *She likes to confound others' expectations about her.*

confront /kən'frʌnt/ *v* [T] to come in front of and deal with (a difficult or threatening situation), or to cause (someone) to deal with something • *Security forces confronted the demonstrators.* ○ *When I took office, I was confronted with new guidelines.* ○ *Becca will have to confront some frightening truths about this disease.*

confrontation /ˌkɑn·frən'teɪ·ʃən/ *n* [C/U] • *He was injured in a confrontation with five teenagers.* [C]

confrontational /ˌkɑn·frən'teɪ·ʃən·əl/ *adj* • *His confrontational style often angers people.*

confuse /kən'fjuːz/ *v* [T] to cause (someone) to feel uncertain or unclear, or to make (something) difficult to understand • *You're confusing me—please repeat the directions more slowly.* • If someone confuses one thing with another, they think the first thing is the second: *You're confusing me with my sister—she's the one who moved to Colorado.*

confused /kən'fjuːzd/ *adj* • *Her confused reaction is understandable.*

confusing /kən'fjuː·zɪŋ/ *adj* • *The directions were confusing, and I got lost.*

confusion /kən'fjuː·ʒən/ *n* [C/U] a lack of understanding, or a state of disorder • *She writes about the confusions of her life.* [C] ○ *In the confusion, I lost my wallet.* [U]

congeal /kən'dʒiːl/ *v* [I] to change from a liquid or soft state to a thick or solid state • *His blood congealed around the wound.*

congenial /kən'dʒiːn·jəl/ *adj* pleasant and friendly; producing a feeling of comfort or satisfaction • *We spent a relaxed evening with congenial friends.*

congenital /kən'dʒen·əṱ·əl/ *adj* [not gradable] existing at or from birth • *a congenital defect*

congested /kən'dʒes·təd/ *adj* too crowded or blocked • *Congested roads are normal on holiday weekends.* • If someone is congested, they cannot breathe through their nose because it is blocked, usually because of a cold.

congestion /kən'dʒes·tʃən/ *n* [U] • *The restaurant would increase traffic congestion and noise.*

conglomerate /kən'glɑm·ə·rət/ *n* [C] a very large company consisting of several smaller companies or divisions that supply varied products or services

conglomeration /kən,glɑm·ə'reɪ·ʃən/ *n* [C] a large group or mass of different things gathered together • *The dish is a wonderful conglomeration of sausage, chicken, seafood, and rice.*

congratulate /kən'græt·ʃ·ə,leɪt, -'grædʒ-/ *v* [T] to praise (someone) by expressing your pleasure at their success or happiness • *I congratulated Jill on winning the award.*

congratulations /kən,græt·ʃ·ə'leɪ·ʃənz, -,grædʒ-/

exclamation, pl n • *"I passed my driving test." "Congratulations!"* ○ *Give him my congratulations when you see him.*

congregate /ˈkɑŋ·grə·geɪt/ *v* [I] to gather together into a large group • *A crowd congregated around City Hall.*

congregation /ˌkɑŋ·grəˈgeɪ·ʃən/ *n* [C] a group of people gathered together for religious worship • *The congregation prayed silently.*

congress MEETING /ˈkɑŋ·grəs/ *n* [C] a formal meeting of representatives from countries or organizations at which ideas are discussed and information is exchanged • *the fourth congress of the European Association for Lexicography*

Congress LAW MAKERS /ˈkɑŋ·grəs/ *n* [U] the elected group of people in the US who are responsible for making the law, consisting of the Senate and the House of Representatives • *Congress has rejected the president's plan.* • A **congressman** (also **representative**) is a male member of a congress, esp. a member of the US House of Representatives. • A **congresswoman** (also **representative**) is a female member of a congress, esp. a member of the US House of Representatives.

congressional /kənˈgreʃ·ən·əl/ *adj* [not gradable] • *a congressional committee*

conical /ˈkɑn·ɪ·kəl/ *adj* • See at CONE.

conifer /ˈkɑn·ə·fər/ *n* [C] any of various types of mostly evergreen trees that produce a CONE

conjecture /kənˈdʒek·tʃər, -ʃər/ *n* [C/U] an opinion or judgment that is not based on proof; a guess • *What lay behind the divorce is open to conjecture.* [U]

conjecture /kənˈdʒek·tʃər, -ʃər/ *v* [I/T] • *Some employees conjecture that it was a money-saving move.* [+ *that* clause]

conjugal /ˈkɑn·dʒə·gəl, kənˈdʒuː-/ *adj* [not gradable] *fml* connected with marriage or the relationship between husband and wife, esp. their sexual relationship • *Prisoners are allowed conjugal visits.*

conjugate /ˈkɑn·dʒə·geɪt/ *v* [I/T] *specialized* to list the forms of a verb in a particular order

conjugation /ˌkɑn·dʒəˈgeɪ·ʃən/ *n* [C] *specialized* the complete set of grammatical forms of a verb • *the conjugation of the French verb "avoir"*

conjunction CONNECTING WORD /kənˈdʒʌŋ·ʃən/ *n* [C] *specialized* (in grammar) a word such as "and," "but," "because," or "although" that connects words, phrases, and clauses in a sentence

conjunction COMBINATION /kənˈdʒʌŋ·ʃən/ *n* [C/U] a combination of events or conditions • *Physicists are working in conjunction with engineers on the project.* [U]

conjure /ˈkɑn·dʒər/ *v* [T] to make (something) appear by magic or as if by magic • *His words conjured images of far-away action.* [T]

conk /kɑŋk, kɔːŋk/ *v* [T] *infml* to hit (someone) on the head • *When he walked in, I conked him.*

◻**conk out** /ˈ-ˈ-/ *v adv* [I] *infml* (of a machine or engine) to stop working or fail suddenly • *My radio conked out again.*

connect JOIN /kəˈnekt/ *v* [I/T] to join together (two things), or to be joined together • *The printer connects to the computer.* [I] ○ *A ferry connects the island to the mainland.* [T] ○ *Is your electricity connected yet* (= has your home been joined to the supply)? [T]

connected /kəˈnek·təd/ *adj* [not gradable] • *the connected parts of a machine*

connecting /kəˈnek·tɪŋ/ *adj* [not gradable] • *They turned down a connecting road.*

connection /kəˈnek·ʃən/ *n* [C] • *a sewer connection* [C]

connect RELATE /kəˈnekt/ *v* [T] to consider (a person or thing) as related in some way to something else • *I connect Roberta Peters with the theater rather than movies.* [T] ○ *He's always found a way to connect with his audience.* [I]

connected /kəˈnek·təd/ *adj* [not gradable] • *some loosely connected stories* • If you are connected, you know important people: *He's a politically connected lawyer.*

connection /kəˈnek·ʃən/ *n* [C] • *There is a connection between cigarette smoking and lung cancer.* ○ *He got the job through connections* (= people who helped him). • *Two men have been arrested* **in connection with** *the theft* (= in some relation to it).

connect TELEPHONE /kəˈnekt/ *v* [T] to make it possible for (someone) to communicate by telephone • *Operator, please connect me with room 1125.*

connect TRANSPORT /kəˈnekt/ *v* [I] (of aircraft, trains, etc.) to arrive before a second vehicle leaves on which passengers can continue their trip • *The flight to Chicago connects with a flight to New York.*

connection /kəˈnek·ʃən/ *n* [C] • *We were delayed and missed our connection.*

conniving /kəˈnɑɪ·vɪŋ/ *adj* planning secretly, esp. in doing something wrong • *a cold, conniving man*

connoisseur /ˌkɑn·əˈsɜr, -ˈsʊr/ *n* [C] a person who has expert knowledge of something, esp. an art, food, or drink, and is qualified to judge and appreciate its quality • *He's become a connoisseur of wine.*

connotation /ˌkɑn·əˈteɪ·ʃən/ *n* [C] a feeling or idea that is suggested by a word in addition to its basic meaning, or something suggested by an object or situation • *"Resolute" means stubborn, but with a more positive connotation.*

conquer /ˈkɑŋ·kər/ *v* [T] to defeat (an enemy), or to take control or possession of (a foreign land) • *I felt like I had conquered the world.* • If you conquer a disease or condition, you succeed in dealing with or fighting against it: *Students have to conquer their initial shyness.*

conqueror /'kaŋ·kə·rər/ *n* [C] • *Alexander the Great was a ruthless conqueror.*

conquest /'kan·kwest, 'kaŋ-/ *n* [C/U] • *The European conquest of South America was a disaster for the people already living there.* [C]

conscience /'kan·tʃəns/ *n* [C/U] the feeling that you know and should do what is right and should avoid doing what is wrong, and that makes you feel guilty when you have done something you know is wrong • *I have a guilty conscience for spending so little time with my kids.* [C]

conscientious /ˌkan·tʃiː'en·tʃəs/ *adj* feeling a moral responsibility to do your work carefully and to be fair to others • *She was a conscientious worker, and I'll miss her.*

conscious AWAKE /'kan·tʃəs/ *adj* awake, aware of what is happening around you, and able to think • *She's out of surgery but not fully conscious yet.* • USAGE: The opposite of conscious is UNCONSCIOUS.

consciousness /'kan·tʃə·snəs/ *n* [U] • *He lost consciousness on the way to the hospital, and regained consciousness the next day.*

conscious NOTICING /'kan·tʃəs/ *adj* noticing the existence or presence of something • *People have become much more conscious of the need to exercise regularly.*

conscious INTENTIONAL /'kan·tʃəs/ *adj* determined and intentional • *Was it a conscious decision to break up the group, or did it just happen?*

consciously /'kan·tʃə·sli/ *adv* • *He consciously seeks out much younger women to date.*

conscious AWARE /'kan·tʃəs/ *adj* [only after n] being especially aware of or worried about something • *Consumers aren't as conscious of prices as they were last year.*

consciousness /'kan·tʃə·snəs/ *n* [U] • *There's definitely a consciousness of the employment market among the students.* • **Consciousness raising** is the effort to increase people's awareness of social and political matters.

conscript /kən'skrɪpt/ *v* [T] to force (someone) to work as a member of a group • *Soldiers conscripted children and old people to build a wall around the city.*

conscript /'kan·skrɪpt/ *n* [C] • *We were volunteers, not conscripts.*

conscription /kən'skrɪp·ʃən/ *n* [U] • *He emigrated from Germany in the 1850s to avoid conscription into the army.*

consecrate /'kan·sə,kreɪt/ *v* [T] to officially make (something) holy and suitable to be used for religious ceremonies • *The church was completed and consecrated in the 1890s.*

consecrated /'kan·sə,kreɪt·əd/ *adj* [not gradable] • *consecrated ground*

consecutive /kən'sek·jəţ·ɪv/ *adj* following one after another without an interruption • *We've had five consecutive days of rain.*

consecutively /kən'sek·jəţ·ɪv·li/ *adv*

consensus /kən'sen·səs/ *n* [U] a generally accepted opinion; wide agreement • *They're trying to build a consensus on the need to improve the city's schools.*

consent /kən'sent/ *n* [U] permission or agreement obtained from someone or something having authority or power • *I asked to leave the room, and the teacher gave his consent.*

consent /kən'sent/ *v* [I] to give permission • *The director consented to change the ending of the movie.* [+ *to* infinitive]

consequence RESULT /'kan·sə·kwəns, -,kwens/ *n* [C usually pl] a result of an action or situation, esp. (in the plural) a bad result • *For someone who is old and weak, the consequences of a broken hip can be serious.*

consequent /'kan·sə·kwənt, -,kwent/ *adj* [not gradable] resulting • *Stock values declined, with consequent financial losses.*

consequently /'kan·sə·kwənt·li, -,kwent·li/ *adv* [not gradable] as a result; therefore • *I was very worried, and consequently I couldn't concentrate.*

consequence IMPORTANCE /'kan·sə·kwəns, -,kwens/ *n* [U] the condition of having a lasting effect; importance • *Last summer there were 15 hurricanes, but only one was of any consequence.*

conservative AGAINST CHANGE /kən'sɜr·vəţ·ɪv/ *adj* tending to emphasize the importance of preserving traditional cultural and religious values, and to oppose change, esp. sudden change • *If you are conservative in your appearance, you wear clothes in traditional colors and styles: He wore a conservative business suit for his interview.*

conservatively /kən'sɜr·vəţ·ɪv·li/ *adv* • *She was conservatively dressed in a gray suit.*

conservative POLITICS /kən'sɜr·vəţ·ɪv/ *adj* tending to emphasize the importance of personal responsibility and traditional values and to oppose depending on government for social services • *conservative Republicans* • Compare LIBERAL POLITICS.

conservative /kən'sɜr·vəţ·ɪv/ *n* [C] • *The Congressional committee had an equal number of conservatives and liberals.*

conservative LOW /kən'sɜr·vəţ·ɪv/ *adj* (of guesses and calculations) likely to be less than the real amount • *Even by conservative estimates, the company will lose $2,000,000 this year.*

conserve /kən'sɜrv/ *v* [T] to keep and protect from waste, loss, or damage; preserve • *In order to conserve fuel, they put in extra insulation.*

conservation /ˌkan·sər'veɪ·ʃən/ *n* [U] • Conservation is a plan for avoiding the unnecessary use of natural materials such as wood, water, or fuel: *The university is saving $300,000 per year by its energy conservation efforts.* • Conservation is also the protection of plants, animals, and natural areas, esp. from the damaging effects of human activity: *wildlife conservation*

conservationist /ˌkɑn·sər'veɪ·ʃə·nəst/ *n* [C] a person who believes in or works for the protection of plants, animals, and natural areas, esp. from the damaging effects of human activity

consider *(obj)* [THINK ABOUT] /kən'sɪd·ər/ *v* to think about (a particular subject or thing) or about doing (something) or about whether to do (something) • *Consider Clara Barton, who founded the American Red Cross.* [T] ∘ *We considered moving to California, but decided not to.* [T] ∘ *We have to consider what to do next.* [+ wh- word]

consideration /kənˌsɪd·ə'reɪ·ʃən/ *n* [C/U] • *Financial considerations were a factor in the decision.* [C] ∘ *You should take his youth into consideration before you punish him.* [U]

considering /kən'sɪd·ə·rɪŋ/ *prep, conjunction, adv* [not gradable] used to mention a condition or fact that has an influence, esp. a disadvantageous one, on something else that you want to mention • *Considering the weather, they were lucky to get here at all.*

consider [CARE ABOUT] /kən'sɪd·ər/ *v* [T] to care about or respect • *Before raising the admission prices, consider the fans.*

considerate /kən'sɪd·ə·rət/ *adj* • *He is always a kind and considerate host.*

consideration /kənˌsɪd·ə'reɪ·ʃən/ *n* [U] • *He showed very little consideration for anyone but himself.*

consider [HAVE AN OPINION] /kən'sɪd·ər/ *v* [T] to believe to be; to think of as • *What some people would consider a personal attack, Andy considers a friendly discussion.*

considerable /kən'sɪd·ə·rə·bəl/ *adj* noticeably large or much • *He exhibited considerable skill in driving through the snowstorm.* • LP VERY, COMPLETELY, AND OTHER INTENSIFIERS

consign /kən'saɪn/ *v* [T] to put (someone) into esp. an unpleasant place or situation • *She refused to consign her children to a life of poverty.*

consignment /kən'saɪn·mənt/ *n* [C/U] the act of sending goods to a business that ordered them • *The last consignment of dresses was shipped yesterday.* [C] • If goods are on consignment, the person or company that has them pays for them only after selling them. [U]

consist of /kən'sɪst·əv, -ʌv, -ɑv/ *v prep* [L] to be something that is made or formed of (various specific things), or to be based on or involve • *The crowd consisted mostly of college kids and office workers.* ∘ *Her responsibilities consist of answering the phone and greeting visitors.*

consistency /kən'sɪs·tən·si/ *n* [C/U] the degree of thickness of a mixture, esp. a liquid • *It had a consistency like that of thick glue.* [C]

consistent [NOT VARYING] /kən'sɪs·tənt/ *adj* always happening or behaving in a similar way

• *The president has been remarkably consistent on economic issues.*

consistency /kən'sɪs·tən·si/ *n* [U] • *The team's success will depend on the consistency of its pitching.*

consistently /kən'sɪs·tənt·li/ *adv* • *His movies are consistently thought-provoking.*

consistent [AGREEING] /kən'sɪs·tənt/ *adj* agreeing with something said or done previously • *The witness's story is consistent with the police report.*

console [COMFORT] /kən'soʊl/ *v* [T] to give comfort and sympathy to (someone who is sad or disappointed) • *The boys consoled one another after their team's first defeat.*

consolation /ˌkɑn·sə'leɪ·ʃən/ *n* [C/U] • *The main consolation for me was that I wouldn't have to leave Boston.* [C] • A **consolation prize** is a small prize given to someone who has taken part in a competition but not won.

console [CONTROLS] /'kɑn·soʊl/ *n* [C] a special area containing a set of controls for electric equipment, esp. on an aircraft or boat • *The jet's console contains dozens of dials, meters, and switches.* • A console is also a cabinet that sits on the floor and contains an electrical unit such as a television.

consolidate /kən'sɑl·ə,deɪt/ *v* [I/T] to bring together or unite (things that were separate) • *Our offices had been spread among three buildings, and then we consolidated into one new high-rise.* [I] • To consolidate is also to make stronger by some action or event: *The governor consolidated his power, getting his allies into key state jobs.* [T]

consolidated /kən'sɑl·ə,deɪt·əd/ *adj* [not gradable] • A **consolidated school** is a public school, esp. in a rural area, formed from several small schools: *She was in charge of a consolidated school district in northern Iowa.*

consolidation /kənˌsɑl·ə'deɪ·ʃən/ *n* [U]

consommé /'kɑn·sə,meɪ/ *n* [U] a thin, clear soup, usually made from juices of boiled meat

consonant /'kɑn·sə·nənt/ *n* [C] a speech sound produced by human beings when the breath that flows out through the mouth is blocked by the teeth, tongue, or lips • A consonant is also a letter that represents a sound produced in this way: *Except for the vowels in English—a, e, i, o, u, and sometimes y—all the letters are consonants.* • Compare VOWEL.

consort /kən'sɔːrt, 'kɑn·sɔːrt/ *v* [I] *usually disapproving* to spend time in the company of (particular people) • *He's more interested in consorting with movie stars than in helping his sister.*

conspicuous /kən'spɪk·jə·wəs/ *adj* easily noticed; obvious • *He was conspicuous as usual with a big yellow bow tie.* • When you say someone or something is **conspicuous by** its **absence**, you are saying that it is strange that it is absent: *Information about the lives of women is conspicuous by its absence in some* *history books.* ° *The police were conspicuous by their absence.*

conspire /kən'spaɪr/ *v* [I] to plan secretly with other people to do something bad, illegal, or against someone's wishes • *Moore conspired with Graham to rob the bank.* [+ *to* infinitive] • To conspire can also mean to make something happen that is difficult to do: *They somehow conspired to keep the theater alive when all government funding ended.* [+ *to* infinitive]

conspiracy /kən'spɪr·ə·si/ *n* [C/U] • *Eight men were charged with conspiracy to smuggle cocaine.* [U]

conspirator /kən'spɪr·əţ·ər/ *n* [C] a person who plans secretly with other people to do something bad, illegal, or against someone's wishes

constable /'kɑn·stə·bəl/ *n* [C] (in the US) an official in a town or village having some of the responsibilities of a police officer

constant /'kɑn·stənt/ *adj* nearly continuous or very frequent • *We had a constant stream of visitors.* • Constant also means not changing, or staying the same: *Even in this age of high technology, the popularity of hunting and fishing remains constant.*

constantly /'kɑn·stənt·li/ *adv* [not gradable] • *They worry constantly about their weight.*

constellation /ˌkɑn·stə'leɪ·ʃən/ *n* [C] a group of stars in the sky that appear to form a pattern and that have a name

consternation /ˌkɑn·stər'neɪ·ʃən/ *n* [U] a feeling of strong annoyance and anger, usually because of something bad that you cannot change or that is completely unexpected • *The power failure caused consternation among local officials.*

constipated /'kɑn·stə,peɪţ·əd/ *adj* unable to excrete the contents of the bowels often enough or in large enough amounts

constipation /ˌkɑn·stə'peɪ·ʃən/ *n* [U] • *A diet that is high in fiber may relieve constipation.*

constituency /kən'stɪtʃ·ə·wən·si/ *n* [C] the voters in a particular area of a country who are represented by an elected official, or the area • *Republican constituencies are mainly in suburban areas.*

constituent /kən'stɪtʃ·ə·wənt/ *n* [C usually pl] a voter in a particular area of a country • *The senator mails a newsletter to his constituents every two months.*

constitute BE CONSIDERED AS /'kɑn·stə,tuːt/ *v* [L] to be or be considered as • *The president said that these policies constitute a threat to the United States.*

constitute EQUAL /'kɑn·stə,tuːt/ *v* [L] to form or make (something); equal • *Asians constitute seven percent of the population in this county.*

constituent /kən'stɪtʃ·ə·wənt/ *n* [C] one of the parts that a substance or mixture is made of • *Oxygen is a constituent of air.*

constitution LAWS /ˌkɑn·stə'tuː·ʃən/ *n* [C] the set of political principles by which a place or organization is governed, or the written document that records it • *The first ten amendments to the Constitution of the United States are called the Bill of Rights.*

constitutional /ˌkɑn·stə'tjuː·ʃən·əl/ *adj* [not gradable] • *Freedom of speech is a constitutional guarantee in the United States.*

constitutionally /ˌkɑn·stə'tuː·ʃən·əl·i/ *adv* [not gradable] according to the rules in a constitution • *We believe that the right to own a gun is constitutionally guaranteed.*

constitutionality /ˌkɑn·stə,tuː·ʃə'næl·əţ·i/ *n* [U] (esp. of a law) legality based on agreement with a constitution • *The Supreme Court upheld the constitutionality of that law.*

constitution HEALTH /ˌkɑn·stə'tuː·ʃən/ *n* [C usually sing] a person's physical condition, esp. as shown by strength and staying well • *a weak constitution*

constraint /kən'streɪnt/ *n* [C] something that limits the range of a person's actions or freedom • *In Egypt, the biggest constraint on new agricultural production is water.*

constrained /kən'streɪnd/ *adj* forced to act or behave in a particular way • *Our opportunities are constrained by lack of money.*

constrict /kən'strɪkt/ *v* [I/T] to make or become tighter and narrower • *Bright sunlight constricts the pupil of the eye.* [T]

constriction /kən'strɪk·ʃən/ *n* [C]

construct /kən'strʌkt/ *v* [T] to build (something made of many parts) • *They approved funds to construct a new ferry terminal.* • To construct is also to put together different parts to form (something new): *to construct a sentence* ° *to construct a new economic theory*

construction /kən'strʌk·ʃən/ *n* [U] • *the construction industry* ° *A new hotel is now under construction* (= being built).

constructive /kən'strʌk·tɪv/ *adj* intended to help someone or improve understanding • *She was my most constructive critic.*

construe /kən'struː/ *v* [T] to understand the meaning of (esp. what someone has said or done) in a particular way • *That comment could be construed in either of two ways.*

construction /kən'strʌk·ʃən/ *n* [C] *fml* • *The construction you are putting on my client's statement is unfair.*

consul /'kɑn·səl/ *n* [C] a government official who lives in a foreign city in order to take care of the people from the official's own country who are traveling or living there and to protect the trade interests of that government

consulate /'kɑn·sə·lət/ *n* [C] the offices or building used by a consul

consult /kən'sʌlt/ *v* [T] to get information or advice from (a person, esp. an expert) or to look at (written material) in order to get information • *If you don't know the meaning of a word, consult a dictionary.* [T] • To consult is also to inform (someone) about a situation, often in order to get their approval about an action you plan to take: *The committee will consult people in the neighborhood before making a recommendation.* [T]

consultant /kən'sʌlt·ªnt/ *n* [C] a person who is a specialist in a particular subject and whose job is to give advice and information to businesses, government organizations, etc. • *The former general now serves as a consultant to the Pentagon.*

consultation /ˌkɑn·səl'teɪ·ʃən/ *n* [C/U] the act of exchanging information and opinions about something in order to reach a better understanding of it or to make a decision, or a meeting for this purpose • *We hope to work in consultation with Congress on how the law should be interpreted.* [U] • A consultation is also a meeting with a doctor who is specially trained to advise you or other doctors about an illness or its treatment: *The consultation with the pathologist convinced me to have surgery right away.* [C]

consume /kən'suːm/ *v* [T] to use (fuel, energy, or time), esp. in large amounts • *Weekend shopping chores consumed much of her time.* • To consume is also to eat or drink: *They consume a lot of alcohol.* • If a fire consumes something, it destroys it completely: *Fire had consumed the whole building.* • Someone can be said to be consumed by/with a feeling if that feeling is extremely strong and is having a great effect on their life: *Consumed with guilt, Charles virtually begs to be punished.*

consumer /kən'suː·mər/ *n* [C] a person who buys goods or services for their own use • *consumer goods/spending* ○ *American consumers are becoming informed about the safety of products made for children.*

consummate COMPLETE /'kɑn·sə·mət, kən 'sʌm·ət/ *adj* perfect; complete in every way • *consummate skill*

consummate /'kɑn·sə,meɪt/ *v* [T] • *The deal was consummated with a handshake.*

consummate HAVE SEX /'kɑn·sə,meɪt/ *v* [T] *literary* to make (a marriage or romantic relationship) complete by having sex

consumption /kən'sʌm·ʃən/ *n* [U] an amount of something that is used, or the process of using something in which less of it remains • *Consumption of electricity is always higher during the summer months because of air-conditioning.* • Consumption is also the using of goods and services in an economy, or the amount of goods and services used.

contact COMMUNICATION /'kɑn·tækt/ *n* [U] communication with someone, or with a group or organization • *Have you kept in contact with your friends from college?* ○ *The pilot was always in contact with an air traffic controller.*

contact /'kɑn·tækt/ *v* [T] • *I tried to contact him at his office but he was out to lunch.*

contact TOUCH /'kɑn·tækt/ *n* [U] the touching of two objects or surfaces • *Don't let that glue come into contact with your skin.* • A contact

lens is a small, round, curved piece of transparent material, esp. plastic, which fits on the surface of an eye to improve sight: *I need new contact lenses.*

contact HELPFUL PERSON /'kɑn·tækt/ *n* [C] a person whom you know and who may be able to help you in a practical way, esp. because of their influence with other people or their knowledge • *He tried to use his contacts to get a better job in advertising.* • A contact is also a person you meet: *My face-to-face contacts outside of the office had been mostly hotel clerks, policemen, and waitresses.*

contagious /kən'teɪ·dʒəs/ *adj* (of a disease) able to be caught by touching someone with the disease or something they have touched or worn, or (of a person) having this type of disease • *a highly contagious strain of flu* • (*fig.*) Contagious also means moving easily from one person to another: *The mood was contagious, and soon everyone was laughing.*

contain HAVE INSIDE /kən'teɪn/ *v* [T] (of an object or area) to have (an amount of something) inside or within it • *How much liquid does this bottle contain?* ○ *Each large crate contains 12 boxes.*

container /kən'teɪ·nər/ *n* [C] a hollow object, such as a box or a bottle, which can be used for holding something esp. for the purposes of carrying or storing • *plastic milk containers*

contain INCLUDE /kən'teɪn/ *v* [T] to have as a part, or be equal to; include • *The information contained on forms would be kept strictly confidential.* ○ *Each food serving contains 95 calories.* ○ *You could retrieve all files that contained certain key words.*

contain CONTROL /kən'teɪn/ *v* [T] to keep within limits; not to allow to spread • *Medical teams were scrambling to contain the illness that has already killed thousands in Latin America.*

contaminate /kən'tæm·ə,neɪt/ *v* [T] to spoil the purity of (something) or make it poisonous • *The disease can be caused by a variety of viruses, bacteria, and other small organisms that contaminate food or water.*

contaminated /kən'tæm·ə,neɪt̬·əd/ *adj* • *contaminated water*

contamination /kən,tæm·ə'neɪ·ʃən/ *n* [U]

contemplate /'kɑnt·əm,pleɪt/ *v* [I/T] to spend time considering (a possible future action), or to consider (one particular thing) for a long time in a serious way • *The owner of the team contemplated moving his football club to another city.* [T] ○ *Sharon is contemplating going to graduate school.* [T]

contemplation /ˌkɑnt·əm'pleɪ·ʃən/ *n* [U]

contemporary EXISTING NOW /kən'tem·pəˌrer·i/ *adj* existing or happening now • *contemporary literature/music*

contemporary OF THE SAME PERIOD /kən'tem·pəˌrer·i/ *adj* belonging to the same or a stated period in the past • *The same style of* *architecture is seen in contemporary churches in the major European cities at that time.*

contemporary /kən'tem·pə,rer·i/ *n* [C] someone living during the same period as another • *Franklin and Jefferson were contemporaries.*

contempt /kən'temt/ *n* [U] a strong feeling of lack of respect for someone or something • *They were bullies, and they showed contempt for everyone and everything.*

contemptible /kən'tem·tə·bəl/ *adj* deserving blame • *His behavior was contemptible.*

contemptuous /kən'tem·tʃə·wəs/ *adj* expressing or feeling a lack of respect • *As one of the senior members of the Senate, he was openly contemptuous of its junior members.*

contemptuously /kən'tem·tʃə·wə·sli/ *adv* • *He spoke contemptuously of his former boss.*

contend COMPETE /kən'tend/ *v* [I] to compete in order to win something or to achieve a position of leadership • *The top tennis players in the world are contending for this title.*

contender /kən'ten·dər/ *n* [C] • *He is a top contender for Senate majority leader.*

contention /kən'ten·tʃən/ *n* [U] • *The big names slowly dropped out of contention at the tournament.* • See also CONTENTION DISAGREEMENT, CONTENTION OPINION.

contend CLAIM /kən'tend/ *v* to state as the truth; claim • *Farmers contended that two drunk officers had raped a local woman.* [+ *that* clause]

□ **contend with** /-'-·-/ *v prep* [T] to try to deal with a difficult situation or solve a problem • *At the age of nine he had to contend with the death of both parents.*

content HAPPY /kən'tent/ *adj* pleased with your situation and not needing or desiring it to be better • *Skating this year with a sprained ankle, he said he was content just to make the Olympic team.*

content /kən'tent/ *v* [T] to make (yourself) accept something as satisfactory, although it could be better • *We had to content ourselves with watching the sea lions from the shore.*

contented /kən'tent·əd/ *adj* • *Our dog leads a happy and contented life.*

contentment /kən'tent·mənt/, **content** *n* [U] • *Her greatest happiness and contentment was found in being a devoted wife, mother, and grandmother.*

content SUBJECT /'kan·tent/ *n* [U] the subject or ideas contained in something written, said, or represented • *The increasingly violent and sexually explicit content of computer and video games is disturbing to a lot of people.*

contents /'kan·tents/ *pl n* • *He went on to cite the contents of that report.*

content AMOUNT /'kan·tent/ *n* [U] the amount of a particular substance contained in something • *This type of milk has a lower fat content.*

contention DISAGREEMENT /kən'ten·tʃən/ *n* [U] disagreement resulting from opposing arguments • *Their refusal to sign the treaty remains a source of contention between the two countries.* • See also **contention** at CONTEND COMPETE.

contentious /kən'ten·tʃəs/ *adj* causing or likely to cause disagreement • *a contentious subject*

contention OPINION /kən'ten·tʃən/ *n* [C] an opinion expressed in an argument • *It's her contention that exercise is almost as important as diet if you want to lose weight.* [+ *that* clause] • See also **contention** at CONTEND COMPETE.

contents /'kan·tents/ *pl n* everything that is contained within something • *They ran through the apartment, pulling out the drawers of the bureaus, tumbling the contents on the floor.*

contest /'kan·test/ *n* [C] a competition to do better than other people, esp. to win a prize or achieve a position of leadership or power • *In the last election, he survived a close contest against a political newcomer.*

contest /kən'test/ *v* [T] to oppose esp. in argument • *The campaign's organizers hotly contest much of the criticism that has been leveled at them.* • To contest is also to claim that a particular action is not fair or is not legal: *The lawyers may decide to contest the fine.*

contestant /kən'tes·tənt/ *n* [C] • *She was once a contestant on a television quiz show.*

context RELATED EVENTS /'kan·tekst/ *n* [C] the influences and events related to a particular event or situation • *In the context of war, many crimes go unpunished.*

context SURROUNDING WORDS /'kan·tekst/ *n* [C] the text or speech that comes immediately before and after a particular phrase or piece of text and that influence how it is used and what it means

continent LAND /'kant·ᵊn·ənt/ *n* [C] one of the seven large land masses on the earth's surface, surrounded or mainly surrounded by sea • *Asia and Africa are the two biggest continents.*

continental /,kant·ᵊn'ent·ᵊl/ *adj* [not gradable]

continent CONTROL /'kant·ᵊn·ənt/ *adj* able to control urination and the excretion of the contents of the bowels

continental breakfast /,kant·ᵊn'ent·ᵊl 'brek·fəst/ *n* [C] a simple breakfast that consists of coffee, bread or pastries, and a fruit juice

contingent GROUP /kən'tɪn·dʒənt/ *n* [C] a group of people representing an organization or country, or a part of a military force • *The conservative contingent walked out of the convention when their plan was rejected.*

contingent DEPENDING /kən'tɪn·dʒənt/ *adj* depending on or influenced by something else • *Buying the new house was contingent on selling the old one.*

contingency /kən'tɪn·dʒən·si/ *n* [C] something that might possibly happen in the future, usually causing problems or making further plans and arrangements necessary • *We must prepare for all possible contingencies.*

continue /kən'tɪn·ju:/ *v* [I/T] to keep happening or to keep doing (something) without stopping • *If it continues to rain, we may have to cancel the outdoor concert.* [+ *to* infinitive] ○ *I will continue to say what I believe.* [+ *to* infinitive] ○ *They continued hoping there would be additional survivors.* • You can also continue to do something or continue doing something if you start to do it again after a pause: *After a break for lunch, they continued their discussions.* [T]

continual /kən'tɪn·jə·wəl/ *adj* [not gradable] happening often; repeating • *There was a continual string of formal parties, dances, and receptions.*

continually /kən'tɪn·jə·wə·li/ *adv* • *I think that we could get by without continually raising taxes.*

continuous /kən'tɪn·jə·wəs/ *adj* [not gradable] without a pause or break • *a continuous line of traffic*

continuously /kən'tɪn·jə·wə·sli/ *adv* [not gradable] • *He spoke continuously for more than two hours.*

continuation /kən,tɪn·jə'weɪ·ʃən/ *n* [C/U] something that is connected to something else, or the state of being continued • *It's really just a continuation of the same street but called by a different name.* [C]

continuity /,kɑnt·ᵊn'u:·ət̬·i/ *n* [U] the state of continuing over time, esp. without change or interruption • *He argued that the country needed to maintain some continuity in foreign policy.*

contorted /kən'tɔːrt̬·əd/ *adj* twisted or bent in a way that does not seem natural • *His face was contorted in anger.*

contour /'kɑn·tʊr/ *n* [C] the shape of a mass of land or other object, esp. of its surface, or the shape formed by its outer edge • *the distinctive contour of Florida's coast*

contraband /'kɑn·trə,bænd/ *n* [U] goods that are secretly or illegally brought into or taken out of a country

contraband /'kɑn·trə,bænd/ *adj* [not gradable] • *contraband cigarettes/guns*

contraception /,kɑn·trə'sep·ʃən/ *n* [U] the planned prevention of pregnancy in a woman who is sexually active, or the methods used to prevent pregnancy • *Coumbaras said that only a small percentage of Russian women use contraception.*

contraceptive /,kɑn·trə'sep·tɪv/ *n* [C] any of various devices or drugs intended to prevent pregnancy • *an oral contraceptive*

contraceptive /,kɑn·trə'sep·tɪv/ *adj* [not gradable] • *a contraceptive device/pill*

contract AGREEMENT /'kɑn·trækt/ *n* [C] a legal document that states and explains a formal agreement between two different people or groups, or the agreement itself • *She already has a contract for her next book with a publisher.*

contract /'kɑn·trækt, kən'trækt/ *v* [T] • *The company had been contracted to build shelters for the homeless.* • To contract out a job is to formally arrange for other people to do it: *The university contracts out the cleaning to a private company.* [M]

contractual /kən'træk·tʃə·wəl/ *adj* [not gradable] • *I have no other contractual obligations.*

contract SHORTEN /kən'trækt/ *v* [I/T] to make or become shorter or narrower, or smaller • *When wet fibers dry, they contract.* [I]

contraction /kən'træk·ʃən/ *n* [C/U] • *the contraction of a muscle* [U] • In the process of giving birth, a contraction is one of the very strong movements of the muscles in the uterus that help to push the baby out. [C] • A contraction is also a shortened form of a word or combination of words: *"Can't" is a contraction of "cannot."* [C]

CONTRACTIONS OF VERBS

In speech and informal writing, some combinations of a verb with a pronoun or with *not* occur in a CONTRACTION (= short form). A mark called an APOSTROPHE goes where the letters from the full form are missing.

Contractions with personal pronouns

CONTRACTION	FULL FORM	EXAMPLES
I'm	I am	*I'm sorry I'm late.*
I've	I have	*I've been sick.*
I'd	I had	*I wish I'd known.*
	I would	*I'd like something to drink.*
I'll	I will	*I'll do it tomorrow.*
he's/she's/it's	he is/she is/it is	*She's writing a letter.* • *It's raining.*
	he has/she has/it has	*He's never been to Japan.* • *It's been a very hot summer.*
he'd/she'd	he had/she had	*I asked if he'd noticed anything unusual.*
	he would/she would	*She'd help you if she could.*

CONTINUED

he'll/she'll/it'll	he will/she will/it will	*He'll be back soon.* • *It'll be ready in a minute.*
you're/we're/they're	you are/we are/they are	*You're welcome.* • *We're still looking.*
you've/we've/they've	you have/we have/they have	*We've been waiting for an hour. They've already left.*
you'd/we'd/they'd	you had/we had/they had / you would/we would/they would	*They thought we'd gotten lost. They'd like to go with us.*
you'll/we'll/they'll	you will/we will/they will	*Do you think you'll buy it?*

The contraction *let's* (= let us) is used for making suggestions that include you and the other person or people: *Let's go outside.*

Contractions with other pronouns and with some other words

CONTRACTION	FULL FORM	EXAMPLES
that's	that is/that has	*I think that's mine.* • *That's been done before.*
here's	here is/here has	*Here's my address.* • *Nothing here's been touched.*
there's	there is/there has	*There's our bus.* • *There's been an accident.*
that's	that will	*That'll be fifty cents, please.*
what's	what is/what has	*What's the matter?* • *What's been happening?*
where's	where is/where has	*Where's the can opener?* • *Where's she been?*
who's	who is/who has	*Who's next?* • *Who's been sleeping in my bed?*
who'd	who would/who had	*Who'd like to be first?* • *I asked him who'd called.*
how's	how is/how has	*How's your mother feeling?* • *How's he been doing?*

Many more contractions are used in spoken English.

My camera's broken. • *Why'd* (= why did) *you do that?* • *This'll* (= this will) *last for a long time.*

When *have* follows an auxiliary verb or a contraction it is often said as *'ve*

I must've been dreaming. • *Really, you shouldn't've bothered.* • *Who'd've expected it?*

Contractions with *not*

CONTRACTION	FULL FORM	CONTRACTION	FULL FORM
I'm not	I am not	hadn't	had not
aren't/-'re not*	are not	isn't/-'s not*	is not
can't	cannot	mustn't	must not
couldn't	could not	shouldn't	should not
didn't	did not	wasn't	was not
doesn't	does not	weren't	were not
don't	do not	won't	will not
hasn't	has not	wouldn't	would not
haven't	have not		

*There are two commonly used contractions for *are not* and *is not*. The second form is used especially when you want to emphasize that the statement is negative: *He's not the person we're looking for.*

The contraction *ain't* is used by some people instead of *am not, is not, are not, has not,* and *have not.* It is not considered to be standard English.

Contractions with *not* are often used in questions.

Aren't you hungry? • *Didn't you talk to him?* • *Can't you find it?*

The full forms of these contractions would not usually be used in questions.

LP Apostrophe [']

---

contract BECOME ILL /kən'trækt/ *v* [T] to catch or become ill with (a disease) • *She contracted pneumonia and was hospitalized.*

contractor /'kɑn,træk·tər/ *n* [C] a person or company that arranges to supply materials or workers, esp. for building

contradict /,kɑn·trə'dɪkt/ *v* [T] (of people) to state the opposite of what someone has said, or (of one fact or statement) to be so different from another fact or statement that one of them must be wrong • *Her testimony contradicted the policeman's testimony, and the jury had to decide who was telling the truth.*

contradiction /,kɑn·trə'dɪk·ʃən/ *n* [C/U] • *(fig.) His life was full of contradictions* (= things that are not likely to appear together). [C]

contradictory /,kɑn·trə'dɪk·tə·ri/ *adj* • *We received contradictory accounts about the success of the military campaign.*

contralto /kən'træl·toʊ/ n [C] pl **contraltos**
a woman's singing voice in the lowest range,
or a singer with this range

contraption /kən'træp·ʃən/ n [C] an awkward or old-fashioned looking device or machine

contrary OPPOSITE /'kɑn,trer·i/ n [U] a fact or
opinion that is the opposite of one already
stated • *We expected the play to be a bore, but
the contrary was true.* • A person might say **on
the contrary** to show that they disagree with
what has just been stated: *"Didn't you think
the movie was great?" "On the contrary, I
thought it was the dullest thing I'd ever seen."*
• **To the contrary** means suggesting the opposite of what has been stated: *Experts predicted the economy would collapse, but, to the
contrary, it continues to do extremely well.*

contrary /'kɑn,trer·i/ adj • *Most people supported the proposal, but Liz expressed a contrary opinion.*

contrary UNREASONABLE /kən'trer·i, 'kɑn,trer·i/
adj (of a person) intentionally wanting to disagree with and annoy other people • *I'm in a
contrary mood—I don't feel like practicing today.*

contrast /'kɑn·træst/ n [C/U] an easily noticed or understood difference between two or
more things • *She is quite petite, in contrast
with her tall sister.* [U] ○ *Contrasts between
Manhattan's rich and poor astonished him.* [C]

contrast /kən'træst, 'kɑn·træst/ v [I/T] to compare (someone or something) with another or
others, or to show the differences between two
or more things • *She contrasted Martin Luther
King's politics with those of Malcolm X.* [T] ○
*His aggressive style contrasts sharply with that
of his low-key predecessor.* [I]

contribute /kən'trɪb·juːt, -jət/ v [I/T] to help
by providing (money or support), esp. when
other people or conditions are also helping •
*Tourism contributes substantially to the local
economy.* [I] • If you contribute something you
wrote or created, you allow it to be published
or shown with pieces by other people: *She soon
began to contribute articles to newspapers and
magazines.* [T]

contributor /kən'trɪb·jət·ər/ n [C] a person
who helps by giving money, or someone whose
writing or art is published or shown with
pieces by other people • *a campaign contributor* ○ *He became a regular contributor to The
New Yorker.*

contribution /,kɑn·trə'bjuː·ʃən/ n [C/U] money, support, or other help • *He made a substantial contribution to the building fund.* [C]

contrite /'kɑn·traɪt, kən'traɪt/ adj feeling regret and guilt for something bad that you have
done • *She seemed genuinely contrite when she
apologized.*

contrition /kən'trɪʃ·ən/ n [U] • *Some of the
worst offenders expressed contrition.*

contrive /kən'traɪv/ v [I/T] to arrange (a sit-

uation) or make (a plan) in order to produce a
result that you want, esp. by being intelligent
or deceiving others • *He contrived to get into
the concert without a ticket.* [I] ○ *They contrived
a way to punish prisoners who didn't work.* [T]

contrived /kən'traɪvd/ adj too obviously designed to produce a particular result, and
therefore not seeming to happen naturally •
The movie's plot was much too contrived.

control /kən'troʊl/ n [C/U] the ability or power to decide or strongly influence the particular way in which something will happen or
someone will behave, or the condition of having such ability or power • *The first few
months he was running the company, Randy
didn't really feel in control.* [U] ○ *The man lost
control of his car and crashed into a tree.* [U]
○ *The fire was out of control for nearly two
hours before firefighters were able to get it under control.* [U] • A control is a rule or law that
sets a limit on something: *She argued for tightening controls on air pollution.* [C] • A **control
tower** is a tall building in an airport from
which air traffic is watched and directed.

control /kən'troʊl/ v [T] **-ll-** • *It's hard to control your temper when you're two years old.* ○
The temperature is controlled by a thermostat.

controller, comptroller /kən'troʊ·lər/ n [C] a
person in a business organization or government who is responsible for managing its
finances • *Perkins was promoted to corporate
controller.*

controls /kən'troʊlz/ pl n devices that are
used to operate a machine, vehicle, or aircraft
• *He was at the controls when the airplane
crashed.*

controversy /'kɑn·trə,vɜr·si/ n [C/U] a disagreement, often a public one, that involves
different ideas or opinions about something •
*The abortion issue is one of the nation's great-
est controversies.* [C] ○ *The president's decisions stirred up a lot controversy.* [U]

controversial /,kɑn·trə'vɜr·ʃəl, -'vɜr·siː·əl/ adj
causing or likely to cause disagreement • *a
controversial theory/movie*

conundrum /kə'nʌn·drəm/ n [C] a problem
that is difficult to deal with • *The best shows
pose moral conundrums that are hard to solve.*

convalesce /,kɑn·və'les/ v [I] to rest in order
to get better after an illness or operation •
*Dad's out of the hospital and convalescing at
home.*

convalescence /,kɑn·və'les·əns/ n [C/U] the
process or period of resting in order to get better after an illness or operation

convalescent /,kɑn·və'les·ənt/ adj [not grad-
able] • A **convalescent home** is a place where
people go when they need medical care but do
not need to be in a hospital.

convene /kən'viːn/ v [I/T] to meet formally as
a group, or to arrange (a meeting) of people or
groups for a serious purpose • *Peace talks will
convene next month.* [I]

convenient /kən'viːn·jənt/ *adj* suitable for your purposes and causing no difficulty for your schedule or plans • *Would 3 o'clock be a convenient time to meet?* ○ *I shop here because it's convenient.* • Convenient can also mean helpful to you but not completely honest: *Both men suffered convenient lapses of memory while testifying.*

conveniently /kən'viːn·jənt·li/ *adv* • *Our house is conveniently located near the station.*

convenience /kən'viːn·jəns/ *n* [C/U] • *I enjoy the convenience of having my groceries delivered.* [U] ○ *Repairs were scheduled at the customer's convenience.* [U] • A convenience is also anything that is easy to use and makes life comfortable: *modern conveniences like a microwave oven* [C] • A **convenience store** is a small store, often open for long hours, that sells food and other goods.

convent /'kɑn·vent, -vənt/ *n* [C] a building or group of buildings in which NUNS (= religious women) live or worship • Compare MONASTERY.

convention MEETING /kən'ven·tʃən/ *n* [C] a large meeting of a group of people who are involved in the same type of work or who have similar interests • *a Baptist convention* ○ *a convention of travel agents* ○ *a Star Trek convention* • A political convention is a meeting of a political party, esp. to choose someone to represent it in an election for a public office: *the Democratic/Republican national convention* • A **convention center** is a large building or group of buildings that is used for conventions.

convention CUSTOM /kən'ven·tʃən/ *n* [C/U] a way of doing something or appearing that is considered usual and correct • *He flouted convention by wearing sneakers with his tuxedo.* [U]

conventional /kən'ven·tʃən·əl/ *adj* following the usual practices of the past • *We were raised in a conventional, middle-class family.* ○ *It's a conventional hot-water heater* (= of the usual type). • Conventional weapons are not nuclear.

conventionally /kən'ven·tʃən·əl·i/ *adv* • *He was conventionally dressed in suit and tie.*

convention AGREEMENT /kən'ven·tʃən/ *n* [C] a formal agreement between countries • *a nuclear arms convention*

converge /kən'vɜrdʒ/ *v* [I] (of lines, roads, or paths) to move toward the same point and come closer together or meet, or (of people or vehicles) to come together and meet • *Six fire trucks converged on the burning factory.*

convergence /kən'vɜr·dʒəns/ *n* [C/U] • *There's a convergence of interests among the US, Canada, and Latin America.* [C]

conversant /kən'vɜr·sənt/ *adj* familiar with, having experience of, or knowing • *She's conversant with US foreign policy.* ○ *John's conver-*

sant in Mandarin (= can use it in conversation.)

conversation /ˌkɑn·vər'seɪ·ʃən/ *n* [C/U] an informal, usually private, talk in which two or more people exchange thoughts, feelings, or ideas, or in which news or information is given or discussed • *We had a brief conversation Friday.* [C] ○ *The topic of conversation was college plans.* [U] • If you make conversation, you cause someone to talk to you, esp. about unimportant matters. [U] • A **conversation piece** is an unusual object that causes people to start talking.

conversational /ˌkɑn·vər'seɪ·ʃən·əl/ *adj* • *He rarely speaks in a normal conversational tone.*

converse /kən'vɜrs/ *v* [I] to talk with someone • *She likes to converse with people from all walks of life.*

conversely /kən'vɜr·sli, 'kɑn,vɜr·sli/ *adv* [not gradable] from a different and opposite way of looking at this • *He was regarded either as too imitative to be considered original or, conversely, as being overly original.*

convert /kən'vɜrt/ *v* [I/T] to change the character, appearance, or operation of (something) • *We converted our oil furnace to gas to save money.* [T] • If someone is converted to something, they are persuaded to accept new preferences or beliefs: *Lateesha converted to Islam.* [I] ○ *My kids are trying to convert me to country music.* [T]

convert /'kɑn·vɜrt/ *n* [C] someone who accepts a new religion or belief • *a convert to Roman Catholicism/vegetarianism*

conversion /kən'vɜr·ʒən/ *n* [C/U] • *Conversion to the metric system has been underway in this country for decades.* [U]

convertible /kən'vɜrt̬·ə·bəl/ *n* [C] a car whose top can be folded back or removed so that there is no roof • A convertible is also a SOFA (= long, soft seat) that can be folded out to make a bed.

convex /kɑn'veks, kən-; 'kɑn·veks/ *adj* curved or swelling out • *a convex lens* • Compare CONCAVE.

convey COMMUNICATE /kən'veɪ/ *v* [T] to express (feelings, thoughts, or information) to other people • *He always conveyed a sense of genuine interest in his students.*

convey TRANSPORT /kən'veɪ/ *v* [T] to take or carry (someone or something) to a particular place • *The Marines were conveyed by helicopter to the battle zone.*

conveyer belt /kən'veɪ·ər·belt/ *n* [C] a continuous moving strip or surface that is used to transport objects from one place to another

convict /kən'vɪkt/ *v* [I/T] to decide officially in a court of law that someone is guilty of a particular crime • *There might not have been enough evidence to convict him.* [T] • USAGE: The opposite of convict is ACQUIT DECIDE NOT GUILTY.

convict /'kɑn·vɪkt/ *n* [C] someone who is in

prison because they have been judged guilty of a crime

conviction /kən'vɪk·ʃən/ n [C/U] • *His criminal record includes convictions for robberies in several states.* [C]

conviction /kən'vɪk·ʃən/ n [C/U] a strong belief that is not likely to change, or the strong feeling that your beliefs are right • *What are her religious/political convictions?* [C] ○ *His followers believed with varying degrees of conviction.* [U]

convince /kən'vɪns/ v [T] to cause (someone) to believe something or to do something • *We tried to convince my grandfather to live with us.* ○ *I'm convinced (that) she's lying.* [+ (that) clause]

convincing /kən'vɪn·sɪŋ/ adj • *North is a pretty convincing actor.* ○ *There are convincing arguments for outlawing tobacco.*

convincingly /kən'vɪn·sɪŋ·li/ adv • *She argued convincingly that the police had no right to stop her.*

convivial /kən'vɪv·iː·əl/ adj pleasant and friendly in manner or attitude • *The talks ended on a convivial note.*

convocation /ˌkɑn·və'keɪ·ʃən/ n [C/U] esp. Cdn a large, formal meeting, esp. for the ceremony at a university at the end of a course of study, or the act of arranging a large, formal meeting • *She was awarded an honorary degree at the spring convocation.* [C]

convoluted /'kɑn·və,luːt̬·əd/ adj (esp. of expression in speech or writing) having a complicated structure and therefore difficult to understand • *a convoluted story/speech/plot*

convoy /'kɑn·vɔɪ/ n [C] a group of ships or vehicles that travel together, esp. for protection • *a convoy of supply ships*

convulse /kən'vʌls/ v [I/T] to shake violently, or to cause (someone) to shake without control • *The audience convulsed with laughter.* [I]

convulsion /kən'vʌl·ʃən/ n [C usually pl] a shaking movement of the body that cannot be controlled, caused by illness or drug use • *The syndrome brought on convulsions.*

convulsive /kən'vʌl·sɪv/ adj • *convulsive laughter/sobs*

coo /kuː/ v [I] he/she/it **coos**, **cooing**, past **cooed** (esp. of some birds, such as PIGEONS) to make a low, soft call, or (of people) to speak in a soft, gentle way • *"Hello again," she cooed in his ear.*

cook /kʊk/ v [I/T] to prepare (food) by heating it in a particular way, or (of food) to be prepared in this way • *I'll cook the steaks on the grill.* [T] ○ *Who's cooking tonight, you or me?* [I] ○ *The potatoes are cooking.* [I]

cook /kʊk/ n [C] • *He's an excellent cook.* • A **cookbook** is a book containing detailed information on how to prepare and cook different foods. • A **cookout** is a meal cooked and eaten outside, often with a group of people.

cooking /'kʊk·ɪŋ/ n [U] the skill or activity of preparing and heating food to be eaten • *My mother always hated cooking.* • Cooking can also refer to a particular style of preparing food: *Southern/Italian cooking*

□ **cook up** obj PREPARE FOOD , **cook** obj **up** /'-'-/ v adv [M] to cook (food), esp. for others • *I know this place where they cook up a nice steak.*

□ **cook up** obj INVENT SOMETHING , **cook** obj **up** /'-'-/ v adv [M] infml to invent (something) imaginatively and sometimes dishonestly • *I'd like to find out who cooked up this scheme.*

cookie FOOD /'kʊk·i/ n [C] a sweet, usually round, flat cake • *She served chocolate chip/oatmeal/peanut butter cookies for dessert.*

cookie PERSON /'kʊk·i/ n [C] slang a person • *She's one tough cookie.*

cool COLD /kuːl/ adj [-er/-est only] slightly cold; of a low temperature • *a cool evening/breeze* ○ *Cereals should be stored in a cool, dry place.*

cool /kuːl/ v [I/T] to lose heat or cause (someone or something) to lose heat • *Remove the pie from the oven and let it cool for 30 minutes.* [I]

boil potatoes   fry eggs

bake a cake

steam vegetables   grill sausages   roast a chicken

cooking methods

○ *He jumped into the pool to cool (himself) off.* [I/T]

cool /kuːl/ *n* [U] • *He loved the cool* (= slight coldness) *of the early morning.*

cooler /'kuː·lər/ *n* [C] a container used for keeping food and drinks cold • *a cooler full of beer* • PIC CAMP

coolness /'kuːl·nəs/ *n* [U] • *There's a slight coolness in the air.*

cool UNFRIENDLY /kuːl/ *adj* [-er/-est only] unfriendly or not showing affection or interest in something or someone • *"Well, that's just too bad," Bill replied in a cool tone.*

coolly /'kuːl·li/ *adv* • *She responded coolly to his suggestion of dinner and a movie.*

coolness /'kuːl·nəs/ *n* [U] • *Grace had felt some coolness between them.*

cool CALM /kuːl/ *adj* [-er/-est only] calm and not anxious or frightened • *What's needed now is calm, cool thinking.* ○ *He made a cool assessment of the situation.*

cool /kuːl/ *n* [U] *infml* the ability to stay calm and not get upset or angry • *He's gone swimming with sharks without losing his cool.*

coolness /'kʊl·nəs/ *n* [U] • *She's known for her coolness under pressure on the tennis court.*

cool /kuːl/ *v* [I/T] to (cause to) become calm or weaker in feeling • *We need to allow time for tempers to cool.* [I] ○ *I wish Casey would cool his enthusiasm for video games.* [T] • (*slang*) **Cool it** means become calmer: *Cool it, man, you don't want to get us in trouble.*

cool GOOD /kuːl/ *adj* [-er/-est only] *infml* excellent; very good • *It's way cool to see you again!* • Cool is also used to show agreement with or acceptance of what someone says: *"He wants to come with us." "Cool."*

□**cool** (*obj*) **down/off, cool down/off** (*obj*) /'-'-'/ *v adv* [I/M] to stop feeling angry, or cause (someone) to stop feeling angry • *She hoped that keeping them apart for a few days might cool down some tempers.* [M] • If you cool down/off after exercising, you continue to exercise gently to prevent injury. [I]

coop /kuːp, kʊp/ *n* [C] a cage where small animals and birds are kept • *a chicken coop*

co-op /'koʊ·ɑp/ *n* [C] *short form of* **cooperative**, see at COOPERATE

cooped up /'kuːp'tʌp, 'kʊp-/ *adj* kept inside, or kept in a place that is too small • *I hate being cooped up in the house all day long.*

cooperate /koʊ'ɑp·ə,reɪt/ *v* [I] to act or work together for a shared purpose, or to help willingly when asked • *The company promised to cooperate fully with the law-enforcement authorities.* ○ *He refused to cooperate.*

cooperation /koʊˌɑp·ə'reɪ·ʃən/ *n* [U] • *Without the cooperation of local residents, this movie could not have been made.*

cooperative /koʊ'ɑp·ə·rəṭ·ɪv/ *adj* • *It was a cooperative effort.*

cooperative /koʊ'ɑp·ə·rəṭ·ɪv/, *short form* **co-op** *n* [C] a company owned and managed by

the people who work in it • *a farmers' cooperative* • A cooperative is also an apartment building in which ownership is shared by all the people living in it.

cooperative /koʊ'ɑp·ə·rəṭ·ɪv/ *adj* [not gradable] • *farm cooperative organizations* ○ *a cooperative day care center*

co-opt /koʊ'ɑpt, 'koʊ·ɑpt/ *v* [T] to persuade (someone who criticizes or disagrees with you) to join your group so that they can no longer oppose you • *The president co-opted journalists by inviting them to private dinners in the White House.* • To co-opt is also to claim something as your own when it was really created by others: *Republicans said the Democrats had co-opted their plan for tax reform.*

coordinate /koʊ'ɔːrd·ən,eɪt/ *v* [T] to make (various, separate things) work together • *Voluntary organizations will need to coordinate their efforts to help the homeless.* ○ *Patients learn how to coordinate movements of their arms and legs.*

coordination /koʊˌɔːrd·ən'eɪ·ʃən/ *n* [U] • *We need better coordination between state and local authorities.*

cop /kɑp/ *n* [C] *slightly infml* a police officer

cope /koʊp/ *v* [I] to deal with problems or difficulties, esp. with a degree of success • *Inside homes, many residents coped with broken glass and collapsed walls and chimneys.* ○ *Victims cope with feelings of anxiety, pain, anger, and fear.*

copilot /'koʊ,paɪ·lət/, **co-pilot** *n* [C] a second PILOT (= person who flies an aircraft) in an aircraft, who helps the pilot who is in charge

copious /'koʊ·piː·əs/ *adj* [not gradable] in large amounts; more than enough • *She took copious notes, filling page after page.*

cop-out /'kɑp·aʊt/, **cop out** *n* [C] *slang* a way or an excuse to avoid responsibility or to avoid doing something • *A plea of temporary insanity is a cop-out and should not be allowed, he said.*

copper METAL /'kɑp·ər/ *n* [U] a soft, red-brown metallic element, widely used in electrical equipment because heat and electricity can flow through it

copper COLOR /'kɑp·ər/ *adj* [not gradable], *n* [U] (of) a bright red-brown color

copter /'kɑp·tər/ *n* [C] *short form of* HELICOPTER

copulate /'kɑp·jə,leɪt/ *v* [I] to have sex

copulation /ˌkɑp·jə'leɪ·ʃən/ *n* [U]

copy PRODUCE /'kɑp·i/ *v* [T] to produce something that is exactly like (another thing), or to do something meant to be like someone or something else • *The design was copied from a 19th-century wallpaper.* ○ *He copied the file onto a diskette.*

copy /'kɑp·i/ *n* [C] • *I always keep copies of letters I have written.* ○ *Please make two copies of this.* • A copy is also a single unit of something produced in large numbers, usually for sale: *I* had a copy of her latest CD somewhere. ○ We ordered ten copies of the book.

copy TEXT /'kɑp·i/ n [U] text that is to be printed, or text that is used to sell a product • She writes advertising copy.

copycat /'kɑp·iːˌkæt/ adj [not gradable] done to copy someone or something • A copycat crime is one that appears to be a copy of a crime because it is so similar.

copyright /'kɑp·iːˌrɑɪt/ n [C/U], © symbol the legal right to control all use of an original work, such as a book, play, movie, or piece of music, for a particular period of time

coral /'kɔːr·əl, 'kɑr-/ n [U] a rocklike substance formed in the sea from masses of shells of very small sea animals, usually orange or red in color

cord THIN ROPE /kɔːrd/ n [C] a length of twisted threads or fibers • She pulled the cord of the Venetian blinds to raise them and let in the sun.

cord WIRE /kɔːrd/ n [C] a length of covered wire that connects electrical equipment to an electrical supply or to other equipment • an electric cord ○ a telephone cord

cordless /'kɔːrd·ləs/ adj (of a device) operated without a wire connected to an electrical supply by using electricity produced by a BATTERY • a cordless phone

cordial /'kɔːr·dʒəl/ adj friendly or pleasant • a cordial greeting/smile ○ cordial relations

cordon /'kɔːrd·ᵊn/ n [C] a line of police, soldiers, vehicles, etc., positioned around an area to guard it or to close it off

cordon off obj, **cordon** obj **off** /'--'-/ v adv [M] • Police cordoned off a four-block area and tried to convince the gunmen to release the hostages.

corduroy /'kɔːrd·əˌrɔɪ/ n [U] a thick, cotton material woven with raised parallel lines on the outside, used esp. for jackets and pants

core CENTER /kɔːr, koʊr/ n [C] the center or most important part of something • Farmers formed the core of traditional party support. ○ Safety concerns are at the core of the new federal policies.

core /koʊr/ adj [not gradable] central; basic • Robertson's remarks encouraged his core supporters, mostly religious conservatives. ○ The notion of love is one of the core values of our civilization. ○ We have to concentrate on the core business, management said.

core FRUIT /koʊr/ n [C] the hard, central part of some fruits, such as apples, which contains the seeds

core /kɔːr, koʊr/ v [T] to remove the core of (fruit)

cork /kɔːrk/ n [C/U] a light material obtained from the BARK (= outer layer) of a tree, or a small, soft cylinder of this material that is pushed into the top of a bottle to close it • The waiter took the cork out of the bottle and poured us each a little wine. [C] • A **corkscrew** is a device for pulling a cork out of a bottle.

corn FOOD /kɔːrn/ n [U] a tall plant grown for its whole yellow or white seeds which are eaten cooked, made into flour, or fed to animals • Let's pick up a half dozen ears of corn for supper. • **Corn bread** is a type of sweetened bread made from **cornmeal**, a rough flour of crushed corn. • A **cornfield** is a field used for growing corn. • **Corn flakes** are a breakfast food of small, dry pieces of crushed corn, often sweetened and served with milk. • **Corn on the cob** is the tubelike part of the corn with its sweet yellow or white KERNELS (= seeds) left on it, served with butter as a cooked vegetable. • **Cornstarch** is a flour made from corn, used to thicken sauces, etc. **Corn syrup** is a sweet, thick liquid made from corn, used esp. in making candy.

corn SKIN /kɔːrn/ n [C] a small, often painful area of hard skin that forms on the foot, esp. on the toes

cornea /'kɔːr·niː·ə/ n [C] the transparent covering of the eye that protects the front of it

corned beef /kɔːrnd'biːf/ n [U] BEEF (= meat from cattle) that has been preserved in salted water and spices

corner /'kɔːr·nər/ n [C] the point or angle formed when two lines or surfaces meet • the corner of a table ○ We could put that chair in the far corner of the room. • A corner is also a place where two streets meet: I'll meet you at the corner of Pine and Market at 7:30. • A corner can also be a part or area of a place: They lived in a remote corner of Wyoming. • A **cornerstone** is a large stone near the base of a corner of a building, often giving information about the building and sometimes put in position with a ceremony: A large group of officials attended a cornerstone laying at that new plant.

corner /'kɔːr·nər/ v [I/T] • If you corner a person or an animal, you force them into a place or situation from which they cannot escape: After a chase, the police cornered him in a hallway. [T] • If an organization or company **corners the market**, it controls the available supply of a type of product or the ability to sell it.

cornerstone /'kɔːr·nərˌstoʊn/ n [C] something of great importance on which everything else depends • Funds for the school system were the cornerstone of his budget proposal. ○ All the parties to the dispute agree that ready access to the law is a cornerstone of democracy.

cornice /'kɔːr·nəs/ n [C] a decorative border of wood or stone at the edge of the ceiling of a room or under the roof of a building

cornrow /'kɔːrn·roʊ/ n [C] one of a number of strips of hair that have been twisted close to the head in thin rows

corny /'kɔːr·ni/ adj infml emotional and obvious from having been used too often • It *sounds corny, but when I get to the beach I feel like a kid again.*

coronary /ˈkɔːr·əˌner·i, ˈkɑr-/ *adj* [not gradable] *medical* relating to the **blood vessels** (= tubes carrying blood) around the heart, or to the heart and diseases of the heart • *coronary artery/heart disease* ○ *the hospital coronary care unit*

coronary /ˈkɔːr·əˌner·i, ˈkɑr-/ *n* [C] a **heart attack**, see at HEART ⟨ORGAN⟩

coronation /ˌkɔːr·əˈneɪ·ʃən, ˌkɑr-/ *n* [C] a ceremony at which a person is made king or queen

coroner /ˈkɔːr·ə·nər, ˈkɑr-/ *n* [C] an official who examines the causes of a person's death, esp. if it was violent or unexpected

corporal /ˈkɔːr·prəl, -pə·rəl/ *n* [C] a person in the military of low rank, below a SERGEANT

corporal punishment /ˈkɔːr·prəlˈpʌn·ɪʃ·mənt, -pə·rəl-/ *n* [C] physical punishment, esp. by hitting with the hand or with a stick • *The state senate voted to outlaw the use of corporal punishment against foster children.*

corporation /ˌkɔːr·pəˈreɪ·ʃən/ (*abbreviation* **Corp.**) *n* [C] an organization, esp. a business, that has a legally separate existence from the people who run it • *multinational corporations* ○ *She was elected to the board of directors of the corporation.*

corporate /ˈkɔːr·pə·rət/ *adj* • *corporate finance/law*

corps /kɔːr, koʊr/ *n* [C] *pl* **corps** /kɔːrz, koʊrz/ a group of people who work together in a particular activity • *The diplomatic corps in Washington includes representatives of most of the countries in the world.* • A corps is also a military unit or a special part of a country's military forces: *the Marine Corps*

corpse /kɔːrps/ *n* [C] a dead body, esp. of a human

corpulent /ˈkɔːr·pjə·lənt/ *adj fml* fat • *a corpulent man*

corpuscle /ˈkɔːr·pʌs·əl/ *n* [C] any of the red or white cells in the blood

corral /kəˈræl/ *n* [C] an area surrounded by a fence for keeping horses or cattle

corral /kəˈræl/ *v* [T] **-ll-** • *A couple of cowboys corralled the horses.* ○ (*fig.*) *The party has to learn how to corral younger voters if it wants to win the next election.*

correct /kəˈrekt/ *adj* in agreement with the true facts or with a generally accepted standard • *It's your responsibility to see that your tax return is correct.* ○ *Do you have the correct time?* ○ *"Did you testify that you recognized this man?" "That's correct."*

correct /kəˈrekt/ *v* [T] to show or fix what is wrong; make right • *He knew she was mistaken but made no effort to correct her.* ○ *It is the policy of this newspaper to correct errors of fact that appear in its news columns.* ○ *Doctors can now use laser surgery to correct certain eye problems.*

correctly /kəˈrek·tli/ *adv* • *Have I pronounced your name correctly?*

correctness /kəˈrekt·nəs/ *n* [U]

correction /kəˈrek·ʃən/ *n* [C/U] a change to make something right or correct, or the act of making such changes • *I made a number of corrections to the manuscript.* [C] ○ *Several errors in this report need correction.* [U]

corrective /kəˈrek·tɪv/ *adj fml* intended to improve something or make it right • *Corrective measures must be taken at once.*

correlation /ˌkɔːr·əˈleɪ·ʃən, ˌkɑr-/ *n* [C] a connection between two or more things • *There is a proven correlation between educational level and income.*

correlate /ˈkɔːr·əˌleɪt, ˈkɑr-/ *v* [I/T] • *Transmission of AIDS is highly correlated with alcohol use.* [T]

correspond ⟨BE SIMILAR⟩ /ˌkɔːr·əˈspɑnd, ˌkɑr-/ *v* [I] to be similar or the same in some way • *Her version of that meeting does not correspond with what I remember* (= I remember it differently).

corresponding /ˌkɔːr·əˈspɑn·dɪŋ, ˌkɑr-/ *adj* [not gradable] • *Income was up compared to the corresponding* (= similar) *period last year.*

correspond ⟨WRITE⟩ /ˌkɔːr·əˈspɑnd, ˌkɑr-/ *v* [I] to exchange letters • *I corresponded with him when he was at school.* ○ *We correspond by e-mail.*

correspondence /ˌkɔːr·əˈspɑn·dəns, ˌkɑr-/ *n* [U] letters written from one person to another, or the activity of writing and receiving letters • *She was behind in her correspondence, and had at least six letters to write.*

correspondent /ˌkɔːr·əˈspɑn·dənt, ˌkɑr-/ *n* [C] • *Willa was not a good correspondent, and often didn't write for months.*

correspondent /ˌkɔːr·əˈspɑn·dənt, ˌkɑr-/ *n* [C] a person employed by a newspaper, magazine, television station, etc., to report news on a particular subject or from a distant place • *He works as a correspondent in Moscow.*

corridor ⟨PASSAGE⟩ /ˈkɔːr·əd·ər, ˈkɑr-, -əˌdɔːr/ *n* [C] a long passage in a building, ship, or train, esp. with rooms on one or both side • *The bathroom is at the end of the corridor.*

corridor ⟨REGION⟩ /ˈkɔːr·əd·ər, ˈkɑr-, -əˌdɔːr/ *n* [C] a long, narrow region between two or more large cities, or an area along a busy road • *the Boston to Washington corridor* ○ *the Route 28 corridor*

corroborate /kəˈrɑb·əˌreɪt/ *v* [T] to add information in support of (an idea, opinion, or statement) • *Recent research seems to corroborate the theory.*

corroboration /kəˌrɑb·əˈreɪ·ʃən/ *n* [U] • *She accused him without corroboration of any kind.*

corrode /kəˈroʊd/ *v* [I/T] to destroy or be destroyed, esp. by acid or RUST, usually over a long period of time • *Rain water corroded the metal pipes.* [T]

corrosion /kə'rou·ʒən/ n [U] • *These alloys protect against corrosion.*

corrosive /kə'rou·sɪv, -zɪv/ adj • *highly corrosive acid*

corrugated /'kɔːr·ə,ɡeɪt̬·əd, 'kɑr-/ adj [not gradable] (esp. of sheets of iron and cardboard) having parallel rows of folds that look like a series of waves when seen from the edge • *corrugated tin/cardboard*

corrupt /kə'rʌpt/ adj dishonest and willing to use your position or power to your own advantage, esp. for money • *It's been called the most politically corrupt city in the nation.* • Corrupt also means bad: *Your philosophy is corrupt.*

corrupt /kə'rʌpt/ v [T] • *Power corrupts, and absolute power corrupts absolutely.* ∘ *Don't let your friends corrupt you* (= have a bad moral influence on you). • If information in a computer is corrupted, it is damaged and can no longer be used.

corruption /kə'rʌp·ʃən/ n [U] • *political corruption*

corsage /kɔːr'sɑʒ, -'sɑdʒ/ n [C] a small group of flowers that a woman pins to her clothes near her chest or wears on her wrist, usually for a special occasion

corset /'kɔːr·sət/ n [C] a tight piece of underwear made from elastic material, worn in the past on the middle part of a woman's body to make her waist appear smaller

cortege /kɔːr'teʒ/ n [C] a slowly moving line of people or cars at a funeral

cortisone /'kɔːrt̬·ə,zoun, -,soun/ n [U] a HORMONE (= chemical produced by some organs of the body) that is used medically, esp. for treating painful joints and skin problems

cosmetic /kɑz'met̬·ɪk/ adj (esp. of changes and improvements) intended to improve the appearance of something without changing its basic structure; SUPERFICIAL • *Whether the change is more cosmetic than concrete is a matter of opinion.* • **Cosmetic surgery** is any medical operation that is intended to improve someone's appearance rather than their health.

cosmetics /kɑz'met̬·ɪks/ pl n substances put on the face or body that are intended to improve its appearance or quality • *Some women spend a fortune on cosmetics.*

cosmonaut /'kɑz·mə,nɔːt, -,nɑt/ n [C] a Soviet or Russian ASTRONAUT (= a person trained to go into space)

cosmopolitan /,kɑz·mə'pɑl·ət̬·ən/ adj containing people and things from many different parts of the world, or having experience of many different places and things • *a cosmopolitan city* ∘ *Gwen's a very cosmopolitan young woman.*

cosmos /'kɑz·məs, -mous/ n [U] the universe considered as a system with an order and pattern

cosmic /'kɑz·mɪk/ adj of or relating to the cosmos rather than to the earth alone • *cosmic dust/rays* • (*infml*) Cosmic also means very great: *a disaster of cosmic proportions*

cost MONEY /kɔːst/ n [C/U] the amount of money needed to buy, do, or make something, or an amount spent for something • *Education costs continue to rise.* [C] ∘ *Most computers come with software included at no extra cost.* [U] ∘ *The area has both high-cost and low-cost housing.* [U] • (*law*) Costs is the money given to a person who wins a legal case to pay for the cost of taking the matter to a law court. [pl] • **At cost** means without a profit: *We were able to buy the furniture from a friend at cost.* • An activity that is **cost-effective** gives you the most value for the amount paid: *It's not cost-effective to heat the whole building if only three people are working here.* • The **cost of living** is the amount of money that a person needs to buy food, housing, and other basic things: *The cost of living is lower in the Midwest.* • LP PRICE

cost /kɔːst/ v [T] *past* **cost** • *The trip will cost (you) $1000.* ∘ *It costs a lot to buy a house these days.* • *The repair work* **cost an arm and a leg/a small fortune** (= was very expensive).

costly /'kɔːs·tli/ adj expensive • *This procedure can be very costly.*

cost SOMETHING GIVEN /kɔːst/ n [U] that which is given, needed, or lost in order to obtain something • *The fire cost 14 people their lives.* • *We realized we had to fight this* **at any cost/ at all costs** (= using everything we have).

cost /kɔːst/ v [T] *past* **cost** • *Drunk driving can cost you your license.*

costly /'kɔːs·tli/ adj • *Her costly mistake allowed the opponents to score.*

costar /'kou·stɑr/ n [C] a famous actor appearing with one or more other famous actors in a film or a play

costar /'kou·stɑr, 'kou'stɑr/ v [I/T] **-rr-** • *Bergman and Bogart costarred in "Casablanca."* [I]

costume /'kɑs·tuːm, -tʃuːm/ n [C/U] a set of clothes worn in order to look like someone else, esp. for a party or as part of an entertainment • *a clown costume* [C] • A costume is also the set of clothes typical of a particular country or period of history: *The dancers dressed in national costume.* [U] • **Costume jewelry** is jewelry that is not expensive or is made from artificial jewels.

cot /kɑt/ n [C] a narrow bed made of strong material attached to a frame, esp. one that can be folded and easily carried

cottage /'kɑt̬·ɪdʒ/ n [C] a small house, usually away from a city or town

cottage cheese /,kɑt̬·ɪdʒ'tʃiːz/ n [U] soft, white, lumpy cheese made from sour milk

cotton /'kɑt̬·ən/ n [U] thread or cloth made from the fiber surrounding the seeds of a tall plant, or these fibers themselves • *a cotton shirt/dress* • **Cotton balls** are small balls of absorbent cotton, used esp. for cleaning the skin. • **Cotton candy** is a large, soft ball of sugar that has been spun in a special machine to form long fibers which are collected on a stick. • A **cotton swab** is a short stick with a small amount of cotton on each end, used for cleaning esp. the ears.

cottonwood /'kɑt·ən,wʊd/ *n* [C] a type of POPLAR tree that grows in North America and produces seeds with soft, white fibers that look like cotton

couch SEAT /kaʊtʃ/ *n* [C] a piece of furniture with a back and usually arms, that two or more people can sit on at once; a SOFA • (*infml*) A **couch potato** is a person who sits and watches a lot of television and does not have an active life.

couch EXPRESS /kaʊtʃ/ *v* [T] to express (something) in a particular way, esp. in order not to upset or anger the person addressed • *They want to couch their response in diplomatic, not threatening, terms.*

cougar /'kuː·ɡər/, **mountain lion, puma, panther** *n* [C] a large, brown, wild cat found in North and South America

cough /kɔːf/ *v* [I] to force air out of your lungs through your throat with a short, loud sound • *The smoke from the bonfire made me cough.* ◦ (*fig.*) *The car engine coughed a few times, but wouldn't start.*

cough /kɔːf/ *n* [C] • *a dry cough* ◦ *There are lots of coughs and colds going around this winter.* • **Cough medicine/syrup** is a liquid that you take to help stop coughing. • **Cough drops** are hard candies that you suck so that you will cough less.

☐ **cough up** *obj* FORCE OUT LIQUID , **cough** *obj* **up** /'-'-/ *v adv* [M] to force (liquid) out of your lungs • *She coughed up a lot of phlegm.*

☐ **cough up** *obj* PAY , **cough** *obj* **up** /'-'-/ *v adv* [M] *infml* to produce (esp. money) unwillingly • *I had to cough up $35 for a parking fine.* [M]

could CAN /kʊd, kəd/ *past simple of* CAN • *You said we could watch television when we finished our homework.* ◦ *When I was younger I could stay up all night and then go to work.*

could ASK PERMISSION /kʊd, kəd/ *v aux* he/she/it **could** used as a more polite form of can when asking for permission • *Could I speak to Mr. Harley, please?* • LP AUXILIARY VERBS

could REQUEST /kʊd, kəd/ *v aux* he/she/it **could** used as a more polite form of can when making a request • *Could you lend me $5?* • LP AUXILIARY VERBS

could BE POSSIBLE /kʊd, kəd/ *v aux* used to express possibility, esp. slight or uncertain possibility • *A lot of crime could be prevented.* ◦ *It could be days before we hear from her.* ◦ *I could have been an actor.* • If you **could care less**, you don't care at all: *Most fans could care less about it.* • *I was so embarrassed* **I could have died** (= I was very embarrassed). • If you say that you **could hardly believe** your **eyes/ears**, you mean that something you saw/

heard was very surprising: *When he said they're getting divorced, I could hardly believe my ears.* • LP AUXILIARY VERBS

could SUGGEST /kʊd, kəd/ *v aux* he/she/it **could** used for making a suggestion • *We could go to the movies.* • If someone or something **could do with** something, they want or need it: *This house could do with a good cleaning.* • LP AUXILIARY VERBS

could SHOULD /kʊd, kəd/ *v aux* he/she/it **could** used for saying what you think someone else should do • *You could try to look a little more enthusiastic.* • LP AUXILIARY VERBS

couldn't /'kʊd·ənt/ *contraction of* could not • *Couldn't you leave on Saturday instead?* • If you **couldn't care less**, you don't care at all. • If you **couldn't agree more/less** about something, you mean you completely agree/disagree: *Bob says it's the government's fault, and I couldn't agree more.*

council /'kaʊn·səl/ *n* [C] a group of people elected or chosen to make decisions or give advice on a particular subject, to represent a particular group of people, or to run a particular organization • *the UN Security Council* ◦ *The council is being pressured to approve the plan.* • A **councilman/councilwoman** is an elected member of a local government.

counsel /'kaʊn·səl/ *v* [T] **-l-** or **-ll-** to give advice, esp. on social or personal problems • *He was counseling athletes not to take steroids.*

counsel /'kaʊn·səl/ *n* [U] *fml* • *The president sought counsel from his advisers.* • (*law*) Counsel is one or more of the lawyers taking part in a case or legally representing a person or organization: *Maloney skipped the meeting on the advice of counsel.*

counselor, counsellor /'kaʊn·sə·lər/ *n* [C] a person whose job is to provide advice, help, or encouragement • *a marriage/guidance counselor* ◦ *a camp counselor* • (*law*) Counselor is used to address a lawyer: *Good afternoon, counselor.*

count CALCULATE /kaʊnt/ *v* [I/T] to say the names of numbers one after the other in order, or to calculate (the number of units in a group) • *By the time I count to three, you'd better be in bed.* [I] ◦ *The teachers counted the students as they boarded the bus.* [T] ◦ *There'll be eight for dinner, counting* (= including) *us.* [T] ◦ *Can you count how many pencils are left?* [+ wh- word] • Something that you **can/could count on one hand** happens very rarely or exists in very small numbers: *I could count the number of times he's been on time on one hand.* • **Don't count your chickens before they hatch** means you should not make plans that depend on something good happening before you know that it has actually happened.

count /kaʊnt/ *n* [C/U] a calculation of the number of units in a group • *We need a count of the number of e-mail inquiries.* [C] • If you **keep/lose count**, you remember/forget a total: *There are so many birds, I've lost count.* [U] • A count is also a scientifically measured amount of something: *a low blood/sperm count* [C] • **On the count of** means after counting to: *On the count of three, run.*

count CONSIDER /kaʊnt/ *v* [I/T] to consider or be considered as • *He counts Lucy as one of his closest friends.* [T] ○ *Does homework count toward my grade?* [I] ○ *Her inexperience may count against her* (= be considered as something bad). [I]

count VALUE /kaʊnt/ *v* [I] to have value or importance • *I've always believed that happiness counts more than money.*

count CRIME /kaʊnt/ *n* [C] *law* a separate item included in a criminal accusation against someone • *She was found guilty on two counts of murder.*

count OPINION /kaʊnt/ *n* [C usually pl] a statement of belief in a discussion or argument • *I think you're wrong on all counts.*

□ **count down** /'-'-/ *v adv* [I] to count backward to zero • *She counts down the top 10 music videos every week.*

countdown /'kaʊnt·daʊn/ *n* [C] an act of counting backward to zero, esp. before sending a spacecraft into space, or a period leading to an important event • *The countdown to Tuesday's primary elections has begun.*

□ **count** *obj* **in** /'-'-/ *v adv* [T] *infml* to include (someone) in an activity or plan • *"We're going to the ballgame—want to come?" "Sure, count me in."*

□ **count on** /'-,-/ *v prep* [T] to depend on (someone) or expect (something) • *You can always count on Michael in a crisis.* ○ *She didn't count on rain, and didn't bring an umbrella.*

□ **count out** /'-'-/ *v adv* [T] to count (each item in a group) one at a time • *The bank clerk counted out $100 in $20 bills.*

□ **count** *obj* **out** /'-'-/ *v adv* [T] *infml* to not include (someone) in an activity • *"Whose coming swimming?" "Count me out—it's too cold."*

countable noun /'kaʊn·ə·bəl/ *n* [C] *specialized* (in grammar) a noun that has both a singular and a plural form and names something that can be counted because there can be one or more of it • *"Book" and "decision" are both countable nouns.* • USAGE: Countable nouns are marked [C] in this dictionary. • Compare UNCOUNTABLE NOUN. LP PLURALS OF NOUNS

countenance FACE /'kaʊnt·ⁿn·əns/ *n* [C/U] *literary* the appearance or expression of someone's face • *Her countenance masked her feelings.* [C]

countenance APPROVE OF /'kaʊnt·ⁿn·əns/ *v* [T] to find (an activity) acceptable; to approve of or give support to (something) • *This school will not countenance drug abuse.*

counter SURFACE /'kaʊnt·ər/ *n* [C] a long, flat, narrow surface in a store, bank, restaurant, etc., at which people are served • *He sat down at the counter of the diner and ordered a cup of*

coffee. • A counter is also a flat surface in a kitchen on which food can be prepared.

counter OPPOSE /'kaʊnt·ər/ *v* [I/T] to react to (something) with an opposing opinion or action; to defend yourself against (something) • *Congress strengthened the role of the FBI to counter the threat to American security.* [T]

counter /'kaʊnt·ər/ *adv* [not gradable] • *David's decision to drop out of school to write plays ran counter to* (= was directly opposite to) *his parent's expectations.*

counteract /,kaʊnt·ə·'rækt/ *v* [T] to reduce or remove the effect of (something) by producing an opposite effect • *The tax must be adjusted upward to counteract inflation.*

counterattack /'kaʊnt·ə·rə,tæk/ *n* [C] an attack intended to stop or oppose an attack by an enemy or competitor

counterattack /'kaʊnt·ə·rə,tæk/ *v* [I] • *Faced with a lawsuit for negligence, he counterattacked by filing charges against his accusers.*

counterclockwise /,kaʊnt·ər'klɑk,waɪz/ *adj, adv* [not gradable] (moving around) in a direction opposite to that of the pointers of a clock or watch • Compare **clockwise** at CLOCK.

counterfeit /'kaʊnt·ər,fɪt/ *adj* [not gradable] copied exactly in order to make someone believe that the copy is the original • *A lot of brand-name merchandise sold on the streets is counterfeit.*

counterfeit /'kaʊnt·ər,fɪt/ *n* [C] • *The bank said this $100 bill was a counterfeit.*

counterfeit /'kaʊnt·ər,fɪt/ *v* [T] • *They were accused of counterfeiting credit cards and selling them.*

counterpart /'kaʊnt·ər,pɑrt/ *n* [C] a person or thing that has the same position or purpose as another person or thing in a different place or organization • *The president will meet with his Brazilian counterpart tomorrow.*

counterproductive /,kaʊnt·ər·prə'dʌk·tɪv/ *adj* having an effect that is the opposite of what you intend or desire • *As a way to improve traffic, widening roads can be counterproductive, as it may just encourage more people to drive.*

countless /'kaʊnt·ləs/ *adj* [not gradable] very many; too many to be counted • *Countless times when I needed someone to talk to, she would listen.*

country POLITICAL UNIT /'kʌn·tri/ *n* [C] an area of land that forms an independent political unit with its own government; a nation considered esp. as a place • *Cuba is my native country, but I now live in Florida.*

country NATURAL LAND /'kʌn·tri/ *n* [U] land that is not in towns, cities, or industrial areas and is either used for farming or left in its natural condition • *I'm spending next weekend in the country with a friend.* • **Country (and western)** is a style of popular music based on traditional music of the western and southern

US. • A **country club** is a private social and sports organization in the countryside, open only to its members and their guests. • **Countryside** is land not in towns, cities, or industrial areas which is either used for farming or left in its natural condition: *Much of Connecticut's countryside is dotted with large estates and horse farms.*

countryman (*pl* **-men**) /ˈkʌn·tri·mən/, **countrywoman** (*pl* **-women**) /ˈkʌn·tri:ˌwʊm·ən/ *n* [C] a person from your own country

county /ˈkaʊnt·i/ *n* [C] the largest political division of most states in the US • *Texas is divided into 254 counties.*

coup /kuː/ *n* [C] *pl* **coups** /kuːz/ an unexpectedly successful achievement • *It was quite a coup for her to get an interview with the First Lady.*

couple SOME /ˈkʌp·əl/ *n* [U] two or a few things that are similar or the same, or two or a few people who are in some way connected • *I'm packing a couple of sweaters in case it gets cold.*

couple TWO PEOPLE /ˈkʌp·əl/ *n* [C] two people who are married or who spend a lot of time together esp. in a romantic relationship • *We're having two couples over for dinner.*

□**couple with** /ˈkʌp·əl/ *v prep* [T] to consider along with or in addition to (something else) • *The new city tax, coupled with Social Security deductions, will take a huge bite out of everybody's paycheck.*

coupon /ˈkuː·pɑn, ˈkjuː-/ *n* [C] a piece of paper that you can use to buy a product or service at a reduced price or to get it free, or to get information, used by businesses as a way to make their name more widely known or to encourage sales • *Send in this coupon with your name and address for a free travel brochure.*

courage /ˈkɜr·ɪdʒ, ˈkʌ·rɪdʒ/ *n* [U] the ability to control fear and to be willing to deal with something that is dangerous, difficult, or unpleasant • *He lacked the courage to tax the American people to pay for his Great Society programs.* ○ *It took me several months to get up the courage to ask her to lunch.*

courageous /kəˈreɪ·dʒəs/ *adj* • *She showed herself to be a courageous journalist.*

courier /ˈkʊr·iː·ər, ˈkɜr·iː-, ˈkʌ·riː-/ *n* [C] a person who carries messages or documents for someone else

course DIRECTION /kɔːrs, koʊrs/ *n* [C] the particular path something such as an aircraft or ship takes as it moves, or the path along which a river flows • *A southern course will take our flight over Texas.*

course DEVELOPMENT /kɔːrs, koʊrs/ *n* [C] the often gradual development of something, or the way something happens, or a way of doing something • *He always chats with waiters and waitresses and becomes their best friends during the course of dinner.* • If you say **of course,**

you mean yes, certainly: *"May I use your telephone?" "Of course, go right ahead."* • If you say **of course not** in answering a question that suggests doing something, you are saying that you are not in any way opposed to what is suggested: *"Do you mind if I have a second helping? It's delicious!" "Of course not, I'm glad you like it."* • **Of course** and **of course not** are often used in speech to say yes or no with emphasis: *"Are you sure you locked the front door?" "Of course."* ○ *"Will they cancel the soccer game if it rains?" "Of course not."*

course CLASSES /kɔːrs, koʊrs/ *n* [C] a set of classes in a subject at a school or university • *He taught a course in film history at Harvard University.*

course SPORTS AREA /kɔːrs, koʊrs/ *n* [C] an area used for a sports event • *a golf course*

course MEAL /kɔːrs, koʊrs/ *n* [C] a part of a meal served separately from the other parts • *the meat course*

court LAW /kɔːrt, koʊrt/ *n* [C/U] the place where trials and other legal cases happen • *He is bringing charges against us and said, "I'll see you in court."* [U] • The **court** is the judge or judges who are in charge of the way a legal case happens and sometimes make decisions about it. [U] ○ *The newspaper agreed to settle the case out of court* (= agreed to a deal that avoided a trial). [U] • A **courthouse** is a building that contains rooms where trials and other legal cases happen: *a county courthouse* • A **courtroom** is a usually large room where trials and other legal cases happen.

court SPORTS /kɔːrt, koʊrt/ *n* [C] a rectangular area used as the playing area in some sports • *a racquetball/tennis court*

court (*obj*) PLEASE /kɔːrt, koʊrt/ *v* to try to please (someone) in the hope of receiving their support, approval, or affection, or to try to get (something) that benefits you • *Both Wilder and Clinton had been courting black voters who are considered pivotal in the Southern primaries.* [T]

courtship /ˈkɔːrt·ʃɪp, ˈkoʊrt-/ *n* [C/U] *dated* the period in which two people have a romantic relationship that often leads to marriage • *They were married in 1923 after a long courtship.* [C]

court RISK /kɔːrt, koʊrt/ *v* [T] to increase the risk of (something bad happening) • *If you drink and drive you are courting disaster.*

courteous /ˈkɜrt̬·iː·əs/ *adj* polite and respectful • *The ticket clerk was courteous and helpful.*

courtesy /ˈkɜrt̬·ə·si/ *n* [C/U] polite behavior, or a polite action • *They should teach drivers to show pedestrians some courtesy.* [U]

court–martial /ˈkɔːrtˌmɑr·ʃəl, ˈkoʊrt-/ *n* [C] *pl* **courts-martial** /ˈkɔːrtˌsmɑr·ʃəl, ˈkoʊrt-/ or **court-martials** a military court, or a trial in a military court, that judges members of the armed forces

court–martial /ˈkɔːrtˌmɑr·ʃəl, ˈkoʊrt-/ *v* [T] •

He was court-martialed for leaving his post without permission.

courtyard /'kɔːrt·jard, 'kourt-/ *n* [C] an area of flat ground outside and partly or completely surrounded by one or more buildings • *Entrance to the apartment building is through a central courtyard.*

cousin /'kʌz·ən/ *n* [C] a child of a person's aunt or uncle • PIC FAMILY TREE

cove /kouv/ *n* [C] a curved part of a coast that partly encloses an area of water; a small BAY

covenant /'kʌv·ə·nənt/ *n* [C] a formal agreement between countries, organizations, or people

cover PLACE OVER /'kʌv·ər/ *v* [T] to put or spread something over (something), esp. in order to hide or protect it, or to lie on the surface of (something) • *Once the rice comes to a boil, turn down the flame and cover the pot.* ○ *She covered the child with a blanket.* • If something covers an area of a particular size, it is equal to an area of that size: *Grand Canyon National Park covers over a million acres.* • A **covered wagon** is a large vehicle with four wheels and a high, covered frame which is pulled by horses or other animals, used in the past to transport people and goods to the western part of the US.

covered wagon

cover /'kʌv·ər/ *n* [C] something that is placed over something, often for protection, or that lies over something else to form a layer • *I keep my computer printer under a plastic cover.* • The cover of a book or magazine is the stiff, outside part of it, usually made of thick paper or cardboard. • A cover is also a layer of a material used to keep a person in bed warm: *On cold days, she pulled the covers up to her chin.* [pl] • If you read something **(from) cover to cover**, you read it all the way through from the beginning to the end. • **Coveralls** are a type of clothing made in one piece that cover and protect most of the body and are worn for doing dirty work. • A **cover charge** is a charge that may be added to the amount that a customer pays for food and drinks in a restaurant or **nightclub** to pay for service or entertainment. • A **cover story** is a report or article connected with the picture on the front of a magazine.

cover TRAVEL /'kʌv·ər/ *v* [T] to travel (a particular distance) • *We covered 600 miles in the last two days.* ○ (*fig.*) *Her lecture covered a lot of ground, from Renaissance art to modern art.*

cover INCLUDE /'kʌv·ər/ *v* [T] to deal with or include (someone or something) • *The travel guide covers all the museums and historic places.*

cover REPORT /'kʌv·ər/ *v* [T] to report or write about (esp. a particular subject) in a continuing way for a newspaper, magazine, television, or radio • *Harold covers sports for the Times, and Joan covers real-estate developments.*

coverage /'kʌv·ə·rɪdʒ/ *n* [U] • *The TV station is trying to improve its coverage of local news.*

cover BE ENOUGH /'kʌv·ər/ *v* [T] to be enough money to pay for • *Will $150 cover your expenses?*

cover PROTECT /'kʌv·ər/ *v* [T] to protect (someone or something) from financial loss, damage, accident, or having something stolen; to INSURE • *Our car insurance covers us up to $250,000 for personal injury.*

coverage /'kʌv·ə·rɪdʒ/ *n* [U] • *I've got $50,000 worth of coverage for the contents of my house.*

cover SHELTER /'kʌv·ər/ *n* [U] shelter or protection, esp. in a dangerous situation • *Police officers took cover behind a bus* (= used a bus to protect them) *as shots rang out.*

cover AIM A GUN /'kʌv·ər/ *v* [T] to aim a gun at (someone) • *I've got you covered—put your hands up!*

cover DO SOMEONE'S JOB /'kʌv·ər/ *v* [I always + adv/prep] to do (someone else's job or duty) when they are absent • *Could you cover the phones while I'm away from the office?* [T]

□ **cover up** (*obj*), **cover** (*obj*) **up** /'--'-/ *v adv* [I/M] to keep (something unpleasant) secret or hidden • *He accused the police of covering up for each other.* [I] ○ *They're trying to cover up the truth.* [M]

coverup /'kʌv·ə,rʌp/ *n* [C] an attempt to prevent the public from discovering information about a serious crime or mistake • *The Watergate coverup led eventually to President Nixon's resignation.*

covert /'kou·vərt, kou'vɜrt/ *adj* hidden or secret • *covert military operations* • USAGE: The opposite of covert is OVERT.

coveted /'kʌv·ət·əd/ *adj* strongly desired by many • *The Caldecott Medal is a coveted children's book award.*

cow ANIMAL /kau/ *n* [C] the adult female of cattle that is kept on a farm to produce milk or meat • A cow is also any of other large female, adult mammals, such as ELEPHANTS or WHALES.

cow FRIGHTEN /kau/ *v* [T] to frighten or control (someone) by using threats or violence • *The dictator has succeeded in cowing his public opponents into near silence.*

coward /'kau·ərd/ *n* [C] *disapproving* a person who is easily frightened or tries to avoid danger, or a person who commits a violent act against someone who is weak or defenseless • *The president denounced the terrorists as cowards.*

cowardly /'kɑʊ·ərd·li/ adj [not gradable] disapproving • a cowardly act

cowardice /'kɑʊ·ərd·əs/ n [U] disapproving the condition of being easily frightened and quick to avoid danger, or the practice of committing acts of violence against people who are weak or defenseless

cowboy /'kɑʊ·bɔɪ/, **cowgirl** /'kɑʊ·gɜrl/ n [C] a person employed to take care of cattle, who usually rides a horse • A **cowboy hat** is a hat with a wide, curved BRIM (= bottom part).

cowboy

cower /'kɑʊ·ər, kɑʊr/ v [I] to bend down or move backward with your head lowered because you are frightened • The dog cowered in the corner, realizing she'd done something wrong.

co–worker, coworker /'kou,wɜr·kər/ n [C] a person working with another worker, esp. as a partner or helper

coy /kɔɪ/ adj [-er/-est only] acting shy, uncertain, or unwilling to say much, often in order to increase interest in something by keeping back information about it • McIntyre is coy about his future in football.

coyly /'kɔɪ·li/ adv [not gradable] • She smiled coyly.

coyote /kaɪ'oʊṭ·i, 'kaɪ·oʊt/ n [C] a doglike wild animal that lives in parts of North America, esp. in the west

cozy /'kou·zi/ adj comfortable, pleasant, and inviting, esp. (of a room or building) because small and warm

CPA n [C] abbreviation for **certified public accountant**, see at CERTIFY

CPR n [U] abbreviation for cardiopulmonary resuscitation (= medical actions performed in an emergency to make the heart and lungs begin to work again)

crab /kræb/ n [C/U] a sea animal that has five pairs of legs and a round, flat body covered by a shell, or its flesh eaten as food

crack DAMAGE /kræk/ v [I/T] to damage (something) by causing thin lines or spaces to ap-

pear on its surface; break slightly • The concrete on the front of the building had begun to crack. [I] ○ The X-ray showed that she had cracked a bone in her foot. [T] • If you **crack a smile**, you smile slightly.

crack /kræk/ n [C] a thin line or space in the surface of something, usually a sign of damage • A series of cracks developed in the road surface. • A crack is also a narrow space: She opened the door a crack. • The **crack of dawn** is the early part of the morning when the sun first appears.

cracked /krækt/ adj • cracked bathroom tiles

crack HIT SOMETHING /kræk/ v [T always + adv/prep] to hit something hard, esp. by accident • He fell backward, his head cracking against a tree.

crack OPEN /kræk/ v [T] to break (something) open, esp. in order to reach or use what is inside • He cracked three eggs into a mixing bowl. • (fig.) If you crack a CODE (= message in symbols), you discover what it means.

crack MAKE A NOISE /kræk/ v [I/T] to make a sudden, sharp noise or to cause (something) to make such a noise • All around us the lightning was cracking. [I] • To **crack the whip** is to act with authority to make someone work harder.

crack /kræk/ n [C] • The crack of a rifle was heard in the woods.

crack LOSE CONTROL /kræk/ v [I] to lose control over your ability to think and act reasonably, esp. because of anxiety or fear • In spite of intense questioning for over eight hours, she never cracked.

crack ATTEMPT /kræk/ n [C] an attempt; a try • I've never tried to cook this before, but I thought I'd have a crack at it.

crack SKILLFUL /kræk/ adj [not gradable] skillful; expert • He was a crack shot (= skillful at shooting). • This software isn't as good as it's cracked up to be (= claimed to be).

crack JOKE /kræk/ v [T] to make (a joke or amusing remark) • Jerry's always cracking jokes.

crack /kræk/ n [C] a joking remark that is critical of someone or slightly insulting • She's always making cracks about how much I eat.

crack DRUG /kræk/ n [U] slang a pure and powerful form of the drug COCAINE

□ **crack down** /'-'-/ v adv [I] to take strong action to stop something from happening • The university is taking steps to crack down on underage drinking on campus.

crackdown /'kræk·dɑʊn/ n [C] • a crackdown on illegal weapons

□ **crack up** (obj), **crack** (obj) **up** /'-'-/ v adv slang to cause (someone) to laugh so much they are not in control of themselves • The stories they told cracked me up. [M]

cracker /'kræk·ər/ n [C] a hard, dry, thin piece of baked bread

crackle /'kræk·əl/ v [I] to make a set of short,

sharp sounds • *The fire spread to an evergreen tree, which crackled with flames.*

crackle /'kræk·əl/ *n* [C] • *the crackle of automatic gunfire*

crackpot /'kræk·pɑt/ *n* [C] *infml* a crazy or strange person • *They obviously think we're a bunch of crackpots.*

cradle [BED] /'kreɪd·əl/ *n* [C] a small bed for a baby, esp. one with raised sides that can be pushed gently so that it moves from side to side • **The cradle of** something means the place or society where it began: *The Near East is considered the cradle of civilization.*

cradle [SUPPORT] /'kreɪd·əl/ *v* [T] to hold (someone or something) gently • *Grady steps out from behind the oak tree, cradling his shotgun in his arm.*

craft [SKILL] /kræft/ *n* [C/U] skill in knowing how to do or make something, or a job or activity needing such skill • *He talked about the craft of writing popular fiction.* [U] ○ *I love to do all kinds of crafts and sewing.* [C]

craft /kræft/ *v* [T] • *The speech was well crafted* (= made with skill).

craftsman (*pl* -**men**) /'kræf·smən/, **craftswoman** (*pl* -**women**) /'kræf,swʊm·ən/ *n* [C] a person who is skilled in a particular craft

craftsmanship /'kræf·smən,ʃɪp/ *n* [U] • *The craftsmanship of the Tiffany lamp was superb.*

craft [TRANSPORT] /kræft/ *n* [C] *pl* **craft** a boat, aircraft, or spacecraft

crafty /'kræf·ti/ *adj* skillful in argument but likely to be dishonest • *a crafty lawyer*

craggy /'kræg·i/ *adj* rocky and rough • *a craggy shoreline* ○ (*fig.*) *His craggy* (= attractively rough) *features seemed at last to relax.*

cram [FORCE] /kræm/ *v* [T always + adv/prep] -**mm**- to force (something) into a small space, or to fill an area with (people) • *Six children were crammed into the back of the car.*

cram [LEARN QUICKLY] /kræm/ *v* [I] -**mm**- to try to learn a lot very quickly before an exam • *She's cramming for her history exam.*

cramp /kræmp/ *n* [C] a sudden, painful tightening of a muscle • *stomach cramps* ○ *a foot cramp*

cramped /kræmt/ *adj* [not gradable] limited in the freedom to move because there is not enough space • *He managed to get a bed in a cramped student apartment.*

cranberry /'kræn,ber·i, -bə·ri/ *n* [C] a small, round red fruit with a sour taste, used esp. to make juice and sauce

crane [MACHINE] /kreɪn/ *n* [C] a large machine with a long, movable part to which is fixed CABLES (= strong wires) for lifting and moving heavy objects

crane [BIRD] /kreɪn/ *n* [C] a large water bird with long, thin legs and a long neck

crane [STRETCH] /kreɪn/ *v* [I/T] to stretch in order to look at something • *We were all craning (our necks) to get a glimpse of the Pope.* [I/T]

crank [PERSON] /kræŋk/ *n* [C] a person who has

strange ideas and behaves strangely • *Some crank called up the TV station to make a bomb threat.*

crank [HANDLE] /kræŋk/ *n* [C] a handle or bar on a machine that you can turn to make another part turn

□ **crank out** *obj*, **crank** *obj* **out** /'kræŋk'aʊt/ *v adv* [M] *infml* to produce (something) in large amounts like a machine • *She cranks out two new books a year.*

□ **crank up** *obj*, **crank** *obj* **up** /'kræŋk'ʌp/ *v adv* [M] *infml* to increase (something), esp. the sound of a radio, television, or STEREO • *The kids cranked up the volume on the stereo.*

cranky /'kræŋ·ki/ *adj* easily annoyed and angry

crap [EXCREMENT] /kræp/ *n* [C/U] *rude slang* excrement, or an act of excreting

crap /kræp/ *v* [I] -**pp**- *rude slang*

crap [NONSENSE] /kræp/ *n* [U] *rude slang* something that is bad or worthless; nonsense • *The principal's speech was just a lot of crap about being good citizens.*

crappy /'kræp·i/ *adj* [-er/-est only] *rude slang* • Crappy also means sick: *He said he was feeling really crappy.*

craps /kræps/ *n* [U] a game played with DICE (= two six-sided playing pieces with different numbers of dots on each of the six sides) for money

crash [ACCIDENT] /kræʃ/ *n* [C] a serious accident in which one or more cars, trucks, or other vehicles hit something, or in which an aircraft hits the ground or another aircraft • *She was killed in an airplane crash in 1983.*

crash /kræʃ/ *v* [I/T] • *The plane crashed into the mountainside, killing all aboard.* [I]

crash [NOISE] /kræʃ/ *n* [C] a loud noise that sounds as if it is caused by something violently breaking apart or hitting something else • *There was a loud crash, and we rushed over to see what had fallen.*

crash /kræʃ/ *v* [always + adv/prep] to fall or hit something in a noisy or violent way • *All the dishes the waitress was carrying crashed to the floor.* [I] • To crash is also to move in a noisy or violent way: *A big black bear came crashing through the underbrush.* [I]

crash [FAILURE] /kræʃ/ *n* [C] a sudden loss of value of investments, or a failure of a business

crash /kræʃ/ *v* [I] • *When the market crashed, everyone lost money.* • If a computer crashes, it suddenly stops operating.

crash [NOT INVITED] /kræʃ/ *v* [T] *infml* to go to (a party or other event) without an invitation • *Some guys tried to crash the party but they weren't allowed in.*

crash [SLEEP] /kræʃ/ *v* [I] *slang* to sleep, or to stay at a place to sleep temporarily • *I was so tired after work, I crashed on the sofa.*

crash [AFTER DRUG USE] /kræʃ/ *v* [I] *slang* to experience unpleasant feelings when a drug no longer has an effect

crash QUICK /kræʃ/ *adj infml* involving great effort to achieve a lot quickly • A **crash course** is a short period of instruction in which much is learned about a subject. • A **crash diet** is a way of losing body weight quickly by eating very little.

crass /kræs/ *adj* [*-er/-est* only] offensive in manner or style • *The Olympics as shown on TV represents crass commercialism, he said.*

crate /kreɪt/ *n* [C] a large wooden box, used esp. for packing, storing, or sending things • *The wooden shipping crates were unloaded at the dock.*

crater /ˈkreɪt̮·ər/ *n* [C] a large hole in the top of a VOLCANO (= mountain made from liquid rock), or a large hole made by something hitting the ground with force • *The bomb blast left a crater six feet deep.*

crave /kreɪv/ *v* [T] to desire (something) strongly • *The neglected kids just crave attention.*

craving /ˈkreɪ·vɪŋ/ *n* [C] a strong or uncontrollable desire • *a craving for alcohol*

crawfish /ˈkrɔː·fɪʃ/, **crayfish** /ˈkreɪ·fɪʃ/ *n* [C/U] a small animal similar to a LOBSTER, that lives in rivers and streams, or its flesh eaten as food

crawl MOVE /krɔːl/ *v* [I] to move slowly with the body stretched out along the ground or (of a human) on hands and knees • *a caterpillar crawling in the grass* ○ *The child crawled across the floor.* ○ *(fig.) The train crawled slowly through the night.*

crawl /krɔːl/ *n* [C usually sing] • *Traffic slowed to a crawl (= a very slow speed).* • **Crawl space** is space in a part of a house, esp. under the bottom floor, that is not high enough for a person to stand in, and where typically equipment for heating water, etc., is kept.

crawl SWIMMING /krɔːl/ *n* [U] a way of swimming fast by lying with your chest down, kicking your legs, and raising first one arm then the other out of the water to move yourself forward

crawling /ˈkrɔː·lɪŋ/ *adj* • If a place is **crawling with** creatures, it is covered with or full of them: *The garbage dump was crawling with rats.*

crayon /ˈkreɪ·ən, -ˌɑn/ *n* [C] a small stick of colored wax used for drawing or writing • *a box of crayons*

craze /kreɪz/ *n* [C usually sing] an activity, style, or fashion that is very popular, usually for a short time • *Cycling shorts were the craze that year.*

crazed /kreɪzd/ *adj* [not gradable] behaving wildly • *He looked at her with a crazed grin like he was about to eat her alive.*

crazy /ˈkreɪ·zi/ *adj* very strange or foolish • *She's the craziest person I've ever met.* ○ *You're crazy to rent the place without seeing it first.* [+ *to* infinitive] • Crazy can mean mentally ill. • Crazy can also mean behaving strangely esp. because of stress, as if you are mentally ill:

The constant whine of the machine nearly drove (= made) *me crazy.* ○ *I think she'll go* (= become) *crazy if she doesn't take a vacation soon.* • If you are **crazy about** someone or something, you like them or it very much: *I was crazy about baseball.* ○ *I'm not that crazy about watching TV.*

crazy /ˈkreɪ·zi/ *n* [C usually pl] *infml* a person who acts in a strange or threatening way, esp. one who is mentally ill • *There have been some crazies who killed people with guns.*

crazily /ˈkreɪ·zə·li/ *adv* [not gradable]

craziness /ˈkreɪ·ziː·nəs/ *n* [U]

creak /kriːk/ *v* [I] to make a high noise, usually caused by a stiff material such as wood or metal that is made to move slightly • *The old floorboards creaked when I walked across the floor.* ○ *He heard a prison cell door creak open and slam shut.*

creak /kriːk/ *n* [C]

creaky /ˈkriː·ki/ *adj* • *a creaky elevator*

cream LIQUID /kriːm/ *n* [U] the thick, yellow-white liquid that forms on the top of milk • *Do you take cream in your coffee?* • Cream is also a pale yellow-white color. • Cream also refers to any of various foods that contain cream or that are smooth like cream: *cream of chicken soup* ○ *chocolate cream pie* • **The cream of the crop** is the best of a group: *The medical school had such a fine reputation that its applicants were the cream of the crop.* • **Cream cheese** is a type of soft, white cheese.

creamy /ˈkriː·mi/ *adj* thick and smooth, like cream

cream THICK SUBSTANCE /kriːm/ *n* [U] a thick, smooth substance that you put on your skin to keep it soft or to treat it medically • *a facial cream*

crease /kriːs/ *n* [C] a line or mark made on material by folding or pressing it, or a line in a person's skin, esp. in the face • *There were tiny creases in her eye shadow.*

crease /kriːs/ *v* [I/T] • *A frown creased Mr. Cuna's boyish face.* [T]

create /kriːˈeɪt/ *v* [T] to cause (something) to exist, or to make (something new or imaginative) • *They worked together to create many popular songs.* ○ *The new hotel is expected to create 200 jobs.*

creation /kriːˈeɪ·ʃən/ *n* [C/U] • *Huge amounts of money went into the creation of a new highway.* [U] • In the Bible, (the) Creation is the making of the world by God. [U] • A creation is something that is made: *The fashion magazine had photos of the latest Paris creations.* [C]

creator /kriːˈeɪ·t̮ər/ *n* [C] a person who creates something • God is sometimes called the Creator.

creative /kriːˈeɪ·t̮ɪv/ *adj* [not gradable] producing or using original and unusual ideas • *a creative designer/person* ○ *creative talents*

creatively /kriːˈeɪ·t̮ɪv·li/ *adv* [not gradable]

creativity /ˌkriː·eɪˈtɪv·ət̮·i, ˌkriː·ə-/ *n* [U] the

creature /ˈkriː·tʃər/ *n* [C] any living thing, esp. an animal • A creature can be a person when an opinion is being expressed about them: *Women were often portrayed as creatures of emotion and treated with condescension.* • If someone is a **creature of habit**, they always want to do the same thing in the same way. • **Creature comforts** are all the things that make life pleasant, such as warmth, good food, and a comfortable home.

creche /kreʃ/ *n* [C] a model of the people and animals present at the birth of Jesus, used as a decoration at Christmas

credence /ˈkriː·dᵊns/ *n* [U] *fml* acceptance, support, or belief that something is true • *New evidence lends credence to his story of police brutality.*

credentials /krɪˈden·tʃəlz/ *pl n* documents that state the abilities and experience of a person and show that they are qualified for a particular job or activity • *I got my teaching credentials from San Jose State.*

credible /ˈkred·ə·bəl/ *adj* able to be believed or trusted • *Investigators found no credible evidence of a crime.*

credibly /ˈkred·ə·bli/ *adv* • *The show credibly portrays the black family experience.*

credibility /ˌkred·əˈbɪl·ə·t̬i/ *n* [U] • *Once his lies were revealed, he lost all credibility as a leader.*

credit PAYMENT LATER /ˈkred·ət/ *n* [U] a method of buying goods or services that allows you to pay for them in the future • *We bought our sofa on credit.* ○ *The bank offers small businesses credit.* • A **credit card** is a small plastic card that you can use to buy something and pay for it in the future. • A **credit rating** is a judgment of whether a person or organization is likely to pay for things purchased using credit: *Late payments give you a bad credit rating.* • A **credit union** is an organization for lending money to its members at low rates of INTEREST (= extra money).

creditor /ˈkred·ət̬·ər/ *n* [C] a country, organization, or person to whom money is owed • *He's trying to earn enough to pay off his creditors.* • Compare **debtor** at DEBT.

credit PRAISE /ˈkred·ət/ *n* [C/U] praise or approval, esp. to recognize achievement • *You have to give him credit for being so honest.* [U] ○ *How can he take credit for work he didn't do?* [U] • *It is to his credit that he's willing to admit he has a problem* (= this should be praised).

credit MONEY AVAILABLE /ˈkred·ət/ *n* [C/U] an amount of money available to you because you paid for something earlier, or a record of this money • *We returned the clothes and got a store credit.* [C] • A credit is also an amount of money you do not have to pay: *a tax credit* [C] • USAGE: The opposite of credit is DEBIT.

credit /ˈkred·ət/ *v* [T] • *I'll be glad to credit your account for the items you returned.*

credit BELIEVE /ˈkred·ət/ *v* [T] to believe or trust (esp. something that may not be true) • *If you can credit what the doctor says, the illness isn't serious.*

creditable /ˈkred·ət̬·ə·bəl/ *adj* • *She gave a creditable performance of a woman in love.*

credit COURSE UNIT /ˈkred·ət/ *n* [C] a unit of measurement of the value contributed by an educational course to a college degree • *Comparative religion is a three-credit course.*

▫ **credit** *obj* **with** *obj* /ˈ--ˌ-/ *v prep* [T] to consider (someone) as having (good qualities or good achievements) • *I credited him with more sense than he showed.*

credits /ˈkred·əts/ *pl n* the list of the names of people and organizations who helped to make a movie or television program which is shown at the beginning or the end of it

credo /ˈkriː·doʊ, ˈkreɪd-/ *n* [C] *pl* **credos** a statement of basic belief • *His credo is "Less is more."*

creed /kriːd/ *n* [C/U] a formal statement or system of esp. religious beliefs • *The law forbids discrimination because of race, color, or creed.* [U]

creek /kriːk, *esp. Northern and Western* krɪk/ *n* [C] a small river or stream

creep MOVE CAREFULLY /kriːp/ *v* [I always + adv/prep] *past* **crept** /krept/ to move quietly and slowly, usually in order to avoid being noticed • *I crept around the corner, hoping my brother wouldn't see me.*

creep MOVE SLOWLY /kriːp/ *v* [I always + adv/prep] *past* **crept** to move very slowly • *We were creeping along in rush-hour traffic.*

creep PERSON /kriːp/ *n* [C] *slang* a person you think is unpleasant and to be avoided • *That guy upstairs is such a creep.*

creeps /kriːps/ *pl n infml* a feeling of fear and disgust • *You give me the creeps.*

creepy /ˈkriː·pi/ *adj infml* strange and slightly frightening • *a creepy old house*

cremate /ˈkriː·meɪt, krɪˈmeɪt/ *v* [T] to burn (a dead person's body)

cremation /krɪˈmeɪ·ʃən/ *n* [C/U] • *The body was sent for cremation.* [U]

crematorium /ˌkriː·məˈtɔːr·iː·əm, ˌkrem·ə-, -ˈtoʊr-/ *n* [C] *pl* **crematoriums** or **crematoria** /ˌkriː·məˈtɔːr·iː·ə, ˌkrem·ə-, -ˈtoʊr-/ a building where dead people's bodies are burnt

Creole LANGUAGE /ˈkriː·oʊl/ *n* [C] any of several languages developed in some Caribbean islands that combine African languages and Indian languages with French or Spanish • *Creole is spoken by most Haitians today.*

Creole PERSON /ˈkriː·oʊl/ *n* [C] a white person who is related to the original group of Spanish or French people who came to the Caribbean or Louisiana, or a black person from some Caribbean islands who is of mixed African and European origin and who speaks esp. French Creole

crepe /kreɪp/ *n* [U] thin cloth with uneven lines on its surface • *a dark blue crepe dress* • **Crepe paper** is thin paper that is not smooth which is used esp. for decoration.

crept /krept/ *past simple and past participle of* CREEP

crescendo /krəˈʃen·doʊ/ *n* [C usually sing] *pl* **crescendos** a gradual increase in loudness, or the moment when a noise or piece of music is at its loudest

crescent /ˈkres·ənt/ *n* [C] a curved shape that has two narrow pointed ends • A **crescent moon** is the moon when more than half the side you can see is dark.

crest /krest/ *n* [C] the top or highest part of something such as a wave or a hill • *We climbed to the crest of the hill.*

crest /krest/ *v* [I] • *The flood waters crested Thursday* (= reached their highest level).

crevice /ˈkrev·əs/ *n* [C] a deep crack or opening in a surface, esp. in rock • *He slipped on the mountain and landed in a crevice.*

crew /kruː/ *n* [C/U] all the people who work together, esp. to operate a ship or aircraft, or all the people of lower rank • *The captain and crew would like to welcome you on board.* [U] ○ *Jack worked on a road-repair crew.* [C]

crew cut /ˈkruː·kʌt/ *n* [C] a hairstyle for men and boys in which the hair is cut very short

crewneck /ˈkruː·nek/ *adj* (of clothing, esp. a SWEATER) having a round, flat, closely fitting opening for the neck

crib /krɪb/ *n* [C] a baby's bed with high sides and usually bars that prevent the baby from falling out • **Crib death** is a baby's death during sleep that cannot be explained by any known illness.

crick /krɪk/ *n* [C] a painful, usually sudden stiffness in the muscles of the neck or back • *I got a crick in my neck from painting the ceiling.*

cricket INSECT /ˈkrɪk·ət/ *n* [C] a brown jumping insect that makes a loud, high, often repeated noise that you hear esp. at night

cricket GAME /ˈkrɪk·ət/ *n* [U] a team sport popular in England and some other countries, played with a small, hard ball and a BAT (= wooden stick)

cried /kraɪd/ *past simple and past participle of* CRY

crime /kraɪm/ *n* [C/U] an action or activity that is against the law, or illegal activity generally • *Violent crime has been reduced.* [U] ○ *It's a crime to yell "fire" in a crowded theater if there isn't one.* [C] ○ *If you commit a crime, you will be punished.* [C] • People say something is a crime if it is wrong: *It's a crime that people go to bed hungry in this country.* [C usually sing] • USAGE: The related adjective is CRIMINAL.

criminal /ˈkrɪm·ən·əl/ *adj* involving or having the character of a crime • *She may face crim-*

inal charges for lying to a grand jury. ○ *He had an extensive criminal record* (= an official record of having committed many crimes). ○ *The way she blames other people for her own mistakes is criminal* (= wrong).

criminal /ˈkrɪm·ən·əl/ *n* [C] a person who has committed a crime or been found guilty of committing a crime • *Violent criminals belong in prison.*

criminally /ˈkrɪm·ən·əl·i/ *adv* [not gradable] • *Parents can be held criminally responsible for their children's actions.*

crimp PRESS /krɪmp/ *v* [T] to press (something) into small folds or curves • *She had her hair crimped.*

crimson /ˈkrɪm·zən/ *adj* [not gradable], *n* [U] (of) a deep red, slightly purple color • *His face was crimson with anger.*

cringe /krɪndʒ/ *v* [I] to feel embarrassed and ashamed about something • *I cringed when I realized what I'd said.* • To cringe is also pull back in fear from someone or something that seems powerful and dangerous: *When their father came home drunk, the children cringed.*

crinkle /ˈkrɪŋ·kəl/ *v* [I/T] to have or cause to have many little lines and folds • *The paper was old and crinkled.* [I]

crinkle /ˈkrɪŋ·kəl/ *n* [C] • *The machine won't take your bills unless you smooth out the crinkles.*

crinkly /ˈkrɪŋ·kə·li, -kli/ *adj* • *I love those crinkly French fries.*

cripple DAMAGE /ˈkrɪp·əl/ *v* [T] to make (something) much less effective; damage • *Economic sanctions have crippled the country's economy.*

crippling /ˈkrɪp·lɪŋ/ *adj* • *The city faces crippling cuts in services.*

cripple INJURED PERSON /ˈkrɪp·əl/ *n* [C] dated a person who because of injury or disease cannot walk or move their legs or arms in the usual way • USAGE: Some people consider this word to be offensive.

cripple /ˈkrɪp·əl/ *v* [T] • *The accident crippled him.*

crippling /ˈkrɪp·lɪŋ, -ə·lɪŋ/ *adj* • *a crippling injury* ○ *crippling pain*

crisis /ˈkraɪ·səs/ *n* [C/U] *pl* **crises** /ˈkraɪ·siːz/ an extremely dangerous or difficult situation • *an economic crisis* [C] ○ *People react in times of crisis, but ignore us the rest of the time.* [U]

crisp HARD /krɪsp/ *adj* (of food) hard enough to be broken easily instead of bent • *crisp bacon* ○ *crisp rolls*

crispy /ˈkrɪs·pi/ *adj* approving • *hot, crispy noodles*

crisp FRESH /krɪsp/ *adj* fresh and clean • *I like to sleep on crisp cotton sheets.* ○ *The teller handed me a crisp hundred-dollar bill.*

crisp COOL /krɪsp/ *adj* (of air) cool, clear, and likely to make you feel awake and active • *Crisp breezes bring out boats of every size.* ○ *It* *was a crisp, midwinter morning in Massachusetts.*

crisp DIRECT /krɪsp/ *adj* (of speech or writing) quick and direct • *I prefer channel 1's crisp presentation of the news.*

crisply /'krɪs·pli/ *adv* • *a crisply written book*

crisp FRIED POTATO /krɪsp/ *n* [C usually pl] *Br* for **potato chip**, see at POTATO

crisscross /'krɪs·krɔːs/ *v* [I/T] to move or exist in a pattern of crossing lines • *From the air, we saw highways crisscrossing the farmland below.* [T]

criterion /krɑɪ'tɪr·i·ən/, *not standard* **criteria** /krɑɪ'tɪr·i·ə/ *n* [C] *pl* **criteria** /krɑɪ'tɪr·i·ə/ a condition or fact used as a standard by which something can be judged or considered • *Eight criteria will be used to select new stadium sites.* ○ (*not standard*) *Is height a criteria for hiring police officers?* • USAGE: The use of criteria as a singular noun is common, esp. in speech.

critic JUDGE OF ENTERTAINMENT /'krɪt·ɪk/ *n* [C] a person whose job is to give their opinion about books, movies, and musical and theatrical performances • *The critics hated it, but it was popular at the box office.*

critical /'krɪt·ɪ·kəl/ *adj* • *The movie was a financial and critical success.*

critically /'krɪt·ɪ·kli/ *adv* • *a critically acclaimed novel*

critic DISAPPROVING PERSON /'krɪt·ɪk/ *n* [C] a person who expresses disagreement with something or disapproval of someone • *He has been one of the most outspoken critics of this administration.*

critical /'krɪt·ɪ·kəl/ *adj* expressing an opinion about something or someone, esp. a negative opinion • *My mother is always so critical of the way I dress!*

critically /'krɪt·ɪ·kli/ *adv* • *Industry spokesmen reacted critically to the report.*

criticism /'krɪt·ə,sɪz·əm/ *n* [C/U] an opinion given about something or someone, esp. a negative opinion, or the activity of making such judgments • *It was meant as a suggestion, not a criticism.* [C] ○ *He was singled out for strong criticism.* [U] • Criticism is also a careful discussion of something in order to judge its quality or explain its meaning: *art criticism* [U]

criticize /'krɪt·ə,sɑɪz/ *v* [I/T] to express disagreement with or disapproval of (something or someone) • *It's a lot easier to criticize (a plan) than to offer useful suggestions.* [I/T]

critical IMPORTANT /'krɪt·ɪ·kəl/ *adj* of the greatest importance • *critical industries* ○ *What happens in the next 48 hours is critical.*

critically /'krɪt·ɪ·kli/ *adv*

critical VERY BAD /'krɪt·ɪ·kəl/ *adj* very bad or dangerous • *He was admitted to Metropolitan Hospital in critical condition.*

critically /'krɪt·ɪ·kli/ *adv* • *She was critically injured in the crash.*

critique /krə'tiːk/ *n* [C] a report that discusses a situation or the writings or ideas of someone and offers a judgment about them • *The book also offers a critique of race relations in the US.*

critter /'krɪt·ər/ *n* [C] *infml* a creature • *That dog's a mean old critter.*

croak MAKE SOUND /kroʊk/ *v* [I/T] (of animals) to make deep sounds such as a FROG makes, or as a person might make because of a very dry throat • *Frogs croaked in the swamp.* [I] ○ *He croaked a greeting, and we realized he could hardly talk.* [T]

croak DIE /kroʊk/ *v* [I] *slang* to die

crochet /kroʊ'ʃeɪ/ *v* [I/T] to make (cloth or clothing) by connecting wool or other thread into joined rows using a single needle with a hook • *My mother crocheted a blanket for the baby.* [T] PIC KNIT

crock CONTAINER /krɑk/ *n* [C] a container made of baked clay • *Dad kept sauerkraut in a twenty-gallon crock.*

crock NONSENSE /krɑk/ *n* [U] *slang* something that is completely false or ridiculous; nonsense • *They claimed they wrote that song? What a crock!*

crockery /'krɑk·ə·ri/ *n* [U] cups, plates, bowls, etc., made of baked clay • *Upstairs we could hear screaming and smashing crockery.*

crocodile /'krɑk·ə,dɑɪl/ *n* [C] a large, hard-skinned REPTILE (= type of animal) with a longer and narrower nose than that of an ALLIGATOR which lives in and near rivers and lakes in hot, wet places

crocus /'kroʊ·kəs/ *n* [C] a small yellow, white, or purple spring flower

croissant /krə'sɑnt, kwɑ'sɑ̃/ *n* [C] a piece of light bread having a curved shape with two narrow pointed ends • *Pick up some croissants for breakfast tomorrow.*

crony /'kroʊ·ni/ *n* [C] *often disapproving* a close friend or companion, esp. someone who may not be honest • *I'd like to see the president and his cronies booted out of office.*

crook BAD PERSON /krʊk/ *n* [C] a person who is dishonest, esp. someone who cheats or steals • *She thinks all politicians are crooks.*

crooked /'krʊk·əd/ *adj* • *Most of the cops in this county are crooked.*

crook BENT PART /krʊk/ *n* [C usually sing] a bent part of something, esp. the inner part • *Grady rested his shotgun in the crook of his elbow.*

crooked /'krʊk·əd/ *adj* not straight or not even; twisted, bent, or uneven • *That dog's tail is crooked.* ○ *Your glasses are on crooked.*

croon /kruːn/ *v* [I/T] to sing or talk in a low, gentle, musical voice • *He held his baby in his arms and crooned softly to her.* [I]

crop PLANT /krɑp/ *n* [C] a plant such as a grain, vegetable, or fruit grown in large amounts by farmers, or the total amount gathered of such a plant • *Apple growers celebrated their biggest* *crop ever last year.* • A crop is also any group of similar things or people: *We've got a new crop of students coming in every year.*

crop CUT /krɑp/ v [T] **-pp-** to make (something) shorter or smaller, esp. by cutting • *The brothers both had their hair cropped.*

□ **crop up** /'-'-/ v adv [I] to happen or appear unexpectedly • *Her name keeps cropping up in their conversations.*

croquet /kroʊ'keɪ/ n [U] a game in which players use MALLETS (= long wooden hammers) to hit wooden balls through small metal arches sunk in the grass

cross GO ACROSS /krɔːs/ v [I/T] to go from one side of (something) to the other • *Look both ways before you cross the street.* [T] • If something **crosses** your **mind**, you think of it: *It crossed my mind yesterday that you might like to join us.* • **Cross-country** sports are those in which competitors travel long distances through natural areas: *cross-country skiing/ running* • **Cross-country** also means across the length of a country: *After college we bought a camper and traveled cross-country for two months.*

crossing /'krɔː·sɪŋ/ n [C] a marked place where a road can be crossed safely; CROSSWALK • *a pedestrian crossing*

cross LIE ACROSS /krɔːs/ v [I/T] to put (one thing) across another, or to lie this way • *Weaver Street crosses the Post Road.* [T] • If you **cross** your **fingers**, you put one finger over another because you hope that something will happen as you want it to happen: *I'll just cross my fingers and hope for the best.* • If someone is **cross-eyed**, each eye seems to be looking over their nose and across the direction the other eye looks in. • *She sat* **cross-legged** (= with each leg crossed under the other).

crossing /'krɔː·sɪŋ/ n [C] a place where a road and a railroad cross

cross MARK /krɔːs/ n [C] a mark or object in the shape of two lines across each other, usually † or X • *He marked off their names with pencilled crosses.* • A cross with a longer vertical line and a shorter horizontal line is the sign of Christianity: *She wears a gold cross around her neck.*

cross /krɔːs/ v [T] • When Christians cross themselves, they move their hand over their body in the shape of a cross.

cross ANNOYED /krɔːs/ adj annoyed or angry • *Don't be cross, I was just joking.*

cross OPPOSE /krɔːs/ v [T] to oppose (someone) by disagreeing with them or by not doing or saying what they want • *I wouldn't cross him if I were you.*

cross MIXTURE /krɔːs/ n [C] a mixture of two different things which have been combined to produce something new • *He's a cross between Clint Eastwood and Cary Grant.*

□ **cross** obj **off** (obj) /'-'-/ v adv [T], v prep to re-

move (someone or something, such as a name) from (a list) by drawing a line through it • *Cross off each item as I put it on the shelf.* [M]

□ **cross out** obj, **cross** obj **out** /'-'-/ v adv [M] to draw a line through (writing) • *Cross out the mistakes.*

cross-examine /ˌkrɔː·sɪg'zæm·ən/ v [T] to ask detailed questions of (someone, esp. during a trial) in order to discover if they have been telling the truth • *Defense attorneys cross-examined the witness.*

cross-examination /ˌkrɔː·sɪg,zæm·ə'neɪ·ʃən/ n [C/U] • *Under cross-examination, she admitted she'd lied.* [U]

crossfire /'krɔːs·fɑɪr/ n [U] the act of firing guns from two or more places at the same time, so that the paths of the bullets cross • *They were trapped by enemy crossfire.*

crossover /'krɔː·soʊ·vər/ n [U] a change from one form to another, or a blending of different types • *There's been a lot of crossover from comic books to movies.* ◦ *His crossover music blends Western and ethnic styles.*

cross-purposes /'krɔː'spɜr·pə·səz/ pl n • If two people or groups are **at cross-purposes**, they do not understand each other because they have different intentions: *They're talking at cross-purposes.*

cross-reference /'krɔːs'ref·rəns/ n [C] (in books) an instruction to look somewhere else in the same book for related information

crossroads /'krɔːs·roʊdz/ n [C] pl **crossroads** a place where two roads meet and cross each other • *(fig.) With funding coming up for review, the program is at a crossroads* (= has reached an important but uncertain stage).

cross-section INSIDE VIEW /'krɔːs,sek·ʃən/ n [C] a part of something cut off from the rest of it in order to be able to see its inside structure, or a drawing of this • *a cross-section of a human heart*

cross-section REPRESENTATIVE GROUP /'krɔːs ,sek·ʃən/ n [C] part of a group which is representative of all the different types within the total group • *A jury should represent a reasonable cross-section of the community.*

crosswalk /'krɔːs·wɔːk/ n [C] a marked place in a street where traffic must stop to allow people to walk across • PIC INTERSECTION

crossword puzzle /'krɔː,swɜrd,pʌz·əl/ n [C] a word game in which you have to guess the answers to CLUES and write the words into numbered squares that go across and down

crotch /krɑtʃ/ n [C] the part of your body where your legs join at the top, or the part of pants or underwear which covers this area

crotchety /'krɑtʃ·ət·i/ adj easily annoyed or angered • *After ten hours in the car, we were all getting crotchety.*

crouch /krɑʊtʃ/ v [I] to bend your knees and lower yourself so that you are close to the ground and leaning forward slightly • *She crouched down behind a bush to hide.*

crouch /kraʊtʃ/ n [C usually sing] • *The goalie waited in a crouch.*

crow BIRD /kroʊ/ n [C] a large, black bird with a loud cry • **Crow's feet** are the lines around the outside corners of a person's eyes.

crow CRY /kroʊ/ v [I] *past* **crowed** (of a male chicken) to make a loud cry • *A rooster crowed repeatedly.* • If someone crows, they express a lot of happiness or pride: *"I told you so," my little brother crowed.*

crowbar /'kroʊ·bɑr/ n [C] a heavy, iron bar with a bent end that is used to lift heavy objects off the ground or to force things open

crowd /kraʊd/ n [C] a large group of people who have gathered together • *A crowd formed outside the club.* ○ *Crowds of people watched the fireworks.* • (*infml*) A crowd is also a group of friends: *I don't know many people in Edsel's crowd.* • A crowd is also a group of people with similar interests: *the art/theater crowd*

crowd /kraʊd/ v [I/T] (of people) to fill a place • *Street vendors crowded the sidewalks.* [T] ○ *As soon as he appeared, reporters crowded around him.* [I] • If you crowd someone, you make them uncomfortable by standing too close to them: *Don't crowd me!* [T] • If people crowd into a place, they fill it completely: *Commuters crowded into the train.* [I]

crowded /'kraʊd·əd/ adj full of people • *By ten o'clock the bar was crowded.*

crown HEAD COVERING /kraʊn/ n [C] a circular decoration for the head, usually made of gold and jewels, worn by a king or queen at official ceremonies • In a sports competition, a crown is a prize or position which you get for beating all the other competitors: *They won six NBA crowns in seven years.* • (*Cdn*) A **crown corporation** is a company that is owned by the Canadian federal government. • (*Cdn*) A **crown prosecutor** is a legal representative of the Canadian federal government who officially accuses someone of committing a crime in a court of law.

crown /kraʊn/ v [T] • *Queen Elizabeth II was crowned in 1953* (= made queen).

crown TOP PART /kraʊn/ n [C] the top part of something, esp. a person's head • *Her hair stuck straight up from her crown.* • The crown of a hat is the part that covers the top of your head. Compare BRIM PART OF HAT.

crown /kraʊn/ v [T] to be on or around the top of (something) • *mountains crowned with snowy caps*

crown BE BEST /kraʊn/ v [T] to be the best or most successful part of (an activity or life) • *He hoped that health-care was the achievement that would crown his administration.*

crowning /'kraʊ·nɪŋ/ adj [not gradable] • *None of my men died in that campaign—it was the crowning glory of my career.*

crown TOOTH /kraʊn/ n [C] an artificial piece used to cover the top and sides of a tooth, esp. if it is damaged • *a gold crown*

crown /kraʊn/ v [T] • *She had her two front teeth crowned.*

crucial /'kru:·ʃəl/ adj (of a decision or event) extremely important because many other things depend on it • *The behavior of the oceans is a crucial aspect of global warming.*

crucially /'kru:·ʃə·li/ adv • *The band wants to win over fans and, more crucially, radio programmers.*

crucifix /'kru:·sə,fɪks/ n [C] a model or picture representing Jesus on a cross • *A crucifix hung on the wall over the bed.*

crucifixion /,kru:·sə'fɪk·ʃən/ n [C/U] the act of killing someone by fixing them to a cross and leaving them to die, or the death of Jesus on a cross

crucify /'kru:·sə,faɪ/ v [T] to kill (someone) by tying or nailing them to a cross and leaving them there to die • (*fig.*) *When Roger wouldn't talk to reporters, they crucified him* (= criticized him severely).

crud /krʌd/ n [U] slang any offensive substance • *You couldn't see a thing with all the crud in the air.*

cruddy /'krʌd·i/ adj slang • *a cruddy book*

crude SIMPLE /kru:d/ adj [-er/-est only] simple and not skillfully done or made • *He made a crude table out of an old crate.* • **Crude (oil)** is oil that has not yet been treated.

crudely /'kru:d·li/ adv • *Crudely painted signs threatened trespassers.*

crude RUDE /kru:d/ adj [-er/-est only] rude and offensive • *Most of his jokes were crude and sexist.*

crudely /'kru:d·li/ adv • *I hope I'm not speaking too crudely when I say you're very attractive.*

cruel /'kru:·əl/ adj extremely unkind and intentionally causing pain • *Her classmates made some cruel remarks.* ○ *Is the death penalty cruel and unusual punishment?* ○ *I think it's cruel to put a dog in a cage.*

cruelly /'kru:·ə·li/ adv • *She treated him cruelly before the divorce.*

cruelty /'kru:·əl·ti/ n [C/U] • *The foundation works to end cruelty to animals.* [U] ○ *Deliberate cruelty will not be tolerated.* [U]

cruise /kru:z/ v [I] to travel at a continuous speed • *The plane is cruising at 240 knots.* • If you cruise in a car, you drive for pleasure: *We went cruising around downtown on Friday night.* • Cruise can also mean to travel on large ships for pleasure.

cruise /kru:z/ n [C] a trip on a large ship for pleasure • *a Caribbean cruise*

cruiser /'kru:·zər/ n [C] a type of boat with an engine, usually used for pleasure

crumb /krʌm/ n [C] a very small piece of bread or cake • *The floor was covered with crumbs after breakfast.*

crumble /'krʌm·bəl/ v [I/T] to break into small pieces • *That old wall is starting to crumble.* [I]

crummy /'krʌm·i/ *adj slang* of very bad quality • *crummy weather* ○ *a crummy job* ○ *a crummy movie*

crumple /'krʌm·pəl/ *v* [I/T] to become full of irregular folds • *Stephanie crumpled up the letter and threw it away.* [M] • If someone crumples, they fall suddenly: *He hit me, and I crumpled to the floor.* [I]

crunch MAKE NOISE /krʌntʃ/ *v* [I/T] to crush (hard food) loudly between the teeth, or to make a sound as if something is being crushed or broken • *She was crunching noisily on an apple.* [I] ○ *The gravel crunched underfoot as we walked up the path.* [I]

crunch /krʌntʃ/ *n* [C usually sing] • *We heard a loud crunch as the car hit the wall.*

crunchy /'krʌn·tʃi/ *adj* (of food) firm and making a loud noise when it is eaten • *crunchy toast*

crunch DIFFICULTY /krʌntʃ/ *n* [U] *slang* a difficult situation which forces you to make a decision or act • *a financial crunch* • **Crunch time** is a point at which something difficult must be done: *He plays fine without pressure, but can he produce at crunch time?*

crunch CALCULATE /krʌntʃ/ *v* [T] to calculate (numbers) or process (information), esp. quickly and in large amounts • *The project seems worthwhile, but you have to crunch the numbers to see if it's affordable.*

crusade /kru:'seɪd/ *n* [C] a long and determined attempt to achieve something you believe in strongly • *She's involved in the crusade for racial equality.*

crusade /kru:'seɪd/ *v* [I] • *He crusaded tirelessly for gay rights.*

crusader /kru:'seɪd·ər/ *n* [C] • *a crusader for social justice*

crush PRESS /krʌʃ/ *v* [T] to press (something) very hard so that it is broken or its shape is destroyed • *The package got crushed in the mail.* ○ *Her car was crushed by a falling tree.*

crush /krʌʃ/ *n* [U] a crowd of people • *I can't stand the crush of holiday shoppers at the mall.*

crush SHOCK /krʌʃ/ *v* [T] to upset or shock (someone) badly • *He was crushed by the news of his wife's death.*

crush DESTROY /krʌʃ/ *v* [T] to defeat (someone) completely • *The army crushed the rebellion.*

crush ATTRACTION /krʌʃ/ *n* [C] *infml* a strong but temporary attraction for someone • *She has a crush on Matthew in sixth grade.*

crust /krʌst/ *n* [C/U] a hard, outer covering, esp. on a loaf of bread or a pastry • *The crust of the earth is its out layer.* [U]

crusty /'krʌs·ti/ *adj* • *fresh, crusty bread*

crustacean /krʌs'teɪ·ʃən/ *n* [C] any of various types of animals that live in water and have a hard outer shell and many legs • *Crabs, lobsters, and shrimps are crustaceans.*

crusty /'krʌs·ti/ *adj* unhappy and easily annoyed • *He's a crusty, old bachelor who lives alone.*

crutch /krʌtʃ/ *n* [C] a stick with a piece that fits under or around the arm which someone leans on for support if they have difficulty walking • *Marty was on crutches for six weeks when he broke his leg.*

crux /krʌks/ *n* [U] the most important problem, question, or part • *The crux of the matter is that most people just don't vote.*

cry PRODUCE TEARS /kraɪ/ *v* [I/T] to produce tears as the result of a strong emotion, such as unhappiness or pain • *I heard someone crying in the next room.* [I] • If you **cry over spilled milk**, you express regret about something that has already happened or cannot be changed: *There's no point in crying over spilled milk.* • (*infml disapproving*) A **crybaby** is someone who cries or complains a lot without good reason.

cry /kraɪ/ *n* [U] • *"Go on, have a good cry," he said.*

cry SHOUT /kraɪ/ *v* [I/T] to call out or speak loudly • *"Help me!" he cried.* [T] ○ *She cried out in pain as she fell.* [I] • To **cry out for** something is to need it badly: *The country is crying out for a change in leadership.* • If you **cry wolf**, you ask for help when you do not need it, which may prevent people from helping you when you do need it.

cry /kraɪ/ *n* [C] • *They were wakened by cries of "Fire!"* • A cry is also the noise that a bird or animal makes: *the cries of an eagle*

crying /'kraɪ·ɪŋ/ *adj* [not gradable] very serious and needing urgent attention • *There's a crying need for better schools.* • If you say that something is a **crying shame**, you mean it is a great misfortune: *It's a crying shame that new mothers have to go back to work after six weeks.*

crypt /krɪpt/ *n* [C] a room or rooms under the floor of a church where people are sometimes buried

cryptic /'krɪp·tɪk/ *adj* mysterious and difficult to understand • *a cryptic message/remark*

crystal ROCK /'krɪs·təl/ *n* [C/U] transparent rock that looks like ice, or a piece of it • Something that is **crystal clear** is very clear or very obvious: *The townspeople have made it crystal clear that they don't want the new highway built.* • (in stories) A **crystal ball** is a transparent ball of crystal or glass that produces images by magic of future events.

crystal GLASS /'krɪs·təl/ *n* [C/U] transparent glass of high quality, usually with its surface cut into patterns that reflect light • A crystal is a transparent glass or plastic cover for a watch or clock. [C]

crystal REGULAR SHAPE /'krɪs·təl/ *n* [C] *specialized* the solid state of many simple substances, which have a regular shape and surfaces arranged in similar patterns

C-section /'siː,sek·ʃən/ *n* [C] *medical abbreviation for* CESAREAN (SECTION)

cub /kʌb/ *n* [C] the young of particular wild animals, such as bears and lions • The **Cub Scouts** is an organization modeled after the **Boy Scouts** but for younger boys, of ages 8 to 10 years old. A **Cub Scout** is a member of the organization.

cubbyhole /'kʌb·iː,hoʊl/ *n* [C] a very small room or space

cube SHAPE /kjuːb/ *n* [C] a solid object with six square sides of equal size

cube NUMBER /kjuːb/ *n* [C] the number made by multiplying a number twice by itself • The cube of 2 (= 2 x 2 x 2) is 8.

cubic /'kjuː·bɪk/ *adj* [not gradable] used in units of volume to show when the length of something has been multiplied by its width and height • A cubic centimeter is a centimeter high, a centimeter long, and a centimeter wide.

cubicle /'kjuː·bɪ·kəl/ *n* [C] a small room, often only large enough for one person, within a larger room or area • a work cubicle

cucumber /'kjuː,kʌm·bər/, short form **cuke** n [C] a long, thin vegetable that has a dark green outer skin and is pale green inside • Cucumbers are usually sliced and eaten raw in salads.

cuddle /'kʌd·əl/ *v* [I/T] to put your arms around (someone) and hold them in a loving way, or (of two people) to hold each other close for affection or comfort • She cuddled the baby in her arms. [T] • To cuddle up is to sit or lie close to someone or something: I like to cuddle up in front of the fireplace with a good book. [I]

cuddle /'kʌd·əl/ *n* [C] I need a cuddle.

cuddly /'kʌd·əl·iː/ *adj* of the kind that you want to put your arms around • a cuddly teddy bear

cue SIGNAL /kjuː/ *n* [C] a signal for someone to do or say something, esp. in a play or movie • She waited for her cue—the ring of the telephone—to come on stage. ○ Being passed over for promotion twice was his cue to start looking for another job. • As if **on cue** (= planned to happen exactly at that moment), we turned to each other and embraced.

cue STICK /kjuː/ *n* [C] in the game of POOL, a long, round, wooden stick held at one end and used to hit a white ball and move it against another or other balls to roll them into holes around the edge of a table covered with cloth • A **cue ball** is the white ball that a player hits with the cue.

cuff MATERIAL /kʌf/ *n* [C] (in a shirt) the thicker material at the end of a sleeve around the wrist, or (in a pair of pants) the turned-up part at the bottom of a leg • A **cuff link** is one of a pair of decorative fasteners used to hold together sleeve cuffs that have a hole for these fasteners instead of a button.

cuff HIT /kʌf/ *v* [T] to hit (someone) with your hand • The boys cuffed Zackie and yanked Constance's hair.

cuff FASTEN /kʌf/ *v* [T] short form of HANDCUFF

cuffs /kʌfs/ pl n short form of HANDCUFFS

cuisine /kwɪ'ziːn, kwiː-/ *n* [U] a style of cooking • Southern/Japanese/Mexican cuisine

cuke /kjuːk/ *n* [C] short form of a CUCUMBER

cul-de-sac /'kʌl·də,sæk, 'kʊl-/ *n* [C] a street that is closed at one end

culinary /'kʌl·ə,ner·i, 'kjuː·lə-/ *adj* [not gradable] connected with cooking, esp. as a developed skill or art • a culinary school

cull /kʌl/ *v* [T] to put together or form (something) by collecting parts or pieces from various places, or to collect (something) from various places • The program was culled from the show's first 13 episodes.

culminate /'kʌl·mə,neɪt/ *v* [I/T] to have as a result or be the final result of (a process) • Secret negotiations culminated in the historic peace accord. [I] ○ The discovery culminated many years of research. [T]

culmination /,kʌl·mə'neɪ·ʃən/ *n* [U]

culottes /'kuː·lɑts, 'kjuː-/ pl n women's pants that end at the knee or just below, and that look like a skirt

culpable /'kʌl·pə·bəl/ adj fml deserving to be blamed or considered responsible for something bad • He was equally culpable for his role in the murder conspiracy.

culpability /,kʌl·pə'bɪl·ət·i/ *n* [U]

culprit /'kʌl·prət/ *n* [C] someone who has committed a crime or done something wrong • A culprit is also anything that causes harm or trouble: The culprit was identified as a microorganism that contaminated mayonnaise.

cult /kʌlt/ *n* [C] a system of religious belief, esp. one not recognized as an established religion, or the people who worship according to such a system of belief • A cult is also any behavior or set of beliefs that is strongly followed as if it were part of a religious duty: the cult of body piercing

cultivate GROW /'kʌl·tə,veɪt/ *v* [T] to prepare (land) and grow crops on it, or to grow (a particular crop) • He cultivated soybeans on most of the land.

cultivation /,kʌl·tə'veɪ·ʃən/ *n* [U] • The vineyard now has 400 acres under cultivation.

cultivate DEVELOP /'kʌl·tə,veɪt/ *v* [T] to create (a new condition) by directed effort • We're trying to help these kids cultivate an interest in science. • To cultivate is also to try to become friendly with someone, esp. because they may be able to help you: to cultivate friendships

cultivated /'kʌl·tə,veɪt·əd/ *adj* well educated • a cultivated accent

culture WAY OF LIFE /'kʌl·tʃər/ *n* [C/U] the way of life of a particular people, esp. as shown in their ordinary behavior and habits, their attitudes toward each other, and their moral and religious beliefs • He studied the culture of the Sioux Indians. [U] • **Culture shock** is a feeling of confusion because of suddenly being in a completely different environment that seems strange to you.

cultural /'kʌl·tʃə·rəl/ *adj* • *The country has a rich cultural heritage.*

culturally /'kʌl·tʃə·rə·li/ *adv*

culture ARTS /'kʌl·tʃər/ *n* [U] the arts of describing, showing, or performing that represent the traditions or the way of life of a particular people or group; literature, art, music, dance, theater, etc.

cultural /'kʌl·tʃə·rəl/ *adj* • *the great cultural centers of Europe*

cultured /'kʌl·tʃərd/ *adj* educated in and familiar with literature, art, music, etc.

culture ARTIFICIAL GROWTH /'kʌl·tʃər/ *n* [C] *specialized* the growing of a group of MICROORGANISMS (= very small organisms) or other cells in an artificial environment for scientific purposes, or a group of organisms so grown • *a tissue culture*

–cum– /kʊm, kʌm/ *combining form* used to join two nouns, showing that a person or thing does two things or has two purposes; combined with • *She appointed the actor-cum-diplomat to the post.*

cumbersome /'kʌm·bər·səm/ *adj* difficult to do or manage and taking a lot of time and effort • *Critics say that the process for amending the Constitution is cumbersome, but others defend it.*

cumulative /'kju:·mjə·lət·ɪv/ *adj* increasing as each new amount is added or as each new fact or condition is considered • *No single development is causing the company's financial trouble—it's the cumulative effect of years of weak leadership.*

cumulatively /'kju:·mjə·lət·ɪv·li/ *adv*

cunning /'kʌn·ɪŋ/ *adj* skillful in planning and ready to deceive people in order to get what you want • *a cunning scheme*

cunning /'kʌn·ɪŋ/ *n* [U] • *They made their way safely back through enemy territory by stealth and cunning.*

cunt /kʌnt/ *n* [C] *taboo slang* the sexual organs on the outside of a woman's body • Cunt is also a very offensive word for any woman or for a woman you do not like.

cup /kʌp/ *n* [C] a small, round container, usually with a handle, used esp. for hot drinks such as coffee and tea • *Would you like a cup of coffee?* • A cup is also a unit of measure of measure equal to ½ PINT and often used in cooking: *a cup of flour* • Something that is not your **cup of tea** is not the type of thing that you enjoy or like: *Watching wrestling matches is not my cup of tea.*

cup /kʌp/ *v* [T] **-pp-** to press (your hands) together to form a ball-like shape with an opening at the top between your thumbs, or to hold (something) gently with a hand or between both hands • *He cupped his hands and dipped*

them in the water to get a drink. ○ *She cupped his face in her hands and kissed him twice.*

cupful /'kʌp·fʊl/ *n* [C] the amount held by a cup

cupboard /'kʌb·ərd/ *n* [C] a piece of furniture or a small part of a room with a door behind which there is space for storing things, usually on shelves • *kitchen cupboards*

cupcake /'kʌp·keɪk/ *n* [C] a small, round cake, usually for one person

cupid /'kju:·pəd/ *n* [C] a statue or painting representing the Roman god of love, a naked baby boy with wings

cur /kɜr/ *n* [C] *dated* a dog considered to be worthless or mean

curable /'kjʊr·ə·bəl/ *adj* • See at CURE MAKE WELL.

curator /'kyʊr,eɪt̬·ər, kjʊ'reɪt̬-/ *n* [C] a person in charge of a department of a MUSEUM or other place where objects of art, science, or historical interest are collected, or a person who organizes and arranges a showing of art or other objects of interest

curb EDGE /kɜrb/ *n* [C] a raised edge along the side of a street, often forming part of a path for people to walk on • *She stood on the curb and waited until the light turned green to cross the street.* • **Curbside** means nearer to the curb: *A uniformed driver had the rear curbside door open for her.* • **Curbside** also means close to the street, esp. in front of your own house: *curbside recycling*

curb CONTROL /kɜrb/ *v* [T] to control the growth or expression of (something) • *You've got to learn to curb your temper.*

curd /kɜrd/ *n* [U] the solid substance that is left when the liquid is removed from milk

curdle /'kɜrd·əl/ *v* [I] to change into CURD, or to become sour • *Her scream was enough to curdle your blood* (= make you extremely frightened).

cure MAKE WELL /kjʊr/ *v* [T] to make (someone who is sick) healthy again, or to cause (an illness) to go away • *She was cured of her migraine headaches when she changed her diet.* ○ *(fig.) He worked to promote programs to cure America's social and economic ills.*

cure /kjʊr/ *n* [C] the process of making a sick person healthy again esp. by treating them, or a treatment that causes a disease to go away • *the effort to find a cure for AIDS* • A **cure-all** is something that cures any illness or solves any problem: *There's a danger in believing that the drug is a cure-all.*

curable /'kjʊr·ə·bəl/ *adj* (of a disease) able to be treated in such a way that it will go away and the person who had it can become well again

cure PRESERVE /kjʊr/ *v* [T] to treat (esp. meat) in a special way to stop it from decaying • *Sodium nitrite is used to cure bacon.*

curfew /'kɜr·fju:/ *n* [C] a rule that some or all people must stay off the streets during particular hours, used esp. to maintain peace during a period of violence • *to impose/lift a curfew*

curio /ˈkjʊr·iˌoʊ/ *n* [C] *pl* **curios** a small and unusual object considered to be of special interest or value • *a curio shop*

curiosity INTEREST /ˌkjʊr·iˈɑs·ət·i/ *n* [U] an eager desire to know or learn about something • *Some people experiment with drugs out of curiosity.*

curiosity STRANGE OBJECT /ˌkjʊr·iˈɑs·ət·i/ *n* [C] something that is interesting because it is rare and unusual • *The museum had a collection of mummies and Egyptian curiosities.*

curious INTERESTED /ˈkjʊr·iː·əs/ *adj* interested in learning about people or things around you • *I'm curious to see what's going to happen on the political scene.* [+ *to* infinitive]

curious UNUSUAL /ˈkjʊr·iː·əs/ *adj* unusual and therefore worth noticing • *A curious figure in a red cape and black boots darted into the building.*

curiously /ˈkjʊr·iː·ə·sli/ *adv* strangely • *Curiously enough, they never explained why they arrived an hour early.*

curl /kɜrl/ *n* [C/U] a piece of hair having a curving shape, like part of a circle, or something else having a circular shape • *He loved that dark curl at the back of her neck.* [C] ○ *We watched the curls of smoke rise from his pipe.* [C]

curl /kɜrl/ *v* [I/T] to form or cause (something) to form a curving or twisted shape • *If I don't curl my hair, it looks too stringy.* [T] • To **curl up** is to lie in a curved position that is comfortable: *Carpenter had slept through most of the trip, curled up on the back seat.*

curler /ˈkɜr·lər/ *n* [C] one of a number of small tubes that are put in a person's hair to make it curl

curly /ˈkɜr·li/ *adj* • *curly hair*
curliness /ˈkɜr·liː·nəs/ *n* [U]

curling /ˈkɜr·lɪŋ/ *n* [U] a game played on ice esp. in Scotland and Canada, in which special flat, round stones are slid toward a mark
curler /ˈkɜr·lər/ *n* [C] • *On Thursday night the rink was taken over by the women curlers.*

currant /ˈkɜr·ənt, ˈkʌ·rənt/ *n* [C] a sour BERRY (= small, round fruit) that grows on bushes, or the plant on which it grows • *red currant jelly* • A currant is also a small RAISIN (= dried fruit) used esp. in baking.

currency MONEY /ˈkɜr·ən·si, ˈkʌ·rən-/ *n* [C/U] the money in use in a particular country • *The US dollar fell yesterday against most foreign currencies.* [C]

currency ACCEPTANCE /ˈkɜr·ən·si, ˈkʌ·rən-/ *n* [U] *fml* the state of being commonly known or accepted, or of being used in many places • *The idea that computer use enhances students' motivation has gained currency in recent years.*

current HAPPENING NOW /ˈkɜr·ənt, ˈkʌ·rənt/ *adj* of the present time or most recent • *Under cur-*

rent state law, students can drop out of school legally at age 17.

currently /ˈkɜr·ənt·li, ˈkʌ·rənt-/ *adv* [not gradable] at the present time; now • *He currently is directing TV sitcoms.*

current MOVEMENT /ˈkɜr·ənt, ˈkʌ·rənt/ *n* [C] a movement of water or air • *The boat drifted with the current until it was miles from shore.* • Electric current is the passage of electricity through a wire.

curriculum /kəˈrɪk·jə·ləm/ *n* [C] *pl* **curricula** /kəˈrɪk·jə·lə/ or **curriculums** all the courses given in a school, college, etc., or a particular course of study in one subject

curry /ˈkɜr·i, ˈkʌ·ri/ *n* [C/U] a dish, originally from India, consisting usually of meat or vegetables cooked in a spicy sauce • *Lamb curry is this restaurant's specialty.* [U]

curse SWEAR /kɜrs/ *v* [I/T] to say rude or offensive words about (something or someone) because you are angry • *I cursed and raved at the stupidity of the Americans who were about to bomb and kill us.* [I]
curse /kɜrs/ *n* [C] • *Finally the soldiers left, muttering curses on the way out.*

curse WISH EVIL /kɜrs/ *v* [T] to wish for something evil or unpleasant to happen to (someone or something), as by asking a magical power • *Curse them! They're animals, beasts!*
curse /kɜrs/ *n* [C] • *In the story, a wicked witch put a curse on the princess.*

cursor /ˈkɜr·sər/ *n* [C] a movable symbol on a computer screen that shows the point where you can change a text or image • *You can move the cursor by using the mouse.*

cursory /ˈkɜr·sə·ri/ *adj* done quickly with little attention to detail • *He gave the picture a cursory glance.*

curt /kɜrt/ *adj* (of a person's manner or speech) rude as a result of being very quick or brief • *He sent a curt, one-sentence letter of resignation to the mayor.*

curtly /ˈkɜrt·li/ *adv* • *She nodded to him curtly and kept talking to someone else.*

curtail /kərˈteɪl/ *v* [T] to reduce or limit (something), or to stop (something) before it is finished • *He had to curtail his speech when time ran out.*

curtailment /kərˈteɪl·mənt/ *n* [U]

curtain /ˈkɜrt·ən/ *n* [C] a piece of cloth or other material that hangs across a window or space to decorate a room or to make it dark or private • *In the restaurant, arches covered with beaded curtains divide the room.* • A **curtain rod** is a pole, often decorative, from which a curtain hangs. • In a theater, the curtain is a large, movable sheet of heavy material that separates the

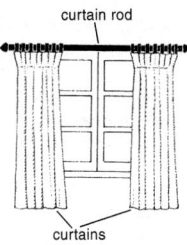
curtain rod

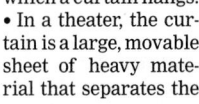
curtains

stage from the area where people are sitting.
• The curtain is also the time at which a performance begins: *The curtain is at 8 o'clock.*

curvaceous /kər'veɪ·ʃəs/ *adj* (of a woman) having a body with attractive curves

curvature /'kɜr·və·tʃər, -,tʃʊr/ *n* [U] the state of being curved or bent • *the curvature of the earth*

curve /kɜrv/ *v* [I/T] to form or move in the direction of a line that turns continuously and has no straight parts, or to cause (something) to do this • *The road curves around the cemetery.* [I]

curve /kɜrv/ *n* [C] • *a curve in a road*

curvy /'kɜr·vi/ *adj* having a shape with a lot of curves • *a curvy road*

cushion /'kʊʃ·ən/ *n* [C] a large, usually square bag filled with soft material, used as a movable part of a chair or SOFA, for sitting on or resting your back against, or a similar but smaller bag used to make yourself more comfortable while sitting • *She sank back against the sofa cushions.*

cushion /'kʊʃ·ən/ *v* [T] • *The soft grass cushioned his fall* (= made it hurt less). • *He lost his job, but he has enough money in the bank to* **cushion the blow** (= make a bad situation less serious).

cushy /'kʊʃ·i/ *adj infml* very easy • *a cushy job*

cuss /kʌs/ *v* [I] *infml* to CURSE SWEAR

custard /'kʌs·tərd/ *n* [U] a soft, usually sweet food made from a mixture of eggs, milk, flavoring, and sugar

custodian /kʌs'toʊd·iː·ən/ *n* [C] a person who has responsibility for the care, protection, or maintaining of something or someone • *King Hussein was recognized as the custodian of Muslim holy sites in East Jerusalem.*

custodial /kʌs'toʊd·iː·əl/ *adj* [not gradable] • *custodial care* ○ *a custodial staff*

custody CARE /'kʌs·təd·i/ *n* [U] the right or duty to care for someone or something, as for a child whose parents have separated or died • *The court awarded custody of the child to the mother.*

custody KEPT BY POLICE /'kʌs·təd·i/ *n* [U] the state of being kept by the police, usually while waiting to go to court for trial • *The police have taken the suspect into custody.*

custom TRADITION /'kʌs·təm/ *n* [C/U] a way of behaving or a belief that has been established for a long time among a group of people • *It was a time-honored custom of the club that blue chairs were reserved for senior members only.* [C] ○ *She's studying the language and customs of the Hopi Indians.* [C]

customary /'kʌs·tə,mer·i/ *adj* • *It was customary for women to wear hats when they went to church.*

custom USUAL ACTIVITY /'kʌs·təm/ *n* [C] something you usually do • *He left the house at nine exactly, as was his custom.*

customary /'kʌs·tə,mer·i/ *adj* usual • *She's not her customary cheerful self today.* ○ *The students sat in their customary classroom seats.*

customarily /,kʌs·tə'mer·ə·li/ *adv* [not gradable] usually • *People who receive gifts do not customarily ask what they cost.*

custom MADE SPECIALLY /'kʌs·təm/ *adj* [not gradable] specially made for a particular buyer • *custom drapes/woodworking* • *His shoes were* **custom-made** (= made specially for him).

customize /'kʌs·tə,maɪz/ *v* [T] • *We will customize existing software to meet our clients' needs.*

customer /'kʌs·tə·mər/ *n* [C] a person who buys goods or a service • *We try to give all our customers good service.*

customs /'kʌs·təmz/ *pl n* money paid to the government when you take particular goods from one country to another

customs /'kʌs·təmz/ *n* [U] the place at a port, airport, or border where travelers' bags are examined for illegal or taxable goods • *customs officials* ○ *It took us ages to get through customs when we got back from Italy.*

cut DIVIDE /kʌt/ *v* [I/T] **cutting,** *past* **cut** to use a sharp tool such as a knife to break the surface of (something), or to divide or make (something) smaller • *Cut the apple in half.* [T] ○ *She wanted to have her hair cut* (= made shorter). [T] ○ *We had to cut two trees down* (= remove them) *to make room for the swimming pool.* [M] ○ *The children cut the pictures out* (= removed them by cutting) *and stuck them in their scrapbooks.* [M] • If a person is cut, they are injured by something sharp that breaks the skin and makes them bleed: *I stepped on a piece of glass and cut my foot.* [T] • If you say something **cuts both ways,** you mean that it has both advantages and disadvantages: *The promotion cuts both ways because though I'll make more money, I'll have to be away from my family more often.* • If you **cut off** your **nose to spite** your **face,** in an effort to punish someone, you hurt yourself more than you hurt them. • If you are at the **cutting edge** of something, you are involved in its most recent stage of development: *His research is at the cutting edge of new therapies for cancer.*

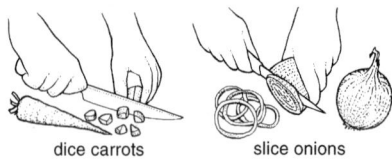

dice carrots   slice onions
cut

cut /kʌt/ *n* [C] something made by cutting • *She went to the butcher's to get a good cut of meat.* • A cut is an injury to the skin made by a sharp object: *She had a nasty cut on her hand.* • A cut is also the particular way clothing looks: *the cut of a suit* • (*infml*) A cut is also a share: *I was part-owner of the business, and when my sister sold it, I said I wanted my cut.*

cut /kʌt/ *adj* [not gradable] • *These cut flowers will last three days in fresh water.* • A **cut-and-dried** solution to a problem is clear and simple and removes any further difficulty: *Unfortunately, there is no cut-and-dried answer to the problem of crime.*

cutting /'kʌt·ɪŋ/ *n* [C] a piece cut from a plant and used to grow a new plant • See also CUTTING.

cut REDUCE /kʌt/ *v* [T] **cutting**, *past* **cut** to make less in size, amount, length, etc. • *We've got to cut costs.* ○ *The original movie was almost four hours long, but it was later cut to two hours.*

cut /kʌt/ *n* [C] • *Many workers had to take a cut in pay.* ○ *For the TV version, they made several cuts in the movie.*

cut MISS /kʌt/ *v* [T] **cutting**, *past* **cut** to stay away from (esp. a class) • *He was cutting classes and getting failing grades.*

cut STOP /kʌt/ *v* [I/T] **cutting**, *past* **cut** to stop or interrupt something, or to stop working suddenly or cause this to happen • *Since his heart attack he's cut out smoking altogether.* [I always + adv/prep] ○ *Because of failing grades, he was cut* (= released) *from the team.* [T] ○ *"Cut!"* (= Stop filming!) *" shouted the director.* [I] • *I was talking to Anne when Joe* **cut in** (= interrupted us). • (*infml*) If a person says **Cut it out** or **Cut that out**, they are annoyed and are telling someone to stop talking or behaving as they are.

cut GROW TEETH /kʌt/ *v* [T] **cutting**, *past* **cut** to grow (a new tooth) • *The baby was cranky last night because she's cutting a tooth.*

cut CROSS /kʌt/ *v* [I always + adv/prep] **cutting**, *past* **cut** to go through or across a place, esp. in order to get somewhere quickly • *To get to school I cut through the field.* • If you **cut corners**, you do something in the easiest, cheapest, or fastest way: *I don't like to cut corners when I have company for dinner.*

cut CARDS /kʌt/ *v* [I/T] **cutting**, *past* **cut** to divide a pile of cards into two parts • *Who's going to cut (the cards)?* [I/T]

cut RECORD /kʌt/ *v* [T] **cutting**, *past* **cut** to make a recording of music or speech on (a record) • *When did Elvis cut his first record?*

cut DEAL WITH /kʌt/ *v* [T] *infml* • If someone cannot **cut it/cut the mustard**, they are not able to deal with problems or difficulties satisfactorily.

◻**cut across** /'--'-/ *v adv* to go beyond (other things to be considered) • *Interest in electronic mail cuts across age groups.*

◻**cut back** /'-'-/ *v adv* to reduce or stop • *He was advised to cut back on his alcohol consumption.*

cutback /'kʌt·bæk/ *n* [C] a reduction, esp. one made to save money • *Cutbacks in public spending are expected in the next budget.*

◻**cut down** /'-'-/ *v adv* to reduce in amount, size, or frequency • *I've decided to cut down on snacks.*

◻**cut off** *obj* STOP , **cut** *obj* **off** /'-'-/ *v adv* [M] to stop or interrupt something suddenly • *We were cut off in the middle of our phone conversation.*

cutoff /'kʌt·ɔːf/ *n* [C] a fixed point or limit at which something is stopped • *The cutoff point for blood donations is usually age 65.* • See also CUTOFF.

◻**cut off** *obj* DRIVE , **cut** *obj* **off** /'-'-/ *v adv* [M] (of a driver or vehicle) to move suddenly in front of another driver or vehicle, leaving too little space • *He claimed that a truck had cut him off just before the accident.*

◻**cut out for** /-'--/ *v adv prep* [T] to be the right type of person to do (a type of work) • *He's just not cut out for politics.*

◻**cut short** *obj*, **cut** *obj* **short** /'-'-/ *v adv* [M] to stop (something) suddenly before it is completed • *We cut short our vacation when we learned of my mother's illness.*

◻**cut through** /'-'-/ *v adv* [T] to understand (something that is not easy to understand) • *She can cut through the confusing statistics and get at the important facts.*

cute CHARMING /kjuːt/ *adj* [*-er/-est* only] (esp. of something or someone small or young) charming and attractive • *She was a really cute baby.* • Something described as cute is attractive and pleasant: *She had a cute apartment with a little garden.*

cute DECEIVING /kjuːt/ *adj* [*-er/-est* only] *disapproving* too carefully designed to get approval or appear attractive, and therefore seeming dishonest • *He thinks it's cute to tell dirty jokes.* [+ *to* infinitive]

cutesy /'kjuːt·si/ *adj* [*-er/-est* only] *slightly disapproving* artificially attractive and charming, esp. in a childlike way • *The house is full of cutesy pictures of kittens.*

cuticle /'kjuːt̬·ɪ·kəl/ *n* [C] the thin skin at the base of the nails on the fingers and toes

cutlery /'kʌt·lə·ri/ *n* [U] knives, forks, and spoons used for eating food; **silverware**

cutlet /'kʌt·lət/ *n* [C] a small slice of meat, esp. from the RIBS, that is usually fried • *veal cutlets*

cutoff /'kʌt̬·ɔːf/ *n* [C] a road that leaves another and provides a shorter route • *We took the cutoff and saved 20 minutes on the trip home.* • See also cutoff at CUT OFF STOP.

cutoffs /'kʌt̬·ɔːfs/, **cutoff jeans** /,kʌt̬,ɔːf'dʒiːnz/ *pl n* a pair of JEANS with the legs removed at or above the knee

cutout /'kʌt̬·ɑut/ *n* [C] a shape cut out, or to be cut out, from something • *This children's book has animal cutouts.*

cut–rate /,kʌt,reɪt/ *adj* [not gradable] available at a lower price than usual • *cut-rate merchandise*

cutthroat /'kʌt·θrout/ *adj* showing no care or

consideration for the harm done to others with whom you are in competition • *He was unhappy working in the cutthroat world of advertising.*

cutting /'kʌt̬·ɪŋ/ *adj* said or done to hurt someone's feelings • *She made a cutting remark about his table manners.* • See also **cutting** at CUT DIVIDE.

CV /si:'vi:/ *n* [C] a written description of your education, achievements, and previous employment, used esp. to show someone who may employ you in a new job, or to qualify for an honor

cyanide /'saɪ·ə‚naɪd/ *n* [U] an extremely powerful poison

cyberspace /'saɪ·bər‚speɪs/ *n* [U] an electronic system that allows computer users around the world to communicate with each other or to access information for any purpose • *Seventeen-year-old Sam is a cyberspace hacker of considerable talent.*

cycle BICYCLE /'saɪ·kəl/ *n* [C] *short form of* BICYCLE • PIC BICYCLE

cycle /'saɪ·kəl/ *v* [I] • *We cycled around campus in the afternoon.*

cyclist /'saɪ·kləst/ *n* [C] a person who rides a bicycle • *There's a special lane for cyclists.*

cycle SERIES /'saɪ·kəl/ *n* [C] a complete set of events that repeat themselves regularly in the same order, or a regularly repeated period of time • *Some economists predict the business cycle will turn downward.*

cyclical /'saɪ·klɪ·kəl, 'sɪk·lə-/, **cyclic** /'saɪ·klɪk, 'sɪk·lɪk/ *adj* • *Changes in the economy often follow a cyclical pattern.*

cyclone /'saɪ·kloʊn/ *n* [C] a violent and often destructive storm in which the wind moves very fast in a circular direction

cylinder SHAPE /'sɪl·ən·dər/ *n* [C] a solid that has long straight sides and circular ends of equal size, or a hollow object shaped like this and often used as a container • *Inside a roll of toilet paper there's a cardboard cylinder.*

cylindrical /sə'lɪn·drɪ·kəl/ *adj* • *cylindrical structures*

cylinder ENGINE PART /'sɪl·ən·dər/ *n* [C] the tube-shaped part of an engine inside of which the PISTON (= part that causes the fuel to produce power) moves up and down • *The engine isn't firing on all its cylinders.*

cymbal /'sɪm·bəl/ *n* [C usually pl] a flat, round musical instrument made of BRASS (= metal) that is hit with a stick or struck against another such instrument to make a loud noise

cynical /'sɪn·ɪ·kəl/ *adj* not trusting or respecting the goodness of other people and their actions, but believing that people are interested only in themselves • *Listening to politicians for too long can make you cynical.* ○ *She's become cynical about men.*

cynic /'sɪn·ɪk/ *n* [C] a person who believes that other people are interested only in themselves and therefore doubts that they can be good

cynicism /'sɪn·ə‚sɪz·əm/ *n* [U] • *He's often been accused of cynicism, but he says he's just realistic.*

cyst /sɪst/ *n* [C] a round growth under the skin or deeper in the body, containing liquid or tissue

czar /zɑr, tsɑr/ *n* [C] (before 1917) the male Russian ruler • (*infml*) A czar is also a person who has a lot of power in a particular activity: *The president has appointed a drug czar to lead the fight on illegal drugs.*

D, d

D LETTER, **d** /diː/ n [C] pl **D's** or **Ds** or **d's** or **ds** the fourth letter of the English alphabet

D MUSICAL NOTE /diː/ n [C/U] pl **D's** or **Ds** the second note in the **major scale** (= series of notes) that begins on the note C, or a set of notes based on this note

D MARK /diː/ n [C] pl **D's** or **Ds** a mark given for an exam, a course, or a piece of work which shows that your work is thought of as below average and that it needs improvement • *I can't believe I got a D in history last semester.*

D NUMBER, **d** /diː/, faɪvˈhʌn·drəd/ *number* the ROMAN NUMERAL for the number 500

D.A. n [C] *abbreviation for* **district attorney**, see at DISTRICT

dab /dæb/ v [I/T] **-bb-** to touch (something) lightly and quickly, usually repeatedly • *He dabbed at his eyes with a tissue.* [I] • If you dab something on a surface, you put a small amount of something on it: *She dabbed a little perfume on her wrists.* [T]

dab /dæb/ n [C] a small amount of a substance • *a dab of lipstick*

dabble /ˈdæb·əl/ v [I] to take a slight and not very serious interest in a subject or try a particular activity for a short period • *I don't paint much, I just dabble.*

dachshund /ˈdɑks·hʊnt, -hʊnd; ˈdɑk·sənd/ n [C] a type of dog that is small and has a long body and short legs

dachshund

dad /dæd/ n [C] *infml* a father • *Can you give me $20, Dad? ○ My dad's a fireman.* • LP TITLES AND FORMS OF ADDRESS

daddy /ˈdæd·i/ n [C] *esp. a child's word for* a father • *Why don't you have any hair on your head, Daddy? ○ Mommy and Daddy are taking me to the circus.* • LP TITLES AND FORMS OF ADDRESS

daddy longlegs /ˌdæd·iˈlɔːŋˌlɛgz/ n [C] pl **daddy longlegs** *infml* a small creature with eight legs that looks like a SPIDER

daffodil /ˈdæf·ə,dɪl/ n [C] a yellow, bell-shaped flower with a long stem, commonly seen in the spring

dagger /ˈdæg·ər/ n [C] a short, pointed knife that is sharp on both sides, used esp. in the past as a weapon

daily /ˈdeɪ·li/ adv, adj [not gradable] happening on or relating to every day, or every working day • *Take the pills twice daily. ○ Exercise is part of my daily routine.*

daily /ˈdeɪ·li/ n [C] a newspaper published every day of the week or every day except the weekend

dainty /ˈdeɪnt·i/ adj small and attractive in a delicate way • *a dainty wrist/hand* ○ *dainty flowers*

dairy /ˈder·i, dær·i/ n [C/U] a place on a farm where milk and cream are kept and cheese and butter are made, a company that supplies milk and products made from milk, or milk and products made from milk • *She eats no meat and very little dairy.* [U] ○ *I'll only buy nonfat dairy products.* [U]

daisy /ˈdeɪ·zi/ n [C] a type of flower with a round, yellow center and a lot of thin, white petals

dally /ˈdæl·i/ v [I] to waste time or do something slowly • *She dallied over her morning coffee.*

dam /dæm/ n [C] a wall built across a river to stop the flow and collect the water, esp. to make a RESERVOIR (= an artificial lake) that provides water for an area or can be used to make electricity

dam /dæm/ v [T] **-mm-** to build a dam across (a river) in order to store the water • *Fish are affected when a river is dammed up.* [M]

damage /ˈdæm·ɪdʒ/ v [T] to harm or spoil (something) • *Many buildings were badly damaged by the earthquake.* ○ *News reports damaged the senator's reputation.*

damage /ˈdæm·ɪdʒ/ n [U] • *The fire did serious damage to the buildings.* ○ *He suffered brain damage in the accident.* • **Damage control** is the process of limiting the damaging effects of an action or mistake: *You can't live on junk food and then attempt dietary damage control with handfuls of vitamins.*

damages /ˈdæm·ɪ·dʒɪz/ pl n *law* money that is paid to someone by a person or organization who was responsible for causing them some injury or loss • *They were awarded $500,000 in damages.*

dame /deɪm/ n [C] *dated slang* a woman • *a fast-talking dame*

damn EXPRESSION /dæm/, **damn it** /ˈdæm·ət, -ɪt/, **dammit** /ˈdæm·ət, -ɪt/ *exclamation infml* an expression of anger or annoyance • *Damn! I spilled coffee on my blouse.* • USAGE: This word may be considered offensive by some people.

damn /dæm/ n [U] *infml* the least amount • *He talks big, but he isn't worth a damn in the game.*

damn /dæm/, **damned** /dæmd/ adj [not gradable] *infml* • *I can't get this damn car to start!*

damn SURPRISE /dæm/ v [T] *infml* used to express surprise • *She's marrying that guy she met last month? Well, I'll be damned!*

damnedest /ˈdæm·dəst/ adj [not gradable] *infml* • *Well, that's the damnedest thing I ever heard!*

damn VERY /dæm/ adv, adj [not gradable] *infml* very; great • *I know damn well you're in* there. ○ *You're a damn fool to try and drive that old car cross-country.*

damnedest /'dæm·dəst/ *n infml* • If you **do/ try** your **damnedest**, you try very hard: *I try my damnedest to produce a good product at a fair price.*

damn BLAME /dæm/ *v* [T] to blame or strongly criticize • *The novel was damned for being too political.* • *No matter what you do in that situation, you're* **damned if** *you* **do and damned if** *you* **don't** (= criticized whatever you decide).

damning /'dæm·ɪŋ/ *adj* very critical, or showing clearly that someone is wrong or guilty • *a damning report/finding*

damn PUNISH /dæm/ *v* [T] (esp. of God) to force (someone) to stay in hell and be punished forever

damned /dæmd/ *pl n* (in the Christian religion) the people who have been sent to hell after their death

damp /dæmp/ *adj* [-er/-est only] slightly wet, esp. in a way that is not pleasant or comfortable • *damp socks* ○ *a cold, damp day*

dampen /'dæm·pən/ *v* [T] • *Rain dampened the tent, but it dried in the sun.* • If something dampens feelings, esp. of excitement or enjoyment, it makes them less strong: *I think the accident dampened his enthusiasm for baseball.*

dampness /'dæmp·nəs/ *n* [U] • *The dampness bothers my arthritis.*

damsel /'dæm·zəl/ *n* [C] *dated literary* a young woman who is not married • *Gallant knights rescue damsels in distress.*

dance /dæns/ *v* [I/T] to move the body and feet in rhythm to music • *Who was she dancing with at the party?* [I] ○ *They danced a waltz.* [T] • If something dances, it moves quickly and easily: *Sunlight danced on the water.* [I]

dance /dæns/ *n* [C/U] an act of dancing, or a particular set of movements • *"May I have this dance?" he asked.* [C] ○ *The next dance will be a waltz.* [C] ○ *Do you take dance lessons?* [U] • A dance is also a social occasion at which people dance: *the eighth-grade dance* [C]

dancer /'dæn·sər/ *n* [C] • *He's a dancer with the New York City Ballet.*

dandelion /'dæn·dəl,aɪ·ən/ *n* [C] a small, bright yellow flower that grows wild and makes light, white, hairlike seeds that are easily blown

dandruff /'dæn·drəf/ *n* [U] small, white bits of dead skin that sometimes gather in the hair or fall on the clothes, esp. on the shoulders

dandy /'dæn·di/ *adj infml* very good • *I'm doing just dandy, thanks.*

danger /'deɪn·dʒər/ *n* [C/U] the possibility of harm or death, or of something unpleasant happening • *I quickly understood the dangers of rock climbing.* [C] ○ *I felt my life was in danger.* [U] ○ *They're in danger of losing the playoffs.* [U] • A danger is also a harmful influence: *the dangers of drugs* [C]

dangerous /'deɪn·dʒə·rəs/ *adj* • *Alcohol can be dangerous for pregnant women.* ○ *He views increased gambling as a dangerous social trend.*

dangerously /'deɪn·dʒə·rə·sli/ *adv* • *dangerously high winds*

dangle /'dæŋ·gəl/ *v* [I/T] to hang loosely, or to cause (something) to hang • *A loose wire was dangling from the wall.* [I] ○ *He dangled the puppet in front her.* [T]

Danish (pastry) /'deɪ·nɪʃ ('peɪ·stri)/ *n* [C/U] a type of sweet pastry for one person, often filled with fruit or cheese

dank /dæŋk/ *adj* [-er/-est only] (esp. of buildings and air) wet, cold, and unpleasant • *For years they lived in a dank, dark basement apartment.*

dapper /'dæp·ər/ *adj* (of a man) looking stylish and neat

dare BE BRAVE /der, dær/ *v* he/she/it **dares** or **dare** to be brave enough to do something difficult or dangerous • *She wouldn't dare go out alone there at night.* [T] ○ *He wanted to touch it, but he didn't dare.* [I] • Dare can also mean foolish enough to do something that you have no right to do: *If he dares to come one step nearer, I'll scream.* [+ *to* infinitive]

daring /'der·ɪŋ, 'dær-/ *adj* showing bravery and willingness to risk danger or criticism • *a daring, experimental performance* ○ *Specially trained troops carried out a daring rescue operation.*

dare ASK /der, dær/ *v* [T] to ask (someone) to do something that involves risk • *I dare you to ask him to dance.*

dare /der, dær/ *n* [C] • *He jumped into the river on a dare.* • A **daredevil** is a person who does dangerous things and takes risks.

dark WITHOUT LIGHT /dɑrk/ *adj* [-er/-est only] with little or no light, or having little brightness • *It was too dark to see much of anything.* ○ *What time does it get dark in the summer?* • Dark colors have less white in them: *a dark blue dress* ○ *dark hair/eyes* • **Dark glasses** are **sunglasses**. See at SUN.

dark /dɑrk/ *n* [U] the absence of light • *Does eating carrots really help you to see in the dark?* ○ *She arrived home well before/after dark* (= before/after the sun had gone down). • *Our boss tends to keep us* **in the dark** (= not informed).

darken /'dɑr·kən/ *v* [I/T] • *The sky darkened as thick smoke billowed from the refinery.* [I] • *She pulled down the shades to darken the room.* [T]

darkness /'dɑrk·nəs/ *n* [U] • *The city was plunged into darkness by the power blackout.*

dark SAD /dɑrk/ *adj* [-er/-est only] unhappy or sad; GLOOMY • *His makes dark predictions about the future.*

dark EVIL /dɑrk/ *adj* [-er/-est only] evil or threatening • *He gave me a dark look when I criticized his work.*

dark horse /'dɑrk'hɔːrs/ *n* [C] *infml* someone

who is not well known but becomes or could become a surprise winner in a competition, esp. an election • *a dark horse in the primaries*

darling /ˈdɑr·lɪŋ/ *n* [C] used to show affection when speaking to someone • *Hello, darling.*

darling /ˈdɑr·lɪŋ/ *adj* [not gradable] much loved • *Here's a picture of my darling child.*

darn EXPRESSION /dɑrn/, **darn it** /ˈdɑr·nət, -nɪt/ *exclamation infml* used instead of DAMN to express annoyance • *Darn it! I missed my bus.*

darn /dɑrn/, **darned** /dɑrnd/ *adj*, *adv* [not gradable] *infml* • *Where's my darn notebook?* • Darn can also mean extremely: *I'm too darn tired to go out tonight.*

darn REPAIR /dɑrn/ *v* [T] to repair (a hole or a piece of clothing) with long stitches across the hole and other stitches woven across them • *to darn socks*

dart WEAPON /dɑrt/ *n* [C] a small, thin object with a sharp point that is thrown by hand in a game, or fired from a gun or blown from a tube when used as a weapon • *poison darts*

darts /dɑrts/ *n* [U] a game in which darts are thrown at a circular board, scoring the number of points marked on the board

dart MOVE QUICKLY /dɑrt/ *v* [I always + adv/prep] to (cause to) move quickly or suddenly • *She darted out from between two parked cars.*

dash MOVE QUICKLY /dæʃ/ *v* [I] to move quickly • *She dashed to the store for some juice.* ○ *Mary's always dashing from one meeting to another.*

dash /dæʃ/ *n* [C usually sing] • *We made a dash for the plane.* • A dash is also a race over a short distance: *a 50-yard dash*

dash HIT /dæʃ/ *v* [I/T] to hit with great force, esp. causing damage • *Waves dashed against the cliffs.* [I] ○ (*fig.*) *Hopes of an economic recovery have been dashed* (= destroyed) *by the latest unemployment statistics.* [T]

dash SMALL AMOUNT /dæʃ/ *n* [C] a small amount of something added to or mixed with something else • *Add a dash of salt to the mixture.*

dash LINE /dæʃ/ *n* [C] a short, horizontal mark (—) used to separate parts of sentences • LP HYPHEN

dashboard /ˈdæʃ·bɔrd, -boʊrd/, *short form* **dash** *n* [C] the part of a car that contains some of the controls used for driving and the devices for measuring esp. speed and distance

dashing /ˈdæʃ·ɪŋ/ *adj dated* attractive and stylish because of being energetic, exciting, and confident • *a dashing young man*

data /ˈdeɪt̬·ə, ˈdæt̬·ə, ˈdɑt̬·ə/ *n* [U] information collected for use • *They had data on health, education, and economic development.* • A **database** is a large amount of information stored in a computer system in such a way that it can be easily looked at or changed. • **Data processing** is the use of a computer to perform calculations on data. • USAGE: Although originally a plural (the rarely used singular is datum) and used with a plural verb, data is

DASH [— OR –]

A dash is a horizontal line that marks a sudden break or pause in a sentence. Dashes are used:

to interrupt a sentence to give extra information or an added thought

Boris took a trip to the San Juan Islands—near Seattle—for his vacation. • *I saw Nicole—you remember her, don't you?—waiting at a bus stop.*

to start a new, independent part of a sentence that follows from the main part, or explains it

We had out tickets, our bags were packed—we were ready to go. • *Local businesses are in financial trouble—hundreds of jobs may be lost.*

In more formal writing, a colon (:), semicolon (;), or period (.) is generally used instead.

to show that the speaker pauses, is interrupted, or is changing what they want to say

"Well—if you insist." • *"I'm sorry I'm late, but—"* • *"Josh, take this to—no, don't bother, I'll take it myself."*

to mean to

During the years 1985–90, prices increased 5–10 percent. • *the Los Angeles–Chicago flight* • *a cost–benefit analysis* • *She won her tennis match, 6–4, 6–3.*

Sometimes a hyphen (-) is used instead of a dash.

now often used as an uncount noun with a singular verb.

date DAY /deɪt/ *n* [C] a numbered day in a month, often given with the name of the month or with the month and the year • *Today's date is June 24, 1998.* ○ *We agreed to meet again at a later date.* ○ *Please fill in your date of birth on the application form.* ○ *I've made a date* (= agreed to a date and time) *to see her about the house.* • *I wrote to you two months ago, but I have not received any response* **to date** (= up to now).

date /deɪt/ *v* [I/T] • *The last letter I received from the insurance company was dated August 30, 1999.* [T] ○ *This signature dates from* (= originated at the time of) *the 1800s.* [I]

date MEETING /deɪt/ *n* [C] a social meeting planned in advance • *We made a date to meet Evelyn and Josie at noon tomorrow for lunch.* • A date is a person you are planning to meet socially and in whom you might have a romantic interest: *Who is your date for the prom?* • **Date rape** is a situation during a date in which a woman is forced to have sex against her will by a man whom she knows.

date /deɪt/ *v* [I/T] • *They dated for five years before they got married.* [I]

date FRUIT /deɪt/ *n* [C] the sweet, brown fruit of various types of PALM tree

COMMON WAYS OF GIVING THE DATE

WRITTEN	SPOKEN
July 18, 1998	*July eighteenth, nineteen ninety-eight*
18 July 1998	*the eighteenth of July, nineteen ninety-eight*

Dates may also be written using numbers only. Notice the difference between the US style and the Canadian and British style.

US	7/18/98	*July eighteenth, nineteen ninety-eight*
	or	or
	7-18-98	*Seven, eighteen, ninety-eight*
Cdn/Br	18/7/98	*the eighteenth of July, nineteen ninety-eight*
	or	
	18.7.98	*eighteen, seven, ninety-eight* or *the eighteenth of the seventh, ninety-eight*

The names of the months

Abbreviations can be used for the names of most months.

Jan.	Apr	.July	Oct.
Feb.	May	Aug.	Nov.
Mar.	June	Sept.	Dec.

The name of the year

The year is usually read by dividing it into two numbers:

| 1984 | *nineteen eighty-four* |

But years that end in -00 through -09 are pronounced differently.

1900	*nineteen hundred*
1909	*nineteen oh nine*
2001	*two thousand and one* or *twenty oh one*

The first two numbers of the year are sometimes omitted.

Where were you in '82? • The Beatles were popular during the '60s (=1960 to 1969).

dated /'deɪt̬·əd/ *adj* showing the facts or style of the past rather than of the present • *This information is dated.*

dative /'deɪt̬·ɪv/ *adj* [not gradable] *specialized* (in grammar) having or relating to the CASE (= form) of a noun, pronoun, or adjective used to show that a word is the **indirect object** *of a verb that has two objects*

daub /dɔːb, dɑb/ *v* [T always + adv/prep] to put (esp. a thick liquid) on or in something with a quick movement • *The children daubed finger paint on large sheets of paper.*

daughter /'dɔːt̬·ər/ *n* [C] a female child in relation to her parents • *We have a son and a daughter.* • PIC FAMILY TREE

daughter–in–law /'dɔːt̬·ə·rən‚lɔː/ *n* [C] *pl* **daughters-in-law** /'dɔːt̬·ər·zən‚lɔː/ the wife of a person's son • PIC FAMILY TREE

daunt /dɔːnt, dɑnt/ *v* [T] to make (someone) feel slightly frightened or worried about their ability to achieve something; to discourage • *She's not at all daunted by criticism.*

daunting /'dɔːnt̬·ɪŋ, 'dɑnt-/ *adj* • *Reforming the welfare system is a daunting task.*

dawdle /'dɔːd·əl/ *v* [I] to do something very slowly, as though you do not want to finish it • *She told her daughter to quit dawdling and get dressed or she'd be late for school.*

dawn /dɔːn, dɑn/ *n* the period in the day when light from the sun begins to appear in the sky • *(fig.) Computers mark the dawn of a new age.* [U]

dawn /dɔːn, dɑn/ *v* [I] • *Winston left his house as the day was dawning.*

□ **dawn on** /'--/ *v prep* [T] to become known or obvious to (someone), often suddenly • *It finally dawned on him that she'd been joking.*

day /deɪ/ *n* [C] a period of 24 hours, esp. from 12 o'clock one night to 12 o'clock the next night, or the part of this period after the sun rises but before it goes down, when there is light • *My husband picks up our son every day after school.* ○ *In summer the days are longer and we have cookouts in the backyard.* ○ *We leave on vacation the day after tomorrow.* • A day is also the part of a period of 24 hours that you spend at work: *He's been working 12-hour days this week.* • Days can mean a long period of time: *In those days* (= that period in history), *people had large families.* • *The same problems keep coming up* **day after day** (= repeatedly). • *The noise is awful—you can hear the traffic* **day and night** (= all the time) • *I do the same things* **day in, day out** (= every day). • *Your* **day-to-day** (= ordinary and regular) *responsibilities will include sorting the mail and making appointments.* • If it is **not** your **day**, you are having a bad day: *I missed my train and forgot my glasses—I guess it's just not my day.* • **Daybreak** is DAWN. • **Day care** is care provided during the day for young children, esp. in order to allow their parents to work. ○ *She ran a* **day-care center** *for working mothers.* • The **Day of Atonement** is YOM KIPPUR.

• **Daytime** is the period between the time when the sun rises and the time it goes down, when there is light. • If you make a **day trip** to a place, you visit it and return home on the same day. ○ *A lot of the people on the beach are* **day-trippers** (= people who are only there for the day).

daydream /ˈdeɪ·driːm/ *n* [C] a set of pleasant thoughts about something that you would like to do or achieve, but which is not likely • *I had a daydream that I'd win the road race.*

daydream /ˈdeɪ·driːm/ *v* [I] • *She would daydream in class about horseback riding and other things she'd rather be doing.*

daylight /ˈdeɪ·laɪt/ *n* [U] natural light from the sun, or the period during a day when there is light • *She had little free time during the daylight hours.* • **Daylight saving time** is the time set usually one hour later in summer so that there is a longer period of daylight in the evening. Compare **standard time** at STANDARD USUAL.

dazed /deɪzd/ *adj* confused or unable to think clearly, esp. as a result of an injury or from shock • *The driver in the accident appeared dazed but not badly hurt.*

daze /deɪz/ *n* [U] • *She was so happy she was in a daze.*

dazzle /ˈdæz·əl/ *v* [T] to cause (someone) to feel strong admiration of something or someone • *He was dazzled by Rome's architectural treasures.* • If a person or animal is dazzled by a light, they cannot see because the light is too bright to look at.

dazzling /ˈdæz·ə·lɪŋ/ *adj* causing or likely to cause strong admiration • *A dazzling smile flashed across his face.*

DDT /ˌdiː·diːˈtiː/ *n* [U] a poisonous chemical used in the past for killing insects

deacon /ˈdiː·kən/ *n* [C] (in some Christian churches) a church official who helps a minister

dead NOT LIVING /ded/ *adj* [not gradable] no longer living • *He was found dead on the bathroom floor, apparently of a heart attack.* • If a piece of machinery or equipment is dead, it is no longer working: *a dead battery* ○ *The phone suddenly went dead.* • (*infml*) If you describe a place as dead, you mean there is not much activity there that interests you: *I love my hometown, but as a teenager I always found it dead.* • *The fox in the road was* (**as**) **dead as a doornail** (= completely dead). • A **dead language** is a language that is no longer spoken by anyone as their main language: *Latin is a dead language.* • **Dead wood** is people, esp. employees, who are no longer useful: *When she took over the agency, she streamlined the operation by getting rid of a lot of dead wood.* •
USAGE: The related noun is DEATH.

dead /ded/ *pl n* people who are no longer living • *Memorial Day honors the dead of our wars.*

deaden /ˈded·ən/ *v* [T] to reduce the severity or effect of (something) • *He asked for some stronger medication to deaden the pain.*

deadly /ˈded·li/ *adj* dangerous and able to kill • *a deadly poison*

dead COMPLETE /ded/ *adj* [not gradable] complete or exact • *The conductor waited for dead silence before lifting his baton.* ○ *He aimed for the dead center of the target.* • A **dead end** is a road that is closed at one end and therefore does not lead anywhere. ○ (*fig.*) *Negotiators have reached a dead end* (= have not been successful and cannot go further) *in their attempts to find a peaceful solution.* • A **dead heat** is a race in which two or more competitors finish at exactly the same time so that there is no single winner: *The two horses finished in a dead heat.* ○ (*fig.*) *Opinion pollsters call the Congressional race a dead heat, saying it is too close to call.*

dead /ded/ *adv* [not gradable] completely or extremely • *After a hard day's work, I was dead tired.* • *She wanted to move to Los Angeles but both her parents were* **dead set against** *it* (= completely opposed to it).

dead /ded/ *n* [U] the deepest or most extreme part of something • The **dead of night** is the middle of the night, when it is very dark. • The **dead of winter** is the middle of winter, when it is very cold.

deadly /ˈded·li/ *adj, adv* • *She was deadly* (= extremely accurate) *with a bow and arrow.* ○ *The movie was deadly* (= very) *dull.*

deadbeat /ˈded·biːt/ *n* [C] a person who is not willing to pay their debts, esp. a father who is no longer living with his children and does not help to support them • *By all means, federal and state governments should get tougher on deadbeat parents.*

deadline /ˈded·laɪn/ *n* [C] a time or day by which something must be done • *The deadline for filing income taxes is April 15th.*

deadlock /ˈded·lɑk/ *n* [C/U] a state or situation in which agreement in an argument cannot be reached because neither side will change its demands or accept the demands of the other side • *The PLO and Israel failed yesterday to break the deadlock over their peace accord.* [U]

deadlocked /ˈded·lɑkt/ *adj* unable to make any progress toward reaching agreement • *A second trial, in 1982, ended in a mistrial with a deadlocked jury.*

deadpan /ˈded·pæn/ *adj, adv* characterized by a serious facial expression, esp. when intended to be humorous • *As an overweight neighbor who drops in periodically, Karen Vaccaro offers a funny deadpan performance.*

deaf /def/ *adj* unable to hear • *She's becoming increasingly deaf.*

deafening /ˈdef·ən/ *adj* (of a sound) extremely loud • *a deafening explosion* ○ *deafening applause*

deal AGREEMENT /diːl/ n [C] an agreement or arrangement, esp. in business • *They bargained with each other but finally agreed to a deal.* ○ *She got a really good deal* (= paid a low price) *on her new car.*

deal /diːl/ v [I/T] *past* **dealt** /delt/ to do business with or be involved with someone or something • *We only deal with companies that have a good credit record.* [I] ○ *They mainly deal in* (= buy and sell) *mutual funds.* [I] • To deal drugs is to sell esp. illegal drugs. [T]

dealer /ˈdiːlər/ n [C] • *an antiques dealer* ○ *a used-car dealer*

dealership /ˈdiːlərˌʃɪp/ n [C] a business that has the right to sell a company's products in a particular area using the company's name • *a Toyota dealership*

dealings /ˈdiːlɪŋz/ pl n activities or relations involving other people, esp. in business • *He was accused of being involved in shady financial dealings.*

deal GIVE OUT /diːl/ v [I/T] *past* **dealt** /delt/ to give or give out (esp. playing cards) • *Whose turn is it to deal (the cards)?* [I/T] ○ *(fig.) Tonight's defeat dealt a blow to* (= damaged) *her hopes of making it to the finals.* [T]

deal /diːl/ n [C] a turn to give out playing cards • *It's your deal.*

deal AMOUNT /diːl/ n [U] a large amount; much • *She used to talk a good deal about her childhood in Indiana.* ○ *A great deal of time and effort went into making the software reliable.*

□ **deal with** MANAGE /ˈ--/ v prep [T] to develop a way to manage or relate to (someone or something) • *We have to deal with problems as they arise.* ○ *She had a marvelous ability to deal with people.*

□ **deal with** BE ABOUT /ˈ--/ v prep [T] to be about or be on the subject of (something) • *She likes novels that deal with serious moral issues.* ○ *The lecture dealt with his trip to South Africa.*

dean /diːn/ n [C] a high-ranking official in a college or university responsible for a department, teachers, students, etc. • *Langer is the dean of the law school.*

dear LOVED /dɪr/ adj [-er/-est only] loved or greatly liked • *She's a dear friend.* • Dear is used at the beginning of a letter to greet the person you are writing to: *Dear Kerrie/Mom and Dad/Ms. Smith/Sir* • Dearest can be used in a letter to greet someone you love: *Dearest Ben, I think of you every day.* • *The charity was dear to his heart* (= very important to him).

dear /dɪr/ n [C] • *Annie's such a dear.* • Dear is used to address someone in a friendly way, esp. someone you love or a child: *Have something to eat, dear.*

dear EXPRESSION /dɪr/ exclamation infml used to express annoyance, disappointment, unhappiness, or surprise • *Oh dear! I've lost my keys again.*

dearly /ˈdɪrˌli/ adv very much • *We would dearly love to move to the country.* ○ *You'll pay dearly for breaking the law in this town.*

dearth /dɜrθ/ n [U] an amount of something that is too small: a lack • *The region is suffering from a dearth of medical specialists.*

death /deθ/ n [C/U] the end of life • *a sudden/natural death* [C] ○ *I hope she finds the peace in death she never found in life.* [U] ○ *Most of the animals burned to death in the fire* (= burned until they died). [U] • To death can mean a lot: *The movie scared the children to death.* • If someone says something on their deathbed, they say it just before their death: *He confessed his love for her on his deathbed.* • A death knell is a warning of the end of something: *Defeat of this bill sounds a death knell for consumer protection.* • The death penalty is the legal punishment of particular crimes by death. • Prisoners on death row are waiting in prison for their legal punishment of death to be carried out. • A death toll is the number of people who died as a result of an event: *The day after the earthquake the death toll had risen to 90.* • A deathtrap is something that is very dangerous and could cause death: *With no fire exits, the nightclub was a deathtrap.* • USAGE: The related adjective is DEAD NOT LIVING.

deathly /ˈdeθˌli/ adj, adv seeming like death • *Madeline looked deathly pale.* ○ *The crowd was deathly silent.*

debase /dɪˈbeɪs/ v [T] to reduce in quality or value • *Television is often blamed for debasing American politics.*

debatable /dɪˈbeɪt̬ˌəˌbəl/ adj not clear, not certain, or not fixed; possibly not true • *It's debatable whether he could get a fair trial here.*

debate /dɪˈbeɪt/ n [C/U] a discussion, esp. one in which several people with different opinions about something discuss them seriously, or the process of discussing something • *Education is always a topic of interest and public debate.* [U]

debate /dɪˈbeɪt/ v [I/T] • *Congress debated for several hours without reaching a vote.* [I]

debilitating /dɪˈbɪlˌəˌteɪt̬ˌɪŋ/ adj causing weakness • *Strokes are a common debilitating condition of old age.*

debit /ˈdebˌət/ n [C/U] *specialized* money taken out of a financial account, or a record of money taken • A debit card is a small plastic card used to make a payment by taking the amount of the payment automatically from your bank account: *The supermarket takes debit cards, credit cards, cash, and checks.* • USAGE: The opposite of debit is CREDIT MONEY AVAILABLE.

debit /ˈdebˌət/ v [T] • *We have debited your account $30.*

debrief /diːˈbriːf/ v [T] to question (someone) in detail to get useful information about something they have done for you • *After every flight, engineers thoroughly debrief the test pilot.* • Compare BRIEF GIVE INSTRUCTIONS.

debris /də'briː, deɪ-/ *n* [U] broken or torn pieces left from the destruction of something larger • *After the tornado, debris from damaged trees and houses littered the town.*

debt /det/ *n* [C] something owed, esp. money • *He managed to pay off his debts in two years.* • If you are in debt, you owe money: *We seem to be perpetually in debt.* • If you go into debt, you borrow money. • If you are **in** someone's **debt**, you are grateful for something they did: *I'm in Senator Glenn's debt for getting my husband a visa.* • See also INDEBTED GRATEFUL; INDEBTED OWING.

debtor /'det·ər/ *n* [C] a country, organization, or person who owes money • *Student loans force students to graduate as debtors.* • Compare **creditor** at CREDIT PAYMENT LATER.

debug /diː'bʌg/ *v* [T] **-gg-** to remove BUGS (= mistakes) from (a computer program) • *He spent weeks debugging the program.*

debunk /diː'bʌŋk/ *v* [T] to show that (something) is not true • *Every week some long-held medical theory is debunked.*

debut /'deɪ·bjuː, deɪ'bjuː/ *n* [C usually sing] a first public appearance or activity • *Cassavetes made his film debut in "Taxi" in 1953.*
debut /'deɪ·bjuː, deɪ'bjuː/ *v* [I/T] • *I'll be debuting this song next Saturday night.* [T]

Dec. *n* [U] *abbreviation for* DECEMBER

decade /'dek·eɪd, de'keɪd/ *n* [C] a period of ten years • *The economy is growing at its fastest rate this decade.* • Decades means a long time: *They're enjoying new popularity after decades of neglect.*

decadence /'dek·əd·ᵊns/ *n* [U] a lowering of standards in a society; social decay
decadent /'dek·əd·ᵊnt/ *adj* • *The US was widely condemned as a decadent society.*

decaf /'diː·kæf/ *n* [C usually sing] coffee that has had the CAFFEINE (= a chemical substance) removed • *Do you have any decaf?*

decaffeinated /diː'kæf·ə,neɪ·təd/, *short form* **decaf** /'diː·kæf/ *adj* [not gradable] • *decaffeinated coffee/tea/cola*

decal /'diː·kæl, dɪ'kæl/ *n* [C] a picture or design on special paper, which can be put onto another surface, such as metal or glass

decal

decanter /dɪ'kænt·ər/ *n* [C] an attractive glass bottle used for storing and serving liquids, esp. wine

decapitate /dɪ'kæp·ə,teɪt/ *v* [T] to cut off the head of (a person or animal) • *a decapitated body*

decathlon /dɪ'kæθ,lɑn/ *n* [C] a competition in which male ATHLETES compete in ten sporting events over two days • Compare HEPTATHLON.

decay /dɪ'keɪ/ *n* [U] damage, or a state that becomes gradually worse • *The dentist says I have a lot of tooth decay.* ○ *There's still too much crime, poverty, and decay in the neighbor-*

hood. ○ *Your attitude just contributes to the growing social decay.*
decay /dɪ'keɪ/ *v* [I/T] • *City services are rapidly decaying.* [I]
decaying /dɪ'keɪ·ɪŋ/ *adj* [not gradable] • *Empty lots stand next to abandoned, decaying buildings.*

deceased /dɪ'siːst/ *adj* [not gradable] dead • *The paintings are by his deceased brother, Dan.*
deceased /dɪ'siːst/ *n* [C] someone who has recently died • *There will be no service, at the deceased's request.*

deceit /dɪ'siːt/ *n* [U] speech or behavior that keeps the truth hidden • *All we hear from them are lies and deceit.*
deceitful /dɪ'siːt·fəl/ *adj* • *She just assumes that elected leaders are cynical and deceitful.*

deceive /dɪ'siːv/ *v* [T] to persuade (someone) that something false is the truth; trick or fool • *Some parents try to deceive school officials and enroll their children in other districts.* • If you deceive yourself, you pretend something is true: *We should not deceive ourselves into thinking this will be the end of it.* • See also DECEPTION.

December /dɪ'sem·bər/ (*abbreviation* **Dec.**) *n* [C/U] the twelfth and last month of the year, after November and before January

decent /'diː·sənt/ *adj* acceptable, satisfactory, or reasonable • *We get good benefits, and the pay is decent.* ○ *It costs $100 to buy a decent sleeping bag.* • Decent also means good or kind: *They're just decent, ordinary people.* • (*infml*) Decent can also mean dressed or wearing clothes: *You can come in now, I'm decent.*
decently /'diː·sənt·li/ *adv* • *Their employer treats them decently.*

decency /'diː·sən·si/ *n* [U] • *She didn't even have the decency to apologize.* [+ *to* infinitive]

decentralize /diː'sen·trə,lɑɪz/ *v* [T] to move or spread (esp. business operations or authority over an activity) from a single, central place to several smaller ones • *The company uses an unusual decentralized distribution system.*
decentralization /,diː,sen·trə·lə'zeɪ·ʃən/ *n* [U] • *Prison security was improved through decentralization.*

deception /dɪ'sep·ʃən/ *n* [C/U] a statement or action that hides the truth, or the act of hiding the truth • *Most advertising involves at least some deception.* [U] • USAGE: The related verb is DECEIVE.
deceptive /dɪ'sep·tɪv/ *adj* • *Appearances can be very deceptive.*
deceptively /dɪ'sep·tɪv·li/ *adv* • *He makes it sound deceptively simple.*

decibel /'des·ə,bel, -bəl/ *n* [C] a unit for measuring the loudness of sound

decide /dɪ'sɑɪd/ *v* to choose between one possibility or another • *I decided I would try it.* ○ *In the end, we decided to go to the theater.* [+ *to* infinitive] ○ *We're trying to decide how to proceed.* [+ *wh-* word] ○ *He decided (that) it was* *his business.* [+ *(that)* clause] • If something decides a result in a competition, it causes that result: *A mistake by our team decided the game against us.* [T] • A **deciding factor** is something so important that it forces a particular decision: *The deciding factor in choosing this school was that it was far from home.*

decided /dɪˈsaɪd·əd/ *adj* clear; certain • *There's been a decided improvement in subway service.*

decidedly /dɪˈsaɪd·əd·li/ *adv* • *He was decidedly careful about what he told me.*

deciduous /dɪˈsɪdʒ·ə·wəs/ *adj* [not gradable] (of a tree) losing its leaves in the fall • Compare EVERGREEN.

decimal /ˈdes·ə·məl/ *adj* [not gradable] of a system of counting or money based on the number ten • A **decimal point** is a mark used in numbers to separate whole numbers from parts of numbers: *To divide by ten, move the decimal point one place to the left.* • LP PERIOD

decimal /ˈdes·ə·məl/ *n* [C] • *Three-fifths expressed as a decimal is 0.6.* • LP FRACTIONS AND DECIMALS

decimate /ˈdes·ə·meɪt/ *v* [T] to destroy large numbers of (something), or to harm (something) severely • *AIDS has decimated whole families.* ○ *We decimated public transportation in the 1950s and 60s.*

decipher /dɪˈsaɪ·fər/ *v* [T] to discover the meaning of (something hard to understand or which contains a hidden message) • *I have a hard time deciphering my phone bill.*

decision /dɪˈsɪʒ·ən/ *n* [C] something you choose; a choice • *The board will make its decision shortly.* ○ *Their decision not to attend the party puzzled everyone.* [+ *to* infinitive]

decisive /dɪˈsaɪ·sɪv/ *adj* making choices quickly and surely, without having any doubts • *In an emergency, decisive action is called for.* • Decisive also means without doubt or question, and of the greatest importance: *DNA test results were decisive in proving his innocence.*

decisively /dɪˈsaɪ·sɪv·li/ *adv* • *We had to act quickly and decisively to put out the fire.*

deck FLOOR /dek/ *n* [C] a wooden floor outside a house, usually with RAILINGS (= a low fence) and without a roof • *In summer, we always eat out on the deck—except when it rains.* • A ship's deck is a floor laid between the sides of the ship: *Waves washed over the deck.*

deck SET OF CARDS /dek/, **pack** *n* [C] a set of cards used for playing card games

deck HIT /dek/ *v* [T] *slang* to hit and knock down • *Jim made a sudden move and decked the guy!*

□ **deck out** *obj* DRESS UP , **deck** *obj* **out** /ˈ-ˈ-/ *v adv* [M] to dress (someone) in special, decorative clothes, or decorate (something) for a special occasion • *Stanton was decked out in cowboy boots and a work shirt.*

declare *(obj)* /dɪˈkler, -ˈklær/ *v* to announce or express (something) clearly and publicly, esp.

officially • *The rebels declared a ceasefire yesterday.* [T] ○ *War can be declared only by Congress.* [T] ○ *People use their license plates to declare their team loyalty.* [T] ○ *I declare that is the best chocolate cake I've ever eaten!* [+ *that* clause]

declaration /ˌdek·ləˈreɪ·ʃən/ *n* [C] an official, public, usually written statement • *a customs declaration* ○ *a declaration of war* ○ *the American Declaration of Independence*

decline GO DOWN /dɪˈklaɪn/ *v* [I] to go down in amount or quality; lessen or weaken • *His interest in the project declined after his wife died.* ○ *Her health declined quickly.*

decline /dɪˈklaɪn/ *n* [C/U] • *Unemployment increased this month after a modest decline.* [C usually sing] ○ *Civilization is in decline.* [U]

decline REFUSE /dɪˈklaɪn/ *v* [I/T] to refuse (something) • *She declined their job offer.* [T]

decode /diːˈkoʊd/ *v* [T] to discover the meaning of (information given in a secret or complicated way) • *Scientists are decoding the genetic sequences in DNA.*

decompose /ˌdiː·kəmˈpoʊz/ *v* [I/T] to destroy (something) by breaking it into smaller parts • *Certain kinds of plastic decompose quickly.* [I]

decongestant /ˌdiː·kənˈdʒes·tənt/ *n* [C] a medicine that helps you to breathe more easily, esp. when you have a COLD ILLNESS

decor /deɪˈkɔːr, dɪ-, ˈdeɪ·kɔːr/ *n* [C/U] the choice of color, style of furniture, and arrangement of objects in a room • *Actually, the ironing board is part of my decor.* [C]

decorate MAKE ATTRACTIVE /ˈdek·əˌreɪt/ *v* [T] to add something to (an object or place), esp. to make it more attractive • *They decorated the table with flowers and candles.*

decoration /ˌdek·əˈreɪ·ʃən/ *n* [C/U] • *The molding has a floral decoration carved into it.* [C] ○ *Some women wear barrettes as decoration.* [U]

decorative /ˈdek·ə·rəṭ·ɪv/ *adj* attractive • *decorative patterns/accessories*

decorator /ˈdek·əˌreɪṭ·ər/ *n* [C] an **interior decorator**, see at INTERIOR

decorate HONOR /ˈdek·əˌreɪt/ *v* [T] to reward or honor (a person) by giving them esp. a MEDAL • *All four firefighters were decorated for bravery.*

decoration /ˌdek·əˈreɪ·ʃən/ *n* [C] • *He received the country's highest decoration for bravery.*

decorum /dɪˈkɔːr·əm, -ˈkoʊr·əm/ *n* [U] *fml* behavior that is socially correct, calm, and polite • *The witness endured the lawyer's badgering with remarkable decorum.*

decoy /ˈdiː·kɔɪ, dɪˈkɔɪ/ *n* [C] something used to trick or confuse a person or animal • *He carves duck decoys for hunters.*

decrease /dɪˈkriːs, ˈdiː·kriːs/ *v* [I/T] to become smaller or make (something) less • *Car sales decreased sharply this year.* [I] • USAGE: The opposite of decrease is INCREASE.

deeply

decrease /'diː·kriːs, dɪ'kriːs/ *n* [C] • *I haven't noticed any decrease in ticket sales.*

decree /dɪ'kriː/ *n* [C] an order or statement of an official decision • *Another military decree closed all libraries.*

decree (obj) /dɪ'kriː/ *v* • *The Olympics charter decrees that the Games be opened by a head of state.* [+ *that* clause]

decrepit /dɪ'krep·ət/ *adj* weak and in poor condition, esp. from age or long use • *The town had two decrepit fire trucks that were constantly breaking down.*

decriminalize /diː'krɪm·ə·nə,laɪz/ *v* [T] to reduce or stop the punishment for (a particular illegal act), esp. by changing a law • *Some people think marijuana should be decriminalized.*

decriminalization /ˌdiː,krɪm·ən·ᵊl·ə'zeɪ·ʃən/ *n* [U] *decriminalization of minor offenses*

decry /dɪ'kraɪ/ *v* [T] to publicly criticize (something) as being regrettable or harmful • *Mitchell decried the high rate of unemployment in the state.*

dedicate /'ded·ə,keɪt/ *v* [T] to give completely (your energy, time, etc.) to something • *He dedicated his life to helping the poor.* • If you dedicate a book, play, performance, etc., to someone or something, you say publicly that it is in their honor: *This book is dedicated to my children, Claire and Tom.*

dedicated /'ded·ə,keɪt̬·əd/ *adj* believing that an activity or idea is important and giving a lot of energy and time to it • *The Boy Scouts organization is dedicated to helping boys become moral and productive adults.*

dedication /ˌded·ə'keɪ·ʃən/ *n* [C/U] the activity of giving a lot of your energy and time to something you think is important • *dedication to worthy causes* [U] • A dedication is also a ceremony in which something is formally opened or made available to the public: *The mayor made a speech at the dedication ceremony for the new school.* [U]

deduce (obj) /dɪ'duːs/ *v* to reach (an answer) by thinking about a general truth and its relationship to a specific situation • *In an attempt to deduce what happened to the jet, investigators are looking at other similar planes.* [+ wh-word]

deduction /dɪ'dʌk·ʃən/ *n* [C/U] the process of learning something by considering a general set of facts and thinking about how something specific relates to them • *Sherlock Holmes was famous for making clever deductions.* [C]

deduct /dɪ'dʌkt/ *v* [T] to take away (an amount or part) from a total • *The company deducts $31.93 each week from my salary for health insurance.* • To deduct is also not to have to pay taxes on an amount that you have earned: *Homeowners can deduct the interest they pay on their mortgages.*

deductible /dɪ'dʌk·tə·bəl/ *adj* [not gradable] • A deductible expense is a cost that you can subtract from the earnings on which you have

to pay income tax: *Mortgage interest is deductible.*

deductible /dɪ'dʌk·tə·bəl/ *n* [C] an amount of money that a person is responsible for paying before their INSURANCE (= protection against loss) will pay them for an expense • *Judy's car insurance policy had a $500 deductible.*

deduction /dɪ'dʌk·ʃən/ *n* [C/U] an amount or part taken away from a total, esp. an expense that you do not have to pay taxes on, or the process of taking away an amount or part • *New tax regulations would cut the deduction for business lunches.* [C]

deed ACTION /diːd/ *n* [C/U] an intentional act, esp. a very bad or very good one • *Whatever his motives, the deed did save a hundred thousand lives.* [C]

deed DOCUMENT /diːd/ *n* [C] *law* a legal document that is an official record and proof of ownership of property • *According to the deed, she owns the land from here to the river.*

deem /diːm/ *v* [T] to consider or judge • *The president asked Congress for authority to take whatever steps he deemed necessary, including the use of force.*

deep DOWN /diːp/ *adj, adv* [-er/-est only] going or being a long way down from the top or surface, or being at a particular distance down from the top • *She had a deep cut on her left arm.* ○ *During the flood, the water in the basement was knee-deep* (= it would reach the knees of an average adult). • Something or someone who has **deep pockets** has a lot of money: *People who fall on a sidewalk often sue the city because it has deep pockets.* • If someone is **in deep (trouble)**, they are in serious trouble. • To **deep-fry** food is to fry it in a lot of oil or fat: *deep-fried chicken* • The **Deep South** is the part of the US that is in the farthest south and east, including South Carolina, Georgia, Alabama, Mississippi, and Louisiana, but usually not including Florida. • USAGE: The related noun is DEPTH DISTANCE DOWN.

deep FRONT TO BACK /diːp/ *adj* [-er/-est only] having a (sometimes stated) distance from front to back • *I want the bookcase shelves to be 12 inches deep.* ○ *The crowd along the parade route was six deep* (= in six rows). • USAGE: The related noun is DEPTH DISTANCE BACKWARD.

deep STRONGLY FELT /diːp/ *adj* [-er/-est only] strongly felt or experienced, or having a strong and lasting effect • *Our deep love for each other will last forever.* ○ *He awoke from a deep sleep.* ○ *Joseph, deep in thought* (= thinking so much that he is not aware of others), *didn't hear Erin enter the room.* • If you feel an emotion **deep down**, it is strongly felt but not often expressed: *You say you forgive him, but deep down, aren't you still angry?*

deepen /'diː·pən/ *v* [I/T] • *Over the years, her love for him deepened.* [I]

deeply /'diː·pli/ *adv* • *Everyone was deeply*

impressed by his performance. • LP VERY, COM-
PLETELY, AND OTHER INTENSIFIERS

deep COMPLICATED /diːp/ *adj* [*-er/-est* only] difficult to understand; complicated • *His book
on how the brain works is too deep for me.*

deep LOW SOUND /diːp/ *adj* [*-er/-est* only] (of a
sound) low • *He was a large man with a deep
voice.*

deep DARK /diːp/ *adj* [*-er/-est* only] (of a color)
strong and dark • *The stain was a deep blood
red.*

deer /dɪr/ *n* [C] *pl* **deer** a large animal, the
males of which have wide horns that stick out
like branches, that lives in forests and eats
grass and leaves

deface /dɪˈfeɪs/ *v* [T] to intentionally spoil the
appearance of (something) by writing on or
marking it • *They used spray paint to deface the
sign.*

de facto /dɪˈfæk·toʊ, deɪ-/ *adj, adv* [not grad-
able] existing in fact, although not necessarily intended or legal • *Legal restrictions on
black activities may have ended, but de facto
segregation remains.*

defame /dɪˈfeɪm/ *v* [T] to damage (someone's
or something's reputation) by saying or writing bad things about them that are not true •
*He was behind the propaganda campaign to de-
fame his political opponent.*

defamation /ˌdef·əˈmeɪ·ʃən/ *n* [U]

default FAIL TO PAY /dɪˈfɔːlt/ *v* [I] to fail to do
something, such as pay a debt, that you legally have to do • *The company defaulted on a $133
million loan.*

default /dɪˈfɔːlt, ˈdiːˌfɔːlt/ *n* [C/U] • *Defaults
rose to 4 percent of all the bank's loans.* [C] • In
sports, to win or lose by default is to win or
lose because one side did not compete: *Humphrey never showed up, so Wilson won by default.* [U]

default STANDARD SETTING /ˈdiːˌfɔːlt, dɪˈfɔːlt/ *n*
[U] *specialized* a standard setting esp. of
computer SOFTWARE, such as of type size or
style • *The default color of text on the screen is
black.*

defeat /dɪˈfiːt/ *v* [T] to oppose and cause
(someone) to lose in a competition or war so
that you can win • *Bill Clinton defeated George
Bush for the presidency in 1992.*

defeat /dɪˈfiːt/ *n* [C/U] success in competition
with an opponent, causing them to lose so that
you can win • *In the American Civil War, the
North's defeat of the South involved tremendous loss of life on both sides.* [U] • A defeat is
also the action or fact of losing a competition
or war: *This was the team's fifth straight defeat.* [C]

defeatism /dɪˈfiːt̬ˌɪz·əm/ *n* [U] a way of thinking or behaving that shows that you expect to
fail • *He criticized his party for defeatism.*

defeatist /dɪˈfiːt̬·əst/ *adj* • *You'll never get
anywhere with a defeatist attitude.*

defecate /ˈdef·əˌkeɪt/ *v* [I] to excrete the contents of the bowels

defecation /ˌdef·əˈkeɪ·ʃən/ *n* [U]

defect SOMETHING WRONG /ˈdiːˌfekt, dɪˈfekt/ *n*
[C] something that is lacking or that is not exactly right in someone or something • *The
cars have a defect in the electrical system that
may cause them to stall.*

defective /dɪˈfek·tɪv/ *adj* • *I replaced the defective light switch.*

defect LEAVE /dɪˈfekt/ *v* [I] to leave a country
or a group you belong to, esp. in order to join
an opposing one • *Some of the mayor's longtime supporters have defected to other candidates.*

defection /dɪˈfek·ʃən/ *n* [C/U] • *There have
been defections to the US by several Cuban baseball players.* [C]

defector /dɪˈfek·tər/ *n* [C] a person who leaves
their own country or group to join an opposing one

defend PROTECT /dɪˈfend/ *v* [T] to protect
(someone or something) from attack or harm
• *She defended herself with a baseball bat.* • To
defend is also to argue in support of (something), esp. when it has been criticized: *She defended her husband against the accusations.*

defendant /dɪˈfen·dənt/ *n* [C] *law* a person in
a court of law who is accused of having done
something wrong • *The prosecutor must prove
beyond a reasonable doubt that the defendant
is guilty.* • Compare PLAINTIFF.

defender /dɪˈfen·dər/ *n* [C] a person who supports someone or something, esp. when attacked or criticized • *She is a defender of wom-
en's rights.*

defensible /dɪˈfen·sə·bəl/ *adj* • Something
that is defensible can be supported, esp. when
criticized: *He's presenting a plan that is morally defensible and politically realistic.*

defend SPORTS /dɪˈfend/ *v* [I/T] (in sports) to
try to prevent the opposition from scoring
points in a competition, or to guard (a goal or
other position) • *Jones is a difficult player to
defend against.* [I]

defender /dɪˈfen·dər/ *n* [C] • *Murray dribbled
past a defender and fired the ball right into the
basket.*

defense PROTECTION /dɪˈfens/ *n* [C/U] the ability to protect against attack or harm, or something used to protect against attack or harm •
*The vaccine strengthens the body's defenses
against infection.* [C] • A defense is also an argument in support of something, esp. when it
has been criticized: *Her defense consisted of denying that she knew anything about the missing check.* [U] • (*law*) The defense is the person
or people in a court who have been accused of
doing something wrong, and their lawyer: *The
defense rests* (= This side has finished giving
its argument). [U]

defensive /dɪˈfen·sɪv/ *adj* intended to protect
against attack or harm • *The Pentagon said it*

defraud

would sell only *defensive weapons* to other countries. • If someone is defensive, they feel they are being criticized and they quickly try to explain themselves: *Don't be defensive—I'm just asking why you didn't vote.*

defensive /dɪˈfen·sɪv/ *n* [U] • If you are **on the defensive**, you are protecting yourself from criticism instead of attacking the position of others: *The speech produced a firestorm of protest, putting him on the defensive.*

defenseless /dɪˈfen·sləs/ *adj* having no way to protect yourself from attack or harm • *How can anyone want to hurt a defenseless child?*

defenselessness /dɪˈfen·slə·snəs/ *n* [U]

defense SPORTS /dɪˈfens, ˈdiː·fens/ *n* [U] (in sports) the ability to prevent the opposition from scoring points in a competition, or, esp. in football, the team without the ball that is trying to prevent its opposition from scoring points • *The team has pretty good scoring ability, but it's weak on defense.* • Compare OFFENSE SCORING ABILITY.

defensive /dɪˈfen·sɪv/ *adj* • *The team's defensive strategy was effective.*

defensively /dɪˈfen·sɪv·li/ *adv*

defer /dɪˈfɜr/ *v* [T] **-rr-** to delay (something) until a later time; to POSTPONE • *You can order the furniture now and defer payment until September.*

deferment /dɪˈfɜr·mənt/ *n* [C/U] (a) temporary delay in taking someone into the military forces • *They got draft deferments as graduate students.* [C]

□ **defer to** /-ˈ-·-/ *v prep* [T] to accept the opinion or judgment of (another person) because you respect that person's experience, knowledge, or age • *I deferred to Brian on the question of what to serve at the party.*

deference /ˈdef·ə·rəns/ *n* [U] respect shown for another person esp. because of their experience, knowledge, age, or power • *In deference to nature lovers, the town refused to grant a permit to builders who would have filled in a swamp used by many birds.*

deferential /ˌdef·əˈren·tʃəl/ *adj* • *A smart lawyer is always deferential to a judge.*

defiance /dɪˈfaɪ·əns/ *n* • See at DEFY.

defiant /dɪˈfaɪ·ənt/ *adj* • See at DEFY.

defiantly /dɪˈfaɪ·ənt·li/ *adv* • See at DEFY.

deficiency /dɪˈfɪʃ·ən·si/ *n* [C/U] the lack of something that is needed in order to meet a particular standard or level of quality, or the thing that is lacking • *Many women suffer from iron deficiency.* [U]

deficient /dɪˈfɪʃ·ənt/ *adj* • *A diet that is deficient (= lacking) in protein is harmful to children.*

deficit /ˈdef·ə·sət/ *n* [C] the amount by which money spent is more than money received • *The theater has been operating at a deficit of over $150,000 a year.*

defied /dɪˈfaɪd/ *past simple and past participle of* DEFY

defile /dɪˈfaɪl/ *v* [T] to spoil (something, esp. something pure or something to be respected) by making it dirty • *Beer cans and paper bags defiled the landscape.*

define EXPLAIN /dɪˈfaɪn/ *v* [T] to describe the meaning of (something, esp. a word or words), or to explain (something) more clearly so that it can be understood • *How would you define "jaded"?*

define SHOW /dɪˈfaɪn/ *v* [T] to show the edge or shape of (something), esp. against a background • *The dark figures are sharply defined on the white background.*

definite /ˈdef·ə·nət/ *adj* fixed, certain, or clear • *We haven't picked a definite date, but it will probably be in June.* • (*specialized*) In grammar, **definite article** is the grammatical name for the word "the" in English, or the words in other languages that have a similar use. Compare **indefinite article** at INDEFINITE. LP ARTICLES

definitely /ˈdef·ə·nət·li/ *adv* without any doubt; certainly • *I don't like that place—I'm definitely not going back there.* ○ *"Are you really going to quit your job?" "Definitely!"* • USAGE: Definitely is often used for emphasis, esp. in speech.

definition EXPLANATION /ˌdef·əˈnɪʃ·ən/ *n* [C] a statement that explains the meaning of a word or phrase • *What is the definition of "mood"?* • If something is so **by definition**, it is so because of its own nature: *Circus performers are, almost by definition, risk takers.*

definition SEEING CLEARLY /ˌdef·əˈnɪʃ·ən/ *n* [U] the degree to which something can be clearly seen or heard • *The tape recorded conversation lacked definition—there was too much background noise.*

definitive /dɪˈfɪn·ət·ɪv/ *adj* firm, final, and complete; not to be questioned or changed • *There is no definitive scientific evidence that coffee is harmful.*

deflate /dɪˈfleɪt/ *v* [I/T] to allow air or gas to escape from within (a container) • *When the roads are icy, you may have to deflate your tires a bit.* [T] • (*fig.*) If someone or something is deflated, they suddenly feel or are considered less important: *The allegations deflate the respect people have for the presidency.* [T]

deflect /dɪˈflekt/ *v* [I/T] to cause (something) to suddenly change direction, or to suddenly go in a different direction • *The ball deflected off the rim of the basket into Larry's hands.* [I] ○ (*fig.*) *The mayor deflected (= did not answer directly) questions about his political plans.* [T]

deformed /dɪˈfɔːrmd/ *adj* spoiled by not having a usual or regular shape or structure • *The child was born with a deformed heart.*

deformity /dɪˈfɔːr·mət·i/ *n* [C/U] • *She was born with a deformity of the spine.* [C]

defraud /dɪˈfrɔːd/ *v* [T] to take or keep something illegally from (someone) by deceiving them • *She is charged with defrauding the Internal Revenue Service.*

defrost /dɪˈfrɔːst/ v [I/T] to become or cause (something) to become free of ice or (esp. of food) no longer frozen • *Take some meat out of the freezer to defrost for supper.* [I]

deft /deft/ adj [-er/-est only] skillful, effective, and quick • *He cut some logs up for firewood with a few deft strokes of his ax.*

deftly /ˈdef·tli/ adv • *She deftly answered the tough questions.*

defunct /dɪˈfʌŋkt/ adj [not gradable] no longer existing • *He was a reporter for the defunct New York Herald newspaper.*

defuse /dɪˈfjuːz/ v [T] to make (a difficult or dangerous situation) calmer • *The two groups are trying to defuse tension in the Middle East.* • If you defuse (a bomb), you prevent it from exploding.

defy /dɪˈfaɪ/ v [T] to refuse to obey or to do (something) in the usual or expected way • *He defied the authorities and refused to surrender his child to his wife.* ○ *It just defies common sense to believe that being exposed to violence would not have an effect, he says.*

defiance /dɪˈfaɪ·əns/ n [U] proud and determined opposition against authority or against someone more powerful than you are • *They are continuing to publish their newspaper, in defiance of government attempts to close it down.*

defiant /dɪˈfaɪ·ənt/ adj • *She is defiant, angry, and tough.*

defiantly /dɪˈfaɪ·ənt·li/ adv • *When I said she might fail, she replied defiantly, "No, I won't!"*

degenerate /dɪˈdʒen·ə‚reɪt/ v [I] to become worse • *Standards of courtesy have degenerated since I was a girl.*

degenerate /dɪˈdʒen·ə·rət/ adj bad or worse in quality or character, or (of a person) morally bad • *He was a lazy, degenerate young man.*

degeneration /dɪ‚dʒen·ə·ˈreɪ·ʃən, ‚diː-/ n [U] the process of becoming worse • *X-rays showed some degeneration of bone.*

degradable /dɪˈɡreɪd·ə·bəl/ adj short form of BIODEGRADABLE

degradation /‚deg·rə·ˈdeɪ·ʃən/ n [U] the process by which something is made worse, esp. the quality of land • *One of the effects of environmental degradation is the absence of fish in that river.*

degrade /dɪˈɡreɪd/ v [T] to cause (someone) to seem to be worth less and lose the respect of others • *A presidential commission said that pornography degraded women.*

degrading /dɪˈɡreɪd·ɪŋ/ adj making you feel ashamed and worth less as a person • *When your commander ordered you to do something, no matter how stupid or degrading it was, you did it.*

degree AMOUNT /dɪˈɡriː/ n [C/U] an amount or level of something • *This job demands a high*

degree of skill. [C] ○ *The house had also been damaged, but to a lesser degree.* [C]

degree UNIT /dɪˈɡriː/, symbol ° n [C] any of various units of measurement, esp. of temperature or angles, usually shown by the symbol ° written after a number • *The temperature is expected to climb to 90° tomorrow.*

degree ACHIEVEMENT /dɪˈɡriː/ n [C] the level of achievement recognized for a student who has completed a course of study at a college or university • *She earned a bachelor's degree in history from Yale.*

dehydrate /‚diː‚haɪˈdreɪt/ v [I/T] to lose water, or to cause (something) to lose water • *The vegetables were dehydrated and frozen.* [T]

dehydration /‚diː‚haɪˈdreɪ·ʃən/ n [U] • *In hot, dry weather you need to drink lots of water to avoid dehydration.*

deign /deɪn/ v [+ to infinitive] to agree to do something although you consider yourself too important to have to do it • *Mr. Clinton did not deign to reply.*

deity /ˈdiː·ət̬·i, ˈdeɪ-/ n [C] a god or GODDESS • *Zeus was an ancient Greek deity.* • The Deity is God.

déjà vu /‚deɪ‚ʒɑˈvuː/ n [U] the strange feeling that in some way you have already experienced what is happening now

dejected /dɪˈdʒek·təd/ adj unhappy, disappointed, or lacking hope • *William felt dejected because he had sprained his ankle and had to sit out the game.*

dejection /dɪˈdʒek·ʃən/ n [U]

delay /dɪˈleɪ/ v [I/T] to cause to be late or to cause to happen at a later time, or to wait before acting • *He wants to delay the meeting until Wednesday.* [T] ○ *The space launch was delayed because of bad weather.* [T] ○ *Don't delay in ordering tickets to the show.* [I]

delay /dɪˈleɪ/ n [C/U] a period when something that might happen does not happen or does not happen quickly enough, or the failure to act quickly • *You need to call back without delay.* [U] ○ *The holiday traffic is likely to cause long delays.* [C] ○ *Any further delay would threaten the entire project.* [C]

delectable /dɪˈlek·tə·bəl/ adj giving great pleasure • *a delectable cake*

delegate CHOSEN PERSON /ˈdel·ə·ɡət/ n [C] a person chosen or elected by a group to represent them, esp. at a meeting • *Each state chooses delegates to the national convention.*

delegate /ˈdel·ə‚ɡeɪt/ v [T] • *Four teachers were delegated to represent the school at the conference.*

delegation /‚del·ə·ˈɡeɪ·ʃən/ n [C] a set of people chosen or elected to represent a larger group

delegate GIVE /ˈdel·ə‚ɡeɪt/ v [I/T] to give (a job or responsibility) to someone in a lower position instead of doing it yourself • *Personnel matters made him uncomfortable, and he increasingly delegated them to others.* [T]

delete /dɪ'liːt/ v [I/T] to remove (part or all of) a written or electronic text • *She accidentally deleted one of her computer files.* [T] ○ *The editor deleted the last three paragraphs.* [T]

deletion /dɪ'liː·ʃən/ n [C/U] a part removed from a written or electronic text, or the act of removing such a part • *You will have to make some deletions to cut the article to 3000 words.* [C]

deli /'del·i/ n [C] pl **delis** short form of DELICATESSEN

deliberate INTENTIONAL /dɪ'lɪb·ə·rət/ adj (of an action or a decision) intentional or planned, often with the result of being harmful to someone • *a deliberate insult* ○ *He accused her of writing deliberate untruths.* • If someone moves, acts, or thinks in a deliberate way, they move, act, or think slowly and usually carefully.

deliberately /dɪ'lɪb·ə·rət·li/ adv • *He did it deliberately to annoy me.*

deliberate CONSIDER /dɪ'lɪb·ə,reɪt/ v [I/T] to think or talk seriously and carefully about (something) • *The jury deliberated for two days before reaching a verdict.* [I]

deliberation /dɪ,lɪb·ə'reɪ·ʃən/ n [C/U] • *After much deliberation, she decided to accept their offer.* [U]

delicacy /'del·ɪ·kə·si/ n [C] something esp. rare or expensive that is good to eat • *a dinner of Vietnamese delicacies*

delicate EASILY DAMAGED /'del·ɪ·kət/ adj needing careful treatment, esp. because easily damaged • *a delicate flower* ○ *delicate jewelry* • Delicate also means needing to be dealt with carefully in order to avoid causing trouble or offense: *The negotiations have reached a delicate stage.* ○ *It's a delicate operation, and you want an experienced surgeon to do it.*

delicately /'del·ɪ·kət·li/ adv • *Please handle the china delicately.*

delicacy /'del·ɪ·kə·si/ n [U] • *We need to discuss a matter of some delicacy* (= needing to be handled carefully in order not to cause trouble or offense).

delicate PLEASANT /'del·ɪ·kət/ adj pleasant but not easily noticed or strong • *a delicate flavor* ○ *We chose a delicate floral pattern for our bedroom curtains.*

delicatessen /,del·ɪ·kə'tes·ən/, short form **deli** n [C] a store that sells foods such as cheeses, types of cold meat, salads, and often cooked foods

delicious /dɪ'lɪʃ·əs/ adj very pleasant, esp. to taste or smell • *Judy's fried chicken is delicious.*

delight /dɪ'laɪt/ n [C/U] great pleasure, satisfaction, or happiness, or something or someone that gives this • *My sister's little boy is a real delight.* [C] ○ *His music teacher expressed delight with his performance.* [U]

delight /dɪ'laɪt/ v [T] • *The songs of coun-*

trypeople and of sailors delight me. ○ *Peter's success at college delighted his family.*

delighted /dɪ'laɪt̬·əd/ adj • *a delighted expression* ○ *I'm delighted to meet you.* [+ to infinitive]

delightful /dɪ'laɪt·fəl/ adj full of pleasure • *We spent a delightful weekend in Maine.*

□ **delight in** /-'-,-/ v prep [T] to enjoy (esp. doing something annoying to someone else) • *My brother always delights in telling me when I make a mistake.*

delineate SHOW BORDER /dɪ'lɪn·iː,eɪt/ v [T] to mark the border of (something) • *The boundary of the park is delineated by a row of trees.*

delineate DESCRIBE /dɪ'lɪn·iː,eɪt/ v [T] to describe (something) completely, including details • *The constitution carefully delineates the duties of the treasurer's office.*

delinquency /dɪ'lɪŋ·kwən·si/ n [U] illegal or unacceptable behavior • *These children witness delinquency, crime, and violence every day in their lives.*

delinquent /dɪ'lɪŋ·kwənt/ adj fml late in paying money owed • *She was delinquent in paying her taxes.*

delirious /dɪ'lɪr·iː·əs/ adj thinking or speaking in a way that is not reasonable because of mental confusion • *He grew feverish and then delirious.* • Delirious also means extremely happy: *delirious with joy*

deliver TAKE TO /dɪ'lɪv·ər/ v [I/T] to take (esp. goods or packages) to people's houses or places of work • *We had the pizza delivered.* [T] ○ *We call our pharmacy with the doctor's prescription and ask them to deliver it.* [T] ○ *We deliver anywhere in the city.* [I]

delivery /dɪ'lɪv·ə·ri/ n [C/U] • *The company gets two deliveries a day.* [C] ○ *You can pay for the rug on delivery* (= when it is received). [U]

deliver GIVE /dɪ'lɪv·ər/ v [T] to give or produce (a speech or result) • *The president is scheduled to deliver a speech on foreign policy.* ○ *The jury delivered a verdict of not guilty.*

delivery /dɪ'lɪv·ə·ri/ n [U] the manner in which someone speaks, esp. in public • *His dialogue was offbeat, his delivery fast.*

deliver GIVE BIRTH /dɪ'lɪv·ər/ v [T] to give birth to (a baby), or to help someone do this • *Dr. Adams delivered all three of my children.*

delivery /dɪ'lɪv·ə·ri/ n [C] • *In a cesarean delivery, a baby is surgically removed through the abdomen.* • The **delivery room** is the part of a hospital in which babies are born.

deliver PRODUCE /dɪ'lɪv·ər/ v [I/T] to achieve or produce (something promised or expected) • *You pay your dues, and you expect the union to deliver.* [I]

delta /'del·tə/ n [C] an area of low, flat land, sometimes shaped approximately like a triangle, where a river divides into several smaller rivers before flowing into the sea • *the Mississippi delta*

delude /dɪ'luːd/ v [T] to fool (yourself) into believing something is true because you want it to be true, when it is actually not true • *He's deluding himself if he thinks he's going to get that promotion.*

deluge LARGE AMOUNT /'del·juːdʒ, -juːʒ/ *n* [C usually sing] a very large volume of something, more than can be managed • *The newspaper received a deluge of complaints about the article.*

deluge /'del·juːdʒ, -juːʒ/ *v* [T] • *The senator's office was deluged with calls asking for clarification.*

deluge RAIN /'del·juːdʒ, -juːʒ/ *n* [C] a very large amount of rain or water

delusion /dɪ'luː·ʒən/ *n* [C] something a person believes to be true because they want it to be true, when it is actually not true • *We have no delusions that these kids are going to play pro basketball, but they are having fun.* [C]

deluxe /dɪ'lʌks/ *adj* [not gradable] of very high quality; luxurious • *a deluxe hotel*

delve into /'del,vin·tə/ *v prep* [T] to search in order to find a thing or information • *She said she was tired of journalists delving into her private life.*

demagogue /'dem·ə,gɑg/ *n* [C] *disapproving* a person, esp. a political leader, who wins support by exciting people's emotions rather than by trying to persuade them

demand /dɪ'mænd/ *v* to ask for forcefully, in a way that shows that refusal is not expected and will not be accepted • *Two hijackers seized a Russian jet and demanded $2 million.* [T] ○ *I demand to see the person in charge.* [+ *to* infinitive] • To demand is also to need something: *The twins demand a lot of attention.* [T]

demand /dɪ'mænd/ *n* [C/U] something asked for forcefully, or something that you accept as necessary • *The union's major demand was for improved benefits.* [C] ○ *The demands of nursing are too great for a lot of people.* [C] • Demand is also need: *We can't meet the demand for tickets to the game.* [C] ○ *Good teachers are always in demand* (= needed). [U] • (*specialized*) Demand is also the desire to buy goods: *There was weak demand for imported goods last month.*

demanding /dɪ'mæn·dɪŋ/ *adj* someone or something that needs a lot of attention, effort, or time • *I'm trying to learn English, and I find it very demanding.*

demean /dɪ'miːn/ *v* [T] to cause to become less respected • *I wouldn't demean myself by asking my father for money.*

demeaning /dɪ'miː·nɪŋ/ *adj* • *It was demeaning to be asked to leave because I was dressed informally.*

demeanor /dɪ'miː·nər/ *n* [U] a way of looking and behaving • *His military demeanor makes some people uneasy.*

demented /dɪ'ment·əd/ *adj* mentally ill

demise /dɪ'maɪz/ *n* [U] the end of the operation or existence of something • *Huge corporate farms have led to the demise of many*

small, family-owned farms. • (*fml*) (of a person) Demise means death.

demo /'dem·oʊ/ *n* [C] *pl* **demos** short form of a **demonstration**, see at DEMONSTRATE SHOW HOW • *I saw several interesting demos at the trade show last week.*

democracy /dɪ'mɑk·rə·si/ *n* [C/U] the belief in freedom and equality between people, or a system of government based on this belief, in which power is either held by elected representatives or directly by the people themselves • *A democracy is a country in which power is held by elected representatives.* [C]

democrat /'dem·ə,kræt/ *n* [C] a person who supports or believes in government by the people or their representatives • *A Democrat is a member or supporter of the* **Democratic Party** (= one of the two main political parties in the US).

democratic /,dem·ə'kræt̬·ɪk/ *adj* • *That country has never had a democratic election* (= an election in which all adults can vote).

demolish /dɪ'mɑl·ɪʃ/ *v* [T] to completely destroy, esp. buildings or other structures • *Most of the town was demolished by the tornado.* ○ *They demolished the old school to build a new one.*

demolition /,dem·ə'lɪʃ·ən/ *n* [C/U] the act of destroying something, such as a building or other structure, esp. intentionally • *They tried unsuccessfully to stop the demolition of the old hotel.* [C]

demon /'diː·mən/ *n* [C] an evil spirit

demonize /'diː·mə,naɪz/ *v* [T] to try to make (someone or a group of people) seem as if they are completely evil • *The mayor demonizes anyone who disagrees with him.*

demonstrate (*obj*) SHOW HOW /'dem·ən ,streɪt/ *v* to show (how to do something); explain • *He demonstrated how to use the new software.* [+ *wh-* word] ○ *The surgeon demonstrated the use of lasers for certain operations.* [T]

demonstration /,dem·ən'streɪ·ʃən/, short form **demo** *n* [C/U] • *Let me give you a demonstration of how the camera works.* [C]

demonstrate (*obj*) PROVE /'dem·ən,streɪt/ *v* to show that something is true; prove • *Research demonstrates that babies can recognize their mother's voice very soon after birth.* [+ *that* clause] ○ *She was eager to demonstrate her skill at chess.* [T]

demonstrate (*obj*) EXPRESS /'dem·ən,streɪt/ *v* [T] to express or show that you have (a feeling, quality, or ability) • *His answer demonstrated a complete lack of understanding of the question.*

demonstration /,dem·ən'streɪ·ʃən/ *n* [C/U] • *Huge crowds followed the funeral procession in a public demonstration* (= show) *of grief.* [C]

demonstrative /dɪ'mɑn·strət̬·ɪv/ *adj* behaving in a way that clearly shows your feelings • *She was always a demonstrative child.*

demonstrate MARCH /ˈdem·ənˌstreɪt/ v [I] (of a group of people) to make a public expression of complaint about a problem or support for something, esp. by marching or meeting

demonstration /ˌdem·ənˈstreɪ·ʃən/ n [C] • *Students staged a protest demonstration in the school gym.*

demonstrator /ˈdem·ənˌstreɪt·ər/ n [C] • *Several demonstrators were arrested when they sat down in the middle of Broadway.*

demonstrative /dɪˈmɑn·strət·ɪv/ adj specialized (in grammar) showing which person or thing is being referred to • *a demonstrative adjective* ○ *In "This is my brother," "this" is a demonstrative pronoun.*

demoralize /dɪˈmɔːr·əˌlaɪz, diː-, -ˈmɑr-/ v [T] to weaken the confidence of (someone) • *The prisoners were hungry, tired, and thoroughly demoralized.*

demote /dɪˈmoʊt/ v [T] to lower (someone) in rank or position • *The day after her boss learned she was gay, he demoted her.* • USAGE: The opposite of demote is PROMOTE ADVANCE.

demotion /dɪˈmoʊ·ʃən/ n [C/U] • *He faces possible demotion.* [U]

demur /dɪˈmər/ v [I] **-rr-** to express disagreement or refusal to do something • *Jack urged me to go, but I demurred.*

demure /dɪˈmjʊr/ adj (esp. of women and girls) quiet and well behaved • *Two demure little girls sat near their mother.*

den /den/ n [C] a room in a home that is used esp. for reading and watching television • *We have a computer in the den.* • A den is also the home of some types of wild animals.

denial /dɪˈnaɪ·əl/ n See at DENY

denigrate /ˈden·əˌgreɪt/ v [T] to say that (someone or something) is not good or important • *Many of his songs denigrate women and promote violence.*

denim /ˈden·əm/ n [U] a thick, strong, cotton cloth, often blue

denomination RELIGIOUS GROUP /dɪˌnɑm·əˈneɪ·ʃən/ n [C] a religious group whose beliefs differ in some ways from other groups in the same religion • *The petition was signed by clergymen from over 20 Protestant denominations.*

denominational /dɪˌnɑm·əˈneɪ·ʃən·əl/ adj [not gradable] • *He avoids denominational rivalries.*

denomination VALUE /dɪˌnɑm·əˈneɪ·ʃən/ n [C] a unit of value, esp. of money • *The machines take coins of any denomination.*

denominator /dɪˈnɑm·əˌneɪt·ər/ n [C] specialized in a FRACTION (= part of a whole number), the number written below the line, showing how many parts the whole contains • Compare NUMERATOR. LP FRACTIONS AND DECIMALS

denote /dɪˈnoʊt/ v [T] to represent (something) • *His angry tone denoted extreme displeasure.*

denounce /dɪˈnaʊns/ v [T] to criticize (some-

one or something) strongly and publicly • *The governor denounced the rally as racist.*

dense THICK /dens/ adj [-er/-est only] close together and difficult to go or see through; thick • *dense fog* ○ *I had trouble getting through the dense crowd.* • Dense can also mean stupid: *There are some really dense people in our class.*

densely /ˈden·sli/ adv • *a densely packed room*

density /ˈden·sət̬·i/, **denseness** /ˈden·snəs/ n [C/U] • *The density of the smoke made it difficult to breathe.* [U]

dense CONTAINING MATTER /dens/ adj [-er/-est only] specialized (of a substance) containing a lot of matter in a small space • *Plutonium is very dense.*

density /ˈden·sət̬·i/ n [C/U] specialized the relationship between the mass of a substance and its size • *Lead has a high density.* [C]

dent /dent/ n [C] a small, hollow mark in the surface of something caused by pressure or being hit • *She ran into my car and put a dent in it.* • If you **make/put a dent in** an amount of esp. money or work, you reduce it: *Buying a new car put a big dent in our savings.*

dent /dent/ v [T] • *I dented the table with my hammer.*

dental /ˈdent̬·əl/ adj [not gradable] relating to the teeth • *dental health* • **Dental floss** is a type of thread that is used for cleaning between the teeth.

dentist /ˈdent̬·əst/ n [C] a person whose job is treating people's teeth

dentistry /ˈdent̬·ə·stri/ n [U] the work or science of treating people's teeth • *Where did Dr. Yee study dentistry?*

dentures /ˈden·tʃərz/ pl n artificial teeth worn by someone who does not have their own teeth • *a set of dentures*

denunciation /dɪˌnʌn·siˈeɪ·ʃən/ n [C/U] a strong, public criticism • *He gave a ringing denunciation of fascism.* [C]

deny (obj) CLAIM TO BE NOT TRUE /dɪˈnaɪ/ v to say that (something) is not true • *The governor denied reports that he will resign.* [T] ○ *She has denied that she is a racist.* [+ that clause]

denial /dɪˈnaɪ·əl/ n [C] • *His statement is not a denial.*

deny REFUSE /dɪˈnaɪ/ v [T] to refuse to permit or allow (someone to do something) • *She denied herself the things that would make her happy.*

denial /dɪˈnaɪ·əl/ n [U] • *Planning staff recommended denial of the project.* • See also SELF-DENIAL.

deny NOT ADMIT /dɪˈnaɪ/ v [T] to fail to admit that you have (knowledge, responsibility, or feelings) • *He denied knowing about the plan.*

denial /dɪˈnaɪ·əl/ n [C] • *He claims he's not sick, but I think he's just in denial.*

deodorant /diːˈoʊd·ə·rənt/ n [C/U] a substance that is used to prevent or hide unpleasant smells, esp. those of the body • *Someone should tell him to use (a) deodorant.* [C/U]

depart /dɪˈpɑrt/ v [I] to go away from a place, esp. on a trip • *The last flight to Cleveland departs at 8 p.m.* ○ *He shook hands and then departed.* • If you depart from your usual or intended activity or behavior, you do something different: *On the last show, they departed from their usual format.*

department /dɪˈpɑrt·mənt/ n [C] any of the divisions or parts of esp. a school, business, or government • *Chavez is the head of the geography department.* ○ *The shoe department is on the fifth floor.* ○ *She lives in Washington and works for the Department of Defense.* ○ (*fig. infml*) I thought buying the tickets was your department (= area of responsibility). • A **department store** is a large store divided into several different areas, each of which sells different types of things.

departmental /dɪˌpɑrtˈment·ᵊl, ˌdiː-/ adj [not gradable] • *a departmental meeting*

departure /dɪˈpɑr·tʃər/ n [C/U] the act of leaving a place, job, etc., or an occasion when this happens • *Departure is scheduled for 2 p.m.* [U] ○ *Our departure was delayed because of bad weather.* [C] • A departure from usual behavior is a change in the way you do something: *His departure from his usual optimism startled his staff.* [C]

depend /dɪˈpend/ v • People say **it/that depends** to show they are not sure: *"Would you lie to your girlfriend?" "It depends."*

□ **depend on/upon** NEED SUPPORT /-ˈ-ˌ-; -ˈ--ˌ-/ v adv [T] to need the support of (someone or something) • *Children depend on their parents.* ○ *The country depends heavily upon foreign aid.*

dependent /dɪˈpen·dənt/ adj needing the support of something or someone in order to continue existing or operating • *She has three dependent children.* ○ *He became dependent on sleeping pills.* • (*specialized*) In grammar, a **dependent clause** is a clause in a sentence that cannot form a separate sentence but can be joined to a main clause to form a sentence.

dependent /dɪˈpen·dənt/ n [C] a person who is financially supported by another person • *Jack and Marion have four dependents.*

dependence /dɪˈpen·dəns/, **dependency** /dɪˈpen·dən·si/ n [U] a state of needing something or someone, esp. in order to continue existing or operating • *drug dependency* ○ *The company is reducing its dependence on foreign markets.*

□ **depend on/upon** HAVE TRUST /-ˈ-ˌ-; -ˈ--ˌ-/ v adv [T] to have confidence in (someone or something); trust • *You can always depend on/upon Michael in a crisis.*

dependable /dɪˈpen·də·bəl/ adj deserving of trust or confidence • *I need a dependable baby-sitter.*

depict /dɪˈpɪkt/ v [T] to represent or show (something) in a picture, story, movie, etc.;

PORTRAY • *The movie depicts his father as a tyrant.*

depiction /dɪˈpɪk·ʃən/ n [C/U] • *It's a wonderful depiction of a female friendship.* [C]

deplete /dɪˈpliːt/ v [T] to reduce (esp. supplies, energy, or money) in size or amount • *Acid rain depletes the region's fish stocks.*

depletion /dɪˈpliː·ʃən/ n [C/U] • *The depletion of our savings is starting to worry me.* [U]

deplore /dɪˈplɔr, -ˈplour/ v [T] to say or think that (something) is very bad; CONDEMN CRITICIZE • *We deplore the recent killings.*

deplorable /dɪˈplɔr·ə·bəl, -ˈplour-/ adj very bad • *The children were raised in deplorable conditions.*

deploy /dɪˈplɔɪ/ v [I/T] to move (something, esp. weapons or military forces) into a position ready for use • *NATO is deploying ground troops.* [T] ○ *When airbags deploy, they save lives.* [I] ○ (*fig.*) *These movies deploy violence in the service of art* (= use it for that purpose). [T]

deployment /dɪˈplɔɪ·mənt/ n [U] • *the deployment of missiles/troops*

deport /dɪˈpɔrt, -ˈpourt/ v [T] to force (a person) to leave a country • *The government hopes to deport the Cuban refugees.*

deportation /ˌdiːˌpɔrˈteɪ·ʃən, -ˌpour-/ n [C/U] • *He ordered the deportation of Jews to death camps during the war.* [U]

deposit MONEY /dɪˈpɑz·ət/ n [C] an amount of money paid into an account • *She made a large deposit last Thursday.* • A deposit is also a sum of money that is given in advance as part of a total payment for something: *Will you get your deposit back if you cancel the trip?* • A deposit is also an additional sum of money that you pay when you rent something to make sure you return the item or to pay for repairs: *The apartment rents for $1200 a month, and we want one month's rent for a deposit.* • A deposit is also an amount paid in addition to the cost of something to make sure you bring its container back when you have used it: *a bottle deposit*

deposit /dɪˈpɑz·ət/ v [T] to put (money) in a bank • *I deposited $500 in my savings account last week.*

depositor /dɪˈpɑz·ət·ər/ n [C] a person who keeps money at a bank • *Depositors will be informed of any change in interest rates.*

deposit LAYER /dɪˈpɑz·ət/ n [C] a layer of a substance • *The flood left a thick deposit of mud on the floor.* ○ *The region has lots of gas and coal deposits.*

deposit LEAVE /dɪˈpɑz·ət/ v [T always + adv/prep] to leave (something) somewhere • *The cat deposited a dead mouse at my door.*

depot /ˈdep·oʊ, ˈdiː·poʊ/ n [C] a building where supplies or vehicles are kept • *a fuel depot* • A depot is also a building that buses and trains leave from.

depraved /dɪˈpreɪvd/ adj morally bad or evil

• *Depraved criminals should not get early parole.*

depravity /dɪˈpræv·ət·i/ *n* [U] • *How could our government support such depravity?*

depreciate /dɪˈpriː·ʃiːˌeɪt, -ˈprɪʃ·iː-/ *v* [T] to cause (something) to lose value, esp. over time • *Malawi's currency was rapidly depreciating.*

depress CAUSE UNHAPPINESS /dɪˈpres/ *v* [T] to cause (a person) to feel unhappy and without hope • *Bad weather depresses a lot of people.* ○ *It depresses me to think about it.*

depressant /dɪˈpres·ənt/ *n* [C] a substance that causes you to feel sad or calm • *Alcohol is a depressant.*

depressed /dɪˈprest/ *adj* • *He's depressed about his divorce.*

depressing /dɪˈpres·ɪŋ/ *adj* • *Life is depressing enough, I don't need depressing movies.*

depressingly /dɪˈpres·ɪŋ·li/ *adv* • *My score was depressingly low.*

depression /dɪˈpreʃ·ən/ *n* [U] a feeling of sadness, or (*medical*) a type of mental illness characterized by long periods of unhappiness • *I'm just beginning to get over the depression from losing my job.* ○ (*medical*) *Tiredness, loss of appetite, and sleeping problems are symptoms of depression.* • See also **depression** at DEPRESS REDUCE, DEPRESS PRESS DOWN.

depress REDUCE /dɪˈpres/ *v* [T] to reduce the value of (esp. money), or to reduce the amount of activity in (esp. a business operation) • *A surplus of corn depressed grain prices.*

depressed /dɪˈprest/ *adj* • *This is an economically depressed area.*

depression /dɪˈpreʃ·ən/ *n* [C] a period in which there is very little business activity and little employment • *My parents lived through the Great Depression of the 1930s.* • See also **depression** at DEPRESS CAUSE UNHAPPINESS, DEPRESS PRESS DOWN.

depress PRESS DOWN /dɪˈpres/ *v* [T] to press down on (something) • *His finger depressed the stop button.*

depression /dɪˈpreʃ·ən/ *n* [C] a part in a surface that is slightly lower than the rest • *There was a depression in the sand where he'd been lying.* • See also **depression** at DEPRESS CAUSE UNHAPPINESS, DEPRESS REDUCE.

deprive *obj* **of** *obj* /dɪˈprɑɪv·əv/ *v prep* [T] to take (esp. something necessary or pleasant) away from (someone) • *He was deprived of food for three days.*

deprived /dɪˈprɑɪvd/ *adj* • *He took pictures in deprived areas of the city.*

deprivation /ˌdep·rəˈveɪ·ʃən/ *n* [C/U] • *There were food shortages and other deprivations during the war.* [C]

depth DISTANCE DOWN /depθ/ *n* [C/U] the distance down from the top surface of something to the bottom • *They were scuba diving at a depth of 22 meters.* [C] ○ *The numbers on the left show the depth in inches.* [U] • USAGE: The related adjective is DEEP DOWN.

depth DISTANCE BACKWARD /depθ/ *n* [C/U] the distance from the front to the back of something • *Bookshelves should be at least nine inches in depth.* [U] • If you are **in the depths** of something, you are in the middle of it: *At the time, America was in the depths of the Depression.* • USAGE: The related adjective is DEEP FRONT TO BACK.

depth STRENGTH /depθ/ *n* [C/U] the strength, quality, or degree of being complete • *It's hard to get a handle on the depth of her knowledge.* [U] • If you are **in the depths of** a negative feeling, you feel it very strongly: *He was in the depths of despair about losing his job.* • See also DEEP STRONGLY FELT.

depth SERIOUSNESS /depθ/ *n* [C/U] the ability to think seriously about something • *Don't look for depth in this show.* [U] • Something done **in depth** is done carefully and in great detail: *I interviewed her in depth.* ○ *an in-depth report/analysis* • See also DEEP COMPLICATED.

deputy /ˈdep·jət·i/ *n* [C] a person who is given the power to act instead of, or to help do the work of, another person • *a deputy chairman* ○ *the deputy editor* ○ *a sheriff's deputy*

derail /dɪˈreɪl, diː-/ *v* [T] to cause (a train) to run off the tracks • (*fig.*) *Renewed fighting threatens to derail the peace talks* (= stop them from continuing).

deranged /dɪˈreɪndʒd/ *adj* behaving in a way that is dangerous or not controlled because of mental illness • *a deranged killer*

derby /ˈdɑr·bi/ *n* [C] a man's hat that has a round, hard top and is usually black

deregulate /diːˈreg·jəˌleɪt/ *v* [T] to remove government controls or rules from (esp. business activity)

deregulation /ˌdiː·reg·jʊˈleɪ·ʃən/ *n* [U] • *The president's advisors recommend further banking-industry deregulation.*

derelict IN BAD CONDITION /ˈder·əˌlɪkt/ *adj* (of buildings or equipment) not cared for and in bad condition

derelict PERSON /ˈder·əˌlɪkt/ *n* [C] a person with no home, job, or money who often lives on the streets • *He stepped over the derelict in the doorway.*

deride /dɪˈrɑɪd/ *v* [T] to show that you think (someone or something) is ridiculous or of no value • *His blustery style is derided by many political pros.*

derision /dɪˈrɪʒ·ən/ *n* [U] • *Talk of tougher laws was met with derision.*

derisive /dɪˈrɑɪ·sɪv, -zɪv/, **derisory** /dɪˈrɑɪ·sə·ri, -zə·ri/ *adj* • *derisive laughter*

derive /dɪˈrɑɪv/ *v* [T always + adv/prep] to get or obtain (something) • *The institute derives all its money from foreign investments.*

□**derive from** /-ˈ--/ *v prep* [T] to originate or come from (something) • *The story derives from a very common folktale.*

derivative /dɪˈrɪv·əṭ·ɪv/ *adj* taken from something else • *Too much of the music feels derivative.*

derivation /ˌder·əˈveɪ·ʃən/ *n* [U] the origin of something • *Does anyone know the derivation of the word OK?*

dermatitis /ˌdɜr·məˈtaɪṭ·əs/ *n* [U] *medical* a red and painful condition of the skin

derogatory /dɪˈrɑg·əˌtɔːr·i, -ˌtoʊr·i/ *adj* critical and insulting • *She was upset by derogatory comments made about her clothes.*

derrick /ˈder·ɪk/ *n* [C] a type of CRANE (= machine with an armlike part) used for moving heavy things esp. on ships, or a tower above a WELL (= hole in the ground) from which oil is taken

descend /dɪˈsend/ *v* [I/T] to go down or come down (something) • *The path descends to the valley below.* [I] ○ *Jane descended the stairs slowly in her wedding gown.* [T]

descent /dɪˈsent/ *n* [C] a way down, such as a path, or an act of coming down • *A steep descent from the peak brings you to a meadow.* ○ *The plane is making its final descent into the airport.*

□ **descend from** /-ˈ--/ *v prep* [T] to have developed from (something or someone in the past) • *Scopes taught that humans had descended from apelike creatures.*

descendant /dɪˈsen·dənt/ *n* [C] a person related to someone from an earlier GENERATION (= all the people of about the same age within a particular family) • *The Pennsylvania Dutch are descendants of early German immigrants.*

descent /dɪˈsent/ *n* [U] • *Their mother is of Irish descent (= family origin).*

□ **descend on/upon** /-ˈ--ˌ-; -ˈ--ˌ-/ *v prep* [T] to visit (someone) or arrive (somewhere) suddenly, without warning or without being invited • *Tourists descend on Prince Edward Island every summer.* ○ (*fig.*) *Homesickness descended upon him.*

descent /dɪˈsent/ *n* [U] the arrival of something or someone, esp. when it is unpleasant or unwanted • *The descent of dozens of motorcycles terrified local residents.*

describe *(obj)* /dɪˈskraɪb/ *v* to say or write what (someone or something) is like • *She was not able to describe her attacker.* [T] ○ *Just describe what happened.* [+ wh- word] ○ *The Democrats describe their rivals as the party of the rich.* [T]

description /dɪˈskrɪp·ʃən/ *n* [C/U] a statement or a piece of writing that tells what something or someone is like • *Your description of Della was hilarious.* [C] ○ *Boats of every description (= of all types) entered the harbor.* [U] ○ *The beauty of the Rockies is beyond description (= is impossible to describe).* [U]

descriptive /dɪˈskrɪp·tɪv/ *adj* • *His poetry skillfully incorporates descriptive details.*

desecrate /ˈdes·əˌkreɪt/ *v* [T] to damage or show a lack of respect toward (esp. something holy) • *Vandals desecrated the temple.*

desecration /ˌdes·əˈkreɪ·ʃən/ *n* [U] • *He denounced the attack as a desecration of the shrine.*

desegregate /diːˈseg·rəˌgeɪt/ *v* [T] to end SEGREGATION (= separation of races) in (schools, housing, organizations, etc.) • *President Truman desegregated the American armed forces in 1948.*

desegregation /ˌdiːˌseg·rəˈgeɪ·ʃən/ *n* [U] • *King's campaign was aimed at the desegregation of all public services, including schools, restaurants, and transportation.*

desert LEAVE BEHIND /dɪˈzɜrt/ *v* [T] to leave (someone or something) without help or in a difficult situation • *He deserted his wife and child for another woman.* • *If you desert the armed forces, you leave without permission and with no intention of returning: He deserted his unit at the start of the battle.*

deserted /dɪˈzɜrt·əd/ *adj* having no people or things in it; empty • *These resort towns are largely deserted in winter.* ○ *We parked in a deserted lot near the river.*

deserter /dɪˈzɜrṭ·ər/ *n* [C] a person who leaves the armed forces without permission and with no intention of returning

desertion /dɪˈzɜr·ʃən/ *n* [U] • *During the war, desertion (= leaving the army without permission) was punishable by death.*

desert SANDY AREA /ˈdez·ərt/ *n* [C/U] a large, dry area where there is very little rain and few plants • *When you live in the desert, water is your most vital resource.* [U]

deserve /dɪˈzɜrv/ *v* to have earned (something) or be given (something) because of your actions or qualities • *These charities deserve your support.* [T] ○ *The American people deserve to know what went wrong.* [+ to infinitive] ○ *I hope those crooks get what they deserve (= receive a punishment that suits their crime).* [T]

design PLAN /dɪˈzaɪn/ *v* [I/T] to make or draw plans for (something) • *A famous engineer designed the new bridge.* [T] ○ *She designs for a dress manufacturer.* [I]

design /dɪˈzaɪn/ *n* [C/U] a plan or drawing • *Have you seen the designs for the new lobby?* [C] • Design is the skill of making plans or drawings for something: *She's an expert in software design.* [U] • Design is also the way in which something is arranged or shaped: *I like the design of this microwave oven.* [U] • A design is also a pattern used to decorate something: *a geometric design*

designer /dɪˈzaɪ·nər/ *n* [C] a person who imagines how something could be made and draws or creates plans for it • *a fashion/graphic designer*

design INTEND /dɪˈzaɪn/ *v* [T] to intend (a result) • *These measures are designed to reduce pollution.*

design /dɪˈzaɪn/ n [U] • If something is done **by design**, it is done with the intention of achieving something: *They are not being educated, and this is being done by design.* • See also DESIGNS.

designate /ˈdez·ɪɡ·neɪt/ v [T] to choose (someone or something) for a special job or purpose, or to state that (something) has a particular character or purpose • *The chairman designated his daughter as his successor.* ○ *North-south streets are designated by numbers.*

designated /ˈdez·ɪɡ·neɪt̬·əd/ adj [not gradable] • *a designated no-smoking area* • A **designated driver** is someone in a group who avoids alcoholic drinks while others are drinking and is then able to drive the others home safely. • Compare ELECT.

designation /ˌdez·ɪɡˈneɪ·ʃən/ n [C/U] • *Associate professor is her official designation* (= title). [C]

designer /dɪˈzaɪ·nər/ n • See at DESIGN PLAN.

designs /dɪˈzaɪnz/ pl n plans to get something or someone for yourself, esp. secret or dishonest plans • *Troop movements suggest the country has designs on its neighbor.*

desire WANT /dɪˈzaɪr/ n [C/U] a strong feeling of wanting something, or something you want • *He claims to have no desire for wealth.* [U] ○ *She expressed a desire to speak with her attorney.* [C] ○ *Teenagers often have a burning desire to look older.* [C] ○ *My desires in life are few.* [C]

desire /dɪˈzaɪr/ v [T] to want (something) strongly • *They don't really seem to desire change.*

desired /dɪˈzaɪrd/ adj wanted • *He dressed carefully, hoping to achieve the desired effect.*

desirable /dɪˈzaɪ·rə·bəl/ adj worth wanting or having • *Good pay and interesting work make this a very desirable job.* ○ *The new store is in a highly desirable location.*

desirability /dɪˌzaɪ·rəˈbɪl·ət̬·i/ n [U] • *Taxes can limit the desirability of home ownership.*

desire SEXUAL NEED /dɪˈzaɪr/ n [C/U] a strong feeling that you want someone sexually • *The further he was from her, the more desire he felt for her.* [U]

desirable /dɪˈzaɪ·rə·bəl/ adj sexually attractive • *She wants men to think of her as attractive and desirable.*

desire /dɪˈzaɪr/ v [T] to want (someone) sexually

desist /dɪˈzɪst, -ˈsɪst/ v [I] fml to stop doing something • *She was ordered to desist from playing music after 11 p.m.*

desk TABLE /desk/ n [C] a type of table for working at, usually one with drawers • *Tommy sits at the desk in front of me in English.* • A **desktop** device is designed to be used on or at a desk: *a desktop computer* • **Desktop publishing** is the process of designing and producing printed material by using a small computer and a high-quality printer.

desk SERVICE AREA /desk/ n [C] a place where you can get information or service, esp. in a hotel, airport, or large store • *The woman at the front desk was very helpful.*

desolate EMPTY /ˈdes·ə·lət/ adj (of a place) having no living things; unpleasantly empty • *a desolate landscape*

desolation /ˌdes·əˈleɪ·ʃən/ n [U] • *It was difficult to describe the emptiness, the desolation of the area.*

desolate SAD /ˈdes·ə·lət/ adj (of a person) extremely sad and feeling alone • *In desolate moments, we have benefited from prayer.*

despair /dɪˈsper, -ˈspær/ n [U] a feeling of being without hope or of not being able to improve a situation • *The refugees are full of hatred and despair.* ○ *She flung up her arms in despair and wailed.*

despair /dɪˈsper, -ˈspær/ v [I] to lose hope or be without hope • *Don't despair—things will improve.* ○ *He began to despair of ever finding a job.*

desperate RISKY /ˈdes·pə·rət/ adj showing a willingness to take any risk in order to change a bad or dangerous situation • *The ads are a desperate attempt to win last-minute votes.* • If someone is desperate, they are willing to be violent, and therefore dangerous: *desperate criminals*

desperation /ˌdes·pəˈreɪ·ʃən/ n [U] the feeling of being in such a bad situation that you will take any risk to change it • *In desperation, they jumped out of the window to escape the fire.*

desperate SERIOUS /ˈdes·pə·rət/ adj very serious or dangerous • *There's a desperate shortage of medical supplies in the area.* ○ *The earthquake survivors are in desperate need of help.*

desperately /ˈdes·pə·rət·li/ adv extremely or very much • *For years they had desperately wanted a child.*

desperate IN NEED /ˈdes·pə·rət/ adj having a very great need • *She was desperate for news of her family.* ○ *I'm desperate for some coffee.*

despise /dɪˈspaɪz/ v [T] to feel a strong dislike for (someone or something) because you think they are bad or worthless • *He adored his daughter, but despised his son.*

despicable /dɪˈspɪk·ə·bəl, ˈdes·pɪk-/ adj deserving to be hated or strongly criticized • *He has a despicable record of human rights abuses.*

despite /dɪˈspaɪt/ prep without being influenced or prevented by • *The game continued despite the rain.* ○ *Despite her illness, she came to work.*

despondent /dɪˈspɑn·dənt/ adj unhappy and discouraged because you feel you are in a hopeless situation • *He grew increasingly despondent when his paintings failed to sell.*

despot /ˈdes·pət, -ˌpɑt/ n [C] a ruler who has unlimited power and often uses it unfairly and cruelly

despotic /des'pɑṭ·ɪk, dɪs-/ *adj* • *a despotic regime*

dessert /dɪ'zɜrt/ *n* [C/U] sweet food eaten at the end of a meal • *He had apple pie with ice cream for dessert.* [U]

destination /ˌdes·tə'neɪ·ʃən/ *n* [C] the place where someone is going or where something is being sent or taken • *The Virgin Islands are a popular tourist destination.*

destined /'des·tənd/ *adj* intended for or being sent to a particular place • *The mail was destined for addresses throughout the Northeast.* • To be destined can mean to happen in a particular way that seems to have been decided in advance: *He was destined to die before he could complete the poem.* [+ *to* infinitive]

destiny /'des·tə·ni/ *n* [C/U] the particular state of a person or thing in the future, considered as resulting from earlier events • *We all want to determine our own destinies.* [C] • Destiny is the force that some people think controls what happens in the future, and which cannot be influenced by people. [U]

destitute /'des·tə·tuːt/ *adj* without money, possessions, or any of the things needed to live • *These groups gathered clothing, bibles, schoolbooks, and medical supplies for the destitute ex-slaves.*

destroy /dɪ'strɔɪ/ *v* [T] to damage (something), esp. in a violent way, so that it can no longer be used or no longer exists • *The goal was to destroy incoming enemy missiles in case of a nuclear attack.* ○ *Losing his job seemed to completely destroy his confidence.* • To destroy an animal is to kill it because it is sick, injured, or dangerous.

destroyer /dɪ'strɔɪ·ər/ *n* [C] a small, fast, military ship that carries weapons

destruction /dɪ'strʌk·ʃən/ *n* [U] the action of destroying something, or the state of being destroyed • *Unusually high winds left widespread destruction over the area.*

destructive /dɪ'strʌk·tɪv/ *adj* • *The child needs help to control his destructive behavior.*

detach /dɪ'tætʃ/ *v* [T] to separate or remove (something) from something else that it is connected to • *Detach the lower half of the form and return it to the above address.*

detached /dɪ'tætʃt/ *adj* • *Their new house has a detached garage.*

detachment /dɪ'tætʃ·mənt/ *n* [C] a group of soldiers who are separated from the main group in order to perform a particular duty • *a detachment of paratroopers*

detached /dɪ'tætʃt/ *adj* (of a person) not emotionally involved in a situation • *As a writer, he took the role of a detached observer of life.*

detail INFORMATION /dɪ'teɪl, 'diː·teɪl/ *n* [C/U] a particular fact or item of information, often noticed only after giving something your close attention, or such facts or items considered as a group • *We have a report of a serious accident on Route 23, but so far no details.* [C] ○ *She*

showed a businesslike attention to detail. [U] ○ *I can't go into much detail, but I've been having some health problems recently.* [U] • **In detail** means by considering all the particular facts about something: *We know roughly what he wants to do, but we haven't had a chance to discuss the matter in detail.*

detail /dɪ'teɪl, 'diː·teɪl/ *v* [T] to give exact and complete information about (something) • *The committee members issued a brief statement detailing their plans.*

detailed /dɪ'teɪld, 'diː·teɪld/ *adj* • *a detailed account/description*

detail GROUP /dɪ'teɪl, 'diː·teɪl/ *n* [C] a small group, esp. of soldiers or police, ordered to perform a particular duty • *A detail of five police officers accompanied the diplomat to his hotel.*

detain /dɪ'teɪn/ *v* [T] to force (someone) officially to stay in a place • *A suspect is being detained by the police for further questioning.* • To detain someone is also to delay them for a short period of time: *We were detained in traffic and arrived at the theater a little late.* • USAGE: The related noun is DETENTION.

detect /dɪ'tekt/ *v* [T] to notice (something that is partly hidden or not clear) or to discover (something), esp. using a special method • *Some sounds cannot be detected by the human ear.* ○ *X-ray procedures can detect a tumor when it is still small.*

detectable /dɪ'tek·tə·bəl/ *adj* • *There has been no detectable change in the patient's condition.*

detection /dɪ'tek·ʃən/ *n* [U] • *These tests can result in the early detection of disease.*

detective /dɪ'tek·tɪv/ *n* [C] a police officer whose job is to discover information about crimes and find out who is responsible for them

detente /deɪ'tɑnt/ *n* [U] an improvement in the relationship between two countries that in the past were not friendly and did not trust each other

detention /dɪ'ten·tʃən/ *n* [C/U] the act or condition of being officially forced to stay in a place • *He claimed that his detention by the immigration authorities was unlawful.* [U] • USAGE: The related verb is DETAIN.

deter /dɪ'tɜr/ *v* [T] **-rr-** to prevent or discourage (someone) from doing something • *High prices are deterring a lot of young couples from buying houses.*

deterrent /dɪ'tɜr·ənt, -'ter-/ *n* [C] • *The company says this alarm is an effective deterrent against theft.*

detergent /dɪ'tɜr·dʒənt/ *n* [C/U] a chemical substance in the form of a powder or a liquid for removing dirt esp. from clothes or dishes

deteriorate /dɪ'tɪr·iː·ə·ˌreɪt/ *v* [I] to become worse • *She went into the hospital when her condition began to deteriorate.*

deterioration /dɪˌtɪr·iː·ə'reɪ·ʃən/ *n* [U] • *a de-*

terioration in relations between the two countries

determine DECIDE /dɪˈtɜr·mən/ *v* to control or influence directly; to decide • *We should be allowed to determine our own future.* [T] ○ *Eye color is genetically determined.* [T] ○ *He determined to find out the real reason.* [+ *to* infinitive]

determine *(obj)* DISCOVER /dɪˈtɜr·mən/ *v* to find out or make certain (facts or information) • *The police never actually determined the cause of death.* [T] ○ *I can't determine why your phone isn't working.* [+ *wh-* word] ○ *The investigation determined that the death was accidental.* [+ *that* clause]

determined /dɪˈtɜr·mənd/ *adj* showing the strong desire to follow a particular plan of action even if it is difficult • *a very determined young man* ○ *She had a determined look on her face.* ○ *I'm determined to finish this book today.* [+ *to* infinitive]

determination /dɪˌtɜr·məˈneɪ·ʃən/ *n* [U] • *She has a lot of determination to succeed.* [+ *to* infinitive]

determiner /dɪˈtɜr·mə·nər/ *n* [C] *specialized* (in grammar) a word that is used before a noun to show which particular example of the noun you are referring to • *In the phrase "my first boyfriend" the word "my" is a determiner.*

deterrent /dɪˈtɜr·ənt, -ˈter-/ *n* See at DETER.

detest /dɪˈtest/ *v* [T] to hate; dislike extremely • *She detested traveling in hot weather.*

DETERMINERS

Determiners are words that go before a noun and identify what the noun refers to. For example, *bread* is a general term for the food made of flour and water, but if someone says **this** *bread* or **my** *bread*, it tells us which particular bread they are talking about, and if they say *some bread*, it tells us they are talking about a quantity of bread.

Adjectives can come between a determiner and a noun (**my** *old coat*), but not before a determiner. Determiners can, however, be qualified by some other determiners.

    all *my money;* **both** *those letters;* **half** *its length;* **twice** *her age;* **such** *a good time*

• **the** is known as the definite article, and refers to a patricular thing known to both the speaker and listener.

    *There's someone at **the** door.*

• **a/an** are known as indefinite articles, and refer to someone or something that is not known to the speaker or listener, or which has not been mentioned before.

    *I need **a** new umbrella.*

LP **Articles**

• **my, her, his, its, our, your,** and **their** show who the person or thing mentioned belongs to or is connected with.

    *Is this **your** coffee?* • *They haven't received **our** check.* • *The bird turned **its** head.* • *Did you meet **her** husband?*

• **this, these, that,** and **those** show which one is referred to.

    *Put it in **this** bag/**these** bags.* • *My grandfather built **that** house/**those** houses.*

• **what, which,** and **whose** in questions ask which one out of a set is referred to.

    ***Whose** books are these?* • ***What** color is her hair?* • ***Which** picture do you like?*

When used in statements, **which, what,** and **whose** show the one that is referred to.

    *The man **whose** coat you took is very angry.* • *I can't remember **which** (or **what**) years he visited us.*

• **whichever** and **whatever** refer to items selected from a group. **Whichever** suggests a more limited choice than **whatever**.

    *Listen to **whatever** kind of music you like.* • *We can go **whichever** day you're free.*

• **either** and **neither** refer to a choice between two items. The following noun is singular.

    *She can write well using **either** hand.* • ***Neither** parent wants to visit the school.*

• **other** and **another** refer to something different, additional, or remaining.

    *There are **other** things you could do.* • *Look in the **other** drawer in my desk.* • *Is there any **other** news?* • *Could I have **another** apple?*

The noun following **another** is singular unless few or a plural number is used.

    *I'll be at this address for **another** two/few months.*

• **every, all, each, both, some, any, many, most, much, a lot of, few, several, (a) little, enough,** and **no** show what quantity or amount is referred to.

LP **Quantity words**

detonate /'det·ᵊn,eɪt/ v [I/T] to explode, or to cause (a bomb) to explode • *A remote control device was used to detonate the bomb.* [T]

detonator /'det·ᵊn,eɪt̬·ər/ n [C] a device used to cause an explosive to detonate

detour /'diː·tʊr/ n [C] a way of getting to a place that is indirect and longer than the usual way, and which is taken in order to avoid a particular problem or to do something special • *You're advised to take a detour to avoid the road construction.* ○ *We made a little detour to drop Sarah off on the way home.*

detour /'diː·tʊr/ v [I] • *We had to detour around the flooded road.*

detoxification /diː,tɑk·sə·fə'keɪ·ʃən/, short form **detox** /'diː·tɑks/ n [U] specialized the process of giving medical treatment to someone in order to remove the effects of poisoning from drinking too much alcohol or taking too many drugs • *a detoxification program/center*

detract (obj) **from** /dɪ'trækt·frəm/ v prep [T] to make (something) seem less valuable or less deserving of admiration • *These small faults, however, do not detract from the overall quality of the book.*

detractor /dɪ'træk·tər/ n [C usually pl] a person who criticizes something or someone, often unfairly • *He is much more popular with his teammates than his detractors would have you believe.*

detriment /'de·trə·mənt/ n [U] harm or damage • *She was very involved with sports at college, to the detriment of her studies.*

detrimental /,de·trə'ment·ᵊl/ adj • *chemicals that have a detrimental effect on the environment*

devastate /'dev·ə,steɪt/ v [T] to cause great damage or suffering to (something or someone), or to violently destroy (a place) • *Waves of corporate downsizing have devastated employee morale.* ○ *I was so devastated I was crying constantly.* ○ *The town was devastated by a hurricane in 1928.*

devastating /'dev·ə,steɪt̬·ɪŋ/ adj • *devastating criticisms* ○ *It will have a devastating impact on the economy.*

develop GROW /dɪ'vel·əp/ v [I/T] to grow or cause to grow or change into a more advanced form • *This exercise will help develop the shoulder and back muscles* (= It will make them stronger). [T] ○ *If Kareem keeps working hard, he could develop into a first-class athlete.* [I] ○ *The tourist industry is continuing to develop in the lake region.* [I] ○ *Your essay is good, but you need to develop your ideas more fully* (= give more details). [T]

developed /dɪ'vel·əpt/ adj • *Sharks have a highly developed sense of smell.*

developing /dɪ'vel·ə·pɪŋ/ adj [not gradable] • *a developing fetus* ○ Developing countries have little industry or wealth but have the ability to grow economically.

development /dɪ'vel·əp·mənt/ n [C/U] • *A good diet and lots of exercise are essential for a child's healthy growth and development.* [U] ○ *I took a history course that dealt with the development of popular culture.* [U] • A development is a recent important event that is the latest in a series of related events: *There is a new development in the murder trial of the three Colorado youths.* [C]

develop START /dɪ'vel·əp/ v [I/T] to bring or come into existence • *Large cracks are developing in the wall of the house.* [I] ○ *George has developed an interest in archaeology.* [T] • If you develop an illness, you catch it or start to suffer from it: *She developed a skin rash.* [T] • If an area of land is developed, it is built on, usually by a company that hopes to make a profit in this way: *We have plans to develop the site.* [T]

developer /dɪ'vel·ə·pər/ n [C] a person or company that makes money by buying land and building new houses, stores, or offices on it • *real estate developers*

development /dɪ'vel·əp·mənt/ n [C/U] • *We were waiting for the development of new plans for the city's convention center.* [U] ○ *I'm in charge of product development* (= the creation and design of new products) *for the company.* [U] ○ *Cotton fields were replaced by housing developments* (= groups of similar houses built at the same time) *as the city experienced rapid growth.* [C] • Development is also the building of houses, stores, or offices, esp. by a company to make a profit, on an area of land where there were none before. [U]

develop PROCESS FILM /dɪ'vel·əp/ v [I/T] to put (film) in chemicals until an image appears

deviant /'diː·viː·ənt/ adj (esp. of people or behavior) not usual, and generally considered to be unacceptable • *deviant behavior*

deviance /'diː·viː·əns/ n [U]

deviate /'diː·viː,eɪt/ v [I] to change from the usual way, or to go in a different direction • *He never deviated from his strict vegetarian diet.* ○ *We need to know when the bus deviates from its scheduled route.*

deviation /,diː·viː'eɪ·ʃən/ n [C/U] • *Any deviation from the party line is seen as betrayal.* [U]

device OBJECT /dɪ'vaɪs/ n [C] an object or machine that has been invented to fulfill a particular purpose • *a contraceptive device* ○ *a safety device* ○ *electronic/mechanical devices* ○ *He invented a device for measuring very small distances exactly.*

device METHOD /dɪ'vaɪs/ n [C] a method that is used to produce a desired effect • *His temper tantrums were just a device for attracting attention.*

devil /'dev·əl/ n [C] an evil being, often represented in human form but with a tail and horns • In Christianity and Judaism, the Devil is the originator of evil and the enemy of God. • The devil can be used to give emphasis to a question: *What the devil are you doing?* •

In an argument or discussion, a **devil's advocate** is a person who supports an unpopular or opposite argument in order to make people think seriously about the matter.

devilish /'dev·ə·lɪʃ/ *adj* slightly bad, but sometimes in an amusing way • *a devilish grin* • Devilish can also mean extremely difficult: *a devilish problem*

devious /'diː·viː·əs/ *adj* using indirect ways to get what you want, esp. without showing your real purpose • *devious methods* • Devious also means indirect: *They went by a devious route.*

devise /dɪ'vaɪz/ *v* [T] to invent (something), esp. with intelligence or imagination • *He devised a new way to treat mental depression.* ○ *The committee is devising an agenda for the upcoming political convention.*

devoid /dɪ'vɔɪd/ *adj* [not gradable] • If someone or something is **devoid of** something, they completely lack it: *He seems to be devoid of any feeling for his parents.*

devote *obj* **to** *obj* /dɪ'voʊt·tə, -,tu, -,tuː/ *v prep* [T] to give (esp. time or effort) wholly to (something you believe in or to a person), or to use (a particular amount of time or energy) doing (something) • *She has devoted her life to helping abused women.* ○ *Over half his speech was devoted to the issue of saving Social Security.*

devotee /,dev·ə'tiː, -'teɪ; dɪ,voʊ'tiː/ *n* [C] a person who strongly admires a particular person or is extremely interested in a subject • *Devotees of jazz won't want to miss this!*

devoted /dɪ'voʊt̬·əd/ *adj* extremely loving and loyal • *a devoted fan/husband/mother*

devotion /dɪ'voʊ·ʃən/ *n* [U] loyalty and affection • *He is a teacher who inspires respect and devotion from his students.* ○ *She knelt in devotion* (= religious worship).

devour /dɪ'vaʊr/ *v* [T] to eat eagerly and in large amounts, so that nothing is left • *He devoured the entire plate of spaghetti.* ○ *(fig.) She devoured* (= read eagerly and quickly) *the novels of Jane Austen.*

devout /dɪ'vaʊt/ *adj* (of people) believing strongly in a religion and obeying all the rules or principles of that religion • *a devout Christian/Jew/Muslim*

devoutly /dɪ'vaʊt·li/ *adv* • *a devoutly religious family*

dew /duː, djuː/ *n* [U] small drops of water that form on the ground and other surfaces outside esp. during the night

dexterity /dek'ster·ət̬·i/ *n* [U] the ability to use the hands skillfully in doing something • *Playing with blocks improves a child's manual dexterity.*

diabetes /,dɑɪ·ə'biːt̬·iːz, -əs/ *n* [U] a disease in which the body cannot control the amount of sugar in the blood

diabetic /,dɑɪ·ə'bet̬·ɪk/ *adj* • *a diabetic patient*

diabetic /,dɑɪ·ə'bet̬·ɪk/ *n* [C] a person who has diabetes

diabolical /,dɑɪ·ə'bɑl·ɪ·kəl/ *adj* very evil but often intelligent • *She devises a diabolical plot to terrorize the two men.*

diagnose /'dɑɪ·ɪg,noʊs, -,noʊz/ *v* [T] to recognize and name (the exact character of a disease or other problem) by making an examination • *He was diagnosed with cancer that year.* ○ *It was not easy to diagnose what was wrong with the business.*

diagnosis /,dɑɪ·ɪg'noʊ·səs/ *n* [C/U] *pl* **diagnoses** /,dɑɪ·ɪg'noʊ,siːz/ the making of a judgment about the exact character of a disease or other problem, esp. after an examination, or such a judgment • *Mammograms have greatly improved the early diagnosis of breast cancer.* [U]

diagnostic /,dɑɪ·ɪg'nɑs·tɪk/ *adj* • *The hospital is doing some diagnostic tests to see if they can figure out why she's running a fever.*

diagonal /dɑɪ'æg·ən·əl/ *adj* (of a line) straight and sloping, so that it is neither horizontal nor vertical • *A diagonal line in a circle is often used as a symbol to show that certain behavior is forbidden.*

diagram /'dɑɪ·ə,græm/ *n* [C] a simple plan drawn to represent something, such as a machine, usually to explain how it works or how it is put together • *The teacher drew a diagram showing how blood flows through the heart.*

dial TELEPHONE /dɑɪl/ *v* [I/T] to make a telephone call by pressing the buttons or turning the disk on a telephone to be connected to (a particular number) • *What number did you dial?* [T] • **Dial tone** is the continuous sound you hear when you pick up the telephone, letting you know that you can now dial a number. • LP TELEPHONE

dial MEASURING DEVICE /'dɑɪl/ *n* [C] the part of a machine or device that shows a measurement, such as of speed or time, often a numbered circle with a moving pointer • A dial is also a part of an instrument that you can turn or move to control it: *Turn the dial of the radio and get some music.*

dialect /'dɑɪ·ə,lekt/ *n* [C/U] a form of a language that is spoken in a particular part of a country or by a particular group of people and that contains some words, grammar, or PRONUNCIATIONS (= the ways in which words are said) that are different from the forms used in other parts or by other groups

dialogue CONVERSATION , **dialog** /'dɑɪ·ə,lɔːg, -,lɑg/ *n* [C/U] conversation between the characters in a story, such as in a book or movie • *Oscar Wilde's plays are famous for their witty dialogue.* [U]

dialogue EXCHANGE OF OPINION , **dialog** /'dɑɪ·ə,lɔːg, -,lɑg/ *n* [C/U] a serious exchange of opinion, esp. among people or groups that disagree • *The president called for a national dialogue on race relations.* [C]

diameter /dɑɪ'æm·ət̬·ər/ *n* [C/U] the distance from one side to the opposite side of a circle, measured by a line passing through the center of the circle • *We need a pipe with a diameter of about six inches.* [C]

diametrically /ˌdaɪ·ə'me·trɪ·kli/ *adv* completely • *Father and son had diametrically opposed views on politics.*

diamond STONE /'daɪ·mənd, -ə·mənd/ *n* [C/U] an extremely hard, valuable stone prized as a jewel and having many uses in industry • *a diamond engagement ring* [U]

diamond SHAPE /'daɪ·mənd, -ə·mənd/ *n* [C] a shape with four straight sides

diamonds /'daɪ·məndz, -ə·məndz/ *pl n* one of the four SUITS (= groups) of playing cards, the symbol for which is a shape with four straight sides • PIC SUITS

diaper /'daɪ·pər, 'daɪ·ə·pər/ *n* [C] a large square of thick, soft, plastic-covered paper or cloth fastened around a baby's buttocks and between its legs to hold its urine and excrement • *Get two boxes of disposable diapers.*

diaphragm /'daɪ·ə,fræm/ *n* [C] a thin piece of material that is stretched across an opening, esp. the muscle that separates the chest from the lower part of the body containing the stomach and bowels • *A diaphragm is also a circular, rubber device that a woman can put inside her vagina before having sex to prevent herself from becoming pregnant.*

diarrhea /ˌdaɪ·ə'riː·ə/ *n* [U] a condition in which a person's solid waste is too watery and is excreted too frequently

diary /'daɪ·ə·ri, 'daɪ·ri/ *n* [C] a person's private record of events, thoughts, feelings, etc., that are written down every day, or a book where such things are recorded • *A diary is also a book in which you keep a personal record of the people you are planning to see or the things you are planning to do: Let me check the doctor's diary and see if she can see you then.*

dice GAME /daɪs/ *pl n* two small CUBES (= square, box-shaped solids) that are the same, each with a different number of spots on each of its six sides, used in games

dice CUT /daɪs/ *v* [T] to cut (food) into small squares • *Peel and dice the carrots.* • PIC CUT

dicey /'daɪ·si/ *adj* dicier, diciest *infml* not certain or safe; risky • *Things are going to be a bit dicey until we know whether the budget was approved.*

dichotomy /daɪ'kɑt̬·ə·mi/ *n* [C] *fml* the division of two things that are completely different • *The minister spoke of the dichotomy between religious conviction and bigotry.*

dick /dɪk/ *n* [C] *taboo slang for* a PENIS

dicker /'dɪk·ər/ *v* [I] to argue with someone, esp. about the price of goods • *She dickered with the driver for several minutes over the fare.*

dictate (obj) GIVE ORDERS /'dɪk·teɪt, dɪk'teɪt/ *v* to give (orders), or state (something) with total authority • *Tennis club rules dictate what kind of footwear may be worn on the courts.* [+

wh- word] • To dictate also means to make necessary: *The threat of terrorist action dictated extreme caution.* [T]

dictate SPEAK /'dɪk·teɪt, dɪk'teɪt/ *v* [I/T] to say (something) aloud for another person or for a machine to record, so that your words can be prepared in writing for use in business or a legal case • *She spent the morning dictating letters.* [T]

dictation /dɪk'teɪ·ʃən/ *n* [U] • *Can we get someone from the agency who takes dictation?* • Dictation is also the reading aloud of a piece of writing in a language being learned in order to test the ability of students to hear and write the language correctly: *a dictation exercise*

dictator /'dɪk,teɪt̬·ər, dɪk'teɪt̬-/ *n* [C] someone who rules a country with complete power, has complete control over the armed forces, and destroys any political opposition

dictatorial /ˌdɪk·tə'tɔːr·iː·əl, -'toʊr-/ *adj* • *dictatorial powers*

dictatorship /dɪk'teɪt̬·ər,ʃɪp/ *n* [C/U] a country ruled by a dictator, or the condition of being so ruled • *A flood of refugees fled the brutal dictatorship then existing in Haiti.* [U]

diction /'dɪk·ʃən/ *n* [U] the manner in which words are pronounced

dictionary /'dɪk·ʃə,ner·i/ *n* [C] a book that lists words alphabetically with their meanings given in the same or in another language, and often includes other information

did /dɪd/ *past simple of* DO

didactic /daɪ'dæk·tɪk/ *adj fml* intended to teach, or to improve morals by teaching • *Children's books possess a practical, didactic purpose—to instill a love for reading.*

didn't /'dɪd·ənt/ *contraction of* did not • *We didn't arrive until after midnight.*

die /daɪ/ *v* [I] dying, *past* died to stop living • *He died of a heart attack.* ○ *She died in her sleep at the age of 94.* ○ *(fig.) The engine just died* (= stopped working). • If you say that you could have/nearly died of a particular feeling, you mean that you felt the feeling very strongly: *I was so embarrassed, I could have died.* • To be dying to do something, or for something, is to be eager to do or to have it: *I'm dying to hear the news.* [+ to infinitive] ○ *I'm dying for a cup of coffee.*

□ **die down** /'-'-/ *v adv* [I] to become reduced in strength • *A storm is expected tonight, but the wind and rain should die down by morning.*

□ **die off** /'-'-/ *v adv* [I] (of a group of people, animals, or plants) to stop living, one by one, until there are none left • *The veterans of World War II are now old and gradually dying off.*

□ **die out** /'-'-/ *v adv* [I] (esp. of a form of life or a custom) to become less common until it stops existing • *Dinosaurs died out millions of years ago.*

diehard /'daɪ·hɑrd/ *adj* [not gradable] unwilling to change or give up your ideas or ways of behaving, even when there are good reasons to do so • *a diehard conservative*

diesel /'diː·zəl/ *n* [U] a type of heavy oil used as a fuel • A diesel is also any vehicle that has an engine using this type of oil as fuel.

diet /'daɪ·ət/ *n* [C/U] the food and drink usually taken by a person or group • *A healthy diet includes fresh vegetables.* [C] • A diet is also the particular food and drink you are limited to when you cannot eat or drink whatever you want to: *a low-salt diet* [C] ○ *I'm going on a diet because I've got to lose some weight.* [C] ○ *(fig.) All you get on TV is a steady diet of violence.* [C]

diet /'daɪ·ət/ *v* [I] to limit the food that you take, esp. in order to lose weight • *He began dieting a month ago and says he has lost ten pounds already.*

diet /'daɪ·ət/ *adj* [not gradable] (of food or drink) containing much less sugar than usual and often sweetened artificially, or containing less fat than usual • *diet Coke/Pepsi*

dieter /'daɪ·ət̬·ər/ *n* [C] • *Studies show there may be as many as 30 million American dieters at one moment.*

differ /'dɪf·ər/ *v* [I] to be not like something else; to be different • *American English and British English obviously differ in pronunciation.* • To differ is also to disagree: *We may differ on what the numbers are, but there is general agreement that we have to do something to cut costs.*

different /'dɪf·rənt, -ə·rənt/ *adj* not the same • *Monet and other Impressionists painted the same scene at different times of day to discover how the colors change in the different light.* ○ *The weather down here is a lot different than it is at home.* ○ *Emily is entirely different from her sister.*

difference /'dɪf·rəns, -ə·rəns/ *n* [C/U] the way in which two things being compared are not the same, or the fact of not being the same • *We try to teach the kids the difference between right and wrong.* [C] ○ *We'd like better seats, but if the difference in price is too much, we'll keep what we have.* [C] • A **difference of opinion** is a disagreement: *There was a difference of opinion about the best way to run the business, and as a result I left the company.* • Differences can be disagreements: *We've had our differences, but we've learned to respect each other's point of view.* [pl]

differently /'dɪf·rənt·li, -ə·rənt·li/ *adv* • *I would have done things differently if I had the chance to do them over again.*

differentiate /ˌdɪf·əˈren·tʃiː·ˌeɪt/ *v* [I/T] to show or find the difference between (one thing) and another, or between things that are compared • *It's the job of the medical examiner to differentiate between accidental death and homicide.* [I always + adv/prep]

difficult /'dɪf·ə·kəlt, -ˌkʌlt/ *adj* not easy or simple; hard to do or to understand • *It's a dif-*

ficult choice, but I've got to decide which job is better.* • Difficult also means having problems: *He's in a difficult situation and could go bankrupt.* • If a person is difficult, they are not easy to deal with: *I loved him, but he could be difficult at times.*

difficulty /'dɪf·ə·kəl·ti, -ˌkʌl·ti/ *n* [C/U] the fact of not being easy, or of being hard to do or understand • *He has some difficulty hearing people when they speak softly.* [U] • A difficulty is also a problem: *In 1986 he experienced financial difficulties and was forced to sell his business.* [C usually pl]

diffuse /dɪˈfjuːz/ *v* [I/T] to spread or cause (something) to spread in many directions • *Television is a powerful means of diffusing knowledge.* [T] • To diffuse is also to make (something) less noticeable or weaker: *The guide tried to diffuse the tension with his grin.* [T]

diffuse /dɪˈfjuːs/ *adj* not dense but spread out over a large area or space • *The smoke may have been too diffuse to detect.*

dig MOVE EARTH /dɪɡ/ *v* **digging**, *past* **dug** /dʌɡ/ to move and break up (earth) using a tool, a machine, or your hands, or to make (a hole, channel, etc.) by moving and breaking up earth • *Friends came with rakes and shovels ready to dig into the earth.* [I] ○ *I was planning to go out and dig up some hibiscus plants.* [M] ○ *Most people out in the country have to dig their own wells.* [T] • If you **dig a hole for** yourself or **dig** yourself **into a hole**, you take an action that is going to cause a lot of trouble for you: *He keeps borrowing more money, and I think he's beginning to dig a hole for himself.*

dig /dɪɡ/ *n* [C] specialized the activity of removing earth to find objects of scientific or historical interest

dig PRESS /dɪɡ/ *v* [T] **digging**, *past* **dug** /dʌɡ/ to press or push strongly • *He dug his hand into his pocket, searching for a quarter.*

dig REMARK /dɪɡ/ *n* [C] a criticism, esp. a remark about someone that does not seem intentional but actually is • *His reference to how busy we were was a dig at us for forgetting to greet him properly.*

□**dig in** /'-'-/ *v adv* [I] *infml* to start eating, esp. eagerly • *The food's getting cold—dig in!*

□**dig out** *obj*, **dig** *obj* **out** /'-'-/ *v adv* [M] to search and find (something) that has been put away for a long time • *There are always people who dig out their old uniforms and put them on for a parade.*

□**dig up** *obj*, **dig** *obj* **up** /'-'-/ *v adv* [M] to discover (information) about someone, esp. damaging information • *Hoover directed his agents in Chicago to see what political dirt they could dig up on David.*

digest EAT /dɪˈdʒest, daɪ-/ *v* [I/T] (of the body of a living creature) to chemically change (food) into smaller forms that the body can absorb and use • *Some people have difficulty digesting milk.* [T]

digestion /dɪ'dʒes·tʃən, daɪ-/ *n* [C/U] the ability of the body to change food chemically so that it can be used

digestive /dɪ'dʒes·tɪv, daɪ-/ *adj* • *the digestive system*

digest UNDERSTAND /dɪ'dʒest, daɪ-/ *v* [T] to take (information) into your mind in a way that gives you the ability to use it • *He could digest an enormous amount of information with amazing speed.*

digest /'daɪ·dʒest/ *n* [C] a short written report containing the most important parts of a longer piece, or a short written report of recent news • *The Sunday newspaper includes a digest of last week's major stories.*

digit NUMBER /'dɪdʒ·ət/ *n* [C] any one of the numbers 0 through 9 • *6735 is a four-digit number.*

digital /'dɪdʒ·ət·ᵊl/ *adj* [not gradable] recording or showing information in the form of numbers, esp. 0 and 1 • *The old movie was re-released with digital sound.* • A digital watch or clock shows the time with numbers that change as the time changes.

digitize /'dɪdʒ·ə,taɪz/ *v* [T] to put (information) into the form of a series of the numbers 0 and 1, usually so that it can be processed electronically • *to digitize sound*

digit FINGER /'dɪdʒ·ət/ *n* [C] *specialized* one of the fingers or toes

dignified /'dɪg·nə,faɪd/ *adj* serious and graceful in manner or style in a way that deserves respect • *a quiet, dignified person*

dignitary /'dɪg·nə,ter·i/ *n* [C] a person who has an important position in a society • *His responsibilities included welcoming visiting dignitaries from foreign countries.*

dignity /'dɪg·nət̬·i/ *n* [U] the quality of a person that makes them deserving of respect, sometimes shown in behavior or appearance • *Laws of privacy are designed to protect the dignity of individuals.*

digress /daɪ'gres/ *v* [I] *fml* (in speech or writing) to move away from the main subject and discuss something else • *He digressed from his subject in order to criticize the accuracy of a newspaper story.*

digression /daɪ'greʃ·ən, dɪ-/ *n* [C] • *His speech was full of digressions about his time in the army.*

dilapidated /də'læp·ə,deɪt̬·əd/ *adj* (esp. of a structure) in bad condition and needing repair • *We still use the dilapidated barn for storing tools.*

dilate /daɪ'leɪt, 'daɪ·leɪt/ *v* [I/T] *esp. medical* to become or make (something, esp. an opening) wider or more open • *The doctor put drops in my eyes to dilate the pupils.* [T]

dilation /daɪ'leɪ·ʃən/ *n* [U] *esp. medical*

dilemma /də'lem·ə, daɪ-/ *n* [C] a situation in which a choice has to be made between possi-

bilities that will all have results you do not want • *The dilemma was over how to protect a charming little island and at the same time allow economic development on it.*

dilettante /'dɪl·ə,tɑnt, -,tænt/ *n* [C] *usually disapproving* a person who is or seems to be interested in a subject, but who is not involved with it in a serious and determined way • *To serious artists, he was merely a dilettante.*

diligent /'dɪl·ə·dʒənt/ *adj* careful and serious in your work, or done in a careful and determined way • *diligent prayer* ○ *They made diligent efforts to carry out their programs.*

diligence /'dɪl·ə·dʒəns/ *n* [U]

dill /dɪl/ *n* [U] an herb whose seeds and leaves are used to flavor foods in cooking

dilute /dɪ'luːt, də-/ *v* [T] to make (a liquid) weaker by mixing it with water or another liquid • *Dilute the bleach in water before adding it to the wash.*

diluted /daɪ'luːt̬·əd, də-/, *esp. specialized* **dilute** /daɪ'luːt, də-/ *adj* • *We let the children have some diluted wine.*

dim /dɪm/ *adj* [-*er*/-*est* only] **-mm-** not bright; not giving or having much light • *A dim bulb provides the only light in the hall.* • Something that is dim is also not clear in your mind or memory or not likely to happen: *I had only a dim memory of a tall, slender man.*

dim /dɪm/ *v* [I/T] **-mm-** to become or make (something) less bright • *In the middle of the storm, the lights suddenly dimmed.* [I]

dimly /'dɪm·li/ *adv* • *a dimly lit hallway*

dime /daɪm/ *n* [C] in the US and Canada, a coin worth ten cents • If you say that something is **a dime a dozen**, you mean that is common and not special: *Books like this are a dime a dozen.*

dimension QUALITY /də'men·tʃən/ *n* [C] a part or quality of a thing or situation that has an effect on the way you think about it • *The new script gave the story a psychological dimension.*

dimension MEASUREMENT /də'men·tʃən/ *n* [C] a measurement of something in a particular direction, esp. its height, length, or width • *The dimensions of the room are 26 feet by 15 feet.*

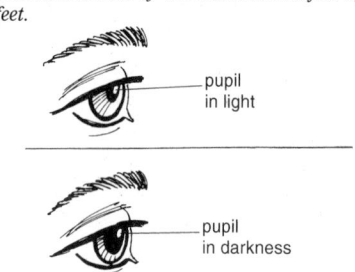

pupil in light

pupil in darkness

dilate

diminish /də'mɪn·ɪʃ/ *v* [I/T] to reduce or be reduced in size or importance • *The threat of inflation is diminishing.* [I] ○ *A single-payer* *system would diminish the bureaucratic cost of health care.* [T]

diminutive /dəˈmɪn·jəṭ·ɪv/ *adj* small • *My grandmother was a diminutive woman, less than 5 feet tall.*

dimly /ˈdɪm·li/ *adv* • See at DIM.

dimple /ˈdɪm·pəl/ *n* [C] a small hollow place, esp. in a person's face and usually considered attractive • *He has a dimple in his chin.*

dimpled /ˈdɪm·pəld/ *adj* • *dimpled cheeks*

din /dɪn/ *n* [U] a loud and unpleasant noise or mixture of noises, esp. one that continues for some time • *The teacher had to yell to be heard over the din.*

dine /daɪn/ *v* [I] to eat, esp. the main meal of the day, usually in the evening • *He dined alone that night.* ○ *This evening we'll be dining out* (= having an evening meal away from home). • A **dining hall** is a large room or building where many people can eat at the same time: *I worked in the dining hall at the college.* • A **dining room** is a room in which meals are eaten.

diner /ˈdaɪ·nər/ *n* [C] someone who eats a meal, esp. in a restaurant • *He comes in very early—he's an early diner.* • A diner is a cheap, informal restaurant that traditionally is long and narrow and looks like part of a train, in which people sit at a COUNTER (= long table) and also in BOOTHS (= partly enclosed areas on either side of a table).

ding–dong /ˈdɪŋ·dɔːŋ, -dɑŋ/ *n* [U] the sound made by a bell

dinghy /ˈdɪŋ·i, -gi/ *n* [C] a small, open boat powered by ROWING (= using long poles with flat ends to push through the water), a motor, or sails, used for pleasure or for moving people to or from a ship

dingy /ˈdɪn·dʒi/ *adj* (of a place or material) dark and unattractive esp. because of being dirty or not cared for • *They met in dingy hotel rooms or cheap restaurants.*

dinky /ˈdɪŋ·ki/ *adj* [-er/-est only] *infml* unpleasantly small or slight • *She had a dinky little apartment.*

dinner /ˈdɪn·ər/ *n* [C/U] the main meal of the day, whether eaten in the evening or in the middle part of the day • *The restaurant is open for dinner from 5 p.m. to 10 p.m.* [U] ○ *What's for dinner* (= What food are we having for our main meal)? [U] ○ *Conversation around the dinner table was always lively.* [U] • A dinner is also a formal social occasion in the evening at which a meal is served: *There will be a black-tie dinner and fund-raiser for Jubilee Housing on April 18th at the Mayflower Hotel.* [C] • A **dinner party** is a social event where a number of people are invited by someone to eat a meal with them, usually in their home. • **Dinnertime** is the time at which the main meal of the day is eaten.

dinosaur /ˈdaɪ·nə,sɔːr/ *n* [C] a creature, some types of which were extremely large, that

stopped existing a very long time ago • A dinosaur is also something that is old and that has not been able to change when conditions have changed and is therefore no longer useful: *The old car was a gas-guzzling dinosaur and we had to get rid of it.*

dint /dɪnt/ *n* • If something is done **by dint of** something else, it is done as a result of that thing: *She achieved her success by dint of hard work.*

diocese /ˈdaɪ·ə·səs, -ˌsiːz, -ˌsiːs/ *n* [C] (in the Roman Catholic Church) the area that is under the control of a BISHOP (= priest of high rank)

diocesan /daɪˈɑs·ə·sən, -zən/ *adj* [not gradable]

dip PUT INTO LIQUID /dɪp/ *v* [T] **-pp-** to put (something) briefly into a liquid • *He dipped his doughnut in the coffee.* • If you **dip into** your money, you spend some of it: *We had to dip into our savings to pay for the repairs.*

dip /dɪp/ *n* [C] • A dip is a thick sauce you can put crackers, raw vegetables, etc., into before eating them. • A dip is also a quick swim: *He took a dip in the pool.*

dip DROP /dɪp/ *v* [I] **-pp-** to go down to a lower level; become less or lower • *Beans and lettuce may suffer if temperatures dip below freezing.* ○ *Stock market prices dipped slightly, losing four points.*

dip /dɪp/ *n* [C usually sing] • *After the yellow house, there's a dip in the road.*

diphtheria /dɪfˈθɪr·i·ə, dɪp-/ *n* [U] a serious infectious disease that causes fever and difficulty in breathing and swallowing

diploma /dəˈploʊ·mə/ *n* [C] a document given by a school, college, or university to show that you have successfully completed a course of study • *It's hard to find a good job if you don't have a high school diploma.*

diplomat /ˈdɪp·lə,mæt/ *n* [C] a person who officially represents their own country's interests in a foreign country • *She is a skilled diplomat and an expert negotiator.*

diplomatic /ˌdɪp·ləˈmæt·ɪk/ *adj* • *He began the diplomatic discussions that resulted in the establishment of NATO.* • If you say that someone is diplomatic, you mean that they are able to control a difficult situation without upsetting anyone: *Lawyers should be diplomatic in dealing with a judge.*

diplomacy /dəˈploʊ·mə·si/ *n* [U] the management of relationships between countries • *Quiet diplomacy is sometimes better than public threats.* • Diplomacy is also the ability to control a difficult situation without upsetting anyone: *It took all her diplomacy to persuade him not to resign.*

dipstick /ˈdɪp·stɪk/ *n* [C] a long, thin stick for measuring the amount of liquid in a container, esp. the oil in a car engine

dire /daɪr/ *adj* very serious or extreme • *Cheating will bring dire consequences.*

direct STRAIGHT /də'rekt, daı-/ *adj* going in a straight line toward somewhere or someone without stopping or changing direction and without anything coming in between • *Is there a direct flight to Madison, or do we have to change planes in Chicago?* ○ *This plant should be kept out of direct sunlight.* • Direct also means without anyone or anything else being involved: *She fired the principal and took direct control of the school.* • Direct also means very honest in saying what you mean: *Her manner was businesslike and direct.* • (*specialized*) In grammar, a **direct object** of a verb is the word or phrase naming who or what the action of the verb is done to: *In the sentence "I saw Mary," "Mary" is the direct object.* Compare **indirect object** at INDIRECT NOT STRAIGHT. See also OBJECT GRAMMAR. LP VERBS WITH TWO OBJECTS at OBJECT GRAMMAR

direct /də'rekt, daı-/ *adv* • *Can I dial this number direct* (= without anything or anyone else being involved) *or do I have to go through the operator?*

directly /d-ə'rek·tli, daı-/ *adv* without anything coming in between • *He went directly home* (= without stopping anywhere first).

directness /də'rekt·nəs, daı-/ *n* [U] a very honest way of saying what you mean

direct AIM /də'rekt, daı-/ *v* [T always + adv/prep] to aim (something) in a particular direction or at particular people • *His criticism was directed at everybody who disagreed with him.* • To direct is also to show someone the particular way to get somewhere: *Can you direct me to the nearest bus stop?*

direct CONTROL /də'rekt, daı-/ *v* [I/T] to control or be in charge of (an activity, organization etc.) • *General Eisenhower directed the allied forces in World War II.* [T] • When someone directs a movie, play, etc., they tell the actors how to play their parts. [I]

direction /də'rek·ʃən, daı-/ *n* [U] the condition of being in charge or in control • *Under her direction, the agency doubled in size.*

director /də'rek·tər, daı-/ *n* [C] a person in charge of an organization or of a particular part of a company's business • *a marketing director* • A director is also a person who tells actors in a movie or play how to play their parts.

direct ORDER /də'rekt, daı-/ *v* [T] to order, esp. officially • *The judge directed the defendant to be quiet.*

directive /də'rek·tɪv, daı-/ *n* [C] • *A federal directive forbids fund-raising in government offices.*

direction /də'rek·ʃən, daı-/ *n* [C] the position toward which someone or something moves or faces • *Cars were facing every direction after slamming into each other on the icy road.* ○ *I glanced in her direction* (= toward her). ○ *You're headed in the direction of* (= toward) *Toronto.*

directions /də'rek·ʃənz, daı-/ *pl n* • *We're lost—let's stop and ask (for) directions* (= to be told how to find the place we are looking for).

directly /də'rek·tli, daı-/ *adv* [not gradable] very soon or immediately • *Dr. Schwartz will be with you directly.*

directory /də'rek·tə·ri, daı-/ *n* [C] a book that gives a list of names, addresses, facts, etc. • *I found your address in the directory of university graduates.*

dirt EARTH /dɜrt/ *n* [U] earth or a substance like it that has gotten on the surface of something such as your skin • *I sat on the ground and got dirt on my pants.* • Dirt is also loose earth on the ground: *After the rain, the woods smelled of wet dirt and greenery.* • Dirt is also the earth considered as a surface: *The basement has a dirt floor.* • Used computers are **dirt cheap** (= very cheap). • A **dirt bike** is a bicycle with wide tires for traveling over rough ground.

dirty /'dɜrt̬·i/ *adj* [*-er/-est* only] having esp. dirt on the surface of something • *He left his dirty towels on the bathroom floor.*

dirty /'dɜrt̬·i/ *v* [T] to allow (something) to get dirt on it • *Don't sit on the ground—you'll dirty your new suit.*

dirt BAD MORALITY /dɜrt/ *n* [U] information about a person's private life that shows them to have done something wrong or to have a bad character, esp. when made public by someone who wants to hurt them • *They are more interested in looking for dirt than in reporting fairly about him.*

dirty /'dɜrt̬·i/ *adj* [*-er/-est* only] unfair or dishonest • *That was a dirty trick—telling me you were out of town when you were right here all the time!* • Dirty is also used to emphasize how strongly you feel that something is wrong or bad: *That's a dirty lie!* • Dirty also means connected with sex esp. in a way that is offensive to some people: *a dirty joke* • (*humorous*) A **dirty word** is also a word that is avoided because it deals with an unpopular subject: *To politicians, "tax" is a dirty word.*

dis /dɪs/ *v* [T] **-ss-** *slang* to say or do something that shows a lack of respect for (someone) and is often intended to insult

disable /dɪs'eɪ·bəl/ *v* [T] to make (something or someone) unable to act in the correct or usual way • *Thieves disabled the museum's alarm system.*

disabled /dɪs'eɪ·bəld/ *adj* lacking one or more of the physical or mental abilities that most people have • *a disabled war veteran* ○ *US law requires that all public buildings be accessible to the disabled.* ○ *They opened a group home for mentally disabled adults.*

disability /ˌdɪs·ə'bɪl·ət̬·i/ *n* [C/U] a physical or mental condition that makes someone unable to act in a way that is considered usual for most people • *The law bars discrimination against those with disabilities.* [C] ○ *The regu-*

lations apply to people unable to work because of disability. [U]

disadvantage /ˌdɪs·əd'vænt·ɪdʒ/ *n* [C] something that makes a successful result less likely, esp. less likely for you than it is for others • *There are disadvantages to living in a rural area.* • If you are **at a disadvantage**, you are in a situation in which you are less likely to succeed than others: *She felt that being so young put her at a disadvantage for the executive position.*

disadvantaged /ˌdɪs·əd'vænt·ɪdʒd/ *adj* (of people) not having the benefits, such as enough money and a healthy social situation, that others have, and therefore having less opportunity to be successful • *Head Start is an educational program for disadvantaged preschool children.*

disaffected /ˌdɪs·ə'fek·təd/ *adj* feeling unhappy about and separate from an organization or idea that you once supported • *Charges of incompetence were made by disaffected members of the club.*

disagree /ˌdɪs·ə'griː/ *v* [I] to have a different opinion or be unable to agree • *I disagree with you about that.* ○ *Most scientists agree there is a risk, but disagree over the exact amount of risk.*

disagreement /ˌdɪs·ə'griː·mənt/ *n* [C/U] a situation in which people have different opinions, or an inability to agree • *The candidates had few disagreements about the major issues.* [C]

□**disagree with** /ˌ--'--/ *v prep* [T] to cause to feel sick • *I must have eaten something that disagreed with me.*

disagreeable /ˌdɪs·ə'griː·ə·bəl/ *adj* unpleasant; unattractive • *The drinking water had a disagreeable oily taste.*

disappear /ˌdɪs·ə'pɪr/ *v* [I] (of a person or thing) to go to a place or into a condition where they cannot be seen • *She disappeared into the house.* ○ *He disappeared for a few hours* (= went somewhere unknown). ○ *They watched the plane until it disappeared* (= could no longer be seen).

disappearance /ˌdɪs·ə'pɪr·əns/ *n* [U] • *The district attorney is looking into the disappearance of the money.* ○ *Her disappearance remains unexplained.*

disappoint /ˌdɪs·ə'pɔɪnt/ *v* [T] to fail to satisfy (someone or their hopes or expectations) • *I hate to disappoint you, but we don't have the book you wanted.*

disappointed /ˌdɪs·ə'pɔɪnt·əd/ *adj* unhappy or discouraged because your hopes or expectations about something or someone were not satisfied • *Obviously, we were disappointed in the jury's verdict.* ○ *I'm disappointed by the way our team played today.* ○ *We were extremely disappointed to receive this information.* [+ to infinitive]

disappointing /ˌdɪs·ə'pɔɪnt·ɪŋ/ *adj* not as good as you had hoped or expected; not satisfactory • *This had been a disappointing Christmas shopping season.* ○ *Kerrigan finished the race a disappointing fifth.*

disappointment /ˌdɪs·ə'pɔɪnt·mənt/ *n* [C/U] the unhappiness or discouragement that results when your hopes or expectations have not been satisfied, or someone or something that is not as good as you had hoped or expected • *Her disappointment showed on her face.* [U] ○ *After two losing seasons, we felt he was a disappointment as a coach.* [C]

disapprove /ˌdɪs·ə'pruːv/ *v* [I] to think that something is wrong, or to have a bad opinion about someone • *His parents disapprove of drinking and smoking.* ○ *They disapproved of his conduct.*

disapproval /ˌdɪs·ə'pruː·vəl/ *n* [U] the expression or feeling that something done or said is wrong • *The boy sensed his mother's disapproval.* ○ *He decided to marry her, to the great disapproval of his father.*

disarm REMOVE WEAPONS /dɪs'ɑrm/ *v* [I/T] to take weapons away from (someone), or give up weapons • *Store security guards disarmed him and held him for the police.* [T] ○ *The revolutionary group refused to disarm.* [I] ○ *Bomb experts disarmed the device* (= made it unable to explode). [T]

disarmament /dɪs'ɑr·mə·mənt/ *n* [U] a reduction in or limitation of the number of weapons in the armed forces of a country • *nuclear disarmament* ○ *disarmament talks*

disarm CHARM /dɪs'ɑrm/ *v* [T] to make (someone) begin to like you, esp. when they had not expected to • *He was disarmed by the older man's wit and intelligence.*

disarming /dɪs'ɑr·mɪŋ/ *adj approving* • *He had a disarming reason for arriving late—he was reading to his children.*

disarray /ˌdɪs·ə'reɪ/ *n* [U] a disorderly or confused condition, showing a lack of organization • *Many party members believe the campaign is in disarray.* ○ *The apartment was in complete disarray.*

disaster /dɪ'zæs·tər, -'sæs·tər/ *n* [C/U] an event causing great harm, damage, or suffering • *financial disaster* [C/U] ○ *disaster aid/relief* [U] ○ *Over 100 people died in the disaster.* [C] ○ *The hurricane may be the costliest natural disaster in US history.* [C] • (*fig.*) A disaster is also a complete failure: *Our last dinner party was an absolute disaster.* [C]

disastrous /dɪ'zæs·trəs, -'sæs·trəs/ *adj* • *It was a disastrous mistake which he lived to regret.* ○ *In 1837, there was a disastrous smallpox epidemic.* • (*fig.*) Something that is disastrous is a complete failure: *His second marriage was equally disastrous.*

disavow /ˌdɪs·ə'vɑʊ/ *v* [T] to say that you know nothing about or have no responsibility for (something) • *He disavowed his earlier confession to the police.*

disband /dɪs'bænd/ v [I/T] (of a group) to stop existing, or to cause (a group) to stop existing • *He was commander of the Havana American Legion post before it (was) disbanded.* [I/T]

disbelief /ˌdɪs·bə'liːf/ n [U] the refusal to believe that something is true • *He shook his head in disbelief when I told him about the crash.*

disc /dɪsk/ n [C] a DISK • Disc is also another name for a musical record or a CD: *This recording is available on disc and on tape.* • A **disc jockey** (also **DJ**) is someone who plays recorded music on the radio or at a dance, party, or other event.

discard /dɪs'kɑrd/ v [T] to throw away or get rid of (something) because you no longer want it • *Cut the melon in half and discard the seeds.* ○ *He makes toys from things people discard.*

discern /dɪs'ɜrn, dɪz-/ v [T] to be able to see, recognize, or understand (something), esp. by separating it from other things • *I could discern a farmhouse not far away.* ○ *The shots came close together and he could not discern who fired first.*

discernible /dɪs'ɜr·nə·bəl, dɪz-/ adj able to be seen, recognized, or understood, esp. by separating one thing from others • *If there was meat in the soup, it was not discernible.*

discerning /dɪs'ɜr·nɪŋ, dɪz-/ adj approving able to make or usually making careful judgments about the quality of similar things • *Marion is a discerning judge of good design.*

discharge ALLOW TO LEAVE /dɪs'tʃɑrdʒ, 'dɪs·tʃɑrdʒ/ v [T] to allow (someone) to leave • *Allen was discharged from the hospital yesterday.* • If someone is discharged from a job, they are asked to leave it.
discharge /'dɪs·tʃɑrdʒ/ n [C/U] • *McCarthy held the rank of captain at the time of his discharge from the army.* [C]

discharge SEND OUT /dɪs'tʃɑrdʒ, 'dɪs·tʃɑrdʒ/ v [I/T] to send out (a substance, esp. waste matter) • *The soapy water from the washing machine will discharge directly into the waste line.* [I]
discharge /'dɪs·tʃɑrdʒ/ n [C/U] • *an oily discharge* [C] • A discharge is also liquid matter that comes from a part of the body. [C/U]

discharge FIRE /dɪs'tʃɑrdʒ, 'dɪs·tʃɑrdʒ/ v [I/T] to fire (a gun) • *In the fight, a gun discharged and wounded a guard.* [I]

discharge PERFORM /dɪs'tʃɑrdʒ, 'dɪs·tʃɑrdʒ/ v [T] fml to perform (a duty, esp. an official one) • *He continued to discharge his duties as administrator of the fund.*

disciple /dɪ'saɪ·pəl/ n [C] a person who believes in the ideas of a leader, esp. a religious or political one, and tries to live according to those ideas • *Jesse Jackson was a disciple of Martin Luther King, Jr.* • The Disciples were the twelve men who followed Jesus during his life.

discipline TRAINING /'dɪs·ə·plən, -ˌplɪn/ n [U] training that produces obedience or self-control, often in the form of rules and punishments if these are broken, or the obedience or self-control produced by this training • *military discipline* • Discipline is also the ability to control a mental activity: *Learning a foreign language requires discipline.*
discipline /'dɪs·ə·plən, -ˌplɪn/ v [T] • *He was disciplined* (= punished) *for his bad conduct.*
disciplinary /'dɪs·ə·plə,ner·i/ adj [not gradable] • *Some disciplinary action was obviously called for.*

discipline SUBJECT /'dɪs·ə·plən, -ˌplɪn/ n [C] a particular area of study, esp. a subject studied at a college or university • *an academic discipline*

disclaim /dɪ'skleɪm/ v [T] to refuse to accept (esp. knowledge of or responsibility for something bad) • *The officers disclaimed any knowledge of the incident.*

disclaimer /dɪ'skleɪ·mər/ n [C] fml a statement that you are not responsible for something, esp. because you did not intend it or did not know about it • *The disclaimer reminded viewers that the movie is a drama, not a documentary.*

disclose /dɪ'skloʊz/ v [T] to give (information) to the public that was not previously known • *Terms of the agreement were not disclosed.*

disclosure /dɪ'skloʊ·ʒər/ n [C/U] *Full financial disclosure is required.* [U] ○ *The report contained disclosures of sexual harassment.* [C]

disco (pl **discos**) /'dɪs·koʊ/ n [C] a place where people dance to modern recorded music for entertainment • *disco dancing*

discolor /dɪs'kʌl·ər/ v [I/T] to cause (a substance or material) to change from its original color when you do not want it to • *Direct sunlight will discolor this fabric.* [T]
discoloration /dɪsˌkʌl·ə'reɪ·ʃən/ n [C/U]

discomfort /dɪs'kʌm·fərt/ n [C/U] the feeling of not being comfortable, either from a physical cause or from a situation, or something that causes this feeling • *These early black entertainers faced danger and discomfort as they traveled from town to town.* [U] ○ *She laughed at his discomfort* (= embarrassment). [U] • Discomfort is also pain, usually not severe: *I could move my arm, but I had a lot of discomfort.* [U]

disconcert /ˌdɪs·kən'sɜrt/ v [T] to make (someone) feel suddenly uncertain or worried • *He was disconcerted by all the attention he was getting.*
disconcerting /ˌdɪs·kən'sɜrt̬·ɪŋ/ adj • *So this deliberate lack of interest in noticing us was most disconcerting.*

disconnect /ˌdɪs·kə'nekt/ v [T] to break (a connection that carries a substance or electricity), or to break such a connection used by (someone or something) • *He disconnected a gas line.* ○ *The doctors wanted to disconnect the patient from life support.* ○ *Our phone was disconnected* (= turned off by the telephone company). • If you are disconnected while speaking on the telephone, the telephone connection is suddenly stopped and you can no longer continue your conversation.

disconnect /ˌdɪs·kə'nekt/ *n* [C] *infml* a lack of connection; a failure of two things to relate • *There's a disconnect between the public and the media.*

discontent /ˌdɪs·kən'tent/ *n* [U] a feeling of not being satisfied with your situation or with the way you are being treated • *Mexican-American leaders expressed discontent with the administration.*

discontented /ˌdɪs·kən'tent·əd/ *adj* • *Discontented with her job, Cassandra often talked of leaving.*

discontinue /ˌdɪs·kən'tɪn·juː/ *v* [T] to stop doing, using, or operating (something) • *Discontinue the medication if you have cramps.* ○ *The airline announced that weekday flights to Kansas City would be discontinued.*

discord /'dɪs·kɔːrd/ *n* [U] a lack of agreement or feeling of trust between people • *The police presence created discord in our community.*

discount REDUCTION /'dɪs·kaʊnt/ *n* [C] a reduction in the usual price for something • *Students receive a 10 percent discount.* ○ *He gets a senior citizen discount at the theater.* • A **discount store** is a store that sells its goods at cheap prices.

discount /dɪs'kaʊnt, 'dɪs·kaʊnt/ *v* [T] • *The airline has discounted domestic fares.*

discount NOT CONSIDER /dɪs'kaʊnt, 'dɪs·kaʊnt/ *v* [T] to decide that (something or someone) is not worth consideration or attention • *He discounted fears about computer programming problems involving the year 2000 as exaggerated.*

discourage MAKE LESS CONFIDENT /dɪs'kɜr·ɪdʒ, -'kʌ·rɪdʒ/ *v* [T] to cause (someone) to feel less confident or less hopeful • *She sometimes got discouraged about her social life, which was going nowhere, she felt.*

discouraging /dɪs'kɜr·ə·dʒɪŋ, -'kʌ·rə-/ *adj* • *It's discouraging to feel that opportunities have passed you by.*

discouragement /dɪs'kɜr·ɪdʒ·mənt, -'kʌ·rɪdʒ-/ *n* [U] • *He had known discouragement and failure, but in the end he persevered and wound up with a successful business.*

discourage PREVENT /dɪs'kɜr·ɪdʒ, -'kʌ·rɪdʒ/ *v* [T] to try to prevent (something from happening or someone from doing something), or to have the effect of making (something) less likely • *We tried to discourage him from spending so much money.* ○ *Higher taxes could discourage business investment.* ○ *The tough competition discourages many athletes from making a serious attempt to make the Olympic team.*

discourse /'dɪs·kɔːrs, -koʊrs/ *n* [C/U] (a) thoughtful spoken or written discussion of a subject • *political discourse* [U] ○ *The play is a wonderful discourse on love.* [C]

discourteous /dɪs'kɜrṱ·iˑəs/ *adj* not caring enough about other people's feelings; not polite • *I felt it was discourteous of him to leave immediately after his talk.*

discourtesy /dɪs'kɜrṱ·əˑsi/ *n* [C/U] • *She was never guilty of the slightest discourtesy.* [C]

discover *(obj)* /dɪ'skʌv·ər/ *v* to find (something for the first time, or something that had not been known before) • *Doctors later discovered (that) he had a cut on his left ankle.* [+ *(that)* clause] ○ *We reviewed enrollment figures to discover exactly when and why the student population declined.* [+ *wh-* word] ○ *Researchers hope to discover new treatments that may help people suffering from migraine headaches.* [T] • To discover is also to realize or learn: *When you go on a trip, you always discover that you forgot a few things.* [+ *that* clause]

discoverer /dɪ'skʌv·ə·rər/ *n* [C] • *The Canadians Frederick Banting and Charles Best were the discoverers of insulin.*

discovery /dɪ'skʌv·ə·ri/ *n* [C/U] the act of finding something that had not been known before • *Many scientific discoveries have been made by accident.* [C] ○ *The discovery of gold in California opened up the west.* [U] • A discovery is also something that you did not know about before: *It was quite a discovery when I came upon this beautiful mountain stream.* [C]

discredit /dɪs'kred·ət/ *v* [T] to give people reason to stop believing (someone) or to doubt the truth of (something) • *The old Soviet economic model has been thoroughly discredited.* ○ *It's the job of the defense to discredit prosecution witnesses.*

discredit /dɪs'kred·ət/ *n* [U] *fml* • *He's brought discredit on himself.*

discreet /dɪ'skriːt/ *adj* (of a person) respectful of other people's privacy and esp. of their secrets, or (of a thing) done in a way that does not attract a lot of attention • *The royal romance might impress one as a delicate account of a discreet courtship.* ○ *There was a discreet knock on the door.*

discreetly /dɪ'skriːt·li/ *adv* • *Some of Nelle's acquaintances discreetly suggested she get a divorce.*

discrepancy /dɪ'skrep·ən·si/ *n* [C] an unexpected difference, esp. in two amounts or two sets of facts or conditions, which suggests that something is wrong and has to be explained • *There were troubling discrepancies between his public and private opinions on how to balance the budget.*

discrete /dɪ'skriːt/ *adj* having an independent existence or form apart from other similar things; separate • *This area has four discrete neighborhoods centered around a school.*

discretion /dɪ'skreʃ·ən/ *n* [U] choice, or the

right to make a choice, based on judgment • *Troopers have discretion in deciding whom to stop for speeding.* ○ *Whether or not to hold the meeting is at the discretion of the president* (= a decision to be made by the president).

discriminate TREAT WORSE /dɪˈskrɪm·ə·ˌneɪt/ *v* [I] to treat a person or particular group of people differently and esp. unfairly, in a way that is worse than the way people are usually treated • *It is illegal to discriminate on the basis of race, sex, national origin, or age.* ○ *They argued that whites in the northwest discriminated against Indians.*

discrimination /dɪˌskrɪm·əˈneɪ·ʃən/ *n* [U] • *Chinese and Japanese immigrants were victims of discrimination.* ○ *The report called racial discrimination in employment one of the most serious causes of family breakdown.* ○ *She claims she is a victim of age discrimination.*

discriminatory /dɪˈskrɪm·ə·nəˌtɔːr·i, -ˌtoʊr·i/ *adj* • *discriminatory practices*

discriminate SEE A DIFFERENCE /dɪˈskrɪm·ə·ˌneɪt/ *v* [I/T] to be able to see the difference between (two things or types of things) • *We need to discriminate between stopgap methods and long-term solutions.* [I]

discriminating /dɪˈskrɪm·ə·ˌneɪt̬·ɪŋ/ *adj* able to judge the quality of something based on its difference from other, similar things • *a discriminating music lover* ○ *discriminating buyers/shoppers*

discrimination /dɪˌskrɪm·əˈneɪ·ʃən/ *n* [U] • *He showed discrimination in his reading habits.*

discus /ˈdɪs·kəs/ *n* [C] a round object shaped like a plate that is thrown in sports competitions, or the sport in which this object is thrown

discuss *(obj)* /dɪˈskʌs/ *v* to talk about (something) to other people, often exchanging ideas or opinions • *We have been discussing the possibility of working together.* [T] ○ *This booklet discusses how to invest money wisely.* [+ wh- word]

discussion /dɪˈskʌʃ·ən/ *n* [C/U] • *The matter is still under discussion* (= being considered). [U] ○ *The council had discussions on issues such as housing and living conditions.* [C]

disdain /dɪsˈdeɪn/ *n* [U] dislike of someone or something that you feel does not deserve your interest or respect • *The mayor's disdain for his opponents was well known.*

disdain *(obj)* /dɪsˈdeɪn/ *v* • *He disdains the flashy trappings of many Dixieland bands, the striped shirts and straw hats and such.* [T]

disease /dɪˈziːz/ *n* [C/U] a condition of a person, animal, or plant in which its body or structure is harmed because an organ or part is unable to work as it usually does; an illness • *Mumps is an infectious disease.* [C] ○ *He suffers from heart disease.* [U] ○ *Hundreds of thousands of trees died from Dutch elm disease.* [U]

disembark /ˌdɪs·əmˈbɑrk/ *v* [I] to leave a ship, aircraft, etc., after a trip • *They disembarked in Seattle.*

disembodied /ˌdɪs·əmˈbɑd·iːd/ *adj* [not gradable] existing without a body • *A disembodied voice crackled from the radio.*

disenchanted /ˌdɪs·ənˈtʃænt·əd/ *adj* no longer believing in the value of something, esp. after having learned of the faults that it has • *I have become disenchanted with politics.*

disengage /ˌdɪs·ənˈɡeɪdʒ/ *v* [I/T] to become separate or not connected, or to cause this to happen • *The US should not disengage from Europe, she said.* [I]

disentangle /ˌdɪs·ənˈtæŋ·ɡəl/ *v* [T] to separate (things that have become joined or confused) • *It's hard to disentangle the truth from all her lies.*

disfigure /dɪsˈfɪɡ·jər/ *v* [T] to spoil completely the appearance of (esp. a person's face) • *She was horribly disfigured by burns.*

disgrace /dɪsˈɡreɪs/ *n* [U] embarrassment and the loss of other people's respect, or behavior that causes this • *He resigned in disgrace.* ○ *He's a disgrace to his family.*

disgraceful /dɪsˈɡreɪs·fəl/ *adj* • *The lies my opponent is telling about me are disgraceful.*

disgruntled /dɪsˈɡrʌnt·ᵊld/ *adj* unhappy, annoyed, and disappointed about something • *a disgruntled employee*

disguise /dɪsˈɡaɪz/ *v* [T] to give a new appearance to (a person or thing), esp. in order to hide its true form • *Two gay men disguised themselves as nuns to visit a friend in a Catholic hospital on his birthday.* • *To disguise an opinion, feeling, etc., is to hide it: I couldn't disguise my unhappiness at this decision.*

disguise /dɪsˈɡaɪz/ *n* [C/U] • *In Shakespeare's plays, many characters appear in disguise.* [U]

disgust /dɪsˈɡʌst/ *n* [U] a strong feeling of disapproval or dislike, or a feeling of becoming ill caused by something unpleasant • *She resigned from the committee in disgust at their inefficiency.* ○ *Something in the kitchen smelled so bad that we all left in disgust.*

disgust /dɪsˈɡʌst/ *v* [T] • *I'm disgusted at/by all the violence on TV.*

disgusted /dɪsˈɡʌs·təd·li/ *adj* • *He gave her a disgusted look.*

disgusting /dɪsˈɡʌs·tɪŋ/ *adj* • *When you burn garbage, you've got some pretty disgusting stuff going up in the atmosphere.*

dish CONTAINER /dɪʃ/ *n* [C] a round, flat container with a raised edge, used for serving or holding food • *The dishes are all the plates, glasses, knives, forks, etc., that have been used during a meal: Who's going to do the dishes* (= clean the plates, glasses, etc.)*?* • *A **dishtowel** is a cloth used for drying dishes.* • *A **dishwasher** is a machine for washing dishes.*

dish FOOD /dɪʃ/ *n* [C] a particular type of food or food prepared in a particular way as part of a meal • *This restaurant serves both Cuban and Chinese dishes.*

□**dish out** *obj*, **dish** *obj* **out** /'-'-/ *v adv* [M] *infml* to give (something), esp. in large amounts • *He's always dishing out criticism.* • To dish out is also to serve food. • If you can **dish it out but** you **can't take it**, you easily criticize other people but don't like it when other people do the same to you.

disheartening /dɪs'hɑrt·ᵊn/ *adj* causing a person to lose confidence, hope, and energy; discouraging • *The new injury, after he had come back from the last, was disheartening.*

disheveled /dɪ'ʃev·əld/ *adj* (of people or their appearance) not neat; messy • *disheveled hair/clothes*

dishonest /dɪs'ɑn·əst/ *adj* not honest • *He's been dishonest with us, and I'll never trust him again.*

dishonesty /dɪs'ɑn·ə·sti/ *n* [U]

dishonor /dɪs'ɑn·ər/ *n* [U] a feeling of embarrassment and loss of people's respect, or something that causes this • *It is no dishonor to lose to a champion.*

dishonorable /dɪs'ɑn·ə·rə·bəl/ *adj* • *He served two years in an army prison and received a dishonorable discharge.*

disillusion /ˌdɪs·ə'luː·ʒən/ *v* [T] to disappoint (someone) by making them realize the unpleasant truth about something or someone they had thought was good • *Two failed marriages disillusioned Florence and made her sick at heart.*

disillusioned /ˌdɪs·ə'luː·ʒənd/ *adj* • *He died a disillusioned man.*

disillusionment /ˌdɪs·ə'luː·ʒən·mənt/ *n* [U]

disinfect /ˌdɪs·ən'fekt/ *v* [T] to clean by using chemicals to kill bacteria that cause disease

disinfectant /ˌdɪs·ən'fek·tənt/ *n* [C/U] a substance that contains chemicals that kill bacteria and is used esp. for cleaning surfaces in bathrooms and kitchens

disingenuous /ˌdɪs·ən'dʒen·jə·wəs/ *adj* (of a person or their behavior) slightly dishonest; not speaking the complete truth • *a disingenuous compliment*

disintegrate /də'sɪnt·əˌgreɪt/ *v* [I] to become weaker or be destroyed by breaking into small pieces • *The spacecraft disintegrated as it entered the earth's atmosphere.*

disintegration /dəˌsɪnt·ə'greɪ·ʃən/ *n* [U]

disinterest /dɪs'ɪn·trəst, -'ɪnt·ə·rəst/ *n* [U] lack of interest; boredom • *He gave an impression of calm disinterest in the world about him.*

disinterested /dɪs'ɪn·trə·stəd, -'ɪnt·əˌres·təd/ *adj* • *Unlike most boys his age, he was totally disinterested in cars or girls.*

disinterested /dɪs'ɪn·trə·stəd, -'ɪnt·əˌres·təd/ *adj* having no personal involvement or receiving no personal advantage, and therefore free to act fairly • *disinterested advice* ○ *a disinterested observer*

disjointed /dɪs'dʒɔɪnt·əd/ *adj* (esp. of words or ideas) not well connected or well ordered, and therefore often confusing • *She gave a disjointed account of getting lost in the woods.*

disk, **disc** /dɪsk/ *n* [C] a flat, circular object • *The dog's name is on a metal disk attached to its collar.* • A disk is also a small piece of CARTILAGE (= strong, elastic body tissue) between the bones of a person's back. • A disk is also a flat, circular device that has a magnetic covering and is used for storing computer information: *a hard disk* • A **disk drive** is a piece of computer equipment that allows information to be stored on and read from a disk. • See also DISC.

diskette /dɪs'ket/ *n* [C] a flat, circular device that has a magnetic covering, used to copy computer information and store it separately from a computer

dislike /dɪs'lɑɪk/ *v* [T] to not like; to find (someone or something) unpleasant, difficult, etc. • *I dislike the idea of leaving him home alone all evening.*

dislike /dɪs'lɑɪk/ *n* [C/U] • *a dislike of flying* [C]

dislocate /dɪs'loʊˌkeɪt/ *v* [T] to force (a bone) suddenly out of its correct position • *He dislocated his elbow in the crash.*

dislodge /dɪs'lɑdʒ/ *v* [T] to remove (esp. a person or people) by force from a position • *Efforts to dislodge the dictator were not successful.*

disloyal /dɪs'lɔɪ·əl/ *adj* not loyal; acting to hurt someone you are expected to support • *His sisters thought that his autobiography was disloyal to the family.*

dismal /'dɪz·məl/ *adj* dark and sad, without hope, or very bad • *The trip was a dismal failure.*

dismantle /dɪs'mænt·ᵊl/ *v* [T] to take (a machine or something complicated) apart, usually to make it unable to work • *The government voted to dismantle its nuclear warheads.* ○ *They worried that dismantling the welfare state would increase poverty.*

dismay /dɪ'smeɪ/ *n* [U] a feeling of shock and unhappiness • *She discovered, to her dismay, that the dog had left a mess on the living room rug.*

dismay /dɪ'smeɪ/ *v* [T] • *They enjoyed the meal but were dismayed by how much it cost.*

dismember /dɪ'smem·bər/ *v* [T] to cut, tear, or pull the arms and legs off (a body)

dismiss NOT CONSIDER /dɪ'smɪs/ *v* [T] to decide that (something or someone) is not important and not worth considering • *Let's not dismiss the idea without discussing it.*

dismissive /dɪ'smɪs·ɪv/ *adj* • *a dismissive, angry look*

dismiss SEND AWAY /dɪ'smɪs/ *v* [T] to formally ask or order (someone) to leave • *The teacher dismissed the class early.* • If someone is dismissed from their job, they are officially told that they no longer have a job.

dismount /dɪˈsmaʊnt/ v [I] to get off a horse or a bicycle

disobedient /ˌdɪs·əˈbiːd·iː·ənt/ adj not doing what you are told to do • a disobedient child

disobedience /ˌdɪs·əˈbiːd·iː·əns/ n [U]

disobey /ˌdɪs·əˈbeɪ/ v [I/T] to intentionally fail to do what you are told or expected to do; not obey • Half of the city's drivers tend to disobey rules and behave poorly. [T]

disorder [CONFUSION] /dɪsˈɔːrd·ər/ n [U] a state in which objects or conditions are in no particular order; lack of system or planned organization • The room was in such disorder that she couldn't find anything.

disorderly /dɪsˈɔːrd·ər·li/ adj

disorder [ILLNESS] /dɪsˈɔːrd·ər/ n [C/U] an illness of the mind or body • a mental/physical disorder [C] ○ She suffers from an eating disorder. [C]

disorder [SITUATION] /dɪsˈɔːrd·ər/ n [U] a situation in which some people behave in a way that threatens the safety of other people or the peace of a neighborhood • public disorder

disorderly /dɪsˈɔːrd·ər·li/ adj • a disorderly crowd ○ He was charged with disorderly conduct.

disorganized /dɪsˈɔːr·ɡəˌnɑɪzd/ adj badly planned and lacking order • According to one officer, things are so disorganized that no one knows who is where.

disorganization /dɪsˌɔːr·ɡə·nəˈzeɪ·ʃən/ n [U]

disorient /dɪsˈɔːr·iːˌent/ v [T] to make (someone) confused about where they are and where they are going • It's easy to get disoriented because all the streets look alike.

disown /dɪsˈoʊn/ v [T] to state that you no longer have any connection with (someone that you used to be closely connected with) • His children disowned him when he remarried.

disparage /dɪˈspær·ɪdʒ/ v [T] to criticize (someone or something) in a way that shows you do not respect or value them • He disparages his business competitors, saying they are all a bunch of amateurs compared to him.

disparaging /dɪˈspær·ə·dʒɪŋ/ adj • Mencken's private diaries revealed a few disparaging references to blacks and Jews.

disparagingly /dɪˈspær·ə·dʒɪŋ·li/ adv • He spoke disparagingly of his political opponent.

disparate /ˈdɪs·pə·rət, dɪˈspær·ət/ adj different in every way • German newspapers have carried reports of sightings in such disparate places as Switzerland, Iran, and Paraguay.

disparity /dɪˈspær·əṭ·i/ n [C/U] a lack of equality and similarity, esp. in a way that is not fair • He will oppose a gross disparity in salary increases between teachers and other state employees. [C]

dispassionate /dɪˈspæʃ·ə·nət/ adj able to think clearly or make good decisions because not influenced by emotions • The book is intended to provide a more dispassionate understanding of recent history.

dispassionately /dɪˈspæʃ·ə·nət·li/ adv

dispatch /dɪˈspætʃ/ v [T] to send (someone or something), esp. quickly and for a particular purpose • Within seconds the university police can identify the exact origin of the alarm and dispatch officers to investigate.

dispatch /dɪˈspætʃ/ n [C/U] • If something is done with dispatch, it is done quickly. [U] • A dispatch is a report sent to you from another place: In her latest dispatch, our correspondent reports on new negotiations. [C] ○ a military dispatch [C]

dispel /dɪˈspel/ v [T] -ll- to remove (fears, doubts, or false ideas), usually by proving them wrong or unnecessary • We need to dispel the myths and establish real facts.

dispensary /dɪˈspen·sə·ri/ n [C] a place where medicines are prepared and given out, often in a hospital or a school

dispense /dɪˈspens/ v [T] to give out or provide (an item or substance) • Is there a tourism agency that dispenses city maps? ○ This gasoline pump is capable of dispensing eight blends of gasoline.

dispenser /dɪˈspen·sər/ n [C] • A dispenser is a machine from which you can get an item, usually by putting coins in it.

□ **dispense with** /-ˈ-·-/ v prep [T] to get rid of or do without (something) • Let's dispense with the formalities and get right down to business.

disperse /dɪˈspɜrs/ v [I/T] to scatter or move away over a large area, or to cause this to happen • It took several hours for the crowd to disperse. [I]

dispersal /dɪˈspɜr·səl/ n [U]

dispirited /dɪˈspɪr·əṭ·əd/ adj not feeling hopeful about a situation or problem • The poor are dispirited.

displace /dɪˈspleɪs/ v [T] to force (something or someone) out of its usual or original place • A major government offensive against rebel groups threatens to displace large numbers of people.

display [SHOW] /dɪˈspleɪ/ v [T] to show (something or a collection of things) in an orderly way for people to see • The museum displays the tools and clothes of native Indians.

display /dɪˈspleɪ/ n [C/U] • Paintings and carvings of birds and animals will be on display in the main ballroom of the hotel. [U]

display [BECOME KNOWN] /dɪˈspleɪ/ v [T] to let (something) become known by what you say or do, or how you look • He doesn't display much emotion.

display /dɪˈspleɪ/ n [C] • It was an impressive display of unity and goodwill among South Africa's diverse legislators.

displease /dɪsˈpliːz/ v [T] to cause (someone) to be annoyed • The city council said it was displeased with the way the mayor had allocated parking spaces.

displeasure /dɪsˈpleʒ·ər/ n [U] • They refused

to work overtime, much to the displeasure of their boss.

disposable /dɪ'spoʊ·zə·bəl/ *adj* intended to be thrown away after use • *disposable diapers*

disposal /dɪ'spoʊ·zəl/ *n* [U] the act of getting rid of something • *the disposal of toxic wastes*

dispose /dɪ'spoʊz/ *v* [T] to make (someone) feel a particular, and often bad, way toward someone else, or to influence (someone) in a particular way • *Her sense of humor disposed me to like her.*

  disposal /dɪ'spoʊ·zəl/ *n* [U] • A person or thing **at** your **disposal** is able to be used by you: *I don't have a car at my disposal.*

  disposed /dɪ'spoʊzd/ *adj* • *We were always well disposed toward my uncle* (= We liked him). • To be disposed to do something is to feel that you may want to do it: *I didn't feel disposed to help her.* [+ *to* infinitive]

□ **dispose of** /-'-'--/ *v prep* [T] to get rid of (something); throw out or destroy • *They are accused of illegally disposing of hazardous materials.* • To dispose of (a matter) is to deal with it so that the matter is finished: *Once the tax bill is disposed of, the House will take up the issue of gun control.*

disposition /ˌdɪs·pə'zɪʃ·ən/ *n* [C] a person's usual way of feeling or behaving; the tendency of a person to be happy, friendly, anxious, etc. • *a cheerful disposition*

dispossess /ˌdɪs·pə'zes/ *v* [T] to force (someone) to give up the possession of a house, land, or other property • *Many people were dispossessed of their homes during the war.*

disproportionate /ˌdɪs·prə'pɔːr·ʃə·nət/ *adj* too great or too small when compared to something else • *The sheer size of the company gave it disproportionate influence in dealing with the Pentagon and Congress.*

  disproportionately /ˌdɪs·prə'pɔːr·ʃə·nət·li/ *adv* • *Unemployment in Iowa is disproportionately high.*

disprove /dɪ'spruːv/ *v* [T] to prove that (an idea, statement, etc.) is not true • *Given the thoroughness of the author's research, the burden rests on critics to disprove the facts he presents.*

dispute /dɪ'spjuːt/ *n* [C/U] an argument or disagreement • *Management and the union are trying to resolve the dispute over working conditions.* [C] • *Her ability is not* **in dispute** (= being doubted), *but I do question her attitude.*

  dispute /dɪ'spjuːt/ *v* [I/T] • *I don't dispute that his films are entertaining, but they don't have much depth.* [+ *that* clause]

disqualify /dɪs'kwɑl·ə·faɪ/ *v* [T] to take away from (someone), often legally, the ability to do or play a part in something, esp. because they are unsuitable or have done something wrong • *He was disqualified from competing in the games after a positive drug test.*

disqualification /dɪsˌkwɑl·ə·fə'keɪ·ʃən/ *n* [C/U]

disquieting /dɪs'kwaɪ·ət·ɪŋ/ *adj* causing anxiety; worrying • *The sheer size of their armed forces is a disquieting factor for neighboring countries.*

disregard /ˌdɪs·rɪ'gɑrd/ *n* [U] lack of consideration or respect • *The writer has shown a reckless disregard for the truth.*

  disregard /ˌdɪs·rɪ'gɑrd/ *v* [T] to not allow (something) to influence you; ignore • *The jury was told to disregard the comments made by the witness.*

disrepair /ˌdɪs·rɪ'per/ *n* [U] the state of being broken or old and needing to be repaired • *The building had fallen into disrepair over the years.*

disreputable /dɪs'rep·jət·ə·bəl/ *adj* having a bad reputation; not honorable • *He hung out in a disreputable bar.*

disrepute /ˌdɪs·rɪ'pjuːt/ *n* [U] *fml* the state of not being respected or trusted • *The judge's behavior, he said, had brought the law profession into disrepute.*

disrespect /ˌdɪs·rɪ'spekt/ *n* [U] lack of respect • *She apologized for not responding to the letter and said she had meant no disrespect.*

  disrespectful /ˌdɪs·rɪ'spekt·fəl/ *adj* • *It is disrespectful to mourners at the funeral to have unruly children running around.*

  disrespectfully /ˌdɪs·rɪ'spekt·fə·li/ *adv*

disrupt /dɪs'rʌpt/ *v* [T] to prevent (esp. a system, process, or event) from continuing as usual or as expected • *A heavy fall of snow disrupted traffic during the rush hour.*

  disruption /dɪs'rʌp·ʃən/ *n* [C/U] • *Strikes threaten more disruptions for the tourist industry.* [C]

  disruptive /dɪs'rʌp·tɪv/ *adj* tending to damage the orderly control of a situation • *disruptive social changes* ○ *The teacher said disruptive behavior would not be tolerated.*

dissatisfied /dɪs'sæt·əs·faɪd/ *adj* not pleased with something; feeling that something is not as good as it should be • *She was dissatisfied with her job and decided to look for a new one.*

  dissatisfaction /dɪsˌsæt·əs'fæk·ʃən/ *n* [U] • *Many of the opinion surveys show deep dissatisfaction with Congress as an institution.*

dissect /dɪ'sekt, daɪ-/ *v* [T] to cut apart (the body of an animal or plant) in order to study its structure • *We had to dissect a frog in our biology class.* • To dissect is also to examine something in detail: *The more experts dissect his tax revision plan, the more inconsistencies turn up.*

disseminate /dɪ'sem·ə·neɪt/ *v* [T] to spread or give out (news, information, ideas, etc.) to many people • *The purpose of a university press is to disseminate knowledge by publishing books and journals.*

  dissemination /dɪˌsem·ə'neɪ·ʃən/ *n* [U] • *the rapid dissemination of new technology*

dissension /dɪˈsen·tʃən/ n [U] strong disagreement, esp. within an organization • *There was a good deal of dissension within women's rights organizations about setting political goals.*

dissent /dɪˈsent/ n [U] strong difference of opinion; disagreement esp. about official decisions • *He claimed the police had prevented them from marching to stifle dissent.* • (law) A dissent is also a legal opinion by a judge in a court that differs from the opinion of most of the other judges of the court.

dissent /dɪˈsent/ v [I] law (of a judge) to offer a legal opinion in a court that differs from the opinion of most of the other judges of the court • *A staunch conservative, he frequently dissented from the court's majority opinion.*

dissertation /ˌdɪs·ərˈteɪ·ʃən/ n [C] a long piece of writing on a particular subject, esp. one that is done for a PH.D. (= high university degree)

disservice /dɪsˈsɜr·vəs/ n [U] an unfair or harmful action • *Calling him a liar does him a great disservice.*

dissident /ˈdɪs·əd·ənt/ n [C] a person who strongly disagrees with and publicly criticizes a government or the official rulings of a group or organization • *Union dissidents have challenged the leadership of the current president.*

dissident /ˈdɪs·əd·ənt/ adj [not gradable] • *dissident views*

dissimilar /dɪsˈsɪm·ə·lər/ adj not similar; different • *Her diagnosis was not dissimilar (= was similar) to that of the previous doctor.*

dissipate /ˈdɪs·əˌpeɪt/ v [I/T] to disappear gradually, or to cause (something) to disappear gradually • *It took months of effort to dissipate the oil spill in the North Sea.* [T]

dissolute /ˈdɪs·əˌluːt/ adj showing a lack of good character and morals; immoral • *a dissolute alcoholic*

dissolution /ˌdɪs·əˈluː·ʃən/ n [U] the ending of esp. an official organization or a legal arrangement • *She has been depressed since the dissolution of her marriage.*

dissolve BE ABSORBED /dɪˈzɑlv, -ˈzɔːlv/ v [I/T] to be absorbed or to cause (a solid) to be absorbed by a liquid, or (of a liquid) to absorb a solid • *Dissolve two teaspoons of yeast in warm water.* [T] • If a situation **dissolves in/into** something, it becomes much worse and often disorderly: *The meeting dissolved into a shouting match between the two sides.*

dissolve END /dɪˈzɑlv, -ˈzɔːlv/ v [I/T] to end (esp. an official organization or a legal arrangement) • *They decided to dissolve the partnership.* [T]

dissuade /dɪˈsweɪd/ v [T] to persuade (someone) not to do something • *The group hopes to dissuade Congress from cutting funds for health programs.*

distance /ˈdɪs·təns/ n [C/U] the amount of space between two places or things • *The distance from San Francisco to Los Angeles is about 400 miles.* [C] • **At/From a distance** (= If you are not too near), *he resembles his mother.* • **In the distance** means at or from a point far away: *We could see the mountains in the distance.*

distance /ˈdɪs·təns/ v [T] • If you distance yourself from something, you try to become less involved or connected with it: *The candidate distanced himself from the extremists in the party.*

distant /ˈdɪs·tənt/ adj far away in space or time • *She dreamed of traveling to distant lands.* ◦ *We could hear the sound of distant thunder.* • Someone whose manner is distant does not show much emotion and is not friendly.

distaste /dɪsˈteɪst/ n [U] a dislike of something because you consider it unpleasant or unacceptable • *He was very selective about the movies he would see because of his distaste for violence.*

distasteful /dɪsˈteɪst·fəl/ adj • *Cutting a player from a team is a distasteful task for any coach.*

distill /dɪˈstɪl/ v [T] to heat (a liquid) until it changes to a gas and then make it liquid again by cooling • *distilled water/whiskey* • To distill something said or written is to reduce it but keep the most important part: *She distilled the report into a paragraph.*

distillation /ˌdɪs·təˈleɪ·ʃən/ n [C/U]

distillery /dɪˈstɪl·ə·ri/ n [C] a factory where strong alcoholic drinks are produced by the process of distilling

distinct DIFFERENT /dɪˈstɪŋt/ adj clearly separate and different • *The two languages are quite distinct from each other.* ◦ *The dogs are of distinct breeds.*

distinctive /dɪˈstɪŋ·tɪv/ adj marking something as clearly different from others • *a distinctive flavor/writing style*

distinction /dɪˈstɪŋ·ʃən/ n [C/U] • *The comment drew/made a false distinction between domestic and foreign affairs, which are really closely related.* [C] ◦ *Martin Luther King, Jr. clearly understood and accepted the distinction between preaching and scholarly criticism.* [U]

distinct NOTICEABLE /dɪˈstɪŋt/ adj not to be ignored; real and present • *There's a distinct possibility of rain today.* ◦ *There were distinct advantages to the first job offer.*

distinctly /dɪˈstɪŋ·tli/ adv • *I distinctly (= clearly) remember asking Ralph not to tell anyone about it.*

distinction QUALITY /dɪˈstɪŋ·ʃən/ n [U] the quality of being excellent or special in some way • *He was a scientist of great distinction.*

distinction HONOR /dɪˈstɪŋ·ʃən/ n [C] honor in recognition of excellence • *Winning a Guggenheim fellowship carries great distinction.*

distinguish SEPARATE /dɪ'stɪŋ·gwɪʃ, -wɪʃ/ v [I/ T] to recognize or understand the difference between two things, or to provide a quality that makes (someone or something) different or special • *It's important to distinguish between scientific fact and fiction.* [I always + adv/prep] ○ *Samuel F. B. Morse distinguished himself both as an inventor and as a painter.* [T]

distinguished /dɪ'stɪŋ·gwɪʃt, -wɪʃt/ adj (of a person or their work) respected and admired for their excellence • *He had a long and distinguished career as a diplomat.* • A person, esp. an older person, might be described as being distinguished in appearance if they look important and respected.

distinguish SEE / HEAR /dɪs'tɪŋ·gwɪʃ, -wɪʃ/ v [T] to see, hear, or experience (something), esp. with difficulty • *In the dark, I could barely distinguish the shape of a person.*

distort /dɪ'stɔːrt/ v [T] to change (something) from its natural or usual shape or condition, esp. in a way that is not desirable, or to change the intended meaning of (a statement, fact, etc.) • *Agony distorted his face.* ○ *There are those who would distort the facts to serve their own political ends.*

distorted /dɪ'stɔːrt̬·əd/ adj • *The article presents a distorted view of life in small-town America.*

distortion /dɪ'stɔːr·ʃən/ n [C/U] • *Dole charged his opponent with making deliberate distortions of his record.* [C]

distract /dɪ'strækt/ v [T] to take (someone's) attention away from what they are doing or should be doing • *She liked to work with the radio playing and said it did not distract her.*

distraction /dɪ'stræk·ʃən/ n [C/U] • *It's impossible to work with all this distraction.* [U]

distraught /dɪ'strɔːt/ adj extremely anxious and upset • *We were all distraught over the deaths of the children.*

distress /dɪ'stres/ n [U] great mental or physical suffering, such as extreme anxiety, sadness, or pain, or the state of being in danger or urgent need • *emotional/financial distress* ○ *Four men were rescued from a fishing boat in distress off the coast.*

distress /dɪ'stres/ v [T] • *Rice appeared distressed about the shooting, and could not talk about it.*

distressing /dɪ'stres·ɪŋ/ adj • *It is distressing that so little progress has been made after all this time.* [+ *that* clause]

distribute /dɪ'strɪb·jət/ v [T] to divide (something) among several or many people, or to spread or scatter (something) over an area • *Food and clothing are being distributed among/to the flood victims.* ○ *Shopping malls are widely distributed across the country.*

distribution /ˌdɪs·trə'bjuː·ʃən/ n [U] • *The bill would prohibit the sale and distribution of firearms.*

distributor /dɪ'strɪb·jət̬·ər/ n [C] a person or company that supplies goods to the businesses that sell them • A distributor in an engine is a device that sends electricity to each of the **spark plugs** (= devices that cause the engine to start).

district /'dɪs·trɪkt/ n [C] an area of a country, state, or city that has been given fixed borders for official purposes, or one having a particular feature that makes it different from surrounding areas • *The theater district in New York is in midtown Manhattan.* • A **district attorney** (*abbreviation* **D.A.**) is a lawyer working in a particular area of the country who represents the government in a trial in a law court.

distrust /dɪs'trʌst/ n [U] lack of trust or confidence • *Many African Americans express deep distrust toward the American legal system.*

distrust /dɪs'trʌst/ v [T] • *According to this history book, John Adams, the second US president, hated and distrusted Britain.*

distrustful /dɪs'trʌst·fəl/ adj

disturb INTERRUPT /dɪ'stɜrb/ v [T] to cause (someone) to stop what they are doing, or to interrupt (an activity) • *Please don't disturb Jimmy—he's trying to do his homework.*

disturbance /dɪ'stɜr·bəns/ n [U] • *I hope I can work today without disturbance.*

disturb WORRY /dɪ'stɜrb/ v [T] to cause (someone) to feel troubled or upset • *This year's election campaign has disturbed a lot of voters who don't like either candidate.*

disturbing /dɪ'stɜr·bɪŋ/ adj • *It is disturbing that so many teenagers are taking up smoking.* [+ *that* clause]

disturb MOVE /dɪ'stɜrb/ v [T] to move or change (something) from its usual position or arrangement • *Be careful not to disturb anything.*

disturbance /dɪ'stɜr·bəns/ n [C] a violent event in a public place or in a way that damages the public peace • *Then the police will come and find the man is drunk, has broken all the windows, beaten up his wife, and created a disturbance.*

disturbed /dɪ'stɜrbd/ adj so mentally confused or ill that special treatment is necessary • *He wrote a book on the treatment of emotionally disturbed children.*

ditch CHANNEL /dɪtʃ/ n [C] a long, narrow, open channel dug in the ground, usually at the side of a road or field, used esp. for supplying or removing water

ditch GET RID OF /dɪtʃ/ v [T] *infml* to get rid of or not continue with (something or someone that is no longer wanted) • *The thief ditched Maxine's purse in a trash can but kept the money.* ○ *Emily plans to ditch her boyfriend* (= end her relationship with him).

dither /'dɪð·ər/ v [I] to be anxious about something and not be able to decide what to do about it • *Both sides in the dispute continue to dither over who should make the first move.*

ditto /'dɪt̬·oʊ/ *adv* [not gradable] *infml* as said before; similarly • *It rained Saturday and it rained Sunday. Ditto Monday.*

ditty /'dɪt̬·i/ *n* [C] a short, simple song

dive MOVE DOWN /daɪv/ *v* [I] *past simple* **dived** or **dove** /doʊv/, *past part* **dived** to jump head first into water, esp. with your arms held straight above your head, or to move down steeply through water or the air • *Mark dove off the cliff into the ocean.* ○ *Dolphins can dive to great depths.* ○ *The plane dived to avoid enemy aircraft fire.* [+ *to* infinitive]

dive /daɪv/ *n* [C] • (*fig.*) *The firm's profits took a dive* (= fell by a large amount) *last quarter.*

diver /'daɪ·vər/ *n* [C] a person who dives into water

diving /'daɪ·vɪŋ/ *n* [U] • *deep-sea diving* • A **diving board** is a board that sticks out over a swimming pool and from which people can dive into the water below.

dive MOVE QUICKLY /daɪv/ *v* [I always + adv/prep] *past simple* **dived** or **dove** /doʊv/, *past part* **dived** to jump or move quickly into or at something • *When the football came loose, he dove at the ball and grabbed it.* ○ *They dived for cover when the shooting started.*

dive /daɪv/ *n* [U] • *White's 1-yard dive with seconds left won the football game.*

dive PLACE /daɪv/ *n* [C] *infml* a cheap, unattractive bar or place for entertainment

diverge /dɪ'vɜrdʒ, daɪ-/ *v* [I] to go in different directions from the same point, or to become different • *The tone of the final report isn't likely to diverge much from the earlier report.*

diverse /dɪ'vɜrs, daɪ-; 'daɪ·vɜrs/ *adj* varied or different • *Lowell, Massachusetts, is noted for its diverse ethnic communities, among them French-Canadians, English, Irish, Greeks, Poles, and Cambodians.*

diversify /dɪ'vɜr·sə,faɪ, daɪ-/ *v* [I/T] • *People are advised to diversify their investments in the stock market to reduce risk.* [T]

diversity /dɪ'vɜr·sət̬·i, daɪ-/ *n* [U] the condition or fact of being different or varied; variety • *There is a wide diversity of opinion on the question of immigration.*

divert CHANGE DIRECTION /dɪ'vɜrt, daɪ-/ *v* [T] to cause (something or someone) to turn in a different direction • *Our flight was diverted from San Francisco to Oakland because of the fog.* • To divert something or someone is also to use them for a different purpose: *The administration had to divert funds from the defense budget to pay for the emergency relief effort.*

diversion /dɪ'vɜr·ʒən, daɪ-/ *n* [C/U] • *A snowstorm closed the airport, and the diversion of air traffic was therefore necessary.* [U]

divert TAKE ATTENTION AWAY /dɪ'vɜrt, daɪ-/ *v* [T] to take (attention) away from something • *Military action now could divert attention from imminent votes in Congress on health-care legis-

lation.* • (*fml*) To divert can also mean to amuse: *The dog kept the children diverted for a while.*

diversion /dɪ'vɜr·ʒən, daɪ-/ *n* [C] an action that takes attention away from something, esp. one that gives pleasure or enjoyment • *This lawyer-bachelor devoted his life to the Senate, his only real diversion being baseball.*

divest /daɪ'vest, dɪ-/ *v* [T] to get rid of (an investment, part of a business, etc.) by selling • *He had encouraged the state to divest such holdings.* • If you divest yourself of a property, you get rid of it, usually by selling: *The company has divested itself of some of its money-losing operations.*

divide SEPARATE /dɪ'vaɪd/ *v* [I/T] to separate into parts or groups, or to cause (something) to separate in such a way • *Divide the cake into six equal parts.* [T] ○ *The votes divided equally for and against the proposal.* [I] • If something divides two areas, it marks the edge or limit of both of them: *A narrow driveway divides our house from the one next door.* [T] • To divide a group of people is to cause them to disagree: *The issue of abortion continues to divide the country.* [T]

divided /dɪ'vaɪd·əd/ *adj* • If you are divided on a matter, you hold opposing opinions about it: *She found herself divided between her love of her brother and her duty toward her husband.* • A **divided highway** is a main road that has an area in the middle that separates traffic moving in opposite directions.

division /dɪ'vɪʒ·ən/ *n* [C/U] the separation of something into parts or groups, or one of the parts or groups that has been separated • *The division of responsibilities among the officers of the company was spelled out in detail.* [U] • A division is a unit of an organization: *An army division is commanded by a major general.* [C] ○ *He was assigned to the narcotics division of the police force.* [C] ○ *The game for the Eastern Division championship of the National Football League is scheduled for tomorrow.* [C]

divisive /dɪ'vaɪ·sɪv, -'vɪs·ɪv/ *adj disapproving* tending to cause disagreements that separate people into opposing groups • *The campaign for the mayor's office was racially divisive.*

divide CALCULATE /dɪ'vaɪd/ *v* [I/T] to calculate the number of times (one number) is contained in another • *10 divided by 5 is/equals 2.* [T] ○ *What do you get if you divide 6 into 18?* [T] • Compare MULTIPLY; SUBTRACT.

division /dɪ'vɪʒ·ən/ *n* [U] the process of finding the number of times one number is contained within another • A **division sign** is the symbol ÷.

dividend /'dɪv·ə,dend, -əd·ənd/ *n* [C] a payment by a company of a part of its profit to the people who own SHARES (= units of ownership) in the company

divine GODLIKE /dɪ'vaɪn/ *adj* [not gradable]

connected with or like God or a god • *divine love*

divinity /dɪ'vɪn·ət̬·i/ *n* [U] the state of being a god • *Christians believe in the divinity of Jesus Christ.* ∘ Divinity is the study of religion: *She has a Doctorate in Divinity from Georgetown University.*

divinely /dɪ'vaɪn·li/ *adv* [not gradable] • *divinely inspired truth*

divine VERY GOOD /dɪ'vaɪn/ *adj infml* extremely good or pleasing • *The dessert was simply divine.*

divinely /dɪ'vaɪn·li/ *adv infml* • *She sings divinely.*

divine (obj) GUESS /dɪ'vaɪn/ *v* to guess (something), or to discover (something) without being told about it • *I divined from his grim expression that the news was bad.* [+ *that* clause]

diving /'daɪ·vɪŋ/ *n* [U] • See at DIVE MOVE DOWN.

division /dɪ'vɪʒ·ən/ *n* • See at DIVIDE SEPARATE, DIVIDE CALCULATE.

divisive /dɪ'vaɪ·sɪv, -'vɪs·ɪv/ *adj* • See at DIVIDE SEPARATE.

divorce /dɪ'vɔːrs, -'voʊrs/ *v* [I/T] to cause a marriage to (a husband or wife) to end by an official or legal process, or to have a marriage ended in this way • *Ford divorced his wife, Anne, in 1964, and married Cristina a year later.* [T] ∘ *He never understood why his parents didn't get divorced* (= end their marriage legally). [T]

divorce /dɪ'vɔːrs, -'voʊrs/ *n* [C/U] • *I got a divorce when the children were small.* [C]

divorcee /dɪ,vɔːr'seɪ, -,voʊr-, -'siː/ *n* [C] a woman whose marriage officially ended while her husband was still alive and who has not married again

□ **divorce** *obj* **from** /-'--/ *v prep* [T] to separate (something) from something else • *I don't see how you can divorce politics from tax policy.*

divulge (obj) /dɪ'vʌldʒ, daɪ-/ *v* to make (something secret) known • *Someone divulged their plans to their competitors.* [T] ∘ *The magazine divulged that several Congressmen were gay.* [+ *that* clause]

divvy up *obj*, **divvy** *obj* **up** /'dɪv·iː'ʌp/ *v adv* [M] *infml* to divide (something) into parts or shares • *They finally decided how to divvy up the money.*

Dixieland (jazz) /'dɪk·siː,lænd ('dʒæz)/ *n* [U] a style of traditional jazz with a two-beat rhythm, which originated in New Orleans in the 1920s

dizzy /'dɪz·i/ *adj* having or causing a feeling of spinning around and being unable to balance • *She was dizzy from drinking too much wine.* ∘ (fig.) *In the computer industry, change comes at a dizzy pace* (= very fast).

dizziness /'dɪz·iː·nəs/ *n* [U]

DJ /'diː·dʒeɪ/ *n* [C] abbreviation for disc jockey, see at DISC

DNA specialized *n* [U] abbreviation for deoxy- ribonucleic acid (= the chemical at the center of the cells of living things that controls the structure and purpose of each cell and carries GENETIC information during reproduction) • A **DNA fingerprint** is the particular way in which GENETIC information is contained in the cells of a person and which is different in every person.

do FOR QUESTIONS / NEGATIVES /duː/ *v aux* he/she/it **does** /dʌz, dəz/, *past simple* **did** /dɪd/, *past part* **done** /dʌn/ used with another verb to form questions and negative sentences • *Where do you work?* ∘ *Why don't we have lunch together on Friday?* ∘ *"Didn't you know Sophie was coming?" "Of course I did." * ∘ *Don't talk about that.* • USAGE: The negative contractions are doesn't, didn't, and don't. • LP AUXILIARY VERBS

do FOR EMPHASIS /duː/ *v aux* he/she/it **does** /dʌz, dəz/, *past simple* **did** /dɪd/ used to give extra force to the main verb • *Do be careful.* ∘ *I did say she was a liar, but I was wrong.* ∘ *"Can I buy stamps here?" "Well, we do sell them, but we're out of them right now." * • LP AUXILIARY VERBS

do TO AVOID REPEATING /duː/ *v aux* he/she/it **does** /dʌz, dəz/, *past simple* **did** /dɪd/, *past part* **done** /dʌn/ used to avoid repeating a verb or verb phrase • *"I don't like either candidate." "Neither do I." * ∘ *He said he'd leave the car in the garage, but he didn't.* ∘ *"May I join you?" "Please do!" * ∘ *"Did you leave the door open?" "Yes, I did." * • Do can also replace the main verb in questions that are added to the end of a sentence: *You met him at a conference, didn't you?* • LP AUXILIARY VERBS

do CAUSE TO HAPPEN /duː/ *v* [T] he/she/it **does** /dʌz, dəz/, *past simple* **did** /dɪd/, *past part* **done** /dʌn/ to cause (something to happen) or be the cause of (something happening); perform or have a part in (an activity) • *Inviting the whole family was a really nice thing to do.* ∘ *What are you doing over the weekend?* ∘ *I've got to stay home and do my homework.* ∘ *The theater club is doing "South Pacific" this year.* ∘ *I'm sorry, there's nothing more to be done* (= nothing else will help). ∘ *It isn't important whether you win or lose—just do your best.* ∘ *It's been a pleasure doing business with you* (= dealing with you). ∘ *The company is counting on each of you to do your part/share.* ∘ *Would you do me a favor* (= help me) *and get some bread while you're out?* ∘ *A little fresh air will do you some good* (= make you feel better). ∘ *What are these toys doing here* (= Why are they here)? ∘ *I've been trying to do* (= solve) *this puzzle for hours.* ∘ *What can I do for you* (= How can I help you)? ∘ *What have you done with my coat* (= Where have you put it)? ∘ *Since she retired, she doesn't know what to do with herself* (= how to keep herself busy). • To do can mean to work at as a regular job: *"What do you do?" "I teach high school math." * • If you ask or say how someone is do-

DO: VERBS MEANING "PERFORM"

There is a small group of verbs that are often used to mean "to perform the action of." They are **give, take, make, have, do, pay**, and **hold**. The noun that acts as the object of the verb shows what action is being performed. For example, the phrase *to take a shower* means "to perform the action of showering."

Phrases like this are common in conversation. They often replace verbs that can sound more formal or abrupt.

I went home and **took a shower.**   rather than   *I went home and* **showered.**

Modifiers can be added before the noun object.

*I took a **quick** shower. • She had a **cold** drink. • She gave him a **big** smile.*

The nouns that commonly act as objects of these verbs are listed below.

DO

the shopping, the cooking, the cleaning, housework, laundry, the dishes, the wash
your homework, a job, work
a drawing, a sketch
harm, damage

Do can be followed by a determiner and the *-ing* form of many verbs.

Have you done **the read**ing *for the course yet? • I did* **some** *paint*ing *over the weekend.*

Do is often used in place of a more specific verb, especially in informal English, to refer to a common activity involving the thing mentioned.

Who did (= cut or styled) *your hair? • She did* (= wrote) *a paper on Macbeth. • This car can do* (= move at a speed of) *over 100 mph.*

Do is the verb used to talk about action in general:

What should I do now?

Give

a push, a kick, a jump, a hug, a kiss • a cough, a cry, a scream, a shout, a shriek • a smile, a laugh, a look, a nod, a shrug • a promise, a warning, permission, an explanation • help, support, protection, advice, encouragement • birth • a performance, a concert, a party

Note that an indirect object often comes before many of these nouns. LP **Verbs with two objects** at TWO.

We gave <u>the car</u> **a push** *to start it. • Could you give <u>me</u>* **a call** *tomorrow morning?*

Take

a chance, a risk, a guess • action, a step, a walk, a stroll • care (of) • a bath, a shower • a trip, a vacation, a break, a rest, a nap • a look, a (deep) breath • a photograph, a picture (= photograph) • a test, a course

Make

a decision, a choice • an effort, a guess • progress, a start • changes, arrangements, plans, payments • a mistake, an error, a correction • a suggestion, an offer, a promise • a speech, a comment, a remark, a sound, a (phone) call • war, peace, love • breakfast, lunch, dinner, a meal (= prepare)

Have

a taste, a bite, a sip • a talk, a conversation, an argument, a fight • a look • a party, a meeting • a dream • a (good) laugh • a game (of cards, chess, etc.) (= play) • a baby (= give birth) • breakfast, lunch, dinner, a drink, a meal (= eat)

Pay

attention • a visit, a call • a compliment

Hold

a conversation, a discussion, talks • a meeting • an election • a trial • a party, a festival

ing, you are asking or saying how they are feeling or what their condition is: *How are you folks doing today?* ○ *Both the mother and her new baby are doing fine.* ○ *We've had some difficult times, but we're doing all right now.* • If you say what's doing or what's doing (at a particular place), you are asking what is happening there: *What's doing at the office?* • If something **does** someone **credit**, they deserve praise because of it: *The teacher's fairness to all her students does her credit.* • To **do** him **justice** (= To be fair to him), *he thought he was helping.* • To **do justice to** someone is to represent them as well as they really are: *This pic-*

ture doesn't really do justice to her (= She looks better than the picture shows). • If something **does more harm than good**, it is intended to improve a situation but instead makes it worse: *Modernizing historic buildings often does more harm than good.* • (*infml*) If something **does the job/trick**, it achieves whatever needed to be done: *I need something to put these papers in—this folder should do the job.* • If someone or something **does wonders for** a person or thing, they make sudden improvements: *That new guy is great—he's done wonders for the company.* [C]

doable /ˈduː·ə·bəl/ *adj* [not gradable] able to be achieved or performed • *The bank officer said that our loan was doable.*

doing /ˈduː·ɪŋ/ *n* [U] • *It was none of my doing* (= My actions were not the cause of this).

dos /duːz/, **do's** *pl n* • **Dos and don'ts** are rules about how people should and should not behave: *Where I work, the old dos and don'ts about how to dress no longer apply.*

do ARRANGE /duː/ *v* [T] he/she/it **does** /dʌz, dəz/, *past simple* **did** /dɪd/, *past part* **done** /dʌn/ to arrange, esp. in an attractive way • *Who does your hair* (= cuts and arranges your hair)?

do TRAVEL /duː/ *v* [T] he/she/it **does** /dʌz, dəz/, *past simple* **did** /dɪd/, *past part* **done** /dʌn/ to travel at (a stated speed) or over (a particular distance) • *We were only doing 70 miles per hour.* ○ *We did 400 miles yesterday.*

do BE ACCEPTABLE /duː/ *v* [I] he/she/it **does** /dʌz, dəz/, *past simple* **did** /dɪd/, *past part* **done** /dʌn/ to be acceptable, suitable, or enough • *"Will this room do?" "Yes, it'll be fine."* ○ *This kind of behavior just won't do.*

▫ **do away with** /ˌ-ˈ-ˈ-/ *v adv prep* [T] to get rid of or destroy • *The governor is proposing to do away with the state transportation department.*

▫ **do** *obj* **in** TIRE /ˈ-ˈ-/ *v adv* [T] *infml* to tire (someone) • *That five-mile hike did me in.*

▫ **do in** *obj* KILL , **do** *obj* **in** /ˈ-ˈ-/ *v adv* [M] *infml* to kill

▫ **do** *obj* **out of** *obj* /-ˈ-ˈ-/ *v adv prep* [T] *infml* to cheat (someone) by preventing them from obtaining or keeping (something of value) • *Con men did him out of over $10,000 of his hard-earned money.*

▫ **do over** *obj*, **do** *obj* **over** /-ˈ-ˈ-/ *v adv* [M] to decorate (a place) in a new way • *We plan to do over the kitchen next year.*

doable /ˈduː·ə·bəl/ *adj* [not gradable] • See at DO CAUSE TO HAPPEN .

doc /dɑk/ *n* [C] *infml* a DOCTOR MEDICINE

docile /ˈdɑs·əl, -ˌɑɪl/ *adj* calm in manner and easy to control • *They have a big dog, but he's real friendly and docile.*

dock STRUCTURE /dɑk/ *n* [C] a structure built out over water in a port along which ships can land to load and unload, or the enclosed area of water between two such structures • *A dock is also a flat, raised area attached to a* building and used for loading and unloading trucks.

dock /dɑk/ *v* [I/T] • *The ship docked in Japan, and he took another to Korea.* [I]

dock REMOVE /dɑk/ *v* [T] to take away a part of (someone's pay) • *I've used up my sick days, and if I take another day off they'll dock me a day's pay.*

docket /ˈdɑk·ət/ *n* [C] *law* a list of cases to be dealt with in a law court

doctor MEDICINE /ˈdɑk·tər/ (*abbreviation* **Dr.**) *n* [C] a person with a medical degree whose job is to treat people who are sick or injured • *This health plan lets you choose your own doctor.* • LP TITLES AND FORMS OF ADDRESS

doctor EDUCATION /ˈdɑk·tər/ (*abbreviation* **Dr.**) *n* [C] a person who has one of the highest-ranking degrees given by a university • A **doctor's degree** is one of the highest-ranging degrees given by a university, esp. the **doctor of philosophy** (*abbreviation* **Ph.D.**). • LP TITLES AND FORMS OF ADDRESS

doctor CHANGE /ˈdɑk·tər/ *v* [T] to change (something) in order to deceive people • *He claimed the photo had been doctored.*

doctrine /ˈdɑk·trən/ *n* [C/U] a belief, theory, or set of beliefs, esp. political or religious, taught and accepted by a particular group • *church doctrine* [U]

docudrama /ˈdɑk·jə،drɑm·ə, -،dræm·ə/ *n* [C/U] a television program whose story is based on an event or situation that really happened, although it is not accurate in every detail

document /ˈdɑk·jə·mənt/ *n* [C] a paper or set of papers with written or printed information, esp. of an official type • *Do you have all your documents in order to apply for a passport?*

document /ˈdɑk·jə،ment/ *v* [T] to record information about (something) by writing about it or taking photographs of it • *The study documents various aspects of Indian life in this period.*

documentary /ˌdɑk·jə·mənt·ə·ri/ *adj* [not gradable] • *documentary evidence*

documentation /ˌdɑk·jə·men·teɪ·ʃən/ *n* [U] official papers, or written material that provides proof of something

documentary /ˌdɑk·jə·mənt·ə·ri/ *n* [C] a film or television or radio program that gives information about a subject and is based on facts • *a documentary on animal communication*

dodge /dɑdʒ/ *v* [I/T] to avoid being hit (by something) by moving quickly to one side • (*fig.*) *We have dodged a bullet a lot of times in the last three or four years.* • To dodge something unpleasant is to avoid it: *Few men still talk about how they dodged the draft.* [T]

dodge /dɑdʒ/ *n* [C] a trick to deceive someone or to avoid doing something that you do not want to do • *She sells antiques as a tax dodge.*

doe /doʊ/ *n* [C] a female deer • Compare BUCK ANIMAL.

does /dʌz, dəz/ *present simple of* DO, used with he/she/it

doesn't /'dʌz·ənt/ *contraction of* **does not** • *Doesn't she look lovely in her wedding gown?*

dog ANIMAL /dɔːg/ *n* [C] an animal with four legs, commonly kept as a pet, and sometimes used to guard things • A **dog-eat-dog** situation is one where everyone is trying to get the best they can for themselves, not caring about what happens to anyone else. • If a person is **in the doghouse**, someone is very angry at them because of something they have done: *If I don't do something for Mother's Day, I'll really be in the doghouse.* • A **dog biscuit** is a hard, baked cracker, often flavored with meat, for dogs to eat. • A **doghouse** is a small shelter outside of a house for a dog to sleep in.

dog PERSON /dɔːg/ *n* [C] *slang* a person of a stated type • *You won $1000? You lucky dog!*

dog FOLLOW /dɔːg/ *v* [T] **-gg-** to follow (someone) closely and continually • *The scandal seems likely to dog him for months to come.*

dog–eared /'dɔː·gɪrd/ *adj* (of a book or paper) with the pages turned down at the corners as the result of a lot of use

dogfight /'dɔːg·faɪt/ *n* [C] a fight between two military aircraft, or any fierce fight • *They are a tough team, and we knew we were in for a real dogfight.*

dogged /'dɔː·gəd/ *adj* determined to do something, even if it is very difficult • *John Regan credited the capture to dogged persistence by police.*

doggedly /'dɔː·gəd·li/ *adv* • *Gove spent much of the last decade of his life doggedly defending his principles.*

doggie /'dɔː·gi/ *n* [C] *a child's word for* a dog

doggone /'dɔː·gɔːn, 'dɑg·ɑn/ *exclamation infml* used to express annoyance • *Doggone it, where's that letter?*

doggy bag /'dɔː·giˌbæg/ *n* [C] a container that a restaurant provides so you can take home any food you have not finished

dogma /'dɔːg·mə, 'dɑg-/ *n* [C/U] a fixed, esp. religious, belief or set of beliefs that people are expected to accept without any doubts • *religious dogma* [U]

dogmatic /dɔːg'mæt̬·ɪk, dɑg-/ *adj* (of a person or a group) certain that they are right and that everyone else is wrong • *He could not accept Freud's dogmatic atheism.*

dog tag /'dɔːg·tæg/ *n* [C] *pl* **dog tags** a small piece of metal worn around the neck by soldiers, which contains their name, official number, and other information

dogwood /'dɔː·gwʊd/ *n* [C/U] a bush or tree that has white or pink flowers in the spring and grows wild or in a garden

doing /'duː·ɪŋ/ *n* [U] • See at DO CAUSE TO HAPPEN.

doldrums /'doʊl·drəmz, 'dɔːl-, 'dɑl-/ *pl n* a state of lack of activity or lack of success • *Business leaders predict a hard year ahead with the economy in the doldrums.*

dole out *obj*, **dole** *obj* **out** /'doʊl'aʊt/ *v adv* [M] to give (money, food, etc.), esp. to several people • *I can't keep doling out money to you kids.*

doleful /'doʊl·fəl/ *adj* very sad • *a doleful expression/look*

doll /dɑl, dɔːl/ *n* [C] a child's toy in the shape of a person, esp. a baby or child • (*infml*) You can call someone a doll to show that you like them or think they are attractive or pleasant: *She's a doll, she's a love, she really is.*

dollar /'dɑl·ər/ *n* [C] a unit of money, used in the US, Canada, Australia, New Zealand, and other countries, that is worth 100 cents • *Could you lend me ten dollars?* • The **dollar sign**, $, is put in front of amounts of money in dollars.

dollop /'dɑl·əp/ *n* [C] a small amount of a substance • *a dollop of whipped cream*

dolly /'dɑl·i, 'dɔː·li/ *n* [C] *a child's word for* a DOLL

dolphin /'dɑl·fən, 'dɔːl-/ *n* [C] a sea mammal that looks like a large fish with a pointed mouth

domain /doʊ'meɪn, də-/ *n* [C] an area of interest or an area over which a person has control • *the domain of polymer science* ○ *public and private domains*

dome /doʊm/ *n* [C] a rounded roof on a building • *The dome of St. Peter's could be seen in the distance.*

domestic HOME /də'mes·tɪk/ *adj* relating to the home, house, or family • *I've never been fond of domestic chores like cooking and cleaning.* • Domestic violence is violence that happens between family members.

domestic /də'mes·tɪk/ *n* [C] *dated* someone paid to help with work that needs to be done in a house, such as cleaning and washing clothes

domesticated /də'mes·təˌkeɪt̬·ɪd/ *adj* [not gradable] (of an animal or plant) brought under human control in order to produce food • *the wild ancestors of our domesticated chickens*

domesticity /ˌdoʊˌmes'tɪs·ət̬·i, -məs-/ *n* [U] the state of being at home a lot with your family • *Since they had their baby, they've settled happily into domesticity.*

domestic COUNTRY /də'mes·tɪk/ *adj* relating to a person's own country • *The president's domestic policy has been more successful than his foreign policy.*

domicile /'dɑm·əˌsaɪl, 'doʊ·mə-/ *n* [C] *law* the place where a person lives • *Any change of domicile should be reported to the proper authorities.*

dominant /'dɑm·ə·nənt/ *adj* more important, strong, or noticeable than anything else of the same type • *a dominant personality* ○ *For years* the Democrats were the dominant party in Congress.

dominance /ˈdɑm·ə·nəns/ n [U] • military dominance

dominate /ˈdɑm·əˌneɪt/ v [I/T] to have control over (a place or a person), or to be the most important person or thing • It was the story that dominated the headlines this week. [T] ○ The Rams dominated the football game in handing the Eagles their second loss. [T]

domination /ˌdɑm·əˈneɪ·ʃən/ n [U] the state of having control over people or a situation • Her domination of the tennis world is undisputed.

domineering /ˌdɑm·əˈnɪr·ɪŋ/ adj having a strong tendency to try to control other people without taking their feelings into consideration • a domineering personality

dominion /dəˈmɪn·jən/ n [C/U] literary control over a country or people, or the land that belongs to a ruler • God has dominion over all his creatures. [U]

domino /ˈdɑm·əˌnoʊ/ n [C] pl **dominoes** one of a set of small rectangular pieces of wood or plastic marked with a particular number of spots on each half of one surface, used in playing a game

dominoes /ˈdɑm·əˌnoʊz/ n [U] a game in which you try to match the spots of a domino put down by another player

donate /ˈdoʊ·neɪt, doʊˈneɪt/ v [I/T] to give (something), esp. to an organization, without wanting anything in exchange • Over $12 million was donated to the building fund. [T] ○ Some businesses have agreed to donate computers to schools. [T]

donation /doʊˈneɪ·ʃən/ n [C/U] • Donations of food and clothing are gratefully accepted. [C]

done /dʌn/ past participle of DO • You can say "done" to show that you agree to something: "I'll give you $25 for the chair." "Done!"

done for /ˈdʌn·fɔːr/ adj [not gradable] about to die or suffer greatly because of a serious difficulty or danger • We thought we were done for when we smelled smoke and the lights went out.

Don Juan /dɑnˈhwɑn, -wɑn, -ˈdʒuː·ən/ n [C] a man who has had sexual or romantic relationships with a lot of women

donkey /ˈdɑŋ·ki, ˈdʌŋ-, ˈdɔːŋ-/ n [C] a gray or brown animal like a small horse with long ears

donor /ˈdoʊ·nər/ n [C] a person who gives money or something else of value to an organization • A large gift from an anonymous donor will allow us to continue our work. • A donor is also someone who gives some of their blood or who agrees to give an organ or part of their body to help someone else.

don't /doʊnt/ contraction of **do not** • Please don't make any noise while they're recording. • "I'm going to tell Billy what you said about him." "**Don't you dare!**" (= I will be very angry at you if you do.)"

donut /ˈdoʊ·nʌt, -nət/ n [C] a DOUGHNUT

doodad /ˈduː·dæd/, **doohickey** /ˈduːˌhɪk·i/ n [C] infml any small device or object whose name you cannot remember or do not know

doodle /ˈduːd·ᵊl/ n [C] a drawing or pattern that you make while you are thinking about something else or when you are bored

doodle /ˈduːd·ᵊl/ v [I]

doom /duːm/ n [U] death, destruction, or any very bad situation that cannot be avoided • A sense of doom hung over the entire country.

doom /duːm/ v [T] to be the certain cause of (someone or something) having a bad end, esp. to die or to fail • The effort is doomed to failure. ○ He was doomed to be a one-term president like Jimmy Carter.

doomsday /ˈduːmz·deɪ/ n [U] the end of the world • Doomsday is also **Judgment Day**. See at JUDGE DECIDE

door /dɔːr, doʊr/ n [C] a flat, usually rectangular, object that is fixed at one edge and is used to close the entrance to something such as a room, building, or vehicle, or the entrance itself • the front/back door ○ We'd like to rent a four-door car. ○ I'll meet you at the main door of the library. ○ Would you open/close/shut the door, please? ○ The door to his bedroom was locked from the inside. ○ Mom, there's someone at the door (= outside the front door). • Door is also used to refer to a house or other building: Sam lives just a few doors away/up/down from us. ○ They live next door to us (= in the house beside ours). • The trip takes an hour **door to door** (= from beginning to end). • A **doorbell** is an electrical device with a button near the outside door of a house or apartment that makes a noise when pressed, to let the people inside know someone is there: He rang the doorbell twice. • A **doorknob** is a round handle that you turn to open a door. • A **doormat** is a rectangular piece of material put on the ground outside a door to a house or apartment so that people coming in can clean their shoes before entering. • A **doorstep** is a step outside the door to a building. • A **doorway** is the space for a door through which you go into and out of a room or building.

doorman /ˈdɔːr·mən, ˈdoʊr-, -ˌmæn/ n [C] pl **-men** /ˈdɔːr·mən, ˈdoʊr-, -ˌmen/ a person whose job is to stand by the door of a hotel or public building and let people in or out, open their car doors, etc.

dope DRUG /doʊp/ n [U] infml any illegal drug • a dope addict

doping /ˈdoʊ·pɪŋ/ n [U] the use of illegal drugs to improve the performance of a person or an animal esp. in a sports competition • For the first time at these Games, doping has been hinted at.

dope PERSON /doʊp/ n [C] infml a stupid or foolish person • You shouldn't have told him, you dope!

dope INFORMATION /doʊp/ n [U] slang information known by only a few people • A new *column of inside dope about the film industry begins next month.*

dork /'dɔːrk/ *n* [C] *slang* a stupid, awkward person • *I felt like a real dork when I realized my mistake.*

dormant /'dɔːr·mənt/ *adj* (of things) not active or growing, but having the ability to be active at a later time • *a dormant volcano* ○ *Most roses being sold now are dormant, and without any soil around their roots.*

dormer (window) /'dɔːr·mər ('wɪn·doʊ)/ *n* [C] a small, roofed structure sticking out from a sloping roof with a vertical window built into it

dormitory /'dɔːr·mə ,tɔːr·i, -,toʊr·i/, *short form* **dorm** /dɔːrm/ *n* [C] a large room or building containing many beds, esp. in a college or BOARDING SCHOOL

dormer

dose /doʊs/ *n* [C] a measured amount of a drug • *She was given large doses of a powerful antibiotic.* • A dose is also an amount of something: *Stories of dramatic cancer cures should be taken with a healthy dose of skepticism.*

dosage /'doʊ·sɪdʒ/ *n* [C] a measured amount of a medicine • *He needed a high dosage to do any good.*

dot /dɑt/ *n* [C] a very small, round mark • *The ducks were black dots in the distance.* • If someone or something arrives **on the dot**, they arrive exactly at the expected time: *Be here at 9 on the dot.* • Dot (*symbol* .) is also used in an INTERNET address to separate its parts: *I keep forgetting you've got a dot org address.*

dot /dɑt/ *v* [T] **-tt-** • When an area is dotted

DOTS [. . .]

Dots are used to show that:

the writer is omitting some of another person's words

According to Thomas Jefferson, "a little rebellion . . . is a good thing." • "A brilliant film . . . extraordinary." ·

a list or an idea has been left incomplete

Old clothes, books, toys, furniture . . . the junk shop has everything.

the speaker pauses, slows down, or changes the subject between words

One of the scientists began the countdown: ten . . . nine . . . eight. . . . • I can't quite remember when we . . . Oh yes, last December.

Three dots are usually used when the omission or pause comes in the middle of the sentence, or when the sentence is incomplete. Four dots are usually used to show that something has been left out at the end of a sentence.

---

with things, it has many of them in different places: *Minnesota is dotted with lakes, especially in the north.* • *The proposal's almost complete—all we have to do now is* **dot the i's and cross the t's** (= finish the details). • A **dotted line** is a line of dots marked or printed on paper: *Please sign your name on the dotted line.*

dote on /'doʊt·ɔːn, -ɑn/ *v prep* [T] to love (someone) very much, sometimes foolishly or too much • *They dote on their grandchild.*

double TWICE /'dʌb·əl/ *adj, adv* [not gradable] twice the size, amount, price, etc., or consisting of two similar things together • *The cost of going to the movies is almost double what it was a few years ago.* ○ *Fold the blanket double* (= so that it is in two layers) *and then you won't be cold.* • If you are seeing **double**, you are seeing two of everything. • A **double bed** is a bed big enough for two people to sleep in. • A **double-breasted** jacket has two sets of buttons and two wide parts at the front, one of which covers the other when the buttons are fastened: *a double-breasted suit* • If you **double-check** something, you make certain it is correct or safe, usually by examining it again: *I always double-check to make sure I locked the door.* • A **double chin** is a fold of skin under the face along the front of the neck, caused by a layer of fat. • To **double-cross** someone is to promise something that they are depending on to help them, and then not doing it or doing something that hurts them instead. • Something that is **double-edged** acts in two ways, often with results that you did not originally intend: *Censorship can be a double-edged sword.* • A **double feature** is the showing of two different movies, one after the other. • **Double figures** means 10 or more but less than 100: *Six players scored in double figures.* • To **double-park** is to leave your car in the street along the side of a car that is already parked, so that your car is blocking other cars from moving along the path they usually go. • A **double room** is a room in a hotel for two people. • If a piece of text is printed **double-spaced**, it has an empty line between each line of writing. • A **double standard** is the habit of treating one group differently than another when to be fair they should be treated the same. • A **double take** is a surprising, delayed act of recognizing someone or something: *With her hair cut short and dyed red, I did a double take at first.* • **Double-talk** is talk that has no real meaning or has more than one meaning and is intended to confuse. • (*infml*) A **double whammy** is a situation that includes two disadvantages or difficulties: *Being deaf and having a substance abuse problem is a double whammy.* • Compare SINGLE ONE.

double /'dʌb·əl/ *v* [I/T] • *Company profits have doubled in the last year.* [I] ○ *For four people, just double the recipe* (= make twice as much). [T] • If something or someone doubles as something or someone else, they have a second use or job: *The kitchen table doubles as my desk.* [I] • If you **double up/over**, you suddenly bend forward and down, usually because of pain or laughter: *A sudden, sharp pain made him double over.* • To **double up** is to share something, esp. a room, with someone else: *The two boys will have to double up in the front bedroom.*

doubles /'dʌb·əlz/ *pl n* (esp. in tennis) a game played with two players on each side

doubly /'dʌb·li/ *adv* [not gradable] twice the amount or degree • *He is doubly talented, as a composer and as a pianist.*

double PERSON /'dʌb·əl/ *n* [C usually sing] a person who looks the same as someone else • *She is a double for Mary Tyler Moore.*

double bass /ˌdʌb·əl'beɪs/, *infml* **bass fiddle** *n* [C/U] a very large, wooden musical instrument with four strings that a player holds up while standing and plays with a BOW (= stick with hairs fixed to it), or this type of instrument generally

doubt /daʊt/ *n* [C/U] a feeling of not knowing what to believe or what to do, or the condition of being uncertain • *If you have any doubt about her ability, don't hire her.* [C] ○ *There's no doubt that the show will be successful.* [+ *that* clause] ○ *The future of the entire project is in some doubt.* [U] ○ *She is without a doubt* (= certainly) *one of the best students I've ever had.* [C]

doubt /daʊt/ *v* [T] to be uncertain about (something or someone), or to have difficulty believing (something) • *He may come back tomorrow with the money, but I doubt it.* [T]

doubtful /'daʊt·fəl/ *adj* uncertain or unlikely • *It was doubtful (that) the money would ever be found.* [+ *(that)* clause] ○ *She gave me a long, doubtful look* (= look full of doubt) *and told me to wait.*

doubtless /'daʊt·ləs/ *adv* [not gradable] very probably • *The film is not rated but would doubtless get an R for violence if it were.*

dough FLOUR /doʊ/ *n* [U] flour mixed with water and other food substances so that it is ready for baking esp. into bread or pastry

dough MONEY /doʊ/ *n* [U] *dated slang* money

doughnut, **donut** /'doʊ·nʌt, -nət/ *n* [C] a small, circular cake, fried in hot fat, sometimes with a hole in the middle

dour /daʊr, dʊr/ *adj* [-er/-est only] (of a person's appearance or manner) very serious and sad, and likely to judge people severely • *a dour look*

douse /daʊs, daʊz/ *v* [T] to stop (esp. a fire) by putting water on it • *Efforts to douse the fire were hampered by high winds.* • To douse is also to make (someone or something) wet by throwing a lot of liquid over them: *They doused him with gasoline and set him on fire.*

dove BIRD /dʌv/ *n* [C] a bird with short legs, a

large body, and a small head, often used as a symbol of peace

dove MOVE DOWN /doʊv/ *past simple of* DIVE

dovetail /'dʌv·teɪl/ *v* [I/T] to fit together well, or to cause (something) to fit together well with something else • *Our plans dovetailed, and we were able to meet that evening.* [I]

dowdy /'daʊd·i/ *adj* (esp. of clothes or the person wearing them) unattractive and not stylish, often because of being old-fashioned

down IN A LOWER POSITION /daʊn/ *prep, adv* [not gradable] in or toward a low or lower position, from a higher one • *There's a bathroom down the stairs and to the right.* ○ *He poured the rest of the coffee down the drain.* ○ *The cat jumped down from the chair.* ○ *Please sit down* (= stop standing and come to a sitting position). ○ *If you feel ill, why don't you lie down* (= stop standing and come to a lying position) *for a while?* • Down also means to the ground, esp. as a result of an action that causes something to fall: *We're going to have to cut down this tree.* • Down also means firmly, in a fixed position, esp. as a result of an action: *Workers in the convention center taped down the edges of the carpets.* ○ *(fig.) We hope to nail down the agreement at tomorrow's meeting.* • If someone's eyes are **downcast**, they are looking down, usually because of shyness or sadness. • **Downhill** means toward the bottom of a hill: *She let the bike coast downhill.* • To **be/go downhill** is to become continually worse: *The job was fine at first, but it's been all downhill since I got a new boss.* • A **downpour** is a lot of rain falling in a short time.

down /daʊn/ *v* [T] to eat or drink (something) quickly • *Okami downed his Scotch and ordered another all in one motion.*

down AT A LOWER LEVEL /daʊn/ *adv, adj* [not gradable] in or toward a lower place or level, a smaller amount, or a simpler state • *Unemployment went down last month, dropping to under 6%.* ○ *Lots of stores are having sales, and prices are coming down.* ○ *He was down to his last $5* (= that was all he had left). • Down is used with a lot of verbs to show that something is becoming smaller, weaker, slower, or less: *The fire burned down.* ○ *She's slimmed down a lot in the past few months.* ○ *Would you please turn down the music—it's too loud.* • If you are **down on** someone, you are angry at them or critical of them: *Dad's down on me since I scraped the car backing out of the garage.* • *(approving)* Someone who is **down-to-earth** is practical and direct in dealing with people: *The players like the coach because he's down-to-earth and straight with them.* • If a situation goes **down to the wire**, the result of it is not known until the end: *I think the election will go right down to the wire.*

down DISTANT /daʊn/ *adv* [not gradable] used, esp. with prepositions, to emphasize that a place is distant from the speaker or in or toward the south • *I'll meet you down at the health club after work.* ∘ *My parents moved down to Florida after they retired.*

down ALONG /daʊn/ *prep* along • *Her office is down the hall on the right.*

down IN WRITING /daʊn/ *adv* [not gradable] in writing or on paper • *He agreed to the deal, but until we get it down on paper, we don't have a legal contract.*

down UNHAPPY /daʊn/ *adj* unhappy • *I'm feeling a little down, I guess because most people have gone home for the holidays and I'm still here.* • **Downhearted** means unhappy, esp. because of a disappointment or failure.

downer /'daʊ·nər/ *n* [C] *infml* an event or experience that makes you unhappy and lacking in hope, confidence, or energy • *Your car's been stolen? That's a real downer!*

down WORSE /daʊn/ *adv, adj* [not gradable] into a worse position or state • *Michigan, down (by) (= losing by) ten points at the half, came back to win the football game.* • Someone or something that is **down-at-the-heels** is poorly dressed or in bad condition, because of a lack of money. • A **downfall** is something that causes the destruction of a person, organization, or government and their loss of power, money, or health: *In the end, ambition was his downfall.* • People who are **downtrodden** have been badly and unfairly treated and therefore feel worthless and unable to act independently. • A **downturn** is a reduction in the amount or success of something, such as economic activity: *a downturn in car sales*

down WHEN BUYING /daʊn/ *adv* [not gradable] at the time of buying • *She paid $100 down and the rest in installments.* • A **down payment** is an amount of money that is only part of the total cost, paid at the time when you buy something.

down NOT IN OPERATION /daʊn/ *adj* [not gradable] (of a system or machine, esp. a computer) not in operation or not working, usually only for a limited period of time • *The network will be down until noon today.* • **Downtime** is the time during which a machine, esp. a computer, is not working or is not able to be used.

down HAIR /daʊn/ *n* [U] small, soft feathers or hair, esp. those of a young bird

downgrade /'daʊn·greɪd/ *v* [T] to reduce (someone or something) to a lower rank or position; to make less important or less valued • *They threatened to downgrade my credit rating if I don't pay the bill immediately.*

download /'daʊn·loʊd/ *v* [T] to copy or move (programs or information) into a computer's memory, esp. from a larger computer

downplay /'daʊn·pleɪ/ *v* [T] to make (something) seem less important or not as bad as it really is • *The mayor is trying to downplay the crisis.*

downright /'daʊn·raɪt/ *adv* [not gradable] ac-

tually or completely • *Their working conditions were downright unhealthy.*

downside /'daʊn·saɪd/ *n* [U] the negative part of a situation • *It's a great plan—the downside is that it's going to cost a lot of money.* • Compare UPSIDE.

downsize /'daʊn·saɪz/ *v* [I] (of a company) to reduce the number of employees, usually as part of a larger change in the structure of an organization • *The company was forced to downsize in order to remain competitive.*

downstairs /'daʊn·sterz, -'stærz/ *adv, adj* [not gradable] on or to a lower floor of a building, esp. the ground floor, or down the stairs • *a downstairs bathroom* ∘ *I hear someone downstairs.*

downstream /'daʊn·striːm/ *adj, adv* [not gradable] in the same direction as the current of a river is flowing • *The boat landing is about half a mile downstream from here.* • Compare UPSTREAM.

downtown /'daʊn·taʊn/ *adj, adv* [not gradable] in or to the business or central part of a city • *downtown Los Angeles*

downtown /'daʊn·taʊn/ *n* [U] • *The hotel is situated two miles north of downtown.*

downward /'daʊn·wərd/, **downwards** /'daʊn·wərdz/ *adv* [not gradable] toward a lower position, level, or amount • *The road slopes gently downward for a mile or two.*

downward /'daʊn·wərd/ *adj* [not gradable] • *The trend has been downward ever since, with donations falling to $143,000 last year.*

downwind /'daʊn·wɪnd/ *adv, adj* in the direction in which the wind is blowing • *We were downwind of the garbage dump and the smell was awful.* • USAGE: The opposite of downwind is UPWIND.

dowry /'daʊr·i/ *n* [C] in some societies, an amount of money or property that a woman's parents give to the man she marries

doze /doʊz/ *v* [I] to have a short period of sleep, esp. during the day • *My cat was dozing in front of the fireplace.* • If you doze off, you start to sleep, esp. during the day: *I must have dozed off, because I don't remember what happened next.*

dozen /'dʌz·ən/ *n* [C] a group or collection of twelve • *a dozen eggs* ∘ *I brought home a half dozen/half a dozen* (= six) *eggs.*

Dr. /'dɑk·tər/ *n pl* **Drs.** *abbreviation for* DOCTOR

drab /dræb/ *adj* [*-er/-est* only] **-bb-** plain and not interesting, or not bright in appearance • *He found London disagreeable, with its thick fog, cold drizzle, and drab food.*

draconian /drə'koʊ·niː·ən/ *adj* (esp. of a rule, law, or punishment) extremely severe • *The governor proposed draconian cuts in state aid to education.*

draft PLAN /dræft/ *n* [C] a piece of writing or drawing that is done early in the development of a work to help prepare it in its final form •

drama

The architects gave us their first draft of the design.

draft /dræft/ *v* [T] to write (something), esp. at an early stage before it is in final form • *She drafted a letter to her lawyer.*

draft CHOOSING PEOPLE /dræft/ *n* [U] the process by which people are ordered by law to become members of the armed forces, or the process by which players are chosen to play for PROFESSIONAL sports teams

draft /dræft/ *v* [T] to order a person to become a member of the armed forces • In sports, to draft is to choose (someone, esp. someone in a college or university) to become available as a player for a team that pays its players: *The Cleveland Cavaliers drafted him in the first round.*

draftee /dræf'ti:/ *n* [C] a person who has been ordered by law to become a member of the armed forces

draft COLD AIR /dræft/ *n* [C] a current of cold air inside a room • *She felt a cold draft every time the door was opened.*

drafty /'dræf·ti/ *adj* full of currents of cold air

draft BEER /dræft/ *adj* [not gradable] (of beer) stored in and served from KEGS (= large containers), usually in bars and restaurants • *We have a large selection of beers* **on draft** (= stored in large containers).

draft BANKING /dræft/ *n* [C] a written order for money to be paid by a bank • *a bank draft*

drag PULL /dræg/ *v* [I/T] **-gg-** to move (something heavy) by pulling it along the ground • *If the box is too heavy to lift, just drag it over here.* [T] • (*fig.*) To drag someone away/out is also to persuade someone to leave or do something when they do not want to do it: *I hate to drag you away from the party, but we really have to go.* [T] • If you drag out an event, you cause it to continue for longer than is necessary or convenient: *They should make a decision now instead of dragging out the discussion.* [M] • If an event drags, it seems to happen very slowly: *The play dragged in the second act.* [I] • If you **drag** your **feet**, you do something slowly or don't start it because you do not want to do it: *He knows he should see a doctor, but he's dragging his feet.*

drag /dræg/ *n* [C] something or someone that slows progress or development, or that makes success less likely • *Keeping a large staff is a drag on our income.*

drag BORING EVENT /dræg/ *n* [U] *infml* someone or something that is unpleasant and boring • *Waiting in a doctor's office is such a drag!*

drag SMOKING /dræg/ *n* [C] *infml* an act of sucking the smoke of burning tobacco into the mouth while smoking, esp. a cigarette • *She took a long drag from her cigarette.*

drag CLOTHES /dræg/ *n* [U] *slang* women's clothes worn by a man • *He appeared in drag, complete with high heels and a blond wig.*

dragon /'dræg·ən/ *n* [C] a large, fierce, imaginary animal, usually represented with wings, a long tail, and fire coming out of its mouth

dragon

dragonfly /'dræg·ən‚flɑɪ/ *n* [C] a flying insect with a long, thin body and two pairs of transparent wings

drag race /'dræg·reɪs/ *n* [C] a race between cars over a flat, straight road from a start at which both cars are not moving

dragonfly

drain /dreɪn/ *v* [I/T] to cause (a liquid) to flow away or cause a liquid to flow away from (something), leaving it dryer, or to become dryer as a liquid flows away • *Wash the lettuce in the sink and let it drain.* [I] ○ *Drain the lettuce and then pat it dry with paper towels.* [T] ○ *Just stir fry the ground beef, and drain (off) the oil.* [T/M] • If something drains you, it makes you very tired: *It drains you to work with a class of 20 four-year-olds, let me tell you.* [T]

drain /dreɪn/ *n* [C] a pipe or channel that carries away waste water or other liquids • *She spilled some sugar in the sink and washed it down the drain.* • Something that is a drain on you takes away a lot of your energy and makes you tired: *Taking care of his sick mother was quite a drain on him.* • If something is a drain on your money or something else, it uses a lot of it or makes it weaker: *Having two mortgages was a tremendous drain on their resources.*

draining /'dreɪ·nɪŋ/ *adj* causing you to lose most of your energy; very tiring • *He found the funeral service emotionally draining.*

drainage /'dreɪ·nɪdʒ/ *n* [U] the process by which water or other liquids flow away into pipes or into the ground • *The swamp has poor drainage throughout.*

drama THEATER /'drɑm·ə, 'dræm·ə/ *n* [C/U] a play, esp. a serious one, written to be performed by actors, the writing of plays, or the art of showing plays • *She's been in several television dramas.* [C] ○ *Arthur Miller, a master of drama, wrote "Death of a Salesman."* [U]

dramatic /drə'mæṭ·ɪk/ *adj* • *He's as good in comedies as he is in dramatic roles.*

dramatist /'drɑm·ət·əst, 'dræm-/ *n* [C] a writer of plays, esp. serious ones

dramatize /'drɑm·ə‚tɑɪz, 'dræm-/ *v* [T] to change (a piece of writing) into a play to be performed • *He was hired by a movie production company to dramatize the novel.*

drama EXCITEMENT /'drɑm·ə, 'dræm·ə/ *n* [U]

excitement and strong interest produced by an unexpected or surprising event or situation • *Watching on television was not the same as experiencing the drama of the event in person.*

dramatic /drə'mæt̬·ɪk/ *adj* (of an event or situation) producing excitement and strong interest because unexpected, surprising, or dangerous • *In a dramatic rescue, 10 crewmen were lifted to a helicopter just minutes before their ship sank.* • Dramatic also means sudden and showing a big change: *There has been a dramatic reduction in crime in New York City.*

dramatically /drə'mæt̬·ɪ·kli/ *adv*

dramatize /'drɑm·ə,tɑɪz, 'dræm-/ *v* [T] to make (something) seem more exciting or surprising than it is • *They dramatized their protest by wearing clothes splattered with red paint that looked like blood.*

drank /dræŋk/ *past simple of* DRINK

drape /dreɪp/ *v* [T] to hang or cover with (something) loosely and often in a decorative way • *She draped a silk scarf over her bare shoulders.*

drapes /dreɪps/, **draperies** /'dreɪ·pə·riːz, -priːz/ *pl n* curtains of thick cloth • *I've ordered new drapes for the living room.*

drastic /'dræs·tɪk/ *adj* (of a change) severe and sudden; extreme • *In the desert there's a drastic change in temperature from day to night.*

drastically /'dræs·tɪ·kli/ *adv* • *Our lives changed drastically when dad died and we had to move.*

draught [COLD AIR] /dræft, drɑːft/ *n* [C] *Br for* DRAFT [COLD AIR]

draught [BEER] /dræft, drɑːft/ *adj Br for* DRAFT [BEER]

draw [PICTURE] /drɔː/ *v* [I/T] *past simple* **drew** /druː/, *past part* **drawn** /drɔːn/ to make a picture of (something or someone) by marking lines with something, esp. a pencil or pen • *The child drew a picture of a dog.* [T] • To **draw the line** is to put a limit on what you will do or allow to happen, esp. because the suggested action is morally wrong: *The teacher allowed the children to talk quietly among themselves, but she drew the line at shouting.*

drawing /'drɔː·ɪŋ/ *n* [C/U] the art or process of making pictures by marking lines, or a picture made in this way • *a beautiful drawing of flowers* [C] ○ *I plan to take a course in drawing next semester.* [U]

draw [MOVE] /drɔː/ *v* [I always + adv/prep] *past simple* **drew** /druː/, *past part* **drawn** /drɔːn/ to move in a particular direction • *As we drew near, a dog started to bark.*

draw [PULL / PULL IN] /drɔː/ *v* [I/T] *past simple* **drew** /druː/, *past part* **drawn** /drɔːn/ to pull or direct (something or someone) in a particular direction, or attract (someone) toward a particular place • *Las Vegas draws millions of tourists to its gambling casinos.* [T] ○ *I would*

like to thank Professor Reynolds for drawing my attention to this article.* [T] • To draw is also to pull together or close (something covering a window), so that no one can see you: *She drew the blinds and sat down on the bed to undress.* [T] • To draw is also to suck in: *He drew deeply on his pipe.* [I]

draw /drɔː/ *n* [C] *infml* someone or something that attracts a lot of interest, esp. of paying customers • *Every team needs a superstar who will be a big draw.*

draw [TAKE OUT] /drɔː/ *v* [T] *past simple* **drew** /druː/, *past part* **drawn** /drɔːn/ to remove (something) • *It was my turn to draw a card.* ○ *He drew his gun and waved it around.* • If you **draw a blank**, you fail to remember something: *He said we'd met before, but I just drew a blank* (= I did not remember him).

draw [DECIDE ON] /drɔː/ *v* [T] *past simple* **drew** /druː/, *past part* **drawn** /drɔːn/ to decide (on something) as a result of thinking about it • *We can draw some conclusions about the causes of this disease.*

draw [CAUSE] /drɔː/ *v* [T] *past simple* **drew** /druː/, *past part* **drawn** /drɔːn/ to cause (a reaction) from someone • *The criticism drew an angry response from the mayor.*

draw [EQUAL] /drɔː/ *n* [C] (in sports and games) a situation in which each side or team has equal points or is in an equal position and neither side wins • *The hockey game ended in a draw, 2 to 2.*

□ **draw out** *obj* [LENGTHEN], **draw** *obj* **out** /'-'-/ *v adv* [M] to cause (something) to last longer than is usual or necessary • *The trial was drawn out because of the need to translate everything.*

drawn–out /'drɔː'nɑut/ *adj* • *Their divorce was a long, drawn-out affair.*

□ **draw out** *obj* [ENCOURAGE], **draw** *obj* **out** /'-'-/ *v adv* [M] to encourage or persuade (someone) to express their thoughts and feelings • *She was good at drawing out young people and getting them to talk about their fears and hopes.*

□ **draw up** *obj* [PREPARE], **draw** *obj* **up** /'-'-/ *v adv* [M] to prepare in writing (something, esp. a formal document) • *The lawyers drew up a contract over the weekend.*

□ **draw** *obj* **up** [STRAIGHTEN] /'-'-/ *v prep* [T] to make (yourself) stand straight with the shoulders back • *She drew herself up like the Statue of Liberty and lifted an arm over her head.*

drawback /'drɔː·bæk/ *n* [C] a disadvantage or problem; the negative part of a situation • *One of the drawbacks of working for a big company is that you have to follow a lot of rules.*

drawer /drɔːr, 'drɔː·ər/ *n* [C] a wide but not very deep container, open at the top, that is part of a piece of furniture and that a person can pull partly out from its front to put things in and then push back to make it even with the front of the furniture • *I keep my socks in the bottom drawer of my dresser.*

drawers /drɔːrz, 'drɔː·ərz/ *pl n dated* UNDER-
PANTS

drawl /drɔːl/ *n* [C] a way of speaking esp. in
the southern US in which some vowel sounds
are lengthened and which therefore seems
slower than usual • *He had bright blue eyes
and a beautiful southern drawl.*

drawn DRAW /drɔːn/ *past participle of* DRAW

drawn TIRED /drɔːn/ *adj* (usually of the face)
appearing tired and anxious or worried • *He's
not as sick as he was, but he still looks thin and
drawn.*

drawn-out /'drɔː'naʊt/ *adj* • See at DRAW OUT
LENGTHEN.

dread /dred/ *n* [U] extreme fear or anxiety
about something that is going to happen or
might happen • *a dread of drowning*

dread /dred/ *v* [T] • *We dreaded hearing the results of the blood tests.*

dreadful /'dred·fəl/ *adj* very bad • *I realized I
had committed a dreadful mistake.*

dreadfully /'dred·fə·li/ *adv* • *He treated her
dreadfully.*

dreadlocks /'dred·laks/ *pl n* a hairstyle in
which long, tightly
twisted lengths of hair
hang down

dream SLEEP /driːm/ *n*
[C] the activities, im-
ages, and feelings ex-
perienced by the mind
during sleep • *In the
dream I had last night,
someone was chasing
me, but I didn't know
who it was.*

dreadlocks

dream /driːm/ *v past* **dreamed** /driːmd, dremt/
or **dreamt** /dremt/ • *What did you dream
about last night?* [I] ○ *I dreamed that I was in
a boat on a big lake, and I was trying to get back
to land.* [+ *that* clause] • If you say that you
would not **dream of** doing something, you
mean that you would not do it, esp. because it
would be wrong: *When I was a girl, my parents
wouldn't dream of letting me stay alone with a
boy.*

dreamily /'driː·mə·li/ *adv* in a way that suggests you are imagining something pleasant
and not giving much attention to what is happening around you • *When I mentioned Dave,
Amanda smiled dreamily.*

dreamlike /'driːm·laɪk/ *adj* • *There was a
strange, dreamlike (= as if imagined while
sleeping) quality to the crash, which seemed to
happen in slow motion.*

dreamy /'driː·mi/ *adj* imagining something
pleasant and not giving much attention to
what is happening around you, or likely to behave this way often • *The music put me into a
dreamy mood and for a moment I forgot where
I was.*

dream HOPE /driːm/ *n* [C] an event or condition that you hope for very much, although it

is not likely to happen • *It was his dream to be
a dancer.* • Dream is sometimes used before a
noun when you want to say that something is
almost perfect: *If there were one more bedroom, it would be my dream house.* • A **dream
come true** is something desired very much
for a long time, and that has now happened:
*For her, making the Olympic team was a dream
come true.*

dream /driːm/ *v* [I] *past* **dreamed** /driːmd,
dremt/ or **dreamt** /dremt/ to desire something
very much and hope that it happens • *Ever
since that defeat, he had dreamed of revenge.*

□ **dream up** *obj*, **dream** *obj* **up** /'-'-/ *v adv* [M]
to invent (something new) by using a lot of imagination • *The Gerbils is an odd name for a
baseball team—who dreamed it up?*

dreary /'drɪr·i/ *adj* unattractive and having
nothing of any interest, and therefore likely
to make you sad • *It was a gray, dreary day,
with periods of rain.*

dredge /dredʒ/ *v* [T] to pull up a lot of sand
or other things from the bottom of an area of
water • *The harbor is being dredged.*

□ **dredge up** *obj*, **dredge** *obj* **up** /'-'-/ *v adv* [M]
to bring to the attention of someone (some-
thing bad that happened in the past) • *Once
this sexual harassment case was settled, people
would dredge up further claims of sexual misbehavior.*

dregs /dregz/ *pl n* the solid bits that sink to
the bottom of some liquids, such as wine or
coffee • If you describe people as the dregs,
you consider them to be the most worthless
type: *the dregs of society*

drench /drentʃ/ *v* [T] to make (someone or
something) extremely wet • *The rain drenched
my clothes.*

dress PIECE OF CLOTHING /dres/ *n* [C] a piece of
clothing for a woman that covers the top of the
body and part or all of the legs • *Cindy wore a
black dress to the party.*

dress PUT ON CLOTHES /dres/ *v* [I/T] to put
clothes on (someone else, esp. a child, or yourself) • *She dresses the kids for school every day.*
[T] • To dress is also to wear clothes of a particular type: *He always dresses neatly.* [I] • To
dress up is to wear more formal clothes than
you usually wear, or to change your appearance by wearing things that are different from
what you usually wear: *You don't need to dress
up for the party.* ○ *The children dressed up as
ghosts for Halloween.* • A **dressing room** is a
room, esp. in a theater, where a person can
dress and get ready for a performance.

dress /dres/ *n* [U] clothes of a particular type
or style • A **dress code** is a particular way that
people must dress in particular places or for
particular events: *The school's dress code does
not permit anyone to wear jeans.*

dressed /drest/ *adj* wearing clothes, or wearing all your usual clothes • *I'm getting
dressed—I'll be ready in a minute.*

dressy /'dres·i/ *adj* (of clothing) suitable for formal occasions • *I have some dressy shoes that I can wear to the wedding.*

dress SALAD /dres/ *v* [T] to add a liquid mixture, such as oil and vinegar, to a salad for additional flavor

dressing /'dres·ɪŋ/ *n* [C/U] **salad dressing**, see at SALAD

dress INJURY /dres/ *v* [T] to treat (an injury) by cleaning it and putting medicine or a protective covering on it • *A doctor in the emergency room dressed the wound.*

dressing /'dres·ɪŋ/ *n* [C] a protective covering put on an injury, esp. when there has been bleeding through the skin • *You have to change the dressing every day.*

dresser /'dres·ər/ *n* [C] a piece of bedroom furniture with drawers, usually with a mirror on top, used esp. for keeping clothes in • *I keep my socks in the bottom drawer of the dresser.*

dressy /'dres·i/ *adj* • See at DRESS PUT ON CLOTHES.

drew /druː/ *past simple of* DRAW

dribble MOVE SLOWLY /'drɪb·əl/ *v* [I] to move or happen slowly in small amounts or a few at a time • *Customers dribbled in and out all day.* • When a liquid dribbles, it escapes slowly in small drops: *Juice dribbled down the baby's chin.*

dribble /'drɪb·əl/ *n* [C] • *There has been only a dribble of tourists since the terrorist attack.*

dribble MOVE BALL /'drɪb·əl/ *v* [I/T] in BASKETBALL, to move (a ball) by using your hand to bounce it against the ground, or (in SOCCER) by kicking it repeatedly

dribble /'drɪb·əl/ *n* [C] • *He took one dribble and then passed the ball.*

dribs /'drɪbz/ *pl n* • **In dribs and drabs** is in small amounts, or a few at a time: *The audience arrived in dribs and drabs.*

dried /draɪd/ *past simple and past participle of* **dry**, see at DRY NOT WET

drier /'draɪ·ər/ *comparative of* DRY • See also **dryer** at DRY NOT WET.

dries /draɪz/ *present simple of* **dry**, see at DRY NOT WET

drift MOVE /drɪft/ *v* [I] to move slowly, esp. as a result of outside forces, with no control over direction • *He stopped rowing and let the boat drift.* • If someone or something drifts, they change in a gradual way that seems to be controlled by outside forces: *I finally drifted off to sleep.*

drift /drɪft/ *n* [C] a gradual change that seems to be controlled by outside forces • *Many people experience a drift toward more conservative politics as they get older.* • A drift is also a pile of something that is made larger by the force of the wind: *The state police closed the highway because of deep snow drifts.*

drifter /'drɪf·tər/ *n* [C] *disapproving* a person who moves from one place to another or from one job to another without any real purpose

drift MEANING /drɪft/ *n* [U] the general meaning or message of something said or written • *After a minute I caught his drift and grinned back.*

driftwood /'drɪf·twʊd/ *n* [U] wood floating in the sea or left on a beach by the action of the waves

drill CUT A HOLE /drɪl/ *v* [I/T] to cut or dig (a hole) into something • *First, drill a small hole in the board.* [T]

drill /drɪl/ *n* [C] a tool or machine that cuts or digs into something to make holes

drill REPEATED ACTIVITY /drɪl/ *n* [C/U] practice involving repetition of an activity in order to improve a skill, or a particular occasion for such practice • *For homework, complete the drill on irregular verbs on pages 30 through 35.* [C]

drill /drɪl/ *v* [T] • *The teacher drills them in arithmetic every day.*

□ **drill** *obj* **into** *obj* /'-'-'--/ *v prep* [T] to tell (something) to (someone) again and again until they know it • *This attention to detail is drilled into the top managers.*

drily /'draɪ·li/ *adv* • See **dryly** at DRY HUMOR.

drink TAKE LIQUID /drɪŋk/ *v* [I/T] *past simple* **drank** /dræŋk/, *past part* **drunk** /drʌŋk/ to take in and swallow (an amount of liquid) through the mouth • *She drinks a glass of orange juice every morning.* [T]

drink /drɪŋk/ *n* [C/U] • *May I have a drink of water?* [C]

drinking /'drɪŋ·kɪŋ/ *n* [U] • **Drinking water** is water that is suitable for drinking. • A **drinking fountain** is a device, usually in a public place, that can send up a flow of water for drinking.

drinker /'drɪŋ·kər/ *n* [C] a person who drinks (a stated type of liquid) • *a coffee drinker*

drink ALCOHOL /drɪŋk/ *n* [C] a liquid containing alcohol that people take for pleasure • *The bartender refused to give him another drink, because he'd already had too much.*

drink /drɪŋk/ *v* [I] *past simple* **drank** /dræŋk/, *past part* **drunk** /drʌŋk/ to take in an alcoholic liquid • *I didn't drink at all when I was pregnant.*

drinking /'drɪŋ·kɪŋ/ *n* [U] • If someone has a **drinking problem**, they regularly drink too much alcohol.

drinker /'drɪŋ·kər/ *n* [C] a person who drinks liquids that contain alcohol, esp. regularly • A **heavy drinker** is someone who drinks a lot of alcohol. • A **social drinker** is someone who drinks alcohol at social events where alcohol is served, and not usually at other times.

□ **drink to** /'--/ *v prep* [T] (of two or more people) to hold your glasses up, often touch them together, and then drink from them to honor or express your good wishes for (something or someone) • *Let's drink to Jessica and wish her well in her new job.*

drip /drɪp/ *v* [I/T] **-pp-** to fall in drops, or let

(liquid) fall in drops • *The sweat dripped down his nose and cheeks.* [I]

drip /drɪp/ *n* [C/U] • *He heard the drip of a leaky faucet.* [U] • If a piece of clothing is **drip-dry**, it is made to be washed and hung up to dry without the need for IRONING (= using a device that presses it to make it flat): *a drip-dry shirt*

dripping /'drɪp·ɪŋ/ *adj* [not gradable] • *She arrived in a rainstorm, dripping wet* (= with her clothes completely wet).

drive USE VEHICLE /draɪv/ *v* [I/T] *past simple* **drove** /droʊv/, *past part* **driven** /'drɪv·ən/ to travel in (a car or other motor vehicle), esp. as the person who operates it, or to travel (a distance) in a motor vehicle • *We drove 40 miles to visit my aunt.* [T] ○ *She drove through Pennsylvania to Ohio.* [I] ○ *She never learned how to drive* (= operate a car). [I] ○ *I'll drive you to the station* (= take you there in my car). [T] • (*law*) If you are **driving while intoxicated** (*abbreviation* **DWI**), you are operating a motor vehicle after having drunk more alcohol than you are legally allowed to. • **Drive-by** means while passing by in a vehicle: *There was a drive-by shooting that left one person dead and two others injured.* • A **drive-in** is a business or part of a business that you can use or visit while staying in your car: *a drive-in restaurant* ○ *I deposited my check at the bank's drive-in window.*

drive /draɪv/ *n* [C] • *We have a 200-mile drive ahead of us.* • A drive is also a road for cars and is sometimes used as part of a name: *Riverside Drive* LP ADDRESSES • A **driveway** is a short, usually private road that leads from a public street to a person's house or GARAGE (= building where a car is kept).

driver /'draɪ·vər/ *n* [C] • *a bus driver* • **Driver's education** is instruction given in schools to teach students how to operate a car. • A **driver's license** is a document that proves that you are legally allowed to drive a car or other motor vehicle: *I got my driver's license when I was 16.*

drive FORCE /draɪv/ *v* [T] *past simple* **drove** /droʊv/, *past part* **driven** /'drɪv·ən/ to force (someone or something) to go somewhere or do something • *He drove a nail into the wall.* ○ *He was driven* (= His actions were caused) *by greed.* • To **drive a hard bargain** is to strongly defend a position that is very much to your advantage when reaching an agreement: *He drives a hard bargain, but we finally made a deal.* • (*infml*) If someone or something **drives** you **crazy/nuts**, it makes you upset: *We love our two-year-old, but sometimes she drives us crazy.*

drive /draɪv/ *n* [C/U] strong determination to do or achieve something • *Intelligence isn't enough—you've got to have the drive to succeed.* [U] • A drive is also a basic human need that

has a strong effect on behavior: *the sex drive* [C]

driving /'draɪ·vɪŋ/ *adj* [not gradable] happening with great power or force • *They arrived in a driving rainstorm.* • A **driving force** is the person or thing that is most important in making something happen: *He was the driving force behind the new ballet company.*

drive PROVIDE POWER /draɪv/ *v* [T] *past simple* **drove** /droʊv/, *past part* **driven** /'drɪv·ən/ to provide the power to make (a machine) operate • *The water pump is driven by a windmill.*

drive PLANNED EFFORT /draɪv/ *n* [C] a planned, usually long-lasting, effort to achieve something • *The university sponsored a blood drive* (= effort to collect blood) *for the Red Cross.*

□ **drive at** /'-,-,-/ *v prep* [T] to try to explain or say (something) • *I can't understand what she's driving at.*

drivel /'drɪv·əl/ *n* [U] something written or said that is completely worthless; nonsense • *The papers are filled with drivel about movie stars.*

drizzle /'drɪz·əl/ *n* [U] a slight rain • *We had fog and drizzle earlier, but now it's sunny.*

drizzle /'drɪz·əl/ *v* [I] • *It's been drizzling on and off all day.*

droll /droʊl/ *adj* [-er/-est] only amusing in an unusual way • *I always loved his droll sense of humor.*

drone /droʊn/ *n* [U] a low, continuous noise • *I could hear the drone of an airplane.*

drone /droʊn/ *v* [I] • *The radio droned in the background while we talked.* • To **drone on** is to talk in a low voice that does not change and is considered boring.

drool /druːl/ *v* [I] to have some SALIVA (= natural, watery liquid) come out of the mouth • *The baby drools and laughs, and it makes me happy.* • (*infml*) To drool is also to show great interest and pleasure: *American businessmen would drool at the thought such low taxes.*

droop /druːp/ *v* [I] to bend or hang down • *The old woman sighed and pushed back a drooping strand of iron-gray hair.*

drop FALL /drɑp/ *v* [I/T] **-pp-** to fall intentionally or unintentionally, or to let (something) fall • *She dropped her keys on a table beside the door.* [T] ○ *The book dropped to the floor.* [I] ○ (*fig.*) *I was so exhausted that I was ready to drop* (= to fall down). [I] • If you **drop a hint**, you suggest something without saying it directly: *He dropped a few hints about some gifts he'd like to get.* • If someone **drops dead**, they die suddenly and unexpectedly. • (*slang*) If you tell someone to **drop dead**, you are telling them that you are very angry with them: *When he said he was too busy to help, I told him to drop dead.*

drop /drɑp/ *n* [C] • **At the drop of a hat** means easily, with little encouragement: *I hate* *to speak in public, but she'll get up on stage at the drop of a hat.*

drop LOWER /drɑp/ *v* [I/T] **-pp-** to move or change to a lower level, or to make (something) lower or less • *The temperature dropped nearly 50 degrees in 24 hours.* [I] ○ *We are going to have to drop our prices.* [T]

drop /drɑp/ *n* [U] • *It's a drop* (= distance down) *of over 150 feet from the top of the Niagara Falls.*

drop STOP /drɑp/ *v* [T] **-pp-** to stop (something you were doing or planning to do) • *After winning a pay raise, the union dropped its other demands.* ○ *He was dropped from* (= taken off) *the team because of his grades.* • If you **drop everything**, you immediately stop what we were doing in order to do something else: *We dropped everything and rushed him to the hospital.*

drop SMALL AMOUNT /drɑp/ *n* [C] a very small amount of a liquid • *I just felt a drop of rain.* • **A drop in the bucket** is something small and unimportant, esp. when compared with something else: *We were paid about $50,000, but that was a drop in the bucket compared to what some other companies got.*

dropper /'drɑp·ər/ *n* [C] a small tube with a rubber container at one end which is pressed and released to draw a liquid into the tube, and which can then be lightly pressed to release very small amounts of the liquid

□ **drop by** /'-'-/ *v adv* [I], *v prep* [T] to come to see someone (sometimes at a stated place), usually briefly and without a specific invitation • *Our neighbor's kids drop by (the house) almost every day.* [I/T]

□ **drop in** /'-'-/ *v adv* [I] to come for a visit, esp. without having received an invitation for a specific time • *Drop in whenever you're in the neighborhood.*

□ **drop off** BEGIN TO SLEEP /'-'-/ *v adv* [I] to begin to sleep • *I must have dropped off during the show, because I don't remember how it ended.*

□ **drop off** *obj* LEAVE, **drop** *obj* **off** /'-'-/ *v adv* [M] to take (someone or something), esp. by car, and leave them at a particular place • *I'm about to leave—can I drop you off somewhere on my way home?*

□ **drop out** /'-'-/ *v adv* [I] to stop going (to) school before finishing the course of instruction • *He dropped out of school when he was 16.*

dropout /'drɑp·ɑut/ *n* [C] a student who leaves school before finishing the course of instruction • *As a high school dropout he'll never get a decent job.*

droppings /'drɑp·ɪŋz/ *pl n* excrement produced by animals or birds • *We found mouse droppings in the garage.*

drought /drɑut/ *n* [C/U] a long period when there is little or no rain

drove /droʊv/ *past simple of* DRIVE

drown /drɑun/ *v* [I/T] to die by being under water and unable to breathe, or to kill (someone) by causing this to happen • *He drowned in a boating accident.* [I] • (*fig.*) If a person drowns themselves or drowns something in a liquid, they drink or use a lot of it: *I was drowning myself in bourbon.* [T always + adv/prep]

□ **drown out** *obj*, **drown** *obj* **out** /'-'-/ *v adv* [M] (of a sound) to be loud enough to block the sound of (something else) • *The sound of the telephone was drowned out by the vacuum cleaner.*

drowsy /'drɑu·zi/ *adj* feeling sleepy esp. when it is not the usual time to sleep • *The room is so warm it's making me drowsy.*

drowsiness /'drɑu·zi·nəs/ *n* [U]

drubbing /'drʌb·ɪŋ/ *n* [C usually sing] a beating or bad defeat, esp. in a sports competition

drudgery /'drʌdʒ·ə·ri/ *n* [U] hard, boring work • *Cleaning the oven is sheer drudgery.*

drug MEDICINE /drʌg/ *n* [C] any chemical that is used as a medicine • *over-the-counter/prescription drugs* • A **drugstore** is a store that sells medicines and usually other goods, esp. products relating to cleaning and caring for the body.

drug /drʌg/ *v* [T] **-gg-** to give (someone or something) a chemical that causes a loss of feeling or of consciousness • *He couldn't talk to us because he had been drugged.*

druggist /'drʌg·əst/ *n* [C] a PHARMACIST

drug ILLEGAL SUBSTANCE /drʌg/ *n* [C/U] any of various chemicals, including illegal substances, that are taken esp. repeatedly for pleasure, to improve someone's performance of an activity, or because a person cannot stop using it • *a drug addict/dealer* [U] ○ *Heroin and cocaine are illegal drugs.* [C] ○ *She began to suspect that her son was on/taking/doing drugs.* [pl] ○ *Drug trafficking* (= Trading in illegal drugs) *is an international problem.* [U]

druggie /'drʌg·i/ *n* [C] *slang* a person who frequently uses illegal drugs

drum INSTRUMENT /drʌm/ *n* [C] a musical instrument, usually with a skin stretched over the end of a hollow tube or bowl, played by hitting with the hand or a stick • A **drumstick** is a stick for beating a drum. See also DRUMSTICK.

drum /drʌm/ *v* [I] **-mm-** to make a rhythmic sound by hitting repeatedly • *The rain drummed on the tin roof.*

drummer /'drʌm·ər/ *n* [C] a musician who plays a drum

drum CONTAINER /drʌm/ *n* [C] a large, cylindrical container usually used for storing liquids • *an oil drum*

□ **drum** *obj* **into** *obj* /'-'--/ *v prep* [T] to teach (something) to (someone) by frequent repeating • *The teacher drummed the names of the state capitals into our heads.*

□ **drum** *obj* **out of** *obj* /'-'--/ *v adv prep* [T] to remove (someone from a job, group, etc.) because of something bad they have done • *The chairman was drummed out of office.*

□ **drum up** *obj*, **drum** *obj* **up** /'-'-/ *v adv* [M] to encourage the development of (something) • *I'm making calls to drum up some business.*

drumstick /'drʌm·stɪk/ *n* [C] the lower part of the leg of a TURKEY (= large bird) or chicken eaten as food • *turkey drumsticks* • See also **drumstick** at DRUM INSTRUMENT.

drunk LIQUID /drʌŋk/ *past participle of* DRINK

drunk TOO MUCH ALCOHOL /drʌŋk/ *adj* unable to speak or act in the usual way because of having had too much alcohol • *After four glasses of wine, he was drunk.* • **Drunk driving** is the act of someone who operates a motor vehicle when they have had too much alcohol and cannot drive safely. ○ *His daughter was killed by a* **drunk driver.**

drunk /drʌŋk/ *n* [C] a person who regularly drinks too much alcohol and often drinks in public or behaves in a drunken way in public • *Now a white-haired, stubborn woman, she shoves drunks out of her doorway and walks to neighborhood church Bingo games.*

drunken /'drʌŋ·kən/ *adj* under the influence of alcohol • *a drunken bum* • **Drunken** can describe a situation in which a lot of alcohol has been drunk: *a drunken brawl*

drunkenness /'drʌŋ·kən·nəs/ *n* [U] • *You don't see much public drunkenness around here.*

dry NOT WET /draɪ/ *adj* [*-er/-est* only] without water or liquid in, on, or around something • *Are the clothes dry yet?* • If hair or skin is dry, it lacks natural oils: *Do you have a shampoo for dry hair?* • If the weather is dry, there is little wetness in the air and no chance of rain. • To **dry-clean** means to clean (clothes) with chemicals, not water. • A **dry cleaner** is a store where clothes are cleaned with chemicals. ○ *Would you pick up my* **dry cleaning** (= clothes cleaned by chemicals)?

dry /draɪ/ *v* [I/T] he/she/it **dries**, **drying**, *past* **dried** • *I can't go out until my hair dries.* [I] ○ *The woman dried her hands on a towel and returned to the table.* [T] ○ *If you don't keep food covered, it dries out.* [I]

dryer, **drier** /'draɪ·ər/ *n* [C] a machine that makes wet things dry • *a hair/clothes dryer*

dryness /'draɪ·nəs/ *n* [U]

dry NO ALCOHOL /draɪ/ *adj* [not gradable] (of a place) not permitting alcoholic drinks to be sold • *Back then, most of Iowa was dry, and you had to drive to Illinois to get a drink.*

dry NOT SWEET /draɪ/ *adj* [*-er/-est* only] (of drinks) not tasting sweet • *dry red wine*

dry NOT INTERESTING /draɪ/ *adj* [*-er/-est* only] not interesting or exciting • *The book is packed with information but it is a little dry.*

dry AMUSING /draɪ/ *adj* [*-er/-est* only] amusing in a way that is not obvious and can be missed • *a dry wit*

dryly, **drily** /'draɪ·li/ *adv* • *Thanks for the warning, Tachi said dryly.*

dry run /'draɪ·rʌn/ *n* [C] an occasion in which you practice a particular activity or performance in preparation for the real event • *We had a dry run of the inauguration ceremony yesterday.*

dual /'duː·əl/ *adj* [not gradable] having two parts, or combining two things • *This room serves a dual purpose—it's both a study and a guest room.* • Someone with dual citizenship has the nationality of two countries at the same time.

dub NAME /dʌb/ *v* [T] **-bb-** to give (something or someone) a particular name, esp. describing what you think of them • *At age 21 Ella Fitzgerald was dubbed "The First Lady of Swing."*

dub CHANGE /dʌb/ *v* [T] **-bb-** to use (different voices, sounds, or images) in a movie, television program, recording, etc., to replace others made originally or as added parts • *She is no singer, and her rock 'n' roll numbers were dubbed.* ○ *The scenery is dubbed into the CD-ROM movie using computer-graphics software.*

dubious /'duː·bi·əs/ *adj* probably not true or not completely true; doubtful • *"The immigrants," they say, "are taking our jobs"—a dubious assertion.* • Dubious can also mean not to be trusted, or not completely moral: *a dubious character*

duchess /'dʌtʃ·əs/ *n* [C] (in some countries) the title of a woman who has a very high social rank, or who is the wife of a DUKE, or the person herself

duck BIRD /dʌk/ *n* [C/U] a bird that lives by water and has short legs with WEBBED feet (= feet with toes joined by skin), or the meat of this bird

duck MOVE /dʌk/ *v* [I/T] to move (your head or the top part of your body) quickly down, esp. to avoid being hit, or to avoid (a hit) by moving your head or bending your body • *Duck your head or you'll bang it on the door frame.* [T] ○ *She ducked below the surface of the rippling water.* [I] • To duck is also to move quickly to a place, esp. in order not to be seen: *When he saw them coming, he ducked into a store.* [I] • To duck a subject or question is to avoid it: *He accused the president of ducking the issue of campaign finance reform.* [T]

duct /dʌkt/ *n* [C] a tube or pipe in a building that carries liquid or air or protects wires • *Air conditioning requires ventilating ducts.* • A duct is also a narrow tube in the body that carries a liquid: *tear ducts*

dud /dʌd/ *n* [C] something that is not successful or is of little value • *The movie turned out to be a dud.*

dude /duːd/ *n* [C] *slang* any man, or one who comes from a city and dresses in a stylish way • A **dude ranch** is a place to go for a vacation where activities such as riding horses are offered.

due OWED /duː/ *adj* [not gradable] owed as a

debt or as a right • *I'm due a refund for the sweater I returned.* ○ *Our thanks are due to everyone who gave so generously.* ○ *The rent is now due* (= should be paid).

dues /duːz/ *pl n* the official payments you make to an organization that you belong to • *Members of the club pay $50 in annual dues.*

due EXPECTED /duː/ *adj* [not gradable] expected (to happen, arrive, etc.) at a particular time • *What time is the next train due?* ○ *The meeting is now due to take place next week.* [+ *to* infinitive]

due RESULTING /duː/ *adj* • **Due to** can mean because of: *Due to computer problems, the checks will be late.* ○ *Due to bad weather, the flight was canceled.*

due USUAL / CORRECT /duː/ *adj* [not gradable] according to the usual custom or the correct process • *Phillips took due note of the key statistics.* ○ *In due course the vineyard became a real money maker.*

duly /ˈduːˑliː/ *adv* [not gradable] • *duly elected officials* ○ *Duly signed by the president, the bill will become law.*

due STRAIGHT /duː/ *adv* [not gradable] (of north, south, east, or west) exactly, straight • *They headed due north.*

duel /ˈduːˑəl/ *n* [C] a formal fight, using guns or SWORDS (= weapons with long, sharp blades), arranged esp. in the past between two people to decide an argument

duet /duːˈet/ *n* [C] two people who sing or play musical instruments together, or a piece of music written for two people • Compare QUARTET, QUINTET, TRIO.

duffel bag, **duffle bag** /ˈdʌfˑəlˌbæg/ *n* [C] a strong bag with a round bottom, often with a string or strap at the top that is used to close it and to carry it

dug /dʌg/ *past simple and past participle of* DIG

dugout /ˈdʌgˑaʊt/ *n* [C] a shelter where baseball players sit when they are not on the field

duh /dʌ/ *exclamation slang* used to express your belief that what was said was extremely obvious • *"A lot of people care about money." "Well, duh."*

du jour /dəˈʒʊr/ *adj* [only after n] (of food in a restaurant) the particular type available today • *The soup du jour is tomato rice.*

duke /duːk/ *n* [C] (in some countries) a title of a man who has a very high social rank or who is the ruler of a small, independent country, or the person himself

dull BORING /dʌl/ *adj* [-er/-est only] not interesting or exciting; boring • *Many of the courtroom events were dull and routine.* ○ *The lecture was dry, dull, and full of statistics.*

dull NOT BRIGHT /dʌl/ *adj* [-er/-est only] not clear, bright, or shiny • *The day started off dull and overcast with a threat of showers.*

dull NOT SHARP /dʌl/ *adj* [-er/-est only] (esp. of sound or pain) not sharp or clear • *a dull knife*

○ *I heard a dull thud from the kitchen.* ○ *She felt a dull ache at the back of her head.*

dull /dʌl/ *v* [T] • *He said he drank to dull his misery.*

duly /ˈduːˑliː/ *adv* [not gradable] • See at DUE USUAL/CORRECT.

dumb STUPID /dʌm/ *adj* [-er/-est only] *infml* stupid • *Don't say anything—just act/play dumb* (= pretend to be stupid or not to know something).

dumb SILENT /dʌm/ *adj* [not gradable] *dated* permanently or temporarily unable to speak

dumbbell /ˈdʌmˑbel/ *n* [C] a short metal bar with a weight on each end that you lift up and down to strengthen your arms and shoulders

dumbfounded /ˈdʌmˌfaʊnˑdəd, dʌmˈfaʊn-/ *adj* [not gradable] so shocked and surprised that you cannot speak • *Ray is dumbfounded at the questions.*

dummy MODEL /ˈdʌmˑiː/ *n* [C] a large model of a human • *They use crash-test dummies in order to improve safety equipment in cars.*

dummy NOT REAL /ˈdʌmˑiː/ *adj* [not gradable] not real but having a similar appearance to something else • *They set up a dummy corporation to try to hide their identities.*

dummy STUPID PERSON /ˈdʌmˑiː/ *n* [C] a stupid or silly person • *Taxpayers are not dummies, and they are going to know how politicians are trying to fool them.*

dump /dʌmp/ *v* [T] to put down or drop (something heavy) in a careless way, or to get rid of (something or someone no longer wanted) • *The ship was accused of dumping garbage overboard.* ○ *She missed too many rehearsals and was dumped from the cast.* • A **dump truck** is a truck with an open container at the back that can be raised at an angle so that its load falls out.

dump truck

dump /dʌmp/, **garbage dump** *n* [C] a place where people are allowed to leave their garbage • *You have to bring household garbage to the town dump.* • (*infml*) A dump is also any place that is messy or that you do not like because it is of low quality: *Why are you staying in this dump?*

dumpling /ˈdʌmˑplɪŋ/ *n* [C] a small ball of DOUGH (= flour and water mixed together) cooked and eaten with soup or meat, or a filling of fruit, meat, or vegetables covered with dough and steamed, baked, or fried

dumps /dʌmps/ *n infml* • If someone is **(down) in the dumps**, they are unhappy: *She's down in the dumps because all her friends are out of town.*

Dumpster /ˈdʌmpˑstər/ *n* [C] *trademark* a large, metal container into which people put garbage or building waste, and which is brought to and taken away from a place by a special truck when requested

dumpy /ˈdʌm·pi/ *adj* short and fat • *Does this dress make me look dumpy?*

dune /duːn/, **sand dune** *n* [C] a hill of sand beside a beach or in a desert

dung /dʌŋ/ *n* [U] solid excrement from animals, esp. cattle and horses; MANURE

dungarees /ˌdʌŋ·ɡəˈriːz/ *pl n* pants or work clothes made of DENIM (= strong cotton cloth)

dungeon /ˈdʌn·dʒən/ *n* [C] an underground prison

dunk /dʌŋk/ *v* [T] to put (a cookie, bread, pastry, etc.) into a liquid such as coffee or soup for a short time before eating it • *She dunked her doughnut in her coffee.* • If you dunk a person, you push them under water: *The kids in the pool kept dunking one another.* • If you dunk a BASKETBALL, you score by jumping high enough to throw the ball down through the goal.

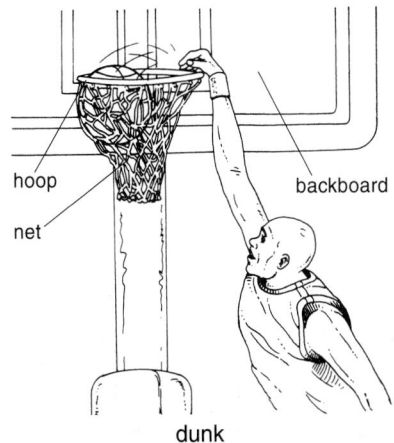

hoop
net
backboard

dunk

dunno /dəˈnoʊ/ *exclamation not standard* (spelled the way it is sometimes spoken) I don't know • *"Where are we exactly?" "Dunno."*

duo /ˈduː·oʊ/ *n* [C] *pl* **duos** a pair, esp. of singers, musicians, or other performers

dupe /duːp/ *v* [T] to cheat (someone) by telling lies or by deceiving them • *They duped me into giving them money by saying it would go to charity.*

dupe /duːp/ *n* [C] someone who has been tricked • *an innocent dupe*

duplex /ˈduː·pleks/ *n* [C] a house having two separate apartments, each with its own entrance • A duplex (or **duplex apartment**) is also an apartment on two floors of a building.

duplicate /ˈduː·plɪˌkeɪt/ *v* [T] to make an exact copy of (something) • *Businesses should make sure important records and files are duplicated and stored in another location.*

duplicate /ˈduː·plɪ·kət/ *adj* [not gradable] • *a duplicate key*

duplicate /ˈduː·plɪ·kət/ *n* [C] • *I lost the original form so they sent me a duplicate.* • If a

form is **in duplicate**, an exact copy has been made of it: *The application has to be completed in duplicate.*

duplication /ˌduː·plɪˈkeɪ·ʃən/ *n* [U]

durable /ˈdʊr·ə·bəl/ *adj* able to last a long time without being damaged • **Durable goods** are items like cars and home APPLIANCES (= large pieces of equipment for the home) that are intended to last several years or longer.

duration /dʊˈreɪ·ʃən/ *n* [U] the length of time that something lasts • *He planned a stay of two years' duration.*

duress /dʊˈres/ *n* [U] threats used to force a person to do something • *He signed the contract under duress.*

during [THROUGH] /ˈdʊr·ɪŋ/ *prep* from the beginning to the end of (a particular period) • *They work during the night and sleep by day.*

during [AT SOME POINT IN] /ˈdʊr·ɪŋ/ *prep* at some time between the beginning and the end of (a period) • *We hope to spend some weekends in the country during the summer.*

dusk /dʌsk/ *n* [U] the time just before night when the day is losing its light but it is not yet dark

dust /dʌst/ *n* [U] dry dirt in the form of powder that covers surfaces inside a building, or very small dry pieces of earth, sand, or other substances • *The furniture was covered with dust.* • A **dust jacket** is a sheet of stiff paper, often in color, wrapped around the cover of a book to protect and advertise it.

dust /dʌst/ *v* [I/T] to remove dry dirt in the form of powder (from a surface) • *I was dusting (her desk) when I noticed the piece of paper.* [I/T] • To **dust off** something is to prepare it for use, esp. after it has not been used for a long time: *Winter is coming, so dust off your skis.*

dusty /ˈdʌs·ti/ *adj* • *Piles of dusty books lay on the floor.*

duty [RESPONSIBILITY] /ˈduːt̬·i/ *n* [C/U] something that you have to do because it is part of your job, or something that you feel is the right thing to do • *Joe is still on jury duty.* [U] ○ *Nobody likes it, but we have a duty to pay taxes.* [C] ○ *One of her duties was to see that all the merchandise was locked away.* [C] • To be **on duty** is to be actively working on your job: *As the diplomatic correspondent of The New York Times, he was on duty all four nights of the debates.*

dutiful /ˈduːt̬·ɪ·fəl/ *adj* (of a person) obedient or (of an action) done because it is necessary or expected • *a dutiful child*

duty [TAX] /ˈduːt̬·i/ *n* [C/U] a tax paid to the government, esp. on things that you bring into a country • **Duty-free** goods are luxury goods that can be bought, esp. in airports, and on which tax does not have to be paid.

dwarf /dwɔːrf/ *n* [C] a person who is much smaller than the usual size, or (in stories for children) a creature like a little man, esp. one having magical powers

dwarf /dwɔːrf/ *v* [T] to make (something) seem small by comparison • *This year's budget dwarfs all previous ones.*

dweeb /dwiːb/ *n* [C] *slang* a person who is physically and socially awkward and lacks confidence

dwell /dwel/ *v* [I always + adv/prep] *past* **dwelt** /dwelt/ or **dwelled** *slightly fml* to live (in a place or in a particular way) • *She dwelt in South Africa for ten years.*

dweller /'dwel·ər/ *n* [C] a person who lives in a particular type of place • *city dwellers*

dwelling /'dwel·ɪŋ/ *n* [C] a place where people live • *The house was a modest one-story dwelling.*

□ **dwell on** /'-,-/ *v prep* [T] to think or talk about (something) a lot of the time • *"Let's not dwell on the past," she said.*

DWI *abbreviation for* **driving while intoxicated**, see at DRIVE USE VEHICLE

dwindle /'dwɪn·dəl/ *v* [I] to become less in number or smaller • *The community had dwindled to a tenth of its former size.*

dye /daɪ/ *v* [T] **dyeing**, *past* **dyed** to change the color of (something) using a special liquid • *He dyed his hair black.* • If someone has **dyed-in-the-wool** opinions, they hold them strongly and will not change them: *Lahti is a dyed-in-the-wool liberal.*

dye /daɪ/ *n* [C/U] a liquid substance for changing the color of things • *She dipped the material into the dye.* [U]

dying /'daɪ·ɪŋ/ *present participle of* DIE

dyke, **dike** /daɪk/ *n* [C] *slang* a homosexual woman; a LESBIAN • USAGE: This word is offensive.

dynamic /daɪ'næm·ɪk/ *adj* having a lot of ideas and enthusiasm; energetic and forceful • *a dynamic person*

dynamism /'daɪ·nə,mɪz·əm/ *n* [U]

dynamics /daɪ'næm·ɪks/ *pl n* forces that produce movement or change • *The fight for the leadership revealed a lot about the group's dynamics.* • (*specialized*) Dynamics is also the scientific study of the forces that produce movement.

dynamite /'daɪ·nə,maɪt/ *n* [U] a type of explosive • *a stick of dynamite* • A subject can be called dynamite if it could have a sudden and important influence on the way many people think or feel: *The Social Security issue is political dynamite.*

dynamite /'daɪ·nə,maɪt/ *v* [T] to use dynamite to destroy or break apart (something) in an explosion • *The rebels dynamited the railroad bridge.*

dynamo /'daɪ·nə,moʊ/ *n* [C] *pl* **dynamos** a device that changes energy of movement into electrical energy • (*fig.*) *She's a real dynamo* (= energetic force).

dynasty /'daɪ·nə·sti, -,næs·ti/ *n* [C] a series of rulers or leaders who are all from the same family, or a period when a country is ruled by them

dysentery /'dɪs·ən,ter·i/ *n* [U] an infectious disease of the bowels that causes the contents to be excreted more often and in a more liquid form than usual

dysfunctional /dɪs'fʌŋ·ʃən·əl/ *adj* not able to operate well; working badly • *a dysfunctional family*

dyslexia /dɪs'lek·si:·ə/ *n* [U] *medical* a difficulty with reading and writing often including a person's inability to see the difference between some letter shapes

dyslexic /dɪs'lek·sɪk/ *adj medical*

E, e

E LETTER , **e** /iː/ *n* [C] *pl* **E's** or **Es** or **e's** or **es**
the fifth letter of the English alphabet

E. EAST *n* [U], *adj abbreviation for* EAST or EAST-
ERN

E MUSICAL NOTE /iː/ *n* [C/U] *pl* **E's** or **Es** the third
note in the **major scale** (= series of notes) that
begins on the note C, or a set of notes based on
this note

e– /iː/ *combining form abbreviation for* ELEC-
TRONIC • *e-commerce* ○ *e-mail*

each /iːtʃ/ *pronoun, adj, adv* [not gradable]
every thing, person, etc., in a group of two or
more, considered separately • *There are five
leaflets—please take one of each.* ○ *Each of the
brothers has a different personality.* ○ *It's 500
miles each way.* ○ *The bill comes to $80, so that's
$20 each.* • LP AMOUNTS, DETERMINERS

each other /iːtʃˈʌð·ər/, **one another** *pronoun*
(not used as the subject of a sentence) the other person, or any or all the other people in a
group • *The couple kept looking at each other
and smiling.* ○ *They're always wearing each
other's clothes.*

EACH OTHER

Each other is used when each member of a
pair or group acts on or is connected to the
other(s) in the same way. *Emilia and Miguel
helped* **each other** *with the homework* means
Emilia helped Miguel and Miguel helped
Emilia.

Two people or more than two people can be
involved.

Jenny and Omar looked at **each other** *and
started to laugh.* • *The four brothers were
always hitting* **each other**.

Some people think that **each other** should be
used only when two are involved, but most people use the expression for two or more than two.

Each other can be used only as the object of a
verb or a preposition, not as the subject of a
verb.

*Anya and I work in the same building but we
hardly ever see* **each other**.

but

We each know what the other likes
not: *We know what each other likes.*

To form the possessive, add **'s** at the end of
other.

The two sisters borrowed **each other's**
clothes.

---

eager /ˈiː·gər/ *adj* [not gradable] having or
showing desire or interest • *Lots of eager volunteers responded to the appeal for help.* •
(*infml*) Someone described as an **eager beaver** is interested, enthusiastic, and willing to
work hard.

eagerly /ˈiː·gər·li/ *adv* [not gradable]
eagerness /ˈiː·gər·nəs/ *n* [U]

eagle /ˈiː·gəl/ *n* [C] a large, strong bird with a
curved beak that eats meat and has good sight
• Someone who is **eagle-eyed** or who has an
eagle eye, has good sight or notices everything.

ear BODY PART /ɪr/ *n* [C] either of the two organs in the head by which people or animals
hear sounds, or the part of this organ that is
outside the head • If someone has **an ear for**
music or languages, they are good at hearing,
repeating, or understanding these sounds. •
An **earache** is a pain in the inside part of your
ear. • An **eardrum** is a thin piece of tissue inside the ear that allows you to hear. • An **earlobe** (also **lobe**) is the soft, round part at the
bottom of the ear. • **Earmuffs** are a pair of
coverings for the ears connected by a curved
strip that goes over the head, and worn to keep
the ears warm. • **Earphones** are an electrical
device that fits over a person's ears, allowing
them to listen to a radio or STEREO. • An **ear-
ring** is a piece of jewelry, usually one of a pair,
worn in a hole in the ear or fixed to the ear by
a fastener. • An **ear-splitting** sound is
extremely loud.

ear PLANT PART /ɪr/ *n* [C] the top part of a grain
plant, such as wheat, which contains the seeds
• *an ear of corn*

earful /ˈɪr·fʊl/ *n* [U] angry, complaining
speech • *I'd better not be late for practice or the
coach will give me an earful.*

early /ˈɜr·li/ *adj, adv* [*-er/-est* only] near the beginning of (a period of time), or before the
usual, expected, or planned time • *I got up early this morning to walk the dog.* ○ *Sheena's in
her early thirties.* ○ *She arrived early for the interview.* ○ *If you finish early* (= before the end
of the allowed time) *you can go home.* ○ *Detroit
has been an automotive center since the early
days/years* (= the beginning time) *of car manufacturing.* ○ *Here's a dish I prepared earlier* (=
I made a short time ago). • **The early bird
gets/catches the worm** means the person
who gets up early or arrives first is the one
who is successful. • *It was a great race for Needles, who took the lead early on* (= shortly after the start). • An **early bird** is a person who
gets up or arrives early. • Compare LATE NEAR
THE END, LATE AFTER.

earmark /ˈɪr·mɑrk/ *v* [T] to intend (something) for a particular purpose • *Ten thousand
dollars of this year's budget is earmarked for
the renovation of the building.*

earn /ɜrn/ *v* [T] to receive (money) as payment
for work that you do, or to get (something) that
you deserve because of your abilities or actions • *This month's raise means that I'll be*

earning $45,000 a year. [T] ○ *After all the work I've done, I've earned a vacation.* [T]

earnings /ˈɜr·nɪŋz/ *pl n* the amount of money that you are paid for the work you do, or the profit that a company makes

earnest /ˈɜr·nəst/ *adj* [not gradable] sincere and serious • *She made an earnest attempt to convert me to her point of view.* • If something is done **in earnest**, it is done seriously.

earnestly /ˈɜr·nəs·tli/ *adv* [not gradable]

earnestness /ˈɜr·nəs·nəs/ *n* [U]

earshot /ˈɪr·ʃɑt/ *n* [U] the range of distance within which you can be heard or hear what someone is saying • *I hope the boss was well out of earshot when you made that nasty remark.*

earth PLANET /ɜrθ/ *n* [U] the planet third in order of distance from the sun, after Venus and before Mars; the world on which we live • *Earth looks incredibly beautiful from space.* ○ *His trainer called him the greatest boxer on earth* (= in the world). • (*infml*) **On earth** is used after the question words how, what, when, where, who, and why when asking how something that seemed impossible really did happen: *How on earth did this happen?* ○ *What on earth is that terrible noise?* • An **earthquake** is a sudden, violent movement of the earth's surface, often causing damage and sometimes loss of life. • If you describe something as **earthshaking** or **earth-shattering**, you mean that it is extreme or very great: *Earthshaking reforms are unlikely in the near future.*

earthly /ˈɜrθ·li/ *adj* [not gradable] happening in or related to the physical world or real life • *All my earthly possessions are in that moving van.*

earth SUBSTANCE /ɜrθ/ *n* [U] the loose substance of which a large part of the surface of the ground is made, and in which plants can grow; the land surface of the earth rather than the sky or sea • *The plowed earth looked dark and fertile.* • An **earthworm** is a common type of WORM (= small animal with a long, narrow, soft body), that moves through the earth.

earthworm

earthy /ˈɜr·θi/ *adj* of or relating to earth • *The cabin has an earthy smell.*

earthly /ˈɜrθ·li/ *adj* [not gradable] (used in questions or negatives) possible • *What earthly reason can she have for being so rude?*

earthy /ˈɜr·θi/ *adj* enjoying and being honest or clear about things connected to life, such as the body and emotions • *Some readers may find his writing offensive because of his earthy humor.*

ease LESSEN /iːz/ *v* [I/T] to make or become less severe, difficult, unpleasant, or painful • *These pills should ease the pain.* [T] • *At last the rain began to ease up* (= gradually stop or become less). [I] • *If his father doesn't ease up on him* (= treat him less severely), *he's going to leave home.* [I]

ease MOVE /iːz/ *v* [I/T] to move (something) slowly and carefully in a particular direction or into a particular position • *I eased through the crowd to the stage.* [I]

ease EASY EFFORT /iːz/ *n* [U] freedom from difficulty, effort, or pain • *She won the match with ease* (= without difficulty). • *He felt completely at ease* (= relaxed and comfortable) *with them.* • Soldiers who are **at ease** stand in a slightly relaxed position with their feet apart and their hands behind their back.

easel /ˈiː·zəl/ *n* [C] a frame, usually with three legs, that holds a picture, esp. one that an artist is painting or drawing

easily /ˈiː·zə·li/ *adv* [not gradable] • See at EASY NOT DIFFICULT.

east /iːst/ (*abbreviation* **E.**) *n* [U] the direction where the sun rises in the morning that is opposite west, or the part of an area or country that is in this direction • *The points of the compass are north, south, east, and west.* ○ *Most of the state's heavy industry is in the east.* • **The East** is Asia, esp. its eastern and southern parts: *She spent her childhood in the East, mostly in China and Japan.* • In the US, **the East** is the part of the country east of the Mississippi River.

east /iːst/ (*abbreviation* **E.**) *adj, adv* [not gradable] • *the east bank* ○ *Texas is east of New Mexico.* • In the US, the **east coast** is the part of the country near the Atlantic Ocean.

easterly /ˈiː·stər·li/ *adj* toward or near the east • *an easterly direction*

eastern /ˈiː·stərn/ (*abbreviation* **E.**) *adj* [not gradable] • *Milwaukee is in the eastern part of Wisconsin.*

easterner /ˈiː·stər·nər, -stə·nər/ *n* [C] a person from the eastern part of a country, or (in the US) a person from the part of the country east of the Mississippi River

eastward /ˈiːs·twərd/ *adj* [not gradable] toward the east • *the eastward trail*

eastward /ˈiːs·twərd/, **eastwards** /ˈiːs·twərdz/ *adv* [not gradable] toward the east • *The storm moved eastward toward Florida.*

Easter /ˈiː·stər/ *n* [C usually sing] a Christian religious holiday that celebrates the death and return to life with God of Jesus • An **Easter egg** is an egg with a painted or decorated shell.

easy NOT DIFFICULT /ˈiː·zi/ *adj, adv* needing little effort; not difficult • *She looked through the test trying to find an easy question.* • *Would a 10 a.m. appointment be easier for you?* ○ *She is very easy to talk to.* [+ *to* infinitive] ○ *Let's run the last two miles at an easy* (= not fast) *pace.* • If something is **(as) easy as pie**, it is very easy: *For Judy, getting a pilot's license was easy as pie.* • *"Why don't you just ask the company to pay?" "That's* **easier said than done** (= easy to suggest but much more difficult to make happen)." • The type of music that is described as **easy listening** is music that is softly played and pleasant to listen to. • (*infml*) *Until he was caught, he used to say that stealing cars was* **easy money** (= money that you get with little effort).

easily /'iː·zə·li/ *adv* • *Ever since his surgery he tires very easily* (= more quickly than usual).

easy COMFORTABLE /'iː·zi/ *adj, adv* [*-er/-est* only] free from worry, pain, or trouble; comfortable or calm • *With three children to support, her life has been far from easy.* ○ *I don't feel easy about leaving him alone in the house all day.* • *He lost most of his investment, but his attitude is* **easy come, easy go** (= Because he got it easily, he is not worried about losing it). • *"Can I put it down now?" "Yes, but it's fragile so* **easy does it** (= do it slowly and carefully)." • An **easy chair** is a big, soft, comfortable chair with arms. • Someone who is **easygoing** manages to accept and stay calm about things that usually anger or worry other people.

eat HAVE FOOD /iːt/ *v* [I/T] *past simple* **ate** /eɪt/, *past part* **eaten** /'iːt·ᵊn/ to put (food) into the mouth, chew it, and swallow it • *He ate a hamburger for lunch.* [T] ○ *When I've got a cold, I don't feel like eating.* [I] ○ *We usually eat* (= have a meal) *at about 7 p.m.* [I] ○ *Let's eat in/out* (= have a meal at home/at a restaurant) *tonight.* [I] • If someone **eats like a bird** or **eats like a horse**, they usually eat a very small amount of food or a lot of food. • If you have someone **eating out of the palm of** your **hand**, they always eagerly do what you ask them to do. • If you **eat** your **words**, you are forced to admit that you were wrong about something. • (*medical*) An **eating disorder** is an illness involving the amounts of food eaten, such as BULIMIA (NERVOSA) or ANOREXIA (NERVOSA).

eat DAMAGE /iːt/ *v* [I/T] *past simple* **ate** /eɪt/, *past part* **eaten** /'iːt·ᵊn/ to damage or destroy (something) • *Running water had gradually eaten into the rock, forming a channel.* [I always + adv/prep]

□ **eat away at** /ˌ--'--/ *v adv prep* [T] (of something bad) to continue to hurt (someone) because they are unable to forget it • *Guilt ate away at him, until he finally turned himself in to the police.*

□ **eat up** /'-ˌ-/ *v adv* [T] to use (something) so that little or nothing is left • *Legal costs ate up most of her savings.*

eaves /iːvz/ *pl n* the edge of a roof that sticks out over the walls

eavesdrop /'iːvz·drɑp/ *v* [I] **-pp-** to listen secretly to someone's private conversation • *The spy satellite will electronically eavesdrop on military and diplomatic communications.*

ebb /eb/ *v* [I] (of the sea or its TIDE) to move away from the coast and fall to a lower level, or, more generally, (of something) to become less or disappear • *He could feel his strength ebbing (away).*

ebb /eb/ *n* [U] • The **ebb and flow** (= frequently changing situation) *of politics in Washington goes on as usual.*

ebony /'eb·ə·ni/ *n* [U] a very hard, dark-colored wood, used esp. for making furniture

ebullient /ɪ'bʊl·jənt, ɪ'bʌl-/ *adj* excited and enthusiastic • *Moody is again ebullient about his church's future.*

eccentric /ɪk'sen·trɪk, ek-/ *adj* strange or unusual, sometimes in an amusing way • *eccentric behavior*

eccentric /ɪk'sen·trɪk, ek-/ *n* [C] • *She was an elderly eccentric who lived with 25 cats.*

eccentricity /ˌek·sen'trɪs·ət·i/ *n* [C/U] • *Although his reputation for eccentricity was well deserved, it was not true that he had asked to be buried in his car.* [U]

ecclesiastical /ɪ,kliː·ziː'æs·tɪ·kəl/, **ecclesiastic** /ɪ,kliː·ziː'æs·tɪk/ *adj* [not gradable] belonging to or connected with the Christian religion • *ecclesiastical history*

echo SOUND /'ek·oʊ/ *n* [C] *pl* **echoes** a sound that is heard again after it has been reflected off a surface such as a wall or a cliff • *The cave was filled with the echoes of our voices.*

echo /'ek·oʊ/ *v* [I] **echoes, echoing,** *past* **echoed** • *The sound of footsteps echoed through the hall.*

echo REPEAT /'ek·oʊ/ *v* [T] **echoes, echoing,** *past* **echoed** to express or think (what someone else has said or thought) • *Brownell's comments echoed the opinion of the majority of the commission members.*

echo /'ek·oʊ/ *n* [C] *pl* **echoes** • *The son's behavior is a clear echo of his father's.*

eclipse SUN / MOON /ɪ'klɪps/ *n* [C] the disappearance from view, either completely or partly, of the sun while the moon is moving between it and the earth, or the darkening of the moon while the SHADOW (= darkness) of the earth moves over it • *a solar/lunar eclipse*

eclipse BLOCK /ɪ'klɪps/ *v* [T] to become much more important and noticeable than (something) • *The state of the economy has eclipsed all other issues during the election campaign.*

ecology /ɪ'kɑl·ə·dʒi/ *n* [U] the relationship of living things to their environment and to each other, or the scientific study of this • *The oil spill caused great damage to the fragile ecology of the coastline.*

ecological /ˌiː·kə'lɑdʒ·ɪ·kəl, ˌek·ə-/ *adj*

ecologist /ɪ'kɑl·ə·dʒəst/ *n* [C] a person who studies the relationship between living things and their environment

economy SYSTEM /ɪ'kɑn·ə·mi/ *n* [C] the system of trade and industry by which the wealth of a country or region is made and used • *Tourism contributes millions of dollars to the region's economy.*

economic /ˌiː·kə'nɑm·ɪk, ˌek·ə-/ *adj* • *economic growth/policies*

economically /ˌiː·kə'nɑm·ɪ·kli, ˌek·ə-/ *adv* [not gradable]

economics /ˌiː·kə'nɑm·ɪks, ˌek·ə-/ *n* [U] the scientific study of the system by which a country's wealth is made and used

economist /ɪ'kɑn·ə·məst/ *n* [C] a person who studies or has a special knowledge of economics

economy SAVING MONEY /ɪ'kɑn·ə·mi/ *n* [U] the careful use and management of money or of time, energy, words, etc. • *For the purpose of economy, you may prefer to use a cheaper cut of meat in this recipe.* • An **economy class** ticket is the cheapest type of ticket for travel on an aircraft. • A package of something that is **economy-sized** is large and costs less for what you get when compared to smaller packages.

economical /ˌiː·kə'nɑm·ɪ·kəl, ˌek·ə-/ *adj* • *With rents so high, it wasn't economical to continue to live in the city.*

economize /ɪ'kɑn·ə·mɑɪz/ *v* [I] to intentionally reduce what you are spending or using • *You could economize on food by not eating in restaurants all the time.*

ecosystem /'iː·koʊ·sɪs·təm, 'ek·oʊ-/ *n* [C] all the plants, animals, and people living in an area considered together with their environment as a system of relationships • *They are working to preserve the delicately balanced ecosystem of these wetlands.*

ecstasy /'ek·stə·si/ *n* [U] a state of extreme happiness or pleasure • *sexual ecstasy*

ecstatic /ɪk'stæt̬·ɪk/ *adj* very happy and excited • *The new president was greeted by an ecstatic crowd.*

ecumenical /ˌek·jə'men·ɪ·kəl/ *adj* tending to support and encourage unity among the various divisions of the Christian religion • *an ecumenical service*

eczema /'ek·sə·mə, 'eg·zə-, ɪg'ziː-/ *n* [U] a skin condition in which areas of the skin become red, rough, and sore

eddy /'ed·i/ *v* [I] (of water, wind, smoke, etc.) to move fast in a circle • *The water eddied ceaselessly in the wake of the boat.*

eddy /'ed·i/ *n* [C]

edge OUTER POINT /edʒ/ *n* [C] the outer or farthest point of something • *the edge of a cliff/table* ○ *They walked down to the water's edge.* ○ (*fig.*) *Hitchcock's films often kept moviegoers at the edge of their seats* (= kept them eagerly interested).

edge LIMIT /edʒ/ *n* [C usually sing] a point beyond which something unpleasant or very noticeable is likely to happen • *It was reported that the company is on the edge of collapse.* ○ *The loss of his job almost pushed him over the edge.*

edge BLADE /edʒ/ *n* [C] the side of a blade that cuts, or any sharp part of an object • *Careful with that open can—it's got a very sharp edge.*

edge MOVE /edʒ/ *v* [always + adv/prep] to move slowly with gradual movements or in gradual stages • *A long line of traffic edged its way forward.* [T] ○ *Inflation has begun to edge up during the last six months.* [I]

edge ADVANTAGE /edʒ/ *n* [U] an advantage • *Because of her experience she has the edge over the other applicants.*

edge NERVOUS CONDITION /edʒ/ *n* [U] • If you are **on edge**, you are nervous and not relaxed.

edgy /'edʒ·i/ *adj* nervous or easily upset • *He paced the hallway looking edgy and impatient.*

edible /'ed·ə·bəl/ *adj* suitable or safe for eating • *Only the leaves of the plant are edible.*

edict /'iː·dɪkt/ *n* [C] *law* a public order given by an authority • *a court edict*

edifice /'ed·ə·fəs/ *n* [C] *fml* a large building • *The state capitol is an imposing edifice topped by a large dome.*

edit /'ed·ət/ *v* [T] to prepare (text or film) for printing or viewing by correcting mistakes, deciding what will be removed, etc., or to be in charge of what is reported in (a newspaper, magazine, etc.) • *He edits the local newspaper.* • If you edit something out, you remove it before it is broadcast or printed: *They edited out the most violent scenes when they showed the film on television.* [M]

editor /'ed·ət̬·ər/ *n* [C] a person who corrects and make changes to texts or films before they are printed or shown, or a person who is in charge of a newspaper, magazine, etc., and is responsible for all of its reports • *a textbook/film editor*

editorial /ˌed·ə'tɔːr·iː·əl, -'toʊr-/ *adj* • *an editorial staff* ○ *He insisted that it was an editorial decision to cut the story.*

editorial /ˌed·ə'tɔːr·iː·əl, -'toʊr-/ *n* [C] a statement in a newspaper or magazine, or on radio or television, that expresses the opinion of the editors or owners on a subject of particular interest • *an editorial on the new tax proposal*

edition /ɪ'dɪʃ·ən/ *n* [C] a particular form in which a book, magazine, or newspaper is published, or the total number of copies of a book, magazine, or newspaper that are published at the same time • *a regional edition of a newspaper* ○ *The book comes in both paperback and hardback editions.*

edu /ˌiːˌdiː'juː, 'ed·juː/ *n* [U] used at the end of US INTERNET addresses to show that the address belongs to a university • *info@harvard.edu*

educate /'edʒ·ə,keɪt/ *v* [T] to teach (someone), esp. by using the formal system of schools and colleges, or to give knowledge or understanding of a particular subject to (someone) • *His application form says he was educated in Germany.* ○ *It's every citizen's responsibility to be educated about his or her rights.*

educated /'edʒ·ə,keɪt̬·əd/ *adj* • *a highly edu-*

EDUCATION IN THE UNITED STATES

Each of the 50 states in the United States controls and directs its own education system. In each city or town a group of citizens decides education policy, and chooses a SUPERINTENDENT (= someone to be in charge of the operation of the public schools).

By law, students must go to school usually between the ages of seven and 16. Public schools are free. Some parents prefer to send their children to a **private school**, which may offer classes in religion, or they may teach their children at home. All schools must meet the standards set by the state in which they are located.

Preschool education is for children younger than six. It is offered by **nursery schools, play groups, child care centers**, the **Head Start program**, and **pre-K** classes. Nursery schools, play groups, and child care centers are usually operated by private owners or social or religious groups, and they usually charge parents money for their services. Head Start is a free program for poor children which is paid for by the Federal government. Pre-K programs operate as part of public schools. **Kindergarten**, a program for five year olds, prepares children for the more formal style of education they will receive in first grade.

Elementary school (also **grade school**) is the first level of formal schooling. It teaches the basics of education—reading, writing, and arithmetic, as well as science, history, art, music, and **physical education**. The aim of elementary education is to develop each child's ability to think as well as their emotional and social skills. Elementary schools are usually divided into **grades** of students who are about the same age. Elementary school grades are usually numbered 1 through 6 or 1 through 8.

Junior high schools were developed for grades 7, 8, and 9 as a way of helping younger children adjust to the different style of learning they will have in high school. Many school systems offer a **middle school** or **intermediate school** to provide this period of adjustment. Middle schools can include students from as young as 4th grade up to 8th grade. Often the size of school buildings and the availability of space for classes influence the decision about which grades are included.

High school traditionally includes grades 9 through 12. If the school system has a junior high program, then grades 10 through 12 are called **senior high school**. Instruction in high school is divided into departments, and students move around the building from class to class. High schools may be general or specialized. Specialized high schools may be **vocational**, preparing students for skilled or technical jobs, or they may be **academic**, offering preparation for college. There are also **magnet schools**, which offer specialized study in subjects like science or music and serve students from a wide area.

A **college** offers education beyond the high school level, usually over a four-year course that leads to a **bachelor's degree**. A **university** offers **graduate** and **undergraduate** degrees. College is also the general word in American English for all formal education beyond high school. Colleges and universities may be private, or they may be operated by a city or state. A **community college** (also **junior college**) offers a two-year course beyond the high school level, either in technical subjects to prepare students for work, or in academic subjects to prepare students to **transfer** (= move) to a four-year college.

---

cated man • An **educated guess** is a guess that is made using judgment and some degree of knowledge and is therefore likely to be correct.

education /ˌedʒ·ə'keɪ·ʃən/ n [U] • a high school/college education • Education is also the study of methods and theories of teaching: She has a master's degree in early childhood education.

educational /ˌedʒ·ə'keɪ·ʃən·əl/ adj • Traveling abroad will be an educational experience for her (= an experience from which she can learn).

educator /'edʒ·əˌkeɪt̬·ər/ n [C] a person whose work is teaching others, or one who is an authority on methods or theories of teaching

eel /iːl/ n [C] a long, thin, snakelike fish, some types of which are eaten

eerie /'ɪr·i/ adj strange in a frightening and mysterious way • Dust lay thick on the furniture, and cobwebs formed eerie patterns in the shadowy corners.

effect RESULT /ɪ'fekt/ n [C/U] the result of a particular influence; something that happens because of something else • The medicine had the effect of making me sleepy. [C] ○ The attempt to prevent protest demonstrations had just the opposite effect, causing riots. [C] ○ The new management actually has not had much effect on us. [U] • Compare AFFECT INFLUENCE.

effective /ɪ'fek·tɪv/ adj producing the intended results, or (of a person) skilled or able to do something well • an effective policy/strategy ○ We've found that giving away samples of our product is the most effective way to promote it. ○ She's an effective administrator and knows how to get things done.

effectively /ɪ'fek·tɪv·li/ adv • Though barely winning election, he governed effectively and was reelected. • Effectively also means having as a certain result in reality, though not in theory: If she loses this match, she's effectively eliminated from the tournament.

effectiveness /ɪˈfek·tɪv·nəs/ n [U] • *The drug's effectiveness is doubtful.*

effect USE /ɪˈfekt/ n [U] (esp. of rules or laws) official or legal use • *Winter parking rules are in effect* (= must be obeyed) *through March.* ○ *All salary increases will take effect* (= begin) *in January.*

effective /ɪˈfek·tɪv/ adj • *The law becomes effective next month.*

effect ACHIEVE /ɪˈfekt/ v [T] to achieve (something) and cause it to happen • *It will take years to effect meaningful changes in the educational system.*

effectual /ɪˈfek·tʃə·wəl/ adj fml successful in producing the intended results • *Unfortunately, efforts to stop the fighting have not been effectual.*

effeminate /ɪˈfem·ə·nət/ adj (of a man) behaving or appearing in a way that is more typical of women than men

efficient /ɪˈfɪʃ·ənt/ adj working or operating in a way that gets the results you want without any waste • *an efficient organization* ○ *They are developing a more fuel-efficient car to save gas.*

efficiently /ɪˈfɪʃ·ənt·li/ adv • *She manages the business efficiently.*

efficiency /ɪˈfɪʃ·ən·si/ n [C/U] the condition or fact of producing the results you want without waste, or a particular way in which this is done • *The use of high-speed machinery improved the efficiency of the factory.* [U] ○ *They reduced costs through production efficiencies.* [C usually pl]

effigy /ˈef·ə·dʒi/ n [C] a model or other object that represents someone, esp. someone in authority who is not liked, usually created in order to pretend to kill them by burning or hanging the model

effluent /ˈef·luː·ənt/ n [C/U] *specialized* liquid waste that is sent out from factories or other places, often into the sea or rivers • *Industrial effluents and sewage remain problems.* [C]

effort /ˈef·ərt/ n [C/U] physical or mental activity needed to achieve something, or an attempt to do something • *They met again in an effort to end the strike and get people back to work.* [C] ○ *It took years to write the book, but it was worth the effort.* [U] ○ *He established the Help Committee to coordinate the relief effort.* [U] ○ *Efforts to reach the senator for comment were not successful.* [C]

effortless /ˈef·ərt·ləs/ adj (of an action or activity) done so well that it seems not to need much mental or physical activity • *Her dancing looks effortless.*

effortlessly /ˈef·ərt·lə·sli/ adv

effusive /ɪˈfjuː·sɪv, -zɪv/ adj strongly expressed, or expressed with a lot of emotion • *Carville delivered his message to reporters in his typical effusive, arm-waving style.*

EFL n [U] abbreviation for **English as a foreign language**, see at ENGLISH

e.g. abbreviation for exempli gratia (= Latin for "for example") • *Eat foods containing a lot of fiber, e.g., fruits, vegetables, and whole grains.* • USAGE: In spoken English, people say "for example" or "such as" instead of "e.g."

egalitarian /ɪˌgæl·əˈter·i·ən/ adj based on the idea that people are equally important and should have the same rights and opportunities • *an egalitarian society*

egg REPRODUCTION /eg, eɪg/ n [C] an oval, rounded object with a hard shell produced by female birds and particular female REPTILES, from which a baby animal is born when it is developed • *An egg is also a cell produced by a woman or female animal from which a baby might develop if it combines with sperm from a male.*

egg FOOD /eg, eɪg/ n [C] the oval or rounded object with a hard shell that is produced by chickens, collected before a baby bird can develop within it, and used as food • *The recipe calls for four eggs and a pint of milk.* ○ *I'd like two scrambled eggs with bacon, please.* • If someone is described as having **egg on** their **face**, it means that they are very embarrassed because of something they said or did: *He told everyone the deal was all but signed, and if it falls through now he'll have egg on his face.* • An **eggshell** is the hard outside covering of an egg, which can break very easily. • **Egg white** or the white of an egg is the transparent part of an egg which becomes white when it is cooked.

▫**egg on** obj, **egg** obj **on** /ˈegˈɔːn, ˈeɪg-, -ˈɑn/ v adv [M] to encourage someone to do something, esp. something foolish or bad • *The mob, egged on by the state's racist governor, had been attempting to prevent the integration of the University of Mississippi.*

eggplant /ˈeg·plænt, ˈeɪg-/ n [C/U] an oval vegetable with a shiny, dark purple skin

ego /ˈiː·goʊ/ n [C] pl **egos** the idea or opinion that you have of yourself, esp. the level of your ability and intelligence, and your importance as a person • *That man has an enormous ego.* ○ *Getting that job should give her ego a boost* (= give her confidence).

egotism /ˈiː·gə·tɪz·əm/ n [U] the tendency to think only about yourself and consider yourself better and more important than other people

egotist /ˈiː·gə·təst/ n [C] • *My brother is such an egotist.*

egotistical /ˌiː·gəˈtɪs·tɪ·kəl/ adj

egregious /ɪˈgriː·dʒəs/ adj (of something bad) extreme; beyond any reasonable degree • *egregious errors of fact* ○ *an egregious example of misrepresentation*

eh /eɪ, e/ exclamation Cdn infml used as a pause in conversation • *So I'm speeding down the TransCanada, eh, and I look in my mirror and see this Mountie, eh.*

eight /eɪt/ *number* 8 • *Eight people are coming to dinner.* • LP NUMBERS

eighth /eɪtθ, eɪθ/ *adj, adv* [not gradable], *n* [C] • *He finished eighth in the race.* ∘ *Clarice was born on the eighth of August.* [C] • An eighth is one of eight equal parts of something. [C]

eighteen /eɪt'tiːn/ *number* 18 • *There are eighteen glasses in the cabinet.* ∘ *an eighteen-hole golf course* • LP NUMBERS

eighteenth /eɪt'tiːnθ/ *adj, adv* [not gradable], *n* [C] • *He ranks eighteenth in the world.* ∘ *Ann-Marie's birthday is the eighteenth of October.* [C] • An eighteenth is one of eighteen equal parts of something. [C]

eighty /'eɪt·i/ *number* 80 • *I bought a package of eighty plastic cups.* ∘ *an eighty-piece puzzle* • LP NUMBERS

eighties, **80s**, **80's** /'eɪt̬·iːz/ *pl n* the numbers 80 through 89 • *The temperature is expected to be in the eighties* (= between 80° and 89°) *tomorrow.* ∘ *Ronald Reagan was president in the eighties* (= between 1980 and 1989). ∘ *My grandmother is in her eighties* (= between 80 and 89 years old).

eightieth /'eɪt̬·iː·əθ/ *adj, adv* [not gradable], *n* [C] • *They finished eightieth out of a hundred.* • An eightieth is one of eighty equal parts of something. [C]

either ALSO /'iː·ðər, 'aɪ-/ *adv* [not gradable] used in negatives instead of also or too • *The restaurant has good food, and it's not expensive either.*

either CHOICE /'iː·ðər, 'aɪ-/ *adj, pronoun, conjunction* one or the other of two • *Either person would be fine for the job.* ∘ *You can go by train or bus—either way it'll take an hour.* ∘ *I left it either at home or in the car.* • You can also use either to mean both: *Smokers were sitting on either side of me.* • LP DETERMINERS

ejaculate SPERM /ɪ'dʒæk·jə,leɪt/ *v* [I] (of a man or male animal) to push out a liquid containing sperm from the penis

ejaculation /ɪ,dʒæk·jə'leɪ·ʃən/ *n* [C/U]

ejaculate SAY /ɪ'dʒæk·jə,leɪt/ *v* [T] to shout or say something suddenly, sometimes unexpectedly

eject /ɪ'dʒekt/ *v* [T] to force (someone) to leave a particular place, or to send out (something) quickly and often with force • *It was difficult to eject squatters from the abandoned building.* • A player who is ejected during a game is told to leave the playing area by the REFEREE because they have done something wrong: *Norman was ejected from the game after he gave Mark Aguirre a two-handed shove high in the chest.*

eke out /'iː·kaʊt/ *v adv* [T] to make a small supply of (something) enough for your needs • *He barely eked out a living* (= earned just enough to live on).

elaborate DETAILED /ɪ'læb·ə·rət/ *adj* containing a lot of connected parts or many complicated details • *an elaborate ceremony* ∘ *an elaborate fireworks display* ∘ *They had created elaborate computer programs to run the system.*

elaborately /ɪ'læb·ə·rət·li/ *adv* • *an elaborately decorated dining room*

elaborate EXPLAIN /ɪ'læb·ə,reɪt/ *v* [I] to add more information or explain something that you have said • *He refused to elaborate on why he had resigned.*

elapse /ɪ'læps/ *v* [I] (of time) to go past • *Four years had elapsed since she last saw him.*

elastic /ɪ'læs·tɪk/ *adj* (of a material) able to stretch and be returned to its original shape or size • *She bunched her ponytail and slipped on an elastic hair band.* • If something that is not a physical object is elastic, it is able or likely to be changed: *Our plans are still very elastic.*

elated /ɪ'leɪt̬·əd/ *adj* extremely happy and excited, often because something has happened or been achieved • *He was elated by the news that he had won a full scholarship.*

elbow /'el·boʊ/ *n* [C] the bony point at which the arm bends, or the part of a piece of clothing which covers this area • *His shirt sleeve was torn at the elbow.* • If you use **elbow grease**, you put a lot of effort into doing something. • **Elbow room** is space in which to move around: *With five people in my little car, there won't be enough elbow room.* • PIC ARM

elbow /'el·boʊ/ *v* [T] to push with an elbow, or to push rudely, esp. to get past someone • *He elbowed his way through the crowd.*

elder /'el·dər/ *n* [C] an older person, esp. one who deserves respect • *You should listen to your elders.* • An elder is also an official in particular religious groups.

elder /'el·dər/ *adj* [not gradable] (of a family member) older • *an elder brother/sister* • An **elder statesman** is an older person who is respected and asked for advice because of their past experience: *He is one of basketball's elder statesmen.*

elderly /'el·dər·li/ *adj* • *William is nearly 50, and his parents are elderly.* • Compare OLD EXISTING A LONG TIME.

elderly /'el·dər·li/ *pl n* old people considered as a group • *The city is building new housing for the elderly.*

eldest /'el·dəst/ *adj* [not gradable] oldest (of three or more people, esp. within a family) • *He's my eldest brother.*

elect /ɪ'lekt/ *v* to decide on or choose, esp. to choose (a person) for a particular job by voting • *We elect representatives every two years.* [T] ∘ *She was elected to the board of directors.* [T] ∘ *He was invited to join them at the concert, but he elected to stay home and watch the ballgame.* [+ *to* infinitive]

elect /ɪ'lekt/ *adj* [only after n] (or a person) who has won a vote but not yet taken office • *the president-elect*

election /ɪ'lek·ʃən/ *n* [C/U] the act or occasion

of being chosen for a particular job, esp. by voting • *congressional/presidential elections* [C] ○ *His election to the Senate was all but assured.* [U] ○ *Election Day is the first Tuesday in November.* [U]

elective /ɪ'lek·tɪv/ *adj* [not gradable] chosen or decided by voting • *an elective office* • Elective also means chosen but not necessary: *elective surgery*

electoral /ɪ'lek·tə·rəl/ *adj* [not gradable] • *The committee endorses electoral reforms for fairer elections.* • In the US, the **electoral college** is a group of people whose votes are determined by how the people vote in each state, and who officially elect the president and vice-president.

electorate /ɪ'lek·tə·rət/ *n* [C] the people who are allowed to vote

electric /ɪ'lek·trɪk/ *adj* powered by electricity • *electric current/power* ○ *an electric light/motor* • Something might be described as electric if it is very exciting: *The aerial acrobats at the circus gave an electric performance.* • The **electric chair** is a special chair used to kill a criminal with a current of electricity. • An **electric fence** is a low electric current that is produced usually around the edge of an area to keep dogs or other animals from leaving it.

electrical /ɪ'lek·trɪ·kəl/ *adj* [not gradable] using electricity for power, involved in the production or movement of electricity, or related in some way to electricity • *electrical equipment*

electrically /ɪ'lek·trɪ·kli/ *adv* [not gradable] • *electrically powered*

electrician /ɪˌlek'trɪʃ·ən/ *n* [C] a person who puts in and maintains wires which carry electricity into a building

electrify /ɪ'lek·trə·faɪ/ *v* [T] to equip with electricity • *They recently electrified this part of the railway line.* • If you electrify a group of people, you do something that makes them very excited: *Her performance electrified the audience.*

electricity /ɪˌlek'trɪs·ət·i/ *n* [U] a form of energy that provides power to motors and devices that create light or heat • *They lived on an island with no electricity and no running water.*

electrocute /ɪ'lek·trə,kjuːt/ *v* [T] to kill by electricity • *Many live wires were downed by the storm, and anyone touching them will almost surely be electrocuted.*

electrocution /ɪˌlek·trə'kjuː·ʃən/ *n* [C/U]

electrode /ɪ'lek,troʊd/ *n* [C] the point at which an electric current enters or leaves something, for example, a BATTERY

electron /ɪ'lek,trɑn/ *n* [C] an extremely small piece of matter with a negative electrical charge • Compare NEUTRON; PROTON.

electronic /ɪˌlek'trɑn·ɪk/ *adj* [not gradable] involving a system of operation that involves the control of a flow of ELECTRONS esp. in var-

ious devices including computers • *electronic components/equipment* ○ *electronic banking* ○ *The huge electronic scoreboard showed a replay of the last goal.* • **Electronic mail** is E-MAIL.

electronics /ɪˌlek'trɑn·ɪks/ *n* [U] • *a degree in electronics* ○ *the electronics industry*

electronically /ɪˌlek'trɑn·ɪ·kli/ *adv* [not gradable]

elegant /'el·ɪ·gənt/ *adj* graceful and attractive in appearance or behavior • *We met a young businesswoman, elegant in a black suit.*

elegantly /'el·ɪ·gənt·li/ *adv* • *elegantly dressed*

elegance /'el·ɪ·gəns/ *n* [U] • *He was known for his elegance and wit.*

elegy /'el·ə·dʒi/ *n* [C] a sad poem or song, esp. remembering someone who has died or something in the past

element PART /'el·ə·mənt/ *n* [C] one of the parts of something that makes it work, or a quality that makes someone or something effective • *the heating element of a toaster* ○ *Having a second income is an important element for most home buyers.* ○ *They had all the elements of a great team.*

element AMOUNT /'el·ə·mənt/ *n* [C] a small amount or degree • *There was an element of truth in what she said, but it was an exaggeration.*

element SUBSTANCE /'el·ə·mənt/ *n* [C] a substance that cannot be reduced to smaller chemical parts • Someone who is **in** their **element** is in a situation they know well and enjoy.

elemental /ˌel·ə'ment·ᵊl/ *adj* basic or simple but powerfully felt • *elemental needs/desires*

elementary /ˌel·ə'men·tri, -'ment·ə·ri/ *adj* simple or easy; basic • *I'm taking a course in elementary Russian.* • An **elementary school** (also **grade school**, **primary school**, or *dated* **grammar school**) is a school that provides the first part of a child's education, usually for children between five and eleven years old. LP EDUCATION IN THE US

elements /'el·ə·mənts/ *pl n* weather conditions, esp. bad ones • *We decided to brave the elements and take a walk.*

elephant /'el·ə·fənt/ *n* [C] a very large, gray animal that has a TRUNK (= long nose) with which it can pick things up • PIC TRUNKS

elevate IMPROVE POSITION /'el·ə,veɪt/ *v* [T] to give (someone) a higher or more important position • *He was elevated to the chairmanship of the House Armed Services Committee.* ○ *They hoped to elevate the position of women in society.*

elevate RAISE /'el·ə,veɪt/ *v* [T] to raise or lift up • *She wore high heels that elevated her a few inches above 5 feet.*

elevation /ˌel·ə'veɪ·ʃən/ *n* [C/U] height above the surface of the earth, or an area that is higher than the surrounding land • *At higher elevations, the air is colder.* [C]

elevator /'el·ə,veɪt̬·ər/ *n* [C] a piece of equipment, usually in the form of a small room, that carries people or goods straight up and down in tall buildings

eleven /ɪ'lev·ən/ *number* 11 • *The child is eleven.* ○ *an eleven-story building* • LP NUMBERS

eleventh /ɪ'lev·ənθ/ *adj, adv* [not gradable], *n* [C] • *We were seated in the eleventh row.* ○ *Today is the eleventh of June.* • An eleventh is one of eleven equal parts of something.

elf /elf/ *n* [C] *pl* **elves** /elvz/ a small, imaginary person, usually shown in pictures dressed in green with pointed ears and a tall hat, and often described in stories as playing tricks and having magical powers

elicit /ɪ'lɪs·ət/ *v* [T] to obtain (esp. information or a reaction) • *His defense of the rights of immigrants elicited cries of outrage from some right-wing politicians.*

eligible /'el·ə·dʒə·bəl/ *adj* having the necessary qualities or fulfilling the necessary conditions • *an eligible voter* ○ *You have to be employed six months to be eligible for medical benefits.* • If you refer to a man or a women as eligible, you mean they are not married and are desirable as a marriage partner: *The magazine listed 50 of the world's most eligible bachelors.*

eligibility /ˌel·ə·dʒə'bɪl·ət·i/ *n* [U]

eliminate /ɪ'lɪm·ə,neɪt/ *v* [T] to remove or take away (something) • *You can never totally eliminate the possibility of human error.*

elimination /ɪ,lɪm·ə'neɪ·ʃən/ *n* [U] • *The agreement calls for the elimination of nuclear weapons.*

elite /eɪ'liːt, ɪ-/ *n* [C] those people or organizations that are considered the best or most powerful compared to others of a similar type

elite /eɪ'liːt, ɪ-/ *adj* • *elite female athletes*

elitist /eɪ'liːt̬·əst, ɪ-/ *adj often disapproving* characteristic of the elite, and esp. not caring about the interests or values of ordinary people • *He denounced the plan as impracticable and elitist.*

elk /elk/ *n* [C] a type of large deer with large, flat horns

elm /elm/ *n* [C/U] a large tree valued for the shade it provides, or the hard wood from this tree

elongated /iː'lɔŋ,geɪt̬·əd, ɪ-/ *adj* longer and thinner than usual, as if stretched • *Giacometti's elongated sculptures of young women*

elope /ɪ'loʊp/ *v* [I] to leave home secretly in order to get married without parental agreement • *She eloped with an army officer.*

elopement /ɪ'loʊp·mənt/ *n* [C]

eloquent /'el·ə·kwənt/ *adj* using language to express ideas or opinions clearly and well, so that they have a strong effect on others • *He made an eloquent defense of his stand against capital punishment.* • Eloquent also means giving a clear, strong message: *The pictures of destruction served as an eloquent reminder of the hurricane's power.*

eloquently /'el·ə·kwənt·li/ *adv*

eloquence /'el·ə·kwəns/ *n* [U] • *I was impressed by her eloquence.*

else /els/ *adv* [not gradable] (after words beginning with any-, every-, no-, and some-, or after how, what, where, who, and why, but not which) other, another, different, additional • *If it doesn't work, try something else* (= something different/another way or thing). ○ *Let's go before anyone else* (= another/an additional person) *arrives.* ○ *The book isn't here— where else* (= In what other place) *should I look?*

elsewhere /'els·hwer, -wer, -hwær, -wær/ *adv* [not gradable] (at, in, from, or to) another place or other places; anywhere or somewhere else • *It's hot and sunny on the coast but not elsewhere.*

elucidate /ɪ'luː·sə,deɪt/ *v* [I/T] *fml* to explain or make clear • *I hope my book will elucidate the complex issues we face.* [T]

elude /ɪ'luːd/ *v* [T] to succeed in avoiding (someone or something), esp. by using tricks • *Her husband eluded capture for two years.* ○ *(fig.) It was simply her misfortune that an Olympic medal eluded her in 1988.*

elusive /ɪ'luː·sɪv, -zɪv/ *adj* • *elusive memories*

elves /elvz/ *pl of* ELF

emaciated /ɪ'meɪ·ʃiː,eɪt̬·əd/ *adj* (esp. of people and animals) very thin and weak, usually because of illness or not eating enough

e–mail /'iː·meɪl/, **electronic mail** *n* [C/U] a system of using computers for sending messages from one place to another • *I have saved all the e-mail I received over the past week.* [U]

emanate /'em·ə,neɪt/ *v* [I/T] to come from or out of • *Angry voices emanated from the next room.* [I always + adv/prep]

emancipate /ɪ'mæn·sə,peɪt/ *v* [T] to free (a person, esp. a SLAVE), allowing them to do what they want and make decisions for themselves

emancipated /ɪ'mæn·sə,peɪt̬·əd/ *adj* • Emancipated also means freed esp. from social limitations: *An emancipated woman can reject fashion without becoming an object of ridicule.*

emancipation /ɪ,mæn·sə'peɪ·ʃən/ *n* [U] • *emancipation from slavery*

embalm /ɪm'bɑm, -'bɑlm/ *v* [T] to treat (a dead body) with chemicals to prevent it from decaying

embankment /ɪm'bæŋk·mənt/ *n* [C] an artificial slope made of earth or stones • *a river embankment*

embargo /ɪm'bɑr,goʊ/ *n* [C] *pl* **embargoes** a government order to temporarily stop trading certain goods or with certain countries • *They put an embargo on imports of steel.*

embark /ɪm'bɑrk/ *v* [I] to go on to a ship or an aircraft • *We embarked at Miami for our Caribbean cruise.*

□ **embark on/upon** /-'-,-; -'--,-/ *v prep* [T] to start (esp. something big or important) • *We've embarked on an exciting new project.*

embarrass /ɪmˈbær·əs/ v [T] to cause (someone) to feel anxious, ashamed, or uncomfortable • *He knew that letter would embarrass him and later he tried to get rid of it.*

embarrassed /ɪmˈbær·əst/ adj • *They sat in embarrassed silence.*

embarrassing /ɪmˈbær·ə·sɪŋ/ adj • *It's embarrassing to be caught telling a lie.* [+ to infinitive]

embarrassingly /ɪmˈbær·ə·sɪŋ·li/ adv • *an embarrassingly poor performance*

embarrassment /ɪmˈbær·ə·smənt/ n [C/U] • *She forgot her lines and blushed with embarrassment.* [U]

embassy /ˈem·bə·si/ n [C] the group of people who officially represent their country in a foreign country, or the building they work in • *I'll be working at the American embassy in Paris.*

embattled /ɪmˈbæt·əld/ adj having a lot of problems or difficulties • *The embattled leaders are trying to hold on to their positions.*

embedded /ɪmˈbed·əd/ adj existing or firmly attached within something or under a surface • *A threat is embedded in the language of the statement.*

embellish /ɪmˈbel·ɪʃ/ v [T] to make (something) more beautiful or interesting by additions or details • *Many early building entrances were richly embellished.* • If you embellish a story or statement, you add details that are not completely true in order to make it more interesting: *He couldn't resist embellishing his account of the African safari.*

ember /ˈem·bərz/ n [C usually pl] a small piece of wood or coal that is burning without a flame • *glowing embers*

embezzle /ɪmˈbez·əl/ v [T] to secretly and illegally take money that is in your care or that belongs to an organization or business you work for

embezzlement /ɪmˈbez·əl·mənt/ n [U] • *They were arrested for the embezzlement of company funds.*

embitter /ɪmˈbɪt̬·ər/ v [T] to make (someone) feel angry and unhappy for a long time • *In his later years, he was embittered by the loss of his money and fame.*

emblazoned /ɪmˈbleɪ·zənd/ adj [not gradable] marked or shown in order to be very noticeable • *The slogan was emblazoned in red paint.*

emblem /ˈem·bləm/ n [C] an object that is used to represent a particular person, group, or idea, or a picture of the object • *A dove is often used as an emblem of peace.*

embody /ɪmˈbɑd·i/ v [T] to be an example of (esp. something good) by your own behavior or personality; represent • *Arthur Ashe embodied the ideals of good sportsmanship.*

embodiment /ɪmˈbɑd·i·mənt/ n [U] • *This cruise ship is the embodiment of luxury.*

embolden /ɪmˈboʊl·dən/ v [T] to make (someone) willing to take more risks, esp. to get what they want • *Those supporting the right to own guns were emboldened by the Republican victories in last month's elections.*

embrace HOLD /ɪmˈbreɪs/ v [I/T] to hold (someone) close to you with your arms to express affection, love, or sympathy, or when greeting or leaving someone • *They embraced (each other) before saying good-bye.* [I/T]

embrace /ɪmˈbreɪs/ n [C] • *They greeted each other with a warm embrace.*

embrace ACCEPT /ɪmˈbreɪs/ v [T] to accept (ideas, beliefs, or opinions) with great interest or enthusiasm • *Anyone who embraced liberal ideals was persecuted.*

embroider DECORATE /ɪmˈbrɔɪd·ər/ v [I/T] to decorate (cloth or clothing) with patterns or pictures sewn directly onto the material, or to create (a pattern or picture) in such a way

embroidery /ɪmˈbrɔɪd·ə·ri/ n [C/U]

embroider ADD /ɪmˈbrɔɪd·ər/ v [T] to make (a story) more entertaining by adding imaginary details to it • *Caroline sometimes embroiders the facts, so don't believe every word she says.*

embroil /ɪmˈbrɔɪl/ v [T] to cause (someone or something) to become involved in an argument or a difficult situation • *The UN was reluctant to get its forces embroiled in another war.*

embryo /ˈem·briˌoʊ/ n [C] pl **embryos** a human being or animal in an early stage of development, either in its mother's uterus or in an egg, or a plant that is developing in a seed

embryonic /ˌem·briˈɑn·ɪk/ adj [not gradable] of or relating to an EMBRYO (= human or animal in an early stage of development) • *the third week of embryonic life* ○ *embryonic tissue* • (fig.) If a plan or process is an embryonic stage, it is in a very early stage of development: *The region's embryonic tourist industry would be damaged by this development.*

emcee /ˈem·siː/ n [C] **master of ceremonies**, see at MASTER CONTROL

emerald /ˈem·ə·rəld/ n [C/U] a bright green, transparent, precious stone often used in jewelry

emerge APPEAR /ɪˈmɜrdʒ/ v [I] to appear by coming out of something or out from behind something • *The runway lights flashed on, and the first models emerged from behind the stage set.* ○ (fig.) *The president emerged unscathed from the scandal* (= He came out of it with no damage to his reputation). ○ (fig.) *We debated which of the candidate will emerge* (= result) *as the winner.*

emerge DEVELOP /ɪˈmɜrdʒ/ v [I] to become known or develop as a result of something • *New business opportunities will emerge with advances in technology.*

emerging /ɪˈmɜr·dʒənt/ adj [not gradable] growing and developing, esp. in business investment • *US government and business must become partners in breaking into these emerging markets.*

emergency /ɪˈmɜr·dʒən·si/ *n* [C] a dangerous or serious situation, such as an accident, that happens suddenly or unexpectedly and needs immediate action • *In an emergency, dial 911 for an ambulance.* • An **emergency room** is the part of a hospital where people who are hurt in accidents or suddenly become sick are taken for treatment.

emery board /ˈem·ə·riˌbɔrd, -ˌboʊrd/ *n* [C] a narrow piece of cardboard with a rough surface, for smoothing and shaping the ends of your finger nails

emigrate /ˈem·əˌɡreɪt/ *v* [I] to leave a country permanently and go to live in another one • *Millions of Germans emigrated from Europe in the nineteenth century.* • Compare **immigrate** at IMMIGRANT.

emigration /ˌem·əˈɡreɪ·ʃən/ *n* [C/U]

emigrant /ˈem·ɪ·ɡrənt/ *n* [C] a person who leaves a country permanently to live in another one • Compare IMMIGRANT.

eminent FAMOUS /ˈem·ə·nənt/ *adj* famous and important • *The commission consisted of fifteen eminent political figures.*

eminence /ˈem·ə·nəns/ *n* [U]

eminent NOTICEABLE /ˈem·ə·nənt/ *adj* noticeable or worth remarking on, or very great • *This shows eminent good sense.*

eminently /ˈem·ə·nənt·li/ *adv* [not gradable] very, or very well • *She's eminently qualified to handle the job.* ○ *The story is eminently worth reading.*

emissary /ˈem·əˌser·i/ *n* [C] a person sent by one government or political leader to another to deliver messages or to take part in discussions

emit /iːˈmɪt, ɪ-/ *v* [T] **-tt-** to send out (light, sound, or a smell, or a gas or other substance) • *The alarm emits a high-pitched sound if anyone tries to break in.*

emission /iːˈmɪʃ·ən, ɪ-/ *n* [C/U] • *The regulations require a reduction in harmful emissions.* [C]

Emmy /ˈem·i/ *n* [C] *trademark* one of a set of American prizes given each year to actors and other people involved in making television programs

emotion /ɪˈmoʊ·ʃən/ *n* [C/U] (a) strong feeling, such as of love, anger, fear, etc. • *He's driven by his emotions, not by careful thought.* [C]

emotional /ɪˈmoʊ·ʃən·əl/ *adj* connected with or showing feelings • *I'm pretty emotional about crime, because I've been a victim.*

emotionally /ɪˈmoʊ·ʃən·əl·i/ *adv* • *The coach appeared emotionally drained after yesterday's loss.*

empathy /ˈem·pə·θi/ *n* [U] the ability to share someone else's feelings or experiences by imagining what it would be like to be in their situation • *He loves children and has a certain empathy with them.*

emperor /ˈem·pə·rər/ *n* [C] a male ruler of an EMPIRE

emphasis /ˈem·fə·səs/ *n* [C/U] *pl* **emphases** /ˈem·fəˌsiːz/ special attention given to something because it is important or because you want it to be noticed, or an example of this • *She paused for emphasis.* [U] ○ *In schools, the emphasis on programming has declined in recent years.* [U]

emphasize /ˈem·fəˌsaɪz/ *v* [T] to state or show that (something) is especially important or deserves special attention • *She emphasized the importance of good nutrition.*

emphatic /emˈfæt̬·ɪk, ɪm-/ *adj* strong and determined in speech or action, so that what is said or done gets attention • *Godard is emphatic about his preference.*

emphatically /emˈfæt̬·ɪ·kli, ɪm-/ *adv* • *He emphatically denied the rumors.*

emphysema /ˌem·fəˈziː·mə, -ˈsiː-/ *n* [U] *medical* a condition in which some parts within the lungs become stretched, causing breathing difficulties

empire /ˈem·paɪr/ *n* [C] a group of countries ruled by a single person, government, or country • *the British/Soviet Empire*

empirical /ɪmˈpɪr·ɪ·kəl, em-/ *adj* based on what is experienced or seen rather than on theory • *We have no empirical evidence that the industry is in trouble.*

employ WORK /ɪmˈplɔɪ/ *v* [T] to pay (someone) to work for or do a job for you • *The factory employs 87 workers.*

employ /ɪmˈplɔɪ/ *n* [U] *fml* • If you are **in** someone's **employ**, you work for them: *Mr. Neil is currently in our employ.*

employee /ɪmˌplɔɪˈiː, em-/ *n* [C] a person who is paid to work for someone else • *Some of their employees do not have insurance.*

employer /ɪmˈplɔɪ·ər/ *n* [C] a person, company, or organization that pays people to work for them • *The Air Force is the largest employer in this area.*

employment /ɪmˈplɔɪ·mənt/ *n* [U] work, esp. for someone else, for which you are paid, or a period of work • *After leaving Pearson, it took Friedman months to find new employment.* • An **employment agency** is a business that is paid for finding jobs for people and for finding people who suit particular jobs.

employ USE /ɪmˈplɔɪ/ *v* [T] to use (something) for a particular purpose • *Jacobs employs this phrase repeatedly.*

employment /ɪmˈplɔɪ·mənt/ *n* [U] the use of something for a particular purpose • *She studied advertisers' employment of images in food ads.*

empower /ɪmˈpaʊ·ər, -ˈpaʊr/ *v* [T] to give (someone) the legal authority or the power to do something • *Voting for Democrats empowers their liberal agenda.*

empowerment /ɪmˈpaʊ·ər·mənt, -ˈpaʊr-/ *n* [U] • *Company programs encourage worker empowerment.*

empty /ˈem·ti/ *adj* having nothing inside • *He*

set the empty glass down. • If a place is empty, no one is using it or is present: *It was past midnight, and the streets were empty.* • Empty also means without any meaning or purpose: *We need jobs, not empty promises.* • *Never take this medicine* **on an empty stomach** (= when you have not eaten anything). • If someone is **empty-handed**, they have not brought anything with them or have not left with anything: *The two would-be robbers fled empty-handed.*

empty /'em·ti/ *v* [I/T] to take out everything from inside (something), or to lose what is inside so that nothing is left • *She emptied her husband's mug in the sink.* [T] ○ *Once the movie ended, the theater emptied quickly.* [I] ○ *The Tombigbee River empties into Mobile Bay* (= its water flows there). [I]

empty /'em·ti/ *n* [C usually pl] a container with nothing in it, esp. one whose contents have been used • *Bring the empties to the recycling center.*

emptiness /'em·ti··nəs/ *n* [U] • *She loves the emptiness of the desert.* ○ *He tried to ignore the feeling of emptiness* (= lack of meaning or purpose).

emulate /'em·jə‚leɪt/ *v* [T] to copy (someone's behavior) or try to be like (someone else) because you admire or respect them • *Officials are looking to emulate successful ideas from other cities.* ○ *He just wants to emulate his dad.*

enable /ɪ'neɪ·bəl/ *v* [T] to make (someone or something) able to do something by providing them with whatever is necessary to achieve it • *Saving enough money now will enable you to retire comfortably.*

enact MAKE LAW /ɪ'nækt/ *v* [T] to make (a law), or to make (an idea) into a law • *Will Congress enact legislation to restrict gun ownership?*

enactment /ɪ'nækt·mənt/ *n* [U] the making of a law, or a particular act of making a law • *Supporters were pleased with the enactment of the bill.*

enamel /ɪ'næm·əl/ *n* [C/U] a glasslike substance used for decoration or protection that is melted onto clay, metal, and glass objects and then left to cool and harden, or an object covered with this substance • *The enamel on the toilet was chipped.* [U] • Enamel is also a type of paint that forms a shiny surface when dry: *I used a blue enamel for the trim.* [C] • Enamel is also the hard, white, shiny substance that forms the covering of a tooth. [U]

enamored /ɪ'næm·ərd/ *adj* liking a lot • *Not everyone is enamored of steak.*

encase /ɪn'keɪs, en-/ *v* [T] to cover or enclose (something) completely • *The medal was encased in clear plastic.*

enchant PLEASE /ɪn'tʃænt/ *v* [T] to charm or please (someone) greatly • *He was enchanted by stories of the Old West.*

enchanting /ɪn'tʃænt·ɪŋ/ *adj* • *Belgium is an enchanting country.*

enchant USE MAGIC /ɪn'tʃænt/ *v* [T] (in stories) to put (someone) completely under your control by using magic

enchanted /ɪn'tʃænt·əd/ *adj* • *The princess lives in an enchanted castle.*

enchilada /‚en·tʃə'lɑd·ə/ *n* [C] a food consisting of a TORTILLA (= type of flat, round bread) wrapped around meat, beans, or cheese, and covered with a sauce that is usually spicy

encircle /ɪn'sɜr·kəl/ *v* [T] to surround or form a circle around (something) • *A parking lot encircles the mall.*

enclave /'en·kleɪv, 'ɑn-/ *n* [C] an area that is different from the larger area or country surrounding it, or a group of people who are different from the people living in the surrounding area • *Yorkville was an enclave of German immigrants.*

enclose SURROUND /ɪn'kloʊz/ *v* [T] to surround • *The garden is enclosed by four walls.*

enclosed /ɪn'kloʊzd/ *adj* (of a place) surrounded by a wall and often covered • *It's the largest fully-enclosed shopping center in the world.*

enclose SEND /ɪn'kloʊz/ *v* [T] to send (something) in the same envelope or package as something else • *Please enclose a stamped, self-addressed envelope.*

enclosure SEPARATE AREA /ɪn'kloʊ·ʒər/ *n* [C] an area surrounded by a fence or other structure in order to be kept separate from other areas • *The dogs are in a fenced enclosure in the backyard.*

enclosure LETTER /ɪn'kloʊ·ʒər/ *n* [C] something extra that is sent in a letter or package with the main message • *You will find two enclosures with this letter—a check and a photograph.*

encompass /ɪn'kʌm·pəs/ *v* [T] to include (several things, esp. different things) • *The plan encompasses repaving the street and planting 40 new trees.*

encore /'ɑn·kɔːr, -koʊr/ *n* [C], *exclamation* the performance of an additional song or piece of music after a show has formally ended, or the word people sometimes call out while clapping to request this performance • *The audience demanded encore after encore.*

encounter /ɪn'kaʊnt·ər/ *v* [T] to meet (someone) unexpectedly, or to experience (esp. something unpleasant) • *In the kitchen I encountered a woman I had never seen before.* ○ *He was shocked by the hostility he encountered.*

encounter /ɪn'kaʊnt·ər/ *n* [C] • *My first encounter with death was when Abraham died.*

encourage /ɪn'kɜr·ɪdʒ, -'kʌ·rɪdʒ/ *v* [T] to help (someone) to feel confident and able to do something, or strongly to advise (someone) to do something • *Our parents always encouraged us to ask questions.* • If something encourages an activity, it supports it or makes it more likely: *The city needs to encourage job creation.*

encouraging /ɪnˈkɜr·ə·dʒɪŋ, -ˈkʌ·rə-/ *adj* • *Early results of the experiment were extremely encouraging.*

encouragement /ɪnˈkɜr·ɪdʒ·mənt, -ˈkʌ·rɪdʒ-/ *n* [U] • *My parents gave me encouragement and support.*

encroach /ɪnˈkroʊtʃ/ *v* [I] to take control or possession of something in a gradual way and often without being noticed • *Farmers encroached on forest land to grow crops.* ○ *These devices are encroaching on people's privacy.*

encroachment /ɪnˈkroʊtʃ·mənt/ *n* [C/U] • *Human encroachment threatens the birds' nesting sites.* [C]

encrusted /ɪnˈkrəs·təd/ *adj* covered with a hard layer or something, or with something decorative • *All our belongings were encrusted with mud.*

encumbered /ɪnˈkʌm·bər/ *adj* prevented from making quick progress by having to carry heavy objects or deal with important duties and responsibilities • *She was encumbered by concern over her husband's health.*

encyclopedia, **encyclopaedia** /ɪnˌsɑɪ·klə ˈpiːd·iː·ə/ *n* [C] a large collection of information about one or many subjects, often arranged alphabetically in articles in a book or set of books, or available through a computer

encyclopedic, **encyclopaedic** /ɪnˌsɑɪ·kləˈpiːd·ɪk/ *adj* covering a large range of knowledge, often in great detail • *He has boundless energy and an encyclopedic memory.*

end LAST PART /end/ *n* [C] the last or farthest part of something or of a period of time, beyond which it does not exist • *She tied one end of the rope a tree.* ○ *The punctuation at the end of this sentence is a period.* ○ *Did you stay to the end of the movie?* ○ *Steve can swim to the far end of the lake and back.* • To be **at an end** is to be finished: *His career was at an end.* • If someone is **at the end of** their **rope/tether**, they have no more patience or strength: *I'm at the end of my rope with these kids!* • **In the end** means after considering everything: *In the end, she chose to go to Oberlin College.* • *She practices the violin for hours* **on end** (= continuously). • *We're hoping to win, but if we finish second it won't be* **the end of the world** (= something unacceptable). • If things are **end to end**, they are all facing in the same direction, with the back end of each against the front end of the next one: *The new cars were lined up end to end.* • An **end product** is what is produced by an industrial process or an activity: *Greed and selfishness are the end products of a system that always puts the individual first.* • The **end result** is what finally happens from a series of events: *I followed the recipe, but the end result was disappointing.* • In football, the **end zone** is the area

the end of the field where a player holding the ball can score a goal.

end /end/ *v* [I/T] • *She ended her speech on an optimistic note.* [T] ○ *Our arguments always end in tears.* [I] • If you end up in a particular place or situation, you reach that place or achieve that situation after other activities: *I usually end up buying something I didn't intend to.* [I] ○ *After two weeks of traveling around Europe, we ended up in Paris.* [I]

ending /ˈen·dɪŋ/ *n* [C] the last part of a process, esp. the way in which something stops existing • *The movie's ending is so romantic!* • (*specialized*) An ending is a part added to a word that changes its meaning: *To make "dog" plural, you add the ending "-s."* LP COMBINING FORMS

endless /ˈen·dləs/ *adj* [not gradable] • If something is endless, it never finishes or seems to never finish because it continues for so long: *When I was a child, the summers seemed endless.*

endlessly /ˈen·dlə·sli/ *adv* [not gradable] • *Education policy is endlessly debated.*

end PART /end/ *n* [C] a specific part or division of an activity • *She takes care of the financial end of the business and I handle the marketing end.*

end INTENTION /end/ *n* [C] something that your actions or efforts are intended to achieve; an aim • *To accomplish that end, you will have to work hard and be lucky, too.*

end FOOTBALL PLAYER /end/ *n* [C] (in football) one of two players who begin play farthest from the ball • *a defensive end*

endanger /ɪnˈdeɪn·dʒər/ *v* [T] to put (someone or something) in a situation in which it is likely to be harmed, damaged, or destroyed • *Revealing that information might endanger our national security.*

endangered /ɪnˈdeɪn·dʒərd/ *adj* • An **endangered species** is a type of animal or plant that might stop existing because there are only a few of this type alive.

endear *obj* **to** *obj* /ɪnˈdɪr·tə, -tʊ, -ˌtuː/ *v prep* [T] to cause (someone) to be liked by (someone) • *His fiery temper did not endear him to his coworkers.*

endearing /ɪnˈdɪr·ɪŋ/ *adj* • *Pickwick is endearing, as so many fools are.*

endeavor /ɪnˈdev·ər/ *n* [C/U] an effort or attempt to do something • *Writing is a very different endeavor than teaching.* [C]

endeavor /ɪnˈdev·ər/ *v* [+ to infinitive] *fml* to try (to do something) • *I endeavored to explain the legal consequences of his action.*

endemic /enˈdem·ɪk, ɪn-/ *adj* (esp. of a disease or social condition) found particularly in a specific area or group • *Some of these problems are endemic to big US cities.*

endive /ˈen·dɑɪv, ˈɑn·diːv/ *n* [U] a plant with long, narrow leaves that curl at the edges and that is eaten in salads

endless /'en·dləs/ *adj* • See at END LAST PART.

endorse SUPPORT /ɪn'dɔːrs/ *v* [T] to make a public statement of your approval or support for (something or someone) • *We're not endorsing tax increases.* ○ *My wife has publicly endorsed Lunny for city council.* • If someone endorses a product, a statement saying they like it or use it is used in advertising the product.
endorsement /ɪn'dɔːr·smənt/ *n* [C/U] • *Both candidates have been seeking the union's endorsement.* [U] • An endorsement is also a public statement, esp. by someone who is famous, that they use or like a particular product: *Some athletes get contracts for product endorsements worth millions of dollars.* [C]

endorse SIGN /ɪn'dɔːrs/ *v* [T] to write your name on (a check) • *He endorsed the check and deposited it in his account.*
endorsement /ɪn'dɔːr·smənt/ *n* [C] • *The bank won't take checks that have no endorsements.*

endow /ɪn'daʊ/ *v* [T] to give money that will provide an income for (a college or university, hospital, or other organization) • *In 1937 Mellon endowed the National Gallery of Art.* • If someone or something is **endowed with** a particular quality or feature, they naturally have that quality or feature: *People think Jefferson was endowed with an almost divine wisdom.*
endowment /ɪn'daʊ·mənt/ *n* [C] • *We are trying to set up an endowment to support the library.*

endure /ɪn'dʊr/ *v* [I/T] to experience and bear (something painful or unpleasant), esp. for a long time, or to continue for a long time • *We had to endure a nine-hour delay at the airport.* [T]○ *Sinatra's popularity endured for decades.*
endurance /ɪn'dʊr·əns/ *n* [U] the physical or mental strength to continue doing something, esp. for a long time or when faced with difficulty or trouble • *These drugs boost an athlete's strength and endurance.*
enduring /ɪn'dʊr·ɪŋ/ *adj* continuing for a long time; lasting • *He believed in the enduring power of love.*

enema /'en·ə·mə/ *n* [C] the forcing of a liquid into the bowels through the RECTUM (= the opening between your buttocks) to empty them

enemy /'en·ə·mi/ *n* [C] a person who hates or opposes another person and tries to harm them • *Some enemies are spreading nasty gossip about her.* ○ *He views the press as the enemy.* • The enemy is a country or the armed forces or people of a country that is at war with your own country: *Prisoners of war were surprised by the enemy's decency.*

energetic /,en·ər'dʒeṭ·ɪk/ *adj* very active physically and mentally • *The president was an energetic campaigner.*
energetically /,en·ər'dʒeṭ·ɪ·kli/ *adv* • *She energetically promotes women's sports.*

energy STRENGTH /'en·ər·dʒi/ *n* the power and ability to be physically and mentally active • *They spent a lot of time and energy on the grant proposal.* [U] ○ *He wrote with a great burst of energy.* [U] • Your energies are the total amount of your physical and mental strength to do something: *All my energies were directed toward establishing an academic career.* [pl]
energize /'en·ər,dʒaɪz/ *v* [T] to make (something) more active • *The candidate is trying to energize voters.*

energy POWER /'en·ər·dʒi/ *n* [U] power to do work that produces light, heat, or motion, or the fuel or electricity used for power • *The cost of energy rose last month.* ○ *Oil prices rose during the energy crisis.*

enervating /'en·ər,veɪṭ·ɪŋ/ *adj* causing you to feel weak and lacking in energy • *We found it enervating to work in the humid jungle heat.*

enforce /ɪn'fɔːrs, -'foʊrs/ *v* [T] to cause (a law or rule) to be obeyed • *We need to enforce the traffic laws.*
enforcement /ɪn'fɔːr·smənt, -'foʊr-/ *n* [U] • *law enforcement*

enfranchise /ɪn'fræn,tʃaɪz/ *v* [T] to give (a person or group of people) the right to vote in elections
enfranchisement /ɪn'fræn,tʃaɪz·mənt/ *n* [U]

engage INTEREST /ɪn'geɪdʒ/ *v* [T] to cause (someone) to become interested or involved in an activity, or to attract (someone's interest) • *He wrote about everything that engaged his interest.*

engage FIT TOGETHER /ɪn'geɪdʒ/ *v* [I/T] (of a machine part) to fit into and move together with another part, or cause (something) to fit into and move together • *The gears won't engage.* [I] ○ *You need to engage second gear.* [T]

engage BEGIN FIGHTING /ɪn'geɪdʒ/ *v* [T] to attack or begin to fight (an enemy) in a military operation • *The marines engaged the enemy.*
engagement /ɪn'geɪdʒ·mənt/ *n* [C] • *a military engagement* • See also **engagement** at ENGAGED, ENGAGEMENT.

engage EMPLOY /ɪn'geɪdʒ/ *v* [T] to arrange to employ (someone); HIRE • *She decided to engage a personal assistant.* ○ *Her family engaged a tutor to teach her French.*

□ **engage in** /-'-,-/ *v prep* [T] to take part in or do (something) • *The school engaged in discrimination by barring women.* ○ *The men were engaged in a heated dispute.*

engaged /ɪn'geɪdʒd/ *adj* [not gradable] publicly promising that you intend to marry someone • *They decided to get engaged.*
engagement /ɪn'geɪdʒ·mənt/ *n* [C] • *They announced their engagement.* • An **engagement ring** is a ring given by a man to a woman as a formal sign that they have decided to get married. • See also **engagement** at ENGAGE BEGIN FIGHTING, ENGAGEMENT.

engagement /ɪn'geɪdʒ·mənt/ *n* [C] an arrangement to do something or meet someone at a particular time and place • *We have a dinner engagement Thursday.* ○ *The Dance Theatre of Harlem began a two-week engagement at the Kennedy Center.* ○ *The governor has numerous speaking engagements* (= arrangements to give formal speeches) *next month.* • See also **engagement** at ENGAGE BEGIN FIGHTING, ENGAGED.

engaging /ɪnˈgeɪ·dʒɪŋ/ *adj* tending to please; attractive • *He has an engaging manner.*

engender /ɪnˈdʒen·dər/ *v* [T] to cause (something) to come into existence • *Your book has engendered much controversy.*

engine /ˈen·dʒən/ *n* [C] a machine that uses the energy from fuel or steam to produce movement • *The car has a four-cylinder engine.* ○ *(fig.) The health-care industry has been an engine of growth.* ○ *The plane was forced to land because of engine problems.* • An engine (also **locomotive**) is a separate part of a train that pulls the other parts of the train.

engineer PERSON /ˌen·dʒəˈnɪr/ *n* [C] a person specially trained to design and build machines, structures, and other things, including bridges, roads, vehicles, and buildings • *He is an engineer at a large electronics company.* • An engineer is also a person whose job is to drive railroad trains.

engineer /ˌen·dʒəˈnɪr/ *v* [T] to plan, design, or build according to scientific principles • *The bridge is engineered to withstand an earthquake.*

engineering /ˌen·dʒəˈnɪr·ɪŋ/ *n* [U] the study of using scientific principles to design and build machines, structures, and other things, including bridges, roads, vehicles, and buildings • *civil/electrical/mechanical engineering* ○ *an engineering firm/degree*

engineer PLAN SKILLFULLY /ˌen·dʒəˈnɪr/ *v* [T] to plan or do (something) in a skillful way • *The administration engineered a compromise.*

English /ˈɪŋ·glɪʃ, -lɪʃ/ *n* [U] the language of the United Kingdom and the United States, used also in many other parts of the world • *American/British/Canadian/Australian English* • **English as a foreign language** (*abbreviation* **EFL**) is English as taught to people whose main language is not English and who live in a country where English is not the official or main language. • **English as a second language** (*abbreviation* **ESL**) is English as taught to people whose main language is not English and who live in a country where English is an official or main language.

English muffin /ˌɪŋ·glɪʃˈmʌf·ən, -lɪʃ-/ *n* [C] a type of small, flat, round bread that is usually cut open and TOASTED (= heated in a way that makes it dry and brown) before being eaten

engrave /ɪnˈgreɪv/ *v* [T] to cut (a picture or design, or letters) into the surface of a hard substance such as metal, wood, or stone • *Engraved in a granite memorial are the names of*

those who died in civil rights marches. • If something is engraved in your memory, mind, or heart, it is something you will never forget.

engraving /ɪnˈgreɪ·vɪŋ/ *n* [C/U] a picture or design printed on paper from a hard, usually metal, surface in which cuts have been made, or this process • *The museum owns many fine 18th-century engravings.* [C] ○ *The book describes the art of engraving.* [U]

engrossed /ɪnˈgroʊst/ *adj* giving all your attention to something • *We were engrossed in conversation.*

engrossing /ɪŋˈgroʊ·sɪŋ/ *adj* taking all your attention; very interesting • *She had written an engrossing and moving story.*

engulf /ɪnˈgʌlf/ *v* [T] to surround and cover completely • *Floodwaters engulfed midwestern farmlands.*

enhance /ɪnˈhæns/ *v* [T] to improve the quality, amount, or strength of (something) • *The marinade enhances the flavor of the fish.* ○ *The county took steps to enhance water quality.*

enhancement /ɪnˈhæn·smənt/ *n* [C/U] • *The new system is a major enhancement in security.* [C] ○ *Enhancement of local transportation is a priority.* [U]

enigma /ɪˈnɪg·mə/ *n* [C] someone or something that is mysterious and impossible to understand • *He is an enigma to most people.*

enigmatic /ˌen·ɪgˈmæt·ɪk/ *adj* • *an enigmatic smile*

enjoin /ɪnˈdʒɔɪn/ *v* [T] to suggest forcefully and esp. with authority to (someone) • *The ad enjoined young people to join the marines.*

enjoy LIKE TO DO /ɪnˈdʒɔɪ/ *v* [T] to feel happy because of doing or experiencing (something) • *We enjoyed the scenery.* ○ *I enjoyed your book very much.* ○ *Enjoy your weekend.* ○ *She liked her job because she enjoyed meeting people.* • To enjoy yourself is to feel happy because of a situation or an event in which you took part: *I really enjoyed myself last night.*

enjoyable /ɪnˈdʒɔɪ·ə·bəl/ *adj* making you feel happy • *The kids had an enjoyable time at the movies.*

enjoyment /ɪnˈdʒɔɪ·mənt/ *n* [U] • *He gets a lot of enjoyment from listening to music.*

enjoy BENEFIT /ɪnˈdʒɔɪ/ *v* [T] to have the benefit of (something) • *The schools here enjoy strong community support.* ○ *She enjoyed good health well into her 90s.*

enjoyment /ɪnˈdʒɔɪ·mənt/ *n* [U] benefit; use • *Public parks are for the enjoyment of all the people.*

enlarge /ɪnˈlɑrdʒ/ *v* [T] to become larger, or to cause (something) to become larger • *The city council voted to enlarge the park.* • If you enlarge a photograph, you print a bigger copy of it.

enlarged /ɪnˈlɑrdʒd/ *adj* [not gradable] • *He suffers from an enlarged heart.*

enlargement /ɪnˈlɑrdʒ·mənt/ *n* [C/U] • *My mother had an enlargement of the photograph* framed. [C] ○ *The new budget would have resulted in enlargement of the deficit.* [U]

▫**enlarge on/upon** /-'-,-; -'--,-/ *v prep* [T] to speak or write about (something) in detail or in more detail • *I was asked to enlarge upon my theory.*

enlighten /ɪn'laɪt·ᵊn/ *v* [I/T] to cause someone to understand something by explaining it to them or by bringing new information or facts to their attention • *The show is meant to both enlighten and entertain.* [I] ○ *We hope the pamphlet will enlighten voters about the issues.* [T]

enlightened /ɪn'laɪt·ᵊnd/ *adj* showing understanding and wisdom in dealing with others • *This company is an enlightened and reasonable employer.* • Enlightened also means open to new ideas and facts based on reason and science rather than following old, false beliefs: *Every enlightened person rejects racism in all its forms.*

enlightening /ɪn'laɪt·ᵊn·ɪŋ/ *adj* • *The discussion was enlightening.*

enlightenment /ɪn'laɪt·ᵊn·mənt/ *n* [U] • *Meditation helps me achieve enlightenment and serenity.* • The Enlightenment was the period in the 18th century in Europe when particular thinkers began to emphasize the importance of science and reason rather than religion and tradition.

enlist JOIN /ɪn'lɪst/ *v* [I] to join (an organization, esp. the armed forces) • *He enlisted in the air force.* • An enlisted man/woman is a person in the armed forces who is not an officer.

enlist ASK FOR HELP /ɪn'lɪst/ *v* [T] to ask (someone) for help or support, or to ask for and obtain (help and support) • *The program enlists businesses in hiring inner city kids.*

enliven /ɪn'laɪ·vən/ *v* [T] to make more interesting or active • *Entertainment enlivened the meeting.*

enmity /'en·mət̬·i/ *n* [U] strong dislike or hate

enormity LARGENESS /ɪ'nɔːr·mət̬·i/ *n* [U] great size or amount • *The enormity of the wilderness awed us.*

enormity EVIL /ɪ'nɔːr·mət̬·i/ *n* [C/U] very great evil, or a very evil act • *The children had no idea of the enormity of their crime.* [U] ○ *Goya's etchings depict in shocking detail the enormities of war.* [C]

enormous /ɪ'nɔːr·məs/ *adj* extremely large or great • *He ate an enormous helping of pasta.* • *The wealthy will get enormous tax cuts under the proposal.*

enormously /ɪ'nɔːr·mə·sli/ *adv* very or very much • *She was enormously rich.*

enough /ɪ'nʌf/ *adj, adv, pronoun* as much as is necessary; in the amount or to the degree needed • *Do we have enough lettuce for a salad?* ○ *He had just enough time to make his train.* ○ *Have you had enough to eat?* [+ *to* infinitive] ○ *I think she's well enough now to make the trip.* [+ *to* infinitive] ○ *You'll find out when*

we're leaving soon enough. • Enough can also mean as much or more than is wanted: *I think we've heard enough.* ○ *I have enough to do without taking on any more work.* [+ *to* infinitive] • If someone says **enough is enough**, they feel that what has been happening is unpleasant and they now want it to stop: *The play was dull and I decided enough is enough and left early.*

enrage /ɪn'reɪdʒ/ *v* [T] to cause (someone) to become very angry • *School curriculum changes enraged a number of parents.* ○ *Enraged readers boycotted the newspaper.*

enrich /ɪn'rɪtʃ/ *v* [T] to improve the quality of (something), esp. by adding something else • *The heritage of Africa has greatly enriched American life.* ○ *Uranium is enriched for use in nuclear reactors.* • To enrich is also to make richer: *The rock music of the 1960s enriched the big recording companies.*

enrichment /ɪn'rɪtʃ·mənt/ *n* [U] • *a course offering language enrichment*

enroll *(obj)* /ɪn'roʊl/ *v* to put (yourself or someone else) on an official list for an activity or for membership in a group, or to accept (someone) in such a list • *We have enrolled eighty children in this day-care program.* [T] ○ *He enrolled at Penn State University.* [I] ○ *She enrolled as a volunteer to tutor adults in English.* [+ *to* infinitive]

enrollment /ɪn'roʊl·mənt/ *n* [C] • *Enrollments at medical schools are down this year.* [C] ○ *Enrollment figures for next year are now available.*

en route /ɑn'ruːt, en-, ɑ̃-/ *adv* [not gradable] on the way to or from somewhere • *The ambulance is en route to the hospital.* ○ *En route from New York to Boston, the bus crashed into a stalled car.*

ensconce /ɪn'skɑns/ *v* [T always + adv/prep] to situate (yourself) in a comfortable place or position • *Dan was ensconced at the bar when I arrived.*

ensemble /ɑn'sɑm·bəl, ɑ̃-/ *n* [C] a group of people who perform together, esp. musically, or a collection of things intended to be used together • *a woodwind ensemble* ○ *I admired her ensemble of coat, hat, and shoes.*

enshrine /ɪn'ʃraɪn/ *v* [T always + adv/prep] to contain or keep in a place that is highly admired and respected • *Only eight second basemen are enshrined in the baseball Hall of Fame.* ○ *This principle is enshrined in the Constitution.*

ensign FLAG /'en·sən/ *n* [C] a flag on a ship showing the country the ship belongs to

ensign OFFICER /'en·sən/ *n* [C] a naval officer of the lowest rank

enslave /ɪn'sleɪv/ *v* [T] to control (someone) by keeping them in a bad or hopeless situation where they are not free, or to make a SLAVE (= person legally owned) of (someone)

ensue /ɪn'suː/ *v* [I] to happen after something

else, esp. as a result of it • *Panic ensued when police opened fire.* ○ *After his outburst, a long silence ensued.*

ensuing /ɪnˈsuː·ɪŋ/ *adj* [not gradable] happening after or following something else • *War has a lasting effect on the ensuing years of a person's life.* ○ *Ensuing tests disclosed an irregular heartbeat.*

ensure *(obj)* /ɪnˈʃʊr/ *v* INSURE MAKE CERTAIN

entail /ɪnˈteɪl/ *v* [T] to involve or make (something) necessary • *Any investment entails risk.*

entangle /ɪnˈtæŋ·ɡəl/ *v* [T] to trap (something) within something else from which it is difficult to escape • *A seal became entangled in the fishing net.* ○ *(fig.) The movie explores the entangled* (= mixed together in many ways) *relationships involving two couples.*

entanglement /ɪnˈtæŋ·ɡəl·mənt/ *n* [C] a situation or relationship that involves you in ways that you are not comfortable with but from which it is difficult to escape • *a legal entanglement* ○ *She wants to avoid any entanglements at the office.*

enter GO IN /ˈent·ər/ *v* [I/T] to come or go into (a place) • *The orchestra entered the hall.* [T] ○ *He entered a shelter for the homeless.* [T] ○ *Half of the museum's visitors are children who enter for free.* [I] • To enter is also to be admitted to or become a member of an organization: *He entered the army at the age of 18.* [I]

enter BEGIN /ˈent·ər/ *v* [I/T] to begin or become involved in (something) • *The president maintained we were about to enter a period of unprecedented economic growth.* [T] ○ *She entered into an exclusive contract with an international sports shoe company.* [I]

enter RECORD /ˈent·ər/ *v* [T] to make a record of (something); list • *Did you enter your names in the guest book?* ○ *Use this computer to enter the data.* ○ *He was entered* (= listed officially as taking part) *in the shot put and discus events.* • *(law)* To enter is to make something, such as a statement or a piece of EVIDENCE, a part of the official record: *He entered a plea of not guilty.*

enterprise /ˈent·ərˌpraɪz/ *n* [C/U] an organization, esp. a business, or a difficult and important plan, esp. one that will earn money • *private enterprise* [U] ○ *The road is bordered by shopping centers, restaurants, retail outlets, and other commercial enterprises.* [C] • Enterprise is also the willingness and energy to do something new that takes a lot of effort: *They've showed a great deal of enterprise in setting up this project.* [U]

enterprising /ˈent·ərˌpraɪ·zɪŋ/ *adj* (of a person) good at thinking of and doing new and difficult things, esp. those that will make money • *The business was started by a couple of enterprising women.*

entertain AMUSE /ˌent·ərˈteɪn/ *v* [I/T] to keep (esp. a group of people) interested or amused • *Children's games and books seek to teach and*

entertain at the same time. [I] ○ *Kerry and Bill entertained listeners of their radio show with tales of their adventures on an ocean cruise.* [T]

entertainer /ˌent·ərˈteɪ·nər/ *n* [C] someone who sings, dances, tells jokes, etc., as a job

entertaining /ˌent·ərˈteɪ·nɪŋ/ *adj* amusing and enjoyable • *an entertaining movie*

entertainment /ˌent·ərˈteɪn·mənt/ *n* [C/U] public shows, performances, or other ways of enjoying yourself • *We try to offer good, clean entertainment.* [U]

entertain INVITE /ˌent·ərˈteɪn/ *v* [I/T] to invite (someone) to your house and give food and drink to them • *She was a good cook and liked to entertain her friends with new dishes.* [T] ○ *We didn't entertain much over the holidays this year.* [I]

entertain THINK ABOUT /ˌent·ərˈteɪn/ *v* [T] to hold in your mind or to be willing to consider or accept • *He entertained some doubts about how truthful the government was.*

enthrall /ɪnˈθrɔːl/ *v* [T] to keep (someone) completely interested • *I was always enthralled by the rotary engine, and thought it was a neat idea.*

enthralling /ɪnˈθrɔː·lɪŋ/ *adj* • *Her performance was enthralling.*

enthuse /ɪnˈθuːz/ *v* [I] to express excitement or interest • *You don't sound too enthused about the party tonight.*

enthusiasm /ɪnˈθuː·ziˌæz·əm/ *n* [C/U] a feeling of energetic interest in a particular subject or activity and an eagerness to be involved in it, or a subject that produces such a feeling • *I find that I'm losing my enthusiasm for the game.* [U] ○ *Parents need to share their enthusiasms with their children.* [C]

enthusiast /ɪnˈθuː·ziˌæst, -əst/ *n* [C] someone who is very interested in and involved with a particular subject or activity • *a computer-games enthusiast*

enthusiastic /ɪnˌθuː·ziˈæs·tɪk/ *adj* • *You don't seem very enthusiastic about the movie.*

enthusiastically /ɪnˌθuː·ziˈæs·tɪ·kli/ *adv* • *She was welcomed enthusiastically by the crowd.*

entice /ɪnˈtaɪs/ *v* [T] to attract (someone) to a particular place or activity by offering something pleasant or advantageous • *People are enticed away from government jobs by higher salaries.*

entire /ɪnˈtaɪr/ *adj* [not gradable] whole or complete, with nothing missing, or continuous, without interruption • *He read the entire book on the flight to Buenos Aires.* ○ *Her entire family gathered for their annual reunion.* ○ *I spent an entire month writing that report.*

entirely /ɪnˈtaɪr·li/ *adv* [not gradable] • *I admit it was entirely my fault.* • LP VERY, COMPLETELY, AND OTHER INTENSIFIERS

entirety /ɪnˈtaɪ·rət̬·i, -ˈtaɪrt̬·i/ *n* [U] • Something in its **entirety** means all of something:

I never read the contract in its entirety, just parts of it.

entitle ALLOW /ɪnˈtaɪt̬·əl/ v [T] to give (someone) the right to do or have something • *He's entitled to his opinion even if you don't agree with him.* ○ *Being over 65 entitles you to a discount at the movies.*

entitlement /ɪnˈtaɪt̬·əl·mənt/ n [C/U] something, often a benefit from the government, that you have the right to have • *Social Security and Medicare are popular entitlement programs in the US.* [U]

entitle GIVE TITLE /ɪnˈtaɪt̬·əl/ v [T] to give (a title) to (a book, movie, etc.) • *Her latest novel, entitled "The Forgotten Child," is arriving in bookstores this week.*

entity /ˈen·t̬ət̬·i/ n [C] something that exists apart from other things, having its own independent existence • *Although the two buildings are in separate locations, the museum they are part of is a single entity.*

entourage /ˌɑn·tʊˈrɑʒ/ n [C] the group of people who travel with and work for an important or famous person • *Her usual entourage includes musicians, backup singers, and technicians.*

entrance WAY IN /ˈen·trəns/ n [C/U] a door, gate, etc., by which you can enter a building or place • *There are two entrances—one at the front and one at the back of the building.* [C] • Entrance is also the right to be admitted to a place or to an organization: *Entrance to the museum is free on Sundays.* [U] ○ *He took the entrance exam to law school yesterday.* [U]

entrance INTEREST /ɪnˈtræns/ v [T] to hold the complete interest and attention of (someone) • *We were entranced by mourners singing in glorious harmony, accompanied by guitar music.*

entrant /ˈen·trənt/ n [C] a person who takes part in a competition, or a new member of a school or organization • *All entrants in the race should go to the starting line now.*

entrap /ɪnˈtræp/ v [T] **-pp-** to arrange a situation so that a particular bad or illegal action is easy to do, allowing the authorities to catch (someone) doing it • *Female police officers have posed as prostitutes to entrap unwary men.*

entrapment /ɪnˈtræp·mənt/ n [U] • *He claimed he was the victim of FBI entrapment.*

entrée /ˈɑn·treɪ/ n [C] the main dish of a meal

entrenched /ɪnˈtrentʃt/ adj esp. disapproving established firmly so that it cannot be changed • *An entrenched bureaucracy stalled Gorbachev's efforts to modernize Soviet society.*

entrepreneur /ˌɑn·trə·prəˈnɜr, -ˈnʊr/ n [C] a person who attempts to make a profit by starting their own company or by operating alone in the business world, esp. when it involves taking risks • *He's an entrepreneur who made his money in computer software.*

entrepreneurial /ˌɑn·trə·prəˈnɜr·i·əl, -ˈnʊr-/ adj

entrust /ɪnˈtrʌst/ v [T always + adv/prep] to make (someone) responsible for (someone or something) • *We entrusted our dog to a neighbor when we went away on a trip.*

entry WAY IN /ˈen·tri/ n [C/U] the act or manner of entering a place or of entering into an organization or relationship with others • *America's entry into the war was delayed.* [U] ○ *Entry to the basement is through a back stairway.* [U] ○ *Police gained entry by breaking a window.* [U] • An **entryway** is an enclosed passage through which you enter a building or a set of rooms within a building.

entry COMPETITION /ˈen·tri/ n [C] a person or thing that is part of a competition • *There were five entries for best picture of the year.*

entry RECORD /ˈen·tri/ n [C] a single written item in a list or collection of records • *an entry in a diary*

entwine /ɪnˈtwaɪn/ v [T] to twist together or around (something) • *The old-fashioned porch was entwined with many creeping plants.* ○ *(fig.) In the old days, moviemaking was entwined with political and social life.*

enumerate /ɪˈnu·məˌreɪt/ v [T] to name (things) separately, one by one • *The salesman enumerated the features of the car.*

enunciate /ɪˈnʌn·siˌeɪt/ v [I/T] fml to state (something) clearly and often officially • *The administration enunciated a new policy on security issues.* [T] • To enunciate is also to pronounce words: *He enunciated his words carefully.* [T]

envelop /ɪnˈvel·əp/ v [T] to cover or surround (something) completely • *The entire area was enveloped in fog.*

envelope /ˈen·vəˌloʊp, ˈɑn-/ n [C] a usually rectangular paper container for a letter • *Don't forget to put a stamp on the envelope.*

enviable /ˈen·vi·ə·bəl/ adj • See at ENVY.

envious /ˈen·vi·əs/ adj • See at ENVY.

environment SURROUNDINGS /ɪnˈvaɪ·rən·mənt, -ˈvaɪrn-/ n [C] the conditions that you live or work in and the way that they influence how you feel or how effectively you can work • *a good business environment* ○ *They provided a smoke-free environment for their employees.*

environment NATURE /ɪnˈvaɪ·rən·mənt, -ˈvaɪrn-/ n [U] the air, water, and land in or on which people, animals, and plants live • *We're trying to protect the environment from pollution.*

environmental /ɪnˌvaɪ·rənˈment·əl, -ˌvaɪrn-/ adj [not gradable] • *We're here to discuss environmental issues.*

environmentally /ɪnˌvaɪ·rənˈment·əl·i, -ˌvaɪrn-/ adv [not gradable]

environmentalist /ɪnˌvaɪ·rənˈment·əl·əst, -ˌvaɪrn-/ n [C] a person who has a specially strong interest in or knowledge of the natural environment, and who wants to preserve it and prevent damage to it • *Environmentalists* *are working to improve the quality of our lakes and rivers.*

environs /ɪnˈvaɪ·rənz, -ˈvaɪ·ɔrnz/ *pl n* the area surrounding a place, esp. a town

envision *(obj)* /ɪnˈvɪʒ·ən/, **envisage** /ɪnˈvɪz·ɪdʒ/ *v* to imagine or expect as a likely or desirable possibility in the future • *He envisioned a partnership between business and government.* [T] ○ *The company envisions adding at least five stores next year.*

envoy /ˈen·vɔɪ, ˈɑn-/ *n* [C] someone who is sent as a representative from one government or organization to another

envy /ˈen·vi/ *v* [T] to wish that you had (a quality or possession) that another person has • *I envy people so much who feel carefree.*

envy /ˈen·vi/ *n* [U] • *His new car is the envy of* (= liked and wanted by) *all his friends.*

enviable /ˈen·vi·ə·bəl/ *adj* (esp. of a quality or advantage) causing you to wish that you also possessed it; desirable • *She has an enviable ability to work under pressure.*

envious /ˈen·vi·əs/ *adj* wanting something another person has • *I'm envious of people that have those big boats.*

enzyme /ˈen·zaɪm/ *n* [C] any of a group of chemical substances that are produced by living cells and which cause particular chemical reactions to happen

ephemeral /ɪˈfem·ə·rəl/ *adj* lasting for only a short time • *ephemeral fame*

epic /ˈep·ɪk/ *n* [C] a book or movie that is long and contains a lot of action, usually dealing with a historical subject • An epic is also a long poem dealing with historical events involving gods or rulers: *The Iliad is the most famous Greek epic.*

epic /ˈep·ɪk/ *adj* happening over a long period and characterized by a lot of difficulties • *an epic struggle to achieve equality for African Americans*

epidemic /ˌep·əˈdem·ɪk/ *n* [C] the appearance of a particular disease in a very large number of people during the same period of time • *a flu epidemic*

epigram /ˈep·əˌɡræm/ *n* [C] a short saying or poem that expresses an idea in an amusing way

epilepsy /ˈep·əˌlep·si/ *n* [U] a disease of the brain that may cause a person to lose consciousness and fall, and to lose control of their movements for a short time

epileptic /ˌep·əˈlep·tɪk/ *adj* [not gradable]

epilogue /ˈep·əˌlɑɡ, -ˌlɔːɡ/ *n* [C] a speech or piece of text added to the end of a play or book, often giving a short statement about what happens to the characters after the play or book finishes

Episcopal /ɪˈpɪs·kə·pəl/ *adj* [not gradable] of a Christian religious group that is one of the Protestant churches • *an Episcopal church/minister*

Episcopalian /ɪˌpɪs·kəˈpeɪl·jən/ *n* [C], *adj* [not gradable] • *George is an Episcopalian.*

episode /ˈep·əˌsoʊd/ *n* [C] a single event or group of related events • *That was an episode in my life that I'd like to forget.* • An episode is also one of the parts of a television or radio program that is given as a series over a period of time.

epitaph /ˈep·əˌtæf/ *n* [C] a short piece of writing or a poem about a dead person, esp. one written on their **tombstone** (= the stone over the place where they are buried)

epithet /ˈep·əˌθet/ *n* [C] a descriptive phrase used esp. to criticize or insult a person or a group of people • *a racial epithet*

epitome /ɪˈpɪt·ə·mi/ *n* [U] the typical or highest example of a stated quality, as shown by a particular person or thing • *He was the epitome of the fashionable gentleman.*

epitomize /ɪˈpɪt·əˌmaɪz/ *v* [T] • *His recordings came to epitomize American popular singing at its finest.*

epoch /ˈep·ək, -ˌɑk/ *n* [C] *pl* **epochs** a long period of time, esp. one in which there are new advances and great change

equal [SAME IN AMOUNT] /ˈiː·kwəl/, *symbol* = *adj* the same in amount, number, size, or quality • *One quart is equal to four cups.* ○ *Divide the class into equal groups.* • An **equal sign** (also **equals sign**) is the symbol =.

equal /ˈiː·kwəl/ *n* [C] • *As an all-around athlete he has no equal* (= no one else is as good).

equal /ˈiː·kwəl/ *v* • *We hope to equal the amount of money we raised last year.* [T] ○ *In mathematics, 10 + 10 = 20 means ten plus ten equals twenty.* [L]

equalize /ˈiː·kwəˌlaɪz/ *v* [T] to bring to the same level or amount • *The law required the state to equalize spending among school districts.*

equally /ˈiː·kwə·li/ *adj* • *The money was shared equally among the three sisters.*

equal [DESERVING THE SAME] /ˈiː·kwəl/ *adj* the same in importance and (of people) deserving the same treatment • *equal rights* ○ *We want a society that promotes equal opportunity for all of its citizens.*

equal /ˈiː·kwəl/ *n* [C] • *In this country, we're all equals with the same rights.*

equality /ɪˈkwɑl·ət·i/ *n* [U] the right of different groups of people to receive the same treatment • *racial equality*

equanimity /ˌek·wəˈnɪm·ət·i, ˌiː·kwə-/ *n* [U] the state of being calm and in control of your emotions, esp. in a difficult situation • *In spite of her financial troubles, she faced the future with equanimity.*

equate /ɪˈkweɪt/ *v* [T always + adv/prep] to consider as the same, or to connect in your mind • *People sometimes equate money with happiness.*

equation /ɪˈkweɪ·ʒən/ *n* [C] a mathematical statement that two amounts, or two symbols or groups of symbols representing an amount, are equal • *In the equation 3x − 3 = 15, x equals 6.*

equator /ɪˈkweɪţ·ər/ n [U] an imaginary line that goes around the middle of the earth and that is an equal distance from the North Pole and the South Pole

equestrian /ɪˈkwes·tri:·ən/ adj [not gradable] connected with the riding of horses • An equestrian statue is a statue of a person on a horse.

equilateral /ˌi:·kwəˈlæţ·ə·rəl, ˌek·wə-/ adj [not gradable] (esp. of triangles), having all sides the same length • *an equilateral triangle*

equilibrium /ˌi:·kwəˈlɪb·ri:·əm, ˌek·wə-/ n [U] a state of balance • *He devised a mathematical method to prove the existence of equilibrium among prices, production, and consumer demand.* • Equilibrium is also a state of mental calmness.

equinox /ˈi:·kwə,nɑks, ˈek·wə-/ n [C] either of the two times during the year when the sun crosses the equator and day and night are of equal length, about March 21st and September 23rd • Compare SOLSTICE.

equip PROVIDE /ɪˈkwɪp/ v [T] **-pp-** to provide (someone or something) with objects that are needed for a particular activity or purpose • *All of our classrooms are equipped with computers.*

equipment /ɪˈkwɪp·mənt/ n [U] the set of tools, clothing, etc., needed for a particular activity or purpose • *computer/electrical/farm equipment*

equip PREPARE /ɪˈkwɪp/ v [T] **-pp-** to prepare (someone or something) with whatever is needed to deal with a particular situation • *The convention center is equipped to handle 20,000 people daily.* ○ *I am not really equipped to discuss international affairs.*

equitable /ˈek·wəţ·ə·bəl/ adj treating everyone equally; fair • *She charged that women are being denied equitable pay.*

equity /ˈek·wəţ·i/ n [U] equal treatment; fairness

equity /ˈek·wəţ·i/ n [C/U] specialized the money value of a property or business after debts have been subtracted • *How much equity do you have in your home?* [U] • An equity is also one of the equal parts, or shares, into which the value of a company is divided. [C]

equivalent /ɪˈkwɪv·ə·lənt/ adj equal to or having the same effect as something else • *A mile is equivalent to about 1.6 kilometers.*

equivalent /ɪˈkwɪv·ə·lənt/ n [C] • *It was the moral equivalent of blackmail.*

equivocal /ɪˈkwɪv·ə·kəl/ adj (of statements) unclear and seeming to have two opposing meanings, or (of actions or ways of behaving) confusing and able to be understood in two different ways • *She gave an equivocal response.*

era /ˈɪr·ə, ˈer·ə, ˈiː·rə/ n [C] a period of time characterized by particular events or developments • *She was one of the more remarkable women of her era.*

eradicate /ɪˈræd·ə,keɪt/ v [T] to get rid of or destroy (something) completely • *A new vaccine eradicated polio.*

erase DESTROY /ɪˈreɪs/ v [T] to destroy or remove (something) completely • *A subdirectory filled with precious data can be erased if you are not careful.*

erase RUB AWAY /ɪˈreɪs/ v [T] to remove (something written or a mark) by rubbing • *I kept changing my mind and erasing my answers on the test.*

eraser /ɪˈreɪ·sər/ n [C] a small piece of rubber that can be used to remove marks, esp. pencil marks on paper

erect BUILD /ɪˈrekt/ v [T] to build (a building or other structure) • *They decided to erect a bridge across the Niagara Gorge.*

erect VERTICAL /ɪˈrekt/ adj in a straight vertical position • *erect posture* • When a part of the body, esp. soft tissue, is erect, it is harder and bigger than usual, often pointing out or up: *an erect penis*

erect /ɪˈrekt/ v [T] to put up or raise to a vertical position • *They're erecting a big circus tent*

erection /ɪˈrek·ʃən/ n [C] • When a man has an erection, his penis is temporarily harder and bigger than usual and points up.

erode /ɪˈroʊd/ v [I/T] to weaken or damage (something) by taking away parts of it gradually, or to become weaker in this way • *Budget cuts could further erode the benefit package provided for by the contract.* [T] • If a natural feature or physical object erodes, it is damaged by the effect of weather. [I]

erosion /ɪˈroʊ·ʒən/ n [U] the weakening or damage done to something by a series of gradual losses of parts of it • *an erosion of academic standards* • Erosion of a natural feature or physical object is damage caused by the effect of weather: *soil erosion*

erotic /ɪˈrɑţ·ɪk/ adj causing or intended to cause someone to feel more interested in sex or to become excited sexually • *erotic dreams/feelings/pictures*

err /er, ɜr/ v [I] to make a mistake • *It's preferable to err on the side of caution* (= to be too careful) *rather than risk disaster.*

errand /ˈer·ənd/ n [C] a short trip for a particular purpose, usually in the neighborhood • *He would clean, do errands, and babysit for their 7-year-old daughter.*

errant /ˈer·ənt/ adj [not gradable] going in a wrong direction actually or morally; done or behaving wrongly • *An errant throw cost them the game.* ○ (slightly humorous) You're dealing with errant husbands and cheating wives.

erratic /ɪˈræţ·ɪk/ adj changing suddenly and unexpectedly • *an erratic schedule*

erroneous /ɪˈroʊ·ni:·əs/ adj based on false

information and therefore wrong; false • *an erroneous assumption*

error /ˈer·ər/ *n* [C/U] a mistake, esp. in a way that can be discovered as wrong, or the making of such mistakes • *a spelling/mathematical error* [C] ○ *Investigators said the train crash was caused by human error rather than mechanical failure.* [U]

erudite /ˈer·jə‚daɪt/ *adj fml* having or showing a lot of knowledge of specialized subjects, esp. from having studied them • *She is a scholarly and erudite person.*

erupt /ɪˈrʌpt/ *v* [I] to burst out suddenly or explode • *The mayor warned that violence might erupt if something wasn't done soon.* ○ *The building erupted in flames when the plane struck it.* • If a VOLCANO (= type of mountain) erupts, it begins to throw out hot rocks and burning substances.

eruption /ɪˈrʌp·ʃən/ *n* [C]

escalate /ˈes·kə‚leɪt/ *v* [I/T] to make or become greater or more serious • *Sending in more troops would escalate the war.* [T] ○ *Our costs escalated considerably over the next few years.* [I]

escalating /ˈes·kə‚leɪt·ɪŋ/ *adj* [not gradable] • *escalating tensions/prices*

escalation /‚es·kə'leɪ·ʃən/ *n* [C/U] the process of becoming greater or more serious, or a particular situation when this happens • *He wanted to avoid any escalation of bloodshed.* [C]

escalator /ˈes·kə‚leɪt·ər/ *n* [C] a set of stairs that moves by electric power and on which people can stand to be taken up and down from one level to another, usually within a building

escapade /ˈes·kə‚peɪd/ *n* [C usually pl] an act or situation that is exciting because it shows behavior that is not controlled as it usually is • *He was better known for his offscreen romantic escapades than his acting.*

escape /ɪˈskeɪp/ *v* [I/T] to become free or get free from, or to avoid (something) • *to escape from prison/a burning house* [I] ○ *The book's faults have not escaped the notice of* (= not been missed by) *critics.* [T]

escape /ɪˈskeɪp/ *n* [C/U] the act or possibility of becoming free or getting away from a place where you are kept esp. by force, or of avoiding a dangerous situation • *The blast knocked me down—it was a narrow escape* (= I was almost hurt badly). [C] • An escape is also an unintentional loss: *an escape of radioactive fuel* [C]

escapism /ɪˈskeɪ‚pɪz·əm/ *n* [U] the avoidance of reality by imagining exciting but impossible activities

eschew /ɪsˈtʃuː/ *v* [T] *fml* to avoid (something) intentionally, or to give up (something) • *The leaders of the organization eschewed the term "union," preferring "guild."*

escort /ɪsˈkɔːrt, es-/ *v* [T] to go with (someone or something) as a companion, guard, or help-er • *He escorted her to her car in the parking lot because it was after dark.*

escort /ˈes·kɔːrt/ *n* [C] a companion or guard for someone or something • *Anytime a clerk transfers money, he is provided with an armed escort.* • An escort is also someone, esp. a young woman, who is paid to go out socially with other people.

Eskimo /ˈes·kə‚moʊ/, **Inuit** *n* [C] *pl* **Eskimos** a member of a group of people who live in the cold northern areas of North America, Russia, and Greenland • USAGE: In Canada and Greenland, the preferred name is Inuit.

ESL *n* [U] *abbreviation for* **English as a second language**, see at ENGLISH • *Luisa teaches ESL in California.*

esophagus /ɪˈsɑf·ə·gəs/ *n* [C] *specialized* the tube in the body that carries food from the mouth to the stomach

esoteric /‚es·ə'ter·ɪk/ *adj* intended for or understandable to only a few people who have special knowledge • *Literary readings can sometimes seem esoteric, but we are trying to make them more attractive to more people.*

esp. *adv abbreviation for* ESPECIALLY

especially /ɪˈspeʃ·li, -ə·li/ *adv* (used to emphasize the importance of one thing among others of its type or to point to one thing among others) very; particularly • *He was especially fond of his youngest brother.* ○ *She campaigned throughout the US, but especially in the northeast.* • LP VERY, COMPLETELY, AND OTHER INTENSIFIERS

espionage /ˈes·pi:·ə‚nɑʒ, *Cdn often* -‚næʒ/ *n* [U] the discovering of a country's or business organization's secrets by using SPIES (= people who secretly gather information within a country or organization) • *industrial espionage*

espouse /ɪˈspaʊz/ *v* [T] *fml* to support (an activity or opinion) • *He espoused conservative political views.*

espresso /esˈpres·oʊ, ɪkˈspres-/ *n* [C/U] *pl* **espressos** coffee made by forcing steam through crushed coffee beans and served without milk, or a small cup filled with this coffee

esprit de corps /es‚priːd·ə'kɔːr, -'koʊr/ *n* [U] the proud and comfortable feeling that you are a member of a group whose purpose you believe in • *People who live on houseboats have a certain esprit de corps.*

essay /ˈes·eɪ/ *n* [C] a short piece of writing on a particular subject, often expressing personal views • In a school test, an essay is a written answer that includes information and discussion, usually to test how well the student understands the subject.

essence IMPORTANCE /ˈes·əns/ *n* [U] the basic meaning or importance of something • *The essence of punk was a revolt against both the sound and the system of popular music.* • **In essence** means that what follows is a brief statement of the basic meaning of something: *In essence, she's saying that she may quit her job.*

essence SMELL / TASTE /'es·əns/ *n* [C] a chemical substance obtained from plants that has a strong smell or taste and can be used to flavor foods or provide a pleasant smell, such as in PERFUMES

essential /ɪ'sen·tʃəl/ *adj* extremely important or necessary • *A knowledge of Spanish is essential for this job.* • Essential also means basic to the nature of someone or something: *There is an essential difference between the two sisters in their approach to life.*

essential /ɪ'sen·tʃəl/ *n* [C usually pl] the basic things you need to live • *The study estimated the cost of essentials for a family of four—its food, shelter, and clothing needs.* • Essentials are also the basic or most important part of something: *the essentials of chemistry*

essentially /ɪ'sen·tʃə·li/ *adv* [not gradable] • *Essentially she's saying that she is not interested in seeing you again.*

establish START /ɪ'stæb·lɪʃ/ *v* [T] to start (something that will last for a long time), or to create or set (something) in a particular way • *He helped to establish the University of California at Berkeley.* ◦ *Once we establish the price, we can begin to market the product.*

establishment /ɪ'stæb·lɪʃ·mənt/ *n* [U] • *She called for the establishment of nationwide academic standards.*

establish *(obj)* PROVE /ɪ'stæb·lɪʃ/ *v* to prove (something) or show (the state of something), esp. by collecting facts or information about it • *The coroner has not yet established the cause of death.* [T] ◦ *We're trying to establish what happened here.* [+ wh- word]

establish ACCEPT /ɪ'stæb·lɪʃ/ *v* [T] to cause (someone or something) to be accepted generally • *She's established herself as a leading authority on urban problems.*

established /ɪ'stæb·lɪʃt/ *adj* generally accepted or familiar, esp. because of having a long history • *an established procedure*

establishment /ɪ'stæb·lɪʃ·mənt/ *n* [C] a business or other organization, or the place where an organization operates • *This establishment does not serve alcoholic beverages.* • The establishment is the people who have most of the power within a country or in a particular activity. [C usually sing]

estate /ɪ'steɪt/ *n* [C] a large, privately owned area of land in the country, often with a large house • *(law)* A person's estate is everything they own when they die. • *(Br)* An estate is a group of houses or factories built in a planned way. • *(Br)* An **estate agent** is a **real estate agent**. See at REAL ESTATE.

esteem /ɪ'stiːm/ *n* [U] respect for or a high opinion of someone • *We held them in high/ low esteem* (= We respected them a lot/very little).

esteemed /ɪ'stiːm/ *adj fml* highly respected • *It is my honor to introduce our esteemed senator.*

esthetic /es'θeṭ·ɪk, ɪs-/ *adj* AESTHETIC

estimable /'es·tə·mə·bəl/ *adj* [not gradable] *fml* considered with respect • *She ran an estimable if obscure publishing house for nearly fifty years.*

estimate /'es·tə·mət/ *n* [C] a judgment or calculation of approximately how large or how great something is • *I can only make a rough estimate* (= an amount that is not exact) *of how many people will attend.* • An estimate is also a statement of the likely cost of building something or doing some other work.

estimate *(obj)* /'es·tə·meɪt/ *v* • *We estimated his wealth at $500 million.* [T] ◦ *Doctors estimate (that) he has a 70 percent chance of recovering.* [+ *(that)* clause]

estimation /ˌes·tə'meɪ·ʃən/ *n* [U] judgment; opinion • *The first novel was successful, whereas the second, in my estimation, was not.*

estranged /ɪ'streɪndʒd/ *adj* [not gradable] (of a husband or wife) not living with the person they are married to • *his estranged wife* • If you are estranged from your family or friends, then you are no longer close or friendly with them and do not see them.

estrogen /'es·trə·dʒən/ *n* [U] a female HORMONE (= chemical substance produced in the body) that is important in sexual development and that causes changes in the uterus

estuary /'es·tʃə·wer·i/ *n* [C] the part of a river or other area of water where it joins the sea, and where fresh water and salt water are mixed

et al. /eṭ'æl/ *adv abbreviation for* (used, esp. in writing, after one or more names) et alii (= and other people) • *The method is described in an article by Feynman et al.*

etc. /et,seṭ·ə·rə, ɪt-, -'se·trə/ *adv abbreviation for* (used after a list) et cetera (= and other similar things) • *The children use computers in many instructional areas, including math, science, language study, etc.*

etch /etʃ/ *v* [T] to cut a pattern, picture, etc., in a surface, esp. wax, covering metal or glass, and allow acid to cut (the pattern, picture, etc.) on the metal or glass surface itself • *(fig.) The scene must have etched itself deeply on Newton's consciousness if he recalled it nine years later.*

etching /'etʃ·ɪŋ/ *n* [C] a picture produced by printing from a metal plate that has been prepared with acid

eternal /ɪ'tɜrn·əl, iː-/ *adj* [not gradable] lasting forever, or seeming to be without end • *Some religions promise their followers eternal life.*

eternally /ɪ'tɜrn·əl·i, iː-/ *adv* [not gradable] • *I'd be eternally grateful if you'd handle it.*

eternity /ɪ'tɜr·nəṭ·i, iː-/ *n* [U] endless time;

time without limits • *At her age, even a few months can seem like an eternity.*

ether /'iː·θər/ *n* [U] a colorless liquid used, esp. in the past, to put people to sleep before an operation

ethereal /ɪ'θɪr·iː·əl/ *adj* extremely light and delicate, as if not of this world • *ethereal music* ○ *an ethereal beauty*

ethic /'eθ·ɪk/ *n* [C usually pl] a system of accepted beliefs that control behavior, esp. such a system based on morals • *Our school promotes an ethic of service to the community.*

ethical /'eθ·ɪ·kəl/ *adj* • *No ethical physician would prescribe that drug.*

ethically /'eθ·ɪ·kli/ *adv* • *Laughing at your clients is ethically wrong.*

ethics /'eθ·ɪks/ *n* [U] the study of what is morally right and wrong, or a set of beliefs about what is morally right and wrong • *They're completely lacking in ethics.*

ethnic /'eθ·nɪk/ *adj* relating to or characteristic of a large group of people who have the same national, racial, or cultural origins, and who usually speak the same language • *an ethnic neighborhood* ○ *She loves ethnic foods, especially Ethiopian and Japanese.* • **Ethnic cleansing** is the organized, often violent attempt by one ethnic group to remove from a country or area all members of a different group.

ethnically /'eθ·nɪ·kli/ *adv* • *an ethnically diverse community*

ethnicity /eθ'nɪs·əṭ·i/ *n* [C/U] • *They place no importance on ethnicity.* [U]

ethos /'iː·θɑs/ *n* [U] the set of moral beliefs, attitudes, habits, etc., that are characteristic of a person or group • *Violence is part of their ethos.*

etiquette /'eṭ·ə·kət/ *n* [U] the set of rules or customs that control accepted behavior in particular social groups or social situations

etymology /,eṭ·ə'mɑl·ə·dʒi/ *n* [C/U] the origin and history of a word or words, or the study of word origins

EU *n* [U] abbreviation for **European Union**, see at EUROPEAN

Eucharist /'juː·kə·rəst/ *n* [U] the Christian ceremony based on Jesus's last meal with his followers, or the bread and wine used in this ceremony

eulogy /'juː·lə·dʒi/ *n* [C/U] a speech or piece of writing containing great praise, esp. for someone who has recently died • *He delivered the eulogy at his father's funeral.* [C]

eunuch /'juː·nək, -nɪk/ *n* [C] *pl* **eunuchs** a man who has been CASTRATED (= had the sex organs that produce sperm removed)

euphemism /'juː·fə,mɪz·əm/ *n* [C] the use of a word or phrase to avoid saying another word or phrase that may be unpleasant or offensive, or the word or phrase used • *"Detained" is their euphemism for "imprisonment."* [C]

euphemistic /,juː·fə'mɪs·tɪk/ *adj* • *euphemistic words for "sex"*

euphoria /jʊ'fɔːr·iː·ə, -'four-/ *n* [U] a feeling of extreme happiness or confidence • *We were caught up in the euphoria of the moment.*

euphoric /jʊ'fɔːr·ɪk, -'fɑr-/ *adj* • *a euphoric expression* ○ *a euphoric mood*

euro /'jʊr·oʊ/ *n* [C] *pl* **euros** the basic unit of money of the European Union

European /,jʊr·ə'piː·ən/ *n* [C], *adj* (a person) of or coming from Europe • The **European Union** (*abbreviation* **EU**) is an group of European countries that act together in political and economic matters.

euthanasia /,juː·θə'neɪ·ʒə/ *n* [U] the killing of someone who is very ill to end their suffering

evacuate /ɪ'væk·jə,weɪt/ *v* [I/T] to remove (people) from a dangerous place • *The school was evacuated because of a bomb threat.* [T]

evacuation /ɪ,væk·jə'weɪ·ʃən/ *n* [C/U] • *A chemical spill prompted the evacuation of area residents.* [U]

evade /ɪ'veɪd/ *v* [T] to avoid (something unpleasant or unwanted), or to manage not to do (something that should be done) • *She's trying to evade my questions.* ○ *He was convicted of evading taxes.*

evasion /ɪ'veɪ·ʒən/ *n* [C/U] • *tax evasion* [U] ○ *a political speech full of evasions* [C]

evasive /ɪ'veɪ·sɪv, -zɪv/ *adj* • *Are you being deliberately evasive?* ○ *The pilot had to take evasive action to avoid the other plane.*

evaluate (*obj*) /ɪ'væl·jə,weɪt/ *v* to judge or calculate the quality, importance, amount, or value of (something) • *Doctors evaluate the patient's condition.* [T] ○ *Have they evaluated what their next step is?* [+ *wh-* word]

evaluation /ɪ,væl·jə'weɪ·ʃən/ *n* [C/U] • *Student evaluations of the class will be collected next week.* [C]

evangelical /,iː,væn'dʒel·ɪ·kəl, ,ev·ən-/ *n* [C], *adj* [not gradable] (a member) of one of the Christian groups that believe biblical teaching and persuading other people to join them are extremely important • *evangelical Christians*

evangelist /ɪ'væn·dʒə·ləst/ *n* [C] a person who tries to persuade people to become Christians, often by traveling and organizing religious meetings or by broadcasting religious programs

evangelism /ɪ'væn·dʒə,lɪz·əm/ *n* [U] • *TV evangelism*

evangelistic /ɪ,væn·dʒə'lɪs·tɪk/ *adj* • *evangelistic services/meetings*

evaporate /ɪ'væp·ə,reɪt/ *v* [I/T] to cause (a liquid) to change to a gas, esp. by heating, or (*fig.*) to disappear • *As water evaporates, the air around it becomes less dry.* [I] ○ (*fig.*) *Your problems are not just going to evaporate.* [I]

evaporation /ɪ,væp·ə'reɪ·ʃən/ *n* [U] • *The storage tank has a lid to prevent evaporation.*

evasion /ɪ'veɪ·ʒən/ *n* [C/U] • See at EVADE.

evasive /ɪˈveɪ·sɪv, -zɪv/ *adj* • See at EVADE.

eve /iːv/ *n* [U] the evening or day before a holiday, or the period immediately before an important event • *New Year's Eve* ○ *the eve of the election*

even EQUAL /ˈiː·vən/ *adj* equal or equally balanced • *The class has a pretty even mix of boys and girls.* ○ *I bought the tickets, so if you pay for dinner we'll be even* (= you will not owe me any money). • If something is **even-handed**, it is fair: *even-handed coverage of a volatile issue*

evenly /ˈiː·vən·li/ *adv* • *Divide the mixture evenly between the two pans.*

even /ˈiː·vən/ *v* [I/T] to make equal • *Tonight's win evens their record at 6-6.* [T] ○ *Minorities should be given special advantages until things even out.* [I] ○ *They won the next night to even up the score.* [M] ○ *Taking me to the movies isn't going to even things out.* [M]

even CONTINUOUS /ˈiː·vən/ *adj* continuous or regular • *We walked at an even pace.*

evenly /ˈiː·vən·li/ *adv* • *She breathed evenly.* • To say something evenly is to speak without showing emotion: *"You have no right to do that," he said evenly.*

even FLAT /ˈiː·vən/ *adj* flat and smooth, or on the same level • *The snow was even with the kitchen doorstep.*

even NUMBER /ˈiː·vən/ *adj* [not gradable] (of numbers) exactly divisible by two • *The result should be an even number.* • Compare ODD NUMBER.

even EMPHASIS /ˈiː·vən/ *adv* [not gradable] used to emphasize a comparison or the unexpected or extreme characteristic of something • *Even smart people can make mistakes.* ○ *She never cried—not even when she was badly hurt.* ○ *Even with a good education, you need some common sense to get ahead.* • **Even if** means whether or not: *Even if you apologize, she still may not forgive you.* • **Even so** means although it is true: *He hates flowers, but even so, he brought some to his mother.* • **Even though** means despite the fact: *Even though he never completed college, he runs a successful software company.*

even MORE EXACTLY /ˈiː·vən/ *adv* [not gradable] used when you want to be more exact or detailed about something you have just said • *I find some of his habits unpleasant, disgusting even.*

evening /ˈiːv·nɪŋ/ *n* [C/U] the part of the day between the afternoon and the night • *We always go to the movies on Friday evenings.* [C] • An **evening dress/gown** is a dress worn to formal evening parties and events. • **(Good) evening** is also a greeting: *Evening, Mr. Hopkins.* LP GREETINGS

event /ɪˈvent/ *n* [C] anything that happens, esp. something important or unusual • *The State Department is keeping an eye on recent events in China.* • An event is also one of a set of races or competitions: *the women's 200-meter event* • **In any event** means whatever happens: *I hope to meet her this afternoon, but in any event I'm leaving town tomorrow.* • **In the event of** means if it should: *In the event of an actual emergency, you will be told what to do.* • **In the event that** (= If it happens that) *the performance is canceled, you can get your money back.*

eventful /ɪˈvent·fəl/ *adj* full of important or interesting happenings • *She led a long and eventful life.*

eventual /ɪˈven·tʃə·wəl/ *adj* [not gradable] happening at a later time or as a result at the end • *The eventual cost of the new facility has not been revealed.*

eventually /ɪˈventʃ·wə·li/ *adv* [not gradable] • *You learn a lot in school, but eventually you forget most of it.*

eventuality /ɪˌven·tʃəˈwæl·əţ·i/ *n* [C] a possible happening or result • *I thought I could cope with any eventuality.*

ever AT ANY TIME /ˈev·ər/ *adv* [not gradable] at any time • *Nothing ever happens here.* ○ *Have you ever been to Europe?* ○ *I thought she was famous, but none of my friends have ever heard of her.* ○ *We are spending more money than ever.* ○ *He hardly ever washes the dishes* (= almost never).

ever ALWAYS /ˈev·ər/ *adv* [not gradable] always, or continuously • *Her record grows ever more impressive over the years.* ○ *There's an ever-increasing demand for new styles.* ○ *He's been depressed ever since his divorce.*

ever EMPHASIS /ˈev·ər/ *adv* [not gradable] used to emphasize an adjective • *I saw the Grateful Dead's last concert ever.* ○ *Was she ever angry* (= She was very angry)*!*

evergreen /ˈev·ərˌgriːn/ *adj* [not gradable] (of a plant, bush, or tree) having leaves for the whole year • Compare DECIDUOUS.

evergreen /ˈev·ərˌgriːn/ *n* [C] • *Spruces, pines, and ivy are evergreens.*

everlasting /ˌev·ərˈlæs·tɪŋ/ *adj* [not gradable] lasting forever, or continuing for a long time • *To his everlasting credit, he's the only one who said it was wrong.* ○ *He believes in everlasting life after death.*

every ALL /ˈev·ri/ *adj* used when referring to all the members of a group of three or more considered separately • *Every employee will receive a bonus this year.* ○ *They're open every day.* ○ *Make sure you eat every bit of dinner.* ○ *Tour guides tend to travelers' every need* (= all their needs). • *Cassandra knows* **every inch** *of Boston* (= all of it). • *I don't need to know* **every last** *detail of his life* (= all the details). • LP AMOUNTS, DETERMINERS

every REPEATED /ˈev·ri/ *adj* used to show that something is repeated regularly • *Computers perform millions of calculations every second.* ○ *In many places, malnutrition affects every third child* (= one child in three). • *The con-*

ference used to be held every year, but now it takes place **every other** *year* (= once in two years). • *We still get together for lunch* **every now and again/then** (= sometimes, but not regularly). • *You meet some really interesting people* **every once in a while/so often** (= sometimes, but not regularly). • LP DETERMINERS

every GREATEST /'ev·ri/ *adj* the greatest possible • *Every effort is being made to fix it.* ○ *She has every right to be proud of herself.* • LP DETERMINERS

everyday /'ev·ri:‚deɪ/ *adj* ordinary, typical, or usual • *The movie is about the everyday lives of working mothers.*

everyone /'ev·ri:·wən/, **everybody** /'ev·ri:‚bɑd·i, -‚bʌd·i/ *pronoun* every person • *You have to wait your turn like everyone else.* ○ *Goodbye, everybody—I'll see you next time.* LP TITLES AND FORMS OF ADDRESS

everything /'ev·ri:‚θɪŋ/ *pronoun* all things • *They lost everything in the fire.* ○ *In spite of everything, I still love him.* ○ *The price of gasoline affects everything else.* ○ *"Is everything all right?" "Everything is fine."* ○ *Money isn't everything* (= it is not the only important thing). ○ *Her children are everything to her* (= the most important part of her life). ○ *They're very busy with their new house and everything* (= all the things connected with it). • *Mike walked into the diner and ordered* **everything but the kitchen sink** (= many or most of the things available).

everywhere /'ev·ri:‚hwer, -‚wer, -‚hwær, -‚wær/, *infml* **everyplace** /'ev·ri:‚pleɪs/ *adv* [not gradable] in or to every place or part • *There were stacks of newspapers everywhere in the apartment.* ○ *We've got relatives in Florida, New Jersey, just about everywhere.*

evict /ɪ'vɪkt/ *v* [T] to force (someone) to leave a place • *Drug dealers are being evicted from city housing.*

eviction /ɪ'vɪk·ʃən/ *n* [C/U] • *He's been threatened with eviction for not paying his rent.* [U]

evidence /'ev·əd· əns/ *n* [U] anything that helps to prove that something is or is not true • *These figures are being given as evidence of economic growth.* ○ *The FBI has found no evidence of a crime.* ○ *The weight of the evidence is against him.* ○ *Juries examine the evidence and decide on the basis of the facts.*

evident /'ev·əd·ənt/ *adj* easily seen or understood; obvious • *It quickly became evident that someone had broken in.* ○ *Twain's interest in Adam is evident in al his work.* • See also SELF-EVIDENT.

evidently /'ev·əd·ənt·li/ *adv* • *I thought she'd want to see me. Evidently, she doesn't.*

evil /'iː·vəl/ *n* [C/U] the condition of being immoral, cruel, or bad, or an act of this type • *a contest between good and evil* [U]

evil /'iː·vəl/ *adj* • *an evil ruler*

evoke /ɪ'voʊk/ *v* [T] to cause (something) to

be remembered or expressed • *The smell of chalk always evokes memories of my school days.*

evocative /ɪ'vɑk·ət̬·ɪv/ *adj* • *The new fashions were evocative of the 1920s.*

evolution /‚ev·ə'luː·ʃən, ‚iː·və-/ *n* [U] a gradual process of change and development • (*specialized*) Evolution is the process by which the physical characteristics of types of creatures change over time, new types of creatures develop, and others disappear.

evolve /ɪ'vɑlv, -'vɑlv/ *v* [I] to change or develop gradually • *These countries are evolving toward more democratic societies.*

ex– /eks/ *combining form* used to show that someone is no longer in the situation or condition they had been in; FORMER EARLIER • *The governor of Minnesota is an ex-wrestler.*

ex /eks/ *n* [C] *pl* **exes** *infml* someone who is no longer a person's wife, husband, or lover • *It was a little embarrassing because both of my exes were at the party.*

exacerbate /ɪg'zæs·ər‚beɪt/ *v* [T] to make (something that is already bad) worse • *Her allergy was exacerbated by the dust.*

exact CORRECT /ɪg'zækt/ *adj* in perfect detail; complete and correct • *The exact distance is 3.4 miles.* ○ *Do you have the exact time?* ○ *"Is it 12 o'clock yet?" "It's 12:03 to be exact."* • Exact is sometimes used to increase emphasis on the following word: *She's going through the exact same things I went through.*

exactly /ɪg'zæk·tli/ *adv* • *We've come exactly 41 miles.* ○ *Make sure you measure the window exactly, otherwise the shade won't fit.* • Exactly is sometimes used to increase emphasis: *The businessmen who work in banking, she thought, all look exactly the same.* ○ *You're exactly right.*

exact OBTAIN /ɪg'zækt/ *v* [T] *fml* to demand and obtain (something), sometimes using threats or force • *to exact revenge*

exacting /ɪg'zæk·tɪŋ/ *adj* demanding a lot of effort, care, or attention • *All our aircraft meet exacting safety standards.*

exaggerate /ɪg'zædʒ·ə‚reɪt/ *v* [I/T] to make (something) seem larger, more important, better, or worse than it really is • *The reports exaggerated the economic benefits of legalized gambling.* [T] ○ *I don't want to exaggerate, but it was a dangerous situation.* [I]

exaggeration /ɪg‚zædʒ·ə'reɪ·ʃən/ *n* [C/U] • *It is no exaggeration to say that she saved my life.* [U]

exalt /ɪg'zɔːlt/ *v* [T] *fml* to praise (someone) a lot, or to raise (someone) to a higher rank or more powerful position • *This hymn exalts the Lord.*

exalted /ɪg'zɔːl·t̬əd/ *adj* • *He felt an exalted sense of power now that he was in line to run the company.*

exaltation /‚eg‚zɔːl'teɪ·ʃən, ‚ek‚sɔːl-/ *n* [U] a

feeling of great happiness • *religious exaltation*

exam /ɪɡ'zæm/, **examination** /ɪɡ,zæm·ə'neɪ·ʃən/ *n* [C] a test of a student's knowledge or skill in a particular subject • *The final exams are scheduled for next week.*

examine /ɪɡ'zæm·ən/ *v* [T] to look at or consider (a person or thing) carefully in order to discover something about the person or thing • *Investigators examined the wreckage for clues about the cause of the explosion.*

examination /ɪɡ,zæm·ə'neɪ·ʃən/, *short form* **exam** *n* [C/U] the act or process of carefully looking at someone or something to learn about its condition or to discover facts • *You have to have a physical examination/exam in order to get life insurance.* [C] ○ *The evidence is still under examination* (= being examined). [U]

example TYPICAL CASE /ɪɡ'zæm·pəl/ *n* [C] something that is typical of the group that it is a member of or that can be used to represent it • *Let me give you an example of what I mean.* ○ *For example* (= as a particular case showing a more general situation), *some states allow one adult to care for as many as 12 infants.*

example GOOD MODEL /ɪɡ'zæm·pəl/ *n* [C] a person or their behavior when considered for their suitability to be copied • *We want our teachers to set a good example.*

example BAD MODEL /ɪɡ'zæm·pəl/ *n* [C] (a person who receives) a punishment that is intended to warn others against doing the thing that is being punished • *The judge made an example of him and sentenced him to prison.*

exasperate /ɪɡ'zæs·pə,reɪt/ *v* [T] to cause anger or extreme annoyance in (someone) • *His assistant's carelessness is exasperating him.*

excavate /'ek·skə,veɪt/ *v* [I/T] to dig a hole or channel in the ground, or to make (a hole or channel) by removing earth • *We'll be excavating here for the foundation of the building.* [I] • To excavate is also to remove earth from a place in order to find old objects buried there: *Archaeologists are excavating a site near the cathedral.* [T]

excavation /,ek·skə'veɪ·ʃən/ *n* [C/U] • *an excavation 40 feet deep* [C]

exceed /ɪk'siːd/ *v* [T] to be greater than (a number or amount), or to go beyond (a permitted limit) • *He was exceeding the speed limit by 15 miles an hour.*

exceedingly /ɪk'siːd·ɪŋ·li/ *adv* to a very great degree; extremely • *He is exceedingly rich.*

excel /ɪk'sel/ *v* [I/T] **-ll-** to do something very well or be highly skilled, and be better than most others • *They all performed well, but the lead dancer really excelled.* [I]

excellent /'ek·sə·lənt/ *adj* extremely good • *The car is in excellent condition.*

excellence /'ek·sə·ləns/ *n* [U] • *The school is known for its excellence.*

except /ɪk'sept/ *prep, conjunction* not including; but not • *It's cool and quiet everywhere except (for) the kitchen.* ○ *Everyone is here except Peter.* • Except also means with this difference or in this case only: *The twins look exactly alike except (that) one is slightly taller.* ○ *I don't drink in the middle of the day at work, except when I have a lunch date.*

except /ɪk'sept/ *v* [T] to not include (something or someone) • *When I say I didn't like the Midwest, I except Chicago.*

excepting /ɪk'sep·tɪŋ/ *prep, conjunction* • *Excepting the two people who left early, I think everyone enjoyed the tour.*

exception /ɪk'sep·ʃən/ *n* [C/U] something that is not included, or the action of not including something • *We don't usually accept late applications, but since you were so sick I'll make an exception* (= do something different from what is usual). [C] ○ *Teen movies usually aren't very good, but this one is an exception to the rule.* [C] ○ *Every apple in the box, without exception, was rotten.* [U]

exceptional /ɪk'sep·ʃən·əl/ *adj* not like most others of the same type; unusual • *This is an exceptional contract, guaranteeing no layoffs.* • Exceptional also means unusually good: *Davis has done an exceptional job of reporting.*

exceptionally /ɪk'sep·ʃən·əl·i/ *adv* • *The drawing had exceptionally fine detail.*

excerpt /'ek·sɜrpt, 'eg·zɜrpt/ *n* [C] a short part taken from a speech, book, etc.

excerpt /ek'sɜrpt, eg'zɜrpt/ *v* [T] • *This article is excerpted from the full report.*

excess /ɪk'ses, 'ek·ses/ *n* [U] an amount that is more than acceptable, expected, or reasonable • *They both eat to excess* (= a lot more than they need). ○ *The company's losses are in excess of* (= more than) *$5 million.*

excess /ɪk'ses, 'ek·ses/ *adj* [not gradable] more than is necessary; too much • *excess baggage*

excesses /ɪk'ses·əz, 'ek,ses·əz/ *pl n* actions beyond the limit of what is acceptable • *His excesses—especially his many affairs with married women—were well known.*

excessive /ɪk'ses·ɪv/ *adj* • *We felt the charges were excessive.*

exchange /ɪks'tʃeɪndʒ/ *v* [T] to change (something) for something else of a similar value or type • *This shirt is too small—can I exchange it for one in a larger size?* ○ *Before we left the meeting, she and I exchanged phone numbers* (= I told her mine and she told me hers).

exchange /ɪks'tʃeɪndʒ/ *n* [C/U] • *an exchange of ideas* [C] ○ *an exchange of prisoners* [C] • An **exchange rate** is the rate at which the money of one country can be changed for the money of another country.

excise TAX /'ek·saɪz/ *n* [U] a tax on some types of goods produced and used within a single country

excise REMOVE /ɪk'saɪz/ *v* [T] *medical* to remove by cutting • *The surgeon excised a small tumor from my leg.*

excite MAKE HAPPY /ɪkˈsaɪt/ *v* [T] to make (someone) have strong feelings, esp. of happiness and enthusiasm • *In some science fiction movies, the music and special effects can really excite audiences.*

excited /ɪkˈsaɪt·əd/ *adj* • *She was excited about the trip because she was going to learn to ski.*

excitedly /ɪkˈsaɪt·əd·li/ *adv* • *She ran excitedly outside to greet her cousins.*

exciting /ɪkˈsaɪt·ɪŋ/ *adj* • *It was an exciting role to play, and I was thrilled to get the part.*

excitement /ɪkˈsaɪt·mənt/ *n* [U] • *Robin's heart was pounding with excitement.*

excite CAUSE TO REACT /ɪkˈsaɪt/ *v* [T] *fml* to cause (a particular reaction) in someone • *The strange noises excited my curiosity.*

excitable /ɪkˈsaɪt·ə·bəl/ *adj* (of a person or an animal) tending to react quickly and strongly to things • *The dog is excitable, so don't come too close.*

exclaim /ɪkˈskleɪm/ *v* to say or shout something suddenly because of surprise, fear, pleasure, etc. • *She exclaimed with delight when she saw the baby.* [I]

exclamation /ˌek·skləˈmeɪ·ʃən/ *n* [C] a sudden expression of pleasure, surprise, agreement, etc. • *exclamations of delight* • An **exclamation point** (also **exclamation mark**) is the mark (!) used in writing immediately after an expression to show that it is sudden or surprising, or that it is a greeting or an order.

EXCLAMATION POINT [!]

An exclamation point (also called an exclamation mark) is used at the end of a sentence. It appears mostly in writing that tries to show how people are speaking. An exclamation point may be used:

to show that the speaker is shouting, or that a noise is loud

"Sarah and David!" she called out. "Time for dinner!" • *Bang! The door behind him shut.*

to show that the speaker feels strong emotion or urgency

"I swear to you I'm telling the truth!" • *"Don't open that package, it might be a bomb!"*

---

exclamation /ˌek·skləˈmeɪ·ʃən/ *n* [C] specialized (in grammar) a word that expresses sudden pain, surprise, anger, excitement, happiness, or other emotion • *"Ouch," "hey," and "wow" are exclamations.*

exclude /ɪkˈsklud/ *v* [T] to keep out or omit (something or someone) • *The advertised price excludes the sales tax.*

excluding /ɪkˈsklud·ɪŋ/ *prep* not including; apart from • *The aircraft carries 250 people, excluding the crew.*

exclusion /ɪkˈsklu·ʒən/ *n* [C/U] • *Her exclusion from the invitation list was a mistake.* [U]

exclusive /ɪkˈsklu·sɪv, -zɪv/ *adj* limited to only one person or group of people • *The pool is for the exclusive use of residents of Springfield.* • A place that is exclusive provides goods and services for a limited number of people, esp. those who are wealthy: *an exclusive club*

exclusively /ɪkˈsklu·sɪv·li, -zɪv·li/ *adv* limited to a specific thing or group • *Our employment agency deals exclusively with the advertising industry.*

excommunicate /ˌek·skəˈmjuː·nə·keɪt/ *v* [T] (of the Christian Church, esp. the Roman Catholic Church) to refuse to allow (someone) to be a member of the church

excrement /ˈek·skrə·mənt/ *n* [U] waste material that leaves the body through the bowels

excrete /ɪkˈskrit/ *v* [I/T] (of humans, animals, or plants) to get rid of (waste material such as excrement or urine) from the body

excretion /ɪkˈskri·ʃən/ *n* [C/U]

excruciating /ɪkˈskru·ʃiːˌeɪt·ɪŋ/ *adj* (of pain) extremely strong • *an excruciating headache*

excursion /ɪkˈskɜr·ʒən/ *n* [C] a short trip usually made for pleasure, often by a group of people • *My class is going on an excursion to Niagara Falls.*

excuse FORGIVE /ɪkˈskjuːz/ *v* [T] to forgive (someone) • *Please excuse me for being so late—there was a lot of traffic.* ○ *It was hard to excuse him for treating me so badly.* • To **excuse** someone **from** something is to give them permission to leave it or not go to it: *I was excused from jury duty because I had to take care of my sick mother.* • The expression **excuse me** is a polite way of attracting the attention esp. of someone you don't know: *Excuse me, where is the bathroom?* LP GREETINGS • **Excuse me** is also used as a way of saying you are sorry for having done something, esp. unintentionally, that might be annoying to other people. • You might also say **excuse me** as a question when you have not heard what someone has said and you want them to repeat it: *"Excuse me? I didn't get the last word."*

excusable /ɪkˈskjuː·zə·bəl/ *adj* • *Considering her difficult childhood, her behavior is excusable.*

excuse EXPLANATION /ɪkˈskjuːs/ *n* [C] the explanation given for bad behavior, absence, etc. • *You're always making excuses for not helping with the housework.*

execute DO /ˈek·sə·kjuːt/ *v* [T] to do or perform (something), esp. in a planned way • *Now that we have approval, we can go ahead and execute the plan.*

execution /ˌek·səˈkjuː·ʃən/ *n* [U] • *The guitarist's execution of the ballad was superb.*

executor /ɪgˈzek·jət·ər/ *n* [C] *law* a person who deals with the wishes expressed in a WILL (= formal statement of what will happen to a dead person's money and property)

execute KILL /ˈek·sə·kjuːt/ *v* [T] to kill (someone) as a legal punishment

execution /ˌek·səˈkjuː·ʃən/ *n* [C/U] • *Execution is done by lethal injection in this state.* [U]

executive /ɪgˈzek·jəţ·ɪv/, *infml* **exec** /ɪgˈzek/ *n* [C/U] someone in a high position, esp. in business, who makes decisions and acts according to them • *a chief executive* [C]

executive /ɪgˈzek·jəţ·ɪv/ *adj* • *In the US, the president is the head of the executive branch of government.*

exemplary /ɪgˈzem·plə·ri/ *adj* extremely good of its type, so that it might serve as a model for others • *He saw action in the Marines, and his performance was exemplary.*

exemplify /ɪgˈzem·plə·faɪ/ *v* [T] to be a typical example of (something) • *American fashion is exemplified by jeans and T-shirts.*

exempt /ɪgˈzempt/ *adj* [not gradable] not having to obey a rule or to do something that is usually necessary • *Nonprofit organizations are exempt from taxes.*

exempt /ɪgˈzemt/ *v* [T] • *The governor plans to exempt small businesses from the tax increase.*

exemption /ɪgˈzem·ʃən/ *n* [C/U] • *He was granted exemption from military service during World War II.* [U] • An exemption is a particular amount of money that is not taxed: *a tax exemption* [C]

exercise HEALTHY ACTIVITY /ˈek·sərˌsaɪz/ *n* [C/U] (a) physical action performed to make or keep your body healthy • *You should get some exercise even when you're pregnant.* [U] ∘ *I do five different exercises every morning to limber up.* [C]

exercise /ˈek·sərˌsaɪz/ *v* [I/T] • *She goes to the gym to exercise every evening.* [I]

exercise PRACTICE /ˈek·sərˌsaɪz/ *n* [C] an action or actions intended to improve something or make something happen • *The military exercises will involve several thousand soldiers.* ∘ *The whole thing was an exercise in futility* (= actions that were useless). • An exercise can be written work that you do to practice something you are learning: *The book has exercises at the end of every chapter.*

exercise USE /ˈek·sərˌsaɪz/ *v* [T] *fml* to use (something) • *Always exercise caution when handling poisonous substances.*

exercise /ˈek·sərˌsaɪz/ *n* [U] • *The exercise of restraint in this situation may be difficult.*

exert USE /ɪgˈzɜrt/ *v* [T] to use (power or the ability to make something happen) • *To cut costs, health-insurance plans are exerting tighter control over paying for medical care.*

exert MAKE AN EFFORT /ɪgˈzɜrt/ *v* [T] to cause (yourself) to make an effort • *She will have to exert herself a lot more if she wants to succeed in this business.*

exertion /ɪgˈzɜr·ʃən/ *n* [C/U] • *Physical exertion isn't always a good thing in a hot climate.* [U]

exhale /eksˈheɪl/ *v* [I/T] to breathe out, or to breathe (esp. air or smoke) out • *She held her breath for a moment and then exhaled.* [I]

exhaust TIRE /ɪgˈzɔːst/ *v* [T] to tire (a person or an animal) greatly • *The long hike up the mountain exhausted us all.*

exhausting /ɪgˈzɔː·stɪŋ/ *adj* [not gradable] • *The pace of twelve-hour days, seven days a week proved exhausting.*

exhaustion /ɪgˈzɔːs·tʃən/ *n* [U] • *Murayama was sidelined shortly after his arrival by what aides said was exhaustion.*

exhaust USE /ɪgˈzɔːst/ *v* [T] to use (something) completely • *After a whole day with the kids, her patience was nearly exhausted.*

exhaustive /ɪgˈzɔː·stɪv/ *adj* [not gradable] detailed and complete • *an exhaustive study of the tax law*

exhaust GAS /ɪgˈzɔːst/ *n* [C/U] the waste gas from an engine, esp. a from a car, or the pipe this gas flows through

exhibit SHOW AN OBJECT /ɪgˈzɪb·ət/ *v* [I/T] to show (something) publicly for competition, sale, or amusement • *The gallery is exhibiting his paintings and watercolors.* [T]

exhibit /ɪgˈzɪb·ət/ *n* [C] • *The museum's exhibits range from Iron Age pottery to Eskimo clothing.* • (*law*) An exhibit is an item used as EVIDENCE (= proof) in a trial.

exhibition /ˌek·səˈbɪʃ·ən/ *n* [C/U] a collection of things shown publicly • *an exhibition of model airplanes* [C]

exhibitionism /ˌek·səˈbɪʃ·ə·nɪz·əm/ *n* [U] a tendency to behave in a way intended to attract attention • Exhibitionism is a mental condition in which someone likes to show their sexual organs in public.

exhibitionist /ˌek·səˈbɪʃ·ə·nəst/ *n* [C]

exhibit SHOW A QUALITY /ɪgˈzɪb·ət/ *v* [T] to show (esp. a quality) by your behavior • *The admiral might have exhibited poor judgment, but he is not guilty of a crime.*

exhilarating /ɪgˈzɪl·əˌreɪţ·ɪŋ/ *adj* [not gradable] causing you to feel excited and happy • *An exhilarating sense of new beginnings swept through him.*

exhort /ɪgˈzɔːrt/ *v* [T] *fml* to strongly encourage or persuade (someone) to do something • *He exhorted business leaders to play their part in improving race relations.*

exhume /ɪgˈzuːm, ɪksˈjuːm/ *v* [T] to remove (a dead body) from the ground after it has been buried

exile /ˈeg·zaɪl, ˈek·saɪl/ *v* [T] to send or keep (someone) away from their own country or home, esp. for political reasons

exile /ˈeg·zaɪl, ˈek·saɪl/ *n* [C/U] the condition being exiled, or a person who is exiled • *Many Cuban exiles live in Florida.* [C]

exist TO BE /ɪgˈzɪst/ *v* [I] to be; have the ability to be known, recognized, or understood • *Can the soul exist independently of the body?* ∘ *Programs like Medicaid for the poor did not exist at that time.*

existence /ɪgˈzɪs·təns/ n [U] • *During the first few years of its existence, the theater had no permanent home.*

exist BE PRESENT /ɪgˈzɪst/ v [I] to be present or be a condition • *We have to stop the violence that exists in some urban neighborhoods.*

existence /ɪgˈzɪz·təns/ n [U] • *the existence of poverty*

existing /ɪgˈzɪs·tɪŋ/ adj [not gradable] • *Under existing conditions, many children are not getting an adequate education.*

exist LIVE /ɪgˈzɪst/ v [I] to be able to live • *No one can be expected to exist on such a low salary.*

existence /ɪgˈzɪs·təns/ n [C usually sing] a way of living, esp. a difficult one • *I lead a rather isolated existence here in Washington.*

exit /ˈek·sət, ˈeg·zət/ n [C] the door through which you might leave a room, building, or large vehicle, or a place on a main road where a vehicle can leave it by taking a smaller road • *In case of fire, use the emergency exit next to the elevator.* ○ *Stay on the freeway until you get to the Ventura exit.* • An exit is also the act of leaving a place, esp. a public place such as the stage of a theater: *She made her exit to rapturous applause.*

exit

exit /ˈek·sət, ˈeg·zət/ v [I/T] • *Please exit (the theater) by the side doors.* [I/T] • If you exit a computer or computer program, you stop using it. [T]

exodus /ˈek·səd·əs, ˈeg·zəd-/ n [C usually sing] the movement of a lot of people from a place at the same time • *The hurricane warning caused a mass exodus.*

exonerate /ɪgˈzɑn·əˌreɪt/ v [T] to show or state that (someone or something) is not to be blamed for something bad that happened • *The police officer was exonerated by a grand jury, but the protests continued.*

exoneration /ɪgˌzɑn·əˈreɪ·ʃən/ n [U]

exorbitant /ɪgˈzɔːr·bət·ənt/ adj [not gradable] (of prices and demands) much too large • *The hotel charges were exorbitant.*

exorcise /ˈek·sɔːrˌsaɪz, ˈek·sər-/ v [T] to force out (an evil spirit) from (a person or a place) by praying or magic

exorcist /ˈek·sɔːr·səst, ˈek·sər-/ n [C]

exotic /ɪgˈzɑt̬·ɪk/ adj [not gradable] unusual and specially interesting because of coming

from a distant country • *exotic pets like snakes and tropical birds*

expand /ɪkˈspænd/ v [I/T] to increase (something) in size, number, or importance • *The air in the balloon expands when heated.* [I] ○ *They expanded their number of stores significantly in the 1990s.* [T]

expansion /ɪkˈspæn·tʃən/ n [U] • *Expansion into new areas of research might be possible.*

□ **expand on/upon** /ɪkˈspænd/ v prep [T] to give more details about (something said or written) • *He studied with Sigmund Freud and expanded upon many of his theories.*

expanse /ɪkˈspæns/ n [C] a very wide space or area • *the vast expanse of Russia*

expansive /ɪkˈspæn·sɪv/ adj wide in area • *The seals form small groups on the expansive beaches where they breed.*

expansive /ɪkˈspæn·sɪv/ adj [not gradable] friendly and willing to talk freely

expatriate /ekˈspeɪ·triː·ət/ n [C] someone who does not live in their own country

expect /ɪkˈspekt/ v to think or believe that (something will happen), or that (someone will arrive) • *We are expecting about 100 people for the lecture.* [T] ○ *His plane is expected to land at about 7:30 this evening.* [T] ○ *We expected to see her here, but I guess she decided not to come.* [+ to infinitive] • To expect is also to ask for (something) to happen because you think you have a right to ask for it: *The boss wants me to work this weekend—that's expecting a lot!* [T] • If you say that a woman is **expecting**, you mean that she is pregnant.

expectancy /ɪkˈspek·tən·si/ n [U] • *There was an air of expectancy as the chairman rose to speak.*

expectant /ɪkˈspek·tənt/ adj [not gradable] • An expectant mother/father/parent is waiting for the birth of their child.

expectantly /ɪkˈspek·tənt·li/ adv [not gradable] • *She looked up at him expectantly.*

expectation /ˌek·spekˈteɪ·ʃən/ n [C/U] the feeling or belief that something will or should happen • *Considering his grades, there is little expectation of his getting into medical school.* [U] ○ *Last year's predictions fell a bit short of expectations.* [C usually pl]

expedient /ɪkˈspiːd·iː·ənt/ adj [not gradable] helpful or useful in a particular situation, and without considering any moral question that might influence your decision • *We thought it expedient not to pay the builder until he finished the work.*

expediency /ɪkˈspiːd·iː·ən·si/, **expedience** /ɪkˈspiːd·iː·əns/ n [U] • *political expediency*

expedite /ˈek·spəˌdaɪt/ v [T] to cause (something) to be done or progress more quickly • *We've got to expedite this order because they need it by tomorrow.*

expedition /ˌek·spəˈdɪʃ·ən/ n [C] a long, organized trip for a particular purpose, or the people, vehicles, or ships making such a trip • *a military expedition*

expel /ɪkˈspel/ *v* [T] **-ll-** to force (someone) to leave a country, organization, or school • *He was arrested for purse snatching at age 12 and expelled from high school four years later.* • USAGE: The related noun is EXPULSION.

expend /ɪkˈspend/ *v* [T] to use or spend (esp. time, effort, or money) • *They expend all their energy fixing up their house.*

expendable /ɪkˈspen·də·bəl/ *adj* [not gradable] not worth keeping or no longer useful • *He was considered expendable and dropped from the team.*

expenditure /ɪkˈspen·də·tʃər/ *n* [C/U] an amount of money, time, or effort that is spent • *a large expenditure of funds* [C]

expense /ɪkˈspens/ *n* [C/U] an amount of money needed or used to do or buy something; cost • *We have to start cutting down on our expenses.* [C] ○ *The house was redecorated at great expense.* [U] • If something is done **at the expense of** someone, or **at** someone's **expense**, it is done in a way that harms or embarrasses them: *They all had a good laugh at her expense.* • An **expense account** is an amount of money that employees can spend to travel or buy things related to their jobs and which their employers will pay for. • LP PRICE

expensive /ɪkˈspen·sɪv/ *adj* [not gradable] costing a lot of money • *Housing in this part of the country is very expensive.*

expensively /ɪkˈspen·sɪv·li/ *adv* [not gradable] • *She was expensively dressed.*

experience /ɪkˈspɪr·iː·əns/ *n* [C/U] (the process of getting) knowledge or skill that is obtained from doing, seeing, or feeling things, or something that happens which has an effect on you • *Do you have any experience working with children?* [U] ○ *I know from experience that it can get quite cold in Maine this time of year.* [U]

experience /ɪkˈspɪr·iː·əns/ *v* [T] • *The community has experienced rapid residential growth.* ○ *She began to experience* (= to feel) *labor pains.*

experienced /ɪkˈspɪr·iː·ənst/ *adj* [not gradable] having the skill and knowledge to do something, esp. because of having done it for a long time • *Martin is an experienced sailor.*

experiment /ɪkˈsper·ə·mənt, -ˈspɪr-/ *n* [C/U] a test done in order to learn something or to discover whether something works or is true • *His experiments were designed to find better methods of using heat energy.* [C]

experiment /ɪkˈsper·ə·ment, -ˈspɪr-/ *v* [I] to test or to try a new way of doing something • *The school is experimenting with new teaching methods.*

experimental /ɪkˌsper·əˈment·ᵊl, -ˌspɪr-/ *adj* [not gradable] using or based on new ideas

experimentation /ɪkˌsper·ə·mənˈteɪ·ʃən, -ˌspɪr-/ *n* [U]

expert /ˈek·spɜrt/ *n* [C] a person having a high level of knowledge or skill in a particular subject • *He is the administration's foreign-policy expert for eastern Europe.*

expert /ˈek·spɜrt, ɪkˈspɜrt/ *adj* [not gradable] • *She's an expert swimmer.*

expertly /ˈek·spɜrt·li, ɪkˈspɜrt·li/ *adv* [not gradable]

expertise /ˌek·spərˈtiːz, -ˈtiːs/ *n* [U] a high level of skill or knowledge • *She was widely known for her expertise as a trial lawyer.*

expire END /ɪkˈspaɪr/ *v* [I] (of something that lasts for a fixed length of time) to end or stop being in use • *My passport will expire next year.*

expiration /ˌek·spəˈreɪ·ʃən/ *n* [U] the end of a period of time during which an agreement or official document can be used • *He stayed on past the expiration of his tourist visa.* • *What is the* **expiration date** *of your credit card* (= the last day on which it can be used)?

expire DIE /ɪkˈspaɪr/ *v* [I] *fml* to die

explain /ɪkˈspleɪn/ *v* [I/T] to make (something) clear or easy to understand by describing or giving information about it • *If there's anything you don't understand, I'll be happy to explain.* [I] ○ *The teacher explained the procedure to the students.* [T] ○ *Bill explained how the program works.* [+ wh- word] • To explain is also to give a reason for doing something: *He couldn't explain why he did it.* [+ wh- word] • If you **explain away** something bad, you try to escape being blamed for it usually by making it seem unimportant: *He tried to explain the error away by saying it was a simple typing mistake.*

explanation /ˌek·spləˈneɪ·ʃən/ *n* [C/U] • *She gave a detailed explanation of the administration's health-care proposal.* [C] • An explanation is also a reason or an excuse for doing something: *He had no explanation for his absence the day before.* [C]

explanatory /ɪkˈsplæn·ə,tɔːr·i, -ˌtoʊr·i/ *adj* [not gradable] helping to make something clear or understandable • *an explanatory note*

expletive /ˈek·splət̬·ɪv/ *n* [C] a rude or offensive word used to express anger, pain, annoyance, etc.

explicit /ɪkˈsplɪs·ət/ *adj* [not gradable] communicated directly in a clear and exact way • *I gave them explicit directions on how to get here.* • Explicit also means showing full details, without anything hidden or suggested: *The magazine had sexually explicit pictures.* • Compare IMPLICIT SUGGESTED.

explicitly /ɪkˈsplɪs·ət·li/ *adv* [not gradable]

explode BURST /ɪkˈsploʊd/ *v* [I/T] to burst violently and usually with a loud noise, or to cause this to happen • *Two persons were killed and 13 injured when a bomb exploded in a mosque.* [I] ○ (*fig.*) *That part of the world could explode into civil war.* [I] • USAGE: The related noun is EXPLOSION BURST.

explode [SHOW EMOTION] /ɪk'sploʊd/ v [I] to show sudden violent emotion, esp. anger • *He exploded in anger when told his luggage had been lost.*

explode [INCREASE] /ɪk'sploʊd/ v [I] to increase very quickly • *The population is exploding in that part of the world.* • USAGE: The related noun is EXPLOSION [INCREASE].

explode [PROVE FALSE] /ɪk'sploʊd/ v [T] to prove to be false or wrong • *Later research exploded the myths that underlay American involvement in Vietnam.*

exploit [USE WELL] /ɪk'splɔɪt, 'ek,splɔɪt/ v [T] to use (something) for your own benefit • *The two companies joined forces to exploit the potential of the Internet.* ○ *The movie industry exploits sex.*

exploit [USE UNFAIRLY] /ɪk'splɔɪt, 'ek·splɔɪt/ v [T] to use (someone) unfairly for your own advantage • *Factories here are coming under criticism for exploiting workers.*

exploitation /,ek,splɔɪ'teɪ·ʃən/ n [U] • *sexual exploitation* ○ *She favors legislation to curb the exploitation of child labor.*

exploit [ACT] /'ek·splɔɪt, ɪk'splɔɪt/ n [C] a brave, interesting, or unusual act • *Since when do we accept as true what an adolescent male says about his sexual exploits?*

explore [TRAVEL] /ɪk'splɔːr, -'sploʊr/ v [I/T] to travel to (a new place) to learn about it or become familiar with it • *They set out to explore the city.* [T]

exploration /,ek·splə'reɪ·ʃən, ,ek,splɔː-/ n [C/U] • *oil/gas exploration* [U] ○ *space exploration* [U]

explorer /ɪk'splɔːr·ər, ɪk'sploʊr·ər/ n [C] • *French explorers traded with the Indians in many parts of North America.*

explore [DISCOVER] /ɪk'splɔːr, -'sploʊr/ v [T] to try to discover; learn about • *We have to explore new ways to market our products.* ○ *Many scholars have explored this issue.*

exploratory /ek'splɔːr·ə,tɔːr·i, ek'sploʊr·ə,tour·i/ adj [not gradable] intended to learn more about something • *After the illness had dragged on for too long, Jake decided that an exploratory operation was necessary.*

explosion [BURST] /ɪk'sploʊ·ʒən/ n [C/U] a violent burst, often with a loud noise • *The fire was caused by a gas explosion.* [C] ○ *The explosion of the space shuttle shocked the nation.* [U] • USAGE: The related verb is EXPLODE [BURST].

explosive /ɪk'sploʊ·sɪv, -zɪv/ n [C] a substance that can be made to burst violently • *Explosives are sometimes used to blast away rock in construction.* ○ *Dynamite is a powerful explosive.*

explosive /ɪk'sploʊ·sɪv, -zɪv/ adj • *an explosive device* ○ *Certain gases are highly explosive.* ○ *(fig.) It was a politically explosive issue.* • Explosive also means difficult to control and likely to be violent: *She has an explosive temper.*

explosion [INCREASE] /ɪk'sploʊ·ʒən/ n [C] a quick and big increase • *Auto dealers report an explosion of interest in family-style vans.* • USAGE: The related verb is EXPLODE [INCREASE].

explosive /ɪk'sploʊ·sɪv, -zɪv/ adj • *There has been an explosive increase in the number households owning a computer.*

expo /'ek·spoʊ/ n [C] *short form of* EXPOSITION [SHOW]

exponent /ɪk'spoʊ·nənt, 'ek,spoʊ-/ n [C] someone who supports an idea, plan, or position • *He was the leading exponent of the behavioral approach to psychology.*

export /ek'spɔːrt, -'spoʊrt/ v [I/T] to send (goods) to another country for sale or use • *Chile exports a large amount of copper to Japan.* [T] • Compare IMPORT [BRING IN].

export /'ek·spɔːrt, -spoʊrt/ n [C/U] something sold and taken out of a country and into another • *Coffee is one of Brazil's main exports.* [C]

exporter /ek'spɔːrt·ər, ek'spoʊrt·ər/ n [C] • *Japan is a major exporter of cars.*

expose [BE SEEN] /ɪk'spoʊz/ v [T] to make (something covered or hidden) able to be seen • *The plaster was removed to expose the original brick wall.*

exposed /ɪk'spoʊzd/ adj • *He left some exposed wires that should be covered up.*

expose [SHOW THE TRUTH] /ɪk'spoʊz/ v [T] to state facts about (someone), esp. publicly, that show they have been dishonest • *He was exposed as a fraud and a liar.*

expose [BE HARMED] /ɪk'spoʊz/ v [T] to create a situation or a condition that makes (someone) likely to be harmed • *His behavior on the Senate floor exposed him to ridicule.* ○ *The article said that children exposed to smoke are more likely to be sick.*

expose [GIVE OPPORTUNITY] /ɪk'spoʊz/ v [T] to create conditions that allow (someone) to have the opportunity to learn or experience new things • *Kate was exposed to new ideas when she went to college.*

exposé /,ek·spoʊ'zeɪ, -spə-/ n [C] a public report about a situation that is shocking or that has been kept secret

exposition [EXPLANATION] /,ek·spə'zɪʃ·ən/ n [C] *fml* a statement that explains something clearly

expository /ɪk'spɑz·ə,tɔːr·i, -,toʊr·i/ adj [not gradable] explaining or describing an event or situation • *expository writing*

exposition [SHOW] /,ek·spə'zɪʃ·ən/, *short form* **expo** n [C] a big public event in which the goods of many different companies or organizations are shown • *the San Francisco exposition*

exposure [HARMFUL CONDITION] /ɪk'spoʊ·ʒər/ n [U] a situation or condition that makes someone likely to be harmed, esp. because they have not been protected from something dangerous • *A federal court jury found the workers* had been harmed by prolonged exposure to asbestos fibers. ○ Avoid prolonged exposure to sunlight.

exposure OPPORTUNITY /ɪkˈspoʊ·ʒər/ n [U] the availability of conditions that create an opportunity to learn or experience new things • Additional exposure to the Japanese language was provided at meals. ○ Students deserve exposure to creative teachers.

exposure PUBLIC ATTENTION /ɪkˈspoʊ·ʒər/ n [U] the attention given to someone or something by television, newspapers, magazines, etc. • Male dominated sports received far more exposure than female athletics on almost every level. ○ He gained wide exposure in both the print and sound media.

exposure SHOWING DANGER /ɪkˈspoʊ·ʒər/ n [U] the act of stating facts publicly that show that someone is dishonest or dangerous • The exposure of a plot to assassinate the prime minister led to a number of arrests.

exposure DIRECTION /ɪkˈspoʊ·ʒər/ n [C usually sing] the condition of facing in (a stated direction) • Our dining room has a southern exposure, so we get plenty of sun. [C]

exposure PHOTOGRAPH /ɪkˈspoʊ·ʒər/ n [C] one of the positions in a strip of film that can produce a photograph • Get a roll of film with 36 exposures.

express SHOW /ɪkˈspres/ v [T] to show (a feeling or idea) by what you say or do or by how you look • She's expressed interest in doing some camping. ○ Several victims expressed disappointment at the small amount of money they were offered. ○ He wrote to express his sympathy after the death of her mother. ○ The program tries to get students to express themselves verbally.

expression /ɪkˈspreʃ·ən/ n [C/U] the act of showing a feeling or idea, or a feeling or idea that is shown • She had such a sad expression on her face that I wondered what was wrong. [C] ○ Freedom of expression is a cherished right in democracies. [U] • See also EXPRESSION.

expressionless /ɪkˈspreʃ·ən·ləs/ adj showing no emotion • His face was expressionless as the verdict was announced.

expressive /ɪkˈspres·ɪv/ adj showing your feelings in your voice, behavior, or appearance • His singing was beautiful and expressive.

express FAST /ɪkˈspres/ adj [not gradable] (esp. of transportation or a service) fast, or direct • The express train makes very few stops.

express /ɪkˈspres/ n [C] a train or bus that does not stop at many places on its route and is therefore faster in getting people to where they want to go • Change here to get the express. • Compare LOCAL VEHICLE.

express CLEAR /ɪkˈspres/ adj clearly and intentionally stated • It was her express wish that art collection be given to the university's museum.

expressly /ɪkˈspres·li/ adv • He wrote the play expressly for her.

expression /ɪkˈspreʃ·ən/ n [C] a word or group of words having a particular meaning or used in a particular way • That was an expression he hadn't heard before, and wondered what it meant. • See also **expression** at EXPRESS SHOW.

expressway /ɪkˈspres·weɪ/ n [C] a wide road built for fast-moving traffic, with a limited number of places where drivers can enter and leave it

expropriate /ekˈsproʊ·priːˌeɪt/ v [T] to take and keep (usually money or property), esp. for public use without payment to the owner

expulsion /ɪkˈspʌl·ʃən/ n [C] the act of forcing someone, or of being forced, to leave somewhere • The government ordered the expulsion of foreign journalists. • USAGE: The related verb is EXPEL.

exquisite /ɪkˈskwɪz·ət, ˈek·skwɪz·ət/ adj especially beautiful or admirable • exquisite Chinese embroideries ○ the most exquisite French cuisine

exquisitely /ɪkˈskwɪz·ət·li, ˈek·skwɪz-/ adv [not gradable] • Their house is exquisitely furnished.

extant /ˈek·stənt, ek·ˈstænt/ adj still existing • Phyllis Wheatley is the author of the earliest extant volume of poetry by an African American.

extemporaneous /ekˌstem·pəˈreɪ·niːˌəs/ adj done or said without preparation • He made some extemporaneous remarks before the award ceremony.

extend REACH /ɪkˈstend/ v [I/T] to reach, continue, or stretch • Farmland extends for miles in every direction. [I] ○ The meeting extended into the late hours of the night. [I] ○ He extended his hand to greet me. [T]

extended /ɪkˈsten·dəd/ adj • There will be extended election day coverage on the evening news. ○ They're taking an extended (= long) vacation. • An **extended family** is a family unit that includes grandparents, aunts, uncles, and others in addition to parents and children. Compare **nuclear family** at NUCLEUS.

extensive /ɪkˈsten·sɪv/ adj covering a large area; having or being a large amount • Extensive roadway repairs are causing traffic problems. • Extensive also means wide in range and including much detailed information: Her knowledge of music is extensive. ○ Foster did extensive research on electromagnetic fields.

extensively /ɪkˈsten·sɪv·li/ adv • The house was extensively rebuilt.

extend INCREASE /ɪkˈstend/ v [T] to add to (something) in order to make it longer; increase • The store has recently extended its hours. ○ I might have extended this essay to include more information. • To extend something is also to increase its range so that it includes more: The proposed law would extend *health insurance to children and pregnant women.*

extension /ɪk'sten·tʃən/ n [C/U] an amount by which something is increased, or something added to something else • *a contract extension* ○ *I applied for an extension to my visa.* ○ *We're building an extension on our house to enlarge the kitchen.* [C] • An **extension cord** is a wire that can be connected to the wire of an electrical device to make it longer.

extend OFFER /ɪk'stend/ v [T] to offer or give • *I would like to extend my thanks to everybody for making this evening a success.* ○ *We'd like to express our condolences to the family.*

extension /ɪk'sten·tʃən/ n [C] any of two or more telephones in the same house that share the same number • *We have an extension in our bedroom.* • An extension is also any of the telephones connected to a central system, esp. in a business.

extent AREA /ɪk'stent/ n [U] the area, length, or size of something • *Approaching the airport, you could see the full extent of the island.*

extent DEGREE /ɪk'stent/ n [U] the degree or limit of something; how great or severe something is • *To some extent it was my fault, though I didn't mean any harm.* ○ *We didn't know the extent of his injuries.* ○ *It makes sense to a certain extent to write down everything.*

extenuating /ɪk'sten·jə,weɪt·ɪŋ/ adj acting to excuse something bad or causing something bad to be judged less seriously • *There were extenuating circumstances.*

exterior /ek'stɪr·i·ər/ adj [not gradable] outer; on or from the outside • *The exterior walls of the house are painted pink.* • Compare INTERIOR.

exterior /ek'stɪr·i·ər/ n [C] • *The exterior of the house needs painting.*

exterminate /ɪk'stɜr·mə,neɪt/ v [T] to kill (all the animals or people in a particular place or of a particular type)

extermination /ɪk,stɜr·mə'neɪ·ʃən/ n [U] • *International measures have been taken to prevent the extermination of whales.*

exterminator /ɪk'stɜr·mə,neɪt·ər/ n [C] a person whose job it is to kill unwanted insects or animals

external /ek'stɜrn·əl/ adj [not gradable] existing, intended for, or happening outside a person, organization, place, country, etc. • *This skin cream is for external use only.* ○ *She handles the company's external relations.* ○ *His paintings show external influences* (= influences coming from other people). • Compare INTERNAL.

externally /ek'stɜrn·əl·i/ adv [not gradable]

extinct /ɪk'stɪŋt/ adj [not gradable] no longer existing • *There is concern that the giant panda will soon become extinct.* • An extinct VOLCANO (= mountain made from burned materials) is one that is no longer active.

extinction /ɪk'stɪŋ·ʃən/ n [U] • *Many species of plants and animals are threatened with extinction.*

extinguish /ɪk'stɪŋ·gwɪʃ, -wɪʃ/ v [T] to stop (a fire or light) from burning • *It took the firefighters four hours to extinguish the flames.*

extol /ɪk'stoʊl/ v [T] **-ll-** to praise highly • *He often extols the virtues of his students.*

extort /ɪk'stɔrt/ v [T] to obtain by force or threat • *The gang is accused of extorting money from local store owners.*

extortion /ɪk'stɔr·ʃən/ n [U] • *He was found guilty of extortion.*

extra /'ek·strə/ adj, adv [not gradable] added, additional, or more than expected • *Some students needed extra help.* ○ *He's been working an extra two hours a day.* ○ *I bought some extra batteries.*

extra /'ek·strə/ n [C] • *We didn't get any extras on our new car except for the CD player.* • An extra is also a person in a movie who does not have a speaking part and is usually in the background or in a crowd.

extract /ɪk'strækt/ v [T] to remove or take out (something) • *The dentist had to extract one of Miguel's teeth.*

extract /'ek·strækt/ n [C/U] a substance removed from another substance, often a food, and containing a basic quality or flavor • *vanilla extract* [U]

extraction /ɪk'stræk·ʃən/ n [C/U] • *a tooth extraction* [C] • If you say that a person is of a particular extraction, you mean that the person originally came from the stated nation or country: *She is of Korean extraction.* [U]

extracurricular /,ek·strə·kə'rɪk·jə·lər/ adj [not gradable] (of activities or subjects) not part of the usual school or college course • *Popular extracurricular activities include pottery, chess, choir, tennis, and swimming.*

extradition /,ek·strə'dɪʃ·ən/ n [U] the return of someone accused of a crime to the country where the crime was committed • *They have applied for his extradition to the United States.*

extradite /'ek·strə,daɪt/ v [T] • *One of the defendants fled to Egypt, which extradited him to the US.*

extramarital /,ek·strə'mær·ət·əl, -'mer-/ adj [not gradable] (of a sexual relationship) with a person other than your marriage partner • *an extramarital affair*

extraneous /ek'streɪ·ni·əs/ adj not directly connected or related to a matter being considered • *We must not be distracted by extraneous issues, she said.*

extraordinary /ɪk'strɔrd·ən,er·i, ,ek·strə'ɔrd-/ adj very unusual and special; different in type or greater in degree than the usual or ordinary • *Being chairman gave him an extraordinary sense of power.* ○ *She was an extraordinary woman, and no one will ever forget her.*

extraordinarily /ɪkˌstrɔːrd·ᵊn'er·ə·li, ˌek·strə
ˌɔːrd-/ *adv* • LP VERY, COMPLETELY, AND OTHER IN-
TENSIFIERS

extraterrestrial /ˌek·strə·tə'res·triː·əl/ *adj*
[not gradable] (coming from) outside the planet earth • *extraterrestrial beings*

extravagant EXPENSIVE /ɪk'stræv·ə·gənt/ *adj*
costing or spending more money than is necessary or reasonable, or characterized by
spending money too freely • *Company executives enjoyed an extravagant lifestyle.* ○ *Top
athletes are showered with extravagant gifts.*

extravagantly /ɪk'stræv·ə·gənt·li/ *adv*

extravagance /ɪk'stræv·ə·gəns/ *n* [C/U] • *In
those days, a second car seemed like a needless
extravagance.* [C]

extravagant UNREASONABLE /ɪkˌstræv·ə·gənt/
adj beyond any reasonable expectation • *Parents who have extravagant hopes for their children are bound to be disappointed.*

extreme GREAT /ɪk'striːm/ *adj* very great; beyond what is usual or what might be expected
• *Use extreme caution, as the steps are very slippery.* ○ *The extreme cold kept most people indoors.*

extreme /ɪk'striːm/ *n* [C] • *The security staff
went to extremes to insure the safety of the
world leaders.*

extremely /ɪk'striːm·li/ *adv* • *She was
extremely intelligent.*

extreme FURTHEST /ɪk'striːm/ *adj* at the furthest point; to the greatest degree • *At the extreme end of the lake there is a hunting lodge.*
• Extreme opinions, ideas, etc., are beyond the
usual range of variety and would seem unreasonable to most people.

extremism /ɪk'striːˌmɪz·əm/ *n* [U] • *political
extremism*

extremist /ɪk'striː·məst/ *n* [C] • *This convention was packed with right-wing extremists.*

extremities /ɪk'strem·ət·iːz/ *pl n* the hands
and feet

extricate /'ek·strə·keɪt/ *v* [T] to remove
(something or someone) from a bad situation,
esp. one in which they are trapped • *They need
education and other economic opportunities in
order to extricate themselves from poverty.* ○
*The president outlined a plan to extricate the
troops if the situation worsened.*

exuberant /ɪg'zuː·bə·rənt/ *adj* (esp. of people
and their behavior) very energetic, and showing the happiness of being alive • *He is an exuberant dancer.*

exuberance /ɪg'zuː·bə·rəns/ *n* [U] • *His exuberance is contagious.*

exude /ɪg'zuːd/ *v* [T] to have a lot of (a particular quality or feeling) • *Sal exudes confidence.* • To exude is also to produce from the
inside and spread out slowly: *Some trees exude
a sap that repels insect parasites.*

exult /ɪg'zʌlt/ *v* [I] to express great pleasure
or happiness, esp. at your success or at someone else's failure • *He exulted in the publicity
he received.*

exultant /ɪg'zʌlt·ᵊnt/ *adj* • *He was exultant at
the news of his team's victory.*

exultation /ˌeg·zəl'teɪ·ʃən/ *n* [U]

exurb /'ek·sɜrb, 'eg·zɜrb/ *n* [C] a region beyond
the SUBURBS (= areas built around cities),
which is not highly developed and where rich
people often live

exurban /ek'sɜr·bən, eg'zɜr-/ *adj* • *an exurban
community*

eye /ɑɪ/ *n* [C] one of the pair of organs of seeing in the faces of humans and animals • *She
has green eyes.* • The eye of a needle is the hole
through which you put the thread. • If you believe in **an eye for an eye**, you believe that a
person who causes another person to suffer
should suffer in an equal amount. • If you cannot **keep/take** your **eyes off** something or
someone, you cannot stop looking at them. •
The **eyeball** is the whole eye, including the
part that cannot usually be seen. • An **eyebrow** is the line of short hairs humans have
above each eye. • **Eye contact** is the act of
looking directly in the eyes of another person
as they look at you. • **Eyeglasses** are **glasses**.
See at GLASS. • An **eyelash** is one of the short
hairs which grow along the edges of the pieces
of skin that you can close over an eye: *She has
long eyelashes.* • An **eyelid** is either of the two
pieces of skin that you can close over each eye.
• (*infml*) If something is an **eye-opener**, you
learn something new from it that is surprising. • **Eye shadow** is a colored cream or powder that is put around the eyes to make them
look larger or more attractive. • **Eyesight** is
the ability to see: *Her eyesight is not as good as
it used to be.*

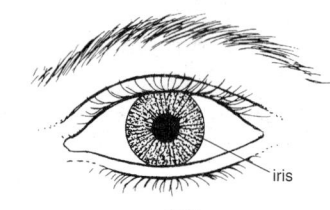

iris

eye

eye /ɑɪ/ *v* [T] **eyeing**, *past* **eyed** • *She eyed the
other passengers* (= looked closely at them).

eyesore /'ɑɪ·sɔːr, -soʊr/ *n* [C] an unpleasant or
ugly sight in a public place • *These billboards
by the side of the road are an eyesore.*

eyewitness /'ɑɪ·wɪt·nəs/ *n* [C] a person who
saw something happen, for example a crime or
an accident • *Police were looking for eyewitnesses.*

F, f

F LETTER , **f** /ef/ *n* [C] *pl* **F's** or **Fs** or **f's** or **fs** the sixth letter of the English alphabet

F MUSICAL NOTE /ef/ *n* [C/U] *pl* **F's** or **Fs** the fourth note in the **major scale** (= series of notes) that begins on the note c, or a set of notes based on this note

F MARK /ef/ *n* [C] *pl* **F's** or **Fs** a mark given for an exam, a course, or a piece of work which shows that your work has failed to meet the lowest acceptable standard • *I'm giving you an F if your paper isn't in by Thursday.*

F TEMPERATURE *n* [U] *abbreviation for* FAHREN- HEIT • *Yesterday the temperature was 90°F.*

fable /'feɪ·bəl/ *n* [C] a short story that tells a moral truth, often using animals as charac- ters • *Latisha loves the fable about the grass- hopper and the ant.*

fabric CLOTH /'fæb·rɪk/ *n* [C/U] cloth or woven material, or a type of this material • *cotton fabric* [U] ○ *Wash delicate fabrics by hand.* [C]

fabric STRUCTURE /'fæb·rɪk/ *n* [U] the structure of something; the parts of something that hold it together and make it what it is • *Ex- treme social activism might rip apart the social fabric.*

fabricate /'fæb·rə,keɪt/ *v* [T] to invent or pro- duce (esp. a story that isn't true) in order to deceive • *She fabricated charges that her boss was stealing money.*

fabrication /,fæb·rə'keɪ·ʃən/ *n* [C] • *That sto- ry is a complete fabrication.*

fabulous GOOD /'fæb·jə·ləs/ *adj infml* very good; wonderful • *This is a fabulous place!*

fabulously /'fæb·jə·lə·sli/ *adv* • *She dressed him fabulously.*

fabulous LARGE /'fæb·jə·ləs/ *adj* great in size or amount • *fabulous profits*

fabulously /'fæb·jə·lə·sli/ *adv* • *They were fabulously successful.*

façade, **facade** /fə'sɑd/ *n* [C] the front of a building • *The façade is made of limestone.* • A person's façade is a way they present them- selves to others: *Behind her façade of gentle- ness was a tough competitor.*

face HEAD /feɪs/ *n* [C] the front of the head in- cluding the eyes, nose, and mouth • *Cal hid his face in his hands.* • If you do something **face- to-face**, you do it looking at another person: *We sat face-to-face.* ○ *(fig.) He's suddenly come face-to-face with his own weakness* (= is dealing with it). • *(slang)* To be **in** someone's **face** is to criticize or annoy them: *One of the man- agers is always in my face.* • If you do some- thing **to** someone's **face**, you do it obviously without worrying what they will think: *I know he's lying and I'll tell him so to his face.* • *She left home* **in the face of** (= despite) *strong op- position from her parents.* • A **facelift** is a med- ical operation that tightens loose skin to make the face look younger. See also **facelift** at FACE FRONT .

facial /'feɪ·ʃəl/ *adj* [not gradable] • *Casey suf- fered a facial cut in the accident.*

facial /'feɪ·ʃəl/ *n* [C] a beauty treatment that cleans and improves the skin of the face with creams, gentle rubbing, etc.

faceless /'feɪ·sləs/ *adj* [not gradable] lacking any particular character; difficult to describe or deal with • *faceless bureaucracy*

face FRONT /feɪs/ *n* [C] the front or surface of an object • *We climbed the north face of Mount Washington.* • The face of a clock or a watch is the surface that has the numbers or marks on it that show what time it is. • *The story seems simple* **on the face of it** (= when first considered), *but it's really pretty complicated.* • A **facelift** is work done on a building to make it look more modern or attractive: *The bank is planning to give its 1930 building a complete facelift.* See also **facelift** at FACE HEAD . • **Face value** is the value or price shown on esp. a stamp, a coin, or a bill. • *I took the offer* **at face value** (= for what it appeared to be) *because I didn't think they would try to trick me.*

face DEAL WITH /feɪs/ *v* [T] to deal with (a diffi- cult situation) • *They are faced with major fi- nancial problems.* ○ *I can't face climbing those stairs again.*

face BE POSITIONED /feɪs/ *v* [I/T] to have the front of something positioned toward, or to turn toward (something or someone) • *The balcony faces south.* [I always + adv/prep] ○ *Please face the front of the room.* [T]

facet /'fæs·ət/ *n* [C] one of the parts or fea- tures of something • *There's always one facet of my golf game that isn't working.*

facetious /fə'si·ʃəs/ *adj* not seriously mean- ing what you say, usually in an attempt to be humorous or to trick someone • *I make so much money that we never have to worry—I'm being facetious.*

facetiously /fə'si·ʃə·sli/ *adv* • *"We could spend all our income on health care," she said facetiously.*

facile /'fæs·əl/ *adj* easy or too easy; not need- ing effort • *He does not permit himself facile answers.*

facilitate /fə'sɪl·ə,teɪt/ *v* [T] to make (some- thing) possible or easier • *To facilitate learn- ing, each class is no larger than 30 students.*

facility ABILITY /fə'sɪl·ət·i/ *n* [U] an ability or skill at doing something • *His facility for mem- orizing dates was astonishing.*

facility BUILDING /fə'sɪl·ət·i/ *n* [C] a place, esp. including buildings, where a particular activ- ity happens • *The new sports facility has a swimming pool.*

facsimile /fæk'sɪm·ə·li/ n [C] an exact copy, esp. of a document • A facsimile is also a FAX.

fact /fækt/ n [C] something known to have happened or to exist • No one disputes the fact that the accident could have been avoided. • **In fact** is used to emphasize something that is true: He was in fact near death by the time they reached him. • A **fact of life** is something unpleasant that cannot be avoided: Driving to work on overcrowded highways is a fact of life for millions of commuters. • The **facts of life** are the details about sex and reproduction.

faction /'fæk·ʃən/ n [C] a group within a larger group, esp. one with slightly different ideas than the main group • The president's advisors represent every faction of his party.

factor /'fæk·tər/ n [C] a fact or situation that influences a result • Economic factors had a lot to do with their decision to sell the company.

factor in obj, **factor** obj **in** /ˌfæk·tər'ɪn/ v prep [M] to consider (information), esp. as something that might influence a result • The children's welfare should be factored in before a divorce is granted.

factory /'fæk·tə·ri, 'fæk·tri/ n [C] a building or buildings where people use machines to produce goods • She worked in a factory that produced air conditioners.

factual /'fæk·tʃə·wəl/ adj based on facts • a factual account

factually /'fæk·tʃə·wə·li/ adv • The newspaper account was factually incorrect.

faculty [COLLEGE TEACHERS] /'fæk·əl·ti/ n [C] the people who teach in a college or university, or in a department of a college or university

faculty [ABILITY] /'fæk·əl·ti/ n [C] any natural ability, such as hearing, seeing, or thinking • Even though she is 102, she still has all of her faculties.

fad /fæd/ n [C] a style or activity that suddenly becomes popular but which usually does not stay popular for very long • He thought computers would be just a fad.

fade /feɪd/ v [I] to lose color, brightness, or strength gradually • If you hang your clothes out in the bright sun, they will fade. • If something fades away/out, it becomes less clear and then disappears: The voice on the radio faded out.

fag /fæg/, **faggot** /'fæg·ət/ n [C] taboo slang a homosexual man • USAGE: This is an offensive word.

Fahrenheit /'fær·ən,haɪt/ (abbreviation **F**) n [U] a scale for measuring temperature in which water freezes at 32° and boils at 212° • The Fahrenheit scale is still used throughout the US. • Compare CELSIUS.

fail [NOT SUCCEED] /feɪl/ v [I] to not be able to do what you are trying to achieve or are expected to do • She applied to Harvard University but failed to get accepted. [+ to infinitive] • If you fail to see/understand what something is, you do not agree with someone's description of a

situation: I fail to see what the problem is (= I don't think there is a problem). [+ to infinitive]

fail [NOT PASS] /feɪl/ v [I/T] to be unsuccessful, or to judge that (someone) has been unsuccessful in (a test or examination) • A lot of people fail (their driving test) the first time. [I/T] ○ She said she would fail any student who misses two exams. [T]

fail [NOT DO] /feɪl/ v [I/T] to not do something that should be done • He promised to help, but failed to send a check. [+ to infinitive] ○ She never fails to meet a deadline. [+ to infinitive] • To fail is also to not help someone when expected to: He failed her when she most needed him. [T]

fail [STOP] /feɪl/ v [I] to become weaker or stop working completely • The bus driver said the brakes failed. • If a business fails, it is unable to continue because of money problems. • A **fail-safe** device is designed so that if one part of it does not work, the whole thing stops working to avoid a dangerous situation.

failing /'feɪ·lɪŋ/ adj [not gradable] • He is in failing health and seldom goes outside any more.

failing [WEAKNESS] /'feɪ·lɪŋ/ n [C] a fault or weakness • His one big failing is that he can't say he's sorry.

failing [WITHOUT] /'feɪ·lɪŋ/ prep used to show what will happen if something is not possible or available • She will very likely be the next president of the company, or failing that, the marketing director.

failure [LACK OF SUCCESS] /'feɪl·jər/ n [C/U] a lack of success in doing something • Their attempt to sail across the Atlantic Ocean ended in failure. [U] ○ He was a failure as a businessman. [C]

failure [SOMETHING NOT DONE] /'feɪl·jər/ n [U] the fact of not doing something you should have done • His failure to return her phone call told her that something was wrong. [+ to infinitive]

failure [SOMETHING NOT WORKING] /'feɪl·jər/ n [C/U] the fact of something not working as it should • He died of heart failure. [U] ○ The new computer system was a complete failure (= It did not work). [C]

faint [LOSE CONSCIOUSNESS] /feɪnt/ v [I] to lose consciousness unexpectedly for a short time • I nearly fainted from the heat.

faint /feɪnt/ adj [-er/-est only] very weak and nearly losing consciousness • He felt faint from hunger.

faint [SLIGHT] /feɪnt/ adj [-er/-est only] not strong or clear; slight • He walked along, guided only by the faint light of the moon.

faintly /'feɪnt·li/ adv • The hospital room smelled faintly of disinfectant.

fair [RIGHT] /fer, fær/ adj [-er/-est only] treating someone in a way that is right or reasonable, or treating people equally and not allowing personal opinions to influence your judgment • All he asks is a fair chance to prove his inno-

cence. • If a game or competition is fair, it is done according to the rules: *It was a fair fight.* • In some sports, esp. baseball, fair means within the playing field: *The umpire ruled it a fair ball.* The opposite of fair is FOUL SPORTS. • If you beat someone **fair and square**, you beat them honestly and according to the rules. • If someone or something is **fair game**, it is considered reasonable to criticize them: *Anyone running for the presidency is fair game.* • If you are **fair-minded**, you treat everyone equally. • **Fair play** is honest behavior, esp. according to established rules. • A **fair share** is the part of something you deserve: *I'm willing to do my fair share of the work.*

fairly /'fer·li, 'fær-/ *adv* • *It's the responsibility of a judge to treat both sides fairly.*

fairness /'fer·nəs, 'fær-/ *n* [U] • *In all fairness, she deserves the award.*

fair AVERAGE /fer, fær/ *adj* [not gradable] neither very good nor very bad • *He's good in physics but only fair in math.*

fair LARGE /fer, fær/ *adj* [not gradable] comparatively large or great • *We still had a fair amount of foreign money when we returned.*

fairly /'fer·li, 'fær-/ *adv* [not gradable] more than a little; to some degree • *I know him fairly well.* ○ *I saw her fairly recently* (= not very long ago).

fair CORRECT /fer, fær/ *adj* [not gradable] likely to be correct; accurate • *The architect's drawing will give you a pretty fair idea of what the completed house will look like.*

fair WEATHER /fer, fær/ *adj* [-er/-est only] (of weather) pleasant and dry • A **fair-weather friend** is someone who can be depended on only when everything is going well.

fair PUBLIC EVENT /fer, fær/ *n* [C] a public event, usually held outside, where goods and sometimes farm animals are shown and sold and where there is often food and entertainment • A county/state fair is one where farm animals and products from that region are shown to compete for prizes and there is food and entertainment. • A street fair is one where a city street is closed to cars so that goods and food can be sold to people walking through it. • A fair is also a show at which producers, sellers, and buyers in a particular industry meet to sell and advertise their products: *a book/antiques/toy fair* • A **fairground/fairgrounds** is a large outside area used for fairs or other public events.

fair PALE /fer, fær/ *adj* [-er/-est only] (of skin) pale, or (of hair) light in color • *If you have fair skin, you'll get a sunburn easily.*

fairy IMAGINARY CREATURE /'fer·i, 'fær·i/ *n* [C] an imaginary creature with magical powers who looks like a small person with wings • A **fairy tale** is a traditional story, usually written for children, which often involves imaginary creatures and magic.

fairy HOMOSEXUAL /'fer·i, 'fær·i/ *n* [C] dated

slang a homosexual man • USAGE: This word is offensive.

faith TRUST /feɪθ/ *n* [U] a high degree of trust or confidence in something or someone • *I have faith that she will do the right thing.* [+ *that* clause]

faithful /'feɪθ·fəl/ *adj* trusted; loyal • *She has been a faithful employee for 30 years.* • If something, such as a copy or recording, is faithful, it is exactly like or very similar to the original: *The painting was a faithful reproduction of the original.* • If a person is faithful to their husband, wife, or usual sexual partner, they do not have a sexual relationship with anyone else.

faithfully /'feɪθ·fə·li/ *adv* • *I always faithfully* (= carefully) *follow the instructions of my doctor when taking medicine.*

faith RELIGION /feɪθ/ *n* [C/U] a particular religion, or belief in God • *the Christian/Jewish/Muslim faith* [C] ○ *We welcome people of all faiths.* [C] ○ *Put your faith in God.* [U]

fake COPY /feɪk/ *n* [C] something that is intended to look like and be mistaken for something else, esp. a copy made in order to deceive • *The toy looked like a real gun, but it was a fake.*

fake /feɪk/ *adj* intended to look like something else, esp. in order to deceive • *He was caught with a fake passport.* ○ *"Is that a real fur coat?" "No, it's fake."*

fake /feɪk/ *v* [T] • *She faked her mother's signature on the permission form.*

fake PRETEND /feɪk/ *v* [I/T] to pretend • *He isn't really crying, he's just faking.* [I]

falcon /'fæl·kən, 'fɔːl-/ *n* [C] a bird with pointed wings and a long tail that hunts and kills other birds and small animals

fall ACCIDENT /fɔːl/ *v* [I] *past simple* **fell** /fel/, *past part* **fallen** /'fɔː·lən/ (of people and animals) to move unintentionally or accidentally onto or toward the ground from a higher place • *He fell and hurt his arm.* ○ *Junior fell backward and landed on his butt.* ○ *I fell down the stairs.* ○ *She fell off the top of the ladder.* ○ *Kathy tripped and fell (flat) on her face* (= fell facing the ground).

fall /fɔːl/ *n* [C usually sing] • *She injured herself in a fall.*

fall MOVE DOWN /fɔːl/ *v* [I] *past simple* **fell** /fel/, *past part* **fallen** /'fɔː·lən/ to move down toward or drop to a lower position • *They expect three inches of snow to fall tonight.* ○ *Tears rolled down her cheeks and fell into her lap.* ○ *Plaster was falling off the walls.* • *(infml)* A **falling star** is a METEOR.

falls /fɔːlz/ *pl n* a **waterfall**, see at WATER

fall SEASON /fɔːl/, **autumn** *n* [C/U] the season of the year between summer and winter, lasting from September to December north of the equator and from March to June south of the equator, when fruits and crops ripen and the leaves fall off the trees • *Fall is my favorite* *time of year.* [U] ∘ *She wants to take a vacation before fall classes start.* [U]

fall BECOME LESS /fɔːl/ v [I] *past simple* **fell** /fel/, *past part* **fallen** /ˈfɔː·lən/ to become less or lower in size, amount, or strength • *Stock prices fell sharply in late March and early April.* ∘ *Her blood sugar levels fell below normal.*

fall /fɔːl/ n [C usually sing] • *a fall in temperature*

fall CHANGE STATE /fɔːl/ v [L] *past simple* **fell** /fel/, *past part* **fallen** /ˈfɔː·lən/ used to show a change from one state to another • *He fell asleep reading the newspaper.* • If you **fall in love** you begin to love someone: *She's fallen in love and made plans to marry.* • If something **falls victim to** something else, it fails or suffers because of that thing: *The movie industry fell victim to its own success.*

fall BE DEFEATED /fɔːl/ v [I] *past simple* **fell** /fel/, *past part* **fallen** /ˈfɔː·lən/ to be defeated or fail • *The city fell to the enemy.* • If soldiers fall, they die: *The statue honors soldiers who fell in battle.* • *I think the stronger groups will flourish and the weaker ones will* **fall by the wayside** (= no longer be active or important). • *Some of the jokes were pretty funny, others* **fell flat** (= were unsuccessful). • If something **falls short**, it doesn't reach a desired amount or standard: *Actual construction usually falls short of what is allowed under land-use plans.*

fall /fɔːl/ n [C usually sing] • *the fall of the Roman Empire*

fall HAPPEN /fɔːl/ v [I] *past simple* **fell** /fel/, *past part* **fallen** /ˈfɔː·lən/ to happen at a particular time • *My birthday falls on a Friday this year.* ∘ *By the time we got home, night had fallen* (= begun).

fall BELONG TO /fɔːl/ v [I always + adv/prep] *past simple* **fell** /fel/, *past part* **fallen** /ˈfɔː·lən/ to belong to a particular group, or to be part of a particular subject • *Archaeology falls under the general subject of natural history.*

fall HANG DOWN /fɔːl/ v [I always + adv/prep] *past simple* **fell** /fel/, *past part* **fallen** /ˈfɔː·lən/ (of hair or cloth) to hang down loosely • *Her long, dark hair fell to her waist.*

□ **fall apart** /ˌ-ˈ-/ v adv [I] to stop working, or to fail completely • *The deal fell apart because of a lack of money.* ∘ *When his wife died, he fell apart* (= was very unhappy). • If an object falls apart, its pieces are no longer attached: *Our furniture is falling apart.*

□ **fall back on** /ˌ-ˈ-ˌ/ v adv prep [T] to use (something) for help because no other choice is available • *The organization has no income and no reserves to fall back on.*

□ **fall behind** /ˌ--ˈ-/ v prep [I/T] to fail to do (something) fast enough or on time • *We fell behind schedule.* [T] ∘ *He fell behind in his work.* [I]

□ **fall for** LOVE /ˈ--/ v prep [T] *infml* to be at-

tracted to (someone) and start to love them • *Mike has fallen for Heather.*

□ **fall for** BE TRICKED /ˈ--/ v prep [T] *infml* to be deceived by (something or someone) • *I said I was an art collector, and they fell for it.*

□ **fall into** /ˈ---, -ˈ--/ v adv [T] to suddenly be in (a condition) • *She fell into a coma.* • *I've worked very hard, and now things have begun to* **fall into place** (= become organized in a positive way). • *I wouldn't want my machine to* **fall into the wrong hands** (= be in the possession of people who should not have it).

□ **fall off** /ˈ-ˈ-/ v adv [I] to become less in number, amount, or quality • *Production fell off last month.*

□ **fall out** /ˈ-ˈ-/ v adv [I] (of objects) to drop from a place where they were attached • *A few pages fell out of the book.*

□ **fall through** /ˈ-ˈ-/ v adv [I] to fail to happen • *The sale of the house fell through.*

fallacy /ˈfæl·ə·si/ n [C] a false belief • *It is a common fallacy that only men are good at math.* [+ *that* clause]

fallacious /fəˈleɪ·ʃəs/ adj [not gradable] • *a fallacious argument*

fall guy /ˈfɔːlˈgɑɪ/ n [C] *infml* a person who is blamed for something bad when others who were also responsible are not blamed • *The cops made him the fall guy, even after they knew he was innocent.*

fallible /ˈfæl·ə·bəl/ adj (of a person) able to fail or likely to make mistakes, or (of an object or system) likely not to work satisfactorily • *Human beings are fallible.*

fallibility /ˌfæl·əˈbɪl·ət·i/ n [U] • *Women are urged to take the test, despite its fallibility.*

fallout EFFECT /ˈfɔːlˌlɑʊt/ n [U] the unpleasant results or effects of an action or event • *He blamed the political fallout from the scandal on the Republicans.*

fallout DUST /ˈfɔːlˌlɑʊt/ n [U] the RADIOACTIVE dust in the air after a nuclear device explodes

false NOT REAL /fɔːls/ adj [not gradable] (of things) not real, but made to look real, or (of information) not true but made to seem true in order to deceive • *Haban used false identification to enter France.* ∘ *He had orders from the CIA to spread false information.* • A **false alarm** is a signal for help given when help is not needed, esp. to fight a fire when there is no fire. • **False pretenses** are lies or statements that hide the truth which are used to achieve something or to get others to do something you want: *Money was collected under false pretenses.* • **False teeth** are artificial teeth used to fill the spaces in a person's mouth where teeth are missing.

falsify /ˈfɔːl·səˌfɑɪ/ v [T] • *She falsified the accounting records.*

false NOT CORRECT /fɔːls/ adj [not gradable] (of information or an idea) not correct or true • *"Three plus three is seven. True or false?" "False."* • In a race, a **false start** is when a competitor starts before the signal has been given. • A **false start** is also an attempt to do something you are not ready or able to do: *She began writing fiction, and after several false starts she wrote "Gone With the Wind."*

falsehood /ˈfɔːls·hʊd/ *n* [C/U] something that is not true; a lie

falsely /ˈfɔːl·sli/ *adv* [not gradable] • *She was falsely accused of shoplifting.*

falsity /ˈfɔːl·sət̬·i/, **falseness** /ˈfɔːl·snəs/ *n* [U] *slightly fml* • *We're trying to determine the truth or falsity of your previous statement.*

false NOT SINCERE /fɔːls/ *adj* [not gradable] (of a person or their manner) dishonest or not sincere • *"I think of myself as great," said Tyler, abandoning false modesty.*

falsetto /fɔːlˈset̬·oʊ/ *n* [C/U] *pl* **falsettos** (esp. of a man) a method of singing in a voice much higher than the singer's usual voice

falsetto /fɔːlˈset̬·oʊ/ *adj, adv* • *He sings a weird falsetto version of "Barbara Ann."*

falter /ˈfɔːl·tər/ *v* [I] to lose strength or purpose and pause or stop • *His career began to falter.* • *To falter is also to move or speak uncertainly.*

faltering /ˈfɔːl·tə·rɪŋ/ *adj* • *faltering speech*

fame /feɪm/ *n* [U] the state of being known for having or doing something important • *She came to the city seeking fortune and fame.* • USAGE: The related adjective is FAMOUS.

familiar KNOWN /fəˈmɪl·jər/ *adj* easy to recognize because previously experienced • *familiar sights ○ a familiar face ○ I'm not familiar with current research in the field.*

familiarity /fə,mɪl·ˈjær·ət̬·i/ *n* [U] • *Harry's familiarity with the city makes him a good tour guide.*

familiarize /fəˈmɪl·jə,rɑɪz/ *v* [T] • *Teachers needed to familiarize themselves with the new software.*

familiar INFORMAL /fəˈmɪl·jər/ *adj* informal or friendly, esp. more than is expected • *Her familiar tone makes her writing more effective.*

familiarly /fəˈmɪl·jər·li/ *adv* • *Greenwich Village is familiarly known as "the Village."*

family PARENTS AND CHILDREN /ˈfæm·ə·li, ˈfæm·li/ *n* [C/U] a social group of parents, children, and sometimes grandparents, uncles, aunts, and other relatives • *Her family moved here when she was eleven.* [C] ○ *Many people cope with the demands of both career and family.* [U] ○ *She wants to get married and have a family* (= have children). [C] • Your **family name** is your **last name**. See at LAST FINAL. • **Family planning** means controlling how many children you have and when you have them: *a family-planning clinic* • A **family room** is a room in a family's home that is used for relaxing, esp. for watching television. • A **family tree** is a drawing that shows all the members of a

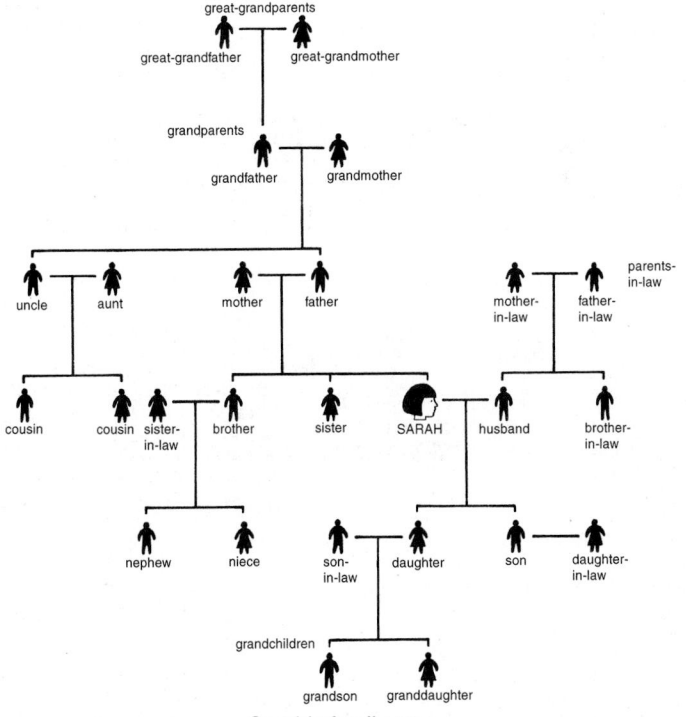

Sarah's family tree

family, esp. over a long period of time, and how they are related to each other.

family BIOLOGICAL TYPE /ˈfæm·ə·li, ˈfæm·li/ *n* [C] *specialized* a large group of related types of animals or plants • *The lion is a member of the cat family.*

famine /ˈfæm·ən/ *n* [C/U] an extreme lack of food in a region, causing suffering and death • *Widespread famine was reported in the region.* [U]

famished /ˈfæm·ɪʃt/ *adj infml* very hungry • *I'm famished! When do we eat?*

famous /ˈfeɪ·məs/ *adj* known by very many or most people • *a famous actor/singer* ○ *Marie Curie is famous for discovering radium.* • USAGE: The related noun is FAME.

famously /ˈfeɪ·mə·sli/ *adv* very well • *Maria and her roommate get along famously.*

fan DEVICE /fæn/ *n* [C] a device to provide a flow of air, either an object that you wave in front of you or a motorized device with blades that turn • *a window fan*

fan /fæn/ *v* [T] **-nn-** • *It was very hot in the car, so I fanned myself with the road map.* • To **fan out** is to spread (something) out or cause something to spread out over a wide area: *The police fanned out over that section of the park.*

fan ADMIRER /fæn/ *n* [C] a person who is very much interested in and spends a lot of time watching or reading about esp. an entertainer or sports team • *a baseball fan*

fanatic /fəˈnæt̬·ɪk/ *n* [C] a person whose strong admiration for something is extreme and unreasonable • *a religious fanatic*

fanatical /fəˈnæt̬·ɪ·kəl/ *adj* • *Her devotion to her pets was fanatical.*

fancy DECORATIVE /ˈfæn·si/ *adj* [-er/-est only] decorative or complicated, or (of restaurants, stores, or hotels) expensive • *I wanted a simple black dress, nothing fancy.* ○ *a fancy hotel*

fancy IMAGINE /ˈfæn·si/ *v* [T] to imagine or think that something is so • *When she was young she fancied herself a rebel.*

fanciful /ˈfæn·sə·fəl/ *adj* • *fanciful ideas/notions*

fancy LIKE /ˈfæn·si/ *v* [T] to like or wish for • *There are two things he fancies—fast cars and thunderous music.*

fancy /ˈfæn·si/ *n* [U] • If something **catches/strikes/tickles** your **fancy**, you decide that you like it: *Look over the clothes in the catalog and see if anything strikes your fancy.*

fanfare /ˈfæn·fer, -ˌfær/ *n* [U] showy activity meant to draw attention to something • *Earth Day was observed without a great deal of fanfare this week.*

fang /fæŋ/ *n* [C] a long, sharp tooth that animals such as snakes and dogs have

fanny /ˈfæn·i/ *n* [C] *infml* a person's buttocks • A **fanny pack** is a small bag fixed to a long strap that you fasten around your waist, and that is used for carrying small objects or money.

fantasize /ˈfæn·t̬əˌsaɪz/ *v* • See at FANTASY.

fantastic GOOD /fænˈtæs·tɪk/ *adj* very good • *You look fantastic in that outfit.*

fantastic NOT REAL /fænˈtæs·tɪk/ *adj* strange and imaginary • *He drew fantastic animals with two heads and large wings.*

fantastic LARGE /fænˈtæs·tɪk/ *adj* (of an amount) very large • *a fantastic sum of money*

fantasy /ˈfæn·t̬ə·si, -zi/ *n* [C/U] a pleasant but unlikely situation that you enjoy thinking about, or the activity of thinking in this way • *sexual fantasies* [C] ○ *She retreated from life into a world of fantasy.* [U]

fantasize /ˈfæn·t̬əˌsaɪz/ *v* [I] • *He fantasized about winning the Nobel Prize.*

far DISTANCE /fɑr/ *adv* **farther** /ˈfɑr·ðər/ or **further** /ˈfɜr·ðər/, **farthest** /ˈfɑr·ðəst/ or **furthest** /ˈfɜr·ðəst/ at, to, or from a great distance in space or time • *One day, perhaps far in the future, you'll regret what you've done.* ○ *How far is it from Los Angeles to San Francisco?* ○ *She doesn't live far from here.* • **As/so far as** means to the degree that: *As far as I know* (= Based on what I know), *he isn't coming until tomorrow.* ○ *She can come whenever she likes, so far as I'm concerned* (= I don't care when she comes). • *We were* **far from** *disappointed* (= we were not at all disappointed) *when they canceled the invitation.* • *Jim, selfish?* **Far from it** (= He's not selfish at all). • Something that is **faraway** is a great distance away: *The story told of strange customs in faraway lands.* • If someone has a **faraway look**, they look as though are thinking about something completely different from what is going on around them. • A time that is **far-off** is a long way from the present, in the past or the future, and **far-off** places are a great distance away. • Something **far-reaching** has a great influence on many people or things: *The effects of the riots will be far-reaching.* • Someone who is **farsighted** can only see objects clearly that are not close to them. Compare **nearsighted** at NEAR. • **Farsighted** also means able to make wise judgments about the results far in the future of an action taken now: *a farsighted proposal*

far /fɑr/ *adj* **farther** /ˈfɑr·ðər/ or **further** /ˈfɜr·ðər/, **farthest** /ˈfɑr·ðəst/ or **furthest** /ˈfɜr·ðəst/ • *the far* (= most distant) *side of the park* ○ *Even the closest stores are pretty far.* • The **far left** is the most LIBERAL political position, and the **far right** is the most CONSERVATIVE one.

far AMOUNT /fɑr/ *adv* [not gradable] much •

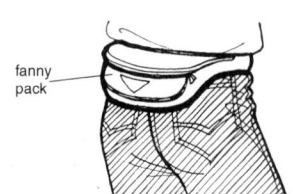

fanny pack

Her new school is far better than the old one. •
She is **by far** (= by a great amount) *the best stu-
dent in the class.* • LP VERY, COMPLETELY, AND
OTHER INTENSIFIERS

farce PLAY /fɑrs/ *n* [C/U] a humorous play in
which the characters become involved in unlikely situations, or the humor in this type of
play

farce SITUATION /fɑrs/ *n* [C] a ridiculous situation or event, or something considered a waste
of time • *The meeting turned out to be a farce
since no one had prepared anything.*

fare PAYMENT /fer, fær/ *n* [C] the money that
you pay for traveling on a vehicle such as a bus
or train • *We shared a taxi and split the fare.*

fare PROGRESS /fer, fær/ *v* [I always + adv/
prep] to progress or to be in a particular condition • *Middle-income families will fare bet-
ter/worse under the new tax laws.*

fare FOOD /fer, fær/ *n* [U] *fml* (in a restaurant)
the type of food that is served • *Middle Eastern fare*

farewell /fer'wel, fær-/ *exclamation, n* [C]
goodbye • *We said our farewells to our dear
friends.*

farewell /fer'wel, fær-/ *adj* [not gradable]
done at the time someone is leaving a place or
job • *a farewell speech* ○ *We gave Latoya a farewell party on her last day.*

far–fetched /'fɑr'fetʃt/ *adj* difficult to believe and unlikely to be true • *Her story about
being chased away from school by wolves seems
pretty far-fetched.*

farm /fɑrm/ *n* [C] an area of land, esp. together with a house and other buildings, used for
growing crops or keeping animals • *A farm
can also be a place where a specific type of animal is raised in large numbers to be sold: a
cattle/mink farm* • *A* **farmhand** *is a person
who is paid to work on a farm.*

farm /fɑrm/ *v* [I/T] • *Their family has farmed
(this land) for three generations.* [I/T]

farmer /'fɑr·mər/ *n* [C] a person who owns or
takes care of a farm

farming /'fɑr·mɪŋ/ *n* [U]

▫ **farm out** *obj*, **farm** *obj* **out** /'-'-, -'-/ *v adv* [M]
to give (work) to other people to do • *Maga-
zines often farm out articles to freelance journalists.*

far–out /'fɑr'aut/ *adj infml* strange and unusual • *They had some far-out ideas.*

fart GAS /fɑrt/ *v* [I] *rude slang* to allow gas
from the bowels to escape through the buttocks, esp. loudly

fart /fɑrt/ *n* [C] *rude slang*

fart PERSON /fɑrt/ *n* [C] *rude slang* a person
you do not like • *He's a pompous old fart.*

▫ **fart around** /ˌ-ˈ-/ *v adv* [I] *rude slang* to
waste time doing silly or useless things • *I
wish you'd stop farting around and help me
clean up.*

farther /'fɑr·ðər/ *adv, comparative of* FAR
DISTANCE; to a greater distance • *How much far-*

ther is it to the airport? ○ *Now that they live farther away we don't see them so often.* • USAGE:
See note at FURTHER GREATER DISTANCE.

farther /'fɑr·ðər/ *adj* • *Birds from farther
north appeared in the fall.*

farthest /'fɑr·ðəst/ *adv, superlative of* FAR
DISTANCE • *What's the farthest you've ever run
in your life?* • USAGE: See note at FURTHEST.

farthest /'fɑr·ðəst/ *adj* • *The farthest landmark visible is about twenty miles away.*

fascinate /'fæs·ə,neɪt/ *v* [T] to have (someone's) complete interest and attention • *Anything to do with airplanes and flying fascinates
him.* ○ *The children were fascinated by the
story.*

fascinating /'fæs·ə,neɪt̬·ɪŋ/ *adj* • *The movie
has a fascinating plot.*

fascination /ˌfæs·əˈneɪ·ʃən/ *n* [U] • *Her fascination with modern art began when she saw
the Picasso show.*

fascism /'fæʃ,ɪz·əm/ *n* [U] a political system
based on a very powerful leader, state control
of social and economic life, and extreme pride
in country and race, with no expression of
political disagreement allowed

fascist /'fæʃ·əst/ *adj* [not gradable] • *fascist
groups*

fascist /'fæʃ·əst/ *n* [C] • *He left Germany when
the fascists took over.*

fashion CUSTOM /'fæʃ·ən/ *n* [C/U] a custom or
way of looking and doing things that characterizes a particular time or place, as in clothing, personal appearance, and polite behavior
• *The program has features on pop music,
sports, and fashion.* [U] ○ *Long skirts are back
in fashion* (= popular) *this season.* [U] ○ *Formal
dinner parties seem to be out of fashion* (= not
popular). [U] ○ *The Sunday newspaper has a
special section called "Fashions of the Times."*
[C]

fashionable /'fæʃ·ə·nə·bəl/ *adj* • *It's not fashionable to wear short skirts this year.* [+ *to* infin-
itive]

fashionably /'fæʃ·ə·nə·bli/ *adv* • *fashionably
dressed*

fashion MANNER /'fæʃ·ən/ *n* [U] a way of doing things • *The sale of the property has to be
conducted in a systematic fashion.*

fashion MAKE /'fæʃ·ən/ *v* [T] to create (something), using the hands or the imagination •
*She fashioned an elaborate sculpture out of
newspapers and glue.*

fast QUICK /fæst/ *adj* [*-er/-est* only] moving or
happening quickly or able to move or happen
quickly • *a fast car* ○ *The fastest way to get
there is by plane.* • *If your watch or clock is
fast, it shows a time later than the real time.* •
He liked to live life **in the fast lane** (= in a
risky and competitive way). • *A* **fastball** *is a
PITCH in baseball that is thrown at the highest
speed.* • **Fast food** *is cheap, often hot food that
is prepared and served quickly in a restaurant.* • *The* **fast track** *is the quickest, but*

usually most competitive, route to success or advancement.

fast /fæst/ *adv* [*-er/-est* only] • *The accident was caused by people driving too fast in bad conditions.* ○ *This type of wilderness area is disappearing fast.*

fast ATTACHED /fæst/ *adv, adj* [not gradable] connected or attached in a way that is not easily unfastened • *Tie the boat fast to the pier.* • Someone who is **fast asleep** is sleeping and cannot easily be awakened.

fast NOT EAT /fæst/ *v* [I] to have a period of time when you eat no food • *We will be fasting until sundown tomorrow.*

fast /fæst/ *n* [C] • *They organized a fast to draw attention to the issue of hunger.*

fasten /ˈfæs·ən/ *v* [I/T] to make or become firmly attached or closed • *This skirt fastens at the back.* [I] ○ *Fasten your seatbelt.* [T]

fastener /ˈfæs·ə·nər/ *n* [C] a button or other device for joining together the separate parts of something, esp. clothes

fastidious /fæsˈtɪd·i·əs/ *adj* having high standards and giving a lot of attention to details • *The restaurant offers elaborate food and fastidious service at high prices.*

fat FLESHY /fæt/ *adj* [*-er/-est* only] **-tt-** having a lot of flesh on the body • *Her weight's normal but she insists she's fat.* • Fat can also mean thick or big: *a fat telephone book* • *"Maybe they'll invite you." "Fat chance!"* (= There is very little or no likelihood of that.)

fattening /ˈfæt·ən·ɪŋ/ *adj* (of food) containing a lot of fat, sugar, etc., that would make you fatter if you ate a lot of it • *I love desserts, but they're so fattening.*

fat SUBSTANCE /fæt/ *n* [C/U] the substance under the skin of humans and animals that stores energy and keeps them warm, or a solid or liquid substance obtained from animals or plants and used esp. in cooking • *This product contains no animal fat.* [U] ○ *Doctors recommend cutting down on saturated fats* (= fats that come from animals). [C] • **Fat-free** foods are ones without any fats in them.

fatty /ˈfæt̬·i/ *adj* containing too much fat • *fatty meat*

fat WEALTHY /fæt/ *adj* [*-er/-est* only] **-tt-** *infml* having or worth a lot of money • *a fat profit* • (*slang*) A **fat cat** is someone who is rich and has a lot of influence.

fatal /ˈfeɪt̬·əl/ *adj* [not gradable] (of illness, accidents, etc.) causing death • *a fatal heart attack* • Fatal can also mean severe enough to produce a very bad result: *a fatal mistake/flaw*

fatally /ˈfeɪt̬·əl·i/ *adv* [not gradable] • *Several people were injured, two fatally.*

fatality /feɪˈtæl·ət̬·i/ *n* [C] • *The first fatalities* (= deaths) *of the war have been civilians.*

fatalism /ˈfeɪt̬·əl·ɪz·əm/ *n* [U] the belief that people cannot change the way events will happen and that esp. bad events cannot be avoided

fatalistic /ˌfeɪt̬·əlˈɪs·tɪk/ *adj*

fate /feɪt/ *n* [C usually sing] something that happens to a person or thing, esp. something final or negative, such as death or defeat • *The fate of numerous smaller buildings is under debate.* ○ *Attendance has not picked up, and the fate of the show is still in doubt.* • Fate is also a power that is considered to cause and control all events, so that people cannot change or control the way things will happen: *When we met again by chance, she said, "It must be fate."* • A **fate worse than death** is something you do not want to experience because it is so unpleasant: *She felt that having to spend another night there would be a fate worse than death.*

fateful /ˈfeɪt·fəl/ *adj* an event or period of time that is very important because of its often negative effect on the future • *In 1971, President Richard Nixon made a fateful decision to install tape recorders in the White House.*

father PARENT /ˈfɑð·ər/ *n* [C] a male parent • *My father retired seven years ago.* • If you describe a man as **the father** of something, you mean that he began it, or first made it important: *Freud was the father of psychiatry.* • A **father figure** is a man who acts toward you as a father would, esp. by giving advice, help, or support. • PIC FAMILY TREE LP TITLES AND FORMS OF ADDRESS

father /ˈfɑð·ər/ *v* [T] to become the father of a child by making a woman pregnant • *to father twins*

fatherhood /ˈfɑð·ər·hʊd/ *n* [U] • *Fatherhood is a lifelong responsibility.*

father-in-law /ˈfɑð·ə·rən·lɔː/ *n* [C] *pl* **fathers-in-law** /ˈfɑð·ər·zən·lɔː/ the father of someone's husband or wife • PIC FAMILY TREE

fatherly /ˈfɑð·ər·li/ *adj* typical of a kind or caring father

Father PRIEST /ˈfɑð·ər/ *n* [C] (the title of) a Christian priest, esp. a Roman Catholic, Episcopal, or Orthodox priest • *Father Randall* ○ *Are you giving a sermon, Father?*

fathom MEASUREMENT /ˈfæð·əm/ *n* [C] a unit of measurement of the depth of water equal to 6 feet or 1.8 meters

fathom UNDERSTAND /ˈfæð·əm/ *v* [T] to discover the meaning of (something) • *I just couldn't fathom what he was talking about.*

fatigue /fəˈtiːɡ/ *n* [U] the condition of being extremely tired • *The doctor said he was suffering from fatigue and work-related stress.*

fatigues /fəˈtiːɡz/ *pl n* the brownish green uniform worn esp. by soldiers when working or fighting • *combat fatigues*

fattening /ˈfæt·ən·ɪŋ/ *adj* • See at FAT FLESHY.

fatty /ˈfæt̬·i/ *adj* • See at FAT SUBSTANCE.

fatuous /ˈfætʃ·ə·wəs/ *adj* foolish or thoughtless • *a fatuous remark*

faucet /ˈfɔː·sət, ˈfɑs·ət/, **tap** *n* [C] a device that controls the flow of liquid, esp. water, out of a pipe • *We have a leaky faucet in the bathroom sink.* • PIC BATHROOM

fault SOMETHING WRONG /fɔːlt/ *n* [C] a quality in

a person that shows that they are not perfect, or a condition of something that shows that it is not working perfectly • *He loves me in spite of my faults.* ○ *Some people find fault in everything they see.* • *Keri is generous* **to a fault** (= more than is necessary).

faultless /ˈfɔːlt·ləs/ *adj* [not gradable] perfect • *He gave a faultless performance at the piano recital.*

faulty /ˈfɔːl·ti/ *adj* [*-er/-est* only] not working correctly, or not correct • *faulty brakes* ○ *His arguments were based on faulty reasoning.*

fault RESPONSIBILITY /fɔːlt/ *n* [U] responsibility for a mistake or for having done something wrong • *I screwed up, so it was my fault we didn't finish on time.* • *The driver was* **at fault** (= responsible) *for the accident—he was going too fast.*

fault /fɔːlt/ *v* [T] to blame (someone) • *Professional athletes cannot be faulted for making millions of dollars when they attract the fans that make the sport popular.*

fault CRACK /fɔːlt/ *n* [C] *specialized* a crack in the earth's surface where the rock is divided into two parts that can move against each other in an **earthquake** (= a sudden, violent movement of the earth's surface)

fauna /ˈfɔː·nə/ *n* [U] *specialized* all the animals of a particular area or period of time • *He studied the fauna of the Galapagos Islands.* • Compare FLORA.

faux pas /ˈfoʊ·pɑ/ *n* [C] *pl* **faux pas** /ˈfoʊ·pɑ, -pɑz/ a remark or action in a social situation that is a mistake and causes embarrassment or offense • *Mentioning his ex-wife was a faux pas.*

favor SUPPORT /ˈfeɪ·vər/ *n* [U] approval or support of someone or something • *In applying for this job, Tiffany has a lot* **in** *her* **favor** (= to her advantage). • *The city council voted* **in favor of** (= in support of) *the proposed housing development.*

favor /ˈfeɪ·vər/ *v* [T] • *Democrats favored a temporary increase in the state sales tax.*

favorable /ˈfeɪ·və·rə·bəl/ *adj* positive or pleasing • *The movie received generally favorable reviews.*

favorably /ˈfeɪ·və·rə·bli/ *adv* • *Consumers responded favorably to the new product.*

favor HELPFUL ACT /ˈfeɪ·vər/ *n* [C] something you do to help someone, often after being asked to • *Will you do me a favor and turn the oven on at four o'clock?*

favor PRESENT /ˈfeɪ·vər/ *n* [C] a small present given to guests at a party • *party favors*

favorite /ˈfeɪ·və·rət, ˈfeɪv·rət/ *adj* best liked or most enjoyed • *This is one of my favorite restaurants.*

favorite /ˈfeɪ·və·rət, ˈfeɪv·rət/ *n* [C] • *Those gold earrings are my favorites.* • A **favorite** is also a competitor likely to win: *The Chicago Bears are 10-point favorites over the Rams in the Super Bowl.*

favoritism /ˈfeɪ·və·rə,tɪz·əm, ˈfeɪv·rə-/ *n* [U] unfair support shown to one person or group, esp. by someone in authority • *The teacher was careful not to show favoritism to any one student.*

fawn DEER /fɔːn/ *n* [C] a young deer

fawn PRAISE /fɔːn/ *v* [I] to give someone a lot of attention and praise in order to get their approval • *Big movie stars are fawned over by the waiters at the restaurant.*

fax /fæks/ *n* [C] a document that is sent by electronic image through a telephone line • *I'll send you a fax of the proposal.* • A **fax** or **fax machine** is the machine that sends or receives such an image: *You can send it by fax to my office.*

fax /fæks/ *v* [T] • *I faxed the changes to my publisher.*

faze /feɪz/ *v* [T] to upset or confuse (someone) • *Speaking in public does not faze her.*

FBI /ˌef,biːˈaɪ/ *n* [U] *abbreviation for* Federal Bureau of Investigation (= the government department that examines certain crimes against federal law)

fear /fɪr/ *n* [C/U] a strong feeling of worry caused by the presence of something dangerous, painful, or unknown • *Even when the boat was rocked by waves, the boy showed no fear.* [U] ○ *The low sales continued, confirming our worst fears.* [C]

fear /fɪr/ *v* • *The cab driver was going so fast, I feared for our safety.* [I] • To **fear** is also to be worried or upset: *They fear that Congress may not allocate the money needed.* [+ *that* clause] • If you **fear the worst**, you feel certain that the worst possible thing has happened or is likely to happen: *When the doctor finally called, she feared the worst.*

fearful /ˈfɪr·fəl/ *adj* • *He was fearful of driving on the icy streets.* ○ *She's fearful that she may lose custody of the children.* [+ *that* clause]

fearless /ˈfɪr·ləs/ *adj* • *He was a tough, fearless soldier.*

feasible /ˈfiː·zə·bəl/ *adj* [not gradable] possible, reasonable, or likely • *It's no longer feasible to fund this research.*

feast /fiːst/ *n* [C] a large, special meal, often for many people, to celebrate someone or something • *a wedding feast* • A **feast** is also a large meal: *We had a feast of fresh seafood.*

feast /fiːst/ *v* [I always + adv/prep] • *The two of us feasted on smoked salmon and champagne.* • I **feasted** *my* **eyes on** (= looked with great enjoyment at) *the beautiful autumn leaves in full color.*

feat /fiːt/ *n* [C] an act that shows skill, strength, or bravery • *a feat of unusual strength* ○ *Getting the house painted was quite a feat.*

feather /ˈfeð·ər/ *n* [C] one of the long, light objects that cover a bird's body, having hair-like material along each side of a thin, stiff, central stem • *The award was another* **feather in** *his* **cap** (= an achievement to be proud of).

feather /'feð·ər/ v • If you **feather** your **(own) nest**, you make yourself rich by wrongly using the power of an important job: *He used inside information to feather his own nest.*

feature CHARACTERISTIC /'fi:·tʃər/ n [C] a noticeable or important characteristic or part • *This car has excellent safety features.* ○ *She has fine, delicate features (= parts of the face).*

feature /'fi:·tʃər/ v [T] to show or advertise (someone or something) as the most important or most obvious part • *Tonight's program features some outstanding performers.*

feature NEWSPAPER / TELEVISION /'fi:·tʃər/ n [C] (in newspapers, magazines, or television) a special or important article or program, esp. one that gives details about something that is not part of the main news • *Tonight we're showing a feature on drug use among school children.* • A feature is also the main movie shown in a movie program.

February /'feb·jə,wer·i, 'feb·rə-/ (*abbreviation* **Feb.**) n [C/U] the second month of the year, after January and before March

feces /'fi:·si:z/ pl n slightly fml solid waste excreted from the bodies of animals and people through the bowels

fed FEED /fed/ past simple and past participle of FEED

fed OFFICER /fed/ n [C usually pl] infml a federal officer or official • *The feds worked with local police on the case.*

federal /'fed·ə·rəl/ adj [not gradable] of or connected with the central government of some countries • *the federal government* ○ *Federal law regulates trade with other countries.*

federalism /'fed·ə·rə,lɪz·əm/ n [U] a system of government in which states unite and give up some of their powers to a central authority

federalist /'fed·ə·rə·ləst/ n [C] someone who believes that a federation is a good system of government, or (*Cdn*) someone who believes Quebec should remain part of Canada

federation /,fed·ə'reɪ·ʃən/ n [C] a group of organizations, states, etc., that have united to form a larger organization or government • *Canada is a federation of provinces and territories.*

fed up /'fed'ʌp/ adj infml annoyed or disgusted by something that you have experienced for too long • *I'm just fed up with his excuses for not getting his work done.*

fee /fi:/ n [C] an amount of money charged for a service or for the use of something • *an admission fee* ○ *The doctor's usual fee is $125.*

feeble /'fi:·bəl/ adj weak • *a feeble joke* ○ *He's pretty feeble, and has to use a cane to get around.* • If someone is **feeble-minded**, they are not able to think carefully: *These regulations will protect the foolish and feeble-minded.*

feed GIVE FOOD /fi:d/ v [I/T] past fed /fed/ to give food to (a person or animal), or (of an animal) to eat • *We fed the kids some leftovers.* [T] ○ *The cows were feeding in the pasture.* [I] • If

you feed a plant, you give it substances that help it grow. [T] • A **feeding frenzy** is a violent activity in which animals, such as SHARKS, attack as a group and eat another animal: (*fig.*) *The judge in this case wants to avoid a media feeding frenzy (= a situation of uncontrolled activity).*

feed /fi:d/ n [U] food for animals, esp. animals that are not kept as pets • *chicken feed*

feeding /'fi:d·ɪŋ/ n [C] a baby's or animal's meal • *She has a midnight feeding, then sleeps until morning.*

feed SUPPLY /fi:d/ v [T] past fed /fed/ to supply (something), esp. regularly or continuously • *We had to keep feeding quarters into the parking meter.* • If you feed someone information, you tell them things that may not be completely true: *They fed him a line about how important this work is to our country.*

feedback /'fi:d·bæk/ n [U] reaction to a process or activity, or the information obtained from such a reaction • *positive/negative feedback* ○ *We're hoping to get feedback on how well the program is working.*

feel EXPERIENCE /fi:l/ v past felt /felt/ to experience or be aware of (something emotional or physical) • *"How are you feeling?" "Oh, I don't feel very good."* [L] ○ *She said she didn't want anyone to feel sorry for her.* [L] ○ *I feel comfortable with you, Nick.* [L] ○ *He felt compelled to report the incident.* [L] ○ *When the anesthesia wore off, I felt a lot of pain.* [T] • If you **feel bad** about something, you believe you have done something wrong and blame yourself: *I feel bad about not inviting him to the party.* • If someone tells you to **feel free** to do something, they mean that you have permission to do it: *Feel free to help yourself to more coffee.* • If you **feel good**, you have satisfaction or pleasure about something: *It feels good to have all the yard work done.* • If you **feel** something **in** your **bones**, you believe it very strongly: *I just know you'll do well on the test, I can feel it in my bones.*

feeling /'fi:·lɪŋ/ n [C/U] a physical or emotional experience or awareness • *My toes were so cold that I lost all feeling in them.* [U] ○ *I have a feeling that I'm not welcome.* [C] • Your feelings are your awareness of the way you should be treated, esp. when you are treated rudely: *He doesn't mean to hurt your feelings.* [pl]

feel TOUCH /fi:l/ v [I/T] past felt /felt/ to touch, esp. with the fingers, in order to examine something • *Feel the softness of the baby's skin.* [T] ○ *She felt around (= searched with her hands) for the light switch.* [I] • If you **feel** your **way**, you move forward without being able to see well, touching your surroundings with your hands: (*fig.*) *This computer program is new, so I'll have to feel my way through it at first (= try it slowly and carefully).*

feel /fi:l/ n [U] • *I love the feel of silk against my skin.*

feeler /ˈfiː·lər/ n [C usually pl] one of the two long parts on an insect's head that it uses to touch things

feel (obj) HAVE OPINION /fiːl/ v past **felt** /felt/ to have as an opinion or belief • I feel (that) I should be doing more to help her. [+ (that) clause]

feeling /ˈfiː·lɪŋ/ n [C] • My feeling is that we should wait until they come back. ○ He has strong feelings about environmental issues.

feel UNDERSTANDING /fiːl/, **feeling** /ˈfiː·lɪŋ/ n [U] an understanding or natural ability • Marcia has a good feel for this kind of work.

□ **feel for** /ˈ--/ v prep [T] to experience sympathy for (someone) • I know she's unhappy, and I feel for her.

□ **feel like** SEEM /ˈ-ˌ-/ v prep [T] to seem to be (something), or (esp. of weather) to seem likely to do (something) • I felt like a fool when I couldn't remember her name. ○ She said she didn't feel like herself today. ○ It feels like rain.

□ **feel like** DESIRE /ˈ-ˌ-/ v prep [T] to have a desire to do or have (something) • He was so rude, I felt like hitting him. ○ I feel like Chinese food.

□ **feel** obj **out** /ˈ-ˈ-/ v adv [T] to try to get information from (someone) without being obvious • Why don't you feel them out to see if they'll invite me over too?

□ **feel up** obj, **feel** obj **up** /ˈ-ˈ-/ v adv [M] rude slang to touch (someone) sexually

□ **feel up to** /-ˈ--/ v adv prep [T] to have the energy to do (something) • I don't feel up to going out tonight.

feet /fiːt/ pl of FOOT BODY PART, FOOT MEASUREMENT

feign /feɪn/ v [T] to pretend to have (a feeling or condition) • He feigned sickness so he wouldn't have to go to school.

feint /feɪnt/ v [I/T] (esp. in sports or in war) to pretend to move (in a particular direction) in order to deceive a competitor • Louis feinted with his left hand and landed a vicious overhand right. [I]

feisty /ˈfaɪ·sti/ adj approving active, forceful, and determined • She's a feisty kid who is not afraid to challenge authority.

feline /ˈfiː·laɪn/ adj [not gradable] of or like an animal of the cat family

fell FALL /fel/ past simple of FALL

fell CUT DOWN /fel/ v [T] to cut down (esp. a tree) • He decided the diseased trees had to be felled. ○ (fig.) He was felled (= killed) by a heart attack.

fella /ˈfel·ə/ n [C] not standard (spelled the way it is often spoken) FELLOW MAN • Where did you meet this fella?

fellow MAN /ˈfel·oʊ, -ə/ n [C] a man • He was a big fellow with broad shoulders.

fellow SHARED /ˈfel·oʊ, -ə/ adj [not gradable] used of people or a person with whom you share something, esp. the same kind of job, interest, or experience • She introduced me to a few of her fellow students.

fellowship /ˈfel·ə.ʃɪp/ n [C/U] people with the same purpose, experience, or interest, or a formal organization of these people • the Fellowship of Christian Athletes [C] • Fellowship is also a friendly feeling that exists between people who have a shared interest or who do something as a group: I like the game, and I enjoy the fellowship of the guys on the team. [U]

fellow MEMBER /ˈfel·oʊ, -ə/ n [C] a member of some groups that you must have special training to join • Dr. Rodriguez is a Fellow of the American College of Physicians.

fellowship /ˈfel·ə.ʃɪp/ n [C] a teaching position at a university for someone who already has a BACHELOR'S DEGREE and is continuing to study to obtain an advanced degree, or the pay for such a position • She applied for a fellowship to continue her studies.

fellow /ˈfel·oʊ, -ə/ n [C] a person who has a teaching fellowship at a university • He was a fellow at Harvard.

felony /ˈfel·ə·ni/ n [C] law a serious crime that can be punished by more than one year in prison • Robbery is a felony.

felon /ˈfel·ən/ n [C] law a person who is guilty of a serious crime • a convicted felon

felt FEEL /felt/ past simple and past participle of FEEL

felt CLOTH /felt/ n [U] a thick cloth made from a pressed mass of wool, hair, or fur • a felt hat • A **felt-tip pen** is a pen that has a point made of fibers.

female /ˈfiː·meɪl/ adj [not gradable] of the sex that can produce eggs and give birth to young • There are now more opportunities for female (= women) athletes in universities. • In plants and flowers, female refers to a plant which produces flowers that will later develop into fruit. • Compare MALE.

female /ˈfiː·meɪl/ n [C] • Almost 60% of poor families are headed by a female.

feminine FEMALE /ˈfem·ə·nən/ adj having qualities traditionally considered to be suitable for a woman • Even with the tailored look of a suit, sometimes I like to have something that's just a little feminine. • Compare MASCULINE MALE.

femininity /ˌfem·əˈnɪn·ət̬·i/ n [U] • Long hair has traditionally been regarded as a sign of femininity.

feminine GRAMMAR /ˈfem·ə·nən/ (abbreviation **fem.**) adj [not gradable] specialized (in grammar) being a noun or pronoun of a type that refers to females, or in some other languages, being a noun of a type that refers to things considered as female

feminism /ˈfem·əˌnɪz·əm/ n [U] the belief that women should have the same economic, social, and political rights as men

feminist /ˈfem·ə·nəst/ n [C] • In the 19th century, feminists argued that women should be allowed to vote.

fence STRUCTURE /fens/ n [C] a structure of

wood or wire forming a wall around a house or a piece of land, often to keep people or animals from coming in or going out • *He put up a fence to keep his dog in the backyard.*

fence /fens/ *v* [T] • *The county requires that all construction sites be fenced (in) as soon as they are built.* [T/M]

fence SPORT /fens/ *v* [I] to take part in the sport of attacking and defending with a weapon having a long blade

fencing /'fen·sɪŋ/ *n* [U] the sport of attacking and defending with a weapon having a long blade

fence CRIMINAL /fens/ *n* [C] a person who buys and sells stolen goods

◻**fend for** /'fend·fər/ *v prep* [T] to take care of and provide for (yourself), without depending on anyone else • *The strike left a million commuters to fend for themselves in getting to work.*

◻**fend off** *obj*, **fend** *obj* **off** /'fend'ɔːf/ *v adv* [M] to push or send away (an attacker or other unwanted person) • *The young woman was attacked by a man in the lobby of her building but managed to fend him off.*

fender /'fen·dər/ *n* [C] the part of a car or other vehicle that covers and protects the wheels

ferment CHANGE CHEMICALLY /fər'ment/ *v* [I/T] to change chemically through the action of living substances, such as YEAST or bacteria, or to use (a substance) to produce a chemical change • *Wine is produced by leaving grape juice to ferment until the sugar has turned to alcohol.* [I]

fermentation /ˌfɜr·men'teɪ·ʃən/ *n* [U]

ferment CONFUSION /'fɜr·ment/ *n* [U] a state of confusion or excited expectation, esp. because of changing conditions that are sudden and disorderly • *He was a central figure in the religious ferment of his time.*

fern /fɜrn/ *n* [C] a green plant with long stems, feathery leaves, and no flowers

ferocious /fə'rou·ʃəs/ *adj* fierce and violent • *ferocious wild dogs*

ferret /'fer·ət/ *n* [C] a type of WEASEL (= small animal with a long, thin body) that usually has black feet and black fur around its eyes

ferret out /'fer·ət,aʊt/ *v adv* [T] to discover (esp. information) after searching • *Officials are attempting to ferret out abuses in the welfare program.*

Ferris wheel /'fer·əs,hwiːl, -,wiːl/ *n* [C] a structure in an **amusement park** that people ride for fun, consisting of a large wheel that turns slowly and has seats attached to its outer edge

ferry /'fer·i/ *n* [C] a boat or ship for taking passengers and often vehicles across an area of water, esp. as a regular service • *There's no bridge around here, but you can take a ferry across the river.*

ferry /'fer·i/ *v* [T always + adv/prep] to transport (someone or something) repeatedly or regularly • *As parents, we seem to spend most*

of our time ferrying the kids to and from their friends' homes.

fertile GROWING PLANTS /'fɜrt·ᵊl/ *adj* (of land) able to produce a large number of high-quality crops • *fertile soil*

fertilize /'fɜrt·ᵊl,aɪz/ *v* [T] to spread a natural or chemical substance on (land) in order to make plants grow well • *You have to fertilize your garden.*

fertilizer /'fɜrt·ᵊl,aɪ·zər/ *n* [C/U] a natural or chemical substance that is spread on land in order to make plants grow well

fertile ABLE TO PRODUCE /'fɜrt·ᵊl/ *adj* (of people or animals) able to produce young • *(fig.)* Someone who has a fertile imagination has an active mind and is able to produce a lot of new and original ideas.

fertility /fər'tɪl·ət·i/ *n* [U] the ability to produce young • *They tried unsuccessfully to have a baby and finally went to a fertility clinic.*

fertilize /'fɜrt·ᵊl,aɪz/ *v* [T] (in plants and animals) to join male and female sexual cells so that young begin to develop • *The sperm fertilizes the egg.*

fertilization /ˌfɜrt·ᵊl·ə'zeɪ·ʃən/ *n* [U]

fervent /'fɜr·vənt/ *adj* showing strong and sincere feelings or beliefs • *She was a fervent supporter of gun control.*

fervently /'fɜr·vənt·li/ *adv* • *He prayed fervently for his sins.*

fervor /'fɜr·vər/ *n* [U] strong, sincere feelings • *The country was swept by patriotic fervor.*

fester /'fes·tər/ *v* [I] (of an injury such as a cut) to become infected and form PUS (= thick yellow liquid) • *(fig.)* If a bad situation such as an argument festers, it becomes worse because it is being ignored: *It was better that she expressed her anger rather than let it fester inside her.*

festival /'fes·tə·vəl/, *infml* **fest** /fest/ *n* [C] an organized set of special events, such as musical performances or plays, usually happening in one place, or a special day or period, usually in memory of a religious event, with its own social activities, food, or ceremonies • *a film/food/music festival* ○ *the Jewish festival of Hanukkah*

festive /'fes·tɪv/ *adj* typical of a holiday when people are in a good humor and expect to have a good time • *The Salts were comfortable in their motor home, which they draped with festive Christmas lights.*

festivities /fes'tɪv·ət·iz/ *pl n* • *Festivities are the parties, meals, and other social activities with which people celebrate a special occasion.*

festoon /fes'tuːn/ *v* [T] to decorate (a room) for a special occasion by hanging chains of colored paper, lights, or flowers around it in curves • *The hall was festooned with Christmas lights.*

fetal /'fiːt̬·ᵊl/ *adj* • See at FETUS.

fetch GET /fetʃ/ *v* [I/T] to go to another place

fiber

to get (something or someone) and bring it or them back • *She's been teaching the dog to fetch* (= get a stick or ball that is thrown and bring it back). [I]

fetch SELL /fetʃ/ *v* [T] to be sold for (a price) • *The collection of paintings fetched over a million dollars.*

fetching /'fetʃ·ɪŋ/ *adj* (of a person or a piece of clothing) attractive in appearance • *Don thought Janice looked rather fetching in her black skating skirt.*

fete /feɪt, fet/ *n* [C] a special celebration, often for a particular purpose, or to honor someone • *The annual fete to raise money for cancer research netted more than $90,000.*

fete /feɪt, fet/ *v* [T] • *The magazine's founding editor was feted with a dinner on her 80th birthday.*

fetish INTEREST /'fet·ɪʃ/ *n* [C] an activity or object that someone is interested in to an extreme degree and that they give an unreasonable amount of time or thought to • *He had a fetish about clothes.* • A fetish is also a strong sexual interest in an object or a part of the body other than the sexual organs: *a foot fetish*

fetish RELIGIOUS OBJECT /'fet·ɪʃ/ *n* [C] an object that is believed to possess a spirit or special magical powers

fetters /'fet·ərz/ *pl n* (esp. in the past) chains that were used to tie prisoners to a place by the legs

fetus /'fiːt̬·əs/ *n* [C] a human being or animal as it is developing in the uterus before birth, after the organs have started to form

fetal /'fiːt̬·ᵊl/ *adj* [not gradable] • *The electronic device monitored the fetal heart rate.* • If a person is in the **fetal position**, they are lying on their side with their legs bent, their knees together and raised against their chest, and their arms around their legs.

feud /fjuːd/ *n* [C] an angry and sometimes violent argument that has continued for a long time between two people, families, or groups • *a feud between rival drug dealers* ○ *(fig.) The mayor has a longstanding feud with the media.*

feud /fjuːd/ *v* [I] • *The two brothers have been feuding for years.*

feudalism /'fjuːd·ᵊl,ɪz·əm/ *n* [U] the social system that developed in western Europe in the eighth and ninth centuries in which people served a man of high rank by working and fighting for him and in exchange were supported and given land and protection

feudal /'fjuːd·ᵊl/ *adj* [not gradable] • *the feudal system*

fever BODY TEMPERATURE /'fiː·vər/ *n* [C/U] a condition in which the body's temperature is higher than usual, esp. as a sign of illness • *The child has a rash and a high fever.* [C] • Fever is also great excitement and interest in something: *Texas was in the grip of football fever.* [U]

feverish /'fiː·və·rɪʃ/ *adj* • *I'm feeling a little feverish—I hope it's not the flu.* • A feverish activity is one that is done as quickly as possible, based on the fear that any delay would cause something bad to happen: *They worked at a feverish pace from dawn to dark.*

feverishly /'fiː·və·rɪʃ·li/ *adv* as quickly as possible, based on the fear that any delay would cause something bad to happen • *Doctors and nurses worked feverishly to save his life.* [+ to infinitive]

fever EXCITEMENT /'fiː·vər/ *n* [U] a state of great excitement or enthusiasm • *Texas was in the grip of football fever.*

few /fjuː/ *adj, pronoun, n* a small number, not many, or not enough (of something) • *He is one of the few (people) I can trust to keep a secret.* • **A few** means a small number of: *I'm going to the supermarket to get a few things.* ○ *We've been having a few problems with the new computer.* ○ *"How many tomatoes do we need?" "Just a few."* • *Sunny, warm weekends have been* **few and far between** *this summer* (= there have not been many). • LP AMOUNTS

fiancé *male, female* **fiancée** /,fiː,ɑnˈseɪ, fiːˈɑn ,seɪ/ *n* [C] a person who has formally promised to marry another • *I'd like you to meet Irene, my fiancée.*

fiasco /fiːˈæs·koʊ/ *n* [C] *pl* **fiascoes** or **fiascos** a complete failure • *The entire political campaign was a fiasco, and at the end he drew only 30% of the votes.*

fiat /'fiː·æt, -ɑt, -ət/ *n* [U] *fml* the giving of orders by someone who has complete authority • *The general ruled by fiat for eight years after seizing power.*

fib /fɪb/ *n* [C] *infml* an unimportant or harmless lie • *Have you been telling fibs about me?*

fib /fɪb/ *v* [I] **-bb-** *infml* • *George was fibbing some to make things seem more exciting.*

fiber MATERIAL /'faɪ·bər/ *n* [C/U] any of the threadlike parts that form plant or artificial material, esp. those that can be made into cloth, or a mass of such parts twisted together • *Police detectives found cloth fibers at the crime scene that matched those from the coat the suspect was wearing.* [C] • Fiber can also refer to the strong, threadlike structures of the body: *muscle fiber* [U] • **Fiberglass** is a material made from small threads of glass twisted together, used within the walls of houses to keep out cold and pressed into hard plastic for use in boats and other structures. • *(specialized)* **Fiber optics** is the use of glass or plastic fibers to send light that contains information or images around curves: *Fiber-optic devices are used in medicine to examine internal organs.* ○ *The cable TV company is laying miles of fiber-optic cables.*

fiber CHARACTER /'faɪ·bər/ *n* [U] the quality of a person's character, esp. its moral strength • *He lacked the moral fiber to be president.*

fiber FOOD /'faɪ·bər/ *n* [U] the part of foods

eaten that is not digested but that passes through the body and is excreted as waste • *Doctors recommend a diet of fruits, vegetables, and grains that are high in fiber.*

fickle /ˈfɪk·əl/ *adj* likely to change your opinion or your feelings suddenly and without a good reason • *He criticized the fickle behavior of football fans who cheer you one week and boo you the next.* • The weather is described as fickle if it tends to change suddenly: *Fickle winds made sailing conditions difficult.*

fickleness /ˈfɪk·əl·nəs/ *n* [U]

fiction /ˈfɪk·ʃən/ *n* [C/U] the type of book or story that is written about imaginary characters and events and does not describe real people or deal with facts, or a false report or statement that you pretend is true • *She wrote detective fiction and made a good living at it.* [U] ○ *It was a fiction, though widely believed, that he had once been rich.* [C usually sing] • Compare NONFICTION.

fictional /ˈfɪk·ʃən·əl/ *adj* [not gradable] • *The characters in the movie are purely fictional.*

fictionalized /ˈfɪk·ʃən·əl‚aɪzd/ *adj* [not gradable] (of a story) based on a real event or character but with imaginary details added or some facts changed • *This is the fictionalized story of the American painter James McNeill Whistler.*

fictitious /fɪkˈtɪʃ·əs/ *adj* [not gradable] invented and not true or existing; false • *He registered at the hotel under a fictitious name.*

fiddle MOVE THINGS /ˈfɪd·əl/ *v* [I always + adv/prep] to move things around or touch things without a particular purpose • *He stood there fiddling with his keys.* ○ (*disapproving*) *I wish they'd quit fiddling (around) with* (= changing) *the tax law.*

fiddle INSTRUMENT /ˈfɪd·əl/ *n* [C] a VIOLIN

fiddler /ˈfɪd·lər, ˈfɪd·əl·ər/ *n* [C] a person who plays the VIOLIN (= small, stringed instrument), esp. in music popular in rural areas

fidelity LOYALTY /fəˈdel·ət·i/ *n* [U] loyalty, esp. (within a marriage) the practice of having sex only with your husband or wife

fidelity ACCURACY /fəˈdel·ət·i/ *n* [U] the degree to which a copy of something shows the true character of the original • *The fidelity of the tape recording was so poor that you could not understand much of what was said.*

fidget /ˈfɪdʒ·ət/ *v* [I] to make continuous small movements because you are restless or bored • *Children can't sit still for long without fidgeting.*

field LAND /fiːld/ *n* [C] an area of land with grass or crops growing on it • *We drove past fields of wheat.* • A field can also be a large area covered by something or having something under its surface: *an oil field* • **The field** is a place where practical work is being done: *He was a working reporter in the field, not some anchorman in a studio.* • **Field glasses** are

BINOCULARS. • A **field trip** is a visit made by students to study something away from their school: *Mrs. Rhines took her class on a field trip to the zoo.* • *Marjorie did a lot of her* **fieldwork** (= testing of scientific theories in the real world) *in the rain forests of Brazil.*

field SPORTS /fiːld/ *n* [C] a grassy area used for playing sports • *He ran laps around the football field after school.* • A **field day** is a special day of organized sports or other outside activities for students. • A **field event** is a competition that involves throwing objects such as a JAVELIN or jumping, but not running races. Compare **track event** at TRACK SPORTS. • In football, a **field goal** is a play in which the ball is kicked and passes between the other team's **goalposts** (= two vertical posts connected by a horizontal pole), and is worth three points. • **Field hockey** is a game in which two teams of 11 players each try to score points by using special sticks to hit a small ball into a net fixed at either end of the field. • A **field house** is a building esp. in a university where sports events can be held inside and where there is equipment that can be used in exercising: *Drake University's field house seats 12,500 people.*

field /fiːld/ *v* [I/T] (in baseball) to catch or pick up the ball after it has been hit in order to prevent the other team from scoring • *He fielded the ball cleanly and threw to first base.* [T] • To field also means to have a person or a team play a sport: *The university fields teams in 14 sports.* [T]

fielder /ˈfiːl·dər/ *n* [C] (in baseball) a person playing defense who tries to catch or pick up the ball after it has been hit

field COMPETITORS /fiːld/ *n* [C/U] all the competitors taking part in a race or activity, or all the competitors other than the leader • *The cross-country race started with a field of 85 competitors.* [C]

field AREA OF INTEREST /fiːld/ *n* [C] an area of activity or interest • *She is an expert in the field of economics.*

field ANSWER /fiːld/ *v* [T] to answer (questions), esp. in a formal situation • *Be prepared to field some tough questions from the senators after your presentation.*

fiend /fiːnd/ *n* [C] *often humorous* an evil or cruel person or spirit • *Who was the fiend who designed such ugly clothes?* • A fiend can also be a person who likes something in an extreme way: *a chocolate fiend* ○ *a dope/drug fiend*

fiendish /ˈfiːn·dɪʃ/ *adj often humorous* getting enjoyment from annoying others • *He took fiendish delight in making them wait.*

fiendishly /ˈfiːn·dɪʃ·li/ *adv* extremely • *The murder mystery had a fiendishly clever plot.*

fierce /fɪrs/ *adj* violent and forceful • *fierce thunderstorms* ○ *The city had been under fierce attack.* • Fierce can also mean severe or extremely strong: *She's a fierce critic of US policies.* ○ *He was a fierce competitor.*

fiercely /'fɪr·sli/ *adv* • *He's fiercely* (= very strongly) *committed to excellence in education.*

fiery FLAMING /'faɪ·ri/ *adj* flaming or extremely bright, hot, or of a red color like fire • *a fiery explosion* ○ *the fiery rays of the sun* ○ (*fig.*) *fiery* (= spicy hot) *chili*

fiery EMOTIONAL /'faɪ·ri/ *adj* emotional or easily made angry • *He's known for his fiery temper.*

fiesta /fiː'es·tə/ *n* [C] a public celebration, esp. on a religious holiday, in Spain or South America

fifteen /fɪf'tiːn/ *number* 15 • *My brother is fifteen.* ○ *a fifteen-story building* • LP NUMBERS

fifteenth /fɪf'tiːnθ/ *adj, adv* [not gradable], *n* [C] • *Our team is ranked fifteenth in the country.* ○ *Her birthday is on the fifteenth of May.* [C] • A fifteenth is one of fifteen equal parts of something. [C]

fifth /fɪfθ, fɪθ/ *adj, adv* [not gradable], *n* [C] (a person or thing) coming immediately after the fourth and before all others • *Leo was fifth in the race.* ○ *Tomorrow is the fifth of September.* [C] • A fifth is one of five equal parts of something. [C] • USAGE: The related number is FIVE. • LP NUMBERS

fifty /'fɪf·ti/ *number* 50 • *My father is fifty.* ○ *a fifty-minute ride* • **Fifty-fifty** means (into) equal halves: *They divided the work fifty-fifty.* • **A fifty-fifty chance** means that a result is equally likely to happen or not happen: *There's only a fifty-fifty chance that she'll survive the operation.* • LP NUMBERS

fifties, 50s, 50's /'fɪf·tiz/ *pl n* the numbers 50 through 59 • *The temperature has been in the fifties* (= between 50° and 59°). • The fifties are the years between 1950 and 1959. ○ *My dad is in his fifties* (= between 50 and 59 years old).

fiftieth /'fɪf·ti·əθ/ *adj, adv* [not gradable], *n* [C] • *a fiftieth wedding anniversary* • A fiftieth is one of fifty equal parts of something. [C]

fig /fɪg/ *n* [C] a tree that grows in warm places, or its soft, sweet edible fruit

fig. *n abbreviation for* FIGURE PICTURE or FIGURATIVE, used esp. in writing

fight /faɪt/ *v* [I/T] *past* **fought** /fɔːt/ to argue with or use force against (esp. another person or group of people), or to oppose (something) • *Rebels have been fighting fierce battles with government forces.* [T] ○ *They're fighting against some powerful organizations.* [I] ○ *She's willing to fight for a more just society.* [I] ○ *Those two little kids were fighting over a toy.* [I] ○ *Gordon has been fighting an uphill battle to attract investors.* [T] • Two people who fight may be boxing: *Lewis will fight Akinwande for the heavyweight title.* [T] • *If someone hits you, you have to* **fight back** (= use force against someone who has used force first). • If you **fight off** a desire or an illness, you try to get rid of it: *I was trying to fight off the*

urge to sneak into the kitchen for something to eat. ○ *Her body couldn't fight the infection off.* • If two people or groups **fight it out**, they argue until they reach a decision: *Let them fight it out.*

fight /faɪt/ *n* [C] • *Isabelle is looking for a fight.* ○ *A patient's attitude is important in the fight against the disease.* ○ *Have you got tickets for the fight* (= a competition between two boxers)?

fighter /'faɪt·ər/ *n* [C] someone who is willing to argue for and put effort into what they believe • *She proved herself to be a real fighter.* ○ *Ali was the greatest fighter* (= boxer) *of all time.* • A fighter is also a small, fast military aircraft.

fighting /'faɪt·ɪŋ/ *n* [U] • *The fighting lasted a long time.* • **A fighting chance** is a small but real possibility of success: *Doctors gave him a fighting chance to make a complete recovery.*

figment /'fɪg·mənt/ *n* • A **figment of** your **imagination** is something imagined or created by your mind: *The people he said he saw were figments of his imagination.*

figurative /'fɪg·jə·rəṭ·ɪv/ (*abbreviation* **fig.**) *adj* [not gradable] (of words and phrases) used not with their basic meaning but to suggest part of that meaning • *literal and figurative meanings*

figuratively /'fɪg·jə·rəṭ·ɪv·li/ *adv* • *Figuratively speaking, negotiators succeeded in building a bridge over a wide river in reaching this agreement.*

figure NUMBER /'fɪg·jər/ *n* [C] a number or an amount • *The school system's enrollment figure was 86,893.*

figure SHAPE /'fɪg·jər/ *n* [C] a shape or form • *geometric/abstract figures* • A **figure eight** is the shape made when drawing an 8: *She skated a perfect figure eight.* • **Figure skating** is a type of **skating** on ice in which the skater's movements include patterns, jumps, and dance steps: *Thirty-five* **figure skaters** *will compete in the national competition.*

figure BODY /'fɪg·jər/ *n* [C] the shape of a person's body, or a body seen not clearly or from a distance • *Her great figure was noticeable even when she wore a simple suit.*

figure PERSON /'fɪg·jər/ *n* [C] • A particular type of figure is a person with that characteristic: *Our consultants are prominent figures in their field.*

figure PICTURE /'fɪg·jər/ (*abbreviation* **fig.**) *n* [C] a picture or drawing, often numbered, in a book or document • *Figure 10.3 shows the maximum length of the bridges.*

figure LANGUAGE /'fɪg·jər/ *n* • A **figure of speech** is an expression that uses words to mean something different than what they usually mean: *You usually use the figure of speech "break a leg" to wish actors good luck.*

figure EXPECT /'fɪg·jər/ *v* [I/T] to expect, believe, decide, or think that something will

□**fill up** *obj*, **fill** *obj* **up** /-'-/ *v adv* [M] to make (something) completely full • *I want to fill up the gas tank.* ○ *That sandwich filled me up.*

□**fill** *(obj)* **with** *obj* /-'--/ *v prep* [T] to cause (a person, place, or period of time) to have a lot of (something) • *His childhood was filled with rage.* ○ *The kitchen is filled with the smell of fresh coffee.*

fillet, **filet** /fɪ'leɪ, 'fɪl·eɪ/ *n* [C/U] a piece of meat or fish without bones

fillet, **filet** /fi'leɪ, 'fɪl·eɪ/ *v* [T] to cut the flesh away from the bones of (a fish) • *The customer wanted her fish filleted.*

filly /'fɪl·i/ *n* [C] a young, female horse • Compare COLT.

film PICTURE /fɪlm/ *v* [I/T] to make pictures of (something) in making a movie, or to make (a movie) • *Her last movie was filmed in Spain.* [T]

film /fɪlm/ *n* [C] a movie • A **filmmaker** is someone who controls the making of a movie, esp. its DIRECTOR.

film MATERIAL /fɪlm/ *n* [U] (a length of) dark plasticlike material on which you can record images as photographs or as moving pictures • *a roll of film* ○ *I didn't get my film developed yet.*

film LAYER /fɪlm/ *n* [C] a thin layer of something on something else • *A film of oil glistened on the surface of the water.*

filter /'fɪl·tər/ *n* [C] a piece of equipment or a device for removing solids from liquids or gases, or for limiting the particular type of light, sound, or electricity going through it • *an oil filter* ○ *a coffee filter*

filter /'fɪl·tər/ *v* [I/T] • *Clams filter water to extract food.* [T] ○ *Devices in the chimneys filter out particles from smoke.* [M] • If something filters down/in/out/through, it appears or happens gradually or to a limited degree: *Reports of the accident began to filter in.* [I always + adv/prep] ○ *Sunlight filtered through the branches.* [I always + adv/prep]

filthy /'fɪl·θi/ *adj* extremely dirty • *Trucks poured out clouds of filthy, black smoke.* • Filthy also means containing offensive words or pictures: *filthy language* • *He was a little embarrassed about being* **filthy rich** (= extremely rich).

filth /fɪlθ/ *n* [U] • *There were beggars in the streets and filth everywhere.* • Filth is also sexually offensive writing or images.

filthiness /'fɪl·θi·nəs/ *n* [U]

fin /fɪn/ *n* [C] a thin, wing-shaped part of a fish that helps it to swim, or a wing-shaped part of a ship, aircraft, or car

finagle /fə'neɪ·gəl/ *v* [I/T] to get (something) by using an indirect method, esp. trickery • *How can I finagle a place on the guest list for the big party?* [T]

final LAST /'faɪn·əl/ *adj* [not gradable] last • *The other team scored twice in the final minute.* ○ *The recommendation will be sent to the City Council for final approval.* ○ *(infml) I'm not coming and that's final* (= I do not want to discuss it any longer).

final (exam) /'faɪn·əl (ɪg'zæm)/ *n* [C] a test taken on a subject at the end of a school year or course • *a math final* ○ *Spring brought final exams and the end of the year.*

finality /faɪ'næl·əţ·i, fə-/ *n* [U] • *The finality of death is sometimes hard to accept.*

finalize /'faɪn·əl,aɪz/ *v* [T] • *Details of the deal are being finalized.*

finally /'faɪn·əl·i, 'faɪn·li/ *adv* [not gradable] at the end, or after some delay • *Finally, I just said, "I don't care."* ○ *We finally got home at midnight.*

final COMPETITION /'faɪn·əl/ *n* [C usually pl] the last in a series of games, races, or competitions, in which the winner is decided • *The women's basketball finals will be on Sunday.*

finalist /'faɪn·əl·əst/ *n* [C] • *a finalist for the award*

finale /fə'næl·i, -'nɑl·i/ *n* [C usually sing] the last part of esp. a musical or theatrical performance • *a grand finale*

finance /fə'næns, 'faɪ·næns/ *n* the management of money, or the money belonging to a person, group, or organization • *corporate/personal finance* [U] ○ *the city's finances* [pl]

finance /fə'næns, 'faɪ·næns/ *v* [T] • *How will you finance a new house* (= provide the money to obtain it)?

financial /fə'næn·tʃəl, faɪ-/ *adj* [not gradable] • *financial problems*

financially /fə'næn·tʃə·li, faɪ-/ *adv* [not gradable] • *We're in fairly good shape financially.*

financier /ˌfɪn·ən'sɪr, ˌfaɪ·næn-/ *n* [C] someone who controls a large amount of money and can give or lend it to people or organizations

finch /fɪntʃ/ *n* [C] a small singing bird with a short, wide, pointed beak

find *(obj)* DISCOVER /faɪnd/ *v past* **found** /faʊnd/ to see where (a thing or person) is, either unexpectedly or by searching, or to begin to understand or know where to get or how to achieve (something); discover • *I found a ten-dollar bill in my pocket.* [T] ○ *I hope I can find a place to live near work.* [T] ○ *The study found that men who took an aspirin a day have fewer heart attacks.* [+ that clause] ○ *Some insects have been found to live several years without water.* [T] ○ *Many plant and animal species are found* (= exist) *only in the rainforests.* [T] • If you find a quality within yourself, you suddenly develop it or learn that you have it: *She found the courage to leave her husband.* [T] • To find someone means to meet someone you can have a close, loving relationship with: *Ellen keeps hoping she'll find a guy she can settle down with.* [T] • If you **find** your**self** somewhere, you learn you have arrived there: *We fell asleep in the back of the car and woke up to find ourselves in Atlanta.* • *I wish I could*

find (the) time (= have enough time) *to do more reading.*

find /faɪnd/ *n* [C] a good or valuable thing or a special person that has been discovered • *She's a real find—singers like her don't grow on trees.*

finding /'faɪn·dɪŋ/ *n* [C usually pl] information that has been discovered esp. by detailed study

find JUDGE /faɪnd/ *v* [I/T] *past* **found** /faʊnd/ *law* to make a judgment in a law court • *She was found guilty of child neglect.* [T]

▫**find out** *(obj)*, **find** *(obj)* **out** /'-'-/ *v adv* [I/T] to obtain knowledge of (something), or to obtain knowledge of the usually dishonest activities of (someone) • *How did you find out about the party?* [I] ○ *I just found out that he was cheating on the test.* [T] ○ *He wondered whether his boss was involved, but he saw no way of finding that out.* [M]

fine SATISFACTORY /faɪn/ *adj, adv* [not gradable] very good or very well; satisfactory or satisfactorily • *I was sick last night, but I feel fine this morning.* ○ *The apartments are very small, which is fine if you're single.* ○ *The car was working fine yesterday.* ○ *"Is something wrong?" "No, everything's just fine, thanks."*

fine EXCELLENT /faɪn/ *adj* [*-er/-est* only] of excellent quality or much better than average • *Although still young, he is already a fine musician.* ○ *California produces some of the finest wines in the world.* • *Fine is sometimes used with an opposite meaning to show that you are annoyed: That's a fine thing to say after all I've done for you.* • **The fine arts** consist of drawings, paintings, and SCULPTURES (= solid objects), and sometimes also music, theater, and dance, that are admired for their beauty.

fine THIN /faɪn/ *adj* [*-er/-est* only] very thin or in very small grains or drops • *fine blond hair* ○ *The paint comes out of the can in a fine spray.* ○ *She has her mother's fine* (= delicate and beautiful) *features.* • *There's sometimes* **a fine line** *between love and hate* (= there is not much difference between them). • *Make sure you examine the* **fine print** (= the details that are printed in small letters) *before you sign any contract.* • If you **fine-tune** something, you make small changes in it in order to make it work as well as possible.

finely /'faɪn·li/, **fine** /faɪn/ *adv* • *finely ground coffee*

fine PUNISHMENT /faɪn/ *n* [C] an amount of money that has to be paid as a punishment for not obeying a rule or law • *If found guilty, he faces six months in jail and a heavy fine.*

fine /faɪn/ *v* [T] • *They fined him $125 for driving through a red light.*

finery /'faɪ·nə·ri/ *n* [U] decorative and expensive clothing and jewelry worn on a special occasion • *The stars arrived for the Oscars dressed in all their finery.*

finesse /fə'nes/ *n* [U] great skill or style • *She has handled these difficult negotiations with real finesse.*

finger /'fɪŋ·gər/ *n* [C] any of the long, thin parts of the hand that bend and hold things, esp. one other than the thumb • *I cut my finger when I was chopping onions.* • A finger is also a part of a GLOVE (= piece of clothing for the hand) that covers a finger. • **Finger-pointing** is saying that particular people are to blame: *The Republicans won, and the finger-pointing among the Democrats began.* • A **fingertip** is the end of a finger. • If you have something **at** your **fingertips**, you have perfect knowledge of it and can bring it to mind immediately: *She had all the facts at her fingertips.* • A **fingernail** is the hard, slightly curved part that covers and protects the top of the end of a finger. • PIC HAND

finger /'fɪŋ·gər/ *v* [T] to touch or feel (something) with the fingers • *He fingered his watch nervously as he waited for the exam to begin.* • (*slang*) If you **finger** someone, you tell the police that they are guilty of a crime.

fingerprint /'fɪŋ·gər,prɪnt/, *short form* **print** *n* [C] the mark left by the pattern of curved lines on the end of a finger or thumb

fingerprint /'fɪŋ·gər,prɪnt/ *v* [T] • *The police fingerprinted the suspects.*

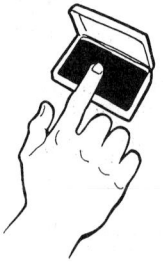

fingerprint

finicky /'fɪn·ɪ·ki/ *adj* giving too much attention to small details; hard to please • *a finicky dresser* ○ *a finicky eater*

finish /'fɪn·ɪʃ/ *v* [I/T] to come to an end, to bring (something) to an end or to completion, or to use (something) completely • *The meeting should finish at four o'clock.* [I] ○ *If you'll let me finish my sentence, I'll explain it to you.* [T] ○ *She didn't win but she did finish* (= end the race) *second.* [I] ○ *Have you finished reading that magazine?* [I] ○ *We may as well finish* (*off*) (= completely use) *the rest of this wine.* [T/ M] ○ *When you finish up* (= complete your work), *come back to the house.* [I] • *The gang warned him not to go to the police or they would* **finish** *him* **off** (= kill him).

finish /'fɪn·ɪʃ/ *n* [C] • *Both candidates are predicting a close finish in this election.* • A **finish** is the appearance of the surface of something or the last covering, as of paint, put onto it: *a glossy finish* • The **finish line** is the line at the end of a race.

finished /ˈfɪn·ɪʃt/ adj [not gradable] • *Raw materials make up only a small part of the cost of the finished* (= completed) *product.* ○ *As a result of this latest scandal, the senator's career is finished* (= brought to an end).

finisher /ˈfɪn·ɪ·ʃər/ n [C usually pl] • *She was one of the top ten finishers in the race.*

finite /ˈfaɪ·naɪt/ adj having a limit or end • *We have only a finite amount of time to complete this project.*

fink on /ˈfɪŋ·kən, -kɔːn/ v prep [T] *slang* to tell secret and damaging information about (someone) • *Someone finked on him to the cops.*

fink out /ˈfɪŋˈkaʊt/ v adv [I] *slang* to fail to do something, esp. something promised • *We'd planned to go camping but at the last minute Ron finked out.*

fir (tree) /fɜr (triː)/ n [C] any of several types of evergreen trees that have needlelike leaves and are grown esp. for their wood or for use as **Christmas trees**

fire FLAMES /faɪr/ n [C/U] the state of burning, or a burning mass of material • *The factory had to be closed because the risk of fire was too great.* [U] ○ *There have been a lot of forest fires because of the drought.* [C] ○ *The library was badly damaged in the fire.* [C] ○ *The theater was destroyed by fire.* [U] ○ *Over a hundred volunteers were needed to put out the fire* (= stop it). [C] • A fire is also a small controlled mass of burning material that is used for heating or cooking: *Light a fire in the fireplace.* [C] • If something is **on fire**, it is burning, esp. when it is not meant to be. • A **fire alarm** is a device that makes a loud continuous noise to warn people that a building is on fire. • A **fireball** is a great mass of fire high in the air, esp. one caused by a powerful explosion. • A **fire department** is an organization working for a city or local government that is in charge of preventing or putting out fires. • A **fire drill** is (the practicing of) a set of actions that should be performed in order to leave a burning building safely. • A **fire engine/truck** is a large vehicle that carries specially trained people and their equipment to a fire. • A **fire escape** is a set of metal stairs, esp. on the outside of a building, that allows people to leave a burning building. • A **fire extinguisher** is a container filled with water or special chemicals that are sprayed onto a fire to stop it from burning. • A **firefighter** (also **fireman**) is a person trained to stop fires and to save people and property from being harmed. • A **fire hydrant** (also **fireplug**) is a device to which firefighters can connect their equipment in order to obtain water from the public

fire hydrant

supply. • A **fireplace** is a space in the wall of a room for a fire to burn in, or the decorated part that surrounds this space: *We usually stack some wood next to the fireplace.* • Something that is **fireproof** will not burn in a fire. • A **fire sale** is a sale of goods at low prices because they have been slightly damaged in a fire. • The part of a room that surrounds a fireplace is called the **fireside**: *She liked to curl up by the fireside with a good book.* • A **fire station/house** is a building where fire engines and equipment are kept and where firefighters are based. • A **firestorm** is a very large, uncontrollable fire that is kept burning by strong winds caused by hot air rising over the burning area: *(fig.) The senator's remarks caused a firestorm of protest* (= a powerful reaction) *from welfare advocates.* • A **firetrap** is a building that would burn easily if a fire started and would be difficult to escape from. • **Firewood** is wood used as fuel for a fire.

fire SHOOT /faɪr/ v [I/T] to shoot bullets or other explosives from (a weapon) • *He fired his gun into the air.* [T] ○ *The gunman began firing into the crowd.* [I] ○ *(fig.) The journalists kept firing questions at the president* (= asking him questions quickly one after the other). [T] ○ *(fig.) "I'd like to ask you some personal questions." "Fire away* (= You can start immediately)*!".* [I] • *He fired off* (= wrote quickly) *an angry letter to his publisher.* • If someone is **on the firing line**, they are being criticized for something they have said or done. • A **firing squad** is a group of soldiers whose job is to shoot someone who is to be killed as a punishment.

fire /faɪr/ n [U] • *The troops were ordered to cease fire* (= stop shooting). ○ *The police opened fire on the fleeing car.* • A **firearm** is a gun that can be carried easily: *Pistols and revolvers are firearms.*

fire LOSE JOB /faɪr/ v [T] to order (someone) to give up their job • *She was fired for stealing from her employer.*

fire EXCITE /faɪr/ v [T] to cause (a strong emotion) in someone • *She's all fired up* (= excited) *about going to college.*

fire /faɪr/ n [U] strong emotion • *The fire in her speech inspired everyone to carry on in spite of recent setbacks.* • **Fire in the belly** is a strong determination to succeed.

firebomb /ˈfaɪr·bɑm/ n [C] a bomb that causes a lot of destruction by spreading fire

firebomb /ˈfaɪr·bɑm/ v [T] • *Members of the cult have threatened to firebomb government buildings.*

firecracker /ˈfaɪrˌkræk·ər/ n [C] a small, usually paper or cardboard container filled with an explosive that makes a loud noise

firefly /ˈfaɪr·flaɪ/, **lightning bug** n [C] a small insect that produces flashes of light when it flies at night

fireworks /ˈfaɪr·wɜrks/ pl n small containers

filled with explosive chemicals that make a loud noise when they explode and sometimes produce bright, colored patterns • Fireworks can also mean the pattern of colorful explosions in the air planned as a show: *What time do the fireworks start?*

firm FIXED /fɜrm/ *adj, adv* [-*er*/-*est* only] set in place and unable or unlikely to move, come loose, or fall over • *The rocks were wet, and we couldn't get a firm footing.* ○ *(fig.) Sometimes it takes more courage to admit you're wrong than to stand firm* (= continue to defend an opinion). ○ *(fig.) The dean is holding firm and refusing to give in to student demands.*

firmly /'fɜrm·li/ *adv* • *Fasten your seatbelt firmly.*

firm HARD /fɜrm/ *adj* [-*er*/-*est* only] not soft when pressed; solid or strong • *a firm mattress* ○ *a firm body* ○ *(fig.) No one seems to have a firm grip on* (= be in control of) *the situation at the moment.*

firmly /'fɜrm·li/ *adv* • *He shook my hand firmly.*

firmness /'fɜrm·nəs/ *n* [U]

firm CERTAIN /fɜrm/ *adj* [-*er*/-*est* only] certain or fixed in a belief, opinion, etc., and unlikely to change, or so certain as to be beyond doubt or question • *a firm believer in the Constitution* ○ *They made a firm commitment to complete the job this week.* ○ *The decision is firm—there will be a strike.* • Firm can also mean showing control and making sure you will be obeyed: *A new teacher has to be firm with her students.*

firmly /'fɜrm·li/ *adv* • *The mayor is firmly committed to reducing crime in the city.*

firmness /'fɜrm·nəs/ *n* [U]

firm BUSINESS /fɜrm/ *n* [C] a company or business • *a law firm*

first /fɜrst/ *adj, adv* [not gradable], *n* [C] (a person or thing) coming before all others in order, time, amount, quality, or importance • *Would you like to go first?* ○ *We leave on the first of August.* [C] • **At first** (= In the beginning) *I thought he was joking but then I realized he meant it.* • **At first blush/glance** means when first considering something, before having a chance to look at it carefully: *At first glance the deal looked wonderful, but after reading the fine print he wasn't so sure.* • **First come, first served** means that only the first people to arrive or ask for something will receive it: *Free tickets will be given out on a first come, first served basis.* • *In spite of her recent success as a novelist, she remains* **first and foremost** (= more than anything else) *a poet.* • **First (of all)/First off** (= Before anything else), *I'd like to ask you a few questions.* • *He said he'd phone back* **first thing** *tomorrow* (= early in the morning). • **First things first** means that more important things should be done or considered before other things: *First things first—was anyone hurt?* • **First aid** is

emergency medical treatment given to someone who is injured or ill. • In baseball, first or **first base** is the place a player runs to after hitting the ball, or the position played by a member of the team on the field: *(fig.) His proposal didn't get to first base with the committee* (= wasn't seriously considered by them). • If a service is **first class**, it is the best that is possible or available: *I upgraded my plane ticket to first class from tourist class.* • **First class** also means excellent: *a first-class education.* • **First class** is also the standard way of sending letters through the mail. • A **first cousin** is a child of someone's aunt or uncle. • **First-degree murder** is the most serious of all crimes involving the killing of a human being. • The **first floor** (also **ground floor**) of a building is the floor at ground level. • In a vehicle, **first (gear)** is the GEAR (= part of the engine) used when starting to move forward: *Put the car in first gear.* • Information that is **first-hand** is obtained directly from its origin: *He has first-hand experience of what war is like.* • The **First Lady** is the wife of the US president or of a governor or other public official. • A person's **first language** is the language they learn from their parents as they are growing up. • A person's **first name** (also **given name**) is a personal name, not a family name: *"James" and "Sarah" are first names.* Compare **last name** at LAST FINAL; **middle name** at MIDDLE. • If you are **on a first-name basis** with someone, you call each other by your first names. • *(esp. Cdn)* The **First Nations** are the people who have a member of their family who belonged to one of the groups of people that originally lived in North America before the Europeans arrived, or political organizations representing these people. • *(specialized)* In grammar, the **first person** is the form of pronouns and verbs people use when speaking or writing about themselves: *"I," "me," and "my" are first person singular pronouns, and "we," "us," and "our" are first person plural pronouns.* ○ *Autobiographies are written in the first person.* ○ Compare **second person** at SECOND POSITION; **third person** at THIRD. • If something is **first-rate**, it is extremely good: *a first-rate performance* • USAGE: The related number is ONE. • LP NUMBERS, WORDS WITH THE MEANING "ONE" at ONE SINGLE

fiscal /'fɪs·kəl/ *adj* [not gradable] relating to public money or other financial matters • *a sound fiscal policy* • A **fiscal year** is a period of twelve months (not always January 1st to December 31st) for which a government or business plans its management of money.

fish ANIMAL /fɪʃ/ *n* [C/U] *pl* **fish** or **fishes** an animal without legs that lives in water, has a soft outer body, uses its tail and FINS to help it swim, and takes in oxygen from the water • *How many fish live in the pond?* [C] ○ *We had fish for dinner.* [U] • Someone who is **a fish out of water** is uncomfortable in the situation

they are in: *I feel like a fish out of water here.*
• A **fishbowl** is a round glass container for pet fish. • A **fishnet** is a net for catching fish: *Fishnets lay on the dock.* • **Fishnet stockings** are clothing that covers the feet and legs and that look like they are made from a net.

fish /fɪʃ/ v [I] to try to catch fish • *We were fishing for tuna.* • If someone says you should **fish or cut bait** they want you to act or admit you are not going to act.

fishing /'fɪʃ·ɪŋ/ n [U] • *I'd like to do a little fishing this weekend.* • A **fishing rod/pole** is a long rod fitted with a strong string with a hook at the end which is used to catch fish.

fish SEARCH /fɪʃ/ v [I/M] to search or to try to get something • *The reporter was fishing around for information.* [I always + adv/prep] • If you **fish** something **out**, you pull or take it out, esp. after searching: *He fished a tissue out of his pocket.* • If you **fish for compliments** you try to get people to say good things about you.

fisherman /'fɪʃ·ər·mən/ n [C] pl **-men** /'fɪʃ·ər·mən/ someone who catches fish, either as their job or as a sport • *Maine fishermen are finding it difficult to make a living.*

fishy /'fɪʃ·i/ adj infml seeming dishonest or false • *There's something fishy going on.*

fission /'fɪʃ·ən, 'fɪʒ-/ n [U] *specialized* the dividing of the NUCLEUS of an atom, producing energy, or the dividing of a living cell

fissure /'fɪʃ·ər/ n [C] a deep crack, esp. one in rock or ice or in the ground

fist /fɪst/ n [C] a hand with the fingers turned in tightly and the thumb held against them • *She clenched her fist.* • The boys got into a **fistfight** (= a fight in which they hit each other).

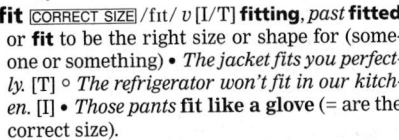
fist

fistful /'fɪst·fʊl/ n [C] • *Anna had a fistful of candy.*

fit CORRECT SIZE /fɪt/ v [I/T] **fitting**, *past* **fitted** or **fit** to be the right size or shape for (someone or something) • *The jacket fits you perfectly.* [T] ○ *The refrigerator won't fit in our kitchen.* [I] • *Those pants fit like a glove* (= are the correct size).

fit /fɪt/ n [U] • *These shoes are a perfect/terrible fit.*

fitted /'fɪt̬·ɪd/ adj • *He bought a fitted suit* (= made to his exact size).

fitting /'fɪt̬·ɪŋ/ n [C] an occasion when you try on clothing being made or adjusted • *a fitting for a wedding gown*

fit SUIT /fɪt/ v [T] **fitting**, *past* **fitted** or **fit** to be suitable for (someone or something) • *The job fits him well.* • *"I'm looking for a fun novel to read on the plane." "This book will* **fit the bill** *(= be suitable)."*

fit /fɪt/ adj [-er/-est only] **-tt-** • *She's not fit to be*

treasurer. • *He was* **fit to be tied** *(= extremely angry) when she showed up an hour late.*

fitness /'fɪt·nəs/ n [U] • *No one questioned her fitness for the job.*

fitting /'fɪt̬·ɪŋ/ adj • *a fitting tribute*

fit HEALTHY /fɪt/ adj [-er/-est only] **-tt-** in good health, esp. as a result of exercise; strong • *You look fit.* • *She's* **fit as a fiddle** *(= in excellent health).*

fitness /'fɪt·nəs/ n [U] • *physical fitness*

fit BRIEF PERIOD /fɪt/ n [C] a sudden, brief period when something uncontrolled happens • *a coughing/sneezing fit* ○ *Epilepsy can cause severe fits* (= uncontrolled muscle contractions). • *The reform process has proceeded in* **fits and starts** (= there have been periods of activity and times when nothing happened).

fitful /'fɪt·fəl/ adj going off and on irregularly • *Her breathing is fitful.*

fitfully /'fɪt·fə·li/ adv • *She slept fitfully.*

fit EMOTIONAL EXPERIENCE /fɪt/ n [C] an experience of a strong emotion or reaction • *a fit of laughter/jealousy* • A fit can be a feeling or expression of great anger: *Your mother will have/throw a fit when she sees this mess.*

▫ **fit in** BE ACCEPTED /-'-/ v adv [I] to belong with other things, or to be accepted by other people in a group • *This chair doesn't fit in with our furniture.* ○ *She fit in well at school.*

▫ **fit in** obj FIND TIME, **fit** obj **in** /'-'-/ v adv [M] to find time to do or to deal with • *The doctor can fit you in at three o'clock.*

five /faɪv/ number 5 • *We work five days a week.* ○ *a five-room apartment* • Five can also mean five o'clock. • USAGE: The related adjective is FIFTH. • LP NUMBERS

fix REPAIR /fɪks/ v [T] to repair or adjust (something) • *I'll fix that broken chair today.*

fix ARRANGE /fɪks/ v [T] to arrange or put in place • *I need to fix my hair.* • To fix something such as a race or game or an election is to illegally arrange who will win.

fix CHOOSE /fɪks/ v [T] to choose (a time or place to do something) • *Let's fix a date for our next meeting.*

fix ATTACH /fɪks/ v [T] to attach in order to keep in one place • *Fix the shelf to the wall with screws.* ○ *I tried to fix the directions in my mind.*

fix BAD SITUATION /fɪks/ n [C usually sing] a situation causing trouble or problems • *He's in a fix and needs our help.*

fix PUNISH /fɪks/ v [T] to hurt or punish (someone) • *She thinks she can steal my boyfriend, but I'll fix her!*

fix PREPARE FOOD /fɪks/ v [T] to cook or prepare (food or drink) • *Will you fix dinner?*

fix AMOUNT TAKEN /fɪks/ n [C] *slang* an amount of a substance, esp. an illegal drug, that someone needs to take • *I need a caffeine fix to get me through this class.*

fix STOP REPRODUCTION /fɪks/ v [T] to remove the reproductive organs of (an animal) • *We had our cat fixed.*

fixated /ˈfɪk·seɪt/ *adj* thinking hard about something all the time • *I am fixated on making tomorrow better.*

fixation /fɪkˈseɪ·ʃən/ *n* [C] • *Jen has a fixation on food.*

fixed /fɪkst/ *adj* [not gradable] not changing • *a fixed stare* ○ *a fixed address*

fixedly /ˈfɪk·səd·li/ *adv* [not gradable] • *She stared fixedly at the screen.*

fixture /ˈfɪks·tʃər/ *n* [C] a piece of equipment that stays attached to a house or other building • *a light fixture* ○ *bathroom fixtures* ○ *(fig.) He became a fixture* (= a regular feature) *on television in the 1980s.*

fizz /fɪz/ *v* [I] (of a liquid) to produce gas bubbles • *The champagne fizzed as she poured it.*

fizz /fɪz/ *n* [U] • *This soda has lost its fizz.*

fizzle /ˈfɪz·əl/ *v* [I] to finish slowly in a way that is disappointing or has become less interesting • *I like the way the movie starts but then it fizzles out.*

flab /flæb/ *n* [U] soft, loose flesh on the body of a person or an animal • *I'm trying to burn off excess flab.*

flabby /ˈflæb·i/ *adj* • *Carol scratched at her flabby upper arm.*

flabbergasted /ˈflæb·ərˌɡæst/ *adj* shocked by the unexpected • *I was absolutely flabbergasted at what she was paid.*

flaccid /ˈflæs·əd, ˈflæk·səd/ *adj* soft and weak; not firm • *flaccid skin* ○ *a politician's flaccid remarks*

flack /flæk/ *n* [U] FLAK

flag SYMBOL /flæɡ/ *n* [C] a piece of cloth with a special color and pattern, used as a symbol esp. to represent a particular country or group • *the American flag* ○ *The man waved a red warning flag.* • A **flagpole** is a long, vertical pole to which a flag can be attached.

flag MARK /flæɡ/ *v* [T] **-gg-** to mark (something) so it can be found easily among other similar things • *She asked me to flag the names that appear on both lists.*

flag BECOME TIRED /flæɡ/ *v* [I] **-gg-** to become tired or less strong • *My interest in the story flagged.*

□ **flag down** *obj*, **flag** *obj* **down** /ˈ-ˈ-/ *v adv* [M] to signal that (a vehicle or person) should stop by waving at them • *A police officer flagged us down.*

flagrant /ˈfleɪ·ɡrənt/ *adj* shocking because of being so bad and so obvious • *a flagrant violation of the rules*

flagrantly /ˈfleɪ·ɡrənt·li/ *adv* • *He flagrantly broke the law.*

flagship SHIP /ˈflæɡ·ʃɪp/ *n* [C] the ship among a group of ships on which the most important officer sails

flagship BEST ONE /ˈflæɡ·ʃɪp/ *n* [C usually sing] the best or most important thing among a group • *The retail chain has its flagship in New York and branches in 19 states.*

flagstone /ˈflæɡ·stoʊn/, **flag** /flæɡ/ *n* [C] a flat piece of stone used esp. outside a building to make floors, stairs, and paths

flail /fleɪl/ *v* [I/T] to wave (esp. arms or legs) energetically but with little or no control • *His hands flailed wildly.* [I]

flair /fler, flær/ *n* [U] the ability to do something well • *Alan has a flair for public speaking.*

flak /flæk/, **flack** *n* [U] *infml* strong criticism or opposition • *She caught some flak from her parents.*

flake THIN PIECE /fleɪk/ *n* [C] a small, thin piece, esp. of a layer on a surface • *Flakes of paint fell from the ceiling.*

flake /fleɪk/ *v* [I] • *Plaster is flaking off the walls.*

flake PERSON /fleɪk/ *n* [C] *infml* a person who does not seem to pay attention and is sometimes silly • *That guy is a real flake.*

flamboyant /flæmˈbɔɪ·ənt/ *adj* intended to be noticed, esp. by being brightly colored • *a flamboyant gesture* ○ *flamboyant clothes*

flame LIGHT /fleɪm/ *n* [C/U] the hot light of a fire • *The logs in the fireplace burst into flame.* [U] • *The house was in flames* (= burning).

flame /fleɪm/ *v* [I] • *The fire suddenly flamed (up).*

flame ANGER /fleɪm/ *v* [I/T] to show anger by turning red • *His face flamed and he started stammering.* [I] • If you **flame** someone you disagree with, you send insulting electronic messages about them over the INTERNET: *He was flamed by several other men in the chat room.* [T]

flamingo /fləˈmɪŋ·ɡoʊ/ *n* [C] *pl* **flamingos** or **flamingoes** a bird with pink feathers, a long neck, and long, thin legs, and which lives near the water in warm places

flammable /ˈflæm·ə·bəl/, **inflammable** /ɪnˈflæm·ə·bəl/ *adj* able to catch fire easily • *This solvent is flammable.* • USAGE: The opposite of flammable is NONFLAMMABLE.

flank /flæŋk/ *v* [T] to be at the side of someone or something • *Secret Service agents flanked the president's car.*

flank /flæŋk/ *n* [C] • *Troops attacked the enemy's left flank.* • A person's or animal's **flanks** are the sides of its body between the RIBS and the hips.

flannel /ˈflæn·əl/ *n* [U] a soft cloth usually made from cotton or wool • *flannel pajamas* ○ *a flannel shirt*

flap WAVE /flæp/ *v* [I/T] **-pp-** (of a bird's wings) to wave up and down while flying, or (of objects that cannot fly) to move quickly from side to side or up and down • *A small bird flapped its wings.* [T] ○ *Flags flapped in the breeze.* [I]

flap /flæp/ *n* [C] • *The bird flew into the air with a flap of its wings.*

flap PIECE /flæp/ *n* [C] a piece of cloth or other material attached along one edge to something else • *a pocket/tent flap*

flap EMOTIONAL STATE /flæp/ *n* [C] a state of excitement or worry • *She caused a big flap when she told her husband about her parents' visit.*

flapjack /ˈflæp·dʒæk/ *n* [C] A PANCAKE

flare BURN /fler, flær/ *v* [I] to burn brightly either for a short time or irregularly • *The candle flared then went out.*

flare /fler, flær/ *n* [C] something that produces a flame or bright light and is usually used as a signal, or the flame or light itself • *The boat is equipped with flares.* ○ *Did you see that flare?*

flare MAKE WIDER /fler, flær/ *v* [I/T] to become wider, or to make (something) wider • *Her skirt flares just below the knee.* [I]

flare HAPPEN SUDDENLY /fler, flær/ *v* [I] to happen in a sudden and often violent way • *The dispute threatens to flare into a lawsuit.* ○ *The argument quieted down then flared up again.*

flareup /ˈfler·ʌp, ˈflær-/ *n* [C] a sudden happening • *A flareup of fighting left seven people dead.*

flash SHINE /flæʃ/ *v* [I/T] to shine suddenly and usually brightly, but only for a short time • *Stop flashing that light in my eyes.* [T]

flash /flæʃ/ *n* [C] • *A flash of lightning lit the sky.* • A **flashlight** is a small electric light a person can carry and that works without being plugged in.

flash HAPPEN QUICKLY /flæʃ/ *v* [I always + adv/ prep] to move or happen quickly • *A fire engine flashed by.*

flash /flæʃ/ *n* [C] • *The answer came to her in a flash* (= suddenly). • If something is a **flash in the pan**, it is interesting for only a short time. • *The heavy rain caused flash floods* (= sudden, severe floods).

flash SHOW /flæʃ/ *v* [I/T] to show (something) quickly or for a short time • *The officer flashed her badge.* [T] ○ *A smile flashed across her face.* [I]

flasher /ˈflæʃ·ər/ *n* [C] someone who shows their sexual organs in public

flash PHOTOGRAPHY /flæʃ/ *n* [C] a device used to produce a bright light for a brief time when taking a photograph

flashback /ˈflæʃ·bæk/ *n* [C] a memory, or a short part of a movie, story, or play describing past events • *This party is like a '70s flashback.*

flash card /ˈflæʃ·kɑrd/ *n* [C] a small piece of stiff paper with a word, picture, or question on it that is to teach something • *She is learning math with flash cards.*

flashy /ˈflæʃ·i/ *adj* [-er/-est only] expensive or stylish, or brightly colored • *He wears flashy clothes.*

flask /flæsk/ *n* [C] a small container, usually with a wide base and a narrow neck • *a flask of whisky*

flat LEVEL /flæt/ *adj* [-er/-est only] **-tt-** level and smooth; having little or no height and not raised or round • *A desk provides a flat surface to work on.* ○ *Campers look for flat ground to put up their tents.* • A drink that is flat has stopped bubbling: *If you don't put the top back*

on the soda bottle, it will go flat. • If a tire is flat, the air has gone out of it so that it does not give the support it should: *One of my tires is flat and I'll have to change it.* • *In some parts of the west, the land is* (**as**) **flat as a pancake** (= very level). • People who are **flat-footed**, or who have **flat feet**, have feet whose bottom part is not curved up in an arch, as is usual, but is level so that almost all of it touches the ground in walking.

flat /flæt/ *n* [C] something flat, esp. a tire that has lost its air, so that it does not give the support that it should • *We pulled off to the side of the road to change a flat.* • **The flat of the hand** is the inside, level part of the hand with the fingers straight: *He hit me hard with the flat of his hand.*

flat /flæt/ *adv* [-er/-est only] **-tt-** • *He hurt his back and could only sleep lying flat on his back* (= with his back down, against the surface on which he was lying).

flatten /ˈflæt·ən/ *v* [I/T] to make or become flat • *In the road race, you go over a few steep hills but then the course flattens out.* [I]

flat COMPLETE /flæt/ *adj* [not gradable] complete and certain • *His request for time off from work was met with a flat refusal.*

flat /flæt/ *adv* [not gradable] • *When he asked for a raise, the boss turned him down flat.* ○ *I'm flat broke* (= I have no money). • If someone goes **flat out**, they are going at full speed and using all of their energy: *He had to go flat out and won the race by inches.*

flatly /ˈflæt·li/ *adv* [not gradable] • *He flatly denied that he saw what had happened.*

flat NOT CHANGING /flæt/ *adj* [not gradable] (esp. of an amount of money) not changing or varying • *We charge a flat rate of $25 per hour.* ○ *Sales are flat* (= low and not changing) *during this time of year.* • A **flat tax** is a tax rate that is the same for everyone, whether their income is high or low.

flat /flæt/ *adv* [only after n; not gradable] exactly • *We managed to get to the station in five minutes flat.*

flat MUSIC /flæt/ *adj, adv* [-er/-est only] **-tt-** (in music) lower than a particular or the correct note • Compare SHARP MUSIC.

flat APARTMENT /flæt/ *n* [C] esp. *Br* an APARTMENT • *They have a house in the country and a flat in London.*

flatter /ˈflæt·ər/ *v* [T] to make (someone) feel important or attractive, or to praise (someone) in order to please them • *They were flattered by the invitation from the mayor.*

flattering /ˈflæt·ə·rɪŋ/ *adj* • *That suit is flattering on you* (= makes you look attractive).

flattery /ˈflæt·ə·ri/ *n* [U] • *Saying I was the best ever was too obvious an attempt at flattery.*

flatulence /ˈflætʃ·ə·ləns/ *n* [U] *fml* the uncomfortable condition of having gas in the stomach and bowels

flatware /ˈflæt·wer, -wær/ *n* [U] objects used

for eating and serving food, esp. utensils; SIL-VERWARE

flaunt /flɔːnt, flɑnt/ v [T] to intentionally make obvious (something you have) in order to be admired • *You go to the mall and you see fourteen-year-old kids flaunting money their parents give them.*

flavor /'fleɪ·vər/ n [C/U] the particular way a substance, esp. food or drink, is recognized from its taste and smell • *We sell 32 different flavors of ice cream.* [C] ○ *This soup doesn't have much flavor.* [U] ○ (fig.) *This brief description should give you a flavor of what the book is like* (= show you the character of the book). [U]

flavor /'fleɪ·vər/ v [T] • *Use some garlic to flavor the stew.*

flavorful /'fleɪ·vər·fəl/ adj having a lot of flavor • *A veal chop was flavorful but too fatty.*

flavoring /'fleɪ·və·rɪŋ/ n [C/U] a substance added to improve or change the taste of something • *A little vanilla flavoring improves the taste of the dessert.* [U]

flaw /flɔː/ n [C] a fault or weakness, esp. one that happens while something is being planned or made and that makes it not perfect • *A flaw in the steering mechanism led to a recall of 200,000 cars.*

flawless /'flɔː·ləs/ adj [not gradable] containing no faults or mistakes; perfect • *The countdown was flawless, and the space missile went off exactly on schedule.*

flea /fliː/ n [C] a very small jumping insect without wings that feeds on the blood of animals and people

flea market /'fliː‚mɑr·kət/ n [C] a place, usually outside, where people sell esp. old or used items at cheap prices • *There's a flea market every Saturday in the school parking lot.*

fleck /flek/ n [C] a small mark, esp. of a different color • *I got a few flecks of paint on the window when I was painting the frames.*

fleck /flek/ v [T] • *Her hair is flecked with gray.*

fled /fled/ past simple and past participle of FLEE

fledgling /'fledʒ·lɪŋ/ adj [not gradable] new and not experienced • *Still in his teens, he pursued his fledgling career in journalism.*

flee /fliː/ v [I/T] past **fled** /fled/ to escape by running away from (a place), esp. because of danger or fear • *An FBI spokesman said Stewart fled before police arrived.* [I]

fleece SHEEP /fliːs/ n [C/U] the wool of a sheep, or a soft, artificial material that looks like wool • *Polyester fleeces are especially popular to provide warmth in coats.* [C]

fleece CHEAT /fliːs/ v [T] to charge (too much money) or cheat (someone) • *He was fleecing investors by setting up bogus companies and then manipulating the price of their stocks.*

fleet SHIPS /fliːt/ n [C] all the ships in the navy of a country, or a number of ships operating as a unit within a navy

fleet VEHICLES /fliːt/ n [C] a number of aircraft, buses, cars, or other vehicles under the control of one company or organization • *He owns a fleet of taxis.*

fleeting /'fliː·t̬ɪŋ/ adj brief or quick • *He had a fleeting moment of panic but quickly recovered.*

flesh /fleʃ/ n [U] the soft part of the body of a person or animal that is between the skin and the bones, or the soft, inner part of a fruit or vegetable • *He rested his hands alongside her neck, gently pressing the soft flesh and the firm muscles beneath.* ○ *Peel the tomatoes and use only the flesh.* • *When you visit a military cemetery, you have to remember these were real* **flesh-and-blood** *people* (= humans physically alive), *not just names on crosses.* • *I've seen her perform on television, but never* **in the flesh** (= in her actual presence). • *If someone is your* **flesh and blood**, *they are members of your family: He treated me as if I were his own flesh and blood.* • **Flesh-colored** *means having approximately the color of white people's skin: flesh-colored tights* • *A* **flesh wound** *is an injury only to the flesh and not to the bones or inner organs: Fortunately it was only a flesh wound, and he was expected to recover completely.*

fleshy /'fleʃ·i/ adj having a lot of flesh • *He extended a broad, fleshy hand before him.*

flesh out obj, **flesh** obj **out** /'fleʃ'aʊt/ v adv [M] to give a more complete account or description of (something) • *Emily should have included these pieces of information to flesh out her argument.*

flew /fluː/ past simple of FLY

flex /fleks/ v [T] to bend (a part of the body, esp. an arm or leg) • *Keep your knees flexed at all times.* • *If someone or something* **flexes** *its* **muscle/muscles**, *it shows its power or strength: Conservatives were beginning to flex their muscles in Utah.*

flexible ABLE TO BEND /'flek·sə·bəl/ adj able to bend or be bent easily without breaking • *The wire has to be flexible enough to go around corners of the room.*

flexible CHANGEABLE /'flek·sə·bəl/ adj able to change or be changed easily according to the situation • *I'm fortunate because my job has flexible hours, and I can come and go pretty much as I want.*

flexibility /‚flek·sə'bɪl·ət̬·i/ n [U] • *The new law gives auto makers more flexibility in meeting lower pollution targets.*

flextime /'flek·staɪm/ n [U] a system of working in which employees can vary the time they start and finish work as long as they work the agreed number of hours

flick MOVE /flɪk/ v [I/T] to make a short, sudden movement that causes (something) to move • *Brina flicked her hair over her shoul-*

der. [T] ○ *He flicked the light switch on/off.* [M] ○ *She flicked through the pages of a magazine* (= turned them quickly). [I always + adv/prep]

flick /flɪk/ *n* [C] • *With a flick of the wrist, he tossed me the Frisbee.*

flick MOVIE /flɪk/ *n* [C] *infml* a movie • *Do you want to go to a flick tonight?*

flicker /'flɪk·ər/ *v* [I] to burn, shine, or move like a flame in quickly changing forms of light and dark • *Candles flickered on all the tables in the restaurant.* ○ *A smile flickered across her face.*

flicker /'flɪk·ər/ *n* [C] any slight and quick expression • *The planes searched the ground for a flicker of movement among the wreckage.*

flier PAPER , **flyer** /'flaɪ·ər/ *n* [C] a piece of paper containing an advertisement or information, usually given out to people walking by • *They handed out fliers asking you to vote for Jane Schumacker.* • See also **flier** at FLY TRAVEL THROUGH AIR.

flier PERSON /'flaɪ·ər/ *n* [C] a **flyer**, see at FLY TRAVEL THROUGH AIR

flight FLYING /flaɪt/ *n* [C/U] an aircraft trip, or the occasion of being a passenger in an aircraft • *We'll be arriving home on Tuesday on flight 147.* [C] ○ *All flights out of Midway have been canceled because of bad weather.* [C] ○ *We had a smooth flight all the way.* [C] • Flight is also the act or process of flying of birds or of other objects: *We watched a flight of geese* (= a group flying together). [C] ○ *Some people think that too much money is spent on space flight.* [U] • A **flight attendant** is a person in an aircraft whose job is to serve passengers and to make sure that safety rules are obeyed. • A **flight recorder** (also **black box**) is a small machine that records information about an aircraft during its flight, and which is used to discover the cause of an accident. • An activity or type of entertainment is described as **in-flight** if it is done or enjoyed during an aircraft flight: *an in-flight movie*

flight ESCAPE /flaɪt/ *n* [U] escape esp. from a dangerous situation • *The book describes the flight of the Jews from Germany at the beginning of World War II.*

flight STAIRS /flaɪt/ *n* [C] a set of stairs connecting one floor and the next in a building or other structure • *We had to climb three flights of stairs.*

flighty /'flaɪt·i/ *adj* not able to keep your attention or interest on one thing for long • *She played the part of a flighty, unsuccessful writer.*

flimsy /'flɪm·zi/ *adj* (of material) very thin, or (of a structure or object) poorly made and weak, and therefore easily broken or destroyed • *a flimsy dress* ○ *a flimsy building* • Flimsy also means weak and not persuasive: *They convicted the defendant on very flimsy evidence.*

flinch /flɪntʃ/ *v* [I] to make a sudden small movement because of pain or fear • *Now I'm going to move the eyepiece right up against your eye for a second—try not to flinch.*

fling THROW /flɪŋ/ *v* [T] *past* **flung** /flʌŋ/ to throw or move (something) suddenly and with force • *I rushed right up to him and flung my arms around his neck and hugged him.* ○ *She flung open the door and greeted us warmly.*

fling PERIOD /flɪŋ/ *n* [C usually sing] *infml* a short period of doing enjoyable things that you usually do not do, esp. having a sexual relationship • *She leaves college with a degree, has a fling with a married professor, and moves to Mississippi.*

flint /flɪnt/ *n* [C/U] a very hard gray or black stone

flip /flɪp/ *v* [I/T] **-pp-** to cause (something) to turn over quickly one or more times, or to cause (something) to move by making a short, quick motion • *I flipped (through) the pages of the dictionary to look up a word.* [I/T] ○ *You just flip a switch to turn on the computer.* [T] ○ *At the beginning of a football game, the referee flips a coin* (= throws it into the air so that it spins in falling) *to see which team gets the ball first.* [T]

flip /flɪp/ *n* [C] • *They settled the issue by a flip of the coin.* • A flip is also a jump in which you swing your legs over your head as your whole body turns around, so that you come down on your feet in the position you started from. • A **flip-flop** is a sudden and complete change of plans or opinion: *They did a complete flip-flop by deciding to have a large wedding rather than getting married secretly.* • The **flip side** of a situation is an opposite or less attractive result of a popular or attractive action: *More homelessness is the flip side of getting people off welfare.*

□**flip out** /'-'-/ *v adv* [I] *slang* to become extremely angry or to lose control of yourself from surprise or shock • *I nearly flipped out when she told me she and David were getting married.*

flippant /'flɪp·ənt/, *infml* **flip** /flɪp/ *adj* showing or having a rude attitude of not being serious esp. by trying to be amusing when most people expect you to be serious • *We had lost thousands of dollars, so we did not appreciate his flippant remark about "better luck next time."*

flipper /'flɪp·ər/ *n* [C] an armlike part used for swimming by any of various sea animals, such as SEALS and PENGUINS • A flipper is also a long, wide rubber shoe used for swimming. • PIC SNORKELING

flirt /flɜrt/ *v* [I] to behave as if sexually attracted to someone, often in a way that is not meant seriously • *He always flirts with waitresses.* ○ *(fig.) If he gets deeper into debt, he's flirting with disaster* (= he is risking very bad trouble). • If you **flirt with** an idea or action, you consider it briefly but are not seriously involved with it: *At one time he flirted with the idea of running for the presidency, though nothing came of it.*

flirt /flɜrt/ n [C] • *Mary has always been something of a flirt.*

flirtation /flərˈteɪ·ʃən/ n [C] • *It was just an office flirtation.* ○ *In his youth he had a brief flirtation with* (= period of being interested in) *communism.*

flirtatious /flərˈteɪ·ʃəs/ adj • *She had a lively, outgoing manner and was a bit flirtatious at times, when she'd had a drink or two.*

flit /flɪt/ v [I always + adv/prep] **-tt-** to fly or move quickly and lightly • *Bees flitted from flower to flower in the garden.*

float MOVE ON LIQUID /floʊt/ v [I/T] to stay or move easily on or over the surface of a liquid, or to cause (something) to move in this way • *An empty bottle will float on water.* [I] ○ *I'd float around for hours, just fishing.* [I] • *Fill the cups with hot coffee and float heavy cream on top.* [T] ○ *We spent a lazy afternoon floating down the river.* [I] • Float also means to move easily through air: *Fluffy white clouds were floating across the sky.* [I] ○ (*fig.*) *She removes the pins and her hair floats* (= moves gracefully) *down around her.* [I] ○ (*fig.*) *Reports have been floating around* (= heard from various people) *that the company might be for sale.* [I] • When he got his test results he was **floating on air** (= very happy).

float /floʊt/ n [C] a piece of light material that stays on the surface of water • *the float in a toilet tank*

float MONEY /floʊt/ v [T] to sell BONDS (= official papers given to people who loan money to a government or company) • *Cities float bond issues that are payable from property taxes.*

float VEHICLE /floʊt/ n [C] a large vehicle that is decorated and used in PARADES (= public celebrations in which people march, walk, and ride along a planned route) • *Marching bands and elaborate floats will be featured in the parade.*

float DRINK /floʊt/ n [C] a sweet drink with ice cream floating in it • *a root beer float*

flock /flɑk/ n [C] a group of sheep, goats, or birds, or a group of people • *a flock of ducks* ○ *a flock of reporters* • A flock is also the people who are members of a church.

flock /flɑk/ v [I] to move or gather together in large numbers • *Tourists flock to the village.* ○ *Crowds of people flocked to see the Picasso exhibition.* [+ to infinitive]

flog /flɑg, flɔːg/ v [T] **-gg-** (esp. in the past) to beat very hard with a stick or a WHIP as a punishment • *He flogged two sailors to death.*

flood COVER WITH WATER /flʌd/ v [I/T] to fill or become covered with water or to cause this to happen to (something) • *A burst pipe flooded the bathroom.* [T] ○ *The basements of many downtown buildings would flood whenever it rained.* [I]

flood /flʌd/ n [C] a large amount of water covering an area that is usually dry • *Kingston was heavily damaged by a flood.*

flooding /ˈflʌd·ɪŋ/ n [U] • *Rain caused flooding that washed out bridges and covered roads.*

flood FILL /flʌd/ v [I/T] to fill or be filled with a large amount or too much of something • *Sunlight floods in through a skylight in the ceiling.* [I always + adv/prep] ○ *In the 1960s, Cuban immigrants began to flood into Florida.* [I always + adv/prep] ○ *He worries that drugs will flood into his country.* [I always + adv/prep] ○ *We don't want them to flood the market with cheap imports.* [T] • If you flood an engine, you fill it with so much fuel that it will not start. [T]

flood /flʌd/ n [C] • *Planners are hoping for a flood of visitors when the center opens.* ○ *He was filled with a flood of new emotions.*

floodlight /ˈflʌd·laɪt/ n [C] a large, powerful electric light used for lighting outside areas, such as sports fields or buildings • *Tonight's game will be played under floodlights.*

floodlit /ˈflʌd·lɪt/ adj lit by FLOODLIGHTS • *The couple was standing in a floodlit aisle.*

floor SURFACE /flɔːr, floʊr/ n [C] the flat surface that you walk on when you are inside a building • *a tile floor* ○ *hardwood floors* ○ *The children sat on the floor.* • A **floorboard** is one of the long straight pieces of wood used to make a floor, or the floor of a car: *The floorboards creaked as we tiptoed across the room.* • A **floor lamp** is an electric light supported by a tall pole with a base on the floor. • A **floor plan** is a drawing that shows the shape, size, and arrangement of rooms in a building when viewed from above.

floor LEVEL OF BUILDING /flɔːr, floʊr/ n [C] a level of a building; a STORY LEVEL • *They rented office space on the second floor.* • USAGE: In the US, the first floor of a building is usually at ground level.

floor BOTTOM /flɔːr, floʊr/ n [C usually sing] the bottom surface of the sea, a forest, a valley, etc. • *Submarines were exploring the ocean floor for signs of the wreck.*

floor OPEN SPACE /flɔːr, floʊr/ n [C usually sing] a public space for having formal discussions • *The proposition was discussed on the Senate floor.* ○ *The chairman said that he would now take questions from the floor* (= from the ordinary people at the meeting).

floor SURPRISE /flɔːr, floʊr/ v [T] to surprise or shock (someone) • *She was completely floored when she heard that he was leaving the country.*

floor GO FAST /flɔːr, floʊr/ v [T] to drive (a car) as fast as it will go • *His buddy started the car and floored it.*

flop FALL /flɑp/ v [I always + adv/prep] **-pp-** to fall or drop heavily • *A newborn baby's head flops backward if you don't support it.*

flub

flop /flɑp/ *n* [U] • *He fell with a flop* (= he dropped heavily) *on the bed.*

flop FAILURE /flɑp/ *n* [C usually sing] *infml* a failure • *The movie was a complete flop.*

flop /flɑp/ *v* [I] **-pp-** • *Her first book flopped, but her second became a bestseller.*

flophouse /'flɑp·haʊs/ *n* [C] *pl* **flophouses** /'flɑp·haʊ·zəz, -səz/ a cheap, usually dirty, hotel • *That area of Manhattan used to be full of flophouses.*

floppy /'flɑp·i/ *adj* soft and easily bent; not able to maintain a firm shape or position • *a floppy hat* ○ *a dog with big, floppy ears* • A **floppy disk** is a round piece of plastic that can bend which is protected by a plastic cover and used to store computer information.

flora /'flɔːr·ə, 'floʊr·ə/ *n* [U] *specialized* all the plants of a particular area or period of time • *the flora of the Hawaiian Islands* • Compare FAUNA.

floral /'flɔːr·əl, 'floʊr·əl/ *adj* made of flowers, or decorated with a flowery pattern • *a floral display* ○ *floral curtains/wallpaper*

florid RED /'flɔːr·əd, 'flɑr·əd/ *adj slightly fml* (of a person's face) too red, esp. in a way that is unhealthy • *a florid complexion*

florid DECORATED /'flɔːr·əd, 'flɑr·əd/ *adj* with too much decoration or detail • *a florid architectural style* ○ *florid prose/speech*

florist /'flɔːr·əst, 'flɑr-/ *n* [C] a person who sells cut flowers and plants for inside the house

floss /flɑs, flɔːs/ *v* [T] to clean between (your teeth) using **dental floss** (= thin thread made especially for this purpose)

floss /flɑs, flɔːs/ *n* [C/U] **dental floss**, see at DENTAL

flotilla /floʊ'tɪl·ə/ *n* [C] a large group of boats or small ships, esp. military ships

flounce /flaʊns/ *v* [I always + adv/prep] to walk quickly with large noticeable movements, esp. to attract attention or show that you are angry • *"Don't expect any help from me!" she said, as she flounced out of the room.*

flounder MOVE AWKWARDLY /'flaʊn·dər/ *v* [I] to move awkwardly or to be in an awkward or difficult situation • *She floundered around in the water.* ○ *He lost the next page of his speech and floundered for a few seconds.* ○ *His business was flourishing, but his marriage was floundering.*

flounder FISH /'flaʊn·dər/ *n* [C/U] *pl* **flounder** a flat fish that is used as food

flour /flaʊr/ *n* [U] powder made from grain, esp. wheat, used for making bread, cakes, pasta, pastry, etc. • *wheat/rye flour* ○ *three cups of flour*

flour /flaʊr/ *v* [T] to put a thin layer of flour on (something) • *Flour the board, then roll out the dough.*

flourish SUCCEED /'flɜr·ɪʃ/ *v* [I] to grow or develop successfully • *Parts of the city continue to flourish.* ○ *This is the perfect environment for our company to flourish and expand in.*

flourish WAVE /'flɜr·ɪʃ/ *v* [T] to move (something) in your hand in order to make people look at it • *She ran up to her father, flourishing her diploma.*

flourish /'flɜr·ɪʃ/ *n* [C] • *I pulled into the driveway with a flourish* (= a noticeable movement).

flout /flaʊt/ *v* [T] to intentionally disobey (a rule or law), or to intentionally avoid (behavior that is usual or expected) • *They think they can flout the law and get away with it.* ○ *He conducted business in his pajamas to flout convention.*

flow /floʊ/ *v* [I] (esp. of liquids, gases, or electricity) to move in one direction, esp. continuously and easily • *Air flows over an aircraft's wing faster than it flows under it.* ○ *Lava from the volcano was flowing down the hillside.* ○ *An electrical current flows from positive to negative.* ○ *Many rivers flow into the Pacific Ocean.* ○ *With fewer cars on the roads, traffic is flowing* (= moving forward) *more smoothly than usual.* • Something can be said to flow if it hangs down loosely and attractively: *Her long, red hair flowed down over shoulders.* ○ *(fig.) My thoughts flow more easily* (= I can think more easily) *if I work on a word processor.*

flow /floʊ/ *n* [C usually sing] • *This drug increases the flow of blood to the heart.* ○ *(fig.) Music interrupted the flow of the conversation* (= the regular exchange between speakers).

flower /'flaʊ·ər, flaʊr/ *n* [C] the part of a plant that is often brightly colored and sometimes has a pleasant smell, or a plant that grows these parts • *to cut/gather/pick flowers* ○ *a bunch/bouquet/vase of flowers* ○ *These flowers bloom in the late spring.* • A **flowerbed** is an area of ground or part of a garden where flowers are planted. • A **flowerpot** is a container usually made of clay or plastic in which a plant is grown. • The related adjective is FLORAL.

flower /'flaʊ·ər, flaʊr/ *v* [I] • *Our shrubs flower* (= produce flowers) *in late summer.*

flowered /'flaʊ·ərd, flaʊrd/ *adj* decorated with pictures of flowers • *flowered curtains* ○ *a flowered dress*

flowery /'flaʊ·ə·ri, 'flaʊr·i/ *adj* covered with pictures of flowers • *a flowery blouse* • *(disapproving)* If a speech or writing style is flowery, it uses too many complicated or unusual words or phrases.

flown /floʊn/ *past participle of* FLY

flu /fluː/, *esp. medical* **influenza** /ˌɪn·fluː'en·zə/ *n* [U] an infectious illness like a very bad cold that also causes a fever • *Robby has a bad case of the flu.*

flub /flʌb/ *v* [I/T] **-bb-** *infml* to fail or make a mistake, esp. when performing • *He really flubbed badly by not catching the ball.* [I] ○ *Sheila flubbed her lines in the second act.* [T]

fluctuate /ˈflʌk·tʃəˌweɪt/ v [I] to change or vary frequently between one level or thing and another • *Vegetable prices fluctuate according to the season.* ○ *I fluctuate between feeling really happy and utterly miserable.*

fluctuation /ˌflʌk·tʃəˈweɪ·ʃən/ n [C/U] • *fluctuations in temperature* [C] ○ *A certain amount of fluctuation in quality is unavoidable.* [U]

flue /fluː/ n [C] a pipe that leads from a fire, STOVE, or heater to the outside of a building, taking smoke, gases, or hot air away

fluent /ˈfluː·ənt/ adj (of a person) able to speak a language easily and well, or (of a language) spoken easily and without many pauses • *She was fluent in French by the time she was five.* ○ *He speaks fluent Chinese.*

fluently /ˈfluː·ənt·li/ adv • *I'd like to speak English fluently.*

fluency /ˈfluː·ən·si/ n [U] • *This job requires fluency in two or more African languages.*

fluff SOFT MASS /flʌf/ n [U] a soft mass of fibers, feathers, or hair • *cotton fluff* ○ *The cat, a ball of white fluff, darted into the house and started to lick its fur.* ○ *We'd lie on our backs and blow the dandelion fluff into the neighbor's yard.*

fluff /flʌf/ v [T/M] to shake (a mass of fibers or feathers) so there is more air between the feathers or fibers, making the mass appear larger • *She fluffed out her hair.* [M] ○ *Make the beds and don't forget to fluff the pillows.* [T]

fluffy /ˈflʌf·i/ adj light and full of air, or soft and furry • *a fluffy mohair sweater* ○ *Beat the eggs and sugar together until they are light and fluffy.*

fluff USELESS INFORMATION /flʌf/ n [U] useless or unimportant information • *Don't expect all fluff—like most good satire, this contains some moments of truth.*

fluid /ˈfluː·əd/ n [C/U] a substance that flows and is not solid • *The doctor drained some fluid from her lungs.* [U] • (*medical*) Fluids are liquids that you drink: *Dr. Tay says I need rest and lots of fluids.* [C]

fluid /ˈfluː·əd/ adj having a flowing or changing quality • *a dancer's fluid movements* ○ *The situation remains fluid—we offered her the job, but she hasn't responded yet.* • A **fluid ounce** (*abbreviation* **fl. oz.**) is a measurement of liquid equal to .03 liter.

fluke /fluːk/ n [C usually sing] something, usually a good thing, that has happened as result of chance instead of skill or planning • *He's trying to prove that his last victory wasn't a fluke.*

flung /flʌŋ/ past simple and past participle of FLING THROW

flunk /flʌŋk/ v [I/T] infml to fail (an exam or course of study) • *I almost flunked chemistry.* [T] • If students **flunk out** of school, they are forced to leave school because their work is not good enough: *She flunked out of high school.* [I]

flunky /ˈflʌŋ·ki/ n [C] a person who does unimportant work or who has few or no important responsibilities and shows too much respect toward their employer • *He could snap his fingers and get his flunky to do it.*

fluorescent /ˌflʊrˈes·ənt, ˌflɔːr-, ˌflɔʊr-/ adj (of a substance) giving off a very bright light when electricity or other waves go through it • *The map was marked with a thin, fluorescent-green line.* • **Fluorescent lights** are very bright, usually tube-shaped electric lights used esp. in offices.

fluoride /ˈflʊr·ɑɪd, ˈflɔːr-, ˈflɔʊr-/ n [U] a chemical substance sometimes added to water or **toothpaste** (= substance for cleaning teeth) in order to help keep teeth healthy

flurry /ˈflɜr·i/ n [C] a sudden light fall of snow, blown in different directions by the wind • *Heavy snow will be tapering off to flurries in the morning.* • A flurry is also a lot of sudden activity: *There was a flurry of excitement as the president walked in.*

flush BECOME RED /flʌʃ/ v [I] (of a person) to become red in the face, esp. as a result of strong emotions, heat, or alcohol • *He felt his face flush as he remembered her kiss.*

flush /flʌʃ/ n [C usually sing] • *a flush of embarrassment*

flushed /flʌʃt/ adj • *Her cheeks were flushed and she was breathing hard.*

flush LEVEL /flʌʃ/ adj, adv on the same level so that no part is higher or lower or sticks out more than another • *The sprinklers are mounted flush with the ceiling.*

flush RICH /flʌʃ/ adj infml having a lot of money • *The Pequot tribe in Connecticut is flush with millions from a new gambling casino.*

flush CARD GAMES /flʌʃ/ n [C] a number of playing cards held by one player that are all from the same SUIT (= type)

flush EMPTY /flʌʃ/ v [I/T] to operate (a toilet) after it has been used by pressing a handle or button, or (of a toilet) to operate in this way • *Why don't you ever flush the toilet after you've used it?* [T] ○ *I can't get the toilet to flush.* [I]

flush /flʌʃ/ n [C] • *The toilet tank empties during a flush.*

□ **flush (out)** obj, **flush** obj **(out)** /ˈ-ˈ-/ v prep [T/M] to clean (something) by forcing a large amount of water on or through it • *Rinse the fabric in cool water to flush out the paint.* [M]

□ **flush out** obj, **flush** obj **out** /ˈ-ˈ-/ v prep [M] to force (a person or animal) to leave a place where they are hiding • *Police prepared to use tear gas to flush the demonstrators out.*

fluster /ˈflʌs·tər/ v [T] to make (someone) nervous or upset, esp. when they are trying to do something • *Don't let that new tax form fluster you—it's not as bad as it looks.*

flustered /ˈflʌs·tərd/ adj • *If I look flustered it's because I'm trying to do 20 things at once.*

flute /fluːt/ n [C/U] a tube-shaped musical instrument with a row of holes along its side that are covered by the fingers to vary the notes and played by blowing into a hole near one end, or this type of instrument generally

flutist /'fluːʈ·əst/ n [C] a flute player

flutter /'flʌʈ·ər/ v [I/T] to move in quick irregular motions, or to cause (something) to move this way • *The flags fluttered in the breeze.* [I] • *If your heart flutters, it beats faster than usual, often from excitement.* [I]

flutter /'flʌʈ·ər/ n [C usually sing] • *There was a flutter of wings overhead.*

flux /flʌks/ n [U] continuous change • *Everything is in a state of flux.*

fly TRAVEL THROUGH AIR /flaɪ/ v [I/T] past simple **flew** /fluː/, past part **flown** /floʊn/ (of creatures, objects, or aircraft) to move through the air, or (of people) to travel by aircraft • *The building just exploded, and glass flew through the air.* [I] ○ *We enjoy watching the birds fly over the water.* [I] ○ *Are you planning to fly or drive to Toronto?* [I] ○ *Some of our pilots have been flying* (= operating an aircraft) *for 20 years.* [I] ○ *What airline are you flying (on)?* (= traveling on as a passenger)? [I/T] • If you **fly by the seat of your pants**, you decide what to do at the time something happens rather than being prepared for it. • A **flying saucer** (also **UFO**) is a strange object shaped like a disk that some people claim they have seen in the sky.

fly /flaɪ/, **fly ball** /'flaɪˈbɔːl/ n [C] in baseball, a ball that has been hit high into the air • *He caught the fly in deep center field.*

flyer, flier /'flaɪ·ər/ n [C] a person who operates an aircraft or travels on one as a passenger

fly MOVE QUICKLY /flaɪ/ v [I] past simple **flew** /fluː/, past part **flown** /floʊn/ to move or go quickly or suddenly • *Theo was startled when the door flew open.* ○ *Saying she was late, Cathy flew by me and ran outside.* ○ *The summer seems to have flown by* (= passed quickly). • If you **fly off the handle** or **fly into a rage**, you suddenly become very angry.

fly INSECT /flaɪ/ n [C] a small insect with two wings • A **fly in the ointment** is something that spoils a situation that could have been pleasant.

fly PANTS /flaɪ/ n [C usually sing] the covered opening at the front of a pair of pants

fly WAVE /flaɪ/ v [I/T] past simple **flew** /fluː/, past part **flown** /floʊn/ to move around in the air while being held at one end, or to cause (something) attached at one end to be moved • *Flags flew from the front of every house.* [I]

fly–by–night /'flaɪˌbɑɪˌnaɪt/ adj [not gradable] *disapproving* (esp. of a business) not able to be trusted, and likely to stop operating without any notice • *a fly-by-night operation*

flyer /'flaɪ·ər/ n [C] a FLIER PAPER • See also **flyer** at FLY TRAVEL THROUGH AIR.

FM /'ef,em, ˌ-'-/ n [U] abbreviation for one of two main types of radio waves used to broadcast in the US • Compare AM RADIO.

foal /foʊl/ n [C] a young horse

foam /foʊm/ n [U] a mass of small, usually white, bubbles formed on the surface of a liquid • *The waves were high and capped with foam.* • Foam is also a type of light material made by adding gas bubbles to a liquid, then letting it cool, used esp. in packaging. • *The cushions are filled with* **foam rubber** (= a soft rubber made with bubbles of gas).

foam /foʊm/ v [I] • *The suds in the sink foamed up when she added hot water.*

focus CENTER /'foʊ·kəs/, **focal point** n [C] pl **focuses** or **foci** /'foʊ·saɪ, -kaɪ/ the central point of something, esp. of attention or interest • *The focus of attention has shifted from the economy to improving the public schools.* ○ *Violence on TV was the focal point of their concern.*

focus /'foʊ·kəs/ v [I/T] to direct attention toward (something or someone) • *Tonight's program focuses on homelessness.* [I]

focus SCIENCE /'foʊ·kəs/, **focal point** n [C/U] pl **focuses** or **foci** /'foʊ·saɪ, -kaɪ/ the point where waves of light, heat, or sound meet after moving toward each other • A photograph or camera that is in focus has a clear image, while one that is out of focus does not have a clear image. [U]

focus /'foʊ·kəs/ v [I/T] to adjust (something) in order to see more clearly • *I focused the binoculars on the bird on a branch of the tree.* [T]

fodder /'fad·ər/ n [U] food given to cows, horses, and other farm animals • *(fig.) The charges of sex in the White House are fodder for* (= have encouraged) *late-evening jokes on television.*

foe /foʊ/ n [C] an enemy, or a competitor • *He appointed a staunch foe of abortion to head the party's platform committee.*

fog /fɔːɡ, faɡ/ n [C/U] a mass of cloud consisting of small drops of water near the surface of the earth • *Heavy fog made driving conditions dangerous.* [U] • If something is **fogbound**, it cannot operate as usual because of fog: *Their flight was canceled because the airport was fogbound.* • A **foghorn** is a loud horn sounded by a ship in a fog as a signal to other ships of its position.

fog /fɔːɡ, faɡ/ v [I/T] **-gg-** • *The airport in Washington was fogged in* (= could not operate because of fog).

foggy /'fɔː·ɡi, 'faɡ·i/ adj • *a cold, foggy day*

□**fog up** (obj), **fog** (obj) **up** /'-'-/ v adv [I/M] to cover (a surface such as glass or a mirror) with small drops of water and make it difficult to see through or reflect an image • *My windshield kept fogging up, and it was hard to see the road.* [I] ○ *The steam fogged my glasses up.* [M]

foible /'fɔɪ·bəl/ n [C usually pl] a small fault or foolish habit • *We all have our little foibles.*

foil METAL SHEET /fɔɪl/ n [U] a very thin sheet

of metal, used esp. for wrapping food • *aluminum foil*

foil PREVENT /fɔɪl/ *v* [T] to prevent (someone or something) from being successful • *An attempted coup against the country's military ruler was foiled yesterday.*

foil COMPARISON /fɔɪl/ *n* [C] someone or something that makes another's good or bad qualities all the more noticeable • *The older, cynical character in the play is the perfect foil for the innocent William.*

foil BLADE /fɔɪl/ *n* [C] a thin, light weapon with a long blade used in the sport of FENCING

foist *obj* **on/upon** *obj* /ˈfɔɪst·ɔːn, -ɑn, -ə,pɑn/ *v prep* [T], **foist** *obj* **off** **on** *obj* /ˈfɔɪstˈɔːfˈɔːn, -ɑn/ *v adv prep* to force (someone) to have or experience (something they do not want) • *She charged that junk food is being foisted on children by TV commercials.*

fold BEND /foʊld/ *v* [I/T] to bend (esp. paper or cloth) so that one part of it lies on the other part, or to be able to be bent in this way • *He took his clothes out of the dryer and carefully folded them.* [T] ○ *She folded up the map and put it back in her bag.* [M] ○ *The tray table folds up so that it fits in a closet.* [I]
• If you fold your hands or arms, you bring them together and cross them: *He folded his arms across his chest.* [T]
• A **folding chair** is a chair that can be folded into a smaller size to make it easier to store or carry.

folding chair

fold /foʊld/ *n* [C] • *If you just make folds along the dotted lines, you can seal it and mail it as an envelope.*

fold FAIL /foʊld/ *v* [I] (of a business) to close because of failure • *Many small businesses fold within the first year.*

fold SHARED BELIEFS /foʊld/ *n* [C/U] the safety or comfort of belonging to a group that shares the same beliefs • *The Democrats attracted many immigrants to the fold.* [U] • A fold is a fenced area on a farm where sheep are kept during the night. [C]

–fold NUMBER /ˌfoʊld/ *combining form* having the stated number of parts, or multiplied by the stated number • *There has been more than a 30-fold increase in Internet users in the past two years.*

▫**fold in** *obj*, **fold** *obj* **in** /ˈ-ˈ-/ *v prep* [M] to mix (a food substance) into another by turning it gently with a spoon • *Fold in the flour and add two eggs.*

folder /ˈfoʊl·dər/ *n* [C] a folded piece of thin cardboard for holding loose papers

foliage /ˈfoʊ·liːˌɪdʒ/ *n* [U] the leaves of a plant or tree • *Dense foliage blocked the path.*

folk /foʊk/ *adj* [not gradable] traditional to or typical of the people of a particular group or country • *folk art/dance* • **Folklore** is the traditional stories, beliefs, and customs of a

group of people. • **Folk music** is the traditional music of a people and a **folk song** a traditional song from the past. • A **folk singer** is someone who specializes in singing folk songs. • A **folktale** is a traditional story.

folks /foʊks/, **folk** /foʊk/ *pl n* people, esp. those of a particular group or type • *Some folks have been waiting over an hour to buy tickets.* • Your folks are your parents: *I'm going home over Thanksgiving to see my folks.* • You can say folks if you want to speak in a friendly way to people you do not know: *Well, folks, thanks for watching Channel 4 news—that's about it for this evening.* • LP TITLES AND FORMS OF ADDRESS

folksy /ˈfoʊk·si/ *adj* [*-er/-est* only] very friendly and informal in style • *His folksy personality sets the tone for the show.*

follicle /ˈfɑl·ɪ·kəl/ *n* [C] any of the very small holes in the skin that a hair grows from

follow MOVE AFTER /ˈfɑl·oʊ/ *v* [I/T] to move along after (someone or something), or to move along (a route or path) • *The dog followed us home.* [T] ○ *He drove ahead and we followed in our own car.* [I] ○ *Follow this road for the next two miles.* [T] • To follow someone is also to move along after them in order to watch where they go: *She had the feeling she was being followed.* [T] • If you **follow in** someone's **footsteps**, you do the same thing as they previously did: *She followed in her mother's footsteps and started her own business.* • To **follow** your **nose** is to go straight in front of you: *There's a gas station up ahead about a mile, so just follow your nose.* • To **follow suit** is to do the same thing: *When one airline reduces its ticket prices, the rest usually follow suit.*

follow HAPPEN AFTER /ˈfɑl·oʊ/ *v* [I/T] to happen after (something else) in order or time • *We were not prepared for what followed.* [I] ○ *A wine-and-cheese reception will follow the meeting, so please stay.* [T]

following /ˈfɑl·ə·wɪŋ/ *adj* [not gradable] • *I'm busy on Thursday, but I'm free the following day.* ○ *The following items were found—a ring, a wallet, and a watch.*

following /ˈfɑl·ə·wɪŋ/ *pl n* • *Will the following please stand—Neal, Crisonino, Druback, Thompson.*

following /ˈfɑl·ə·wɪŋ/ *prep* • *Following the ballgame, there will be a fireworks display.*

follow OBEY /ˈfɑl·oʊ/ *v* [T] to obey (someone), or to act according to (something) • *Follow the instructions in taking the medicine.* ○ *I decided to follow her advice.* ○ *If you follow the signs, you will have no trouble finding the airport.*

follower /ˈfɑl·ə·wər/ *n* [C] someone who obeys or supports another person or their ideas • *He discouraged his followers from using violence to achieve their demands.*

following /ˈfɑl·ə·wɪŋ/ *n* [C] • *The religious group has a large following among young people.*

follow [UNDERSTAND] /'fɑl·oʊ/ v [T] to understand • *He spoke so rapidly we could hardly follow what he said.*

follow [INTERESTED IN] /'fɑl·oʊ/ v [T] to be actively interested in (something), or to give your attention to (something) • *Do you follow football?* ○ *We've followed her political career for many years.*

follower /'fɑl·ə·wər/ n [C]

follow [BE RESULT] /'fɑl·oʊ/ v [I] to happen as a result, or to be a likely result • *If he has been violent before, it follows that he will be violent again.* [+ *that* clause]

□ **follow through** /'--'-/ v adv [I] to continue something until it is completed • *The city has raised the money for more teachers—now it has to follow through and hire them.* • In sports, to follow through is to continue a swinging motion of the arms or legs when making a play: *You can't drive the golf ball unless you follow through after hitting it.*

follow-through /'fɑl·oʊˌθruː/ n [U] • *They made a good start at improving prison conditions, but unless there's follow-through, the reforms won't last.* • In sports, a follow-through is the continuation of a swinging motion of the arms or legs when making a play: *My tennis instructor says I need to have better follow-through on my backhand.*

□ **follow** obj **up** /'--'-/ v adv [T], **follow up on** /ˌ--'-ˌ-/ v adv prep to discover more about (something) or to take further action connected with it • *As a news reporter, when something important happens, I have to follow it up.*

follow-up /'fɑl·oʊˌʌp/ n [C] something done after an earlier event that is connected with it • *I've got to go in for a follow-up to the dentist next week.*

follow-up /'fɑl·oʊˌʌp/ adj [not gradable] • *a follow-up visit* ○ *Reporters can have one follow-up question.*

folly /'fɑl·i/ n [C/U] foolishness, or a foolish action or belief • *It would be folly to attempt a trip in this snowstorm.* [+ *to* infinitive]

foment /foʊ'ment/ v [T] *fml* to cause (something bad or illegal) to develop • *to foment revolution*

fond /fɑnd/ adj [-er/-est only] having feelings of affection for someone or something, or having a liking for an activity • *I'm really fond of my aunt and enjoy seeing her.* ○ *She had fond memories of her childhood.* ○ *Charles is fond of driving, so I'm happy just to be a passenger.*

fondly /'fɑn·dli/ adv • *He smiled fondly at his wife.*

fondness /'fɑnd·nəs/ n [U] • *Ruth has a real fondness (= liking) for old houses.*

fondle /'fɑn·dəl/ v [T] to touch in a gentle and loving way, or to touch in a sexual way • *He fondled the baby's feet.* ○ *She accused him of fondling her in the back of a taxi.*

font [LETTERS] /fɑnt/ n [C] a set of printed letters, numbers, and other symbols of the same style • *The printer can produce a variety of fonts in virtually any type size.*

font [CONTAINER] /fɑnt/ n [C] a container for the water used in BAPTISM (= religious ceremony)

food /fuːd/ n [C/U] something that can be taken in by an animal and used to keep it alive and allow it to grow or develop, or such things considered as a whole • *baby/cat food* [U] ○ *There were a lot of frozen foods in the refrigerator.* [C] • Sometimes food means only the solid material eaten by animals, and not liquids: *He has had no food or drink for 24 hours.* [U] • If something is **food for thought**, it is something to seriously think about. • A **food chain** is a series of living things in which each group eats organisms from the group lower than itself in the series. • **Food poisoning** is an illness caused by eating food that contains harmful bacteria. • A **food processor** is an electric machine that cuts, slices, or mixes food quickly. • **Food stamps** are specially printed pieces of paper worth specific dollar amounts which the US government provides to poor people for buying food. • A **foodstuff** is any substance used as food.

fool /fuːl/ n [C] a person who behaves in a silly way, or someone who lacks judgment • *Crazy I may be, but I try not to be a fool.* ○ *I know I'm making a fool of myself, but I can't help it.* ○ *They never fail to make Americans out as a bunch of damn fools.*

fool /fuːl/ v [I/T] • *She tries to fool* (= deceive) *people about her age by wearing heavy makeup and coloring her hair.* [T] ○ *You don't owe me a penny, I was only fooling* (= joking). [I] • To **fool around** is to behave in a silly way: *She fools around a lot—she's always joking or laughing.* • If you **fool around** you do something you enjoy: *We have a real good garden, and we enjoy fooling around with it.* • If someone **fools around**, they have sex with someone other than their husband, wife, or usual sexual partner: *Some people think that women just want commitment and men just want to fool around.* • If you **fool with** something you handle it, esp. for no particular purpose: *The sheriff sat in the car for a few moments, fooling with some papers on a clipboard.* • To **fool with** something can also mean to work with something difficult or dangerous: *I just don't like to fool with these computers.*

fool /fuːl/ adj [not gradable] *not standard* • *I made a damn fool* (= stupid) *mistake, but I'll never do it again.*

foolish /'fuː·lɪʃ/ adj stupid or unwise • *She was afraid that she would look foolish if she refused to go along with her friends.* ○ *It would be foolish of us to assume that everything will work out fine.*

foolishly /'fuː·lɪʃ·li/ adv • *I would just like to know that my taxes are not being foolishly spent.*

foolishness /'fuː·lɪʃ·nəs/ *n* [U] • *My father was not one to tolerate foolishness.*

foolhardy /'fuːl,hɑrd·i/ *adj* [-*er*/-*est* only] foolishly brave, or taking unnecessary risks • *He made a foolhardy attempt to climb the tree to recover his kite.*

foolproof /'fuːl·pruːf/ *adj* [not gradable] (of a plan, method, or machine) designed to be easily done or operated without possibility of mistake or failure • *It's not a foolproof system and it never will be.*

foot BODY PART /fʊt/ *n* [C] *pl* **feet** /fiːt/ the part of the body at the bottom of the leg on which a person or animal stands • *I've got a blister on my left foot.* ○ *He got to/jumped to/rose to his feet* (= stood up) *to get a better look at the parade passing by.* • *I've been* **on** *my* **feet** (= standing) *all day serving customers.* • *The driver of the stolen car fled the scene* **on foot** (= walking). • *The doctor said he'd be* **(back) on** *his* **feet** *again soon* (= he would soon be healthy). • A **footbridge** is a bridge used by people who are walking. • A **foothold** is a place where you can safely put your feet, esp. when climbing: *She searched desperately for a foothold in the steep rock.* • A **foothold** is also a strong position from which you can achieve what you want: *In buying their business, the company gains a major foothold in a market it considers critical to the future of the industry.* • A **footpath** is a path for walking. • A **footprint** is a mark left on a surface by a foot: *There was not a single footprint in the sand.* • **Footsteps** are the movements or the sounds made by a person when walking: *We never saw anyone in the building, but sometimes we heard footsteps down the hall.* • A **footstool** is a low piece of furniture that supports a person's feet when they are sitting. • **Footwear** is shoes, boots, or other outer coverings for the human foot. • **Footwork** is the use of the feet in sports and dancing, esp. when it is skillful: *He was one of the all-time great boxers with his quick jab and dazzling footwork.*

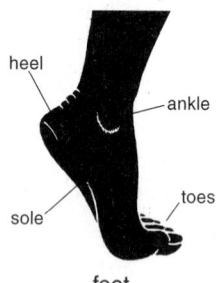

heel

ankle

sole

toes

foot

foot MEASUREMENT /fʊt/ (*abbreviation* **ft.**, *symbol* **'**) *n* [C] *pl* **foot** or **feet** /fiːt/ a unit of measurement of length equal to 12 inches or 0.348 meter

foot BOTTOM /fʊt/ *n* [U] the bottom or end of a space or object • *She dreamed she saw someone* standing at the foot of her bed. • **Foothills** are low hills at the base of a mountain or mountain range. • **Footlights** are a row of lights along the bottom at the front of a stage in a theater. • A **footnote** is a note at the bottom of a page that gives extra information about something in the text on that page.

foot PAY /fʊt/ *v* • To **foot the bill** is to pay an amount of money: *His parents can't afford to foot the bill for his college education.*

footage /'fʊt·ɪdʒ/ *n* [U] film or **videotape** that shows a single event or place • *Footage showing entire city blocks in flames flickered nightly on TV.*

football /'fʊt·bɔːl/ *n* [C/U] (the oval ball used in) a game played by two teams in which each team tries to kick, run with, or throw the ball across the opposing team's goal line to score points. American and Canadian football differ in the number of players, the size of the field, and some rules of play. • *Mom bought me a football.* [C] ○ *Let's play football after lunch.* [U] • Football also means SOCCER in most of the world. [C/U]

footing FEET /'fʊt·ɪŋ/ *n* [U] a firm position of the feet • *He lost his footing and tumbled into the water.*

footing CONDITION /'fʊt·ɪŋ/ *n* [U] a position or condition on which something exists • *Both sides need to begin negotiations on equal footing.*

footlocker /'fʊt,lɑk·ər/ *n* [C] a large, rectangular container used to hold clothing and personal possessions

footloose /'fʊt·luːs/ *adj* free to do what pleases you or go where you like • *I'm jealous of those footloose women who have been following their hearts all these years I've been raising children.*

for TO BE GIVEN /fɔːr, fər/ *prep* intended to be given to • *There's a phone message for you on your desk.* ○ *There will be a prize for the best costume at the Halloween party.*

for PURPOSE /fɔːr, fər/ *prep* having the purpose of • *What do you imagine he uses this old thing for?* ○ *Why don't you take an aspirin for your headache* (= to stop it)? • If you say or do something **for effect**, you do it to get a particular reaction from someone. • *You can have that book* **for keeps** (= to have forever). • *The lamps on the top shelf are not* **for sale** (= available to be bought). • *Her name's Alexandria, or Alex* **for short** (= using a short form). • *I drove my van across country just* **for the hell of** *it* (= without any purpose except amusement). ○ (*infml*) *He signed a new contract and got a $500,000 signing bonus* **for starters** (= as the first thing with others to follow).

for BECAUSE OF /fɔːr, fər/ *prep* because of; as a result of (doing something) • *She was stopped for speeding.* ○ *The things we do for love!* ○ *For some reason, she isn't interested in going out at all tonight.* ○ *Certain Chicago restaurants are* famous for their deep-dish pizza. • (*infml*) If you say that you would not do something **for anything (in the world)** it means that you certainly would not do it: *It was a fantastic party—I wouldn't have missed it for anything.* • If you do something **for old times' sake**, you do it as a reminder of the times you did it in the past: *We get together once a year for old times' sake.*

for INSTEAD OF /fɔːr, fər/ *prep* instead of; to help • *Let me carry those groceries to the car for you.*

for TIME / DISTANCE /fɔːr, fər/ *prep* showing amount of time or distance • *We drove for miles.* ○ *She's out of town for a few days on business.* • If something happens **for good** it is permanent: *She says she's leaving him for good.* • "*Hodge's argument is utterly rotten,*" he said, and that was **for openers** (= the first thing he said).

for OCCASION /fɔːr, fər/ *prep* on the occasion of or at the time of • *What are you getting mom and dad for Christmas?* ○ *We're planning a party for Stephen's birthday.* ○ *The neighbors invited us for dinner* (= to eat with them). ○ *What's for lunch* (= what will we eat)*?* • People say **for crying out loud** when they are annoyed: *Oh, for crying out loud, would you stop leaving your magazines all over the house!* • *The union voted not to strike* **for the time being/for the moment/for now** (= at this time).

for CONSIDERING /fɔːr, fər/ *prep* considering (something or someone with reference to things or people as they usually are) • *This winter has been mild for Canada.* ○ *I think Kristy is very mature for her age.* • *The book's range is broad, covering not just the main branches of science,* **for example** (= considering one item like this), *but more specialized areas as well.* • You say **for goodness/Pete's/heaven's/pity's sake** when you are giving an order or making a request to show that you are angry or have lost patience: *For goodness' sake, don't let her know I told you!* • *Can you tell us a little of your background?* **For instance** (= As an example), *where were you born?*

for SUPPORT /fɔːr, fər/ *prep* in support of or agreement with • *I voted for her in the last election.* ○ *We thought about moving, and I was all for it, but my wife didn't want to.*

for IN RELATION TO /fɔːr, fər/ *prep* in relation to (someone or something) • *Her feelings for him were obvious.* ○ *That jacket is a bit big for you.* • **For all** (= Despite) *those years of lessons, she doesn't play the piano very well.* ○ *Once the rollercoaster got going, we were hanging on* **for dear life** (= as if we feared we would die). • *I'm certainly not attracted to him—***for one thing** (= one reason is), *he's too old.* • (*infml*) When something is **for real** it is not false and is what it appears to be: *Is this letter a joke or is it for real?* • People say **for what it's worth** when they care about something but don't

think the person they are talking to will care about it: *You may not want to see me again, but for what it's worth, I want you to know I still love you.*

for PAYMENT /fɔːr, fər/ *prep* (getting) in exchange • *If I take the car in, it'll be $45 for a tuneup.* • (*infml*) *She bought that antique chest* **for a song** (= very cheaply). • *She said the table was mine* **for nothing/for the asking/for free** (= without payment or effort).

for REPRESENTING /fɔːr, fər/ *prep* representing (an organization or country) • *Michael works for a Washington-based foundation.* ○ *She carried the flag for the US at the opening ceremonies.*

for TOWARD /fɔːr, fər/ *prep* toward; in the direction of • *Just follow signs for the airport once you're on the highway.* • *The new teacher made a lot of changes, mostly* **for the better** (= they improved things). • *The doctor says her condition has changed* **for the worse** (= it has become worse).

for MEANING /fɔːr, fər/ *prep* meaning; representing • *What's another word for "happy"?*

for TO GET /fɔːr, fər/ *prep* in order to get or have • *I had to wait half an hour for the bus.* ○ *Call the phone number below for more information.* • If you know something **for sure/certain** you know it is true: *I saw him and knew for sure that he had come to see me.* • *It looks like we're* **in for** *rain* (= going to get it).

for DUTY /fɔːr, fər/ *prep* the duty or responsibility of • *It's not for her to say whether I should cut my hair.*

for BECAUSE /fɔːr, fər/ *conjunction* because; as • *She told the truth, for she had nothing to lose.*

forage /ˈfɔːr·ɪdʒ, ˈfɑr-/ *v* [I/T] to go searching, esp. for food • *Wild dogs roam the streets, foraging for food.* [I]

foray /ˈfɔːr·eɪ, ˈfoʊr-/ *n* [C] a brief attempt at or involvement in an activity outside a person's or organization's usual range of activities • *The opera company has made curious forays into contemporary music in recent seasons.* • A foray is also a sudden and quick attack by a group of soldiers on an enemy area.

forbear /fɔːrˈber, -ˈbær/ *v* [I] *past simple* **forbore** /fɔːrˈbɔːr, -ˈboʊr/, *past part* **forborne** /fɔːr·ˈbɔːrn, -ˈboʊrn/ *dated literary* to prevent yourself from saying or doing something, esp. in a way that shows patience • *We must forbear to take the Lord's name in vain.* [+ *to* infinitive]

forbearance /fɔːrˈber·əns, -ˈbær-/ *n* [U] *literary* • *He had been sustained by his wife's love and forbearance* (= patience).

forbid /fərˈbɪd, fɔːr-/ *v* [T] **forbidding**, *past simple* **forbade** /fərˈbæd, fɔːr-, -ˈbeɪd/ *or* **forbid**, *past part* **forbidden** /fərˈbɪd·ᵊn, fɔːr-/ to not allow (something), or to order (someone) not to do something • *You can't forbid me to go.* • If you say **heaven/God forbid** you mean you hope what you say does not happen: *If the* *building exploded, God forbid, we'd be able to respond to the disaster.*

forbidden /fər'bɪd-ᵊn, fɔːr-/ *adj* not permitted, esp. by rule or law • *Automobiles are forbidden on the island.* ○ *Smoking is strictly forbidden.*

forbidding /fər'bɪd-ɪŋ, fɔːr-/ *adj* appearing unfriendly, threatening, or difficult • *The mountains looked dark and forbidding.*

force PHYSICAL POWER /fɔːrs, foʊrs/ *n* [C/U] physical, often violent, strength or power • *The force of the wind knocked down many trees during the hurricane.* [U] ○ *She had to use force to get the old window open.* [U] • (*specialized*) In science, a force is a power that causes an object to move or that changes movement. [C/U] • *Because of the threat of violence, the police are out* **in force** *tonight* (= there are many of them out).

force /fɔːrs, foʊrs/ *v* [T] • *If the piece won't fit in the hole, don't force it.* ○ *He forced his way through the crowd to reach the exit.* • To force a lock, door, window, etc., is to break it in order to get in: *I forgot my house key, so I had to force a window.* • If you **force-feed** a person or an animal, you make them eat and drink, often sending food to the stomach through a tube in the mouth: (*fig.*) *Children should not be force-fed this nonsense in school* (= made to learn it).

forced /fɔːrst, foʊrst/ *adj* [not gradable] • *There were no obvious signs of forced entry into the house.*

forcible /'fɔːr·sə·bəl, 'foʊr-/ *adj* • *The youths had been arrested for homicide, forcible rape, and robbery.*

forcibly /'fɔːr·sə·bli, 'foʊr-/ *adv* • *The Ponca Indians were forcibly removed from their lands in 1877.*

force INFLUENCE /fɔːrs, foʊrs/ *n* [C/U] (a person or thing with) strong influence and energy • *The sheer force of her words kept the audience glued to their seats.* [U] ○ *He was a powerful force in national politics for 30 years.* [C] • If an organization or a person is described as **a force to be reckoned with** they are powerful and have a lot of influence.

forceful /'fɔːrs·fəl, 'foʊrs-/ *adj approving* • *He developed a forceful, emotional preaching style.*

forcefully /'fɔːrs·fə·li, 'foʊrs-/ *adv approving* • *He argues his case forcefully.*

force DO UNWILLINGLY /fɔːrs, foʊrs/ *v* [T] to do (something difficult or unpleasant) or cause (something difficult) to be done, esp. by threatening or not offering the possibility of choice • *I hate string beans, so I had to force myself to eat them.* ○ *Anderson was forced to leave the game with a bruised knee.* [+ to infinitive] ○ *I didn't actually want any more dessert, but Julia forced it on me.*

force /fɔːrs, foʊrs/ *n* • If something is done **by force of habit**, it is not thought about much but is done simply because it is a habit: *By force of habit I always hung the house keys on*

a hook next to the front door.

forced /fɔːrst, foʊrst/ *adj* [not gradable] • *The plane made a forced landing in Denver* (= was unexpected but necessary). • Forced laughter or a forced smile is produced with effort and not sincerely felt.

forcible /'fɔːr·sə·bəl, 'foʊr-/ *adj* • *A federal court refused to allow the forcible return of the refugees to their homeland.*

force OPERATION /fɔːrs, foʊrs/ *n* • If laws, rules, or systems are **in force**, they exist and are being used: *New regulations limiting fishing on this river are now in force.*

force GROUP /fɔːrs, foʊrs/ *n* [C] a group of people who do the same job, esp. an organized and trained military or police group • *a sales force* ○ *the Air Force* ○ *the police force* ○ *the armed forces* ○ *UN forces continue to provide relief in the war-torn region.* • If a person or group joins or combines forces with another person or group, they agree to work together.

forceps /'fɔːr·səps, -seps/ *pl n* a medical instrument used for holding things firmly

ford /fɔːrd, foʊrd/ *n* [C] a place in a river where the water is not deep, making it possible to get across

ford /fɔːrd, foʊrd/ *v* [T] • *The horses forded the river without any problems.*

fore /fɔːr, foʊr/ *n* • Something or someone that comes **to the fore** is brought to an obvious position that is impossible to ignore: *The presidential campaign has brought the issue of big political contributions to the fore.*

forearm /'fɔːr·ɑrm, 'foʊr-/ *n* [C] the lower part of the arm, between the wrist and the ELBOW • PIC ARM

forebear, forbear /'fɔːr·ber, 'foʊr-, -bær/ *n* [C usually pl] an ANCESTOR

foreboding /fɔːr'boʊd·ɪŋ, foʊr-/ *n* [U] the feeling that something bad is going to happen • *The gloomy weather gave me a sense of foreboding.*

forecast /'fɔːr·kæst, 'foʊr-/ *n* [C] a statement of what is likely to happen in the future • *The forecast is heavy rain for tomorrow.*

forecast /'fɔːr·kæst, 'foʊr-/ *v* [T] *past* **forecast** or **forecasted** • *The government is forecasting that unemployment will continue to fall.*

forecaster /'fɔːr₁kæs·tər, 'foʊr-/ *n* [C] • *a weather forecaster*

foreclose /fɔːr'kloʊz, foʊr-/ *v* [I] *specialized* (esp. of banks) to take control of the property of owners because they did not pay back the bank's money borrowed to pay for it

forefathers /'fɔːr₁fɑð·ərz, 'foʊr-/ *pl n* members of a family, national, or religious group who lived in the past • *Mario is spending the summer in Italy, the land of his forefathers.*

forefinger /'fɔːr₁fɪŋ·ər, 'foʊr-/ *n* [C] the finger next to the thumb; INDEX FINGER • *He held a tiny seed between his thumb and forefinger.*

forefront /'fɔːr·frʌnt, 'foʊr-/ *n* [U] the most

important or leading position • *She was in the forefront on many social issues of her day.*

forego /fɔːrˈgoʊ, foʊr-/ *v* [T] • See at FORGO.

foregone conclusion /ˌfɔːrˌgɔːnˈkənˈkluː-ʒən, ˌfoʊr-, -ˌgɑn-/ *n* [C] a result that is obvious before it happens • *Democrats so outnumber Republicans here that if you are nominated as a Democrat, it's a foregone conclusion you will be elected.*

foreground /ˈfɔːrˈgraʊnd, ˈfoʊr-/ *n* [C] the things in a picture that seem nearest to you • *The children are in the foreground in front of our house.* • Compare BACKGROUND THINGS BEHIND.

forehand /ˈfɔːrˈhænd, ˈfoʊr-/ *n* [C] (in sports such as tennis) a way of hitting the ball in which the inside part of the hand that is holding the RACKET (= piece of equipment) faces the direction of movement of the ball, or the player's ability to perform this hit • Compare BACKHAND.

racket

forehand / backhand

forehead /ˈfɑrˈəd, ˈfɔːr-; ˈfɔːrˈhed, ˈfoʊr-/ *n* [C] the flat part of the face, above the eyes and below the hair

foreign /ˈfɔːrˈən, ˈfɑr-/ *adj* [not gradable] belonging or connected to a country that is not your own or is not the one you are in • *a foreign country* ○ *a foreign language*

foreigner /ˈfɔːrˈə·nər, ˈfɑr-/ *n* [C] a person who comes from another country

foreman /ˈfɔːrˈmən, ˈfoʊr-/, **forewoman** /ˈfɔːr-ˌwʊm·ən, ˈfoʊr-/ *n* [C] *pl* **-men** /ˈfɔːrˈmən, ˈfoʊr-/ or **-women** /ˈfɔːrˌwɪm·ən, ˈfoʊr-/ (esp. for people who work with their hands) a skilled person who is in charge of a group of workers • *After four years on the job, he was promoted to foreman.* • (*law*) In a court of law, the foreman on the JURY is the person who reports the group's decision to the judge.

foremost /ˈfɔːrˈmoʊst, ˈfoʊr-/ *adj* [not gradable] best known or most important • *He was one of the foremost actors of his day.*

forensic /fəˈren·sɪk, -zɪk/ *adj* [not gradable] using the methods of science to provide information about a crime • *forensic medicine*

foreplay /ˈfɔːrˈpleɪ, ˈfoʊr-/ *n* [U] sexual activity such as kissing and touching each other before having sex

forerunner /ˈfɔːrˌrʌn·ər, ˈfoʊr-/ *n* [C] an early,

often less advanced model of something • *His machine was a forerunner of the modern computer.*

foresee /fɔːrˈsiː, foʊr-/ *v* [T] *past simple* **foresaw** /fɔːrˈsɔː, foʊr-/, *past part* **foreseen** /fɔːr ˈsiːn, foʊr-/ to realize or understand (something) in advance or before it happens • *He foresaw the need for cars that would be less polluting.*

foreseeable /fɔːrˈsiː·ə·bəl, foʊr-, fər-/ *adj* [not gradable] able to be understood in advance • *Unfortunately, he was likely to remain in power for the foreseeable future* (= for a long time, beyond which no one could say what would happen).

foreshadow /fɔːrˈʃæd·oʊ, foʊr-/ *v* [T] (of a past event) to suggest the happening of (a future event) • *Low unemployment may foreshadow wage and price increases.*

foresight /ˈfɔːrˈsaɪt, ˈfoʊr-/ *n* [U] the ability to judge correctly what is going to happen • *She had the foresight to sell her house just before prices came down.* [+ *to* infinitive]

foreskin /ˈfɔːrˈskɪn, ˈfoʊr-/ *n* [C] the loose skin that covers the end of the penis

forest /ˈfɔːrˈəst, ˈfɑr-/ *n* [C/U] a large area full of trees, usually wild • *We camped out in a clearing in the forest.*

forestry /ˈfɔːrˈə·stri, ˈfɑr-/ *n* [U] the science of caring for forests • *He studied forestry at Colorado State University.*

forestall /fɔːrˈstɔːl, foʊr-/ *v* [T] to prevent (something) from happening by acting first • *Many doctors prescribe aspirin to forestall second heart attacks.*

foretaste /ˈfɔːrˈteɪst, ˈfoʊr-/ *n* [C] an experience that lets you know in advance what something will be like • *Her job as an intern during the summer gave her a foretaste of the world of work.*

forever /fəˈrev·ər, fɔː-; *esp. Southern* fəˈev·ər/ *adv* [not gradable] for all time, without end • *Nobody lives forever.* • Forever can also mean always or frequently: *She was forever late for appointments.* ○ *He was forever saying that he'd pay me back, but he never did.*

foreword /ˈfɔːrˈwərd, ˈfoʊr-/ *n* [C] an introduction to a book, sometimes by someone who is not the person who wrote the book

forfeit /ˈfɔːrˈfət, -fɪt/ *v* [T] to give up or lose (something) because you cannot do something that the rules or the law says you must do • *She had to forfeit the tennis match after she fell and hurt her wrist.*

forfeit /ˈfɔːrˈfət, -fɪt/ *n* [C/U] • *Throwing objects on the field, the umpire said, would result in the forfeit of the game by the home team.* [C]

forgave /fərˈgeɪv, fɔːr-/ *past simple of* FORGIVE

forge COPY ILLEGALLY /fɔːrdʒ, foʊrdʒ/ *v* [T] to make an illegal copy of (something) in order to deceive • *He was accused of forging his father's signature on the check.*

forger /'fɔːr·dʒər, 'four-/ *n* [C] • *He was the forger of a painting sold as a Rembrandt.*

forgery /'fɔːr·dʒə·ri, 'four-/ *n* [C/U] • *These twenty-dollar bills are forgeries.* [C] ○ *He was convicted of forgery.* [U]

forge MAKE /fɔːrdʒ, fourdʒ/ *v* [T] to make or produce, esp. with difficulty • *Baker had worked for months to forge a peace plan that both sides could accept.*

forge MOVE /fɔːrdʒ, fourdʒ/ *v* [I always + adv/ prep] to move forward in a determined way although progress is difficult • *She forged ahead with her plans to stage a protest in Washington.*

forge WORK AREA /fɔːrdʒ, fourdʒ/ *n* [C] a working area with a fire for heating metal until it is soft enough to be beaten into different shapes • *a blacksmith's forge*

forget /fər'get, fɔːr-/ *v* [I/T] **forgetting**, *past simple* **forgot** /fər'gɑt, fɔːr-/, *past part* **forgotten** /fər'gɑt·ən, fɔːr-/ or **forgot** to be unable to remember; fail to remember • *You'd better not forget your mother's birthday.* [T] ○ *She forgot (that) she had a dental appointment.* [+ (that) clause] ○ *Don't forget to lock the car.* [+ to infinitive] • To forget (about) is to stop thinking about someone or something, or to stop thinking about doing something: *I wish I could forget him but I can't.* [T] ○ *I'm afraid we'll have to forget about going to the beach—it's raining.* [I] • When you tell someone to **forget about** something, you are saying no or telling them not to do it: *"Let's go to a movie tonight." "Forget about it—I've got too much work to do."* • **Forget (about) it** means don't worry about it or it's not important: *"I'm sorry I was late." "Forget it."*

forgetful /fər'get·fəl, fɔːr-/ *adj* likely to forget things • *She worries because her father is getting forgetful.*

forget–me–not /fər'get·miː,nɑt, fɔːr-/ *n* [C] a plant having small blue flowers

forgive /fər'gɪv, fɔːr-/ *v* [T] *past simple* **forgave** /fər'geɪv, fɔːr-/, *past part* **forgiven** /fər 'gɪv·ən, fɔːr-/ to stop being angry with (someone who has done something wrong) • *She apologized and he forgave her.* ○ *I can't forgive someone who has treated me so badly.*

forgiveness /fər'gɪv·nəs, fɔːr-/ *n* [U] • *The minister said we must ask God for forgiveness for our sins.*

forgo, forego /fɔːr'goʊ, four-/ *v* [T] he/she/it **forgoes, forgoing**, *past simple* **forwent** /fɔːr 'went, four-/, *past part* **forgone** /fɔːr'gɔːn, four-, -'gɑn/ to give up or do without • *She decided to forgo flowers at the funeral and asked people to send money to a charity instead.*

fork TOOL /fɔːrk/ *n* [C] a common tool used in eating and consisting of usually three or four stiff, wirelike points attached to a handle • *The knives and forks go in the middle drawer.*

fork DIVISION /fɔːrk/ *n* [C] the place where a single thing divides into two or more parts, or one of the parts • *a fork in the road*

fork /fɔːrk/ *v* [I] • *You'll come to our house just before the road forks.*

▫**fork over** *obj*, **fork** *obj* **over** /'-'--/ *v adv* [M] *infml* to give away (something), esp. on demand • *He had to fork over $125 for the traffic ticket.*

forklift /'fɔːr,klɪft/ *n* [C] a vehicle with two bars sticking out in the front for moving and lifting heavy goods

forlorn /fɔːr'lɔːrn, fər-/ *adj* looking or feeling alone and sad because you need help but do not expect to get it • *As I left little Bobby on his first day of school, he gave me such a forlorn look.*

forklift

form COME TOGETHER /fɔːrm/ *v* [I/T] to come together and make (a particular order or shape) • *A crowd formed to watch the fire.* [+ to infinitive] ○ *Please form a single line.* [T] ○ *The geese flying overhead formed a V-shaped pattern.* [T]

form /fɔːrm/ *n* [C] the shape or appearance of something • *The stadium was in the form of a circle.*

formation /fɔːr'meɪ·ʃən/ *n* [C/U] the process by which something comes into existence or begins to have a particular order or shape • *They called for the formation of a committee to investigate corruption.* [U] • A formation is the particular form that something has taken, or the things or people having this form: *unusual cloud formations* [C] ○ *The soldiers marched in formation* (= in an orderly arrangement). [U]

formative /'fɔːr·mət·ɪv/ *adj* [not gradable] developing and not yet completely formed • *the formative years of adolescence*

form BEGIN HAVING /fɔːrm/ *v* [T] to begin to have • *I formed the opinion that I was not really welcome there any more.*

form BEGIN /fɔːrm/ *v* [T] to begin (something), esp. involving organizing people or things • *We formed a community group to help people who are sick or disabled.* ○ *They formed a new publishing company.*

form TYPE /fɔːrm/ *n* [C] a type or kind of something, or the particular way in which something exists • *Of all the forms of government, democracy is the best.* ○ *She has a mild form of the flu and should be OK in a few days.* ○ *The medicine comes in the form of a liquid or pills.*

form DOCUMENT /fɔːrm/ *n* [C] something, usually paper, that has spaces marked where you fill in information • *Fill out an application form and we will let you know if a job opens up.*

form BEHAVIOR /fɔːrm/ *n* [U] the way in which someone does something • *He was in great form and won the golf tournament by 7 strokes.*

formal /'fɔːr·məl/ *adj* using an agreed and often official or traditional way of doing things

• *There are formal procedures for applying to become a US citizen.* • If a social occasion is formal, you wear traditional or dressy clothes: *It was a formal affair, and men were supposed to wear dark suits or tuxedos.* • Formal language is the language used esp. in writing in situations that are official and where accuracy is more important than simplicity, and which is therefore often more difficult than the language used in ordinary conversation. • Formal education/training is the learning of a subject or skill from courses in a school: *His formal education ended at the sixth grade, but he became a millionaire at the age of thirty.*

formal /'fɔːr·məl/ *n* [C] a dance at which women wear fashionable, expensive dresses and men wear TUXEDOS or similar clothes

formally /'fɔːr·mə·li/ *adv* • *You will receive a letter formally confirming* (= officially stating) *your appointment as professor of English.*

formalize /'fɔːr·mə,lɑɪz/ *v* [T] to make (something) official • *The trade agreement was formalized with Congress's approval of the bill.*

formality /fɔːr'mæl·əṭ·i/ *n* something done because it follows the usual or accepted way of doing things, although it may not be important • *There were only a few legal formalities to be finished, and he would be free to leave the country.* [C] ○ *It was just a mere formality.* [C] • Formality is also formal behavior or appearance. [U]

format /'fɔːr·mæt/ *n* [C] the way in which something is shown or arranged • *The two candidates could not agree on the format of the TV debate.*

format /'fɔːr·mæt/ *v* [T] **-tt-** • If you format (a text or a disk) on a computer, you organize it according to chosen patterns.

former EARLIER /'fɔːr·mər/ *adj* [not gradable] of an earlier time, but not now • *Her former husband has remarried.*

formerly /'fɔːr·mər·li/ *adv* [not gradable] before the present time or in the past • *Formerly, he had gone regularly to Europe, but now he seldom traveled.*

former FIRST /'fɔːr·mər/ *n* [U] the first of two people, things, or groups previously mentioned • *Of the two suggestions, I prefer the former.* • Compare LATTER SECOND

formidable /'fɔːr·məd·ə·bəl, fɔːr'mɪd-, fər'mɪd-/ *adj* strong and powerful, and therefore difficult to deal with if opposed to you • *There were formidable obstacles to reaching an early settlement of the dispute.*

formula /'fɔːr·mjə·lə/ *n* [C/U] the exact chemical parts that a mixture consists of • *The company announced that it was changing its soft-drink formula to make it sweeter.* [C] • Formula is a liquid food mixture that is fed to babies instead of mother's milk. [U] • A formula is also any plan or method for doing something well: *The formula for success in business, he said, is a willingness to take risks.* [C usually

sing] • In mathematics, a formula is a set of numbers and letters that express a rule. [C]

formulate /'fɔːr·mjə,leɪt/ *v* [T] to create (something), esp. by putting together different parts • *The Administration said it was formulating a new policy for the Middle East.* ○ *New drugs are being formulated to combat AIDS.*

fornicate /'fɔːr·nə,keɪt/ *v* [I] *disapproving* to have sex with someone you are not married to **fornication** /,fɔːr·nə'keɪ·ʃən/ *n* [U]

forsake /fər'seɪk, fɔːr-/ *v* [T] *past simple* **forsook** /fər'sʊk, fɔːr-/, *past part* **forsaken** /fər'seɪ·kən, fɔːr-/ *fml* to leave forever or to give up completely • *Nobody respects a mother who forsakes her children.*

fort /fɔːrt, foʊrt/ *n* [C] a building or group of buildings contained in an area enclosed by a strong wall and designed to be used by soldiers in defending against attack

forte /'fɔːr·teɪ, fɔːrt, foʊrt/ *n* [C usually sing] something that a person can do well; a strong ability • *Singing is definitely her forte.*

forth /fɔːrθ, foʊrθ/ *adv* [not gradable] out so that it can be seen or heard • *A round of applause burst forth.*

forthcoming SOON /fɔːrθ'kʌm·ɪŋ, foʊrθ-/ *adj* [not gradable] happening soon • *the forthcoming conference*

forthcoming WILLING /fɔːrθ'kʌm·ɪŋ, foʊrθ-/ *adj* willing to give information or to talk; friendly and helpful • *He has not been forthcoming about the details of his divorce.*

forthcoming SUPPLIED /fɔːrθ'kʌm·ɪŋ, foʊrθ-/ *adj* [not gradable] supplied or offered when wanted • *No explanation for his absence was forthcoming.*

forthright /'fɔːr·θrɑɪt, 'foʊr-/ *adj* honest or direct in expressing one's thoughts or feelings • *forthright comments* ○ *She's pretty forthright about her opinions.*

fortieth /'fɔːrṭ·i·əθ/ *adj, adv, n* • See at FORTY

fortify /'fɔːrṭ·ə,fɑɪ/ *v* [T] to strengthen, esp. in order to protect • *Property owners have to fortify their oceanfront homes against weather damage.* ○ *These reforms are aimed at fortifying the political system.*

fortified /'fɔːrṭ·ə,fɑɪd/ *adj* • *Children should not eat highly fortified cereals* (= ones with added healthful substances). • A fortified town has strong walls that can be defended against enemies.

fortification /,fɔːrṭ·ə·fə'keɪ·ʃən/ *n* • *I had some wine as fortification for the afternoon's work.* [U] ○ *Those towers were part of the city's fortifications* (= buildings, walls, etc., built as protection). [pl]

fortitude /'fɔːrṭ·ə,tuːd/ *n* [U] bravery when dealing with pain or difficulty, esp. over a long period • *Throughout his illness, he showed great fortitude.*

fortnight /'fɔːrt·nɑɪt, 'foʊrt-/ *n* [C usually sing] *Br* a period of two weeks

fortress /'fɔːr·trəs/ n [C] a large, strong building or group of buildings that can be defended from attack

fortuitous /fɔːr'tuː·ət·əs/ adj (esp. of something to your advantage) happening by chance • *We made a fortuitous escape.* ○ *The discovery of the files was fortuitous.*

fortuitously /fɔːr'tuː·ət·ə·sli/ adv • *They had fortuitously been out of the house when the fire started.*

fortunate /'fɔːr·tʃə·nət/ adj receiving or bringing a good thing that was uncertain or unexpected • *a fortunate choice* ○ *You're fortunate to have found such a pleasant house.* [+ to infinitive] ○ *It was fortunate that you left in time.* [+ that clause]

fortunately /'fɔːr·tʃə·nət·li/ adv [not gradable] • *Fortunately we were already home when it started to snow.*

fortune WEALTH /'fɔːr·tʃən/ n [C] a very large amount of money or property • *They made a fortune in real estate.* ○ *This dress cost a (small) fortune* (= a lot of money).

fortune CHANCE /'fɔːr·tʃən/ n [C/U] the set of good or bad events that happen to you and have an effect on your life • *He had the good fortune to be awarded a scholarship.* [U] • If you tell someone's fortune, you try to discover what will happen to them in the future, for example by looking at the lines on their hands or using a special set of cards. [C] • A **fortune cookie** is a cookie containing a message, usually about your future, that you get at Chinese restaurants in the US. • A **fortune teller** is a person who tells you what they think will happen to you in the future.

forty /'fɔːrt̬·i/ number 40 • *Forty children have signed up for the trip.* ○ *a forty-gallon tank* • LP NUMBERS

forties, 40s, 40's /'fɔːrt̬·iz/ pl n the numbers 40 through 49 • *The temperature will be in the forties* (= between 40° and 49°) *today.* ○ *Our house was built in the forties* (= between 1940 and 1949). ○ *They are both in their forties* (= between 40 and 49 years old).

fortieth /'fɔːrt̬·i·əθ/ adj, adv [not gradable], n [C] • *He married in his fortieth year.* • A fortieth is one of forty equal parts of something. [C]

forum /'fɔːr·əm, 'four-/ n [C] an occasion or a place for talking about a matter of public interest • *The university sponsored a forum on affirmative action.*

forward LEADING /'fɔːr·wərd/ adj [not gradable] directed toward the front or in the direction you are facing, or directed toward the future • *a forward motion* ○ *the forward part of an airplane* • Someone who is **forward-looking** or **forward-thinking** plans for the future.

forward /'fɔːr·wərd/, **forwards** /'fɔːr·wərdz/ adv [not gradable] toward the front, toward the direction in which you are facing, or toward a future time or better condition • *I leaned forward and glared at her.* ○ *The project moved forward slowly.* ○ *Set your clocks forward one hour to daylight saving time.* ○ (fig.) *Because of the story in the paper, a woman came forward* (= spoke to authorities). • Compare BACKWARD TOWARD THE BACK.

forward TOO CONFIDENT /'fɔːr·wərd/ adj too noticeable or confident; rude • *It was awfully forward of him to invite himself over for dinner.*

forward SEND /'fɔːr·wərd/ v [T] to send (something), esp. from an old address to a new address • *The post office will forward my mail while I'm away.* • A **forwarding address** is where you want your mail sent after you have left the place to which it was originally sent.

forward SPORTS /'fɔːr·wərd/ n [C] a player whose position is nearer the opposing team's goal in team sports such as BASKETBALL, SOCCER, and HOCKEY

forwent /fɔːr'went, four-/ past participle of FORGO

fossil /'fɑs·əl/ n [C] part of a plant or animal, or its shape, that has been preserved in rock or earth for a very long period • **Fossil fuels** are fuels such as gas, coal, and oil that have been produced in the earth from plants and animals.

foster TAKE CARE OF /'fɔːs·tər, 'fɑs-/ v [T] to take care of (a child) as if it were your own, usually for a limited time, without being the child's legal parent • Compare ADOPT TAKE CHILD.

foster /'fɔːs·tər, 'fɑs-/ adj [not gradable] • *A social service agency placed the child with a foster family.*

foster ENCOURAGE /'fɔːs·tər, 'fɑs-/ v [T] to encourage the development or growth of (ideas or feelings) • *I try to foster an appreciation for classical music in my students.*

fought /fɔːt/ past simple and past participle of FIGHT

foul UNPLEASANT /faʊl/ adj [-er/-est only] extremely unpleasant • *a foul odor* ○ *a foul mood* • Many movies these days are full of violence and **foul language** (= swearing). • If someone is **foul-mouthed**, they use rude and offensive language a lot. • **Foul play** is a violent criminal act, esp. murder: *The police have ruled out foul play in the drowning.*

foul SPORTS /faʊl/ n [C] (esp. in BASKETBALL) an act that is against the rules of a sport, sometimes causing injury to another player, or a punishment given to a player for breaking the rules • *an intentional foul* ○ *a flagrant foul* • In baseball, a foul or **foul ball** is a ball hit outside the playing field on either side. • In BASKETBALL, a **foul shot** (also **free throw**) is an opportunity or attempt to score one or more points without opposition because of a foul committed by a member of the other team.

foul /faʊl/ v [I/T] • *Sahlstrom was fouled after the shot.* [I]

foul MAKE DIRTY /faʊl/ v [T] to pollute (something) or make it dirty • *The oil slick fouled the California coastline.*

□ **foul up** (obj), **foul** (obj) **up** /'-'-/ v adv [I/M] *infml* to spoil or damage (something), esp. by making a mistake or doing something stupid • *I think the antipollution devices really foul up a lot of engines.* [M]

foul-up /'faʊ·lʌp/ n [C] *infml* • *I do not allow any foul-ups in this company.*

found FIND /faʊnd/ *past simple and past participle of* FIND

found BEGIN /faʊnd/ v [T] to bring (something) into existence • *She donated money to help found a wildlife refuge.* ○ *New Orleans was founded by the French in 1718.* • A **founding father** (also **founder**) of a country, organization, or idea is a person who establishes it: *The Founding Fathers of the United States were the men who wrote and approved the US Constitution in 1787.*

foundation /faʊn'deɪ·ʃən/ n [U] • *The foundation of the children's home was made possible by a generous contributor.*

founder /'faʊn·dər/ n [C] • *She is the founder and managing director of the company.* • See also FOUNDER.

found BASE /faʊnd/ v [T always + adv/prep] to base (a belief, claim, idea, etc.) on something • *This case was founded on insufficient evidence.*

foundation /faʊn'deɪ·ʃən/ n [U] • *These charges are completely without foundation (= false).*

foundation BASE /faʊn'deɪ·ʃən/ n [C] the base that is built below the surface of the ground to support a building • *a concrete foundation* ○ (fig.) *The two leaders have laid the foundations of a new era of cooperation between their countries.*

foundation ORGANIZATION /faʊn'deɪ·ʃən/ n [C] an organization that has been established to provide financial support for socially important or beneficial activities • *the Ford Foundation*

founder /'faʊn·dər/ v [I] to fill with water and sink, or (fig.) to fail • *The ship foundered in a heavy storm.* ○ (fig.) *Plans for a new airport have foundered because of budget cuts.* • See also **founder** at FOUND BEGIN.

foundry /'faʊn·dri/ n [C] a factory where metal is melted and poured into specially shaped containers to produce machine parts

fountain /'faʊnt·ᵊn/ n [C] a stream of water that is forced up into the air through a small hole, esp. for decorative effect, or the structure from which this flows • *the fountain in Central Park*

four /fɔːr, foʊr/ *number* 4 • *A square has four sides.* ○ *a four-part television series* • Four can also mean four o'clock. • A **four-leaf clover**

is a small plant that has four leaves rather than the usual three and is thought to bring good luck. • A **four-letter word** is a short swear word that is considered to be extremely rude or offensive. • If a vehicle has **four-wheel drive** its engine supplies power to all four wheels rather than the usual two, so that the vehicle can travel easily over rough ground. • LP NUMBERS

fourth /fɔːrθ, foʊrθ/ adj, adv [not gradable], n [C] • *Mark finished fourth in the race.* ○ *My birthday is on the fourth of December.* [C] • A fourth is one of four equal parts of something. [C] • The **Fourth of July** (also **Independence Day**) is the national holiday in the US that celebrates its independence from Great Britain in 1776: *The Fourth of July is traditionally celebrated with fireworks.*

fourteen /fɔːrt'tiːn, foʊrt-/ *number* 14 • *Fourteen people will be coming to dinner.* ○ *a fourteen-week program* • LP NUMBERS

fourteenth /fɔːrt'tiːnθ, foʊrt-/ adj, adv [not gradable], n [C] • *the fourteenth edition of the book* ○ *Could we arrange a meeting for the fourteenth of April?* [C] • A fourteenth is one of fourteen equal parts of something. [C]

fowl /faʊl/ n [C/U] pl **fowl** or *old use* **fowls** a bird of a type that is used to produce meat or eggs • *I now eat more fish and fowl and less red meat.* [U]

fox ANIMAL /fɑks/ n [C/U] a wild mammal belonging to the dog family which has a pointed face and ears, a wide furry tail, and often red-brown fur, or the fur of this animal • *A fox who had smelled the chickens came out of the woods into the yard.* [C]

foxy /'fɑk·si/ adj • *The company's foxy (= quick and intelligent) chairman outmaneuvered his competitors.*

fox PERSON /fɑks/ n [C] *infml* a sexually attractive young person • *Doug's girlfriend is quite a fox.*

foxy /'fɑk·si/ adj *infml* • *McGovern plays a foxy babe in the film.*

foxhole /'fɑks·hoʊl/ n [C] a hole dug in the ground and used by soldiers as a shelter from enemy attack

foyer /'fɔɪ·ər, 'fɔɪ·eɪ/ n [C] a large, open area just inside the entrance of a public building such as a theater or hotel; LOBBY • A foyer is also the room in a house or apartment that leads from the front door to other rooms.

fracas /'freɪ·kəs, 'fræk·əs/ n [C] a noisy argument or fight • *The players got into a scuffle, both benches cleared, and some fans joined the fracas.*

fraction /'fræk·ʃən/ n [C] a number that results from dividing one **whole number** (= a number with no part of a number after it) by another, or a very small part or amount of something • *¼ and 0.25 are different ways of representing the same fraction.* ○ *Counterfeits are sold at a fraction of the cost of the genuine*

FRACTIONS AND DECIMALS

SYMBOLS	WORDS	SPOKEN
½	one-half	a half
⅓	one-third	a third
¼	one-quarter *or* one fourth	a quarter *or* a fourth
¾	three-quarters	
⅗	three-fifths	
3⅞	three and seven-eighths	
¹⁄₆₄	one sixty fourth	a sixty-fourth
¹⁄₁₀₀	one one-hundredth	a hundredth
0.62	sixty-two hundredths	(zero) point six two
1.5	one and five-tenths *or* one and a half	one point five
2.15	two and fifteen one-hundredths	two point one five

articles. ○ *Juries often hear only a fraction of the story.*

fractious /ˈfræk·ʃəs/ *adj* tending to argue, fight, or complain, and hard to control • *fractious relationships* ○ *the fractious nature of politics*

fracture /ˈfræk·tʃər/ *v* [I/T] to crack or break (esp. a bone) • *She fractured her skull in the accident.* [T]

fracture /ˈfræk·tʃər/ *n* [C] • *He had a hairline fracture of the toe* (= a thin crack in the bone).

fragile /ˈfrædʒ·əl, -ɑɪl/ *adj* easily damaged, broken, or harmed • *a fragile piece of metal* ○ *These events remind us just how fragile race relations are in America.* ○ *I feel fragile, as if a breath of wind could knock me over.*

fragility /frəˈdʒɪl·ət̬·i/ *n* [U] • *She was a strong woman, with no hint of fragility about her.*

fragment /ˈfræɡ·mənt/ *n* [C] a small piece or part, esp. one that is broken off of something • *a bone fragment* ○ *a fragment of Indian pottery* ○ *She read a fragment of the story.*

fragmented /ˈfræɡ,ment·əd/ *adj* separated into or consisting of several parts • *a fragmented narrative* ○ *a country fragmented by social strife*

fragmentary /ˈfræɡ·mən,ter·i/ *adj* existing only in small parts and not complete • *Tom talks in images that are fast and fragmentary.* ○ *The surviving evidence is fragmentary.*

fragrance /ˈfreɪ·ɡrəns/ *n* [C] a sweet or pleasant smell • *The shampoo has a light fragrance of herb and plant extracts.*

fragrant /ˈfreɪ·ɡrənt/ *adj* • *the fragrant bouquet of roses*

frail /freɪl/ *adj* [-er/-est only] physically weak, or easily damaged, broken, or harmed • *He's always in frail health.* ○ *The shirt is old and frail, and the threads look ready to part.*

frailty /ˈfreɪl·ti/ *n* [C/U] • *Despite his frailty, he continued to travel.* [U] • Frailty also means moral weakness: *human frailties such as selfishness and greed* [C]

frame ⌊BORDER⌋ /freɪm/ *n* [C] a border that en-

closes and supports a picture, mirror, etc. • *She put his picture in a silver frame.*

frame /freɪm/ *v* [T] to fix a border around (a picture, photograph, etc.), often with glass in front of it • *We had our wedding pictures framed.* ○ (*fig.*) *Her small face was framed by the open door.*

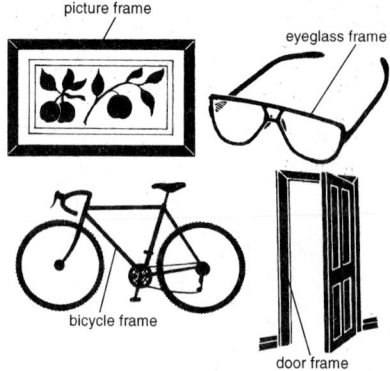

picture frame

eyeglass frame

bicycle frame

door frame

frames

frame ⌊STRUCTURE⌋ /freɪm/ *n* [C] a structure that holds the parts of an object in position and gives them support • *The houses have wood frames built on concrete slabs.* • A **frame of reference** is a set of ideas or facts accepted by a person which influences their behavior, opinions, or decisions: *The report provided a common frame of reference for discussing public policy.* • A **framework** is a supporting structure around or over which something is built: *the steel framework of a bridge* • A **framework** is also the structure of an organization or plan: *They're operating within the framework of a military bureaucracy.* ○ *The agreement outlines a framework and schedule for resolving the issues.*

frames /freɪmz/ *pl n* the part of a pair of eyeglasses that holds the LENSES (= parts that you see through) in position

frame BODY /freɪm/ *n* [C] a person's body when referring to its size or structure • *He eased his lean frame into a chair.*

frame EXPRESS /freɪm/ *v* [T] to express (an idea, suggestion, etc.) in a particular way, esp. after careful consideration, or plan a course of action • *Their conclusions are framed in such a way that if one piece of evidence were shown to be false, the argument would be suspect.*

frame /freɪm/ *n* • Someone's **frame of mind** is their mood or their particular way of thinking or feeling about something: *That music puts me in a romantic frame of mind.*

frame MAKE GUILTY /freɪm/ *v* [T] *infml* to make (a person) seem to be guilty of a crime by providing false information • *It looked like somebody was trying to frame him.*

franchise BUSINESS /ˈfræn·tʃaɪz/ *n* [C] a right to sell a company's products in a particular area using the company's name

franchise VOTE /ˈfræn·tʃaɪz/ *n* [U] the right to vote • *Women in the US won the franchise in 1920.*

frank /fræŋk/ *adj* honest, sincere, and truthful, even if there is a risk of offending someone • *To be perfectly frank, I don't think you are as well qualified as some of the other candidates.*

frankly /ˈfræŋ·kli/ *adv* • *She spoke frankly about her troubled marriage.* ○ *Frankly, I'm worried.*

frankness /ˈfræŋk·nəs/ *n* [U] • *We appreciate your frankness.*

frankfurter /ˈfræŋk,fɜrt̬·ər/, *short form* **frank** /ˈfræŋk/ *n* [C] a long, tube-shaped, cooked SAUSAGE (= meat cut into very small pieces), usually eaten after being put in a long bread loaf that has been cut lengthwise; HOT DOG • *I'll have a frankfurter with mustard and sauerkraut.*

frantic HURRIED /ˈfrænt̬·ɪk/ *adj* done in a very great hurry and often in a state of excitement or confusion • *Rescuers made frantic efforts to dig out people buried by the mudslide.*

frantic EMOTIONAL /ˈfrænt̬·ɪk/ *adj* extremely upset, esp. because of anxiety or fear • *Under the bombardment, frantic women and children run for the safety of shelters.*

fraternal /frəˈtɜrn·əl/ *adj* relating to brothers, or friendly like brothers • *He's a member of a fraternal order/organization* (= organized group of men). • **Fraternal twins** are two children born to the same mother at the same time who come from different eggs, may be of different sexes, and do not always look exactly like each other. Compare **identical twins** at IDENTICAL.

fraternity /frəˈtɜr·nət̬·i/, *infml* **frat** /fræt/ *n* [C] a social organization for male students at a college or university • A fraternity is also a group of people who have the same job or interest: *the coaching fraternity* • Compare SORORITY.

fraternize /ˈfræt̬·ər,naɪz/ *v* [I] to meet socially with someone who belongs to a different or opposing group • *The soldiers were told not to fraternize with any of the local people.*

fraud CRIME /frɔːd/ *n* [U] the crime of obtaining money or property by deceiving people • *Convicted of tax fraud, he was sentenced to two years in prison.*

fraudulent /ˈfrɔː·dʒə·lənt/ *adj* • *There's been a rise in fraudulent insurance claims.*

fraud FALSE /frɔːd/ *n* [C] a person or thing that is not what it claims or pretends to be • *He says he's been everywhere and done everything, but I think he's a fraud.*

fraudulent /ˈfrɔː·dʒə·lənt/ *adj* • *fraudulent advertising*

fraught /frɔːt/ *adj* full of (unpleasant things such as problems or dangers) • *Writing about science at a popular level is a task fraught with difficulty.*

fray LOOSEN /freɪ/ *v* [I/T] to become or to cause the threads in (cloth or rope) to become slightly separated and loose at the edge or end • *All his shirts are fraying at the collar.* [I] ○ (*fig.*) *My nerves are getting frayed* (= I am becoming nervous) *from the constant noise around here.* [I]

fray FIGHT /freɪ/ *n* [U] a fight or argument, esp. one in which several people take part • A fray is also a situation in which people or organizations compete forcefully: *A third buyer has entered the fray.*

frazzled /ˈfræz·əld/ *adj* tired and nervous or anxious, often because of having to deal with too many things at the same time • *She was a bit frazzled from all the media attention.*

freak UNUSUAL /friːk/, **freakish** /ˈfriː·kɪʃ/ *adj* [not gradable] extremely unusual or unlikely • *She died in a freak automobile accident.* ○ *A freak midsummer hailstorm caught us all by surprise.*

freak /friːk/ *n* [C] someone or something that is strange or unusual and not like others of its type • *In my school, everyone thought you were some kind of freak if you didn't like sports.*

freak ENTHUSIAST /friːk/ *n* [C] *infml* a person who is enthusiastic about the stated thing • *My eight-year-old grandson is a real sports freak.* ○ *This guy is a control freak* (= wants to control everything).

freak (*obj*) **out** /friːˈkaʊt/ *v adv* [I/T] *slang* to be or cause (someone) to be very excited or emotional • *Here in Texas they don't have snow, and they don't know what snow is, so they freak out when there's snow on the ground.* [I] ○ *Her latest album just freaked me out.* [T]

freckle /ˈfrek·əl/ *n* [C] a small brown spot on the skin, esp. on a light-skinned person • *The brothers were in their early teens, and both had reddish hair and freckles.* • A person who is **freckle-faced** has a lot of freckles on their face.

freckled /ˈfrek·əld/ *adj* *a freckled nose*

free NOT LIMITED /fri:/ *adj, adv* [*-er/-est* only] not limited or controlled • *You are free to come and go as you please.* [+ *to* infinitive] ○ *Please feel free to ask questions.* [+ *to* infinitive] ○ *Free elections will be held in two months.* • The atmosphere in our office is **free and easy** (= relaxed and informal). • **Free enterprise** is an economic system in which private businesses compete with each other to sell goods and services in order to make a profit. • A **free-for-all** is an argument or fight in which many people take part: *Someone threw a chair over the bar, and it was a free-for-all.* • If someone has a **free hand**, they have the authority to do whatever they consider necessary: *The company has given me a free hand to negotiate a deal with the Japanese.* • A **free market** is an economic system with only a small amount of government control, in which prices and earnings are decided by the level of demand for, and production of, goods and services: *a free-market economy* • **Free rein** is freedom to act, esp. complete freedom: *The young filmmakers were given free rein to experiment with new themes and techniques.* • **Free speech** is the right to express your opinions publicly. • In BASKETBALL, a **free throw** is a **foul shot**. See at FOUL SPORTS. • **Free trade** is the buying and selling of goods, without limits on the amount of goods that one country can sell to another, and without special taxes on the goods bought from a foreign country: *a free-trade agreement* • **Free will** is the ability to decide what to do independent of an outside influence: *She signed the confession of her own free will.*

free /fri:/ *v* [T] • *The inheritance freed him to travel.* [+ *to* infinitive]

freely /'fri:·li/ *adv* • *The animals are allowed to roam freely instead of being kept in cages.* ○ *Everyone is encouraged to speak freely* (= talk honestly).

free NOT IN PRISON /fri:/ *adj, adv* not or no longer a prisoner or a SLAVE (= person legally owned by someone else) • *She left the court a free woman.* ○ *New Orleans was home to both slave and free black communities.*

free /fri:/ *v* [T] • *The gunmen agreed to free the hostages.*

free NO CHARGE /fri:/ *adj, adv* [not gradable] costing nothing; not needing to be paid for • *When you buy a dinner for over $10, you get a soda free.* • *They paid off the mortgage and own their house* **free and clear** (= without debt). • A **free lunch** is something you get free that you usually have to work or pay for: *There's no such thing as a free lunch.* ○ *This is a fiercely competitive business, and don't expect free lunches.* • A **free ride** is the acceptance of your plans or ideas without having anyone question or criticize them: *No one has seriously examined the president's trade policy—he's gotten a free ride so far.*

-free /fri:/ *combining form* • *tax-free* ○ *toll-free* ○ *The superintendent lives here rent-free.*

free NOT BUSY /fri:/ *adj* [not gradable] not doing anything planned or important, or not being used • *We have plans for Friday night but we're free the rest of the weekend.* ○ *I do a lot of reading in my free time.*

free NOT HELD /fri:/ *adj, adv* [*-er/-est* only] not held in a fixed position or not joined to anything • *He grabbed the free end of the rope.* ○ *Mechanics checked the plane to see if any of the bolts had worked themselves free.* • If something is in **free fall**, it is moving down fast under the influence of GRAVITY (= the natural force that attracts things toward the earth) without any other force acting on it to reduce its speed: *The parachutists are briefly in free fall before opening their parachutes.* ○ (*fig.*) *The government had to act to keep the dollar from going into free fall* (= losing value quickly) *against other currencies.* • If something is **freestanding**, it is not fixed to anything and stands alone: *a freestanding sculpture*

free /fri:/ *v* [T] • *They worked to free the man trapped in the wreckage of his car.*

freely /'fri:·li/ *adv* • *The steering wheel should move freely.*

free WITHOUT /fri:/ *adj* [*-er/-est* only] not having something that is unwanted or unpleasant • *After many months of treatment, she was declared free of disease.* • *We will install your washing machine* **free of charge** (= without cost).

free /fri:/ *v* [T always + adv/prep] to release • *He longed to be freed of all his obligations.*

□ **free up** /'-'-/ *v* [T] to make (something) available to be used • *I need to free up some time this weekend to finish the report.*

freebie /'fri:·bi/ *n* [C] *infml* something that is usually sold but that is given to you without your having to pay for it • *They're giving out freebies of a new diet drink.*

freedom /'fri:d·əm/ *n* [U] the condition or right of being able or allowed to do whatever you want to, without being controlled or limited • *freedom of speech* ○ *If children aren't allowed some freedom, they won't learn to be independent.* ○ *We were promised freedom from persecution.* • Freedom is also the state of not being in prison or in the condition of SLAVERY (= condition of being legally owned by someone else).

freehand /'fri:·hænd/ *adj, adv* [not gradable] (of a design or picture) drawn while holding a pen, pencil, etc., without the help of any special equipment • *She made a freehand sketch of the layout of the apartment.*

freelance /'fri:·læns/ *adj, adv* [not gradable] working independently usually for various organizations rather than as an employee of a particular one • *a freelance musician/photographer/writer*

freelance /'friː·læns/ v [I] • *She freelanced for years while her children were in school.*

freelancer /'friː,læn·sər/, **freelance** /'friː·læns/ n [C]

freeloader /'friː,loʊd·ər/ n [C] *disapproving* a person who has the advantage of something given, such as money, food, or a place to stay, without offering anything in exchange

freely /'friː·li/ adv • See FREE [NOT LIMITED], FREE [NOT HELD]

freestyle /'friː·staɪl/ n [U] a sports competition, esp. a swimming race, in which each competitor can use any style or method they choose, or a style of swimming in which you lie on your front and move first one arm then the other over your head, while kicking your legs

freeway /'friː·weɪ/ n [C] a wide road for fast moving traffic traveling long distances, with a limited number of places at which drivers can enter and leave it • *the Santa Monica freeway in California*

freewheeling /'friː·hwiː·lɪŋ, -'wiː·l-/ adj [not gradable] willing to experiment and take risks by going beyond the usual rules or accepted ways of doing things • *There is an independence and freewheeling spirit in Alaska.*

freeze /friːz/ v [I/T] *past simple* **froze** /froʊz/, *past part* **frozen** /'froʊ·zən/ to become solid, or to make (a liquid, esp. water) solid, because of very low temperatures • *The rainwater froze overnight, leaving the roads icy.* [I] • If you freeze food, you preserve it by storing it at a very low temperature so that it becomes or remains solid. [T] • If someone such as a police officer says freeze, they are ordering you not to move except as they tell you: *Freeze! Drop the gun and put your hands up!* [I] • To freeze something such as pay or prices is to fix them at a particular level and not allow any increases: *The company has frozen salaries.* [T] • To freeze money or property is to officially and legally prevent it from being used or moved: *The government froze his assets.* [T] • By January, the lake had started to **freeze over** (= become covered with ice). • To **freeze-dry** something, esp. food, is to preserve it by freezing and then drying it: *freeze-dried instant coffee*

freeze /friːz/ n [C] a period when the air temperature is low enough so that water will freeze • *The first freeze didn't come until mid-December.* • A freeze is a temporary stopping of something: *The company has imposed a wage/hiring freeze.*

freezing /'friː·zɪŋ/ adj [not gradable] • *We can expect freezing temperatures all week.* • (*fig.*) Freezing also means very cold: *It's freezing in here—turn off the air conditioner!* • The **freezing point** of a liquid is the temperature at which it becomes solid: *The freezing point of water is 32°F or 0°C.* Compare **boiling point** at BOIL [HEAT].

freezer /'friː·zər/ n [C] an electrically powered container or part of a REFRIGERATOR that freezes foods so that they can be preserved safely for a long time • *Put the steaks in the freezer.*

□ **freeze out** obj, **freeze** obj **out** /'-'-'/ v adv [M] *infml* to intentionally prevent (someone) from being involved in an activity • *They tried to freeze me out of the bonus money.*

freight /freɪt/ n [U] goods that are transported from one place to another by ship, aircraft, train, or truck • *Most planes carry both freight and passengers.* • A **freight train** is a train that carries only goods.

freighter /'freɪt·ər/ n [C] a large ship or aircraft for carrying goods

French bread /'frentʃ·bred/ n [U] a type of usually white bread in the form of a long, thin loaf with a hard CRUST (= outer layer)

French Canadian /'frenʃ·kə'neɪd·i·ən/ n [C], adj [not gradable] (a person) of or coming from the part of Canada where French is the most important language

French fries /'frentʃ·fraɪz/, **fries** /'fraɪz/, **French-fried potatoes** /'frentʃ,fraɪd·pə'teɪt·əz, -oʊz/ pl n long, thin pieces of potato that are fried and eaten hot • *I'd like a hamburger and French fries.*

French horn /'frentʃ'hɔːrn/ n [C/U] a BRASS musical instrument shaped in a circle, with keys that are pressed to vary the notes and played by blowing into it, or this type of instrument generally; a HORN

French kiss /'frentʃ'kɪs/ n [C] a kiss with the lips apart and the tongues touching

French toast /'frentʃ'toʊst/ n [U] bread that has been put in a mixture of egg and milk and then fried, and which is usually eaten at breakfast

frenetic /frə'net·ɪk/ adj involving a lot of movement or activity; extremely active, excited, or uncontrolled • *Americans like fast cars, fast-food restaurants, and a frenetic pace of life.*

frenzy /'fren·zi/ n [C/U] uncontrolled, excited, and sometimes violent behavior or emotion • *Duncan's game-winning shot sent the crowd into a frenzy.* [C usually sing] ○ *People go into a spending frenzy at Christmastime.* [C usually sing]

frenzied /'fren·ziːd/ adj • *a frenzied crowd*

frequency /'friː·kwən·si/ n [C] the number of times that a wave, esp. a sound or radio wave, is produced within a particular period, esp. within one second • *Dogs can hear very high frequencies.*

frequent [COMMON] /'friː·kwənt/ adj happening often; common • *She makes frequent trips home to Beijing.* • A **frequent flier** is someone who can get special benefits for flying a lot on a particular company's aircraft.

frequently /'friː·kwənt·li/ adv • *I frequently disagree with him.* ○ *I moved much more frequently than I wanted to.*

frequency /'friː·kwən·si/ *n* [U] the number of times something is repeated, or the fact of something happening often • *Houses are sold here with greater frequency than in most other parts of the country.*

frequent VISIT /friːˈkwent, ˈfriː·kwənt/ *v* [T] to often be in or often visit (a particular place) • *They go to clubs frequented by artists.*

fresh RECENTLY GROWN / COOKED /freʃ/ *adj* [-er/ -est only] (of food or flowers) recently picked, made, or cooked • *fresh fruit/vegetables* ○ *fresh-baked bread* ○ *Elise is in the garden cutting some fresh flowers for the table.* ○ *There's a fresh pot of coffee on the stove.* • Fresh food is also food in a natural condition rather than artificially preserved by a process such as freezing.

fresh RECENT /freʃ/ *adj* [-er/-est only] recently made or done, and not yet changed by time • *The events of last year are still fresh in people's minds.* • If someone is **fresh from** or **fresh out of** somewhere, they have just arrived from there: *We hired her fresh out of college.* • If you are **fresh out** of something, you have just finished or sold all of it: *We're fresh out of oranges, would you like an apple?*

freshly /'freʃ·li/ *adv* [not gradable] • *I just love the smell of freshly cut grass.*

fresh DIFFERENT /freʃ/ *adj* different or additional; replacing what exists • *He's got a fresh way of looking at old material.* • A **fresh start** is an opportunity to begin something again: *Andujar looks forward to a fresh start with his new team.*

freshen /'freʃ·ən/ *v* [T] • *Can I freshen your drink (= fill your glass again)?*

fresh COOL /freʃ/ *adj* [-er/-est only] (of air) clean and cool, in a way thought typical of air away from cities and outside buildings • *How can we keep the kids indoors when they want to play in the fresh air?*

freshen /'freʃ·ən/ *v* [I/T] • *The wind freshened (= became stronger and cooler) and dragged my hair across my eyes.* [I]

fresh CLEAN /freʃ/ *adj* [-er/-est only] clean and pleasant • *fresh bed linens* ○ *the fresh pine smell of Christmas trees*

freshen /'freʃ·ən/ *v* [T] • *These mints are supposed to freshen your breath.* • *Sally, would you like to freshen up (= make yourself clean)?*

fresh NOT SALTY /freʃ/ *adj* [not gradable] (of water) from rivers and lakes and therefore not salty • *Rainfall is the sole source of the island's fresh water.* • *The village is near a freshwater pond.*

fresh NOT TIRED /freʃ/ *adj* [-er/-est only] energetic and enthusiastic; not tired • *I awoke feeling fresh and ready to go.*

fresh TOO CONFIDENT /freʃ/ *adj* [-er/-est only] being too confident and showing a lack of respect • *Don't get fresh with me, young woman!*

freshman /'freʃ·mən/ *n* [C] *pl* **-men** /'freʃ·mən/ a student in the first year of a program of study in a college, university, or HIGH SCHOOL (= a school for students aged 14 to 18) • *She is a freshman at Harvard.*

fret WORRY /fret/ *v* [I] **-tt-** to worry or be unhappy about something • *Don't fret—I'm sure we'll find the kitten.*

fretful /'fret·fəl/ *adj* • *She fell into a fretful sleep.*

fret RAISED BAR /fret/ *n* [C] a thin, slightly raised metal bar, several of which are positioned across the NECK (= long, narrow part) of some stringed musical instruments, such as a guitar

Freudian /'frɔɪd·iː·ən/ *adj* [not gradable] relating to the ideas or methods of Sigmund Freud about the way in which people's hidden thoughts and feelings influence their behavior • A **Freudian slip** is the act of saying something you do not mean to say that shows your hidden thoughts.

friar /'frɑɪ·ər, frɑɪr/ *n* [C] (esp. in the past) a man belonging to one of several Roman Catholic religious groups whose members often worked as teachers and showed their love of god by staying poor

friction FORCE /'frɪk·ʃən/ *n* [U] the force that makes it difficult for one object to slide along the surface of another or to move through a liquid or gas • *A gasoline engine loses over 70 percent of its energy to friction and heat.*

friction DISAGREEMENT /'frɪk·ʃən/ *n* [U] disagreement or unfriendliness caused by people having different opinions • *There's less friction in relationships when you use teamwork.*

Friday /'frɑɪd·i, -eɪ/ (*abbreviation* **Fri.**) *n* [C/U] the day of the week after Thursday and before Saturday

fridge /frɪdʒ/ *n* [C] *infml* a **refrigerator**, see at REFRIGERATE

friend /frend/ *n* [C] a person you know well and like a lot, but who is usually not a member of your family • *I dreamed my school friends were being chased by a whale.* ○ *Today I got a call from a friend of mine.* ○ *Chloë was her best friend.* ○ *I moved to California, made friends (= became friends with people), and started dating.* • Friend can also be used when you are speaking to someone: *Well, friends, I think it's time to go.* • A person or organization that is a friend to/of a group or organization helps and supports them: *He was no friend to slavery.* ○ *The Senator was a friend of business interests.* • If you have **friends in high places**, you know important people whom you can ask for support and help in getting what you want.

friendly /'fren·dli/ *adj* having an attitude or acting in a way that shows that you like people and want them to like and trust you • *They were friendly people.* ○ *She had a bright, friendly smile.* • If you describe a place as friendly, you mean that it is pleasant and comfortable: *It's a very friendly city.* • If countries or organizations are friendly, they are willing to help each other: *Sometimes an ambassador will get too friendly with the local dictator.* • Friendly is also used as a combining form to mean easy to be comfortable with or not damaging: *user-friendly technology* ○ *a family-friendly film*

friendship /'frend·ʃɪp/ *n* [C/U] a friendly relationship, or the state of being friends • *Their friendship goes back 25 years.* [C] ○ *I value friendship above all else.* [U]

fries /fraɪz/ *pl n* FRENCH FRIES

frieze /friːz/ *n* [C] a narrow strip of decoration, often cut from stone or wood and usually placed at the top of a wall

frigate /'frɪg·ət/ *n* [C] a small, fast military ship

frigging /'frɪg·ən, -ɪŋ/ *adj, adv* [not gradable] *rude slang* used to give force to an expression of annoyance or anger • *You frigging idiot!*

fright /fraɪt/ *n* [C/U] the feeling of fear, esp. if felt suddenly, or an experience of fear which happens suddenly • *When the rescue team reached him, he was shaking with fright.* [U] ○ *You gave her a fright turning the lights out like that.* [C usually sing] • *Hearing the explosion gave me* **the fright of** *my* **life** (= a very severe fright).

frighten /'fraɪt·ᵊn/ *v* [T] • *Be quiet or you'll frighten the deer.*

frightened /'fraɪt·ᵊnd/ *adj* • *She was too frightened to enter the room alone.*

frightening /'fraɪt·ᵊn·ɪŋ/ *adj* • *a frightening situation* • Frightening can also mean extreme: *My car insurance payments are frightening.*

frighteningly /'fraɪt·ᵊn·ɪŋ·li/ *adv* • *His heart rate changed frighteningly.*

frightful /'fraɪt·fəl/ *adj* shocking or extremely unpleasant • *People sometimes do frightful things to their pets.*

frightful /'fraɪt·fəl/ *adj* great or extreme • *The weather is just too frightful to go out.*

frightfully /'fraɪt·fə·li/ *adv* • *She's frightfully smart.*

frigid COLD /'frɪdʒ·əd/ *adj* extremely cold • *frigid weather/air/water* ○ *It's frigid in here—could you turn down the air-conditioning?*

frigid DISLIKING SEX /'frɪdʒ·əd/ *adj* (usually of a woman) having difficulty in becoming sexually excited

frill DECORATION /frɪl/ *n* [C] a long, narrow strip of folded cloth that is sewn along the edge of a piece of clothing or material for decoration

frilly /'frɪl·i/, **frilled** /frɪld/ *adj* • *She wore a frilly white dress.*

frill ADDITIONAL ITEM /frɪl/ *n* [C] something additional that is not necessary • *The frills on that car are nice, but except for air-conditioning, I don't want them.*

fringe EDGE /frɪndʒ/ *n* [C] the outer or less important part of an area, group, or activity • *There is some industry on the fringes of the city.* ○ *His organization is a fringe group* (= one that

represents the views of a small number of people). • A **fringe benefit** is something useful you get because of your job in addition to your pay: *Fringe benefits here include health insurance, three weeks' vacation, and tuition reimbursement.*

fringe /frɪndʒ/ *v* [T] • *The coast is fringed with islands and beaches.*

fringe DECORATION /frɪndʒ/ *n* [C] a decorative edge of narrow strips of material or threads on a piece of clothing or material

fringed /frɪndʒd/ *adj* [not gradable] • *The waitress came by in her little fringed skirt.*

Frisbee /'frɪz·bi/ *n* [C/U] *trademark* a plastic disk that is thrown between people as a game, or the game of throwing this disk • *Do you want to play Frisbee?* [U]

frisk /frɪsk/ *v* [T] to use your hands to search (someone's clothes and body) for hidden objects or weapons • *The teenager was frisked by police officers who found a concealed handgun.*

frisky /'frɪs·ki/ *adj* (of a person or an animal) playful or very active • *a frisky puppy*

frisk /frɪsk/ *v* [I] to move around in a happy, energetic way • *The dog ran ahead, frisking in the brush.*

fritter /'frɪt·ər/ *n* [C] pieces of fried BATTER (= a mixture of flour, egg, and milk) usually containing fruit, vegetables, or meat • *corn/potato/apple fritters*

fritter away *obj*, **fritter** *obj* **away** /'frɪt·ər·ə 'weɪ/ *v adv* [M] *disapproving* to waste (money, time, or an opportunity) carelessly • *Retirees must plan how to fill their hours or they risk frittering the time away.*

frivolous /'frɪv·ə·ləs/ *adj* (of people) behaving in a silly and foolish way, or (of activities or objects) silly or unimportant • *I'm very frivolous—I just like to have fun.* ○ *With our justice system there are a lot of frivolous cases that go to court.*

frivolously /'frɪv·ə·lə·sli/ *adv* • *We don't have a monthly budget, but we don't spend frivolously either.*

frivolity /frɪ'vɑl·ət·i/ *n* [C/U] foolish behavior, or something silly or unimportant • *You shouldn't treat such a serious subject with frivolity.* [U]

frizzy /'frɪz·i/ *adj* (of hair) having small, tight curls and not being smooth or shiny

frizz /frɪz/ *v* [I/T] *infml* • *The rain frizzes my hair.* [T]

frizz /frɪz/ *n* [U] • *She had a huge frizz of red hair.*

frog /frɔːg, frɑg/ *n* [C] a small animal that has smooth skin, lives in water and on land, has long powerful back legs with which it jumps from place to place, and has no tail • If someone has **a frog in** their **throat**, they have difficulty speaking because their throat feels dry.

frolic /'frɑl·ɪk/ *v* [I] **frolicking**, *past* **frolicked** to behave in a happy and playful way • *A group* *of children were frolicking on the beach.*

frolic /ˈfrɑl·ɪk/ *n* [C] • *Some people think of skiing as a wintertime frolic.*

from PLACE /frʌm, frɑm, frəm/ *prep* used to show the place where someone or something starts moving or traveling • *He took a handkerchief from his pocket.* ○ *She ran away from home.* • *People came from far and wide to see the parade* (= their journeys began in many places). • *Look from side to side* (= to the left and right) *before you cross the road.*

from TIME /frʌm, frɑm, frəm/ *prep* used to show the time when something starts or the time when it was made or first existed • *Here's a song from the 60s.* ○ *I'm leaving a week from Thursday* (= one week after Thursday). • *I never know what I'll be doing from one day to the next* (= before each day happens). • *The lecture ends at 2:30 and from then on* (= starting at that time and then continuing) *I'll be at the library.* • *I still think of her from time to time* (= irregularly).

from DISTANCE /frʌm, frɑm, frəm/ *prep* used to show the distance between two places • *We're about a mile from home.* • *She was dressed in red from head to toe* (= completely). • *They cleaned the house from top to bottom* (= completely).

from ORIGIN /frʌm, frɑm, frəm/ *prep* used to show the origin of something or someone • *I heard music coming from my room.* ○ *Someone from the bank just called.* ○ *Where are you from?* ○ *US Route 1 runs from Maine to Florida.* • If something is done **from scratch**, it is done completely from the beginning: *Can we fix the current computer system, or would it be better to start from scratch?* • *I'll always love you, and I mean it* **from the bottom of** *my* **heart** (= very sincerely). • *Her speech came* **from the heart** (= was sincere). • If you hear something **(straight) from the horse's mouth,** you hear it from the person who has direct personal knowledge of the matter.

from MATERIAL /frʌm, frɑm, frəm/ *prep* used to show the material of which something is made; OF • *The desk is made from pine.*

from RANGE /frʌm, frɑm, frəm/ *prep* used to show where a range of numbers, prices, or items begins • *Tickets will cost from $10 to $45.* ○ *Everyone from the oldest to the youngest had a good time.* • *This manual explains everything about our operations from A to Z* (= including all possible subjects).

from CHANGE /frʌm, frɑm, frəm/ *prep* used to show the original state of someone or something that is changing or has changed • *She has been promoted from manager to vice president.* ○ *Things went from bad to worse.*

from CAUSE /frʌm, frɑm, frəm/ *prep* used to show the cause of something or the reason why something happens • *Your child will benefit from piano lessons.*

from CONSIDER /frʌm, frɑm, frəm/ *prep* used to

show the facts or opinions you consider before making a judgment or decision • *From looking at the clouds, I would say it's going to rain later.* ○ *It's cheap, but not very good from a quality standpoint.*

from REDUCE /frʌm, frɑm, frəm/ *prep* used to show that a larger amount is being reduced by a smaller amount • *Three from sixteen is thirteen.*

from DIFFERENCE /frʌm, frɑm, frəm/ *prep* used to show a difference between two people or things • *It's hard to tell one sister from the other.*

from PROTECTION /frʌm, frɑm, frəm/ *prep* used to show what someone is being protected against • *They found shelter from the storm under a large oak tree.*

from PREVENTION /frʌm, frɑm, frəm/ *prep* used to show what someone cannot do or know, or what cannot happen • *High rents keep us from moving to a larger apartment.*

frond /frɑnd/ *n* [C] a large, usually divided, leaf, esp. of a FERN or PALM TREE

front PLACE /frʌnt/ *n* [C] the most forward position or most important side of an object or surface • *The front of the house faces Peach Street.* ○ *My little boy can't eat ice cream without most of it dripping down the front of his shirt.* ○ *You'll find the date of publication in the front of the book.* ○ *I like to sit near the front of the plane so that I can be among the first to get off.* ○ *Do you want me to lie on my front* (= the side of my body that faces forward) *or on my back?* ○ *Would you like me to sit in the front* (= most forward seat) *or the back of the car?* • *Dad pushed Matthew in the stroller while David and Stephen walked* **in front** (= farther forward than the others). • Someone or something that is **in front of** something else is in a position close to the most forward or most important part of it: *They chatted for a while in front of the apartment house.* • If someone is **in front of** someone else, they are directly forward of them: *Carla and Bob were sitting in front of me at the movie.* • If you do or say something **in front of** other people, you do or say it when they are present: *Why did you have to embarrass me in front of all those people?*

front /frʌnt/ *adj* [not gradable] • *I'd like seats in the front row of the balcony.* ○ *Alice designed the front cover of the book.* • The **front burner** is a place where something, such as a political program, is put when you want action on it or want it to be noticed: *The White House is making an effort to keep human rights on the front burner.* • The **front door** of a building, esp. a house, is the door on the side of the building that faces the street, or the main entrance door.

front /frʌnt/ *v* [I/T] to face or be next to (something) • *Houses fronting (on) the ocean are the most expensive.* [I/T]

frontal /ˈfrʌnt·əl/ *adj* [not gradable] at, from,

frustrate

or toward the front • *a frontal attack/assault* ○ *frontal nudity*

front AREA OF ACTIVITY /frʌnt/ *n* [C usually sing] a particular area of activity • *Now let's take a look at news on the health front.* ○ *I'm not having much luck on the job front.* • During a war, a front is a particular place of directed military activity.

front APPEARANCE /frʌnt/ *n* [U] an appearance that a person chooses to show to others instead of showing their true feelings • *Even though he doesn't like his in-laws, he always puts on a cheerful front when they come to visit.* • A front can also be a person, group, or thing used to hide the real character of a secret or illegal activity: *The society was a front for making illegal political contributions.*

front WEATHER /frʌnt/ *n* [C] the advancing edge of a mass of cold or warm air • *a cold/ warm front*

front POLITICAL GROUP /frʌnt/ *n* [C] an organization of political groups united to put forward ideas or programs that they share • *The National Liberation Front fought American troops in the Vietnam War.*

frontage /'frʌnt·ɪdʒ/ *n* [C] the front part of a building or land that faces a road or river

frontier /frʌn'tɪr/ *n* [C] a border between two countries, or (esp. in the past in the US) a border between developed land where white people live and land where Indians live or land that is wild • *It was a movie about the hardships of frontier life in the northwest.* • (fig.) A frontier is also a border between what is known and what is not known: *the frontiers of knowledge*

front–runner /'frʌnt'rʌn·ər/ *n* [C] the person, idea, or product that seems most likely to succeed • *With polls showing Schaefer ahead by 20 percentage points, he's clearly the front-runner.*

frost COLD /frɔːst/ *n* [U] a white, powdery, layer that sometimes forms on outside surfaces when it is cold enough for water to freeze, or freezing temperatures • *There was frost on the grass in the early morning.* ○ *An early frost killed some of my tomatoes.*

frost /frɔːst/ *v* [I/T] • *The windshield frosted up overnight.* [I]

frosty /'frɔː·sti/ *adj* covered with frost, or with something that looks like frost • *We each had a root beer served in a frosty glass with a big handle.*

frost COVER CAKE /frɔːst/, **ice** *v* [T] to cover (a cake) with a thin layer of sugar mixed with a liquid

frosting /'frɔː·stɪŋ/ *n* [U] • *chocolate/vanilla frosting*

frostbite /'frɔːst·baɪt/ *n* [U] injury to body tissues, esp. the fingers and toes, caused by freezing

frostbitten /'frɔːst·bɪt·ən/ *adj* (of body tissues) injured from having been frozen • *Res-*

cuers found two of the mountain climbers alive but badly frostbitten.

frosted /'frɔː·stəd/ *adj* [not gradable] (of glass) having a roughened surface so that it is not transparent • *frosted glass*

frosty /'frɔː·sti/ *adj* unfriendly or not welcoming • *a frosty manner*

froth /frɔːθ/ *n* [U] a mass of small bubbles, esp. on the surface of a liquid

frown /fraʊn/ *v* [I] to bring your **eyebrows** together so that lines appear on your face above your eyes, in an expression of anger, disapproval, or worry • *She noticed that whenever she spoke up at a faculty meeting, some of the men present would invariably frown or look unhappy.* • If you **frown on** something, you disapprove of it: *You can wear jeans, but I think they frown on shorts and sneakers.*

frown /fraʊn/ *n* [C] • *Pierre's mouth tightened with a small frown.*

froze /froʊz/ *past simple of* FREEZE

frozen /'froʊ·zən/ *past participle of* FREEZE

frugal /'fruː·gəl/ *adj* careful in spending money • *Lungren, a fiscal conservative when it comes to spending taxpayers' money, is frugal in his personal life as well.*

fruit PLANT PART /fruːt/ *n* the usually sweet and edible product of a plant or tree that contains the seeds • *We eat a lot of fruits and vegetables at our house.* [C] ○ *I usually eat a piece of fresh fruit with my lunch.* [U] • A **fruitcake** is a cake containing small dried or candied fruit, nuts, and spices. See also FRUITCAKE.

fruity /'fruː·t̬i/ *adj* tasting or smelling like fruit • *The wine has a pleasant, fruity flavor.*

fruit RESULT /fruːt/ *n* [C usually pl] the result of work or actions, esp. if pleasant or successful • *The fruits of economic growth are starting to make a difference in the lives of many workers.*

fruitful /'fruːt·fəl/ *adj* producing good results • *He had a long and fruitful career as a research chemist.*

fruitless /'fruːt·ləs/ *adj* unsuccessful or not productive • *After months of fruitless negotiations with team owners, the city withdrew its offer to build a new stadium.*

fruit PERSON /fruːt/ *n* [C] dated slang a male homosexual • Many people consider this word offensive.

fruitcake /'fruːt·keɪk/ *n* [C] slang a crazy or unusual person • *He's crazy as a fruitcake.* • See also **fruitcake** at FRUIT PLANT PART.

fruition /fruː'ɪʃ·ən/ *n* [U] fml the successful completion of an activity or plan • *The governor plans to use his considerable influence to bring the museum to fruition.*

fruity /'fruː·t̬i/ *adj* • See at FRUIT PLANT PART.

frustrate ANNOY /'frʌs·treɪt/ *v* [T] to annoy (someone) or cause them to be disappointed or discouraged • *People are frustrated with the politicians.* ○ *Activists went into the woods to* *frustrate hunters, shooing geese and ducks out of shotgun range by beating pots and pans.*

frustrated /'frʌs,treɪt·əd/ *adj* • *You just get so frustrated when everything in your vegetable garden is ripe and then the bugs get at them.* ○ *Frustrated residents protested the situation.*

frustrating /'frʌs,treɪt·ɪŋ/ *adj* • *I guess job opportunities at the top are improving for women, but it's such a slow process that it's frustrating.*

frustration /frʌs'treɪ·ʃən/ *n* [C/U] disappointment or discouragement, or a discouraging situation • *He finally quit in frustration.* [U] ○ *The teacher confirmed widespread frustration with the lack of up-to-date textbooks.* [U] ○ *You have to learn to cope with these frustrations.* [C]

frustrate [BLOCK] /'frʌs·treɪt/ *v* [T] to block (something from being achieved); prevent the success of (a plan or effort) • *North Vietnam frustrated President Johnson's hopes for a quick victory,*

frustrated /'frʌs,treɪt·əd/ *adj* [not gradable] desiring something but not able to achieve it • *I'm a frustrated songwriter at heart.*

frustration /frʌs'treɪ·ʃən/ *n* [U] • *All her efforts to save her marriage met with frustration, as John refused even to talk to her.*

fry /fraɪ/ *v* [I/T] to cook (food) in hot oil or fat • *She was frying eggs and getting the coffee ready.* [T] • A **frying pan** (also **skillet**) is a flat metal pan with a long handle, used for frying food. [PIC] PANS • [PIC] COOKING METHODS

frying pan

fried /fraɪd/ *adj* [not gradable] • *We had fried chicken and mashed potatoes for supper.*

fries /fraɪz/ *pl n short form of* FRENCH FRIES

ft. *n* [C] *pl* **ft.** *abbreviation for* FOOT [MEASUREMENT]

fuck [HAVE SEX] /fʌk/ *v* [I/T] *taboo slang* to have sex (with someone)

fuck /fʌk/ *n* [C] *taboo slang* the act of having sex

fuck [ANGER] /fʌk/ *exclamation taboo slang* used when expressing anger or annoyance to add force to what is being said • *The car just died—what the fuck am I supposed to do now?*

fucking /'fʌk·ɪŋ, 'fʌk·ən/ *adj* [not gradable] *taboo slang* • *That was a fucking waste of time.*

▫**fuck up** (*obj*), **fuck** (*obj*) **up** /'-'-/ *v adv* [I/M] *taboo slang* to harm or upset (someone) very much, or to do (something) very badly • *She's been really fucked up since her parents' divorce.* [M] ○ *He didn't know how to install it properly and really fucked up (his computer).* [I/M]

fuck–up /'fʌk·ʌp/ *n* [C] *taboo slang* • *It's been one fuck-up after another since she took charge.*

fudge [CANDY] /fʌdʒ/ *n* [U] a soft, creamy candy made from sugar, milk, butter, and chocolate or other flavoring

fudge [CHEAT] /fʌdʒ/ *v* [I/T] to cheat about (something) slightly, esp. by not reporting

facts accurately or not telling the exact truth • *I think the company fudged the figures to make their losses look less than they were.* [T]

fuel /'fju:·əl, fju:l/ *n* [C/U] a substance such as oil or gas that is used to provide heat or power, usually be being burned

fuel /'fju:·əl, fju:l/ *v* [T] to provide power to (something) • *The heating system is fueled by natural gas.*

fugitive /'fju:·dʒət·ɪv/ *n* [C] a person who is running away, esp. from the police • *Three men escaped from the prison and were being sought as fugitives.*

fulcrum /'fʊl·krəm, 'fʌl-/ *n* [C] *specialized* the point of support for a LEVER (= bar used to move or raise something)

fulfill [MAKE HAPPEN] /fʊl'fɪl/ *v* [T] to do (something) as promised or intended, or to satisfy (your hopes or expectations) • *She said the president had failed to fulfill his campaign promises.* ○ *He stayed an extra semester to fulfill his graduation requirements.* ○ *At the age of 45, she finally fulfilled her ambition to run a marathon.*

fulfillment /fʊl'fɪl·mənt/ *n* [U] • *Morales said that owning his own home was the fulfillment of a dream.*

fulfill [DEVELOP] /fʊl'fɪl/ *v* [T] to succeed in developing (abilities or qualities) to their fullest degree • *Her immediate goal was to complete her novel, but her long-term goal was to fulfill her potential as a writer.*

fulfilling /fʊl'fɪl·ɪŋ/ *adj* • *I hope you can find a job that's really fulfilling.*

fulfillment /fʊl'fɪl·mənt/ *n* [U] • *Workaholics can only find fulfillment in their work.*

full [CONTAINING A LOT] /fʊl/ *adj* having or containing a lot • *The glass is full, so be careful not to spill it.* ○ *This sweater is full of holes.* ○ *You're always so full of energy.* ○ *Don't talk with your mouth full* (= with food in your mouth)! ○ *I have a full schedule* (= a lot of activities planned) *next week.* • *When we arrived, the party was* **in full swing** (= there was a lot of activity). • *I doubt he even thought about your needs, he's so* **full of** *himself* (= his opinion of himself is too positive). • (*rude slang*) *If you say someone is* **full of shit/full of crap/full of it** *you mean that what they are saying isn't true.*

full [ATE ENOUGH] /fʊl/ *adj* having eaten so much that you do not want to eat any more • *I'm so full I couldn't eat another bite.* • *You might get sick if you go jogging* **on a full stomach** (= soon after you have eaten).

full [WHOLE] /fʊl/ *adj* [not gradable] including all of something or everything; whole • *What should we do on our last full day in New York?* • *If someone or something moves* **full circle** *it returns to a previously held belief or position: His funeral would bring his influence on my life full circle.* • *To come* **full circle** *is also to change to an opposing belief or opinion: We* used to think the family was not important, and now we've come full circle. • Aspirin reduces your chances of having a **full-blown** stroke (= one with all the physical problems). • If something is **full-fledged**, it is complete: She's a full-fledged member of the community. • **Full-length** means being as tall as a person or a room: a full-length mirror ○ full-length windows • **Full-length** clothing ends just above your feet: full-length coats • **Full-length** also means giving complete treatment or being the usual amount of time: a full-length biography ○ a full-length movie • Geoff swam under a full **moon** (= the complete disk of the moon could be seen). • (Cdn and Br) A **full stop** is a PERIOD MARK. • She was a **full-time** student (= She did this for all the hours people usually work).

full /fʊl/ adv [not gradable] • The biting wind was blowing full in his face. • You know **full well** (= without doubt) that you're not supposed to go there without asking me!

fullness /'fʊl·nəs/ n [U] • Life today doesn't have that fullness and beauty that it did when I was a young woman. • **In the fullness of time** (= After a suitable period), everything would be all right.

fully /'fʊl·i, -li/ adv [not gradable] • Have you fully recovered from your illness? ○ If you're not fully satisfied with your purchase, we'll refund your money.

full GREATEST POSSIBLE /fʊl/ adj [not gradable] the greatest possible; MAXIMUM • We don't make full use of our basement. • She was roaring up the freeway at **full throttle** (= traveling at the highest possible speed). • My roommate's stereo was on **full blast** (= as loudly as possible). • This will be a big dog when it's **full-grown** (= grown as large as possible). • For opening night we're expecting a **full house** (= every seat in the theater will be filled). • The police have begun a **full-scale** investigation (= one using all their power and authority).

fully /'fʊl·i, -li/ adv [not gradable] • Carrie has always participated fully in the life of the school. • LP VERY, COMPLETELY, AND OTHER INTENSIFIERS

full LARGE /fʊl/ adj [-er/-est only] (of clothing) loose or containing a lot of material, or (of the body) large and rounded • full face/lips/mouth ○ The dress was tight at the waist with a very full skirt and puffy sleeves. • If something is **full-sized** it is larger than other things of its type: They bought a full-sized station wagon.

fullness /'fʊl·nəs/ n [U] • Her bright red lipstick emphasized the fullness of her lips.

full STRONG /fʊl/ adj [-er/-est only] (of a flavor, sound, or smell) strong or deep • A cello has a fuller sound than a violin. • These dark beans make a **full-bodied** cup of coffee (= coffee with a lot of strength and flavor).

fumble /'fʌm·bəl/ v [I/T] to feel around awkwardly, esp. with your hands • Jack fumbled in

his pocket for the keys. [I] ○ My mind went blank, and I began to fumble for words. [I] • In some sports, esp. football, if you fumble the ball you fail to hold it after touching or carrying it. [I/T]

fume /fjuːm/ v [I] to be very angry, sometimes without expressing it • Days after the argument, he was still fuming.

fumes /fjuːmz/ pl n harmful or strong-smelling gases or smoke • Neighbors complain about fumes from the nearby sewage treatment plant.

fumigate /'fjuː·mə·ɡeɪt/ v [I/T] to remove harmful insects, bacteria, or disease, using chemical gas or smoke • We had to fumigate the house to get rid of cockroaches. [T]

fumigation /ˌfjuː·mə'ɡeɪ·ʃən/ n [U]

fun /fʌn/ n [U] pleasure, enjoyment, amusement, or someone or something that causes this • Everybody had a lot of fun at the party. ○ It's no fun having to work on Saturdays. ○ He studies French just for fun/for the fun of it. • I only said it **in fun** (= as a joke). • Being a comedian is not all **fun and games** (= enjoyable activities).

fun /fʌn/ adj [not gradable] infml • Going camping would be a really fun thing to do. ○ Cindy is a fun person (= enjoyable to be with).

function PURPOSE /'fʌŋk·ʃən/ n [C/U] a purpose or duty, or the way something or someone works • The function of the veins is to carry blood to the heart. [U] ○ One of your functions as receptionist is to answer the phone. [C]

function /'fʌŋk·ʃən/ v [I] • She quickly learned how the office functions. ○ I'm so tired today, I can barely function. • Our spare bedroom also functions as a study (= is also used for that purpose).

functional /'fʌŋk·ʃən·əl/ adj intended to be used; practical rather than attractive • Our furniture isn't very fancy, but it's functional. ○ Is the plumbing functional yet (= does it work)?

function CEREMONY /'fʌŋk·ʃən/ n [C] a social event or official ceremony • Morse went to the White House for a ceremonial function.

fund /fʌnd/ n [C] a sum of money saved and made available for a particular purpose • a scholarship fund for college students ○ the company's pension fund • A **fund-raiser** is a person or event that collects money: The Boy Scouts collect cans as a fund-raiser.

fund /fʌnd/ v [T] • He plans to donate money to fund health centers that treat Vietnam veterans.

funding /'fʌn·dɪŋ/ n [U] money made available for a particular purpose • Doug is trying to get funding for his research.

funds /fʌndz/ pl n money, often money for a specific purpose • I'm short of/low on funds at the moment. ○ The Brownies sold cookies to raise funds for their troop.

fundamental /ˌfʌn·də'ment·əl/ adj being the

most basic or most important thing on which other things depend • *fundamental beliefs/ principles* ○ *We need to make fundamental changes in the way we treat our environment.*

fundamentally /ˌfʌn·dəˈment·ᵊl·i/ *adv* [not gradable] • *Their economy was fundamentally* (= basically) *in good shape.*

fundamentals /ˌfʌn·dəˈment·ᵊlz/ *pl n* • *In the early grades, children learn the fundamentals of reading.*

fundamentalism /ˌfʌn·dəˈment·ᵊl·ɪz·əm/ *n* [U] the belief that the traditional principles of a religion should be maintained, and that what is taught in a holy book should be obeyed

fundamentalist /ˌfʌn·dəˈment·ᵊl·əst/ *n* [C] • *The governor hopes to get the support of Christian fundamentalists.*

fundamentalist /ˌfʌn·dəˈment·ᵊl·əst/ *adj* • *fundamentalist groups*

funeral /ˈfju·nə·rəl/ *n* [C] a ceremony honoring someone who has recently died, which happens before burying or burning the body • A **funeral home** (also **mortuary**) is a place where the bodies of dead people are prepared to be buried or burned, and where part of the ceremony can take place.

fungus /ˈfʌŋ·gəs/ *n* [C/U] *pl* **fungi** /ˈfʌn·dʒaɪ, ˈfʌŋ·gaɪ/ a plant without leaves, flowers, or color that lives on other plants or on decaying matter • *Fungus grows in damp, dark places.* [U]

funk UNHAPPY /fʌŋk/ *n* [U] the state of being unhappy and without hope • *Christmas sometimes gets me in a funk.*

funk MUSIC /fʌŋk/ *n* [U] a style of music related to jazz, with a strong rhythm

funky /ˈfʌŋ·ki/ *adj* • *a funky beat*

funky /ˈfʌŋ·ki/ *adj* in a style that is informal and unusual • *Darcy usually wears really funky clothes.*

funnel TUBE /ˈfʌn·ᵊl/ *n* [C] a tube with a wide opening at the top, sides that slope inward, and a narrow opening at the bottom, used for pouring liquids or powders into containers that have small openings • *Pour the batter through a funnel into hot oil.* • A **funnel cloud** is a TORNADO.

funnel MOVE /ˈfʌn·ᵊl/ *v* [I/T] **-l-** or *also* **-ll-** to move or be moved through a narrow space, or to put (something) in a place or use (something) for a particular purpose • *The crowd funneled into the theater.* [I] ○ *We've been funneling our money into renovations.* [T]

funny AMUSING /ˈfʌn·i/ *adj* [*-er/-est* only] amusing; causing laughter • *Jerome is so funny.* ○ *She told me the funniest joke.*

funnies /ˈfʌn·iz/ *pl n* (in a newspaper) one or more pages that have groups of amusing drawings, each of which tell a story or joke • *the Sunday funnies* • See also **comic strip** at COMIC MAGAZINE].

funny STRANGE /ˈfʌn·i/ *adj* [*-er/-est* only] strange or surprising, or difficult to explain

or understand • *The washing machine is making funny noises again.* ○ *Something funny is going on next door.* ○ *That's funny—I'm sure I left my keys here, but now I can't find them.* ○ *It's funny how Pat always disappears whenever there's work to be done.* [+ *wh-* word] • If you feel funny, you feel slightly sick: *He felt a little funny after taking a pill on an empty stomach.*

funny bone /ˈfʌn·iˌboʊn/ *n* [C usually sing] the part of the ELBOW that hurts a lot if it is hit even lightly

fur /fɜr/ *n* [C/U] the soft, thick hair that covers the bodies of some animals, or the hair-covered skin of animals, removed from their bodies • *Persian cats have long fur.* [U] ○ *My jacket is lined with fur.* [U] ○ *She wore diamonds and furs and always looked glamorous.* [C]

furry /ˈfɜr·i/ *adj* covered with fur, or feeling or looking like fur • *a furry animal* ○ *She was wearing her bathrobe and pink, furry slippers.*

furious ANGRY /ˈfjʊr·iː·əs/ *adj* extremely angry • *Sandy was furious with me for forgetting to pick her up.*

furiously /ˈfjʊr·iː·ə·sli/ *adv* • *She marched out of the house furiously.*

furious VIOLENT /ˈfjʊr·iː·əs/ *adj* violent or forceful • *Furious winds rocked the coastal town.*

furiously /ˈfjʊr·iː·ə·sli/ *adv* energetically • *I was furiously taking notes during the lecture.*

furl /fɜrl/ *v* [T] (esp. of a flag, sail, or UMBRELLA) to roll or fold up and fasten • *He took down the flag and furled it carefully.*

furlong /ˈfɜr·lɔːŋ/ *n* [C] a unit of length equal to 1/8 mile or 201 meters, used esp. in horse racing • *a six-furlong race*

furlough /ˈfɜr·loʊ/ *n* [C] a time allowed for a person to be absent, esp. from the army or a prison • *I'm home on furlough.*

furnace /ˈfɜr·nəs/ *n* [C] a container for holding burning substances, usually to heat buildings or to melt metals and other materials

furnish ADD FURNITURE /ˈfɜr·nɪʃ/ *v* [T] to put furniture in (a place) • *They furnished their home with antiques.*

furnished /ˈfɜr·nɪʃt/ *adj* [not gradable] • *She's trying to rent a furnished apartment* (= one that has furniture in it).

furnishings /ˈfɜr·nɪ·ʃɪŋz/ *pl n* furniture and decorative items, such as curtains and floor coverings

furnish SUPPLY /ˈfɜr·nɪʃ/ *v* [T] to supply or provide (something needed) • *Jeanne's catering company furnished all the food for the party.*

furniture /ˈfɜr·nɪ·tʃər/ *n* [U] items such as chairs, tables, and beds that are used in a home or office • *office/bedroom/lawn furniture*

furor /ˈfjʊr·ɔːr, -oʊr, -ər/ *n* [U] a sudden expression of excitement or anger by a lot of people, esp. in reaction to something • *She created a* *furor* with a comment many saw as insulting to Puerto Ricans.

furrow /'fɜr·oʊ, 'fʌ·roʊ/ *n* [C] a long, narrow cut or fold in the surface of something • *The plow sped along the furrow, turning over the earth.* ○ *He tried to smooth the furrow out of his jacket.*

furrow /'fɜr·oʊ, 'fʌ·roʊ/ *v* [T] • *When Tony's deep in thought, he furrows his brow.*

furry /'fɜr·i/ *adj* • See at FUR.

further [MORE] /'fɜr·ðər/ *adj, adv* [not gradable], *comparative of* FAR [AMOUNT]; more, extra, or additional • *Call your local library for further information.* ○ *To further complicate things, Bev learned she was pregnant.* ○ *Not only did I arrive at my conclusions after careful thought, I took a further step and tested them.* • If you say that something could not be **further from the truth**, you are saying that what has been suggested is not true: *I'm certainly not in love with him—nothing could be further from the truth!* • USAGE: Both further and farther are comparatives of FAR [DISTANCE] and FAR [AMOUNT]. Farther is more commonly used when referring to physical distances. Further is more commonly used when referring to greater amounts, to additional time, or to changes in a situation.

further [GREATER DISTANCE] /'fɜr·ðər/ *adj, adv* [not gradable], *comparative of* FAR [DISTANCE]; to a greater distance in space or time • *I can't run any further.* ○ *Read a little further and it will begin to make sense.* • USAGE: See Usage note at FURTHER [MORE].

further [ENCOURAGE] /'fɜr·ðər/ *v* [T] to help (something) to succeed; to advance (something) • *She says she would kill to further her cause.*

furthermore /'fɜr·ðər,mɔr, -,moʊr/ *adv* [not gradable] (used to add information) also and more importantly • *I don't know what happened to Roberto, and furthermore, I don't care.*

furthest [DISTANCE] /'fɜr·ðəst/ *adj, adv* [not gradable], *superlative of* FAR [DISTANCE] • *The furthest west I've ever gotten is the Grand Canyon.* • USAGE: Both furthest and farthest are used as adverbs and adjectives. Farthest is more commonly used when referring to distances. Furthest is more often used when the intended meaning is figurative.

furthest [AMOUNT] /'fɜr·ðəst/ *adj, adv* [not gradable], *superlative of* FAR [AMOUNT] • *At that time, the countries furthest along in terms of economic development were Chile, Mexico, and Venezuela.* • There have been rumors of me resigning, but that's **the furthest thing** from the truth (= not true).

furthest /'fɜr·ðəst/ *pronoun* • *This is the furthest our soccer team has advanced in the playoffs.*

furtive /'fɜrt̬·ɪv/ *adj* done or acting secretly and quietly to avoid being noticed • *They exchanged furtive gestures and words of encouragement.*

furtively /'fɜrt̬·ɪv·li/ *adv* • *She glanced furtively at the papers on his desk.*

fury /'fjʊr·i/ *n* [C/U] extreme anger or force; fierceness • *The battle raged with mounting fury.* [U]

fuse [SAFETY DEVICE] /fjuːz/ *n* [C] a safety device for protecting an electrical system which contains a material that will melt if too much electricity passes through the system • A **fuse box** is a container that holds several fuses, esp. for a home.

fuse [EXPLOSIVE DEVICE] /fjuːz/ *n* [C] a cord or tube along which a flame moves to light FIREWORKS or bomb, or a device inside a bomb that causes it to explode at a particular time or when it hits something

fuse [JOIN] /fjuːz/ *v* [I/T] to join or become combined, or to cause (things) to join • *Genes determine how we develop from the moment the sperm fuses with the egg.* [I] ○ *The heat of the fire fused many of the machine's parts together.* [T]

fusion /'fjuː·ʒən/ *n* [C/U] • *His innovative albums feature a fusion of progressive rock and soul.* [C] • Fusion is also the technique of joining atoms in a reaction that produces energy: *nuclear fusion* [U] • Compare FISSION.

fuselage /'fjuː·sə,lɑʒ, -zə-/ *n* [C] the main part of an aircraft

fusillade /'fjuː·sə,lɑd, -zə-, -,leɪd/ *n* [C] a number of bullets fired at the same time or one after another quickly • *The gunman cut loose with a five-round fusillade.*

fuss /fʌs/ *n* [U] excitement, annoyance, or dissatisfaction about something, esp. about something that is not very important • *Let's see what all the fuss is about.* [U] ○ *She learned to make good food without too much fuss.* [U] ○ *Why are they suddenly making a fuss about this* (= becoming excited about it)? [C]

fuss /fʌs/ *v* [I] to become upset or excited • *She was never one to fuss about insignificant things.* ○ *Some people like to be fussed over* (= receive a lot of attention). ○ *She sat there fussing with her bright red dress* (= touching and moving it nervously).

fussy [NOT SATISFIED] /'fʌs·i/ *adj disapproving* not easily satisfied or pleased; worried or careful about unimportant details • *She's really fussy about who she goes out with.* ○ *Kevin's a fussy eater.*

fussy [TOO DECORATED] /'fʌs·i/ *adj* having too much decoration or too many details • *My new dress is sophisticated but not too fussy.*

futile /'fjuːt̬·əl, 'fjuː·taɪl/ *adj* [not gradable] achieving no result; not effective or successful • *The plane detoured north in a futile attempt to avoid the bad weather.*

futility /fjuː'tɪl·ət̬·i/ *n* [U] • *A sense of futility and powerlessness infected her.*

futon /'fuː·tɑn/ *n* [C] a MATTRESS (= large, flat,

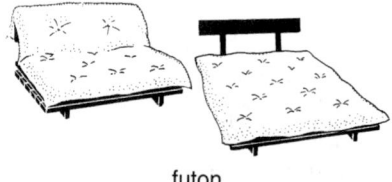

futon

firm bag filled with soft material and used for sleeping on) which is used on the floor or on a wooden frame that can often be folded to make a seat • *a futon sofa*

future TIME /'fjuː·tʃər/ *n* [C/U] time which is to come, or something that will happen or exist later • *What are your plans for the future?* [U] ○ *We hope to buy a house in the foreseeable future.* [U] ○ *He faces an uncertain future.* [C] ○ *I really don't expect any change in the near future.* [U] • *I'll be sure to observe the speed limit* **in the future** (= the next time).

future /'fjuː·tʃər/ *adj* [not gradable] • *She was aware that her writings might speak to future generations of African Americans.*

futuristic /ˌfjuː·tʃəˈrɪs·tɪk/ *adj* relating to the future, or very modern or advanced • *Her latest novel is a futuristic thriller, set in the twenty-first century.* ○ *The mall is noted for its futuristic, glass-steel-and-concrete construction.*

future CONDITION /'fjuː·tʃər/ *n* [C/U] the con-ditions for success • *In 1903, Ford realized that the future of automobiles lay in making them faster and cheaper.* [U] ○ *Candidates always promise a brighter future for Americans.* [C usually sing]

future GRAMMAR /'fjuː·tʃər/ *adj* [not gradable] *specialized* (in grammar) having the tense of the verb used to describe actions, events, or states that will happen or exist later • *In the sentence, "Who will look after the dog?", the phrase "will look" is in the future tense.* • The **future perfect** is a tense formed using "will have" or "shall have" with a past participle to show that an action will be completed by a particular time in the future: *"I will have left by noon" is in the future perfect.* • LP TENSES

fuzz /fʌz/ *n* [U] *infml* light, loose hairs or fibers, or a covering or mass of these • *He's got a little adolescent fuzz on his upper lip.* ○ *Nylon doesn't create fuzz like natural fibers.*

fuzzy /'fʌz·i/ *adj* • *I peel peaches because I don't like their fuzzy skins.*

fuzzy /'fʌz·i/ *adj* not clear or not easily heard, seen, or understood • *Is the picture always fuzzy on your TV?* ○ *The basic facts of the story are starting to emerge though the details are still fuzzy.*

FYI *abbreviation for* for your information • *FYI, tomorrow's staff meeting is scheduled for 10 A.M.*

G, g

G [LETTER] , **g** /dʒiː/ *n* [C] *pl* **G's** or **Gs** or **g's** or **gs** the seventh letter of the English alphabet

G [MUSICAL NOTE] /dʒiː/ *n* [C/U] *pl* **G's** or **Gs** the fifth note in the **major scale** (= series of notes) that begins on the note C, or a set of notes based on this note

g [WEIGHT] *n* [C] *pl* **g** *abbreviation for* GRAM

G [MOVIE] /dʒiː/ *adj abbreviation for* GENERAL, used in the US for movies considered suitable for all people, including children of any age • Compare NC-17; PG; R [MOVIE]; X [SEXUAL].

gab /gæb/ *v* [I] *-bb- infml* to talk continuously and eagerly, esp. about unimportant matters • *The two of us were always gabbing away.*

gab /gæb/ *n* [U] • *Along with his gift for gab, he has a great grasp of human nature.*

gable /ˈgeɪ·bəl/ *n* [C] the triangular top end of the wall of a building where it meets the sloping parts of a roof

gadget /ˈgædʒ·ət/ *n* [C] a small device or machine with a particular purpose • *This handy gadget separates egg yolks from whites.*

gaffe /gæf/ *n* [C] an embarrassing mistake • *His failure to consult with the county's black leadership was a major gaffe.*

gag [PIECE OF CLOTH] /gæg/ *n* [C] a piece of cloth that is put over or in a person's mouth to stop them from speaking, shouting, or calling for help • *Her hands and feet were tied and a gag placed over her mouth.* • A **gag order/rule** is an official order not to discuss something, esp. a legal case.

gag /gæg/ *v* [T] *-gg-* • *He was bound and gagged and left in a cell for three days.*

gag [ALMOST VOMIT] /gæg/ *v* [I] *-gg-* to experience the sudden, uncomfortable feeling of tightness in the throat and stomach that makes you feel you are going to vomit • *The smell of burning rubber made him gag.*

gag [JOKE] /gæg/ *n* [C] *infml* a joke, esp. one told by an actor or COMEDIAN • *He used to write gags for a talk-show host.*

gaggle /ˈgæg·əl/ *n* [C] a group of GEESE, or a group of people, esp. if they are noisy or silly • *A gaggle of kids followed him down the street.*

gaiety /ˈgeɪ·ət·i/ *n* [U] happiness and excitement • *She loved the gaiety of the holiday season.* • USAGE: The related adjective is GAY [HAPPY].

gaily /ˈgeɪ·li/ *adv* happily or brightly • *gaily colored blouses*

gain [OBTAIN] /geɪn/ *v* [T] to obtain (something useful, advantageous, or positive), esp. over a period of time • *He gained control of the business.* ○ *You've got nothing to lose and everything to gain.* ○ *He hoped to gain an advantage by beginning his campaign early.*

gain /geɪn/ *n* [C/U] • *The commissioner denied having used his office for personal gain.* [U]

gain [INCREASE] /geɪn/ *v* [I/T] to increase in weight, speed, height, or amount • *I've gained weight, and I'm going on a diet.* [T] ○ *The campaign has been gaining momentum ever since the television ads started to run.* [T] ○ *Step on the gas—they're gaining on us* (= getting nearer to us). [I] • If a clock or watch gains or gains time, it works too quickly and shows a time that is later than the real time. [I/T]

gain /geɪn/ *n* [C/U] • *Stock prices rose again today after yesterday's gains.* [C]

gait /geɪt/ *n* [C] a particular way of walking • *He walked with a slow, stiff gait.*

gal [GIRL] /gæl/ *n* [C] *infml* a GIRL

gal. [VOLUME] *n* [C] *pl* **gal.** or **gals.** *abbreviation for* GALLON

gala /ˈgeɪ·lə, ˈgæl·ə/ *n* [C] a special public occasion at which there is a lot of entertainment • *a gala affair*

galaxy /ˈgæl·ək·si/ *n* [C] one of the large, independent groups of stars in the universe • A galaxy is sometimes used to describe a gathering of famous people: *a galaxy of Hollywood stars*

gale /geɪl/ *n* [C] a very strong wind • *I could hear* **gales of laughter** (= a lot of loud laughter) *coming from downstairs.*

gall [ANNOY] /gɔːl/ *v* [T] to make (someone) feel annoyed, esp. because they feel they have not been respected • *It galls him to take orders from a less experienced colleague.*

galling /ˈgɔː·lɪŋ/ *adj* • *He found his reduced status galling.*

gall [RUDENESS] /gɔːl/ *n* [U] rudeness and inability to understand that your behavior or what you say is not acceptable to other people • *I don't know how she can have the gall to accuse other people of being lazy when she comes in late every day!* [+ to infinitive]

gallant [BRAVE] /ˈgæl·ənt/ *adj* showing no fear of dangerous or difficult things • *She made a gallant effort to win, even if her effort fell short.*

gallant [POLITE] /gəˈlɑnt, gəˈlænt, ˈgæl·ənt/ *adj* (of a man) polite to women, esp. when in public • *He was always charming and gallant toward women.*

gall bladder /ˈgɔːlˌblæd·ər/ *n* [C] a small, bag-like bodily organ connected to the LIVER which stores a liquid substance that helps you to digest food

gallery [BUILDING] /ˈgæl·ə·ri/ *n* [C] a room or building that is used for showing or selling works of art • *There are some contemporary art galleries you should visit.*

gallery [RAISED AREA] /ˈgæl·ə·ri/ *n* [C] a raised area around the sides or at the back of a large room that provides extra space for people to sit or stand

galley /ˈgæl·i/ n [C] a kitchen in a ship or aircraft

gallivant /ˈgæl·ə,vænt/ v [I] *humorous* to visit or go to a lot of different places, enjoying yourself and having few worries or responsibilities • *I don't go gallivanting around like this every night.*

gallon /ˈgæl·ən/ (*abbreviation* **gal.**) n [C] a unit of measurement of volume of liquid equal to 4 quarts or 3.78 liters

gallop /ˈgæl·əp/ v [I/T] (of a horse) to run fast so that all four feet come off the ground together in each act of forward movement

gallop /ˈgæl·əp/ n [C] • *The horse suddenly broke into a gallop.*

galloping /ˈgæl·ə·pɪŋ/ adj [not gradable] increasing or developing at a very fast and often uncontrollable rate • *galloping inflation*

gallows /ˈgæl·oʊz/ n [C] pl **gallows** a raised, wooden structure used, esp. in the past, for hanging and killing criminals as a punishment

galore /gəˈlɔːr, -ˈloʊr/ adj [only after n; not gradable] in great amounts or numbers • *Down South you get biscuits and gravy and fried foods galore.*

galoshes /gəˈlɑʃ·əz/ pl n large, waterproof shoes, usually made of rubber, for wearing over ordinary shoes esp. during snowy weather

galvanize /ˈgæl·və,naɪz/ v [T] to cause (someone) to suddenly take action, esp. by shocking or exciting them in some way • *Why not use the media to galvanize the community into action?*

gambit /ˈgæm·bət/ n [C] something that you do or say that is intended to achieve an advantage and usually involves taking a risk • *The arrest of the political leader was seen as the opening gambit in a move to take control of the government.*

gamble /ˈgæm·bəl/ v to risk losing money in the hope of winning a lot more money, esp. if the result of a future event happens as you hope • *She spent her day gambling at the slot machines in a Las Vegas casino.* [I] ○ *He gambled away most of his money.* [M] • To gamble is also to do something that you think is worth doing although it might not succeed or you might lose money: *We're gambling that enough people will show up at the concert to cover our expenses.* [+ *that* clause]

gamble /ˈgæm·bəl/ n [C usually sing] • *Starting up a new business is always a gamble.*

gambler /ˈgæm·blər/ n [C] • *His father was a gambler who bet on the horses.* • A compulsive gambler is someone who cannot stop risking and usually losing their money in the hope of winning a lot more money.

gambling /ˈgæm·blɪŋ/ n [U] • *Gambling in the form of state lotteries is used to raise money for education.*

game ENTERTAINMENT /geɪm/ n [C] an enter-taining activity, esp. one played by children, or a sports competition • *a baseball/basketball/ football/soccer game* ○ *The kids are playing a computer game.* ○ *I told the children to put away their toys and games* (= equipment for an entertaining activity). • In some activities such as tennis, a game is one part of a competition: *I'm ahead, 3 games to 2.* ○ *Love is just a game to him* (= something that is not treated seriously). ○ *Not telling the whole truth is one of the games that people play* (= one of the ways in which they behave in order to get an advantage). • A **game plan** is a plan for achieving success: *Cutting costs is part of our game plan.* • A **game show** is a television program in which people compete for money and prizes, often by answering questions.

games /geɪmz/ pl n an organized competition consisting of different sporting events • *the Olympic Games*

game WILLING /geɪm/ adj willing to do new or risky things • *The ocean water's cold but I'm going in anyway—are you game?*

game ANIMALS /geɪm/ n [U] wild animals and birds that are hunted for food or sport • *Deer and pheasant are types of game.*

gamut /ˈgæm·ət/ n [U] the whole range of things that can be included in something • *Her stories express the gamut of emotions from joy to despair.*

gander BIRD /ˈgæn·dər/ n [C] a male GOOSE (= a large bird)

gander LOOK /ˈgæn·dər/ n [U] *infml* a quick look • *I heard she had a new car, so I went out to take a gander at it.*

gang CRIMINALS /gæŋ/ n [C] a group of criminals or of people, esp. young men and women, who spend time together and cause trouble • *A gang of armed robbers was involved in a shootout with police yesterday.* ○ *Fights among rival gangs account for most murders in the city.*

gang GROUP /gæŋ/ n [C] a group of people who are friendly with each other or are involved in the same activity • *I went out with the usual gang on Friday night—all my friends from college.*

gang up on /-ˈ-,-/ v adv prep [I] *infml* to unite as a group against someone • *Johnnie says the girls in his class are ganging up on him and teasing him.*

gangly /ˈgæŋ·gli/, **gangling** /ˈgæŋ·glɪŋ/ adj tall, thin, and awkward in movement • *Susan showed up with a tall, gangly boy.*

gangplank /ˈgæŋ·plæŋk/, **gangway** /ˈgæŋ·weɪ/ n [C] a board or similar object put between a ship and the land so that people can get on and off

gangplank

gangrene /ˈgæŋ·griːn, ˌgæŋˈgriːn/ n [U] decay

of part of a person's body because the blood has stopped flowing there • *Doctors were afraid gangrene might set in.*

gangster /ˈɡæŋ·stər/ *n* [C] a member of an organized group of violent criminals

gangway /ˈɡæŋ·weɪ/ *n* [C] a passage for walking, esp. on a ship, or a GANGPLANK

gangway /ˈɡæŋˈweɪ/ *exclamation* used to ask people to move so that you can go past quickly

gap /ɡæp/ *n* [C] an empty space or opening in the middle of something or between two things • *Picking up speed, she closed the gap between them.* ○ *She has a gap between her front teeth.* • A gap can be a period in which something does not exist: *After a gap of five years, Juanita decided to go back to work full-time.* • A gap can also be something missing: *Some people read to fill in gaps in their education.* • A gap can also be a difference between people: *He was trying to bridge the gap between elders and youth, the middle class and poor.*

gape /ɡeɪp/ *v* [I] to look in great surprise at someone or something, esp. with an open mouth • *We all stood gaping at the bear in our backyard.*

gaping /ˈɡeɪ·pɪŋ/ *adj* open wide • *He had a gaping wound and we called for an ambulance.*

garage /ɡəˈrɑʒ, -ˈrɑdʒ, *Cdn* ɡəˈræʒ, -ˈrædʒ/ *n* [C] a building where a car or cars are kept, esp. one that is next to or part of a house • *The car wasn't in the garage so I thought you weren't home.* • A garage is also a place where you can have your car repaired. • A **garage sale** (also **tag sale** or **yard sale**) is an occasion when people sell things, often in their garage or outside their house, that they no longer want.

garb /ɡɑrb/ *n* [U] *slightly fml* clothes that are in a particular style • *She was dressed in nun's garb.*

garbage WASTE /ˈɡɑr·bɪdʒ/ *n* [U] waste material, esp. unwanted food, or a container in which waste is kept • *There will be no regular garbage collection Monday.* ○ *She threw the cheese in the garbage.* • A **garbage bag** is a large plastic bag used to hold waste when it is ready to be collected or a smaller plastic bag used inside a container in the home. • A **garbage can** is a large container made of metal or hard plastic, used to hold waste and usually kept outside. • A **garbage disposal** is an electrical device fitted under a kitchen SINK

that cuts up food waste into very small pieces so that it can be washed away with water. • A **garbageman** is a person whose job is to collect the garbage from containers outside houses and other buildings. • A **garbage truck** is a large vehicle that collects the garbage from containers outside houses and other buildings.

garbage NONSENSE /ˈɡɑr·bɪdʒ/ *n* [U] nonsense, or worthless ideas or things • *He was talking a lot of garbage about women being unfit to serve in the military.*

garbanzo (bean) /ɡɑrˈbɑn·zoʊ (ˈbiːn)/ *n* [C] *pl* **garbanzos** a CHICKPEA

garbled /ˈɡɑr·bəld/ *adj* (of something said) confused and unclear, or giving a false idea • *He left a garbled message on my answering machine.*

garden /ˈɡɑrd·ən/ *n* [C] a piece of land, usually near a home, where flowers and other plants are grown • *We have a vegetable garden.* • Gardens are also public places where flowers, trees, and other plants are grown for people to enjoy. • The **garden variety** of something is the most common or ordinary kind: *a garden-variety wine*

garden /ˈɡɑrd·ən/ *v* [I] • *You've probably never gardened in your life.*

gardener /ˈɡɑrd·nər, -ən·ər/ *n* [C] someone who takes care of a garden either as a hobby or as a regular job

gardening /ˈɡɑrd·nɪŋ, -ən·ɪŋ/ *n* [U] the activity or hobby of taking care of a garden • *I don't do very much gardening.*

gardenia /ɡɑrˈdiːn·jə/ *n* [C] a plant with large white or yellow flowers that have a sweet smell

gargantuan /ɡɑrˈɡæn·tʃə·wən/ *adj* very large • *He has a gargantuan ego.*

gargle /ˈɡɑr·ɡəl/ *v* [I] to wash your mouth or throat by holding liquid in your mouth, keeping your head back, and breathing out slowly through the mouth • *For a sore throat, gargle with warm salt water.*

gargoyle /ˈɡɑr·ɡɔɪl/ *n* [C] a stone object in the shape of the head of an ugly creature, usually seen on the roofs of old churches and other buildings

garish /ˈɡær·ɪʃ, ˈɡer-/ *adj* showy or too brightly colored • *The coffee shop, painted a garish pink, is a landmark in the neighborhood.*

garland /ˈɡɑr·lənd/ *n* [C] a circle made of flowers and leaves worn around the neck or head as a decoration

garlic /ˈɡɑr·lɪk/ *n* [U] a plant of the onion family that has a strong taste and smell and is used in cooking to add flavor • **Garlic bread** is bread that has been spread with a mixture of butter, garlic, and sometimes herbs before being heated.

garment /ˈɡɑr·mənt/ *n* [C] *slightly fml* a piece of clothing • *He's fussy about how a garment fits him.* • A **garment bag** is a long, flat bag

garbage truck

in which suits and other clothes can be kept while traveling.

garner /ˈgɑr·nər/ v [T] to get or earn (something valuable or respected), often with difficulty • *Coppola garnered several Oscars for his movie, "The Godfather."*

garnet /ˈgɑr·nət/ n [C] a dark red stone used in jewelry • *a garnet ring*

garnish /ˈgɑr·nɪʃ/ v [T] to decorate (food) with a small amount of a different food • *Garnish the dish with lemon wedges.*

garnish /ˈgɑr·nɪʃ/ n [C] • *Use chopped parsley for a garnish.*

garret /ˈgær·ət/ n [C] a small room at the top of a house

garrison /ˈgær·ə·sən/ n [C] a group of soldiers living in or defending a town or building, or the buildings that the soldiers live in

garrulous /ˈgær·ə·ləs, ˈgær·jə-/ adj having the habit of talking a lot, esp. about unimportant things • *I had talked too much about myself and felt like a garrulous old fool.*

garter /ˈgɑrt̬·ər/ n [C] a narrow piece of elastic used for holding up a STOCKING or sock

garter snake /ˈgɑrt̬·ər·sneɪk/ n [C] a small snake with a pattern of long, thin marks along its body whose bite is not poisonous

gas MATTER /gæs/ n [C/U] a form of matter that is neither solid nor liquid and can increase in size to fill any container • *Air is a mixture of gases.* [C] • Gas is also the usual word used to talk about **natural gas**: *Do you have an electric stove or do you use gas for cooking?* [U] • Gas is also a feeling of fullness in the stomach that you sometimes get after eating a lot, or the airlike substance such eating produces. [U] • A **gas mask** is a device worn over the face to prevent you from breathing in poisonous gases.

gas /gæs/ v [T] **-ss-** to kill or injure (people or animals) by making them breathe poisonous gas • *Hundreds of thousands of soldiers were gassed in World War I.*

gaseous /ˈgæs·i·əs, ˈgæʃ·əs/ adj consisting of gases • *the gaseous atmosphere of Uranus*

gassy /ˈgæs·i/ adj feeling that your stomach is full of gas

gas LIQUID FUEL /gæs/, **gasoline** /ˈgæs·ə₁liːn, ₁--ˈ-/ n [U] a liquid obtained from PETROLEUM (= dark, thick oil), used esp. as a fuel for cars and other vehicles • *We're running low on gas.* • A **gas station** is a place where drivers can buy fuel and oil.

□**gas up** (obj), **gas** (obj) **up** /ˈ-ˈ-/ v adv [I/M] to fill (a vehicle's fuel container) with gas • *I want to gas up when we get to the next service area.* [I] ○ *Be sure to gas it up before you start on the trip.* [M]

gash /gæʃ/ v [T] to make a long deep cut in (esp. flesh) • *She gashed her knee when she slipped on a rock.*

gash /gæʃ/ n [C] • *He suffered a deep gash on his hand from the broken glass.*

gasket /ˈgæs·kət/ n [C] a flat piece of soft material or rubber put between two joined metal surfaces to prevent gas, oil, or steam from escaping

gasoline /ˈgæs·ə₁liːn, ₁gæs·əˈliːn/ n [U] GAS LIQUID FUEL

gasp /gæsp/ v [I/T] to take a short quick breath through the mouth, esp. because of surprise, pain, or shock • *When he collapsed on stage, the audience gasped.* [I] ○ *"Help me!" he gasped.* [T]

gasp /gæsp/ n [C] • *The circus acrobats drew gasps from the crowd.*

gassy /ˈgæs·i/ adj See at GAS MATTER.

gastric /ˈgæs·trɪk/ adj [not gradable] medical of the stomach • *gastric juices* ○ *a gastric ulcer*

gate /geɪt/ n [C] a section of a fence or outer wall that can swing open to let you through • *I pushed open the gate and went into the backyard.* • A gate is also the door at an airport that you go through to get on an aircraft: *All passengers for flight 103 please proceed to gate D4.*

gate–crasher /ˈgeɪt₁kræʃ·ər/ n [C] a person who goes to a party although they have not been invited to it • *The party was ruined by a couple of gate-crashers who got very drunk.*

gateway /ˈgeɪt·weɪ/ n [C] a place through which you have to go to get to another place, esp. a tall and wide entrance through a wall • *(fig.) The new airport is regarded as the most convenient gateway to southeast Asia.*

gather COLLECT /ˈgæð·ər/ v [T] to collect or obtain (things), esp. from different places • *I went to several libraries to gather information.* ○ *We gathered blackberries from the nearby fields.* • If something gathers momentum/speed, it gradually becomes faster or stronger: *Pressure for reform of the health-care system is gathering momentum.* • If something is **gathering dust**, it is not being used regularly: *My tennis racket has just been gathering dust since I hurt my back.*

gather COME TOGETHER /ˈgæð·ər/ v [I] (of people or animals) to come together in a group • *A crowd gathered to hear her speak.*

gathering /ˈgæð·ə·rɪŋ/ n [C] • *We're having a little social gathering (= meeting of people) tonight and hope you can come.*

gather (obj) UNDERSTAND /ˈgæð·ər/ v slightly fml to understand or believe (something) as a result of something that has been said or done • *From the look on their faces, she gathered (that) they were annoyed with her.* [+ (that) clause]

gator /ˈgeɪt̬·ər/ n [C] short form of ALLIGATOR

gauche /ɡoʊʃ/ adj behaving in a way that offends other people, esp. because of not knowing what is correct or not caring about their feelings • *It was gauche to invite them just two days before the party.*

gaudy /ˈgɔːd·i, ˈɡɑd·i/ adj having too many bright colors • *He was wearing a gaudy Hawaiian shirt.*

gauge /geɪdʒ/ v [T] to calculate (an amount) by using a measuring device or by your own judgment, or to make a judgment about (people's feelings) • *It was not easy to gauge his height from this distance, but he seemed pretty tall.* ○ *It's difficult to gauge how they'll react when they hear the news.* [+ *wh-* word]

gauge /geɪdʒ/ n [C] a device for measuring the amount or size of something • *She used a pressure gauge to measure the air pressure in her bicycle tires.* ○ *The test is simply a gauge of* (= a way of judging) *how well they will do in college.* • A gauge is also a measure of the thickness of a wire or of the opening inside the BARREL (= long part) of a gun: *a 12-gauge shotgun*

gaunt /gɔːnt, gɑnt/ adj very thin, esp. because of illness or hunger • *He's always been thin, but now he looks gaunt, his skin stretched tight over his bones.*

gauntlet /'gɔːnt·lət, 'gɑnt-/ n [C] a long thick GLOVE (= covering for the hand), worn for protection

gauze /gɔːz/ n [U] a very thin, light cloth used for making clothing and for covering cuts in the skin • *a gauze skirt* ○ *a sterile gauze bandage*

gave /geɪv/ past simple of GIVE

gavel /'gæv·əl/ n [C] a small hammer used by an official in charge of a meeting for hitting a wooden block or table in order to get people's attention • *The judge banged her gavel and said, "Quiet, please!"*

gawk /gɔːk/ v [I] to look at something or someone in a foolish way without thinking • *Don't stand there gawking at her, give her a hand!*

gay [HOMOSEXUAL] /geɪ/ adj homosexual • *gay rights* ○ *Mark knew he was gay by the time he was fourteen.* • Sometimes gay refers only to men: *the lesbian and gay community*

gay /geɪ/ n [C] • *The law banned discrimination against gays.*

gay [HAPPY] /geɪ/ adj [-er/-est only] dated (of a person) happy, or (of a place) bright and attractive • *Her gay, lively personality made her attractive to everyone who knew her.* • USAGE: The related noun is GAIETY.

gaze /geɪz/ v [I] to look at something or someone for a long time, esp. in surprise, admiration, or because you are thinking about something else • *He spends hours gazing out of the window when he should be working.*

gaze /geɪz/ n [U] • *I felt his gaze on me as I walked out the door.*

gazebo /gə'ziː·boʊ/ n [C] pl **gazebos** a small, often decorated shelter with no walls, usually in an open space, used for rest and relaxation

gazelle /gə'zel/ n [C] an animal like a small deer that lives in Africa or Asia

gazette /gə'zet/ n [C usually sing] (used only in the titles of newspapers) a newspaper • *the Montreal Gazette*

gazpacho /gə'spɑtʃ·oʊ/ n [U] a spicy soup made from TOMATOES (= juicy, red vegetable) and other vegetables and eaten cold

GDP n [U] abbreviation for gross domestic product, see at GROSS [TOTAL]

gear [MACHINE PART] /gɪr/ n (in a machine) a wheel having pointed parts around the edge that come together with similar parts of other wheels to control how much power from an engine goes to the moving parts of a machine • In a vehicle, a gear is any of several limited ranges of power that are used for different speeds: *Use second gear going up a steep hill.* [U] • A **gearshift** (also **stick shift**) is a metal rod or handle that you use to change from one gear to another in a vehicle.

gear [MAKE READY] /gɪr/ v [always + adv/prep] to make something ready or suitable for a particular purpose • *Our program is geared to the needs of children.* [T] ○ *Politicians are already gearing up* (= preparing) *for the next election.* [I]

gear [EQUIPMENT] /gɪr/ n [U] equipment or clothes used for a particular activity • *camping gear*

GED n [C] abbreviation for general equivalency diploma (= a document given to someone who did not complete HIGH SCHOOL but has passed an examination on those school subjects)

gee /dʒiː/ exclamation an expression of surprise, enthusiasm, annoyance, etc. • *Gee, I'm so glad you called!*

geese /giːs/ pl of GOOSE [BIRD]

gee whiz /dʒiː'wɪz, -'hwɪz/ exclamation an expression of surprise, enthusiasm, annoyance, etc. • *Gee whiz, where'd you get that hat?*

geezer /'giː·zər/ n [C] an old man • USAGE: This word is sometimes considered offensive.

Geiger counter /'gaɪ·gər,kaʊnt·ər/ n [C] an electronic device for finding and measuring the level of RADIOACTIVITY (= harmful atomic energy)

geisha /'geɪ·ʃə, 'giː-/ n [C] a Japanese woman trained in music and dancing whose job is entertaining men

gel /dʒel/ n [U] a thick, soft, partly liquid substance • *hair gel*

gel /dʒel/ v [I] -ll- (of a liquid) to become thick • *As the pudding cooled, it began to gel.*

gelatin /'dʒel·ət·ən/ n [U] a clear substance obtained by boiling animal bones, skin, etc., and used to make some foods and other substances such as glue

gelding /'gel·dɪŋ/ n [C] a male horse that has had its TESTICLES (= sexual organs that produce sperm) removed

gem /dʒem/ n [C] a precious stone, esp. when cut into a regular shape; jewel • *The necklace was studded with diamonds, rubies, and other gems.* • If you say that something or someone is a gem, you mean that you value them highly for their quality or beauty: *The building was an architectural gem.*

Gemini /'dʒem·ə,naɪ/ n [C/U] the third sign of the ZODIAC, covering the period May 21 to June 21 and represented by TWINS, or a person born during this period

gender SEX /'dʒen·dər/ n [C/U] the male or female sex, or the state of being either male or female • *Discrimination on the basis of gender is not allowed.* [U]

gender GRAMMAR /'dʒen·dər/ n [C/U] specialized (in grammar) the divisions, usually MASCULINE, FEMININE, and NEUTER, into which nouns are separated in some languages • *French has two genders and German has three.* [C]

gene /dʒiːn/ n [C] a specific chemical pattern on a CHROMOSOME (= cell structure) that is received from the parents and controls the development of particular characteristics in an animal or plant • *You inherit half your genes from your mother and half from your father.* • A **gene pool** is all the genes of a particular group of people.

genealogy /,dʒiː·niː'ɑl·ə·dʒi, -'æl-/ n [C/U] the study of the history of the past and present members of a family, or a particular history of this type • *He has produced a genealogy of his family going back to 1732.* [C]

genealogical /,dʒiː·niː·ə'lɑdʒ·ɪ·kəl/ adj [not gradable]

genera /'dʒen·ə·rə/ pl of GENUS

general COMMON /'dʒen·rəl, -ə·rəl/ adj involving or relating to most people, things, or conditions, esp. when these are considered as a unit; not particular or specific • *the general standard of living* ○ *This book is intended for the general reader* (= one who is not a specialist). ○ *He has only a general knowledge of anatomy* (= does not have detailed information about it). • **In general** (= In most cases), *women live longer than men.* • A **general anesthetic** is a drug used to make a person unconscious so that they do not feel pain during an operation. • **General delivery** is a department in a post office that will receive and hold mail for a person to pick up. • A **general election** is a national or state election, rather than a local one. • A **general store** is a store, usually in a rural area, where many different products, including food, are sold.

generality /,dʒen·ə'ræl·ət·i/ n [C usually pl] a statement without details and sometimes without much meaning • *The candidate's speech was full of generalities and never focused on the issues.*

generally /'dʒen·rə·li, -ə·rə·li/ adv • *It was generally believed at the time that both men were guilty.* ○ *The baby generally* (= usually) *wakes up twice during the night.*

generalize /'dʒen·rə,laɪz, -ə·rə-/ v [I] to make a statement that relates to many people, things, or conditions, esp. when based on limited facts • *You can't generalize about a continent as varied as Africa.*

generalization /,dʒen·rə·lə'zeɪ·ʃən, -ə·rə-/ n [C/U] • *The report is full of sweeping generalizations* (= statements that lack facts or details and may be wrong). [C]

general OFFICER /'dʒen·rəl, -ə·rəl/ n [C] a military officer of the highest rank

generate /'dʒen·ə,reɪt/ v [T] to cause to exist; produce • *The new construction project will generate 500 new jobs.* ○ *Her latest book has generated a lot of excitement.* ○ *The power plant generates electricity for the eastern part of the state.*

generation /,dʒen·ə'reɪ·ʃən/ n [U] • *the generation of electricity*

generator /'dʒen·ə,reɪt·ər/ n [C] a machine that produces electricity

generation /,dʒen·ə'reɪ·ʃən/ n [C] all the people of about the same age within a society or within a particular family, or the usual period of time from a person's birth to the birth of his or her children • *the last/next generation* ○ *There were three generations at the wedding—grandparents, parents, and children.* ○ *This farm has been in the family for generations.* • A generation is also a group of products or machines that are all at the same stage of development: *a new generation of AIDS drugs* ○ *third-generation computers* • A **generation gap** is a lack of understanding between older and younger people that results from their different experiences of life. • **Generation X** (also **short form Gen X**) refers to people born in the US in the second half of the 1960s or the early part of the 1970s.

generic /dʒə'ner·ɪk/ adj relating to or shared by a whole group of similar things; not specific to any particular thing • *Christmas has become a sort of generic holiday that is celebrated by people of various religions.* • Generic also means not having a trademark: *a generic drug*

generic /dʒə'ner·ɪk/ n [C] a product, esp. a drug, that is no longer owned or legally controlled by a particular company

generous /'dʒen·ə·rəs/ adj (of someone) willing to give help or support, esp. more than is usual or expected, or (of something) larger than usual or expected • *a generous donor* ○ *food in generous portions*

generosity /,dʒen·ə'rɑs·ət·i/ n [U] • *She is admired for her generosity.*

generously /'dʒen·ə·rə·sli/ adv • *Please give generously to those in need.*

genesis /'dʒen·ə·səs/ n [U] the time when something came into existence; the beginning or origin • *the genesis of life on earth* • In the Bible, Genesis is the first book of the Old Testament, describing how God created the world.

genetic /dʒə'neţ·ɪk/ adj relating to the biological process by which the characteristics of living things are passed from parents to children • *Some diseases are caused by genetic de-*

fects. • **Genetic engineering** is the science of changing the structure of the GENES (= specific chemical patterns) of a living thing, used esp. in developing new food products and in medicine.

genetics /dʒə'net·ɪks/ *n* [U] the study in biology of how the characteristics of living things are passed through the GENES (= specific chemical patterns) from parents to children
genetically /dʒə'net·ɪ·kli/ *adv* • *genetically engineered plants*

genial /'dʒiːn·jəl/ *adj* friendly and pleasant • *a genial personality*

genie /'dʒiː·ni/ *n* [C] a spirit, esp. a magical spirit who will do whatever the person who controls it asks it to do

genitals /'dʒen·ət·ᵊlz/, **genitalia** /ˌdʒen·ə'teɪl·jə/ *pl n* the sex organs, esp. the penis and vagina
genital /'dʒen·ət·ᵊl/ *adj* [not gradable] • *the genital organs*

genius /'dʒiːn·jəs/ *n* [C/U] a very great and rare natural ability of the mind, or a person having this ability • *Einstein was a scientific genius.* [C] ○ *His idea was a stroke of genius!* [U] ○ (*slightly fml*) *She has a genius* (= special skill) *for raising money.* [U]

genocide /'dʒen·ə,saɪd/ *n* [U] the intentional killing of all of the people of a nation, religion, or racial group

genre /'ʒɑn·rə, 'ʒɑ̃·rə/ *n* [C] a type of literature, art, or music characterized by its particular subject or style • *the genre of landscape painting*

genteel /dʒen'tiːl/ *adj* polite and correct in manner, or trying to be polite and correct in order to appear to be of a high social class • *When in company, they affected genteel table manners.*

gentile /'dʒen·taɪl/ *n* [C] a person who is not Jewish

gentle /'dʒent·ᵊl/ *adj* calm, kind, or soft; not violent or severe • *a gentle smile* ○ *a gentle breeze* ○ *The path has a gentle* (= gradual) *slope.*
gently /'dʒent·li/ *adv* • *He gently lifted the baby out of the crib.*
gentleness /'dʒent·ᵊl·nəs/ *n* [U]

gentleman /'dʒent·ᵊl·mən/ *n* [C] *pl* **-men** /'dʒent·ᵊl·mən/ a man who is polite and behaves well toward other people • *a perfect gentleman* • Gentleman is often used as a polite way of referring to any man: *This gentleman has a question.* ○ *Ladies and gentlemen, may I have your attention.* [LP] TITLES AND FORMS OF ADDRESS • (*infml*) In speech, a gentleman often means simply a man: *The gentleman involved had a long history of this type of offense.*

gentrification /ˌdʒen·trə·fə'keɪ·ʃən/ *n* [U] the process by which a poor neighborhood in a city is changed by people who have money, including esp. the improvement or replacement of buildings • USAGE: This word is now

sometimes used in a disapproving way, but was originally considered positive.
gentrify /'dʒen·trə,faɪ/ *v* [T] • *The area where he grew up has been gentrified and lost all its old character.*

gentry /'dʒen·tri/ *pl n* people of high social class • *His diaries provide an intimate look at the life of the gentry in 18th-century Virginia.*

genuflect /'dʒen·jə,flekt/ *v* [I] to bend one knee or touch one knee to the floor as a sign of worship or respect • *The people genuflected as they passed in front of the altar.*
genuflection /ˌdʒen·jə'flek·ʃən/ *n* [C]

genuine /'dʒen·jə·wən, -,waɪn/ *adj* being what something or someone appears or claims to be; real, not false • *genuine leather* ○ *a genuine masterpiece* ○ *She showed genuine* (= sincere) *sorrow at the news.*
genuinely /'dʒen·jə·wən·li, -,waɪn·li/ *adv* • *I'm genuinely* (= sincerely) *sorry if I offended you.*
genuineness /'dʒen·jə·wən·nəs/ *n* [U] • *No one doubts the genuineness of your concern.*

genus /'dʒiː·nəs/ *n* [C] *pl* **genera** /'dʒen·ə·rə/ *specialized* a group of animals or plants that share some characteristics in a larger biological group

geography /dʒiː'ɑg·rə·fi/ *n* [U] the study of the features and systems of the earth's surface, including continents, mountains, seas, weather, and plant life, and of the ways in which countries and people organize life within an area
geographic /ˌdʒiː·ə'græf·ɪk/, **geographical** /ˌdʒiː·ə'græf·ɪ·kəl/ *adj* [not gradable] • *a geographic region*

geology /dʒiː'ɑl·ə·dʒi/ *n* [U] the study of the rocks and physical processes of the earth in order to understand its origin and history
geological /ˌdʒiː·ə'lɑdʒ·ɪ·kəl/ *adj* [not gradable] • *a geological survey*

geometry /dʒiː'ɑm·ə·tri/ *n* [U] the area of mathematics relating to the study of space and the relationships between points, lines, curves, and surfaces
geometric /ˌdʒiː·ə'me·trɪk/, **geometrical** /ˌdʒiː·ə'me·trɪ·kəl/ *adj* consisting of shapes such as squares, triangles, or rectangles • *a geometric pattern*

geranium /dʒə'reɪ·ni:·əm/ *n* [C] a plant with red, pink, or white flowers and round leaves

gerbil /'dʒɜr·bəl/ *n* [C] a small, furry animal that has long back legs and a thin tail, and is often kept as a pet

geriatric /ˌdʒer·i:'æ·trɪk/ *adj* relating to the medical care and treatment of old people • *geriatric medicine/patients* • (*often disapproving*) Geriatric also means old: *This place attracts a geriatric crowd.* ○ *Ballplayers are geriatric at 36.*

geriatrics /ˌdʒer·i:'æ·trɪks/ *n* [U] the area of study in medicine that deals with the care and treatment of old people and the diseases of old age

germ ORGANISM /dʒɜrm/ *n* [C usually pl] a very small organism that causes disease • *The patient has little natural resistance to germs.* • **Germ warfare** is **biological warfare**. See at BIOLOGY.

germ ORIGIN /dʒɜrm/ *n* [C] the origin of something that develops, esp. a cell from which grain grows or the beginning of an idea • *Alejandro's suggestion was the germ of an idea.*

German measles /ˈdʒɜr·mənˈmiː·zəlz/, *medical* **rubella** *n* [U] an infectious virus that causes a fever, a cough, and small red spots on your skin

German shepherd /ˈdʒɜr·mənˈʃep·ərd/ *n* [C] a type of dog that is large and is often used as a guard dog, for police work, and to lead the blind

germicide /ˈdʒɜr·məˌsɑɪd/ *n* [C] a substance that kills GERMS (= very small organisms that cause disease)

germinate /ˈdʒɜr·məˌneɪt/ *v* [I/T] to start growing, or to cause (a seed) to start growing • *This community is where the seeds of Gandhi's philosophy germinated.* [I]

gerrymander /ˈdʒer·iːˌmæn·dər/ *v* [T] to divide (an area) into election DISTRICTS (= special areas of voters who elect someone) in a way that gives an unfair advantage to one group or political party

gerrymandering /ˈdʒer·iːˌmæn·də·rɪŋ/ *n* [U] • *Enlarging the district to dilute the Latino vote is a blatant example of gerrymandering.*

gerund /ˈdʒer·ənd/ *n* [C] *specialized* (in grammar) a word ending in "-ing" that is made from a verb and is used like a noun • *In the sentence "Everyone enjoyed Tyler's singing," the word "singing" is a gerund.* • LP THE -ING FORM OF VERBS at PRESENT GRAMMAR

gestation /dʒeˈsteɪ·ʃən/ *n* [U] (the period of) the development of a child or young animal inside its mother's uterus • *The gestation period of rats is 21 days.*

gesticulate /dʒeˈstɪk·jəˌleɪt/ *v* [I] to make movements with your hands or arms, esp. to help express something when you are speaking

gesture MOVEMENT /ˈdʒes·tʃər/ *n* [C] a movement of the body, hands, arms, or head to express an idea or feeling • *He made a rude gesture to the crowd after his tennis match.*

gesture /ˈdʒes·tʃər/ *v* [I] • *When I asked where the children were, she gestured toward the beach.*

gesture SYMBOLIC ACT /ˈdʒes·tʃər/ *n* [C] an action that expresses your feelings or intentions, although it might have little practical effect • *Her warm thank-you note was a nice gesture.*

gesundheit /ɡəˈzʊntˌhɑɪt/ *exclamation* used to wish good health to someone after they have sneezed

get OBTAIN /ɡet/ *v* [T] **getting**, *past* **got** /ɡɑt/, *past part* **gotten** /ˈɡɑt·ᵊn/ or **got** to take (something) into your possession, or have (something) happen that you accept or receive • *He climbed over the fence to get his ball back.* ○ *Monique raised her hand to get the teacher's attention.* ○ *Can I get you a drink?* ○ *Dad keeps telling me to get a job.* ○ *What did you get on the test* (= What mark did you receive)? ○ *I think she gets* (= earns) *about $10 an hour.* ○ *We don't get much snow in this part of the country* (= It does not often snow). • To **get** something often means to buy or pay for it: *He went to the store to get milk.* • **Get a grip on** *your*self (= control your emotions) *and tell me what happened.* • If someone tells you to **get a life,** they mean you are boring. • *Where do these kids get hold of* (= obtain) *these drugs, anyway?* • To **get** your **money's worth** is to receive good value for something you have paid for: *Those sneakers lasted for four years—he really got his money's worth from them.* • *She's an excellent coach and she knows how to get results* (= succeed). • To **get the better/best of** someone is to defeat them: *She played well, but her opponent got the better of her.* • To **get wind of** information is to learn about it, esp. when it has been a secret: *We have a crisis on our hands and don't want the press get wind of it.*

get BECOME /ɡet/ *v* [L] **getting**, *past* **got** /ɡɑt/, *past part* **gotten** /ˈɡɑt·ᵊn/ or **got** to become or start to be • *Your coffee is getting cold.* ○ *He's gotten so big, I hardly recognized him.* ○ *They're getting married later this year.* ○ *Tom got lost in the woods.* ○ *What time do you get off work?* ○ *We'd better get going/moving or we'll be late.* • To **get better** is to improve. • *After she left me, all I thought about was how I could get even with her* (= punish her by doing something equally bad to her). • (*slang*) *Those kids were mean—they told the new girl to get lost* (= go away). • *He and his friend tried to start a band but it never got off the ground* (= started). • If something **gets underway,** it begins to happen: *The Democratic convention gets underway tomorrow in Chicago.* • A **get-well card** is a card that expresses the wish that someone who has been ill will become healthy again soon.

get BECOME ILL WITH /ɡet/ *v* [T] **getting**, *past* **got** /ɡɑt/, *past part* **gotten** /ˈɡɑt·ᵊn/ or **got** to become ill with (a disease) • *Everyone seems to be getting the flu.*

get CAUSE /ɡet/ *v* [T] **getting**, *past* **got** /ɡɑt/, *past part* **gotten** /ˈɡɑt·ᵊn/ or **got** to cause (something) to be done or persuade (someone) to do something • *The bed is too wide—we'll never get it through the door.* ○ *I can't get this printer to work!* • (*infml*) *Hey, Francine, get a move on* (= hurry) *or you'll be late!* • When you **get** your **feet wet,** you are beginning a new experience or becoming used to a new situation: *I worked as a substitute teacher for a while, just to get my feet wet.* • *I haven't talked to her in years and wouldn't know how to get*

GET, HAVE, AND OTHER VERBS USED TO MEAN "CAUSE"

to cause someone to do something

The verbs **get, have,** and **make** are often used in the following patterns with the meaning "to cause someone to do something."

get	*I finally* **got** *the doctor* **to** *come.*	= persuade; often suggests the other person was unwilling
	We **got** *her talking about the past.*	= cause or persuade; used esp. of actions that continue
have	*I* **had** *him fill out an application.*	= request or tell
	Could you **have** *her call me back?*	= request or tell
	The clown **had** *us all laughing.*	used esp. of actions that continued; often suggests the action was unexpected
make	*She* **made** *him apologize.*	= force or require
	You'll **make** *me miss my train.*	= cause
	The dust **made** *me sneeze.*	= cause

When **have** and **make** are followed by an infinitive, *to* is not used. But when **make** is used in passive sentences, *to* is required:

He was **made to** *apologize.*

Have is not used in this way in passive sentences.

cause	*Ice* **caused** *the driver* **to** *lose control.*	slightly formal; used esp. of results that are bad
keep	*Sorry to* **keep** *you waiting.*	= cause to continue
lead	*What* **led** *the police* **to** *suspect him?*	= influence or cause

to cause something to happen

These verbs are also used with things as objects in most of the same patterns, with the meaning "to cause something to happen."

I can't **get** *this door* **to** *stay closed.* • *We'll* **get** *this bus moving in just a few minutes.* • *Don't worry—I'll* **have** *it working in no time.* • *The onions* **made** *my eyes tear.*

to cause a state

These verbs are also used with people as objects and an adjective, noun, or other object following, to express the meaning "to cause something to be in a particular state."

I have to **get** *the kids ready for school.*
This medicine might **make** *you sleepy.*
The committee **made** *him treasurer.*
Here's more work to **keep** *you busy.*
This plan will **cause** *us trouble.*

LP **Verbs with two objects**

---

hold of *her anymore* (= communicate with her). • *Let the kids run around a little longer, maybe they'll* **get** *it* **out of** *their* **system** (= do it enough so they will not want to do it any longer). • If you **get rid of** something or someone, you find a way to make them leave or free yourself from something unwanted: *I can't wait to get rid of that ugly old couch.* • *(infml)* *If we're going to be on time, we'd better* **get this show on the road** (= begin what we have planned). • When people **get** their **wires crossed**, they have a different understanding of the same situation: *We must have got our wires crossed—I thought she was arriving tomorrow, not today.*

get PREPARE /get/ v [T] **getting,** past **got** /gɑt/, past part **gotten** /ˈgɑt·ᵊn/ or **got** to prepare (a meal) • *Why don't you* **get** *supper ready?*

get MOVE /get/ v [always + adv/prep] **getting,** past **got** /gɑt/, past part **gotten** /ˈgɑt·ᵊn/ or **got** to move in a particular direction • *Get away from that wet paint!* [I] ○ *He got down on*

his hands and knees to look for his contact lens. [I] ○ *Her throat was so sore that she had trouble getting the medicine down* (= swallowing it). [T] ○ *I hit my head as I was getting into the car.* [I] ○ *Momma said we have to get these wet clothes off* (= remove them). [M] • To **get off** a road when you are driving means to turn onto another road: *Get off the expressway at exit 43.* [I] • To **get off** a train, bus, or aircraft is to leave it: *Get off at Union Station.* [I] ○ *Get your feet off the couch* (= move them off it). [T] • To **get in on the act** means to take advantage of something that someone else started: *We designed the Web page, and now everyone else in our class wants to get in on the act.* • If you **get** something **off** your **chest**, you express something that has been worrying you and that you have wanted to say: *I thought these meetings would help the kids air their concerns and get it off their chests.*

get TRAVEL /get/ v [T] **getting,** past **got** /gɑt/, past part **gotten** /ˈgɑt·ᵊn/ or **got** to go into (a vehicle or aircraft) for traveling • *We could call for a taxi or get the bus.*

get ARRIVE /get/ *v* [I always + adv/prep] **getting**, *past* **got** /gɑt/, *past part* **gotten** /'gɑt·ᵊn/ or **got** to arrive at a place or reach a stage in a process • *We only got as far as Denver when the car broke down.* ○ *What time does he normally get home from work?* ○ *We're not getting very far* (= not advancing) *with this computer program, are we?* • If someone says that they are **getting somewhere**, it means they are making progress, obtaining desired results, or achieving a goal. If they are **not getting anywhere**, they are not achieving anything: *After months of talks, negotiators think they'll finally getting somewhere.* ○ *His parents tried to talk him out of enlisting, but didn't get anywhere.*

get UNDERSTAND /get/ *v* [T] **getting**, *past* **got** /gɑt/, *past part* **gotten** /'gɑt·ᵊn/ or **got** to understand • *I think I got the general idea of the sermon.* ○ *The music was loud and I didn't get what he said.* ○ *I never dated Leanne—you've got it all wrong* (= you are confused about this matter). • If you **get the hang of** something, you learn how to do it, esp. when it is not simple or obvious: *I'll teach you how to use this program—you'll get the hang of it after a while.* • *I ignore him every time I see him, so you'd think he'd get the message/get the point* (= understand the intended meaning). • To **get** someone **wrong** is to be offended because you do not understand them correctly: *Don't get me wrong—I like your haircut, I'm just surprised.*

get CALCULATE /get/ *v* [T] **getting**, *past simple* **got** /gɑt/, *past part* **gotten** /'gɑt·ᵊn/ or **got** to calculate (the answer to a mathematical problem) • *What do you get if you divide 20 by 4?*

get ANSWER /get/ *v* [T] **getting**, *past* **got** /gɑt/, *past part* **gotten** /'gɑt·ᵊn/ or **got** to answer (a ringing telephone, a knock at the door, etc.) • *Hey, Juan, someone's at the door—would you get it, please?*

get HIT /get/ *v* [T] **getting**, *past* **got** /gɑt/, *past part* **gotten** /'gɑt·ᵊn/ or **got** to hit (someone), esp. with something thrown or a bullet • *His first shot missed, but the second got him in the leg.*

get ANNOY /get/ *v* [T] **getting**, *past* **got** /gɑt/, *past part* **gotten** /'gɑt·ᵊn/ or **got** *infml* to cause (someone) to feel annoyance • *It gets me when I have to both cook dinner and clean the dishes.* • If someone **gets** your **goat** or **gets under** your **skin**, they make you very annoyed or angry: *When I park in her space, it really gets her goat.* • If someone **gets in** your **hair**, they annoy you, usually by being present all the time when you wish they weren't: *The children have been getting in my hair all afternoon.* • If you **get on** someone's **nerves**, you annoy them a lot.

get CAUSE EMOTIONS /get/ *v* [T] **getting**, *past*

got /gɑt/, *past part* **gotten** /'gɑt·ᵊn/ or **got** *infml* to have an emotional effect on (someone) • *That scene in the movie, when the father and daughter are reunited, always gets me.* • If something **gets** you **down**, you feel unhappy.

get PUNISH /get/ *v* **getting**, *past simple* **got** /gɑt/, *past part* **gotten** /'gɑt·ᵊn/ or **got** *infml* • If you **get it/get yours/get what's coming to you**, you are punished: *When Mom finds out you skipped school yesterday, you're going to get it.*

□ **get across** *obj*, **get** *obj* **across** /ˌ·-'-/ *v adv* [M] to cause (an idea or message) to be communicated successfully • *I hoped to get across the idea that a community is more than just a bunch of people living in one place.*

□ **get ahead** /ˌ·-'-/ *v adv* [I] to achieve success, often in your work or in society • *You've got to take risks if you want to get ahead.*

□ **get along/on** /ˌ·-'-, -'-/ *v adv* [I] to have a good relationship or deal successfully with a situation • *Alexis and her roommate are getting along better.* ○ *She doesn't get on well with her father.*

□ **get around** DEAL WITH /ˌ·-'-/ *v adv* [T] to find a way of dealing with or avoiding (a problem) • *He was trying to get around paying tax on that income.*

□ **get around** (*obj*) TRAVEL /ˌ·-'-/ *v adv* [I/T] to travel or move from place to place • *You need a car to get around town.* [T] ○ *During her last few years, Edna couldn't get around very well.* [I] ○ *It didn't take long for the rumor that he was leaving to get around the office.* [T]

□ **get around to** /ˌ·-'--/ *v adv prep* [T] to find time to do (something that you have intended or would like to do) • *I wanted to see that movie but never got around to it.*

□ **get at** SUGGEST /'·ˌ-, '--/ *v prep* [T] to suggest or express (something) in a way that is not direct or clear • *You mean I shouldn't come tonight—is that what you're getting at?*

□ **get at** REACH /-'-/ *v prep* [T] to reach (something) • *I keep cleaning supplies on a high shelf where my three-year-old can't get at them.*

□ **get away** /ˌ·-'-/ *v adv* [I] to leave or escape • *Wouldn't it be nice to get away for a weekend?*
getaway /'get·ə·weɪ/ *n* [C] • *The men made their getaway in a car parked outside the bank.* • A getaway is also a place where or a time when you escape for relaxation or a vacation: *a getaway in the Poconos*

□ **get away with** /ˌ·-'--/ *v adv prep* [T] to escape blame or punishment when you do something wrong, or to avoid criticism or harm when you do something risky • *She thought she could get away with cheating on her taxes.*

□ **get back** RETURN /-'-/ *v adv* [I] to return, esp. to your home • *When did you get back from Hawaii?*

□ **get back** *obj* OBTAIN AGAIN , **get** *obj* **back** /-'-/ *v adv* [M] to obtain (something) again after loss or separation • *She was thrilled to get her old job back.*

▢ **get back at** /-'-,-/ *v adv prep* [T] to punish (someone) because they have done something wrong to you • *I think he's trying to get back at her for what she said in the meeting.*

▢ **get back to** START AGAIN /-'--/ *v adv prep* [T] to continue doing (something) that you started earlier • *I'd better get off the phone—I have to get back to making supper.*

▢ **get back to** COMMUNICATE /-'--/ *v adv prep* [T] to communicate with (someone) at a later time • *He can't find the phone number right now, but promised to get back to me with it.*

▢ **get by** /-'-/ *v adv* [I] to manage or continue to exist in a state or situation where something is lacking • *When we were students we got by on very little money.*

▢ **get down to** /-'--/ *v adv prep* [T] to start to direct your efforts and attention to (esp. some work) • *We've got to get down to business, folks, or we'll never get the newsletter out on time.*

▢ **get in** ARRIVE /-'--/ *v adv* [I] to arrive at a place • *What time did you say his plane gets in?*

▢ **get in** BE ELECTED /-'--/ *v adv* [I] to be elected to a political position • *If Archer gets in as mayor, he's likely to raise taxes.*

▢ **get in** *obj* FIND TIME , **get** *obj* **in** /-'-, '-,-/ *v adv* [M] to manage to find time for doing (something) or dealing with (someone) • *I'd like to get in some skiing while we're in Colorado.*

▢ **get in** *obj* SAY , **get** *obj* **in** /'-,-/ *v adv* [M] to succeed in saying (something), often in a situation where other people talk a lot too • *She tried to get her suggestion in at the start of the meeting.* • To **get a word in edgewise** means to have an opportunity to speak: *Harold talked so much that nobody could get a word in edgewise.*

▢ **get** *(obj)* **off** /-'-/ *v adv* [I/T] to escape legal punishment, or to help (someone) escape legal punishment • *She was charged with fraud, but her lawyer got her off.* [T]

▢ **get off on** /-'-,-/ *v adv prep* [T] to become excited by (something) • *He really gets off on those little porcelain figurines.*

▢ **get on** /-'-/ *v adv* [I] to grow old • *Uncle Meade's getting on in years—he's 76.* • See also GET ALONG/ON.

▢ **get on with** /-'--/ *v adv prep* [T] to continue doing (something) after stopping • *We don't have all day to finish this job, so can we just get on with it?*

▢ **get out of** AVOID /-'--/ *v adv prep* [T] to avoid doing something that you do not want to do, or to escape responsibility for something • *If I can get out of going to the meeting tonight, I will.*

▢ **get** *(obj)* **out of** *obj* STOP /-'--/ *v adv prep* [T] to stop doing (a regular activity) • *I used to work out every day, but I've gotten out of the habit.* • *Hey, get out of the way* (= move), *I want to put these boxes there.*

▢ **get** *obj* **out of** *obj* FORCE /-'--/ *v adv prep* [T] to obtain (esp. money or information) from (someone) by force or persuasion • *It was not easy to get the truth out of her.*

▢ **get** *obj* **out of** *obj* OBTAIN /-'--/ *v adv prep* [T] *infml* to obtain (esp. a good feeling) by (doing something) • *Anna sometimes gets pleasure out of torturing her kid sister.*

▢ **get over** /-'--/ *v prep* [T] to return to your usual state of health or happiness after having (esp. an illness or bad experience) • *She's just getting over the flu.* ○ *I can't get over how short he is* (= it surprised me). • If you say someone will **get over it**, you mean that they will accept a fact or situation in time: *They're upset that you didn't call, but they'll get over it.*

▢ **get** *obj* **over with** /-'---,-/ *v adv prep* [T] to finish or reach the end of (usually some unpleasant work or duty) • *I'll be glad to get these exams over with.*

▢ **get** *(obj)* **through** *obj* FINISH /-'-/ *v prep* [T] to reach the end of or finish (something) • *Once we get through exams, we'll have three weeks off.* • To get someone through something is to make it possible for them to deal successfully with a difficult or painful experience, and come to the end of it: *My friendship with Carla got me through those tough months just after we moved.*

▢ **get through** COMMUNICATE /-'-/ *v adv* [I] to communicate with someone, esp. by telephone • *I tried phoning her, but I couldn't get through.*

▢ **get** *(obj)* **through** *(obj)* BE UNDERSTOOD /-'-/ *v adv* [I/T] to be understood or believed, or to cause (someone) to understand or believe you • *I just don't seem to be able to get through to him.* [I] • *(infml) How can I get it through your thick head/skull that it's dangerous to swim that far out in the ocean?*

▢ **get to** CAUSE BAD FEELINGS /'--/ *v prep* [T] *infml* to cause feelings, esp. suffering or disgust, in (someone) • *The heat was beginning to get to me so I went indoors.*

▢ **get to** HAVE CHANCE /'--/ *v aux* to have an opportunity to do something • *I never get to see her now that she's moved to California.*

▢ **get to** BEGIN /'--/ *v aux* to begin to do or be • *You're getting to be just like your mother.* • *(infml)* If you do not **get to first base** with something or someone, you are not able to start doing what you intend to do: *We need financing for this project, but we can't get to first base with the banks.* ○ *(infml) I think she's attractive, but I never got to first base* (= developed a sexual relationship) *with her.* • To **get to know** someone or something is to spend time with them so that they become familiar: *I'd like to get to know you better—could we have dinner sometime?* • If you **get to the bottom of** something, you discover the real but sometimes hidden reason that it exists or happens: *Investigators are trying to get to the bottom of what went wrong.*

□**get** *(obj)* **together** /ˌ--ˈ--/ *v adv* [I/T] to have a meeting or a party • *Why don't we all get together on Friday.* [I] • If you **get it together** or **get** your **act together** you make a decision or take positive action: *We would have liked to have gone, but we couldn't get it together to drive there.*

get–together /ˈget·tə,geð·ər/ *n* [C] • *She went home for a family get-together over the weekend.*

□**get** *(obj)* **up** RISE /-ˈ-/ *v adv* [I/T] to rise from bed, or to cause (someone) to rise from bed • *I get the boys up at 7 a.m.* [T] • *Dad* **got up on the wrong side of bed** (= awoke in a bad mood), *and he's been grumpy all day.*

□**get up** *obj* MAKE STRONGER , **get** *obj* **up** /ˈ-ˌ-/ *v adv* [M] to make (your feelings or your determination) stronger in order to do something • *He couldn't get up his courage/nerve to ask her for a date.*

getaway /ˈget·ə,weɪ/ *n* [C] • See at GET AWAY.

get–together /ˈget·tə,geð·ər/ *n* [C] • See at GET TOGETHER.

getup /ˈget·ʌp/ *n* [C] *infml* the particular clothing, esp. when strange or unusual, that someone is wearing • *He was in a weird getup with a red wig.*

get–up–and–go /ˌget,ʌp·ən'goʊ/ *n* [U] *infml* the quality of being energetic, determined, and enthusiastic • *We need someone with real get-up-and-go to run this office.*

geyser /ˈgaɪ·zər/ *n* [C] a pool of hot water that sends a column of water and steam into the air on a regular or irregular schedule

ghastly /ˈgæst·li/ *adj* frightening and shocking • *It was a ghastly crime.*

ghetto /ˈget·oʊ/ *n* [C] *pl* **ghettos** or **ghettoes** a very poor area of a city in which people of the same race or religion live, or a part of a society or group that is in some way set apart • *She lived in the Jewish ghetto on New York's Lower East Side.* ○ *The area is one of the nation's most devastated black ghettos.*

ghost /goʊst/ *n* [C] the spirit of a dead person imagined as visiting the living and usually appearing as a pale, almost transparent form of the dead person • *Do you believe in ghosts?* • *There's* **not a ghost of a chance** *that he'll be promoted* (= It is not possible). • A **ghost town** is a town that was busy in the past but is now empty or nearly empty because the activities that kept people there have stopped.

ghostwrite /ˈgoʊ·straɪt/, **ghost** /goʊst/ *v* [T] **ghostwriting**, *past simple* **ghostwrote** /ˈgoʊ·stroʊt/, *past part* **ghostwritten** /ˈgoʊ,strɪt·ᵊn/ to write (a book, article, or speech) for another person to use as their own

ghostwriter /ˈgoʊ,straɪt̬·ər/ *n* [C] • *Carol worked as a ghostwriter for that radio talk-show host.*

ghoul /ɡuːl/ *n* [C] an evil spirit or frightening creature who enjoys thinking about dead bodies and other such unpleasant things

ghoulish /ˈɡuː·lɪʃ/ *adj* • *Casey likes that ghoulish book about the guy who gets eaten by rats.*

GI /dʒiːˈaɪ/ *n* [C] *pl* **GI's** or **GIs** a soldier in the US army

giant LARGE PERSON / ORGANIZATION /ˈdʒaɪ·ənt/ *n* [C] a person, either real or imaginary, who is extremely large and strong, or a very large or powerful organization • *He was a giant of a man, over six and a half feet tall.* ○ *The merger makes them a giant in the publishing business.*

giant /ˈdʒaɪ·ənt/ *adj* [not gradable] • *a giant corporation* ○ *a giant-size box of cornflakes* ○ *Admitting the problem is a giant* (= large and important) *step forward in your recovery.* • See also GIGANTIC.

giant LEADING PERSON /ˈdʒaɪ·ənt/ *n* [C] a person of great ability, power, or influence • *She was one of the intellectual giants of this century.*

gibberish /ˈdʒɪb·ə·rɪʃ/ *n* [U] confused or meaningless speech or writing • *See if you can make out what he's saying—it sounds like gibberish to me.*

gibe, jibe /dʒaɪb/ *n* [C] an insulting remark intended to make someone look foolish • *racist gibes*

giblets /ˈdʒɪb·ləts/ *pl n* the neck and some other parts, such as the LIVER, of a bird that may be removed before the bird is cooked, or that may be cooked and eaten themselves or used as a flavoring

giddy /ˈgɪd·i/ *adj* having a slight feeling of spinning around or being unable to balance; slightly DIZZY • *After two glasses of wine, she felt giddy and lightheaded.*

gift PRESENT /gɪft/ *n* [C] something that is given, esp. to show your affection; a present • *I have to get my sister a gift for her birthday.* • A present that is **gift-wrapped** is covered with decorative paper, ready for giving.

gift ABILITY /gɪft/ *n* [C] a special or unusual ability; a TALENT • *He has a gift for music—he plays the piano and sings beautifully.*

gifted /ˈgɪf·təd/ *adj* having a special ability • *a gifted artist* • Gifted can also be used more generally to mean intelligent or having a great range of abilities.

gigantic /dʒaɪˈgænt·ɪk/ *adj* extremely large • *a gigantic shopping center*

giggle /ˈgɪg·əl/ *v* [I] to laugh esp. in a childish way, often at something silly • *We couldn't stop giggling.*

giggle /ˈgɪg·əl/ *n* [C] • *There were a few nervous giggles from people in the audience.*

gill /gɪl/ *n* [C usually pl] the organ through which fish and other water creatures breathe

gilt /gɪlt/ *adj* [not gradable] covered with a thin layer of gold or a substance that looks like gold • *gilt-rimmed eyeglasses* • Something that is **gilt-edged** is of the highest quality: *gilt-edged bonds*

gimme /ˈgɪm·i/ *n* [C] *slang* something so easy

to do that it seems as if you only have to reach out and take it • *Though everyone expected the victory by the world champions to be a gimme, in fact it was a close contest.*

gimmick /'gɪm·ɪk/ *n* [C] something invented esp. for the purpose of attracting attention and that has no other purpose or value • *The proposal to cut taxes was nothing but a campaign gimmick.*

gin /dʒɪn/ *n* [U] a type of colorless, strong alcoholic drink

ginger /'dʒɪn·dʒər/ *n* [U] the spicy root of a tropical plant, used esp. as a powder in cooking and baking • **Ginger ale** is a sweet, bubbly drink containing the flavor of ginger. • **Gingerbread** is a type of cake, often dark brown, that contains ginger. • A **gingerbread man** is a spicy cookie that contains ginger and is shaped like a person.

gingerly /'dʒɪn·dʒər·li/ *adv* in a slow, careful way • *Gingerly, he moved the heavy vase.*

gingham /'gɪŋ·əm/ *n* [U] a cotton cloth that has a pattern of woven colored squares on a white background • *a gingham dress*

giraffe /dʒə'ræf/ *n* [C] a large African animal with a very long neck and long legs

girder /'gɜrd·ər/ *n* [C] a long, thick piece of steel or concrete that supports a roof, floor, bridge, or other large structure

girdle /'gɜrd·əl/ *n* [C] a piece of elastic underwear worn around the waist and buttocks, esp. in the past by women, to shape the body

girl /gɜrl/ *n* [C] a female child or, more generally, a female of any age • *Two little girls showed us around the kindergarten.* ○ *The girls' basketball team is undefeated.* • Girl sometimes means daughter: *We have two girls, a six-year-old and an eight-year-old.* • The **Girl Scouts** is an organization for girls that encourages them to take part in different activities and to become responsible and independent. A **Girl Scout** is a member of the organization. • USAGE: Many adult women consider it offensive to be called girls by other people, esp. men, although this was common in the past, and they might still call themselves or their friends girls.

girlhood /'gɜrl·hʊd/ *n* [U] • *She lived in Chicago during her girlhood* (= when she was a child).

girlfriend /'gɜrl·frend/ *n* [C] the female person with whom a male has a romantic or sexual relationship, or the female friend of another female • *I've never met his girlfriend.* ○ *Susan was going out to lunch with her girlfriends.* • Compare BOYFRIEND.

girth /gɜrθ/ *n* [U] the distance around the outside of a thick or fat object, like a tree or a body • *He was a man of massive girth.*

gist /dʒɪst/ *n* [U] the main subject, without details, of a piece of information • *The gist of what she said was that I didn't know what I was talking about.*

give OFFER /gɪv/ *v* [T] **giving**, *past simple* **gave**, *past part* **given** to offer (something of your own) to another person or thing, or to allow (something you own or control) to be owned or used by another • *We're collecting for the Red Cross—please give what you can.* ○ *We're giving Helen a salad bowl/We're giving a salad bowl to Helen as a wedding present.* ○ *Give me back my book/Give my book back* (= Return my book). ○ *Give her enough time* (= Allow her to have enough time) *to finish the exam.* • (*infml*) If you say **give** me **a break**, you are asking someone to relax and let you do something or let something happen: *Give her a break—she was only late by five minutes.* • If you would **give anything/a lot/the world**/your **eyeteeth**/ your **right arm** for something or to do something, you want it very much: *I'd give anything to see the pyramids of Egypt.* • If you **give** someone **a piece of** your **mind**, you are angry with them and are telling them why: *I'd like to give her a piece of my mind.* • If you **give** something **a whirl**, you try it for the first time: *I've never done cross-country skiing before, but I thought I'd give it a whirl this winter.* • (*infml*) If someone **gives** you **hell**, they criticize or punish you severely: *The boss gave me hell for not telling him about it.* • **Give or take** means a little more or a little less compared to the amount mentioned: *The army spent two billion dollars, give or take a few million, to develop the new fighter plane.* • If you **give** someone **the benefit of the doubt**, you accept what they say as true although it is not certain: *She said she was late because her regular train was canceled, and we gave her the benefit of the doubt.* • If someone **gives** you **the cold shoulder**, you are intentionally ignored or treated in an unfriendly way. • If you would **give** someone **the shirt off** your **back**, you would be willing to do anything to help someone. • If you would not **give** someone **the time of day**, you are not friendly to them and will not speak to them or help them: *He kept pestering me to go out with him, but I wouldn't give him the time of day.*

give PRODUCE /gɪv/ *v* [T] **giving**, *past simple* **gave**, *past part* **given** to produce (something, esp. something that is not a physical object) • *He gave her a hard push.* ○ *Give me a phone call when you get home.* ○ *The president is giving a speech tonight.* ○ *The fresh air gave us an appetite* (= made us hungry). ○ *We're giving a birthday party for Kareem.* ○ *He gave me the impression* (= He made me think) *that the deal would go through.* ○ *This car has given* (= caused) *me lots of trouble ever since I got it.* • (*infml*) To **give a damn** or to **give a hoot** is to care: *Don't tell me your problems—I don't give a damn!* ○ *I don't give a hoot what he does.* • *He'll* **give** *them* **a run for** *their* **money** (= compete and have a chance of winning). • To **give birth** is to produce a baby. • (*slightly fml*) To **give rise to** is to lead to: Birth control gave rise to a new era where sex and marriage were no longer linked. • To **give (some) thought to** is to think about or consider carefully: *You should give some thought to how you're going to pay for your son's education.* • To **give way** is to break apart or fall away: *The wooden seats gave way under the weight of the crowd.* • [LP] DO: VERBS MEANING "PERFORM"

give [STRETCH] /gɪv/ *v* [I] **giving**, *past simple* **gave**, *past part* **given** to stretch or become looser • *New shoes will give a little after you've worn them a few times.* ○ *(fig.) The negotiations are completely deadlocked, and neither side will give an inch* (= they refuse to change their positions even a little).

give /gɪv/ *n* [U] • *A cotton sweater doesn't have much give.*

□ **give away** *obj* [TELL] , **give** *obj* **away** /ˌ--'-/ *v adv* [M] to tell (a secret) or show (your feelings) unintentionally • *The look on her face gave her away* (= showed her real feelings).

giveaway /'gɪv·ə,weɪ/ *n* [C usually sing] • *The look on his face when her name is mentioned is a dead giveaway* (= makes his real feelings obvious).

□ **give away** *obj* [SUPPLY FREE] , **give** *obj* **away** /ˌ--'-/ *v adv* [M] to supply at no charge • *They're giving away shopping bags.*

giveaway /'gɪv·ə,weɪ/ *n* [C] something given at no charge, or for which nothing is expected in return

□ **give in** /-'-/ *v adv* [I] to decide to do what someone else wants • *Our kids kept begging us to take them to the beach, and finally we gave in.*

□ **give off** /-'-/ *v prep* [T] to produce (something) as a result of a natural process • *The forest fire gave off thick black smoke.*

□ **give out** [NOT CONTINUE] /-'-/ *v adv* [I] to last no longer, or to work no longer • *Food supplies will give out by the end of the week.*

□ **give out** *obj* [SUPPLY] , **give** *obj* **out** /-'-/ *v adv* [M] to give (something) to each of a number of people • *They're giving out free tickets to the circus.*

□ **give up** *(obj)*, **give** *(obj)* **up** /-'-/ *v adv* to stop doing or to stop having • *He gave up alcohol after his heart attack.* [M] • To give up also means to lose or be defeated: *Although behind in the chess match, he refused to give up.* [I] ○ *Can you guess what actor I'm pretending to be? No, I give up* (= I can't guess). [I] • To **give up on** someone is to expect them to fail: *Most people were ready to give up on him when he left school, but he later returned and earned his degree.*

give–and–take /ˌgɪv·ən'teɪk/ *n* [U] a free exchange of ideas or opinions • *We were simply told what to do—there wasn't any give-and-take.* • **Give-and-take** is also a situation in which people do not agree on everything and so decide to let one side make some of the choices and the other side make the other

choices: *Any successful negotiation involves some give-and-take.*

giveaway /'gɪv·ə,weɪ/ *n* [C] • See at GIVE AWAY [SUPPLY FREE].

given [GIVE] /'gɪv·ən/ *past participle of* GIVE

given [ACCEPTED FACT] /'gɪv·ən/ *n* [C] something that is certain to happen or to be • *It's a given that if he is defeated for reelection, he'll be offered a position in the administration.*

given [KNOWING] /'gɪv·ən/ *prep* considering • *Given his age, he's in excellent physical condition.*

given [ARRANGED] /'gɪv·ən/ *adj* [not gradable] already decided, arranged, or agreed • *At any given time* (= at any particular time), *the jury may reach a verdict, so we'd better stay nearby.* • A **given name** is a **first name**: *His given name is John, but everyone calls him Jack.* See at FIRST.

gizmo /'gɪz·moʊ/ *n* [C] *pl* **gizmos** *infml* any small device • *The store is full of gizmos like pagers and cellular telephones.*

glacier /'gleɪ·ʃər/ *n* [C] a large mass of ice that moves slowly over land, esp. down the side of a mountain, often moving rocks with it and changing the shape of the land

glad /glæd/ *adj* [*-er/-est* only] **-dd-** pleased and happy • *We were glad (that) she succeeded.* [+ *(that)* clause] ○ *You don't have to thank us—we were glad to help.* [+ *to* infinitive]

gladly /'glæd·li/ *adv* [not gradable] • *I'd gladly show her around, but I'll be on vacation next week.*

gladden /'glæd·ən/ *v* [T] to make (someone) happy • *A visit to Disneyland is sure to gladden the heart of any 8-year-old.*

gladiator /'glæd·iː,eɪt̬·ər/ *n* [C] in ancient Rome, a man who fought another man or an animal as a public entertainment

gladiolus /ˌglæd·iː'oʊ·ləs/, **gladiola** /ˌglæd·iː'oʊ·lə/ *n* [C] *pl* **gladioli** /ˌglæd·iː'oʊ·li, -ˌlɑɪ/ or **gladiolas** a tall garden plant that has long, thin leaves and a stem with many brightly colored flowers

glamour, **glamor** /'glæm·ər/ *n* [U] a quality of someone or something that causes excitement and admiration because of its style or attractive appearance • *Hollywood glamour* ○ *The downhill race was one of the glamour events of the Winter Olympics.*

glamorous /'glæm·ə·rəs/ *adj* • *glamorous fashion models* ○ *a glamorous job*

glamorize /'glæm·ə,rɑɪz/ *v* [T] to make (something) more exciting and attractive • *The ad glamorized life in the army, emphasizing travel and adventure.*

glance /glæns/ *n* [C] a quick look at someone or something • *The driver gave a glance back as he moved into the passing lane.* • **At a glance** means almost immediately: *She could see/tell at a glance that something was seriously wrong.*

glitz

glance /glæns/ *v* [I always + adv/prep] • *She glanced around the room to see who was there.*

glancing /'glæn·sɪŋ/ *adj* [not gradable] touching or hitting you quickly and lightly from the side rather than from the front, and usually not doing much damage • *He never saw the ball coming, but fortunately it gave him only a glancing blow.*

gland /glænd/ *n* [C] an organ of the body that produces chemicals that influence various bodily activities, such as growth and sexual desire, and that have an important effect on the organism's health • *sweat glands*

glandular /'glæn·dʒə·lər/ *adj* [not gradable] • *glandular secretions*

glare LOOK /gler, glær/ *v* [I] to look at someone angrily and without moving your eyes • *He kept talking during the concert, and people were glaring at him.*

glare /gler, glær/ *n* [C] • *an angry glare*

glare SHINE /gler, glær/ *v* [I] to shine too brightly • *The sun glared on the snow and the effect was blinding.*

glare /gler, glær/ *n* [U] • *A tinted windshield cuts down on glare.*

glaring /'gler·ɪŋ, 'glær-/ *adj* (of something bad) very obvious • *It was glaring mistake.*

glass /glæs/ *n* [C/U] a hard, transparent material that is used to make windows, bottles, and other objects • *A glass is a small container of glass, usually round and without a handle, for holding a liquid that you can drink, or the liquid held by such a container: She poured some milk into a glass.* [C] ○ *May I have a glass of water?* [C]

glass /glæs/ *adj* [not gradable] made of glass • *a glass jar/bottle* • *A glass ceiling is an upper limit of power or responsibility that prevents someone, esp. a woman, from achieving a top position, esp. when the agreement to limit power is understood rather than stated: The fact that no woman has managed one of the branch offices is pretty strong evidence of a glass ceiling.*

glasses /'glæs·əz/, **eyeglasses** *pl n* two small pieces of specially made glass or transparent plastic worn in front of the eyes to improve sight and held in place with a frame that reaches back over the ears • *a pair of glasses* • PIC BRIDGE

glassful /'glæs·fʊl/ *n* [C] the amount of something that is needed to fill a glass • *Drink a glassful of water with this medicine.*

glassy /'glæs·i/ *adj* [-er/-est] only smooth and shiny like glass • *the glassy surface of the water* • Someone who has glassy eyes or a glassy stare has a fixed expression and seems unable to see anything: *When he arrived at the hospital, his eyes were glassy and he didn't seem to know where he was.*

glassware /'glæs·wer, -wær/ *n* [U] objects made of glass, esp. containers for drinking

glaze /gleɪz/ *n* [C] a shiny surface given to an object or a food, esp. by covering it with a liquid that shines when it dries • *The pottery was famous for the rich glaze of its vases and jugs.*

glaze /gleɪz/ *v* [I/T] • *The cake was glazed with raspberry syrup.* [T] • When someone's eyes glaze over, they become fixed and shiny, as if they are not seeing anything: *By the fourth act of the opera, his eyes had glazed over.* [I]

gleam /gliːm/ *v* [I] to shine with a soft light • *Christmas lights gleamed brightly on the tree.*

gleam /gliːm/ *n* [C] • *the gleam of silver candlesticks* • If you have **a gleam in** your **eye**, your eyes show that you are amused or that you have a secret.

glean /gliːn/ *v* [T] to collect (esp. information) in small amounts and often with difficulty • *From what I was able to glean, the news isn't good.*

glee /gliː/ *n* [U] happiness or great pleasure • *Malone pumped his fist with glee after scoring the game-winner.*

gleeful /'gliː·fəl/ *adj* • *gleeful children*

gleefully /'gliː·fə·li/ *adv* • *She talks gleefully about her adventures.*

glee club /'gliː·klʌb/ *n* [C] a group organized to sing together, often at a school or university

glib /glɪb/ *adj* **-bb-** easy and confident in speech, with little thought or sincerity • *He's not flashy, and he doesn't know how to be glib.*

glide /glaɪd/ *v* [I always + adv/prep] to move easily and continuously, as if without effort • *She glided along on her skates.*

glider /'glaɪd·ər/ *n* [C] an aircraft without an engine that flies by using its long, fixed wings to ride on air currents

glimmer /'glɪm·ər/ *v* [I] (of light) to shine weakly or not continuously • *A candle glimmered faintly in the darkened room.*

glimmer /'glɪm·ər/ *n* [C] • *a glimmer of light* • A glimmer is also a slight sign: *The treaty offered a glimmer of hope to the region.*

glimpse /glɪmps/ *n* [C] a brief look at someone or something • *He caught a glimpse of her face.*

glimpse /glɪmps/ *v* [I/T] • *I glimpsed her walking back from town.* [T]

glint /glɪnt/ *v* [I] to produce or reflect small, bright flashes of light • *sun glinting off a windshield*

glint /glɪnt/ *n* [C] • *a glint in your eye*

glisten /'glɪs·ən/ *v* [I] (esp. of wet surfaces) to shine brightly • *His eyes glistened with tears.*

glitch /glɪtʃ/ *n* [C] *infml* a problem or fault • *a technical glitch* ○ *a minor glitch*

glitter /'glɪt·ər/ *v* [I] to shine with little, bright flashes of reflected light • *The grass glittered like jewels.*

glitter /'glɪt·ər/ *n* [U] • *the glitter of moonlight on the lake* • Glitter is also very small pieces of shiny material used to decorate a surface.

glitz /glɪts/ *n* [U] the showy quality of something • *the glitz and glamour of Hollywood*

glitzy /ˈglɪt·si/ *adj* • *a glitzy restaurant*

gloat /gloʊt/ *v* [I always + adv/prep] to feel or show much pleasure because of your own success or good luck, or because of someone else's misfortune • *You may have won, but don't gloat about it.*

glob /glɑb/ *n* [C] a round mass of a thick liquid or a soft substance • *a glob of wax*

globe WORLD /gloʊb/ *n* [U] the world • *The Olympic Games will be seen around the globe.*

global /ˈgloʊ·bəl/ *adj* relating to the whole world • *We hope an era of peace and global cooperation has begun.* • **Global warming** is a gradual increase in the earth's temperature, caused by gases, esp. **carbon dioxide**, surrounding the earth.

globally /ˈgloʊ·bə·li/ *adv* • *The company is trying to compete globally.*

globe ROUND OBJECT /gloʊb/ *n* [C] an object shaped like a ball, or such an object having a map of the world on its outer surface

gloom SADNESS /gluːm/ *n* [U] a feeling of hopelessness and sadness • *Gloom and anger replaced her earlier upbeat mood.*

gloomy /ˈgluː·mi/ *adj* • *Despite gloomy predictions, the stock market remains strong.*

gloomily /ˈgluː·mə·li/ *adv* • *He watched gloomily as the bus drove off.*

gloom DARKNESS /gluːm/ *n* [U] darkness or near darkness • *Up ahead they could see lights in the gloom.*

gloomy /ˈgluː·mi/ *adj* • *It was another gray, gloomy day.*

glop /glɑp/ *n* [U] *infml* a sticky, thick substance, such as food, that appears unpleasant • *I can't believe they served us this glop.*

glorify /ˈglɔːr·əˌfɑɪ, ˈgloʊr-/ *v* [T] to praise or honor (someone or something), or to make (someone or something) seem more excellent than is actually true • *Our society glorifies violence.* ○ *He has been glorified in the press.*

glorification /ˌglɔːr·ə·fəˈkeɪ·ʃən, ˌgloʊr-/ *n* [U] • *the glorification of wealth*

glory ADMIRATION /ˈglɔːr·i, ˈgloʊr·i/ *n* [U] great admiration, honor, and praise that you earn by achieving something, or something which deserves admiration or honor • *He basked in the glory of his victory.* ○ *She dedicated her work to the glory of God.* ○ *Winning the championship was the crowning glory of her career* (= it was her highest achievement).

glorious /ˈglɔːr·iː·əs, ˈgloʊr-/ *adj* deserving admiration, praise, and honor • *She thought it was a grand and glorious country.*

gloriously /ˈglɔːr·iː·ə·sli, ˈgloʊr-/ *adv* • *The meanings of his paintings are gloriously elusive.*

glory in /ˈ---/ *v prep* [T] to be greatly pleased or proud about (something) • *I ran easily, every muscle glorying in its strength.*

glory BEAUTY /ˈglɔːr·i, ˈgloʊr·i/ *n* [C/U] great beauty, or something that is very beautiful or excellent • *They are restoring the church to its*

former glory. [U] ○ *the glories of ancient Egypt* [C usually pl]

glorious /ˈglɔːr·iː·əs, ˈgloʊr-/ *adj* • *July was a beautiful month of glorious sun.*

gloss SHINE /glɑs, glɔːs/ *n* [U] a smooth shine on the surface of something • *The floor was waxed and buffed to a high gloss.*

glossy /ˈglɑs·i, ˈglɔː·si/ *adj* [-er/-est only] • *He has straight, glossy black hair.* • A glossy magazine or photograph is one printed on shiny paper.

gloss EXPLANATION /glɑs, glɔːs/ *n* [C] an explanation of a word or phrase in a text

gloss /glɑs, glɔːs/ *v* [T] • *Special senses of words are glossed in this dictionary.*

▢**gloss over** /ˈ-ˈ--/ *v adv* [T] to treat (something) in a way that fails to recognize its importance or its faults • *Popular writing sometimes glosses over important facts.*

glossary /ˈglɑs·ə·ri, ˈglɔː·sə-/ *n* [C] an alphabetical list of difficult, technical, or foreign words in a text along with explanations of their meaning

glove /glʌv/ *n* [C] a covering for the hand and wrist, with separate parts for the thumb and each finger, that provides warmth or protection • *leather/rubber gloves* ○ *a pair of gloves* • A **glove compartment** (also **glove box**) is a small container facing the front passenger seat in a car which is used for storing small items.

glow LIGHT /gloʊ/ *n* [U] continuous light, esp. light from something that is heated • *the glow of embers from a fire*

glow /gloʊ/ *v* [I] • *A nightlight glowed dimly in the bedroom.*

glowing /ˈgloʊ·ɪŋ/ *adj* [not gradable] • *the glowing tip of a cigar*

glow LOOK /gloʊ/ *n* [U] a red or warm look • *Her face has a natural, healthy glow.* • A glow is also a positive feeling: *The glow of romance seemed to have worn off.*

glow /gloʊ/ *v* [I] • *His cheeks glowed after the workout.*

glower /ˈglɑʊ·ər, ˈgloʊ-/ *v* [I] to look angry or annoyed • *Grant glowered at the kids crossing his lawn.*

glowing /ˈgloʊ·ɪŋ/ *adj* full of enthusiastic praise • *glowing reviews* ○ *a glowing evaluation*

glowingly /ˈgloʊ·ɪŋ·li/ *adv* • *Engineers speak glowingly of the device.*

glue /gluː/ *n* [U] a sticky substance used for joining things

glue /gluː/ *v* [T] • *I'll just glue the handle back on the cup.* • *During football season, he's **glued** to the TV* (= he watches it a lot).

glum /glʌm/ *adj* [-er/-est only] **-mm-** sad and hopeless • *a glum expression*

glumly /ˈglʌm·li/ *adv* • *Marty nodded glumly.*

glut /glʌt/ *n* [C] a supply or amount that is much greater than necessary • *a glut of new housing* ○ *a glut of information*

glutton /'glʌt·ən/ n [C] a person who regularly eats too much • *What a glutton—he ate a whole pizza by himself.*

gnarled /narld/ adj rough and twisted in shape • *ancient gnarled trees* ○ *gnarled hands*

gnash /næʃ/ v [T] to bring (your top and bottom teeth) together quickly • If you **gnash** your **teeth**, you feel very angry or express anger publicly: *Petersen is gnashing his teeth over his inability to prove his innocence.*

gnat /næt/ n [C] a small flying insect that bites

gnaw [BITE] /nɔː/ v [I/T] to bite or chew (something) repeatedly • *The cat began to gnaw at the towel beneath him.* [I]

gnaw [FEEL ANXIOUS] /nɔː/ v [I always + adv/ prep] to cause someone to feel continual anxiety or pain

gnawing /'nɔː·ɪŋ/ adj • *He has gnawing doubts about his loyalties.*

gnome /noʊm/ n [C] (in children's stories) an imaginary, very small old man who lives underground and guards gold and other valuable objects

go [TRAVEL] /goʊ/ v [I] he/she/it **goes, going,** *past simple* **went** /went/, *past part* **gone** /gɔːn, gɑn/ to move or travel to another place • *Let's go home now.* ○ *Are you going away for your vacation?* ○ *He's going to his country house for the weekend.* ○ *We don't go to the movies much.* ○ *You go on (ahead) and I'll be along in a minute.* ○ *Are you planning to go by car or are you flying?* • To go **back** is to return: *When do you go back to school?* • To go **back** is also to have existed since some time in the past: *Their friendship goes back to when they were in college together.* • If something **goes up** or **down,** it increases or is reduced: *My rent is going up 6% this year.* • To **be going** or to **go for** a particular activity is to move to the place of the activity or to begin to do it: *to go for a walk/ swim* ○ *Why don't we go for a drive* (= have a ride in a car)*?* ○ *We're going shopping at the mall.* • To **have gone** to do a particular activity is to have left to do it and not yet returned: *They've gone sailing on the lake.* ○ *The payroll checks have gone out* (= were sent) *a week later than usual.* ○ *I'm just going over* (= making a visit) *to Pete's for half an hour.* ○ *My son is planning to go into* (= get a job in) *journalism.* ○ *Where did my keys go* (= I can't find them)*?* ○ *A considerable amount of money and effort has gone into* (= been used in preparing) *this exhibition.* • To **go a long way** or **go far** is to be successful: *Maria's a talented writer—she'll go far.* • *You can give her advice, but it just* **goes in one ear and out the other** (= It is immediately forgotten and has no effect).* • If you **go out of your way,** you try especially hard: *They really went out of their way to make us feel welcome.* • If you **go to bed,** you get into bed in order to sleep. • If you **go to bed with** someone, you have sex with them. • If alcohol **goes to** your **head,** it makes you feel slightly drunk.

• If a success **goes to** someone's **head,** it makes them feel more successful or powerful than they are, and they become unpleasant to deal with. • (*rude slang*) If you tell someone to **go to hell,** you are swearing at them and angrily telling them to stop talking and go away. • To **go to the bathroom** is to urinate or excrete waste from the bowels.

–goer /ˌgoʊ·ər/ *combining form* a person who goes to the stated type of place • *Regular moviegoers like to compare notes about the latest movies.*

go [MOVE TOWARD] /goʊ/ v [I] he/she/it **goes, going,** *past simple* **went** /went/, *past part* **gone** /gɔːn, gɑn/ to be or continue moving, esp. in a particular way or direction • *We were going (at) about 65 miles an hour.* ○ *I had a wonderful weekend but it went awfully quickly.* ○ *If you take the bus, you go over the bridge, but the train goes through the tunnel.* ○ *There's still three months to go before he has surgery, but he's already nervous about it.* ○ *The flu is going around right now* (= It's moving from person to person)*.* ○ *I was going up/down the stairs when the phone rang.* ○ *He went up to her* (= approached her) *and asked for her autograph.* ○ *On summer evenings we often sat on the porch and watched the sun go down.* • To **go by** is to move past or beyond: *We sat on the shore and watched the sailboats go by.* ○ *Several months went by, and still he had no word from her.*

going /'goʊ·ɪŋ/ n [U] • *It was slow going because of ice on the roads.*

go [LEAVE] /goʊ/ v [I] he/she/it **goes, going,** *past simple* **went** /went/, *past part* **gone** /gɔːn, gɑn/ to leave a place, esp. in order to travel to somewhere else • *It's time to go.* ○ *Please close the door when you go.* ○ *She wasn't feeling well, so she went home early* (= left early to go home).* ○ *She's gone off with my umbrella* (= She took it by accident).* ○ *I always go out* (= leave my home and travel to another place, esp. for entertainment) *on Saturday night.* • If something is **gone,** none of it is left: *I can't believe the milk is gone already.* • The sea or TIDE **goes out** when the water leaves the beach or coast to return to a lower level. Compare **come in** at COME [ARRIVE]. • If you tell someone to **go jump in a/the lake,** you are angry or annoyed with them and want them to leave. • To **go out** is to have a romantic relationship with someone else: *How long have you been going out with him?* • If you are in a restaurant and buy food **to go,** you want it wrapped up so you can take it with you instead of eating it in the restaurant: *I'd like a cheeseburger and a strawberry milk shake to go, please.*

going /'goʊ·ɪŋ/ n [C] • *There were a lot of comings and goings at the apartment next door.*

go [LEAD] /goʊ/ v [I always + adv/prep] he/she/ it **goes, going,** *past simple* **went** /went/, *past part* **gone** /gɔːn, gɑn/ (of a road, path, etc.) to lead in a particular direction • *Does I-70 go to*

Denver? • If something goes a particular length, it is that long: *The well goes down at least 30 feet.*

go BECOME /goʊ/ *v* he/she/it **goes, going,** *past simple* **went** /went/, *past part* **gone** /gɔːn, gɑn/ to become or be in a certain condition • *Her father is going blind.* [L] ○ *If anything goes wrong, you can call our emergency hotline.* [L] ○ *Because of lack of evidence, the police were forced to let him go free.* [L] ○ *If you keep applying ice, the swelling will go down* (= become smaller). [I] ○ *The computer went down* (= stopped operating) *twice last week.* [I] ○ *The electricity suddenly went off* (= stopped operating). [I] ○ *One of these days I'll have to go on a diet* (= start to be on one). [I] ○ *I was so exhausted I went to sleep* (= started sleeping) *immediately.* [I] ○ *It was feared for a while that the two countries would go to war* (= start to fight a war) *over this dispute.* [I] ○ *It wasn't a bad hospital, as hospitals go* (= compared with the usual standard of hospitals), *but I still hated being there.* [I] • If a situation **goes from bad to worse,** a situation that was worrying you has become very bad. • If something **goes haywire,** it stops working correctly: *His heart had gone haywire.* • If someone **goes overboard** in doing something, they are extreme in doing it: *I went overboard decorating my house for Christmas this year.* • If you **go to bat for** someone, you support them when they need help: *The government will go to bat for companies that pay lots of taxes.* • (*infml*) If someone or something **goes to pot,** it is not cared for and its condition becomes very bad as a result: *The old neighborhood has gone to pot.* • To **go to sleep** can mean to get in bed in order to sleep: *I normally go to sleep at midnight.* • If a person who has committed a crime decides to **go straight,** they decide to change their behavior and live in a way that is legal from then on. • To **go together** or (*dated*) **go steady** is to have a romantic relationship for a long period. • If a situation is **going to the dogs,** it is becoming much worse: *Ever since Joe retired, the business has been going to the dogs.* • To **go wrong** is to make a mistake: *If you just follow the signs to the park, you can't go wrong.*

go CHANGE /goʊ/ *v* [I always + adv/prep] he/she/it **goes, going,** *past simple* **went** /went/, *past part* **gone** /gɔːn, gɑn/ to do something to cause a change or create a new condition • *I'd love to come to dinner, but I don't want you to go to any trouble* (= do a lot of work). • If you **go from one extreme to the other,** you cannot decide what to do, and first do one thing and then the opposite.

go WEAKEN /goʊ/ *v* [I] he/she/it **goes, going,** *past simple* **went** /went/, *past part* **gone** /gɔːn, gɑn/ to become weak or damaged, esp. from use, or to stop working • *Her hearing is starting to go, but otherwise she's in good shape.*

go START /goʊ/ *v* [I] he/she/it **goes, going,** *past simple* **went** /went/, *past part* **gone** /gɔːn, gɑn/ to start doing or using something • *I'll just connect the printer to the computer and we'll be ready to go.* • To **go it alone** is to decide to do something by yourself and without help from other people: *I decided to go it alone and set up my own business at home.*

go OPERATE /goʊ/ *v* [I] he/she/it **goes, going,** *past simple* **went** /went/, *past part* **gone** /gɔːn, gɑn/ to operate (in the right way) • *My watch was going fine up until a few minutes ago, but then it stopped running.* • Something that is **(still) going strong** has existed for a long time and is still successful or working well: *After one hundred years of service as a public institution, the state university system is still going strong.* ○ *His father is still going strong* (= active and well) *at 94.*

going /ˈgoʊ·ɪŋ/ *adj* [not gradable] operating successfully or without difficulty • *The advertising agency was a going concern when she headed it.*

go MAKE SOUND /goʊ/ *v* [I/T] he/she/it **goes, going,** *past simple* **went** /went/, *past part* **gone** /gɔːn, gɑn/ to produce (a noise) • *Somebody's car alarm went off at 3 in the morning and woke me up.* [I]

go MOVE BODY /goʊ/ *v* [I always + adv/prep] he/she/it **goes, going,** *past simple* **went** /went/, *past part* **gone** /gɔːn, gɑn/ to move a part of the body in a particular way or in the way that is shown • *Try making your foot go backwards and forwards.*

go DIVIDE /goʊ/ *v* [I] he/she/it **goes, going,** *past simple* **went** /went/, *past part* **gone** /gɔːn, gɑn/ (of a number) to fit (into another number), esp. resulting in a whole number • *Three goes into 12 four times.*

go BE SITUATED /goʊ/ *v* [I always + adv/prep] he/she/it **goes, going,** *past simple* **went** /went/, *past part* **gone** /gɔːn, gɑn/ to belong in a particular place, esp. as the usual place • *Tell the moving men that the sofa goes against that wall.*

go HAPPEN /goʊ/ *v* [I always + adv/prep] he/she/it **goes, going,** *past simple* **went** /went/, *past part* **gone** /gɔːn, gɑn/ to happen or develop • *The doctor said the operation went well.* ○ *What's going on here* (= Explain what is happening)?

go BE SOLD /goʊ/ *v* [I] he/she/it **goes, going,** *past simple* **went** /went/, *past part* **gone** /gɔːn, gɑn/ to be sold or be available • *The painting is expected to go for at least a million dollars.* • If someone has something going for them, that thing causes them to have a lot of advantages and to be successful: *They've got a happy marriage, great careers, and wonderful children— in fact they've got everything going for them.*

go BE EXPRESSED /goʊ/ *v* [I] he/she/it **goes, going,** *past simple* **went** /went/, *past part* **gone**

/gɔːn, gɑn/ to be expressed, sung, or played • *I can never remember how that song goes.*

go BE SUITABLE /gou/ *v* [I] he/she/it **goes, going,** *past simple* **went** /went/, *past part* **gone** /gɔːn, gɑn/ to be acceptable or suitable • *Do you think my new brown scarf goes with my black coat?*

going /ˈgou·ɪŋ/ *adj* [not gradable] (of a price or a charge) usual or suitable at the present time • *What's the going rate for this kind of work?*

go BE KNOWN /gou/ *v* [I always + adv/prep] he/she/it **goes, going,** *past simple* **went** /went/, *past part* **gone** /gɔːn, gɑn/ to be known (by a particular name) • *He went under the name of Platt, but that was not his real name.*

go DEPEND ON /gou/ *v* [I always + adv/prep] he/she/it **goes, going,** *past simple* **went** /went/, *past part* **gone** /gɔːn, gɑn/ to have an opinion, decision, or judgment depend on something • *There were no witnesses to the crime, and so far the police don't have much to go on.*

go BE TRUE /gou/ *v* [I] he/she/it **goes, going,** *past simple* **went** /went/, *past part* **gone** /gɔːn, gɑn/ to be true • *What Mary just said goes for me as well* (= I agree with what she said). • If something **goes without saying,** it is obviously true: *If you got an "A" in the course, it goes without saying you did well on the final exam.*

go BE FINAL /gou/ *v* [I] he/she/it **goes, going,** *past simple* **went** /went/, *past part* **gone** /gɔːn, gɑn/ to be final; not to be questioned • *In my parents' day, nobody ever argued with their father—whatever he said went.*

go PLAY /gou/ *v* [I] he/she/it **goes, going,** *past simple* **went** /went/, *past part* **gone** /gɔːn, gɑn/ to do something at a particular time or in a particular order, before or after other people; have a turn • *Who goes next?*

go ENERGY /gou/ *n* [U] the condition of being energetic and active • *Elise is always on the go* (= busy). • A **go-getter** is someone who is energetic and works hard to be successful: *We like go-getters who bring in new customers.*

□ **go about** /ˈ-ˌ-, ˌ-ˈ-/ *v prep* [T] to begin to do (something) • *We'd like to help but we're not sure what's the best way to go about it.*

□ **go against** /ˌ--ˈ-/ *v prep* [T] to be opposed to or in disagreement with (something) • *What you're asking me to do goes against everything I believe in.*

□ **go ahead** /ˌ--ˈ-/ *v adv* [I] to begin or continue an action or plan of action without waiting, esp. after a delay • *The meeting will go ahead as planned.*

go-ahead /ˈgou·əˌhed/ *n* [U] • *We're ready to start the project but we're still waiting for the go-ahead.*

□ **go along** /ˌ--ˈ-/ *v adv* [I] to agree or be willing to accept something • *Alex has already agreed, but it's going to be harder persuading Mike to go along.*

□ **go around** /ˌ--ˈ-/ *v adv* [I] to be enough for everyone • *There won't be enough pizza to go around if you take two pieces.*

□ **go back on** /ˈ-ˌ-ˌ-/ *v adv prep* [T] to fail to keep (a promise), or to change (a decision or agreement) • *Jason is totally unreliable and always goes back on his word.*

□ **go by** /ˈ--/ *v prep* [T] to follow or use information provided by (something or someone) • *Don't go by what she says—she's always wrong.* • If you **go (strictly) by the book,** you do everything exactly according to rules or the law.

□ **go down** /ˈ-ˈ-/ *v adv* [I always + adv/prep] to be remembered or recorded (in a particular way) • *Hurricane Hugo will go down as one of the worst storms of the century.*

□ **go for** TRY /ˈ-ˌ-, ˈ--/ *v prep* [T] to try to have or achieve (something) • *He'll be going for his third straight Olympic gold medal in the 200-meter dash.* • If you want it, **go for it** (= do what you need to do in order to obtain it).

□ **go for** CHOOSE /ˈ-ˌ-, ˈ--/ *v prep* [T] to choose • *Offered the choice between a higher salary and more vacation time, I know which one I'd go for.*

□ **go for** LIKE /ˈ-ˌ-, ˈ--/ *v prep* [T] *infml* to like or admire • *I don't go for action movies with lots of violence.*

□ **go in for** /ˈ-ˌ-ˌ-, ˈ-ˈ--/ *v adv prep* [T] to do (something) regularly, or to enjoy (something) • *I've never gone in for spending all day at the beach.*

□ **go into** /ˈ-ˈ--, ˈ-ˌ--/ *v prep* [T] to discuss, describe, or explain (something), esp. in a detailed or careful way • *This is the first book to go into her personal life as well as her work.*

□ **go off** /ˈ-ˈ-/ *v adv* [I] to explode or (of a gun) to fire bullets • *A local newspaper received an anonymous warning twenty minutes before the bomb went off.*

□ **go on** /ˈ-ˈ-/ *v adv* [I] to continue • *I won't go on working in this job forever, he said.* ○ *Go on, tell me what happened next.*

□ **go over** EXAMINE /ˈ-ˈ--, ˈ-ˈ--/ *v prep* [T] to examine or look at (something) in a careful or detailed way • *Remember to go over your essay to check for grammar and spelling mistakes.*

going-over /ˌgou·ɪŋˈou·vər/ *n* [C usually sing] *pl* **goings-over** /ˌgou·ɪŋˈzou·vər/ • *Police gave the apartment a thorough going-over but failed to find any illegal drugs.*

□ **go over** STUDY /ˈ-ˈ--, ˈ-ˈ--/ *v prep* [T] to study or explain (something) again • *Let's go over the rules once more before we begin.*

□ **go over** BE RECEIVED /ˈ-ˈ--, ˈ-ˈ--/ *v adv* [I always + adv/prep] to be received in a particular way • *Do you think my speech went over OK?*

□ **go through** EXPERIENCE /ˈ--, ˈ-ˈ-/ *v prep* [T] to experience (something, esp. something unpleasant or difficult) • *She's been going through a difficult time since her divorce.* • *We went through hell during the flood* (= had an extremely bad experience).

□ **go through** USE /ˈ--/ *v prep* [T] to use (something that cannot be used again) • *She went* *through all the money from her paycheck in one day.*

□ **go through** BE ACCEPTED /-'-/ *v adv* [I] to be officially accepted or approved • *We're hoping that the proposal for the new mall won't go through.*

□ **go through** PRACTICE /'--/ *v prep* [T] to do (something) in order to practice or as a test • *Let's go through it once more to make sure you know what to say.*

□ **go through** EXAMINE /'--, -'-/ *v prep* [T] to examine (a collection of things) carefully in order to organize them or find something • *I'm going through my clothes and throwing out all the stuff I don't wear any more.*

□ **go through with** /-'--/ *v adv prep* [T] to complete (something begun or promised) • *He'd threatened to quit many times, but I never thought he'd go through with it.*

□ **go under** /-'--/ *v adv* [I] (of a business) to fail financially • *Nothing could be done to keep the bank from going under.*

□ **go up** /-'-/ *v adv* [I] to burn or explode • *The house went up in flames.* • Something that **goes up in smoke** is wasted: *When the business went bankrupt, twenty years of hard work went up in smoke.*

□ **go without** /,--'-, '--,-/ *v adv* [I/T], *v prep* to not have (something) or to manage to live despite not having (something) • *If you don't want fish, then you'll just have to go without (your dinner).* [I/T]

goad /goʊd/ *v* [T] to cause (someone) to do something by frequently annoying them • *His brother goaded him into a wrestling match.*

go–ahead /'goʊ·ə,hed/ *n* [U] • See at GO AHEAD.

goal GAME /goʊl/ *n* [C] (in many sports) a point scored when a player sends a ball or other object into a particular area of play or into a netted structure that is defended by the opposing team • *Lanzo missed scoring a goal by inches.* • In some sports, a goal is also the area or netted structure into which a player sends a ball or other object in order to score a point. • In some sports, such as SOCCER and HOCKEY, a **goalkeeper** (also *infml* **goalie**) is the player whose responsibility is to prevent the other team from scoring. • A **goalpost** is one of two vertical posts, often connected by a horizontal bar, between which a ball or other object must go in order to score points in some sports.

goal AIM /goʊl/ *n* [C] an aim or purpose • *My goal is to lose ten pounds before the summer.*

goalie /'goʊ·li/ *n* [C] *infml* a **goalkeeper**, see at GOAL GAME

goat ANIMAL /goʊt/ *n* [C] a horned animal related to the sheep, which is kept to provide milk, meat, or wool

goat PERSON BLAMED /goʊt/ *n* [C] *infml disapproving* a person who is blamed for causing a failure or defeat, esp. in a team sports competition • *Jefferson's three errors made him the goat of last night's game.*

goatee /goʊ'tiː/ *n* [C] a small BEARD (= the hair on the lower part of a man's face) grown on the middle, but not the sides, of the lower part of the face

gob /gɑb/ *n* [C] a small piece or lump of something • *a gob of butter* • (*infml*) *He's got gobs of money* (= large amounts of it).

gobble EAT /'gɑb·əl/ *v* [T] to eat quickly and sometimes noisily • *Nowadays people gobble pills like peanuts.* [T] ○ *She gobbled up/down her lunch and hurried back.* [M]

gobble MAKE NOISE /'gɑb·əl/ *v* [I] to make the sound of a male TURKEY (= a large bird)

gobbledygook, **gobbledegook** /'gɑb·əl·di ,guk, -,guːk/ *n* [U] *disapproving* language that sounds important and official but is difficult to understand • *This computer manual is gobbledygook.*

goblin /'gɑb·lən/ *n* [C] a small, imaginary, usually ugly creature who plays tricks on people

go–cart /'goʊ·kɑrt/ *n* [C] a small, low racing car with an open frame

God CREATOR /gɑd/ *n* [U] (esp. in Christian, Jewish, and Muslim belief) the being that created and rules the universe, the earth, and its people • *Do you believe in God?* • **God/My God/Oh (my) God** are used to express surprise, or for emphasis: *My God, what a terrible shock that must have been!* • **God bless (you)** is said to show you hope good things happen to someone. • (*infml*) **God only knows** (= It's impossible to say) *how he managed to find out where I lived.* • People use **in God's name** in a question to add emphasis: *If you knew you had to go out, why in God's name didn't you tell us?* • A **godchild** (*female* **goddaughter**, *male* **godson**) is a child whose moral and religious development in the Christian religion is partly the responsibility of the child's godparents. • A **godparent** (*male* **godfather**, *female* **godmother**) is an adult who is partly responsible for their godchild's moral and religious development. See also GODFATHER. • (*dated*) Someone who is **God-fearing** is religious and tries to live in the way they believe God would wish them to. • LP CAPITAL LETTERS

godless /'gɑd·ləs/ *adj* [not gradable] not showing belief in, or respect for, God

god SPIRIT /gɑd/, *female* **goddess** /'gɑd·əs/ *n* [C] a spirit or being believed to control some part of the universe or life and often worshiped for doing so, or a representation of this being • *the god of war* • A god can also be someone who is admired a lot or too much: *Dr. Tay is a god to me.*

god–awful /gɑd'ɔː·fəl/ *adj infml* very bad • *That was a god-awful meal.*

goddamn, **goddam** /'gɑd·dæm/, **goddamned** /'gɑd·dæmd/ *exclamation, adj, adv* [not gradable] *infml* used to add force to what is being said, or to express unhappiness • *Don't drive so goddamn fast!* ○ *Goddamn (it)!* • USAGE: This word is considered offensive by some people.

godfather /ˈgɑdˌfɑð·ər/ *n* [C] *slang* the leader of a criminal group • See also **godfather** at GOD [CREATOR].

godforsaken /ˈgɑd·fərˌseɪ·kən/ *adj* (of places) not containing anything interesting or attractive, and far from other people • *Why would you come to this godforsaken place?*

godsend /ˈgɑd·send/ *n* [C] something good that happens unexpectedly and at a time when it is especially needed • *That savings account was a real godsend when she lost her job.*

goes /goʊz/ *present simple of* GO, used with he/she/it

gofer /ˈgoʊ·fər/ *n* [C] *infml* a person whose job is to take messages or to collect and deliver things for other people

goggle–eyed /ˈgɑg·əˌlɑɪd/ *adj* having eyes that are wide open, esp. in surprise • *Goggle-eyed tourists stared at the nude bathers.*

goggles /ˈgɑg·əlz/ *pl n* special glasses that fit close to the face to protect the eyes • *safety goggles* ○ *swimming goggles*

going /ˈgoʊ·ɪŋ/ *n, adj* • See at GO [MOVE TOWARD], GO [LEAVE], GO [OPERATE], GO [BE SUITABLE].

going on /ˌgoʊ·ɪŋˌɑn, -ˌɔːn/ *adv* [not gradable], *prep* nearly; almost • *Leslie is 16 going on 17.*

going–over /ˌgoʊ·ɪŋˈoʊ·vər/ *n* • See at GO OVER [EXAMINE].

goings–on /ˌgoʊ·ɪŋˈzɑn, -ˈzɔːn/ *pl n* unusual events or activities • *There were some strange goings-on in that house.*

going to /ˈgoʊ·ɪŋˌtuː, -tə/ *phrasal auxiliary* intending to do something in the future, or being certain or expecting to happen in the future • *Are you going to go to Claire's party?* ○ *The radio said it was going to be hot and sunny tomorrow.*

gold [METAL] /goʊld/ *n* [U] a soft, yellow metal that is highly valued and used esp. in jewelry and as a form of wealth • *The price of gold reached a new high Thursday.* • A **gold medal** is a large disk-shaped prize made of or covered with gold that is given to a person or team that wins a competition. Compare **silver medal** at SILVER [METAL]; **bronze medal** at BRONZE [METAL]. • A **gold mine** is a place where gold is removed from the ground: *(fig.) In the eyes of real estate developers, this property was truly a gold mine* (= an opportunity for making money).

gold /ˈgoʊl·dən/ *adj* [not gradable] • *She wears lots of gold jewelry.*

golden /ˈgoʊl·dən/ *adj* [not gradable] • *a golden chain*

gold [COLOR] /goʊld/ *adj* [not gradable], *n* [U] (of) a bright yellow color • *a gold dress* ○ *His uniform was scarlet and gold.* [U]

golden /ˈgoʊl·dən/ *adj* • *Bake about seven minutes, or until golden.*

golden /ˈgoʊl·dən/ *adj* advantageous, successful, or promising • *the golden days of youth* • A **golden age** is a period of time, sometimes imaginary, when everyone was happy, or when everything is thought to have been better than it is now: *the golden age of boxing* • A **golden anniversary** is a celebration of the 50th year of esp. a marriage's continuation. Compare **silver anniversary** at SILVER [METAL]. • A **golden opportunity** is an especially good opportunity to do something: *They had several golden opportunities to score.*

goldfish /ˈgoʊld·fɪʃ/ *n* [C] *pl* **goldfish** a small, gold or orange-colored fish often kept as a pet

golf /gɑlf, gɔːlf/ *n* [U] a game in which players use a set of sticks to hit small, round, hard balls into a series of nine or 18 small holes on an area of grassy land using as few hits as possible • *Do you play golf?* • A **golf club** is one of a set of wooden or metal sticks with long handles used for hitting a golf ball. • A **golf club** is also a private organization that owns land on which members and their guests can play golf. • A **golf course** is a large area of grassy land with a series of nine or 18 holes, used for playing golf.

golfer /ˈgɑl·fər, ˈgɔːl-/ *n* [C] • *a professional golfer*

golly /ˈgɑl·i/ *exclamation infml* used to express surprise, or to emphasize what you are saying • *"He broke his arm and he'll be out for weeks." "Golly, that's terrible."*

gondola [CONTAINER] /ˈgɑn·də·lə, gɑnˈdoʊ-/ *n* [C] a container in which passengers travel, esp. one hung from a thick wire which moves up a mountain • *The gondolas seat 12 skiers and move at 14 miles per hour.*

gondola [BOAT] /ˈgɑn·də·lə/ *n* [C] a long, narrow boat with a flat bottom and raised points at both ends, moved along by a person with a pole at the back end

gone [GO] /gɔːn, gɑn/ *past participle of* GO

gone [DEAD] /gɔːn, gɑn/ *adj* [not gradable] no longer living; dead • *Both her parents are gone.*

goner /ˈgɔː·nər, ˈgɑn·ər/ *n* [C usually sing] *infml* a person or thing that has no chance of succeeding or continuing to live or exist • *He reckoned he was a goner when he heard enemy soldiers approaching.*

gong /gɑŋ, gɔːŋ/ *n* [C] a piece of metal hanging from a frame which is hit with a stick to produce a hollow, ringing sound • *a dinner gong*

gonna /ˌgɔː·nə, ˌgoʊ·nə, gən·ə/ *phrasal auxiliary not standard* (spelled the way it is often spoken) GOING TO • *What are you gonna do about it?* • USAGE: In written English "gonna" is usually used to report or approximate speech.

gonorrhea /ˌgɑn·əˈriː·ə/, *slang* **clap** *n* [U] a disease of the sex organs, caught during sexual activity

goo /guː/ n [U] *infml* a thick, sticky substance • *Mudslides left goo all over the highway.*

good SATISFACTORY /gʊd/ adj **better** /ˈbeṭ·ər/, **best** /best/ of a kind that is pleasing or enjoyable, or of high quality • *Let's go on a picnic tomorrow if the weather's good.* ○ *That was a really good meal.* ○ *Dogs have a very good sense of smell.* ○ *Now would be a good time* (= a suitable time) *to talk to Andy about the promotion.* ○ *He's a good swimmer* (= an able and skillful swimmer). ○ *Did they have a good time on their vacation?* ○ *She makes good money in her new job* (= earns a high income). • **(It's) a good thing** means it is lucky: *A good thing they didn't go camping last weekend—the weather was terrible.* • If something is **(as) good as new**, it is in very good condition: *Yussef fixed my computer and now it's good as new.* • **Good and** means completely: *She won't drink coffee if it's not good and hot.* • The expression **good for** you is used to show approval for someone's success or good luck: *She passed her driving test? Good for her!* • If someone says **good riddance**, they are expressing happiness because something unwanted has gone: *At last the Joneses and their nasty dogs have moved out—good riddance!* • If something or someone is **no good/not so good**, they are useless or of low quality: *Their seats were no good because they were so far from the stage they couldn't see anything.* • A **good-for-nothing** is a worthless person: *She's a lazy good-for-nothing.* • If someone is **good-humored**, they have a friendly and happy personality. • A person who is **good-looking** is attractive and pleasant to look at.

good MORALLY RIGHT /gʊd/ adj **better** /ˈbeṭ·ər/, **best** /best/ morally right, or admirable because kind, thoughtful, or honest • *José is a genuinely good person.* ○ *If you're a good boy* (= if you behave well) *at the dentist, I'll buy you some ice cream later.* ○ *He's always been good to his mother.* • **Good** can be used as part of an exclamation: *Good heavens! You mean they still haven't arrived?* • **The good book** is the Bible. • In the Christian religion, **Good Friday** is the day Jesus is believed to have died, the Friday before Easter Sunday. • Someone who is **good-hearted** is kind and wants to be helpful. • Someone who is **good-natured** has a friendly and welcoming attitude toward other people. • A **Good Samaritan** is someone who helps someone in trouble.

good /gʊd/ n [U] • *Even a small donation can do a lot of good.*

goodness /ˈgʊd·nəs/ n [U] • *I believe in the basic goodness of human nature.* • See also GOODNESS.

good GREETING /gʊd/ adj [not gradable] used in greetings • **Good afternoon** and **good evening** are sometimes said when people meet in the afternoon or evening: *Good evening, welcome to our restaurant.* • **Good morning** is often the first thing people say when they meet in the morning: *Good morning, how are you?* • **Good night** is said when people leave each other in the evening or before going to bed or to sleep. • LP GREETINGS

good HEALTH /gʊd/ adj **better** /ˈbeṭ·ər/, **best** /best/ useful for health, or in a satisfactory condition • *Make sure you eat plenty of good, fresh vegetables.*

good LARGE /gʊd/ adj [not gradable] large in number or amount • *We had to walk a good way in the airport to reach our gate.* ○ *There was a good-sized crowd on hand.* • **A good** means this much or more (of a stated amount): *It's a good half hour's walk to the fair grounds from here.* • **A good deal** means a lot: *There was a good deal of discussion about whether the police had acted properly.* • **A good many** means a lot of: *There were a good many people at the concert.*

goodbye /gʊdˈbaɪ, gə-/, short form **bye** /ˈbaɪ/, *infml* **bye-bye** /baɪˈbaɪ/ exclamation, n [C/U] said when you are going away from someone else, or the act of saying this when you are going away • *Goodbye, Roberto, and thanks again for a great dinner.* [U] ○ *Don't go without saying goodbye to me, will you?* [U]

goodness /ˈgʊd·nəs/ n [U] used in many fixed expressions to show emotion, esp. surprise • *Goodness! I thought you'd gone home already!* • See also **goodness** at GOOD MORALLY RIGHT.

goods /gʊdz/ pl n items for sale, or possessions that can be moved • *They sell leather goods such as wallets, purses, and briefcases.*

goodwill /ˈgʊdˈwɪl/ n [U] a friendly attitude in which you wish that good things happen to people • *We hope the negotiations will take place in an atmosphere of openness and goodwill.*

goody FOOD /ˈgʊd·i/ n [C usually pl] *infml* something pleasant to eat, such as a piece of candy

goody EXPRESSION /ˈgʊd·i/ exclamation used, esp. by children, to show pleasure • *Oh goody! Chocolate cake.*

goody–goody /ˈgʊd·i,gʊd·i/, **goody–two-shoes** /,gʊd·iˈtuː,ʃuːz/ n [C] someone who is too ready to behave in a way intended to please people in authority • *She's a real goody-goody—I hate her!*

gooey /ˈguː·i/ adj **gooier**, **gooiest** (of a substance) thick and sticky • *a gooey dessert*

goof /guːf/ v [I] *infml* to make a foolish or embarrassing mistake • *The governor showed up and no one was there to meet him—somebody goofed!*

goof /guːf/ n [C] *infml* • *Forgetting to bring my driver's license was a major goof.*

▢**goof off** /ˈ-ˈ-/ v adv [I] *infml* to avoid work or waste time • *You'd better not let the boss catch you goofing off!*

goon /guːn/ n [C] a man who is paid to threaten or hurt people • *The strikers were beaten by a bunch of hired goons.*

goop /guːp/ *n* [U] *infml* a messy, slightly liquid substance, esp. one whose contents are not known • *He puts this goop on his hair to make it stand up straight.*

goose BIRD /guːs/ *n* [C] *pl* **geese** /giːs/ a large bird that lives by water • If your **goose** is **cooked**, you have no chance of succeeding in what you are trying to do: *When he got an F on the final exam, he knew his goose was cooked.*

goose PUSH FINGER /guːs/ *v* [T] *infml* to push a finger or thumb suddenly between the buttocks of (someone) in order to surprise them • *He jumped up as if he'd been goosed.*

goose bumps /'guːs·bʌmps/, **goose flesh** /'guːs·fleʃ/, **goose pimples** /'guːs,pɪm·pəlz/ *pl n* a temporary condition in which small raised swellings appear on the skin because of cold, fear, or excitement • *Let's move out into the sun—I'm getting goose bumps.*

GOP *n* [U] *abbreviation for* Grand Old Party (= a name for the Republican Party) • *The symbol of the GOP is an elephant.*

gopher /'goʊ·fər/ *n* [C] a North American animal that lives in holes it makes in the ground

gore INJURE /gɔːr, goʊr/ *v* [T] (of an animal) to cause an injury with the horns or TUSKS (= long, curved teeth) • *The bullfighter was almost gored to death.*

gore BLOOD /gɔːr, goʊr/ *n* [U] blood that has come from an injury and become thick • *It's a great movie, but there's lots of blood and gore in it* (= it shows people bleeding badly from injuries).

gory /'gɔːr·i, 'goʊr·i/ *adj* • *I'm afraid most operations look pretty gory.* • The **gory details** of a situation are the unpleasant but interesting facts about someone's private life: *Come on, I want to know all the gory details about what caused them to split up.*

gorge VALLEY /gɔːrdʒ/ *n* [C] a deep, narrow valley with steep sides, usually formed by a river or stream cutting through rock • *The only way to cross the gorge was over a flimsy wooden bridge.*

gorge EAT /gɔːrdʒ/ *v* [I/T] to eat or fill (yourself with food) until you are unable to eat any more • *She sat in front of the television, gorging herself on chocolates.* [T]

gorgeous /'gɔːr·dʒəs/ *adj* beautiful and attractive • *What a gorgeous dress!* ○ *The bride looked gorgeous.*

gorilla /gə'rɪl·ə/ *n* [C] a large APE (= animal like a monkey) that comes from western Africa

gory /'gɔːr·i, 'goʊr·i/ *adj* • See at GORE BLOOD.

gosh /gɑʃ, gɔʃ/ *exclamation infml* used to express surprise • *Gosh, I didn't expect to see you here!*

gospel (music) /'gɑs·pəl ('mjuː·zɪk)/ *n* [U] a style of Christian religious music originally

developed and performed by African-Americans • *gospel singers*

gospel /'gɑs·pəl/ *n* [C] any of the four books of the Bible that contain details of the life of Jesus • The **gospel (truth)** is the complete truth: *I don't know what happened to the money, that's the gospel truth.*

gossip /'gɑs·əp/ *n* [C/U] talk about other people's private lives • *Have you heard the latest gossip* (= what is being said about someone)? [U] • A gossip is also someone who enjoys talking about other people's private lives: *Charlie is a real gossip.* [C]

gossip /'gɑs·əp/ *v* [I] • *Don't mind us—we're just gossiping!*

got /gɑt/ *past simple and past participle of* GET • Got is also used with "have" or "has" to show that someone has or possesses something: *Brandon's got* (= now has) *a new pair of glasses.* • If someone says you **got them**, you confused them by saying something they do not understand or cannot explain: *I don't know why the wrong number is on it—you've got me there.* • Compare GOTTEN.

gotcha /'gɑtʃ·ə/ *exclamation not standard* (spelled the way it is often spoken) got you • *"Gotcha* (= caught you), *you little thief!" she cried, as I tried to snatch a cookie from the table.* • Gotcha also means I understand what you are trying to say: *"So be sure you get here by three." "Gotcha."*

gotta /'gɑt·ə/ *v* [I] *not standard* (spelled the way it is often spoken) got to • *"I gotta go now."* ○ *"He's gotta be kidding."*

gotten /'gɑt·ən/ *past participle of* GET • *If you hadn't gotten sick, we'd be in Hawaii now.* ○ *She's gotten used to having me around.* • Gotten is also used with "have" to show that someone has come to possess something they did not have before: *I've gotten* (= I recently bought) *a new pair of glasses.* • Compare GOT.

gouge DIG /gaʊdʒ/ *v* [T] to make (a hole) in something, or remove (something) from a hole using a sharp, pointed object • *The bomb had gouged a huge hole in the roadway.*

gouge CHEAT /gaʊdʒ/ *v* [T] to charge (someone) far too much money for something done or something sold • *We didn't know the value of the foreign money, and the taxi driver gouged us.*

goulash /'guː·lɑʃ/ *n* [U] a dish originally from Hungary consisting of meat cooked in a sauce with vegetables and PAPRIKA (= a red spice)

gourd /gɔːrd, goʊrd, gʊrd/ *n* [C] a round or bottle-shaped fleshy fruit that has a hard shell and that cannot usually be eaten, or the shell of this fruit, used as a container

gourmet /'gʊr·meɪ, gʊr'meɪ/ *n* [C] a person who knows a lot about food and cooking, and who enjoys eating good food • *She is a gourmet cook.*

gout /gaʊt/ *n* [U] a painful disease of the joints, esp. a toe or finger

gov /ˌdʒiːˌoʊ'viː, gʌv/ *n* [U] used at the end of US INTERNET addresses to show that the address belongs to a federal or state government department • *info@hhs.gov*

govern RULE /'gʌv·ərn/ *v* [I/T] to control and be responsible for the public business of (a country, state, city, or other organized group) • *A small group of military leaders seized control and are now governing the country.* [T]

government /'gʌv·ərn·mənt, -ər·mənt/ *n* [C/U] the offices, departments, and groups of people that control a country, state, city, or other political unit • *She works for the government.* [U] ○ *The new tax law affects the budgets of both state and local governments.* [C] • Government is also a particular system of managing a country, state, city, etc.: *democratic government* [U]

governor /'gʌv·ə·nər, -ər·nər/ *n* [C] a person in charge of an organization or of a particular political unit, esp. a US state • *Governors from most of the 50 states will meet in Omaha this weekend.* ○ *The board of governors of the hospital meets every month.*

govern INFLUENCE /'gʌv·ərn/ *v* [T] to have a direct effect or controlling influence on (something) • *Prices of manufactured goods are governed largely by the cost of raw materials and labor.*

governess /'gʌv·ər·nəs/ *n* [C] (esp. in the past) a woman who lives with a family and educates the children at home

gown /gɑʊn/ *n* [C] a woman's dress, esp. a long one worn on formal occasions, or a long, loose piece of clothing worn over other clothes for a particular purpose • *She wore a beautiful satin gown to the senior prom.* ○ *Students wore black gowns for the graduation ceremonies.*

GP *n* [C] *abbreviation for* general practitioner (= a doctor who provides general medical treatment)

GPA *n* [C] *abbreviation for* **grade-point average**, see at GRADE MEASURE/MARK

grab /græb/ *v* [T] **-bb-** to take or take hold of (something or someone) suddenly • *A man tried to grab her handbag as she was walking through the park.* ○ *We'd better get there early, or someone else will grab the best seats* (= take them first). ○ *(infml) Let's grab a sandwich* (= get it and eat it quickly) *before we leave.*

grab /græb/ *n* [C] • *The two children both made a grab for* (= made a sudden attempt to take) *the same piece of cake.* • A **grab bag** is any mixed collection of things, some of which are not very attractive or useful: *The musical was a grab bag of old, tired songs and a few gems.*

grace BEAUTY /greɪs/ *n* [U] simple beauty of movement or form • *The skaters moved over the ice with effortless grace.*

graceful /'greɪs·fəl/ *adj* • *The dancers formed graceful, whirling combinations.*

gracefully /'greɪs·fə·li/ *adv* • *He gracefully skis down the slopes.*

grace POLITENESS /greɪs/ *n* [U] the charming quality of politeness or pleasantness, or a willingness to be fair and honorable • *She always handles her clients with tact and grace.*

graceful /'greɪs·fəl/ *adj* • *I want to make a graceful exit when it's time to leave.*

gracefully /'greɪs·fə·li/ *adv* • *A lot of people grow old gracefully.*

grace RELIGION /greɪs/ *n* [U] a prayer of thanks to God that is said before and sometimes after a meal • *Before we eat, I want to ask Cory to say grace.* • Grace is also approval, acceptance, or protection given by God: *By the grace of God, I hope to stay drug-free.*

grace TIME /greɪs/ *n* [U] an added period of time allowed before something must be done or paid • *The landlord gave us a week's grace to pay the rent.* • *You have a* **grace period** (= extra time) *after the due date to pay the insurance premium.*

gracious PLEASANT /'greɪ·ʃəs/ *adj* pleasant, kind, and polite • *You're a gracious host.*

graciously /'greɪ·ʃə·sli/ *adv* • *You should learn to accept criticism graciously.*

gracious COMFORTABLE /'greɪ·ʃəs/ *adj* characterized by great comfort and luxury made possible by wealth • *He was used to gracious living.*

gracious SURPRISE /'greɪ·ʃəs/ *exclamation slightly dated* used to express surprise or to emphasize what is being said • *My goodness gracious, that was a huge repair bill.*

grad /græd/ *n* [C] *short form of* GRADUATE • *a Harvard grad* • *a* **grad student** • *She spent five years in* **grad school**.

gradation /greɪ'deɪ·ʃən, grə-/ *n* [C] a gradual change, or one stage in a series of changes • *There are many gradations of color in a rainbow.*

grade MEASURE / MARK /greɪd/ *n* [C] a measure of the quality of a student's performance, usually represented by the letters A (the best) through F (the worst) • *She always gets good grades.* • A grade is also a measure or mark of quality, amount, or degree: *high-grade musicianship* ○ *He's suffering from a low-grade infection.* • A **grade-point average** (*abbreviation* **GPA**) is a number giving the average quality of a student's work, used to calculate rank in class: *To get into the best colleges you need a grade-point average between 3.0 and 4.0.*

grade /greɪd/ *v* [T] to judge and give a mark to (a student, exam, etc.) • *The essays were graded on clarity of expression.* • To grade is also to separate things according to quality or size: *Eggs are usually graded by size.*

grade SCHOOL /greɪd/ *n* [C] a school class or group of classes in which all the children are of a similar age or ability • *James is in the seventh grade this year.* • A **grade school** is an

elementary school. See at ELEMENTARY. • LP EDUCATION IN THE US

–grader /ˈɡreɪd·ər/ *combining form* • *Katy is a fifth-grader.*

grade SLOPE /ɡreɪd/ *n* [C] the degree of slope of land or of a road or path • *In hilly San Francisco, many streets have a steep grade.*

gradual /ˈɡrædʒ·ə·wəl/ *adj* changing or developing slowly or by small degrees • *He has suffered a gradual decline in health over the past year.*

gradually /ˈɡrædʒ·ə·wə·li/ *adv* • *Sales of the product are improving gradually.*

graduate /ˈɡrædʒ·ə·wət/, *short form* **grad** /ɡræd/ *n* [C] a person who has successfully completed studies at a school or received a degree from a college or university • *a Yale graduate/a graduate of Yale* • A **graduate school** (*short form* **grad school**) is a division of a university where you work toward a specialized degree beyond the one you receive after four years of study. • A **graduate student** (*short form* **grad student**) is someone studying for a graduate degree. • LP EDUCATION IN THE US

graduate /ˈɡrædʒ·ə·weɪt/ *v* [I/T] • *Although he never graduated from high school, he became a successful businessman.* [I]

graduation /ˌɡrædʒ·ə·ˈweɪ·ʃən/ *n* [C/U] the formal event at which a person who has successfully completed a course of study at a school, college, or university gets a document stating this fact, or the successful completion of a course of study • *We'll be attending two graduations this weekend.* [C] ◦ *After graduation, she wants to travel around Europe.* [U]

graduated /ˈɡrædʒ·ə·weɪt̬·əd/ *adj* arranged in regular small stages or degrees • *With a graduated income tax, people who make more money pay a higher rate.*

graffiti /ɡrəˈfiːt̬·i/ *n* [U] writings or drawings made on surfaces in public places • *Someone had scrawled rude graffiti on the bathroom wall.*

graft INFLUENCE /ɡræft/ *n* [U] (esp. in politics) the obtaining of money or advantage through the dishonest use of power and influence • *His administration was marked by widespread graft and crime.*

graft TISSUE /ɡræft/ *n* [C] a piece of healthy skin or bone cut usually from a person's own body and used to repair a damaged part on that person • *skin/bone grafts* • A graft is also a piece cut from a living plant and fixed to another plant so that it grows there.

graft /ɡræft/ *v* [T] • *Surgeons grafted skin from her hip onto her leg.*

grain SEED /ɡreɪn/ *n* [C/U] a seed from a plant, esp. a grasslike plant such as wheat, or the crop from such a plant • *Wheat and rye are two common grains used in making bread.* [C] ◦ *Grain is one of the main exports of the American Midwest.* [U]

grain SMALL PIECE / AMOUNT /ɡreɪn/ *n* [C] a very small piece of a hard substance, or a small amount of something • *grains of sand* ◦ *There was a grain of truth in what she said.* ◦ *You haven't got a grain of sense.*

grainy /ˈɡreɪ·ni/ *adj* (of a picture) appearing to be made up of a lot of spots • *a grainy newspaper photo*

grain PATTERN /ɡreɪn/ *n* [U] the natural pattern of lines in the surface of a material, such as wood or rock, or the direction in which the fibers that form these substances lie • *Polishing the wood brings out its grain.*

gram /ɡræm/ (*abbreviation* **g**) *n* [C] a unit of measurement of weight equal to 0.001 kilogram

grammar /ˈɡræm·ər/ *n* [U] the study or use of the rules about how words change their form and combine with other words to express meaning • *She memorized the vocabulary but is having trouble with the grammar.* • (*dated*) A **grammar school** is an **elementary school**. See at ELEMENTARY.

grammatical /ɡrəˈmæt̬·ɪ·kəl/ *adj* [not gradable] • *grammatical structure* ◦ *Your sentence is not grammatical* (= the words it contains do not combine correctly).

Grammy /ˈɡræm·i/ *n* [C] *trademark* one of a set of prizes given in the US each year to people in the music industry

grand IMPORTANT /ɡrænd/ *adj* important and large in degree or size • *When I mess up, I mess up on a grand scale.* • (*law*) A **grand jury** is a group of people who decide whether a person who has been accused of a crime should be given a trial in court or should be released. • A **grand opening** is a celebration of the opening of esp. a business: *The new postal facility's grand opening is scheduled for Friday.* • A **grand piano** is a large piano with horizontal strings and is the kind usually used in public performances. • A **grand prize** is the largest prize in a competition: *The grand-prize winner will be given $10,000.* • In baseball, a **grand slam** is the hitting of a HOME RUN with runners at all three BASES, so that four points are scored. • In tennis and golf, a **grand slam** is the act of winning all of a series of important competitions. • A **grand total** is the complete amount after everything has been added up: *Andre's sold a grand total of 11 copies of the book.*

grand ATTRACTIVE /ɡrænd/ *adj* attractive in style and appearance • *A grand staircase leads to the second floor.*

grand MONEY /ɡrænd/ (*abbreviation* **G**) *n* [C] *pl* **grand** *slang* $1000 • *He lost three grand in the gambling casino last night.*

grandchild /ˈɡræn·tʃaɪld/ *n* [C] *pl* **grandchildren** /ˈɡræn,tʃɪl·drən/ the child of a person's son or daughter • PIC FAMILY TREE

granddaughter /ˈɡræn,dɔːt̬·ər/ *n* [C] the

grandeur /ˈgræn·dʒər, -ˌdʒʊr/ *n* [U] a quality of great beauty and size which attracts admiration • *We were struck by the silent grandeur of the desert.*

grandfather /ˈgrænd·fɑð·ər/, *infml* **granddad** /ˈgræn·dæd/, **grandpa** /ˈgræm·pɔ, -pɑ/ *n* [C] the father of a person's mother or father • A **grandfather clock** is a clock in a tall wooden case that stands on the floor. • ⓟⓘⓒ FAMILY TREE ⓁⓅ TITLES AND FORMS OF ADDRESS

grandiose /ˈgræn·diˌoʊs, ˌgræn·diˈoʊs/ *adj* very large or wonderful, or intended to seem great and important • *grandiose buildings* ○ *grandiose plans*

grandmother /ˈgrændˌmʌð·ər/, *infml* **grandma** /ˈgræm·ɔ, ˈgræn·mɑ/, **granny** /ˈgræn·i/ *n* [C] the mother of a person's father or mother • ⓟⓘⓒ FAMILY TREE ⓁⓅ TITLES AND FORMS OF ADDRESS

grandparent /ˈgrændˌpær·ənt, -ˌper-/ *n* [C] the father or mother of a person's father or mother

grandson /ˈgrænd·sʌn/ *n* [C] the son of a person's son or daughter • ⓟⓘⓒ FAMILY TREE

grandstand /ˈgræn·stænd/ *n* [C] a large area containing many seats arranged in rising rows, sometimes covered by a roof, from which people can watch sports or other events

grandstanding /ˈgrænˌstæn·dɪŋ/ *n* [U] *disapproving* acting or speaking in a way intended to attract attention and to influence the opinion of people who are watching • *Experts criticized the program as mere grandstanding by corporations and local officials.*

granite /ˈgræn·ət/ *n* [U] a hard gray, pink, or black rock, used in buildings

granny /ˈgræn·i/ *n* [C] *infml* GRANDMOTHER

granola /grəˈnoʊ·lə/ *n* [U] a food made of grains, nuts, and dried fruit, often eaten for breakfast

grant MONEY /grænt/ *n* [C] a sum of money given by the government, a university, or a private organization to another organization or person for a special purpose • *a research/ study grant*

grant GIVE /grænt/ *v* [T] to give, agree to give, or do something that another person has asked for, esp. as an official or formal act • *She was granted American citizenship.*

grant ACCEPT /grænt/ *v* [T] to accept that something is true, often before expressing an opposite or disapproving opinion • *I grant you (that) it must have been upsetting, but even so I think he made too big a deal of it.* [+ (that) clause]

granulated /ˈgræn·jəˌleɪt̬·əd/ *adj* [not gradable] (esp. of sugar) in small grains • *Granulated sugar is coarser than powdered sugar.*

grape /greɪp/ *n* [C] a small, round fruit, usually pale green, purple, or red, that grows on a VINE and is eaten raw, made into juice, or used for making wine • *a bunch of grapes* ○ *grape juice* • A **grapevine** is the climbing plant that grapes grow on. • The **grapevine** is an unofficial, informal way of getting information by hearing about it from someone who heard it from someone else: *I heard through the grapevine that he's been fired—is it true?*

grapefruit /ˈgreɪp·fruːt/ *n* [C] *pl* **grapefruit** or **grapefruits** a yellow fruit that is larger than an orange but tastes less sweet

graph /græf/ *n* [C] a drawing that shows, usually by lines or curves, how two sets of amounts are related • *a bar/line graph* ○ *A graph would show this information more clearly.* • **Graph paper** is paper with small squares printed on it that can be used to draw some types of graphs.

graphic CLEAR /ˈgræf·ɪk/ *adj* producing very clear and detailed mental images • *a graphic description of a murder*

graphically /ˈgræf·ɪ·kli/ *adv* in a very clear and detailed manner • *The accident graphically illustrates the importance of wearing seat belts.*

graphic DRAWING /ˈgræf·ɪk/ *adj* [not gradable] having to do with drawing or images • *She first worked as a graphic designer.* ○ *The network has upgraded the graphic look of the show.* • The **graphic arts** are the arts that include drawing and printing.

graphic /ˈgræf·ɪk/ *n* [C] • *Choose a graphic from the clip-art file, add your text, and you've made your own birthday card.* • A graphic can also be printing shown on television that gives additional information: *Let's take a look at the graphic of that quote.*

graphite /ˈgræf·ɑɪt/ *n* [U] a soft, dark gray form of carbon used in the center of pencils which makes a mark when pressed against something

grapple /ˈgræp·əl/ *v* [I] to hold someone while fighting with them • *He briefly grappled with the police officer.* ○ *Bad news is something it becomes necessary to grapple with* (= deal with).

grasp HOLD /græsp/ *v* [I/T] to take (something) quickly, esp. in your hand, and hold it firmly • *I grasped his arm to keep from falling.* [T] • If someone is **grasping at straws**, they are trying to solve a problem in a way that is unlikely to succeed because they have no other solutions available: *If we weren't so deeply in debt, we wouldn't be grasping at straws.*

grasp /græsp/ *n* [U] power to achieve or control something • *A full partnership at last seemed to be within her grasp.*

grasp UNDERSTAND /græsp/ *v* [T] to understand (esp. something difficult) • *It was hard to grasp what the professor was getting at.*

grasp /græsp/ *n* [U] • *I'm afraid my grasp of economics is weak.*

grasping /ˈgræs·pɪŋ/ *adj disapproving* always

eager to get more of something, esp. money • *He's a grasping, insensitive executive.*

grass /græs/ *n* [U] a low, green plant with narrow leaves growing naturally over much of the earth's surface • *a blade of grass* ○ *Are you going to cut the grass?* • (*slang*) Grass is also MARIJUANA. • A **grass-hopper** is a plant-eating insect having long back legs that make it able to jump high. • A **grassland** is a large area of land covered with grass: *Conservation groups are restoring grasslands in the Midwest.*

grasshopper

grassy /ˈgræs·i/ *adj* • *a grassy hillside*

grass roots /ˈgræsˈruːts/ *pl n* the ordinary people in a society, movement, or organization • *Washington politicians have to get back to the grass roots.*

grass–roots /ˌgræsˈruːts/ *adj* [not gradable] • *a grass-roots movement*

grate METAL STRUCTURE /greɪt/ *n* [C] a structure made of iron bars for holding wood or other fuel, esp. in a fireplace • A grate is also a structure of metal bars that covers an opening: *They have grates across every window.*

grating /ˈgreɪt·ɪŋ/ *n* [C] a structure made of metal bars • *an iron grating*

grate RUB TOGETHER /greɪt/ *v* [I] (of two hard objects) to rub together, often making an unpleasant sound, or to make an unpleasant sound of this kind • *The trolley's wheels grated horribly as it went around the curve.*

grating /ˈgreɪt·ɪŋ/ *adj* • *I turned on the car's engine, and there was that familiar grating sound.*

grate ANNOY /greɪt/ *v* [I] to have an annoying or painful effect • *His constant whining for attention is beginning to grate on my nerves.*

grate COOKING /greɪt/ *v* [T] to rub (food) against the rough surface of a metal device having holes through which small pieces of the food fall as they break off • *Would you grate the cheese?* ○ *Add the grated carrots to the salad.*

grater /ˈgreɪt·ər/ *n* [C] a metal device with holes surrounded by sharp edges, used to cut food into small pieces • *a cheese grater*

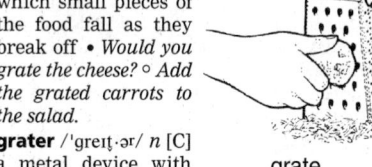
grate

grateful /ˈgreɪt·fəl/ *adj* showing or expressing thanks, esp. to another person • *I'm grateful for your love and support.*

gratefully /ˈgreɪt·fə·li/ *adv* • *We gratefully acknowledge the support of the Lincoln Fund.*

gratify /ˈgræt·əˌfɑɪ/ *v* [T] to please (someone), or to satisfy (a wish or need) • *He was gratified to see how well his students had done.* [+ to infinitive]

gratifying /ˈgræt·əˌfɑɪ·ɪŋ/ *adj* • *It was a big game for us, and a very gratifying win.*

gratis /ˈgræt·əs, ˈgrɑt-/ *adv, adj* [not gradable] free; not costing anything • *Drinks were gratis.*

gratitude /ˈgræt·əˌtuːd/ *n* [U] a strong feeling of appreciation to someone or something for what they have done to help you • *Many of his patients gave works of art to Dr. Klein in gratitude.*

gratuitous /grəˈtuː·ət·əs/ *adj* not necessary; with no reasonable cause • *The movie contains lots of cursing, nudity, sex, and gratuitous violence.*

gratuity /grəˈtuː·ət·i/ *n* [C] *fml* an amount of money given as a reward for a service; TIP

grave BURYING PLACE /greɪv/ *n* [C] a place where a dead person or dead people are buried, esp. when under the ground and marked by a stone • A **gravestone** is a **tombstone**. See at TOMB. • A **graveyard** is a place where dead people are buried.

grave SERIOUS /greɪv/ *adj* [-*er*/-*est* only] urgent and very bad; serious • *It was the gravest political crisis of his career.*

gravely /ˈgreɪv·li/ *adv* • *She is gravely ill.*

gravity /ˈgræv·ət·i/ *n* [U] • *I don't think you understand the gravity of the situation.* • See also GRAVITY.

gravel /ˈgræv·əl/ *n* [U] very small, rounded stones, often mixed with sand • *Gravel covers the driveway.*

gravelly /ˈgræv·ə·li/ *adj* (of a voice) low and rough

gravitate /ˈgræv·əˌteɪt/ *v* [I always + adv/prep] to be attracted to or move toward something • *People tend to gravitate to the beaches here.*

gravity /ˈgræv·ət·i/ *n* [U] the force that makes objects fall toward the earth • See also **gravity** at GRAVE SERIOUS.

gravy FOOD /ˈgreɪ·vi/ *n* [U] a sauce made from meat juices, often mixed with flour

gravy EXTRA /ˈgreɪ·vi/ *n* [U] *infml* something extra that you became having and often did not expect to get • *This business took care of all our expenses, and the revenue from other ads and subscriptions was gravy.*

gray, *esp. Cdn and Br* **grey** /greɪ/ *adj* [-*er*/-*est* only], *n* [C/U] (of) the color that is a mixture of black and white, the color of clouds on a rainy day • *a gray coat* ○ *She was dressed in gray.* [U] • Gray can also refer to hair that has changed color to gray: *He's already beginning to turn gray.* • If the weather is gray, there are a lot of clouds in the sky. • A **gray area** is a situation that is not clear or where the rules are not known: *Criminal negligence is a gray area.*

graze HURT SLIGHTLY /greɪz/ *v* [T] to touch and rub against (something) while passing it, causing slight damage • *The bullet only grazed his leg.*

graze EAT /greɪz/ *v* [I/T] (of animals) to eat

grass, or to cause (animals) to feed on grass • *Cows grazed in the field.* [I]

grease /griːs/ *n* [U] animal fat that is soft after melting • *There's always a lot of grease when you cook lamb.* • Grease is also any thick, oily substance: *You ought to put some grease on that hinge.*

grease /griːs, griːz/ *v* [T] • *Grease the pan.*

greasy /ˈgriː·si, -zi/ *adj* covered with or full of grease • *These French fries are too greasy.* • (*slang*) A **greasy spoon** is a small, cheap restaurant, esp. one that sells a lot of fried food.

greasepaint /ˈgriːs·peɪnt/ *n* [U] makeup as used by actors in the theater

great LARGE /greɪt/ *adj* [-er/-est only] large or unusually large in amount or degree • *the Great Lakes* ○ *He went on to great success as an actor.* • *He offered me* **a great deal** *of money* (= a lot of money). • *There were* **a great many** *people* (= a lot of people) *in the ballpark.*

greatly /ˈgreɪt·li/ *adv* [not gradable] very much • *Her piano-playing has improved greatly.* • LP VERY, COMPLETELY, AND OTHER INTENSIFIERS

great IMPORTANT /greɪt/ *adj* [-er/-est only] important, powerful, or famous • *a great president* ○ *a great athlete* • *Keeping the house really clean* **a great deal** *to me* (= was very important to me).

great /greɪt/ *n* [C] a famous person in a particular area of activity • *This sports facility is named after the tennis great Arthur Ashe.*

greatness /ˈgreɪt·nəs/ *n* [U] • *Her greatness as a writer is beyond question.*

great GOOD /greɪt/ *adj* [-er/-est only] *infml* very good or very effective; excellent • *We had a great time.* ○ *She has a great voice.* ○ *This stuff is great for cleaning windows.*

great– FAMILIES /ˌgreɪt/ *combining form* used with a word for a relative, such as grandmother, to mean one GENERATION older than such a relative • *great-grandmother* • PIC FAMILY TREE

greed /griːd/ *n* [U] a strong desire to continually get more of something, esp. money • *He was motivated by pure greed.*

greedy /ˈgriː·di/ *adj* • *He was greedy for power.*

Greek /griːk/ *n* • If someone says that something is **Greek to me**, they mean it is not possible to understand it: *Modern poetry is all Greek to me.*

green COLOR /griːn/ *adj, n* [C/U] (of) the color that is a mixture of blue and yellow; the color of grass • *a green dress* ○ *I don't like that green.* [C] • *When I heard about his new job I was* **green with envy** (= desired what he had). • A **greenback** is any piece of US paper money that is printed in green on the back: *He took out a thick wad of greenbacks.* • **Green beans** (also **string beans**) are a type of long, green, edible bean. • A **green card** is a document giving a foreigner permission to live and work in the United States. • A **green light** is a traffic signal in which the part that is green is brighter

as a symbol that it is safe for the people facing it to go: *Wait for the green light before crossing the street.* Compare **red light** at RED. • If you get or are given the **green light**, you have official permission to do something: *She had the green light to hire three more people.*

green PLANTS /griːn/ *adj* [-er/-est only] of or relating to grass, trees, and other plants • *I'd like a green salad* (= LETTUCE and other leafy vegetables). • Someone who has a **green thumb** is good at making plants grow. • A **greenhouse** is a building with a roof and sides made of glass or other transparent material, used for growing plants that need warmth and protection. • The **greenhouse effect** is a gradual warming of the earth because of heat trapped by **carbon dioxide** and other gases in the ATMOSPHERE.

green /griːn/ *n* [C] *regional* an area planted with grass, esp. for use by the public • *The fair will be held on the green behind the library.* • A green is also an area of smooth grass surrounding a hole on a golf course.

greenery /ˈgriː·nə·ri/ *n* [U] green plants, or branches that have been cut off from plants, esp. when used as decoration

greens /griːnz/ *pl n* the leaves of green vegetables such as LETTUCE or SPINACH when eaten as food

green POLITICAL /griːn/ *adj* [-er/-est only] relating to the protection of the environment • *green politics*

green NOT READY /griːn/ *adj* [-er/-est only] not experienced or trained • *I was pretty green when I joined this company.*

greenhorn /ˈgriːn·hɔːrn/ *n* [C] a person who is not experienced • *I'm a greenhorn when it comes to skiing.*

greet /griːt/ *v* [T] to welcome (someone) with particular words or a particular action, or to react to (something) in the stated way • *The men greeted each other warmly.* ○ *The mayor was greeted with shouts of anger.*

greeting /ˈgriː·t̬ɪŋ/ *n* [C] • *Jennifer sends birthday greetings* (= good wishes for your birthday). • A **greeting card** is a card containing a message of good wishes, usually sent to someone to celebrate an event such as a birthday.

gregarious /grɪˈgær·i·əs, -ˈger-/ *adj* liking to be with other people • *Leo was an open, gregarious, kind individual, who loved people.*

gremlin /ˈgrem·lən/ *n* [C] an imaginary creature that gets inside things, esp. machines, and causes problems

grenade /grəˈneɪd/ *n* [C] a small bomb thrown by hand or shot from a gun

grew /gruː/ *past simple of* GROW

grey /greɪ/ *adj esp. Cdn and Br for* GRAY

greyhound /ˈgreɪ·haʊnd/ *n* [C] a type of dog that has a thin body and long legs, and that can run very fast

grid /grɪd/ *n* [C] a pattern of horizontal and

GREETINGS

attracting someone's attention

• **If you know the person** you can begin by saying their name or with **excuse me**. You can also say **hey** in informal situations.

Kevin, . . . • Excuse me, Sylvia . . . • (formal) Ms. Sikorsky, . . . • (formal) Excuse me, Mr. McDermott, . . . • Hey, you guys, wait for me!

The use of titles like **Mr.** and **Ms.** is formal, and people quickly begin to address each other by first name in most situations.

Ⓛ🄿 **Titles and forms of address**

• **If you don't know the person** you can begin by saying **excuse me, pardon me,** or **hi**.

Excuse me, do you know where Somerset Mall is? • Pardon me, I think you dropped your glove. • (formal) Excuse me, Sir/Ma'am/Miss, . . . • Hi, I'm sorry to bother you, but could you tell me the time?

• **If you are angry or annoyed, or want to give a warning,** you can begin by saying **hey** or **look**.

Hey! Watch where you're going! • Look, I don't want to have to tell you this twice.

greeting someone

There are many words and phrases that can be used to greet people. A person's name can be added to any of these greetings.

Hi! • Hello • (informal) Hiya! • Hi, Michael, how are you? • (informal) How (are) you doing? • (Good) morning. • (informal) What's up?

(Good) afternoon and **(good) evening** are used mostly to greet people you do not know, such as people working in stores or restaurants.

When someone new comes to a place, or when someone visits you at your home or office, you can greet them by saying **welcome**.

"Hi, I'm Jean Bleisch, I've just transferred to your class." "Welcome, Ms. Bleisch. Please find a seat."

• **Special greetings** may be used on holidays or a person's birthday.

Merry Christmas! • Happy New Year! • Happy birthday!

replying to a greeting

When someone greets you, a short greeting is often repeated in response.

"Hi, Sean." "Hi, Julia. How are you?" • "Happy New Year!" "Happy New Year to you, too!"

asking how someone is

People often ask someone how they are as part of a greeting. The reply is usually short unless the two people know each other well. **Thank you** can be used instead of **thanks** but is more formal.

"How are you?" "Fine, thank you." • "How are things?" "OK, thanks." • "How's everything?" "Great!" • (informal) "How (are) you doing?" "Can't complain." • (informal) "How's it going?" "Not bad/Pretty good, thanks."

The first speaker might then be asked how they are.

Fine, thanks, and you? • (And) how are you? • How are things with you?

---

vertical lines that cross each other to make a set of squares • A grid is also a system of wires through which electricity is connected to different parts of a region: *a power grid*

griddle /ˈgrɪd·əl/ *n* [C] a flat metal surface of a stove heated from below for cooking, or a flat metal pan • *Some bacon was cooking on the griddle.*

gridiron /ˈgrɪd·ɑɪ·ərn/ *n* [C] a football field

gridlock /ˈgrɪd·lɑk/ *n* [U] a situation where streets that meet and cross become so blocked by cars that it is impossible for any traffic to move

grief /griːf/ *n* [U] very great sadness, esp. at the death of someone • *It took her years to get over her grief at the death of her mother.* ○ *(fig.)*

I had no idea that forgetting my driver's license would cause me so much grief (= trouble).

grievance /ˈgriː·vəns/ *n* [C] a complaint or a strong feeling that you have been treated unfairly • *A special committee investigates prisoners' grievances.*

grieve /griːv/ *v* [I/T] to feel a great sadness, esp. because of the death of someone • *The entire community is grieving for the loss of the four children.* [I]

grievous /ˈgriː·vəs/ *adj* having very serious effects or causing great pain • *It was a grievous head wound, and he was not expected to survive.*

grievously /ˈgriː·və·sli/ *adv* • *He was grievously injured.*

grill COOK /grɪl/ v [T] to cook (something) by direct heat, esp. on a frame of metal bars over a gas or coal fire • *We love to grill outside and eat on the back porch in the summer.* • PIC COOKING METHODS

grill /grɪl/ n [C] a frame of metal bars on which food is cooked over a fire

grill QUESTION /grɪl/ v [T] to ask (someone) a lot of questions for a long time • *After being grilled by the police for eight hours, Johnson signed a confession.*

grim NOT GOOD /grɪm/ adj [-er/-est only] -mm- not good; having no chance of a good result • *The outlook for a full recovery was grim.*

grim SERIOUS /grɪm/ adj [-er/-est only] -mm- very serious and sad • *Not until recently were white students made aware of the grim realities of slavery.* ○ *He looked at us with a grim expression.*

grimace /ˈgrɪm·əs, grɪˈmeɪs/ n [C] an expression of pain or disgust in which the muscles of the face are tightened and the face looks twisted

grimace /ˈgrɪm·əs, grɪˈmeɪs/ v [I] • *He grimaced in pain as the surgeon removed his bandages.*

grime /graɪm/ n [U] a layer of dirt on skin or a building • *The building is covered with grime.*

grimy /ˈgraɪ·mi/ adj • *a grimy face*

grin /grɪn/ n [C] a wide smile • *He flashed a big grin and gave us a thumbs up.*

grin /grɪn/ v [I] -nn- • *He grinned and waved to us.* • To **grin and bear it** is to accept something without complaining: *This cast will be on my arm for six weeks, so I'll just have to grin and bear it.*

grind CRUSH /graɪnd/ v [T] *past* **ground** /graʊnd/ to crush (a substance) between hard, moving surfaces into small pieces or a powder • *Every morning I go to the kitchen and grind some coffee.* • USAGE: The related noun is **grounds**, see at GROUND CRUSH.

grinder /ˈgraɪn·dər/ n [C] a machine for crushing or cutting something into very small pieces • *a meat grinder*

grind RUB /graɪnd/ v [T] *past* **ground** /graʊnd/ to rub (an object) against a hard surface in order to make it sharper, thinner, or smoother • *Laborers grind and shape steel bars into decorative fences.* • If you grind two sets of objects, you press and rub them together in a way that makes an unpleasant noise: *Ursula grinds her teeth at night.* • A **grindstone** is a large, round stone that is turned by a machine and is used to make tools sharper.

grind ACTIVITY /graɪnd/ n [U] *infml* difficult or unpleasant activity that is tiring or repetitious • *Karen came to the hotel for a rest from the daily grind.*

grind /graɪnd/ v [I/M] *infml* • *The speeches ground on for hours.* [I] ○ *Small-towns life can grind you down.* [M] • If something **grinds to a halt** it stops or no longer works well: *Traffic ground to a halt.* ○ *The country's economy is slowly grinding to a halt.*

grinding /ˈgraɪn·dɪŋ/ adj • Something that is grinding causes people or activities to lose energy and spirit: *He was brought up in grinding poverty.*

gringo /ˈgrɪŋ·goʊ/ n [C] *pl* **gringos** a foreigner in a Latin American country, esp. one who speaks only English • USAGE: This word is usually considered offensive.

grip /grɪp/ v [I/T] **gripping**, *past* **gripped** to hold (something) tightly, or stick to something • *The baby gripped my finger.* [T] ○ *Worn tires don't grip very well on wet roads.* [I] • If an emotion grips you, you feel it strongly: *Brady was gripped by fear.* [T]

grip /grɪp/ n [C usually sing] a way of holding something, or a tight hold • *She has a strong/firm/weak grip.* ○ *He lost his grip on Nancy's arm.* ○ *(fig.) They were in the grip of a tropical storm* (= suffering its effects).

gripe /graɪp/ n [C] *infml* a strong complaint • *My biggest gripe about living here is the hot weather.*

gripe /graɪp/ v [I] • *People gripe about doing yard work.*

gripping /ˈgrɪp·ɪŋ/ adj interesting or exciting • *a gripping story*

grisly /ˈgrɪz·li/ adj extremely unpleasant or disgusting, and usually causing fear • *It was a grisly murder involving sexual assault.*

gristle /ˈgrɪs·əl/ n [U] a part of a piece of meat that is very hard to chew

grit STONES /grɪt/ n [U] very small pieces of stone or sand • *I cleaned the grit off my bike.*

gritty /ˈgrɪt̬·i/ adj • *gritty dust*

grit BRAVERY /grɪt/ n [U] bravery and strength of character • *Emma is enthusiastic, all grit and determination.*

gritty /ˈgrɪt̬·i/ adj • *a gritty, no-nonsense approach*

grit PRESS /grɪt/ v [T] -tt- to press (your top and bottom teeth) together • *I grit my teeth because I'm trying not to moan.* • If you **grit** your **teeth** you accept a situation although it is difficult or unpleasant: *Many fans grit their teeth about the baseball strike.*

grits /grɪts/ *pl* n a roughly crushed type of corn, usually boiled in water and eaten esp. for breakfast

grizzly (bear) /ˈgrɪz·li (ˌber, ˌbær)/ n [C] a large, grayish brown bear from North America

groan /groʊn/ n [C] a low, sad sound that is continued for a while and that is made by someone who is suffering from pain or unhappiness • *Nick let out a groan.*

groan /groʊn/ v [I] • *He would often groan in his sleep.* ○ *(fig.) The tires of the pickup truck groaned under the weight* (= made sounds because of the pressure).

grocer /ˈgroʊ·sər/ *n* [C] a person who owns or works in a store selling food

groceries /ˈgroʊ·sə·riːz/ *pl n* the food and other items that you buy in a food store or SUPERMARKET • *My wife wrote a check to pay for groceries.*

grocery (store) /ˈgroʊ·sə·ri (ˌstɔːr, ˌstoʊr)/ *n* [C] a store where food and small items for the house are sold

groggy /ˈgrɑg·i/ *adj* weak and unable to think clearly or walk correctly, usually because of illness or being tired • *The drug made her groggy.*

groin /grɔɪn/ *n* [C] the place at the front of your body where your legs meet • *Jeff pulled a muscle in his groin.*

groom MAKE READY /gruːm, grʊm/ *v* [I/T] to make (yourself) ready to be seen; put in order • *The girls groomed their hair.* [T] ○ *He's gone upstairs to finish grooming.* [I] ○ *They're grooming the ski runs at Snow Basin* (= preparing them for use). [T]

groom PREPARE /gruːm, grʊm/ *v* [T] to prepare (someone) for a special job or activity • *The record company groomed performers to fit the music's image.*

groom MAN /gruːm, grʊm/, **bridegroom** *n* [C] a man who is about to get married or just got married • *The bride and groom were posing for pictures.*

groom CLEAN /gruːm, grʊm/ *v* [T] to clean (an animal), often by brushing its fur • *I've groomed horses for years.*

groom /gruːm, grʊm/ *n* [C] a person whose job is to take care of and clean horses

groove /gruːv/ *n* [C] a long, narrow, hollow space cut into a surface • *The window slides along a groove in the frame.*

groovy /ˈgruː·vi/ *adj dated slang* very fashionable and interesting • *groovy music*

grope /groʊp/ *v* [I/T] to search for something you cannot see or find easily, esp. by feeling with your hands • *She stands on her toes and gropes around on the closet shelf.* [I] • (*infml*) If someone gropes someone else, they touch that person's body in a sexual way: *A group of men groped and fondled the women as they came through.* [T]

gross EXTREME /groʊs/ *adj* [-er/-est only] (esp. of something bad or wrong) extreme or obvious • *The birds die from hunger, thirst, and gross overcrowding.*

grossly /ˈgroʊ·sli/ *adj* • *Medical insurance can be grossly expensive.*

gross UNPLEASANT /groʊs/ *adj* [-er/-est only] *infml* rude or offensive • *She watches these really gross movies.* ○ *"Gross!" Pamela says as she wipes the goo off her fingers.*

gross TOTAL /groʊs/ *adj* [not gradable] (of earnings) total, before tax is paid or costs are subtracted • *Investors have earned gross income of $780 million.* • The **gross domestic product** (*abbreviation* **GDP**) is the total value of goods and services produced by a country in one year.

gross /groʊs/ *n* [C usually sing] • *On a gross of $28 million, the company netted $7 million.*

gross /groʊs/ *v* [T] • *The film grossed over $200 million.*

gross NUMBER /groʊs/ *n* [C] *pl* **gross** a group of 144 items

□ **gross out** *obj*, **gross** *obj* **out** /'-'-/ *v adv* [M] *infml* to make (someone) uncomfortable because something is very unpleasant • *It grosses people out when I wear shorts.*

grotesque /groʊˈtesk/ *adj* strange and often frightening in appearance or character • *She had a grotesque, protruding stomach.*

grotesquely /groʊˈtes·kli/ *adv* • *His face was grotesquely scarred.*

grotto /ˈgrɑt·oʊ/ *n* [C] *pl* **grottoes** or **grottos** a small cave or an artificial structure that is like a cave, esp. one used for religious purposes

grouch /graʊtʃ/ *n* [C] a person who complains a lot even when there is little reason to complain

grouchy /ˈgraʊ·tʃi/ *adj* • *You're awfully grouchy today.*

ground LAND /graʊnd/ *n* [U] the surface of the earth or of a piece of land • *We laid a blanket on the ground for our picnic.* • The **ground floor** (also **first floor**) of a building is the floor that is nearest the level of the ground. • *Can someone tell me how you get* **in on the ground floor** (= involved at the start) *of a deal like that?* • **Groundwater** is water that collects below the surface of the earth.

ground /graʊnd/ *v* [T] to put or keep on the ground • *All flights have been grounded because of the snowstorm.*

grounds /graʊnz/ *pl n* land that surrounds a building • *We strolled around the hospital grounds.* • See also **grounds** at GROUND CRUSH.

ground AREA OF KNOWLEDGE /graʊnd/ *n* [U] an area of knowledge or experience; a subject • *This teacher just keeps going over the same ground again and again.*

ground CAUSE /graʊnd/ *n* [C usually pl] a reason, cause, or argument • *He refused to answer on the grounds that he'd promised to keep it secret.* [+ *that* clause]

ground /graʊnd/ *v* [T] • *His beliefs are grounded in his experience.*

groundless /ˈgraʊnd·ləs/ *adj* • *Your concerns are groundless.*

ground PUNISH /graʊnd/ *v* [T] *infml* to punish (an older child) by not allowing them to go out and have their usual social activities • *My parents grounded me for a week.*

ground CRUSH /graʊnd/ *past simple and past participle of* GRIND • **Ground beef** is meat from cows which has been cut up into very small pieces.

grounds /graʊnz/ *pl n* wet grains of coffee

beans from which coffee was made • See also
grounds at GROUND LAND .

ground WIRE /graʊnd/ *n* [C] a connection between a piece of electrical equipment and the
earth, or a wire that makes this connection

groundbreaking /'graʊnd,breɪ·kɪŋ/ *adj* original and important; showing a new way of doing or thinking about things • *This groundbreaking work changed the way historians
looked at slavery.*

groundhog /'graʊnd,hɔːg, -,hɑg/ *n* [C] a
WOODCHUCK • In the US, **Groundhog Day** is
February 2nd, which is believed to be the first
day the groundhog wakes up after sleeping
through the winter. According to this story, if
the groundhog sees its SHADOW on this day,
there will be six more weeks of winter, and if
it does not, spring will start early.

ground rules /'graʊnd·ruːlz/ *pl n* the basic
rules for doing something • *We set very strict
ground rules for the interviews.*

groundwork /'graʊn·dwɜrk/ *n* [U] work done
in preparation for something that will happen
later • *The planning committee will lay the
groundwork for the conference.*

group /gruːp/ *n* [C] a number of people or
things that are together or considered as a
unit • *a group of trees* ○ *I'm meeting a group of
friends for dinner.* • A group is also a number
of people who play music together, especially
popular music: *a rock/soul group*

group /gruːp/ *v* [T] • *She grouped the children
by height for the class photograph.*

groupie /'gruː·pi/ *n* [C] *infml* a person who admires someone famous, esp. a popular musician, and tries to meet them • *Groupies were
hanging around the entrance while he was
recording here.*

grouse COMPLAIN /graʊs/ *v* [I] *infml* to complain • *He's always grousing about how hard
he has to work.*

grouse BIRD /graʊs/ *n* [C/U] *pl* **grouse** a
small, fat bird that is hunted, or the flesh of
this bird eaten as meat

grove /groʊv/ *n* [C] a group of trees growing
close together

grovel /'grʌv·əl, 'grɑv·əl/ *v* [I] to lie facing the
ground, esp. in fear, or to behave toward someone in a way that shows that you are small and
unimportant and they are powerful • *My dog
grovels at my feet when she's done something
wrong.* ○ *I'll apologize, but I won't grovel just
because I made a mistake.*

grow INCREASE /groʊ/ *v* [I/T] *past simple* **grew**
/gruː/, *past part* **grown** /groʊn/ to increase in
size or amount, or to allow or encourage
(something) to increase in size or to become
more advanced or developed • *The population
is growing rapidly.* [I] ○ *She's grown a lot since
we last saw her.* [I] ○ *He began to grow a beard.*
[T] ○ *The economy is expected to grow by 2%
next year.* [I]

growing /'groʊ·ɪŋ/ *adj* [not gradable] increas-

ing in size or amount • *There is a growing
awareness of the seriousness of this disease.* •
Growing pains are emotional difficulties or
confusion experienced by a young person
nearing adulthood. • If an organization has
growing pains, it experiences temporary difficulties when it first starts or when it develops a new area of activity.

grow DEVELOP /groʊ/ *v* [I/T] *past simple* **grew**
/gruː/, *past part* **grown** /groʊn/ to provide (a
plant) with the conditions it needs to develop,
or to develop from a seed or small plant • *This
plant grows best in the shade.* [I] ○ *We're growing some herbs on the windowsill.* [T]

grower /'groʊ·ər/ *n* [C] a person or company
that cultivates a particular plant or crop in order to sell it • *citrus growers*

grow BECOME /groʊ/ *v past simple* **grew** /gruː/,
past part **grown** /groʊn/ to develop gradually,
or to start to do something gradually • *I grew
too old to be interested.* [L] ○ *She has grown to
like him.* [+ *to* infinitive]

▫ **grow into** BEGIN TO FIT /-'--/ *v prep* [T] to become tall enough or big enough to fit (esp.
clothes) • *Never buy a bike that's too big and
expect your child to grow into it.*

▫ **grow into** DEVELOP /'-,--/ *v prep* [T] to become
(a more fully developed type of person) • *We
want these children to grow into responsible
adults.*

▫ **grow on** /'--/ *v prep* [T] to become increasingly liked or enjoyed by (someone) • *Living in a
small town was tough at first, but the place
grows on you.*

▫ **grow out of** STOP FITTING /-'--/ *v adv prep* [T]
to become too tall or too big to fit into (esp.
clothes) • *Mom said she wasn't going to buy me
something I was going to grow out of next
week.*

▫ **grow out of** STOP LIKING /-'--/ *v adv prep* [T]
to stop having (an interest) or stop doing
(something you have done) as you become older • *He wants to be a rap singer, but I hope he
grows out of it.*

▫ **grow out of** DEVELOP /-'--/ *v adv prep* [T] (of
ideas) to develop from (an existing idea or
experience) • *His music grew out of black life.*

▫ **grow up** /-'-/ *v prep* [I] to change from being
a child to being an adult • *She grew up on a
Pennsylvania farm.* • If you tell someone to
grow up, you are telling them to stop behaving in a childish way.

growl /graʊl/ *v* [I] to make a low, rough sound,
usually in anger • *The dog growled at her.* • If
your stomach growls, it is making a low, continuous noise because you are hungry.

growl /graʊl/ *n* [C] • *I heard a growl outside
our tent, and prayed that whatever was out
there would go away.*

grown /groʊn/ *adj* [not gradable] adult • *a
grown woman/man* • A **grownup** is an adult:
*The grownups sat inside while the children
played in the yard.*

growth /grouθ/ n [C/U] the process of developing or of increasing in size • *Plant growth is most noticeable in spring.* [U] ○ *His budget is designed to promote economic growth in this country.* [U] • A growth is also tissue growing on the outside or inside of a person, animal, or plant which is caused by a disease. [C]

grub FOOD /grʌb/ n [U] *slang* food • *The food was just good, greasy grub.*

grub ASK FOR /grʌb/ v [T] **grubbing**, past **grubbed** *slang* to ask someone to give you (something) • *Can I grub a cigarette?*

grub (worm) /'grʌb (wɜrm)/ n [C] an insect in the stage when it has just come out of its egg

grubby /'grʌb·i/ adj dirty or messy • *grubby old clothes*

grudge /grʌdʒ/ n [C] a strong feeling of anger and dislike for a person who treated you badly • *He wasn't one to hold a grudge, but he wasn't going to be friendly.*

grudging /'grʌdʒ·ɪŋ/ adj done or offered unwillingly • *Her hard work won the grudging respect of her boss.*

grudgingly /'grʌdʒ·ɪŋ·li/ adv • *Grudgingly, Congress approved the funds.*

grueling /'gruː·ə·lɪŋ, 'gruː·lɪŋ/ adj extremely tiring and difficult, and demanding great effort and determination • *a grueling 50-mile run*

gruesome /'gruː·səm/ adj extremely unpleasant and shocking • *The movie was pretty gruesome.*

gruff /grʌf/ adj [-er/-est only] dealing with people in a way that lacks patience and seems unfriendly • *He has that gruff exterior, but underneath he's very kind.* • If a person's voice is gruff, it sounds low and slightly damaged.

gruffly /'grʌf·li/ adv • *"You drive," Casey gruffly told Jack.*

grumble /'grʌm·bəl/ v [I] to complain in an annoyed way • *There's no point in grumbling about the hotel—we're only here for one night.*

grumpy /'grʌm·pi/ adj infml being in a slightly angry mood because you are annoyed at something or are feeling tired • *Dad is always grumpy on Monday mornings.*

grunge /grʌndʒ/ adj connected with a type of ROCK music, popular in the early 1990s, or with a style of clothing that gives the appearance of being dirty and careless

grungy /'grʌn·dʒi/ adj slang (of a person) feeling dirty and that you need to wash, or (of a thing) dirty • *After a 15-hour flight, I felt really grungy.*

grunt /grʌnt/ v [I] to make a short, low noise, esp. in surprise, pain, or pleasure, or to show that you do not want to talk • *I tried to start a conversation, but he just grunted and continued reading.*

grunt /grʌnt/ n [C] • *The weightlifter raised the bar over his head with a grunt.*

G-string /'dʒiː·strɪŋ/ n [C] a narrow piece of cloth worn between a person's legs to cover their sexual organs and held in place by a piece of string around their waist • *When the stripper finished her act she was wearing only a G-string.*

guacamole /ˌgwɑk·ə'moʊ·li/ n [U] a thick mixture of AVOCADO (= an oily, green tropical fruit), TOMATO, onion, and spices, usually eaten cold with Mexican food and sometimes offered as a food before meals

guarantee /ˌgær·ən'tiː, 'gær·ən,tiː/ n [C/U] a promise that something will be done or will happen, esp. a written promise by a company to repair or change a product that develops a fault within a particular period of time • *The vacuum cleaner comes with a two-year guarantee.* [C] • Guarantee is also the certainty of a particular result: *No matter how many stars you have in the show, there's no guarantee* (= it is not certain that) *it will be a success.* [U]

guarantee /ˌgær·ən'tiː, 'gær·ən,tiː/ v [T] • *The freezer is guaranteed for three years.* • If you guarantee something, you promise that a particular thing will happen or exist: *I guarantee (you) that our team will play hard and have a shot at winning the championship.* [+ (that) clause] • If something is guaranteed to happen or have a particular result, it is certain that it will happen or have that result: *Eating all that rich food is guaranteed to give you indigestion.* [+ to infinitive]

guard /gɑrd/ n [C] a person or group of people whose job it is to protect a person, place, or thing from danger or attack, or to prevent a person such as a criminal from escaping • *prison guards* ○ *Armed guards were posted at every exit.* • In sports, a guard is a player who supports and defends other players of his or her team. • If you are **on (your) guard**, you are careful and aware because a situation might be dangerous: *She was warned to be on (her) guard against pickpockets.*

guard /gɑrd/ v [T] • *Soldiers guarded* (= protected) *the buildings against terrorist attacks.* • If you **guard against** something, you take careful action in order to try to prevent it from happening: *The best way to guard against financial problems is to avoid getting into debt.*

guarded /'gɑrd·əd/ adj careful in speech in order to avoid giving information • *The president made a guarded, lawyerly response.*

guardian /'gɑrd·i·ən/ n [C] a person who has the legal right and responsibility of taking care of someone who cannot take care of themselves, such as a child whose parents have died • (*slightly fml*) A guardian is also someone who protects something: *She characterized the department as the guardian of the nation's forests.* • A **guardian angel** is a spirit who is believed to protect and help a particular person.

guava /'gwɑv·ə/ n [C] a round, yellow, tropical fruit with pink or white flesh and hard seeds

gubernatorial /ˌguː·bər·nəˈtɔːr·iː·əl, -ˈtoʊr-/ *adj* [not gradable] relating to a governor of a US state • *a gubernatorial election*

guerrilla /gəˈrɪl·ə/ *n* [C] a member of an unofficial military group that is trying to change the government by making sudden, unexpected attacks on the official army forces • *guerrilla warfare*

guess /ges/ *v* [I/T] to give (an answer) to a question when you do not have all the facts and so cannot be certain if you are right • *I didn't know the answer, so I had to guess.* [I] ○ *He guessed (that) she was about 50.* [+ (that) clause] • To guess can also mean to give the correct answer: *She guessed the right answer.* [T] • To guess also means to think or believe: *My plane leaves in an hour, so I guess I'd better be going.* [T] ○ *"Is he going to call you back?" "I guess so."* [T]

guess /ges/ *n* [C] an attempt to give the right answer when you are not certain if you are right • *Go on, take a guess.* • Someone's guess is also their opinion about something, formed without any knowledge of the situation: *I don't know why she's late, but my guess is she got off at the wrong exit.* • If you say that something is **anyone's/anybody's guess**, you mean it is not possible for anyone to really know: *He has a plan, but whether it will work or not is anyone's guess.* • If you say that someone's **guess is as good as mine**, you mean that you have no way of knowing exactly what happened or what will happen: *Will she run again for the governorship? I don't know—your guess is as good as mine.* • **Guesswork** is the process of making a guess when you do not know all the facts: *She had to rely on pure guesswork in deciding how much food to order.*

guesstimate /ˈges·tə·mət/ *n* [C] a calculation of the size or amount of something when you do not know all the facts • *Current guesstimates are that the company's profits will increase by 10% this year.*

guest /gest/ *n* [C] a person who is staying with you in your home, or a person whom you have invited to a social occasion, such as a party or a meal • *dinner/wedding guests* • A person who is staying in a hotel is also called a guest. • If you are someone's guest, they are paying for you: *Four senators and their families were flown to Martinique as guests of the oil company.*

guff /gʌf/ *n* [U] *infml* (of speech or writing) nonsense • *All that talk about an economic crisis is a lot of guff.*

guffaw /gəˈfɔː/ *v* [I] to laugh loudly but briefly • *Kruger guffawed as though Ray had told him a particularly lewd joke.*

guffaw /gəˈfɔː/ *n* [C] • *a loud guffaw*

guide /gaɪd/ *n* [C] a person whose job it is to show a place or a route to visitors • *Our tour guide in Rome was a lovely young woman who spoke perfect English.* • A guide is also a book or piece of information that gives advice or help on how to do or understand something: *a travel guide* ○ *a guide to the best restaurants* ○ *a tax guide* • A **guidebook** is a book that gives information for visitors about a place, such as a city or region of a country: *We bought a guidebook for the New England area.* • A **guideline** is a piece of information that suggests how something should be done: *The article gives guidelines on how to invest your money safely.*

guide /gaɪd/ *v* [T] • *She guided me into her living room and offered me a seat on her couch.* ○ *If you want to learn how to use the computer, it has a program that will guide you through it* (= show you how to use it). ○ *We took a guided tour of* (= A guide showed us) *the historic houses in Newport.* • To guide someone or something can also mean to control or influence them: *Public policy must be guided by the best information available.* • A **guided missile** is an explosive weapon whose direction is controlled by radio signals during its flight.

guidance /ˈgaɪd·ᵊns/ *n* [U] help and advice about how to do something or about how to deal with problems • *She never got any guidance when she needed it.* • A **guidance counselor** is a person employed to help students with plans for their futures or personal problems.

guild /gɪld/ *n* [C] an organization of people who do the same job or have the same interests • *the Screen Actors Guild*

guile /gaɪl/ *n* [U] *slightly fml* the practice of deceiving people or using other dishonest methods to achieve your aims, or the ability to deceive people for this purpose • *He is a simple, honest man, totally lacking in guile.*

guileless /ˈgaɪl·ləs/ *adj* honest and direct • *He was completely guileless and trusting.*

guillotine /ˈgɪl·əˌtiːn; ˈgiː·əˌtiːn/ *n* [C] a device, invented in France, consisting of a sharp blade in a tall frame that was used for killing a person by cutting off his or her head

guillotine /ˈgɪl·əˌtiːn; ˈgiː·əˌtiːn/ *v* [T] • *During the French Revolution, thousands of people were guillotined.*

guilt /gɪlt/ *n* [U] the fact or state of having done something wrong or committed a crime • *In the US, people accused of a crime are presumed to be innocent until their guilt is proven.* • Guilt is also a feeling of anxiety or unhappiness that you have done something immoral or wrong, such as causing harm to another person: *She was tormented by feelings of guilt after putting her mother in a nursing home.* • (*infml*) A **guilt trip** is a strong feeling of having done something wrong in a particular situation: *Hector is going through a major guilt trip over his divorce.*

guilty /ˈgɪl·ti/ *adj* • *He pleaded guilty* (= He formally admitted his guilt in court). • If you feel guilty, you feel that you have done something wrong: *I feel so guilty about forgetting your birthday.* • If someone has a **guilty conscience**, they are unhappy because of something they feel they have done wrong.

guinea pig /'gɪn·iː,pɪg/ *n* [C] a small, furry animal with rounded ears, short legs, and no tail, often kept as a pet and for use in scientific experiments • (*fig.*) A guinea pig is also a person used in a test, esp. one to discover how effective a new drug or process is: *Her own son accused her of having used him as a guinea pig to test her theories about the education of children.*

guise /gaɪz/ *n* [U] the appearance of someone or something, esp. when intended to deceive • *The men who arrived in the guise of drug dealers were actually undercover police officers.*

guitar /gə'tɑr, gɪ-, *esp. Southern* 'gɪ·tɑr/ *n* [C/U] a musical instrument with usually six strings and a flat back that is held on the knee or by a strap worn over the shoulder and played by moving the fingers or a small piece of plastic across the strings, or this instrument generally • *an acoustic/electric guitar* [C]

guitarist /gə'tɑr·əst, gɪ-, *esp. Southern* 'gɪ,tɑr·əst/ *n* [C] a person who plays the guitar

guitar

gulch /gʌltʃ/ *n* [C] a narrow, rocky valley or channel with steep sides, made by a fast-flowing stream

gulf AREA /gʌlf/ *n* [C] an area of sea surrounded on three sides by land • *the Gulf of Mexico/the Gulf Coast* ○ *the Gulf Stream*

gulf DIFFERENCE /gʌlf/ *n* [C] an important difference between two things or groups of people • *There is a widening gulf between the rich and the poor.*

gull /gʌl/, **sea gull** *n* [C] a large bird that is black or gray and white and that lives near the sea

gullible /'gʌl·ə·bəl/ *adj* easily deceived or tricked, and too willing to believe everything that other people say • *a gullible young man*

gully /'gʌl·iː/ *n* [C] a channel cut by running water, which is usually dry except after heavy rain

gulp /gʌlp/ *v* [I/T] to eat or drink (food or liquid) quickly by swallowing it in large amounts, or to make a swallowing movement because of fear, surprise, or excitement • *Ray gulped (down) the last of his coffee and pushed back his chair.* [T/M] ○ *When his agent asked for a five-year contract worth $30 million, I gulped and said nothing.* [I]

gulp /gʌlp/ *n* [C] • *He swallowed his drink in one gulp.*

gum MOUTH /gʌm/ *n* [C usually pl] either of the two areas of firm, pink flesh inside the mouth that covers the bones to which the teeth are attached

gum STICKY SUBSTANCE /gʌm/ *n* [U] a sticky substance obtained from the stems of some trees and plants that is used in industry and for sticking things together • Gum is also **chewing gum**: *Most teachers don't allow their students to chew gum in class.* See at CHEW.

gum /gʌm/ *v* **-mm-** • If something **gums up the works**, it causes something to work badly or not work at all: *The case was going well so far, but if his client had to testify, it would only gum up the works.*

gumbo /'gʌm·boʊ/ *n* [C/U] *pl* **gumbos** a thick soup made with OKRA (= a green vegetable) and meat or fish

gumdrop /'gʌm·drɑp/ *n* [C] a chewy candy that comes in many different colors and is usually fruit-flavored

gumption /'gʌmp·ʃən/ *n* [U] the strong will and determination to do something risky • *She had the gumption to write directly to the company president.*

gun WEAPON /gʌn/ *n* [C] a weapon from which bullets or SHELLS (= explosive containers) are fired through a metal tube • *She took the gun from its drawer and loaded it.* • **Gunfire** is the shooting of one or more guns: *At the sound of gunfire, we ran into a building.* • A **gunman** is a criminal who uses a gun: *The gunman ordered the couple to toss their cash onto the floor.* • **Gunpowder** is a substance in powder form that is used in making explosive devices. • A **gunshot** is the firing of a gun or the sound this makes: *He suffered a gunshot wound in the thigh.*

gunner /'gʌn·ər/ *n* [C] a soldier or sailor in the armed forces who helps to operate a large gun

gun OPERATE ENGINE /gʌn/ *v* [T] **-nn-** to make (an engine) operate at high speed • *Tom gunned the engine and sped off into the night.*

□ **gun down** *obj*, **gun** *obj* **down** /'-'-/ *v adv* [M] to shoot and kill or badly injure (someone) • *A 19-year-old man was gunned down in a parking lot Sunday night.*

□ **gun for** /'--/ *v adv* [T] to make a great effort to defeat or hurt (someone) • *We know all the other teams are gunning for us.* • If someone is gunning for someone else, they can also be trying to shoot or attack them: *Government troops went gunning for the rebels.*

gung-ho /gʌŋ'hoʊ/ *adj infml* extremely enthusiastic • *I have a grandson who is gung-ho for football.*

gunk /gʌŋk/ *n* [U] any thick, sticky, unpleasant substance • *There was a lot of gunk on my bike chain.*

gunnysack /'gʌn·iː,sæk/ *n* [C] a large bag made of rough cloth • *She put the sticks in a gunnysack that she dragged along behind her.*

gunpoint /'gʌn·pɔɪnt/ *n* • Something that is done **at gunpoint** is done while threatening to use a gun: *He forced her at gunpoint to drive into the mountains.*

gurgle /'gɜr·gəl/ *v* [I] to make a bubbling

sound like that of water flowing unevenly • *A stream gurgled over the rocks.*

gurgle /'gɜr·gəl/ *n* [C] • *I said something that sounded like a gurgle.*

gurney /'gɜr·ni/ *n* [C] a flat table, or a light frame covered with cloth, which has wheels and is used for moving people who are ill or injured • *A nurse wheeled the gurney away.*

guru /'gʊr·uː, 'guː·ruː/ *n* [C] an expert in a particular subject who gives advice • *I've become the computer guru in our department.*

gush FLOW /gʌʃ/ *v* [I] to flow or pour out suddenly in large amounts • *Water gushed out of the broken pipe.*

gush /gʌʃ/ *n* [U] • *There was a gush of water from the hose.*

gush EXPRESS /gʌʃ/ *v* to express admiration, praise, or pleasure, in such a strong and enthusiastic way that it does not seem sincere • *"This is the best party I've ever had," Taylor gushed.* ○ *Mom gushed over the baby.* [I]

gust /gʌst/ *n* [C] a sudden, strong wind that blows for a very short time • *A sudden gust lifted his trailer and tossed it on its side.*

gust /gʌst/ *v* [I] • *Winds are gusting up to 55 miles per hour.*

gusty /'gʌs·ti/ *adj* • *gusty winds*

gusto /'gʌs·toʊ/ *n* [U] eager enjoyment experienced when doing something • *We ate and drank with gusto.*

gut STOMACH /gʌt/ *n* [C/U] the bowels or the stomach • *I had a feeling of sickness deep in the gut.* [U] ○ *Guts dangled from the just-butchered hogs.* [C usually pl] • *Your gut is also the front part of your body near the waist: He'd added a few extra pounds to his gut.* [C usually sing] • The guts of a machine are its inner, necessary parts: *The front panel was attached to the guts of the unit by three color-coded wires.* [pl]

gut FEELING /gʌt/ *adj* [not gradable] coming from or having to do with your emotions, not from thought • *My gut reaction is we'd better not get involved.* • *The movie ends with a gut-wrenching* (= emotionally painful) *scene where the lovers part forever.*

gut DESTROY /gʌt/ *v* [T] **-tt-** to destroy, esp. by fire, or remove the inside parts of (a building) • *The warehouse was gutted—only the charred walls remained.*

guts /gʌts/ *pl n infml* bravery and determination • *I don't think I'd have the guts to say that to his face.* [+ to infinitive]

gutsy /'gʌt·si/ *adj infml* • *Suing your employer is a gutsy move.*

gutter CHANNEL /'gʌt·ər/ *n* [C] a channel at the lower edge of a roof for carrying away rain, or a side of a road that is lower than the center of the road, where water and garbage col-

lects • *Every fall we have to clean leaves out of the gutters.*

gutter

gutter BAD MORALITY /'gʌt·ər/ *n* [U] a condition of very low moral standards • *The campaign went right into the gutter once the candidates started debating.* • **Gutter talk** is offensive language.

guy /gɑɪ/ *n* [C] *infml* a man • *Who's that guy?* ○ *Three guys and three girls left the room.* • Sometimes *guys* means people, both men and women: *Are you guys coming to lunch?* • LP TITLES AND FORMS OF ADDRESS

guzzle /'gʌz·əl/ *v* [T] *infml* to drink or eat (something) eagerly or in large amounts • *He sat at the bar, guzzling beer.*

gym BUILDING /dʒɪm/ *n* [C] *short form of* GYMNASIUM • *I work out at the gym every day.*

gym SCHOOL ACTIVITY /dʒɪm/ *n* [U] **physical education**, see at PHYSICAL BODY • *We have gym after recess.*

gymnasium /dʒɪmˈneɪ·ziː·əm/, *short form* **gym** /dʒɪm/ *n* [C] a building or room designed and equipped for various sports, physical training, and exercise

gymnast /'dʒɪm·næst, -nəst/ *n* [C] a person who is skilled at performing controlled physical exercises, often on special equipment, sometimes in sports competitions

gymnastics /dʒɪmˈnæs·tɪks/ *n* [U] physical exercises that increase the body's strength, balance, and ability to move gracefully, often using special equipment, or the competitive sport of performing such exercises

gynecology /ˌgɑɪ·nəˈkɑl·ə·dʒi/ *n* [U] the area of medicine that deals with women's physical health and treatment of diseases, esp. of the female reproductive organs

gynecological /ˌgɑɪ·nə·kəˈlɑdʒ·ɪ·kəl/ *adj* [not gradable] • *a gynecological examination*

gynecologist /ˌgɑɪ·nəˈkɑl·ə·dʒəst/ *n* [C] a doctor who specializes in gynecology

gyp /dʒɪp/ *v* [T] **-pp-** *infml* to cheat (someone) • *I think the taxpayers are getting gypped.*

Gypsy /'dʒɪp·si/ *n* [C] a member of a group of people who travel from place to place esp. in Europe and who originally came from northern India, or anyone who travels often and does not live in one place for long

gyrate /'dʒɑɪ·reɪt/ *v* [I] to swing repeatedly around a fixed point • *She recites a poem while a dancer gyrates next to her.*

gyration /dʒɑɪˈreɪ·ʃən/ *n* [C/U] • *The men pack the room to watch Tina's gyrations* (= twisting movements). [C]

H, h

H, h /eɪtʃ/ n [C] pl **H's** or **Hs** or **h's** or **hs** the eighth letter of the English alphabet

ha, hah /hɑ/ exclamation used to express surprise, interest, or victory • *Ha! So you see I was right after all!*

habit /ˈhæb·ət/ n [C/U] a particular act or way of acting that you tend to do regularly • *Judy is in the habit of sleeping late on Sundays.* [U] ○ *I have the habit of checking my e-mail as soon as I log on to my computer.* [U] ○ *Eating between meals is a bad habit.* [C] ○ *He denied having a drug habit* (= taking illegal drugs regularly). [C]

habitable /ˈhæb·ət·ə·bəl/ adj suitable to be lived in • *The houses have been vacant and need repairs to make them habitable.*

habitat /ˈhæb·ə,tæt/ n [C] the natural surroundings in which an animal or plant usually lives

habitation /ˌhæb·ə'teɪ·ʃən/ n [U] fml the act of living in a place • *Wilderness areas are not intended for human habitation.*

habitual /hə'bɪtʃ·ə·wəl/ adj [not gradable] usual or repeated • *Longer prison sentences will help keep habitual criminals off the streets.*

habitually /hə'bɪtʃ·ə·wə·li/ adv [not gradable] • *She was habitually late.*

hack CUT /hæk/ v [I/T] to cut (something or someone) roughly or unevenly • *The two men were hacked to death.* [T] ○ *He hacked away at the logs, splitting enough wood for a fire.* [I]

hack PERSON /hæk/ n [C] a person who willingly works or acts mostly for money or other rewards without considering their own independence, beliefs, or reputation • *a political/party hack* • A hack is also a writer who produces a lot of work for money without caring very much about its quality.

hack COMPUTING /hæk/ v [I] to access someone else's computer system without permission in order to obtain or change information • *Some schoolkid managed to hack into a government database.*

hacker /ˈhæk·ər/ n [C] • *Hackers are a major defense department concern.*

hack MANAGE /hæk/ v infml • If you cannot **hack it**, you are no longer able to deal with a difficult situation: *I guess I'm burned out and I just can't hack it anymore.*

hacker /ˈhæk·ər/ n [C] a person who is skilled in the use of computer systems, often one who illegally obtains access to private computer systems

hackneyed /ˈhæk·ni:d/ adj used or said so often that it seems ordinary, meaningless, or not sincere • *a hackneyed plot*

hacksaw /ˈhæk·sɔ:/ n [C] a small SAW (= a cutting tool with sharp points along a flat blade) used for cutting metal

had HAVE /hæd, həd, əd, d/ past simple and past participle of HAVE • *We had a dog when I was growing up.* • If someone says you **had better** do something, they mean you should do it: *You'd better get moving if you want to catch your train.*

had TRICKED /hæd/ adj infml • To be **had** is to be tricked or made to look foolish: *If you paid more than $20 for that picture frame, you've been had.* ○ *I think I was had.*

haddock /ˈhæd·ək/ n [C/U] an edible sea fish

hadn't /ˈhæd·ənt/ contraction of had not • *I hadn't seen Patty since we were in high school.*

hag /hæg/ n [C] an ugly old woman, esp. an unpleasant or evil one

haggard /ˈhæg·ərd/ adj (of a person) having dark areas around the eyes and lines on the face, esp. from being tired or from suffering • *His face was haggard, and his eyes were bloodshot.*

haggle /ˈhæg·əl/ v [I] to argue, esp. about the price of something • *He hated to haggle over prices.*

ha ha /hɑ'hɑ, 'hɑ'hɑ/ exclamation used in writing to represent laughter

hail ICE /heɪl/ n [U] small, hard balls of ice that fall from the sky like rain • A hail of things is a lot of them directed toward someone: *He fell amid a hail of bullets.* • A **hailstorm** is a storm with hail.

hail /heɪl/ v [I] • *It hailed for a few minutes this morning.*

hail CALL /heɪl/ v [T] to call (someone) in order to attract their attention • *You wait here with our bags while I hail a taxi.*

hail PRAISE /heɪl/ v [T] to publicly praise or show approval for (a person or an achievement) • *Heppner has been hailed as one of the finest tenors in the operatic world today.*

□ **hail from** /'--/ v prep [T] to live (somewhere) or to have come from there originally • *Both John and Leeza hail from South Carolina.*

hair /her, hær/ n the mass of threadlike structures on the head of a person, or any of these structures that grow out of the skin of a person or animal • *blond/curly/wavy hair* [U] ○ *I already have a few gray hairs.* [C] ○ *I have to get my hair cut this week.* [U] • Something that is **hair-raising** is frightening or shocking: *She told us a hair-raising story about suddenly meeting a black bear on her camping trip.* • A **hairbrush** is a brush used for making the hair on your head neat. PIC BRUSH • A **haircut** is an occasion of cutting the hair, or the style in which it is cut. • A **hairdresser** is a person who cuts and styles hair. • A **hair dryer** is an electrical device that blows hot air for drying and styling a person's hair. • A person's **hairline** is the edge of their hair along the top of the face. • A **hairpiece** is an artificial covering of hair used to hide an area of the head where hair no longer grows. • **Hair spray** is a liquid that is sprayed onto the hair to hold it in position. • A **hairstyle** or **hairdo** is the style in which a person's hair is arranged.

hairy /ˈher·i, ˈhær·i/ *adj* having a lot of hair, esp. on parts of the body other than the head • *hairy arms*

hairline /ˈher·lɑɪn, ˈhær-/ *adj* [not gradable] (of cracks or lines) very narrow • *a hairline fracture of a bone in the hand*

hairy /ˈher·i, ˈhær·i/ *adj infml* difficult, risky, or frightening • *The roads were really icy, and it was definitely a hairy situation even going slow.*

hale /heɪl/ *adj* [not gradable] • If someone is **hale and hearty**, they are healthy and strong: *My grandfather is in his nineties and still hale and hearty.*

half /hæf/ *n* [C/U], *pronoun pl* **halves** /hævz/ either of the two equal or nearly equal parts that together make up a whole • *Half of 12 is 6.* [U] ○ *Half (of) the students are Spanish.* [U] ○ *Cut the apple in half* (= into two equal parts). [U] ○ *The recipe calls for a pound and a half of ground beef.* [C] • In sports, a half is one of two equal periods of play, often with a short pause for rest between them. [C] • When you say that something is **half the battle**, you mean that it is a large part of the effort or work: *For jobs like that, getting an interview is half the battle.* • LP DETERMINERS

half /hæf/ *adj, adv* [not gradable] • *Each talk should last about a half hour/half an hour* (= 30 minutes). ○ *We need half a dozen* (= six) *eggs.* • Half also means partly or not completely: *She was still sleepy and only half aware of what was happening.* ○ *I half expected* (= almost expected) *to see her at the party.* • (*rude slang*) **Half-assed** means not carefully considered or planned: It's another one of her half-assed ideas for getting rich. • An idea or plan that is **half-baked** has not been considered carefully enough: *It was some half-baked scheme to get people off welfare.* • A **half-dollar** is a coin worth 50 cents. • A person or action that is **half-hearted** shows a lack of enthusiasm: *He made a half-hearted attempt to keep up with us, but soon fell back.* • If a flag is at **half-mast**, it has been lowered to a point half the way down the pole as an expression of sadness at someone's death. • Your **half-sister** or **half-brother** has one of the same parents as you do, but their other parent is different from yours. • **Half-time** is a short rest period between the two parts of a sports game. • A **half-truth** is a statement that is intended to deceive by telling only part of the truth.

halfback /ˈhæf·bæk/ *n* [C] (in football) a player who plays in the middle of the field, and (in SOCCER and **field hockey**) a player who plays near the forward line

halfway /ˈhæfˈweɪ/ *adj, adv* [not gradable] (being) at a place that is equally distant from two other places, or in the middle of something • *We're almost halfway there.* ○ *At the halfway point of the race, he began to pull away.* ○ *We're about halfway through the renovation.*

halibut /ˈhæl·ə·bət, ˈhɑl-/ *n* [C] a large, flat, edible sea fish

hall PASSAGE /hɔl/, **hallway** /ˈhɔl·weɪ/ *n* [C] a passage in a building, or the area just inside the main entrance of a building • *Her office is just down the hall.*

hall BUILDING /hɔl/ *n* [C] a building or large room used for events involving a lot of people • *a concert/lecture hall* • A hall can also be a building at a college or university. • A **hall of fame** is a building that contains images of famous people and items that are connected with them.

hallelujah /ˌhæl·əˈluː·jə/ *exclamation* an expression of great happiness, praise, or thanks • *Hallelujah, praise the Lord!*

hallmark /ˈhɔl·mɑrk/ *n* [C] a typical characteristic or feature of a person or thing • *An independent press is one of the hallmarks of a free society.*

hallowed /ˈhæl·oʊd/ *adj fml* holy or highly respected • *hallowed traditions*

Halloween, **Hallowe'en** /ˌhæl·əˈwiːn, ˌhɑl-/ *n* [U] the evening of October 31, when children wear special clothes and often MASKS to hide their faces and go from house to house asking for candy

hallucinate /həˈluː·səˌneɪt/ *v* [I] to see or hear something that does not exist • *Police said the suspect was yelling incoherent statements as if he was hallucinating.*

hallucination /həˌluː·səˈneɪ·ʃən/ *n* [C/U] • *a drug-induced hallucination* [C]

hallucinogen /həˈluː·sə·nəˌdʒən/ *n* [C] a drug that causes people to HALLUCINATE (= see or hear things that do not exist)

hallucinogenic /həˌluː·sə·nəˈdʒen·ɪk/ *adj* • *The drug can be hallucinogenic.*

hallway /ˈhɔl·weɪ/ *n* [C] a HALL PASSAGE

halo /ˈheɪ·loʊ/ *n* [C] *pl* **halos** or **haloes** a ring of light around or above the head of a holy person in a religious drawing or painting

halt /hɔlt/ *v* [I/T] to stop (something), or to bring (something) to a stop • *"Halt!" ordered the guard.* [I] ○ *Congress voted additional funds in an effort to halt the spread of AIDS.* [T] ○ *Nationwide, mail delivery was halted by the strike.* [T]

halt /hɔlt/ *n* [U] • *All work had come to a halt and everyone was standing silently at their desks.*

halting /ˈhɔl·tɪŋ/ *adj* (esp. of speech or movement) slow, stopping and starting repeatedly,

hand

as if lacking confidence • *His mind is clear, but his speech is slow and halting.*

halve /hæv/ *v* [T] to divide something into two equal parts, or to reduce something to half of its original size, number, or degree • *The doctor decided to halve the dose of the drug.*

halves /hævz/ *pl of* HALF • *Cut the chicken breasts into halves.*

ham MEAT /hæm/ *n* [C/U] meat from a pig's leg or shoulder • *a boiled ham* [C] ○ *ham and eggs* [U]

ham ACTOR /hæm/ *n* [C] an actor who tends to perform with too much obvious expression

ham /hæm/ *v* -mm- • To **ham it up** is to act with too much obvious expression: *The old vaudeville comedians always hammed it up.*

ham RADIO /hæm/ *n* [C] a person who operates a radio station as a hobby • *a ham radio operator*

hamburger /'hæm,bɜr·gər/ *n* [C/U] very small pieces of BEEF (= meat from cattle), or this meat pressed into a round, flat shape, cooked, and usually eaten as a sandwich in a small, round ROLL (= piece of bread) • *a pound of hamburger (meat)* [U] ○ *I'll take a hamburger and French fries, please.* [C]

hamburger

hamlet /'hæm·lət/ *n* [C] a small village

hammer /'hæm·ər/ *n* [C] a tool with a heavy metal top attached to a straight handle, used for hitting an object such as a nail into a substance that holds it firmly in place

hammer

hammer /'hæm·ər/ *v* [I/T] to hit (something) repeatedly with, or as if with, a hammer • *I hammered the nail into the wall.* [T] • To hammer is also to repeat again and again esp. to persuade other people about something: *Martin Luther King, Jr. hammered at the theme that the civil rights movement must avoid violence.* [I always + adv/prep] ○ *His attorneys hammered away at the idea that the police department was incompetent.* [I always + adv/prep]

□**hammer out** /'--'-/ *v adv* [T] to arrive at (an agreement or solution) after a lot of argument or discussion • *The delegates to the United Nations Conference on Women's Rights hammered out a statement on family planning.*

hammock /'hæm·ək/ *n* [C] a net or strong piece of cloth, wide enough for a person to lie

hammock

on, hanging between two poles or trees to which it is attached

hamper MAKE DIFFICULT /'hæm·pər/ *v* [T] to make (an action intended to achieve something) more difficult • *High winds hampered efforts to put out the fire.*

hamper CONTAINER /'hæm·pər/ *n* [C] a large container, often a BASKET (= container made of strips of wood), with a lid • *a laundry/picnic hamper*

hamster /'hæm·stər/ *n* [C] a small, furry animal with a short tail, often kept as a pet

hamstring PREVENT /'hæm·strɪŋ/ *v* [T] *past* **hamstrung** /'hæm·strʌŋ/ to prevent an activity, or to block the effectiveness of (someone or something) • *The company is hamstrung by its traditional but inefficient ways of doing business.*

hamstring MUSCLE /'hæm·strɪŋ/ *n* [C] a muscle at the back of the upper part of the leg • *I played the whole game with a pulled hamstring* (= injured muscle in the leg).

hand BODY PART /hænd/ *n* [C] the part of the body at the end of the arm that includes the fingers and is used for holding, moving, touching, and feeling things • *Keep both hands on the steering wheel.* ○ *When eating, most Americans hold the fork in their right hand.* ○ *He took my hand* (= held it with his hand) *as we walked along.* • If something is **at hand**, it is ready and available for use: *I feel safer having a gun at hand.* • Something that happens **at the hands of** someone else happens because of their actions: *The boy suffered at the hands of his brother.* • *Please deliver the message* **by hand** (= personally). • Something that is made

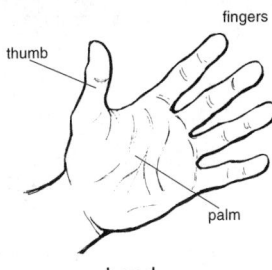
hand

by hand is made by a person, not a machine. • *I saw Pat and Chris walking* **hand in hand** (= holding each other's hand) *the other day.* • **Hands down** means definitely: *If we had a race, he'd win hands down.* • When a person says **hands off**, they mean you should not touch something: *Hey! Hands off my camera!* • If a situation is **in hand**, someone in a position of authority has control of it: *The police have the situation well in hand.* • If something is **in** someone's **hands** or moved **into** someone's **hands**, it is in their control or they are responsible for it: *Florida passed into American hands in 1821.* ○ *You'll be in good hands with her—she's a terrific lawyer.* • He always kept a supply of firewood **on hand** (= ready and available). • A **handgun** is a small gun that is held in one hand when used. • Something **handmade** or **hand-crafted** was made as a separate item by a person working with their hands and was not made by a machine with a lot of other similar objects: *handmade jewelry* • Someone who is **hand-picked** has been carefully chosen for a special job or purpose: *He was the mayor's hand-picked choice to lead the investigation.* • A **handshake** is a greeting or expression of agreement in which two people who are facing each other take hold of each other's right hands and sometimes also move them up and down. • Someone with a **hands-on** way of managing and organizing things in a business or project is closely involved with other workers in making decisions: *She's a hands-on manager.* • A **handstand** is an action in which you move your body upside down to balance vertically with your hands on the ground and your legs pointing up in the air.

hand /hænd/ *v* [T] to put (something) from your hand into someone else's hand • *Would you please hand me a pencil?*

hand POINTER /hænd/ *n* [C] a narrow pointer on a clock or watch that shows the time • *the hour/minute hand*

hand CARDS /hænd/ *n* [C] the set of cards that a player is given in a game • *a winning/losing hand*

hand HELP /hænd/ *n* [C usually sing] help with doing something • *Can I give you a hand with those bags?*

hand WORKER /hænd/ *n* [C] a person who does physical work, esp. as one of a team or group • *a farm hand*

hand CLAPPING /hænd/ *n* [C usually sing] a period of clapping to show enjoyment of a performance • *Let's give this band a big hand.*

□ **hand back** *obj*, **hand** *obj* **back** /'-'-/ *v adv* [M] to return (something) to the person it belongs to after they have given it to you • *You'll have to hand these books back at the end of the school year.*

□ **hand down** *obj* GIVE , **hand** *obj* **down** /'-'-/ *v adv* [M] to give (something) to a younger member of your family when you no longer need it, or to arrange for them to get it after you have died • *My grandmother handed down this necklace to my mother.*

□ **hand down** DECIDE /'-'-/ *v adv* [T] *law* to make (a legal decision) publicly known with an official statement • *The appeals court handed down its decision yesterday.*

□ **hand in** *obj*, **hand** *obj* **in** /'-'-/ *v prep* [M] to give (something) to someone in charge • *She handed her term paper in late.*

□ **hand out** *obj*, **hand** *obj* **out** /'-'-/ *v adv* [M] to give (something) to a each of a number of people • *Would you please hand out the balloons to the children?*

handout /'hæn·daʊt/ *n* [C] a document given to each of the people who are present, usually to give information about a particular subject • *There aren't enough handouts, so you'll have to share.* • A handout is also something such as food, clothing, or money that is given free to someone who needs it: *government handouts*

□ **hand over** *obj*, **hand** *obj* **over** /'-'--/ *v adv* [M] to give (something) to someone else, esp. after being asked or told • *I've got a gun! Hand over your wallet!*

handbag /'hænd·bæg/ *n* [C] a bag, often with a handle or a strap going over the shoulder, used esp. by women for carrying money, keys, and small personal items such as makeup; PURSE

handbook /'hænd·bʊk/ *n* [C] a book that contains advice about how to do something or information about esp. an organization • *The student handbook describes all the campus activities.*

handcuffs /'hænd·kʌfs/, *short form* **cuffs** *pl n* two metal rings, joined by a short chain, that are locked around a prisoner's wrists to prevent free movement • *She was taken away in handcuffs.*

handcuff /'hænd·kʌf/, *short form* **cuff** *v* [T] • *On the plane, he was handcuffed to an FBI agent.*

handful VERY FEW /'hænd·fʊl/ *n* [C usually sing] a very few, esp. when compared to a larger group • *A handful of professional athletes make millions, but most do not do so well.*

handful SMALL AMOUNT /'hænd·fʊl/ *n* [C] an amount of something that can be held in one hand • *He scooped up a handful of soil and examined it carefully.*

handful PROBLEM /'hænd·fʊl/ *n* [C usually sing] *infml* a person or thing that is difficult to control or manage • *Sam was an easygoing baby, but Rory is a real handful.*

handicap PHYSICAL CONDITION /'hæn·di:ˌkæp/ *n* [C] a physical or mental condition that makes ordinary activities more difficult than they are for other people • *His loss of hearing was a severe handicap.*

handicapped /'hæn·di:ˌkæpt/ *adj* • *a handi-*

capped person ○ *Buildings have to provide access for the handicapped.* • USAGE: This word is considered offensive by some people, who prefer the words "challenged" or "impaired."

handicap DIFFICULTY /ˈhæn·diˌkæp/ *n* [C] something that causes unusual difficulties • *Their lack of knowledge of computer programming was not much of a handicap for them.*

handicap /ˈhæn·diˌkæp/ *v* [T] **-pp-** • *Rescue efforts have been handicapped by bad weather.*

handicap DISADVANTAGE /ˈhæn·diˌkæp/ *n* [C] (in a sports competition) a disadvantage given to a strong competitor in order to give weaker competitors a better chance of winning • *a golf handicap*

handiwork /ˈhæn·diˌwɜrk/ *n* [U] work done skillfully with the hands • *He built his own telescope, and he was proud of his handiwork.* • Handiwork is also the effects of any action: *These dead bodies are the handiwork of terrorists.*

handkerchief /ˈhæŋ·kər·tʃəf, -tʃɪf, -ˌtʃiːf/ *n* [C] a square piece of cloth used for blowing the nose or for cleaning the face or eyes

handle TOUCH /ˈhæn·dəl/ *v* [T] to lift (something) and touch, hold, or move it with your hands • *Please handle the old photographs carefully.*

handle /ˈhæn·dəl/ *n* [C] a part of an object designed for holding, moving, or carrying the object • *the handle of a shovel* ○ *I can't pick the pot up—the handle's too hot.* • **Handlebars** are a bar along the front of a bicycle or **motorcycle** that a rider holds in order to balance and turn. PIC BICYCLE

handle DEAL WITH /ˈhæn·dəl/ *v* [T] to deal with, have responsibility for, or be in charge of (something) • *Who handles the marketing in your company?* ○ *Some managers have no idea how to handle people.*

handler /ˈhæn·dlər, ˈhæn·dəl·ər/ *n* [C] a person who trains and takes care of animals, esp. as a job • *a dog handler*

hand–me–down /ˈhænd·miːˌdaʊn/ *n* [C] a piece of clothing given to a younger relative or friend because the person who owns it no longer wants it or it no longer fits • *Claudia had three older sisters, so she wore a lot of hand-me-downs.*

handout /ˈhæn·daʊt/ *n* [C] • See at HAND OUT.

handsome ATTRACTIVE /ˈhæn·səm/ *adj* (esp. of a man) physically attractive • *He was handsome, brilliant, witty, and generally the center of attention wherever he was.*

handsome GENEROUS /ˈhæn·səm/ *adj* (esp. of money) large in amount • *a handsome salary*

handwriting /ˈhænˌdraɪt·ɪŋ/ *n* [U] a person's style of writing done with a pen or pencil • *His handwriting is so sloppy it's hard to read.*

handwritten /ˈhænˌdrɪt·ən/ *adj* [not gradable] written by someone using a pen or pencil • *a handwritten thank-you note*

handy USEFUL /ˈhæn·di/ *adj* useful or convenient • *We found it handy to have a cellular phone.* ○ *When I'm cooking something new, I like to keep the cookbook handy* (= in a convenient place).

handy SKILLFUL /ˈhæn·di/ *adj* skillful with the hands or with using tools, esp. in making or repairing things • *Eduardo is handy with power tools.* • A **handyman** is a man who works at many small jobs, such as repairing and making things.

hang ATTACH AT TOP /hæŋ/ *v* [I/T] *past* **hung** /hʌŋ/ to put (something) so that it is supported at the top, leaving the other part parts free, or (esp. of cloth) to be held in this way • *There was no wind, and the flag hung straight down.* [I] ○ *I plan to hang this picture in the hall.* [T] • If you **hang** your **head**, you let it bend forward so you are facing down, esp. because you are feeling embarrassed or guilty: *I hung my head like a guilty child.* • If a situation **hangs in the balance**, the result has not yet been decided one way or another: *The game hung in the balance until the last seconds.* • (*infml*) **Hang in there** means do not give up despite difficulties: *Hang in there—exams are almost over.* • A **hang glider** is an aircraft consisting of a light frame over which cloth or similar material is stretched in order to catch the wind when a person holding it jumps off a cliff.

hang KILL /hæŋ/ *v* [I/T] *past* **hanged** or **hung** /hʌŋ/ to kill (someone) by fixing a rope around their neck which is tied to something above them and allowing their body to drop down suddenly • *He was sentenced to die and was hanged the next morning.* [T]

hanging /ˈhæŋ·ɪŋ/ *n* [C/U] • *He was present at the hangings of dozens of outlaws in the 1860s.* [C]

hang STAY /hæŋ/ *v* [I] *past* **hung** /hʌŋ/ to stay in the air • *Smoke from the campfires hung in the air.* • If something **hangs over** your **head**, its existence makes you unable to relax or enjoy yourself: *I've got those darn credit card bills hanging over my head.*

hang TURN /hæŋ/ *v* [T] *past* **hung** /hʌŋ/ *infml* to turn to (the left or right) • *Hang a left/right at the next corner.*

□ **hang around** /ˌ-ˈ-/ *v adv* [I/T] to wait at (a place), or to stay near (a place or person), often for no particular reason • *We were just hanging around the mall.* [T] ○ *She hangs around with some tough kids.* [I]

□ **hang on** HOLD /-ˈ-/ *v adv* [I] to hold or continue holding onto something • *He was driving so fast I had to hang on tight whenever he turned.*

□ **hang on** WAIT /-ˈ-/ *v adv* [I] *infml* to wait • *Hang on—I'll be with you in a minute!*

□ **hang on** LISTEN /ˈ-ˌ-/ *v prep* [T] to listen very carefully to (someone's speech) • *She hung on every word he said.*

□**hang onto** /'-'--/ *v adv* [T] to keep (something) • *Our team was just trying to hang onto the lead.*

□**hang out** /'-'-/ *v adv* [I] *infml* to spend a lot of time in a place or with someone • *Who is he hanging out with these days?*

hangout /'hæŋ·aʊt/ *n* [C] *infml* a place where someone or a particular group spends a lot of time • *a student hangout*

□**hang up** *obj* [CLOTHING] , **hang** *obj* **up** /'--, -'-/ *v adv* [T] to place (esp. clothing) on a hook or HANGER • *Hang your coat up and come on in.* • See also HANG-UP.

□**hang up** [TELEPHONE] /'-'-/ *v adv* [I] to end a telephone conversation by stopping the connection, usually by putting down the RECEIVER (= the part you hold to your mouth and ear) • *Don't hang up—there's something else I want to say.* • If you **hang up on** someone, you end a telephone conversation suddenly: *She hung up on me in the middle of a sentence.* • See also HANG-UP.

hangar /'hæŋ·ər/ *n* [C] a large building in an airport in which aircraft are kept

hanger /'hæŋ·ər/ *n* [C] a frame of wire, wood, or plastic on which clothes are hung to keep them neat when you are not wearing them

hanger-on /'hæŋ·ə,rɔːn, -,rɑn/ *n* [C] *pl* **hangers-on** /'hæŋ·ər,zɔːn, -,zɑn/ a person who tries to be friendly and spend time with rich or important people to get some advantage • *Wherever there are rock stars, there are always hangers-on.*

hangout /'hæŋ·aʊt/ *n* [C] • See at HANG OUT.

hangover /'hæŋ,oʊ·vər/ *n* [C] a feeling of illness you get the day after drinking too much alcohol

hang–up /'hæŋ·ʌp/ *n* [C] *infml* a permanent and unreasonable feeling of anxiety esp. about yourself • *Some people have hang-ups about sex.* • See also HANG UP [CLOTHING] HANG UP [TELEPHONE].

hanker /'hæŋ·kər/ *v* [I] to have a strong desire for something • *I've been hankering for a hot dog.* ○ *I always hankered to go to Nashville.* [+ to infinitive]

hankering /'hæŋ·kə·rɪŋ/ *n* [C] • *She's got a hankering to write plays.*

hanky, **hankie** /'hæŋ·ki/ *n* [C] a small, often decorative HANDKERCHIEF (= square piece of cloth)

hanky–panky /,hæŋ·ki'pæŋ·ki/ *n* [U] *infml* dishonest or immoral behavior, esp. involving sexual activity or cheating • *financial hanky-panky*

Hanukkah /'hɑn·ə·kə, 'xɑn-/, **Chanukah** *n* [U] a Jewish holiday celebrated for eight days in December

haphazard /hæp'hæz·ərd/ *adj* lacking order or purpose; not planned • *Haphazard record-keeping made it difficult for the agency to keep track of its clients.*

hapless /'hæp·ləs/ *adj* unlucky • *hapless victims of war*

happen [HAVE EXISTENCE] /'hæp·ən/ *v* [I] (of a situation or event) to come into existence; OCCUR • *If you want to know what is happening in the world, you have to read the newspapers.* ○ *No one knows exactly what happened, but several people have been hurt.* • If a situation or event happens to someone or something, it has an effect on them: *What happened to Phil? I thought he would be here by now.*

happening /'hæp·ə·nɪŋ/ *n* [C usually pl] • *Earl had been alerted to the happenings of the day before.*

happening /'hæp·ə·nɪŋ/ *adj* [not gradable] *slang* (of a place or event) newly exciting or fashionable • *a happening neighborhood*

happen [CHANCE] /'hæp·ən/ *v* [I] to do or be by chance • *I happened to come across this book I think you would like.* [+ to infinitive] ○ *I happen to think he's right* (= I do, although others may not). [+ to infinitive] • If you happen on/upon someone or something, you meet them or find it by chance: *I happened on the perfect dress for the party.*

happy [PLEASED] /'hæp·i/ *adj* feeling, showing, or causing pleasure or satisfaction • *To tell the truth, I've never been happier in my whole life.* ○ *People want movies to have happy endings.* ○ *I'm happy (that) everything is working out for you.* [+ (that) clause] ○ *I've been very happy with* (= satisfied with) *the education that my boys have gotten through scouting.* • Happy is used as a polite way to express your willingness to do something: *I'm driving that way and I'd be happy to drop you off at your home.* [+ to infinitive] ○ *It was no trouble at all—I was happy to be of help.* [+ to infinitive] • Happy is also used in greetings for special occasions, expressing good wishes: *Happy birthday!* ○ *Happy New Year* [LP] GREETINGS • *(infml)* If someone is **not a happy camper**, they are very annoyed by their situation: *The dog is sick, Jessie sprained her ankle, and the car won't start—I am not a happy camper!* • If someone is **happy-go-lucky**, they don't worry or become anxious easily. • A **happy hour** is a period of time during which a bar sells drinks at a reduced price. • A **happy medium** is a way of acting or thinking that avoids being extreme: *Somewhere in the debate over abortion, there has to be a happy medium.*

happily /'hæp·ə·li/ *adv* • *happily married*

happiness /'hæp·iː·nəs/ *n* [U] • *Our children have brought us so much happiness.*

happy [LUCKY] /'hæp·i/ *adj slightly fml* (of a condition or situation) lucky • *By a happy coincidence, we found ourselves on the same flight.*

harangue /hə'ræŋ/ *v* [T] to speak to (someone or a group of people), often for a long time, in a forceful and sometimes angry way, esp. to persuade them or to express disapproval • *He kept haranguing the crowd about the decline in morality in modern society.*

harangue /həˈræŋ/ *n* [C] • *The coach delivered his regular half-time harangue to the team.*

harass /həˈræs, ˈhær·əs/ *v* [T] to annoy or trouble (someone) repeatedly • *He claimed that the police continued to harass foreign journalists.* ○ *She felt she was being harassed by his constant demands.*

harassment /həˈræs·mənt, ˈhær·ə·smənt/ *n* [U] • *He was accused of sexual harassment* (= offensive sexual suggestions or actions).

harbor WATER /ˈhɑr·bər/ *n* [C] a protected area of water next to the land where ships and boats can be safely kept

harbor HAVE IN MIND /ˈhɑr·bər/ *v* [T] to have in mind (a thought or feeling), usually over a long period • *He harbored the suspicion that someone in the agency was spying for the enemy.*

harbor HIDE /ˈhɑr·bər/ *v* [T] to protect (someone) by giving them a place to hide • *They were accused of harboring a fugitive.*

hard SOLID /hɑrd/ *adj* [-er/-est only] firm and solid, or not easy to bend, cut, or break • *It hadn't rained in a long time, and the ground was hard.* ○ *He chewed on something hard and was afraid he'd broken a tooth.* • Something that is **hard-and-fast** does not change: *a hard-and-fast rule* • When an egg is **hard-boiled**, it has been boiled in its shell until both the white and yellow parts are solid. Compare **soft-boiled** at SOFT NOT HARD. • **Hard copy** is information from a computer that has been printed on paper. • A **hard disk** is a magnetized disk on which a large amount of information can be stored and used by a computer. • A **hard hat** is a hat made of a strong substance which is worn to protect the head, esp. of someone who works as a builder. • **Hardcover** (also **hardback**) is the stiff covers of a book, or a book that has stiff covers: *This book was originally published in hardcover.* ○ *a hardcover book*

harden /ˈhɑr·ən/ *v* [I/T] to become firm or solid, or to cause (something) to become firm or solid • *In a few hours the cement will harden.* [I]

hardness /ˈhɑrd·nəs/ *n* [U]

hard DIFFICULT /hɑrd/ *adj* [-er/-est only] difficult to understand or do • *hard questions to answer* ○ *It's hard to say which of them is lying.* [+ *to* infinitive] ○ *It's hard being a single mother.* ○ *Her handwriting is hard to read.* [+ *to* infinitive] ○ *She always does things the hard way* (= makes things more difficult to do). • If someone says that something is **hard to swallow**, they mean it is not believable, or it is difficult to agree with. • *She's finding the bad news* **hard to take** (= difficult to accept). • *I find her books* **hard going** (= difficult and tir-

ing). • If someone is **hard of hearing**, they cannot hear well. • Someone who is **hard up** lacks money. • To be **hard-pressed** (also **hard-put**) means to have a lot of difficulty: *Most people would be hard-pressed to name all their elected officials.*

hard USING EFFORT /hɑrd/ *adj* [-er/-est only] needing or using a lot of physical or mental effort • *Qualifying as a surgeon is hard work.* ○ *We had fun cycling, but it was hard to go up the hills.*

hard /hɑrd/ *adv* [-er/-est only] • *You have to push the door hard to open it.* • If something is **hard-earned**, it is deserved because a lot of work was done: *a hard-earned vacation* • If something is **hard-won**, it was achieved only after a lot of effort: *a hard-won victory* • Someone who is **hardworking** always works with a lot of effort: *a hardworking employee*

hard SEVERE /hɑrd/ *adj* [-er/-est only] not pleasant or gentle; severe • *She's had a hard life.* ○ *His boss is giving him a hard time* (= is being unpleasant to him). ○ *Don't be too hard on her—she's just learning the job.* • If someone is hard on a piece of clothing, they tend to damage it quickly: *I'm very hard on shoes.* • If water is hard, it contains MINERALS (= chemical substances) that prevent soap from producing bubbles and cleaning easily. • Someone who is **(as) hard as nails** does not show or feel emotion. • *We may disagree, but let's not have any* **hard feelings** (= bad feelings between us). • A person who is **hard-boiled** does not seem to have any emotions or weaknesses: *a hard-boiled detective* • Someone or something that is **hard-core** does not change in condition or belief: *hard-core poverty* ○ *a hard-core conservative* • **Hard-core** can also mean showing sexual acts clearly and in detail: *hard-core pornography* • **Hardheaded** (also **hard-nosed**) means practical and determined: *a hardheaded approach to a problem* • If someone is **hardhearted**, they are not kind or sympathetic. Compare **softhearted** at SOFT GENTLE. • **Hard labor** is a punishment for criminals that involves tiring physical work. • A **hard line** is an opinion or position that is fixed and will not change: *The president has taken a hard line on the budget.* • **Hard rock** is a type of ROCK music (= popular music) with a strong beat in which drums and electric guitars are played very loudly. • A **hard sell** is a way of trying to sell something by being very forceful.

hard /hɑrd/ *adv* [-er/-est only] • *They took the defeat hard.* ○ *It's raining hard.* ○ *She slapped him hard.*

harden /ˈhɑr·ən/ *v* [I/T] to make or become stronger or more severe • *As the war progressed, attitudes on both sides hardened.* [I]

hardened /ˈhɑr·ənd/ *adj* • *The judge called him a hardened criminal* (= one who will not stop his criminal activity).

hard [DRUG] /hɑrd/ *adj* [-*er*/-*est* only] (of a drug) dangerous and ADDICTIVE (= giving you the habit of taking it), or (of a drink) containing a large amount of alcohol • *Heroin and cocaine are hard drugs.* • *For those who prefer* **hard liquor,** *the bar serves whiskey, vodka, and gin.*

hard [FACTUAL] /hɑrd/ *adj* [-*er*/-*est* only] able to be proven; factual • *hard evidence*

hardiness /ˈhɑrd·iː·nəs/ *n* [U] • See at HARDY.

hardly [ONLY JUST] /ˈhɑrd·li/ *adv* [not gradable] only just or almost not • *Hardly a day passes that I don't think about it.* ◦ *You've hardly eaten anything.* ◦ *Something is wrong with the phone—I can hardly hear you.* ◦ *I can hardly wait for your visit.* ◦ *We hardly ever see them anymore.*

hardly [CERTAINLY NOT] /ˈhɑrd·li/ *adv* [not gradable] certainly not • *It's hardly surprising that he was angry.*

hardship /ˈhɑrd·ʃɪp/ *n* [C/U] a condition of life that causes difficulty or suffering • *The 1930s were a time of high unemployment and economic hardship.* [U]

hardware [TOOLS] /ˈhɑrd·wer, -wær/ *n* [U] metal objects, materials, and equipment, such as tools • *a hardware store*

hardware [COMPUTER] /ˈhɑrd·wer, -dwær/ *n* [U] the physical and electronic parts of a computer, rather than the instructions it follows • Compare SOFTWARE.

hardwood /ˈhɑr·dwʊd/ *n* [U] the strong, heavy wood of particular trees such as OAK, used esp. to make furniture

hardy /ˈhɑrd·i/ *adj* able to bear difficult or extreme conditions; strong and healthy • *a hardy group of campers* • *A hardy plant can live through the winter without protection from the weather.*

hardiness /ˈhɑrd·iː·nəs/ *n* [U]

hare /her, hær/ *n* [C] a small, furry animal with long ears that is like a large rabbit and can run fast

harebrained /ˈher·breɪnd, ˈhær-/ *adj* (of plans or people) foolish; not practical • *a harebrained scheme*

harem /ˈhær·əm, ˈher-/ *n* [C] esp. in the past, the women in a Muslim home, including the wives and other family members and sexual partners of a man, or the part of a house in which these women live

hark /hɑrk/, **hearken** /ˈhɑr·kən/ *v* [I] to listen closely or give attention to something • *Hark, I hear music.* • To **hark back** is to remember or to cause to remember something from the past: *The director's latest film harks back to the era of silent movies.*

harm /hɑrm/ *n* [U] physical or other injury or damage • *Missing a meal once in a while won't do you any harm.* ◦ *Fortunately, she didn't come to any harm when the car skidded.* ◦ *Maybe Jim can help you—there's no harm in ask-ing (= no one will be annoyed and you might benefit).*

harm /hɑrm/ *v* [T] • *The tornado blew out the windows of a nearby school, but none of the children were harmed.* ◦ *News reports of the extramarital affair harmed his reputation.*

harmful /ˈhɑrm·fəl/ *adj* • *This group of chemicals is known to be harmful to the environment.*

harmless /ˈhɑrm·ləs/ *adj* not able or likely to cause harm • *Some think television hurts children and others regard it as harmless entertainment.*

harmonica /hɑrˈmɑn·ɪ·kə/ *n* [C/U] a small, rectangular musical instrument with spaces along one side that are blown into to play notes, or this type of instrument generally

harmony [MUSIC] /ˈhɑr·mə·ni/ *n* [C/U] (in a piece of music) notes that are played or sung with the main tune and that make the piece more complicated and interesting

harmonize /ˈhɑr·mə,nɑɪz/ *v* [I/T] to add a harmony • *I can sing a tune, but I find it hard to harmonize.* [I]

harmony [AGREEMENT] /ˈhɑr·mə·ni/ *n* [U] agreement of ideas, feelings, or actions, or a pleasing combination of different parts • *He imagined a society in which all races lived together in harmony.*

harmonious /hɑrˈmoʊ·ni·əs/ *adj* • *a harmonious blend of colors*

harmonize /ˈhɑr·mə,nɑɪz/ *v* [I/T] • *We need to harmonize the different approaches into a unified plan.* [T]

harness /ˈhɑr·nəs/ *n* [C] a piece of equipment, including straps for fastening it, used to control an animal such as a horse or attach it to a load to be pulled, or a set of straps used to hold a person in place • *a horse's harness* ◦ *a parachute harness*

harness /ˈhɑr·nəs/ *v* [T] • *He harnessed the baby into her car seat.* ◦ *The dam harnesses water power* (= controls and uses it) *to generate electricity.*

harp [INSTRUMENT] /hɑrp/ *n* [C/U] a usually large, triangle-shaped musical instrument with strings stretched across it that you PLUCK (= pull with the fingers) to play notes, or this type of instrument generally

harp [REPEAT] /hɑrp/ *v* [I always + adv/prep] to repeat or esp. complain about something many times in an annoying way • *I'm tired of these people who keep harping on what is wrong with the country.*

harpoon /hɑrˈpuːn/ *n* [C] a long, sharp weapon that is fixed to a rope and shot from a gun or thrown, used for hunting WHALES and other sea animals

harpsichord /ˈhɑrp·sɪ,kɔːrd/ *n* [C/U] a large musical instrument, similar to a piano and used esp. in the 17th and 18th centuries, with a row of keys that are pressed with the fingers to play notes, or this type of instrument generally

harried /'hær·iːd/ *adj* anxious or worried because you have too many things to do • *I've been feeling very harried at work.*

harrowing /'hær·ə·wɪŋ/ *adj* extremely upsetting because connected with suffering • *His book tells the harrowing story of how they climbed Mt. Everest.*

harsh UNKIND /hɑrʃ/ *adj* [-er/-est only] unkind or cruel • *harsh criticism*

harshly /'hɑrʃ·li/ *adv* • *Violators are being dealt with harshly.*

harshness /'hɑrʃ·nəs/ *n* [U]

harsh SEVERE /hɑrʃ/ *adj* [-er/-est only] severe and unpleasant • *a harsh winter* ○ *harsh lighting*

harshness /'hɑrʃ·nəs/ *n* [U] • *We weren't aware of the harshness of our condition.*

harshly /'hɑrʃ·li/ *adv* • *harshly lit images*

harvest /'hɑr·vəst/ *n* [C/U] the activity or time of gathering a crop, or a crop that is gathered • *We picked the corn that had been missed during harvest.* [U] ○ *He had a large garden and loved to share his harvest with others.* [C]

harvest /'hɑr·vəst/ *v* [I/T] • *They couldn't get anyone to harvest their crop.* [T]

has /hæz, həz, əz, in "has to" often hæs/ *v* HAVE, used with he/she/it

has–been /'hæz·bɪn/ *n* [C] a person who was famous, important, admired, or good at something in the past, but is no longer any of these • *She's a has-been TV star.*

hash /hæʃ/ *n* [U] a mixture of meat and potatoes cut into small pieces and baked or fried • *hash and eggs* • **Hash browns** are small pieces of potato pressed flat and fried.

hash out *obj*, **hash** *obj* **out** /'-'-/ *v adv* [M] *infml* to talk about (something) with someone else in order to reach agreement about it • *You two hash out the details of the presentation.*

hashish /'hæʃ·iːʃ, -ɪʃ/, **hash** /hæʃ/ *n* [U] a drug, illegal in many countries, made from the CANNABIS plant and usually smoked

hasn't /'hæz·ənt/ *contraction of* **has not** • *He hasn't visited in years.*

hassle /'hæs·əl/ *n* [C] *infml* a situation that causes difficulty or trouble, or an argument • *Bad weather was the major hassle during our trip.* ○ *I got into a hassle with my father about being late.*

hassle /'hæs·əl/ *v* [T] *infml* • *The kids keep hassling me about going to Disney World.*

haste /heɪst/ *n* [U] great speed • *In spite of all their haste, they didn't have time to finish.* • *Officials acted* **in haste** (= too quickly), *without understanding the situation.*

hasten /'heɪ·sən/ *v* to hurry, or to make (something) go or happen faster • *They didn't get what they were after—thanks to you, I hasten to add.* [+ *to* infinitive] ○ *To hasten softening, place the cream cheese in the oven for a few minutes.* [T]

hasty /'heɪ·sti/ *adj* • *Don't make a hasty decision.*

hastily /'heɪ·stə·li/ *adv* • *hastily constructed houses*

hat /hæt/ *n* [C] a piece of clothing for the head • *a straw/fur hat* ○ *a cowboy hat*

hatch BREAK EGG /hætʃ/ *v* [I/T] to break an egg so a baby animal can come out • *The birds hatched out the next afternoon.* [I]

hatch PLAN /hætʃ/ *v* [T] to create or decide on (a plan, esp. a secret plan) • *They hatched a plan to steal drugs.*

hatch OPENING /hætʃ/ *n* [C] an opening through a floor or wall, or the cover for an opening, esp. on a ship • *a cargo hatch* • A **hatchback** is a large door in the back of a car that opens by being lifted up, allowing wide things to be put inside, or a car that has such a door.

hatchet /'hætʃ·ət/ *n* [C] a tool with a blade that cuts which is attached to a short handle; a small AX • *She chased a neighbor, waving her grandson's hatchet.* • (*infml*) A **hatchet man** is someone who does unpleasant jobs or attacks competitors in unfair ways.

hate /heɪt/ *v* [I/T] to strongly dislike someone or something • *Kelly hates her teacher.* [T] ○ *I have always hated speaking in public.* [T] ○ *I hate to say it, but I don't think Leo is the right man for the job.* [+ *to* infinitive] • To **hate** someone's **guts** is to hate them very much.

hate /heɪt/ *n* [U] • *She seems to be full of hate and bigotry.*

hateful /'heɪt·fəl/ *adj* filled with or causing strong dislike • *She said some hateful things about me.*

hatred /'heɪ·trəd/ *n* [U] a strong feeling of dislike; hate • *He has an intense hatred of Americans.*

haughty /'hɔːt̬·i/ *adj* unreasonably proud and unfriendly • *They show a haughty contempt of others.*

haughtily /'hɔːt̬·ᵊl·i/ *adv*

haul MOVE /hɔːl/ *v* [T/M] to pull (something heavy) slowly and with effort, or to transport (something) esp. over long distances • *They use these trucks to haul freight.* [T] ○ *A tractor was used to haul away the fallen tree.* [M] • (*rude slang*) If you **haul ass** you move quickly. • (*infml*) If officials **haul** someone **in** or **haul** someone **off**, they force them to go somewhere: *Iris got hauled into court again for speeding.* • (*infml*) If you **haul off**, you pull your arm back in order to hit someone or something: *He said hello, then hauled off and punched me.*

haul /hɔːl/ *n* [C usually sing] a distance over which something is transported • *short-haul flights* ○ *It's a long haul to Minnesota.*

haul AMOUNT /hɔːl/ *n* [C] an amount of something that was obtained illegally, esp. after it has been taken by the authorities • *Police say it is the largest cocaine haul in years.*

haunch

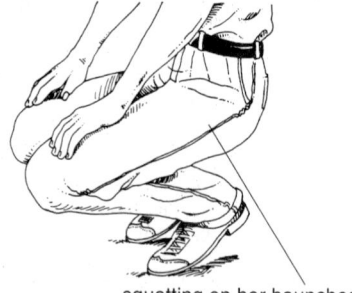

squatting on her haunches

haunch /hɔːntʃ, hɑntʃ/ n [C] the top part of the leg between the knee and the waist

haunt APPEAR /hɔːnt, hɑnt/ v [T] to often appear (somewhere), or to appear to (someone) in the form of a GHOST (= spirit of a dead person)

haunted /'hɔːnt·əd, 'hɑnt·əd/ adj [not gradable] • a haunted house

haunt WORRY /hɔːnt, hɑnt/ v [T] to cause (someone) to worry or feel anxiety because of being thought about too often • His experiences in Vietnam still haunt him.

haunted /'hɔːnt·əd, 'hɑnt·əd/ adj • haunted eyes

haunting /'hɔːnt·ɪŋ, 'hɑnt·ɪŋ/ adj staying in the mind • a haunting melody

haunt PLACE /hɔːnt, hɑnt/ n [C] a place often visited • This bar was one of our old haunts.

have PERFECT TENSE /hæv, həv, əv, v/ v aux he/she/it **has** /hæz, həz, əz/, past **had** /hæd, həd, əd/ used with the past participle of other verbs to form PERFECT tenses • I have heard that story before. ○ "Have we been invited?" "Yes, we have." • If you say you **have had it** or **have had enough**, you mean that you are not able or willing to continue doing something: We've been to three museums today and I've just about had it. • (infml) This old vacuum cleaner **has had it** (= no longer works and cannot be repaired). • To **have heard of** someone or something is to have some knowledge about them or it: Have you heard of the artist Bazile? • If something **has seen better days**, it is now old and in bad condition: This jacket's seen better days. • LP AUXILIARY VERBS

have POSSESS /hæv, həv/, **have got** /hæv'gɑt, həv-/ v [T] he/she/it **has** /hæz, həz, əz/, past **had** /hæd, həd, əd/ to own or possess (something) • We have a dog. ○ Have you got a cold? ○ I've got a big nose. ○ Have you got any money on you (= Are you carrying money with you)? • Have can also mean to be related to, or to know: Carol has six sisters. ○ I've got a friend who could lend us a car. • If a store has something, it is available to be bought: While you're there, see if they have any toothpicks. • If you **don't have a clue**, you have no knowledge about something: I don't have a clue about how to deal with this. • To **have a (good) head for**

an activity or skill is to have a natural ability to do it well: Kim has a head for numbers. • If you **have an eye for** something, you have an ability to notice it: She has a good eye for detail. • (infml) She **has** her **eye** on that new bike at Miller's Toys (= She has been admiring it and wants it). • Please let me go to the party— **have a heart** (= show some kindness and sympathy)! • If you **have an axe to grind** you have a personal, often selfish, reason for wanting something to happen, or a particular idea or belief that you are always trying to persuade other people to agree with: The study should be conducted by a firm that has no axe to grind. • (infml) If someone **has another think coming**, they are mistaken: If you expected him to pat you on the back, you had another think coming. • (infml) If you say someone **has a screw loose**, you mean they seem crazy. • To **have** your **cake and eat it too** is to get two things you want when it does not seem possible to have both. • (infml) To **have dibs on** something is to have the first right to use it, before anyone else: I've got dibs on the sofa. • His speech was really funny—we didn't know he **had it in** him (= possessed this ability). • (infml) She **has it in for** me (= dislikes me). • (infml) If you **have it made**, you are or will be successful or rich: Everyone thinks if you're in a hit movie, you've got it made. • If you **have nothing to lose** by doing something, your situation could improve by doing it and will not be any worse for you if you fail at it: Since I had nothing to lose, I accepted the offer. • If you do not **have the heart** to do something, you think it would be mean or unkind to do it: I don't have the heart to kick her out because she's too friendly. • If you **have the hots for** someone, you are strongly attracted to them in a sexual way: He's got the hots for Sue. • If you **have the last/final word on** something, you can make a decision without asking anyone else: Carol has the last word on whether we go. • Do you **have the time?** (= Do you know what time it is?) • Will you **have time** to finish the report today (= Can you do it in the amount of time available to you)? • **have what it takes** is to have the qualities or character needed to be successful: She doesn't have a college degree, but I think she has what it takes. • If someone **has** their **work cut out for** them, they have something difficult to do: If she has to finish that report by tomorrow, she has her work cut out for her. • They settled the lawsuit because they did **not have a leg to stand on** (= had no good arguments to support their case.) • USAGE: "Have got" is often used, but only in the present tense.

have CONTAIN /hæv, həv/, **have got** /hæv'gɑt, həv-/ v [T] **has** /hæz, həz, əz/, past **had** /hæd, həd, əd/ to contain or include (something), esp. as a part • The Chicago area has a population of about eight million. ○ Our house has three *bedrooms and two baths.* ∘ *We have a few min-utes left before the end of class.* • *My question* **has to do with** *last week's assignment* (= is about this subject).

have DO /hæv/ v [T] he/she/it **has** /hæz, həz, əz/, *past* **had** /hæd, həd, əd/ to do (an action) • *We didn't have a Halloween party this year.* ∘ *The baby is having her nap.* • Have can also mean eat or drink: *We're going to have lunch.* • To have a baby is to give birth: *Glennis had a girl.* • To **have a go at** something is to attempt to do it: *Let me have a go at getting that window open.* • If you **have** your **feet on the ground/have both feet on the ground**, you are practical and able to take care of yourself.
• LP DO: VERBS MEANING "PERFORM"

have RECEIVE /hæv/ v [T] he/she/it **has** /hæz, həz, əz/, *past* **had** /hæd, həd, əd/ to receive or accept (something), or to allow (something) to happen • *I'll have some more coffee.* ∘ *I just had a phone call from Judy.* ∘ *I won't have those kids running through my flower bed.* • (*infml*) If you say someone **has it coming**, you mean they deserve what happens to them: *He got caught speeding, and he had it coming to him.*

have CAUSE /hæv/ v [T] he/she/it **has** /hæz, həz, əz/, *past* **had** /hæd, həd, əd/ to cause (some-thing) to happen, or to cause (someone) to do something • *We're having the house painted.* ∘ *She had her parents come to her house for Thanksgiving.* ∘ *We often have friends over.* • If you **have (got) a hand in** something, you are involved with it or influence it. • If you **have (got)** your **heart set on** something, you want to have it a lot and will be very disappointed if you do not get it: *She's got her heart set on dance lessons.* • If you **have (got) only** your-**self to blame**, only you are responsible for something bad that has happened: *He didn't study, so he's got only himself to blame if he fails.* • LP GET, HAVE, AND OTHER VERBS USED TO MEAN "CAUSE"

have EXPERIENCE /hæv/ v [T] he/she/it **has** /hæz, həz, əz/, *past* **had** /hæd, həd, əd/ to expe-rience (something) • *We had a wonderful va-cation.* ∘ *She had her car stolen last week.* • **Have a good/nice day** and (*infml*) **Have a good one** are polite phrases that people say to someone who is about to leave. • *I have had my* **fill** *of violent movies* (= do not want to expe-rience any more of them). • If you **have had** your **share/more than** your **share of** some-thing, you have had a lot or too much of it: *We've had our share of problems with the new computer system.* • To **have (got)** your **hands full** is to be very busy or involved with some-thing: *I've got my hands full right now with a sick baby.*

▫ **have (got) on** obj WEAR , **have (got)** obj **on** /-'-, -'-'-/ v adv [M] *infml* to be wearing (clothes) • *She had on a blue hat.*

▫ **have (got)** obj **on** obj KNOW /-'-, --'-'-/ v prep [T] to know (secret or damaging information)

about (someone) • *She threatened to go to the newspapers, but she hasn't got anything on me.*

▫ **have (got) on** obj OPERATE , **have (got)** obj **on** /-'-, --'-'-/ v adv [M] to be operating or used • *She's always got the TV on while she irons.*

▫ **have to** /'hæf·tuː, 'hæv-, -tə/, **have got to** /'gɑt̬,tuː, həv-, -tə/ v aux (used with the infin-itive form of another verb) to need to or be forced to; must • *I have to go to Vermont tomor-row.* • If you say someone or something **has (got) to be** something, you mean that you be-lieve it must be: *That has got to be the stupidest excuse I've ever heard.* • If you say you **have (got) to hand it to** someone, you mean that person deserves respect for what they did: *You've got to hand it to her, she built that cab-in herself.* • *The mess those kids made* **had to be seen to be believed** (= was difficult to be-lieve, but really did exist). • LP AUXILIARY VERBS

haven /'heɪ·vən/ n [C] a safe or peaceful place

haven't /'hæv·ənt/ *contraction of* **have not** • *I haven't finished eating.*

havoc /'hæv·ək/ n [U] confusion and lack of order that result in damage or trouble • *The storm created complete havoc in the park.*

Hawaiian shirt /hə'wɑɪ·ən'ʃɜrt, -'wɔɪ-/ n [C] a loose, informal shirt with colorful patterns on it

hawk BIRD /hɔːk/ n [C] a type of large bird that catches small birds and animals for food • Someone who is **hawk-eyed** sees very well.

hawk SELL /hɔːk/ v [T] to sell goods in public places, esp. by calling out to people • *She was hawking flowers at the parking lot exit.*

hay /heɪ/ n [U] tall grass that is cut, dried, and used as animal food or as covering material • *a bale of hay* • **Hay fever** is a physical reac-tion to the POLLEN of plants which causes some people to have problems with their eyes, nose, throat, and lungs. • A **hayride** is a social event in which a group of people take a ride in a hay-filled open vehicle. • A **haystack** is a large pile of hay in a field.

hazard DANGER /'hæz·ərd/ n [C] something dangerous and likely to cause damage • *a health/fire hazard*

hazardous /'hæz·ərd·əs/ adj • *a hazardous road*

hazard RISK /'hæz·ərd/ v [T] to risk making (a guess or suggestion) • *She wouldn't hazard a guess about the meaning of the event.*

haze FOG /heɪz/ n [C/U] fog caused by water, smoke, or dust, or an effect of heat that pre-vents things being seen clearly • *A brownish haze hung over the field.* [C]

hazy /'heɪ·zi/ adj • *a hazy day/sky* • Hazy al-so means not clear: *I'm hazy about what hap-pened after the accident.*

haze TREAT BADLY /heɪz/ v [T] to force (people new to a group, esp. a college social group or sports team) to take part in activities that are very embarrassing and sometimes harmful

hazing /ˈheɪ·zɪŋ/ *n* [U] • *Ten fraternity members had their heads shaved during hazing last week.*

hazel TREE /ˈheɪ·zəl/ *n* [C] a small tree that produces edible nuts

hazel COLOR /ˈheɪ·zəl/ *adj* [not gradable] (esp. of eyes) a green-brown or yellow-brown color

H–bomb /ˈeɪtʃ·bɑm/ *n* [C] a **hydrogen bomb**, see at HYDROGEN

he /hiː, iː/ *pronoun male* the male being spoken about, who has already been mentioned • *Don't ask Andrew, he won't know.* • He is also used to refer to a person whose sex is not known: *Today a person can travel anywhere he likes.* ○ Some people find this use of he to be offensive.

he /hiː/ *n* [C] *male* • *Is your turtle a he or a she?*

head BODY PART /hed/ *n* [C/U] the part of the body that contains the eyes, nose, mouth, ears, and the brain • *She nodded her head in agreement.* [C] • A head is also the approximate length of a head used as a measurement: *Carlos is almost a head taller than Manuel.* [C] • If someone or something is **head and shoulders above** other people or things, they are much better than them: *Natasha is head and shoulders above the other dancers in her age group.* • (*infml*) If you laugh, talk, etc., your **head off**, you do it very strongly or for a long time. • If someone goes **head over heels**, their body rolls forward, esp. when falling: *She tripped on the curb, and went head over heels into the bushes.* • If someone is **head over heels in love**, they love another person very much: *Laura fell head over heels in love with Chris.* • A **headache** is a pain you feel inside your head. • A **headache** is also something that causes you difficulty or worry: *Finding a babysitter for New Year's Eve is going to be a real headache.* • A **headband** is a narrow strip of material worn around the head, usually to keep the hair back from the face. • A **head count** is the exact number of people in a place that you discover by counting, or the act of counting them: *A quick head count revealed an audience of 56 people.* • A **headdress** is a decorative covering for the head: *The Indian warrior was dressed in brilliantly beaded buckskin and wore an eagle-feather headdress.* • If you go **headfirst**, you move forward with your head in front: *She dived headfirst into the pool.* • **Headgear** is any type of covering for the head: *Protective headgear for hockey players is now required.* • When vehicles hit **head-on**, they are going in opposite directions when the front parts meet: *The head-on collision left three people dead.* • **Headphones** are a device with parts that cover each ear through which you can listen to something, such as music, without other people hearing. • **Headroom** is the space above your head when you are inside something, esp. while sitting in a car: *There's not enough headroom to wear a hat.* •

A **head start** is the advantage of beginning before others in a competition or other situation: *If we leave early, we can get a head start on the holiday traffic.* • If two things go **head-to-head**, they oppose each other in direct competition: *The two giant aircraft companies went head-to-head for the $2 billion order.* ○ *head-to-head competition*

head MIND /hed/ *n* [C] the mind and mental abilities • *She has a good head for figures.* ○ *If you'd just use your head* (= think clearly or practically), *you would realize that you are better off living where you are.* ○ *Someone offered me the ticket, and your name popped into my head.* • If someone is **headstrong**, they are determined to do or think what they want: *a headstrong teenager*

head TOP /hed/ *n* [C/U] a position or part at the top, front, or beginning • *They were early enough to get a place at the head of the line.* [U] ○ *As the guest of honor, he sat at the head of the table* (= the more important end). [U] • The head of a plant is the top part where a flower or leaves grow: *I bought two heads of lettuce.* [C] • A **headlight** is a light, usually one of a pair, at the front of a vehicle. PIC CAR • A **headline** is a word or words printed in large letters at the top of a story in a newspaper and serving as its title. • A **headstone** is a **tombstone**. See at TOMB. • A **headwind** is a wind blowing directly against you as you move forward: *The boats had to battle a strong headwind over the last part of the race.*

head /hed/ *v* [T] • *Currently, her name heads* (= is at the top of) *the list of candidates for the job.*

heading /ˈhed·ɪŋ/ *n* [C] a word or words put at the top of a page or section of text as a title • *He looked at the listings under the heading, "Help wanted," hoping to find a job.*

head LEADER /hed/ *n* [C] someone who leads or is in charge of an organization or group, or this position of leadership • *In 1990 he was made head of the engineering division.* • A **headhunter** is a person whose job is to find people qualified for and willing to take esp. important jobs: *She was contacted by a headhunter and invited to apply for the position.* • **Headquarters** are the main offices or center of operations of an organization, such as the army, police, or a company.

head /hed/ *adj* [not gradable] main or most important • *In his first season as head coach, McGuire guided his team to the regional championship.* • The **headmaster** is the man and the **headmistress** is the woman who is the leader of a private school.

head /hed/ *v* [T/M] to be in charge of • *He was appointed by the governor to head (up) the investigation.* [T/M]

head GO /hed/ *v* [I] to go in a particular direction • *I was heading out the door when the phone rang.* ○ *We decided to head back/home* (=

return to where we started) *before it got too dark.* ○ *(fig.)* *He's headed for trouble if he gets involved with her.* • If you **head** someone **off/head off** someone, you block their movement by getting in front of them and forcing them to stop or turn: *Police were sent ahead to head off the bank robbers at the next exit.*

headlong /'hed'lɔːŋ/ *adj, adv* [not gradable] very quick or quickly without considering what you are doing • *When you break up with someone, the temptation is to rush headlong into a new relationship.* • Headlong also means moving forward with your head first: *a headlong plunge into the lake*

heads /hedz/ *pl n* the side of a coin that has a picture of the head of a person on it • To decide something by chance, you might ask someone, "Heads or tails?" and have them guess which side of a coin that is thrown into the air will land face up. • USAGE: The opposite of heads is TAILS.

heady /'hed·i/ *adj* producing a feeling of high energy, confidence, and excitement • *Home sales remained steady in August, although running slightly below July's heady pace.*

heal /hiːl/ *v* [I/T] to make or become healthy or whole again • *As people age, they tend to heal more slowly.* [I] ○ *Steroids are produced by the body to help heal damaged tissue.* [T]

healer /'hiː·lər/ *n* [C] a person or thing that heals • *Time is a great healer.*

health /helθ/ *n* [U] the condition of the body or mind and the degree to which it is free from illness, or the state of being well • *Her health was much improved after she gave up smoking.* • If you are in good/poor health, your physical condition is healthy or is not healthy: *He's in excellent health.* ○ *(fig.)* *The health of the economy is still causing concern.* • **Health care** is the providing of medical services: *She claimed that women and minority-group members frequently receive inferior health care.* ○ *Hospitals and other health care providers are having difficulty charging enough to meet their expenses.* • **Health food** is food that is naturally grown or prepared, without artificial substances or processes. • A **health maintenance organization** (*abbreviation* **HMO**) is an organization that employs doctors and other medical people to provide health care to people who pay a fixed amount to the organization rather than an amount based on each service they get.

healthy /'hel·θi/ *adj* having, showing, or encouraging good health • *As long as the baby is healthy, I don't care if it's a boy or a girl.* • Healthy can mean positive: *She had a healthy attitude toward life and was fun to be with.* • Something is described as healthy if it is financially successful and strong: *The real-estate market is much healthier today than it was ten years ago.* • A healthy amount is a large

amount: *Their business showed a healthy profit in its first year.*

healthful /'helθ·fəl/ *adj* helping to produce good health • *A healthful diet includes plenty of green vegetables.*

heap /hiːp/ *n* [C] a messy pile of things • *A heap of dirty laundry lay at the foot of his bed.* • *(infml)* **A heap of/heaps of** something is a lot of it: *Isako is making heaps of money now that she's in business for herself.*

heap /hiːp/ *v* [T] to put (things) in a pile • *They heaped their plates with food.*

heaping /'hiː·pɪŋ/ *adj* [not gradable] (of an amount of something esp. in a spoon) filling it to a rounded level above the top • *a heaping teaspoon of sugar*

□ **heap** *obj* **on** *obj* /'--, -'-/ *v prep* [T] to express (a strong opinion) by making many remarks about (someone or something) • *He heaped scorn on the idea that good intentions were enough to produce good results.*

hear RECEIVE SOUND /hɪr/ *v* [I/T] *past* **heard** /hɜrd/ to receive or become aware of (sounds) with your ears • *I can't hear you with the TV on.* [T] ○ *After a long trip on a plane, I don't hear very well for a few hours.* [I]

hearing /'hɪr·ɪŋ/ *n* [U] the ability to hear sounds • *Since he's gotten older, his hearing isn't what it used to be.* • A **hearing aid** is a small device worn inside or next to the ear that makes sounds louder for people who cannot hear well.

hear LISTEN /hɪr/ *v* [T] *past* **heard** /hɜrd/ to listen to (what someone is saying or sounds being made) • *I heard him interviewed on the radio this morning.* ○ *Have you heard the group's latest recording?* • To **hear** someone **out** is to listen to them until they are finished speaking: *Hear me out and then decide whether I acted wisely or not.*

hearing /'hɪr·ɪŋ/ *n* [C] an official meeting that is held to gather the facts about an event or problem • *A Senate subcommittee is holding hearings about pornography on the Internet.*

hear BE TOLD /hɪr/ *v* [I/T] *past* **heard** /hɜrd/ to be told or informed (about) • *Have you heard the news?* [T] ○ *I hadn't heard about that.* [I] ○ *I hear (that) your house is up for sale.* [+ *(that)* clause] ○ *I've heard a lot about you from my sister and am glad to meet you.* [T] • If you **hear from** someone, you get a letter, a telephone call, etc., from them: *We haven't heard from her for ages.* • If Mary gets that promotion, we'll *never/we won't* **hear the end of it** (= she will talk about it for a long time).

hearsay /'hɪr·seɪ/ *n* [U] information you have heard that might or might not be true • *He said that the murder was ordered by a mob boss, but he admitted that it was just hearsay.*

hearse /hɜrs/ *n* [C] a special car used to carry a body in a COFFIN (= long box) esp. to a funeral

heart ORGAN /hɑrt/ *n* [C] the organ inside the

chest that sends the blood around the body • *heart disease* ○ *The paramedics took his pulse to see if his heart was still beating.* • A **heart attack** is a sudden and serious physical change in which the heart does not get enough blood, causing damage to the heart and sometimes death: *He'd survived two heart attacks and was very careful about what he ate.* • A **heartbeat** is the regular movement or sound that the heart makes as it pushes blood around the body. • **Heartburn** is an unpleasant burning feeling in the lower part of the chest caused by difficulty in digesting food.

heart EMOTIONS /hɑrt/ *n* [C/U] the center of a person's emotions, or their general character • *He has a good/kind heart* (= is a kind and generous person). [C] ○ *Our hearts were broken* (= We were very sad) *at the news of the accident.* [C] ○ *Homelessness is a subject close/near to her heart* (= is important to her and is a subject she feels strongly about). [C] ○ *In his heart* (= According to his true feelings), *he knew she was right.* [U] • *She can be abrupt with people at times, but* **at heart** (= basically) *she's a good person.* • If you know something or the words of something **by heart**, you can say it from memory: *If you say the Pledge of Allegiance every morning, you soon know it by heart.* • *My* **heart goes out to** *Carla* (= I sympathize with her), *with a sick husband and three kids to look after.* • *We still have a relationship, but somehow my* **heart isn't in it** anymore (= I no longer feel that it is exciting or interesting). • *He plays the part of a tough cop on TV who really has* **a heart of gold** (= is very generous and kind). • *My* **heart sank** (= I was very disappointed) *when I opened the letter and realized I had not been accepted into graduate school.* • *He comes across to his students as demanding at times, but his* **heart is in the right place** (= his intentions are good). • A **heartache** is great sadness or worry: *Their rebellious son has caused them so much heartache.* • **Heartbreak** is a feeling of great sadness: *They endured the heartbreak of losing two of their children to illness.* ○ *The end of Shakespeare's "Romeo and Juliet" is* **heart-breaking** (= causes you to feel very sad). ○ *Alexis was* **heartbroken** (= very disappointed) *when she was dropped from the team.* • If something is **heartfelt**, it is strongly felt and sincere: *His goodbye was awkward but his good wishes were heartfelt.* • If something is **heartrending**, it causes great sympathy or sadness: *The pictures of starving children on television were heartrending.* • If you are **heartsick**, you are very sad: *When the vet said that her cat was too badly hurt to survive, Keri was heartsick.* • A talk or discussion that is **heart-to-heart** is one in which two people talk honestly and in a serious way about their feelings: *We had a good, heart-to-heart talk about where our relationship was heading.* • If

something is **heartwarming**, it causes feelings of pleasure and happiness: *The response from the public to our calls for donations has been really heartwarming.*

heartless /ˈhɑrt·ləs/ *adj* cruel or unkind • *She denounced the cutbacks on aid to the poor as heartless and shortsighted policies.*

heart CENTER /hɑrt/ *n* [C/U] the central or most important part • *Protestors marched through the heart of the city.* [C usually sing] • *The heart of a vegetable, esp. a leafy one, is its firm, central part: artichoke hearts* [C] • The **heartland** is the central or most important part of an area: *The Midwest is the agricultural heartland of the US.*

heart SHAPE /hɑrt/ *n* [C] a shape used to represent the heart, esp. as a symbol of love

hearten /ˈhɑrt·ən/ *v* [T] to encourage and make confident and happy • *We were heartened by the news that Jason is feeling so much better.*

hearth /hɑrθ/ *n* [C] the floor of a fireplace, and often also the area in front of it

hearts /hɑrts/ *pl n* one of the four SUITS (= groups) of playing cards, the symbol for which is the rounded shape used to represent the heart as a symbol of love • PIC SUITS

hearty ENTHUSIASTIC /ˈhɑrt·i/ *adj* enthusiastic and strong • *a hearty handshake* ○ *a hearty laugh*

heartily /ˈhɑrt·əl·i/ *adv* • *He heartily approved of the changes in policy.*

hearty LARGE /ˈhɑrt·i/ *adj* [-er/-est only] generous or large • *We ate a hearty breakfast before we set off on our hike.* • Hearty is also used to mean satisfying to the taste: *a hearty red wine*

heat TEMPERATURE /hiːt/ *n* [U] warmth, esp. a lot of warmth • *the heat of the sun* • The heat can also mean hot weather: *I thought I'd like living in Florida, but the heat was too much for me.* • The heat is also the system in a building or a stove that controls the temperature: *I'm freezing—can you turn up the heat?* ○ *Lower the heat when the water starts to boil.* • A **heat wave** is a period of days when the weather is much hotter than usual.

heat /hiːt/ *v* [T/M] to make (a place) warm enough for comfort, or to make (something) hot • *It costs a lot to heat this house.* [T] ○ *Shall I heat up some soup for lunch?* [M]

heater /ˈhiːt·ər/ *n* [C] a device that heats esp. water or an enclosed space

heat EMOTION /hiːt/ *n* [U] a state of strong emotion, esp. excitement or anger • *The heat of his own argument swept him away.* • *John apologized for the remarks he had made* **in the heat of the moment** (= while he was angry or excited).

heated /ˈhiːt·əd/ *adj* • *a heated argument/exchange*

heat RESPONSIBILITY /hiːt/ *n* [U] responsibility

or blame • *We took a lot of heat for showing that on TV.*

heat COMPETITION /hiːt/ *n* [C] a competition, esp. a race, in which it is decided who will compete in the final event

heat SEX /hiːt/ *n* • If an animal, esp. a female, is **in heat**, it is in a state of sexual excitement and ready to breed.

heathen /ˈhiːðən/ *adj disapproving* (used, esp. in the past, of people or their way of life, activities, and ideas) having no religion, or belonging to a religion that is not Christianity, Judaism, or Islam

heathen /ˈhiːðən/ *n* [C] *pl* **heathen** or **heathens** *disapproving* • *Those folks are heathens.*

heave MOVE /hiːv/ *v* [I/T] to pull, push, lift, or throw something heavy • *He leaned his weight against the door and heaved it open.* [T always + adv/prep] • If something heaves, it moves up and down: *After the race she was covered in sweat, her chest heaving.* [I]

heave /hiːv/ *n* [C] • *With a great heave, they rolled the boulder out of the way.*

heave FEEL HAPPY /hiːv/ *v* • If you **heave a sigh of relief**, you are happy because a situation that could have ended badly has had a good result: *I heaved a sigh of relief when my dog came home.*

heave VOMIT /hiːv/ *v* [I] *infml* to feel as if you are going to vomit, or to vomit

heaven /ˈhev·ən/ *n* [U] (in some religions) the place where God or the gods live or where good people are believed to go after they die, sometimes thought to be in the sky • Heaven is also something that gives you great pleasure: *It was heaven lying there in the sunshine listening to the birds sing.* • People say **in heaven's name** to add emphasis to something that has been said: *If you knew you had to go out, why in heaven's name didn't you tell us?*

heavenly /ˈhev·ən·li/ *adj* of or from heaven, or giving great pleasure • *It was a good party and the food was heavenly.*

heavens /ˈhev·ənz/ *pl n literary* the sky • *They rolled their eyes toward the heavens.* • **(Good/My) heavens** is used to express surprise or anger, or to add emphasis: *"Does your mother live here?" "Heavens, no—that's all I need."*

heavy WEIGHING A LOT /ˈhev·i/ *adj* [-er/-est only] weighing a lot • *The piano's much too heavy for one person to lift.* ◦ *Bob's much heavier than the last time I saw him.* • In boxing, a **heavyweight** is a competitor who weighs more than 175 pounds, or 79.5 kilograms, and is in the heaviest group. • A **heavyweight** is also someone who is important in a particular business or activity: *a political heavyweight*

heavy SOLID /ˈhev·i/ *adj* [-er/-est only] thick, strong, solid, or looking that way • *heavy clouds* ◦ *heavy cream* ◦ *It's too hot today for a heavy meal* (= a large, cooked meal that is hard to digest). • **Heavy-duty** machines and equipment are strongly made so that they can be

used a lot, esp. in difficult conditions: *heavy-duty tools* • **Heavy industry** is the business of making or working with materials such as coal and steel. • **Heavy metal** is a style of ROCK music with a strong beat, played loudly on electric instruments. • Someone who is **heavy-set** has a large, wide body: *The blond, heavy-set waitress seemed to know Bob well.*

heavy GREAT DEGREE /ˈhev·i/ *adj* [-er/-est only] (esp. of something unpleasant) of great force, amount, or degree • *heavy snowfall/rain/fog* ◦ *a heavy fine* • Heavy breathing is loud, deep breathing, usually because of being tired, sick, or sexually excited. • A heavy day/schedule is one that is full of activity which will require a lot of work. • A heavy drinker/smoker is someone who drinks or smokes a lot. • Heavy traffic is a lot of vehicles traveling on the same road. • A heavy sleeper is someone who is able to sleep without being awakened by noise. • If something is **heavy-handed**, it is done in an unnecessarily forceful way: *These songs have a heavy-handed, moralistic tone.*

heavily /ˈhev·ə·li/ *adv* • *heavily armed* ◦ *She's heavily involved in politics.* ◦ *The news weighed heavily on his mother.* • LP VERY, COMPLETELY, AND OTHER INTENSIFIERS

heck /hek/ *exclamation slang* an expression of annoyance or surprise, or a way of adding emphasis to a statement or question; HELL • *Where the heck have you been?* • *You only paid 20 dollars for it? That's* **a heck of** *a good deal* (= a very good deal).

heckle /ˈhek·əl/ *v* [I/T] to interrupt a public speaker or entertainer with loud, unfriendly statements or questions

heckler /ˈhek·lər, ˈhek·ə·lər/ *n* [C] • *A heckler tried to disrupt the ceremony.*

hectic /ˈhek·tɪk/ *adj* busy, fast, and full of activity • *a hectic schedule* ◦ *the hectic pace of city life*

he'd /hiːd, iːd/ *contraction of* **he had** or **he would** • *He'd* (= He had) *already spent all his money by the second day of the trip.* ◦ *He'd* (= He would) *be able to do it if he would just try.*

hedge BUSHES /hedʒ/ *n* [C] a line of bushes or small trees planted close together, esp. along the edge of a yard or road

hedge PROTECTION /hedʒ/ *n* [C] a means of protection, control, or limitation • *She invested in foreign companies as a hedge against inflation.*

hedge /hedʒ/ *v* [I/T] • *Congressmen were warned against hedging their support for the missile program.* [T] • To hedge is also to try to avoid giving an answer or taking any action: *Officials continued to hedge on exactly when the program would begin.* [I] • If you **hedge your bets**, you protect yourself against loss by preparing for more than one possible result: *We are hedging our bets because we are unsure of the demand.*

heed /hiːd/ v [T] to listen to and follow (advice) • *The airline failed to heed warnings about security.*

heed /hiːd/ n [U] • *Voters are dissatisfied, and Congress should take heed* (= consider this).

heedless /ˈhiːd·ləs/ adj not giving attention to a risk or difficulty • *Heedless of the hurricane warnings, they took the small boat out into open water.*

heel BODY PART /hiːl/ n [C] the rounded back part of the foot • *I've got a splinter in my heel.* • The heel of your hand is the raised, inside part close to the wrist. • If you are on someone's **heels**, you are following closely behind them. • If one event or situation follows **on the heels of** another, it happens soon after the first: *For Brad, disaster followed on the heels of his initial success.* • PIC FOOT

heel /hiːl/ v [I] • If you say "Heel!" to a dog, you are ordering it to walk close to you.

heel FOOT COVERING /hiːl/ n [C] the part of a sock or shoe that covers the rounded back part of the foot, or the part of the bottom of a shoe that lifts the back of the foot higher than the front

heel PERSON /hiːl/ n [C] *infml* a person who treats other people badly and unfairly • *I felt like a real heel when I saw how upset she was.*

heft /heft/ v [T always + adv/prep] to lift, hold, or carry something heavy using your hands • *I watched him heft the heavy sack onto his shoulder.*

hefty /ˈhef·ti/ adj [-er/-est only] large in amount or size • *a hefty fine/bonus* ○ *a hefty steak dinner* ○ *a hefty, pink-faced baby*

heifer /ˈhef·ər/ n [C] a young cow that has not yet given birth to a CALF

height /haɪt, haɪtθ/ n [C/U] the distance from the top to the bottom of something, or the quality of being tall • *The heights of the two World Trade Center skyscrapers are equal.* [C] ○ *She's of average height* (= neither unusually short nor tall). [U] • Height also refers to the distance that something is above a surface: *You can adjust the height of the chair with this lever.* [U] • **The height of** a condition or event is when it is most full of activity or when it is at its top level of achievement: *She was at the height of her career when they met.* • **The height of** also means an extreme example of: *the height of luxury/power/stupidity*

heights /haɪts/ pl n high places, or the tops of hills • *Don't go up there if you're afraid of heights.* ○ (fig.) *Stock prices reached new heights yesterday.*

heighten /ˈhaɪt·ᵊn/ v [I/T] to increase (esp. an emotion or effect) • *As the excitement heightened, the audience began stamping their feet.* [I] ○ *A strong police presence heightened tensions.* [T]

Heimlich maneuver /ˈhaɪm·lɪk·məˈnuː·vər/ n [U] an emergency method of removing something that is stuck in a person's throat and is preventing them from breathing, performed by putting sudden pressure on the person's stomach

Heimlich Maneuver

heinous /ˈheɪ·nəs/ adj (esp. of a crime) extremely bad or evil • *heinous murders*

heir /er, ær/, *female* **heiress** /ˈer·əs, ˈær·əs/ n [C] a person who will receive or already has received money or property from another person at the time of that other person's death • *My cousin Robert is the only heir to my uncle's fortune.*

heirloom /ˈer·luːm, ˈær-/ n [C] a valuable object that has been given by an older member of a family to a younger member of the same family, esp. one given several times in this way • *family heirlooms*

heist /haɪst/ n [C] *slang* a crime in which property is taken illegally and often violently from a place or person

held HOLD /held/ past simple and past participle of HOLD

held CARRIED /held/ adj [not gradable] carried, kept, or maintained • *a hand-held computer* ○ *firmly held beliefs*

helicopter /ˈhel·əˌkɑp·tər, ˈhiː·lə-/, *short form* **copter** n [C] a type of aircraft without wings but with large blades that spin on top

helicopter

helium /ˈhiː·liː·əm/ n [U] a gas, one of the chemical elements, that is lighter than air and will not burn

hell PLACE /hel/ n [U] (in some religions) the place where some people are believed to go after death to be punished forever for the bad things they have done • *As a Christian, I'm concerned about whether we end up in heaven or hell.*

hell CONDITION /hel/ *n* [U] an extremely unpleasant or difficult place, situation, or experience • *Holidays are hell for me.*

hellish /'hel·ɪʃ/ *adj* very bad or unpleasant • *a hellish experience*

hell EXPRESSION /hel/ *exclamation slang* used to express anger, or to give emphasis to an expression • *Oh hell, I forgot my keys!* ○ *"Did you apologize?" "Hell, no, it was his fault!"* • After driving for 12 hours, I'm tired **as hell** (= extremely tired). • If you say something will happen when, or won't happen until, **hell freezes over**, you mean it will probably never happen: *I'll fight this till hell freezes over.* • People say **hell of a** (also **helluva**) to add emphasis: *He's one hell of a nice guy.* ○ *We had a helluva time getting home last night.* • People add **the hell** to a question to show they are angry, annoyed, or frightened: *What the hell was that noise?* • If something or someone annoys or frightens **the hell out of** you, it makes you extremely annoyed or frightened. • To beat, knock, etc., **the hell out of** someone is to hit them with great force. • If you wish or hope **to hell** that something is true or that it will happen, you are saying strongly that you want it to be true or to happen. • If you say **to hell with** someone or something, you are saying that you no longer care about them.

he'll /hiːl, iːl, hɪl/ *contraction of* **he will** or **he shall** • *I'm sure he'll help you if he can.*

hello /həˈloʊ, helˈoʊ/ *exclamation, n* [C] *pl* **hellos** used when meeting or greeting someone • *"Hello, Paul," she said, "I haven't seen you for months."* ○ *I know her vaguely—we've exchanged hellos a few times.* ○ *Come and say hello to my friends* (= meet them). • Hello is also said at the beginning of a telephone conversation. • Hello is also used to attract someone's attention: *She walked into the shop and called out, "Hello! Is anybody here?"* • LP GREETINGS

helm /helm/ *n* [C] the handle or wheel that controls the direction in which a ship or boat travels • If someone is **at the helm** of a group or organization, they control it: *She is the first woman to be at the helm of this corporation.*

helmet /'hel·mət/ *n* [C] a hard hat that covers and protects the head • *a soldier's helmet* ○ *a motorcycle/bicycle helmet*

help MAKE EASIER /help/ *v* [I/T] to make it possible or easier for (someone) to do something • *How can I help you?* [T] ○ *Please help those less fortunate than you are.* [T] ○ *Avoiding fatty foods and salt can help to bring down your blood pressure.* [+ *to* infinitive] • If something helps a difficult or painful situation, it improves it or makes it easier or less painful: *Aspirin will help relieve the pain.* [T] • You shout *"Help!"* in an emergency when you need the immediate support of someone else. [I] • If you **can't/couldn't help** something, you are not able to control or stop it: *"Stop giggling!" "I can't help it!"* • If you **help** someone **out**, you do some work for them or provide them with something they need: *Blair helps (us) out at the store when we're busy.* • (*specialized*) In grammar, a **helping verb** is an **auxiliary verb**. See at AUXILIARY.

help /help/ *n* [U] • *Do you need help with those boxes?* ○ *My parents gave us financial help when we bought our first house.*

helper /'hel·pər/ *n* [C] a person who helps • *The driver or a helper picks up the trash.*

helpful /'help·fəl/ *adj* giving help • *He made several helpful suggestions.*

helpless /'hel·pləs/ *adj* unable to care for yourself or protect yourself esp. against danger • *a helpless infant*

helplessly /'hel·plə·sli/ *adv* [not gradable]

helplessness /'hel·plə·snəs/ *n* [U]

help GIVE / TAKE /help/ *v* [T] to serve something to (someone), or to take something for (yourself) • *Help yourself to more cake.*

helping /'hel·pɪŋ/ *n* [C] an amount of food served to a person at one time • *He took another helping of dessert.*

helter–skelter /ˌhel·tərˈskel·tər/ *adj, adv* [not gradable] hurried and not organized • *People were running helter-skelter out of the building.*

hem EDGE /hem/ *n* [C] the bottom edge of a piece of cloth, folded up and sewn, on an item of clothing • A **hemline** is the bottom edge or the length of a skirt, dress, or coat.

hem /hem/ *v* [T] **-mm-** • *She was busy hemming her skirt.*

hem SOUND /hem/ *v* **-mm-** • If you **hem and haw** when speaking, you pause because you are not certain or slightly embarrassed about something: *The supervisor hemmed and hawed before telling me that Judy was getting promoted but I wasn't.*

▫ **hem in** *obj*, **hem** *obj* **in** /'-'-/ *v adv* [M] to surround (someone or something) closely • *Her car was hemmed in between two other vehicles.*

hemisphere /'hem·ə,sfɪr/ *n* [C] half of a sphere, or half of the earth • *The equator divides the earth into the northern and southern hemispheres.*

hemlock /'hem·lɑk/ *n* [C/U] a poisonous plant that has small white flowers • Hemlock is also a type of evergreen tree or its wood. [C/U]

hemoglobin /'hiː·mə,gloʊ·bən/ *n* [U] *specialized* a red substance in the red blood cells that contains iron and carries oxygen around the body

hemophilia /ˌhiː·məˈfɪl·iː·ə/ *n* [U] a rare blood disease, usually of males, in which the body lacks a chemical that thickens and stops the flow of blood when a VESSEL is injured

hemophiliac /ˌhiː·məˈfɪl·iˌæk/ *n* [C] a person who suffers from hemophilia

hemorrhage /'hem·ə·rɪdʒ/ *n* [C/U] a large

flow of blood from a damaged **blood vessel** (= tube that carries blood around the body)

hemorrhage /'hem·ə·rɪdʒ/ *v* [I] • *He hemorrhaged as a result of the beating.* ○ *(fig.) The company was allowed to hemorrhage money* (= lose a lot of money) *for more than two years before the government closed it down.*

hemorrhoids /'hem·ə·rɔɪdz/ *pl n* swollen VEINS (= tubes carrying blood) at or near the ANUS (= the hole where solid waste is excreted), a condition that can be painful

hemp /hemp/ *n* [U] a plant used to make rope and strong, rough cloth

hen /hen/ *n* [C] an adult female chicken that is often kept for its eggs, or the female of any bird

hence THEREFORE /hens/ *adv* [not gradable] *slightly fml* for this reason; therefore • *A better working environment improves people's performance, and hence productivity.*

hence FROM NOW /hens/ *adv* [not gradable] *fml* from this time • *The project should be completed by next March, six months hence.*

henceforth /'hens,fɔːrθ, -,foʊrθ/ *adv* [not gradable] *fml* starting from this time • *Henceforth, attendance will be taken in all classes.*

henchman /'hentʃ·mən/ *n* [C] *pl* **-men** *disapproving* a person who is loyal to and works for someone in a position of authority and is willing to help them even by hurting others or by committing crimes • *Although the president kept himself above the fray, his henchmen were blaming everyone.*

hepatitis /,hep·ə'taɪt̬·əs/ *n* [U] a disease of the LIVER (= an organ in the body)

heptathlon /hep'tæθ,lɑn/ *n* [C] a competition in which women ATHLETES compete in seven sporting events • Compare DECATHLON.

her POSSESSIVE /hɜr, hər/ *pronoun female* belonging to or connected with the person mentioned; the possessive form of she, used before a noun • *Her name is Linda.* ○ *She met her husband in college.* • LP DETERMINERS

hers /hɜrz/ *pronoun female* belonging to her, or that which belongs to her • *I've been a friend of hers for years.* ○ *Hers is the second house.*

her OBJECTIVE /hɜr, hər/ *pronoun female* the female being spoken about, who has already been mentioned; the objective form of she • *I saw her yesterday.*

herself /hər'self/ *pronoun female* the female being spoken about, the reflexive form of she • *She kept telling herself that nothing was wrong.* • Herself is sometimes used to emphasize a female subject or object of a sentence: *She herself was to blame.* • If a woman or girl does something **by herself**, she does it alone or without help from anyone: *Holly wrote her name (all) by herself.* • If a woman or girl is **not herself**, she is not in her usual mental or physical condition: *Janeen hasn't been herself recently.* • If a woman or girl has something **to**

herself, she has it for her own use only: *She's got the house (all) to herself while her husband is away.* • LP REFLEXIVE PRONOUNS

herald /'her·əld/ *v* [T] to announce or signal that (something) is approaching • *The trade agreement heralded a new era of economic development.*

herb /ɜrb, hɜrb/ *n* [C] a type of plant with a soft stem, used in cooking and medicine

herbal /'ɜr·bəl, 'hɜr-/ *adj* [not gradable] relating to herbs, or made from herbs • *herbal tea*

herculean /,hɜr·kjə'liː·ən, hər'kjuː·liː·ən/ *adj* [not gradable] having or needing great strength or effort • *She had the herculean task of bringing up four children single-handedly.*

herd /hɜrd/ *n* [C] a large group of animals of the same type that feed, travel, or are kept together • *a herd of elephants*

herd /hɜrd/ *v* [T] to move together as a group, or to cause (animals or people) to move together in a group • *The teachers herded the children into buses.*

here /hɪr/ *adv* [not gradable] in, at, or to this place • *I've lived here in Atlanta all my life.* ○ *Please step over here for a minute.* ○ *It hurts here, just above my ankle.* • Here can be used at the beginning of a statement to call attention to someone or something: *Here's the money I owe you.* ○ *Here she is now.* • You can say **here you are/here you go** when you are giving something to someone: *"Would you please pass the sugar?" "Here you are."* • *(infml)* People sometimes say **here goes** just before they do something brave or new: *I've never been on Rollerblades before, but here goes!* • People sometimes say **here's to** when drinking to the health or success of someone or something: *Here's to the happy couple!* • If something is **here to stay**, it is generally accepted and is permanent: *Cell phones are here to stay.*

hereafter IN THE FUTURE /hɪr'æf·tər/ *adv* [not gradable] *fml* starting from this time; in the future • *I will let you in this time, but hereafter you have to get permission in advance.*

hereafter AFTER DEATH /hɪr'æf·tər/ *n* [U] life after death • *She firmly believes in the hereafter.*

hereby /hɪr'baɪ, 'hɪr·baɪ/ *adv* [not gradable] *fml* by this statement, action, or law • *I hereby pronounce you man and wife.*

heredity /hə'red·ət̬·i/ *n* [U] the natural process by which parents pass on to their young through their GENES the characteristics that make them related

hereditary /hə'red·ə,ter·i/ *adj* [not gradable] caused by or having to do with heredity • *Baldness in men is hereditary.*

herein /hɪr'ɪn/ *adv* [not gradable] *fml* in this • *All opinions expressed herein are solely those of the author.*

heresy /'her·ə·si/ *n* [C/U] a belief opposed to the official belief of a church and that is considered wrong, or the condition of having such beliefs • *(fig.) Her views on gun control were heresy (= unusual opinions considered completely wrong) here in Montana.* [U]

heretic /'her·ə‚tɪk/ n [C] a person who has beliefs that are opposed to the official belief of a church and that the church considers wrong

herewith /hɪr'wɪð, -'wɪθ/ adv [not gradable] *fml* with this letter or other official written material • *I enclose three documents herewith.*

heritage /'her·əţ·ɪdʒ/ n [U] features belonging to the culture of a particular society, such as traditions, languages, or buildings, which still exist from the past and have historical importance • *The organization is devoted to preserving our cultural heritage.*

hermetically /hər'meţ·ɪ·kli/ adv [not gradable] tightly closed so that air cannot enter or escape • *The space vehicle must be hermetically sealed.*

hermit /'hɜr·mət/ n [C] a person who lives alone and apart from society

hernia /'hɜr·ni·ə/ n [C] a medical condition in which part of an organ, such as the IN- TESTINES, pushes through a layer of muscle that encloses it

hero (pl **heroes**) /'hɪr·oʊ, 'hiː·roʊ/, *female* **heroine** /'her·ə·wən/ n [C] a person admired for bravery, great achievements, or good qualities, or the main character of a story, play, or movie

heroic /hɪ'roʊ·ɪk, hiː-/ adj [not gradable] • *The ceremony at City Hall honored the heroic acts of firefighters who lost their lives.*

heroics /hɪ'roʊ·ɪks, hiː-/ pl n unusual actions or achievements that are far greater than what is expected • *He won a medal for his wartime heroics as a fighter pilot.*

heroism /'her·ə‚wɪz·əm, 'hɪr-/ n [U] great bravery • *an act of heroism*

hero (sandwich) /'hɪr·oʊ, 'hiː·roʊ/, *regional* **submarine (sandwich)**, **hoagie**, **grinder**, **poor boy** n [C] pl **heroes** *regional* a long, narrow sandwich filled with such things as meat, cheese, and vegetables

heroin /'her·ə·wən/ n [U] a powerful drug taken illegally for pleasure

heroine /'her·ə·wən/ n [C] • See at HERO.

heron /'her·ən/ n [C] a large bird with long legs and a long neck that lives near water

herpes /'hɜr·piːz/ n [U] any of several infectious diseases in which painful red sores appear on the skin, esp. of the face or in the area of the sexual organs

heron

herring /'her·ɪŋ/ n [C/ U] a long silver fish that swims in large groups in the sea and is used as food

hers /hɜrz/ pronoun • See at HER POSSESSIVE.

he's /hiːz, iːz/ *contraction of* **he is** or **he has** • *He's* (= He is) *late.* ○ *He's* (= He has) *got $12 left.*

hesitate /'hez·ə‚teɪt/ v [I] to pause before you do or say something, often because you are uncertain or nervous about it • *If you need anything, don't hesitate to call me.* [+ to infinitive]

hesitation /‚hez·ə'teɪ·ʃən/ n [U] • *There was some hesitation about inviting him.*

hesitant /'hez·ə·tənt/ adj • *The bank manager is hesitant to approve the loan.* [+ to infinitive]

heterogeneous /‚heţ·ə·rə'dʒiː·niː·əs, -njəs/ adj *fml* consisting of different parts or types • *With many ethnic groups represented, the student body is very heterogeneous.* • Compare HO- MOGENEOUS.

heterosexual /‚heţ·ə·rə'sek·ʃə·wəl/, *infml* **hetero** /'heţ·ə‚roʊ/ n [C] a person who is sexually attracted to people of the opposite sex • Compare HOMOSEXUAL.

heterosexual /‚heţ·ə·rə'sek·ʃə·wəl/ adj [not gradable] • *She had both gay and heterosexual friends.*

hew CUT /hjuː/ v [T] *past simple* **hewed**, *past part* **hewed** or **hewn** /hjuːn/ to cut (something) by hitting it repeatedly with a cutting tool • *The monument was hewn out of stone.*

hew OBEY /hjuː/ v [I] *past simple* **hewed**, *past part* **hewed** to obey or behave according to (rules, principles, or expectations) • *He never states his own opinion but hews to the party line.*

hexagon /'hek·sə‚gɑn/ n [C] a flat shape that has six straight sides

hey /heɪ/ *exclamation infml* used to get someone's attention, or to express surprise, pleasure, or questioning • *Hey, you guys, wait for me!* • LP GREETINGS

heyday /'heɪ·deɪ/ n [C usually sing] a period of great success, popularity, or power • *In its heyday, Pittsburgh was a center of the steel and coal industries.*

hi /haɪ/ *exclamation* used as an informal greeting • *Hi, how are you doing?* • LP GREETINGS

hiatus /haɪ'eɪţ·əs/ n [C usually sing] a short pause in which nothing happens, or a space where something is missing • *Peace talks resumed this week after a five-month hiatus.*

hibernate /'haɪ·bər‚neɪt/ v [I] (of some animals) to spend the winter months in a state like sleep

hibernation /‚haɪ·bər'neɪ·ʃən/ n [U]

hiccup, hiccough /'hɪk·ʌp, -əp/ n [C usually pl] one of a series of sudden, explosive releases of air from the throat, which are difficult to control but usually stop after a short time • *I've got the hiccups.*

hiccup, hiccough /'hɪk·ʌp, -əp/ v [I] **-p-** or **-pp-** • *She couldn't stop hiccuping.*

hick /hɪk/ n [C] *disapproving* a person from a rural area who has little knowledge of culture and city life • *A hick town is a rural town with few attractions.*

hickory /'hɪk·ə·ri/ n [C/U] a small tree from

North America or east Asia that has edible nuts, or the hard wood from this tree

hide PREVENT FINDING /haɪd/ *v* [I/T] *past simple* **hid** /hɪd/, *past part* **hidden** /ˈhɪd·ᵊn/ to put (something or someone) in a place where they cannot be seen or found, or to put (yourself) somewhere where you cannot be seen or found • *She used to hide her diary under her pillow.* [T] ○ *Tommy ran and hid behind his dad.* [I] • If you hide your feelings, you do not show them: *She tried to hide her disappointment.* [T] • If you hide information from someone, you do not let that person know it: *He said nothing is wrong, but I think he's hiding something.* [T] • If you **hide out**, you stay somewhere where you cannot be found: *Criminals often hide out in these empty apartments.* • **Hide-and-seek** is a game in which several children hide while one child counts to a particular number without watching the others and then tries to find them.

hiding /ˈhaɪd·ɪŋ/ *n* • Someone who is **in hiding** or goes **into hiding** has secretly gone somewhere so they cannot be found.

hide SKIN /haɪd/ *n* [C/U] the strong thick skin of an animal that is used for making leather • *He began scraping the hide to prepare it for tanning.* [C] • A person's hide is their self, esp. when they are in trouble: *He expects me to save his hide every time he screws up.* [C]

hideaway /ˈhaɪd·əˌweɪ/ *n* [C] a place where someone goes when they want to relax and get away from their usual surroundings • *a country hideaway*

hideous /ˈhɪd·iː·əs/ *adj* offensive, extremely ugly, or shocking • *The bathroom was pink and green and silver—it was absolutely hideous.*

hideout /ˈhaɪd·aʊt/ *n* [C] a secret place where someone can go when they do not want to be found by other people • *We made our hideout under the bushes.*

hierarchy /ˈhaɪ·əˌrɑr·ki, ˈhaɪˌrɑr-/ *n* [C] a system in which people or things are put at various levels or ranks according to their importance • *He rapidly rose in the corporate hierarchy.*

hieroglyphics /ˌhaɪ·ə·rəˈɡlɪf·ɪks, ˌhaɪ·rə-/ *pl n* pictures or symbols that represent words, used in the writing system of ancient Egypt

hifalutin /ˌhaɪ·fəˈluːt·ᵊn/ *adj infml* HIGHFA-LUTIN

hi–fi /ˈhaɪˈfaɪ/ *n* [C/U] *slightly dated* the sound produced by electronic equipment that plays recorded music very accurately, or the equipment itself

high DISTANCE /haɪ/ *adj* [-er/-est only] (esp. of things that are not living) being a large distance from top to bottom or a long way above the ground, or having the stated distance from top to bottom • *Mount Everest is the highest mountain in the world.* ○ *We had to climb over a wall that was ten feet high.* • A **high chair** is

a long-legged chair for a baby or a small child, usually with a small table connected to it for the child to eat from. • **High heels** or **high-heeled shoes** are shoes usually worn by women that have a very tall piece on the bottom that lifts the back of the foot higher than the front. • The **high jump** is a sport in which competi-

high chair

tors try to jump over a bar that can be raised. • **High noon** is exactly twelve o'clock in the middle of the day, when the sun should be at its highest point in the sky. • A **high-rise** is a tall, modern building with a lot of floors. • **High tide** is the time when the sea or a river reaches its highest level and comes furthest up the beach or the bank.

high /haɪ/ *adv* [-er/-est only] • *The Concorde flies much higher than most airplanes.* • **High and low** means everywhere: *I searched high and low for my keys and I still can't find them.*

high ABOVE AVERAGE /haɪ/ *adj* [-er/-est only] greater than the usual level • *high standards of quality* ○ *high salaries* ○ *a high level of concentration* ○ *She was driving at high speed on a wet road.* • A person or thing that is in **high gear** is very active and productive: *The movie really goes into high gear when Williams appears on screen.* • Someone who is **high-strung** worries about things unnecessarily, is easily upset, and finds it difficult to relax. • (*infml*) If it is **high time** that someone did something, it should have been done sooner or a long time ago: *It's high time you had your gimpy knee looked at.* • **High beams** are the lights on the front of a car when they are switched to their brightest level. Compare **low beams** at LOW SMALLER THAN USUAL. • **High blood pressure** is a medical condition in which the measurement of how strongly the blood is pushing against the walls of the VEINS as it travels through in the body is greater than is considered healthy. • If something is described as **high-class**, it is of good quality: *a high-class hotel* • **High fidelity** (*short form* **hi-fi**) is the sound produced by electronic equipment of very good quality that plays recorded music very accurately. • A person who is **high-minded** has moral standards that are above average. • Something's **high point** is the time when it is the most successful, enjoyable, important, or valuable: *The high point of my week is arriving home from work on a Friday evening.* • Something that is **high-powered** has a lot of power or strength: *a high-powered microscope* • If a person is **high-powered**, the things that they do are important and need a lot of energy, skill, experience, knowledge, or responsibility: *He's one of the most high-powered men in the capital.* • A **high-pressure** system or tool has or uses more force than usual: *a high-pressure air mass* • A **high-pressure** situation is one in which people expect success from you: *a high-pressure job* • Someone or something that has a **high profile** receives a lot of attention and interest from the public: *He has many high-profile clients.* • A **high roller** is someone who spends a lot of money, esp. someone who risks money to win money when they have little chance of winning. • Something that is **high-speed** moves or operates at a fast rate: *a high-speed drill* • Something that is **high-tech** (also **hi-tech**) uses the most advanced and developed machines and methods: *Only a few teaching hospitals have those new, high-tech devices.* • A **high tension wire** has very strong electric current moving through it. • **High-tops** are a type of SNEAKERS (= cloth shoes) that cover the feet and the bottoms of the legs: *I liked the high-tops I wore.* • A **high-voltage** wire or system is one that has very strong electric current moving through it.

high– /haɪ/ *combining form* • *a high-protein diet* ○ *high-quality printers*

high /haɪ/ *n* [C] • *Interest rates have reached an all-time high.*

higher /ˈhaɪ·ər/ *adj* [not gradable] more developed or advanced • *higher species of animals* • **Higher education** is education at a college or university where subjects are studied in great detail and at an advanced level.

highly /ˈhaɪ·li/ *adv* • *a highly paid job* ○ *We need a highly skilled, highly educated workforce.*

high IMPORTANT /haɪ/ *adj* [-er/-est only] having power, great influence, or an important position • *He is an officer of high rank.* • *She has a lot of friends* **in high places** (= in positions of power). • (*infml*) The **high court** is the US Supreme Court. • If a person or event is **high-level**, they are very important: *He's a very high-level scientist.* • **High treason** is an act of war against the government or leader of your country or an attempt to help an enemy take control of your country.

high /haɪ/ *adv* [-er/-est only] • Someone who is living **high on/off the hog** is living in great comfort with a lot of money.

highly /ˈhaɪ·li/ *adv* • *The statement was made by a highly placed official* (= a person in an important position). • LP VERY, COMPLETELY, AND OTHER INTENSIFIERS

high SOUND /haɪ/ *adj* [-er/-est only] near or at the top of the range of sounds • *Dog whistles play notes that are too high for human beings to hear.* • A voice or noise that is **high-pitched** is high and sometimes also loud or unpleasant: *The combination of Pierce's tenor sax and Roney's high-pitched trumpet was exciting.*

high FEELING HAPPY /haɪ/ *adj* [-er/-est only] feeling extremely happy, excited, or full of energy as a result of taking drugs, drinking alcohol, being successful, or having a religious experience • *He was high on drugs and couldn't think straight.* • If someone is **in high spirits**, they are extremely happy and enjoying themselves: *She was in high spirits after scoring the winning basket.* • Someone or something that is **high-spirited** is energetic and happy: *The play is a youthful, high-spirited, and fast-moving piece.*

high /haɪ/ *n* [C usually sing] • *There are lots of highs and lows in this job.*

highbrow /ˈhaɪ·braʊ/ *adj* (of literature, art, music, films, or plays) serious and intended for intelligent educated people who are knowledgeable about these forms of art, or (of people) intelligent and knowing a lot about such things • *highbrow entertainment* ○ *a highbrow intellectual* • Compare LOWBROW; MIDDLEBROW.

highfalutin, highfaluting, hifalutin /ˌhaɪ·fəˈluːt·ən/ *adj infml* trying to seem very important or serious without having a good reason for doing so; PRETENTIOUS • *highfalutin language*

high jinks, hijinks /ˈhaɪ·dʒɪŋks/ *n* [U] slightly dated energetic behavior in which people do amusing or entertaining things or sometimes behave slightly badly • *The dancers let loose with some fancy footwork and high jinks.*

highlands /ˈhaɪ·lənz/ *pl n* a mountainous area of a country • *Melting snow in the highlands is causing flooding in the valley.*

highlight BEST PART /ˈhaɪ·laɪt/ *n* [C] the best, most important, or most interesting part • *The highlight of our trip to New York was going to the top of the Empire State Building.*

highlight EMPHASIZE /ˈhaɪ·laɪt/ *v* [T] to attract attention to or emphasize (something important) • *The report highlights the need for increased funding.*

highlight BRIGHT AREA /ˈhaɪ·laɪt/ *n* [C usually pl] a bright or lighter-colored area on the surface of something, esp. on a painting

highlighter /ˈhaɪ·laɪt·ər/ *n* [C] a pen with a wide writing end and bright, transparent ink which is used to color parts of a text to make them easier to find later

Highness /ˈhaɪ·nəs/ *n* [C] *fml* a title used when referring to an important member of a family that rules a country • *His Royal Highness Prince Michael*

high school /ˈhaɪ·skuːl/ *n* [C/U] a school for children who are about 15 to 18 years old that is usually divided into GRADES nine through twelve or ten through twelve • *Cory will be starting high school in September.* [U] • LP EDUCATION IN THE US

highway /ˈhaɪ·weɪ/ *n* [C] a road, esp. a big road that joins cities or towns together • *The interstate highways are usually faster, but smaller roads can be more scenic.*

hijack /ˈhaɪ·dʒæk/ *v* [T] to force someone to give you control of (a vehicle, aircraft, or ship that is in the middle of a trip) • *Gunmen tried to hijack their truck.* • If someone hijacks someone else's ideas or plans, they use those ideas as their own: *The movie hijacks some of its style from "Blade Runner."*

hijacker /'haɪˌdʒæk·ər/ *n* [C] a person who takes control of a vehicle by force

hijacking /'haɪˌdʒæk·ɪŋ/ *n* [C/U] • *He's a leading suspect in the hijacking of the jetliner.* [U]

hike WALK /haɪk/ *v* [I] to walk a long distance, esp. in the countryside • *We plan to hike from lake to lake.* ○ *I've got to hike back to my car to get my jacket.*

hike /haɪk/ *n* [C] • *a 10-mile hike*

hiker /'haɪ·kər/ *n* [C] • *The wooded area is attractive to hikers and hunters.*

hike INCREASE /haɪk/ *n* [C] an increase in the cost of something, esp. a large or unwanted increase • *a tax hike*

hike /haɪk/ *v* [T] • *Dairies have hiked milk prices again.*

hilarious /hɪl'er·iː·əs, -'ær-/ *adj* extremely amusing and causing a lot of laughter • *Her jokes are absolutely hilarious.*

hill /hɪl/ *n* [C] an area of land that slopes up to a point higher than the surrounding land and then slopes down again, but which is smaller than a mountain • *They built a house on the top of a hill, overlooking the town.* ○ *The highway runs through rolling hills* (= land that gradually slopes up and down). • (*infml*) **The Hill** is **Capitol Hill**. See at CAPITOL. • A **hillside** is the sloping surface of a hill between its top and bottom.

hilly /'hɪl·i/ *adj* • *The plane crashed in a hilly, heavily wooded area.*

hillbilly /'hɪl,bɪl·i/ *n* [C] *disapproving* a person from a rural area who lacks knowledge and familiarity with modern ideas and popular culture, esp. someone who lives in the mountains or far from cities or towns in the southeastern US

hilt /hɪlt/ *n* [C] the handle of a sharp, pointed weapon, esp. of a SWORD • Something that is done **to the hilt** is done completely and without limitation: *We're already being taxed to the hilt.*

him /hɪm, ɪm/ *pronoun male* the male being spoken about, who has already been mentioned; the objective form of he • *Why don't you give him his present?* ○ *We've just got a new cat, but we haven't thought of a name for him yet.* • Him is also used to refer to a person whose sex is not known: *If anyone causes a problem, get rid of him.* ○ *Some people find this use of him to be offensive.*

himself /hɪm'self, ɪm-/ *pronoun male* the male being spoken about; the reflexive form of he • *Larry bought himself a new coat.* • Himself is sometimes used to emphasize a male subject or object of a sentence: *I got to meet the president himself.* • Himself is also used to refer to a person whose sex is not known: *I hope nobody's hurt himself.* ○ *Some people find this use of him to be offensive.* • If a man or boy

does something **by himself**, he does it alone or without help from anyone else: *Jamie made that snowman all by himself.* • If a man or boy is **not himself**, he is not in his usual mental or physical condition: *Hugh hasn't been himself since the accident.* • If a man or boy has something **to himself**, he has it for his own use only: *He's got the house (all) to himself tonight.* • LP REFLEXIVE PRONOUNS

hind /haɪnd/ *adj* [not gradable] at the back of an animal's body • *Phil's dog stands on her hind legs to greet me.*

hinder /'hɪn·dər/ *v* [T] *slightly fml* to limit the ability of (someone) to do something, or to limit the development of (something) • *A poor diet can hinder mental and physical growth.* ○ *I don't know if these changes are going to help or hinder the team.*

hindrance /'hɪn·drəns/ *n* [C/U] *slightly fml* • *Often his training has proved a hindrance rather than a help.* [C]

hindquarters /'haɪndˌkwɔːrt̬·ərz/ *pl n* the back part of a four-legged animal

hindsight /'haɪnd·saɪt/ *n* [U] the ability to understand, after something has happened, why or how it was done and how it might have been done better • *They are ideas that, in hindsight, often seem hair-brained.*

Hindu /'hɪn·duː/ *n* [C], *adj* [not gradable] (a member) of or belonging to the main religion of India, which is based on four holy texts, has a very long history, and supports the belief that when a person or creature dies, their spirit returns to life in another body • *a Hindu god* ○ *There are more than 500 million Hindus in the world.*

Hinduism /'hɪn·duːˌɪz·əm/ *n* [U] the Hindu religion

hinge /hɪndʒ/ *n* [C] a folding device, usually made of metal, that is attached to a door, gate, or lid on one side, allowing it to open and close

hinge on/upon /'-ˌ-; '-ˌ-,-/ *v prep* [T] to depend on (something), or to need (something) in order to be successful • *The case hinges on the evidence of a single eyewitness.*

hint INDIRECT STATEMENT /hɪnt/ *n* [C] a statement or action that suggests indirectly what a person thinks or wants • *When he yawned and looked at his watch, I took it as a hint that we should leave.* [+ *that* clause] • A hint is also a piece of advice that helps you to do something: *hints on ways to save money*

hint /hɪnt/ *v* [I/T] • *My parents have hinted that they'll pay for a European vacation after I graduate from college.* [+ *that* clause]

hint SMALL AMOUNT /hɪnt/ *n* [C usually sing] a small amount of something • *It was the first cool day of September, and there was a hint of autumn in the air.*

hinterland /'hɪnt·ər,lænd, -lənd/ *n* [U], **hinterlands** *pl n* a region in the middle part of a country, esp. a large country, that is far from cities or the coast • *The touring theater group took its production into the hinterland.*

hip [BODY PART] /hɪp/ *n* [C] the part on either side of the body where the legs are attached to the upper part of the body, or either of the joints at the PELVIS (= bowl-shaped bones) where the legs are attached • *Arthritis is causing pain and stiffness in your hips.*

hip [KNOWING] /hɪp/ *adj* **-pp-** *approving slang* knowing a lot about what the most modern fashions are, esp. in music, social behavior, and styles of clothes

hip–hop /'hɪp·hɑp/ *n* [U] a type of popular, African-American music with songs about politics and society, and words spoken rather than sung

hippie, **hippy** /'hɪp·i/ *n* [C] a young person, esp. in the late 1960s and early 1970s, who typically had long hair, believed in peace, opposed many accepted ideas about how to live, often lived in groups, and took drugs

hippopotamus /ˌhɪp·ə'pɑt̬·ə·məs/, *short form* **hippo** /'hɪp·oʊ/ *n* [C] a large, dark gray animal of Africa that lives in or near rivers and that has a big head, short legs, and thick skin

hire /hɑɪr/ *v* [T] to start to employ (someone) • *You ought to hire a lawyer to handle your taxes.*

hire /hɑɪr/ *n* [C] an employee • *Those retiring will be replaced by new hires.*

his /hɪz, ɪz/ *pronoun male* belonging to or connected with the person mentioned; the possessive form of he, often used before a noun • *Joe left his car parked with the lights on.* ○ *Isn't this Kevin's umbrella? I think it's his.* • His is also used to refer to a person whose sex is not known: *Anyone who drives his car that fast is asking for trouble.* ○ Some people find this use of his to be offensive. • [LP] DETERMINERS

Hispanic /hɪ'spæn·ɪk/ *adj* [not gradable], *n* [C] connected with a person who lives in the US but who originally came from or whose family came from Spanish-speaking Latin America • *The US Hispanic population totaled more than 22 million in 1990.* • A **Hispanic-American** is an American citizen of Hispanic origin.

Hispanic /hɪ'spæn·ɪk/ *n* [C] • *Hispanics make up a large proportion of the population of Miami.*

hiss /hɪs/ *v* [I] to make a noise like the sound of the letter "s"

hiss /hɪs/ *n* [C] • *We heard the loud hiss of escaping gas.*

history [PAST EVENTS] /'hɪs·tə·ri, -tri/ *n* [C/U] (the study of) past events considered together, esp. events or developments of a particular period, country, or subject • *I'm taking a course in American history.* [U] ○ *I'm reading a history of jazz* (= a book that describes the development of this music). [C]

historian /hɪ'stɔːr·i·ən, -'stoʊr-/ *n* [C] someone who writes about or studies history

historic /hɪ'stɔːr·ɪk, -'stɑr-/ *adj* [not gradable] (of a thing or event) important when studied as part of the past • *historic buildings and monuments*

historical /hɪ'stɔːr·ɪ·kəl, -'stɑr-/ *adj* [not gradable] connected with the study or representation of things from the past • *The library has an important collection of historical documents.*

history [REPEATED HAPPENINGS] /'hɪs·tə·ri, -tri/ *n* [C usually sing] something that has been done or experienced by a particular person or thing repeatedly over a long period • *He has a history of alcoholism and drug abuse.*

histrionic /ˌhɪs·tri·'ɑn·ɪk/ *adj* (of behavior) showing a lot of emotion in order to persuade others or attract attention • *a histrionic performance*

histrionics /ˌhɪs·tri·'ɑn·ɪks/ *pl n* loud, emotional behavior that does not seem sincere • *Both lawyers indulged in courtroom histrionics.*

hit [TOUCH] /hɪt/ *v* [T] **hitting**, *past* **hit** to touch quickly and forcefully, with the hand or an object • *Don't hit your little brother!* ○ *They were throwing rocks, and one of the rocks hit a window and broke it.* ○ *She must have fallen asleep, and the car hit a tree.* • If something hits part of your body, or you hit it, you come up against it by accident: *He's so tall he keeps hitting his head when he goes through a doorway.* • To hit is also to shoot a weapon and cause a bullet or other object to touch (something or someone) quickly and forcefully and usually hurt them, sometimes very badly: *One journalist was hit in the leg by a stray bullet.* • Something that is **hit-or-miss** seems to happen by chance rather than by planning: *It's a hit-or-miss situation, with some qualified people being rejected and some people with no experience landing jobs.* • (*infml*) If you **hit the books**, you begin to study in a serious and determined way. • If you **hit the brakes** of a vehicle, you cause it to slow down or stop suddenly. • If someone **hits the ground running**, they begin something new, such as a job, and have already started learning the skills to do it well: *She studied the reports over the weekend so she could hit the ground running when the meeting began.* • If you **hit the jackpot**, you do something very successfully: *I think we hit the jackpot with the telemarketing campaign—our sales have doubled.* • If someone says that you have **hit the nail on the head**, they mean that you have expressed their opinion exactly and clearly. • A **hit-and-run** accident is an accident in which a car hits and injures a person and the driver leaves the area without trying to get help or telling the police.

hit /hɪt/ *n* [C] • *The hospital took a direct hit from a bomb.* • A **hit list** is a list of people, groups, or organizations that someone, esp. in politics, intends to take unpleasant action against: *He's on the president's hit list because he helped defeat the tax bill.*

hit HURT /hɪt/ *v* [T] **hitting**, *past* **hit** to have an unpleasant or negative effect on (a person or thing) • *Commuters are going to be hit hard by the rise in gasoline prices.* • (*infml*) If an important fact hits you, you suddenly understand the meaning of it: *It just hit me that once she leaves, I may never see her again.*

hit ARRIVE AT /hɪt/ *v* [T] **hitting**, *past* **hit** *infml* to arrive at (a place, position, or state) • *The company's profits hit an all-time high last year.* • If you **hit the ceiling/roof**, you become extremely angry: *Dad will hit the roof when he finds out I dented a fender of the car.* • If you **hit the deck**, you lie down quickly and suddenly so that you are hidden from view or sheltered from something dangerous. • (*infml*) If you **hit the hay/sack**, you go to bed in order to sleep: *I've got a busy day tomorrow, so I think I'll hit the sack.* • *The full horror of the war* **hit home** (= became completely understood) *when we started seeing pictures of the wounded on TV.* • If you **hit the road**, you leave a place or begin a journey: *I'd love to stay longer but it's really time to hit the road.* • (*infml*) *That ice cream sandwich really* **hit the spot** (= was exactly what I needed)*!*

hit SUCCESS /hɪt/ *n* [C] someone or something that is very popular or successful • *The musical "Cats" is one of the biggest hits on Broadway.*

hit /hɪt/ *v* **hitting**, *past* **hit** • If two people **hit it off**, they meet and begin to like each other immediately: *We had similar ideas about the show, and the two of us hit it off right away.*

hit BASEBALL /hɪt/ *v* [T] (in baseball) to make (a play) by hitting the ball within the playing area • *Rodriguez hit a high pop-up fly that was caught by the shortstop.* ◦ *Last time at bat he hit a home run.*

hit /hɪt/ *n* [C] a **base hit**, see at BASE BASEBALL • *Jason had three hits in four times at bat.*

hitter /'hɪt̬·ər/ *n* [C] (in baseball) a player who hits the ball with the BAT (= long, shaped stick held in the hands) • *Babe Ruth is famous as one of the best hitters in baseball.*

□ **hit back** /'-'-/ *v adv* [I] to attack someone who has attacked you • *In tonight's speech, the attorney general is expected to hit back at critics who have attacked her handling of the crisis.*

□ **hit on** /'-,-/ *v prep* [T] *slang* to show (someone) in a direct way that you are sexually attracted to them • *I hate parties where guys are hitting on you the whole time.*

□ **hit on/upon** /'-,-; '--,-/ *v prep* [T] to think of (an idea) unexpectedly or unintentionally • *When we first hit on the idea, everyone told us it would never work.*

□ **hit up** *obj*, **hit** *obj* **up** /'-'-/ *v adv* [M] *infml* to ask (someone) for something, esp. money • *She tried to hit me up for a loan till payday, but I didn't have any money to give her.*

hitch DIFFICULTY /hɪtʃ/ *n* [C] a difficulty or troubling fact esp. in a situation that is generally positive • *I finally did get a job offer that sounded perfect—the only hitch was the low salary.* ◦ *The taping at Channel 4 went off without a hitch* (= perfectly).

hitch RIDE /hɪtʃ/ *v* [T] to get (a free ride in someone else's road vehicle) as a way of traveling • *Nancy hitched a ride with her husband's cousin.*

hitch FASTEN /hɪtʃ/ *v* [T] to fasten (something) to another thing, such as a vehicle • *We just need to hitch the trailer to the car and then we can go.*

hitchhike /'hɪtʃ·hɑɪk/ *v* [I] to travel by getting a free ride in someone else's road vehicle • *It took us days to hitchhike across Minnesota.*

hitchhiker /'hɪtʃ·hɑɪ·kər/ *n* [C]

hi–tech /'hɑɪ'tek/ *adj* **high-tech**, see at HIGH ABOVE AVERAGE

hither /'hɪð·ər/ *adv* [not gradable] *old use* to or toward this place • *Come hither!*

hitherto /'hɪð·ər,tuː/ *adv* [not gradable] *fml* until now or until a particular time • *Economic aid has been offered to hitherto depressed people.*

HIV *n* [U] *abbreviation for* human immunodeficiency virus (= the virus that is believed to cause AIDS) • If a person is HIV or **HIV-positive**, they are infected with HIV, although they might not have AIDS, or might not develop it for a long time.

hive /hɑɪv/ *n* [C] a place where bees live, esp. a **beehive** (= boxlike container), or the group of bees living there

hives /hɑɪvz/ *n* [U] a condition in which a person's skin develops swollen red areas, often suddenly, esp. as a reaction to something the person has eaten • *Eating shellfish makes me break out in hives.*

hm, h'm, hmm /hᵊm/ *exclamation* a sound made when someone is thinking about something or needs more time to decide what to say

HMO *n* [C] *pl* **HMOs** *abbreviation for* **health maintenance organization**, see at HEALTH

hoard /hɔːrd, hoʊrd/ *v* [T] to collect (a large supply of something), more than you need now, often because you think you will not be able to get it later • *Many people hoarded food in wartime.*

hoarse /hɔːrs, hoʊrs/ *adj* (of a voice) sounding weak and not very well controlled, often because it has been used too much or the speaker has a cold • *He was hoarse from shouting.*

hoax /hoʊks/ *n* [C] a plan to deceive a large group of people; a trick • *It is a cruel hoax, she said, to encourage people to think they have a real chance to win the lottery.*

hobble /'hɑb·əl/ *v* [I/T] to walk with difficulty in an awkward way, or to cause (someone) to walk in this way, usually because of an injury to the feet or legs • *He hobbled over on crutches.* [I always + adv/prep]

hobby /'hɑb·i/ *n* [C] an activity that you do for pleasure when you are not working • *Sonya's hobbies include traveling, sailing, and reading fiction.*

hobnob /'hɑb·nɑb/ *v* [I always + adv/prep] -**bb-** to spend time being friendly with someone who is important or famous • *She often gets her picture in the papers, hobnobbing with the rich and famous.*

hobo /'hoʊ·boʊ/ *n* [C] *pl* **hobos** or **hoboes** a person who does not have a job or a house to live in, and so moves from one place to another

hock /hɑk/ *v* [T] *infml* to exchange in return for borrowing money; PAWN • *to hock jewelry*

hock /hɑk/ *n* • To be **in hock** is to have a debt: *The state itself is already in hock, running a $13 billion deficit.*

hockey /'hɑk·i/, **ice hockey** *n* [U] a game played on ice between two teams of eleven players who each have a curved stick with which they try to put the PUCK (= small, hard, rubber disk) into the other team's goal

hocus–pocus /ˌhoʊ·kə'spoʊ·kəs/ *n* [U] tricks used to deceive or words used to hide what is happening, esp. by making the actual situation difficult to understand • *Like so many politicians, he relies on a lot of statistical hocus-pocus.*

hodgepodge /'hɑdʒ·pɑdʒ/ *n* [C usually sing] a confused mixture of different things • *It was a hodgepodge of theories.*

hoe /hoʊ/ *n* [C] a garden tool with a long handle and a short blade, used to remove WEEDS (= unwanted plants) and break up the surface of the ground

hog ANIMAL /hɑg, hɔːg/ *n* [C] a pig, esp. one allowed to grow large so that it can be used as food

hog PERSON /hɑg, hɔːg/ *n* [C] *infml disapproving* a person who takes more than they should of something, esp. food • *Don't be a hog—take only as much as you can eat.*

hog /hɑg, hɔːg/ *v* [T] -**gg-** *infml disapproving* • *He's always hogging the newspaper* (= using it so that no one else can read it).

hogwash /'hɑg·wɑʃ, 'hɔːg·wɔːʃ/ *n* [U] nonsense, or words intended to deceive • *His answer was pure hogwash.*

ho–hum /'hoʊ'hʌm/ *adj infml* not interesting; boring • *The chess match was a ho-hum affair, ending in a draw.*

hoist /hɔɪst/ *v* [T] to lift (something heavy), often with special equipment • *Tomorrow the final section of the bridge will be hoisted into place.*

hokey /'hoʊ·ki/ *adj infml* too emotional or artificial and not believable • *The ending of the movie was hokey, but otherwise it was OK.*

hokum /'hoʊ·kəm/ *n* [U] nonsense • *This report on the causes of crime is pure hokum.*

hold TAKE FIRMLY /hoʊld/ *v* [I/T] *past* **held** /held/ to take and keep (something) in your hand or arms • *The nurse held the child in her arms.* [T] ○ *Hold tight* (= firmly) *to the railing.* [I] • If you hold your nose, you press your nose tightly between thumb and finger to close it. [T] • When two people **hold hands**, each one takes the other person's hand in their hand, esp. to show affection. • *Her latest book* **can't hold a candle to** (= is of much lower quality than) *her earlier works.*

hold /hoʊld/ *n* [U] • *Don't lose hold of the dog's leash.* ○ *If you can get/grab/take hold of that end of the box, I'll take this end and we'll lift it.*

hold MOVE AWAY /hoʊld/ *v* [always + adv/prep] *past* **held** /held/ to move (something) away from your body • *Rosie held an apple out to the horse.* [M] ○ *Close your eyes and hold out your hands.* [M] ○ *All those who agree, please hold your hand up.* [M]

hold KEEP IN PLACE /hoʊld/ *v* [always + adv/prep] *past* **held** /held/ to keep (something) in a particular place or position • *Could you hold the door open for me, please?* [M] ○ *I can't fasten this skirt unless I hold my stomach in* (= keep it tight with my muscles so that it does not stick out). [M] ○ *Each wheel is held on by/with four bolts.* [M] ○ *Individual parts are held together with glue.* [M] ○ *Hold still* (= Do not move)*!* [I]

hold /hoʊld/ *n* [C] (in some sports) a position in which one person prevents another from moving • *In karate, beginners learn several simple holds.*

holder /'hoʊl·dər/ *n* [C] a device for putting objects in or for keeping them in place • *a cigarette/paper towel holder*

hold CONTINUE /hoʊld/ *v* [I/T] *past* **held** /held/ to continue or cause to continue in the same way as before • *If the weather holds, we can go sailing.* [I] ○ *The ship held its course.* [T] ○ *She seemed to hold the note she was singing for more than a minute.* [T] • If something **holds true**, it continues to be true: *Einstein's theories still hold true today.* • If you **hold** your **own**, you maintain your position or condition despite difficulties: *She can hold her own in any argument.* ○ *He was very ill, but now he's holding his own.*

hold DELAY /hoʊld/ *v* [I/T] *past* **held** /held/ to stop (something) from happening, or to delay (something) temporarily • *How long can you hold your breath?* [T] • If someone on the telephone asks you to hold, they want you to wait until they or someone else can speak to you: *Her line is busy, would you like to hold?* [I] • If you hold something that is usually included in food, you do not include it: *I'd like a salad, but hold the dressing.* [T] • **Hold it** (= Stop and do not continue)*! You're putting too much pepper* *in the stew.* • If you **hold** your **tongue,** you stop yourself from speaking.

hold /hoʊld/ *n* • If something is **on hold,** it is intentionally delayed: *The space launch is on hold until the weather clears.* • If you are **on hold** when using the telephone, you are waiting to speak to someone: *His line is busy—can I put you on hold?*

hold CONTAIN / SUPPORT /hoʊld/ *v* [T] *past* **held** /held/ to support or contain (something) or be able to contain or support (it) • *This bottle holds exactly one pint.* ○ *Modern computers can hold* (= store) *huge amounts of information.* ○ *Will the rope be strong enough to hold the weight?* • If something **holds promise,** it is likely to be successful: *The new drug holds promise for relieving addiction.* • If a reason, argument, or explanation **holds water,** it is true: *Her alibi seems to hold water.*

hold CONTROL /hoʊld/ *v* [T] *past* **held** /held/ to keep control or possession of (something) • *His speech held the audience's attention for over an hour.* ○ *He was held hostage for three days.* ○ *After many days of fighting, the rebels now hold the town.* ○ *The champion held the lead until the last lap.* • If someone who committed a crime is **held,** they are kept guarded in a police station. • If you **hold** a job or a financial account, you have it: *He currently holds the position of managing editor.* ○ *She holds three different accounts with the same bank.* • If someone **holds all the cards,** they have a big advantage: *Management holds all the cards when it comes to negotiations.* • If a person **holds the fort,** they have responsibility for something while someone is absent: *She held the fort for two weeks while the boss was away.*

hold /hoʊld/ *n* [U] • *The team is strengthening its hold on first place.* ○ *She has a strong hold on her daughters.*

holder /ˈhoʊl·dər/ *n* [C] • *property holders* ○ *Competition benefits credit card holders.*

hold CAUSE TO HAPPEN /hoʊld/ *v* [T] *past* **held** /held/ to organize or cause (a meeting, election, or social event) to happen • *The election will be held on the 8th of November.* ○ *We're holding our annual New Year's Day party again.* • LP DO: VERBS MEANING "PERFORM"

hold (*obj*) BELIEVE /hoʊld/ *v past* **held** /held/ to believe (an idea or opinion) to be correct, or to state that (something) is true • *He holds unpopular views on many subjects.* [T] ○ *I hold him responsible for the damage to my car.* [T] ○ *Murphy's law holds that if anything can go wrong, it probably will.* [+ *that* clause]

hold SPACE /hoʊld/ *n* [C] the space in a ship or aircraft where goods are carried

▫ **hold** *obj* **against** *obj* /ˈ--ˈ-/ *v prep* [T] to allow (something) to cause you to have a bad opinion about (someone or something) • *He made a mistake, but I don't hold it against him—we all make mistakes.*

▫ **hold back** (*obj*), **hold** (*obj*) **back** /ˈ-ˈ-/ *v adv* [I/M] to stop (something) from happening or advancing, or to keep (someone) from doing something • *She held back from interfering in their arguments.* [I] ○ *Sandbags will hold back the flood waters for a while.* [M] ○ *A lack of computer skills is holding many graduates back.* [M] ○ *He admitted that something had gone wrong, but he held back the details* (= stopped himself from telling the complete truth). [M]

▫ **hold down** REMAIN WORKING /ˈ-ˈ-/ *v adv* [T] to remain working in (a job) • *He's never been able to hold down a steady job.*

▫ **hold down** *obj* MAINTAIN LEVEL , **hold** *obj* **down** /ˈ-ˈ-/ *v adv* [M] to maintain (something) at a low level • *Hold down the noise in there, kids!*

▫ **hold forth** /ˈ-ˈ-/ *v adv* [I] to express your opinions for a long time • *She held forth all through lunch on a variety of subjects.*

▫ **hold off** (*obj*), **hold** (*obj*) **off** /ˈ-ˈ-/ *v prep* [I/M] to stop (something) from happening, or to be delayed • *They're hoping to hold off surgery until he's stronger.* [M] ○ *I hope the rain holds off until we get home.* [I]

▫ **hold on** /ˈ-ˈ-/ *v prep* [I] to wait for someone to speak to you after you telephone them • *She's on the other line—can you hold on?*

▫ **hold on/tight** /ˈ-ˈ-/ *v adv* [I] *infml* to continue doing something or staying somewhere although it is difficult or unpleasant to do so • *Hold on and I'll go and get some help.*

▫ **hold onto** /ˈ-ˈ--/ *v prep* [I] to continue to keep (something) • *Two local representatives held onto their seats in yesterday's election.* ○ *The team held onto first place with a 4-3 win last night.*

▫ **hold out** OFFER AS POSSIBILITY /ˈ-ˈ-/ *v adv* [T] to offer (something) as a possibility • *Few people hold out any hope of finding more survivors.*

▫ **hold out** CONTINUE EXISTING /ˈ-ˈ-/ *v adv* [I] to continue existing • *They won't be able to hold out much longer against these attacks.* • If someone **holds out** for something, they continue to demand it although they have been told they cannot have it: *The workers are holding out for a pay increase.*

▫ **hold out on** /-ˈ-,-/ *v adv prep* [T] to refuse to give help, information, or something of value to (someone) • *Don't hold out on me—I need to know who did it.*

▫ **hold** *obj* **to** *obj* /ˈ--/ *v prep* [T] to make (someone) act on (a promise or agreement) • *They're holding him to the exact terms of the contract.*

▫ **hold together** (*obj*), **hold** (*obj*) **together** /ˈ--ˈ--/ *v adv* [I/M] to keep (a group or organization) complete or in its original state or condition • *Social relationships held the Crow people together into the 20th century.* [M] ○ *We ought to do everything we can to get marriages to hold together.* [I]

▫ **hold up** *obj* DELAY , **hold** *obj* **up** /ˈ-ˈ-/ *v adv* [M] to delay (someone or something) • *Traffic* *was held up for several hours by the accident.* ○ *Sorry to hold you up—my train was late.*

□ **hold up** *obj* STEAL , **hold** *obj* **up** /'-'-/ *v adv* [M] to try to steal money or property from (a bank, store, etc.) by using violence or threats • *They held up the store at gunpoint.*

holdup /'hoʊl·dəp/ *n* [C] • *a bank holdup*

□ **hold up** CONTINUE /'-'-/ *v prep* [I] to continue to operate or be able to do things, esp. after being fixed or ill • *I hope the spare tire holds up until we can get to a garage.* ○ *She is holding up well despite her problems.* • If information holds up, it is proved to be true: *The evidence may not hold up in court.*

□ **hold up** *obj* GIVE EXAMPLE , **hold** *obj* **up** /'-'-/ *v adv* [M] to offer (something) as an example • *Her parents always held her sister up to her as the kind of person she should be.*

holdings /'hoʊl·dɪŋz/ *pl n* [C] something valuable that is owned, esp. investments in a company • *He's got several car dealerships and banks among his holdings.*

hole SPACE /hoʊl/ *n* [C] an empty space or opening in an object • *We dug a hole to plant the tree.* ○ *My sweater has a hole in it.* • A hole is also something that has been left out or not explained: *The new proposal is full of holes.* • In golf, a hole is one of the small hollow spaces in the ground into which the ball is hit, or one of the usually 18 areas of play: *the seventh hole* • A **hole-in-the-wall** is a very small place, usually a store or apartment.

hole DIFFICULTY /hoʊl/ *n* [C usually sing] a difficult situation • *Without their starting quarterback, the team is in a (bit of a) hole.* • If someone is **in the hole**, they are in debt: *We're still in the hole on our credit cards.*

hole up /'-'-/ *v adv* [I] to stay in a safe place, often as a way of escape • *While writing his book, he holed up for a year at a cabin in the woods.*

holiday /'hɑl·ə,deɪ/ *n* [C] a day for celebration when many people are allowed to stay away from work or school • *a national holiday* • (*Cdn and Br*) A holiday is a VACATION.

holiness /'hoʊ·li:·nəs/ *n* [U] • See at HOLY GOOD.

holistic /hoʊ'lɪs·tɪk/ *adj* relating to the whole of something or to the total system instead of just to its parts • **Holistic medicine** attempts to treat the whole person, including mind and body, not just the injury or disease.

holler /'hɑl·ər/ *v* [I/T] *infml* to shout or call loudly • *She hollered "Stop!" just before the collision.* [T]

holler /'hɑl·ər/ *n* [C] *infml* • *He let out a holler when he fell.*

hollow EMPTY /'hɑl·oʊ/ *adj* having an empty space inside or on the surface of an object • *a hollow tree* ○ *His hollow cheeks and paleness made him look ill.* • If a sound is hollow, it sounds as if it were made by hitting an empty container: *the low, hollow rumble of thunder*

hollow /'hɑl·oʊ/ *n* [C] an empty space inside something; a hole • A hollow is also a small valley: *We hiked along Bear Hollow last weekend.*

hollow out *obj*, **hollow** *obj* **out** /'hɑl·ə,waʊt/ *v adv* [M] to remove the inside of (something) • *We hollowed out the tree trunk to make a canoe.*

hollow WITHOUT VALUE /'hɑl·oʊ/ *adj* (of situations, feelings, or words) lacking value; not true or sincere • *a hollow victory* ○ *hollow promises* ○ *Their objections had a hollow ring* (= did not seem sincere).

holly /'hɑl·i/ *n* [C/U] an evergreen bush with pointed, shiny green leaves and small, red fruit which are often used for Christmas decorations.

Hollywood /'hɑl·i:,wʊd/ *n* [U] an area in Los Angeles, California, that is considered the center of the movie industry in the US

holocaust /'hɑl·ə,kɔːst, 'hoʊ·lə-, -,kɑst/ *n* [C] a large amount of destruction, esp. by fire or heat, or the killing of large numbers of people • *a nuclear holocaust* • **The Holocaust** was the systematic murder of many people, esp. Jews, by the NAZIS during World War II.

hologram /'hɑl·ə,græm, 'hoʊ·lə-/ *n* [C] an image made with a LASER beam, in which the objects shown look like they have depth rather than appearing flat and can seem to move

holster /'hoʊl·stər/ *n* [C] a leather container that holds a gun, usually fixed on a belt or a strap

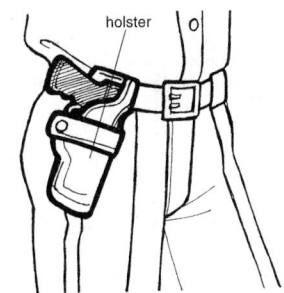

holster

holy GOOD /'hoʊ·li/ *adj* considered to be pure or good because of being related to what a religion values • *holy scriptures* ○ *Jerusalem is a holy city to Christians, Muslims, and Jews.*

holiness /'hoʊ·li:·nəs/ *n* [U] • *This temple is a place of great holiness.* • Holiness is also a title used of or to the leader of the Roman Catholic Church: *We do not know the views of His Holiness on the subject.*

holy EMPHASIS /'hoʊ·li/ *adj infml* used to emphasize another word, and sometimes to avoid swearing • *My nephew is a* **holy terror** (= a child who behaves very badly). • (*infml*) **Holy cow**, **holy mackerel**, **holy smoke**, and (*rude slang*) **holy shit** are exclamations of surprise.

homage /'ɑm·ɪdʒ, 'hɑm-/ *n* [U] an expression of great respect and honor • *We pay homage to him for his achievements in medical research.*

home HOUSE /hoʊm/ *n* [C/U] a structure in which a person lives, esp. a house or apartment • *Phone me at home after four o'clock.* [U] ○ *We have a country home and a city home.* [C] • A home also refers to the family that lives together there: *a happy home* [C] • A home is also a place where a group of people live who need special care: *a nursing home* [C] • Your **home address** is the address of the place where you live. • A **homemaker** is a person who manages a home and family instead of earning money from employment. • A **homeowner** is a person who owns the house or apartment in which they live. • **Homework** is studies for school that teachers tell students to do at home: *(fig.) It was obvious that she had done her homework* (= made a lot of preparations) *and thoroughly researched the backgrounds of her clients.* • USAGE: "House" is the more usual word for a building that one family lives in. The word "home" also refers to the life that goes on in that building.

home /hoʊm/ *adj* [not gradable] done or made in the place where you live • *home cooking* • Something **homemade** is made at home rather than bought from a store: *homemade bread* • For a sports team, home refers to the city or the building or STADIUM where that team usually plays: *a home game*

home /hoʊm/ *adv* [not gradable] to or toward the place where you live • *going home*

homeless /'hoʊm·ləs/ *adj* [not gradable] having no place to live • *a homeless person*

homeless /'hoʊm·ləs/ *pl n* • *The homeless sometimes have to sleep in the streets.*

homelessness /'hoʊm·lə·snəs/ *n* [U] • *Homelessness is a major problem in large cities.*

homeward /'hoʊm·wərd/, **homewards** /'hoʊm·wərdz/ *adv* toward home • *Now that our vacation is over, it's time to head homeward.*

home ORIGIN /hoʊm/ *n* [C/U] a place of origin, or the place where a person feels they belong • *Australia is the home of the kangaroo.* [C] ○ *I've lived here for two years, but it still doesn't feel like home.* [U] • When you are **at home** in a place or situation, you are comfortable and relaxed there: *She's beginning to feel at home in her new job.* ○ *Go into the living room and make yourself at home.* • *(infml)* If you are **home free**, you have finished the difficult or dangerous part of an activity and are sure of success: *Once you get past the essay questions on the test, you're home free.* • A **homecoming** is a person's arrival home after being away for a long time, or a celebration held at a school or college to honor people who were students there earlier. • Your **homeland** is the country where you were born. • A **home page** is the opening image on the computer when you look at someone's description of themselves

on the INTERNET. • If you are **homesick**, you are unhappy because of being away from home: *She was homesick during her first semester at college.* ○ *I was almost overcome with* **homesickness**. • The **home stretch** is the last part of a race or other activity: *We've been on this project for three months, but we're in the home stretch now.* • Your **hometown** is the town or city you are from, esp. the one in which you were born and lived while you were young.

home in on /'-'-,-/ *v adv prep* [T] *infml* to aim for and move directly toward (something) • *The missile homed in on the ship.*

homeboy /'hoʊm·bɔɪ/, **homey** /'hoʊ·mi/ *n slang* someone from your own town, or someone who is a close friend or a member of your GANG

homely /'hoʊm·li/ *adj* unattractive in appearance

homeopathy /,hoʊ·mi:'ɑp·ə·θi/ *n* [U] a system of treating disease by giving extremely small amounts of natural substances that, if given in larger amounts to healthy people, would produce the same effects as the disease

homeopathic /,hoʊ·mi:·ə'pæθ·ɪk/ *adj* [not gradable] • *homeopathic medicine*

home run /hoʊm'rʌn/, **homer** /'hoʊ·mər/ *n* [C] (in baseball) a play in which a player hits the ball and scores, usually by hitting the ball a long way so that it comes down beyond the playing area • *(fig.) The movie didn't just make money, it hit a home run* (= was extremely successful).

homespun /'hoʊm·spʌn/ *adj* simple and ordinary • *homespun wisdom*

homestead /'hoʊm·sted/ *n* [C] a house and the surrounding area of land, esp. land obtained from the government which is lived on and used for farming

homey COMFORTABLE /'hoʊ·mi/ *adj* pleasant and comfortable • *It's a small hotel with a homey atmosphere.*

homey PERSON /'hoʊ·mi/ *n* [C] a HOMEBOY

homicide /'hɑm·ə,saɪd, 'hoʊ·mə-/ *n* [C/U] the crime of killing a person; murder • *He was convicted of homicide.* [U]

homicidal /,hɑm·ə'saɪd·əl, ,hoʊ·mə-/ *adj* likely to murder • *a homicidal maniac*

homogeneous /,hoʊ·mə'dʒiː·ni:·əs/ *adj* consisting of parts or having qualities that are the same • *Like the other valley towns, this was once a fairly homogeneous Anglo community.* • Compare HETEROGENEOUS.

homogenized /hə'mɑdʒ·ə,naɪzd/ *adj* [not gradable] (of a substance) mixed together so that it is of the same thickness in all parts • *homogenized milk*

homonym /'hɑm·ə,nɪm, 'hoʊ·mə-/ *n* [C] specialized a word that is spelled the same as another word but that does not have the same meaning • *"Close" as a verb and "close" as an adjective are homonyms.* • A homonym is also a HOMOPHONE. • LP WORDS THAT ARE SPELLED THE SAME at SPELL FORM WORDS

homophobia /ˌhoʊ·məˈfoʊ·biː·ə/ *n* [U] hate of homosexuals

homophobic /ˌhoʊ·məˈfoʊ·bɪk/ *adj*

homophone /ˈhɑm·əˌfoʊn, ˈhoʊ·mə-/ *n* [C] *specialized* a word which is pronounced the same as another word, but which has a different meaning or spelling • *The words "so" and "sew" are homophones.* • LP WORDS THAT SOUND SIMILAR at SOUND SOMETHING HEARD

homosexual /ˌhoʊ·məˈsek·ʃə·wəl/ *n* [C] a person who is sexually attracted to people of the same sex • Compare HETEROSEXUAL.

homosexual /ˌhoʊ·məˈsek·ʃə·wəl/ *adj* [not gradable] • *a homosexual couple/relationship*

homosexuality /ˌhoʊ·məˌsek·ʃəˈwæl·ət̬·i/ *n* [U]

hone /hoʊn/ *v* [T] to direct (something such as an ability) to make it more effective • *He helps performers hone their skills as dancers and singers.* • To hone (an object) is to make it sharper: *to hone scissors*

honest /ˈɑn·əst/ *adj* (of a person) truthful or able to be trusted; not likely to steal, cheat, or lie, or (of actions, speech, or appearance) showing these qualities • *an honest man* ○ *an honest answer* ○ *To be honest* (= To tell the truth), *I didn't like the movie.*

honestly /ˈɑn·əs·tli/ *adv* • *We always try to deal honestly with our customers.*

honesty /ˈɑn·ə·sti/ *n* [U] the quality of being honest • *The judge praised the girl's honesty.*

honestly /ˈɑn·əs·tli/ *adv* [not gradable] used to emphasize that you are telling the truth • *I honestly don't know what I did to upset her.* ○ *Honestly, I wish I had time to do more reading.*

honey SWEET SUBSTANCE /ˈhʌn·i/ *n* [U] a sweet, sticky, yellow substance made by bees and used as food • A **honeybee** is a bee that produces honey. • A **honeycomb** is a structure bees make in which to store honey, having many small separate areas, or (*fig.*) any space divided into many small, separate areas or paths: *The building was a honeycomb of private offices.*

honey PERSON /ˈhʌn·i/ *n* [C] *infml* used as an affectionate way to address a person • *Hi, honey, I'm home.*

honeymoon /ˈhʌn·iːˌmuːn/ *n* [C] a vacation or trip taken by two people who have just been married • *We went to Hawaii on our honeymoon.* • A honeymoon is also an early period in a relationship when criticism is not given: *The first year of the presidency is regarded as a honeymoon.*

honeymoon /ˈhʌn·iːˌmuːn/ *v* [I always + adv/prep] • *They are honeymooning in Jamaica.*

honeymooners /ˈhʌn·iːˌmuː·nərz/ *pl n* • *This resort is popular with honeymooners.*

honeysuckle /ˈhʌn·iːˌsʌk·əl/ *n* [U] a climbing plant with white, yellow, or red flowers that smell sweet

honk /hɑŋk, hɔːŋk/ *v* [I/T] to make a short, loud noise, or to sound (a horn) to make such a noise • *The cars honking (their horns) kept us awake half the night.* [I/T]

honor RESPECT /ˈɑn·ər/ *n* [U] great respect for someone, or the feeling of pride and pleasure resulting when respect is shown to you • *It is an honor to meet you.* • *The dinner is* **in honor of** (= to show respect for) *a colleague who is leaving.* • **Your/His/Her Honor** is a title of respect for a judge or MAYOR (= elected official).

honor /ˈɑn·ər/ *v* [T] • *We are honored that you have come to speak to our students.*

honor CHARACTER /ˈɑn·ər/ *n* [U] a good character, or a reputation for honesty and fair dealing • *David has always been a man of honor.* ○ *On my honor* (= Asking you to trust my reputation for honesty), *I never said that.*

honorable /ˈɑn·ə·rə·bəl/ *adj* • *The neighbors are decent, honorable people.*

honorably /ˈɑn·ə·rə·bli/ *adv* • *The general served his country honorably for 32 years.*

honor REWARD /ˈɑn·ər/ *n* [C] a public reward to show appreciation for unusual achievement • *She received the Presidential Medal of Freedom, the country's highest civilian honor.* • An **honor roll** is a list of students who have earned high marks in their studies. • An **honor student** is a student whose high marks have earned a place on a school's honor roll.

honor /ˈɑn·ər/ *v* [T] • *Today we honor those who died defending our country.*

honorable /ˈɑn·ə·rə·bəl/ *adj* deserving public praise or reward • An **honorable discharge** from the armed forces is a release from your duties with praise from those in authority.

honorary /ˈɑn·əˌrer·i/ *adj* given as a reward, without qualifying in a standard way • *The university awards honorary degrees to various distinguished people each year.*

honors /ˈɑn·ərz/ *pl n* • *He was buried with full military honors.* • An honors course or program is one or more courses of a high standard for advanced students. • If a student qualifies for a degree **with honors** from a school, college, or university, they have done work of an unusually high standard.

honor FULFILL /ˈɑn·ər/ *v* [T] to fulfill an existing agreement or promise, or to accept a form of payment • *The governor honored her pledge to cut taxes.*

hood CLOTHING /hʊd/ *n* [C] a part of a coat or jacket that can be used to cover the head • *The raincoat comes with a detachable hood.*

hood

hood CAR /hʊd/ *n* [C] the metal cover over the engine of a car • PIC CAR

hoodlum /ˈhuːd·ləm,

'hʊd-/, *infml* **hood** /'hʊd/ *n* [C] a criminal, esp. one who is member of a group • *Hoodlums assaulted and robbed two people in a convenience store, police said.*

hoodwink /'hʊd·wɪŋk/ *v* [T] to deceive or trick (someone) • *We were hoodwinked into believing that we had won a lot of money.*

hoof /hʊf, huːf/ *n* [C] *pl* **hooves** /hʊvz, huːvz/ or **hoofs** the hard part of the foot of an animal such a horse

hook /hʊk/ *n* [C] a curved device used for catching hold of something or for hanging something on • *Hang your coat on one of the hooks in the hall.* ○ *I need to change the hook on my fishing line.* • *We'll get there* **by hook or by crook** (= in one way or another).

hook

• If you say that someone believed a story **hook, line, and sinker**, you are surprised or pleased that they believed it because it was intended to deceive them: *I forged the note and the teacher fell for it hook, line, and sinker.* PIC BARB

hook /hʊk/ *v* [T] to use (something) like a hook, or to put (something) so that it is supported at one end and hangs • *She hooked her arm through his.* ○ *He hooked his cane over the back of the chair.* • To hook fish means to catch them on hooks: *We hooked some bass.*

□ **hook up** *obj*, **hook** *obj* **up** /'-'-/ *v adv* [M] to connect (something), usually to a system or to a piece of equipment • *We just moved and I haven't hooked up my stereo yet.* ○ *He hooked the trailer up to his car.*

hookup /'hʊk·ʌp/ *n* [C] the connection between a supply of something and its user, or a connection between two or more pieces of equipment • *Each campsite has complete electric, water, and sewage hookups.*

hooked /hʊkt/ *adj* [not gradable] *infml* strongly attracted to something or someone • *We were afraid she was getting hooked on painkillers, so we changed the medication.* ○ *During the Olympics, we all got hooked on ice dancing.*

hooker /'hʊk·ər/ *n* [C] *slang* a PROSTITUTE

hoop /huːp, hʊp/ *n* [C] a ring of wood, metal, or plastic • *Dad put up a basketball hoop in the driveway on the front of the garage.* • PIC DUNK

hoopla /'huː·plɑ, 'hʊp·lɑ/ *n* [U] busy excitement or a lot of public attention for an event or activity • *She loved the rush she got from the shows, the elegant parties, the attention, the hoopla.*

hooray /hʊ'reɪ, hə-/ *exclamation* HURRAH **hoorah**

hoot SOUND /huːt/ *n* [C] the sound an OWL (= type of bird) makes, or a shout showing anger or amusement • *There were some hoots from the audience at these so-called experts.*

hoot /huːt/ *v* [I/T] • *He hooted with laughter.* [I]

hoot AMUSING PERSON / THING /huːt/ *n* [C] *infml* an amusing person or thing • *Matt's a real hoot.*

Hoover /'huː·vər/ *v* [I/T] *trademark Br for* VACUUM

hooves /huːvz, hʊvz/ *pl of* HOOF

hop /hɑp/ *v* [I/T] **-pp-** to make small jumps on one or two feet, or to move along in this way • *A bird hopped across the lawn.* [I] ○ *Nikki hopped the fence* (= jumped over it). [T] ○ (*fig.*) *Come on, hop in* (= get in), *I've got plenty of room in the car.* [I]

hop /hɑp/ *n* [C] • (*fig.*) *It's just a short hop to Pittsburgh by plane.*

hope /hoʊp/ *n* [C/U] the feeling that something desired can be had or will happen • *We never entirely gave up hope.* [U] ○ *This research offers hope of developing better ways to treat cancer.* [U] ○ *He had hopes of being chosen for the leading part in the play.* [C]

hope /hoʊp/ *v* to express the feeling or wish that something desired will happen • *I'm hoping the company gives us a bonus this year.* [I] ○ *We hope to see you soon.* [+ *to* infinitive] ○ *I hope (that) his plane won't be delayed.* [+ (*that*) clause]

hopeful /'hoʊp·fəl/ *adj* having hope or causing you to hope; believing or causing you to believe that something desired will happen • *I'm hopeful that when both sides understand the situation better, they will agree to meet and cooperate.* [+ *that* clause] ○ *The fact that he's eating with a good appetite is a hopeful sign.*

hopeful /'hoʊp·fəl/ *n* [C] a person who wants to achieve a position of power • *Five presidential hopefuls were invited to speak.*

hopefully /'hoʊp·fə·li/ *adv* • *"Do you have a cigarette?" he asked hopefully.* ○ *Hopefully* (= I/ we hope that), *dad will get home before his supper gets cold.*

hopeless /'hoʊ·pləs/ *adj* without hope • *We tried to save the building, but it was a hopeless task* (= it could not succeed).

hopelessly /'hoʊ·plə·sli/ *adv* completely • *We got hopelessly lost in Rome.*

horde /hɔrd, hoʊrd/ *n* [C] a large group, esp. of people • *A horde of reporters waited on the lawn outside the White House.*

horizon /hə'rɑɪ·zən/ *n* the place in the distance where the earth and sky seem to meet • *We watched the horizon as the sun set.* [U] • A person's horizons are the limit of their ideas, knowledge, and experience: *Spending her junior year abroad has broadened her horizons.* [pl]

horizontal /ˌhɔːr·ə'zɑnt·ᵊl, ˌhɑr-/ *adj* [not gradable] flat or level; parallel with the ground • *Keep the patient in a horizontal position with her feet slightly raised.* • Compare VERTICAL.

hormone /'hɔːr·moʊn/ *n* [C] any of various chemicals in the body that are carried by the blood and that influence the body's growth and how it works • *Dairy cows are often given hormones to promote milk production.*

horn ANIMAL /hɔːrn/ *n* [C/U] a hard, pointed part, usually one of a pair, on the head of cows, goats, and other animals

horny /ˈhɔːr·ni/ *adj* consisting of, or feeling hard like horn • *Birds have horny beaks.* • See also HORNY.

horn MUSIC /hɔːrn/ *n* [C/U] any of various musical instruments consisting of a long curved metal tube that is narrow at the end you blow into and wider at the other end, or this type of instrument generally

horn VEHICLE /hɔːrn/ *n* [C] a device on a vehicle that is used to make a loud sound as a warning or signal • *Angry drivers were honking their horns.*

horn in /ˈ-ˈ-/ *v adv* [I] to interrupt or try to become involved in something when you are not welcome • *Julie is always trying to horn in on our conversations.*

hornet /ˈhɔːr·nət/ *n* [C] a large flying insect that can give a severe sting

horny /ˈhɔːr·ni/ *adj slang* easily excited sexually, or feeling sexually excited • *When we were young college kids in Milwaukee, we were so horny.* • See also **horny** at HORN ANIMAL.

horoscope /ˈhɔːr·əˌskoʊp, ˈhɑr-/ *n* [C] a description of what is going to happen to you, based on the position of the stars and planets at the time of your birth

horrendous /həˈren·dəs/ *adj* so bad as to be shocking; extremely unpleasant • *Conditions in the refugee camps are horrendous.*

horrible /ˈhɔːr·ə·bəl, ˈhɑr-/ *adj* very bad, unpleasant, or disgusting • *There was a horrible smell outside the factory.*

horribly /ˈhɔːr·ə·bli, ˈhɑr-/ *adv* very badly • *They suffered horribly during the war.* • LP VERY, COMPLETELY, AND OTHER INTENSIFIERS

horrid /ˈhɔːr·əd, ˈhɑr-/ *adj* very bad or unpleasant • *It was a horrid purple color which she detested.*

horrify /ˈhɔːr·əˌfaɪ, ˈhɑr-/ *v* [T] to cause (someone) to experience shock, fear, or disgust • *The public was horrified by the brutal murder of an entire family.* ○ (*fig.*) *He was horrified to find that I had never been to a county fair.*

horrifying /ˈhɔːr·əˌfaɪ·ɪŋ, ˈhɑr-/ *adj* • *She has been through the horrifying experience of being raped.*

horrific /həˈrɪf·ɪk/ *adj* so bad as to be shocking • *The report detailed the horrific conditions in the prison.*

horror /ˈhɔːr·ər, ˈhɑr·ər/ *n* [C/U] a strong feeling of fear, shock, or disgust, or an event that produces such a feeling • *the horrors of war* [C] ○ *People cried out in horror as they watched the building burn.* [U] • A **horror story** is a situation in which something bad happens unexpectedly, resulting in a lot of trouble, danger, or expense: *I've heard a lot of horror sto-*

ries about people driving their car and suddenly the steering wheel won't turn.

hors d'oeuvre /ɔːrˈdɜrv/ *n* [C] a small amount of food served before a meal, or at a party

horse /hɔːrs/ *n* [C] a large animal with four legs that people ride on and which, esp. in the past, was used for pulling vehicles and carrying loads • *She taught him how to ride a horse.* • *He set out* on horseback (= riding a horse). • *I went* horseback riding (= riding on a horse, esp. for enjoyment) *with my brother.* • A **horseshoe** is a U-shaped metal object that is fixed to the bottom of a horse's HOOF (= foot) to protect it. • **Horseshoes** is a game in which horseshoes are thrown at a metal rod in the ground.

horse around /ˌ-ˈ-/ *v adv* [I] *infml* to behave in a silly and noisy way • *This fellow at work keeps horsing around.*

horsefly /ˈhɔːrsˌflaɪ/ *n* [C] any of various large, flying insects that bite

horseplay /ˈhɔːrˌspleɪ/ *n* [U] noisy, physically active behavior, esp. when people push each other as a joke • *No running or horseplay in the halls.*

horsepower /ˈhɔːrˌspaʊ·ər/ *n* [C/U] *pl* **horsepower** a unit for measuring the power of an engine • *a 170-horsepower engine* [C]

horseradish /ˈhɔːrsˌræd·ɪʃ/ *n* [U] a plant with a long, white root that has a strong taste

horticulture /ˈhɔːrt̬·əˌkʌl·tʃər/ *n* [U] the study or activity of growing plants, esp. for decoration

hose PIPE /hoʊz/ *n* [C] a long, usually plastic or rubber pipe that can be bent and is used to move water or other substances • *a fire hose* ○ *a garden hose* ○ *a radiator hose*

hose /hoʊz/ *v* [T/M] to clean (something) with water from a hose • *They have to hose down the streets.* [M]

hose CLOTHING /hoʊz/, **hosiery** /ˈhoʊ·ʒə·ri, -zə-/ *pl n* STOCKINGS or PANTYHOSE

hoser /ˈhoʊ·zər/ *n* [C] *Cdn slang* a man, esp. one who works at a job that uses physical rather than mental skills and whose habits are slightly offensive but amusing • *You hoser—leave some beer for the rest of us!*

hospice /ˈhɑs·pəs/ *n* [C] a place or an organization that provides care for people who are dying

hospitable /hɑsˈpɪt̬·ə·bəl/ *adj* friendly and welcoming to guests or visitors • *a hospitable host* ○ *She retired to a more hospitable climate* (= a more comfortable place).

hospital /ˈhɑsˌpɪt̬·əl/ *n* [C/U] a place where people who are very sick or injured are treated by doctors and nurses • *She spent a week in the hospital last year.* [U]

hospitalize /ˈhɑsˌpɪt̬·əlˌaɪz/ *v* [T] to take (someone) to stay in a hospital because of illness or injury • *Did he have to be hospitalized?*

hospitalization /ˌhɑsˌpɪt̬·əl·əˈzeɪ·ʃən/ *n* [U]

hospitality /ˌhɑs·pəˈtæl·ət̬·i/ *n* [U] kindness and friendly behavior, esp. to guests • *Thank you for your hospitality.*

host PARTY ORGANIZER /hoʊst/, *female* **hostess** /ˈhoʊ·stəs/ *n* [C] someone who gives a party or has guests • *Lucy was a gracious host.* ○ *Vancouver played host to the conference* (= the event happened there).

host /hoʊst/ *v* [T] • *Which country is hosting the next Olympics?*

host BROADCASTER /hoʊst/, *female* **hostess** /ˈhoʊ·stəs/ *n* [C] a person who introduces guests and performers on television or radio • *a talk-show host*

host PLANT / ANIMAL /hoʊst/ *n* [C] a plant or animal that another plant or animal lives on as a PARASITE

host LARGE NUMBER /hoʊst/ *n* [C usually sing] a large number • *They cared for wounded soldiers and performed a host of other duties.*

hostage /ˈhɑs·tɪdʒ/ *n* [C] someone who is made a prisoner in order to force other people to do something • *Inmates at the jail held 12 hostages and demanded to meet the governor.*

hostel /ˈhɑs·t̬əl/ *n* [C] a large house where people can stay free or cheaply • *a youth hostel*

hostile UNFRIENDLY /ˈhɑs·t̬əl, -taɪl/ *adj* showing strong dislike; unfriendly • *Her parents were openly hostile to me.*

hostility /hɑˈstɪl·ət̬·i/ *n* [U] • *He tried to hide his hostility.*

hostile DIFFICULT /ˈhɑs·t̬əl, -taɪl/ *adj* difficult or not suitable for living or growing • *The Nevada desert is one of the most hostile regions in America.*

hostile WARLIKE /ˈhɑs·t̬əl, -taɪl/ *adj* [not gradable] connected with an enemy or an act of war • *The enemy was preparing to take hostile action.*

hostilities /hɑˈstɪl·ət̬·iz/ *pl n fml* • *Both sides were trying to avoid further hostilities.*

hot VERY WARM /hɑt/ *adj* [-er/-est only] **-tt-** having a high temperature • *a hot day* ○ *a hot meal* ○ *It's hotter in Ohio than it is here.* • If you are **in hot water** or you get **into hot water**, you are in a difficult situation and in danger of being punished: *Making this complaint could get you into hot water.* • (*infml*) **Hot air** is speech that does not really mean anything or is not sincere: *His promises turned out to be a lot of hot air.* • A **hot-air balloon** is an aircraft consisting of a very large bag filled with heated air, with a container hanging under it in which people can ride. • A **hot cake** is a PANCAKE. • *Matt makes his little sister* **hot chocolate** (= a warm drink made with chocolate). • If a woman has a **hot flash**, she suddenly feels hot and uncomfortable because of the effects of MENOPAUSE (= the time when she stops being able to have children). • A **hotplate** is a small, movable, electric device on which food is cooked. • (*infml*) A **hot potato** is a situation or subject that people disagree strongly about

and that no one wants to deal with: *The issue became a political hot potato.* • A **hot tub** is a large container full of heated water in which more than one person can sit. • A **hot water bottle** is a rubber container that you fill with hot water and use to warm a bed or part of your body. • *We put in a new* **hot-water heater** (= device to make water in a building hot).

hot SPICY /hɑt/ *adj* [-er/-est only] **-tt-** (of food) causing a feeling in the mouth like burning or TINGLING (= as if a lot of sharp points are being put in quickly and lightly) • *If you like curry really hot, you can add some hot peppers and hot sauce.*

hot CLOSE /hɑt/ *adj* [-er/-est only] **-tt-** close • *He drove off, with the police* **in hot pursuit** (= following closely behind).

hot ANGRY /hɑt/ *adj* [-er/-est only] **-tt-** easily excited, or angry • *She's hot-tempered.* ○ *I got really hot about them not recycling.*

hotly /ˈhɑt·li/ *adv* • *She hotly denied having taken the money.* ○ *The race for district leader was hotly contested* (= the competition was strong).

hot GOOD /hɑt/ *adj* [-er/-est only] **-tt-** *infml* very good and having energy • *Right now the stock market is hot.* ○ *The show isn't so hot.* ○ *He doesn't feel so hot.* • A **hot spot** is a place that is popular: *This summer's vacation hot spot is Alaska.*

hot STOLEN /hɑt/ *adj* [not gradable] *slang* (of goods) stolen and therefore difficult to sell • *Those CD players are so cheap, they must be hot.*

hot DANGEROUS /hɑt/ *adj* [-er/-est only] **-tt-** *infml* (of a situation) risky • *Things got a lot hotter when the military took over.* • A **hot spot** is a place where war or other fighting is likely to happen: *She sees the Middle East as a real hot spot.*

hot SEXY /hɑt/ *adj* [-er/-est only] **-tt-** *slang* sexually attractive, or sexually excited • *I think she's the hottest actress around.* ○ *You get me so hot.*

hotbed /ˈhɑt·bed/ *n* [C] a place or situation where a lot of a particular activity is happening or might happen • *Seattle is a hotbed of software publishing.*

hot dog /ˈhɑt·dɔːɡ/ *n* [C] a long, cooked SAUSAGE (= tube-shaped meat), usually eaten after being put in a small bread loaf that has been cut lengthwise • *a hot dog with mustard*

hotel /hoʊˈtel/ *n* [C] a building where you pay to have a room to sleep in • *a luxury hotel*

hotfoot /ˈhɑt·fʊt/ *v infml* • If you **hotfoot it** somewhere, you go there quickly: *You should hotfoot it down to your video store and rent this movie.*

hothead /ˈhɑt·hed/ *n* [C] *disapproving* someone who gets angry too quickly and reacts without thinking carefully first

hotheaded /ˈhɑt·hed·əd/ *adj disapproving* • *a hotheaded young fool*

hotline /'hɑt·laɪn/ n [C] a special telephone number for emergencies or for a particular service • *a hotline for complaints*

hotshot /'hɑt·ʃɑt/ n [C] someone who is skillful and successful at something • *He's a hotshot lawyer from New York.*

hot–wire /'hɑt·wɑɪr/ v [T] *slang* to start (a car engine) without using the key, esp. in order to steal the car

hound /haʊnd/ v [T] to chase (someone) or refuse to leave them alone, esp. because you want to get something from them • *Socialists were hounded by the FBI in the 1950s.*

hound (dog) /'haʊnd (dɔːg)/ n [C] any of several types of dog used for hunting

hour /aʊr/ n [C] a period of 60 minutes • *Take this an hour after eating.* ○ *It's open 24 hours a day.* ○ *He works long hours* (= starts work early and finishes late). • An hour can be a period of time, not necessarily 60 minutes, when you do something: *a lunch hour* • An hour can be the distance you can travel in 60 minutes: *San Francisco is only a couple of hours away.* • *He gets paid* **by the hour** (= for each hour worked). • (*infml*) **Hours (and hours)** means a long time: *I spent hours filling out forms.* • **Hour after hour** or **hour upon hour** mean for a long time: *The dog just sits there hour after hour and watches these hamsters.* • *Buses pull out every hour* **on the hour** (= at the time an hour begins). • An **hourglass** is a glass container filled with sand that moves from an upper to a lower part through a narrow opening in the middle in one hour.

hourglass

hourly /'aʊr·li/ adj [not gradable] • *hourly pay* (= pay for every hour worked) ○ *hourly bus service* (= service once an hour)

hourly /'aʊr·li/ adv [not gradable] • *Tours are offered hourly* (= once an hour).

house [HOME] /haʊs/ n [C] pl **houses** /'haʊ·zəz, -səz/ a building in which people, usually one family, live • *to buy/rent a house* ○ *a brick/clapboard house* ○ *my/your/grandma's house* • A house can also be a building where animals are kept: *a dog house* • A **house** (also **household**) can be all the people living in a house: *Try not to wake the whole house when you come in!* • **House arrest** is the legal act of forcing someone to stay in their home instead of a prison: *Kitty's father was placed under house arrest.* • A **houseboat** is a boat that people can use as their home. • *Ever since the accident she's been* **housebound** (= unable to leave home). • If a pet, esp. a dog, is **housebroken**, it has been taught to go outside to excrete waste matter. • A **housefly** is a small, common **FLY** (= type of insect) often found in houses. • A **housekeeper** is a person, usually a woman, whose job is to take care of another

person's house, esp. by cleaning for them: *She does some light* **housekeeping** (= cleaning) *for us.* • If you **house-sit**, or are a **house-sitter**, you stay in someone's house while they are away in order to keep it safe. • A **housewarming (party)** is a party that you give when you move into a new home. • A **housewife** is a woman whose work is cleaning, cooking, and taking care of her children at home. • **Housework** is the work of keeping a house clean and neat.

house /haʊz/ v [T] • *Homeless families have been housed* (= given a place to live) *in motels.* ○ *The building houses the library* (= gives it space).

housing /'haʊ·zɪŋ/ n [U] buildings that people live in, or the providing of places for people to live • *affordable/expensive housing* • A **housing project** (also **project** or **the projects**) is a group of houses or apartments, usually provided by the government for families who have very low incomes.

house [BUSINESS] /haʊs/ n [C] pl **houses** /'haʊ·zəz, -səz/ a business or organization • *a publishing/fashion house* • A house can also be a building or part of a building which is used by an organization: *the Metropolitan Opera House* • If you have something **on the house**, it is given to you free by a business, esp. a bar or restaurant: *Drinks are on the house!*

house [POLITICS] /haʊs/ n [C] pl **houses** /'haʊ·zəz, -səz/ an organization that makes laws, or its meeting place • In the Congress of the United States, the lower house is the **House of Representatives** (*infml* **the House**) and the upper house is the SENATE. • In Canada, the **House of Commons** (*infml* **Commons**) makes laws, and the SENATE advises.

house [THEATER] /haʊs/ n [C] pl **houses** /'haʊ·zəz, -səz/ the seats in a theater, or the people watching a performance • *The opera played to a full/empty house.*

household /'haʊs·hoʊld/ n [C] a group of people, often a family, who live together • *She became part of his household.* • A **household name/word** is a famous person or organization: *Overnight, his name was a household word.*

housewares /'haʊs·wɛrz, -swɛrz/ pl n equipment esp. for the kitchen that is sold in a store

hovel /'hʌv·əl, 'hɑv-/ n [C] a small home, esp. one that is dirty and in bad condition • *Their house was little more than a hovel.*

hover /'hʌv·ər, 'hɑv-/ v [I] to stay in the air in one place • *A helicopter hovered overhead.* • If a person hovers, they stand near someone, waiting for attention: *She hovered outside her boss's door.*

how /haʊ/ adv [not gradable] in what way or state, to what amount or degree, or for what reason • *How do we get to the interstate highway from here?* ○ *How did you hear about the concert?* ○ *How is your mother?* ○ *How did you* *like the movie? ○ How much does this cost? ○ How old is his daughter? ○ She didn't say how far it is to her house. ○ How long are you going to be at the gym?* • How is sometimes used for emphasis: *How nice to see you!* • **How are you?** is used as a greeting: *"Hi, how are you?" "Fine, thanks, how are you?"* • **How are things?/How's everything?/How's it going?** are informal greetings. • *(infml)* **How come** *you got invited and I didn't* (= Why did that happen)? • People say **how dare you** when they are shocked by someone's behavior: *How dare you show up at my wedding?* • **How do you do?** is a formal greeting: *"I'm Jack Stewart." "How do you do, I'm Angela Black."* • *(infml)* How is used for making suggestions: **How about** *going* (= Would you like to go) *for a drink after work?* • LP GREETINGS

how /haʊ/ *conjunction* the way or condition in which • *Do you know how this machine works? ○ Roz doesn't know how to ride a bicycle.* [+ *to* infinitive] ○ *I was horrified to hear about how she had been treated.*

howdy /'haʊd·i/ *exclamation infml* used as a greeting; HELLO • *Howdy, folks! When did you all get here?*

however DEGREE /haʊ'ev·ər/ *adv* [not gradable] to whatever amount or degree • *However fast we drive, we're not going to get there in time. ○ If Emma likes something she'll buy it, however much it costs.*

however WAY /haʊ'ev·ər/ *adv* [not gradable] in whatever way • *However you look at it, it's still a mess.*

however /haʊ'ev·ər/ *conjunction* • *You can do it however you like, it really doesn't matter.*

however DESPITE /haʊ'ev·ər/ *adv* [not gradable] despite this; NEVERTHELESS • *There may, however, be other reasons that we don't know about.*

howl /haʊl/ *v* [I] to make a long, high, crying sound, like that of a dog • *I kicked Toby as hard as I could in the shins, and he howled in pain. ○ The wind howled. ○ (fig.) Sarah kept howling* (= loudly complaining) *that she could wait no longer, the baby was coming.* [+ *that* clause]

howl /haʊl/ *n* [C] • *(fig.)* A howl of a person or a group can mean a complaint that is strongly expressed: *The loudest howl seemed to come from farmers in the Midwest.*

hr. *n* [C] *abbreviation for* HOUR

HTML *n* [U] *abbreviation for* hypertext markup language (= a way of marking text for display on computers)

hub /hʌb/ *n* [C] the central part of something, esp. of a wheel, or a center of activity • *Chicago is a major transportation hub, with the busiest airport in the US.* • A **hubcap** is a round cover that fits over the center of the outside of a car's wheel to hide the BOLTS (= screwlike parts) that hold the wheel in place.

hubbub /'hʌb·ʌb/ *n* [U] a mixture of contin-

uing noises producing a feeling of busy activity or confused excitement • *There is always quite a hubbub in the hallways between class periods when students are moving from one room to another.*

huckleberry /'hʌk·əl,ber·i/ *n* [C] a small, round, dark blue fruit, or the low North American bush on which it grows

huckster /'hʌk·stər/ *n* [C] *disapproving* a person who sells things or puts forward ideas in a very determined way that is often not completely honest

huddle /'hʌd·əl/ *v* [I always + adv/prep] to come close together in a group, or to hold your arms and legs close to your body, esp. because of cold or fear • *Everyone huddled around the fire to keep warm.*

huddle /'hʌd·əl/ *n* [C] • *The football players formed a huddle.*

hue /hjuː/ *n* [C] a color, or the particular degree of lightness or darkness of a color • *In the waters of the Caribbean there are fish of every hue.*

huff BREATHE /hʌf/ *v* [I] to breathe loudly, esp. after physical exercise • *He huffed and puffed going up the stairs.*

huff ANGER /hʌf/ *n* [C] • To be **in a huff** is to be angry and upset: *When Julia criticized his art, Giraldo left in a huff.*

hug /hʌg/ *v* [I/T] -gg- to hold (someone or something) close to your body with your arms, esp. to show affection • *Maria hugged her dog.* [T] ○ *As the verdict of not guilty was announced, he leaped up and hugged his lawyer.* [T] ○ *(fig.) Some fish hug* (= stay close to) *the bottom of the lake.* [T]

hug /hʌg/ *n* [C] • *My little boy always gets a kiss and a hug before he goes to bed.*

huge /hjuːdʒ, juːdʒ/ *adj* [-er/-est only] extremely large in size or amount • *a huge forest ○ a huge parking lot ○ They made huge profits in real estate.*

hugely /'hjuːdʒ·li, 'juːdʒ-/ *adv* • *Their business has been hugely successful.* • LP VERY, COMPLETELY, AND OTHER INTENSIFIERS

huh /hʌ̃, hə̃m/ *exclamation* said to show that you have not heard or understood something, or used at the end of a statement to question it • *"Huh? What did you say?" ○ "You called right in middle of dinner." "Great timing, huh?"*

hulk BROKEN THING /hʌlk/ *n* [C] the body of an old ship, car, or large piece of equipment, which is broken and no longer used • *The rusted hulk of an abandoned car sat at the side of the road.*

hulk LARGE PERSON /hʌlk/ *n* [C] a large, heavy person or thing • *He was a huge hulk of a man, about six and a half feet tall.*

hull SHIP /hʌl/ *n* [C] the body or frame of a ship, most of which lies under the water

hull PLANT COVERING /hʌl/ *n* [C] the outer covering of a seed or fruit, such as the shell of a nut

hullabaloo /ˌhʌl·ə·bəˈluː/ *n* [C] *pl* **hullaba-loos** *infml* a loud noise made by people, often because they are angry, or a situation in which many people are angry or upset • *They finally stopped production of the play because of all the hullabaloo it caused.*

hum /hʌm/ *v* [I/T] -**mm**- to make a continuous, low sound, or to sing (a tune) with closed lips • *Debbie always hums to herself when she listens to music.* [I] ○ *I've forgotten how that tune goes—could you hum it for me?* [T] • (*fig.*) If something is humming, it is very busy and full of activity: *Factories that make paper products are humming at 97% of capacity.* [I]

hum /hʌm/ *n* [C usually sing] • *We could hear the constant hum of traffic outside the window.*

human /ˈhjuː·mən, ˈjuː-/ *adj* of or typical of people • *the human body* ○ *Of course I make mistakes, I'm only human* (= not perfect). ○ *The accident was due to human error* (= a person's mistake). • **Human nature** is the behavior common to most people. • The **human race** is all people. • **Human resources** (also **personnel**) is the department within a company or organization that is responsible for its relationship with its employees, esp. new employees, and for following the laws dealing with employment. • **Human rights** are the basic rights to fair and moral treatment, esp. by government, that every person is believed to have.

human (being) /ˈhjuː·mən (ˈbiː·ɪŋ,, ˈjuː-/ *n* [C] a person

humanity /hjuːˈmæn·ət·i, juː-/ *n* [U] all people in the world as a whole, or the qualities characteristic of people • *The former general was put on trial for crimes against humanity.* • See also **humanity** at HUMANE.

humanize /ˈhjuː·məˌnɑɪz, ˈjuː-/ *v* [T] to make (someone or something) kinder, gentler, or more agreeable • *If people were just a little more courteous, it would humanize this city a lot.*

humanly /ˈhjuː·mən·li, ˈjuː-/ *adv* • *They did everything humanly possible to help her* (= They did everything they could).

humane /hjuːˈmeɪn, juː-/ *adj* showing kindness, care, and sympathy toward others, esp. those who are suffering • *She felt it was more humane to kill the injured animal quickly than to let it suffer.*

humanely /hjuːˈmeɪn·li, juː-/ *adv*

humanity /hjuːˈmæn·ət·i, juː-/ *n* [U] understanding and kindness toward other people • *He showed his humanity by giving generously to charities.* • See also **humanity** at HUMAN.

humanism /ˈhjuː·məˌnɪz·əm, ˈjuː-/ *n* [U] a system of thought and reasoning based on human values and interests, often without accepting the beliefs of religion

humanitarian /hjuːˌmæn·əˈter·iː·ən, juː-/ *adj*

involved in or connected with improving people's lives and reducing suffering • *humanitarian aid in the form of food supplies*

humanitarian /hjuːˌmæn·əˈter·iː·ən, juː-/ *n* [C] • *She was regarded by many as a compassionate humanitarian.*

humanities /hjuːˈmæn·ət·iz, juː-/ *pl n* literature, language, history, PHILOSOPHY, and other subjects that are not sciences, or the study of these subjects

humankind /ˈhjuː·mənˌkɑɪnd, ˈjuː-/ *n* [U] the whole of the human race, including both men and women

humanly /ˈhjuː·mən·li, juː-/ *adv* • See at HUMAN.

humble NOT PROUD /ˈhʌm·bəl/ *adj* tending to consider yourself as having no special importance that makes you better than others; not proud • *He's a humble man and he's not comfortable talking about his own achievements.*

humble /ˈhʌm·bəl/ *v* [T] • *Seeing the courage and skill of the disabled athletes was a humbling experience.*

humbly /ˈhʌm·bli/ *adv* • *I humbly ask your pardon.*

humble LOW IN RANK /ˈhʌm·bəl/ *adj* low in rank or position; poor • *She rose from humble origins to become one of the best-known political writers in the world.*

humbly /ˈhʌm·bli/ *adv* • *They live humbly* (= simply).

humdrum /ˈhʌm·drʌm/ *adj* lacking excitement and interest; ordinary • *We lead such a humdrum life/existence.*

humid /ˈhjuː·məd, juː-/ *adj* (of air and weather) containing extremely small drops of water in the air • *New York is very hot and humid in the summer.*

humidify /hjuːˈmɪd·əˌfɑɪ, juː-/ *v* [T] to make (air) wetter • *The doctor says we need to humidify the air in the baby's room because it's too dry.*

humidifier /hjuːˈmɪd·əˌfɑɪ·ər, juː-/ *n* [C] a machine that adds water to the air

humidity /hjuːˈmɪd·ət·i, juː-/ *n* [U] a measure of how wet the air is • *Tomorrow will be hot, with high humidity.*

humiliate /hjuːˈmɪl·iːˌeɪt, juː-/ *v* [T] to make (someone) feel ashamed or lose their respect for themselves • *They called him an old fool in public just to humiliate him.*

humiliating /hjuːˈmɪl·iːˌeɪt·ɪŋ, juː-/ *adj* • *It was humiliating to see all my possessions piled on the street.* [+ to infinitive]

humiliation /hjuːˌmɪl·iːˈeɪ·ʃən, juː-/ *n* [C/U] • *the humiliation of defeat* [U]

humility /hjuːˈmɪl·ət·i, juː-/ *n* [U] the feeling or attitude that you have no special importance that makes you better than others; lack of pride • *Grandma was a religious woman of deep humility.*

hummed /hʌmd/ *past simple and past participle of* HUM

humming /'hʌm·ɪŋ/ *present participle of* HUM

hummingbird /'hʌm·ɪŋ͵bɜrd/ *n* [C] a very small, brightly colored bird with a long beak that it uses to drink NECTAR (= sweet liquid) from flowers

humongous /hju:'mʌŋ·gəs, ju:-/ *adj infml* very large • *We had our picture taken in New Mexico before a humongous cactus.*

humor AMUSEMENT /'hju:·mər, 'ju:-/ *n* [U] the ability to be amused by something seen, heard, or thought about, sometimes causing you to smile or laugh, or the quality in something that causes such amusement • *He has a wonderful sense of humor.* ○ *Fortunately, she saw the humor in the situation.*

humorist /'hju:·mə·rəst, 'ju:-/ *n* [C] a person who regularly writes or tells amusing stories, esp. as part of their job

humorous /'hju:·mə·rəs, 'ju:-/ *adj* • *Mark Twain was known for his humorous short sketches.*

humorously /'hju:·mə·rə·sli, 'ju:-/ *adv*

humorless /'hju:·mər·ləs, 'ju:-/ *adj* unable to see humor in things when most others do • *His father was humorless, embittered man.*

humor AGREE WITH /'hju:·mər, 'ju:-/ *v* [T] to agree to (someone's wishes) in order to help their mood improve or to avoid upsetting them • *Phil seems a bit cranky today, so just humor him.*

hump /hʌmp/ *n* [C] a large, round, raised lump or part • *The car swerved when it hit a hump in the road.* • A hump is also a round, raised part on a person's or animal's back: *a camel's hump*

hunch IDEA /hʌntʃ/ *n* [C] an idea that is based on feeling and for which there is no proof • *I had a hunch that you'd be here.* [+ *that* clause]

hunch BEND /hʌntʃ/ *v* [I/T] to lean forward with your shoulders raised or to bend (your back and shoulders) into a rounded shape • *We gathered in a circle and hunched over the fire to get warm.* [I]

hunchback /'hʌntʃ·bæk/ *n* [C] a person who has a back with a large, round lump on it and therefore looks as if they are bent over

hundred /'hʌn·drəd/ *number* 100 • *We've driven a/one hundred miles in the last two hours.* ○ *This area of the coast is home to hundreds of bird species.* • **A/one hundred percent** means completely: *I agree with you a hundred percent.* • LP NUMBERS

hundredth /'hʌn·drətθ/ *adj, adv* [not gradable], *n* [C] • *She reached her hundredth birthday.* • A hundredth is one of a hundred equal parts of something. [C]

hung /hʌŋ/ *past simple and past participle of* HANG

hunger FOOD /'hʌŋ·gər/ *n* [U] the uncomfortable or painful feeling in your stomach caused by the need for or lack of food • *Mother Teresa devoted her life to fighting hunger in the poorest parts of the world.* • A **hunger strike** is a refusal to eat by someone, usually to show opposition to a policy or program of a government or authority.

hunger DESIRE /'hʌŋ·gər/ *n* [U] a strong wish or desire • *a hunger for adventure/power*

hunger /'hʌŋ·gər/ *v* [I always + adv/prep] • *She had always hungered for a starring role in a musical.*

hungry NEEDING FOOD /'hʌŋ·gri/ *adj* feeling the need to eat because there has been a period of time when you have not eaten • *The children are always hungry when they get home from school.* ○ *They were poor and often went to bed hungry* (= did not get enough to eat at night).

hungry EAGER /'hʌŋ·gri/ *adj* having a strong desire; eager • *Kim is so hungry for success that she'll do anything to achieve it.*

hung up /hʌŋ'ʌp/ *adj infml* feeling unreasonably anxious, esp. about yourself • *Don't be so hung up about your weight—you look fine.*

hunk PIECE /hʌŋk/ *n* [C] a large, thick piece, esp. of food • *a hunk of bread/cheese/meat*

hunk MAN /hʌŋk/ *n* [C] *slang* a large, strong man, esp. one who is attractive • *Who was that gorgeous hunk you were with last night?*

hunker down /'hʌŋ·kər/ *v adv* [I] to sit with your knees bent in front of you so that your buttocks are almost resting on your heels • *We hunkered down near the campfire.* • To hunker down is also to be prepared to stay in a particular place or situation for as long as necessary, esp. for protection or to achieve something: *We hunkered down in the cellar while the storm raged outside.* ○ *Members of Congress were hunkered down for weeks of debate on the health-care issue.*

hunky–dory /͵hʌŋ·kiːˈdɔːr·i, -'dour·i/ *adj infml* (esp. of a situation) satisfactory and pleasant • *You can't lose your temper with everyone like that and then expect everything to be hunky-dory.*

hunt CHASE /hʌnt/ *v* [I/T] to chase or search for (a wild animal or bird) with the intention of killing or catching it for food, sport, or profit • *He hunts every weekend.* [I] ○ *Cats like to hunt mice and birds.* [T]

hunt /hʌnt/ *n* [C] • *a deer hunt*

hunter /'hʌnt·ər/ *n* [C] a person or animal that hunts animals for food or sport

hunting /'hʌnt·ɪŋ/ *n* [U] • *My father and I both enjoy hunting.*

hunt SEARCH /hʌnt/ *v* [I/T] to search for (something or someone) • *I've hunted everywhere for the missing keys.* [I] • If the police **hunt** someone **down**, they find them after much searching: *Detectives have finally managed to hunt down the killer.*

hunt /hʌnt/ *n* [C] • *The hunt for the injured climber continued through the night.*

–hunting /͵hʌnt·ɪŋ/ *combining form* • *job-hunting* ○ *house-hunting* ○ *a book-hunting expedition*

hurdle /ˈhɜrd·ᵊl/ n [C] a frame for jumping over in a race • A hurdle is also a difficulty to be dealt with: *There are a lot of hurdles to overcome before the contract can be signed.*

hurdle /ˈhɜrd·ᵊl/ v [I/T] • *The boys hurdled the fence* (= jumped over it). [T]

hurdler /ˈhɜrd·lər, -ᵊl·ər/ n [C] a competitor in a race over a series of hurdles

hurl /ˈhɜrl/ v [T] to throw (something) forcefully • *Demonstrators hurled rocks at the troops.* ○ *He hurled* (= shouted) *racial obscenities at a black officer.*

hurrah, hoorah /həˈrɑ, -ˈrɔː/, **hooray** /hʊˈreɪ, hə-/ exclamation used to express excitement, pleasure, or approval • *Hurrah for American enterprise!*

hurricane /ˈhɜr·əˌkeɪn, ˈhʌ·rə-/ n [C] a violent storm with strong circular winds, esp. in the western Atlantic Ocean

hurry /ˈhɜr·i, ˈhʌ·ri/ v [I/T] to move or act quickly, or to cause (someone) to move or act quickly • *We have to hurry if we're going to make it there in time.* [I] ○ *I hurried the kids through their breakfasts.* [T] • **Hurry up** and **hurry it up** mean do something more quickly: *Hurry up, or we'll miss the bus!* ○ *He wished that Lily would hurry it up.*

hurry /ˈhɜr·i, ˈhʌ·ri/ n [U] • *We've got plenty of time—what's the hurry* (= Why hurry)*?* • *He's* **in a hurry** *to get to a meeting* (= anxious to get there quickly). • *I'm* **in no hurry/not in any hurry** *for the book—keep it as long as you want.*

hurried /ˈhɜr·id, ˈhʌ·rid/ adj [not gradable] done quickly • *We left early, after a hurried breakfast.*

hurriedly /ˈhɜr·əd·li, ˈhʌ·rəd-/ adv • *The man hurriedly walked away.*

hurt /ˈhɜrt/ v [I/T] *past* **hurt** to feel pain, or to cause pain or injury to (yourself or someone else) • *Tell me where it hurts.* [I] ○ *My leg hurts.* [I] ○ *Stop! You're hurting me!* [T] ○ *Emilio hurt his back when he fell off a ladder.* [T] • To hurt also means to cause harm or difficulty: *A lot of businesses are being hurt by high interest rates.* [T] ○ *His lack of experience may hurt his chances of getting the job.* [T] • To hurt someone can also mean to upset them or make them unhappy: *I didn't mean to* **hurt** *your* **feelings.** [T] • *It* **won't/wouldn't hurt** *you* **to** *do the ironing for once* (= You should do it).

hurt /ˈhɜrt/ adj [not gradable] feeling pain or being upset • *I saw you fall—are you hurt?* ○ *Naomi was hurt by your criticism.*

hurt /ˈhɜrt/ n [U] *esp. literary* emotional pain • *It's a hurt that he has tried all his life to heal.*

hurtful /ˈhɜrt·fəl/ adj [not gradable] causing emotional pain • *a hurtful remark*

hurtle /ˈhɜrt̬·ᵊl/ v [I always + adv/prep] to move very fast, esp. in what seems a dangerous way • *The truck hurtled along at breakneck speed.*

husband /ˈhʌz·bənd/ n [C] the man to whom a woman is married; a married man • Compare WIFE. PIC FAMILY TREE

hush /ˈhʌʃ/ n [U] quiet or silence, esp. after noise • *A hush fell over the crowd.* • (*infml*) If something is **hush-hush**, it is secret: *I can't tell you anything about it—it's all hush-hush.*

hush /ˈhʌʃ/ exclamation • *Hush! You'll wake the baby!*

hushed /ˈhʌʃt/ adj [not gradable] • *hushed tones/voices*

hush up obj, **hush** obj **up** /ˈ-ˈ-/ v adv [M] to prevent (something) from becoming known • *The mayor tried to hush up the fact that he had been in prison.*

husk /ˈhʌsk/ n [C] the dry, outer covering of some fruits and seeds • *corn husks*

husky VOICE /ˈhʌs·ki/ adj (esp. of a person's voice) low and sounding slightly damaged • *The singer had a husky voice.*

husky STRONG /ˈhʌs·ki/ adj (esp. of boys or men) big and strong • *Rennett was a husky, broad-shouldered kid.*

husky DOG /ˈhʌs·ki/ n [C] a type of dog that is strong and furry and is used for pulling SLEDS in cold regions of the world

hustle ACT QUICKLY /ˈhʌs·əl/ v [I] to act quickly and with energy • *If we really hustle, we can finish the job by lunchtime.*

hustle /ˈhʌs·əl/ n [U] energetic action • *The team showed a lot of determination and hustle.* • *They love the* **hustle and bustle** *of the city* (= its energy and excitement).

hustle PUSH /ˈhʌs·əl/ v [T always + adv/prep] to push or force (someone) along • *The demonstrators were hustled out of the hall.*

hustle SELL /ˈhʌs·əl/ v [T] *infml* to sell (something unwanted) to someone, or to cheat or deceive (someone), esp. in order to get money from them • *On weekends they hustle tourists on the waterfront.*

hustle /ˈhʌs·əl/ n [C] *infml* a dishonest way of making money • *Advertising turns every achievement into a hustle.*

hustler /ˈhʌs·lər/ n [C] someone who tries to obtain esp. money by dishonest or illegal methods

hut /ˈhʌt/ n [C] a small, simple house or shelter • *a thatched hut*

hutch CAGE /ˈhʌtʃ/ n [C] a cage or box to keep small animals in

hutch CABINET /ˈhʌtʃ/ n [C] a cabinet with doors or drawers on the bottom and usually open shelves on the top

hyacinth /ˈhaɪ·əˌsɪnθ/ n [C] a pleasant-smelling plant with a lot of small flowers growing closely around a thick stem

hybrid /ˈhaɪ·brɪd/ n [C] a plant or animal that has been produced from two different types of plant or animal • A hybrid is also anything that is a mixture of two or more things: *The architecture is a hybrid of classical and modern styles.*

hydrant /ˈhaɪ·drənt/ n [C] *short form of* **fire**

hydrant, see at FIRE FLAMES • PIC⟩ FIRE HYDRANT

hydraulic /haɪˈdrɔː·lɪk/ *adj* [not gradable] (of a device) operated by water pressure or by pressure from another liquid • *The plane's hydraulic systems can withstand incredibly high temperatures.*

hydroelectric /ˌhaɪ·droʊ·ɪˈlek·trɪk/ *adj* [not gradable] of or related to electricity produced from the energy of fast-moving water • *a hydroelectric power plant*

hydrogen /ˈhaɪ·drə·dʒən/ *n* [U] the lightest gas, one of the chemical elements, and having no color, taste, or smell • A **hydrogen bomb** (also **H-bomb**) is a type of nuclear bomb. • **Hydrogen peroxide** is a liquid chemical used to kill bacteria or to make hair lighter in color.

hyena /haɪˈiː·nə/ *n* [C] a wild animal of Africa and Asia that looks like a dog and makes a laughing sound

hygiene /ˈhaɪ·dʒiːn/ *n* [U] the practice or principles of keeping yourself and your environment clean in order to maintain health and prevent disease • *He doesn't care much about personal hygiene.*

hygienic /haɪˈdʒiː·nɪk, -ˈdʒen·ɪk/ *adj* [not gradable] clean and unlikely to cause disease

hymn /hɪm/ *n* [C] a song of praise, esp. to God

hymnal /ˈhɪm·nəl/, **hymnbook** /ˈhɪm·bʊk/ *n* [C] a book of hymns

hype /haɪp/ *n* [U] *infml* information that makes something seem very important or exciting • *The big-name, big-money New York art world is full of hype.*

hype (up) *obj*, **hype** *obj* **(up)** /ˈhaɪp (ˈʌp)/ *v* [T/M] *infml* to make (something) seem more exciting or important than it is • *No sports event is more hyped than the Super Bowl.* [T]

hyped (up) /haɪpt, ˈhaɪpˈtʌp/ *adj infml* emotionally excited, nervous, or anxious • *I was really hyped up on my new car, so it was disappointing when I had to keep bringing it in for repairs.*

hyper– TOO MUCH /ˌhaɪ·pər/ *combining form* having a lot or too much of the stated quality • *hypercritical* ○ *hyperintelligent*

hyper EXCITABLE /ˈhaɪ·pər/ *adj infml* extremely excited or nervous • *I was so hyper it took me over an hour to get to sleep.*

hyperactive /ˌhaɪ·pəˈræk·tɪv/ *adj* [not gradable] (esp. of children) extremely or unusually active • *She wanted to keep her hyperactive son busy.*

hyperbole /haɪˈpɜr·bə·li/ *n* [U] a way of speaking or writing that makes someone or something sound much bigger, better, smaller, worse, more unusual, etc., than they are • *Although he's not given to hyperbole, Ron says we are light-years ahead of our time.*

hypersensitive /ˌhaɪ·pərˈsen·sət·ɪv/ *adj* [not gradable] very easily changed or damaged by

physical conditions, or easily upset • *He's hypersensitive about his height.*

hypertension /ˌhaɪ·pərˈten·tʃən/ *n* [U] *medical* unusually high blood pressure

hyperventilate /ˌhaɪ·pərˈvent·ᵊl,eɪt/ *v* [I] to breathe too quickly, causing too much oxygen to enter the blood

hyphen /ˈhaɪ·fən/ *n* [C] the mark (-) used in writing to join two words together, or between the syllables of a word when it is divided at the end of a line of text

hyphenate /ˈhaɪ·fə,neɪt/ *v* [T] • *She hyphenates her first name, Anne-Marie.*

HYPHEN [-]

A hyphen is used when a word has to be divided between two lines. A hyphen is also used to join together words to make a new combination. The following kinds of combinations are formed with the help of hyphens:

words that combine two or more different words

baby-sit
brother-in-law
do-it-yourselfer
government-funded
head-on
rent-free
well-being
well-known
X-ray

words made of a word and a prefix
Sometimes the hyphen is dropped.

post-Depression
pre-war (or prewar)
re-elect (or reelect)

compounds in which the words together mean a relationship rather than a single thing
Sometimes a short dash is used instead.

I need a decent French-English dictionary.
How much is a Caracas-New York City ticket?
The movie is about a father-son relationship.

numbers between 21 and 99 and fractions when they are written out

seventy-eight • *two-thirds* • *six and one-half*

to mean "to" in a range of numbers or dates
Sometimes a short dash is used instead.

There were 6-8 climbers on the team
The vacation period is June-August.

to separate groups of numbers
Our mailing zip code is 10011-4211.

---

hypnosis /hɪpˈnoʊ·səs/ *n* [U] an artificially produced state of mind similar to sleep in which a person can be influenced to say or do things

hypnotic /hɪpˈnɑt·ɪk/ *adj* [not gradable] relating to or causing hypnosis • *a hypnotic trance* ○ *the hypnotic rhythm of the waves*

hypnotize /ˈhɪp·nəˌtaɪz, -mə-/ v [T] to produce hypnosis in (someone), or to completely influence (someone) • *The crowd sits hypnotized by Harper's trumpet.*

hypnotism /ˈhɪp·nəˌtɪz·əm, -mə-/ n [U] the act of causing hypnosis

hypochondria /ˌhaɪ·pəˈkɑn·driː·ə/ n [U] unnecessary anxiety about and attention to your health

hypochondriac /ˌhaɪ·pəˈkɑn·driːˌæk/ n [C] • *Elderly hypochondriacs were generally complainers in their youth.*

hypocrisy /hɪˈpɑk·rə·si/ n [U] *disapproving* pretending to be what you are not, or pretending to believe something that you do not • *Critics are accusing him of hypocrisy and deceit.*

hypocrite /ˈhɪp·əˌkrɪt/ n [C] • *The biggest hypocrites in sports are owners who yell about players' salaries.*

hypocritical /ˌhɪp·əˈkrɪt̬·ɪ·kəl/ adj [not gradable] • *It's hypocritical for states that run the lottery to tell people they shouldn't open a gambling operation.*

hypodermic /ˌhaɪ·pəˈdɜr·mɪk/ adj [not gradable] (of medical tools) used to INJECT drugs under a person's skin • *a hypodermic needle/ syringe*

hypotenuse /haɪˈpɑt·ᵊnˌuːs, -ˌuːz/ n [C] specialized the longest side of a triangle that has one angle of 90°

hypothermia /ˌhaɪ·pəˈθɜr·miː·ə, -poʊ-/ n [U] *medical* a dangerous condition in which a person's body temperature is unusually low

hypothesis /haɪˈpɑθ·ə·səs/ n [C] pl **hypotheses** /haɪˈpɑθ·əˌsiːz/ an idea or explanation for something that is based on known facts but has not yet been proven • *Several hypotheses for global warming have been suggested.*

hypothetical /ˌhaɪ·pəˈθet̬·ɪ·kəl/ adj [not gradable] of or based on a HYPOTHESIS • *He dismissed the questions as purely hypothetical.*

hysterectomy /ˌhɪs·təˈrek·tə·mi/ n [C] a medical operation to remove part or all of a woman's uterus

hysteria /hɪˈster·iː·ə, hɪˈstɪr-/ n [U] excitement or emotion that is uncontrollable • *One woman, close to hysteria, grabbed my arm.*

hysterical /hɪˈster·ɪ·kəl/ adj • *Calm down, you're getting hysterical.* ○ *She broke into hysterical laughter* (= laughter that is not controlled). ○ (*infml*) *That joke was hysterical* (= extremely amusing).

hysterically /hɪˈster·ɪ·kli/ adv [not gradable] • *Gillian was laughing/crying hysterically.*

hysterics /hɪˈster·ɪks/ pl n a state of uncontrolled excitement or emotion • *I told her she couldn't have it and she went into hysterics.*

I, i

I LETTER , **i** /aɪ/ *n* [C] *pl* **I's** or **i's** the ninth letter of the English alphabet

I NUMBER , **i** /aɪ, wʌn/ *number* the ROMAN NUMERAL for the number 1

I PERSON /aɪ/ *pronoun* the person speaking • *I can see her car.*

ice FROZEN WATER /aɪs/ *n* [U] water that has frozen solid, or pieces of this • *Don't slip on the ice.* ○ *I'd like a ginger ale with no ice.* • An **ice-breaker** is a strong ship that can move through ice. • An **icebreaker** is also something such as a game, joke, or story that makes people who don't know each other feel more comfortable together. • *The water off the coast here is always ice-cold* (= extremely cold). • **Ice cream** is a sweet, frozen food made from milk and cream: *chocolate ice cream* ○ *Who wants an ice cream cone* (= a cone-shaped, edible container with ice cream in it)*?* • An **ice cube** is a small block of ice, esp. one put into a drink to make it cold. • **Ice hockey** is another name for HOCKEY. • **Ice water** is water that has been made very cold, esp. by putting ice in it.

iced /aɪst/, **ice** /aɪs/ *adj* [not gradable] (of drinks that are often drunk hot) very cold, or with ice added • *iced tea*

icy /'aɪ·si/ *adj* • *an icy sidewalk* (= covered with ice) ○ *icy winds* (= extremely cold winds) • See also ICY.

ice COVER CAKE /aɪs/ *v* [T] FROST COVER CAKE

iceberg /'aɪs·bɜrg/ *n* [C] a very large mass of ice that floats in the sea

ice skate /'aɪs·skeɪt/ *n* [C usually pl] a special shoe with a metal blade attached to the bottom that you wear to slide over ice • USAGE: PIC SKATES

ice–skate /'aɪs·skeɪt/ *v* [I] • *Vivian loves to ice-skate.*

ice skating /'aɪs·skeɪt̬·ɪŋ/ *n* [U]

icicle /'aɪ·sɪk·əl/ *n* [C] a pointed stick of ice that hangs down from something

icing /'aɪ·sɪŋ/, **frosting** *n* [U] the sweet, thick mixture of sugar, liquid, and flavoring that is used to cover cakes • *He was delighted to have his story published—getting paid for it was just icing on the cake* (= an unexpected additional good thing).

icky /'ɪk·i/ *adj a child's word for* unpleasant or disgusting • *Rory thinks peas are icky.*

icon REPRESENTATION /'aɪ·kɑn/ *n* [C] a famous person or thing that represents something of importance • *The US Capitol building is an American icon.*

icon COMPUTER SYMBOL /'aɪ·kɑn/ *n* [C] a picture on a computer screen that represents a program, **disk drive**, file, or instruction • *Click on the icon to open the program.*

icon HOLY PAINTING /'aɪ·kɑn/ *n* [C] (esp. in some

christian religions) a painting of Jesus Christ or of a holy person

icy /'aɪ·si/ *adj* unfriendly and showing dislike • *an icy stare* • See also **icy** at ICE.

I'd /aɪd/ *contraction of* **I had** or **I would** • *I'd* (= I had) *just got in the shower when the phone rang.* ○ *I'd* (= I would) *love to see you.*

ID /aɪˈdiː/ *n* [C/U] any official card or document with your name and other information on it that you use to prove who you are • *You need two pieces of ID to cash a check.* [U]

idea SUGGESTION /aɪˈdiː·ə/ *n* [C] a suggestion, thought, or plan • *"Let's go swimming." "Good idea!"* ○ *She's full of bright ideas.*

idea KNOWLEDGE /aɪˈdiː·ə/ *n* [C/U] knowledge or understanding about something • *Can you give me a rough idea of the cost* (= tell me approximately how much it will cost)*?* [C] ○ *You have no idea how hard it is to raise a child all by yourself.* [U]

idea BELIEF /aɪˈdiː·ə/ *n* [C] a belief about something • *They have some unusual ideas about parenting.*

idea PURPOSE /aɪˈdiː·ə/ *n* [C usually sing] a purpose or reason for doing something • *The idea behind the state lottery is to raise money for education.*

ideal PERFECT /aɪˈdiː·l/ *adj* [not gradable] perfect, or the best possible • *In an ideal world, no one would go hungry.*

ideal /aɪˈdiː·l/ *n* [U] • *She's my ideal of beauty* (= perfectly beautiful).

ideally /aɪˈdiː·li/ *adv* [not gradable] • *This job is ideally suited to her skills.*

idealize /aɪˈdiː·ə·laɪz/ *v* [T] to think of or represent (someone or something) as perfect • *Thoreau seemed to idealize the women close to him.*

ideal PRINCIPLE /aɪˈdiː·l/ *n* [C] a principle that sets a high standard for behavior • *I think most people share the same ideals and basic beliefs.*

idealism /aɪˈdiː·ə·lɪz·əm/ *n* [U] • *He wrote about America's lost idealism* (= belief in principles).

idealist /aɪˈdiː·l·əst/ *n* [C] a person who values principles above practical behavior

idealistic /aɪˌdiː·ə·ˈlɪs·tɪk/ *adj* • *She sacrificed idealistic dreams for conventional reality.*

identical /aɪˈdent·ɪ·kəl/ *adj* [not gradable] exactly the same, or very similar • *The test is identical to the one you took last year.* • **Identical twins** are two people who come from the same egg, are the same sex, and look extremely similar. Compare **fraternal twins** at FRATERNAL.

identically /aɪˈdent·ɪ·kli/ *adv* [not gradable] • *The two sisters dressed identically.*

identification /aɪˌdent·ə·fəˈkeɪ·ʃən/ *n* [U]

recognition of or the ability to name someone or something • *Identification of the victims of the plane crash still is not complete.* • Identification is also proof of who someone or something is, usually in the form of documents: *We were asked to show identification at the airport check-in.*

identify /aɪˈdent·ə‚faɪ/ *v* [T] to recognize or be able to name (someone or something), or to prove who or what (someone or something) is • *Small babies can identify their mothers.* ○ *The police officer refused to identify himself.* • If you **identify with** someone or something, you think you understand their feelings: *I don't identify with those beautiful, thin models in magazines.* • If someone is **identified with** something, it is connected with them in people's minds: *Jerry Lewis became closely identified with an annual TV fundraiser.*

identifiable /aɪ‚dent·ə'faɪ·ə·bəl/ *adj* • *In her bright yellow coat, she was easily identifiable* (= you could recognize her).

identity /aɪˈdent·ət·i/ *n* [C/U] who a person is, or the qualities of a person or group that make them different from others • *As a journalist she refuses to reveal the identity of her source.* [C] • An **identity crisis** is a feeling that you are not sure of who you are or what you should do.

ideology /‚aɪd·iˈɑl·ə·dʒi, ‚ɪd-/ *n* [C/U] a theory or set of beliefs, esp. one on which a political system, party, or organization is based

ideological /‚aɪd·iː·əˈlɑdʒ·ɪ·kəl, ‚ɪd-/ *adj* • *They voted along ideological lines.*

idiom /ˈɪd·iː·əm/ *n* [C] a group of words whose meaning considered as a unit is different from the meanings of each word considered separately • *Mastering the use of idioms can be hard for a learner.* ○ *"Shoot yourself in the foot" is an idiom that means to do something that hurts yourself.* • An idiom is also the particular style or manner of expression used by a person or group: *Curse words simply aren't a part of his idiom.* [C usually sing]

idiomatic /‚ɪd·iː·əˈmæt̬·ɪk/ *adj* • *an idiomatic expression* • (of speech or writing) Idiomatic also means natural in expression, correct without being too formal: *His English is fluent and idiomatic.*

idiosyncrasy /‚ɪd·iː·əˈsɪŋ·krə·si/ *n* [C] a strange or unusual habit, way of behaving, or feature • *One of her many idiosyncrasies is always smelling a book before opening it.*

idiot /ˈɪd·iː·ət/ *n* [C] a foolish person, esp. someone who has done something stupid • *I felt like an idiot.*

idiotic /‚ɪd·iːˈɑt̬·ɪk/ *adj* • *Whose idiotic idea was it to go camping?*

idle /ˈaɪd·əl/ *adj* not working, not active, or doing nothing • *idle factories* ○ *The machines are standing idle because there are no spare parts.* • Idle also means not useful or not based on fact: *idle speculation*

idle /ˈaɪd·əl/ *v* [I] • If an engine idles, it is operating but not doing any work: *Let the engine idle for a minute before you put the car in gear.* • If you **idle away** time, you spend it doing very little: *We idled away the hours playing cards.*

idleness /ˈaɪd·əl·nəs/ *n* [U]

idly /ˈaɪd·li, -əl·i/ *adv* • *I will not stand idly by while my business is being destroyed.*

idol /ˈaɪd·əl/ *n* [C] a person who is greatly loved, admired, or respected • *Basketball players are his idols.* • An idol is also an object or picture that is worshipped as a god.

idolize /ˈaɪd·əl‚aɪz/ *v* [T] • *Her young fans idolize her* (= admire her greatly).

i.e. *abbreviation for* id est (= Latin for "that is"), used esp. in writing after a general statement to introduce specific information or examples • *The hotel is closed during the off season, i.e., from October to March.*

if IN THAT SITUATION /ɪf/ *conjunction* used to say that a particular thing can or will happen when, only when, or after something else happens or becomes true • *We'll have the party in the backyard if the weather's good.* ○ *If anyone calls for me, just say I'll be back at 4 o'clock.* ○ *Would you mind if I opened the window* (= May I open it)*?* • If is also used to talk about the amount or degree of something: *This time of year we get little, if any, rain* (= almost none). • If can mean when: *If I don't have a cup of coffee in the morning, I'm useless.* • If can also mean in case it is true that: *I'm sorry if I've offended you.* • **If all else fails** (= If what was planned cannot happen), *we can always spend the weekend at home.* • **If and when** emphasizes that something may not happen at all: *We'll deal with that problem if and when it arises.* • When you say **if it weren't for/ hadn't been for** something, you mean if it were not true or had not happened, the situation would be different: *If it weren't for your help, we would never have finished in time.* • **If I were you** means imagining myself in your situation: *If I were you, I'd accept his apology.* • *I think you should get a job, if only* (= the reason being) *to have something to do.* • **If need be** (= If it is necessary), *we can take two cars.* • **If only** *I had more money* (= I wish I had more money)*!* • **If only** also means that doing something simple would have made it possible to avoid something unpleasant: *If only she had listened to me, she wouldn't be in this mess.* • When you say to someone **if the shoe fits**, you are suggesting that a criticism made in general may fit their own behavior. • **If worse/worst comes to worst** means if a bad situation becomes even worse: *If worst comes to worst, we can ask Dad to send us some more money.* • (*fml*) **If you will** is a way of suggesting that what you have just said may not be exactly the way you would prefer to say it:

I did very well in school, with a "genius IQ," if you will.

if /ɪf/ *n* [C] • *The plan contains a lot of ifs* (= arrangements that need to be made).

iffy /ˈɪf·i/ *adj* • *Our plans are iffy* (= uncertain).

if WHETHER /ɪf/ *conjunction* (used to introduce a clause, often when reporting what someone else said) whether • *Mrs. Kramer called to ask if her cake was ready.*

igloo /ˈɪg·luː/ *n* [C] *pl* **igloos** a circular house made of blocks of hard snow, esp. one built by the Inuit people of northern North America

ignite /ɪgˈnɑɪt/ *v* [I/T] to start burning, or to cause (something) to start burning • *The fire began when he fell asleep while smoking and his cigarette ignited the bedding.* [T] ○ (*fig.*) *to ignite a controversy* [T]

ignition /ɪgˈnɪʃ·ən/ *n* [C/U] the act of starting to burn • *An engine's ignition is the electrical system that starts the engine.* [C usually sing]

ignominious /ˌɪg·nəˈmɪn·i·əs/ *adj* (esp. of events or behavior) embarrassing • *an ignominious defeat*

ignorant /ˈɪg·nə·rənt/ *adj* having no knowledge or awareness of something or of things in general • *We were very young, ignorant, unskilled men.*

ignorance /ˈɪg·nə·rəns/ *n* [U] • *You have to assume that incoming students have an almost total ignorance of the rules of grammar.*

ignore /ɪgˈnɔːr, -ˈnoʊr/ *v* [T] to give no attention to (something or someone) • *They ignored our warnings.* ○ *The mayor ignored the hecklers and went on with her speech.*

iguana /ɪˈgwɑn·ə/ *n* [C] a large, gray-and-green LIZARD (= hairless animal)

ill NOT HEALTHY /ɪl/ *adj* **worse, worst** having a disease or feeling as if your body or mind has been harmed by not being able to work as it should • *I felt ill, so I went home.*

illness /ˈɪl·nəs/ *n* [C/U] a condition in which the body or mind is harmed because an organ or part is unable to work as it usually does; a disease or sickness • *mental illness* [U] ○ *He died at home after a long illness.* [C]

iguana

ill BADLY /ɪl/ *adv* [not gradable] badly, with great difficulty, or certainly not • *They could ill afford to lose all that money.* • *If you are ill at ease, you feel anxious and not relaxed.* • Someone or something that is **ill-advised** is unwise or foolish. • If someone or something is **ill-equipped** to do something, they do not have the ability or equipment necessary to do it well: *Young parents are sometimes ill-equipped to cope with a child.* • You say that something is **ill-fated** when it experiences failure or bad luck.

ill /ɪl/ *adj* [not gradable] • *Did you experience any ill effects from the treatment?*

I'll /ɑɪl/ *contraction of* **I will** or **I shall** • *I'll want to see your tax records.* ○ *I'll be on vacation next week.*

illegal /ɪˈliː·gəl/ *adj* against the law • *Selling liquor without a license is illegal.* • An illegal immigrant/alien is a person who has entered a country without government permission.

illegality /ˌɪl·ɪˈgæl·ət̬·i/ *n* [U] the quality of being against the law

illegally /ɪˈliː·gə·li/ *adv* • *illegally obtained handguns*

illegible /ɪˈledʒ·ə·bəl/ *adj* (of writing or print) impossible or difficult to read because it is unclear • *illegible handwriting*

illegitimate /ˌɪl·ɪˈdʒɪt̬·ə·mət/ *adj* [not gradable] born of parents not married to each other • *an illegitimate child* • Illegitimate can also mean not legal: *an illegitimate ruler*

illicit /ɪˈlɪs·ət/ *adj* illegal or socially disapproved of • *illicit drugs* ○ *an illicit love affair*

illiterate /ɪˈlɪt̬·ə·rət/ *adj* not knowing how to read and write

illiteracy /ɪˈlɪt̬·ə·rə·si/ *n* [U]

illness /ˈɪl·nəs/ *n* • See at ILL NOT HEALTHY.

illogical /ɪˈlɑdʒ·ɪ·kəl/ *adj* not reasonable, wise, or practical • *It was an illogical decision, but I was in love.*

illuminate /ɪˈluː·məˌneɪt/ *v* [T] to put light in or on (something) • *The buildings were illuminated at night.* • If you illuminate (a subject), you explain it: *This article illuminates the basic principles of economics.*

illuminating /ɪˈluː·məˌneɪt̬·ɪŋ/ *adj* • *She tells the story in illuminating detail* (= explaining it completely).

illumination /ɪˌluː·məˈneɪ·ʃən/ *n* [U] • *The only illumination* (= light) *was from a skylight in the roof.*

illusion /ɪˈluː·ʒən/ *n* [C] an idea or belief that is not true, or something that is not what it seems to be • *We have no illusions about how difficult the job will be.* ○ *I was under the illusion that trains ran frequently on weekends* (= I wrongly believed this). [+ *that* clause] ○ *They managed to create the illusion of space in a tiny apartment.*

illusory /ɪˈluː·sə·ri, -zə·ri/ *adj* • *Her fears were illusory.*

illustrate /ˈɪl·əˌstreɪt/ *v* [T] to add pictures to (something, such as a book) • *She writes children's books and also illustrates them.* • To illustrate is also to show the meaning or truth of (something) more clearly, esp. by giving examples: *To illustrate her point, she told a story about how her family felt when they moved here.*

illustration /ˌɪl·əˈstreɪ·ʃən/ *n* [C/U] a picture • *Look at the illustration on page 37.* [C] • An illustration is also an example that makes something easier to understand, or the giving of such examples: *That's a perfect illustration of the problem.* [C]

illustrator /ˈɪl·əˌstreɪt̬·ər/ *n* [C] a person who draws pictures, esp. for books

illustrious /ɪˈlʌs·triː·əs/ *adj fml* famous because of its excellence • *an illustrious career*

I'm /aɪm/ *contraction of* I am • *I'm sorry I'm late.*

image IDEA /ˈɪm·ɪdʒ/ *n* [C] an idea, esp. a mental picture, of what something or someone is like • *I had an image of Texas in my head that was totally different from how it really is.* • Someone's image is the idea that other people have of them, esp. an idea created by advertising and by newspaper and television stories: *He's trying to project a more presidential image.* • An image is also a description of something or someone: *The book presented an image of life on a farm in the 19th century.*

imagery /ˈɪm·ɪdʒ·ri/ *n* [U] the use of pictures or words to create images, esp. to create an impression or mood • *The film contains strong sexual imagery.*

image PICTURE /ˈɪm·ɪdʒ/ *n* [C] a picture, esp. one seen in a mirror or through a camera • *moving images on a TV screen*

imagine /ɪˈmædʒ·ən/ *v* [T] to form or have a mental picture or idea of (something or someone) • *Imagine Tom as a child—that's what John looks like.* ○ *I imagine* (= expect) *(that) they charge extra for dessert.* [+ that clause] • If you imagine (something) that is not real or true, you think that it exists, has happened, or is true: *"Did you hear a noise?" "No, you're imagining things."*

imaginable /ɪˈmædʒ·ə·nə·bəl/ *adj* possible, or able to be imagined • *They sell every flavor of ice cream imaginable.*

imaginary /ɪˈmædʒ·əˌner·i/ *adj* existing only in the mind; not real • *All her worries were imaginary.*

imagination /ɪˌmædʒ·əˈneɪ·ʃən/ *n* [U] • *Rafael has a very active imagination* (= has many ideas).

imaginative /ɪˈmædʒ·ə·nət̬·ɪv/ *adj* new, original, and showing a quick intelligence • *an imaginative little girl*

imaginatively /ɪˈmædʒ·ə·nət̬·ɪv·li/ *adv*

imbalance /ɪmˈbæl·əns/ *n* [C] a condition in which two or more things are not equally or fairly divided or spread • *a trade imbalance*

imbecile /ˈɪm·bə·səl, -ˌsɪl/ *n* [C] a stupid person

imbibe /ɪmˈbaɪb/ *v* [T] *slightly fml* to drink (esp. alcohol)

imbue *obj* **with** *obj* /ɪmˈbjuː·wɪθ, -, -wɪθ/ *v prep* [T] to fill (something or someone) with (a quality or feeling) • *Her poetry was imbued with a love of the outdoors.*

imitate /ˈɪm·əˌteɪt/ *v* [T] to copy (someone's speech or behavior), or to copy (something) as a model • *My four-year-old daughter is always*

trying to imitate her older sister. ○ *He imitated her accent perfectly.*

imitation /ˌɪm·əˈteɪ·ʃən/ *n* [C/U] something copied, or the act of copying • *Freya does a pretty good imitation of her science teacher.*

imitation /ˌɪm·əˈteɪ·ʃən/ *adj* [not gradable] not real but produced as a copy of something real • *imitation leather* [C]

immaculate /ɪˈmæk·jə·lət/ *adj* perfectly clean or in perfect condition • *My aunt's kitchen was always immaculate.*

immaculately /ɪˈmæk·jə·lət·li/ *adv* • *She was immaculately dressed.*

immaterial /ˌɪm·əˈtɪr·iː·əl/ *adj* [not gradable] not important; not likely to make a difference • *It's immaterial whether the trial is in San Diego or Los Angeles or anyplace else.*

immature /ˌɪm·əˈtʃʊr, -ˈtʊr/ *adj* not completely developed physically, mentally, or emotionally, or lacking the expected type of responsible behavior for your age • *Some of the boys in my class are so immature—they're always doing silly things.*

immaturity /ˌɪm·əˈtʃʊr·ət̬·i, -ˈtʊr-/ *n* [U] • *physical/emotional immaturity*

immediate NO DELAY /ɪˈmiːd·iː·ət/ *adj* happening or done without delay or very soon after something else • *She made an immediate impact when she arrived to coach the team.* ○ *Emotional outbursts followed in the immediate aftermath of Stewart's death.*

immediately /ɪˈmiːd·iː·ət·li/ *adv* • *The plane began to turn to the left almost immediately after takeoff.*

immediacy /ɪˈmiːd·iː·ə·si/ *n* [U] the quality or feeling of being directly involved • *Recording before a live audience captures the immediacy of the performance.*

immediate NEAREST /ɪˈmiːd·iː·ət/ *adj* nearest in space or relationship • *There are three schools in the immediate area.* • Your **immediate family** includes your closest family members, such as your parents, children, husband or wife, and brothers and sisters.

immediately /ɪˈmiːd·iː·ət·li/ *adv* • *Turn left, and the bathroom is immediately on the right.*

immense /ɪˈmens/ *adj* extremely large; great in size or degree • *He inherited an immense fortune.* ○ *Did you see that guy? He was immense!*

immensely /ɪˈmen·sli/ *adv* [not gradable] • *Country music is immensely popular.* • LP VERY, COMPLETELY, AND OTHER INTENSIFIERS

immensity /ɪˈmen·sət̬·i/ *n* [U] • *He realized the immensity of the risk he was taking.*

immerse /ɪˈmɜrs/ *v* [T] to involve (someone) completely in an activity • *She immersed herself wholly in her work.* • To immerse something is also to put it completely under the surface of a liquid: *Immerse the egg in boiling water.*

immersion /ɪˈmɜr·ʒən, -ʃən/ *n* [U] • *The course offers total immersion in English.*

immigrant /ˈɪm·ə·grənt/ *n* [C] a person who

has come into a foreign country in order to live there • *My grandparents arrived here as immigrants from Russia in 1910.* • Compare **emigrant** at EMIGRATE.

immigrate /ˈɪm·ə‚greɪt/ *v* [I] • *His family immigrated to the United States in 1928.* • Compare EMIGRATE.

immigration /‚ɪm·əˈgreɪ·ʃən/ *n* [U] the process by which people come in to a foreign country to live there, or the number of people coming in • *Immigration increased by 25% last year.*

imminent /ˈɪm·ə·nənt/ *adj* (esp. of something unpleasant) likely to happen very soon • *A rain storm was imminent.*

immobile /ɪˈmoʊ·bəl/ *adj* [not gradable] not moving, or not able to move or be moved • *He is in a cast to keep his spine immobile.*

immobilize /ɪˈmoʊ·bə‚laɪz/ *v* [T] • *He was immobilized, tied hand and foot.*

immoral /ɪˈmɔːr·əl, ɪˈmɑr-/ *adj* not following accepted standards of morally right behavior or thought • *Discrimination on the basis of race is immoral.*

immorality /‚ɪm·ɔːˈræl·ət·i/ *n* [U] • *the immorality of sexual abuse*

immortal /ɪˈmɔːrt̬·ˀl/ *adj* [not gradable] living or lasting forever, or so famous as to be remembered for a very long time • *I told him to pray for his immortal soul.* ○ *Churchill made his immortal speech about the Iron Curtain in Missouri.*

immortality /‚ɪm·ɔːrˈtæl·ət̬·i/ *n* [U] • *A place in history is the only kind of immortality open to us.*

immortalize /ɪˈmɔːrt̬·ˀl‚aɪz/ *v* [T] to cause (someone) to be remembered for a very long time • *He was immortalized in song.*

immovable /ɪˈmuː·və·bəl/ *adj* [not gradable] fixed in place and impossible to move • *Without the help of heavy equipment, that large rock is immovable.*

immune /ɪˈmjuːn/ *adj* protected against a particular disease or illness by particular substances in the blood • *Some people are immune to poison ivy.* • Immune also means protected from or unable to be influenced by something, esp. something bad: *She says her mother is immune to disgrace.* • Your **immune system** is the ways in which your body naturally fights diseases and illnesses.

immunity /ɪˈmjuː·nət̬·i/ *n* [U] • *Breast-feeding provides natural immunity against some childhood infections.* • (*law*) Immunity is also the condition of being protected from the law: *Rowe was promised immunity from prosecution if he cooperated.*

immunize /ˈɪm·jəˌnaɪz/ *v* [T] to protect (someone) against a particular disease or infection by introducing special substances into the body, esp. by INJECTION • *All children should be immunized against childhood illnesses.*

immunization /‚ɪm·jə·nəˈzeɪ·ʃən/ *n* [U] • *immunization against polio*

immutable /ɪˈmjuːt̬·ə·bəl/ *adj* [not gradable] *fml* not changing or unable to be changed • *The laws of physics are assumed to be immutable.*

impact FORCE /ˈɪm·pækt/ *n* [U] the force with which one thing hits another or with which two things hit each other • *The impact of the crash destroyed the car.* • *The bullet explodes* **on impact** (= at the moment when it hits something).

impact EFFECT /ˈɪm·pækt/ *n* [U] the strong effect or influence that something has on a situation or person • *These charges will have a damaging impact on the army's reputation.* ○ *The environmental impact of this project will be enormous.*

impact /ɪmˈpækt/ *v* [I/T] • *A big decline in exports will impact (on) the country's economy.* [I/T]

impair /ɪmˈper, -ˈpær/ *v* [T] to damage or weaken (something) so that it is less effective • *Lack of sleep impaired her ability to think clearly.*

impaired /ɪmˈperd, -ˈpærd/ *adj* • *She attended a school for the visually impaired* (= people who cannot see well). ○ *He was driving while impaired by alcohol.*

impairment /ɪmˈper·mənt, -ˈpær-/ *n* [C/U] • *The law bans discrimination against anyone with a mental or physical impairment.* [C]

impale /ɪmˈpeɪl/ *v* [T] to push a sharp pointed object through (something, esp. an animal's or person's body) • *Walruses sometimes use their tusks to impale seals for food.*

impart /ɪmˈpɑrt/ *v* [T] *slightly fml* to give (a feeling or quality) to something, or to make (information) known to someone • *If the movie has any lesson to impart, it's that parents shouldn't aim for perfection.*

impartial /ɪmˈpɑr·ʃəl/ *adj* able to judge or consider something fairly without allowing your own interest to influence you • *The jury has to give an impartial verdict after listening to all of the evidence.*

impartially /ɪmˈpɑr·ʃə·li/ *adv* • *Many people do not believe that complaints against the police are impartially handled.*

impartiality /ɪm‚pɑrˈʃiː·æl·ət̬·i/ *n* [U] • *scientific impartiality*

impassable /ɪmˈpæs·ə·bəl/ *adj* [not gradable] (esp. of a road) impossible to travel on or over • *Mudslides made the coast highway impassable.*

impasse /ˈɪm·pæs/ *n* [C usually sing] a point in a process at which further progress is blocked, esp. by disagreement • *We have reached an impasse in the negotiations—neither side will budge.*

impassioned /ɪmˈpæʃ·ənd/ *adj* expressed with strong feeling • *She went on television to make an impassioned plea for the release of her child.*

impassive /ɪmˈpæs·ɪv/ *adj* not showing or

feeling any emotion • *Nick kept his face impassive but his mind was racing.*

impassively /ɪmˈpæs·ɪv·li/ *adv* • *Even as the guilty verdict was read, he stared impassively ahead.*

impatient /ɪmˈpeɪ·ʃənt/ *adj* not willing to wait for something to happen and becoming annoyed at delays • *Don't be impatient, you'll get your turn.* ○ *She grew impatient with the others.* • Impatient can also mean eager for something to happen: *He was impatient to become the new boss.* [+ *to* infinitive]

impatience /ɪmˈpeɪ·ʃəns/ *n* [U] • *The horse snorted with impatience.*

impatiently /ɪmˈpeɪ·ʃənt·li/ *adv* • *Unable to sleep, he waited impatiently for the dawn to arrive.*

impeach /ɪmˈpiːtʃ/ *v* [T] *law* to formally accuse (a public official) of a serious crime in connection with their job

impeachment /ɪmˈpiːtʃ·mənt/ *n* [U] • *The federal judge faces impeachment.*

impeccable /ɪmˈpek·ə·bəl/ *adj* [not gradable] faultless or without mistakes; perfect • *impeccable manners/taste*

impeccably /ɪmˈpek·ə·bli/ *adv* [not gradable] • *She was always impeccably dressed.*

impede /ɪmˈpiːd/ *v* [T] to slow (something) down or prevent (an activity) from making progress at its previous rate • *Shortages of medicine were impeding the effort to control diseases.*

impediment /ɪmˈped·ə·mənt/ *n* [C] • *The lack of funds is a major impediment to research.*

impel /ɪmˈpel/ *v* [T] **-ll-** *fml* to force (someone) to do something • *When I see them eating, I feel impelled to eat, too.* [+ *to* infinitive]

impending /ɪmˈpen·dɪŋ/ *adj* [not gradable] (esp. of something unpleasant) about to happen soon • *The impending crisis over trade made everyone nervous.*

impenetrable /ɪmˈpen·ə·trə·bəl/ *adj* impossible to enter or go through • *an impenetrable jungle* • If language is described as impenetrable, it is impossible to understand: *Too many scholarly books are written in an impenetrable jargon.*

imperative URGENT /ɪmˈper·ət·ɪv/ *adj* extremely important or urgent • *It is imperative that sales of cigarettes to children be prevented.* [+ *that* clause]

imperative /ɪmˈper·ət·ɪv/ *n* [C] • *He argued that it was a moral imperative to increase funding for AIDS.*

imperative GRAMMAR /ɪmˈper·ət·ɪv/ *n* [U], *adj* [not gradable] *specialized* (in grammar) the MOOD (= form) of a verb used for giving orders • *In the phrase "Leave him alone," the verb "leave" is in the imperative.*

imperceptible /ˌɪm·pərˈsep·tə·bəl/ *adj* [not gradable] (of an action or change) so slight that it cannot be noticed • *When they brought*

her in to the emergency room, her breathing was imperceptible.

imperceptibly /ˌɪm·pərˈsep·tə·bli/ *adv* • *Imperceptibly, the day grew darker.*

imperfect /ɪmˈpɜr·fɪkt/ *adj* not perfect or not complete • *Our rule of law is still imperfect, but it's better than having no laws at all.*

imperfection /ˌɪm·pərˈfek·ʃən/ *n* [C/U] • *Investigators suspect the engine broke because of a tiny imperfection in one of the parts.* [C]

imperial /ɪmˈpɪr·i·əl/ *adj* [not gradable] *usually disapproving* relating to a government or country that controls or rules other countries • *imperial expansion of American power* ○ *the imperial tradition of Britain*

imperialism /ɪmˈpɪr·i·ə·lɪz·əm/ *n* [U] *usually disapproving* the attempt of one country to control another country, esp. by political and economic methods • *France was accused of economic imperialism because of its trade policies.*

imperialist /ɪmˈpɪr·i·ə·ləst/ *n* [C] *usually disapproving* • *Roosevelt believed that he was a benevolent imperialist.*

imperialistic /ɪmˌpɪr·i·əˈlɪs·tɪk/, **imperialist** /ɪmˈpɪr·i·ə·ləst/ *adj usually disapproving* • *They denounced the war as an imperialistic exploitation of oppressed peoples.*

imperil /ɪmˈper·əl/ *v* [T] *slightly fml* to put (something or someone) in danger • *Withdrawing the medical team would imperil the effort to control the spread of malaria.*

imperious /ɪmˈpɪr·i·əs/ *adj slightly fml* with an attitude of authority and expecting obedience • *She was a very imperious, arrogant woman.*

impersonal /ɪmˈpɜr·sən·əl/ *adj* lacking or not showing any interest or feeling • *The congressman gave a short, impersonal speech and left soon afterward.*

impersonate /ɪmˈpɜr·sə·neɪt/ *v* [T] to intentionally copy (another person's) speech, appearance, or behavior, esp. in order to entertain or deceive people • *to impersonate a movie star* ○ *He was charged with impersonating a police officer.*

impertinent /ɪmˈpɜrt·ən·ənt/ *adj* not showing enough respect; rude • *Don't be impertinent—you're in no position to tell your boss what to do.*

imperturbable /ˌɪm·pərˈtɜr·bə·bəl/ *adj slightly fml* staying calm and controlled despite problems or difficulties • *He was imperturbable in a crisis.*

impervious /ɪmˈpɜr·vi·əs/ *adj* not able to be influenced, hurt, or damaged • *He seems to be impervious to pain.* ○ *Granite is almost impervious to acid rain damage.*

impetuous /ɪmˈpetʃ·ə·wəs/ *adj* acting or done suddenly without much thought • *Then, impetuous and stupid young guy that I was, I jumped out of the car and tapped the bear on the head with a shovel.*

impetus /ˈɪm·pət̬·əs/ n [U] a force that encourages a particular action or makes it more energetic or effective • *Often the impetus for change in education has had to come from outside the school establishment.*

impinge on/upon /ɪmˈpɪndʒ/ v prep [T] to have an effect on (something), often by limiting it in some way • *The Supreme Court will decide if the new communications bill impinges on the Constitutional right to free speech.*

impish /ˈɪm·pɪʃ/ adj suggesting behavior that is playful but likely to upset other people • *He had an impish grin on his face.*

implacable /ɪmˈplæk·ə·bəl/ adj unable to be changed, satisfied, or stopped • *an implacable enemy*

implant /ɪmˈplænt/ v [T] to fix firmly, esp. to put (an organ, group of cells, or device) into the body in a medical operation • *He had a new heart valve implanted.* ○ *(fig.) It is now accepted that memories of sexual abuse can be implanted* (= fixed in the mind).

implant /ˈɪm·plænt/ n [C] • *breast implants*

implausible /ɪmˈplɔː·zə·bəl/ adj difficult to believe; not probable • *The plot of the movie, involving a 23-year-old brain surgeon, is implausible to begin with.*

implement USE /ˈɪm·plə·ment/ v [T] to put (a plan or system) into operation • *Congress refused to pass the bill that would implement tax reforms.*

implement TOOL /ˈɪm·plə·mənt/ n [C] a tool or other piece of equipment for doing work • *farm implements*

implicate /ˈɪm·plə·keɪt/ v [T] to show that (someone) is involved in a crime or partly responsible for something bad that has happened • *A lot of people were implicated in the scandal.*

implication /ˌɪm·pləˈkeɪ·ʃən/ n [U] • *Implication of his co-workers in the fraud was crucial to the defendant's case.*

implication /ˌɪm·pləˈkeɪ·ʃən/ n [C/U] a suggestion of something that is made without saying it directly • *There was no implication that they were divorcing.* [U] ○ *What are the implications* (= possible effects) *of the new regulations?* [C]

implicit SUGGESTED /ɪmˈplɪs·ət/ adj suggested but not communicated directly • *We interpreted his silence as implicit agreement.* ○ *Implicit in the poem's closing lines are the poet's religious doubts.* • Compare EXPLICIT.

implicitly /ɪmˈplɪs·ət·li/ adv • *The report implicitly questioned his competence.*

implicit COMPLETE /ɪmˈplɪs·ət/ adj [not gradable] (esp. of trust and belief) complete and without any doubts • *implicit faith*

implicitly /ɪmˈplɪs·ət·li/ adv • *He feels secure only with associates who obey him implicitly.*

implore /ɪmˈplɔːr, -ˈploʊr/ v [T] to ask (someone) in a determined, sincere, and sometimes emotional way to do or not to do something, or to ask for (something) in this way • *She implored him not to leave her.*

imply /ɪmˈplaɪ/ v [T] to suggest (something) without saying it directly, or to involve (something) as a necessary part or condition • *He implied (that) the error was mine.* [+ (that) clause] ○ *Democracy implies free elections.*

impolite /ˌɪm·pəˈlaɪt/ adj rude; not POLITE

import BRING IN /ɪmˈpɔːrt, -ˈpoʊrt/ v [T] to bring in (products, goods, etc.) from another country for sale or use • *We import a large number of cars from Japan.* • (specialized) To import information into a program or computer is to copy it from another program or form of storage. • Compare EXPORT.

import /ˈɪm·pɔːrt, -poʊrt/ n [C] something bought and taken into a country from another • *Imports of foreign cars are at an all-time high.*

import IMPORTANCE /ˈɪm·pɔːrt, -poʊrt/ n [U] *fml* the importance given to something • *It is still too early to judge the political import of his speech.*

important /ɪmˈpɔːrt·ənt/ adj of great value, meaning, or effect • *an important discovery* ○ *It's important that you tell the doctor all your symptoms.* [+ that clause] • Important also means having great influence: *an important modern artist*

importantly /ɪmˈpɔːrt·ənt·li/ adv • *She has a pleasant personality, but more importantly, she is well qualified for the job.*

importance /ɪmˈpɔːrt·əns/ n [U] • *He stressed the importance of fruits and vegetables in the diet.*

impose MAKE RULES /ɪmˈpoʊz/ v [T] to establish (something) as a rule to be obeyed, or to force the acceptance of (something) • *Settlers often imposed their culture on the peoples of the countries they conquered.*

impose INCONVENIENCE /ɪmˈpoʊz/ v [I] to cause inconvenience to someone or to force your presence on them when it is not wanted • *She's always imposing on people for favors.* ○ *I hope I'm not imposing by staying another night.*

imposing /ɪmˈpoʊ·zɪŋ/ adj noticeable because of large size, appearance, or importance • *an imposing mansion*

imposition INCONVENIENCE /ˌɪm·pəˈzɪʃ·ən/ n [C] something done that causes inconvenience to another person • *I hope the drive to the airport isn't an imposition.*

imposition MAKING RULES /ˌɪm·pəˈzɪʃ·ən/ n [U] the act of establishing a rule or law to be obeyed • *the imposition of new taxes*

impossible NOT POSSIBLE /ɪmˈpɑs·ə·bəl/ adj [not gradable] unable to exist, happen, or be achieved; not possible • *an impossible goal* ○ *It's almost impossible to get them to agree on anything.* [+ to infinitive]

impossibility /ɪmˌpɑs·ə·ˈbɪl·ət̬·i/ n [C] something that is not possible • *What you're asking for is an impossibility.*

impossible VERY DIFFICULT /ɪmˈpɑs·ə·bəl/ *adj* very difficult to deal with • *Traffic at rush hour is just impossible.*

impossibly /ɪmˈpɑs·ə·bli/ *adv* [not gradable] • *She had to work impossibly long hours.*

impostor, **imposter** /ɪmˈpɑs·tər/ *n* [C] a person who pretends to be someone else in order to deceive others

impotent LACKING POWER /ˈɪm·pət·ənt/ *adj* lacking the power or ability to change or improve a situation; powerless

impotence /ˈɪm·pət·əns/ *n* [U]

impotent SEXUAL PROBLEM /ˈɪm·pət·ənt/ *adj* [not gradable] (of a man) unable to have sex because the penis cannot harden or stay hard

impotence /ˈɪm·pət·əns/ *n* [U]

impound /ɪmˈpɑʊnd/ *v* [T] to take possession of (something) by legal right • *The police impounded personal property belonging to the drug dealers.*

impoverished /ɪmˈpɑv·ə·rɪʃt/ *adj* extremely poor • *an impoverished family*

impractical /ɪmˈpræk·tɪ·kəl/ *adj* not effective or reasonable, or (of people) not able to provide effective or simple solutions • *an impractical plan* ○ *It's impractical to buy things just because they're on sale.*

imprecise /ˌɪm·prɪˈsɑɪs/ *adj* not accurate or exact • *As all the data have not yet been collected, the figures are still imprecise.*

impregnable /ɪmˈpreg·nə·bəl/ *adj* so strongly made that it cannot be broken into or taken by force • *an impregnable fortress*

impregnate MAKE PREGNANT /ɪmˈpreg·neɪt/ *v* [T] to make (a woman or female animal) pregnant

impregnate ABSORB /ɪmˈpreg·neɪt/ *v* [T] to cause (a substance) to absorb a liquid substance • *This cloth is impregnated with a cleaning solution.*

impress /ɪmˈpres/ *v* [T] to cause (someone) to feel admiration or respect • *She impressed us with her sincerity.* • If you impress something on someone, you cause them to understand its importance or value: *He always impressed on us the need to do our best.*

impressive /ɪmˈpres·ɪv/ *adj* • *an impressive performance*

impressively /ɪmˈpres·ɪv·li/ *adv* • *an impressively large collection of medals*

impression OPINION /ɪmˈpreʃ·ən/ *n* [C] an idea or opinion of what someone or something is like • *It makes a bad impression if you're late for an interview.* ○ *I get the impression that she's rather shy.* [+ that clause] ○ *I was under the impression that you didn't like your job (= I was wrong to think that you did not like your job).* [+ that clause]

impression EFFECT /ɪmˈpreʃ·ən/ *n* [U] effect or influence on the way someone feels or thinks • *All our warnings made little impression on him.*

impressionable /ɪmˈpreʃ·ə·nə·bəl/ *adj* easily influenced • *He's at an impressionable age.*

impression MARK /ɪmˈpreʃ·ən/ *n* [C] a mark made on the surface of something by pressing an object into it • *The bookcase had left an impression in the rug.*

imprint /ɪmˈprɪnt/ *v* [T] to mark (a surface) by pressing something into it, or to fix (something) firmly in the memory • *The terrible scene has been deeply imprinted on my mind.*

imprint /ˈɪm·prɪnt/ *n* [C] • *The children enjoyed leaving the imprints of their feet in the wet sand.*

imprison /ɪmˈprɪz·ən/ *v* [T] to put (someone) in prison or in a situation that is like prison • *He was imprisoned for attempted murder.* ○ *After weeks of snow, she felt imprisoned in her own home.*

imprisonment /ɪmˈprɪz·ən·mənt/ *n* [U]

improbable /ɪmˈprɑb·ə·bəl/ *adj* not likely to be true or to happen; not PROBABLE • *an improbable excuse*

improbably /ɪmˈprɑb·ə·bli/ *adv*

improbability /ɪmˌprɑb·əˈbɪl·ət·i/ *n* [C/U]

impromptu /ɪmˈprɑm·tuː/ *adj* [not gradable] done or said without earlier planning or preparation • *an impromptu speech*

improper DISHONEST /ɪmˈprɑp·ər/ *adj* being against a law or a rule; dishonest or illegal • *The treasurer denied accepting any improper payments.*

improper WRONG /ɪmˈprɑp·ər/ *adj* not suitable or correct for a particular use or situation • *an improper choice of words*

improperly /ɪmˈprɑp·ər·li/ *adv* • *If handled improperly, some chemicals used for cleaning can cause severe skin irritation.*

impropriety /ˌɪm·prəˈprɑɪ·ət·i/ *n* [C/U] dishonesty, or a dishonest act • *He said he regretted the appearance of impropriety and resigned.* [U] ○ *There have been charges of financial improprieties.* [C]

improve /ɪmˈpruːv/ *v* [I/T] to get better, or to make (something) better • *Her grades have improved greatly this semester.* [I] ○ *He did a lot to improve conditions for factory workers.* [T] • If you improve on something, you succeed in doing or making it better: *The company is hoping to improve on last year's sales figures.* [I]

improvement /ɪmˈpruːv·mənt/ *n* [C/U] • *We made some improvements to the house before selling it.* [C] ○ *There's been no improvement in his condition.* [U]

improvise /ˈɪm·prəˌvɑɪz/ *v* [I/T] to invent or provide (something) at the time when it is needed without having already planned it, or to invent (what you are going to say or play as music) as it is performed • *We improvised a mattress from a pile of blankets.* [T] ○ *Hughes encourages young actors to improvise during rehearsals.* [I]

impudent /ˈɪm·pjəd·ənt/ *adj* rude and not respectful • *an impudent child*

impudence /'ɪm·pjəd·əns/ *n* [U]

impugn /ɪm'pjuːn/ *v* [T] *fml* to cause people to doubt or not trust (someone's character, honesty, or ability) • *He could no longer work as a doctor because his reputation had been impugned.*

impulse DESIRE /'ɪm·pʌls/ *n* [C/U] a sudden, strong desire to do something • *I had this impulse to dye my hair red.* [+ *to* infinitive] • If you do something on impulse, you do it because you suddenly want to: *I bought this expensive sweater on impulse.* [U]

impulsive /ɪm'pʌl·sɪv/ *adj* acting or done suddenly without any planning or consideration of the results • *She's an impulsive shopper and often buys things she doesn't need.*

impulsively /ɪm'pʌl·sɪv·li/ *adv*

impulse SIGNAL /'ɪm·pʌls/ *n* [C] a short electrical signal that carries information or instructions between the parts of a system • *nerve impulses*

impunity /ɪm'pjuː·nət̬·i/ *n* [U] *slightly fml* freedom from punishment for something that has been done that is wrong or illegal • *It was an area where drug dealing was carried on with impunity in broad daylight.*

impure /ɪm'pjʊr/ *adj* mixed with other substances and therefore harmful or lower in quality • *impure drinking water*

impurity /ɪm'pjʊr·ət̬·i/ *n* [C] • *Impurities are removed from the blood by the kidneys.*

in WITHIN /ɪn/ *prep, adv* [not gradable] positioned inside or within the limits of something, or contained, surrounded, or enclosed by something • *There's a cup in the cabinet.* ○ *Anne is still in bed.* ○ *Don't stand in the driveway.* ○ *He's always looking at himself in the mirror.* ○ *Clarice lives in Orlando.* ○ *He was in prison* (= a prisoner). ○ *Erika is still in school* (= still a student). ○ *He has a pain in his shoulder.* • If you are **in and out** of a place, you go there and leave, often repeatedly: *Since the accident, she's been in and out of the hospital several times.* • (*infml*) Something that is **in between** has the qualities of two different things: *This suit isn't gray or blue, it's in between.* • **In-house** work is done by employees or people working at a place of business, and not by people working independently: *in-house designers/lawyers*

in MOVING TOWARD /ɪn/ *prep* into or toward • *Get in the car.* ○ *She stepped in the batter's box.* ○ *He looked in my direction.*

in FROM OUTSIDE /ɪn/ *adv* [not gradable] from outside, or toward the center • *Could you bring the clothes in for me?* ○ *The roof of their house caved in during a hurricane.* • An **in-box** is a container where letters and other documents are put when they arrive in a person's office.

in INCLUSION /ɪn/ *prep, adv* [not gradable] being a member or forming a part of something • *Who's the woman in that painting?* ○ *Mr.*

Harper is in a meeting. ○ *I've been waiting in line for two hours.* ○ *Do you take milk in your coffee?* • *I wasn't* **in on** (= taking part in) *planning the party.* • If you are **in with** someone, you are taking part in some activity with them: *He owns a small restaurant and his brother wants to go in with him on it.*

in CONNECTED WITH /ɪn/ *prep* involved or connected esp. with a job or interest • *I never knew you were in publishing.* ○ *I'm taking a course in economics next semester.*

in WEARING /ɪn/ *prep* wearing, covering, or decorated with • *Do you recognize that man in the gray suit?* ○ *The living room is done in blue and green.*

in USING /ɪn/ *prep* said, made, or done using something • *Fill out the application in ink.* ○ *They spoke in Russian the whole time.*

in DURING /ɪn/ *prep* during part or all of a period of time or an event • *We're going to Arizona in April.* ○ *What was it like to be a student in 1968?* ○ *See you in the morning.* ○ *How many people died in the war?* ○ *She's in her forties* (= between 40 and 49 years old). • In can also mean no longer than a particular period of time: *Can you finish the job in two weeks?* • In can also mean at the end of a particular period of time: *I should be there in half an hour.* • Something that is **in-flight** happens or is available during a flight: *We hope you will enjoy your in-flight movie.*

in SITUATION /ɪn/ *prep, adv* [not gradable] experiencing a situation, condition, or feeling • *We watched in horror as the cars crashed.* ○ *I'd like to talk to you in private.* ○ *He left in a hurry.* ○ *Have you ever been in love?* ○ *He's always in a bad mood on Monday mornings.* ○ *Temperatures tomorrow will be in the 70s* (= between 70 and 79 degrees).

in ARRANGEMENT /ɪn/ *prep* used to show how something is arranged or divided • *We sat in a circle around the campfire.* ○ *The potatoes will bake faster if you cut them in half.*

in COMPARING AMOUNTS /ɪn/ *prep* used to compare a part of an amount of something with the total amount of it; out of • *The survey found that one person in ten has a reading problem.* ○ *The chance of that happening is one in a million.*

in CHARACTERISTIC /ɪn/ *prep* used to show which characteristic of a person or thing is being described • *She's deaf in her left ear.* ○ *Canned vegetables are not very rich in vitamins.* ○ *I wasn't using the word "guarantee" in its strict legal sense.*

in CAUSE /ɪn/ *prep* used to show that doing one thing is the cause of another thing happening • *The government banned tobacco advertising near schools, and in doing so hopes to reduce smoking among young people.* ○ *It might be made of plastic, in which case it will be light enough to carry.*

in AT PLACE /ɪn/ *adv* at a place, esp. at home or

a place of work • *Why is it that whenever I call, you are never in?* ○ *Danielle was out sick last week—do you know if she'll be in today?*

in PLACE /ɪn/ *adv* [not gradable] used to show that a space or place exists where something can be put or added • *Just pencil in your answers on the attached sheet.* ○ *The text is finished, but the pictures need to be pasted in.* • For many sports, if a ball is in, it has not gone outside the edges of the area on which the game is played.

in POLITICS /ɪn/ *adv* into an elected position or office • *She's been voted in for a second term as treasurer.*

in FASHIONABLE /ɪn/ *adj, adv infml* fashionable or popular • *That new jazz club is the in place to go.* ○ *High heels came in again this season.* • An **in-group** is a social group whose members share interests or characteristics that people outside the group do not. • An **in-joke** is a private joke understood only by the people who know what the joke refers to.

in ADVANTAGE /ɪn/ *n* [C] an advantage resulting from a good relationship with someone powerful • *Sal has an in with someone at the theater.*

in. MEASUREMENT *n* [C] *pl* **in.** abbreviation for INCH MEASUREMENT

in– LACKING /ɪn/ *combining form* used to add the meaning not, lacking, or the opposite of to adjectives and to words formed from adjectives • *incomplete/incompletely*

inability /ˌɪn·əˈbɪl·ət̬·i/ *n* [C/U] a lack of ability to do something • *an inability to read and write* [C usually sing]

inaccessible /ˌɪn·ɪkˈses·ə·bəl/ *adj* difficult or impossible to reach • *The place is inaccessible except by trail.*

inaccurate /ɪnˈæk·jə·rət/ *adj* not correct, or not exact • *Your information is inaccurate—I was born in 1956, not 1965.* ○ *inaccurate measurements*

inaccurately /ɪnˈæk·jə·rət·li/ *adv* • *an inaccurately worded question*

inaccuracy /ɪnˈæk·jə·rə·si/ *n* [C/U] • *Rose says the story was loaded with inaccuracies.* [C]

inaction /ɪnˈæk·ʃən/ *n* [U] failure to do anything that might provide a solution to a problem • *The mayor was criticized for his inaction on problems affecting the city's poor.*

inactive /ɪnˈæk·tɪv/ *adj* doing nothing • *Knee surgery will keep him physically inactive for two months.* ○ *About half of the church members are regarded as inactive.*

inactivity /ˌɪn·ækˈtɪv·ət̬·i/ *n* [U] • *The journey was long, and he found the inactivity boring.*

inadequate /ɪnˈæd·ɪ·kwət/ *adj* too low in quality or too small in amount; not enough • *an inadequate income/offer* ○ *I feel inadequate when I talk to Miranda about art because she knows so much.*

inadequately /ɪnˈæd·ɪ·kwət·li/ *adv* • *The research is inadequately funded.*

inadequacy /ɪnˈæd·ɪ·kwə·si/ *n* [C/U] • *She's frustrated by the inadequacies of language.* [C]

inadmissible /ˌɪn·ədˈmɪs·ə·bəl/ *adj* [not gradable] unable to be accepted, esp. in a law court • *The lie detector test was inadmissible as evidence in the case.*

inadvertent /ˌɪn·ədˈvɜrt·ənt/ *adj* done or happening unintentionally • *an inadvertent mistake*

inadvertently /ˌɪn·ədˈvɜrt·ənt·li/ *adv* • *I inadvertently gave her change for $20, but she'd only given me $10.*

inadvisable /ˌɪn·ədˈvɑɪ·zə·bəl/ *adj* likely to have unwanted results and therefore to be avoided • *It is inadvisable to generalize from the results of a single experiment.*

inalienable /ɪnˈeɪl·jə·nə·bəl/ *adj* • **Inalienable rights** are freedoms that cannot be taken away: *The right to survival has to be the first on any list of inalienable rights for every human being.*

inane /ɪˈneɪn/ *adj* extremely silly or lacking real meaning or importance • *There are so many inane programs on television!*

inanimate /ɪˈnæn·ə·mət/ *adj* [not gradable] possessing none of the characteristics of life that an animal or plant has • *an inanimate object*

inappropriate /ˌɪn·əˈproʊ·priː·ət/ *adj* unsuitable, esp. for the particular time, place, or situation • *His casual clothes were inappropriate for such a formal occasion.*

inarticulate /ˌɪn·ɑrˈtɪk·jə·lət/ *adj* unable to express feelings or ideas in words, or communicated in a way that is difficult to understand • *He refers to them as inarticulate mountain people.* ○ *inarticulate cries of rage*

inasmuch as /ɪn·əzˈmʌtʃ·əz/ *conjunction fml* used to show why or in what limited way the other part of the sentence is true • *Inasmuch as funding is not available, building plans have been delayed.*

inattentive /ˌɪn·əˈtent·ɪv/ *adj* not listening to what is being said or giving your attention to what is happening • *Barbara has been inattentive in class lately.*

inaudible /ɪˈnɔːd·ə·bəl/ *adj* [not gradable] unable to be heard • *The noise of the machinery made her voice inaudible.*

inaudibly /ɪˈnɔːd·ə·bli/ *adv* • *Music was playing almost inaudibly backstage.*

inaugurate /ɪˈnɔː·gjə·reɪt/ *v* [T] to put (something) into use or action, or to put (a person) into an official position with a ceremony • *He wants to inaugurate his museum with elaborate opening ceremonies.* ○ *The nation prepares to inaugurate its new president.*

inauguration /ɪˌnɔː·gjə·ˈreɪ·ʃən/ *n* [C/U] • *She's a journalist who has covered six presidential inaugurations.* [C]

inaugural /ɪˈnɔː·gjə·rəl/ *adj* [not gradable] • *What was the theme of her inaugural address?*

inauspicious /ˌɪn·ɔːˈspɪʃ·əs/ *adj* suggesting

that success is not likely • *After an inauspicious start, our team went on to win the game 30 to 24.*

inborn /'ɪn·bɔːrn/ *adj* [not gradable] possessed as a characteristic from birth • *Research suggests that some people have an inborn tendency to develop certain types of cancer.*

inbred BASIC /'ɪn·bred/ *adj* [not gradable] having as a basic part of your character • *Americans have an inbred hostility toward government.*

inbred RELATED /'ɪn·bred/ *adj* [not gradable] produced by breeding between closely related plants, animals, or people

Inc. /ɪŋk/ *adj short form of* **incorporated**, see at INCORPORATE MAKE A COMPANY • *Automated Document Systems, Inc.*

incalculable /ɪn'kæl·kjə·lə·bəl/ *adj* [not gradable] too large to be calculated or measured, or extremely large • *The consequences of a nuclear war are incalculable.*

incandescent /ˌɪn·kən'des·ənt/ *adj* [not gradable] producing a bright light after being heated to a high temperature • *an incandescent light/bulb*

incandescence /ˌɪn·kən'des·əns/ *n* [U] • *At night, Los Angeles looked like a vast carpet of incandescence.*

incantation /ˌɪn·kæn'teɪ·ʃən/ *n* [C/U] the saying of words believed to have a magical effect when spoken or sung • *She recited an incantation designed to protect the planet.* [C]

incapable /ɪn'keɪ·pə·bəl/ *adj* unable to do something • *She's incapable of hurting a fly.*

incapacitate /ˌɪn·kə'pæs·ə,teɪt/ *v* [T] to remove (someone's) ability to do something • *The accident incapacitated me for seven months.*

incapacitating /ˌɪn·kə'pæs·ə,teɪt·ɪŋ/ *adj* • *an incapacitating illness*

incapacity /ˌɪn·kə'pæs·ət·i/ *n* [U] • *The novel tells the story of a man's incapacity for love.*

incarcerate /ɪn'kɑr·sə,reɪt/ *v* [T] to put or keep (someone) in prison • *The governor announced his plan to incarcerate repeat violent offenders.*

incarceration /ɪn,kɑr·sə'reɪ·ʃən/ *n* [U] • *We're spending billions of dollars on drug wars and incarceration.*

incarnation /ˌɪn,kɑr'neɪ·ʃən/ *n* [C/U] the human form of a spirit, or the human representation of a principle or idea • *When he dances, he's the incarnation of gracefulness.* [U] • *An incarnation is also, according to some religious beliefs, one of the several lives people have over time.* [C] See also REINCARNATION. • *An incarnation can also be a new or different form or condition of something: This movie is the latest incarnation of an old French fairy tale.* [C]

incarnate /ɪn'kɑr·nət, -ˌneɪt/ *adj* [not grad-

able] in human form • *One man described his jailer as the devil incarnate.*

incendiary FIRE /ɪn'sen·diː,er·i/ *adj* [not gradable] designed to cause fires • *an incendiary bomb/device* ○ *(fig.) Thai food often is incendiary* (= spicy hot).

incendiary CAUSING ANGER /ɪn'sen·diː,er·i/ *adj* likely to cause violence or strong feelings of anger • *He gave an incendiary speech at last night's rally.*

incense SUBSTANCE /'ɪn·sens/ *n* [U] a substance that is burned to produce a sweet smell

incense ANGER /ɪn'sens/ *v* [T] to cause (someone) to be extremely angry • *The editor felt readers would be incensed by my article on illegal adoption.*

incentive /ɪn'sent·ɪv/ *n* [C/U] something that encourages a person to do something • *Tax incentives are sometimes effective in encouraging people to save money.* [C] ○ *These kids have no incentive to learn.* [U]

inception /ɪn'sep·ʃən/ *n* [U] the establishment of an organization or official activity • *Since its inception in 1968, the company has been at the forefront of computer development.*

incessant /ɪn'ses·ənt/ *adj* [not gradable] (esp. of something unpleasant) never stopping • *The city endured weeks of incessant bombing.*

incessantly /ɪn'ses·ənt·li/ *adv* [not gradable] • *Bob talks incessantly about their new baby.*

incest /'ɪn·sest/ *n* [U] sexual activity between people who are too closely related to marry

incestuous /ɪn'ses·tʃə·wəs/ *adj* [not gradable] • *an incestuous relationship*

inch MEASUREMENT /ɪntʃ/ *(abbreviation* **in.**, *symbol* ″*) n* [C] a unit of measurement of length equal to 1/12 foot or 2.54 centimeters • *Detectives searched the murder scene* **inch by inch** (= in a lot of small stages).

inch MOVE /ɪntʃ/ *v* [always + adv/prep] to move very slowly, or in a lot of short stages • *Stock prices inched higher throughout the afternoon.* [I] ○ *Mike inched the bookcase into position.* [T]

incidence /'ɪn·səd·əns, -sə,dens/ *n* [U] the rate at which something happens • *There's been an increased incidence of cancer in the area.*

incident /'ɪn·səd·ənt, -sə,dent/ *n* [C/U] an event, esp. one that is either unpleasant or unusual • *Two youths were shot and killed in separate incidents early this morning.* [C] ○ *The demonstration took place without incident.* [U]

incidental /ˌɪn·sə'dent·ə l/ *adj* happening by chance, or in connection with something of greater importance • *His influence on younger employees was incidental, not intentional.* ○ *Will I be reimbursed for incidental expenses at the conference?*

incidentally /ˌɪn·sə'dent·ə l·i, -'dent·li/ *adv* [not gradable] *"Ain't"* was mentioned only incidentally in an article about nonstandard words. • *Incidentally is also used to introduce something additional that is not as important: She, incidentally, was an enormous woman.*

incidentals /ˌɪn·sə'dent·ᵊlz/ *pl n* unimportant facts • *She may be wrong on incidentals, but she's never wrong in substance.* • Incidentals are also small expenses: *I need money for incidentals like coffee.*

incinerate /ɪn'sɪn·ə₁reɪt/ *v* [T] to burn (something) completely • *The company is accused of incinerating hazardous waste without a license.*

incinerator /ɪn'sɪn·ə₁reɪt̬·ər/ *n* [C] a device for burning waste material

incipient /ɪn'sɪp·i·ənt/ *adj slightly fml* just beginning or just coming into existence • *He has a black mustache and an incipient pot-belly.*

incision /ɪn'sɪʒ·ən/ *n* [C] *medical* a cut made in the surface of the skin or in other body tissue

incisive /ɪn'saɪ·sɪv/ *adj* expressing an idea or opinion clearly and in a persuasive manner • *The guide's incisive comments give us a new perspective on the painting.*

incisor /ɪn'saɪ·zər/ *n* [C] one of the sharp teeth at the front of the mouth that cut food when you bite into it • Compare MOLAR.

incite /ɪn'saɪt/ *v* [T] to encourage (someone) to do or feel something unpleasant or violent, or to cause (violent or unpleasant actions) • *He was trying to incite people to stir up a rebellion.*

incitement /ɪn'saɪt·mənt/ *n* [U] • *The film was described as an incitement to violence.*

inclement /ɪn'klem·ənt/ *adj* (of weather) unpleasant, esp. cold or stormy • *The concert in the park was postponed because of the inclement weather.*

inclination /ˌɪn·klə'neɪ·ʃən/ *n* [C] a preference or tendency, or a feeling that makes a person want to do something • *Tony has a strong inclination toward the arts.* ○ *If I were in your situation, my inclination would be to look for another job.*

inclined /ɪn'klaɪnd/ *adj* • *I'm inclined to agree with you.*

incline /ɪn'klaɪn/ *v* [I/T] to lean down, or to place (something) with one part toward the ground and the opposite part raised • *Marge inclined her head to whisper something to me.* [T]

incline /'ɪn·klaɪn/ *n* [C] a slope • *The road has a steep incline for the next ten miles.*

inclined /ɪn'klaɪnd, 'ɪn·klaɪnd/ *adj* • *an inclined roof/roadway/surface*

include /ɪn'kluːd/ *v* [T] (of something) to have (something smaller) as a part of it, or to make (something smaller) part of it • *The hotel room charge includes breakfast.* ○ *The encyclopedia includes the names of all Nobel Prize winners.* ○ *Sheila asked to be included among the people going on the tour.*

including /ɪn'kluːd·ɪŋ/ *prep* • *The book has 360 pages, including the index.*

inclusion /ɪn'kluː·ʒən/ *n* [U] the act of including something as a part of something else •

The inclusion of offensive words in the dictionary was discussed.

incoherent /ˌɪn·koʊ'hɪr·ənt/ *adj* not expressed in a way that can be understood, or not able to talk clearly • *He seemed dazed and incoherent, apparently from blood loss.*

income /'ɪn·kʌm, -kəm/ *n* [C/U] money that is earned from doing work or received from investments • An **income tax** is a tax on a person's income: *federal, state, and local income taxes*

incoming /'ɪn₁kʌm·ɪŋ/ *adj* [not gradable] arriving at, coming into, or entering a place • *Incoming flights are being delayed because of bad weather.*

incomparable /ɪn'kɑm·pə·rə·bəl, ˌɪn·kəm'pær·ə·bəl/ *adj* [not gradable] so good or great that nothing else could achieve the same standard • *the incomparable achievement of Einstein*

incompatible /ˌɪn·kəm'pæt̬·ə·bəl/ *adj* not able to exist or work with another person or thing • *Any new video system that is incompatible with existing ones has little chance of success.*

incompatibility /ˌɪn·kəm₁pæt̬·ə'bɪl·ət̬·i/ *n* [U]

incompetent /ɪn'kɑm·pət̬·ənt/ *adj* lacking the skills or knowledge to do a job or perform an action correctly or to a satisfactory standard • *Cowden was incompetent and incapable of administering the duties of secretary of the association.*

incompetent /ɪn'kɑm·pət̬·ənt/ *n* [C] • *The business failed because it was run by a bunch of incompetents.*

incompetence /ɪn'kɑm·pət̬·əns/ *n* [U] • *Local politicians accused the federal government of incompetence in failing to respond more quickly to the emergency.*

incompetently /ɪn'kɑm·pət̬·ənt·li/ *adv*

incomplete /ˌɪn·kəm'pliːt/ *adj* lacking some parts, or not finished • *The polls have closed but the results of the election are still incomplete.*

incomplete /ˌɪn·kəm'pliːt/ *n* [C] a mark, usually temporary, received when some of the work for a class has not been finished • *He failed to hand in his term paper, so he got an incomplete for the course.*

incomprehensible /ɪn₁kɑm·prɪ'hen·sə·bəl/ *adj* impossible or extremely difficult to understand • *The writing ability of some of the students was so poor that their essays were almost incomprehensible.*

inconceivable /ˌɪn·kən'siː·və·bəl/ *adj* impossible to imagine or think of • *Politicians always say that a tax increase is inconceivable.*

inconclusive /ˌɪn·kən'kluː·sɪv, -zɪv/ *adj* not giving or having a result or decision; uncertain • *The evidence is inconclusive, and no arrest is warranted.*

incongruous /ɪn'kɑŋ·grə·wəs/ *adj* appearing strange or wrong within a particular situation • *Having a picnic in a graveyard struck some as incongruous.*

inconsequential /ˌɪnˌkɑn·sɪ'kwen·tʃəl/ *adj* not important; able to be ignored • *Changes in the stock market were pretty inconsequential during the past week.*

inconsiderate /ˌɪn·kən'sɪd·ə·rət/ *adj* not caring about other people or their feelings; selfish • *She thought it was inconsiderate of him not to have asked her friend to the party.*

inconsistent NOT AGREEING /ˌɪn·kən'sɪs·tənt/ *adj* (of an argument or opinion) containing elements that are opposed and do not match, so that it is difficult to imagine how both can be true • *These findings are inconsistent with those of previous studies.*

inconsistency /ˌɪn·kən'sɪs·tən·si/ *n* [C/U] a situation in which two things do not match and are opposed • *There appear to be inconsistencies in her alibi.* [C]

inconsistent CHANGEABLE /ˌɪn·kən'sɪs·tənt/ *adj disapproving* changing in character; not staying the same • *The team's play is inconsistent—winning one day and losing the next.*

inconspicuous /ˌɪn·kən'spɪk·jə·wəs/ *adj* not easily noticed or seen; not attracting attention • *Agents placed the camera on a wall in an inconspicuous place.*

incontestable /ˌɪn·kən'tes·tə·bəl/ *adj* [not gradable] impossible to question because obviously true • *There is now incontestable evidence that the victim was murdered.*

incontinent /ɪn'kɑnt·ᵊn·ənt/ *adj* unable to control the excretion of urine or the contents of the bowels • *Many of our elderly patients are incontinent.*

incontinence /ɪn'kɑnt·ᵊn·əns/ *n* [U]

incontrovertible /ˌɪnˌkɑn·trə'vɜrt·ə·bəl/ *adj* [not gradable] *slightly fml* impossible to doubt because obviously true • *incontrovertible proof*

inconvenience /ˌɪn·kən'viːn·jəns/ *n* [C/U] something that causes trouble or difficulty and is annoying but not serious, or the condition of being in such an annoying situation • *Changing planes was an inconvenience, but there were no direct flights.* [C]

inconvenience /ˌɪn·kən'viːn·jəns/ *v* [T] • *The postal strike inconvenienced many people.*

inconvenient /ˌɪn·kən'viːn·jənt/ *adj* not convenient • *He scheduled the meeting for an inconvenient time, and few people could attend.*

incorporate INCLUDE /ɪn'kɔːr·pə‚reɪt/ *v* [T] to include (something) within something else • *This aircraft incorporates several new safety features.*

incorporate MAKE A COMPANY /ɪn'kɔːr·pə‚reɪt/ *v* [I/T] to make (a business) into a CORPORATION (= business protected by specific laws)

incorporated /ɪn'kɔːr·pə‚reɪt·əd/ (*abbreviation* **Inc.**) *adj* [only after n; not gradable] • *McLaughlin Glass, Incorporated*

incorrect /ˌɪn·kə'rekt/ *adj* not CORRECT; not accurate • *He charged that the news story was factually incorrect and demanded an apology.*

incorrectly /ˌɪn·kə'rekt·li/ *adv* • *For each question on the test that is answered incorrectly, you will lose two points.*

incorrigible /ɪn'kɔːr·ɪ·dʒə·bəl, -'kɑr-/ *adj* [not gradable] (of people and their behavior) impossible to improve or correct • *an incorrigible liar*

increase /ɪn'kriːs, 'ɪn·kriːs/ *v* [I/T] to become or make (something) larger or greater • *They've increased the price of gas by two cents a gallon.* [T] ○ *Pressure is increasing to make health insurance more widely available.* [I] USAGE: The opposite of increase is DECREASE.

increase /'ɪn·kriːs/ *n* [C/U] • *There was a slight increase in unemployment last month.* [C] • *Homelessness is* **on the increase** (= increasing) *in many cities.*

increasingly /ɪn'kriː·sɪŋ·li/ *adv* [not gradable] more often or to a greater degree • *She turned increasingly to radical diets to lose weight.*

incredible /ɪn'kred·ə·bəl/ *adj* impossible or very difficult to believe • *She showed incredible courage and determination in coming back from her injuries to compete again at the international level.* • Incredible is also used to emphasize that something is unusually good or bad: *It was an incredible bargain.*

incredibly /ɪn'kred·ə·bli/ *adv* • *Incredibly, no one was hurt in the accident.* • Incredibly also means extremely: *He was incredibly rude.* LP VERY, COMPLETELY, AND OTHER INTENSIFIERS

incredulous /ɪn'kredʒ·ə·ləs/ *adj* not wanting or not able to believe, and usually showing this • *"Why am I here?" the witness responded in an incredulous tone.*

increment /'ɪŋ·krə·mənt, 'ɪn-/ *n* [C] one of a series of amounts that increase a total • *She was in the habit of saving in small increments each week.*

incremental /ˌɪŋ·krə'ment·ᵊl, ˌɪn-/ *adj* [not gradable] • *Workers were promised two incremental pay increases a year.*

incriminate /ɪn'krɪm·ə‚neɪt/ *v* [T] to make (someone) seem guilty, esp. of a crime • *He refused to say anything on the grounds that he might incriminate himself.*

incriminating /ɪn'krɪm·ə‚neɪt̬·ɪŋ/ *adj* • *incriminating evidence/statements*

incubate /'ɪŋ·kjə‚beɪt, 'ɪn-/ *v* [I/T] to keep (esp. birds' eggs) warm until the young come out, or (of eggs) to develop to the stage at which the young come out

inculcate /ɪn'kʌl‚keɪt, 'ɪn·kʌl-/ *v* [T] *fml* to cause someone to have (particular beliefs or values) by repeating them frequently • *The goal is to inculcate in students a tolerance for people of other religions and races.*

incumbent PERSON /ɪn'kʌm·bənt/ *n* [C] (referring to the present time) a person who has a particular office or position, esp. an elected one • *Senator Smith, the incumbent, faces a tough fight for reelection next year.*

incumbent NECESSARY /ɪn'kʌm·bənt/ *adj fml*

• If it is **incumbent on/upon** you to do something, it is necessary for you to do it: *She felt it incumbent upon her to raise the subject of the safety of the children.* [+ *to* infinitive]

incur /ɪnˈkɜr/ *v* [T] **-rr-** to become responsible for or experience (esp. something bad) as a result of actions taken • *We incurred heavy expenses to repair the poor work done by the builder.*

incurable /ɪnˈkjʊr·ə·bəl/ *adj* [not gradable] not able to be cured • *Before antibiotics the disease was incurable.* • If you describe someone as incurable, you mean that nothing that happens can change them: *Marjorie is an incurable optimist.*

incursion /ɪnˈkɜr·ʒən/ *n* [C] a sudden and unwanted entrance to a place or area controlled by others, esp. in a military attack

indebted GRATEFUL /ɪnˈdet·əd/ *adj* • If you are **indebted to** someone, you are grateful to them because of help given: *For her encouragement and support, I am especially indebted to my wife, Nancy.*

indebted OWING /ɪnˈdet·əd/ *adj* owing money • *Heavily indebted farms are still struggling.*

indecent /ɪnˈdiː·sənt/ *adj* morally offensive, esp. in a sexual way • *The university prohibits gambling, pornography, and other materials that it considers indecent.*

indecision /ˌɪn·dɪˈsɪʒ·ən/, **indecisiveness** /ˌɪn·dɪˈsɑɪ·sɪv·nəs/ *n* [U] the quality of being unable to make a decision or having a lot of difficulty in deciding something • *I tossed and turned all night in a frenzy of indecision.*

indecisive /ˌɪn·dɪˈsɑɪ·sɪv/ *adj* • *As a leader during the war, he was indecisive and ineffectual, and was eventually relieved of his command.*

indeed /ɪnˈdiːd/ *adv* [not gradable] (used to emphasize something said or about to be said) really; truly • *If he has indeed quit his job, I asked myself, why is he still here?* ○ *From a medical standpoint, the discovery may turn out to be very big news indeed.* ○ *Indeed* (= When you really think about it), *why should you follow a doctor's advice to the letter when you feel like Superman?* • Indeed is also used to clarify or add to something you have just said: *It was impossible to find work and, indeed, it became increasingly hard to keep looking for a job.*

indefatigable /ˌɪn·dɪˈfæt·ə·gə·bəl/ *adj* slightly *fml* never becoming tired • *For many years Annie has been an indefatigable campaigner for human rights.*

indefensible /ˌɪn·dɪˈfen·sə·bəl/ *adj* (of behavior) so bad that it cannot be defended against criticism • *His actions in destroying the tapes were indefensible.*

indefinable /ˌɪn·dɪˈfɑɪ·nə·bəl/ *adj* impossible to clearly describe or explain • *She had about her an indefinable quality that charmed everyone.*

indefinite /ɪnˈdef·ə·nət/ *adj* not exact or not clear; without clear limits • *It was a wonderful opportunity, but it meant leaving family and friends for an indefinite period, perhaps forever.* • (*specialized*) In grammar, **indefinite article** is the grammatical name for the words "a" and "an" in English or words in other languages that have a similar use. Compare **definite article** at DEFINITE. LP ARTICLES

indefinitely /ɪnˈdef·ə·nət·li/ *adv* • *In the light of recent disclosures, the business deal has been postponed indefinitely.*

indelible /ɪnˈdel·ə·bəl/ *adj* [not gradable] impossible to remove by washing or by any other method • *an indelible mark* ○ (*fig.*) *His performance of Hamlet left an indelible impression on all who saw it.*

indelicate /ɪnˈdel·ɪ·kət/ *adj* showing a lack of awareness of socially correct behavior • *There was an embarrassed silence after his indelicate remark about her age.*

indemnity /ɪnˈdem·nət·i/ *n* [C/U] *law* protection against possible damage or loss, esp. a promise of payment, or the money paid if there is such damage or loss

indent /ɪnˈdent/ *v* [T] to begin (a line of written or printed text) after leaving extra space, compared with the place where other lines begin • *Normally each new paragraph is indented.*

indentation /ˌɪn·denˈteɪ·ʃən/ *n* [C] a part of a surface that curves inward • *If a surgeon takes out too much fat, he may leave indentations in the skin.*

independent /ˌɪn·dɪˈpen·dənt/ *adj* not influenced or controlled by other people but free to make your own decisions • *an independent thinker* ○ *Congress called for the appointment of an independent counsel to investigate the president.* ○ *Now that Jean's got a job, she's financially independent* (= she does not need money from other people). • If a country becomes independent, it is no longer governed or ruled by another country. • (*specialized*) In grammar, an **independent clause** is a clause in a sentence that would form a complete sentence by itself. • An **independent contractor** is a person who agrees to do a particular job for someone else for an agreed amount of money but who is not an employee: *She used to be on staff, but now she's an independent contractor.*

independence /ˌɪn·dɪˈpen·dəns/ *n* [U] • *Most college students who live on a campus are enjoying independence from their families for the first time in their lives.* ○ *Juan is in favor of Puerto Rican independence* (= the condition of not being governed by another country). • In the US, **Independence Day** is the official name for the **Fourth of July** holiday. See at FOUR.

independently /ˌɪn·dɪˈpen·dənt·li/ *adv* • *The discovery of the AIDS virus was made independently in France and the United States.*

indescribable /ˌɪn·dɪˈskraɪ·bə·bəl/ *adj* [not gradable] impossible to describe, esp. because extremely good or bad • *The stench was indescribable.*

indestructible /ˌɪn·dɪˈstrʌk·tə·bəl/ *adj* [not gradable] impossible to destroy or break • *The fireproof material used is virtually indestructible.*

indeterminate /ˌɪn·dɪˈtɜr·mə·nət/ *adj* not clearly determined or established • *Juvenile criminals are sometimes sentenced to indeterminate prison terms rather than a fixed length of time.*

index LIST /ˈɪn·deks/ *n* [C] *pl* **indexes** /ˈɪn·dek·səz/ or **indices** /ˈɪn·də·siːz/ an alphabetical list, such as one printed at the back of a book showing on which page a name or subject appears, or computer information ordered in a particular way • *If you want to find the place in the text that Henry James is mentioned, look it up in the index.*

index /ˈɪn·deks/ *v* [T] • *He organized and indexed the material by computer.*

index COMPARISON /ˈɪn·deks/ *n* [C] *pl* **indices** /ˈɪn·də·siːz/ or **indexes** /ˈɪn·dek·səz/ a number used to show the value of something by comparing it to something else whose value is known • *a wage/price index* ○ *(fig.) The rate of consumer spending is often thought to be an index of public confidence* (= show the state of the public's confidence) *in the health of the economy.*

index /ˈɪn·deks/ *v* [T] • *Social Security payments are indexed to* (= adjusted to allow for) *inflation every year.*

index finger /ˈɪn·deksˈfɪŋ·gər/ *n* [C] the finger next to the thumb; FOREFINGER • *He pointed his index finger at me and cried out, "I mean you!"*

Indian /ˈɪn·diː·ən/ *n* [C], *adj* [not gradable] (an) **American Indian**, see at AMERICAN • Indian also means a person from India, or relating to India.

Indian summer /ˈɪn·diːənˈsʌm·ər/ *n* [C] a period of warm weather happening in the fall when you expect cooler weather

indicate (*obj*) /ˈɪn·dəˌkeɪt/ *v* to show or signal (a direction or warning), or to make (something) clear • *These statistics might indicate quality problems.* [T] ○ *She did not move or indicate that she had heard him.* [+ *that* clause]

indication /ˌɪn·dəˈkeɪ·ʃən/ *n* [C/U] • *Is that nod an indication of your agreement?* [C] ○ *The jury gave no indication of their decision as they came back into the courtroom.* [U]

indicative /ɪnˈdɪk·ət̬·ɪv/ *adj* • *Resumption of the talks is indicative of an improved relationship between the countries.*

indicator /ˈɪn·dəˌkeɪt̬·ər/ *n* [C] • *Housing permits are an indicator of the state's economic health.* ○ *The car's speedometer and temperature indicator were broken.*

indicative /ɪnˈdɪk·ət̬·ɪv/ *n* [U], *adj* [not gradable] *specialized* (in grammar) the MOOD (= form) of a verb used in ordinary statements and questions • *In the sentence "We walked home," the verb "walked" is in the indicative.*

indices /ˈɪn·dəˌsiːz/ *pl of* INDEX

indict /ɪnˈdaɪt/ *v* [T] *law* to accuse (someone) officially of a crime • *Five people were indicted on drug charges.*

indictment /ɪnˈdaɪt·mənt/ *n* [C] *law* a formal statement of accusation • An indictment is also a reason for giving blame: *The high level of adult illiteracy is seen as an indictment of the country's education policy.*

indifferent NOT INTERESTED /ɪnˈdɪf·rənt/ *adj* [not gradable] lacking in interest or feeling • *an indifferent student* ○ *She was utterly indifferent to his irritation.*

indifference /ɪnˈdɪf·rəns/ *n* [U] • *Her indifference to sports bothered him.*

indifferent NOT GOOD OR BAD /ɪnˈdɪf·rənt/ *adj* [not gradable] neither very good nor very bad • *No matter how good or bad or indifferent Foster is, he'll always be my friend.*

indigenous /ɪnˈdɪdʒ·ə·nəs/ *adj* [not gradable] existing naturally or having always lived in a place; NATIVE • *The Navajos are among the indigenous people of North America.* ○ *Are there any species of frog indigenous to the area?*

indigent /ˈɪn·dɪ·dʒənt/ *adj* [not gradable] *slightly fml* (of a person) having no money or anything else of value

indigestible /ˌɪn·dəˈdʒes·tə·bəl, ˌɪn·daɪ-/ *adj* (of food) difficult or impossible to change into smaller forms that the body can absorb after eating it • *The meat was so tough, it was almost indigestible.*

indigestion /ˌɪn·dəˈdʒes·tʃən, ˌɪn·daɪ-/ *n* [U] an uncomfortable condition caused when your body cannot DIGEST food after you have eaten it • *Greasy food gives me indigestion.*

indignant /ɪnˈdɪg·nənt/ *adj* angry because of something that is wrong or not fair • *She wrote an indignant letter to the paper complaining about the mayor's actions.*

indignantly /ɪnˈdɪg·nənt·li/ *adv* • *"Your assumption is entirely incorrect," he declared indignantly.*

indignation /ˌɪn·dɪgˈneɪ·ʃən/ *n* [U] • *They reacted with shock and indignation when they were accused of cheating.*

indignity /ɪnˈdɪg·nət̬·i/ *n* [C/U] loss of respect, or something that causes this • *She describes the indignities that rape victims bear after the crime.* [C]

indirect ADDITIONAL /ˌɪn·dəˈrekt, ˌɪn·daɪ-/ *adj* happening in addition to an intended result • *Several other people died as an indirect result of his violence.*

indirect NOT STRAIGHT /ˌɪn·dəˈrekt, ˌɪn·daɪ-/ *adj* not following a straight line, or not connected in a simple way • *an indirect route* ○ *Ransom thought the best approach in defending truth is the indirect one.* • *(specialized)* In grammar, an

indirect object is the person or thing that receives the effect of the action of a verb that has two objects: *In the sentence "Give Jason some cake," "Jason" is the indirect object.* Compare **direct object** at DIRECT STRAIGHT. See also OBJECT GRAMMAR. LP VERBS WITH TWO OBJECTS at OBJECT GRAMMAR • (*specialized*) **Indirect speech** is **reported speech**. See at REPORT TELL.

indirectly /ˌɪn·də'rek·tli, ˌɪn·daɪ-/ *adv* • *She controls the company indirectly, through a hand-picked board of directors.*

indiscreet /ˌɪn·dɪ'skriːt/ *adj* not careful in saying or doing things that should be kept secret • *It was indiscreet of you to mention the party—she hasn't been invited.*

indiscretion /ˌɪn·dɪ'skreʃ·ən/ *n* [C/U] • *youthful indiscretions* [C] ○ *This sort of indiscretion is unforgivable!* [U]

indiscriminate /ˌɪn·dɪ'skrɪm·ə·nət/ *adj* not showing careful thought or planning, esp. so that harm results • *Breast cancer is completely indiscriminate in whom it strikes.*

indiscriminately /ˌɪn·dɪ'skrɪm·ə·nət·li/ *adv* • *Words like "organic" and "natural" are used so indiscriminately that they are often meaningless.*

indispensable /ˌɪn·dɪ'spen·sə·bəl/ *adj* too important not to have; necessary • *None of our players is indispensable.*

indisputable /ˌɪn·dɪ'spjuːt̬·ə·bəl/ *adj* [not gradable] obviously true • *an indisputable fact*
indisputably /ˌɪn·dɪ'spjuːt̬·ə·bli/ *adv* [not gradable] • *He is indisputably one of the finest baseball players ever.*

indistinct /ˌɪn·dɪ'stɪŋt/ *adj* not clear • *an indistinct shape/sound/recollection*

indistinguishable /ˌɪn·dɪ'stɪŋ·gwɪʃ·ə·bəl, -wɪʃ-/ *adj* [not gradable] impossible to notice differences when compared to another similar thing • *The fish's markings make it virtually indistinguishable from the sand it swims over.*

individual /ˌɪn·də'vɪdʒ·ə·wəl/ *n* [C] a single person or thing, esp. when compared to the group or set to which it belongs • *We will remember him as an individual who always tried to make people happy.*

individual /ˌɪn·də'vɪdʒ·ə·wəl/ *adj* [not gradable] • *Every company has its own individual style.*
individually /ˌɪn·də'vɪdʒ·ə·wə·li/ *adv* [not gradable] • *The children will first sing individually and then as a group.*

individuality /ˌɪn·də,vɪdʒ·ə'wæl·ət̬·i/ *n* [U] • *His individuality* (= That which makes him different) *really comes out when he dances.*

individualism /ˌɪn·də'vɪdʒ·ə·wə,lɪz·əm/ *n* [U] the idea that each person should think and act independently rather than depending on others • *Many Americans believe strongly in individualism.*

individualist /ˌɪn·də'vɪdʒ·ə·wə·ləst/ *n* [C] a person who is different and original in their

thoughts and actions • *Even though she's part of the mainstream, McCardell remains an individualist who thinks for herself.*
individualistic /ˌɪn·də,vɪdʒ·ə·wə'lɪs·tɪk/ *adj* • *Americans are highly individualistic and self-concerned.*

indivisible /ˌɪn·də'vɪz·ə·bəl/ *adj* [not gradable] not able to be divided into parts

indoctrinate /ɪn'dɑk·trə,neɪt/ *v* [T] *esp. disapproving* to persuade (someone) to accept an idea by repeating it and showing it to be true • *These groups are trying to indoctrinate our society with racial and religious hatred.*

indolent /'ɪn·də·lənt/ *adj slightly fml* without real interest or effort; LAZY • *I was an indolent creature who could not imagine action.*

indomitable /ɪn'dɑm·ət̬·ə·bəl/ *adj* (of a person) strong, brave, and impossible to defeat or make frightened • *an indomitable spirit/will*

indoor /ˌɪn,dɔːr, -,dour/ *adj* [not gradable] happening, used, or being inside a building • *indoor sports* ○ *indoor plumbing* ○ *an indoor swimming pool* • USAGE: The opposite of indoor is OUTDOOR.

indoors /ɪn'dɔːrz, -'dourz/ *adv* [not gradable] • *Come indoors, it's cold outside.* • USAGE: The opposite of indoors is OUTDOORS.

induce /ɪn'duːs/ *v* [T] to persuade (someone) to do something, or to cause (something) to happen • *They induced her to take the job by offering her a bonus.* • *If doctors induce labor, they cause a baby to be born before its natural time.*
inducement /ɪn'duːs·mənt/ *n* [C] • *If you want me to stay, you're going to have to offer me some inducement.*

induct /ɪn'dʌkt/ *v* [T] to introduce (someone) formally or with a special ceremony to an organization or group • *She was inducted into the army.*
inductee /ˌɪn,dʌk'tiː/ *n* [C] • *Basketball Hall of Fame inductee Cheryl Miller will be there.*
induction /ɪn'dʌk·ʃən/ *n* [C/U] • *He refused induction into the Army on religious grounds.* [U]

indulge /ɪn'dʌldʒ/ *v* [I/T] to allow yourself or someone else to have something enjoyable • *When I get my first paycheck I'm going to indulge in a shopping spree.* [I] ○ *He indulged his passion for skiing whenever he could.* [T]
indulgence /ɪn'dʌl·dʒəns/ *n* [C/U] • *Heavy indulgence in alcohol should be avoided.* [U] ○ *I do not much like self-quotation, but I shall ask your indulgence.* [C]
indulgent /ɪn'dʌl·dʒənt/ *adj* • *He was indulgent to his grandchildren.*

industry PRODUCTION /'ɪn·də·stri, 'ɪn,dʌs·tri/ *n* [U] the companies and activities involved in the production of goods for sale, esp. in a factory • *business and industry*
industrial /ɪn'dʌs·tri·əl/ *adj* • *industrial output* ○ *It's an industrial city* (= one that has

many factories). • An **industrial park** is a special area for factories and businesses.

industrialist /ɪnˈdʌsˌtriːəˌləst/ *n* [C] an owner or an employee in a high position in industry

industrialized /ɪnˈdʌsˌtriːəˌlaɪzd/ *adj* • *industrialized nations*

industry TYPE OF WORK /ˈɪnˌdəˌstri, ˈɪnˌdʌsˌtri/ *n* [C] a type of business • *She's worked in the banking and computer industries.*

industry HARD WORK /ˈɪnˌdəˌstri, ˈɪnˌdʌsˌtri/ *n* [U] the quality of working hard • *It takes industry and determination to complete a Ph.D.*

industrious /ɪnˈdʌsˌtriːəs/ *adj* • *Every employee is expected to be competent and industrious.*

inebriated /ɪˈniːbriˌeɪt̮əd/ *adj* having drunk too much alcohol • *In her inebriated state she was ready to agree to anything.*

inedible /ɪˈnedəbəl/ *adj* not suitable as food • *The potato plant produces inedible fruit that looks like green tomatoes.*

ineffective /ˌɪnəˈfekˌtɪv/ *adj* not producing the results that are wanted; not effective • *Those pills were ineffective—I still have a headache.*

ineffectual /ˌɪnəˈfekˌtʃəwəl/ *adj* not able to produce good results • *an ineffectual teacher*

inefficient /ˌɪnəˈfɪʃˌənt/ *adj* wasteful of time, money, energy, or other valuable possessions or qualities • *Many of their industries are hopelessly inefficient.*

inefficiently /ˌɪnəˈfɪʃˌəntˌli/ *adv* • *He uses his time inefficiently.*

inefficiency /ˌɪnəˈfɪʃˌənˌsi/ *n* [U] • *She promised to end government inefficiency.*

inelegant /ɪnˈelɪˌɡənt/ *adj* not graceful and attractive in character or appearance • *inelegant writing*

ineligible /ɪnˈelədʒəbəl/ *adj* [not gradable] not allowed by the rules • *After serving two terms, the president was ineligible to run again.* [+ *to* infinitive]

inept /ɪˈnept/ *adj* not skilled or effective • *He was always pretty inept at sports.*

ineptitude /ɪˈnepˌtəˌtuːd/ *n* [U] • *political/social/economic ineptitude*

inequality /ˌɪnɪˈkwɑlˌət̮i/ *n* [C/U] a lack of equality or fair treatment in the sharing of wealth or opportunities • *social/racial inequality* [U]

inequity /ɪˈnekˌwət̮i/ *n* [C/U] *slightly fml* the quality of being unfair, or something that is not fair or equal • *We're working to reduce the inequities in school funding.* [C]

inert NOT MOVING /ɪˈnɜrt/ *adj* not moving or not able to move • *The inert figure of a man lay in the front of the car.*

inert CHEMISTRY /ɪˈnɜrt/ *adj* [not gradable] not reacting chemically with other substances • *an inert gas*

inertia /ɪˈnɜrˌʃə/ *n* [U] the tendency not to change what is happening • *Many teachers were reluctant to use computers in their classrooms simply out of inertia.* • (*specialized*) In physics, inertia is the force that causes something moving to tend to continue moving, and that causes something not moving to tend to continue not to move.

inescapable /ˌɪnəˈskeɪpəbəl/ *adj* [not gradable] not avoidable • *The inescapable truth is that cigarette smokers cause their own illness.*

inevitable /ɪˈnevˌət̮əbəl/ *adj* [not gradable] certain to happen • *Accidents are the inevitable result of carelessness.*

inevitably /ɪˈnevˌət̮əbli/ *adv* [not gradable] • *He inevitably orders iced tea with his lunch.*

inexact /ˌɪnɪɡˈzækt/ *adj* not known in detail or not completely accurate • *Economics is an inexact science.*

inexcusable /ˌɪnɪkˈskjuːzəbəl/ *adj* (of behavior) too bad to be accepted • *It was inexcusable for them to leave so early.*

inexhaustible /ˌɪnɪɡˈzɔːstəbəl/ *adj* [not gradable] existing in such large amounts that it cannot be used completely or cannot come to an end • *There's a nearly inexhaustible supply of people willing to buy those homes.*

inexorable /ɪˈnekˌsərəbəl, ɪˈneɡˌzə-/ *adj* [not gradable] continuing without any possibility of being stopped • *Aging is an inexorable process.*

inexpensive /ˌɪnɪkˈspenˌsɪv/ *adj* costing little money • *an inexpensive hotel*

inexperience /ˌɪnɪkˈspɪrˌiːəns/ *n* [U] lack of practice in a particular activity • *He has been criticized for his inexperience in foreign affairs.*

inexperienced /ˌɪnɪkˈspɪrˌiːənst/ *adj* • *She's relatively inexperienced with computers.*

inexplicable /ˌɪnɪkˈsplɪkəbəl, ɪˈnekˌsplɪk-/ *adj* that cannot be explained or understood • *an inexplicable accident*

inexplicably /ˌɪnɪkˈsplɪkəbli, ɪˈnekˌsplɪk-/ *adv* • *He inexplicably started to undress.*

inextricable /ˌɪnɪkˈstrɪkəbəl, ɪˈnekˌstrɪk-/ *adj* [not gradable] unable to be separated, freed, or escaped from • *People say sex and love are inextricable.*

inextricably /ˌɪnɪkˈstrɪkəbli, ɪˈnekˌstrɪk-/ *adv* • *The Louis Armstrong legend is inextricably linked with his recordings.*

infallible /ɪnˈfæləbəl/ *adj* [not gradable] never wrong, or never failing • *Memory is not infallible.*

infallibly /ɪnˈfæləbli/ *adv* [not gradable] • *My car infallibly starts in cold weather.* • Infallibly also means always: *He is infallibly cheerful.*

infallibility /ɪnˌfæləˈbɪlˌət̮i/ *n* [U] • *His stubborn belief in his own infallibility kept him from listening to others.*

infamous /ˈɪnˌfəˌməs/ *adj* well known for something bad; NOTORIOUS • *He is infamous for saying that cheating is the way the game is played.*

infamy /ˈɪnˌfəˌmi/ *n* [U] • *Franklin Roosevelt*

spoke of Japan's attack on Pearl Harbor as "a day that will live in infamy."

infant /'ɪn·fənt/ *n* [C] a baby

infancy /'ɪn·fən·si/ *n* [U] the state or period of being a baby, or (*fig.*) the early stage of growth or development of something • (*fig.*) *Bird research on the island is still in its infancy.*

infantile /'ɪn·fən,taɪl/ *adj* of or relating to babies • *infantile diarrhea* • If you describe the behavior of an older child or adult as infantile, you mean that it is foolish and is typical of a young child: *infantile humor*

infantry /'ɪn·fən·tri/ *n* [U] soldiers who fight on foot

infatuated /ɪn'fætʃ·ə,weɪt̬·əd/ *adj* having a strong but unreasonable feeling of love or attraction for someone or something • *Susan was infatuated with her friend's brother.*

infatuation /ɪn,fætʃ·ə'weɪ·ʃən/ *n* [C/U] • *It's just an infatuation—she'll get over it.* [C]

infect /ɪn'fekt/ *v* [T] to cause disease in (someone) by introducing organisms such as bacteria or viruses • *He infected at least three women with the AIDS virus.* ○ (*fig.*) *He felt that racism had infected almost every aspect of American life.*

infected /ɪn'fek·təd/ *adj* [not gradable] • *an infected toe*

infection /ɪn'fek·ʃən/ *n* [C/U] • *a sinus infection* [C]

infectious /ɪn'fek·ʃəs/ *adj* [not gradable] • *infectious diseases* • If something is infectious, it quickly spreads or influences others: *an infectious laugh*

infer (*obj*) /ɪn'fɜr/ *v* -rr- to reach an opinion from available information or facts • *He inferred from her letter that she was not interested in a relationship.* [+ *that* clause]

inference /'ɪn·fə·rəns, -frəns/ *n* [C] • *His inference was that I had been promoted because of my father.*

inferior /ɪn'fɪr·iː·ər/ *adj* worse than average, or not as good as others of the same type • *She felt inferior to her older sister.* • Compare SUPERIOR BETTER.

inferiority /ɪn,fɪr·iː'ɔːr·ət̬·i, -'ɑr-/ *n* [U] • *feelings of inferiority* • If you have an **inferiority complex**, you feel you are less important, intelligent, or skillful than other people.

infertile /ɪn'fɜrt·ᵊl/ *adj* [not gradable] (of people or animals) not able to produce young, or (of land) of poor quality for growing crops • *an infertile couple* ○ *infertile soil*

infertility /,ɪn·fər'tɪl·ət̬·i/ *n* [U] • *After a year of trying to get pregnant, she sought treatment for infertility.* ○ *There are two million couples with infertility problems.*

infest /ɪn'fest/ *v* [T] (of insects and some animals) to be present in large numbers, sometimes causing disease or damage • *When we first moved in, the apartment was infested with cockroaches.*

infidelity /,ɪn·fə'del·ət̬·i/ *n* [C/U] the act of having sex with someone who is not your husband or wife • *marital infidelity* [U]

infield /'ɪn·fiːld/ *n* [U] (in baseball) the part of the playing field enclosed by the BASES, or the four players whose positions are near the bases • Compare OUTFIELD.

infielder /'ɪn,fiːl·dər/ *n* [C] any of the four players positioned in the infield

infighting /'ɪn,faɪt·ɪŋ/ *n* [U] arguments or competition between members of a group for power or influence • *Infighting continues among union and management representatives on the board.*

infiltrate /ɪn'fɪl,treɪt, 'ɪn·fɪl-/ *v* [I/T] to become a member of (a group or organization) esp. to get information secretly about its activities • *The FBI had successfully infiltrated the neo-Nazi group.* [T]

infinite /'ɪn·fə·nət/ *adj* [not gradable] without limits; extremely large or great • *infinite space* ○ *God's infinite love*

infinitely /'ɪn·fə·nət·li/ *adv* [not gradable] very much • *Downtown traffic is infinitely worse than when we first moved to L.A.*

infinitesimal /,ɪn·fɪn·ə'tes·ə·məl/ *adj* extremely small • *Even in infinitesimal amounts, this poison can kill you.*

infinitive /ɪn'fɪn·ət̬·ɪv/ *n* [C] specialized (in grammar) the basic form of a verb, usually following "to" or another verb form • *In the sentences "I had to go" and "I must go," "go" is an infinitive.*

infinity /ɪn'fɪn·ət̬·i/ *n* [C/U] unlimited space, time, or amount, or a number large beyond any limit

infirm /ɪn'fɜrm/ *adj* physically or mentally weak, esp. because of old age or illness

infirmity /ɪn'fɜr·mət̬·i/ *n* [C/U] (a) physical or mental weakness

infirmary /ɪn'fɜr·mə·ri/ *n* [C] a hospital, or a room in a school or prison, where the sick are given care or treatment

inflame /ɪn'fleɪm/ *v* [T] to excite (someone's) strong feelings or make them stronger • *The defense objected to the graphic pictures, claiming they were meant merely to inflame the jury.*

inflamed /ɪn'fleɪmd/ *adj* (of a part of the body) red, sore, and often swollen, esp. because of infection • *An inflamed tendon in his right shoulder kept him out of the game.*

inflammation /,ɪn·flə'meɪ·ʃən/ *n* [C/U] • *Tennis elbow is an inflammation of the ligaments below the elbow.* [C]

inflammable /ɪn'flæm·ə·bəl/ *adj* FLAMMABLE

inflammatory /ɪn'flæm·ə,tɔːr·i, -,toʊr·i/ *adj* likely to excite strong feelings, esp. of anger • *He wrote an inflammatory headline, "Big Brave Men Beat a Tired Beast to Death."*

inflate ⟨FILL WITH AIR⟩ /ɪn'fleɪt/ *v* [I/T] to cause (an object) to increase in size and shape by filling it with air or gas, or (of an object) to become larger as a result of this process • *to* *inflate balloons* [T] ○ *Air bags in cars are designed to inflate automatically on impact.* [I]

inflatable /ɪnˈfleɪt̬·ə·bəl/ *adj* [not gradable] • *an inflatable mattress*

inflate MAKE GREATER /ɪnˈfleɪt/ *v* [T] to make (a number or value) higher or greater than it should be, or to make (something) seem more important than it really is • *Company officials misled the public in order to inflate the value of the company's stock.* ○ *The story was inflated by the media.*

inflation /ɪnˈfleɪ·ʃən/ *n* [U] a continuing rise in prices caused by an increase in the money supply and demand for goods

inflationary /ɪnˈfleɪ·ʃəˌner·i/ *adj* • *Inflationary pressures seem to be building in the economy.*

inflection SPEECH /ɪnˈflek·ʃən/ *n* [U] change in the quality of the voice, often showing an emotion • *Phyllis replies without any particular inflection in her voice, "I guess I'm lazy."*

inflection GRAMMAR /ɪnˈflek·ʃən/ *n* [C] specialized (in grammar) a change in a word form or ending to show a difference in the word's meaning or use • *"Gets," "got," and "gotten" are inflections of the verb "get."*

inflexible NOT CHANGING /ɪnˈflek·sə·bəl/ *adj* fixed and unable or unwilling to change • *Some officials think the law is too harsh and inflexible, and they argue it should be changed.*

inflexible STIFF /ɪnˈflek·sə·bəl/ *adj* [not gradable] (of a substance) stiff and hard, and not able to be bent • *an inflexible material*

inflict /ɪnˈflɪkt/ *v* [T] to force someone or something to experience (something unpleasant) • *Why would anyone inflict harm on a helpless animal?*

influence /ˈɪn·fluˌəns, Southern also ɪnˈfluː-/ *v* [T] to cause (someone) to change their behavior or the way they think about something, or to cause (something) to be changed • *Businesses make large contributions to members of Congress, hoping to influence their votes on key issues.* ○ *She was influenced by the common-sense views of her grandparents.* ○ *That speech influenced the course of American history.*

influence /ˈɪn·fluˌəns, Southern also ɪnˈfluː-/ *n* [C/U] the power to have an effect on people or things, or someone or something having such power • *The kid next door is a bad/good influence on Kevin.* [C] ○ *She used her influence to get her son a summer job.* [U]

influential /ˌɪn·fluˈen·t̬əl/ *adj* having a lot of influence • *Dr. Carter is an influential member of the board.*

influenza /ˌɪn·fluˈen·zə/ *n* [U] esp. medical FLU

influx /ˈɪn·flʌks/ *n* [U] the arrival of a large number of people or things • *The border patrol has been increased to curb the influx of illegal immigrants.*

info /ˈɪn·foʊ/ *n* [U] short form of INFORMATION • *For additional info, call this number.*

inform /ɪnˈfɔːrm/ *v* [T] to tell (someone) about something • *Keep me informed about any job opportunities.* ○ *She informed her tenants that she was raising the rent.*

informant /ɪnˈfɔːr·mənt/ *n* [C] a person who tells esp. the police or newspaper reporters about something • *He was working as an undercover drug informant for police.*

informative /ɪnˈfɔːr·mət̬·ɪv/ *adj* providing useful knowledge or ideas • *The dietician's talk was very informative.*

informer /ɪnˈfɔːr·mər/ *n* [C] a person who tells esp. the police about someone's criminal activities

informal /ɪnˈfɔːr·məl/ *adj* not formal or official, or not suitable for official or special occasions • *an informal gathering* ○ *Informal talks resumed today in an attempt to end the strike.*

informally /ɪnˈfɔːr·mə·li/ *adv* • *It's OK to dress informally for the dinner party.*

informality /ˌɪn·fɔːrˈmæl·ət̬·i/ *n* [U]

information /ˌɪn·fərˈmeɪ·ʃən/, short form **info** *n* [U] news, facts, or knowledge • *an important piece of information* ○ *Can you give us some information on tours to Alaska?* ○ *Information about upcoming local events is printed in the newspaper.* • The **information superhighway** is an electronic network for exchanging information quickly and over large distances using advanced computers and other systems.

infraction /ɪnˈfræk·ʃən/ *n* [C] *fml* a breaking of a rule or law • *a minor infraction*

infrared /ˌɪn·frəˈred/ *adj* [not gradable] specialized describing light at the red end of the SPECTRUM (= set of colors into which light is separated), which cannot be seen by human beings, and which gives out heat

infrastructure /ˈɪn·frəˌstrʌk·tʃər/ *n* [C] the basic structure of an organization or system which is necessary for its operation, esp. public water, energy, and systems for communication and transport

infrequent /ɪnˈfriː·kwənt/ *adj* not happening often; rare • *Wiggins made one of his infrequent trips into Manhattan.*

infrequently /ɪnˈfriː·kwənt·li/ *adv*

infringe /ɪnˈfrɪndʒ/ *v* [I/T] to act in a way that is against (a law) or that limits (someone's rights or freedom) • *Copying videos infringes copyright law.* [T] ○ *The senator is opposed to any laws that infringe on a citizen's right to bear arms.* [I always + adv/prep]

infringement /ɪnˈfrɪndʒ·mənt/ *n* [C/U] • *copyright/patent infringement* [U]

infuriate /ɪnˈfjʊr·iˌeɪt/ *v* [T] to make (someone) extremely angry • *The referee's calls infuriated the home team fans.*

infuriating /ɪnˈfjʊr·iˌeɪt̬·ɪŋ/ *adj* causing anger and annoyance • *It's infuriating to be kept waiting this long!*

infuse /ɪnˈfjuːz/ *v* [T] to cause (someone or

something) to take in and be filled with a quality or a condition of mind • *His landscape paintings were infused with a warm, subtle light.*

infusion /ɪnˈfjuːˌʒən/ n [C] an inward flow that helps to fill something • *An infusion of funds is desperately needed.*

ingenious /ɪnˈdʒiːnˌjəs/ adj (of a person) skilled at inventing new ways to do something and esp. to solve problems, or (of ideas or things) original, and showing esp. the ability to solve problems • *an ingenious engineer/songwriter* ○ *She devised an ingenious solution to the problem.*

ingenuity /ˌɪnˌdʒəˈnuːˌəṭˌi/ n [U] the skill of thinking, performing, or using things in new ways, esp. to solve problems • *With a little ingenuity, meals can be tasty as well as inexpensive.*

ingest /ɪnˈdʒest/ v [T] *fml* to take (food or liquid) into the stomach • *These mushrooms are poisonous if ingested.*

ingrained /ˈɪnˌɡreɪnd/ adj [not gradable] (of beliefs, attitudes, or habits) so established that they are difficult to change • *The incident only served to stir up the ingrained hatred of poor and blue-collar whites.*

ingratiate /ɪnˈɡreɪˌʃiːˌeɪt/ v [T] *disapproving* to try to make (yourself) especially pleasant in order to get someone to like or approve of you, and often to influence them to do something for you • *He tries to ingratiate himself with the boss by saying that all her ideas are brilliant.*

ingratitude /ɪnˈɡræt̬ˌəˌtuːd/ n [U] lack of appreciation for help that has been given

ingredient /ɪnˈɡriːdˌiːˌənt/ n [C] one of the parts in a mixture • *Combine all the ingredients for the stew.* ○ *(fig.) She viewed color as an essential ingredient of good design.*

ingrown /ˈɪnˌɡroʊn/ adj [not gradable] growing into the flesh • *an ingrown toenail*

inhabit /ɪnˈhæbˌət/ v [T] to live in (a place) • *These remote islands are inhabited only by birds and animals.*

inhabitant /ɪnˈhæbˌəṭˌənt/ n [C] a person or animal living in a place

inhale /ɪnˈheɪl/ v [I/T] to breathe in (something) • *She inhaled (the fresh air) deeply.* [I/T]

inhalation /ˌɪnˌhəˈleɪˌʃən, ˌɪnˌəlˈeɪ-/ n [U] • *Two firefighters were treated for smoke inhalation.*

inhaler /ɪnˈheɪˌlər/ n [C] a small device for breathing in a medicine, used esp. by people who have ASTHMA (= disease that can make breathing difficult)

inherent /ɪnˈhɪrˌənt, -ˈher-/ adj [not gradable] existing as a natural and permanent quality of something or someone • *The drug has certain inherent side effects.*

inherently /ɪnˈhɪrˌəntˌli, -ˈher-/ adv [not gradable] • *The oldest nuclear reactors are inherently unsafe.*

inherit /ɪnˈherˌət/ v [T] to receive (money, property, or possessions) from someone after

they have died, or to be born with (characteristics) that a parent, grandparent, or other relative has • *Who will inherit the house when he dies?* ○ *She inherits her musical ability from her father.*

inheritance /ɪnˈherˌəṭˌəns/ n [C/U] money, land, or possessions received from someone after they have died

inhibit /ɪnˈhɪbˌət/ v [T] to take an action that makes (something) less likely to happen, or that discourages (someone) from doing something • *He argued that the university's attempt to ban sexist and racist writing would inhibit free speech.* ○ *Fear of further abuse inhibited her from speaking out.*

inhibition /ˌɪnˌhəˈbɪʃˌən, ˌɪnˌə-/ n [C/U] an inability to act naturally esp. because of a lack of confidence • *After a couple of drinks he loses his inhibitions.* [C]

inhuman /ɪnˈhjuːˌmən, -ˈjuː-/ adj [not gradable] extremely cruel; lacking in or not influenced by human feeling • *In those days war movies always portrayed the enemy as fanatical, even inhuman.*

inhumanity /ˌɪnˌhjuːˈmænˌəṭˌi, -juː-/ n [U] inhuman treatment or behavior

inhumane /ˌɪnˌhjuːˈmeɪn, -juː-/ adj [not gradable] cruel to people or animals in not caring about their suffering or about the conditions under which they live • *Prisoners were confined in tiny cells without toilets in inhumane conditions.*

inimitable /ɪˈnɪmˌəṭˌəˌbəl/ adj [not gradable] *slightly fml* impossible to copy because of being of very high quality or a particular style • *Louis Armstrong's inimitable gravelly voice*

initial ~BEGINNING~ /ɪˈnɪʃˌəl/ adj [not gradable] of or at the beginning; first • *She failed her driving test on the initial try, but passed the next time.* ○ *The president's initial popularity soon disappeared.*

initially /ɪˈnɪʃˌəˌli/ adv [not gradable] • *The ceremony, initially planned for this month, was postponed.*

initial ~FIRST LETTER~ /ɪˈnɪʃˌəl/ n [C] the first letter of a name, esp. when used to represent a name • *Your initials are the first letters of each of your names: They will put your initials on the luggage for another $15.* • ~LP~ PERIOD

initial /ɪˈnɪʃˌəl/ v [T] to write your initials on (something) • *Please initial each document.*

initiate ~BEGIN~ /ɪˈnɪʃˌiːˌeɪt/ v [T] to cause (something) to begin • *The peace talks were initiated by a special envoy.*

initiation /ɪˌnɪʃˌiːˈeɪˌʃən/ n [U] • *The initiation and carrying out of such a measure, he wrote, is absolutely necessary.*

initiative /ɪˈnɪʃˌəṭˌɪv/ n [C] a new attempt to achieve a goal or solve a problem, or a new method for doing this • *The defense secretary announced a major initiative to upgrade our military preparedness.*

initiate ~ACCEPT IN GROUP~ /ɪˈnɪʃˌiːˌeɪt/ v [T] to

signal the acceptance of (someone) into a group by a special ceremony • *The rite of baptism initiates people into the Christian faith.*

initiation /ɪˌnɪʃ·iːˈeɪ·ʃən/ *n* [C/U] a special ceremony or responsibility that signals the acceptance of someone into a group • *One fraternity's initiation required new members to run around the campus in their underwear.* [C] ○ *Sailors who charter a boat must pay a $495 initiation fee to join the club.* [U]

initiative /ɪˈnɪʃ·ət̬·ɪv/ *n* [U] the ability to judge what needs to be done and take action, esp. without suggestion from other people • *Lisa showed initiative on the job and was soon promoted.*

inject /ɪnˈdʒekt/ *v* [T] to force (a liquid) into someone or something, esp. to use a needle to put a drug into (a person's body) • *The morphine took effect almost as soon as it was injected.* • If you inject something into an organization, conversation, or exchange, you add it purposefully: *The contest was intended to inject some friendly competition into the proceedings.*

injection /ɪnˈdʒek·ʃən/ *n* [C/U] • *an insulin injection* [C] ○ *vaccines given by injection* [U]

injunction /ɪnˈdʒʌŋ·ʃən/ *n* [C] *law* an official order given by a court, usually to stop someone from doing something • *The court has issued an injunction to prevent distribution of the book.* [+ *to* infinitive]

injure /ˈɪn·dʒər/ *v* [T] to hurt (a living creature), esp. to cause physical harm to (someone) • *The bus careened out of control, injuring several people.*

injured /ˈɪn·dʒərd/ *adj* • *She was told to rest her injured back.*

injury /ˈɪn·dʒə·ri/ *n* [C/U] physical harm or damage done to a living thing • *He was removed from the game with a knee injury.* [C] ○ *They were lucky to escape injury.* [U]

injustice /ɪnˈdʒʌs·təs/ *n* [C/U] unfairness and lack of justice, or an action that is unfair • *racial injustice* [U] ○ *I was falsely arrested, so there was definitely an injustice done.* [C] • USAGE: The related adjective is UNJUST.

ink /ɪŋk/ *n* colored liquid used for writing, printing, and drawing • *colored inks* [C] ○ *Please write in ink, not pencil.* [U]

inky /ˈɪŋ·ki/ *adj* colored or covered with ink, or having this appearance • *the inky blue of the night sky*

inkling /ˈɪŋ·klɪŋ/ *n* [U] a slight idea that something is true or likely to happen, although it is not certain • *She saw the look on Nick's face but had no inkling of what it meant.*

inland /ˈɪn·lænd, -lənd/ *adj, adv* away from the sea • *We left the coast and headed inland.*

in-law /ˈɪn·lɔː/ *n* [C] a person you are related to by marriage, esp. the parents and other members of your husband's or wife's family • *He's spending Christmas with his in-laws.*

inlay /ˈɪn·leɪ/ *n* [C/U] a decorative pattern made of pieces set into the surface of an object • *a pine table with mahogany inlay* [U]

inlet /ˈɪn·let, -lət/ *n* [C] a narrow channel of water that goes from a sea or lake into the land or between islands

in-line skate /ˌɪn·lɑɪnˈskeɪt/, *trademark* **Rollerblade** *n* [C usually pl] a type of shoe with a single row of small wheels on the bottom which you wear in order to travel along quickly for enjoyment, sports, or exercise • (PIC) SKATES

inmate /ˈɪn·meɪt/ *n* [C] a person who is forced by law to stay in a prison or hospital • *The inmates were living in terrible conditions.*

inn /ɪn/ *n* [C] a hotel, esp. a small, rural hotel, or a bar

innards /ˈɪn·ərdz/ *pl n infml* the inner organs of a person or animal, or the inside parts of a machine • *the innards of radios* ○ *frogs' innards*

innate /ɪˈneɪt/ *adj* [not gradable] (of a quality) which you are born with, or which is present naturally • *Her dance expresses the innate beauty of the human spirit.*

innately /ɪˈneɪt·li/ *adv* • *Power is innately seductive.*

inner /ˈɪn·ər/ *adj* [not gradable] inside or contained within something else • *These islands lie between the bay's outer and inner sections.* ○ *She met life's challenges with courage and inner strength* (= the strength of her character or spirit). • *Simpson was part of the club's* **inner circle** (= the most powerful group). • The **inner city** is the older, central part of a city where there are poor people and bad housing: *There are more problems in large, inner-city school districts.* • An **inner tube** is a round, rubber tube filled with air that fits inside a car or bicycle tire.

innermost /ˈɪn·ərˌmoʊst/ *adj* [not gradable] (of thoughts) most strongly felt and most private, or (of objects) nearest to the center • *They told her their innermost secrets.*

inning /ˈɪn·ɪŋ/ *n* [C] a numbered period of play in a game of baseball in which both teams BAT (= try to hit the ball), or one team's turn to bat in one of these periods • *Cleveland scored three times in the ninth inning.*

innkeeper /ˈɪnˌkiː·pər/ *n* [C] *esp. old use* a person who owns or manages an INN (= a hotel)

innocent /ˈɪn·ə·sənt/ *adj* (of a person) not guilty of a particular crime, or having no knowledge of the unpleasant and evil things in life, or (of words or an action) not intended to cause harm • *He pleaded innocent to drunken driving charges.* ○ *It was a totally innocent kind of mistake.* • There were reports that soldiers were beating **innocent bystanders** (= people who were not involved but who were there by chance).

innocence /ˈɪn·ə·səns/ *n* [U] • *He acts like he doesn't have to prove his innocence* (= lack of guilt).

innocently /ˈɪn·ə·sənt·li/ *adv* • *Some people innocently drove into the contaminated area.*

innocuous /ɪˈnɑk·jə·wəs/ *adj* completely harmless • *an innocuous statement* ○ *innocuous activities*

innovative /ˈɪn·əˌveɪt̬·ɪv/ *adj* (of ideas and methods) new and different • *Gwen introduced a number of innovative solutions.*

innovation /ˌɪn·əˈveɪ·ʃən/ *n* [C/U] • *The recording industry is driven by constant innovation.* [U] ○ *His latest innovation is a theater company that will perform for schools.* [C]

innuendo /ˌɪn·jəˈwen·doʊ/ *n* [C/U] *pl* **innuendos** or **innuendoes** a remark that suggests something but does not refer to it directly, or this type of remark in general • *sexual innuendo* [U]

innumerable /ɪˈnuː·mə·rə·bəl/ *adj* [not gradable] too many to be counted, or very many • *Roland sent her innumerable love letters.*

inoculate /ɪˈnɑk·jəˌleɪt/ *v* [T] to give (a person or animal) a VACCINE (= substance to prevent disease)

inoculation /ɪˌnɑk·jəˈleɪ·ʃən/ *n* [C/U] • *a cholera inoculation* [C]

inoffensive /ˌɪn·əˈfen·sɪv/ *adj* not causing any harm or offense • *Their music is upbeat and inoffensive.*

inoperable DISEASE /ɪˈnɑp·ə·rə·bəl/ *adj* [not gradable] (of an illness, esp. CANCER) that doctors are unable to treat or remove by an operation

inoperable NOT WORKING /ɪˈnɑp·ə·rə·bəl/ *adj* [not gradable] not able to be done or made to work • *Most of the weapons were inoperable.*

inopportune /ɪˌnɑp·ərˈtuːn/ *adj* slightly *fml* happening or done at a time that is not suitable or convenient • *Difficulties seem to crop up at the most inopportune times.*

inordinate /ɪˈnɔːrd·ᵊn·ət/ *adj* unreasonably or unusually large in size or degree

inordinately /ɪˈnɔːrd·ᵊn·ət·li/ *adv* • *She seemed to be inordinately fond of her dog.*

inorganic /ˌɪn·ɔːrˈɡæn·ɪk/ *adj* [not gradable] not consisting of living material, or relating to substances that do not contain living material • *Rocks and metals are inorganic.* ○ *inorganic chemistry* • Compare ORGANIC LIVING.

inpatient /ˈɪnˌpeɪ·ʃənt/ *n* [C] a person who stays one or more nights in a hospital in order to receive medical care • *His insurance company is unwilling to pay for inpatient treatment.* • Compare OUTPATIENT.

input /ˈɪn·pʊt/ *n* [C/U] information, money, or energy that is put into a system, organization, or machine so it can operate • *The city plans to get input from local community groups.* [U] ○ *This unit has three audio inputs* (= places to connect other devices). [C]

input /ˈɪn·pʊt/ *v* [T] **inputting**, *past* **input** or **inputted** • *keyboard operators inputting data*

inquest /ˈɪn·kwest/ *n* [C] an official examination of facts in an attempt to discover the cause of something, esp. of a sudden or violent death • *a coroner's inquest*

inquire, **enquire** /ɪnˈkwaɪr/ *v* to ask for information • *Officials from around the country have called to inquire about the program.* [I] ○ *Phil inquired whether I wanted to meet his roommate.* [+ *wh-* word] • If you **inquire into** something, you try to discover the facts about it: *He thought the committee had no right to inquire into his politics.*

inquiring, **enquiring** /ɪnˈkwaɪ·rɪŋ/ *adj* • *You have a very inquiring mind.*

inquiry, **enquiry** /ɪnˈkwaɪ·ri, ˈɪn·kwə·ri/ *n* [C/U] • *I've made inquiries about the cost of a ticket.* [C] • An inquiry is also an official attempt to discover the facts about something. [C]

inquisition /ˌɪn·kwəˈzɪʃ·ən/ *n* [C usually sing] a detailed questioning, esp. of someone's beliefs

inquisitive /ɪnˈkwɪz·ət̬·ɪv/ *adj* (of a person or their behavior) eager to know a lot about people or things • *an inquisitive mind* ○ *Our neighbors are too inquisitive.*

inroads /ˈɪn·roʊdz/ *pl n* direct and noticeable effects on something • *Women have made major inroads into this profession over the last 20 years.*

ins and outs /ˈɪn·zənˈaʊts/ *pl n* the details or facts relating to something • *She knows the ins and outs of the law.*

insane /ɪnˈseɪn/ *adj* extremely unreasonable, or mentally ill • *You'd have to be insane to spend $200 on dinner!* ○ *Fisher went totally insane, shooting seven of his colleagues before killing himself.*

insanely /ɪnˈseɪn·li/ *adv* • *She's insanely* (= extremely unreasonably) *jealous of her husband.*

insanity /ɪnˈsæn·ət̬·i/ *n* [U] • *The jury found him innocent on the grounds of temporary insanity* (= mental illness).

insatiable /ɪnˈseɪ·ʃə·bəl/ *adj* (of a desire or need) too great to be satisfied • *an insatiable appetite* ○ *insatiable curiosity*

inscribe /ɪnˈskraɪb/ *v* [T] to write (words) in a book or cut (words) onto the surface of an object • *She inscribed the book, "To my number-one fan."*

inscription /ɪnˈskrɪp·ʃən/ *n* [C] • *Wind and rain wore away the inscriptions on the gravestones.*

inscrutable /ɪnˈskruːt̬·ə·bəl/ *adj* very difficult to understand or get to know • *an inscrutable smile* ○ *He believes that a certain portion of life must remain inscrutable.*

insect /ˈɪn·sekt/ *n* [C] a type of very small animal with six legs, a body divided into three parts, and often two pairs of wings • *Ants, beetles, butterflies, and flies are all insects.* ○ *an insect bite*

insecticide /ɪnˈsek·təˌsaɪd/ *n* [C/U] a chemical substance for killing insects • Compare PESTICIDE.

insecure NOT CONFIDENT /ˌɪn·sɪˈkjʊr/ *adj* (of people) lacking confidence and doubtful about their own abilities • *Eleanor was shy and insecure as a child.*

insecure NOT SAFE /ˌɪn·sɪˈkjʊr/ *adj* (of objects or situations) not fixed or safe • *The stairs seemed kind of rickety and insecure.*

inseminate /ɪnˈsem·əˌneɪt/ *v* [T] to put a male's sperm into (a female) and make her pregnant

insemination /ɪnˌsem·əˈneɪ·ʃən/ *n* [U] • *artificial insemination*

insensitive /ɪnˈsen·sət̬·ɪv/ *adj* not aware of other people's feelings, or not showing sympathy for the feelings of other people • *The governor apologized for his insensitive remarks about the homeless.* • Insensitive can also mean not noticing the effects of something or unable to feel something: *His feet seem to be insensitive to pain.*

insensitivity /ɪnˌsen·səˈtɪv·ət̬·i/ *n* [U] • *I find your insensitivity to my needs insulting.*

inseparable /ɪnˈsep·ə·rə·bəl/ *adj* (of two or more people) such good friends that they spend most of their time together, or (of two or more things) so closely connected that they cannot be considered separately • *When we were kids Zoe and I were inseparable.*

insert /ɪnˈsɜrt/ *v* [T] to put (something) in something else • *Insert your ATM card in the slot to begin your transaction.*

insert /ˈɪn·sɜrt/ *n* [C] • *newspaper advertising inserts* (= extra pieces placed inside)

insertion /ɪnˈsɜr·ʃən/ *n* [U] • *Software can automate the insertion of SGML codes in texts.*

inset /ˈɪn·set/ *n* [C] something positioned within a larger object • *The city map has an inset in the corner showing the downtown area in more detail.*

inside INNER PART /ɪnˈsaɪd, ˈɪn·saɪd/ *n* the inner part, space, or side of (something) • *the inside of a car* [U] ○ *the inside of your wrist* [U] • (*infml*) Your insides are your stomach and other digestive organs. [pl] • *She put her sweater on* **inside out** (= with the inside part facing the outside). • *He knows the city* **inside out** (= completely and in detail). • Compare OUTSIDE OUTER PART.

inside /ɪnˈsaɪd, ˈɪn·saɪd/ *adv* [not gradable], *prep, adj* [not gradable] • *What's inside the big box?* ○ *I'll work inside and you work outside.* ○ *People* **inside** (= working for) *the White House get an us versus them mentality.* • If you get inside an idea or someone's mind, you understand it or them: *He tried to get inside her mind.* • If you do something **inside of** a particular time, you do it using less than that amount of time: *I should be back inside of two hours.*

inside SECRET /ˈɪn·saɪd/ *adj* [not gradable] (of information) known only by people in a group, organization, or company; secret • *Maloney had inside information about the investigation.*

insider /ɪnˈsaɪd·ər, ˈɪn·saɪd-/ *n* [C] someone

who is an accepted member of a group • *His books have made him an insider in the music world.*

insidious /ɪnˈsɪd·i·əs/ *adj* (of something unpleasant or dangerous) gradually and secretly causing harm • *Drug dependency is an insidious disease.*

insidiously /ɪnˈsɪd·i·ə·sli/ *adv* • *"Pornography," he said, "insidiously corrupts a society's attitude toward women."*

insight /ˈɪn·saɪt/ *n* [C/U] a clear, deep, and sometimes sudden understanding of a complicated problem or situation, or the ability to have such an understanding • *Hurston's writings were recognized for their insights.* [C] ○ *His work shows originality and insight.* [U]

insightful /ˈɪn·saɪt·fəl, ɪnˈsaɪt-/ *adj* • *an insightful observation*

insignia /ɪnˈsɪg·ni·ə/ *n* [C] an object or mark which shows that a person belongs to a particular organization or has a particular rank • *a Cub Scout insignia*

insignificant /ˌɪn·sɪgˈnɪf·ɪ·kənt/ *adj* not important or thought to be valuable • *Her problems seemed pretty insignificant compared to her brother's.*

insignificance /ˌɪn·sɪgˈnɪf·ɪ·kəns/ *n* [U] • *My colleagues despised this man for his insignificance.*

insincere /ˌɪn·sɪnˈsɪr/ *adj disapproving* not feeling, believing, or meaning something although you pretend to; not sincere • *an insincere promise/offer*

insincerity /ˌɪn·sɪnˈser·ət̬·i/ *n* [U] • *There's often a bit of insincerity in these speeches.*

insinuate (*obj*) /ɪnˈsɪn·jəˌweɪt/ *v* to express but not directly state (something) • *What exactly are you insinuating?* [T] ○ *She insinuated (that) I'm getting fat.* [+ *that*) clause]

insinuation /ɪnˌsɪn·jəˈweɪ·ʃən/ *n* [C/U] • *Contrary to your insinuation, we are not being unreasonable.* [C]

insipid /ɪnˈsɪp·əd/ *adj* (of food) lacking a strong taste or character, or (of people, activities, or entertainment) lacking in interest or energy • *an insipid flavor* ○ *insipid TV sitcoms*

insist /ɪnˈsɪst/ *v* to state or demand forcefully, esp. despite opposition • *She insisted on seeing her lawyer.* [I] ○ *Greg still insists (that) he did nothing wrong.* [+ *that*) clause]

insistence /ɪnˈsɪs·təns/ *n* [U] • *At his insistence, I continued living with my mother.* ○ *Her insistence that he bring her took him by surprise.*

insistent /ɪnˈsɪs·tənt/ *adj* • *I heard a soft, insistent rapping at the door.*

insistently /ɪnˈsɪs·tənt·li/ *adv* • *She was insistently cheerful.*

insofar as /ˌɪn·səˈfɑr·əz/ *adv* [not gradable] *slightly fml* to the degree that • *She had done her best to comfort him, insofar as she was able.*

insolent /ˈɪn·sə·lənt/ *adj* (of a person or their behavior) intentionally and rudely showing no respect • *Students were often inattentive, sometimes even insolent, and showed relatively little interest in their work.*

insolently /ˈɪn·sə·lənt·li/ *adv*

insoluble DIFFICULT TO SOLVE /ɪnˈsɑl·jə·bəl/ *adj* [not gradable] (of a problem) so difficult that it is impossible to solve • *Traffic congestion in big cities seems to be an insoluble problem.*

insoluble IMPOSSIBLE TO MIX /ɪnˈsɑl·jə·bəl/ *adj* (of a substance) impossible to dissolve • *Sand is insoluble in water.*

insolvent /ɪnˈsɑl·vənt, -ˈsɔːl-/ *adj* (esp. of a company) unable to pay what you owe because you do not have enough money • *When it discovered the loans could not be repaid, the bank became insolvent.*

insomnia /ɪnˈsɑm·ni·ə/ *n* [U] the condition of being unable to sleep

inspect /ɪnˈspekt/ *v* [T] to look at (something or someone) carefully in order to discover information, esp. about quality or correctness • *After the accident both drivers got out and inspected their cars for damage.* • If an official person inspects a thing, place, or a group of people, they look at it carefully in order to make certain it is in good condition and that rules are being obeyed: *Someone from the Health Department will inspect the restaurant this afternoon.*

inspection /ɪnˈspek·ʃən/ *n* [C/U] • *At first she suspected that the letter was a forgery, but on closer inspection* (= looked at more carefully), *it appeared to be genuine.* [U] • An inspection is also a careful examination by an official to make certain that something is in good condition or that rules are being obeyed: *He made an inspection of the elevators in the building.* [C]

inspector /ɪnˈspek·tər/ *n* [C] • *a safety inspector* • An inspector is also a police officer of high rank.

inspire /ɪnˈspaɪr/ *v* [T] to fill (someone) with confidence and eagerness, esp. so that they feel they can achieve something difficult or special • *She inspired her students to do the best they could.* • If something or someone inspires something else, it causes, suggests, or leads to it: *A successful TV program inspires many imitations.*

inspiration /ˌɪn·spəˈreɪ·ʃən/ *n* [C/U] • *She has been an inspiration to us all* (= a good example for all). [C usually sing] • An inspiration is also a sudden good idea: *She had the inspiration to turn the play into a musical.* [+ *to* infinitive]

inspirational /ˌɪn·spəˈreɪ·ʃən·əl/ *adj* • *He gave an inspirational talk on overcoming obstacles in life.*

inspiring /ɪnˈspaɪr·ɪŋ/ *adj approving* causing you to feel confident about yourself or eager to learn or do something • *She was an inspiring teacher and a gifted scientist.*

instability /ˌɪn·stəˈbɪl·ət̬·i/ *n* [U] the condition of being likely to change, esp. unexpectedly •

Teenagers often go through periods of emotional instability.

install PUT IN /ɪnˈstɔːl/ *v* [T] to put (esp. equipment) in its place so that it is ready for use, usually involving a lot of work or skill • *We're having a new tile floor installed in the kitchen.* • When you install computer SOFTWARE, you copy it onto your computer so that it can be used.

installation /ˌɪn·stəˈleɪ·ʃən/ *n* [C/U] • *Do you have to pay extra for installation?* [U]

install PLACE IN JOB /ɪnˈstɔːl/ *v* [T] to place (someone) formally in an official job of high rank • *The new president of the university was installed before the graduation ceremony.*

installment /ɪnˈstɔːl·mənt/ *n* [C] one of a number of payments that you make over a period of time to pay for something that you can use while you are paying for it • *We paid for the car in monthly installments over two years.* • An installment is also one of the parts of something, such as a show, that is experienced as part of a series over a period of time: *a TV miniseries with five installments*

instance /ˈɪn·stəns/ *n* [C] a particular situation, event, or fact • *There were several instances of computer failure before we got the system to work properly.* ○ *Usually this kind of skin condition is caused by a food allergy, but in this instance it may be caused by the medicine you are taking.*

instant /ˈɪn·stənt/ *n* [C usually sing] a very short moment of time, or a particular point in time • *At that instant, someone knocked on the door.* ○ *Call me the instant you get home* (= as soon as you get to your home).

instant /ˈɪn·stənt/ *adj* [not gradable] happening immediately • *I took an instant liking to him.* • An instant food or drink is one, usually in dried or powdered form, that can be prepared easily and quickly, esp. by adding hot water: *instant coffee* • **Instant replay** is the showing again on television of a play in a sports event immediately after the play happened: *When they showed the instant replay, it looked like he had caught the ball out of bounds.*

instantly /ˈɪn·stənt·li/ *adv* [not gradable] • *The force of the explosion killed him instantly.*

instantaneous /ˌɪn·stənˈteɪ·ni·əs/ *adj* [not gradable] happening or completed immediately, without any delay • *TV has conditioned us to expect instantaneous answers to difficult questions.*

instantaneously /ˌɪn·stənˈteɪ·ni·ə·sli/ *adv* [not gradable]

instead /ɪnˈsted/ *adv* [not gradable] rather than; as an ALTERNATIVE • *If we don't go to Europe this summer, where would you like to go instead* (= what other place would you like to go)? ○ *We went by train instead of by car.*

instep /ˈɪn·step/ *n* [C] the curved upper part of the foot between the toes and the heel

instigate /'ɪn·stə,ɡeɪt/ v [T] to cause (an event or situation) to happen by your actions • *He denied instigating violence during the demonstration.*

instigation /,ɪn·stə'ɡeɪ·ʃən/ n [U] • *The inquiry was begun at the instigation of Senator Hyde* (= he asked for it).

instill /ɪn'stɪl/ v [T] to put (a feeling, idea, or principle) gradually into someone's mind, so that it has a strong influence on the way they live • *My parents instilled in me a love of reading.*

instinct /'ɪn·stɪŋt/ n [C/U] a natural ability that helps you decide what to do or how to act without thinking • *He lacked the instinct for quick action.* [U] ○ *His biggest asset may be his political instincts.* [C] • Instinct is also the ability to behave in a particular way that has not been learned: *the maternal instinct* [U]

instinctive /ɪn'stɪŋ·tɪv/ adj • *Many Americans seem to have an instinctive distrust of authority.*

instinctively /ɪn'stɪŋ·tɪv·li/ adv • *She instinctively understood how I felt.*

institute ORGANIZATION /'ɪn·stə,tuːt/ n [C] an organization whose purpose is to advance the study of a particular subject • *The National Institutes of Health fund medical research in many areas.*

institute START /'ɪn·stə,tuːt/ v [T] to put into effect; cause to be used • *These are some of the safety guidelines we've instituted in our hotels.*

institution ORGANIZATION /,ɪn·stə'tuː·ʃən/ n [C] an organization that exists to serve a public purpose such as education or support for people who need help • *a charitable/educational/scientific institution* • An **institution of higher learning** is a college or university.

institutional /,ɪn·stə'tuː·ʃən·əl/ adj of or typical of an institution • *The hospital provides typically awful institutional food.*

institutionalize /,ɪn·stə'tuː·ʃən·əl,aɪz/ v [T] to send (someone) to stay or live in an institution, esp. a hospital for people who are mentally ill • *Martin had to be institutionalized for several months during his last depression.*

institution CUSTOM /,ɪn·stə'tuː·ʃən/ n [C] a custom or practice that has existed for a long time and is accepted as an important part of a society • *the institution of marriage*

instruct ORDER /ɪn'strʌkt/ v [T] to order or tell (someone) to do something, esp. in a formal way • *The police have been instructed not to let anyone leave the area.* [+ *to* infinitive]

instruction /ɪn'strʌk·ʃən/ n [C usually pl] • *The general received instructions to attack at dawn.* [+ *to* infinitive]

instruct TEACH /ɪn'strʌkt/ v [T] to teach (someone) how to do something • *I need someone to instruct me on how to use the computer.*

instruction /ɪn'strʌk·ʃən/ n [C/U] • *The course gives you basic instruction in car maintenance and repairs.* [U] ○ *Didn't the VCR come with*

any instructions (= information on how to use it)*?* [pl]

instructive /ɪn'strʌk·tɪv/ adj giving useful or interesting information • *It would be instructive to follow up the opinion poll with another one after the election.*

instructor /ɪn'strʌk·tər/ n [C] a person whose job is to teach people a skill • *a driving/ski/swimming instructor* • An instructor is also a teacher at a college or university, ranking lower than a PROFESSOR.

instrument MUSIC /'ɪn·strə·mənt/ n [C] an object, such as a piano, guitar, or FLUTE, which is played to produce musical sounds • *He plays saxophone, trumpet, and several other instruments.* • PIC GUITAR, KEY, TROMBONE, TRUMPET

instrumental /,ɪn·strə'ment·əl/ adj [not gradable] performed with musical instruments only and not voices

instrument TOOL /'ɪn·strə·mənt/ n [C] a tool or other device used for doing a particular piece of work • *surgical instruments*

instrumental /,ɪn·strə'ment·əl/ adj important in causing something to happen • *As secretary of state, he was instrumental in the creation of NATO.*

insubordination /,ɪn·sə,bɔːrd·ən'eɪ·ʃən/ n [U] the refusal to obey someone who is in a higher position than you and who has the authority to tell you what to do • *She had recently been fired from her job for insubordination.*

insubstantial /,ɪn·səb'stæn·tʃəl/ adj of little value or importance, or lacking strength, solidity, or size • *He was popular during the early part of the 20th century, but today his work seems dated and insubstantial.*

insufferable /ɪn'sʌf·ə·rə·bəl/ adj extremely unpleasant and therefore difficult to bear • *George is an insufferable bore, and you know it.*

insufficient /,ɪn·sə'fɪʃ·ənt/ adj [not gradable] not enough in amount, strength, or quality; less than is needed • *There was insufficient evidence, so we had to find him not guilty.*

insufficiently /,ɪn·sə'fɪʃ·ənt·li/ adv [not gradable] • *Many of the students got low grades because they were insufficiently prepared.*

insular /'ɪn·sə·lər, -sjə-/ adj interested only in your own country or group and not willing to accept different or foreign ideas or people

insulate COVER /'ɪn·sə,leɪt/ v [T] to use a material to cover or go around (the surface of something) in order to prevent heat, electricity, etc., from escaping or entering • *We've saved a lot on our heating bills by insulating the attic.*

insulation /,ɪn·sə'leɪ·ʃən/ n [U] the substance used in insulating • *Rubber is better insulation than cloth for electric wiring.*

insulate PROTECT /'ɪn·sə,leɪt/ v [T] to protect (someone or something) from outside influences • *As a member of a rich and powerful family, she was insulated from ordinary life.*

insulin /'ɪn·sə·lən/ n [U] *medical* a HORMONE (= chemical substance) in the body that controls the amount of sugar in the blood • *She has to have insulin injections for her diabetes.*

insult /ɪnˈsʌlt/ *v* [T] to act in a way or say something that is offensive or rude to (someone) • *All her life, she said, men had belittled and insulted her because she was not thin and beautiful.*

insult /ˈɪnˌsʌlt/ *n* [C] an offensive remark or action • *Offering me so little money was an insult.*

insulting /ɪnˈsʌltɪŋ/ *adj* • *an insulting remark*

insure *(obj)* MAKE CERTAIN, **ensure** /ɪnˈʃʊr/ *v* to make (something) certain or to be certain about (something) • *Because of the importance of the game, we wanted to insure (that) it would be televised.* [+ *(that)* clause] ○ *We had reporters check to insure the accuracy of the story.* [T]

insure PROTECT /ɪnˈʃʊr/ *v* [T] to protect (yourself or your property) against damage or loss by making regular payments to a company that will pay for the damage or loss if it happens • *We've insured our house for $100,000.*

insurance /ɪnˈʃʊr·əns, *Southern also* ˈɪnˌʃʊr-/ *n* [U] the agreement or the amount by which you are insured • *fire/health/life insurance*

insurgent /ɪnˈsɜr·dʒənt/ *n* [C] a person who is a member of a group that is fighting against the government of their country

insurmountable /ˌɪn·sərˈmaʊnt·ə·bəl/ *adj* [not gradable] (esp. of a problem or a difficulty) so great that it cannot be dealt with successfully • *As the election returns came in, it was clear that his opponent had an insurmountable lead.*

insurrection /ˌɪn·səˈrek·ʃən/ *n* [C/U] an organized attempt by a group of people to defeat their government or ruler and take control of the country, usually by violence

intact /ɪnˈtækt/ *adj* complete and in the original state • *He emerged from the investigation with his reputation largely intact* (= not damaged).

intake /ˈɪnˌteɪk/ *n* [U] the amount of something such as food, breath, or a liquid that is taken in by someone or something • *the intake of fuel in a vehicle* ○ *a deep intake of breath*

intangible /ɪnˈtæn·dʒə·bəl/ *adj* influencing you but not able to be seen or physically felt • *There is the intangible benefit of playing a home game before a friendly crowd.*

intangible /ɪnˈtæn·dʒə·bəl/ *n* [C] • *Common sense and creativity are some of the intangibles we're looking for in the people we hire.*

integer /ˈɪnt·ə·dʒər/ *n* [C] *specialized* a whole number and not a FRACTION • *The numbers 5, 3, and 0 are integers.*

integral /ˈɪnt·ə·grəl, ɪnˈteg·rəl/ *adj* necessary and important as a part of a whole, or contained within it • *Taking a ride on the canals of Venice is an integral part of experiencing that city.*

integrate /ˈɪnt·əˌgreɪt/ *v* [T] to take an action that causes (an organization or group) to bring into it people, esp. of a different race, who have been kept separated previously, or to cause such a separation to end in (a place) • *Until President Truman integrated the armed forces in 1948, African-American soldiers served in segregated army units.* • To integrate is also to combine (something) with something else to form a new whole thing: *We were taught how to integrate computer use into normal classroom procedures.*

integration /ˌɪnt·əˈgreɪ·ʃən/ *n* [U]

integrity HONESTY /ɪnˈteg·rət·i/ *n* [U] the quality of being honest and having strong moral principles • *He was a man of the highest personal integrity.*

integrity UNITY /ɪnˈteg·rət·i/ *n* [U] wholeness and unity • *The integrity of the play would be ruined by changing the ending.*

intellect /ˈɪnt·əlˌekt/ *n* [C/U] a person's ability to think and understand esp. ideas at a high level • *The stroke left her partially paralyzed, but her intellect was not affected.* [C]

intellectual /ˌɪnt·əlˈek·tʃə·wəl/ *adj* relating to the ability to think and understand ideas at a high level, or involving ideas • *He was among the political and intellectual leaders of his time.*

intellectual /ˌɪnt·əlˈek·tʃə·wəl/ *n* [C] a person whose life or work centers around the study or use of ideas, such as in teaching or writing

intelligence THINKING ABILITY /ɪnˈtel·ə·dʒəns/ *n* [U] the ability to understand and learn well, and to form judgments and opinions based on reason • *He's a child of normal intelligence but he's emotionally immature.* • An **intelligence test** is a test that measures the ability of a person to understand and learn by comparing it with the ability of other people. Compare **achievement test** at ACHIEVE.

intelligent /ɪnˈtel·ə·dʒənt/ *adj* • *a highly intelligent woman*

intelligence INFORMATION /ɪnˈtel·ə·dʒəns/ *n* [U] a government department or other group that gathers information about other countries or enemies, or the information that is gathered • *the Central Intelligence Agency*

intelligible /ɪnˈtel·ə·dʒə·bəl/ *adj* (of speech and writing) clear enough to be understood • *It was a poor telephone connection, and only some of his words were intelligible.*

intend *(obj)* /ɪnˈtend/ *v* to have as a plan or purpose • *We intend to go to Australia next year to visit our daughter.* [+ *to* infinitive] ○ *The remark was intended as a compliment.* [T]

intent /ɪnˈtent/ *n* [U] *fml* something that you intend or intended to do • *There was clearly no intent to cause harm, and the judge ruled that the injury was accidental.* • See also INTENT GIVING ATTENTION, INTENT DETERMINED.

intention /ɪnˈten·tʃən/ *n* [C/U] something that you want and plan to do; an aim • *I have*

no intention of selling this house. [U] ◦ *He had good intentions* (= He meant to be kind)*, but unfortunately things just didn't work out.* [C]
intentional /ɪn'ten·tʃən·ᵊl/ *adj* • *Do you think the insult was intentional?*

intentionally /ɪn'ten·tʃən·ᵊl·i/ *adv* • *The company was accused of intentionally dumping garbage into the river.*

intense /ɪn'tens/ *adj* (of physical and emotional feelings) extreme • *intense heat/cold* ◦ *a look of intense joy* • Intense work or thought requires a lot of effort: *an intense 13-week course* • If a person is intense, they are very forceful and have strong emotions and opinions: *He was young and intense, and silly, too.*

intensely /ɪn'ten·sli/ *adv* • *intensely personal songs* ◦ *He lives every aspect of life intensely.* •
LP VERY, COMPLETELY, AND OTHER INTENSIFIERS

intensify /ɪn'ten·sə‚fɑɪ/ *v* [I/T] • *He intensified his training, running 45 miles a week.* [T] ◦ *Fighting around the capital has intensified.* [I]

intensity /ɪn'ten·sət̬·i/ *n* [U] • *Simone sings with emotional intensity.* ◦ *The light hit us with such intensity that we ducked.*

intensive /ɪn'ten·sɪv/ *adj* needing or using great energy or effort • *We're in the midst of intensive negotiations.* ◦ *an intensive workout* • Intensive study or training deals with a lot of information in a short period of time: *a month-long intensive course in Spanish* • In a hospital, **intensive care** is continuous treatment provided for PATIENTS who are seriously ill or have just had an operation.

intensifier /ɪn'ten·sə‚fɑɪ·ər/, **intensive** /ɪn'ten·sɪv/ *n* [C] *specialized* (in grammar) a word, esp. an adverb, that is used to add force to another word or phrase • *In "extremely large" and "I strongly object," "extremely" and "strongly" are intensifiers.* • LP VERY, COMPLETELY, AND OTHER INTENSIFIERS

intent GIVING ATTENTION /ɪn'tent/ *adj* giving all your attention to something • *an intent look* • See also **intent** at INTEND.

intently /ɪn'tent·li/ *adv* • *The boys played intently.*

intent DETERMINED /ɪn'tent/ *adj* • If you are **intent on** doing something, you are determined to do it: *The climbers were intent on reaching the mountaintop.* • See also **intent** at INTEND.

intention /ɪn'ten·tʃən/ *n* • See at INTEND.

intentional /ɪn'ten·tʃən·ᵊl/ *adj* • See at INTEND.

intentionally /ɪn'ten·tʃən·ᵊl·i/ *adv* • See at INTEND.

inter BURY /ɪn'tɜr/ *v* [T] **-rr-** *slightly fml* to put (a dead body) in the earth; bury

inter– BETWEEN /‚ɪnt·ər/ *combining form* between or among • *an interfaith church service*

interact /‚ɪnt·ə'rækt/ *v* [I] to communicate with or react to each other • *He does not interact well with the other students.*

interaction /‚ɪnt·ə'ræk·ʃən/ *n* [C/U] • *drug interactions* [C]

interactive /‚ɪnt·ə'ræk·tɪv/ *adj* • *The ocean and the atmosphere form an interactive system.* • An interactive computer program involves the user in the exchange of information while the computer is in operation: *interactive software/technology*

intercede /‚ɪnt·ər'siːd/ *v* [I] to use your influence to persuade someone in authority not to punish or harm someone or to do something for someone • *Some pharmacists will intercede on your behalf with doctors.*

intercept /‚ɪnt·ər'sept/ *v* [T] to stop or catch (something or someone) that is on the way from one place to another so that it does not reach the intended place • *to intercept a letter* ◦ *The ball was intercepted by Grady.*

interception /‚ɪnt·ər'sep·ʃən/ *n* [C] (esp. in football) the act of catching a ball intended for someone on the opposing team • *He's thrown 122 passes without an interception.*

interchange EXCHANGE /'ɪnt·ər‚tʃeɪndʒ/ *n* [C/U] an exchange, esp. of ideas or information, between different people or groups • *They hope to encourage the free interchange of ideas.* [U]

interchangeable /‚ɪnt·ər'tʃeɪn·dʒə·bəl/ *adj* able to be exchanged with each other without making any difference or without being noticed • *interchangeable machine parts*

interchange ROAD /'ɪnt·ər‚tʃeɪndʒ/ *n* [C] a connection between two roads that allows vehicles to move from one road to the other without crossing the flow of traffic • PIC CLOVERLEAF

intercom /'ɪnt·ər‚kɑm/ *n* [C] a set of communications devices that allows people in different parts of a building, aircraft, ship, etc., to speak to each other

intercontinental /‚ɪnt·ər‚kɑnt·ᵊn'ent·ᵊl/ *adj* [not gradable] between continents • *intercontinental flights*

intercourse /'ɪnt·ər‚kɔːrs, -‚koʊrs/ *n* [U] the sexual activity in which the male's penis enters the female's vagina, or the sexual activity in which a male's penis enters another male's or a female's ANUS

interdependent /‚ɪnt·ər·dɪ'pen·dənt/ *adj* [not gradable] depending on each other • *an interdependent relationship*

interest INVOLVEMENT /'ɪn·trəst, 'ɪnt·ə·rəst/ *n* [C/U] a feeling of having your attention held by something, or of wanting to be involved with and learn more about something • *an interest in chess* [C] ◦ *I lost interest halfway through the book.* [U] • Your interests are the activities that you enjoy doing and the subjects that you like to spend time learning about. [C] • If something is **of interest**, it holds your attention and makes you want to learn more about it: *Nothing much of interest was discussed.*

interest /'ɪn·trəst, 'ɪnt·ə·rəst/ *v* [T] • *Sailing has never really interested me.* • Someone might ask if they can **interest** you **in** something when they are trying to persuade you to buy or take something: *Can I interest you in a cup of coffee?*

interested /'ɪn·trə·stəd, 'ɪnt·ə·rə·stəd/ *adj* • *He didn't seem interested in coming.* ○ *I'd be interested to learn why he likes her.* [+ to infinitive]

interesting /'ɪn·trə·stɪŋ, 'ɪnt·ə,res·tɪŋ/ *adj* holding one's attention • *An interesting thing happened on the trip back.*

interestingly /'ɪn·trə·stɪŋ·li, 'ɪnt·ə,res·tɪŋ-/ *adv* • Interestingly can introduce a piece of information that the speaker finds surprising and interesting: *Interestingly enough, he never actually said that he was innocent.*

interest ADVANTAGE /'ɪn·trəst, 'ɪnt·ə·rəst/ *n* [C] something that gives you what is important or necessary to you in some way • *A union looks after the interests of its members.* • *I was only acting in your interest* (= to achieve what would help you).

interest MONEY /'ɪn·trəst, 'ɪnt·ə·rəst/ *n* [U] money that is charged, esp. by a bank, when you borrow money, or money that is paid to you for the use of your money • *My savings account is earning 5% interest.*

interface /'ɪnt·ər,feɪs/ *n* [C] the place where two systems come together and have an effect on each other, or a connection between two computers or between a person and a computer • *Amphibians live at the interface of land and sea.* ○ *To simplify software, you improve its interface.*

interface /'ɪnt·ər,feɪs/ *v* [I/T] to communicate or cause (someone or something) to communicate • *Neighborhood groups here interface very well with police.* [I]

interfere /,ɪnt·ər'fɪr/ *v* [I] to involve yourself in matters connected with other people without being asked or needed • *Interfering in other people's arguments is always a mistake.* • If something or someone interferes with a situation or a process, it spoils it or prevents its advancement: *Even a little noise interferes with my concentration.*

interference /,ɪnt·ər'fɪr·əns/ *n* [U] • *She seems to regard any advice from me as interference.* • On the radio, television, or telephone, interference is noise, lines, etc., that prevent a clear sound or picture from being received. • In sports, interference is an action that is against the rules which prevents an opposing player from completing a play.

interim /'ɪnt·ə·rəm/ *adj* [not gradable] temporary; intended for a short period only • *an interim government*

interim /'ɪnt·ə·rəm/ *n* [U] • *I started writing two years ago, and other books on the subject have come out in the interim* (= during this period).

interior /ɪn'tɪr·iː·ər/ *adj* [not gradable] inner; on or from the inside • *The interior surface of seashell was smooth.* • Compare EXTERIOR.

interior /ɪn'tɪr·iː·ər/ *n* [C/U] the inside part of something • *a car's interior* [U] • An **interior decorator** is a person whose job is to decorate the insides of buildings, etc. • Compare EXTERIOR.

interject /,ɪnt·ər'dʒekt/ *v* [T] to say (something) that interrupts someone who is speaking • *He interjected questions throughout the discussion.*

interjection /,ɪnt·ər'dʒek·ʃən/ *n* [C] specialized (in grammar) a word or phrase that is used as a short, sudden expression of emotion • *"Hey!" "Ouch!" and "Cut that out!" are interjections.*

interlock /,ɪnt·ər'lɑk/ *v* [I/T] to join together firmly, esp. by fitting one part into another

interlocking /,ɪnt·ər'lɑk·ɪŋ/ *adj* • *interlocking rings*

interloper /'ɪnt·ər,loʊ·pər/ *n* [C] someone who becomes involved in an activity or a social group without being asked or wanted, or who enters a place without being allowed • *We felt like interlopers when we tried to join the game.*

interlude /'ɪnt·ər,luːd/ *n* [C] a period or event that comes between two others and is different from them • *The ferry trip was a relaxing interlude during the drive.*

intermarriage /,ɪnt·ər'mær·ɪdʒ/ *n* [U] marriage between people who are of different groups, esp. racial or religious groups

intermediary /,ɪnt·ər'miːd·iː,er·i/ *n* [C] someone who acts to arrange an agreement between people who are unwilling or unable to communicate directly

intermediate /,ɪnt·ər'miːd·iː·ət/ *adj* [not gradable] being or happening between two other related things, levels, or points • *a student of English at the intermediate level* • An **intermediate school** is a school for children who are about 12 to 14 years old to which they go after **elementary school** and before HIGH SCHOOL. LP EDUCATION IN THE US

interminable /ɪn'tɜr·mə·nə·bəl/ *adj* continuing for too long and seeming never to end • *interminable arguments*

interminably /ɪn'tɜr·mə·nə·bli/ *adv* • *They talked interminably.*

intermingle /,ɪnt·ər'mɪŋ·gəl/ *v* [I] to become mixed together • *The spices intermingle to produce an unusual flavor.*

intermission /,ɪnt·ər'mɪʃ·ən/ *n* [C/U] a brief period between the parts of a performance

intermittent /,ɪnt·ər'mɪt·ᵊnt/ *adj* not happening regularly or continuously; stopping and starting repeatedly or with long periods in between

intermittently /,ɪnt·ər'mɪt·ᵊnt·li/ *adv* • *It rained intermittently all day.*

intern PUNISH /ɪn'tɜrn, 'ɪn·tɜrn/ *v* [T] to put (someone) in prison for political or military reasons

intern STUDENT /'ɪn·tɜrn/ *n* [C] someone who

is receiving training by obtaining practical experience of a type of work

internship /'ɪn,tɜrn,ʃɪp/ *n* [C] • *He served his internship at a local hospital.*

internal /ɪn'tɜrn·ªl/ *adj* [not gradable] existing, intended for, or happening inside a person, organization, place, country, etc. • *the internal organs of the body* ○ *The bank will conduct an internal investigation.* • **Internal medicine** is the part of medical science that deals with illnesses inside the body, esp. of the organs. • The **Internal Revenue Service** is the IRS. • Compare EXTERNAL.

internally /ɪn'tɜrn·ªl·i/ *adv* [not gradable] • *This medicine should not be taken internally.*

international /,ɪnt·ər'næʃ·ən·ªl/ *adj* [not gradable] involving more than one country • *international affairs/trade* • The **International Phonetic Alphabet** (*abbreviation* **IPA**) is a system of symbols for showing the speech sounds of a language.

internationally /,ɪnt·ər'næʃ·ən·ªl·i/ *adv* [not gradable] • *an internationally acclaimed scientist*

Internet /'ɪnt·ər,net/, **Net** *n* [U] the large system of connected computers around the world which people use to communicate with each other • *I learned about it on the Internet.*

internist /'ɪn,tɜr·nəst/ *n* [C] a doctor who specializes in **internal medicine** (= medicine dealing with illnesses inside the body)

internship /'ɪn,tɜrn,ʃɪp/ *n* [C] • See at INTERN STUDENT.

interpersonal /,ɪnt·ər'pɜr·sən·ªl/ *adj* [not gradable] involving relationships between people

interplanetary /,ɪnt·ər'plæn·ə,ter·i/ *adj* [not gradable] between planets • *interplanetary travel*

interplay /'ɪnt·ər,pleɪ/ *n* [U] the action between two or more things or the effect they have on each other • *the interplay of light and shadow in a photograph*

interpret FIND MEANING /ɪn'tɜr·prət/ *v* [T] to describe the meaning of (something); examine in order to explain • *It's difficult to interpret these statistics without knowing how they were obtained.*

interpretation /ɪn,tɜr·prə'teɪ·ʃən/ *n* [C/U] • *We had different interpretations of the survey results.* [C] • An interpretation by an actor or musician is the expression by their performance of their understanding of the part they are playing: *Masur's interpretation of the Brahms symphony was masterful.* [C]

interpret CHANGE LANGUAGE /ɪn'tɜr·prət/ *v* [I/T] to change (the words, esp. spoken words) into the words of another language; TRANSLATE • *I had to ask someone to interpret for me because I don't know any Italian.* [I]

interpreter /ɪn'tɜr·prət·ər/ *n* [C] • *The Chinese witness testified with the help of an interpreter.*

interracial /,ɪnt·ə'reɪ·ʃəl/ *adj* [not gradable]

involving people of different races • *an interracial marriage*

interrelated /,ɪnt·ə·rɪ'leɪt·əd/ *adj* connected in such a way that each thing has an effect on the others • *He saw all aspects of society as interrelated.*

interrogate /ɪn'ter·ə,geɪt/ *v* [T] to ask (someone) many questions in a formal situation, often in a forceful way that can be seen as threatening • *We were stopped at the border and interrogated for hours by the police.*

interrogation /ɪn,ter·ə'geɪ·ʃən/ *n* [C/U] • *Police brought in the suspect for a lengthy interrogation.* [C]

interrupt /,ɪnt·ə'rʌpt/ *v* [T] to stop (someone) from speaking, esp. by speaking while they are speaking, or to cause (an activity or event) to stop briefly • *Please don't interrupt until I'm finished.* [I] ○ *The picnic was interrupted by a rain shower.* [T]

interruption /,ɪnt·ə'rʌp·ʃən/ *n* [C/U] • *I need to get some work done without interruption this afternoon.* [U]

interscholastic /,ɪnt·ər·skə'læs·tɪk/ *adj* [not gradable] involving two or more schools • *interscholastic sports*

intersect /,ɪnt·ər'sekt/ *v* [I] (esp. of two lines or paths) to cross • *Weaver Street intersects Palmer Avenue at the next corner.*

intersection /'ɪnt·ər,sek·ʃən/ *n* [C] a place where streets meet or cross each other • *Times Square is one of New York's busiest intersections.*

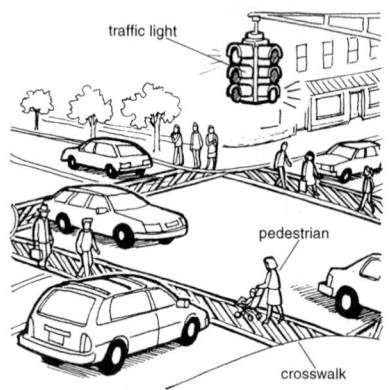

traffic light

pedestrian

crosswalk

intersection

intersperse /,ɪnt·ər'spɜrs/ *v* [T] to put (things of one type) in different parts or places among other things • *Framed pictures of her children were interspersed among the books in the bookcase.*

interstate /,ɪnt·ər'steɪt/ *adj* [not gradable] involving two or more US states • *interstate commerce*

interstate (highway) /'ɪnt·ər,steɪt ('haɪ·weɪ)/ *n* [C] one of the main roads that are part of a

US system of large roads that go across states to connect many cities • *You'll get here quicker if you take the interstate, I-95.*

intertwined /ˌɪnt·ər'twaɪnd/ *adj* twisted together or closely connected so as to be difficult to separate • *Our fates seemed to be intertwined.*

interval /'ɪnt·ər·vəl/ *n* [C] a period between two events or times, or the space between two points • *If there is a fire, the alarm will sound at 15-second intervals.* ○ *We've positioned guards around the embassy at intervals of 10 feet.* • (*Br*) An interval is an INTERMISSION.

intervene GET INVOLVED /ˌɪnt·ər'viːn/ *v* [I] to become involved intentionally in a difficult situation in order to change it or improve it, or prevent it from getting worse • *The superpowers began to intervene in local struggles in Africa.*

intervention /ˌɪnt·ər'ven·tʃən/ *n* [C/U] • *The intervention by UN troops failed to prevent fighting from breaking out.* [C]

intervene COME BETWEEN /ˌɪnt·ər'viːn/ *v* [I] to happen between two events, or to prevent something from happening by happening first • *Two decades intervened between the completion of the design and the opening of the theater.*

interview /'ɪnt·ər,vjuː/ *n* [C] a formal meeting at which a person who is interested in getting a job or other position is asked questions to learn how well they would be able to do it • *a job interview* • An interview is also a formal meeting at which reporters try to get information, esp. from a famous person or public official: *an interview with the British prime minister*

interview /'ɪnt·ər,vjuː/ *v* [T] • *We interviewed dozens of applicants, and have narrowed the job search down to two.* • To interview is also to ask questions of (someone) to get information: *She interviewed voters as they left the polls.*

interviewer /'ɪnt·ər,vjuː·ər/ *n* [C] a person who manages an interview and asks the questions

interweave /ˌɪnt·ər'wiːv/ *v* [T] **interweaving**, *past simple* **interwove**, *past part* **interwoven** to put together or combine (two or more things) so that they cannot be separated easily • *The author skillfully interweaves fiction and history in her novel.*

intestines /ɪn'tes·tənz/, **bowels** *pl n* a long tube through which food travels while it is being digested after leaving the stomach

intestinal /ɪn'tes·tən·əl/ *adj* [not gradable] • *intestinal flu*

intimate PERSONAL /'ɪnt·ə·mət/ *adj* being a close, personal friend, or having a close, personal relationship • *an intimate friend* • An intimate relationship can also refer to a romantic or sexual relationship: *They had been good friends, but they had never in any way*

been intimate. • Intimate can also mean private and personal: *Roseanne on TV talks about her intimate gynecological problems.*

intimacy /'ɪnt·ə·mə·si/ *n* [C/U] • *He was always polite, but he shunned intimacy.* [U]

intimate /'ɪnt·ə·mət/ *n* [C] a close friend • *George was never one of the president's intimates.*

intimate EXPERT /'ɪnt·ə·mət/ *adj* expert and detailed • *an intimate knowledge of cattle farming*

intimate (*obj*) SUGGEST /'ɪnt·ə,meɪt/ *v* to suggest that something will happen or is true, without saying so directly • *He intimated that they had thought about getting married.* [+ that clause]

intimidate /ɪn'tɪm·ə,deɪt/ *v* [T] to frighten or threaten (someone), usually in order to persuade them to do something against their wishes • *Anti-abortion forces, she said, use tactics designed to intimidate women.*

intimidation /ɪn,tɪm·ə'deɪ·ʃən/ *n* [U] • *a campaign of intimidation against striking workers*

into INSIDE /'ɪn·tuː, -tə/ *prep* toward the inside or middle of something and about to be contained, surrounded, or enclosed by it • *Pour some sugar into the bowl.* ○ *They went into the backyard.*

into CONNECTED WITH /'ɪn·tuː, -tə/ *prep* connected with or involved in a condition or activity • *My father went into the army the day after the war began.* ○ *An investigation into the accident is underway.* ○ *I know I should do my taxes but I just don't want to get into it now.* • (*infml*) Into also means strongly interested in or involved with something: *Jeanne is heavily into drugs.* ○ *Ken is into long-distance running.*

into CHANGE /'ɪn·tuː, -tə/ *prep* used to show when a person or thing is changing from one form or condition to another • *Peel the potatoes and chop them into small cubes.* ○ *We made the extra bedroom into an office.* ○ *Her novels have been translated into nineteen languages.*

into COME TOGETHER /'ɪn·tuː, -tə/ *prep* used to show movement that involves two things coming together with force • *The driver apparently fell asleep and his car slammed into a tree.* ○ (*fig.*) *Guess who I ran into* (= met unexpectedly) *at the shopping mall!*

into DIVISION /'ɪn·tuː, -tə/ *prep* used when referring to the division of one number by another number • *5 into 10 is 2.*

intolerable /ɪn'tɑl·ə·rə·bəl/ *adj* too bad or difficult to bear or to be accepted • *It was a brutal dictatorship that brought intolerable misery to the peoples who came under its control.* ○ *This hot weather is becoming intolerable.*

intolerant /ɪn'tɑl·ə·rənt/ *adj* disapproving of or refusing to accept people, behavior, or ideas that are different from your own • *It seems to me that the Democrats have been intolerant of diverse views on the issue for years.*

intolerance /ɪn'tɑl·ə·rəns/ *n* [U] • *With the rise*

of Hitler in Germany he began to speak out against racism and intolerance.

intonation /ˌɪn·təˈneɪ·ʃən/ *n* [C/U] the sound changes produced by the rise and fall of the voice when speaking

intone /ɪnˈtoʊn/ *v* [I/T] to say (something) slowly and seriously in a voice that does not rise or fall much • *"Say after me," he would intone, and the class dutifully repeated whatever he said.* [I]

intoxicated /ɪnˈtɑk·sə·keɪt̬·əd/ *adj slightly fml* drunk • *He was arrested and charged with driving while intoxicated.*

intoxicating /ɪnˈtɑk·sə·keɪt̬·ɪŋ/ *adj* making you feel a little drunk, as if you are in a pleasant dream • *After being cooped up in the overheated room all day, we took a stroll and found the fresh air intoxicating.*

intractable /ɪnˈtræk·tə·bəl/ *adj* difficult or impossible to manage or control • *intractable problems* ◦ *an intractable child*

intramural /ˌɪn·trəˈmjʊr·əl/ *adj* [not gradable] happening within or involving the members of one school • *At college she was active in intramural sports.*

intransigent /ɪnˈtræn·zə·dʒənt/ *adj fml* refusing to change an opinion • *Although the legislature overwhelmingly voted to legalize gambling, the governor was intransigent and vowed to veto the bill.*

intransitive /ɪnˈtræn·zət̬·ɪv/ *adj* [not gradable] *specialized* (in grammar) (of a verb) needing no **direct object** (= the thing the verb acts on) • *In the sentence "I ran with him to the store," "ran" is an intransitive verb.* • Compare TRANSITIVE. [LP] TRANSITIVE AND INTRANSITIVE VERBS

intravenous /ˌɪn·trəˈviː·nəs/ (*abbreviation* **IV**) *adj* [not gradable] put directly into a VEIN (= one of the tubes in the body that carry blood to the heart) • *an intravenous drug*

intravenously /ˌɪn·trəˈviː·nə·sli/ *adv* [not gradable] • *The antibiotic was given in a fluid intravenously.*

intrepid /ɪnˈtrep·əd/ *adj slightly fml* very brave and willing to risk being in dangerous situations • *an intrepid explorer*

intricate /ˈɪn·trɪ·kət/ *adj* having a lot of small parts or pieces arranged in a complicated way, and therefore sometimes difficult to understand in detail • *The novel's intricate plot will not be easy to translate into a movie.*

intricately /ˈɪn·trɪ·kət·li/ *adv* • *The antique silver teapot is intricately engraved.*

intricacy /ˈɪn·trɪ·kə·si/ *n* [C usually pl] a detail that is part of something complicated • *No one could understand all the intricacies of the deal.*

intrigue INTEREST /ɪnˈtriːg/ *v* [T] (of something or someone) to make you want to discover more esp. because there is something unusual about it or them • *I was intrigued by his slow, deliberate way of talking and the serious look in his eyes.*

intriguing /ɪnˈtriː·gɪŋ/ *adj* • *She has written an intriguing account of growing up on a farm as one of ten children.*

intrigue SECRET /ˈɪn·triːg, ɪnˈtriːg/ *n* [C/U] the making of a secret plan to do something, esp. something that will harm someone • *In that tale of political intrigue, he combined great dialogue with an interesting plot and a surprise ending.* [U]

intrinsic /ɪnˈtrɪn·zɪk/ *adj* basic to a thing, being an important part of making it what it is • *Each human being has intrinsic dignity and worth.*

intro /ˈɪn·troʊ/ *n* [C] *pl* **intros** *infml* an INTRODUCTION

introduce MEET SOMEONE /ˌɪn·trəˈduːs/ *v* [T] to arrange for (you) to meet and learn the name of (another person) • *I'd like to introduce you to my friend, Sally.* ◦ *George, I'd like to introduce my friend, Sally.* • To introduce is also to make a formal announcement of (someone) esp. to a public group: *It's my distinct honor to introduce the president of the United States of America.*

introduction /ˌɪn·trəˈdʌk·ʃən/ *n* [C] • *Let me do the introductions* (= introduce everyone to each other).

introduce BEGIN TO USE /ˌɪn·trəˈduːs/ *v* [T] to put (something) into use for the first time, or to put (something) into a new place • *When were music CDs first introduced?* ◦ *These trees were introduced into New England from Europe.*

introduction /ˌɪn·trəˈdʌk·ʃən/ *n* [U] • *The introduction of express buses is scheduled for July.*

introduction /ˌɪn·trəˈdʌk·ʃən/ *n* [C] a short speech or piece of writing that comes before a longer speech or written text, usually giving basic information about what is to follow • *The author's introduction explains the organization of the book.*

introductory /ˌɪn·trəˈdʌk·tə·ri/ *adj* [not gradable] coming before something else • *introductory remarks*

intrude /ɪnˈtruːd/ *v* [I] to go into a place or be involved in a situation where you are not wanted or do not belong • *Sorry to intrude, but I wanted to insure that this got to your attention.* ◦ *Students who live in a dorm regard any curfew as intruding on their rights.*

intruder /ɪnˈtruːd·ər/ *n* [C] someone who enters a place without permission, esp. in order to commit a crime

intrusion /ɪnˈtruː·ʒən/ *n* [C/U] • *They complained of the unwarranted intrusion into their home by federal agents.* [U]

intuition /ˌɪn·təˈwɪʃ·ən/ *n* [C/U] an ability to understand or know something without needing to think about it or use reason to discover it, or a feeling that shows this ability • *You should trust your intuition in making your decision.* [U] ◦ *Hank's intuitions were right.* [C]

intuitive /ɪnˈtuː·əţ·ɪv/ *adj* • *Most people have an intuitive sense of right and wrong.*

intuitively /ɪnˈtuː·əţ·ɪv·li/ *adv* • *People all over the world respond intuitively to the movie* (= understood it without using reason).

Inuit /ˈɪn·ə·wət, -jə-/ *n* [C] *pl* **Inuit** or **Inuits** *esp. Cdn* an ESKIMO

inundate /ˈɪn·ən,deɪt/ *v* [T] to bring to (a place or person) so much of something, so that it cannot be dealt with • *Inner cities were inundated with unprecedented levels of drugs.* ○ *We were inundated with complaints when the show had to be canceled.* • To inundate is also to flood (an area) with water: *Floods inundated various Indian communities.*

invade /ɪnˈveɪd/ *v* [I/T] to enter (a place) by force, often in large numbers • *The Allies were poised to invade Germany.* [T] ○ *(fig.) I think that the opportunity is definitely there for people to invade your privacy when they want to* (= find out personal things about you against your wishes). [T]

invasion /ɪnˈveɪ·ʒən/ *n* [C] • *the invasion of the Normandy coast on D-day* ○ *(fig.) I certainly regarded the tapping of my phone as an invasion of (my) privacy.*

invalid NOT ACCEPTABLE /ɪnˈvæl·əd/ *adj* [not gradable] not true or acceptable, or not correctly thought out • *The results of the election were declared invalid by the court.*

invalidate /ɪnˈvæl·ə,deɪt/ *v* [T] • *A few minor factual errors should not invalidate the theory* (= make it not true).

invalid WEAK PERSON /ˈɪn·və·ləd, -,lɪd/ *n* [C] a person who is ill or injured for a long time and usually has to be cared for by others • *My dad's mother is an invalid, and she lives with my aunt and uncle.*

invaluable /ɪnˈvæl·jə·bəl, -jə·wə·bəl/ *adj* [not gradable] extremely useful • *Alejandro said the tutoring he received was invaluable.*

invariable /ɪnˈver·iː·ə·bəl, -ˈvær-/ *adj* [not gradable] never changing; staying the same • *an invariable response* ○ *an invariable rule*

invariably /ɪnˈver·iː·ə·bli, -ˈvær-/ *adv* [not gradable] always • *There's no point in rushing—she's invariably late.* ○ *High blood pressure is almost invariably accompanied by high blood cholesterol.*

invasion /ɪnˈveɪ·ʒən/ *n* • See at INVADE.

inveigle /ɪnˈveɪ·gəl/ *v* [T] to persuade (someone) to do something, esp. in a dishonest way • *Nomo meant to inveigle him into helping out.*

invent /ɪnˈvent/ *v* [T] to design or create (something that did not exist before) • *Gutenberg invented movable type in the 15th century.* • To invent is also to create a story or explanation which is not true: *I don't know what I really saw and what I've invented.*

invention /ɪnˈven·tʃən/ *n* [C/U] something newly designed or created, or the activity of designing or creating new things • *The mountain bike was a California invention.* [C] ○ *The invention of the pressure cooker provided a method for cooking quickly.* [U] ○ *His story of being kidnapped and held prisoner was an invention* (= something represented as being true which is not true). [C]

inventive /ɪnˈvent·ɪv/ *adj* approving having or showing the ability to design or create something new • *He is famous for his zany, inventive books for children.*

inventor /ɪnˈvent·ər/ *n* [C] • *Alfred Nobel was the inventor of dynamite.*

inventory /ˈɪn·vən,tɔːr·i, -,tour·i/ *n* [C/U] goods that are readily available, or a detailed list of goods, property, etc. • *large inventories of oil and gasoline* [C] ○ *The store is closed* *while we're taking inventory* (= counting and listing all the goods). [U]

inverse /ɪnˈvɜrs, ˈɪn·vɜrs/ *adj* [not gradable] changing in an opposite direction in relation to something else, esp. an amount • *in inverse proportion* ∘ *an inverse relationship*

inversely /ɪnˈvɜr·sli, ˈɪn·vɜr-/ *adv* [not gradable] • *By and large, your ability to cope with change varies inversely with age.*

invert /ɪnˈvɜrt/ *v* [T] to put (something) upside down or in the opposite order or position • *Invert the cake onto a wire rack and let it cool.*

invest /ɪnˈvest/ *v* [I/T] to put (money or effort) into something to make a profit or achieve a result • *She tends to invest a lot of energy in her work.* [T] ∘ *I think it's time to invest in* (= buy) *a new washing machine.* [I]

investment /ɪnˈvest·mənt/ *n* [C/U] • *real estate investments* [C] ∘ *There's an awful lot of foreign investment in the US.* [U]

investor /ɪnˈves·tər/ *n* [C] a person or group of people that puts its money into a business or other organization in order to make a profit • *Many stock-market investors who wanted to sell couldn't find any buyers.*

investigate /ɪnˈves·təˌɡeɪt/ *v* [I/T] to examine (something, such as an event or situation) carefully, esp. to discover the truth about it • *There was a suspicious man near the playground, and we asked the police to investigate.* [I] ∘ *The school created an independent review board to investigate charges of misconduct.* [T]

investigation /ɪnˌves·təˈɡeɪ·ʃən/ *n* [C/U] • *a criminal investigation* [C] ∘ *The cause of the fire is under investigation* (= is being examined). [U]

investigator /ɪnˈves·təˌɡeɪt·ər/ *n* [C] • *She hired a private investigator to check into her husband's activities.*

inveterate /ɪnˈveṭ·ə·rət/ *adj usually disapproving* done as a habit and not likely to change • *an inveterate liar*

invidious /ɪnˈvɪd·iː·əs/ *adj slightly fml* likely to cause unhappiness or offense • *We are not going to seek for invidious comparisons between governments.*

invigorate /ɪnˈvɪɡ·əˌreɪt/ *v* [T] to give new energy or strength to (someone or something) • *They argued that a cut in the tax rate would invigorate the economy.*

invigorating /ɪnˈvɪɡ·əˌreɪṭ·ɪŋ/ *adj* • *The fresh air was invigorating.*

invincible /ɪnˈvɪn·sə·bəl/ *adj* [not gradable] impossible to defeat or prevent from doing what is intended • *an invincible army* ∘ *She seemed nearly invincible on the tennis court this year.*

invisible /ɪnˈvɪz·ə·bəl/ *adj* [not gradable] impossible to see • *Invisible bacteria can lead to food poisoning.* ∘ *She was so unimportant in their lives that she was almost invisible to them.*

invisibility /ɪnˌvɪz·əˈbɪl·əṭ·i/ *n* [U]

invite ASK /ɪnˈvaɪt/ *v* [T] to ask (someone) in a polite or friendly way to come somewhere, such as to a party, or to formally ask (someone) to do something • *I should invite her over for coffee.* ∘ *Architects were invited to submit their designs for a new city hall.*

invitation /ˌɪn·vəˈteɪ·ʃən/, *not standard* **invite** /ˈɪn·vaɪt/ *n* [C] • *We received their wedding invitation today.* ∘ *He accepted the invitation to join the committee.*

invite ENCOURAGE /ɪnˈvaɪt/ *v* [T] to cause (something, esp. something bad) to happen • *If you're scared of an animal, make a lot of noise, because running away usually invites problems.*

invitation /ˌɪn·vəˈteɪ·ʃən/ *n* [U] • *Leaving your house unlocked is an open invitation to burglars* (= encourages them).

inviting /ɪnˈvaɪṭ·ɪŋ/ *adj* attractive • *The kitchen is cheerful and inviting.*

invoice /ˈɪn·vɔɪs/ *n* [C] a statement listing goods or services provided and their prices, used in business as a record of sale • *You need to have a copy of your original invoice if you want a refund.*

invoice /ˈɪn·vɔɪs/ *v* [T] • *When they ship the CDs, the company will invoice you* (= send you a request for payment).

invoke CALL FOR HELP /ɪnˈvoʊk/ *v* [T] to ask (esp. God) for help • *Barry repeatedly invoked God during his discussion of his alcoholism.*

invoke USE /ɪnˈvoʊk/ *v* [T] to cause (something) to be used; bring into effect • *The administration is willing to invoke trade sanctions against Japan if negotiations fail.*

involuntary /ɪnˈvɑl·ənˌter·i/ *adj* not done willingly, or not done intentionally • *A sharp tap beneath the knee usually causes an involuntary movement of the lower leg.* ∘ *The driver of the vehicle was charged with involuntary manslaughter.*

involve INCLUDE /ɪnˈvɑlv, -ˈvɔːlv/ *v* [T] to include (someone or something) in an activity • *The accident involved two cars and a truck.* ∘ *The operation involves inserting a small tube into the heart.*

involvement /ɪnˈvɑlv·mənt, -ˈvɔːlv-/ *n* [C/U] • *He was accused of involvement in the murder.* [U]

involve MAKE INTERESTED /ɪnˈvɑlv, -ˈvɔːlv/ *v* [T] to make (someone) interested in taking part in something • *A good teacher tries to involve children in activities where they interact with each other.*

involved /ɪnˈvɑlvd, -ˈvɔːlvd/ *adj* interested in or taking part in an activity or event • *The couple was having a loud argument, and I was afraid to get involved.* ∘ *Maria was so involved in her work that she didn't hear me come in.* • If someone is **involved with** someone else, they have a close, personal, often sexual relationship: *She's involved with a married man.*

involved /ɪnˈvɑlvd, -ˈvɔːlvd/ *adj* difficult to

understand or deal with; complicated • *His story was so involved that I couldn't follow it.*

inward /'ɪn·wərd/ *adj* [not gradable] on or toward the inside • *the inward curve of her waist* • Inward also means directed toward your self, your mind, or your spirit: *an inward spiritual quest* • Compare OUTWARD AWAY FROM.

inward /'ɪn·wərd/, **inwards** /'ɪn·wərdz/ *adv* [not gradable] • *Fold the edges of the paper inward.* ○ *We turned inward to our own thoughts.*

inwardly /'ɪn·wərd·li/ *adv* [not gradable] • *She inwardly hoped he would fail.*

iodine /'aɪ·ə,daɪn, -əd·ən/ *n* [U] a chemical element found in small amounts in sea water, and used in medicine and photography

ion /'aɪ,ɑn, -ən/ *n* [C] *specialized* an atom that has a positive or negative electrical charge as the result of adding or taking away an ELECTRON

iota /aɪ'oʊt̬·ə/ *n* [U] a very small amount • *All this bragging does not detract one iota from the fact that Henryk is an extraordinary man.*

IOU *n* [C] *pl* **IOUs** or **IOU's** *abbreviation for* I owe you (= a written promise to pay back money owed) • *I'll give you an IOU for the loan.*

IPA *n* [U] *abbreviation for* **International Phonetic Alphabet**, see at INTERNATIONAL

ipso facto /,ɪp·soʊ'fæk·toʊ/ *adv* [not gradable] by that fact or act • *If he is right, then anyone who disagrees with him is, ipso facto, wrong.*

IQ *n* [C] *abbreviation for* intelligence quotient (= a person's level of intelligence measured by standardized tests which are adjusted for age) • *a high/low IQ* ○ *an IQ test*

IRA /'aɪ·rə/ *n* [C] *abbreviation for* individual retirement account (= a special bank account in which you invest money to use when you are older and stop working)

irascible /ɪ'ræs·ə·bəl/ *adj* (of a person) easily made angry • *a cranky, irascible artist*

irate /aɪ'reɪt/ *adj* very angry • *We've been getting some irate calls from customers.*

ire /aɪr/ *n* [U] anger • *The team drew the ire of local politicians when it moved to a new stadium outside the city.*

iris FLOWER /'aɪ·rəs/ *n* [C] a tall plant with large, colorful, often yellow or purple flowers and long pointed leaves

iris EYE /'aɪ·rəs/ *n* [C] the colored, circular part of an eye surrounding the black PUPIL (= central part) • *When you say someone is blue-eyed, you are referring to the color of their irises.* • PIC EYE

irk /ɜrk/ *v* [T] to annoy (someone) • *Her comments really irked me.*

iron METAL /'aɪ·ərn/ *n* [U] a common, silver-colored, metal element that is magnetic and strong, is used in making steel, and is found in small amounts in blood and in all living things • *Iron rusts easily.* ○ *Liver is a rich source of dietary iron.* • Something that is

ironclad cannot be doubted: *The new contract provides employees with ironclad job security.*

iron /'aɪ·ərn/ *adj* [not gradable] • *iron ore* ○ *an iron railing along the steps* ○ *(fig.) Her success depended on physical strength and an iron will* (= strong determination).

iron DEVICE /'aɪ·ərn/ *n* [C] a device with a handle and a flat metal base that can be heated and pressed against cloth to make the cloth smooth

iron /'aɪ·ərn/ *v* [T] • *I have to iron this skirt* (= make it smooth using an iron). ○ *Let me iron out the wrinkles in this tablecloth.* [M]

ironing /'aɪ·ər·nɪŋ/ *n* [U] • *I do the ironing once a week.* • An **ironing board** is a board covered with cloth, usually with folding legs, on which clothes and other items can be made smooth with an iron.

▫ **iron out** *obj*, **iron** *obj* **out** /'-'-/ *v adv* [M] to put something into a finished state by solving or removing (something causing a problem) • *They met to iron out the details of the contract.*

irony /'aɪ·rə·ni, 'aɪ·ər·ni/ *n* [C/U] a type of usually humorous expression in which you say the opposite of what you intend • *He had a powerful sense of irony, and you could never be absolutely sure when he was serious.* [U] • Irony is also something that has a different or opposite result from what is expected: *It is one of the ironies of life that by the time you have earned enough money for the things you always wanted, you no longer have the energy to enjoy them.* [C] • Compare SARCASM.

ironic /aɪ'rɑn·ɪk/, **ironical** /aɪ'rɑn·ɪ·kəl/ *adj* • *The play was full of witty, ironic banter.* ○ *It's really ironic that I would be asked to write about pets today because just yesterday our dog ran away.* [+ *that* clause]

ironically /aɪ'rɑn·ɪ·kli/ *adv* in a way that is different or opposite from the result you would expect • *Ironically, his ability as an inventor made him a poor administrator, and he had one business failure after another.*

irrational /ɪ'ræʃ·ən·əl/ *adj* not based on reason or clear thinking; not reasonable • *One of her main themes is the irrational nature of love.*

irrefutable /,ɪr·ɪ'fjuːt̬·ə·bəl, ɪ'ref·jət̬-/ *adj* [not gradable] *slightly fml* that cannot be proved wrong • *irrefutable evidence/proof*

irregardless /,ɪr·ɪ'gɑrd·ləs/ *adv not standard* without attention to, or despite the conditions or situation; REGARDLESS • *Irregardless of whether he gives me a raise, I'm quitting at the end of this week.*

irregular SHAPE /ɪ'reg·jə·lər/ *adj* not regular in shape or form; having parts of different shapes or sizes • *an irregular surface*

irregular TIME / SPACE /ɪ'reg·jə·lər/ *adj* not happening at regular times, or not having usual or regular spaces in between • *There are irregular spaces between the words.* ○ *He showed up at irregular intervals.*

irregular RULE /ɪˈreg·jə·lər/ *adj* (of behavior or actions) not according to usual rules or what is expected • (*specialized*) In grammar, an irregular verb, noun, adjective, or other type of word does not obey the usual rules in the language for changing word endings.

irrelevant /ɪˈrel·ə·vənt/ *adj* not related to what is being discussed or considered • *These documents are totally irrelevant to the investigation.*

irreligious /ˌɪr·ɪˈlɪdʒ·əs/ *adj* having no interest in religion, or generally opposed to religion

irreparable /ɪˈrep·ə·rə·bəl/ *adj* [not gradable] impossible to repair or make right again • *irreparable damage*

irreparably /ɪˈrep·ə·rə·bli/ *adv* [not gradable]

irreplaceable /ˌɪr·ɪˈpleɪ·sə·bəl/ *adj* [not gradable] too special, unusual, or valuable to replace with something else, or of which no others like it exist • *irreplaceable documents* ○ *No one on this team is irreplaceable, the new manager insisted.*

irrepressible /ˌɪr·ɪˈpres·ə·bəl/ *adj* full of energy and enthusiasm; impossible to hold back • *irrepressible high spirits*

irresistible /ˌɪr·ɪˈzɪs·tə·bəl/ *adj* impossible to refuse, oppose, or avoid because too pleasant, attractive, or strong • *an irresistible smile* ○ *I wasn't going to have dessert, but the pie proved irresistible.*

irrespective /ˌɪr·ɪˈspek·tɪv/ *adv* [not gradable] without considering; not needing to allow for • *The rules apply to everyone, irrespective of how long they have been with the company.*

irresponsible /ˌɪr·ɪˈspɑn·sə·bəl/ *adj* not thinking carefully enough or not caring about what might result from actions taken • *It would have been irresponsible to let Claire drive home after all she had to drink.* [+ to infinitive]

irresponsibly /ˌɪr·ɪˈspɑn·sə·bli/ *adv*

irreverent /ɪˈrev·ə·rənt/ *adj* lacking the expected respect for official, important, or holy things • *The television program takes an irreverent look at the medical profession.*

irreverence /ɪˈrev·ə·rəns/ *n* [U]

irreversible /ˌɪr·ɪˈvɜr·sə·bəl/ *adj* [not gradable] impossible to change or to return to a previous condition • *Technology has had an irreversible impact on society.*

irrevocable /ɪˈrev·ə·kə·bəl, ˌɪr·ɪˈvoʊ·kə-/ *adj* [not gradable] (esp. of a decision) impossible to change • *The court's ruling is irrevocable.*

irrigate /ˈɪr·əˌgeɪt/ *v* [T] to supply (land) with water so that crops and plants will grow or grow better • *to irrigate farmland*

irrigation /ˌɪr·əˈgeɪ·ʃən/ *n* [U] • *an irrigation system*

irritate ANNOY /ˈɪr·əˌteɪt/ *v* [T] to annoy or make angry • *After a while the noise began to irritate him.*

irritable /ˈɪr·ət·ə·bəl/ *adj* • *The baby has really been irritable today.*

irritating /ˈɪr·əˌteɪt·ɪŋ/ *adj* • *There was one irritating delay after another.*

irritation /ˌɪr·əˈteɪ·ʃən/ *n* [C/U] • *minor irritations* [C]

irritate MAKE SORE /ˈɪr·əˌteɪt/ *v* [T] to make (something) sore or painful or cause an uncomfortable physical reaction • *At first my contact lenses irritated my eyes.*

irritant /ˈɪr·ə·tənt/ *n* [C] a cause of an uncomfortable physical reaction • *Especially in the spring, plant pollen is an irritant that makes the eyes and throat itchy and can cause breathing problems.*

irritation /ˌɪr·əˈteɪ·ʃən/ *n* [C/U] a sore or reddened area on the skin or other part of the body • *a skin irritation* [C]

IRS *n* [U] *abbreviation for* Internal Revenue Service (= the part of the US Treasury Department that collects most taxes owed to the federal government, including income tax)

is /ɪz, əz/ *v* BE, used with he/she/it • *She is a lawyer.*

Islam /ɪzˈlɑm, ˈɪz·lɑm/ *n* [U] a religion based on a belief in one god and the teaching of Muhammad • *Islam is the religion of the Muslims.*

Islamic /ɪzˈlɑm·ɪk, -ˈlæm-/ *adj* [not gradable] • *Islamic art* ○ *an Islamic country*

island /ˈaɪ·lənd/ *n* [C] a piece of land completely surrounded by water • *Manhattan is an island.*

isle /aɪl/ *n* [C] an ISLAND, esp. a small one

isn't /ˈɪz·ənt/ *contraction of* is not • *He isn't coming until tomorrow.*

isolate /ˈaɪ·səˌleɪt/ *v* [T] to separate (something) from other things, or to keep (something) separate • *They tried to isolate the cause of the problem.* ○ *A high wall isolated the house from the rest of the neighborhood.*

isolated /ˈaɪ·səˌleɪt·əd/ *adj* • *Only a few isolated cases of measles have been reported.*

isolation /ˌaɪ·səˈleɪ·ʃən/ *n* [U] • *The prisoner was kept in isolation for three days.*

issue SUBJECT /ˈɪʃ·uː, *esp. Southern* ˈɪʃ·ə/ *n* [C] a subject or problem that people are thinking and talking about • *There continues to be a great deal of debate over the abortion issue.* ○ *Isn't the need to hire more staff what's really at issue here* (= the subject of the disagreement)? ○ *I like my hair this way, I don't see why you have to make an issue of it* (= cause it to be a problem).

issue SUPPLY /ˈɪʃ·uː, *esp. Southern* ˈɪʃ·ə/ *v* [T] to give, supply, or produce (something official) • *Reporters gathered on the White House lawn, hoping that the president would issue a statement.*

issue /ˈɪʃ·uː, *esp. Southern* ˈɪʃ·ə/ *n* [C] a group or series, or one of a group or series, of things that are supplied, made available, or printed at the same time • *A new issue of postage stamps was released to honor women in the mil-*

itary. ○ *He picked up an old issue of Life magazine.*

isthmus /'ɪs·məs/ *n* [C] a narrow piece of land that has water on either side and joins two larger areas of land • *the Isthmus of Panama*

it /ɪt, ət/ *pronoun* the thing or animal being spoken about, that has already been mentioned • *I can't find the newspaper. Do you know where it is?* ○ *Someone is at the door. Find out who it is.* • It is sometimes used to introduce a statement that does not involve a particular event or person: *It's supposed to rain tomorrow.*

its /ɪts, əts/ *pronoun* belonging to or connected with the thing or animal mentioned; the possessive form of it, used before a noun • *The horse flicked its tail at the flies.* ○ *The movie has its flaws, but it is interesting nevertheless.* • See also IT'S. LP DETERMINERS

itself /ɪt'self, ət-/ *pronoun* the thing or animal being spoken about; the reflexive form of it • *The cat licked itself all over.* • Itself can also used for emphasis: *The company itself is 15 years old, but the mail order business is new.* ○

That in itself (= without considering anything else) *was quite an achievement.* • LP REFLEXIVE PRONOUNS

italics /ɪ'tæl·ɪks, ɑɪ-/ *pl n* a style of printing in which the letters lean to the right • *This sentence is printed in italics.* LP ITALICS (p. 466)

italic /ɪ'tæl·ɪk, ɑɪ-/ *adj* • *italic type*

italicize /ɪ'tæl·ə,sɑɪz, ɑɪ-/ *v* [T] • *Sometimes words are italicized for emphasis.*

itch /ɪtʃ/ *v* [I] to have an uncomfortable feeling on the skin that makes you want to rub it with something hard • *My insect bites are itching.* • To be itching to do something means to want to do it very much and as soon as possible: *The kids are itching to go out and play.* [+ to infinitive]

itch /ɪtʃ/ *n* [C usually sing] • *I have an itch on the back of my neck.* ○ *He has an itch* (= desire) *to travel.* [+ to infinitive]

itchy /'ɪtʃ·i/ *adj* [-er/-est only] • *an itchy sweater*

it'd /'ɪt̬·əd, ɪd/ *contraction of* it would or it had • *It'd* (= It would) *be great if we could finish*

IT

It is often used in a way that does not refer to a particular thing, person, etc. It is used as the subject in:

• sentences giving the time, the date, the weather, and distances

   It's three o'clock. • It *was Tuesday.* • It*'s March 5.* • It *rained all day.* • It*'s 230 miles to New Orleans.*

   It is also used in these question forms:

   What time/day/date is it? • *What's it like out/outside?* • *How far is it to New Orleans?*

• sentences with a linking verb [L] and an adjective describing conditions in a place

   It*'s dark outside.* • It *seems very crowded in here.* • It *was too noisy in the restaurant.*

• sentences with an adjective, noun, or verb followed by:

   a to infinitive

   It *was* **good to** *see you.* • It *isn't* **easy to** *find a cheap apartment.* • *How much does* it **cost to** *rent a movie?* • It *never* **occurred** *to me* **to** *ask.*

   a that or (that) clause

   It*'s* **unlikely (that)** *the train will be on time.* • It*'s* **important that** *you see a doctor quickly.* • It *seems* **strange that** *no one is here yet.*

   an -ing form

   It *was good talking to you.* • It*'s* **no use knocking**—*she can't hear you.* • *Is* it **difficult being** *a single parent?*

   a wh- word

   It*'s* **amazing wh**at *people will do to get on TV.* • It **surprised** *me* **how** *quickly the time passed.*

• sentences with **if, as if, as though,** or **like**

   It *wouldn't* **surprise** *me* **if** *he already knew.* • It **sounds as if** *you had a difficult time.* • It **looks like** *we made the right decision.* • It *isn't* **as though** *you can't afford it.*

• sentences intended to emphasize something

   Compare these sentences:

   Paul came here in September.

   It *was Paul* **who** *came here in September.* (emphasizes Paul)

   It *was in September* **that** *Paul came here.* (emphasizes September)

The verbs **be, appear, seem, look, sound, take, happen,** and **occur to** often take it as a subject. Some of these verbs can also take **there** as a subject. **There**, not it, is used when you want to say that something exists or to emphasize where it is.

LP **There**

ITALICS

In printed text italics are used:

to emphasize something important

This emergency door must be kept clear *at all times.* • She spent *over thirty years* of her life in prison.

Underlining is used instead when the text is written by hand or typed.

for the titles of books, magazines, plays, movies, and works of art

Melville's *Moby-Dick* • a stack of *Time*s and *Newsweek*s • today's *Daily News* • a new production of *The Buried Child* • Bob Dylan's *Blowin' in the Wind* • Leonardo's *Mona Lisa*

Quotation marks are sometimes used instead.

for the names of ships, aircraft, and spacecraft

the *Titanic* • *Apollo 13*

for foreign words that might not be familiar to the reader

A *carioca* is someone from Rio de Janeiro. • Did life on earth begin *ex nihilo*?

But: I cooked pasta for dinner.

for difficult or technical words when they are first used

The *bole* of a tree is its trunk; the *crown* is its thick upper foliage. • I use the word *tribe* to mean any distinct group of people living together.

today. ∘ *It'd* (= It had) *been left in the yard all week.*

item /ˈaɪt̬·əm/ *n* [C] one thing that is a part of a list or a collection of things • *There were several more items on the agenda.* • An item is also a particular thing considered as one among others of its type: *a news item in this morning's newspaper* ∘ *basic food items such as butter*

itemize /ˈaɪt̬·əˌmɑɪz/ *v* [T] to list (particular things) separately • *I always itemize deductions on my income tax.*

itinerant /ɑɪˈtɪn·ə·rənt/ *adj* (of a person) traveling from one place to another, usually to work for a short period • *itinerant farm workers*

itinerary /ɑɪˈtɪn·əˌrer·i/ *n* [C] a detailed plan or route of a trip • *We planned our itinerary several weeks before the trip.*

it'll /ˈɪt̬·əl/ *contraction of* it will • *It'll be hard to find someone to help.*

it's /ɪts, əts/ *contraction of* it is *or* it has • *It's* (= It is) *my turn to do it.* ∘ *It's* (= It has) *been a long day and I'm tired.* • See also **its** at IT.

I've /ɑɪv/ *contraction of* I have • *I've decided not to go.*

ivory /ˈɑɪ·və·ri, ˈɑɪv·ri/ *n* [U] the hard white substance of the TUSKS (= long teeth growing outside the mouth) of some animals, such as ELEPHANTS • *an ivory statue* • Ivory is also a yellow-white color.

ivory tower /ˌɑɪv·riːˈtɑʊ·ər/ *n* [C] an imaginary place where you are protected from unpleasant facts and have little practical knowledge of the real world • *They all live in their ivory towers and have no idea what it takes to win a football conference title.*

ivory–tower /ˌɑɪv·riːˌtɑʊ·ər/ *adj* [not gradable] • *They were essentially realists, not ivory-tower dreamers.*

ivy /ˈɑɪ·vi/ *n* [C/U] an evergreen plant that often grows along the surface of trees or buildings • **The Ivy League** is a group of established colleges in the northeastern US with a good reputation: *Yale and Harvard are Ivy League schools.*

J, j

J, j /dʒeɪ/ *n* [C] *pl* **J's** or **Js** or **j's** or **js** the tenth letter of the English alphabet

jab /dʒæb/ *v* [I/T] **-bb-** to push at (something) hard and quickly, esp. with a sharp or pointed object • *I jabbed my finger on the needle.* [T] ○ *He jabbed at his food with his fork.* [I]

jab /dʒæb/ *n* [C] • *He gave his opponent a quick jab in the ribs.*

jabber /'dʒæb·ər/ *v* [I] to speak or say something quickly in a way that is difficult to understand • *Jay was jabbering on about this and that.*

jack [DEVICE] /dʒæk/ *n* [C] a device used to raise and hold something heavy off the ground, esp. one for raising a vehicle so that a tire can be changed

jack [CARD] /dʒæk/ *n* [C] a playing card that has a picture of a man on it and has a lower value than the cards showing a king or queen • *the jack of diamonds*

jack [ELECTRICITY] /dʒæk/ *n* [C] a hole into which a wire connected to a piece of electrical equipment can be plugged so that the equipment can operate • *a microphone jack*

□ **jack up** *obj* [RAISE] , **jack** *obj* **up** /'-'-/ *v adv* [M] to raise (something heavy) off the ground • *I had the car jacked up on blocks.*

□ **jack up** *obj* [INCREASE] , **jack** *obj* **up** /'-'-/ *v adv* [M] to increase (a price) • *Ad rates will be jacked up to $3600 a month.*

jackal /'dʒæk·əl/ *n* [C] any of several types of wild dog of Asia and Africa that hunt and travel in groups

jackass [PERSON] /'dʒæk·æs/ *n* [C] *infml* a foolish person • *Why is Russ behaving like such a jackass?*

jackass [ANIMAL] /'dʒæk·æs/ *n* [C] a male DONKEY (= small horselike animal)

jacket [CLOTHING] /'dʒæk·ət/ *n* [C] a short coat • *a leather/denim jacket* ○ *a suit/sports jacket*

jacket [COVERING] /'dʒæk·ət/ *n* [C] a protective outer covering for something, esp. a bullet or wire

jackhammer /'dʒæk·hæm·ər/ *n* [C] a powerful tool, held in the hands and operated by air pressure, that is used for breaking hard surfaces such as rock and roads

jack–in–the–box /'dʒæk·ɪn·ðə·bɑks/ *n* [C] a toy consisting of a box from which a model of a person suddenly appears when the top of the box is raised

jackknife [KNIFE] /'dʒæk·nɑɪf/ *n* [C] a knife with one or more blades that fold into the handle, which fits into a person's pocket

jackknife [MAKE AN ANGLE] /'dʒæk·nɑɪf/ *v* [I] to bend in half, or bend so the parts make a sharp angle • *A truck jackknifed on Route 80 this morning.*

jack–of–all–trades /ˌdʒæk·ə·vɔːl'treɪdz/ *n* [U] someone who can do many different jobs • *An artist with the right technology can become a jack-of-all-trades.*

jack–o'–lantern /'dʒæk·ə,lænt·ərn/ *n* [C] a PUMPKIN that has been hollowed out and cut with holes shaped like eyes, a nose, and a mouth, and lit with a candle inside, which is made at HALLOWEEN

jackpot /'dʒæk·pɑt/ *n* [C] the largest prize offered in a competition, or a prize that is added to until it is won • *I dreamt that I won/hit the jackpot.*

jackrabbit /'dʒæk,ræb·ət/ *n* [C] a type of large HARE (= animal like a rabbit) of N America, with long ears and long back legs

jacks /dʒæks/ *n* [U] a children's game in which the player bounces a small ball into the air and tries to pick up a number of small metal or plastic objects with the same hand before catching the ball again

Jacuzzi /dʒə'kuː·zi/ *n* [C] *trademark* a bath or pool into which warm water flows through small holes, producing a pleasant, bubbling effect

jade /dʒeɪd/ *n* [U], *adj* [not gradable] a precious, usually green stone from which jewelry is made, or a blue-green or yellow-green color

jaded /'dʒeɪd·əd/ *adj* [not gradable] lacking interest or desire because of experiencing too much of something • *Business travel is exciting at first, but you soon become jaded.*

jagged /'dʒæg·əd/ *adj* [not gradable] rough and uneven, with sharp points • *a jagged piece of glass* ○ *a jagged edge*

jaguar /'dʒæg·wɑr, -jə,wɑr/ *n* [C] a large, wild cat of Central and S America with black spots

jail /dʒeɪl/ *n* [C/U] a place where criminals are kept as a punishment for their crime or while waiting for trial • *County jails are already overcrowded.* [C] ○ *He was sentenced to six months in jail.* [U]

jail /dʒeɪl/ *v* [T] • *He was jailed for three years.*

jailer /'dʒeɪ·lər/ *n* [C] a person in charge of a jail or of the prisoners there

jalopy /dʒə'lɑp·i/ *n* [C] *infml humorous* an old car in bad condition

jam [PUSH] /dʒæm/ *v* [T always + adv/prep] **-mm-** to push (something) hard with sudden effort • *She jammed on the brakes when the light turned red.* [M]

jam [PACK] /dʒæm/ *v* [T always + adv/prep] **-mm-** to pack tightly into a small space • *He jammed the boxes into the trunk of the car.*

jammed /dʒæmd/, **jam–packed** /'dʒæm'pækt/ *adj* • *The room was jammed.* ○ *a jam-packed meeting*

jam [BECOME STUCK] /dʒæm/ *v* [I/T] **-mm-** to become stuck and unable to move, or to be stuck

in (something) • *My key jammed in the lock.* [I]
∘ *Paper was jamming the printer.* [T]

jammed /dʒæmd/ *adj* [not gradable] • *This drawer is jammed.*

jam SITUATION /dʒæm/ *n* [C] *infml* a difficult situation • *She expects her parents to bail her out whenever she gets in a jam.*

jam MUSIC /dʒæm/ *v* [I] **-mm-** to play popular music informally with other people, without planning it or practicing together • *He once jammed with Charlie Parker.*

jam FOOD /dʒæm/ *n* [U] a soft, sweet food made by cooking fruit with sugar • *strawberry/ raspberry jam on toast*

jamboree /ˌdʒæm·bəˈriː/ *n* [C] a large social gathering • *a country music jamboree* ∘ *a Boy Scout jamboree*

Jane Doe /ˈdʒeɪnˈdoʊ/ *n* [C] *female* JOHN DOE

jangle /ˈdʒæŋ·gəl/ *v* [I/T] to make a noise like metal hitting metal • *The phone jangled insistently.* [I]

janitor /ˈdʒæn·ət̬·ər/ *n* [C] a person whose job is to clean and take care of a building

January /ˈdʒæn·jəˌwer·i/ (*abbreviation* **Jan.**) *n* [C/U] the first month of the year, after December and before February

jar CONTAINER /dʒɑr/ *n* [C] a cylindrical container, usually made of glass, with a wide top opening, and used esp. for storing food, or the amount held by such a container • *a jar of pickles/mayonnaise* ∘ *He poured half the jar into his cup.*

jar SHAKE /dʒɑr/ *v* [T] **-rr-** to give a sudden shake to (someone or something) • *He kind of jars people when he tackles them.* • *If a noise jars you, it shocks you: The train's rumbling jarred them out of their sleep.*

jar CAUSE ACTION /dʒɑr/ *v* [I/T] to cause (action or activity), or to have an effect • *He was jarred into political action by events on the national scene.* [T]

jargon /ˈdʒɑr·gən/ *n* [U] words and phrases used by particular groups of people, esp. in their work, that are not generally understood • *technical jargon* ∘ *legal/computer jargon*

jarring /ˈdʒɑr·ɪŋ/ *adj* different from surrounding or usual things, or disagreeing with others, and therefore surprising or upsetting • *a jarring succession of images* ∘ *The band took a new, if jarring, approach to this music.*

jaundice /ˈdʒɔːn·dəs, ˈdʒɑn-/ *n* [U] a disease of the blood that causes the skin and the white part of the eyes to turn yellow

jaundiced /ˈdʒɔːn·dəst, ˈdʒɑn-/ *adj*

jaundiced /ˈdʒɔːn·dəst, ˈdʒɑn-/ *adj* [not gradable] showing negative feelings or ideas • *He has a jaundiced view of middle-class life.*

jaunt /dʒɔːnt, dʒɑnt/ *n* [C] a short trip for pleasure • *a weekend jaunt*

jaunty /ˈdʒɔːnt̬·i, ˈdʒɑnt̬·i/ *adj* [-er/-est only] happy and confident

jauntily /ˈdʒɔːnt̬·ᵊl·i, ˈdʒɑnt̬-/ *adv* • *He scampered jauntily down the stairs.*

javelin /ˈdʒæv·ə·lən/ *n* [C/U] a long, pointed stick that is thrown in sports competitions, or the sport in which this stick is thrown

jaw /dʒɔː/ *n* [C] either of the two bony parts bordering the mouth that hold your teeth in place • *the upper/lower jaw* • The **jawbone** is either of the two bones that form the lower jaw. • If your **jaw drops**, you are very surprised: *When I saw him make that shot, my eyebrows went up and my jaw dropped.*

jaws /dʒɔːz/ *pl n* the mouth, including the teeth • *The lion opened its jaws and roared.*

jaywalk /ˈdʒeɪ·wɔːk/ *v* [I] to walk across a street at a place where you are not allowed to cross

jaywalking /ˈdʒeɪˌwɔː·kɪŋ/ *n* [U] • *You got ticketed for jaywalking?*

jazz /dʒæz/ *n* [U] a type of music of African-American origin with a strong rhythm in which the players IMPROVISE (= invent music that has not been written)

jazzy /ˈdʒæz·i/ *adj* [-er/-est only] • *There's a jazzy quality to her voice.*

jazz up *obj*, **jazz** *obj* **up** /ˈ-ˈ-/ *v adv* [M] *infml* to make (something) more interesting or exciting • *He jazzed up the food with a spicy sauce.*

jazzy /ˈdʒæz·i/ *adj* [-er/-est only] *infml* exciting or showy • *a jazzy tie/dress*

jealous WANTING QUALITIES /ˈdʒel·əs/ *adj* unhappy and slightly angry because you wish you had someone else's qualities, advantages, or success • *Ron was jealous of his colleague's promotion.*

jealousy /ˈdʒel·ə·si/ *n* [C/U] • *petty jealousies* [C] ∘ *Jealousy over a colleague's success is considered unprofessional.* [U]

jealous FEARFUL ABOUT LOVE /ˈdʒel·əs/ *adj* fearful that someone you love loves someone else or is loved by someone else • *Anna is jealous of any woman who comes near her boyfriend.*

jealousy /ˈdʒel·ə·si/ *n* [C/U] • *Grace felt jealousy flare in her stomach when she saw them dancing.* [U]

jealous PROTECTIVE /ˈdʒel·əs/ *adj* very protective of someone or something • *Her parents kept a jealous watch over her.*

jealously /ˈdʒel·ə·sli/ *adv* • *He jealously guarded his privacy.*

jeans /dʒiːnz/ *pl n* pants made of DENIM (= strong, cotton cloth) • *I don't usually wear blue jeans to work.*

Jeep *trademark* /dʒiːp/ *n* [C] a strongly built, four-wheeled motor vehicle designed for travel over rough ground

jeer /dʒɪr/ *v* [I/T] to laugh or shout insults at (someone); to ridicule • *Striking workers jeered at those who crossed the picket line.* [I]

jeer /dʒɪr/ *n* [C] • *We were surprised to hear jeers from our own fans.*

jeez /dʒiːz/ *exclamation slang* used to express

surprise, anger, or annoyance • *Jeez, what took you so long?*

Jehovah's Witness /dʒəˌhoʊˈvɑzˈwɪt·nəs/ *n* [C] a member of a Christian religious group who distribute religious literature to people's homes and on the street • *the Jehovah's Witnesses*

jell /dʒel/, **gel** *v* [I] (of a substance) to change from a liquid to a partly solid state, or (of ideas or plans) to become more clear and certain • *Refrigerate the mixture till it jells.* ○ *I'll let you know as soon as our plans jell.*

Jell-O, jello /ˈdʒel·oʊ/ *n* [U] *trademark* a soft, colored, sweet food made from GELATIN, sugar, and fruit flavoring

jelly /ˈdʒel·i/ *n* [U] a soft, sweet, slightly solid food made by boiling fruit juice with sugar • *grape/apple jelly* ○ *a peanut butter and jelly sandwich* • Jelly is also a substance that is almost solid: *petroleum jelly*

jellybean /ˈdʒel·iːˌbiːn/ *n* [C] a small, brightly colored, bean-shaped candy that is soft in the middle and covered with hard sugar

jellyfish /ˈdʒel·iːˌfɪʃ/ *n* [C] *pl* **jellyfish** a sea animal with a soft, round, almost transparent body with TENTACLES that can sting

jeopardize /ˈdʒep·ərˌdaɪz/ *v* [T] to cause (something) to be harmed or damaged, or to put (something) in danger • *She knew that failing her exams could jeopardize her whole future.*

jeopardy /ˈdʒep·ərd·i/ *n* [U] • Something **in jeopardy** is in danger of being damaged or destroyed: *Bad investments have put the company's future in jeopardy.*

jerk MOVE /dʒɜrk/ *v* [always + adv/prep] to make a short, sudden movement, or to cause someone or something to move in this way • *She jerked the phone out of his hands.* [T] ○ *The bus jerked to a halt.* [I]

jerk /dʒɜrk/ *n* [C] • *He gave the dog's leash a jerk.*

jerky /ˈdʒɜr·ki/ *adj* • *jerky movements*

jerk PERSON /dʒɜrk/ *n* [C] *slang* a foolish, annoying person • *What a jerk—he parked in my spot!*

□ **jerk around** *obj*, **jerk** *obj* **around** /ˈ--ˈ-/ *v adv* [M] *infml* to intentionally cause difficulty for (someone) • *I don't think she really likes Colten—she's just jerking him around.*

□ **jerk off** *(obj)*, **jerk** *(obj)* **off** /ˈ-ˈ-/ *v adv* [I/M] *rude slang* to rub the sexual organs of (yourself or a male) with the hand to give pleasure

jerky /ˈdʒɜr·ki/ *n* [U] strips of dried, salty meat • *beef jerky*

jersey /ˈdʒɜr·zi/ *n* [C] a KNITTED shirt, esp. one that is part of a uniform • *I have to wash my daughter's softball jersey.* • Jersey is also a type of soft, KNITTED cloth: *She was dressed in a jersey top and tight-fitting jeans.*

jest /dʒest/ *n* [C] a joke • If you say something **in jest**, you are not serious about it: *His remarks about the Beatles were in jest.*

jester /ˈdʒes·tər/ *n* [C] (in earlier times) a man whose job was to tell jokes and make people laugh • *a court jester*

Jesuit /ˈdʒeʒ·ə·wət, ˈdʒez-/ *n* [C] a Roman Catholic priest who is a member of the Society of Jesus (= a religious group begun in 1540)

Jesus (Christ) RELIGIOUS LEADER /ˈdʒiː·zəs (ˈkraɪst), -zəz/, **Christ** *n* [U] the Jewish religious teacher believed by his followers to be the son of God, whose teachings and life Christianity developed from

Jesus (Christ) EXPRESSION /ˈdʒiː·zəs (ˈkraɪst), ˌ-zəz/, **Christ** *exclamation* used to express anger or surprise • *Jesus Christ, Irene, close the door when you come in!* • USAGE: This use is considered offensive by religious people.

jet CONTINUOUS FLOW /dʒet/ *n* [C] a strong, narrow, continuous flow, esp. of water or gas, that is forced out of a small hole • *The whale blew a jet of water into the air.* • A **jet engine** is an engine that moves an aircraft forward by sending hot air and gases under pressure out behind it. • If an engine is **jet-propelled**, it has a jet engine.

jet AIRCRAFT /dʒet/ *n* [C] a fast aircraft with a JET engine • *He owns a private jet.* • **Jet lag** is the feeling of being tired you experience after a long journey in an aircraft to a place where the time is different from the place that you left.

jet /dʒet/ *v* [I always + adv/prep] **-tt-** to travel in a jet aircraft • *I'm jetting off to LA next week.*

jet STONE /dʒet/ *n* [U] a hard, black, shiny stone that is used to make jewelry • If something is **jet-black**, it is pure black: *jet-black hair*

jettison /ˈdʒeṭ·ə·sən, -zən/ *v* [T] to throw away or get rid of (something that is not wanted or needed) • *Some of her material will probably be jettisoned for the TV show.* ○ *The bombs were jettisoned over the English Channel.*

jetty /ˈdʒeṭ·i/ *n* [C] a structure built out from the land into the water as a landing place for boats or as protection from waves

Jew /dʒuː/ *n* [C] a person whose religion is Judaism, or a person related by birth to the ancient peoples of Israel

Jewish /ˈdʒuː·ɪʃ/ *adj* [not gradable] of or related to Jews

jewel /ˈdʒuː·əl/ *n* [C] a precious stone, such as a DIAMOND or RUBY, or a decorative object with such a stone or several stones in it • *a jewel necklace*

jeweler /ˈdʒuː·ə·lər, ˈdʒuː·lər/ *n* [C] a person who sells and sometimes repairs jewelry and watches

jewelry /ˈdʒuː·əl·ri, ˈdʒuː·l·ri/ *n* [U], **jewels** *pl n* decorative objects worn on clothes or on the body, such as rings and NECKLACES, often made from valuable metals and containing precious stones • *costume jewelry*

jibe INSULT /dʒaɪb/ *n, v* GIBE

jibe AGREE /dʒaɪb/ *v* [I] to agree with something else • *Her story just doesn't jibe with what the other witnesses say.*

jiffy /'dʒɪf·i/ *n* [U] *infml* a very short time • *I'm on the phone, but I'll be with you in a jiffy.*

jig /dʒɪg/ *n* [C] an energetic, traditional dance of Great Britain and Ireland, or the music that is played for such a dance

jigger /'dʒɪg·ər/ *n* [C] a small, round, metal container used for measuring strong alcoholic drinks, or the amount of alcohol that this container holds • *a jigger of whiskey*

jiggle /'dʒɪg·əl/ *v* [I/T] to move (something) or cause something to move from side to side or up and down with quick short movements • *If the toilet won't stop flushing, jiggle the handle.* [T]

jigsaw puzzle /'dʒɪg,sɔː,pʌz·əl/ *n* [C] a game consisting of a lot of differently shaped pieces of cardboard or wood that you try to fit together in order to show the complete picture that the pieces make when they are all used • *We spent the evening working on the jigsaw puzzle of the Monet painting.*

jilt /dʒɪlt/ *v* [T] to end a romantic relationship with (someone) suddenly • *He jilted her for another woman.*

Jim Crow /'dʒɪm'kroʊ/ *n* [U] the US laws and customs that kept black people apart from white people and prevented them from having opportunities available to white people from the 1800s to the 1960s

jingle RING /'dʒɪŋ·gəl/ *v* [I/T] to make a repeated gentle ringing sound, or to cause (an object) to make a ringing sound • *He jingled the coins in his pocket.* [T]

jingle /'dʒɪŋ·gəl/ *n* [U] • *the jingle of bells*

jingle TUNE /'dʒɪŋ·gəl/ *n* [C] a short, simple tune, often with words, that is easy to remember and is used to advertise a product on radio or television

jinx /dʒɪŋks/ *v* [T] to cause (a person or group) to experience bad luck • *I didn't want to say anything to him—I was afraid I might jinx him.*

jinx /dʒɪŋks/ *n* [C usually sing] a person or thing that brings bad luck, or a period of bad luck • *There must be a jinx on our team—four of our best players were injured yesterday.*

jitney /'dʒɪt·ni/ *n* [C] a small bus that follows a regular route

jitters /'dʒɪt·ərz/ *pl n* a feeling of nervousness that you experience before something important happens • *I always get the jitters the morning before an exam.*

jittery /'dʒɪt·ə·ri/ *adj* • *Gwen always felt jittery when she got up on stage.*

jive /dʒaɪv/ *n* [U] *slang* dishonest talk intended to deceive • *Don't give me this jive.*

job EMPLOYMENT /dʒɑb/ *n* [C] the regular work that a person does to earn money • *a full-time/ part-time/permanent/temporary job* ○ *to get/ quit a job* ○ *The new supermarket will create 50*

new jobs in the area. ○ *She's applied for a job with an insurance company.* ○ *How long have you been out of a job* (= unemployed)? • If you do something **on the job**, you do it while at work: *He keeps falling asleep on the job.* ○ *The company provides on-the-job training* (= training while you work).

jobless /'dʒɑb·ləs/ *adj* [not gradable] without a job • *He's been jobless for more than six months.*

job PIECE OF WORK /dʒɑb/ *n* [C] a particular piece of work • *I should have this job done by lunchtime.* ○ *A microwave oven makes the job of preparing meals a lot easier.* • (*infml*) A job can be work done on or to something to improve or repair it: *a paint job* • If you do a good/bad job, you do a piece of work of that quality: *Jamie did a wonderful job on that sales presentation.*

job DUTY /dʒɑb/ *n* [C] a responsibility or duty • *I know it's not my job to tell you how to run your life, but I do think you've made a mistake.* [+ *to* infinitive]

job CRIME /dʒɑb/ *n* [C] *slang* a crime in which money or goods are stolen • *a bank job* ○ *an inside job* (= a crime committed by someone who works for the company it was committed against)

jock /dʒɑk/ *n* [C] *infml* a person, esp. a young man, who is extremely enthusiastic about and good at sports • *Everyone on campus thought I was just another dumb jock.* • A **jockstrap** (also **jock**) is a tight piece of clothing worn by men under their pants or shorts to support and protect their sex organs esp. while playing sports.

jockey HORSE RIDER /'dʒɑk·i/ *n* [C] a person whose job is riding horses in races

jockey GET ADVANTAGE /'dʒɑk·i/ *v* [I always + adv/prep] to attempt to obtain power or get into a more advantageous position than other people by using any methods you can • *TV news cameramen jockeyed for position near the podium.*

jocular /'dʒɑk·jə·lər/ *adj* amusing or intended to cause amusement • *a jocular mood*

jog RUN /dʒɑg, dʒɔːg/ *v* [I] **-gg-** to run at a slow regular speed, esp. as a form of exercise • *Bill jogs for 30 minutes every morning before breakfast.*

jog /dʒɑg, dʒɔːg/ *n* [U] • *I think I'll go out for a jog.*

jogger /'dʒɑg·ər, 'dʒɔː·gər/ *n* [C] • *The park was full of joggers, bicyclists, and skaters.*

jogging /'dʒɑg·ɪŋ, 'dʒɔː·gɪŋ/ *n* [U] • *The president goes jogging several times a week.*

jog CAUSE TO REMEMBER /dʒɑg, dʒɔːg/ *v* **-gg-** • If something or someone **jogs** your **memory**, they cause you to remember something: *Seeing her again jogged my memory, and I recalled my life as a child on a farm in Minnesota.*

john TOILET /'dʒɑn/ *n* [C] *infml* a toilet or bathroom • *Excuse me, where's the john?*

john PERSON /'dʒɑn/ *n* [C] *slang* a man who is the customer of a PROSTITUTE (= a woman who has sex for money)

John Doe *male* /'dʒɑn'doʊ/, *female* **Jane Doe** /'dʒeɪn'doʊ/ *n* [U] *law* a name used in a law court for a person whose real name is not known • John Doe is also an average or typical man, and Jane Doe is an average or typical woman.

johnny–come–lately /ˌdʒɑn·iːˌkʌm'leɪt·li/ *n* [C] *disapproving* a person who starts a job or activity later than other people and sometimes uses the experience and knowledge of these people to obtain an advantage over them • *Riley, whose father founded the industry, calls her competitors johnny-come-latelies.*

join DO WITH /dʒɔɪn/ *v* [I/T] to do something with or be with (someone or something) • *Why don't you ask your sister if she would like to join us for dinner?* [T] ○ *I'm sure everyone will join me in wishing you a very happy birthday.* [T] ○ *Won't you join with us in combating racism in the workplace?* [I] • To **join in** (an activity) is to become actively involved in it: *Please let's all join in when I sing the National Anthem.*

join BECOME A MEMBER /dʒɔɪn/ *v* [I/T] to become a member of (an organization) • *I've decided to join a gym.* [T] ○ *It's a great club—why don't you join?* [I] • (*infml*) If you say **join the club**, you mean you are in the same bad situation as the person you are talking to: *"I've got no money till payday." "Join the club!"* • If you **join up**, you become a member of one of the military forces.

join FASTEN /dʒɔɪn/ *v* [I/T] to cause (something) to be attached or fastened to another thing, or to bring (two or more things) together in this way; connect • *A long suspension bridge joins the island with the mainland.* [T] • If roads or rivers join, they meet at a particular point: *The Missouri River and Mississippi River join north of St. Louis.* [I] • If two or more people **join hands**, they hold each other's hands, esp. before doing some activity: *This folk dance begins with everyone joining hands to form a circle.*

joint SHARED /dʒɔɪnt/ *adj* [not gradable] belonging to or shared between two or more people • *Do you and your husband have a joint bank account or separate accounts?* ○ *In court, the parents were awarded joint custody of their son* (= the right to care for him was shared between them). • The **Joint Chiefs of Staff** are the leaders of the armed forces in the United States. • A **joint venture** is a business that gets its money from two or more partners.

jointly /'dʒɔɪnt·li/ *adv* [not gradable] • *Construction of the new high school will be jointly funded by the city and the state.*

joint BODY PART /dʒɔɪnt/ *n* [C] a place in the body where two bones meet • *Good running*

shoes are supposed to reduce the stress on the ankle, knee, and hip joints.

joint CONNECTION /dʒɔɪnt/ *n* [C] a place where two things are joined together • *Metal joints in the bridge allow it to expand or contract with changes in air temperature.*

joint PLACE /dʒɔɪnt/ *n* [C] *slang* a cheap bar or restaurant • *a hamburger joint* • A joint is also a place where people go for some type of entertainment: *a strip joint*

joint DRUG /dʒɔɪnt/ *n* [C] *slang* a cigarette containing MARIJUANA (= an illegal drug)

joke AMUSING /dʒoʊk/ *n* [C] something, such as an amusing story or trick, that is said or done in order to make people laugh • *He told a joke about a farmer and a priest that made Nicholas burst into laughter.* • If **the joke is on** you, you have tried to make someone look foolish but have made yourself look foolish instead.

joke /dʒoʊk/ *v* to say things in an amusing or playful manner • *He joked about how I was always cleaning.* [I] ○ *They've always joked that the place is so wet, and the bullfrogs have to sit on the fences.* [+ *that* clause] • If you say someone **must be joking/has got to be joking**, you mean that you doubt that what they said is true or cannot believe they meant it seriously.

joke RIDICULOUS /dʒoʊk/ *n* [U] *infml* something considered to be so bad or worthless that it is ridiculous • *The playing conditions on the muddy field were a joke.* ○ *The midterm exam was a joke* (= too easy).

joker /'dʒoʊ·kər/ *n* [C] an annoying person • *It costs $60,000 a year to keep some joker in prison.*

joker /'dʒoʊ·kər/ *n* [C] (in some card games) a special playing card that can be given any value and used instead of any other card

jolly /'dʒɑl·i/ *adj* happy and pleasant • *That clown looks pretty jolly.*

jolt /dʒoʊlt/ *v* [T] to cause (something or someone) to move suddenly and violently, or to surprise (someone) unpleasantly • *I was jolted out of bed by the earthquake.* ○ *He was jolted by the sight of bodies lying in the lobby.*

jolt /dʒoʊlt/ *n* [C] a sudden, violent movement or force, or a large and unpleasant surprise • *jolts of electricity* ○ *She bumped into him, and the jolt sent his books to the ground.* ○ *Jack realized with a jolt of fear that he was helpless.*

jostle /'dʒɑs·əl/ *v* [I/T] to push against (someone) in order to move past them or get more space when you are in a crowd of people • *Someone jostled her from behind.* [T]

jot /dʒɑt/ *v* [T] **-tt-** to write (something) quickly in a short note • *The guard jotted down the van's license plate number.* [M]

journal MAGAZINE /'dʒɜrn·əl/ *n* [C] a magazine or newspaper, esp. one that deals with a specialized subject • *a scientific journal* ○ *The Wall Street Journal*

journal RECORD /'dʒɜrn·əl/ *n* [C] a record of what you have done, or of descriptions or thoughts, written each day or frequently over a long period; a DIARY • *He kept a journal for over 50 years.*

journalism /'dʒɜrn·ˀl,ɪz·əm/ n [U] the work of collecting, writing, and publishing or broadcasting news stories and articles • *broadcast journalism* ○ *print journalism*

journalist /'dʒɜrn·ˀl·əst/ n [C] someone who collects and writes news stories and articles for newspapers, magazines, radio, and television • *a freelance journalist* ○ *a TV journalist* ○ *a Mexican journalist*

journalistic /,dʒɜrn·ˀl'ɪs·tɪk/ adj [not gradable] • *Normal journalistic standards don't allow for this kind of abuse.*

journey /'dʒɜr·ni/ n [C] a trip, esp. over a long period or a great distance • *He was planning a six-week journey to China.*

journey /'dʒɜr·ni/ v [I always + adv/prep] • *As we journeyed north, the weather improved.*

jovial /'dʒoʊ·vi:·əl/ adj showing or feeling good humor; friendly • *a jovial smile*

jowls /dʒaʊlz/ pl n loose skin and flesh that hangs below the JAW (= the lower part of the face)

 — jowls

joy /dʒɔɪ/ n [C/U] great happiness or pleasure • *My heart was full of pure joy.* [U] • A joy is a person or thing that causes happiness: *His daughters were the joys of his life.* [C] ○ *She's a joy to work with.* [C]

joyful /'dʒɔɪ·fəl/ adj having or causing great happiness • *joyful news*

joyfully /'dʒɔɪ·fə·li/ adv

joyless /'dʒɔɪ·ləs/ adj being without happiness or pleasure • *a joyless marriage*

joyous /'dʒɔɪ·əs/ adj full of joy • *a joyous occasion*

joyously /'dʒɔɪ·ə·sli/ adv

joyride /'dʒɔɪ·raɪd/ n [C] an act of driving around for enjoyment in a car, esp. one that was taken without permission and is driven in a dangerous manner

joystick /'dʒɔɪ·stɪk/ n [C] a vertical handle that is moved to control the direction or height of an aircraft or to control the action in some computer games

Jr. /'dʒuːn·jər/ adj abbreviation for junior (= used at the end of a man's name to show that he is the son of a man with the same name) • *Martin Luther King, Jr.*

jubilant /'dʒuː·bə·lənt/ adj feeling or showing great happiness, esp. because of a success • *Jubilant crowds shouted, "It's liberation day!"*

jubilation /,dʒuː·bə'leɪ·ʃən/ n [U] a feeling of great happiness

Judaism /'dʒuː·d·ə,ɪz·əm, -iː,ɪz-/ n [U] a religion based on a belief in a single God and on the TALMUD (= a collection of writings explaining Jewish law and customs) and parts of

the Bible • USAGE: The related adjective is **Jewish**, see at JEW.

judge LAW /dʒʌdʒ/ n [C] a person who is in charge of a court of law • *The judge dismissed the charge after a preliminary hearing.*

judgment, judgement /'dʒʌdʒ·mənt/ n [C/U] a decision in a court of law

judge DECIDE /dʒʌdʒ/ v [I/T] to have or give an opinion, or to decide about (something or someone), esp. after thinking carefully • *He seems to be handling the job well, but it's really too soon to judge.* [I] ○ *It's hard to judge how old he is.* [+ wh- word] ○ *I'm hopeless at judging distances* (= guessing how far it is between places). [T] ○ *What gives you the right to judge people* (= decide how good or bad they are)? [T] • To judge a competition is to decide officially who will be the winner. [T] • **Judging by/ judging from** or **to judge by/to judge from** refers to the reasons you have for thinking something: *Judging by their home, they seem to be quite wealthy.*

judge /dʒʌdʒ/ n [C] a person who is qualified to form or give an opinion about something • *a good judge of character* • A judge is also a person who officially decides the winner of a competition.

judgment, judgement /'dʒʌdʒ·mənt/ n [C/U] the ability to make decisions or to make good decisions, or the act of developing an opinion, esp. after careful thought • *to show good/poor judgment* [U] ○ *They questioned his judgment in buying land he had never seen.* [U] • A judgment is a decision: *We were asked to make a number of difficult judgments.* [C] • A **judgment call** is a decision you make that is based on your feelings and personal experience. • According to some religions, **Judgment Day** is the time when the world ends and everyone is judged by God for the way they lived.

judgmental /dʒʌdʒ'ment·ˀl/ adj tending to form opinions too quickly, esp. when disapproving of someone or something • *I'm trying not to be judgmental about my daughter's new boyfriend.*

judiciary /dʒʊ'dɪʃ·iː,er·i, -'dɪʃ·ə·ri/ n [U] the part of a country's government that is responsible for its legal system and that consists of all the judges in its courts of law

judicial /dʒʊ'dɪʃ·əl/ adj [not gradable] • *the judicial branch of government*

judicious /dʒʊ'dɪʃ·əs/ adv having or showing good judgment in making decisions • *The law allows for the judicious use of force in some situations.*

judiciously /dʒʊ'dɪʃ·ə·sli/ adv • *Spend your money a little more judiciously.*

judo /'dʒuː·d·oʊ/ n [U] a sport in which two people fight with their arms and legs, using skill more than strength, in trying to throw each other to the ground

jug /dʒʌɡ/ n [C] a large container for liquids

that usually has a handle and a narrow opening at the top

juggle /'dʒʌg·əl/ v [I/T] to throw (several objects) into the air, catch them, and keep them moving so that at least one is always in the air • (fig.) Many women find it hard to juggle a family and a career (= to arrange their lives so that they have time for both). [T]

juggler /'dʒʌg·lər/ n [C]

jugular (vein) /'dʒʌg·jə·lər (ˌveɪn)/ n [C] any of several large VEINS (= tubes that carry blood to the heart) in the neck

juice LIQUID /dʒuːs/ n [C/U] the liquid that comes from fruits and vegetables • orange/ tomato juice [U] ○ fruit juices [C]

juices /'dʒuː·səz/ pl n infml liquid in meat or in a person's body • the digestive juices

juicy /'dʒuː·si/ adj full of juice or juices and therefore enjoyable to eat • a juicy orange/ steak • (infml) Juicy can also mean very interesting or exciting: a bit of juicy gossip

juiciness /'dʒuː·si·nəs/ n [U]

juice ELECTRICITY /dʒuːs/ n [U] slang electricity • I've fixed the wiring, so you can turn the juice back on.

jukebox /'dʒuːk·bɑks/ n [C] a machine that plays recorded music when a coin is put into it

July /dʒʊ'lɑɪ, dʒə-/ (abbreviation **Jul.**) n [C/U] the seventh month of the year, after June and before August

jumble /'dʒʌm·bəl/ n [U] a confused mixture or mass of things • a jumble of papers on the desk

jumble /'dʒʌm·bəl/ v [T] • The events of the last few weeks are all jumbled up in my mind.

jumbo /'dʒʌm·boʊ/ adj [not gradable] infml extremely large • a jumbo size box of cereal • A **jumbo jet** is a very large aircraft that can fly long distances.

jump RAISE UP SUDDENLY /dʒʌmp/ v [I/T] to push yourself off the ground and into the air using your legs and feet • The kids were jumping up and down with excitement. [I] ○ The cats jumped up onto the table. [I] • To jump sometimes means to lift yourself off the ground in order to go over something: Can you jump this fence? [T] • If you **jump through hoops**, you go to a lot of trouble to achieve something: We had to jump through hoops to get Dad admitted into a hospital.

jump /dʒʌmp/ n [C] • The skater's jump was high but not graceful. • A **jump rope** is a thick cord that you jump over as a game or exercise: We grabbed our jump rope and headed for the playground.

jump

jumper /'dʒʌm·pər/ n [C] • To dunk a basketball when you're just six feet tall, you have to be a great jumper.

jump MOVE QUICKLY /dʒʌmp/ v [I] to move suddenly or quickly • A man jumped out of the bushes. ○ He jumped to his feet and ran out the door. • If a noise or action causes you to jump, your body makes a sudden movement because of surprise or fear: The thunder made us all jump. • To **jump at** something is to accept it eagerly: She jumped at the chance to go to Paris. • If someone accused of a crime **jumps bail**, they fail to appear in court and lose the money they gave in exchange for being released until the trial. • When I said he was wrong, he really **jumped down** my **throat** (= spoke suddenly and angrily to me). • To **jump on/jump all over** someone is to criticize them suddenly and severely: When I showed him my report card, Dad jumped all over me and said I wasn't working hard enough. • If someone **jumps the gun**, they act too soon or before the right time: They only met three weeks ago—isn't it jumping the gun to start talking about marriage? • If a car **jumps the light**, it starts moving past a traffic light while the light is still red.

jump OMIT STAGES /dʒʌmp/ v [I/T] to move up or go across suddenly from one point or stage to another, often missing what comes between • Her book jumped from fifth place to first place on the best-seller list. [I always + adv/prep] ○ The forest fire jumped the road and spread to the other side. [T] • If you **jump to conclusions**, you judge a situation quickly and emotionally without having all the facts: It's not fair to jump to conclusions about a whole group of people based on one incident.

jump /dʒʌmp/ n [C] • He made a big jump from general manager to president of the company.

jump INCREASE /dʒʌmp/ v [I] to increase suddenly by a large amount • Home prices in the area have jumped to an all-time high.

jump ATTACK /dʒʌmp/ v [T] infml to attack suddenly • He was jumped and robbed by two guys on his way home from work.

jumper /'dʒʌm·pər/ n [C] a dress without sleeves that is usually worn over a shirt • (Br) A jumper is a SWEATER.

jumper cables /'dʒʌm·pər'keɪ·bəlz/ pl n two wires that carry electrical power from one car's engine to help start another that has a BATTERY with no power

jump–start /'dʒʌmp·stɑrt/ v [T] to start or improve (something) more quickly by giving it extra help • These recordings jump-started her career. • If you jump-start a car, you start its engine by using wires to carry electric power from another car's engine.

jumpy /'dʒʌm·pi/ adj nervous or anxious • Stop watching him, it makes him jumpy.

junction /'dʒʌŋ·ʃən/ n [C] a place where things, esp. roads and railroads, meet or join

• *The shopping center is near the junction of the New Jersey Turnpike and Garden State Parkway.*

juncture /'dʒʌŋ·tʃər/ *n* [U] *fml* a particular point in time or stage in a series of events • *Negotiations are at a critical juncture.*

June /dʒuːn/ (*abbreviation* **Jun.**) *n* [C/U] the sixth month of the year, after May and before July

jungle /'dʒʌŋ·gəl/ *n* a forest in one of the hottest regions of the earth, where trees and plants grow very densely

junior LESS ADVANCED /'dʒuːn·jər/ *adj* less advanced, or lower in rank • *the junior varsity* ○ *Alfredo is a junior partner in the law firm.* • A **junior college** is a **community college**. See at COMMUNITY. • A **junior high (school)** is a school for children who are 12 to 15 years old. LP EDUCATION IN THE US • Compare SENIOR MORE ADVANCED.

junior SCHOOL /'dʒuːn·jər/ *n* [C] a student in the third year of a program of study in a college, university, or HIGH SCHOOL (= a school for students aged 14 to 18) • LP EDUCATION IN THE US

junior /'dʒuːn·jər/ *adj* • *They met in their junior year of college and married soon after they graduated.*

junior YOUNGER /'dʒuːn·jər/ *adj* [not gradable] younger • *He was born in April, so he's three months my junior* (= he is three months younger). • See also JR.

junk /dʒʌŋk/ *n* [U] things that are considered to be useless, worthless, or of low quality • *I cleared all the junk out of the garage.* • **Junk food** is food that is not good for your health because it is high in fat, sugar, or artificial substances. • **Junk mail** is mail, usually advertising products or services, that is sent to people although they have not asked to receive it: *There's a letter for you and the rest is junk mail.* • A **junkyard** is a place, often a large open area, where useless or unwanted items are left and stored, and sometimes sold.

junk /dʒʌŋk/ *v* [T] *infml* to throw out (something) because it is does not work well or is worthless • *Why don't we junk this old TV and get a new one?*

junket /'dʒʌŋ·kət/ *n* [C] *disapproving* an unnecessary trip by a government official which is paid for with public money • *The senator is off on another junket to Hawaii at taxpayers' expense.*

junkie, junky /'dʒʌŋ·ki/ *n* [C] *slang* a person who regularly takes and is dependent on illegal drugs, esp. HEROIN • (*humorous*) A junkie is also a person who enjoys or is interested in a particular activity so much that they do it a lot: *If you want to follow politics, basically you have to become a talk-show junkie.*

junta /'hʊn·tə, 'dʒʌnt·ə, 'hʌn·tə/ *n* [C] a small group, esp. of military officers, that rules a country after taking power by force

Jupiter /'dʒuː·pəṭ·ər/ *n* [U] the planet fifth in order of distance from the sun, after Mars and before Saturn

jurisdiction /,dʒʊr·əs'dɪk·ʃən/ *n* [U] the official authority to make (esp. legal) decisions and judgments • *The Supreme Court ruled that the US government had no jurisdiction over crimes committed on Indian lands.*

jurist /'dʒʊr·əst/ *n* [C] *fml* an expert in law, esp. a judge

jury /'dʒʊr·i/ *n* [C/U] a group of people who have been chosen to listen to the facts of a trial in a law court and to decide whether a person is guilty or not guilty, or whether a claim has been proved • *a trial by jury/a jury trial* [U] ○ *My husband served on a jury in a criminal case a few months ago.* [C] • A jury is also a group of people chosen to judge a competition: *The jury chose an unexpected winner for the literary prize.* [C] • If you say **the jury is still out** on a situation, you mean that no decision or agreement about it has yet been made, often because there is not enough information: *The jury is still out on whether welfare reform will work.*

juror /'dʒʊr·ər, -ɔːr/ *n* [C] a member of a jury • *A majority of the jurors were women.*

just NOW /dʒʌst, dʒəst/ *adv* [not gradable] now or (almost) at the same time, or very soon, or very recently • *He just left—if you run, you can catch him.* ○ *It was just past* (= very soon after) *midnight.* ○ *We got the children off to school just as the bus was about to leave.* ○ *We're just about to begin* (= We will begin very soon). ○ *The doctor will see you in just a minute/moment/second* (= very soon). • **Just a minute/moment/second** (= Wait a short period of time)—*I've nearly finished.* • *Who was that at the door just now* (= a short time ago)?

just EXACTLY /dʒʌst, dʒəst/ *adv* [not gradable] exactly • *Beth looks just like her mother.* ○ *It was just what I expected.* [+ *wh-* word]

just ONLY /dʒʌst, dʒəst/ *adv* [not gradable] only; simply • *I'll just check my e-mail, then we can go for coffee.* ○ *I just called to wish you a happy birthday.* ○ *We'll just have to wait and see what happens.* • Just can be used to make a statement stronger: *He just won't listen to me.* • *I'll take my car too* **just in case** (= if it happens that) *we need it.* • If you say it's **just one of those things**, you mean that something has happened that you must accept even if you do not like it: *The traffic was awful and I missed my flight—it was just one of those things.*

just ALMOST /dʒʌst, dʒəst/ *adv* [not gradable] almost not or almost • *We arrived at the airport just in time to catch the plane.* ○ *Matthew weighed just* (= slightly) *over seven pounds at birth.* ○ *"Are you finished yet?" "Just about."*

just VERY /dʒʌst, dʒəst/ *adv* [not gradable] very; completely • *You look just wonderful!* ○

It's just amazing how powerful the new computers are.

just [FAIR] /dʒʌst/ *adj* morally correct; fair • *a just verdict*

justly /'dʒʌs·tli/ *adv* • *We agreed that he was justly condemned to life imprisonment.* • Justly also means with good reason or rightly: *Kenji Mizoguchi is justly recognized as one of Japanese cinema's greatest figures.*

justice [FAIRNESS] /'dʒʌs·təs/ *n* [U] the condition of being morally correct or fair • *He accused the police of brutality and demanded justice.*

justice [LAW] /'dʒʌs·təs/ *n* [U] the system of laws by which people are judged and punished • *the criminal justice system*

justice [JUDGE] /'dʒʌs·təs/ *n* [C] a judge, esp. of one of the higher courts of law • *a justice of the US Supreme Court* • A **justice of the peace** is a public officer who judges local and less important legal cases, and marries people.

justify /'dʒʌs·tə,faɪ/ *v* [T] to show that (something) is reasonable, right, or true • *Her fears of a low voter turnout were justified when fewer than half of the people voted.*

justifiable /'dʒʌs·tə,faɪ·ə·bəl/ *adj* able to be explained or shown to be reasonable; understandable • *The jury decided that the shooting was justifiable because Rogers thought his own life was in danger.*

justifiably /'dʒʌs·tə,faɪ·ə·bli/ *adv* • *His parents were justifiably proud of his achievements.*

justification /,dʒʌs·tə·fə'keɪ·ʃən/ *n* [C/U] • *There is no justification for sexist or racist behavior,* she said. [U]

jut /dʒʌt/ *v* [I always + adv/prep] **-tt-** to stick out, esp. above or beyond the edge or surface of something • *A large ship was docked at the pier that jutted out into the harbor.*

juvenile /'dʒuː·və,naɪl, -vən·ᵊl/ *adj esp. law* of, by, or for a young person who is not yet an adult • *He studied both adult and juvenile crime.* • A **juvenile delinquent** is a young person, usually under 18, who commits a crime. ○ *Keeping our young people from dropping out of school is one way to fight* **juvenile delinquency.**

juxtapose /,dʒʌk·stə'poʊz/ *v* [T] to put (things or people) next to each other, esp. in order to compare them • *The exhibition juxtaposes architectural drawings with photographs of the buildings as constructed.*

juxtaposition /,dʒʌk·stə·pə'zɪʃ·ən/ *n* [C/U] • *The juxtaposition of the original painting with the fake clearly showed up the differences.* [C]

K, k

K [LETTER] , **k** /keɪ/ *n* [C] *pl* **K's** or **Ks** or **k's** or **ks** the eleventh letter of the English alphabet

K [SCHOOL] /keɪ/ *n abbreviation for* KINDER-GARTEN

kaleidoscope /kəˈlaɪd·ə‚skoʊp/ *n* [C] a tube-shaped device containing loose pieces of colored glass or plastic and mirrors which reflect changing patterns as the tube is turned

kangaroo /‚kæŋ·gəˈruː/ *n* [C] *pl* **kangaroos** a type of large, Australian mammal with a long, thick tail, short front legs, and long powerful back legs, that moves by jumping

kaput /kəˈpʊt, kɑ-/ *adj* [not gradable] *infml* severely damaged, broken, or not working correctly • *His credibility is kaput.*

karat /ˈkær·ət/ (*abbreviation* **kt.**, **k.**) *n* [C] a unit for measuring the purity of gold • Compare CARAT.

karate /kəˈrɑt̬·i/ *n* [U] a method of fighting that originated in Japan and uses fast, hard hits with the hands or feet

karma /ˈkɑr·mə/ *n* [U] (in the Buddhist and Hindu religions) the force produced by a person's actions in one of their lives which influences what happens to them in their future lives

kayak /ˈkaɪ·æk/ *n* [C] a small, light, narrow boat, pointed at both ends, with a covering over the top, which is moved by using a PADDLE (= short pole with a wide, flat part)

kayak

KB *n* [C] *pl* **KB** *abbreviation for* KILOBYTE

keel /kiːl/ *n* [C] the long piece of wood or steel put along the bottom of a boat from front to back that supports the frame

keel over /ˈkiːlˈoʊ·vər/ *v adv* [I] to fall over suddenly • *Jasper keeled over dead.*

keen [STRONGLY FELT] /kiːn/ *adj* [-er/-est only] (esp. of emotions and beliefs) strongly felt • *a keen interest in painting*

keen [DEVELOPED] /kiːn/ *adj* [-er/-est only] (of an awareness or ability) very developed, or (of the mind) very quick to understand • *a keen eye for detail* ○ *a keen sense of smell*

keen [EAGER] /kiːn/ *adj* [-er/-est only] eager, interested, and enthusiastic • *Theresa isn't too keen on pets.*

keep [POSSESS] /kiːp/ *v* [T] *past* **kept** /kept/ to be in or continue to be in someone's possession • *Can I keep this photo?* ○ *"Keep the change,"* she told the driver. ○ *We keep aspirin in the kitchen* (= have it there for future use).

• If you **keep** a diary or record, you write about events or record information.

keeper /ˈkiː·pər/ *n* [C] someone responsible for guarding or taking care of a person, animal, or thing • *an animal keeper* ○ *Each of the contest judges was assigned a keeper.*

keep [DO] /kiːp/ *v* [T] *past* **kept** /kept/ to do (something you promised or had scheduled) • *I kept my promise.* ○ *Did she keep her appointment?* ○ *Can you keep a secret* (= not tell other people)?

keeping /ˈkiː·pɪŋ/ *n* • *There will be no flowers at the funeral,* **in keeping with** (= following) *the family's wishes.*

keep [STAY] /kiːp/ *v past* **kept** /kept/ to stay or cause to stay or continue in a particular place, direction, or condition • *keep left* [L] ○ *keep quiet* [L] ○ *It's hard to keep cool in this weather.* [L] ○ *Sorry to keep you waiting.* [T] • To **keep** someone **company** is to stay with them so they are not alone: *I kept him company while he was waiting for the bus.* • If you **keep** your **eyes open/peeled/out** for something, you watch carefully for it: *I try to always keep my eyes open for good recipes.* • If you **keep** an **eye on** something or someone, you watch them or stay informed about their behavior, esp. so they do not get in trouble: *I'd better keep an eye on you.* • If you **keep** your **head above water,** you are just able to continue doing what you do: *The business is in trouble, but we're keeping our heads above water.* • *He told her to* **keep** her **mouth shut** (= say nothing). • If you **keep** something **quiet/keep quiet about** something, you say nothing about it: *She managed to keep the operation quiet for a while.* • (*infml*) If you tell someone to **keep** their **shirt on,** you mean they should relax and stop being upset: *Keep your shirt on—I'll be right there.* • **Keep** it to **yourself** means do not tell anyone. • *I found it hard to* **keep** my **temper** (= not become angry) *with so many things going wrong.*

• [LP] GET, HAVE, AND OTHER VERBS USED TO MEAN "CAUSE"

keep [CONTINUE DOING] /kiːp/ *v* [T] *past* **kept** /kept/ to continue doing (something) without stopping, or to do it repeatedly • *I keep thinking I've seen her somewhere before.* • If you **keep a tight rein on** someone or something, you control them carefully: *He doesn't earn very much but keeps a tight rein on his budget.* • *We're* **keeping** our **fingers crossed** (= hoping strongly) *for a complete recovery.* • If you **keep** someone **guessing,** you do not give them the information they want: *The idea was to keep the enemy guessing until the attack had actually begun.* • *The doctors* **kept** me **posted** about her condition (= made certain I stayed informed about it). • If you **keep track,** you make certain you know what is happening to someone or something: *My sister's had so many jobs, I can't keep track anymore.*

keep STAY FRESH /kiːp/ *v* [I] *past* **kept** /kept/ (of food) to stay fresh and in good condition • *Milk keeps longer in the refrigerator.*

▫**keep at** /'-'-/ *v prep* [T] to continue to do or work on (something) • *I kept at it and finally finished at three this morning.*

▫**keep down** *obj* STOP INCREASING , **keep** *obj* **down** /'-'-/ *v adv* [M] to prevent (something) from increasing • *We need to keep down our costs.* • **Keep it down** in there (= Be quieter).

▫**keep down** NOT VOMIT , **keep** *obj* **down** /'-'-/ *v adv* [M] to prevent (something eaten) from being vomited up • *After the operation I couldn't keep my food down.*

▫**keep** (*obj*) **from** *obj* PREVENT YOURSELF /'--/ *v prep* [T] to prevent (yourself) from doing (something) • *We couldn't keep (ourselves) from laughing.*

▫**keep** *obj* **from** *obj* PREVENT SOMEONE ELSE /'--/ *v prep* [T] to prevent (someone else) from learning about (something) • *He's seriously ill, and I don't think it's right to keep it from the children.*

▫**keep** (*obj*) **off** (*obj*) /'-'-/ *v prep* [I/T] to prevent something from touching or being on something else • *He wears a hat to keep the sun off his head.* [T] ○ *The sign says, Keep off.* [I]

▫**keep out** (*obj*), **keep** (*obj*) **out** /'-'-/ *v prep* [I/M] to prevent something from entering a place • *Danger! Keep out!* [I] ○ *The car windows were tinted to keep out the sun.* [M]

▫**keep** (*obj*) **out of** *obj* /'-'--/ *v adv prep* [T] to prevent (something) from happening, or to avoid or not become involved with (someone or something) • *You can't keep the dirt out of the tent.* ○ *Don't use credit cards and you'll keep out of debt.* • (*infml*) *I know what I'm doing— just* **keep** *your* **nose out of** *it* (= do not become involved).

▫**keep to** /'--/ *v prep* [T] to limit yourself to (a subject or activity) • *I can never keep to a diet.* • *He* **keeps to** *himself* (= does not talk much to other people).

▫**keep up** STAY LEVEL /'-'-/ *v prep* [I] to stay level or equal with someone or something • *You run too fast—I can't keep up.*

▫**keep up** *obj* CONTINUE , **keep** *obj* **up** /'-'-/ *v prep* [M] to continue to do or have (something) • *Keep up the good work.*

▫**keep** *obj* **up** PREVENT SLEEP /'-'-/ *v prep* [T] to prevent (someone) from sleeping • *I hope I'm not keeping you up.*

keepsake /'kiːp·seɪk/ *n* [C] something that helps you remember a person, place, or occasion • *Her aunt gave her a little wooden elephant as a keepsake.*

keg /keg/ *n* [C] a small BARREL (= container with a circular top and bottom and curved sides) usually used for storing beer

kennel /'ken·ᵊl/ *n* [C] a place where animals are bred and trained and where people pay to leave their dogs to be taken care of while they are away

kept KEEP /kept/ *past simple and past participle of* KEEP

kept PROVIDED FOR /kept/ *adj* [not gradable] (of a person) given money and a place to live, esp. as part of a sexual relationship • *a kept woman*

kerb /kɜrb/ *n* [C] *Br for* CURB EDGE

kerchief /'kɜr·tʃəf, -ˌtʃiːf/ *n* [C] a square piece of cloth worn on the head or around the neck

kernel /'kɜrn·ᵊl/ *n* [C] the edible part of a nut that is inside the shell, or the whole seed of a grain plant • (*fig.*) *There's a kernel of truth in what he said* (= some small part of it is true).

kerosene /'ker·əˌsiːn, ˌker·əˈsiːn/ *n* [U] a type of clear oil that is used as a fuel, esp. in heaters and lights

ketchup /'ketʃ·əp, 'kætʃ-/, **catsup** *n* [U] a thick, red sauce made from TOMATOES that is eaten on other foods • *Do you want ketchup for your French fries?*

kettle /'ket·ᵊl/ *n* [C] a covered container with a handle and a SPOUT (= opening for pouring), used for boiling water

key METAL SHAPE /kiː/ *n* [C] a piece of metal cut into a special shape to fit into a lock where it can be turned to open something, such as a door, or to start something, such as a car engine • *I put the key into the ignition.* • A **keyhole** is a hole in a lock into which a key fits. • A **key ring** is a metal ring used for keeping your keys together.

key to a lock   piano keys

key MOVABLE PART /kiː/ *n* [C] any of the set of movable parts that you press with your fingers on a computer or other machine to produce letters, numbers, or symbols, or on a musical instrument to produce sound • *piano keys* ○ *Press the shift key to write in capital letters.* • A **keyboard** is the set of keys arranged in rows used to operate a computer, or the row of keys on a piano or similar musical instrument. • A **keyboard** is also a musical instrument having keys like a piano: *Steve plays keyboards, drums, and saxophone.* • A **keystroke** is the act of pressing down on a key on a computer: *I can add the date with a single keystroke.*

key in *obj*, **key** *obj* **in** /'-'-/ *v adv* [M] to put (information) into a computer using a keyboard • *It will take about two hours to key in all this data.*

key IMPORTANT PART /kiː/ *n* [U] the most important part of achieving something or explaining a situation • *Luck is the key to winning at gambling.*

key /kiː/ *adj* • *Deception is a key element of military strategy.*

key MUSICAL NOTES /kiː/ *n* [C] a set of musical notes based on one particular note • *the key of C*

key LIST OF SYMBOLS /kiː/ *n* [C] a list of the symbols used in a map or book with explanations of what they mean • *The key is printed at the bottom of the page.*

keyed up /ˈkiːˈdʌp/ *adj* excited or nervous • *She was too keyed up to sleep.*

keynote /ˈkiːˌnoʊt/ *n* [C] the most important part, esp. of an event, or something that is emphasized strongly • *a keynote speaker/speech* ○ *Luxury is the keynote here.*

kg *n* [C] *pl* **kg** *abbreviation for* KILOGRAM

khaki /ˈkæk·i, ˈkɑk·i, *Cdn often* ˈkɑr·ki/ *adj* [not gradable], *n* [C/U] a pale yellow-brown color, or a type of cloth that is this color and is often used to make uniforms for soldiers • *I bought a new pair of summer khakis* (= pants made of this cloth). [pl]

kibbutz /kɪˈbʊts, -ˈbuːts/ *n* [C] *pl* **kibbutzim** /kɪˌbʊtˈsiːm, -ˌbuːt-/ (in Israel) a place, usually a farm, where a group of people live and work and where all duties are shared

kick HIT /kɪk/ *v* [I/T] to hit (someone or something) with the foot, or to move the feet and legs suddenly and violently • *I kicked the ball as hard as I could.* [T] ○ *I kicked at them and screamed for help.* [I] • (*infml*) If you **kick** an idea **around** you consider it. • *You can't kick me around* (= treat me badly). • (*slang*) When *Dad finds out what you did, he's going to kick your butt/ass* (= hit you or punish you). • *We couldn't get the door open so Mike just kicked it in/down* (= opened it by kicking it very hard). • When something **kicks off** it begins: *We like to kick off the summer with a barbecue.* • *Why don't we leave before they kick us out of here* (= no longer allow us to stay)? • (*slang*) To **kick the bucket** or **kick off** is to die: *When did Al kick the bucket?* • If you **kick a/the habit** you give up something that you have done for a long time: *She used to smoke but she kicked the habit last year.* • If you say you could **kick** yourself, you mean you are annoyed because you did something stupid or missed a chance: *When I realized what I had done I could have kicked myself.*

kick /kɪk/ *n* [C] • *She gave him a kick in the shins.* • If you say that someone should get a **kick in the pants/ass** you think they are acting badly and should improve their behavior: *He needs a good kick in the pants.*

kick EXCITEMENT /kɪk/ *n* [C] a strong feeling of excitement and pleasure • *We got a kick out of that show.*

kick INTEREST /kɪk/ *n* [C usually sing] a new interest, esp. one that does not last long • *He's been on an exercise kick lately.*

kickback /ˈkɪk·bæk/ *n* [C] payment made to someone, esp. illegally, for providing help, a job, or a piece of business • *Bankhead got a contract to supply computers to the department in exchange for a kickback.*

kickoff /ˈkɪk·ɔːf/ *n* [C/U] the time when a football game starts, or a kick of the ball that starts play during a game • *Kickoff is at 6:30.* [U] ○ *Patterson hurt his ankle on the opening kickoff.* [C]

kid CHILD /kɪd/ *n* [C] a child, or a young adult • *I took the kids to the park.* ○ *He's only 19, just a kid.* • A **kid brother/kid sister** is a younger brother or sister. • (*disapproving*) **Kid stuff** is something easy or suitable for children: *This class is kid stuff.*

kid ANIMAL /kɪd/ *n* [C/U] a young goat, or very soft leather made from the skin of a young goat

kid JOKE /kɪd/ *v* [I/T] **-dd-** *infml* to say something as a joke, often making (someone) believe something that is not true • *You're kidding around, aren't you?* [I] ○ *Casey's just kidding you.* [T] • If you **kid** yourself, you believe that something you want to be true is true although it probably is not: *He thinks she'll come back, but I think he's kidding himself.* • If you say someone **has got to be kidding/must be kidding** you doubt or are surprised by what they said: *You want me to drive into the city? You've got to be kidding.*

kiddie, **kiddy** /ˈkɪd·i/ *n* [C] *infml* a young child • *We have soda for the kiddies.*

kidnap /ˈkɪd·næp/ *v* [T] **-pp-** or **-p-** to illegally take (a person) away by force, usually in order to demand money in exchange for releasing them • *The wife of a prominent businessman was kidnapped today.*

kidnapper, **kidnaper** /ˈkɪdˌnæp·ər/ *n* [C]

kidney /ˈkɪd·ni/ *n* [C] either of a pair of small organs in the body that remove waste matter from the blood and produce urine, or these organs from an animal, which are used as food

kidney bean /ˈkɪd·niˌbiːn/ *n* [C] a small, dark red, edible bean that is shaped like a KIDNEY.

kill /kɪl/ *v* [I/T] to cause (someone or something) to die • *Her parents were killed in a car crash.* [T] ○ *Just a tiny drop of this poison is enough to kill.* [I] ○ (*fig.*) *If you tell Mom, I'll kill you* (= I will be extremely angry with you). [T] • To kill something can also mean to hurt, damage, remove, or destroy it: *It wouldn't kill you to apologize.* [T] ○ *The doctor gave her something to kill the pain.* [T] • If you **kill off** something, you destroy it completely: *The natives were soon killed off by the settlers.* • If you **kill time** or a period of time, you are waiting for something to happen: *We had an hour to kill before going to dinner.* [T] • *I can bring your suit to the cleaner's when I pick up the kids and*

479 kiss

kill two birds with one stone (= achieve two things at once).

kill /kɪl/ *n* [U] an animal that has been hunted and killed • *The leopard seized its kill and dragged it into the bush.*

killer /'kɪl·ər/ *n* [C] • *The police haven't found the killer yet.* ○ *Heart disease is a killer* (= cause of death). • (*infml*) If something is described as a killer, it is very difficult: *The test was a real killer.* • (*infml*) A killer is also someone or something that is very entertaining or skilled: *Dizzy was a killer on the trumpet.* • The killer is the most interesting or amusing part of a story: *It took her six hours to get there, and the killer is, she went to the wrong place!*

killing /'kɪl·ɪŋ/ *n* [C] • *She took part in the killing.*

kiln /kɪln, kɪl/ *n* [C] a type of large OVEN (= box in which things are cooked or heated) used for making bricks and clay objects hard after they have been shaped

kilobyte /'kɪl·ə,baɪt, 'kiː·lə-/ (*abbreviation* **KB**) *n* [C] a unit of measurement of computer storage space equal to 1024 BYTES

kilogram /'kɪl·ə,græm/ (*abbreviation* **kg**, *short form* **kilo** /'kiː·loʊ/) *n* [C] a unit of measurement of weight equal to 1000 grams or 2.2 pounds

kilometer /kə'lɑm·ət·ər, 'kɪl·ə,miːt·ər/ (*abbreviation* **km**) *n* [C] a unit of measurement of length equal to 1000 meters or 0.62 mile

kilowatt /'kɪl·ə,wɑt/ (*abbreviation* **kW**) *n* [C] a unit of power equal to 1000 WATTS

kilt /kɪlt/ *n* [C] a skirt with many folds, made from TARTAN cloth and traditionally worn by Scottish men and boys, but also worn by women and girls

kimono /kə'moʊ·nə, -noʊ/ *n* [C] *pl* **kimonos** a long, loose piece of outer clothing with very wide sleeves, traditionally worn by the Japanese

kin /kɪn/ *pl n* family and relatives • *They're not any kin of mine.*

kind GOOD /kaɪnd/ *adj* [*-er/-est* only] generous, helpful, and caring about other people's feelings • *She's a kind, thoughtful person.* ○ *It was kind of you to give me your seat.* • A kind-hearted person is one who cares about other people.

kindly /'kaɪnd·li/ *adv, adj* • *a kindly man* ○ *They treated me kindly.*

kindness /'kaɪnd·nəs/ *n* [C/U] • *Acts of kindness are rare.* [U]

kind TYPE /kaɪnd/ *n* [C] a group with similar characteristics, or a particular type • *What kind of thing is it?* ○ *They talked about all kinds of stuff.* ○ *It's the largest organization of its kind in history.* • *Where books are concerned, Tyler and Chloë are two of a kind* (= similar). • (*infml*) Kind of means slightly, or is used to show that you are not certain about something: *We have to dress kind of nice at work.* ○ *I guess I kind of take her for granted.*

kinda /'kaɪn·də/ *adv* [not gradable] *not standard* (spelled the way it is often spoken) kind of (= slightly) • *I was kinda sorry to see him go.*

kindergarten /'kɪn·dər,gɑrt·ən, -,gɑrd·ən/ *n* [C/U] a class for young children, usually children four and five years old, which is often the first year of formal education • *Callie will start kindergarten in September.* [U] • LP EDUCATION IN THE US

kindle /'kɪn·dəl/ *v* [T] to cause (a fire) to start burning • (*fig.*) *Romantic love kindled their imaginations* (= made them work).

kindling /'kɪn·dlɪŋ, -lɪŋ/ *n* [U] small, dry sticks or other materials used to start a fire

kindred /'kɪn·drəd/ *adj* [not gradable] being related, esp. by having the same opinions, feelings, and interests • *We recognized each other as kindred spirits as soon as we met.*

kinfolk /'kɪn·foʊk/, **kinfolks** /'kɪn·foʊks/ *pl n* family; KIN

king /kɪŋ/ *n* [C] a man who rules a country because he has been born into a family which by tradition or law has the right to rule, or the title given to such a man • *King Philip IV of Spain* • A king is a playing piece in the game of CHESS and each player's most important piece. • A king is also a playing card with a picture of a king on it: *the king of hearts* • If someone or something is called the king of an activity, they are the best or the most important in that activity: *He was baseball's home-run king.* • Something that is **king-sized** (also **king-size**) is larger than the ordinary size, and usually the largest size: *a king-size bed* ○ Compare **queen-sized** at QUEEN WOMAN.

kingdom /'kɪŋ·dəm/ *n* [C] a country ruled by a king or queen • *She was queen of an ancient kingdom in Egypt.* • A kingdom is also one of the groups into which natural things can be divided, depending on their type: *the animal/plant kingdom*

kingpin /'kɪŋ·pɪn/ *n* [C] the most important person in an organization • *He was the kingpin of the Democratic organization in Chicago.*

kink /kɪŋk/ *n* [C] a sharp twist or bend in something such as a wire or rope • *There was a kink in the hose and the water wouldn't come through.* • A kink is also a small problem: *The system will work fine once we work out a few kinks.*

kinky /'kɪŋ·ki/ *adj* [*-er/-est* only] • *kinky hair* (= hair with many small, tight bends in it)

kinky /'kɪŋ·ki/ *adj infml* connected with or having a preference for unusual sexual activities • *kinky sex*

kiosk /'kiː·ɑsk/ *n* [C] a small structure where things such as newspapers, magazines, and candy are sold

kiss /kɪs/ *v* [I/T] to touch or press your lips against another person, esp. their lips or CHEEK, as a greeting or to express love • *The two women hugged and kissed (each other).* [I/T] ○ *He kissed the children goodbye.* [T] • If you

kiss something **goodbye**, you lose it or you lose the opportunity to have it: *If you lend him money, you can kiss it goodbye.*

kiss /kɪs/ *n* [C] • *Give grandma a kiss and say goodnight.* • If you describe something as the **kiss of death**, you mean it will cause something else to fail: *His failure to raise enough money for the political campaign was the kiss of death.*

kit /kɪt/ *n* [C] a set of things, such as tools or equipment, used for a particular purpose or activity • *We keep a first-aid kit in the office for emergencies.* • A kit is also a set of parts sold ready to be put together: *a model airplane kit*

kitchen /'kɪtʃ·ən/ *n* [C] a room where food is prepared and cooked

kite /kaɪt/ *n* [C] a light frame covered with plastic, paper, or cloth that is flown in the wind at the end of a long string, esp. for amusement • *On windy days the kids fly their kites in the park.*

kitsch /kɪtʃ/ *n* [U] showy art or cheap, decorative objects that are attractive to people who are thought to lack any appreciation of style or beauty • *She collects all sorts of kitsch, like these ceramic figurines of movie stars.*

kitten /'kɪt·ən/ *n* [C] a young cat • *Our cat just had six kittens.*

kitty MONEY /'kɪt̬·i/ *n* [C usually sing] money to be used for a particular purpose that has been collected from a number of people • *We each put $20 a week into the kitty to cover the cost of food.*

kitty CAT /'kɪt̬·i/ *n* [C] a cat or KITTEN

kiwi (fruit) /'kiː·wiː/ (,fruːt)/ *n* [C] an oval fruit with brown, hairy skin and green flesh

KKK *n* [U] *abbreviation for* KU KLUX KLAN

Kleenex /'kliː·neks/ *n* [C/U] *trademark* a type of thin, soft paper that comes in separate sheets, or one of these sheets • *She dried her eyes with a Kleenex.* [C]

klutz /klʌts/ *n* [C] *infml* a person who moves awkwardly and often drops things • *Don't expect Mark to catch the ball, he's a klutz.*

km *n* [C] *pl* **km** *abbreviation for* KILOMETER

knack /næk/ *n* [U] an ability or special method for doing something easily and well • *There's a knack to using this corkscrew.*

knapsack /'næp·sæk/ *n* [C] a small bag with straps that can hold it against a person's back, leaving the arms free

knead /niːd/ *v* [T] to press (esp. clay or a mixture for making bread) firmly and repeatedly with the hands • *Knead the dough until it is smooth.*

knee /niː/ *n* [C] the middle joint of the leg • *Her skirt came to just above the knee.* ○ *He got down on his hands and knees to look for his contact lens.* • If something is **knee-**

knead

deep, it reaches from the ground up to your knees: *The snow was knee-deep.* ○ *(fig.) I'm knee-deep in work* (= have a lot of work). • Something described as **knee-jerk** is not thought about but is done automatically as a result of habit: *When asked about crime, the mayor's knee-jerk reaction is to call for longer prison sentences.*

knee /niː/ *v* [T] to force your knee violently into (someone) • *She kneed him in the groin.*

kneecap /'niː·kæp/ *n* [C] the round bone at the front of the knee

kneel /niːl/ *v* [I] *past* **knelt** /nelt/ or **kneeled** to go down into, or stay in, a position where one or both knees are on the ground • *She knelt down to look under the bed for her doll.* ○ *He prayed, kneeling in front of the altar.*

knew /nuː/ *past simple of* KNOW

knickers /'nɪk·ərz/ *pl n* short, loose pants that fit tightly below the knee, worn esp. in the past • (*Br*) Knickers are women's and girl's UNDER-PANTS.

knickknack /'nɪk·næk/ *n* [C] a small, decorative object, esp. in a house • *The room was filled with knickknacks.*

knife /naɪf/ *n* [C] *pl* **knives** /naɪvz/ a tool or weapon used for cutting, usually consisting of a metal blade and a handle • *a sharp knife* ○ *We took plastic knives and forks on our picnic.*

knife /naɪf/ *v* [T] to push a knife into (someone) to hurt them • *She had been knifed to death.*

knight /naɪt/ *n* [C] (in the past) a man of high rank who was trained to fight as a soldier on a horse • *I'm reading about King Arthur and his knights.* • A knight is a playing piece in the game of CHESS that is often shaped like a horse's head.

knight /naɪt/ *v* [T] in Britain, to give (a person) a rank of honor because of their special achievements • *He was knighted by Queen Elizabeth II.*

knighthood /'naɪt·hʊd/ *n* [C]

knit MAKE CLOTHES /nɪt/ *v* [I/T] **knitting**, *past* **knitted** or **knit** to make (cloth or clothing) by connecting YARN (= fiber threads) into rows with two long needles, or to do this with a machine • *She's knitting a scarf for her daughter.* [T]

crochet   knit

knitting /'nɪt̬·ɪŋ/ *n* [U] something being made by the act of knitting • *She takes her knitting with her everywhere.* • *You need size eight* **knitting needles** (= long needles used to knit) *to make this cardigan.*

knit JOIN /nɪt/ *v* [I/T] **knitting**, *past* **knitted**

or **knit** to join together • *She's got a break in this bone, but the ends of the bones will knit without the need for surgery.* [I]

knob /nɑb/ *n* [C] a round handle or a small, round device for controlling a machine or electrical equipment • *Turn the knob on the left to start the washer.*

knobby /'nɑb·i/ *adj* having knobs on the surface, or shaped like a knob • *knobby knees*

knock MAKE NOISE /nɑk/ *v* [I] to repeatedly hit something, producing a noise • *Someone is knocking at the door.* ○ *Jane knocked on the window to attract his attention.* • If an engine is knocking, it makes a repeated noise because of a mechanical problem. • People say **knock on wood** when they want to continue to have good luck in something they are talking about: *I never have trouble with my car, knock on wood.*

knock /nɑk/ *n* [C] • *There was a loud knock at the door.*

knocker /'nɑk·ər/ *n* [C] a metal object attached to the outside surface of a door in such a way that it can be hit against the door to make a noise, getting the attention of those inside

knock MOVE /nɑk/ *v* [T] to push into (something or someone), often forcefully, causing them to move • *Alice accidentally knocked the pot off the table.* ○ *The blast knocked him off his feet.* • If something or someone **knocks you for a loop**, you are so surprised that you do not how to react: *Marguerite knocked me for a loop when she said she and Pete had been secretly married.* • If you tell someone to **knock it off**, you want them to stop doing something that annoys you.

knock /nɑk/ *n* [C] • *He got a nasty knock on the head from the side of the pool when he misjudged the turn.* ○ *(fig.) Joey has had a lot of hard knocks (= bad luck).*

knock CRITICIZE /nɑk/ *v* [T] *infml* to criticize, esp. unfairly • *She knocks every suggestion I make.*

▫ **knock down** *obj* CAUSE TO FALL , **knock** *obj* **down** /'-'-/ *v adv* [M] to cause to fall to the ground or to a lower place by hitting or by other forceful action • *Try not to knock the fence down when you back out of the driveway.*

▫ **knock down** *obj* DESTROY , **knock** *obj* **down** /'-'-/ *v adv* [M] to destroy and remove, usually a building or wall • *The city is going to knock the old train station down and build a new library.*

▫ **knock down** *obj* REDUCE , **knock** *obj* **down** /'-'-/ *v adv* [M] to reduce the price of (something) • *He wanted $300 for the ring, but we got him to knock it down to $250.*

▫ **knock off** STOP /'-'-/ *v adv* [I/T], *v prep* to stop working or doing (something) • *We knocked off (work) at six o'clock.* [I/T]

▫ **knock off** *obj* REMOVE , **knock** *obj* **off** /'-'-/ *v adv* [M], *v prep* to remove by pushing, hitting, or other forceful action • *A low branch*

knocked her off her horse. ○ *One of the side mirrors on the truck got knocked off.*

▫ **knock** *(obj)* **off** *(obj)* REDUCE /'-'-/ *v adv* [T], *v prep* to reduce the price of something by (a particular amount) • *The manager knocked ten bucks off because the dress had a few buttons missing.* [M] ○ *The manager knocked ten bucks off the price.*

▫ **knock out** *obj* HIT , **knock** *obj* **out** /'-'-/ *v adv* [M] to hit (someone) so that they become unconscious, or to cause (someone) to go to sleep • *His fall from the ladder knocked him out.* ○ *Those sleeping pills knocked me out.* • If something such as a piece of equipment is knocked out by something else, it stops operating: *The lightning knocked out our electricity.* • If you **knock yourself out**, you work hard to succeed at something: *Pat has really knocked herself out for this dinner.*

knockout /'nɑk·ɑʊt/ *(abbreviation* **KO**) *n* [C] (in boxing) a situation in which a fighter falls after being hit and cannot get up in ten seconds • *He won by a knockout in the tenth round.* • See also KNOCKOUT.

▫ **knock out** *obj* REMOVE , **knock** *obj* **out** /'-'-/ *v adv* [M] to remove (something), esp. by hitting it with force • *Sean fell off his bike and knocked two teeth out.* • If a person or team is knocked out of a competition, they are defeated and no longer can take part: *A loss in today's game will knock our team out of the playoffs.*

▫ **knock over** *obj*, **knock** *obj* **over** /'-'-/ *v adv* [M] to hit and cause to be no longer standing • *Who knocked over the chair?* • *You could have knocked me over with a feather (= I was extremely surprised).*

▫ **knock up** *obj*, **knock** *obj* **up** /'-'-/ *v adv* [M] *slang* to make a woman pregnant

knock-down drag-out /'nɑk,dɑʊn'dræɡ,ɑʊt/ *adj* [not gradable] *infml* (of an argument or physical fight) lasting a long time and fiercely fought • *We had knock-down drag-out fights, but when I really needed him on the big issues, he was helpful.*

knockoff /'nɑk·ɔːf/ *n* [C] *infml* a cheaper copy of an expensive and widely known product • *She bought a knockoff of a designer suit.*

knockout /'nɑk·ɑʊt/ *n* [C] *slang* a very attractive person or thing • *She was a real knockout.* • See also **knockout** at KNOCK OUT HIT.

knoll /noʊl/ *n* [C] a small hill with a rounded top

knot FASTENING /nɑt/ *n* [C] a fastening made by tying together a piece or pieces of string, rope, cloth, etc. • *Wrap this string around the package and then tie a knot.* ○ *(fig.) She's so nervous, her stomach is in knots (= feels tight and uncomfortable).*

knot /nɑt/ *v* [I/T] *-tt-* • *He knotted his tie carefully.* [T]

knot GROUP /nɑt/ *n* [C] a group of people or

things • *After the game, disappointed knots of people drifted away.*

knot WOOD /nɑt/ *n* [C] a hard, dark area on a tree or piece of wood where a branch was joined to the tree

knotty /'nɑt̬·i/ *adj* • *knotty pine*

knot MEASUREMENT /nɑt/ *n* [C] *specialized* a measure of speed for ships, aircraft, or movements of water and air equal to approximately 6076 feet (1·85 kilometers) an hour

know HAVE INFORMATION /noʊ/ *v* [I/T] *past simple* **knew** /nu:/, *past part* **known** /noʊn/ to have (information) in your mind; to be aware of (something) • *"Where did he go?" "I don't know."* [I] ∘ *Do you know the answer?* [T] ∘ *She knows the name of every kid in school.* [T] ∘ *Do you know how to tap dance?* [+ *wh-* word] ∘ *We don't know when he's arriving.* [+ *wh-* word] ∘ *I knew (that) something was wrong from the start.* [+ *(that)* clause] ∘ *I want to know how much this will cost.* [+ *wh-* word] • If someone **knows better**, they are wise enough to behave in a more responsible or acceptable way: *You know better than to interrupt when someone else is talking.* • If someone **knows best**, they know what should be done better than other people: *Dad knows best when it comes to investing money.* • If you **know of** someone or something, you have experience of them or information about them: *Do you know of a good doctor?* • If you **know what's what**, you know the facts of a situation or the results of an action: *I wanted someone to tell me everything, say here you go, now you know what's what.* • If you **know what** you **are doing**, you have the knowledge that is necessary to act: *Don't worry about me—I know what I'm doing!* • If you **know what** you **are talking about**, you understand a subject because of your experience or training: *He doesn't know what he's talking about—he's never even been to Alaska.* • If someone says you do **not know** one thing **from** another, they mean you are stupid: *She doesn't know her left shoe from her right.* • If you do **not know the first thing about** someone or something, you have no information about them or it: *I don't know the first thing about physics.* • If you do **not know what hit** you, you are suddenly shocked and confused by something: *When Nancy said she wanted a divorce, I didn't know what hit me.* • (*infml*) **Know-how** is practical knowledge and ability: *technical/financial know-how* • (*infml disapproving*) A **know-it-all** is a person who thinks that they know everything.

know /noʊ/ *n* • If someone is **in the know**, they have information about something: *Ask Keith—he's always in the know about upcoming projects.*

knowing /'noʊ·ɪŋ/ *adj* [not gradable] having or showing knowledge of private or secret information • *My mother gave me a knowing smile.*

knowingly /'noʊ·ɪŋ·li/ *adv* [not gradable] while understanding the meaning of what you are doing • *Many of them knowingly broke the law.*

know *(obj)* HAVE UNDERSTANDING /noʊ/ *v past simple* **knew** /nu:/, *past part* **known** /noʊn/ to agree with or understand the reasons for (an action or opinion) • *I don't know what all the fuss is about.* [+ *wh-* word] ∘ *"What a stupid movie!" "I know what you mean."* [+ *wh-* word] • To **know what it is (like) to** be or do something is to understand because you have personally experienced it: *She knows what it's like to go bankrupt—it happened to her 20 years ago.*

known /noʊn/ *adj* [not gradable] generally understood or proven • *There is no known reason for the accident.* ∘ *It is a known fact that he was married before.* ∘ *These substances are known to cause skin problems.* [+ *to* infinitive]

know BE FAMILIAR WITH /noʊ/ *v* [I/T] *past simple* **knew** /nu:/, *past part* **known** /noʊn/ to be familiar with (a person or place) • *I've known Vince since we were in elementary school.* [T] ∘ *She grew up in Hawaii so she knows it well.* [T] ∘ *Knowing Debbie (= from my experience of her in the past), she'll do a good job.* [T] • If you **know** your **way around**, you are familiar with a place, subject, or system, and therefore can act effectively.

know *(obj)* FEEL CERTAIN /noʊ/ *v past simple* **knew** /nu:/, *past part* **known** /noʊn/ to feel certain • *I know (that) I took those library books back.* [+ *(that)* clause] ∘ *I don't know whether or not I should go to college.* [+ *wh-* word]

know RECOGNIZE /noʊ/ *v* [T] *past simple* **knew** /nu:/, *past part* **known** /noʊn/ to recognize (someone or something), or to recognize the difference between (two people or things) • *That's Pete—I'd know him anywhere.* ∘ *I know a bargain when I see one!*

knowledge /'nɑl·ɪdʒ/ *n* [U] awareness, understanding, or information that has been obtained by experience or study, and that is either in a person's mind or possessed by people generally • *How will we use our increasing scientific knowledge?* ∘ *A lack of knowledge on the part of teachers is a real problem.* ∘ *He has a limited knowledge of French.* ∘ *The owner claims the boat was being used without her knowledge.* ∘ *It was common knowledge that Lucy was superstitious about the number 13.*

knowledgeable /'nɑl·ɪdʒ·ə·bəl/ *adj* [not gradable] • *He's very knowledgeable about Native American art.* ∘ *She's a knowledgeable person.*

knuckle /'nʌk·əl/ *n* [C] one of the joints of the fingers

□ **knuckle down** /ˌnʌk·əl'daʊn/ *v adv* [I] *infml* to start working hard • *You're going to have to knuckle down and catch up on your schoolwork.*

□ **knuckle under** /ˌ-'--/ *v adv* [I] *infml* to give

up power or control • *The other side is not ready to negotiate, but we won't knuckle under to their demands.*

KO *n* [C] *pl* **KOs** *abbreviation for* **knockout**, see at KNOCK OUT HIT

koala (bear) /koʊˈɑl·ə ('ber, 'bær)/ *n* [C] an Australian animal like a small bear with gray fur which lives in trees and eats leaves

kook /kuːk/ *n* [C] *infml* a strange or crazy person • *There's some kook outside who says he's your long-lost husband.*

kooky /ˈkuː·ki/ *adj infml* • *I love her in spite of her kooky ways.*

Koran /kəˈræn, -ˈrɑn/ *n* [U] the holy book of the Islamic religion • *There are many verses in the Koran which emphasize that life is sacred.*

kosher /ˈkoʊ·ʃər/ *adj* [not gradable] (of food or places where food is kept) prepared or kept in conditions that follow the rules of Jewish law • *kosher food* ○ *a kosher restaurant* • Kosher can also mean acceptable or correct: *It's kosher for a politician to make a fortune when he leaves office, but not when he's in office.*

kowtow /ˈkaʊˌtaʊ/ *v* [I] *disapproving* to show too much respect or obedience • *People say he kowtowed to the white establishment to get elected.*

Kremlin /ˈkrem·lən/ *n* [U] the government of Russia and (in the past) of the Soviet Union, or the buildings where the Russian government meets • *They provided leaders in the Kremlin with information.*

kt. *n* [C] *abbreviation for* KARAT

kudos /ˈkuː·dɑs, -doʊs/ *n* [U] praise, admiration, and fame received for an achievement • *Women's organizations have been getting kudos for their service activities.*

Ku Klux Klan /ˌkuːˌklʌksˈklæn/ (*abbreviation* **KKK**) *n* [U] a secret organization of white, Protestant Americans, esp. in the southern part of the United States, who oppose people of other races or religions • *He's spent his life fighting the Ku Klux Klan in Alabama.*

kung fu /kʌŋˈfuː/ *n* [U] a method of fighting without weapons that originated in China and involves using your hands and feet

kW *n* [C] *pl* **kW** *abbreviation for* KILOWATT

Kwanzaa, Kwanza /ˈkwɑn·zə/ *n* [C] an African-American cultural celebration lasting from December 26 to January 1

L, l

L LETTER , **l** /el/ *n* [C] *pl* **L's** or **Ls** or **l's** or **ls** the twelfth letter of the English alphabet

L NUMBER , **l** /el/ *number* the ROMAN NUMERAL for the number 50

l VOLUME *n* [C] *pl* **l** *abbreviation for* LITER

L SIZE /el/ *adj* [not gradable] *abbreviation for* LARGE, used esp. on clothing to show its size

lab /læb/ *n* [C] *short form of* LABORATORY • *a research lab* ○ *a lab technician*

label /ˈleɪ·bəl/ *n* [C] a piece of paper, cloth, or other material that is attached to an object, telling you what the object is, how to use it, to whom it belongs, or other information • *The label on the bottle says not to take more than six tablets a day.* • A label can also mean the name or symbol of a company that produces goods for sale: *Everything we produce goes out under our own label.* • A label can also be a name or a phrase used to describe the characteristics or qualities of people, activities, or things: *It's hard to say whether to apply the label "jazz" or "rock" to her music.*

label /ˈleɪ·bəl/ *v* [T] • *She labeled all the packages and sent them out the same afternoon.* • To label (something or someone) is also to characterize them with a name: *He didn't want to be labeled a complainer, so he didn't raise any objection to the extra work.*

labor WORK /ˈleɪ·bər/ *n* [U] practical work, esp. that which involves physical effort • *The car parts themselves are not expensive—it's the labor that costs so much.* • Labor also refers to the workers themselves, esp. those who do practical work with their hands: *skilled/unskilled labor* • A **labor camp** is a place where people are kept as prisoners and forced to do hard physical work. • **Labor Day** is a public holiday that honors workers, and is celebrated in the United States on the first Monday in SEPTEMBER. • A **labor-saving** device or method is one that saves a lot of effort and time. • A **labor union** (also **union**) is an organization of workers that protects their rights and represents them in discussions with employers over such matters as pay and working conditions.

labor /ˈleɪ·bər/ *v* [I] to do hard physical work • *Hours after the explosion, rescue teams were still laboring to free those trapped.* [+ *to* infinitive]

laborer /ˈleɪ·bə·rər/ *n* [C] a person who does physical work • *a farm/factory laborer*

laborious /ləˈbɔːr·i·əs, -ˈboʊr-/ *adj* needing a lot of time and effort • *a laborious task*

labor BIRTH /ˈleɪ·bər/ *n* [U] the last stage of pregnancy when the muscles of the uterus start to push the baby out of the body, usually lasting until the baby appears • *She went into* (= started) *labor at twelve o'clock last night.*

laboratory /ˈlæb·rə,tɔːr·i, -,toʊr-/, *short form* **lab** *n* [C] a room or building with equipment for doing scientific tests or for teaching science, or a place where chemicals or medicines are produced • *a physics laboratory*

labyrinth /ˈlæb·ə·rɪnθ/ *n* [C] a confusing set of connecting passages or paths in which it is easy to get lost

lace MATERIAL /leɪs/ *n* [U] a decorative cloth that is made by weaving thin thread into delicate patterns having small spaces within them • *a lace curtain/handkerchief*

lacy /ˈleɪ·si/ *adj* • *a lacy white blouse*

lace CORD /leɪs/ *n* [C usually pl] *short form of* a cord used to close a shoe or boot; shoelace • *Your laces are untied.*

lace /leɪs/ *v* [T] • *She laced (up) her boots.* [T/M]

lacerate /ˈlæs·ə,reɪt/ *v* [T] to cut or tear (something, esp. flesh) • *His face and hands were lacerated by the flying glass.*

laceration /ˌlæs·əˈreɪ·ʃən/ *n* [C/U] • *Justina was treated for a scalp laceration.* [C]

lack /læk/ *n* [U] a condition of not having any or enough of something, esp. something necessary or wanted • *a lack of ambition/confidence/knowledge* ○ *a lack of money* ○ *She certainly has no lack of friends* (= She has a lot of friends).

lack /læk/ *v* [T] • *What we lack in this house is space to store things.* ○ *He's totally lacking a sense of humor.*

lackadaisical /ˌlæk·əˈdeɪ·zɪ·kəl/ *adj* lacking enthusiasm and effort • *The food wasn't bad but the service was lackadaisical.*

lackluster /ˈlæk,lʌs·tər/ *adj* lacking energy and effort • *a lackluster performance*

laconic /ləˈkɑn·ɪk/ *adj* using very few words to express what you mean • *"I might," was the laconic reply.*

lacquer /ˈlæk·ər/ *n* [U] a shiny, hard substance that is painted on wood or metal to protect its surface

lacrosse /ləˈkrɔːs/ *n* [U] a game played by two teams in which the players each use a long stick with a net at the end to catch, carry, and throw a small ball, and try to get the ball in the other team's goal

lacy /ˈleɪ·si/ *adj* • See at LACE MATERIAL.

lad /læd/ *n* [C] *dated* a boy or young man

ladder /ˈlæd·ər/ *n* [C] a piece of equipment used for climbing up and down, and consisting of two vertical bars joined by a set of horizontal steps • (*fig.*) *In only a few years she managed to climb up the corporate ladder* (= achieve success in the business world) *to become a vice president.*

laden /ˈleɪd·ən/ *adj* carrying or holding a lot of something • *a table laden with food*

ladle /ˈleɪd·ᵊl/ *n* [C] a big spoon with a long handle and a deep, cup-shaped part, used esp. to move liquids from one container to another • *a soup ladle*

ladle /ˈleɪd·ᵊl/ *v* [T] • If you ladle (out) soup or other liquid food, you use a ladle to put it into bowls to give to people: *to ladle out stew* [T/M]

lady WOMAN /ˈleɪd·i/ *n* [C] a woman who is polite and behaves well toward other people • *Try to act like a lady.* • Lady is often used as a polite way of addressing or referring to any woman: *This lady has a question.* ○ *Ladies and gentlemen, may I have your attention.* • Lady can be a form of address, sometimes considered rude, to a woman whose name you do not know: *Hey, lady, what's the rush?* LP TITLES AND FORMS OF ADDRESS • A **ladies' room** (also **women's room**) is a toilet for women in a public building. Compare **men's room** at MEN. • Ladylike means suitable for a lady: *Mom still thinks it isn't ladylike to drink beer from a bottle.*

lady TITLE /ˈleɪd·i/ *n* [U] (in some countries) the title of a woman who has, or is the wife of a man who has, a specially high social rank, or the person herself • Compare LORD TITLE.

ladybug /ˈleɪd·iːˌbʌg/ *n* [C] a small, round, red BEETLE (= type of insect) with black spots

ladybug

lag /læg/ *v* [I] **-gg-** to move or advance so slowly that you are behind other people or things • *John's always lagging behind the others in the class.*

lag /læg/ *n* [C/U] a delay in the period of time in which events happen • *There is often a lag between becoming infected and the first signs of the illness.* [C]

lagoon /ləˈguːn/ *n* [C] an area of sea water separated from the sea by a REEF (= a line of rocks and sand)

laid /leɪd/ *past simple and past participle of* LAY • *He laid the book on the table.* • USAGE: (*not standard*) In speech, many people use laid instead of lay as the past simple of lie: *He laid down and went to sleep.*

laid-back /ˈleɪdˈbæk/ *adj* not tending to get anxious about behavior or things that need to be done • *It's a laid-back company—you can choose your own hours and the dress is very casual.*

lain /leɪn/ *past participle of* LIE POSITION

lair /ler, lær/ *n* [C] a place where certain kinds of wild animals live, often underground and hidden, or a place where a person hides • *a fox's lair* ○ *a thieves' lair*

laissez faire, laisser faire /ˌles·eɪˈfer, ˌleɪˌseɪ-, -ˈfær/ *n* [U] an economic theory or plan in which a government does not have many laws or rules to control the buying and selling of goods and services

laity /ˈleɪ·ət·i/ *n* • See at LAY NOT TRAINED.

lake /leɪk/ *n* [C] a large area of water that is not salty and is surrounded by land • *Lake Michigan*

lamb /læm/ *n* [C/U] a young sheep, or the flesh of a young sheep eaten as meat

lambaste /læmˈbeɪst, -ˈbæst/ *v* [T] to criticize (someone or something) severely • *His first novel was lambasted by the critics.*

lame UNABLE TO WALK /leɪm/ *adj* [*-er/-est* only] not able to walk correctly because of physical injury or weakness of the legs or feet • In politics, a **lame duck** is a person who has an elected position and will not be elected to it again, either because they do not want to continue in public office or because someone else has been elected to take the position.

lame NOT SATISFACTORY /leɪm/ *adj* [*-er/-est* only] (esp. of an excuse or argument) weak and not deserving to be believed • *Saying she'd lost her homework was a pretty lame excuse, if you ask me.*

lament /ləˈment/ *v* [T] to express sadness and regret about (something) • *He lamented his students' lack of interest in the classics.*

lament /ləˈment/ *n* [C] an expression of sadness over something, or a complaint • *Baker's lament was that his schedule kept him away from his family too often.*

lamentable /ləˈment·ə·bəl, ˈlæm·ənt·ə-/ *adj fml* regrettable • *a lamentable failure of nerve*

laminated /ˈlæm·əˌneɪt̬·əd/ *adj* [not gradable] consisting of several thin layers of wood, plastic, glass, etc., stuck together, or covered with a thin, protective layer of plastic • *laminated plywood* ○ *laminated diplomas*

lamp /læmp/ *n* [C] a device for giving light, esp. one with a covering that the light shines through or around • *a floor lamp* • A **lampshade** is a covering that is put over or around a light to reduce brightness or to direct the light, and also to look attractive.

land DRY SURFACE /lænd/ *n* [U] the surface of the earth that is not covered by water • *It is cheaper to drill for oil on land than at sea.* • Land is also a particular area of the earth's surface: *They just bought 150 acres of land in Idaho.* • The land refers to farms, farming, and the countryside: *My parents worked (on) the land all their lives.* • A country that is **landlocked** is surrounded by the land of other countries and has no sea coast. • A **land mine** is a bomb that is hidden in the ground and explodes when a person steps on it or a vehicle is driven over it. • A **landowner** is someone who owns land, often a lot of land. • A **landslide** is a mass of rock and earth moving suddenly and quickly down a steep slope. See also LANDSLIDE.

land NATION /lænd/ *n* [C] a country • *Ireland was my mother's native land.*

land ARRIVE /lænd/ *v* [I/T] to arrive or cause (something) to arrive at a place, esp. after moving down through the air • *The pilot said we would land in about 20 minutes.* [I] • To land is also to arrive in a boat: *We'd been sailing for three weeks by the time we landed at Miami.* [I] • If you **land on** your **feet**, you return to a good situation after experiencing difficulties: *She was very upset when she lost her job, but she landed on her feet and found another one a week later.*

landed /'læn·dəd/ *adj* • (*Cdn*) A **landed immigrant** is someone who has come to Canada to live, but who is not yet a citizen.

landing /'læn·dɪŋ/ *n* [C] • *We had a smooth takeoff and the flight was great, but our landing was a bit rough.*

land UNLOAD /lænd/ *v* [T] to unload (people or things) from a ship or aircraft onto the ground • *The general's plan involved landing troops behind enemy lines.*

land ACHIEVE /lænd/ *v* [T] *infml* to get or achieve (something desirable) • *to land a job*

landfill /'lænd·fɪl/ *n* [C/U] a place where garbage is buried • *The shopping center was built on landfill.* [U]

landing /'læn·dɪŋ/ *n* [C] a floor between two sets of stairs or at the top of a set of stairs • *There is another bathroom on the landing between the first and second floors.*

landlord /'lænd·lɔːrd/, **landlady** /'lænd,leɪd·i/ *n* [C] a person who owns a building or an area of land and is paid by other people for the use of it • *The street got much worse about two years ago when a landlord let prostitutes and drug dealers move in.*

landmark PLACE /'lænd·mɑrk/ *n* [C] a building or place that is easily recognized, esp. one that you can use to judge where you are • *I couldn't pick out any familiar landmarks in the dark and got completely lost.* • A landmark is also a building or other structure that is considered especially important as an example of its type: *a landmark skyscraper*

landmark STAGE /'lænd·mɑrk/ *n* [C] an important stage in the development of something • *The invention of the silicon chip is a landmark in the history of technology.*

landscape COUNTRYSIDE /'lænd·skeɪp/ *n* [C] a large area of countryside, usually one without many buildings or other things that are not natural • A landscape is also a view or picture of the countryside: *She collects early twentieth century landscapes.*

landscape CHANGE APPEARANCE /'lænd·skeɪp/ *v* [T] to change the appearance of (an area of land), esp. by planting trees, flowers, and other plants • *The park was beautifully landscaped.*

landslide /'lænd·slaɪd/ *n* [C] the winning of an election with an extremely large number of votes • *a landslide victory* ○ *The senator won by a landslide last year.* • See also **landslide** at LAND DRY SURFACE.

lane PATH /leɪn/ *n* [C] one of two or more

marked paths in a road to keep vehicles traveling in the same direction a safe distance apart • *That section of Interstate 95 is a four-lane highway, with two northbound lanes and two southbound lanes.* • A lane in a running track or swimming pool is a narrow section marked to keep the competitors apart.

lane ROAD /leɪn/ *n* [C] a narrow road, esp. in the countryside or in a small town

language /'læŋ·gwɪdʒ, -wɪdʒ/ *n* [C/U] a system of communication by speaking, writing, or making signs in a way that can be understood, or any of the different systems of communication used in particular regions • *the English language* [C] ○ *American Sign Language* [C] ○ *He speaks six foreign languages.* [C] ○ *Her language skills are excellent.* [U] • Language is also a particular type of expression: *beautiful language* [U] ○ *foul language* (= offensive words) [U] • In computer programming, a language is a system of writing instructions for computers. [C]

languid /'læŋ·gwəd/ *adj* lacking energy, or causing a lack of energy or enthusiasm • *He sat on the porch enjoying the delicious, languid warmth of a summer afternoon.*

languish /'læŋ·gwɪʃ/ *v* [I] to exist in an unpleasant or unwanted situation, often for a long time • *to languish in prison*

lanky /'læŋ·ki/ *adj* [-er/-est only] tall and thin and often tending to move awkwardly as a result • *He shifted his lanky body uncomfortably in the cramped airplane seat.*

lantern /'lænt·ərn/ *n* [C] a light enclosed in a container that has a handle for holding it or hanging it up, or the container itself

lap LEGS /læp/ *n* [C usually sing] the top surface of the upper part of the legs of a person who is sitting down • *Come and sit on my lap and I'll read you a story.*

lap DRINK /læp/ *v* [T] **-pp-** to drink (a liquid) by taking it in small amounts into the mouth with a lot of short quick movements of the tongue • *The cat lapped (up) the water.* [T/M]

lap HIT GENTLY /læp/ *v* [I/T] **-pp-** (of waves) to hit (something) gently, producing low sounds • *Waves lapped (at) the shore.* [I/T]

lap RACING /læp/ *n* [C] one complete trip around a race track or from one end of a swimming pool to the other • *Each lap of the track is 400 meters.*

lapel /lə'pel/ *n* [C] a strip of cloth that is attached to the collar and front opening of a jacket or similar piece of clothing and is folded back over it • *wide lapels*

lapse FAILURE /læps/ *n* [C] a failure to do something that happens as a particular event at a particular time • *a memory lapse* ○ *She had a momentary lapse in concentration and lost the game.*

lapse PERIOD /læps/ *n* [U] a period of time after an event or between two events • *Owing to* the lapse of time since the crimes, none of the original witnesses could be found.

lapse END /læps/ v [I] to end something, either intentionally or accidentally, that might be continued or that should continue • I must have let my subscription lapse, because I haven't received any issues of the magazine in months.

▫ **lapse into** /'-ˌ--/ v prep [T] to end an activity and change to (something easier or a less active state) • He had difficulty with English and often lapsed into his native German. ○ He lapsed into silence.

laptop (computer) /'læp·tɑp (kəm'pjuːṭ·ər)/ n [C] a computer small and light enough to be carried around • If I had a laptop, I could work on the train.

larceny /'lɑr·sə·ni/ n [C/U] law the crime of taking something that does not belong to you, but not in a way that involves force or the threat of force • As a pickpocket, he was charged with larceny. [U]

lard /lɑrd/ n [U] a soft, white, creamy substance made from the fat of pigs and used in cooking and baking

large /lɑrdʒ/ adj [-er/-est only] of more than a typical or average size or amount • They have a large house in the suburbs. ○ This apartment is much larger than our last one. ○ It was the largest bug I had ever seen. ○ This computer stores large amounts of data. ○ I'd like a large soda. • Large (abbreviation L) is a size of clothing or other product that is bigger than average: The shirt is available in small, medium, and large (sizes). • **At large** can mean generally: Society at large will benefit from this. • If a person or an animal is **at large**, they are dangerous and in an area where they can harm people: The escaped prisoners are still at large. • There are a few things that I don't like about my job, but **by and large** (= when everything about my job is considered together) it's very enjoyable. • The characteristics of someone or something that is **larger than life** are much more obvious than usual: His superhuman strength gives the story a larger-than-life quality, like a fable. • If something is **large-scale**, it involves many people or things, or happens over a large area: Technological changes prompted a shift to large-scale milk production plants. • USAGE: The opposite of large is SMALL.

largely /'lɑrdʒ·li/ adv [not gradable] to a great degree, or generally • My advice was largely ignored. ○ His early novels went largely unnoticed.

lark BIRD /lɑrk/ n [C] a small brown bird with a pleasant song

lark ACTIVITY /lɑrk/ n [C] an activity done for enjoyment or amusement • He started hang-gliding years ago as a lark.

larva /'lɑr·və/ n [C] pl **larvae** /'lɑr·viː/ a young insect that has left its egg but has not yet developed wings, or the young of some animals

laryngitis /ˌlær·ən'dʒɑɪṭ·əs/ n [U] an infection of the LARYNX, which often makes speaking painful • Carol's flu developed into laryngitis.

larynx /'lær·ɪŋks/ n [C] pl **larynxes** or **larynges** /lə'rɪn·dʒiːz/ an organ in the throat which contains the **vocal cords** (= tissue that moves to produce the voice) • Smokers are more likely to have cancer of the larynx than non-smokers.

lasagna, **lasagne** /lə'zɑn·jə/ n [U] a dish consisting of layers of thin, wide pasta combined with cheese, TOMATO sauce, and sometimes meat

lascivious /lə'sɪv·iː·əs/ adj esp. disapproving feeling, expressing, or causing a desire for sexual activity • She thought his comments were lewd and lascivious.

laser /'leɪ·zər/ n [C] a device that produces a powerful, highly controlled, narrow beam of light • a laser beam ○ Doctors destroyed the tumor with a laser.

lash HIT /læʃ/ v [I/T] to hit (someone or something) with a lot of force, esp. using a stick or leather strip, or to move forcefully against something • Prisoners were beaten, kicked, and sometimes lashed. [T] ○ Ice storms lashed across the state. [I] • If someone **lashes out**, they suddenly attack someone or something physically or with words: Nixon went out of his way to lash out at his critics.

lash /læʃ/ n [C] • She saw a woman whipped till blood trickled from every stroke of the lash (= thin leather strip).

lash TIE /læʃ/ v [T always + adv/prep] to tie or fasten together tightly and firmly • Lash the boat to the rail.

lash HAIR /læʃ/ n [C] an eyelash, see at EYE • She has enormous wide-set eyes with thick lashes.

lasso /'læs·oʊ, -uː/ n [C] pl **lassos** or **lassoes** a long rope with one end tied in a circle that can be tightened, used for catching horses and cattle

lasso /'læs·oʊ, læ'suː/ v [T] **lassoes**, **lassoing**, past **lassoed** • The terrified pony was finally lassoed (= caught).

last FINAL /læst/ adj, adv [not gradable], n [U] (the person or thing) after everyone or everything else • Our house is the last one on the left. ○ In math tests, American students came in last (= ranked the lowest). ○ He was last in line for tickets. ○ Heather was the last to go to bed and the first to get up. ○ Despite recent wins, the team is still in last place (= lowest in rank among its competitors). • I would like to thank my publisher, my editor, and **last but not least** (= importantly, despite being mentioned after everyone else), my husband for his encouragement during the writing of my book. • The **last minute** is the latest possible opportunity for doing something: He always leaves his homework until the last minute. ○ Our babysitter canceled at the last minute. • **The last word** is the final remark in an argument or discussion: No matter what we're talking about, Cheryl has to have the last word. • **The last word** is also the best or most complete statement or treatment of a subject: In 1945, punch cards were the last word in data processing. • A **last-ditch** or **last-gasp** effort is a final try to achieve something before it is too late: In a last-ditch attempt to win the election, he promised sweeping tax cuts. • Your **last name** is the name that comes after the name(s) you are given, and is usually the name of your father's family: His first name is Julio, but I can't remember his last name. ○ Compare **first name** at FIRST; **middle name** at MIDDLE. • A **last resort** is the only choice available: As a last resort, we could ask your mother to help.

last /ˈlæst/, **lastly** /ˈlæst·li/ adv [not gradable] (in ending a set of items or a series of thoughts) finally • The men begin the dance, then the women enter, and last, the children join in.

last NO MORE /læst/ adj [not gradable], n [U] (being) the only one or part that is left • I need to borrow some money—I'm down to my last dollar. ○ Mark ate the last of the ice cream. • Something that is **on** its **last legs** is weak or in very bad condition: This mower's on its last legs, but it still cuts the grass.

last MOST RECENT /læst/ adj, adv [not gradable], n [U] (being) the most recent or the one before the present one • last night/week/month/year ○ last spring/summer/fall/winter ○ These last five years have been very difficult for him. ○ Kristal said in her last letter that she might come to visit. ○ When was the last time you had a cigarette? ○ We last saw Grandma in 1994. ○ We had lunch together the week/month before last (= two weeks/months ago). ○ The last we heard, she was teaching English overseas. ○ Each of her novels seems better than the last.

last NOT DESIRABLE /læst/ adj [not gradable] being the least desirable or least likely • Traveling across the country with two small children is the last thing I want to do.

last CONTINUE /læst/ v to continue for a period of time, or to continue to exist • The tour lasts about an hour. [I] ○ She's into soccer at the moment, but it won't last. [I] • To last is also to continue in a situation although it is difficult: Her previous secretary only lasted a month. [L] • To last is also to continue to work well or stay in good condition: I'd rather pay a little more and buy clothing that's going to last. [I] • If you **wouldn't last five minutes** or **wouldn't last long** in a situation, you would not be successful in it: I wouldn't last five minutes as a cop— it's far too tough a job for me.

lasting /ˈlæs·tɪŋ/ adj continuing to exist or have an effect for a long time • These poems

have won him a lasting reputation as Puerto Rico's finest love poet.

latch /lætʃ/ n [C] a fastening device for a door or gate

latch /lætʃ/ v [I/T] • Make sure the cabinet door is latched so the cat can't get in. [T]

□ **latch onto** /ˈ-ˈ-/ v prep [T] infml (esp. of living things) to become firmly attached to (someone or something) • Antibodies latch onto proteins on the surfaces of the virus. • If people latch onto something, they accept it: We don't latch onto new Christmas carols easily.

late NEAR THE END /leɪt/ adj, adv [-er/-est only] (happening or being) near the end of a period or in the recent past • I expect him home late this afternoon. ○ I'd better get going—I had no idea it was so late! ○ It's too late to call now [+ to infinitive] ○ I think Jody's in her late twenties. ○ He is a celebrated painter of the late 19th century. • See also LATEST. Compare EARLY.

lately /ˈleɪt·li/ adv [not gradable] recently • My wife hasn't been feeling well lately.

late AFTER /leɪt/ adj, adv [-er/-est only] (happening or arriving) after the planned, expected, usual, or necessary time • Sorry I'm late—I was caught in traffic. ○ You'll be later than you already are if you don't hurry up. ○ This is the latest she's ever worked. ○ Summer came late this year (= The weather became warm after the usual time). ○ It's too late to do anything about it now. • A **latecomer** is a person who arrives late: Latecomers will not be admitted until intermission. • See also LATEST. Compare EARLY.

lateness /ˈleɪt·nəs/ n [U] • My boss doesn't tolerate lateness.

late DEAD /leɪt/ adj [not gradable] no longer alive, esp. having recently died • She gave her late husband's clothes to charity.

latent /ˈleɪt·ᵊnt/ adj [not gradable] present, but not yet active, developed, or obvious • Latent ethnic tensions exploded into the open yesterday.

later NEAR THE END /ˈleɪt·ər/ adv [not gradable], comparative of LATE NEAR THE END • He was successful later in his career.

later AFTER /ˈleɪt·ər/ adv [not gradable], comparative of LATE AFTER; after the present, expected, or usual time • She said she would speak to me later. ○ Why don't you call back later on, when he's sure to be here?

lateral /ˈlæt·ə·rəl/ adj [not gradable] relating to the sides of an object or to sideways movement • The bird spread its wings for lateral stability.

latest /ˈleɪt·əst/ adj [not gradable] newest, most recent, or most modern • Did you see her latest movie?

latest /ˈleɪt·əst/ n • **The latest** is the most recent news: Have you heard the latest about Celine and Michael?

latex /ˈleɪ·teks/ n [U] a white liquid produced by particular plants, esp. rubber trees, or an artificial substance similar to this, used esp. in paint, glue, and cloth • *latex paint* ○ *latex gloves*

lather /ˈlæð·ər/ *n* [U] a mass of small white bubbles produced esp. when soap is mixed with water • If you are **in a lather**, you are upset or excited: *Why was everybody getting into such a lather over this?*

lather /ˈlæð·ər/ *v* [I/T] • *I lathered and shaved quickly.* [I]

Latin American /ˈlæt·ᵊn·əˈmer·ə·kən, -ˈmær-/, **Latin** /ˈlæt·ᵊn/ *n* [C], *adj* [not gradable] (a person) of or coming from South America, Central America, or Mexico • *Latin American coffee producers will be hurt by the embargo.*

Latino *male* (*pl* **Latinos**) /læˈtiː·noʊ/, *female* **Latina** (*pl* **Latinas**) /læˈtiː·nə/ *n* [C] a person who lives in the US whose family is from Latin America, or a person who lives in Latin America • *a Latino community leader* ○ *There are 57 black students, about 600 Anglos, and more than 15,000 Latinos in the school district.*

latitude DISTANCE /ˈlæt·əˌtuːd/ *n* [C/U] the distance north or south of the equator measured from 0° to 90° • Compare LONGITUDE.

latitude FREEDOM /ˈlæt·əˌtuːd/ *n* [U] freedom to behave, act, or think in the way you want to • *Judges now have considerable latitude in sentencing.*

latrine /ləˈtriːn/ *n* [C] a toilet, esp. a simple one such as a hole in the ground, used in a military area or when CAMPING (= living in a tent for a short period)

latter SECOND /ˈlæt·ər/ *n* [U] *slightly fml* the second of two people, things, or groups previously mentioned • *He directed "The Wizard of Oz" and "Gone with the Wind," receiving an Oscar for the latter.* • Compare FORMER FIRST.

latter END /ˈlæt·ər/ *adj* [not gradable] near or toward the end of something • *He was in the news during the latter part of the Watergate scandal.* • **Latter-day** means having a new form of a person or thing from the past: *He acts like a latter-day cowboy armed with ideas.*

laud /lɔːd/ *v* [T] *fml* to praise (someone or something) • *The president lauded the rise of market economies around the world.*

laudable /ˈlɔːd·ə·bəl/ *adj fml* • *Recycling is a laudable activity.*

laudatory /ˈlɔːd·əˌtɔːr·i, -ˌtoʊr·i/ *adj fml* expressing praise • *Patients speak of Dr. Goertzen in laudatory terms.*

laugh /læf/ *v* [I] to make the sounds and movements of the face and body that express happiness or amusement, or that sometimes express ridicule or anxiety • *The audience just laughed and laughed.* ○ *That guy always makes me laugh.* ○ *When I made a face at Drew, he laughed out loud.* ○ *We were laughing at the clown.* • Sometimes when you laugh at someone, you are ridiculing them: *I don't want to be laughed at by my classmates.* • *It's not easy*

to **laugh off** *an accusation like that* (= pretend that it is less serious than it really is).

laugh /læf/ *n* [C] • *Holly has a very strange laugh—it sounds like she's screaming.* • (*infml*) A laugh is also an amusing or ridiculous situation or person: *You should have seen Sean trying to stay on the skateboard—what a laugh!*

laughable /ˈlæf·ə·bəl/ *adj* amusing or ridiculous • *Efforts to prevent teen pregnancy remain laughable to most teenagers.*

laughingstock /ˈlæf·ɪŋˌstɑk/ *n* [C] a person or group that is ridiculed • *This team has become the laughingstock of the league.*

laughter /ˈlæf·tər/ *n* [U] the act or sound of laughing • *Laughter from the living room kept me awake past midnight.*

launch SEND /lɔːntʃ, lɑntʃ/ *v* [T] to send (something) out, esp. a vehicle into space or a ship onto water • *On the last shuttle mission, the crew launched a communications satellite.*

launch /lɔːntʃ, lɑntʃ/ *n* [C] • *The launch of the space shuttle was delayed by bad weather.* • A **launch pad** (also **launching pad**) is a special area from which ROCKETS or MISSILES are launched.

launch BEGIN /lɔːntʃ, lɑntʃ/ *v* [I/T] to begin, or to introduce (a new plan or product) • *We're planning to launch a new Internet services company next month.* [T] ○ *He launched into a verbal attack on her handling of the finances.* [I always + adv/prep]

launch /lɔːntʃ, lɑntʃ/ *n* [C usually sing] • *Frank went to the launch* (= introduction) *of Hibichu's new flat-screen TV.*

launch BOAT /lɔːntʃ, lɑntʃ/ *n* [C] a large open or partly enclosed motor boat

launder WASH CLOTHES /ˈlɔːn·dər, ˈlɑn-/ *v* [I/T] *slightly fml* to clean (clothes, bed sheets, etc.) by washing them • *The sweater should be laundered by hand or dry-cleaned.* [T]

launder MOVE MONEY /ˈlɔːn·dər, ˈlɑn-/ *v* [T] to move (money which has been obtained illegally) through banks and other businesses to make it seem to have been obtained legally

laundromat /ˈlɔːn·drəˌmæt, ˈlɑn-/ *n* [C] *trademark* a place where the public may wash and dry their clothes in machines that operate when coins are put in them

laundry /ˈlɔːn·dri, ˈlɑn-/ *n* [C/U] clothing, bed sheets, etc., that have been or need to be washed • *piles of dirty laundry* [U] • A laundry is also a room in a house where clothes, etc., are washed, or a business that washes clothes, etc., for customers. [C] • A **laundry list** is a large group of items that do not seem related: *He's got a whole laundry list of ailments to tell the doctor about.*

laureate /ˈlɔːr·iː·ət, ˈlɑr-/ *n* [C] a person who has been given an important job or a prize because of their achievement in a particular subject • *a Nobel laureate*

laurel /ˈlɔːr·əl, ˈlɑr-/ *n* [C/U] a small evergreen tree that has shiny, dark green leaves and black BERRIES (= small round fruit)

lava /'lɑv·ə, 'læv·ə/ *n* [U] hot liquid rock that comes out of a VOLCANO, or the solid rock formed when liquid rock cools

lavatory /'læv·ə,tɔːr·i, -,tour·i/ *n* [C] a room equipped with a toilet and sink • *Smoking is not permitted in the plane's lavatories.*

lavender PLANT /'læv·ən·dər/ *n* [U] a plant with gray-green, needlelike leaves and small, pale purple flowers that has a pleasant smell, or its dried flowers and stems which are sometimes kept with sheets and clothes to make them smell pleasant

lavender COLOR /'læv·ən·dər/ *adj, n* [U] (of) a pale purple color • *a lavender shirt*

lavish /'læv·ɪʃ/ *adj* spending, giving, or using more than is necessary or reasonable; more than enough • *The team has the most lavish training facility in the league.*

lavishly /'læv·ɪʃ·li/ *adv* • *They live in a lavishly furnished apartment overlooking Central Park.*

lavish *obj* **on** *obj* /'læv·ɪʃ,ɔːn, -,ɑn/ *v prep* [T] to give a lot or too much (of something) to (someone or something) • *She lavishes more attention on that dog than she does on her children.*

law RULE /lɔː/ *n* [C/U] a rule made by a government that states how people may and may not behave in society and in business, and that often orders particular punishments if they do not obey, or a system of such rules • *civil/criminal law* [U] ∘ *federal/state law* [U] ∘ *We have a law in this state that drivers must wear seatbelts.* [C] ∘ *She's studying law at Georgetown University.* [U] ∘ *Playing loud music late at night is against the law.* [U] • The law is also the police: *He got in trouble with the law as a young man.* [U] • Someone who is **law-abiding** obeys the law: *a law-abiding citizen* • **Law and order** is the condition of a society in which laws are obeyed, and social life and business go on in an orderly way. • A **lawbreaker** is a person who does not obey the law, esp. intentionally and often. • **Law enforcement** is the government activity of keeping the public peace and causing laws to be obeyed: *Several law enforcement officers were sent to Mexico to bring the prisoner back.* • A **lawmaker** is someone, such as a politician, who is responsible for making and changing laws. • A **lawsuit** is a claim brought in a court of law by a person or an organization stating that they have been illegally injured by the action of another: *A lawsuit for sexual harassment was brought by two women against their former employer.*

lawful /'lɔː·fəl/ *adj* [not gradable] permitted by law; legal • *The judge concluded that the search of the house had been lawful.*

lawless /'lɔː·ləs/ *adj* [not gradable] not permitted by law or not obeying the law; illegal • *The university promised better police protec-*tion at football games to stop the lawless behavior of some beer-drinking fans.*

law PRINCIPLE /lɔː/ *n* [C] a general rule that states what always happens when the same conditions exist • *the laws of physics*

lawn /lɔːn, lɑn/ *n* [C] an area of grass, esp. near a house or in a park, which is cut regularly to keep it short • A **lawnmower** is a machine used for cutting grass.

lawyer /'lɔɪ·ər, 'lɔː·jər/ *n* [C] someone whose job is to give advice to people about the law and speak for them in court • *Following his arrest, he demanded to see his lawyer before making any statement.*

lax /læks/ *adj* lacking care, attention, or control; not severe or strong enough • *Security at the airport seemed lax.*

laxity /'læk·sət·i/, **laxness** /'læk·snəs/ *n* [U] • *Laxity in enforcing safety regulations can cost lives.*

laxative /'læk·sət·ɪv/ *n* [C] a substance that helps a person get rid of the contents of their bowels

lay PUT DOWN /leɪ/ *v* [T] *past* **laid** /leɪd/ to put (something) down, esp. into a flat or horizontal position • *He laid his coat on a chair.* ∘ *She laid the baby (down) in her crib.* • To lay is also to put down in a careful or systematic way for a particular purpose: *We're having a new carpet laid in the hall next week.* • If you **lay a finger/hand on** *her* (= touch her in a harmful or threatening way), *you'll live to regret it!* • To **lay** someone **to rest** is to bury them: *She was laid to rest in Mt. Zion Cemetery.* • *(fig.)* *I hope what he said has* **laid** *your fears to rest* (= removed them). • Compare LIE POSITION.

lay PREPARE /leɪ/ *v* [T] *past* **laid** /leɪd/ to prepare (something) • *The initial negotiations laid the groundwork for more detailed talks later on.*

lay NOT TRAINED /leɪ/ *adj* [not gradable] not trained in or not having a detailed knowledge of a particular subject • *To a lay audience, the mathematics would be difficult.* • A **layman** (also **layperson**) is a person who is not trained in or does not have a detailed knowledge of a particular subject: *The book is supposed to be the layman's guide to home repair.*

laity /'leɪ·ət·i/ *n* [U] the ordinary people who are involved with a church but who do not hold official religious positions • *The clergy and the laity are both participating in the program.*

lay PRODUCE EGGS /leɪ/ *v* [I/T] *past* **laid** /leɪd/ (of an animal or bird) to produce (eggs) from out of its body

lay HAVE SEX /leɪ/ *v* [T] *past* **laid** /leɪd/ *rude slang* to have sex with (someone)

lay RISK /leɪ/ *v* [T] *past* **laid** /leɪd/ to risk (something) on the result of an event • *I'll lay odds* (= risk money) *that she won't show up.*

lay EXPRESS /leɪ/ *v* [T] *past* **laid** /leɪd/ to put or express • *He laid emphasis on the fact that he* *had never been found guilty of a crime.* ○ *She's trying to lay the blame on someone else* (= blame someone else).

lay LIE /leɪ/ *past simple of* LIE POSITION

□ **lay down** *obj* STOP USING , **lay** *obj* **down** /'-'-/ *v adv* [M] to put away or stop using • *Lay down your weapons and surrender.* • To **lay down** your **life** is to die for something you believe in: *Today we remember those who laid down their lives for their country.*

□ **lay down** STATE /'-,-/ *v adv* [T] to state (something) plainly esp. as an official rule • *The coach laid down the rules from the first day of practice.* • If someone **lays down the law**, they state forcefully what they want to happen: *She laid down the law—no smoking in her house at any time.*

□ **lay in** *obj*, **lay** *obj* **in** /'-'-/ *v adv* [M] to obtain and store • *We'd better lay in plenty of food for the winter months.*

□ **lay into** /-'--/ *v prep* [T] *infml* to attack (someone) physically or with words • *The critics laid into her for a weak and lackluster performance.*

□ **lay off** *obj* NOT EMPLOY , **lay** *obj* **off** /-'-/ *v adv* [M] to stop employing (a worker), esp. for reasons that have nothing to do with the worker's performance • *She was laid off along with many others when the company moved to California.*

layoff /'leɪ·ɔːf/ *n* [C] • *Layoffs are expected when business slows after Christmas.*

□ **lay off** STOP /'-,-, -'-/ *v adv* [I/T] *infml* to stop using or dealing with (something or someone) • *You're going to have to lay off salt.* [T]

□ **lay out** *obj* ARRANGE , **lay** *obj* **out** /'-'-/ *v adv* [M] to arrange in a pattern or design; plan (something) by showing how its parts fit together • *The designer laid out the book with pictures on every page.*

layout /'leɪ·aʊt/ *n* [C] • *We're not happy with the layout of the apartment—the bathroom is too far from the bedroom.*

□ **lay out** SPEND /'-,-/ *v adv* [T] to spend (money), esp. if it seems like a large amount • *He laid out $100 for the flowers and $50 for two bottles of wine.*

□ **lay up** *obj*, **lay** *obj* **up** /'-'-/ *v adv* [M] to force to stay in bed • *She's been laid up with the flu for a week.*

layer /'leɪ·ər/ *n* [C] a thin sheet of a substance on top of a surface, or a level of material that is different from the material on either side • *We put on two layers of paint.* ○ *The road was built up with layers of crushed stone and asphalt.*

layover /'leɪ,oʊ·vər/ *n* [C] a short stay at a place in the middle of a trip • *We had a three-hour layover in San Francisco and had to change planes on the way to Hawaii.*

lazy /'leɪ·zi/ *adj* [-er/-est] only] not willing or not wanting to work or use effort to do something • *If you weren't so lazy we could start fixing up the house.* • If you describe an activity

as lazy, you mean that it is slow and gentle, or does not involve much effort: *a lazy breeze* ○ *We spent a lazy afternoon sunbathing on the beach.*

laziness /'leɪ·zi:·nəs/ *n* [U]

lb. *n* [C] *pl* **lb.** or **lbs.** *abbreviation for* POUND WEIGHT

lead CONTROL /liːd/ *v* [T] *past* **led** /led/ to manage or control (a group of people); to be the person who makes decisions that other people choose to follow or obey • *The minister led us in prayer.* ○ *I've asked George to lead the discussion.*

lead /liːd/ *n* [C] • *Who will play the lead* (= be the main actor) *in the show?*

leader /'liːd·ər/ *n* [C] a person who manages or controls other people, esp. because of his or her ability or position • *a business/financial/ political leader*

leadership /'liːd·ər,ʃɪp/ *n* [U] the quality or ability that makes a person a leader, or the position of being a leader • *The company was extremely successful under Murphy's leadership.* • Leadership is also the people who are in charge of a government or group: *the Democratic leadership in Congress*

lead SHOW WAY /liːd/ *v* [I/T] *past* **led** /led/ to show the way to (someone or something that follows), esp. by going first • *She led the children along the path out of the forest.* [T] ○ *That research group leads the way in the development of new software.* [T] • If something such as a road or sign leads somewhere, it goes toward something else or shows you how to get to a particular place: *A flight of narrow stairs leads to the kitchen.* [I] ○ *Just follow the signs and they will lead you to the exit.* [T]

lead /liːd/ *n* [C] a piece of information that allows a discovery to be made or a solution to be found • *The lead the detectives were following led to several arrests.*

lead CAUSE /liːd/ *v* [I/T] *past* **led** /led/ to prepare the way for (something) to happen; cause • *Ten years of scientific research led to the development of the new drug.* [I] ○ *The fact that the victim had $10,000 in cash and was not robbed led the police to assume that robbery was not the motive.* [T] • To **lead up to** something is to prepare slowly or indirectly for it: *I wonder what all this talk about the sorry state of our schools is leading up to.* • A period of time that **leads up to** an event or activity comes before it: *We're going to be real busy in the weeks leading up to final exams.* • LP) GET, HAVE, AND OTHER VERBS USED TO MEAN "CAUSE"

lead BE FIRST /liːd/ *v* [I/T] *past* **led** /led/ (esp. in sports or other competitions) to be in front, be first, or be winning • *With only three minutes to go in the football game, New Orleans led (Dallas), 24 to 21.* [I/T]

lead /liːd/ *n* [U] • *She took the lead* (= went in front) *with ten meters to go in the race.* • A lead is also the amount or distance by which someone is in front: *After five games, she was still ahead by a point in the chess tournament, but her lead was shrinking.*

leader /'li:d·ər/ *n* [C] someone or something that is the first or the most important • *Her company is a leader in the women's clothing industry.*

leading /'li:d·ɪŋ/ *adj* first or most important • *She is a leading expert on the art of ancient Greece.*

lead METAL /led/ *n* [U] a dense, soft, dark gray metal, used esp. in combination with other metals and in BATTERIES (= devices that produce electricity) • *Lead pipes in many older houses have been replaced by copper ones.* ○ (*fig.*) *The day after running a marathon, my legs felt like lead* (= heavy and tired). • *Some types of paint can contribute to* **lead poisoning** (= an illness caused by lead) *in children.*

leaden /'led·ən/ *adj* like lead in color or weight; gray or heavy • *They said goodbye under a leaden sky.*

lead PENCIL /led/ *n* [U] the black writing material made of GRAPHITE, used esp. in the center of a pencil

lead LIVE /li:d/ *v* [T] *past* **led** /led/ to live (a particular type of life) • *She retired to Florida and still leads a busy life.*

lead ANIMAL /li:d/ *n* [C] a LEASH

▢ **lead off** /'-'-/ *v adv* [I/T] to be the first of a series of people to do something • *"Who's the first speaker in the sales conference?" "Sally is leading off."* [I]

leaf PLANT /li:f/ *n* [C] *pl* **leaves** /li:vz/ any of the flat, usually green parts of a plant that are joined at one end to the stem or branch • *By early November it's getting cold and the trees are starting to lose their leaves.*

leafy /'li:·fi/ *adj* • *You should include plenty of green leafy vegetables in your diet.*

leaf PAPER /li:f/ *n* [C] *pl* **leaves** /li:vz/ a thin flat substance, esp. a sheet of paper, or a layer of something • *Some of the leaves of the old book had come loose.* • *A leaf of a table is an extra flat piece that can be added to the top surface to make the table larger.*

leaf /li:f/ *v* [I always + adv/prep] to turn pages quickly and read only a little • *Three patients sat leafing through magazines in the doctor's waiting room.*

leaflet /'li:·flət/ *n* [C] a piece of paper, or several pieces of paper folded together, that gives information or advertises something • *They were handing out leaflets outside the supermarket about the school board election.*

league SPORTS /li:g/ *n* [C] a group of teams or players in a sport who take part in competitions against each other • *Our team has the worst record in the league.* ○ *Do you belong to a bowling league?* • A league is also a group in which all the players, people, or things are on approximately the same level: *His new movie*

is just not in the same league as his last one (= not as good as the one before).

league ORGANIZATION /li:g/ *n* [C] a group of people or countries that join together because they have the same interest • *the League of Nations* • (*fml*) If someone is **in league with** someone else, they have agreed secretly to do something, esp. something illegal or wrong: *They were in league with their accountants to cheat the government by hiding their real income.*

leak /li:k/ *v* [I/T] (of a liquid or gas) to escape from a hole or crack in a pipe or container, or (of a container) to allow (liquid or gas) to escape • *He heard the sound of dripping and saw water leaking from a pipe overhead.* [I] ○ *The ship ran aground off the coast and began to leak oil.* [T] • To leak is also to give out information privately esp. when people in authority do not want it to be known: *Someone had leaked the news of the ambassador's resignation to the press.* [T]

leak /li:k/ *n* [C] • *Little jets of water shot out of the leaks in her garden hose.* • A leak is also the act of giving out information privately, esp. when people in authority do not want it to be known: *The Justice Department was investigating security leaks.*

leakage /'li:·kɪdʒ/ *n* [U] the condition of leaking • *The cause of the leakage of the chemical is under investigation, he said.*

leaky /'li:·ki/ *adj* [-er/-est only] • *There's a leaky radiator in the bedroom.*

lean SLOPE /li:n/ *v* [I/T] *past* **leaned** /li:nd/ to move your body away from a vertical position so that it is bent forward or resting against something, or to place (something) in a sloping position against something • *The conductor leaned over us and asked for our tickets.* [I always + adv/prep] ○ *She paused for a moment to rest and leaned against a large rock.* [I always + adv/prep] ○ *He leaned the rifle against a tree.* [T] • To **lean over backwards** is to make every effort to do something: *We lean over backwards to be give people with disabilities a chance, she said.*

lean THIN /li:n/ *adj* [-er/-est only] (of a person) thin and in good physical condition • *Her body is lean, taut, athletic.* • When you describe meat as lean, you mean that it does not have much fat in it: *lean hamburger meat* • A lean period is a time during which there is not enough of something, esp. money or food: *It is a particularly lean year for science funding.* • When you say that a company or business is lean, you mean that it has the fewest employees it needs to do its work.

▢ **lean on** /'-,-/ *v prep* [T] to depend on (someone or something) • *They had leaned on the dictionary as the authority that answered all their questions.*

▢ **lean toward** /'-,-/ *v prep* [T] to be interested in something and be likely to do (a particular activity) • *He said he was leaning toward entering the race for governor.*

leaning /'liː·nɪŋ/ *n* [C usually pl] a tendency to have positive feelings or attitudes about beliefs or opinions of a particular kind • *Conservative groups rated Congressional members for their liberal leanings.*

leap /liːp/ *v* [I/T] *past* **leaped** /liːpt, lept/ or **leapt** /lept/ to make a large jump or sudden movement, or to jump over (something) • *He leaps to his feet when the phone rings.* [I] ○ *Flames were leaping into the sky.* [I] ○ *The dog leaped the fence.* [T] ○ *(fig.) Americans want change, but they don't want to leap into the unknown* (= move quickly into unknown situations). [I] • If your heart leaps, you have a sudden, strong feeling of pleasure or fear: *My heart leaps when I hear his voice.* [I] • If you **leap at** an opportunity, you accept it quickly and eagerly: *I leapt at the chance to go to the concert.* • PIC JUMP

leap /liːp/ *n* [C] a large jump • If something increases **by leaps and bounds**, it increases very quickly: *Church membership is growing by leaps and bounds this year.* • A **leap of faith** is an act of believing something that is not easily believed: *It takes a leap of faith to believe that bankers have your interests at heart.* • A **leap year** happens once every four years and has February 29th as an extra day.

leapfrog /'liːp·frɔːg, -frɑg/ *n* [U] a children's game in which each player jumps over another who is bending over

leapfrog /'liːp·frɔːg, -frɑg/ *v* [I/T] **-gg-** to improve your position by moving quickly past or over something that blocks your way • *We're going to leapfrog the rest of the market in technology.* [T]

leapfrog

learn /lɜrn/ *v* [I/T] to get knowledge or understanding of facts or ideas or of how to do things • *We're learning algebra.* [T] ○ *He's not much of a cook, but he's learning.* [I] ○ *We were shocked when we learned of his death.* [I] ○ *I hope you'll learn from your mistakes .* [I] ○ *I learned to drive when I was 16.* [+ *to* infinitive] ○ *First you must learn how to use this computer.* [+ *wh-* word] • If someone has **learned** their **lesson**, they have suffered from a bad experience and will not do it again: *The kid made a mistake and got arrested, but he's learned his lesson.* • If you **learn** something **the hard way**, you discover what you need to know through experience or by making mistakes.

learned /'lɜr·nəd/ *adj fml* having or showing much knowledge • *a learned scholar*

learner /'lɜr·nər/ *n* [C] • *a fast/slow learner*

learning /'lɜr·nɪŋ/ *n* [U] the activity of getting knowledge • *This technique makes learning fun.* • A **learning disability** is an inability of a child to learn a skill at the expected time because of a problem of development.

lease /liːs/ *v* [T] to use or allow someone else to use (land, property, etc.) for an agreed period of time in exchange for money • *I leased my new car instead of buying it.*

lease /liːs/ *n* [C] • *The lease on this office expires in two years.*

leash /liːʃ/, **lead** *n* [C] a strap, chain, etc., fastened to a dog or other animal, esp. at its collar, in order to lead or control it • *Dogs must be kept on a leash in this park.*

least /liːst/ *adj, adv* [not gradable], *pronoun, superlative of* LITTLE NOT MUCH; less than anything or anyone else; (of) the smallest amount or number • *I'm not the least bit concerned.* ○ *That's the answer I least wanted to hear.* ○ *Which car costs the least?* • **At (the very) least** means not less than: *It will cost at least $1000.* ○ *I'll be gone for two weeks, at the very least.* • **At least** is also used to reduce the effect of a statement: *I can handle it—at least, I think so.* • **At least** is also used to emphasize that something is good in a bad situation: *The car was damaged, but at least he wasn't hurt.* • If you say that something is **the least** you **could do**, you mean you are doing something you feel you must do: *"Do I have to do as he says?" "Yeah, since it's his house, it's the least you can do."* • *No one believed her,* **least of all** *me* (= especially not me). • LP AMOUNTS, COMPARING

leather /'leð·ər/ *n* [U] animal skin that has been treated in order to preserve it and is used to make shoes, bags, clothes, equipment, etc. • *a leather jacket*

leathery /'leð·ə·ri/ *adj* • *His skin was tough and leathery.*

leave GO AWAY /liːv/ *v* [I/T] *past* **left** /left/ to go away from (someone or something that stays in the same place) • *I'll be leaving tomorrow.* [I] ○ *He left the house by the back door.* [T] ○ *The bus leaves (the station) in five minutes.* [I/T] • If you leave a job, you stop working at a place: *He left work in June.* [T] ○ *She's left her husband* (= stopped living with him). [T] • If you leave home, you stop living in your parents' home. [T] • *I've simply decided to quit—let's* **leave it at that** (= not continue discussing it).

leave NOT TAKE /liːv/ *v* [T] *past* **left** /left/ to not take (something) with you • *I mistakenly left my checkbook at home.* ○ *Hurry up or you'll get left behind the other hikers.* • You can leave something somewhere for a purpose: *I've left dinner for you on the stove.* • If you leave something to someone after you die, you have arranged for them to receive it then: *She left all her money to her children.*

leave CAUSE TO STAY /liːv/ *v* [T] *past* **left** /left/ to allow or cause (something) to stay in a particular place, position, or state • *The dog left muddy tracks on the carpet.* ○ *He left a message for me at the office.* ○ *Leave the window open.* ○ *Her rudeness left us all speechless.* ○ *He left the engine running.* • If you leave some activity that involves work, you wait before you do it: *I'll leave the cleaning for tomorrow.* • If something **leaves a bad taste (in** your **mouth)**, you have an unpleasant memory of it: *Our experience there left a bad taste in my mouth.* • Something that **leaves a lot to be desired** is not as good as it could be. • If something **leaves** you **cold**, it does not make you feel interested or excited: *His kisses leave me cold.* • If you **leave** someone **hanging**, you keep them waiting for your decision about something. • If you **leave** someone **high and dry**, they are forced to deal with an inconvenient or difficult situation: *They pulled out of the deal at the last minute, leaving us high and dry.* • If you **leave** someone **in the lurch**, you do not do what you had promised you would do for them: *He said he would help with the rent, but he left me in the lurch.* • To **leave** your **mark** is to have a permanent effect: *The heart attack left its mark on him, and he was never quite the same after it.* • If you feel **left out (in the cold)**, you feel you do not belong to a particular group of people and are not wanted by them. • To **leave well enough alone** is to allow something to stay as it is because doing more might make things worse: *I could rewrite it, but I decided to leave well enough alone.*

leave MAKE AVAILABLE /liːv/ *v* [T] *past* **left** /left/ to make (something) available after some part has been taken or used • *There are only four cookies—please leave one for me.* ○ *Five from twelve leaves seven* (= Seven is the result of taking five from twelve). • If something is **left (over)**, it was not previously used or eaten: *There's some pasta left over from dinner.*

leave GIVE RESPONSIBILITY /liːv/ *v* [T] *past* **left** /left/ to allow someone to make a choice or decision about (something), or to make (someone) responsible for something • *Leave it to me—I'll see what I can do.* ○ *I'll leave it up to you to choose the gift.* • If you are **left to** your **own devices**, you are allowed to make your own decisions about what to do.

leave VACATION /liːv/ *n* [U] time permitted away from work, esp. for a medical condition or illness or for some other special purpose • *maternity leave* • *She asked for a* **leave of absence** (= a permitted period of time away from work) *to care for her ailing father.*

leave PERMISSION /liːv/ *n* [U] *fml* permission to do something • *He took it without my leave.*

□ **leave** *obj* **alone, leave alone** *obj* /'--'-/ *v adv* [M] • If you **leave** someone or something **alone**, you don't touch or annoy them: *You shouldn't pick at the scab, just leave it alone.* ○ *He won't leave me alone—he's always calling.*

□ **leave out** *obj*, **leave** *obj* **out** /'-'-/ *v adv* [M] to fail to include (something); omit • *You left out the best parts of the story.*

leaves /liːvz/ *pl of* LEAF

lecherous /'letʃ·ə·rəs/ *adj disapproving* (esp. of men) always interested in sex

lectern /'lek·tərn/, **podium** *n* [C] a tall, narrow piece of furniture having a sloping part that holds a book or papers to be read from while standing

lecture FORMAL TALK /'lek·tʃər/ *n* [C] a formal, prepared talk given to a group of people, esp. students • *a lecture on astronomy* • Compare SEMINAR.

lecture /'lek·tʃər/ *v* [I] • *She's lecturing on the geology of the region.*

lecturer /'lek·tʃə·rər/ *n* [C]

lecture CRITICISM /'lek·tʃər/ *n* [C] a serious talk given to advise and criticize someone • *She gave him a lecture about his table manners.*

lecture /'lek·tʃər/ *v* [T] • *He lectured me on the need to keep accurate records.*

led /led/ *past simple and past participle of* LEAD

ledge /ledʒ/ *n* [C] a narrow, flat area like a shelf that sticks out from a building, cliff, or other vertical surface • *a window ledge*

ledger /'ledʒ·ər/ *n* [C] a book in which items are regularly recorded, esp. business activities and money received or paid

leech /liːtʃ/ *n* [C] a fat WORM that lives in wet places and fastens itself onto the bodies of humans and animals to suck their blood • (*disapproving*) A leech is also a person who gets money or support from someone, giving little or nothing in return.

leek /liːk/ *n* [C] a vegetable in the onion family with long, straight leaves that are white at the bottom and dark green at the top

leer /lɪr/ *v* [I] to look at someone in an unpleasant way that suggests sexual interest or bad intentions • *He leered at her and made lewd comments.*

leeway /'liː·weɪ/ *n* [U] freedom to act within certain limits • *The law gives companies more leeway to decide whether to accept or reject an offer.* [+ *to* infinitive] • Leeway is also additional time or money: *Homeowners need some leeway to buy a new house after they sell the old one.*

left DIRECTION /left/ *adj, adv* [not gradable], *n* [C/U] (in or toward) a position that is the opposite of right and on the side of your body that contains the heart • *He injured his left eye.* ○ *Turn left at the stop sign.* ○ *Make a left at the corner.* [C] ○ *My sister is third from the left in the back row.* [U] • If someone or something is **out in left field**, they are strange, unusual, or completely wrong: *His ideas look like they're from out in left field to me.* • **Left-hand** means on or to the left: *the left-hand side* • Someone who is **left-handed** or is a **left-hander** uses their left hand to write with and to do most things. • Something **left-handed** is designed to be used by such a person or is done with the left hand: *a left-handed pitch* • USAGE: The opposite of left is RIGHT DIRECTION.

left POLITICS /left/ *n* [U] political groups that believe governments should provide a higher level of social services and support laws to bring about greater economic and social equality • If someone is **left-wing**, they support the political opinions of the left, and a **left-winger** is a person who has these beliefs. • Compare RIGHT POLITICS.

left LEAVE /left/ *past simple and past participle of* LEAVE

leftover /ˌlef.tou·vər/ *adj* [not gradable] that has not been eaten or used during a meal • *left-over meatloaf*
leftovers /ˈlef.tou·vərz/ *pl n* • *We ate the leftovers cold the next day.*

leg BODY PART /leg/ *n* [C/U] one of the parts of a human or animal body that is used for standing or walking, or one of the thin, vertical parts on which a piece of furniture stands • *He broke his leg skiing.* [C] ○ *The table has carved legs.* [C] ○ *We had leg of lamb for dinner.* [U] • The leg of a piece of clothing is the part you put your leg into. [C] • **Legroom** is the amount of space available for your legs when seated.

leggy /ˈleg·i/ *adj* [*-er/-est* only] having long legs • *a leggy redhead*

leg STAGE /leg/ *n* [C] a part of a trip, competition, or activity that has several stages • *the last leg of the race*

legacy /ˈleg·ə·si/ *n* [C] something that is a result of historical events • *the bitter legacy of a civil war* • A legacy is also money or property left to a person by someone who has died.

legal /ˈliː·gəl/ *adj* [not gradable] connected with or allowed by the law • *the legal profession* ○ *the legal right to vote* • A **legal holiday** is a day on which government offices and many businesses are closed. • **Legal tender** is the official money used in a country.
legally /ˈliː·gə·li/ *adv* • *The contract is legally binding.*
legality /liːˈgæl·ət·i/ *n* [U] the fact or state of being allowed by law • *Attorneys questioned the legality of the police officer's actions.*
legalize /ˈliː·gəˌlaɪz/ *v* [T] to allow by law; make legal
legalization /ˌliː·gə·ləˈzeɪ·ʃən/ *n* [U] • *the legalization of marijuana*

legend STORY /ˈledʒ·ənd/ *n* [C/U] an old story or set of stories from ancient times, or the stories that people tell about a famous event or person • *Cajun legend suggests that white alligators are a symbol of prosperity.* [U]
legendary /ˈledʒ·ənˌder·i/ *adj* [not gradable] • *legendary tales*

legend FAME /ˈledʒ·ənd/ *n* [C] someone who is very famous and admired, usually because of their ability in a particular area • *Louis Armstrong is a jazz legend.*
legendary /ˈledʒ·ənˌder·i/ *adj* • *the legendary magician Houdini*

legend EXPLANATION /ˈledʒ·ənd/ *n* [C] the words written on or next to a picture, map, coin, etc., that explain what it is about or what the symbols on it mean

leggings /ˈleg·ɪŋz/ *pl n* tight pants made from a material that stretches easily, usually worn by women

leggy /ˈleg·i/ *adj* • See at LEG BODY PART.

legible /ˈledʒ·ə·bəl/ *adj* (of writing or print) able to be read easily • *The letter was faded and barely legible.*
legibly /ˈledʒ·ə·bli/ *adv*

legion /ˈliː·dʒən/ *n* [C] a very large group of soldiers who form part of an army, esp. of an ancient Roman army, or any large group of people • *Legions of fans attended the concert.*

legislate /ˈledʒ·əˌsleɪt/ *v* [I] to make laws • *to legislate against cigarette advertising*
legislation /ˌledʒ·əˈsleɪ·ʃən/ *n* [U] a law or set of laws that is being created • *New legislation offers a tax break for young families.*
legislative /ˈledʒ·əˌsleɪt·ɪv/ *adj* [not gradable] relating to the making of laws • *Congress is the legislative branch of government.*
legislator /ˈledʒ·əˌsleɪt·ər/ *n* [C] a member of an elected group of people who have the power to make or change laws
legislature /ˈledʒ·əˌsleɪ·tʃər/ *n* [C] an elected group of people who have the power to make and change laws in a state or country

legitimate /ləˈdʒɪt·ə·mət/, *infml short form* **legit** /ləˈdʒɪt/ *adj* allowable according to law, or reasonable and acceptable • *a legitimate tax deduction* ○ *legitimate concerns/questions*
legitimacy /ləˈdʒɪt·ə·mə·si/ *n* [U]
legitimize /ləˈdʒɪt·əˌmaɪz/, **legitimate** /ləˈdʒɪt·əˌmeɪt/ *v* [T] to make (something) legal or acceptable

legwork /ˈleg·wɜrk/ *n* [U] *infml* practical work that needs to be done, as in gathering information, and that usually involves a lot of walking from place to place • *Months of legwork enabled detectives to uncover a new lead.*

leisure /ˈliː·ʒər, ˈleʒ·ər/ *n* [U] the time when you are free from work or other duties and can relax • *She has a limited amount of leisure time.* • *You can study the documents* **at your leisure** (= when you want to and have the time).
leisurely /ˈliː·ʒər·li, ˈleʒ·ər-/ *adj* • *a leisurely stroll on the beach*

lemon /ˈlem·ən/ *n* [C/U] a yellow, oval fruit whose juice has a sour taste • (*infml*) A lemon is a device or machine that does not work well: *That car I bought is a real lemon.* [C]

lemonade /ˌlem·əˈneɪd/ *n* [U] a drink made with the juice of lemons, water, and sugar

lend /lend/ *v* [T] *past* **lent** /lent/ to give (something) to someone for a short period of time, expecting it to be given back • *Can you lend me a few dollars till payday?* • If you **lend a hand**, you provide help: *Marcia has taught her children to lend a hand when it comes to cleaning up after meals.* • (*fml*) If something **lends itself to** something, it can be considered in that way: *The story lends itself to different interpretations.*

lender /'len·dər/ n [C] a person or business, such as a bank, that lends money

length DISTANCE /leŋθ, lenθ/ n [C/U] the measurement of something from end to end or along its longest side, or a measurement of a particular part of something • *a length of rope* [C] ○ *The boat is 20 feet in length.* [U] • The length of a piece of writing, such as a book or story, is a measure of the material it contains: *The length of the poem was 30 lines.* [U]

lengthen /'leŋ·θən, 'len-/ v [I/T] to make (something) longer, or to become longer • *I'll have to lengthen this skirt.* [T] ○ *In the late afternoon, the shadows of the haystacks lengthened.* [I]

lengthwise /'leŋθ,wɑɪz, 'lenθ-/ adv [not gradable] in the direction of the longest side • *Cut the pickles lengthwise.*

length TIME /leŋθ, lenθ/ n [U] an amount of time • *The movie is nearly three hours in length.* ○ *George went on about his illnesses at great/some length* (= for a long time).

lengthen /'leŋ·θən, 'len-/ v [I/T] to make (something) take longer to happen, or to become longer • *There is a plan to lengthen the summer theater workshop to eight weeks.* [T]

lengthy /'leŋ·θi, 'len-/ adj [-er/-est only] taking a long time • *a lengthy speech*

lenient /'liːn·jənt/ adj not as severe or strong in punishment or judgment as would be expected • *Some felt that five years in prison was lenient, considering the suffering he had caused.*

leniently /'liːn·jənt·li/ adv

leniency /'liːn·jən·si/ n [U] • *The defense lawyer asked for leniency for her young client.*

lens GLASS /lenz/ n [C] a piece of glass or plastic having a curved surface in order to change the images that are received after going through it, usually to make them larger, smaller, or clearer • *a camera lens* ○ *Her eyeglasses have thick lenses.*

lens EYE /lenz/ n [C] a curved, transparent part of the eye that helps you to see clearly by directing images of light onto the RETINA (= the back surface of the eye)

lent LEND /lent/ past simple and past participle of LEND

Lent RELIGION /lent/ n [U] in Christian religions, the 40 days before Easter

lentil /'lent·əl/ n [C] a small, round, flat seed, cooked and eaten in soups and other dishes

Leo /'liː·oʊ/ n [C/U] pl **Leos** the fifth sign of the ZODIAC, covering the period July 23 to August 22 and represented by a lion, or a person born during this period

leopard /'lep·ərd/ n [C] a large, wild cat that has yellow fur with black spots and that lives in Africa and south Asia

leotard /'liː·ə,tɑrd/ n [C] a piece of clothing that fits tightly over the body from the shoulders to the tops of the legs, worn esp. by dancers and people exercising

leper /'lep·ər/ n [C] a person who has LEPROSY (= a disease of the nerves and skin)

leprosy /'lep·rə·si/ n [U] an infectious disease that damages a person's nerves and skin

lesbian /'lez·bi·ən/ n [C] a woman who is sexually attracted to other women

lesion /'liː·ʒən/ n [C] *medical* an injury to a person's body or to an organ

less SMALLER AMOUNT /les/ adv, adj [not gradable], *comparative of* LITTLE NOT MUCH; a smaller amount of (something), to a smaller degree, or not as much • *We've got to spend less money.* ○ *It was less than a mile to the nearest gas station.* ○ *She had less reason to complain than I.* • If something happens **less and less**, it gradually becomes smaller in degree or amount: *I seem to see her less and less.* ○ *There were no less than* (= as many as) *a thousand people buying tickets.* ○ *I think he was less than honest* (= not completely honest). • LP AMOUNTS, COMPARING

lessen /'les·ən/ v [I/T] to become or make (something) smaller in amount or degree • *Keeping your weight down can lessen the risk of heart disease.* [T]

lesser /'les·ər/ adj [not gradable] not as great in size, amount, or importance as something else • *Texas and, to a lesser degree, Oklahoma will be affected by the drought.* • If something is **the lesser of two evils** it is bad, but not as bad as something else.

less SUBTRACT /les/ prep MINUS SUBTRACTION; after subtracting • *$30, less the discount of 15%, is $25.50.*

lesson /'les·ən/ n [C] a period of time during which something is taught • *Have you ever taken piano lessons?* • A lesson is also a useful piece of information learned through experience: *Losing his job was a lesson he never forgot.*

let ALLOW /let/ v [T] **letting**; past **let** to allow (something to happen or someone to do something) by giving permission or by not doing anything to stop it from happening • *Fraya's parents let her go to the movie.* ○ *He decided to let his hair grow long.* ○ *She opened the door and let me in* (= allowed me to enter). ○ *After questioning him for six hours, the police finally let him go* (= released him). • If you **let** someone or something **alone**/**let** someone or something **be**, you don't touch them or annoy them: *Why don't you let her alone?* • If you **let go** or **let** your **hair down**, you behave more freely than usual and enjoy yourself: *I got out on the dance floor and let myself go.* • If you **let off steam**, you do something to release anger or energy: *She jogs after work to let off steam.*

let CAUSE /let/ v [T] **letting**, past **let** to cause (something) to happen or to be in a particular condition, or to cause (someone) to understand something • *He let the pool empty.* ○ *Let me know if you need help.* ○ *He let out a shout* (= He shouted). • **Let alone** is used to say that something is not at all likely to happen, because something more likely has never happened: *Brian would never even read a newspaper, let alone a book.* • To **let** something **be known** is to make certain that people are aware of it: *She let it be known that she did not want to run again for Congress.* • To **let go** or to **let go of** something is to stop holding it: *When you try to rescue someone who is drowning, they may panic and hit you, but you just can't let go of them.* • If you **let** someone **have it**, you attack them, either with words or physically: *When Joe finally got home three hours late, Lea let him have it.*

let SUGGEST /let/ *v* [T] used to express a suggestion that includes you and another person or people; used to give an order or to make a request • *Let's ask John and Rebecca over to dinner tonight.* • **Let's face it** (= We should accept the truth), *you're never going to be a great artist.* • You say **let's see** or **let me see** when you want to think carefully about something or are trying to remember something. • USAGE: Let's means let us, but you would never say "let us" except in a formal situation: *Let us pray.*

let RENT /let/ *v* [T] **letting**, *past* **let** *fml* to allow (housing) to be lived in or used by someone in exchange for a payment made regularly • *She has a room to let in her house.*

□ **let down** *obj*, **let** *obj* **down** /'-'-/ *v adv* [M] to cause (someone) to be disappointed, often because you have failed to do what you have promised • *You'll be there tomorrow—you won't let me down, will you?*

letdown /'let·daʊn/ *n* [C usually sing] • *It was quite a letdown when Joyce only got a grade of C on the final exam.*

□ **let** *obj* **in on** /-'-,-/ *v adv prep* [T] to tell (someone) something, esp. private information, that others already know • *My children never want to let me in on what they do in school.*

□ **let off** *obj*, **let** *obj* **off** /'-'-/ *v adv* [M] to fail to punish (someone) when they expect to be punished, or to fail to punish (someone) severely enough • *The boys were let off with a reprimand.*

□ **let on** /-'-'/ *v adv* [I] to tell other people about something that you know, esp. when it is a secret • *If he did know the truth, he didn't let on.*

□ **let out** FINISH /-'-/ *v adv* [I] (of a class of school) to end or be finished • *My history class lets out at 4:15.* ○ *When does your school let out for the summer?*

□ **let out** *obj* WIDEN , **let** *obj* **out** /'-'-/ *v adv* [M] to make (a piece of clothing) wider or larger by changing where it is sewn or adding more cloth • *Can this skirt be let out?*

□ **let up** /-'-/ *v adv* [I] (esp. of something unpleasant) to become less strong or stop • *When the rain lets up we'll go for a walk.*

letup /'let·ʌp/ *n* [U] • *Since the mall was built, there's been no letup in traffic.*

lethal /'liː·θəl/ *adj* able to cause or causing death; extremely dangerous • *a lethal weapon*

lethargic /ləˈθɑr·dʒɪk/ *adj* lacking in energy; feeling unwilling or unable to do anything

lethargy /'leθ·ər·dʒi/ *n* [U]

let's /lets/ *contraction of* let us • See at LET SUGGEST

letter MESSAGE /'let·ər/ *n* [C] a written or printed message from one person to another, usually put in an envelope and delivered as mail • *I got a letter from the bank this morning.* • (*Br*) A **letterbox** is a **mailbox**. See at MAIL. • A **letter carrier** is a person who works for the government service responsible for delivering mail to homes and offices. • A **letterhead** is the printing at the top of a piece of writing paper telling the name and address of the person or business sending the letter.

AUTOMATED DOCUMENT SYSTEMS
1324 Locust Street • Philadelphia, PA 19107 • (215) 735-4254

letterhead

letter SYMBOL /'let·ər/ *n* [C] any of the set of symbols used to write a language, representing a sound in the language • *She wrote her name on the board in large letters.* • LP SILENT LETTERS

lettering /'let·ə·rɪŋ/ *n* [U] written letters • *The perfume comes in a black box with gold lettering.*

lettuce /'let·əs/ *n* [U] a plant of large, green leaves, eaten raw in salads

letup /'let·ʌp/ *n* [U] • See at LET UP.

leukemia /luˈkiː·miː·ə/ *n* [U] a disease in which the body produces too many white blood cells, causing weakness and sometimes leading to death

level HORIZONTAL /'lev·əl/ *adj* (of a surface) not rising or falling or higher on one side, but even in all directions; horizontal or flat • *The table wobbles because the floor is not level.* • Something that is level with something else is at the same height: *The top of the tree is level with his bedroom window.* • A level spoon or cup is filled with something just to the top edge. • If you speak in a level voice, you speak in a calm and controlled way. • If someone is **on the level**, they are being honest or speaking truthfully: *I know he's lied to you before, but I really think he's on the level this time.* • With the quality of high schools varying so much, how can everyone start college on a **level playing field** (= with all the same advantages and disadvantages)? • If you describe someone as **level-headed**, you mean that they are calm and able to deal easily with difficult situations.

level /'lev·əl/ *v* [T] to make (something) level • *We had to level the backyard before putting up the pool.* • To level (buildings or other structures) is to destroy them by causing them to fall down: *Her grandfather survived the 1906* *earthquake that leveled San Francisco.* • (*infml*) To level (someone) is to cause them to fall down: *Giordano leveled him with a punch to the jaw.* • If something **levels off**, it stops rising or falling: *Housing prices have leveled off this year.* ○ *The plane climbed to 36,000 feet before leveling off.*

level /'lev·əl/ *n* [C] a tool containing a tube of liquid with an air bubble in it, which shows whether a surface is horizontal by the position of the bubble

level POSITION /'lev·əl/ *n* [C/U] a particular position, degree, or amount of something, esp. compared with other possible positions, degrees, or amounts • *The water level in the lake is higher after a heavy rain.* [C] ○ *The big debate is whether more decisions should be made at the local level or at the national level.* [U] ○ *He achieved a high level of skill as an interpreter.* [C] ○ *We publish a dictionary for intermediate level students.* [U] • A level is also one of several floors at different heights in a building: *The reception area is on the ground level.* [C]

level AIM /'lev·əl/ *v* [T] to aim or direct (something, esp. a weapon or criticism) at someone or something • *She leveled the gun at me.* ○ *Allegations of brutality were leveled against three police officers.*

◻**level with** /'--,-/ *v prep* [T] to tell (someone) the truth, esp. when it may be unpleasant • *I'll level with you—the salary is not particularly good.*

lever /'lev·ər, 'liː·vər/ *n* [C] a handle that you move to control the operation of a machine, or a bar, moving around a fixed point, that when pressed down at one end can move or lift something at the other end • *He pushed the lever into the "on" position and started the machine.*

leverage /'lev·ə·rɪdʒ, 'liː·və-/ *n* [U] the power to influence results • *financial/political leverage* ○ *The US has very little leverage in that part of the world.*

leverage /'lev·ə·rɪdʒ, 'liː·və-/ *v* [T] specialized to use (borrowed money) for investments, esp. in order to buy a large enough part of a business so that you can control it • *They can leverage a very small investment into millions of dollars.*

levity /'lev·əṭ·i/ *n* [U] amusement or lack of seriousness • *a moment of levity*

levy /'lev·i/ *n* [C] an amount of money, such as a tax, that you have to pay to a government or organization • *A levy was imposed on wine imports.*

levy /'lev·i/ *v* [T] • *They are going to levy a new tax on cigarettes.*

lewd /luːd/ *adj* [-er/-est only] (esp. of behavior or speech) sexual in an obvious and socially unacceptable way • *He was accused of making lewd remarks and inappropriately touching women subordinates.*

lexicon /'lek·sə,kɑn/ *n* [C] all the words used

in a particular language or subject, or a dictionary

liability /ˌlɑɪ·ə'bɪl·əṭ·i/ *n* [C/U] the responsibility of a person, business, or organization to pay or give up something of value • *He denies any liability in the accident.* [U] ○ *The business has liabilities of $5 million.* [C usually pl] • A liability is also anything that hurts your chances of success or that causes difficulties: *Not having our own delivery trucks is a liability in our business.* [C] • Compare ASSET.

liable LIKELY /'lɑɪ·ə·bəl, 'lɑɪ·bəl/ *adj* [+ *to* infinitive] likely to do, happen, or experience something • *If you don't take care of yourself, you're liable to get sick.* ○ *He's liable to say anything that comes into his head.*

liable RESPONSIBLE /'lɑɪ·ə·bəl/ *adj* [not gradable] *law* having legal responsibility for something • *He is still liable for repaying his student loan.*

liaison /liː'eɪ,zɑn, 'liː·ə-/ *n* [C/U] communication between groups and the beneficial relationship that this creates, or a person who does the communicating between the groups • *There is an unfortunate lack of liaison between the departments.* [U] • A liaison is also a sexual relationship, esp. between two people not married to each other. [C]

liar /'lɑɪ·ər/ *n* [C] a person who has just told a lie or who regularly lies

libel /'lɑɪ·bəl/ *n* [C/U] a piece of writing that says bad, false, and harmful things about a person, or the legal claim you make when you accuse someone in court of writing such things about you • *The whole story was a vicious libel.* [C] ○ *Angry at what the newspaper had printed, she sued for libel.* [U] • Compare SLANDER.

libel /'lɑɪ·bəl/ *v* [T] **-l-** • *She libeled him by writing that he had been a drug dealer.*

libelous /'lɑɪ·bə·ləs/ *adj* • *libelous articles*

liberal OPEN TO THE NEW /'lɪb·ə·rəl/ *adj* allowing many different types of beliefs or behavior • *a liberal society/church/person* • The **liberal arts** are college or university subjects, including history, languages, and literature, that are not technical. • Compare CONSERVATIVE AGAINST CHANGE.

liberalize /'lɪb·ə·rə,lɑɪz/ *v* [I/T] • *They have plans to liberalize the prison system* (= make it less severe). [T]

liberalization /ˌlɪb·ə·rə·lə'zeɪ·ʃən/ *n* [U] • *political/trade liberalization*

liberal POLITICS /'lɪb·ə·rəl/ *adj* tending to emphasize the need to make new laws when necessary because of changing conditions and to depend on the government to provide social services • *a liberal policy/position* • Compare CONSERVATIVE POLITICS.

liberal /'lɪb·ə·rəl/ *n* [C] • *Liberals in Congress support the bill.*

liberalism /'lɪb·ə·rə,lɪz·əm/ *n* [U] • *She opposes liberalism and big-government solutions.*

liberal GENEROUS /'lɪb·ə·rəl/ *adj* giving or given generously • *Some merchants offer very liberal return policies, but others are strict.*

liberally /'lɪb·ə·rə·li/ *adv* • *The food was liberally seasoned with salt.*

liberal NOT EXACT /'lɪb·ə·rəl/ *adj* without attention to or interest in small details • *They're not as liberal as we are in our interpretation of the Bible.*

liberate /'lɪb·ə,reɪt/ *v* [T] to release (someone) from control, duties, limits, or prison • *Muñoz Rivera helped liberate Puerto Rico from Spain.*

liberated /'lɪb·ə,reɪt̬·əd/ *adj* • *liberated nations/people*

liberation /,lɪb·ə'reɪ·ʃən/ *n* [U] • *Summer vacation means liberation for school children but not for their parents.*

liberty /'lɪb·ərt̬·i/ *n* [C/U] the freedom to live as you wish and go where you want • *individual liberties* [C] ○ *Our group is fighting for independence, liberty, democracy, and peace.* [U] • If someone is **at liberty** to do something, they have permission to do it: *I'm not at liberty to discuss this with you.*

Libra /'liː·brə/ *n* [C/U] the seventh sign of the ZODIAC, covering the period September 23 to October 23 and represented by a pair of measuring SCALES, or a person born during this period

library /'laɪ,brer·i, 'laɪ·brər·i/ *n* [C] a building, room, or organization that has a collection esp. of books, musical recordings, and electronically stored information for people to read, use, or borrow • *a library book* ○ *a public library*

librarian /laɪ'brer·iː·ən/ *n* [C] a person who works in a library, esp. someone with special training for this type of work

libretto /lə'bret̬·oʊ/ *n* [C] *pl* **librettos** *specialized* the words that are sung or spoken in an opera or similar musical performance

lice /laɪs/ *pl of* LOUSE

license DOCUMENT /'laɪ·səns/ *n* [C] an official document that gives you permission to own, do, or use something • *a gun/fishing/export/driver's/liquor license* • A **license plate** is the metal sign with numbers on it that you to attach to the front or back of your car. PIC CAR

license /'laɪ·səns/ *v* [T] • *She's licensed to teach elementary school.*

license FREEDOM /'laɪ·səns/ *n* [U] the freedom to break rules or principles, or to change facts, esp. when producing a literary or artistic work • *poetic/artistic license*

lick MOVE TONGUE /lɪk/ *v* [T] to move the tongue across the surface of something as a way of eating it or making it wet or clean • *to lick a stamp/lollipop* [T] • If you **lick** your **lips**, you feel and show pleasure at the thought of something: *She was licking her lips in anticipation of getting the prize money.* • If you **lick** your **wounds**, you spend time getting back your strength or happiness after a defeat or bad experience: *Farmers were licking their wounds after crop prices dropped by 50%.*

lick /lɪk/ *n* [C] • *Can I have a lick of your ice cream cone?*

lick DEFEAT /lɪk/ *v* [T] *infml* to defeat (someone or something), or to solve (a difficult problem) • *He has licked the cancer.*

licking /'lɪk·ɪŋ/ *n* [C] *infml* • *Our team really gave them a licking last night.*

lick SMALL AMOUNT /lɪk/ *n* [C] *infml* a small amount • *Chuck couldn't read a lick.* • If you give something **a lick and a promise**, you do it quickly and carelessly.

licorice /'lɪk·ə·rɪʃ/ *n* [U] the dried root of a plant used for flavoring food, particularly candy, or candy with this flavor

lid /lɪd/ *n* [C] a cover that can be lifted up or removed from a container • If you **put/keep a lid on** something, you keep it under control: *We've got to keep a lid on our credit-card purchases.*

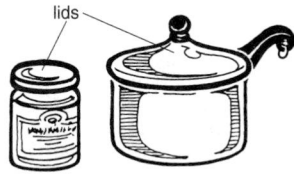

lids

lie POSITION /laɪ/ *v* **lying** /'laɪ·ɪŋ/ *or not standard* **laying** /'leɪ·ɪŋ/, *past simple* **lay** /leɪ/ *or not standard* **laid** /leɪd/, *past part* **lain** /leɪn/ to be in or move into a horizontal position on a surface • *The mechanic was lying on his back underneath my car.* [I always + adv/prep] ○ *I love to lie down in front of the fire and read.* [I always + adv/prep] ○ *He lies awake at night, worrying.* [L] • If something **lies** in a particular place, position, condition, or direction it is in that place, position, condition, or direction: *The river lies 40 miles to the south of us.* [I always + adv/prep] ○ *You shouldn't leave that check lying around* (= not in its place). [I always + adv/prep] • *We don't know what* **lies ahead** (= is in the future). [I always + adv/prep] • *I wonder what* **lay behind** *his decision to quit school* (= what caused this decision). • If you **lie low** you hide so you will not be found: *The gunmen were lying low until the sheriff left town.* • USAGE: Compare LAY PUT DOWN.

lie SPEAK FALSELY /laɪ/ *v* [I/T] **lying** /'laɪ·ɪŋ/, *past* **lied** to say something that is not true in order to deceive • *Both witnesses lied to the police about what happened.* [I] ○ *She lied her way past the guards.* [T always + adv/prep] • See also LIAR.

lie /laɪ/ *n* [C] • *Her report is full of lies and misinformation.* • A **lie detector** (also **polygraph**) is a piece of equipment used to try to discover if someone is lying.

lieu /luː/ *n slightly fml* • **In lieu of** means instead of: *Grandma wanted people to make* *donations to a charity in lieu of sending flowers to her funeral.*

lieutenant /lu:'ten·ənt/ *n* [C] a naval officer of middle rank, above an ENSIGN; or a military officer of the lowest rank • A **lieutenant governor** is a state government official whose rank is just below that of governor.

life TIME BEING ALIVE /laɪf/ *n* [C/U] *pl* **lives** /laɪvz/ the period between birth and death, or the state of being alive • *Life is too short to worry about money!* [U] ○ *Cats are supposed to have nine lives.* [C] • Life is also anything that is alive: *animal/plant life* [U] • If you believe in **life after death**, you believe that a person continues to exist in some way after dying. • **Life insurance** is a system in which you make regular payments to an INSURANCE company in exchange for a fixed amount of money that will be paid after you die to someone you chose. • Something that is **lifelong** lasts for the whole of a person's life: *It's so hard to stop smoking when it's been a lifelong habit.* • A **life-size** or **life-sized** work of art is the same size as the person or thing that it represents: *a life-size statue* • **Life support** or a **life-support system** is the equipment used to keep a person alive when they are dangerously ill. • Something that is **life-threatening** can cause death: *a life-threatening experience/illness* • A **lifetime** is the period of time during which someone lives or something exists: *The watch is high quality and should last a lifetime.*

lifeless /'laɪf·fləs/ *adj* dead or appearing to be dead • *a lifeless body* ○ *(fig.) The performance was boring and lifeless* (= lacking interest or energy).

lifelike /'laɪf·flaɪk/ *adj* seeming real or seeming to be alive • *The mask was so lifelike it was frightening.*

life EXPERIENCE /laɪf/ *n* [C/U] a particular type or part of someone's experience • *She appreciates life in the United States.* [U] ○ *A vacation is a pleasant change from daily/everyday life.* [U] ○ *He rarely talks about his private/sex life.* [C] • A **lifestyle** is the particular way a person or group decides to live and the values and ideas that they support in this way of living: *a healthy/gay/single lifestyle*

life TIME SOMETHING WORKS /laɪf/ *n* [U] the period during which a machine or object that produces power works • *The newer batteries have a much longer life—up to 100 hours.*

life ENERGY /laɪf/ *n* [U] energy or enthusiasm • *The show was full of life.*

lifeblood /'laɪf·blʌd/ *n* [U] the thing that is most important to the continuing success and existence of something else • *Tourism is the lifeblood of Hawaii's economy.*

lifeboat /'laɪf·boʊt/ *n* [C] a large boat that is kept ready to take out to sea and save people who are in danger, or a smaller boat kept on a ship for people to leave in if the ship is not safe or might sink

lifeguard /'laɪf·ɡɑrd/ *n* [C] a person on a beach or at a swimming pool whose job is to make certain that the swimmers are safe and to save them if they are in danger

life jacket /'laɪf·dʒæk·ət/, **life vest** /'laɪf·vest/ *n* [C] a piece of equipment that looks like a jacket without sleeves and that is filled with air or light material designed to help someone float if they fall into the water

lifeline /'laɪf·flaɪn/ *n* [C] something, esp. a way of getting help, on which you depend • *Airplanes are this Alaskan town's lifeline.*

life preserver /'laɪf·prɪˌzɜr·vər/ *n* [C] a large ring or sleeveless jacket made of material that floats and that you can put around your chest to keep you from sinking in the water

lift RAISE /lɪft/ *v* [I/T] to move (something) from a lower to a higher position • *I can't lift you up—you're a big boy now!* [T] ○ *The top of the stool lifts off* (= can be removed) *so you can store things in it.* [I always + adv/prep] ○ *She lifted the baby out of her chair.* [T] ○ *(fig.) Nothing, it seemed, could lift his spirits* (= make him feel happier). [T] • *He just watches TV all evening and never **lifts a finger*** (= makes any effort) *to help with the dishes.*

lift /lɪft/ *n* [C] • *(fig.) She'd been feeling depressed, but hearing that she got the job gave her spirits a lift* (= made her happier). [C] • *(Br)* A lift is an ELEVATOR. • **Liftoff** is the moment when a space vehicle leaves the ground.

lift JOURNEY /lɪft/ *n* [C] *infml* a free trip in another person's vehicle, esp. a car • *Can I give you a lift home?*

lift GO AWAY /lɪft/ *v* [I] (of fog or rain) to go away until none is left • *The morning mist had lifted and the sun was shining.*

lift END /lɪft/ *v* [T] to end (a rule or law) • *They finally lifted the ban on baggy jeans at my school.*

lift STEAL /lɪft/ *v* [T] *infml* to steal (something) • *He lifted whole paragraphs verbatim from my book.*

ligament /'lɪɡ·ə·mənt/ *n* [C] any of the strong strips of tissue in the body that connect various bones together, that limit movements in joints, and that support muscles and other tissue • *She tore a ligament in her knee while she was playing basketball.*

light ENERGY /laɪt/ *n* [C/U] the energy from the sun or fire and from electrical devices that allows you to see clearly • *Light was streaming through the windows.* [U] ○ *The light was so bright that it hurt my eyes.* [U] • A light is also anything which provides light, esp. an electric LAMP: *Don't forget to turn off the lights when you leave.* [C] • A light is also a **traffic light**: *Let's go—you've got a green light.* See at TRAFFIC MOVING THINGS. [C] • **In (the) light of** (= Because of) *the situation, we have no alternative but to raise prices.* • If there is a **light at the end of the tunnel**, there is hope of success, happiness, or help after a long period of difficulty: *After four years as an impoverished grad student, Sujata saw the light at the end of the tunnel.* • A **light bulb** is a rounded glass container that fits into a LAMP and produces light when an electric current is passed through it. • (*specialized*) A **light year** is the distance that light travels in one year. • **Light years** is also an extremely large amount: *When I was a young man, being 50 seemed light years away.*

light /laɪt/ *v* [T] *past* **lit** /lɪt/ *or* **lighted** • *The church was lit with candles for the ceremony.* • *Rosa's face* **lit up** (= She looked happy) *when she saw the presents under the Christmas tree.*

light /laɪt/ *adj* [-er/-est only] • *It was still light out at eight in the evening.*

lighting /ˈlaɪt̬·ɪŋ/ *n* [U] the lights in a room or on a stage, or the effects of those lights • *The lighting in the living room is too dim.*

light FLAME /laɪt/ *n* [U] a device used to produce a flame, such as a MATCH • *Excuse me, have you got a light?*

light /laɪt/ *v* [I/T] *past* **lit** /lɪt/ *or* **lighted** • *I can't get the barbecue to light.* [I] ○ *He lit another cigarette.* [T] • To **light up** is to light a cigarette. • If you **light a fire under** someone, you get them to act quickly or forcefully: *Coach tried to light a fire under the team with a rousing halftime speech.*

lighter /ˈlaɪt̬·ər/ *n* [C] a small device that provides a flame to light esp. tobacco

light NOT HEAVY /laɪt/ *adj* [-er/-est only] having little weight; not heavy • *This suitcase is pretty light.* ○ *Ty's a few pounds lighter than he used to be.* • Clothes that are light are made of thin material which allows you to be cool: *a light summer dress* • A light meal is a small one: *a light snack* • *You're* (**as**) **light as a feather** (= extremely light). • If you are **light-headed**, you feel as if you are spinning around and about to lose your balance: *She'd had a couple of glasses of champagne and was starting to feel lightheaded.*

lighten /ˈlaɪt̬·ən/ *v* [T] to reduce (the weight of something) • *He lost 30 pounds to lighten the burden on his knee.* • To lighten is also to make (an amount of work or a responsibility) less heavy: *To lighten the load, he decided to divide the job between two people.*

light NOT FAT , **lite** /laɪt/ *adj* (of food) having less fat or fewer CALORIES than usual • *light beer*

light NOT SERIOUS /laɪt/ *adj* [-er/-est only] intended to entertain; not serious • *Take along some light reading for the trip.* • **Lighthearted** means happy, amusing, and not serious: *The documentary takes a lighthearted look at the world of filmmaking.*

lighten /ˈlaɪt̬·ən/ *v* [T] to become or make (someone) happier and less anxious • *Being with friends lightened her mood.* • If you tell someone to **lighten up**, you are criticizing

them for being too serious: *Why don't you just relax and enjoy the situation? Lighten up!*

lightly /ˈlaɪt·li/ *adv* without serious consideration • *Bomb threats are never taken lightly by the police.*

light NOT A LOT /laɪt/ *adj* [-er/-est only] not great in strength or amount; slight • *a light rain* ○ *light traffic* ○ *The doctor said it was OK to take light exercise, such as walking.* • A light sentence in prison is a short one. • Alcoholic drinks described as light are not strong in flavor or do not have a lot of alcohol in them: *a light, fruity wine* • A light **eater/drinker/ smoker** eats, drinks, or smokes only a little.

lightly /ˈlaɪt·li/ *adv* • *She patted the dog lightly on the head.* • If food is lightly cooked, it is cooked for only a short time.

light PALE /laɪt/ *adj, adv* [-er/-est only] (of colors) pale • *a light-colored car* ○ *The walls were light green.*

lighten /ˈlaɪt·ən/ *v* [T] • *Do you think he lightens his hair?*

lighter /ˈlaɪt·ər/ *n* • See at LIGHT FLAME.

lighthouse /ˈlaɪt·hɑʊs/ *n* [C] *pl* **lighthouses** /ˈlaɪt·hɑʊ·zəz, -səz/ a tower or other tall structure by the sea with a flashing light that warns ships of dangerous rocks or shows them the way into a port

lighting /ˈlaɪt·ɪŋ/ *n* • See at LIGHT ENERGY.

lightning ELECTRIC FLASH /ˈlaɪt·nɪŋ/ *n* [U] a flash of bright light in the sky produced by electricity moving within or between clouds, or between clouds and the ground • *That tree was struck by lightning in a recent thunderstorm.* • A **lightning bolt/bolt of lightning** is a particular flash of bright light seen in the sky. • A **lightning rod** is a strip of metal that prevents lightning from damaging a building by directing the electricity into the ground. • Someone who is a **lightning rod** attracts criticism or anger that would be directed at someone else: *Darman, more liberal than his colleagues, continues to be the administration's lightning rod, drawing criticism from conservatives.*

lightning FAST /ˈlaɪt·nɪŋ/ *adj* [not gradable] very fast • *She moves at lightning speed.*

lightweight LESS WEIGHT /ˈlaɪt·weɪt/ *adj* (esp. of clothes) weighing little and therefore not warm • *a lightweight jacket*

lightweight NOT IMPORTANT /ˈlaɪt·weɪt/ *adj* (of a person) of little importance, or (of ideas) without serious thought or purpose • *The movie was a lightweight comedy.*

lightweight /ˈlaɪt·weɪt/ *n* [C] • *She's changed from a lightweight into a tough competitor.*

like ENJOY /laɪk/ *v* [T] to enjoy or approve of (something or someone), or to prefer (something) a particular way • *I like your new haircut.* ○ *Do you like fish?* ○ *I like taking my time in the morning.* ○ *I like my music loud.* • Like can be used with "how" when asking for someone's reaction to something: *How do you like* *my new shoes?* • If you do not **like the looks/ sound of** something, it worries you: *"The radio says there'll be rain turning into snow." "Ooh, I don't like the sound of that."*

likable, **likeable** /ˈlaɪ·kə·bəl/ *adj* easy to like • *Cassius was a likable, friendly youngster.*

likes /laɪks/ *pl n* the things that you enjoy • *She knows her children's likes and dislikes.*

liking /ˈlaɪ·kɪŋ/ *n* [U] • *The dessert was a bit sweet to my liking.*

like WANT /laɪk/ *v* [I/T] used with "would" to politely ask for something or say that you want something • *I'd like the chicken soup, please.* [T] ○ *The commissioner would like to say thanks to everyone who's helped.* [+ to infinitive] ○ *Would you like* (= Do you want) *something to drink?* [T]

like SIMILAR TO /laɪk/ *prep, conjunction* similar to; in the same way or manner as • *I've got a sweater just like yours.* ○ *Stop acting like a jerk!* ○ *She looks just like her father.* • If you ask what something is like, you are asking someone to describe it or compare it to something: *What's your new job like?* ○ *What does it taste like?* • So far, everything had worked **like clockwork** (= very regularly). • *Mark's working* **like crazy/mad** (= extremely hard) *to get the house painted by the end of the week.* • If something happens **like gangbusters**, it happens with enthusiasm and great success: *The new sales pitch is working like gangbusters.* • If you do something **like hell**, you do it quickly or with a lot of energy: *We ran like hell.* • If something sells **like hot cakes**, people buy it quickly and eagerly: *The new video game is going like hot cakes.* • If two people, groups, or activities are **like oil and water**, they are not friendly with each other or do not combine easily. • (*infml*) **Like** *I* **said** (= As I have already said), *I'm not interested in buying insurance at the moment.* • If something moves **like wildfire**, it moves quickly in a way that cannot be controlled: *News of the layoffs spread like wildfire through the company.* • People who are **like-minded** share the same opinions, ideas, or interests: *A dedicated football fan herself, she started the magazine for like-minded women.*

like /laɪk/ *n* [U] • *There are courts for tennis and badminton and* **the like** (= similar things). • *We haven't seen* **the likes of** *Muhammad Ali* (= someone who equals him) *since he retired.*

–like /ˌlaɪk/ *combining form* • *with catlike quickness* ○ *a ball-like shape*

likeness /ˈlaɪk·nəs/ *n* [C] a similarity • *Sandy bears a much stronger likeness to her mother than to her father.* • A painting, photograph, or other representation described as a good likeness looks very similar to the person or thing it represents.

like WILLING TO /laɪk/ *prep* willing to; in the mood for • *I don't feel like going out tonight.*

like TYPICAL OF /laɪk/ *prep* typical or characteristic of; to be expected of • *It's not like you to be so quiet—are you all right?*

like SUCH AS /laɪk/ *prep* such as; for example • *I prefer natural fabrics like cotton and wool.* ○ *Alonzo is not the kind of guy who would do something like this.*

likes /laɪks/, **like** /laɪk/ *pl n* • *They're competing with* **the likes of** (= items such as) *IBM and Unisys.*

like AS IF /laɪk/ *prep, conjunction* as if it will or was; in a way that suggests • *It looks like rain.* ○ *It sounds to me like you ought to change jobs.* • *The minute he got paid, he started spending money* **like there's no tomorrow** (= without considering future needs).

like PAUSE /laɪk/ *adv* [not gradable] not standard used in conversation to emphasize what follows, or when you cannot express your exact meaning • *He's, like, really friendly—someone you can talk to.* ○ *It was, like, getting pretty late but I didn't want to go home yet.* • Like is also used in conversation to introduce someone else's words or your own words: *So I'm telling Patti about my date and she's like, No way, and I'm like, It happened.*

likely /ˈlaɪ·kli/ *adj* expected to happen; probable • *If I don't write it down, I'm likely to forget.* [+ to infinitive] • *"He said he got them free from some guy he knows." "(That's)* **a likely story** (= I don't believe that)*!"*

likely /ˈlaɪ·kli/ *adv* probably • *I'll most likely get there at about ten o'clock.*

likelihood /ˈlaɪ·kliː,hʊd/ *n* [U] probability • *There's little likelihood of a compromise.*

likewise /ˈlaɪ·kwaɪz/ *adv* [not gradable] in the same way or manner; similarly • *We put up a fence, and other neighbors did likewise.*

lilac /ˈlaɪ·lək, -læk, -lɑk/ *n* [C] a bush or small tree with sweet-smelling purple or white flowers

lilting /ˈlɪl·tɪŋ/ *adj* (of a voice or a piece of music) rising and falling in a regular or rhythmic way • *"It's about time you showed up," he says to Eddie in a lilting, teasing voice.*

lily /ˈlɪl·i/ *n* [C] a plant with large, usually bell-shaped flowers on long stems

lima bean /ˈlaɪ·mə,biːn/ *n* [C] an edible, flat, pale green bean

limb ARM OR LEG /lɪm/ *n* [C] *slightly fml* an arm or leg of a person or animal, or an animal's wing

limb BRANCH /lɪm/ *n* [C] a large branch of a tree

limber /ˈlɪm·bər/ *adj* able to bend and move easily • *Kirsty had the lithe, limber body of a dancer.*

limber up (*obj*), **limber** (*obj*) **up** /ˈ--ˈ-/ *v adv* [I/M] to stretch your muscles by exercise esp. in preparation for sports • *We limber up with a few tosses back and forth.* [I]

limbo /ˈlɪm·boʊ/ *n* [U] • If someone or something is **in limbo**, they are in a situation where they do not know what will happen or when something will happen: *She refused to answer and kept him in limbo for weeks.*

lime FRUIT /laɪm/ *n* [C/U] a green, oval fruit whose juice has a sour taste

lime CHEMICAL /laɪm/ *n* [U] a white powdery substance used in building materials and to improve earth for crops

limelight /'laɪm·laɪt/ *n* [U] public attention and interest • *He always tried to avoid the limelight.*

limerick /'lɪm·ə·rɪk/ *n* [C] a humorous poem with five lines, the first two lines having the same final sound as the last line

limit /'lɪm·ət/ *n* [C] the greatest amount, number, or level allowed or possible • *There's a limit to her patience.* ○ *Two cups of coffee are my limit.* ○ *Spending limits were imposed by the mayor.*

limit /'lɪm·ət/ *v* [T] to control (something) so that it is not greater than a particular amount, number, or level • *I have to limit my talk to 20 minutes.*

limitation /ˌlɪm·əˈteɪ·ʃən/ *n* [C/U] the act of controlling, or something that controls • *The major limitation of early record players was the short playing time of the records.* [C] ○ *They favor anything that involves limitation of government control.* [U]

limited /'lɪm·ət·əd/ *adj* • *There are a limited* (= small) *number of bikes available in that store.* • Limited also means kept within a particular size, range, time, or group: *The advanced course is limited to those who have already taken the introductory course.*

limousine /ˌlɪm·əˈziːn, 'lɪm·əˌziːn/, *short form* **limo** /'lɪm·oʊ/ *n* [C] a large, luxurious car, or a small bus that takes people to and from an airport

limp WALK /lɪmp/ *v* [I] to walk with an irregular step, esp. because your foot or leg is hurt • *Jackson limped off the field after injuring his ankle.*

limp /lɪmp/ *n* [U] • *He walks with a slight limp.*

limp NOT FIRM /lɪmp/ *adj* [-er/-est only] not firm or stiff • *The lettuce in this salad is completely limp.*

linchpin /'lɪntʃ·pɪn/ *n* [C] a person or thing that is the most important part of a group or system's operation • *Germany is the linchpin of the European Union.*

line LONG MARK /laɪn/ *n* [C] a long, thin mark on the surface of something • *Draw a straight line.* ○ *You shouldn't drive across the double yellow lines.* ○ *As I grow older, lines and wrinkles show on my face.*

linear /'lɪn·iː·ər/ *adj* [not gradable] consisting of or related to straight lines • *The garden has very linear paths.* • See also LINEAR LENGTH, LINEAR REASONABLE.

line EDGE /laɪn/ *n* [C] a real or imaginary mark that forms the edge, border, or limit of something • *The police caught him before he crossed the state line.* • A line is also a mark on a sports field which shows where things can or cannot happen, or which measures the field: *the foul line* ○ *the 50-yard line* ○ *the free-throw line* ○ *the* **line of scrimmage** (= an imaginary line along which football teams face each other at the start of each play) • If you say something is **on the line**, you mean there is a risk of loss involved: *His job is on the line.* ○ *Firefighters regularly put their lives on the line.*

line STRING /laɪn/ *n* [C] a length of string, rope, or wire that is used to support something • *fishing line* ○ *Would you help me hang the wash out on the line?*

line ROW /laɪn/ *n* [C] a row of people or things • *There was a long line at the movie theater.* • In football, the lines are the two front rows of opposing players who face one another at the start of a play: *the offensive/defensive line* • *Just get* **in line** *(regional on line)* and wait your turn. • *I'm* **in line for** (= likely to get) *a promotion.* • *We try to keep our prices* **in line with** (= similar to) *our competitors.* • If something comes/gets/falls or is brought **into line**, it begins or is forced to follow usual standards: *Raises would bring their salaries into line with their coworkers.*

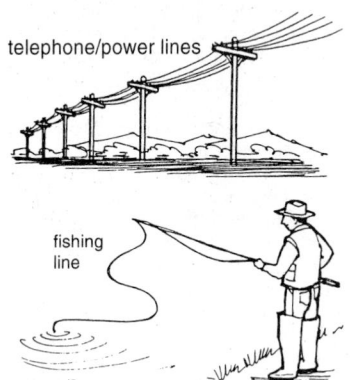

telephone/power lines

fishing line

clothesline

line of people

line /laɪn/ *v* [T] • *People lined the streets along the parade route.* ○ *The long driveway was lined with trees.* • *Please* **line up** (= form a line) *behind the rail.* • If you **line up** people or things, you arrange them in lines: *The photographer lined the family members up for a picture.* • To **line up** something also means to organize or arrange for something to be done: *Did you line anyone up to cater the Christmas party?*

line SERIES /laɪn/ *n* [C usually sing] a series of people, esp. members of the same family, following one another in time • *He comes from a long line of doctors.*

line COVER /laɪn/ *v* [T] to cover the inside surface of (an object) with another material • *I lined the kitchen cabinets with shelf paper.* • If you **line** your **pocket(s)**, you make money esp. by using dishonest, immoral, or illegal methods: *Some of these lawyers are only interested in lining their pockets.*

lining /ˈlaɪ·nɪŋ/ *n* [C] material that covers the inside surface of something • *The lining of my jacket is torn.*

line MILITARY /laɪn/ *n* [C] a row of defensive positions, particularly the ones closest to enemy positions • *the front line* ○ *behind enemy lines*

line WIRE / CONNECTION /laɪn/ *n* [C] an electrical or telephone wire or connection • *Power lines were down after the storm.* ○ *That line is busy—may I take a message?*

line PIPE /laɪn/ *n* [C] a system of pipes • *a water/gas line*

line RAILROAD /laɪn/ *n* [C] a train route, or a railroad track • *rail/commuter lines*

line COMPANY /laɪn/ *n* [C] a company that has an organized system of transport by ship, truck, aircraft, or bus • *a shipping line*

liner /ˈlaɪ·nər/ *n* [C] a large ship operated by a transport company • *an ocean/cruise liner*

line WORDS /laɪn/ *n* [C] a row of words that form part of a text • *Limericks are humorous five-line poems.* • A line is also a short written message: *Drop me a line when you get a chance.* • A line is also a remark that is intended to amuse, persuade, or deceive: *He gave me some line about how his father is the mayor.* • Lines are also the words that actors speak when performing.

line DIRECTION /laɪn/ *n* [C usually sing] a direction or path • *Fortunately, the pedestrian wasn't in the line of fire.*

line WAY OF DEALING /laɪn/ *n* [C] a way of dealing with or thinking about something or someone • *I couldn't follow his line of reasoning.*

line JOB /laɪn/ *n* [C] a job, interest, or activity • *"What line of work are you in?" "I'm a teacher."* • *A police officer was killed in the line of duty* (= while working).

line GOODS /laɪn/ *n* [C] a type of goods • *Our new swimwear line will be in stores shortly.*

linear LENGTH /ˈlɪn·iː·ər/ *adj* [not gradable] relating to length, rather than area or volume • *This carpet costs $12 per linear foot.* • See also **linear** at LINE LONG MARK.

linear REASONABLE /ˈlɪn·iː·ər/ *adj* (esp. of stories or ideas) continuing reasonably from one part to the next • *The book offers excitement, linear plot development, and dramatic descriptions.* • See also **linear** at LINE LONG MARK.

linebacker /ˈlaɪnˌbæk·ər/ *n* [C] (in football) a defensive player who stands behind the first line of defenders and tries to stop players from the other team from moving the ball along the field • *a middle/outside linebacker*

linen /ˈlɪn·ən/ *n* [U] strong cloth that is woven from plant fibers • *a linen jacket* • Linens are cloth items for the home, such as sheets and **tablecloths**, made from linen or a similar material like cotton.

lineup /ˈlaɪ·nʌp/ *n* [C] a group of people that has been brought together to form a team or take part in an event • *the starting lineup for today's game* ○ *a star-studded lineup of guests on the show* • A lineup is also a row of people brought together by the police so that a person who saw a crime can recognize the criminal among them.

linger /ˈlɪŋ·ɡər/ *v* [I] to take longer than usual to leave or disappear • *His hand lingered briefly on hers.* ○ *The smell lingered in the kitchen for days.*

lingering /ˈlɪŋ·ɡə·rɪŋ/ *adj* [not gradable] • *She has lingering doubts about his faithfulness.*

lingerie /ˌlɑn·dʒəˈreɪ, ˌlɑ̃·ʒə-, -ˈriː/ *n* [U] women's underwear or clothing worn in bed

lingo /ˈlɪŋ·ɡoʊ/ *n* [C] *pl* **lingoes** *infml* language containing slang or technical expressions, or a foreign language • *In typical Hollywood lingo, he said, "This is gonna be big."*

linguist /ˈlɪŋ·ɡwəst/ *n* [C] someone who studies the structure and development of language, or someone who knows several languages

linguistic /lɪŋˈɡwɪs·tɪk/ *adj* [not gradable] connected with language or the study of language • *linguistic analysis*

linguistics /lɪŋˈɡwɪs·tɪks/ *n* [U] the study of the structure and development of language in general or of particular languages

lining /ˈlaɪ·nɪŋ/ *n* • See at LINE COVER.

link CHAIN /lɪŋk/ *n* [C] one of the rings in a chain

link CONNECTION /lɪŋk/ *n* [C] a connection between two things • *There is a clear link between poverty and malnutrition.* ○ *A high-speed rail link brings you to the airport.*

link /lɪŋk/ *v* [I/T] • *Various activities have been linked to global warming.* [I] ○ *This is the only bridge linking the island with the mainland.* [T] • To **link up** is to connect or combine: *My computer links up to the office network.* • (*specialized*) In grammar, a **linking verb** is a verb that links the properties of an object or person to that object or person: *In the sentence*

LINKING VERBS

Linking verbs like **be** and **become** are followed by an adjective or a noun.

The meal was *delicious.* • *She* became *a photographer.* • *You* look *great.*

They do not have an object, because they refer to a state or process and not to an action or activity that is done to an object. Linking verbs are marked [L] in this dictionary.

Linking verbs are followed:

- **by a noun or adjective** or by a noun phrase or adjective-like phrase

The apartment was *a mess.*	*The apartment* was *messy.*
He later became *a famous writer*	*He later* became *famous as a writer.*
Can we stay/remain *friends?*	*Can we* stay/remain *friendly with each other?*

  Some linking verbs can be followed by a limited set of nouns but are normally followed by an adjective:

I'm really starting to feel *my age.*	*I'm starting to* feel *old.*
It seems *a shame to waste all this food.*	*It* seems *unfortunate to waste all this food.*

- **only by an adjective** or adjective-like phrase

  It's getting *dark out.* • *Your voice* sounds *different over the phone.* • *The soup* smells *wonderful.* • *Please* keep *quiet.* • *The problem is* growing *worse.* • *Hundreds of chairs in the hall* stood *empty.*

  Many linking verbs follow this pattern.

- **only by a noun** or noun phrase

  You'll make *a good doctor.* • *The company* consists of *five young women.* • *A mile* equals *1.6 kilometers.* • *The package* weighed *three pounds.*

  Only a small number of verbs follow this pattern.

Linking verbs are:

- **not followed by an adverb**

  She looked happy. not *She looked happily.*

- **often used in phrases beginning with it and there**

  There seems *to be a mistake.* • *It's* getting *late.*

[LP] **It** and **There**

"My suitcase weighs 45 pounds," "weighs" is a linking verb.

linkage /'lɪŋ·kɪdʒ/ *n* [C/U] a connection, or the action of connecting • *There's a direct linkage between cultural values and the way people live.* [C]

linoleum /lə'noʊ·li:·əm/ *n* [U] a hard, smooth floor covering

lint /lɪnt/ *n* [U] small, loose cloth fibers or pieces of thread • *My black sweater is covered with lint.*

lion /'laɪ·ən/, *female* **lioness** /'laɪ·ə·nəs/ *n* [C] a large, strong animal of the cat family from Africa and Asia which has yellow-brown fur, the male having a large MANE (= long neck fur) • *She didn't do much, but she got* the lion's share *of the attention* (= the largest part of it).

lip BODY PART /lɪp/ *n* [C] either of the two edges of flesh around the opening of the mouth • *She licked/pursed/puckered her lips.* • To **give/pay lip service to** (something) is to publicly support or approve of it, while actually taking no action to produce it. • If your **lips are sealed**, you will keep something secret: *"I want the party to be a surprise." "Don't worry, my lips are sealed."* • **Lip gloss** is a makeup applied to someone's lips to make them shiny. • To **lipread** is to understand what someone is

saying by watching the movements of their mouth. • **Lipstick** is a waxy makeup for coloring a person's lips that is usually shaped like a rod and enclosed in a tube.

lip EDGE /lɪp/ *n* [C] the edge of a container or opening, esp. the part of the edge used for pouring

lip SPEECH /lɪp/ *n* [U] *slang* speech that is rude and not respectful • *Don't give me any more of your lip.*

liquefy, liquify /'lɪk·wə,faɪ/ *v* [I/T] to become or make (something) liquid • *Gases liquefy under pressure.* [I]

liqueur /lɪ'kɜr, -'kjʊr, -'kʊr/ *n* [C] any of several strong, sweet alcoholic drinks that are usually drunk in small amounts after a meal

liquid SUBSTANCE /'lɪk·wəd/ *n* [C/U] a substance that flows easily and is neither a gas nor a solid • *Water, oil, and milk are all liquids.* [C]

liquid /'lɪk·wəd/ *adj* [not gradable] • *liquid oxygen/hydrogen* ◦ *The metal mercury is liquid at room temperature.*

liquid MONEY /'lɪk·wəd/ *adj* [not gradable] in the form of money, rather than investments or property, or able to be changed into money easily • *liquid assets*

liquidate /'lɪk·wə,deɪt/ *v* [T] • *Investors have*

started to liquidate their mutual funds (= sell them). • If someone liquidates a business, they close it and sell what it owns.

liquidation /ˌlɪk·wə'deɪ·ʃən/ n [U] • The company was forced into liquidation.

liquidate /'lɪk·wə,deɪt/ v [T] to kill or make powerless • If you go on fighting against us we shall liquidate you.

liquify /'lɪk·wə,faɪ/ v to LIQUEFY

liquor /'lɪk·ər/ n [U] an alcoholic drink, esp. one that has been DISTILLED (= heated to a gas, then cooled to a liquid) • He stays away from hard liquor like whiskey and rum.

lisp /lɪsp/ v [I/T] to pronounce "s" and "z" sounds like "th," so that "sin" sounds like "thin" and "Zen" sounds like "then"

lisp /lɪsp/ n [C] • I was teased at school because I spoke with a lisp.

list RECORD /lɪst/ n [C] a record of short pieces of information usually arranged one below the other so that they can be read easily or counted • I have a long list of things we need to get for our new house.

list /lɪst/ v [T] • The professor gave us a handout in which she listed the books we were supposed to read for the course.

listing /'lɪs·tɪŋz/ n [C] an item in a list of information that is published regularly • To find the correct TV channel, check the listings in your local newspaper.

list LEAN /lɪst/ v [I] (esp. of a ship) to lean to one side • The tanker is listing badly and may sink.

listen /'lɪs·ən/ v [I] to give attention to something you can hear or to a person who is speaking • Can you really listen to music while you do your homework? ○ Listen, we really need to do something about having this place painted. • If you **listen in**, you listen to something, esp. secretly, without saying anything: I think someone is listening in on my phone conversations.

listener /'lɪs·ə·nər/ n [C] • For many listeners, the music of the Beatles summed up the sentiments of the 1960s.

listless /'lɪst·ləs/ adj tired and weak, and lacking energy or interest • As the tennis match continued in the 90° heat, his play grew listless and he made a number of errors.

lit /lɪt/ past simple and past participle of LIGHT • a dimly lit room (= a room without much light)

litany /'lɪt·ən·i/ n [C] a long list spoken or given to someone, esp. to someone who has heard or seen it before or finds it boring • She had to hear once again his litany of complaints over how badly he was treated.

lite /laɪt/ adj [not gradable] infml containing less fat or sugar than similar types of food and therefore less likely to make you increase your weight • lite beer • USAGE: This spelling of light is used in advertising products. If used

otherwise, it is usually intended to be humorous.

liter /'liːt̬·ər/ (abbreviation **l**) n [C] a unit of measurement of volume equal to 1.057 quarts

literacy /'lɪt̬·ə·rə·si/ n [U] the ability to read and write • She was actively involved in programs to increase adult literacy. • Literacy is also a basic skill or knowledge of a subject: computer literacy ○ scientific literacy

literate /'lɪt̬·ə·rət/ adj able to read and write • The man was barely literate and took a long time to write his name. • Literate also means having a good education or showing it in your writing: He wrote a literate, colorful column and reviewed plays. • Literate also means having a basic skill or knowledge of a subject: They wanted to make sure their child was computer literate.

literal /'lɪt̬·ə·rəl/ adj having exactly the same meaning as the basic or original meaning of a word or expression • a literal interpretation of the Bible • A literal translation of a phrase in another language gives the meaning of each separate word.

literally /'lɪt̬·ə·rə·li/ adv • Beginning students tend to translate too literally.

literally /'lɪt̬·ə·rə·li/ adv [not gradable] used for emphasizing how large or great an amount is • There were literally hundreds of pages to read in the contract. • Literally is also used to emphasize a statement and suggest that it is surprising: I literally (= really) had no idea you and Sophie were coming.

literary /'lɪt̬·ə,rer·i/ adj connected with literature • She contributed poems to literary magazines.

literature WRITING /'lɪt̬·ə·rə·tʃər, -,tʃʊr/ n [U] writing that has lasting, artistic value • The course in English literature covers Shakespeare's plays.

literature INFORMATION /'lɪt̬·ə·rə·tʃər, -,tʃʊr/ n [U] all the information written about a subject, esp. by specialists • The medical literature is full of examples of accidental discoveries that led to important advances in science. • Literature is also printed material published by a company that informs people about its products or services: They handed out literature at the meeting about their new software.

lithe /laɪð, laɪθ/ adj (of a body) thin and attractive, and able to move easily and gracefully • She had a marvelously lithe dancer's body.

litigate /'lɪt̬·ə,geɪt/ v [I/T] law to cause (an argument between people or groups) to be discussed in a law court so that a judgment can be made

litigation /ˌlɪt̬·ə'geɪ·ʃən/ n [U] law the process of taking an argument between people or groups to a court of law • Both sides agreed to the settlement to avoid the expense of litigation.

litmus test /'lɪt·məs,test/ n [C] a specific decision or opinion that is thought to show what you believe about other, more general, subjects • *The president's policy on abortion is regarded as a litmus test of his views on women's rights.*

litre /'liːt̬·ər/ *n* [C] a LITER

litter WASTE /'lɪt̬·ər/ *n* [U] pieces of paper and other small objects that have been thrown out and are left on the ground in public places • (*disapproving*) A **litterbug** is someone who leaves paper, plastic, etc., on the ground in public places.

litter /'lɪt̬·ər/ *v* [T] • *The park was littered with bottles and soda cans after the concert.*

litter YOUNG ANIMALS /'lɪt̬·ər/ *n* [C] a group of animals born at the same time and having the same mother

little SMALL /'lɪt̬·əl/ *adj* [-*er*/-*est* only] small in size or amount, or brief in time • *She has a little room on the top floor where she works on her computer.* ○ *They have very little money.* ○ *It'll take me a little while longer to get ready.* • Little can be used with approving words for emphasis: *They have a nice little house.* • A **little finger** (also **pinkie** or **pinky**) is the smallest of the four fingers on a hand. • A **little toe** is the smallest of the five toes on a foot.

little /'lɪt̬·əl/ *pronoun, n* [U] a small amount • *I could understand very little of what he said.* • **A little** means a small amount of (something): *"Do we have any sugar left?" "A little."*

little NOT MUCH /'lɪt̬·əl/ *adv* **less** /les/, **least** /liːst/ not much • *The county has done little to improve the traffic problem.* ○ *It's a little-known fact that ticks are not insects.* • **A little** means slightly: *She was a little frightened.* ○ *You're walking a little too fast for me.* • LP AMOUNTS

little YOUNG /'lɪt̬·əl/ *adj* [-*er*/-*est* only] young • *When you were little, you and your brother were always fighting.* ○ *My little brother/sister* (= younger brother or sister) *is seven years old.* ○ *He stayed home from work today because his little boy/girl* (= young son or daughter) *is sick.* • **Little League** is an organization of baseball teams in the US for children between the ages of 8 and 12.

little NOT IMPORTANT /'lɪt̬·əl/ *adj* [not gradable] not important or not serious • *I had a little problem with my car, but it's fixed now.*

liturgy /'lɪt̬·ər·dʒi/ *n* [C/U] a set of words, music, and actions regularly used in religious ceremonies

liturgical /lə'tɜr·dʒɪ·kəl/ *adj* [not gradable]

livable, **liveable** /'lɪv·ə·bəl/ *adj* (esp. of a place) acceptable or good enough • *The apartment is far from perfect, but it's livable.*

live HAVE LIFE /lɪv/ *v* [I] to be alive or have life, or to continue in this state • *Rembrandt lived in the 17th century.* ○ *This oak tree has been living for over 200 years.* • A **living room** is the room in a house or apartment where people sit or relax together but do not usually eat or sleep.

live /laɪv/ *adj* [not gradable] • *There was a tank of live lobsters in the restaurant.*

living /'lɪv·ɪŋ/ *adj* [not gradable] • *Are any of your grandparents living* (= still alive)*?* • Living is also used in some expressions to make them stronger: *He's the living image of his father* (= looks exactly like his father). • A **living will** is a written document in which a person states the kind of medical treatment they refuse to have if they become so sick that they will die soon and have lost the ability to communicate.

living /'lɪv·ɪŋ/ *pl n* people who are still alive • *On this anniversary of the tragedy we remember the living as well as the dead.*

live HAVE A HOME /lɪv/ *v* [I always + adv/prep] to have as your home or as the place where you stay or return, esp. to sleep • *Where do you live?* ○ *We live in St. Louis now but we used to live in Cincinnati.* ○ *Freshmen are required to live on campus.* ○ *My brother lives with four other people in a big house.* • If two people **live together/with each other**, they share a home and have a sexual relationship but are not married: *Joe and Rebecca lived together for two years before they got married.* • **Live-in** means living in the home of your employer: *We have a live-in nanny who takes care of the children.*

live STAY ALIVE /lɪv/ *v* [I] to stay alive by getting enough money to pay for food, a home, clothing, etc., or to stay alive by eating a particular food • *She's so poor—I wonder how she lives.* ○ *While he's studying for the finals, he lives on junk food.* ○ *He's living off the money he inherited from his father.*

living /'lɪv·ɪŋ/ *n* [C] the way you earn money; your job • *What do you do for a living?* ○ *She's not happy working at the hospital but at least it's a living.*

live SPEND LIFE /lɪv/ *v* [always + adv/prep] to spend (your life) in a particular way • *After a while you get used to living alone.* [I] ○ *On his income, they can afford to live well.* [I] ○ *She lived her whole life in a little town in New Mexico.* [T] • To live can also mean to have the full experience that life can offer: *If you haven't been to Alaska, you haven't lived.* [I] • **Live and let live** means that we should accept the way other people live and behave, and not try to make them change, even if they are very different from us. • If you **live it up**, you spend a lot of money to enjoy yourself with the knowledge that it is a special time: *The kids are away at school, so we thought we'd live it up and go to Bermuda.*

live AS IT HAPPENS /laɪv/ *adj, adv* [not gradable] (of a performance) shown or broadcast to people watching or listening as it is happening, rather than being recorded to be shown or broadcast later • *This evening at seven there will be a live telecast of the debate.* ○ *There will* *be live music* (= people playing music) *at the party.*

live ELECTRICITY /laɪv/ *adj* [not gradable] carrying or charged with electricity • *You'd better test the electric outlet first to see if it's live.* • If you say someone is a **live wire,** you mean they are very energetic and active.

live EXPLODE /laɪv/ *adj* [not gradable] able to explode • *The army is using live ammunition on these maneuvers.*

□ **live down** *obj,* **live** *obj* **down** /ˈlɪvˈdaʊn/ *v adv* [M] to stop feeling uncomfortable about (something embarrassing or bad that you have done), by either waiting long enough for other people to forget it, or by behaving well • *If you show up with green hair, your parents will never let you live it down.*

□ **live for** /ˈlɪvˈfɔːr/ *v prep* [T] to enjoy (something) more than anything else you do • *My son lives for sports.*

□ **live through** /ˈlɪvˈθruː/ *v prep* [T] to experience (something difficult or painful) and continue to live • *He may not live through the operation, but it's his only chance.*

□ **live up to** /lɪvˈʌpˌtuː, -tə/ *v adv prep* [T] to achieve (what is expected, esp. high standards) • *We expected a lot of her, and her performance lived up to our expectations.*

□ **live with** /ˈlɪvˈwɪθ, -wɪð/ *v prep* [T] to experience and accept (something unpleasant that is lasting) • *When you get arthritis at your age, it's just something you have to live with.*

liveable /ˈlɪvˈə·bəl/ *adj* LIVABLE

livelihood /ˈlaɪvˈliːˌhʊd/ *n* [C/U] the way you earn the money you need to pay for food, a place to live, clothing, etc. • *They earn their livelihood from farming.* [C]

lively /ˈlaɪvˈli/ *adj* having or showing a lot of energy and enthusiasm, or showing interesting and exciting thought • *We have a lively group of seniors who meet to discuss the books they've read.* ○ *Imelda takes a lively interest in politics.*

liveliness /ˈlaɪvˈliːˈnəs/ *n* [U]

liven up *obj,* **liven** *obj* **up** /ˌlaɪ·vəˈnʌp/ *v adv* [M] to make (something) more interesting or attractive • *New wallpaper would help to liven up the kitchen.*

liver /ˈlɪvˈər/ *n* [C/U] a large organ in the body that cleans the blood, or this organ from an animal used as meat • *He ordered calves' liver with onions.* [U]

lives /laɪvz/ *pl of* LIFE

livestock /ˈlaɪvˈstɑk/ *pl n* animals kept on a farm, such as cows, sheep, chickens, and pigs

livid ANGRY /ˈlɪvˈəd/ *adj* extremely angry • *The rude letter from his mother-in-law made him livid.*

livid COLOR /ˈlɪvˈəd/ *adj* (esp. of marks on the skin) of a purple or dark blue color, usually caused by an injury • *There was a livid bruise on her upper arm where she had fallen.*

living /ˈlɪvˈɪŋ/ *adj, n* • See at LIVE HAVE LIFE, LIVE STAY ALIVE.

lizard /ˈlɪzˈərd/ *n* [C] a REPTILE (= a type of animal that produces eggs) that has a long body, four short legs, and a long tail • PIC IGUANA

llama /ˈlɑm·ə/ *n* [C] a South American animal with a long neck and long hair, used to carry loads and to provide wool

load AMOUNT CARRIED /loʊd/ *n* [C] the amount or weight of something carried by a vehicle, a structure such as a bridge, or a person or animal • *The truck had a load of bricks.* ○ *The maximum load for this elevator is eight persons.* • *(infml)* A **load/loads of** means much or many: *There were loads of people on the train and no empty seats.* • A **load of** can also be used to express your disapproval of something: *(rude slang)* That's a load of crap/shit!

load /loʊd/ *v* [T] to put a load of something in or on (something) • *Let's load (up) the car and then we can go.* [T/M] • If you are **loaded down with** things, you are carrying or trying to carry a lot of things: *She was loaded down with two heavy pieces of luggage and was trying to look after three children.*

load AMOUNT OF WORK /loʊd/ *n* [C] the amount of work to be done by a person • *The normal teaching load at this university is three courses each semester.*

load PUT INTO /loʊd/ *v* [T] to put into a piece of equipment (something it uses to make it work) • *She loaded the camera* (= put film in it). ○ *He loaded the gun* (= put bullets in it). ○ *You need to load the new software before you can use the computer.*

loaded /ˈloʊdˈəd/ *adj* [not gradable] • *It's dangerous to leave a loaded gun* (= one with bullets in it) *lying around.*

loaded NOT FAIR /ˈloʊdˈəd/ *adj* not fair, esp. by being especially helpful to one side and not the other, or (of a question) by intentionally using words that will likely produce a particular answer • *The report is loaded in favor of the tobacco companies.*

loaded RICH /ˈloʊdˈəd/ *adj infml* having a lot of money; rich • *The old guy never spends a dime but believe me, he's loaded.*

loaded DRUNK /ˈloʊdˈəd/ *adj slang* drunk

loaf BREAD /loʊf/ *n* [C] *pl* **loaves** /loʊvz/ bread that is shaped and baked in a single piece and can be sliced for eating • *Get a loaf of white bread from the corner store.*

loaf AVOID WORK /loʊf/ *v* [I] *infml* to avoid activity, esp. work • *He just wanted to loaf for a while before beginning the new job.*

loafer /ˈloʊˈfər/ *n* [C] trademark a type of shoe with stitches around the top and without shoelaces (= strings used to tie shoes)

loafers

loan /loʊn/ *n* [C/U] an act

of lending something, esp. a sum of money that that has to be paid back with INTEREST (= an additional amount of money that is a percentage of the amount borrowed), or an amount of money that has been lent • *Thanks for the loan of your bike.* [U] ○ *My brother repaid his student loan within five years.* [C] • *The painting is* on loan *to the Metropolitan Museum of Art* (= has been lent to it, esp. for more than a short period of time). • (*infml disapproving*) A loan shark *is a person who charges a very large amount of interest for lending money.*

loan /loʊn/ *v* [T] to lend (something, esp. money) • *Can you loan me $10 until payday?*

loath /loʊθ, loʊð/ *adj* [+ *to* infinitive] unwilling; RELUCTANT • *She'd be loath to admit it, but she doesn't really like opera.*

loathe /loʊð/ *v* [T] to feel strong hate, dislike, or disgust for (someone or something) • *I loathe doing housework.* ○ *"Do you like fish?" "No, I loathe it."*

loathing /ˈloʊ·ðɪŋ/ *n* [U] • *He's full of loathing and despair.*

loaves /loʊvz/ *pl of* LOAF BREAD

lob /lɑb/ *v* [T] -bb- to hit or throw (something, esp. a ball) in a high curve • *Smith lobbed a perfect pass over the basket to Watkins.*

lobby SPACE /ˈlɑb·i/ *n* [C] a large, open space just inside the main entrance of a public building such as a hotel, office building, or theater • *As you enter the lobby, you'll see the elevators on your right.*

lobby PERSUADE /ˈlɑb·i/ *v* [I/T] to try to persuade (someone, esp. an elected official) to take a particular action or change a law • *They have been lobbying Congress to change the gun laws.* [T]

lobby /ˈlɑb·i/ *n* [C] a group of people who represent a particular industry or interest in dealing with a politician, official, etc. • *the environmental lobby*

lobbyist /ˈlɑb·i·əst/ *n* [C] • *lobbyists for the tobacco industry*

lobe /loʊb/ *n* [C] an earlobe, see at EAR BODY PART

lobster /ˈlɑb·stər/ *n* [C/U] an animal that lives in the sea and has a shell-like covering on its body, two large CLAWS, and eight legs, or the flesh of this animal when used as food • *We had lobster for dinner.* [U]

claws

lobster

local AREA /ˈloʊ·kəl/ *adj* [not gradable] from, existing in, or serving a particular place or small area • *the local population* ○ *the local newspaper* ○ *local phone calls* ○ *local government* • (*medical*) Local also means limited to a particular part of the body: *a local anesthetic*

local /ˈloʊ·kəl/ *n* [C] a person who lives in the particular small area you are talking about • *If you're lost and need directions, just ask one of the locals.*

localize /ˈloʊ·kə,laɪz/ *v* [I/T] • *The infection seems to have localized in the foot.* [I]

locally /ˈloʊ·kə·li/ *adv* [not gradable] • *locally grown vegetables*

local VEHICLE /ˈloʊ·kəl/ *n* [C] a train or bus that stops at all or most of the places on its route where passengers can get on or off • Compare EXPRESS FAST

locale /loʊˈkæl/ *n* [C] an area or place, esp. one where something special happens • *The film's locale is Venice in the summer of 1957.*

locality /loʊˈkæl·ət̬·i/ *n* [C] a particular area or neighborhood • *The schools work with states, localities, teachers, and parents.*

locate PUT IN PLACE /ˈloʊ·keɪt, loʊˈkeɪt/ *v* [I/T] to put or establish (something) in a particular place • *The company decided to locate its headquarters in Denver.* [T]

locate FIND POSITION /ˈloʊ·keɪt, loʊˈkeɪt/ *v* [T] to find or discover the exact position of (something) • *Archeologists have located the remains of an ancient temple.*

location /loʊˈkeɪ·ʃən/ *n* [C] a particular place or position • *a good location for a bookstore* ○ *The map showed the location of an old mine.* • If a movie is filmed on location, it is made in an actual place: *The documentary was filmed on location in San Francisco.*

lock DEVICE TO FASTEN /lɑk/ *n* [C] a device that keeps something, such as a door or drawer, fastened, usually needing a key to open it • *The company has been sold* lock, stock, and barrel (= including everything). • A locksmith *is a person who makes and repairs locks and supplies keys.*

lock /lɑk/ *v* [I/T] • *Be sure to lock all the doors when you leave.* [T] ○ *The garage door doesn't lock.* [I] • If you lock something somewhere, you make it safe by putting it in a special place and fastening it closed with a lock: *He locked the documents in his filing cabinet.* [T] • *The door slammed with our keys inside, so we were* locked out (= unable to get in because the door was locked). • *Please* lock up *when you leave* (= make the building safe by locking the doors). • *People who commit serious crimes should be* locked up (= put into prison) *for a long time.*

lock NOT ALLOW CHANGE /lɑk/ *v* [I/T] to be or hold something in a position or condition where movement, escape, or change is not possible • *They're locked in a lawsuit with their former employer.* [T] ○ *The cars crashed and the bumpers locked, making it impossible to move.* [I] ○ *The bank won't lock in our mortgage rate.* [M]

lock /lɑk/ *n* [C] • *The candidate has a lock on the nomination* (= has control of it).

lock WATER /lɑk/ *n* [C] a length of water with

gates at either end where the level of water can be changed to allow boats to move between parts of a CANAL or river that are at different heights

lock HAIR /lɑk/ n [C] a curl of hair, or a group of hairs

locker /ˈlɑk·ər/ n [C] a cabinet, often tall and made of metal, in which someone can lock their possessions and leave them for a period of time • A **locker room** is a room with lockers, esp. near a GYMNASIUM, where people can change their clothes.

locket /ˈlɑk·ət/ n [C] a small item of jewelry that opens to show a picture of someone or a piece of hair, which is usually worn on a chain around the neck

lockout /ˈlɑk·ɑʊt/ n [C] an action taken by an employer to stop workers from going into their place of work until they agree to particular conditions given by the employer

locomotion /ˌloʊ·kəˈmoʊ·ʃən/ n [U] the ability to move; movement

locomotive /ˌloʊ·kəˈmoʊt·ɪv/ n [C] the engine of a train that pulls it along

locust /ˈloʊ·kəst/ n [C] any of several types of large **grasshoppers** (= insects with wings and long back legs) found esp. in hot areas • a *swarm of locusts*

lodge BECOME FIXED /lɑdʒ/ v [always + adv/prep] to become fixed or cause (something) to become fixed in a place or position • *A fish bone had lodged in her throat.* [I] ○ *The explosion lodged some metal fragments in his leg.* [T]

lodge MAKE /lɑdʒ/ v [T] to formally make (a statement, esp. a complaint) to an official • *to lodge a complaint/protest*

lodge STAY /lɑdʒ/ v [I always + adv/prep] to stay in a place temporarily, usually paying rent to do so • *Mrs. Brown rents rooms—you can lodge with her for a few weeks.*

lodging /ˈlɑdʒ·ɪŋ/ n [U] • *The price includes board and lodging* (= a room to sleep in).

lodge BUILDING /lɑdʒ/ n [C] a small building used by people during a particular sports season • *a hunting lodge* • A lodge is also a type of hotel in the countryside or mountains.

loft ROOF SPACE /lɔːft/ n [C] a space at the top of a building under the roof, used for storage or sometimes made into a room, or a raised area built over part of a room that is used esp. for sleeping • A loft can also be an apartment in a building that was previously used for industry: *She lives in a converted loft.*

loft HIT /lɔːft/ v [T] to hit (a ball) high in the air • *The batter lofted the ball into right field.*

lofty /ˈlɔːf·ti/ adj slightly fml high • *lofty mountains* • If someone's ideas or words are lofty, they show high principles or standards: *lofty sentiments/ideals*

log WOOD /lɔːg, lɑg/ n [C] a thick piece of tree trunk or branch • *Stack the logs near the fireplace.* • A **log cabin** is a small house made from tree trunks.

log /lɔːg, lɑg/ v [I/T] **-gg-** to cut down trees for their wood • *Timber companies logged these mountains for years.* [T]

logging /ˈlɔː·gɪŋ, ˈlɑg·ɪŋ/ n [U] • *There's a lot of logging in the region.*

log RECORD /lɔːg, lɑg/ n [C] a full, written record of a trip, a period of time, or an event • *a ship's log*

log /lɔːg, lɑg/ v [T] **-gg-** to put (information) into a written record • *The police have logged several complaints about loud parties in that building.* [T] ○ *He has logged over 1500 hours of flying time* (= flown and recorded this amount). [T] • When you **log in/on** to a computer system, you start using it, esp. by giving a PASSWORD (= a secret word by which the system recognizes an approved user). When you **log out/off**, you finish using the system.

loggerheads /ˈlɔː·gər,hedz, ˈlag·ər-/ pl n • If you are **at loggerheads** with someone, you strongly disagree with them: *The company's two divisions were said to have been at loggerheads frequently.*

logic REASONABLE THINKING /ˈlɑdʒ·ɪk/ n [U] a particular way of thinking, esp. one that is reasonable and based on good judgment • *I fail to see the logic of your argument.*

logical /ˈlɑdʒ·ɪ·kəl/ adj • *After the children were grown, moving to a smaller house was the logical thing to do.*

logically /ˈlɑdʒ·ɪ·kli/ adv • *Related material has been grouped logically.*

logic FORMAL THINKING /ˈlɑdʒ·ɪk/ n [U] a formal, scientific method of examining or thinking about ideas

logistics /ləˈdʒɪs·tɪks/ pl n the careful organization of a complicated military, business, or other activity so that it happens in a successful and effective way • *The logistics of getting five kids off to school in the morning are pretty complex.*

logjam /ˈlɔːg·dʒæm, ˈlag-/ n [C] something that blocks the ability to do other things • *They broke the logjam by starting a series of discussions.*

logo /ˈloʊ·goʊ/ n [C] pl **logos** a small picture or design that a company or organization uses as its symbol • *Athletes are all wearing the sneaker company's logo.*

loin /lɔɪn/ n [C] a piece of meat from the back of an animal near the tail or from the top part of the back legs • *a pork loin*

loincloth /ˈlɔɪn·klɔːθ/ n [C] a piece of cloth that hangs down from the waist and covers the LOINS, sometimes worn by men in hot countries

loins /lɔɪnz/ pl n esp. literary the sexual organs, or the part of the body around them

loiter /ˈlɔɪt̬·ər/ v [I] to stay in a public place without an obvious reason to be there • *drunks loitering in the park*

loitering /ˈlɔɪt̬·ə·rɪŋ/ n [U] • *He was arrested for loitering.*

loll /lɑl/ v [I always + adv/prep] to lie or sit in a relaxed, informal way, or (esp. of the tongue) to hang loosely • *She lolled in an armchair.* ○ *The patient lay with her mouth open, her tongue lolling out.*

lollipop /ˈlɑl·iː,pɑp/ n [C] a hard candy on the end of a small stick

lone /loʊn/ adj [not gradable] being the only one in a place or situation; standing alone • *A lone mourner stood at the grave.*

loner /ˈloʊ·nər/ n [C] someone who prefers to be alone and to do things without other people

lonely /ˈloʊn·li/ adj (of someone) feeling sad because you are alone, or (of something) causing this feeling • *a lonely child* ○ *my lonely room* • A lonely place has no people, buildings, etc.: *a lonely and deserted road*

loneliness /ˈloʊn·li·nəs/ n [U] • *Some elderly people live in isolation and loneliness.*

lonesome /ˈloʊn·səm/ adj (of someone) feeling sad because you are alone or are apart from someone, or (of something) causing this feeling • *She was feeling lonesome for her family.* ○ *the lonesome whistle of a distant train*

long DISTANCE /lɔːŋ/ adj [-er/-est only] being a distance between two points that is more than average or usual, or being of a particular length • *There was a long line at the post office.* ○ *When I was young I wore my hair long.* ○ *We're still a long way from the station* (= a great distance). • A long piece of writing, such as a book or story, has many words: *It's a long book—over 600 pages.* • **Long-distance** means traveling or separated by a large distance: *a long-distance phone call* • **Long underwear** (also **long johns**) is warm, tight-fitting underwear reaching to the feet and hands. • A **long shot** is something that is not likely to succeed: *It's a long shot, but you could try phoning him at home.*

long TIME /lɔːŋ/ adj [-er/-est only] being an amount of time that is more than average or usual, or being of a particular amount of time • *The days are longer in summer than in winter.* ○ *We had to wait a long time to see the doctor.* ○ *We went away for a long weekend in April* (= a weekend and an extra day or days). • If something has **a long way to go** to reach a goal, it requires a lot of time and effort to reach it: *You've got a ling way to go before you're ready to compete at the national level.* • **At long last** (= Finally, after much waiting) *the government is starting to listen to our problems.* • *You may want to quit school now, but* **in the long run** (= at some time in the future), *you'll regret it.* • Over **the long haul** (= a period of years), *you're better off putting your money in municipal bonds.* • If someone or something is described as **longtime**, it has existed or lasted for many years: *a longtime friend* • Something **long-term** happens, ex-

ists, or continues for many years or far into the future: *Scientists warned of the long-term effects of global warming.*

long /lɔːŋ/ adv [-er/-est only] • *Have you been waiting long?* ○ *I've known her longer than you have.* ○ *I don't want to stay any longer* (= for any more time). • Someone or something that is **long-lost** has not been seen for many years: *A long-lost diary was discovered among his papers.* • Something **long-running** continues to happen for a period of time that is more than usual: *a long-running Broadway musical* • Something **long-standing** has existed for a great period of time: *It's been our long-standing policy not to admit latecomers to the show.*

long WANT /lɔːŋ/ v [I] to want something very much • *She longed to move out of the city.* [+ to infinitive]

longing /ˈlɔː·ŋɪŋ/ n [C] a strong desire • *a longing for peace and quiet*

longevity /lɑnˈdʒev·ət̬·i, lɔːn-/ n [U] a long life • *He attributed his longevity to exercise and a healthy diet.*

longhand /ˈlɔːŋ·hænd/ n [U] writing done by hand usually with a pen or pencil • *He wrote the confession in longhand and signed it.*

longitude /ˈlɑn·dʒə,tuːd/ n [C/U] the position to the east or west of an imaginary circle around the earth that goes through the North Pole, the South Pole, and Greenwich, England • Compare LATITUDE DISTANCE.

longshoreman /ˈlɔːŋˈʃɔːr·mən, -ˈʃoʊr-/ n [C] pl **-men** a person whose job is loading and unloading ships

look SEE /lʊk/ v [I] to direct your eyes in order to see • *Come look at what I've found.* ○ *She looked at her brother.* ○ *He looked out (of) the window of the bus.* • *I forgot I had a date with her, and now I'm afraid to* **look** *her* **in the eye/face** (= I feel ashamed). • To **look right through** someone is to pretend not to see them even while your eyes are directed toward them: *I smiled at him but he looked right through me.* • LP SEE, LOOK, AND WATCH at SEE USE EYES

look /lʊk/ n [C usually sing] • *Take a look at this picture and see if you recognize anyone.*

look SEARCH /lʊk/ v [I always + adv/prep] to try to find something • *Please help me look for my keys.* ○ *We looked everywhere but couldn't find it.* ○ *I'll look for a present for Tracy while I'm at the mall.* • If someone is **looking for trouble**, they are acting foolishly in a way that will cause them problems: *Parking illegally in front of the police station is looking for trouble.* • *If you don't believe me, you can* **look** *it* **up** (= check it in a written text).

look /lʊk/ n [C usually sing] • *I'll take a look and see if you left the keys in the kitchen.* ○ *After a brief look around, the police left.*

look SEEM /lʊk/ v [L] to seem or appear to be • *The roads look icy.* ○ *That dress looks nice on you.* ○ *He looked friendly.* ○ *He has started to* *look his age* (= appear as old as he really is). ○ *It looks like* (= It is likely that) *we'll be finished by January.* ○ *It looks like snow* (= It seems likely to snow). ○ *She looked like she hadn't slept all night.*

look /lʊk/ *n* [C] an expression of the face, or a particular appearance • *a joyful/sad look* ○ *I didn't like the look of the place and left as soon as I could.* ○ *He had good looks and lots of money.* [pl] • A **lookalike** is someone whose physical appearance is similar to someone else's, esp. to someone famous: *an Elvis Presley lookalike*

–looking /'lʊk·ɪŋ/ *combining form* having a stated type of appearance • *a good-looking woman* ○ *an odd-looking man*

look EXAMINE /lʊk/ *v* [I always + adv/prep] to examine or study, often quickly or informally • *Would you look over these numbers to see if I've made a mistake?* ○ *I don't go there to shop—I just like to look around and see what they have.*

look /lʊk/ *n* [C usually sing] • *I'm worried about this skin rash and I want my doctor to have a look at it.*

look FACE /lʊk/ *v* [I] to be in or view a particular direction; face • *The garden looks east.* ○ *The porch looks out over the lake.*

look GETTING ATTENTION /lʊk/ *exclamation* used to get someone's attention, often to express anger or annoyance • *Look, I've already told you that I'm not lending you any more money.*

□ **look after** /-'-/ *v prep* [T] to care for or be in charge of (someone or something) • *He looks after his son during the day.* ○ *Annie can look after herself.*

□ **look ahead** /,--'-/ *v adv* [I] to think of and decide about the future • *We need to look ahead to when the children are grown.*

□ **look back** /-'-/ *v adv* [I] to think of or remember what has happened in the past • *George looked back on his career in government with a great deal of satisfaction.*

□ **look down on** *obj* /-'-,-/ *v adv prep* [T] to feel that (someone) is less important than you or does not deserve respect • *I always felt that we were looked down on because we could never afford a new car or meals in restaurants.*

□ **look forward to** *obj* /-'---/ *v adv prep* [T] to feel pleasure because (an event or activity) is going to happen • *I'm looking forward to my vacation.*

□ **look into** *obj* /'-,--/ *v prep* [T] to try to find out about (something) • *I'll look into the reasons for the decision.*

□ **look like** *obj* /'-,-/ *v prep* [T] to be similar in appearance to (someone) • *The twins look like their mother.*

□ **look on/upon** *obj* /'-,-; '--,-/ *v prep* [T] to consider or think of (someone or something) in a stated way • *We looked on her as a daughter.*

□ **look out** /-'-/ *v adv* [I] to watch what is happening and be careful • *Please look out when you're crossing streets.*

lookout /'lʊk·aʊt/ *n* [C] a person whose job is to watch for someone or something to appear • *The lookout was standing on the corner watching for police.* • A lookout is also a place where you can have a special view, esp. of the countryside.

□ **look up** *obj* VISIT , **look** *obj* **up** /'-'-/ *v adv* [M] to come and see (someone); visit • *Look me up the next time you're in Los Angeles.*

□ **look up** IMPROVE /'-'-/ *v adv* [I] to get better; improve • *I hope things will start to look up in the new year.*

□ **look up to** *obj* /'-'--/ *v adv prep* [T] to admire and respect (someone) • *We always looked up to our Aunt Ginny.*

loom APPEAR /luːm/ *v* [I] to appear, esp. when seeming large and threatening • *Record budget deficits, now running well above $200 billion a year, loom over the recovery.* • If something **looms large**, it becomes important and often causes worry: *Questions of how to control development loom large in many of these towns.*

loom DEVICE /luːm/ *n* [C] a piece of equipment on which thread is woven into cloth

loonie /'luː·ni/ *n* [C] *Cdn infml* a Canadian coin worth one dollar

loony /'luː·ni/ *adj* [-er/-est only] foolish or crazy • *He has loony ideas.*

loop /luːp/ *n* [C] a circular shape made by something long and narrow in which the two ends cross each other, leaving an open space within • *A loop of thread from my sweater caught on a nail.* ○ *The exit ramp makes a loop under the elevated highway.*

loop /luːp/ *v* [I/T] • *The nature trail loops around and comes back to where you start.* [I always + adv/prep]

loophole /'luːp·hoʊl/ *n* [C] an opportunity to legally avoid an unpleasant responsibility, usually because of a mistake in the way rules or laws have been written • *The new law is designed to close most of the tax loopholes.*

loose NOT ATTACHED /luːs/ *adj* [-er/-est only] not firmly fixed in place • *I'd better sew that loose button before it comes off.* ○ *A few loose sheets of paper were lying around.* • If an animal is loose, it is not tied up or caged in. • If someone is **at loose ends**, they are very upset and do not know how they should act to solve their problems. • **Loose ends** are things that still need to be done or explained: *My research is done, but I have some loose ends to tie up.* • **Loose-leaf** describes pieces of paper that are not attached to each other and are easily removed and replaced: *a loose-leaf notebook*

loosely /'luː·sli/ *adv* • *The package was loosely wrapped.*

loosen /'luː·sən/ *v* [I/T] to become or make (something) less firmly fixed • *The screws holding the light fixture have loosened, and it's* *dangling from the ceiling.* [I] ∘ *(fig.) When immigration laws were loosened, the number of immigrants shot up.* [T]

loose NOT TIGHT /luːs/ *adj* [-er/-est only] not tight; not fitting closely to the body or the thing that is covered • *Wear comfortable, loose clothing to your exercise class.* • Loose can also mean not closely following something original, or not exact: *The film is a loose adaptation of Conrad's novel.*

loosely /ˈluːsli/ *adv* • *a loosely knit sweater*
loosen /ˈluːsən/ *v* [T] • *It was hot in the room so I loosened my tie.* • To **loosen up** is to stretch your muscles, esp. by doing special exercises before a hard physical activity: *He always spent 20 minutes loosening up before going for his morning run.* • To **loosen up** is also to relax, esp. after being nervous: *She was nervous at the beginning of the interview but loosened up after a while.*

loose IMMORAL /luːs/ *adj* [-er/-est only] *dated* (of a woman) lacking in morals, esp. sexually free

loot /luːt/ *v* [I/T] (said esp. of large numbers of people) to steal from stores • *Riot police were sent to prevent the mob from looting.* [I] • To loot (something) is also to take a lot of money away from it that does not belong to you: *The officers of the corporation looted the company of millions of dollars.* [T]

loot /luːt/ *n* [U] money or valuable objects that have been stolen • *Three men have been sentenced to prison for taking part in the robbery, but the loot was never recovered.*

lop /lɑp/ *v* [T] **-pp-** to cut (a piece from something) with a single quick action • *We've got to lop off the lower branches of this tree.* [M] ∘ *(fig.) The city council lopped thousands of dollars from the budget.*

lope /loʊp/ *v* [I] (of a person or animal) to run with long, relaxed steps

lopsided /ˈlɑpˈsaɪd·əd/ *adj* with one side or part much bigger or higher than the other; uneven • *The Yankees won by the lopsided score of 17 to 2.*

loquacious /loʊˈkweɪ·ʃəs/ *adj* having the habit of talking a lot

lord TITLE /lɔːrd/ *n* [C] (in some countries) a title of a man who has a specially high social rank, or the person himself • A lord is also a man who has a lot of power in a particular area: *Several alleged drug lords were arrested.* If you **lord it over** someone, you behave as if you are more important and have a right to tell that person what to do: *He likes to lord it over his little sister.* • Compare LADY TITLE.

Lord GOD /lɔːrd/ *n* [U] (in the Christian and Jewish religions) God • Some people say Lord to express surprise, shock, or worry: *Oh Lord! I've forgotten the tickets!*

lore /lɔːr, loʊr/ *n* [U] knowledge and stories, usually traditional, about a subject • *He pub-*

lished several books on Indian lore and hunting.

lorry /ˈlɔːr·i/ *n* [C] *Br for* TRUCK

lose NOT BE ABLE TO FIND /luːz/ *v* [T] *past* **lost** /lɔːst/ to not be able to find (something) • *I lost my keys somewhere in the house.* ∘ *Two officers chased the suspect, but he turned down an alley and they lost sight of him* (= could no longer see him). • *I've lost count of* (= cannot remember) *how many times she's been late for work this month.* • If you **lose sight** of something, you do not consider it, or you forget about it: *We cannot lose sight of the need to ensure public safety.* • If you **lose track** of something, you do not know any longer where it is, or you cannot remember it: *I've lost track of most of my old college friends, unfortunately.*

lose NO LONGER POSSESS /luːz/ *v* [T] *past* **lost** /lɔːst/ to no longer have (something), because it has been taken away from you, either by accident or purposely • *Workers will lose their jobs if the plant closes.* ∘ *He lost his leg in a car accident.* • When a person loses their life, they die or are killed: *George lost his wife in 1990* (= she died then). • If you lose money you have risked, you do not make a profit and do not get your money back. • A business that is losing money is spending more money than it is receiving. • *These are difficult days, but this is no time to lose heart* (= weaken in determination or hope).

lose BE DEFEATED /luːz/ *v* [I/T] *past* **lost** /lɔːst/ to fail to succeed in (a game or competition) • *If we lose again, we're out of the playoffs.* [I] ∘ *Anderson lost the election by a narrow margin.* [T] • If you **lose face**, you become less respected: *She had to accept defeat without losing face.* • *(infml)* If you **lose out**, you suffer a defeat or disadvantage: *If you don't read the newspaper, you lose out on an awful lot.*

loser /ˈluː·zər/ *n* [C] a person who is defeated, or someone who regularly fails • *No one ever asks me out—I'm such a loser!*

lose NOT MAINTAIN /luːz/ *v* [T] *past* **lost** /lɔːst/ to not maintain or no longer have control over (a quality or ability) • *She used to play tennis regularly, but lately she's lost interest in it.* ∘ *The driver lost control of her car.* ∘ *The dog is losing her eyesight/hearing/sense of smell.* ∘ *Carl lost his balance and fell down the stairs.* • If you lose time or an opportunity, you waste it. • If a clock loses time, it goes more slowly than it should. • If you **lose** your **temper** or *(infml)* **lose it/lose** your **cool/lose** your **head**, you fail to maintain control of yourself: *When he saw his wife dancing with another man, Dave really lost it.* • *(infml)* If someone **loses** their **mind**, they are acting crazy, or becoming mentally ill: *I'm going to lose my mind if I have to stay here any longer.* • If you **lose** your **touch**, your ability is not as effective as it once was: *The director seems to have lost his touch for subtlety.* • If you **lose touch** with someone, you are not communicating with them as you once did: *I lost touch with Katie after she moved to Canada.*

lose HAVE LESS OF /luːz/ *v* [T] *past* **lost** /lɔːst/ to have less of (something), esp. in the body • *to lose blood/weight* • To **lose sleep over** something is to stay awake because you worry about it a lot.

lose CONFUSE /luːz/ *v* [T] *past* **lost** /lɔːst/ to confuse (someone) • *I'm sorry, you've lost me—would you go over that again?*

loss NOT HAVING /lɔːs/ *n* [C/U] the action or state of not having or keeping something any more • *The company's losses over the last few years have been staggering.* [C] • Loss may mean death: *They never got over the loss of their son.* [U]

loss NOT CONTROLLING /lɔːs/ *n* [C/U] the action or state of not maintaining or having control over something any more • *He suffered a gradual loss of memory in his later years.* [C] • If you are **at a loss**, you do not know what to do: *I'm at a loss to know how I can help you.* ○ *I was so embarrassed that I was at a loss for words* (= I didn't know what to say).

lost CANNOT BE FOUND /lɔːst/ *adj* (of a person) unable to find your way, or (of an item) not to be found • *a lost child/pet/earring* ○ *We got lost on the way home.* ○ (*fig.*) *I'd be lost without you* (= I would not know what to do). • A **lost cause** is something that cannot be achieved: *It rained all weekend, so painting the house was a lost cause.*

lost CONFUSED /lɔːst/ *adj* confused, or not able to understand or appreciate • *His explanation was so complicated, I got lost after the first example.* ○ *Everyone else thought it was funny, but that joke was lost on me.*

lost LOSE /lɔːst/ *past simple and past participle of* LOSE

lot LARGE AMOUNT /lɑt/ *n infml* • **A lot of** or **lots of** means a large amount or number of something: *I saved a lot of money with those coupons.* ○ *They hope to have lots of children.* • **A lot** can mean much or often: *You look a lot like your sister.* ○ *We eat out a lot.* • LP AMOUNTS

lot LAND /lɑt/ *n* [C] an area of land • *They purchased a lot last summer and built a house on it the following year.*

lotion /ˈloʊ-ʃən/ *n* [C/U] a liquid that is put on your skin in order to protect it, improve its condition, or make it smell pleasant • *She applied some hand/suntan lotion and rubbed it in.* [U]

lottery /ˈlɑt-ə-ri/ *n* [C] a system of selling numbered tickets and giving prizes to those people whose numbers are chosen by chance • *Even if she won the lottery, Paige says she'd still keep her job.*

loud NOISY /laʊd/ *adj, adv* [-er/-est only] having or producing a large amount of sound • *a loud noise* ○ *Would you speak a little louder, please?* • If something is **loud and clear**, it is

easily understood: *We need to get our message through loud and clear.* • A **loudmouth** is a person who talks too noisily or too much, esp. in an offensive or stupid way. • A **loudspeaker** is a device that changes electrical signals into sounds loud enough to be heard at a distance.

loudly /ˈlaʊd-li/ *adv* • *"What does she want now?" he asked loudly.*

loudness /ˈlaʊd-nəs/ *n* [U] • *Differences in loudness are measured in decibels.*

loud BRIGHT /laʊd/ *adj* [-er/-est only] (of colors) unpleasantly bright • *a loud tie/pattern*

lounge ROOM /laʊndʒ/ *n* [C] a public room for relaxing or waiting in, or a bar or **nightclub** • *a faculty lounge* ○ *a cocktail lounge*

lounge RELAX /laʊndʒ/ *v* [I] to stand or sit in a relaxed way • *She was lounging on the beach.*

louse /laʊs/ *n* [C] *pl* **lice** /laɪs/ a small insect that lives on the bodies of people and animals

louse up *obj*, **louse** *obj* **up** /ˈlaʊˈsʌp/ *v adv* [M] *infml* to spoil or make (something) worse • *There isn't a mechanic alive who doesn't louse up a job once in a while.*

lousy /ˈlaʊ-zi/ *adj* [-er/-est only] *infml* bad or unpleasant • *The city does a lousy job of snow removal.* ○ *I thought the movie was lousy.*

lout /laʊt/ *n* [C] *infml* a rude, stupid, or awkward man • *She married a lout.*

love LIKE SOMEONE /lʌv/ *v* [T] to have a strong affection for (someone), which can be combined with a strong romantic and sexual attraction to them • *Susan loved her brother dearly.* ○ *"I love you and want to marry you, Emily," he said.*

love /lʌv/ *n* [U] • *Our love will last forever.* ○ *Children need lots of love.* ○ *"I'm seeing Laura next week." "Oh, please give/send her my love"* (= Tell her I am thinking about her with affection). • You can write love/love from/all my love/lots of love before your name at the end of letters to family and friends. • A person who is **in love** is experiencing a romantic attraction for another person. • A **love affair** is a sexual relationship between two people who are not married to each other.

lovable, **loveable** /ˈlʌv-ə-bəl/ *adj* easy to love • *Owen's a lovable little kid with lots of energy.*

lover /ˈlʌv-ər/ *n* [C] a partner in a romantic or sexual relationship, esp. one you are not married to

loving /ˈlʌv-ɪŋ/ *adj* • *a loving home/relationship*

lovingly /ˈlʌv-ɪŋ-li/ *adv* • *Grandma lovingly kissed the baby.*

love LIKE SOMETHING /lʌv/ *v* to like (something) very much • *My kids love cartoons.* [T] ○ *We'd love to own our own home.* [+ *to* infinitive]

love /lʌv/ *n* [C/U] • *I don't share my boyfriend's love for sports.* [U] ○ *Music is Stephen's greatest love.* [C]

lover /ˈlʌv-ər/ *n* [C] a person who likes or enjoys a particular thing • *The remote island is ideal for nature lovers.*

loving /'lʌv·ɪŋ/ *adj* • *He described his work in loving detail.*

lovely /'lʌv·li/ *adj* [-er/-est only] attractive and beautiful, or pleasant and enjoyable • *You look lovely in that dress.* ○ *Thank you for a lovely evening.*

loveliness /'lʌv·li:·nəs/ *n* [U]

love seat /'lʌv·si:t/ *n* [C] a small SOFA (= soft seat with a back and arms) that is only long enough for two people

loving /'lʌv·ɪŋ/ *adj* • See at LOVE LIKE SOMEONE, LOVE LIKE SOMETHING.

lovingly /'lʌv·ɪŋ·li/ *adv* • See at LOVE LIKE SOMEONE.

low NOT HIGH /loʊ/ *adj, adv* [-er/-est only] not high or tall; close to the ground or near the bottom of something • *a low fence/ceiling* ○ *Until I'm a better skier, I'll stay on the lower slopes.* ○ *That plane is flying awfully low.* • Clothing that is **low-cut** does not cover the upper part of the chest: *a low-cut blouse* • **Low-lying** land is at or near the level of the sea. • **Low tide** is the time when the sea has reached its lowest level.

lower /'loʊ·ər/ *v* [T] to let or bring (someone or something) down, or make (something) less high • *She lowered the blinds to block out the afternoon sun.*

low SMALLER THAN USUAL /loʊ/ *adj, adv* [-er/-est only] smaller than the usual or average size, number, value, or amount • *They have the lowest food prices in town.* ○ *Temperatures will dip lower near the end of the week.* ○ *Believe it or not, this dessert is low in calories.* • If a supply of something becomes low, you have very little of it left: *We're running low on gas.* • Low can also mean producing only a small amount of sound, heat, or light: *They spoke in low voices.* ○ *She turned the lights/heat down low.* • Low can also mean of bad quality: *My test results were disappointingly low.* • **Low beams** are the lights on the front of a car when they are on but not switched to their brightest level. Compare **high beams** at HIGH ABOVE AVERAGE. • If something is **low-key**, it is simple, controlled, and not intended to attract attention: *The wedding will be a low-key affair, with fewer than thirty guests.*

low /loʊ/ *n* [C] a smaller than usual amount or level, or the smallest amount or level • *Enrollment at the college reached new lows this fall.* ○ *The temperature in Boston reached a record low last night.*

lower /'loʊ·ər/ *v* [I/T] to reduce (something), or to become less • *They lowered the asking price of their house.* [T] ○ *Please lower your voice* (= speak more softly). [T]

low NOT IMPORTANT /loʊ/ *adj* [-er/-est only] not important, or not of high rank • *low social status* • **Low-level** means having little impor-

tance or rank: *a low-level job* • A **lowlife** is someone of bad character.

lowly /'loʊ·li/ *adj* not having importance or rank • *Steve worked his way up in the hotel business, from a lowly porter to a senior manager.*

low SOUND /loʊ/ *adj* (of a sound or voice) near or at the bottom of the range of sounds • *a low voice/note* • If a sound is **low-pitched**, it is at the bottom of the range of sounds: *He gave a low-pitched whistle and his dog came running.*

low NOT KIND /loʊ/ *adj* [-er/-est only] (of behavior or speech) mean or unfair • *What a cruel comment—how low can you get?* • A **low blow** is something unexpected and unfair: *Criticizing his wife's family was a low blow.*

lower /'loʊ·ər/ *v* [T] • If you **lower** your**self**, you behave in a way that is dishonest or immoral: *I never expected him to lower himself by stealing.*

low UNHAPPY /loʊ/ *adj* [-er/-est only] unhappy or discouraged • *She's feeling pretty low because she failed her driver's test.*

lowbrow /'loʊ·braʊ/ *adj disapproving* (of literature, art, music, movies, or plays) not serious and intended for people who are not knowledgeable about these forms of art, or (of people) not intelligent and not knowing a lot about such things • *lowbrow tastes* ○ *lowbrow readers* • Compare HIGHBROW; MIDDLEBROW.

lowdown /'loʊ·daʊn/ *n* [U] the most important facts and information about something • *Our fashion editor gives you the lowdown on winter coats for this season.*

lowercase /ˌloʊ·ər'keɪs/ *n* [U] the small form of letters when they are printed or written • Compare UPPERCASE.

lowercase /ˌloʊ·ər'keɪs/ *adj* [not gradable]

loyal /'lɔɪ·əl/ *adj* always supportive • *People close to Woodruff are fiercely loyal and quick to shower her with superlatives.*

loyalty /'lɔɪ·əl·ti/ *n* [C/U] • *My loyalties to my family come before my loyalties to my work.* [C]

lozenge /'lɑz·əndʒ, 'lɑs-/ *n* [C] a small, flavored candy, often containing medicine, which dissolves when sucked in the mouth

LP /el'pi:/ *n* [C] a record that plays for about 20 minutes a side

LSD, *slang* **acid** *n* [U] *abbreviation for* lysergic acid diethylamide (= an illegal drug taken for pleasure)

lubricate /'lu:·brəˌkeɪt/, *infml* **lube** /lu:b/ *v* [T] to put oil or an oily substance on or in something so that its parts move easily • *to lubricate gears/machinery*

lubricant /'lu:·brə·kənt/, *infml* **lube** /lu:b/ *n* [C/U] a substance that is used to make parts move easily

lubrication /ˌlu:·brə'keɪ·ʃən/, *infml* **lube** /lu:b/ *n* [U] • *engine lubrication*

lucid /'lu:·səd/ *adj* (of speech or writing) clearly expressed and easy to understand, or (of a person) thinking or reasoning clearly • *The* author's style is lucid and sober. ○ He didn't seem very lucid after the accident.

luck /lʌk/ n [U] chance, or that which happens to you as the result of chance • It was just by luck that she got the job. • Luck is also the amount of success experienced: She had bad luck in the last race, finishing fourth. ○ Jean had good luck in finding her great-grandmother's birth records. • Luck is also success: I've got a job interview today, so wish me luck. • "Do you have any tickets for tonight's game?" "You're in/out of luck (= They are available/ not available)."

lucky /'lʌk·i/ adj [-er/-est only] having good things happen by chance • For ten games, the Orioles have gotten every conceivable lucky break. ○ Today is my lucky day!

luckily /'lʌk·ə·li/ adv • I was late getting to the airport, but luckily for me, the plane was delayed.

□ **luck into** /'lʌk·ɪn·tuː, -tə/ v adv [T] infml to get or experience something good by chance • We lucked into tickets for the Super Bowl because we knew the coach's cousin.

□ **luck out** /'-'-/ v adv [I] infml to have something good happen by chance • Marj really lucked out when she won the raffle.

lucrative /'luː·krəṭ·ɪv/ adj producing much money or making a large profit • The owner and general manager offered the player a lucrative lifetime contract.

ludicrous /'luː·də·krəs/ adj ridiculous or foolish; laughable because unreasonable or unsuitable • The charges seemed ludicrous at first, but damning evidence kept piling up.

lug /lʌg/ v [T] -gg- to carry or pull (something heavy) with much effort • I lugged my suitcase to the check-in counter.

luggage /'lʌg·ɪdʒ/ n [U] the bags or other containers that you take your possessions in when traveling; BAGGAGE • The luggage of our tour group was piled up next to the bus.

lukewarm /'luː·kwɔːrm/ adj [not gradable] (esp. of a liquid) only slightly warm • How can you drink lukewarm coffee? • A reaction that is lukewarm is not enthusiastic: His support for the civil rights measures was lukewarm.

lull /lʌl/ v [T] to cause (someone) to feel calm, sleepy, or safe • The music lulled the infant to sleep. ○ Carrying a weapon lulled him into a false sense of security.

lull /lʌl/ n [C] a period of quiet or reduced activity • a lull in the conversation

lullaby /'lʌl·ə,baɪ/ n [C] a quiet, gentle song sung to children to help them go to sleep

lumber WOOD /'lʌm·bər/ n [U] wood that has been cut into various lengths for building • A **lumberjack** (also **logger**) is a person whose job is to cut down trees and transport the LOGS. • A **lumberyard** is a place where lumber is stored and sold.

lumber MOVE /'lʌm·bər/ v [I always + adv/ prep] to move in a slow, awkward, and heavy way • A noisy, old, pickup truck lumbered past.

luminary /'luː·mə,ner·i/ n [C] a person who is famous and important in a particular area of activity • The speaker is a luminary in the field of cancer research.

luminous /'luː·mə·nəs/ adj producing or reflecting light, esp. in the dark • The snowy landscape was growing luminous in the late afternoon light.

lump /lʌmp/ n [C] a solid mass without a regular shape • The gravy had lumps of flour in it. • A lump is also a swelling under the skin: She found a lump in her breast. • **A lump in** your **throat** is a tight feeling in your throat because of emotion. • A **lump sum** is a single payment of an amount rather than several payments of smaller amounts.

lump /lʌmp/ v [T] to consider or deal with as a group • Children of various abilities are lumped together in one class.

lumpy /'lʌm·pi/ adj • a lumpy pillow

lunar /'luː·nər/ adj [not gradable] of or relating to the moon • a lunar eclipse

lunatic /'luː·nə,tɪk/ n [C] a foolish or crazy person • He drives like a lunatic.

lunatic /'luː·nə,tɪk/ adj [not gradable] • A **lunatic fringe** is the members of a group whose opinions are extreme and different from those of the rest of the group: The violence was the work of a lunatic fringe.

lunacy /'luː·nə·si/ n [U] extreme foolishness or mental illness • It would be lunacy to try and climb the mountain in this weather.

lunch /lʌntʃ/ n [C/U] a meal eaten in the middle of the day, or the food prepared for this meal • We had soup and sandwiches for lunch. [U] ○ I take my lunch to work. [C] • **Lunchtime** is the time around the middle of the day when lunch is usually eaten.

lunch /lʌntʃ/ v [I] • We lunched on crackers and cheese.

luncheon /'lʌn·tʃən/ n [C] a formal lunch • The president hosted a luncheon for the press group.

luncheonette /,lʌn·tʃə'net/ n [C] a small restaurant serving simple, light meals

lung /lʌŋ/ n [C] either of the two breathing organs in the chest of people and some animals

lunge /lʌndʒ/ v [I always + adv/prep] to move forward with sudden force • The goalkeeper lunged at the ball and knocked it away.

lunge /lʌndʒ/ n [C] a sudden forward movement

lurch /lɜrtʃ/ v [I] to move in an irregular way, esp. making sudden movements forward or to the side • When he put the truck into gear, it lurched forward.

lure /lʊr/ n [C/U] anything that attracts people or animals, or the qualities that make something attractive • The lure of easy money led them to commit fraud. [U] • A lure is an object used to attract fish or wild animals in order to catch them. [C]

lure /lʊr/ v [T] to attract (a person or animal) • *The university hopes to lure a new coach with an attractive salary package.*

lurid /ˈlʊr·əd/ adj shocking because involving violence or sex • *She told me all the lurid details of her divorce.*

lurk /lɜrk/ v [I] to stay around a place secretly, or to stay hidden, waiting to attack or appear • *When I was four, I was convinced there was a monster lurking in my closet.*

lurking /ˈlɜr·kɪŋ/ adj [not gradable] • (*fig.*) *She had a lurking suspicion* (= a feeling that stayed in her mind) *that he wasn't telling the truth.*

luscious /ˈlʌʃ·əs/ adj [not gradable] having a pleasant sweet taste or smell • *luscious fruit tarts and cream pies* • Luscious can also mean pleasing to see, hear, or feel: *She slipped into her luscious pale pink silk pajamas.* • Someone luscious is sexually attractive: *a luscious woman*

lush /lʌʃ/ adj [-er/-est only] (of plants, or an area of land with plants) growing densely • *The lake, with its lush scenery, is a favorite with canoeists.*

lust /lʌst/ n [U] strong sexual desire • *It was a steamy drama of lust, greed, and betrayal in a New England family.* • Lust is also any strong desire: *a lust for power and fame*

lust /lʌst/ v [I always + adv/prep] • *I lusted after one kind of man, but married the kind my mother wanted me to marry.* • To lust after or for something is also to have a strong desire for it: *Cathie has been lusting for my job for a long time.*

luster BRIGHTNESS /ˈlʌs·tər/ n [U] the brightness of a smooth or shiny surface • *The polished furniture had a rich luster.*

lustrous /ˈlʌs·trəs/ adj [not gradable] • *This conditioner will give your hair a lustrous glow.*

luster SPECIAL QUALITY /ˈlʌs·tər/ n [U] the quality of being attractive or special • *The commercial district around the theater had lost its luster, becoming a magnet for the homeless and driving moviegoers elsewhere.*

lusty /ˈlʌs·ti/ adj healthy, strong, and energetic • *Her lusty, alto voice has seldom sounded better.*

lustily /ˈlʌs·tə·li/ adv [not gradable] • *The baby cried lustily.*

Lutheran /ˈluː·θə·rən/ n [C], adj [not gradable] (a member) of a Christian religious group that is one of the Protestant churches • *a Lutheran church* ○ *a Lutheran minister*

luxuriant /ləɡ'ʒʊr·iː·ənt, lək'ʃʊr-/ adj having a thick and healthy appearance • *Her luxuriant hair fell around her shoulders.*

luxury /ˈlʌk·ʃə·ri, ˈlʌɡ·ʒə-/ n [C/U] great comfort, esp. as provided by expensive and beautiful possessions, surroundings, or food, or something enjoyable and often expensive but not necessary • *a life of luxury* [U] ○ *a luxury hotel* [U] ○ *Having an extra bathroom was at first a luxury, but after we had children it became a necessity.* [C] • A luxury is also any unusual, enjoyable activity: *Sleeping late was a real luxury.* [C]

luxurious /ləɡ'ʒʊr·iː·əs, lək'ʃʊr-/ adj • *luxurious accommodations* ○ *a luxurious hotel/resort*

lying /ˈlaɪ·ɪŋ/ present participle of LIE

lynch /lɪntʃ/ v [T] (of a group of people) to kill (someone, often someone accused of a crime) without a trial, esp. by HANGING them (= putting a rope around their neck and letting them fall to break their neck) • *In the 1890s, white Americans lynched an average of one African American every two or three days.*

lyric /ˈlɪr·ɪk/, **lyrical** /ˈlɪr·ɪ·kəl/ adj [not gradable] expressive esp. of emotions, and often having the quality of a song • *lyric poetry*

lyrics /ˈlɪr·ɪks/ pl n the words of a song

M, m

M LETTER , **m** /em/ *n* [C] *pl* **M's** or **Ms** or **m's** or **ms** the 13th letter of the English alphabet

M NUMBER , **m** /em/ *number* the ROMAN NUMERAL for the number 1000

m MEASUREMENT *n* [C] *pl* **m** *abbreviation for* METER MEASUREMENT

M SIZE /em/ *adj* [not gradable] *abbreviation for* MEDIUM AVERAGE , used esp. on clothing to show its size

ma /mɑ/ *n* [C] *infml* mother • *She was thrilled when her baby said, "Ma."* • LP TITLES AND FORMS OF ADDRESS

M.A. *n* [C] *abbreviation for* **Master of Arts**, see at MASTER SKILLED PERSON • *My brother has an M.A. in linguistics.* • LP EDUCATION IN THE US

ma'am /mæm/ *contraction of* MADAM WOMAN • *Can I help you, ma'am?*

macabre /məˈkɑb·rə, -ˈkɑb/ *adj* causing shock and fear because connected with death, esp. strange or cruel death • *Retrieving the mangled bodies from the wreckage was a macabre task.*

macaroni /ˌmæk·əˈroʊ·ni/ *n* [U] a type of pasta in the shape of small tubes • *macaroni and cheese*

Mace /meɪs/ *n* [U] *trademark* a chemical in a container which, when sprayed into a person's face, causes their eyes to sting and become full of tears

machete /məˈʃeṭ·i/ *n* [C] a big knife with a wide blade • *You'd need a machete to clear a path through this undergrowth.*

machinations /ˌmæk·əˈneɪ·ʃənz, ˌmæʃ-/ *pl n* complicated and secret plans, esp. in obtaining or using power • *She complained about the machinations political candidates employed to win.*

machine /məˈʃiːn/ *n* [C] a device with moving parts that uses power to do work of a particular type • *a sewing/washing machine* ○ *an answering machine* • A machine is also a group of people who control a political organization: *He was a product of an old-line party machine.* • A **machine gun** is an automatic gun that can fire a lot of bullets one after the other very quickly. • Information that is **machine-readable** is in a form can be used by a computer.

machinery /məˈʃiː·nə·ri/ *n* [U] a group of machines, or the movable parts of a machine • *farm machinery* ○ *Some of the older machinery breaks down frequently.*

machinist /məˈʃiː·nəst/ *n* [C] a person whose job is operating or repairing machines

machismo /mɑˈtʃiːz·moʊ, -ˈkiːz-, -ˈkɪz-/ *n* [U] strong pride in behaving in a way that is thought to be typically male, esp. by showing strength and power

macho /ˈmɑtʃ·oʊ/ *adj* behaving in a way that is thought to be typical of a man, esp. by seeming strong and powerful but also seeming too determined to avoid showing weakness and sympathy • *He's too macho to admit that a woman can do his job as well as he can.*

mackerel /ˈmæk·rəl/ *n* [C/U] *pl* **mackerel** an edible sea fish

macro– /ˈmæk·roʊ/ *combining form* large, or relating to the whole of something and not just its parts • *macroeconomics* • Compare MICRO–.

mad ANGRY /mæd/ *adj* [-er/-est only] **-dd-** angry or annoyed • *I get so mad at her I sometimes start screaming.*

maddening /ˈmæd·ən·ɪŋ/ *adj* annoying • *Airlines make you wait in maddening ticket counter lines for hours on end.*

mad NOT CONTROLLED /mæd/ *adj* [-er/-est only] **-dd-** (of an activity) wild, fast, or excited and not well controlled • *We made a mad dash for the school bus.*

madly /ˈmæd·li/ *adv* • *Just before my in-laws arrived, I rushed around madly trying to clean the place up.*

mad ENTHUSIASTIC /mæd/ *adj* [-er/-est only] **-dd-** *infml* very enthusiastic and interested • *Jeanne's mad about old Woody Allen movies.*

madly /ˈmæd·li/ *adv* • *She says she's madly in love with him.*

mad MENTALLY ILL /mæd/ *adj* [-er/-est only] **-dd-** mentally ill, or unable to behave in a reasonable way; INSANE • *In his years as a prisoner of war, he often felt as if he might go mad.* • If you call a place a **madhouse**, you mean it is wild and noisy, with too many activities going on: *I can't study here, this place is a madhouse!* • A **madman** is someone who is mentally ill, or who behaves in a way that is seems strange or not controlled.

madness /ˈmæd·nəs/ *n* [U] • *There was a history of madness (= mental illness) in her family.* ○ *It would be sheer madness (= crazy) to ignore the symptoms and do nothing.*

madam WOMAN /ˈmæd·əm/, *contraction* **ma'am** *n* [U] *fml* a polite word used to address a woman, or a title for a woman used before a position • *"May I help you, madam?"* ○ *Madam President* • Compare SIR MAN . LP TITLES AND FORMS OF ADDRESS

madam SEX WORKER /ˈmæd·əm/ *n* [C] a woman who is in charge of a BROTHEL (= place where men pay to have sex with women)

madcap /ˈmæd·kæp/ *adj* foolish but often amusing, and usually involving doing something risky or dangerous • *The madcap antics of the clowns made us laugh.*

made /meɪd/ *past simple and past participle of* MAKE • If two people are **made for each other**, they are suited to be romantically involved. • Someone who is **made of money** is very rich.

made–to–order /ˌmeɪd·təˈɔːrd·ər/ adj [not gradable] (esp. of clothing) created especially for a particular person • *made-to-order boots* • A situation that is made-to-order is perfect: *The weather on this vacation has been made-to-order so far.*

made–up WEARING MAKEUP /ˈmeɪdˈʌp/ adj wearing esp. a lot of makeup • *She was heavily made-up and wearing a wig.*

made–up INVENTED /ˈmeɪdˈʌp/ adj (of stories) created by the imagination, or invented and not true • *We thought the child's story about being kidnapped was made-up, but we were wrong.*

Madison Avenue /ˈmæd·ə·səˈnæv·əˌnuː, -ˌnjuː/ n [U] the advertising industry in the US

madly /ˈmæd·li/ adv • See at MAD NOT CONTROLLED, MAD ENTHUSIASTIC.

madness /ˈmæd·nəs/ n • See at MAD MENTALLY ILL.

Madonna /məˈdɑn·ə/ n [C/U] the mother of Jesus, or a picture or statue of her

maelstrom /ˈmeɪl·strəm, -ˌstrɑm/ n [C] a situation in which there is great confusion, disagreement, or violence • *It was a country in turmoil, caught up in a maelstrom of change.*

maestro /ˈmaɪ·stroʊ/ n [C] pl **maestros** a person who is very skilled in CONDUCTING (= directing the performance of) music or writing music

Mafia /ˈmɑf·iː·ə, ˈmæf-/ n [U] a large criminal organization, esp. a secret criminal organization that is active in the US and Italy

magazine /ˌmæg·əˈziːn/ n [C] a type of thin book with a paper cover that is published regularly and usually contains articles and photographs • *a weekly/monthly magazine* • A magazine on television is a regularly broadcast program that reports about news events or other true stories.

magenta /məˈdʒent·ə/ adj, n [C/U] (of) a dark, purple-red color

maggot /ˈmæg·ət/ n [C] a creature like a very small WORM (= an animal with a soft body and no arms or legs) that later develops into a flying insect

magic IMAGINARY POWER /ˈmædʒ·ɪk/ n [U] (esp. in stories for children) the use of special powers to make things happen that would usually be impossible • *a tale of witchcraft and magic* • Magic is also the skill of performing tricks to entertain people, such as making things seem to appear and disappear, or the tricks performed: *My daughter loves doing magic.*

magical /ˈmædʒ·ɪ·kəl/ adj • *It's a story about a timid schoolteacher who obtains magical powers after he's hit by a lightning bolt.*

magician /məˈdʒɪʃ·ən/ n [C] a person who performs tricks as entertainment, such as making things seem to appear and disappear

magic SPECIAL QUALITY /ˈmædʒ·ɪk/ n [U] a spec-

ial, exciting quality that makes something or someone different and better than others • *As an actress, she has lost none of her magic, and she still is thrilling to watch.*

magical /ˈmædʒ·ɪ·kəl/ adj • *There was something magical about that evening that I will never forget.*

Magic Marker /ˈmædʒ·ɪkˈmɑr·kər/ n [C] trademark a type of pen available in many colors of ink that has a thick writing end made of fiber

magistrate /ˈmædʒ·əˌstreɪt/ n [C] a judge in a law court who deals with crimes that are not serious

magnanimous /mægˈnæn·ə·məs/ adj generous and honorable, esp. toward a competitor or enemy • *The Yankees' manager was magnanimous in defeat, praising Seattle for its fine play.*

magnate /ˈmæg·nət, -neɪt/ n [C] a person who is very successful, powerful, and rich, esp. in a particular business • *a real estate/media magnate*

magnesium /mægˈniː·ziː·əm/ n [U] a silver-white metallic element that burns very brightly and is used in making FIREWORKS (= explosions producing colored patterns for entertainment)

magnet /ˈmæg·nət/ n [C] an object, esp. a piece of iron, that is able to attract iron and steel objects toward itself • *Magnets are used to attach the toy train's cars to the engine.* ○ *We use a refrigerator magnet* (= small decorative magnet that will stick to a steel door) *to hang our kids' latest drawings.* ○ *(fig.) New York City remains a magnet for tourists* (= it attracts them). • A **magnet school** is a special school that is designed to offer a high-quality education and to attract students from all racial and economic groups in an area. LP EDUCATION IN THE US

magnetic /mægˈnet·ɪk/ adj • *Leni was playing with the magnetic letters on the refrigerator.* ○ *(fig.) She has a magnetic personality* (= it is powerfully attractive). • A **magnetic tape/strip** is a plastic strip covered with a substance that makes it act like a magnet and on which sound, images, or computer information can be recorded.

magnetism /ˈmæg·nəˌtɪz·əm/ n [U] the power of a magnet to attract other objects • *(fig.) Elvis's animal magnetism* (= powerful physical attraction) *made him a beloved celebrity to millions.*

magnificent /mægˈnɪf·ə·sənt/ adj causing admiration esp. because of an unusual quality such as great size or beauty • *New Orleans is famous for its magnificent old oak trees.*

magnificence /mægˈnɪf·ə·səns/ n [U] • *the magnificence of nature*

magnify /ˈmæg·nəˌfaɪ/ v [T] to make (something) look larger than it is, esp. by looking at it through a special piece of glass • *Although* *your skin looks smooth, when magnified you can see a lot of little bumps and holes.* • (fig.) To magnify something is also to make it seem more important or more serious than it really is: *He always magnifies the problems and inconveniences of travel.* • A **magnifying glass** is a special piece of glass, usually with a handle attached, that you can hold over something to make objects under it appear larger than they are.

magnification /ˌmæg·nə·fəˈkeɪ·ʃən/ *n* [C/U] the act of making something look larger than it is, or the degree to which it does look larger

magnitude /ˈmæg·nə·tuːd/ *n* [U] large size or great importance • *The magnitude of the task would have discouraged an ordinary man.*

magnolia /mægˈnoʊl·jə/ *n* [C] a type of tree with large, sweet-smelling, usually white or pink flowers, esp. common in the southeastern US

magpie /ˈmæg·paɪ/ *n* [C] a bird with black-and-white feathers and a long tail

mahogany /məˈhɑg·ə·ni/ *n* [U] a type of tree that grows in hot regions of the earth, or its dark, red-brown wood used esp. to make furniture • *a mahogany chest of drawers*

maid /meɪd/ *n* [C] a woman who is employed to clean hotel rooms and make them neat, or a woman who is a servant in a person's home • *We left a note in our room for the maid to give us extra towels.*

maiden WOMAN /ˈmeɪd·ⁿn/, **maid** /meɪd/ *n* [C] *literary or old use* a girl or young woman • *In the story, the prince woos the fair maiden.* • A woman's **maiden name** is the family name she has before she gets married.

maiden FIRST /ˈmeɪd·ⁿn/ *adj* [not gradable] (esp. of a trip by a ship or vehicle) first • *a maiden voyage/flight*

maid of honor /ˌmeɪd·əˈvɑn·ər/ *n* [C] (at a wedding) a girl or woman who is the most important BRIDESMAID (= woman who helps the woman getting married)

mail /meɪl/ *n* [U] the letters and packages that are transported and delivered to your home or the place you work, esp. those delivered by the government's system • *She spent the morning reading and answering mail.* ○ *The mail is usually delivered before noon.* • A **mailbox** is a metal container along a street or in another public place in which you can put a letter you are sending by mail, or a box outside a person's house where letters are delivered. • A **mailman** is a male **letter carrier**. See at LETTER MESSAGE. • **Mail order** is a way of buying goods in which you choose what you want, usually from a CATALOG (= a special book showing what goods are available), and it is sent to you: *I often buy clothes by mail order.*

mail /meɪl/ *v* [T] to send (esp. letters or packages) by the mail system • *She mailed the letter last week but it still hasn't arrived.*

mailing /ˈmeɪ·lɪŋ/ *n* [C] • *The museum sent out a mailing* (= a lot of letters sent at one time) *asking for donations.* • A **mailing list** is a list of names and addresses kept by an organization so that it can send information or advertisements to the people on the list.

maim /meɪm/ *v* [I/T] to injure (a person) so severely that a part of their body will no longer work correctly or is completely lacking • *Many civilians have been maimed by land mines.* [T]

main MOST IMPORTANT /meɪn/ *adj* [not gradable] most important or larger • *The main thing is to keep calm and don't get angry.* ○ *The main social event of the summer was a dance and reception.* • (*slang*) *There's a great little restaurant just off the main drag* (= the town's most important street). • The **mainland** is the main part of a country or continent, not including the islands around it: *the Japanese mainland* ○ *The island is accessible by ferry from the mainland.* • **Main Street** in a town is the street with the most important stores and businesses.

mainly /ˈmeɪn·li/ *adv* [not gradable] usually, or to a large degree • *The group is mainly made up of young people.*

main PIPE /meɪn/ *n* [C] a large pipe that is part of the system carrying water or gas from one place to another • *A water main burst and flooded the street.*

mainframe /ˈmeɪn·freɪm/ *n* [C] a large computer that can be used to do several things at once and which is usually used by a number of people

mainstay /ˈmeɪn·steɪ/ *n* [C] the most important part of something, providing support for everything else • *In the early 1900s, farming was the mainstay of the national economy.*

mainstream /ˈmeɪn·striːm/ *adj* (of beliefs or behavior) common and shared by most people, or representing such beliefs or behavior • *The story was largely ignored by the mainstream press.*

mainstream /ˈmeɪn·striːm/ *n* [U] most of a society • *New laws will allow more disabled people to enter the mainstream.*

mainstream /ˈmeɪn·striːm/ *v* [T] to place (children with special needs) in regular classes at school • *The district was ordered to mainstream more children with disabilities.*

maintain CONTINUE TO HAVE /meɪnˈteɪn/ *v* [T] to continue to have; keep in existence, or not allow to become less • *Despite living in different states, the two families have maintained a close friendship.* ○ *You have to maintain a minimum balance in your checking account.*

maintain PRESERVE /meɪnˈteɪn/ *v* [T] to keep (a road, machine, building, etc.) in good condition • *A large house costs a lot to maintain.*

maintenance /ˈmeɪnt·ⁿn·əns/ *n* [U] • *Bridges require a lot of maintenance.*

maintain (*obj*) EXPRESS /meɪnˈteɪn/ *v* to express strongly your belief that something is true • *She maintains (that) she's being criticized simply for telling the truth.* [+ (*that*) clause]

maize /meɪz/ *n* [U] corn

majestic /mə'dʒes·tɪk/ *adj* (of something) having the quality of causing you to feel great admiration and respect for it because of its size, power, or beauty • *We flew over the majestic Sierra Nevada mountains.*

majesty /'mædʒ·ə·sti/ *n* [U] • *A whale passed by in all its majesty.*

Majesty /'mædʒ·ə·sti/ *n* [C] a title used to speak to or about a king or queen or other ruler with a similar title • *Her Majesty, the Empress of Japan*

major IMPORTANT /'meɪ·dʒər/ *adj* [not gradable] more important, bigger, or more serious than others of the same type • *Fresh fruits are a major source of vitamin C.* ○ *We awaited major new developments in the peace talks.* • A **major league** is an organized group of sports teams that have the best players in the sport, and whose players are paid for playing: *He's happy to finally be playing in the major leagues.* ○ (*fig.*) *She hired a major-league attorney* (= one who is highly paid and considered to be among the best). • Compare MINOR UNIMPORTANT.

major OFFICER /'meɪ·dʒər/ *n* [C] a military officer of middle rank, above a CAPTAIN

major MUSIC /'meɪ·dʒər/ *adj* (of music) based on a SCALE (= series of notes) in which there is a whole STEP (= sound difference) between each note and the next except between the third and fourth notes and the seventh and eighth notes • *a major chord* • A **major scale** is a series of eight notes in which there is a half STEP between the third and fourth notes and between the seventh and eighth notes.

major SPECIAL SUBJECT /'meɪ·dʒər/ *n* [C] the most important subject that a college or university student is studying, or the student studying that subject • *an English major*

major in /'meɪ·dʒə·rɪn/ *v prep* [T] • *She majored in earth sciences at Arizona State.*

majority /mə'dʒɔːr·əţ·i, -'dʒɑr-/ *n* [U] more than half of a total number or amount; the larger part of something • *A majority of the people voted against the bill to raise school taxes.* • A majority is also the difference in the number of votes in an election between the winning person or group and the one that has the second highest number: *The Republicans won by a small majority.* [C] • Compare MINORITY.

make PRODUCE /meɪk/ *v* [T] *past* made /meɪd/ to bring (something) into existence, esp. using a particular substance or material; produce • *Does that company make computers?* ○ *Butter is made from cream.* ○ *My wedding ring is made of gold.* ○ *He made us some coffee.* • Make-

work is unimportant work given to someone to keep them busy.

make /meɪk/ *n* [C] a particular product, or the name of the company that made it • *What make of air conditioner do you recommend?*

maker /'meɪ·kər/ *n* [C] • *The makers of music videos show a fantasy world.*

make CAUSE /meɪk/ *v* [T] *past* made /meɪd/ to cause (something) • *The kids made a mess in the kitchen.* ○ *Don't make any noise.* • *When I hear stories of cruelty to animals, it* makes *my* blood boil (= causes me to be very angry). • If you **make do** or **make** something **do**, you use what is available although it is not enough or what you wanted: *Can you make do with $5 for now and I'll give you the rest tomorrow?* • *It's not easy to* **make ends meet** (= have enough money to pay our expenses) *with a big family, but somehow we manage.* • To **make headway** is to begin to succeed: *There's little evidence that the city has made any headway in its goal of attracting new businesses.* • To **make waves** is to cause trouble: *You'll only make trouble for yourself if you complain—don't make waves.* • To **make way** is to be taken away to provide space for something else: *The tenements are being torn down to make way for a new parking garage.* • LP GET, HAVE, AND OTHER VERBS USED TO MEAN "CAUSE"

make CAUSE TO BE /meɪk/ *v* [T] *past* made /meɪd/ to cause (something) to be, become, or appear in a particular way • *If you open some windows, you'll make it cooler.* ○ *He said something that made her angry.* ○ *We can sit closer together and make room* (= provide space) *for one more.* ○ *We're making our attic into a spare bedroom.* • To **make a difference** or **make all the difference** is to improve a situation or condition in an important way: *Let me tell you, not having a two-hour commute makes a difference.* • If you **make a face**, you move your mouth, nose, and eyes in strange ways to show you are upset, worried, or annoyed: *She stepped in something, made a face, and looked down.* • If someone **makes a face at/makes faces at** someone, they move their mouth, nose, and eyes in a silly or ugly way to amuse or annoy someone: *Johnnie's making faces at me—make him stop!* • If you **make a habit of** something, you begin to do it regularly, often without thinking about it: *He made a habit of ignoring me whenever we had guests.* • If you **make allowances for** something, you plan for or accept a condition: *We try to make allowances for our students' different backgrounds.* • If you **make a mountain out of a molehill**, you cause something unimportant to seem important. • To **make believe** is to pretend: *Johnny likes to make believe he's a pirate.* • If you **make fun of** someone, you are unkind to them and laugh at them or cause others to do so: *You're always making fun of me!* • If you **make light of** something, you act as if it is not serious: *He makes light of his divorce, but I think he was very hurt by it.* • If you **make no apologies** for something you have done, you firmly support it: *The network makes no apologies for broadcasting the controversial film.* • If you **make no bones about** something, you do not try to hide it or say you are sorry about it: *He makes no bones about his sloppiness.* • If something **makes no difference** or **does not make any difference**, it will not cause a change that leads to a different result: *It doesn't make any difference now what he says—it's too late for apologies.* • She has the power to **make or break** your career (= cause it to be successful or a failure). • If something **makes sense**, it is reasonable or can be understood: *This last paragraph doesn't make any sense.* • If you **make short work of** (something or someone), you deal with them quickly and effectively, esp., in a sports competition, to defeat them easily. • If you **make sure** of something, you find out whether it is really so or you take special care to do it: *Make sure you're home by midnight.* • *I'll have a steak—no,* **make that** (= change it to) *an omelet.* • If you **make the most of** something, you use or enjoy it as much as possible: *We're only in Paris for a day so let's make the most of it.* • *I try to* **make time** (= be certain there is enough time) *to run twice a week.*

make PERFORM /meɪk/ *v* [T] *past* **made** /meɪd/ to perform (an action) • *I've got to make a (phone) call to Ricardo.* ○ *We must make a decision by tomorrow.* ○ *Someone has made a mistake.* ○ *Latisha is making progress in her reading.* ○ *Can I make a suggestion?* ○ *We might as well make use of the car, since we've got it for the whole weekend.* • *When he came in and saw me there, he* **made a beeline for** *the door* (= moved quickly and directly toward it). • (*fml*) *I'm very pleased to* **make** *your* **acquaintance** (= meet you). • To **make a pass at** someone is to do or say something to them that is obviously intended as an invitation to have a sexual relationship. • If you **make a point of** doing something, you always do it or you take particular care to do it: *She makes a point of sending thank-you notes.* • To **make love** is to have sex. • To **make (up) the bed** is to put sheets and covers to keep you warm on a bed so that it is ready for someone to sleep in, or to straighten them after someone has slept in it.
• LP DO: VERBS MEANING "PERFORM"

make FORCE /meɪk/ *v* [T] *past* **made** /meɪd/ to force (someone or something) to do something • *He said the police made him sign a confession, and declared he was innocent.*

make BE OR BECOME /meɪk/ *v* [L] *past* **made** /meɪd/ to be or become (something), esp. by having the necessary characteristics • *I don't think he will ever make a good lawyer.* ○ *Hector and Wanda make a delightful couple.* ○ *He worked really hard, but he didn't make the*

team (= was not chosen to be a member of it). • *We sent her to school hoping she'd* **make friends** (= get to know and like people who get to know and like her). • If you **make good**, you become successful and usually rich: *He's a boy from a poor background who made good on Wall Street.* • (*infml*) If someone **makes it (big)**, they become famous or successful. • If you **make the grade**, you are good enough to be successful at something: *He hoped to make the grade as a chef.*

make /meɪk/ *n infml* • If someone is **on the make**, they are trying hard to become rich and powerful: *He's a young man on the make.*

makings /ˈmeɪ·kɪŋz/ *pl n* • *I think the plan has (all) the makings of a disaster* (= is likely to be one).

make TOTAL /meɪk/ *v* [L] *past* **made** /meɪd/ to add up to (a total) • *6 and 6 make 12.*

make EARN /meɪk/ *v* [T] *past* **made** /meɪd/ to earn or get • *She makes $70,000 a year.* ○ *Can you make a living as a painter?*

make ARRIVE /meɪk/ *v* [T] *past* **made** /meɪd/ *infml* to arrive at or reach • *We should make Whitefish Bay by nightfall.* ○ *He made it to the bed and then collapsed.* • If you **make good time**, you complete a trip quickly.

make HAVE SEX /meɪk/ *v* [T] *past* **made** /meɪd/ *slang* to have sex with (someone)

□ **make** *obj* **of** *obj* /ˈ--/ *v prep* [T] to understand (the meaning) of (a statement or action), or to have (an opinion) about (something or someone) • *What do you make of the new boss?* • *We couldn't* **make heads or tails of** *your directions* (= could not understand them at all). • If you **make much of** something, you give a lot of importance to it: *Don't make too much of the test results.*

□ **make off with** /-ˈ--/ *v adv prep* [T] to steal (something) • *Somebody broke into the store and made off with several VCRs.*

□ **make out** SUCCEED /ˈ-ˈ-/ *v adv* [I] to continue or succeed in life or in business • *How is Fran making out in her new job?*

□ **make** (*obj*) **out** (*obj*) CLAIM /ˈ-ˈ-/ *v adv* [I/T] to claim, usually falsely, that something is true • *He made himself out to be a millionaire.* [T]

□ **make out** *obj* UNDERSTAND , **make** *obj* **out** /ˈ-ˈ-/ *v adv* [M] to see, hear, or understand (something or someone) with difficulty • *I couldn't make out what he said.*

□ **make out** *obj* WRITE , **make** *obj* **out** /ˈ-ˈ-/ *v adv* [M] to write all the necessary information on (an official form, document, etc.) • *Make the check out to Hommocks School PTA.*

□ **make out** SUCCEED SEXUALLY /ˈ-ˈ-/ *v adv* [I] *infml* to succeed sexually with (someone) • *All he's interested in is making out.*

□ **make up** *obj* INVENT , **make** *obj* **up** /ˈ-ˈ-/ *v adv* [M] to invent (an excuse, a story, etc.), often in order to deceive • *I was trying to make up a good excuse for being late.*

□ **make up** *obj* PREPARE , **make** *obj* **up** /ˈ-ˈ-/ *v* *adv* [M] to prepare or arrange (something) by putting different things together • *Could you make up a list of what we need at the supermarket?* ○ *The maid will make up your room* (= clean it).

□ **make up** *obj* PROVIDE , **make** *obj* **up** /'-'-/ *v adv* [M] to provide (something, esp. an amount) so that a total is reached • *We're $5 short, but I'll make up the difference.*

□ **make up** BECOME FRIENDS /'-'-/ *v adv* [I] to forgive someone and become friends with them again after an argument or disagreement • *We argue all right, but we always make up before long.*

□ **make up** FORM /'-'-/ *v prep* [T] (of a number of things) to form (something) as a whole • *The book is made up of several different articles.* • If you **make up** your **mind**, you decide what to do: *She's made up her mind to take dance lessons.*

makeup /'meɪ·kʌp/ *n* [C usually sing] a combination of things that form something • *The committee's membership does not reflect the city's racial makeup.* • See also MAKEUP.

□ **make up for** /-'--/ *v adv prep* [T] to take the place of (something lost or damaged); to receive something good because of having suffered from (something bad) • *The good years make up for the bad ones.* • *After seven years in prison, he's home with his kids and* **making up for lost time** (= doing many things as quickly as possible that he was not able to do before).

□ **make** *obj* **up to** *obj* /-'--'/ *v adv prep* [T] to give something to or do something for (someone who is owed something) • *You've done an awful lot for me, and I don't know how I can ever make it up to you.*

make–believe /'meɪk·bə,liːv/ *n* [U] a state of mind in which you pretend to believe that conditions are real, esp. because that reality would be more pleasant than the actual one • *Disneyland creates a world of make-believe.*

make–believe /'meɪk·bə,liːv/ *adj* [not gradable] (used esp. in children's play) representing something that you agree to pretend is real for the purpose of playing • *They dueled with make-believe swords and climbed make-believe cliffs.*

makeshift /'meɪk·ʃɪft/ *adj* temporary and of low quality, but used because of a sudden need • *We pulled into a makeshift parking area.*

makeup /'meɪ·kʌp/ *n* [U] colored substances used on your face to improve or change its appearance • *She always wears a lot of makeup.* • See also **makeup** at MAKE UP FORM .

malady /'mæl·əd·i/ *n* [C] *slightly fml* a disease, or a problem in the way something works • *Smoking has been linked to lung cancer and other maladies.*

malaise /mə'leɪz, mæ-, -'lez/ *n* [U] a general feeling of bad health or lack of energy in a person, group, or society • *Many think there's a growing moral malaise in society.*

malaria /mə'ler·i·ə/ *n* [U] a disease, esp. of the hotter regions of the earth, caused by the bite of an infected MOSQUITO (= small flying insect)

male /meɪl/ *adj* [not gradable] of the sex that produces a natural substance that can make an egg develop into young • *a male gorilla* ○ *Male and female soldiers serve in the same units.* • Compare FEMALE.

male /meɪl/ *n* [C] • *The target audience is young males 20 to 30 years old.*

malevolent /mə'lev·ə·lənt/ *adj* causing or wanting to cause harm or evil • *a malevolent juvenile delinquent*

malfunction /mæl'fʌŋk·ʃən/ *v* [I] (of a machine, piece of equipment, or organ) to fail to work correctly • *The equipment malfunctions at temperatures below freezing.*

malfunction /mæl'fʌŋk·ʃən/ *n* [C] • *a computer malfunction*

malice /'mæl·əs/ *n* [U] *law* the intention to do something wrong and esp. to cause injury • *If the killing had been planned in any way, it was committed with malice.*

malicious /mə'lɪʃ·əs/ *adj* intending to cause harm, esp. by hurting someone's feelings or reputation • *She denied the report that she appeared on the movie set drunk, saying it was a malicious story put out by people envious of her success.*

malign /mə'laɪn/ *v* [T] to say things about (someone or something) that are harmful and usually not true • *He said he had been unfairly maligned by a few board members who wanted him fired.*

malignant /mə'lɪg·nənt/ *adj medical* (of a disease or tissue growing because of a disease) leading to death • *The pathologist's report said the tumor was malignant.* • Compare BENIGN.

malignancy /mə'lɪg·nən·si/ *n* [C/U] *medical* tissue that is growing because of a disease process and that is likely to cause death • *If this type of malignancy is discovered early enough, the outlook is pretty good.* [C]

mall /mɔːl/, **shopping mall** *n* [C] a very large building or buildings containing a lot of stores and often restaurants, and usually with space around it outside for parking • *Judy likes to hang out at the mall with her friends.* • A mall is also a street in a city or town with a lot of stores and that is closed to traffic.

mallard /'mæl·ərd/ *n* [C] a common, wild DUCK (= type of water bird)

malleable /'mæl·i·ə·bəl/ *adj* easily influenced, trained, or controlled • *Mother wanted me to be a malleable girl who would take her advice.* • A substance that is malleable is easily bent and shaped.

mallet /'mæl·ət/ *n* [C] a hammer with a large, flat end made of wood or rubber

malnourished /mæl'nɜr·ɪʃt/ *adj* weak and in bad health because of a lack of food or a lack of food that is good for you • *By the time we saw the child, she was extremely malnourished.*

malnutrition /ˌmæl·nuːˈtrɪʃ·ən/ *n* [U] physical weakness and bad health caused by a lack of food or by a lack of food that is good for you

malpractice /mælˈpræk·təs/ *n* [U] *law* the failure of a doctor or other PROFESSIONAL to do their job with a reasonable degree of skill, esp. when their actions or failure to act causes injury or loss • *He was sued for medical malpractice.*

malt /mɔːlt/ *n* [U] grain, usually BARLEY, that has been left in water until it starts to grow and is then dried, used in making beer and other alcoholic drinks

malted (milk) /ˈmɔːl·təd (ˈmɪlk)/ *n* [C] a drink made from milk, BARLEY, flavoring, and ice cream

mama, mamma, momma /ˈmɑm·ə/ *n* [C] *a child's word for* mother • *(disapproving)* A **mama's boy** is a boy or man who others think behaves as his mother tells him to. • LP TITLES AND FORMS OF ADDRESS

mammal /ˈmæm·əl/ *n* [C] any animal in which the female gives birth to babies, not eggs, and feeds them on milk from her own body

mammogram /ˈmæm·əˌgræm/ *n* [C] an X-RAY photograph of a woman's breasts, used to find signs of disease

mammoth /ˈmæm·əθ/ *adj* [not gradable] extremely large • *Building the dam was a mammoth construction project.*

man MALE /mæn/ *n* [C] *pl* **men** /men/ an adult male human being • *a young man* ○ *the men's 400-meter race* ○ *John can solve anything—the man's a genius.* • A man is also a male employee without particular rank or title, or a member of the military who has a low rank: *The gas company sent a man to fix the heating system.* • *(infml)* Man is sometimes used when addressing an adult male human being: *Hey, man, got a light?* • *(infml)* Man is sometimes used as an exclamation, esp. when the speaker is expressing a strong emotion: *Man, what a storm!* • When a minister or other official at a wedding says a man and a woman have become **man and wife**, it means they are now married to each other. • If you talk to someone **man to man**, or if you have a **man-to-man** talk with them, you talk seriously and honestly together as equals.

manhood /ˈmæn·hʊd/ *n* [U] the condition or time of being a man • *a boy on the brink of manhood* • Manhood is also the qualities that are considered typical of a man: *He feels he has to do dangerous things to prove his manhood.*

manly /ˈmæn·li/ *adj* having qualities such as strength and bravery that people think a man should have • *The boy was told that it wasn't manly to cry.*

manliness /ˈmæn·liː·nəs/ *n* [U] • *We no longer equate aggression with manliness.*

mannish /ˈmæn·ɪʃ/ *adj* (of a woman) having characteristics typical of a man • *Her short haircut and severe suit gave her a mannish appearance.*

man PERSON /mæn/ *n* [C/U] *pl* **men** /men/ the human race, or any member or group of it • *prehistoric man* [U] ○ *This poison is one of the most dangerous substances known to man.* [U] ○ *All men are equal in the sight of the law.* [C] • The **man in the street** is a person or people who think like most other people: *To win the election she needs to understand what the man in the street wants.* • Dogs are sometimes called **man's best friend.** • If something is **man-made**, it is produced or developed by humans rather than coming directly from nature: *man-made fibers* ○ *a man-made lake* • USAGE: Some people dislike this use of man because it does not seem to give women equal importance with men. They prefer to use other words, such as humanity, humankind, people, and person.

man OPERATE /mæn/ *v* [T] **-nn-** to be present in order to operate (something, such as equipment or a service) • *Man the pumps!* ○ *The phones are manned 24 hours a day.* • USAGE: Some people dislike this use of man because it does not seem to give women equal importance with men. They prefer to use other words, such as operate and staff.

man PIECE /mæn/ *n* [C] *pl* **men** /men/ any of the pieces that are played with in games such as CHESS

manacles /ˈmæn·ə·kəlz/ *pl n* HANDCUFFS

manage SUCCEED /ˈmæn·ɪdʒ/ *v* [I/T] to succeed in doing (esp. something difficult) • *The pilot managed to land the plane safely.* [+ *to* infinitive] ○ *We managed to live on very little money.* [+ *to* infinitive] ○ *Don't worry about us—we'll manage.* [I]

manageable /ˈmæn·ɪdʒ·ə·bəl/ *adj* easy or possible to deal with • *The people at the workshop were divided into small, manageable groups.*

manage CONTROL /ˈmæn·ɪdʒ/ *v* [T] to control or organize (someone or something, esp. a business) • *Does she have any experience managing large projects?* • **Managed care** is a system in which medical costs are controlled by a company or the government by controlling the services that doctors and hospitals offer and limiting the charges they can make.

management /ˈmæn·ɪdʒ·mənt/ *n* [U] the control of the way an organization operates, esp. by controlling the way people are used and money is spent • *He assumed management of a large real-estate company.* • Management is also the people in charge of a business organization: *Negotiators tried all weekend to get labor and management back to the bargaining table.*

manager /ˈmæn·ɪdʒ·ər/ *n* [C] • *the manager of a supermarket* ○ *He is manager of the New York City Ballet.*

managerial /ˌmæn·ə'dʒɪr·i:·əl/ *adj* [not gradable] • *managerial skills*

mandate /'mæn·deɪt/ *n* [C] authority to act in a particular way given to a government or a person, esp. as a result of a vote or ruling • *The president secured a congressional mandate to send troops to Bosnia.* [+ *to* infinitive]

mandate /'mæn·deɪt/ *v* [T] to make (something) necessary, esp. as a rule • *The law mandated a minimum six-year sentence for violent crimes.*

mandatory /'mæn·də,tɔːr·i, -,tour·i/ *adj* [not gradable] made necessary, usually by law or by some other rule • *If you are a driver and are involved in an accident, a drunk-driving test is mandatory.*

mandolin /ˌmæn·də'lɪn/ *n* [C/U] a musical instrument with eight strings and a rounded back that is held in the hands or on the knee and played by moving the fingers across the strings, or this instrument generally

mane /meɪn/ *n* [C] the long, thick hair that grows along the top of a horse's neck or around the face and neck of a male lion

maneuver MILITARY OPERATION /mə'nuː·vər/ *n* [C] a planned and controlled movement of military forces

maneuvers /mə'nuː·vərz/ *pl n* military operations by the armed forces for training purposes

maneuver PLANNED ACTION /mə'nuː·vər/ *n* [C] a planned action that is intended to obtain an advantage • *A clever maneuver by the chairman secured a valuable contract for the company.*

maneuver /mə'nuː·vər/ *v* [T] to cause (someone) to act in a particular way • *The management tried to maneuver her into resigning.*

maneuver HANDLE /mə'nuː·vər/ *v* [I/T] to handle and move (something) carefully or with difficulty • *I maneuvered the grocery cart around piles of boxes to the checkout counter.* [T]

manger /'meɪn·dʒər/ *n* [C] an open box from which horses, cows, and other animals feed

mangle /'mæŋ·gəl/ *v* [T] to destroy (something) by twisting it with force or tearing it so that its original form is changed • *His car was mangled when it slammed head-on into a semitrailer truck.* ○ (*fig.*) *The text was so mangled in translation that it was impossible to be sure of the meaning.*

mango /'mæŋ·gou/ *n* [C] *pl* **mangoes** or **mangos** a fruit grown in the hotter parts of the earth, having an oval shape, a large seed, and juicy, orange-yellow flesh

mangy /'meɪn·dʒi/ *adj* [-*er*/-*est* only] (esp. of dogs and cats) having an infectious disease that makes hair fall out and causes areas of rough skin • *a mangy-looking dog* • Mangy also means old and dirty: *Throw away that mangy rug.*

manhandle /'mæn,hæn·dᵊl/ *v* [T] to handle (someone) with force or by pushing them around, often when taking them somewhere • *Security guards had manhandled some of the fans.*

manhole /'mæn·houl/ *n* [C] an opening in a street usually covered by a heavy, metal lid, for allowing workers to reach underground pipes and wires

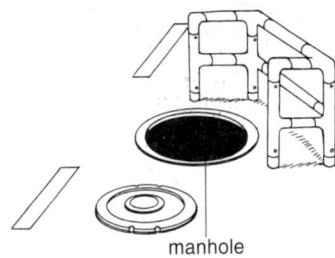

manhole

manhood /'mæn·hud/ *n* • See at MAN MALE.

manhunt /'mæn·hʌnt/ *n* [C] an organized search for a person, esp. a criminal

mania STRONG INTEREST /'meɪ·ni:·ə/ *n* [C] an unusually strong and continuing interest in an activity or subject • *He was surprised by his wife's sudden mania for exercise.*

maniac /'meɪ·ni:,æk/ *n* [C] a person who has an unusually strong interest in an activity or subject • *My brother is a maniac when it comes to football.*

mania MENTAL ILLNESS /'meɪ·ni:·ə/ *n* [U] *medical* a mental illness that causes a person to be in a state of extreme physical and mental activity, often characterized by a loss of judgment

maniac /'meɪ·ni:,æk/ *n* [C] a person who seems unable to control their behavior and may commit violent acts • *a homicidal maniac*

manic /'mæn·ɪk/ *adj* excited or anxious in a way that causes a lot of physical activity • *She was a manic talker.* • A person who suffers from **manic depression** varies between extreme excitement and deep, hopeless sadness. ○ *treatment for a* **manic-depressive** *disorder*

manicure /'mæn·ə,kjur/ *n* [C] a treatment for the hands that involves softening the skin and making the nails look better by cutting, smoothing, and possibly painting them

manifest /'mæn·ə,fest/ *v* [T] to show (something, esp. an emotion or idea) clearly, through signs or actions • *Kipper manifested no joy or disappointment, but remained in his chair, calm and unconcerned.*

manifest /'mæn·ə,fest/ *adj* easily noticed or obvious • *He listed a host of symptoms manifest in individuals who had survived Nazi persecution.*

manifestly /'mæn·ə,fest·li/ *adv* • *Blaming the victim for the crime is manifestly unjust.*

manifestation /ˌmæn·ə·fə'steɪ·ʃən, -,fes'teɪ-/ *n*

[C] a sign showing the existence of a particular condition • *His refusal to see us was a manifestation of his guilt.*

manifesto /ˌmæn·ə'fes·toʊ/ n [C] pl **manifestos** or **manifestoes** a written statement of the beliefs or aims esp. of a political party

manifold /'mæn·ə,foʊld/ adj [not gradable] *fml* many and of different types • *Our organization's problems are manifold—too few members, too little money, and poor management.*

manila /mə'nɪl·ə/ adj [not gradable] made of strong, stiff, usually light brown paper • *She removed a manila folder from a desk drawer and handed it to me.*

manipulate INFLUENCE /mə'nɪp·jə,leɪt/ v [T] to influence or control (someone) to your advantage, often without their knowing it • *Her success is partly due to her ability to manipulate the media.*

manipulative /mə'nɪp·jə·lət·ɪv, -,leɪt·ɪv/ adj • *He is resourceful, smart, skillful, ingenious, and savvy, but he also can be manipulative.*

manipulation /mə,nɪp·jə'leɪ·ʃən/ n [U] • *They have been accused of illegal manipulation of the stock market.*

manipulate TOUCH /mə'nɪp·jə,leɪt/ v [T] to control (something) by using the hands • *The wheelchair is designed to be easy to manipulate.*

manipulation /mə,nɪp·jə'leɪ·ʃən/ n [C/U] • *Often a dislocated finger can be fixed by manipulation.* [U]

mankind /'mæn'kaɪnd/ n [U] the whole of the human race, including both men and women

manliness /'mæn·li:·nəs/ n • See at MAN MALE.

manly /'mæn·li/ adj • See at MAN MALE.

mannequin /'mæn·ə·kɪn/ n [C] an artificial model made in the form of a human being, used esp. to show clothes in a store

manner WAY /'mæn·ər/ n [U] the way in which something is done • *Please exit the building in an orderly manner.* • **In a manner of speaking** means in one way of expressing something or thinking about something: *His old self died, in a manner of speaking, and he was born again as a devout Christian.*

manner BEHAVIOR /'mæn·ər/ n [U] the usual way in which you behave toward other people, or the way you behave on a particular occasion • *His manner was formal, though friendly.* ○ *She had a warm smile and an engaging manner.*

mannered /'mæn·ərd/ adj • *The children are well mannered.* • (disapproving) A mannered way of speaking or behaving is one that is artificial, or intended to achieve a particular effect: *He continued to write, but his mannered prose was not well received.*

mannerism /'mæn·ə,rɪz·əm/ n [C] something that a person does repeatedly with their face, hands, or voice, esp. a habit that they are not aware of • *We've spent so much time together that we've picked up each other's mannerisms.*

manners /'mæn·ərz/ pl n ways of behaving toward people that are socially correct and show respect for their comfort and their feelings; politeness • *He had the bad manners to keep interrupting whoever was speaking.*

mannish /'mæn·ɪʃ/ adj • See at MAN MALE.

manpower /'mæn,paʊ·ər, -,paʊr/ n [U] the supply of people who are able to work • *For years there was a shortage of manpower in engineering.*

mansion /'mæn·tʃən/ n [C] a very large and usually expensive house • *Mansions line the shore around the lake.*

manslaughter /'mæn,slɔːt·ər/ n [U] *law* the crime of killing someone unintentionally or without having planned to do it • *He was found guilty of manslaughter and sentenced to two years in prison.*

mantelpiece /'mænt·ə l,pi:s/, short form **mantel** /'mænt·ə l/ n [C] a shelf above a fireplace, usually part of a frame that surrounds the fireplace

mantle COVERING /'mænt·ə l/ n [C] *literary* a covering, or a layer of something that covers a surface • *They escaped under the mantle of darkness.*

mantle POSITION /'mænt·ə l/ n [C usually sing] a position of authority or responsibility • *He inherited the mantle of leadership at the Transit Authority in the early 1980s.*

mantra /'mæn·trə, 'mɑn-/ n [C] a word or sound that is repeated as a prayer • *A mantra is also any word or expression used repeatedly: "Moderate" is the new Republican mantra,* he said.

manual DONE BY HAND /'mæn·jə·wəl/ adj [not gradable] done or operated with the hands • *The mail can be sorted faster by machine then by manual sorting.* • If a machine is manual, it does not use electricity to operate: *We all used manual typewriters in those days.* • Manual labor is work that involves mostly physical rather than mental effort.

manually /'mæn·jə·wə·li/ adv • *a manually operated pump*

manual BOOK /'mæn·jə·wəl/ n [C] a book that gives you practical instructions on how to do something or how to use something • *Get the computer manufacturer's operating manual.*

manufacture PRODUCE /ˌmæn·jə'fæk·tʃər/ v [T] to produce (goods) in large numbers, esp. in a factory using machines • *He works for a company that manufactures toys.*

manufacture /ˌmæn·jə'fæk·tʃər/ n [U] • *Oil is used in the manufacture of synthetic fabrics.*

manufacturer /ˌmæn·jə'fæk·tʃə·rər/ n [C] • *Canadian liquor manufacturers held a press conference advocating lower taxes on alcohol.*

manufacture INVENT /ˌmæn·jə'fæk·tʃər/ v [T] to invent (something) esp. to deceive someone • *The president said this is a political crisis manufactured by Republicans.*

manure /mə'nʊr, -'njʊr/ n [U] excrement from

animals, esp. horses and cattle, often used as a FERTILIZER (= material added to earth to help plants grow)

manuscript /ˈmæn·jəˌskrɪpt/ n [C] the original copy of a book or article before it is printed • *The author's manuscript ran to over 1000 pages.*

many /ˈmen·i/ adj, pronoun **more**, **most** a large number (of), or a lot (of) • *Many people bought tickets for the concert.* ○ *Rachel has so many friends that I couldn't invite them all.* ○ *How many years have you worked here?* ○ *Not everyone could get a seat, and many (of the people) were unhappy with having to stand.* • USAGE: Many is used with countable nouns. Compare MUCH GREAT. • LP) AMOUNTS

map /mæp/ n [C] a drawing that represents a region or place by showing the various features of it, such as rivers and roads, and the distances between them, so that people can get help in finding their way from one place to another • *a map of California* ○ *a New York City subway map* ○ *According to this road map, it's 740 miles from Charlotte, North Carolina to Miami, Florida.*

map /mæp/ v [T] **-pp-** to draw (a representation of a place) • *Archaeologists have mapped the old Roman city using aerial photography.* • To **map out** what will be done: *She's mapped out her entire college curriculum.*

maple /ˈmeɪ·pəl/ n [C/U] a type of large tree that grows in northern areas of the world, or the wood of this tree • **Maple syrup** is a sticky, sweet liquid produced from maple trees: *pancakes with maple syrup*

mar /mɑr/ v [T] **-rr-** to spoil (something), making it less good or less enjoyable • *Water will mar the finish of polished wood.*

marathon /ˈmær·əˌθɑn/ n [C] a long race, run on roads, of 26.2 miles or 42.2 kilometers • *The New York City marathon begins in Staten Island and ends in Manhattan's Central Park.* • A marathon is also an activity that continues for a very long time: *a dance marathon*

marathon /ˈmær·əˌθɑn/ adj [not gradable] • *a marathon runner* • A marathon activity is one that continues for a very long time: *The marathon negotiating session lasted all night.*

marble ROCK /ˈmɑr·bəl/ n [U] a type of hard stone, often with a pattern of irregular lines going through it, that is used as a building material and in statues • *polished marble floors*

marble GLASS BALL /ˈmɑr·bəl/ n [C] a small glass ball, often of various colors

marbles /ˈmɑr·bəlz/ n [U] a child's game in which marbles are rolled along the ground

March MONTH /mɑrtʃ/ (abbreviation **Mar.**) n [C/U] the third month of the year, after February and before April

march WALK /mɑrtʃ/ v [I] to walk with regular steps of equal length, esp. with other people who are all walking in the same way • *The band marched through the downtown streets.* • If you march, you walk quickly with purpose and determination: *She marched up to the customer service desk and demanded her money back.*

march /mɑrtʃ/ n [C] (of a military unit) the act of walking together in formation

march MUSIC /mɑrtʃ/ n [C] a piece of music with a strong, regular rhythm written for marching to • *The parade was led by the high school band, playing a series of marches.*

march PUBLIC EVENT /mɑrtʃ/ n [C] an event in which many people walk through a public place to express their support of something, often in disapproval of an official position • *a protest march*

march /mɑrtʃ/ v [I] • *They marched to protest police brutality against African Americans.*

Mardi Gras /ˈmɑrd·iˌɡrɑ, -ˌɡrɔ/ n [C usually sing] the last day before Lent, or the large public celebration on this day • *In New Orleans, Mardi Gras marks the end of a carnival period.*

mare /mer, mær/ n [C] an adult female horse • Compare STALLION.

margarine /ˈmɑr·dʒə·rən/ n [U] a yellow substance that is made from vegetable or animal fat and is often used instead of butter

margin BORDER /ˈmɑr·dʒən/ n [C] the border of empty space around the written or printed text on a page • *She was in the habit of making notes in the margins of her textbooks.*

margin AMOUNT / DEGREE /ˈmɑr·dʒən/ n [C] the amount or degree of difference between a higher amount and a lower amount • *He was reelected by a wide margin.* • A **margin for error** is the amount by which you can make a mistake without risking complete failure: *There is no margin for error—it's got to work the first time.* • A **margin of error** is the degree to which a calculation can be wrong without changing the useful accuracy of the final result: *When dating ancient objects, scientists allow a margin of error of several hundred years.* ○ *The poll had a margin of error of plus or minus 4%.*

marginal /ˈmɑr·dʒən·əl/ adj small in amount or effect • *The difference between the two bids was marginal.*

marigold /ˈmær·əˌɡoʊld/ n [C] a plant with bright yellow or orange flowers

marijuana, **marihuana** /ˌmær·əˈwɑn·ə, -ˈhwɑn·ə/ n [U] an illegal drug that is made from the dried leaves and flowers of the HEMP plant and is smoked for pleasure

marina /məˈriː·nə/ n [C] a small port that is designed for small pleasure boats • *Our sailboat is docked at the marina.*

marinate /ˈmær·əˌneɪt/ v [T] to put (fish, meat, or vegetables) in a mixture esp. of oil, vinegar or wine, and spices, in order to flavor it or make it softer

marine SEA /məˈriːn/ adj [not gradable] of or

near the sea • *a marine biologist* ○ *The oil slick threatened marine life around the islands.*

mariner /ˈmær·ə·nər/ *n* [C] *literary* a person who works on a ship; a SAILOR

Marine ⟨SOLDIER⟩ /məˈriːn/ *n* [C] a member of the United States Marine Corps, a part of the US military forces that consists of soldiers who operate on land and sea

marionette /ˌmær·iː·əˈnet/ *n* [C] a small model of a person or animal, controlled from above by strings attached to its movable body parts and used as characters on small stages as an entertainment

marital /ˈmær·ət̬·əl/ *adj* [not gradable] *slightly fml* connected with marriage • *marital problems*

maritime /ˈmær·əˌtaɪm/ *adj* [not gradable] connected with ships or the sea, or being near the sea • *a maritime museum*

mark ⟨SMALL AREA⟩ /mɑrk/ *n* [C] a small area on the surface of something that is damaged, dirty, a different color, or in some other way not like the rest of the surface • *You've got paint marks on your shirt.* ○ *There were skid marks where the car had gone off the road.*

mark /mɑrk/ *v* [T] • *Sale items are marked in red on the tags.*

marking /ˈmɑr·kɪŋ/ *n* [C] noticeable spots or areas on a surface • *One of the fishes had blue and white markings.*

mark ⟨WRITING⟩ /mɑrk/ *n* [C] a written or printed symbol • *a punctuation mark* ○ *a check mark* ○ *Put a mark in the box that corresponds to the correct answer.* • ⟨LP⟩ SYMBOLS, SIGNS, AND MARKS

mark /mɑrk/ *v* [T] • *The trail is marked by numbered signs.*

marker /ˈmɑr·kər/ *n* [C] a symbol or object that gives information • *When the boats reached the halfway marker, the wind started to pick up.* • A marker is also a type of pen that makes a thick line: *She used a yellow, felt-tip marker to highlight certain words.*

mark ⟨SIGN⟩ /mɑrk/ *n* [C] an action that is understood to represent a characteristic or feeling • *As a mark of respect for those who died, there will be a minute of silence.*

mark ⟨REPRESENT⟩ /mɑrk/ *v* [T] to represent (something) that has happened in the past or is about to happen • *A guided tour will be held to mark the opening of the new school.* ○ *Today marks my tenth anniversary with this company.*

mark ⟨JUDGMENT⟩ /mɑrk/ *n* [C] a letter or number used as a measure of how good a student's work is, usually given by a teacher; a GRADE • *I got a decent mark on my final exam and wound up with a B for the course.* • *(fig.)* If you give someone high/low marks for something, you judge them to be good or bad in a particular way: *I'd certainly give him high marks for perseverance, but he doesn't have much talent.*

mark /mɑrk/ *v* [T] to put a number or letter on

(a student's work) that shows how good it is • *I have a stack of exam papers to mark.*

mark ⟨OBJECT⟩ /mɑrk/ *n* [C] the object you are aiming at • *US officials said three missiles went wide of the mark* (= missed the object aimed at) *and caused civilian casualties.* ○ *(fig.)* Her criticisms were wide of the mark.

□ **mark down** *obj*, **mark** *obj* **down** /ˈ-ˈ-/ *v adv* [M] to reduce the price of (something) • *In August they begin to mark down summer suits.*

markdown /ˈmɑrk·daʊn/ *n* [C] a reduction in price • *a 25% markdown on swimsuits*

marked /mɑrkt/ *adj* obvious or noticeable • *There was a marked improvement in my health when I gave up smoking.*

markedly /ˈmɑr·kəd·li/ *adv* • *Eyewitness accounts differed markedly from police reports of the incident.*

market ⟨AREA⟩ /ˈmɑr·kət/ *n* [C] an open area, building, or event at which people gather to buy and sell goods or food • A **marketplace** is a place, usually in an open area, where goods or food is sold.

market ⟨DEMAND⟩ /ˈmɑr·kət/ *n* [C] the demand for products or services • *Are you sure there's a market for something like this?* • A market is also an area or particular group that goods can be sold to: *the teenage/adult market* ○ *domestic/foreign markets* • A market is also the business or trade in a particular type of goods or services: *the job/housing/ market* • *Thanks for the offer, but I'm not* in the market for (= interested in buying) *another car at the moment.* • On the market means available for sale: *We put our house on the market last spring.* • The marketplace is the system of trading in competitive conditions: *Analysts question whether the company can survive in a highly competitive marketplace.* • Market research is the collection and examination of information about what people prefer to buy.

market ⟨ADVERTISE⟩ /ˈmɑr·kət/ *v* [T] to advertise and offer (goods) for sale • *It's a product that will sell if we can find the right way to market it.*

marketing /ˈmɑr·kət̬·ɪŋ/ *n* [U] • *marketing strategies* ○ *She's the director of marketing.*

marketable /ˈmɑr·kət̬·ə·bəl/ *adj* easily sold • *marketable products/skills*

marksman /ˈmɑrk·smən/, **markswoman** /ˈmɑrk·swʊm·ən/ *n* [C] *pl* **-men** /ˈmɑrk·smən/ or **-women** /ˈmɑrk·swɪm·ən/ someone skilled at shooting accurately

marksmanship /ˈmɑrk·smənˌʃɪp/ *n* [U] skill in shooting • *The competitors display their marksmanship at targets along the ski route.*

markup /ˈmɑr·kʌp/ *n* [C] an increase in price, esp. the amount by which the cost of an item for sale is increased to provide a profit for the seller • *The markup on books has to be at least 30%.*

marmalade /ˈmɑr·məˌleɪd/ *n* [U] a soft food

made by cooking fruit, esp. oranges, with sugar • *She spread marmalade on her toast.*

maroon /mə'ruːn/ *adj* [not gradable], *n* [U] (of) a dark brown-red color • *a maroon tie*

marooned /mə'ruːnd/ *adj* [not gradable] left in a place from which you cannot escape • *My flight was canceled because of a snowstorm and I was marooned at the Denver airport.*

marquee /mɑr'kiː/ *n* [C] a covered entrance to a theater with a sign that shows the names of the movies or play that you can see

marrow /'mær·oʊ/, **bone marrow** *n* [U] the soft, fatty tissue in the center of bones

marry /'mær·i,'mer-/ *v* [I/T] to become the legally accepted husband or wife of (someone) in an official or religious ceremony • *He married Lori, his girlfriend from high school.* [T] • To marry is also to perform the ceremony for (two people) that makes them legally married: *Judge Wilcox married us at City Hall.* [T]

married /'mær·iːd, 'mer-/ *adj* [not gradable] • *a married couple* ○ *We plan to get married next June.*

marriage /'mær·ɪdʒ, 'mer-/ *n* [C/U] a legally accepted relationship between a man and a woman in which they live as husband and wife, or the official ceremony which results in this • *a long and happy marriage* [C]

Mars /mɑrz/ *n* [U] the planet fourth in order of distance from the sun, after the earth and before Jupiter

Martian /'mɑr·ʃən/ *adj* [not gradable] relating to the planet Mars • *the Martian atmosphere*

marsh /mɑrʃ/ *n* [C/U] an area of low, wet land, usually covered with tall grasses • *The marshes along the coast are home to many shorebirds.* [C]

marshy /'mɑr·ʃi/ *adj* • *marshy ground*

marshal [ORGANIZE] /'mɑr·ʃəl/ *v* [T] to gather or organize (people or things), esp. in order to achieve a particular aim • *The president is trying to marshal support for his plan.*

marshal [OFFICIAL] /'mɑr·ʃəl/ *n* [C] an official who arranges and controls a public ceremony • *The mayor was the honorary grand marshal of the St. Patrick's Day parade.*

marshal [LAW] /'mɑr·ʃəl/ *n* [C] a government official who is responsible for putting the decisions of a law court into effect • *He was conducted to the airport by federal marshals and deported.* • In some parts of the US, marshal is also a title used for police or fire department officers of high rank.

marshmallow /'mɑrʃ,mæl·oʊ, -,mel-/ *n* [C/U] a soft, often white, candy made mainly of sugar • *We roasted marshmallows over the campfire.* [C]

mart /mɑrt/ *n* [C] a market or place where goods are sold • *I'll pick up some snacks at the food mart on the corner.*

martial /'mɑr·ʃəl/ *adj* [not gradable] of or suitable for war • **Martial arts** are the traditional skills of fighting or defending yourself,

such as JUDO and KARATE, which originated in Asian countries. • **Martial law** is temporary rule by the military, esp. during a war or an emergency.

Martian /'mɑr·ʃən/ *n* [C] • See at MARS.

martini /mɑr'tiː·ni/ *n* [C] an alcoholic drink usually made with GIN

martyr /'mɑrṭ·ər/ *n* [C] a person who suffers greatly or is killed because of their political or religious beliefs • *a Christian martyr*

martyr /'mɑrṭ·ər/ *v* [T] to be killed or be made to suffer because of your beliefs

martyrdom /'mɑrṭ·ər·dəm/ *n* [U] a martyr's suffering or death • *the martyrdom of St. Catherine*

marvel /'mɑr·vəl/ *v* [I always + adv/prep] to show or experience great surprise or admiration • *Tourists marvel at the panoramic view.* ○ *I marvel at her patience with the children.*

marvel /'mɑr·vəl/ *n* [C] a person or thing that is very surprising or admirable • *This gadget is a technological marvel.*

marvelous /'mɑr·və·ləs/ *adj* [not gradable] extremely good • *This marvelous invention will help many disabled people.* ○ *We've had some marvelous results with this drug.*

marvelously /'mɑr·və·lə·sli/ *adv* • *Jackie is marvelously well organized.*

Marxism /'mɑrk,sɪz·əm/ *n* [U] a social, political, and economic theory based on the writings of Karl Marx

Marxist /'mɑrk·səst/ *n* [C] a supporter of Marxism

mascara /mæs'kær·ə/ *n* [U] facial makeup used to make **eyelashes** appear darker and thicker

mascot /'mæs·kɑt/ *n* [C] a person, animal, or object used esp. by a group as a symbol, and believed to bring good luck • *Their team's mascot is a goat.*

masculine [MALE] /'mæs·kjə·lən/ *adj* [not gradable] having qualities traditionally considered to be suitable for a man • *It was a movie likely to appeal to a masculine audience.* • Compare FEMININE [FEMALE].

masculinity /,mæs·kjə'lɪn·əṭ·i/ *n* [U] • *They are trying to prove their masculinity by having sex with as many girls as possible.*

masculine [GRAMMAR] /'mæs·kjə·lən/ (*abbreviation* **masc.**) *adj* [not gradable] *specialized* (in grammar) being a noun or pronoun of a type that refers to males, or in some other languages, being a noun of a type that refers to things considered as male

mash /mæʃ/ *v* [T] to beat or crush (esp. cooked food) into a soft mass • *Mash the potatoes, adding warm milk and butter.*

mashed /mæʃt/ *adj* [not gradable] • *mashed potatoes*

mask /mæsk/ *n* [C] a covering for all or part of the face, worn for protection or to hide the face • *a gas mask* ○ *an exhibit of African masks* ○ *The children all wore Halloween masks that* *were supposed to frighten us.*

mask /mæsk/ *v* [T] to prevent (something) from being seen or noticed • *The tastelessness of the meat was masked by a heavy gravy.* • **Masking tape** is a strip of sticky material that is used esp. when painting to cover surfaces on which you do not intend to paint.

masochist /'mæs·ə·kəst/ *n* [C] a person who gets pleasure, sometimes sexual pleasure, from being hurt by another person • Compare SADIST.

masochistic /,mæs·ə'kɪs·tɪk/ *adj* [not gradable] • *(fig.) Running in ultramarathons seems somewhat masochistic to me.*

masochism /'mæs·ə,kɪz·əm/ *n* [U]

mason /'meɪ·sən/ *n* [C] a person who is trained to work with bricks and stones used in buildings

masonry /'meɪ·sən·ri/ *n* [U] something, esp. the walls of a building, made of bricks or stone

masquerade /,mæs·kə'reɪd/ *n* [C] a party or dance in which people wear MASKS (= coverings for the face) • *There were dozens of masquerade balls, parades, street dances, and fancy dress parties.* • A masquerade is also a false show or appearance: *I'm afraid we will not have a fair election but another masquerade.*

masquerade /,mæs·kə'reɪd/ *v* [I always + adv/prep] to pretend or appear to be • *In this business, there are a lot of unqualified people masquerading as experts.*

mass LARGE AMOUNT /mæs/ *n* [C] a large amount or number • *All roads were clogged with a mass of refugees.* ○ *We had to wade through masses of seaweed.*

mass /mæs/ *adj* [not gradable] involving or having an effect on a large number of people or things • *Nuclear weapons can cause mass destruction.* • The **mass media** are the newspapers, magazines, television, and radio that reach large numbers of people. • A **mass murderer** is someone who has murdered a lot of people. • If you **mass-produce** something, you make a lot of it, esp. with machinery. • **Mass transit** is a system of public transportation, esp. buses or trains in a city.

mass /mæs/ *v* [I/T] to come or bring together in large numbers • *The crowd massed around the entrance to the exhibition.* [I]

masses /'mæs·əz/ *pl n* [C] the ordinary people who form the largest group in a society • *The candidate won the support of the masses.*

mass MATTER /mæs/ *n* [C] *specialized* the amount of matter in any solid object or in any volume of liquid or gas

Mass CEREMONY /mæs/ *n* [C/U] (esp. in the Roman Catholic Church) a religious ceremony based on Jesus's last meal with his followers, or music written for the parts of this ceremony

massacre /'mæs·ə·kər/ *n* [C] the killing of a large number of people, esp. people who are

not involved in any fighting or have no way of defending themselves • *The massacre in the village left 29 people dead, including 12 children.*

massacre /'mæs·ə·kər/ *v* [T] • *Guerrilla troops are thought to have massacred some 500 elderly men, women, and children.*

massage /mə'sɑʒ, -'sɑdʒ/ *v* [T] to rub or press (someone's body), usually with repeated hand movements, in order to reduce stiffness or pain in their joints or muscles • *She massaged his aching neck.*

massage /mə'sɑʒ, -'sɑdʒ/ *n* [C/U] • *A massage would do wonders for my back.* [C]

masseur *male* /mæ'sɜr/, *female* **masseuse** /mæ'suːz/ *n* [C] a person whose job it is to give MASSAGES to people

massive /'mæs·ɪv/ *adj* very large in size, amount, or degree • *a massive building* ○ *He took massive doses of vitamin C.* ○ *She died of a massive heart attack.*

mast /mæst/ *n* [C] a tall pole used to support a ship's sails

mastectomy /mæs'tek·tə·mi/ *n* [C] the removal of a woman's breast by a medical operation

master CONTROL /'mæs·tər/, *female* **mistress** *n* [C] a person who controls something or someone • *I always wanted to start my own business, because I like being my own master.* • A **master key** is a key that can be used to open a number of different locks. • A **master of ceremonies** (*abbreviation* **MC** or **emcee**) is a person who is in charge of an official event and introduces the speakers or performers.

master /'mæs·tər/ *v* [T] • *Now that she's mastered* (= learned to control) *her fear of flying, she travels by air whenever possible.*

mastery /'mæs·tə·ri/ *n* [U] complete control • *It was a lifelong battle to gain mastery over his passions, which often got him into trouble.*

master SKILLED PERSON /'mæs·tər/ *n* [C] a person who is very skilled in a particular job or activity • *The terrorist was a master of disguise.* ○ *This painting is clearly the work of a master.* ○ *He is a master chef/craftsman.* • A **masterpiece/masterwork** is something made or done with great skill, esp. an artist's greatest work. • A **Master of Arts/Science** or **master's degree** is a second level college or university degree, above a BACHELOR'S DEGREE and below a **doctor's degree**.

master /'mæs·tər/ *v* [T] to become more skilled at (something) • *She quickly mastered the art of interviewing people.*

masterful /'mæs·tər·fəl/ *adj* • *It was a masterful analysis of the causes of the Civil War.*

mastery /'mæs·tə·ri/ *n* [U] • *Louis Armstrong's mastery of the trumpet is legendary.*

master ORIGINAL /'mæs·tər/ *n* [C] an original of something, such as a document, recording, or film, from which copies can be made

mastermind /'mæs·tər,mɑɪnd/ *v* [T] to plan

and direct (a difficult activity) • *Oliver masterminded the takeover of his top business competitor.*

mastermind /'mæs·tər,maɪnd/ *n* [C] • *The mastermind behind the escape has never been identified.*

masthead /'mæst·hed/ *n* [C] a list of the names of the most important people involved in producing and writing for a magazine or newspaper • *Hirth, listed on the masthead as publisher, wrote several articles in each issue.*

masturbate /'mæs·tər,beɪt/ *v* [I/T] to rub or touch the sex organs of (yourself or someone else) for sexual pleasure

masturbation /,mæs·tər'beɪ·ʃən/ *n* [U]

mat /mæt/ *n* [C] a flat piece of material that covers and protects part of a floor, or provides a soft surface • *The kids slept on straw mats on the floor of the den downstairs.*

matador /'mæt̬·ə,dɔːr/ *n* [C] the person in a **bullfight** who is skilled in killing the BULL (= the male form of cattle)

match COMPETITION /mætʃ/ *n* [C] a sports competition or event in which two people or teams compete against each other • *a tennis/wrestling match* ○ *(fig.) They got into a shouting/ shoving match* (= they were arguing or fighting).

match STICK /mætʃ/ *n* [C] a short, thin stick of wood or cardboard, covered at one end with a material that will burn when rubbed against a rough surface • *A* **matchbook** (also **book of matches**) is a small folded piece of cardboard containing cardboard matches.

match SUITABLE /mætʃ/ *v* [I/T] to be similar to or the same (as something), or to combine well with (someone or something else) • *The shirt and pants match perfectly.* [I] ○ *Her fingerprints matched the prints that were taken from the crime scene.* [T]

match /mætʃ/ *n* [U] • *This tie is a perfect match for your shirt and suit.* ○ *I think Ross and Rhonda are a good match.*

match EQUAL /mætʃ/ *v* [I/T] to be equal to (another person or thing) in some quality • *It would be difficult to match the service this airline gives its customers.* [T] • If something **matches up to** something else, it is as good as it: *The sequel didn't match up to the original movie.*

match /mætʃ/ *n* [U] • *The teams were a good match when it came to ability.*

matchless /'mætʃ·ləs/ *adj* [not gradable] of a standard or quality that cannot be equaled • *The museum has a matchless collection of Rembrandt etchings.*

matchmaker /'mætʃ,meɪ·kər/ *n* [C] a person who tries to arrange romantic relationships between other people, esp. that lead to marriage

mate FRIEND /meɪt/ *n* [C] *infml Br for* a friend, or a person you work with

mate PARTNER /meɪt/ *n* [C] an animal's sexual partner • *Swans keep the same mate for life.* • A mate is also a husband or wife.

mate /meɪt/ *v* [I/T] to have sex and produce young, or to cause (a male and female animal) to do this • *Zoo officials are hoping the pandas will mate.* [I]

mate PAIR /meɪt/ *n* [C] either of a pair of matched objects • *I can't find the mate to this sock.*

material PHYSICAL THING /mə'tɪr·iː·əl/ *n* [C] a type of physical thing, such as wood, stone, or plastic, having qualities that allow it to be used to make other things • *a hard/soft material* ○ *The sculpture was made of various materials, including steel, copper wire, and rubber.*

material CLOTH /mə'tɪr·iː·əl/ *n* [C/U] cloth that can be used to make clothes, curtains, etc. • *What kind of material are you going to use for the curtains?* [U]

material SUPPLIES /mə'tɪr·iː·əl/ *n* [C/U] equipment or supplies needed for a particular activity • *The money will be spent on educational materials.* [C usually pl]

material INFORMATION /mə'tɪr·iː·əl/ *n* [C/U] information used when writing something such as a book, or information produced to help people or to advertise products • *He is working in the library gathering material for the article he is writing.* [U]

materialism /mə'tɪr·iː·ə,lɪz·əm/ *n* [U] the belief that money, possessions, and comfort are the most important things to obtain in life

materialistic /mə,tɪr·iː·ə'lɪs·tɪk/ *adj* • *I was a materialistic person, very career-oriented, with a large ego.*

materialize /mə'tɪr·iː·ə,laɪz/ *v* [I] (of ideas and wishes) to become real or true • *Her hopes of owning her own restaurant never materialized.* • If a person or object materializes, it appears suddenly: *They listened to the footsteps, then watched the figure materialize in the doorway.*

maternal /mə'tɜrn·əl/ *adj* behaving or feeling as a mother does toward her child • *maternal instincts* • Maternal also means related by way of the mother: *Alice's maternal grandmother* (= her mother's mother) *will be 90 next month.* • Compare PATERNAL.

maternity /mə'tɜr·nət̬·i/ *n* [U] the state of being a mother • *issues of reproduction, maternity, and women's health*

maternity /mə'tɜr·nət̬·i/ *adj* [not gradable] relating to a period during which a woman is pregnant and has a baby, and often to a period following this • *Anita passed along some used maternity clothes* (= clothes worn when she was pregnant). ○ *She asked about the company's maternity benefits.* • **Maternity leave** is a period in which a woman is allowed to be absent from work in the weeks before and after she gives birth.

mathematics /,mæθ·ə'mæt̬·ɪks, mæθ'mæt̬-/, *short form* **math** /mæθ/ *n* [U] the science of numbers, forms, amounts, and their relationships

mathematical /ˌmæθ·ə·'mæt̬·ɪ·kəl, mæθ'mæt̬-/ *adj* [not gradable] • *a mathematical formula*

mathematician /ˌmæθ·ə·mə'tɪʃ·ən/ *n* [C] a person skilled in mathematics

matinee, matinée /ˌmæt·ᵊn'eɪ/ *n* [C] an afternoon performance of a movie or play

matriarch /'meɪ·tri·ˌɑrk/ *n* [C] a powerful and usually older woman in charge of a family, or the female leader of a society in which women hold power • Compare PATRIARCH.

matriarchal /ˌmeɪ·tri·'ɑr·kəl/ *adj* • *a matriarchal society*

matriarchy /'meɪ·tri·ˌɑr·ki/ *n* [C] a society in which women have most of the authority and power, or a society in which property belongs to women rather than men

matriculate /mə'trɪk·jə·ˌleɪt/ *v* [I] to be formally admitted to study at a university or college • *Are you just auditing the course or are you a matriculated student?*

matrimony /'mæ·trə·ˌmoʊ·ni/ *n* [U] *fml* the state of being married • *They were joined in holy matrimony.*

matrimonial /ˌmæ·trə·'moʊ·ni:·əl/ *adj* [not gradable] • *matrimonial advice*

matrix /'meɪ·trɪks/ *n* [C] *pl* **matrices** /'meɪ·trə·ˌsi:z/ or **matrixes** /'meɪ·trɪk·səz/ *specialized* (in mathematics) a group of numbers or other symbols arranged in a rectangle that can be used to solve particular mathematical problems

matron WOMAN /'meɪ·trən/ *n* [C] *dated* a married woman who is old enough and of a high enough social class to have the respect of others

matronly /'meɪ·trən·li/ *adj* (of a woman) middle-aged and a little fat • *She plays a matronly black housekeeper named Cassie.*

matron MANAGER /'meɪ·trən/ *n* [C] a woman who manages a service or is in charge of women or children at a hospital, prison, or school • *She was a matron at the Women's Correctional Center.*

matted /'mæt̬·əd/ *adj* twisted or pressed into a dense mass • *His hair was matted on his forehead.*

matter SITUATION /'mæt̬·ər/ *n* [C] a situation or subject that is being dealt with or considered • *Her arrival complicates matters even further.* ○ *The Pill made birth control a simple matter for millions of women.* • *In a matter of seconds* (= after only a few seconds), *the building was in flames.* • *Cooking lasagna isn't difficult—it's just a matter of following a recipe* (= this is all that need to be done). • *Don't worry about missing your bus—it's not a matter of life and death* (= extremely serious). • *Choosing the best ballplayer of all time is really a matter of opinion* (= a personal preference).

matter BE IMPORTANT /'mæt̬·ər/ *v* to be impor-

tant • *"What did you say?" "Oh, it doesn't matter." [I]* ○ *It no longer mattered what happened.* [+ *wh-* word]

matter PROBLEM /'mæt̬·ər/ *n* [U] the reason for pain or worry • *What's the matter? Why are you so upset?*

matter SUBSTANCE /'mæt̬·ər/ *n* [U] *specialized* physical substance in the universe • *Matter is also a particular type of substance:* printed matter ○ waste matter

matter-of-fact /ˌmæt̬·ə·rə'fækt/ *adj* not showing feelings or emotion, esp. in a situation when emotion would be expected • *He spoke in a very matter-of-fact way about the accident.*

matter-of-factly /ˌmæt̬·ə·rə'fæk·tli/ *adv* • *She announced the news matter-of-factly.*

mattress /'mæ·trəs/ *n* [C] the part of a bed that you lie on, made of a strong cloth cover filled with firm but bouncy material

mature GROW PHYSICALLY /mə'tʊr, -'tʃʊr/ *v* [I] to become completely grown • *Humans take longer to mature than most other animals.*

mature /mə'tʊr, -'tʃʊr/ *adj* • *The forest has a lot of mature oak trees.* • Mature can also be a polite way of saying older: *The jeans were marketed to mature women.*

maturity /mə'tʊr·ət̬·i, -'tʃʊr-/ *n* [U] • *How long does it take for the chicks to grow to maturity?*

mature DEVELOP MENTALLY /mə'tʊr, -'tʃʊr/ *v* [I/T] to become more developed mentally and emotionally and behave in a responsible way, or to cause (someone) to do this • *When you are the oldest child of a large family, you mature pretty quickly, because you have to take care of your younger brothers and sisters.* [I]

mature /mə'tʊr, -'tʃʊr/ *adj* mentally and emotionally well-developed, and therefore responsible • *He just wasn't mature enough to keep a dog.*

maturity /mə'tʊr·ət̬·i, -'tʃʊr-/ *n* [U] • *It takes maturity to be a leader.*

mature FINANCE /mə'tʊr, -'tʃʊr/ *v* [I] (of some types of investment) to become ready to be paid • *When her bonds matured, she moved the money into stocks.*

maul /mɔːl/ *v* [T] to physically attack (a person or animal) and hurt them badly • *A jogger was mauled by a huge bear.*

mauve /moʊv, mɔːv/ *adj* [not gradable], *n* [U] (of) a pale purple color

maven /'meɪ·vən/ *n* [C] *infml* a person with good knowledge or understanding of a subject • *Walter's a baseball maven and knows Hank Aaron's statistics by heart.*

maverick /'mæv·ə·rɪk/ *n* [C] a person who thinks and acts independently of and differently from others • *She is considered a political maverick.*

max /mæks/ *adj slang* MAXIMUM • *"How much will it cost?" "Ten bucks max."*

max /mæks/ *n slang* • **To the max** means to

the highest degree or level: *He had the volume up to the max and didn't hear the phone ring.*

max out *(obj)*, **max** *(obj)* **out** /ˈmækˈsaʊt/ *v adv* [I/M] *slang* to reach the greatest level or amount of (something) • *We had seven credit cards and we maxed them out.* [M] ° *My car maxes out at about 80 miles an hour.* [I]

maxim /ˈmæk·səm/ *n* [C] a brief statement of a general truth, principle, or rule for behavior • *She lived by the maxim, "Do right, risk consequences."*

maximum /ˈmæk·sə·məm/ *adj* [not gradable] being the largest amount or number allowed or possible • *a maximum penalty/sentence* ° *The stereo was turned up to maximum volume.* • The opposite of maximum is MINIMUM.

maximum /ˈmæk·sə·məm/ *n* [C] • *The temperature will reach a maximum of 88° today.*

maximize /ˈmæk·sə,maɪz/ *v* [T] to make (something) as great in amount, size, or importance as possible • *Most people try to maximize their gains and minimize their losses.*

may POSSIBILITY /meɪ/ *v aux* he/she/it **may**, *past simple* **might** /maɪt/ used to express possibility • *She said she may decide to accept the job offer and may not.* • Compare MIGHT POSSIBILITY. LP AUXILIARY VERBS

may PERMISSION /meɪ/ *v aux* he/she/it **may**, *past simple* **might** /maɪt/ *slightly fml* used to ask or give permission • *May I use your telephone?* • LP AUXILIARY VERBS

may SUGGESTION /meɪ/ *v aux* he/she/it **may**, *past simple* **might** /maɪt/ used to make a suggestion or suggest a possibility in a polite way • *You may want to have a bite to eat before you leave.* • *There's nothing to lose so you may as well* (= there is no reason not to) *do whatever you want to do.* • Compare MIGHT SUGGESTION. LP AUXILIARY VERBS

May MONTH /meɪ/ *n* [C/U] the fifth month of the year, after April and before June

maybe /ˈmeɪ·bi/ *adv* [not gradable] used to show that something is possible or that something might be true • *Maybe I can get the yard mowed before it rains.* ° *There were maybe* (= approximately) *50 people there when I left.* • Maybe can also be used to avoid giving a clear or certain answer to a question: *"Are you still going to join me for dinner?" "Maybe."* • Maybe can also be used to introduce a possible explanation: *I thought maybe my phone message had scared him off.*

mayday /ˈmeɪ·deɪ/ *n* [C] a call for help sent from a ship or aircraft by radio, esp. in an emergency

mayhem /ˈmeɪ·hem/ *n* [U] a situation characterized by confused activity or excitement, sometimes involving destructive violence • *The movie includes a considerable amount of violence and mayhem.*

mayonnaise /ˈmeɪ·ə,neɪz/, *short form* **mayo** /ˈmeɪ·oʊ/ *n* [U] a thick, creamy, cold sauce that

is added to foods and is made from oil, vinegar, and the yellow part of eggs

mayor /ˈmeɪ·ər/ *n* [C] the elected leader of a city or town • *The mayor announced a reorganization of the police department.*

mayoral /ˈmeɪ·ə·rəl/ *adj* [not gradable] • *mayoral elections*

maze /meɪz/ *n* [C] a complicated and confusing network of passages • *He felt like a rat in a maze.* ° *(fig.) You have to weed through the maze of complex rules in order to fill out your tax forms.*

M.B.A. *n* [C] *abbreviation for* Master of Business Administration (= an advanced university degree in business)

MC *n* [C] *abbreviation for* **master of ceremonies**, see at MASTER CONTROL • *Who's the MC for the awards ceremony?*

M.D. *n* [C] *abbreviation for* Doctor of Medicine (= an advanced university degree needed to work as a medical doctor) • *Steven Tay, M.D.*

me /miː/ *pronoun* the person speaking; the objective form of I • *Pass me that book/Pass that book to me.* • *"I want to go to the store." "Me, too"* (= I also want to do this). • *"I'd never go there alone at night." "Me neither"* (= I also would not).

meadow /ˈmed·oʊ/ *n* [C] an area of land with grass and other wild plants in it • *We walked through fields and meadows.*

meager /ˈmiː·gər/ *adj* very small in amount or number; only as much or not as much as is needed or thought to be suitable • *The food in jail was meager and barely edible.*

meal FOOD /miːl/ *n* [C] an occasion when food is served or eaten, esp. breakfast, lunch, or dinner, or the food itself on such an occasion • *I don't enjoy preparing three meals a day everyday.* • A **meal ticket** is someone or something that provides you with the money you need to live: *The role has been a generous meal ticket for this actress.* • **Mealtimes** (= The times meals were eaten) *were silent unless Dad had something to say.*

meal POWDER /miːl/ *n* [U] a substance that has been crushed to make a rough powder, esp. plant seeds crushed to make flour or for animal food

mean *(obj)* EXPRESS /miːn/ *v past* **meant** /ment/ to represent or express (something intended), or to refer to (someone or something) • *"What does 'rough' mean?" "It means 'not smooth, or uneven.'"* [T] ° *These figures mean that almost 7% of the population is unemployed.* [+ *that* clause] ° *"Do you see that girl over there?" "Do you mean the one with short blond hair?"* [T]

meaning /ˈmiː·nɪŋ/ *n* [C/U] what something represents or expresses • *Do you know the meaning of this word?* [C] ° *The word has several meanings.* [C]

meaningless /ˈmiː·nɪŋ·ləs/ *adj* • *The leaflet*

was full of meaningless (= not expressing anything) *information.*

mean *(obj)* HAVE RESULT /miːn/ *v past* **meant** /ment/ to have as a result • *Lower costs mean higher profits.* [T] ○ *If she doesn't answer the phone, it means (that) she's out in the garden.* [+ *(that)* clause]

mean HAVE IMPORTANCE /miːn/ *v* [T] *past* **meant** /ment/ to have the importance or value of • *My grandmother's ring wasn't valuable, but it meant a lot to me.*

meaning /'miː·nɪŋ/ *n* [U] importance or value • *Life had lost its meaning for her.*

meaningful /'miː·nɪŋ·fəl/ *adj* • *She found it difficult to form meaningful relationships.*

meaningless /'miː·nɪŋ·ləs/ *adj* without purpose; useless • *a meaningless gesture*

mean INTEND /miːn/ *v* [I/T] *past* **meant** /ment/ to say or do (something) intentionally; intend • *I think she meant 8 o'clock, although she said 7 o'clock.* [T] ○ *I've been meaning to call you but I've been so busy I never got around to it.* [I] • Mean can also be used to add emphasis to what you are saying: *She means what she says.* [T] • If you **mean business**, you are serious about taking action that will be unpleasant for someone if they do not do something: *You've got to tell the students that you mean business—if they don't do the reading you assign, they won't pass the course.* • If you **mean well**, you try to be helpful, although you might unintentionally cause problems: *He means well, but he keeps interfering when he just ought to let us handle things.*

mean NOT KIND /miːn/ *adj* [-er/-est only] unkind or not caring • *I felt a little mean when I said I couldn't visit her in the hospital until Saturday.*

mean GOOD /miːn/ *adj* [-er/-est only] *slang* very good • *She plays a mean bass fiddle.*

meander /miː'æn·dər/ *v* [I] to follow a route that is not straight or direct • *Hikers can meander along the path next to the river for several miles.*

means METHOD /miːnz/ *pl n* a method or way of doing something • *They had no means of letting him know that the flight was canceled.* • **A means to an end** is something you do in order to achieve something else: *Going to college for many is just a means to an end, a way to get a better job.* • **By all means** is used to mean yes, certainly: *"May I come in and have a seat?" "By all means, make yourself comfortable."* • **By means of** is used to show the method used: *Students are selected for scholarships by means of an open, national competition.* • **By no means** or **not by any means** are used to mean not exactly or not completely: *It is by no means clear what the president can do to end the strike.*

means MONEY /miːnz/ *pl n* money or income that allows you to buy things or services • *They simply don't have the means to send their*

children to private schools. [+ *to* infinitive] • *A man of means is a rich man.*

meantime /'miːn·taɪm/ *n* • **In the meantime** means while something else is happening or until something else happens: *Rick wants to be an actor, but in the meantime he's working as a waiter.*

meanwhile /'miːn·waɪl, -ʰwaɪl/ *adv* [not gradable] until something expected happens, or while something else is happening • *It's going to take several days for my car to be repaired—meanwhile I'm renting one.*

measles /'miː·zəlz/ *n* [U] an infectious disease, esp. of children, which produces small red spots all over the body

measly /'miːz·li/ *adj* [not gradable] too small in size or amount; not generous • *We got a measly 2% raise last year.*

measure SIZE /'meʒ·ər/ *v* to discover the exact size, amount, etc., of (something), or to be of a particular size • *"Will the table fit in here?" "I don't know—I'll measure it."* [T] ○ *The sofa measures* (= is of the size of) *3 feet by 7 feet.* [L] • If something or someone doesn't **measure up**, they are not as good as expected or needed: *Production targets are set for each branch, and branch managers who don't measure up don't last long.*

measure /'meʒ·ər/ *n* [C/U] a way of measuring, or a way of showing how much or how great something is • *a system of weights and measures* [C] ○ *It is a measure of his popularity that he got over 70% of the vote.* [U] • Measure can also mean amount or degree: *There was a large measure of luck in his quick promotion to company vice president.* [U] • A measure is also a BAR MUSIC. [C]

measurement /'meʒ·ər·mənt/ *n* [C/U] the act of measuring • *The test is based on the measurement of blood sugar.* [U] • A measurement is the length, height, width, etc., of something, which you discover by measuring it: *The measurements of several of the drawings were identical.* [C]

measure METHOD /'meʒ·ər/ *n* [C] a way to achieve something; a method • *Medicare was a measure intended to guarantee health care for everyone over the age of 65.*

meat /miːt/ *n* [U] the flesh of an animal when it is used for food • *Get a pound of chopped meat from the supermarket on your way home.* • If something is described as **meat-and-potatoes**, it is more basic or important than other things: *For many unions, the meat-and-potatoes issue is no longer pay increases but job security.* • A **meatball** is a small ball made of meat that has been cut into small pieces, pressed together, and cooked: *spaghetti and meatballs* • **Meat loaf** is meat cut into small pieces, mixed with other things, cooked in a container, and then cut into slices to be eaten.

meaty /'miːt̬·i/ *adj* containing a lot of meat • *a meaty meal*

mecca /ˈmek·ə/ *n* [C] a place to which many people are attracted • *Historic Creek Street, lined with shops and restaurants, has become a tourist mecca.*

mechanical MACHINES /məˈkæn·ɪ·kəl/ *adj* [not gradable] of machines or their parts • *a mechanical problem*

mechanic /məˈkæn·ɪk/ *n* [C] someone who repairs or works with machines, esp. as a job • *an auto mechanic*

mechanical WITHOUT THOUGHT /məˈkæn·ɪ·kəl/ *adj* without thinking about what you are doing, esp. because you do it often • *The garbagemen worked in a slow, mechanical way.*

mechanics OPERATION /məˈkæn·ɪks/ *n* [U] the particular way something works or happens • *You have to be familiar with the mechanics of the criminal justice system to understand why so many criminals don't spend much time in jail.*

mechanics PHYSICAL FORCES /məˈkæn·ɪks/ *n* [U] *specialized* the study of the effect of physical forces on objects and their movement

mechanism MACHINE PART /ˈmek·ə,nɪz·əm/ *n* [C] a part of a machine, or a set of parts that work together • *Automatic cameras have a special focusing mechanism.*

mechanism SYSTEM /ˈmek·ə,nɪz·əm/ *n* [C] a way of doing something, esp. one that is planned or part of a system • *The mechanism for collecting taxes needs revising.*

medal /ˈmed·ᵊl/ *n* [C] a small metal disk given to someone usually in a public ceremony to recognize a brave action or special service, or the winning of a competition esp. in sports • *She won three Olympic gold medals.* • *The* **Medal of Honor** *is the highest military honor in the US.*

medalist /ˈmed·ᵊl·əst/ *n* [C] a person who has won a medal in a sport • *She's the gold/silver/bronze medalist* (= She got the medal for finishing in first/second/third place) *in foil fencing.*

medallion /məˈdæl·jən/ *n* [C] a metal disk worn as a decoration on a chain around the neck or attached to a vehicle to show that it can be legally used for a special purpose • *He drove a medallion taxi while he attended college at night.* • *A medallion is also a round piece of meat: medallions of lamb/veal*

meddle /ˈmed·ᵊl/ *v* [I] *disapproving* to try to change or have an influence on things that are not your responsibility • *I don't want my parents meddling in my affairs by telling me how I should run my life.*

media NEWSPAPERS /ˈmiːd·iː·ə/ *pl n* newspapers, magazines, television, and radio, considered as a group • *the news media* • *There was a tremendous amount of media coverage of the funeral of Princess Diana.* • See also MEDIUM METHOD.

media MEDIUM /ˈmiːd·iː·ə/ *pl of* MEDIUM METHOD

median /ˈmiːd·iː·ən/, **median strip** /ˌmiːd·iː·ən ˈstrɪp/ *n* [C] a narrow strip of land or concrete between the two sides of a large road, separating the vehicles moving in opposite directions • *The car went out of control, jumped the median, and hit a truck head on.*

mediate /ˈmiːd·iː·eɪt/ *v* [I/T] to help solve (a disagreement) by talking to the separate people or groups involved, or to communicate information between people • *to mediate a dispute* [T]

mediation /ˌmiːd·iː·ˈeɪ·ʃən/ *n* [U] • *Last-minute attempts at mediation failed, and the workers went on strike.*

mediator /ˈmiːd·iː·ˌeɪt·ər/ *n* [C] • *The governor appointed a mediator and asked both sides to return to the bargaining table.*

medic /ˈmed·ɪk/ *n* [C] *infml* a person who belongs to the part of the armed forces that gives medical help to soldiers

Medicaid /ˈmed·ɪ,keɪd/ *n* [U] a government service in the US for poor people that pays for their medical treatment • Compare MEDICARE.

medical /ˈmed·ɪ·kəl/ *adj* [not gradable] of or relating to medicine, or for the treatment of disease or injury • *She is in her final year of medical school.* ○ *Medical research has led to better treatment for AIDS patients.* • A **medical examiner** is a doctor who examines dead bodies to discover the cause of death.

medically /ˈmed·ɪ·kli/ *adv* [not gradable] • *Staying another night in the hospital was not medically necessary, so she was discharged.*

Medicare /ˈmed·ɪ,ker, -,kær/ *n* [U] a government service in the US for people who are 65 years old and older that pays for medical treatment • Compare MEDICAID.

medicate /ˈmed·ɪ,keɪt/ *v* [T] to treat (someone) with a medicine • *Patients are usually medicated with tranquilizers before having anesthesia.*

medication /ˌmed·ɪˈkeɪ·ʃən/ *n* [C/U] any substance used to treat an illness or disease, esp. a drug • *Are you taking any medications now?* [C] ○ *I'm on medication for my heart condition.* [U]

medicated /ˈmed·ɪ,keɪt·əd/ *adj* [not gradable] containing a medical substance • *medicated shampoo*

medicine TREATMENT /ˈmed·ə·sən/ *n* [U] the science dealing with the preserving of health and with the prevention and treatment of disease or injury • *Pediatrics is a branch of medicine.* ○ *She continued to practice medicine until she was in her eighties.*

medicine SUBSTANCE /ˈmed·ə·sən/ *n* [C/U] a substance taken into the body in treating an illness • *Take two spoonfuls of cough medicine.* [U] ○ *This antibiotic should not be taken with other medicines.* [C] • A **medicine cabinet/chest** is a small cabinet, usually with a mirror on the front, which is attached to the

wall in a bathroom and contains medicines.
PIC BATHROOM

medicinal /məˈdɪs·ən·ᵊl/ *adj* • *The Indians used the plant as a medicinal substance.*

medieval /ˌmiːdˈiːˈiː·vəl, medˈiː·vəl/ *adj* [not gradable] of or from the MIDDLE AGES (= the period in the past from about 500 to 1500) • *a medieval church*

mediocre /ˌmiːdˈiːˈoʊ·kər/ *adj* [not gradable] just acceptable but not good; not good enough • *The movie's plot is predictable, the dialogue is second-rate, and the acting is mediocre.*

mediocrity /ˌmiːdˈiːˈɑk·rət̬·i/ *n* [U] • *He urged educators to combat mediocrity in the classroom.*

meditate /ˈmed·ə̣teɪt/ *v* [I] to think seriously about something, esp. over a period of time • *They decided to meditate on the matter for an additional week or so.* [always + adv/prep] • If you meditate, you give your attention to one thing, and do not think about anything else, usually as a religious activity or as way of calming or relaxing your mind.

meditation /ˌmed·ə̣ˈteɪ·ʃən/ *n* [C/U]

medium AVERAGE /ˈmiːd·iː·əm/ *adj* [not gradable] being in the middle between an upper and lower amount, size, or degree; average • *He was a man of medium height.* ○ *The shirt is available in small, medium, and large sizes.* • Medium is also used to refer to a way of cooking meat so that it is no longer red in the middle: *Would you like your steak rare, medium, or well-done?*

medium METHOD /ˈmiːd·iː·əm/ *n* [C] *pl* **mediums** or **media** /ˈmiːd·iː·ə/ a method or way of expressing something • *the broadcasting/print medium* ○ *The work of art was done in mixed media* (= using different substances), *and included wood shavings, pieces of metal, glue, and oil paint.*

medium PERSON /ˈmiːd·iː·əm/ *n* [C] *pl* **mediums** a person who says that they can receive messages from people who are dead

medley /ˈmed·li/ *n* [C] a mixture of different things, such as tunes put together to form a longer piece of music • *He played a medley of popular songs on the piano.*

meek /miːk/ *adj* [-er/-est only] quiet and unwilling to disagree or fight or to strongly support personal ideas and opinions • *He's slight, meek, and balding, and hardly heroic.*

meekly /ˈmiː·kli/ *adv* • *Ed meekly accepted his father's rages.*

meet COME TOGETHER /miːt/ *v* [I/T] *past* **met** /met/ to come together (esp. with another person) • *We agreed to meet on Tuesday at six.* [I] ○ *They're meeting with their advisers to work out a new plan.* [I] ○ *The doctor unexpectedly met one of her patients in the supermarket.* [T] ○ *Will we meet Joyce's plane* (= be at the airport when she arrives)? [T] ○ *The teams met twice this season* (= competed against each other twice). [I] • If you **meet** someone **halfway**,

you do part of what they want if they will do part of what you want: *Mary asked me to stay another month, and I only want to stay two weeks, but I met her halfway and offered to stay three weeks.* • *Let's* **meet up** *after work* (= get together, esp. informally). • If someone or something **meets with** an event or action, it happens or is experienced: *She met with an accident on her way to school.* ○ *The announcement was met with applause.*

meeting /ˈmiːt̬·ɪŋ/ *n* [C] an occasion when people come together • *We scheduled the meeting for Friday.* • A **meeting house** is a Christian place of worship.

meet BECOME FAMILIAR WITH /miːt/ *v* [I/T] *past* **met** /met/ to become familiar with (someone) for the first time • *They met at work.* [I] ○ *I'd like you to meet my friend Laura.* [T]

meet JOIN /miːt/ *v* [I/T] *past* **met** /met/ (esp. of objects) to join or touch • *The curtains don't meet in the middle of the window.* [I]

meet FULFILL /miːt/ *v* [T] *past* **met** /met/ to fulfill, satisfy, or achieve • *We haven't found office space that meets our needs.* ○ *Do you think she'll be able to meet the deadline?*

meet SPORTS EVENT /miːt/ *n* [C] a sports event at which several teams or people compete • *a track meet* ○ *a swimming meet*

meeting /ˈmiːt̬·ɪŋ/ *n* • See at MEET COME TOGETHER.

mega– /ˈmeg·ə/ *combining form* used to add the meaning "extremely big" or "a large amount" to nouns • *His last movie made him a megastar.* ○ *They're making megabucks* (= a lot of money).

megabyte /ˈmeg·ə̣baɪt/ (*abbreviation* **MB**) *n* [C] a unit of measurement of computer storage space equal to 1,048,576 BYTES

megalomania /ˌmeg·ə·ləˈmeɪ·niː·ə/ *n* [U] the belief that you are much more important and powerful than you really are

megaphone /ˈmeg·ə̣foʊn/ *n* [C] a hollow, cone-shaped device, open at both ends, that makes your voice sound louder when you speak into its smaller end

melancholy /ˈmel·ən̩kɑl·i/ *adj* feeling or expressing sadness • *a melancholy song* ○ *Larry is in a very melancholy mood.*

melee /ˈmeɪ̩leɪ, meɪˈleɪ/ *n* [C] a situation that is confused and not under control, esp. a fight involving a number of people • *Sometime during the melee, three shots were fired.*

mellow SMOOTH /ˈmel·oʊ/ *adj* pleasing because of being smooth, soft, or well developed and not too sharp, bright, new, or rough • *a mellow flavor/tone*

mellow /ˈmel·oʊ/ *v* [I] • *The bright orange of the fresh paint mellowed as it dried.*

mellow RELAXED /ˈmel·oʊ/ *adj* (of a person or mood) relaxed and pleasant • *He looks mellow on stage, but he's always tense before the show.*

mellow /ˈmel·oʊ/ *v* [I/T] • *She used to be very*

impatient, but she's mellowed. [I] • (*slang*) *You need to* **mellow out** (= become more relaxed).

melodrama /'mel·ə‚drɑm·ə, -‚dræm·ə/ *n* [C/U] a play or style of acting in which the characters behave and show emotion in a more noticeable way than real people usually do **melodramatic** /‚mel·ə·drə'mæṭ·ɪk/ *adj* tending to behave or show emotion noticeably • *I've always been a little melodramatic.*

melody /'mel·əd·i/ *n* [C] the main tune in a piece of music, often forming part of a larger piece of music • *Could you play the melody for me?*
melodic /mə'lɑd·ɪk/ *adj* relating to a tune, or having a pleasant tune • *a melodic theme*
melodious /mə'loʊd·i·əs/ *adj* pleasant and relaxing to listen to

melon /'mel·ən/ *n* [C/U] any of several types of large, round, sweet fruit with a thick skin and seeds • *I put orange, banana, and melon in the fruit salad.* [U]

melt /melt/ *v* [I/T] to change (something) or cause something to change from solid to liquid, esp. by making it warmer • *The sun was hot and melted the snow.* [T] ○ *The ice cream was starting to melt by the time I got it home.* [I] • If you melt something down, you heat it until it becomes liquid: *Mat melted down the wax and poured it into a mold.* [M] • If something **melts away**, it leaves or disappears: *The frost melted away.* ○ *Her anger melted away.* • If food **melts in** your **mouth**, it is prepared well and tastes good. • A **melting pot** is a place or situation where the people and cultures of many different places mix together: *The mayor said New York was not a melting pot but a beautiful mosaic.*

meltdown /'melt·dɑʊn/ *n* [C/U] a dangerous accident in which the fuel melts in a nuclear REACTOR (= device that produces energy)

member PERSON /'mem·bər/ *n* [C] a person or thing that is part of a group • *She's a member of our team.* ○ *The lion is a member of the cat family.*
membership /'mem·bər‚ʃɪp/ *n* [C/U] the state of belonging to an organization, or an agreement by which someone joins an organization • *We applied for membership in the country club.* [U] ○ *Some fitness clubs sell lifetime memberships.* [C] • *The membership is all the members of an organization: We asked the membership to vote on the issue.* [U]

member BODY PART /'mem·bər/ *n* [C] a part or organ of a body, such as an arm, leg, or lung
membrane /'mem·breɪn/ *n* [C] a thin, soft layer of tissue that covers organs or connects parts of living things, or the outer covering of a cell • *the nasal membrane* ○ *a cell membrane*

memento /mə'ment·oʊ/ *n* [C] *pl* **mementos** or **mementoes** an object that you keep to help you remember a person or a special event

memo /'mem·oʊ/ *n* [C] *pl* **memos** short form

of MEMORANDUM • *He put his conclusions in a memo to Bethel.*

memoir /'mem·wɑr, -wɔːr/ *n* [C] a written record of a person's knowledge of events or of their own experiences • *She wrote a memoir about her years as a war correspondent.* ○ *He's writing his memoirs* (= the story of his life).

memorabilia /‚mem·ə·rə'bɪl·i:·ə/ *pl n* objects that are collected because they are connected with a person or event that you want to remember

memorable /'mem·ə·rə·bəl/ *adj* likely to be remembered or worth remembering • *a memorable song/story* ○ *Dizzy Dean was one of baseball's most memorable personalities.*
memorably /'mem·ə·rə·bli/ *adv* • *The part was played memorably by Humphrey Bogart.*

memorandum /‚mem·ə'ræn·dəm/, *short form* **memo** *n* [C] *pl* **memoranda** /‚mem·ə'ræn·də/ or **memorandums** a written report prepared especially for a person or group of people and containing information about a particular matter • *Ann will send a memorandum to the staff outlining the new procedures.*

memorial /mə'mɔːr·i:·əl, -'moʊr-/ *n* [C] an object made in order to honor a person or event • *The statue is a memorial to those who died in the war.* • **Memorial Day** is a US holiday on the last Monday in May honoring members of the military who died in war. • A memorial/**memorial service** is also an event held to remember a person who has died.

memory ABILITY TO REMEMBER /'mem·ə·ri/ *n* [C/U] the ability to remember things • *After the accident he suffered from loss of memory.* [U] ○ *She has an excellent memory for names.* [C] ○ *Each of the children recited a short poem from memory* (= by remembering it). [U] • A computer's memory is the part of a computer in which information is stored, or its ability to store information. [U]
memorize /'mem·ə‚rɑɪz/ *v* [T] to learn (something) so that you will remember it exactly • *She memorized her friends' phone numbers.*

memory WHAT IS REMEMBERED /'mem·ə·ri/ *n* [C] something that you remember from the past • *She has vivid memories of her trip to Los Angeles 20 years ago.* ○ *That song brings back memories* (= makes me remember past events). • *A service was held* **in memory of** (= to remember) *those who died in the earthquake.*

men /men/ *pl of* MAN MALE • A **men's room** is a toilet for men in a public building. Compare **ladies' room** at LADY WOMAN.

menace /'men·əs/ *n* [C/U] danger, or someone or something that is likely to cause harm • *There was an air of controlled menace about him.* [U] ○ *That boy is a menace to himself and his friends.* [C]

menace /'men·əs/ *v* [T] • *A hurricane menaced the east coast yesterday.*

menacing /'men·ə·sɪŋ/ *adj* • *a menacing gesture*

menacingly /'men·ə·sɪŋ·li/ *adv* • *She glared menacingly at him.*

menagerie /mə'nædʒ·ə·ri, -'næʒ-/ *n* [C] a collection of different animals that are kept, usually for people to see

mend REPAIR /mend/ *v* [T] to repair (cloth that is torn or something that is damaged) • *Could you mend this hole in my shirt?* ○ *The country is seeking to mend relations with the US.* • *He's messy but has promised to try to mend his ways* (= behave better).

mend BECOME WELL /mend/ *v* [I/T] to become well again after an illness or injury • *The bones in my broken wrist took eight weeks to mend.* [I]

mend /mend/ *n* • If you are **on the mend**, you are becoming healthy after an illness.

menial /'miː·ni·əl/ *adj* (of work) needing little skill or education • *a menial job*

meningitis /ˌmen·ən'dʒaɪt̬·əs/ *n* [U] a swelling of the outer MEMBRANE (= thin layer of tissue) of the brain caused by an infection

menopause /'men·ə.pɔːz/ *n* [U] the time in a woman's life when she gradually stops MENSTRUATING (= having a regular flow of blood from her uterus)

menorah /mə'nɔːr·ə, -'nour·ə/ *n* [C] a nine-branched candle holder used during the Jewish celebration of Hanukkah

menstruate /'men·strə.weɪt/ *v* [I] to have a flow of blood from the uterus, usually for three to five days every four weeks, in women who are not pregnant

menstruation /ˌmen·strə'weɪ·ʃən/ *n* [U] the flow of blood from a woman's uterus

menstrual /'men·strəl, -strə·wəl/ *adj* [not gradable] • *a menstrual cycle/period*

menswear /'menz·wer, -wær/ *n* [U] clothing for men • *designer menswear*

mental /'ment̬·əl/ *adj* [not gradable] of or about the mind, or involving the process of thinking • *Stress can affect both your physical and mental health.* ○ *Many people suffer from some form of mental illness during their lives.* ○ *I made a mental note of her address* (= I will try to remember it).

mentally /'ment̬·əl·i/ *adv* [not gradable] • *mentally ill*

mentality /men'tæl·ət̬·i/ *n* [U] a person's or group's way of thinking about things • *They buy everything on credit—they have this play now, pay later mentality.*

menthol /'men·θɔːl/ *n* [U] a natural substance made from PEPPERMINT (= a plant with a fresh, strong smell) and used in medicines and as a flavoring

mention (*obj*) /'men·tʃən/ *v* to speak about (something), esp. briefly and without giving much detail • *Has he mentioned (that) he's leaving his job?* [+ (*that*) clause] ○ *I promised never to mention the incident again.* [T]

mention /'men·tʃən/ *n* [C/U] • *There was no mention of the robbery in today's newspaper.* [U]

mentor /'men·tɔːr/ *n* [C] an experienced and trusted person who gives another person advice and help, esp. related to work, over a period of time

menu /'men·juː/ *n* [C] a list of the dishes served at a meal, esp. in a restaurant • *There are several vegetarian dishes on the menu.* • A menu is also a list of items shown on a computer screen from which the user can choose an operation for the computer to perform.

meow /miː'aʊ/ *n* [C] the crying sound a cat makes

meow /miː'aʊ/ *v* [I]

mercenary /'mɜr·sə.ner·i/ *n* [C] a soldier who fights for a foreign country or group for pay

mercenary /'mɜr·sə.ner·i/ *adj* interested only in the money that can be obtained from a situation • *I don't trust his motives—he's too mercenary.*

merchandise /'mɜr·tʃən.daɪs/ *n* [U] goods that are bought and sold • *This store has a wide selection of merchandise for sale.*

merchandising /'mɜr·tʃən.daɪ·zɪŋ/ *n* [U] the activity of advertising or selling goods

merchant /'mɜr·tʃənt/ *n* [C] a person whose business is buying and selling goods for profit • The **merchant marine** means a country's ships that are involved in trade.

mercury METAL /'mɜr·kjə·ri/ *n* [U] a heavy, silver-colored metal that is liquid at ordinary temperatures • *Mercury is used in thermometers.*

Mercury PLANET /'mɜr·kjə·ri/ *n* [U] the planet nearest in distance to the sun

mercy KINDNESS /'mɜr·si/ *n* [U] kindness and forgiveness shown toward someone whom you have the right or power to punish • *divine mercy* ○ *The soldiers showed no mercy toward their prisoners.* • **Mercy killing** is EUTHANASIA.

merciful /'mɜr·sɪ·fəl/ *adj* kind and forgiving • *She believed in a just and merciful God.*

merciless /'mɜr·sɪ·ləs/ *adj* showing no kindness or forgiveness; cruel • *a merciless enemy*

mercilessly /'mɜr·sɪ·lə·sli/ *adv* • *He was teased mercilessly at school.*

mercy LUCK /'mɜr·si/ *n* [U] something that is considered lucky because it is not as bad as it had been or could have been • *It's a mercy that no one was hurt in the fire.*

mercifully /'mɜr·sɪ·fli, -fə·li/ *adv* luckily • *His speech was mercifully brief.*

mere /mɪr/ *adj* [not gradable] nothing more than; nothing more important than • *He flew into a rage at the mere mention of her name.* ○ *The city receives a mere 20% of the parking revenues.*

merely /'mɪr·li/ *adv* [not gradable] only; and nothing more • *I merely said that I was tired.* ○ *These columns have no function and are merely decorative.*

merge /mɜrdʒ/ v [I/T] to combine or join together • *Route 9A splits off from Route 9, but they merge after 5 more miles.* [I]

merger /'mɜr·dʒər/ n [C] the combining of two or more companies or organizations into one

meridian /mə'rɪd·i·ən/ n [C] an imaginary line that passes from the North Pole to the South Pole through any place on the surface of the earth, used to show the position of places on a map

meringue /mə'ræŋ/ n [C/U] a mixture of sugar and the beaten white part of eggs, baked until firm, or the light, sweet cake made of this

merit /'mer·ət/ n [C/U] the quality of being good and deserving praise, or a good quality • *Judged on artistic merit, it was a success.* [U] ∘ *Being able to work at home has its merits.* [C] • If something is judged **on its (own) merits**, it is judged on the qualities it possesses rather than by people's opinions of it.

merit /'mer·ət/ v [T] to deserve (something) • *These recommendations merit careful attention.*

mermaid /'mɜr·meɪd/ n [C] an imaginary creature with the upper body of a woman and the tail of a fish

merry /'mer·i/ adj happy or showing enjoyment • You say **Merry Christmas** to wish people a happy time at Christmas. ⒧ GREETINGS

merry–go–round /'mer·i·ˌgoʊˌraʊnd/, **carousel** n [C] a circular stage with brightly colored artificial animals that children can ride on while it turns around and around as music plays

mesh ⌈NET⌉ /meʃ/ n [U] a material loosely woven of wire, plastic, or thread so that it has spaces in it like a net • *Pour the liquid through a strainer of fine mesh.*

mesh ⌈JOIN⌉ /meʃ/ v [I/T] (of two or more things) to fit together or be suitable for each other • *The teeth of the smaller and larger gears mesh with each other.* [I] ∘ *Their ideas on how to run the company never really meshed.* [I]

mesmerize /'mez·mə·ˌraɪz/ v [T] to hold completely the attention or interest of (someone) • *Her beautiful voice mesmerized the audience.*

mesmerizing /'mez·mə·ˌraɪ·zɪŋ/ adj • *a mesmerizing performance*

mess ⌈DISORDER⌉ /mes/ n [C usually sing] a disorderly and confused condition, or something in that condition • *They left the kitchen (in) a mess.* ∘ *We sat in traffic for two hours while they cleaned up the mess from the accident.* • A mess is also a dirty condition: *The puppy's made a mess on the dining room rug.* • A mess is also a situation that is full of problems and difficulties: *Her life was a mess after her husband walked out.*

mess /mes/ v [I/T] infml • *Don't kiss me—*

you'll mess (up) my lipstick. [I/T] • If you **mess around**, you join in a relaxed, aimless activity: *The kids were just messing around at the mall.* • If you **mess** something **up**, you deal with it badly and cause it to fail: *I messed up my chances of getting into a good school.* • If you **mess up**, you do something badly or make a mistake: *I messed up on the measurements, and now the piece won't fit.* • If you **mess with** something harmful, you become involved with it: *He warned the kids not to mess with drugs.*

messed–up /'mest'ʌp, 'mest·ʌp/ adj infml unhappy and emotionally confused • *a messed-up teenager*

messy /'mes·i/ adj dirty, unpleasant, or lacking order • *I hate a messy kitchen.* • A messy situation is one that is confused and unpleasant: *He's going through a messy divorce.*

mess ⌈ROOM⌉ /mes/, **mess hall** /'mes·hɔːl/ n [C] a room or building in which members of the military eat their meals • *the officers' mess*

message ⌈INFORMATION⌉ /'mes·ɪdʒ/ n [C] a short piece of written or spoken information that is given or sent to someone • *If I'm not there when you phone, leave a message.* ∘ *She's not here—can I take a message?*

message ⌈IDEA⌉ /'mes·ɪdʒ/ n [C] the main idea that an artist, writer, speaker, or group is trying to communicate • *The message of the movie seems to be that only the most ruthless people can get ahead in politics.*

messenger /'mes·ən·dʒər/ n [C] a person who carries a message

messiah /mə'saɪ·ə/ n [C] a person who is expected to come and save the world • In the Christian religion, the Messiah is Jesus. • In the Jewish religion, the Messiah has not yet come.

met /met/ past simple and past participle of MEET

metabolism /mə'tæb·ə·ˌlɪz·əm/ n [C] the chemical and physical processes by which a living thing uses food for energy and growth

metal /'met·əl/ n [C/U] a generally hard and shiny chemical element, such as iron or gold, or a mixture of such elements, such as steel, which usually allows electricity and heat to travel through it • A **metal detector** is an electronic device that finds metal, used esp. at airports to search passengers for weapons.

metallic /mə'tæl·ɪk/ adj made of or similar to metal, or showing a quality of metal • *a loud metallic sound*

metamorphosis /ˌmet·ə'mɔːr·fə·səs/ n [C/U] pl **metamorphoses** /ˌmet·ə'mɔːr·fə·ˌsiːz/ a complete change of character, appearance, or condition • *She underwent a metamorphosis from a steady player into a ruthless aggressor on the court.* [C] • (*specialized*) Metamorphosis is the process by which the young form of insects, FROGS, etc., develops into the adult form. [U]

metaphor /'meṭ·ə,fɔːr, -fər/ n [C/U] an expression that describes a person or object by referring to something that is considered to possess similar characteristics • *"A heart of stone" is a metaphor.* [C]

metaphorical /,meṭ·ə'fɔːr·ɪ·kᵊl, -'fɑr-/ adj • *metaphorical expressions*

metaphysical /,meṭ·ə'fɪz·ɪ·kəl/ adj relating to the part of PHILOSOPHY that deals with existence and knowledge • *metaphysical questions about the nature of the universe*

meteor /'miːṭ·iː·ər, -,ɔːr/, **shooting star** n [C] a small piece of matter that falls from space with great speed, producing a bright light as it enters the earth's ATMOSPHERE (= the air surrounding it)

meteoric /,miːṭ·iː'ɔːr·ɪk, -'ɑr-/ adj [not gradable] of or like a meteor • *meteoric rock* • If something is described as meteoric, it is sudden and usually brief: *a meteoric rise to fame*

meteorite /'miːṭ·iː·ə,raɪt/ n [C] a piece of matter from space that has landed on earth • *Meteorites striking land usually vaporize instantly.*

meteorology /,miːṭ·iː·ə'rɑl·ə·dʒi/ n [U] the scientific study of the earth's ATMOSPHERE (= the air surrounding it) and how it causes changes in weather conditions

meteorological /,miːṭ·iː·ə·rə'lɑdʒ·ɪ·kəl/ adj [not gradable]

meteorologist /,miːṭ·iː·ə'rɑl·ə·dʒəst/ n [C]

mete out obj, **mete** obj **out** /'miːṭ'aʊt/ v adv [M] fml to give or order (a punishment) • *The prison sentence is the toughest meted out to any of the seven athletes who have pleaded guilty.*

meter [MEASUREMENT] /'miːṭ·ər/ (abbreviation **m**) n [C] a unit of measurement of length equal to 100 centimeters or 39.37 inches

metric /'me·trɪk/ adj [not gradable] of or using the meter or a system of measurement based on it • The **metric system** is a system of measurement based on the meter, the gram, and the liter as the basic units of length, weight, and volume.

meter [DEVICE] /'miːṭ·ər/ n [C] a device that measures the amount of gas, water, or electricity used • In a TAXI (= car whose driver you pay to take you somewhere), a meter is the device that measures the distance or the amount of time spent traveling and records how much you have to pay.

meter [RHYTHM] /'miːṭ·ər/ n [C/U] the rhythm of a poem, produced by the arrangement of syllables according to the number and type of beats in each line

methadone /'meθ·ə,doʊn/ n [U] a drug given to a person to lessen their pain, or to a person who is trying to stop using HEROIN

methane /'meθ·eɪn/ n [U] a gas having no color or smell which is often used as fuel

method /'meθ·əd/ n [C] a way of doing something • *New teaching methods encourage children to think for themselves.* ○ *Automated tel-*

ephone answering service is one method being used to cut business costs.

methodical /mə'θɑd·ɪ·kəl/ adj controlled and systematic • *The economy's slow, methodical growth is likely to continue into next year.*

methodically /mə'θɑd·ɪ·kli/ adv • *We methodically recorded the details of how the new division would work.* ○ *He methodically gunned down all six people.*

Methodist /'meθ·əd·əst/ n [C], adj [not gradable] (a member) of a Christian religious group that is one of the Protestant churches • *a Methodist church* ○ *a Methodist minister*

methodology /,meθ·ə'dɑl·ə·dʒi/ n [C] a set of methods used in a particular area of study or activity • *The two researchers are using different methodologies.*

meticulous /mə'tɪk·jə·ləs/ adj giving or showing careful attention to every detail • *a meticulous housekeeper* ○ *meticulous research*

metric /'me·trɪk/ adj • See at METER [MEASUREMENT].

metro /'me·troʊ/ adj short form of METROPOLITAN • *the Atlanta metro area* ○ *the metro section in today's newspaper*

metronome /'me·trə,noʊm/ n [C] a device that produces a regular beat at a desired speed to help musicians keep the correct rhythm

metropolis /mə'trɑp·ə·ləs/ n [C] a large city, esp. the main city of a country or region • *Chicago is a major metropolis.*

metropolitan /,me·trə'pɑl·ət·ᵊn/ adj of or in a large city • *the Boston metropolitan area* ○ *the Metropolitan Museum of Art*

mettle /'meṭ·ᵊl/ n [U] bravery and determination • *The climb to the summit in a blizzard would test their mettle.*

mezzanine /'mez·ə,niːn, ,mez·ə'niːn/ n [C] a floor that comes between two other floors of a building, usually directly above the main floor

mg n [C] pl **mg** abbreviation for MILLIGRAM

mi. n [C] pl **mi.** abbreviation for MILE

mic /maɪk/ n [C] short form of MICROPHONE

mice /maɪs/ pl of MOUSE

mick, Mick /mɪk/ n [C] taboo slang a person from Ireland • USAGE: This word is offensive when used to or about an Irish person or a person whose family was originally from Ireland.

Mickey Mouse /,mɪk·iː'maʊs/ adj infml disapproving (of an organization, place, object, or activity) too small and simple; not to be taken seriously • *I don't get paid enough to put up with that Mickey Mouse sort of stuff.*

micro– /,maɪ·kroʊ, ,maɪ·krə/ combining form very small • *a microbrewery* • Compare MACRO–.

microbe /'maɪ·kroʊb/ n [C] a very small living thing, esp. one that causes disease, and which is too small to see without a MICROSCOPE (= device that makes very small objects look larger)

microbiology /,maɪ·kroʊ·baɪ'ɑl·ə·dʒi/ n [U]

the study of very small living things, such as bacteria

microcosm /'maɪ·krə,kɑz·əm/ n [C/U] a small place, society, or situation that has the same characteristics as something much larger • *What's happened to us is a microcosm of what's happened to industry in America.* [C]

microfiche /'maɪ·krə,fiːʃ/ n [C/U] a small sheet of film on which information is photographed in a reduced size

microfilm /'maɪ·krə,fɪlm/ n [C/U] (a length of) film containing photographed information in a reduced size

micron /'maɪ·krɑn/ n [C] a unit of measurement of distance equal to 0.000001 meter

microorganism /,maɪ·kroʊ'ɔːr·gə,nɪz·əm/ n [C] a living thing that is too small to be seen without a MICROSCOPE (= device that makes very small objects look larger)

microphone /'maɪ·krə,foʊn/, *infml* **mike**, *short form* **mic** n [C] a device that records sound or increases the loudness of sounds by changing the sound waves into electrical waves

microscope /'maɪ·krə,skoʊp/ n [C] a device that makes very small objects look larger, esp. so that they can be scientifically examined and studied

microscopic /,maɪ·krə'skɑp·ɪk/ adj extremely small, esp. so small that it can only be seen with a microscope • *microscopic dust* ○ *microscopic organisms*

microwave (oven) /'maɪ·krə,weɪv ('ʌv·ən)/ n [C] a machine that cooks food quickly with energy waves that produce heat within the food

microwave /'maɪ·krə,weɪv/ v [I/T] • *Microwave on high power for 12 minutes.* [I]

mid– /mɪd/ *combining form* the middle of • *midweek* ○ *mid-March* ○ *He's in his mid-thirties.*

midair /mɪd'er, -'ær/ n [U] a point in the air, not on the ground • *She caught the ball in midair.*

midday /'mɪd·deɪ, -'deɪ/ n [U] the middle of the day, at or near 12 o'clock; NOON

middle /'mɪd·əl/ n [C usually sing] a point, position, or part that is not on one side or the other but is equally far from things on either side; the central point, position, or part • *This is my class photo—I'm the one in the middle.* • The middle of a period of time is a point between the beginning and the end of that period: *The noise woke us up in the middle of the night.* • *(infml)* Your middle is your waist. • *When she called, I was* in the middle of (= busy with) *bathing the baby.* • If you describe a place as being (in) the middle of nowhere, you mean that it is very far from towns and cities and does not have many services. • A person, organization, opinion, or type of entertainment that is middle-of-the-road is not

extreme and is acceptable to or liked by most people.

middle /'mɪd·əl/ adj [not gradable] • *In the sequence a, b, c, d, e, the middle letter is c.* • Middle age (also midlife) is the period of your adult life, usually between 40 and 60 years old, when you are no longer young but are not yet old: *a middle-aged couple* • Middle America is the part of American society that is neither rich nor poor and does not have extreme political or religious opinions. • Middle America (also the Middle West) is also the MIDWEST. • The middle class is the people in a society who are not of high social rank or extremely rich but are not poor. • Your middle finger is your longest finger. • A middleman is a person who buys goods from a producer and makes a profit by selling them to a store or a user. • Middle management is the people within a company who are in charge of departments or groups but who are below those who are in control of the company as a whole. • A middle name is the name some people have between their first name and their last name. Compare first name at FIRST; last name at LAST. • A middle school is a school for children between the ages of about 10 and 14. ⓛⓟ EDUCATION IN THE US

Middle Ages /,mɪd·əl'eɪ·dʒəz/ pl n the period in European history, approximately between the years 500 and 1500, when the power of kings, people of high rank, and the Christian church was strong

middlebrow /'mɪd·əl,braʊ/ adj (of music, literature, art, or film) of good quality, interesting, and often popular, but not needing very much thought to understand • Compare HIGHBROW; LOWBROW.

middling /'mɪd·lɪŋ, -lən/ adj [not gradable] medium or average; neither very good nor very bad • *a middling amount*

midget /'mɪdʒ·ət/ n [C] an unusually small person

midlife /'mɪd·laɪf/ n [U] middle age, see at MIDDLE • A midlife crisis is feelings of unhappiness, anxiety, and disappointment that some people experience when they are about 40 years old.

midnight /'mɪd·naɪt/ n [U] 12 o'clock in the middle of the night • ⓛⓟ TIME

midpoint /'mɪd·pɔɪnt/ n [C usually sing] a point half the distance along something, esp. a line, or a point in the middle of a period of time • *the midpoint of the season*

midriff /'mɪd·rɪf/, **midsection** /'mɪd,sek·ʃən/ n [C] the part of the human body between the chest and the waist

midst /mɪdst, mɪtst/ n • In the midst of means in the middle of or surrounded by: *Long Beach is in the midst of a revival.* ○ *The pear tree stood in the midst of a rainbow of flowers.*

midstream /'mɪd'striːm/ n [U] the middle of

a river where the water flows fastest, or (*fig.*) the middle of an activity • (*fig.*) *Never switch software in midstream.*

midterm /'mɪd·tɜrm/ *adj* [not gradable] being at the end of the first half of a TERM (= fixed period of time) • *midterm elections* ○ *Midterm exams start next week.*

midterm /'mɪd·tɜrm/ *n* [C] a test given at the end of the first half of a school TERM

midway /'mɪd·weɪ, -'weɪ/ *adv* [not gradable] in the middle between two places, or in the middle of a process or period of time • *Milwaukee is about midway between Chicago and Green Bay.* ○ *She stopped working midway through her pregnancy.*

midweek /'mɪd·wiːk, -'wiːk/ *n* [U] the middle of the week

Midwest /mɪd'west/, **Middle America**, **Middle West** *n* [U] the north central part of the US which includes Ohio, Indiana, Michigan, Illinois, Wisconsin, Iowa, Minnesota, Nebraska, Missouri, and Kansas • *The drought has destroyed grain crops across much of the Midwest.*

midwife /'mɪd·waɪf/ *n* [C] *pl* **midwives** /'mɪd·waɪvz/ a person, usually a woman, who is not a doctor and who has been trained to help women when they are giving birth

midwifery /mɪd'wɪf·ə·ri, -'waɪ·fə-/ *n* [U] the techniques or activity of helping women give birth without doctors

miffed /mɪft/ *adj* annoyed, esp. at someone's behavior toward you • *I was miffed because she didn't call all week.*

might MAY /maɪt/ *past simple of* MAY

might POSSIBILITY /maɪt/ *v aux* he/she/it **might** used to express the possibility that something will happen or be done or is true, although it may not be very likely • *We might come visit you in Atlanta in the spring.* ○ *He's very fast and he might even finish in the top three.* ○ *The Beach Boys might well have been the most talented act to perform at the Monterey Pop Festival.* • Compare MAY POSSIBILITY. LP AUXILIARY VERBS

might SUGGESTION /maɪt/ *v aux* he/she/it **might** used to make a suggestion or suggest a possibility in a polite way • *I thought you might like to join me for dinner.* • Compare MAY SUGGESTION. LP AUXILIARY VERBS

might SHOULD /maɪt/ *v aux* he/she/it **might** used to suggest, esp. angrily, what someone should do to be pleasant or polite • *You might at least try to look like you're enjoying yourself!* • LP AUXILIARY VERBS

might POWER /maɪt/ *n* [U] power, strength, or force • *She struggled with all her might to lift the rock.*

mighty /'maɪt̬·i/ *adj, adv* • *a mighty* (= powerful) *river* ○ (*infml*) *I'd be mighty* (= very) *grateful if you looked in on my mother while I'm away.*

mightn't /'maɪt·ənt/ *contraction of* **might not**

migraine /'maɪ·greɪn/ *n* [C/U] a severe continuous pain in the head, often with vomiting and difficulty in seeing

migrate /'maɪ·greɪt, maɪ'greɪt/ *v* [I] to move from one country or region to another, often temporarily • *Farm workers migrate at harvest time.* ○ *In September these birds migrate south.*

migrant /'maɪ·grənt/ *n* [C] • *migrant workers*

migration /maɪ'greɪ·ʃən/ *n* [C/U] • *She's interested in bat migration.* [U]

migratory /'maɪ·grə,tɔːr·i, -,toʊr·i/ *adj* [not gradable] having the characteristic of moving regularly to another place • *migratory birds*

mike /maɪk/ *n* [C] *infml* a MICROPHONE

mild /maɪld/ *adj* [-*er*/-*est* only] not violent, severe, or extreme; slight or gentle • *mild criticism* ○ *a mild case of the flu* ○ *She has a very mild temperament.* • If the flavor of food or a smell is described as mild, it is not very strong. • Mild weather is not very cold or not as cold as usual.

mildly /'maɪld·li/ *adv* • *We were mildly surprised to see him again.* ○ *"I think you've made a mistake," he said mildly.*

mildew /'mɪl·duː/ *n* [U] a soft, usually white, green, or black area caused by a FUNGUS that sometimes grows on things such as plants, food, paper, or buildings, esp. if the conditions are warm and wet

mile /maɪl/ (*abbreviation* **mi.**) *n* [C] a unit of measurement of distance equal to 1760 YARDS or 1.6 kilometers • **Miles** can mean a very long distance: *They live way out in the country, miles from anywhere.*

mileage, **milage** /'maɪ·lɪdʒ/ *n* [U] the distance that a vehicle has traveled • *What's the mileage on your car?* • Mileage is also the distance a vehicle can travel using a particular amount of fuel: *Smaller cars get better mileage.*

milestone /'maɪl·stoʊn/ *n* [C] an important event in the development or history of something or in someone's life • *We've been married now for 20 years, a real milestone.*

milieu /mɪl'juː, -'juː/ *n* [C] *pl* **milieus** or **milieux** /mɪl'juː, -'juːz, -'juː, -'juːz/ the people and the physical and social conditions and events that provide a background in which someone acts or lives • *the Irish-Catholic milieu of Chicago* ○ *a cultural milieu*

militant /'mɪl·ə·tənt/ *adj* active, determined, and often willing to use force • *a militant environmentalist*

militant /'mɪl·ə·tənt/ *n* [C] • *Militants fired at a tour bus.*

military /'mɪl·ə,ter·i/ *adj* [not gradable] relating to or belonging to the armed forces • *military spending/intervention/forces* • A **military academy/school** is a place where soldiers are trained to become officers. • A **military academy/school** is also a private school or college that expects obedience to rules, has uniforms, and is generally run like the armed forces.

military /'mɪl·ə,ter·i/ n [U] the armed forces of a country • *My Dad was in the military.*

militarism /'mɪl·ə·tə,rɪz·əm/ n [U] the belief that it is necessary to have strong armed forces and that they should be used in order to win political or economic advantage

militaristic /,mɪl·ə·tə'rɪs·tɪk/ adj • *a hard-line militaristic regime*

militia /mə'lɪʃ·ə/ n [C] a military force that operates only some of the time and whose members are not soldiers in a permanent army • *Each militia represents one of the country's political factions.*

milk /mɪlk/ n [U] the white liquid produced esp. by cows which people drink • *cookies and milk* • Milk is also the white liquid produced by female mammals used for their young: *Breast milk is the best nourishment for a baby.* • The white liquid obtained from some plants is also called milk: *coconut milk* • **Milk chocolate** is sweet chocolate that contains milk. • A **milk shake** is a drink made of milk, **ice cream**, and fruit, chocolate, or some other flavoring, all mixed together in a machine until it is full of bubbles.

milk /mɪlk/ v [T] • *Milking a cow by hand is harder than it looks.* • To milk something or someone is to get as much from it or them as possible: *The newspapers milked the story dry.*

milky /'mɪl·ki/ adj having the color or thickness of milk • *a milky white vase* • The **Milky Way** is the pale strip of stars across the sky that forms part of the GALAXY (= star system) that includes the earth.

mill /mɪl/ n [C] a building with machinery for crushing grain into flour • A mill is also a factory where a particular materials or substances are processed: *a paper/steel mill* • A mill is also a device for crushing a solid substance into powder: *a coffee/pepper mill* • A **millstone** is one of a pair of large, circular, flat stones used, esp. in the past, to crush grain into flour. • A millstone or **a millstone around** your **neck** is a continuing difficult responsibility or problem: *The huge mortgage has become a millstone around his neck.*

mill around/about /,-'-'-/ v adv [I] (of a group of people) to move around with no obvious purpose • *There were people milling around the entrance to the stadium.*

millennium /mə'len·i·əm/ n [C] pl **millennia** /mə'len·i·ə/ or **millenniums** a period of 1000 years • *Big celebrations are planned for the arrival of the next millennium (= the beginning of the 21st century).*

millennial /mə'len·i·əl/ adj [not gradable]

milligram /'mɪl·ə,græm/ (*abbreviation* **mg**) n [C] a unit of measurement of weight equal to 0.001 gram

milliliter /'mɪl·ə,li:ṭ·ər/ (*abbreviation* **ml**) n [C] a unit of measurement of volume equal to 0.001 liter

millimeter /'mɪl·ə,mi:ṭ·ər/ (*abbreviation* **mm**) n [C] a unit of measurement of length equal to 0.001 meter

millinery /'mɪl·ə,ner·i/ n [U] women's hats and other related goods

million /'mɪl·jən/ *number* 1,000,000 • *The tourist attraction brings in over a million people a year.* ○ *a million-dollar project* ○ (*fig.*) *I have a million things (= a lot of things) to do tomorrow.* • LP NUMBERS

millionth /'mɪl·jənθ/ adj, n [C] • *In 1988 Honda produced its millionth car in America.* • A millionth is one of a million equal parts of something.

millionaire /,mɪl·jə'ner, -'nær/ n [C] someone who has more than a MILLION dollars (= $1,000,000) in property, possessions, or savings

mime /maɪm/ n [C/U] the art of acting without speech, or a person who is skilled at performing this art, esp. in a theater • *In the game of charades, you have to convey the title of a movie or book through mime.* [U]

mime /maɪm/ v [I/T] to use actions without speech to communicate (something), or to pretend to speak by moving your lips but without making any sound • *The illusion of live music was created by singers miming to their records.* [I]

mimic /'mɪm·ɪk/ v [T] **mimicking**, *past* **mimicked** to copy (the way someone speaks and moves), esp. in order to amuse or insult people • *She was mimicking the various people in our office.* • To mimic is also to have the same or similar effect as something else: *This substance mimics calcium and can replace it in bones.*

mimic /'mɪm·ɪk/ n [C] • *He was a fine mimic.*

mimicry /'mɪm·ɪ·kri/ n [U] • *The mockingbird is known for its mimicry of other birds.*

min. n [C] *abbreviation for* MINUTE TIME

mince CUT /mɪns/ v [T] to cut (food) into very small pieces • *Mince the onion and sauté it in butter.*

minced /mɪnst/ adj [not gradable] • *minced garlic/onions/parsley*

mince SPEAK /mɪns/ v • To **mince words** is to say things carefully and indirectly, esp. in order not to upset people: *The report does not mince words, describing the situation as extremely serious.*

mincemeat /'mɪn,smiːt/ n [U] a sweet, spicy mixture of small pieces of apple, RAISINS, and other fruit that is cooked in pastry

mind THINKING /maɪnd/ n [C] the part of you that has the ability to think, feel emotions, and be aware of things • *His mind was open to new ideas.* ○ *I just said the first thing that came into my mind.* • Your mind is also your attention or thoughts: *His mind began to wander during the lecture.* ○ *Joanna has a lot on her mind at the moment (= has much to think about).* •

Your mind is also your intelligence and ability to reason: *a brilliant/logical mind* • Your mind is also your ability to remember: *My mind went blank on that exam question.* • To **bear/keep** something **in mind** is to consider it when you are doing something because it may influence how you do it: *"You're always welcome to stay with us when you're in town." "Thanks, I'll keep it in mind."* • **Mind over matter** is the power of the mind to control the body and the physical world generally: *My grandfather believed that he had cured his own cancer through mind over matter.* • People sometimes say **in** their **mind's eye**, meaning in their memory of how something looked: *In my mind's eye she remains a little girl of six although she's a grown woman.* • (*infml*) If something is **mind-blowing/mind-boggling**, it is surprising, shocking, and often difficult to understand or imagine: *The movie's special effects are mind-blowing.* • A **mind-set** is a person's attitudes or opinions resulting from earlier experiences: *Teenagers often complain about the shortcomings or their parents' mind-set.*

mindless /'maɪn·dləs/ *adj* [not gradable] not reasonable or understandable • *There's a lot of mindless violence in this movie.*

mind CARE FOR /maɪnd/ *v* [T] to watch carefully and care for (someone or something) • *She asked me if I'd mind the children for an hour.* ○ *Could you mind my bag while I go to the restroom?* • When you **mind** your **own business**, you only take an interest in your own matters: *If she asks where we're going, tell her to mind her own business.*

mind BE CAREFUL /maɪnd/ *v* [T] to be careful (of); give attention (to) • *Mind how you cross the highway.* [+ *wh-* word] ○ *Mind your manners!* (= Be polite!) ○ *Don't mind him* (= Do not worry about him)—*he's harmless.*

mindful /'maɪnd·fəl/ *adj* [not gradable] giving attention (to) • *Mindful of the poor road conditions, she drove slowly.*

mind OPPOSE /maɪnd/ *v* [I/T] (often used in requests and negative sentences) to find annoying or offensive, or to oppose • *I wouldn't mind seeing a movie tonight* (= I would like to see a movie). [T] ○ *Would you mind turning the radio down* (= Please would you turn it down)? [T] ○ *Do you mind if I smoke* (= May I smoke)? [I]

mine BELONGING TO ME /maɪn/ *pronoun* belonging to me, or that which belongs to me • *"Whose bag is this?" "It's mine."* ○ *Your hair is longer than mine.* ○ *She's an old friend of mine.*

mine HOLE /maɪn/ *n* [C] a deep hole in the ground made for the removal of coal and other substances by digging • *a gold mine* • A mine is also where something originates: *Belinda is a mine of information about home decorating.*

mine /maɪn/ *v* [I/T] • *They mine copper in this area.* [T]

miner /'maɪ·nər/ *n* [C] a person who works in a mine

mining /'maɪ·nɪŋ/ *n* [U] the industry or activity of removing coal and other substances from the earth

mine BOMB /maɪn/ *n* [C] a bomb put underground or in the sea that explodes when vehicles, ships, or people go over or near it • A **mine detector** is a device used to discover whether there are mines in a particular area. • A **minefield** is an area of land or water that contains mines, or (*fig.*) a situation that contains hidden problems and dangers: (*fig.*) *Their anger escalates, turning the living room into an emotional minefield.* • A **minesweeper** is a ship that is used to discover and remove mines that are under water.

mine /maɪn/ *v* [T] to hide mines in (an area) • *The desert has been heavily mined.*

mineral /'mɪn·ə·rəl/ *n* [C] a chemical substance that has formed naturally in foods, in water, or in the ground, or any substance that is obtained from the earth by MINING • *Minerals and timber are the state's main natural resources.* • **Mineral water** is natural water containing dissolved minerals.

mingle MIX /'mɪŋ·gəl/ *v* [I/T] to mix (with); combine • *Her excitement at starting the new job was mingled with fear.* [T]

mingle BE WITH /'mɪŋ·gəl/ *v* [I] to be with or among other people, esp. talking to them • *He seems to be mingling with the other guests.*

mini SKIRT /'mɪn·i/ *n* [C] *short form of* MINISKIRT

mini– SMALL /'mɪn·i/ *combining form* smaller than others of the same type • *a minivan*

miniature /'mɪn·i:·ə,tʃʊr, -tʃər/ *adj* [not gradable] very small • *She has dollhouse filled with miniature furniture.*

miniature /'mɪn·i:·ə,tʃʊr, -tʃər/ *n* [C/U] (of an object) the state of being much smaller than the thing it represents, or such an object • *She bought a model of the Empire State Building in miniature.* [U]

minibus /'mɪn·i:,bʌs/ *n* [C] a small bus, usually for transporting people short distances

minimum /'mɪn·ə·məm/ *adj* [not gradable] being the smallest amount or number allowed or possible • *Her lawyer asked the judge to give her the minimum sentence.* • A **minimum wage** is the lowest pay for an hour's work that can legally be paid to a worker: *They want to raise the minimum wage to $8 an hour.* • USAGE: The opposite of minimum is MAXIMUM.

minimum /'mɪn·ə·məm/ *n* [C] • *We need a minimum of ten people to play this game.* ○ *Expenses must be kept to a minimum.*

minimal /'mɪn·ə·məl/ *adj* [not gradable] as small as possible • *Fortunately, damage to the heart was minimal.*

minimally /'mɪn·ə·mə·li/ *adv* [not gradable]

slightly • *The factory was only minimally damaged by the fire.*

minimize /'mɪn·ə,maɪz/ v [T] to reduce (something) to the smallest possible level or amount • *We do all that we can to minimize the risk of infection.* • To minimize something is also to make it seem less important or smaller than it really is: *He minimized his involvement in the scandal.*

mining /'maɪ·nɪŋ/ n • See at MINE HOLE.

miniscule /'mɪn·ə,skjuːl/ adj [not gradable] MINUSCULE

miniseries /'mɪn·iː,sɪr·iːz/ n [C] pl **miniseries** a television program broadcast in several parts over a short period of time

miniskirt /'mɪn·iː,skɜrt/, *short form* **mini** n [C] a very short skirt, ending well above the knee

minister PRIEST /'mɪn·ə·stər/ n [C] (in various Christian churches) a person who leads religious ceremonies

ministry /'mɪn·ə·stri/ n [U] the job of being a religious leader • *He felt called to the ministry.*

minister POLITICIAN /'mɪn·ə·stər/ n [C] (in many countries) a high government official who is in charge of or has an important position in a particular department • *the foreign minister*

ministerial /,mɪn·ə'stɪr·iː·əl/ adj [not gradable] • *Social justice has concerned him since his first ministerial assignment.*

ministry /'mɪn·ə·stri/ n [C] a government department led by a minister • *All the ministries were represented at the meeting—justice, foreign affairs, economic affairs, and the interior.*

minivan /'mɪn·iː,væn/ n [C] a large vehicle that looks like a small bus, usually with three rows of seats, the last of which can be removed or folded flat to transport large objects

mink /mɪŋk/ n [C] pl **minks** or **mink** a small brown animal from Europe, North America, and Asia, or its fur, used to make expensive coats and other items of clothing • *a mink coat*

minnow /'mɪn·oʊ/ n [C] a very small fish found in lakes and rivers

minor UNIMPORTANT /'maɪ·nər/ adj [not gradable] lesser in size or importance • *She suffered minor injuries in the accident.* ○ *Waiting another half hour was only a minor inconvenience.* • Compare MAJOR IMPORTANT.

minor YOUNG PERSON /'maɪ·nər/ n [C] a person under the age at which he or she legally becomes an adult

minor SPECIAL SUBJECT /'maɪ·nər/ n [C] the second most important subject that a college student is studying • *I'm taking two courses in my minor, chemistry.*

minor /'maɪ·nər/ v [I] • *I minored in Spanish in college.*

minority /mə'nɔːr·ət̬·i, maɪ-, -'nɑr-/ n [C/U] less than half of a total number or amount; the smaller part of something • *Only a minority of people support military action.* [U] ○ *Tra-*ditional families are in the minority in this neighborhood* (= there are not many). [U] • Compare MAJORITY.

minority (group) /mə'nɔːr·ət̬·i (,gruːp), maɪ-, -'nɑr-/ n [C] a group of people who share some characteristic by birth that makes their group smaller than some other groups in a society and may cause others to treat them unfairly • *He argued that African Americans and other minorities were not getting a fair deal in sports and elsewhere in society.* ○ *Jews and Roman Catholics belonged to religious minorities.*

minstrel show /'mɪn·strəl/ n [C] (in the past in the US) a show of dance and song, originally, in the time of SLAVERY, by white people who darkened their faces to look like black people, and represented them as silly, simple, and happy, to amuse the white people who came to see it

mint PLANT /mɪnt/ n [C/U] an herb whose leaves have a clean smell and taste, used to flavor food, drinks, and candy • A mint is also a candy with this strong, fresh flavor. [C]

mint COIN FACTORY /mɪnt/ n [C] a place where the new coins and paper money of a country are made • (*infml*) A mint is also a very large amount of money: *The new roof cost us a mint.*

mint /mɪnt/ v [T] to make (a new coin)

mint /mɪnt/ adj [not gradable] • If something is in **mint condition**, it is in excellent condition, as if new: *Alex's old Cadillac is in mint condition.*

minus SUBTRACTION /'maɪ·nəs/, *symbol* – prep reduced by (the stated number) • *Five minus one is four.* • Minus can also mean without: *He published the novel minus the offensive words.*

minus /'maɪ·nəs/, *symbol* – adj [not gradable] (of a number or amount) less than zero • *Temperatures will be dropping to minus 10°.* • A mark such as B-minus (B–) or C-minus (C–) given to a student's work means that the work is slightly worse than if it were given the B or C mark. • A minus sign is the symbol –.

minus DISADVANTAGE /'maɪ·nəs/ n [C] pl **minuses** a disadvantage • *Not having any experience is a big minus.*

minuscule /'mɪn·ə,skjuːl, mə'nʌs,kjuːl/, **miniscule** /'mɪn·ə,skuːl/ adj extremely small • *Salaries are a minuscule part of the budget.*

minute TIME /'mɪn·ət/ n (*abbreviation* **min.**) [C] any of the 60 parts that an hour is divided into; 60 seconds • *It takes me 20 minutes to get to work.* • A minute is also a very short time: *Just a minute—I'm almost ready.* ○ *When you've got a minute, I'd like a word with you.* • The minute (that) (= As soon as) *I saw him, I knew something was wrong.*

minute SMALL /maɪ'nuːt, mə-/ adj extremely small • *minute amounts/quantities* • *She examined the contract in minute detail* (= looking at all the details of it).

minutes /'mɪn·əts/ pl n the written record of

what was said at a meeting • *Harry will take the minutes.*

miracle /'mɪr·ɪ·kəl/ *n* [C] an unusual and mysterious event that is thought to have been caused by God, or any surprising and unexpected event • *Some people think the human body is God's greatest miracle.* ○ *It's a miracle (that) he wasn't killed in that car crash.* [+ (that) clause]

miraculous /mə'ræk·jə·ləs/ *adj* unusual and mysterious because of being caused by God, or very surprising and unexpected • *He made a miraculous recovery from heart disease.*

mirage /mə'rɑʒ/ *n* [C] an image, produced by very hot air, of something that seems to be far away but does not really exist • *Up ahead she saw a slight shimmer that looked like water, a road mirage.*

mire /maɪr/ *n* [C usually sing] an area of deep, wet, sticky earth, or (*fig.*) any messy situation • *The cart's wheels sank in the red mire.*

mire /maɪr/ *v* [T] to cause (something) to sink in deep, wet, sticky earth, or (*fig.*) to cause (someone or an activity) to become trapped in a difficult situation • (*fig.*) *At the time the country was mired in the Great Depression.*

mirror GLASS /'mɪr·ər/ *n* [C] a piece of glass with a shiny, metallic back that reflects light, producing an image of whatever is in front of it • *a rear-view mirror* ○ *a hand mirror* • *The apartment next door is a* **mirror image** *of ours* (= it is exactly the same except that the left and right sides have changed positions).

mirror REPRESENT /'mɪr·ər/ *v* [T] to be a copy of (something); be similar to (something)

mirror /'mɪr·ər/ *n* [C] • *The law is a mirror of the nation's character.*

mirth /mɜrθ/ *n* [U] *esp. literary* laughter or amusement • *Chen could not contain his mirth.*

misadventure /ˌmɪs·əd'ven·tʃər/ *n* [C/U] bad luck, or an experience with a bad result

misapprehension /mɪsˌæp·rɪ'hen·tʃən/ *n* [C] a failure to understand something, or an understanding or belief about something that is not correct • *He was under the misapprehension that those chemicals were banned.*

misappropriate /ˌmɪs·ə'prou·priˌeɪt/ *v* [T] to steal (something that you have been trusted to manage) and use it for your own benefit • *He misappropriated $30,000 to pay for personal travel.*

misbehave /ˌmɪs·bɪ'heɪv/ *v* [I] to behave badly • *There will always be some kids who misbehave.*

misbehavior /ˌmɪs·bɪ'heɪ·vjər/ *n* [U] • *You can be suspended from school for that sort of misbehavior.*

miscalculate /mɪs'kæl·kjəˌleɪt/ *v* [I/T] to calculate (an amount) wrongly, or to judge (someone or something) wrongly • *Swensen badly miscalculated the time it would take.* [T]

miscalculation /mɪsˌkæl·kjə'leɪ·ʃən/ *n* [C] •

They thought they could win the war, and that was a horrible miscalculation.

miscarriage /'mɪsˌkær·ɪdʒ/ *n* [C/U] an early, unintentional end to a pregnancy in which the developing baby is unable to live • A **miscarriage of justice** is a wrong decision in a court of law, or any unfair decision: *He spent nine years in prison for a crime he didn't commit— it was a great miscarriage of justice.*

miscarry /ˌmɪs'kær·i/ *v* [I] to unintentionally end a pregnancy early because the baby is unable to live

miscellaneous /ˌmɪs·ə'leɪ·ni:·əs/ *adj* [not gradable] consisting of a mixture of various things that are not necessarily connected with each other • *His bedroom is full of guitars, keyboards, and miscellaneous instruments.*

mischief /'mɪs·tʃəf/ *n* [U] behavior, esp. of a child, that is slightly bad or causes trouble but is not intended to harm anyone • *Some of the neighborhood kids like to get into mischief.* ○ *She's a cute little girl, but full of mischief.*

mischievous /'mɪs·tʃə·vəs; *not standard* mɪs 'tʃiː·vəs, -viː·əs/ *adj* (of behavior) slightly annoying or slightly bad, esp. in a playful way, or (of someone's appearance) looking likely to do something bad • *a mischievous prank* ○ *a mischievous smile*

misconception /ˌmɪs·kən'sep·ʃən/ *n* [C] an idea that is wrong because it is based on a failure to understand a situation • *It's a common misconception that Americans think only about money.* [+ that clause]

misconduct /mɪs'kɑnˌdʌkt/ *n* [U] wrong or immoral behavior of someone in a position of authority or responsibility • *sexual misconduct* ○ *criminal misconduct* ○ *official misconduct*

misconstrue /ˌmɪs·kən'struː/ *v* [T] *slightly fml* to form a false understanding of the meaning or intention of (something that someone does or says) • *Johnson complained that his statements were misconstrued.*

misdeed /mɪs'diːd/ *n* [C usually pl] an act that is criminal or bad • *I cannot be held responsible for the misdeeds of others.*

misdemeanor /ˌmɪs·də'miː·nər, 'mɪs·dəˌmiː·/ *n* [C] a crime considered to be one of the less serious types of crime • *Possession of small amounts of marijuana is a misdemeanor.*

miser /'maɪ·zər/ *n* [C] someone who has a great desire to possess money and hates to spend it, sometimes living like a poor person because of this • *On environmental spending, the president is a miser.*

miserly /'maɪ·zər·li/ *adj* • *My father was pretty miserly.*

miserable UNHAPPY /'mɪz·ə·rə·bəl/ *adj* very unhappy, or causing much unhappiness • *They can make your life miserable if they want to.*

miserably /'mɪz·ə·rə·bli/ *adv* • *She groaned miserably and trembled with anger.*

miserable LOW VALUE /'mɪz·ə·rə·bəl/ *adj* very low in quality or value • *The forecast is for miserable weather today.*

miserably /'mɪz·ə·rə·bli/ *adv* • *Our leaders have failed miserably* (= completely failed).

misery /'mɪz·ə·ri/ *n* [C/U] great unhappiness • *The war brought misery to Vietnam.* [U] • **Misery loves company** means that people who are unhappy like to share their troubles with others. • USAGE: The related adjective is MISERABLE UNHAPPY.

misfire /mɪs'faɪr/ *v* [I] (of a gun or other weapon) to fail to fire, or to fail to fire as intended • *Conchas's gun misfired after three shots.*

misfit /'mɪs·fɪt/ *n* [C] someone who is not accepted socially by other people because his or her behavior is unusual or strange • *I was a social misfit, the kind of kid no one played with.*

misfortune /mɪs'fɔːr·tʃən/ *n* [C/U] bad luck, or an unlucky event • *Never take delight in someone's personal misfortunes.* [C] ○ *The school nurse was as mean a lady as you'd ever have the misfortune to meet.* [U]

misgiving /mɪs'gɪv·ɪŋ/ *n* [C usually pl] a feeling of doubt, uncertainty, or worry about a future event • *Cheung spoke of his deep misgivings about graduate school.*

misguided /mɪs'gaɪd·əd/ *adj* unreasonable or unsuitable because of being based on a bad judgment of a situation or on information or beliefs that are wrong • *"The Red Shoes" was a misguided attempt to turn a ballet film into a musical.*

mishandle /mɪs'hæn·dəl/ *v* [T] to deal with (something) without the necessary care or skill • *Bonds was slain when teenagers mishandled a gun.*

mishap /'mɪs·hæp/ *n* [C/U] an accident or unlucky event • *The parade took place without mishap.* [U]

mishmash /'mɪʃ·mæʃ, -mɑʃ/ *n* [C usually sing] a badly organized mixture • *The movie is a mishmash of past and present.*

misinform /ˌmɪs·ən'fɔːrm/ *v* [T] to tell (someone) information that is not correct • *I was misinformed about the meeting—it was yesterday, not today.*

misinformation /ˌmɪs·ɪn·fər'meɪ·ʃən/ *n* [U]

misinterpret /ˌmɪs·ən'tɜr·prət/ *v* [T] to understand (something) wrongly • *She felt that her comments had been misinterpreted.*

misjudge /mɪs'dʒʌdʒ/ *v* [T] to form an unfair or wrong judgment about (a person or thing) • *He grabbed for her hand, but he misjudged her quickness.*

mislay /mɪs'leɪ/ *v* [T] *past* **mislaid** /mɪs'leɪd/ to lose (something) temporarily by forgetting where you put it • *Could I borrow your pen? I seem to have mislaid mine.*

mislead /mɪs'liːd/ *v* [T] *past* **misled** /mɪs'led/ to cause (someone) to believe something that is not true • *We're not misleading people, and we're not pretending to be something we're not.*

misleading /mɪs'liːd·ɪŋ/ *adj* • *misleading information* ○ *a misleading story*

mismanage /mɪs'mæn·ɪdʒ/ *v* [T] to manage (something) badly • *Many of these health-care plans have been mismanaged.*

mismanagement /mɪs'mæn·ɪdʒ·mənt/ *n* [U] *Officials are facing charges of mismanagement.*

misnomer /mɪs'noʊ·mər/ *n* [C usually sing] a name that is not correct or does not suit what it refers to, or a use of such a name • *Dry cleaning is a misnomer, since the clothes are cleaned in a fluid.*

misogynist /mə'sɑdʒ·ə·nəst/ *n* [C] someone, usually a man, who hates women or believes that men are much better than women

misogyny /mə'sɑdʒ·ə·ni/ *n* [U] • *There's a disturbing misogyny in his films.*

misplace /mɪs'pleɪs/ *v* [T] to lose (something), esp. temporarily, by forgetting where you put it • *I am always misplacing my eyeglasses.*

misplaced /mɪs'pleɪst/ *adj* wrongly or unwisely directed toward someone or something • *Their life together was full of misplaced trust and repressed emotion.*

misprint /'mɪs·prɪnt/ *n* [C] a mistake in a printed text • *There was a misprint in the ad—it should have read $10,000, not $1000.*

mispronounce /ˌmɪs·prə'naʊns/ *v* [T] to pronounce (a word or sound) wrongly • *I always mispronounce his name.*

mispronunciation /ˌmɪs·prə·nʌn·si:'eɪ·ʃən/ *n* [C/U] a wrong sound used when saying a word, or the habit of pronouncing words or sounds wrongly • *I don't speak Russian well and when I made a slight mispronunciation, she didn't understand me.* [C]

misquote /mɪs'kwoʊt/ *v* [T] to repeat (something someone has said or written) in a way that is not accurate • *Lines from his essay were misquoted in the book.*

misread /mɪs'riːd/ *v* [T] *past* **misread** /mɪs'red/ to make a mistake when reading (something), or (*fig.*) to form a wrong understanding or judgment of (something) • *Please correct me if I misread anything.* ○ (*fig.*) *I'm sorry I got angry—I simply misread the situation.*

misrepresent /mɪs·rep·rɪ'zent/ *v* [T] to represent (something or someone) falsely, often in order to obtain an advantage • *He misrepresented facts about his legal experience on his application.*

Miss TITLE /mɪs/ *n* [U] a title for a girl or a woman who has never been married, used before the family name or full name • *Miss Green* • Miss is also used as a form of address to get the attention of a girl or woman: *Hey, Miss, you dropped a glove!* • A woman who has won a beauty competition is often given the title "Miss" and the name of the place that she represents: *Miss Alaska/Miss America* • LP TITLES AND FORMS OF ADDRESS

miss NOT HIT /mɪs/ *v* [I/T] to fail to hit or to

avoid hitting (something) • *The plane narrowly missed power lines as it landed.* [T] ○ *He threw a snowball at me, but he missed.* [I]

miss /mɪs/ *n* [C] • *Scurry blocked eight shots and caused misses on numerous others.*

miss NOT DO /mɪs/ *v* [T] to fail to do, see, or experience (something, esp. something planned or expected) when it is available • *I wanted to see that movie, but I missed it.* ○ *If you don't hurry you'll miss your plane* (= fail to get on it before it leaves). ○ *You should leave early if you want to miss rush hour* (= avoid it). • (*infml*) To **miss the boat** is to lose an opportunity to do something by being slow to act: *After I decided not to buy the house, I felt I missed the boat.*

miss REGRET /mɪs/ *v* [T] to feel sad because you cannot see (a person or place) or do (something) • *Luis says he misses Puerto Rico very much.*

miss NOT FIND /mɪs/ *v* [T] to notice that (something) is lost or absent • *He didn't miss his wallet until the waiter brought the check.*

missing /'mɪs·ɪŋ/ *adj* [not gradable] (of a person or possession) not found where you expect to find them; lost or absent • *He disappeared on his way to school and has been missing for over a year.* ○ *When did you realize the money was missing?*

▫**miss out** /-'-'-/ *v adv* [I] to fail to use an opportunity to enjoy or benefit from something • *We're having a few people over to watch the game, and we'll just serve finger food so we won't miss out on anything.*

misshapen /mɪs'ʃeɪ·pən/ *adj* having a shape that is not natural • *His knee is badly misshapen from years of football and seven operations.*

missile /'mɪs·əl/ *n* [C] a flying weapon that has its own engine and can travel a long distance before exploding at the place at which it has been aimed • *a nuclear missile* ○ *a guided missile* • A missile can also be any object that is thrown with the intention of causing injury or damage: *Rioters hurled missiles at the police.*

mission /'mɪʃ·ən/ *n* [C] the action of sending someone to a place to do a particular job, esp. one for a government or religious organization, or the job they are sent to do • *They were sent on a secret political mission to the Middle East.* ○ (*fig.*) *She's a woman on a mission* (= She is strongly determined) *to teach those children to read.* • A mission is also a group of people who are sent to another place to do a particular job or to represent their country, organization, or religion, or the place where they go to do this work: *A trade mission was sent to South Africa.* ○ *The Methodist mission* (= place for those who are poor and need help) *is located near the railroad yards.*

missionary /'mɪʃ·ə,ner·i/ *n* [C] a person who has been sent to a place, usually a foreign country, to teach their religion to the people who live there • *Pearl Buck was raised in China, where her parents were Christian missionaries.*

misspell /mɪs'spel/ *v* [T] to spell (a word) wrongly • *Edgar Allan Poe's middle name is often misspelled as Allen.*

misspelling /mɪs'spel·ɪŋ/ *n* [C] • *This essay is full of misspellings.*

mist /mɪst/ *n* [C/U] a light rain or a collection of very small drops of water in the air that is like a fog • *In the mornings, a mist covered the surface of the lake.* [C]

misty /'mɪs·ti/ *adj* slightly wet • *His eyes grew misty as he remembered her.*

mistake /mə'steɪk/ *n* [C] an action or decision that is wrong or produces a result that is not correct or not intended • *We all make mistakes.* ○ *It was a mistake to come to this restaurant without a reservation.* [+ to infinitive] • **By mistake** means unintentionally: *I'm sorry—I must have dialed your number by mistake.*

mistake /mə'steɪk/ *v* [T] *past simple* **mistook** /mə'stʊk/, *past part* **mistaken** /mə'steɪ·kən/ to be wrong about or fail to recognize (something or someone) • *I called Karen and mistook her mother for her* (= I thought I was speaking to Karen when I was speaking to her mother). [T always + adv/prep]

mistaken /mə'steɪ·kən/ *adj* [not gradable] wrong • *I was mistaken about how much it would cost.*

mister /'mɪs·tər/ *n* [U] MR. • (*infml*) Mister is also of a way of getting the attention of a man you do not know: *Hey, Mister, do you know what time it is?*

mistletoe /'mɪs·əl,toʊ/ *n* [U] an evergreen plant with small white fruits and pale yellow flowers • *Mistletoe is used as a Christmas decoration and is hung up so that people will kiss each other when they meet under it.*

mistreat /mɪs'triːt/ *v* [T] to treat (a person or animal) badly or cruelly • *Both parents denied that they had ever mistreated their child.*

mistreatment /mɪs'triːt·mənt/ *n* [U] • *The sad condition of the horses suggested a long period of mistreatment and neglect.*

mistress /'mɪs·trəs/ *n* [C] a woman who has a sexual relationship with a man who is not her husband, esp. a married man, over a long period of time

mistrial /'mɪs·traɪl/ *n* [C] *law* a trial that is ended by a judge because no decision can be reached or because mistakes in law have been made that make a fair trial impossible • *After the jury had deliberated for two weeks without reaching a verdict, the judge declared a mistrial.*

mistrust /mɪs'trʌst/ *v* [T] to have doubts about the honesty of (someone) or be unable to trust (something) • *I've always mistrusted leaders who make too many promises.*

mistrust /mɪs'trʌst/ *n* [U] • *Their mistrust of*

lawyers remained with them long after the lawsuit was settled.

misty /'mɪs·ti/ *adj* • See at MIST.

misunderstand /mɪs,ʌn·dər'stænd/ *v* [I/T] *past* **misunderstood** /mɪs,ʌn·dər'stʊd/ to fail to understand (something or someone) • *I think she misunderstood what I meant.* [T]

misunderstanding /mɪs,ʌn·dər'stæn·dɪŋ/ *n* [C/U] a failure to understand, or an argument resulting from the failure of two people or two sides to understand each other • *The whole thing was just a misunderstanding, he said, as he had no intention of breaking into the middle of the line.* [C]

misuse /mɪs'juːz/ *v* [T] to use (something) in an unsuitable way or in a way that was not intended • *She's been accused of misusing federal funds to pay for her son's private school expenses.*

misuse /mɪs'juːs/ *n* [C/U] • *This new computer system is completely unnecessary and a misuse of taxpayers' money.* [C]

mitigate /'mɪt̬·ə,geɪt/ *v* [T] to make (something) less severe or less unpleasant • *Getting a lot of sleep and drinking plenty of fluids can mitigate the effects of the flu.*

mitt /mɪt/ *n* [C] a type of GLOVE in which all the fingers but the thumb are in one section, and which is used to protect the hand from injury under special conditions • *Use the mitt to take the pot out of the oven.*

mitten /'mɪt·ᵊn/ *n* [C] a type of GLOVE with a single part for all the fingers but the thumb, which is in a separate part • *She bought a pair of woolen mittens and a matching scarf.*

mix COMBINE /mɪks/ *v* [I/T] to combine different substances, esp. so that the result cannot easily be separated into its parts, or to cause (different substances) to combine in this way • *Oil and water don't mix.* [I] ○ *Mix two eggs into the flour.* [T] ○ *He mixed the blue paint with white to lighten it.* [T] • To mix is also to combine or put in the same place: *The report mixed together a lot of different ideas in a confusing way.* [T]

mix /mɪks/ *n* [C/U] a combination of different things or people • *There was an interesting mix of people at Jean's party.* [C usually sing] • A mix is also a food substance that you can buy and to which a liquid, such as water or milk, can be added later when preparing to cook something: *a cake mix* [C]

mixed /mɪkst/ *adj* • Mixed often means combining positive and negative features: *I have mixed emotions/feelings about moving across the country—it's exciting, but I'll miss my old friends.* • Mixed can also mean combining people of a different races or religions: *My children go to a racially mixed school.* • (*infml*) A **mixed bag** is a situation that involves something good and something bad: *Being in a single-sex dorm was a mixed bag, because yes, you could relax more, but life wasn't as interesting.*

• A **mixed blessing** is an event or situation that is good but that has some disadvantages: *Making the team is a mixed blessing, because though it's an honor and all that, I'll have to spend a lot of time training.* • (*dated*) **Mixed company** is a group where both males and females are present. • A **mixed drink** is an alcoholic drink made by mixing at least two liquids, one of which contains alcohol: *Gin and tonic is a mixed drink.*

mixer /'mɪk·sər/ *n* [C] a machine in which you mix things, esp. food substances • *Whip the cream by hand or with an electric mixer.*

mix SOCIALIZE /mɪks/ *v* [I] (of a person) to be comfortable being with or talking to other people in social situations, esp. people you do not know • *She is very shy and has trouble mixing at parties.*

□ **mix up** *obj* MISTAKE , **mix** *obj* **up** /'-'-/ *v adv* [M] to mistake (someone or something) for someone or something else, or not know which one of (two people or things) each one is • *It's easy to mix up the twins.* ○ *I mix them up all the time.*

mix-up /'mɪk·sʌp/ *n* [C] a mistake • *She said that because of a mix-up, our check was sent to the wrong address.*

□ **mix up** *obj* MESS , **mix** *obj* **up** /'-'-/ *v adv* [M] to put (objects) in the wrong order or place • *If you mix up the photos in my family album, I'll never forgive you!*

mixed up CONFUSED /mɪk'stʌp, 'mɪk-/ *adj* temporarily confused • *I just got mixed up, and thought she wanted us to come early.*

mixed up INVOLVED /mɪk'stʌp/ *adj* [not gradable] involved, esp. with someone or something bad or dangerous • *Though her son was convicted of murder, his mother said he was a good boy, but he just got mixed up with a bad crowd.*

mixture /'mɪks·tʃər/ *n* [C] a combination of substances resulting from mixing them together so that they cannot be easily separated • *It's a highly explosive mixture and has to be handled carefully.* • A mixture is also any combination of different things: *Good fashion designers often rely on a mixture of the old and the new.*

ml /mɪl/ *n* [C] *pl* **ml** *abbreviation for* MILLILITER • *As little as 3 ml of this poison is enough to cause death.*

mm *n* [C] *pl* **mm** *abbreviation for* MILLIMETER

moan /moʊn/ *v* [I] to make a long, low sound because of pain or suffering, or to say something in a complaining way • *We could hear someone moaning within the rubble of the collapsed building.*

moan /moʊn/ *n* [C] • *He tried to forget his wartime experience, but in his dreams he heard again the moans of the dead and dying.*

mob /mɑb/ *n* [C] a large group of people gathered together and often disorderly or violent • *Police escorted the convicted murderer*

through an angry mob to a waiting police car.
• The mob is also an organization of criminals, esp. the MAFIA.

mob /mɑb/ *v* [T] **-bb-** to gather in a large group around (someone) to express admiration, interest, or anger • *She was mobbed by her fans.* ○ *The department stores are always mobbed* (= very crowded) *just before Christmas.*

mobile /'moʊ-bəl, -baɪl/ *adj* able to move freely or be easily moved • *The Marines are a highly mobile force and can get anywhere fast.* • A **mobile home** (also **motor home**) is a small house, usually long and narrow, that can be attached to a vehicle and moved.

mobile home

mobile /'moʊ-biːl/ *n* [C] a decoration or work of art that has parts that move freely, often because each one is hung by a thread • *We hung a mobile over the baby's crib, and she loves to look at it when it moves.*

mobility /moʊ'bɪl-ət̬-i/ *n* [U] the ability to move freely • *Because of severe arthritis, her mobility was limited.*

mobilize *(obj)* /'moʊ-bə,laɪz/ *v* to organize (people) to support something or to make (a part of an organization) ready for a special purpose • *They are trying to mobilize public opinion to oppose the construction of new nuclear waste-disposal facilities.* [T]

mobster /'mɑb-stər/ *n* [C] a person, esp. a man, who belongs to an organization of criminals

moccasin /'mɑk-ə-sən/ *n* [C] a light shoe made completely of soft leather and having stitches around the top

mock INSULT /mɑk, mɔːk/ *v* [T] to copy (someone or a characteristic of someone) in an amusing but unkind way that makes other people laugh, or to try to make (someone or something) seem foolish or ridiculous • *Some of the boys in the dorm loved to mock Roger's British accent.*

mockery /'mɑk-ə-ri, 'mɔː-kə-/ *n* [U] unkind, critical remarks or actions, or something so foolish that it can be easily criticized • *The renewed fighting made a mockery of the peace agreement* (= made it look ridiculous).

mock ARTIFICIAL /mɑk, mɔːk/ *adj* [not gradable] intended to seem real; artificial or pretended • *She gave a little scream in mock surprise when she opened the door and saw us.*

mockingbird /'mɑk-ɪŋ,bɜrd, 'mɔː-kɪŋ-/ *n* [C] a

North American bird that copies the sounds made by other birds

modal verb /'moʊd-əl'vɜrb/, **modal auxiliary** /'moʊd-əl,ɔːg'zɪl-jə-ri/ *n* [C] *specialized* (in grammar) a verb used with another verb to express an idea such as possibility that is not expressed by the main verb • *The modal verbs in English are "can," "could," "may," "might," "must," "ought," "shall," "should," "will," and "would."*

mode /moʊd/ *n* [C] a way of operating, living, or behaving • *Good teachers get their students into a learning mode.* ○ *Each department has its own mode of operation.*

model REPRESENTATION /'mɑd-əl/ *n* [C] something built or drawn esp. to show how something much larger would look • *The architect showed us a model of the planned hotel.* • A model is also a representation of something in words or numbers that can be used to tell what is likely to happen if particular facts are considered as true: *a statistical model predicting population growth*

model /'mɑd-əl/ *v* [T] to form (something) from a plastic substance such as clay, or to use (a plastic substance) to make a form of something • *to model a face* ○ *She modeled the clay into a sculpture.*

model GOOD EXAMPLE /'mɑd-əl/ *n* [C] someone or something that is an extremely good example of its type, esp. when a copy can be based on it • *She was a model of loyalty and stuck by him even after he went to jail.*

model /'mɑd-əl/ *adj* [not gradable] • *They were model parents and were loved by the whole community.*

model /'mɑd-əl/ *v* [T] to create (something) by basing its form or appearance on something else • *The state building was modeled on the US Capitol in Washington, D.C.*

model PERSON /'mɑd-əl/ *n* [C] a person employed to wear esp. new, fashionable clothes to show how the clothes look and to make them look attractive • *Models paraded down the ramp to show off the latest fashions of Paris and New York.* • A model is also a person employed to show his or her body, clothed or naked, to be drawn or photographed by those studying the human form.

model /'mɑd-əl/ *v* [T] • *She will be modeling the new line of spring coats.*

model MACHINE /'mɑd-əl/ *n* [C] a particular type of device or machine that is different in quality, style, or some other feature from others that have the same use • *This car comes in a two-door and a four-door model.* ○ *We were shown large and small models of air conditioners.*

modem /'moʊd-əm, 'moʊ-dem/ *n* [C] an electronic device that allows one computer to send information to another over telephone wires

moderate MEDIUM /'mɑd-ə-rət/ *adj* being

within a middle range in size, amount, or degree; neither great nor little • *The rent has gone up over the years, but in moderate amounts.* ○ *The company was of moderate size, with about 50 employees.*

moderately /'mɑd·ə·rət·li/ *adv* • *The new apartment complex will be moderately priced for middle-income people.*

moderation /ˌmɑd·ə'reɪ·ʃən/ *n* [U] • *My doctor advised me to eat anything I want as long as it's in moderation.*

moderate SOME /'mɑd·ə·rət/ *adj* some, but not as much or as great as desired • *There has been moderate improvement in her health since she began the treatment.*

moderately /'mɑd·ə·rət·li/ *adv* to some degree • *He was moderately successful, making a living but hardly getting rich.*

moderate NOT EXTREME /'mɑd·ə·rət/ *adj* (of opinions) not extreme • *When she was young she was a radical, but her political views have become more moderate as she has gotten older.*

moderate /'mɑd·ə·rət/ *n* [C] • *Of the seven members of the committee, five were political moderates.*

moderate LOSE STRENGTH /'mɑd·ə,reɪt/ *v* [I/T] to lose strength or force, or to make (something) less strong • *The weather prediction is for strong winds, moderating by evening.* [I]

moderate MANAGE /'mɑd·ə,reɪt/ *v* to manage (a public discussion) • *The local TV anchorman is going to moderate (the debate).* [I/T]

moderator /'mɑd·ə,reɪţ·ər/ *n* [C] • *The moderator allowed each side two minutes to sum up at the end of the televised debate.*

modern /'mɑd·ərn/ *adj* existing in the present or a recent time, or using or based on recently developed ideas, methods, or styles • *modern life* ○ *modern architecture/art*

modernistic /ˌmɑd·ər'nɪs·tɪk/ *adj* designed in a way that is obviously modern • *The Denver airport has a modernistic design.*

modernize /'mɑd·ər,naɪz/ *v* [I/T] to make or become more modern • *We decided to modernize our kitchen and installed a new sink and dishwasher.* [T]

modest NOT LARGE /'mɑd·əst/ *adj* not large in size or amount, or not great in value • *a modest increase in salary* ○ *a modest house*

modestly /'mɑd·əst·li/ *adv* • *He lives in a modestly furnished apartment.*

modest QUIETLY SUCCESSFUL /'mɑd·əst/ *adj* tending not to talk about or make obvious your own abilities and achievements • *Although an outstanding scientist, he's a modest man.*

modestly /'mɑd·əst·li/ *adv* • *She spoke modestly about her work.*

modesty /'mɑd·ə·sti/ *n* [U] • *Sosa's modesty and sportsmanship made him a fan favorite.*

modest CORRECT /'mɑd·əst/ *adj* (of behavior and clothes) correct or socially acceptable,

and not wild, sexy, or showing too much of your body

modestly /'mɑd·əst·li/ *adv* • *She modestly hid her legs behind full-length skirts.*

modesty /'mɑd·ə·sti/ *n* [U] • *"Put on some clothes," he yells. "Show some modesty."*

modicum /'mɑd·ɪ·kəm, 'moʊd-/ *n* [U] a small amount • *He achieved a modicum of success.*

modify CHANGE /'mɑd·ə,faɪ/ *v* [T] to change (something) slightly, esp. to improve it or make it more acceptable or less extreme • *The school board decided to modify its existing employment policy.*

modification /ˌmɑd·ə·fə'keɪ·ʃən/ *n* [C/U] • *behavior modification* [U] ○ *Several modifications have been made in the proposals.* [C]

modify GRAMMAR /'mɑd·ə,faɪ/ *v* [T] *specialized* (in grammar) to limit or add to the meaning of (a word or phrase)

modifier /'mɑd·ə,faɪ·ər/ *n* [C] *specialized* (in grammar) a word or phrase that limits or adds to the meaning of another word or phrase • *In the sentence "The little girl ran quickly," the adjective "little" and the adverb "quickly" are modifiers.*

modulate /'mɑdʒ·ə,leɪt/ *v* [T] to vary the strength, quality, or amount of (something) • *Teachers modulate the way they work in response to their students' needs.* ○ *Modulate your tone of voice when speaking in court.*

module /'mɑdʒ·uːl/ *n* [C] one of a set of separate parts that can be joined together to form a larger object • *The reactor was built in modules that were assembled later at the site.* • A module is also a part of a spacecraft that can operate independently from the main part.

modular /'mɑdʒ·ə·lər/ *adj* [not gradable] • *modular homes* ○ *modular classrooms*

mogul /'moʊ·gəl/ *n* [C] an important person who has great wealth or power • *a media mogul*

mohair /'moʊ·her, -hær/ *n* [U] soft cloth made from ANGORA

moist /mɔɪst/ *adj* slightly wet • *moist blueberry muffins* ○ *rich, moist soil*

moisten /'mɔɪ·sən/ *v* [I/T] • *Moisten the shirts before ironing.* [T]

moisture /'mɔɪs·tʃər/ *n* [U] very small drops of water, either in the air or on a surface • *It was a clear day with little moisture in the air.*

moisturize /'mɔɪs·tʃə,raɪz/ *v* [T] • *This new makeup protects and moisturizes the skin.*

moisturizer /'mɔɪs·tʃə,raɪ·zər/ *n* [C] a thick liquid put on the skin to make it soft and less dry

molar /'moʊ·lər/ *n* [C] any of the large teeth at the back of the mouth, used for crushing and chewing food • Compare INCISOR.

molasses /mə'læs·əz/ *n* [U] a thick, dark, sweet liquid made from sugar plants

mold SHAPE /moʊld/ *n* [C] a hollow container into which you pour a soft or liquid substance so that it will cool or harden into the shape of the container • *The pieces are made in a mold and I just paint them.* • If someone or something is **in the mold of** someone or something else, they share some important characteristics: *Lewis was not an inventor in the mold of Edison.*

mold /mould/ *v* [T] to shape (something) into a particular form • *She molded the clay into little animals.* • If someone molds someone else, they have an important influence on how that person develops: *Parents help mold a child's character.*

molding /'moul·dɪŋ/ *n* [C/U] a line of wood, plastic, or PLASTER used as a decoration around the edge or along the top of something

mold GROWTH /mould/ *n* [U] a soft green, gray, or black growth that develops on old food or on objects that have been left too long in warm, slightly wet places

moldy /'moul·di/ *adj* • *moldy cheese*

mole ANIMAL /moul/ *n* [C] a small, dark, furry mammal that lives in passages it digs under the ground

mole SPOT /moul/ *n* [C] a small, dark, permanent spot or lump on a person's skin

mole PERSON /moul/ *n* [C] a person who works within an organization, such as a government department, and secretly reports information about its activities to its enemy

molecule /'mɑl·ə,kjuːl/ *n* [C] the smallest unit into which a substance can be divided without chemical change, usually a group of two or more atoms

molecular /mə'lek·jə·lər/ *adj* [not gradable] • *molecular biology*

molest /mə'lest/ *v* [T] to wrongly touch or force sexual activity on (someone, esp. a child) • *She claims that he sexually molested her.*

molestation /,mou,les'teɪ·ʃən/ *n* [U] • *child molestation*

molester /mə'les·tər/ *n* [C]

mollify /'mɑl·ə,faɪ/ *v* [T] to make (someone) less angry or upset, or to make (something) less severe or more gentle • *She was not mollified by his apology.*

mollusk, mollusc /'mɑl·əsk/ *n* [C] any of a large group of animals that have soft bodies, no SPINE (= supporting bones), and usually a hard shell • *Oysters, clams, and snails are mollusks.*

molt /moult/ *v* [I] (of a bird or animal) to lose feathers, skin, or hair as a natural process before a new growth of feathers, skin, or hair

molten /'moult·ən/ *adj* [not gradable] (esp. of metal or rock) melted or made liquid by being heated to very high temperatures

mom /mɑm/ *n* [C] *infml for* MOTHER PARENT • *Can I borrow the car, Mom?* • LP TITLES AND FORMS OF ADDRESS

moment SHORT TIME /'mou·mənt/ *n* [C] a very short period of time • *Hold still for a moment while I tie your shoe.* ∘ *I'll be ready in just a moment.*

momentary /'mou·mən,ter·i/ *adj* [not gradable] • *There was a momentary lull in the conversation.*

momentarily /,mou·mən'ter·ə·li/ *adv* [not gradable] • *I was momentarily confused.* ∘ *The train will be leaving momentarily* (= very soon).

moment OCCASION /'mou·mənt/ *n* [C] a particular time or occasion • *I'm waiting for the right moment to tell her the good news.* ∘ *Just at that moment, the phone rang.* • A moment is also a special time or opportunity: *You know that when that curtain goes up, it's going to be your big moment.* • *Are you staying with your mother* **at the moment** (= now)?

momentous /mou'ment·əs/ *adj* very important, esp. because of the effects on future events • *a momentous decision/event*

momentum /mou'ment·əm/ *n* [U] the force or speed of an object in motion, or the increase in the rate of development of a process • *A falling object gains momentum as it falls.* ∘ *Technology seems to create its own momentum—if something can be done, it will be.*

momma /'mɑm·ə/ *n* MAMA

mommy /'mɑm·i/ *n* [C] *infml for* MOTHER PARENT • *The little girl misses her mommy.* ∘ *Mommy, I want some candy.* • LP TITLES AND FORMS OF ADDRESS

Mon. *n abbreviation for* MONDAY

monarch /'mɑn·ərk, -ɑrk/ *n* [C] a nation's king or queen

monarchy /'mɑn·ər·ki, -,ɑr·ki/ *n* [C/U] a system of government that has a king or queen, or a country that has this system of government

monastery /'mɑn·ə,ster·i/ *n* [C] a building or group of buildings in which MONKS (= religious men) live and worship • Compare CONVENT.

monastic /mə'næs·tɪk/ *adj* of or related to MONASTERIES or MONKS

Monday /'mʌn·di, -deɪ/ (*abbreviation* **Mon.**) *n* [C/U] the day of the week after Sunday and before Tuesday

monetary /'mɑn·ə,ter·i/ *adj* [not gradable] relating to money, esp. the money supply of a country • *monetary policy*

money /'mʌn·i/ *n* [U] the coins or bills with their value on them that are used to buy things, or the total amount of these that someone has • *I need a dollar—have you got any money on you?* ∘ *There's not much money in our savings account.* ∘ *We spent a lot of money redecorating the house.* ∘ *I save money on groceries by using coupons.* ∘ *He makes a lot of money as a contractor.* ∘ *The job wasn't exciting, but the money* (= amount of pay) *was good.* • **Money talks** means that wealthy people receive special treatment or have more power and influence. • If something is **(right) on the money**, it is exact or correct: *Her prediction was right on the money.* • A **moneymaker** is a person who is successful at obtaining large amounts of money, or something that produces a large profit. • The **money market** is the system in which banks and other similar organizations buy, sell, lend, or borrow money for profit. • A **money order** is a type of check that you buy at a bank or post office and use for payment of a particular amount. • LP PRICE

mongrel /'mɑŋ·grəl, 'mʌŋ-/, *infml* **mutt** *n* [C] a dog of mixed breed

moniker /'mɑn·ɪ·kər/ *n* [C] *slang* a name or NICKNAME (= informal name)

monitor SCREEN /'mɑn·əṭ·ər/ *n* [C] a device with a screen on which words or pictures can be shown • *a computer monitor*

monitor WATCH /'mɑn·əṭ·ər/ *v* [T] to watch and check (something) carefully over a period of time • *They hired an accountant to help monitor cash flow.* ○ *The nurse is monitoring his heart rate and respiration.*

monitor /'mɑn·əṭ·ər/ *n* [C] a person who has the job of watching or checking particular things, or a machine that regularly tests or records things • *United Nations monitors were prevented from entering the area.* ○ *A fetal monitor records an unborn baby's heartbeat.* • In school, a monitor is a student with special duties who helps the teacher: *the attendance monitor*

monk /mʌŋk/ *n* [C] a man who is a member of a group of religious men who live a simple life apart from general society, usually in a MONASTERY

monkey /'mʌŋ·ki/ *n* [C] any of a group of mammals that usually have flat faces and long tails, esp. any of the smaller mammals in this group • **Monkey business** is tricky or dishonest behavior: *There's been some monkey business connected with his tax returns.*

monkey /'mʌŋ·ki/ *v infml* • If you **monkey around**, you behave in a silly, playful way: *The kids were just monkeying around, throwing things at each other.* • If you **monkey (around) with** something, you play with or use something carelessly: *Who's been monkeying around with my tools?*

monkey wrench /'mʌŋ·ki:,rentʃ/ *n* [C] a tool that can be adjusted to hold or turn NUTS and BOLTS (= metal fasteners that screw together) of different widths

mono /'mɑn·oʊ/ *n* [U] *short form of* MONONU-CLEOSIS

monogamy /mə'nɑg·ə·mi/ *n* [U] the condition or custom of being married to only one person at a time or of having only one sexual partner for a period of time
monogamous /mə'nɑg·ə·məs/ *adj* • *Our relationship has been monogamous.*

monogram /'mɑn·ə,græm/ *n* [C] a design made of two or more letters, usually the first letters of a person's names, used esp. on clothing and writing paper

monogrammed /'mɑn·ə,græmd/ *adj* [not gradable] • *a monogrammed shirt*

monolingual /,mɑn·ə'lɪŋ·gwəl, -gjə·wəl/ *adj* [not gradable] speaking or using only one language • Compare BILINGUAL.

monolithic /,mɑn·ə'lɪθ·ɪk/ *adj* very large, united, and difficult to change • *People think of "the media" as this great monolithic thing that's out there.* • A monolithic building or rock is large and solid.

monologue /'mɑn·əl,ɔ:g, -,ɑg/ *n* [C] a long speech by one person, esp. in a play, movie, or television show

mononucleosis /,mɑn·ə,nu:'kli:'oʊ·səs/, *short form* **mono** *n* [U] a disease that causes a sudden fever, swelling of organs that produce white blood cells, and a sore throat, and which can make a person feel weak and ill for a long time

monopoly /mə'nɑp·ə·li/ *n* [C] complete control of the supply of particular goods or services, or a company or group that has such control • *The Postal Service is guaranteed a monopoly on all first-class letters.* ○ *(fig.) California has no monopoly on strangeness* (= is not the only strange place).
monopolistic /mə,nɑp·ə'lɪs·tɪk/ *adj* • *a monopolistic system*

monopolize /mə'nɑp·ə,laɪz/ *v* [T] to have or take complete control of (something) so that others are prevented from sharing it • *Rockefeller monopolized oil refining in the 1800s.* ○ *She has a habit of monopolizing the conversation.*

monorail /'mɑn·ə,reɪl/ *n* [C] a railway system in which trains travel along a single RAIL (= metal bar), usually above ground level

monosodium glutamate /,mɑn·ə,soʊd·i:·əm'glu:ṭ·ə,meɪt/ *(abbreviation* **MSG**) *n* [U] a chemical that is sometimes added to food to improve its taste

monotheism /'mɑn·ə,θi:,ɪz·əm/ *n* [U] the belief that there is only one God

monotonous /mə'nɑt·ᵊn·əs/ *adj* boring because of never changing • *She stood all day ironing a monotonous succession of clothes and sheets.*

monotony /mə'nɑt·ᵊn·i/ *n* [U] boring sameness • *He drove for hours with nothing to break the monotony.*

monotone /'mɑn·ə,toʊn/ *n* [U] a sound or voice that stays on the same note • *He spoke in a boring monotone.*

monsoon /mɑn'su:n/ *n* [C] the season of heavy rain, the wind that brings rain, or the heavy rain that falls during the summer in hot Asian countries

monster CREATURE /'mɑn·stər/ *n* [C] any imaginary frightening creature, esp. one that is large and strange

monster EVIL PERSON /'mɑn·stər/ *n* [C] a person who does very cruel and evil acts • *the* monster who killed defenseless animals in the zoo

monstrous /'mɑn·strəs/ *adj* • *monstrous deeds*

monster BIG /'mɑn·stər/ *adj* [not gradable] very big, or too big • *a monster shark*

monster /'mɑn·stər/ *n* [C] • *a monster of a movie, over four hours long*

monstrous /'mɑn·strəs/ *adj* very bad, esp. because too big • *After the flood she was faced with monstrous repair bills.*

monstrosity /mɑn'strɑs·əţ·i/ *n* [C] something that is very ugly and usually large • *That new office building is a real monstrosity.*

month /mʌnθ/ *n* [C] a period of about four weeks, esp. one of the twelve periods into which a year is divided • *I'll be away for the whole month of June.* ○ *The puppy is two months old.*

monthly /'mʌnθ·li/ *adj, adv* [not gradable] • *If you ride the bus a lot, you should buy a monthly ticket.* ○ *We're paid monthly.*

monthly /'mʌnθ·li/ *n* [C] a newspaper or magazine that is published once a month

monument /'mɑn·jə·mənt/ *n* [C] an object, esp. large and made of stone, built to remember and show respect for a person or group of people, or a special place made for this purpose • *While in Washington, D.C., we visited a number of historical monuments.* ○ (fig.) *The annual arts festival is a monument to* (= is a result of) *her vision and hard work.*

monumental /ˌmɑn·jə'ment·ᵊl/ *adj* very big or very great • *Rebuilding the bridge proved to be a monumental job.*

moo /muː/ *n* [C] *pl* **moos** (esp. in children's books) a written representation of the noise that a cow makes

moo /muː/ *v* [I] **moos, mooing,** *past* **mooed**

mood FEELING /muːd/ *n* [C] the way you feel at a particular time • *She's in a good/bad mood today.* ○ *"Do you want to go to the movies?" "No, I'm not in the mood* (= not interested in that)*."*

moody /'muːd·i/ *adj* (of a person) often sad, or changing from being happy to sad, often for no clear reason

mood GRAMMAR /muːd/ *n* [C] *specialized* (in grammar) the forms of verbs used to show whether the person speaking intends to express a fact, an order, or a hope • *the indicative/imperative/subjunctive mood*

moon OBJECT IN SPACE /muːn/ *n* [C/U] the object, similar to a planet, that moves through the sky, circling the earth once every 28 days, and which can often be seen clearly at night when it shines with the light coming from the sun • *the full moon* [U] • *A moon is also a similar object that moves around another planet: Jupiter has at least sixteen moons.* [C] • **Moonlight** is the pale light of the moon. See also MOONLIGHT.

moonless /'muːn·ləs/ *adj* [not gradable] • *If a night is moonless, you cannot see the moon in the sky at night.*

moon LACK PURPOSE /muːn/ *v* [I always + adv/prep] *infml* to move or spend time in a way that shows a lack of care and interest and no clear purpose • *She's been mooning around the house all weekend.*

moonlight /'muːn·lɑɪt/ *v* [I] *past* **moonlighted** to work at an additional job, esp. without telling your main employer • *In addition to her teaching job, she moonlights as a waitress on weekends.*

moonshine /'muːn·ʃɑɪn/ *n* [U] *slang* alcoholic drink made illegally

moor /mʊr/ *v* [I/T] to cause (esp. a boat) to stay in the same position on the sea or a lake or river by tying it to something on the land or at the bottom of the sea • *We moored (the boat) further up the river.* [I/T]

mooring /'mʊr·ɪŋ/ *n* [C usually pl] a place to tie a boat or aircraft, or the ropes or chains that keep esp. a boat from moving away from a particular place

moose /muːs/ *n* [C] *pl* **moose** a type of large deer of North America and northern Europe, having large, flat horns

moot NOT WORTH CONSIDERING /muːt/ *adj* [not gradable] *law* having no practical use or meaning • *Because the claim of negligence was denied, seeking an award for damages was moot.*

moot NOT DECIDED /muːt/ *adj* [not gradable] (of a matter being considered) that has not been decided and can therefore still be discussed • *Whether or not to make the school coeducational is still a moot point, and we'll be discussing it over the next few months.*

mop /mɑp/ *n* [C] a stick having at one end a mass of thick, cloth strings or a SPONGE (= soft substance) that you slide along a floor to spread or absorb a liquid in cleaning the floor • *A mop of hair is a lot of hair in a thick mass: The child's face was framed by a mop of brown curls.*

mop /mɑp/ *v* [I/T] **-pp-** • *I can go as soon as I finish mopping (the floor).* [I/T] • If you **mop** the SWEAT (= liquid produced because you are hot) from your face, you use your hand or a piece of cloth to remove it. [T] • To **mop up** is to finish a job after most of it has been completed: *The battle had been won, but two infantry units were left behind to mop up.*

mope /moʊp/ *v* [I] to be unhappy and unwilling to think or act positively, esp. because of a disappointment • *Don't sit in the house moping—go out and enjoy yourself.*

moped /'moʊ·ped/ *n* [C] a small, motorized, two-wheeled vehicle with PEDALS like those on a bicycle, which can be used when starting it or traveling up a hill

moral /'mɔːr·əl, 'mɑr-/ *adj* relating to standards of good behavior, honesty, and fair dealing, or showing high standards of this type • *a highly moral man* ○ *It's her moral obligation to tell the police what she knows.*

morals /'mɔːr·əlz, 'mɑr-/ *pl n* standards for good or bad character and behavior • *a man of low morals*

morality /mə'ræl·ət·i/ *n* [C/U] a personal or social set of standards for good or bad behavior and character, or the quality of being right and honest • *Technology is neutral—its morality is determined by its political or social use.* [U]

morally /'mɔːr·ə·li, 'mɑr-/ *adv* considered from a moral position • *morally wrong* • If you act morally, you act in a way that you or people in general consider to be right, honest, or acceptable.

moral /'mɔːr·əl, 'mɑr-/ *n* [C] a message about how people should or should not behave, contained in a story, event, or experience • *The moral of the story is that honesty is the best policy.*

moralistic /ˌmɔːr·ə'lɪs·tɪk, ˌmɑr-/ *adj* involved with judging other people's morals and telling them how to behave • *American foreign policy had been rigidly moralistic.*

moralize /'mɔːr·ə,lɑɪz, 'mɑr-/ *v* [I] *disapproving* to make judgments about right and wrong, esp. in a way that does not consider other people's ideas or opinions • *A good teacher manages to educate without moralizing.*

morale /mə'ræl/ *n* [U] the amount of confidence felt by a person or group of people, esp. when in a dangerous or difficult situation • *Low morale in the police department was a continuing problem.*

morass /mə'ræs/ *n* [C usually sing] something that is extremely complicated and difficult to deal with, making any advance almost impossible • *The morass of rules and regulations is delaying the start of the project.*

moratorium /ˌmɔːr·ə'tɔːr·iː·əm, ˌmɑr-, -'toʊr-/ *n* [C] a stopping of an activity for an agreed period of time • *They are proposing a five-year moratorium on whaling.*

morbid /'mɔːr·bəd/ *adj* too interested in unpleasant subjects, esp. death • *He has a morbid sense of humor.*

more /mɔːr, moʊr/ *adj, adv, comparative of* MANY *or* MUCH; a larger or extra number or amount (of) • *You need to listen more and talk less.* ○ *There were no more seats on the bus, so we had to stand.* ○ *DisneyWorld was more fun than I expected.* • More is used to form the comparative of many adjectives and adverbs: *You couldn't be more wrong.* ○ *He finds physics far/much more difficult than biology.* ○ *Would you play the song once more* (= again)? • It gets **more and more** (= increasingly) *difficult to understand what is going on.* • *It weighs 50 pounds,* **more or less** (= approximately). • **More than** is also used to mean very: *It's more than likely that she got a ride home with Harry.* ○ *We will be more than happy to help you in any way we can.* • Compare MOST. ⓛⓟ COMPARING

more /mɔːr, moʊr/ *pronoun* • *She kept asking me if I wanted more to eat.* ○ *More than 20,000 people attended the concert.* • **The more** he insisted he was innocent (= As he continued to say this again many times,) *the less they seemed to believe him.* • Compare MOST.

moreover /mɔːr'oʊ·vər, moʊr-/ *adv* [not gradable] (used to add information) also and more importantly • *It was a good car and, moreover, the price was quite reasonable.*

mores /'mɔːr·eɪz, 'moʊr-/ *pl n* the traditional customs and ways of behaving that are typical of a particular society • *The novel examines the mores of nineteenth-century Boston society.*

morgue /mɔːrg/ *n* [C] a building, or a room in a hospital, where dead bodies are kept to be examined or until buried

Mormon /'mɔːr·mən/ *n* [C], *adj* [not gradable] (a member) of a religious group called the Church of Jesus Christ of Latter-day Saints • *the Mormon church* ○ *a Mormon missionary*

morning /'mɔːr·nɪŋ/ *n* [C/U] the part of the day from the time when the sun rises until the middle of the day • *Sunday/tomorrow morning* [U] ○ *I work three mornings a week at the bookstore.* [C] • **(Good) morning** is also a greeting: *Morning, Mr. Hopkins.* ⓛⓟ GREETINGS • Morning is also the half of the day between 12 o'clock at night and 12 o'clock in the middle of the day: *The murder took place at four in the morning.* [U] • **Morning sickness** is a feeling that some pregnant women have of wanting to vomit soon after waking, experienced esp. during the first months of pregnancy.

moron /'mɔːr·ɑn, 'moʊr-/ *n* [C] a stupid person

morose /mə'roʊs/ *adj slightly fml* unhappy or annoyed and unwilling to speak, smile, or be pleasant to people • *He recalls his father as a morose, moody man with a violent temper.*

morphine /'mɔːr·fiːn/ *n* [U] a drug used medically to stop people from feeling pain

morphology /mɔːr'fɑl·ə·dʒi/ *n* [U] *specialized* the scientific study of the structure and form of animals and plants

morsel /'mɔːr·səl/ *n* [C] a very small piece of food • *She ate every last morsel on her plate.*

mortal /'mɔːrt·əl/ *adj* [not gradable] (of living things, esp. people) unable to continue living forever; having to die • *Humans are mortal and we all eventually die.* • *As the ship began to sink, they realized they were in mortal danger* (= they might die).

mortal /'mɔːrt·əl/ *n* [C] *literary* a human, or an ordinary person • *mere mortals*

mortality /mɔːr'tæl·ət·i/ *n* [U] the condition of being mortal • *A sense of her own mortality overcame her.* • Mortality is also the number of deaths within a particular society and within a particular period of time: *infant mortality*

mortally /'mɔːrt·əl·i/ *adv* • *He fell, mortally wounded.*

mortar MIXTURE /'mɔːrt·ər/ *n* [U] a mixture of

sand, water, and CEMENT or LIME that is used to join bricks or stones to each other when building walls

mortar GUN /'mɔːrt̬·ər/ *n* [C] a gun with a short, wide BARREL (= part shaped like a tube) that can fire bombs high in the air

mortarboard /'mɔːrt̬·ər,bɔːrd, -,boʊrd/ *n* [C] a black hat with a square, flat top, worn by some students and teachers on formal school occasions • *Following the ceremony, the graduating seniors all threw their mortarboards into the air.*

mortgage /'mɔːr·gɪdʒ/ *n* [C] an agreement that allows you to borrow money from a bank or similar organization by offering something of value, esp. in order to buy a house or apartment, or the amount of money itself • *They took out a $90,000 mortgage to buy the house.*

mortgage /'mɔːr·gɪdʒ/ *v* [T] to offer (something of value) in order to borrow money from a bank or similar organization • *They had to mortgage their home to borrow enough money to pay for their children's education.*

mortician /mɔːr'tɪʃ·ən/ *n* [C] an UNDERTAKER

mortify /'mɔːrt̬·ə,fɑɪ/ *v* [T] to cause (someone) to feel extremely ashamed or embarrassed • *He was mortified when his mother turned up drunk for his piano recital.*

mortuary /'mɔːr·tʃə,wer·i/ *n* [C] a **funeral home**, see at FUNERAL

mosaic /moʊ'zeɪ·ɪk/ *n* [C] a pattern or picture of many small pieces of colored stone or glass • *a mosaic floor*

mosey /'moʊ·zi/ *v* [I always + adv/prep] *infml* to walk or go slowly, usually without a special purpose • *I think I'll mosey on down to the beach for a while.*

Moslem /'mɑz·ləm, 'mɑs-/ *n* [C], *adj* [not gradable] MUSLIM

mosque /mɑsk/ *n* [C] a building for Islamic religious activities and worship

mosquito /mə'skiːt̬·oʊ/ *n* [C] *pl* **mosquitoes** or **mosquitos** a small flying insect that bites people and animals, and sucks their blood

moss /mɔːs/ *n* [U] a small green or yellow plant that grows esp. in wet earth or on rocks, walls, and tree trunks

most /moʊst/ *adj, adv, superlative of* MANY or MUCH; the biggest number or amount (of), or more than anything or anyone else • *Which of you earns the most money?* ○ *The kids loved the circus, and most of all the clowns.* • Most is used to form the superlative of many adjectives and adverbs: *Joanne is the most intelligent person I know.* • Most also means almost all: *I like most vegetables.* • Most also means very: *He argued his case most persuasively.* • Compare MORE. LP AMOUNTS, COMPARING

most /moʊst/ *pronoun* • *Most of the players are coming on the next bus.* • Compare MORE.

mostly /'moʊs·tli/ *adv* [not gradable] in large degree or amount • *The story seemed to be*

mostly true. ○ *The group is mostly teenagers, with a few younger children.*

motel /moʊ'tel/ *n* [C] a hotel for people who arrive in their own cars, typically with all the rooms on one floor or a few floors, and with parking spaces near their rooms

moth /mɔːθ/ *n* [C] an insect with wings which is similar to a BUTTERFLY and flies esp. at night • A **mothball** is a small ball made of material that has a strong smell, used esp. to protect wool clothing from moths.

moth

mother PARENT /'mʌð·ər/ *n* [C] a female parent • *My mother was 20 when I was born.* ○ (*slightly fml*) *Mother, where's my red blouse?* • **Mother Nature** is nature or weather considered as a force that has power over human beings. • **Mother's Day** is the second Sunday in May in North America, when people express their love and appreciation for their mothers. • A **mother-to-be** is a pregnant woman. • PIC FAMILY TREE LP TITLES AND FORMS OF ADDRESS

mother /'mʌð·ər/ *v* [T] to treat (someone) with kindness and affection and try to protect them from danger or difficulty • *Leave me alone—I don't need to be mothered.*

motherhood /'mʌð·ər,hʊd/ *n* [U] the state of being a mother

mother–in–law /'mʌð·ə·ə·rɪn,lɔː/ *n* [C] *pl* **mothers-in-law** /'mʌð·ər·zɪn,lɔː/ the mother of someone's wife or husband • PIC FAMILY TREE

motherly /'mʌð·ər·li/ *adj* typical of a kind or caring mother

mother EXTREME THING /'mʌð·ər/ *n* [U] the largest or most extreme example of something • *They got caught in a mother of a storm.*

motherfucker /'mʌð·ər,fʌk·ər/, **mother** /'mʌð·ər/ *n* [C] *taboo slang* a person whom you do not like and do not respect because you think they are bad or worthless, or something annoying and unpleasant • USAGE: This word is considered offensive by many people.

mother–of–pearl /,mʌð·ə·ə·rəv'pɜrl/ *n* [U] a hard, shiny, white substance inside the shells of some sea animals that is used for decoration

motif /moʊ'tiːf/ *n* [C] a pattern or design • *We chose curtains with a flower motif.* • A motif is also an idea that appears repeatedly in a piece of writing or music.

motion MOVEMENT /ˈmoʊ·ʃən/ n [C/U] the act or process of moving, or a particular movement • *The rocking motion of the ship upset her stomach.* [U] ∘ *She moved her finger in a circular motion.* [C] • Something that is moving or operating or has started: *The alarm rang and suddenly everyone was in motion.* ∘ *The governor's request set in motion the process for receiving federal funds.* • A **motion picture** is a movie. • **Motion sickness** is illness, esp. a need to vomit, caused by movement when traveling in a boat, car, or aircraft.

motionless /ˈmoʊ·ʃən·ləs/ adj [not gradable] not moving

motion SIGNAL /ˈmoʊ·ʃən/ v [always + adv/prep] to make a signal to (someone), usually with your hand or head • *He motioned me to sit down.* [T] ∘ *I saw him motion to the man at the door.* [I]

motion FORMAL REQUEST /ˈmoʊ·ʃən/ n [C] a formal request, usually one made, discussed, and voted on at a meeting • *Someone made a motion to increase the membership fee.* [+ to infinitive] • A motion is also a request made to a judge in court for something to happen.

motive /ˈmoʊt̬·ɪv/ n [C] a reason for doing something • *Does he have a motive for lying about where he was?* ∘ *Judy moved to Florida because she likes it there, not for any ulterior motive* (= secret reason).

motivate /ˈmoʊt̬·əˌveɪt/ v [T] • *She's motivated by a desire to help people.*

motivated /ˈmoʊt̬·əˌveɪt̬·əd/ adj • *The lawsuit was politically motivated.* ∘ *Heather is a highly motivated student* (= she works hard).

motivation /ˌmoʊt̬·əˈveɪ·ʃən/ n [C/U] willingness to do something, or something that causes such willingness • *One motivation for reducing the staff was the need to cut costs.* [C] ∘ *You need a lot of motivation to succeed.* [U]

motley /ˈmɑt·li/ adj consisting of many different types, parts, or colors that do not seem to belong together • *A motley crew of educators and students gathered at the seminar.*

motor ENGINE /ˈmoʊt̬·ər/ n [C] an engine that makes a machine work or a vehicle move • *an electric/diesel motor.* • A **motorbike** is a small motorcycle. • A **motorboat** is a small boat that is powered by an engine. • A **motorcycle** is a two-wheeled vehicle powered by an engine. • A **motor home** is a recreational vehicle, see at RECREATION. • (*fml*) A **motor vehicle** is a car, bus, truck or other vehicle powered by a motor that uses roads.

motorized /ˈmoʊt̬·əˌraɪzd/ adj [not gradable] • *a motorized wheelchair/telescope*

motorist /ˈmoʊt̬·ə·rəst/ n [C] someone who drives a car or other road vehicle

motor BODY MOVEMENT /ˈmoʊt̬·ər/ adj [not gradable] relating to muscles that produce movement and the nerves and parts of the brain that control these muscles • *motor skills*

motorcade /ˈmoʊt̬·ərˌkeɪd/ n [C] a group of cars or other vehicles traveling together, usually one behind the other • *a presidential motorcade*

motorway /ˈmoʊt̬·ərˌweɪ/ n [C] Br for EXPRESSWAY

mottled /ˈmɑt̬·əld/ adj marked with areas of different colors in an irregular pattern • *mottled skin*

motto /ˈmɑt̬·oʊ/ n [C] pl **mottos** or **mottoes** a word, phrase, or sentence that expresses the principles or belief of a person, group, country, or organization • *The motto printed on US currency is "In God We Trust."*

mound /maʊnd/ n [C] a rounded pile of dirt, sand, stones, or other material, or a raised area of earth • *We're using that mound of sand to level the ground for our new pool.* • A mound is also a rounded mass of something: *a mound of spaghetti*

mount GET ONTO /maʊnt/ v [I/T] to get onto (something) • *The winners mounted the podium.* [T] ∘ *When the horses were saddled we mounted up and rode away.* [I]

mount GO UP /maʊnt/ v [T] to go up (something) • *Reaching the porch, he mounted the steps.*

mount INCREASE /maʊnt/ v [I] to increase, rise, or get bigger • *Excitement mounted as the racers neared the finish.* ∘ *Watch what you eat, because those calories really mount up.*

mounting /ˈmaʊnt̬·ɪŋ/ adj [not gradable] • *There's been mounting international criticism of the move.*

mount ORGANIZE /maʊnt/ v [T] to prepare and produce; to organize • *He has the support needed to mount a successful campaign.*

mount ATTACH /maʊnt/ v [T] to attach (something) to something else so that it can be seen • *Don's planning to mount these photographs.*

Mount MOUNTAIN /maʊnt/ (*abbreviation* **Mt.**) n [U] (used esp. as part of the name of a place) a high hill or mountain • *Mount Saint Helens* ∘ *Mt. Fuji*

mountain HIGH PLACE /ˈmaʊnt̬·ən/ n [C] a raised, often rocky part of the earth's surface, larger than a hill • *the Blue Ridge Mountains* ∘ *We're spending the weekend in the mountains* (= an area with mountains). • A **mountain bike** is a bicycle with thick tires and straight **handlebars** made for riding on hills and rough ground. • A **mountain lion** is a COUGAR. • *The Rockies form the biggest North American* **mountain range** (= group of mountains). • *A thick haze covered the* **mountainside** (= the sloping side of the mountain).

mountainous /ˈmaʊnt̬·ən·əs/ adj having many mountains • *mountainous terrain*

mountain LARGE AMOUNT /ˈmaʊnt̬·ən/ n [C] a large amount of something • *I've got mountains of work to do.* ∘ *You'll never eat that mountain of food.*

Mountie /ˈmaʊnt̬·i/ n [C] *infml* a member of the Royal Canadian Mounted Police

mourn /mɔːrn, moʊrn/ v [I/T] to feel or express deep sadness, esp. because of someone's death • *Frank is mourning the death of his father.* [T]

mourner /'mɔːr·nər, 'moʊr-/ n [C] a person who is feeling or expressing sadness, or who is at a funeral

mournful /'mɔːrn·fəl, 'moʊrn-/ adj • *We heard the mournful cry of a wolf.*

mournfully /'mɔːrn·fə·li, 'moʊrn-/ adv • *He gazed mournfully out the window.*

mourning /'mɔːr·nɪŋ, 'moʊr-/ n [U] • *The family is in morning.*

mouse ANIMAL /maʊs/ n [C] pl **mice** /maɪs/ a type of small RODENT (= small mammal with sharp teeth) that has short, usually brown, gray, or white hair, a pointed face, and a long tail • *a field mouse* ○ *pet mice* • A **mousetrap** is a small device used for catching and usually killing mice.

mouse COMPUTER DEVICE /maʊs/ n [C] pl **mice** /maɪs/ a small device with a ball inside that is moved by hand across a flat surface to control the movement of the CURSOR (= pointer) on a computer screen

mousse FOOD /muːs/ n [C/U] a light food made from eggs mixed together with cream and other things, such as fruit, chocolate, or fish, and served cold • *a chocolate mousse* [C]

mousse BEAUTY SUBSTANCE /muːs/ n [U] a light, creamy substance that is put on the hair or skin to improve its appearance or condition • *styling/conditioning mousse*

moustache /'mʌs·tæʃ, mə'stæʃ/ n [C] a MUSTACHE

mousy, mousey /'maʊ·si, -zi/ adj (of hair) not shiny or attractive, or (of people) quiet and not interesting • *mousy brown hair* ○ *He's a meek, short, mousey man.*

mouth BODY PART /maʊð/ n [C] the opening in the face used by a person or animal to eat food • *I wish you wouldn't chew with your mouth open.* • A **mouthpiece** is the part of a musical instrument, telephone, or other device that goes near, on, or between the lips. • A **mouthpiece** is also a person or a newspaper that expresses the opinions of others: *He's a mouthpiece for the pharmaceutical industry.* • **Mouth-to-mouth (resuscitation)** is a way to help get air into the lungs of a person who is not breathing by blowing into their mouth. • **Mouthwash** is a liquid used for keeping the mouth clean and smelling fresh. • If something is **mouth-watering**, it looks or smells as if it will taste good.

mouth /maʊð, maʊθ/ v [T] to move the lips as if speaking (a word) • *I mouthed a single word, "Please."* • If you **mouth off**, you express your opinions or complain, esp. loudly and in a way that shows no thoughtfulness or respect: *Clark was mouthing off in the locker room after the loss.*

mouthful /'maʊθ·fʊl/ n [C] the amount of food or drink that fills your mouth, or that you put

into your mouth at one time • *Marj forked up a mouthful of pie.* • (*infml*) A mouthful is also a long word or sentence, or something said that has a lot of meaning: *He has a mouthful to say on the subject.*

mouth OPENING /maʊθ/ n [C usually sing] the opening of a hole or cave • *We looked down into the mouth of the volcano.* • The mouth of a river is the place where it flows into the sea. • The opening of a bottle or JAR is also called a mouth.

move CHANGE BODY PLACE /muːv/ v [I/T] to change the place or position of (your body or a part of your body), or to cause (someone's body) to do this • *They moved out of the way to let us past.* [I] ○ *"Can you move your fingers?" the doctor asked.* [T] ○ *I could hear someone moving around upstairs.* [I] ○ *The police moved the crowd along.* [T] ○ *We should get moving* (= start to leave). [I] • *There will be room for Joan, if you* **move over** (= go further to the side).

move /muːv/ n [U] • *I hate the way my boss watches my every move* (= everything I do). • *I'm sorry I didn't call—I've been* **on the move** *all day* (= busy all day).

movement /'muːv·mənt/ n [C/U] • *the movements of the dancers* [C] ○ *There was no movement in his legs.* [U]

move CHANGE POSITION /muːv/ v [I/T] (of a thing) to change position or place, or to cause (something) to change its position or place • *Will you help me move this table?* [T] ○ *There was no wind, and the flags were not moving at all.* [I] • *If Brian wants something, his parents will* **move heaven and earth** (= do everything possible) *to get it for him.*

move /muːv/ n [C] a change of the position of one of the pieces in a game, or a player's turn to move their piece • *It's your move.*

movable, moveable /'muː·və·bəl/ adj [not gradable] able to be moved • *We have movable screens dividing our office into working areas.*

movement /'muːv·mənt/ n [C/U] • *Fire doors should be kept closed to prevent the movement of fire from one area to another.* [U]

moving /'muː·vɪŋ/ adj [not gradable] • *This machine has a lot of moving parts* (= parts that change their position).

move GO /muːv/ v [I/T] to go to live or work in a different place, or to cause (someone) to do this • *We're moving next week.* [I] ○ *I've decided to move to the country.* [I] • To move can mean to change (a person's position) in an organization or system, or to cause (a person) to be changed in this way: *He's moving from the publicity department to sales.* [I] ○ *Carol has been moved (up) to a more advanced karate class.* [T]

move /muːv/ n [C] the act or process of moving • *The office move is scheduled for March.*

mover /'muː·vər/ n [C usually pl] a person or a company whose business is to move furniture and other possessions to a different place

moving /ˈmuː·vɪŋ/ *n* [U] • *Any moving expenses will be paid by the company.*

move CHANGE CONDITIONS /muːv/ *v* [I/T] to change (a situation or event), or to change (the way something happens or is done) • *The meeting has been moved from Tuesday to Wednesday.* [T] ○ *People are moving toward buying products that don't harm the environment.* [I]

movement /ˈmuːv·mənt/ *n* [C/U] • *There has been a movement toward smaller families.* [C]

move ACT /muːv/ *v* [I/T] to take action, or to cause (someone) to take action • *OK, everybody, let's get things moving!* [I] ○ *If we don't move quickly on this deal, we'll lose it.* [I] ○ *I can't imagine what could have moved me to do such a thing.* [T] • To move is also to progress, or to cause (something) to progress: *The building project is finally moving ahead.* [I]

move /muːv/ *n* [C] an action taken to cause something to happen • *What do you think our next move should be?* ○ *Buying that property was a good/smart move.*

movement /ˈmuːv·mənt/ *n* [C] a group of people with a particular set of aims • *The women's movement works for better job opportunities for women.*

mover /ˈmuː·vər/ *n* [C] • A person who is a **mover and shaker** is someone who is willing to make big changes to get things done: *The new director of the company is a real mover and shaker.*

move FEEL /muːv/ *v* [T] to cause (someone) to have strong feelings, such as sadness or sympathy • *Their kindness really moved me.* ○ *The film moved him to tears* (= made him cry).

moving /ˈmuː·vɪŋ/ *adj* [not gradable] • *I found the novel deeply moving.*

move (*obj*) SUGGEST /muːv/ *v fml* to suggest (something), esp. formally at a meeting or in a court of law • *I move that the proposal be accepted.* [+ *that* clause]

move EXCRETE /muːv/ *v* [I/T] to excrete the contents of (the bowels)

▢ **move away** /-ˈ--ˈ-/ *v adv* [I] to leave the place where you have been living to go to a different place • *My best friend moved away.*

▢ **move in** /-ˈ-/ *v adv* [I] to begin to live in a new place • *When are you moving in to your new apartment?* ○ *We moved in in January.*

▢ **move in on** /-ˈ-ˌ-/ *v adv prep* [T] to threaten or attempt to take control of (something or someone) • *The police are moving in on the student demonstrators.*

movie /ˈmuː·vi/ *n* [C] a series of moving pictures, often telling a story, usually shown in a theater or on television; film • A **moviegoer** is someone who goes to movies, esp. frequently. • A **movie theater** is a building in which movies are shown.

movies /ˈmuː·viːz/ *pl n* the showing of movies at a theater • *We went to the movies last night.*

mow /moʊ/ *v* [T] *past simple* **mowed**, *past part* **mown** /moʊn/ or **mowed** to cut (esp.

grass or grain) with a machine or tool with a blade • *You can't mow the grass if it's wet.* [T] • If you **mow down** someone, you kill or seriously injure them: *The car went out of control and mowed down pedestrians on the sidewalk.* [M]

mph *abbreviation for* miles per hour (= the number of miles a vehicle travels in one hour, a measure of its speed) • *The speed limit is 55 mph.*

Mr. /ˈmɪs·tər/ *n* [U] a title for a man, used before the family name or full name, or sometimes before a position • *Mr. Kaplan/Mr. David Kaplan* ○ *Good afternoon, Mr. Mendoza.* ○ *I'm afraid I can't agree with what's just been said, Mr. Chairman.* • LP TITLES AND FORMS OF ADDRESS

Mrs. /ˈmɪs·əz, -əs, *Southern also* mɪz, mɪs/ *n* [U] a title for a married woman, used before the family name or full name • *Mrs. Schultz/Mrs. Doris Schultz* ○ *Hello, Mrs. Taylor, how are you today?* • LP TITLES AND FORMS OF ADDRESS

Ms. /mɪz/ *n* [U] a title for a woman, used before the family name or full name • *Ms. McCracken/Ms. Elizabeth McCracken* ○ *What can I do for you, Ms. Jackson?* • LP TITLES AND FORMS OF ADDRESS

M.S. *n* [C] *abbreviation for* **Master of Science**, see at MASTER SKILLED PERSON. • *Marj has an M.S. in biology.* • LP EDUCATION IN THE US

MSG *n* [U] *abbreviation for* MONOSODIUM GLUTAMATE

much GREAT /mʌtʃ/ *adj, adv* **more** /mɔːr, moʊr/, **most** /moʊst/ great in amount, degree, or range • *Mark's got too much work to do.* ○ *I don't have much money to spend.* ○ *Jody doesn't eat very much.* ○ *It doesn't matter that much to me whether we go or not.* ○ *Thank you so/very much.* ○ *She doesn't go out much* (= often). ○ *He's feeling much better/worse* (= a lot better or worse). ○ *Rita would much rather have her baby at home than in a hospital* (= She would greatly prefer it). • **Much less** means and even less (do something else): *Tony can't boil an egg, much less cook dinner* (= he certainly cannot cook dinner). • USAGE: Much is used with singular, uncountable nouns. Compare MANY. • LP AMOUNTS, VERY, COMPLETELY, AND OTHER INTENSIFIERS

much /mʌtʃ/ *n* [U], *pronoun* a great amount, degree, or range • *There's not much to do around here.* ○ *He's still recovering, and sleeps much of the time.*

much AMOUNT /mʌtʃ/ *n* [U] an amount or degree of something • *How much sugar do you take in your coffee?* ○ *How much are these shoes?/How much do these shoes cost?* • LP AMOUNTS

much NEARLY /mʌtʃ/ *adv* **more** /mɔːr, moʊr/, **most** /moʊst/ nearly; approximately • *The two schools are much the same.* ○ *She is so much like her mother.*

muck /mʌk/ *n* [U] wet, sticky dirt • *It was hard to walk in the muck.*

mucus /ˈmjuː·kəs/ *n* [U] sticky, wet liquid produced inside your nose and other parts of the body

mud /mʌd/ *n* [U] wet, sticky earth • *The car got stuck in the mud.* • **Mud-slinging** is the act of saying insulting or unfair things about someone else, esp. to damage their reputation: *It was a dirty, mud-slinging political campaign.*

muddy /ˈmʌd·i/ *adj* • *a muddy road*

muddy /ˈmʌd·i/ *v* [T] • To **muddy the waters** is to make a situation unnecessarily complicated and less clear: *We had almost reached agreement when he came along and muddied the waters.*

muddled /ˈmʌd·əld/ *adj* confusing and not clearly reasoned • *the movie's muddled plot* ○ *On the subject of dating coworkers, Ellen's opinions were somewhat muddled.*

muddle /ˈmʌd·əl/ *v* [I always + adv/prep] • If you **muddle along**, you continue doing something without a clear purpose or plan. • If you **muddle through**, you manage to do something although you are not organized and do not know how to do it: *I don't know how to keep score—I'll just have to muddle through.*

muddle /ˈmʌd·əl/ *n* [C] a messy and confused state • *Her life was in a muddle.*

muff /mʌf/ *v* [T] *infml* to fail to catch (a ball), or do (something) badly • *She muffed her lines in her first stage appearance.*

muffin /ˈmʌf·ən/ *n* [C] a small, round, usually sweet bread, baked in a pan

muffle /ˈmʌf·əl/ *v* [T] to make (a sound) quieter and less clear • *Ted and I looked at each other with open mouths and muffled our laughs in our sleeves.*

muffled /ˈmʌf·əld/ *adj* [not gradable] • *I could hear muffled voices next door, but couldn't make out any words.*

muffler /ˈmʌf·lər/ *n* [C] a device on a vehicle which reduces noise

muffler /ˈmʌf·lər/ *n* [C] a long strip of cloth, often of wool, worn around the neck for warmth; SCARF

mug CUP /mʌg/ *n* [C] a large cup with a handle on the side, used esp. for hot drinks, and usually used without a SAUCER (= plate below it)

mug ATTACK /mʌg/ *v* [T] **-gg-** to attack (a person), using force or threats of force to steal their money or possessions • *He was mugged in broad daylight.*

mugger /ˈmʌg·ər/ *n* [C] • *You've got to look out for muggers if you walk in the park at night.*

muggy /ˈmʌg·i/ *adj* (of weather) very warm and HUMID (= containing a lot of very small drops of water in the air)

mulatto /mʊˈlɑt̬·oʊ, mjʊ-/ *n* [C] *dated* a person who has one black parent and one white parent or whose parents are any mixture of black and white

mulberry /ˈmʌlˌber·i/ *n* [C] a tree with wide, dark green leaves, or its small purple or white fruit

mulch /mʌltʃ/ *n* [C/U] a covering, esp. of decaying leaves, grass, or plant material, used to keep water in the earth near plants or to protect them from WEEDS (= unwanted plants)

mule /mjuːl/ *n* [C] an animal whose mother is a horse and whose father is a DONKEY, used esp. for transporting loads

mull over *obj*, **mull** *obj* **over** /ˈmʌlˈoʊ·vər/ *v adv* [M] to think carefully about (something) for a period of time • *I need a few days to mull things over before I decide.*

mullah /ˈmʌl·ə, ˈmʊl·ə/ *n* [C] an Islamic religious teacher or leader

multicultural /ˌmʌl·tiːˈkʌl·tʃə·rəl, ˌmʌlˌtɑɪ-/ *adj* [not gradable] relating to a number of different cultures, esp. to the traditions of people of different religions and races • *The school board strongly endorsed a curriculum that reflected a multicultural education.*

multiculturalism /ˌmʌl·tiːˈkʌl·tʃə·rəˌlɪz·əm, ˌmʌlˌtɑɪ-/ *n* [U]

multilateral /ˌmʌl·tiːˈlæt̬·ə·rəl, ˌmʌlˌtɑɪ-/ *adj* [not gradable] involving more than two groups or countries • *a multilateral trade agreement*

multimedia /ˌmʌl·tiːˈmiːd·iː·ə, ˌmʌlˌtɑɪ-/ *n* [U] the use of a combination of pictures, sound, and words, used esp. in computers or entertainment • *a multimedia production*

multinational /ˌmʌl·tiːˈnæʃ·ən·əl, ˌmʌlˌtɑɪ-/ *adj* [not gradable] involving or relating to different countries, or (of a business) operating in different countries • *multinational corporations*

multiple MANY /ˈmʌl·tə·pəl/ *adj* [not gradable] consisting of or involving many things or types of things • *Make multiple copies of the report.* • A **multiple-choice** question on an exam is one in which you are given a list of possible answers and you have to choose the right one.

multiple NUMBER /ˈmʌl·tə·pəl/ *n* [C] a number that results from multiplying one number by another when at least one of them is a **whole number** (= a number with no part of a number after it) • *18 is a multiple of 3, because 6×3=18.*

multiplex /ˈmʌl·təˌpleks/ *n* [C] a large movie theater building that has several separate movie theaters inside it • *What's playing at the multiplex?*

multiplicity /ˌmʌl·təˈplɪs·ət̬·i/ *n* [U] a large number or wide range of items • *She knew a multiplicity of languages.*

multiply /ˈmʌl·təˌplɑɪ/ *v* [I/T] to increase greatly in number, or (in mathematics) to increase (a number) by itself a particular number of times • *The viruses multiply within the* *body.* [I] ∘ *If you multiply 7 by 15 you get 105.* [T] • Compare DIVIDE CALCULATE.

multiplication /ˌmʌl·tə·plə'keɪ·ʃən/ *n* [U] • *Emma's learning multiplication* (= how to multiply numbers) *in school.* • A **multiplication sign** is the symbol × or the symbol ·.

multitude /'mʌl·tə·tuːd/ *n* a large number of things • *Two large circles are surrounded by a multitude of small, colorful squares.* [U] ∘ *As manager of the restaurant, his job is to feed the multitudes* (= large numbers of people). [pl]

mum SILENT /mʌm/ *adj* [not gradable] silent in order not to tell anyone what you know • *The governor is keeping mum about his plans.*

mum FLOWER /mʌm/ *n* [C] *short form of* CHRYSANTHEMUM

mumble /'mʌm·bəl/ *v* [I/T] to speak unclearly or quietly so that the words are difficult to understand • *She mumbled a prayer for their safe return.* [T] ∘ *He often mumbles in Yiddish.* [I]

mumbo jumbo /ˌmʌm·bou'dʒʌm·bou/ *n* [U] words or activities that are unnecessarily complicated or mysterious and seem meaningless • *Financial information is just mumbo jumbo to me.*

mummy /'mʌm·i/ *n* [C] (esp. in ancient Egypt) a dead body that has been preserved from decay, esp. by being treated with special substances before being wrapped in cloth

mumps /mʌmps/ *n* [U] an infectious disease that causes painful swellings in the neck and throat and a fever

munch /mʌntʃ/ *v* [I/T] to eat (esp. something hard) noisily and without trying to be quiet, or to SNACK (= eat a small amount of food between meals) • *He was munching on an apple.* [I]

munchies /'mʌn·tʃiːz/ *pl n* small amounts of food, esp. sweet or salty food eaten between meals • *Do you have any munchies—maybe potato chips or crackers?*

mundane /mʌn'deɪn, 'mʌn·deɪn/ *adj* ordinary and not interesting in any way • *The show was just another mundane family sitcom.*

municipal /mjʊ'nɪs·ə·pəl/ *adj* [not gradable] of or belonging to a town or city • *municipal services*

municipality /mjʊˌnɪs·ə'pæl·əṭ·i/ *n* [C] a city or town with its own local government, or this local government itself

munitions /mjʊ'nɪʃ·ənz/ *pl n* military weapons such as guns and bombs

mural /'mjʊr·əl/ *n* [C] a large picture painted on a wall

murder /'mɜrd·ər/ *n* [C/U] the crime of intentionally killing a person • *There were three murders in the town last year.* [C] ∘ *Two sisters have been convicted of murder.* [U] • If you say that something is murder, you mean it is very difficult or takes a lot of work: *It's murder finding a parking space in this neighborhood.* [U]

murder /'mɜrd·ər/ *v* [T] • *Gunmen murdered her husband.*

murderer /'mɜrd·ə·rər/ *n* [C] • *The convicted murderer was executed in Texas yesterday.*

murderous /'mɜrd·ə·rəs/ *adj* • *She experienced the murderous* (= deadly) *brutality of the Nazi regime.*

murk /mɜrk/ *n* [U] darkness or a thick cloud, which prevents you from seeing clearly • *a dense murk of smog*

murky /'mɜr·ki/ *adj* • *murky waters* ∘ *The movie has dumb characters and a murky plot* (= it is difficult to understand).

murmur /'mɜr·mər/ *v* [I/T] to speak or say very quietly • *"I love you," she murmured.*

murmur /'mɜr·mər/ *n* [C] • *a murmur of voices*

muscle /'mʌs·əl/ *n* [C/U] a mass of tissue in the body, often attached to bones, that can tighten and relax to produce movement • *He strained a muscle in his leg.* [C] • Muscle is also the power to do things or to make people behave in a certain way: *Republicans are flexing some political muscle.* [U] • If you are **muscle-bound**, you have trouble moving because your muscles are too well developed.

muscle /'mʌs·əl/ *v* [always + adv/prep] to force your way into a place or situation • *Starks muscled his way to the basket.* [T] ∘ *Amanda muscled in on our meeting.* [I]

muscular /'mʌs·kjə·lər/ *adj* having well-developed muscles • *muscular arms/legs*

muse THINK /mjuːz/ *v* [I/T] to think about something carefully and for a long time • *At breakfast, he allowed himself to muse about his presidency.* [I always + adv/prep]

muse IMAGINARY FORCE /mjuːz/ *n* [C/U] an imaginary force that gives someone ideas and helps them to write, paint, or make music, or a physical representation of this force

museum /mjʊ'ziː·əm/ *n* [C] a building where people can go to view objects of historical, scientific, or artistic interest • *an art/science/natural history museum*

mush /mʌʃ/ *n* [U] any thick, soft substance, such as food that has been boiled too long • *The rain turned the ground into clay and then to mush.*

mushy /'mʌʃ·i/ *adj* [-er/-est only] • *The yard's still too mushy to mow the grass.*

mushroom PLANT /'mʌʃ·ruːm, -rʊm/ *n* [C] any one of many types of fast-growing FUNGUS (= plants without leaves or flowers) with a round top and short stem, many of which are used as food • *wild mushrooms* ∘ *mushroom soup* ∘ *a pizza with mushrooms*

mushroom GROW /'mʌʃ·ruːm, -rʊm/ *v* [I] to grow quickly • *If your business were to mushroom, would you be happy?*

music /'mjuː·zɪk/ *n* [U] a pattern of sounds made by instruments or by singing or a by combination of both, or the written symbols representing these sounds • *classical/folk/*

country/rap music ○ *Music blared from a juke-box.* ○ *She started composing music when she was 14.* • If something is **music to** your **ears**, you are pleased to hear it: *When she said they would make a profit, it was music to Richard's ears.*

musical /'mju:·zɪ·kəl/ *adj* • *Musical instruments hang from the walls of the restaurant.* ○ *Everyone in our family is musical* (= can sing or play an instrument, or likes music a lot).

musician /mju'zɪʃ·ən/ *n* [C] a person who is skilled in playing music, usually as their job • *a jazz/classical/rock musician*

musk /mʌsk/ *n* [U] a natural substance with a strong, sweet smell

musky /'mʌs·ki/ *adj* • *Her skin had a warm, musky odor.*

musket /'mʌs·kət/ *n* [C] a type of gun with a long BARREL that was used in the past

Muslim /'mʌz·ləm, 'mʊs-, 'mʊz-/, **Moslem** *n* [C], *adj* [not gradable] (a member) of the religion of ISLAM • *a Muslim mosque*

muslin /'mʌz·lən/ *n* [U] a type of thin cotton material • *a muslin shirt/blouse*

muss /mʌs/ *v* [T] to make messy • *Don't muss my hair (up)—I just had it styled.*

mussel /'mʌs·əl/ *n* [C] a small, edible sea animal that has a dark shell with two parts that close tightly together

must NECESSARY /mʌst, məst/ *v aux* he/she/it **must** used to show that it is necessary or important that something happen in the present or future • *Seeing what others have and she lacks, she believes that she must have more.* ○ *We must not surprise them* (= it is wrong, dangerous, or forbidden). • If you say that you must do something, you can mean that you have a firm intention to do something in the future: *I must call my sister later.* • Must is sometimes used for emphasis: *I must admit I enjoy these movies.* • LP⟩ AUXILIARY VERBS

must /mʌst/ *n* [C] something that is necessary • *If you live in the suburbs a car is a must.*

must PROBABLY /mʌst, məst/ *v aux* he/she/it **must** used to show that something is likely, probable, or certain to be true • *Death must be better than this.* ○ *"It must have been fun." "No, it wasn't."* • LP⟩ AUXILIARY VERBS

mustache /'mʌs·tæʃ, mə'stæʃ/, **moustache** *n* [C] hair that grows above the upper lip • *He's a slender man with a trim mustache.*

mustard /'mʌs·tərd/ *n* [U] a yellow or brown thick liquid that tastes spicy and is eaten in small amounts, esp. on meat and sandwiches • *a hot dog with mustard*

muster PRODUCE /'mʌs·tər/ *v* [T] to produce or encourage (esp. an emotion or support) • *I shouted with all the lung power I could muster.*

muster GATHER /'mʌs·tər/ *v* [I/T] to gather together as a group or force, or to cause (a force) to gather, esp. in preparation for a fight • *Op-*

ponents will have to muster at least 23 votes to defeat the bill. [T]

musty /'mʌs·ti/ *adj* [*-er/-est* only] smelling unpleasantly old and slightly wet • *a musty room*

mutation /mju'teɪ·ʃən/ *n* [C/U] the change that happens in an organism's GENES which produces differences that are passed to its young, or the process of this change • *These genes will be compared with others in an attempt to find mutations.* [C]

mute /mju:t/ *adj* [not gradable] (of a person) completely unable or unwilling to speak, or (of a place, object, or activity) silent • *He stood mute before the judge.* ○ *The decay of Dawson City bore mute testimony to the end of the gold rush era.*

muted /'mju:t·əd/ *adj* not loud, or not enthusiastic • *Her reaction was muted.* • Muted colors are not bright.

mutilate /'mju:t·əl·eɪt/ *v* [T] to damage (someone or something) very seriously, esp. by violently removing a part • *She was raped and mutilated.*

mutilation /ˌmju:t·əl'eɪ·ʃən/ *n* [C/U] • *Some of the beatings and mutilations had occurred in police headquarters.* [C]

mutiny /'mju:t·ən·i/ *n* [C/U] refusal to obey orders, or a violent attempt to take control from people in authority, esp. in the military or on a ship • *Walker's superiors charged him with mutiny.* [U]

mutiny /'mju:t·ən·i/ *v* [I] • *The crew mutinied and killed the captain.*

mutinous /'mju:t·ən·əs/ *adj* • *Mutinous troops failed to overthrow the government.*

mutt /mʌt/ *n* [C] *infml* a MONGREL

mutter /'mʌt·ər/ *v* [I/T] to speak quietly and in a voice that is not easy to hear, often when you are anxious or complaining about something • *He muttered to himself as he walked.* [I] ○ *I heard him mutter something.* [T] *"There has to be another way," he muttered.*

mutton /'mʌt·ən/ *n* [U] the meat from an adult sheep

mutual /'mju:·tʃə·wəl/ *adj* [not gradable] (of two or more people or groups) feeling the same emotion, or doing the same thing to or for each other • *The organization promotes mutual understanding between peoples.* ○ *We let the subject drop, by mutual agreement.* • A **mutual friend** is someone who is a friend of each of two or more other people: *They were gossiping about parties and mutual friends.*

mutually /'mju:·tʃə·wə·li/ *adv* [not gradable] • *A lot of people still think brains and beauty are mutually exclusive* (= cannot exist together at the same time).

mutual fund /'mju:·tʃə·wəl,fʌnd/ *n* [C] a company that sells shares to the public and invests the money obtained in many different companies or lends it to governments

muzzle ANIMAL NOSE /'mʌz·əl/ *n* [C] the mouth and nose of an animal, esp. a dog or a horse

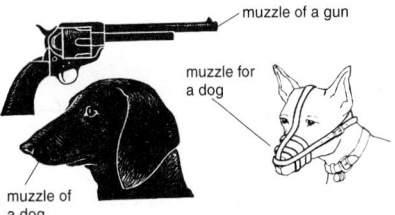

muzzle of a gun

muzzle for a dog

muzzle of a dog

muzzle

or a covering put over this in order to prevent the animal from biting

muzzle /ˈmʌz·əl/ v [T] • *Dangerous dogs should be muzzled.*

muzzle ‾PREVENT EXPRESSION‾ /ˈmʌz·əl/ v [T] to prevent (someone) from speaking or expressing their thoughts • *Frank will continue to muzzle his critics.*

muzzle ‾GUN PART‾ /ˈmʌz·əl/ n [C] the end of a gun BARREL (= the cylindrical part of a gun), where the bullets come out

my /mɑɪ/ pronoun belonging to or connected with me; the possessive form of I, used before a noun • *I think about my father and my mother.* ○ *He wanted to be my friend.* ○ *My mind went absolutely blank.* • If you say **be my guest**, you mean that you are very willing to do something that someone has asked you to do: *"Can I take this seat?" "Be my guest."* • **My/my, my/my, oh, my** are used to express surprise or pleasure: *My, this food is wonderful.* ○ *My, oh, my, what a strange haircut!* • **My own** is used to emphasize that something belongs to or is connected with me and no one else: *I bit my own hand.* • ‾LP‾ DETERMINERS

myself /mɑɪˈself, mə-/ pronoun the person speaking; the reflexive form of I • *I bought myself a new coat.* • Myself is sometimes used to emphasize I as the subject of a sentence: *I myself prefer to skip lunch.* • Myself is sometimes used instead of I or me: *They very kindly invited my sister and myself to the party.* • *I live* **by myself** (= alone) *in a small apartment in Brooklyn.* • *I had to do the whole job* **by myself** (= alone and without help from anyone). • *I never get an hour* **to myself** (= for my own use).

myopic *fml* /mɑɪˈɑp·ɪk, -ˈoʊ·pɪk/, **near-sighted** adj unable to see distant things clearly

myriad /ˈmɪr·iː·əd/ n [C usually sing] a very large number • *There's a myriad of insects on the island.*

myriad /ˈmɪr·iː·əd/ adj [not gradable] • *A cloud of dust was raised by their myriad feet.*

mystery /ˈmɪs·tə·ri, -tri/ n [C/U] something strange or unknown which has not yet been explained or understood • *Despite years of study, sleepwalking remains a mystery.* [C] ○ *The details of the scandal are shrouded in mystery.* [U] • A mystery is also a book, movie, or play about a crime or other event that is difficult to explain: *a murder mystery* [C] • *It's a* **mystery to me** (= I do not understand) *why she married him in the first place!*

mysterious /mɪsˈtɪr·iː·əs/ adj • *He tried to convince this mysterious woman to go out with him.*

mysteriously /mɪsˈtɪr·iː·ə·sli/ adv • *The light mysteriously came on, although no one was near the switch.*

mysticism /ˈmɪs·tə‚sɪz·əm/ n [U] the belief that it is possible to directly obtain truth or achieve communication with God or other forces controlling the universe by prayer and CONTEMPLATION (= serious, quiet consideration)

mystic /ˈmɪs·tɪk/ n [C] a person who tries to communicate directly with God or other forces controlling the universe • *His ideas might sound familiar to New Age mystics today.*

mystical /ˈmɪs·tɪ·kəl/, **mystic** /ˈmɪs·tɪk/ adj • *Meditation can lead to a total mystical experience.*

mystify /ˈmɪs·tə‚fɑɪ/ v [T] to confuse (someone) or make them uncertain by doing or involving them in something difficult to explain • *Doctors were mystified by her high fever and headaches.*

mystique /mɪsˈtiːk/ n [U] a quality of mysterious attraction • *Men never seem to show any emotion, and that's part of the male mystique.*

myth /mɪθ/ n [C/U] a traditional story, esp. one which explains the early history or a cultural belief or practice of a group of people, or explains a natural event • *Kids like the stories about the gods and goddesses of Greek and Roman myths.* [C] • A myth is also a commonly believed but false idea: *Equal opportunity continues to be a myth for many.* [C]

mythical /ˈmɪθ·ɪ·kəl/ adj • *Grandpa tells stories about dragons and other mythical creatures.* • Mythical also means imaginary or not real: *I'd like to see that mythical girlfriend he's always talking about.*

mythology /mɪˈθɑl·ə·dʒi/ n [U] myths in general • *We're studying classical mythology in English.*

mythological /‚mɪθ·əˈlɑdʒ·ɪ·kəl/ adj [not gradable] • *mythological tales*

N, n

N <u>LETTER</u> , **n** /en/ *n* [C] *pl* **N's** or **Ns** or **n's** or **ns**
the 14th letter of the English alphabet

N. <u>NORTH</u> , **No.** *n* [U], *adj abbreviation for* NORTH
or NORTHERN

nab /næb/ *v* [T] **-bb-** *infml* to catch (someone)
or take (something) suddenly • *The thief was
nabbed as he left the store.*

nag /næg/ *v* [I/T] **-gg-** to annoy (a person) by
making continual criticisms or suggestions •
*My mom's always nagging me to get my hair
cut.* [T]

nagging /'næg·ɪŋ/ *adj* • *She has a nagging
cough* (= a cough that worries you because it
does not completely stop).

nail <u>METAL</u> /neɪl/ *n* [C] a thin piece of metal
having a pointed end that is forced into wood
or another substance by hitting the other end
with a hammer, and is used esp. to join two
pieces or to hold something in place

nail /neɪl/ *v* [T] to attach or fasten with a nail
or nails • *Workmen were nailing down the carpet.* [M] • If you nail something shut, you put
nails in it to fasten it so that it cannot easily
be opened: *He nailed the box shut.* • (*infml*) To
nail someone is to catch them in a dishonest
or illegal act: *We finally nailed the guys dumping garbage in the park.* • If you **nail down**
something/**nail** something **down**, you make
it final: *After an all-night meeting, representatives from the two sides finally nailed down the
deal.*

nail <u>BODY PART</u> /neɪl/ *n* [C] the hard, smooth
part at the upper end of each finger and toe •
A **nailbrush** is a small, stiff brush used for
cleaning your nails. • A **nail file** is a strip of
metal with a rough surface, for smoothing and
shaping the ends of your nails. <u>PIC</u> FILE • **Nail
polish** is a shiny liquid substance that some
women put on their nails as a decoration.

naive /nɑɪˈiːv/ *adj* too ready to believe someone or something, or to trust that someone's
intentions are good, esp. because of a lack of
experience • *It was naive of her to think that
she would ever get her money back.*

naked /'neɪ·kəd/ *adj* [not gradable] not wearing any clothes

name /neɪm/ *n* [C] a word or words that a person or thing is known by • *Hello, my name is
Beth.* ○ *Do you remember the name of that town
we visited in Maine?* • A name is also a reputation, esp. a good one: *She had made a name for
herself as an architect by the time she was thirty.* • A name is also a famous person or thing:
He's a big name in the field of fashion. ○ *They
wanted a name band for the wedding.* • *I'm
looking for someone* **by the name of** (= known
as) *Stephen Weinberg.* • If someone or something is called something **in name only**, the
name does not accurately describe what they

are: *It's an island in name only, since it's been
joined to the mainland now by landfill.* • **In the
name of** means in serving the cause of: *In the
name of common decency, let him spend the
night here.* • **The name of the game** is the
main purpose of an activity: *In professional
sports, winning is the name of the game.* • (*disapproving*) **Name-dropping** is the habit of
mentioning the names of famous or important people that you know or pretend to know
in order to make yourself seem more important. • <u>LP</u> CAPITAL LETTERS

name /neɪm/ *v* [T] to give a name to (someone
or something) • *They decided to name their
first child Benjamin.* • To name is also to
choose or to state publicly: *The president has
yet to name a new ambassador to Russia.* • *David was* **named after** (= given the same name
as) *his grandfather.* • To **name names** is to tell
the names of people who are involved in something bad or illegal: *She said she had been the
victim of sexual harassment by several Congressmen, and she was prepared to name
names.*

nameless /'neɪm·ləs/ *adj* [not gradable] • If
someone is nameless, their name is not given
publicly: *We are pleased to report a large gift to
the school from someone who wishes to remain
nameless.*

namely /'neɪm·li/ *adv* [not gradable] to be
specific • *He suggested that these so-called contributions are something else, namely taxes.*

namesake /'neɪm·seɪk/ *n* [C usually sing] a
person or thing with the same name as another person or thing

nanny /'næn·i/ *n* [C] a woman employed to
take care of children in the children's home •
*She relied on a nanny to care for her baby dur-
ing the week.*

nap /næp/ *n* [C] a brief sleep, esp. during the
day

nap /næp/ *v* [I] **-pp-** • *While the children nap
after lunch, their teachers will get a break.*

nape /neɪp/ *n* [C usually sing] the back of the
neck • *She kissed the
nape of his neck.*

napkin /'næp·kən/, *also Cdn* **serviette** *n* [C] a
piece of cloth or paper
used at meals to pro-
tect your clothes and
to clean your lips or
fingers

nappy /'næp·i/ *n* [C]
Br for DIAPER

nape

narcotic /nɑrˈkɑt̬·ɪk/ *n* [C] a type of drug that
causes sleep and that is used medically to reduce the strength of pain, and that in some
forms is also used illegally

narcotic /nɑr'kɑt·ɪk/ *adj* • *narcotic drugs*

narrative /'nær·ət·ɪv/ *n* [C] a story or a description of events • *The novel is a wonderful narrative of wartime adventure.*

narrator /'nær·eɪt̬·ər/ *n* [C] a person who tells a story, or a person who speaks during a film or television program not as an actor but to describe or discuss the pictures being shown • *Michael Caine is the narrator in the documentary film.*

narrate /'nær·eɪt, nær'eɪt/ *v* [I/T] to act as a narrator for (something shown) • *We have to hire a professional to narrate the video.* [T]

narration /nær'eɪ·ʃən/ *n* [C/U] the telling of a story or the work of a narrator

narrow SMALL /'nær·oʊ/ *adj* having a small distance from one side to the other • *Scenes from the movie were filmed in some of Rome's ancient, narrow streets.* • Narrow also means slight, esp. as a measure of difference: *He was defeated in the election by a narrow margin.* ○ *It was a narrow victory/defeat, with the golf tournament decided by a single stroke.* • Narrow also means only just successful: *He had a narrow escape, getting out of the car just before it burst into flames.*

narrow /'nær·oʊ/ *v* [I/T] to become or make (something) narrower or smaller • *The road narrows from four lanes to two when you leave town.* [I] ○ *Senate leaders met again to try to narrow the budget deficit.* [T]

narrowly /'nær·ə·li/ *adv* • *The proposal to ban the sale of liquor was narrowly defeated* (= it lost but nearly won).

narrow LIMITED /'nær·oʊ/ *adj* limited in range • *The local newspaper tends to focus on narrow regional issues.* • If someone is **narrow-minded**, they are unwilling to accept or consider ideas and behavior that are different from their own.

NASA /'næs·ə/ *n* [U] *abbreviation for* National Aeronautics and Space Administration (= the US government organization that plans and controls space travel and the scientific study of space)

nasal /'neɪ·zəl/ *adj* of or related to the nose • *This medicine is supposed to relieve nasal congestion.* • If a person's voice is nasal, the sound is produced through the nose: *He had a high, unpleasant, nasal voice.*

nasty /'næs·ti/ *adj* mean, unpleasant, or offensive • *He was, to be honest, a nasty man, with never a kind word for anyone.* ○ *I got a rather nasty* (= severe) *cut from the garage door.*

nation /'neɪ·ʃən/ *n* [C] a country, esp. when thought of as a large group of people living in one area with their own government, language, and traditions • *Most industrialized nations of the world will be represented at the conference.* ○ *Throughout the nation today people will go to the polls to elect a new government.* • A nation is also an American In-

dian group, esp. one that is a member of an American Indian FEDERATION.

national /'næʃ·ən·əl/ *adj* [not gradable] relating to all parts of a nation or to a nation as a whole rather than to any part of it • *National headquarters of the company are in Atlanta, with branches throughout the country.* ○ *National news goes on the front page of the newspaper, with local news in the second section.* • A **national anthem** is a country's official song, often played on public occasions. • The **National Guard** is the state military force that is available for service in state and federal emergencies. • A **national park** is an area of a country that is owned and maintained by the government because of its natural beauty or historical importance: *Yellowstone National Park*

national /'næʃ·ən·əl/ *n* [C usually pl] a citizen of a particular country • *The group of Mexican nationals requested a hearing before the immigration officer.*

nationality /ˌnæʃ·ə'næl·ət̬·i/ *n* [C/U] the state of belonging to a particular country or being a citizen of a particular nation • *"What's your nationality?" "I'm from Brazil."* [C] ○ *New York City is home to people of many nationalities.* [C]

nationally /'næʃ·ən·əl·i/ *adv* • *The football game, to be nationally televised, will begin at 9.*

nationalism /'næʃ·ən·əl,ɪz·əm/ *n* [U] the feelings of affection, loyalty, and pride that people have for their country • Nationalism is also the desire for political independence in a country that is controlled by or part of another country: *The government is alarmed at the rise of nationalism among its ethnic minorities.*

nationalist /'næʃ·ən·əl·əst/ *adj* supporting political independence for a group within a nation • *His views were those of the nationalist Quebec government.*

nationalistic /ˌnæʃ·ən·əl'ɪs·tɪk/ *adj* strongly supporting your country or its political independence • *A series of nationalistic speeches prepared the country for going to war.*

nationalize /'næʃ·ən·əl,aɪz/ *v* [T] to bring (business, industry, or land) under the control or ownership of the government • *The program's huge cost makes it unlikely that Congress will try to nationalize health care in the near future.*

nationwide /ˌneɪ·ʃən'waɪd/ *adj* [not gradable] existing or happening in all parts of a particular country • *A nationwide survey of mothers revealed some very interesting things about what mothers want from fathers.*

nationwide /ˌneɪ·ʃən'waɪd/ *adv* [not gradable] • *The performances were taped for telecasting nationwide.*

native /'neɪt̬·ɪv/ *adj* [not gradable] of or relating to the place where you were born, or (of plants and animals) growing naturally in a particular region • *This was his first visit to his native land in 30 years.* • If someone or something is native to a place, they were born or started to develop there: *Corn is native to North America.* ○ *Larry is a native Texan* (= He was born in Texas). • Native can also mean first, or coming before any others: *His native language is Spanish, but he speaks English without a trace of an accent.* • A **Native American** (also **American Indian**) is someone who has a member of their family who belonged to one of the groups of people that originally lived in North America before the Europeans arrived.

native /'neɪt̬·ɪv/ *n* [C] a person born in a particular place • *He was a native of Indianapolis and a graduate of Indiana University.* • *(dated)* (used esp. by western Europeans) A native is also a person, usually someone who is not white, who was born and lived in a country before the Europeans began to visit and live there: *Nineteenth-century missionaries tried to convert the natives to Christianity.* The use of the word with this meaning is offensive.

Nativity /nə'tɪv·ət̬·i/ *n* [U] the birth of Jesus, celebrated by Christians at Christmas • *A Nativity scene was displayed on the mantelpiece.*

NATO, Nato /'neɪt̬·oʊ/ *n* [U] *abbreviation for* North Atlantic Treaty Organization (= an international organization that includes the US, Canada, and several European countries, formed in 1949 for military defense)

natural NOT ARTIFICIAL /'næt̬·ə·rəl/ *adj* from nature; not artificial or involving anything made or caused by people • *Cotton is a natural fiber.* ○ *He died of natural causes* (= because he was old or ill). ○ *Floods and earthquakes are natural disasters.* • A natural ability or characteristic is one that you were born with: *a natural athlete* ○ *a natural blonde* • If food or drink is described as natural, it means it has no artificial chemical substances added to it. • **Natural childbirth** is a method of giving birth in which there is little or no use of drugs. • **Natural gas** is gas found underground that is used as a fuel. • **Natural resources** are materials such as coal and wood that exist in nature and can be used by people. • **Natural selection** is the process by which animals and plants that are best suited to their environment will tend to continue to exist.

natural /'næt̬·ə·rəl/ *n* [C] *infml* a person born with the characteristics or abilities needed for doing something • *She won't have any trouble learning to ride a horse—she's a natural.*

naturalist /'næt̬·ə·rə·ləst/ *n* [C] a person who studies plants and animals

naturally /'næt̬·ə·rə·li/ *adv* • *naturally curly hair* ○ *a naturally talented artist* • If a particular skill comes naturally to you, you are able to do it easily, without much effort or learning: *Exercising should come as naturally as brushing your teeth.*

naturalness /'næt̬·ə·rəl·nəs/ *n* [U] • *I admire his naturalness on stage.*

natural EXPECTED /'næt̬·ə·rəl/ *adj* to be expected; usual • *a natural reaction* ○ *It's only natural to be upset when your dog dies.* [+ to infinitive]

naturally /'næt̬·ə·rə·li/ *adv* • *Naturally, we have to arrive early to get the best seats.* ○ *"You will be polite when you speak to her, won't you?" "Naturally* (= Yes, obviously)*."*

naturalize /'næt̬·ə·rə,laɪz/ *v* [T] to make (someone) a legal CITIZEN of a country that they were not born in

naturalization /,næt̬·ə·rə·lə'zeɪ·ʃən/ *n* [U] • *She's applied for naturalization.*

nature LIFE /'neɪ·tʃər/ *n* [U] all the animals and plants in the world and all the features, forces, and processes that exist or happen independently of people, such as the weather, the sea, mountains, reproduction, and growth • *As a young man he loved hiking and being close to nature.* ○ *This technique of growing cells copies what actually happens in nature.* • The force that is responsible for physical life is often called nature, and is sometimes spoken of as a person: *Feeling stressed is Nature's way of telling you to relax.* • If **nature takes its course**, something happens independent of people: *It's a rare farmer who will let nature take its course.* • A **nature preserve** or **nature reserve** is a protected area of land where animals and plants live.

nature TYPE /'neɪ·tʃər/ *n* [C/U] the type or main characteristic (of something) • *The problem is delicate in nature.* [U] ○ *Nothing of a secret nature can happen in that household.* [C] • *There are problems in every relationship—it's in* **the nature of things** (= the usual and expected characteristics of life).

nature CHARACTER /'neɪ·tʃər/ *n* [C/U] the character of a person, or the characteristics a person is born with • *She's always had a sunny nature.* [C] ○ *She is by nature a gentle soul.* [U]

naught /nɔːt, nɑt/ *n* [U] *literary* nothing • *All our effort was for naught.*

naughty /'nɔːt̬·i, 'nɑt̬·i/ *adj* (esp. of children) behaving badly and not being obedient, or (esp. of behavior or language) not socially acceptable • *a naughty girl* ○ *a naughty word*

nausea /'nɔː·ziː·ə, 'nɔː·ʒə, 'nɔː·ʃə/ *n* [U] a feeling of illness in the stomach that makes you think you are going to vomit

nauseated /'nɔː·ziː,eɪt̬·əd/ *adj* • *He didn't become nauseated by the treatments at all.*

nauseating /'nɔː·ziː,eɪt̬·ɪŋ/ *adj* • *The TV news can be pretty nauseating at times.*

nauseous /'nɔː·ʃəs, 'nɔː·ziː·əs/ *adj* (of people) sick and likely to vomit, or (of things) causing such feelings • *He felt nauseous and dehydrated.* ○ *unpleasant, nauseous odors*

nautical /'nɔːt̬·ɪ·kəl, 'nɑt̬-/ *adj* [not gradable] relating to ships, sailing, or sailors • A **nautical mile** is a unit of distance used at sea which is equal to 6076 feet in the US system. Compare MILE.

naval /'neɪ·vəl/ *adj* [not gradable] belonging to a country's navy, or relating to military ships • *A major naval battle was fought near here.*

navel /'neɪ·vəl/, *infml* **belly button** *n* [C] the small round part or hollow place in the middle of the stomach which is left after the UMBILICAL CORD (= long tube of flesh joining the baby to its mother) has been cut at birth

navigable /'næv·ɪ·gə·bəl/ *adj* deep and wide enough for a ship to go through • *a navigable stretch of river*

navigate /'næv·ə,geɪt/ *v* [I/T] to direct the way that (a vehicle, esp. a ship or aircraft) will travel, or to find a direction across, along, or over (an area of water or land) • *He learned to navigate these waters.* [T] ○ *Whales navigate by visual means.* [I] ○ (*fig.*) *Cyberspace is an environment in which computers navigate.* [I]

navigation /,næv·ə'geɪ·ʃən/ *n* [U] • *a satellite navigation system*

navigator /'næv·ə,geɪt̬·ər/ *n* [C] a person in a vehicle who decides on the direction in which the vehicle travels

navy /'neɪ·vi/ *n* [C] the part of a country's armed forces that is trained to operate at sea

navy (blue) /'neɪ·vi ('blu:)/ *adj* [not gradable], *n* [U] dark blue

Nazi /'nɑt·si, 'næt-/ *n* [C] a member of the National Socialist German Workers' Party that controlled Germany from 1933 to 1945 under Adolf Hitler, or someone who believes in FASCISM (= state control of social and economic life and extreme pride in country and race, with no political disagreement allowed)

Nazi /'nɑt·si, 'næt-/ *adj* [not gradable]

NBA *n* [U] *abbreviation for* National Basketball Association (= the main organized group of US BASKETBALL teams that have players who are paid for playing)

NC-17 /,en,si:,sev·ən'ti:n/ *adj* [not gradable] used in the US for movies that no one under the age of 17 will be admitted to see • Compare G MOVIE; PG; R MOVIE; X SEXUAL.

N.E. *n* [U], *adj abbreviation for* NORTHEAST or NORTHEASTERN

Neanderthal, **Neandertal** /ni:'æn·dər,tɔːl, -,θɑːl/ *adj* of a type of people who lived in Europe and Asia in the ancient past, or (of modern people or beliefs) like a person from the ancient past in mentality or behavior

near /nɪr/, **near to** /'nɪr·tə, -tu:/ *prep* close to; not far away from in distance, time, or relationship • *We live near the school.* ○ *She asked to sit nearer the front of the classroom.* ○ *It will probably be near midnight by the time we get home.* ○ *We couldn't park anywhere near the theater.*

near /nɪr/ *adv* [-*er*/-*est* only] • *I wish we lived nearer.* ○ *I was standing near enough to hear what they were saying.* • Someone who is **near-**

sighted can see clearly only objects that are close to them. Compare **farsighted** at FAR DISTANCE.

near /nɪr/ *adj* [-*er*/-*est* only] • *in the near future* ○ *The nearest library is in the next town.* • A **near miss** is a situation in which an accident almost happened and was only just avoided: *That was a near miss—he must have come within 50 feet of the other plane.*

near /nɪr/ *v* [I/T] to come closer to (something), or to approach • *As the big day nears, I'm starting to get nervous.* [I] ○ *The project is nearing completion.* [T]

nearly /'nɪr·li/ *adv* [not gradable] almost but not quite; close to • *I've nearly finished that book you lent me.* ○ *She's nearly as tall as her father now.* ○ *The problem isn't nearly as bad as you think.*

nearness /'nɪr·nəs/ *n* [U] • *I'm surprised by the nearness of her.*

nearby /nɪr'bɑɪ, 'nɪr·bɑɪ/ *adv, adj* [not gradable] not far away in distance; close • *A police officer was standing nearby.* ○ *We walked to a nearby park.*

neat ARRANGED /ni:t/ *adj* [-*er*/-*est* only] arranged well, with everything in its place • *neat handwriting* ○ *She keeps her room neat and clean.* • A neat person likes everything to be clean and well arranged. • Neat can also mean skillful or effective: *a neat trick/solution*

neatly /'ni:t·li/ *adv* • *neatly folded clothes*

neatness /'ni:t·nəs/ *n* [U]

neat NOTHING ADDED /ni:t/ *adj* [not gradable] (of alcoholic drinks) with nothing added; STRAIGHT BASIC

neat GREAT /ni:t/ *adj* [-*er*/-*est* only] *infml* great • *The party was really neat.* ○ *What a neat bike!*

nebulous /'neb·jə·ləs/ *adj* (esp. of ideas) unclear and lacking form; VAGUE • *a nebulous concept*

necessary /'nes·ə,ser·i/ *adj* needed in order to achieve a particular result • *Don't take any more luggage than is strictly necessary.* ○ *He lacks the necessary skills for the job.* ○ *If necessary, we can always change the date of our trip.* • Necessary can be used in negatives and questions to show that you disapprove of something and do not think it should be done: *Was it really necessary to say that?* [+ *to* infinitive] • A **necessary evil** is something unpleasant that must be accepted in order to achieve a particular result: *Bed checks and strip searches are a necessary evil in prison.*

necessarily /,nes·ə'ser·ə·li/ *adv* [not gradable] (esp. in negatives) in all cases; as an expected result • *Money doesn't necessarily buy happiness.* ○ *"These cheap glasses will break easily." "Not necessarily."*

necessitate /nə'ses·ə,teɪt/ *v* [T] to make (something) necessary • *An important meeting necessitates my being in Houston on Friday.*

necessity /nə'ses·ət̬·i/ *n* [C/U] the need for something, or something that is needed •

Don't you understand the necessity of eating a balanced diet? [U] ○ *She was forced to take the job out of necessity.* [U] ○ *In my work, a computer is a necessity.* [C]

neck BODY PART /nek/ *n* [C] the part of the body that joins the head to the shoulders • *She rubbed her neck.* • The neck of a piece of clothing is the part that goes around a person's neck: *His shirt was open at the neck.* • A neck is also a narrow part near the top of an object such as a bottle: *a vase with a long neck* • A neck is also the long, narrow part of a string instrument, such as a guitar, on which the strings are pressed in order to produce different notes. • If two people who are competing against each other are **neck and neck**, they have an equal chance of winning. • (*infml*) If someone is **in** a particular **neck of the woods**, they are in a particular place or area: *I'm surprised to see you in this neck of the woods.* • A **neckline** is the shape made by the edge of a dress or shirt at the front of the neck or on the chest: *a low-cut/plunging neckline* • A **necktie** is a **tie**. See at TIE FASTEN.

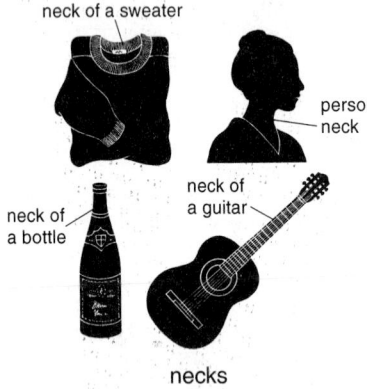

neck of a sweater

person's neck

neck of a guitar

neck of a bottle

necks

neck KISS /nek/ *v* [I] *infml dated* to kiss and hold a person in a sexual way for a length of time

necklace /'nek·ləs/ *n* [C] a piece of jewelry worn around the neck, such as a chain or a string of decorative stones or BEADS

nectar /'nek·tər/ *n* [U] a sweet liquid produced by flowers and collected by bees • *The bee turns nectar into honey.* • Nectar is also a drink made from some fruits: *apricot nectar*

nectarine /ˌnek·təˈriːn/ *n* [C] a type of PEACH (= a fruit) with a smooth skin

née /neɪ/ *adj* [not gradable] used after a woman's married name to show the family name by which she was known before she married • *Anne Timberlake, née Logan*

need MUST HAVE /niːd/ *v* [T] to be necessary to have (something), or to want (something) very much • *To make pastry, you need flour, fat, and water.* ○ *Do we need anything from the store?* ○ *Will I be needed in the office tomorrow?* ○ *I need*

you to advise me on what to wear. ○ *I need a rest.* • (*infml*) If you say that you don't need something, it can mean that you do not want it because it is causing you trouble: *I don't need all this arguing.* • If you say that someone or something needs something, you can mean that they should have it or would benefit from having it: *What you need is some hot soup to warm you up.* ○ *She needs her hair washed.*

need /niːd/ *n* [U] something that you must or should have, or the lack of this • *There's a growing need for low-cost housing.* • Need can be a reason: *I don't think there's any need to worry.* [+ *to* infinitive] • Need is also a feeling or state of greatly wanting something: *a desperate need to be loved* [+ *to* infinitive] ○ *We have no need for your sympathy.* • Need is also the state of being necessary: *Help yourself to supplies as the need arises.* ○ *There's no need to buy any more food.* [+ *to* infinitive] • People who are **in need** do not have enough money or need some type of help: *The money will go to those who are most in need.* • If someone is **in need of** something, they must or should have it: *They're in need of help.* ○ *You look as if you're in need of a bath.*

needs /niːdz/ *pl n* the things you must have for a satisfactory life • *the special needs of the disabled*

needy /'niː·di/ *adj* • If people are needy, they are very poor.

need MUST DO /niːd/ *v* he/she/it **needs** or **need** to have to take an action • *He needs to lose weight.* [+ *to* infinitive] ○ *Before we make a decision, we need to consider our options.* [+ *to* infinitive] ○ *I need to do some shopping on my way home.* [+ *to* infinitive] ○ *I don't think we need ask him.* ○ *Nothing need be done about this before next week.* ○ *As it turned out, I didn't need to buy any extra material* (= I did it, although I didn't have to). [+ *to* infinitive] • *Mike did the cooking—* **need I say more?** (= you know what to expect after I have told you that)

needless /'niːd·ləs/ *adj* [not gradable] completely unnecessary • *a needless waste of time* • People say **needless to say** when making a remark that gives information that is expected and not at all surprising: *Needless to say, because of the accident he won't be at work for a while.*

needlessly /'niːd·lə·sli/ *adv* [not gradable] • *You're worrying needlessly—they'll be fine.*

needle TOOL /'niːd·əl/ *n* [C] a thin, solid, metal piece with a sharp point at one end, esp. one used for sewing that has a hole to hold thread • *Can you thread this needle for me?* • A needle is also any pointed or hooked stick used to make stitches: *knitting needles* • A needle is also a thin metal tube with a sharp pointed end that can be stuck into the skin to put a medicine or drug into the body, or, specifically, the sharp, pointed end. PIC SYRINGE • **A needle in**

neon

a haystack is something that is extremely difficult to find.

needle POINTER /'ni:d·ᵊl/ *n* [C] the thin, moving part on a compass or measuring instrument that points in a particular direction or to a particular value

needle LEAF /'ni:d·ᵊl/ *n* [C] one of the thin, stiff, green leaves of some evergreen trees • *pine needles*

needle ANNOY /'ni:d·ᵊl/ *v* [T] *infml* to purposely annoy (someone) by making critical remarks or jokes • *I hate to be needled about my weight.*

needless /'ni:d·ləs/ *adj* • See at NEED MUST DO.

needlessly /'ni:d·lə·sli/ *adv* • See at NEED MUST DO.

needn't /'ni:d·ᵊnt/ *contraction of* **need not** • *You needn't be shy.*

needs /ni:dz/ *pl n* • See at NEED MUST HAVE.

needy /'ni:d·i/ *adj* • See at NEED MUST HAVE.

negate /nɪ'geɪt/ *v* [T] to show (something) to be wrong or to be the opposite of what was thought, or to cause (something) to have no effect • *The increase in sales was negated by the rising cost of materials.*

negative NO /'neg·ət̬·ɪv/ *adj* expressing no or not, or expressing refusal • *We received a negative answer to our request.* Compare AFFIRMATIVE. • A negative sentence or phrase is one that contains a word such as *no, not, nor, never,* or *nothing.* • A medical test that is negative shows that you do not have that disease or condition. Compare POSITIVE MEDICAL TEST.

negative /'neg·ət̬·ɪv/ *n* [C/U] • *The governor replied in the negative.* [U] • USAGE: The opposite of negative is AFFIRMATIVE.

negative NOT HAPPY /'neg·ət̬·ɪv/ *adj* not happy, hopeful, or approving; tending to consider only bad things • *a negative attitude* ○ *All the candidates in the mayoral campaign ran negative ads* (= advertising saying bad things about each other). • USAGE: The opposite of negative is POSITIVE HAPPY.

negative ELECTRICITY /'neg·ət̬·ɪv/ *adj* [not gradable] of the type of electrical charge carried by ELECTRONS • Compare POSITIVE ELECTRICITY.

negative PHOTOGRAPH /'neg·ət̬·ɪv/ *n* [C] a piece of film in which light areas appear dark and dark areas appear light, the opposite of how they will appear in the photograph made from it

negative LESS THAN ZERO /'neg·ət̬·ɪv/ *adj* [not gradable] (of a number or amount) less than zero • *negative numbers* • USAGE: The opposite of negative is POSITIVE MORE THAN ZERO.

neglect /nɪ'glekt/ *v* [I/T] to fail to give needed care or attention to (someone or something) • *As a smoker and heavy drinker, he had neglected his health for years.* [T] ○ *He neglected to tell his employer that he would be taking the day off.* [I]

neglect /nɪ'glekt/ *n* [U] • *The park was in a sorry state of neglect.*

negligee /ˌneg·lə'ʒeɪ, 'neg·lə,ʒeɪ/ *n* [C] a light, thin, loose piece of women's clothing, worn by someone who is not completely dressed or is dressing

negligent /'neg·lə·dʒənt/ *adj* failing to be careful enough or to give enough attention to your responsibilities, esp. when this results in harm or loss to others

negligence /'neg·lə·dʒəns/ *n* [U] • *She charged her landlord with negligence for not repairing leaks that ruined her rugs.*

negligible /'neg·lɪ·dʒə·bəl/ *adj* too slight or small in amount to be important • *The effect on sales was negligible.*

negotiate DISCUSS /nɪ'goʊ·ʃiː,eɪt/ *v* [I/T] to have formal discussions with someone in order to reach (an agreement) • *We want to negotiate a settlement that is fair to both sides.* [T]

negotiation /nɪ,goʊ·ʃiː'eɪ·ʃən/ *n* [C/U] • *Negotiations remained at a standstill.* [C usually pl]

negotiable /nɪ'goʊ·ʃə·bəl, -ʃiː·ə-/ *adj* • *At this stage, everything is negotiable* (= can be discussed or changed).

negotiator /nɪ'goʊ·ʃiː,eɪt̬·ər/ *n* [C]

negotiate MOVE /nɪ'goʊ·ʃiː,eɪt/ *v* [T] to move carefully or with difficulty past, through, or along (something) • *She was able to negotiate the climb with some help from younger campers.*

Negro /'ni:·groʊ/ *n* [C] *pl* **Negroes** *dated* a person of African origin with dark skin • USAGE: Negro is now considered offensive by most people, and black or African American is used instead. See note at BLACK DARK SKIN.

neigh /neɪ/ *n* [C] a long, loud, high sound that horses make when excited or frightened

neighbor /'neɪ·bər/ *n* [C] someone who lives near you • *Elie is my next-door neighbor.*

neighborhood /'neɪ·bər,hʊd/ *n* [C] an area with characteristics that make it different from other areas, or the people who live in a particular area • *This is a nice, quiet neighborhood, with modest single-family homes.* • *We hope to get something in the neighborhood of* (= at approximately) *$150,000 for our house.*

neighboring /'neɪ·bə·rɪŋ/ *adj* [not gradable] (of places) next or near to each other • *Kentucky and Tennessee are neighboring states.*

neighborly /'neɪ·bər·li/ *adj* friendly and helpful, esp. to those living near by

neither /'ni:·ðər, 'naɪ-/ *adj* [not gradable], *pronoun, conjunction* not one and not the other of two things or people • *They have two TVs but neither one works.* ○ *Neither of my brothers could come to the party.* ○ (*infml*) *"I don't feel like going out tonight." "Me neither."* • Something that is **neither here nor there** is not important, or not connected with the subject being discussed. • LP DETERMINERS

neon /'ni:·ɑn/ *n* [U] a colorless gas, one of the

chemical elements, that is often used in signs because it produces a bright light when an electric current goes through it • *a neon sign*

neonatal /ˌniː·ouˈneɪt̬·əl/ *adj* [not gradable] *medical* of or for babies that were just born • *a nurse specializing in neonatal care*

neophyte /ˈniː·ə̩faɪt/ *n* [C] someone who has recently become involved in an activity and is still learning about it • *This computer course is for neophytes.*

nephew /ˈnef·juː/ *n* [C] a son of someone's brother or sister, or a son of someone's husband's or wife's sister or brother • Compare NIECE. PIC FAMILY TREE

nepotism /ˈnep·ə̩tɪz·əm/ *n* [U] the activity of unfairly give good jobs or advantages to members of your family

Neptune /ˈnep·tuːn/ *n* [U] the planet eighth in order of distance from the sun, after Uranus and before Pluto

nerd /nɜrd/ *n* [C] *infml* a person who lacks social skills, esp. someone interested in technical things • *Gina's brother is a complete nerd.*

nerdy /ˈnɜrd·i/ *adj infml* • *He was a short, nerdy guy with glasses.*

nerve BODY FIBER /nɜrv/ *n* [C] a group of long, thin fibers in the body, esp. in the brain, which send and receive messages that control how the body reacts to signals it receives, such as to changes in temperature or pressure against the skin

nervous /ˈnɜr·vəs/ *adj* • *a nervous condition/ disorder* • An animal's **nervous system** consists of its brain and all the nerves in its body that together make movement and feeling possible.

nerve BRAVERY /nɜrv/ *n* [U] bravery or confidence necessary to do something difficult or unpleasant • *It takes a lot of nerve to get up in front of a class when you're not used to it.* • Nerve also means the ability to do something rude without caring about other people's feelings: *She has some nerve.* • Something that is **nerve-racking/nerve-wracking** is difficult to do and causes you a lot of worry or anxiety: *This was a nerve-racking experience for me, being back in the employment search.*

nervous /ˈnɜr·vəs/ *adj* worried or slightly frightened • *I was nervous during my driving test.* • A **nervous breakdown** is an illness that causes a person to suffer from anxiety and to have difficulty living and working as they usually do.

nerves /nɜrvz/ *pl n* [C] worry or anxiety • *an attack of nerves*

nervously /ˈnɜr·və·sli/ *adv* • *He laughed nervously.*

nest /nest/ *n* [C] a structure or other place where creatures, esp. birds, give birth or leave their eggs to develop • A **nest egg** is money saved or kept for a special purpose.

nest /nest/ *v* [I] • *Swallows are nesting in our apple tree.*

nestle /ˈnes·əl/ *v* [I/T] to be or put (someone or something) into a comfortable or protected position • *She nestled in his arms.* [I]

net MATERIAL /net/ *n* [C] a piece of material made of long, narrow strips woven so that there are spaces between them • *fishing nets* ∘ *a volleyball net* • PIC DUNK

net /net/ *v* [T] **-tt-** (in sports) to hit (the ball) into a net instead of over it • *He netted an easy backhand in the fifth game to lose the tennis match.* • To net is also to catch (something) in a net: *They netted five crabs.*

net LEFT OVER /net/ *adj* [not gradable] (of money received from selling something) left after you have subtracted the cost of what you are selling, and other expenses related to it • *net income/profit* ∘ *(fig.) The net result* (= result after everything has been considered) *of the changes will be fewer trains for most suburban commuters.* • **Net weight** is the weight of something contained in a package, without including the weight of the package.

net /net/ *v* [T] **-tt-** • *Smithsonian, on a gross of $28 million, netted $7 million with one magazine.*

net GET /net/ *v* [T] **-tt-** to succeed in getting (something of value), esp. as the result of a plan of action • *The drug seizure netted the police 606 pounds of cocaine.*

Net COMPUTER SYSTEM /net/ *n* [U] *short form of* INTERNET • Net is also used at the end of US INTERNET addresses to show that the address belongs to a network: *info@sover.net*

network /ˈnet·wɜrk/ *n* [C] a group formed from parts that are connected together • *a transportation network* • A network is also a company that provides programs to a group of television or radio stations, or this company and the group considered together: *the ABC television network* • A network is also a group of computers that are connected and can share information. • A network is also a group of people with the same interests: *a network of political advisers*

network /ˈnet·wɜrk/ *v* [I/T] • To network is also to make an effort to meet and talk to a lot of people, esp. in order to get information that can help you. [I]

networking /ˈnet̩wɜr·kɪŋ/ *n* [U] • Networking is also the process of meeting and talking to a lot of people, esp. in order to get information that can help you: *Students find networking essential to finding the right job.*

neurology /nʊrˈɑl·ə·dʒi/ *n* [U] the study of the structure and diseases of the brain and the nervous system

neurological /ˌnʊr·əˈlɑdʒ·ɪ·kəl/ *adj* [not gradable] • *a neurological disorder*

neurosis /nʊˈrou·səs/ *n* [C] *pl* **neuroses** /nʊˈrou̩siːz/ a mental condition resulting in unreasonable anxiety and unusual behavior

neurotic /nʊˈrɑt̬·ɪk/ *adj* related to or having a

mental condition characterized by unreasonable anxiety or unusual behavior • *a deep-seated neurotic fear of women*

neurotic /nʊˈrɑt̬·ɪk/ *n* [C] a neurotic person

neuter GRAMMAR /ˈnuːt̬·ər/ *adj* [not gradable] *specialized* (in grammar) being a noun or pronoun of a type that refers to things; not MASCULINE or FEMININE

neuter REMOVE SEX ORGANS /ˈnuːt̬·ər/ *v* [T] to remove part of the sex organs of (an animal) so that it cannot reproduce • *We took our dog to the animal hospital to be neutered.*

neutral NO OPINION /ˈnuː·trəl/ *adj* not expressing an opinion or taking actions that support either side in a disagreement or war • *Switzerland remained neutral during the war.*

neutrality /nuːˈtræl·ət̬·i/ *n* [U] the condition of being neutral

neutral NOT BRIGHT /ˈnuː·trəl/ *adj* (of colors) not bright, and therefore not likely to attract attention • *He wanted the office painted in neutral colors.* • In chemistry, a substance that is neutral is neither an acid nor a ALKALI. • In physics, something that is neutral has no electrical charge.

neutralize /ˈnuː·trəˌlaɪz/ *v* [T] to produce an effect that removes the effect of (something else) • *Raising the sales tax will neutralize the tax cut.*

neutron /ˈnuː·ˌtrɑn/ *n* [C] a part of an atom that has no electrical charge • Compare ELECTRON; PROTON.

never /ˈnev·ər/ *adv* [not gradable] not at any time, or not on any occasion • *I've never been to Europe.* ○ *He was never seen again.* ○ *She never had acting lessons* ○ *In all the years I knew him, I never heard him curse.* ○ *Hal Willner? Never heard of him.* ○ *I never forget a face.* • *"I lost that wallet you gave me." "Well, never mind* (= don't worry about it)*, I can always buy you another one."*

nevertheless /ˌnev·ər·ðəˈles/, **nonetheless** *adv* [not gradable] despite what has just been said or referred to • *Their team hadn't lost a game the entire season. Nevertheless, we beat them by a huge margin last night.*

new RECENTLY CREATED /nuː/ *adj* [-er/-est only] recently created or having started to exist recently • *His newest book will be out next month.* ○ *She's always coming up with new ideas.* • A **newborn** is a child or young animal who has recently been born.

newly /ˈnuː·li/ *adv* [not gradable] • *a newly waxed floor* ○ *She plans to begin touring with a newly formed band in July.* • A **newlywed** is someone who has recently married.

newness /ˈnuː·nəs/ *n* [U] • *Kids lose their enthusiasm for things when the sense of newness wears off.*

new DIFFERENT /nuː/ *adj* [-er/-est only] different from the one that existed earlier • *Have you met Carlos's new assistant?* ○ *"What's new* (= What is different in your life)*?" "Not much,*

what's new with you?" • **New Age** beliefs or activities relate to a way of life and thinking that stresses awareness of your inner life: *Meditation, alternative medicine, and astrology are part of the New Age movement.* • **New blood** is people who have just started working or living somewhere who are energetic, enthusiastic, and, often, young: *The new boss brought in some new blood.* • The **New Testament** is the second of the two main parts of the Christian Bible: *The New Testament describes the life and work of Jesus Christ.* Compare **Old Testament** at OLD PREVIOUS . • The **New World** is North, Central, and South America, esp. at the time when people from Europe first began to visit and try to control it. Compare **Old World** at OLD PREVIOUS . • The **New Year** is the beginning of the year that is about to begin or has just begun: *Happy New Year!* • **New Year's Day** is the first day of the year and is a public holiday in many countries. • **New Year's Eve** is the last day of the year, and esp. the evening of the last day, when many people celebrate.

new NOT FAMILIAR /nuː/ *adj* [-er/-est only] not yet familiar or experienced • *Don't ask me how to get there, I'm new around here.* • A **newcomer** is someone who has recently arrived in a place, or a person or organization that has recently become involved in an activity: *The company is a relative newcomer to the personal computer industry.*

new NOT USED /nuː/ *adj* [-er/-est only] not previously used or owned • *They sell new and used cars/books/clothing.*

new RECENTLY DISCOVERED /nuː/ *adj* [-er/-est only] recently discovered or made known • *This new treatment offers hope to many sufferers.* ○ *Astronomers reported finding millions of new stars.* • If someone or something is **newfound**, they have recently happened or been discovered by you: *newfound friends* ○ *newfound respect*

newfangled /ˈnuːˈfæŋ·ɡəld/ *adj* [not gradable] *esp. disapproving* recently created or invented • *I hate those newfangled alarm clocks that buzz.*

news INFORMATION /nuːz/ *n* [U] recent information about people you know • *Why don't you call them and see if there's any news?* ○ *I've got some bad news for you.* ○ *We just heard the good news—congratulations on your engagement!* • *She's expecting a baby? That's news to me* (= I am very surprised).

newsy /ˈnuː·zi/ *adj* full of news • *a long, newsy letter*

news REPORTS /nuːz/ *n* [U] a printed or broadcast report of information about important events in the world, the country, or the local area • *the nightly news* ○ *I'm pretty disgusted with TV news coverage.* ○ *Where were you when the news of the assassination broke?* • A **newscast** is a radio or television program consisting of news reports. A **newscaster** is someone who reads the reports on a television or radio news program. • A **news conference** is a meeting in which someone makes a statement to reporters or answers questions from them. • A **newsletter** is a printed document with information about the activities of a group, sent regularly to members or friends. • A **newspaper** is a regularly printed document consisting of news reports, articles, photographs, and advertisements that are printed on large sheets of paper folded together but not permanently joined. • A **newsstand** is a small structure where newspapers and magazines are sold. • If something is **newsworthy**, it is considered important enough to be in news reports.

newt /nuːt/ *n* [C] a small animal with a long body and tail, short, weak legs, and cold, wet skin; a type of SALAMANDER

next /nekst/ *pronoun, adj* [not gradable] being the first one after the present one or after the one just mentioned, or being the first after the present moment • *Go straight at the traffic light and then take the next right.* ○ *The next time you want to borrow my dress, ask me first.* ○ *She was next in line after me.* ○ *They're getting married next week/month/year.* ○ *The next day/morning we left for Calgary.* • *If I can't have cake, ice cream is the* **next best thing** (= almost as good). • If you live **next door** to someone, no one else's home is between your home and their home: *next-door neighbors* • Something that is **next door** to something else is in the space directly to one side of it: *I can hear everything the guy in the cubicle next door says.* • Someone's **next of kin** are their closest relatives, who will be informed if they die.

next /nekst/ *adv* [not gradable] immediately following in time • *What happened next?* • Two people or things that are **next to** each other are very close to each other with nothing in between them: *My friend and I sat next to each other on the bus.* • Sometimes **next to** means almost: *They pay me next to nothing but I really enjoy the work.*

NFL *n* [U] *abbreviation for* National Football League (= the main organized group of US football teams that have players who are paid for playing)

NHL *n* [U] *abbreviation for* National Hockey League (= the main organized group of US and Canadian HOCKEY teams that have players who are paid for playing)

nibble /ˈnɪb·əl/ *v* [I/T] to eat (something) by taking a lot of small bites • *Ben stopped nibbling his apple.* [T] ○ *Keep vegetables handy to nibble on.* [I] • You can nibble something by moving your teeth against it without eating it: *She nibbled his ear.* [T]

nibble /ˈnɪb·əl/ *n* [C] • (*fig.*) *The real-estate agent says she's gotten some nibbles for our*

house (= some people have expressed interes in it).

nice PLEASANT /naɪs/ *adj* [-*er*/-*est* only] pleasant, enjoyable, or satisfactory • *Have a nic day!* ○ *It was nice talking to you.* ○ *That's a re ally nice restaurant.* ○ *She plans to start run ning more when the weather gets nicer.*

nicely /ˈnaɪ·sli/ *adv* • *That's a nicely tailore jacket.* ○ *Elise and her new baby are both doin nicely* (= They are healthy).

nice KIND /naɪs/ *adj* [-*er*/-*est* only] kind o friendly • *I wish you'd be nice to your brothe* ○ *He's very smart, but he isn't very nice.*

nicely /ˈnaɪ·sli/ *adv* • *Even though I was ne at school, they treated me very nicely.*

niche POSITION /nɪtʃ/ *n* [C] a job, position, o place that is very suitable for someone • *She never quite found her niche on television.*

niche HOLLOW /nɪtʃ/ *n* [C] a hollow made in wall, esp. one designed to put a statue in s that it can be seen

nick /nɪk/ *n* [C] a small cut in a surface or a edge • *The car was covered with nicks anc scratches.* • If something happens **in the nick of time**, it happens at the last possible mo ment: *She fell in the river and was rescued i the nick of time.*

nick /nɪk/ *v* [T] • *He nicked himself shaving*

nickel COIN /ˈnɪk·əl/ *n* [C] (in the US and Can ada) a coin worth five cents

nickel /ˈnɪk·əl/ *v* • If you **nickel and dime** someone, you force them to make many smal payments: *The companies were being nickel and-dimed to death by settling lawsuits all over the country.* • You can also **nickel and dime** someone by making them give their attention to many unimportant things: *The other team just nickel-and-dimed us to death, throwing short passes all afternoon.*

nickel METAL /ˈnɪk·əl/ *n* [U] a silver-white, me tallic element • *Nickel is useful because of its resistance to corrosion.*

nickname /ˈnɪk·neɪm/ *n* [C] an informal name for someone or sometimes something, used esp. to show affection, and often based on their name or a characteristic that they have

nickname /ˈnɪk·neɪm/ *v* [T] • *He was so opti mistic that his staff nicknamed him Twinkle toes.*

nicotine /ˈnɪk·əˌtiːn/ *n* [U] a poisonous chem ical found in tobacco

niece /niːs/ *n* [C] a daughter of someone's brother or sister, or a daughter of someone's husband's or wife's brother or sister • Com pare NEPHEW. PIC FAMILY TREE

nifty /ˈnɪf·ti/ *adj infml* good, pleasing, or effec tive • *What a nifty little gadget—you can use it for all kinds of things.*

nigger /ˈnɪg·ər/ *n* [C] *taboo slang* a black per son • USAGE: This is an extremely offensive word when used to or about a black person by a person who is not black.

niggling /ˈnɪg·lɪŋ/ *adj* (of thoughts, worries,

or details) unimportant but demanding one's attention in an annoying way • *She had no niggling doubts like the ones that plagued me.*

nigh /naɪ/ *adv* [not gradable], *prep literary or dated* near in time or space • *She believes that the end of the world is nigh.*

night /naɪt/ *n* [C/U] the part of every 24-hour period when it is dark because there is no direct light from the sun • *I'll be in Pittsburgh on Tuesday night.* [C] ○ *There was a fire last night in the Tremont section of the Bronx.* [C] ○ *It often gets cold here at night.* [U] • *The howling of the neighbors' dogs kept him awake* **night after night** (= every night). • *He says he wants to be with me* **night and day** (= all the time). • A **nightclub** is a place that is open in the evening where people can go to dance or see musical performances and to drink. • **Nightfall** is the time at the end of the day when it becomes dark. • A **nightgown** is a comfortable piece of clothing like a loose dress worn by a woman or a girl in bed. • **Nightlife** is the entertainment, dancing, and drinking that happen esp. in nightclubs in the evening. • A **nightlight** is a light that is not bright and is left on through the night, esp. for a child. • (*infml*) A **night owl** is a person who prefers to be awake and active at night. • **Night school** is a series of classes held in the evening, esp. for adults who work during the day. • **Nighttime** is the time in every 24-hour period when it is dark. The opposite of nighttime is **daytime**, see at DAY.

nightly /ˈnaɪt·li/ *adj*, *adv* [not gradable] happening every night • *a nightly news program*

nights /naɪts/ *adv* [not gradable] • *She works nights* (= at night) *at the hospital.*

nightmare /ˈnaɪt·mer, -mær/ *n* [C] a very upsetting or frightening dream, or an extremely unpleasant event or experience

nightmarish /ˈnaɪt,mer·ɪʃ, -,mær-/ *adj* • *a nightmarish traffic jam*

nil /nɪl/ *n* [U] nothing • *He went to a dating service in September because his social life was nil.*

nimble /ˈnɪm·bəl/ *adj* quick and exact in movement or thought; AGILE • *a nimble mind* ○ *He tried to catch his friend, but she was too nimble.*

nincompoop /ˈnɪŋ·kəm,puːp/ *n* [C] *infml* a foolish or stupid person

nine /naɪn/ *number* 9 • *My sister is nine.* ○ *a nine-month prison sentence* • Nine can also mean nine o'clock. • LP NUMBERS

ninth /naɪnθ/ *adj*, *adv* [not gradable], *n* [C] • *She currently ranks ninth in the world.* ○ *Election day falls on the ninth of November this year.* [C] • A ninth is one of nine equal parts of something. [C]

nineteen /naɪnˈtiːn, naɪnt-/ *number* 19 • *Nineteen of the passengers were injured.* ○ *a nineteen-car train* • LP NUMBERS

nineteenth /naɪnˈtiːnθ, naɪnt-/ *adj*, *adv* [not gradable], *n* [C] • *I was nineteenth in line to renew my driver's license.* ○ *Our next meeting is on the nineteenth of June.* [C] • A nineteenth is one of nineteen equal parts of something. [C]

ninety /ˈnaɪnt·i, ˈnaɪn·di/ *number* 90 • *Grandma just turned ninety.* ○ *a ninety-year-old woman* • LP NUMBERS

nineties, 90s, 90's /ˈnaɪnt·iːz, ˈnaɪn·diːz/ *pl n* the numbers 90 through 99 • *It's expected to be in the nineties* (= between 90° and 99°) *tomorrow.* ○ *Inflation was held in check in the nineties* (= between 1990 and 1999). ○ *I know only two people in their nineties* (= between 90 and 99 years old).

ninetieth /ˈnaɪnt·i·əθ, ˈnaɪn·diː-/ *adj*, *adv* [not gradable], *n* [C] • *He finished ninetieth in the marathon.* ○ *Mine was the ninetieth signature on the petition.* • A ninetieth is one of ninety equal parts of something. [C]

ninny /ˈnɪn·i/ *n* [C] *infml* a foolish person

ninth /naɪnθ/ *adj*, *adv*, *n* • See at NINE.

nip PRESS /nɪp/ *v* [I/T] **-pp-** to press (something) hard between two often sharp objects, such as teeth or the nails on fingers • *The puppy kept nipping (at) her ankles.* [I/T] • If you **nip** something **in the bud**, you stop it before it has an opportunity to develop: *They searched for a way to nip the spiraling arms race in the bud.*

nip /nɪp/ *n* [C] • If a competition is **nip and tuck**, first one side seems to be winning and then the other, so that the result is uncertain: *The vote was nip and tuck in the mayoral election.*

nip COLD /nɪp/ *n* • A **nip in the air** is a feeling of cold: *There's a real nip in the air this morning.*

nippy /ˈnɪp·i/ *adj* [*-er/-est* only] • *It's a bit nippy outside.*

nipple /ˈnɪp·əl/ *n* [C] the dark part of the skin that sticks out from the breast, and through which females can supply milk to their young

nit /nɪt/ *n* [C] the egg of an insect, esp. a LOUSE

nite /naɪt/ *n* [C] NIGHT

nitpicking /ˈnɪt,pɪk·ɪŋ/ *n* [U] the tendency to look for slight mistakes or faults • *This constant nitpicking is hard on your friends.*

nitrate /ˈnaɪ·treɪt/ *n* [C/U] a chemical that is used esp. as a FERTILIZER (= substance that helps plants grow)

nitrogen /ˈnaɪ·trə·dʒən/ *n* [U] a gas, one of the chemical elements, that has no color or taste, is a part of all living things, and forms about 78 percent of the earth's ATMOSPHERE (= mixture of gases surrounding it)

nitty–gritty /,nɪt·i·ˈɡrɪt·i/ *n* [U] *infml* the basic facts of a situation • *Let's get down to the nitty-gritty of the actual building costs.*

nitwit /ˈnɪt·wɪt/ *n* [C] a foolish or stupid person

nix /nɪks/ *v* [T] *infml* to stop, forbid, or refuse

no 574

to accept (something) • *I hoped to get the day off, but the boss nixed it.*

no NOT ANY /noʊ/ *adj* [not gradable] not any; not one; not a • *There's no butter left.* ○ *No trees grow near the top of the mountain.* ○ *There's no chance of us getting there by eight.* ○ *She no longer writes to me* (= does not continue to write to me). • In signs and official notices, "no" is used to show that something is not allowed: *No hunting/smoking/swimming* • *Now that we're on the interstate highway, we'll be there* in no time (= very quickly). • If there are no/not any buts about it, there is no possibility of doubt, disagreement, or discussion about something: *You are grounded, and there are no buts about it.* • No end means a lot: *The twins were no end of trouble.* • Someone who is no fool is not easily deceived: *The teacher's never going to believe that the dog ate your homework—he's no fool.* • If something is no go, it is impossible or hopeless: *She tried to get into med school, but it was no go.* • No hard feelings means that you are not upset: *Yvonne wanted to show there were no hard feelings over my having won the contest.* • I want no ifs, ands, or buts (= no excuses or doubts)—*just pay up now.* • If something is no joke, it is a difficult or serious matter: *It's no joke when a virus corrupts your computer files.* • No mean means very good: *Getting the job finished so quickly was no mean achievement.* • No news is good news means that you would have been told if anything bad had happened: *We haven't heard anything from the hospital today, but I suppose no news is good news.* • If something is no object, it is not a difficulty that will prevent something from happening: *When he wanted something, money was no object.* • (*infml*) If someone asks you to do something or thanks you for doing it, and you answer no problem, you mean that you can easily do it or that it was not much trouble to do it: *"Can you pick me up at noon?" "No problem."* • If someone says there is no saying/telling, they mean it is not possible to know what will happen: *There's no telling how her parents will react to the news.* • If you are no stranger to something, you are familiar with it: *She's no stranger to hard work.* • (*slang*) If you say that something is no sweat, you do not think it is a difficulty: *"Will you be able to fix the light?" "Yeah, no sweat."* • If something is no use, it has no chance of success: *People tried to stop her, but it was no use.* ○ *I wanted her to like me, but it's no use.* • If you say there are no two ways about it, you mean that there is no doubt about a decision or a situation: *My mom is going to have to come live with us—there's no two ways about it.* • If an action or event happens to no avail, it does not succeed or have any effect: *Many appealed to the governor to spare the life of Johnson, con-*

demned to death, but to no avail. • (*slang*) A **no-brainer** is something so simple or obvious that you do not need to think much about it: *Taking that job over the one I had was a no-brainer.* • If something is **no-frills**, it is basic, without details or extras: *He opted for a no-frills flight to save on expenses.* • **No one** (also **nobody**) means not one person: *There was no one in the room.* • LP AMOUNTS

no NEGATIVE ANSWER /noʊ/ *adv* [not gradable] used to give negative answers • *"Are you hurt?" "No, I'm OK."* ○ *"Would you like some coffee?" "No, thank you."*

no /noʊ/ *n* [C] *pl* **noes** • *The answer is no.* • (*infml*) A **no-no** is something that is thought to be unsuitable or unacceptable: *Wearing shorts to work is a no-no.*

no NOT /noʊ/ *adv* [not gradable] not • *It's no colder today than it was yesterday.* • **No doubt** means certainly: *He will no doubt tell you all about his vacation.* • *Being late for a job interview is* **no laughing matter** (= It is serious). • If something is done **no questions asked**, a person is not questioned about the matter: *If you are not satisfied with your purchase, we will refund your money, no questions asked.* • If something is **no sooner said than done**, it is done immediately: *I asked for it to be delivered, and it was no sooner said than done.* • If **no sooner** had one thing happened **than** a second thing happens, the second thing happens immediately after the first: *No sooner had I started mowing the lawn, than it started raining.* • (*infml*) You say **no way** when you want to emphasize that you mean no or not in any way: *No way was I going to pay that much for an old, beat-up car.* • (*law*) A **no-fault** agreement is one where blame does not have to be proved before action can be taken, esp. paying money: *no-fault insurance* • **No holds barred** means without limits or controls. • A **no-man's-land** is an area or strip of land that no one owns or controls, such as a strip of land between two countries' borders, esp. in a war. • **No-nonsense** means serious and practical: *The manager has a quiet, no-nonsense manner of conducting business.* • A **no-show** is a person who is expected, because they have made arrangements, but does not arrive: *Airlines overbook some flights because they count on a certain number of no-shows.* • When a situation is described as **no-win**, it means success is impossible.

no. NUMBER /ˈnʌm·bər/ *n* [C] *pl* **nos.** *abbreviation for* number

No. NORTH *n* [U], *adj abbreviation for* NORTH or NORTHERN

noble MORAL /ˈnoʊ·bəl/ *adj* having or showing high moral qualities or character • *It was a noble effort to achieve a peaceful settlement to the conflict.*

noble HIGH RANK /ˈnoʊ·bəl/ *adj* [not gradable]

having a high social rank, esp. from birth • *a noble family related to the queen*

noble /ˈnoʊ·bəl/ *n* [C] a person of high social rank, esp. from birth

nobility /noʊˈbɪl·ət̬·i/ *n* [U] the class or group of people who have a high social rank, esp. from birth

nobody /ˈnoʊ·bɑd·i, -ˌbɑd·i/ *pronoun, n* [C] not anyone; no person • *Nobody was around to answer the phone.* ○ *If he can't fix your computer, nobody can.* • A nobody is also someone who is considered unimportant: *There were celebrities there, but I sat between two nobodies.*

nocturnal /nɑkˈtɜrn·əl/ *adj* of the night, or active during the night • *Most bats and owls are nocturnal.*

nod MOVE HEAD /nɑd/ *v* [I/T] **-dd-** to move (the head) down and then up again quickly, esp. to show agreement, approval, or greeting • *The teacher nodded (his head) in agreement.* [I/T]

nod /nɑd/ *n* [C usually sing] • *He gave her a nod of recognition.*

nod SLEEP /nɑd/ *v* [I] **-dd-** to let your head fall forward when you are beginning to sleep • If you **nod off**, you begin to sleep, esp. while sitting up: *I nodded off once or twice during the movie.*

node /noʊd/ *n* [C] a lump of tissue • *a lymph node*

noes /noʊz/ *pl of* NO NEGATIVE ANSWER

noise /nɔɪz/ *n* [C/U] (a) sound, esp. when it is unwanted, unpleasant, or loud • *I heard background noise on the phone line.* [U] ○ *If the washing machine gets out of balance, it makes a horrible noise.* [C]

noisy /ˈnɔɪ·zi/ *adj* [*-er/-est* only] • *The garbage truck is so noisy it wakes me up in the morning.*

nomad /ˈnoʊ·mæd/ *n* [C] a member of a group of people who move from one place to another, rather than living in one place all of the time

nomadic /noʊˈmæd·ɪk/ *adj* • *nomadic people*

nomenclature /ˈnoʊ·mən·kleɪ·tʃər/ *n* [C] a system for naming things, esp. in a particular area of science • *the nomenclature of nuclear physics*

nominal NOT IN REALITY /ˈnɑm·ən·əl/ *adj* [not gradable] in name or thought, but not in reality • *He's the nominal head of the university.*

nominal SMALL /ˈnɑm·ən·əl/ *adj* [not gradable] (of a sum of money) very small compared to an expected price or value • *There is a nominal fee for the workshop.*

nominate /ˈnɑm·ə· neɪt/ *v* [T] to officially suggest (someone) for a position, an honor, or election • *She was nominated by the president to serve on the Supreme Court.* • If someone or something is nominated for a prize, it is one of the official competitors for it.

nomination /ˌnɑm·əˈneɪ·ʃən/ *n* [C/U] • *Three candidates are seeking the Democratic nomination for the presidency.* [U]

nominative /ˈnɑm·ə·nət̬·ɪv/ *adj* [not gradable] *specialized* (in grammar) having or relating to the CASE (= form) of a noun, pronoun, or adjective used to show that a word is the subject of a verb

nominee /ˌnɑm·əˈniː/ *n* [C] a person who has been officially suggested for a position, an honor, or election • *He is a nominee for best actor.*

non– /nɑn/ *combining form* used to add the meaning "not" to adjectives and nouns • *non-alcoholic* ○ *nonflammable* ○ *nonpartisan*

nonchalant /ˌnɑn·ʃəˈlɑnt/ *adj* [not gradable] behaving in a calm manner, showing that you are not worried or frightened • *She waited her turn to audition, trying to look nonchalant.*

nonchalance /ˌnɑn·ʃəˈlɑns/ *n* [U]

nonchalantly /ˌnɑn·ʃəˈlɑnt·li/ *adv* [not gradable] • *Once on a safari Charles found 14 female lions walking nonchalantly across an open field.*

noncombatant /ˌnɑn·kəmˈbæt·ənt/ *n* [C] a person who is part of a military group, but whose job does not include fighting • *Medics, chaplains, and other noncombatants were part of the regiment.*

noncommittal /ˌnɑn·kəˈmɪt̬·əl/ *adj* [not gradable] not expressing a clear opinion or decision • *The ambassador was noncommittal about the introduction of further sanctions.*

nonconformist /ˌnɑn·kəmˈfɔːr·məst/ *n* [C] a person who does not live and think according to accepted customs and standards

nondescript /ˌnɑn·dɪˈskrɪpt/ *adj* [not gradable] having no interesting or unusual features; ordinary • *A nondescript couple sat next to her in the waiting room.*

none /nʌn/ *pronoun* not one, or not any • *None of my children has blue eyes.* ○ *"Is there any more wine?" "I'm sorry there's none left."* • You can say **none other (than)** someone or something) when you want to emphasize that they are a special or surprising choice: *The speech was given by none other than the vice president.*

none /nʌn/ *adv* [not gradable] • If you are **none the wiser**, you are not any wiser: *I read the computer manual, but I'm still none the wiser.* • **None the worse** means no worse because of something: *It was cold and windy during the parade but it was none the worse for that.* • **None too** means not very: *He seemed none too happy at the prospect of meeting the family.*

nonentity /nɑnˈent·ət̬·i/ *n* [C] a person or thing of no importance • *It's a low-budget film full of nonentities.*

nonetheless /ˌnʌn·ðəˈles/ *adv* [not gradable] despite what has just been said or referred to; NEVERTHELESS • *There are risks, but nonetheless, we feel it's a sound investment.*

nonexistent /ˌnɑn·ɪgˈzɪs·tənt/ *adj* [not gradable] completely absent • *Crime is virtually nonexistent around here.*

nonfiction /ˌnɑnˈfɪk·ʃən/ *n* [U] the type of book or other writing that deals with facts about real people or events, not imaginary stories • Compare FICTION.

nonflammable /nɑnˈflæm·ə·bəl/ *adj* not able to burn • *nonflammable clothing*

nonpayment /ˈnɑnˈpeɪ·mənt/ *n* [U] failure to pay an amount that is expected • *He has a long record of nonpayment of traffic violations.*

nonplussed /nɑnˈplʌst/ *adj* surprised, confused, and not certain how to react • *The aggressive questioning at the job interview left her nonplussed.*

nonprofit /ˈnɑnˈprɑf·ət/ *adj* [not gradable] not established to make a profit • *nonprofit organizations*

nonproliferation /ˌnɑn·prə‚lɪf·ə·reɪˈʃən/ *n* [U] the effort to stop the increase in nuclear weapons

nonsectarian /ˌnɑn‚sekˈter·iː·ən/ *adj* [not gradable] not associated with any specific religion • *The court permitted graduation prayers provided they were nonsectarian.*

nonsense /ˈnɑn·sens, -sɑns/ *n* [U] foolish words or actions • *Those accusations are pure/sheer nonsense.* ○ *What's all this nonsense about quitting school?* • Nonsense is also language that cannot be understood or that has no meaning.

nonsensical /nɑnˈsen·sɪ·kəl/ *adj* [not gradable]

non sequitur /nɑnˈsek·wət·ər/ *n* [C] a statement that does not reasonably relate to the previous statement

nonsmoker /nɑnˈsmoʊ·kər/ *n* [C] a person who does not smoke cigarettes or other tobacco products

nonsmoking /nɑnˈsmoʊ·kɪŋ/ *adj* [not gradable] (of a place) where smoking is not permitted • *Let's sit in the nonsmoking section.*

nonstandard /nɑnˈstæn·dərd/ *adj* [not gradable] not standard; different from a standard, and often considered not correct • *"Drownded" is a nonstandard pronunciation for "drowned."*

nonstop /ˈnɑnˈstɑp/ *adj, adv* [not gradable] (of travel) without any stops, or (of an action) done without stopping • *We got on a nonstop flight from New York to Denver.* ○ *He talked nonstop about his new book.*

nonviolent /nɑnˈvaɪ·ə·lənt/ *adj* [not gradable] not using violent methods, esp. to cause a political or social change • *The protest demonstration was nonviolent, although the marchers were heckled throughout by onlookers.*

nonviolence /nɑnˈvaɪ·ə·ləns/ *n* [U] the use of methods that are not violent to cause a political or social change

nonwhite /nɑnˈhwaɪt, -ˈwaɪt/ *adj* [not gradable] not belonging to a race that has pale skin

noodle /ˈnuːd·əl/ *n* [C usually pl] a long, thin strip of pasta made from flour, water, and sometimes eggs, and cooked esp. in boiling water or soup

nook /nʊk/ *n* [C] *literary* a small space that is hidden or partly sheltered • Every **nook and cranny** means every part of a place: *Every nook and cranny of the house was stuffed with souvenirs from trips abroad.*

noon /nuːn/ *n* [U] 12 o'clock in the middle of the day; MIDDAY • *My first class is at noon.* • ⓁⓅ TIME

no one /ˈnoʊ·wən, -wʌn/ *pronoun* not any person • *I called twice, but no one answered.*

noontime /ˈnuːn·taɪm/ *n* [U], *adj* [not gradable] (happening at) noon • *He frequents the restaurant at noontime.*

noose /nuːs/ *n* [C] one end of a rope tied to form a circle which can be tightened around something, such as a person's neck to HANG them (= kill them)

nope /noʊp/ *adv* [not gradable] *infml* (esp. used in spoken answers) no • *"Are you coming along?" "Nope."*

nor /nɔːr, nər/ *conjunction* used before the second or last of a series of negative possibilities that usually begin with "neither" • *Neither Michael nor his wife was injured in the crash.*

nor'easter /nɔːrˈiː·stər/ *n* [C] **northeaster**, see at NORTHEAST

norm /nɔːrm/ *n* [C] an accepted standard or a way of being or doing things • *Illness has become the norm for her.*

normal /ˈnɔːr·məl/ *adj* ordinary or usual; as would be expected • *He seemed perfectly normal to me.* ○ *The temperature is above/below normal today.*

normality /nɔːrˈmæl·ət·i/, **normalcy** /ˈnɔːr·məl·si/ *n* [U] the state of being normal

normalize /ˈnɔːr·mə‚laɪz/ *v* [I/T] to return to the normal, usual, or generally accepted situation • *They hope to normalize relations with the US.* [T]

normally /ˈnɔːr·mə·li/ *adv* usually or regularly • *She doesn't normally stop working to have lunch.*

north /nɔːrθ/ (*abbreviation* **N.**, **No.**) *n* [U] the direction that is opposite south, or the part of an area or country which is in this direction • *The points of the compass are north, south, east, and west.* • In the US, the North is the part of the country in the north and east: *Ken grew up in Mississippi but settled in the North after college.* • In the US Civil War, the North was the group of states that fought to keep the US together.

north /nɔːrθ/ (*abbreviation* **N.**, **No.**) *adj, adv* [not gradable] • *the north coast* ○ *She lives about forty miles north of here.* • The **North Pole** is the point on the earth's surface that is farthest north. • A **north wind** is a wind coming from the north.

northerly /ˈnɔːr·ðər·li/ *adj* toward or near the north • *a northerly route*

northern /ˈnɔːr·ðərn/ (*abbreviation* **N.**, **No.**) *adj* [not gradable] • *Tom lives in the northern part of the state.* • The **Northern Lights** are patterns of colors that can be seen at night in skies over the most northerly parts of the world.

northerner /'nɔːr·ðər·nər, -ðə·nər/ *n* [C] a person from the northern part of a country, or (in the US) a person from the part of the country in the north and east

northward /'nɔːrθ·wərd/ *adj* [not gradable] toward the north • *northward migration*

northward /'nɔːrθ·wərd/, **northwards** /'nɔːrθ·wərdz/ *adv* [not gradable] • *He headed northward.*

northeast /nɔːr'θiːst/ (*abbreviation* **N.E.**) *n* [U] the direction between north and east, or the part of an area or country which is in this direction • *A snowstorm brought an inch of snow to the northeast.*

northeast /nɔːr'θiːst/ (*abbreviation* **N.E.**) *adj, adv* [not gradable] • *Betsy lives in the northeast corner of Vermont.*

northeastern /nɔːr'θiː·stərn/ (*abbreviation* **N.E.**) *adj* [not gradable] • *northeastern Arizona*

northeaster /nɔːr'iː·stər, nɔːrθ-/, **nor'easter** /nɔːr'iː·stər/ *n* [C] a storm with northeast winds, or a strong wind coming from the northeast

northwest /nɔːrθ'west/ (*abbreviation* **N.W.**) *n* [U] the direction between north and west, or the part of an area or country which is in this direction • *Seattle is in the northwest.*

northwest /nɔːrθ'west/ (*abbreviation* **N.W.**) *adj, adv* [not gradable] • *The plane crashed six miles northwest of the airport.*

northwestern /nɔːrθ'wes·tərn/ (*abbreviation* **N.W.**) *adj* [not gradable] • *northwestern Mexico*

nose BODY PART /noʊz/ *n* [C] the part of a person's or animal's face above the mouth through which they breathe and smell • *Kate wrinkled her nose* (= contracted the muscles in her nose to show disgust or annoyance). ○ *I have a runny nose* (= liquid coming out of the nose). ○ *She blew her nose* (= breathed out powerfully through the nose to clear it). • (*infml*) If you have your **nose to the grindstone**, you work very hard without resting: *After a year of keeping your nose to the grindstone, you finally get a vacation.* • If a statement or number is **on the nose**, it is exactly correct or the exact amount: *He weighs 174 pounds on the nose.* • (*infml*) If you **stick/poke/put** your **nose into** something, you try to discover things which do not involve you: *You're always sticking your nose into my business.* • A **nosebleed** is a condition in which blood comes out of a person's nose. • USAGE: The related adjective is NASAL. PIC BRIDGE

nose FRONT /noʊz/ *n* [C] the front of a vehicle, esp. an aircraft or spacecraft

nose /noʊz/ *v* [always + adv/prep] to move forward slowly and carefully • *The car nosed out into traffic.* [I]

nose SEARCH /noʊz/ *v* [I always + adv/prep] *infml* to look around or search in order to discover something, esp. something that other people do not want you to find • *I don't want you nosing around in my drawers.*

nosedive /'noʊz·dɑɪv/ *n* [C] (esp. of an aircraft) a fast and sudden fall to the ground with the front pointing down • (*fig.*) *Stock prices took a nosedive* (= a sudden fall in value).

nosedive /'noʊz·dɑɪv/ *v* [I] • (*fig.*) *Profits nosedived in the last quarter.*

nosh /nɑʃ/ *n* [U] *infml* a small amount of food eaten between meals or as a meal

nosh /nɑʃ/ *v* [I] *infml* • *We noshed on pretzels during the game.*

nostalgia /nə'stæl·dʒə, nə-; nə'stɑl-/ *n* [U] a feeling of pleasure and sometimes slight sadness at the same time as you think about things that happened in the past • *Hearing her voice again filled him with nostalgia.*

nostalgic /nə'stæl·dʒɪk, nə-; nə'stɑl-/ *adj* • *Jenny grew nostalgic for home on Thanksgiving day.*

nostril /'nɑs·trəl/ *n* [C] either of the two openings in the nose through which air moves

nosy, **nosey** /'noʊ·zi/ *adj* too interested in what other people are doing and wanting to discover too much about them • *I was a nosy kid.*

not /nɑt/ *adv* [not gradable] used to make a word or group of words negative, or to give a word or words an opposite meaning • *Her life was not happy.* ○ *If it's not yours, whose is it?* ○ *He's not bad-looking* (= He is attractive). • When answering questions, **not at all** and **not in the least** mean I do not: *"Do you mind if I sit here?" "Not at all."* • If something is **not much**, it is not very good or important, or not interesting or attractive: *My car's not much to look at, but it runs well.* • *She was not only an inspiring teacher but* (**also**) *a brilliant researcher* (= she was both these things). • If someone is **not** them**self** they do not feel well or are acting strangely: *Pay no attention to her, she's just not herself today.* • **Not that** *I mind* (= I do not mind), *but why didn't you call yesterday?* • People say **not to mention** before adding something to a discussion to emphasize that it should be considered: *Bananas were scarce, not to mention mangoes.* • A **not-too-distant** time is one in the near future or recent past: *They plan to have children in the not-too-distant future.* • LP CONTRACTIONS OF VERBS

notable /'noʊt̬·ə·bəl/ *adj* important and deserving attention • *She worked with many notable musicians.*

notably /'noʊt̬·ə·bli/ *adv* • *Other sports have had work stoppages, most notably baseball.*

notary (public) /'noʊt̬·ə·ri ('pʌb·lɪk)/ *n* [C] *pl* **notaries (public)** *law* an official who has the legal authority to say that documents are correctly signed or truthful

notarize /'noʊt̬·ə,rɑɪz/ *v* [T] *law* • *Do these signatures have to be notarized?*

notation /nou'teɪ·ʃən/ n [C/U] a system of written symbols, used esp. in mathematics or to represent musical notes, or a short piece of writing • *musical notation* [U] ○ *Make notations on the card.* [C]

notch CUT /natʃ/ n [C] a cut in a hard surface • *The rope had jammed in a V-shaped notch.*
notch /natʃ/ v [T] • *He notched the end of the beam.*

notch POSITION /natʃ/ n [C] an imaginary point or position in a comparison of amounts or values; degree • *Suddenly he raised his voice a notch.*

notch RECORD /natʃ/ v [T] to achieve or keep a record of (something) • *Her band notched another Grammy Award last night.*

note WRITING /nout/ n [C] a short piece of writing • *a handwritten note* ○ *Make a note to phone him* (= Write it down so you remember). • **Notes** are written information: *Be sure to take notes in class.* • A **notebook** is a book of paper for writing on: *She wrote everything down in her notebook.* See also NOTEBOOK.

note SOUND /nout/ n [C] a single sound, esp. in music, or a written symbol which represents this sound • *(fig.) The meeting ended on an optimistic note* (= it had this feeling).

musical notes

handwritten note

notes

note *(obj)* NOTICE /nout/ v to take notice of, give attention to, or make a record of (something) • *Please note that we will be closed on Saturday.* [+ *that* clause]

note IMPORTANCE /nout/ n • If something is **of note**, it has importance or fame: *There was nothing of note in the report.*

noted /'nout·əd/ adj • *a noted scholar*

notebook /'nout·buk/ n [C] a small, light computer about the size and shape of a book • See also **notebook** at NOTE WRITING.

noteworthy /'nout,wɜr·ði/ adj deserving attention because of being important or interesting • *Two noteworthy films open this week.*

nothing /'nʌθ·ɪŋ/ pronoun not anything • *There's nothing in the drawer—I took every-*

thing out. ○ *Money means nothing to him* (= is not important). ○ *The score is Yankees three, Red Sox nothing* (= no points). • People say something is nothing as a polite answer when they are thanked: *"Thanks for the tickets." "Oh, it's nothing."* • The story was **nothing but** (= only) *lies.* • **Nothing less than** is used to emphasize how important or desirable something is: *Her dream was nothing less than to become a star.* • *"What's up?" "Nothing much* (= Very little)*."* • *Dinner was nothing special* (= neither very good nor very bad)*.* If something is **nothing** to someone, it has little meaning or value to them: *Losing a thousand bucks is nothing to him.* • If someone or something has **nothing to do with** something else, they are not involved with it: *That has nothing to do with me.* • If you say that something, esp. an amount of money, is **nothing to sneeze at**, you mean that it is a large enough amount to be worth having: *An extra two thousand bucks a year is nothing to sneeze at.*

nothing /'nʌθ·ɪŋ/ adv [not gradable] • *Instant coffee is OK, but it's nothing like* (= not as good as) *the real thing.* • *The party was nothing short of/nothing less than* (= it was) *a disaster.*

nothingness /'nʌθ·ɪŋ·nəs/ n [U] a state or place where nothing is present, or where nothing important is present

notice SEE /'nout·əs/ v to become aware of, esp. by looking; to see • *Mary waved but he didn't seem to notice.* [I] ○ *He noticed that she was staring at him.* [+ *that* clause]

notice /'nout·əs/ n [U] slightly fml • *Twain first attracted notice* (= attention) *as a humorist.*

noticeable /'nout·ə·sə·bəl/ adj easy to see and recognize • *There's a noticeable improvement in your grades.*

noticeably /'nout·ə·sə·bli/ adv • *It's gotten noticeably colder this week.*

notice INFORMATION /'nout·əs/ n [C/U] something written or printed that gives information or instructions • *We got a notice about recycling in the mail.* [C] ○ *This building is closed until further notice* (= until official instructions are given). [U] • Notice is also warning that something will happen or needs to happen: *I can't cancel my plans on such short notice/at a moment's notice* (= immediately). [U] • Notice is also an official statement saying you are leaving your job or telling you your job has ended: *I got my 30-day notice yesterday at work.* [U]

notify /'nout·ə,faɪ/ v [T] to tell (someone) officially about something • *Contest winners will be notified by postcard.*

notification /,nout·ə·fə'keɪ·ʃən/ n [C/U] • *Final notification should reach teachers by March 15.* [U]

notion /'nou·ʃən/ n [C] a belief or idea • *Nast*

helped form the American notion of Santa Claus.

notoriety /ˌnoʊt̬·əˈraɪ·ət̬·i/ *n* [U] the state of being famous for doing something, esp. something immoral or bad • *He gained notoriety for his erotic poetry.*

notorious /nəˈtɔːr·iː·əs, -ˈtoʊr-/ *adj* famous for something immoral or bad • *The canal is notorious for its pollution.*

notoriously /nəˈtɔːr·iː·ə·sli, -ˈtoʊr-/ *adv*

notwithstanding /ˌnɑt·wɪθˈstæn·dɪŋ, -wɪð-/ *prep, adv* not considering or being influenced by; despite • *Injuries notwithstanding, this season has been a disappointment to me.*

noun /naʊn/ *n* [C] *specialized* (in grammar) a word that refers to a person, place, thing, event, substance, or quality • *"Doctor," "party," and "beauty" are nouns.*

nourish /ˈnɜr·ɪʃ, ˈnʌ·rɪʃ/ *v* [T] to provide (people or animals) with food in order to make them grow and keep them healthy

nourishing /ˈnɜr·ɪ·ʃɪŋ, ˈnʌ·rɪ·ʃɪŋ/ *adj* • *Candy isn't very nourishing.*

nourishment /ˈnɜr·ɪʃ·mənt, ˈnʌ·rɪʃ-/ *n* [U] • *A young baby gets its nourishment from its mother's milk.*

novel BOOK /ˈnɑv·əl/ *n* [C] a long, printed story about imaginary characters and events • *literary/romance novels*

novelist /ˈnɑv·əl·əst/ *n* [C] a person who writes novels

novel NEW /ˈnɑv·əl/ *adj* new and original; not like anything seen before • *a novel idea/suggestion*

novelty /ˈnɑv·əl·ti/ *n* [C/U] the quality of being new or unusual, or a new or unusual experience • *The novelty of the toys soon wore off.* [U]

November /noʊˈvem·bər/ (*abbreviation* **Nov.**) *n* [C/U] the eleventh month of the year, after October and before December

novice /ˈnɑv·əs/ *n* [C] a person who is beginning to learn a job or an activity and has little or no experience or skill in it • *I'm just a novice at making videos.*

now AT PRESENT /naʊ/ *adv* [not gradable] at the present time rather than in the past or future, or immediately • *She used to work in an office, but now she works at home.* ○ *It's now 7 o'clock, time to get up or you'll be late for work.* • Just now means either a very short time ago or at the present time: *I can't stop to talk just now, but give me a call when you get home.* • If you do something (every) now and then/again, you do it sometimes but not very often: *We still meet for lunch now and then, but not as often as we used to.*

now /naʊ/ *n* [U] the present moment or time • *That's all for now* (= until a future point in time). ○ *From now on* (= Starting at this moment and continuing in the future), *the front door will be locked at midnight.*

now (that) /ˈnaʊ (ðət)/ *conjunction* • You use

now that to give an explanation of a new situation: *Now that I live only a few blocks from work, I walk to work and enjoy it.*

now IN SPEECH /naʊ/ *adv* [not gradable] used in statements and questions to introduce or give emphasis to what you are saying • *Now where was I before you interrupted me?* • You say **now, now** to someone when you want to make them feel better or give them a gentle warning: *Now, now, don't cry.*

nowadays /ˈnaʊ·əˌdeɪz/ *adv* [not gradable] at the present time, in comparison to the past • *Nowadays people don't dress up as much as they used to.*

nowhere /ˈnoʊ·hwer, -wer, -ˈhwær, -wær/ *adv* [not gradable] in, at, or to no place; not anywhere • *Nowhere in the statement did he apologize for what he had done.* ○ *Nowhere else will you find such wonderful beaches.* • If you **get/go nowhere (fast)** you completely fail to achieve something: *He was trying to persuade her to let him drive, but he was getting nowhere fast.* • **Nowhere near** means far from (something) or not nearly: *The surgery had already been going on for eight hours, and it was nowhere near finished.* • If someone or something is **nowhere to be found**, you cannot see them: *We looked for her everywhere, but she was nowhere to be found.*

noxious /ˈnɑk·ʃəs/ *adj* (esp. of a gas) poisonous or harmful • *noxious gases*

nozzle /ˈnɑz·əl/ *n* [C] a narrow piece attached to the end of a tube so that the liquid or air that comes out can be directed in a particular way • *Attach the nozzle to the garden hose before turning on the water.*

nuance /ˈnuː·ɑns/ *n* [C] a quality of something that is not easy to notice but may be important • *Actors have to study the nuances of facial expression to show the whole range of emotions.*

nuclear /ˈnuː·kliː·ər, *not standard* ˈnuː·kjə·lər/ *adj* [not gradable] of or relating to a process by which the NUCLEUS (= central part) of an atom is divided or joined to another nucleus, resulting in the release of energy, which can be used to produce power, such as electricity, or to produce weapons • *a nuclear reaction* ○ *nuclear power* • **Nuclear disarmament** is the giving up or removing of a country's nuclear weapons. • **Nuclear waste** is the unwanted RADIOACTIVE material made when producing nuclear power. • A **nuclear reactor** is a large device that produces nuclear energy.

nucleus /ˈnuː·kliː·əs/ *n* [C] *pl* **nuclei** /ˈnuː·kliːˌaɪ/ the central part of something • People or things that form the nucleus of something are the most important part of it: *These two people will form the nucleus of a new management team to promote sales in South America.* • In physics, a nucleus is the central part of an atom. • In biology, a nucleus is the part of a cell that controls its growth.

nuclear /ˈnuːˌkli·ər, *not standard* ˈnuːˌkjə·lər/ *adj* • A **nuclear family** is two parents and their children: *In earlier times children usually grew up near their aunts, uncles, cousins, and grandparents, but now a nuclear family is likely to have no other relatives nearby.* • Compare **extended family** at EXTEND ⟨REACH⟩.

nude /nuːd/ *adj* [not gradable] not wearing any clothes • *As a young actress she posed nude for a magazine.*

nude /nuːd/ *n* [C] a picture or other piece of art showing a person who is not wearing any clothes • If you are **in the nude**, you are not wearing any clothes: *The model for our art class posed in the nude.*

nudist /ˈnuːd·əst/ *n* [C] a person who believes that not wearing clothes is healthy and who is often part of a group of people who meet to practice their belief • *a private beach for nudists*

nudity /ˈnuːd·əţ·i/ *n* [U] the state of wearing no clothes • *There is brief nudity in the movie but not a lot of sex.*

nudge /nʌdʒ/ *v* [T] to push (someone or something) gently, sometimes to get someone's attention • *My wife nudged me to tell me to get off the phone so that she could use it.*

nudge /nʌdʒ/ *n* [C] • *I gave him a nudge to wake him up.*

nugget /ˈnʌɡ·ət/ *n* [C] a small, unevenly shaped lump, esp. of gold • *a gold nugget*

nuisance /ˈnuː·səns/ *n* [C] something or someone that annoys you or causes trouble for you • *It's a nuisance filling out all these forms.*

nuke /nuːk/ *v* [T] *infml* to bomb with nuclear weapons • (*slang*) To nuke (food) is to cook it in a MICROWAVE OVEN.

nuke /nuːk/ *n* [C] *infml* a nuclear weapon • *Signs reading "No nukes!" were everywhere.*

null and void /ˈnʌl·ənd·ˈvɔɪd/ *adj* [not gradable] *law* (of an agreement or contract) having no legal effect and to be considered therefore as if it did not exist

nullify /ˈnʌl·ə,fɑɪ/ *v* [T] to cause (an agreement or result) to be no longer effective or consider it as not existing • *The referee nullified the goal.*

numb /nʌm/ *adj* [-er/-est only] (of a part of the body) unable to feel anything • *My fingers are so cold, they're numb.* • If you are numb with a strong emotion, you are not able to feel anything else or to think clearly: *At the sound of breaking glass, she went numb with fear.*

numbness /ˈnʌm·nəs/ *n* [U]

number ⟨SYMBOL⟩ /ˈnʌm·bər/ (*abbreviation* **no.**) *n* [C] a unit or its symbol that forms part of a system of counting and calculating, and that represents an amount or position in a series • *You can write numbers in words, such as six, seven, and eight, or with symbols, such as 6, 7, and 8.* • A number is also a specific set of symbols in a particular order that represent someone or something so that they can be recognized: *Please put down your Social Security number.* • A number can also be a position in a series: *We're up to 10—who has the next number?* • (*infml*) If someone's **number is up**, they are going to die: *When the plane started to shake, Charles thought his number was up.* • (*slang*) **Number crunching** is mathematical work, usually that takes a long time, and is performed either by people or by computers: *I'm only a number cruncher in the accounting department.* • A person or organization that is **number one** is the best: *She's still number one in tennis.*

number /ˈnʌm·bər/ *v* [T] to give a different number to (each of two or more things), esp. in a particular order • *The software automatically numbers the footnotes.*

number ⟨AMOUNT⟩ /ˈnʌm·bər/ *n* [C/U] an amount or total • *A large number of tickets were sold almost immediately.* [C] ○ *Large numbers of people* (= A lot of people) *crowded the streets.* [C] ○ *Quite a number of* (= Many) *cases of the flu have been reported already.* [U] • A **number of** things is several of them: *There were a number of causes for the accident.* [U] • **Any number of** things is a lot of them: *He'd already heard any number of excuses.* [U]

number /ˈnʌm·bər/ *v* [L] to be (a total) • *The crowd numbered over 100,000.*

number ⟨SONG⟩ /ˈnʌm·bər/ *n* [C] a song, dance, or other part in a performance • *The last number she sang was a beautiful, slow ballad.*

numeral /ˈnuː·mə·rəl/ *n* [C] a symbol that represents a number • *the numeral 5*

numerator /ˈnuː·mə,reɪţ·ər/ *n* [C] a number above the line in a FRACTION (= a division of a whole number) • *In the fraction ¾, 3 is the numerator.* • Compare DENOMINATOR. ⟨LP⟩ FRACTIONS AND DECIMALS

numerical /nuːˈmer·ɪ·kəl/ *adj* [not gradable] involving or expressed in numbers • *numerical ability* ○ *Keep your files in numerical order.*

numerous /ˈnuː·mə·rəs/ *adj* many • *She is the author of three books and numerous articles.*

nun /nʌn/ *n* [C] a member of a female religious group whose members promise to obey the orders of the leader of the group and not to marry

nuptial /ˈnʌp·ʃəl, -tʃəl/ *adj* [not gradable] *fml* relating to marriage • *nuptial vows*

nuptials /ˈnʌp·ʃəlz, -tʃəlz/ *pl n fml* a marriage ceremony; a wedding • *The nuptials will take place in a church in the bride's home town.*

nurse ⟨PERSON⟩ /nɜrs/ *n* [C] a person trained to care for people who are sick or not able to care for themselves because of injury or old age, and who may also help doctors in treating people • *The hospital has at least five nurses on duty in the pediatrics ward all the time.*

nurse /nɜrs/ *v* [T] to care for (someone) when they are sick or cannot care for themselves because of injury or old age • *After my mother's operation, she stayed with us for a while until*

NUMBERS

Cardinal Numbers		Ordinal Numbers	
SYMBOL	WORD	SYMBOL	WORD
0	zero		
1	one	1st	first
2	two	2nd	second
3	three	3rd	third
4	four	4th	fourth
5	five	5th	fifth
6	six	6th	sixth
7	seven	7th	seventh
8	eight	8th	eighth
9	nine	9th	ninth
10	ten	10th	tenth
11	eleven	11th	eleventh
12	twelve	12th	twelfth
13	thirteen	13th	thirteenth
14	fourteen	14th	fourteenth
15	fifteen	15th	fifteenth
16	sixteen	16th	sixteenth
17	seventeen	17th	seventeenth
18	eighteen	18th	eighteenth
19	nineteen	19th	nineteenth
20	twenty	20th	twentieth
21	twenty-one	21st	twenty-first
22	twenty-two	22nd	twenty-second
23	twenty-three	23rd	twenty-third
30	thirty	30th	thirtieth
40	forty	40th	fortieth
50	fifty	50th	fiftieth
60	sixty	60th	sixtieth
70	seventy	70th	seventieth
80	eighty	80th	eightieth
90	ninety	90th	ninetieth
100	one hundred *infml* a hundred	100th	(one) hundredth *infml* a hundredth
101	one hundred (and) one *infml* a hundred (and) one	101st	(one) hundred (and) first *infml* a hundred (and) first
110	one hundred (and) ten *infml* a hundred (and) ten	110th	(one) hundred (and) tenth *infml* a hundred (and) tenth
200	two hundred	200th	two hundredth
1000	one thousand *infml* a thousand	1000th	one thousandth *infml* a thousandth
1001	one thousand (and) one *infml* a thousand (and) one	1001st	one thousand (and) first *infml* (a) thousand (and) first
1200	one thousand two hundred twelve hundred	1200th	twelve hundredth
2000	two thousand	2000th	two thousandth
10,000	ten thousand	10,000th	ten thousandth
100,000	one hundred thousand *infml* a hundred thousand	100,000th	one hundred thousandth *infml* a hundred thousandth
1,000,000	one million *infml* a million	1,000,000th	one millionth *infml* a millionth
1,000,000,000	one billion *infml* a billion	1,000,000,000th	one billionth *infml* a billionth

Cardinal numbers are used in counting and to refer to amounts

the ten most popular magazines • All fifty states were affected.

Ordinal numbers show the order of something, or its position in a series

They're celebrating their fiftieth wedding anniversary. • It's on the corner of Broadway and 116th Street. • We live on the second floor.

LP Zero

we nursed her back to health. • If you nurse (an injury), you rest it to help it get better: *Robert stayed home today, nursing a bad back.*

nursing /'nɜr·sɪŋ/ *n* [U] the job of being a nurse • *She studied nursing at Northwestern University.* • A **nursing home** is a place where old people live and receive care when they can no longer care for themselves, and where people who have recently had operations may stay temporarily.

nurse [FEED A BABY] /nɜrs/ *v* [I/T] (of a woman) to feed (a baby) from the breast, or (of a baby) to drink from a woman's breast • *I'm planning to nurse (the baby) for at least three months.* [I/T]

nurse [LAST LONGER] /nɜrs/ *v* [T] to make (something) last a long time • *He sat at the bar, nursing his drink, hoping Lisa would show up.*

nursery [CHILD CARE] /'nɜr·sə·ri/ *n* [C] a place where young children and babies are cared for while their parents are somewhere else • *The store has a nursery where you can leave your children while you shop.* • (*dated*) A nursery is also a child's room in a house. • A **nursery rhyme** is a short poem or song for young children. • A **nursery school** is a school for children between about three and five years old.

[LP] EDUCATION IN THE US

nursery [PLANTS] /'nɜr·sə·ri/ *n* [C] a place where plants and trees are grown, usually for sale

nurture /'nɜr·tʃər/ *v* [T] to feed and care for (a child), or to help (someone or something) develop by encouraging them • *As a record company director, his job is to nurture young talent.*

nut [FOOD] /nʌt/ *n* [C] the dry fruit of some trees, consisting of an edible seed within a hard, outer shell, or the seed itself • A **nutcracker** is a tool for breaking the shell of a nut, so that you can get to the softer, edible part inside.

nutty /'nʌt̬·i/ *adj* [-er/-est only] • *a nutty flavor*

nut [METAL OBJECT] /nʌt/ *n* [C] a small ring of metal that a BOLT (= a screwlike object) can be screwed into to hold something in place • *a wing nut* (= a nut with flat edges for turning) • The **nuts and bolts** of something are the basic facts or practical things that need to be understood or done: *He was a genius on paper, but when it came to the nuts and bolts of running a business, he was a failure.*

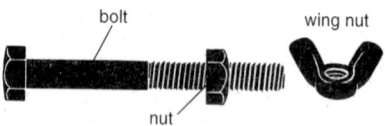

bolt   wing nut

nut

nut [PERSON] /nʌt/ *n* [C] *infml* a person who is crazy, foolish, or strange • *What kind of nut would leave a computer in his car overnight with the doors unlocked?* • (*humorous*) A nut is also a person who is extremely enthusiastic about a particular activity or thing: *Joyce is a nut for antiques—we've got a house full of them.*

nuts /nʌts/ *adj* [not gradable] *infml* crazy, foolish, or strange • *You're nuts if you think you can go mountain climbing in a snowstorm.* • If you are nuts about/over someone or something, you are very enthusiastic about them: *He's nuts about his new granddaughter.*

nutty /'nʌt̬·i/ *adj* [-er/-est only] very foolish, esp. because not practical • *It sounds nutty, but she can make it work.*

nutmeg /'nʌt·meg/ *n* [U] a brown powder made from the fruit of a tree and used as a spice

nutrient /'nu·tri··ənt/ *n* [C] *specialized* any substance that plants or animals need in order to live and grow

nutrition /nu·'trɪʃ·ən/ *n* [U] the process by which the body takes in and uses food, esp. food that it needs to stay healthy, or the scientific study of this process • *Nutrition experts have been urging people to eat less fatty food.*

nutritional /nu·'trɪʃ·ən··əl/, **nutritive** /'nu··trət̬·ɪv/ *adj* [not gradable] relating to nutrition, or containing a food substance your body can use • *Artificial sweeteners have no nutritional value.*

nutritious /nu·'trɪʃ·əs/ *adj* (of food or drink) containing substances your body needs and can use to stay healthy • *In general, raw vegetables are more nutritious than cooked vegetables.*

nuts /nʌts/ *adj* • See at NUT [PERSON].

nutshell /'nʌt·ʃel/ *n* [U] the hard, outer covering of a nut of a tree • **In a nutshell** means very briefly, giving only the main points: *"What went wrong?" "In a nutshell, everything."*

nutty /'nʌt̬·i/ *adj* • See at NUT [FOOD], NUT [PERSON].

nuzzle /'nʌz·əl/ *v* [I/T] to touch, rub, or press (someone) gently and affectionately, esp. with the head or nose • *She loved to nuzzle her dog and scratch him behind the ears.* [T]

N.W. *n* [U], *adj*, *adv* [not gradable] *abbreviation for* NORTHWEST or NORTHWESTERN

nylon /'naɪ·lɑn/ *n* [U] an artificial substance used esp. to make clothes, ropes, and brushes • *The fishing line is made of nylon and it's very strong.* • Nylons are women's nylon STOCKINGS: *Most women these days wear pantyhose instead of nylons.* [pl]

O, o

O LETTER , **o** /oʊ/ *n* [C] *pl* **O's** or **Os** or **o's** or **os** the 15th letter of the English alphabet

O EMOTION /oʊ/ *exclamation old use* used when addressing someone or something, or when expressing strong emotion • *"O! Canada" is the Canadian national anthem.* • Compare OH.

O ZERO /oʊ/ *n* [U] *not standard* (spelled the way it is often spoken) ZERO NUMBER • LP) ZERO

oaf /oʊf/ *n* [C] a big, stupid, awkward person, esp. a man

oak /oʊk/ *n* [C/U] a large tree common in northern countries, or the hard wood of this tree • *The wine is aged in barrels made of oak.* [U]

oar /ɔːr, oʊr/ *n* [C] a long pole with a wide, flat part at one end which is used to ROW a boat (= move it through water) • Compare PADDLE.

oasis /oʊˈeɪ·səs/ *n* [C] *pl* **oases** /oʊˈeɪˌsiːz/ an area in a desert where there is water and trees can grow

oath PROMISE /oʊθ/ *n* [C] a serious promise that you will tell the truth or that you will do what you have said • *Presidents take an oath to uphold the Constitution.*

oath RUDE WORD /oʊθ/ *n* [C] *dated or literary* an offensive word, esp. one that uses a name for God

oatmeal /ˈoʊt·miːl/ *n* [U] crushed OATS, esp. cooked as a breakfast food

oats /oʊts/ *pl n* a grass-like plant cultivated for its edible grains

obedient /oʊˈbiːd·iː·ənt/ *adj* doing or willing to do what you have been asked or ordered to do by someone in authority • *an obedient child* • USAGE: The related verb is OBEY.

obedience /oʊˈbiːd·iː·əns/ *n* [U] • *She demands absolute obedience to the rules.*

obese /oʊˈbiːs/ *adj* extremely fat

obesity /oʊˈbiːˌsət̬·i/ *n* [U] • *Obesity and lack of exercise are bad for the heart.*

obey /oʊˈbeɪ/ *v* [I/T] to do what you are told or expected to do according to (someone in authority or a rule or law) • *The toddler refused to obey.* [I] ○ *Residents are expected to obey the house rules.* [T] • USAGE: The related adjective is OBEDIENT.

OB–GYN /ˌoʊ·biːˌdʒiːˌwaɪˈen/ *n* [U] *medical abbreviation for* obstetrics and gynecology (= a medical specialty that deals with pregnancy, birth, and diseases of the female reproductive system)

obituary /oʊˈbɪtʃ·əˌwer·i/, *infml* **obit** /oʊˈbɪt, ˈoʊ·bət/ *n* [C] a notice, esp. in a newspaper, of a person's death, usually with details about their life

object THING /ˈɑb·dʒɪkt/ *n* [C] a thing that can be seen, held, or touched, usually not a living thing • *Distant objects look blurry to me.*

object PURPOSE /ˈɑb·dʒɪkt/ *n* [C] a purpose or aim of some effort or activity • *The object of the game of chess is to checkmate your opponent.*

object PERSON DIRECTED TO /ˈɑb·dʒɪkt/ *n* [C] a person or thing to which thoughts, feelings, or actions are directed • *She was surprised to learn she was the object of his affection.*

object GRAMMAR /ˈɑb·dʒɪkt/ *n* [C] *specialized* (in grammar) a noun, pronoun, or noun phrase that represents the person or thing toward which the action of a verb is directed or to which a preposition relates • *In the sentence, "Give the book to me," "book" is the direct object of the verb "give," and "me" is the indirect object.* LP) VERBS WITH TWO OBJECTS

object OPPOSE /əbˈdʒekt/ *v* to feel or express opposition, dislike, or disapproval • *I don't think anyone will object to leaving early.* [I] ○ *She objected that the price was too high.* [+ that clause]

objection /əbˈdʒek·ʃən/ *n* [C] • *A couple of people raised/voiced objections to the plan.* ○ *Does anyone have any objections?*

objectionable /əbˈdʒek·ʃə·nə·bəl/ *adj* causing offense or opposition • *objectionable behavior*

objective GRAMMAR /əbˈdʒek·tɪv, ɑb-/ *adj* [not gradable] *specialized* (in grammar) having or relating to the CASE (= form) of a noun, pronoun, or adjective, used to show that a word is the object of a verb

objective AIM /əbˈdʒek·tɪv, ɑb-/ *n* [C] something that you aim to do or achieve • *long-term objectives* ○ *His main objective this semester is to improve his grades.*

objective FAIR OR REAL /əbˈdʒek·tɪv, ɑb-/ *adj* not influenced by personal beliefs or feelings; fair or real • *an objective opinion* • USAGE: The opposite of objective is SUBJECTIVE.

objectively /əbˈdʒek·tɪv·li, ɑb-/ *adv* • *Jurors must weigh the evidence in the case objectively.*

objectivity /ˌɑbˌdʒekˈtɪv·ət̬·i/ *n* [U] • *The newspaper has a reputation for objectivity and fairness.*

obligate /ˈɑb·ləˌɡeɪt/ *v* [T] to make (someone) feel morally or legally forced to do something • *I'm in favor of obligating welfare recipients to do more.*

obligated /ˈɑb·ləˌɡeɪt̬·əd/ *adj* • *I felt obligated to speak up and defend my friend's reputation.* [+ to infinitive]

obligation /ˌɑb·ləˈɡeɪ·ʃən/ *n* [C/U] something that a person feels morally or legally forced to do • *The government has an obligation to assist relief efforts.* [C] ○ *You can just look— you're under no obligation to buy.* [U]

oblige FORCE /əˈblaɪdʒ/ *v* [T] *slightly fml* to force or make it expected for (someone) to do something • *Circumstances obliged him to leave town.*

VERBS WITH TWO OBJECTS

Some verbs, such as *give, buy*, and *offer*, can have two objects. In the sentence *I gave Sarah a present*, the present is what I gave, and Sarah is the person I gave it to. The main object (*a present*) is called the **direct object**. The other object (*Sarah*) is called the **indirect object**. The indirect object typically refers to a person to or for whom something is done.

Verbs can have two objects if both objects are nouns, as in *I gave Sarah a present*, or if the indirect object is a pronoun, as in *I gave her a present*. If the direct object is a pronoun, the indirect object cannot be a noun. In that case, it is necessary to use a preposition before the indirect object: *I gave it to Sarah* (not "I gave Sarah it"). This pattern is also more common when both objects are pronouns: *I gave it to her*.

Most verbs like this can be used to say exactly the same thing in a different way by putting a preposition in front of one of the objects, usually the indirect object: *I gave a present to Sarah*. The prepositions most commonly used are *to* and *for*. In the lists below, verbs marked * can use more than one preposition.

USED WITH *to*

Some verbs can be used either with two objects or with the preposition *to* before the indirect object. These verbs often express the idea of giving or exchanging something.

give, sell, hand, feed, bring*, take, send, teach, tell, read, write*

> **Give** *them a hand.* • *He tried to* **sell** *me his camera.* • *Could you* **hand** *me the sugar?* • *We* **fed** *the chickens some corn.* • *Karen* **brought** *us news from home.* • *He* **sent** *me a postcard from Alaska.* • *My mother started to* **teach** *me the piano when I was five.* • *I* **told** *Martine the news.* • *Will you* **read** *me another story?* • *I* **wrote** *my aunt a long letter.*

Notice that **tell** is not used with *to* in most situations.

🄻🄿 **Say, tell, talk, and speak.**

USED WITH *for*

Some verbs can be used either with two objects or with the preposition *for* before one of the objects, usually the indirect object. These verbs often express the idea of doing something that another person wants.

buy, win, keep, save, get, bring*, find, cook, make, cut, build, draw, write*, cause, leave

> *She* **bought** *us lunch.* • *Mario's serve* **won** *us the game.* • *Please* **save** *me a seat on the train.* • *If you're going to the post office, could you* **get** *me some stamps?* • *He's trying to* **find** *us a room. Should I* **make** *you something to eat?* • *He* **cut** *everyone a big slice of cake.* • *We* **built** *the children a play house.* • *I'll* **draw** *you a map of the area.* • *He* **wrote** *her a poem.* • *Will the change in schedule* **cause** *you any problems?* • *Will that* **leave** *us enough time to get there?*

USED WITH OTHER PREPOSITIONS

ask

> *I* **asked** *him a question.* / *I* **asked** *a question* **of** *him.*

NOT USED WITH A PREPOSITION

With some verbs, neither of the objects can be expressed with a preposition. For example, you can say *They charged me $50* but not "They charged $50 to me."

bet, cost, charge, allow, refuse

> *I* **bet** *you $10 Nora gets the job.* • *It* **cost** *me $40.* • *She* **was charged** *$50 for a haircut.* • *They only* **allow** *you an hour to complete the test.* • *Officials* **refused** *him entry into the U.S.*

Verbs followed by an object and a noun or adjective

With some verbs, the object can be followed by a noun or noun phrase that does not refer to a separate person or thing and is therefore not a second object.

> *We* **made** *him dinner* (= we made dinner for him).   two objects: *dinner, him*
> *We* **made** *him chairman* (= he is now chairman).   one object: *him*

Verbs like **make** in the second example above usually name or describe someone or something or give a person a title, and the noun after the object refers to the name, description, or title.

> *I* **named** *my dog Hamlet.* • *She* **called** *him a liar.* • *She was* **elected** *president of the society.*

Sometimes the object can be followed by an adjective or an adjective-like phrase. These verbs often describe, give an opinion of, or show a change in someone or something.

> *Did you* **find** *the book interesting?* • *They* **painted** *the house green.* • *Things like that* **make** *me so angry.* • *Your questions are* **driving** *me crazy!*

obligatory /ə'blɪg·ə,tɔːr·i, -,tour·i/ *adj* [not gradable] • *Everybody who goes to England makes the obligatory trip to Stonehenge.*

obliged /ə'blaɪdʒd/ *adj* • *He was obliged to call the nurse to help him up again.* [+ *to* infinitive]

oblige HELP /ə'blaɪdʒ/ *v* [I/T] to please or help (someone), esp. by doing something they have asked you to do • *We needed a guide and he was only too happy to oblige.* [I]

obliging /ə'blaɪ·dʒɪŋ/ *adj* willing or eager to help • *He found an obliging doctor who prescribed the drugs he needed.*

obligingly /ə'blaɪ·dʒɪŋ·li/ *adv* • *She obligingly offered us a lift.*

oblique INDIRECT /ou'bliːk, ə-, -'blaɪk/ *adj* indirectly expressed • *He made an oblique reference to their relationship.*

oblique DIAGONAL /ou'bliːk, ə-, -'blaɪk/ *adj* having a sloping direction, angle, or position • *the oblique rays of the afternoon sun*

obliterate /ə'blɪt̬·ə,reɪt, ou-/ *v* [T] to remove all signs of (something); destroy • *The hurricane virtually obliterated this small coastal town.*

oblivion MENTAL STATE /ə'blɪv·iː·ən, ou-/ *n* [U] the state of being unconscious or lacking awareness of what is happening around you • *He sought oblivion in drugs.*

oblivion FORGOTTEN BY OTHERS /ə'blɪv·iː·ən, ou-/ *n* [U] the state of being completely forgotten by the public • *He wrote one extraordinary book and then faded into oblivion.*

oblivious /ə'blɪv·iː·əs, ou-/ *adj* not aware of or not noticing something, esp. what is happening around you • *She was often oblivious to the potential consequences of her actions.*

oblong /'ɑb·lɔːŋ/ *n* [C] a shape that is longer than it is wide, esp. a rectangle that is not a square

obnoxious /əb'nɑk·ʃəs, ɑb-/ *adj* very unpleasant or offensive • *Can't you express your opinions without being obnoxious?*

oboe /'ou·bou/ *n* [C/U] a tube-shaped musical instrument that is played by blowing through two REEDS (= thin pieces of wood), or this type of instrument generally; a WOODWIND

obscene /əb'siːn, ɑb-/ *adj* offensive, rude, or disgusting according to accepted moral standards, esp. in relation to sexual matters • *obscene pictures/phone calls* ○ *The money he's paid is obscene* (= morally offensive).

obscenity /əb'sen·ət̬·i, ɑb-/ *n* [C/U] behavior or language that is offensive, rude, or disgusting • *His first novel was banned for obscenity.* [U] ○ *Sprewell answered by shouting obscenities* (= offensive words). [C]

obscure UNKNOWN /əb'skjur, ɑb-/ *adj* not known to many people • *an obscure 18th-century painter*

obscurity /əb'skjur·ət̬·i, ɑb-/ *n* [U] • *She worked in obscurity for years.*

obscure UNCLEAR /əb'skjur, ɑb-/ *adj* unclear and difficult to understand or see • *Official*

policy has changed for reasons that remain obscure.

obscure /əb'skjur, ɑb-/ *v* [T] • *Bad writing just obscures your point.* ○ *Two large trees obscured the view.*

obscurity /əb'skjur·ət̬·i, ɑb-/ *n* [U] • *Many movie reviewers confuse obscurity with quality.*

obsequious /əb'siː·kwiː·əs, ɑb-/ *adj* too eager to serve or obey someone • *She is embarrassingly obsequious to anyone in authority.*

observatory /əb'zɜr·və,tɔːr·i, -,tour·i/ *n* [C] a building equipped for studying the planets and the stars

observe (*obj*) WATCH /əb'zɜrv/ *v* to watch (something or someone) carefully • *She spent her career observing animal behavior.* [T] ○ *On their field trip, the students observed how a newspaper was put together.* [+ *wh-* word]

observation /,ɑb·zər'veɪ·ʃən/ *n* [U] • *scientific observation* ○ *He was admitted to the hospital for observation after complaining of chest pains.*

observer /əb'zɜr·vər/ *n* [C] a person who watches what happens but has no active part in it • *Political observers say it's going to be a close election.*

observe NOTICE /əb'zɜrv/ *v* [T] to notice (something or someone) • *Jack observed a look of panic on his brother's face.* [T]

observable /əb'zɜr·və·bəl/ *adj* [not gradable] • *There's no observable connection between the two events.*

observant /əb'zɜr·vənt/ *adj* quick to notice things • *Carrie has a clear, observant eye.*

observation /,ɑb·zər'veɪ·ʃən/ *n* [U] • *He has remarkable powers of observation.*

observe REMARK /əb'zɜrv/ *v* [I] to remark about something • *"It's raining again," he observed.*

observation /,ɑb·zər'veɪ·ʃən/ *n* [C] • *She made an interesting observation about the poet's intentions.*

observe OBEY /əb'zɜrv/ *v* [T] to obey (a law or rule), or celebrate (a holiday or religious event) • *You must observe the law.* ○ *Do you observe Passover* (= celebrate it in the traditional way)?

observance /əb'zɜr·vəns/ *n* [C/U] • *Religious observances mark the Christmas season.* [C] ○ *Financial markets will be closed Monday in observance of Labor Day.* [U]

observant /əb'zɜr·vənt/ *adj* careful in obeying laws, rules, or customs • *an observant Jew*

obsessed /əb'sest, ɑb-/ *adj* unable to stop thinking about something • *She is obsessed with thoughts of her dead husband.*

obsession /əb'seʃ·ən, ɑb-/ *n* [C/U] the control of one's thoughts by a continuous, powerful idea or feeling, or the idea or feeling itself • *His love for her turned to obsession.* [U] ○ *They have an obsession with making money.* [C]

obsessive /əb'ses·ɪv, ɑb-/ *adj* • *She is obsessive about punctuality.*

obsessively /əbˈses·ɪv·li, ab-/ *adv* • *Sue exercises obsessively.*

obsolescence /ˌab·səˈles·əns/ *n* [U] the process of becoming no longer useful or needed • *Older versions had passed into obsolescence and a new version was already on the market.*

obsolete /ˌab·səˈliːt/ *adj* [not gradable] no longer used or needed, usually because something newer and better has replaced it • *Typewriters have been rendered obsolete by computers.*

obstacle /ˈab·stɪ·kəl/ *n* [C] something that blocks your way so that movement or progress is prevented or made more difficult • *We suddenly encountered an obstacle along the trail.* ○ *Money seems to be no obstacle.* • An **obstacle course** is an area with a series of obstacles that people climb over or go under or through as a form of exercise or in a race.

obstetrics /əbˈste·trɪks, ab-/ *n* [U] the area of medicine that deals with pregnancy and the birth of babies

obstetrician /ˌab·stəˈtrɪʃ·ən/ *n* [C] a doctor with special training in how to care for pregnant women and help in the birth of babies

obstinate /ˈab·stə·nət/ *adj* unwilling to change your opinion or action despite argument or persuasion; STUBBORN • *an obstinate two-year-old* • An obstinate thing or problem is difficult to deal with, remove, or defeat.

obstinately /ˈab·stə·nət·li/ *adv* • *The engine obstinately refused to start.*

obstinacy /ˈab·stə·nə·si/ *n* [U] • *the obstinacy of the human spirit*

obstruct /əbˈstrʌkt, ab-/ *v* [T] to block or get in the way of (something or someone), or to prevent (something) from happening or progressing by causing difficulties • *Demonstrators obstructed the entrance to the building.* ○ *Trees obstructed our view of the ocean.*

obstruction /əbˈstrʌk·ʃən, ab-/ *n* [C/U] • *Doctors found an obstruction in one of his arteries* (= something was blocking it). [C] • (*law*) **Obstruction of justice** is the act of preventing the police or law courts from doing their job.

obtain /əbˈteɪn, ab-/ *v* [T] *slightly fml* to get (something), esp. by a planned effort • *to obtain knowledge* ○ *She was finally able to obtain legal possession of the house.*

obtainable /əbˈteɪ·nə·bəl, ab-/ *adj* [not gradable] *slightly fml* • *That drug is now obtainable without a prescription.*

obtrusive /əbˈtruː·sɪv, ab-, -zɪv/ *adj* noticeable in a way that is unpleasant or unwanted • *The soldiers wore civilian clothes to make their presence less obtrusive.*

obtuse ANGLE /əbˈtuːs, ab-/ *adj* (of an angle) more than 90° and less than 180° • Compare ACUTE ANGLE

obtuse STUPID /əbˈtuːs, ab-/ *adj* stupid or slow to understand • *I'm not trying to be obtuse, but I don't get it.*

obvious /ˈab·viː·əs/ *adj* easily seen, recognized, or understood • *an obvious solution* ○ *For obvious reasons, he needs to find work soon.*

obviously /ˈab·viː·ə·sli/ *adv* • *They were obviously exhausted after the game.* ○ *Obviously, you won't be needing my help.*

occasion PARTICULAR TIME /əˈkeɪ·ʒən/ *n* [C] a particular time when something happens • *We've been saving the wine for a special occasion.* ○ *She has lied on several occasions.* ○ *A funeral is hardly an occasion* (= a suitable time) *for jokes.* • **On occasion** means sometimes but not often: *He has, on occasion, had too much to drink.*

occasion REASON /əˈkeɪ·ʒən/ *n* [U] a reason or cause • *I've never had occasion to worry about my children's school work.*

occasional /əˈkeɪ·ʒən·əl/ *adj* [not gradable] not happening often or regularly • *occasional snowstorms* ○ *His job requires occasional trips to the West Coast.*

occasionally /əˈkeɪ·ʒən·əl·i/ *adv* [not gradable] • *Stir occasionally while the pasta is cooking.* ○ *I occasionally watch TV.*

occult /əˈkʌlt, ˈak·ʌlt/ *adj* [not gradable] relating to mysterious or SUPERNATURAL powers and activities • *Witchcraft and astrology are occult sciences.*

occult /əˈkʌlt, ˈak·ʌlt/ *n* [U] • *He dabbled in the occult.*

occupancy /ˈak·jə·pən·si/ *n* [U] *slightly fml* the act or state of living in or using a particular place • *Her occupancy of the apartment lasted only six months.*

occupant /ˈak·jə·pənt/ *n* [C] someone who lives in a particular place • *The occupants of the building are unhappy about the rent increase.* • An occupant of a car, room, seat, or other space is a person who is in it.

occupation JOB /ˌak·jəˈpeɪ·ʃən/ *n* [C] *slightly fml* a person's job • *He listed his occupation on the form as "teacher."* • An occupation is also a regular activity: *Sailing was his favorite weekend occupation.*

occupational /ˌak·jəˈpeɪ·ʃən·əl/ *adj* [not gradable] relating to or caused by a person's work or activity • *Occupational training is absolutely essential.*

occupation CONTROLLING FORCE /ˌak·jəˈpeɪ·ʃən/ *n* [U] the act of controlling a foreign country or region by armed force • *the occupation of France during World War II*

occupy FILL /ˈak·jə·paɪ/ *v* [T] to fill, use, or exist in (a place or a time) • *A large couch occupies most of the space in the living room.*

occupied /ˈak·jə·paɪd/ *adj* full, in use, or busy • *The bathroom is occupied at the moment.* ○ *Organized sports can keep teenagers occupied.*

occupy TAKE CONTROL /ˈak·jə·paɪ/ *v* [T] (of an army or group of people) to move into and take control or possession of (a place) • *Nationalist forces now occupy more than 70% of the country.*

occupied /ˈɑk·jə,pɑɪd/ *adj* [not gradable] • *occupied territories*

occupier /ˈɑk·jə,pɑɪ·ər/ *n* [C]

occur HAPPEN /əˈkɜr/ *v* [I] **-rr-** (esp. of unexpected events) to happen • *The incident occurred shortly after the plane took off.*

occurrence /əˈkɜr·əns/ *n* [C] • *Break-ins are an everyday occurrence in this neighborhood.*

occur EXIST /əˈkɜr/ *v* [I] **-rr-** to exist or be present • *The condition occurs primarily in older adults.* ○ *Helium occurs as a byproduct of natural gas.*

occurrence /əˈkɜr·əns/ *n* [U] • *The tests can detect the occurrence of certain cancers.*

▫ **occur to** /-ˈ-·-/ *v prep* [T] (of a thought or idea) to come into (someone's) mind • *Didn't it occur to you to phone the police?* ○ *It never occurred to her that her parents might be worried.*

ocean /ˈoʊ·ʃən/ *n* [C/U] the large mass of salt water that covers most of the earth's surface • *These mysterious creatures live at the bottom of the ocean.* [U] • Ocean is also used in the name of the world's five main divisions of this mass of water: *the Atlantic/Pacific/Indian/Arctic/Antarctic Ocean* [C]

oceanic /,oʊ·ʃiːˈæn·ɪk/ *adj* [not gradable] • *oceanic conditions*

o'clock /əˈklɑk/ *adv* [not gradable] used after a number from one to twelve to state the time • *She called at nine o'clock this morning.*

octagon /ˈɑk·tə,gɑn/ *n* [C] a flat shape with eight straight sides and eight angles

octagonal /ɑkˈtæg·ən·əl/ *adj* [not gradable]

octane /ˈɑk·teɪn/ *n* [C] a chemical substance in GASOLINE (= liquid fuel) which is used as a measure of its quality

octave /ˈɑk·tɪv/ *n* [C] *specialized* the space between two musical notes that are eight musical notes apart

October /ɑkˈtoʊ·bər/ (*abbreviation* **Oct.**) *n* [C/U] the tenth month of the year, after September and before November

octopus /ˈɑk·tə·pəs, -,pʊs/ *n* [C] *pl* **octopuses** or **octopi** /ˈɑk·tə,pɑɪ/ a sea creature with a soft oval body and eight TENTACLES (= arms)

octopus

OD /oʊˈdiː, ˈoʊˈdiː/ *v* [I] **OD'ing**, *past* **OD'd** or **ODed** *slang abbreviation* to take an OVERDOSE (= too much) of a drug • *She OD'd on heroin.*

odd STRANGE /ɑd/ *adj* [**-er/-est** only] strange or unexpected • *an odd person* ○ *That's odd—I thought I left my glasses on the table but they're not here.*

oddity /ˈɑd·ət·i/ *n* [C] someone or something that is strange and unusual • *As one of the few women in engineering in the 1950s, she was considered an oddity.*

oddly /ˈɑd·li/ *adv* • *an oddly shaped house* ○ *Yet oddly enough, some of the most impassioned pleas against capital punishment are based on religion.*

odd SEPARATED /ɑd/ *adj* [not gradable] (of something that should be in a pair or set) separated from its pair or set • *He's got a whole drawer full of odd socks.* • **Odd jobs** are small jobs of different types, esp. those that involve repairing or cleaning things: *He's been doing odd jobs this summer to earn a little extra money.*

odd NUMBER /ɑd/ *adj* [not gradable] (of numbers) not able to be divided exactly by 2 • *Some examples of odd numbers are 1, 3, 5, and 7.* • Compare EVEN NUMBER.

odd APPROXIMATELY /ɑd/ *adv* [not gradable] used after a number, esp. a number that can be divided by 10, to show that the exact number is not known • *He holds another 50-odd acres of land in reserve, providing plenty of room for expansion.*

oddball /ˈɑd·bɔːl/ *n* [C] a person whose behavior is unusual and strange

odds /ɑdz/ *pl n* the probability that a particular thing will or will not happen • *She was sick yesterday, so the odds are she won't be in today.* • The odds are also the probability expressed as a number when making a BET: *The odds against my horse winning are 7 to 1.* • *The two brothers were always* **at odds** (= disagreeing).

odds and ends /,ɑd·zəˈnenz/ *pl n* various items of different types, usually small and unimportant or of little value • *We've moved most of the furniture to the new house, but there are still a few odds and ends to bring over.*

odious /ˈoʊd·iː·əs/ *adj* extremely unpleasant; causing and deserving hate • *an odious person/task*

odometer /oʊˈdɑm·ət·ər/ *n* [C] a device in a vehicle that measures and shows the distance the vehicle travels

odor /ˈoʊd·ər/ *n* [C] a particular smell, esp. a bad one • *the stale odor of cigarettes and spilled beer*

odorless /ˈoʊd·ər·ləs/ *adj* [not gradable] having no smell • *an odorless gas*

odyssey /ˈɑd·ə·si/ *n* [C usually sing] a long trip or period involving a lot of different and exciting activities, esp. while searching for something • *The movie follows one man's odyssey to find the mother he was separated from at birth.*

of POSSESSION /ʌv, ɑv, əv/ *prep* used to show possession, belonging, or origin • *She is a friend of mine.* ○ *The color of his tie matches* *his suit.* ○ *Have you read the novels of John Updike?*

of CONTAINING /ʌv, ɑv, əv/ *prep* containing or consisting of • *a bag of groceries* ○ *a book of short stories* ○ *a forest of pine trees* ○ *a bunch of grapes*

of AMOUNT /ʌv, ɑv, əv/ *prep* used after words or phrases expressing amount, number, or a particular unit • *a drop of rain* ○ *two pounds of potatoes* ○ *hundreds of people*

of POSITION /ʌv, ɑv, əv/ *prep* used in expressions showing position • *I left the book on top of my desk.* ○ *I've never been north of Montreal.*

of RESULT /ʌv, ɑv, əv/ *prep* resulting from or having to do with • *the joy of sex* ○ *the fear of failure*

of RELATING TO /ʌv, ɑv, əv/ *prep* about, or relating to • *Speaking of Elizabeth, here she is.* ○ *There's a chapter on the use of herbs for medicinal purposes.*

of CAUSED BY /ʌv, ɑv, əv/ *prep* used to show the cause of something • *He died of a heart attack.* ○ *Penny is frightened of spiders.* ○ *I'm tired of all this criticism.*

of THAT IS / ARE /ʌv, ɑv, əv/ *prep* that is/are • *Sales tax of 7% is included in the price.* ○ *She could read by the age of five.*

of COMPARING /ʌv, ɑv, əv/ *prep* used when comparing related things • *He's the oldest of three brothers.* ○ *Of all his films, this one is my favorite.*

of DONE TO /ʌv, ɑv, əv/ *prep* done to or involving • *the destruction of the rain forests* ○ *the graduation of the class of 2001*

of DISTANCE FROM /ʌv, ɑv, əv/ *prep* used in expressions showing distance from something in place or time • *We live within a mile of the school.* ○ *She came within two seconds of beating the world record.*

of TIME /ʌv, ɑv, əv/ *prep* used in saying what the time is • *It's ten (minutes) of five* (= ten minutes before five o'clock).

of DAYS /ʌv, ɑv, əv/ *prep* used to describe a particular day • *the eleventh of March* ○ *the first of the month*

off NOT OPERATING /ɔːf/ *adj, adv* [not gradable] (esp. of machines, electrical devices, lights, etc.) not operating because they are not switched on • *Was the computer on or off when you left?* ○ *Turn the engine off.*

off AWAY FROM /ɔːf/ *adv, adj* [not gradable], *prep* away from a place or position, esp. the present place or position • *He drove off at high speed.* ○ *She's off to Canada next week.* ○ *The sign says, "Keep off the grass."* • To be **off balance** is to temporarily lose control over the position of your body: *The blow knocked him off balance, and he almost fell.* • If an aircraft or ship is **off course**, it is not following the path it is meant to take. • If a place is **off the beaten path/track**, it is not a place where a lot of people go: *We wanted to find a camping site that was a little bit off the beaten path.* • Money that is earned **off the books** is money that a person does not report as income to the government, in order to avoid paying taxes on it. • If someone, esp. a public official, says something **off-the-record**, they do not want it to be reported. • *(slang)* **Off-the-wall** means intentionally unusual, unexpected, and shocking: *off-the-wall jokes* • If something is **offshore**, it is away from or at a distance from the land: *an offshore oil rig*

off REMOVED /ɔːf/ *adv* [not gradable], *prep* used with actions in which something is removed or removes itself from another thing • *I think I'll take my jacket off.* ○ *I can't get the lid off this jar.* ○ *He fell off his bike.* • *Did you leave the phone off the hook* (= not put back in such a way that a call is ended)?

off NOT AT /ɔːf/ *adv, adj* [not gradable] not at work or school, esp. being at home or on vacation • *I'm going to take a week off to work on my house.* ○ *I'm off next week.* ○ *The kids get off early from school today.* • To be **off duty** is not to be working, usually because you have finished work for the day: *She goes off duty at midnight.* ○ *An off-duty police officer on his way home interrupted a crime in progress.*

off NEAR TO /ɔːf/ *prep* near to • *The island is just off the coast of Florida.*

off TAKEN AWAY /ɔːf/ *adv* [not gradable] in such a way as to be taken away or removed, esp. because of having been used or killed • *to pay off debts* ○ *Exercise burns off fat.* ○ *They were all killed off by disease.*

off BELOW USUAL LEVEL /ɔːf/ *adv, adj* [not gradable] below the usual standard or rate • *Sales have been off this month.* ○ *He's a good tennis player but had an off day and lost in straight sets.* ○ *They took 10% off* (= below the usual price) *because I paid in cash.* • **Off-color** refers to remarks or jokes that deal with sex and that some people would think offensive. • **Off-season** refers to a period of the year when there is less activity in business.

off DISTANT /ɔːf/ *adv* [not gradable], *prep* distant (from) in time or space • *Graduation is still a long way off.* ○ *That's not the right answer, but you're not far off.*

off STOPPED /ɔːf/ *adj, adv* [not gradable] (of an arranged event) stopped or given up in advance • *Last night's baseball game was called off because of rain.* • If something happens **off and on** (also **on and off**), it does not happen all the time.

off CLOSED /ɔːf/ *adv* [not gradable] in such a way as to be separated • *to mark off 10 feet* ○ *The children's play area is fenced off for safety reasons.*

offbeat /ˈɔːfˌbiːt, ɔːfˈbiːt/ *adj* unusual and therefore surprising or noticeable • *an offbeat sense of humor*

offend /əˈfend/ *v* [T] to cause to be upset or to hurt the feelings of (someone), esp. by being rude or showing a lack of respect • *I think she was offended that she wasn't invited to the party.*

offender /əˈfen·dər/ *n* [C] a person who is guilty of a crime • *Well, in Washington state, if you're a habitual sexual offender, they just don't let you out.*

offense BAD FEELINGS /əˈfens/ *n* [U] the condition of having your feelings hurt esp. because of someone's rudeness or lack of respect • *Do you think he took offense* (= was upset) *at the joke about his age?*

offensive /əˈfen·sɪv/ *adj* causing someone to be upset or to have their feelings hurt • *offensive comments/jokes* • Offensive can be used more generally to mean unpleasant: *an offensive odor*

offense CRIME /əˈfens/ *n* [C] an illegal act; crime • *He was charged with the offense of driving without a license.*

offense SCORING ABILITY /ˈɔː·fens, ˈɑf·ens, əˈfens/ *n* [U] (in sports) the ability to score points in a competition, or, esp. in football, the team that has the ball and is trying to score points • Compare DEFENSE SPORTS.

offensive /ˈɔːˌfen·sɪv, ˈɑf·en-, əˈfen-/ *adj* [not gradable] • *Bob made the team as an offensive guard.*

offensive /əˈfen·sɪv/ *n* [C] a planned military attack • *They launched the land offensive in the middle of the night.*

offensive /əˈfen·sɪv/ *adj* • *an offensive action*

offer AGREE TO GIVE /ˈɔː·fər, ˈɑf·ər/ *v* [I/T] to ask (someone) if they would like to have (something) or if they would like you to do something • *She was offered a new job.* [T] ○ *Can I offer you* (= Would you like) *something to drink?* [T] ○ *My father offered to take us to the airport.* [I]

offer /ˈɔː·fər, ˈɑf·ər/ *n* [C] • *I appreciate your offer to help.* [+ *to* infinitive] ○ *The offer of $5000 was too good to refuse.*

offering /ˈɔː·fə·rɪŋ, ˈɑf·ə-/ *n* [C] something that a person gives, esp. to a god or to a religious organization, often during a religious ceremony

offer PROVIDE /ˈɔː·fər, ˈɑf·ər/ *v* [T] to provide or supply (something) • *The organization offers free legal advice to low-income people.* ○ *He offered excuses but no real explanation.*

offhand /ˈɔːfˈhænd/ *adv* now, without looking for information or without taking the time to consider carefully • *I can't tell you the exact number offhand, but it was something like $25,000.*

offhand /ˈɔːfˈhænd/ *adj* not showing or not done with much thought or consideration • *offhand remarks* ○ *His offhand manner disturbed us.*

office WORK PLACE /ˈɔː·fəs, ˈɑf·əs/ *n* [C] a place in a building where a business is carried on by people working at DESKS (= special tables) used for writing and for holding telephones

and computers • *an office building* ○ *I didn't leave the office until nearly 8 o'clock.* • An office is also the place of business where a doctor, lawyer, or other PROFESSIONAL sees people: *The doctor's office was filled with people.*

officer /ˈɔː·fə·sər, ˈɑf·ə-/ *n* [C] a person who has an important job in a company • *the chief financial officer*

office GOVERNMENT DEPARTMENT /ˈɔː·fəs, ˈɑf·əs/ *n* [C] a part of a government department • *the Office of Management and Budget* ○ *the Patent Office*

office RESPONSIBILITY /ˈɔː·fəs, ˈɑf·əs/ *n* [C/U] a position of authority and responsibility in a government or other organization • *elective office* [U] ○ *the office of executive vice president* [C] ○ *The governor retired after 12 years in office.* [U]

officer /ˈɔː·fə·sər, ˈɑf·ə-/ *n* [C] a person in the armed forces who has a position of authority • *Mike's father was an officer in the US Marines.* • An officer is also a member of a police force.

official /əˈfɪʃ·əl/ *n* [C] a person who has a position of responsibility in an organization • *a senior official*

official /əˈfɪʃ·əl/ *adj* connected with or arranged by someone in a position of responsibility • *an official announcement*

officially /əˈfɪʃ·ə·li/ *adv* • *The name of the new director will be officially announced in June.*

officiate /əˈfɪʃ·iːˌeɪt/ *v* [I] to be in charge of a sports event and make decisions about the rules of play, or to lead a ceremony or other public event • *Lambert was a football official for three decades and officiated in ten postseason games.* ○ *A judge officiated at the wedding.*

offing /ˈɔː·fɪŋ, ˈɑf·ɪŋ/ *n* [U] • Something that is **in the offing** is going to happen soon: *With an election in the offing, the mayor is anxious to boost his popularity.*

off-key /ˈɔːfˈkiː/ *adv* singing the wrong notes • *He was singing off-key, and it was painful to hear.*

offset /ɔːfˈset/ *v* [T] **offsetting**, *past* **offset** to balance (one influence) against an opposing influence so that no great difference results • *The extra cost of commuting to work from the suburbs is offset by cheaper rents.*

offshoot /ˈɔːf·ʃuːt/ *n* [C] something that has developed from something larger that already existed • *Overeaters Anonymous and other groups that try to change destructive behavior are offshoots of Alcoholics Anonymous.*

offspring /ˈɔːf·sprɪŋ/ *n* [C] *pl* **offspring** the young of an animal, or a person's children • *Champion horses have numerous offspring.*

offstage /ˈɔːfˈsteɪdʒ/ *adv* [not gradable] behind or at the side of the stage, so that people who are watching cannot see • *We could hear someone shouting offstage.*

often /ˈɔː·fən, ˈɔːf·tən/ *adv* a lot or many

times; frequently • *She was often late for class.* ○ *I don't see my parents as often as I'd like to.*

ogle /'oʊ·gəl/ *v* [I/T] to look at (someone) with obvious and esp. sexual interest • *They sat around ogling every passing woman.* [T]

ogre /'oʊ·gər/ *n* [C] a frightening, fierce, or ugly person

oh /oʊ/ *exclamation* used to express a variety of emotions, such as surprise, disappointment, and pleasure, often as a reaction to something someone has said • *Oh, I didn't know they were married.* ○ *Oh, my God, I forgot my purse!*

ohm /oʊm/ *n* [C] *specialized* the standard unit of electrical RESISTANCE (= the degree to which electrical flow is prevented)

oil FAT /ɔɪl/ *n* [C/U] thick, liquid fat obtained from plants which does not mix with water and is used esp. in cooking and beauty products • *vegetable/corn/olive oil* [U] ○ *bath oil* [U] ○ *I like oil and vinegar on my salad.* [U] ○ *These cookies are made with soybean and palm oils.* [C] • **Oil paint** (also **oils**) is a type of paint made by adding color to oil and used for painting pictures. An **oil painting** (also **oil**) is a picture made with oil paints.

oil /ɔɪl/ *v* [T] to put oil on (a pan or other surface that you cook on) to keep things from sticking to it • *Lightly oil the grill.*

oily /'ɔɪ·li/ *adj* like oil, or containing or covered with oil • *an oily liquid* ○ *oily skin/hair*

oil CHEMICAL SUBSTANCE /ɔɪl/ *n* [U] a thick, liquid substance that burns and is used as fuel or as a LUBRICANT (= substance that helps connecting parts move easily), or the thick liquid taken from under the ground which oil, GASOLINE, and other products are made from • *motor oil* ○ *fuel/heating oil* ○ *Change your car's oil every 12,000 miles.* • An **oil slick** is a layer of oil floating on water.

oil /ɔɪl/ *v* [T] to add oil to something so it works better • *Oil the door hinges so they stop squeaking.*

oily /ɔɪ·li/ *adj* covered in or containing a lot of oil • *an oily rag*

oink /ɔɪŋk/ *n* [C] the sound made by a pig

ointment /'ɔɪnt·mənt/ *n* [C/U] a thick, oily substance, usually containing medicine, that is put on the skin to treat soreness or injury • *germicidal ointment* [U]

OJ /'oʊ·dʒeɪ/ *n* [U] *abbreviation for* orange juice

OK AGREED , **okay** /oʊ'keɪ/ *adj* [not gradable], *exclamation* agreed or acceptable; ALL RIGHT AGREED • *Is it OK if I bring a friend to the party?* ○ *"Will you lend me ten bucks?" "OK."*

OK, okay /oʊ'keɪ/ *v* [T] **OKing** or **okaying**, *past* **OKed** or **okayed** • *Did the boss OK your proposal?*

OK, okay /oʊ'keɪ/ *n* [C] agreement about or permission to do something • *We'll start building as soon as we get the OK from the owner.*

OK SATISFACTORY , **okay** /oʊ'keɪ/ *adj, adv* in a satisfactory state or of a satisfactory quality; ALL RIGHT SATISFACTORY • *Are you OK? You look pale.* ○ *I hope you got home OK.* • OK is used to mean not bad but also not very good: *Her voice is OK, but it's nothing special.*

OK EXPRESSION , **okay** /oʊ'keɪ, 'oʊ'keɪ/ *exclamation infml* used as a way of showing that you are going to take action or start doing or saying something new • *OK, let's go.*

okra /'oʊ·krə/, **gumbo** *n* [U] a green, conical seed container that is used as a vegetable, or the plant it grows on

old EXISTING A LONG TIME /oʊld/ *adj* [-er/-est only] having lived or existed for a long time in comparison to others of the same kind • *An old man lives there with his dog.* ○ *They have a beautiful old farm house in the country.* ○ *She got very depressed in her old age* (= the time of her life when she was old). • (*slang*) Something **old hat** is not modern, or is familiar and not interesting: *Parents often expect older kids to treat a new school year as old hat.* • (*disapproving*) An **old maid** is a woman who is not young and has not married. • (*infml*) An **old-timer** is someone who has lived a long time, or someone who has been or worked in a place for a long time. • An **old wives' tale** is a traditional story or belief. • Compare **elderly** at ELDER.

old KNOWN A LONG TIME /oʊld/ *adj* [-er/-est only] (esp. of a friend) known for a long time • *She's one of my oldest friends.* • (*infml*) Old is also used to show that you know and like someone: *Poor old Frank broke his arm.*

old AGE /oʊld/ *adj* [-er/-est only] having a particular age, or an age suited to a particular activity or condition • *a 14-year-old* ○ *Charlie is older than I.* ○ *You're old enough to know better.*

old PREVIOUS /oʊld/ *adj* [-er/-est only] from a previous time or a period in the past; FORMER EARLIER • *Our old house in Lakewood burned down.* ○ *Sharon gave her old skates to her younger cousin.* • The **Old Testament** is the holy writings of the Jewish people that form the first part of the Christian Bible. Compare **New Testament** at NEW DIFFERENT. • The **Old World** is Europe, Asia, and Africa, or people and customs that came from there. Compare **New World** at NEW DIFFERENT.

olden /'oʊl·dən/ *adj* [not gradable] from a long time ago • *olden times/days*

old–fashioned /'oʊld'fæʃ·ənd/ *adj* not modern; belonging to or typical of a time in the past • *old-fashioned clothes/ideas/music* ○ *She's old-fashioned* (= her views are typical of the past, not the present).

oldie /'oʊl·di/ *n* [C] *infml* someone or something, esp. a song, movie, or joke, that was popular long ago • *That radio station plays only golden oldies.*

Olestra /oʊ'les·trə/ *n* [U] *trademark* an artificially produced substance that replaces fat in some foods

olive /ˈɑl·ɪv/ *n* [C/U] a small, oval fruit eaten raw or cooked or pressed to make oil, or the evergreen tree on which this fruit grows • Olive is also a dark, yellow-green color. [U]

Olympics /əˈlɪm·pɪks, oʊ-/, **Olympic Games** /ə ˌlɪm·pɪk ˈɡeɪmz, oʊ-/ *pl n* international winter and summer sports competitions, each taking place every four years, but not in the same year • *She won a gold medal at the Winter Olympics in Nagano, Japan, in 1998.*

Olympic /əˈlɪm·pɪk, oʊ-/ *adj* [not gradable] • *Olympic athletes/competitions* ○ *an Olympic gold medalist*

Olympian /əˈlɪm·piː·ən, oʊ-/ *n* [C] a competitor in the Olympics

ombudsman /ˈɑmˌbʊdz·mən, -bədz-/ *n* [C] *pl* **-men** someone who works for a government or large organization and deals with the complaints made against it

omelet, **omelette** /ˈɑm·lət/ *n* [C] eggs with their yellow and transparent parts mixed together, cooked in a pan, and usually folded over some other food • *a cheese/mushroom omelet*

omen /ˈoʊ·mən/ *n* [C] an event that is thought to tell something about the future • *Scoring that goal was an omen of things to come.*

ominous /ˈɑm·ə·nəs/ *adj* suggesting something unpleasant will happen • *a ominous silence*

ominously /ˈɑm·ə·nə·sli/ *adv* • *Clouds had gathered ominously.*

omit /oʊˈmɪt, ə-/ *v* [T] **-tt-** to fail to include or do (something) • *I'd be upset if my name were omitted from the list of contributors.*

omission /oʊˈmɪʃ·ən, ə-/ *n* [C/U] • *The omission of black artists from the show is wrong.* [U]

omnipotent /ɑmˈnɪp·ət̬·ənt/ *adj* [not gradable] having the power to do anything • *Belief in an omnipotent creator is a feature of many religions.*

omnipotence /ɑmˈnɪp·ət̬·əns/ *n* [U] • *America had illusions of omnipotence in the 1950s.*

omniscient /ɑmˈnɪʃ·ənt/ *adj* [not gradable] having or seeming to have unlimited knowledge • *They give the impression that the magazine is omniscient.*

omniscience /ɑmˈnɪʃ·əns/ *n* [U]

omnivorous /ɑmˈnɪv·ə·rəs/ *adj* [not gradable] eating both plants and meat • *Bears are omnivorous.*

on SUPPORTED BY /ɔːn, ɑn/ *adv* [not gradable], *prep* supported by or resting at the top of another thing • *There is snow on the ground.* ○ *You put pudding in the pie crust and then put whipped cream on.*

on ATTACHED TO /ɔːn, ɑn/ *adj, adv* [not gradable], *prep* attached to or forming a part of another thing • *Read the instructions on the*

bag. ○ *Hang your coat on that hook.* ○ *Don't screw the lid on so tight.*

on COVERING /ɔːn, ɑn/ *adj, adv* [not gradable], *prep* covering or wrapping another thing • *The child had no shoes on her feet.* ○ *You should put a coat on.* ○ *That man's got nothing on (= is not wearing anything)!*

on AT /ɔːn, ɑn/ *prep* at, near, or next to a particular place, thing, or person • *They live on Carlisle Street.* ○ *Which page is that cheesecake recipe on?* ○ *El Paso is on the Mexican border.* ○ *Princess Caroline was seated on my left.*

on STORED AS /ɔːn, ɑn/ *prep* used to show the form in which information is stored or recorded for use with an electronic device • *How much data can you store on your hard disk?* ○ *That movie just came out on video.*

on BROADCAST /ɔːn, ɑn/ *adj, adv* [not gradable], *prep* being broadcast • *What's on TV tonight?* ○ *I wish there were more jazz on the radio.*

on USING /ɔːn, ɑn/ *prep* showing what tool, instrument, system, etc., is used to do or achieve something • *I made this chart on my computer.* ○ *I'm on the telephone.* ○ *You'll cut yourself on that knife if you're not careful.*

on TAKING /ɔːn, ɑn/ *prep* showing that a drug is taken or used • *My doctor put me on antibiotics.* ○ *Parker was on heroin at the time.*

on NEEDING HELP FROM /ɔːn, ɑn/ *prep* used after some verbs and adjectives to show that help is needed from a person or thing • *We're counting on you to drive us to the airport.*

on EXISTING /ɔːn, ɑn/ *prep* used to show that a condition or process exists or is being experienced • *The musicians are on strike.* ○ *Are winter coats on sale?*

on INVOLVED IN /ɔːn, ɑn/ *prep* involved in or doing a particular thing • *I'm working on a new book.* ○ *She's on a diet.* • On is also used to show that someone is doing something they were chosen to do: *There was a guard on duty.*

on CONNECTED WITH /ɔːn, ɑn/ *prep* connected with or part of a group or process • *Have you ever served on a jury?* ○ *There are two women on the committee.*

on ABOUT /ɔːn, ɑn/ *prep* about or having something as a subject • *Did you see that documentary on volcanoes last night?* ○ *Sarita's thesis is on George Crumb.*

on PAYING FOR /ɔːn, ɑn/ *prep* showing that something is paid for or how something is paid for • *I've wasted a lot of money on this car.* ○ *Lunch is on me.*

on WHEN /ɔːn, ɑn/ *prep* used to show when something happens • *What are you doing on Friday?* ○ *My birthday's on May 30th.* ○ *The flight arrived on time (= at the time it was expected).*

on TRAVEL BY /ɔːn, ɑn/ *adv, adj* [not gradable], *prep* used to show a method of travel; VIA • *It's easy to get to the beach on foot.* ○ *Two people rode by on horseback.* • On is also sometimes used to show you are getting in a vehicle: *It's time to get on the bus.*

on COMPARED WITH /ɔːn, ɑn/ *prep* used to make a comparison • *This week's sales figures are down on last week's.* ○ *He's got two inches on me* (= is two inches taller).

on HAVING AN EFFECT /ɔːn, ɑn/ *prep* used to show that something has happened to someone • *Marty is always playing jokes on people.* ○ *My car broke down on me this morning.*

on POSSESSING /ɔːn, ɑn/ *prep* possessing, carrying, or having something with you now • *Do you have any money on you?* ○ *I don't have my driver's license on me.*

on NOT STOPPING /ɔːn, ɑn/ *adv* [not gradable] continuing or not stopping • *If her line's busy, keep on trying.* • *The noise just went* **on and on** (= continued for a long time).

on TOWARD /ɔːn, ɑn/ *adv* [not gradable] toward or to something or someone • *You go on and I'll meet you at the lake.* ○ *Pass the newsletter on to Emily.*

on OPERATING /ɔːn, ɑn/ *adj, adv* [not gradable] operating or made to start operating • *Would you turn the TV on?* ○ *The electricity hasn't been turned back on yet.* • (*infml*) When someone is on, they are either performing very well or they are in a situation where they must be aware of everything that is happening and ready to act: *Andy was really on last night—I haven't heard him sing like that in months.* ○ *The thing about breast-feeding a baby is that you have to be on all the time.*

on HAPPENING /ɔːn, ɑn/ *adj* [not gradable] happening or planned • *I have nothing on for tomorrow.* ○ *Is the party still on?* • If something happens **on and off** (also **off and on**), it does not happen all the time.

on–board /ˌɔːnˌbɔːrd, ˌɑn-, -ˌboʊrd/ *adj* [not gradable] existing among the parts that make up or come with a vehicle • *an on-board computer*

once AT ONE TIME /wʌns/ *adv* [not gradable] on or at a single time • *I went to Disney World once.* ○ *The book club meets once a month.* • *You've got to phone him* **at once** (= immediately). • **At once** also means at the same time: *Everything happened at once—she graduated, got a job, and got married, all in June!* • *They settled the matter* **once and for all** (= completely and finally). • **Once in a blue moon** means rarely: *Once in a blue moon he'd call, but for months at a time we heard nothing.* • *We see each other (every)* **once in a while** (= sometimes). • *I'll explain it* **once again/once more** (= another time). • *Going to the Olympics is a* **once-in-a-lifetime** *opportunity* (= a rare and valuable one). • LP WORDS WITH THE MEANING "ONE" at ONE SINGLE

once IN THE PAST /wʌns/ *adv* [not gradable] in the past, but not now • *I lived in Milwaukee once.* ○ *Computers are much cheaper now than they once were.*

once AS SOON AS /wʌns/ *conjunction* as soon as, or when • *Once you've tried their ice cream, you'll be back for more.*

once–over /ˈwʌnˌsoʊ·vər/ *n* [C usually sing] *infml* a quick examination of someone or something • *The security guards gave me the once-over.*

oncoming /ˈɔːnˌkʌm·ɪŋ, ˈɑn-/ *adj* [not gradable] moving toward or approaching you • *His car was struck by an oncoming vehicle.*

one NUMBER /wʌn/ *number* 1 • *I have one brother and two sisters.* ○ *Paula rented a one-room studio apartment.* • One can also mean one o'-clock. • Things that happen **one after another/one after the other** happen in a series: *He ate one chocolate after another until the box was finished.* • **One-on-one** means having direct, personal communication: *Smaller class sizes mean that children get more one-on-one teacher attention.* • A **one-man/one-woman** show is a show of artistic work by a single person. • **One-upmanship** or **one-upsmanship** is the effort to get an advantage over someone, esp. by making them believe they are at a disadvantage: *There has been the usual boasting and one-upsmanship that accompany heavyweight fights.* • USAGE: The related adjective is FIRST. • LP NUMBERS

one SINGLE /wʌn/ *adj* [not gradable], *pronoun* not two or more • *There are too many of us to fit in just one car.* • **One by one** means singly and one after the other: *The children filed out of the bus, one by one.* • If you do something **one step at a time**, you do a little at a time: *He wanted to rush through the job, but I encouraged him to take it one step at a time.* • (*slang*) A **one-night stand** is a single act of sex, without a continuing relationship. • **One-shot** means only once: *The tryouts are a one-shot deal, so you either you get the part or you don't.* • If something is **one-sided**, it is not balanced or fair: *The book presents a one-sided view of history.* • Of a competition, **one-sided** means by a large amount: *a one-sided victory, 10-3.* • **One-time** means only once: *The gym charges a separate, one-time fee to join.* • Someone who has a **one-track mind** tends to think about or be interested in a single subject. • **One-way** describes something that travels or allows travel in only a single direction: *a one-way street* ○ *He bought a one-way ticket to Miami.*

one ONLY /wʌn/ *adj* [not gradable] used when saying there is no other person or thing • *He's the one person you can rely on in an emergency.* • *This may be your* **one and only** (= single) *opportunity to meet her.*

one PARTICULAR THING / PERSON /wʌn/ *adj* [not gradable], *pronoun* used to refer to a particular thing or person within a group or range of things or people • *There are lots of flavors—which one would you like?* ○ *Which one of you knows the way to Millie's house?* ○ *Kayla is the one with dark brown hair.* ○ *The twins look*

WORDS WITH THE MEANING "ONE"

Words used to count one thing or person are **one**, **single**, **only**, **sole**, **alone**, and **first**.

One is used before a noun when you want to emphasize that there is only one person or thing, or for contrast.

Will all the books fit on **one** *shelf?* · *I can't tell* **one** *sister from the other.*

One is also used with *of* to refer to a member of a group.

One of *my cousins is coming to visit.* · *Guangzhou is* **one of** *the largest cities in China.*

Single can be used before a noun to emphasize the idea of there being no more than one person or thing.

A **single** *candle burned in the window.*

Only is used before a noun to show there are no others of the same type or in the same situation. Usually, *the* or a possessive pronoun is used before it.

Math is the **only** *subject I really like.* · *Julio was the* **only** *one who brought a gift.*

Sole has the same meaning as *only*, but sounds a little more formal.

He was the **sole** *survivor of the crash.*

Alone can be used after a noun to emphasize that the statement refers to that person or thing and no others.

She **alone** *knew where the money was hidden.*

First is used for a thing or person that comes before all others. **Very** can be put before it for emphasis.

He was the **first** *person to arrive.* · *She was the* **very first** *person I met in college.*

Words used to count one event are **once**, **only**, and **first**.

Once means one time.

I've been to Mexico **once**. · *She calls her sister* **once** *a week.*

Only can be used to emphasize that there have been no other such occasions.

The **only** *time I was on a boat I got sick.*

First is used for an event that comes before all others of the same type.

Is this your **first** *time on a plane?* · *I* **first** *visited Tokyo in 1990.*

LP) **Definite and indefinite articles**

identical—it's hard to tell **one** *from the other.* ○ *She is* **one** *beautiful woman* (= she is very beautiful). ○ *Why don't we meet for lunch* **one** *day next week?* · *I'd like to go to Mexico again* **one day** (= at some time in the future). · To be **one** *of* a group of people or things is to be a member of that group: *It's* **one of** *the most popular songs.* · If someone or something is **one of a kind**, there is no other person or thing like

them: *In the world of ballet, she was* **one of a kind**. · *She hangs out with her brothers' friends, like* **one of the boys** (= a member of their group). · *These bills have to be paid* **one way or another** (= in some possible way). · You say **on the one hand** but **on the other hand** when you are comparing two opposing opinions: *On the one hand, I'd like a job that pays more, but on the other hand I enjoy the work I'm doing now.* · **One another** means EACH OTHER. · **One-time** means at some time in the past, but no longer: *The one-time Olympic track star is now a coach.*

one [ANY PERSON] /wʌn/ *pronoun fml* any person, but not a particular person · *One ought to make the effort to vote.*

oneself /wʌn'self, wən-/ *pronoun fml* · *One needs to take care of oneself.* · LP) REFLEXIVE PRONOUNS

onerous /'an·ə·rəs, 'oʊ·nə-/ *adj* causing great difficulty or trouble · *The tax bill was aimed at lifting the onerous tax burden from the backs of the middle class.*

ongoing /'ɔːn,goʊ·ɪŋ, 'an-/ *adj* [not gradable] continuing to exist, happen, or develop · *The investigation is ongoing.*

onion /'ʌn·jən/ *n* [C] a plant with a round, edible root having a strong smell and flavor

on–line /'ɔːn'laɪn, 'an-/, **online** *adj, adv* [not gradable] using a computer to communicate with other computers, or of or about a computer that is connected to another computer · *I went on-line to see if I got any e-mail.* ○ *The computer isn't on-line now, so the phone line is available.*

onlooker /'ɔːn,lʊk·ər, 'an-/ *n* [C] someone who watches something happening but is not involved in it · *The building was demolished before a crowd of nearly 200 onlookers.*

only [SINGLE] /'oʊn·li/ *adj* [not gradable] being a particular one or that one and no other; single · *As the only surviving relative, he will someday inherit a lot of money.* ○ *The only solution is stop drinking completely.* · An **only child** is a child with no sisters or brothers. · LP) WORDS WITH THE MEANING "ONE" on this page.

only [NO MORE THAN] /'oʊn·li/ *adv* [not gradable] no more than or no other than; as much or as great as (something) but no more; just · *She was only 27 when she died.* ○ *These shoes only cost $40.* ○ *I was only trying to help.* ○ *I was only going to say that I was sorry.* · Only can mean and no one else: *Only she knew the truth.* ○ *This club is for members only.* ○ *I got paid only* (= as recently as) *yesterday.* · You can use **only just** to refer to something that happens almost immediately after something else: *She only just arrived in town.* · **Only just** can also mean almost not: *She only just had enough money to pay for the taxi.* · **Only too** means very: *There are some people who would be only too happy to cheat on their tax returns.*

only 594

only [IN THIS WAY] /'oʊn·li/ *adv* [not gradable] for this reason or in this way and no other • *You only said that to annoy me.* ○ *It only happened because he forgot to lock the front door.*

only [BUT] /'oʊn·li/ *conjunction* but; except that • *This fabric is similar to wool, only cheaper.* ○ *I would have left earlier, only you didn't want to.*

onset /'ɔːn·set, 'ɑn-/ *n* [U] the beginning of something • *We have to get the roof fixed before the onset of winter.*

onslaught /'ɑn·slɔːt, 'ɔːn-/ *n* [C] a violent and forceful attack • *(fig.)* *On the day before Christmas, department stores were bracing themselves for the onslaught of last-minute shoppers.*

onto /'ɔːn·tə, 'ɑn-, -tuː/ *prep* into a position on • *Gennaro tossed his newspaper onto the table.* • To **be onto** something or someone is to be aware of information related to it or them, esp. when they are trying to deceive you: *Everybody is onto your game—why don't you admit you lied?*

onus /'oʊ·nəs/ *n* [U] the responsibility or duty to do something • *The onus is on the administration to come up with a balanced budget.*

onward /'ɔːn·wərd, 'ɑn-/, **onwards** /'ɔːn·wərdz, 'ɑn-/ *adv, adj* [not gradable] further on in place or time • *The geese continued onward, heading south.*

oodles /'uːd·ᵊlz/ *pl n infml* very large amounts • *She inherited oodles of money.*

oops /ʊps, uːps/ *exclamation infml* used to express surprise or regret about a mistake or slight accident

ooze /uːz/ *v* [I/T] to flow slowly out through a small opening, or to slowly produce (a liquid) through such an opening • *Pus oozed from her ears.* [I always + adv/prep] ○ *The wound oozed blood.* [T] ○ *(fig.)* *The candidate just oozes confidence* (= shows much confidence). [T]

ooze /uːz/ *n* [U] soft, sticky earth

opaque /oʊ'peɪk/ *adj* [not gradable] (of a substance) preventing light from traveling through, and therefore not allowing you to see through it • *opaque watercolors* • Opaque also means difficult to understand: *The majority of readers found his poetry difficult, even opaque.* • Compare TRANSLUCENT; TRANSPARENT.

op-ed /'ɑp'ed/ *n* [U] a page or section of a newspaper with signed articles expressing personal opinions, usually opposite the page of EDITORIALS (= statements of the newspaper's opinions)

open [POSITIONED FOR ACCESS] /'oʊ·pən/ *adj, adv* being in a position that allows things to pass through or that allows for immediate use; not closed or fastened • *The window was wide open.* ○ *The trunk of his car had been pried open.* • A problem or legal matter that is **open-and-shut** is easy to prove or answer: *Our lawyer thinks that we have an open-and-shut case.*

• **Open-heart surgery** is a medical operation in which the heart is repaired while the body's blood is kept flowing by a machine.

open /'oʊ·pən/ *v* [I/T] • *She opened a window to let in some air.* [T] ○ *You can open your eyes now.* [T] ○ *These cans open easily.* [I] ○ *That door opens (out) onto the porch.* [I] • If you **open** someone's **eyes**, you show them something, esp. something surprising or shocking that they had not known about or understood before: *She opened my eyes to how foolish I'd been.* • *(infml)* *I was so scared that I never opened my mouth* (= said anything). • If something or someone **opens the floodgates**, it allows action to be taken that has not previously been allowed, or feelings to be expressed that have previously been controlled: *When neighboring states allow casinos, our state will open the floodgates.*

opener /'oʊ·pə·nər/ *n* [C] a device for opening closed containers • *a bottle/can opener*

opening /'oʊ·pə·nɪŋ/ *n* [C] a hole or space • *The children crawled through an opening in the fence.*

open [READY FOR USE] /'oʊ·pən/ *adj* [not gradable] ready to be used or to provide a service • *The supermarket is open till 9 p.m.*

open /'oʊ·pən/ *v* [I/T] to become or make (something) ready to provide a service • *The cleaners opens (up) around seven.* [I] ○ *They opened the exhibit to the public yesterday.* [T]

opening /'oʊ·pə·nɪŋ/ *n* [C] • *A huge crowd turned out for the opening of the new show.*

open [NOT DECIDED] /'oʊ·pən/ *adj* not decided or certain • *I want to keep my options open until I have all the facts.* ○ *Whether we'll go is still an open question.* • *You should keep an open mind* about your new school (= not form any opinions) *until you've been there.* • *She's a cheerful, curious,* **open-minded** *young girl* (= willing to listen to other people and consider new ideas, suggestions, and opinions).

open [NOT SECRET] /'oʊ·pən/ *adj* not secret • *Open warfare has broken out in Yugoslavia.* • A person who is open is honest and not secretive: *He is quite open about his weaknesses.*

open /'oʊ·pən/ *n* • Something that is **in the open** is no longer secret: *I hope we can finally get our feelings out into the open.*

openly /'oʊ·pən·li/ *adv* • *She talked about her cancer quite openly.*

open [BEGIN] /'oʊ·pən/ *v* [I/T] to begin (something) or cause it to begin • *I would like to open the meeting by asking each of you to introduce yourself.* [T] ○ *They're opening up a new restaurant in about a month.* [M] ○ *The film opens (= will be shown for the first time) next week.* [I] • *Do not open fire* (= begin shooting) *until you hear the command.*

opening /'oʊ·pə·nɪŋ/ *adj* [not gradable] • *He made some opening remarks, then introduced the main speaker.* • The **opening night** of play, movie, etc., is the first night it is performed or shown.

opening /'oʊ·pə·nɪŋ/ n [C] • *The opening* (= beginning) *of the symphony is by far the best part.*

opener /'oʊ·pə·nər/ n [C] *infml* the first in a series of competitions or items • *The team played their season opener a couple of nights ago.*

open NOT COVERED /'oʊ·pən/ *adj* not enclosed or covered • *The park is one of the city's largest open spaces.* • The **open air** is anywhere which is not inside a building: *It's nice to get out in the open air.*

open /'oʊ·pən/ n [U] • *After being at work all day, it's good to get (out) in the open* (= somewhere outside a building).

open AVAILABLE /'oʊ·pən/ *adj* [not gradable] available; not limited • *Are there any positions open in the marketing department?* ○ *This library is open to the general public.* • If something is **open to** a specific condition, it is not protected against it: *Their behavior left them open to criticism.* • *I'm* **open to** (= willing to consider) *any reasonable suggestion.* • An **open house** is a party at which visitors are welcome in your home, or an occasion when an organization such as a school or college allows members of the public in to see what happens there: *We're having an open house on Sunday.* • An **open house** is also a time when a house or apartment that is being sold or is available for rent can be looked at by the public. • The **open market** is a trading situation in which anyone can be involved and prices are not controlled: *These guns are being sold on the open market.* • **Open season** is the period in the year when it is legal to hunt particular animals, or *(fig.)* a situation in which a particular group of people is attacked: *(fig.) The mayor has declared open season on jaywalkers.*

opening /'oʊ·pə·nɪŋ/ n [C] an available position or job • *I hear you have an opening in sales.*

▫ **open up** LET IN /ˌ--'-/ v adv [I] (used as an exclamation) let me in; open the door • *"Open up!" Sam shouted, banging on the door.*

▫ **open up** MAKE AVAILABLE /'--'-/ v adv [T] to make (something) available • *Robinson, the first black player, opened up a wealth of opportunity for others.*

▫ **open up** *obj* MAKE LARGER, **open** *obj* **up** /'--'-/ v adv [M] to make larger or less enclosed • *We're going to open up the kitchen by knocking down that wall.*

▫ **open up** SPEAK /'--'-/ v adv [I] to talk about your personal thoughts or feelings • *I felt I couldn't open up to anybody.*

opera /'ɑp·rə, 'ɑp·ə·rə/ n [C/U] a formal play in which all or most of the words are sung, or this type of play generally

operatic /ˌɑp·ə'ræt̬·ɪk/ *adj*

operate WORK /'ɑp·əˌreɪt/ v [I/T] to work or cause (something) to work, be in action, or have an effect • *How do you operate the remote control unit?* [T] ○ *Changes are being introduced to make the department operate more efficiently.* [I]

operation /ˌɑp·ə'reɪ·ʃən/ n [C/U] • *Several printing presses are in operation* (= working) *at the moment.* [U] ○ *Setting a mousetrap is a delicate operation* (= act of doing something). [C] • An operation is also an activity planned to achieve something: *a rescue operation* [C]

operational /ˌɑp·ə'reɪ·ʃən·əl/ *adj* [not gradable] • *Repairs have already begun and we expect the plant to soon be fully operational* (= working correctly and completely).

operative /'ɑp·ə·rət̬·ɪv/ *adj slightly fml* working, or in existence • *Our computerized stock-control system is now operative.* ○ *I'm looking for a large, affordable apartment—and "affordable" is the operative word* (= it has special importance).

operator /'ɑp·əˌreɪt̬·ər/ n [C] a person who makes something work or puts something into action • *a computer/machine operator* • An operator is also a person who works on a telephone SWITCHBOARD: *Dial zero for the operator.* • (*esp. disapproving*) An operator is a person who is often successful but seems too intelligent or speaks and acts too quick and may not always be honest: *He's a smooth operator.*

operate MEDICAL PROCESS /'ɑp·əˌreɪt/ v [I] to cut a body open in order to repair, remove, or replace an unhealthy or damaged part • *Doctors will operate on her tomorrow morning.* • An **operating room** (*abbreviation* **OR**) is a specially equipped room in a hospital in which people are operated on.

operation /ˌɑp·ə'reɪ·ʃən/ n [C] • *She underwent a six-hour open-heart operation.*

operetta /ˌɑp·ə'ret̬·ə/ n [C/U] an amusing play in which many or all of the words are sung and which often includes some dancing, or this type of play generally

ophthalmologist /ˌɑf·θəl'mɑl·ə·dʒəst, ˌɑp-/ n [C] *medical* a doctor who specializes in treatment of the eye

opinion /ə'pɪn·jən/ n [C/U] the ideas that a person or a group of people have about something or someone, which are based mainly on their feelings and beliefs, or a single idea of this type • *Many people have strong opinions about/on capital punishment.* [C] ○ *McGuinness was expressing his personal opinion.* [C] ○ *Her writings influenced public opinion.* [U] ○ *I think you're wrong, though you're certainly entitled to your opinion.* [C]

opinionated /ə'pɪn·jəˌneɪt̬·əd/ *adj* having strong opinions and expressing them freely • *She's seven years old and she's already pretty opinionated.*

opium /'oʊ·piː·əm/ n [U] a drug made from

POPPY plants and used in medicine to control pain or help people sleep, sometimes taken illegally for its temporarily pleasant effects

opossum /ə'pɑs·əm/, *short form* **possum** *n* [C] a small animal that lives in trees and has thick fur, a long nose, and no hair on its tail

opponent OPPOSING POSITION /ə'pou·nənt/ *n* [C] a person who disagrees with something and speaks against it or tries to change it • *Opponents of the project fear it will attract undesirables.*

opponent COMPETITOR /ə'pou·nənt/ *n* [C] a person you are competing against, esp. in politics or sports • *His chief opponent in the November election will be Jim Crowley.*

opportune /ˌɑp·ər'tuːn/ *adj* happening at a time which is likely to give success or which is convenient • *You couldn't have arrived at a more opportune time.*

opportunist /ˌɑp·ər'tuː·nəst/ *n* [C] *disapproving* a person who takes advantage of every chance they have for success without thinking about the effects of their actions on other people • *There will always be opportunists ready to play on the public's fears and prejudices.*

opportunistic /ˌɑp·ər·tuː'nɪs·tɪk/ *adj* • *Our team was pretty opportunistic and took advantage of some mistakes.*

opportunity /ˌɑp·ər'tuː·nət̬·i/ *n* [C/U] an occasion or situation which makes it possible to do something that you want to do or have to do, or the possibility of doing something • *She was given the opportunity to manage a day care center.* [C] ○ *The university is not providing enough recreational opportunities for the community.* [C] ○ *He had ample opportunity to examine the car.* [U]

oppose /ə'pouz/ *v* [T] to disagree with (something), often by speaking or fighting against it • *The governor adamantly/vehemently opposes raising taxes.* • USAGE: The related noun is OPPONENT OPPOSING POSITION.

opposed /ə'pouzd/ *adj* • *He was opposed to slavery.* • *I'd prefer to go in May,* **as opposed to** (= rather than) *September.*

opposing /ə'pou·zɪŋ/ *adj* [not gradable] • *The opposing sides failed to reach agreement today.*

opposite DIFFERENT /'ɑp·ə·zət/ *adj* [not gradable] completely different • *We turned and walked in the opposite direction.* ○ *People often believe the exact opposite of what you tell them.* ○ *His efforts to intimidate his enemies produced just the opposite effect* (= made them braver).

opposite /'ɑp·ə·zət/ *n* [C/U] • *My father is a very calm person, but my mother is just the opposite.* [U] ○ *Do you think it's true that opposites are attracted to each other?* [C]

opposite FACING /'ɑp·ə·zət/ *adj, adv* [not gradable], *prep* being in a position on the other side; facing • *The two settlements are on opposite sides of the river.* ○ *We're in the building opposite the gas station.* ○ *She asked the man sitting opposite if she could borrow his newspaper.*

opposition /ˌɑp·ə'zɪʃ·ən/ *n* [U] disagreement with something, often by speaking or fighting against it, or (esp. in politics) the people or group who are not in power • *The proposal faces strong opposition.* ○ *They expect to defeat the opposition.*

oppress RULE /ə'pres/ *v* [T] to govern (people) in an unfair and cruel way and prevent them from having opportunities and freedom • *He says that white society keeps black men oppressed and deprived and ignorant.*

oppression /ə'preʃ·ən/ *n* [U] • *There's less oppression and freer speech here now.*

oppressive /ə'pres·ɪv/ *adj* • *an oppressive government*

oppressor /ə'pres·ər/ *n* [C] • *They're not the powerful oppressors that society says they are.*

oppress MAKE UNCOMFORTABLE /ə'pres/ *v* [T] to make (a person) feel uncomfortable or anxious • *He's just as confused and oppressed by love as I am.*

oppressive /ə'pres·ɪv/ *adj* • *an oppressive sense of guilt* • *Oppressive weather is hot, with a lot of wetness in the air.*

oppressively /ə'pres·ɪv·li/ *adv* • *It was oppressively hot on the bus.*

opt /ɑpt/ *v* [I] to make a choice, esp. for one thing or possibility in preference to any others • *Some guys opt for boxer shorts.* ○ *He opted out of the health insurance plan* (= chose not to be a part of it).

optical /'ɑp·tɪ·kəl/ *adj* [not gradable] connected with the eyes or sight, or connected with or using light • *an optical telescope* • An **optical illusion** is something you think you see, but which is not really there: *Some sort of optical illusion makes these things seem to travel faster than they really do.*

optic /'ɑp·tɪk/ *adj* [not gradable] *medical* referring to the eyes • *the optic nerve*

optician /ɑp'tɪʃ·ən/ *n* [C] a person who makes LENSES for eyeglasses or sells eyeglasses

optics /'ɑp·tɪks/ *n* [U] the study of light

optimal /'ɑp·tə·məl/ *adj* OPTIMUM

optimism /'ɑp·tə,mɪz·əm/ *n* [U] the tendency to be hopeful and to emphasize or think of the good part in a situation rather than the bad part, or the feeling that in the future good things are more likely to happen than bad things • *There was a note of optimism in his voice as he spoke about his recovery.* • USAGE: The opposite of optimism is PESSIMISM.

optimist /'ɑp·tə·məst/ *n* [C] • *She was an optimist in the face of adversity.*

optimistic /ˌɑp·tə'mɪs·tɪk/ *adj* • *I'm optimistic that they can work things out.*

optimistically /ˌɑp·tə'mɪs·tɪ·kli/ *adv* • *White optimistically predicted success.*

optimum /'ɑp·tə·məm/, **optimal** *adj* [not gradable] being the best or most likely to bring success or advantage • *For optimum flavor, prepare just before serving.*

option /'ɑp·ʃən/ *n* [C] one thing that can be

chosen from a set of possibilities, or the freedom to make a choice • *The program helps students explore career options.* • An option is also a part of a contract that allows for something to happen in the future: *He decided to exercise an option to break the team's lease on the stadium.* • If someone **keeps/leaves** their **options open**, they wait before making a choice: *I haven't signed a contract—I'm leaving my options open.*

optional /ɑpˈʃən·əl/ *adj* [not gradable] not necessary or demanded but possible or available; depending on what you decide to do • *I think military service should be completely optional.*

optometrist /ɑpˈtɑm·ə·trəst/ *n* [C] a person trained to test the sight of people and to decide how best to improve their sight, if necessary, by ordering eyeglasses or **contact lenses** for them

optometry /ɑpˈtɑm·ə·tri/ *n* [U] • *She decided to study optometry.*

opulent /ˈɑp·jə·lənt/ *adj* rich in appearance; showing great wealth • *He lived the life of a playboy in an opulent Chicago mansion.*

opulence /ˈɑp·jə·ləns/ *n* [U]

or [POSSIBILITIES] /ɔr, ər/ *conjunction* used to connect different possibilities • *Is today Tuesday or Wednesday?* ○ *You can get that blouse in blue, gray, or white.* ○ *There were ten or twelve people in the room* (= approximately that number of people). ○ *We'd better make a decision soon or the whole deal will fall through.* • After a negative verb, or can also continue the negative meaning of the verb: *He won't eat meat or fish* (= and will not eat fish either). • **Or else** is a stronger way of saying or: *We'd better be there by eight or else we'll miss the beginning.* • When **or else** is spoken at the end of an order you give someone, it is a threat, but it can also be meant humorously: *You'd better remember to bring the baby bottles this time, or else!* • **Or other** is used after words such as some, someone, something, or somewhere when you cannot be exact about what you are saying: *The event will be held in some park or other.* • **Or so** means approximately: *We raised $500 or so for charity.*

or [EXPLAIN] /ɔr, ər/ *conjunction* used to show that a word or phrase means the same as, or explains or corrects, another word or phrase • *Photons, or individual particles of light, travel huge distances in space.* ○ *Things were going well, or seemed to be, but the relationship had already begun to change.*

oral [SPOKEN] /ˈɔr·əl, ˈoʊr-, ˈɑr-/ *adj* [not gradable] spoken; not written • *an oral agreement/exam*

orally /ˈɔr·ə·li, ˈoʊr-, ˈɑr-/ *adv* [not gradable] • *She decided to give the report orally rather than in writing.*

oral [MOUTH] /ˈɔr·əl, ˈoʊr-, ˈɑr-/ *adj* [not gradable] of, taken by, or done to the mouth • *oral*

contraceptives ○ *oral surgery* • **Oral sex** is the activity of using the tongue, lips, and mouth to give pleasure to someone's sexual organs.

orally /ˈɔr·ə·li, ˈoʊr-, ˈɑr-/ *adv* [not gradable] • *This medicine is to be taken orally.*

orange [COLOR] /ˈɑr·əndʒ, ˈɔr-/ *adj* [not gradable], *n* [U] (of) the color that is a mixture of red and yellow • *an orange jacket* ○ *The setting sun made the sky orange.*

orange [FRUIT] /ˈɑr·əndʒ, ˈɔr-/ *n* [C/U] a round, orange-colored fruit that is valued mainly for its sweet juice

orangutan, orangutang /əˈræŋ·ə,tæŋ, -,tæn/ *n* [C] a large APE (= animal like a monkey) with red-and-brown hair and long arms

oratory /ˈɔr·ə,tɔr·i, ˈɑr-, -,toʊr·i/ *n* [U] the activity of giving skillful and effective speeches in public

oration /ɔˈreɪ·ʃən/ *n* [C] a formal public speech about a serious subject • *a funeral oration*

orator /ˈɔr·ət·ər, ˈɑr-/ *n* [C] • *Daniel Webster was famous as an orator.*

orbit /ˈɔr·bət/ *n* [C/U] the curved path through which objects in space move around a planet or star that has GRAVITY (= a pulling force) • *The spacecraft was launched and went into orbit last week.* [U]

orbit /ˈɔr·bət/ *v* [I/T] • *The spacecraft is orbiting (the earth) at a height of several hundred miles.* [I/T]

orchard /ˈɔr·tʃərd/ *n* [C] an area of land where fruit trees are grown • *an apple orchard*

orchestra /ˈɔr·kə·strə, -,kes·trə/ *n* [C] a large group of musicians playing different instruments and usually organized to play together and led by a CONDUCTOR • *the New York Philharmonic Orchestra* • The orchestra of a theater is the part on the main floor: *We've got seats in the fifth row of the orchestra.* • In a theater, the **orchestra pit** is the area in front of the stage where the musicians sit.

orchestral /ɔrˈkes·trəl/ *adj* [not gradable] • *an orchestral arrangement*

orchestrate /ˈɔr·kə,streɪt/ *v* [T] to arrange or write (a piece of music) to be played by an orchestra

orchestration /ˌɔr·kəˈstreɪ·ʃən/ *n* [C/U]

orchestrate /ˈɔr·kə,streɪt/ *v* [T] to plan and organize (something) carefully and sometimes secretly in order to achieve a desired result • *There was a worldwide protest, orchestrated mainly by liberals and the left wing.*

orchid /ˈɔr·kəd/ *n* [C] a plant with three-part flowers, or one of its flowers, which can be white or of several different colors

ordain /ɔrˈdeɪn/ *v* [T] to make (someone) officially a priest, minister, or rabbi in a religious ceremony • USAGE: The related noun is ORDINATION.

ordeal /ɔrˈdiːl/ *n* [C] an experience that is very painful, difficult, or tiring • *Her seven-month stay in the hospital was quite an ordeal.*

order INSTRUCTION /'ɔːrd·ər/ *n* [C] something you are told to do by someone else and which you must do • *The Third Infantry Division received the order to attack at 4 a.m.* [+ *to* infinitive] ○ *His defense was that he was only obeying orders.*

order /'ɔːrd·ər/ *v* [T] (esp. of a person in authority) to tell (someone) to do something • *They ordered him to leave the room.*

order REQUEST /'ɔːrd·ər/ *v* [I/T] to ask for (something) to be made, supplied, or delivered • *Are you ready to order, or do you need a little more time?* [I] ○ *I ordered some pasta and a mixed salad.* [T] ○ *After looking through the catalog, she called the store and ordered new sheets and towels.* [T]

order /'ɔːrd·ər/ *n* [C] • *Can I take your order now or would you like to have a drink first?* ○ *I would like to place* (= make) *an order for the new software.* • An order is also the thing that has been requested: *The store phoned to say your order has come in.* • If something is **on order**, you have asked for it to be obtained but have not yet received it: *The lamp has been on order for several weeks.*

order ARRANGEMENT /'ɔːrd·ər/ *n* [U] the way in which people or things are arranged in relation to one another or according to a particular characteristic • *Please arrange the books in alphabetical order by author.* ○ *I can't find the files I need because they're all out of order* (= they are not arranged in the correct way). • If you leave/put things in order, you make them neat: *I want to leave my desk in order before I go on vacation.*

order /'ɔːrd·ər/ *v* [T] • *The records are ordered by date.*

orderly /'ɔːrd·ər·li/ *adj* well arranged or organized • *During the fire drill, the children were asked to proceed in an orderly way down the stairs and out of the building.*

order PURPOSE /'ɔːrd·ər/ *n* [U] • **In order** means with the stated aim or purpose: *He came home early in order to see the children before they went to bed.* ○ *In order for us to win, we'll all have to try a little harder.*

order CORRECT BEHAVIOR /'ɔːrd·ər/ *n* [U] a situation in which rules are obeyed and people do what they are expected to do • *As the demonstration began to turn violent, the police were called in to restore order.*

order USABLE CONDITION /'ɔːrd·ər/ *n* [U] the state of working correctly or of being suitable for use • *The set of power tools are all in good working order.* ○ *Are your immigration papers in order* (= legally correct)? ○ *The elevator is out of order* (= not working).

order SYSTEM /'ɔːrd·ər/ *n* [C] a social or political system • *a new economic order*

orderly /'ɔːrd·ər·li/ *n* [C] a hospital worker who does jobs for which no training is necessary, such as helping nurses or carrying heavy things

ordinal (number) /'ɔːrd·ən·əl ('nʌm·bər)/ *n* [C] a number like 1st, 2nd, 3rd, that shows the position of something in a list of items • *In "She was fifth in the race," "fifth" is an ordinal number.* • Compare CARDINAL (NUMBER). LP NUMBERS

ordinance /'ɔːrd·ən·əns/ *n* [C] a law or rule made by a government or authority • *A city ordinance forbids the parking of cars in this area.*

ordinary /'ɔːrd·ən,er·i/ *adj* not different, special, or unexpected in any way; usual • *His music was of the sort that ordinary Americans could relate to.* ○ *Computers are now widely available in ordinary school settings.*

ordinarily /,ɔːrd·ən'er·ə·li/ *adv* usually; most often • *We ordinarily get paid on Friday, but because Friday is a holiday, we're getting paid on Thursday instead.*

ordination /,ɔːrd·ən'eɪ·ʃən/ *n* [C/U] a religious ceremony at which someone is officially made a priest • USAGE: The related verb is ORDAIN.

ore /ɔːr, oʊr/ *n* [C/U] a substance formed naturally in the ground and from which metal can be obtained • *iron ore* [U]

oregano /ə'reg·ə,noʊ/ *n* [U] an herb whose dried leaves are used in cooking

org /,oʊ,ar'dʒiː, ɔːrg/ *n* [U] used at the end of US INTERNET addresses to show that the address belongs to a group or company that is not established to make a profit • *dictionaries@cup.org*

organ BODY PART /'ɔːr·gən/ *n* [C] a part of the body of a person, animal, or plant that performs a special job • *The ear is an external organ.* ○ *The heart, lungs, and kidneys are internal organs.*

organ INSTRUMENT /'ɔːr·gən/ *n* [C/U] a musical instrument with one or more rows of keys that are pressed with the fingers to play notes produced electronically or by forcing air through pipes of different sizes, or this type of instrument generally • *She plays the organ for her church.* [U]

organist /'ɔːr·gə·nəst/ *n* [C] • *He is the organist at Washington Cathedral.*

organic LIVING /ɔːr'gæn·ɪk/ *adj* [not gradable] consisting of or relating to living plants and animals, or the substances of which they are made • *organic chemistry* • Compare INORGANIC.

organic NO CHEMICALS /ɔːr'gæn·ɪk/ *adj* not using artificial chemicals in the production of plants and animals for food • *organic fruits and vegetables*

organism /'ɔːr·gə,nɪz·əm/ *n* [C] a single living plant, animal, or other living thing • *Some viruses and bacteria are disease-causing organisms.*

organization /,ɔːr·gə·nə'zeɪ·ʃən/ *n* [C] a group whose members work together for a shared purpose in a continuing way • *the*

National Organization of Women ○ *Labor organizations have contributed heavily to the Democratic campaigns.*

organize PLAN /'ɔːr·gə,naɪz/ *v* [T] to make the necessary plans for (something) to happen; arrange • *The group organizes theater trips once a month.* ○ *They organized a meeting between the students and teachers.*

organization /,ɔːr·gə·nə'zeɪ·ʃən/ *n* [U] • *He didn't want to be involved in the organization of the conference.*

organizer /'ɔːr·gə,naɪ·zər/ *n* [C] • *a union organizer*

organize MAKE A SYSTEM /'ɔːr·gə,naɪz/ *v* [T] to do or arrange (something) according to a particular system • *She had organized her work so that she could do some of it at home.*

organization /,ɔːr·gə·nə'zeɪ·ʃən/ *n* [U] arrangement according to a particular system • *An organization by subject rather than by date seems to make sense.*

organized /'ɔːr·gə,naɪzd/ *adj* • If someone is organized, they plan things carefully and keep things in a neat way: *We are looking for a person who is well organized.* • Organized also means relating to groups or people who are members of large and often powerful organizations in a particular area of activity: *organized crime* ○ *organized labor* ○ *organized religion*

orgasm /'ɔːr,gæz·əm/ *n* [C/U] the moment of greatest pleasure and excitement in sexual activity

orgy /'ɔːr·dʒi/ *n* [C] an occasion when a group of people have a lot of sex with little or no control

Orient ASIA /'ɔːr·iː·ənt, 'oʊr-/ *n* [U] the countries in the east and southeast of Asia

oriental /,ɔːr·iː'ent·əl, ,oʊr-/ *adj* [not gradable] • *oriental cuisine/art*

orient FIND DIRECTION /'ɔːr·iː·ənt, 'oʊr-, -,ent/, *esp. Br* **orientate** /'ɔːr·iː·ən,teɪt, 'oʊr-/ *v* [T] to discover the position of (yourself) in relation to your surroundings • *After she came out of the station, she paused to orient herself.*

orientation /,ɔːr·iː·ən'teɪ·ʃən, ,oʊr-/ *n* [U] position of something in relation to its surroundings • *The church has an east-west orientation* (= has one main side facing east and the opposite side facing west).

orient MAKE FAMILIAR /'ɔːr·iː·ənt, 'oʊr-, -,ent/, *esp. Br* **orientate** /'ɔːr·iː·ən,teɪt, 'oʊr-/ *v* [T] to make (someone) familiar with a new place • *Incoming freshmen have advisers to help orient them to the university.*

orientation /,ɔːr·iː·ən'teɪ·ʃən, ,oʊr-/ *n* [C/U] • *There's an orientation* (= meeting to help you become familiar with a new place) *for freshmen tonight.* [C]

orientation /,ɔːr·iː·ən'teɪ·ʃən, ,oʊr-/ *n* [U] the particular interests, activities, or aims of a person or an organization • *He considered it an invasion of privacy to be asked about his sexual orientation* (= the sex of the people whom he was sexually attracted to).

–oriented /,ɔːr·iː,ent·əd, ,oʊr-/ *combining form* showing the direction in which something is aimed • *Hotels are a service-oriented industry.*

origin /'ɔːr·ə·dʒən, 'ɑr-/ *n* [C/U] the thing from which something comes, or the place where it began • *the origins of language* [C] ○ *He studied the origin and development of the nervous system.* [U] • A person's origin is the country from which they come: *The population is of Indian or Pakistani origin.* [U]

original /ə'rɪdʒ·ən·əl/ *n* [C] the first one made and not a copy • *Send a copy of your receipt, but keep the original.* • An original is also a piece of work by an artist or designer and not a copy by someone else. • If someone is an original, they behave or speak in a way that is not like other people.

original /ə'rɪdʒ·ən·əl/ *adj* [not gradable] in the earliest form of something, or in the form that existed at the beginning • *The original plans have been changed.* • Original can also mean different from anything or anyone else and therefore new and interesting: *Our teacher said we'd better come up with something original.* • An original piece of work, such as a painting or drawing, is produced by the artist or writer and is not a copy.

originality /ə,rɪdʒ·ə'næl·əṭ·i/ *n* [U] • *The essays will be judged on the basis of style and originality* (= the degree to which they are new and different).

originally /ə'rɪdʒ·ən·əl·i/ *adv* [not gradable] • *It was a bedroom originally* (= in the beginning), *but we turned it into a study.* ○ *They now live in California, but originally they came from Mexico.*

originate /ə'rɪdʒ·ə,neɪt/ *v* [I] to come from or begin in a particular place or situation • *Jazz originated in the US and is now popular throughout the world.*

originator /ə'rɪdʒ·ə,neɪṭ·ər/ *n* [C] • *Morton was the originator of Arbor Day.*

oriole /'ɔːr·iː·əl, 'oʊr-/ *n* [C] a bird found in many parts of North America, the male of which has bright black and orange or black and yellow feathers

ornament /'ɔːr·nə·mənt/ *n* [C] an object that is decorative rather than useful • *Christmas tree ornaments*

ornament /'ɔːr·nə,ment/ *v* [T] • *A diamond ornamented his left ear.*

ornamental /,ɔːr·nə'ment·əl/ *adj* • *The buttons on the sleeves are just ornamental.*

ornate /ɔːr'neɪt/ *adj* having a lot of decoration • *ornate jewelry/buildings*

ornery /'ɔːr·nə·ri/ *adj infml* tending to get angry and argue with people • *He's ornery and opinionated, but he doesn't lie.*

ornithology /,ɔːr·nə'θɑl·ə·dʒi/ *n* [U] the study of birds

ornithologist /ˌɔːr·nəˈθɑl·ə·dʒəst/ *n* [C] someone who scientifically studies birds

orphan /ˈɔːr·fən/ *n* [C] a child whose parents are dead

orphan /ˈɔːr·fən/ *v* [T] • *She was orphaned at an early age.*

orphanage /ˈɔːr·fə·nɪdʒ/ *n* [C] a home for children whose parents are dead or unable to care for them

orthodontist /ˌɔːr·θəˈdɑnt·əst/ *n* [C] a DENTIST who specializes in correcting the position of the teeth

orthodox /ˈɔːr·θəˌdɑks/ *adj* (of beliefs, ideas, or activities) following generally accepted beliefs or standards • *orthodox methods of teaching* • The **Orthodox Church** is a Christian religious group with many members in Greece and eastern Europe: *a Greek/Russian Orthodox church*

orthopedics /ˌɔːr·θəˈpiːd·ɪks/ *n* [U] the medical specialty that deals with the treatment of bones that did not grow correctly or are damaged

orthopedic /ˌɔːr·θəˈpiːd·ɪk/ *adj* [not gradable] • *an orthopedic surgeon*

Oscar /ˈɑs·kər/ *n* [C] *trademark* an **Academy Award**, see at ACADEMY • *He won an Oscar for best supporting actor.*

oscillate /ˈɑs·əˌleɪt/ *v* [I] to move repeatedly from side to side or up and down between two points, or to vary between two feelings or opinions • *She oscillates between cooperation and hostility.*

oscillation /ˌɑs·əˈleɪ·ʃən/ *n* [C/U]

osmosis /ɑzˈmoʊ·səs, ɑs-/ *n* [U] *specialized* (in animals and plants) the process by which a liquid passes gradually from one part to another through a MEMBRANE (= tissue that covers cells) • Osmosis is also the process by which ideas and information are absorbed without conscious effort: *Children often learn by osmosis.*

ostensible /ɑˈsten·sə·bəl/ *adj* [not gradable] appearing or claiming to be one thing when it is really something else • *Rous published 60 scientific papers after his ostensible retirement.*

ostensibly /ɑˈsten·sə·bli/ *adv* [not gradable] • *American forces attacked the nation, ostensibly to rescue American students trapped between warring factions.*

ostentation /ˌɑs·tənˈteɪ·ʃən/ *n* [U] a show of wealth, possessions, or power intended to attract admiration or notice

ostentatious /ˌɑs·tənˈteɪ·ʃəs/ *adj* intended to attract admiration or notice • *ostentatious jewelry* ○ *ostentatious gestures*

ostentatiously /ˌɑs·tənˈteɪ·ʃə·sli/ *adv* • *She waved her hand about, ostentatiously displaying her large diamond ring.*

osteoporosis /ˌɑs·tiːˌoʊ·pəˈroʊ·səs/ *n* [U] a medical condition that causes the bones to weaken and become easily breakable

ostracize /ˈɑs·trəˌsaɪz/ *v* [T] to prevent (someone) from being part of a group because you dislike them or disapprove of something they have done • *She was ostracized by fellow officers after bringing charges against her partner.*

ostracism /ˈɑs·trəˌsɪz·əm/ *n* [U] • *Those who refused to conform risked ostracism.*

ostrich /ˈɑs·trɪtʃ/ *n* [C] a very large bird from Africa that has a long neck and long legs and cannot fly

other PART OF A SET /ˈʌð·ər/ *pronoun* the second of two things or people, or the item or person that is left from a group or set of things • *Hold the racket in one hand and the ball in the other.* ○ *Some people like living in big cities, but others prefer the suburbs.*

other /ˈʌð·ər/ *adj* [not gradable] • *Where's the other key to the back door?* ○ *I've found one glove—have you seen the other one?* • The **other end/side** means the opposite end or side: *Put this chair at the other end of the table.* ○ *Jeanne was waiting on the other side of the street.* • LP DETERMINERS

other MORE /ˈʌð·ər/ *adj* [not gradable] more of the same kind as the item or person already mentioned • *In addition to the microwave oven, the kitchen has several other modern appliances.* ○ *There is one other point I would like to discuss with you.* ○ *Are there any other people you want to invite?* • Other can be used at the end of a list to show that there are more items without being exact about what they are: *milk, cheese, and other dairy products* • LP DETERMINERS

others /ˈʌð·ərz/ *pronoun* • *I only know about this book, but there might be others* (= other books). ○ *This one is broken—can you find any others?* • Others also refers to people in general, not the person you are talking to or about: *You shouldn't expect others to do your work for you.*

other DIFFERENT /ˈʌð·ər/ *adj* [not gradable] different from the item or person already mentioned • *I'm going to have to take the car—there's no other way to get there.* ○ *Ask me some other time, when I'm not so busy.* • He was economical with the truth—**in other words** (= to explain it more clearly), *he was lying.* • **On the other hand** calls attention to the fact that a second thing is different from the first thing you mentioned: *My husband likes only classical music—I, on the other hand, like all kinds.* • **Other than** means except: *The form cannot be signed by anyone other than you.* • You say **the other day/night** to refer to a time in the recent past without saying exactly which day or night it was: *I saw him (just) the other day.* ○ *She phoned me the other night.* • LP DETERMINERS

otherwise /ˈʌð·ərˌwaɪz/ *adv* [not gradable] differently, or in another way • *Samuel Clemens, otherwise known as Mark Twain* ○ *Parts of the company will be sold or otherwise dismantled.* • Otherwise is also used to give an exception to what has just been mentioned: *I like working outside when it's warm, but otherwise I stay indoors.*

otherwise /'ʌð·ər‚waɪz/ *conjunction* if not; or else • *Tell me if you want it, otherwise I'll give it to Freya.*

otter /'ɑt̬·ər/ *n* [C] a water mammal with four legs and dark brown fur, which eats fish and is related to the WEASEL

ouch /aʊtʃ/ *exclamation* used to express sudden pain • *Ouch, you're hurting me!*

ought DUTY /ɔːt, ɑt/ *v aux* [+ *to* infinitive] he/she/it **ought** used to say that it is necessary, desirable, or advisable to perform the action expressed in the verb • *We ought to clean up before we go home.* ○ *She really ought to apologize.* • LP AUXILIARY VERBS

ought PROBABLE /ɔːt, ɑt/ *v aux* [+ *to* infinitive] he/she/it **ought** used to say that the action expressed in the verb is probable or expected • *He ought to be home by seven o'clock.* ○ *The curtains ought to be ready on Monday.* ○ *At his age, he ought to have known better.* • LP AUXILIARY VERBS

ounce WEIGHT /aʊns/ (*abbreviation* **oz.**) *n* [C] a unit of measurement of weight equal to ¹⁄₁₆ pound or 28 grams • *An ounce is also a very small amount:* *If he's got an ounce of common sense, he'll realize that this project is bound to fail.*

ounce VOLUME /aʊns/ (*abbreviation* **oz.**) *n* [C] a **fluid ounce**, see at FLUID

our /aʊr, ɑr/ *pronoun* [pl] belonging to or connected with us; the possessive form of we, used before a noun • *These are our children.* ○ *Our plans have changed.* • LP DETERMINERS

ours /aʊrz, ɑrz/ *pronoun* [pl] belonging to, or that which belongs to us • *He's a cousin of ours.* ○ *That's their problem—not ours.* ○ *I think these seats are ours.*

ourselves /aʊr'selvz, ɑr-/ *pronoun* [pl] the person speaking and one or more others; the reflexive form of we • *We promised ourselves a long vacation this year.* ○ *It's a big garden, but we do the gardening (all by) ourselves* (= without help). ○ *Everyone else is busy, so we'll have to go (all) by ourselves* (= without other people). ○ *We had the swimming pool all to ourselves* (= we did not have to share it). • LP REFLEXIVE PRONOUNS

oust /aʊst/ *v* [T] to force (someone) out of a job or position • *The school board voted to oust the school superintendent.*

ouster /'aʊ·stər/ *n* [U] • *She publicly called for his ouster as chairman.*

out FROM INSIDE /aʊt/ *adv* [not gradable], *prep* from within to a place or position that is not inside a building or not enclosed or contained • *I'm going out for a walk.* ○ *He leaned out the window and waved.* ○ *Our office looks out on a public park.* • See also OUT OF OUTSIDE.

out BEYOND /aʊt/ *adv* [not gradable] in the area beyond a building or room, or OUTDOORS (=

not in a building) • *It's cold out today.* ○ *They camped out.* ○ *Keep out* (= Do not enter). • See also OUT OF OUTSIDE.

out AWAY /aʊt/ *adj, adv* [not gradable], *prep* away or absent from your home or place of work • *I'll be out tomorrow.* ○ *Leo went out to lunch* (= went away to eat lunch). See also **out to lunch** at OUT NOT AWARE. ○ *We often eat out* (= at restaurants). ○ *Bill asked me out* (= to go somewhere enjoyable together). • If something is out, it is not where it is usually kept or belongs: *I checked at the library and that book is out.* • See also OUT OF OUTSIDE.

out REMOVED /aʊt/ *adv* [not gradable] to the point where something is removed or disappears • *The stain on my tie won't come out.* ○ *Cross out the second number.*

out FROM A PLACE /aʊt/ *adv* [not gradable], *prep* away from a place or starting point, or far away • *They moved out to the country.* ○ *We sent our Christmas cards out early.* • If someone or something is **out in left field**, they are strange, unusual, or completely wrong: *His ideas look like they're from out in left field to me.* • See also OUT OF OUTSIDE.

out COMPLETELY /aʊt/ *adv* [not gradable] completely, or as much as possible • *She stretched out on the bed.* ○ *We were tired out.*

out ALOUD /aʊt/ *adv* [not gradable] aloud, so other people can hear • *Her mother called out to us.* ○ *I laughed out loud* (= aloud).

out AVAILABLE /aʊt/ *adj, adv* [not gradable] (esp. of a book, movie, or recording) available to the public • *Is his new novel out yet?*

out MADE KNOWN /aʊt/ *adj, adv* [not gradable] made known to the public • *The secret's out about her retirement.*

out SEEN /aʊt/ *adj, adv* [not gradable] able to be seen • *It stopped raining and the sun came out.*

out NOT OPERATING /aʊt/ *adj, adv* [not gradable] no longer operating or working • *The electricity went out during the storm.* • If something that burns is out, it is no longer burning: *Be sure the fire is out.* • See also OUT OF NOT IN A STATE OF.

out NOT AWARE /aʊt/ *adj, adv* [not gradable] unconscious, sleeping, or not aware • *He passed out* (= became unconscious). ○ *Matt was so tired, he's out cold* (= in a deep sleep). • *Dina looks like she's out of it* (= not aware of what is happening). • (*infml*) If you say someone is **out to lunch**, you mean they are not aware or are not thinking clearly. • See also OUT OF NOT IN A STATE OF.

out COMPLETELY USED /aʊt/ *adj, adv* [not gradable] (coming) into a condition in which something has been used and no more of it is left • *Our money ran out.* ○ *His luck was running out.* ○ *Renew your membership before the month is out.* • See also OUT OF NOT HAVE.

out NOT ACCEPTABLE /aʊt/ *adj* [not gradable] not acceptable, not possible, or not allowed •

Thursday is out so let's meet Friday. • See also OUT OF NOT IN A STATE OF.

out NOT FASHIONABLE /aʊt/ *adj, adv* [not gradable] *infml* not fashionable or popular • *Long hair is out.* • See also OUT OF NOT IN A STATE OF.

out INTENDING /aʊt/ *adj* [not gradable] *infml* intending to do or get something • *He's just out for a good time.* ○ *The mayor is out to get some publicity.*

out BASEBALL /aʊt/ *adj* [not gradable] failing or having failed to reach a BASE • *He was out on a close play at second base.* • Compare SAFE BASEBALL.

out /aʊt/ *n* [C] • *He made an out on a fly ball.*

out EXCUSE /aʊt/ *n* [C usually sing] *infml* an excuse or reason for avoiding an unpleasant situation • *The kids need to get home, so we have an out if we need it.*

out of OUTSIDE /'--/ *prep* from a place or position inside something to a place or position that is beyond it or not part of it • *I jumped out of bed and ran downstairs.* ○ *My daughter just got out of the hospital.* • If you are out of an activity, you are no longer involved in it: *He decided to get out of teaching.* • In a sport, if a person or thing is **out of bounds**, it is not in the playing area: *The ball was ruled out of bounds.* ○ *The ball fell out-of-bounds.* • If someone's behavior is **out of bounds**, it is beyond the usual limits of acceptable behavior or the usual standards: *Sexual remarks are out of bounds in the workplace.* • If something is **out of sight**, it is too far away to be seen or is hidden by something else. • (*infml*) The price of the house we really want is **out of sight** (= far beyond what we can pay). • **Out of the frying pan into the fire** means changing from a bad or difficult situation to one that is worse. • *I can relax when this term paper is* **out of the way** (= completed). • A place that is **out-of-the-way** is far away from areas that are central: *Train service to out-of-the-way locations is limited.* • If you are **out of the woods**, you no longer have a problem or difficulty: *Membership in the society has increased but we're not out of the woods yet.* • *On nice days in summer, we sometimes eat* **out-of-doors** (= outside) *in the backyard.* • *We had dinner at a little,* **out-of-the-way** *place* (= one away from where people usually go).

out of NOT IN A STATE OF /'--/ *prep* not in the best or in a correct state, or not in a particular state or condition • *The picture was out of focus.* ○ *James has been out of work for over a month.* • If a person's behavior is **out of character**, it is very different from their usual way of behaving: *Swearing would be completely out of character for Charles.* • Something that is **out of commission** is not working or no longer in use: *My car is out of commission.* • If you are **out of condition/shape**, you are not physically healthy enough for difficult exercise because you have not been involved in physical

activities. • Someone or something **out of control** is difficult to manage: *The weeds in the flower bed are out of control.* • If something is **out-of-date**, it is no longer useful or modern: *out-of-date information* See also OUTDATED. • Something that is **out-of-doors** is not in a building: ○ *The kids are playing out-of-doors.* • Something said or done that is **out of line** is beyond what is considered acceptable behavior: *You can disagree with her, but calling her dishonest was out of line.* • *You must be* **out of your mind** (= crazy). • Something that is **out of order** is not operating because it is broken: *I'm afraid you will have to walk up the stairs—the elevator is out of order.* • Something **out of place** is not where it belongs or does not suit the situation or surroundings: *The picture looks out of place here.* • A book that is **out of print** is no longer available from the publisher. • When a fruit or vegetable is **out of season**, it is a time of the year when it does not usually grow locally and must be obtained from another region or country: *Tomatoes are out of season now.* • If you feel **out of sorts**, you are in an unhappy mood: *Peter overslept this morning and has been out of sorts all day.* • To be **out of step with** something is to live in a way or have ideas that are very different from the ideas of most people: *A TV program that makes fun of overweight people is simply out of step with the times.* • *This dress is* **out of style** (= no longer fashionable). • Someone who is **out of the closet** lets people know they are HOMOSEXUAL. • Something **out of the question** is not possible or not allowed: *The class ends at 2 and leaving before then is out of the question.* • To be **out of the running** is to have no chance of being successful: *He wasn't able to raise enough money for his campaign and declared himself out of the running.* Compare **in the running** at RUN POLITICS. • Something **out of this world** is extremely good. • Someone who is **out of touch** is not aware of or does not have information about something.

out of WITH /'--/ *prep* with the help of • *I paid for the computer out of my savings.*

out of BY USING /'--/ *prep* (of a material or substance) by using, to produce something • *The dress was made out of velvet.*

out of NOT HAVE /'--/ *prep* in a condition in which you have no more of something, esp. because it has all been used • *We'll soon be out of gas.* ○ *I'm out of patience with her.* ○ *We're out of time—we've got to leave right now.*

out of ORIGINATING FROM /'--/ *prep* originating or coming from • *She copied the pattern out of a magazine.* • *My old roommate called me from* **out of the blue** (= unexpectedly). • *I was watching TV when I saw something move* **out of the corner of** *my eye* (= without looking at it directly). • **Out of thin air** means from nowhere or from nothing: *She seemed to appear out of thin air.*

out of BECAUSE OF /'--/ *prep* because of • *She volunteered out of a sense of duty.*

out of FROM AMONG /'--/ *prep* from among a group or a particular number • *The poll showed that six out of ten people approved of the job the president is doing.*

out-and-out /'aʊt·ᵊn,aʊt/ *adj* [not gradable] complete; in all ways • *He's an out-and-out fraud.*

outbreak /'aʊt·breɪk/ *n* [C] a sudden appearance of something, esp. of a disease or something else dangerous or unpleasant • *an outbreak of cholera* ○ *the outbreak of war*

outburst /'aʊt·bɜrst/ *n* [C] a sudden, violent expression of emotion, esp. anger

outcast /'aʊt·kæst/ *n* [C] a person who is not accepted or has no place in society or in a particular group • *a social outcast*

outclass /aʊt'klæs/ *v* [T] to be much better than (someone or something) • *Jason outclasses everyone on the team.*

outcome /'aʊt·kʌm/ *n* [C] the result or effect of an action, situation, or event • *It's too early to predict the outcome of the election.*

outcry /'aʊt·kraɪ/ *n* [C] a strong expression of public anger and disapproval • *Plans to tear down the old courthouse led to a public outcry.*

outdated /aʊt'deɪt̬·əd/, **out-of-date** *adj* no longer useful or modern • *an outdated computer system* ○ *This handbook is outdated.*

outdistance /aʊt'dɪs·təns/ *v* [T] to go faster or farther than, esp. in a race • *He easily outdistanced the other runners.*

outdo /aʊt'duː/ *v* [T] he/she/it **outdoes** /aʊt'dʌz/, *past simple* **outdid** /aʊt'dɪd/, *past part* **outdone** /aʊt'dʌn/ to do more or be better than (someone else) • *He always tries to outdo his teammates.*

outdoor /,aʊt,dɔːr, -,doʊr/ *adj* [not gradable] existing, happening, or done outside a building • *The city's outdoor pools open June 19th.*

outdoors /aʊt'dɔːrz, -'doʊrz/, **out-of-doors** *adv* [not gradable] out in the air, not in a building • *We'll eat outdoors.* ○ *The kids are playing outdoors.*

outdoors /aʊt'dɔːrz, -'doʊrz/, **out-of-doors** *n* [U] • *Mike enjoys the outdoors.*

outer /'aʊt̬·ər/ *adj* [not gradable] on the outside, or at a greater distance from the center or inside • *an outer covering/layer* ○ *A line of trees marks the outer edge of the property.* • **Outer space** is the universe beyond the earth's ATMOSPHERE (= the air surrounding the earth).

outermost /'aʊt̬·ər,moʊst/ *adj* [not gradable] farthest away, or farthest from the center or from the inside • *We took a ferry ride to the outermost island.*

outfield /'aʊt·fiːld/ *n* [C/U] (in baseball) the part of the playing field beyond the BASES, or

the three players whose positions are in this area • Compare INFIELD.

outfielder /'aʊt,fiːl·dər/ *n* [C]

outfit CLOTHES /'aʊt·fɪt/ *n* [C] a set of clothes worn for a particular occasion or activity • *Susan wore a black outfit.* • An outfit is also a set of equipment for a particular purpose: *She got a complete ski outfit for Christmas.*

outfit /'aʊt·fɪt/ *v* [T] to provide (someone) with clothes or other equipment • *I found a place that can outfit us for the canoe trip.*

outfit ORGANIZATION /'aʊt·fɪt/ *n* [C] an organization or group • *Our company merged with another consulting outfit.*

outflow /'aʊt·floʊ/ *n* [C] the flow from something • *an outflow of waste water*

outgoing FRIENDLY /'aʊt,goʊ·ɪŋ/ *adj* friendly and willing to meet new people • *Sherry is a very outgoing person.*

outgoing LEAVING /'aʊt,goʊ·ɪŋ/ *adj* [not gradable] leaving a particular job, office, or position • *the outgoing chairman*

outgrow /aʊt'groʊ/ *v* [T] *past simple* **outgrew** /aʊt'gruː/, *past part* **outgrown** /aʊt'groʊn/ to grow too large for (something) • *Our teenager has outgrown most of his clothes.* ○ *The company outgrew its office space.*

outgrowth /'aʊt·groʊθ/ *n* [C usually sing] a result or further development of something • *The new emphasis on science teaching is an outgrowth of a report that criticized the way science had been taught.*

outhouse /'aʊt·haʊs/ *n* [C] *pl* **outhouses** /'aʊt,haʊ·zəz, -səz/ a small building containing a seat over a hole that is used as a toilet, used esp. by people who live in houses that do not have water moving in pipes

outing /'aʊt̬·ɪŋ/ *n* [C] a short trip, taken for pleasure or entertainment • *a family outing* ○ *an outing to the beach*

outlandish /aʊt'læn·dɪʃ/ *adj* strange and unusual • *She liked to dress in outlandish clothes.*

outlast /aʊt'læst/ *v* [T] to exist or operate longer than (someone or something) • *This type of battery outlasts the ordinary kind.*

outlaw /'aʊt·lɔː/ *n* [C] a criminal, esp. one who is trying to avoid being caught

outlaw /'aʊt·lɔː/ *v* [T] to make (something) illegal • *The bill outlaws smoking in restaurants.*

outlay /'aʊt·leɪ/ *n* [C] an amount of money spent, esp. at the beginning of a planned activity or business • *This year's advertising outlay was over $250,000.*

outlet OPENING /'aʊt·lət, -let/ *n* [C] an opening through which something, usually a liquid or gas, can come out • *an outlet to the sea* ○ *The plumber tightened the outlet valve.*

outlet METHOD OF EXPRESSION /'aʊt·lət, -let/ *n* [C] a method by which emotions, energy, or abilities can be expressed • *Drawing classes provided an outlet for her creativity.*

outlet STORE /'aʊt·lət, -let/ n [C] a store selling the goods of a particular company or goods of a particular type, often one selling goods at prices that are lower than usual • *a factory outlet* ○ *The company has more than 1200 retail outlets nationwide.*

outlet ELECTRICITY /'aʊt·lət, -let/ n [C] a device connected to the electricity system that a plug fits into in order to supply electricity to something • *a wall outlet*

plug

outlet

outline STATEMENT /'aʊt·laɪn/ n [C] a statement of the main facts, ideas, or items • *The House approved the broad outlines of the president's budget.*

outline /'aʊt·laɪn/ v [T] • *I've outlined my research paper and begun writing the first draft.*

outline LINE /'aʊt·laɪn/ n [C] a line or lines showing the main shape of something • *She drew the outline of a face.*

outlive /aʊt'lɪv/ v [T] to live or exist longer than (someone or something) • *At 90, I've outlived most of my friends.*

outlook FUTURE SITUATION /'aʊt·lʊk/ n [C usually sing] the likely future situation • *The economic outlook is good.*

outlook ATTITUDE /'aʊt·lʊk/ n [C usually sing] a person's general attitude or way of thinking about something • *He has a positive outlook on life.*

outlying /'aʊt·laɪ·ɪŋ/ adj away from the center or main area • *Many of the students come from outlying areas.*

outmaneuver /ˌaʊt·mə'nuː·vər/ v [T] to obtain an advantage over (esp. a competitor) in a skillful or intelligent way • *He outmaneuvered the competition.*

outmoded /aʊt'moʊd·əd/ adj old-fashioned; no longer modern, useful, or necessary • *The city is replacing its outmoded sewage-treatment plant.*

outnumber /aʊt'nʌm·bər/ v [T] to be greater in number than (someone or something) • *Girls outnumbered boys by a margin of 2 to 1.*

outpatient /'aʊt,peɪ·ʃənt/ n [C] a person who receives medical care from a hospital but who does not stay in the hospital for one or more nights • *Anna had foot surgery as an outpatient.* • Compare INPATIENT.

outperform /ˌaʊt·pər'fɔːrm/ v [T] to perform better or do better than (someone or something) • *Technology stocks are outperforming the rest of the market.*

outplay /aʊt'pleɪ/ v [T] to play better than (another person or team)

outpost /'aʊt·poʊst/ n [C] a small town or group of buildings in a distant place, usually established as a center for military or trade operations

outpouring /'aʊt,pɔːr·ɪŋ, -,poʊr·ɪŋ/ n [C] something that flows out in large amounts or with strong force, esp. emotion • *an outpouring of love/sympathy*

output /'aʊt·pʊt/ n [U] an amount that a person, machine, or organization produces • *agricultural/industrial output*

outrage /'aʊt·reɪdʒ, aʊt'reɪdʒ/ v [T] to cause (someone) to feel very angry, shocked, or upset • *The proposed pay cut outraged the staff*

outrage /'aʊt·reɪdʒ/ n [C/U] a strong feeling of anger and shock, or an act or event that causes these feelings • *The terrible living conditions of migrant workers, he said, were an outrage.* [C]

outrageous /aʊt'reɪ·dʒəs/ adj unacceptable, offensive, violent, or unusual • *He made outrageous claims.*

outrageously /aʊt'reɪ·dʒə·sli/ adv

outrank /aʊt'ræŋk/ v [T] to have greater importance than (someone or something), or to have a higher rank than (someone) • *She outranks the other officers involved in the investigation.*

outreach /'aʊt·riːtʃ/ n [U] an effort to bring services or information to people where they live or spend time • *The center was awarded a grant for counseling and outreach to the homeless.*

outright /'aʊt·raɪt/ adv [not gradable] directly and plainly, or immediately instead of in stages • *They bought their car outright.* ○ *I told him outright that I think he is making a mistake.*

outright /'aʊt·raɪt/ adj [not gradable] • *The Surgeon General lobbied for an outright ban on cigarette advertising.*

outrun /aʊt'rʌn/ v [T] **outrunning**, past simple **outran** /aʊt'ræn/, past part **outrun** to run faster than (someone), or to increase faster or do better than (something) • *Martha can outrun everyone on the team.*

outs /aʊts/ pl n infml • People who are **on the outs** are in a state of disagreement or unfriendliness: *Dick is on the outs with his father.*

outset /'aʊt·set/ n [C usually sing] the start or beginning • *From the outset we planned to conduct our research together.*

outside OUTER PART /aʊt'saɪd, 'aʊt·saɪd/ n [U] the outer part of something, or the area or side that faces out or can be seen • *She stood in the snow on the outside, watching him.* • Compare INSIDE INNER PART.

outside /aʊt'saɪd, 'aʊt·saɪd/ adv [not gradable], prep, adj [not gradable] • *Hordes of cats howled outside the window.*

outside NOT PART OF SOMETHING /aʊt'saɪd, 'aʊt·saɪd/ adv [not gradable], prep, adj [not gradable] not within or part of something • *I live just outside (of) Baltimore.* ○ *Cars, movies, and radio linked small towns to the outside world.*

• **Outside of** means other than or except for:

Outside of a department store, she had never seen so many lovely clothes!

outside /aʊtˈsaɪd, ˈaʊtˌsaɪd/ *n* [U] • *People looking from the outside would say I had a dream childhood.*

outsider /aʊtˈsaɪd·ər/ *n* [C] a person who is not involved with a particular group of people or an organization, or who does not live in a particular place • *I moved here three years ago, but I still feel like an outsider.*

outside SLIGHT /aʊtˈsaɪd, ˈaʊtˌsaɪd/ *adj* slight, small, or unlikely • *There's an outside chance that Boston will make it to the playoffs.*

outskirts /ˈaʊtˌskɜrts/ *pl n* (of cities and towns) the areas that form the edge • *the outskirts of town*

outsmart /aʊtˈsmɑrt/ *v* [T] to obtain an advantage over (someone) by using your intelligence and often by using a trick; to OUTWIT • *You think you can outsmart me?*

outspoken /aʊtˈspoʊ·kən/ *adj* (of a person) expressing strong opinions very directly without worrying if other people will be upset by them • *Men are threatened by a woman who's witty and outspoken.*

outstanding EXCELLENT /aʊtˈstæn·dɪŋ, ˈaʊtˌstæn-/ *adj* very much better than usual; excellent • *You've done an outstanding job.*

outstanding NOT FINISHED /aʊtˈstæn·dɪŋ, ˈaʊtˌstæn-/ *adj* not yet done, solved, or paid • *My credit cards usually have an outstanding balance.*

outstretched /aʊtˈstretʃt/ *adj* stretched as far as possible or held out in front • *outstretched arms*

outstrip /aʊtˈstrɪp/ *v* [T] **-pp-** to be or become greater than (something or someone) in amount, degree, or success • *Car dealers worry that demand will outstrip their supply.*

outta /ˈaʊt̬·ə/ *prep not standard* (spelled the way it is often spoken) out of • *I gotta get outta here.*

outward SEEMING /ˈaʊt·wərd/ *adj* [not gradable] relating to how people, situations, or things seem to be, rather than how they are inside • *There were no outward signs that she was injured.*

outwardly /ˈaʊt·wərd·li/ *adv* [not gradable] • *Outwardly, he seemed confident, but he was full of doubt.*

outward AWAY FROM /ˈaʊt·wərd/, **outwards** /ˈaʊt·wərdz/ *adv* [not gradable] away from a particular place or toward the outside • *The door opens outward.* • Compare INWARD.

outweigh /aʊtˈweɪ/ *v* [T] to be likely to be more important than or have an effect on (something else) • *The benefits of increased immigration outweigh the costs.*

outwit /aʊtˈwɪt/ *v* [T] **-tt-** to obtain an advantage over (someone) by being more intelligent; to OUTSMART • *It is impossible to negotiate if one side feels that the other side is trying to outwit them.*

oval /ˈoʊ·vəl/ *adj* shaped like a circle that is flattened with two long, straight sides and round ends, or shaped like an egg • *an oval table*

oval /ˈoʊ·vəl/ *n* [C] • *The sculptor created patterns of cylinders, cones, and ovals.*

ovary /ˈoʊ·və·ri/ *n* [C] either of the pair of organs in a woman's body that produce eggs, or the part of any female animal or plant that produces eggs or seeds

ovarian /oʊˈver·i·ən/ *adj* [not gradable] • *ovarian cysts/cancer*

ovation /oʊˈveɪ·ʃən/ *n* [C] loud clapping that expresses a crowd's great enjoyment or approval of something • *At the end of the program, the dancers received a thunderous ovation.*

oven /ˈʌv·ən/ *n* [C] part of a stove that is box-shaped with a door, in which food is baked or heated, or a separate device with this shape and use • *Roast the turkey in a 325° oven for four hours.* ∘ *a toaster/microwave oven*

over ABOVE /ˈoʊ·vər/ *prep* in, to, on, or at a position above or higher than something else, sometimes so that one thing covers the other; above • *The sign over the door said, "Private."* ∘ *He put a sweater on over his shirt.* ∘ *The horse jumped over the fence.* ∘ *I couldn't hear what she said over the sound of the music* (= The music was louder than her voice). • *Most of that lecture was over my head* (= too difficult for me to understand). • Compare UNDER LOWER POSITION. • PIC on p. 606

over /ˈoʊ·vər/ *adv* [not gradable] • *We repaired the cracks in the wall and painted over them.*

over ACROSS /ˈoʊ·vər/ *prep* across from one side to the other, esp. by going up and then down • *Once we get over the bridge we'll stop for lunch.* ∘ *She tripped over the rug.* ∘ *The car went over the cliff* (= across the edge of it). • Over also means on the other side of: *Their house is just over the river.*

over /ˈoʊ·vər/ *adv* [not gradable] • *She leaned over and kissed me.* ∘ *Who's that man over there?* ∘ *When is Howard coming over* (= coming to your house)*?* • Over also describes the way an object moves or is moved so that a different part of it is facing up: *The dog rolled over onto its back.* PIC on p. 606

over MORE THAN /ˈoʊ·vər/ *prep* more than • *Most of these rugs cost over $1000.* ∘ *Children over 12* (= older than 12) *pay full price.* • If someone or something goes over a limit or point, it increases beyond it: *Construction costs are already $25 million over budget.* • Compare UNDER LESS THAN.

over– /ˌoʊ·vər/ *combining form* too much or more than usual • *overpriced* ∘ *overdressed* ∘ *He's always been an overachiever.*

over DOWN /ˈoʊ·vər/ *adv* [not gradable] from a higher to a lower position; down • *The little boy fell over and started to cry.*

a sign over the door

She knocked the bottle over.

The show is over.

over USING /'oʊ·vər/ *prep* using a device such as a telephone • *They spoke over the phone.* ○ *We transfer files over the Internet.*

over DURING /'oʊ·vər/ *prep* during a period of time, or while doing something • *She made a lot of changes over the past six months.* ○ *Can we discuss this over lunch?*

over AUTHORITY /'oʊ·vər/ *prep* greater in authority, power, or position than • *Parents want to have control over their children.*

over ABOUT /'oʊ·vər/ *prep* about or connected with • *There's no point in arguing over this.*

over FINISHED /'oʊ·vər/ *adj* [not gradable] (esp. of an event) finished, completed, or ended • *I'll be glad when the meeting is over.* ○ *The game was over by 5 o'clock.* • If someone is **over the hill**, they are no longer considered useful, esp. because they are old: *I don't think of myself as being over the hill.*

over /'oʊ·vər/ *prep* (esp. of illness) no longer suffering from • *Is he over the flu yet?* ○ *His wife died last year and he's still not over it.*

over AGAIN /'oʊ·vər/ *adv* [not gradable] again or repeatedly • *You've ruined it—now I'll have to do it over.* • If you do something or if something happens **over and over (again)**, you do it or it happens many times: *Words such as love lose their impact because they've been said over and over again.*

overall /ˌoʊ·vəˈrɔːl/ *adj, adv* [not gradable] in general rather than in particular, or including all the people or things in a particular group or situation • *The overall situation is good.* ○ *The second act was a little long, but overall it was a good performance.*

overalls /'oʊ·vəˌrɔːlz/ *pl n* a pair of pants with an extra piece of cloth that covers the chest and is held in place by a strap over each shoulder

overbearing /ˌoʊ·vərˈber·ɪŋ, -ˈbær-/ *adj* too confident and too determined to tell other people what to do, in a way that is unpleasant and not easy to like • *an overbearing father*

overboard /'oʊ·vərˌbɔːrd, -ˌboʊrd/ *adv* [not gradable] over the side of a boat or ship and into the water • *Someone fell overboard.*

overburdened /ˌoʊ·vərˈbɜrd·ᵊnd/ *adj* having too much to carry, contain, or deal with • *We're trying to stop development in areas with overburdened roads and schools.*

overcast /'oʊ·vərˌkæst, ˌoʊ·vərˈkæst/ *adj* cloudy and therefore not bright and sunny • *an overcast sky/day*

overcoat /'oʊ·vərˌkoʊt/ *n* [C] a long coat, esp. a thick one used in cold weather

overcome DEAL WITH /ˌoʊ·vərˈkʌm/ *v* [I/T] *past simple* **overcame** /ˌoʊ·vərˈkeɪm/, *past part* **overcome** to defeat or succeed in controlling or dealing with (something) • *I eventually overcame my shyness in class.* [T] ○ *I believe that we will overcome in the end.* [I]

overcome UNABLE TO ACT /ˌoʊ·vərˈkʌm/ *v* [T]

past simple **overcame** /ˌoʊ·vərˈkeɪm/, *past part* **overcome** to prevent (someone) from being able to act or think in the usual way • *He was overcome by smoke before he could get out of the apartment.*

overcompensate /ˌoʊ·vərˈkɑm·pən·seɪt/ *v* [I] to try too hard to produce a usual or correct state from one that is not usual, and therefore produce a new difficulty or lack of balance • *Chris overcompensates for his lack of height by being a clown.*

overcrowded /ˌoʊ·vərˈkraʊd·əd/ *adj* containing too many people or things • *The prisons are overcrowded.*

overcrowding /ˌoʊ·vərˈkraʊd·ɪŋ/ *n* [U] • *Overcrowding in classrooms is an important issue in this election.*

overdo /ˌoʊ·vərˈduː/ *v* [T] he/she/it **overdoes** /ˌoʊ·vərˈdʌz/, *past simple* **overdid** /ˌoʊ·vərˈdɪd/, *past part* **overdone** /ˌoʊ·vərˈdʌn/ to do, use, or say (something) in a way that is too extreme • *They should get the attention they need without overdoing it.*

overdone /ˌoʊ·vərˈdʌn/ *adj* (esp. of meat) cooked too long • *The steak was dry and overdone.*

overdose /ˈoʊ·vərˌdoʊs/ *n* [C] (of a drug) an amount that is too large • *an overdose of sleeping pills*

overdose /ˌoʊ·vərˈdoʊs/ (*slang abbreviation* **OD**) *v* [I] • *She overdosed on heroin.*

overdrawn /ˌoʊ·vərˈdrɔːn/ *adj* (of a person) having taken more money out of a bank account than the account contained, or (of a bank account) having had more money taken from it than was originally in it • *Your account is overdrawn.*

overdrive /ˈoʊ·vərˌdraɪv/ *n* [U] a state of great activity, effort, or hard work • *The show's cast went into overdrive to prepare for the first performance.*

overdue /ˌoʊ·vərˈduː/ *adj* not done or happening when expected or when needed; late • *She feels she's overdue for a promotion.*

overeat /ˌoʊ·vəˈriːt/ *v* [I] *past simple* **overate** /ˌoʊ·vəˈreɪt/, *past part* **overeaten** /ˌoʊ·vəˈriːt·ᵊn/ to eat more food than your body needs, esp. so that you feel uncomfortable • *You're supposed to overeat on Thanksgiving.*

overestimate /ˌoʊ·vəˈres·təˌmeɪt/ *v* [I/T] to think that (something) is or will be greater, more extreme, or more important than it really is • *I'm afraid Theresa is forever overestimating her strength.* [T]

overflow /ˌoʊ·vərˈfloʊ/ *v* [I/T] (of a liquid) to flow over the edges of (something, esp. a container) because there is too great an amount to be held, or (of something containing liquid) to have liquid flowing over the edges • *Because of the heavy rains, the river overflowed its banks.* [T] ○ *The sink quickly overflowed, flooding the room.* [I] ○ (*fig.*) *The train platform was overflowing with passengers.* [I]

overflow /ˈoʊ·vərˌfloʊ/ *n* [C] • *There is sewer overflow due to the storm.* ○ (*fig.*) *The old barn is being used to house the overflow of guests.*

overgrown COVERED /ˌoʊ·vərˈɡroʊn/ *adj* covered with plants that are growing thickly and wildly • *The playground is overgrown with weeds.*

overgrown TOO LARGE /ˌoʊ·vərˈɡroʊn/ *adj* *disapproving* (of people) grown large or too large • *Even Professor Adams looked like an overgrown schoolboy beside him.*

overhand /ˈoʊ·vərˌhænd/ *adj, adv* [not gradable] (esp. of a throw) made with the hand and part or all of the arm moving above the shoulder • *an overhand pitch* ○ *Throw the ball overhand.*

overhang /ˌoʊ·vərˈhæŋ/ *v* [T] *past* **overhung** /ˌoʊ·vərˈhʌŋ/ (of something at a high level) to stick out farther than something at a lower level and therefore not to have any support from below, or to hang over • *The balcony overhangs the patio, creating a shady place to sit.*

overhang /ˈoʊ·vərˌhæŋ/ *n* [C] • *The house has a deep overhang facing the southern sun.*

overhaul /ˌoʊ·vərˈhɔːl/ *v* [T] to examine in a detailed way and repair (esp. a machine or vehicle), or make improvements to (a system, idea, or program) • *They repaired and maintained aircraft and overhauled their engines.* ○ *Congressional leaders are considering overhauling the Clean Air Act.*

overhaul /ˈoʊ·vərˌhɔːl/ *n* [C] • *I think our justice system needs a major overhaul.*

overhead IN AIR /ˈoʊ·vərˌhed/ *adj, adv* [not gradable] at a level higher than a person's head; in the air or the sky above the place where you are • *overhead lighting* ○ *A flock of geese flew overhead.*

overhead EXPENSES /ˈoʊ·vərˌhed/ *n* [U] the regular and necessary costs, such as rent, heat, electricity, and telephone, involved in operating a business • *overhead expenses*

overhear /ˌoʊ·vərˈhɪr/ *v* [I/T] *past* **overheard** /ˌoʊ·vərˈhɜrd/ to hear (what other people are saying) unintentionally and without their knowledge • *I overheard a funny conversation on the bus this morning.* [T] ○ *They were so loud, I couldn't help overhearing.* [I]

overjoyed /ˌoʊ·vərˈdʒɔɪd/ *adj* extremely pleased and happy • *They were overjoyed to learn that their son had not been injured in the accident.* [+ *to* infinitive]

overkill /ˈoʊ·vərˌkɪl/ *n* [U] much more of something than is needed or suitable • *Running so fast with the competition so far behind might seem like overkill, but that's Gardner.*

overland /ˈoʊ·vərˌlænd, -lənd/ *adj, adv* [not gradable] (of travel) across the land, and not by sea or air • *They're taking an overland trip across Canada.*

overlap /ˌoʊ·vərˈlæp/ *v* [I/T] **-pp-** to partly cover (something) with a layer of something else • *The edges of the wallpaper should over-lap slightly.* [I]

The shingles and boards overlap.

overload /ˌoʊ·vər'loʊd/ *v* [T] to put too great a load in or on (something) • *Don't overload the washer or it won't work properly.* ○ (*fig.*) *I can't go out tonight—I'm overloaded with work* (= I have a lot of work to do). • If you overload an electrical system, you put too much electricity through it.

overlook VIEW /ˌoʊ·vər'lʊk/ *v* [T] to have or give a view of (something) from above • *Our hotel room overlooked the harbor.*

overlook /'oʊ·vər,lʊk/ *n* [C] a place that provides a good view of what is below, esp. an area of natural beauty

overlook NOT NOTICE /ˌoʊ·vər'lʊk/ *v* [T] to fail to notice (something) • *His film was nominated for an Oscar, but Reiner himself was overlooked as best director.* • To overlook is also to forgive (bad behavior): *We'll overlook your absence this time, but don't let it happen again.*

overly /'oʊ·vər·li/ *adv* [not gradable] too; very • *Sales forecasts were overly optimistic.*

overnight /ˌoʊ·vər'naɪt/ *adj*, *adv* [not gradable] for or during the night • *You can stay overnight with us if you want to.* ○ (*fig.*) *The book was an overnight success* (= a sudden success).

overpass /'oʊ·vər,pæs/ *n* [C] a bridge that carries a road or railroad over another road

overpopulated /ˌoʊ·vər'pɑp·jə,leɪt̬·əd/ *adj* having too many people or animals for the amount of food, materials, and space available

overpopulation /ˌoʊ·vər,pɑp·jə'leɪ·ʃən/ *n* [U]

overpower /ˌoʊ·vər'paʊ·ər, -'paʊr/ *v* [T] to defeat (someone) by having greater strength or power • *Inmates overpowered the prison guards in the dining hall.*

overpowering /ˌoʊ·vər'paʊ·ə·rɪŋ, -'paʊ·rɪŋ/ *adj* • *The stench from the sewage treatment plant was overpowering.*

overpriced /ˌoʊ·vər'praɪst/ *adj* offered for sale at too high a price • *I think these coats are overpriced.*

overran /ˌoʊ·vər'ræn/ *past simple of* OVERRUN

overrated /ˌoʊ·vər'reɪt̬·əd/ *adj* (of something) considered to be better than it really is • *After seeing the award-winning movie, we decided it was overrated.*

overreact /ˌoʊ·vər·ri'ækt/ *v* [I] to react too strongly • *She overreacted when I said she'd made a mistake.*

overreaction /ˌoʊ·vər·ri'æk·ʃən/ *n* [C/U]

override /ˌoʊ·vər'raɪd/ *v* [T] *past simple* **overrode** /ˌoʊ·vər'roʊd/, *past part* **overridden** /ˌoʊ·vər'rɪd·ən/ to ignore or refuse to accept (a suggestion, idea, or method) that already exists or operates • *The legislature voted to override the presidential veto.*

overriding /ˌoʊ·vər'raɪd·ɪŋ/ *adj* [not gradable] most important; main • *The government's overriding concern is to reduce inflation.*

overrule /ˌoʊ·vər'ruːl/ *v* [T] to make a decision that opposes and changes (another decision or suggestion) from a position of higher authority • *The judge was constantly overruling the objections of the prosecution.*

overrun /ˌoʊ·vər'rʌn/ *v* [T] **overrunning**, *past simple* **overran** /ˌoʊ·vər'ræn/, *past part* **overrun** to spread over (an area) quickly and in large numbers • *The city has become increasingly unpleasant because it is overrun with tourists.*

overseas /ˌoʊ·vər'siːz/ *adj*, *adv* [not gradable] in, from, or to countries that are across the sea • *The Air Force was recalling troops from overseas bases.* ○ *I've had to travel overseas fairly often.*

oversee /ˌoʊ·vər'siː/ *v* [T] *past simple* **oversaw** /ˌoʊ·vər'sɔː/, *past part* **overseen** /ˌoʊ·vər'siːn/ to watch and manage (a job or activity) • *As marketing manager, her job is to oversee all the company's advertising.*

overshadow /ˌoʊ·vər'ʃæd·oʊ/ *v* [T] to cause (someone or something) to seem less important or noticeable • *Karen has always been overshadowed by her older sister.*

overshoot /ˌoʊ·vər'ʃuːt/ *v* [T] *past* **overshot** /ˌoʊ·vər'ʃɑt/ to go past or beyond (a limit or stopping place) • *The plane overshot the runway and wound up in a cornfield.*

oversight MISTAKE /'oʊ·vər,saɪt/ *n* [C] a mistake caused by a failure to notice or do something • *Because of a bank oversight, the money had not been credited to my account.*

oversight MANAGEMENT /'oʊ·vər,saɪt/ *n* [U] management of an operation or process • *The FBI provided technical expertise and general oversight to the investigation.*

oversimplify /ˌoʊ·vər'sɪm·plə,faɪ/ *v* [I/T] to state (something) in such a simple way that it is no longer accurate • *The issue has been oversimplified for political purposes.* [T]

oversimplification /ˌoʊ·vər,sɪm·plə·fə'keɪ·ʃən/ *n* [C/U]

oversleep /ˌoʊ·vər'sliːp/ *v* [I] *past* **overslept** /ˌoʊ·vər'slɛpt/ to sleep longer or later than you intended to • *I missed the bus because I overslept.*

overstate /ˌoʊ·vər'steɪt/ *v* [T] to state (something) too strongly, or to state that it is greater than it really is • *The prospect of a trade war is vastly overstated.*

overstep /ˌoʊ·vərˈstep/ *v* [T] **-pp-** to go beyond (what is permitted or acceptable) • *He overstepped his authority in agreeing to those terms.*

overt /oʊˈvɜrt/ *adj* [not gradable] done or shown obviously or publicly; not hidden or secret • *There are no overt signs of damage.*

overtly /oʊˈvɜrt·li/ *adv* [not gradable] • *The speech was described as overtly racist.*

overtake GO PAST /ˌoʊ·vərˈteɪk/ *v* [T] *past simple* **overtook** /ˌoʊ·vərˈtʊk/, *past part* **overtaken** /ˌoʊ·vərˈteɪ·kən/ to go beyond (something) by being a greater amount or degree, or to come from behind and move in front of • *In the 1500-meter race, he finished with a late rush to overtake Barbosa in 1 minute, 44.84 seconds.* ○ *The Bruins got within three points late in the game but just couldn't overtake the Cowboys.*

overtake HAPPEN /ˌoʊ·vərˈteɪk/ *v* [T] *past simple* **overtook** /ˌoʊ·vərˈtʊk/, *past part* **overtaken** /ˌoʊ·vərˈteɪ·kən/ (esp. of unpleasant emotions or events) to happen suddenly and unexpectedly • *The family was overtaken by tragedy several years ago.*

over–the–counter /ˌoʊ·vər·ðəˈkɑʊnt·ər/ *adj* [not gradable] (of drugs) legally sold without a PRESCRIPTION (= special written instruction from a doctor) • *The painkiller is available as an over-the-counter drug.*

overthrow /ˌoʊ·vərˈθroʊ/ *v* [T] *past simple* **overthrew** /ˌoʊ·vərˈθruː/, *past part* **overthrown** /ˌoʊ·vərˈθroʊn/ to remove from power, esp. by force • *He allegedly plotted to overthrow the government.*

overthrow /ˈoʊ·vərˌθroʊ/ *n* [C] • *The overthrow of the dictatorship occurred in 1922.*

overtime /ˈoʊ·vərˌtɑɪm/ *n* [U] time worked in addition to your usual job hours • *Overtime is also the period of time in a game, such as football or* BASKETBALL, *in which play continues if neither team has won in the usual time allowed for the game.*

overtime /ˈoʊ·vərˌtɑɪm/ *adv, adj* [not gradable] • *I'm working overtime this week.*

overtly /oʊˈvɜrt·li/ *adv* • See at OVERT.

overtone /ˈoʊ·vərˌtoʊn/ *n* [C usually pl] a quality, attitude, or emotion that is suggested in addition to what is stated • *The movie is rated R for graphic violence, nudity, and sexual overtones.*

overtook /ˌoʊ·vərˈtʊk/ *past simple of* OVERTAKE

overture MUSIC /ˈoʊ·vərˌtʃʊr, -tʃər/ *n* [C] a piece of music that is an introduction to a longer piece, such as an opera

overture APPROACH /ˈoʊ·vərˌtʃʊr, -tʃər/ *n* [C] an approach made to someone in order to discuss or establish something • *The country's leaders rejected all overtures for a peace settlement.*

overturn /ˌoʊ·vərˈtɜrn/ *v* [I/T] to turn over, or to cause (something) to turn over • *The truck overturned, spilling its cargo.* [I] • When a decision, judgment, or belief is overturned, a higher authority decides that it should not be effective: *The court of appeals overturned her conviction and ordered a new trial.* [T]

overuse /ˌoʊ·vərˈjuːz/ *v* [T] to use (something) too often or too much • *We all tend to overuse certain expressions.*

overuse /ˌoʊ·vərˈjuːs/ *n* [U] • *Utah is a national leader in the overuse of Caesarean section births.*

overview /ˈoʊ·vərˌvjuː/ *n* [C] a short description of something that provides general information but no details • *I'll give you a brief overview of what the job involves.*

overweight /ˌoʊ·vərˈweɪt/ *adj* too heavy or too fat • *He's at least 20 pounds overweight.*

overwhelm /ˌoʊ·vərˈwelm, -ˈhwelm/ *v* [T] to make (something or someone) powerless by using force or by introducing too much or too many of something • *The number of refugees overwhelmed the relief agencies in the area.* • To overwhelm can also mean to cause (someone) to feel helpless because of strong emotion: *He was overwhelmed by feelings of remorse for what he had done.*

overwhelming /ˌoʊ·vərˈwel·mɪŋ, -ˈhwel·mɪŋ/ *adj* very great or strong • *An overwhelming majority voted in favor of the proposal.* ○ *I felt an overwhelming sense of relief when the semester was over.*

overwhelmingly /ˌoʊ·vərˈwel·mɪŋ·li, -ˈhwel-/ *adv* [not gradable]

overwork /ˌoʊ·vərˈwɜrk/ *v* [I/T] to work or make (a person or animal) work too hard or too long • *She overworks her staff.* [T]

overwork /ˌoʊ·vərˈwɜrk/ *n* [U] • *Her headaches are likely caused by overwork.*

overworked /ˌoʊ·vərˈwɜrkt/ *adj* • *I feel overworked and underpaid.*

ow /ɑʊ/ *exclamation* used to express sudden pain • *Ow, stop it, you're hurting me!*

owe HAVE A DEBT /oʊ/ *v* [I/T] to have the responsibility to pay or give back (something) you have received from someone • *Don't forget—you owe me ten dollars.* [T] • If someone tells you that you **owe it to yourself** to do something, they feel you deserve it: *You owe it to yourself to take a long vacation.*

owe BE GRATEFUL /oʊ/ *v* [T] to be grateful to (someone or something) because of what they provided or made possible • *I owe a lot to my parents, who have always supported and encouraged me.*

owing to /ˈ---/ *prep fml* because of • *The performance has been canceled owing to the strike.*

owl /ɑʊl/ *n* [C] a bird with a flat face, large round eyes, a hook-shaped beak, and strong, curved nails, that hunts small mammals at night

own /oʊn/ *adj* belonging to or done by a particular person or thing • *Mary has her own car.* ○ *You'll have to fix your own dinner.* ○ *The police testified that the woman left of her own accord* (= she chose to do it without being forced or advised). • *Tell us what happened* **in** *your* **own words** (= in your own way). • *I don't mind going to the movies* **on** *my* **own** (= alone). • *Bridget learned to tie her shoes* **on** *her* **own** (= without help from anyone else).

own /oʊn/ *v* [T] to have or possess (something) • *We own some property in Texas.*

owner /'oʊ·nər/ *n* [C] • *Will the owner of the gray Ford parked in front of the restaurant please move it?*

ownership /'oʊ·nər,ʃɪp/ *n* [U] the right or state of being an owner • *His business interests include ownership of a county newspaper.*

▫ **own up** /'-'-/ *v adv* [I] to admit that you are to blame for something • *C'mon, own up—you did it, didn't you?*

OX /ɑks/ *n* [C] *pl* **oxen** /'ɑk·sən/ an adult an-imal of the cattle family, esp. a male that has had its sexual organs removed

oxide /'ɑk·saɪd/ *n* [C/U] a chemical combination of oxygen and one other element • *ni-trogen/iron oxide* [U]

oxygen /'ɑk·sə·dʒən/ *n* [U] a colorless gas, one of the chemical elements, that forms a large part of the air on earth and is needed to keep most living things alive and to create fire

oyster /'ɔɪ·stər/ *n* [C] a water creature that grows within a shell, some types of which can be eaten, and other types of which produce PEARLS (= small, round, white stones used in jewelry)

oz. *n* [C] *pl* **oz.** or **ozs.** *abbreviation for* OUNCE

ozone /'oʊ·zoʊn/ *n* [U] a colorless gas that is a form of oxygen • The **ozone layer** is a layer of ozone above the earth that protects the earth from the sun's harmful ULTRAVIOLET light.

P, p

p LETTER , **p** /piː/ n [C] pl **P's** or **Ps** or **p's** or **ps** the 16th letter of the English alphabet

p. PAGE n [C] pl **pp.** abbreviation for PAGE PAPER • See "Sleepwalking Through History," p. 368.

pa /pɑ, pɔː/ n [C] infml father • Do you know where pa went? • LP TITLES AND FORMS OF ADDRESS

PAC /pæk/ n [C] pl **PACs** abbreviation for **political action committee**, see at POLITICAL

pace SPEED /peɪs/ n [U] the speed at which someone or something moves, or with which something happens or changes • She walks four miles every day at a brisk pace. ○ You seem to be working at a slower pace than normal. ○ (fig.) The Orioles won their ninth straight game to keep pace with Boston (= stay in the same position compared to them).

pace /peɪs/ v [T] • It was a cheaply produced film, sluggishly paced and poorly acted. • To pace (someone) is to lead them: Smith scored 17 points to pace North Springs to a 78-38 victory.

pace WALK /peɪs/ v [I/T] to walk in one direction and then in the opposite direction, often because you are worried or waiting for something to happen • She paced back and forth outside the courtroom. [I]

pacemaker /'peɪs,meɪ·kər/ n [C] a small, electronic device that is put near a person's heart, usually under the skin, in order to control the rate at which the heart beats

pacifier /'pæs·ə,faɪ·ər/ n [C] a rubber or plastic object with a part that sticks out like a NIPPLE and that is given to a baby to suck, usually to calm them

pacifism /'pæs·ə,fɪz·əm/ n [U] the belief that war and violence are wrong

pacifist /'pæs·ə·fəst/ n [C] • Einstein was an ardent pacifist who promoted the cause of world peace.

pacify /'pæs·ə,faɪ/ v [T] to cause (esp. someone who is angry or upset) to be calm and satisfied • The governor later apologized, but union members weren't pacified. • To pacify a place is to bring it into a state of peace, esp. when it has been in a state of war: The US plans to send troops to pacify the country.

pack PUT INTO /pæk/ v [I/T] to put (items) into a container, esp. for transporting them or for storage • You'd better start packing. [I] ○ I forgot to pack my socks. [T] ○ Pack your bag, we're leaving tonight. [T]

pack /pæk/ n [C] a number of things usually of the same kind that are tied together or stored in a container, or the container itself • a pack of bubble gum ○ a pack of cigarettes • A pack is also a BACKPACK.

packer /'pæk·ər/ n [C] a person whose job is

wrapping or tying items or putting them in containers • a meat packer

packing /'pæk·ɪŋ/ n [U] the act of putting things in containers for travel or storage • We still have a lot of packing to do before our trip.

pack FILL /pæk/ v [T] to fill (a space), or to crowd (people or things) together, esp. in large numbers • People packed Times Square, waiting for the new year to begin. [T] ○ The cooler was packed with cans of soda. ○ (fig.) How much can you pack into a short vacation? • If an entertainment or event packs people in, it attracts large numbers of people. [M] • (infml) To **pack it in** is to stop doing something: When it started to rain again, we decided to pack it in and go home.

packed /pækt/ adj • Several people in the packed courtroom were crying.

pack PRESS TOGETHER /pæk/ v [T] to press (something consisting of a lot of small pieces) together so that they form a solid mass • Nina packed the snow into a hard snowball.

pack GROUP /pæk/ n [C] a group of animals • Wolves live and hunt in packs.

□ **pack off** obj, **pack** obj **off** /'-'-/ v adv [M] to send (someone) somewhere else • We packed the kids off to their grandparents for the weekend.

□ **pack up** /'-'-/ v adv [I] to stop doing an activity • It's 5:30, time to pack up and head home.

package /'pæk·ɪdʒ/ n [C] a box or container in which something is put, esp. to be sent or sold, or a groxup of objects wrapped together • a package of frozen spinach ○ She went to the post office to mail a package. • A package is also a group of objects, plans, or arrangements that are related and offered as a unit: a retirement package ○ a five-night ski package • A **package store** is a store where you can buy bottles of wine and other alcoholic drinks that you open and drink somewhere else.

package /'pæk·ɪdʒ/ v [T] to put (something) in a box or container, or to wrap (things) together, esp. to be sold • The book and CD are packaged together. • To package (someone or something) is also to represent it in a way to make it seem attractive: You have an idea, but how do you package it?

packaging /'pæk·ɪ·dʒɪŋ/ n [U] • frozen food packaging ○ It came shrink-wrapped in its original packaging.

packed /pækt/ adj • See at PACK FILL.

packer /'pæk·ər/ n [C] • See at PACK PUT INTO.

packet /'pæk·ət/ n [C] a small, thin package or envelope, or a collection of things in it • a packet of stamps

packing /'pæk·ɪŋ/ n [U] • See at PACK PUT INTO.

pact /pækt/ n [C] a formal agreement between two people or groups of people • a peace pact

pad

pad PAPER /pæd/ *n* [C] a number of sheets of paper glued along one edge so that they can be easily carried about together but separated as needed • *He gave me a pencil and laid a pad on my bed for me to write on.*

pad SOFT MATERIAL /pæd/ *n* [C] a flat piece of soft material used to protect a surface, to prevent injury to a person, or to give a fuller shape to clothing • *Hockey players wear these pillow-thick leg pads.* ○ *A carpet and pad on the floor help insulate against the cold.*

pad /pæd/ *v* [T] **-dd-** • *Old-fashioned Valentine's cards were often padded with satin.* • If you pad (a document or report), you add something extra that is unnecessary or not correct: *Lawyers occasionally pad their hours.*

padding /'pæd·ɪŋ/ *n* [U] • *We put some padding around the sides of the baby's crib.*

pad WALK /pæd/ *v* [I] **-dd-** to walk with a soft, light step • *She padded silently into his bedroom.*

pad HOUSE /pæd/ *n* [C] slang a person's house or apartment • *a bachelor pad*

paddle /'pæd·əl/ *n* [C] a short pole with a wide, flat part at one or both ends, used for moving a small boat through the water • A paddle is also a flat blade held with a short handle that is used in some games such as **table tennis** for hitting a small ball. • PIC CANOE, KAYAK

paddle /'pæd·əl/ *v* [I/T] • *She paddled her canoe across the lake.* [T]

padlock /'pæd·lɑk/ *n* [C] a movable lock with a U-shaped part that is pushed into another part to close and is usually opened with a key • *One of the gates has a padlock on it.*

padlock /'pæd·lɑk/ *v* [T] • *After ten p.m. the doors are padlocked.*

pagan /'peɪ·gən/ *adj* belonging to or used in a religion that worships many gods • *Those altars were used in pagan worship.*

page PAPER /peɪdʒ/ (*abbreviation* **p.**) *n* [C] one side of a sheet of paper in a book, newspaper, magazine, etc. • *What page are the baseball standings on?* ○ *It's a terrific novel, but it's over 800 pages long.* ○ *The article is continued on page 43* (= a side of a sheet of paper numbered 43).

page COMMUNICATE /peɪdʒ/ *v* [T] to communicate with (a person) by having their name announced publicly or by sending a signal to an electronic device they are carrying • *Doctors are paged by their answering services at all hours.*

pager /'peɪ·dʒər/ *n* [C] a small electronic device that you carry or wear that makes a noise or shows a message to tell you that someone wants you to telephone them; a BEEPER

pageant /'pædʒ·ənt/ *n* [C] a show, celebration, or PARADE (= a large number of people walking or marching together), esp. one in which people wear special clothing or act out historical events • *the Miss Chinatown pag-eant* ○ *Our school held a Pageant of Great Women.*

pageantry /'pædʒ·ən·tri/ *n* [U] • *Between games, the traditional pageantry includes the Parade of Champions.*

pagoda /pə'goud·ə/ *n* [C] a tower that is used for religious worship in Asia, each floor of which has its own curved and decorated roof

paid /peɪd/ *past simple and past participle of* PAY

pail /peɪl/ *n* [C] a container, usually with a curved handle attached to opposite sides at the top edge • *She carried a pail of water.*

pain /peɪn/ *n* [C/U] a bad or unpleasant physical feeling, often caused by injury or illness that you want to stop, or an emotional feeling of this type • *Your whole perspective on life changes when you're in pain.* [U] ○ *He was admitted to the hospital with chest pains.* [C] • (*infml*) Someone or something described as a **pain** or **a pain in the neck** is annoying or difficult to deal with • *One of my students is a real pain in the neck.* • (*rude slang*) A person or thing that is **a pain in the ass** is very annoying. • A **painkiller** is a pill or other medicine used to reduce or remove physical pain.

pain /peɪn/ *v* [T] *slightly fml* • *It pained him when he did not make the high school football team.*

painful /'peɪn·fəl/ *adj* • *A painful leg injury forced her to withdraw from the competition.*

painfully /'peɪn·fə·li/ *adv* • *We were painfully* (= unpleasantly but clearly) *aware of the money that we had lost already.* • Painfully is also used to emphasize a quality or situation that is unpleasant or not desirable: *He's a bright boy, but painfully shy.*

painless /'peɪn·ləs/ *adj* without pain, or causing no pain • *Laser treatments for this condition are simple and painless.* ○ *The company tried to make the layoffs as painless as possible.*

painstaking /'peɪn,steɪ·kɪŋ/ *adj* (esp. of work) very careful and needing a lot of attention • *It took many months of painstaking research, but he was now ready to write the book.*

paint /peɪnt/ *n* [C/U] a colored liquid that is put on a surface to protect or decorate it • *acrylic/oil paints* [C] ○ *We need some white paint for the kitchen.* [U] • A **paintbrush** is a brush used for putting paint on a surface. PIC BRUSH • A **paint roller** is a handle attached to a tube covered with a soft material that absorbs paint and spreads it over a surface when rolled against it.

paint /peɪnt/ *v* [I/T] • *We hired three men to paint the outside of our house.* [T] • If someone paints, they may make a picture by using paints: *She always loved to paint.* [I] • If you **paint a picture** of something, you de-

paint roller

scribe it in a particular way: *The statistics do not paint an optimistic picture.*

painter /'peɪnt·ər/ *n* [C] an artist who uses paint to create pictures, or a worker whose job is to cover parts of buildings with paint

painting /'peɪnt·ɪŋ/ *n* [C/U] a picture created by putting paint on a surface, or the activity or skill of creating pictures by using paint • *oil paintings* [C] ○ *In later years, he took up painting as a hobby.* [U]

pair /per, pær/ *n* [C] *pl* **pairs** or **pair** two things of the same appearance and size that are intended to be used together, or something that consists of two parts joined together • *a pair of gloves/shoes* ○ *a pair of pants/scissors* ○ *Each package contains three pairs of socks.*

pair /per, pær/ *v* [I/T] to make or become one of a pair • *Famous paintings have been paired with poems by Sandburg, Angelou, and others.* [T] • *The skaters, six girls and six boys,* **paired off** (= formed pairs) *and started across the ice.*

paisley /'peɪz·li/ *adj* [not gradable] (esp. of cloth) having a pattern of curved, colored shapes • *a paisley tie*

pajamas /pə'dʒɑm·əz, -'dʒæm·əz/, *infml* **pj's** *pl n* clothes worn in bed,

paisley

consisting of a loosely fitting shirt and pants • *I need a new pair of pajamas.*

pal /pæl/ *n* [C] *infml* a friend • *The two politicians were never really pals.*

palace /'pæl·əs/ *n* [C] a large, highly decorated house, esp. one that is the official home of a king or queen • *Most of the palace is open to the public as a museum.* • USAGE: The related adjective is PALATIAL.

palatable /'pæl·əṭ·ə·bəl/ *adj* good enough to eat or drink • *They could make powdered eggs into palatable omelets.* • If something is palatable, it is acceptable: *The city council has tried to make property taxes more palatable by giving homeowners more time to pay them.*

palate /'pæl·ət/ *n* [C] the top part of the inside of your mouth • *A person's palate is also their ability to taste and judge good food and drink: I let my palate dictate what I eat.*

palatial /pə'leɪ·ʃəl/ *adj* (of a house or other property) large and highly decorated; like a PALACE • *They lived in a palatial apartment.*

pale /peɪl/ *adj* [-er/-est only] (of a person's face) having less color than usual, or (of a color or light) not bright or strong • *a pale blue scarf* ○ *A pale young man answered the door.*

pale /peɪl/ *v* [I] to become lighter than usual in color • *Madeleine sickened and paled during the next two days.* • If something **pales by/in comparison with** something else, it is not nearly as good as the other thing: *The paintings he made later pale in comparison with his earlier work.*

palette /'pæl·ət/ *n* [C] a thin board that painters use to hold and mix paints before

putting them on the picture surface, or a range of colors, esp. those typically used by an artist • *Van Gogh's palette included brilliant yellows and blues.*

pall COVERING /pɔːl/ *n* [C] a dark, thick covering or cloud that blocks light • *A heavy pall of smoke from the forest fires blotted out the sun.* • A pall can also be a feeling of being unhappy or hopeless: *News of his death cast a pall over the evening.*

pall BECOME LESS GOOD /pɔːl/ *v* [I] to become less interesting or enjoyable • *The joy of being his own boss began to pall after working 70-hour weeks.*

pallbearer /'pɔːl,ber·ər, -,bær·ər/ *n* [C] a person who helps to carry a COFFIN (= a box that holds a dead body) at a funeral or who walks beside it

pallid /'pæl·əd/ *adj* pale and slightly sickly-looking • *He looked pallid and bloated a few years ago.*

pallor /'pæl·ər/ *n* [U] the condition of being pale • *The pallor of his skin contrasted with his dark hair.*

palm /pɑm, pɑlm/ *n* [C] the inside part of your hand from your wrist to the base of your fingers • *I wiped my palm on my shirt.* • If you have someone **in the palm of** your **hand**, you have complete control over them: *The audience was fascinated—he had them in the palm of his hand.* • A **palm reader** is someone you pay to tell you your future by looking at the lines on the inside of your hands. • PIC HAND

palm off *obj*, **palm** *obj* **off** /'-'-/ *v adv* [M] to persuade someone to accept (something you do not want or something that has no value) • *They produced fake stamps and palmed them off as genuine.*

palm (tree) /'pɑm (,triː), 'pɑlm/ *n* [C] a tree growing in warm regions and having a tall, straight trunk, no branches, and a mass of long, pointed leaves at the top

palm trees

Palm Sunday /'pɑm'sʌn·di, 'pɑlm-, -deɪ/ *n* [C/U] the Sunday before Easter in the Christian year

palpable /'pæl·pə·bəl/ *adj* so obvious that it can easily be seen or known, or (of a feeling) so strong that it seems as if it can be touched or physically felt • *In the Bosnian Serb capital, Pale, the climate of fear is palpable.*

palpitations /ˌpæl·pəˈteɪ·ʃənz/ *pl n* fast and strong beating of the heart

paltry /ˈpɔːl·tri/ *adj* less than expected or needed; too small or slight • *I don't think my paltry student grants are enough for us to live on.*

pamper /ˈpæm·pər/ *v* [T] to treat with too much kindness and attention • *Our children are pampered by their grandparents.*

pamphlet /ˈpæm·flət/ *n* [C] a few sheets of paper folded together to form a thin magazine that contains information or opinions about something • *a voter's information pamphlet* ○ *She wrote the pamphlet, "Why My Child Is Gay."*

pan CONTAINER /pæn/ *n* [C] any of various types of metal containers, usually not deep, used for cooking food • *a frying pan* ○ *Louise moved around some pots and pans on the stove.*

pans

pan CRITICIZE /pæn/ *v* [T] **-nn-** *infml* to severely criticize (esp. a movie, book, or show) • *Critics panned the concert.*

pan MOVE SLOWLY /pæn/ *v* [I] **-nn-** *specialized* (of a movie camera) to move gradually in one direction • *Opening scenes panned the crowded, cluttered street.*

□**pan out** /ˈ-ˈ-/ *v adv* [I] to develop or be successful • *Not all his ideas have panned out as he would have liked.*

panacea /ˌpæn·əˈsiː·ə/ *n* [C] something that will solve all problems or cure all illnesses • *Books are not meant to be a panacea for an illness or loss.*

pancake /ˈpæn·keɪk/, **flapjack**, **hot cake** *n* [C] a thin, flat, usually round cake made from a mixture of flour, milk, and egg that is fried on both sides and usually eaten for breakfast • *He poured the maple syrup on his stack of pancakes.*

pancreas /ˈpæŋ·kriː·əs/ *n* [C] an organ in the body that produces INSULIN (= a chemical substance that controls the amount of sugar in the blood) and substances that help to digest food

panda /ˈpæn·də/ *n* [C] a large black-and-white mammal, similar to a bear, that lives in forests in China and eats BAMBOO (= stems of a type of grass)

pandemonium /ˌpæn·dəˈmoʊ·niː·əm/ *n* [U] noisy confusion and wild excitement • *Pandemonium erupted in the courtroom when members of the victim's family started shouting "Kill him!"*

pander to /ˈpæn·dər·tuː, -ˌtʊ, -tə/ *v prep* [T] to do (what someone else wants), even if the action is wrong or is below your standards, to get some personal advantage • *TV stations have to pander to the tastes of mass audiences.*

pane /peɪn/ *n* [C] a flat piece of glass used in a window or door • *a window pane* ○ *a pane of glass*

panel PART /ˈpæn·əl/ *n* [C] a flat section in the shape of a rectangle that is part of or fits into something larger • *We sanded down the insides of the door panels.*

panel /ˈpæn·əl/ *v* [T] • *The hall has been tastefully paneled in cherrywood.*

paneling /ˈpæn·əl·ɪŋ/ *n* [U] • *My den had dark wood paneling at one end.*

panel CONTROL DEVICE /ˈpæn·əl/ *n* [C] a surface with devices that a person uses to control or get information about the operation of one or more machines • *The car's instrument panel has buttons that give off a little blue-green light at night.*

panel TEAM /ˈpæn·əl/ *n* [C] a small group of people chosen to give advice, make a decision, or publicly discuss their opinions • *A panel of experts was formed to look into the causes of the fire.*

panelist /ˈpæn·əl·əst/ *n* [C] a member of a panel, esp. on a television or radio show • *He was a panelist on the popular television show "Meet the Press."*

pang /pæŋ/ *n* [C] a sudden, sharp feeling of pain or painful emotion • *hunger pangs* ○ *pangs of remorse*

panhandle ASK /ˈpæn,hæn·dəl/ *v* [I] to ask for money, esp. in a public place; to BEG • *A homeless man often panhandles in front of the bank.*

panhandle AREA /ˈpæn,hæn·dəl/ *n* [C] a long, narrow piece of land joined to a larger area • *The Oklahoma panhandle extends over Texas.*

panic /ˈpæn·ɪk/ *n* [C/U] a sudden, strong feeling of anxiety or fear that prevents reasonable thought and action and may spread to influence many people • *When fire broke out, 602 people died in the panic that ensued.* [U] • *Panic is also used to describe any behavior that is sudden, extreme, and results from fear: A brief panic overtook the financial markets in October.* [C] • (*slang*) If a person **hits/presses/pushes the panic button**, they let unreasonable fears make them react to a situation in an extreme way: *Despite two consecutive losses, our coach isn't about to push the panic button.* • **Panic-stricken** (= Very frightened) *people ran from the scene.*

panic /ˈpæn·ɪk/ *v* [I/T] **panicking**, *past* **panicked** • *The driver who hit him panicked and fled.* [I]

panicky /ˈpæn·ɪ·ki/ *adj* • *a panicky feeling*

panorama /ˌpæn·ə'ræm·ə, -'ram·ə/ *n* [C] a view from a great distance that covers a very large area • *From the top floor of the hotel you get a panorama of the whole city.*

panoramic /ˌpæn·ə'ræm·ɪk/ *adj* • *a panoramic view of the city*

pansy PLANT /'pæn·zi/ *n* [C] a small garden plant with flowers of many different colors

pansy PERSON /'pæn·zi/ *n* [C] *dated rude slang* a man who behaves in a way that is considered to be more typical of a woman, or a male homosexual • USAGE: This word is considered offensive by most people.

pant /pænt/ *v* [I] to breathe quickly and loudly through your mouth, usually because you have been doing something energetic • *Blake was panting hard after running up the hill.*

panther /'pæn·θər/ *n* [C] a black LEOPARD (= large wild cat) or a COUGAR

panties /'pænt·iːz/ *pl n* underwear worn by women and girls that covers the area between the waist and the tops of the legs

pantomime /'pænt·ə,maɪm/ *n* [C/U] the art or act of expressing thoughts and emotions with movement rather than speech; MIME

pantry /'pæn·tri/ *n* [C] a small room or storage area near a kitchen, where food is kept

pants /pænts/ *pl n* a piece of clothing covering the lower part of the body from the waist to the foot, and including separate sections, joined at the top, for each leg • *I need a new pair of gray pants to go with this jacket.* • (*Br*) Pants are UNDERPANTS. • A **pants/pant leg** is either of the separate sections covering a leg in a pair of pants. • A **pantsuit** is a matching jacket and pair of pants worn by women.

pantyhose /'pænt·iː,houz/ *pl n* a piece of clothing made of a thin material that stretches to cover the body below the waist, including the legs and feet, and that is usually worn under dresses or skirts by women and girls • *She bought a new pair of pantyhose.*

papa /'pɑp·ə/ *n* [C] *slightly dated infml* father; DAD • LP TITLES AND FORMS OF ADDRESS

papacy /'peɪ·pə·si/ *n* [U] the position of the POPE (= leader of the Roman Catholic Church)

papal /'peɪ·pəl/ *adj* [not gradable] • *a papal audience/Mass*

papaya /pə'paɪ·ə/ *n* [C/U] a large, oval fruit that grows on trees in hotter regions of the world, having a yellow skin and sweet, orange flesh

paper /'peɪ·pər/ *n* [C/U] a thin, flat material made from crushed wood or cloth used esp. for writing and printing on and in packaging • *a piece/sheet of paper* [U] ○ *a paper bag/towel* [U] ○ *paper cups/napkins/plates* [U] • A paper is also a newspaper: *I read it in the paper.* [C] • A paper is also a piece of writing by a student for a course: *One of the course requirements is a 20-page paper.* [C] • **On paper** means written: *They laughed at stuff that didn't look*

all that funny on paper. • **On paper** also means according to theory: *It's one of those things that look good on paper, but making it happen is a whole different ball game.* • A **paperback** is a book with a cover made of thick paper: *I want to get a paperback to read on the plane.* • A **paper clip** is a small piece of bent wire or plastic used for holding pieces of paper together. • If something is **paper-thin**, it is very thin: *You can hear every word our neighbors say through these paper-thin walls.* • A **paperweight** is a small, heavy object, often decorative, placed on papers to keep them together. • *She liked everything about her job but the* **paperwork** (= the activity of keeping records and writing reports).

paper /'peɪ·pər/ *v* [T] to put WALLPAPER (= decorative paper) on a surface, esp. a wall • *We plan to paper the dining room.*

papers /'peɪ·pərz/ *pl n* • *The guard asked to see my papers* (= official documents).

papier-mâché /ˌpeɪ·pər·mə'ʃeɪ, ˌpɑp,yeɪ·mə-/ *n* [U] paper mixed with glue or flour and water that can be shaped to make decorative objects or models that become hard when dry • *a papier-mâché mask*

paprika /pə'priː·kə, pæ-/ *n* [U] a red powder used as a spice to give a slightly hot flavor to food, esp. in meat dishes

Pap test /'pæp·test/, **Pap smear** /'pæp·smɪr/ *n* [C] an examination of cells contained in the thick liquid on the surface of a woman's CERVIX (= entrance to the uterus) to discover if there is CANCER (= a disease)

par EQUAL /pɑr/ *n* • Something that is **on a par with** something else is equal or similar to it: *In my opinion, none of the new jazz trumpeters are on a par with Louis Armstrong.*

par STANDARD /pɑr/ *n* [U] the usual standard or condition • *About half the teachers are good, and the rest are clearly below par.* • In golf, par is the expected number of times a good player should have to hit the ball in order to get it into a hole or into all the holes: *Walker shot a par 72 for the victory.* • *The school budget is going to be cut again this year, but then that's* **par for the course** (= what can be expected from past experience).

par. TEXT *n* [C] *abbreviation for* PARAGRAPH

parable /'pær·ə·bəl/ *n* [C] a simple story told because it represents a basic moral truth or religious principle

parachute /'pær·ə,ʃuːt/ *n* [C] a large, usually circular piece of special cloth fastened to someone or something so that when they are dropped from an aircraft, it will catch the wind like a sail to make them fall slowly and safely to the ground

parachute

parachute /'pær·ə,ʃuːt/ *v*

[I/T] • *When the plane went down, three of the crewmen parachuted to safety.* [I]

parade /pə'reɪd/ *n* [C] a large number of people marching, walking, or riding in vehicles, all moving in the same direction, usually in a formal way as part of a public celebration • *We used to go and see the Thanksgiving Day parade in New York.* • A parade is also a military ceremony in which soldiers march in front of important officials or as part of a public celebration.

parade /pə'reɪd/ *v* [I/T] • *The Saint Patrick's Day marchers paraded up Fifth Avenue.* [I] ○ *These men parade their women past each other* (= show them to each other). [T] ○ *We all paraded down to the cellar to carry up the Christmas ornaments* (= went there together). [I]

paradigm /'pær·ə,daɪm/ *n* [C] *slightly fml* a very clear or typical example used as a model • *His ruthless accumulation of wealth stands as a paradigm of greed in the business world.*

paradise /'pær·ə,daɪs, -,daɪz/ *n* [U] a place or condition of great happiness where everything is exactly as you would like it to be • *His idea of paradise is to spend the day sailing.* ○ (*infml*) *This place is a shopper's/children's/pickpocket's paradise* (= a place where the conditions are exactly right for them). • Paradise is another word for heaven.

paradox /'pær·ə,daks/ *n* [C] a statement or situation that may be true but seems impossible or difficult to understand because it contains two opposite facts or characteristics • *It's a strange paradox that people who say you shouldn't criticize the government criticize it as soon as they disagree with it.*

paradoxical /,pær·ə'dak·sɪ·kəl/ *adj* • *a paradoxical quality*

paradoxically /,pær·ə'dak·sɪ·kli/ *adv* • *The hot thing in video equipment is, paradoxically, sound.*

paragon /'pær·ə,gan, -gən/ *n* [C] a person or thing that is an example of excellence or perfection • *a paragon of virtue*

paragraph /'pær·ə,græf/ (*abbreviation* **par.**) *n* [C] a short part of a text that begins on a new line and consists of one or more sentences dealing with a single idea

parakeet /'pær·ə,kiːt/ *n* [C] a small PARROT (= type of tropical bird) with a long tail

parallel POSITION /'pær·ə,lel, -ləl/ *adj* [not gradable] (of two or more straight lines) being the same distance apart along all their length • *The wood was marked with parallel dark bands.*

parallel /'pær·ə,lel, -ləl/ *n* [C] one of the imaginary lines around the earth that are parallel to the equator • *the 40th parallel*

parallel /'pær·ə,lel, -ləl/ *adv* [not gradable] • *Maple Street runs parallel to State Street.*

parallel /'pær·ə,lel, -ləl/ *v* [T] • *The highway parallels the river for about 20 miles.*

parallel SIMILARITY /'pær·ə,lel, -ləl/ *n* [C] some-thing very similar to something else, or a similarity between two things • *There's an incredible parallel between the talking blues of 50 years ago and today's rap music.* ○ *The black experience in America has been without parallel in the experience of other peoples.*

parallel /'pær·ə,lel, -ləl/ *adj* similar or matching • *Parallel experiments are being conducted in Europe and the United States.*

parallel /'pær·ə,lel, -ləl/ *v* [T] • *Her account of the incident closely parallels what others have reported.*

paralysis /pə'ræl·ə·səs/ *n* [U] the state of being unable to move or act • *Some spinal cord injuries can cause permanent paralysis.*

paralyze /'pær·ə,laɪz/ *v* [T] to cause (a person or animal) to lose the ability to move or feel part of the body, or to cause (someone or something) to be unable to act or operate correctly • *He was paralyzed from the waist down.* ○ *Commuter traffic paralyzes the city's roads every morning.*

paramedic /,pær·ə'med·ɪk/ *n* [C] a person who is trained to give medical help, especially in an emergency, but who is not a doctor or a nurse

parameter /pə'ræm·ət·ər/ *n* [C usually pl] a fixed limit that establishes how something should be done • *Aspin outlined the parameters of the debate between Congress and the Pentagon.*

paramilitary /,pær·ə'mɪl·ə,ter·i/ *adj* [not gradable] similar to an army, but not official and sometimes not legal • *paramilitary forces*

paramount /'pær·ə,maʊnt/ *adj* [not gradable] more important than anything else • *Everybody agrees that education is the paramount issue.*

paranoia /,pær·ə'nɔɪ·ə/ *n* [U] a strong tendency to feel that you cannot trust other people or that they have a bad opinion of you, or (*medical*) a mental illness that causes extreme feelings that others are trying to harm you

paranoid /'pær·ə,nɔɪd/ *adj* anxious because you do not feel you can trust others, or (*medical*) suffering from PARANOIA • *My husband is very paranoid about making sure everything's locked.*

paraphernalia /,pær·ə·fə'neɪl·jə, -fər-/ *n* [U] a collection of objects, esp. equipment needed for or connected with a particular activity • *drug paraphernalia*

paraphrase /'pær·ə,freɪz/ *v* [T] to state (something written or spoken) in different words, esp. in a shorter and simpler form to make the meaning clearer • *I'll have to paraphrase it because I didn't get a chance to memorize it.*

paraplegic /,pær·ə'pliː·dʒɪk/ *n* [C] a person who has lost the ability to move the legs and lower part of the body, usually because of a severe injury to the SPINE (= bones in the back)

parasite /'pær·ə,saɪt/ *n* [C] an animal or plant that lives on or in another animal or plant of a different type and feeds from it • (*fig.*) *Many people believe that lawyers are parasites* (= useless people who live off others).

parasol /ˈpær·əˌsɔːl, -ˌsɑl/ *n* [C] a type of UMBRELLA (= round cloth-covered frame on a stick) carried by women, esp. in the past, for protection from the sun

paratrooper /ˈpær·əˌtruː·pər/ *n* [C] a soldier who is trained to be dropped from an aircraft with a PARACHUTE • *French paratroopers held war games last week.*

parcel /ˈpɑr·səl/ *n* [C] an object or collection of objects wrapped in paper; a package • *a food parcel* • A parcel of land is an area of it: *a 50-acre parcel on Lake Mead* • **Parcel post** is the cheapest way to send packages through the mail.

parcel out *obj*, **parcel** *obj* **out** /ˈ--ˈ-/ *v prep* [T] to divide (something) and give it in parts to different people • *More than $13,000 in awards will be parceled out, with $6000 going to the first-prize winner.*

parched /pɑrtʃt/ *adj* dried out because of too much heat • *My lips were parched.*

parchment /ˈpɑrtʃ·mənt/ *n* [C/U] the dried, pale, yellowish skin of some animals which was used in the past for writing on, or a paper made to look like this • *I found a scrap of parchment dating from the 17th century.* [U]

pardon /ˈpɑrd·ən/ *v* [T] to forgive (someone) for something • *I think they were, pardon the phrase, all in bed together.* • If someone who has committed a crime is pardoned, they are officially forgiven and their punishment is stopped: *He was convicted of murder, but was later pardoned by the governor.* • **Pardon me** is sometimes used as a way of saying you are sorry for behaving in a slightly rude way, such as accidentally pushing someone or BURPING, or when you are trying to move past someone in a small space. • **Pardon me** is a polite way of attracting someone's attention: *Pardon me, does this train go to Oakland?* • **Pardon me** is also a polite way of asking someone to repeat something: *Pardon me, but I didn't catch your name.* • **Pardon me** can also be used to show respect before disagreeing with someone: *Pardon me, but I think you've got it backwards.*

pardon /ˈpɑrd·ən/ *n* [C] forgiveness • *He had actively sought a pardon* (= official forgiveness) *from the president.*

pardon /ˈpɑrd·ən/ *exclamation* said when you have not heard what someone has said to you and you want them to repeat it • *"The train leaves at 2:15." "Pardon?"*

pardonable /ˈpɑrd·ən·ə·bəl/ *adj* able to be forgiven • *a pardonable mistake*

pare /per, pær/ *v* [T] to cut away the thin outer layer of (something, esp. food), or to reduce (something), esp. by a large amount • *He turned the blade to pare off a piece of cheese.* [M] ○ *We have to pare down and eliminate the*

waste and inefficiency. [M] ○ *Simon had to pare the play.* [T]

parent /ˈpær·ənt, ˈper-/ *n* [C] a person who gives birth to or raises a child, or an animal or plant that produces another • *His parents live in New York.* • A **Parent-Teacher Association** (*abbreviation* **PTA**) is an organization of parents and teachers at a school which tries to help the school, esp. by arranging activities that raise money for it.

parentage /ˈpær·ənt·ɪdʒ, ˈper-/ *n* [U] one's parents or origins • *She's of Puerto Rican parentage.*

parental /pəˈrent·əl/ *adj* [not gradable] • *parental guidance*

parenthood /ˈpær·əntˌhʊd, ˈper-/ *n* [U] • *Just barely newlyweds, they now have to confront the harsh realities of parenthood.*

parenting /ˈpær·ənt·ɪŋ, ˈper-/ *n* [U] the raising of children and all the responsibilities and activities involved in it • *parenting skills*

parents–in–law /ˈpær·ən·sənˌlɔː/ *pl n* the parents of someone's husband or wife

parenthesis /pəˈren·θə·səs/ *n* [C usually pl] *pl* **parentheses** /pəˈren·θəˌsiːz/ either of a pair of marks (), or the information inside them, used in a piece of writing to show that what is inside these marks should be considered as separate from the main part • *Dates in parentheses indicate when the film was reviewed.*

PARENTHESES ( )

Parentheses are used to give extra information that does not change the meaning. The extra information can be an explanation, an example, a thought, a date, or a number.

Ozone (a form of oxygen) occurs naturally in the atmosphere. • *The figures given earlier (see p. 76) show a clear increase in sales.* • *Some birds (ostriches, for example) cannot fly.* • *The building will be open tomorrow. (Visitors are welcome.)* • *Haydn (1732-1809) wrote over 100 symphonies.* • *Telephone: (212) 924-3900*

Parentheses go around numbers or letters in a list or series.

(1) Insert a cassette. (2) Press the PLAY and RECORD buttons.
The war was (a) expensive, (b) unpopular, and (c) unsuccessful.

Brackets [ ] are used in place of parentheses for special purposes. They can be used inside a pair of parentheses or when parentheses are already being used for something else.

Call me soon (my phone number is [509] 257-8803). • *"Wonder (which is the seed of knowledge)" [Francis Bacon]*

---

parenthetical /ˌpær·ənˈθeţ·ɪ·kəl/, **parenthetic** /ˌpær·ənˈθeţ·ɪk/ *adj* [not gradable] written in PARENTHESES, or said in addition to the main part of what you are saying • *He added a parenthetical comment to his original statement.*

par excellence /ˌpɑrˌek·səˈlɑns, -ˈlɑs/ *adj* [only after n; not gradable] of the best quality of its type • *He praised her as the teacher par excellence.*

pariah /pəˈrɑɪ·ə/ *n* [C] a person who is avoided or not accepted by a social group, esp. because he or she is not liked, respected, or trusted; an OUTCAST • *Smokers are treated as pariahs these days.*

parish /ˈpær·ɪʃ/ *n* [C] an area that a church provides for • *She lived her whole life in this parish.* • A parish is also a political division within the state of Louisiana. • USAGE: The related adjective is PAROCHIAL [OF A CHURCH].

parishioner /pəˈrɪʃ·ə·nər/ *n* [C] a member of a particular parish, esp. one who frequently goes to its church

parity /ˈpær·əṭ·i/ *n* [U] equality, esp. of pay or position • *Washington, DC, hopes to achieve political parity with the states.*

park [AREA OF LAND] /pɑrk/ *n* [C] a large area of land with grass and trees which is maintained for the pleasure of the public • *a picnic in the park* ○ *Central Park*

park [STOP] /pɑrk/ *v* [I/T] to leave (a vehicle) in a place where it can stay for a period of time, or (*fig. infml*) to put (yourself or something) in a particular place for a period of time • *Where did you park?* [I] ○ *Just park your car out front.* [T] ○ (*fig. infml*) *He parked himself in front of the TV.* [T]

parking /ˈpɑr·kɪŋ/ *n* [U] the act of parking, or the spaces in which cars are parked • *There's lots of parking available at the theater.* • A **parking garage** is a building, or an area under a building, where cars can be parked. • A **parking lot** is an open area where cars can be parked. • A **parking meter** is a device that you put money into so that you can park next to it for a particular period of time.

parka /ˈpɑr·kə/ *n* [C] a long, often waterproof, warm jacket with a HOOD (= covering for the head)

parkway /ˈpɑr·kweɪ/ *n* [C] a wide, usually divided, road with an area of grass and trees on both sides

parliament /ˈpɑr·lə·mənt/ *n* [C/U] the group of people who make the laws in some countries

parliamentary /ˌpɑr·ləˈment·ə·ri, -ˈmen·tri/ *adj* [not gradable] • *a parliamentary election*

parlor [STORE] /ˈpɑr·lər/ *n* [C] a store that sells a stated product, or a business that provides a stated service • *an ice cream parlor* ○ *a funeral parlor*

parlor [ROOM] /ˈpɑr·lər/ *n* [C] *dated* a room in a private house used esp. for entertaining guests • *the front parlor*

Parmesan (cheese) /ˈpɑr·məˌzɑn (ˈtʃiːz, -ˌʒɑn/ *n* [U] a hard, dry, Italian cheese that is usually GRATED

parochial [OF A CHURCH] /pəˈroʊ·kiː·əl/ *adj* [not gradable] connected with a PARISH (= an area that a church provides for) or with a church • *a parochial school*

parochial [LIMITED] /pəˈroʊ·kiː·əl/ *adj* limited t a narrow or local range of matters • *The U coverage of the summit has been extreme parochial.*

parody /ˈpær·əd·i/ *n* [C/U] a piece of writin or music that copies the style of a seriou piece in a way that is intentionally humorou • *Brando did a parody of the character h played in "The Godfather."* [C]

parody /ˈpær·əd·i/ *v* [T] • *Downey started th show by parodying a performance artist.*

parole /pəˈroʊl/ *n* [U] the release of a prisone before that person's period in prison is fir ished, with the agreement that the person wi behave well • *a life sentence without parole*

parole /pəˈroʊl/ *v* [T] • *He was paroled afte serving ten years.*

paroxysm /ˈpær·əkˌsɪz·əm, pəˈrɑk-/ *n* [C] sudden and powerful expression of stron feeling • *The mention of his name can send pe ple into paroxysms of anger.*

parquet /pɑrˈkeɪ/ *n* [U] floor covering tha consists of small blocks of wood arranged i a pattern

parrot [BIRD] /ˈpær·ət/ *n* [C] a tropical bird wit a curved beak and usually colorful feathers some of which can be taught to repeat word

parrot /ˈpær·ət/ *v* [T] to repeat (somethin said by someone else) without thought or ur derstanding • *She just parrots anything h says.*

parsley /ˈpɑr·sli/ *n* [U] an herb with curly o flat green leaves, used to add flavor to food o to decorate it

parsnip /ˈpɑr·snəp/ *n* [C] a long, cream-col ored root eaten as a vegetable

part [SOME] /pɑrt/ *n* [C/U] some but not all o something larger or greater • *I could only ea part of my dinner.* [U] ○ *Parts of the movie wer good.* [C] ○ *Surgeons had to remove part of hi lung.* [U] ○ *Part of the problem is that she does n't like her boss very much.* [U]

part /pɑrt/ *adj, adv* [not gradable] • *She's par scientist and part artist.* ○ *Al is a part owner o a restaurant* (= one of the owners).

partly /ˈpɑrt·li/ *adv* [not gradable] • *The hous is partly owned by her father.*

part [SEPARATE PIECE] /pɑrt/ *n* [C] a separat piece or unit of something, esp. a piece tha combines with other pieces to form the whol of something • *The garage stocks auto part from all current car models.* • A part is also on of two or more equal measures of something *Mix one part vinegar with three parts olive oi* • A part is also a single broadcast of a serie of television programs or a division of a sto ry: *Part three will be broadcast Tuesday.* • (*spe cialized*) In grammar, a **part of speech** is any of the groups into which words are divided de pending on their use, such as verbs, nouns and adjectives.

part SEPARATE /part/ v [I/T] to cause to separate, or to come apart • *The curtains parted, revealing a darkened stage.* [I]

parting /'part·ɪŋ/ n [C/U] the act of leaving or of moving apart • *It was a sad parting, because we knew it was the last time we would see each other.* [C] • If you and another person have a **parting of the ways**, you now have different ideas about something, disagree, or decide to no longer work together.

parting /'part·ɪŋ/ adj [not gradable] • *She gave him a parting kiss.* • A **parting shot** is a critical remark made as you are leaving, so that it has a stronger effect: *"And the dress that you bought me doesn't fit either!" was her parting shot.*

part INVOLVEMENT /part/ n [C usually sing] involvement in or responsibility for an activity or action • *He admitted his part in the robbery.* ○ *It was a mistake on Julia's part* (= she was responsible). • A part in a movie or play is one of its characters, or the words written for that character: *She plays the part of Lady MacBeth.* ○ *Ben is learning his part for the school play.*

part HAIR /part/ n [C] a line formed by the hair on a person's head where the hair is divided

part /part/ v [T] • *I've always parted my hair on the left side.*

□**part with** /'-,-/ v prep [T] to throw out (something, esp. a possession) that you enjoy having • *I just couldn't part with my old car, even though it uses too much gas.*

partake /par'teɪk/ v [I] *past simple* **partook** /par'tʊk/, *past part* **partaken** /par'teɪ·kən/ *slightly fml* to become involved with or take part in something with other people • To partake of food or drink is to eat or drink some of it: *Feel free to partake of the food and drink displayed on tables.*

partial NOT COMPLETE /'par·ʃəl/ adj [not gradable] not complete • *He made a partial repayment of the loan.*

partially /'par·ʃə·li/ adv [not gradable] • *The accident left him partially paralyzed.*

partial PREFERENCE /'par·ʃəl/ adj to have a particular preference or liking for someone or something • *I'm partial toward the larger dogs.*

partiality /,par·ʃiːˈæl·ət·i/ n [U] an unfair preference for one person or group over another • *Some parents complained about the partiality of the teacher toward certain students.*

participant /par'tɪs·ə·pənt/ n [C] a person who takes part in or becomes involved in a particular activity • *Participants in the experiment also keep track of what they eat and drink over three days so their eating habits can be evaluated.*

participate /par'tɪs·ə,peɪt/ v [I] to take part in or become involved in an activity • *The teacher tries to get everyone to participate in the classroom discussion.*

participation /par,tɪs·əˈpeɪ·ʃən/ n [U] • *Participation in the program was voluntary.*

participle /'part·ə,sɪp·əl/ n [C] specialized (in grammar) a form of a verb, often ending in "-ed" or "-ing" and used with auxiliary verbs to make verb tenses, or to form adjectives • LP THE -ING FORM OF VERBS at PRESENT GRAMMAR

particle /'part·ɪ·kəl/ n [C] an extremely small piece of matter • *dust particles*

particular SPECIAL /pər'tɪk·jə·lər, pə'tɪk-/ adj special or single, or this and not any other • *Is there a particular restaurant you'd like to eat at?* ○ *What in particular* (= special things) *did you like about the last apartment that we saw?*

particularly /pər'tɪk·jə·lər·li, pə'tɪk-/ adv very or very much; especially • *We're particularly interested in hearing from people who are fluent in both Spanish and English.*

particulars /pər'tɪk·jə·lərz, pə'tɪk-/ pl n details or information about a person or an event • *We're going to discuss a little bit more about the particulars of the case.*

particular CAREFUL /pər'tɪk·jə·lər, pə'tɪk-/ adj wanting to make choices carefully because you are not easily satisfied • *She's very particular about what she eats.*

partisan /'part·ə·zən, -sən/ adj characterized by loyal support of a person, principle, or political party • *partisan politics*

partition /par'tɪʃ·ən/ n [C/U] the division of something into smaller parts, or something that divides a space • *Both sides agreed to the partition of the disputed territory.* [U] • A partition is also a wall that separates one part of a room or building from another. [C]

partition /par'tɪʃ·ən/ v [T] • *Germany was partitioned after World War II.*

partly /'part·li/ adv • See at PART SOME.

partner /'part·nər/ n [C] one of two people who do something together or are closely involved in some way • *Children, hold your partner's hand when you cross the street.* • A partner in a company is one of the owners. • A partner is also one of two people who dance together or who play a sport or a game together, esp. when they play as a team. • A person's partner can also be the person to whom they are married, or to whom they are not married but with whom they live and have a sexual relationship.

partnership /'part·nər,ʃɪp/ n [C/U] • *a business partnership* [C]

partook /par'tʊk/ *past simple of* PARTAKE

part–time /'part'taɪm/ adj, adv [not gradable] (of an activity or work) done for periods of time shorter than the usual hours or schedule • *She got a part-time job working three days a week.* ○ *Joe works part-time.*

part–timer /'part'taɪ·mər/ n [C] • *We have a full-time staff of three, plus two part-timers.*

party SOCIAL GATHERING /'part·i/ n [C] a social gathering at which people talk, eat, drink, and enjoy themselves • *a birthday party* ○ *Sally is having a party at her place tonight.*

party /'parţ·i/ *v* [I] *infml* to enjoy yourself at a party with others, esp. by drinking alcohol, dancing, etc. • *My mom thinks that everyone in college spends all of their time partying.*

party POLITICAL GROUP /'parţ·i/ *n* [C] a political group with particular beliefs and aims and which supports members who are trying to get elected to public office • *the Democratic/Republican Party* ○ *a political party*

party PARTICULAR GROUP /'parţ·i/ *n* [C] a particular group of people who are involved in an activity • *I made a dinner reservation for a party of eight.*

party ONE INVOLVED /'parţ·i/ *n* [C] one of the people or sides involved in a formal agreement or argument, esp. a legal one • *The UN called on all parties to lay down their arms.*

pass GO PAST /pæs/ *v* [I/T] to go past (something or someone) or move beyond it or them • *A car passed us doing 70 miles per hour.* [T] ○ *I was just passing by and stopped to say hello.* [I]

passable /'pæs·ə·bəl/ *adj* able to be traveled on or through • *It's snowing, but the roads are passable.*

passing /'pæs·ɪŋ/ *adj* [not gradable] • If something is said **in passing**, it is said while talking about something else and is not the main subject of a conversation: *Leo mentioned in passing that you are going on vacation next week.*

pass GO THROUGH /pæs/ *v* [I/T] to cause (something) to go around, across, through, etc., something else, or to be positioned in such a way • *Pass the wire through the slot and pull it out from the other side.* [T] ○ *The causeway passes across the bay and takes you to the mainland.* [I always + adv/prep]

passage /'pæs·ɪdʒ/ *n* [U] • *Passage through the Panama Canal will take a number of hours.* • See also PASSAGE.

pass GIVE /pæs/ *v* [I/T] to give (something) to (someone) • *Please pass the bread.* [T] • In team sports played with a ball, if you pass, you throw, kick, or hit the ball to someone on your team. [I/T] • If you **pass the buck**, you leave a difficult problem for someone else to deal with. • If you **pass the hat**, you ask people to give money for something, esp. because you have entertained them: *The clown in front of the museum passed the hat when he finished his act.*

pass /pæs/ *n* [C] the act of giving or sending the ball to another player on your own team • *The receiver dropped the pass.*

pass DO WELL /pæs/ *v* [I/T] to be successful in (a test, exam, or course), or to judge (someone) as having been successful in it • *The professor said that if I passed the final exam, she'll pass me.* [T]

pass /pæs/ *n* [C] a mark given to show that a

student has successfully completed a course or an exam • If an exam or course is **pass-fail**, students can pass or fail but no other mark is given.

passable /'pæs·ə·bəl/ *adj* satisfactory but not excellent • *Angie can speak passable Russian.*

pass TIME /pæs/ *v* [I/T] to go past or through a period of time • *The hours passed quickly.* [I] • If you **pass the time**, you do something for enjoyment or while waiting to do something else you have planned: *We passed the time playing cards.* [T]

passage /'pæs·ɪdʒ/ *n* [U] • *Memory fades with the passage of time.* • See also PASSAGE.

pass APPROVE /pæs/ *v* [I/T] to approve or be approved by (a group having authority), esp. by voting • *The bill passed both houses of Congress and was signed by the president.* [T] ○ *The bill passed unanimously.* [I]

passage /'pæs·ɪdʒ/ *n* [U] • *The speaker urged passage of the tax bill.* • See also PASSAGE.

pass GIVE OPINION /pæs/ *v* [T] • If you **pass judgment on** (someone or something), you express your opinion about them or it: *Don't pass judgment on Lori until you hear what happened.*

pass NOT DO /pæs/ *v* [I] to choose not to do, have, take part in, or take a turn at something • *I think I'll pass on going to the movies.*

pass DOCUMENT /pæs/ *n* [C] an official document or ticket showing that you have the right to go somewhere or do something • *We bought three-day passes to the amusement park.* ○ *The children get bus passes to travel to and from school.*

pass BE ACCEPTED /pæs/ *v* [I] to be accepted as being something that you are not, esp. something better or more attractive • *Marion looks so young she could pass for 30.* ○ *Do this jacket and skirt match well enough to pass as a suit?*

□ **pass away** /ˌ·-'-/ *v adv* [I] to die • *Her father passed away last week.*

□ **pass off** *obj*, **pass** *obj* **off** /'·'-/ *v adv* [M] to pretend that (someone or something) is something other than what they are • *Maurice is trying to pass himself off as a journalist to get admitted to the press conference.*

□ **pass on** *obj*, **pass** *obj* **on** /'·'-/ *v adv* [M] to bring (something) to someone's attention • *No one passed the news on to me.*

□ **pass out** UNCONSCIOUS /·'-/ *v adv* [I] to become unconscious • *He passed out from the heat.*

□ **pass out** *obj* GIVE /'·'-/, **pass** *obj* **out** *v adv* [M] to give (something) to each person in a group • *Jeff, please pass out the test booklets.*

□ **pass over** *obj*, **pass** *obj* **over** /'·'--/ *v adv* [M] to ignore or to not give attention to (someone or something) • *They passed Sal over for promotion.*

□ **pass up** *obj*, **pass** *obj* **up** /'·'-/ *v adv* [M] to fail to take advantage of (an opportunity) • *I can't believe she passed up the chance to go to South America.*

passage CONNECTING WAY /'pæs·ɪdʒ/, **passage-way** /'pæs·ɪdʒ,weɪ/ n [C] a usually long and narrow part of a building with rooms on one or both sides, or an enclosed path that connects places • *A narrow passage led through the house to the yard.* • A passage is also an entrance or opening: *the nasal passages* • See also **passage** at PASS GO THROUGH, PASS TIME, PASS APPROVE.

passage PART /'pæs·ɪdʒ/ n [C] a short piece of writing or music that is part of a larger piece • *a short passage for a trumpet solo* • See also **passage** at PASS GO THROUGH, PASS TIME, PASS APPROVE.

passage TRAVEL /'pæs·ɪdʒ/ n [U] the right to travel or to leave a place • *We booked passage on a cruise ship.* ◦ *He was guaranteed safe passage to the border.* • See also **passage** at PASS GO THROUGH, PASS TIME, PASS APPROVE.

passé /pæ'seɪ/ adj no longer fashionable • *Writing personal letters, unfortunately, is passé.*

passenger /'pæs·ən·dʒər/ n [C] a person who is traveling in a vehicle but is not operating it or working as an employee in it • *airline passengers* ◦ *Taxis are allowed to carry no more than four passengers.*

passer–by /,pæs·ər'baɪ/ n [C] pl **passers-by** /,pæs·ərz'baɪ/ someone who is going past a particular place • *A passer-by saw smoke and called the fire department.*

passing /'pæs·ɪŋ/ n [U] fml someone's death • *We note with sorrow the passing of Raymond Wilson, a member of the board.*

passion EMOTION /'pæʃ·ən/ n [C/U] a powerful emotion or its expression, esp. the emotion of love, anger, or hate • *sexual passion* [U] ◦ *Passions were running high in the aftermath of the racial incident.* [C]

passionate /'pæʃ·ə·nət/ adj full of emotion • *a passionate embrace*

passion STRONG INTEREST /'pæʃ·ən/ n [C] something that you are strongly interested in and enjoy • *She has two passions in life—her cats and opera.*

passive BEHAVIOR /'pæs·ɪv/ adj not reacting to what happens, or not acting or taking part • *They attack people who are too weak or too passive to resist.* • **Passive resistance** is a way of showing your opposition to a law or official activity without acting violently. • **Passive smoking** is the act of breathing in other people's cigarette smoke.

passively /'pæs·ɪv·li/ adv • *She watched passively as the children ran wild.*

passive GRAMMAR /'pæs·ɪv/ adj [not gradable] specialized (in grammar) describing a verb or sentence in which the subject is the person or thing to which something stated is done • *In the sentence, "I was given a gift by Alex," the verb "give" is passive, or in the passive voice.* • USAGE: In English, passive verbs or sentences

are formed with a form of the verb "to be" and a past participle. • Compare ACTIVE GRAMMAR.

Passover /'pæs,oʊ·vər/ n [U] a Jewish celebration in March or April, lasting seven or eight days, in memory of the escape of the Jews from Egypt

passport /'pæs·pɔːrt, -poʊrt/ n [C] an official document provided by the government of a particular country which shows that the owner is a citizen of that country and allows them to travel to foreign countries

password /'pæs·wɜrd/ n [C] a secret word or phrase that is used to obtain access to a place, information, or a computer system

past TIME BEFORE /pæst/ n [C/U] the period before and until, but not including, the present time • *In the past, a streetcar line ran down 13th Avenue.* [U] • A person's past is their life before the present time: *He never talks about his past.* [C]

past /pæst/ adj [not gradable] • *I've been working out regularly for the past six months.* ◦ *Rising temperatures signal that the worst of winter is past* (= finished).

past GRAMMAR /pæst/ adj [not gradable] specialized (in grammar) having the tense used to describe actions, events, or states that happened or existed before the present time • *The past tense of "change" is "changed."* • A **past participle** is a form of a verb that is used to show past action or to make PERFECT tenses and adjectives: *"Sung" is the past participle of the verb "sing."* • The **past perfect** is a tense usually formed with "had" that is used to refer to actions or events that happened in a period of time before another time or event: *The sentence, "She had broken her leg once before," is in the past perfect.* • LP TENSES

past FAR SIDE /pæst/ prep, adv [not gradable] on the far side of something, or from one side to the other • *They live just past the post office.* ◦ *Three boys went past us on bikes.*

past BEYOND /pæst/ prep, adv [not gradable] beyond or above a particular point • *Melissa is past the age where she needs a babysitter.* ◦ *It's already past noon.*

pasta /'pɑs·tə, 'pæs-/ n [U] a food made of flour, water, and sometimes egg which is formed into a variety of shapes that are hard when dry and soft when cooked

paste /peɪst/ n [U] a thick, wet substance used for sticking things together, or any soft, wet mixture of powder and liquid • *Use paste, glue, or tape to attach the pictures.* ◦ *tomato paste*

paste /peɪst/ v [T always + adv/prep] to stick (something) to something else • *She pasted a heart onto the valentine.*

pastel COLOR /pæs'tel/ adj (of colors) pale and soft

pastel /pæs'tel/ n [C] • *Her room is decorated in pink and pastels.*

pastel COLORED STICK /pæs'tel/ n [C] a colored

stick of soft, waxy material that is used for drawing, or a picture made using these sticks

pasteurize /'pæs·tʃə,raɪz/ v [T] to heat (esp. milk) to a high temperature for a period of time in order to kill bacteria

pasteurization /,pæs·tʃə·rə'zeɪ·ʃən/ n [U] • ultra-high temperature pasteurization

pastime /'pæs·taɪm/ n [C] an activity that is done for enjoyment • Hockey is Canada's national pastime.

pastor /'pæs·tər/ n [C] a minister of a Christian church, esp. one that is Protestant

pastoral /'pæs·tə·rəl/ adj • pastoral work/ duties

pastoral /'pæs·tə·rəl/ adj (of a piece of art, writing, or music) having or representing the pleasant, traditional features of the countryside • a pastoral scene

pastrami /pə'strɑm·i/ n [U] spicy smoked BEEF (= meat from a cow), usually cut in slices • a pastrami sandwich on rye

pastry /'peɪ·stri/ n [C/U] a mixture of flour, fat, and water which is used as a base or covering for other foods and baked • pie pastry [U] • A pastry is a sweet, baked food made of a mixture of flour, fat, and water and often filled with fruit or cream: We were offered a selection of pastries for dessert. [C]

pasture /'pæs·tʃər/ n [C/U] land covered with grass or similar plants suitable for animals, such as cows and sheep, to eat • The best places to find bluebirds are open pastures. [C]

pasty /'peɪ·sti/ adj (of someone's skin) pale and unhealthy looking • a pasty face

pat [TOUCH] /pæt/ v [T] -tt- to touch (someone or something) lightly and repeatedly with an open hand • He patted me on the shoulder. ○ Pat the vegetables dry with a paper towel.

pat /pæt/ n [C] • You've done a great job and you deserve a pat on the back (= praise).

pat [PIECE] /pæt/ n [C] a small, flat piece of butter

pat [WITHOUT THINKING] /pæt/ adj, adv [not gradable] usually disapproving (esp. of an answer) having been already prepared and therefore said without thinking much about the question • You've got a pat response to every question that comes along.

patch [AREA] /pætʃ/ n [C] a comparatively small part of a surface that is different in some way from the area around it • Watch for patches of ice on the road. ○ We have a small vegetable patch (= area for growing vegetables).

patchy /'pætʃ·i/ adj happening or existing in small areas • patchy rain/fog • If information is patchy, only small parts of it are known: My knowledge of physics is pretty patchy.

patch [PIECE OF MATERIAL] /pætʃ/ n [C] a piece of material put over a damaged area or hole to repair, strengthen, or cover it • His old jeans are covered with patches. • **Patchwork** is cloth consisting of smaller pieces of differently patterned cloth that are sewn together: a patchwork quilt

patch /pætʃ/ v [T] • to patch a tire • If you **patch** something **up**, such as a relationship you make it better after a disagreement: The next morning, they patched up their differences.

pate /peɪt/ n [C] dated or humorous the top of a person's head • A hat covered his bald pate

pâté /pɑ'teɪ, pæ-/ n [C/U] a thick, smooth, soft savory mixture made from ground meat or fish

patent [LEGAL RIGHT] /'pæt·ᵊnt/ n [C] the legal right to be the only one who can make, use, or sell an invention for a particular number of years

patent /'pæt·ᵊnt/ v [T] • Otis patented a steam elevator in 1861.

patent [OBVIOUS] /'pæt·ᵊnt, 'peɪt-/ adj (of ideas or characteristics) obvious • He felt the notion of absolute equality was patent nonsense.

patently /'pæt·ᵊnt·li, 'peɪt-/ adv • She finds the nude scenes patently offensive.

patent leather /'pæt·ᵊnt 'leð·ər/ n [U] leather with a hard, shiny surface • black patent leather shoes

paternal /pə'tɜrn·ᵊl/ adj behaving or feeling as a father does toward his child • His father gave him a good-humored, paternal smile. • Paternal also means related by way of the father: paternal grandparents • Compare MATERNAL.

paternity /pə'tɜr·nət·i/ n [U] the fact or state of being a father

paternalism /pə'tɜrn·ᵊl,ɪz·əm/ n [U] the practice of controlling esp. employees or citizens in a way that is similar to that of a father controlling his children, by giving them what is beneficial but not allowing them responsibility or freedom of choice

paternalistic /pə,tɜrn·ᵊl'ɪs·tɪk/ adj • a paternalistic employer

path /pæθ/ n [C] a way or track made by or for people walking on the ground, or a line along which something moves • a bike path ○ The forest fire burned everything in its path. • A path is also a set of actions that lead to a result or goal: Ashe pioneered the path of black tennis players to the top of the game.

pathetic [SAD] /pə'θeṭ·ɪk/ adj causing feelings of sadness or sympathy • I think it's pathetic that only half of the eligible voters tend to vote.

pathetically /pə'θeṭ·ɪ·kli/ adv • a pathetically small dog

pathetic [UNSUCCESSFUL] /pə'θeṭ·ɪk/ adj unsuccessful, useless, or worthless • a pathetic excuse ○ Bernie's hitting was pretty pathetic!

pathological /,pæθ·ə'lɑdʒ·ɪ·kəl/ adj (of a person) unreasonable, or unable to control part of their behavior • a pathological fear of heights ○ a pathological liar

pathology /pə'θɑl·ə·dʒi, pæ-/ n [U] the scientific study of disease

pathological /,pæθ·ə'lɑdʒ·ɪ·kəl/ adj of or caused by disease • a pathological laboratory

pathos /'peɪ·θɑs, -θoʊs, -θɔːs/ *n* [U] a quality in life or art that causes feelings of sadness or sympathy • *The dying girl's speech generates genuine pathos.*

pathway /'pæθ·weɪ/ *n* [C] a PATH • *a rough pathway on the mountainside*

patience /'peɪ·ʃəns/ *n* [U] the ability to accept delay, suffering, or annoyance without complaining or becoming angry • *He's a man of great patience.* ○ *Her constant complaining was beginning to test/try my patience.*

patient /'peɪ·ʃənt/ *adj* • *Just be patient—dinner's almost ready.*

patiently /'peɪ·ʃənt·li/ *adv* • *He waited patiently for his name to be called.*

patient /'peɪ·ʃənt/ *n* [C] a person who is receiving medical care, esp. in a hospital, or who is cared for by a particular doctor or DENTIST when necessary

patio /'pæt·iː·oʊ/ *n* [C] *pl* **patios** an outside area with a solid floor next to a house, where people can sit

patriarch /'peɪ·triː·ɑrk/ *n* [C] a powerful and usually older man in charge of a family, or the male leader of a society in which men hold power • Compare MATRIARCH.

patriarchal /ˌpeɪ·triː·ɑr·kəl/ *adj* • *a patriarchal society*

patriarchy /'peɪ·triː·ɑr·ki/ *n* [C/U] the attitude that it is right for men to have most of the authority and power in society, or a society in which power and property belongs to men rather than women

patriot /'peɪ·triː·ət, -ˌɑt/ *n* [C] a person who loves their country and defends it when necessary

patriotic /ˌpeɪ·triː·ˈɑt̬·ɪk/ *adj* • *Candidates love to associate themselves with patriotic values.*

patriotism /'peɪ·triː·ə·ˌtɪz·əm/ *n* [U] • *This really calls into question his patriotism.*

patrol /pə'troʊl/ *v* [I/T] **-ll-** to go around (an area or a building), esp. regularly, to check that it is free from trouble or danger • *Security guards patrol the building at night.* [T]

patrol /pə'troʊl/ *n* [C/U] • *State troopers make regular patrols of the highway.* [C] ○ *Aircraft are on patrol in the region.* [U] • A **patrol car** is a **squad car**, see at SQUAD.

patron $\boxed{\text{SUPPORTER}}$ /'peɪ·trən/ *n* [C] a person or group that gives money or support to a person, an activity, or an organization • *Auchincloss is a longtime patron of the arts.*

patron $\boxed{\text{CUSTOMER}}$ /'peɪ·trən/ *n* [C] a customer of a store, restaurant, hotel, etc., esp. a regular customer

patronage /'pæ·trə·nɪdʒ, 'peɪ-/ *n* [U] • *We would like to thank all of our customers for their patronage.*

patronize /'peɪ·trə·ˌnaɪz, 'pæ-/ *v* [T] • *Local writers and artists patronize the coffee house.*

patronage /'pæ·trə·nɪdʒ, 'peɪ-/ *n* [U] esp. disapproving the power to give someone an important job or advantages in exchange for

their help or support • *New rules would minimize the effects of political patronage.*

patronize /'peɪ·trə·ˌnaɪz, 'pæ-/ *v* [T] disapproving to treat (someone) in a manner that shows you consider yourself to be better or more important than they are • *She's angry, smart, and not about to be patronized.*

patronizing /'peɪ·trə·ˌnaɪ·zɪŋ, 'pæ-/ *adj* disapproving • *a patronizing manner/attitude*

patsy /'pæt·si/ *n* [C] slang a person who is easily cheated or made to suffer • *He claimed he was a patsy being framed by the police.*

patter $\boxed{\text{TALK}}$ /'pæt̬·ər/ *n* [U] fast, continuous talk, esp. that of an entertainer or someone trying to sell things • *Phinizy's clever patter kept his audience in a good mood.*

patter $\boxed{\text{SOUND}}$ /'pæt̬·ər/ *n* [U] the sound of quick, light hits or steps • *Now that she's older, we have the patter of little feet in our hallways.*

pattern $\boxed{\text{WAY}}$ /'pæt̬·ərn/ *n* [C] a recognizable way in which something is done or organized, or in which something happens • *Our weather pattern comes from the northwest.* ○ *A whole variety of behavior patterns affect infants.*

pattern $\boxed{\text{SHAPES}}$ /'pæt̬·ərn/ *n* [C] a regular arrangement of lines, shapes, or colors • *A human fingerprint can be viewed as a geometric pattern.* • A pattern is also a design or set of shapes that show how to make something: *a dress pattern* • $\boxed{\text{PIC}}$ PAISLEY, POLKA DOTS

patterned /'pæt̬·ərnd/ *adj* • *a rose and black patterned skirt*

patty /'pæt̬·i/ *n* [C] pieces of food, esp. meat, formed into a thin, circular shape and then usually cooked • *hamburger patties*

paucity /'pɔː·sət̬·i/ *n* [U] *fml* the condition of having very little or not enough of something • *The authorities had to cope with the paucity of information about this new terrorist organization.*

paunch /pɔːntʃ, pɑntʃ/ *n* [C] a fat stomach

paunch

pauper /'pɔː·pər/ *n* [C] *dated* a very poor person

pause /pɔːz/ *n* [C] a moment in which something, such as a sound or an activity, stops before starting again • *There was a long pause during which we all wondered what he would say next.*

pause /pɔːz/ *v* [I] • *She paused to catch her breath.*

pave /peɪv/ *v* [T] to cover (an area of ground or a road) with materials such as stone, concrete, or bricks that will form a hard, level surface • If something **paves the way** to something else, it prepares for and makes the other thing possible: *Data from the space flight should pave the way for a more detailed exploration of Mars.*

pavement /ˈpeɪv·mənt/ *n* [C/U] the hard surface of a road, a SIDEWALK (= path next to a road), or other area of ground • *The umbrella fell to the pavement with a clatter.* [U]

pavilion /pəˈvɪl·jən/ *n* [C] a large, open structure or tent, providing shelter esp. in a park or at a FAIR (= temporary public event) • A pavilion is also one of a group of related buildings, such as a hospital.

paw /pɔː/ *n* [C] the foot of an animal, such as a cat, dog, or bear, that has CLAWS or nails

paw /pɔː/ *v* [I/T] • *The dog was pawing (at) the door to be let in.* [I/T] • *(infml)* If a person paws someone else, they feel or touch them, often in a sexual way, that is too forceful. [T]

pawn MONEY /pɔːn/ *v* [T] to leave (a possession) with someone in order to borrow money from them, with the understanding that if you do not pay it back within the agreed time, they can keep your possession and sell it • A **pawnshop** is a store where you can leave possessions to borrow money, or buy objects that have been pawned and are now for sale.

pawn GAME PIECE /pɔːn/ *n* [C] any of the eight least valuable pieces in the game of CHESS • A pawn is also a person who is controlled by others and used for their own advantage: *She felt she had been used as a political pawn.*

pay GIVE MONEY FOR /peɪ/ *v* [I/T] *past* **paid** /peɪd/ to give (money) to (someone) for goods or services • *We paid a lot of money for that table.* [T] ○ *Would you prefer to pay by credit card?* [I] ○ *(fig.) We all eventually pay for our mistakes* (= suffer or are punished because of our mistakes). [I] • To pay is also to give someone or something money for (an amount you owe): *We've got to pay the rent.* [T] ○ *We have so many bills to pay.* [T] • To **pay** your **dues** is to earn the right to something because of your work or suffering: *I've paid my dues for the last 25 years and now I'm ready for a comfortable retirement.* • If you **pay through the nose** for something, you pay too much money for it. • A **pay phone** is a public telephone which is made to operate by putting coins into it or by using a **credit card.** LP TELEPHONE

payable /ˈpeɪ·ə·bəl/ *adj* [not gradable] • *Please make your check payable to Broadway Antiques.*

payee /peɪˈiː/ *n* [C] a person to whom money is given or owed

payer /ˈpeɪ·ər/ *n* [C] a person who pays or owes money that should be paid

payment /ˈpeɪ·mənt/ *n* [C/U] an amount of money paid, or the act of paying • *When is the first payment due?* [C] ○ *Usually we ask for payment when the order is placed.* [U]

pay GIVE EARNINGS /peɪ/ *v* [I/T] *past* **paid** /peɪd/ to give (money) to (someone) that they earn for work they do • *We pay our salespeople a salary plus a bonus based on their sales.* [T] ○ *Construction jobs generally pay well.* [I]

pay /peɪ/ *n* [U] • *I asked the boss for a raise in pay.* • A **paycheck** is a check used to pay an employee the amount of money they earned. • **Payday** is the day on which employees receive their pay. • A **payroll** is a list of a company's employees and the amount each earns, or the total earnings a business gives to its employees.

pay PROFIT /peɪ/ *v* [I] *past* **paid** /peɪd/ to give a profit, advantage, or benefit • *It never pays to take risks where human safety is concerned.* [+ *to* infinitive] ○ *The moral is, "Crime doesn't pay."*

pay PROVIDE /peɪ/ *v* [T] *past* **paid** /peɪd/ to provide or do (something) • *Please pay attention.* ○ *It's always nice to be paid a compliment.* • *Why don't you* **pay** *us* **a visit** *next time you're in town* (= visit us when you are here next)? • LP DO: VERBS MEANING "PERFORM"

□ **pay back** *obj*, **pay** *obj* **back** *(obj)* /ˈ-ˈ-/ *v adv* [M] to return (money) to (someone) from whom you have borrowed it • *I'll pay you back as soon as I get my next paycheck.*

□ **pay off** *obj* GIVE MONEY OWED , **pay** *obj* **off** /ˈ-ˈ-/ *v adv* [M] to give all of or the last part of (an amount you owe) • *I expect to pay the debt off within two years.*

□ **pay off** HAVE SUCCESS /ˈ-ˈ-/ *v adv* [I] to result in success • *I hope this investment pays off.*

payoff /ˈpeɪ·ɔːf/ *n* [C] *infml* a result that rewards you for your effort or work • *After years of study, the payoff is supposed to be a good job.*

□ **pay off** *obj* PAY FOR DISHONESTY , **pay** *obj* **off** /ˈ-ˈ-/ *v adv* [M] to give (someone) money, often illegally, as a reward for having done something dishonest to help you • *He paid off the inspectors with bribes of $500.*

payoff /ˈpeɪ·ɔːf/ *n* [C] • *He denied receiving any kickbacks or payoffs for giving a large contract to the company.*

□ **pay out** *(obj)* /ˈ-ˈ-/ *v adv* [I/T] to spend money for (something) • *The federal government paid out $7.7 billion as a result of damage caused by hurricanes this year.* [T]

□ **pay up** /ˈ-ˈ-/ *v adv* [I] to give all the money that is owed • *Some ballplayers charge fans $10 for autographs, and the fans, incredibly enough, pay up.*

payload /ˈpeɪ·loʊd/ *n* [C] the amount of explosive that a MISSILE carries, or the equipment carried in a spacecraft

payment /ˈpeɪ·mənt/ *n* [C/U] • See at PAY GIVE MONEY FOR.

PC COMPUTER, **pc** /piːˈsiː/ *n* [C] *abbreviation for* **personal computer**, a small computer used in homes and offices

PC CORRECT *adj abbreviation for* **politically correct**, see at POLITICAL

pea /piː/ *n* [C] an edible, round, green seed, that grows with others in a POD (= outer covering), from which they are removed to be cooked as a vegetable

peace NO VIOLENCE /piːs/ *n* [U] (a period of) freedom from war or violence, esp. when people live and work together without violent disagreements • *The country has been* **at peace** *for 25 years* (= not involved in war during this period). • **Peacekeeping** is the maintaining of peace, esp. the use of armed forces not involved in the disagreement to prevent fighting in an area. • A **peacemaker** is a person who tries to influence people, organizations, or countries to stop fighting or arguing. • **Peacetime** is a period when a country is not at war.

peaceful /ˈpiːs·fəl/ *adj* [not gradable] • *The US is promoting a peaceful and rapid solution to the present crisis.*

peaceable /ˈpiː·sə·bəl/ *adj* [not gradable] not liking or involving fighting or argument • *The group supports peaceable, nonviolent protest.*

peaceably /ˈpiː·sə·bli/ *adv*

peace CALM /piːs/ *n* [U] calm and quiet; freedom from worry or annoyance • *I need peace and quiet to study.* • *She seems* **at peace** *with herself* (= not troubled). • If a person has **peace of mind**, they are not worried or confused: *For everyone's peace of mind, please check that the door is locked.*

peaceful /ˈpiːs·fəl/ *adj* [not gradable] • *It's so peaceful by the lake.*

peacefully /ˈpiːs·fə·li/ *adv* [not gradable] • *She died peacefully in her sleep at the age of 90.*

peacefulness /ˈpiːs·fəl·nəs/ *n* [U]

peach FRUIT /piːtʃ/ *n* [C] a round fruit with sweet, juicy, yellow flesh, soft red and yellow skin, and a large seed in its center

peach COLOR /piːtʃ/ *adj* [not gradable], *n* [U] (of) a pink-orange color • *a set of peach towels*

peacock /ˈpiː·kɑk/ *n* [C] a large bird with long, bright, showy, blue and green tail feathers that it can spread out

peak REACH HIGHEST POINT /piːk/ *v* [I] to reach the highest point, value, or level • *Official figures show unemployment peaked in November.*

peak /piːk/ *n* [C] • *Kelly is at the peak of her skating career.*

peak /piːk/ *adj* [not gradable] • *During the peak season, the population swells with over 50,000 tourists.*

peak MOUNTAIN TOP /piːk/ *n* [C] the pointed top of a mountain, or the mountain itself

peaked /ˈpiː·kəd/ *adj* [not gradable] (of a person) looking slightly ill and often pale

peal /piːl/ *v* [I] to sound loudly • *The bells pealed from the church tower.*

peal /piːl/ *n* [C] a loud sound • *A peal of thunder woke him up.*

peanut /ˈpiː·nət, -nʌt/ *n* [C] a small nut that grows in a shell under the ground • **Peanut butter** is a soft food made of crushed, ROASTED peanuts, that is often spread on bread.

peanuts /ˈpiː·nəts, -nʌts/ *pl n infml* a very small amount of money • *They expect us to work for peanuts.*

pear /per, pær/ *n* [C] a sweet, juicy, yellow or green fruit with a round base and slightly pointed top

pearl /ˈpɜrl/ *n* [C] a small, shiny, hard ball, usually white or blue-gray, that forms around a grain of sand inside some OYSTER shells and is valued as a jewel • *a string of pearls*

peasant /ˈpez·ənt/ *n* [C] a member of a low social class of small farmers or farm workers

peat /piːt/ *n* [U] partly decayed plant matter, used to improve garden dirt or as fuel

pebble /ˈpeb·əl/ *n* [C] a small stone, made smooth by the action of water

pecan /pɪˈkɑːn, -ˈkæn/ *n* [C] an edible nut with a smooth shell

peck /pek/ *v* [I/T] (of a bird) to hit, bite, or pick up (something) with the beak • *Erin just* **pecked at** *her food* (= ate only small amounts of it). • A **pecking order** is the order of importance of people in a group: *But the teachers were so low in the social and economic pecking order that their voices were rarely heeded.*

peck /pek/ *n* [C] • A peck is also a quick kiss: *Aunt Velma gave me a peck on the cheek.*

peculiar STRANGE /pɪˈkjuːl·jər/ *adj* [not gradable] unusual and strange • *The copy editor will check type size and technical details to see if anything looks peculiar.*

peculiarity /pɪˌkjuː·liːˈær·əṭ·i/ *n* [C/U] • *The owners love the house in spite of its peculiarities* (= strange characteristics). [C]

peculiar BELONGING TO /pɪˈkjuːl·jər/ *adj* [not gradable] characteristic especially of a particular person, group, or thing • *Katherine Hepburn's way of talking was peculiar to her.*

peculiarly /pɪˈkjuːl·jər·li/ *adv* [not gradable] • *He identifies this social practice as peculiarly Irish.*

peculiarly /pɪˈkjuːl·jər·li/ *adv* [not gradable] very or specially • *She's a peculiarly attractive woman.*

pedagogical /ˌped·əˈgɑdʒ·ɪ·kəl, -ˈgoʊdʒ-/ *adj specialized* relating to the practice of teaching and its methods • *The book describes current pedagogical methods used in teaching reading.*

pedal /ˈped·əl/ *n* [C] a small part of a machine or vehicle that you can press down with your foot to operate the machine or make the vehicle move • *bicycle pedals* ○ *You have to press* down hard on the gas pedal to get this car up hills. • PIC BICYCLE

pedal /'ped·ᵊl/ v [I/T] • He struggled to pedal (his bike) up the hill. [I/T]

pedantic /pɪ'dænt·ɪk/ adj caring too much about unimportant rules or details and not enough about understanding or appreciating a subject • Professor Harris had a narrow, pedantic approach to history that put us to sleep.

peddle /'ped·ᵊl/ v [T] to sell (things), esp. by taking them to different places • Mrs. Cawthorn peddled vegetables out of the back of a pickup truck to earn a living.

peddler /'ped·lər/ n [C] a person who sell things on the street or by going to people's houses • He's a suspected drug peddler.

pedestal /'ped·ə·stəl/ n [C] a base for a statue, or a base for a column • Museum staff plan to replace the cracked pedestal under the statue. • If someone is **on a pedestal**, they are treated with too much respect and admiration: We put athletes and movie stars on a pedestal.

pedestrian WALKER /pə'des·tri:·ən/ n [C] a person who is walking, esp. in an area where vehicles go • Bicyclists and pedestrians use the path. • PIC INTERSECTION

pedestrian NOT INTERESTING /pə'des·tri:·ən/ adj showing little imagination; not interesting • The lyrics are pretty pedestrian.

pediatrics /ˌpiːd·i:'æ·trɪks/ n [U] the area of medicine that deals with children

pediatrician /ˌpiːd·i·ə'trɪʃ·ən/ n [C] a doctor with special training in medical care for children

pedicure /'ped·ɪˌkjʊr/ n [C] a treatment for the feet that involves cutting and sometimes painting the nails, and softening or MASSAGING (= rubbing) the skin

pedigree /'ped·əˌgriː/ n [C] the parents, grandparents, etc., of a particular animal, or a record of them • a dog's pedigree • The pedigree of a person, idea, or activity is its history: Populism and conservatism have strong Southern pedigrees.

pee /piː/ v [I] infml to urinate • Do you have to pee again?

pee /piː/ n [U] infml • Rick is taking a pee.

peek /piːk/ v [I] to look, esp. for a short time or while trying to avoid being seen • Close your eyes and don't peek. • If something peeks out or up, it can be partly seen: The dog's head peeked out from behind the tree.

peek /piːk/ n [C] • She took a peek down the hall.

peek-a-boo /'piː·kəˌbuː/ n [U], exclamation a game played with very young children in which you hide your face, esp. with your hands, and then suddenly take your hands away, saying "peek-a-boo"

peel REMOVE VEGETABLE SKIN /piːl/ v [T] to remove the skin of (fruit and vegetables) • Peel, core, and chop the apples.

peel /piːl/ n [C/U] • banana peels [C] ○ strips of lemon peel [U]

peeler /'piː·lər/ n [C] a utensil for removing the skin of fruit and vegetables • a vegetable peeler

peel REMOVE COVERING /piːl/ v [I/T] to remove (a covering) slowly and carefully, or (of a covering) to come off • We peeled the wallpaper off the walls. [T always + adv/prep] ○ My back is peeling from that sunburn I got last weekend. [I] • If you peel off clothing, you take it off: Ramon peeled his sweaty shirt off and hung it on a chair to dry. [M]

peel

peep LOOK /piːp/ v [I] to look quickly and often secretly • He peeped over his shoulder to see if anyone was watching. • If something peeps up or out, it has just begun to appear: Daisies were peeping through the turf. • (disapproving) A **peeping Tom** is a man who tries to secretly watch women when they are dressing or naked.

peep /piːp/ n [C usually sing] • Take a peep at this (= Look quickly at it). • A **peephole** is a small hole in a door or a wall through which you can see who or what is on the other side.

peep SOUND /piːp/ n [C] a sound, or a spoken word • She's too scared to make a peep.

peer LOOK /pɪr/ v [I always + adv/prep] to look carefully or with difficulty • The judge peered over his glasses at the jury.

peer EQUAL /pɪr/ n [C] a person of the same age, the same social position, or having the same abilities as other people in a group • Getting help from a peer is easier than asking a teacher. • **Peer pressure** is the strong influence of a group on members of that group to behave in the same way, even if the behavior is not good: There is tremendous peer pressure among teenagers to go out on dates.

peerless /'pɪr·ləs/ adj [not gradable] slightly fml better than all others • peerless beauty/ability

peg HANGING DEVICE /peg/ n [C] a small, shaped piece of wood or other material on which objects can be hung • She hung her apron on the peg.

peg ATTACHING TOOL /peg/ n [C] a device used to attach something or hold it in place

pegs

peg FIX AMOUNT /peg/ v [T] **-gg-** to fix the amount or value of (something) in relation to something else • *There's talk of trying to peg the value of the peso to the dollar.*

peg DISCOVER /peg/ v [T] **-gg-** *infml* to recognize or discover what (something) is; IDENTIFY • *They had you pegged as a sucker the minute you walked in.*

peg down /'-'-/ v adv [M] to fix (something) in place • *The tent's ropes were pegged down by two-foot stakes.*

pejorative /pɪˈdʒɔːr·ət·ɪv, -ˈdʒɑr-/ *adj slightly fml* (of words) insulting, disapproving, or suggesting that something is not good or is of no importance • *Is "Yankee" a pejorative term?*

pelican /ˈpel·ɪ·kən/ n [C] a large, fish-eating bird with a baglike throat

pellet /ˈpel·ət/ n [C] a small, hard, ball-shaped or tube-shaped piece of any substance • *shotgun pellets* ○ *plastic pellets*

pelt THROW /pelt/ v [I/T] to throw a number of things quickly at (someone or something) • *Youths tried to pelt them with stones.* [T]

pelt SKIN /pelt/ n [C] the skin and fur of a dead animal, or the skin with the fur removed • *rabbit pelts*

pelvis /ˈpel·vəs/ n [C] the bones that form a bowl-shaped structure in the area below the waist at the top of the legs, to which the leg bones and SPINE (= row of bones in the back) are joined

pelvic /ˈpel·vɪk/ *adj* [not gradable] • *a pelvic examination*

pen WRITING DEVICE /pen/ n [C/U] a thin device with a point used for writing or drawing with ink • *a fountain/ballpoint/felt-tip pen* [C] ○ *You must fill out the application in pen* (= using a pen). [U] • **Penmanship** is the ability to write neatly, or the activity of learning to do this. • A **pen name** is an invented name used by a writer when publishing works: *John Steinbeck published under the pen name Amnesia Glasscock.* • A **pen pal** is someone with whom you exchange letters as a hobby, esp. someone in another country.

pen /pen/ v [T] **-nn-** • *She penned* (= wrote) *a thank-you note.*

pen ENCLOSED SPACE /pen/ n [C] a small area surrounded by a fence in which animals are kept, or (*slang*) a prison or JAIL

pen /pen/ v [T] **-nn-** • *Sheep are penned behind the barn.* ○ *A fence would pen us in like animals.*

penal /ˈpiːn·əl/ *adj* [not gradable] of or connected with punishment given by law • *the penal system* • A **penal code** is the system of legal punishment in a particular place: *the Penal Code of Pennsylvania* ○ *the Swedish Penal Code*

penalize /ˈpiːn·əlˌɑɪz, ˈpen-/ v [T] to punish (someone), esp. for breaking the law or a rule • *The new law penalizes fathers who fail to make child support payments.* ○ *Boone was pe-*nalized for swearing and thrown out of the game.*

penalty /ˈpen·əl·ti/ n [C] a punishment, esp. the usual one, for breaking a law • *Repeat offenders should face stiff/tough penalties.* • A penalty is also a type of punishment for breaking an agreement or not following rules: *If you pay off the loan early, they'll charge an extra month's interest as a prepayment penalty.* ○ *When a football team gives up 143 yards in penalties, they deserve to lose.*

penance /ˈpen·əns/ n [C/U] activity that shows you regret some previous action, sometimes for religious reasons • *They are doing penance for their sins.* [U]

penchant /ˈpen·tʃənt/ n [C usually sing] a liking for or a habit of doing something, esp. something that other people might not like • *Ives had a penchant for musical experimentation.*

pencil /ˈpen·səl/ n [C/U] a thin, usually wooden, tube-shaped device for writing or drawing which has colored material in the center and a point at one end • *colored pencils* [C] ○ *a number 2 pencil* (= one with a center of a particular hardness) [C] ○ *Make your corrections in pencil* (= using a pencil). [U] • A **pencil sharpener** is an electric, mechanical, or small hand-held device for sharpening pencils.

pencil /ˈpen·səl/ v [T] **-l-** or *also* **-ll-** • *She penciled* (= wrote) *the name "Sloan" inside a circle.* [T] ○ *Bill spent a couple of hours penciling in corrections.* [M] • If you **pencil** something **in**, you expect it but understand that it might need to be changed later: *The team had penciled in Morton as a key player this season.*

pendant /ˈpen·dənt/ n [C] a piece of jewelry worn around the neck consisting of a long chain with an object hanging from it, or the object itself

pending /ˈpen·dɪŋ/ *adj* [not gradable] about to happen or waiting to happen • *His divorce was still pending.*

pending /ˈpen·dɪŋ/ *prep* until after • *Flights were suspended pending an investigation of the crash.*

pendulum /ˈpen·dʒə·ləm/ n [C] a device consisting of a weight hanging on a rod or cord that moves from one side to the other, esp. one that forms a part of a clock • A pendulum is also power or control of an activity that changes from one group to another: *In labor-management relations, the pendulum has swung wildly in the direction of the players.*

penetrate MOVE /ˈpen·əˌtreɪt/ v [I/T] to move into or through (something) • *The drill isn't sharp enough to penetrate into the rock.* [I] ○ *Women have begun to penetrate a lot of fields that were dominated by men for centuries.* [T]

penetration /ˌpen·əˈtreɪ·ʃən/ n [U] • *The program's penetration in Utah schools varies from district to district.*

penetrate UNDERSTAND /'pen·ə‚treɪt/ v [I/T] to understand (something), or to be understood as a result of study or INVESTIGATION • *Her writing penetrated to the heart of contemporary life.* [I]

penetrating /'pen·ə‚treɪt̬·ɪŋ/ adj showing a very good understanding; knowledgeable • *a penetrating critique* ○ *penetrating observations* • Someone with **penetrating eyes** or a **penetrating gaze** seems able to understand or know you just by looking at you.

penetrating /'pen·ə‚treɪt̬·ɪŋ/ adj very loud • *I heard a penetrating scream.*

penguin /'pen·gwən, 'peŋ-/ n [C] a black-and-white sea bird found in cold, southern parts of the world which cannot fly and swims using its small wings

penguin

penicillin /‚pen·ə'sɪl·ən/ n [U] a type of ANTIBIOTIC (= medicine that kills bacteria)

peninsula /pə'nɪn·sə·lə/ n [C] an area of land mostly surrounded by water but connected to a larger piece of land • *the Monterey Peninsula*

penis /'piː·nəs/ n [C] a tube-shaped organ of male mammals that is used for urinating and for sex and that is on the outside of the body between the legs

penitence /'pen·ə·təns/ n [U] regret for a mistake and willingness to correct it • *He expressed his penitence for what he had done.*

penitentiary /‚pen·ə'ten·tʃə·ri/ n [C] a prison • *a federal/state penitentiary*

penknife /'pen·naɪf/ n [C] a small knife with a blade that folds into its handle

pennant /'pen·ənt/ n [C] a flag shaped like a triangle

penny /'pen·i/ n [C] in the US and Canada, a coin worth 1/100th of a dollar; a cent • *I keep pennies in a jar.* • A penny can also mean the smallest amount of money possible or the total cost of something: *Our insurance didn't cover a penny of our medical bills.* ○ *It was an expensive meal but worth every penny.* • You can say **a penny for your thoughts** when you want to know what another person is thinking, usually because they have been quiet for a while.

penniless /'pen·i·ləs/ adj, adv without any money at all • *a penniless youth*

pension /'pen·tʃən/ n [C] a sum of money paid regularly to a person who has RETIRED (= stopped working because of having reached a certain age) • A **pension fund** is a supply of money that many people pay into, which is invested in order to provide them with a pension. • A **pension plan** is an employer's system for investment that allows you to receive a pension.

pensive /'pen·sɪv/ adj quiet and thinking seriously • *James was more pensive than usual.*
pensively /'pen·sɪv·li/ adv • *He gazed pensively out the window.*

pentagon SHAPE /'pent·ə‚gɑn/ n [C] a flat, five-sided shape with five angles

Pentagon BUILDING /'pent·ə‚gɑn/ n [U] the building where the US Defense Department is based, or the US Defense Department itself

Pentecostal /‚pent·ə'kɑs·təl, -'kɔːs-/ n [C], adj [not gradable] (a member) of a Christian group that believes everything written in the Bible is true • *a Pentecostal preacher*

penthouse /'pent·haʊs/ n [C] pl **penthouses** /'pent‚haʊ·zəz, -‚səz/ a luxurious apartment or set of rooms at the top of a hotel or tall building

pent–up /'pent'ʌp/ adj (of feelings) not expressed or released • *His pent-up anger and frustration burst forth.*

peony /'piː·ə·ni/ n [C] a plant with large red, pink, or white flowers

people PERSONS /'piː·pəl/ pl of PERSON; men, women, and children generally; human beings • *There were a lot of people there.* ○ *Some people were hurt.* • People can refer to a particular group mentioned: *young/old people* ○ *poor/rich people* ○ *Those people look as if they're lost.* • When you say the people, you mean the large number of ordinary men and women who do not have positions of power: *The president wanted to take his message directly to the people.* • USAGE: See note at PERSON.

people /'piː·pəl/ v [T] • If a place is peopled by a particular type of people, they have moved there or live there: *Honolulu is peopled by native Hawaiians, Japanese, Chinese, Filipinos, white Americans, and others.*

people NATION /'piː·pəl/ n [C] a culture or nation • *It is a custom shared by many native American peoples.*

pep /pep/ n [U] *infml* energy or enthusiasm • *That morning she felt full of pep and decided to go for a long walk.* • A **pep rally** is a gathering of people who want to show their support and enthusiasm for a sports team or a person involved in a competitive situation, such as a politician. • A **pep talk** is a short speech intended to encourage people to work harder or to try to win a game or competition: *The coach just gave them a good old-fashioned pep talk at halftime.*

pep up obj, **pep** obj **up** /'-'-/ v adv [M] to make (something) more exciting or interesting • *The boss said I had to pep up the ad and make it more lively.*

pepper SPICE /'pep·ər/ n [U] a black or cream-colored spice, often used in powdered form, that gives a spicy hot taste to food

pepper VEGETABLE /'pep·ər/ n [C] a vegetable that is green, red, or yellow, having a rounded shape, that is hollow with seeds in the middle

pepper ATTACK /'pep·ər/ v [T] to direct something suddenly and repeatedly at (someone), as if attacking them • *The mayor was peppered with questions from reporters about the municipal corruption scandal.* • To pepper is also to add to (something) in many places: *He peppered his speech with jokes.*

peppermint /'pep·ər,mɪnt/ n [C/U] a strong, fresh flavoring from a type of MINT plant • A peppermint is a candy that has the flavor of peppermint. [C]

pepperoni /,pep·ə'rou·ni/ n [U] a type of Italian SAUSAGE • *Do you want pepperoni on your pizza?*

per /pɜr, pər/ prep for each • *The speed limit is 55 miles per hour.* ○ *This dish is 225 calories per serving.*

perceive THINK OF /pər'siːv/ v [T] to think of (something) in a particular way • *The way people perceive the real world is strongly influenced by the language they speak.* ○ *In those days, crime wasn't even perceived as a problem.*

perceive NOTICE /pər'siːv/ v [T] to notice (something or someone) by using sight, sound, touch, taste, or smell • *I perceived something moving in the shadows.*

percent, **per cent** /pər'sent/ adv [not gradable] (of rates) for or out of every 100 • *You got 20 percent of the answers right—that's one out of five.* • The symbol used for percent is %: *Only 48% of registered voters actually voted in the election.*

percentage /pər'sent·ɪdʒ/ n [C] an amount showing how much something is when compared to a total amount represented by 100 • *TV ratings are based on the percentage of sets tuned to a particular program.*

percentage /pər'sent·ɪdʒ/ n [U] an improvement or advantage, esp. when considered against other possibilities • *There's no percentage in working long hours if you don't plan to stay in that job.*

perceptible /pər'sep·tə·bəl/ adj that can be seen, heard, felt, tasted, smelled, or noticed • *His pulse was barely perceptible* (= difficult to feel) *upon arrival at the hospital.*

perception BELIEF /pər'sep·ʃən/ n [C] a thought, belief, or opinion, often held by many people and based on appearances • *Even though he had done nothing illegal, the public's perception was that he had acted dishonestly, and he was forced to resign.*

perception AWARENESS /pər'sep·ʃən/ n [U] an awareness of things through the physical SENSES, esp. sight

perceptive /pər'sep·tɪv/ adj • If someone is perceptive, they notice and understand things that many people do not notice: *Her books are full of perceptive insights.*

perch /pɜrtʃ/ v [I/T] (of a bird) to rest on a branch or other object, or (of a person or thing) to sit or be on (the edge or top of something) • *A baseball cap, turned backwards, was perched on his head.* [T]

perch /pɜrtʃ/ n [C] • *From their perches in the towers, the prison guards could see the entire prison yard.*

percolate /'pɜr·kə,leɪt/ v [I] (of a liquid) to move through a substance by going through very small spaces within it • *Underground water had percolated through the soil to form puddles.*

percolator /'pɜr·kə,leɪt·ər/ n [C] a device for making coffee that boils water and forces it up a tube and through crushed coffee beans held in a container

percussion /pər'kʌʃ·ən/ n [U] musical instruments, such as drums, that are played by being hit with an object or with the hand

peremptory /pə'remp·tə·ri/ adj fml having the expectation of immediate and complete obedience, or to be obeyed without explanation • *In his usual peremptory manner, he ordered us all into the conference room.*

perennial TIME /pə'ren·i·əl/ adj lasting a long time, or happening repeatedly or all the time • *Each year, the nation's marketers try to answer the perennial question, What do consumers really want?*

perennial PLANT /pə'ren·i·əl/ n [C] a plant that lives for more than two years • Compare ANNUAL PLANT; BIENNIAL.

perfect RIGHT /'pɜr·fɪkt/ adj complete and right in every way; having nothing wrong • *The car is two years old but it's in perfect condition.* • You can also use perfect to mean complete and emphasize the noun that comes after it: *I felt like a perfect fool when I forgot her name.*

perfect /pər'fekt/ v [T] to make (something) perfect • *She practices tennis whenever she can, hoping to perfect her serve.*

perfectly /'pɜr·fɪk·tli/ adv extremely well; in a perfect way • *He managed everything perfectly.* • Perfectly can also mean very or completely: *I want to make it perfectly clear that I have no intention of selling this company.* • LP VERY, COMPLETELY, AND OTHER INTENSIFIERS

perfection /pər'fek·ʃən/ n [U] • *She is a superb violinist, and combines technical perfection with an exciting performance style.* • If something is done to perfection, it is done very well and happens exactly as planned: *In the last few minutes of the football game, they tried a trick play, and it worked to perfection.*

perfectionist /pər'fek·ʃə·nəst/ n [C] a person who wants very much to get every detail exactly right • *As a film director, Alfred Hitchcock had the reputation of a perfectionist.*

perfect BEST /'pɜr·fɪkt/ adj exactly right for a particular purpose or situation; being the best possible • *It was a warm, sunny day, a perfect afternoon for a ballgame.*

perfect GRAMMAR /'pɜr·fɪkt/ adj [not gradable] specialized (in grammar) having the tense of a verb that shows action that has happened in the past or before another time or event and has continued up to the present or up to a particular point • See **present perfect** at PRESENT GRAMMAR; **past perfect** at PAST GRAMMAR; **future perfect** at FUTURE GRAMMAR. LP TENSES

perforated /ˈpɜr·fəˌreɪţ·əd/ *adj* [not gradable] (of a surface) having a hole or holes in it • *He was taken to the hospital to have emergency surgery for a perforated stomach ulcer.* **perforation** /ˌpɜr·fəˈreɪ·ʃən/ *n* [C] • *The perforations* (= very small holes) *make it easy to remove checks from your checkbook.*

perform DO /pərˈfɔːrm/ *v* [I/T] to do (an action or piece of work) • *The operation was performed with the patient under general anesthesia.* [T] • If something performs well or badly, it operates satisfactorily or does not operate satisfactorily: *The car performed poorly during the tests.* [I]

performance /pərˈfɔːr·məns/ *n* [U] the act of doing something, such as your job • *If the accident happened during the performance of his regular duties, he's covered by disability insurance.* • Performance also refers to how well an activity or job is done: *With a record of 2 wins and 3 defeats, the team's performance has been disappointing.*

perform ENTERTAIN /pərˈfɔːrm/ *v* [I/T] to entertain people esp. by doing something they have specially come to see • *The magician performed a number of tricks that had us gasping in surprise.* [T]

performance /pərˈfɔːr·məns/ *n* [C] • *Her performance in the play won rave reviews.*

performer /pərˈfɔːr·mər/ *n* [C] • *By the age of 12, she was a seasoned circus performer.*

performing /pərˈfɔːr·mɪŋ/ *adj* [not gradable] • The **performing arts** are acting, singing, dancing, and other forms of public entertainment.

perfume /ˈpɜr·fjuːm, pərˈfjuːm/ *n* [C/U] a liquid produced and sold for its strong, pleasant smell, often used on the skin • *She put a few drops of perfume on the back of her neck.* [U]

perfunctory /pərˈfʌŋ·tə·ri/ *adj* done quickly and without showing that you care or have much interest • *She asked a few perfunctory questions about my family and then ended the conversation.*

perhaps /pərˈhæps, pəˈræps/ *adv* [not gradable] used to show that something is possible or that you are not certain about something; MAYBE • *Perhaps the greatest swimming coach in history, Kiphuth retired after 41 years at Yale.* ○ *Soon, perhaps as early as this week, she is to testify in the trial.*

peril /ˈper·əl/ *n* [C/U] *fml* danger, or something that is dangerous • *The president said that we are entering a time of great peril.* [U] **perilous** /ˈper·ə·ləs/ *adj fml* dangerous

perimeter /pəˈrɪm·əţ·ər/ *n* [C] the outer edge of an area or the border around it • *Several bombs landed near the perimeter of the airport.*

period TIME /ˈpɪr·iː·əd/ *n* [C] a length of time • *The study will be carried out over a six-month period.* • A period in the life of a person or in history is a particular time during that life or history: *The period after World War II was marked by rapid economic growth.* • A period is a division of time in an event of fixed length, such as a day at school or a game: *There was no scoring in the second period.* • Period costume/dress/furniture is the clothing or furniture of a particular time in history: *At the Revolutionary War theme park, everyone was wearing period costumes.*

periodic /ˌpɪr·iːˈɑd·ɪk/, **periodical** /ˌpɪr·iːˈɑd·ɪ·kəl/ *adj* [not gradable] happening repeatedly although not necessarily frequently • *He suffers periodic mental breakdowns.* **periodically** /ˌpɪr·iːˈɑd·ɪ·kli/ *adv* [not gradable] • *The equipment should be tested periodically* (= repeatedly at regular times).

period BLEEDING /ˈpɪr·iː·əd/, **menstrual period** /ˈmen·strəl ˌpɪr·iː·əd, -strə·wəl-/ *n* [C] the bleeding from a woman's uterus that happens approximately every four weeks when she is not pregnant

period MARK /ˈpɪr·iː·əd/ *n* [C] a mark (.) used in writing to show where the end of a sentence

---

PERIOD [.]

A **period** (sometimes called a *point* or a *dot*) is used to end sentences and phrases that are not questions.

I'll meet you at the theater entrance. • *Of course.* • *If necessary.*

Notice that a comma (,) can mark the end of a sentence when it is in quotation marks and forms part of another sentence.

"I think this bag is yours," she said.

A period is also used after abbreviations and initials.

no. (= number) • *Feb. 17* • *U.S.A.* • *an H.M.O.* • *e.g.* • *Dr. Wong* • *Mrs. Albino* • *H.G. Wells*

Periods are used after numbers and letters in lists and outlines.

name your choices:
1. _____
2. _____
3. _____

Periods are used as the decimal point in numbers and money amounts.

6.75 miles (said as "six point seven five") • *$8.50* ("eight dollars and fifty cents" or "eight fifty")

Periods form part of e-mail and Web site addresses.

Contact us at dictionaries@cup.org ("dictionaries at c u p dot org")

A period is not used in American English to separate long numbers. Use a comma instead.

The city has a population of 4,500,000.

is, or to show that the letters before it are an abbreviation • (*infml*) You can say period at the end of a statement as way of adding emphasis: *There will be no more shouting, period!*

periodical /ˌpɪr·iˈɑd·ɪ·kəl/ *n* [C] a magazine that is published regularly • *The library subscribes to a number of periodicals dealing with the arts and sciences.*

periphery /pəˈrɪf·ə·ri/ *n* [C usually sing] the outer edge of an area • *We've planted 50 small trees around the periphery of the property.*

peripheral /pəˈrɪf·ə·rəl/ *adj* not central or of main importance • *First of all, we had to find out who the thief was—getting the money back was a peripheral issue.* • **Peripheral vision** is what you can see to the sides of what you are looking at.

peripheral /pəˈrɪf·ə·rəl/ *n* [C] a piece of equipment, such as a printer, that can be connected to a computer

periscope /ˈper·əˌskoʊp/ *n* [C] a vertical tube containing mirrors that can give you a view of what is above you when you look through the bottom of the tube • *The periscope of the submarine was visible just above the surface of the water.*

perish /ˈper·ɪʃ/ *v* [I] to die, esp. as a result of an accident, violence, or war • *Without this assistance, thousands of refugees would perish from hunger and neglect.*

perishable /ˈper·ɪ·ʃə·bəl/ *adj* • Food that is perishable has to be used quickly or it will decay so that you cannot eat it: *He owns one of the largest distributors of perishable foods.*

perjury /ˈpɜr·dʒə·ri/ *n* [U] *law* the crime of telling a lie in court after promising formally to tell the truth

perjure /ˈpɜr·dʒər/ *v* [T] *law* • *Perjuring yourself* (= Telling a lie in court) *is a criminal offense.*

perk ADVANTAGE /pɜrk/ *n* [C] *infml* a special advantage or benefit, in addition to the money you are paid, that you are given because of your job • *Free child care for preschool children of employees was a popular perk.*

perk MAKE COFFEE /pɜrk/ *v* [I/T] (of boiling water or coffee) to move up a tube in a PERCOLATOR (= a type of coffee maker) when the coffee is being made • *The coffee had begun to perk.* [I]

□ **perk up** (*obj*), **perk** (*obj*) **up** /ˈ-ˈ-/ *v adv* [I/M] (of a thing) to make or become more interesting or exciting, or (of a person) to make or become more active or energetic, or happier • *The city is trying to perk up the business district by planting trees.* [M] ○ *She perked up considerably when her sister arrived.* [I]

perky /ˈpɜr·ki/ *adj* showing a lot of energy in a happy, confident way • *Kimberly burst in with a crowd of perky teenagers.*

perm /pɜrm/, **permanent (wave)** /ˈpɜr·mə·nənt (ˈweɪv)/ *n* [C] a chemical process that makes a person's hair wavy or curly

perm /pɜrm/ *v* [T] • *Tiffany got her hair permed.*

permanent /ˈpɜr·mə·nənt/ *adj* [not gradable] lasting for a long time or forever • *Are you looking for a temporary job or something permanent?* ○ *He entered the United States in 1988 as a permanent resident with a green card.*

permanently /ˈpɜr·mə·nənt·li/ *adv* [not gradable] • *The accident left him permanently paralyzed.*

permanence /ˈpɜr·mə·nəns/ *n* [U]

permeate /ˈpɜr·miˌeɪt/ *v* [T] to spread through (something) and be present in every part of it • *The smell of detergent and bleach permeated the air.*

permission /pərˈmɪʃ·ən/ *n* [U] the act of allowing someone to do something, or of allowing something to happen • *Parents have to give their permission for their children to go on school trips.* ○ *We had to get permission* (= approval) *from the city to build an extension to our house.* [+ *to* infinitive]

permissible /pərˈmɪs·ə·bəl/ *adj* • *It is no longer permissible for athletic programs in universities to give a lot more money for men's sports than for women's sports.*

permissive /pərˈmɪs·ɪv/ *adj esp. disapproving* allowing a wide range of choices, esp. in an area where there have traditionally been rules that had to be obeyed • *In the 1960s, many Americans became more permissive about sexual behavior.*

permissiveness /pərˈmɪs·ɪv·nəs/ *n* [U]

permit /pərˈmɪt/ *v* [T] **-tt-** to allow (something), or make (something) possible • *Smoking is not permitted in any part of this building.*

permit /ˈpɜr·mɪt, pərˈmɪt/ *n* [C] an official document that allows you to do something • *Do you have a permit to park here?*

permitting /pərˈmɪt̬·ɪŋ/ *adj* [only after n] used to show that an activity depends on an uncertain condition • *Weather permitting* (= if the weather is good enough), *the picnic will be next Saturday.*

pernicious /pərˈnɪʃ·əs/ *adj* having a very harmful effect or influence • *The book focuses on the pernicious effects of slavery.*

peroxide /pəˈrɑkˌsaɪd/ *n* [U] **hydrogen peroxide**, see at HYDROGEN

perpendicular /ˌpɜr·pənˈdɪk·jə·lər/ *adj* [not gradable] standing straight up, or being at an angle of 90° to another line or surface • *The cliff was nearly perpendicular and impossible to climb.* ○ *Two perpendicular lines form a right angle.*

perpetrate /ˈpɜr·pəˌtreɪt/ *v* [T] to commit (a crime or other harmful act) • *Deadly terrorist attacks have been perpetrated by extremists.*

perpetrator /ˈpɜr·pəˌtreɪt̬·ər/ *n* [C] • *He promised vigorous action against the perpetrators of this crime.*

perpetual /pərˈpetʃ·ə·wəl/ *adj* [not gradable]

continuing forever, or happening all the time
• *They lived in perpetual fear of being discovered.* ○ *She resented his perpetual complaining about her cooking.*

perpetually /pər'petʃ·ə·wə·li/ *adv* [not gradable] • *She is perpetually late.*

perpetuate /pər'petʃ·ə,weɪt/ *v* [T] to cause (esp. something bad) to continue • *The movie perpetuates stereotypes of African American life.*

perpetuity /,pɜr·pə'tuː·əṱ·i/ *n fml* • Something that is done **in perpetuity** goes on forever: *Wildlife areas have to be maintained in perpetuity.*

perplex /pər'pleks/ *v* [T] to cause (someone) to be confused or uncertain over something that is not understood • *The symptoms of the disease have continued to perplex her doctors.*

perplexed /pər'plekst/ *adj* • *Just when it appeared that interest rates were headed up, they fell, leaving some analysts clearly perplexed.*

per se /pɜr'seɪ/ *adv* [not gradable] by or of itself • *It's not the violence per se that I object to, it's the way it was shown.*

persecute /'pɜr·sɪ,kjuːt/ *v* [T] to treat (someone) unfairly or cruelly over a period of time because of their race, religion, etc. • *The rebels' supporters fear they'll be persecuted by the army.*

persecution /,pɜr·sɪ'kjuː·ʃən/ *n* [U] • *political/religious persecution*

persecutor /'pɜr·sɪ,kjuː·ṱ·ər/ *n* [C] • *Given the chance, victims may seek revenge on their persecutors.*

persevere /,pɜr·sə'vɪr/ *v* [I] to try to do or continue doing something in a determined way, despite difficulties • *If I had persevered, I probably would have gotten the job.*

perseverance /,pɜr·sə'vɪr·əns/ *n* [U] • *Perseverance accounts for much of their success.*

persist /pər'sɪst, -'zɪst/ *v* [I] to continue to exist past the usual time, or to continue to do something in a determined way even when facing difficulties or opposition • *If the pain persists, consult a doctor.* ○ *Although the meeting had ended, she persisted in trying to question the mayor.*

persistence /pər'sɪs·təns, -'zɪs-/ *n* [U] • *Her book details the persistence of racism.* ○ *His persistence paid off—he won the contract.*

persistent /pər'sɪs·tənt, -'zɪs-/ *adj* • *a persistent cough* ○ *persistent rumors*

persistently /pər'sɪs·tənt·li, -'zɪs-/ *adv* • *The rains persistently fell.*

person /'pɜr·sən/ *n* [C] *pl* **people** /'piː·pəl/ or **persons** a man, woman, or child • *Neil Armstrong was the first person to set foot on the moon.* ○ *The auditorium can seat about 500 people.* ○ *The plane crashed just after takeoff, killing all 29 persons aboard.* • Person is also used when describing someone's character or personality: *I don't think of him as a book person* (= someone who likes books). ○ *She's nice*

enough *as a person, but she's not right for the job.* • To do something **in person** means to be physically present: *You must apply for the license in person.* • USAGE: In formal writing, the plural "persons" is sometimes preferred over "people," but "persons" is also used in news reports—*At least 30 persons are dead or missing*—and in the phrase "person or persons" when the number of people is not known—*We expect to catch the person or persons responsible.*

persona /pər'soʊ·nə/ *n* [C] *pl* **personae** /pər'soʊ·niː, -,nɑɪ/ or **personas** the particular type of character that a person seems to have, which is often different from their real or private character • *the senator's public persona*

personable /'pɜr·sə·nə·bəl/ *adj* having a pleasing and attractive manner • *She is an intelligent and personable young woman.*

personal /'pɜr·sən·əl/ *adj* relating or belonging to a single or particular person • *I think you have a personal responsibility to know when to stop.* ○ *That's my personal opinion.* ○ *He was given one hour to pack his personal belongings and leave.* • Personal is also used to refer to your body: *Students are taught about personal hygiene.* • A personal action is one that is done by someone directly rather than by someone else: *The governor made a personal appearance at the hospital.* • Personal also means private or relating to someone's private life: *Simon's songs are intensely personal.* ○ *He's got problems in his personal life.* • Personal also refers to an intentionally offensive or critical remark about someone's character or appearance: *There's no need to get personal.* • A **personal (ad)** is a short advertisement about yourself that you put in a newspaper or magazine in order to meet a romantic partner. • A **personal computer** (*abbreviation* PC) is a small computer used in homes and offices. • (*specialized*) In grammar, a **personal pronoun** is a word, such as "I," "you," or "they," that refers to a person in speech or in writing.

personalize /'pɜr·sən·əl,ɑɪz/ *v* [T] to make (something) specially suitable for a particular person • *We try to personalize these stories for the people who are listening.* • If you personalize an issue, you talk about how it relates to particular people: *In his description, he personalizes the plight of the homeless.* • Objects that are personalized have your name or something else you choose on them: *personalized checks* ○ *personalized license plates* • If you personalize an argument or discussion, you start to criticize the other person's faults instead of discussing the facts: *We shouldn't personalize these negotiations.*

personally /'pɜr·sən·əl·i/ *adv* • Personally can refer to yourself or your own opinion: *Personally, I think their marriage won't last.* ○ *I haven't been there personally, but I've read a lot* *about it.* • If you do something personally, you do it yourself rather than asking someone else to do it: *He plans to personally direct the fund-raising drive.* ○ *He believes that parents should be made personally responsible for their children's behavior.* • Personally also refers to an intentionally offensive remark about someone's character or appearance or which is understood as being critical: *Please don't take this personally, but I think you've had enough to drink.*

personality /ˌpɜr·səˈnæl·əṭ·i/ *n* [C/U] the special combination of qualities in a person that makes them different from others, as shown by the way they behave, feel, and think • *She has a cheerful, attractive personality.* [C] ○ *Personality is formed at a very early age.* [U] • A personality is also a famous person, esp. in popular entertainment or sports: *a TV personality* [C]

personify /pərˈsɑn·əˌfɑɪ/ *v* [T] to be a person who is a perfect example of (a thing or quality) • *The senator personifies Washington, DC, to many people.* • If a particular quality or idea is personified, it is represented in the form of a person: *In Greek myth, love is personified by the goddess Aphrodite.*

personification /pərˌsɑn·ə·fɪˈkeɪ·ʃən/ *n* [U] • *Satan is the personification of evil.*

personnel /ˌpɜr·səˈnel/ *pl n* the people working in an organization or for a particular type of employer • *Saturday was the most convenient day for students, parents, and school personnel.* ○ *military personnel*

personnel /ˌpɜr·səˈnel/, **human resources** *n* [U] the department within a company or organization that is responsible for its relationship with its employees, esp. new employees, and for following the laws dealing with employment

perspective [VIEW] /pərˈspek·tɪv/ *n* [C/U] a particular way of viewing things that depends on one's experience and personality • *He brings a new perspective to the job.* [C] ○ *From a scientific perspective, evolution has no goal.* [C] • Perspective also means the ability to consider things in relation to one another accurately and fairly: *With more maturity and experience, you will gradually acquire perspective.* [U] • If something is **in perspective**, it is considered as part of a complete situation so that you have an accurate and fair understanding of it: *Putting the past in perspective is an enormous task.*

perspective [ART] /pərˈspek·tɪv/ *n* [U] (in art) the method by which solid objects painted on a flat surface are given the appearance of depth and distance

perspire /pərˈspaɪr/ *v* [I] *slightly fml* to excrete a salty, colorless liquid through the skin which cools the body; SWEAT

perspiration /ˌpɜr·spəˈreɪ·ʃən/ *n* [U] *slightly*

fml • *Beads of perspiration glistened on his forehead.*

persuade /pərˈsweɪd/ *v* [T] to cause (someone) to do or believe something, esp. by explaining why they should • *The government is trying to persuade consumers to save more.* ○ *She tried to persuade them that they should leave.*

persuasion /pərˈsweɪ·ʒən/ *n* [U] • *Most of the time he gets what he wants with gentle persuasion.*

persuasive /pərˈsweɪ·sɪv, -zɪv/ *adj* • *a persuasive argument*

persuasion /pərˈsweɪ·ʒən/ *n* [C] a particular set of beliefs, esp. religious or political ones • *People of all religious persuasions are welcome.*

pert /pɜrt/ *adj* [not gradable] (esp. of a young woman) energetic, enthusiastic, and confident • Pert can also mean small and attractive: *a pert nose* • Pert can also mean too confident and not very respectful: *a pert reply*

pertain to /pərˈteɪn/ *v prep* [T] to relate to or have a connection with (something) • *regulations pertaining to high-tech industries* ○ *Seaweed's properties, as they pertain to skin care, are still in dispute.*

pertinent /ˈpɜrt·ən·ənt/ *adj* relating directly to the subject being considered; RELEVANT • *a pertinent question*

perturbed /pərˈtɜrbd/ *adj slightly fml* worried or troubled • *Ms. McCurdy was too perturbed to pay attention.*

peruse /pəˈruːz/ *v* [T] to read or look at (something) in a relaxed way • *He opened the newspaper and perused the sports pages.* • Peruse can also mean to read carefully in a detailed way.

pervade /pərˈveɪd/ *v* [T] to spread through all parts of (something) • *The influence of the early jazz musicians pervades American music.*

pervasive /pərˈveɪ·sɪv, -zɪv/ *adj* • *a pervasive smell of insecticide* ○ *pervasive political corruption*

perverse /pərˈvɜrs/ *adj* having the effect of being, or intended to be, the opposite of what is ordinarily expected or considered reasonable • *Sometimes I think he refuses to cooperate just to be perverse.* ○ *She took a perverse pleasure in her sister's divorce.*

pervert [CHANGE] /pərˈvɜrt/ *v* [T] to change (something) from its proper use or original purpose • *These journalists are perverting the news.* ○ *The will of the people is being perverted by their elected representatives.*

perverted /pərˈvɜrṭ·əd/ *adj* • *He used a perverted form of nationalism to incite racial hatred.*

perversion /pərˈvɜr·ʒən/ *n* [C/U] • *What we're being shown here is not intimacy, it's a perversion of that.* [C]

pervert [UNNATURAL PERSON] /ˈpɜr·vɜrt/ *n* [C] a

person whose sexual behavior is considered unnatural and morally wrong

perverted /pər'vɜrt̬·əd/ *adj* • *Homosexuality has frequently been regarded as perverted sexual behavior.*

perversion /pər'vər·ʒən/ *n* [C/U] sexual behavior that is considered unnatural and morally wrong • *All manner of perversions can be found in the big city.* [C]

pesky /'pes·ki/ *adj infml* annoying or troublesome • *No matter how often I weed the garden, those pesky weeds keep coming back.*

pessimism /'pes·ə,mɪz·əm/ *n* [U] the tendency to see the bad side of things or to expect the worst in any situation • *There has been a mood of growing pessimism about the nation's economy.* • Compare OPTIMISM.

pessimist /'pes·ə·məst/ *n* [C] • *How come you're such a pessimist?*

pessimistic /,pes·ə'mɪs·tɪk/ *adj* • *She's pretty pessimistic about her chances* (= thinks her chances are not good).

pest /pest/ *n* [C] an insect or small animal that is harmful or damages crops • *The aphid is a garden pest.* • (*infml*) A pest is also an annoying person, esp. a child: *My brother is such a pest.*

pester /'pes·tər/ *v* [T] to annoy (someone) by doing or asking for something repeatedly • *The kids keep pestering me to buy them a new video game.*

pesticide /'pes·tə,saɪd/ *n* [C] a chemical substance used to kill harmful insects, small animals, wild plants, and other unwanted organisms • Compare INSECTICIDE.

pestilence /'pes·tə·ləns/ *n* [C/U] *slightly fml* a disease that spreads quickly and kills large numbers of people

pesto /'pes·toʊ/ *n* [U] a green sauce used in Italian cooking, esp. on pasta

pet ANIMAL /pet/ *n* [C] an animal that is kept in the home as a companion and treated affectionately • *She has several interesting pets, including a couple of snakes.*

pet LIKED /pet/ *adj* [not gradable] especially liked or personally important • *The legislation will face strong opposition from senators whose pet projects would be cut back.* • A **pet name** is an informal, affectionate name given to someone by their family or friends: *Her dad's pet name for her was "Babe."* • A **pet peeve** is something that especially annoys you: *Weak coffee is one of my pet peeves.*

pet TOUCH /pet/ *v* [I/T] **-tt-** to touch (an animal or person) kindly or lovingly with the hands • *Our dog loves to be petted and tickled behind the ears.* [T] • If two people are petting, they are kissing and touching each other in a sexual way. [I]

petal /'pet̬·əl/ *n* [C] any of the usually brightly colored parts that together form most of a flower • *rose petals*

peter out /,pi:t̬·ə'raʊt/ *v adv* [I] to be reduced

gradually so that nothing is left • *We thought the storm would peter out.*

petite /pə'ti:t/ *adj* (of a woman or girl) small and attractively thin • Petite is also a size of clothing for small, thin women.

petition /pə'tɪʃ·ən/ *n* [C] a document signed by a large number of people requesting some action from the government or another authority, or (*law*) a formal letter to a court of law requesting a particular legal action • *More than 2000 people signed a petition to protect a wildlife area from development.* ○ (*law*) *She's filing a petition for divorce.*

petition /pə'tɪʃ·ən/ *v* [I/T] • *They plan to petition the governor to increase funding for the project.* [T]

petrified /'pet·rə,faɪd/ *adj* very frightened • *As soon as they got on the stage they were petrified with fright.*

petrochemical /,pe·troʊ'kem·ɪ·kəl/ *n* [C] any chemical substance obtained from PETROLEUM or natural gas

petrol /'pe·trəl/ *n* [U] *Br for* GAS LIQUID FUEL

petroleum /pə'troʊ·li:·əm/ *n* [U] a dark, thick oil obtained from under the ground and made into fuels such as GAS and heating oil, and used in making plastics

petty SMALL /'pet̬·i/ *adj* small or of lesser importance • *a petty thief* ○ *I don't have time for petty matters like that.* • **Petty cash** is a small amount of money kept for buying cheap items.

petty SELFISH /'pet̬·i/ *adj* selfish and mean, esp. because of having too much interest in small and unimportant matters • *The women in the story are petty and hateful.*

pettiness /'pet̬·i·nəs/ *n* [U]

petulant /'petʃ·ə·lənt/ *adj* easily angered or annoyed, esp. in a childish way • *He plays the part of a petulant young man in the film.*

petunia /pɪ'tu:n·jə/ *n* [C] a plant with white, pink, or purple, bell-shaped flowers

pew /pju:/ *n* [C] a long, wooden seat with a back in a church, usually forming one of a number of rows facing the ALTAR in the front

pewter /'pju:t̬·ər/ *n* [U] a blue-gray metal that is a mixture of TIN and LEAD

PG *adj abbreviation for* parental guidance, (= used in the US for movies that some parents might think unsuitable for their children) • **PG-13** is used in the US for movies that some parents might think unsuitable for their children under the age of 13. • Compare G MOVIE; NC-17; R MOVIE; X SEXUAL.

phallic /'fæl·ɪk/ *adj* suggesting a penis esp. in appearance • *a phallic shape*

phantom /'fænt·əm/ *n* [C] something that appears or seems to exist but is not real or is imagined • A phantom is also a GHOST.

pharmaceutical /,far·mə'su:t̬·ɪ·kəl/ *adj* [not gradable] connected with the science, preparation, and production of medicines • *the pharmaceutical industry*

pharmacist /ˈfɑr·mə·səst/, **druggist** *n* [C] a person who is trained in the preparation of medicines • *Rachel is studying to be a pharmacist.*

pharmacy /ˈfɑr·mə·si/ *n* [C] a store or a part of a store where medicines are prepared and sold

phase /feɪz/ *n* [C] any stage in a series of events or in a process of development • *The project is only in its first phase of planning, so we haven't yet established the cost.* • The phases of the moon are the regular changes in its shape as it appears to people on earth.

phase /feɪz/ *v* [M] • If you **phase** something **in/out**, you introduce it gradually, in stages, or you gradually stop using it: *Many airlines have begun to phase out* (= stop using) *airplanes 20 years old or older.*

Ph.D. *n* [C] *abbreviation for* doctor of philosophy (= the highest college degree or a person having this) • *He earned a Ph.D. in physics from Northwestern University.*

pheasant /ˈfez·ənt/ *n* [C/U] a large bird with a rounded body and long tail, sometimes hunted as a sport and eaten as food

phenomenon [EXPERIENCE] /fɪˈnɑm·əˌnɑn, -nən/ *n* [C] *pl* **phenomena** /fɪˈnɑm·ə·nə/ anything that is or can be experienced or felt, esp. something that is noticed because it is unusual or new • *We discussed the ever-growing popularity of talk radio, and wondered how to explain this phenomenon.*

phenomenon [SPECIAL PERSON / THING] /fɪˈnɑm·əˌnɑn, -nən/ *n* [C usually sing] *pl* **phenomenons** someone or something special, esp. because it is entirely different or extremely unusual • *He was a kind of phenomenon, an actor running for president.*

phenomenal /fɪˈnɑm·ən·ᵊl/ *adj* unusually great; much more or much better • *Angela can do a phenomenal amount of work in one day.* ○ *He has a phenomenal memory.*

phenomenally /fɪˈnɑm·ən·ᵊl·i/ *adv* • *Her first play was phenomenally successful.*

philanderer /fɪˈlæn·dər·ər/ *n* [C] a man who has sex with many different women without having a lasting emotional relationship with any of them • *His own brothers know he is a drinker and philanderer and always will be.*

philanthropic /ˌfɪl·ənˈθrɑp·ɪk/ *adj* showing generosity toward other people and a sincere wish to help them, esp. by giving money • *a philanthropic organization*

philanthropist /fɪˈlæn·θrə·pəst/ *n* [C]

philistine /ˈfɪl·əˌstiːn, fəˈlɪsˌtiːn/ *n* [C] *disapproving* a person who enjoys only popular entertainment but does not appreciate art, literature, or music of high quality

philodendron /ˌfɪl·əˈden·drən/ *n* [C] a climbing plant with leaves that are usually green and heart-shaped

philosophy /fəˈlɑs·ə·fi/ *n* [C/U] the study of the nature of reality and existence, of what it is possible to know, and of right and wrong behavior, or a particular set of beliefs of this type • *the philosophy of Kant* [C] ○ *I'd like to take a course in philosophy next semester.* [U] • The philosophy of a subject is a group of theories and ideas related to the understanding of that subject: *the philosophy of religion/science* [U] • A philosophy is also the beliefs you have about how you should behave in particular situations in life: *It was always my philosophy to pay my debts promptly.* [C]

philosopher /fəˈlɑs·ə·fər/ *n* [C] • *Plato, Aristotle, and the other Greek philosophers*

philosophical /ˌfɪl·əˈsɑf·ɪ·kəl/ *adj* • To be philosophical about something, esp. something disappointing, is to accept it calmly: *You just have to be philosophical about losing some games, because you can't win them all.*

philosophize /fəˈlɑs·əˌfaɪz/ *v* [I] • *That's when she'll start philosophizing about the notion of time.*

phlegm /flem/ *n* [U] a thick, liquid substance produced in the throat and nose esp. when you are sick with a cold

phlegmatic /flegˈmæt·ɪk/ *adj* not easily excited or emotional; calm • *He is a retired lawyer with a solid, phlegmatic manner.*

phobia /ˈfoʊ·biː·ə/ *n* [C] an extreme fear of a particular thing or situation, esp. one that cannot be reasonably explained • *a phobia about heights*

phone /foʊn/ *n* [C] *short form of* TELEPHONE • *The phone is ringing—would you answer it?* • A **phone book** is a book containing the telephone numbers of people and businesses in a particular area. • A **phone card** is a card that you buy for various amounts and can use to operate a public telephone, using the value you bought. • A **phone number** is a series of numbers which you use to call a particular telephone. • [LP] TELEPHONE

phone /foʊn/ *v* [I/T] • *Fernando phoned just after lunch.* [I]

phonetic /fəˈnet·ɪk/ *adj* [not gradable] *specialized* relating to the sounds made in speaking

phonetics /fəˈnet·ɪks/ *n* [U] *specialized* the study of the sounds made by the human voice in speech

phony /ˈfoʊ·ni/ *adj* represented as real but actually false; intended to deceive • *They were accused of submitting phony claims to insurers, including Medicare.*

phony /ˈfoʊ·ni/ *n* [C] *infml* a person who falsely pretends to be something • *I think he's a phony.*

phosphate /ˈfɑs·feɪt/ *n* [C] a chemical COMPOUND (= substance consisting of at least two elements) that contains PHOSPHORUS • *a phosphate-free detergent* ○ *The plant fertilizer contains phosphates.*

phosphorescent /ˌfɑs·fəˈres·ənt/ *adj* giving off or shining with light, and giving off little or no heat

phosphorescence /ˌfɑs·fəˈres·əns/ *n* [U]

phosphorus /ˈfɑs·fə·rəs/ *n* [U] a poisonous, yellow-white chemical element that shines in the dark and burns when in the air

photo /ˈfoʊt̬·oʊ/ *n* [C] *pl* **photos** *short form of* PHOTOGRAPH • *Giraldo takes a lot of photos.* • A **photo finish** in a race is a situation where competitors finish so close that a photograph must be examined to decide the winner.

photocopier /ˈfoʊt̬·əˌkɑp·iː·ər/ *n* [C] a machine using a photographic process to make copies of pages with printing, writing, or drawing on them

photocopy /ˈfoʊt̬·əˌkɑp·i/ *n* [C] a copy of a document made on a photocopier

photocopy /ˈfoʊt̬·əˌkɑp·i/ *v* [T]

photogenic /ˌfoʊt̬·əˈdʒen·ɪk, -ˈdʒiː·nɪk/ *adj* having an appearance that is attractive in photographs

photograph /ˈfoʊt̬·əˌɡræf/, *short form* **photo** *n* [C] an image of a person, object, or view that is produced by using a camera and film • *col-or/black-and-white photographs*

photograph /ˈfoʊt̬·əˌɡræf/ *v* [T] • *We photographed the house to document the damage done by the storm.*

photographer /fəˈtɑɡ·rə·fər/ *n* [C] • *a fashion/newspaper photographer*

photographic /ˌfoʊt̬·əˈɡræf·ɪk/ *adj* [not gradable] • *photographic equipment* ○ *You can store photographic images on your computer's hard drive.*

photography /fəˈtɑɡ·rə·fi/ *n* [U] the skill or activity of taking or processing photographs

photosynthesis /ˌfoʊt̬·əˈsɪn·θə·səs/ *n* [U] *specialized* the process by which a plant uses energy from the light of the sun to produce its own food from water and **carbon dioxide**

phrase /freɪz/ *n* [C] a group of words expressing a particular idea or meaning • *I think the phrase "bundle of energy" describes Mara very well.* • *(specialized)* In grammar, a phrase is a group of words forming a part of a sentence: *In "He was a man of great wealth," "of great wealth" is a prepositional phrase.*

phrase /freɪz/ *v* [T] to express (something) in a particular way when speaking or writing • *The wording of his resignation was carefully phrased to avoid any admission of guilt.*

phrasal /ˈfreɪ·zəl/ *adj* • *(specialized)* In grammar, a **phrasal verb** is a combination of a verb and an adverb or a verb and a preposition, or both, in which the combination has a meaning different from the meaning of the particular words considered separately: *"Catch on" is a phrasal verb meaning to understand.*

physical BODY /ˈfɪz·ɪ·kəl/ *adj* connected with the body • *physical strength/disabilities* ○ *She tries to keep herself in good physical condition* • Physical can also mean sexual: *There's obviously a strong physical attraction between them.* • **Physical education** (also **gym**, *abbreviation* **phys. ed.**) refers to the classes at school in which children exercise and learn to play sports, or the area of study relating to such classes. • **Physical therapy** (also **physiotherapy**) is the treatment of stiffness, muscle weakness, and pain, esp. by rubbing and moving the sore parts and through exercise. A person whose job is treating people using physical therapy is a **physical therapist** (also **physiotherapist**). • See also **physical** at PHYSICS. Compare MENTAL.

physical (examination) /ˈfɪz·ɪ·kəl (ɪɡˌzæm·əˈneɪ·ʃən)/ *n* [C] a careful look at a person's body by a doctor in order to discover if that person is healthy, sometimes done before a person can be accepted for a particular job • *They found the cancer during a routine physical.*

physically /ˈfɪz·ɪ·kli/ *adv* • *She works out at a gym and is very physically fit.* • People who are physically disabled/handicapped/challenged lack the full use of their body.

physical MATERIAL /ˈfɪz·ɪ·kəl/ *adj* existing as or connected with things that can be seen or touched • *The physical dimensions of the theater are smaller than I thought.*

physician /fəˈzɪʃ·ən/ *n* [C] a medical doctor, esp. one who is not a SURGEON

physics /ˈfɪz·ɪks/ *n* [U] the scientific study of matter and energy and the effect that they have on each other • *nuclear/particle/theoretical physics*

physical /ˈfɪz·ɪ·kəl/ *adj* connected with physics • The **physical sciences** are the sciences such as physics, chemistry, and ASTRONOMY that examine matter and energy and the way the universe behaves. • See also PHYSICAL BODY.

physicist /ˈfɪz·ə·səst/ *n* [C] a person who studies physics or whose job is connected with physics

physiology /ˌfɪz·iːˈɑl·ə·dʒi/ *n* [U] the scientific study of the way in which the bodies of animals and plants work • *the physiology of the brain*

physiotherapy /ˌfɪz·iː·oʊˈθer·ə·pi/ *n* [U] physical therapy, see at PHYSICAL BODY

physiotherapist /ˌfɪz·iː·oʊˈθer·ə·pəst/ *n* [C] a physical therapist, see at PHYSICAL BODY

physique /fəˈziːk/ *n* [C] the appearance, esp. shape and size, of a human body • *a small/large physique* ○ *a dancer's physique*

piano /piːˈæn·oʊ/ *n* [C/U] *pl* **pianos** a large musical instrument with a row of black and white keys that are pressed with the fingers to play notes, or this type of instrument gener-

PHRASAL VERBS

Phrasal verbs are combinations of two or more words—a verb followed by an adverb, a verb followed by a preposition, or a verb followed by an adverb and a preposition. Adding the adverb or preposition changes the basic meaning of the verb.

HOW TO FIND THEM IN THE DICTIONARY

Each phrasal verb is given a separate entry for each meaning of the combination. Think of it as a new verb that is made up of two or three words.

Phrasal verb entries are marked with a small box just to the left of the entry. They follow the entries for basic verbs in the alphabetical order of the dictionary. For example, **look after** and **look forward to** are shown after all the definitions for **look**.

GRAMMAR AND WORD ORDER

There are five basic grammatical types of phrasal verbs.

intransitive verbs with an adverb: *v adv* [I]

set off *v adv* [I]
What time do we **set off** *tomorrow?*

transitive verbs followed by an adverb that can go in only one position: *v adv* [T]

gloss over *v adv* [T]
Popular writing sometimes **glosses over** *important facts.*

Sometimes, the object of the verb comes between the verb and the adverb. In these cases, the object is shown as part of the word.

set *obj* **apart** *v adv* [T]
Her original ideas **set** *her* **apart** *from other students.*

Sometimes, phrasal verbs of this type can take two objects, one between the verb and adverb, and another following the adverb. In these cases, the objects are shown as part of the word. If one of the objects is not necessary, it is put in parentheses.

set *obj* **back** *(obj) v adv* [T]
Our vacation **set** *us* **back** *over $3000.*

transitive verbs followed by a movable adverb (one that goes either before or after the object): *v adv* [M]

Most transitive verbs with an adverb are of this type. Usually the adverb can appear either before or after the object without any change in meaning. When all uses of a verb follow this pattern, the two possible positions of the object are shown as part of the word.

pass out *obj*, **pass** *obj* **out** *v adv* [M] to give (something) to each person in a group • *Jeff, please* **pass out** *the test booklets.*

Notice that when the object is a <u>pronoun</u> like *me, him, it,* or *myself,* the pronoun must go <u>before the adverb</u>. **Turn off** *the light* and **Turn** *the light* **off** are both possible, but with *it* you can say only **Turn** *it* **off**.

verbs with a preposition: *v prep* [T] or *v prep* [I]

These are usually [T], meaning that the object can go in only one position. If the object always follows the preposition, the verb is shown this way:

deal with *v prep* [T] to develop a way to manage or relate to (someone or something) • *We have to* **deal with** *problems as they arise.*

Sometimes, phrasal verbs of this type can take two objects, one between the verb and preposition and another following the preposition. In these cases, the objects are shown as part of the word. If one of the objects is not necessary, it is put in parentheses.

hold *obj* **against** *obj* to allow (something) to cause you to have a bad opinion about (someone or something) • *He made a mistake, but don't* **hold** *it* **against** *him—we all make mistakes.*

verbs with an adverb and a preposition: *v adv prep* [T]

Some verbs are followed by both an adverb and a preposition.

How can you **put up with** *all that noise?*

Sometimes, phrasal verbs of this type can take two objects, one between the verb and adverb and another following the preposition. In these cases, the objects are shown as part of the word. If one of the objects is not necessary, it is put in parentheses.

[LP] **Verbs: Transitive and Intransitive Grammer Patterns**

piano

ally • *a grand/upright piano* [C] ∘ *I play piano.*
[U] • PIC KEY

pianist /pi:ˈæn·əst, ˈpiː·ə·nəst/ *n* [C] someone
who plays the piano • *a concert/jazz pianist*

piccolo /ˈpɪk·əˌloʊ/ *n* [C/U] *pl* **piccolos** a very
small musical instrument that is like a FLUTE
and plays high notes, or this type of instrument generally

pick CHOOSE /pɪk/ *v* [T] to take some things
and leave others • *She's been picked for the
Olympic team.* ∘ *We finally picked February 14
as the date for our wedding.* • If you **pick a
fight** with someone, you intentionally start it:
*Some kids were staring at him, trying to get him
to look back so they could pick a fight.* • If you
pick and choose you take only the things you
want: *People want to pick and choose their own
religious life.* • *Charlie* **picked** *his* **way**
through the crowd (= carefully chose where to
walk).

pick /pɪk/ *n* [C/U] a choice, or something that
is chosen • *Mick gets first pick of where to sit.*
[U] ∘ *Here are my picks for the ten best restaurants.* [C] • If something is described as **the
pick of** a group of things, it is the best in the
group: *This puppy was the pick of the litter.*

picky /ˈpɪk·i/ *adj* liking only a few things and
therefore difficult to please • *a picky eater*

pick REMOVE /pɪk/ *v* [T] to remove or move
(something) with your fingers or hands • *I
picked a piece of lint off my suit.* ∘ *We picked
apples yesterday.* ∘ *The child continued picking
her nose* (= trying to remove things from inside it with her finger). • If you **pick** someone's **brain** you ask their advice about a subject they know a lot about: *Can I pick your
brain about how you got rid of those trees?* • If
someone **picks** your **pocket** they steal small
objects, esp. money, from your pockets or bag.

picker /ˈpɪk·ər/ *n* [C] a person or machine that
picks crops • *fruit pickers*

pick MUSICAL TOOL /pɪk/ *n* [C] a thin piece of
plastic or metal used to pull at the strings of a
guitar

pick DIGGING TOOL /pɪk/ *n* [C] a PICKAX, or a
sharp, pointed tool • *They worked with a pick
and shovel.*

▫ **pick at** /ˈ--/ *v adv* [T] to eat (food) in small

pieces and without enjoyment • *She only
picked at her dinner.*

▫ **pick off** *obj*, **pick** *obj* **off** /ˈ-ˈ-/ *v adv* [M] to
shoot (a person or animal chosen out of a
group), esp. from a distance • *Snipers picked
the soldiers off one by one.*

▫ **pick on** /ˈ-ˌ-/ *v prep* [T] to repeatedly treat unfairly, criticize, or punish (someone) • *He gets
picked on because he's small.*

▫ **pick out** *obj*, **pick** *obj* **out** /ˈ-ˈ-/ *v adv* [M] to
choose, find, or recognize (something) in a
group • *From all the puppies, we picked out the
smallest one to take home.* ∘ *We could pick our
parents out easily in the old photos.*

▫ **pick over** *obj*, **pick** *obj* **over** /ˈ-ˈ-/ *v adv* [M]
to examine (a group of things) carefully in or-
der to choose the ones you want • *She picked
over the strawberries, selecting the largest ones.*

▫ **pick up** *obj* LIFT, **pick** *obj* **up** /ˈ-ˈ-/ *v adv* [M]
to lift (something or someone) • *He picked his
briefcase up and headed for the door.* ∘ *She
picked up the little boy and kissed him.*

▫ **pick up** *obj* TAKE, **pick** *obj* **up** /ˈ-ˈ-/ *v adv* [M]
to get or bring (someone or something) from
somewhere • *Whose turn is it to pick up the
kids from school?* ∘ *A truck picks up the recycling once a week.* • If the police pick someone
up, they arrest them: *Cops picked up the suspect a few miles away.*

pickup /ˈpɪk·ʌp/ *n* [C] the act of getting something or someone • *Trash pickups are on Tuesdays and Fridays.* ∘ *We arranged the pickup for
ten o'clock.* • A **pickup (truck)** is a vehicle
with an open part at the back in which things
can be carried.

▫ **pick up** *obj* OBTAIN, **pick** *obj* **up** /ˈ-ˈ-/ *v adv*
[M] to obtain or receive (something) • *I pick
some ideas up from those cooking shows.* ∘
*While you're in town, would you pick up a book
for me?* ∘ *Can you pick up the Yankees game up
here* (= receive broadcasts of it)? ∘ *She picked
up her soccer skills from her older brother* (=
learned them informally). ∘ *Gwen picked up a
cold on her trip* (= started to suffer from it). •
If someone **picks up the bill/tab**, they pay
for something, esp. for what someone else has
bought or used: *The company will pick up the
tab for this trip.*

▫ **pick up** *obj* MEET, **pick** *obj* **up** /ˈ-ˈ-/ *v adv* [M]
infml to meet (someone) for the first time and
invite them to have esp. a sexual relationship
with you • *Is that the girl who picked him up
from the bar last week?*

▫ **pick up** *obj* IMPROVE / INCREASE /ˈ-ˈ-/ *v adv* [I/T] to
improve (an activity) or increase (an amount)
• *Retailers are starting to see sales pick up
again.* [I] ∘ *The truck picked up speed slowly.*
[T] • To **pick up steam** is to start working or
producing at a faster rate or more effectively:
*After a slow start, the project began to pick up
steam.*

pickup /ˈpɪk·ʌp/ *n* [U] the power of a vehicle

to increase its rate of speed • *The car is easy to turn but it lacks pickup.*

❑ **pick up** *(obj)* START AGAIN , **pick** *(obj)* **up** /'-'-/ *v adv* [I/M] to start again after an interruption • *The author picks up the theme again on page ten.* [M] ○ *Tomorrow we'll pick up where we left off.* [I]

❑ **pick up on** /-'-,-/ *v adv prep* [T] to choose (something previously said) as being worth discussion, or to give (something) particular attention • *I want to pick up on a point that Susan made about role models.* ○ *He was pretty nervous, but they didn't seem to pick up on it.*

pickax, **pickaxe** /'pɪk·æks/, **pick** *n* [C] a tool with a long wooden handle fitted into the middle of a curved metal bar with a sharp point

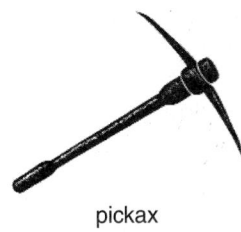

pickax

picket /'pɪk·ət/, **picketer** /'pɪk·ət·ər/ *n* [C] a person or group of people who have a disagreement with a company, usually the one where they work, and who walk around in a line outside the place of business to tell other people not to enter until the problem is solved • *Three pickets stood at the factory gate.* • *Truck drivers refused to cross the* **picket line** (= a group of pickets).

picket /'pɪk·ət/ *v* [I/T] • *The women picketed (outside) the factory for three months.* [I/T]

picket fence /'pɪk·ət'fens/ *n* [C] a low fence made of a row of flat, vertical sticks, pointed at the top, usually with space between them and connected by a few horizontal sticks

pickle /'pɪk·əl/ *n* [C] a CUCUMBER (= a green, tube-shaped vegetable) that has been preserved in a liquid containing salt and other spices or vinegar • *a sweet/dill pickle*

pickle /'pɪk·əl/ *v* [T] to preserve in a liquid containing salt or vinegar

pickled /'pɪk·əld/ *adj* • *pickled tomatoes/herring*

pick-me-up /'pɪk·miː,ʌp/ *n* [C] *infml* something, often food or drink, that makes you feel better when you are sick or tired • *I need a little pick-me-up in the middle of the afternoon.*

pickpocket /'pɪk,pɑk·ət/ *n* [C] a thief who steals things out of pockets or bags, esp. in a crowd

picky /'pɪk·i/ *adj* See at PICK CHOOSE

picnic /'pɪk·nɪk/ *n* [C] a meal you take to a place outside to be eaten there in an informal way, or an occasion on which such a meal is eaten • *a church picnic* • *(infml)* A picnic is also any pleasant activity: *Did you think law*

school *would be a picnic?* ○ *Filing tax returns is no picnic.*

picnic /'pɪk·nɪk/ *v* [I] **picnicking**, *past* **picnicked** • *We can picnic in the park.*

pictorial /pɪk'tɔːr·iː·əl, -'tour-/ *adj* [not gradable] consisting of or having the form of a picture or pictures • *a pictorial history of America*

picture REPRESENTATION /'pɪk·tʃər/ *n* [C] a representation of someone or something produced by drawing, painting, or photographing • *He drew/painted a picture of my dog.* ○ *Brian takes lots of pictures* (= photographs). • A picture is also an image seen on a television or movie screen: *It's an old set, and the picture is a little fuzzy.* • A picture is also a movie: *It won an Academy Award for best picture.* • If you describe someone as **the picture of** something, you mean that they give a very clear appearance of it: *He's the picture of health.*

picture /'pɪk·tʃər/ *v* [T] to imagine (how something looks) • *Try to picture yourself lying on a beach in the hot sun.*

picture DESCRIPTION /'pɪk·tʃər/ *n* [C/U] a description of a situation, or the situation itself • *Do news reports give an accurate picture of events?* [C] ○ *They're looking at individuals and not at the overall picture.* [U] ○ *Don't say any more—I get the picture* (= understand the situation). [U] ○ *Marilyn's mother more or less stayed out of the picture* (= was not involved). [U] • To paint a picture is to describe a situation: *The statistics do not paint an optimistic picture.* [C]

picturesque /,pɪk·tʃə'resk/ *adj* (esp. of a place) attractive in appearance • *We strolled through the picturesque streets of the old city.*

piddling /'pɪd·lɪŋ, -lən/ *adj infml* very small or unimportant • *a piddling amount/figure*

pidgin /'pɪdʒ·ən/ *n* [C] a language that has developed from a mixture of two or more languages and is used for communicating by people who do not speak each other's language

pie /pɑɪ/ *n* [C/U] a round pastry with a filling such as fruit, meat, or vegetables • *a blueberry pie* [C] ○ *We're having sweet potato pie for dinner.* [U] • **Pie in the sky** is something desirable that is unlikely to happen: *For some, religion offers only pie in the sky.* • A **pie chart** is a circle that is divided into several parts to show how a total amount is divided up. • A **piecrust** is the pastry on the top or bottom of a pie.

piece PART /piːs/ *n* [C] a part of something • *a piece of cake/chicken/pizza* • *The vase lay on the floor* **in pieces** (= broken into small parts). • *She was so angry that she ripped/tore the letter* **to pieces** (= into small parts). • If someone **goes/falls to pieces**, they become unable to think clearly and control their emotions because of something unpleasant or difficult that they have experienced: *She fell to pieces at the funeral.* • *(infml)* If something is **a piece**

of cake, it is easy to do: *For him, schoolwork is a piece of cake.* • (*infml*) **A piece of the action** is a part of the profits or advantages that come from an activity: *When it comes to lawsuits, everyone seems to want a piece of the action.*

piece together *obj*, **piece** *obj* **together** /'--'--/ *v adv* [M] to put (the parts of something) into place • *Archeologists have pieced together fragments of the pottery.* • If you piece together facts or information, you collect them in order to understand a situation: *Investigators are trying to piece together what happened just before the accident.*

piece ITEM /piːs/ *n* [C] a single item that is one of other similar items • *a piece of furniture/ equipment/luggage/paper* ○ *I have an important piece of information for you.* • A piece can be something created by an artist, writer, or musician: *He's written a new piece of music.* • **Piecework** is work for which the amount of pay depends on the number of items completed rather than the time spent making them.

piecemeal /'piːˌsmiːl/ *adv, adj* [not gradable] not done according to a plan but done at different times in different ways • *Do we fix it all now, or do we approach it piecemeal over time?*

pier STRUCTURE /pɪr/ *n* [C] a structure built out over the water on posts, along which boats can land • *a fishing pier*

pier COLUMN /pɪr/ *n* [C] a thick, strong column used to support a structure such as a bridge

pierce /pɪrs/ *v* [T] to go in or through (something), esp. with a pointed object, making a hole • *Pierce the potatoes with a fork to see if they're done.* ○ *She got her ears pierced.*

piercing /'pɪr·sɪŋ/ *adj* feeling or seeming very sharp or powerful • *He had piercing blue eyes.* ○ *She let out a piercing* (= loud) *shriek.*

piety /'paɪ·ət·i/ *n* [U] a strong belief in God or a religion, shown by your worship and dutiful behavior • USAGE: The related adjective is PIOUS.

pig ANIMAL /pɪg/ *n* [C] a farm or wild animal with pink, brown, or black skin, short legs, and a SNOUT (= flat nose) • A **pigpen/pigsty** is an enclosed area where pigs are kept, or (*fig.*) a dirty or messy place: *Your bedroom is a pigsty!*

piggy, **piggie** /'pɪg·i/ *n* [C] *a child's word for* pig • A **piggy bank** is a container, sometimes in the shape of a pig, which holds coins and is used esp. by children for saving money.

pig PERSON /pɪg/ *n* [C] *infml* a person who is messy, selfish, or rude, or someone who eats too much • If someone is **pigheaded**, they refuse to change their opinion or behavior: *Not even somebody as pigheaded as Ira could argue about it.*

pig out /'-'-/ *v adv* [I] *infml* to eat too much • *We just pigged out on chips while we watched a movie.*

pigeon /'pɪdʒ·ən/ *n* [C] a large, usually gray-and-white bird that lives esp. in cities • *We feed the pigeons in the park.* • A person who is **pigeon-toed** walks with their feet pointed in toward each other.

pigeonhole /'pɪdʒ·ən.hoʊl/ *v* [T] to put (someone or something) into a group or type, often unfairly • *He's was pigeonholed early on in his career as a gospel singer.*

piggyback /'pɪg·iːˌbæk/ *adj, adv* [not gradable] on someone's back • *Uncle Sean loves to give Tyler piggyback rides.*

piglet /'pɪg·lət/ *n* [C] a young pig

pigment /'pɪg·mənt/ *n* [C/U] a natural substance that produces color in animals and plants, such as of skin, hair, and leaves, or the substance in a paint or DYE that gives it its color

pigmentation /ˌpɪg·mən'teɪ·ʃən/ *n* [U] • *skin pigmentation*

pigtail /'pɪg·teɪl/ *n* [C usually pl] one of usually two lengths of hair gathered at each side of the head, either hanging loose or in a BRAID • *a little girl in pigtails*

pike FISH /paɪk/ *n* [C] *pl* **pike** a large fish with sharp teeth that lives in lakes and rivers

pike ROAD /paɪk/ *n* [C] *short form of* TURNPIKE • *Traffic is slow along Rockville Pike.*

pile THINGS /paɪl/ *n* [C] a number of things lying on top of each other • *a pile of newspapers* ○ *After dinner there is always a pile of dishes to be washed.* • (*infml*) A pile or piles can also be a lot of something: *I've got piles of homework.*

pile /paɪl/ *v* [always + adv/prep] to put (things) many on top of each other, or to collect in this way • *Magazines just pile up on my desk at work.* [I] ○ *I asked her to pile on extra potatoes.* [M]

pile MOVE /paɪl/ *v* [I always + adv/prep] (of a group of people) to move together, esp. in a disorderly way • *About ten kids piled into the room, all talking at once.* ○ *Someone yelled "Fire!" and we all piled out into the street.*

pile SURFACE /paɪl/ *n* [U] the soft surface of short threads on a CARPET (= material for covering a floor) or on some types of cloth • *carpets with a deep pile*

□**pile up** /-'-/ *v adv* [I] to increase in amount • *The work was piling up, and I decided I had to go in to the office on the weekend.*

pileup /'paɪl·ʌp/ *n* [C] a traffic accident involving several vehicles • *Police reported a ten-car pileup on an icy road.*

pilfer /'pɪl·fər/ *v* [I/T] to steal things of little value or in small amounts • *Neighborhood kids were pilfering (candy) from the corner store.* [I/T]

Pilgrim HISTORICAL PERSON /'pɪl·grəm/ *n* [C] a member of the group of English people who sailed to America and began living in Plymouth, Massachusetts, in 1620

pilgrim RELIGIOUS TRAVELER /'pɪl·grəm/ *n* [C] a

person who travels to a holy place as a religious act

pilgrimage /ˈpɪl·grə·mɪdʒ/ n [C/U] a trip, often a long one, made to a holy place for religious reasons

pill /pɪl/ n [C] a small, solid substance that a person swallows whole, esp. as medicine • *a sleeping pill* • **The pill** is a pill taken regularly by a woman to prevent her from becoming pregnant.

pillage /ˈpɪl·ɪdʒ/ v [I/T] *slightly fml* to steal (something) from (a place or a person) by using violence, esp. during war • *Rioters pillaged and set fire to downtown buildings.* [T]

pillar /ˈpɪl·ər/ n [C] a strong vertical column made of stone, metal, or wood that supports part of a building or stands alone for decoration • A pillar is also someone or something that is an important part of a group, place, or activity: *He's a pillar of the Dallas business community.*

pillow /ˈpɪl·oʊ/ n [C] a cloth bag filled with feathers or soft artificial fibers that supports a person's head when they are resting or sleeping • *I was asleep the minute my head hit the pillow.* • A **pillowcase** is a cloth cover for a pillow.

pilot PERSON /ˈpaɪ·lət/ n [C] a person who flies an aircraft, or someone who directs a ship safely through an area of water • *an airline pilot* ○ *a harbor pilot*

pilot /ˈpaɪ·lət/ v [T] • *He piloted the ship through the busy harbor.*

pilot TEST /ˈpaɪ·lət/ adj [not gradable] (of a plan, product, or system) done as a test before introducing it • *From the pilot episode, this looks to be one of the best new shows we'll see this fall.*

pilot /ˈpaɪ·lət/ v [T] • *Our district is piloting a day-care program.*

pilot (light) /ˈpaɪ·lət (ˈlaɪt)/ n [C] a small flame that burns continuously in a gas device, such as a stove or water heater, and lights a larger flame when the device is turned on

pimp /pɪmp/ n [C] a man who controls PROSTITUTES (= people who are paid to have sex) and takes some of the money that they earn

pimple /ˈpɪm·pəl/ n [C] a small, raised spot on the skin

pimply /ˈpɪm·pə·li/ adj • *a pimply teenager*

pin FASTENER /pɪn/ n [C] a thin piece of stiff wire with a pointed end that you can stick through two things to fasten them together • *Mary put a pin in her hair to hold her hat on.* • A pin can also be decorative and used as jewelry: *She wore a beautiful gold pin on her coat.* • **Pins and needles** is an uncomfortable feeling of being stuck by a lot of sharp points, which may happen when you have not moved an arm or a leg for a long time or have kept it pressed against something. • If someone is **on pins and needles**, they are worried or anxious about something that is going to happen:

Don't keep Margaret on pins and needles, give her a call. • A **pincushion** is a small bag filled with soft material into which pins are partly pushed until they are needed. • A **pinhole/pinprick** is a very small hole made by a pin or by something like it.

pin /pɪn/ v [T] **-nn-** • *She kept a map of Manhattan pinned on the wall.*

pin HOLD FIRMLY /pɪn/ v [T always + adv/prep] **-nn-** to hold (someone or something) firmly in the same position or place • *The terrorist attack on the embassy building left a number of people pinned in the wreckage.* ○ *(fig.) No one could pin the label of "conservative" on him* (= call him that).

□ **pin down** obj SHOOT AT , **pin** obj **down** /ˈ-ˈ-/ v adv [M] to shoot at (someone who is protected by an object) and therefore prevent them moving from behind it • *Soldiers were pinned down by enemy fire.*

□ **pin** obj **down** QUESTION /ˈ-ˈ-/ v adv [T] to force (someone) to be specific or make their intentions known, esp. by asking a lot of questions • *I tried to pin him down on where the money would come from.*

□ **pin down** DISCOVER /ˈ-ˈ-/ v adv [T] to discover the exact details about (something) • *The fire department is trying to pin down the cause of Wednesday's fire.*

□ **pin** obj **on** obj /ˈ-ˌ-/ v prep [T] to give (responsibility for something) to (someone or something) • *They pinned their hopes on the new technology.*

PIN (number) /ˈpɪn (ˈnʌm·bər)/ n [C] *abbreviation for* personal identification number (= a secret number that can be read by a computer to prove who you are) • *I punched my PIN number into the ATM machine and took out $100.*

pinball /ˈpɪn·bɔːl/ n [U] a game played on a machine in which the player tries to prevent a ball from rolling off the end of a sloping surface by causing the ball to bounce between devices that score points • *a pinball machine*

pinch PRESS /pɪntʃ/ v [I/T] to press (esp. someone's skin) strongly between your finger and thumb, or between two surfaces • *He pinched his nose together and breathed through his mouth.* [T] ○ *I had to pinch myself so I'd know I wasn't dreaming.* [T] • *She should continue to write plays, even if she has to* **pinch pennies** (= spend as little money as possible) *to do it.*

pinch /pɪntʃ/ n [C usually sing] • *He gave her a playful pinch on the cheek.* • **In a pinch** means if it is really necessary, although it is not the best choice: *You should use broccoli, but in a pinch celery will do.*

pinch AMOUNT /pɪntʃ/ n [C] a small amount of something, esp. the amount that you can hold between your finger and thumb • *a pinch of nutmeg/pepper*

pinched /pɪntʃt/ adj (of someone's face) thin and anxious, or (of clothing) narrow • *Nora* *was short, with a pinched face, and wore thick glasses with wire rims.* ○ *Her dress was pinched at the waist.* • If a person or organization is pinched, they do not have enough money: *The space program is pinched.*

pinch–hit /'pɪntʃ'hɪt/ *v* [I] (in baseball) to take another player's turn to hit
pinch hitter /'pɪntʃ'hɪt·ər/ *n* [C] • *They took me out for a pinch hitter.*

pine TREE /paɪn/ *n* [C/U] an evergreen tree that has thin leaves like needles and that grows in cool northern regions, or the wood of these trees • **Pine cones** are the hard, oval fruit of the pine tree which open and release seeds.

pine DESIRE /paɪn/ *v* [I always + adv/prep] to strongly desire esp. something that is difficult or impossible to obtain • *Braley pined for his wife, who was far away.*

pineapple /'paɪˌnæp·əl/ *n* [C/U] a large, juicy fruit that grows in hotter regions, having a rough skin, a short stem, and pointed leaves on the top, or its sweet, yellow flesh

ping /pɪŋ/ *n* [C] a short, metallic sound

Ping–Pong /'pɪŋ·pɔːŋ, -pɑŋ/ *n* [U] *trademark* **table tennis**, see at TABLE FURNITURE

pineapple

pinion /'pɪn·jən/ *v* [T] to hold or tie (someone), esp. by the arms, to prevent them from moving • *Two burly men pinioned Josef's arms behind his back.*

pink /pɪŋk/ *adj, n* [C/U] (of) a pale red color • *a pink hat* ○ *The bridesmaid wore pink.* [U] • If someone is **in the pink**, they are healthy. • A **pink slip** is a notice from an employer informing an employee that they no longer have a job: *Management started issuing pink slips yesterday.*

pinkeye /'pɪŋ·kaɪ/ *n* [U] an infectious illness of the eyes in which the eye and the surrounding area become red and swollen, a condition that is easily spread from one person to another

pinkie, pinky /'pɪŋ·ki/ *n* [C] the smallest finger of a person's hand

pinnacle SUCCESSFUL POINT /'pɪn·ɪ·kəl/ *n* [C usually sing] the most successful point • *The Olympics represent the pinnacle of athletic achievement.*

pinnacle TOP /'pɪn·ɪ·kəl/ *n* [C usually pl] a small pointed structure on top of a building, or a pointed top on a mountain • *The volcanic range is extremely rugged, with many cliffs, gorges, canyons, and pinnacles.*

pinpoint /'pɪn·pɔɪnt/ *v* [T] to discover or establish (something) exactly • *They were unable to pinpoint the source of the noise.*

pinstripe /'pɪn·straɪp/ *n* [C] a narrow line of a light color in the design of a cloth, or the

cloth itself with such parallel lines • *a dark blue suit and pants with gray pinstripes*

pin–striped /'pɪn·straɪpt/, **pin–stripe** /'pɪn·straɪp/ *adj* [not gradable] • *a pin-striped suit*

pint /paɪnt/ (*abbreviation* **pt.**) *n* [C] a unit of measurement of volume equal to ½ quart or about 0.47 liter • If someone or something is **pint-sized/pint-size**, they are small: *a pint-sized actress*

pin–up /'pɪn·ʌp/ *n* [C] a picture of a sexually attractive, usually famous person, suitable for hanging on a wall, or a person shown in such a picture

pioneer /ˌpaɪ·ə'nɪr/ *n* [C] a person who is among the first to study or develop something • *He was a pioneer in big-band jazz.* • A pioneer is also a person who is among the first to enter and live in an area, esp. in the western US: *The pioneers made their way across the desert.*

pioneer /ˌpaɪ·ə'nɪr/ *v* [T] • *He pioneered the design of the Internet.*

pious /'paɪ·əs/ *adj* strongly believing in God or a particular religion, and living in a way that shows this belief • USAGE: The related noun is PIETY.

pipe TUBE /paɪp/ *n* [C] a tube through which liquids or gases can flow • *You have to remember to shut off the water in winter or the pipes will freeze and burst.* • A **pipeline** is a series of connected tubes for transporting gas, oil, or water, usually over long distances. • If something is **in the pipeline**, it is being made ready for action but has yet to be dealt with: *Twenty-eight lawsuits were filed this week, and another 200 cases are in the pipeline.*

pipe /paɪp/ *v* [T always + adv/prep] • *Hot water is piped to all the apartments from the boiler.*

piping /'paɪ·pɪŋ/ *n* [U] pipes, or a system of pipes • See also PIPING.

pipe DEVICE FOR SMOKING /paɪp/ *n* [C] a short, narrow tube with a small bowl at one end, used for smoking esp. tobacco • *My dad smoked a pipe.* • If an idea or a plan is a **pipe dream**, it is not practical or possible: *The idea of Africa becoming food self-sufficient is not a pipe dream.*

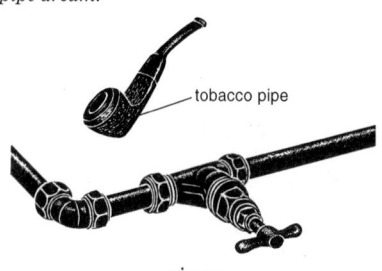

tobacco pipe

pipes

pipe MUSICAL INSTRUMENT /paɪp/ *n* [C] a musical instrument consisting of a short, narrow tube that is played by blowing through it • Pipes are also the metal or wood tubes in an ORGAN (= a large musical instrument with a keyboard) that produce sound.

□ **pipe down** /ˈpɑɪpˈdɑʊn/ *v adv* [I] *infml* to stop making noise; become quieter • *You kids better pipe down in there!*

□ **pipe up** /ˈpɑɪ·pʌp/ *v adv* [I] to speak suddenly, esp. in an excited way • *"I'll bet you dropped it," Cherry piped up.*

piping /ˈpɑɪ·pɪŋ/ *n* [U] a folded strip of cloth, often enclosing a cord, used to decorate the edges of clothes or furniture • *Contrasting fabric was used for the cushion's piping.* • See also PIPING at PIPE TUBE.

piping hot /ˈpɑɪ·pɪŋˈhɑt/ *adj* [not gradable] (of food or drinks) very hot • *I like my soup piping hot.*

pipsqueak /ˈpɪp·skwiːk/ *n* [C] *infml* a small or unimportant person • *I'm not afraid of that little pipsqueak!*

piquant /ˈpiː·kənt, piːˈkɑnt/ *adj* having a strong, slightly sour, slightly spicy taste or smell • *a piquant sauce*

pique EXCITE /piːk/ *v* [T] to excite or cause (interest) • *Labor law piqued his interest in law school.*

pique ANGER /piːk/ *n* [U] anger or annoyance • *He stormed from the room in a fit of pique.*
pique /piːk/ *v* [T] • *Something piqued him and he had words with our coach.*

piranha /pəˈrɑn·ə/ *n* [C] *pl* **piranha** or **pirhanas** a small, South American river fish with sharp teeth, that attacks and eats small animals

pirate TAKE ILLEGALLY /ˈpɑɪ·rət/ *v* [T] to take or use (someone's work) without permission, esp. by copying and then selling it • *A lot of this software is pirated.*
pirate /ˈpɑɪ·rət/ *n* [C] • *Video pirates are stealing movie company revenues.*
piracy /ˈpɑɪ·rə·si/ *n* [U] • *The agency tries to halt piracy of copyrighted recordings.*

pirate SEA THIEF /ˈpɑɪ·rət/ *n* [C] a person who sails on the sea and attacks and steals from other ships
piracy /ˈpɑɪ·rə·si/ *n* [U] the practice of attacking and stealing from ships at sea

pirouette /ˌpɪr·əˈwet/ *n* [C] a fast turn of the body on the toes or the front part of the foot, performed esp. by a BALLET dancer
pirouette /ˌpɪr·əˈwet/ *v* [I] • *Dancers pirouetted across the stage.*

Pisces /ˈpɑɪ·siːz, ˈpɪs·iːz/ *n* [C/U] *pl* **Pisces** the twelfth sign of the ZODIAC, covering the period February 19 to March 20 and represented by two fish, or a person born during this period

piss /pɪs/ *v* [I/T] *rude slang* to urinate
piss /pɪs/ *n* [C/U] *rude slang* urine, or the act of urinating

□ **piss away** *obj*, **piss** *obj* **away** /ˈ-ˈ-/ *v adv* [M] *rude slang* to waste (something) • *They pissed away the money Grandma left them.*

□ **piss off** *obj*, **piss** *obj* **off** /ˈ-ˈ-/ *v adv* [M] *rude*

slang to anger or annoy (someone) • *It pisses me off when she doesn't call.*

pissed (off) /ˈpɪst (ˈɔːf)/ *adj* [not gradable] *rude slang* • *I get pissed off when people do stupid things.*

pistachio /pəˈstæʃ·iː·oʊ/ *n* [C/U] *pl* **pistachios** an edible green nut with a hard shell • Pistachio is also a pale green color. [U]

pistol /ˈpɪs·təl/ *n* [C] a small gun which can be held in and fired from one hand

piston /ˈpɪs·tən/ *n* [C] an engine part, usually a short, solid tube or round, flat object, which moves up and down or forward and backward inside a cylinder, and causes other parts of an engine or machine to move

pit HOLE /pɪt/ *n* [C] a large hole in the ground, or a hollow in any surface • *The trash had been buried in a six-foot-deep pit.* ○ *a fire pit* • A pit is an **orchestra pit**. See at ORCHESTRA. • **The pit of** your **stomach** is the center of your body, where you feel esp. fear and anxiety: *I got a sick feeling in the pit of my stomach before the performance.* • (*infml*) If something is **the pits** it is the worst of its kind, or a very bad or unpleasant thing: *Life with kids sounds like it's just the pits, but it's not all that bad.* • A **pit (mine)** is a hole with steep sides from which natural substances, such as rocks and MINERALS, are dug.
pitted /ˈpɪt̬·əd/ *adj* (of a surface) covered with holes • *Their cars have been pitted by acid rain.*

pit SEED /pɪt/ *n* [C] a large, hard seed that grows inside some types of fruit and vegetables • *a peach/plum/cherry pit*
pitted /ˈpɪt̬·əd/ *adj* [not gradable] having the seed removed • *pitted cherries/olives*

pit REPAIR AREA /pɪt/ *n* [C] an area on the side of a TRACK on which cars race, where the cars are given fuel or repaired during a race • *The car made its second* **pit stop** (= brief stop for fuel or repairs). • A **pit stop** is also a brief stop during a car trip to get food, fuel, or use the bathroom.

□ **pit** *obj* **against** *obj* /ˈ-,-ˈ-/ *v prep* [T] to put (someone or something) in competition with (someone or something else) • *That talk show is always pitting men against women.*

pita (bread) /ˈpiːt̬·ə (ˈbred)/ *n* [C] a round or oval flat bread that is hollow and can be filled with other food

pit bull (terrier) /ˈpɪt·bʊl (ˈter·iː·ər)/ *n* [C] a type of small dog with a wide chest and short hair, known for its strength and sometimes trained to fight

pitch THROW /pɪtʃ/ *v* [T] to throw (something), esp. forcefully • *She pitched a stone into the river.*

pitch THROW BASEBALL /pɪtʃ/ *v* [I/T] (in baseball) to throw a baseball toward a player from the opposing team who tries to hit it with a baseball BAT
pitch /pɪtʃ/ *n* [C] • *Wait for a good pitch before you swing.*

pitcher /'pɪtʃ·ər/ *n* [C] a person who pitches the baseball to a BATTER • See also PITCHER.

pitch FALL /pɪtʃ/ *v* [always + adv/prep] to fall suddenly • *The bus stopped suddenly, pitching everyone forward.* [T]

pitch SOUND QUALITY /pɪtʃ/ *n* [C/U] the degree to which a sound has a high or low quality

pitch /pɪtʃ/ *v* [T] • *He pitched his voice just so, making them pay attention.*

pitch PERSUASION /pɪtʃ/ *n* [C] a speech that attempts to persuade someone to buy or do something • *a sales pitch*

pitch RAISE /pɪtʃ/ *v* [T] to raise (a tent) and fix it in place • *We pitched our tent in a sheltered area.*

pitch SLOPE /pɪtʃ/ *n* [U] the degree of slope, esp. of a roof

pitched /pɪtʃt/ *adj* [not gradable] • *a pitched roof*

pitch BLACK SUBSTANCE /pɪtʃ/ *n* [U] a thick, black, sticky substance used to make ships and roofs waterproof, and to cover cracks in roads • **Pitch-dark** means completely dark: *In winter it was already pitch-dark by 5.* • **Pitch-black** means completely black: *a moonless, pitch-black night*

pitch SPORTS FIELD /pɪtʃ/ *n* [C] *Br for* FIELD SPORTS

□**pitch in** /-'-/ *v adv* [I] to become involved in esp. something helpful • *If we all pitch in, the cleanup shouldn't take long.*

pitcher /'pɪtʃ·ər/ *n* [C] a container for liquids with a handle on one side and a shaped opening at the top of the other side for pouring • See also **pitcher** at PITCH THROW BASEBALL.

pitchfork /'pɪtʃ·fɔːrk/ *n* [C] a tool with a long handle and two or three large points used for moving HAY (= cut dried grass) or STRAW (= cut dried stems of crops)

pitfall /'pɪt·fɔːl/ *n* [C] an unexpected danger or difficulty • *Who knows what kind of pitfalls they're going to run into.*

pithy /'pɪθ·i/ *adj* (of speech or writing) brief and full of meaning • *pithy comments* ○ *a pithy quote*

pittance /'pɪt·əns/ *n* [C usually sing] a very small amount of money • *He couldn't live on the pittance his mother sent him.*

pity /'pɪt·i/ *n* [U] sympathy and understanding for someone else's suffering or troubles • *She did not want his pity.* • If something is described as a pity, it is a cause for regret: *It's a pity you can't come to the party.*

pity /'pɪt·i/ *v* [T] • *I pity people who have to work with statistics.*

pitiful /'pɪt·ɪ·fəl/, **pitiable** /'pɪt·iː·ə·bəl/ *adj* • *She made a pitiful plea for acceptance.* • Something described as pitiful is not considered to be satisfactory or deserving of respect: *He's a bum, a pitiful excuse for a human being.*

pitifully /'pɪt·ɪ·fə·li, -fli/, **pitiably** /'pɪt·iː·ə·bli/ *adv* [not gradable] • *I was pitifully ill-informed.*

pitiless /'pɪt·ɪ·ləs/ *adj* [not gradable] having or showing no pity • *a pitiless dictator*

pivot /'pɪv·ət/ *n* [C] a fixed point supporting something which turns or balances, or a person or thing on which something else depends • *Boston was the pivot of his emotional and intellectual life.*

pivot /'pɪv·ət/ *v* [I/T] **-tt-** to turn or twist • *She pivots her left foot.* [T] ○ *He pivoted on his heels and headed out.* [I] ○ *Future deals will pivot on easing commercial conflicts* (= they will depend on this). [I]

pivotal /'pɪv·ət·ʰl/ *adj* [not gradable] important because other things depend on it • *She played a pivotal role in the civil rights movement.*

pixel /'pɪk·səl/ *n* [C] *specialized* the smallest unit of an image on a television or computer screen

pixie /'pɪk·si/ *n* [C] (esp. in children's stories) a small, imaginary person

pizazz, pizzazz /pɪ'zæz/ *n* [U] *infml approving* excitement, energy, or style • *I want food that's low in fat but that has some pizazz.*

pizza /'piːt·sə/ *n* [C/U] a flat, usually round bread that is baked covered with TOMATO sauce, cheese, and often pieces of vegetables or meat • *a slice of pizza* [U] ○ *I phoned for a pizza.* [C]

pj's /'piː·jeɪz/ *pl n infml* PAJAMAS

placard /'plæk·ərd, -ɑrd/ *n* [C] a notice or sign hung in a public place or carried by people • *Foley's placard read, "Go home."*

placate /'pleɪ·keɪt, 'plæk·eɪt/ *v* [T] to stop (someone) from feeling angry • *She's more easily placated then her husband.*

place AREA /pleɪs/ *n* [C] an area, a building, or a city, town, or village • *Airports are usually busy places.* ○ *Larchmont is a nice place to live.* • Your place is your home: *We can meet at my place.* • (*slightly fml*) A place is also an area or building used for a specific purpose: a place of worship/business

place POSITION /pleɪs/ *n* [C] a particular position • *That's the best place for the piano.* ○ *The librarian put the book back in its place* (= in the right position). • A place is also a space for a person, as in a theater, at a table, or in a line: *Will you hold my place in line for a minute?* • If plans are **in place**, they have been made: *I think everything's in place for the wedding.* • A **place in the sun** is a position of importance: *When will Nigeria take its proper place in the sun?* • A **place mat** is a piece of cloth, paper, or plastic on a table on which someone's plate and eating utensils are put.

place /pleɪs/ *v* [T] • *Flowers had been placed on all the tables.*

placement /'pleɪ·smənt/ *n* [U] • *The placement of the furniture makes it hard to walk around.*

place RANK /pleɪs/ *n* [C] the rank someone or something has • *Our team finished in second place.*

place /pleɪs/ v [I] • *She placed high on the tests.*

placement /'pleɪ·smənt/ n [U] • *Churches have the social placement to be influential in politics.*

place JOB /pleɪs/ n [C] a job, or acceptance at a school or college • *Ann just got a place at Yale.*

place /pleɪs/ v [T] • *The agency is usually able to place temporary workers for the summer.*

placement /'pleɪ·smənt/ n [U] • *There are students for whom this school is not the best possible placement.* • A **placement test** measures someone's ability in order to put them in a particular class or group.

place RECOGNIZE /pleɪs/ v [T] to recognize (someone or something) because of memory or past experience • *She looks familiar, but I can't place her.*

place DUTY /pleɪs/ n [U] a person's duty or position of authority • *It's not your place to tell me what to do.* [+ to infinitive]

place PUT /pleɪs/ v [T] to put (someone) in a situation • *They placed him in a nursing home.* ○ *She was placed under arrest.*

place INVEST /pleɪs/ v [T] to invest or BET (= risk) money • *He placed a bet on his favorite horse.*

place GIVE /pleɪs/ v [T] to give (an order) to a supplier • *I placed an order for three CDs.*

placebo /plə'siː·boʊ/ n [C] pl **placebos** a substance that is not medicine, but that is given to someone who is told that it is a medicine, used to test the effect of a drug or to please a patient

placenta /plə'sent·ə/ n [C] pl **placentas** an organ that develops inside the uterus of a pregnant woman or animal and provides food for the developing baby

placid /'plæs·əd/ adj calm and peaceful • *a placid child* ○ *The placid lake was perfect for canoeing.*

plagiarize /'pleɪ·dʒə,raɪz/ v [I/T] to use (another person's idea or a part of their work) and pretend that it is your own

plagiarism /'pleɪ·dʒə,rɪz·əm/ n [U] • *She's been accused of plagiarism.*

plague CAUSE DIFFICULTY /pleɪɡ/ v [T] to cause (someone or something) difficulty or suffering, esp. repeatedly or continually • *Financial problems have been plaguing the company.* ○ *That pain in my shoulder is plaguing me again.*

plague DISEASE /pleɪɡ/ n [C/U] a serious disease which kills many people • A plague is also a large number of insects or animals which cause damage or unpleasant conditions in an area: *Trees throughout the Northeast are being attacked by a plague of gypsy moths.* [C]

plaid /plæd/ n [U] a pattern of different colored straight lines crossing each other at 90° angles, or a cloth with this pattern

plain WITH NOTHING ADDED /pleɪn/ adj [-er/-est only] not decorated in any way; with nothing

added • *The catalog was sent in a plain brown envelope.* ○ *The food is pretty plain* (= prepared simply and without strong flavors)*, but there's lots of it.* • Someone dressed in **plainclothes** is not wearing the uniform that is connected with their job: *plainclothes detectives/policemen*

plainly /'pleɪn·li/ adv • *a plainly furnished room*

plain CLEAR /pleɪn/ adj [-er/-est only] obvious, or clear and easy to see or understand; not complicated • *A group of wild horses was in plain view* (= We could see them clearly)*.* ○ *Why can't they write these instructions in plain English?*

plain /pleɪn/ adv [not gradable] infml • *It was just plain stupid to give him your telephone number.*

plainly /'pleɪn·li/ adv clearly or obviously • *Plainly, the new tax rules are a major headache.*

plain NOT BEAUTIFUL /pleɪn/ adj [-er/-est only] (esp. of a woman or girl) not beautiful • *She always thought of herself as plain, and as a result she was extremely shy.*

plain LAND /pleɪn/ n [C usually pl] a large area of flat land • *A number of paintings by Western artists show Indian settlements in the plains.*

plaintiff /'pleɪnt·əf/ n [C] law a person who accuses someone else in a law case of having done something illegal that has harmed them • Compare **defendant** at DEFEND PROTECT

plaintive /'pleɪnt·ɪv/ adj (esp. of a sound) having a sad quality • *I love the plaintive sound of the bagpipes.*

plait /pleɪt, plæt/ v, n esp. Br for BRAID HAIR

plan METHOD /plæn/ n [C/U] a method for doing or achieving something, usually involving a series of actions or stages, or something you have arranged to do • *The financial plan calls for growth of 5% next year.* [C] ○ *They had plans to have dinner at a local restaurant.* [C] • A plan is also an arrangement for investment: *a pension/savings plan* [C] • If something goes according to plan, it happens the way you wanted it to: *Producing a new movie rarely goes exactly according to plan.* [U]

plan /plæn/ v [I/T] **-nn-** to think about and decide on a method for doing or achieving (something) • *She's planning to visit her sister in Australia next year.* [+ to infinitive] ○ *He planned on taking his vacation in July.* [I always + adv/prep] ○ *You've got to plan ahead and save your money for your retirement.* [I always + adv/prep]

plan MAP /plæn/ n [C] a drawing that shows the shape, size, and position of important details of a building or other structure, or of objects within it • *The floor plan showed us exactly where everyone's office would be.*

plan /plæn/ v [T] **-nn-** • *Few American cities*

were planned—they just grew larger in all directions.

planner /'plæn·ər/ *n* [C] a person whose job is to plan something, esp. how land in a particular area is to be used and what should be built on it • *a city planner* ◦ *an urban planner*

plane AIRCRAFT /pleɪn/ *n* [C] a vehicle that is designed for air travel and that has wings and one or more engines • *Shelley's plane is due in at 10, but it's a half-hour late.*

plane LEVEL /pleɪn/ *n* [C] a level or standard • *Once we got a new financial manager, our business meetings were conducted on a much higher plane.*

plane TOOL /pleɪn/ *n* [C] a tool with a blade in a flat surface that is rubbed against wood to cut away rough parts and make it smooth

planet /'plæn·ət/ *n* [C] a large, spherical mass of matter, such as the earth or Mars, that moves in a circular path around the sun or another star

planetarium /ˌplæn·ə'ter·iː·əm/ *n* [C] a building specially equipped to show images of the stars in the sky and other objects in space on a curved ceiling

plank FLAT PIECE /plæŋk/ *n* [C] a long, flat piece of wood or other material, esp. one wide enough and strong enough to walk on • *They walked across the creaky, wooden-plank floor of the old house.*

plank PRINCIPLE /plæŋk/ *n* [C] an important principle on which the activities of a political or other group are based • *He prepared the peace plank in the Democrats' 1864 presidential platform.*

plant LIVING THING /plænt/ *n* [C] a living thing that usually produces seeds and typically has a stem, leaves, roots, and sometimes flowers • *We brought a house plant as a gift when we spent the weekend with our friend Sylvia.*

plant /plænt/ *v* [T] to put (a seed or plant) into the ground or into a container of earth so that it will grow • *We've planted some trees along the back of our property.*

planter /'plænt·ər/ *n* [C] a large container in which esp. decorative plants are grown • *The sidewalk is lined with planters overflowing with flowers.* • A planter is also someone who owns a PLANTATION (= large farm in a hot part of the world).

plant PUT /plænt/ *v* [T always + adv/prep] to put (something) firmly in a particular place • *He planted a kiss on her forehead.* • To plant an idea or story is to cause it to exist: *Defense lawyers try to plant doubts in the minds of the jurors about what actually happened.*

plant PUT SECRETLY /plænt/ *v* [T] to put (something or someone) in a position secretly, esp. in order to deceive • *She insisted that the drugs had been planted in her car by the police.*

plant FACTORY /plænt/ *n* [C] a factory and the machinery in it used to produce or process something • *a manufacturing plant*

plantain /'plænt·ən/ *n* [C] a fruit of the hotter regions that looks like a BANANA and is usually cooked before being eaten

plantation /plæn'teɪ·ʃən/ *n* [C] a large farm, esp. in a hot part of the world, on which a particular crop is grown • *a coffee/rubber plantation*

plaque /plæk/ *n* [C] a flat sign usually made to be permanent and attached to a wall or other surface • *A bronze plaque on the wall informed us that the house had been built in 1830.*

plasma /'plæz·mə/ *n* [U] *specialized* the liquid part of blood that carries the blood cells

plaster WALL COVERING /'plæs·tər/ *n* [U] a substance that is used esp. for spreading on walls and ceilings because it makes a smooth, hard surface after it dries • **Plaster of Paris** is a mixture of a white powder and water that becomes hard quickly as it dries and is used esp. to make CASTS (= protective coverings) for broken bones or to make copies of objects such as statues.

plaster /'plæs·tər/ *v* [T] • *Someone will come in tomorrow to plaster the wall where the plumber had to make a hole.* • (*infml*) To plaster a surface or an object with something is to cover it completely or thickly: *She has plastered her bedroom walls with posters of pop singers.*

plaster INJURY PROTECTION /'plæs·tər/ *n* [C] *Br for* BAND-AID

plastered /'plæs·tərd/ *adj slang* very drunk • *They got plastered.*

plastic MATERIAL /'plæs·tɪk/ *n* [C/U] a chemically made material that is widely used because it is strong, light in weight, hard, and cheap to produce, and because when it is being made it can be shaped into many different forms for different uses • *The cover of the book is actually made of plastic, though it looks like cloth.* [U] ◦ *Plastics can be produced in the form of fibers or sheets and are used in building materials as well as in consumer goods.* [C]

plastic /'plæs·tɪk/ *adj* [not gradable] • *a plastic bag/bottle/container*

plastic SOFT /'plæs·tɪk/ *adj* soft enough to be shaped into different forms • *Clay is a plastic material.* • **Plastic surgery** is the medical operations used to bring a damaged or badly formed area of skin or bone back to a better condition, or to improve a person's appearance.

plate DISH /pleɪt/ *n* [C] a flat dish on which food is served or from which it is eaten • A plate (also **plateful**) is an amount of food on a plate: *Dominic helped himself to a plate of spaghetti.*

plate FLAT PIECE /pleɪt/ *n* [C] a flat piece of something that is hard, does not bend, and is usually used to cover something • *Large, metal plates covered the trench in the roadway.* • **Plate glass** is large sheets of glass used esp. as windows and doors in stores and offices: *a plate-glass window*

plate ADD THIN LAYER /pleɪt/ *v* [T] to cover (a metal object) with a thin layer of another metal, esp. gold or silver • *gold plated*

plate /pleɪt/ *n* [U] • *The knives and forks are silver plate.*

plateau /plæ'toʊ/ *n* [C] a large, flat area of land that is higher than the land around it • A plateau is also a period during which there are no big changes: *The crime rate in the city reached a plateau in the 1980s and then declined.*

plateau /plæ'toʊ/ *v* [I] to reach a level and stay there, rather than rising or falling • *The population increase is expected to plateau in the year 2007.*

platform /'plæt·fɔːrm/ *n* [C] a flat, raised area or structure • *We waited on the platform for the train to arrive from Boston.* • A politician's or political party's platform is the things they say they believe in and that they will achieve if they are elected: *He campaigned on a platform of reducing taxes and cutting the costs of government.*

platinum /'plæt·ᵊn·əm/ *n* [U] a valuable metal that is silver in color, does not react easily with other elements, and is used in jewelry and in industry

platitude /'plæt·ə,tuːd/ *n* [C] a statement that has been repeated so often that it is meaningless • *They nodded at every platitude about making sacrifices today for a better tomorrow.*

platonic /plə'tɑn·ɪk/ *adj* (of a relationship or emotion) affectionate but not sexual • *He insisted that his relationship with his friend's wife had always been platonic.*

platoon /plə'tuːn/ *n* [C] a military unit consisting of a group of about 20 soldiers who are all members of a COMPANY

platter /'plæt·ər/ *n* [C] a large plate used for serving food • In a restaurant, a platter is a dish with a variety of foods on it: *I'd like the seafood platter, please.*

plaudit /'plɔːd·ət/ *n* [C usually pl] *fml* an expression of approval; praise • *She won plaudits for her toughness during tense labor negotiations.*

plausible /'plɔː·zə·bəl/ *adj* possibly true; able to be believed • *a plausible excuse/explanation*

play ENJOY /pleɪ/ *v* [I] to spend time doing something enjoyable or amusing • *The children spent the afternoon playing.* • To **play hooky/hookey** is to stay away from school without permission: *They played hooky and went fishing.* • To **play with** something is to handle it without giving it your attention: *Stop playing with your food.* • *I'm warning you that if you get mixed up with him, you're* **playing with fire** (= doing something very dangerous).

play /pleɪ/ *n* [U] • *Play is an important educational activity for preschool children.* • A **playground** is an outside area designed for children to play in, esp. at a school: *a school*

playground • A **playmate** is a friend, esp. another child, with whom a child often plays: *We were childhood playmates.* • A **playpen** is a small structure with bars or a net around the sides but open at the top, within which a baby can be left to play. • A **play on words** is an amusing use of a word with more than one meaning. • A **plaything** is a child's toy. • *(fig.)* A **plaything** is also a person or thing used only for someone's amusement: *Fancy cars and diamond jewelry were the playthings of the rich.*

playful /'pleɪ·fəl/ *adj* done as a form of play rather than intended seriously, or wanting to have a good time and not feeling serious • *She gave him a playful push.* ○ *My mother was in a playful mood that day.*

play COMPETE /pleɪ/ *v* [I/T] to take part in (a game or other organized activity) • *He loves playing football.* [T] ○ *What team does she play for?* [I] • If you play a person or team, you compete against them: *We're going to the stadium to see New York play Chicago.* [T] • If you play the ball or a shot, you hit or kick the ball: *In golf, you have to take time to decide how to play difficult shots.* [T] • In a card game, to play a card is to choose it from the ones you are holding and put it down on the table. [T] • *(infml)* To **play ball** is to agree to work with or help someone in the way they have suggested: *The family wanted a full-time nurse but the insurance company refused to play ball.* • *If you* **play your cards right** (= act wisely), *you could make a lot of money out of this.* • *(infml)* To **play hardball** is to be determined to get what you want, even if you have to behave in an unpleasant, threatening way: *He's a nice guy but he can play hardball when he has to.* • *The snowstorm is really* **playing havoc with** *rush-hour traffic* (= making it much more difficult or confusing). • A **playing card** is one of a set of 52 small, rectangular pieces of stiffened paper, each with a number or face and one of four signs printed on it, used in games. • A **playing field** is an open, outside area for sports. • A **playing field** is also an area within which there is competition: *All we ask is that there be a level playing field for everyone bidding for the work.* • **Playoffs** are a series of games played after the regular season to decide which teams will advance to play for the CHAMPIONSHIP (= compete to be recognized as the best team): *the basketball playoffs* ○ *a playoff game*

play /pleɪ/ *n* • *Play was suspended because of a heavy rainstorm.* [U] • If a ball or something else is in play, it is in a position where it can be used as part of the regular action in a game or sport, and if it is out of play, it is not in such a position: *She put the ball in play in midfield.* [U] • In sports, a play can also be a particular action or a plan for a specific set of actions:

The school football team has been practicing new plays all week. [C]

player /'pleɪ·ər/ *n* [C] someone who takes part in a sport or game • *This basketball team has a lot of talented players.* ○ (*fig.*) *The company is one of the leading players* (= organizations taking part) *in the deal.*

play ACT /pleɪ/ *v* [I/T] to perform as (a character) in a play or movie, or (of a performance) to be shown • *She played the part of a beautiful and brilliant scientist.* [T] ○ *What's playing at* (= being shown at) *the local movie theaters?* [I] • To play is also to behave or pretend in a particular way, esp. to produce an effect or result: *Don't play dumb with me* (= pretend you don't know anything)—*you know very well what happened!* • To play can mean to influence or have an effect on: *The president denied that politics played any part in his decision to appoint a woman to the Supreme Court.* • *"I can't tell you what to expect." "Don't worry, I'll* **play it by ear** (= decide what to do when I see what is happening, rather than planning in advance)." • *Let's* **play it safe** (= be careful) *and allow an extra ten minutes to get there.* • To **play a joke/trick on** someone is to deceive them for amusement or in order to get an advantage: *She loves to play jokes on her friends.*

play /pleɪ/ *n* [C] a story that is intended to be acted out before people who have come to see it • *She starred in many Broadway plays in her career.* • A **playhouse** is a theater. • A **playwright** is a person who writes plays.

play PRODUCE SOUNDS / PICTURES /pleɪ/ *v* [I/T] to perform (music) on (an instrument), or to cause (something that produces sound or a picture) to operate • *She plays (the piano) brilliantly.* [I/T] ○ *I was just playing my stereo.* [T]

player /'pleɪ·ər/ *n* [C] someone who plays a musical instrument • *a cello/flute player* • A player is also a machine: *a CD/record player*

play RISK MONEY /pleɪ/ *v* [T] to risk money, esp. on the results of (races or business deals), hoping to win money • *He plays the stock market.*

□ **play around** /ˌ--'-/ *v adv* [I] to have a sexual relationship with someone other than your husband, wife, or main partner

□ **play back** *obj*, **play** *obj* **back** /'-'-/ *v adv* [M] to hear or see (a sound recording or film) that has been previously recorded • *She taped the Olympic speed skating final so that she could play it back later.*

□ **play down** *obj*, **play** *obj* **down** /'-'-/ *v adv* [M] to make (something) seem less important than or not as bad as it really is • *The doctor tried to play down the seriousness of my father's illness, but we weren't fooled.*

□ **play up** *obj*, **play** *obj* **up** /'-'-/ *v adv* [M] to make (something) seem more important or better than it really is, esp. to get an advantage • *The report plays up the benefits of the plan, but doesn't say much about the costs.*

playboy /'pleɪ·bɔɪ/ *n* [C] a rich man who spends his time and money on luxuries and a life of pleasure, esp. with women

playful /'pleɪ·fəl/ *adj* • See at PLAY ENJOY.

plaza /'plæz·ə, 'plɑz·ə/ *n* [C] an open, public area in a city or town, or a group of buildings with stores, often including an open, public area • *New York City's Rockefeller Plaza*

plea REQUEST /pliː/ *n* [C] an urgent and emotional request • *The president made a strong plea to Congress to ban semiautomatic weapons as part of the crime bill.*

plea STATEMENT /pliː/ *n* [C] *law* the answer that a person gives in court to the accusation that they have committed a crime • *He received a sentence of 25 years to life for his guilty plea to second-degree murder.* • A **plea bargain** is an agreement to allow someone who has been accused of a crime to admit that they are guilty of a less serious crime in order to avoid being tried for the more serious one. • **Plea bargaining** is the legal discussion that may result in a plea bargain.

plead REQUEST /pliːd/ *v* [I] *past* **pleaded** or **pled** /pled/ to make an urgent, emotional statement or request for something • *She appeared on television to plead with the kidnappers to release her husband.*

plead (*obj*) STATE /pliːd/ *v past* **pleaded** or **pled** /pled/ *fml* to give (an official answer) to an accusation in a law court • *to plead guilty/ not guilty* [T]

pleasant /'plez·ənt/ *adj* enjoyable or attractive, or (of a person) friendly and easy to like • *We spent a pleasant afternoon at the beach.* ○ *She had a pleasant manner and was popular with everyone.*

pleasantly /'plez·ənt·li/ *adv* • *Mohammed was pleasantly surprised to get a B in history.*

pleasantry /'plez·ən·tri/ *n* [C usually pl] *slightly fml* a polite remark, usually made by people when they first meet to show they are friendly • *The officials shook hands and exchanged pleasantries about the weather before getting down to business.*

please POLITE REQUEST /pliːz/ *exclamation* commonly used in order to make a request more polite, or, sometimes, to make it stronger or urgent • *Could I please have some ketchup for my hamburger?* ○ *Please be sure to take all your personal belongings when you leave the train.* ○ *Please do as I say and don't ask questions.* ○ *"Would you like some more salad?" "Please* (= yes, I would)."

please MAKE HAPPY /pliːz/ *v* [I/T] to make (someone) feel happy or satisfied, or to give (someone) pleasure • *He did what he could to please her, but she was hard to please.* [I/T] ○ *I'm pleased to report that sales have increased by 15%.* [T] ○ *She'll listen to what you say, but in the end she'll do as/what she pleases* (= what she wants to do). [I]

pleased /pliːzd/ *adj* happy or satisfied • *a*

pleased expression ○ *Mom was not pleased when she saw my grades.* • A person may say **(I'm) pleased to meet you** as a polite way of greeting someone they meet for the first time. LP GREETINGS

pleasing /'pliː·zɪŋ/ *adj* giving a feeling of satisfaction or enjoyment • *a pleasing performance/design*

pleasure /'pleʒ·ər/ *n* [C/U] a feeling of enjoyment or satisfaction, or something that produces this feeling • *The boy's visits gave his grandparents a great deal of pleasure.* [U] ○ *It's always a pleasure to see you.* [C usually sing]

pleasurable /'pleʒ·ə·rə·bəl/ *adj slightly fml* pleasant • *The hotels were not so good, but on the whole the trip was a pleasurable experience.*

pleat /pliːt/ *n* [C] a flat, usually narrow, fold made in a piece of cloth by pressing or sewing two parts of the cloth together

pleated /'pliːt̬·əd/ *adj* • *a pleated skirt*

pleated skirt

pled /pled/ *past simple and past participle of* PLEAD

pledge /pledʒ/ *n* [C] a formal promise, or something that is given as a sign that you will keep a promise • *a pledge of friendship* ○ *The telethon raised $150,000 in pledges for leukemia research.* • The **pledge of allegiance** is a promise to be loyal to the US that is said esp. by children at school at the start of each day.

pledge /pledʒ/ *v* • *Many countries have pledged food and funds to aid the region.* [T] ○ *The police pledged to arrest those responsible.* [+ *to* infinitive]

plenary /'pliː·nə·ri, 'plen·ə-/ *adj* [not gradable] *slightly fml* having all the members of a group or organization present • *a plenary session*

plenty /'plent̬·i/ *n* [U] an amount or supply that is enough or more than enough, or a large number or amount • *This car has plenty of power.* ○ *I didn't eat them all—there's plenty left for you.* ○ (*infml*) *This car cost me plenty* (= a lot of money).

plenty /'plent̬·i/ *adv* [not gradable] *infml* • *He was plenty mad.* • *Have another sandwich—there's* **plenty more where** *that* **came from** (= a lot more available).

plentiful /'plent̬·ɪ·fəl/ *adj* • *Strawberries are in plentiful supply this year.*

plethora /'pleθ·ə·rə/ *n* [U] a very large

amount of something, esp. a larger amount than you need, want, or can deal with • *a plethora of excuses/agencies/diet books*

pliable /'plaɪ·ə·bəl/, **pliant** /'plaɪ·ənt/ *adj* (of a substance) easily bent without breaking or cracking, or (of a person) easily influenced or controlled by others • *soft, pliable materials* ○ *A more pliant leader would compromise.*

pliers /'plaɪ·ərz/ *pl n* a small tool used for pulling, holding, or cutting that has two handles that you press together in order to bring together two specially shaped pieces of metal at the other end

plight /plaɪt/ *n* [C usually sing] an unpleasant condition, esp. a serious, sad, or difficult one • *My problems aren't much compared with the plight of a single mother.*

plod WALK /plɑd/ *v* [I always + adv/prep] **-dd-** to walk taking slow steps as if your feet are heavy • *Danny plodded through the store behind his wife.*

plod WORK /plɑd/ *v* [I always + adv/prep] **-dd-** to work or do something slowly and continuously in a tiring or boring way • *I sat at my desk, plodded ahead doggedly, and finished the paper before noon.*

plodding /'plɑd·ɪŋ/ *adj* • *I'll try not to bore you with a lot of plodding details.*

plop SOUND /plɑp/ *n* [C] a soft sound like that of something dropping lightly into a liquid

plop PUT /plɑp/ *v* [always + adv/prep] **-pp-** to sit down or land heavily, or to put (something) down heavily without taking care • *He came over and plopped down next to me.* [I] ○ *He plopped the sandwich into the pan.* [T]

plot SECRET PLAN /plɑt/ *n* [C] a secret plan to do something that is wrong, harmful, or illegal • *Okami discovered a plot to assassinate the prince.*

plot /plɑt/ *v* **-tt-** • *The officers were accused of plotting the overthrow of the government.* [T] ○ *They were plotting to blow up the church.* [+ *to* infinitive]

plotter /'plɑt̬·ər/ *n* [C] • *One of the coup plotters was charged with treason.*

plot STORY /plɑt/ *n* [C] the plan or main story of a book, film, play, etc. • *The novel has a complicated plot that is sometimes difficult to follow.*

plot MARK /plɑt/ *v* [T] **-tt-** to mark or draw (lines showing a route) on a piece of paper or a map, or to put (numbers) on a piece of paper to show how amounts are related • *He plotted a course between Hawaii and Tahiti.* ○ *We measured and plotted the amounts of chemicals that were released in the countryside.*

plot GROUND /plɑt/ *n* [C] a small piece of land that has been marked or measured for a particular purpose • *a garden plot*

plow TOOL /plaʊ/ *n* [C] a large farming tool with blades that dig into the earth, or a large, curved blade fixed to the front of a vehicle that moves snow or sand

plow /plaʊ/ v [I/T] • *It rained so much I thought I'd have to plow the crops under.* [T] ○ *I won't be able to drive to the store until they plow.* [I]

plow FORCE /plaʊ/ v [always + adv/prep] to force (your way), or to advance slowly although it is difficult • *His truck left the road and plowed through some small trees.* [I] ○ *He picked the book up again and plowed his way through two more chapters.* [T]

plow INVEST /plaʊ/ v [T always + adv/prep] to invest (money) in a business, esp. to help make it successful or in order to make more money • *If we're hit by higher taxes, we'll have a little less to plow back into the business.*

ploy /plɔɪ/ n [C] something that is done or said, often dishonestly, in order to get an advantage; a trick • *a marketing ploy*

pluck REMOVE /plʌk/ v [T] to remove (something), esp. with a sudden movement • *Astronauts plan to use the shuttle's robot arm to pluck the satellite out of space.* • If you pluck something, you remove hair or feathers from it by pulling: *She plucked her eyebrows.* ○ *I don't think I could pluck a chicken.*

pluck BRAVERY /plʌk/ n [U] bravery and a strong desire to succeed • *Her 80-plus years have not dulled her pluck.*

plucky /ˈplʌk·i/ adj brave • *Terriers are plucky little dogs with independent spirits and reckless courage.*

pluck PULL AT /plʌk/ v [I/T] to pull at (something) with your fingers and then release it • *Jenkins's idea of swinging is plucking violins.* [T] ○ *(fig.) Her stories are designed to pluck at your heartstrings.* [I]

plug ELECTRICAL DEVICE /plʌg/ n [C] a small plastic or rubber device with metal pins that connects the end of a wire on a piece of electrical equipment to a supply of electricity • A plug is also a **spark plug**. See at SPARK. • A **plug-in** device is one that can be fitted into a machine, esp. a computer. • PIC OUTLET

plug /plʌg/ v [I/T] **-gg-** • *All you have to do is plug in the computer.* [M] ○ *I'd like to plug the stereo into that outlet.* [T] ○ *These systems plug into TV sets and run games.* [I]

plug HOLE BLOCK /plʌg/ n [C] a small piece of esp. rubber or plastic that fits into a hole in order to block it • *I was trying to fill the bathtub, but Matthew kept pulling out the plug.*

plug /plʌg/ v [T] **-gg-** • *You'll have to plug (up) the leak in that pipe.* [T/M]

plug ADVERTISE /plʌg/ v [T] **-gg-** to mention (esp. a product or service) on a radio or television program or in print in order to praise or advertise it

plug /plʌg/ n [C] • *He took the opportunity to put in a plug for his new book.*

plug SHOOT /plʌg/ v [T] **-gg-** slang to shoot (someone) with a gun

□**plug away** /ˈ--ˈ-/ v adv [I] to keep working hard in a determined way, esp. at something

that you find difficult • *She's been plugging away at that novel for years.*

plum FRUIT /plʌm/ n [C] a small, round fruit with a smooth, usually red-purple skin, sweet flesh, and a single large seed

plum SOMETHING GOOD /plʌm/ n [C] something that is very good and worth having

plum /plʌm/ adj [not gradable] • *Senior staff members get all the plum assignments.*

plumbing /ˈplʌm·ɪŋ/ n [U] the system of pipes and other devices that carry water in a building • *bathroom plumbing* • PIC PIPES

plumber /ˈplʌm·ər/ n [C] someone whose job is to supply, connect, and repair water pipes and devices

plume /pluːm/ n [C] a long, large feather • *She wore a hat with a tall white plume.* • A plume of something like smoke, steam, or dust is a long mass of it that rises up into the sky: *A black plume of smoke rose from the ship.*

plumage /ˈpluː·mɪdʒ/ n [U] the feathers that cover a bird • *a parrot with bright plumage*

plummet /ˈplʌm·ət/ v [I] to fall very quickly and suddenly • *Temperatures plummeted last night.* ○ *The parachute failed to open and he plummeted to the ground.*

plump /plʌmp/ adj [-er/-est only] having a soft, rounded shape; slightly fat • *plump hands* ○ *a plump, middle-aged woman* ○ *The berries are plump and juicy.*

plump /plʌmp/ v [T] • *The nurse plumped (up) the pillows* (= shook them to make them bigger and softer). [T/M]

□**plump for** /ˈ--ˈ-/ v prep [T] infml to support (someone or something) enthusiastically • *Marcy had been writing campaign speeches and plumping for McCarthy since December.*

plunder /ˈplʌn·dər/ v [I/T] to steal goods forcefully from a place, esp. during a war or an attack • *They raped, plundered, and slaughtered.* [I] ○ *(fig.) He plundered* (= took from) *his ballet scores in writing his later operas.* [T]

plunder /ˈplʌn·dər/ n [U] • *We met after school and divided our plunder so each boy would have about the same amount.*

plunge /plʌndʒ/ v [I/T] to move or fall suddenly forward or down, esp. into water, or to push or throw (something) forcefully into something else • *Her car plunged off the cliff.* [I] ○ *He plunged into the crowd, smiling and shaking hands.* [I] ○ *She plunged the knife into her assailant's arm.* [T always + adv/prep] • If a value or price plunges, it suddenly becomes less: *Rumors on Wall Street have caused stock prices to plunge.* [I] • If a person or group plunges into an activity, or a place plunges into a condition, it suddenly experiences it: *The US was in danger of plunging into war with Russia.* [I always + adv/prep] ○ *The storm cut power lines, plunging the town into darkness.* [T always + adv/prep]

plunge /plʌndʒ/ n [C] • *A tree broke his plunge downhill.* ○ *The plunge of the Mexican peso* *against the US dollar has been tough on investors.*

plunger /ˈplʌn·dʒər/ *n* [C] a device consisting of a cup-shaped piece of rubber on the end of a stick, used to remove substances blocking a pipe, esp. in a kitchen or bathroom

plunk PUT /plʌŋk/ *v* [T always + adv/prep] to put (something) down heavily or suddenly • *She plunked the trashcan down in the driveway.* [M] ∘ *He returned to the bar and plunked his butt on the counter.* • If you plunk money down, you pay it: *She plunked down most of her savings to buy the house.* [M]

plunk SOUND /plʌŋk/ *n* [U] a sound like that made when a hollow object is dropped • *The stone dropped in the lake with a satisfying plunk.*

pluperfect /pluˈpɜr·fɪkt/ *n, adj specialized* **past perfect,** see at PAST GRAMMAR

plural /ˈplʊr·əl/ *adj* [not gradable] *specialized* (in grammar) being the form of a word used to talk about more than one thing • *a plural verb* ∘ *"Cats" and "cattle" are plural nouns.* • Compare SINGULAR GRAMMAR.

plural /ˈplʊr·əl/ *n* [C/U] *specialized* • *"Geese" is the plural of "goose."* [U]

pluralize /ˈplʊr·əˌlaɪz/ *v* [T] *specialized* to make (a word) plural in form • *Certain nouns, such as "information," cannot be pluralized.*

pluralism /ˈplʊr·əˌlɪz·əm/ *n* [U] the existence of people of different races, religious beliefs, and cultures within the same society, or the belief that this is a good thing • *religious pluralism* ∘ *political pluralism*

pluralistic /ˌplʊr·əˈlɪs·tɪk/, **pluralist** /ˈplʊr·ə·lɪst/ *adj* • *the pluralistic American system*

plurality /plʊˈræl·əṭ·i/ *n* [C/U] (in elections involving three or more people) the difference between the number of votes received by the winner and that received by the person who is second, or a number of votes or places in a legislature that is more than any other party has but less than half the total number • *Jenson won by a plurality of 2000 votes over her nearest rival.* [C]

plus ADDITION /plʌs/, *symbol* **+** *prep* with the ad-

dition of, or and in addition • *Six plus four is ten.* ∘ *That will be $16.99, plus tax.*

plus /plʌs/, *symbol* **+** *adj* [not gradable] • *Those cars cost $30,000 plus* (= more than that amount). ∘ *They earn $100 an hour, plus or minus 10%.* • A mark such as B-plus (B+) or C-plus (C+) given to a student's work means that the work is slightly better than if it were given the B or C mark. • A **plus sign** is the symbol +.

plus /plʌs/ *conjunction* and also • *The four of us, plus my son's girlfriend, went out to dinner.*

plus ADVANTAGE /plʌs/ *n* [C] *pl* **pluses** or **plusses** an advantage or a good feature • *Your teaching experience will be a plus in this job.*

plush LUXURIOUS /plʌʃ/ *adj* [-er/-est only] expensive, comfortable, and of high quality; luxurious • *a plush hotel room*

plush CLOTH /plʌʃ/ *n* [U] thick, soft cloth, with a surface like short fur, that is used esp. for covering furniture

Pluto /ˈpluː·t̬oʊ/ *n* [U] the planet ninth in order of distance from the sun, after Neptune

plutonium /pluˈtoʊ·ni·əm/ *n* [U] a metallic element that is used esp. as a fuel in the production of nuclear power, and in nuclear weapons

ply LAYER /plaɪ/ *n* [U] a layer of something such as wood or paper, or a thread that is wrapped with other threads to form YARN (= wool cord) or rope • *two-ply facial tissue* • **Plywood** (also **ply**) is a wooden sheet made of several thin layers of wood glued together: *plywood bookshelves*

ply WORK /plaɪ/ *v* [T] to work at (something) regularly • *Franklin Square Park was a place where prostitutes plied their trade and drug dealers sold their wares.*

ply TRAVEL /plaɪ/ *v* [I/T] to travel over (distances) regularly by boat or other form of transport • *Large numbers of vessels plied the waters between New York and Cape Hatteras.* [T]

▫**ply** *obj* **with** *obj* /ˈ-ˌ-/ *v prep* [T] to continue to give (something) to (someone), or to continue to ask (questions) of (someone) • *We were*

PLURALS OF NOUNS

Regular plurals

Most nouns have a plural form. These nouns are marked [C] for "countable." Usually the plural is regular, and it is not given in the dictionary. Nouns such as *furniture* or *assistance* that have no plural are marked [U] for "uncountable"—you cannot count them. Here are the rules for spelling regular plurals:

noun ends in	change	examples
-s/-ss/-sh/-ch/-x/-z	+ es	bus, buses • class, classes • wish, wishes • match, matches • box, boxes • quiz, quizzes (Note that a final *z* may be doubled.)
consonant + yy • i	+ es	baby, babies • university, universities
other regular nouns	+ s	hand, hands • store, stores • play, plays • monkey, monkeys

Nouns for which the plural is the same as the singular

aircraft, craft [TRANSPORT], deer, moose, offspring, reindeer, sheep, and the names of some fish

CONTINUED

PLURALS OF NOUNS (continued)

Noun endings that sometimes have irregular plurals

Some irregular plurals are replaced by regular forms, especially in situations that are informal or not specialized. Words like this are marked * in the following table.

singular ending	regular plurals	irregular plurals
-a	agendas, areas, dilemmas, diplomas, encyclopedias, eras, guerrillas, quotas	**-ae** algae, antennae*, larvae, vertebrae*
-ex/-ix	Almost all these nouns have an **-es** plural: apexes, complexes, mixes, sixes.	**-ices** appendices*, indices*
-f/-fe	beliefs, chiefs, cliffs, handkerchiefs, proofs, roofs, safes. Roofs is sometimes pronounced /ru:vz/.	**-ves** calves, halves, hooves*, knives, leaves, lives, loaves, scarves*, selves, shelves, thieves, wives, wolves-
is	irises, metropolises	**-es** analyses, axes, bases, crises, diagnoses, hypotheses, neuroses, oases, parentheses, psychoses, syntheses, theses
-o	Many nouns form the plural with **-s**: autos, memos, photos, pianos, radios, solos, studios, videos, zoos. The following common nouns take **-es**: echoes, embargoes, heroes, potatoes, tomatoes, vetoes. Some nouns can take either **-es** or **-s**: cargoes or cargos, mosquitoes or mosquitos, mottos or mottoes, tornados or tornadoes, volcanoes or volcanos, zeros or zeroes.	
-on	Almost all **-on** nouns add **-s**: aprons, electrons, lions, moons, nations.	**-a** criteria, phenomena
-um	Most nonspecialized words: albums, forums, gymnasiums, museums, premiums. Some nouns are usually regular, but also have irregular plurals with **-a**: aquariums or aquaria, mediums or media (= methods).	**-a** Mainly specialized or formal words: bacteria, curricula*, memoranda*, millennia*, spectra*, strata
-us	Most **-us** nouns add **-es**: bonuses, campuses, choruses, geniuses, prospectuses, surpluses, viruses.	**-i** Mainly specialized words: alumni, cacti*, foci*, fungi, nuclei, radii, stimuli. Notice: **genus, genera**.

Other irregular plurals

child, children • ox, oxen • foot, feet • tooth, teeth • goose, geese • man, men • woman, women • mouse, mice • louse, lice • person, people or persons

---

plied with coffee, doughnuts, and refreshments. ○ Anxious to hear firsthand the latest about the outside world, they plied us with questions.

p.m., P.M. /pi:'em/ adv [not gradable] used when referring to a time between twelve o'clock in the middle of the day and twelve o'clock at night; in the afternoon or evening or at night • Our plane is due to arrive at 8:30 p.m. • Compare A.M. LP TIME

PMS n [U] abbreviation for **premenstrual syndrome**, see at PREMENSTRUAL

pneumatic /nʊ'mæt·ɪk/ adj [not gradable] operated by air pressure, or containing air • pneumatic tires • A **pneumatic drill** is a JACKHAMMER.

pneumonia /nʊ'moʊn·jə/ n [U] a serious illness in which one or both lungs become red and swollen and filled with liquid • The patient died of pneumonia.

P.O. n [U] abbreviation for POST OFFICE • A **P.O. Box** is a post office box. See at POST OFFICE.

poach COOK /poʊtʃ/ v [T] to cook (something) in water or another liquid that is almost boiling • poached eggs

poach TAKE ILLEGALLY /poʊtʃ/ v [I/T] to catch or kill (an animal) without permission on someone else's property, or to kill animals illegally to get (valuable parts of them) • Anybody you see with a piece of ivory has poached it. [T] ○ Foreign fishing boats were caught poaching offshore. [I]

poacher /'poʊ·tʃər/ n [C]

pocket BAG /'pɑk·ət/ n [C] a small bag, usually made of cloth, sewn on the inside or outside of a piece of clothing and used to hold small objects • coat/pants/shirt pockets ○ She took her keys out of her pocket. ○ I paid for my ticket out of my own pocket (= with my own money). • A pocket is also a small container that is part of or attached to something else: The map is in the pocket on the car door. • In the game of POOL, the pockets are the holes around the edge of the table into which the balls are hit. • A **pocketknife** is a small knife with one or more blades that can be folded into its handle for keeping it in a pocket. • *When we go to the museum you should bring some* **pocket money** (= a small amount of money). • Something **pocket-size/pocket-sized** is small and usually fits in a pocket: *a pocket-size book*

pocket /'pɑk·ət/ *v* [T] to put (something) in your pocket, or (fig.) to take (money) esp. when it has been obtained unfairly or illegally • *He pocketed his change.* ◦ (fig.) *Some sold nonexistent land and pocketed all the cash.*

pocket /'pɑk·ət/ *adj* [not gradable] small enough to be kept in a pocket • *a pocket diary* ◦ *a pocket watch*

pocketful /'pɑk·ət,fʊl/ *n* [C] • *a pocketful of coins*

pocket PART /'pɑk·ət/ *n* [C] a small part of something larger that is considered separate because of a particular quality • *It remained a pocket of poverty within a generally affluent area.*

pocketbook /'pɑk·ət,bʊk/, **bag**, **handbag**, **purse** *n* [C] a bag, often with a handle or a strap going over the shoulder, used esp. by women for carrying money and small items such as keys • *I have a map in my pocketbook.* • Someone's pocketbook is their finances or ability to pay for something: *The sales tax hits consumers in the pocketbook.*

pockmark /'pɑk·mɑrk/ *n* [C] a small hollow on the skin caused by a disease

pockmarked /'pɑk·mɑrkt/ *adj* • *a pockmarked face* • A surface that is pockmarked has a lot of hollows in it: *a pockmarked wall*

pod /pɑd/ *n* [C] a long seed container that grows on some plants • *a pea/bean pod*

podiatrist /pə'dɑɪ·ə·trəst/ *n* [C] a person trained in the treatment of problems and diseases of people's feet

podiatry /pə'dɑɪ·ə·tri/ *n* [U]

podium /'poʊd·iː·əm/ *n* [C] a small, low box or stage that someone stands on so they can be seen by a group of people, esp. to speak or CONDUCT music • *The conductor mounted the podium.* • A podium is also a LECTERN.

poem /'poʊ·əm, 'poː·ɪm/ *n* [C] a piece of writing in which the words are carefully chosen for the images and ideas they suggest, and in which the sounds of the words when read aloud often follow a particular rhythmic pattern

poet /'poʊ·ət/ *n* [C] someone who writes poems

poetic /poʊ'eṭ·ɪk/ *adj* of or suggesting poets or poems • *poetic language* • **Poetic license** is a writer's freedom to change such things as facts or the usual rules of good writing for artistic effect.

poetry /'poʊ·ə·tri/ *n* [U] poems, esp. as a form of literature • *the poetry of John Donne* • Compare PROSE.

poetic justice /poʊ,eṭ·ɪk'dʒʌs·təs/ *n* [U] a punishment or a reward that you feel is just, esp. when it is unexpected or unusual

pogrom /pə'grɑm, -'grʌm; 'poʊ·grəm/ *n* [C] organized killing of a large group of people, esp. Jews, because of their religion or race

poignant /'pɔɪn·jənt/ *adj* causing a feeling of sadness • *The monument is a poignant reminder of those who died in the war.*

poignantly /'pɔɪn·jənt·li/ *adv*

poinsettia /,pɔɪn'seṭ·ə, -'seṭ·iː·ə/ *n* [C] a Central American plant with groups of bright red leaves that look like flowers

point SHARP END /pɔɪnt/ *n* [C] the sharp or narrow end of something, such as a knife or pin • *I stuck myself with the point of the needle.* • A point is also a narrow piece of land that stretches out into the sea.

pointed /'pɔɪnt·əd/ *adj* • *a pointed arch* • See also POINTED.

pointy /'pɔɪnt·i/ *adj* [-er/-est only] • *pointy shoes*

point SHOW /pɔɪnt/ *v* [I/T] to direct other people's attention to (something or someone) by signaling toward it or them, esp. with your finger • *"Look," she said, pointing at the sign.* [I] ◦ *Which one is your sister—would you point her out to me?* [M] • If something points in a particular direction, it is turned toward that direction: *The arrow points left.* [I] • To **point the way** is to show how something can be done: *New research is pointing the way to developing more efficient vaccines.*

pointer /'pɔɪnt·ər/ *n* [C] any of various things used for pointing, esp. a long, thin stick • *The lecturer used a pointer to show what part or the diagram he was referring to.* • A pointer is also a helpful piece of advice or information: *The booklet gives some useful pointers for getting around in Washington.*

point IDEA EXPRESSED /pɔɪnt/ *n* [C] an idea, opinion, or piece of information that is said or written • *He made some good points in his speech.* ◦ *The lawyers reviewed the issues point by point.* ◦ *You have a point* (= What you say is reasonable). • The point is the main or most important idea: *He doesn't have much money, but that's not the point.*

point CHARACTERISTIC /pɔɪnt/ *n* [C] a particular quality or characteristic • *Truthfulness is not one of his strong points.*

point TIME OR PLACE /pɔɪnt/ *n* [C] a particular time, place, or stage reached in a process • *She felt that they were at a critical point in their marriage.* • The **point of no return** is the stage where it is too late to change what you are doing and must continue: *Once the contract is signed, we've reached the point of no return.* • A **point of view** (also **viewpoint**) is a person's opinion or their particular way of thinking about something: *We're interested in hearing all points of view.*

point ADVANTAGE /pɔɪnt/ *n* [U] purpose or

usefulness • *What's the point of leaving at six in the morning?*

pointless /'pɔɪnt·ləs/ *adj* having no useful purpose • *a pointless argument* ○ *The trip seemed pointless.*

point UNIT /pɔɪnt/ *n* [C] a unit for measuring or counting • *Our team won by seven points.* ○ *Interest rates dropped two percentage points.*

point POSITION /pɔɪnt/ *n* [C] an exact position, or a small mark showing an exact position • *Find the point in the map where Broadway intersects 15th Street.*

□ **point out** *obj*, **point** *obj* **out** /'-'-/ *v adv* [M] to direct attention toward (something) • *Angela pointed out some spelling errors in my paper.*

□ **point up** /'-,-/ *v prep* [T] (esp. of an event) to make clearer; show • *But that only points up how sensitive people are about racial issues.* [+ wh- word]

point–blank /'pɔɪnt'blæŋk/ *adv* [not gradable] aimed or fired directly at from a close position • *He was shot in the back, point-blank.* ○ (*fig.*) *He asked me point-blank* (= directly) *if I was lying.*

pointed /'pɔɪnt·əd/ *adj* having special esp. critical meaning • *He made a pointed remark about her unwillingness to volunteer.* • See also **pointed** at POINT SHARP END.

pointedly /'pɔɪnt·əd·li/ *adv* in an obvious and intentional way • *She pointedly ignored him.*

pointer /'pɔɪnt·ər/ *n* • See at POINT SHOW.

pointless /'pɔɪnt·ləs/ *adj* • See at POINT ADVANTAGE.

pointy /'pɔɪnt·i/ *adj* • See at POINT SHARP END.

poise /pɔɪz/ *n* [U] behavior or a way of moving that shows calm confidence • *"I think it was a credit to our team that we kept our poise," the coach said, "even when we were down by 21 points."*

poised /pɔɪzd/ *adj* • *Angela is a polite, poised young woman.*

poised /pɔɪzd/ *adj* [not gradable] ready to move, or prepared and waiting for something to happen • *The lion was poised to strike.*

poison SUBSTANCE /'pɔɪ·zən/ *n* [C/U] a substance that causes illness or death if swallowed, absorbed, or breathed into the body • *poison gas* [U] ○ *Some cleaning products are poisons.* [C] ○ *He injected his victims with poison.* [U] • **Poison ivy** is a North American plant that can cause soreness on the skin if you touch it.

poison /'pɔɪ·zən/ *v* [T] to cause (a person or animal) to take in poison, or to add poison to (food or a liquid) • *He thinks someone is trying to poison him.* ○ *Her tea was poisoned.*

poisonous /'pɔɪ·zə·nəs/ *adj* • *The mushrooms they picked were poisonous.*

poison CAUSE HARM /'pɔɪ·zən/ *v* [T] to cause serious harm to (something) • *Jealousy poisoned our relationship.* ○ *I don't see why you think TV poisons people's minds* (= influences them in a bad way).

poison /'pɔɪ·zən/ *n* [U] • *the poison of racism*

poke PUSH /pouk/ *v* [I/T] to push something esp. a finger, into (someone or something), or to push something through or past (someone or something) • *Quit poking me to move ahead—there are people in front of me.* [T] ○ *Josie poked her head around the corner to see what made the noise.* [T] • If you **poke fun at** someone, you make them seem ridiculous by making jokes about them.

poke /pouk/ *n* [C] • *He gave his brother a poke in the arm.*

poke INVOLVE /pouk/ *v* [I always + adv/prep] to involve yourself or take part in (something) that is not your responsibility or does not involve you • *He's always poking into other people's business.* • *Don't poke your nose in* (= involve yourself) *where you don't belong.*

poker GAME /'pou·kər/ *n* [U] a game played with cards in which people try to win money from each other • Someone with a **poker face** does not show what they are thinking or feeling. ○ *He stared at us poker-faced* (= without any expression).

poker TOOL /'pou·kər/ *n* [C] a long, metal pole that you can stick in a fire to move wood or coal so that it will burn better

polarize /'pou·lə,rɑɪz/ *v* [I/T] to cause (people in a group) to have opposing positions • *The gay-rights issue polarized the city council.* [T]

Polaroid /'pou·lə,rɔɪd/ *n* [C] *trademark* a camera that takes a picture and prints it after a few seconds, or a photograph taken with this type of camera

pole STICK /poul/ *n* [C] a long, usually round piece of wood or metal, often used to support something • *a telephone pole* ○ *a tent pole* • The **pole vault** is a sports competition in which you hold a long, stiff pole near one end and force it to bend so that when it straightens, it pushes you up over a high bar.

pole PLACE /poul/ *n* [C] either of the two points at the most northern and most southern ends of the earth or another planet, around which the planet turns • *the North/South Pole*

polar /'pou·lər/ *adj* [not gradable] of or near the area around the most northern or most southern points of the earth • *the polar ice cap* ○ *a polar expedition* • A **polar bear** is a large, white bear that lives in the cold regions of the north.

pole ELECTRICITY /poul/ *n* [C] either of the two ends of a magnet or two parts of a BATTERY (= device that produces electricity) which have opposite charges • Two things **poles apart** are far apart: *Labor and management are poles apart on the salary issue.*

polar /'pou·lər/ *adj* • (*fig.*) *The play's main characters are polar opposites* (= They are completely opposite).

polarity /pou'lær·əṭ·i/ *n* [U] *specialized* the quality in an object that produces opposite magnetic or electric charges

polemic /pə'lem·ɪk/ n [C] *slightly fml* a piece of writing or a speech in which a person argues forcefully for or against someone or something

polemical /pə'lem·ɪ·kəl/ *adj slightly fml* • *a series of polemical essays*

police /pə'liːs/ *pl n* an official force whose job is to maintain public order, deal with crime, and make people obey the law, or the members of this force • *I think you should call the police.* ○ *Police arrested two people in connection with the robbery.* • A **police department** is an organization of police in a city, region, or state. • The **police force** is the group of people who are employed as police in a city, region, or state. • A **police officer** (*male* **policeman**, *female* **policewoman**) is a member of the police force. • A **police station** is the office of the local police force. • (*disapproving*) A **police state** is a country controlled by the government police.

police /pə'liːs/ *v* [T] to control or maintain order, esp. with police • *Security forces policed the border.* ○ *It's up to the government to police the financial markets.*

policy PLAN /'pɑl·ə·si/ *n* [C] a set of ideas or a plan for action followed by a business, a government, a political party, or a group of people • *The White House said there will be no change in policy.*

policy DOCUMENT /'pɑl·ə·si/ *n* [C] a document showing an agreement you have made with an INSURANCE company • *a life-insurance policy*

polio /'poʊ·liː,oʊ/, *medical* **poliomyelitis** /,poʊ·liː·oʊ,maɪ·ə'laɪt·əs/ *n* [U] a serious, infectious disease of the nerves of the SPINE, that can cause temporary or permanent PARALYSIS (= inability to move the body)

polish /'pɑl·ɪʃ/ *v* [T] to make (something) smooth and shiny by rubbing • *He polished the hardwood floor.* • (*fig.*) If you polish something, you improve it: *I've got to polish (up) my French before the trip.* [T/M] • If you polish your nails, you paint them with a colored or colorless liquid to make them shine.

polish /'pɑl·ɪʃ/ *n* [U] • *I'll just give my shoes a quick polish.* • Polish is a cream or other substance that you use to clean or shine something: *shoe/furniture/silver polish* • Someone or something with polish has great skill or perfect style: *The rest of the cast comes nowhere near equaling his polish onstage.*

polished /'pɑl·ɪʃt/ *adj* [not gradable] • *highly polished furniture* • Someone who is polished is characterized by politeness, grace, and style: *He's suave, polished, and charming.* • Something that is polished shows great skill: *a polished performance*

polish off *obj*, **polish** *obj* **off** /'--'-/ *v adv* [M] *infml* to finish (something) quickly and easily • *He polished off two burgers and a mountain of French fries.*

polite /pə'laɪt/ *adj* behaving in a way that is socially correct and shows respect for other people's feelings • *She was too polite to point out my mistake.*

politely /pə'laɪt·li/ *adv* • *He politely asked them to leave.*

politeness /pə'laɪt·nəs/ *n* [U] • *With unfailing politeness he answered their questions.*

politic /'pɑl·ə,tɪk/ *adj* wise or practical • *It would not be politic for you to be seen there.*

political /pə'lɪt·ɪ·kəl/ *adj* [not gradable] relating to politics • *political parties* ○ *a political speech* ○ *Differences between men and women can be a political issue* (= one involving advantages and power). • A **political action committee** (*abbreviation* **PAC**) is an organization that gives money and support to politicians in order to influence them. • A **political prisoner** is a person who has been put in prison because they have criticized the government. • **Political science** is the study of government and political systems.

politically /pə'lɪt·ɪ·kli/ *adv* [not gradable] • *They encourage African Americans to become more politically active.* • (*disapproving*) If someone's actions or language is **politically correct** (*abbreviation* **PC**), they try extremely hard to show fairness and consideration for men and women of all races, ages, and physical abilities: *The politically correct term "firefighter" is used instead of "fireman."*

politics /'pɑl·ə,tɪks/ *n* the activities of the government, politicians, or political parties, or the study of these activities • *She got involved in local politics.* [U] • A person's politics are their opinions about how a country should be governed: *His politics are becoming increasingly liberal.* [pl] • Politics are also the activities of people who are trying to obtain an advantage within a group or organization: *I don't like to get involved in office politics.* [pl]

politician /,pɑl·ə'tɪʃ·ən/ *n* [C] a person who is active in politics, esp. as a job

politicize /pə'lɪt·ə,saɪz/ *v* [T] to make (an organization, individual, or activity) political or more aware of political matters • *Law enforcement should not be politicized.*

polka /'poʊl·kə, 'poʊ-/ *n* [C] a fast, active dance that originated in eastern Europe, or a piece of music for this dance

polka dot /'poʊ·kə,dɑt/ *n* [C usually pl] one of many round spots that form a pattern on cloth • *a polka-dot bow tie*

polka dots

poll OPINION /poʊl/ *n* [C] a study of a group's opinion on a subject, in which people are questioned and their answers examined • *an opinion poll* ○ *We took a poll this week.*

poll /poʊl/ *v* [T] • *Almost 86% of the parents polled said yes, and only 7% said no.*

poll RECEIVE VOTES /poʊl/ *v* [T] to receive (a

particular number of votes) in an election • *Bob Friedman polled 67% of the vote.*

polls /poulz/ *pl n* the places where people vote in a political election • *The polls close in an hour.*

pollen /'pɑl·ən/ *n* [U] a powder produced by the male part of a flower that causes the female part of other flowers of the same type to produce seeds • A **pollen count** is a measurement of the amount of pollen in the air.

pollinate /'pɑl·ə,neɪt/ *v* [T] to carry POLLEN from a male part of a flower to the female part of another flower of the same type • *Insects, birds, and the wind all pollinate plants.*

pollster /'poul·stər/ *n* [C] a person whose job is to ask people their opinions on a subject, as part of a POLL (= opinion study)

pollute /pə'luːt/ *v* [T] to make (air, water, or earth) dirty or harmful to people, animals, and plants, esp. by adding harmful chemicals or waste • *Chemical fertilizers and pesticides are polluting the groundwater.*

pollutant /pə'luːt·ᵊnt/ *n* [C] • *Maybe there's some kind of chemical pollutant in their drinking water.*

polluter /pə'luːt·ər/ *n* [C] a person or organization that pollutes

pollution /pə'luː·ʃən/ *n* [U] the act of polluting, or the substances that pollute • *air pollution* ○ *Pollution from the factory could be contaminating nearby wells.*

polo /'pou·lou/ *n* [U] a game in which players riding horses use wooden hammers with long handles to hit a ball into the opposing team's goal

polo shirt /'pou·lou,ʃɜrt/ *n* [C] a shirt with short sleeves, a collar, and some buttons at the neck

polyester /,pɑl·iː'es·tər/ *n* [U] a cloth made from artificial substances • *polyester pants*

polygamy /pə'lɪg·ə·mi/ *n* [U] the custom or condition of being married to more than one person at the same time • Compare MONOGAMY.

polygon /'pɑl·i,gɑn/ *n* [C] *specialized* a flat shape with three or more straight sides • *Triangles and squares are polygons.*

polygraph /'pɑl·i,græf/ *n* [C] *specialized* a lie detector, see at LIE SPEAK FALSELY

polymer /'pɑl·ə·mər/ *n* [C] *specialized* a natural or artificial substance made from many smaller MOLECULES (= groups of combined atoms)

polyp /'pɑl·əp/ *n* [C] a small mass of tissue that grows in the body

polytechnic /,pɑl·ə'tek·nɪk/ *n* [C] a college where students study scientific and technical subjects • Compare UNIVERSITY.

polytheism /,pɑl·i'θiː,ɪz·əm/ *n* [U] the belief in or worship of more than one god

polyunsaturated fat /,pɑl·iː,ʌn'sætʃ·ə,reɪt·əd/ *n* [C] a fat or oil with a chemical structure that does not easily change into CHOLESTEROL

(= a fatty substance that can cause heart disease) in the blood

pomegranate /'pɑm·ə,græn·ət, 'pʌm,græn-/ *n* [C] a round, thick-skinned fruit with a center full of large, juicy, edible seeds

pomp /pɑmp/ *n* [U] showy, formal ceremony, esp. on public occasions • *Pomp and pageantry accompanied the royal couple on their state visit.*

pompom /'pɑm·pɑm/, **pompon** /'pɑm·pɑn/ *n* [C] a small ball of loose strings or pieces of YARN used as a decoration, esp. on the top of a hat, or a ball of loose strips of paper or plastic waved at sports events

pompous /'pɑm·pəs/ *adj disapproving* feeling or showing that you think you are better or more important than other people • *I regarded him as somewhat pompous and opinionated.*

pomposity /pɑm'pɑs·əṭ·i/, **pompousness** /'pɑm·pə·snəs/ *n* [U] *disapproving* • *the pomposity of New York society*

poncho /'pɑn·tʃou/ *n* [C] *pl* **ponchos** an outer piece of clothing without sleeves which hangs from your shoulders, made of a large piece of material with a hole in the middle for your head

pond /pɑnd/ *n* [C] a still area of water smaller than a lake, often artificially made

ponder /'pɑn·dər/ *v* [I/T] to consider (something) carefully for a long time • *She ponders the reaction she'll receive.* [T] ○ *The bathtub is a place where one can ponder.* [I]

ponderous /'pɑn·də·rəs/ *adj* slow and awkward because of being very heavy or large, or (esp. of speech or writing) boring and difficult • *a ponderous pace* ○ *ponderous dialogue*

pontiff /'pɑnt·əf/ *n* [C] a POPE (= leader of the Roman Catholic Church)

pontificate /pɑn'tɪf·ɪ,keɪt/ *v* [I] to speak in an important manner as if only your opinion was correct • *Experts get on the tube and pontificate about the economy.*

pontoon /pɑn'tuːn/ *n* [C] a small, flat boat or similarly shaped metal structure esp. used to form or support a temporary floating bridge

pony /'pou·ni/ *n* [C] a small type of horse • The **pony express** was a system for carrying mail using horses and riders that existed in the American West in the 1800s.

ponytail /'pou·niː,teɪl/ *n* [C] a hairstyle in which the hair is gathered and fastened at the back of the head so that it hangs down loosely

pooch /puːtʃ/ *n* [C] *infml* a dog

poodle /'puːd·ᵊl/ *n* [C] a type of dog with curly hair that is usually cut only on parts of its body

ponytail

pool LIQUID /puːl/ n [C] a small area of usually still water, or a small amount of liquid • *pools of water in the gutter* ○ *a pool of blood* • A pool is also a **swimming pool**. See at SWIM.

pool COLLECTION /puːl/ n [C] an amount of money or a number of people or things collected together for shared use by several people or organizations • *Their profits get plowed back into a pool to pay subscribers' claims.* • A pool is also the total amount of money risked by people on the result of a card game or sports event: *an office Super Bowl pool*

pool /puːl/ v [T] • *The kids pooled their money to buy their parents plane tickets.*

pool GAME /puːl/ n [U] a game played by two or more people in which a CUE (= long, round, wooden stick) is used to hit a white ball against other balls in order to roll them into one of six holes around the edge of a special table • *a pool table*

poop /puːp/ n [U] *rude slang* excrement

poop /puːp/ v [I] *rude slang* • *The puppy pooped on the carpet.*

□**poop out** /ˈpuːpˈaʊt/ v [I] *infml* to become very tired • *I just poop out if I stay up too late.*

pooped /puːpt/ adj *infml* very tired • *Students are pooped because they're juggling classes, studying, and activities.*

pooper–scooper /ˈpuː�·pərˈskuː·pər/ n [C] a small tool used for picking up dog excrement from public places

poor NO MONEY /pʊr, pɔʊr/ adj [-er/-est only] having little money or few possessions, or lacking something important • *He came from a poor, immigrant family.* ○ *Most of the world's poorest countries are in Africa.* ○ *The country is poor in natural resources.*

poor /pʊr, pɔʊr/ pl n poor people • *She gives a lot of money to the poor.*

poor BAD /pʊr, pɔʊr/ adj [-er/-est only] of a very low quality or standard; not good • *poor eyesight* ○ *poor grades* ○ *He's in very poor health.*

poorly /ˈpʊr·li, ˈpɔʊr-/ adv [not gradable] • *Critics say the plan was poorly conceived.* ○ *The kids are doing poorly at school.*

poor DESERVING SYMPATHY /pʊr, pɔʊr/ adj [not gradable] deserving sympathy • *That poor dog looks like it hasn't been fed in a while.*

pop SOUND /pɑp/ v [I/T] **-pp-** to make a short little explosive sound, often by bursting something, or to cause this to happen • *The kids were popping all the birthday balloons.* [T]

pop /pɑp/ n [C] • *There was a loud pop as the cork came out of the bottle.*

pop MOVE /pɑp/ v [I always + adv/prep] **-pp-** to move or appear quickly, suddenly, or when not expected • *McEnroe hits it and the ball pops over his shoulder.* ○ *There are lots of good young players popping up these days.*

□**pop in** /ˈ-ˈ-/ v prep [I] *infml* to visit briefly • *Why don't you pop in and see us this afternoon?*

□**pop (obj) in/into** obj /ˈ-ˈ-; ˈ-ˈ--/ v prep [T] *infml*

to put (something) quickly in (something else) • *Pop the CD-ROM into a personal computer.* ○ *Just pop your supper in the microwave.* ○ *This just popped into my head.*

pop POPULAR /pɑp/ adj [not gradable] of or for the general public • *pop art* ○ *pop culture* ○ *pop music*

pop FATHER /pɑp/ n [C] *infml* a father • *Hey Pop, can I borrow the car?* • LP TITLES AND FORMS OF ADDRESS

pop DRINK /pɑp/, dated **soda pop** n [C/U] *regional* a **soft drink**, see at SOFT WEAK

pop EACH /pɑp/ n *infml* • **A pop** means each: *The tickets cost $200 a pop.*

pop. PEOPLE n [U] *abbreviation for* POPULATION (= number of people living in a place) • *Devil's Lake, N.D. (pop. 7442)*

popcorn /ˈpɑp·kɔːrn/ n [U] seeds of corn that are heated until they burst, becoming light, white balls that are usually eaten with salt and butter or a sweet covering on them

pope /poʊp/ n [C/U] the leader of the Roman Catholic Church • *Pope John Paul II* [U]

poplar /ˈpɑp·lər/ n [C] a tall, straight, fast-growing tree with soft wood

poplin /ˈpɑp·lən/ n [U] a plain, closely woven cloth with a slightly shiny surface

poppy /ˈpɑp·i/ n [C] a plant with large, usually red flowers, and small, black, edible seeds

Popsicle /ˈpɑp·sɪk·əl/ n [C] *trademark* a sweet, flavored ice on a stick

populace /ˈpɑp·jə·ləs/ n [U] the people who live in a particular country or place, or ordinary people • *It seemed as if the town's entire populace had turned out for the parade.*

popular LIKED /ˈpɑp·jə·lər/ adj liked, enjoyed, or admired by many people or by most people in a particular group • *In-line skating is increasingly popular.*

popularity /ˌpɑp·jəˈlær·ət̬·i/ n [U] • *The governor's popularity will probably guarantee his reelection.*

popularize /ˈpɑp·jə·ləˌrɑɪz/ v [T] to cause (something) to become known, admired, or used by many people • *He helped to popularize the hard-bop style of jazz in the mid-1950s.*

popular GENERAL /ˈpɑp·jə·lər/ adj involving or relating to ordinary people or to all the people who live in a country or area • *Contrary to popular belief, air travel is less dangerous than travel by car.* • **Popular music** is the kind of music with a strong rhythm that many young people enjoy listening and dancing to, or any music that is not CLASSICAL music.

popularize /ˈpɑp·jə·ləˌrɑɪz/ v [T] to make (something) known or understood to ordinary people • *His books helped popularize the study of language.*

popularly /ˈpɑp·jə·lər·li/ adv by most people • *In the 1970s, so many Russian immigrants came to live in Brighton Beach that it became popularly known as Little Odessa.*

population /ˌpɑp·jəˈleɪ·ʃən/ (*abbreviation*

pop.) *n* [C/U] all the people living in a particular country, area, or place • *What is the population of Toronto* (= how many people live there)*?* [U] • Population is also used to refer to all the people or animals of a particular type or group who live in a particular place: *The deer population has increased dramatically in the northeast.* [U]

populated /ˈpɑp·jəˌleɪt/ *adj* lived in • *densely populated cities*

populous /ˈpɑp·jə·ləs/ *adj* (of a country, area, or place) having a lot of people living there • *populous metropolitan areas*

porcelain /ˈpɔːr·sə·lən/ *n* [U] a hard but delicate, shiny, white substance made by heating a special type of clay to a high temperature, used esp. to make cups, plates, and small, decorative objects • *a porcelain figurine*

porch /pɔːrtʃ/ *n* [C] a covered area next to the entrance of a house, sometimes open to the air and sometimes surrounded by a SCREEN (= wire net) • *The back porch looks out on our garden.*

porcupine /ˈpɔːr·kjəˌpaɪn/ *n* [C] a small, brown mammal with a protective covering of QUILLS (= long, sharp points) on its back

pore /pɔːr, poʊr/ *n* [C] one of many very small holes in the skin of people or other animals or on the surface of plants

▢ **pore over** /ˈpɔːrˈoʊ·vər, ˈpoʊr-/ *v prep* [T] to look at and study (a book, document, etc.) carefully • *She spends a lot of time poring over the historical records of the church.*

pork /pɔːrk/ *n* [U] meat from a pig, eaten as food • *pork chops*

pork barrel /ˈpɔːrkˌbær·əl/, **pork** /pɔːrk/ *n* [U] the spending of federal or state government money for local improvements to help a politician win popularity with local voters • *pork-barrel politics*

pornography /pɔːrˈnɑg·rə·fi/, *infml* **porn** /pɔːrn/ *n* [U] pictures, movies, or writing that show or describe sexual acts or naked people for the purpose of exciting people sexually, and usually for no other purpose

pornographer /pɔːrˈnɑg·rə·fər/ *n* [C] a person who makes or sells pornography

pornographic /ˌpɔːr·nəˈgræf·ɪk/, *infml* **porn** /pɔːrn/, **porno** /ˈpɔːr·noʊ/ *adj*

porous /ˈpɔːr·əs, ˈpoʊr·əs/ *adj* allowing liquid or air to pass through • *porous soil*

porpoise /ˈpɔːr·pəs/ *n* [C] a large mammal that lives in the sea and swims in groups

porridge /ˈpɔːr·ɪdʒ, ˈpɑr-/ *n* [U] *dated* a thick, soft food made from OATS (= a type of grain) boiled in water or milk; OATMEAL

port CITY /pɔːrt, poʊrt/ *n* [C/U] a city or town that has a HARBOR (= sheltered area of water where ships can load or unload) on the sea or a river, or the harbor itself • *a fishing/naval port* [C]

port CONNECTION /pɔːrt, poʊrt/ *n* [C] *specialized* a part of a computer where wires can be con-

nected in order to control other pieces of equipment, such as a printer

port LEFT /pɔːrt, poʊrt/ *n* [U] *specialized* the left side of a ship or aircraft as you are facing forward • Compare STARBOARD.

portable /ˈpɔːrt·ə·bəl, ˈpoʊrt-/ *adj* [not gradable] small and light enough to be carried or moved easily, and not attached by electric wires • *a portable phone/radio*

portal /ˈpɔːrt·ᵊl, ˈpoʊrt-/ *n* [C] *slightly fml* a large and often highly decorated entrance to a building • *We entered the Romanesque side portal of Verona Cathedral.*

portend /pɔːrˈtend, poʊr-/ *v* [T] *fml* to be a sign that (something, esp. something bad) is likely to happen in the future • *It was a major scandal whose full exposure portended the end of a popular presidential reign.*

porter /ˈpɔːrt·ər, ˈpoʊrt-/ *n* [C] a person whose job is to carry travelers' bags at railroad stations and airports • A porter is also a person whose job is to clean, esp. in a large building.

portfolio CONTAINER /pɔːrtˈfoʊ·liːˌoʊ, poʊrt-/ *n* [C] *pl* **portfolios** a large, flat container used for carrying large drawings, documents, or other papers • A portfolio is also a collection of drawings, designs, or other papers that represent a person's work.

portfolio INVESTMENTS /pɔːrtˈfoʊ·liːˌoʊ, poʊrt-/ *n* [C] *pl* **portfolios** a collection of investments that are owned by a particular person or organization • *a stock portfolio*

porthole /ˈpɔːrt·hoʊl, ˈpoʊrt-/ *n* [C] a small, usually round, window in the side of a ship

portico /ˈpɔːrt·ɪˌkoʊ, ˈpoʊrt-/ *n* [C] *pl* **porticoes** or **porticos** an open structure with a roof supported by columns, which serves as an entrance, usually to a large house or a public building

portion /ˈpɔːr·ʃən, ˈpoʊr-/ *n* [C] a part or share of something larger • *She read large portions of the manuscript and offered many useful suggestions.* ○ *A portion of my paycheck was withheld for taxes.* • A portion is also the amount of food served to or suitable for a person: *They serve children's portions at half price.*

portly /ˈpɔːrt·li, ˈpoʊrt-/ *adj* slightly fat • *a tall, portly man*

portrait /ˈpɔːr·trət, ˈpoʊr-/ *n* [C] a painting, photograph, or drawing of a person • A portrait is also a description or representation of something: *The book paints a grim portrait of wartime suffering.*

portray /pɔːrˈtreɪ, poʊr-/ *v* [T] to represent or describe (someone or something), esp. in writing or in a movie, often as having particular qualities • *The book portrayed him as somebody who was uncaring, even bigoted.* ○ *The writer portrays life in a working-class community at the turn of the century.* • To portray is also to act the part of someone in a movie or play: *Michael Douglas portrays the president of the United States.*

portrayal /pɔːrˈtreɪ·əl, pour-/ *n* [C] • *A lot of people felt the film wasn't quite an accurate portrayal.*

pose CREATE /pouz/ *v* [T] to cause (esp. a problem or difficulty) to exist • *Does this defendant really pose a threat to the community?* • To pose a question is to bring attention to a problem, often in the form of a question: *Joanna poses the question, "How do we accomplish these goals?"*

pose POSITION /pouz/ *v* [I] to move into and stay in a particular position, usually so that you can be photographed or have your picture drawn or painted • *We all posed for our photographs in front of the Lincoln Memorial.*

pose /pouz/ *n* [C] the position in which someone stands or sits when they are posing • *Can you hold that pose?*

pose PRETEND /pouz/ *v* [I] to pretend to be (someone else) in order to deceive others • *The detective posed as a drug dealer.*

posh /pɑʃ/ *adj* luxurious and of high quality • *a posh hotel/restaurant*

position PLACE /pəˈzɪʃ·ən/ *n* [C/U] the place where something or someone is, often in relation to other things • *I've switched the positions of the sofa and the chair.* [C] • In sports, a position is the place where you play on your team, or the responsibilities of someone who plays in that place: *He played the shortstop position when he started in baseball.* [C]

position /pəˈzɪʃ·ən/ *v* [T] • *The Secret Service men quickly positioned themselves around the president.*

position RANK /pəˈzɪʃ·ən/ *n* [C] a rank or level in a company, competition, or society • *She's devoted her life to improving the position of women in society.* • A position in a company or organization is also a job: *He applied for the position of marketing manager.*

position SITUATION /pəˈzɪʃ·ən/ *n* [C usually sing] a situation or condition • *a shaky financial position* ○ *She found herself in a difficult position and didn't know what to say.* • If you are in a position to do something, you are able to do it, usually because you have the necessary power or money: *Do you think she's in a position to help you?* [+ to infinitive]

position OPINION /pəˈzɪʃ·ən/ *n* [C] a way of thinking about a particular matter; opinion • *Our position is that we've made a very fair offer to settle this dispute.*

position ARRANGEMENT OF BODY /pəˈzɪʃ·ən/ *n* [C] the way in which the body is arranged • *My knees gets stiff when I sit in the same position for a long time.*

positive CERTAIN /ˈpɑz·ət̬·ɪv/ *adj* without any doubt; certain • *I'm absolutely positive that's he's the man I saw.*

positively /ˈpɑz·ət̬·ɪv·li/ *adv* • *I positively will be there.*

positive HAPPY /ˈpɑz·ət̬·ɪv/ *adj* happy or hopeful, or giving cause for happiness or hope • *It's important to have a positive attitude when you have a serious illness.* • USAGE: The opposite of positive is NEGATIVE NOT HAPPY.

positively /ˈpɑz·ət̬·ɪv·li/ *adv* • *I just don't respond positively to being bossed around.*

positive MEDICAL TEST /ˈpɑz·ət̬·ɪv/ *adj* [not gradable] (of a medical test) showing the presence of the disease or condition for which the person is being tested • *Her pregnancy test was positive.* • Compare NEGATIVE NO.

positive COMPLETE /ˈpɑz·ət̬·ɪv/ *adj* [not gradable] (used to add force to an expression) complete • *She was a positive joy to have around.*

positively /ˈpɑz·ət̬·ɪv·li/ *adv* [not gradable] • *You look positively gorgeous in that outfit!*

positive MORE THAN ZERO /ˈpɑz·ət̬·ɪv/ *adj* [not gradable] (of a number or amount) more than zero • *Two is a positive number.* • USAGE: The opposite of positive is NEGATIVE LESS THAN ZERO.

positive ELECTRICITY /ˈpɑz·ət̬·ɪv/ *adj* [not gradable] of the type of electrical charge carried by PROTONS • Compare NEGATIVE ELECTRICITY.

posse /ˈpɑs·i/ *n* [C] a group of people following a person in order to catch him or her • *In a lot of old westerns, the sheriff gathers a posse to chase the bad guy.*

possess OWN /pəˈzes/ *v* [T] to have or own (something), or to have (a particular quality) • *Those states are the countries that possess nuclear weapons.* ○ *She possesses the unusual talent of knowing when to say nothing.*

possession /pəˈzeʃ·ən/ *n* [C/U] something that you own, or the condition of owning something • *She couldn't take possession of the house until the current occupants moved out.* [U] ○ *Meanwhile, all her possessions were in storage.* [C] • To be in possession of something is to have it with you: *He was in possession of an illegal drug.*

possessive /pəˈzes·ɪv/ *adj* • If you are possessive about something that you own, you do not like sharing it: *He's very possessive about his car.* • Someone who is possessive in their feelings and behavior toward another person wants all of that person's love and attention: *It's a movie about a possessive husband and his unfaithful wife.* • See also POSSESSIVE.

possessor /pəˈzes·ər/ *n* [C usually sing] • *I am now the proud possessor of a driver's license!*

possess CONTROL /pəˈzes/ *v* [T] (of a desire or an idea) to take control over (a person's) mind, making that person behave in a strange way • *I don't know what possessed me to start yelling like that.*

possessive /pə'zes·ɪv/ *adj* [not gradable] *specialized* (in grammar) having or relating to the CASE (= form) of a word used to show who or what something belongs to • See also **possessive** at POSSESS OWN. LP APOSTROPHE

possible ACHIEVABLE /'pɑs·ə·bəl/ *adj* [not gradable] that can be done or achieved, or that can exist • *Is it possible to get an earlier flight?* [+ to infinitive] ○ *If possible I'd like to get there before noon.* ○ *We need to send that letter off as soon as possible.*

possibly /'pɑs·ə·bli/ *adv* [not gradable] • *He can't possibly mean what he says.*

possibility /ˌpɑs·ə'bɪl·ət̬·i/ *n* [C] • *One possibility is to hire more people.*

possible NOT CERTAIN /'pɑs·ə·bəl/ *adj* [not gradable] that might or might not happen or exist • *It's possible (that) Mary will turn up tonight.* [+ (that) clause]

possibly /'pɑs·ə·bli/ *adv* [not gradable] • *"Do you think this skirt might be too small for her?" "Possibly, she has put on weight."*

possibility /ˌpɑs·ə'bɪl·ət̬·i/ *n* [U] • *There's a possibility of snow tonight.*

possum /'pɑs·əm/ *n short form of* OPOSSUM

post POLE /poʊst/ *n* [C] a vertical pole stuck in the ground, usually to support something or to mark a position • *Al leaned against a fence post.*

post JOB /poʊst/ *n* [C] a job, esp. one in which someone is performing an official duty • *Novello was the first woman and first Hispanic to hold the post of surgeon general.*

post /poʊst/ *v* [T] • *Police officers will be posted at some abortion clinics.*

post MAKE KNOWN /poʊst/ *v* [T] to make (information) known to the public, or to put up (signs) on land or other property • *Snow advisories were posted for Ohio and Pennsylvania.* ○ *All over town, for-sale signs are posted in front of houses.*

post PAY /poʊst/ *v* [T] to pay (money) to a law court, as a formal promise that a person released from prison will return for their trial • *McLaughlin posted $3000 bail after his arrest.*

postage /'poʊ·stɪdʒ/ *n* [U] the money charged or paid for sending letters and parcels by mail

postal /'poʊ·stəl/ *adj* [not gradable] relating to the delivery of mail, or to or about the POST OFFICE • *Two postal workers were accused of theft.*

postcard /'poʊst·kɑrd/ *n* [C] a small, rectangular card, often with a picture on one side, that can be sent in the mail without an envelope • *a picture postcard*

postcode /'poʊst·koʊd/ *n* [C] *Br for* zip code, see at ZIP MOVE FAST

postdate /poʊs'deɪt/ *v* [T] to write a DATE (= day, month, and year) that is later than the present on (a check, letter, or document)

poster /'poʊ·stər/ *n* [C] a large printed picture or notice put up for advertising or decoration • *She had a poster of some rock star on the wall.*

posterior /pɑ'stɪr·iː·ər, poʊ-/ *n* [C] *often humorous infml* a person's buttocks • *Park your posterior on that seat.*

posterity /pɑ'ster·ət̬·i/ *n* [U] the people who will exist in the future • *Their recollections were recorded for posterity.*

postgraduate /ˌpoʊst'grædʒ·ə·wət/ *n* [C] a student who is doing advanced studies after already obtaining one degree • LP EDUCATION IN THE US

postgraduate /ˌpoʊst'grædʒ·ə·wət/, **graduate** *adj* [not gradable] • *postgraduate studies*

posthumous /'pɑs·tʃə·məs/ *adj* [not gradable] happening after a person's death

posthumously /'pɑs·tʃə·mə·sli/ *adv* [not gradable] • *Dillon was posthumously awarded a Silver Star.*

Post–It (note) /'poʊ·stət ('noʊt)/ *n* [C] *trademark* a piece of paper with a sticky strip on the back that allows it to be stuck temporarily to smooth surfaces

postmark /'poʊst·mɑrk/ *n* [C] an official mark on letters or packages, showing the place and day, month, and year of mailing

postmark /'poʊst·mɑrk/ *v* [T] • *Contest entries must be postmarked no later than July 16.*

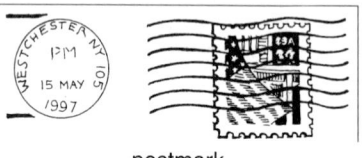

postmark

postmaster *male* /'poʊst,mæs·tər/, **postmistress** /'poʊst,mɪs·trəs/ *n* [C] a person in charge of a POST OFFICE • *He's the local postmaster.*

post–mortem /poʊst'mɔrt̬·əm/ *n* [C] a medical examination of a dead body to discover the cause of death, or a discussion of an event after it has happened • *The disease can be confirmed only in a post-mortem.* ○ *a post-mortem on Harkin's presidential campaign*

postnatal /poʊst'neɪt̬·əl/ *adj* [not gradable] relating to the period of time immediately after a baby has been born • *a postnatal exercise program* • Compare PRENATAL.

post office /'poʊ,stɔr·fəs, -,stɑf·əs/ *n* [C] a place where you can mail letters or packages and buy stamps, or *(infml)* the US Postal Service • A **post office box** (*abbreviation* **P.O. Box**) is a small, numbered, locked box at a post office to which letters are delivered.

postpartum /poʊst'pɑrt̬·əm/ *adj* [not gradable] following the birth of a child • *They offer the full package of prenatal, delivery, and postpartum care.*

postpone /poʊst'poʊn/ *v* [T] to delay (an event) or arrange for it to take place at a later time • *The trip has been postponed twice.*

postponement /poʊst'poʊn·mənt/ *n* [C/U] •

THE POSSESSIVE FORM

how to form the possessive

The possessive form of a noun is usually formed by adding **'s**.

Pat's • Jane's • Max's • my aunt's • your father's • his niece's • women's

Regular plurals ending in *s* take an apostrophe (') with no extra *s*.

a boys' school

With singular nouns and names ending in *s*, an extra *s* is usually added after the apostrophe, but sometimes the extra *s* is omitted.

James's shoes or *James' shoes*

using the possessive

The possessive form of a noun is used to show:

- ownership, qualities, parts of the body
  Paul's house • the old woman's courage • the cat's whiskers
- relationships, intended users
  Hamid's brother • children's books
- things produced, events
  the committee's report • cow's milk • my grandmother's fall • a bird's cry

Appearing alone, a possessive noun functions like the pronouns *mine, hers,* etc.

"Whose camera is this?" "Sasha's." • Don't use that plate, it's the cat's.

The **'s** is added to the last word of a phrase that acts as a unit.

the King of Spain's daughter • the chairman of the board's office • my son-in-law's car

It is also possible for a possessive noun to come before another possessive noun, especially if the possessive nouns are single words.

Lilli's brother's car

with nouns for people, animals, and groups

The possessive form is most typically used with nouns for people and animals (see the examples above), including groups of people or animals.

the crowd's reaction • the group's leader

It is also used with:

- Political groups, business companies, and places
  the Republican Party's foreign policy • New York's largest park
- Names of owners to refer to their businesses
  I need to go to the hairdresser's/butcher's/doctor's.
- Names of people to refer to their homes
  I'm going to stop by my aunt's tonight. • We're invited to the Chens' for dinner.

with other types of nouns

When words for parts like *front, back, top, bottom, middle,* and *end* are used, a phrase with *of* is generally used instead of the possessive form.

the front of the building • the bottom of the page • the end of the book

Possessives are also used:

- In time expressions
  in a week's time • an hour's walk from here • a good night's sleep • at Tuesday's meeting
- In some idioms
  I saw it in my mind's eye • In heaven's name

when the possessive form is not used

English often does not use a possessive form when some other languages do. Sometimes, a compound noun or combination of two nouns is used instead.

a family friend • a company car • a shirtsleeve • a chair leg • a truck driver • a rose petal

It is also common in English to use a phrase with a preposition instead of a possessive form.

the color of the sky • the pages in the book • the smile on her face • the money in my account

Rain forced (a) postponement of the match. [C/U]

postscript /ˈpoʊs·skrɪpt/ *n* [C] an extra message added at the end of a story or letter • *There is a postscript to this story.*

postulate *(obj)* /ˈpɑs·tʃə,leɪt/ *v fml* to suggest or accept that (a theory, idea, etc.) is true, esp. as a starting point for reasoning or discussion • *Astronomers postulate that the comet will reappear in 4000 years.* [+ *that* clause]

postulate /ˈpɑs·tʃə·lət, -,leɪt/ *n* [C] *fml* • *He suggested an original and interesting postulate.*

posture POSITION OF BODY /ˈpɑs·tʃər/ *n* [C/U] a position of the body, or the way in which someone holds their body when standing, sitting, or walking • *Newton sat back in a reclining posture.* [C] ○ *She's got good/bad posture.* [U]

posture ACT FALSELY /ˈpɑs·tʃər/ *v* [I] to act falsely in order to attract attention or achieve an effect • *This trial turned into a carnival, with everybody posturing and playing to the camera.*

postwar /ˈpoʊs·twɔːr/ *adj* [not gradable] happening or existing in the period after a war, esp. World War II

pot CONTAINER /pɑt/ *n* [C] a round container used for cooking, serving, storing, and other purposes • *a clay/brass pot* ○ *a flower pot* ○ *We need space for our pots and pans.* • A pot is also the substance contained in a pot: *The pot was simmering.* ○ *He made a new pot of coffee.* • If someone's actions are an example of **the pot calling the kettle black**, they are accusing someone else of bad behavior although they have done something bad themselves. • A **potholder** is a small piece of thick material for protecting your hands when holding hot pots or pans. • A **pot pie** is a pastry filled with vegetables and usually meat: *a chicken pot pie* • A **pot roast** is a piece of BEEF (= meat from cattle) cooked whole in a covered pot.

pot /pɑt/ *v* [T] **-tt-** to put (a plant) into a pot • *We should be potting the roses.*

pot DRUG /pɑt/ *n* [U] *infml* MARIJUANA • *She saw him smoking pot.*

pot AMOUNT /pɑt/ *n* [C] *infml* a large amount, esp. of money • *There are pots of money involved in this deal.* • A pot is also all the money being risked at a single time in a card game: *Frank won this pot, but his luck wouldn't last all night.*

potassium /pəˈtæs·i·əm/ *n* [U] a soft, silver-white metallic element that burns quickly in the air and is used in special hard glasses and FERTILIZERS (= substances that help crops grow better)

potato /pəˈteɪt·oʊ/ *n* [C/U] *pl* **potatoes** a white vegetable with a brown or reddish skin which grows underground and is used for food, or the plant on which this grows • *a baked potato* [C] ○ *mashed potato* [U] • **Potato chips** are very thin slices of potatoes fried until stiff, and sometimes flavored.

potbelly /ˈpɑtˌbel·i/ *n* [C] a noticeably fat, round stomach

potbellied /ˈpɑtˌbel·iːd/ *adj* • *a small, potbellied old man* • A **potbellied stove** is an old-fashioned round stove that uses wood or COAL for fuel.

potent /ˈpoʊt·ənt/ *adj* powerful, persuasive, or effective • *She kept some potent Canadian ale in the basement.* ○ *Her voice has been a potent force on concert stages for more than 30 years.*

potency /ˈpoʊt·ən·si/ *n* [U] • *Scientists are testing the potency of the new drug.*

potential /pəˈten·tʃəl/ *adj* [not gradable] possible but not yet achieved • *He was eager to talk with potential customers.*

potential /pəˈten·tʃəl/ *n* [U] • *He saw little potential* (= possibility) *for change.* • Someone's potential is an ability they have not yet developed: *She keeps saying I should live up to my potential.*

potentially /pəˈten·tʃə·li/ *adv* [not gradable] • *Potentially dangerous products are often recalled by their manufacturers.*

pothole /ˈpɑt·hoʊl/ *n* [C] a hole in the surface of a road caused by traffic and bad weather

potion /ˈpoʊ·ʃən/ *n* [C] a drink that is believed to have medicinal, poisonous, or magical powers • *We don't have a magic potion to make you tell the truth.*

pot luck /ˈpɑt'lʌk/ *adj* [not gradable] offering whatever is available or what others bring • *Our church suppers are always pot luck.*

potpourri /ˌpoʊ·pəˈriː/ *n* [C/U] a mixture of dried flower petals and spices, used to make a room or drawer smell pleasant • *She liked the scent of floral potpourri.* [U] • A potpourri is also a mixed grouping of things: *a potpourri of scenes* [C]

potshot /ˈpɑt·ʃɑt/ *n* [C] a criticism made without careful thought • *Her opponent has taken potshots at her for not being tough enough.*

pottery /ˈpɑt·ə·ri/ *n* [U] dishes, bowls, and other objects made from baked clay

potty /ˈpɑt·i/ *n* [C] a small toilet, used by children when they are being trained to use a toilet • *Melissa, do you need to go potty* (= use the toilet)*?*

pouch /paʊtʃ/ *n* [C] a bag or soft container • *The raincoat is folded inside a small waterproof pouch.* • A pouch is also a pocket of skin on the lower part of the body of some female animals, such as KANGAROOS, in which they carry their young.

poultry /ˈpoʊl·tri/ *n* [U] birds, such as chickens, kept for their meat or eggs, or the meat from these birds • *Mediterranean diets favor fish and poultry over red meat.*

pounce /paʊns/ *v* [I] to attack suddenly, esp. by jumping or flying down to catch or take hold of something or someone • *The mountain lion pounced onto the back of an elk.*

pound WEIGHT /paʊnd/ (*abbreviation* **lb.**, *symbol* **#**) *n* [C] a unit of measurement of weight equal to 0.453 kilogram • The **pound sign** is the symbol #.

pound HIT /paʊnd/ *v* [I/T] to hit repeatedly with force, or to crush by hitting repeatedly • *The speaker pounded his fists on the table.* [T] ○ *Waves were pounding at the rocks.* [I] • If your heart pounds, it beats very strongly: *My heart was still pounding after we nearly crashed on the Interstate.* [I]

pounding /'paʊn·dɪŋ/ *n* [C/U] the sound, feeling, or action of something beating repeatedly • *The pounding in her chest was loud.* [U] ○ *All that pounding from running really isn't good for your knees.* [U] ○ (*fig.*) *The dollar's going to take a pounding* (= its value will be damaged). [C]

pound PLACE /paʊnd/ *n* [C] a place where pets that are lost or not wanted are kept • *We got this mutt at the pound.*

pound MONEY /paʊnd/, *symbol* **£** *n* [C] the standard unit of money in the United Kingdom and some other countries

pound cake /'paʊnd·keɪk/ *n* [C] a type of cake made with flour, butter, sugar, and eggs

pour CAUSE TO FLOW /pɔːr, poʊr/ *v* [T] to make (a substance) flow, esp. out of a container and usually into another container • *Pour the sugar into the bowl.* [T] ○ *Would you like me to pour you some wine?* [T] • If someone pours out something to you, they tell you all about it: *I poured my heart out to him* (= told him my feelings). [M]

pour FLOW QUICKLY /pɔːr, poʊr/ *v* [always + adv/prep] to flow quickly and in large amounts, or to cause (something) to flow in large amounts • *Water poured into the basement.* [I] ○ *When the movie ended, the crowd poured into the street.* [I] • If you say about the weather that it is pouring, you mean that it is raining heavily: *You'd better take an umbrella—it's pouring out there.* [I]

pout /paʊt/ *v* [I] to show annoyance esp. by pressing the lips together or pushing out the lower lip • *Our four-year-old pouts whenever she doesn't get what she wants.*

poverty /'pɑv·ərt̬·i/ *n* [U] the condition of being poor • *He grew up in poverty.* • The **poverty level/line** is the amount of income a person or family needs in order to maintain an acceptable standard of living, and below which they are considered poor. • **Poverty-stricken** means extremely poor: *My grandparents arrived in this country as poverty-stricken immigrants.*

POW PRISONER *n* [C] *abbreviation for* **prisoner of war**, see at PRISON

pow NOISE /paʊ/ *exclamation* (a word representing) a sudden loud noise, as that of an explosion or of a gun being fired • *All of a sudden we heard pow! pow! pow!—like shots being fired.*

powder /'paʊd·ər/ *n* [C/U] a loose, dry substance of extremely small pieces, usually made by breaking up something into smaller parts and crushing them • *During the raid, police found four packages of white powder, believed to be cocaine.* [U] • Powder is also any of various loose, dry, usually pleasant-smelling substances that people put on their skin as a help in healing or as makeup: *talcum powder* [U] • Powder is also **gunpowder**. See at GUN WEAPON. • A **powder keg** is a situation that is dangerous and that could become violent: *Tension was high following the shooting of another black teenager by a white police officer, and some African-American leaders called the inner city a powder keg.* • (*dated*) A **powder room** is a bathroom for women.

powdered /'paʊd·ərd/ *adj* [not gradable] being in the form of a powder • *powdered milk*

powdery /'paʊd·ə·ri/ *adj* having the form of powder

power CONTROL /'paʊ·ər/ *n* [U] the ability or right to control people and events, or to influence the way people act or think in important ways • *The election results showed that the Democrats had lost power, with Republicans taking over five more Democratic seats.* • (*law*) A **power of attorney** is a legal document in which someone gives another person the right to act for them, esp. in financial or legal matters.

powerful /'paʊ·ər·fəl/ *adj* having a lot of power • *He's in a powerful position as an adviser of the president.*

powerless /'paʊ·ər·ləs/ *adj* without the power to do something or to prevent something from happening • *The government seems powerless to do anything about the trade in illegal drugs.* [+ *to* infinitive]

power PERSON WHO CONTROLS /'paʊ·ər/ *n* [C] someone or something, such as an organization or country, that has control over others, often because of authority, importance, or wealth • *She is a power in the field of medical education.* • A **powerhouse** is a person, organization, or country with a lot of energy, power, or influence: *Germany is the economic powerhouse of the European Union.*

power NATURAL ABILITY /'paʊ·ər/ *n* [C/U] a natural skill or ability to do something • *She was so shocked that for a moment she lost the power of speech.* [U] ○ *The doctor did everything in her power to save him.* [C]

power STRENGTH /'paʊ·ər/ *n* [U] physical strength or force • *He's a good baseball player—he hits with a lot of power.*

power /'paʊ·ər/ *v* [T] • *At the start of the race, she dived into the pool and quickly powered her way into the lead.*

powerful /'paʊ·ər·fəl/ *adj* strong • *The picture quality is bad because the TV signal isn't powerful enough.* • Things that are powerful have a strong effect: *a powerful drug*

powerfully /ˈpɑʊ·ər·fə·li, -fli/ *adv* • *Dewayne is powerfully built* (= has a strong body).

power ENERGY /ˈpɑʊ·ər/ *n* [U] the ability to produce energy, or the energy produced • *electrical/nuclear/solar power* • Power is also electricity: *Whenever there's a storm in these parts, you can expect a power outage* (= a loss of electrical power). • A **powerboat** is a small, fast boat often used in racing. • **Power steering** is a system that lets the driver of a vehicle easily change the direction in which it is moving by using power from the engine. • A **power plant** is a building where electricity is produced.

power /ˈpɑʊ·ər/ *v* [T] to provide (something) with the energy it needs to operate • *Many buses and trucks are powered by diesel fuel.* [T] • To **power up** is to provide (something) or be provided with electricity so that something can begin to operate: *The computer takes a few seconds to power up after it's been switched on.*

powerful /ˈpɑʊ·ər·fəl/ *adj* • *Do you really need a car with such a powerful engine?*

power MATHEMATICS /ˈpɑʊ·ər/ *n* [U] *specialized* the number of times that a number is to be multiplied by itself, or the number that is the result of multiplying a number by itself • *Three to the fourth power can be written 3^4.*

powwow /ˈpɑʊ·wɑʊ/ *n* [C] an American Indian meeting or gathering for making decisions or for ceremonies or celebrations • *In South Dakota each summer, a Sioux powwow attracts dancers from all over the US.* ○ *(fig.) I'm going home for a family powwow* (= discussion) *this weekend.*

pp. *pl n abbreviation for* PAGES • *There is a detailed discussion on pp. 101-123.*

PR *n* [U] *abbreviation for* **public relations**, see at PUBLIC INVOLVING PEOPLE

practicable /ˈpræk·tɪ·kə·bəl/ *adj* able to be done or put into action • *A detailed report on the cause of the accident will be made public as soon as practicable.*

practical ACTUAL / REAL /ˈpræk·tɪ·kəl/ *adj* relating to actual experience or to the use of knowledge in activities rather than to knowledge only or ideas • *I know you've been trained as a teacher, but do you have any practical teaching experience?* • If you say that a person is practical, you mean they behave in ways that relate more to the realities of the world than to their ideas or desires: *You've got to learn to be practical and save your money.* • A **practical joke** is a joke intended to make someone seem foolish and involves a physical action rather than words: *She glued that cup and saucer together as a practical joke.*

practicalities /ˌpræk·tɪˈkæl·əṭ·iːz/ *pl n* the particular conditions of a situation; the actual facts • *I know you have to be in Paris tomorrow, but you have to understand the practicalities of arranging transportation on such short notice.*

practical EFFECTIVE /ˈpræk·tɪ·kəl/ *adj* fitting the needs of a particular situation in a helpful way; helping to solve a problem or difficulty; effective or suitable • *We didn't want to spend the night at a motel, but it just wasn't practical to do the trip in one day.* ○ *In some cities, it isn't practical to keep the subways operating all night because there aren't enough passengers.* • When used of objects such as clothes, practical can mean directed only to the goal of doing their intended work, and often plain in style or character: *I wear clothes that are practical rather than fashionable.*

practically /ˈpræk·tɪ·kli/ *adv* • *Many people have offered help, but there's little they can practically do.*

practically /ˈpræk·tɪ·kli/ *adv* [not gradable] almost or very nearly • *Practically everybody will be at the party.* ○ *It's practically impossible to get home in less than an hour.*

practical nurse /ˌpræk·tɪ·kəlˈnɜrs/ *n* [C] a person who is trained to care for the sick but who is not as qualified as a **registered nurse**

practice ACTION /ˈpræk·təs/ *n* [U] action rather than thought or ideas • *It seemed like a good idea, but in practice it was a disaster.* ○ *How soon will the new procedures be put into practice?*

practice REGULAR ACTIVITY /ˈpræk·təs/ *n* [C/U] something that is usually or regularly done, often as a habit, tradition, or custom • *It was his usual practice to buy a newspaper every morning on the way to the office.* [U]

practice, *esp. Cdn and Br* **practise** /ˈpræk·təs/ *v* [T] • *The right to practice religion as you choose is guaranteed by the US Constitution.* • If you **practice what** you **preach**, you do the things that you advise other people to do: *Why don't you try practicing what you preach?*

practicing, *esp. Cdn and Br* **practising** /ˈpræk·tə·sɪŋ/ *adj* [not gradable] following the rules esp. of a religion • *a practicing Catholic/Jew/Muslim*

practice TRAIN , *esp. Cdn and Br* **practise** /ˈpræk·təs/ *v* [I/T] to do or play (something) regularly or repeatedly in order to become skilled at it • *I'm good at tennis but I need to practice my serve.* [T]

practice /ˈpræk·təs/ *n* [C/U] • *I need more practice before I take my driving test.* [U]

practice WORK , *esp. Cdn and Br* **practise** /ˈpræk·təs/ *v* [I/T] to do (a particular kind of work, esp. law or medicine) for which a lot of training is necessary • *The firm has been practicing law for over a hundred years.* [T]

practice /ˈpræk·təs/ *n* [C] • *He gave up the practice of medicine when he came to the United States.*

practicing, *esp. Cdn and Br* **practising** /ˈpræk·tə·sɪŋ/ *adj* [not gradable] • *He remained a practicing architect until he died at the age of 89.*

practitioner /prækˈtɪʃ·ə·nər/ *n* [C] someone whose regular work has involved a lot of training • *Dr. Goldstein is a family/general practitioner* (= a medical doctor who treats general conditions).

pragmatic /præg'mæt̬·ɪk/ *adj* based on practical judgments rather than principles • *He made a pragmatic decision to settle the lawsuit because in the end it would cost more to try it in court.*

prairie /'prer·i/ *n* a wide area of flat land, covered with grass, esp. a large area in central North America that was originally covered by grass and is now mainly farming land • A **prairie dog** is a small animal that is a kind of SQUIRREL and that lives in western North America.

praise SHOW APPROVAL /preɪz/ *v* [T] to express strong admiration for or approval of (a person or something done) • *The "Times" praised the mayor's decision to reappoint the parks commissioner.*

praise /preɪz/ *n* [U] • *His economic policies have won praise from fellow Republicans.*

praise GOD /preɪz/ *v* [T] to honor, worship, and express admiration for (God or a god) • *Praise God/the Lord.*

prance /præns/ *v* [I] to walk or dance in an energetic way, with high, kicking steps • *In the square dance, each couple took turns prancing together under the linked arms of the other couples.*

prank /præŋk/ *n* [C] a trick that is intended to be amusing and often to make someone look foolish • *She's always playing pranks on her little brother.*

pray /preɪ/ *v* to speak to God or a god either privately or in a religious ceremony esp. to express thanks or to ask for help • *Then the minister said, "Let us pray."* [I] ∘ *We often prayed (that) the war would end.* [+ (*that*) clause] • To pray also means to hope: *I prayed (that) she wouldn't discover my secret.* [+ (*that*) clause]

prayer /prer, prær/ *n* [C/U] the act or ceremony of speaking to God or a god, esp. to express thanks or to ask for help, or the words used in this act • *She knelt in prayer.* [U] ∘ *Before each meal someone says the blessing, a short prayer to thank God for the food.* [C]

praying mantis /'preɪ·ɪŋ'mænt̬·əs/ *n* [C] a large, green insect that holds its front legs in a way that makes it look as if it is praying

pre- /ˌpri/ *combining form* before (a time or an event) • *precooked food* ∘ *a preexisting condition*

preach SPEAK IN CHURCH /priːtʃ/ *v* [I/T] to give (a religious speech), esp. in a church • *The minister preached a sermon on the need for forgiveness.* [T]

preacher /'priː·tʃər/ *n* [C] a person who gives a religious speech, esp. one whose job is to do this

preach PERSUADE /priːtʃ/ *v* [I/T] to try to persuade other people to do or accept (something) • *Should Liddy be allowed to preach hatred?* [T] • To preach is also to give unwanted advice, esp. about moral matters, in an annoying way: *My mother's always preaching at me about studying harder.* [I] • *For the most part, Adams was preaching to the converted* (= trying to persuade people who already agree with him).

preamble /'priːˌæm·bəl/ *n* [C] an introduction to a speech or piece of writing • *the preamble to the Constitution*

prearranged /ˌpriː·ə'reɪndʒd/ *adj* [not gradable] arranged in advance • *a prearranged plan*

precarious /prɪ'kær·i·əs, -'ker-/ *adj* in danger because not firmly fixed; likely to fall or suffer harm • *I climbed onto a precarious platform to get a better view.*

precariously /prɪ'kær·i·ə·sli, -'ker-/ *adv* • *The vase was precariously perched on a narrow shelf next to the door.*

precaution /prɪ'kɔː·ʃən/ *n* [C] an action taken to prevent something unpleasant or dangerous from happening • *Homeowners should take the basic precaution of locking their doors and windows.*

precautionary /prɪ'kɔː·ʃəˌner·i/ *adj* [not gradable] • *The company has withdrawn the drug as a precautionary measure while further testing is done.*

precede /prɪ'siːd/ *v* [T] to be or go before (someone or something) in time or space • *John Adams preceded Thomas Jefferson as president.* ∘ *Nouns are often preceded by adjectives*

preceding /prɪ'siː·dɪŋ/ *adj* [not gradable] • *The table on the preceding page shows the test results.*

precedence /'pres·əd·əns/ *n* [U] the condition of being dealt with before other things or of being considered more important than other things • *What takes precedence here, environmental cost or consumer convenience?*

precedent /'pres·əd·ənt/ *n* [C/U] a previous action, situation, or decision that can be used as a reason or example for a similar action or decision at a later time • *Conditions have changed enormously, and the past is not much of a precedent.* [C] ∘ *Precedent indicated that a change would take place sooner rather than later.* [U]

precept /'priː·sept/ *n* [C] a rule for action or behavior, esp. one based on moral consideration • *common precepts of decency*

precinct /'priː·sɪŋt/ *n* [C] a division of a city or town, esp. an area protected by one police station, or a division used for electoral purposes • *The precincts of a place are the areas that surround it, esp. when enclosed: the sacred precincts of the temple*

precious VALUABLE /'preʃ·əs/ *adj* of very great value or worth • *precious memories* ∘ *Children are our most precious resource.* • Precious metals are gold, silver, and PLATINUM. • A precious stone is a jewel: *Diamonds and rubies are precious stones.*

precious VERY /ˈpreʃ·əs/ adv infml very • He earns precious little money.

precipice /ˈpres·ə·pəs/ n [C] a very steep side of a cliff or mountain • We stood at the edge of the precipice and looked down at the sea.

precipitate /prɪˈsɪp·əˌteɪt/ v [T] slightly fml to make (something) happen suddenly or sooner than expected • An invasion would certainly precipitate a war.

precipitate /prɪˈsɪp·ə·ət/ adj slightly fml • We were alarmed by his precipitate actions.

precipitation /prɪˌsɪp·əˈteɪ·ʃən/ n [U] water that falls from the clouds toward the ground, esp. as rain or snow

precipitous /prɪˈsɪp·ət·əs/ adj very steep, or falling a long way very fast • precipitous cliffs ○ New fads could result in a precipitous drop in sales.

précis /ˈpreɪ·si, preɪˈsiː/ n [C] pl **précis** /ˈpreɪ·siːz, preɪˈsiːz/ a short form of a text that gives only the important parts

precise /prɪˈsaɪs/ adj exact and accurate in form, time, detail, or description • The precise recipe is a closely guarded secret. ○ Years of doing this research had made her very precise in her working methods. ○ There was a good turnout for the meeting—twelve of us, to be precise.

precisely /prɪˈsaɪ·sli/ adv • Tell me precisely what happened. ○ He works slowly and precisely, whereas I tend to rush things and make mistakes. • Precisely is also used to emphasize the accuracy of what you are saying: Armed conflict is precisely what the government is trying to avoid.

precision /prɪˈsɪʒ·ən/ n [U] • Great precision is required to grind the lenses accurately. ○ She writes with clarity and precision.

preclude /prɪˈkluːd/ v [T] slightly fml to prevent (something) or make it impossible • Although your application was not accepted, it doesn't preclude the possibility of your applying again later.

precocious /prɪˈkoʊ·ʃəs/ adj showing unusually early mental development or achievement • Lucy was a verbally precocious child.

preconceived /ˌpriː·kənˈsiːvd/ adj [not gradable] (of an idea or opinion) formed too early, esp. without enough consideration or knowledge • Since I'm new, I have no preconceived notions about how it should be done.

preconception /ˌpriː·kənˈsep·ʃən/ n [C] an idea or opinion formed before enough information is available to form it correctly • These people shared many of the racial preconceptions common among whites.

precondition /ˌpriː·kənˈdɪʃ·ən/ n [C] something that must be or be true before it is possible for something else to happen • Sound financial policies are a precondition for economic growth.

precursor /prɪˈkɜr·sər, ˈpriːˌkɜr-/ n [C] something that comes before another and may lead to it or influence its development • Opponents fear this would be a precursor to development of the entire canyon.

predate /priːˈdeɪt/ v [T] to have existed or happened before (another thing) • These burial mounds predated the arrival of Europeans in North America.

predator /ˈpred·əţ·ər/ n [C] an animal that hunts and kills other animals for food

predatory /ˈpred·əˌtɔːr·i, -ˌtoʊr-/ adj • a predatory bird • If a person or organization is predatory, they tend to use others for their own advantage: Larger companies, which played a predatory role, swooped down to cash in on the new fad.

predecessor /ˈpred·əˌses·ər, ˈpriːd-/ n [C] a person who had a job or position before someone else, or a thing that comes before another in time or in a series • My predecessor worked in this job for twelve years. ○ The latest model is faster and sleeker than its predecessors.

predestination /priːˌdes·təˈneɪ·ʃən/ n [U] the belief that events in life are decided in advance by God or by FATE and cannot be changed

predicament /prɪˈdɪk·ə·mənt/ n [C] an unpleasant or confusing situation that is difficult to get out of or solve • With no money and no job, he found himself in a real predicament.

predicate GRAMMAR /ˈpred·ɪ·kət/ n [C] (in grammar) the part of a sentence that gives information about the subject • In the sentence "We went to the airport," "went to the airport" is the predicate.

predicate (obj) STATE /ˈpred·əˌkeɪt/ v fml to state that (something) is true • One cannot predicate that the disease is caused by a virus on the basis of current evidence. [+ that clause] • If an idea or argument is **predicated on** something, it depends on the existence or truth of that thing: The sales forecast is predicated on a growing economy.

predict /prɪˈdɪkt/ v to say that (an event or action) will happen in the future • Astronomers can predict the exact time of an eclipse. [T] Who could have predicted that she would win the election? [+ that clause] ○ The storm is predicted to reach the Florida coast tomorrow morning. [+ to infinitive] ○ No one can predict when the disease will strike again. [+ wh- word]

predictable /prɪˈdɪk·tə·bəl/ adj acting or happening in a way that is expected • Comets usually appear at predictable times. ○ She's so predictable—she always wants to go to the same old restaurant.

predictably /prɪˈdɪk·tə·bli/ adv • Predictably, the movie was a hit.

prediction /prɪˈdɪk·ʃən/ n [C/U] • We are not yet able to make accurate predictions about earthquakes. [C]

predilection /ˌpred·əlˈek·ʃən, ˌpriːd-/ n [C] a strong liking or preference • a predilection for spicy foods

predispose /ˌpriːd·ɪˈspoʊz/ v [T] to influence (someone) to behave or think in a particular way or to have a particular condition • *Individualism predisposes many people to look for individual solutions to social problems.* ○ *There is a medical test to determine if a woman is predisposed toward breast cancer.*

predisposition /ˌpriː.dɪs.pəˈzɪʃ.ən/ *n* [C] • *She has an annoying predisposition to find fault with everything.* ○ *There is evidence that a predisposition toward asthma runs in families.*

predominant /prɪˈdɑm.ə.nənt/ *adj* [not gradable] being the most noticeable or largest in number, or having the most power or influence • *Women have a predominant role as health care professionals.*

predominantly /prɪˈdɑm.ə.nənt.li/ *adv* [not gradable] • *This neighborhood is now predominantly Hispanic.*

predominance /prɪˈdɑm.ə.nəns/ *n* [U] • *The predominance of white males in powerful school positions sends a signal to youngsters about who is going to be successful in life.*

predominate /prɪˈdɑm.əˌneɪt/ *v* [I] to be the most important or the greatest in number • *We live in an area in which livestock, poultry, and dairy farming predominate.*

preeminent /priˈem.ə.nənt/ *adj* [not gradable] more important or powerful than all others • *He was the preeminent scientist of his day.*

preeminence /priˈem.ə.nəns/ *n* [U] • *Before the 19th century, China's preeminence in Asia was never challenged.*

preempt /priˈempt/ *v* [T] to prevent (something) from happening by taking action first • *State laws preempted local governments from restricting newspaper displays.* • If a broadcast is preempted, it is replaced by another, usually more important broadcast: *One station preempted its Friday night schedule to televise the high school playoffs.*

preemptive, pre-emptive /priˈemp.tɪv/ *adj* [not gradable] • *a preemptive air strike on an enemy base*

preen /priːn/ *v* [I/T] (of a bird) to clean and arrange (its feathers) using its beak • If a person preens, they make themself more attractive: *As they preened in the sun, Evelyn snapped photos of them.* [I]

prefabricated /priˈfæb.rəˌkeɪt.əd/, *infml* **prefab** /ˈpriːˌfæb/ *adj* [not gradable] built from parts that have been made in a factory and can be put together quickly • *Our school is using prefabricated buildings for extra classrooms.*

preface /ˈpref.əs/ *n* [C] something that comes before and introduces a more important thing, esp. an introduction at the beginning of a book that explains its aims • *an author's preface*

preface /ˈpref.əs/ *v* [T] • *He didn't preface the bad news with, "I don't know how to tell you this but."*

prefer /prɪˈfɜr/ *v* **-rr-** to choose or want (one thing) rather than another • *We have tea and coffee, but perhaps you'd prefer a cold drink.* [T]

○ *He prefers watching baseball to playing it.* [T]
○ *She prefers that we meet at the station.* [+ *that* clause] ○ *Would you prefer to leave?* [+ *to* infinitive]

preferable /ˈpref.ə.rə.bəl/ *adj* [not gradable] better or more desirable • *We could take a later flight if it would be preferable.* ○ *Surely a diplomatic solution is preferable to war.*

preferably /ˈpref.ə.rə.bli/ *adv* [not gradable] • *We're looking for a new house, preferably one closer to the school.*

preference /ˈpref.ə.rəns/ *n* [C/U] • *What are your preferences in music?* [C] ○ *It's not up to me to say what someone's sexual preference should be.* [C] • A preference is also an advantage given to someone: *The city gives preference to job applicants who live there.* [U]

preferential /ˌpref.əˈren.tʃəl/ *adj* better than that given to others • *Some prisoners had apparently received preferential treatment.*

prefix /ˈpriː.fɪks/ *n* [C] *specialized* (in grammar) a letter or group of letters added to the beginning of a word to change the meaning or make a new word • *In the words "unknown" and "unusual," "un-" is a prefix meaning "not."* • Compare SUFFIX. ⟨LP⟩ COMBINING FORMS

pregnant ⟨DEVELOPING YOUNG⟩ /ˈpreg.nənt/ *adj* [not gradable] (of female mammals) having young developing in the uterus • *She's seven months pregnant.*

pregnancy /ˈpreg.nən.si/ *n* [C/U] • *She experienced morning sickness during her first months of pregnancy.* [U]

pregnant ⟨HAVING MEANING⟩ /ˈpreg.nənt/ *adj* filled with meaning that has not been expressed • *There followed a pregnant pause in which each knew what the other was thinking but neither knew what to say.*

preheat /priˈhiːt/ *v* [T] to heat (something) before using it • *Preheat the oven to 350°F.*

prehistoric /ˌpriː.hɪsˈtɔːr.ɪk, -ˈtɑr-/ *adj* [not gradable] happening in the period of human history before there were written records • *Painting originated in prehistoric times with murals drawn on cave walls.*

prejudge /priˈdʒʌdʒ/ *v* [T] to form an opinion about (someone or something) before knowing or examining all the facts • *I am not prejudging your guilt or innocence.*

prejudice /ˈpredʒ.əd.əs/ *n* [C/U] an unfair and unreasonable opinion or feeling formed without enough thought or knowledge • *racial prejudice* [U] ○ *The experience merely confirmed all his prejudices about foreigners.* [C]

prejudice /ˈpredʒ.əd.əs/ *v* [T] to unfairly influence (a person or matter) so that an unreasonable opinion or decision results • *Both sides pledged not to do anything to prejudice the final outcome.*

prejudiced /ˈpredʒ.əd.əst/ *adj* • *Now someone will accuse me of being a hateful, prejudiced homophobe.*

prejudicial /ˌpredʒ.əˈdɪʃ.əl/ *adj* • *An official*

investigation would have a prejudicial effect on the company's reputation.

preliminary /prɪˈlɪm·ə₁ner·i/ *adj* [not gradable] coming before a more important action or event, esp. introducing or preparing for it • *preliminary talks* ○ *a preliminary investigation* ○ *The preliminary rounds of negotiation went well.*

preliminary /prɪˈlɪm·ə₁ner·i/ *n* [C usually pl] • *Her time of 12:32 took four seconds off the mark she set in Friday's preliminaries.*

prelude INTRODUCTION /ˈprel·juːd, ˈpreɪ·luːd/ *n* [C usually sing] something that comes before a more important event or action and introduces or prepares for it • *The dinner was only a prelude to a much larger meeting.*

prelude MUSIC /ˈprel·juːd, ˈpreɪ·luːd/ *n* [C] a piece of music that introduces a longer piece of music, or a short piece of music written esp. for the piano

premarital /priːˈmær·əṱ·ᵊl/ *adj* [not gradable] before marriage • *premarital sex*

premature /₁priː·məˈtʊr, -ˈtʃʊr/ *adj* happening or done too soon, esp. before the natural or desired time • *a premature death at age 50* ○ *A spokesman said it was premature to comment on the negotiations.*

prematurely /₁priː·məˈtʊr·li, -ˈtʃʊr-/ *adv* • *Twins often are born prematurely.* ○ *Tony is getting prematurely gray* (= his hair is becoming gray).

premed /priːˈmed/ *adj* [not gradable] being in a university course that prepares students for medical school • *He was a premed student at the University of California.*

premeditated /priːˈmed·ə₁teɪṱ·əd/ *adj* [not gradable] thought of or planned before being done • *The police believe the killing was premeditated.*

premenstrual /priːˈmen·strə·wəl/ *adj* [not gradable] of the time just before a woman's PERIOD (= monthly bleeding from her uterus) • **Premenstrual syndrome** (abbreviation **PMS**) is pains and feelings of unhappiness or annoyance that some women experience a few days before their monthly flow of blood from the uterus begins.

premier BEST /prɪˈmɪr, ˈpriː·mɪr, ˈprem·ɪr/ *adj* [not gradable] best or most important • *He was widely regarded as one of the world's premier authorities on heart disease.*

premier LEADER /prɪˈmɪr, ˈpriː·mɪr, ˈprem·ɪr/ *n* [C] the leader of the government of some countries, or the leader of the government of a part of a country • *the premier of Ontario*

premiere, **première** /prɪmˈjɪr, prɪˈmɪr/ *n* [C] the first public showing of a play, opera, movie, television program, or other entertainment • *The season premieres of two of my favorite TV shows are on Wednesday.*

premiere /prɪmˈjɪr, prɪˈmɪr/ *v* [T] • *The three-part BBC program will premiere in the United States on the Discovery Channel on Sunday.*

premise /ˈprem·əs/ *n* [C] an idea or theory on which a statement or action is based • *We don't accept the premise that cutting taxes will necessarily lead to increased economic productivity.* [+ *that* clause]

premises /ˈprem·ə·səz/ *pl n* a house or other building and the land on which it is built • *The bread sold here is baked on the premises.*

premium PAYMENT /ˈpriː·miː·əm/ *n* [C] an amount of money paid at regular times to INSURE (= protect against risk) your health or life, or your home or possessions • *That could mean higher Medicare premiums for retirees.*

premium EXTRA /ˈpriː·miː·əm/ *n* [C] something extra given or an extra amount charged • *You get a lipstick as a premium with the purchase of this makeup.* ○ *Our customers are willing to pay a premium for a superior product.* • A premium is also a great amount of importance: *The admissions office places a premium on a student's character in the selection process.* • If you get something **at a premium**, you pay a high price for it, esp. because it is not easily available: *It's possible to get a large apartment, but only at a premium.*

premium /ˈpriː·miː·əm/ *adj* [not gradable] of higher than usual quality or value • *premium gasoline*

premonition /₁prem·əˈnɪʃ·ən, ₁priː·mə-/ *n* [C] a feeling that something, esp. something unpleasant, is going to happen • *a premonition of danger*

prenatal /priːˈneɪṱ·ᵊl/ *adj* [not gradable] happening or existing before birth • *prenatal care*

prenuptial /priːˈnʌp·ʃəl, -tʃəl/ *adj* [not gradable] before getting married • A **prenuptial agreement** is a legal document signed by two people before they marry stating what will happen to their money and possessions if they DIVORCE (= legally end their marriage).

preoccupy /priːˈɑk·jə₁paɪ/ *v* [T] to be the main thought in (someone's mind), causing other things to be forgotten • *The wedding next month preoccupied her.*

preoccupied /priːˈɑk·jə₁paɪd/ *adj* • *He's been preoccupied lately because of problems at school.*

preoccupation /priː₁ɑk·jəˈpeɪ·ʃən/ *n* [C/U] the thing you think about most • *His preoccupation with sports is affecting his grades.* [U]

prep /prep/ *v* [T] **-pp-** *infml* to prepare • *The president's advisers are busy prepping him for the debate.* • (*medical*) To prep is also to get a person in a hospital ready for an operation.

prepare /prɪˈper, -ˈpær/ *v* [I/T] to make or get (something or someone) ready for something that will happen in the future • *Keane is preparing a film version of the play.* [T] ○ *The Southeast prepared for the worst as the hurricane turned toward the Atlantic coast.* [I]

prepared /prɪˈperd, -ˈpærd/ *adj* • *Everything looked prepared for the party.* ○ *The press representative read a prepared statement* (= one already written).

preparedness /prɪˈper·əd·nəs, -ˈpær·əd-/ *n* [U] • *military preparedness*

preparation /ˌprep·əˈreɪ·ʃən/ *n* [C/U] the state of being ready for something that will happen, or an action taken to become ready • *The teacher said my preparation for the exam was inadequate.* [U] ○ *By April, war preparations were moving ahead.* [C] ○ *A platform had been set up in preparation for the ceremony.* [U]

preparatory /prɪˈpær·əˌtɔːr·i, -ˈper-, -ˌtour·i/ *adj* [not gradable] • *Plans for building a new school are under way, but so far only in the preparatory stage.* • A **preparatory school** (also *short form* **prep school,** *abbreviation* **prep.**) is a private school for children over the age of eleven that prepares them to go to college: He went to St. John's Prep.

preponderance /prɪˈpɑn·də·rəns/ *n* [U] the largest part or greatest amount • *The preponderance of evidence suggests the crash was an accident and not a terrorist attack.*

preposition /ˌprep·əˈzɪʃ·ən/ *n* [C] *specialized* (in grammar) a word that connects a noun, a noun phrase, or a pronoun to another word, esp. to a verb, another noun, or an adjective • *In the sentence, "We jumped in the lake," "in" is a preposition, and in the sentence, "I heard the sound of loud music," "of" is a preposition.*

prepositional /ˌprep·əˈzɪʃ·ən·əl/ *adj* [not gradable] *specialized* • A **prepositional phrase** is a combination of a preposition and a noun or pronoun that is its object.

preposterous /prɪˈpɑs·tə·rəs/ *adj* completely unreasonable and ridiculous; not to be believed • *It was a preposterous idea, and no one took it seriously.*

preppie /ˈprep·i/, **preppy** *n* [C] a person who is or was a student at a **preparatory school** (= private school that prepares students for college), or someone who dresses in the traditional, upper-class style of such students • *Dressed like a preppie, she wears a pleated wool plaid pinafore dress and white cotton shirt with white knee socks.*

prep school /ˈprep·skuːl/ *n short form* **preparatory school,** see at PREPARE

prerequisite /priːˈrek·wə·zət/ *n* [C] something that must exist or happen before something else can exist or happen • *Introductory physics is a prerequisite for any of the advanced courses in physics.*

prerogative /prɪˈrɑg·ət·ɪv/ *n* [C] a special advantage that allows some people the freedom to do or have something that is not possible or allowed for everyone • *It's the president's prerogative to nominate judges who share his political philosophy.*

Pres. /prez/ *n* [C] *abbreviation for* PRESIDENT POLITICS

Presbyterian /ˌprez·bəˈtɪr·iː·ən/ *n* [C], *adj* [not gradable] (a member) of a Christian religious group that is one of the Protestant churches • *a Presbyterian church* ○ *a Presbyterian minister*

preschool /ˈpriː·skuːl/ *n* [C/U] a school for children who are younger than five years old

preschooler /ˈpriːˌskuː·lər/ *n* [C]

prescribe GIVE MEDICAL TREATMENT /prɪˈskraɪb/ *v* [T] to order (treatment) for someone, or to say what someone should do or use to treat an illness or injury • *Many doctors prescribe aspirin to forestall second heart attacks.* ○ *My doctor prescribed rest and gave me a painkiller for my knee.*

prescribe GIVE RULE /prɪˈskraɪb/ *v* [T] to tell someone (what they must have or do), or to give as a rule • *A secretary of education cannot and should not prescribe the curriculum of the nation's colleges.*

prescription MEDICINE /prɪˈskrɪp·ʃən/ *n* [C] a doctor's written direction for the medicine that someone needs and how it is to be used, or the medicine itself • *The doctor gave me prescriptions for antibiotics and cough syrup.* ○ *The drugstore called to say your prescription is ready to be picked up.*

prescription RULES /prɪˈskrɪp·ʃən/ *n* [C] rules or a situation that will have a particular effect • *The company's reorganization could be a prescription for disaster.*

prescriptive /prɪˈskrɪp·tɪv/ *adj* tending to say what someone should do or how something should be done • *His basic attitude toward language is highly prescriptive.*

present SOMETHING GIVEN /ˈprez·ənt/ *n* [C] something that is given without being asked for, esp. on a special occasion, to show friendship, or to say thank you; a GIFT • *a birthday/Christmas present* ○ *Did you wrap the present?*

present PROVIDE /prɪˈzent/ *v* [T] to give, show, provide, or make known • *The mayor presented five firefighters with medals for saving people's lives.* ○ *Two clubs in the neighborhood present jazz on Thursdays.* ○ *Dr. Gottlieb will present her research in a series of lectures this spring.* • If you **present yourself,** you go to someone or make yourself known to someone: *Paul Groncki presented himself to the receptionist on the 41st floor.* • If something presents itself, it happens or takes place: *An opportunity suddenly presented itself.*

present CAUSE /prɪˈzent/ *v* [T] to cause (esp. something bad) • *Falling tax revenues present a problem for the city.*

present NOW /ˈprez·ənt/ *n* [U] this period of time, not the past or the future; now • *The story moves back and forth between the past and the present.*

present /ˈprez·ənt/ *adj* [not gradable] • *the present situation* • *The story takes place in* **present-day** (= modern) *Greece.*

presently /ˈprez·ənt·li/ *adv* [not gradable] at this time • *Three of the ten boats are presently being repaired.* • See also PRESENTLY.

present GRAMMAR /'prez·ənt/ *adj* [not gradable] *specialized* (in grammar) having the tense of a verb used to describe actions, events, or states that are happening or existing at this time • *Her book is written entirely in the present tense.* • A **present participle** is a form of a verb that ends in "ing" and comes after another verb to show continuous action: *In the sentence "The children are watching television," "watching" is a present participle.* • The **present perfect** is the tense you use to refer to actions or events that have been completed or have happened in a period of time up to now: *The sentence "She has broken her leg" is in the present perfect.* • LP TENSES

present PLACE /'prez·ənt/ *adj* [not gradable] in a particular place • *The mayor was present during the entire meeting.*

presence /'prez·əns/ *n* [C/U] • *We shouldn't discuss Jeff's progress in the presence of the other students* (= when the other students are there). [U] ○ *Those who disagreed with the funding proposal made their presence felt* (= made their opinions known). [U] • Presence is also a person's ability to make their character known to others: *He writes better, he reports better, and his presence on camera is better.* [U] • If a country or organization has a presence somewhere, some of its members are there. [C usually sing] • **Presence of mind** is the ability to make good decisions and to act quickly and calmly in a difficult situation or an emergency.

present INTRODUCE /prɪ'zent/ *v* [T] *fml* to introduce (a person) • *I'm pleased to present my son, Charles.*

presentable /prɪ'zent·ə·bəl/ *adj* looking suitable or good enough, esp. in the way you are dressed • *You need to look presentable for the interview.* ○ *A coat of paint made the house presentable.*

presentation /ˌprez·ən'teɪ·ʃən, ˌpriː·zen-/ *n* [C/U] the act of giving or showing something, or the way in which something is given or shown • *a multimedia presentation* [C] ○ *After the sales presentation, the board had a number of questions.* [C] ○ *Presentation of the awards takes place at a banquet in June.* [U] ○ *Both the food and its presentation were excellent.* [U]

presently /'prez·ənt·li/ *adv* [not gradable] soon; not at this time but after a short time in the future • *We will be leaving presently.* • See also **presently** at PRESENT NOW.

preserve KEEP /prɪ'zɜrv/ *v* [T] to keep (something) as it is, esp. in order to prevent it from decaying or to protect it from being damaged or destroyed • *The committee will suggest ways to preserve historically important buildings in the downtown area.* • To preserve food is to treat it in a particular way so it can be kept for a long time without going bad: *My grandmother preserved cherries in syrup.*

preserve /prɪ'zɜrv/ *n* [C usually pl] fruit cooked with sugar • *apricot preserves*

preservative /prɪ'zɜr·vəˌɪv/ *n* [C/U] • *artificial/natural preservatives* [C]

preservation /ˌprez·ər'veɪ·ʃən/ *n* [U] • *Janet is very interested in historic preservation* (= protecting places of historic importance).

preservationist /ˌprez·ər'veɪ·ʃə·nəst/ *n* [C] • *Preservationists were outraged at the proposal to tear down a historic theater.*

preserve SEPARATE ACTIVITY /prɪ'zɜrv/ *n* [C] an activity that only one person or a particular type of person does or is responsible for • *The gardening is Jeanne's special preserve.*

preserve SEPARATE PLACE /prɪ'zɜrv/ *n* [C] an area of land kept in its natural state, esp. for hunting and fishing or for raising animals and fish • *a wildlife preserve*

preside /prɪ'zaɪd/ *v* [I] to be in charge of or to control a meeting or event • *The vice president will preside at today's meeting.*

president POLITICS /'prez·əd·ənt, -əˌdent/ (*abbreviation* **Pres.**) *n* [C] the highest political position in the United States and some other countries, usually the leader of the government • *Several people are considering running for president, but none have announced their candidacy yet.*

presidential /ˌprez·ə'den·tʃəl/ *adj* • *a presidential candidate*

presidency /'prez·əd·ən·si, -əˌden-/ *n* [C] the position of being president, or the length of time during which someone is president • *the office of the presidency* ○ *Franklin D. Roosevelt's presidency lasted more than 12 years.*

president ORGANIZATION /'prez·əd·ənt, -əˌdent/ *n* [C] a person who has the highest position in a company or organization • *The company's board of directors will name a new president at its next meeting.*

press PUSH /pres/ *v* [I/T] to push firmly against (something that is fixed in position) • *I pressed the button on the VCR.* [T] ○ *The crowd pressed up against the doors.* [I always + adv/prep] ○ *He pressed down hard on the accelerator, and the car shot ahead.* [I always + adv/prep] • When you press clothes, you use an IRON (= a heavy device with a flat base) to make them smooth. [T] • If you **press ahead**, you continue to do something although there is opposition to it: *The firm pressed ahead with plans to build the skyscraper.* • If you **press on**, you continue working or traveling: *We didn't have time to stop, and pressed on into Arizona.*

press PERSUADE /pres/ *v* [T] to try to persuade or cause (someone) to do something, or to act in a determined way to cause (something) to be accepted • *The police pressed her to identify the man she had seen.* ○ *Marquez will visit Washington to press his country's case.* ○ *She decided not to press charges against him* (= make an official complaint).

press DEVICE /pres/ *n* [C] any of various de-

THE -ING FORM OF VERBS

the present participle

Most verbs have an **-ing** form. One important use of the **-ing** form is to form continuous (or progressive) tenses. When used in this way, it is called the present participle or **-ing** participle.

Alicia was working in the garden.

Other uses for the -ing participle are:

- **Following intransitive verbs**
  Some intransitive verbs can be followed by an **-ing** participle.
  He came rushing over when I fell (= He came when I fell, and he was rushing.) • *We sat in the cafe chatting for hours* (= We sat in the cafe, and we were chatting).
  Verbs with this grammar pattern usually describe the movement or position of someone:
  arrive, come, go, lie, remain, run, rush, sit, stand, stay

- **Following the object of transitive verbs**
  The object of some transitive verbs can be followed by an **-ing** participle.
  I heard the children opening their presents (= I heard the children, and they were opening their presents). • *I'm sorry to keep you waiting* (= for making you wait for a long time).
  Verbs that can be used this way include:
  bring, catch, discover, excuse, feel, find, get, hate, have, hear, imagine, keep, leave, like, notice, observe, picture, prevent, remember, reveal, see, send, set, show, start, stop, take, want, watch

- **Used as adjectives**
  It is common to use an **-ing** participle form of a verb as an adjective.
  She is a growing girl. • *The news was very disturbing.*
  These adjectives often express the idea of activity or change in progress, or describe the thing or person that causes a feeling.
  Pour out some of the boiling water (= the water that is boiling). • *It's a really exciting film* (= a film that excites you).
  Compare them with **-ed** (or **-en**) adjectives, which often express the idea of the result of activity or describe how you feel.
  I'd like a pound of boiled ham (= ham that has been boiled). • *The children were really excited* (= Something had excited the children).

the -ing form used like a noun

The **-ing** form can also be used in ways that are like a noun. Some grammar books call this use of the **-ing** form a GERUND. Compare the following pairs of sentences:

Fast cars are dangerous.
Driving too fast is dangerous.

The actors were terrible.
The acting was terrible.

I like trains.
I like traveling by train.

Thank you for the meal.
Thank you for cooking us a meal.

Do you mind my questions?
Do you mind my asking something?

An **-ing** form of this type is frequently used after other verbs and after prepositions. It is also used after some adjectives and nouns.

---

vices that use force • *a pants press* ∘ *a garlic press* ∘ *a printing press*

press NEWSPAPERS /pres/ *n* [U] newspapers, magazines, and other businesses that communicate news to the public by print, television, or radio, or the people who work to prepare and present the news • *Is the press too conservative?* • Good/bad press is the positive or negative reaction of newspapers, magazines, etc., to a person or thing: *At some point, every president has complained about bad press.* • A **press conference** is a meeting at which government or business officials make a public statement and reporters can ask questions. • A **press release** is a public statement given to the press.

press PUBLISHER /pres/ *n* [C] a business that prints and produces books or other printed material • *Cambridge University Press*

pressing /'pres·ɪŋ/ *adj* urgent or needing to be dealt with immediately • *a pressing need/issue*

pressure FORCE /'preʃ·ər/ *n* [C/U] the force produced by pressing against something •

air/blood/water pressure [U] • A **pressure cooker** is a container with a tightly fitting lid that cooks food quickly in steam.

pressure INFLUENCE /ˈpreʃ·ər/ n [C/U] a strong, often threatening influence on an organization or person • *Competitive pressures will force the company to sell off its factories.* [C] • If you put pressure on someone, you try to cause them to do something by persuading or threatening them: *They put a lot of pressure on him to resign.* [U]

pressure /ˈpreʃ·ər/ v [T] • *She was pressured into signing the agreement.*

pressure WORRY /ˈpreʃ·ər/ n [U] worry and fear caused by the feeling that you have too many responsibilities and cares • *I like this job—there's not so much pressure to produce every day.*

prestige /presˈtiːʒ, -ˈtiːdʒ/ n [U] respect and admiration given to someone or something, usually because of a reputation for high quality, success, or social influence • *No one would go into this sort of work for the prestige.*

prestigious /presˈtɪdʒ·əs/ adj • *a prestigious school*

presume *(obj)* BELIEVE /prɪˈzuːm/ v to believe (something) to be true because it is likely, although not certain • *I presume (that) they're not coming, since they haven't replied to the invitation.* [+ *(that)* clause] ○ *People accused of a crime are presumed innocent until proven guilty.* [T]

presumably /prɪˈzuː·mə·bli/ adv [not gradable] • *Presumably they can afford to buy an apartment, or they wouldn't be looking.*

presume BE RUDE /prɪˈzuːm/ v [I] to be rude by doing something you know that you do not have a right to do • *The Japanese may reasonably ask how we can presume to give them advice.* [+ *to* infinitive]

presumption BELIEF /prɪˈzʌmp·ʃən/ n [C] a belief that something is true because it is likely, although not certain • *There is no scientific evidence to support such presumptions.*

presumption RUDENESS /prɪˈzʌmp·ʃən/ n [U] behavior that is rude or shows that you expect too much • *What presumption, to assume that I'd pay for everyone!*

presumptuous /prɪˈzʌmp·tʃə·wəs/ adj rude because of doing something although you know you do not have a right to do it • *It would be presumptuous of me to speak for the others.*

presuppose *(obj)* /ˌpriː·səˈpoʊz/ v *slightly fml* to think that (something) is true in advance without having any proof, or to consider that (something) is necessarily true if something else is true • *You're presupposing that he told her—but he may not have.* [+ *that* clause] ○ *Teaching presupposes a formal education.* [T]

pretax /ˈpriːˈtæks/ adj [not gradable] before tax is paid • *pretax income/earnings/profit*

pretend /prɪˈtend/ v [I/T] to behave as if something is true when you know that it is

not, esp. in order to deceive people or as a game • *Tom pretends to care.* [+ *to* infinitive] ○ *The children pretended (that) they were di nosaurs.* [+ *(that)* clause]

pretend /prɪˈtend/ adj [not gradable] • *a pretend tea party*

pretense /ˈpriː·tens, prɪˈtens/ n [U] a way of behaving that is intended to deceive people • *He made no pretense of looking for work.*

pretension /prɪˈten·tʃən/ n [C/U] the appearance of being more important or more serious than there is reason for • *Leonard's paintings have a real freedom from pretension.* [U] • A pretension is also a claim or belief that you can succeed or that you are important or have serious value: *He has no pretensions for higher office.* [C usually pl]

pretentious /prɪˈten·tʃəs/ adj *disapproving* trying to give the appearance of great importance, esp. in a way that is obvious • *pretentious restaurants* ○ *pretentious, silly poetry*

pretext /ˈpriː·tekst/ n [C] a pretended reason for doing something that is used to hide the real reason • *He called her on the pretext of needing help with his homework.*

pretty PLEASANT /ˈprɪt̬·i/ adj [*-er/-est* only] pleasant to look at, or (esp. of girls or women or things connected with them) attractive or charming in a delicate way • *a pretty view* ○ *My older sister is prettier than I am.*

prettiness /ˈprɪt̬·i·nəs/ n [U] • *Her prettiness was matched by her intelligence.*

pretty TO A LARGE DEGREE /ˈprɪt̬·i/ adv [not gradable] (used to give emphasis) to a large degree; to some degree • *I've got a pretty clear idea of what's going on.* ○ *She was pretty tired.* ○ *"How are you feeling?" "Pretty good, thanks."* • **Pretty much** means almost completely: *I've pretty much finished packing now.*

pretzel /ˈpret·səl/ n [C] a kind of hard or chewy bread, usually with salt on it, that is baked in the shape of a loose knot or stick

prevail /prɪˈveɪl/ v [I] to exist and be accepted among a large number of people, or to get a position of control and influence • *Let's hope that common sense prevails.* ○ *In spite of injuries, our team prevailed and went on to win.* • To **prevail on/upon** is to persuade: *My father prevailed on some friends to house us temporarily.*

prevailing /prɪˈveɪ·lɪŋ/ adj [not gradable] existing and accepted • *The prevailing view is that economic growth is likely to slow down.*

prevalent /ˈprev·ə·lənt/ adj existing commonly or happening frequently • *Violent crime is not as prevalent as it was a few years ago.*

prevalence /ˈprev·ə·ləns/ n [U] • *He was surprised by the prevalence of middle-aged women among the job seekers.*

prevent /prɪˈvent/ v [T] to stop (something) from happening or (someone) from doing something • *The police tried to prevent him* *from leaving.* ○ *Can this type of accident be prevented?*

preventable /prɪ'vent·ə·bəl/ *adj* • *Fortunately, the suffering caused by ulcers is entirely preventable.*

prevention /prɪ'ven·tʃən/ *n* [U] • *crime prevention*

preventive /prɪ'vent·ɪv/, **preventative** /prɪ'vent·əṭ·ɪv/ *adj* [not gradable] intended to stop something before it happens • *preventive measures* ○ *preventative health care*

preview /'pri·vju:/ *n* [C] an advance showing of something such as a movie or play before its formal opening, or the showing of a few parts of a movie or television program as an advertisement

preview /'pri·vju:/ *v* [T] • *Members got a chance to preview the new show at the museum.*

previous /'pri·vi·əs/ *adj* [not gradable] happening or existing before the one mentioned • *The previous owner of the house added a back porch.*

previously /'pri·vi·ə·sli/ *adv* [not gradable] • *She was previously employed as a tour guide.*

prewar /'pri·'wɔːr/ *adj* [not gradable] existing or happening before a war, esp. World War II • Compare POSTWAR.

prey /preɪ/ *n* [U] a creature that is hunted and killed for food by another animal • *The prey had been sighted.* • *He is* **prey to** *superstition and ignorance* (= influenced by it).

prey on /'preɪ·ɔːn, -ɑn/ *v prep* [T] to kill and eat (an animal) • *(fig.) Beggars work the airport, where they prey on tourists* (= unfairly get things from them).

price /praɪs/ *n* [C] the amount of money for which something is sold or offered for sale • *high/low prices* ○ *The price of gas went up five cents a gallon.* • If you can obtain something **at/for a price**, you either have to pay a lot of money or be involved in something unpleasant in order to get it: *You can get anything you want there—for a price.* • A **price tag** is a piece of paper attached to something for sale that shows how much it costs, or the cost of something: *The price tag for restoring the building will be around $150 million.*

price /praɪs/ *v* [T] • *The car is priced at $24,000.*

priceless /'praɪ·sləs/ *adj* more valuable than any amount of money; precious • *He has a priceless collection of antique silver.*

pricey /'praɪ·si/ *adj* **pricier, priciest** expensive • *That restaurant's too pricey for me.*

prick MAKE HOLES /prɪk/ *v* [T] to make a small hole or holes in the surface of (something) • *The nurse pricked his finger to draw blood.*

prick BODY PART /prɪk/ *n* [C] *taboo slang* a penis

prick MAN /prɪk/ *n* [C] *rude slang* a man you do not like • *She hated this curly-haired, egotistical prick.*

□ **prick up** /'-'-/ *v adv* [T] (of an animal) to cause (its ears) to straighten because it is listening carefully to something • *Both hunting dogs pricked up their ears.* ○ *(fig.) When I heard my name, I pricked up my ears.*

prickle /'prɪk·əl/ *n* [C] a stinging feeling as if made by a sharp point • *A prickle of fear ran up the back of my neck.* • A prickle is also a sharp point that sticks out of a plant or animal.

prickle /'prɪk·əl/ *v* [I/T] • *She lay on the dry grass, which prickled the back of her legs.* [T]

prickly /'prɪk·li/ *adj* having sharp points that stick out, or causing a stinging feeling • *a prickly cactus* ○ *The wool felt prickly and itchy against his skin.*

pride FEELING OF SATISFACTION /praɪd/ *n* [U] a feeling of pleasure and satisfaction that you get because you or people connected with you have done something good • *Their son's outstanding academic record was a source of great pride to them.* ○ *We take pride in the high quality of our food.* • *Those flowers are her* **pride**

PRICE

Price, cost, charge, and expense all refer to the amount of money needed to buy something.

- **Price** usually refers to the amount of money asked or given for an object or product, as in a store.

  I hear the price of coffee is going up. • *We thought the price they asked for the house was too high.*

- **Charge** usually refers to the amount of money asked for a service or activity.

  Is there a charge for admission to the museum?

  It is also common as a verb.

  They charged five dollars for postage and handling.

- **Cost** can refer to the amount of money needed to do or make something, as well as to buy something. It is common as both a noun and verb.

  The cost of building the new center is expected to be over $2 million. • *How much did that cost?* • *This suit cost me $200.*

- **Expense** refers to the spending of money for a purpose.

  We were worried about the expense of sending our son to college.

  It is often used in the plural to refer to the money spent to doing a job or to maintain a house.

  Her employer reimbursed her for travel expenses. • *The three roommates shared household expenses.*

- The **value** of something is what it is worth, and might be different from its cost.

  I bought this painting for $100, and now its value is over $500. • *Property values in the area have fallen since the new airport was built.*

and joy (= give her a feeling of pleasure and satisfaction). • The related adjective is PROUD SATISFIED.

pride FEELING OF WORTH /praɪd/ *n* [U] your feelings of your own worth and respect for yourself • *Out of pride, he refused an offer to take over his business.* • (*disapproving*) Pride is also the belief that you are better or more important than other people. • The related adjective is PROUD RESPECTING YOURSELF.

pride /praɪd/ *v* [T] • If you **pride** your**self** on something, you value a skill or special quality that you have: *He prides himself on his singing.*

pride GROUP /praɪd/ *n* [C] a group of lions

priest /priːst/ *n* [C] a person, usually a man, who has been trained to perform religious duties in some Christian churches, esp. the Roman Catholic Church, or (*female* **priestess**) a person with particular duties in some other religions • *a Catholic priest*

priesthood /ˈpriːst·hʊd/ *n* [U] the position of being a priest • *He left the priesthood in order to get married.*

prim /prɪm/ *adj* formal, neat, and socially correct • *She wore a silk gown and prim white gloves.*

prima donna /ˌprim·əˈdɑn·ə, ˈpriː·mə-/ *n* [C] *pl* **prima donnas** the most important female singer in an opera company, or (*disapproving*) a person who is difficult to please and who expects to be treated better than anyone else • *The performance was met with enough applause to please the most demanding prima donna.*

primal /ˈpraɪ·məl/ *adj* [not gradable] characteristic of the earliest time in the existence of a person or thing; basic • *The appeal of music is primal.*

primary MOST IMPORTANT /ˈpraɪˌmer·i, -mə·ri/ *adj* [not gradable] more important than anything else; main • *The primary goal of the space flight was to recover a satellite.* • A **primary color** is one of the three colors—red, yellow, or blue— that can be mixed together in various ways to make any other color.

primarily /praɪˈmer·ə·li/ *adv* [not gradable] • *The company's failure was primarily due to weak sales.*

primary EDUCATION /ˈpraɪˌmer·i, -mə·ri/ *adj* [not gradable] relating to the first part of a child's education • *the primary grades* • A **primary school** is a school for children from the ages of about five to nine, or an **elementary school**. See at ELEMENTARY. • LP EDUCATION IN THE US

primary EARLIEST /ˈpraɪˌmer·i, -mə·ri/ *adj* [not gradable] happening first • *the primary stages of development* • (*medical*) **Primary care** is basic medical care that is available when someone first wants to be helped: *a primary care physician*

primary ELECTION /ˈpraɪˌmer·i, -mə·ri/ *n* [C] an election in which people who belong to a political party choose who will represent that party in an election for political office

primate /ˈpraɪ·meɪt/ *n* [C] *specialized* a member of the most developed and intelligent group of mammals, including humans, monkeys, and APES

prime MAIN / BEST /praɪm/ *adj* [not gradable] most important, or of the best quality • *You're a prime candidate to be spending money on foolish things.* ○ *This is a prime example of native Utah architecture.* ○ *The hospital is located on prime Upper East Side property.* • A **prime minister** is the leader of the government in some countries. • (*specialized*) A **prime number** is a number that cannot be divided by any other number except itself and the number 1. • **Prime time** is the period between 8 and 11 at night when the largest number of people are watching television: *prime time programs*

prime /praɪm/ *n* [U] • If you are **in your prime/in the prime of** your **life**, you are in the best possible condition or are most successful or most powerful: *She died young, snatched away in her prime.*

prime PREPARE /praɪm/ *v* [T] to prepare (someone or something) for the next stage in a process • *Their teachers are getting those kids primed for the tests.* • To prime a surface is to cover it with a special paint before the main paint is put on.

primer /ˈpraɪ·mər/ *n* [C/U] a type of paint put on a surface before putting on the main paint

primer /ˈprɪm·ər/ *n* [C] a basic text for teaching something • *As a primer for Navaho thinking, this book is a good place to start.*

primeval /praɪˈmiː·vəl/ *adj* existing at or from a very early time; ancient • *primeval forests*

primitive /ˈprɪm·əṭ·ɪv/ *adj* of or typical of an early stage of development; not advanced or complicated in structure • *primitive art/tools* ○ *The pioneers who settled the west had to cope with primitive living conditions.*

primordial /praɪˈmɔːrd·iː·əl/ *adj* existing at or since the beginning of the world or the universe • *primordial gases*

primrose /ˈprɪm·roʊz/ *n* [C] a wild plant with pale yellow flowers

prince /prɪns/ *n* [C] a member of a ROYAL family, esp. a son of a king or queen • A prince is also a male ruler of a small country.

princely /ˈprɪn·sli/ *adj* [not gradable] (esp. of money) very large in amount • *Advertisers pay a princely sum for prime-time commercials.*

princess /ˈprɪn·səs, -ses/ *n* [C] a member of a ROYAL family, esp. a daughter of a king or queen • A princess is also the wife of a PRINCE.

principal MAIN /ˈprɪn·sə·pəl/ *adj* [not gradable] first in order of importance • *Iraq's principal export is oil.*

principally /ˈprɪn·sə·pli/ *adv* [not gradable] more than anything or anyone else; mainly •

The advertising campaign is aimed principally at women.

principal PERSON /'prɪn·sə·pəl/ *n* [C] a person in charge of a school

principal MONEY /'prɪn·sə·pəl/ *n* [C usually sing] an amount of money that is lent, borrowed, or invested, apart from any additional money such as INTEREST

principality /ˌprɪn·sə'pæl·ət·i/ *n* [C] a country ruled by a PRINCE

principle MORAL RULE /'prɪn·sə·pəl/ *n* [C/U] a moral rule or standard of good behavior or fair dealing • *It's a well-established principle that the guilt for war crimes is shared not only by those who pull the trigger but by those who command them.* [C] ○ *He refused to compromise his principles.* [C] • If you believe or act **on principle**, you are following a personal standard of behavior: *He opposed the death penalty on principle* (= because he believed it was wrong).

principled /'prɪn·sə·pəld/ *adj* based on principles, or (of a person) having good personal standards of behavior • *She was known among her colleagues as a principled professional.*

principle BASIC TRUTH /'prɪn·sə·pəl/ *n* [C often pl] a basic truth that explains or controls how something happens or works • *the principles of Newtonian physics* • If someone agrees to something **in principle**, they agree with the idea, although they may not agree with using the idea to bring about practical changes: *In principle I agree that mothers should spend as much time as possible with their young children, but it isn't easy.*

print MAKE TEXT /prɪnt/ *v* [T] to put letters or images on (paper or another material) by pressing a surface, esp. a surface covered with ink, against it, or to produce (books, magazines, newspapers, etc.) in this way • *The newspaper printed my letter to the editor.* • To print is also to write without joining the letters together: *Please print your name clearly below your signature.* • To print something out is to print text or images from a machine attached to a computer: *Just print out the first two pages.* [M]

print /prɪnt/ *n* [U] text or images that are produced on paper or other material by printing • If something is **in print**, it is published. • If a book is **in/out of print**, it is available or no longer available from a publisher: *I'm afraid you can't get that book—it's out of print.* • A **printout** is a paper copy of text and images produced by a machine attached to a computer.

printing /'prɪnt·ɪŋ/ *n* [C/U] the process or business of producing printed material • A printing is the number of copies of a book printed at one time: *The first printing will be 25,000 copies.* [C] • A **printing press** is a machine that prints text or images on paper or

another material, esp. to produce books, magazines, and newspapers.

printer /'prɪnt·ər/ *n* [C] a machine connected to a computer that prints onto paper using ink • *a laser printer* • A printer is also a person whose job is to print material, esp. by using a **printing press**.

print PICTURE /prɪnt/ *n* [C] a single photograph made from film, or a photograph of a painting or other work of art • *We made extra prints of the baby to send out with the birth announcement.* • A print is also a picture made by pressing paper or other material against a special surface covered with ink: *woodcut prints*

print /prɪnt/ *v* [T] • *Photographs are better if they are printed from the original negative.*

print PATTERN /prɪnt/ *n* [C] a pattern produced on a piece of cloth, or cloth having such a pattern • *a print dress*

print MARK /prɪnt/ *n* [C] a mark left on a surface where something has been pressed on it • *The dog left prints all over the kitchen floor.* • A print is also a **fingerprint**. See at FINGERPRINT.

prior /'praɪ·ər/ *adj, adv* [not gradable] coming before in time, order, or importance • *She denied prior knowledge of the meeting.* • *Friends may call at the chapel an hour* **prior to** (= before) *the funeral service.*

priority /praɪ'ɔːr·ət·i, -'ɑr-/ *n* [C/U] something that is considered more important than other matters • *The president vowed to make education one of his top priorities.* [C] • If something **has/takes priority over** something else, it is more important: *Getting fresh water and food to the flood victims takes priority over dealing with their insurance claims.* [U]

prioritize /praɪ'ɔːr·ə,taɪz, -'ɑr-/ *v* [I/T] to arrange in order of importance so that you can deal with the most important things before the others • *You have to prioritize in this job because you can't do everything.* [I]

prism /'prɪz·əm/ *n* [C] a transparent object, often glass, that separates white light into different colors

prison /'prɪz·ən/ *n* [C/U] a building where criminals are kept as a punishment • *He was sent to prison for life.* [U]

prisoner /'prɪz·ə·nər/ *n* [C] a person who is kept in prison as punishment • A prisoner is also someone who is not physically free because they are under the control of someone else: *We were held/taken prisoner by the gunmen.* • A **prisoner of war** (*abbreviation* **POW**) is a member of the armed forces who has been caught by enemy forces during a war.

pristine /'prɪs·tiːn, prɪ'stiːn/ *adj* [not gradable] original and pure; not spoiled or worn from use • *The car seemed to be in pristine condition.*

private PERSONAL /'praɪ·vət/ *adj* for the use of or belonging to one particular person or group only, or not shared or available to other people • *The sign on the gate said "Private Property—*

Keep Out." ◦ Let's go somewhere private so we can talk freely. • If you do something **in private**, you do it without other people present: *I asked if I could talk to her in private.* • **Private parts** are the sexual organs.

privately /ˈpraɪ·vət·li/ *adv* [not gradable] • *Could I speak with you privately* (= without other people present)*?* ◦ *Despite his public support, privately* (= in his own mind) *he was worried.*

privacy /ˈpraɪ·və·si/ *n* [U] the state of being alone, or the right to keep one's personal matters and relationships secret • *A fence would give us more privacy in the backyard.*

private INDEPENDENT /ˈpraɪ·vət/ *adj* [not gradable] belonging to or managed by a person or independent company rather than the government • *The governor visited Ireland as a private citizen* (= not as an official). • **Private enterprise** is the businesses owned and controlled independently and not by government, or the system that encourages such businesses. • A **private investigator** or **private detective** (*infml* **private eye**) is a person whose job it is to discover information about people, but who is not a member of a police force. • A **private school** is a school that does not receive its main financial support from the government. LP EDUCATION IN THE US • *The project will be financed by the government and the* **private sector** (= businesses owned and controlled independently of government).

privately /ˈpraɪ·vət·li/ *adv* [not gradable] • *She was privately educated at an exclusive girls' school.*

privatize /ˈpraɪ·və·taɪz/ *v* [T] (of an industry, company, or service) to change from being owned by a government to being owned and controlled independently

privatization /ˌpraɪ·vət·ə·ˈzeɪ·ʃən/ *n* [U]

private RANK /ˈpraɪ·vət/ *n* [C] a person in the military of the lowest rank, below a CORPORAL

privilege /ˈprɪv·ə·lɪdʒ/ *n* [C/U] a special advantage or authority possessed by a particular person or group • *As a senior executive, you will enjoy certain privileges.* [C] ◦ *I had the privilege* (= the honor) *of interviewing the prime minister of Canada.* [C]

privileged /ˈprɪv·ə·lɪdʒd/ *adj* [not gradable] • *As an old friend of the president, he enjoys privileged status.* • (*specialized*) Information that is privileged is secret: *A person's medical history is privileged information.*

privy /ˈprɪv·i/ *adj* [not gradable] *fml* • Someone who is **privy to** information has knowledge about something secret: *Only top management was privy to the proposed merger.*

prize /praɪz/ *n* [C] a reward for victory in a competition or game • *David won first prize in the school science fair.* • A **prizefight** is a sports competition in which two men trained to fight try to hit each other before people who pay to see them.

prize /praɪz/ *adj* [not gradable] given as a prize, or having won or deserving to win a prize • *prize money*

prize /praɪz/ *v* [T] to value greatly • *The Japanese prize personal relationships in doing business.* • A **prized** possession is one that is very important to you.

pro SPORTS PERSON /proʊ/ *n* [C] *pl* **pros** *infml* a person who receives money for playing a sport • *a tennis pro* • A **pro** is also someone who is very good at something: *Debbie is a real pro at arranging flowers.*

pro ADVANTAGE /proʊ/ *n* [C] *pl* **pros** an advantage or a reason for doing something • **Pros and cons** are advantages and disadvantages: *We considered all the pros and cons carefully before deciding to buy a bigger house.*

pro– SUPPORT /proʊ/ *combining form* supporting or approving of something • *pro-American* • Compare ANTI-.

probable /ˈprɑb·ə·bəl/ *adj* likely to be true or likely to happen • *The doctor said that the most probable cause of death was heart failure.*

probably /ˈprɑb·ə·bli/ *adv* [not gradable] • *I'll probably be home about midnight.*

probability /ˌprɑb·ə·ˈbɪl·ət·i/ *n* [C/U] the likelihood of something happening or being true • *There's a higher probability of now having a state income tax* (= the tax is more likely now). [C] • **In all probability** *he would never see her again* (= very likely he would not see her again).

probation /proʊ·ˈbeɪ·ʃən/ *n* [U] a period during which a person's behavior or performance on a job or in a school is watched closely to see whether they are good enough to stay • *I'm on probation this semester, so I've really got to study hard.* • Probation is also the condition of a criminal who is allowed to remain free if they commit no more crimes and meet regularly with their **probation officer** (= officer whose job is to manage criminals in this condition).

probe /proʊb/ *v* [I/T] to search into or examine (something) • *Investigators are probing into drug dealing in the area.* [I] • To probe something with a tool is to examine it: *Using a special instrument, the doctor probed the wound for the bullet.* [T]

probe /proʊb/ *n* [C] a careful and detailed examination • *The probe explored allegations of corruption in the police department.* • A probe is also a long, thin tool used by doctors in medical examinations or operations.

probing /ˈproʊ·bɪŋ/ *adj* (of a question) difficult to answer without telling the truth • *probing questions*

problem /ˈprɑb·ləm/ *n* [C] something that causes difficulty or that is hard to deal with • *Financing the camp's athletic program is a problem.* ◦ *He has a serious drinking problem.* ◦ *I'm having problems with my in-laws again.* • A problem is also a question to be answered or solved, esp. by reasoning or calculating: *math problems*

problematic /ˌprɑb·lə'mæt̬·ɪk/ *adj* • *Social interactions are really problematic with a lot of children.*

procedure /prə'siː·dʒər/ *n* [C/U] an order or method of doing something • *It's standard procedure for those at the top of the list to be called first.* [U]

proceed /prə'siːd, prou-/ *v* [I] to start or continue an action or process • *The building project is proceeding smoothly.* ○ *You should ask a lawyer for advice on how to proceed.* • To proceed is also to move forward or travel in a particular direction: *The warning signs said "Proceed with caution."*

proceedings /prə'siːd·ɪŋz, prou-/ *pl n* a series of actions that happen in a planned and controlled way • *As the president was sworn in, the nation watched the proceedings on TV.*

proceeds /'prou·siːdz/ *pl n* the amount of money received from a particular sale or event • *All proceeds from the auction will be donated to charity.*

process /'prɑs·es, 'prou·ses/ *n* [C] a series of actions or events performed to make something or achieve a particular result, or a series of changes that happen naturally • *Completing his degree at night was a long process.* ○ *Graying hair is part of the aging process.* • *We are still in the process of redecorating the house* (= working to decorate it). • A process is also a method of doing or making something, as in industry: *A new process has been developed for removing asbestos.*

process /'prɑs·es, 'prou·ses/ *v* [T] to deal with (something) according to a particular set of actions • *Your insurance claim will take about a month to process.* • If a computer processes information, it performs a series of operations on it. • To process food or raw materials is to prepare, change, or treat them as part of an industrial operation.

processed /'prɑs·est, 'prou·sest/ *adj* [not gradable] (of food) treated with chemicals that preserve it or give it extra taste or color • *processed cheese/meat*

processor /'prɑs·es·ər, 'prou·ses-/ *n* [C] a person, device, or business that processes things • *a food processor*

procession /prə'sef·ən/ *n* [C] a line of people, vehicles, or objects moving forward in an orderly manner, esp. as part of a ceremony • *a funeral procession*

processional /prə'sef·ən·ᵊl/ *adj* [not gradable] • *There was tight security along the processional route.*

pro–choice /'prou'tʃɔɪs/ *adj* [not gradable] supporting the belief that a pregnant woman should have the freedom to choose an ABORTION (= an operation to end a pregnancy) if she does not want to have a baby • Compare PRO-LIFE.

proclaim /prə'kleɪm, prou-/ *v* [T] to announce (esp. something positive) publicly or officially • *She confidently proclaimed victory even as the first few votes came in.*

proclamation /ˌprɑk·lə'meɪ·ʃən/ *n* [C] a public announcement, or the act of making it

procrastinate /prə'kræs·tə,neɪt/ *v* [I] to delay doing something • *When it comes to housework, I tend to procrastinate.*

procreate /'prou·kriː,eɪt/ *v* [I] to reproduce sexually

procreation /ˌprou·kriː'eɪ·ʃən/ *n* [U]

procure /prə'kjur, prou-/ *v* [T] to obtain (something), esp. after an effort • *We procured maps and directions from the tourist office.*

procurement /prə'kjur·mənt, prou-/ *n* [U] • *the city's procurement process*

prod /prɑd/ *v* [I/T] **-dd-** to push (something or someone) with your finger or with an object, or to encourage (someone) to take action, esp. when they are slow or unwilling • *The barber prodded the back of Ray's head.* [T] ○ *No matter how much I prod he will not tell me what happened.* [I]

prod /prɑd/ *n* [C] • *Religion should be a prod to your spiritual life.*

prodigal /'prɑd·ɪ·gəl/ *adj esp. literary* tending to spend or use something without thinking of the future • *He was prodigal with his talents.*

prodigious /prə'dɪdʒ·əs/ *adj* extremely great in ability, amount, or strength • *Americans are the world's most prodigious consumers.*

prodigiously /prə'dɪdʒ·ə·sli/ *adv* • *a prodigiously gifted artist*

prodigy /'prɑd·ə·dʒi/ *n* [C] a child who shows a great ability at a young age • *a child prodigy on the piano*

produce MAKE /prə'duːs/ *v* [T] to create (something) or bring into existence • *Bukowski produced poetry and novels.* ○ *Dairy goods and beef are produced locally.*

producer /prə'duː·sər/ *n* [C] a company, country, or person that makes things, usually for sale, esp. things made by an industrial process or grown or obtained from the ground • *a producer of automobiles/wheat*

produce ORGANIZE A SHOW /prə'duːs/ *v* [T] to organize the financial and other practical matters connected with the making of (a movie, play, television show, or other entertainment program) • *He produced a couple of wonderful films.* • Compare DIRECT CONTROL.

producer /prə'duː·sər/ *n* [C] • *a movie/record producer*

produce BRING OUT /prə'duːs/ *v* [T] to bring (something) out and show it • *He walked up and produced his passport.*

produce CAUSE /prə'duːs/ *v* [T] to cause (a reaction or result) • *Too much coffee can produce unwanted side-effects.*

produce FOOD /'prɑd·uːs, 'proud·uːs/ *n* [U]

food that is grown or raised through farming, esp. fruits and vegetables • *local produce*

product THING MADE /'prɑd·əkt, -ʌkt/ *n* [C] something that is made to be sold, esp. something produced by an industrial process or something that is grown or raised through farming • *industrial products* ○ *A new product can require two years to develop.*

production /prə'dʌk·ʃən/ *n* [U] the process of making or growing goods to be sold, or the amount of goods made or grown • *mass production* ○ *Agricultural production has increased dramatically this year.*

product RESULT /'prɑd·əkt, -ʌkt/ *n* [C] a result obtained from experiencing something • *She's a product of the city's public schools.* • In mathematics, a product is the number you get when you multiply numbers: *The product of 6 and 3 is 18.*

production /prə'dʌk·ʃən/ *n* [C/U] a movie, television program, play, or other entertainment, or the work of organizing the practical matters involved in a show • *a terrific production of "The Wizard of Oz"* [C] ○ *She's hoping to get into television production.* [U]

productive /prə'dʌk·tɪv/ *adj* causing or providing a good result or a large amount of something • *We had a very productive meeting—a lot of problems were solved.* ○ *What was once desert has become productive farmland.*

productively /prə'dʌk·tɪv·li/ *adv* • *Her students worked less productively than the teacher hoped.*

productivity /ˌprou·ˌdʌk'tɪv·ət·i, ˌprɑd·ək-/ *n* [U] the rate at which a person, company, or country does useful work • *A pleasant working environment increases productivity.*

Prof. /prɑf/ *n abbreviation for* PROFESSOR, used in writing before a name • *Prof. Linda Chen*

profane /prə'feɪn, prou-/ *adj* (esp. of words) offensive because of not respecting religion, or offensive because of being rude or taboo • *Who's more profane—a candidate who says the word "damn," or a president who doesn't give a damn?* ○ *profane language* • Compare SACRED.

profanity /prə'fæn·ət·i, prou-/ *n* [C/U] • *The film contains profanity and violence.* [U] ○ *They shouted profanities at us.* [C usually pl]

profess /prə'fes, prou-/ *v* to claim (something), sometimes falsely • *They professed to have no knowledge of the event.* [+ *to* infinitive] ○ *She continues to profess her innocence.* [T]

professed /prə'fest/ *adj* [not gradable] • *a professed belief*

profession /prə'feʃ·ən/ *n* [C] • *His professions of regret were not sincere.*

profession /prə'feʃ·ən/ *n* [C/U] any type of work, esp. one that needs a high level of education or a particular skill • *the medical/teaching profession* [C] ○ *I'm a writer by profession.* [U]

professional /prə'feʃ·ən·əl/ *adj* done as a job, or relating to a skilled type of work • *a professional athlete* ○ *professional sports* ○ *He spent his professional career at the University of Pennsylvania.* • Professional also means having the qualities of skilled and educated people, such as effectiveness and seriousness of manner: *Wearing jeans to work is not looked upon as being professional.* • Compare AMATEUR.

professional /prə'feʃ·ən·əl/ *n* [C] a person who has a job that needs skill, education, or training • *Don't you wish you had hired a professional to paint your house?* ○ *Many of these homes have been restored by young professionals.*

professionally /prə'feʃ·ən·əl·i/ *adv* • *I always wanted to sing professionally.*

professionalism /prə'feʃ·ən·əl·ɪz·əm/ *n* [U] the qualities connected with trained and skilled people • *We were impressed with the professionalism of the staff.*

professor /prə'fes·ər/ *n* (*abbreviation* **Prof.**) *n* [C] a teacher of high rank in an American university or college • *Professor W. B. Ofuatey-Kodjoe* ○ *a history professor/professor of history*

proficient /prə'fɪʃ·ənt/ *adj* skilled and experienced • *a proficient swimmer* ○ *He studied Chinese and became proficient in the language.*

proficiency /prə'fɪʃ·ən·si/ *n* [U] • *Morgan has great proficiency as a jazz saxophonist.*

profile SIDE VIEW /'prou·faɪl/ *n* [C/U] a side view of a person's face • *I'd seen her profile on a billboard.* [C] ○ *A face in profile never looks at the viewer.* [U]

profile DESCRIPTION /'prou·faɪl/ *n* [C] a description of someone containing all the most important or interesting facts about them •

profile

There's a profile of producer Hal Willner in "New York" magazine.

profile /'prou·faɪl/ *v* [T] • *Gilbert was recently profiled by a Washington business magazine.*

profile ATTENTION /'prou·faɪl/ *n* [C usually sing] the amount of public attention that someone or something receives • *He keeps a low profile and doesn't go after headlines.* ○ *The victim in this case doesn't have as high a profile as her attacker.*

profit /'prɑf·ət/ *n* [C/U] money that a business earns above what it costs to produce and sell goods and services • *Any profit made on the sale is taxable.* [U] ○ *A lot of businesses are reaping huge profits.* [C] • Profit can also mean benefit: *He could see little profit in arguing with them.* [U] • A **profit margin** is the amount that is made in a business after the costs have been subtracted: *Many farmers claim that the profit margin for growing trees* *remains slim.* • **Profit sharing** is a system in which the people who work in a company are given part of the profits in addition to their regular pay.

profit /'praf·ət/ *v* [I/T] • *It's sickening that somebody would profit off her death* (= earn money from it). [I] ∘ *(slightly fml)* *What will it profit us to make this bargain* (= How will we benefit)? [T]

profitable /'praf·əṭ·ə·bəl/ *adj* resulting in or likely to result in a profit or a benefit • *a profitable business* ∘ *I try to make profitable use of my time.*

profitably /'praf·əṭ·ə·bli/ *adv* • *We can operate profitably within that market.*

profitability /ˌpraf·əṭ·ə'bɪl·əṭ·i/ *n* [U] • *He revealed plans to restore the magazine's profitability.*

profligate /'praf·lɪ·gət, -ˌgeɪt/ *adj* wasteful, esp. with money • *profligate spending*

profound EXTREME /prə'faʊnd/ *adj* felt or experienced strongly; extreme • *The speech had a profound influence on her.*

profoundly /prə'faʊn·dli/ *adv* • *Having foreigners criticize us is profoundly offensive to Americans.*

profound SHOWING UNDERSTANDING /prə'faʊnd/ *adj* showing a clear and deep understanding of serious matters • *You're touching on a very profound question.*

profuse /prə'fjuːs/ *adj* large in amount

profusely /prə'fjuː·sli/ *adv* • *a profusely illustrated book* ∘ *Quinn was bleeding profusely.*

profusion /prə'fjuː·ʒən/ *n* [U] • *a profusion of beautiful flowers*

progeny /'pradʒ·ə·ni/ *n* [U] the young of a person, animal, or plant; OFFSPRING • *Housewives chased their progeny out-of-doors.*

prognosis /prag'noʊ·səs/ *n* [C] *pl* **prognoses** /prag'noʊˌsiːz/ a doctor's judgment of the likely or expected development of a disease, or a statement of what the likely future situation is • *After successful surgery his prognosis was good.*

program ACTIVITIES /'proʊ·græm, -grəm/ *n* [C] a group of activities or things to be achieved • *a training program* ∘ *the university basketball program* ∘ *a pilot recycling program*

program BROADCAST /'proʊ·græm, -grəm/ *n* [C] a broadcast or series of broadcasts on television or radio • *What's your favorite program?*

program COMPUTER /'proʊ·græm, -grəm/ *n* [C] a series of instructions that make a computer perform an operation • *a word processing program*

program /'proʊ·græm, -grəm/ *v* [T] **-mm-** to instruct (a computerized device or system) to operate in a particular way or at a particular time • *The CD player can be programmed to play the songs in any order.*

programmer /'proʊˌgræm·ər/ *n* [C] a person whose job is to write computer programs

programmable /'proʊˌgræm·ə·bəl/ *adj* • *a programmable thermostat*

program THIN BOOK /'proʊ·græm, -grəm/ *n* [C] a thin book or piece of paper giving information about a play or musical or sports event

progress /'prag·rəs, -res/ *n* [U] advancement to an improved or more developed state, or to a forward position • *The talks failed to make any progress toward a settlement.* • If something is **in progress**, it is happening or being done now: *The show was already in progress when I turned it on.*

progress /prə'gres/ *v* [I] • *Construction is progressing well.* ∘ *As the game progressed I was bouncing in my chair.*

progression /prə'greʃ·ən/ *n* [U] • *The show examines one woman's progression from youth to old age.*

progressive /prə'gres·ɪv/ *adj* • *His papers show a progressive* (= gradually advancing) *change in style.* • A progressive disease is one that gets increasingly worse. • Progressive ideas or systems encourage change in society or in the way things are done: *She worked for women's rights, labor reforms, and other progressive causes.*

progressively /prə'gres·ɪv·li/ *adv* • *My eyesight has gotten progressively worse over the years.*

prohibit /prə'hɪb·ət, proʊ-/ *v* [T] to forbid (something), esp. by law, or to prevent (an activity) by making it impossible • *The law prohibits smoking in most restaurants.* ∘ *Loud music prohibited serious conversation.*

prohibition /ˌproʊ·hə'bɪʃ·ən, ˌproʊ·ə-/ *n* [C/U] • *Are you proposing a prohibition on bilingual signs?* [C] ∘ *Prohibition of free speech is forbidden by the Constitution.* [U] • In the US, Prohibition was the period from 1920 to 1933 when the production and sale of alcohol was illegal. [U]

prohibitive /prə'hɪb·əṭ·ɪv/ *adj* (of costs) too expensive to pay • *The cost of a nursing home is prohibitive.*

prohibitively /prə'hɪb·əṭ·ɪv·li/ *adv* • *Fees are prohibitively expensive.*

project PIECE OF WORK /'pradʒ·ekt, -ɪkt/ *n* [C] a piece of planned work or activity that is completed over a period of time and intended to achieve a particular aim • *a research project* ∘ *construction projects* ∘ *Painting the bedroom is Steve's next project.*

project BUILDING /'pradʒ·ekt, -ɪkt/ *n* [C usually pl] a **housing project**, see at HOUSE HOME

project *(obj)* CALCULATE /prə'dʒekt/ *v* to calculate (an amount or result expected in the future) from information already known • *The hotels are projecting big profits.* [T] ∘ *They project (that) 31 billion people will watch the World Cup.* [+ *(that)* clause]

projected /prə'dʒek·təd/ *adj* [not gradable] • *The projected population growth will keep doctors busy.*

projection /prə'dʒek·ʃən/ n [C] • *Sales projections made last year were too optimistic.*

project STICK OUT /prə'dʒekt/ v [I] to stick out beyond the edge of something • *The hotel dining room projects (out) over the water.*

projection /prə'dʒek·ʃən/ n [C] • *It was a strange-looking house, with little projections off the sides.*

project MAKE AN IMAGE /prə'dʒekt/ v [T] to cause (a picture or light) to appear on a surface • *We don't have a screen but we can project the slides onto the back wall.* • If you **project an image**, you represent yourself in a particular way through your speech, behavior, and appearance: *He's trying to project a more confident image.*

projection /prə'dʒek·ʃən/ n [C/U] • *A projection of his face appeared on the back wall.* [C]

projector /prə'dʒek·tər/ n [C] a device for showing movies or other images on a screen or other surface

projectionist /prə'dʒek·ʃə·nəst/ n [C] a person whose job is to operate a projector in a movie theater

project DIRECT FORWARD /prə'dʒekt/ v [T] to direct (esp. your voice) forward, with force • *Singers are used to projecting their voices.* • If you project something into the air, you throw it.

projectile /prə'dʒek·təl, -,taɪl/ n [C] an object that is thrown or fired, esp. from a weapon

pro–life /'proʊ'laɪf/ adj [not gradable] supporting the belief that it is immoral for a pregnant woman to have the freedom to choose to have an ABORTION (= an operation to end a pregnancy) if she does not want to have a baby • Compare PRO-CHOICE.

proliferate /prə'lɪf·ə,reɪt/ v [I] to increase greatly in number or amount, usually quickly • *Gambling is proliferating in America.*

proliferation /prə,lɪf·ə'reɪ·ʃən/ n [U] • *the proliferation of nuclear weapons*

prolific /prə'lɪf·ɪk/ adj producing a great number or amount of something • *He was probably the most prolific songwriter of his generation.*

prologue /'proʊ·lɔːɡ, -lɑɡ/ n [C] a part at the beginning of esp. a play, story, or long poem that introduces it • *The essay provides a prologue to the book.*

prolong /prə'lɔːŋ/ v [T] to make (something) last a longer time • *They're trying to prolong their lives.*

prolonged /prə'lɔːŋd/ adj • *Grasslands were damaged by the prolonged drought.*

prom /prɑm/ n [C] a formal party held at the end of the school year for older students in HIGH SCHOOL • *Who are you taking to the senior/junior prom?*

promenade /,prɑm·ə'neɪd, -'nɑd/ n [C] a wide path for walking on, esp. one built next to a sea, lake, or river • *We strolled along the promenade.*

promenade /,prɑm·ə'neɪd, -'nɑd/ v [I] *dated* to walk slowly along a street or path, usually where you can be seen by many people, for relaxation and pleasure

prominent /'prɑm·ə·nənt/ adj very noticeable, important, or famous • *She plays a prominent role in the organization.* • If something is prominent, it sticks out from a surface or can be seen easily: *She has a prominent chin/nose.*

prominently /'prɑm·ə·nənt·li/ adv • *prominently displayed pictures*

prominence /'prɑm·ə·nəns/ n [U] • *Despite his prominence, he was never able to make a living.*

promiscuous /prə'mɪs·kjə·wəs/ adj *disapproving* (of a person) having a lot of different sexual partners or sexual relationships, or (of sexual habits) involving a lot of different partners • *She wasn't promiscuous, and she didn't do drugs.*

promiscuity /,prɑm·ə'skjuː·ət·i/ n [U] • *Public school programs discourage promiscuity.*

promise STATE CERTAINLY /'prɑm·əs/ v [I/T] to state to (someone) that you will certainly do something • *We promised the kids (that) we'd take them to the zoo.* [T] ○ *She promised to be careful.* [+ *to* infinitive]

promise /'prɑm·əs/ n [C] a statement that you will certainly do something • *I'll try to get back in time, but I'm not making any promises.* ○ *He broke his promise to* (= said he would but did not) *give his art collection to the county museum.*

promise LIKELY SUCCESS /'prɑm·əs/ n [U] the likelihood of success or achievement • *She shows great promise as a fiction writer.*

promise /'prɑm·əs/ v to seem likely • *The new movie promises to be one of the biggest money-makers of all time.* [+ *to* infinitive]

promising /'prɑm·ə·sɪŋ/ adj showing signs of future success or achievement • *a promising career*

promote ADVERTISE /prə'moʊt/ v [T] to advertise (something) in order to sell it • *The new model cars are being heavily promoted on television.*

promotion /prə'moʊ·ʃən/ n [C/U] advertising intended to increase the sales of a product or service

promotional /prə'moʊ·ʃən·əl/ adj [not gradable] • *We picked up some promotional material on holiday tours to Europe.*

promote ENCOURAGE /prə'moʊt/ v [T] to encourage or support (something), or to help (something) become successful • *A new campaign has been launched to promote safe driving.*

promoter /prə'moʊt·ər/ n [C] a person or company that organizes or finances a sports event or a performance, esp. of musical entertainment

promote ADVANCE /prə'moʊt/ v [T] to advance (someone) to a more important rank or position • *She was promoted to division manager last year.* • If a student is promoted, they advance to the next GRADE (= level of schooling). • USAGE: The opposite of promote is DEMOTE.

promotion /prə'moʊ·ʃən/ *n* [C/U] • *She's been recommended for (a) promotion.* [C/U]

prompt QUICK /prɑmt/ *adj* [*-er*/*-est* only] (of an action) done quickly and without delay, or (of a person) acting quickly or arriving at an arranged time • *The agency sent back a prompt reply to my inquiries.*

promptly /'prɑm·tli/ *adv* • *She arrived promptly at 9 o'clock.*

prompt CAUSE /prɑmt/ *v* [T] to cause (someone) to say or do something • *What prompted you to say that?* [+ *to* infinitive] • If you prompt an actor or speaker, you help them when they forget by quietly saying the next word or phrase.

prompt /prɑmt/ *n* [C] • On a computer screen, a prompt is a sign that shows that the computer is ready to receive your instructions.

prone LIKELY /proʊn/ *adj* likely to do, get, or suffer from something • *As a child, he was prone to ear infections.* ○ *Carol's kind of accident-prone* (= seems to have a lot of accidents).

prone LYING DOWN /proʊn/ *adj* [not gradable] lying on your chest, with your face looking down • *The body was found in a prone position on the bed.*

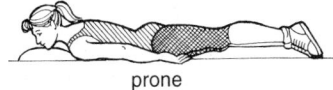

prone

prong /prɔːŋ, prɑŋ/ *n* [C] one of two or more long pointed parts at the end of a tool, electric plug, or other object

pronged /prɔːŋd, prɑŋd/ *adj* [not gradable] • A two/three-pronged plan involves two/three different ways of achieving the same aim: *The government has launched a two-pronged attack against teenagers' smoking.*

pronoun /'proʊ·naʊn/ *n* [C] *specialized* (in grammar) a word that is used instead of a noun or a noun phrase • *Pronouns are often used to refer to a noun that has been previously mentioned.* ○ *"She," "it," "them," and "who" are all examples of pronouns.*

pronounce MAKE SOUND /prə'naʊns/ *v* [T] to say a word or a letter in a particular way or in a correct way • *In these parts, cement is pronounced SEE-ment.* ○ *How do you pronounce your last name?* • USAGE: The related noun is PRONUNCIATION.

pronounce TO STATE /prə'naʊns/ *v* [T] to state (something) officially or formally • *One person was pronounced dead at the scene.*

pronouncement /prə'naʊn·smənt/ *n* [C] an official or formal statement

pronounced /prə'naʊnst/ *adj* easily noticeable; obvious • *The need for strong leadership is more pronounced* (= clearer) *during wartime.*

pronto /'prɑn·toʊ/ *adv* [not gradable] *infml* quickly and without delay • *When you get fresh corn, eat it pronto.*

pronunciation /prə,nʌn·si:'eɪ·ʃən/ *n* [C/U] the way in which a word or letter is said, or said correctly, or the way in which a language is spoken • *Her pronunciation of English is improving.* [U] ○ *There are two acceptable pronunciations for the word "either."* [C] • USAGE: The related verb is PRONOUNCE MAKE SOUND.

proof FACTS /pruːf/ *n* [U] facts or documents that can be used to show that something is true or believable • *We insist that young people show us proof of their age before we serve them alcohol.*

proof PRINTED COPY /pruːf/ *n* [C] a printed copy of written material that is examined and corrected before final copies are printed • *Page proofs went out yesterday to all the contributors to the book.*

proof AMOUNT OF ALCOHOL /pruːf/ *n* [U] a measure of the percentage of alcohol in an alcoholic drink, equal to twice the actual percentage of alcohol • *Liquor that is 50 proof is 25% alcohol.*

proofread /'pruː·friːd/ *v* [I/T] to read and correct (a piece of written work) • *Tondra proofreads (books) for a small publishing company.* [I/T]

prop SUPPORT /prɑp/ *v* [T] **-pp-** to support (something) by putting something else under or against it • *She propped the door open with a footstool.* ○ *He was reading in bed, propped up by pillows.* • (*fig.*) To prop up something/prop something up is to support something that would fail or become weaker without such help: *The US joined with other nations in a coordinated effort yesterday to prop up the value of the dollar.* [M]

prop /prɑp/ *n* [C] an object used to support something or hold it in position

prop THEATER / MOVIES /prɑp/ *n* [C usually pl] an object that is used on a theater stage or in a movie • *The only props used in the show are a table, a chair, and a glass of water.*

propaganda /ˌprɑp·ə'gæn·də/ *n* [U] information or ideas that are methodically spread by an organized group or government to influence people's opinions, esp. by not giving all the facts or by secretly emphasizing only one way of looking at the facts

propagate /'prɑp·ə,geɪt/ *v* [I/T] to produce (a new plant) from a parent plant, or (of a plant or animal) to reproduce • To propagate (ideas, opinions, or customs) is to spread them among people, or to spread them to other places. [T]

propane (gas) /'proʊ·peɪn ('gæs)/ *n* [U] a colorless gas used as a fuel • *Camps for mobile homes usually provide propane gas for cooking and heating.*

propel /prə'pel/ *v* [T] **-ll-** to cause (something) to move forward • *Seals use their fins and flippers to propel them through the water with* *great force.* ○ *(fig.) If the team won the next two games, they would be propelled into the number one ranking in collegiate football.*

propeller /prə'pel·ər/ *n* [C] a device with two or more blades that spin around to produce a force for moving the ship or aircraft to which it is attached

propensity /prə'pen·sət·i/ *n* [U] *fml* a tendency to behave in a particular way • *The poll confirmed Americans' growing propensity to invest in the stock market.* [+ *to* infinitive]

proper SUITABLE /'prɑp·ər/ *adj* fitting or right for a particular situation; suitable • *We didn't have the proper tools to do the job right.* ○ *With proper treatment she should recover completely.* • *(specialized)* In grammar, a **proper noun** is the name of a particular person, place, or thing, and it is spelled with a beginning capital letter: *"San Francisco" and "White House" are proper nouns.* Compare **common noun** at COMMON SHARED. LP CAPITAL LETTERS

properly /'prɑp·ər·li/ *adv* • *If the plants are tended properly, they'll thrive in this climate.*

proper CORRECT /'prɑp·ər/ *adj* [not gradable] correct, or considered to be correct • *The coach showed him the proper way to hold a bat.*

properly /'prɑp·ər·li/ *adv* [not gradable] • *To learn to speak a language properly, you have to live in the country where that language is spoken.*

proper SOCIALLY ACCEPTABLE /'prɑp·ər/ *adj* according to socially accepted standards of behavior • *I didn't think it was proper to just invite myself in.*

properly /'prɑp·ər·li/ *adv* • *I expect you to behave properly at the restaurant.*

proper CENTRAL /'prɑp·ər/ *adj* [only after n; not gradable] being in the central or main part or place • *They live in the suburbs, not in Boston proper.*

property THINGS OWNED /'prɑp·ərt·i/ *n* [C/U] a thing or things owned by someone; a possession or possessions • *The books are the property of the public library.* [U] • Property is also land and buildings: *He owns some valuable waterfront properties.* [C]

property QUALITY /'prɑp·ərt·i/ *n* [C] a quality that something has • *Wool has excellent properties for clothing, since it can keep you warm while letting air in.*

prophecy /'prɑf·ə·si/ *n* [C] a statement that tells what will happen in the future • *biblical prophecies*

prophesy /'prɑf·ə,saɪ/ *v* [T] to say (what will happen in the future) • *He prophesied a Democratic defeat in the next election.*

prophet /'prɑf·ət/ *n* [C] a person who speaks for God or a god, or a person who tells what will happen in the future

prophetic /prə'fet·ɪk/ *adj* accurately saying what will happen • *His predictions about how computer technology would revolutionize the workplace were prophetic* (= true).

propitious /prə'pɪʃ·əs/ *adj* likely to result in

success, or showing signs of success • *With economic conditions so uncertain, he felt it was not a propitious time to make a big investment.*

proponent /prə'poʊ·nənt/ *n* [C] a person who supports an idea, plan, or cause • *Long a proponent of government health insurance, he pointed out that millions of Americans have no health insurance at all.*

proportion /prə'pɔːr·ʃən/ *n* [C/U] a part or share of the whole, or the relationship between one thing and another in size, amount, or degree • *The proportion of the population that is over 65 has been growing.* [C] ○ *The occurrence of the disease has reached epidemic proportions.* [pl] • Proportion is also the right relationship between one thing and another: *His anger was out of all proportion to the offense* (= was much too strong). [U]

proportional /prə'pɔːr·ʃən·əl/, **proportionate** /prə'pɔːr·ʃə·nət/ *adj* in correct relation to • *The degree of punishment is meant to be proportional to the seriousness of the crime.*

propose SUGGEST /prə'poʊz/ *v* to suggest or state (a possible plan or action) for consideration • *She proposed to keep the schools open all summer.* [+ *to* infinitive] ○ *It has often been proposed that the president be elected by direct popular vote.* [+ *that* clause] • If you propose to someone, you ask them to marry you: *She felt sure he was going to propose.* [I]

proposal /prə'poʊ·zəl/ *n* [C] a suggestion for a possible plan or action • *The president's proposal was to tax a percentage of Social Security benefits for high-income people.*

propose INTEND /prə'poʊz/ *v fml* to intend to do something • *How do you propose to complete the project in such a short time?* [+ *to* infinitive]

proposition /,prɑp·ə'zɪʃ·ən/ *n* [C] a suggestion or statement for consideration • *The chairman was advised that it was a risky business proposition.*

proposition /,prɑp·ə'zɪʃ·ən/ *v* [T] to suggest having sex with (someone) • *She was propositioned by a stranger at the bar.*

proprietor /prə'praɪ·ət·ər/ *n* [C] a person who owns a business and usually manages it themselves • *He is the proprietor of one of the best hotels in Orlando.*

proprietary /prə'praɪ·ə,ter·i/ *adj* [not gradable] owned and legally controlled by a particular company • *This is proprietary software, and you have no right to copy it without a license from the owner.*

propriety /prə'praɪ·ət·i/ *n* [U] moral correctness of behavior, or the suitability of something • *Critics questioned the propriety of the senator's appearance at a political fundraiser with a convicted criminal.*

propulsion /prə'pʌl·ʃən/ *n* [U] the force produced by a system for moving a vehicle or other object • *jet propulsion*

prosaic /proʊ'zeɪ·ɪk/ *adj* ordinary and not especially interesting or unusual • *Only a few* *prosaic tables and chairs remained by the time we got to the auction.*

proscribe /prou'skraɪb/ *v* [T] to forbid (an action or practice) officially, esp. because it is harmful or dangerous • *The sale of materials that could be used in making nuclear weapons is proscribed by US law.*

prose /prouz/ *n* [U] written language in its ordinary form rather than in the form of poems • Compare **poetry** at POET.

prosecute /'pras·ɪ,kju:t/ *v* [I/T] to officially accuse (someone) of committing an illegal act, esp. a crime, and to bring a case against them in a court of law • *The banker was prosecuted for fraud.* [T]

prosecution /,pras·ɪ'kju:·ʃən/ *n* [C/U] • *She was granted full immunity from prosecution by the state in return for her testimony.* [U] • *(law)* The prosecution refers to the lawyers in a trial who try to prove that a person accused of committing a crime is guilty of that crime. [U]

prosecutor /'pras·ɪ,kju:t̬·ər/ *n* [C] a legal representative who officially accuses someone of committing a crime in a court of law • *Federal prosecutors intend to retry the case.*

proselytize /'pras·ə·lə,taɪz/ *v* [I/T] to try to persuade (someone) to change their religious beliefs, political party, etc., to your own • *Missionaries proselytize among the less enlightened.* [I]

prospect POSSIBILITY /'pras·pekt/ *n* [C/U] the possibility or likelihood that something will happen • *Losing the elections is a prospect that still appears unlikely.* [C] ○ *She smiled at the prospect of seeing him again.* [U] ○ *Prospects* (= Chances for success) *in the computer industry are excellent.* [pl]

prospective /prə'spek·tɪv/ *adj* [not gradable] • *There were offers from several prospective buyers.*

prospect SEARCH /'pras·pekt/ *v* [I] to search for gold, oil, or other valuable substances on or under the surface of the earth

prospector /'pras,pek·tər/ *n* [C] • *a prospector searching for gold*

prospectus /prə'spek·təs/ *n* [C] a small book that describes a college, school, etc., and its activities, or a document that advertises a planned business, investment opportunity, etc.

prosper /'pras·pər/ *v* [I] to be successful, esp. financially • *As the company prospered, we prospered.*

prosperity /pras'per·ət̬·i/ *n* [U] • *a period of increasing prosperity*

prosperous /'pras·pə·rəs/ *adj* • *a prosperous business*

prostate (gland) /'pras·teɪt ('glænd)/ *n* [C] an organ in males that surrounds the URETHRA and produces a liquid that mixes with and carries sperm

prosthesis /pras'θi:·səs/ *n* [C] *pl* **prostheses** /pras'θi:,si:z/ an artificial body part, such as an arm or leg, which replaces a missing part

prosthetic /pras'θet̬·ɪk/ *adj* [not gradable] • *prosthetic devices*

prostitute /'pras·tə,tu:t/ *n* [C] someone, usually a woman, who has sex with people for money

prostitute /'pras·tə,tu:t/ *v* [T] • *She prostituted herself because she needed the money.* ○ *Some critics say that he is prostituting his writing talent* (= using it in a way that does not deserve respect, esp. to earn money).

prostitution /,pras·tə'tu:·ʃən/ *n* [U] the business of having sex for money

prostrate /'pras·treɪt/ *adj* lying flat with the face down • *She lay there prostrate and lifeless.*

protagonist /prou'tæg·ə·nəst/ *n* [C] an important character in a story or play

protect /prə'tekt/ *v* [T] to keep (someone or something) safe from injury, damage, or loss • *He says he was protecting his home and family.* ○ *A citizens' group worked to protect forest areas.*

protected /prə'tek·təd/ *adj* • *a protected environment* ○ *a protected species*

protection /prə'tek·ʃən/ *n* [U] • *Their tent offered little protection against the storm.* ○ *These laws may not provide enough protection for some endangered species.*

protective /prə'tek·tɪv/ *adj* • *Firefighters wear protective clothing to reduce the risk of being burned.* ○ *She is fiercely protective of her family.*

protector /prə'tek·tər/ *n* [C] • *After his parents died, he became the protector of his sisters.* ○ *A $20 surge protector can save your computer.*

protégé /'prout·ə,ʒeɪ/ *n* [C] someone who is helped, taught, or protected by an important or more experienced person

protein /'prou·ti:n/ *n* [C/U] any of a large group of chemicals that are a necessary part of the cells of all living things • *Meat, milk, and nuts are good sources of protein.* [U]

protest /'prou·test/ *n* [C/U] a strong complaint expressing disagreement, disapproval, or opposition • *Three board members walked out of the meeting in protest.* [U] ○ *A protest against capital punishment was held outside the courthouse.* [C]

protest /prə'test, 'prou·test/ *v* [I/T] • *Groups of students have been protesting (against) the tuition increase.* [I/T]

Protestant /'prat̬·ə·stənt/ *n* [C], *adj* [not gradable] (a member) of one of the major Christian divisions to which a number of different religious groups belong • *a Protestant minister* ○ *Methodists, Baptists, and Lutherans are all Protestants.*

Protestantism /'prat̬·ə·stənt,ɪz·əm/ *n* [U] the beliefs of the Protestant religions

protocol RULES /'prout·ə,kɔ:l, -,kɑl/ *n* [C/U] the formal system of rules for correct behavior on official occasions • *According to protocol, the new ambassador will present his credentials to the president.* [U] • *(specialized)* A protocol is also the rules to be followed when doing a scientific study or an exact method for giving medical treatment: *medical protocol* [U] ○ *a treatment protocol* [C]

protocol AGREEMENT /'proʊṭ·ə,kɔːl, -,kɑl/ *n* [C] a formal international agreement

proton /'proʊ·tɑn/ *n* [C] a part of an atom that has a positive electrical charge • Compare ELECTRON; NEUTRON.

protoplasm /'proʊṭ·ə,plæz·əm/ *n* [U] the transparent liquid that is inside all living cells

prototype /'proʊṭ·ə,tɑɪp/ *n* [C] the original model of something from which later forms are developed

prototypical /,proʊṭ·ə'tɪp·ɪ·kəl/ *adj* [not gradable] • *a prototypical jazz singer*

protracted /proʊ'træk·təd/ *adj* lasting for a long time, or made to continue longer than necessary • *Their protracted legal battle may soon be resolved.*

protractor /proʊ'træk·tər/ *n* [C] a device for measuring and drawing angles, usually shaped in a half circle and marked with degrees

protrude /prə'truːd/ *v* [I/T] to stick out from something • *Tufts of gray hair protruded from under his hat.* [I] ○ *The snake protruded its tongue and hissed loudly.* [T]

protrusion /prə'truː·ʒən/ *n* [C/U] • *A protrusion on the cliffs looks like a human head.* [C]

proud SATISFIED /praʊd/ *adj* [-er/-est only] feeling satisfaction and pleasure because of something that you have achieved, possess, or are a part of • *He's very proud of his daughters.* ○ *The company is proud of its environmental record.* ○ *I am proud to have played a part in what this team achieved.* [+ *to* infinitive]

proudly /'praʊd·li/ *adv* • *We proudly announce the birth of our son, Logan.*

proud RESPECTING YOURSELF /praʊd/ *adj* [-er/ -est only] having respect for yourself, or showing feelings of your own worth • *Americans are a proud people.* ○ *He might be poor but he's too proud to accept charity.* • People may also be unpleasantly proud and have too high an opinion of themselves: *She is too proud to admit that she could ever be wrong.* [+ *to* infinitive] • USAGE: The related noun is PRIDE FEELING OF WORTH.

proudly /'praʊd·li/ *adv* • *Crow warriors rode proudly through the village.*

prove SHOW /pruːv/ *v past part* **proved** or **proven** /'pruː·vən/ to show after a time or by experience that something or someone has a particular quality • *The dispute over rights to the song could prove impossible to resolve.* [L] ○ *The new safety procedures have so far proven to be satisfactory.* [+ *to* infinitive] • *As a newcomer, I felt I had to prove myself* (= show I am skilled).

proven /'pruː·vən/ *adj* [not gradable] • *You can't trust him—he's a proven liar.*

prove (*obj*) MAKE CLEAR /pruːv/ *v past part* **proved** or **proven** /'pruː·vən/ to make it clear that (something) is or is not true • *They sus-*

pected she killed him but could never prove it. [T] ○ *I had to take all my records to the bank to prove (that) the mistake was theirs.* [+ (*that*) clause] ○ *Under our legal system, you're innocent until proven guilty.* [T]

proverb /'prɑv·ɜrb/ *n* [C] a short statement usually known by many people for a long time, that gives advice or expresses some common truth • *The Chinese proverb says that the longest journey begins with a single step.*

proverbial /prə'vɜr·biː·əl/ *adj* [not gradable] • *Yelling at me was the proverbial straw that broke the camel's back.*

provide GIVE /prə'vɑɪd/ *v* [T] to give something that is needed or wanted to someone • *The company provides medical benefits to all employees.* ○ *I can provide you with directions to their house.* • If someone **provides for** someone else, they give them the things they need to live: *Prisoners must learn to provide for themselves once they've left the halfway house.*

provider /prə'vɑɪd·ər/ *n* [C] • *The company's medical plan allows you to choose your healthcare provider.* ○ *He is the main provider in the family* (= earns most of the family's money).

provide STATE /prə'vɑɪd/ *v* (of a law or contract) to state that something must happen or be done • *The new statute provides for life imprisonment without parole.* [I] ○ *Many loan agreements provide that the interest rate will change.* [+ *that* clause]

provided (that) /prə'vɑɪd·əd (ðət, ,ðæt)/, **providing (that)** /prə'vɑɪd·ɪŋ (ðət, ,ðæt)/ *conjunction* if; only if • *I know what to do, provided that nobody asks me.*

providence /'prɑv·əd·əns, -ə,dens/ *n* [U] the care and control of God or of a force that is not human in origin • *He trusts in divine providence.*

province REGION /'prɑv·əns/ *n* [C] a division of a country that has its own government • *The province of Quebec has voted several times on independence from Canada.* • The provinces are the parts of a country outside its capital or most important city.

provincial /prə'vɪn·tʃəl/ *adj* of or relating to a province, or to the parts of a country outside its capital or most important city • *provincial governments* • (*disapproving*) A provincial person has limited ideas and is not willing to understand or accept new ideas or ways of behaving.

province SUBJECT /'prɑv·əns/ *n* [U] *fml* a subject or activity of special interest, knowledge, or responsibility • *Architecture is within the province of the art department.*

provision SOMETHING NEEDED /prə'vɪʒ·ən/ *n* [C/U] something that is needed or wanted, or the act of considering the need for something and arranging for it • *When designing buildings in California, you have to make some provision for earthquakes.* [U] ○ *Ample provisions for aircraft stability have been made.* [C] • Provisions are also supplies of food and other necessary items: *Provisions had to be flown in by helicopter.* [pl]

provision AGREEMENT /prə'vɪʒ·ən/ *n* [C] a statement in an agreement or a law that a particular thing must happen or be done • *Her contract contains a provision covering additional expenses.*

provisional /prə'vɪʒ·ən·ᵊl/ *adj* for the present time but likely to change; temporary • *a provisional government*

provisionally /prə'vɪʒ·ə·nə·li/ *adv* • *I was provisionally accepted at Stanford.*

provocation /ˌprɑv·ə'keɪ·ʃən/ *n* [C/U] an action that is intended to cause a reaction, esp. anger or annoyance • *a deliberate act of provocation* [U]

provocative /prə'vɑk·ət·ɪv/ *adj* • *a provocative speech* ○ *provocative advertisements* • If behavior or clothing is provocative, it is intended to cause sexual desire.

provocatively /prə'vɑk·ət·ɪv·li/ *adv* • *She swung her hips provocatively as she walked.*

provoke ANGER /prə'voʊk/ *v* [T] to try to make (a person or an animal) angry or annoyed • *I see these men in uniform provoking people into violence.*

provoke CAUSE REACTION /prə'voʊk/ *v* [T] to cause (a particular reaction or feeling) • *I'm trying to make people think, provoke their emotions.* ○ *His death provoked huge demonstrations.*

provost /'proʊ·voʊst/ *n* [C] an official of high rank at a college or university

prow /praʊ/ *n* [C] the front part of a boat or ship; BOW

prowess /'praʊ·əs/ *n* [U] great ability or skill • *athletic prowess*

prowl /praʊl/ *v* [I/T] to move around (an area) quietly and secretly, as when hunting • *At night, scorpions prowl the desert for insects.* [T] ○ *There have been reports of a man prowling in the neighborhood.* [I]

prowl /praʊl/ *n* [U] • If someone is on the **prowl**, they are moving and looking for something or someone: *Those girls were powdered and perfumed and on the prowl.*

proximity /prɑk'sɪm·ət·i/ *n* [U] nearness in space or time • *Mexico is a popular vacation spot because of its proximity to California.*

proxy /'prɑk·si/ *n* [C/U] authority given to a person to act for someone else, as by voting for them in an election, or the person to whom this authority is given

prude /pruːd/ *n* [C] *disapproving* a person who is easily shocked by rude things, esp. in sexual matters

prudish /'pruːd·ɪʃ/ *adj disapproving* • *We were all naked, but none of us acted the least bit prudish.*

prudent /'pruːd·ᵊnt/ *adj* showing good judgment in avoiding risks and uncertainties; careful • *His decision was prudent and timely.*

prudence /'pruːd·ᵊns/ *n* [U] • *A little prudence would be appropriate.*

prune CUT /pruːn/ *v* [T] to cut off unwanted branches from (a tree, bush, etc.), esp. so that it will grow better • *We need to prune (back) the roses.* [T/M]

prune FRUIT /pruːn/ *n* [C] a dried whole PLUM (= fruit)

prurient /'prʊr·iː·ənt/ *adj* having or showing an unpleasantly strong sexual interest in things • *a prurient fascination with young men*

pry OPEN /praɪ/ *v* [T always + adv/prep] to open, move, or lift (something) by force, esp. by putting one end of a tool under it and pushing down on the other end • *She pried the oyster open.* • *(fig.)* To pry is also to get something with much effort: *They pried the information out of him.*

pry ASK QUESTIONS /praɪ/ *v* [I] to try to obtain private facts about a person • *Reporters were prying into her personal life.*

P.S. *n abbreviation for* POSTSCRIPT, added at the end of a letter when you want to write something more • *P.S. Best wishes to your father.*

psalm /sɑm, sɑlm/ *n* [C] a religious poem or song

pseudonym /'suːd·ᵊn,ɪm/ *n* [C] a name that a person, esp. a writer, uses instead of their real name on their work • *Samuel Clemens used the pseudonym Mark Twain.*

psych STUDY OF THE MIND /saɪk/ *n short form of* PSYCHOLOGY

psych PREPARE MENTALLY /saɪk/ *v* [T] *infml* to prepare (yourself) mentally to be strong and confident about something difficult that you must do • *I really tried to get myself psyched (up) to do it.* [T/M] • To psych someone out is to cause them to lose confidence in dealing with a difficult situation: *He hit a couple of bad shots at the start and I think it just psyched him out.* [M]

psyche /'saɪ·ki/ *n* [C] the mind, or the deepest thoughts, feelings, or beliefs of a person or group • *the male/female psyche*

psychedelic /ˌsaɪ·kə'del·ɪk/ *adj* causing unusually strong experiences of color, sound, smell, taste, and touch, and other mental effects such as feelings of deep understanding or HALLUCINATION (= imagining things that do not exist), usually caused by a plant or drug • *psychedelic drugs* ○ *a psychedelic experience* • Psychedelic also means likely to produce a strong effect because of having bright colors or patterns.

psychiatry /saɪ'kaɪ·ə·tri/ *n* [U] the medical study and treatment of mental illness

psychiatric /ˌsaɪ·ki'æ·trɪk/ *adj* [not gradable] • *psychiatric treatment*

psychiatrist /saɪ'kaɪ·ə·trəst/ *n* [C] a doctor with special training in treating mental illness

psychic /'saɪ·kɪk/ *adj* having to do with the mind and the emotions rather than with the body • *Regular exercise has psychic as well as physical benefits.* • If a person, experience, or event is said to be psychic, the person's abilities or the nature of the experience or event cannot be explained by modern science: *psychic phenomena*

psychic /'saɪ·kɪk/ *n* [C] a person believed to have abilities, esp. involving a knowledge of the future, that cannot be explained by modern science

psycho /'saɪ·koʊ/ *n pl* **psychos** *infml* a PSY-CHOPATH

psychoanalysis /,saɪ·koʊ·ə'næl·ə·səs/ *n* [U] a theory and method of treating mental illness in which a person is encouraged to talk about private thoughts and events to someone trained in this method

psychoanalyst /,saɪ·koʊ'æn·ᵊl·əst/, *short form* **analyst** *n* [C] a person with special training in psychoanalysis

psychology /saɪ'kɑl·ə·dʒi/, *short form* **psych** *n* [U] the scientific study of how the mind works and how it influences behavior, or the influence of a particular person's character on their behavior • *She took a course in abnormal psychology.*

psychological /,saɪ·kə'lɑdʒ·ɪ·kəl/ *adj* • *psychological testing* ○ *Her problems were psychological.* • Psychological also means having an effect on or involving the mind: *psychological stress/well-being* ○ *Her new novel is a psychological thriller.*

psychologist /saɪ'kɑl·ə·dʒəst/ *n* [C] someone who studies the mind and emotions and their relationship to behavior

psychopath /'saɪ·kə,pæθ/, *infml* **psycho** *n* [C] a person who is likely to commit violent criminal acts because of mental illness characterized by the lack of any feelings of guilt

psychopathic /,saɪ·kə'pæθ·ɪk/ *adj* • *a psychopathic killer*

psychosis /saɪ'koʊ·səs/ *n* [C/U] *pl* **psychoses** /saɪ'koʊ,siːz/ *medical* a severe mental illness

psychotic /saɪ'kɑt̬·ɪk/ *adj medical* • *psychotic delusions*

psychosomatic /,saɪ·koʊ·sə'mæt̬·ɪk/ *adj* relating to a physical problem caused by emotional anxiety and not by illness, infection, or injury • *The doctor thinks Leo's symptoms are psychosomatic.*

psychotherapy /,saɪ·koʊ'θer·ə·pi/ *n* [C/U] any of various methods of treating mental illness in which the people who are ill are encouraged to talk about themselves to each other or to a person trained in the method being used

psychotherapist /,saɪ·koʊ'θer·ə·pəst/ *n* [C]

pt. *n* [C] *pl* **pt.** *abbreviation for* PINT

PTA *n* [C] *abbreviation for* **Parent-Teacher Association,** see at PARENT

pub /pʌb/ *n* [C] a BAR DRINKING PLACE

puberty /'pjuː·bərt̬·i/ *n* [U] the stage in a person's life when they develop from a child into an adult because of changes in their body that make them able to have children

pubic hair /'pjuː·bɪk/ *n* [U] the hair on the body near the sexual organs

public INVOLVING PEOPLE /'pʌb·lɪk/ *adj* [no gradable] relating to or involving people in general, rather than being limited to a particular group of people • *public opinion* ○ *There is increased public awareness of the dangers of smoking.* ○ *His ideas have very little public support.* ○ *The results won't be made public* (= told to people in general). • **Public relations** (*abbreviation* **PR**) is the activity of keeping good relationships between an organization and the people outside it.

public /'pʌb·lɪk/ *n* [U] all the people, esp. all those in one place or country • *The park is open to the public from sunrise to sunset.* • The public is also the people who do not belong to a particular group or organization: *The book is not yet available to the general public.* • Your public is the people involved with you or your organization, esp. in a business relationship *The newspapers publish the stories they know their public wants to read.*

publicly /'pʌb·lɪ·kli/ *adv* [not gradable] by or among ordinary people • *publicly traded stock*

public OPEN /'pʌb·lɪk/ *adj* allowing anyone to see or hear what is happening • *a public performance* ○ *a public display of temper* • Something done **in public** is done where anyone can see or hear it: *He was afraid to be seen in public for some time after the incident.*

publicly /'pʌb·lɪ·kli/ *adv* • *She spoke out publicly in opposition to US participation in the war.*

public BY THE GOVERNMENT /'pʌb·lɪk/ *adj* [not gradable] involving or provided by the government, usually for the use of anyone • *public transportation* ○ *a public park* ○ *public housing* • Public also means supported by government funds, sometimes also by money given by private citizens: *public broadcasting/radio/television* • A **public defender** is a lawyer paid for by the government to represent an accused person who cannot pay for a private lawyer. • **Public health** is the system for providing for the health needs and services of all the people of a country or region, and is the responsibility of a government: *The county's public health officer urged parents to keep their children home from school when they have the flu.* • A **public school** is a free school, supported by taxes, and managed by local representatives. LP EDUCATION IN THE US • The **public sector** is the offices and responsibilities of government: *She worked in the public sector for years before returning to private practice in her old law firm.* • **Public servants** are elected officials and people employed by local or national government, and **public service** is the work they do for the benefit of the public.

publicly /'pʌb·lɪ·kli/ *adv* [not gradable] • *The new airport will not be publicly funded.*

publication /,pʌb·lə'keɪ·ʃən/ *n* [C/U] a book, magazine, newspaper, or document, or the act of making information or writing available, esp. in a printed form • *His writing appears* frequently in French, Mexican, and Canadian publications. [C] ○ *The publication of the marathon finishers will be in next Sunday's newspaper.* [U]

publicity /pə'blɪs·əṭ·i/ *n* [U] the activity of making certain that someone or something attracts a lot of interest or attention from many people, or the attention received as a result of this activity • *The publicity surrounding the case made jury selection difficult.* ○ *His speech attracted a lot of publicity.*

publicist /'pʌb·lə·səst/ *n* [C] someone whose job is to draw attention to events and give information to reporters and broadcasters

publicize /'pʌb·lə·sɑɪz/ *v* [T] to make information available about (someone or something) • *Luna has helped publicize the problem of homelessness.*

publish /'pʌb·lɪʃ/ *v* [I/T] to make available to the public, usually by printing, a book, magazine, newspaper, or other document • *She was 29 when her first novel was published.* [T] ○ *We plan to begin publishing a newsletter on the Internet.* [T]

publisher /'pʌb·lɪʃ·ər/ *n* [C] an organization that publishes books, magazines, or newspapers • Publisher is also the title of a person in a company who is responsible for publishing particular books, magazines, or newspapers.

puck /pʌk/ *n* [C] a small, hard, rubber disk used in HOCKEY (= a game played on ice)

pucker /'pʌk·ər/ *v* [T] to press together and form small folds, esp. on the lips or in cloth • *She puckered her lips.* ○ *This hem is all puckered up.* [M]

pucker /'pʌk·ər/ *n* [C] • *Puckers were sewn in the sleeves of the blouse.*

pudding /'pʊd·ɪŋ/ *n* [C/U] a sweet dish, often made from sugar, milk, flour, and flavoring, and usually eaten after a meal • *I'll make rice pudding for dessert.* [U]

puddle /'pʌd·əl/ *n* [C] a pool of liquid on the ground or floor, formed by filling up the holes in uneven surfaces • *You have to step around the puddles in the street after a rain shower.*

pudgy /'pʌdʒ·i/ *adj* short and fat • *He jabbed a pudgy finger at me.*

pueblo /'pweb·loʊ, puː'eb-/ *n* [C] *pl* **pueblos** a group of flat-roofed, connected buildings made of pressed, dried earth or stone, built by American Indians in the southwestern US • *While in New Mexico we visited the ruins of an ancient pueblo.*

pueblo

puff BREATHE /pʌf/ *v* [I] to breathe quickly and with a lot of force, usually as a result of an activity that needs a lot of physical effort • *Ricardo was puffing hard after he raced up five flights of stairs.* • To puff is also to breathe in and blow out smoke from a cigarette, CIGAR (= rolled tobacco), or PIPE (= device for smoking): *Lynn sat reading the newspaper and puffing on a cigarette.*

puff /pʌf/ *n* [C] • *The professor spoke to us between puffs on his pipe.*

puff SMALL BURST /pʌf/ *n* [C] a small burst of smoke, air, or something that can rise into the air in a small cloud • *We felt a puff of wind as the door open and closed.*

puff /pʌf/ *v* [I] • *The volcano continued to puff out poisonous gases.*

puff SWELL /pʌf/ *v* [I/T] to swell or increase in size • *One eye was puffed and her cheek was bruised dark as a coal smear.* [T] ○ *The child held a deep breath and puffed her cheeks until they turned red.* [T]

puffy /'pʌf·i/ *adj* swollen to a size slightly larger than usual • *His eyes were red and puffy.*

puff CAKE /pʌf/ *n* [C] a small, round cake or other food, esp. one made from pastry with a filling inside • *a cream puff* • **Puff pastry** is a light pastry made in layers with butter between them.

puffin /'pʌf·ən/ *n* [C] a sea bird that lives in northern parts of the world and has a large, brightly colored beak

pugnacious /pʌg'neɪ·ʃəs/ *adj* ready to fight or to argue very forcefully • *a pugnacious politician*

puke /pjuːk/ *v* [I/T] *slang* to vomit • *It makes me want to puke, just thinking about it.* [I]

puke /pjuːk/ *n* [U] *slang* vomit

pull MOVE TOWARD YOU /pʊl/ *v* [I/T] to move (something) toward yourself, sometimes with great physical effort • *Could you help me move this bookcase over there? You pull and I'll push.* [I] ○ *Alice lay down and pulled a blanket over her.* [T] ○ *The little girl pulled at his sleeve* (= moved it slightly and repeatedly toward her). [I] • To **pull strings** is to use important or influential people to help you achieve something: *Wilson is a very important man who can pull strings from a long distance.*

pull /pʊl/ *n* [C/U] • *Give the rope a hard pull.* [C]

pull REMOVE FROM SOMEWHERE /pʊl/ *v* [T] to take (something) out of or away from a place, esp. using physical effort • *The dentist had to pull two of my teeth out.* [M] ○ *I spent the morning pulling up weeds in the garden.* [M] ○ *She's asking companies to pull their ads from the program.* • If someone **pulls** a weapon **on** you, they take it from a hidden place and threaten you with it: *How did I know she was going to pull a gun on me?* • When you **pull out all the stops**, you make a lot of effort to do something well: *They're pulling out all the stops for a* *fund-raising dinner.* • If someone **pulls the plug** on someone or something, they stop providing support for it: *Network executives threatened to pull the plug on the show.* • If someone or something **pulls the rug out (from under** you), you are prevented from doing what you were going to do: *If you change the terms for Social Security, you'll pull the rug out from under those who are now receiving benefits.*

pull BRING BEHIND YOU /pʊl/ v [I/T] to hold or be attached to the front of (something) and cause it to move with you • *The car was pulling a trailer.* [T] ○ *Elise sat on the sled while Carol pulled.* [I] • Someone who does not **pull** their **weight** does not do their fair share of the work.

pull MOVE IN A DIRECTION /pʊl/ v [I/M] to move or move (something) in the stated direction • *Her car pulled out into traffic.* [I] ○ *The sun was so strong we had to pull down the blinds.* [M] ○ *He pulled his wet clothes off and laid them out to dry.* [M] • If a group of people **pull together**, they help each other to achieve a particular result. • If you **pull** your**self together**, you behave in a less emotional way and take control of what you are doing. • If you **pull up a chair**, you move a chair so you can sit with other people: *Pull up a chair and join us.*

pull MOVE YOUR BODY /pʊl/ v [I/T] to move your body or a part of your body • *She screamed and pulled away from him.* [I] ○ *He pulled his arm out just as the doors were closing.* [T always + adv/prep] ○ *She pulled herself up onto the rock.* [T always + adv/prep]

pull OPERATE A DEVICE /pʊl/ v [T] to operate (a device that makes a piece of equipment work) • *She took out a quarter, dropped it into the slot machine, and pulled the lever.* ○ *He raised the gun and pulled the trigger.*

pull ATTRACT /pʊl/ v [T] to attract (a person or people) • *She was able to pull more votes than the other candidates.* ○ *The networks are grabbing for any edge that pulls in viewers.* [M]

pull /pʊl/ n [U] • *Our bodily processes are influenced by the moon's gravitational pull.*

pull INFLUENCE /pʊl/ n [U] *infml* influence, esp. with important people • *The manufacturer used political pull to get the application approved.*

pull INJURE /pʊl/ v [T] to injure (esp. a muscle) • *Marie pulled a hamstring and couldn't play in the finals.*

pull /pʊl/ n [C] • *a muscle pull*

pull BE DISHONEST /pʊl/ v [T] *slang* to perform (an action that is dishonest or intended to deceive) • *Mikey was pulling his usual stunt of feeding most of his lunch to the cat.* ○ *Why would you try to pull a trick/prank like that on her?* • If you **pull a fast one** you trick someone. • (*infml*) If someone **pulls** your **leg**, they deceive you in a way that is intended to be humorous: *Stop pulling my leg—you didn't have*

lunch with Elvis! • *I'm not as stupid as you think—you can't* **pull the wool over** *my* **eyes** (= deceive me).

□ **pull away** /ˌ-ˈ-/ v adv [I] (esp. in sports) to increase (a score) or improve (a rank) • *The Cowboys hit five shots in a row to pull away from Marquette.*

□ **pull down** obj DESTROY , **pull** obj **down** /ˈ-ˈ-/ v adv [M] to destroy (esp. a building) • *Many of those old buildings will soon be pulled down.*

□ **pull down** EARN /-ˈ-/ v adv [T] *infml* to earn (an amount of money) • *She's pulling down over $100,000 a year.*

□ **pull off** obj, **pull** obj **off** /ˈ-ˈ-/ v adv [M] *infml* to succeed in doing (something difficult or unexpected) • *He won five straight games and pulled off one of the tournament's biggest upsets.*

□ **pull out** (obj), **pull** (obj) **out** /ˈ-ˈ-/ v adv [I/M] to leave or no longer be involved in something or to cause (someone) to stop doing something • *They'll be pulling the rest of the troops out by next spring.* [M] ○ *She's considering a run for governor but is stalling to see who else may jump in or pull out.* [I]

pullout /ˈpʊl-aʊt/ n [C] • *a troop pullout* ○ *Hi. pullout from the race leaves her the likely winner.*

□ **pull** (obj) **through** (obj) /ˈ-ˈ-/ v adv [I/T] to help (someone or something) to continue to exist or live after a serious problem or illness • *He pulled the city through a financial crisis.* [T] ○ *I didn't think he'd survive, but he pulled through.* [I] ○ *Some people pull through things that seem impossible.* [T]

□ **pull up** STOP A VEHICLE /-ˈ-/ v prep [I] to stop a vehicle • *The boat pulled up at the dock.* ○ *I was at the gas station, and he pulled up next to me.*

□ **pull up** obj GET INFORMATION , **pull** obj **up** /ˈ-ˈ-/ v adv [M] to get (information), esp. on a computer screen • *When officers pull over a speeding motorist, they can punch in the license plate number and pull up the owner's record.*

pulley /ˈpʊl-i/ n [C] a piece of equipment for moving heavy objects up or down, consisting of a small wheel over which a rope or chain attached to the object can be easily pulled or released slowly

pullover /ˈpʊl-oʊ-vər/ n [C] a piece of clothing, esp. made of warm material, that is worn on the top part of the body and put on by pulling it over your head

pulmonary /ˈpʊl-mə-ner-i/ adj [not gradable] *medical* relating to the lungs • *a test of pulmonary function*

pulp /pʌlp/ n [U] a soft, wet mass, often produced by pressing things until they lose their shape and firmness • *Mash the bananas to a pulp and then mix in the yogurt.* • Pulp is also a mixture of water and small pieces of paper, cloth, or wood that is used for making paper: *wood pulp*

pulpit /ˈpʊl-pət, ˈpʌl-/ n [C] a raised place in

church, with steps leading up to it, from which a minister or priest speaks

pulsate /'pʌl·seɪt/ v [I] to make sounds or movements with a regular rhythm • *A light pulsates in the distance.*

pulse /pʌls/ n [C] a regular rhythm made by blood being moved through your body by your heart, esp. when it is felt at the wrist or side of the neck • *a strong/weak pulse* ○ *A nurse took her pulse* (= measured its rate).

pulse /pʌls/ v [I] to move with a regular beat • *The music pulses with soul, Creole, and Cuban rhythms.*

pulverize /'pʌl·vəˌraɪz/ v [T] to press or crush (something) until it becomes powder or a soft mass • *Seashells were pulverized by the ocean's waves.* ○ *(infml) Our team aims to pulverize the competition* (= badly defeat them).

puma /'pjuː·mə, 'puː-/ n [C] a COUGAR (= large wild cat)

pummel /'pʌm·əl/ v [T] **-l-** or **-ll-** to hit (someone or something) repeatedly, esp. with your FISTS • *He pummeled her face until her glasses broke.* ○ *(fig.) Taxes are pummeling the middle class* (= hurting them).

pump DEVICE /pʌmp/ n [C] a piece of equipment used to cause liquid, air, or gas to move from one place to another • *a gas/water pump*

pump /pʌmp/ v [T] • *You have to pump your own gasoline at that station.* ○ *He ran toward us, pumping his arms* (= moving them up and down energetically). ○ *She pumped her bike tires up* (= filled them with air). [M] • If you pump money into something, you spend a lot of money trying to make it successful: *We're pumping millions into this new program.* • *(infml)* When you pump someone, you ask them for information, esp. in an indirect way: *I pumped him for details about the deal.* • *(infml)* To **pump iron** is to lift heavy weights for exercise.

pump SHOE /pʌmp/ n [C usually pl] a women's shoe with no fasteners

▢**pump up** obj, **pump** obj **up** /'-'-/ v adv [M] *infml* to make (someone) more confident or more enthusiastic • *Myerson spent a lot of time trying to pump up his partners.*

pumpernickel /'pʌm·pərˌnɪk·əl/ n [U] a type of dark brown bread made from RYE

pumpkin /'pʌmp·kən, 'pʌŋ·kən/ n [C] a large, round vegetable with hard yellow or orange flesh

pun /pʌn/ n [C] an amusing use of a word or phrase that has several meanings or that sounds like another word • *People groan at a pun if it's told correctly.*

pun /pʌn/ v [I] • *She kept punning on "whole" and "hole."*

punch HIT /pʌntʃ/ n [C] a forceful hit with a FIST (= hand with the fingers closed tight) • *She gave him a punch in the nose.*

punch /pʌntʃ/ v [I/T] • *She punched the pillow, trying to fluff it up.* [T] • If you **punch a clock,**

you record the times you arrive at and leave work, using a special machine. • A **punching bag** is a bag filled with air or material that is hung from a frame or fixed to a stand and hit for exercise or boxing practice.

punch EFFECT /pʌntʃ/ n [U] the power to be interesting and have a strong effect on people • *His acting gives the show its emotional punch.* • A **punch line** is the last part of a joke or a story that explains the meaning of what has happened previously or makes it amusing.

punch DRINK /pʌntʃ/ n [C/U] a cold or hot drink made by mixing fruit juices, pieces of fruit, and sometimes wine or other alcoholic drinks • *Would you like a glass of punch?* [U]

punch TOOL /pʌntʃ/ n [C] a piece of equipment that cuts holes in a material by pushing a piece of metal through it • *a hole/leather punch*

punch /pʌntʃ/ v [T] • *The rod came loose, punching a hole in the box.*

▢**punch in** obj PRESS BUTTONS , **punch** obj **in** /'-'-/ v adv [M] to press (buttons or keys) to put information into a computer or other device • *Trev lifted the receiver and punched in a set of seven numbers.*

▢**punch in** RECORD HOURS /-'-/ v adv [I] to use a special machine to record the time you start working • *I punched in on the time clock.*

▢**punch out** /-'-/ v adv [I] to record the time you finish working on a special machine • *I punched out and walked out the door.*

punctual /'pʌŋ·tʃə·wəl/ adj arriving, doing something, or happening at the expected or correct time; not late • *Please try to be punctual, so we can start the meeting on time.*

punctually /'pʌŋ·tʃə·wə·li/ adv • *We arrived punctually at 8.*

punctuality /ˌpʌŋ·tʃəˈwæl·əṭ·i/ n [U] • *He's obsessive about punctuality.*

punctuate /'pʌŋ·tʃəˌweɪt/ v [T] to regularly interrupt (something that is happening) • *His comments were punctuated by shouts from hecklers.*

punctuation /ˌpʌŋ·tʃəˈweɪ·ʃən/ n [U] special marks that are placed in a text to show the divisions between phrases and sentences, or the use of these marks • *Check your spelling and punctuation.* • A **punctuation mark** is a mark that you add to a text to show the divisions between different parts of it: *Periods, commas, semicolons, question marks, and parentheses are all punctuation marks.* • LP APOSTROPHE, CAPITAL LETTERS, COMMA, DASH, DOTS, EXCLAMATION POINT, HYPHEN, PARENTHESES, PERIOD, QUESTION MARK, QUOTATION MARKS, SEMICOLON, SLASH

punctuate /'pʌŋ·tʃəˌweɪt/ v [T] • *I would punctuate that sentence differently.*

puncture /'pʌŋ·tʃər/ n [C] a small hole made by a sharp object

puncture /'pʌŋ·tʃər/ v [I/T] • *Hot-air balloons are made so that they won't puncture easily.* [I]

○ *The bullet hadn't punctured any vital organs.* [T]

pundit /ˈpʌn·dət/ n [C] a person who knows a lot about a particular subject, or someone who gives opinions in a way that makes them sound knowledgeable • *Wall Street pundits are divided over whether the economy is slowing down.*

pungent /ˈpʌn·dʒənt/ adj (of a smell or taste) very strong, sometimes in an unpleasant way • *pungent odors*

punish /ˈpʌn·ɪʃ/ v [T] to cause (someone who has done something wrong or committed a crime) to suffer for what they have done, esp. by making them do something they don't want to do or sending them to prison • *She was punished for smoking in school.*

punishable /ˈpʌn·ɪʃ·ə·bəl/ adj • *Swimming in the Potomac is punishable by a fine.*

punishment /ˈpʌn·ɪʃ·mənt/ n [C/U] • *Serving your community is seen as a punishment these days.* [C]

punishing /ˈpʌn·ɪʃ·ɪŋ/ adj extremely difficult or tiring • *a punishing schedule*

punitive /ˈpju:·nət·ɪv/ adj intended as a punishment • *No punitive action was taken against Dawkins after he smashed the backboard during warmups.*

punk CULTURE /pʌŋk/ n [U] a style or culture popular among young people, esp. in the late 1970s, expressing opposition to authority through shocking behavior, clothes, and hair, and through fast, loud music • *punk music/ rock*

punk CRIMINAL /pʌŋk/ n [C] slang a young person who fights and is involved in criminal activities • *Some punk tried to steal my coat.*

punt /pʌnt/ v [T] (in football) to kick (the ball) after you have dropped it from your hands and before it touches the ground

punt /pʌnt/ n [C] • *I caught the punt and started running.*

puny /ˈpju:·ni/ adj [-er/-est only] small and weak, or not effective • *Don't tell me you're afraid of that puny little kid.* ○ *In 1981, computers were puny compared with today's machines.*

pup /pʌp/ n [C] the young of particular animals, or a PUPPY DOG • *a seal pup*

pupil STUDENT /ˈpju:·pəl/ n [C] a person who is being taught, esp. a child at school

pupil EYE PART /ˈpju:·pəl/ n [C] the circular, black area in the center of the eye that gets larger and smaller and lets in light • PIC DILATE

puppet /ˈpʌp·ət/ n [C] a type of toy that looks like a person or animal and is moved by a person using strings or putting their hand inside it • (disapproving) A puppet is also a person or group whose actions are controlled by someone else: *The mayor is a puppet who does what business leaders tell him to.*

puppeteer /ˌpʌp·əˈtɪr/ n [C] a person who makes or uses puppets

puppy (dog) /ˈpʌp·i (ˌdɔːg)/, **pup** n [C] a young dog

puppy love /ˈpʌp·iːˌlʌv/ n [U] romantic love that a young person feels for someone else

purchase /ˈpɜr·tʃəs/ v [T] to buy (something) • *To qualify for this fare, you must purchase your ticket 21 days in advance.*

purchase /ˈpɜr·tʃəs/ n [C/U] • *The makeover is free with a $50 purchase.* [C] • Purchase can also mean the act of buying: *New restrictions have been placed on the purchase of guns.* [U]

purchaser /ˈpɜr·tʃə·sər/ n [C] • *Software purchasers have reported problems with the product.*

pure NOT MIXED /pjʊr/ adj [-er/-est only] not mixed with anything else • *The scarf is pure silk.* ○ *It was a moment of pure joy.* ○ *The mountain air was fresh and pure* (= not polluted)

purify /ˈpjʊr·əˌfaɪ/ v [T] to rid (something) of dirty or harmful substances • *Flower growers here are required to purify all their runoff water.*

purification /ˌpjʊr·ə·fəˈkeɪ·ʃən/ n [U]

purist /ˈpjʊr·əst/ n [C] a person who believes that it is important to speak, write, or do things in a correct or traditional way • *Some purists complain that the buildings are not being accurately restored.*

purity /ˈpjʊr·ət·i/ n [U] • *The purity of the city's water is checked regularly at its reservoirs.*

pure MORALLY GOOD /pjʊr/ adj [-er/-est only] morally good • *His motives were pure, but his approach was tactless.*

purify /ˈpjʊr·əˌfaɪ/ v [T] • *In his prayer he strove to purify his own heart to have more compassion for others.*

purity /ˈpjʊr·ət·i/ n [U] • *purity of heart*

pure COMPLETE /pjʊr/ adj [not gradable] complete; only • *Getting the job was pure luck.* • LP VERY, COMPLETELY, AND OTHER INTENSIFIERS

purely /ˈpjʊr·li/ adv [not gradable] only; just • *Meeting Gail in the airport was purely coincidental.*

puree, purée /pjʊˈreɪ, -ˈriː/ v [T] to crush (food) into a thick, soft sauce • *Puree the bananas thoroughly in a blender.*

puree, purée /pjʊˈreɪ, -ˈriː/ n [C/U] • *Add two tablespoons of tomato puree.* [U]

purge RID /pɜrdʒ/ v [T] to rid (a group or organization) of unwanted people • *They purged the senior ranks of the department by offering them generous retirement packages.*

purge /pɜrdʒ/ n [C] • *The purge of alleged Communists and progressives had started as early as April.*

purge REMOVE /pɜrdʒ/ v [T] to remove by cleaning or purifying • *The system is designed to purge impurities from the city's drinking water.*

Puritan, puritan /ˈpjʊr·ət·ən/ n [C] a member of an English religious group in the 16th and 17th centuries who wanted to make church ceremonies simpler and emphasized morality

puritanical /ˌpjʊr·əˈtæn·ɪ·kəl/ adj [not gradable] having standards of moral behavior that forbid many pleasures • *Voicing his own deep* set puritanical nature, he damned Londoners for such sins as smoking, drinking, and enjoying sex.

purple /'pɜr·pəl/ *adj, n* [C/U] (of) the color that is a mixture of red and blue • *a purple dress* ∘ *The walls are a pale purple.* [C]

purport /pər'pɔːrt, -'poʊrt/ *v* [+ *to* infinitive] *fml* to claim that something is true, but without proof • *The story purports to explain the origin of the game of chess.*

purported /pər'pɔːrt̬·əd, -'poʊrt̬-/ *adj* [not gradable] claimed but not proved to be true • *The new brand of potato chips is purported to be lower in cholesterol, fat, and calories.* [+ *to* infinitive]

purpose REASON /'pɜr·pəs/ *n* [C/U] an intention or aim; a reason for doing something or for allowing something to happen • *For budgeting purposes, you really have to start estimating costs now.* [C] ∘ *The delay really served no good purpose and may have harmed the negotiation.* [C] • Purpose is also determination: *The project gave him a renewed sense of purpose.* [U] • If you do something **on purpose**, you do it intentionally: *This is the second time in a row that he didn't show up, and I believe he did it on purpose.*

purposeful /'pɜr·pəs·fəl/ *adj* aimed at achieving something; determined • *He desired to lead a more purposeful life.* • Purposeful also means intentional: *the purposeful destruction of historic sites*

purposely /'pɜr·pə·sli/ *adv* [not gradable] with a specific intent • *I purposely spoke loud enough to be overheard.*

purpose RESULT /'pɜr·pəs/ *n* [C] an intended result or use • *These assault weapons, she said, are developed for one purpose and one purpose only, which is to kill people.*

purr /pɜr/ *v* [I] (of a cat) to make a soft, low, continuous sound, or (of a machine) to make a similar sound • *After a tune-up, the car just purred like new.*

purse BAG /pɜrs/ *n* [C] a bag, often with a handle or a strap going over the shoulder, used esp. by women for carrying money, keys, and small personal items such as makeup; a POCKETBOOK • **Purse strings** means your control over how much money you spend: *Retailers are hoping that American consumers will loosen their purse strings next year* (= spend more money).

purse AMOUNT OF MONEY /pɜrs/ *n* [C] an amount of money offered as a prize in a sporting competition, or the total amount of money available for spending • *Yesterday's race had a purse worth over $100,000.*

purse MOVE LIPS /pɜrs/ *v* [T] to bring (your lips) tightly together so that they form a rounded shape • *She pursed her lips and said nothing.*

pursue FOLLOW /pər'suː/ *v* [I/T] to follow or search for (someone or something), in order to catch them or attack them • *The police pursued on foot, but lost him in the crowd.* [I]

pursue ATTEMPT /pər'suː/ *v* [T] to try to achieve • *She single-mindedly pursued her goal of earning a law degree.*

pursue CONTINUE /pər'suː/ *v* [T] to continue to do • *The hobbies that I pursue in my spare time are crafts—woodworking, mainly.* • To pursue is also to continue to consider: *I don't think the idea is worth pursuing.*

pursuit ACT OF FOLLOWING /pər'suːt/ *n* [C/U] the act of following or searching for someone or something, in order to catch them or attack them • *Police are in pursuit of an armed man who held up a convenience store.* [U]

pursuit ATTEMPT /pər'suːt/ *n* [U] an attempt to achieve something • *The Declaration of Independence states that life, liberty, and the pursuit of happiness are basic human rights.*

pursuit ACTIVITY /pər'suːt/ *n* [C usually pl] an activity that you spend time and energy doing • *scholarly pursuits*

purvey /pər'veɪ/ *v* [T] *fml* to provide food, services, or information, esp. as a business • *The two mall shops purvey nearly identical merchandise.*

purveyor /pər'veɪ·ər/ *n* [C] *fml* • *Radio stations are purveyors of music, information, and companionship.*

pus /pʌs/ *n* [U] thick, yellow liquid that forms in and comes out from infected body tissue

push USE FORCE AGAINST /pʊʃ/ *v* [I/T] to put a continuing force against (something) to cause it to move forward or away from you • *We should be able to move this table if we both push together.* [I] ∘ *She pushed her plate away.* [T] • To push is also to cause something to move or change in a stated direction: *Rising demand tends to push prices up.* [M] • When someone says something will happen if **push comes to shove**, they mean it will happen when you cannot avoid really dealing with a problem: *Only a few people will really come through for you when push comes to shove.* • A **push-up** is a type of physical exercise performed by lying with your face down and, while keeping your body stiff, using your arms only to raise and lower your head and shoulders.

push /pʊʃ/ *n* [C] • *She gave her daughter a push on the swing.* • (*Br*) A **pushchair** is a STROLLER.

push MOVE FORCEFULLY /pʊʃ/ *v* [I/T] to move forcefully through a group of people or things • *Stop pushing and wait your turn!* [I] ∘ *Rescuers pushed their way through the rubble to reach survivors.* [T always + adv/prep]

push PERSUADE FORCEFULLY /pʊʃ/ *v* [T] to persuade (someone) forcefully to do or accept something • *She's pushing me for an answer.* ∘ *The administration is pushing its new trade agreement with Mexico.* ∘ (*infml*) *This restaurant is pushing its carrot soup today* (= trying to get people to order it). • (*slang*) To push (drugs) is to sell illegal drugs.

push /pʊʃ/ *n* [C] • *Florida is making a major push to attract tourists.* [+ *to* infinitive]

pusher /ˈpʊʃ·ər/ *n* [C] *slang* a person who sells illegal drugs

pushy /ˈpʊʃ·i/ *adj disapproving* trying too hard to persuade someone to do something • *The salesman was a little too pushy, and we felt uncomfortable.*

▫**push** *obj* **around** /ˈ--ˈ-/ *v adv* [T] to use greater strength or power to treat (someone) in a rude and threatening way • *When we were kids, my older brother liked to push me around.*

▫**push for** /ˈ--ˈ/ *v prep* [T] to demand that (something be done) or to take strong action to cause (something to happen) • *The unions are pushing for job security even if it means settling for modest wage increases.*

▫**push off** /ˈ-ˈ-/ *v adv* [I] *infml* to leave • *I'd better be pushing off now—I've got work to do.*

▫**push on** /ˈ-ˈ-/ *v adv* [I] to continue in a determined way • *We decided to push on to the summit while there was still daylight.*

pushover /ˈpʊʃ·oʊ·vər/ *n* [C] *infml* something easy to do or win, or someone who is easily persuaded, influenced, or defeated • *Krista gets whatever she wants—her parents are real pushovers.*

pussy CAT /ˈpʊs·i/, **pussycat** /ˈpʊs·i·ˌkæt/ *n* [C] a child's word for a cat

pussy VAGINA /ˈpʊs·i/ *n* [C/U] *taboo slang* a woman's vagina, or sex with a woman

pussyfoot /ˈpʊs·iˌfʊt/ *v* [I] to be careful about expressing an opinion or taking action, esp. because you might hurt someone's feelings • *Quit pussyfooting around and tell me what you really think.*

pussy willow /ˈpʊs·iˌwɪl·oʊ/ *n* [C] a small tree which has gray, furry flowers in the spring

put MOVE /pʊt/ *v* [T always + adv/prep] **putting**, *past* **put** to move (something or someone) into the stated place, position, or direction • *She put her arm around him.* ○ *Put your clothes in the closet.* ○ *When you set the table, put the soup spoons next to the knives.* ○ *She put her coffee cup on the table.* ○ *The film was so frightening that she put her hands over her eyes.* • If you **put down roots**, you become established in a place: *Very quickly, settlers in Oregon built towns and put down roots.* • *Something seemed to be wrong, but I couldn't **put** my **finger on** it* (= say exactly what it was). • To **put** your **foot down** is to use your authority to stop something from happening: *When she started borrowing my clothes without asking, I had to put my foot down.* • To **put** your **foot in** your **mouth** is to say or do something that you should not have said or done: *I really put my foot in my mouth—I asked her when the baby was due and she wasn't even pregnant.* • If you **put** someone **in** their **place**, you make it clear that they are less important than they think they are: *When he tried to take charge, she soon put him in his place.* • If you **put** yourself in someone's **place/position/shoes**, you imagine that you are in the difficult situation that they are in: *Put yourself in my place—what else could I have done?* • If you **put** someone

to bed, you dress them in the clothes they wear for sleeping and see that they get in bed • *I'll call back after I put the kids to bed.* • If you say that someone is **putting words in** your **mouth**, you mean they are saying you meant one thing when you really meant something else. • (*infml*) If you say you **wouldn't put it past** someone to do something bad, it means that you would not be surprised if they did it • *I wouldn't put it past Helena to pass secrets to our competitors.*

put WRITE /pʊt/ *v* [T always + adv/prep] **putting**, *past* **put** to write down or record • *Put your name on the list if you want to go.* ○ *Put an answer in the space provided.*

put EXPRESS /pʊt/ *v* [T] to express (something) in words • *She wanted to tell him that she didn't want to see him any more, but she didn't know how to put it.* ○ *He has difficulty putting his feelings into words.* • If you put something in a particular way, you express it that way: *To put it bluntly, Pete, you're just no good at the job.* ○ *Dad was annoyed, to put it mildly.*

put CONDITION /pʊt/ *v* [T] **putting**, *past* **put** to cause (something) to be in the stated condition or situation • *Are you prepared to put your children at risk?* ○ *This puts me in a very difficult position.* ○ *What put you in such a bad mood?* • If you **put an end to** something, you cause it to stop existing or happening: *Mrs. Carroll said she was going to put an end to all the talking and fooling around in our class.* • After working all week, you deserve to **put** your **feet up** (= relax and do very little). • If you **put** someone or something **out of** your **mind**, you do not think about them: *Karen can't put the burglary out of her mind.* • To **put the brakes on** something is to cause it to slow down or not to develop: *Raising taxes now would put the brakes on economic recovery.* • If you **put the squeeze on** something, you cause it to be less active: *Budget cuts are putting the squeeze on scientific research.* • If you **put** something **to the test**, you find out how good it is: *Those icy roads certainly put my driving to the test.*

put JUDGE /pʊt/ *v* [T always + adv/prep] **putting**, *past* **put** to judge (something or someone) in comparison with other similar things or people • *I'd put him among the top six tennis players of all time.* ○ *The value of the painting has been put at $1.5 million.* ○ *He always puts his family first.*

▫**put aside** *obj* IGNORE, **put** *obj* **aside** /ˈ--ˈ-/ *v adv* [M] to ignore or not deal with (a subject) • *Let's put aside our differences.*

▫**put aside** *obj* SAVE, **put** *obj* **aside** /ˈ--ˈ-/ *v adv* [M] to save (something, esp. money) for use at a later time • *We're putting aside $20 a week for our vacation.* ○ *He puts some time aside each evening to read to his children.*

▫**put away** *obj* EAT, **put** *obj* **away** /ˈ--ˈ-/ *v adv* [M] *infml* to eat (a lot of food) • *He put away a whole pie in one sitting.*

▫**put away** *obj* STORE, **put** *obj* **away** /ˈ--ˈ-/ *v* *adv* [M] to store (things) where they are usually stored • *You never put away your toys.*

□ **put away** *obj* MOVE INTO CARE , **put** *obj* **away** /'-'-/ *v adv* [M] *infml* to move (someone) into prison, a mental hospital, or a home for old people • *He deserves to be put away for life.*

□ **put back** *obj*, **put** *obj* **back** /'-'-/ *v adv* [M] to move (something) to a place or position it was in before • *Will you put the books back when you're finished with them?*

□ **put** *obj* **behind** *obj* /'--'-/ *v prep* [T] to try to forget or ignore (something unpleasant) • *I'm going to put all this behind me and think about the future.*

□ **put down** *obj* STOP CARRYING , **put** *obj* **down** /'-'-/ *v adv* [M] to stop carrying or holding (someone or something) • *I have to put this bag down—it's too heavy.* ○ *Put me down, Daddy!* • *It was such a good book that I couldn't put it down* (= felt I had to read it without stopping until I reached the end).

□ **put down** *obj* PAY , **put** *obj* **down** /'-'-/ *v adv* [M] to pay (money, esp. part of a total payment) • *She put $1000 down on an apartment this afternoon.*

□ **put down** *obj* INSULT , **put** *obj* **down** /'-'-/ *v adv* [M] *infml* to make (someone) feel foolish and unimportant • *They never put down other companies in their commercials.* ○ *Did you have to put me down in front of everybody?*

put-down /'pʊt·daʊn/ *n* [C] *infml* • *Calling American workers lazy was a mean-spirited put-down.*

□ **put down** *obj* STOP , **put** *obj* **down** /'-'-/ *v adv* [M] to stop or limit (forces opposing an authority or government), usually by using force • *He helped put down the rebellion.*

□ **put forward/forth** *obj*, **put** *obj* **forward/forth** /'-'--; '-'-/ *v adv* [M] to suggest (an idea) for consideration • *None of the ideas that I put forward have been accepted.* ○ *He put forth a clear, logical argument.*

□ **put in** *obj* INCLUDE , **put** *obj* **in** /'-'-/ *v prep* [M] to include (something), esp. in a piece of writing or a broadcast • *Kids like this computer program because they can put in things that they create.* ○ *We put an ad in the paper to sell our car.*

□ **put in** *obj* OFFER , **put** *obj* **in** /'-'-/ *v adv* [M] to offer (something or yourself) for consideration • *She put in an application to the college.* • *If you put in a good word with someone, you tell them positive things about someone else.*

□ **put in** *obj* MAKE READY , **put** *obj* **in** /'-'-/ *v adv* [M] to bring (a device) somewhere and make it ready to operate • *They're putting Paul's new stove in next week.*

□ **put in** *obj* DO , **put** *obj* **in** /'-'-/ *v adv* [M] to do (work), use (effort), or spend (time) • *She's put in a lot of effort on this proposal.*

□ **put** *obj* **into** *obj* /'-'--/ *v prep* [T] to give (money or effort) to (an activity) • *We put all our profits back into the company.* ○ *She's put a lot of energy into making the house look nice.*

□ **put off** *obj* DELAY , **put** *obj* **off** /'-'-/ *v adv* [M] to delay or move (an activity) to a later time, or to stop or prevent (someone) from doing something • *The meeting has been put off for a week.* ○ *He keeps asking me out, and I keep putting him off.*

□ **put off** *obj* DISLIKE , **put** *obj* **off** /'-'-/ *v adv* [M] to cause (someone) to dislike someone or something, or to discourage (someone) from doing something • *I was put off by his appearance.* ○ *The experience put me off politics.*

□ **put on** *obj* WEAR , **put** *obj* **on** /'-'-/ *v adv* [M] to move (something you wear) onto your body • *Put your shoes on.* ○ *She put on too much makeup.*

□ **put on** *obj* ADD , **put** *obj* **on** /'-'-/ *v adv* [M] to add or increase (an amount or action) • *I put on weight when I gave up smoking.* ○ *I put on my brakes too fast, and the car skidded.* ○ *The school puts a lot of emphasis on music and art.* ○ *He's putting pressure on me to change my mind.*

□ **put on** *obj* START , **put** *obj* **on** /'-'-/ *v adv* [M] to start (a piece of equipment), or to place (a recording) in a device that will play it • *I put the heat on, but it will take a minute for the car to warm up.* ○ *Put on that Ella Fitzgerald CD.*

□ **put on** *obj* DO , **put** *obj* **on** /'-'-/ *v adv* [M] to do (an activity, esp. one that others can watch) • *The second graders want to put a play on.* ○ *The experience of putting on a campaign was exciting.*

□ **put on** *obj* PRETEND , **put** *obj* **on** /'-'-, '-,-/ *v adv* [M] to appear to have (a feeling or way of behaving that is not real or not natural for you) • *I can't tell whether he's really upset or if he's just putting it on.* • *If you put someone on you deceive them: "I hear Joe's left his wife." "You're putting me on!"*

□ **put out** *obj* MOVE AWAY , **put** *obj* **out** /'-'-/ *v adv* [M] to move (a part of your body) away from the rest of you • *She put out her hand to shake mine.*

□ **put out** *obj* INJURE , **put** *obj* **out** /'-'-/ *v adv* [M] to injure (a part of the body) by pulling or twisting it • *I put my back out last week when I fell.*

□ **put out** *obj* STOP BURNING , **put** *obj* **out** /'-'-/ *v adv* [M] to stop (something burning) from continuing to burn • *Put out that cigarette!*

□ **put out** *obj* MAKE KNOWN , **put** *obj* **out** /'-'-/ *v adv* [M] to make (information) more generally known • *The senator has put out a statement denying the allegations.* • *To put out feelers is to try to get information about something or let others know you are available: I'll put out some feelers and see if there are any jobs.*

□ **put out** *obj* ANNOY , **put** *obj* **out** /'-'-/ *v adv* [M] to annoy, upset, or inconvenience (someone) • *Would you be put out if we came tomorrow instead of today?*

□ **put out** *obj* SPEND , **put** *obj* **out** /'-'-/ *v adv* [M] to spend (money) • *I'll be putting a lot of money out when I buy my house.*

□ **put** *obj* **over on** *obj* /-'---,-/ *v adv prep* [T] *infml* to cause (something that is not true) to be believed by (someone) • *My dad's really smart—you can never put anything over on him.*

□ **put** *obj* **through** *obj* CAUSE TO EXPERIENCE /-'-/ *v adv* [T] to cause, allow, or pay for (someone) to experience or do (something) • *I'm sorry to have to put you through this.* ○ *She's putting herself through college.* • If you **put** someone or something **through** their **paces**, you make them show their qualities and abilities: *I like to put a new car through its paces.*

□ **put through** *obj* CONNECT TELEPHONES , **put** *obj* **through** /'-,-, -'-/ *v adv* [M] to connect (a caller) to the person they have telephoned • *Hold the line a minute, I'll put you through to Mrs. Barnhart.*

□ **put** *obj* **to** *obj* /'--/ *v prep* [T] to cause (someone) to experience (an emotion or activity) • *Your generosity puts me to shame.* ○ *He was put to death.*

□ **put together** *obj* COMBINE , **put** *obj* **together** /'--'--/ *v adv* [M] to combine (people or things), or organize (something) • *Put two and two together and you get four.* ○ *She earns more than all three of us put together.* ○ *After his first band failed, he put together a second orchestra.*

□ **put together** *obj* MAKE WHOLE , **put** *obj* **together** /'--'--/ *v adv* [M] to repair (something broken) or make (something) out of parts • *The bowl broke into so many pieces that I can't put it back together again.* ○ *The bombs were being put together in a basement.*

□ **put** *obj* **toward** *obj* /'-,--, -'-/ *v adv* [T] to use (money) to help pay the cost of (something) • *Grandma told me to put that money toward my college education.*

□ **put up** *obj* ATTACH , **put** *obj* **up** /'-'-/ *v adv* [M] to attach (something) esp. to a wall • *We put up some new pictures in the living room.*

□ **put up** *obj* RAISE , **put** *obj* **up** /'-'-/ *v adv* [M] to raise (something) to a higher position • *I put my hands up.* ○ *A statue of him was put up in Gramercy Park.*

□ **put up** *obj* BUILD , **put** *obj* **up** /'-'-/ *v adv* [M] to build (a structure) in an empty space • *They're planning to put a hotel up where the museum used to be.*

□ **put up** SHOW FEELINGS /'-,-/ *v adv* [T] to show or express (your feelings about something) • *I'm not going to let them build a road here without putting up a fight.* ○ *Little Rory always puts up such a fuss around bedtime.*

□ **put up** *obj* PROVIDE HOUSING , **put** *obj* **up** /'-'-/ *v adv* [M] to provide (someone) with a place to stay temporarily • *Sally is putting me up for the weekend.*

□ **put up** *obj* PROVIDE MONEY , **put** *obj* **up** /'-'-/ *v adv* [M] to provide or lend (money) so that an aim can be achieved • *Dad put $1000 up to help me buy a car.*

□ **put** *obj* **up to** *obj* /'-'--/ *v adv prep* [T] to encourage (someone) to do (something, esp. something wrong) • *She never stole anything before—maybe her friends put her up to it.*

□ **put up with** /-'--/ *v adv prep* [T] to be willing to accept (something that is unpleasant or not desirable) • *I don't know why she puts up with him.*

putrefy /'pjuː·trə,faɪ/ *v* [I] *slightly fml* to decay, producing a strong, unpleasant smell

putrid /'pjuː·trəd/ *adj* very decayed and having an unpleasant smell • *a putrid garbage dump*

putt /pʌt/ *v* [I/T] to hit (a golf ball) gently across an area of short and even grass toward or into a hole

putt /pʌt/ *n* [C] • *She won with an impressive six-yard putt.*

putter /'pʌt̬·ər/ *v* [I] to move around without hurrying and in a relaxed and pleasant way • *He really enjoys puttering in the garden.*

putty /'pʌt̬·i/ *n* [U] a soft, oily, claylike substance which is used esp. for fixing glass into window frames or for filling small holes in wood

put–upon /'pʊt̬·ə,pɑn/ *adj infml* treated unfairly by others who want you to help them • *Parents often feel put-upon by the school fund-raisers.*

puzzle /'pʌz·əl/ *n* [C] something that is difficult to understand • *Their son is a puzzle to them.* ○ *The police are trying to solve the puzzle of who sent them the letter.* • A puzzle is also a game or toy in which you have to fit separate pieces together, or a problem or question which you have to answer by using your skill or knowledge: *a jigsaw/crossword puzzle*

puzzle /'pʌz·əl/ *v* [I/T] • *It puzzles me why she said that.* [T] ○ *We puzzled over what it meant.* [I always + adv/prep]

puzzled /'pʌz·əld/ *adj* • *She looked puzzled, then suspicious.*

Pygmy, **Pigmy** /'pɪg·mi/ *n* [C] a member of one of several groups of very small people who live in central Africa

pygmy, **pigmy** /'pɪg·mi/ *adj* [not gradable] (of an animal or bird) one of a type which is smaller than animals or birds of that type usually are • *a pygmy hippopotamus*

pylon /'paɪ·lɑn/ *n* [C] a tall, metal structure used as a support • *Bomb attacks were made on railway lines and power pylons.*

pyramid /'pɪr·ə,mɪd/ *n* [C] a solid object with a flat, square base and four flat, triangular sides which slope inward and meet to form a point at the top • A pyramid is also a pile of things that has a triangular shape: *The acrobats formed a pyramid by standing on each other's shoulders.*

pyre /paɪr/ *n* [C] a large pile of wood on which a dead body is burned in some types of funerals

Pyrex /'paɪ·reks/ *n* [U] *trademark* a type of glass that is used to make containers for cooking because it does not break when it is heated

python /'paɪ·θɑn, -θən/ *n* [C] a very large snake that kills animals for food by wrapping itself around them and crushing them

Q, q

Q, q /kjuː/ *n* [C] *pl* **Q's** or **Qs** or **q's** or **qs** the 17th letter of the English alphabet

qt. *n* [C] *pl* **qt.** *abbreviation for* QUART

Q–tip /'kjuː·tɪp/ *n* [C] *trademark* a short stick with a small amount of cotton on each end, used for cleaning esp. the ears

quack SOUND /kwæk/ *v* [I] to make the sound DUCKS make • *The ducks started quacking.*

quack FALSE DOCTOR /kwæk/ *n* [C] a person who falsely pretends to have medical skills or knowledge

quad /kwɑd/, **quadrangle** /'kwɑd,ræŋ·gəl/ *n* [C] a square or rectangular outside area with buildings on all four sides, often part of the land of a college or university

quadrangle /'kwɑd,ræŋ·gəl/ *n* [C] a flat shape with four straight sides • *Squares and rectangles are forms of quadrangles.*

quadriplegic /ˌkwɑd·rə'pliː·dʒɪk/ *n* [C] a person who is permanently unable to move any of their arms or legs • *The riding accident injured his spine and left him a quadriplegic.*

quadruped /'kwɑd·rə,ped/ *n* [C] *specialized* any animal that has four feet • *Horses and dogs are quadrupeds.*

quadruple /kwɑ'druː·pəl, -'drʌp·əl/ *v* [I/T] to become or make (something) four times greater • *The number of students at the college quadrupled in the last ten years.* [I]

quadruple /kwɑ'druː·pəl, -'drʌp·əl/ *adj* [not gradable] consisting of four parts, or four times greater in amount, number, or size • *My father had quadruple bypass heart surgery.*

quadruplet /kwɑ'druː·plət, -'drʌp·lət/, *short form* **quad** /kwɑd/ *n* [C] any of four children who are born to the same mother at the same time

quagmire /'kwæg·mɑɪr, 'kwɑg-/ *n* [C] a situation that can easily trap you so that you become involved with problems from which it is difficult to escape • *When I tried to get my tax situation straightened out with the government, I ran into a bureaucratic quagmire.*

quail /kweɪl/ *n* [C/U] a small brown bird with a short tail, sometimes hunted as a sport and eaten as a food

quaint /kweɪnt/ *adj* [-er/-est only] attractive because of being unusual and esp. old-fashioned • *In Spain, we visited a cobblestone plaza with quaint little cafés around its perimeter.*

quake SHAKE /kweɪk/ *v* [I] to shake, esp. because you are frightened • *He quaked with fear at the thought.*

quake EARTH MOVEMENT /kweɪk/ *n* [C] *short form of* **earthquake**, see at EARTH PLANET

Quaker /'kweɪ·kər/ *n* [C] a member of a Christian group called the Society of Friends, which believes that a person can experience God directly and which does not have formal ceremonies or ministers, and whose meetings often include periods of silence

qualification SKILL /ˌkwɑl·ə·fə'keɪ·ʃən/ *n* [C usually pl] knowledge, skill, or some other characteristic that gives a person the ability or the right to do or have something • *I assume my qualifications for the job will be considered along with theirs.* • A qualification is also a level of skill or ability that you have to achieve to be allowed to do something: *Passing the advanced Red Cross life-saving course is a qualification for all our lifeguards.*

qualification LIMITATION /ˌkwɑl·ə·fə'keɪ·ʃən/ *n* [C/U] the act of limiting the use or range of a statement you make, or a particular limitation to a statement • *I can recommend Helen Hefferman for this position without qualification.* [U]

qualify REACH A STANDARD /'kwɑl·ə,fɑɪ/ *v* [I/T] to achieve or have the standard of skill, knowledge, or ability that is necessary for doing or being something, or to cause (someone) to reach that standard • *She was qualified to teach high school mathematics and physics.* [+ to infinitive] ○ *Derrick won his tennis match and qualified for the semifinals.* [I] ○ *James hopes to qualify as a nurse practitioner.* [I] • To qualify is also to have the legal right to have or do something: *She doesn't qualify for maternity leave because she hasn't worked there long enough.* [I]

qualified /'kwɑl·ə,fɑɪd/ *adj* • *She was extraordinarily well qualified to run the State Department.*

qualify LIMIT /'kwɑl·ə,fɑɪ/ *v* [T] to limit the strength or meaning of (a statement) • *The press secretary later qualified the president's remarks by saying he hadn't been aware of all of the facts.*

qualitative /'kwɑl·ə,teɪt·ɪv/ *adj* relating to the quality of an experience or situation rather than to facts that can be measured • *There's a qualitative difference between seeing a live performance in a theater and watching a movie.* • Compare QUANTITATIVE.

quality EXCELLENCE /'kwɑl·ət·i/ *n* [U] the degree of excellence of something, often a high degree of it • *Our company guarantees the quality of our merchandise.* • Quality often refers to how good or bad something is: *The wine was of the best quality.* • A person's **quality of life** is the level of satisfaction they have based on the comforts and conditions of their life: *Our quality of life improved tremendously once we finished paying for our kid's college education.*

quality /'kwɑl·ət·i/ *adj* • *This is a quality product* (= an excellent product).

quality CHARACTERISTIC /'kwɑl·ət·i/ *n* [C] a

characteristic or feature of someone or something • *We're looking for someone who loves children and has the qualities of a good teacher.*

qualm /kwɑm, kwɑlm/ *n* [C usually pl] an uncomfortable feeling of doubt about whether you are doing the right thing • *Unfortunately, he said, there are people who have no qualms about bringing in replacement workers for strikers.*

quandary /ˈkwɑn·dri/ *n* [C usually sing] a state of not being able to decide what to do about a situation in which you are involved • *I've had two job offers, and I'm in a real quandary about/over which one to accept.*

quantify /ˈkwɑnt·ə‚faɪ/ *v* [T] to measure or judge the amount or number of (something) • *It's difficult to quantify how many people will have to pay higher taxes.*

quantifier /ˈkwɑnt·ə‚faɪ·ər/ *n* [C] *specialized* (in grammar) a word or phrase that is used before a noun to show the amount of it that is being considered • *"Some," "many," "a lot of," and "a few" are examples of quantifiers used in English.*

quantitative /ˈkwɑnt·ə‚teɪt̬·ɪv/ *adj* relating to an amount that can be measured • *Our employees receive a quantitative rating based on the dollar value of their sales.* • Compare QUALITATIVE.

quantity /ˈkwɑnt·ət̬·i/ *n* [C/U] the amount or number of something, or a fixed amount or number • *a large/small quantity* [C] ○ *She served each of us a vast quantity of spaghetti.* [C]

quantum leap /ˈkwɑnt·əm‚liːp/, **quantum jump** /ˈkwɑnt·əm‚dʒʌmp/ *n* [C] a great improvement or important advance in something • *It was a revolutionary generation of computers that was a quantum leap beyond anything on the market.*

quarantine /ˈkwɑr·ən‚tiːn, ˈkwɔːr-/ *n* [U] a period of time during which a person or animal that might have a disease is kept away from other people or animals so that the disease cannot spread • *The horse had to spend several months in quarantine when it reached this country.*

quarantine /ˈkwɑr·ən‚tiːn, ˈkwɔːr-/ *v* [T] • *He was quarantined with mumps, which is highly contagious.*

quark /kwɑrk, kwɔːrk/ *n* [C] *specialized* one of the most basic forms of matter that make up atoms

quarrel /ˈkwɑr·əl, ˈkwɔːr-/ *n* [C] an angry disagreement between people, groups, or countries • *A big family quarrel left Judith and me in tears.*

quarrel /ˈkwɑr·əl, ˈkwɔːr-/ *v* [I] • *We often heard our neighbors quarreling about/over money.* • If you quarrel with facts or judgments, you do not accept them as true: *While we may quarrel with his conclusions, there is no reason to doubt his sincerity.*

quarry PLACE /ˈkwɑr·i, ˈkwɔːr·i/ *n* [C] a large hole in the ground that workers dig in order to use the stone and sand for building material

quarry /ˈkwɑr·i, ˈkwɔːr·i/ *v* [T] • *The gray limestone in this area was once quarried for use in bridges and buildings.*

quarry PERSON / ANIMAL /ˈkwɑr·i, ˈkwɔːr·i/ *n* [U] a person, animal, or group being hunted or looked for • *The Coast Guard, searching for drug smugglers, spotted a fast boat but then lost their quarry in the fog.*

quart /kwɔːrt/ (*abbreviation* **qt.**) *n* [C] a unit of measurement of volume equal to 2 PINTS or about 0.95 liter

quarter FOURTH PART /ˈkwɔːrt̬·ər/ *n* [C] one of four equal or almost equal parts of something • *My house is one and three-quarter miles/a mile and three-quarters from here.* • A quarter of/to the hour means 15 minutes before the stated hour: *It's a quarter to three.* • A quarter past/after the hour means 15 minutes after the stated hour: *I'll meet you at a quarter past five.* • A quarter is one of four equal or nearly equal periods of time into which an activity is divided: *Many universities divide the school year into quarters rather than two semesters.* ○ *After three quarters of football, the score was tied at 14.* • A **quarterfinal** is any of the four games in a competition that decides which players or teams will play in the two SEMIFINALS.

quarter /ˈkwɔːrt̬·ər/ *v* [T] to divide (something) into four pieces of approximately the same size • *Peel and quarter the tomatoes and put them in the stew.*

quarterly /ˈkwɔːrt̬·ər·li/ *adj, adv* [not gradable] (happening) four times a year • *a quarterly journal* ○ *It's published quarterly.*

quarterly /ˈkwɔːrt̬·ər·li/ *n* [C] a magazine that is published four times a year

quarter MONEY /ˈkwɔːrt̬·ər/ *n* [C] in the US and Canada, a coin worth 25 cents

quarter AREA /ˈkwɔːrt̬·ər/ *n* [C] an area of a city or place having a special history or character • *We stayed in the French Quarter in New Orleans.*

quarterback /ˈkwɔːrt̬·ər‚bæk/ *n* [C] (in football) the player who receives the ball at the start of every play and tries to move it along the field by carrying it or throwing or handing it to other members of the team

quarters /ˈkwɔːrt̬·ərz/ *pl n* a place where someone lives or has their business • *In 1998 he moved his company to larger quarters on State Street.*

quartet /kwɔːrˈtet/ *n* [C] four people who sing or play musical instruments together, or a piece of music written for four people • *A string quartet was playing Mozart.* • Compare DUET, QUINTET, TRIO.

quartz /ˈkwɔːrts/ *n* [U] a MINERAL (= hard substance formed naturally in the ground) used in making electronic equipment and watches and clocks

quash /kwɑʃ/ v [T] to stop or block (something) from happening • *The Secretary of Defense tried to quash speculation that he was planning to resign following the disastrous military defeat.*

quasi– /ˌkweɪˌzɑɪ, ˌkwɑzˌiː/ *combining form* to a degree, but not completely • *The governor appointed a quasi-independent commission to review police brutality.*

quaver /ˈkweɪ·vər/ v [I] (of a person's voice) to sound shaky, esp. because of emotion • *Her voice quavered as she began reading the names of those who had died of AIDS.*

quay /kiː, keɪ, kweɪ/ n [C] a long, usually stone structure beside water, where boats can be tied up and their goods can be loaded or unloaded

queasy /ˈkwiː·zi/ *adj* feeling as if you are going to vomit • *I'm a little queasy this morning.*

queen WOMAN /kwiːn/ n [C] a woman who rules a country because she has been born into a family which by tradition or law has the right to rule, or the title given to such a woman • *Queen Elizabeth II of Great Britain* • A queen is also a woman who is considered to be the best in some way: *the reigning queen of crime writers* ○ *a beauty queen* • In the game of CHESS, the queen is the most powerful piece on the board. • A queen is also a playing card with a picture of a queen on it: *the queen of hearts* • In a group of insects, a queen is a large female that produces eggs: *a queen bee* • If something is **queen-sized**, it is larger than the ordinary size: *a queen-sized bed* ○ Compare **king-sized** at KING.

queen HOMOSEXUAL /kwiːn/ n [C] *slang* a homosexual man, esp. an older man, whose manner is artificially like a woman's • USAGE: This word is usually considered offensive.

queer HOMOSEXUAL /kwɪr/ *adj* [-er/-est only] *slang* homosexual • USAGE: This word is considered offensive when used by someone who is not homosexual.

queer /kwɪr/ n [C] *slang* • *He was afraid of being called a queer.*

queer STRANGE /kwɪr/ *adj* [-er/-est only] *dated* unusual or strange • *She had a queer expression on her face.*

quell /kwel/ v [T] to stop (esp. something violent) from happening or developing, esp. by using force • *The police were called in to quell the riot.* • If you quell doubts, fears, etc., you calm them: *He's been unable to quell his wife's suspicions.*

quench /kwentʃ/ v [T] to satisfy (a thirst) by drinking liquid, or to stop (fire) from burning • *We quenched our thirst at a mountain spring.* ○ *Heavy rains quenched the fire.*

query /ˈkwɪr·i, ˈkwer·i/ n [C] a question, often one expressing doubt about something or looking for information

query /ˈkwɪr·i, ˈkwer·i/ v [T] • *Lawyers queried Ann about what she wore that day.*

quest /kwest/ n [C] a long search for something that is difficult to find • *a quest for the meaning of life*

question SOMETHING ASKED /ˈkwes·tʃən/ n [C] a word or words used to find out information • *May I ask you a personal question?* ○ *Our help line will answer your questions about patient care.* • A **question mark** is a mark (?) used in writing that is put at the end of a word or group of words to show that it is a question.

question (obj) /ˈkwes·tʃən/ v • *Mom's always questioning me about my friends.* [T] ○ *The police questioned several men about the burglary.* [T] • If you question something, you express doubt or uncertainty about it: *The book questions whether people today are better off than their parents were.* [+ wh- word]

questionable /ˈkwes·tʃə·nə·bəl/ *adj* not certain, or probably wrong in some way • *It is questionable whether that investment will pay off.* [+ wh- word] ○ *His comments were in questionable taste.*

questioner /ˈkwes·tʃə·nər/ n [C] a person who asks a question

---

QUESTION MARK [?]

A question mark is used at the end of a direct question.

How much does it cost? • *"You're studying law, aren't you?" I asked.* • *The question is, will present trends continue?*

A question that is part of a longer sentence, with changes in grammar to make it fit into the longer sentence, does not end with a question mark.

She asked how much it cost. • *I asked if she was studying law.*

A question mark is also used to show that a sentence that has the form of a statement is meant as a question.

I beg your pardon? • *So, you're ready to go?*

Question marks are also used to show doubt about a figure, date, or fact.

The actress Mae West (1893?-1980) was always vague about her age. • *The older man (your father?) left you a phone message.* • *the wisdom (?) of the majority* • *Kevin? Is that you?*

---

question PROBLEM /ˈkwes·tʃən/ n [C/U] a matter to be dealt with or discussed, or a problem to be solved • *Your article raises the question of human rights.* [C] ○ *It's simply a question of getting your priorities straight.* [C] ○ *The question is, are they telling the truth?* [C] ○ *I was at home on the night in question.* [U] • In an exam, a question is a problem that tests a person's knowledge: *Answer as many questions as you can.* [C]

question DOUBT /ˈkwes·tʃən/ n [U] doubt or uncertainty • *He's competent—there's no ques-*

tion about that. ○ *Her loyalty is beyond question.*

questionnaire /ˌkwes·tʃəˈner, -ˈnær/ *n* [C] a written list of questions that people are asked so that information can be collected

queue /kjuː/ *n* [C] *esp. Br* a line of people or things waiting for something • *There was a long queue for tickets at the theater.* • PIC LINE

queue /kjuː/ *v* [I] • *Fans queued up to buy tickets.*

quibble /ˈkwɪb·əl/ *v* [I] to argue or complain about small and unimportant details • *The issue is too important to quibble over.*

quibble /ˈkwɪb·əl/ *n* [C] • *My only quibble with the movie is that it's too long.*

quiche /kiːʃ/ *n* [C/U] an open pastry filled with a mixture of eggs, cheese, and other foods • *a spinach quiche* [C]

quick /kwɪk/ *adj* [-er/-est only] done, happening, or moving fast; lasting only a short time • *She cast a quick glance in the mirror.* ○ *You're back already—that was quick!* ○ *He made a quick profit.* ○ *John was quick to point out the error.* [+ *to* infinitive] • (*infml*) Something described as **quick and dirty** has been done fast and carelessly: *a quick-and-dirty job of snow removal* • A **quick fix** is an easy but temporary solution to a problem: *Managers are looking for a quick fix.* • A **quick-witted** person is mentally fast.

quick /kwɪk/ *adv* not standard • *We bought it quick, before someone else could.*

quick /kwɪk/ *exclamation* • *Quick! Close the door before the dog gets out!*

quicken /ˈkwɪk·ən/ *v* [I/T] to become or make faster or more active • *His pulse quickened when he saw her.* [I] ○ *Computers have quickened the pace of communications.* [T]

quickly /ˈkwɪk·li/ *adv* • *Emergency workers were on the scene quickly.*

quickness /ˈkwɪk·nəs/ *n* [U] • *She moves with quickness, balance, and grace.*

quicksand /ˈkwɪk·sænd/ *n* [U] a mass of wet sand into which people and objects can sink

quid pro quo /ˌkwɪdˌproʊˈkwoʊ/ *n* [C] *pl* **quid pro quos** something that is given or received in return for something else • *Contributors expect a quid pro quo for their donations.*

quiet NO NOISE /ˈkwaɪ·ət/ *adj* making very little or no noise • *Our new dishwasher is very quiet.* • A quiet person is one who does not talk much: *a shy, quiet child* • **Be quiet** (= Stop making noise)*!*

quiet /ˈkwaɪ·ət/ *v* [I/T] • *He quieted the crowd by raising his hand.* [T] ○ *After a great deal of crying, the baby quieted down.* [I] ○ *I tried to quiet him down.* [M]

quietly /ˈkwaɪ·ət·li/ *adv* • *"It's time," he said quietly.*

quiet /ˈkwaɪ·ət/ *n* [U] • *Let's have some quiet in here!*

quietness /ˈkwaɪ·ət·nəs/ *n* [U] • *I need sustained quietness to write.*

quiet NO ACTIVITY /ˈkwaɪ·ət/ *adj* [-er/-est only] without much activity or many people • *a quiet neighborhood* ○ *a quiet candlelit dinner*

quiet /ˈkwaɪ·ət/ *n* [U] • *After a hard day at work, all she wanted was some peace and quiet.*

quietly /ˈkwaɪ·ət·li/ *adv* without attracting attention • *The church quietly increased security.*

quill /kwɪl/ *n* [C] a long, sharp point on a PORCUPINE, or a large feather with a sharpened end that was used, esp. in the past, as a pen

quilt /kwɪlt/ *n* [C] a covering for a bed, made of two layers of cloth with a layer of soft filling between them, and stitched in lines or patterns through all the layers • *a patchwork quilt*

quilted /ˈkwɪl·təd/ *adj* • *a quilted coat*

quintessential /ˌkwɪnt·əˈsen·tʃəl/ *adj* [not gradable] representing the most perfect or most typical example of something • *a quintessential small town* ○ *a quintessential athlete*

quintessentially /ˌkwɪnt·əˈsen·tʃə·li/ *adv* [not gradable] • *She is quintessentially American.*

quintet /kwɪnˈtet/ *n* [C] a group of five people who sing or play musical instruments together, or a piece of music written for five people • Compare DUET; QUARTET; TRIO.

quintuplet /kwɪnˈtʌp·lət, -ˈtuː·plət/ *n* [C] any of five children born at the same time to the same mother • Compare QUADRUPLET; TRIPLET; TWIN.

quip /kwɪp/ *n* [C] a quick, intelligent, and often amusing remark

quip /kwɪp/ *v* [T] **-pp-** • *When asked why he seemed so relaxed, he quipped, "It's the drugs."*

quirk /kwɜrk/ *n* [C] an unusual habit or type of behavior, or something that is strange and unexpected • *a personality quirk* ○ *It's just one of the quirks of living there.*

quirky /ˈkwɜr·ki/ *adj* [-er/-est only] • *a quirky, offbeat sense of humor*

quit /kwɪt/ *v* [I/T] **quitting,** *past* **quit** to leave (a job or a place), or to stop doing (something) • *Her assistant quit without an explanation.* [I] ○ *I quit smoking ten years ago.* [T] ○ *Quit worrying about him—he'll be fine!* [T]

quite VERY /kwaɪt/ *adv* [not gradable] to a large degree • *School is quite different from what it once was.* • **Quite a** is used before some nouns to emphasis the large number, amount, or size of the subject referred to: *We've had quite a lot of rain this year.* ○ *There were quite a few* (= a lot) *of people waiting in line.* ○ *She had quite a bit* (= a lot) *to say to him when he finally showed up.* ○ *I hadn't seen Rebecca in quite a while* (= for a long time). • LP VERY, COMPLETELY, AND OTHER INTENSIFIERS

quite COMPLETELY /kwaɪt/ *adv* [not gradable] completely • *Quite frankly, the thought of performing terrifies me.* ○ *I'm not quite done yet.* ○ *I'm not quite sure I understand.*

quite REALLY /kwaɪt/ *adv* [not gradable] really or truly • *Winning this contest was quite an accomplishment.* ◦ *It was quite a remarkable speech.*

quiver /ˈkwɪv·ər/ *v* [I] to shake slightly; TREMBLE • *The dog quivered with fear.*

quiver /ˈkwɪv·ər/ *n* [C] • *A quiver of excitement ran through the crowd.*

quixotic /kwɪkˈsɑt̬·ɪk/ *adj slightly fml* having intentions or ideas that are admirable but not practical • *Many think these attempts to make lawyers behave are quixotic.*

quiz /kwɪz/ *n* [C] a short, informal test • *We had a history quiz today.*

quiz /kwɪz/ *v* [T] **-zz-** • *Reporters quizzed the jurors about their verdict.*

quizzical /ˈkwɪz·ɪ·kəl/ *adj* expressing slight uncertainty or amusement • *a quizzical look/smile*

quorum /ˈkwɔːr·əm, ˈkwoʊr-/ *n* [C] the number of members who must be present at a meeting in order for decisions to be officially made

quota /ˈkwoʊt̬·ə/ *n* [C] a number, amount, or share that is officially allowed or necessary • *an import quota* ◦ *He thinks racial quotas are ineffective in dealing with discrimination.*

quote SAY /kwoʊt/ *v* [I/T] to repeat words that someone else has said or written • *She quoted him as saying he couldn't care less.* [T] ◦ *He's always quoting from the Bible.* [I] • If you quote a fact or example, you refer to it to provide proof of something: *The judge quoted several cases to support his opinion.* [T] • You can say quote or **quote unquote** to show that you are repeating someone else's words, or to show that something is called a particular word or phrase: *He hailed the performance as, quote, an extraordinary achievement.* ◦ *He's on a quote unquote high-protein diet.*

quotation /kwoʊˈteɪ·ʃən/, **quote** /kwoʊt/ *n* [C] a group of words from a book, play, speech, etc., that are repeated by someone who did not write them • *A quotation from Shakespeare prefaces the novel.* • **Quotation marks** (also **quotes**) are a pair of marks (" ") used before and after a word or group of words to show that they are spoken or that someone else originally wrote them. • LP CAPITAL LETTERS

quote STATE A PRICE /kwoʊt/ *v* [T] to state (a price or amount that something will cost) • *The roofer quoted $3000 to fix the roof.*

QUOTATION MARKS ["..." AND '...']

Quotation marks are put at the beginning and end of a word, sentence, or paragraph to show that the words were said by someone or written by someone else. Double quotation marks— "..."—are usual in the United States and Canada.

Quotation marks are used to enclose direct quotations.

"My car broke down," the stranger said. • *"Do you want some help?" I offered.* • *She kept saying, "Hurry up."* • *"A man cannot be comfortable," Mark Twain wrote, "without his own approval."*

When a quotation is given within another quotation, it is enclosed in single quotation marks.

The host said, "I'll pour coffee until you say 'Enough'."

Quotation marks are also used to show that the words within them are someone else's way of describing something. Sometimes they show that the writer thinks these words are questionable, amusing, or not true.

The daily "rest period" was often a time of lively activity. • *Invaders "liberated" the countryside and "pacified" areas where they met resistance.* • *Why didn't your "friends" help you out when you needed them?*

Quotation marks are used to enclose slang words or words the writer thinks are unusual.

The industry is in a "crunch." • *The electricity, or "juice," came on again that night.*

Quotation marks are also used to enclose titles of short works like poems, articles, short stories, and television programs. When italics are not used, quotation marks are also used for titles of books and movies.

Robert Frost's "The Gift Outright" • *Did you watch "Friends" last night?*

quotation /kwoʊˈteɪ·ʃən/, **quote** /kwoʊt/ *n* [C] • *He called back to say the price quotes were "not accurate."*

quotient /ˈkwoʊ·ʃənt/ *n* [C] the degree, rate, or amount of something • *King had a full quotient of faults.* • (*specialized*) A quotient is also the result you get when you divide one number by another.

R, r

R [LETTER] , **r** /ɑr/ *n* [C] *pl* **R's** or **Rs** or **r's** or **rs** the 18th letter of the English alphabet

R [MOVIE] *adj* [not gradable] *abbreviation for* RE-STRICTED, used in the US for movies that people under the age of 17 will not be allowed in to see except if they are with an adult • Compare G [MOVIE]; NC-17; PG; X [SEXUAL].

rabbi /'ræb·aɪ/ *n* [C] (the title of) a Jewish religious leader or a teacher of Jewish law

rabbit /'ræb·ət/ *n* [C] a small animal with long ears and a short tail, that lives in holes in the ground

rabble /'ræb·əl/ *n* [U] *disapproving* the mass of people who are ordinary, unimportant, and poor, and sometimes threatening • A **rabble-rouser** is a person who excites others to anger, hate, or violence.

rabid /'ræb·əd, 'reɪ·bəd/ *adj* having RABIES (= serious disease of the nervous system) • If a person is described as rabid, they are extremely enthusiastic or have extreme feelings or opinions: *rabid football fans* ○ *rabid anti-Semites*

rabies /'reɪ·biːz/ *n* [U] a disease of the nervous system of animals that can be spread to humans, usually by a bite of an infected animal, and that causes death if not treated quickly

raccoon /ræ'kuːn/ *n* [C] a North American animal whose fur is mainly gray and brown, but black around the eyes, and with a thick tail

race [COMPETITION] /reɪs/ *n* [C] a competition between people or animals to see who can get from the starting place to the finish before all the others • *a horse race* ○ *She won the 100-meter race in 11.06 seconds.* • (*fig.*) A race is also an urgent effort: *It was a race against time to get the project finished by Friday's deadline.* [+ to infinitive] • A race is also a competition to be elected to a political position: *The governor of California plans to enter the presidential race.* • A **racehorse** is a horse bred and trained for racing. • A **racetrack** is a usually oval path on which esp. horses or cars compete.

race /reɪs/ *v* [I/T] to compete in a race or run a race with (someone) • *He's been racing (cars) for over ten years.* [I/T] ○ (*fig.*) To race is also to move fast or to happen quickly: *The boys came racing across the playground.* [I always + adv/prep] ○ *Last summer seemed to race by.* [I always + adv/prep]

racing /'reɪ·sɪŋ/ *n* [U] • *thoroughbred/harness racing*

race [PEOPLE] /reɪs/ *n* [C/U] any group into which humans can be divided according to their shared physical characteristics, such as skin color or hair color and type, or their common GENETIC characteristics, such as blood type • *Discrimination because of race is against the law.* [U]

racial /'reɪ·ʃəl/ *adj* [not gradable] of or involving a particular race or different races • *racial discrimination/equality* ○ *He opposed awarding scholarships and jobs based on racial preference* (= preference given a particular race over others).

racially /'reɪ·ʃə·li/ *adv* [not gradable] • *They lived in a racially mixed neighborhood.*

racism /'reɪ,sɪz·əm/ *n* [U] the belief that some races are better than others, or the unfair treatment of someone because of their race

racist /'reɪ·səst/ *n* [C] a person who believes that some races are better than others, or who acts unfairly to someone because of their race

racist /'reɪ·səst/ *adj* • *a racist society*

rack [FRAME] /ræk/ *n* [C] a frame, often with bars or hooks, for holding or hanging things • *a bike rack* ○ *a towel rack*

rack [CAUSE PAIN] /ræk/ *v* [T] to cause (someone) great physical or mental pain • *Even near the end, when cancer racked his body, he remained hopeful.* • To **rack** your **brain** is to try very hard to think of or remember something: *I've been racking my brains all day trying to remember her name.*

▫ **rack up** *obj*, **rack** *obj* **up** /'-'-/ *v adv* [M] *infml* to obtain, achieve, or score • *The airline was racking up losses of $1.5 million a day.* ○ *He racked up 31 percent of the Asian vote in the election.*

racket [SPORTS] , **racquet** /'ræk·ət/ *n* [C] an object consisting of a net fixed tightly to an oval frame with a long handle, used in various sports for hitting a ball • *a tennis/squash racket* • [PIC] FOREHAND/BACKHAND

racket [NOISE] /'ræk·ət/ *n* [U] *infml* a loud, annoying noise • *Who's making such a racket?*

racket [ILLEGAL ACTIVITY] /'ræk·ət/ *n* [C] *infml* a dishonest or illegal activity that makes money • *They ran an extensive racket in stolen cars.*

racketeer /,ræk·ə'tɪr/ *n* [C] a person who makes money through dishonest or illegal activities

racketeering /,ræk·ə'tɪr·ɪŋ/ *n* [U]

racquetball /'ræk·ət,bɔːl/ *n* [U] a game played in an enclosed playing area between two or four people who use RACKETS to hit a small rubber ball against a wall

racy /'reɪ·si/ *adj* [-er/-est only] exciting and interesting, possibly because sex is mentioned or suggested • *a racy story*

radar /'reɪ·dɑr/ *n* [C/U] a device or system for finding the position or speed of objects, such as aircraft, that cannot be seen, by measuring the direction and timing of short radio waves that are sent out and reflect back from the objects

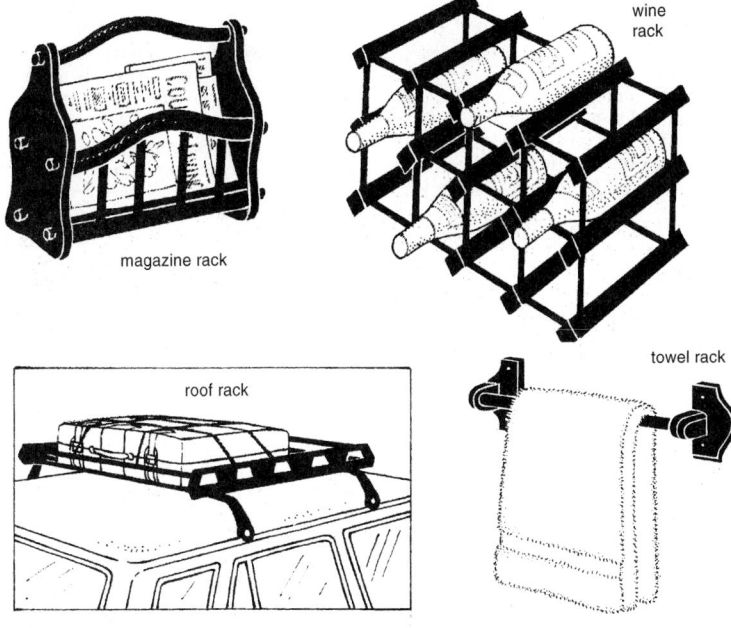

wine
rack

magazine rack

towel rack

roof rack

racks

radial (tire) /'reɪd·i·əl ('taɪr)/ *n* [C] a tire that has cords arranged across the edge of the wheel at an angle of 90° • *Radials make a vehicle easier to control on wet surfaces.*

radiate SEND OUT HEAT / LIGHT /'reɪd·iː,eɪt/ *v* [I/T] to send out (heat or light), or (of heat or light) to be sent out • *The little stove radiated a surprising amount of heat.* [T]

radiant /'reɪd·iː·ənt/ *adj* • *Plants absorb radiant energy from sunlight.*

radiance /'reɪd·iː·əns/ *n* [U] • *We basked in the radiance of the afternoon sun.*

radiation /ˌreɪd·iː'eɪ·ʃən/ *n* [U] (the sending out of) heat, light, or energy in waves • *solar radiation*

radiate EXPRESS /'reɪd·iː,eɪt/ *v* [I/T] to express strongly (an emotion or quality), or (of an emotion or quality) to be expressed strongly by someone • *He simply radiates integrity.* [T]

radiant /'reɪd·iː·ənt/ *adj* expressing great happiness, hope, or beauty • *The bride looked radiant on her wedding day.*

radiance /'reɪd·iː·əns/ *n* [U]

radiate SPREAD /'reɪd·iː,eɪt/ *v* [I always + adv/prep] to spread out from a central point • *The major avenues of the city all radiate from this point.*

radiator /'reɪd·iː,eɪt·ər/ *n* [C] a device for heating rooms in buildings, consisting of a series of pipes through which steam or hot water passes • In a motor vehicle, a radiator is a device for cooling the engine.

radical SUPPORTING CHANGE /'ræd·ɪ·kəl/ *adj* believing or expressing the belief that there should be great or extreme social, economic, or political change • *White's political orientation was decidedly liberal, but hardly radical.*

radical /'ræd·ɪ·kəl/ *n* [C] a person who supports great social, economic, or political change

radical EXTREME /'ræd·ɪ·kəl/ *adj* causing or being an example of great change; extreme • *During bad economic times, radical steps may be necessary to restore the confidence of the consumer.*

radically /'ræd·ɪ·kə·li/ *adv* • *Her views are not radically different from my own.*

radii /'reɪd·iː,aɪ/ *pl of* RADIUS

radio /'reɪd·iː,oʊ/ *n* [C/U] *pl* **radios** a device for receiving, and sometimes broadcasting, sound messages, or the receiving or sending of sound messages • *I listen to the radio in the morning to get the weather report.* [C] • Radio is also the work of broadcasting sound programs for the public to listen to. [U]

radio /'reɪd·iː,oʊ/ *v* [I/T] **radioing**, *past* **radioed** to send a message to (someone) by radio • *They radioed (their base) for help.* [I/T]

radioactive /ˌreɪd·iː·oʊ'æk·tɪv/ *adj* possessing or producing energy from the breaking up of atoms, or resulting from the production of such energy • *radioactive waste*

radioactivity /ˌreɪd·iː,oʊ·æk'tɪv·ət·i/ *n* [U]

radiology /ˌreɪd·iː'ɑl·ə·dʒi/ *n* [U] the scientific study of the medical use of RADIATION (= type of energy), esp. X-RAYS

radiologist /ˌreɪd·iˈɑl·ə·dʒəst/ *n* [C] a doctor who specializes in the medical use of RADIA-TION, esp. X-RAYS

radiotherapy /ˌreɪd·iˈoʊˈθer·ə·pi/ *n* [U] the use of controlled amounts of RADIATION (= type of energy), aimed at a particular part of the body, to treat disease

radish /ˈræd·ɪʃ/ *n* [C] a small, red or white vegetable that grows as a root and is eaten raw, esp. in salads

radium /ˈreɪd·i·əm/ *n* [U] a chemical element that is RADIOACTIVE (= producing energy from the breaking up of atoms)

radius /ˈreɪd·i·əs/ *n* [C] *pl* **radii** /ˈreɪd·i·ˌɑɪ/ (the length of) a straight line from the center of a circle to its edge • *The supermarket, shopping mall, and school are all within a one-mile radius of the house* (= are all less than a mile away from it).

raffle /ˈræf·əl/ *n* [C] a system of selling numbered tickets and then giving prizes to those people whose numbers are chosen by chance, often used by groups in order to make money

raffle /ˈræf·əl/ *v* [T] • *The club is going to raffle (off) a car for charity.* [T/M]

raft FLOATING STRUCTURE /ræft/ *n* [C] a flat, floating structure made of pieces of wood tied together, often attached to the bottom of a river or lake for use by swimmers • *A raft is also a small rubber or plastic boat that can be filled with air.*

rafting /ˈræf·tɪŋ/ *n* [U] the use of a rubber raft to travel with the current of a river, esp. as a sport • *The camp offered bicycle tours, river rafting, fishing, and hiking.*

raft A LOT /ræft/ *n* [C] a large number or collection; a lot • *We've identified a whole raft of problems affecting traffic flow.*

rafter /ˈræf·tər/ *n* [C] any of the large, specially shaped pieces of wood that support a roof

rag /ræg/ *n* [C] a piece of usually old, torn cloth • *They were dressed* **in rags** (= in old, torn pieces of clothing). • A **rag doll** is a child's DOLL (= toy in the shape of a person) made of a soft, cloth material so that the arms and legs swing freely. • **Rags-to-riches** is used to describe what happens to a person who was poor but becomes rich: *Hers was a rags-to-riches success story.*

rage /reɪdʒ/ *n* [C/U] extreme or violent anger, or a period of feeling such anger • *I had never seen him in such a rage before.* [C]

rage /reɪdʒ/ *v* [I always + adv/prep] • *He raged at me for sending the letter out before he had seen it.* • If something destructive rages, it happens in a way that cannot be controlled: *The fire broke out and raged for four days, destroying most of the old city.*

ragged IN BAD CONDITION /ˈræg·əd/ *adj* (of clothes) torn and usually in bad condition from too much use, or (of people) wearing clothes in this condition • *A group of ragged children appeared, begging for coins.*

ragged UNEVEN /ˈræg·əd/ *adj* not straight or even • *His scalp had a ragged gash.*

ragtag /ˈræg·tæg/ *adj* consisting of parts or pieces that are in no particular order or system • *He transformed a ragtag militia into a capable, well-disciplined fighting force.*

ragtime /ˈræg·tɑɪm/ *n* [U] a type of popular music, developed about 1900, with a strong beat

raid /reɪd/ *n* [C] a planned attack by a military group that is done suddenly and unexpectedly and is intended to destroy or damage something • *an air raid ◦ a bombing raid* • A raid is also a planned but sudden and unexpected entering of a place by the police in order to find illegal drugs or to stop an illegal activity.

raid /reɪd/ *v* [T] • If the police raid a place, they enter it suddenly and unexpectedly in order to find illegal drugs or to stop an illegal activity: *The FBI said it had no plans to raid the suspect's farm.* • To raid is also to unfairly or secretly take something for your own use or benefit: *The movie company was accused of raiding talent from other studios.*

rail TRAINS /reɪl/ *n* [C/U] one of the two metal bars fixed to the ground on which trains travel • Rail also means railroad: *rail transportation* [U] *◦ Commuter rail and subway lines will be linked.* [U]

rail ROD /reɪl/ *n* [C] a straight bar or rod fixed in position, esp. to a wall or to vertical posts, used to enclose something or as a support • *The car swerved out of control and crashed through a guard rail on the bridge.*

rail COMPLAIN /reɪl/ *v* [I always + adv/prep] to complain angrily • *He railed against the injustices of the system.*

railing /ˈreɪ·lɪŋ/ *n* [C] a type of fence made of one or more usually metal or wooden bars attached to posts, often along the edge of a path or at the side of stairs for safety and to provide support • *The iron railing at the edge of the boardwalk was some six feet above the beach.*

railroad TRANSPORTATION /ˈreɪl·roʊd/, **railway** /ˈreɪl·weɪ/ *n* [C] a system of transportation using special vehicles whose wheels turn on metal bars fixed to the ground, or a particular company using such a system • *railroad tracks ◦ a railroad station ◦ the Pennsylvania Railroad*

railroad FORCE /ˈreɪl·roʊd/ *v* [T always + adv/prep] to force (something to happen or someone to do something), esp. quickly and unfairly • *We feel our client was railroaded into pleading guilty.*

rain /reɪn/ *n* [U] drops of water that fall from clouds • *It looks like rain* (= as if rain is going to fall). • A **rain check** is a part of a ticket to a game, activity, etc., that can be used to see another game, etc., if rain prevents the original one from happening. • A **rain check** is also an offer or request to do or get something at a later time than was originally intended: *I'm busy now, but can I take a rain check on that cup of coffee?* • A **raincoat** is a coat worn for protection against rain. • **Rainfall** is the amount of rain that falls: *Heavy rainfall is expected in the northwest.* • A **rain forest** is a forest in a hot area of the world that receives a lot of rain. • A **rainstorm** is a period with strong winds and heavy rain. • **Rainwater** is water that has fallen as rain.

rain /reɪn/ v [I] • *It's raining hard* (= heavily). • Rain can also mean to fall in a large amount: *Debris from the explosion rained down.* • If you say that it's **raining cats and dogs**, you mean that it is raining very heavily. • *The tennis match was rained out* (= stopped because of rain).

rainy /ˈreɪ·ni/ adj • *a rainy afternoon* • *She had saved some money for* **a rainy day** (= a time when money might unexpectedly be needed).

rainbow /ˈreɪn·boʊ/ n [C] an arch of many colors sometimes seen in the sky for a short time after rain, esp. when the sun is shining

raise LIFT /reɪz/ v [T] to cause (something) to be lifted up or become higher • *He raised the window shades.* ○ *Stephie raised her hand to ask the teacher a question.*

raise BECOME BIGGER /reɪz/ v [T] to cause (something) to become bigger or stronger; increase • *I had to raise my voice to be heard over the noise in the classroom.* ○ *There are no plans to raise taxes, the president said.* ○ *I don't want to raise your hopes too much, but I think the worst of the flooding is over.*

raise /reɪz/ n [C] an increase in the amount money you earn • *She asked her boss for a raise.*

raise DEVELOP /reɪz/ v [T] to take care of (children or young animals) until completely grown • *They raised a family and now want to enjoy their retirement.*

raise BRING ABOUT /reɪz/ v [T] to bring (something) to your attention; cause to be noticed • *This raises a number of important issues.* • To raise money is to succeed in getting it: *I want to start my own business if I can raise enough money.* • If you **raise hell**, you cause trouble: *They drank beer and generally raised hell.*

raisin /ˈreɪ·zən/ n [C] a dried GRAPE (= a small, round fruit)

rake /reɪk/ n [C] a garden tool with a long handle and pointed, usually plastic, wooden, or metal parts sticking out in a row at the bottom, used for making earth level or for gathering leaves or cut grass

rake /reɪk/ v [I/T] • *I have to rake (up) the dead leaves.* [T/M] • If you **rake in** money, you earn a lot of it: *She's really raking it in.*

rally MEETING /ˈræl·i/ n [C] a public meeting of a large group of people, esp. to show support for a particular opinion, political party, or sports team • *He helped organize the first national rally against the war.*

rally /ˈræl·i/ v [I/T] to bring or come together in order to provide support or make a shared effort • *African-American groups rallied around the president when he was under attack.* [I]

rally IMPROVE /ˈræl·i/ v [I/T] to return or bring to a better condition; improve or cause to succeed • *Cleveland rallied in the fourth quarter to beat Washington, 111-102.* [I] ○ *The dollar rallied against the yen in trading today.* [I]

rally /ˈræl·i/ n [C] • *Stock prices fell again today after yesterday's rally.* • In baseball, a rally is a period during which a team scores a lot of RUNS (= points), esp. when it has been losing.

ram PUSH /ræm/ v [I/T] **-mm-** to hit or push with force • *Someone rammed (into) my car in the parking lot.* [I/T] ○ (*fig.*) *The governor tried to ram the budget through in the last days of the legislative session.* [T] • *I'm tired of having his opinions rammed down my throat* (= forced on me).

ram ANIMAL /ræm/ n [C] an adult male sheep

RAM COMPUTER /ræm/ n [U] *abbreviation for* random-access memory (= a type of computer memory that can be searched in any order and changed as necessary)

Ramadan /ˈrɑm·əˌdɑn, ˌræm-/ n [C] the ninth month of the Muslim year, during which believers take no food or drink during the day from the time the sun appears in the morning until it can no longer be seen in the evening

ramble WALK /ˈræm·bəl/ v [I] to walk for pleasure, esp. in the countryside • *I love to ramble through the woods.*

ramble /ˈræm·bəl/ n [C] • *We took a ramble through the park.*

ramble TALK /ˈræm·bəl/ v [I] to talk or write in a confused way, often for a long time • *It was hard to listen to her ramble on and on about her vacation.*

rambunctious /ræmˈbʌŋ·ʃəs/ adj full of energy and difficult to control • *Driving a long distance with four rambunctious children is not exactly fun.*

ramification /ˌræm·ə·fəˈkeɪ·ʃən/ n [C usually pl] the possible result of a decision or action • *Have you considered all the ramifications of changing careers at this stage of your life?*

ramp /ræmp/ n [C] a surface connecting a higher and a lower level; a slope • *Wide ramps flanked the stairs at the entrance.* • A ramp is also a road that lets you drive onto or leave a large road, such as an EXPRESSWAY: *an entrance/exit ramp* PIC EXIT

rampage /ˈræm·peɪdʒ/ v [I] to move, run, and do things in a wild, violent way • *Youths rampaged through the downtown district.*

rampage /ˈræm·peɪdʒ/ n [C] • *He went on a rampage, killing four people.*

rampant /ˈræm·pənt/ *adj* [not gradable] happening a lot or becoming worse, usually in an uncontrolled way • *Disease is rampant in the overcrowded refugee camps.*

ramshackle /ˈræmˌʃæk·əl/ *adj* badly made and likely to break or fall down easily • *a ramshackle building with a sagging roof*

ran /ræn/ *past simple of* RUN

ranch /ræntʃ/ *n* [C] a type of large farm on which animals are kept • *a cattle ranch* • A **ranch house** is style of house that has one level.

rancher /ˈræn·tʃər/ *n* [C] someone who owns or works on a ranch

rancid /ˈræn·səd/ *adj* (of food containing a fat such as butter or oil) tasting or smelling unpleasant because it is not fresh

rancor /ˈræŋ·kər/ *n* [U] *slightly fml* bitterness and hatred • *Can we settle this disagreement without rancor?*

rancorous /ˈræŋ·kə·rəs/ *adj* slightly *fml* • *a rancorous debate*

random /ˈræn·dəm/ *adj* happening, done, or chosen by chance rather than according to a plan or pattern • *a random sample* ○ *random drug testing* ○ *She was the victim of a random attack.* • **At random** means by chance, or without any organization or plan: *Dylan picked several books at random.*

randomly /ˈræn·dəm·li/ *adv* • *The people I interviewed were chosen randomly.*

rang /ræŋ/ *past simple of* RING [SOUND]

range [LIMIT] /reɪndʒ/ *n* [C/U] the level to which something is limited, or the area within which something operates • *a wide range of subjects* [C] ○ *The coat was beautiful, but way out of my price range.* [C] ○ *I like temperatures in the 60s and 70s, somewhere in that range.* [C] • Range is also the period of time within which something happens, or the distance something travels: *the short/intermediate/long range* [U] ○ *He was shot at very close range.* [U] • A vehicle's or aircraft's range is the distance that it can travel without having to stop for more fuel. [C]

range /reɪndʒ/ *v* [I always + adv/prep] • *Prices range from $50 to $250.* ○ *Our discussions ranged over many issues.*

range [SET] /reɪndʒ/ *n* [C] a set of similar or related things • *We offer a wide range of options.* ○ *The clinic provides a full range of medical services.* • A range (also **line**) is a group of products of a particular type.

range [MOUNTAINS] /reɪndʒ/ *n* [C] a group of mountains or hills • *the San Juan Range*

range [PRACTICE AREA] /reɪndʒ/ *n* [C] an area where people can practice shooting guns or hitting golf balls, or where bombs or other weapons can be tested • *a driving range* ○ *a rifle range*

range [LAND] /reɪndʒ/ *n* [C] a large area of land for animals to feed on, or the region a type of

animal or plant comes from and is most often found in

range /reɪndʒ/ *v* [I always + adv/prep] to move or travel freely • *The hikers ranged over the hills all day.*

range [STOVE] /reɪndʒ/ *n* [C] a stove used for cooking that has a top surface with burners for heating pots and pans and usually an OVEN (= enclosed cooking space) • *gas/electric range*

ranger /ˈreɪn·dʒər/ *n* [C] a person whose job is to care for or protect a forest, park, or public lands

rank [POSITION] /ræŋk/ *n* [C/U] a position in relation to others higher or lower, showing the importance or authority of the person having it • *You get more privileges if you have a higher rank.* [C] ○ *He rose quickly in rank.* [U] • The **rank and file** are the soldiers who are not officers, or the members of an organization who are not part of the leadership.

rank /ræŋk/ *v* [I/T] • *Sylvia ranks in the top 5 percent in her class.* [I] ○ *The tennis association ranks her second.* [T]

ranking /ˈræŋ·kɪŋ/ *adj* [not gradable] having the highest rank or standing in relation to others of the same kind • *The Senator is the ranking Republican on the committee.*

ranks /ræŋks/ *pl n* the members of a group or organization, or members of the armed service who are not officers • *He rose through the ranks to become a director of the company.*

rank [SMELLY] /ræŋk/ *adj* smelling very unpleasant • *a rank odor*

rankle /ˈræŋ·kəl/ *v* [I/T] to cause annoyance or anger that lasts a long time • *The way she left him still rankles.* [I]

ransack /ˈræn·sæk/ *v* [T] to completely search (a place) for something, esp. something valuable to steal, and usually leaving the place in a mess • *Burglars ransacked the house.*

ransom /ˈræn·səm/ *n* [C/U] a sum of money demanded in exchange for someone or something that has been taken • *The kidnappers demanded a huge ransom.* [C] ○ *The boy was held for ransom.* [U]

ransom /ˈræn·səm/ *v* [T] to free (someone who has been taken away) by paying money • *The executive was ransomed for a million dollars.*

rant /rænt/ *v* [I] to speak or shout in a loud, uncontrolled, or angry way • *He keeps ranting and raving about pornography.*

rap [HIT] /ræp/ *v* [I/T] **-pp-** to hit suddenly and forcefully • *We heard him rap on the door.* [I] ○ *She rapped the table to get everyone's attention.* [T]

rap /ræp/ *n* [C] • *He got a nasty rap on the head.*

rap [MUSIC] /ræp/ *n* [U] a type of popular music of African American origin that features rhythmic speaking set to a strong beat

rap /ræp/ *v* [I] **-pp-** • *If he wants to rap about gangsters and whores, that's his business.*

rap [ACCUSATION] /ræp/ *n* [C usually sing] *slang*

an accusation that someone has committed a crime, or punishment for a crime • *He was jailed on a drug rap.* • A **rap sheet** is a list of crimes a person has committed or been accused of that is kept by the police.

rap REPUTATION /ræp/ *n* [C usually sing] *slang* a judgment, report, or reputation • *The smell of the Great Salt Lake has given it a bad rap.*

rape /reɪp/ *v* [T] to have sex with (someone) when they are unwilling, esp. by using force • *The girl was raped.* ○ (*fig.*) *Developers are raping the countryside* (= destroying it).

rape /reɪp/ *n* [C/U] • *He was convicted of rape.* [U]

rapist /'reɪ·pəst/ *n* [C] a man who rapes someone

rapid /'ræp·əd/ *adj* quick or sudden • *rapid growth* ○ *There's been rapid change in China.* ○ *We kept up a rapid pace.*

rapidly /'ræp·əd·li/ *adv* • *Males grow more rapidly than females.*

rapids /'ræp·ədz/ *pl n* a fast-flowing part of a river

rapport /ræ'pɔːr, rə-, -'poʊr/ *n* [U] agreement or sympathy between people or groups • *She has a good rapport with her staff.*

rapprochement /ˌræp·roʊʃ'mɑ̃, -ˌrɔːʃ-/ *n* [C/U] *fml* agreement reached by opposing groups or people • *Both countries have agreed to seek a rapprochement.* [C]

rapt /ræpt/ *adj* receiving someone's full interest, or complete • *I haven't been following the conversation with rapt attention.*

rapture /'ræp·tʃər/ *n* [C/U] extreme pleasure and happiness • *Life was rapture for a little while.* [U]

rare NOT COMMON /rer, rær/ *adj* not common and therefore sometimes valuable • *rare species of birds* ○ *Success like that is extremely rare.* ○ *She's usually positive, but on rare occasions disappointment shows through.* ○ *With rare exceptions, the families in this town have lived here for generations.*

rarely /'rer·li, 'rær-/ *adv* • *I rarely have time to read the newspaper.*

rarity /'rer·ət·i, 'rær-/ *n* [C/U] something rare, or the state of being rare • *Snow in Florida is a rarity.* [C]

rare SLIGHTLY COOKED /rer, rær/ *adj* [-*er*/-*est* only] (esp. of meat) not cooked for very long and still red inside • *rare steak*

rarefied /'rer·əˌfaɪd, 'rær-/ *adj* not ordinary, esp. because of being related to wealth, high social position, or artistic or literary subjects • *You get a very rarefied view of things living on a college campus.*

raring /'rer·ɪŋ, 'rær-, -ən/ *adj* [+ *to* infinitive] *infml* very enthusiastic or eager • *Everyone is raring to go.*

rascal /'ræs·kəl/ *n* [C] a person who behaves badly or dishonestly but who is usually likable • *The group includes thieves, politicians, and rascals of every sort.*

rash WITHOUT THOUGHT /ræʃ/ *adj* without thought for what might happen or result; careless or unwise • *a rash statement* ○ *It was rash of them to get married so quickly.*

rash SKIN CONDITION /ræʃ/ *n* [C] a group of spots or a raised area on the skin resulting from illness or from touching a harmful substance • *an itchy rash*

rash LARGE NUMBER /ræʃ/ *n* [C usually sing] a large number, esp. of something happening in a short period of time • *There's been a rash of robberies in the valley.*

rasp /ræsp/ *n* [U] an unpleasant sound, like something roughly rubbed

raspy /'ræs·pi/ *adj* [-*er*/-*est* only] • *His voice had dwindled to a raspy croak.*

raspberry /'ræz·ˌber·i, -bə·ri/ *n* [C] a small, soft, red fruit that grows on a bush

rat ANIMAL /ræt/ *n* [C] a small animal that looks like a large mouse • *A rat was sniffing around the trash.*

rat PERSON /ræt/ *n* [C] *infml* an unpleasant person who deceives or is not loyal • *"I knew I wouldn't understand, so I started speaking in Spanish." "Oh, you dirty rat!"* • *I love the city, but sometimes it's a* **rat race** (= a situation or way of life in which there is severe competition).

ratchet /'rætʃ·ət/ *v* [I/T] to change (an activity, amount, or feeling) by degrees • *Interest rates always ratchet down in an election year.* [I] ○ *Critics are trying to ratchet up public pressure on lawmakers.* [M]

rate MEASUREMENT /reɪt/ *n* [C] a measurement of the speed at which something happens or changes, or the number of times it happens or changes, within a particular period • *We have relatively low unemployment rates these days.* ○ *If we improve students' self-esteem, we could reduce the dropout rate.*

rate PAYMENT /reɪt/ *n* [C] an amount or level of payment • *Interest rates may rise soon.* ○ *Rental rates vary depending on the size of the car.*

rate VALUE /reɪt/ *v* to judge the value or worth of something • *Half of those surveyed rated his work as good.* [T] ○ *The movie is rated R.* [L] ○ *Mark Twain has rated as an enduring author for 100 years.* [I] • (*disapproving*) *If you say something or someone doesn't rate, you mean it or they are of poor quality or not worth consideration.* [I]

rating /'reɪt̬·ɪŋ/ *n* [C] • *Chez Paul got a three-star rating from our restaurant reviewer.* • A rating is a record of the number of people who watch or listen to a particular broadcast: *Advertisers are interested in ratings.*

rather PREFERABLY /'ræð·ər, 'rɑð-, 'rʌð-/ *adv* [not gradable] in preference to, or as a preference • *She wants us to meet her here rather than go to her apartment.* ○ *I'd rather wear the black shoes.* ○ *She's saying things that many would rather not hear.*

rather TO SOME DEGREE /'ræð·ər, 'rɑð-, 'rʌð-/

adv, adj [not gradable] to a noticeable degree; SOMEWHAT • *It all seems rather unimportant.*

rather MORE EXACTLY /'ræð·ər, 'rɑð-, 'rʌð-/ *adv* [not gradable] more accurately; more exactly • *These were not common criminals, but rather enemies of the state.*

ratify /'ræṭ·ə,faɪ/ *v* [T] (esp. of governments or organizations) to agree in writing to (a set of rules), or to officially approve (a decision or plan) • *Four countries have now ratified the agreement.*

ratification /,ræṭ·ə·fə'keɪ·ʃən/ *n* [U] • *The Senate will consider ratification of the treaty in July.*

ratio /'reɪ·ʃiː,oʊ/ *n* [C] *pl* **ratios** a relationship between two groups or amounts that expresses how much bigger one is than the other • *a low student-teacher ratio* ○ *The ratio of men to women at the conference was ten to one.* • LP COLON

ration /'ræʃ·ən, 'reɪ·ʃən/ *n* [C] a limited amount (of something) that one person is allowed to have, esp. when there is not much of it available • *Rations of rice were distributed to the refugees.*

ration /'ræʃ·ən, 'reɪ·ʃən/ *v* [T] • *Even their clothing is rationed.*

rationing /'ræʃ·ə·nɪŋ, 'reɪ·ʃə-/ *n* [U] • *food rationing*

rations /'ræʃ·ənz, 'reɪ·ʃənz/ *pl n* the food given to someone at one time, esp. to soldiers • *He fed prisoners the same rations he fed his own troops.*

rational /'ræʃ·ən·əl/ *adj* showing clear thought or reason • *a rational decision* ○ *Obviously, he wasn't rational.*

rationally /'ræʃ·ən·əl·i/ *adv* [not gradable] • *It's hard to behave rationally at such times.*

rationality /,ræʃ·ə'næl·əṭ·i/ *n* [U] • *You have too much faith in rationality* (= reason).

rationale /,ræʃ·ə'næl/ *n* [C/U] the reasons or intentions for a particular set of thoughts or actions • *I don't understand your rationale.* [C]

rationalize /'ræʃ·ən·əl,ɑɪz/ *v* [I/T] to provide an explanation, esp. one based on reason • *You can rationalize your way out of anything.* [T]

rationalization /,ræʃ·ən·əl·ə'zeɪ·ʃən/ *n* [C/U] • *Parents are fed up with rationalizations about why schools don't work.* [C]

rattle /'ræṭ·əl/ *v* [I/T] to make a noise consisting of quickly repeated knocks • *The windows rattled when the wind blew.* [I] ○ *Manny slammed the door, rattling the cups on the shelf.* [T]

rattle /'ræṭ·əl/ *n* [C/U] • *We could hear the rattle of stones as they fell down the well.* [U] • A rattle is also a baby's toy that rattles when it is shaken. [C] • A **rattlesnake** (also **rattler**) is a poisonous snake of the southwest-

rattlesnake

ern US and Mexico that produces a noise by shaking its tail.

□**rattle off** *obj*, **rattle** *obj* **off** /'--'-/ *v adv* [M] to say (something) quickly • *She rattled off the names of everyone coming to the party.*

rattled /'ræṭ·əld/ *adj* worried or nervous • *Walter got rattled when they didn't call.*

raucous /'rɔː·kəs/ *adj* loud, excited, and not controlled, esp. unpleasantly so • *raucous laughter*

raunchy /'rɔːn·tʃi, 'rɑn-/ *adj infml* rude or offensive because of showing or talking about sex in an obvious way • *raunchy language/humor*

ravage /'ræv·ɪdʒ/ *v* [T] to cause great damage to (something or someone) • *Hurricane Mitch ravaged the tiny Central American country.*

ravages /'ræv·ɪ·dʒəz/ *pl n* • *They survived the ravages of disease and malnutrition.*

rave ENTHUSIASTIC /reɪv/ *adj* admiring; giving praise • *The show has received rave reviews.*

rave /reɪv/ *n* [C] • *Her speech drew raves from everyone.*

rave /reɪv/ *v* [I] *infml* • *Everyone is raving about that new Vietnamese restaurant.*

rave SPEAK FOOLISHLY /reɪv/ *v* [I] to speak or shout in an uncontrolled way, usually because of anger or mental illness • *She was wild and raving, tearing up her books.*

raven /'reɪ·vən/ *n* [C] a large, black bird that is bigger than a CROW

ravenous /'ræv·ə·nəs/ *adj* [not gradable] extremely hungry • *We were ravenous after hiking all day.*

ravine /rə'viːn/ *n* [C] a deep, narrow valley with steep sides

raving /'reɪ·vɪŋ/ *adj, adv* [not gradable] complete or extreme, or completely or extremely • *He was raving mad near the end of his life.*

ravioli /,ræv·iː'oʊ·li/ *pl n* small squares of pasta, often filled with meat or cheese, that are cooked in boiling water

raw NOT COOKED /rɔː/ *adj* [not gradable] not cooked • *raw fish/oysters*

raw NOT PROCESSED /rɔː/ *adj* [not gradable] not processed or treated; in its natural condition • *raw milk* ○ *raw silk* ○ *Raw sewage ran in ditches along the streets of the village.* • If a person or their qualities are raw, they have not been developed or trained: *Even when she first started skating, you could see the determination and the raw talent.* ○ *Alex was just a raw recruit when he was handed this job.* • A **raw material** is any material, such as oil, cotton, or sugar, in its natural condition, before it has been processed for use: *The cost of raw materials was going up.*

raw SORE /rɔː/ *adj* sore because the skin has been rubbed or damaged

raw COLD /rɔː/ *adj* [not gradable] (of weather) cold and wet • *It was a raw, wintry day with a cold wind.*

raw UNFAIR /rɔː/ *adj* [not gradable] • A **raw**

deal is unfair treatment or arrangements: *He felt he had gotten a raw deal but didn't complain.*

ray BEAM /reɪ/ *n* [C] a narrow beam of light, heat, or energy

ray AMOUNT /reɪ/ *n* [C] a slight amount or signal of something good • *One couple seems interested in buying our house, which is a ray of hope after all these months.*

rayon /'reɪ·ɑn/ *n* [U] smooth, shiny material made from CELLULOSE (= wood fibers)

raze /reɪz/ *v* [T] to destroy (a building, structure, etc.) completely • *Developers razed the old buildings on the site to make way for new construction.*

razor /'reɪ·zər/ *n* [C] a device with a sharp blade for removing hair from the skin's surface • *an electric razor* • A **razor blade** is a very thin, sharp blade that can be used in a razor: *She used a razor blade to cut out newspaper articles.* • **Razor-sharp** means very sharp: *These animals have razor-sharp teeth.* • **Razor-thin** means very thin or small: *The administration's economic program was approved by a razor-thin margin in the Senate.*

razzle–dazzle /ˌræz·əl'dæz·əl/ *n* [U] *infml* showy appearance or performance, intended to attract attention or cause confusion • *The razzle-dazzle in this movie doesn't make up for the lackluster plot.*

RCMP *n* [U] *abbreviation for* Royal Canadian Mounted Police (= a Canadian police force known for special police services and for ceremonial appearances in red uniform and on horses)

Rd. *n* [U] *abbreviation for* road • *The center is located at 1065 Edwards Rd.*

re ABOUT /reɪ, riː/ *prep* (esp. in business letters) about; on the subject of • *Re your memo July 10, I have indeed received the order.*

re– DO AGAIN /riː/ *combining form* used esp. with verbs to add the meaning "do again" • *remarry* ○ *redecorate*

reach ARRIVE /riːtʃ/ *v* [T] to arrive (somewhere) • *The storm continues to move west and is expected to reach the east coast of Florida tomorrow.*

reach BECOME HIGHER /riːtʃ/ *v* [T] to become higher or greater so as to equal (a particular level) • *The temperature is expected to reach 90° today.* ○ *The government fears unemployment will reach 10%.* • To reach is also to develop to a stage in order to achieve (a particular result): *We hope to reach agreement soon on the new trade policy.* ○ *They reached the conclusion that nothing further could be done.*

reach PUT OUT ARM /riːtʃ/ *v* [I/T] to put out your arm to its full length, esp. in order to take or touch (something) • *Our little girl isn't tall enough to reach the light switches.* [T] ○ *The receptionist reached for the phone.* [I always + adv/prep] ○ *She reached across the table and took his hand.* [I always + adv/prep] • If an ob-

ject reaches something, the top or bottom of it touches that thing: *The ladder won't quite reach the roof.* [T] • To reach someone is to communicate with them, esp. by telephone: *I've been trying to reach you all afternoon, but the line's been busy.* [T] • If you **reach out**, you make an effort to communicate with people or to give them your support: *He said the Republican Party has to reach out to the people to make its message known.*

reach /riːtʃ/ *n* [U] the distance to which you can put out your arm and touch something • *All medicines should be kept out of the reach of children.* • Your reach is also the limit of your ability to achieve something: *An expensive trip like that would be completely beyond our reach.*

react /riː'ækt/ *v* [I] to act in a particular way as a direct result of something else • *How do you think she'll react when she hears the news?* ○ *The State Department reacted favorably to the proposal.* • (*specialized*) If substances react, they change when brought together.

reaction /riː'æk·ʃən/ *n* [C] behavior, a feeling, or an action that is a direct result of something else • *My initial reaction was to call off the party.* ○ *Senator, what is your reaction to the proposal to cut Medicare benefits?* • A reaction is also a change that opposes a previous opinion or behavior: *His art is a reaction against photographic realism.* • A reaction can also be an unpleasant effect on the body resulting from something eaten or taken, such as a drug: *Some people have an allergic reaction to penicillin.* • (*specialized*) A chemical reaction is the change that happens when two or more substances are mixed with each other.

reactionary /riː'æk·ʃəˌner·i/ *n* [C] a person who opposes political or social change

reactionary /riː'æk·ʃəˌner·i/ *adj* [not gradable] • *Reactionary forces opposed to the president's reforms could move to oust him.*

reactor /riː'æk·tər/ *n* [C] a **nuclear reactor**, see at NUCLEAR

read OBTAIN MEANING /riːd/ *v* [I/T] *past* **read** /red/ to obtain meaning or information from written words or symbols, esp. by looking at them as printed or written on (something) • *I read the book over the weekend.* [T] ○ *She couldn't read or write.* [I] ○ *Did you read about the plan to build a new road to the airport?* [I] ○ *I read that the job market for teachers is excellent.* [+ *that* clause] • If you read to others, you say aloud the words you are reading: *She read (the story) to the class.* [I/T] • To read is also to know a language or symbol system enough to understand its meaning: *He reads French/music.* [T] • To **read up on** something is to learn about it by reading: *It's a good idea to read up on a publisher before sending in a manuscript.*

readable /'riː·də·bəl/ *adj* easy or enjoyable to read • *Reviewers praised it as a highly readable and rewarding book.*

reader /'ri:d·ər/ *n* [C] a person who reads • *Both of my parents were great readers* (= they read a lot). ○ *The local newspaper welcomes comments from its readers.*

reading /'ri:d·ɪŋ/ *n* [C/U] • *Reading is my favorite pastime.* [U] • Reading is also text to be read: *These books are required reading for architecture students.* [U] • A reading is an occasion when a literary work or formal text is read aloud to a group of people: *a poetry reading* [C]

read UNDERSTAND /ri:d/ *v* [I/T] to understand the meaning or intent of something • *If I've read the situation right, we'll soon have agreement on a contract.* [T] • To **read between the lines** is to find meanings that are intended but that are not directly expressed in something said or written. • To **read** something **into** a statement or situation is to add to its intended meaning: *I think you're reading more into their refusal than is justified.* • To **read** someone's **mind** is to know what they are thinking without them telling you: *How did you know I wanted that CD for my birthday—you must have read my mind.*

reading /'ri:d·ɪŋ/ *n* [C] the way in which you understand something • *My reading of the situation is that John wanted an excuse to resign.*

read SHOW / STATE /ri:d/ *v past* **read** /red/ to show or state (information) • *The sign read, "No parking here to corner."* [L] • If you read a device, you look at the measurement it shows: *The gas company sends someone to read the meter every month.* [T]

reading /'ri:d·ɪŋ/ *n* [C] • *Temperature readings in the area are in the 30s.*

readjust /ˌri:·ə'dʒʌst/ *v* [I] to change the way you live or behave to fit a new or different situation • *The government program was established to help soldiers returning from World War II readjust to civilian life.*

readjustment /ˌri:·ə'dʒʌs·mənt/ *n* [C] • *Retirement is a readjustment—no question about it.*

readout /'ri:d·aʊt/ *n* [C] information produced by electronic equipment and shown in print on a screen

ready PREPARED /'red·i/ *adj* [not gradable] prepared and suitable for action or use • *Dinner is ready.* ○ *The twins are getting ready for bed.* ○ *I'm ready to go now.* [+ *to* infinitive] ○ *"Are you ready to order?" the waiter asked.* [+ *to* infinitive] • If something is **ready-made**, it is in finished form, or is available to use immediately: *I didn't sew these curtains—they came ready-made.*

readily /'red·əl·i/ *adv* quickly or easily • *The complete collection is now readily available to researchers through the Internet.*

readiness /'red·i:·nəs/ *n* [U] the state of being ready or prepared • *Military readiness is the country's overriding concern.*

ready WILLING /'red·i/ *adj* [not gradable] willing • *My friends are always ready to help me out.*

readily /'red·əl·i/ *adv* [not gradable] • *Cory readily admits he was hired because of his contacts.*

ready QUICK /'red·i/ *adj* [not gradable] quick, esp. in answering or in thinking of what to say • *He had a ready reply to every question.*

reaffirm /ˌri:·ə'fɜrm/ *v* [T] to state something as true again, or to state your support for something again • *This album reaffirms his reputation as a splendid songwriter and guitarist.*

real ACTUAL /ri:l/ *adj* existing in fact; not imaginary • *There is a real possibility that he will lose his job.* ○ *This is a true story about real people.*

realism /'ri:·ə,lɪz·əm/ *n* [U] a tendency to accept and deal with people and situations as they are

realist /'ri:·ə·ləst/ *n* [C] a person who tends to accept and deal with people and situations as they are

realistic /ˌri:·ə'lɪs·tɪk/ *adj* having or showing a practical awareness of things as they are • *She is realistic about her chances of winning.* • Realistic also means appearing to be existing or happening in fact: *The scene in the movie where the dinosaur hatches from the egg is incredibly realistic.*

realistically /ˌri:·ə'lɪs·tɪ·kli/ *adv* [not gradable] • *Realistically, we can't afford a piano.*

reality /ri:'æl·ət·i/ *n* [C/U] • Reality is the actual state of things, or the facts involved in such a state: *The reality is I'm not going to be picked for the team.* [U] ○ *The realities of parenthood were overwhelming at first.* [C] • **In reality** means what actually happened or what the actual situation is: *He told us he was out of town, but in reality, he wasn't invited to the party.* • A **reality check** is an occasion when someone must consider the unpleasant truth about something: *The disappointing results of the last election were a reality check for the Republicans.*

really /'ri:·li/ *adv* [not gradable] • *What really happened that day?* ○ *I just don't know if we would really use it that much.* • See also **really** at REAL VERY GREAT, REALLY SINCERELY, REALLY EXPRESSING SURPRISE.

real NOT FALSE /ri:l/ *adj* being what it appears to be; GENUINE • *Are those flowers real or fake?* ○ *The chest of drawers is a real antique.* • If someone or something is **the real McCoy**, they or it is the original or true person or thing, and not a copy: *We've seen so many reproductions of the Mona Lisa, and when we were in Paris we saw the real McCoy.*

real VERY GREAT /ri:l/ *adj* [not gradable] very great or to a great degree • *He's a real gentleman.* ○ *The current situation is a real mess.*

real /ri:l/ *adv* [not gradable] *infml* • *I get cold real easy.* ○ *It's real nice to meet you.*

really /'ri:·li/ *adv* [not gradable] • *That was a really good movie.* ○ *This room is really hot.* • See also **really** at REAL ACTUAL; REALLY SINCERELY, REALLY EXPRESSING SURPRISE. LP VERY, COMPLETELY, AND OTHER INTENSIFIERS

real estate /'ri:·lə,steɪt/ *n* [U] property in the form of land or buildings • A **real estate agent** is a person whose business is to arrange the selling or renting of houses, land, offices, or buildings for their owners.

realize BECOME AWARE /'ri:·ə,laɪz/ *v* [T] to become aware of or understand (a situation) • *He realized the store would be closing in a few minutes.* ○ *Suddenly I realized (that) I was lost.* [+ (*that*) clause]

realization /,ri:·ə·lə'zeɪ·ʃən/ *n* [C usually sing] • *You soon come to the horrible realization that the flat skinny letters mean No, you are not accepted.*

realize ACHIEVE /'ri:·ə,laɪz/ *v* [T] to achieve (esp. hopes or plans) • *They finally realized their goal of buying a summer home.*

realization /,ri:·ə·lə'zeɪ·ʃən/ *n* [U] • *Playing in the major leagues was the realization of his dreams.*

really SINCERELY /'ri:·li/ *adv* [not gradable] sincerely; truly • *I'm really telling the truth this time.* ○ *If she really cared about me, she would have called by now.* • See also **really** at REAL ACTUAL, REAL VERY GREAT, REALLY EXPRESSING SURPRISE.

really EXPRESSING SURPRISE /'ri:·li/ *exclamation* used to express interest, surprise, or annoyance • *"Debbie and I are getting married." "Really? When?"* ○ *Really, Jen, you should have let me know sooner.* • See also **really** at REAL ACTUAL, REAL VERY GREAT; REALLY SINCERELY.

realm /relm/ *n* [C] an area of interest or activity • *the economic/political realm* ○ *the realm of art/literature/music*

realtor /'ri:l·tər, 'ri:·lət̬·ər/ *n* [C] a **real estate agent**, see at REAL ESTATE • (*trademark*) A Realtor is also a member of the National Association of Realtors, an organization of **real estate agents.**

ream /ri:m/ *n* [C] a standard measure of paper equal to 500 sheets

reams /ri:mz/ *pl n infml* a very large amount of something • *They had reams of data to prove their point.*

reap /ri:p/ *v* [I/T] to obtain or receive (something) as a result of your own actions • *They didn't reap any benefits from that deal.* [T] • If you reap a crop, you cut and collect it. [I/T]

reaper /'ri:·pər/ *n* [C] a machine that cuts and collects crops, or a person who cuts and collects crops by hand

rear AT THE BACK /rɪr/ *adj* [not gradable] at or near the back of something • *I had the rear brakes on the car redone.* ○ *She entered the school through an unlocked rear door.* ○ *Our dog hurt his rear left leg.* • *Supporters trying to*

keep the museum open are fighting a **rearguard action** (= making final and probably hopeless efforts to succeed). • A **rear-view mirror** is a mirror inside a car in which the driver can see what is happening behind the car.

rear /rɪr/ *n* [C/U] • *The bus driver told us to move to the rear.* [U] • (*infml*) Your buttocks are sometimes called your rear. [C]

rear CARE FOR /rɪr/ *v* [T] to care for (young children or animals) until they are able to care for themselves • *She reared eight children.*

rear RISE /rɪr/ *v* [I/T] to rise up or to lift up • *The horse suddenly reared (up) on its hind legs.* [I] • *Racism once again reared its (ugly) head* (= appeared).

rear end /rɪr'end/ *n* [C] the back of something • *A bomb blew off the rear end of the car.* ○ (*infml*) Roy walked over and swatted her rear end (= buttocks).

rear–end /rɪr'end/ *v* [T] to hit (esp. the back of) a vehicle) from behind • *A truck rear-ended a car stopped in traffic on the expressway.*

rearrange /,ri:·ə'reɪndʒ/ *v* [T] to change the order, position, or time of (arrangements already made) • *Our bedrooms are so small we can't rearrange the furniture.*

rearrangement /,ri:·ə'reɪndʒ·mənt/ *n* [C/U] • *There was a last-minute rearrangement of the schedule.* [C]

reason EXPLANATION /'ri:·zən/ *n* [C/U] the cause of an event or situation, or something suggested as an explanation • *She had never stopped by before for any reason.* [C] ○ *There must be a reason why she's not here yet.* [C] ○ *Adams had good reason to fire Pickering.* [U]

reason JUDGMENT /'ri:·zən/ *n* [U] the ability to think and make judgments, esp. good judgments • *Meditation seemed to have improved her ability to reason.*

reason /'ri:·zən/ *v* • *He reasoned (that) he had only four or five years left as an athlete.* [+ (*that*) clause] • To reason with someone is to argue with and try to persuade them: *Grace kept her voice gentle, as if she were reasoning with a child.* [I]

reasonable /'ri:·zə·nə·bəl/ *adj* based on or using good judgment, and therefore fair and practical • *Johnson was a reasonable man.* ○ *It seemed like a reasonable question/explanation.* • Reasonable also means not expensive: *You can still get a good house for a very reasonable price.* • Reasonable also means satisfactory or not bad: *He could read French with reasonable fluency.*

reasonably /'ri:·zə·nə·bli/ *adv* • *He kept talking slowly and reasonably* (= in a way that showed good judgment). ○ *I was reasonably certain she would be home* (= it seemed likely).

reasoned /'ri:·zənd/ *adj* using judgment • *He offered reasoned responses to our questions.*

reasoning /'ri:·zə·nɪŋ/ *n* [U] • *I didn't follow her reasoning.*

reassure /ˌriː·əˈʃʊr/ v [T] to comfort (someone) and stop them from worrying • *Her smile didn't reassure me.*

reassuring /ˌriː·əˈʃʊr·ɪŋ/ adj • *His reassuring manner convinced her she was safe.*

reassuringly /ˌriː·əˈʃʊr·ɪŋ·li/ adv • *I bent down and patted the dog reassuringly.*

reassurance /ˌriː·əˈʃʊr·əns/ n [C/U] • *We need reassurances our company isn't going to be closed.* [C] ○ *The boy looked at his parents for reassurance.* [U]

rebate /ˈriː·beɪt/ n [C] money that is returned to you after you pay for goods or services, done in order to make the sale more attractive • *Chrysler announced cash rebates of $1000 on some trucks.*

rebel /ˈreb·əl/ n [C] a person who refuses to accept their government's power and uses force to oppose it, or a person who opposes authority and thinks or behaves differently • *The government tried to set up talks with the rebels.* ○ *Though he dressed unusually, he never meant to be a rebel.* • Soldiers fighting for the southern states in the American Civil War were called rebels.

rebel /rəˈbel/ v [I] **-ll-** • *Indians rebelled against being forced onto reservations.*

rebellion /rəˈbel·jən/ n [C/U] violent action organized by a group of people who refuse to accept their government's power and are willing to use force to oppose it • *The slave leader Nat Turner led an 1831 rebellion.* [C] • Rebellion is also a feeling of strong disagreement with an organization or with people in authority: *Many students were in rebellion against the older generation.* [U]

rebellious /rəˈbel·jəs/ adj • *A peace agreement was signed yesterday between the republic and its rebellious region.* ○ *He was a rebellious student in school.*

rebirth /ˈriːˈbɜrθ/ n [U] a new period of growth of something or an increase in popularity of something that was popular in the past • *Spring is the season of rebirth.* ○ *This production was hailed as a rebirth of Swedish theater.*

rebound /ˈriːˈbaʊnd, rɪˈbaʊnd/ v [I] to return to an earlier and better condition; improve • *Older athletes find it harder to rebound from injuries.* • If a ball or other object rebounds, it bounces back after hitting a hard surface.

rebound /ˈriːˈbaʊnd/ n [C/U] • *The artist is on the rebound from his midcareer slump.* [U]

rebuff /rɪˈbʌf/ v [T] to refuse to accept (a suggestion or an offer to help), esp. in a quick or unfriendly way • *Our request for assistance has been rebuffed.*

rebuff /rɪˈbʌf/ n [C] • *Boren's idea took a sharp rebuff.*

rebuild /ˈriːˈbɪld/ v [I/T] past **rebuilt** /ˈriːˈbɪlt/ to build (something) again that has been damaged or destroyed • *The church was completely rebuilt after it had burned down.* [T] • If you rebuild a system or organization, you develop

it so that it works effectively: *The company is rebuilding under new management.* [I]

rebuke /rɪˈbjuːk/ v [T] *slightly fml* to criticize (someone) strongly because you disapprove of what they have said or done • *The senator was publicly rebuked for his insensitive remarks about women.*

rebuke /rɪˈbjuːk/ n [C/U] *slightly fml* • *an angry/harsh/sharp rebuke* [C]

rebut /rɪˈbʌt/ v [T] **-tt-** *slightly fml* to argue that (a statement or claim) is not true • *He appeared on TV to rebut charges that he had an extramarital affair.*

rebuttal /rɪˈbʌt̬·əl/ n [C] *slightly fml* a statement that a claim or criticism is not true • *She issued a rebuttal of the charges.*

recalcitrant /rɪˈkæl·sə·trənt/ adj unwilling to do what you are asked or ordered to do, even if it is reasonable • *One recalcitrant smoker paid a $100 fine rather than put out a butt.*

recall (obj) REMEMBER /rɪˈkɔːl/ v to bring (the memory of a past event) into your mind • *I can vividly recall our first kiss.* [T] ○ *He recalled that he had sent the letter over a month ago.* [+ that clause] ○ *Can you recall what happened last night?* [+ wh- word]

recall /rɪˈkɔːl, ˈriːˈkɔːl/ n [U] the ability to remember things • *He has perfect/total recall.*

recall ASK TO RETURN /rɪˈkɔːl/ v [T] to order the return of (a product made by a company) because of a fault in the product

recall /ˈriːˈkɔːl/ n [C usually sing] • *The government ordered a recall of the garment, saying it could burst into flames.*

recant /rɪˈkænt/ v [I/T] to announce in public that your past beliefs or statements were wrong or not true and that you no longer agree with them • *Anderson recanted, saying his brother had told him to lie.* [I]

recap /ˈriːˈkæp, rɪˈkæp/ v [I/T] **-pp-** short form of RECAPITULATE • *We saw a video recapping her early career.* [T] ○ *To recap, we expect sunny skies in the morning, rain by nightfall.* [I]

recap /ˈriːˈkæp/ n [C] • *They give a quick recap of the top news stories.*

recapitulate /ˌriːˈkəˈpɪtʃ·əˌleɪt/ v [I/T] *fml* to repeat (the main points of an explanation or description) • *The passage recapitulates the version he offers in his prologue.* [T]

recapture /riːˈkæp·tʃər/ v [T] to take (something or someone) into your possession again, esp. by force • *American troops recaptured Guam in July 1944.* • If something recaptures an emotion, it allows you to experience that emotion again: *They're bent on recapturing their past glory.*

recede /rɪˈsiːd/ v [I] to move further away into the distance, or to become less clear • *McLaughlin expects to go home again when the flood waters recede.* • If a man has a **receding hairline**, he is losing the hair from the front of his head.

receipt PAPER /rɪˈsiːt/ n [C] a piece of paper

which proves that money or goods have been received • *Ask the taxi driver for a receipt.*

receipt RECEIVING /rɪˈsiːt/ *n* [U] *fml* the act of receiving something, esp. of money or goods • *We are awaiting receipt of your check.*

receipts /rɪˈsiːts/ *pl n* the amount of money received during a particular period by a business or government • *tax receipts* ○ *box-office receipts*

receive GET /rɪˈsiːv/ *v* [T] to get or be given (something) • *She received a letter from her son.* ○ *I'll receive my bachelor's degree in the spring.* • When a radio or television receives signals, it changes them into sounds or pictures. The related noun is RECEPTION RADIO/ TELEVISION. • To be **on/at the receiving end** of something is to suffer something unpleasant when you have done nothing to deserve it: *She was on the receiving end of abuse all her life.*

receiver /rɪˈsiː·vər/ *n* [C] a piece of equipment that changes radio and television signals into sounds and pictures, or that changes electrical signals into sound • *a telephone receiver* ○ *a stereo receiver* • In football, a receiver is one of the players who can catch the ball on the team that is trying to score points. • See also SO RECIPIENT.

receive WELCOME /rɪˈsiːv/ *v* [T] *fml* to welcome (someone or something) • *The president received Fulbright cordially.* • USAGE: The related noun is RECEPTION WELCOME.

recent /ˈriː·sənt/ *adj* having happened or having been done a short time ago • *He sent me a copy of his most recent article.* ○ *A recent study shows that most of the country-music audience is female.*

recently /ˈriː·sənt·li/ *adv* • *We just recently moved to Texas.*

receptacle /rɪˈsep·tɪ·kəl/ *n* [C] *slightly fml* a container for holding things or that you can put things in • *a trash receptacle*

reception WELCOME /rɪˈsep·ʃən/ *n* [C] the way in which people react to something or someone • *The proposed jail has received a cool/ lukewarm reception from local residents.* ○ *American musicians found a warm reception in Europe in the 1960s.* • A reception is also a formal party: *a cocktail/wedding reception* • USAGE: The related verb is RECEIVE WELCOME.

reception RADIO / TELEVISION /rɪˈsep·ʃən/ *n* [U] the degree to which radio or television sounds and pictures are clear • *We get poor reception around here.* • USAGE: The related verb is RE-CEIVE GET.

receptionist /rɪˈsep·ʃə·nəst/ *n* [C] a person who works in an office, store, or hotel, helping visitors or giving information

receptive /rɪˈsep·tɪv/ *adj* willing to listen to and accept new ideas and suggestions • *I think you're more receptive to new ideas when you're younger.*

recess PAUSE /ˈriː·ses, rɪˈses/ *n* [C] a period of time in which an organized activity such as

study or work is temporarily stopped • *Congress returns from its August recess next week.* ○ *After lunch, the kids have recess.*

recess SECRET PLACE /ˈriː·ses, rɪˈses/ *n* [C usually pl] a secret or hidden place • *He spent hours in the dark recesses of bars.* • A recess is also an ALCOVE.

recession /rɪˈseʃ·ən/ *n* [C/U] a period when the economy of a country is not doing well, industrial production and business activity are at a low level, and there is a lot of unemployment • *The country is mired in recession.* [U] ○ *The Japanese economy is experiencing its worst recession in 20 years.* [C]

recharge /riːˈtʃɑrdʒ/ *v* [T] to give (a BATTERY) the ability to supply electricity again by connecting it to a piece of electrical equipment and filling it with electricity

rechargeable /riːˈtʃɑr·dʒə·bəl/ *adj* [not gradable] • *a rechargeable electric razor*

recipe /ˈres·ə·piː/ *n* [C] a set of instructions telling you how to prepare and cook a particular food, including a list of what foods are needed for this • *When I make pies, I don't need to follow a recipe.* • A **recipe for** something is an idea, situation, or method that is likely to result in this: *Telling stories of people who go from rags to riches is a sure-fire recipe for success.*

recipient /rɪˈsɪp·iː·ənt/ *n* [C] a person who receives something • *Lund was the first female recipient of an artificial heart.* • See also **receiver** at RECEIVE GET.

reciprocal /rɪˈsɪp·rə·kəl/ *adj slightly fml* (of two people or things) operating for both, esp. equally or to a similar degree • *They share a truly reciprocal relationship.*

reciprocate /rɪˈsɪp·rə·ˌkeɪt/ *v* [I/T] *slightly fml* to do (something) for someone because they have done something similar for you • *We gave them information, but they didn't reciprocate.* [I] ○ *Hemingway loved Stein and she reciprocated his love.* [T]

recital /rɪˈsaɪt̬·ᵊl/ *n* [C] a performance of music or dance, usually given by one person or a small group of people • *a piano recital*

recite /rɪˈsaɪt/ *v* [I/T] to say (a piece of writing) aloud from memory, or to state in public (a list of things) • *He was nervous about reciting in front of the class.* [I] ○ *The children recite the pledge of allegiance every morning.* [T]

recitation /ˌres·əˈteɪ·ʃən/ *n* [C] *slightly fml* • *a recitation of facts*

reckless /ˈrek·ləs/ *adj* showing a lack of care about risks or danger, and acting without thinking about the results of your actions • *These punks have a reckless disregard for the law.* ○ *He pleaded innocent to reckless driving charges.*

recklessly /ˈrek·lə·sli/ *adv* • *She spends her money recklessly.*

recklessness /ˈrek·lə·snəs/ *n* [U] • *I showed my recklessness by joining their gang.*

reckon (obj) CALCULATE /'rek·ən/ v to calculate (an amount) based on facts or on your expectations • *Do you reckon this watch has a little value?* [T] ○ *Brusca reckons that the value of all goods and services produced declined last quarter.* [+ that clause]

reckoning /'rek·ə·nɪŋ/ n [U] • *By my reckoning, we should get there in another hour or so.*

reckon CONSIDER /'rek·ən/ v [T] to consider or have the opinion that something is as stated • *She reckoned they were both equally responsible.* ○ *She was widely reckoned to be the best actress of her generation.* ○ *I reckon I better be goin' now.* • If you **reckon with** someone or something, you consider the effect they will have: *Experts did not reckon with his determination.* ○ *This was an important story, something to be reckoned with.*

reclaim /rɪ'kleɪm/ v [T] to take back (something that was yours) • *The tribe set out to reclaim their lost lands.* ○ *Residents want to reclaim their streets from drug dealers.*

recline /rɪ'klaɪn/ v [I/T] to lean or lie back with the upper part of your body in a nearly horizontal position, or to cause (something) to lean back • *Hacker was reclining leisurely in an office chair, his legs propped up on a desk.* [I] • If a seat reclines, you can change the position of its back so that it is in a leaning position: *The bus has air conditioning and seats that recline/reclining seats.* [I]

recluse /'rek·luːs, rə'kluːs/ n [C] a person who lives alone and avoids going outside or talking to other people

recognition KNOWLEDGE /ˌrek·ɪg'nɪʃ·ən/ n [U] the fact of knowing who a person is or what a thing is because of having seen or had experience with them before • *Dole obviously had the greatest name recognition of all the Republican candidates.* • USAGE: The related verb is RECOGNIZE KNOW.

recognition APPRECIATION /ˌrek·ɪg'nɪʃ·ən/ n [U] public appreciation for a person's or group's achievements • *She gained recognition as an expert in energy conservation.* • Recognition also refers to the acceptance of something as true: *Charges were dropped in recognition of the fact that there simply wasn't enough evidence.* • USAGE: The related verb is RECOGNIZE ACCEPT AS TRUE.

recognize KNOW /'rek·ɪg,naɪz/ v [T] to know (someone or something) because you have seen or had experience with them before • *I recognized my old high school teacher from the photograph.* ○ *Doctors are trained to recognize the symptoms of different diseases.* • USAGE: The related noun is RECOGNITION KNOWLEDGE.

recognizable /'rek·ɪg,naɪ·zə·bəl/ adj • If a person or thing is recognizable, they are familiar to others and can be recognized: *The cartoon character was instantly recognizable to millions of children.*

recognizably /'rek·ɪg,naɪ·zə·bli/ adv • *At seven weeks, an embryo is recognizably human.*

recognize ACCEPT AS TRUE /'rek·ɪg,naɪz/ v [T] to accept that (something) is true, important, or legal • *We recognize the problems you've faced and sympathize with you.* [T] ○ *He recognized that it was unlikely he would ever see her again.* [+ that clause] • To recognize is also to show public appreciation for (the achievements of someone, or a person or group): *With this medal, we would like to recognize Lynn Jennings for excellence in women's running.* [T] • USAGE: The related noun is RECOGNITION APPRECIATION.

recoil /rɪ'kɔɪl/ v [I] to make a sudden movement away from something esp. because of fear or disgust • (fig.) *Sun-worshipers might recoil in horror at the chilling winds and rough seas, but we loved the place.*

recoil /'riː·kɔɪl, rɪ'kɔɪl/ n [U] the sudden, backward movement that a gun makes when it is fired

recollect /ˌrek·ə'lekt/ v [I/T] to remember (something) • *There were five young men in the car, as near as I can recollect.* [I]

recollection /ˌrek·ə'lek·ʃən/ n [C/U] a memory of something, or the ability to remember past events • *I have fond recollections of the times our families vacationed together in Vermont.* [C]

recommend /ˌrek·ə'mend/ v [T] to suggest that (someone or something) would be good or suitable for a particular job or purpose, or to suggest that (a particular action) should be done • *Can you recommend a hotel in San Francisco?* ○ *I recommend that you go on a diet.* [+ that clause]

recommendation /ˌrek·ə·mən'deɪ·ʃən, -ˌmen-/ n [C/U] a statement that someone or something would be good or suitable for a particular job or purpose, or the act of making such a statement • *I have to get five letters of recommendation to support my application to medical school.* [U]

recompense /'rek·əm,pens/ n [U] fml payment given to someone for an injury suffered, or for the loss of or damage to property • *The government seized the land without recompense to the owners.*

reconcile /'rek·ən,saɪl/ v [T] to adjust the way you think about (a fact or situation that is opposed to another fact or situation) so that you can accept both • *Hurston tells the story of a country preacher struggling to reconcile his love for his wife with his attraction to other women.* • If two people are reconciled, they become friendly again after having argued so seriously that they kept apart: *After two years of not speaking to one another, the two brothers were finally reconciled.* • To reconcile (yourself) to a situation is to accept it even if it is unpleasant or painful, because it cannot be changed: *After the death of her husband, she* *found it difficult to reconcile herself to a life alone.*

reconciliation /ˌrek·ən·ˌsɪl·iˈei·ʃən/ *n* [C/U] the process of making two people or groups of people friendly again after they have argued seriously or fought and kept apart from each other, or a situation in which this happens

reconnaissance /rɪˈkɑn·ə·səns, -zəns/ *n* [U] *specialized* the process of obtaining information about enemy forces or positions by sending out small groups of soldiers or by using aircraft • *Aerial reconnaissance showed the location of the enemy's tanks.*

reconsider /ˌriː·kənˈsɪd·ər/ *v* [I/T] to think again about (a decision or opinion) and decide whether you want to change it • *He begged her to reconsider.* [I]

reconstruct /ˌriː·kənˈstrʌkt/ *v* [T] to build or create again (something that has been damaged or destroyed) • *If you reconstruct something that happened in the past, you combine a lot of details to try to get a clear idea of what happened: Detectives tried to reconstruct the crime by comparing all the statements of the eyewitnesses.*

reconstruction /ˌriː·kənˈstrʌk·ʃən/ *n* [C/U]

record STORE INFORMATION /rɪˈkɔːrd/ *v* [T] to keep (information) for the future by writing it down or storing it on a computer • *She carefully recorded the events of the meeting.* • To record is also to use a device to measure (an amount, rate of speed, etc.) and show it: *Wind gusts of up to 50 miles per hour were recorded.*

record /ˈrek·ərd/ *n* [C/U] a piece of information or a description of an event that is written on paper or stored in a computer • *Did anyone make a record of what the president said at that meeting?* [C] ○ *All medical records are kept confidential.* [C] ○ *She has a long criminal record* (= There is official information about many crimes she has done.). [C] ○ *This summer has been the hottest on record* (= the hottest summer known about). [U] • A person's or organization's record is the actions they have done in the past, and esp. how well or badly they have done them: *During his twenty years as a football coach, he compiled an outstanding record.* [C]

record STORE SOUNDS / IMAGES /rɪˈkɔːrd/ *v* [T] to put (sounds or pictures) onto usually a magnetic TAPE using electronic equipment so that they can be heard or seen later • *The Beatles recorded many terrific albums over the years.* ○ *When I tried to phone her, all I got was a recorded message.*

record /ˈrek·ərd/ *n* [C] a flat, plastic disk on which music is recorded • A **record player** is a machine on which records can be played.

recording /rɪˈkɔːrd·ɪŋ/ *n* [C] a disk or TAPE used to record sounds or pictures that can be heard or seen when played in a machine

record BEST /ˈrek·ərd/ *n* [C] the best or fastest ever done • *She set a new world record in the*

high jump. ○ *Christmas sales this season broke/shattered the record* (= were better than ever before). • If something is **record-breaking**, it is better than anything else: *In terms of profit, this is going to be a record-breaking year for the company.*

record /ˈrek·ərd/ *adj* [not gradable] at a higher level than ever achieved before • *Farmers in the Midwest are reporting a record harvest this year.*

recorder /rɪˈkɔːrd·ər/ *n* [C/U] a musical instrument consisting of a wooden tube with holes along its length that are covered by the fingers to vary the notes and played by blowing into one end, or this type of instrument generally

recount DESCRIBE /rɪˈkaʊnt/ *v* [T] to describe the particular events of (an experience), or to tell (a story) • *She recounted some of her experiences working as a nurse in a hospital emergency room.*

recount COUNT /ˈriː·kaʊnt/ *n* [C] a second or another count, esp. of the number of votes in an election • *The final vote was so close that they demanded a recount.*

recoup /rɪˈkuːp/ *v* [T] to get back (money that has been spent or lost) • *It takes a while to recoup your initial costs when you begin a new business.*

recourse /ˈriː·kɔːrs, -koʊrs/ *n* [U] *slightly fml* a way of dealing with a difficult or unpleasant situation • *If the company won't pay me, the only recourse left to me is to sue them.*

recover /rɪˈkʌv·ər/ *v* [I/T] to get better after an illness or a period of difficulty or trouble • *It took her a while to recover after the operation.* [I] • To recover (something) is to find or get back the use of (something lost or taken away): *The police recovered her handbag, but her wallet was gone.* [T]

recovery /rɪˈkʌv·ə·ri/ *n* [C/U] the act or process of getting better; improvement • *The economy is showing signs of recovery.* [U] ○ *The story deals with the recovery of* (= getting back) *stolen jewelry.* [U]

recreation /ˌrek·riˈei·ʃən/ *n* [C/U] something done for pleasure or relaxation, or such activities generally • *Sarah's favorite recreation is shopping for antiques.* [C]

recreational /ˌrek·riˈei·ʃən·əl/ *adj* • *Recreational facilities include a swimming pool, gym, and fully-equipped exercise center.* • A **recreational vehicle** (abbreviation **RV**) is a large motor vehicle in which you can sleep, store a lot of equipment, and often cook.

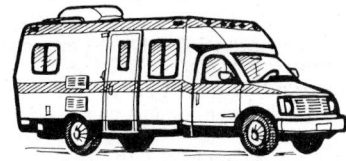

recreational vehicle

recrimination /rɪˌkrɪm·əˈneɪ·ʃən/ n [C/U] argument between people who are blaming each other, or the particular way they blame each other • *Western leaders, instead of presenting a coherent policy, have repeatedly lapsed into finger-pointing and recrimination.* [U]

recruit /rɪˈkruːt/ v [T] to persuade (someone) to become a new member of an organization • *The coach spends a lot of time recruiting the top high school athletes.*

recruit /rɪˈkruːt/ n [C] a new member of an organization, esp. a military organization

rectal /ˈrek·təl/ adj • See at RECTUM.

rectangle /ˈrekˌtæŋ·gəl/ n [C] a flat shape with four straight sides at 90° angles, and with opposite sides of equal length

    rectangular /rekˈtæŋ·gjə·lər/ adj • *The painting consists of four rectangular blocks of color.*

rectify /ˈrek·təˌfaɪ/ v [T] to correct or make right • *I hadn't meant to cause trouble, and asked what I could do to rectify the situation.*

rector /ˈrek·tər/ n [C] (in some Christian groups) a priest in charge of a PARISH (= area) • *A rector can also be the person in charge of a university or school.*

rectory /ˈrek·tə·ri/ n [C] a house in which a rector or other priest lives

rectum /ˈrek·təm/ n [C] the lowest end of the bowels, through which excrement passes as it leaves the body

    rectal /ˈrek·təl/ adj [not gradable] • *She took the baby's temperature with a rectal thermometer.*

recuperate /rɪˈkuː·pəˌreɪt/ v [I] to become stronger and better again after an illness or injury • *After leaving the hospital, he continued to recuperate at home.*

    recuperation /rɪˌkuː·pəˈreɪ·ʃən/ n [U] • *a lengthy recuperation*

recur /rɪˈkɜr/ v [I] **-rr-** to happen again or happen many times • *If the problem recurs, I'll see my doctor about it.*

    recurring /rɪˈkɜr·ɪŋ/, **recurrent** /rɪˈkɜr·ənt/ adj [not gradable] • *He suffered recurring nightmares that someone was chasing him.*

    recurrence /rɪˈkɜr·əns/ n [C/U]

recycle /riːˈsaɪ·kəl/ v [I/T] to collect and treat (used objects and materials that are ready to be thrown out) in order to produce materials that can be used again • *The law requires us to recycle paper products, glass bottles, soda cans, and some kinds of plastic.* [T]

    recyclable /riːˈsaɪ·klə·bəl/ adj able to be recycled • *Are plastic bottles recyclable or do they go in the garbage?*

red /red/ adj, n [C/U] **-dd-** (of) the color of fresh blood • *red gloves* ○ *She wore red.* [U] ○ *These reds don't match.* [C] • If you are **in the red**, you owe money. Compare **in the black** at BLACK [COLOR]. • The **red carpet** is specially good or respectful treatment that is given to an important guest: *They rolled out the red car-*

pet for the head of the International Olympic Committee. • A **red herring** is a fact, idea, or subject that is intended to take people's attention away from the central point being considered: *The charge that race was a factor in the arrest was a red herring, the district attorney said.* • **Red tape** means official rules and processes that seem unnecessary and delay the getting of results: *My mortgage application is stuck in red tape.* • A **redcap** is a person whose job it is to help travelers carry their bags in an airport or to a train or bus. • The **Red Cross** and the **Red Crescent** are international organizations that take care of people suffering because of war, hunger, illness, etc. • A **redhead** is a person whose hair is red or a brown color that is partly red. • A **red light** is a traffic signal in which the part that is red is brighter as a symbol of danger and to tell people facing it to stop. Compare **green light** at GREEN [COLOR]. • The **red-light district** of a city is the part where people, esp. women, have sex with other people, usually men, for money. • **Red meat** is meat from cows and sometimes also sheep or pigs, which is dark brown in color after it has been cooked.

reddish /ˈred·ɪʃ/ adj slightly red • *The leaves turn bright yellow or reddish-orange in the fall.*

redden /ˈred·ən/ v [I/T] to make or become red • *His face reddened with embarrassment.* [I]

redeem [IMPROVE] /rɪˈdiːm/ v [T] to do something that makes other people have a better opinion of (you), esp. after you have behaved badly or failed at something • *After his poor performance in the golf tournament two weeks before, he was determined to redeem himself by playing well.* ○ *Very few TV talk shows have any redeeming values* (= have good qualities that make their bad qualities less important).

redeem [BUY BACK] /rɪˈdiːm/ v [T] to buy back (something), or to exchange (something) for money or for goods or services • *You can redeem the bond at any time, but you will lose some interest.*

redemption /rɪˈdem·ʃən/ n [U] the state of being kept from evil or of improving morally • *The political leadership in that state is so corrupt that it's beyond redemption* (= it will always be morally bad).

redneck /ˈred·nek/ n [C] slang a poor, white person without education, esp. one living in the countryside in the southern US, who has **prejudiced** (= unfair and unreasonable) ideas and beliefs • USAGE: This word is usually considered offensive.

redouble /riːˈdʌb·əl/ v [T] to make (something) much stronger; increase • *We must redouble our efforts to find a cure for AIDS.*

redress /rɪˈdres/ v [T] fml to correct (a wrong) • *Affirmative action to help minorities is intended to redress wrongs.*

reduce /rɪˈduːs/ v [T] to make (something) less in size, amount, degree, importance, or price

• *A low-fat diet can reduce the risk of heart disease.* ○ *Grunn employs 17,900 people, but that number will be reduced by 500 workers.* ○ *All electronic equipment in the store has been reduced* (= lowered in price). • To reduce someone or something to a particular state is to bring them to that state: *Without any information, we've been reduced to guessing what happened.* ○ *The town was reduced to rubble in the fighting.*

reduction /rɪˈdʌkˌʃən/ *n* [C/U] • *a 2% reduction in the budget* [C] ○ *There will be no reduction in services.* [U]

redundant /rɪˈdʌnˌdənt/ *adj* more than what is usual or necessary, esp. using extra words that mean the same thing • *"A single unmarried woman" is a redundant phrase.* • (*Br*) A person who is redundant has become unemployed because they are no longer needed at their place of work.

redundancy /rɪˈdʌnˌdənˌsi/ *n* [U] • *They're trying to cut the redundancy of some federal programs.*

redwood /ˈredˌwʊd/ *n* [C/U] an evergreen tree that grows esp. in California and can become very tall, or the valuable brown-red wood of this tree

reed /riːd/ *n* [C] a type of tall, stiff grass that grows near water • A reed is also a thin strip of wood in some musical instruments, such as the CLARINET or OBOE, that produces sound when air is blown over it.

reef /riːf/ *n* [C] a line of rocks or sand at or near the surface of the sea • *a coral reef*

reefer /ˈriːfər/ *n* [C] *slang* a cigarette that contains the drug MARIJUANA

reek /riːk/ *v* [I] to have a strong, unpleasant smell • *His breath reeked of alcohol.*

reek /riːk/ *n* [U] • *the reek of dead fish*

reel HOLDER /riːl/ *n* [C] a round or cylindrical device on which a rope, wire, film, or other long, thin strip or object is rolled, or the amount of something stored on this • *a reel of film*

reel MOVE /riːl/ *v* [I] to move from side to side as if you are going to fall while walking or standing • *Reeling a bit, he tripped and fell.* • If you reel, or your mind or brain reels, you feel very confused or shocked: *Our team is reeling from five straight losses.*

□ **reel in/out** *obj*, **reel** *obj* **in/out** /ˈ-ˈ-/ *v adv* [M] to move (something) by using a REEL • *to reel in a fish* ○ *The firemen reeled the hoses out.*

□ **reel off** *obj*, **reel** *obj* **off** /ˈ-ˈ-/ *v adv* [M] to say or repeat (something, esp. a list of things) quickly and easily, or to do (something) repeatedly • *He reeled off the names of his grandchildren.* ○ *The Hawks reeled off nine straight points.*

reelect /ˌriːəˈlekt/ *v* [T] to elect (someone) again • *He was reelected despite some concerns about his personal life.*

reelection /ˌriːəˈlekˌʃən/ *n* [C/U] • *Reelection seemed unlikely after her arrest.* [U]

reenact /ˌriːəˈnækt/ *v* [T] to perform (actions that happened in the past), esp. in order to entertain or instruct • *The show reenacts medical emergencies.*

reenactment /ˌriːəˈnæktˌmənt/ *n* [C] • *a reenactment of Civil War battles*

reenter /riːˈentˌər/ *v* [I/T] to enter (a place), or to join (an activity) again • *She reentered the game shortly after being injured.* [T]

reentry /riːˈenˌtri/ *n* [C/U] • *The program offers single mothers an avenue for reentry into the world of education.* [U]

ref /ref/ *n* [C] *short form of* REFEREE

refer to MENTION /rɪˈfɜrˌtuː, -tə/ *v prep* [T] to mention or talk about (someone or something) • *I don't know which of his sisters he was referring to.*

reference /ˈrefˌrəns/ *n* [C/U] • *Avoid making any reference to his accident.*

refer to RELATE /rɪˈfɜrˌtuː, -tə/ *v prep* [T] to relate to or involve (someone or something) • *The town's name may refer to a nearby underground spring.*

reference /ˈrefˌrəns/ *n* [U] • *His story was in reference to a stupid question someone asked.*

refer to LOOK AT /rɪˈfɜrˌtuː, -tə/ *v prep* [T] to look at (something) for information or help • *He referred to the dictionary for the correct spelling of the word.*

reference /ˈrefˌrəns/ *n* [C/U] • *These books are for reference only and may not be checked out of the library.* [U] ○ *There is a list of the author's references at the end of the article.* [C] • A **reference book** is a book of facts, such as a dictionary or an ENCYCLOPEDIA, which you look at to get information. • See also REFERENCE.

refer *obj* **to** *obj* SEND /rɪˈfɜrˌtuː, -tə/ *v prep* [T] to send (someone or something) to (a different place or person) for information, treatment, a decision, etc. • *The librarian referred me to several books on the subject.*

referral /rɪˈfɜrˌəl/ *n* [C] • *Her doctor gave her a referral to a specialist.*

referee /ˌrefˌəˈriː/, *short form* **ref** *n* [C] (in some sports) a person who controls a game and makes sure the rules are followed, or (more generally) a person who helps to find a fair solution to a disagreement • *Fans booed the referee's call.*

referee /ˌrefˌəˈriː/ *v* [I/T] • *He volunteered to referee the game.* [T]

reference /ˈrefˌrəns/ *n* [C] a written statement describing your character and abilities, esp. when you are trying to get a new job, or the person who writes this statement • *She has excellent references.* ○ *Could I list you as a reference on my application?* • See also REFERENCE at REFER TO.

referendum /ˌrefˌəˈrenˌdəm/ *n* [C] *pl* **referendums** or *fml* **referenda** /ˌrefˌəˈrenˌdə/ a vote in which all the people in a country or an area decide on an important question

referral /rɪˈfɜr·əl/ *n* [C] • See at REFER TO SEND.

refill /riːˈfɪl/ *v* [T] to fill (esp. a container) again • *He refilled their glasses with ice-cold lemonade.*

refill /ˈriː·fɪl/ *n* [C] • *The waitress asked if I wanted a refill of coffee.* • A refill is also a container, esp. for the ink in a pen, that can be replaced.

refine /rɪˈfaɪn/ *v* [T] to make (a substance) pure by removing unwanted material • *Sugar and oil are refined before use.* • To refine something also means to improve it by making small changes: *We haven't finished refining the plan yet.*

refined /rɪˈfaɪnd/ *adj* • *Regional exports include refined oil and copper.* • If someone is refined, they are polite, graceful, and aware of quality and style: *The hotel lobby reflects the refined taste of the owners.*

refinement /rɪˈfaɪn·mənt/ *n* [C/U] • *The accuracy of the machine has been increased through a number of refinements.* [C] ○ *The refinement of raw opium yields drugs such as morphine.* [U] ○ *She grew up in a home environment of culture and refinement* (= politeness and quality). [U]

refinery /rɪˈfaɪ·nə·ri/ *n* [C] a factory where raw substances, such as sugar, oil, or metal, are made pure

reflect SEND BACK /rɪˈflekt/ *v* [I/T] to send back (light, heat, or sound) from a surface • *Light-colored clothing reflects the sun's heat rather than absorbing it.* [T] ○ *Moonlight reflected off the surface of the lake.* [I]

reflective /rɪˈflek·tɪv/ *adj* • *Joggers should wear reflective clothing at night.* • See also **reflective** at REFLECT THINK.

reflection /rɪˈflek·ʃən/ *n* [C] an image seen in a mirror or other shiny surface • *Standing on the dock, we could see the reflection of the sky in the still water.*

reflector /rɪˈflek·tər/ *n* [C] • *His new lighting system uses lamps and reflectors.*

reflect SHOW /rɪˈflekt/ *v* [T] to show, express, or be a sign of (something) • *His blank face reflected his boredom.* • *When one player behaves badly, it reflects on* (= gives a similar reputation to) *the whole team.*

reflection /rɪˈflek·ʃən/ *n* [C] • *Their finely decorated home is a reflection of their good taste.* ○ *The team's losses of late seem to be a reflection on the coaching.*

reflect THINK /rɪˈflekt/ *v* [I] to think carefully • *She felt she needed time to reflect on what to do next.*

reflection /rɪˈflek·ʃən/ *n* [C/U] • *Her reflections on life are recorded in her journal.* [C] ○ *After much reflection, he decided to return to teaching.* [U]

reflective /rɪˈflek·tɪv/ *adj* • *In my more reflec-*

tive moments, I write poetry. • See also **reflective** at REFLECT SEND BACK.

reflex /ˈriː·fleks/ *n* [C usually pl] a sudden, automatic reaction to something, esp. a physical reaction • *He's strong, always has good positioning, and his reflexes are fantastic.*

reflexive /rɪˈflek·sɪv/ *adj* [not gradable] specialized (in grammar) showing that the action of the verb is directed back on the subject • *In the sentence "He hurt himself," "hurt" is a reflexive verb and "himself" is a reflexive pronoun.*

reform /rɪˈfɔːrm/ *v* [I/T] to become better, or to make (something) better by making corrections or removing any faults • *As governor, he reformed election procedures.* [T] ○ *She was a heavy smoker for years, but she finally reformed.* [I]

reform /rɪˈfɔːrm/ *n* [C/U] • *The administration is proposing welfare reform.* [U]

reformation /ˌref·ərˈmeɪ·ʃən/ *n* [C/U] • *reformation of the health care system* [U]

reformed /rɪˈfɔːrmd/ *adj* • *a reformed alcoholic*

reformer /rɪˈfɔːr·mər/ *n* [C] a person who works for political, social, or religious change

refrain NOT DO /rɪˈfreɪn/ *v* [I] to not let yourself do something • *Please refrain from talking during the lecture.*

refrain SONG /rɪˈfreɪn/ *n* [C] a short part of a song or poem that is repeated, esp. at the end of each longer part, or any phrase that is often repeated • *Every year we hear the same refrain, that women are making great strides in business.*

refresh /rɪˈfreʃ/ *v* [T] to give new energy and strength to (someone) • *A good night's sleep will refresh you.* • *She reread her notes to refresh her memory* (= help her remember).

refresher /rɪˈfreʃ·ər/ *n* [C] • *Lemonade is a good refresher on a hot summer day.* • A **refresher course** is a training course that keeps people informed about new developments in their area of interest or skill.

refreshing /rɪˈfreʃ·ɪŋ/ *adj* • *a refreshing breeze on a hot day* ○ *It's refreshing to see so many young families moving into the neighborhood.* [+ *to* infinitive]

refreshingly /rɪˈfreʃ·ɪŋ·li/ *adv* • *a refreshingly honest statement*

refreshment /rɪˈfreʃ·mənt/ *n* [C/U] a small amount of food or drink • *Light refreshments will be available after the meeting.* [C]

refrigerate /rɪˈfrɪdʒ·ə·reɪt/ *v* [T] to make or keep (esp. food or drink) cold so that it stays fresh, esp. in a REFRIGERATOR • *Refrigerate the mayonnaise after opening the jar.*

refrigeration /rɪˌfrɪdʒ·əˈreɪ·ʃən/ *n* [U] • *The food will spoil without refrigeration.*

refrigerator /rɪˈfrɪdʒ·ə·reɪt·ər/, *infml* **fridge** *n* [C] a large piece of equipment that uses electricity to preserve food at a cold temperature • Compare **freezer** at FREEZE.

REFLEXIVE PRONOUNS

The singular reflexive pronouns are **myself**, **yourself**, **himself**, **herself**, **itself**, and (*formal*) **one-self**. The plural reflexive pronouns are **ourselves**, **yourselves**, and **themselves**.

A reflexive pronoun is used when the subject and object of a verb refer to the same person or thing.

*He describes **himself** as a socialist.* • *It was dark and they found **themselves** in a strange part of town.* • *The city defended **itself** from attack.*

The reflexive form of *you* has both a singular and a plural form.

*If you don't drive more carefully you'll get **yourself** killed.* • *Help **yourselves** to more cake, everybody!*

Reflexive pronouns can also be used as the object of a preposition.

*Can you tell me something about **yourself**?* • *I caught a glimpse of **myself** in the mirror.* • *Sitting around feeling sorry for **yourself** won't help the situation.*

Reflexive forms often are not used after prepositions when it is clear that the subject of the verb and the object of the preposition refer to the same person.

I brought a friend with me.

Other uses for reflexive pronouns

for emphasis

Reflexive pronouns are often used to give special attention to the person, animal, or thing being referred to.

*The president **himself** will attend the meeting.* • *The apartment **itself** is nothing special, but the view is spectacular.*

The reflexive pronoun can appear either directly after the noun or pronoun it emphasizes or at the end of the clause if the clause is relatively short.

*I **myself** don't happen to like hamburgers./I don't happen to like hamburgers **myself**.*

When a reflexive pronoun is used to emphasize that an action is done by one particular person instead of or without the help of another, it usually appears at the end of the clause.

*Don't wash my cup—I'll do it **myself**.* • *Did you make those curtains **yourself**?*

to mean "alone" or "without help"

The phrases by **myself**, by **herself**, by **themselves**, etc., mean either "alone" or "without help from anyone else." They can often be replaced by *alone* or *on my own, on her own*, etc.

*Do you live in that big house (all) by **yourself**?* • *I'm sure I can fix this by **myself**.*

to mean "for one's own use"

The phrases to **myself**, to **herself**, to **themselves**, etc., can mean "for my/her/their own use only."

*We had the whole beach to **ourselves**.*

to mean "behaving as usual"

If someone **is himself** or **herself** or **seems like herself** or **himself**, the person is in his or her usual mental or physical condition.

*Marie hasn't **been herself** since the accident.* • *Just **be yourself** at the interview.*

in place of other pronouns

Reflexive pronouns are sometimes used in place of other personal pronouns, especially in spoken English.

*It should be easy for an experienced skier like **yourself**.* • *"Who's going?" "Just my brother and **myself**."*

---

refuge /'ref·juːdʒ, -juːʒ/ *n* [C/U] protection or shelter from danger, trouble, etc., or a place that provides this • *Residents took refuge in their basements during the tornado.* [U] ○ *The bay is also a wildlife refuge for large numbers of birds.* [C]

refugee /ˌref·jʊˈdʒiː, ˈref·jʊˌdʒiː/ *n* [C] a person who leaves their home or country to find safety, esp. during a war or for political or religious reasons

refund /rɪˈfʌnd, ˈriː·fʌnd/ *v* [T] to pay back (money received or spent) • *The theater re-* funded our money when the performance was canceled.

refund /ˈriː·fʌnd/ *n* [C] • *If you overpaid, you should demand a refund.*

refurbish /rɪˈfɜr·bɪʃ/ *v* [T] to make (esp. a room or building) look fresh and clean again • *You've refurbished the kitchen.*

refuse SAY NO /rɪˈfjuːz/ *v* [I/T] to say or show that you are not willing to do, accept, or allow something • *She asked him for a loan, but he refused.* [I] ○ *We were refused admission to the* *building.* [T] ∘ *On cold mornings, the car may refuse to start.* [+ *to* infinitive]

refusal /rɪˈfjuː·zəl/ *n* [C/U] • *His refusal to contribute money angered the organizers.* [C]

refuse GARBAGE /ˈref·juːs, -juːz/ *n* [U] worthless or unwanted objects or materials; garbage • *We separate refuse from recyclables.*

refute /rɪˈfjuːt/ *v* [T] to prove (a statement, opinion, or belief) to be wrong or false • *Are you refuting the evidence?*

regain /rɪˈɡeɪn/ *v* [T] to get (something) back again • *I had to move out to regain my sanity.*

regal /ˈriː·ɡəl/ *adj* suitable for or in the manner of a king or queen • *a regal bearing*

regale /rɪˈɡeɪl/ *v* [T] to entertain (someone) with stories or jokes • *Grandpa regaled us with tales of his small-town childhood.*

regalia /rɪˈɡeɪl·jə/ *n* [U] special clothes and decorations, esp. those used at official ceremonies • *He wore the full regalia of a Kiowa chieftain.*

regard /rɪˈɡɑrd/ *v* [T always + adv/prep] to consider or think about (something) in a particular way, or to look carefully at (someone or something) • *Laura is highly regarded by her colleagues.* ∘ *The dog regarded me with suspicion as I approached the door.*

regard /rɪˈɡɑrd/ *n* [U] • *She has no regard for other people's feelings.* ∘ *The boss holds her opinions in high regard.* • *I am calling* **in/with regard to** (= in relation to) *your recent inquiry.*

regarding /rɪˈɡɑrd·ɪŋ/ *prep* in relation to; about • *I have a question regarding your last statement.*

regardless /rɪˈɡɑrd·ləs/ *adv* [not gradable] despite what has been said or done • *We want tax cuts, but regardless, we need to limit expenditures.* • *I tell them the truth,* **regardless of** (= without attention to) *what they want to hear.*

regards /rɪˈɡɑrdz/ *pl n* greetings and expressions of affection • *Please give my regards to your sister.*

regatta /rɪˈɡɑt̬·ə, -ˈɡæt̬·ə/ *n* [C] a boat race or series of races

regenerate IMPROVE /riːˈdʒen·ə·ˌreɪt/ *v* [T] to improve (a place or system) so that it is active or producing good results again • *As president of the college, he regenerated a failing institution.*

regenerate GROW AGAIN /riːˈdʒen·ə·ˌreɪt/ *v* [I/T] to grow again, or to make (something) grow again • *Tissue regenerates after skin is scratched.* [I]

regent /ˈriː·dʒənt/ *n* [C] (in the US) a member of the governing group of a university or educational system • *the Board of Regents*

reggae /ˈreɡ·eɪ, ˈreɪ·ɡeɪ/ *n* [U] a type of popular music from Jamaica with a strong second and fourth beat

regime /reɪˈʒiːm, rə-/ *n* [C] *esp. disapproving* a particular government, or a system or method of government • *a Communist/totalitarian regime*

regimen /ˈredʒ·ə·mən/, **regime** /reɪˈʒiːm, rə-/ *n* [C] a set of rules about food, exercise, or behavior that someone follows, esp. in order to improve their health • *His doctor put him on a strict regimen of exercise and low-fat food.*

regiment /ˈredʒ·ə·mənt/ *n* [C] a large group of soldiers combining several BATTALIONS

regimented /ˈredʒ·əˌment·əd/ *adj* extremely controlled • *They lead a very regimented life.*

regimentation /ˌredʒ·ə·mənˈteɪ·ʃən, -ˌmen-/ *n* [U] • *He hated the regimentation of boarding school.*

region /ˈriː·dʒən/ *n* [C] a particular area or part of a state, country, or the earth's surface • *Wheat is the major crop of this region.* • A region is also a particular area or part of the body: *He's complaining of pain in the lower abdominal region.* • *The temperature yesterday was* **(somewhere) in the region of** (= approximately) *-30°C.*

regional /ˈriː·dʒən·əl/ *adj* [not gradable] • *a regional trade and rail center*

regionalism /ˈriː·dʒən·əlˌɪz·əm/ *n* [C] a word or expression characteristic of a particular area • *"Spider" is a New England regionalism for a type of frying pan.*

register RECORD /ˈredʒ·ə·stər/ *v* [I/T] to record (someone's name or ownership of property) on an official list • *I registered the car in my name.* [T] ∘ *Voters have until February 16 to register to vote in the primary.* [+ *to* infinitive] ∘ *Students are currently registering for summer courses.* [I] • If you register a letter or parcel when you mail it, you pay extra to have it recorded and receive special care in delivery. [T]

register /ˈredʒ·ə·stər/ *n* [C] a book containing an official list or record • *She found the entry for her grandparents' marriage in the church register.*

registered /ˈredʒ·ə·stərd/ *adj* [not gradable] • *Only registered voters can be picked for jury selection.* • If you send a letter or parcel by **registered mail**, you pay extra to have it recorded so that it will be delivered carefully and not lost. • A **registered nurse** (*abbreviation* **R.N.**) is a nurse who has formally trained and passed an exam and is officially qualified to perform nursing duties. • A **registered trademark** (*symbol* ®) is a sign or name of a producer of goods which is officially recorded and cannot be used by others.

registration /ˌredʒ·əˈstreɪ·ʃən/ *n* [C/U] • *Keep your car registration with the vehicle.* [C] ∘ *With an election approaching, both political parties are encouraging voter registration.* [U]

registry /ˈredʒ·ə·stri/ *n* [C] an official list or record, or a place where official records are kept • *a registry of sex offenders*

register MEASURE /ˈredʒ·ə·stər/ *v* [I/T] (of an instrument) to measure and record an amount

• *The thermometer registered 79°F.* [T] ○ *The tremor barely registered on the Richter scale.* [I]

register SHOW /'redʒ·ə·stər/ *v* [T] to show (an emotion) by your facial expression • *Her face registered shock at the news.*

register HAVE EFFECT /'redʒ·ə·stər/ *v* [I] to have some effect • *The loss of her home has not really registered on her yet.*

register RANGE /'redʒ·ə·stər/ *n* [C] all the notes that a voice or musical instrument can produce, from the highest to the lowest

register MONEY /'redʒ·ə·stər/ *n* [C] short form of **cash register**, see at CASH

register DEVICE /'redʒ·ə·stər/ *n* [C] a device that controls the flow of air from a heating or cooling system through an opening into a room

registrar /,redʒ·ə'strɑr/ *n* [C] a person who keeps records, esp. a college or university official who is responsible for students' records of classes and marks

regress /rɪ'gres/ *v* [I] to return to a previous and less advanced or worse state • *Our team improved in the second half, while our opponents regressed.*

regression /rɪ'greʃ·ən/ *n* [U] • *Learning a language requires regression to childlike simplicity.*

regret /rɪ'gret/ *v* **-tt-** to feel sorry or unhappy about (something you did or were unable to do) • *He regretted his decision to leave school.* [T] ○ *I regret (that) I didn't buy more when they were on sale.* [+ (that) clause] ○ *I'm going to regret eating all those nachos.* [T] • (slightly fml) Regret is also used to express politely that you feel sorry about something: *My husband regrets (that) he couldn't be here tonight.* [+ (that) clause] ○ *The weather, I regret to say, is getting worse.* [+ to infinitive]

regret /rɪ'gret/ *n* [C/U] • *I have no regrets about quitting.* [C] ○ *She expressed regret for letting her friends down.* [U]

regretful /rɪ'gret·fəl/ *adj* feeling or expressing sadness or disappointment • *a regretful sigh*

regretfully /rɪ'gret·fə·li/ *adv* • *"We never spoke of it," Anne regretfully acknowledged.*

regrettable /rɪ'gret̬·ə·bəl/ *adj* causing or deserving sadness or disappointment • *The omission of a sponsor's name on the program was a regrettable error.*

regrettably /rɪ'gret̬·ə·bli/ *adv* • *Regrettably, he died before he could see her again.*

regroup /riː'gruːp/ *v* [I/T] to organize again in order to make a new effort, esp. after a defeat • *They lost their first game, but then regrouped and beat Detroit and Hartford.* [I]

regular REPEATED /'reg·jə·lər/ *adj* happening repeatedly in a fixed pattern, with equal or similar amounts of space or time between one and the next • *a regular heartbeat* ○ *working regular hours* ○ *Trees were planted at regular intervals along the avenue.*

regularly /'reg·jə·lər·li/ *adv* • *We meet regularly each morning for coffee.* • See also **regularly** at REGULAR OFTEN.

regularity /,reg·jə'lær·ət̬·i/ *n* [U] • *The regularity of the design gets boring after a while.* • See also **regularity** at REGULAR OFTEN.

regular USUAL /'reg·jə·lər/ *adj* usual or customary; NORMAL • *He drove his regular route to work.* ○ *Her regular assistant is on vacation.* • Regular also means of an average or standard size: *That minivan is longer than a regular station wagon.* • If you describe a man as a **regular guy**, you mean that he is an ordinary, likable person: *He wanted to prove he was a regular guy by going fishing.* • The **regular army** is the permanently organized army of a country. • (specialized) In grammar, a regular verb, noun, adjective, or other type of word follows the usual rules in the language for changing word endings.

regular OFTEN /'reg·jə·lər/ *adj* doing the same thing or going to the same place often • *a regular contributor to the magazine* ○ *a regular customer*

regular /'reg·jə·lər/ *n* [C] • *He's one of the regulars at the club.*

regularly /'reg·jə·lər·li/ *adv* • *She appears regularly on national TV.* • See also **regularly** at REGULAR REPEATED.

regularity /,reg·jə'lær·ət̬·i/ *n* [U] • *She watches those shows with amazing regularity.* • See also **regularity** at REGULAR REPEATED.

regular EQUAL /'reg·jə·lər/ *adj* shaped equally on all sides • *Her teeth are small and regular.*

regulate (obj) /'reg·jə,leɪt/ *v* to control (an activity or process) by rules or a system • *A computer system regulates production.* [T] ○ *Their parents regulate how much TV the children can watch.* [+ wh- word] • Regulate also means to adjust something to a desired level or standard: *As a diabetic, she regulates her sugar intake carefully.* [T]

regulation /,reg·jə'leɪ·ʃən/ *n* [C/U] • *federal safety regulations* [C] ○ *She favors government regulation of health-care systems.* [U]

regulation /,reg·jə'leɪ·ʃən/ *adj* [not gradable] • *Soldiers wear a regulation uniform.*

regulatory /'reg·jə·lə,tɔːr·i, -,toʊr·i/ *adj* • *a regulatory agency* ○ *federal regulatory standards*

regurgitate /rɪ'gɜr·dʒə,teɪt/ *v* [I/T] to repeat (information) without understanding it • *People are just regurgitating what they see on TV.* [+ wh- word] • Regurgitate also means to vomit. [I/T]

rehabilitate /,riː·hə'bɪl·ə,teɪt, ,riː·ə-/, short form **rehab** /'riː·hæb/ *v* [T] to return (someone) to a healthy or usual condition or way of living, or to return (something) to good condition • *The aim is to rehabilitate the prisoners so that they can lead productive lives when they are released.* ○ *That builder rehabilitates older housing which he then sells for a profit.*

rehabilitation /ˌriː·hə·bɪl·əˈteɪ·ʃən, ˌriː·ə-/, short form **rehab** /ˈriː·hæb/ n [U] • *She's in rehabilitation, trying to kick a drug habit.* ◦ *How much rehabilitation will your knee require?*

rehash /ˈriː·hæʃ/ v [T] to present (something old) in a new way or form without any real change or improvement • *The kids keep rehashing the same old argument about whose turn it is.*

rehash /ˈriː·hæʃ/ n [C] • *The new season's fashions seem like a rehash of last year's.*

rehearse /rɪˈhɜrs/ v [I/T] to practice (something, such as music or a speech), or lead (a person or group) in practicing it, in order to prepare for a public performance • *We rehearse all day and do the show that evening.* [I]

rehearsal /rɪˈhɜr·səl/ n [C/U] • *Zubin Mehta will conduct several rehearsals as well as the actual concert.* [C] ◦ *The play is in rehearsal.* [U]

reign /reɪn/ v [I] to rule a country, or to have power or control

reign /reɪn/ n [C] • *the reign of Louis XIV*

reimburse /ˌriː·əmˈbɜrs/ v [T] to pay back money to (someone), esp. for expenses • *They're going to reimburse me for the airfare.*

reimbursement /ˌriː·əmˈbɜr·smənt/ n [C/U] the act of paying back, or the money that is paid back

rein /reɪn/ n [C usually pl] a long thin piece of material, esp. leather, used to control a horse

rein in /reɪˈnɪn/ v prep [T] to control (something) esp. by preventing it from growing or from growing too fast • *The federal government is attempting to rein in health care costs.*

reincarnation /ˌriː·ɪnˈkɑrˈneɪ·ʃən/ n [C/U] the belief that the spirit of a dead person returns to life in another body or form, or a person or thing that has returned or been brought back

reincarnate /ˌriː·ɪnˈkɑrˌneɪt/ v [T] to live again in a different form after having died

reindeer /ˈreɪn·dɪr/ n [C] pl **reindeer** a type of deer that has horns like branches and lives in colder, northern parts of the world

reinforce /ˌriː·ənˈfɔrs, -ˈfoʊrs/ v [T] to make (something) stronger, usually by adding more material or another piece • *Building codes in California required that steel rods be used to reinforce cinder-block construction.* • Something that reinforces an idea or opinion provides proof or support: *But let me just cite one other fact to reinforce what you're saying.* • To reinforce an army is to provide it with more soldiers or weapons.

reinforcement /ˌriː·ənˈfɔr·smənt, -ˈfoʊr-/ n [U] something added to provide more strength or support • *The dam urgently needs reinforcement.* • Reinforcements are soldiers sent to join an army to make it stronger. [pl] • Reinforcement is also a way of influencing behavior through rewards and punishments: *positive/negative reinforcement*

reinstate /ˌriː·ənˈsteɪt/ v [T] to put (someone) back in a job or position they previously had, or to put (a law or rule) back into effect • *The state of California has reinstated the death penalty.* ◦ *The hospital suspended Goldstein during the investigation but reinstated him when the report cleared him of any wrongdoing.*

reinvent /ˌriː·ənˈvent/ v [T] to change (someone or something) so much that they or it seems completely new • *He promised to reinvent government if elected.* • To **reinvent the wheel** is to waste time learning how to do something when it is already known how to do it.

reissue /riːˈɪʃ·uː/ v [T] to print or produce again • *The recording was reissued on CD.*

reiterate /riːˈɪt·əˌreɪt/ v [T] *slightly fml* to say (something) again • *He reiterated his view that it was time to withdraw from Southeast Asia*

reject /rɪˈdʒekt/ v [T] to refuse to accept, use or believe (something or someone) • *The school rejects a third of all applicants.* • To reject someone is also to treat them in a way that shows you do not feel affection for them: *As a child, she had felt rejected by her mother.* • (*medical*) If your body rejects tissue or an organ that comes from another person, your body has a dangerous physical reaction to it

reject /ˈriː·dʒekt/ n [C] a damaged or faulty object, or a person who has had many jobs because of not being successful at any of them • *In desperation the hockey team picked up a 35-year-old reject as a backup goalie.*

rejection /rɪˈdʒek·ʃən/ n [C/U] • *fear of rejection* [U] ◦ *I applied for ten jobs and got ten rejections.* [C]

rejoice /rɪˈdʒɔɪs/ v [I] *fml* to feel or show great happiness • *Everyone rejoiced at the news of his safe return.*

rejoin /riːˈdʒɔɪn/ v [T] to return to (a person or group) • *She rejoined her husband in Toronto*

rejoinder /rɪˈdʒɔɪn·dər/ n [C] *fml* a quick answer, often given in a way that is competitive or amusing • *The reviewer's mistakes were so flagrant that Gove drafted a strong rejoinder.*

rejuvenate /rɪˈdʒuː·vəˌneɪt/ v [T] to make (someone) look or feel young and energetic again • *She felt rejuvenated by her vacation.* To rejuvenate an organization or place is to improve the way it works or looks and make it seem fresh: *They can do much to rejuvenate old neighborhoods and keep the city from declining again.*

relapse /rɪˈlæps/ v [I] to return to a previous bad condition or a worse way of life after making an improvement • *She had stopped using cocaine for a month but relapsed.*

relapse /rɪˈlæps, ˈriː·læps/ n [C] the return of an illness suffered previously

relate CONNECT /rɪˈleɪt/ v [I/T] to be connected with (something else), or to show that (something) is connected with something else • *The point I'm making now relates to what I said be-*

fore. [I always + adv/prep] ○ *There is a tradition in American public life of relating Christian values to public life.* [T]

related /rɪˈleɪt̬·əd/ *adj* [not gradable] connected • *We discussed inflation, unemployment, and related issues.* ○ *Police said the murder was drug related* (= connected with drugs). • See also RELATED.

relation /rɪˈleɪ·ʃən/ *n* connection or similarity • *There was little relation between the book and the movie.* [U] • Relations are the connections between people, groups, organizations, or countries: *diplomatic relations* [pl] ○ *business/economic relations* [pl] • *The drug is being studied for possible beneficial effects* **in relation to** (= connected with) *migraine headaches, rheumatoid arthritis, and breast cancer.* • **In relation to** also means compared with: *She checked the map to see where Miami is in relation to Orlando.*

relationship /rɪˈleɪ·ʃənˌʃɪp/ *n* [C] the way in which people behave or feel toward each other, or the way in which things work together or are connected • *The two men have a good working relationship.* ○ *Write an essay on the economic relationship between farming and transportation.* • A relationship is also a close romantic friendship between two people, which is often sexual: *She's just broken off a six-year relationship.*

elate *(obj)* ⟨TELL⟩ /rɪˈleɪt/ *v* to tell (a story) or describe (a series of events) • *She related the story over dinner.* [T] ○ *In this article, the author relates what it felt like to return to school at the age of 47.* [+ *wh*- word]

relate to /-ˈ--/ *v prep* [T] to understand and sympathize with (someone) • *The kids need a teacher who can relate to them.* • If someone says I can relate to that, they mean that they understand and sympathize with the situation being described, usually because they also have experienced it.

elated /rɪˈleɪt̬·əd/ *adj* [not gradable] belonging to the same family • *Of course Elise and Linda are related—they're cousins.* ○ *José and Alfonso are related by marriage.* • See also **related** at RELATE ⟨CONNECT⟩.

relation /rɪˈleɪ·ʃən/ *n* [C] a person who is a member of the same family as another person • *The funeral was attended by her many friends and relations.*

elative ⟨COMPARED WITH⟩ /ˈrel·ət̬·ɪv/ *adj* [not gradable] as judged or measured in comparison with something else • *We considered the relative merits of flying to Washington or taking the train.* ○ *Relative to* (= Considering) *birthweight, the newborns were doing well.* • *(specialized)* In grammar, a **relative clause** is a clause in a sentence that cannot exist independently, begins with a **relative pronoun**, and describes a noun that comes before it: *In the sentence "The movie that we saw was very good," "that we saw" is a relative clause.* • *(spe-*

cialized) In grammar, a **relative pronoun** is a pronoun such as "which," "who," or "that," used to begin a **relative clause**: *In the sentence "The movie that we saw was very good," "that" is a relative pronoun.*

relatively /ˈrel·ət̬·ɪv·li/ *adv* [not gradable] • *The stereo was relatively inexpensive.*

relative ⟨FAMILY⟩ /ˈrel·ət̬·ɪv/ *n* [C] a member of your family • *All her relatives came to the wedding.*

relativity /ˌrel·əˈtɪv·ət̬·i/ *n* [U] *specialized* a two-part theory in physics describing motion and the relationships between space, time, and energy • *Einstein's theory of relativity*

relax /rɪˈlæks/ *v* [I/T] to become or cause (someone) to become comfortably calm, and not worried or nervous, or to become or cause (a muscle or the body) to become less tight • *She saw a need for a downtown club where women could relax.* [I] ○ *This exercise will help you to relax your neck muscles.* [T] ○ *He relaxed his grip on my arm* (= held it less tightly). [T] • When rules or controls are relaxed, they are made less severe. [T]

relaxation /ˌriː·lækˈseɪ·ʃən/ *n* [U] • *The senator and his family flew to West Palm Beach for golf and relaxation.*

relaxed /rɪˈlækst/ *adj* comfortable and informal • *It's a very relaxed atmosphere on campus.*

relay /riːˈleɪ, ˈriː·leɪ/ *v* [T] to tell (something) you heard • *I relayed the news to the others.*

relay (race) /ˈriː·leɪ (ˈreɪs)/ *n* [C] a running or swimming race between two or more teams usually of four members, each of whom goes a part of the distance • *the Penn Relays*

release ⟨MAKE FREE⟩ /rɪˈliːs/ *v* [T] to give freedom to (someone) • *The new government immediately released all political prisoners.* • If you release a device, you move it from a locked position and allow it to move freely: *She released the brake and the car rolled forward.*

release /rɪˈliːs/ *n* [C usually sing] • *Diplomatic efforts were underway to secure the release of the two Americans being held.*

release ⟨STOP HOLDING⟩ /rɪˈliːs/ *v* [T] to drop, or to stop carrying, holding, or containing (something) • *The dog brought the ball back to us but wouldn't release it.* ○ *The company was charged with releasing toxic gases into the atmosphere.*

release ⟨MAKE PUBLIC⟩ /rɪˈliːs/ *v* [T] to let (something) be shown in public or made available for use • *The police released a drawing of the suspected rapist.*

release /rɪˈliːs/ *n* [C] • *The release of the movie was delayed till the Christmas season.*

relegate /ˈrel·əˌɡeɪt/ *v* [T] *slightly fml* to put (something or someone) into a lower or less important rank or position • *In the past when African-American men worked as sailors aboard ships, they were often relegated to jobs as cooks and stewards.*

relent /rɪ'lent/ v [I] to do something you had refused to do before, or to allow someone to do something that you had refused to allow before • *For days we begged him to see a doctor about his cough, and finally he relented.*

relentless /rɪ'lent·ləs/ adj continuing in a determined way without any interruption • *the relentless pursuit of wealth and power*

relevant /'rel·ə·vənt/ adj related to a subject or to something happening or being discussed • *We turned over relevant documents to the investigating team.*

relevance /'rel·ə·vəns/, **relevancy** /'rel·ə·vən·si/ n [U] • *the relevance of railroads to the development of the American west*

reliable /rɪ'laɪ·ə·bəl/ adj deserving trust; DEPENDABLE • *My car is old but it's reliable.*

reliably /rɪ'laɪ·ə·bli/ adv • *His whereabouts were unknown, but he was reliably reported to be alive.*

reliability /rɪˌlaɪ·ə'bɪl·ət·i/ n [U] • *The reliability of this smoke detector is guaranteed.*

reliance /rɪ'laɪ·əns/ n [U] the condition of depending on something or someone • *She said that there is too much reliance on meat in our diet.*

reliant /rɪ'laɪ·ənt/ adj • *The nation is still reliant on imported oil.*

relic /'rel·ɪk/ n [C] an object from the past, esp. one that has no modern use but is often valued for its historic meaning or importance • *The ship was a relic of the Spanish-American War.* • A relic is also a part of the body or clothing or one of the belongings of a SAINT (= holy person).

relief HAPPINESS /rɪ'liːf/ n [U] a feeling of happiness that something unpleasant has not happened or has ended • *She breathed a sigh of relief when she finished her exams.* • Relief also means the reduction or end of pain: *Aspirin may give you some relief.*

relief HELP /rɪ'liːf/ n [U] food, money, or services for people in need • *disaster relief*

relief WORK OF ART /rɪ'liːf/ n [C/U] the building up of parts of a surface to form a picture or design that can be seen above the background, or a work of art made by this method • *the reliefs of the Parthenon* [C] • To be **in relief** is to be easily noticeable.

relieve LESSEN PAIN /rɪ'liːv/ v [T] to make (something bad or painful) less severe • *The addition to the school will relieve overcrowding.* ○ *She was given morphine to relieve the pain.* • To relieve yourself is to urinate.

relieved /rɪ'liːvd/ adj happy that something unpleasant has not happened or has ended • *She was immensely relieved when the medical test proved to be negative.*

relieve REPLACE /rɪ'liːv/ v [T] to arrive or come in order to take the place of (another person) • *The guard is relieved at 6 p.m. by the night watchman.*

□ **relieve** *obj* **of** /-'--/ v prep [T] to take from

(someone) something they have, esp. a responsibility • *After the charges of sexual harassment surfaced, the captain was relieved of his command.*

religion /rɪ'lɪdʒ·ən/ n [C/U] the belief in and worship of a god or gods, or any such system of belief and worship

religious /rɪ'lɪdʒ·əs/ adj • *a religious holiday* ○ *He is deeply religious.*

religiously /rɪ'lɪdʒ·ə·sli/ adv • If you do something religiously, you do it regularly: *I exercise religiously, I really do.*

relinquish /rɪ'lɪŋ·kwɪʃ/ v [T] to give up (esp. a responsibility or claim) • *He refused to relinquish control of his company.*

relish ENJOY /'rel·ɪʃ/ v [T] to like or enjoy (something) • *I enjoyed our vacation, but didn't relish the twenty-hour trip back home.*

relish /'rel·ɪʃ/ n [U] the enjoyment you get from doing something

relish SAUCE /'rel·ɪʃ/ n [C/U] a type of sauce, usually made of vegetables cut into small pieces, vinegar, and spices, that adds flavor to food • *We have relish for the hamburgers and hot dogs.* [U]

relive /riː'lɪv/ v [T] to remember (an experience) clearly • *Rape is often not reported because victims do not want to relive the trauma.*

relocate /riː'loʊ·keɪt/ v [I/T] to move to a new place • *The company will relocate, but a new home has not been chosen yet.* [I]

reluctant /rɪ'lʌk·tənt/ adj not wanting to do something and therefore slow to do it • *She had trouble sleeping but was reluctant to take sleeping pills.* [+ *to* infinitive]

reluctantly /rɪ'lʌk·tənt·li/ adv • *He reluctantly resigned.*

reluctance /rɪ'lʌk·təns/ n [U]

rely on/upon /rɪ'laɪˌɔːn, -ˌɑn; -əˌpɔːn, -əˌpɑn/ v prep [T] to depend on or trust (someone or something) • *You can't rely on good weather for the whole trip.* ○ *The system relies too heavily on one means of financing.*

remain /rɪ'meɪn/ v to stay in the same place or in the same condition • *The doctor said he should remain in bed for a few days.* [I] ○ *She remained silent.* [L] • If something remains, it continues to exist when other parts or things no longer do: *Only the foundation of the ancient temple remains.* [I] • *How much things will change* **remains to be seen** (= is not yet certain).

remainder /rɪ'meɪn·dər/ n [C usually sing] the part that is left after the other parts are gone, used, or taken away • *It rained the first day but was sunny for the remainder of the trip.* • In mathematics, a remainder is the amount left when one number cannot be exactly divided by another.

remaining /rɪ'meɪ·nɪŋ/ adj [not gradable] • *Use half the dough and keep the remaining half covered.*

remains /rɪ'meɪnz/ pl n • *Rescue workers*

searched *the remains of the house.* • *A person's* remains are *that person's dead body.*

remake /riː'meɪk/ v [T] *past* **remade** /riː 'meɪd/ to make (esp. a movie or song) again with different people performing

remake /'riː·meɪk/ n [C] • *Have you seen the remake of "King Kong"?*

remark /rɪ'mɑrk/ v to give a spoken statement of an opinion or thought • *She remarked (that) she'd be home late.* [+ (*that*) clause] • If you remark on something, you notice it and say something about it: *All his friends remarked on the change in him.* [I]

remark /rɪ'mɑrk/ n [C] • *His racist remarks offended me.*

remarkable /rɪ'mɑr·kə·bəl/ adj approving unusual and surprising • *He's a remarkable young man.*

remarkably /rɪ'mɑr·kə·bli/ adv approving • *They were remarkably calm after the crash.*

remedial /rɪ'miːd·iː·əl/ adj [not gradable] (of an activity) intended to correct or improve something, esp. skills • *Students can enroll in remedial English classes.*

remedy /'rem·əd·i/ n [C] a substance or method for curing an illness, or a way of dealing with a problem or difficulty • *cold remedies*

remedy /'rem·əd·i/ v [T] • *We're working to remedy these shortcomings.*

remember /rɪ'mem·bər/ v [I/T] to be able to bring a piece of information back into your mind, or to keep (a piece of information) in your memory • *Naomi vividly remembers the day her daughter was born.* [T] ○ *I've been a Tiger fan as long as I can remember.* [I] ○ *Williams will be remembered for his generosity.* [T] ○ *Can you remember where we parked the car?* [+ *wh-* word] ○ *You have to remember that these things take time.* [+ *that* clause] ○ *Remember to buy some stamps.* [+ *to* infinitive] • USAGE: Compare REMIND.

remembrance /rɪ'mem·brəns/ n [C/U] • *The video makes a nice remembrance of the party.* [C]

remind /rɪ'maɪnd/ v [T] to make (someone) aware of something they have forgotten or might have forgotten, or to bring back a memory to (someone) • *Remind him to call me.* ○ *Anna reminds me of her mother.* • USAGE: Compare REMEMBER.

reminder /rɪ'maɪn·dər/ n [C] something that helps someone remember • *She kept the shells as a reminder of our days together.* ○ *The park serves as a reminder that nature is worth preserving.* [+ *that* clause]

reminisce /,rem·ə'nɪs/ v [I] to talk or write about past experiences that you remember with pleasure • *Grandpa likes to reminisce about his years in the navy.*

reminiscence /,rem·ə'nɪs·əns/ n [C/U] • *She published reminiscences of her life in China.* [C]

reminiscent /,rem·ə'nɪs·ənt/ adj • *That tune is reminiscent of a song my mother used to sing.*

remiss /rɪ'mɪs/ adj careless and not doing a duty well enough • *I would be remiss if I didn't mention it.*

remission /rɪ'mɪʃ·ən/ n [C/U] a period of time when an illness is less severe • *Her leukemia is in remission.* [U]

remit /rɪ'mɪt/ v [T] **-tt-** *slightly fml* to send (money) to someone • *Please remit payment by the 15th of the month.*

remnant /'rem·nənt/ n [C] a small piece or amount of something that is left from a larger, original piece or amount • *a carpet remnant*

remodel /riː'mɑd·əl/ v [I/T] **-l-** or **-ll-** to give a new shape or form to (esp. a room or house) • *We remodeled the kitchen.* [T]

remorse /rɪ'mɔːrs/ n [U] a strong feeling of guilt and regret about something you have done • *He felt no remorse for the shooting.*

remorseful /rɪ'mɔːrs·fəl/ adj • *I'm still remorseful for having broken it.*

remorseless /rɪ'mɔːr·sləs/ adj • *a remorseless tyrant*

remote /rɪ'moʊt/ adj far away in distance, time, or relation; not close • *Ben grew up in a remote part of Montana.* ○ *It happened in the remote past.* • If someone's behavior is remote, they are not friendly or interested in others. ○ *There is a remote possibility* (= slight chance) *that we won't be able to make the trip.* • A **remote (control)** is a device for controlling something from a distance: *Is this remote for the TV or the VCR?* ○ **Remote-controlled** *cameras monitor the entrance.*

remotely /rɪ'moʊt·li/ adv [not gradable] • *He isn't even remotely* (= in any way) *like his brother.* ○ *a remotely operated car*

remove /rɪ'muːv/ v [T] to take (something) away from an object, group, or place • *Please remove your books from the counter.* ○ *Club soda will remove that stain.* ○ *He was removed from office* (= forced to leave an official position). ○ *Space flight is pretty far removed from* (= not part of) *most people's experience.*

removal /rɪ'muː·vəl/ n [U] • *He ordered the immediate removal of the troops.*

remover /rɪ'muː·vər/ n [U] • *paint remover*

remuneration /rɪ,mjuː·nə'reɪ·ʃən/ n [U] *slightly fml* pay for work or services

renaissance /'ren·ə,sɑns, -,zɑns/ n [C] a new growth or interest in something, esp. art, literature, or music • *a poetry renaissance* • The Renaissance was a period of growth and activity in the areas of art, literature, and ideas in Europe during the 14th, 15th, and 16th centuries.

rend /rend/ v [T] *past* **rent** /rent/ *literary* to break (something) violently; tear • *I would rend the heavens for her.*

render CAUSE /'ren·dər/ v [T] to cause (someone or something) to be in a particular state •

New technology renders a computer obsolete in a year.

render REPRESENT /'ren·dər/ v [T] to represent (something) in a work of art or a performance • *The drawing was rendered in muted pastels.*

rendering /'ren·də·rɪŋ/ n [C] • *a watercolor rendering*

render GIVE /'ren·dər/ v [T] *fml* to give (something) to someone • *She renders service unto God.*

rendezvous /'ran·dɪ,vuː, -deɪ-/ n [C] *pl* **rendezvous** /'ran·dɪ,vuːz, -deɪ-/ a meeting at a particular place and time • *a secret rendezvous* • A rendezvous is also a particular place where people often meet: *This restaurant is a popular rendezvous for local artists.*

rendezvous /'ran·dɪ,vuː, -deɪ-/ v [I] • *Shall we rendezvous around 6 p.m.?*

rendition /ren'dɪʃ·ən/ n [C] a particular way in which music is performed or a drawing or painting is produced or appears • *new renditions of old Beatles tunes*

renegade /'ren·ɪ,geɪd/ n [C] a person who has changed their loyalties, esp. from one political, religious, or national group to another one • *a renegade priest* ∘ *She's always been a renegade.*

renege /rɪ'nɪg, -'neg/ v [I] to not do what you previously agreed to do; to fail to keep a promise or agreement • *He reneged on his offer.*

renew INCREASE ACTIVITY /rɪ'nuː/ v [T] to begin doing (something) again or with increased strength • *She renewed her efforts to contact her sister.*

renewed /rɪ'nuːd/ adj [not gradable] • *renewed interest/enthusiasm*

renew CONTINUING USE /rɪ'nuː/ v [T] to increase the period of time that something can be used or is in effect • *to renew a passport/subscription*

renewable /rɪ'nuː·ə·bəl/ adj [not gradable] • *a renewable agreement* • Renewable substances can be used and easily replaced: *renewable energy resources*

renewal /rɪ'nuː·əl/ n [C/U] • *renewal of a license* [U]

renounce /rɪ'nɑʊns/ v [T] to say publicly that you no longer own, support, believe in, or have a connection with (something) • *Gandhi renounced the use of violence.* • USAGE: The related noun is RENUNCIATION.

renovate /'ren·ə,veɪt/ v [T] to repair and improve (esp. a building)

renovation /,ren·ə'veɪ·ʃən/ n [C/U] • *The museum is closed for renovations.* [C]

renown /rɪ'nɑʊn/ n [U] *slightly fml* the state of being famous • *an artist of national renown*

renowned /rɪ'nɑʊnd/ adj • *The region is renowned for its natural beauty.*

rent PAYMENT /rent/ n [C/U] a fixed amount of money paid or received regularly for the use of usually an apartment, house, or business space • *Rents in this building are ridiculously*

high. [C] ∘ *How much rent do you pay?* [U] ∘ *Are there were any apartments for rent* (= available) *there?* [U]

rent /rent/ v [T] • *I rented a car for the trip to Boston.*

rental /'rent·ʔl/ n [C/U] the act of renting, an amount paid in rent, or something rented • *boat/car rental* [U]

rent TORN /rent/ *past simple and past participle of* REND

renunciation /rɪ,nʌn·siː'eɪ·ʃən/ n [C] the act or RENOUNCING (= no longer supporting) something • *the renunciation of the use of force*

rep SALES /rep/ n [C] *short form of* **sales representative**, see at SALE SELL

rep REPUTATION /rep/ n [C usually sing] *short form of* REPUTATION • *I wouldn't spend time with him—he's got a bad rep.*

Rep. CONGRESS n [C] *abbreviation for* **Representative**, see at REPRESENT ACT FOR

repaid /rɪ'peɪd/ *past simple and past participle of* REPAY

repair /rɪ'per, -'pær/ v [T] to put (something damaged, broken, or not working correctly) back into good condition or make it work again • *Surgeons repaired the severed artery.*

repair /rɪ'per, -'pær/ n [C/U] • *My car is in the garage for repairs.* [C] ∘ *Our building is in poor repair* (= bad condition). [U] • A **repairman** is someone whose job is to make things that are broken work correctly: *a TV repairman*

reparation /,rep·ə'reɪ·ʃən/ n [C/U] payment for harm or damage • *The company paid reparations to the victims of the explosion.* [C]

repatriate /riː'peɪ·triː,eɪt, -'pæ·triː-/ v [T] to send or bring (someone or something) back to their own country

repatriation /riː,peɪ·triː'eɪ·ʃən, -,pæ·triː-/ n [U] • *Repatriation of refugees is essential to rebuilding the country.*

repay /rɪ'peɪ/ v [T] *past* **repaid** /rɪ'peɪd/ to pay (someone) money that was borrowed, or to reward (someone) • *How can I ever repay you for your kindness.*

repayment /riː'peɪ·mənt/ n [C/U] • *They expect repayment of the loan over three years.* [U]

repeal /rɪ'piːl/ v [T] (of a government) to make (a law) no longer a law • *Legislators repealed the sales tax.*

repeal /rɪ'piːl/ n [U] • *Senators called for the law's repeal.*

repeat /rɪ'piːt/ v [T] to say, tell, or do (something) again • *She repeated the question.* ∘ *Listen to the tape and repeat each word.*

repeat /rɪ'piːt, 'riː·piːt/ n [C] • *We're hoping to avoid a repeat of last year's disaster.*

repeated /rɪ'piːt̬·əd/ adj [not gradable] happening again and again • *repeated attempts/warnings*

repeatedly /rɪ'piːt̬·əd·li/ adv [not gradable] • *He has repeatedly denied being there.*

repel /rɪ'pel/ v [T] **-ll-** to force away (something unwanted) • *This coat repels moisture.* • Repel can also mean disgust: *Even the idea of him repels her.*

repellent /rɪ'pel·ənt/ *n* [C/U] • *Bring insect repellent along on the hike.* [U]

repent /rɪ'pent/ *v* [I/T] to be sorry you did or did not do something • *He repented for his sins.* [I]

repercussion /ˌriː·pər'kʌʃ·ən, ˌrep·ər-/ *n* [C usually pl] the usually bad effect of an event, action, or decision • *The repercussions of her comments could be serious.*

repertoire /'rep·ər,twɑr/ *n* [C] all the music, plays, dances, operas, etc., that a person or a group can perform, or that exist in a particular type of artistic activity • *Americans don't know the American repertoire, aside from Gershwin.*

repertory /'rep·ər,tɔːr·i, -,toʊr·i/ *n* [C/U] a series of performances by a group of actors or dancers presenting several different works during a particular period, or a REPERTOIRE

repetitive /rɪ'pet·əṭ·ɪv/ *adj* expressed or happening in the same way many times • *a repetitive task* ○ *a series of repetitive motions* • The related verb is REPEAT.

repetitious /ˌrep·ə'tɪʃ·əs/ *adj* • *The movie got a little repetitious after the third car chase.*

repetition /ˌrep·ə'tɪʃ·ən/ *n* [C/U] • *It takes time, patience, and repetition to learn a language.* [U]

rephrase /riː'freɪz/ *v* [T] to say or write (something) again in a different way • *Could you rephrase your question?*

replace CHANGE FOR /rɪ'pleɪs/ *v* [T] to take the place of (something) or put in the place of (something or someone else) • *We replaced our old air conditioners.* ○ *The ailing actress was replaced by her understudy.*

replacement /rɪ'pleɪs·mənt/ *n* [C/U] • *The replacement of typewriters by computers happened quickly.* [U]

replace PUT BACK /rɪ'pleɪs/ *v* [T] to put (something) back where it was before • *After dusting the vase, she replaced it on the shelf.*

replay REPETITION /'riː·pleɪ/ *n* [C usually sing] a repetition of an earlier event • *Interest rates were lowered to avoid a replay of the stock market crash.*

replay REPEAT PLAYING /'riː·pleɪ/ *n* [C] a playing for a second time, sometimes at a slower speed, of a recording, esp. of an event shown on television • *News programs broadcast endless replays of the shooting.*

replay /riː'pleɪ/ *v* [T] • *I replayed the night in my mind.*

replenish /rɪ'plen·ɪʃ/ *v* [T] to fill (something) again, or return (something) to its earlier condition • *We need to replenish our cookie supply.*

replete /rɪ'pliːt/ *adj slightly fml* • **Replete with** means full of: *a heart replete with affection*

replica /'rep·lɪ·kə/ *n* [C] a copy of an object

replicate /'rep·lə,keɪt/ *v* [I/T] to copy or repeat (something) • *Researchers tried to replicate the original experiment.* [T]

reply /rɪ'plaɪ/ *v* to answer a question • *She asked him how old he was but he didn't reply.* [I] ○ *He replied that he wasn't interested.* [+ that clause]

reply /rɪ'plaɪ/ *n* [C/U] • *Mary's reply was carefully considered.* [C] ○ *When he made no reply, she continued.* [U]

report *(obj)* TELL /rɪ'pɔːrt, -'poʊrt/ *v* to give a description of (something) or information about (something) to someone • *We called the police to report the theft.* [T] ○ *The accident was reported in all the newspapers.* [T] ○ *She reported that her teacher hit her.* [+ that clause] • *(specialized)* **Reported speech** (also **indirect speech**) is a description of what someone has said without using the exact words they used: *The sentence, "He told me that he would like to go" is an example of reported speech.*

report /rɪ'pɔːrt, -'poʊrt/ *n* [C] • *a financial report* ○ *I have to write a report on immigration.* ○ *According to reports there has been an earthquake in Los Angeles.* • A **report card** is a teacher's written statement about a student's performance at school.

reportedly /rɪ'pɔːrṭ·əd·li, -'poʊrṭ-/ *adv* [not gradable] • *New York is reportedly a very exciting place to live* (= People say that it is).

reporter /rɪ'pɔːrṭ·ər, -'poʊrṭ·ər/ *n* [C] a person whose job is to discover information about news events and describe them for a newspaper or magazine or for radio or television

report GO SOMEWHERE /rɪ'pɔːrt, -'poʊrt/ *v* [I always + adv/prep] to go to a place and say that you are there or inform someone about what you are doing • *I report for work/duty at 8 a.m. every morning.* ○ *In this job you'll be reporting directly to* (= working for) *the president.*

repository /rɪ'pɑz·ə,tɔːr·i, -,toʊr·i/ *n* [C] a place where things are stored • *a nuclear waste repository* ○ *(fig.) The proverbs amounted to a repository of wisdom.*

reprehensible /ˌrep·rɪ'hen·sə·bəl/ *adj* [not gradable] deserving blame; recognized as bad • *A spokeswoman for the Methodist Church called the national lottery morally reprehensible.*

represent ACT FOR /ˌrep·rɪ'zent/ *v* [T] to speak, act, or be present officially for (a person or group) • *His law firm is representing a dozen of the families involved in that disaster.*

representation /ˌrep·rɪ·zen'teɪ·ʃən, -zən-/ *n* [U] • *People too poor to pay for legal representation get a public defender.*

representative /ˌrep·rɪ'zent·əṭ·ɪv/ *adj* [not gradable] • *Democracy is a representative system of government.*

representative /ˌrep·rɪ'zent·əṭ·ɪv/ *n* [C] a person who represents another person or a group • *The company has representatives in most European capitals.* • A **Representative** *(abbreviation* **Rep.**) is also a member of the US

House of Representatives, or of a state law-making group.

represent [DESCRIBE] /ˌrep·rɪ'zent/ v [T] to show or describe (something); be a sign or symbol of (something) • *The memorial represents the sacrifice of the men and women who gave their lives in the Vietnam War.*

representative /ˌrep·rɪ'zent·ət·ɪv/ adj [not gradable] serving to describe, esp. a larger group of the same type • *A good political poll is based on a representative sampling of voters.*

represent [BE] /ˌrep·rɪ'zent/ v [L] to be (something), or to be the result of (something) • *China and India represent 40% of the world's population.* ○ *This represents years of work.*

repress /rɪ'pres/ v [T] to prevent (feelings, desires, or ideas) from being expressed • *In the end, it was impossible to repress his sexuality totally.* ○ *The government repressed all dissent.*

repressed /rɪ'prest/ adj • *In the play, George has the role of a repressed homosexual.*

repression /rɪ'preʃ·ən/ n [U] • *sexual repression* ○ *The report dealt with the exploitation and repression of women.*

repressive /rɪ'pres·ɪv/ adj • *The military regime was repressive and corrupt.*

reprieve /rɪ'priːv/ n [C] an official order to delay or stop a prisoner's punishment, esp. the punishment of death • *The warden notified Shaw of his reprieve.* • A reprieve is also any delay that is welcomed: *The play, about to close, was granted a four-week reprieve.*

reprieve /rɪ'priːv/ v [T]

reprimand /'rep·rə,mænd/ v [T] to tell (someone), esp. officially, that their behavior is wrong and not acceptable • *The committee reprimanded and censured him for his uncooperative attitude.*

reprimand /'rep·rə,mænd/ n [C] • *His boss gave him a severe reprimand for being late again.*

reprint /riː'prɪnt/ v [T] to print (a book) again • *The first edition sold out, so it is being reprinted.*

reprint /'riː·prɪnt/ n [C]

reprisal /rɪ'praɪ·zəl/ n [C/U] an act of damage or injury against an enemy in reaction to an act of damage or injury done to you • *Military action might bring reprisals against UN troops in the region.* [C]

reprise /rɪ'priːz/ n [C] a repeat of something • *The government feared a reprise of the bloody riots that followed sharp food price increases in 1977.*

reprise /rɪ'priːz/ v [T] to repeat (a song, performance, or set of actions) • *I was to play the doctor, reprising a role I'd done years earlier.*

reproach /rɪ'proʊtʃ/ v [T] to criticize or find fault with (someone) • *He's still reproaching himself for the accident.*

reproach /rɪ'proʊtʃ/ n [C/U] • *The child's behavior was above/beyond reproach (= blameless).* [U]

reproduce [PRODUCE YOUNG] /ˌriː·prə'duːs/ v [I/T] (of living things) to produce young • *Bacteria reproduce themselves by cell division.* [T]

reproduction /ˌriː·prə'dʌk·ʃən/ n [U] the act or process of producing young

reproductive /ˌriː·prə'dʌk·tɪv/ adj [not gradable] • *the reproductive organs*

reproduce [COPY] /ˌriː·prə'duːs/ v [I/T] to produce a copy of (something), or to show or do (something) again • *The design was reproduced on T-shirts.* [T]

reproduction /ˌriː·prə'dʌk·ʃən/ n [C/U] • *The poster is a reproduction of a Monet painting.* [C]

reptile /'rep·təl, -taɪl/ n [C] any of various animals whose blood temperature changes with the outside temperature and whose bodies are covered with SCALES or PLATES (= hard material) • *Snakes, turtles, and crocodiles are all reptiles.*

republic /rɪ'pʌb·lɪk/ n [C] a country that is governed by elected representatives and an elected leader

republican /rɪ'pʌb·lɪ·kən/ n [C] a person who supports or believes in representative government • A Republican is a member or supporter of the **Republican Party** (= one of the two main political parties in the US).

repudiate /rɪ'pjuː·diˌeɪt/ v [T] *fml* to refuse to accept or obey (something or someone); REJECT • *Southerners should repudiate their legacy of slavery, segregation, and racism.*

repudiation /rɪˌpjuː·diˈeɪ·ʃən/ n [U]

repugnant /rɪ'pʌg·nənt/ adj [not gradable] causing a feeling of strong dislike or disgust • *Torture was morally repugnant.*

repulse /rɪ'pʌls/ v [T] to successfully stop (esp. an attack), or to push away or refuse (someone or something unwanted) • *The enemy attack was quickly repulsed.* • If something repulses you, it causes you to have a strong feeling of dislike or disgust.

repulsion /rɪ'pʌl·ʃən/ n [U] • *When she was pregnant, certain foods produced a feeling of repulsion in her.*

repulsive /rɪ'pʌl·sɪv/ adj causing a feeling of strong dislike or disgust • *The movie contains a repulsive scene that lingers on the vicious beating of a helpless woman.*

reputation /ˌrep·jə'teɪ·ʃən/ n [C] the general opinion that people have about someone or something • *a good/bad reputation* ○ *His work in Congress won him a reputation as reliable and industrious.*

reputable /'rep·jət·ə·bəl/ adj having a good reputation • *Call a reputable heating contractor to inspect your furnace.*

reputed /rɪ'pjuːt·əd/ adj [not gradable] generally reported or believed • *The restaurant is reputed to be the best of its kind in the city.* [+ to infinitive]

reputedly /rɪ'pjuːt·əd·li/ adv [not gradable] • *At one time he was reputedly the richest man in America.*

request /rɪˈkwest/ n [C/U] an act of asking for something, or the thing asked for • *The library gets a lot of requests for books about new babies.* [C] ○ *An application will be sent to you upon request* (= if you ask). [U]

request (obj) /rɪˈkwest/ v • *The caller requested that his name not be mentioned on the air.* [+ that clause]

require NEED /rɪˈkwaɪr/ v [T] to need (something), or to make (something) necessary • *If you require assistance with your bags, I'll be glad to get someone to help you.* ○ *This game requires total concentration.*

requirement /rɪˈkwaɪr·mənt/ n [C] something needed or necessary • *Previous experience is one of the requirements for the job.*

require ORDER /rɪˈkwaɪr/ v to order or demand (something), or to order (someone) to do something, esp. because of a rule or law • *We're required to check your identification before letting you in.* [+ to infinitive] ○ *A building permit is required.* [T]

requisite /ˈrek·wə·zət/ adj [not gradable] *fml* needed for a particular purpose or result • *I worked to develop the requisite skills for a managerial position.*

requisition /ˌrek·wəˈzɪʃ·ən/ n [C/U] a formal or official request for something needed • *The staff made a requisition for new desks.* [C]

requisition /ˌrek·wəˈzɪʃ·ən/ v [T] to officially request or take (something) • *The army requisitioned all the trucks in the region.*

reroute /riːˈruːt, -ˈraʊt/ v [T] to change the route of (someone or something) • *Traffic is being rerouted due to construction.*

rerun /riːˈrʌn/ v [T] **rerunning**, *past simple* **reran** /riːˈræn/, *past part* **rerun** to show (esp. a television program) that has been shown previously

rerun /ˈriː·rʌn/ n [C] • *There's nothing on TV but reruns.*

reschedule /riːˈskedʒ·uːl, -əl/ v [T] to arrange (something) for a different time • *I rescheduled my doctor's appointment for later in the week.*

rescind /rɪˈsɪnd/ v [T] *fml* to make (a law, order, or decision) no longer have any legal effect • *The vote rescinds zoning decisions made earlier in the decade.*

rescue /ˈres·kjuː/ v [T] to save (someone or something) from a dangerous, harmful, or difficult situation • *Medical teams immediately rushed in to rescue persons trapped in buildings and give medical aid.*

rescue /ˈres·kjuː/ n [C/U] • *Rescue workers arrived at the scene within minutes.* [U]

rescuer /ˈres·kjuː·ər/ n [C] • *Rescuers in helicopters and on foot continued their search for survivors.*

research /rɪˈsɜrtʃ, ˈriː·sɜrtʃ/ n [U] a detailed study of a subject in order to discover information or achieve a new understanding of it • *medical/scientific research* ○ *The US*

government has funded some research on high-speed trains. ○ *I like doing research.*

research /rɪˈsɜrtʃ, ˈriː·sɜrtʃ/ v [I/T] • *Obviously they didn't research it and get enough information.* [T]

researcher /rɪˈsɜr·tʃər, ˈriː·ˌsɜr-/ n [C]

resemble /rɪˈzem·bəl/ v [T] to be similar to (someone or something) • *Several of the women resemble one another closely enough to be sisters.*

resemblance /rɪˈzem·bləns/ n [C/U] • *There is a clear resemblance between the two breeds of dogs.* [C]

resent /rɪˈzent/ v [T] to dislike or be angry at (something or someone) because you have been hurt or not treated fairly • *She bitterly resented her father's new wife.*

resentful /rɪˈzent·fəl/ adj • *Marshall was resentful that he had made almost nothing from his discovery.*

resentment /rɪˈzent·mənt/ n [U] • *There was a lot of resentment towards the Americans.*

reservation /ˌrez·ərˈveɪ·ʃən/ n [C/U] a doubt or reason for not accepting or agreeing with something completely • *We have reservations about letting the children stay home alone.* [C]

reserve /rɪˈzɜrv/ v [I/T] to keep (something) for a particular purpose or time • *He reserved the right to veto any future plans.* [T] • If you reserve something such as a table in a restaurant or a room in a hotel, you arrange for it to be kept for your use at a later time: *It's a popular restaurant, and you'll have to reserve well in advance.* [I] ○ *I'm sorry, this seat is reserved.* [T]

reservation /ˌrez·ərˈveɪ·ʃən/ n [C] an arrangement to have something kept for a person or for a special purpose • *I made a reservation at the restaurant for 7 o'clock.* • A reservation is also an area of land set apart for a particular group of people to live on, esp. American Indians.

reserve /rɪˈzɜrv/ n [C/U] • *I have a reserve of food in case of emergency.* [C] ○ *The book is on reserve and can't be checked out.* [U] • A reserve (also **preserve**) is also an area of land kept for the protection of animals and plants: *a nature/game reserve* [C] • The reserves are a part of a country's armed forces that are not always on active duty but are available in an emergency. [pl] • *She keeps a little money* **in reserve** (= for use if and when needed).

reserved /rɪˈzɜrvd/ adj tending to keep your feelings or thoughts private rather than showing them • *Marcus is more reserved than his brother.*

reservoir /ˈrez·ər·ˌvwɑr, -ər·ˌvwɔːr/ n [C] a natural or artificial lake for storing and supplying water for an area • A reservoir is also a large supply of something that could be used if needed: *There's a tremendous reservoir of goodwill out there.*

reshuffle /riːˈʃʌf·əl/ v [T] to change the positions of people or things within (a group) • *It is rumored that the president will reshuffle his Cabinet.*

reside /rɪˈzaɪd/ v [I always + adv/prep] *fml* to live (in a place) • *The family resides in Arkansas.*

residence /ˈrez·əd·əns/ n [C/U] the place where someone lives, or the condition of living somewhere • *That big building is the Governor's official residence* (= home). [C] ○ *She took up residence in Boston* (= began living there). [U]

residency /ˈrez·əd·ən·si/ n [C/U] • *You have to establish residency requirements* (= live in a place long enough) *before you can apply for citizenship.* [U] • A residency is also a period of work, usually in a hospital, for a doctor to get practical experience and training in a special area of medicine. [C]

resident /ˈrez·əd·ənt/ n [C] someone who lives in a place • *The local residents were angry at the lack of parking spaces.* • A resident is also a doctor who is working, usually in a hospital, to get practical experience and training in a special area of medicine. [C]

residential /ˌrez·əˈden·tʃəl/ adj [not gradable] of or relating to houses where people live rather than to places where they work • *Glen Oaks is a residential neighborhood.*

residue /ˈrez·əˌduː/ n [C] something that is left after the main part is no longer present • *A residue of bitterness remained in the aftermath of the war.*

residual /rɪˈzɪdʒ·ə·wəl/ adj [not gradable] resulting or left from something that was previously present • *Residual oil has to be cleaned up.*

resign /rɪˈzaɪn/ v [I/T] to give up (a job or position) • *He resigned from the committee.* [I]

resignation /ˌrez·ɪgˈneɪ·ʃən/ n [C/U] • *a letter of resignation* [U] ○ *The athletic director announced his resignation.* [C]

◻**resign** *obj* **to** *obj* /-ˈ--/ v prep [T] to make (yourself) accept (something unpleasant) that cannot be changed • *He was resigned to living alone.*

resignation /ˌrez·ɪgˈneɪ·ʃən/ n [U] • *She received the disappointing news with resignation.*

resigned /rɪˈzaɪnd/ adj [not gradable] showing acceptance of something unpleasant • *They are resigned to losing money for at least the first year.*

resilient /rɪˈzɪl·jənt/ adj [not gradable] able to improve quickly after being hurt or being ill • *a tough and resilient enemy*

resilience /rɪˈzɪl·jəns/, **resiliency** /rɪˈzɪl·jən·si/ n [U]

resin /ˈrez·ən/ n [U] a clear, yellow, sticky substance produced by some trees and plants and used to make VARNISH, medicine, or plastics, or a similar substance produced chemically for use in industry

resist /rɪˈzɪst/ v [I/T] to fight against or oppose (something or someone) • *Students want to discover the truth themselves, and they resist having conclusions forced upon them.* [T] • To resist is also to keep or stop yourself from doing something: *I couldn't resist laughing at him.* [T]

resistance /rɪˈzɪs·təns/ n [U] • *A good diet helps the body to build up resistance to disease.* • (specialized) Resistance is the degree to which a substance prevents the flow of electricity through it: *Copper has low resistance.*

resistant /rɪˈzɪs·tənt/ adj not easily changed or damaged, or not accepting of (something) • *fire resistant* ○ *Why are you so resistant to change?*

resolute /ˈrez·əˌluːt/ adj determined in character, action, or ideas • *I admired her resolute optimism in those difficult times.*

resolutely /ˈrez·əˌluːt·li, ˌrez·əˈluːt-/ adv • *She resolutely refuses to lower her standards.*

resolution SOLUTION /ˌrez·əˈluː·ʃən/ n [C/U] the act of solving a problem or finding a way to improve a difficult situation • *Negotiators are working tirelessly for a swift resolution of this crisis.* [C]

resolution DECISION /ˌrez·əˈluː·ʃən/ n [C] a formal statement of decision or opinion • *The United Nations adopted a resolution to increase aid to the Third World.* [+ to infinitive] • If you make a resolution, you promise yourself to do something: *I made a New Year's resolution to lose ten pounds.* [+ to infinitive]

resolve SOLVE /rɪˈzɑlv, -ˈzɔːlv/ v [T] to solve or end (a problem or difficulty) • *The couple resolved their differences.*

resolve DECIDE /rɪˈzɑlv, -ˈzɔːlv/ v to make a determined decision • *They resolved that they would never argue over money.* [+ that clause] ○ *I resolved to run a mile a day.* [+ to infinitive]

resolve /rɪˈzɑlv, -ˈzɔːlv/ n [U] strong determination • *The experience increased her resolve to change careers.*

resolved /rɪˈzɑlvd, -ˈzɔːlvd/ adj • *He was resolved to quit smoking.* [+ to infinitive]

resonate /ˈrez·əˌneɪt/ v [I] to produce or be filled with clear, continuing sound • *The noise of the bell resonated through the building.*

resonance /ˈrez·ə·nəns/ n [U]

resonant /ˈrez·ə·nənt/ adj (of sound) clear and continuing • *a resonant voice*

resort /rɪˈzɔːrt/ n [C] a place where people can go on vacations for relaxation or for an activity they enjoy • *a ski resort*

resort to /rɪˈzɔːrtˌtuː, -tə/ v prep [T] to do or use (something) not because you prefer it but because there is no other choice available • *There's hope the countries will reach a settlement without resorting to armed conflict.*

resound /rɪˈzaʊnd/ v [I] to sound loudly or for

a long time, or (of a place) to be filled with sound • *The air resounds with the delightful music of birds.*

resounding /rɪ'zaʊn·dɪŋ/ *adj* very great; complete • *The remake of the movie was a resounding success.*

resource /'riː·sɔːrs, -zɔːrs/ *n* [C] something that can be used to help you • *The library was a valuable resource, and he frequently made use of it.* • Resources are natural substances such as water and wood which are valuable in supporting life: *The earth has limited resources, and if we don't recycle them we use them up.* [pl] • Resources are also things of value such as money or possessions that you can use when you need them: *The government doesn't have the resources to hire the number of teachers needed.* [pl]

resourceful /rɪ'sɔːrs·fəl, -'zɔːrs-/ *adj* able to find and use different ways to help achieve your goals • *She plays the part of a tough, resourceful newspaper reporter.*

respect ADMIRATION /rɪ'spekt/ *n* [U] admiration for someone or something that you believe has good ideas or qualities • *I believe people had more respect for teachers back then.*

respect /rɪ'spekt/ *v* [T] to admire (an ability or good quality), or to admire (someone) for their ability or qualities • *While I respected his deep knowledge of American history, he wasn't a very effective teacher.*

respect POLITE ATTITUDE /rɪ'spekt/ *n* [U] the polite attitude shown toward someone or something that you consider important • *Some drivers don't have any respect for other motorists.* • Respects are polite expressions of greeting, friendship, or sympathy: *Give my respects to your parents.* [pl] ○ *We stopped by the funeral home to pay our respects.* [pl]

respect /rɪ'spekt/ *v* [T] • *We should try to respect one another no matter what we believe.*

respectful /rɪ'spekt·fəl/ *adj* • *The protestors were respectful and polite.*

respectfully /rɪ'spekt·fə·li/ *adv* • *Most old acquaintances address him respectfully as "Governor."*

respect FEATURE /rɪ'spekt/ *n* [C] a particular feature or detail • *In some respects, I had to admit, I had behaved foolishly.*

respectable /rɪ'spek·tə·bəl/ *adj* socially acceptable because of having a good character or appearance or behaving in a way that is approved of • *It was hard to find a clean shirt that looked respectable enough to be seen in.* • Respectable also means large enough or good enough to be acceptable: *a respectable income* ○ *Her school has a respectable basketball program.*

respectability /rɪˌspek·tə'bɪl·ət·i/ *n* [U] • *Everything in the hotel had an air of old-time respectability.*

respectively /rɪ'spek·tɪv·li/ *adv* [not gradable] (of two or more items) with each relating to something previously mentioned, in the same order as first mentioned • *George and Kenneth were married in 1980 and 1985, respectively.*

respective /rɪ'spek·tɪv/ *adj* [not gradable] • *Barkley and Jordan are the two best players on their respective* (= separate) *teams.*

respiratory /'res·pə·rəˌtɔːr·i, -ˌtoʊr·i/ *adj* [not gradable] of or relating to breathing • *respiratory infections*

respirator /'res·pəˌreɪt·ər/ *n* [C] a device that forces air into a person's lungs to help them to breathe when they cannot breathe independently • *Miya was hooked up to a respirator at University Hospital.*

respiration /ˌres·pə'reɪ·ʃən/ *n* [U] *medical* the process of breathing

respite /'res·pət, rɪ'spaɪt/ *n* [C/U] a pause or rest from something difficult or unpleasant • *The center provides a respite for teens in trouble.* [C usually sing]

resplendent /rɪ'splen·dənt/ *adj slightly fml* (esp. of a person's clothes or jewelry) beautiful and seeming to shine, esp. because they are fashionable and expensive • *a white hat resplendent with red velvet flowers*

respond /rɪ'spɑnd/ *v* [I] to say or do something as a reaction to something that has been said or done • *I want to respond to something that Norman said.* • If a disease responds to treatment, the harmful effects of the disease begin to lessen.

response /rɪ'spɑns/ *n* [C/U] something said or done as a reaction to something that has been said or done; an answer or reaction • *She's applied for admission and is still waiting for a response from the school.* [C] • *The law was passed by the town council* **in response to** (= acting as a result of) *complaints from residents.*

responsive /rɪ'spɑn·sɪv/ *adj* quick to act, esp. to meet the needs of someone or something • *He had promised a government responsive to the people.*

responsible DUTY /rɪ'spɑn·sə·bəl/ *adj* having the duty of taking care of something • *The government's Energy Regulatory Board is responsible for nuclear safety.* • A responsible job/position is an important one involving control and authority over something.

responsibility /rɪˌspɑn·sə'bɪl·ət·i/ *n* [C/U] • *With this promotion, Jorge's responsibilities will be increased.* [C] ○ *Parents must assume responsibility for their children.* [U]

responsible BLAME /rɪ'spɑn·sə·bəl/ *adj* being the cause of a particular action or situation, esp. a harmful or unpleasant one • *We are not responsible for things getting lost in the mail.*

responsibility /rɪˌspɑn·sə'bɪl·ət·i/ *n* [U] • *A terrorist group claimed responsibility for the attack.*

responsible GOOD JUDGMENT /rɪ'spɑn·sə·bəl/ *adj* having good judgment and the ability to act correctly and make decisions on your own • *We want to be responsible citizens.*

responsibly /rɪˈspɑn·sə·bli/ *adv* • *Parties are permitted, so long as everyone behaves responsibly.*

rest RELAX /rest/ *v* [I/T] to stop being active for a period of time in order to relax and get back your strength, or to cause (someone or something) to stop doing an activity so that they can get back their strength • *We hiked for five miles and then rested for a while.* [I] ○ *The coach decided to rest some of the team's starters tomorrow night.* [T] ○ *I just need to sit down and rest my legs.* [T] • **Rest in peace** is a religious phrase people say to show respect for a dead person: *the late Pat McLaughlin, may he rest in peace*

rest /rest/ *n* [C/U] • *What you need is a nice long rest.* [C] ○ *The doctor told him to get plenty of rest and drink lots of fluids.* [U] • **At rest** means not doing anything active or not moving: *The cat seemed coiled to spring, even when it was at rest.* • A **restroom** is a room in a public building in which there are toilets. • A **rest area/rest stop** is a place beside a large road where a vehicle can stop and where toilets, food, and fuel are often available.

restful /ˈrest·fəl/ *adj* causing a feeling of calmness • *The island was quiet and restful and so beautiful.*

restless /ˈrest·ləs/ *adj* moving around because you are unable to relax, esp. because you are worried or bored, or (of an activity) characterized by a lot of movement • *He dozed off to a restless sleep.* ○ *The audience began to get restless.* • Restless can also mean not satisfied with your situation and wanting a change: *The opposition parties provide no clear alternative for restless voters.*

restlessly /ˈrest·lə·sli/ *adv* • *I wandered restlessly around the apartment.*

restlessness /ˈrest·lə·snəs/ *n* [U] • *He went hunting out of sheer restlessness.*

rest STAY /rest/ *v* [I] to be or stay under the control of a particular person or organization • *The final decision rests with the City Council.* • *You can* **rest assured** *that you're going to get a good deal* (= feel certain this will happen).

rest SUPPORT /rest/ *v* [I/T] to lie or lean on something, or to put (something) on something else so that its weight is supported • *She rested her head against my belly.* [T] • **To rest on** something is to depend on it: *Our whole legal system rests on the notion of personal responsibility.* • *The company can hardly afford to* **rest on** *its* **laurels** (= feel comfortable because it has been successful in the past).

rest OTHER PART /rest/ *n* [U] the other things, people, or parts that are left • *I want to do something else with the rest of my life.*

restaurant /ˈres·tə·rɑnt, -tə-rɑnt/ *n* [C] a place of business where people can choose a meal to be prepared and served to them at a table, and

for which they pay, usually after eating • *c Chinese/Italian/Mexican restaurant*

restaurateur /ˌres·tə·rəˈtɜr/ *n* [C] a person who owns or manages a restaurant

restitution /ˌres·təˈtuː·ʃən/ *n* [U] *law* payment for damage or loss of property, or the return of items stolen or lost • *The company ha. agreed to make restitution of $44,930 and to pay an equal fine.*

restive /ˈres·tɪv/ *adj* slightly *fml* unwilling to be controlled or be patient • *The crowd began to get restive during the long wait for the con cert to begin.*

restore /rɪˈstɔːr, -ˈstoʊr/ *v* [T] to return (something or someone) to an earlier condition or position, or to bring (something) back into existence • *Power company crews were work ing yesterday to restore electrical service t homes in the area.* ○ *Surgeons restored the sigh. in her right eye.*

restoration /ˌres·təˈreɪ·ʃən/ *n* [C/U] the act or the process of returning something to its orig inal condition, or to a state similar to its orig inal condition • *She is in charge of the restora tion of paintings in the collection.* [U] ○ *Elis has worked on a number of 19th-century build ing restorations.* [C]

restrain /rɪˈstreɪn/ *v* [T] to control (the actions or behavior of someone) by force, esp. in or der to stop them from doing something • *Sea mons got into a shouting match and had to be restrained by his teammates.* ○ *I could hardl restrain my laughter.* • To restrain is also to limit the growth or force of something: *Politi cians are reluctant to restrain spending.*

restrained /rɪˈstreɪnd/ *adj* • *Considering the abuse they receive from fans, athletes are re markably restrained* (= calm and controlled).

restraint /rɪˈstreɪnt/ *n* [C/U] determined con trol over behavior in order to prevent the strong expression of emotion or any violent action • *You really have to show a lot of re straint to stay out of debt.* [U] • A restraint is something that limits freedom of movement action, or growth: *Social restraints seem to have become dangerously unrestrictive.* [C]

restrict /rɪˈstrɪkt/ *v* [T] to limit (an intended action) esp. by setting the conditions under which it is allowed to happen • *The state legis lature voted to restrict development in the area.* ○ *Efforts are under way to further restrict ciga rette advertising.*

restricted /rɪˈstrɪk·təd/ *adj* • *Many events are free, so families on restricted budgets can par ticipate.*

restriction /rɪˈstrɪk·ʃən/ *n* [C/U] • *You can ge a discount fare, but some restrictions* (= rules about limits) *apply.* [C]

restrictive /rɪˈstrɪk·tɪv/ *adj* • *She campaigned against restrictive immigration laws.*

restructure /riːˈstrʌk·tʃər/ *v* [T] to change (the jobs and responsibilities within an organization), usually in order to make the organization operate more effectively • *The commission developed guidelines for restructuring the city's police department.*

result /rɪˈzʌlt/ *n* [C] something that happens or exists because of something else • *The mayor says crime is lower as a result of good police work.* ○ *A lot of people survived the crash as a direct result of the excellent training our pilots and flight attendants receive.* • Results are what you discover after examining something: *The election results show that the governor is not as popular as she was two years ago.* ○ *Results of the medical tests showed no sign of cancer.*

result /rɪˈzʌlt/ *v* [I] • *Weeks of negotiations resulted in an agreement.* ○ *The flight delay resulted from mechanical problems.*

resume /rɪˈzuːm/ *v* [I/T] to start (something) again after a pause or period of time • *Almost half of smokers who quit resume smoking.* [T] ○ *Government officials hoped talks will resume.* [I]

résumé, resume /ˈrez·əˌmeɪ/ *n* [C] a written statement of your educational and work experience, used esp. when you are trying to get a new job

resumption /rɪˈzʌmp·ʃən/ *n* [U] the act of starting something again after a pause or period of time • *He worked for the resumption of economic ties between Vietnam and the US.*

resurface COVER /riːˈsɜr·fəs/ *v* [T] to put a new surface on (a road) • *Expect delays while they resurface the highway.*

resurface APPEAR /riːˈsɜr·fəs/ *v* [I] to appear again after not being seen or heard • *His ex-girlfriend suddenly resurfaced.*

resurgence /rɪˈsɜr·dʒəns/ *n* [C/U] an increase of activity or interest in a particular subject or idea which had been forgotten for some time • *There's been a resurgence of criticism of the president.* [C usually sing]

resurrect /ˌrez·əˈrekt/ *v* [T] to bring (someone) back to life, or bring (something) back into use or existence after it disappeared • *Buckley enjoys resurrecting some of the more obscure words of the English language.*

resurrection /ˌrez·əˈrek·ʃən/ *n* [U] • *the resurrection of his political career* • In the Christian religion, the Resurrection is Jesus Christ's return to life after his death.

resuscitate /rɪˈsʌs·əˌteɪt/ *v* [I/T] to bring (someone who is dying or unconscious) back to life or consciousness, or bring (something) back into use or existence • *You should learn how to resuscitate a person whose breathing has stopped.* [T] ○ *He led the effort to resuscitate the local newspaper.* [T]

retail /ˈriː·teɪl/ *n* [U] the activity of selling goods to the public, usually in small amounts, for their own use • Compare WHOLESALE SELLING.

retail /ˈriː·teɪl/ *adj, adv* [not gradable] • *Retail*

sales are rising. ○ *The company has three retail outlets/stores in the Washington area.*

retail /ˈriː·teɪl/ *v* [I/T] to sell (goods) to the public, usually in small amounts, for their own use • *Country Miss makes and retails sportswear.* [T] ○ *The wine retails for $11.* [I]

retailer /ˈriː·teɪ·lər/ *n* [C] • *If you bought it there, you can't take it back to another retailer.*

retain /rɪˈteɪn/ *v* [T] to keep or continue to have (something) • *Francis retained control of the company.* ○ *His capacity to retain* (= remember) *facts was as keen as ever, but he had trouble remembering people's names.*

retake /riːˈteɪk/ *v* [T] *past simple* **retook** /riːˈtʊk/, *past part* **retaken** /riːˈteɪ·kən/ to take (something) into possession again, esp. by force • *He ordered his troops to prepare to retake the town.*

retaliate /rɪˈtæl·iːˌeɪt/ *v* [I] to hurt someone or do something harmful to them because they have done or said something harmful to you • *The pitcher threw at a couple of our guys and hit one of them, but we didn't retaliate.*

retaliation /rɪˌtæl·iːˈeɪ·ʃən/ *n* [U] • *The enemy attacked air bases in retaliation for the bombing.*

retard /rɪˈtard/ *v* [T] to make (something) slower • *Reductions in pollution levels could retard global warming.*

retard /ˈriː·tard/ *n* [C] *rude slang* a person you do not like and consider stupid

retarded /rɪˈtard·əd/ *adj* having a slower mental development than other people of the same age • *mentally/emotionally retarded* • USAGE: Because retarded has sometimes been used as a term of insult, it is now less often used as a specialized term in the care of people with slow mental development.

retardation /ˌriː·tarˈdeɪ·ʃən/ *n* [U] *fml* the process of making something happen or develop slower than it should

retch /retʃ/ *v* [I] to make the sound and action of vomiting, esp. when nothing is actually vomited

retention /rɪˈten·tʃən/ *n* [U] the ability to keep or continue having something • *Officials are focusing on job creation, not job retention.*

retentive /rɪˈtent·ɪv/ *adj* • *a retentive memory*

rethink /riːˈθɪŋk/ *v* [T] *past* **rethought** /riːˈθɔːt/ to think again about (something, such as a plan) in order to change or improve it • *It's time to rethink whether we need a part-time or full-time mayor.*

reticent /ˈret·ə·sənt/ *adj* unwilling to speak about your thoughts or feelings • *At first she was reticent, but later she relaxed and was more forthcoming.*

reticence /ˈret·ə·səns/ *n* [U] • *Due to his reticence, little is known about his personal life.*

retina /ˈret·ən·ə/ *n* [C] the area at the back of the eye that receives light and sends an image to the brain so that seeing can happen

retinue /ˈret·ənˌuː/ *n* [C] *slightly fml* a group

of helpers and followers who travel with an important person • *He jets around the country with a retinue of aides and attorneys.*

retire STOP WORKING /rɪˈtaɪr/ *v* [I/T] to leave your job or stop working because of having reached a particular age or because of ill health, or to cause (someone or something) to stop being employed or used • *He worked in television after retiring from baseball.* [I] ○ *I'll be retiring soon.* [I] ○ *The aircraft was retired in 1990.* [T]

retired /rɪˈtaɪrd/ *adj* [not gradable] • *He is a retired airline pilot.*

retirement /rɪˈtaɪr·mənt/ *n* [C/U] the point at which someone stops working, esp. because of having reached a particular age or because of ill health, or the period in someone's life after they have stopped working • *He announced his retirement in September.* [C]

retiree /rɪˌtaɪˈriː/ *n* [C] • *Florida and Arizona are the most popular states for retirees* (= people who have stopped working).

retire LEAVE A PLACE /rɪˈtaɪr/ *v* [I] *fml* to leave a room or group of people and go somewhere quiet or private • *The judge retired to her study to review the case.* • *To retire also means to go to bed.*

retiring /rɪˈtaɪr·ɪŋ/ *adj* unwilling to be noticed or to be with other people • *He's a shy, retiring sort of person.*

retort /rɪˈtɔːrt/ *v* [T] to make a quick answer that is often amusing and sometimes expresses anger or annoyance • *When the telephone operator called him boy, he retorted, "That's Mr. Boy to you!"*

retort /rɪˈtɔːrt/ *n* [C]

retouch /riːˈtʌtʃ/ *v* [T] to make small changes to (esp. a picture or photograph) in order to improve it • *Photographs do not lie, unless they are retouched.*

retrace /riːˈtreɪs/ *v* [T] to go back over (a path or a series of past actions) • *This trail is not circular, so you have to retrace your steps back to the start.*

retract /rɪˈtrækt/ *v* [I/T] to say publicly that you will not do (something you had said you would do), or to admit that (something that you had said was true is false) • *She had to retract statements in published articles.* [T] • To retract is also to pull something back or in: *The pilot retracted the landing gear soon after takeoff.* [T]

retractable /rɪˈtræk·tə·bəl/ *adj* [not gradable] • *Cats have retractable claws* (= they can be pulled back).

retread /ˈriː·tred/ *n* [C] a worn tire that has had a new rubber surface joined to its outer part

retreat /rɪˈtriːt/ *v* [I] to move back and away from someone or something, esp. because you are frightened or want to be alone • *She burst into tears and retreated to the bedroom.* • To retreat is also to go away from a person or place

because you are unwilling to fight any more: *Under heavy fire, the soldiers retreated.*

retreat /rɪˈtriːt/ *n* [C/U] the act of going away from a person or place because you are unwilling to fight any more or are frightened • *Rebel soldiers were in (full) retreat.* [U] • A retreat is also a private and safe place where you can be alone. [C]

retrial /ˈriː·traɪl/ *n* [C] a new trial of a law case • *The appeals court ordered a retrial.*

retribution /ˌre·trəˈbjuː·ʃən/ *n* [U] *fml* deserved punishment • *He was seeking retribution for the crime committed against him.*

retrieve /rɪˈtriːv/ *v* [T] to find and bring back (something) • *Her grandson had jumped into a nearby yard to retrieve a ball when he was attacked by the dogs.*

retrieval /rɪˈtriː·vəl/ *n* [U] • *information storage and retrieval*

retroactive /ˌre·trouˈæk·tɪv/ *adj* [not gradable] (of a law or other agreement) having effect from the time before the law or agreement was approved • *I'm getting a retroactive salary increase.*

retroactively /ˌre·trouˈæk·tɪv·li/ *adv* [not gradable] • *The courts cannot apply a new rule retroactively.*

retrospect /ˈre·trəˌspekt/ *n* • When something that happened in the past is considered **in retrospect**, it is thought about now: *In retrospect, I think their marriage was doomed from the beginning.*

retrospective /ˌre·trəˈspek·tɪv/ *adj* looking back over the past • *He was the subject of a retrospective exhibit.*

return GO BACK /rɪˈtɜrn/ *v* [I] to come or go back to a previous place, subject, activity, or condition • *He returned to New York last week.* ○ *He worked at other jobs but kept returning to mining.* ○ *She was returning home from a business trip when the plane crashed.*

return /rɪˈtɜrn/ *n* [C] • *She looked forward to the return of spring.* ○ *On her return* (= When she came back), *she decided to take a few days off.*

return /rɪˈtɜrn/ *adj* [not gradable] • *return postage* • A **return address** is the address from which a letter is being sent.

return PUT BACK /rɪˈtɜrn/ *v* [T] to put, send, or give (something) back to where it came from • *Emily returned the blouse because it didn't fit.*

return EXCHANGE /rɪˈtɜrn/ *v* [T] to give, do, or get (something) in exchange • *She just doesn't return phone calls.*

return /rɪˈtɜrn/ *n* • **In return for** means as an exchange for: *We got someone to do housekeeping in return for room and board.*

return DECIDE /rɪˈtɜrn/ *v* [T] *fml* to decide on (something such as a judgment or decision) • *The jury returned a verdict of not guilty.*

returns /rɪˈtɜrn/ *pl n* the results of voting in an ELECTION (= a political competition) • *Officials haven't finished counting the returns yet.*

reunion /riː'juːn·jən/ n [C] a gathering of people who have been together before, esp. as a special event at a planned time • *a family reunion* ○ *a high school reunion*

reunite /ˌriː·juˈnɑɪt/ v [I/T] to bring together again • *He was reunited with his sister after 14 years.* [T]

reuse /riː'juːz/ v [T] to use (something) again • *We reuse our grocery bags.*

reusable /riː'juː·zə·bəl/ adj [not gradable] • *reusable containers*

rev /rev/ v [I/T] **-vv-** to increase the speed of (the engine of a vehicle) while the vehicle is not moving • *He was revving (up) his engine.* [T/M]

revamp /riː'væmp/ v [T] to change (something), or to make or arrange (something) differently, in order to improve it • *This country's health care system needs revamping.*

reveal *(obj)* /rɪ'viːl/ v to make known or show (something usually secret or hidden) • *She revealed her sexual history to him because she thought it was important.* [T] ○ *X-rays revealed that my ribs had been cracked but not broken.* [+ *that* clause]

revealing /rɪ'viː·lɪŋ/ adj showing more of the body than is usual • *a revealing blouse* • Revealing also means explaining more than you might expect: *The book provides a revealing glimpse of how the organization works.*

revel /'rev·əl/ v [I] **-l-** or **-ll-** literary or humorous to dance, drink, sing, and enjoy yourself with others, esp. in a noisy way • *Cowboys from miles around come here to drink, gamble, and revel.* • To **revel in** a situation or an activity is to get great pleasure from it: *They reveled in their success.*

revelry /'rev·əl·ri/ n [C] the activity of a noisy party or other celebration

revelation /ˌrev·ə'leɪ·ʃən/ n [C/U] the act of making known something that was secret, or a fact that has been made known • *What a revelation it was to discover that even thieves can be victims of theft.* [C]

revenge /rɪ'vendʒ/ n [U] harm that you do to someone as a punishment for harm that they have done to you • *He had been seeking a chance for revenge against those who had helped oust him from his leadership position in Congress.*

revenue /'rev·ə,nuː/ n [C/U] the income that a business or government receives regularly, or an amount representing such income • *state/federal revenues* [C usually pl] ○ *Company revenue rose 4% last year.* [U]

reverberate /rɪ'vɜr·bə,reɪt/ v [I] (of sound) to continue to be heard; to ECHO repeatedly • *The rifle shot reverberated in the mountains.*

revere /rɪ'vɪr/ v [T] slightly fml to greatly respect and admire (someone or something) • *Nelson Mandela is widely revered for his courage and leadership.*

reverence /'rev·ə·rəns/ n [U] • *Most Ameri-*

cans have little reverence for their political leaders.

Reverend /'rev·rənd, -ə·rənd/ *(abbreviation* **Rev.)** n [C] a title for a member of the Christian CLERGY (= official workers of the church) • *I'd like you to meet Reverend Smith.*

reverie /'rev·ə·ri/ n [C/U] literary (a state of having) pleasant dreamlike thoughts • *She was lost in reverie.* [U]

reversal /rɪ'vɜr·səl/ n [C/U] a complete change of direction, order, or position • *In a significant reversal of earlier trends, people are moving back to Salt Lake City.* [C]

reverse /rɪ'vɜrs/ v [I/T] to cause (something) to go in the opposite direction, order, or position • *The group is trying to reverse the trend toward developing the wetlands.* [T]

reverse /rɪ'vɜrs/ n [C/U] • *A car came down the street in reverse.* [U] • A reverse is also a defeat or failure: *He suffered a series of financial reverses in the 1980s.* [C]

reverse /rɪ'vɜrs/ adj [not gradable] • *Repeat the steps in reverse order to shut the system off.* • **Reverse discrimination** is the practice of giving an unfair advantage to people who are thought to have been treated unfairly in the past, such as African-Americans or women.

reversible /rɪ'vɜr·sə·bəl/ adj • *a reversible condition* • Something that is reversible can be placed or worn with either side out: *a reversible jacket*

reversion /rɪ'vɜr·ʒən/ n [U] fml a change back to a previous and often worse condition • *Reversion to the wild isn't easy for a captive animal.*

revert to /rɪ'vɜrt/ v prep [T] to go back to (a previous condition) • *The money will revert to the state general fund if it isn't claimed.*

review /rɪ'vjuː/ v [I/T] to consider (something) in order to make changes in it, study it, or give an opinion about it • *Officials have to review the text before it's made public.* [T] ○ *Pauline Kael reviewed (movies)* (= wrote opinions about movies) *for "The New Yorker".* [I/T] ○ *She spent half the night reviewing her notes for the French test* (= studying them again). [T]

review /rɪ'vjuː/ n [C/U] • *The proposed budget is under review.* [U] ○ *Cash's work got rave reviews* (= published opinions of it were good). [C] ○ *The teacher devoted the last week of the semester to (a) review* (= studying again what was taught). [C/U]

reviewer /rɪ'vjuː·ər/ n [C] someone who writes articles expressing their opinion of a book, play, movie, etc. • *She's the restaurant reviewer for "The Times".*

revile /rɪ'vɑɪl/ v [T] to criticize (someone) strongly • *Works of art are often reviled when they are first produced.*

revise /rɪ'vɑɪz/ v [I/T] to change or correct (something, esp. a piece of writing) • *With the final exam, you don't revise it after the teacher* *reads it.* [T] • (*Br*) To revise is to study again what you have been learning in order to prepare for an exam. [I/T]

revised /rɪˈvaɪzd/ *adj* [not gradable] • *Her book is available in a new revised edition.*

revision /rɪˈvɪʒ·ən/ *n* [C/U] the act of changing or correcting (something, esp. a piece of writing), or the thing that has been changed or corrected • *The Senate is expected to act on tax revision.* [U]

revitalize /riːˈvaɪt̬·ᵊlˌaɪz/ *v* [T] to put new life or energy into (something) • *to revitalize a city/the economy*

revive /rɪˈvaɪv/ *v* [I/T] to come back to life, health, existence, or use, or bring (something) back to such a state • *She tried to revive the unconscious woman.* [T] ○ *My plants revived as soon as I gave them a little water.* [I]

revival /rɪˈvaɪ·vəl/ *n* [C/U] • *There's been a revival of ancient disputes in the region.* [C] • A revival is also a performance of a play which has not been seen for a long time: *a revival of Pinter's 1960 play* [C] • A revival or **revival meeting** is a Christian religious meeting: *People sang loudly and clapped their hands at the revival.* [C]

revoke /rɪˈvoʊk/ *v* [T] to say officially that (an agreement, permission, or law) is no longer effective • *His license was revoked after two drunk-driving convictions.*

revolt FIGHT /rɪˈvoʊlt/ *v* [I] to take violent action against authority, or to refuse to be controlled or ruled • *Californians may be ready to revolt against broad cuts in government services.*

revolt /rɪˈvoʊlt/ *n* [C/U] • *a spirit of revolt* [U] ○ *The punk movement was a revolt against both the sound and the system of popular music.* [C]

revolt DISGUST /rɪˈvoʊlt/ *v* [T] to make (someone) feel disgusted • *I was revolted by his cruelty.*

revolting /rɪˈvoʊl·tɪŋ/ *adj* • *She finds the idea of shooting animals really revolting.*

revolution /ˌrev·əˈluː·ʃən/ *n* [C/U] a sudden and great change, esp. the violent change of a system of government • *The country seems to be heading toward revolution.* [U] ○ *The discovery of penicillin produced a revolution in medicine.* [C] • See also **revolution** at REVOLVE.

revolutionary /ˌrev·əˈluː·ʃəˌner·i/ *adj* relating to a complete change in a system of government, or bringing or causing great change • *a revolutionary leader/program/idea* ○ *Computers have brought revolutionary changes to publishing.*

revolutionary /ˌrev·əˈluː·ʃəˌner·i/ *n* [C] a person who supports or takes part in a revolution

revolutionize /ˌrev·əˈluː·ʃəˌnaɪz/ *v* [T] to produce a very great or complete change in (something) • *Newton's discoveries revolutionized physics.*

revolve /rɪˈvɑlv, -ˈvɔːlv/ *v* [I/T] to move in a circle or a curve around a central point, or to cause (something) to do this • *The plane revolved 162 degrees onto its back.* [T] ○ *The earth revolves around the sun, roughly in a circle.* [I] ○ (*fig.*) *His life revolves around* (= He is only interested in) *football.* [I] • A **revolving door** is a set of doors which you go through by pushing them around in a circle.

revolving door

revolution /ˌrev·əˈluː·ʃən/ *n* [C/U] • *The moon makes one revolution around the earth in about 29.5 days.* [C] • See also REVOLUTION.

revolver /rɪˈvɑl·vər, -ˈvɔːl-/ *n* [C] a small gun that is held in one hand and can be fired several times before needing more bullets

revue /rɪˈvjuː/ *n* [C] a theatrical show with songs, dances, jokes, and short plays, often about recent events

revulsion /rɪˈvʌl·ʃən/ *n* [U] a strong, often sudden, feeling of dislike or disgust • *Most of us feel only revulsion from such crimes.*

reward /rɪˈwɔːrd/ *n* [C/U] something given in exchange for a useful idea, good behavior, excellent work, etc. • *Students hoped for more reward than an announcement in the school paper of their achievement.* [U] ○ *The rewards* (= benefits) *of motherhood outweigh the difficulties.* [C] • A reward is also an amount of money given to someone who gives information about a crime to the police or who helps to return lost or stolen property to its owner. [C]

reward /rɪˈwɔːrd/ *v* [T] • *He was rewarded for his bravery with a medal from the president.*

rewarding /rɪˈwɔːrd·ɪŋ/ *adj* satisfying or beneficial • *a rewarding experience*

rewind /riːˈwaɪnd/ *v* [T] *past* **rewound** /riːˈwaʊnd/ to put (a TAPE recording) back to the beginning

rework /riːˈwɜrk/ *v* [T] to change (esp. a speech, other writing, or drawing) to make it better or more suitable for a particular purpose

rewrite /riːˈraɪt/ *v* [T] *past simple* **rewrote** /riːˈroʊt/, *past part* **rewritten** /riːˈrɪt·ᵊn/ to write (a book, speech, etc.) again to improve or change it or to correct information in it

rewrite /ˈriːˌraɪt/ n [C] • *The producer says the last scene in the play needs a rewrite.*

rhapsody /ˈræp·səd·i/ n [C] a piece of music written without a formal structure that expresses powerful feelings and emotional excitement • *Gershwin's "Rhapsody in Blue"*

rhetoric /ˈret̬·ə·rɪk/ n [U] speech or writing that is effective and persuasive • *(disapproving)* Rhetoric is also language, esp. speech, that contains few ideas or lacks real meaning, even though it sounds good: *The candidate's speech was full of empty rhetoric.*

rhetorical /rɪˈtɔːr·ɪ·kəl, -ˈtɑr-/ adj • A **rhetorical question** is a statement made in the form of a question with no expectation of an answer.

rhetorically /rɪˈtɔːr·ɪ·kli, -ˈtɑr-/ adv • *"Why did this happen to me?" she asked rhetorically.*

rheumatism /ˈruː·məˌtɪz·əm/ n [U] a medical condition that causes stiffness and pain in the joints or muscles

rhinestone /ˈraɪnˌstoʊn/ n [C] a bright, colorless, artificial jewel that looks like a DIAMOND

rhinoceros (*pl* **rhinoceroses** or **rhinoceros**) /raɪˈnɑs·ə·rəs/, *short form* **rhino** /ˈraɪ·noʊ/ n [C] a very large, thick-skinned animal that eats plants and has one or two horns on its nose

rhododendron /ˌroʊd·əˈden·drən/ n [C] a large evergreen bush with flat, glossy leaves and bright pink, purple, or white flowers

rhubarb /ˈruː·bɑrb/ n [U] the long red stems of a plant that are prepared in a pie or as a sweet fruit dish

rhyme /raɪm/ v [I/T] (of words) to have the same final sound, or to use (words) that have the same final sound • *"Love" and "above" rhyme.* [I]

rhyme /raɪm/ n [C/U] • *Can you think of a rhyme for "orange"?* [C] ○ *She does not use rhyme in her poems.* [U] • If something has no **rhyme or reason**, it means that there is no obvious explanation for it: *Her strange behavior is without rhyme or reason.*

rhythm /ˈrɪð·əm/ n [C/U] a regularly repeated pattern of sounds or beats used in music, poems, and dances • *a jazz rhythm* [C] ○ *You need a sense of rhythm to be a good dancer.* [U] • Rhythm is also a regular movement: *The rhythm of a boat rocking in the water lulled him to sleep.* [C] • Rhythm is also a regular pattern of change: *Waking and sleeping are examples of biological rhythms.* [C] • **Rhythm and blues** (also **R & B**) is a type of popular music with a strong beat and jazz influence, developed by African-Americans in the 1940s and 1950s.

rhythmic /ˈrɪð·mɪk/, **rhythmical** /ˈrɪð·mɪ·kəl/ adj • *The rhythmic sound of the rain on the roof put the child to sleep.*

rib BONE /rɪb/ n [C] one of the bones that curve around from the SPINE (= the line of bones down the center of the back) on each side of the upper part of the body to form the chest •

A rib is also a piece of meat taken from this part of an animal: *barbecued ribs* • Ribs are also the thin, curved pieces of metal or wood that shape and support the sides and bottom of a boat or the top of an umbrella. • A person's or animal's **rib cage** is the part of the chest supported by the ribs that surrounds and protects the heart and lungs.

rib JOKE /rɪb/ v [T] **-bb-** *infml* to laugh at or joke about (someone) in a friendly way; TEASE • *His brothers ribbed him about his new girlfriend.*

ribald /ˈrɪb·əld, ˈraɪ·bɔːld/ adj (of language) rude and humorous, often in reference to sex

ribbon /ˈrɪb·ən/ n [C/U] a long, narrow strip of material used to tie things together or as a decoration • *He tied the present with ribbon.* [U] ○ *(fig.) A ribbon of road stretched before us.* [C] • A ribbon is also the narrow strip of material that contains the ink for a TYPEWRITER or computer PRINTER. [C]

rice /raɪs/ n [U] the small brown or white seeds produced by a grass plant that are a major food source in many countries, or the plant itself, which is grown in warm, wet places • A **rice paddy** is a flooded field in which rice is grown. • **Rice pudding** is a sweet dish made by cooking rice in milk and sugar.

rich WEALTHY /rɪtʃ/ adj [-er/-est only] having a lot of money or valuable possessions; wealthy • *a rich man* ○ *The United States is one of the world's richest nations.* • Rich also means made of something luxurious and costly; expensive, valuable: *a rich brocade jacket*

rich /rɪtʃ/ pl n people who have a lot of money or valuable possessions • *The resort is crowded with the rich and famous in winter.*

riches /ˈrɪtʃ·əz/ pl n great wealth

rich HAVING A LOT /rɪtʃ/ adj [-er/-est only] having or containing a large amount of something desirable or valuable • *The country is rich in oil, minerals, and timber.* ○ *Orange juice is rich in vitamin C.* ○ *The island has a rich and complex history* • Earth that is rich contains a large amount of substances that help plants to grow. • If the style or decoration of something, such as a piece of furniture or a building, is rich, it has a large amount of costly and beautiful decoration.

riches /ˈrɪtʃ·əz/ pl n a large amount of something desirable or valuable • *oil/mineral/cultural riches*

richly /ˈrɪtʃ·li/ adv [not gradable] to a great degree • *a richly stocked wine cellar* ○ *a richly deserved reward* ○ *a richly decorated church*

richness /ˈrɪtʃ·nəs/ n [U] • *the richness of detail* ○ *the richness of Mexico's history*

rich FOOD /rɪtʃ/ adj [-er/-est only] (of food) containing a large amount of oil, butter, eggs, or cream • *This chocolate butter cream is too rich for me.*

richness /ˈrɪtʃ·nəs/ n [U] • *The richness of the food made him feel slightly ill.*

736

rich COLOR / SOUND /rɪtʃ/ *adj* [*-er/-est* only] (of a color, sound, smell, or taste) strong in a pleasing or attractive way • *The fields were bathed in a rich, red-gold light from the setting sun.* ○ *He has a rich, resonant voice.*

rickety /'rɪk·ət̬·i/ *adj* in bad condition or weak and therefore likely to break • *a rickety old chair*

ricochet /'rɪk·ə,ʃeɪ/ *v* [I] (of a ball, bullet, or other small object) to bounce off a surface • *The ball ricocheted off the goalie's foot and into the net.*

ricochet /'rɪk·ə,ʃeɪ/ *n* [C] • *He was downed by a ricochet during the shootout.*

ricotta /rə'kɑt̬·ə/ *n* [U] soft, white Italian cheese that does not have a strong flavor

rid /rɪd/ *v* [T] *past* **rid** to free (a person or place) of something unwanted or harmful • *In the city, it is hard to rid a building permanently of pests.*

riddle QUESTION /'rɪd·əl/ *n* [C] a word puzzle in the form of a question, or something that remains a mystery or is hard to explain • *Scholars have not completely solved the riddle of the sphinx.*

riddle MAKE HOLES /'rɪd·əl/ *v* [T] to make a lot of holes in (something) • *Gunfire from the ground riddled the plane with bullets.*

riddled /'rɪd·əld/ *adj* [not gradable] full of (something unwanted) • *an old sweater riddled with holes* ○ *a book riddled with errors*

ride /raɪd/ *v* [I/T] *past simple* **rode** /roʊd/, *past part* **ridden** /'rɪd·ən/ to sit on (a horse, bicycle, etc.) and travel on it while controlling its movements, or to travel in a vehicle, such as a car, bus, or train • *I ride to work on my bike.* [I] ○ *We rode the subway from Coney Island to the Bronx.* [T] • To ride someone is to criticize them, esp. to push them to do more or to do what you want: *Your boss rides you much too hard.* [T] • To **ride a wave of** something is to be carried along by it: *The healthy economy has allowed the president to ride a wave of popularity.* • If one thing **rides on** another, its result depends entirely on something else: *The future of the company is riding on the new management.* If someone or something **rides out** a difficult or dangerous situation, they get through it: *The ship managed to ride out the storm.* • If an item of clothing **rides up**, it moves up out of position: *That sweater rides up at the back.* • If someone is **riding high**, they are very successful.

ride /raɪd/ *n* [C] a trip on an animal or bicycle, etc., or in a vehicle • *It's a short bus ride to the airport.* • A ride is also a machine in an amusement park which moves people esp. in circles or along a track for entertainment: *My favorite ride is the Ferris wheel.*

rider /'raɪd·ər/ *n* [C] a person in a vehicle, or on an animal, bicycle, etc.

ridership /'raɪd·ər,ʃɪp/ *n* [U] the number of passengers on a transportation system • *This*

month, ridership on the Chicago subway went down again.

riding /'raɪd·ɪŋ/ *n* [U] the sport or activity of riding horses • See also RIDING.

ridge /rɪdʒ/ *n* [C] a long, narrow, raised part of a surface, esp. a high edge of a hill or mountain • *a mountain ridge* ○ *Plowed ridges looked like stripes across the field.* • A ridge of high pressure is a narrow air mass that brings good weather. • The ridge of a roof is where the sloping parts or sides come together at the top.

ridicule /'rɪd·ə,kjuːl/ *n* [U] words or actions that make someone or something seem foolish or stupid • *He was an unhappy figure of ridicule, not a figure of fun, among his colleagues.*

ridicule /'rɪd·ə,kjuːl/ *v* [T] to laugh at (someone or something) in an unkind way • *She was ridiculed for her old-fashioned ideas.*

ridiculous /rə'dɪk·jə·ləs/ *adj* foolish or unreasonable and deserving to be laughed at • *Don't be ridiculous—there's no way I can buy a car.*

riding /'raɪd·ɪŋ/ *n* [C] *Cdn* a particular area of a country which is represented by an elected official • See also **riding** at RIDE.

rife /raɪf/ *adj* [not gradable] (of something unpleasant) very common or frequent • *Graft and corruption were rife in city government.* • If a place is rife with something unpleasant, it is full of it: *The office is rife with rumors that many of us will be fired.*

riff /rɪf/ *n* [C] (in popular music) a simple tune that is used as a pattern for creating more complicated musical patterns

riffraff /'rɪf·ræf/ *pl n disapproving* people with a bad reputation or of a low social class • *She warned her son to keep away from such riffraff.*

rifle GUN /'raɪ·fəl/ *n* [C] a type of gun with a long BARREL (= cylindrical part) which is fired from the shoulder

rifle SEARCH /'raɪ·fəl/ *v* [I/T] to search quickly through (something), esp. in order to steal • *He rifled through the safe, but the diamonds were gone.* [I]

rifle /'raɪ·fəl/ *v* [T] (in sports, esp. baseball and hockey) to hit or throw (a ball) very hard • *By the game's end, he had rifled two balls out of the ball field.*

rift /rɪft/ *n* [C] something that divides partners or friends • *The border dispute caused a rift between Canada and the US.*

rig ARRANGE /rɪg/ *v* [T] **-gg-** to arrange (an event or amount) in a dishonest way • *The station had rigged gasoline prices.* ○ *Until this year, all elections were rigged by the ruling party.*

rig FIX IN PLACE /rɪg/ *v* [T] to fix (a piece of equipment) in place, or to put (something) together quickly, for temporary use • *I rigged up a TV antenna from a coat hanger.* [M]

rig STRUCTURE /rɪg/ *n* [C] a structure used to support machinery and equipment for a particular purpose • *an oil rig* ○ *a camera/plow rig*

rigging /'rɪg·ɪŋ/ *n* [U] the ropes that hold and control the sails on a boat or ship

rig TRUCK /rɪg/ *n* [C] a large truck consisting of at least two sections, including an engine to drive it and another part to hold a load • *A huge rig, a sixteen-wheeler, rolling downhill, flew right by me.*

rigamarole /'rɪg·ə·mə,roʊl/ *n* [U] RIGMAROLE

right CORRECT /rɑɪt/ *adj, adv* correct, true, or exact • *He said the trip would take two hours and he was absolutely/exactly right.* ○ *My watch has stopped—do you have the right time?* ○ *Ellen is the right person for the job.* ○ *She got every answer right.* • USAGE: The opposite of right is WRONG NOT CORRECT.

rightly /'rɑɪt·li/ *adv* [not gradable] • *I think these people don't rightly know what they're doing.*

right WISE /rɑɪt/ *adj* having or showing good judgment; wise • *The president was right to veto that bill.* [+ *to* infinitive] ○ *I think we reached the right conclusion.*

rightly /'rɑɪt·li/ *adv* [not gradable] • *You did have the opportunity, and rightly or wrongly, you didn't follow up on it.*

right SUITABLE /rɑɪt/ *adj, adv* suitable or desirable, or as it should be • *He thought the time was right to expand his new business.* [+ *to* infinitive] ○ *That hat looks just right on you.* • If you start off or get off **on the right foot** when doing something new, you make a successful start: *He really got off on the right foot with my mother.* • USAGE: The opposite of right is WRONG NOT SUITABLE.

right MORAL RULE /rɑɪt/ *n* [U] what is considered to be morally good or acceptable or fair • *You know the difference between right and wrong.* ○ *You have no right* (= You are wrong) *to criticize me.* [+ *to* infinitive] • Someone who is **in the right** is morally or legally correct. • USAGE: The opposite of right is WRONG IMMORAL.

right /rɑɪt/ *adj, adv* [not gradable] considered fair or morally acceptable by most people • *It isn't right to tell a lie.* • (*slang*) **Right on** is an expression of agreement or approval.

right /rɑɪt/ *v* [T] • *Lawsuits were brought to right wrongs* (= to correct unfair situations) *in the workplace.*

rightly /'rɑɪt·li/ *adv* [not gradable] • *She rightly protested against the idea that women can't succeed in politics.*

right LEGAL OPPORTUNITY /rɑɪt/ *n* [C] your opportunity to act and to be treated in particular ways that the law promises to protect for the benefit of society • *civil/human rights* ○ *You have a right to a trial by jury.* ○ *He claimed that his right to express religious views were being trampled.* [+ *to* infinitive] ○ *The dispute is over fishing rights.* • If someone has or is something **in** their **own right**, they have

earned or obtained it themselves: *Her husband has money, but she's wealthy in her own right.*

rightful /'rɑɪt·fəl/ *adj* [not gradable] • *The stolen property was returned to the rightful owners.*

rightfully /'rɑɪt·fə·li/ *adv* [not gradable] • *This portion of land is rightfully theirs.*

rights /rɑɪts/ *pl n* the legal authority to publish, copy, or make available a work such as a book, movie, recording, or work of art • *electronic/reprint rights*

right DIRECTION /rɑɪt/ *adj, adv* [not gradable], *n* [C/U] the side of the body opposite the side that contains the heart, or the direction that is the opposite of left • *Most people throw a ball with their right hand.* ○ *Our house is on the right.* ○ *After you go over the bridge, make a right* (= turn to the right). [C] • A **right angle** is an angle of 90°: *A square has four right angles.* • **Right-hand** means on or to the right: *The picture is on the right-hand page.* • Someone who is **right-handed** or is a **right-hander** uses their right hand to write with and to do most things. • USAGE: The opposite of right is LEFT DIRECTION.

right POLITICS /rɑɪt/ *n* [U] political groups that believe in limited government and economic controls, private ownership of property and wealth, and traditional social attitudes • If someone is **right-wing**, they support the political opinions of the right, and a **right-winger** is a person who has these beliefs. • Compare LEFT POLITICS.

right HEALTHY /rɑɪt/ *adj, adv* [not gradable] healthy, or working correctly • *I haven't felt right all day.*

right AGREEMENT /rɑɪt/ *exclamation* used to express agreement with someone or to show that you have understood what someone has said • *"Robert, be sure to pick up Susan on your way home." "Right."*

right EXACTLY /rɑɪt/ *adv* [not gradable] exactly; just • *I'm too busy to talk right now but I'll get back to you later.* ○ *He sat right behind me.* ○ *I'll be right back* (= I will return very soon). • **Right away** means immediately: *I need this right away.*

righteous /'rɑɪ·tʃəs/ *adj* behaving in a morally correct way, or considered morally correct • *a righteous man*

rigid NOT VARYING /'rɪdʒ·əd/ *adj* not permitting any variation • *rigid rules of behavior* ○ *I keep to a rigid schedule.*

rigid STIFF /'rɪdʒ·əd/ *adj* not able to be bent • *rigid plastic*

rigmarole /'rɪg·mə,roʊl/, **rigamarole** *n* [U] a long, complicated, or silly process • *You have to go through this whole rigmarole before you can register for a course.*

rigorous /'rɪg·ə·rəs/ *adj* severe or difficult, esp. because at a high level • *rigorous standards of accuracy* ○ *The Manhattan district* *attorney's office had a pretty rigorous training program.*

rigor /'rɪg·ər/ *n* [C/U] careful control in following high standards in doing something • *intellectual rigor* [U] • Rigors refers to difficult conditions, esp. of weather: *They survived the rigors of the winter.* [C]

rile /raɪl/ *v* [T] to annoy or make angry • *Sharply higher cigarette prices have riled smokers.* ○ *Your loud parties rile up the neighbors.* [M]

rim /rɪm/ *n* [C] the outer edge of something, esp. of something curved or circular • *The rim of this cup is chipped.*

rims

rind /raɪnd/ *n* [C/U] the hard outer layer or covering of some fruits and foods • *lemon/orange/melon rind* [U]

ring CIRCLE /rɪŋ/ *n* [C] a circular piece, esp. of jewelry worn on a finger • *a gold wedding ring* • A ring is also any group of things or people in a circular shape or arrangement: *A ring of people joined hands in the dance.* ○ *a key ring*

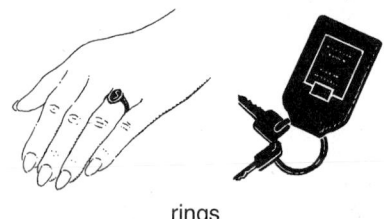

rings

ring /rɪŋ/ *v* [T] to surround (something) • *The island is ringed with rocks.*

ring SOUND /rɪŋ/ *v* [I/T] *past simple* **rang** /ræŋ/, *past part* **rung** /rʌŋ/ to make a sound, esp. the sound made when metal is hit, or to cause (a bell) to make a sound • *The telephone rang.* [I] ○ *I rang the doorbell but nobody answered.* [T] ○ *My ears are ringing* (= I hear a noise that is not really there). [I] • If something you hear **rings a bell**, it is familiar to you: *His name rang a bell, but I don't know where I met him.*

ring /rɪŋ/ *n* [C usually sing] • A ring is also a telephone call: *I'll give Sophia a ring.*

ringer /'rɪŋ·ər/ *n* [C usually sing] • *I turned the ringer off on my phone so I could get some sleep.*

ring GROUP /'rɪŋ,liːd·ər/ *n* [C] a group of people who work together, often secretly in criminal activities • *a drug/spy ring* • A **ringleader** is the leader of a group of people who cause trouble or commit crimes.

ring SPACE /rɪŋ/ *n* [C] a space where people perform or compete that is separated from, and usually at the center of, the space where

people can watch the event • *a boxing ring* ○ *a one-ring/three-ring circus* • **Ringside** is the area just outside the space where people compete or perform: *They had ringside seats.*

▫ **ring up** *obj* SELL , **ring** *obj* **up** /'-'-/ *v adv* [M] to record (items being bought) and calculate the cost, using a **cash register** (= calculating machine with a drawer to hold money) • *He finished ringing up a sale and handed Mrs. Drummond her change.*

▫ **ring up** *obj* TELEPHONE , **ring** *obj* **up** /'-'-/ *v adv* [M] to telephone (someone) • *She rang me up at home.*

ringworm /'rɪŋ·wɜrm/ *n* [U] a disease caused by a FUNGUS that leaves red rings on the skin

rink /rɪŋk/ *n* [C] a large, separate area having a flat surface specially prepared, sometimes with ice, for SKATING, or a building having such an area • *an ice-skating/roller-skating rink*

rinse /rɪns/ *v* [T] to use water to clean (soap or dirt) from (something) • *Rinse the silverware before drying it.* ○ *Don't forget to rinse the dishes off.* [M] ○ *Did you rinse out your bathing suit?* [M]

rinse /rɪns/ *n* [C usually sing] • *I put the clothes through a cold rinse in the washing machine.* • A rinse is also a temporary coloring for hair.

riot /'raɪ·ət/ *n* [C] a noisy and violent public gathering • *The streets in this district include South Central Los Angeles, where the riots broke out two years ago.* • (*infml*) A riot is also something very amusing: *The show was a riot.* [C usually sing]

riot /'raɪ·ət/ *v* [I] • *Inmates rioted yesterday at a prison in West Virginia.*

rioter /'raɪ·ət̬·ər/ *n* [C] • *The rioters killed at least 200 people.*

rip TEAR /rɪp/ *v* [I/T] **-pp-** to tear (something) quickly and with force, or to break apart (something) • *I ripped my sleeve.* [T] ○ *The wind ripped the flag to shreds.* [T] ○ *The letter made me so angry, I ripped it up.* [M] ○ *He lost control of the car and it ripped down a fence.* [M] • To rip out something is to remove it: *The previous owner ripped out the fireplace.* [M]

rip MOVE QUICKLY /rɪp/ *v* [I always + adv/prep] to move quickly or violently • *A hurricane ripped through Rhode Island yesterday.*

▫ **rip off** *obj*, **rip** *obj* **off** /'-'-/ *v adv* [M] *infml* to cheat (someone) by charging them too much money • *We got ripped off buying our new car.*

rip-off /'rɪp·ɔːf/ *n* [C] *slang* • *Don't eat in the museum restaurant—it's a rip-off.*

ripe /raɪp/ *adj* wholly developed, esp. of fruit ready to be collected or eaten • *The tomatoes aren't ripe.* • (*fig.*) A ripe old age is a very old age: *My grandmother lived to the ripe old age of 95.* • If a condition is **ripe for** something, it is ready or in a good condition for that to happen: *The time seems ripe for Canadian Football League expansion in the United States.*

ripen /'raɪ·pən/ v [I/T] • *Mangoes need to ripen at room temperature until the fruit yields to the touch.* [I]

ripple /'rɪp·əl/ n [C] a small wave or a slight movement of a surface, esp. the surface of water • *The stone hit the water and caused a ring of ripples to spread out.* • A ripple is also a sound or feeling that is slight

ripples

but is noticed: *A ripple of laughter ran through the crowd.* ○ *The story created ripples of alarm here in Washington.* • A **ripple effect** is a series of things that happen as the result of a particular action or event: *It is hoped the arts center will have a ripple effect by attracting retailers and other arts-related activities.*

ripple /'rɪp·əl/ v [I/T] • *A breeze rippled the water.* [T] • Something that ripples moves in a way that is not obvious but is noticeable: *A shy smile rippled nervously over his features.* [I always + adv/prep]

rise MOVE UP /raɪz/ v [I] *past simple* **rose** /roʊz/, *past part* **risen** /'rɪz·ən/ to move up from a lower to a higher position, or to become higher • *Smoke rose from the campfire.* ○ *The trail rises gently to the top of the ridge.* ○ *We watched the sun rise over the bay.* ○ *New buildings are rising* (= becoming higher as they are built) *throughout the city.* ○ *On a clear day, you can see the mountains rising* (= appearing high) *in the distance.* • To rise is also to stand up: *She rose to welcome us.* • To rise is also to get out of bed, esp. in the morning.

rise /raɪz/ n [C] a small hill or slope • *The house is built on a rise.*

riser /'raɪ·zər/ n [C] • *Paul is an early riser* (= gets out of bed early).

rise INCREASE /raɪz/ v [I] *past simple* **rose** /roʊz/, *past part* **risen** /'rɪz·ən/ to become more or greater in amount, size, or degree; increase • *Real estate prices have risen rapidly.* ○ *The temperature rose to 80° by midday.* ○ *Our hopes rose when the doctors told us that she was conscious and alert.* ○ *A murmur rose from the crowd* (= began to be heard). • To rise is also to move into a more important rank or position: *He rose to fame in the 1940s.* • To **rise above** an unpleasant situation is not to allow yourself to become involved with it, esp. because you have more important things to do: *In politics, you have to rise above petty quarreling and look at the big picture.* • To **rise to** something difficult is to succeed in doing it: *It was a tough competition, but Jean rose to the challenge and rode her horse beautifully.*

rise /raɪz/ n [C/U] • *a rise in temperature* [C] ○ *Inflation is on the rise* (= increasing). [U]

rise FIGHT /raɪz/ v [I always + adv/prep] *past simple* **rose** /roʊz/, *past part* **risen** /'rɪz·ən/ to begin to oppose or fight (esp. a bad government or ruler) as a group • *He urged his followers to rise up against the oppressive regime.*

risk /rɪsk/ n [C/U] danger, or the possibility of danger, defeat, or loss • *There's a risk of an accident happening in this fog.* [C] ○ *I was afraid to take the risk of quitting my job before I had another one lined up.* [C] ○ *We want clean rivers and lakes, where you can swim without risk to your health.* [U] ○ *It was a high/low risk situation* (= a situation with a lot of/very little danger). [U] • A risk is also someone or something that could cause a problem or loss: *Teenage drivers are considered higher risks.* [C] • To be **at risk** is to be in danger: *A child who hasn't been vaccinated is at risk.*

risk /rɪsk/ v [T] to do (something) or to enter a situation where there is a possibility of (being hurt) or of (a loss or defeat) • *He risked his life helping another man escape the fire.* ○ *We risk losing the business if we don't pay off the loan on time.*

risky /'rɪs·ki/ adj • *The business investment was a risky proposition.*

risqué /rɪ'skeɪ/ adj slightly shocking, esp. because of being connected with sex

rite /raɪt/ n [C] a set of fixed words and actions, esp. as part of a religious ceremony • *the marriage rite* • A **rite of passage** is a particular event that represents the beginning of an important, new stage in your life.

ritual /'rɪtʃ·ə·wəl/ n [C/U] a set of actions or words performed in a regular way, esp. as part of a religious ceremony • A ritual is also any act done regularly, usually without thinking about it: *My morning ritual includes reading the newspaper while I drink my coffee.* [C]

ritzy /'rɪt·si/ adj [-er/-est only] *infml* expensive and luxurious • *They had a ritzy wedding.*

rival /'raɪ·vəl/ n [C] a person, group, or organization competing with others for the same thing or in the same area • *business/political rivals*

rival /'raɪ·vəl/ adj [not gradable] • *rival political organizations* ○ *rival claims*

rival /'raɪ·vəl/ v [T] to equal or be as good as • *No computer can rival a human brain.*

rivalry /'raɪ·vəl·ri/ n [C/U] a serious and often continuing competition • *Jerusalem was the scene of more passions and rivalries than any other city on earth.* [C]

river /'rɪv·ər/ n [C] water that flows naturally through a wide channel that is surrounded by land • *the Mississippi River* ○ *We went swimming in the river.* • A river is also any large flow of a liquid: *Rivers of sweat ran down his back.* • The **riverbank/riverside** is the land at either side of a river. A **riverbed** is the low ground over which a river flows.

rivet /'rɪv·ət/ n [C] a metal pin used to fasten together flat pieces of metal or other thick materials such as leather

rivet /'rɪv·ət/ v [T] • *Parts of the aircraft are*

riveted together. • If something rivets some-one, it attracts and keeps their attention: *Her murder trial has riveted the nation.*

riveting /ˈrɪv·ət̬·ɪŋ/ *adj* extremely interesting • *a riveting TV show*

R.N. *n* [C] *abbreviation for* **registered nurse**, see at REGISTER RECORD • *Ruth Retallack, R.N.*

roach /roʊtʃ/ *n* [C] *short form of* COCKROACH

road /roʊd/ *n* [C/U] a route for traveling be-tween places by vehicle, esp. one that has been specially surfaced and made flat • *a gravel/ dirt/paved road* [C] • Road (*abbreviation* **Rd.**) is often used in the names of roads: 82 Mill Road [U] LP ADDRESSES • *The band spends three months a year* **on the road** (= traveling to different places). • *The doctors say she's* **on the road to** *recovery* (= likely to achieve this). • A **roadblock** is a temporary structure put across a road to stop traffic, or anything that stops the progress of something: *a police road-block* ∘ *Emotional roadblocks can complicate childbirth.* • **Road rage** is dangerous behav-ior by drivers who are not patient and become angry. • The **roadside** is the edge of the road. • A **road test** is an official test of driving skill that must be passed in order to obtain a LI-CENSE to drive. • A **road trip** is a long trip tak-en for pleasure, business, or by a sports team so it can play games against other teams in places where the other teams usually play. • The **roadway** is the part of the road on which vehicles drive. • If a vehicle is **roadworthy**, it is in good condition for driving.

roadrunner /ˈroʊdˌrʌn·ər/ *n* [C] a fast-run-ning bird from the southwestern US, Mexico, and Central America which has a long tail and feathers that stand up on the top of its head

roam /roʊm/ *v* [I/T] to walk or travel without any real purpose or direction • *Our dog just likes to roam.* [I]

roar /rɔːr, roʊr/ *v* [I] to make a long, loud, deep sound • *Lions were roaring in their cages.* ∘ *The crowd roared with laughter.* • If a vehicle roars somewhere, it moves there quickly mak-ing a lot of noise: *His truck roared down the steep mountain.*

roar /rɔːr, roʊr/ *n* [C/U] • *Living near the high-way, we hear the constant roar of traffic.* [U]

roaring /ˈrɔːr·ɪŋ, ˈroʊr-/ *adj, adv* • *a roaring river* • A roaring fire is very large, noisy, and bright.

roast /roʊst/ *v* [I/T] to cook (meat or other food) by dry heat in an OVEN or over a fire • PIC COOKING METHODS, PANS

roast /roʊst/, **roasted** /ˈroʊ·stəd/ *adj* [not grad-able] • *roast beef/turkey*

roast /roʊst/ *n* [C] a large piece of meat cooked in an OVEN • *a pork roast* • A roast is also an outside event at which food is cooked over a fire: *a pig roast*

rob /rɑb/ *v* [T] **-bb-** to take money or property from (a person or place) illegally • *Two armed men robbed the store last night.* • If someone

is robbed of a quality, it is taken away from them: *Prisoners should not be robbed of their dignity.*

robber /ˈrɑb·ər/ *n* [C] a person who takes mon-ey or property illegally

robbery /ˈrɑb·ə·ri/ *n* [C/U] • *armed robbery* [U] ∘ *He's accused of several bank robberies.* [C]

robe /roʊb/ *n* [C] a long, loose-fitting piece of clothing, esp. one worn at home • *I had on pa-jamas and a robe.*

robin /ˈrɑb·ən/ *n* [C] a brown North American bird with a red chest

robot /ˈroʊ·bɑt, -bət/ *n* [C] a mechanical de-vice that works automatically or by computer control • *Industrial robots are replacing peo-ple.*

robotic /roʊˈbɑt̬·ɪk/ *adj* • *He spoke in a robot-ic monotone.*

robotics /roʊˈbɑt̬·ɪks/ *n* [U] the science of de-signing and operating ROBOTS

robust /roʊˈbʌst/ *adj* (of a person, animal, or plant) strong and healthy, or (of food or drink) full of flavor • *She was in robust health.* ∘ *The house blend of coffee is particularly robust.*

rock STONE /rɑk/ *n* [C/U] a large mass of stone that sticks up out of the ground or the sea, or a separate piece of stone • *This is some of the oldest rock on the earth's surface.* [U] ∘ *Waves crashed against the rocks.* [C] ∘ *Demonstrators were hurling rocks at the police.* [C] • (*slang*) A rock is also a DIAMOND or other jewel. [C] • (*infml*) If something is **on the rocks**, it is fail-ing: *Their marriage is on the rocks.* • If an al-coholic drink is **on the rocks**, it is served with ice. • (*infml*) **Rock bottom** means at the low-est possible level or in the worst situation: *rock-bottom prices* ∘ *The team hit rock bottom, losing 12 games in a row.*

rocky /ˈrɑk·i/ *adj* covered with, or consisting of, stones • *a rocky path* • See also ROCKY.

rock MOVE /rɑk/ *v* [I/T] to move (something) or cause something to move backward and for-ward or from side to side • *He rocked the baby to sleep.* [T] ∘ *If you rock back on that chair, you're going to break it.* [I] • If a building or area rocks, it shakes it violently: *An earth-quake rocked the downtown area today.* [T] • If a person or place is rocked, it is surprised, up-set, or excited: *The university was rocked by the scandal.* [T] • (*infml*) If you **rock the boat**, you do or say something that upsets people or causes problems. • A **rocking chair** (also **rocker**) is a chair built on two pieces of curved wood so that you can rock when you sit in it. • A **rocking horse** is a toy horse that a child sits and rocks on.

rocker /ˈrɑk·ər/ *n* [C] a **rocking chair** (= a chair built on two pieces of curved wood), or one of the two curved pieces under the chair that allow it to move forward and backward

rock MUSIC /rɑk/, **rock-and-roll** /ˌrɑk·ən'roʊl/, **rock 'n' roll** *n* [U] a type of popular music with a strong beat, which is usually played with electric guitars and drums

rocker /ˈrɑk·ər/ n [C] *infml* someone who performs or likes ROCK music

rocket /ˈrɑk·ət/ n [C] a cylindrical device containing material that explodes, sending the device through the air • *The rocket was launched yesterday.* • (*humorous*) If you say **you don't have to be a rocket scientist/it doesn't take a rocket scientist** to understand or do something, you mean that it is simple enough for anyone to understand or do.

rocket /ˈrɑk·ət/ v [I/T] to travel by rocket, or to rise, increase, or move very quickly • *The astronauts were rocketed into space.* [T] ○ *A train rocketed by.* [I] ○ *Anna rocketed to fame in the late 1980s.* [I]

rocky /ˈrɑk·i/ adj difficult or uncertain • *Their season got off to a rocky start with three straight losses.* • See also **rocky** at ROCK [STONE].

rod /rɑd/ n [C] a long, thin pole made of wood, metal, or other material • *a fishing/curtain rod*

rode /roʊd/ *past simple of* RIDE

rodent /ˈroʊd·ᵊnt/ n [C] a type of small mammal with sharp front teeth • *They expect to catch rodents, mostly mice.*

rodeo /ˈroʊd·iːˌoʊ, rəˈdeɪ·oʊ/ n [C] *pl* **rodeos** a public performance or competition in which COWBOYS (= people who take care of cattle) show their skill at riding cattle and wild horses and at catching cattle with ropes

roe /roʊ/ n [U] the mass of eggs inside a female fish, which is eaten as food

rogue /roʊg/ n [C] a person, organization, or country that does not behave in the usual or acceptable way • *Buzzy's a fun-loving teenage rogue.*

rogue /roʊg/ adj [not gradable] • *A rogue employee might tap into the computer.*

role [DUTY] /roʊl/ n [C] the duty or use that someone or something usually has or is expected to have • *Bouchard hopes to play a pivotal/major/key role in Quebec's future.* • A **role model** is a person whose behavior is copied by others.

role [REPRESENTATION] /roʊl/ n [C] the person whom an actor represents in a movie or play • *Astin plays the role of Radford, the store's owner.*

roll [MOVE] /roʊl/ v [I/T] to move in a direction by turning over and over or by traveling on wheels, or to cause (something) to move in this way • *The coin rolled off the table.* [I] ○ *I rolled the spare tire around to the side of the car.* [T] ○ *Tears rolled down his cheeks.* [I] • If you **roll** a car window up or down, you turn a handle or press a button that opens or closes the window. [M] • If you **roll around**, you move in a way that is not controlled: *Whenever she turned the corner we rolled around in the backseat.* • If a time or event **rolls around**, it hap-

pens: *Will you still be here when spring rolls around?* • If someone **rolls back** a price or rate, they reduce it: *The governor plans to roll property taxes back.* • If you **roll** your **eyes** when someone says or does something stupid or foolish, you move them around in a circle. • If something **rolls in**, it arrives: *Fog rolled in overnight.* • (*infml*) If money **rolls in**, it arrives in large amounts: *Business was great and the money was rolling in.* • (*infml*) The comedian had the audience **rolling in the aisles** (= laughing loudly). • If you **roll over**, you turn your body: *Bob rolled over onto his stomach.*

roll /roʊl/ n [C/U] • *I wouldn't bet it all on one roll of the dice.* [C] • (*infml*) If someone is **on a roll**, they are experiencing a period of success or good luck: *They've won nine games in a row, so they're obviously on a roll.*

roller /ˈroʊ·lər/ n [C] a cylinder or wheel that turns over and over in order to move something along

roll [FORM ROUNDED SHAPE] /roʊl/ v [T] to form (something soft) into a rounded shape • *He rolled the clay into a ball.* ○ *She rolled up her pants so they wouldn't get wet.* [M] • *He is a businessman, community leader, and family man* (**all**) **rolled into one** (= He is all of these). • *New York* **rolled out the red carpet** *for the astronauts* (= gave them special treatment). • (*infml*) If you **roll up** your **sleeves**, you prepare for hard work.

roll /roʊl/ n [C] a long piece of something that bends, formed into a cylinder • *a roll of film/tape/toilet paper* • A roll is also a rounded mass of something: *rolls of fat*

roll [SMOOTH] /roʊl/ v [T] to make (something) smooth and flat, by pushing a cylindrical object or tool over it • *Roll (out) the pastry and place it in a pie pan.* [T/M] • A **rolling pin** is a cylinder that you move over DOUGH or pastry to flatten it.

roller /ˈroʊ·lər/ n [C] a cylinder used for shaping something, or for spreading something over a surface • *hair rollers* ○ *a paint roller*

roll [SOUND] /roʊl/ v [I/T] to make a continuous repeated sound • *Thunder rolled in the distance.* [I]

roll /roʊl/ n [C usually sing] • *a drum roll*

roll [LIST] /roʊl/ n [C] an official list of names • *a roll of eligible voters* • A **roll call** is the act of reading aloud the names of all the people on a list to check if they are present.

roll [BREAD] /roʊl/ n [C] a small loaf of bread

Rollerblade /ˈroʊ·lərˌbleɪd/ n [C] *trademark* an IN-LINE SKATE

roller coaster /ˈroʊ·lərˌkoʊ·stər/ n [C] *pl* **roller coasters** a small railroad, esp. in an amusement park, with open cars that travel quickly along a steep, curved track • A roller coaster is also a feeling, situation, or experience that changes very quickly: *an emotional roller coaster*

roller skate /ˈroʊ·lərˌskeɪt/ n [C usually pl] a

boot with wheels on the bottom that lets you roll quickly over a smooth surface

roller–skate /'roʊ·lər,skeɪt/ v [I] • *Jessica loves to roller-skate in the park.*

rollicking /'ral·ɪ·kɪŋ/ adj [not gradable] (esp. of an experience or story) happening with a lot of fast action and good humor and often noise • *a rollicking adventure movie*

rolling /'roʊ·lɪŋ/ adj [not gradable] (of hills) gently rising and falling

Roman Catholic /ˌroʊ·mən'kæθ·ə·lɪk/ n [C], adj [not gradable] (a member) of the largest Christian religion • *a Roman Catholic priest* ○ *the Roman Catholic church*

Roman Catholicism /ˌroʊ·mən·kə'θɑl·ə,sɪz·əm/ n [U] the beliefs of the Roman Catholic religion

romance /roʊ'mæns, 'roʊ·mɑns/ n [C/U] a close relationship between two people who are in love with each other • *Their three-year romance never went smoothly.* [C] • Romance is also the feeling of comfort and pleasure you experience in a relationship with someone you love: *Without romance, marriage is a lot like an old habit.* [U] • Romance is also a quality of excitement or mystery connected with an experience or place: *He loves the romance of traveling by train.* [U] • A romance is a story of love between two people that is very imaginative: *He is the successful author of rollicking historical romances.* [C]

Roman numeral /ˌroʊ·mən'nuː·mə·rəl/ n [C] one of the letters that the ancient Romans used to write numbers • *Written in Roman numerals, 14=XIV and 2001=MMI.* • Compare ARABIC NUMERAL

romantic /roʊ'mænt·ɪk/ adj relating to love or to an affectionate, loving relationship • *a romantic comedy/novel* • If something is romantic, it is exciting and mysterious and has a strong effect on your emotions: *I think Egypt is an incredibly romantic country.* • If someone is romantic, their ideas are not practical or related to real life: *She has a romantic idea of what it's like to be an actor.*

romantic /roʊ'mænt·ɪk/ n [C] • *You're such an old-fashioned romantic, always bringing me flowers.*

romantically /roʊ'mænt·ɪ·kli/ adv • *Their names have been romantically linked.*

romanticize /roʊ'mænt·ə,saɪz/ v [T] to believe that (something) is better, more interesting, or more exciting than it really is • *He romanticized the life of a spy, not knowing how boring and lonely it can be.*

romp /rɑmp, rɔːmp/ v [I] to play or run in a happy, excited, and noisy way • *The puppy and children romped together in the yard.* • To romp is also to succeed or win easily: *The unbeaten Charlottesville Crackers romped past the Beantown Beanies 68-26.*

romp /rɑmp, rɔːmp/ n [C usually sing] • *The film is a comic romp.* • A romp is also an easy

victory over an opponent: *Nothing could stop his romp to the nomination.*

roof /ruːf, rʊf/ n [C] the covering that forms the top of a building, vehicle, or other object • *The school has a flat roof.* • The roof of your mouth is the mouth's upper, inside surface: *Peanut butter sticks to the roof of your mouth.* • To have a **roof over** your **head** is to have a place to live: *It is hard to keep a roof over your head and food in the fridge.* • A **roof rack** is a device attached to the roof of a car which is used to carry things. • A **rooftop** is the top surface of a building or vehicle.

roof /ruːf, rʊf/ v [T] • *They roofed the house with old-fashioned shingles.*

roofing /'ruː·fɪŋ, 'rʊf·ɪŋ/ n [U] material used for roofs, or the process of building roofs • PIC OVERLAP

rook /rʊk/, **castle** n [C] (in the game of CHESS) a piece that can move in a straight line in any direction but not on a diagonal

rookie /'rʊk·i/ n [C] a person with little experience who is just starting to work in a job or to play on a sports team • *a rookie goalie/cop*

room PLACE /ruːm, rʊm/ n [C] an area within a building that has its own walls, floor, ceiling, and door • *The house has a laundry room.* • **Room and board** means a charge for renting a room and the cost of meals: *I pay each semester for room and board at college.* • **Room service** is a hotel service that provides food and drink to guests in their rooms.

room /ruːm, rʊm/ v [I always + adv/prep] to share a room with someone, esp. a rented room • *I roomed with Anita in college.*

room SPACE /ruːm, rʊm/ n [U] space available for something • *Is there any room for me in the car?* ○ *(fig.)* *She writes better, but there is still room for improvement.*

roomy /'ruː·mi, 'rʊm·i/ adj [not gradable] having a lot of space • *Her new apartment is very roomy.*

roommate /'ruːm·meɪt, 'rʊm-/ n [C] a person with whom you share a room, apartment, or house

roost /ruːst/ n [C] a place, such as a branch of a tree, where birds rest or sleep

roost /ruːst/ v [I] • *In the city, pigeons roost on the ledges of buildings.*

rooster /'ruː·stər/, **cock** n [C] an adult male chicken

root PLANT PART /ruːt, rʊt/ n [C] the part of a plant which grows down into the earth • *The root of a hair, tooth, or nail is the part of it that is inside the body.* • **Root beer** is a sweet, bubbly drink, flavored with the roots of various plants, that is not alcoholic. • A **root canal** is a treatment for a tooth where the infected roots are removed and replaced by a hard substance.

root /ruːt, rʊt/ v [I/T] • *The trees I just planted did not root.* [I] • To **root out** something is to get rid of it: *No one rooted out mistakes in the article.*

root ORIGIN /ruːt, rʊt/ *n* [C] the origin or source of something • *We must get to the root of this problem.*

rooted /'ruːt·əd, 'rʊt-/ *adj* [not gradable] • *deeply rooted loyalty*

roots /ruːts, rʊts/ *pl n* family origins, or the particular place you come from and the experiences you have had living there • *Somehow, I had forgotten my roots in Kansas.*

rootless /'ruːt·ləs, 'rʊt-/ *adj* [not gradable] having no family origins or connections, or having no feeling of belonging to a particular place

root WORD /ruːt, rʊt/ *n* [C] the basic form of a word, to which prefixes or endings can be added • *The root of the word "sitting" is "sit."*

▫**root for** /'--/ *v prep* [T] to give your support to (someone), or to show your support for (someone) • *The crowd noisily rooted for the home team.*

rope /roʊp/ *n* [C/U] a strong, thick cord made of twisted fibers • **The ropes** are the practices or rules you need to know in order to get something done: *I spent a day in our warehouse showing the new guy the ropes.* • If someone is **on the ropes**, they are in serious trouble, or if something is **on the ropes**, it is likely to fail: *For a while, our business was on the ropes.*

rope /roʊp/ *v* [T] to tie (something) with rope • *We roped the box to the top of the car.* • To rope something off is to put rope or cord around it to keep it separate: *The police roped off the area where the shooting took place.* [M] • If you **rope** someone **in** or **into** something, you persuade them to do it: *I was roped into playing softball last night.*

rosary /'roʊ·zə·ri/ *n* [C] a series of prayers said by Roman Catholics, or a string of BEADS (= little balls) used to count prayers

rose RISE /roʊz/ *past simple of* RISE

rose PLANT /roʊz/ *n* [C] a plant with pleasant-smelling flowers and THORNS (= sharp points) on its stems, or a flower from this plant • *a bunch of roses* ○ *I am planting roses this year.*

rose COLOR /roʊz/ *adj* [not gradable], *n* [U] (of) a light red-purple color • *a rose dress* ○ *painted in rose* [U] • If someone sees or looks at things through **rose-colored glasses**, they have a happy or positive attitude toward life.

rosy /'roʊ·zi/ *adj* [-er/-est only] of a pale red or pink color • *sunset's rosy glow* • Rosy also means optimistic, bright, happy: *Our future looks rosy.*

rosemary /'roʊz,mer·i/ *n* [U] an herb whose leaves are used to flavor foods and to make PERFUME (= pleasant-smelling liquids)

Rosh Hashanah /ˌroʊʃ·hə'ʃoʊ·nə, ˌrɑʃ-, -'ʃɑn·ə/, **Rosh Hashana** *n* [U] the Jewish New Near, celebrated in early fall, either on the first or second day of the first month of the Jewish year

roster /'rɑs·tər/ *n* [C] a list of people's names and sometimes their work schedules, esp. for a military unit or a sports team

rostrum /'rɑs·trəm/ *n* [C] a PODIUM

rot /rɑt/ *v* [I/T] **-tt-** to decay, or to cause (something) to decay or weaken • *The fallen apples rotted on the ground.* [I] ○ *Dampness rotted the old wood.* [T]

rot /rɑt/ *n* [U] • *Rot weakened the beams in the house.*

rotten /'rɑt·ᵊn/ *adj* • *The room smelled of rotten eggs.* • Rotten also means bad: *a rotten trick* ○ *rotten behavior* ○ *That kid is rotten to the core* (= completely bad)*!*

rotary /'roʊt·ə·ri/ *adj* [not gradable] turning in a circle around a fixed point, or having one or more parts that turns in this way • *a rotary motor/mower*

rotary /'roʊt·ə·ri/ *n* [C] a **traffic circle**, see at TRAFFIC MOVING THINGS

rotate TURN /'roʊ·teɪt/ *v* [I/T] to turn around a fixed point, or to cause (something) to do this • *The wheel rotates on an axle.* [I]

rotation /roʊ'teɪ·ʃən/ *n* [C/U] • *Two rotations of the dial opens the lock.* [C]

rotate TAKE TURNS /'roʊ·teɪt/ *v* [I/T] to happen in turns, or to cause (something) to happen in a particular order • *Every 30 days we rotate shifts.* [T]

rotation /roʊ'teɪ·ʃən/ *n* [U] • *crop rotation*

rote /roʊt/ *n* [U] the process of learning something by repetition, rather than by really understanding it • *She learned multiplication by rote.*

rotisserie /roʊ'tɪs·ə·ri/ *n* [C] a device that turns meat around slowly to cook it over a flame or in an oven

rotten /'rɑt·ᵊn/ *adj* See at ROT.

rotund /roʊ'tʌnd/ *adj* rounded or fat • *a rotund piglet/man*

rotunda /roʊ'tʌn·də/ *n* [C] a building or part of a building that is round in shape, and often has a DOME (= rounded roof)

rouge /ruːʒ, *esp. Southern* ruːdʒ/ *n* [U] BLUSH MAKEUP

rough UNEVEN /rʌf/ *adj* [-er/-est only] (of a surface) not even or smooth • *It was a rough road, full of potholes.* ○ *Her laugh was rough and loud.* • **Rough-hewn** means not gentle in manner: *The hero in the film is a rough-hewn detective.*

roughen /'rʌf·ən/ *v* [T] to make or become rough • *I roughened the edges and glued them together.*

rough VIOLENT /rʌf/ *adj* [-er/-est only] violent or stormy • *The sea was too rough for sailing.* ○ *They live in a rough neighborhood.* • **Rough-and-tumble** means disorderly or very competitive: *rough-and-tumble play/politics*

rough /rʌf/ *adv* [not gradable] • *The team had a reputation for playing rough.*

roughly /'rʌf·li/ *adv* [not gradable] • *He pushed the luggage roughly to the side.*

rough DIFFICULT /rʌf/ *adj* [-er/-est only] difficult or unpleasant • *She's had a rough year—she lost her job, then her father died.*

rough /rʌf/ *v* • To **rough it** means to live without comforts, esp. running water, heat, etc.: *We roughed it until our house was repaired.*

rough NOT EXACT /rʌf/ *adj* [-er/-est only] not exact or detailed; approximate • *I quickly made a rough table from some boards.* ○ *Can you give us a rough estimate of the cost?*

roughly /'rʌf·li/ *adv* [not gradable] • *The town's population has roughly doubled.*

□ **rough up** *obj*, **rough** *obj* **up** /'-'-/ *v adv* [M] to attack (someone) physically • *Who roughed this guy up in the parking lot?*

roughhouse /'rʌf·haʊs, -haʊz/ *v* [I] to play in a rough and noisy way • *The boys roughhoused outdoors.*

roughshod /'rʌf·ʃɑd/ *adv* • If you **ride/run roughshod over** someone, you act without thought for their interests or feelings: *In a democracy, the majority should not ride roughshod over the minority.*

round CIRCULAR /raʊnd/ *adj* [-er/-est only] shaped like a circle or having a surface like part of a ball • *They sat at a round table.* ○ *She held up a round mirror.* ○ *Carlos was a round-cheeked boy.* • A **round trip** is a trip from one place to another and back to where you started: *I drive 45 miles round trip every day for work.* ○ *I'd like a* **round-trip** *ticket to Baltimore, please.*

rounded /'raʊn·dəd/ *adj* curved • *rounded pebbles*

round APPROXIMATE /raʊnd/ *adj* [not gradable] (of a number) not exact but approximate, and ending in zero • *In round numbers, about three million tourists visit each year.*

round MOVE AROUND /raʊnd/ *v* [T] to go around (something) and arrive on the other side • *The car rounded the corner and stopped in front of the house.*

round /raʊnd/ *adv* around • *The children spun* **round and round** *(= in a circle) until they made themselves dizzy.* • *He requires* **round the clock** *(= continual) care.*

round SINGLE EVENT /raʊnd/ *n* [C] a single event or a small group of similar events that are part of a larger series of events • *The first round of negotiations got nowhere.* • In many sports, a round is a stage in a competition: *They lost in the first round of the tournament.* • In golf, a round is a complete game. • In boxing, a round is one of the periods during which the competitors fight. • *Let's give this band a nice* **round of applause** *(= period of clapping).* • *I ordered another* **round of drinks** *(= a drink for each of us).* • A **round-robin** is a competition in which everyone competes at least once against each other competitor: *a round-robin tennis tournament* • A **round-table discussion** is an event where several people talk about something as equals:

The writers will take part in round-table discussions and read from their works.

round BULLET /raʊnd/ *n* [C] a bullet or other piece of AMMUNITION (= something that can be shot from a weapon or exploded) • *They fired several rounds, then fled.*

□ **round out** *obj*, **round** *obj* **out** /'-'-/ *v adv* [M] to complete (something) • *A bit more research is needed to round out the article.*

□ **round up** *obj*, **round** *obj* **up** /'-'-/ *v adv* [M] to gather (people, animals, or things) together into one place • *The brothers set about rounding up the horses.*

roundup /'raʊn·dʌp/ *n* [C] a gathering together of people, animals, or things • *a cattle roundup* ○ *a roundup of suspected terrorists*

roundabout NOT DIRECT /'raʊn·də,baʊt/ *adj* not simple, direct, or quick • *She was telling him in her roundabout way that she loved him.*

roundabout CIRCLE /'raʊn·də,baʊt/ *n* [C] *Br for* **traffic circle**, see at TRAFFIC MOVING THINGS

rounds /raʊndz/ *pl n* a work activity that regularly involves going to several different places • *Doctors made their daily rounds, visiting patients in the hospital.*

rouse /raʊz/ *v* [T] to wake (someone) or make (someone) more active or excited • *She roused him from his sleep.*

rousing /'raʊ·zɪŋ/ *adj* enthusiastic, or causing enthusiasm • *a rousing speech* ○ *They gave him a rousing welcome.*

rout /raʊt/ *v* [T] to defeat (an enemy or competitor) completely

rout /raʊt/ *n* [C usually sing] • *Washington defeated Orlando in a 141-104 rout.*

route /ruːt, raʊt/ *n* [C] a particular way or direction between places • *The most direct route is to take the expressway.* • A route is also a fixed path for regularly moving or delivering people or things: *bus routes* ○ *a supply route*

route /ruːt, raʊt/ *v* [T always + adv/prep] • *The airline thinks my bags were routed (= sent) to Portland, Oregon instead of Portland, Maine.*

routine /ruː'tiːn/ *n* [C/U] a usual set of activities or way of doing things • *Getting coffee and a bagel was part of my daily routine.* [C] • A routine is also a particular set of activities performed to entertain others: *a comedy/skating routine* [C]

routine /ruː'tiːn/ *adj* [not gradable] • *The test is part of a routine six-month checkup.*

routinely /ruː'tiːn·li/ *adv* [not gradable] • *She routinely attends a prayer group.*

rove /roʊv/ *v* [I/T] to move, travel, or look around (an area), without having a particular place you intend to go to • *He roved around town, looking for work.* [I]

row LINE /roʊ/ *n* [C] a line of things arranged next to each other • *Everybody lined up in a neat little row.* ○ *I want to sit in the front row.* • If something happens a number of times **in**

a row, it happens that many times without interruption: *They've won six games in a row.* • A **row house** is a house in a city that is joined to others like it on either side.

row MOVE IN WATER /roʊ/ *v* [I/T] to cause (a boat) to move by pushing against the water with OARS (= long poles with flat ends), or to move (people in a boat) in this way • *Dad rowed us back to shore.* [T] • A **rowboat** is a small boat that is moved by rowing.

rowing /ˈroʊ·ɪŋ/ *n* [U] • *Sarah won an Olympic medal in rowing.*

rowdy /ˈrɑʊd·i/ *adj* noisy and seeming likely to become violent • *The theater was full of rowdy teenagers throwing popcorn and yelling.*

royal /ˈrɔɪ·əl/ *adj* [not gradable] belonging or connected to a king or queen • *Sweden's royal family* • The **Royal Canadian Mounted Police** (*infml* **Mounties**) is Canada's national police force.

royalty PEOPLE /ˈrɔɪ·əl·ti/ *n* [U] kings or queens and their families as a group, or the rank or power of these people • *They treated her like royalty.*

royalty PAYMENT /ˈrɔɪ·əl·ti/ *n* [C usually pl] a payment made esp. to writers and musicians every time their books or songs are bought or used by others

rpm *n abbreviation for* revolutions per minute (= a measurement of the number of times something goes around during a minute) • *a 78 rpm record*

RSVP *v* [I] *abbreviation for* répondez s'il vous plaît (= French for "please answer"), often written on invitations • *RSVP by October 9th.*

rub /rʌb/ *v* [I/T] **-bb-** to press or be pressed against (something) with a repeated circular, side to side, or up and down movement • *I rubbed the place where I bumped my head.* [T] ◦ *If you rub linseed oil into the wood, it will protect it.* [T] • If you **rub elbows with** someone, you spend time with them in a friendly way: *He loved to rub elbows with the rich and famous.* • To **rub it in** is to make someone feel worse than they did about something they already feel foolish about: *I know I shouldn't have paid that much for the poster—don't rub it in, OK?* • If they said it was true and I knew it wasn't, that would really **rub** me **the wrong way** (= make me angry or unhappy).

rub /rʌb/ *n* [C] • *Give my neck a rub.* • The **rub** is something that prevents success: *She got good reviews for her original cooking, but the rub was that people wanted very traditional dishes.*

▢**rub down** *obj*, **rub** *obj* **down** /ˈ-ˈ-/ *v adv* [M] to rub or press (someone's body) in order to dry them or reduce muscle stiffness or pain • *After the game the trainer was rubbing my arm down.*

rubdown /ˈrʌb·dɑʊn/ *n* [C] • *I got a rubdown after my workout.*

▢**rub off on** /ˈ-ˈ-/ *v adv prep* [T] to pass along a skill, an interest, or a quality to (someone) without making an active effort to do so • *I like to think that our love of reading will rub off on our children.*

rubber /ˈrʌb·ər/ *n* [C/U] an elastic, waterproof substance made either from the juice of a tree that grows in hotter parts of the world or artificially • *rubber boots/gloves* [U] ◦ *Tires are made of rubber.* [U] • (*slang*) A rubber is a CONDOM. [C] • (*Br*) A rubber is an ERASER. [C] • Rubbers are waterproof shoes made of rubber, which are worn over regular shoes to keep them dry: *Wear your rubbers—it's raining.* [pl] • A **rubber band** is a thin ring of rubber used for holding things together: *She brought five or six pencils and put a rubber band around them.*

rubbery /ˈrʌb·ə·ri/ *adj* elastic and difficult to break, like rubber • *I don't like squid, it's too rubbery.* • Rubbery also means feeling weak: *His legs were rubbery.*

rubbernecking /ˈrʌb·ər,nek·ɪŋ/ *n* [U] the act of slowing down while driving to look at something interesting, esp. an accident • *There are delays due to rubbernecking at the scene of the accident.*

rubber stamp /ˈrʌb·ər·stæmp/ *n* [C] a device with raised letters, numbers, or pictures made of an elastic substance such as rubber that you cover with ink and press against a surface for printing them, or the printed letters, etc., made in this way • *The guard marked my pass with a rubber stamp.* • (*disapproving*) A rubber stamp is also an approval given without much thought: *You want the minority community to give this proposal its rubber stamp.*

rubber–stamp /ˈrʌb·ər·stæmp/ *v* [T] *disapproving* to approve (something) without giving it much thought • *Congress is not going to simply rubber-stamp any policy the president proposes.*

rubbish /ˈrʌb·ɪʃ/ *n* [U] worthless and unwanted things or ideas; garbage • *All that was left of the property was a pile of rubbish nine feet high.* ◦ *I can't believe they broadcast such rubbish.*

rubble /ˈrʌb·əl/ *n* [U] broken wood, stones, bricks, etc., that are left when a building falls down or is destroyed

rubella /ruːˈbel·ə/ *n* [U] *medical* GERMAN MEASLES

ruby /ˈruː·bi/ *n* [C] a dark red jewel • *a ruby ring*

ruckus /ˈrʌk·əs/ *n* [C usually sing] *infml* a noisy situation or argument • *He caused quite a ruckus.*

rudder /ˈrʌd·ər/ *n* [C] a flat blade at the back of a boat or aircraft that is moved from side to side in order to control the direction of travel

ruddy /ˈrʌd·i/ *adj* (of a white person's skin) having a red color, often suggesting good health • *a ruddy-cheeked girl*

rude NOT POLITE /ruːd/ *adj* [*-er/-est* only] behaving in a way that hurts other people's feelings; not polite • *I apologized for Ted's rude behavior.* ○ *I thought it was rude of him not to introduce me.*

rudely /'ruːd·li/ *adv*

rudeness /'ruːd·nəs/ *n* [U] • *He asked too many questions, and his curiosity verged on rudeness.*

rude SUDDEN /ruːd/ *adj* [*-er/-est* only] sudden and unpleasant • *I've lived in Texas most of my life, so it was a rude awakening when I moved to New York.*

rudimentary /,ruːd·ə'ment·ə·ri, -'men·tri/ *adj* only basic, and not deep or detailed • *She has only a rudimentary grasp of the language.*

rudiments /'ruːd·ə·məns/ *pl n* the simplest and most basic facts • *the rudiments of grammar*

rue /ruː/ *v* [T] *esp. literary* to feel sorry about an event and wish it had not happened; regret • If you **rue the day** you did something, you regret it very much: *She'll rue the day she bought that house.*

rueful /'ruː·fəl/ *adj* • *She gave him a rueful smile.*

ruffle MAKE UPSET /'rʌf·əl/ *v* [I/T] to make (someone) upset or reduce their calmness or confidence • *It ruffled her composure, and she did not know how to respond.* [T] • To **ruffle feathers** is to cause someone to be upset.

ruffled /'rʌf·əld/ *adj* [not gradable] • *We spent a lot of time soothing the author's ruffled feelings.*

ruffle MAKE UNEVEN /'rʌf·əl/ *v* [T] to make (something that is smooth) uneven • *A sudden, strong breeze ruffled the women's skirts in the stands.*

ruffle FOLD /'rʌf·əl/ *n* [C] a series of small folds made in a piece of cloth or sewn into it as decoration • *lace ruffles*

ruffled /'rʌf·əld/ *adj* [not gradable] • *a blouse with a ruffled neck*

rug /rʌg/ *n* [C] a shaped piece of thick cloth for covering part of a floor • *The rug we bought for the living-room has a beautiful red and gold pattern.*

rugby /'rʌg·bi/ *n* [U] a game played between two teams using an oval-shaped ball that is kicked or carried to goals at either end of a field

rugged STRONG /'rʌg·əd/ *adj* strong or powerful; not delicate • *rugged individualism* • If you describe a man's face as rugged, you mean it is strong and rough: *rugged good looks*

rugged UNEVEN /'rʌg·əd/ *adj* (of land) uneven and wild; not easy to travel over • *rugged terrain/cliffs*

ruin /'ruː·ən, -ɪn/ *v* [T] to spoil or destroy (something) • *It would be a shame to ruin such a beautiful place.* ○ *That guy isn't going to ruin my life.*

ruin /'ruː·ən, -ɪn/ *n* [C/U] • *an ancient Mayan* ruin (= destroyed building) [C] • *The city lies* **in ruins** (= destroyed).

ruinous /'ruː·ə·nəs/ *adj* [not gradable] causing permanent and severe harm • *ruinous costs*

rule INSTRUCTION /ruːl/ *n* [C] an accepted principle or instruction that states the way things are or should be done, and tells you what you are allowed or are not allowed to do • *The university is strictly enforcing its rules against alcohol and drug use.* ○ *If you broke the rule, you're going to be punished for it.* ○ *Smoking is against the rules.* • A **rule of thumb** is a method of judging a situation or condition that is not exact but is based on experience: *As a rule of thumb, the ice on the lake should be at least two inches thick to support one person.*

rule DECIDE /ruːl/ *v* [I/T] to decide officially • *A lower court ruled in favor of the society.* [I] ○ *The judge ruled that the defendant be taken back to Virginia.* [+ *that* clause]

ruling /'ruː·lɪŋ/ *n* [C] an official decision • *The US Supreme Court refused to review the state court's ruling.*

rule CONTROL /ruːl/ *v* [I/T] to control, or be the person in charge of (a country) • *The prince ruled wisely and well.* [I]

rule /ruːl/ *n* [U] • *This area was under Polish rule until the start of World War II.*

ruler /'ruː·lər/ *n* [C] • *a military ruler*

ruling /'ruː·lɪŋ/ *adj* [not gradable] • *the ruling party*

▫ **rule out** *obj*, **rule** *obj* **out** /'-'-/ *v adv* [M] to stop considering (something) as a possibility • *It's unlikely that he'll run for president, but you can never rule anything out.*

ruler /'ruː·lər/ *n* [C] a narrow, flat object with straight edges you can use to draw straight lines and having markings you can use to measure things

rum /rʌm/ *n* [U] a strong alcoholic drink made from MOLASSES (= sweet liquid from sugar plants)

rumble /'rʌm·bəl/ *v* [I] to make a continuous, low sound, or to move slowly while making such a sound • *My stomach is rumbling.* ○ *The trucks rumbled across the field.*

rumble /'rʌm·bəl/ *n* [C usually sing] • *We could hear the rumble of distant thunder.*

ruminate /'ruː·mə,neɪt/ *v* [I] *fml* to think slowly and carefully • *He ruminated over his loss.*

rummage /'rʌm·ɪdʒ/ *v* [I always + adv/prep] to search for something by moving things around without care and looking into, under, and behind them • *She rummaged through the drawer, looking for a pen.*

rummage sale /'rʌm·ɪdʒ'seɪl/ *n* [C] a sale of used clothing, books, toys, etc.

rummy /'rʌm·i/ *n* [U] any of various card games in which two or more players try to collect cards that have the same value or whose numbers follow an ordered series

rumor /'ruː·mər/ *n* [C/U] an unofficial, interesting story or piece of news that might be true or invented, and that is communicated quickly from person to person • *Rumors about her are circulating at school.* [C]

rumored /ˈruː·mərd/ *adj* [not gradable] • *She was rumored to be the leader of the gang.*

rump /rʌmp/ *n* [C] the back end of an animal, or a person's buttocks • *a rump steak*

rumple /ˈrʌm·pəl/ *v* [T] to cause (something smooth) to become messy with unwanted folds • *You'll rumple your jacket if you don't hang it up.*

rumpled /ˈrʌm·pəld/ *adj* • *a rumpled suit*

run GO QUICKLY /rʌn/ *v* **running**, *past simple* **ran** /ræn/, *past part* **run** to move your legs faster than when walking, with the weight of your body pressing forward • *They ran for the bus and got there just in time.* [I] ○ *Hugh runs five miles a day.* [T] ○ *We want a place with a big backyard with room for the kids to run around.* [I] ○ (*fig.*) *I've got to run now* (= hurry away) *because I'm late for my appointment.* [I] • If you **run an errand**, you do a small job such as buying or delivering things in the neighborhood: *I've got to run a few errands and then stop by my mother's.* • (*infml*) *The Japanese took that technology and ran with it* (= worked at it so that it produced something).

run /rʌn/ *n* [C] • *She goes for a three-mile run every evening after work.* • *He eats on the run* (= while busy), *downing an apple in his car.* • If criminals are **on the run**, they are trying to avoid being caught.

runner /ˈrʌn·ər/ *n* [C] • *Distance runner Gwyn Coogan is a favorite in the marathon.* • See also RUNNER SHOE, RUNNER BLADE.

running /ˈrʌn·ɪŋ/ *n* [U] • *Running is a very popular form of exercise.* • A **running back** is a football player who carries the ball when it is not thrown or kicked. • See also **running** at RUN OPERATE; RUN POLITICS.

run TRAVEL / GO /rʌn/ *v* [I/T] **running**, *past simple* **ran** /ræn/, *past part* **run** to travel or go, to move (something), or to be positioned in a particular way • *The bus runs three times a day between here and Albuquerque.* [I] ○ *I'm going to run down to the bank to cash my check.* [I] ○ *Trains are running twenty minutes late because of the weather.* [I] ○ *The car skidded on the ice and ran off the road.* [I] ○ *A shiver of fear ran through her.* [I] ○ *John said he'd run me back to school* (= take me there in his car). [T] ○ *A deep creek runs through the property.* [I] ○ *The road runs along the coast.* [I] • If you run your finger or hand down/over something, you move it quickly: *She ran her fingers along the edge of the desk.* [T] • If you run something through your hair, you move it quickly and easily: *He ran a comb through his hair.* [T] • If a driver or a vehicle runs a sign or signal to stop, the vehicle continues without stopping: *Our taxi ran a red light and a truck rammed us in the side.* [T] • To **run the gamut** is to cover the whole range of possible things or emo-

tions, esp. from one extreme to the other: *Their projects run the gamut from mobile homes to luxury condos.*

run /rʌn/ *n* [C] a trip • *The train made its final run in 1986.*

run OPERATE /rʌn/ *v* [I/T] **running**, *past simple* **ran** /ræn/, *past part* **run** to manage or operate (something), esp. in a particular way • *She runs the business out of her home.* [T] ○ *She left the engine running while she went into the store.* [I] ○ *Can you run both of these programs at once?* [T] ○ *They're running tests on his heart functions.* [T] • If something runs on a particular type of energy, it uses that type of energy to operate: *Some calculators run on solar power.* [I] • When you're creative, you **run the risk of** *being silly* (= this is a possible result of such behavior). • If you **run a fever/temperature**, your body is hotter than it usually is because you are sick.

running /ˈrʌn·ɪŋ/ *n* [U] the management or operation of something • *The running of a large household is not easy.* • See also **running** at RUN GO QUICKLY; RUN POLITICS.

run FLOW /rʌn/ *v* [I/T] **running**, *past simple* **ran** /ræn/, *past part* **run** to cause (a liquid) to flow, or to produce a liquid that flows • *He ran a little cold water into the sink.* [T] ○ *He has a cold and his nose is running.* [I] ○ *Tears were running down her face.* [I] • *The summer homes on the island have no running water* (= water supplied by pipes).

runny /ˈrʌn·i/ *adj infml* producing a lot of liquid, or (of a substance) partly liquid • *a runny nose* ○ *runny eggs*

run LOSE COLOR /rʌn/ *v* [I] **running**, *past simple* **ran** /ræn/, *past part* **run** (of colors) to come out of material and mix with other colors, so that the original colors are lost • *If you wash the dress in hot water, the colors will run.*

run POLITICS /rʌn/ *v* [I] **running**, *past simple* **ran** /ræn/, *past part* **run** to try to get elected; be a CANDIDATE • *Kutukas ran unsuccessfully for sheriff.*

run /rʌn/ *n* [C] • *Gunter made a run for the US Senate.* • A **runoff** is a second or final election held to decide the winner when no one gets enough votes to win an election.

running /ˈrʌn·ɪŋ/ *n* [U] • To be **in the running** is to have a chance of being successful for a job or political office: *She's still in the running for Treasurer.* Compare **out of the running**. • A **running mate** is someone who is trying to get elected to the second of two top positions: *Eisenhower's running mate became vice president when Eisenhower won the presidency.* • See also **running** at RUN GO QUICKLY; RUN OPERATE.

run BE / CONTINUE /rʌn/ *v* **running**, *past simple* **ran** /ræn/, *past part* **run** to be, become, or continue in a particular way • *The doctor is running a bit late.* [L] ○ *We're running low on gas.* [L] ○ *Inflation is running at 4%.* [I always +

adv/prep] ∘ *The show ran on Broadway for six weeks before closing.* [I always + adv/prep] • If someone **runs afoul of** a rule or authority, they do something they are not allowed to do: *Foreigners who run afoul of the law will be arrested.* • To **run amok** is to have no control and act in a wild or dangerous manner: *There were 50 little kids running amok at the snack bar.* • If a skill or quality **runs in** your **family**, it is present in a lot of your relatives: *I guess a love of music runs in the family.*

run /rʌn/ *n* [C] a period during which something happens or continues • *The movie starts a two-week run tonight.*

run SHOW /rʌn/ *v* [T] **running**, *past simple* **ran** /ræn/, *past part* **run** to show (something) in a newspaper or magazine, or on television • *The magazine doesn't run cigarette ads.*

run POINT /rʌn/ *n* [C] (in baseball) a single point, scored by touching each of the four BASES (= positions on a square) in the correct order

run HOLE /rʌn/ *n* [C] a long, vertical hole in particular types of cloth, esp. STOCKINGS (= thin, tight-fitting clothing for a woman's feet and legs)

run /rʌn/ *v* [I] **running**, *past simple* **ran** /ræn/, *past part* **run** • *My pantyhose ran!*

□ **run across** /'--,-/ *v prep* [T] to meet (someone) unexpectedly or to experience (something unexpected) • *You don't run across many people who don't own a TV.*

□ **run after** /-'--/ *v prep* [T] to chase (someone or something) • *I ran after her, trying to get her attention.*

□ **run around** /,--'-/ *v prep* [I] to exist or do something in the stated condition • *I'm tired of running around on crutches.*

□ **run around with** /,--'-,-/ *v adv prep* [T] to spend a lot of time with (someone) • *Mom likes to know what kind of crowd I'm running around with.*

□ **run away** /'---/ *v adv* [I] to leave a place or person secretly and suddenly • *Vinnie ran away from home when he was 16.*

runaway /'rʌn·ə,weɪ/ *n* [C] a young person who has left their home without permission • See also RUNAWAY.

□ **run** *obj* **by** *obj* /'-,-/ *v prep* [T] to tell (something) to (someone), esp. in order to discover their opinion of it • *Would you run that by me again?*

□ **run down** *obj* HIT , **run** *obj* **down** /'-'-/ *v adv* [M] (of a vehicle or its driver) to hit and hurt (a person or animal), esp. intentionally • *Some people drive like they're trying to run you down.*

□ **run down** (*obj*) WEAKEN , **run** (*obj*) **down** /'-'-/ *v adv* [I/T] to lose energy, power, or strength, or to cause (someone or something) to use everything available • *By 1923 the radio boom seemed to be running down.* [I] ∘ *With only a*

minute left in the basketball game, Providence decided to **run down the clock**. [M]

run-down /rʌn'daʊn/ *adj* weak or in bad condition • *an old run-down factory* ∘ *She was run-down, thin, with no appetite.* • See also RUNDOWN.

□ **run down** *obj* FIND , **run** *obj* **down** /'-,-/ *v adv* [M] to find (someone) or learn the facts about (something) after searching for them • *The Border Patrol tries to run those illegals down and take them back.*

□ **run down** *obj* CRITICIZE , **run** *obj* **down** /'-,-/ *v adv* [M] to criticize (someone), often unfairly • *Those people are always running down our country and our values.*

□ **run** (*obj*) **into** *obj* HIT /'-,--/ *v prep* [T] to unintentionally drive (a vehicle) into (something) • *He ran his car into a ditch.*

□ **run into** *obj* MEET /,-'--/ *v prep* [T] to meet (someone) by chance, or to experience (esp. something unpleasant) unexpectedly • *I ran into Mike on Seventh Avenue.* ∘ *The center ran into some financial trouble and had to borrow money.*

□ **run** (*obj*) **off** (*obj*) LEAVE /'-'-/ *v adv* [I/T] to leave suddenly and unexpectedly, or to cause (someone) to leave suddenly • *She punched me in the shoulder and ran off.* [I] ∘ *Barlow wouldn't leave unless she ran him off.* [T]

□ **run off** *obj* PRODUCE , **run** *obj* **off** /'-'-/ *v adv* [M] to print (copies of something) • *She downloaded it, printed it, and ran off copies for her friends.* • If a team **runs off** points in a competition, they score quickly: *Iowa ran off 12 straight points to take the lead.*

□ **run off with** /'-'-/ *v adv prep* [T] to take (something that does not belong to you); borrow or steal • *The dog ran off with my shoe.* • If a person **runs off with** someone else, they leave their partner or home and begin a new sexual relationship: *Her husband ran off with her best friend.*

□ **run out** /-'-/ *v adv* [I] to use something completely so that nothing is left • *He just ran out of ideas.* ∘ *Time was running out* (= There was only a little time left).

□ **run over** *obj* HIT , **run** *obj* **over** /'-'--/ *v adv* [M] (of a vehicle or its driver) to hit and drive over (someone or something) • *Pfeifer tried to run him over, then shot him.*

□ **run over** REPEAT /'-,--/ *v prep* [T] to repeat the action of checking (facts or a statement) • *They ran over the list to make sure there were no mistakes.*

□ **run through** PRACTICE /'-'-/ *v prep* [T] to practice (something); to REHEARSE • *The director wants us to run through the first act this morning.*

□ **run through** EXAMINE /'-'-/ *v prep* [T] to look at, examine, think of, or deal with (a set of things), esp. quickly • *I mentally ran through what I had eaten since Thursday.*

□ **run through** EXIST /'-'-/ *v prep* [T] to exist as

part of (esp. a group of things) • *The blues runs through all of Clapton's music.*

□ **run to** /'--/ *v prep* [T] to reach (a particular amount, level, or size) • *Its 1992 budget ran to over $1 billion.*

□ **run up** *obj*, **run** *obj* **up** /'-'-/ *v adv* [M] to make (an amount you owe) increase • *He ran up huge bills on clothes.*

□ **run up against** /-'--,-/ *v adv prep* [T] to experience (an unexpected difficulty), or to meet (someone who is difficult to deal with) • *He's the slickest talker I've ever run up against.*

runaround /'rʌn·ə,raʊnd/ *n* [U] a series of actions or answers to questions that prevent someone from achieving what they want to do • *He expected to get the runaround, but surprisingly, the store offered him a refund.*

runaway /'rʌn·ə,weɪ/ *adj* [not gradable] being or seeming to be out of control, or happening suddenly and strongly • *runaway health-care costs* ○ *From the moment he launched the Boy Scout movement in 1908, it was a runaway success.* • See also **runaway** at RUN AWAY.

rundown /'rʌn·daʊn/ *n* [C] a detailed report • *This guide gives a rundown on the basics of backpacking.* • See also **run-down** at RUN DOWN WEAKEN.

rung RING /rʌŋ/ *past participle of* RING SOUND

rung STEP /rʌŋ/ *n* [C] any of the short bars that form the steps of a LADDER (= a device used for climbing), or *(fig.)* a level or stage of progress • *(fig.) Community colleges occupy the lower rung of the state's higher education system.*

run-in /'rʌn·ɪn/ *n* [C] *infml* an argument, disagreement, or fight • *She'd had a run-in with the dog before.*

runner BLADE /'rʌn·ər/ *n* [C] a long, narrow blade designed to slide over ice easily, fixed to the bottom of SKATES (= a type of boot) or snow vehicles • See also **runner** at RUN GO QUICKLY.

runner SHOE /'rʌn·ər/ *n* [C usually pl] a SNEAKER • See also **runner** at RUN GO QUICKLY.

runner-up /'rʌn·ə,rʌp/ *n* [C] *pl* **runners-up** /'rʌn·ər,zʌp/ a person or team that finishes second in a race or competition • *Madison is the Eastern Region champion and last year's state runner-up.*

running /'rʌn·ɪŋ/ *n* • See at RUN GO QUICKLY; RUN OPERATE; RUN POLITICS.

runny /'rʌn·i/ *adj* • See at RUN FLOW.

run-up /'rʌn·ʌp/ *n* [U] the period before an important event • *Wolfson is playing a key role in the run-up to the elections.*

runway /'rʌn·weɪ/ *n* [C] a long, level piece of ground at an airport, having a smooth, hard surface on which aircraft can take off and land

rupture /'rʌp·tʃər/ *v* [I/T] to burst or break, or to cause (something) to burst or break • *High winds caused the oil tank to rupture.* [I]

rupture /'rʌp·tʃər/ *n* [C] • *There is a rupture in confidence in government.*

rural /'rʊr·əl/ *adj* in, of, or like the COUNTRY (= land not in cities) • *She grew up in rural Utah.* • Compare URBAN.

ruse /ruːz/ *n* [C] a trick intended to deceive someone • *You didn't fall for my ruse.*

rush /rʌʃ/ *v* [I/T] to do something or move very quickly, or to cause (someone) to act in such a way; hurry • *She rushed toward me, talking and laughing.* [I] ○ *You shouldn't rush out and buy one.* [I] ○ *We rushed her to the hospital.* [T] ○ *She never rushes her students.* [T]

rush /rʌʃ/ *n* [C/U] something moving quickly, or the need for quick action • *a rush of cold air* [C] ○ *There's no rush, I can wait.* [U] • A rush is also a sudden strong emotion or physical feeling: *a rush of excitement* [C] • *"It's like this," she said* **in a rush** (= quickly). • The **rush hour** is one of the busy parts of the day, either when people are traveling to work in the morning or when they are traveling home from work in the evening: *Take alternate routes during the morning rush hour.*

rust /rʌst/ *n* [U] a red-brown substance that forms on the surface of iron and steel as a result of decay caused by reacting with air and water

rust /rʌst/ *v* [I/T] • *Stainless steel won't rust.* [I]

rusty /'rʌs·ti/ *adj* • *People would toss their soda cans into rusty old barrels.* • See also RUSTY.

rustic /'rʌs·tɪk/ *adj* typical of the COUNTRY (= land not in cities), esp. because of being attractively simple • *We stayed in rustic cabins, with no electricity.*

rustle MAKE NOISE /'rʌs·əl/ *v* [I/T] to make soft sounds, or to cause (esp. cloth, paper, or leaves) to make soft sounds • *A sudden breeze rustled the leaves.* [T]

rustle /'rʌs·əl/ *n* [C usually sing] • *We heard the rustle of her dress.*

rustling /'rʌs·ə·lɪŋ/ *n* [C/U] • *the rustling of papers on the desk* [U]

rustle STEAL /'rʌs·əl/ *v* [T] to steal (esp. cattle, horses, etc.)

rustler /'rʌs·lər, -ə·lər/ *n* [C] • *Some rustlers had made off with half of their horses during the night.*

□ **rustle up** *obj*, **rustle** *obj* **up** /'--'-/ *v adv* [M] *infml* to make (esp. food) quickly • *Give me a minute and I'll rustle up some scrambled eggs.*

rusty /'rʌs·ti/ *adj* (esp. of a person) not as good at knowing or doing something as you once were, because you have not practiced it in a long time • *We're a little rusty after having the summer off.* • See also **rusty** at RUST.

rut /rʌt/ *n* [C] a narrow channel, esp. one that has been unintentionally cut into the ground by a wheel • If a person or organization is **in a rut**, they have not changed what they do or how they do it for a very long time: *I was in a rut and couldn't get out of it.*

ruthless /'ruːθ·ləs/ *adj* cruel, or determined to succeed without caring about others • *a ruthless terrorist group* ○ *To compete abroad requires ruthless cost-cutting at home.*

RV *n* [C] *abbreviation for* **recreational vehicle**, see at RECREATION

Rx /'ɑr'eks/ *symbol* a medical PRESCRIPTION (= a doctor's written order for the medicine a person should receive)

rye /raɪ/ *n* [U] a type of grasslike plant, the grain of which is used to feed animals and to make flour for bread • **Rye (whiskey)** is a type of strong alcoholic drink made with this grain.

S, s

S LETTER , **s** /es/ *n* [C] *pl* **S's** or **Ss** or **s's** or **ss** the 19th letter of the English alphabet

S. SOUTH , **So.** *n* [U], *adj abbreviation for* SOUTH or SOUTHERN

S SIZE *adj* [not gradable] *abbreviation for* SMALL LESS, used esp. on clothing to show its size

Sabbath /'sæb·əθ/ *n* [C] the day of the week set aside by some religions as a day of rest and worship

sabbatical /sə'bæt̬·ɪ·kəl/ *n* [C/U] time away from work given to college or university teachers, esp. to do research, study, or travel • *Professor Logan will be on sabbatical this term.* [U]

saber /'seɪ·bər/ *n* [C] a weapon with a sharp blade, used esp. in the past by soldiers on horses

sable /'seɪ·bəl/ *n* [C] *pl* **sables** or **sable** a small animal from cold regions that has very soft, dark brown fur, or the fur of this animal used esp. to make luxurious coats

sabotage /'sæb·ə,tɑʒ/ *v* [T] to intentionally damage or destroy (property) • *Enemy agents had sabotaged the bridge.* ○ (*fig.*) *The bombing was meant to sabotage the peace talks.*

sabotage /'sæb·ə,tɑʒ/ *n* [U] • *The explosion was not an accident, it was sabotage.*

sac /sæk/ *n* [C] *specialized* a part inside a plant or animal which is like a small bag and contains liquid or air

saccharin /'sæk·ə·rən/ *n* [U] an artificial sweetener, used to replace sugar

saccharine /'sæk·ə·rən, -ə,rɑɪn/ *adj disapproving* too pleasant or charming, with too much feeling to be believed • *Longfellow's later poems are regarded as saccharine.*

sack BAG /sæk/ *n* [C] a bag, or the amount contained in a bag • *plastic sacks* ○ *a sack of flour*

sack FOOTBALL /sæk/ *v* [T] (in football) to bring (the other team's QUARTERBACK) to the ground before he can complete a play

sack STEAL /sæk/ *v* [T] to steal all the valuable things from (a place) and destroy it, usually during a war • *Villages were sacked and burned by the raiders.*

▫ **sack out** /'sæk'ɑʊt/ *v adv* [I] *infml* to go to sleep • *She sacked out in the front seat of the car.*

sacrament /'sæk·rə·mənt/ *n* [C] (in Christianity) an important religious ceremony, such as marriage, BAPTISM, or CONFIRMATION

sacred /'seɪ·krəd/ *adj* holy and deserving respect • *sacred writings/music* ○ *The rabbi plans to restore the sacred scroll.* ○ (*fig.*) *Art was sacred to her* (= extremely important and deserving respect). • A **sacred cow** is something accepted or believed without question: *Defense spending is a sacred cow in Congress.* • Compare PROFANE.

sacrifice GIVE UP /'sæk·rə,fɑɪs/ *v* [T] to give up (something) for something else considered more important • *He sacrificed his vacations to work on his book.*

sacrifice /'sæk·rə,fɑɪs/ *n* [C/U] • *My parents made many sacrifices to pay for my college education.* [C]

sacrifice OFFER A LIFE /'sæk·rə,fɑɪs/ *v* [I/T] to offer the life of (an animal or a person) to a god or gods in the hope of pleasing them, usually in a ceremonial killing

sacrifice /'sæk·rə,fɑɪs/ *n* [C/U] • *The Aztecs in Mexico practiced human sacrifice.* [U]

sacrilege /'sæk·rə·lɪdʒ/ *n* [C/U] the failure to treat something holy with the respect it should have, or an example of this • *Many thought it was sacrilege to move the bones to another place.* [U]

sacrilegious /,sæk·rə'lɪdʒ·əs/ *adj* • *Is it sacrilegious to ask whether there is a god or not?*

sacrosanct /'sæk·roʊ,sæŋt/ *adj* so important that there cannot be any change or question • *His time with his children was sacrosanct.*

sad NOT HAPPY /sæd/ *adj* **-dd-** showing, feeling, or causing unhappiness or regret • *I've just heard the saddest news.*

sadly /'sæd·li/ *adv* • *She spoke sadly about the loss of her home.*

sadness /'sæd·nəs/ *n* [U] • *There was a look of great sadness in his eyes.*

sadden /'sæd·ən/ *v* [T] • *It saddened me to learn of your father's death.*

sad UNPLEASANT /sæd/ *adj* **-dd-** very bad or regrettable • *The sad fact is that all the trees have got the virus.* • A **sad state of affairs** is a situation to be regretted: *It is a sad state of affairs when a doctor is killed for helping patients.* • **Sad to say** means that something is a cause for regret: *Sad to say, the violin was never found.*

sadly /'sæd·li/ *adv* • *If you think she doesn't care, you're sadly mistaken.*

saddle /'sæd·əl/ *n* [C] a seat, usually made of leather, fastened on the back of a horse for a rider • A saddle is also a seat on a bicycle or **motorcycle.** • If someone is **in the saddle**, they are in charge or in control: *The chairman is back in the saddle after his heart attack.*

saddle /'sæd·əl/ *v* [I/T] • *She saddled (up) the horse for her daughter.* [T/M]

▫ **saddle** *obj* **with** *obj* /'--,-/ *v prep* [T] to give (a job or responsibility) to (someone), although they do not want it • *They saddled me with cleaning up after the party.*

sadist /'seɪd·əst, 'sæd·/ *n* [C] a person who gets pleasure from hurting another person • Compare MASOCHIST.

sadistic /sə'dɪs·tɪk/ *adj* • *a sadistic killer*

sadism /'seɪˌdɪz·əm, 'sæd,ɪz-/ n [U] • *The violence and sadism in the film were horrific.*

sadly /'sæd·li/ adv • See at SAD NOT HAPPY, SAD UNPLEASANT.

sadness /'sæd·nəs/ n • See at SAD NOT HAPPY.

safari /sə'fɑr·i/ n [C] pl **safaris** a trip to watch, photograph, or hunt wild animals in their natural environment • *For his vacation, he plans to go on safari in Kenya.*

safe FREE FROM DANGER /seɪf/ adj free from danger or harm, or not causing danger or harm • *Have a safe trip.* ○ *Is this medicine safe for children?* ○ *I feel safe here.* • Safe also means not involving any risk or disagreement: *She's looking for some safer investments.* ○ *With most of the votes counted now, I think it's safe to say that we won.* [+ to infinitive] • People say **to be on the safe side** when they do something to avoid risk: *Maybe it won't rain, but to be on the safe side, take your umbrella.* • **Safe and sound** means not hurt or damaged: *Three days later, the hikers were found safe and sound.* • A **safe haven** is an officially protected place in an area of military activity, or any safe or peaceful place in a dangerous area. • **Safe sex** is the use of CONDOMS or other preventive methods to avoid catching a sexual disease, esp. AIDS.

safely /'seɪ·fli/ adv • *The plane landed safely in the storm.*

safe BOX /seɪf/ n [C] a strong box, usually made of steel, with a door and lock, where valuable things, esp. money or jewels, can be kept • A **safe deposit box** (also **safety deposit box**) is a strong box in a bank where you can keep valuable things, esp. documents or jewelry.

safe BASEBALL /seɪf/ adj [not gradable] (of a player in the game of baseball) having successfully reached a BASE • Compare OUT BASEBALL.

safeguard /'seɪf·gɑrd/ v [T] to protect (someone or something) from harm or destruction • *Judges have an obligation to safeguard our right to free speech and a free press.*

safeguard /'seɪf·gɑrd/ n [C] • *The best safeguard against someone stealing your car is to lock it.*

safekeeping /'seɪf'kiː·pɪŋ/ n [U] protection from harm or loss • *My friend left her jewelry with me for safekeeping when she went on vacation.*

safely /'seɪ·fli/ adv • See at SAFE FREE FROM DANGER.

safety /'seɪf·ti/ n [U] the condition of not being in danger or of not being dangerous • *For your safety, keep your seat belt securely fastened.* ○ *Fire officials worry about the safety of those heaters.* • A **safety belt** is a **seat belt**. See at SEAT FURNITURE. • A **safety deposit box** is a **safe deposit box**. See at SAFE BOX. • A **safety net** is something, esp. a government program, that protects or helps people:

Unemployment insurance is a safety net for people who lose their jobs. • A **safety pin** is a pin with a round end to hold the sharp point so that it will not stick you and will stay fastened. • A **safety razor** is a device for removing hair, esp. from the face, which has a blade that is partly covered to prevent you from unintentionally cutting the skin. • A **safety valve** is a device on a machine which allows steam or gas to escape if there is too much pressure: *(fig.) For people with stressful jobs, weekends in the country can be a good safety valve.*

sag /sæg/ v [I] **-gg-** to bend or sink lower • *It was a ramshackle building and its roof sagged.* ○ *Her shoulders sagged wearily.* • Sag also means to become weaker or less firm: *Muscles sag when you reach your 50s.* ○ *The economy is sagging.*

saga /'sɑg·ə/ n [C] a long, detailed story of connected events • *The Gold Rush was just one chapter in the saga of the old West.*

sage WISE /seɪdʒ/ adj [not gradable] esp. literary wise, esp. as a result of long experience • *sage advice*

sage /seɪdʒ/ n [C] literary a wise person, esp. an old man

sage PLANT /seɪdʒ/ n [U] an herb with gray-green leaves that is used to flavor foods in cooking

Sagittarius /ˌsædʒ·ə'ter·iː·əs/ n [C/U] the ninth sign of the ZODIAC, covering the period November 22 to December 21 and represented by a creature with a human upper body and horse's lower body, or a person born during this period

said /sed/ past simple and past participle of SAY

sail /seɪl/ v [I/T] to travel across water in a boat or ship, or to operate (a boat or ship) on the water • *He is not fun to sail with.* [I] ○ *I sail a small racing boat.* [T] • Sail also means to leave on a boat or ship: *When do we sail?* [I] • If you **sail through** something, you do it easily and confidently: *She sailed through Senate confirmation last year.*

sail /seɪl/ n [C] a sheet of material used to catch the wind and move a boat or ship • *I restored an old wooden boat and got a new canvas sail for it.* • A **sailboat** is a boat with one or more sails used to move it.

sailing /'seɪ·lɪŋ/ n [U] the sport or activity of using boats with sails • *I never really got into sailing.*

sailor /'seɪ·lər/ n [C] a person who operates or works on a boat or ship, or a person in the navy who is not an officer • *My dad is a sailor.*

saint /seɪnt/ (abbreviation **St.**) n [C] a holy person, esp. one who has been officially honored with this title by a Christian church • *Elizabeth Seton was the first person born in the US to be made a saint by the Roman Catholic Church.* • A saint is also a good, kind, and patient person: *His mother was a saint to everyone who knew her.*

saintly /'seɪnt·li/ *adj* • *He seemed the gentle, saintly man everyone said he was.*

sake ADVANTAGE /seɪk/ *n* [C] an advantage or benefit • *For his sake, I hope he has some protection.* ○ *She tried to look healthy, for her husband's sake.*

sake PURPOSE /seɪk/ *n* [U] purpose or reason • *He is unwilling to oppose it just for the sake of opposing.*

salacious /sə'leɪ·ʃəs/ *adj* causing or showing an unpleasantly strong interest in sexual matters • *a salacious joke/comment*

salad /'sæl·əd/ *n* [C/U] a mixture of raw vegetables, usually covered with a DRESSING (= liquid mixture) • *a green salad* [C] ○ *Lunches include soup or salad.* [U] • A salad is also a dish of small pieces of cold food, usually mixed with a sauce such as MAYONNAISE (= a creamy sauce of oil, vinegar, and eggs): *tuna/ egg/potato/macaroni salad* [U] • A **salad bar** is a table in a restaurant or store where you serve yourself from a variety of salads. • **Salad dressing** is a liquid mixture, such as oil, vinegar, and spices, added to vegetable salads to give them flavor.

salamander /'sæl·ə,mæn·dər/ *n* [C] a small AMPHIBIAN (= animal that lives in water and on land) that has a long, narrow body, four short legs, a long tail, and soft, wet skin

salami /sə'lɑm·i/ *n* [U] a large, strongly flavored SAUSAGE (= meat cut into small pieces and shaped in a tube) that is usually eaten cold in slices

salary /'sæl·ə·ri/ *n* [C] a fixed amount of money paid to someone for the work they are employed to do, esp. the amount paid every year • *a meager/generous salary* ○ *Teachers' salaries would rise an average of $1000 under the proposal.*

salaried /'sæl·ə·ri:d/ *adj* [not gradable] • *All our salaried employees have agreed to take a pay cut.*

sale SELL /seɪl/ *n* [C/U] an act of exchanging something for money • *You pay tax on the profits from the sale of buildings.* [U] ○ *The school raised money from book sales, bake sales, and individual contributors.* [C] ○ *When I bought this house, there were many, many homes for sale.* [U]

sales /seɪlz/ *pl n* the number of items sold • *US car sales got off to a hot start in January.* [C] • Sales is also the department that sells a company's products: *He works in sales.* • A **sales clerk** is someone who works in a store and sells goods to customers. • A **salesperson** (*male* **salesman**/*female* **saleswoman**) is someone who sells something. • A **sales representative** (also **sales rep**) is someone who travels to different places selling a company's products. • **Sales tax** is tax on things people buy in stores.

sale LOWER PRICE /seɪl/ *n* [C] an occasion when goods are sold at a lower price than usual • *a clearance sale* • *Are these dresses on sale (= reduced in price)?*

salient /'seɪ·li:·ənt/ *adj* [not gradable] most noticeable or important • *The salient fact about the case is that it involves an American.*

saline /'seɪ·li:n, -laɪn/ *adj medical* containing or consisting of salt • *a saline solution*

saliva /sə'laɪ·və/ *n* [U] the natural, watery liquid in the mouth that keeps it wet and helps prepare food for digestion

salivate /'sæl·ə,veɪt/ *v* [I] to produce saliva

sallow /'sæl·oʊ/ *adj* pale yellow and unhealthy looking • *a sallow face*

salmon /'sæm·ən/ *n* [C/U] *pl* **salmon** a medium-size fish with pink flesh which lives in the sea • *smoked/canned salmon* [U] ○ *They went salmon fishing.* [U]

salmonella /,sæl·mə'nel·ə/ *n* [C/U] *pl* **salmonella** a group of bacteria, some types of which live in food and cause illness in people who eat the food, or the illness caused by this bacteria

salon STORE /sə'lɑn, 'sæl·ɑn/ *n* [C] a store where you can obtain esp. a beauty service or fashionable clothes • *a beauty/tanning/hair salon*

salon MEETING /sæ'lɔː, sə'lɑn/ *n* [C] a regular meeting of important or influential people, esp. of writers or artists at the house of someone famous • *the Paris salon of Gertrude Stein*

saloon /sə'lu:n/ *n* [C] a place where alcoholic drinks are sold and drunk; a bar

salt FOOD /sɔːlt/ *n* [U] a common, white substance, found in sea water and in the ground, used to add flavor to food or to preserve it • *a grain of salt* ○ *Please pass the salt and pepper.* ○ *Add a pinch of salt (= small amount of it).* • A **saltshaker** is a small container for salt with holes in the top so the salt can be shaken out of it.

salt /sɔːlt/ *v* [T] • *She salted and peppered her stew.*

salt /sɔːlt/ *adj* [not gradable] containing or tasting of salt, or preserved with salt • *a salt pond/lake* ○ *salt pork/cod* • **Saltwater** is water containing salt, and often means having to do with or living in the sea: *saltwater fish/ plants* ○ *saltwater lakes*

salted /'sɔːl·təd/ *adj* [not gradable] • *salted nuts/pretzels*

salty /'sɔːl·ti/ *adj* tasting or smelling like salt • *salty popcorn* ○ *salty sea air*

salt CHEMICAL /sɔːlt/ *n* [C] *specialized* a chemical substance made with an acid • *potassium salts* • Salt is used to melt ice on roads and SIDEWALKS in the winter.

salt /sɔːlt/ *v* [T] • *Work crews were busy plowing and salting roads.*

□ **salt away** *obj*, **salt** *obj* **away** /'--'-/ *v adv* [M] to save (esp. money) to use at a later time • *She's salting away more money for retirement.*

salutary /'sæl·jə,ter·i/ *adj fml* causing improvement of behavior or character • *The effects of such a decision would not be salutary.*

salutation /ˌsæl·jəˈteɪ·ʃən/ *n* [C/U] a greeting in words or actions, or the words used at the beginning of a letter or speech • *Start your letter with the salutation "Dear Friends."* [C]

salute RECOGNIZE /səˈluːt/ *v* [I/T] to recognize or show respect for a member of the armed forces of higher rank than yourself, usually by raising the right hand to the side of the head • *When you see an officer, you must salute.* [I]

salute /səˈluːt/ *n* [C] • *Uniformed soldiers gave him a salute.* • A salute is also the firing of guns by a military organization to show respect for someone: *a 21-gun salute*

salute HONOR /səˈluːt/ *v* [T] to honor or express admiration publicly • *We salute the important work done by the association.*

salute /səˈluːt/ *n* [C] • *The Film Institute held a salute to Jack Nicholson.*

salvage /ˈsæl·vɪdʒ/ *v* [T] to save (something valuable) from damage, destruction, or loss • *After the storm, we were able to salvage some of our belongings, but the house was destroyed.*

salvation /sælˈveɪ·ʃən/ *n* [U] something that prevents danger, loss, or harm • *That blanket was my salvation when my car broke down in the snow.* • In some religions, salvation is the state of complete belief in God that will save believers from the punishment of God for evil or immoral acts. • The **Salvation Army** is an international Christian organization whose members work to help poor people.

salvo /ˈsæl·voʊ/ *n* [C] *pl* **salvos** or **salvoes** a firing of several guns at the same time, either in a war or in a ceremony, or a statement in an exchange of opinions • *His opening salvo in the debate sparked a war of words.*

samba /ˈsæm·bə, ˈsɑm-/ *n* [C/U] a rhythmic style of dance from Brazil, or the music for this dance • *Fans jumped up and danced the samba.* [U]

same EXACTLY LIKE /seɪm/ *adj* [not gradable] exactly like another or each other • *My sister and I have the same color hair.* ○ *Our grades were exactly the same.* • **By the same token** is used to mean that something you are about to say is also true, for the same reasons as what has just been said: *Players are happy to be in the news, but by the same token, they must not be distracted from their studies.* • (*infml*) **Same difference** is used when you think the difference between two things or choices is unimportant: *"They lowered the income tax, but raised the sales tax." "Same difference."*

same /seɪm/ *pronoun* • *Life was never the same again once the children started school.* ○ *It took longer to lose weight the second time, even though my diet was exactly the same.* • *"I thought that movie was awful." "Same here* (= I agree)*."*

sameness /ˈseɪm·nəs/ *n* [U] • *The fall TV line-up promises another season of sameness.*

same NOT ANOTHER /seɪm/ *adj* [not gradable] this one; not another, different one • *She keeps saying the same thing over and over.* ○ *Production is down by 80% from the same period last year.* ○ *She started studying languages and became interested in travel at the same time.* • *I can't hear what either of you is saying when you talk* **at the same time** (= together at once). • *No one likes war, but* **at the same time** (= despite this) *we are making money out of it.* • To be **in the same boat** is to be in the same difficult situation: *None of us has any money, so we're all in the same boat.* • If something is **the same old thing** or (*infml*) **the same old same old**, it has not changed: *You get tired of eating the same old thing for breakfast.*

sample /ˈsæm·pəl/ *n* [C] a small amount of something which shows what the rest is or should be like • *a free sample* ○ *a blood/urine sample* ○ *The booklet contains sample questions and answers.* • A sample of people is a small group that is tested to obtain information about the larger group: *The poll is based on a random sample of Montgomery voters.*

sample /ˈsæm·pəl/ *v* [T] to take or try (a small amount of something) • *He sampled a little of each dish.* ○ *Buma sampled opinions from people in both countries.*

sanatorium /ˌsæn·əˈtɔːr·iː·əm, -ˈtoʊr-/ *n* a SANITARIUM

sanctify /ˈsæŋk·təˌfaɪ/ *v* [T] to make holy • *Their marriage was sanctified by the church.*

sanctimonious /ˌsæŋk·təˈmoʊ·niː·əs/ *adj* disapproving morally better, or more religious • *Spare me your sanctimonious comments.*

sanction APPROVAL /ˈsæŋk·ʃən/ *n* [U] slightly *fml* approval or permission, esp. formal or legal • *To be just, a government must have the sanction of the governed.*

sanction /ˈsæŋk·ʃən/ *v* [T] • *The UN sanctioned intervention in the crisis.*

sanction PUNISHMENT /ˈsæŋk·ʃən/ *n* [C usually pl] an official action taken against a government to force it to behave in a particular way or as punishment for not doing so • *trade/ economic sanctions*

sanctity /ˈsæŋk·tət·i/ *n* [U] holiness, or a condition of deserving great respect • *the sanctity of life*

sanctuary /ˈsæŋk·tʃəˌwer·i/ *n* [C/U] protection or a safe place, esp. for someone or something being chased or hunted • *Fugitives took sanctuary in the church.* [U] ○ *Soldiers attacked an enemy sanctuary.* [C] • A sanctuary is a place where birds or animals can live and be protected: *a wildlife/bird sanctuary* [C]

sand SMALL GRAINS /sænd/ *n* [U] a mass of very small grains that at one time were rock and now form deserts and beaches • A **sandbag** is a strong, cloth bag filled with sand that is used as a defense against flooding and explosions

Thousands of sandbags were piled along the riverbank. • A **sandbox** is a square area filled with sand in which children can play. • A **sandcastle** is a model building of sand, often made by children on the beach. • A **sand dune** is a DUNE. • The **sandman** is an imaginary man who puts sand in children's eyes to make them go to sleep. • **Sandstone** is a soft, yellow or red rock, often used as a building material. • A **sandstorm** is a strong wind in a desert carrying a large amount of sand.

sandy /'sæn·di/ *adj* • *Cactuses grow well in sandy soil.* • Sandy hair is pale brown.

sand MAKE SMOOTH /sænd/ *v* [T] to make (a surface, esp. wood) smooth by rubbing it with SANDPAPER (= paper with sand stuck to it) or with a special tool • *The bookcase has to be sanded and stained.*

sandal /'sæn·dəl/ *n* [C] a light shoe consisting of a bottom part held onto the foot by straps • *a pair of sandals*

sandpaper /'sænd,peɪ·pər/ *n* [U] strong paper with a layer of sand or a similar rough substance stuck to one side, used for rubbing a surface in order to make it smooth

sandpaper /'sænd,peɪ·pər/ *v* [T] to rub (a surface, esp. wood) with sandpaper to make it smooth

sandwich /'sæn·dwɪtʃ/ *n* [C] slices or pieces of meat, cheese, salads, etc., put between two pieces of bread that are held together by the person who picks them up when ready to eat • *a bacon, lettuce, and tomato sandwich* ○ *My kids always eat peanut butter and jelly sandwiches for lunch.*

sandwich /'sæn·dwɪtʃ/ *v* [T always + adv/prep] to put (something or someone) in a small space between two other, usually bigger, things or people • *She lived in a skinny Victorian house sandwiched between two brownstones in Cambridge.*

sandy /'sæn·di/ *adj* • See at SAND SMALL GRAINS.

sane /seɪn/ *adj* [-er/-est only] having a reasonable or healthy mind, or showing good judgment and understanding • *Your work, he said, is the one thing that keeps you sane in this crazy world.*

sanity /'sæn·ət̬·i/ *n* [U] • *He was beginning to doubt his own sanity.*

sang /sæŋ/ *past simple of* SING

sanguine /'sæŋ·gwən/ *adj* (of someone or their character) positive and hopeful • *Some people expect the economy to continue to improve, but others are less sanguine.*

sanitarium /,sæn·ə'ter·iː·əm/, **sanatorium** /,sæn·ə'tɔːr·iː·əm, -'toʊr-/ *n* [C] (esp. in the past) a type of hospital for people who needed long periods of rest and treatment for their illnesses • *She died of tuberculosis at a sanitarium in Saranac Lake, N.Y., in 1914.*

sanitary /'sæn·ə,ter·i/ *adj* relating to health, esp. to standards of cleanliness and the protection of health by the removal of dirt and waste, including human waste • *He worked to improve sanitary conditions in New Orleans.* • A **sanitary napkin** is a soft, absorbent paper product worn by a woman between her legs during her **menstrual** period (= monthly bleeding).

sanitation /,sæn·ə'teɪ·ʃən/ *n* [U] the system used to keep healthy standards of cleanliness in a place where people live, esp. by removing waste products and garbage safely • *the Department of Sanitation* ○ *Sanitation workers are picking up the garbage.*

sanitize /'sæn·ə,taɪz/ *v* [T] to change (a story, record, or representation of something) to make it less shocking or upsetting, esp. by not showing or expressing everything • *Some critics want to sanitize the exhibition by removing graphic photographs of the bomb's effect on people.*

sanity /'sæn·ət̬·i/ *n* • See at SANE.

sank /sæŋk/ *past simple of* SINK

Santa Claus /'sænt·ə,klɔːz/, **Santa** /'sænt·ə/ *n* [C] an imaginary old man with white hair, a long white BEARD, and a red coat who, children are told, brings them presents at Christmas

sap WEAKEN /sæp/ *v* [T] **-pp-** to gradually weaken (someone's strength) • *Depression can sap the energy and self-esteem from an individual.*

sap LIQUID /sæp/ *n* [U] the liquid within a plant that carries food to all parts of it

sap PERSON /sæp/ *n* [C] *dated* a foolish person

sapling /'sæp·lɪŋ/ *n* [C] a young tree

sapphire /'sæf·aɪr/ *n* [C] a transparent precious stone that is usually bright blue

sarcasm /'sɑr,kæz·əm/ *n* [U] remarks that mean the opposite of what they say, made to criticize someone or something in a way that is amusing to others but annoying to the person criticized • *biting/heavy sarcasm*

sarcastic /sɑr'kæs·tɪk/ *adj* • *sarcastic comments*

sardine /sɑr'diːn/ *n* [C] a small, edible fish, often packed in large numbers in flat metal containers • *The train was so crowded, we were packed in like sardines* (= too close together).

sardonic /sɑr'dɑn·ɪk/ *adj* showing an amused attitude toward someone or something that suggests a criticism but does not express it • *a sardonic smile* ○ *Mildly sardonic, the chairman's soft-spoken cross-examination embarrassed hostile witnesses without humiliating them.*

sari /'sɑr·i/ *n* [C] a dress consisting of a very long piece of cloth wrapped around the body, worn esp. by Indian and Pakistani women

SASE *n* [C] *abbreviation for* self-addressed stamped envelope (= an envelope that has a stamp on it and the address of the person who sends it)

sash CLOTHING /sæʃ/ *n* [C] a long, narrow piece of cloth worn around the waist, or a strip of cloth worn over the shoulder and across the chest

sash WINDOW /sæʃ/ *n* [C] the frame of a window or door around a piece of glass

sassy /'sæs·i/ *adj* [-*er*/-*est* only] rude but not seriously offensive • *I was a sassy kid who sometimes talked back to my mother.*

SAT TEST /,es,eɪ'tiː/ *n* [C] one of two tests for entry into college that measure students' abilities and skills

sat SIT /sæt/ *past simple and past participle of* SIT

Sat. DAY OF THE WEEK *n* [U] *abbreviation for* SATURDAY

Satan /'seɪt·ən/ *n* the main evil spirit; the DEVIL (= the originator of evil and the enemy of God)

satanic /sə'tæn·ɪk, seɪ-/ *adj* evil, or done in worship of Satan • *satanic rituals*

satellite /'sæt·əl,aɪt/ *n* [C] a natural object moving around a larger object in space, or an artificial object sent up into space to travel around the earth • *a spy/weather satellite* ○ *The moon is a satellite of the earth.* • A **satellite dish** is a CONCAVE (= curved inward), circular object that receives television or other electronic signals.

satin /'sæt·ən/ *n* [U] a type of cloth that is shiny on one side but not on the other • *a satin dress*

satire /'sæ·taɪr/ *n* [C/U] a humorous way of criticizing people or ideas to show that they have faults or are wrong, or a piece of writing or a play that uses this style • *The play is a satire on corporate culture.* [C]

satirical /sə'tɪr·ɪ·kəl/ *adj* • *satirical humor*

satirist /'sæt·ə·rəst/ *n* [C] a person who writes or performs satires

satirize /'sæt·ə,raɪz/ *v* [T] • *Garry Trudeau would satirize him in his Doonesbury comic strip.*

satisfaction /,sæt·əs'fæk·ʃən/ *n* [C/U] the pleasant feeling you get when you receive something you wanted, or when you have done or are doing something you wanted to do • *She looked at the finished painting with satisfaction.* [U] ○ *He had the satisfaction of knowing he had done the right thing.* [U] ○ *The job had to be done to our satisfaction* (= to a standard that we approved). [U] • Satisfaction is also the fulfillment of a desire or need: *sexual satisfaction* [U]

satisfactory /,sæt·əs'fæk·tə·ri/ *adj* good or good enough, esp. for a particular need or purpose • *We did not feel the response was satisfactory and asked for more information.* ○ *Her progress so far has been satisfactory, and we expect a full recovery.*

satisfactorily /,sæt·əs'fæk·tə·rə·li/ *adv* • *The heating system is working satisfactorily now.*

satisfy /'sæt·əs,faɪ/ *v* [T] to please (someone) by giving them what they want or need, or to make (someone) feel pleased because a particular result they desired has happened • *Giving the baby her bottle seemed to satisfy her, and*

she stopped crying. ○ *I am not really satisfied with the job you did.* • To satisfy a standard is to show that you are qualified for it: *I'd like to go to that college if I can satisfy the entrance requirements.* • To be satisfied is also to be sure, with all your doubts removed: *I'm satisfied that the doctors did all they could to save her.* [+ *that* clause]

satisfying /'sæt·əs,faɪ·ɪŋ/ *adj* giving pleasure, esp. by taking care of a need or desire • *It's very satisfying to know that we were the ones who brought Sarah and Stephen together.* [+ *to* infinitive]

saturate /'sætʃ·ə,reɪt/ *v* [T] to make (something or someone) completely wet, or to make (a place) completely full of something • *Water thoroughly to saturate the soil.* ○ *Contemporary U.S. culture is completely saturated with technology.*

saturation /,sætʃ·ə'reɪ·ʃən/ *n* [U]

Saturday /'sæt·ər·di, -,deɪ/ (*abbreviation* **Sat.**) *n* [C/U] the day of the week after Friday and before Sunday • *Do you want to go out Saturday night?* [U] ○ *Saturdays are the only days I get to sleep late.* [C] • A **Saturday night special** is any small gun that is cheap, often bought illegally and used by criminals.

Saturn /'sæt·ərn/ *n* [U] the planet sixth in order of distance from the sun, after Jupiter and before Uranus

sauce /sɔːs/ *n* [C/U] a thick liquid prepared and served with food to add flavor • *barbecue/tomato sauce* [U] • A **saucepan** is a deep cooking pan with a long handle. PIC PANS

saucer /'sɔː·sər/ *n* [C] a small plate that goes under a cup • *a cup and saucer*

saucy /'sɔː·si, 'sæs·i/ *adj* [-*er*/-*est* only] rude and lacking respect • *a saucy child* • Saucy also means confident and full of energy in an entertaining, slightly sexual way: *a saucy musical review*

sauerkraut /'saʊr·kraʊt/ *n* [U] CABBAGE (= large, leafy vegetable) that has been cut into small pieces and preserved in its own salted juice • *Do you want sauerkraut on your frankfurter?*

sauna /'sɔː·nə, 'saʊ·nə/ *n* [C] a room or small building, often with wooden walls, that is heated to a high temperature and in which people sit for their health

saunter /'sɔːnt·ər, 'sɑnt-/ *v* [I always + adv/prep] to walk in a slow and relaxed way • *My cousin stood up, yawning, and sauntered away toward the door.*

sausage /'sɔː·sɪdʒ/ *n* [C/U] a food made of meat that has been cut into very small pieces, mixed with spices, and put into a thin and usually edible tube

sauté /sɔː'teɪ/ *v* [T] to fry (food) in a little oil or fat, usually until it is brown

savage FIERCE /'sæv·ɪdʒ/ *adj* (of an animal) wild and fierce, or (of a remark or action) violently cruel • *savage criticism* ○ *A savage beating left him in a coma.*

savage /'sæv·ɪdʒ/ *v* [T] to criticize (someone) cruelly • *The performance was savaged by the media.*

savagely /'sæv·ɪdʒ·li/ *adv* • *savagely attacked*
savagery /'sæv·ɪdʒ·ri/ *n* [U] violent cruelty

savage PERSON /'sæv·ɪdʒ/ *n* [C] *dated* someone who is thought to be in a wild state and to have no experience of a CIVILIZED society (= highly developed society) • USAGE: This word is often considered offensive.

save MAKE SAFE /seɪv/ *v* [T] to make or keep (someone or something) safe from danger or harm, or to bring (something) back to a satisfactory condition • *She jumped into the pool and saved the child from drowning.* ○ *His leg was partly crushed in the accident but the surgeon was able to save it.* ○ *Smoke detectors can save lives.* • To **save face** is to take an action to avoid having others lose respect for someone: *We said he left "to pursue other interests" to save face, but actually we fired him.*

save KEEP /seɪv/ *v* [I/T] to keep (money or something else) for use in the future • *I'm saving (up) for a new bike and I've got almost $100.* [I] ○ *If you save the receipts from your business trip, the company will reimburse you.* [T] ○ *I forgot to get milk—will you save my place in line while I get it?* [T] • (*specialized*) To save information on a computer is to store it in a computer file. [T]

savings /'seɪ·vɪŋz/ *pl n* the money you keep, esp. in a bank or other financial organization • *I'm going to put some of my savings into a down payment on a car.* • A **savings account** is money you put in a bank or similar financial organization to earn INTEREST (= a kind of profit).

save NOT WASTE /seɪv/ *v* [I/T] to prevent (time, money, or effort) from being lost or spent, or to help (someone) by taking an action to prevent time, money, etc., from being lost • *You'll save time if you take the car.* [T] ○ *The governor claims he can save the taxpayers $10 million a year.* [T] ○ *If you'd stop and pick up the kids on your way home, it will save me from having to do it later.* [T] • *I don't know why I bother talking to you—I might as well save my breath* (= not talk, because I know you are not listening).

save SPORTS /seɪv/ *n* [C] (in some sports) the stopping of the ball or other object from going into the goal you are defending • *We watched a soccer game on TV, and the goalie made several spectacular saves.*

save EXCEPT /seɪv/, **save for** /'seɪv·fɔːr, -fər/ *prep* but or except (for) • *They found all the lost documents save one.* ○ *The walls were bare save for a poster.*

savior /'seɪv·jər/ *n* [C] a person who saves someone from danger or harm • In Christianity, the Savior is a name for Jesus.

savor /'seɪ·vər/ *v* [T] to enjoy (food or an expe-

rience) slowly, in order to appreciate it as much as possible • *He wanted to savor his time with Henrietta and their grown children.*

savvy /'sæv·i/ *n* [U] *infml* practical knowledge and ability • *She has a lot of marketing savvy.*
savvy /'sæv·i/ *adj infml* • *He's a politically savvy guy.*

saw SEE /sɔː/ *past simple of* SEE

saw TOOL /sɔː/ *n* [C] a tool that has a blade with sharp points along one edge, used for cutting hard materials, such as wood or metal • *a circular saw* ○ *a hand-held saw* • **Sawdust** is the very small grains that are produced when you cut wood. • A **sawmill** is a place where wood is cut into boards or other forms, usually with heavy machinery.

saw /sɔː/ *v* [I/T] *past simple* **sawed**, *past part* **sawn** /sɔːn/ or **sawed** to cut with a saw • *I sawed off the end of the plank.* [M]

saxophone /'sæk·sə,foʊn/, *short form* **sax** /sæks/ *n* [C/U] a musical instrument that is played by blowing through a REED (= thin piece of wood), or this instrument generally

say SPEAK /seɪ/ *v* [T] *past* **said** /sed/, he/she/it **says** /sez/ to speak or pronounce (words) • *How do you say your name?* ○ *The child said her prayers every night.* LP SAY, TELL, SPEAK p. 758.

say EXPRESS /seɪ/ *v* [I/T] *past* **said** /sed/, he/she/it **says** /sez/ to express (something) in words, or to tell someone (something) • *What did you say to him?* [T] ○ *Mom said to meet her in front of the building.* [I] • To say also means to communicate without using words, esp. in music and art: *What do you think the artist said in this painting?* [T] • If you **say** something **to yourself** you think it: *I said to myself, I'd better take care of that now.* • *It says a lot for her determination* (= shows how determined she is) *that she practices the piano so much.* • **Say what you will** means no matter what can be said about someone or something: *Say what you will about them, they are always willing to help when you need them.* • People will tell you to **say when** if they are serving you food or drink and want you to tell them when to stop giving you more. • **Says who?** is used to show that what someone has just said to you is not likely to happen: *"I'm going to win for sure." "Says who?"* • **To say the least** is used to show that what you are saying is not as much as you could say about something: *She's embarrassed about her bad temper, to say the least.*

say STATE AN OPINION /seɪ/ *v* [I/T] *past* **said** /sed/, he/she/it **says** /sez/ to state (an opinion) • *If they're late, I say (that) we go without them.* [+ (that) clause] • Say can also mean imagine: *Say (that) you won the lottery—what would you do?* [+ (that) clause]

say /seɪ/ *n* [U] the right or opportunity to give your opinion or be involved in making decisions • *I have no say in hiring and firing.*

say GIVE INFORMATION /seɪ/ *v* [I/T] *past* **said** /sed/, he/she/it **says** /sez/ (of a sign or writ-

SAY, TELL, TALK, AND SPEAK

say and tell

Say and tell are used for direct speech. **Say** is more common in this use.

"Hi," she **said**. *"I'm Melissa."* • *"I'm Melissa," she* **told** *him.*

With **tell**, the listener must be mentioned. The listener is not usually mentioned with **say**, but if it is, *to* is required.

"Hi," she **said to** *him. "I'm Melissa."*

Both **say** and **tell** can be used with orders or instructions.

Max **said**, *"Be careful with those boxes!"* • *"Be careful with those boxes!" Max* **told** *me.*

Say can be used with questions, exclamations, and other forms of speech, though the common verb used with questions is *ask*.

Then I **said**, *"How do you know?"* • *"Good grief!" he* **said**. *"You nearly killed me."* • *She* **said** *"hi."*

Say and tell are also used for reported speech. With **tell** the listener is usually mentioned.

She **said** *that her name was Melissa.* • *She* **told** *him where she worked.*

Tell is often used with instructions or orders.

Max **told** *me to be careful with the boxes.* • **Tell** *her to come back at three o'clock.*

Both **say** and **tell** can be used in passive sentences.

She **is said** *to earn $100,000.* • *We* **were told** *(that) she earns $100,000.*

Say and tell can be used to mean "to give information."

The sign **said** *that the road was closed.* • *The label* **told** *us nothing about the contents.*

Tell can be used with a noun object that refers to the information given.

Tell *me your problem.* • *Did he* **tell** *you the answer?*

Say can be used to mean "to express an idea" or "to pronounce a word or phrase."

He **said** *yes.* • *How do you* **say** *"please" in Greek?* • *How do you* **say** *your last name?*

Tell is used in some common expressions to describe the character of the words or the type of speech used. These expressions can include the listener or not.

I think she was **telling** *the truth.* • *He* **told** *me a lie.* • *Grandpa* **told** *a story.* • **Tell** *me a joke.*

talk and speak

Talk and speak are usually used without an object. **Talk** is the word generally used to describe people having a conversation.

A couple of men **were talking** *in the hallway.* • *She* **spoke** *slowly and clearly.* • *My daughter is learning* **to talk/speak**.

Talk, speak, and tell can be used with *about* and *of* (*of* is more formal).

We **talked** ***about*** *the future.* • *He* **spoke** ***of*** *his plans for the company.* • *He* **told** *me* ***about*** *his trip to Mexico.*

Talk, speak, and say can be used with to. **Speak** can also be used with *with*.

The little girl **talked** ***to*** *herself as she played.* • *I'd like to* **talk/speak** ***to*** *you for a minute.* • *Can I* **speak** ***to/with*** *Andy, please?* • **Say** *something* ***to*** *him.*

Talk and speak can be used with languages. Note that only **speak** is used for the ability to talk in a language.

I (can) **speak** *a little Spanish.* • *Do you* **speak** *Japanese?* • *They were* **talking/speaking** *(in) French.*

Talk is used in some common expressions that describe the character of of what is being said.

Whenever they get together, they **talk** *politics.* • *When are you going to start* **talking** *sense* (= saying something reasonable)? • *He's* **talking** *nonsense.*

ing) to give information or instructions • *What does that sign say?* [T]

aying /'seɪ·ɪŋ/ *n* [C] a well-known expression or wise statement • *I hate T-shirts with sayings on them.*

ay–so /'seɪ·soʊ/ *n* [U] *infml* authority or approval to do something • *A coach's responsibility is to have the final say-so on any subject.*

cab SKIN COVERING /skæb/ *n* [C] a hard covering of dry blood that forms over a cut or sore • *Don't pick at your scab!*

cab WORKER /skæb/ *n* [C] someone who takes the place of a worker who is STRIKING (= joining in an organized refusal to work)

cads /skædz/ *pl n infml* a large number or amount • *There were scads of dogs, all sizes, shapes, and colors.*

caffold /'skæf·əld, -oʊld/ *n* [C] a structure workers can stand on while working on a building, or a structure from which to HANG (= kill by hanging from a rope around the neck) criminals sentenced to death

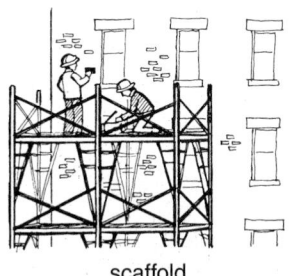

scaffold

caffolding /'skæf·əl·dɪŋ, -ˌoʊl·dɪŋ/ *n* [U] a raised structure that supports workers and materials during work on a building • *The scaffolding rises 10 stories above the street.*

calawag /'skæl·ə,wæg/ *n* [C] someone who causes trouble in a playful way, or a charming person who is slightly dishonest • *That's the last time that scalawag is going to steal from me.*

cald /skɔːld/ *v* [T] to burn (someone) with very hot liquid or steam • *The liquid spilled out and scalded his hand.* • To scald a liquid is to heat it until it almost boils: *scald the milk*

scalding /'skɔːl·dɪŋ/ *adj, adv* • *You can wash off the wax with scalding water.*

cale MEASURING SYSTEM /skeɪl/ *n* [C] a range of numbers used as a system to measure or compare things • *Restaurant ratings are on a scale of zero to five stars.*

cale SERIES OF MARKS /skeɪl/ *n* [C] a series of marks in a line with regular spaces between them for measuring, or an object for measuring marked in this way • *The two scales show inches and centimeters.*

cale SIZE / LEVEL /skeɪl/ *n* [U] the size or level of something in comparison to what is average • *Our problems are like those in the city, just on a smaller scale.*

scale WEIGHING DEVICE /skeɪlz/ *n* [C] a device for weighing people or things • *a baby scale* ○ *a postal scale*

scale SIZE RELATIONSHIP /skeɪl/ *n* [C/U] the relationship of the size of a map, drawing, or model of something to the size of the actual thing • *The model was built at a 1-inch-to-1-foot scale.* [C]

scale MUSIC /skeɪl/ *n* [C] a set of musical notes in which each note is higher or lower than the previous one by a particular amount • *Tyler practices scales on the piano every day.* • PIC NOTES

scale SKIN /skeɪl/ *n* [C usually pl] any of the thin pieces of hard skin covering the bodies of fish, snakes, and LIZARDS

scaly /'skeɪ·li/ *adj* [-er/-est only] • *Reptiles have scaly skin.* • If a person's skin is scaly, it is very dry.

scale CLIMB /skeɪl/ *v* [T] to climb up something steep, such as a cliff or wall • *He scaled a steep cliff beside the river.*

□ **scale back/down** (*obj*), **scale** (*obj*) **back/down** /'-'-/ *v adv* [I/M] to reduce (something) in size or amount • *Sid will have to scale back his plans.* [M]

scallion /'skæl·jən/ *n* [C] a small, thin onion with a white bottom and a green stem and leaves, which is eaten in salads and other dishes

scallop /'skɑl·əp, 'skæl-/ *n* [C] a sea creature with two joined, flat, round shells, or the thick, round muscle of this animal eaten as food

scalp HEAD /skælp/ *n* [C] the skin on the upper part of the head where the hair grows • *His hair was cut so short you could see his scalp.*

scalp /skælp/ *v* [T] • *Cody killed the Cheyenne chief and then scalped him* (= cut off the skin on his head).

scalp SELL /skælp/ *v* [T] to sell (tickets) unofficially at increased prices

scalper /'skæl·pər/ *n* [C] • *We tried to get tickets, but the scalpers wanted $150 per ticket.*

scalpel /'skæl·pəl/ *n* [C] a small, very sharp knife used for exact cutting, esp. for an operation

scam /skæm/ *n* [C] *infml* a dishonest or illegal plan or activity, esp. one for making money • *She was involved in an insurance scam, collecting on false accident claims.*

scamper /'skæm·pər/ *v* [I always + adv/prep] (esp. of small children and animals) to run with small, quick steps • *The kitten scampered around the kitchen, chasing a ball.*

scan /skæn/ *v* [I/T] **-nn-** to examine (something) carefully • *This technique is used to scan for defective genes.* [I] • If an image or text on paper is scanned into a computer, it is changed into electronic information by a special device: *A little hand-held device beeps as soon as it has scanned a bar code.* [T] • If you scan a text you read it quickly: *I scanned a few pages* *of the book and thought it looked interesting.* [T]

scan /skæn/ *n* [C] • *A quick scan of my calendar shows that I'm pretty busy this week.* • A scan is an examination of the inside of something, such as part of the body or a package, using a computerized device to produce an image of what cannot be seen with the eyes: *a medical scan of the head* ∘ *a security scan of passengers' bags*

scanner /'skæn·ər/ *n* [C] a device that changes images or text into electronic form • *a supermarket checkout scanner* ∘ *An MRI scanner makes images of the brain, spinal cord, and other organs.*

scandal /'skæn·dᵊl/ *n* [C/U] an action or event that is considered immoral, causing the public to react with shock or anger • *She was at the center of scandals involving adultery and drugs.* [C]

scandalize /'skæn·də,laɪz/ *v* [T] to shock (someone) with an action or opinion thought of as immoral or wrong • *His novel scandalized readers with his description of sex-for-power swaps in Washington.*

scandalous /'skæn·də·ləs/ *adj* • *She has a reputation for spreading scandalous gossip.*

scant /skænt/ *adj* [not gradable] very little or not much • *I paid scant attention to the movie's plot.* • Scant can also mean not quite a full measure of something: *Pour the batter by scant ¼ cups onto the hot griddle.*

scanty /'skænt·i/ *adj* • *a scanty dress* ∘ *Help has been scanty.*

scantily /'skænt·ᵊl·i/ *adv* • *This young woman was very scantily attired.*

scapegoat /'skeɪp·goʊt/ *n* [C] someone who is blamed or punished for another's faults or actions • *When things don't go well, people always look for a scapegoat.*

scar /skɑr/ *n* [C] a mark left on the skin by a cut or burn that has healed • *(fig.) The loss of a parent causes permanent scars for many children.*

scar /skɑr/ *v* [T] **-rr-** • *She was badly scarred by the fire.*

scarce /skers, skærs/ *adj* [-er/-est only] not available in necessary amounts, or rare • *Jobs are scarce.*

scarcity /'sker·sət·i, 'skær-/ *n* [C/U] a lack of something • *A scarcity of flour makes bread, cake, and other baked goods more expensive.* [C]

scarcely ONLY JUST /'sker·sli, 'skær-/ *adv* [not gradable] only just or almost not • *I could scarcely move my arm after the accident.*

scarcely NOT /'sker·sli, 'skær-/ *adv* [not gradable] *slightly fml* certainly not • *He would scarcely have broken it on purpose.*

scare /sker, skær/ *v* [I/T] to feel frightened, or to cause (someone) to feel frightened • *Snakes scare me.* [T] ∘ *Jesse doesn't scare easily.* [I] • If you **scare the daylights out of** someone,

scare someone **to death**, or **scare the he**▮ **out of** someone, you frighten them very much • *The area was under attack, and it scared th*▮ *daylights out of us.* ∘ *She is scared to death o*▮ *thunderstorms.*

scare /sker, skær/ *n* [C] • *You gave me a rea*▮ *scare.* • **Scare tactics** are a way to achieve ▮ particular result by frightening people s▮ much that they do what you want them to do▮ *They teach kids not to take drugs by using scar*▮ *tactics.*

scared /skerd, skærd/ *adj* • *I was scared, and*▮ wanted to go home.

scary /'sker·i, 'skær·i/ *adj* [-er/-est only] • *Neu*▮ *York isn't very scary.*

□ **scare away/off** *obj*, **scare** *obj* **away/off** /'--'-' '-'-/ *v adv* [M] to cause (a person or animal) t▮ go or stay away • *I wished I could scare thos*▮ *crows away.* ∘ *A show like that could scare of*▮ *advertisers.*

□ **scare up** *obj*, **scare** *obj* **up** /'-'-/ *v adv* [M▮ *infml* to find or obtain (something) despite dif▮ ficulties • *She's campaigning hard, trying t*▮ *scare up votes.* ∘ *I'll scare up something for u*▮ *to eat.*

scarecrow /'sker·kroʊ, 'skær-/ *n* [C] an objec▮ that looks like a person dressed in rags and stands in a garden or field to frighten birds away

scarf CLOTH /skɑrf/ *n* [C] *pl* **scarves** /skɑrvz▮ or **scarfs** /skɑrfs/ a piece of cloth that cover▮ the shoulders, neck, or head for warmth or ap▮ pearance • *A heavy woolen scarf hid most o*▮ *his face.*

scarf EAT /skɑrf/ *v* [I/T] *infml* to eat a lot o▮ food quickly • *In no time, I scarfed down two*▮ *hamburgers, French fries, and something t*▮ *drink.* [I]

scarlet /'skɑr·lət/ *adj, n* (of) a bright red color • *scarlet roses* ∘ *She was dressed in scarlet.* [U▮

scary /'sker·i, 'skær·i/ *adj* • See at SCARE.

scat /skæt/ *exclamation infml* said to make an animal go away quickly • *Go on—scat! Get of*▮ *my chair!*

scathing /'skeɪ·ðɪŋ/ *adj* severely and unkind▮ ly critical • *He delivered a scathing attack on*▮ *the president.*

scatter /'skæt̬·ər/ *v* [I/T] to move apart in many directions, or to throw (something) in different directions • *We grew up in a smal*▮ *town, but now we're scattered all over the coun*▮ *try.* [I]

scattered /'skæt̬·ərd/ *adj* • *There will be scat*▮ *tered showers throughout the afternoon.*

scavenge /'skæv·əndʒ/ *v* [I/T] to search for and collect (unwanted food or objects), or (of animals or birds) to feed on decaying flesh • *We scavenged a table and chairs someone had*▮ *thrown out.* [T] ∘ *The crows scavenged on the dead carcass.* [I]

scavenger /'skæv·ən·dʒər/ *n* [C] an animal, bird, or person who scavenges • *A* **scavenger hunt** *is a game in which people must collect a* *number of specified items in a given period of time without buying them.*

scenario /sə'nær·i:,ou, -'ner-, -'nɑr-/ *n* [C] *pl* **scenarios** a description of possible events, or a description of the story of a movie, play, or other performance • The worst-case scenario is the worst situation that can be imagined: *In the worst-case scenario, the whole coast would be under water.*

scene PLAY / MOVIE /si:n/ *n* [C] a part of a play or movie in which the action stays in one place for a continuous period • *The opening scene of the movie was filmed in New York City.*

scene VIEW /si:n/ *n* [C] a view or picture of a place • *The scene from the mountaintop was breathtaking.* ○ *He painted a street scene.*

scene PLACE /si:n/ *n* [C usually sing] a place where an actual or imagined event happens • *Bloodstains were found at the scene of the crime.* ○ *Minutes after the gunshot, police were on the scene* (= they arrived at the place quickly).

scene EVENT /si:n/ *n* [C] an event, actual or imaginary • *Scenes of violence in the street were captured by cameramen.*

scene AREA /si:n/ *n* [U] a particular area of activity or way of life • *the fashion/music/drug scene* ○ *He disappeared from the political scene after failing to win reelection.*

scene SHOW /si:n/ *n* [C] a show of emotion or anger • *She made a scene at the checkout when I wouldn't buy her any candy.*

scenery COUNTRYSIDE /'si:·nə·ri/ *n* [U] the general appearance of natural surroundings, esp. when these are beautiful • *We stopped at the top of the hill to admire the scenery.*

scenic /'si:·nɪk/ *adj* [not gradable] having or showing beautiful natural surroundings • *They took the scenic route on the way home.*

scenery THEATER /'si:·nə·ri/ *n* [U] the painted backgrounds used on a theater stage to represent the place where the action is

scent /sent/ *n* [C/U] a smell, esp. when pleasant, or a smell left behind by an animal or person • *The scent of lilacs permeated the air.* [C] ○ *The dogs were onto the lost boy's scent* (= were following his smell). [C] • Scent is also PERFUME (= liquid with a pleasant smell). [U]

scent /sent/ *v* [T] • *Perfume scented the air* (= filled the air with a smell). ○ *The dogs eventually scented the fox* (= discovered it by smelling). • If you scent something, you have a feeling that something exists or is present: *We could scent danger/trouble/success.*

scented /'sent·əd/ *adj* [not gradable] • *scented perfume/soap/candles*

scepter /'sep·tər/ *n* [C] a decorated stick that is carried by a queen or king as a symbol of power, esp. at state ceremonies

schedule /'skedʒ·u:l, -əl; *Cdn often* 'ʃedʒ-/ *n* [C/U] a list of planned activities or things to be done at or during a particular time • *Amid her hectic schedule, she found time to stop by.* [C] ○

The work schedule for this month is posted on the staff bulletin board. [C] ○ *The construction was completed ahead of/on/behind schedule* (= early/on time/late). [U] ○ *Everything went according to schedule* (= as planned). [U] • An airline/bus/train schedule (also **timetable**) is a list of days and times that aircraft/buses/trains leave and arrive at particular places. [C]

schedule /'skedʒ·u:l, -əl; *Cdn often* ʃedʒ-/ *v* [T] to plan something for a particular time • *The meeting has been scheduled for tomorrow afternoon.* ○ *The film is scheduled to begin production in August.*

scheme /ski:m/ *n* [C] a plan for doing or organizing something • *The committee came up with a creative fundraising scheme.* ○ *The yellow and white color scheme brightened up the kitchen.* • A scheme is also a secret and dishonest plan: *They devised a scheme to defraud the government of millions of dollars.* [+ to infinitive] • *Being invited to the White House is unimportant* **in the scheme of things** (= considering everything).

scheme /ski:m/ *v* [I] to make a plan, esp. a secret and dishonest one • *He was scheming to get the top job from the moment he joined the company.* [+ to infinitive]

schemer /'ski:·mər/ *n* [C] *disapproving*

schism /'sɪz·əm, 'skɪz-/ *n* [C] a division of a group into two opposing groups, esp. in a church

schizo /'skɪt·sou/ *n, adj short form of* **schizophrenic**, see at SCHIZOPHRENIA

schizophrenia /,skɪt·sə'fri:·ni:·ə/ *n* [U] *medical* a mental illness in which a person's thoughts and feelings are not related to reality

schizophrenic /,skɪt·sə'fren·ɪk/, *short form* **schizo** /'skɪt·sou/ *adj* [not gradable]

schizophrenic /,skɪt·sə'fren·ɪk/, *short form* **schizo** /'skɪt·sou/ *n* [C] a person who has schizophrenia

schlep CARRY /ʃlep/, **schlepp, shlep** *v* [T] **-pp-** *infml* to carry (an object) with effort • *We schlepped our suitcases into the airport.* [I]

schlep GO /ʃlep/ *v* [I] to go or move around with effort • *I've been schlepping all over town looking for just the right present.*

schlock /ʃlɑk/ *n* [U] *slang* anything cheap or of low quality • *The jewelry she bought on the street was real schlock.*

schmaltzy, schmalzy /'ʃmɔːlt·si, 'ʃmɑlt-/ *adj infml disapproving* causing extreme emotions of love or sadness, esp. in the arts • *They spend a lot of time together listening to schmaltzy love songs.*

schmaltz, schmalz /ʃmɔːlts, ʃmɑlts/ *n* [U] *infml* • *His writing is full of schmaltz.*

schmooze, shmooze /ʃmuːz/ *v* [I] *infml* to talk informally with someone • *Mike's out on the porch schmoozing with the neighbors.*

schmuck /ʃmʌk/ *n* [C] *slang* a stupid or fool-

ish person • USAGE: This word is considered offensive by some, esp. by people who speak Yiddish.

schnapps /ʃnæps, ʃnɑps/ n [U] a colorless alcoholic drink, usually made from grain, potato, or fruit

scholar /'skɑl·ər/ n [C] a person with great knowledge, usually of a particular subject • A scholar is also a student who has been given a college or university SCHOLARSHIP (= money to pay for their studies).

scholarly /'skɑl·ər·li/ adj relating to, or typical of scholars • John is more serious and scholarly than his brother. ○ Her research was published in a scholarly journal.

scholarship /'skɑl·ərˌʃɪp/ n [C/U] the qualities, methods, or achievements of a scholar • Recent scholarship has addressed this scientific issue. [U] • A scholarship is also money given to a person to help pay for their education. [C]

scholastic /skə'læs·tɪk/ adj [not gradable] relating to school and education • Laura's scholastic achievements won her acceptance into Harvard.

school EDUCATION /skuːl/ n [C/U] a place where people, esp. young people, are educated • a nursery / grade / elementary / secondary / graduate school [C] ○ What school do you go to? [C] ○ The kids walk to school. [U] ○ The whole school knew about the incident (= all the students and teachers at the school knew about it). [C] • School also means the time spent in school: School is out early today. [U] • School also means the process of being educated in a school: Krista starts school in the fall. [U] ○ I've got one more year of school left. [U] • A school is also a part of a college or university specializing in a particular subject or group of subjects: Johns Hopkins School of Advanced International Studies [C] • A school is also a place where a particular subject or skill is taught: a driving/dancing/art school [C] • School is also a college or university: We went to school together in Atlanta. [U] • If you learn something in the school of hard knocks, you learn it as a result of difficult experience. • A schoolteacher is a person who teaches school. • Schoolwork is studying done at school or at home. • LP EDUCATION IN THE US

school /skuːl/ v [T] to train or teach • She was schooled locally and then went away to college.

schooling /'skuː·lɪŋ/ n [U] training or education • He had little formal schooling (= education at school).

school GROUP /skuːl/ n [C] a group of artists, writers, or thinkers, whose styles, methods, or ideas are similar • Her painting belongs to the Impressionist school. • A school of thought is a set of ideas or opinions about a matter shared by a group of people: There are two schools of thought on reducing unemployment.

school SEA ANIMALS /skuːl/ n [C] a large number of fish or other sea animals swimming in a group

schooner /'skuː·nər/ n [C] a sailing ship with two or more MASTS, and sails parallel to the length of the ship

science /'sɑɪ·əns/ n [C/U] (knowledge obtained from) the systematic study of the structure and behavior of the natural and physical world, by observation and experiment • Advances in medical science mean that people are living longer. [U] ○ She shows a talent for math and science. [U] • Sciences are also particular areas of science, such as biology, chemistry, and physics. [C] • Science also refers to subjects which are studied like a science: political/computer science [U] • **Science fiction** (also infml **sci-fi**) is writing about imagined developments in science and their effect on life esp. in the future.

scientific /ˌsɑɪ·ən'tɪf·ɪk/ adj • The biotechnology center is on the cutting edge of scientific research. • Scientific also means using organized methods, like those of science: I haven't been very scientific about the design of the garden.

scientifically /ˌsɑɪ·ən'tɪf·ɪ·kli/ adv

scientist /'sɑɪ·ən·təst/ n [C] an expert in science, esp. in the physical or natural sciences

sci–fi /'sɑɪ'fɑɪ/ n [U] short form of science fiction, see at SCIENCE

scintillating /'sɪnt·ᵊlˌeɪt·ɪŋ/ adj exciting and intelligent • It was a superb script and a scintillating production.

scion /'sɑɪ·ən/ n [C] fml a young member of a rich and famous family

scissors /'sɪz·ərz/ pl n a cutting device consisting of two blades, each with a ring-shaped handle, which are joined in the middle so that their sharp edges move against each other, used esp. for cutting paper or cloth • a pair of scissors

scoff /skɑf, skɔːf/ v [I] to speak about someone or something in a way which shows that you have no respect for them • The coach scoffed at the notion that he was about to resign.

scold /skoʊld/ v [T] to criticize angrily (someone who has done something wrong) • His mother scolded him for breaking the window.

scolding /'skoʊl·dɪŋ/ n [C/U] • I got a scolding for coming home late. [C]

scone /skoʊn, skɑn/ n [C] a small, usually round, soft bread made with flour, milk, and fat

scoop TOOL /skuːp/ n [C] a tool with a handle and a curved, open end, used to dig out and move an amount of something • an ice-cream scoop • A scoop is also the amount held by a scoop: Just one scoop of mashed potatoes for me, please.

scoop /skuːp/ v [T] • Scoop out the melon with a spoon. ○ He scooped the sand into a bucket.

scoop NEWS /skuːp/ n [C usually sing] a news story discovered and published by one newspaper before all the others • The scoop is also the most recent information or details: *What's the scoop on the new boss?*

scoop /skuːp/ *v* [T] • *Another paper scooped the story, just as we were about to publish it.*

scoot /skuːt/ *v* [I] *infml* to go quickly • *I need to scoot over to the post office.* • To scoot is also to slide while sitting: *Scoot over and make room for your sister.*

scooter TOY /ˈskuːt̬·ər/ *n* [C] a child's vehicle with two or three small wheels joined to the bottom of a narrow board and a long vertical handle fixed to the front wheel. The rider stands with one foot on the board and pushes against the ground with the other foot, while turning the handle to direct movement.

scooter MOTOR VEHICLE /ˈskuːt̬·ər/ *n* [C] a motor vehicle with two wheels, that is similar to, but smaller than, a **motorcycle**

scope RANGE /skoʊp/ *n* [U] the range of matters considered or dealt with • *We are going to widen the scope of the investigation.*

scope OPPORTUNITY /skoʊp/ *n* [U] the opportunity for activity • *There is limited scope for further reducing the workforce.*

scorch /skɔːrtʃ/ *v* [I/T] to burn (a surface) slightly, causing it to change color • *The iron was too hot and scorched the shirt.* [T]

scorch /skɔːrtʃ/ *n* [C] a burn mark on a surface

scorcher /ˈskɔːr·tʃər/ *n* [C] *infml* an extremely hot day • *Yesterday was a real scorcher.*

scorching /ˈskɔːr·tʃɪŋ/ *adj, adv* [not gradable] (of the weather) very hot • *I don't want to be outside in this scorching heat.* ○ *It was scorching hot at the beach.*

score WIN /skɔːr, skoʊr/ *v* [I/T] to win or obtain (a point or something else that gives you an advantage) in a competitive activity, such as a sport, game, or test • *Has either team scored yet?* [I] ○ *The Packers scored a touchdown with two minutes to go in the football game.* [T] ○ *A student from Gettysburg scored a perfect 1600 points on the college entrance exam.* [T] ○ *(fig.) Nearly every bomb scored a hit* (= destroyed something). [T] • *(rude slang)* (esp. of men) To score is to succeed in having sex with someone. [I] • To **score points** is to make someone think better of you because of something you have done: *I don't think you'll score any points with your clients if you don't return their calls.*

score /skɔːr, skoʊr/ *n* [C] the number of points achieved or obtained in a game or other competition • *The final score was 103-90.* ○ *Who's going to keep score when we play bridge?* ○ *(infml) So what's the score* (= what are the facts of this situation)*, doctor? Is it serious?* • A **scoreboard** is a large board or screen, sometimes electronic, on which the score of a game is shown.

scoreless /ˈskɔːr·ləs, ˈskoʊr-/ *adj* [not gradable] • *After eight innings, the game was still a*

scoreless tie (= neither team had made any points).

scorer /ˈskɔːr·ər, ˈskoʊr-/ *n* [C] someone who scores a point or points • *Patrick is his team's leading scorer.*

score MUSICAL TEXT /skɔːr, skoʊr/ *n* [C] a piece of written music showing the parts for all the different instruments and voices, or the music written for a movie or other entertainment

score MATTER /skɔːr, skoʊr/ *n* [C usually sing] a particular matter among others related to it • *I'll let you have the money, so there's nothing to worry about on that score.*

score NUMBER /skɔːr, skoʊr/ *n* [C] (a set or group of) 20 • *Brandon received cards from scores of* (= many) *local well-wishers.*

scorn /skɔːrn/ *n* [U] a strong feeling that someone or something is of little or no worth and deserves no respect • *She feels nothing but scorn for people who sympathize more with criminals than with their victims.*

scorn /skɔːrn/ *v* [T] to treat with a great lack of respect, or to refuse (something) because you think it is wrong or not acceptable • *As the first African-American in the previously all-white school, he was a second-class citizen, scorned by his teachers and classmates.*

scornful /ˈskɔːrn·fəl/ *adj* • *a scornful laugh/ look*

Scorpio /ˈskɔːr·piː̩oʊ/ *n* [C/U] *pl* **Scorpios** the eighth sign of the ZODIAC, covering the period October 24 to November 21 and represented by a SCORPION, or a person born during this period

scorpion /ˈskɔːr·piː·ən/ *n* [C] a small, insect-like creature that lives in hot, dry areas of the world and has a long body and a curved tail with a poisonous sting

scotch /skɑtʃ/ *v* [T] to prevent (something) from being believed or being done • *The company hoped to scotch the rumors of a takeover.*

Scotch (whiskey) /ˈskɑtʃ (ˈwɪs·ki, ˈhwɪs-)/ *n* [C/U] a strong alcoholic drink made in Scotland

Scotch tape /ˈskɑtʃˈteɪp/ *n* [U] *trademark* a long, usually transparent strip of material with a sticky substance on one side, used for attaching two pieces of paper or fixing a torn place

scot–free /skɑtˈfriː/ *adv* [not gradable] without receiving the punishment deserved • *She agreed to testify against her boyfriend and got off scot-free.*

scoundrel /ˈskaʊn·drəl/ *n* [C] a person, esp. an elected official, who treats others badly and cannot be trusted

scour CLEAN /skaʊr/ *v* [T] to clean (something, esp. a utensil) by rubbing it with something having a rough surface • *We scoured the pots and pans with pads of steel wool.*

scour SEARCH /skaʊr/ *v* [T] to search (a place or thing) very carefully • *Police are scouring the countryside for the missing child.*

scout BOY / GIRL /skaʊt/ *n* [C] a **Boy Scout**, see at BOY, or **Girl Scout**, see at GIRL

scout SEARCH /skaʊt/ *v* [I/T] to go to look in (various places) for something you want or to check for possible danger • *Retired folks were scouting for homes in Florida.* [I] • In sports, to scout is to have the job of trying to find young players with good athletic ability: *I scouted for the Angels baseball team for about 15 years.* [I]

scout /skaʊt/ *n* [C] someone whose job is to look for people with particular skills, esp. in sports or entertainment • A scout is also a person, esp. a soldier, sent out to get information about the enemy.

scowl /skaʊl/ *v* [I] to make a facial expression that shows anger, esp. at someone • *When I asked the boss for a day off, he just scowled and told me to get back to work.*

scowl

scowl /skaʊl/ *n* [C] • *She is clearly annoyed, as you can tell from the scowl on her face.*

scrabble /'skræb·əl/ *v* [I] to move your hands or fingers quickly to find and pick up something, esp. something that you cannot see • *She scrabbled around in her bag, trying to find her keys.*

scram /skræm/ *v* [I] **-mm-** *infml* to leave quickly; get away • *We'd better scram!*

scramble MOVE QUICKLY /'skræm·bəl/ *v* [I] to move or climb quickly but with difficulty, often using the hands • *She scrambled to safety away from the fighting.* ○ *(fig.) Poultry farmers scrambled* (= worked hard and fast) *to provide water to their flocks as pipes burst in Georgia's coldest weather this century.* [+ *to* infinitive]

scramble /'skræm·bəl/ *n* [U] • *(fig.) There was a mad scramble* (= many people moving at once) *for the best seats in the theater.*

scramble MIX EGGS /'skræm·bəl/ *v* [T] to mix together and cook (the transparent and yellow parts of eggs) • *We had bacon and scrambled eggs for breakfast.*

scramble CHANGE SIGNAL /'skræm·bəl/ *v* [T] to change (a radio or telephone signal) while it is being sent so that it cannot be understood unless you have a special device

scrap THROW AWAY /skræp/ *v* [T] **-pp-** to get rid of (something no longer useful or wanted) • *Over 60% of all Georgians want to keep the present flag and only 29% want to scrap it.*

scrap MATERIALS /skræp/ *n* [U] old or used material, esp. metal, that has been collected in one place, often in order to be treated so that it can be used again • *He was charged with stealing copper tubing, which he then sold as scrap metal.*

scrap SMALL PIECE /skræp/ *n* [C] a small and often irregular piece of something, or a small amount of something • *He jotted it down on a*

scrap of paper. ○ *She picked up scraps of information about her husband's whereabouts, but nothing definite.* [pl]

scrapbook /'skræp·bʊk/ *n* [C] a book with empty pages where you can stick newspaper articles, pictures, etc., that you have collected and want to keep

scrape /skreɪp/ *v* [I/T] to remove (something) by rubbing something rough or sharp against it, or to rub (part of your body) against something rough that tears away or injures your skin • *Jackie scraped her knee on the wall as she was climbing over it.* [T] ○ *Sheila scraped the snow off the windshield of her car.* [T] ○ *The metal gate scraped along the ground when I opened it.* [I]

scrape /skreɪp/ *n* [C] a slight injury caused by having your skin rubbed against something rough • *She had a few scrapes from the accident in the parking lot, but nothing serious.* • *(infml)* A scrape is also a difficult situation that you are in because of your own actions: *Oh, he's had a few scrapes with the law when he was younger, but he's straightened his life out now.*

▫ **scrape by** /'-'-'-/ *v prep* [I] to have only enough money to buy the basic things you need to live • *Even with both of us working, we earn just enough to scrape by.*

▫ **scrape together/up** *obj*, **scrape** *obj* **together/up** /'--'--, '-'-'/ *v adv* [M] to gather (things) together with difficulty • *My grandfather told me that, during the depression, at times the most the family could scrape up was ten cents.*

scrappy /'skræp·i/ *adj* [*-er/-est* only] *approving* very competitive and willing to oppose others without fear to achieve something • *They were a scrappy team—you had to go all out to beat them.*

scratch CUT /skrætʃ/ *v* [I/T] to cut or damage (a surface) with something sharp or rough, or to rub (a part of your body) with something sharp or rough • *He used a penknife to scratch his initials into the bark of the tree.* [T] ○ *You can hold the cat—she won't scratch.* [I] • If you scratch your skin, you rub it with the nails of your fingers: *I know they itch, but don't scratch your mosquito bites.* [T] ○ *(fig.) A lot of people must be* **scratching** *their* **heads** (= thinking very hard) *and trying to figure out what happened.* • To **scratch the surface** is to deal with only a small part of a subject or a problem: *All the loan payments we've paid so far have hardly scratched the surface in terms of what we've still got to pay.*

scratch /skrætʃ/ *n* [C] • *Upon his arrest as a rape suspect, police noticed deep scratches on his face and arms.*

scratch REMOVE /skrætʃ/ *v* [I/T] to remove (yourself or another person or an animal) from a competition before the start • *Mary Slaney scratched from the 1500-meter run because of an Achilles tendon problem.* [I] • To scratch is also to decide not to do (something that you had planned to do); to CANCEL: *We were going to remodel our kitchen, but we had to scratch that when I lost my job.* [T]

scrawl /skrɔːl/ *v* [T] to write (something) in a fast, careless way • *Someone had scrawled graffiti on the side of our garage.*

scrawl /skrɔːl/ *n* [C] • *I had trouble reading the uneven scrawl of his signature.*

scrawny /ˈskrɔː·ni/ *adj* (of a person's or animal's body) very thin because not fed enough, so that you can see the shape of the bones under the skin • *The store had only a few scrawny chickens left.*

scream /skriːm/ *v* [I/T] to cry or say (something) loudly and usually on a high note, esp. because of strong emotions such as fear, excitement, or anger • *The children screamed in delight as they sledded down the hill.* [I] ○ *Some people still trapped in the wreckage screamed for help.* [I]

scream /skriːm/ *n* [C] • *screams of joy/laughter/pain* • (*slang*) A scream is someone or something that is very entertaining: *Josie's a real scream—she's never serious.*

screech /skriːtʃ/ *v* [I] to make a long, loud, high noise • *They clapped their hands and screeched with laughter.* ○ *A semitrailer truck screeched to a halt* (= stopped suddenly with a long, loud, high noise of its BRAKES).

screech /skriːtʃ/ *n* [C] • *The truck stopped with a screech of brakes.*

screen PICTURE /skriːn/ *n* [C] a flat surface in a theater, on a television, or on a computer system on which pictures or words are shown • *I spend most of the day working in front of a computer screen.* • The screen sometimes means the movies: *Her ambition is to write for the screen.* ○ *a screen actor/actress* • A **screenplay** is a story written with the words to be spoken by actors on television or in a movie. • A **screenwriter** is someone who writes the story for a movie.

screen /skriːn/ *v* [T] to show or broadcast (a movie or television program) • *His new movie got rave reviews when it was screened at Cannes.*

screen EXAMINE /skriːn/ *v* [T] to test or examine (someone or something) to discover if there is anything wrong with them • *All applicants for the teaching jobs have to be screened to see whether they have a criminal record.* ○ *The company president's secretary screens all his calls* (= answers them first to prevent some from getting through).

screen THING THAT SEPARATES /skriːn/ *n* [C] something that blocks you from seeing what is behind it, esp. a stiff piece of material that you can stand up like part of a wall and move around • *Jennifer has a beautiful screen decorated with Japanese art.* • A screen is also a stiff, wire net that has very small holes and is fixed within a frame, put in windows esp. in warm weather to let in air and keep insects

out. ○ *In summer we keep the front door open and just keep the* **screen door** (= a door that is the frame for a screen) *closed.*

screen /skriːn/ *v* [T] • *She raised her hand to screen her eyes from the sun.*

screw METAL FASTENER /skruː/ *n* [C] a thin piece of metal, usually with a pointed end and a flat top shaped to hold a tool, that is forced into wood or metal by turning, and is used esp. to join two pieces or to hold something in place • A **screwdriver** is a tool for turning screws that has a handle at one end and a metal rod shaped at the other end to fit in the top of a screw. • A container with a **screw top** has a cover that fastens by being turned.

screw /skruː/ *v* [T] to fasten (objects) with a screw • *The shelves were screwed to the wall.* • To screw also means to attach to something by turning: *Screw the lid onto the jar.* ○ *He doesn't even know how to screw in a light bulb.* [M]

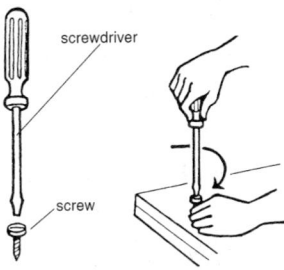

screwdriver

screw

screw CHEAT /skruː/ *v* [T] *slang* to cheat or deceive (someone) • *He really got screwed on that stock tip.*

screw HAVE SEX /skruː/ *v* [I/T] *rude slang* to have sex, or to have sex with (someone) • People say **screw it** to show they do not care what happens: *She didn't want to go, but I thought, screw it, I'm going anyway.* • **Screw you** is an expression of anger or annoyance: *You don't like it? Well, screw you!*

▫ **screw around** /ˈ--ˈ-/ *v adv* [I] *slang* to waste time • *Stop screwing around and finish your work.*

▫ **screw up** *obj* TWIST , **screw** *obj* **up** /ˈ-ˈ-/ *v adv* [M] to twist (a part of the face) • *"This milk is sour," she said, screwing up her face.*

▫ **screw up** (*obj*) DAMAGE , **screw** (*obj*) **up** /ˈ-ˈ-/ *v adv* [I/M] *infml* to spoil or destroy (something), or to damage (someone), by causing them to become anxious or confused • *Their parents' divorce really screwed the kids up.* [M] ○ *You couldn't screw up much worse than I did.* [I]

▫ **screw up** *obj* STRENGTHEN , **screw** *obj* **up** /ˈ-ˈ-/ *v adv* [M] to strengthen or make more powerful (a feeling of bravery) • *Every day she screwed up her courage and went to work.*

screwball /ˈskruː·bɔːl/ *n* [C] *slang* a person who is strange and amusing

screwball /ˈskruː·bɔːl/ *adj* [not gradable] • *screwball ideas*

screwy /'skruː·i/ *adj* [*-er/-est* only] *infml* very strange, foolish, or unusual • *She had some weird ideas, but her brother was even screwier.*

scribble /'skrɪb·əl/ *v* [I/T] to write or draw (something) quickly or carelessly, or to make meaningless marks • *I scribbled a few words to her on a postcard.* [T]

scribble /'skrɪb·əl/ *n* [C/U] • *His scribble is completely illegible.* [U]

scribe /skraɪb/ *n* [C] a person who made written copies of documents, before the invention of printing

scrimp /skrɪmp/ *v* [I] to spend as little money as possible • *We scrimp on schools but spend a lot on weapons.*

script TEXT /skrɪpt/ *n* [C] a text that is written for a movie, play, broadcast, or speech • *They gave me the script and I only had five lines.* • A **scriptwriter** is someone who writes texts for movies, television programs, etc.

scripted /'skrɪp·təd/ *adj* [not gradable] (of a speech, conversation, meeting, or public appearance) written or arranged in advance • *The meeting was scripted, which means there was no real discussion.*

script WRITING /skrɪpt/ *n* [C/U] writing, esp. writing done by hand in which the letters of a word are joined to each other • *a neat, legible script* [C] • Script is also the special set of letters used in writing a language: *Arabic/Hebrew script* [U]

scripture /'skrɪp·tʃər/ *n* [C/U] the holy writings of a religion • *sacred Scriptures* [C] • Scripture or the Scriptures refers to the Bible, including the Old and New Testaments. [U]

scroll MOVE TEXT /skroʊl/ *v* [I] to move text or pictures up or down on a computer screen to view different parts of them • *Scroll to the end of the document.*

scroll PAPER /skroʊl/ *n* [C] a long roll of paper or similar material, usually with official writing on it • *parchment/ancient scrolls* ○ *a painted Japanese scroll*

scrotum /'skroʊt̬·əm/ *n* [C] (in most male mammals) a bag of skin near the penis which contains the TESTICLES (= ball-shaped male sex organs)

scrounge /skraʊndʒ/ *v* [I/T] *infml* to get (something) by asking for it instead of buying it or working for it, or to gather (something you want or need) from what is available • *Baxter scrounged furniture and equipment from local businesses.* [T] ○ *A black cat scrounged through piles of litter.* [I]

scrub CLEAN /skrʌb/ *v* [I/T] **-bb-** to rub (something) hard to clean it, esp. with a stiff brush, soap, and water • *After the tomato sauce boiled over, I had to scrub the stove.* [T] ○ *You scrub and scrub, but those marks never come off.* [I]

scrub PLANTS /skrʌb/ *n* [U] low trees and bushes that grow in dirt that is not especially good or where it is windy and dry

scruff /skrʌf/ *n* • If you hold a person or an-imal **by the scruff of the neck**, you hold the back of their neck: *She grabbed the dog by the scruff of his neck and hung on to him.*

scruffy /'skrʌf·i/ *adj* old and dirty; messy • *a scruffy denim jacket*

scrumptious /'skrʌmp·ʃəs/ *adj* tasting extremely good; DELICIOUS • *a scrumptious breakfast*

scrunch /skrʌntʃ/ *v* [I/T] to press or crush (something) together • *He scrunched down to hide in a nearby doorway.* [I]

scruple /'skruː·pəl/ *n* [C/U] a strong belief about what is right or wrong that governs your actions • *He has scruples about going out with his students.* [C]

scrupulous /'skruː·pjə·ləs/ *adj* extremely careful to do what is right or moral • *She managed to get a copy of the report through a friend who wasn't so scrupulous about sharing information.* • Scrupulous also means extremely accurate and exact: *Her report is scrupulous in its detail.*

scrutinize /'skruːt̬·ənˌaɪz/ *v* [T] to examine (someone or something) very carefully • *All new products are scrutinized by the laboratory.*

scrutiny /'skruːt̬·ən·i/ *n* [U] • *Will the candidates stand up under all that scrutiny?*

scuba diving /'skuː·bə,daɪ·vɪŋ/ *n* [U] the sport of swimming under water with special equipment for breathing

scuff /skʌf/ *v* [T] to damage slightly by leaving a mark on (a smooth surface, esp. a shoe or floor) • *Always wear sneakers in the gym to avoid scuffing the floor.* • If you scuff your feet, you do not lift them as you walk.

scuffle /'skʌf·əl/ *n* [C] a short fight that is filled with confusion • *In the scuffle, a gun went off, and a guard was wounded.*

sculpture /'skʌlp·tʃər/ *n* [C/U] the art of creating objects out of material such as wood, clay, metal, or stone, or a work of art of this type • *In the ruins they found ancient stone sculptures.* [C]

sculpt /skʌlpt/, **sculpture** /'skʌlp·tʃər/ *v* [T] • *Picasso sculpted the "Venus of Lapigue."*

sculpted /'skʌlp·təd/, **sculptured** /'skʌlp·tʃərd/ *adj* • *Dramatically sculpted red and gray sandstone cliffs came into view.*

sculptor /'skʌlp·tər/ *n* [C] • *The sculptor supervised the placement of his newest sculpture in the garden.*

scum LAYER ON LIQUID /skʌm/ *n* [U] a thin layer that forms on the surface of a liquid • *The tea was nasty-tasting stuff that looked like pond scum.* ○ *I wish you wouldn't leave soap scum in the bathtub.*

scum BAD PEOPLE /skʌm/ *n* [U] *rude slang* very bad, worthless people • *The scum who own those companies aren't about to help us.*

scumbag /'skʌm·bæg/ *n* [C] *rude slang* a very bad or immoral person

scurrilous /'skɜr·ə·ləs/ *adj* rude and cruel,

and sometimes damaging • *scurrilous re-marks*

scurry /'skɜr·i, 'skʌ·ri/ *v* [I always + adv/prep] to move quickly, esp. with small running steps • *Mice scurried around the attic.*

scuttle RUN /'skʌt̬·əl/ *v* [I always + adv/prep] to move quickly, with small, short steps • *We heard rats scuttling by in the dark.*

scuttle GIVE UP /'skʌt̬·əl/ *v* [T] to give up (a plan or activity), or spoil (a possibility for success) • *Angry workers scuttled all hope of quick agreement on a new contract.*

scuttle SINK /'skʌt̬·əl/ *v* [T] to intentionally sink (a ship) by opening a hole in the bottom or sides

scuttlebutt /'skʌt̬·əl,bʌt/ *n* [U] *infml* information that may or may not be true; RUMOR • *Scuttlebutt around the office has it that he's been fired.*

scythe /saɪð, saɪ/ *n* [C] a tool with a long curved blade and a long handle, used esp. to cut down tall grass

S.E. *n* [C], *adj, adv abbreviation for* SOUTHEAST or SOUTHEASTERN

sea /siː/ *n* [C/U] a large area of salt water that is partly or completely surrounded by land, or the salt water that covers most of the surface of the earth • *the Caribbean/Mediterranean Sea* [C] ○ *The seas are filled with creatures we know nothing about.* [C] • If you travel by sea, you go in a ship. [U] • *With no data they could depend on, they were utterly* **at sea** (= confused). • A **sea of** something is a lot of it: *a sea of faces* • The **seabed** is the bottom of the sea. • A **seaboard** is a large strip of land next to the sea: *the eastern seaboard* • The **seacoast** is the edge of the land next to the sea. • **Seafood** is fish or SHELLFISH eaten as food. • A **sea gull** is a large bird that lives near salt water. • A **sea horse** is a type of fish whose head and neck look like those of a horse. • **Sea level** is the average level of the sea where it meets the land: *The town is 300 feet above sea level.* • A **sea lion** is a large SEAL ANIMAL that has ears. • A **seaman** is a sailor who is not an officer in the US Coastguard or Navy. • A **seaplane** is an aircraft that can land on and take off from water. • A **seaport** is a town or city on the water where ships load and unload goods. • **Seashells** are the empty shells of animals from the sea. • The **seashore** is the land at the edge of the sea. • If someone traveling on a boat becomes **seasick** or suffers from **seasickness**, they vomit or feel as if they will vomit because of the movement of the boat. • The **seaside** is a place near the water: *a seaside resort* • **Seaweed** is a green, brown, or dark red plant that grows in the sea.

sea horse

seal ANIMAL /siːl/ *n* [C] a large, fish-eating mammal that has very thick fur and lives in

seal

the sea • *Seals are sometimes hunted for their valuable fur.*

seal OFFICIAL MARK /siːl/ *n* [C] an official mark on a document that shows that it is legal or actually what it claims to be • *Diplomas are stamped with the state seal.* • A **seal of approval** means that something has been proven to be good or is very pleasing: *My brother's girlfriend got my mom's seal of approval.*

seal /siːl/ *v* [T] • If you seal an agreement, you formally approve or agree to it: *They sealed the agreement with their signatures.*

seal COVERING /siːl/ *n* [C] anything that prevents the escape of liquid or gas from a container or pipe • *The oil seal broke, and all the oil leaked from the engine.* ○ *Don't use that jar of baby food if the seal is broken.*

seal /siːl/ *v* [T] • *Rubber seals jars tightly.* ○ *He sealed the envelope and put a stamp on it.* ○ *Broiling with high heat seals in the flavor of the meat.* [M] ○ *The police sealed off the area to search it.* [M] • If official documents are sealed, they are cannot be seen or are closed to the public.

seam JOINT /siːm/ *n* [C] a line where two things join, esp. where two pieces of cloth or other material have been sewn together • *My jacket came apart at the back seam.*

seamless /'siːm·ləs/ *adj* [not gradable] • *seamless tube socks* • Seamless can also mean without noticeable change from one part to the next: *The department hopes this will be a seamless transition from one computer system to another.*

seam LAYER /siːm/ *n* [C] a long, thin layer of rock or another substance that formed between layers of other rocks • *a coal seam*

seamstress /'siːm·strəs/ *n* [C] a woman whose job is sewing, esp. clothes

seamy /'siː·mi/ *adj* [-er/-est only] mean, unpleasant and often connected with violence • *She tells a seamy, sordid tale.*

séance /'seɪ·ɑns, -ɑ̃s/ *n* [C] a meeting where people try to communicate with the dead, often with the help of someone who claims to have special powers to do this

sear /sɪr/ *v* [T] to burn the surface of (something) with very high heat, or to cook (meat) quickly at a high temperature to keep in the juices and flavor • *He seared the steaks on the grill.*

searing /'sɪr·ɪŋ/ *adj* very hot • *searing*

temperatures • Searing also means very powerful: *Gary felt searing pain in his leg.*

search /sɜrtʃ/ *v* [I/T] to look (somewhere) carefully in order to find something • *Dogs were brought in to search the area for survivors.* [T] ○ *Teens are often searching for their identity.* [I]

search /sɜrtʃ/ *n* [C/U] • *After a long search, they finally found the lost child.* [C] ○ *It's a book about the search for love.* [U] • A **searchlight** is a device that puts out a very bright beam of light and can turn in any direction. • A **search party** is a group of people who look for someone who is lost. • A **search warrant** is an official document that gives the police the authority to search a place for a list of things connected with a particular crime, such as stolen property, drugs, and important papers or notes.

searching /'sɜr·tʃɪŋ/ *adj* intended to discover the hidden truth • *Fran stared hard, her searching gaze trying to get him to admit what he knew.*

season PART OF YEAR /'siː·zən/ *n* [C] one of the four parts a year is divided into; spring, summer, fall, or winter

seasonable /'siː·zə·nə·bəl/ *adj* expected at or suitable for a particular season • *seasonable weather*

seasonal /'siː·zən·ᵊl/ *adj* • *seasonal jobs/work*

season PERIOD /'siː·zən/ *n* [C] a period of time during the year, esp. a period that happens every year at the same time • *the Christmas/holiday season* ○ *The baseball season lasts from April to October.* • A fruit or vegetable that is **in season** is available fresh locally at that time: *Strawberries are in season.*

seasonal /'siː·zən·ᵊl/ *adj* • *seasonal fruits and vegetables* ○ *seasonal decorations*

season FLAVOR /'siː·zən/ *v* [T] to improve (the flavor of food) by adding small amounts of salt, herbs, or spices • *Season the soup with fresh tarragon, salt, and pepper.*

seasoning /'siː·zə·nɪŋ/ *n* [C/U] • *Adjust the seasoning to taste.* [U]

seasoned /'siː·zənd/ *adj* having much experience and knowledge of a particular activity • *seasoned travelers/journalists*

seat FURNITURE /siːt/ *n* [C] a piece of furniture designed to be used for sitting, or the part of a piece of furniture on which a person sits • *She left her jacket on the back of her seat.* ○ *There's a piece of gum stuck under the seat of the chair.* ○ *Please have/take a seat* (= sit down). • A seat is also a ticket allowing you to use a seat on an aircraft or at a show: *I got a seat on the flight to New York.* • The **seat** of your **pants** is the part of your pants you sit on. • If you do something **by the seat of** your **pants**, you guess how to do it: *We started a magazine by the seat of our pants, without any of the market testing that's done today.* • A **seat belt** is a strap in a vehicle or aircraft that fas-

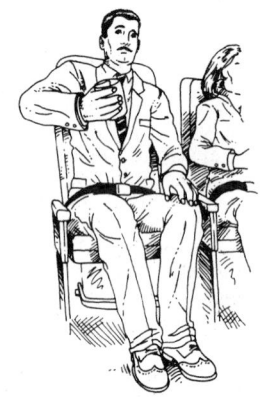

seat belt

tens around a person, holding them in their seat to reduce the risk of injury in an accident.

seat /siːt/ *v* [T] to have or be given (a place to sit) • *I was seated between Jasmine and Emily.* ○ *The concert hall seats 350.* ○ *Our group is still waiting to be seated for dinner.* ○ *Please be seated* (= sit down).

seating /'siː·t̬·ɪŋ/ *n* [U] the seats provided in a place • *The seminars are free but seating is limited.* ○ *The kids couldn't agree on the seating arrangement in the car* (= where they would sit).

seat OFFICIAL POSITION /siːt/ *n* [C] an official position as a member of a legislature or group of people who control an organization • *She decided to run for a seat on the school board.*

seat PLACE /siːt/ *n* [C] a place that is a center for an important activity, esp. government • *Pittsburgh is the county seat of Alleghany County.*

sec /sek/ *n* [C] *short form of* SECOND TIME • *Hang on a sec, Brian, I've got another call.*

secede /sɪ'siːd/ *v* [I] to decide not to continue to be part of a larger group or organization • *The American Civil War began when the South seceded from the Union.*

secession /sɪ'seʃ·ən/ *n* [U] • *Dabney had opposed secession at first.*

secluded /sɪ'kluː·d·əd/ *adj* away from people and busy activities, and often hard to reach • *a secluded area/beach*

seclusion /sɪ'kluː·ʒən/ *n* [U] • *She spent her days in the seclusion of her room.*

second POSITION /'sek·ənd/ *adj, adv* [not gradable], *n* [C] (a person or thing) coming immediately after the first • *He missed only 2 of 11 shots in the second half.* ○ *Rent is due the second of every month.* [C] • In baseball, second or **second base** is the second place a player has to touch in order to score, or a position near this place played by a member of the team on the field. • Someone or something **second-class** is thought to be less important or of lower quality than others: *He treats the ESL* students like second-class citizens. • To **second-guess** someone is to criticize them after something has happened, or to guess what someone will do or what will happen: *It's kind of hard to second-guess the decision.* • **Secondhand** means owned or used in the past by someone else: *a secondhand car* • If you learn something **secondhand** or **at second hand**, you learn about it indirectly or from someone else: *I'm familiar with racing only at second hand.* • **Secondhand smoke** is tobacco smoke you inhale because someone else is smoking. • Something that is **second nature** to someone is so familiar it is done without having to think about it: *Using the computer is second nature to me now.* • (*specialized*) In grammar, the **second person** is the form of pronouns and verbs people use when speaking or writing to someone else: *"You" and "your" are second person pronouns*: Compare **first person** at FIRST; **third person** at THIRD. • **Second-rate** means not good: *a second-rate hotel* • A **second thought** is a change in a decision or opinion: *He apparently had second thoughts about that remark.* ○ *On second thought, I would like a glass of water.* • Your **second wind** is a return of strength or energy that makes it possible to continue in an activity or start again: *I was tired, but I ignored it until I got my second wind.* • USAGE: The related number is TWO. • ⟨LP⟩ NUMBERS

seconds /'sek·ənz/ *pl n* an extra serving of food given after the first serving has been eaten • *Would anybody like seconds?*

secondly /'sek·ən·dli/, **second** *adv* [not gradable] • *First, what does it cost? And secondly, who's it for?*

second TIME /'sek·ənd/, *short form* **sec** *n* [C] any of the 60 parts that a minute is divided into • *She won by 22 seconds.* • A second is also any short period of time: *I'll be back in a second.*

second SUPPORT /'sek·ənd/ *v* [T] to make a formal statement of support for a suggestion made by someone else during a meeting in order to allow a discussion or vote • *I second the motion to adjourn.*

secondary LESS IMPORTANT /'sek·ən,der·i/ *adj* [not gradable] less important than related things • *A coach's first responsibility is to the team—everything else is secondary.*

secondary EDUCATION /'sek·ən,der·i/ *adj* [not gradable] relating to the education of children approximately between the ages of 12 and 18 • *The secondary curriculum will have to be drastically improved.* • A **secondary school** is a HIGH SCHOOL.

secondary COMING AFTER /'sek·ən,der·i/ *adj* [not gradable] developing from something similar that existed earlier • *Someone who's been treated for cancer can get a secondary tumor 20 years later.*

seconds /'sek·ənz/ • See at SECOND POSITION.

secret /'siː·krət/ *n* [C] a piece of information that is not generally known or is not known by someone else and should not be told to others • *We don't keep secrets from each other.* ○ *Don't tell anyone—it's a secret.* • *What's* **the secret of** *your success* (= How was it achieved)*?*

secret /'siː·krət/ *adj* known, done, or kept without others knowing • *secret information* ○ *She has a secret boyfriend.* • A government's **secret police** is a police organization that keeps information about its country's citizens and prevents opposition to the government. • The **Secret Service** is a US government organization responsible for the safety of important politicians, esp. the president.

secretive /'siː·krət̬·ɪv/ *adj* not wanting others to know, or done privately so that others do not know • *She's secretive about her age.* ○ *secretive dealings*

secretly /'siː·krət·li/ *adv* • *They secretly took photographs of Jack.*

secrecy /'siː·krə·si/ *n* [U] • *What's the reason for all this secrecy?*

secretary OFFICE WORKER /'sek·rə,ter·i/ *n* [C] a person who works in an office and prepares letters, keeps records, schedules meetings, and makes other arrangements for a particular person or for an organization

secretarial /,sek·rə'ter·iː·əl/ *adj* [not gradable] • *She does mostly secretarial work.*

secretary GOVERNMENT OFFICIAL /'sek·rə,ter·i/ *n* [C] the head of a government department • *the Secretary of the Treasury*

secretary WRITER /'sek·rə,ter·i/ *n* [C] an official in an organization who is responsible for writing notes about what happens at meetings and sending official letters • *Freya is running for secretary of the student council.*

secrete /sɪ'kriːt/ *v* [T] *specialized* to produce and release liquid, esp. from the cells or body • *The thyroid gland secretes hormones that affect growth.*

secretion /sɪ'kriː·ʃən/ *n* [C/U] *specialized* • *nasal secretions* [C]

secretive /'siː·krət̬·ɪv/ *adj* • See at SECRET.

secretly /'siː·krət·li/ *adv* • See at SECRET.

sect /sekt/ *n* [C] a religious group with beliefs that make it different from a larger or more established religion it has separated from • *a Christian sect*

sectarian /sek'ter·iː·ən/ *adj* [not gradable] • *More than 600 people were killed in sectarian fighting.*

section /'sek·ʃən/ *n* [C] a part of something • *Dad always reads the sports section of the newspaper.* ○ *He lived in a poor section of town.* ○ *You'll find ice cream in the frozen food section of the supermarket.*

□ **section off** *obj*, **section** *obj* **off** /'--'-/ *v adv* [M] • *The floor is sectioned off into squares.*

sector /'sek·tər/ *n* [C] a part of society that can be separated from other parts because of its own special character • *the farm sector* ○

the nonprofit sector ∘ She works in the private/public sector (= for a business/government) • A sector is also an area of land or sea that has been divided from other areas: The buildings are in an industrial sector in the southern part of the city.

secular /'sek·jə·lər/ adj not having any connection with religion • secular society/music/education

secure FREE FROM RISK /sɪ'kjʊr/ adj free from risk and the threat of change for the worse • a secure job ∘ People want to feel secure economically. ∘ The museum has a large endowment, so its future is relatively secure. • Secure can also mean confident and free from worry: Children need to feel secure in order to do well at school.

security /sɪ'kjʊr·ət·i/ n [U] • financial/job security • See also **security** at SECURE FREE FROM DANGER, SECURITY INVESTMENT, SECURITY MONEY.

secure FREE FROM DANGER /sɪ'kjʊr/ adj free from danger or the threat of harm or unwanted access; safe • Troops were sent to make the border secure. ∘ He questioned whether the government's computer database was secure from hackers. ∘ For some time after the robbery we could not feel secure, even in our own home.

secure /sɪ'kjʊr/ v [T] • The wall was originally built to secure the town from attack.

security /sɪ'kjʊr·ət·i/ n [U] freedom from danger; safety • For security reasons, for the protection of the White House and the president, they felt it necessary to close the avenue. ∘ A convicted spy, he sold information that may have damaged our national security. • Security is also the group of people responsible for keeping buildings or other areas safe: If anyone gives you trouble, just call security. • A **security blanket** is a small BLANKET (= bed cover) sometimes carried by a child to provide a feeling of safety. • See also **security** at SECURE FREE FROM RISK, SECURITY INVESTMENT, SECURITY MONEY.

secure FIXED /sɪ'kjʊr/ adj fixed, fastened, or locked into a position that prevents movement • That ladder doesn't look very secure to me. ∘ Just check that the door is secure—the lock doesn't always work.

secure /sɪ'kjʊr/ v [T] to fasten (something) firmly • Secure the boat to the dock.

securely /sɪ'kjʊr·li/ adv • Please make sure that your seatbelts are securely fastened.

secure OBTAIN /sɪ'kjʊr/ v [T] to obtain (something), sometimes with difficulty • She managed to secure a loan from the bank.

security INVESTMENT /sɪ'kjʊr·ət·i/ n [C usually pl] specialized an investment in a company or in government debt that can be traded on the financial markets • See also **security** at SECURE FREE FROM RISK, SECURE FREE FROM DANGER; SECURITY MONEY.

security MONEY /sɪ'kjʊr·ət·i/ n [U] money you pay someone that can be legally used by them

if your actions cause them to lose money, but that will be returned to you if they do not • You have give the landlord an extra month's rent as security when you sign the lease. • See also **security** at SECURE FREE FROM RISK, SECURE FREE FROM DANGER; SECURITY INVESTMENT.

sedan /sɪ'dæn/ n [C] a type of car with two or four doors and seats for at least four people • PIC CAR

sedate /sɪ'deɪt/ adj calm and controlled, and often traditional in habit or manner • She preferred standard ballads and sedate pop tunes to rock music.

sedative /'sed·ət·ɪv/ n [C] a drug that has a calming effect • If your pet is unaccustomed to car travel, consider a mild sedative to help relieve its anxiety.

sedentary /'sed·ᵊn,ter·i/ adj involving little exercise or physical activity • Marilyn leads a more sedentary lifestyle now that she works at home.

sediment /'sed·ə·mənt/ n [C/U] solid material, such as dirt or MINERALS, that falls to the bottom of a liquid

sedition /sɪ'dɪʃ·ən/ n [U] language or behavior intended to persuade other people to oppose their government and change it, sometimes by using violence • He himself was tried for sedition and sentenced to ten years in jail.

seditious /sɪ'dɪʃ·əs/ adj

seduce HAVE SEX /sɪ'duːs/ v [T] to use your charm to persuade (someone) to have sex with you • Several of his students said that he had tried to seduce them.

seduction /sɪ'dʌk·ʃən/ n [C/U] • The movie depicts the seduction of a schoolgirl by a middle-aged man. [U]

seductive /sɪ'dʌk·tɪv/ adj • a seductive voice

seduce PERSUADE /sɪ'duːs/ v [T] to persuade or trick (someone) into doing something by making it very attractive • Nowadays you have to seduce students into learning through colorful graphics, fantasy, or exciting adventure themes.

seduction /sɪ'dʌk·ʃən/ n [C/U] • A recovering alcoholic, Gully is determined to save others from the seduction of alcohol. [U]

see USE EYES /siː/ v [I/T] past simple **saw** /sɔː/, past part **seen** /siːn/ to be aware of (what is around you) by using your eyes; look at (something) • From the kitchen window, I can see the kids playing in the backyard. [T] ∘ Can you see what is happening? [+ wh- word] ∘ The agent said they could see the house at 3 p.m. [T] ∘ Did you see that documentary about homelessness on TV last night? [T] • **Seeing is believing** means that if you see something yourself, you will believe it to exist or be true, despite the fact that it is unlikely: I never thought he'd shave off his beard, but seeing is believing! • If you **see red**, you become very angry. • If you **see stars**, you are partly unconscious because you have been hit on the head. • If you are **see-**

SEE, LOOK, AND WATCH

To **see** is to notice something or to be aware of what is around you by using your eyes. To **look** is to direct your eyes in order to see. To **watch** is to look at something for a period of time, esp. something that is moving or changing or is expected to do so.

*I **looked** out the window but didn't **see** anything. • She **watched** as the snow fell on the garden.*

In general, when you direct attention to people or things that move or change, you **watch** them. However, you **see** complete events such as movies or plays that happen in public.

*I was trying to **watch** the movie, but the person in front of me kept asking me questions. • He says he's **seen** Jurassic Park five times. • Would you like to **see** a play on Saturday?*

Notice that you **watch** television, but you can either **see** or **watch** a particular program.

*I want to **see**/**watch** that new comedy on Channel 5 tonight.*

All three verbs can be used intransitively.

*I can't **see** very well without my glasses. • I **looked** around but no one was there. • They all **watched** as she opened the envelope.*

The verbs **see** and **watch** can be used transitively.

*I **see** three or four empty seats in the back. • I **watched** TV for a couple of hours.*

Look must be followed by a preposition (commonly *at*) before you can say what will be seen.

Look at all this stuff on the floor.

---

ing things, you are imagining that things are present or happening when they are not: *Didn't Maria come in just now? I must be seeing things. •* Something which is **see-through** is transparent or almost transparent: *She wore a see-through blouse.*

see UNDERSTAND /siː/ *v* [I/T] *past simple* **saw** /sɔː/, *past part* **seen** /siːn/ to understand, know, or be aware • *"It's easier if you hold it this way." "Oh, I see."* [I] ○ *I can't see any reason why they would object.* [T] ○ *I can see why you didn't want to go out with him.* [+ *wh*-word] • If you **can't see the forest for the trees,** you are unable to get a general understanding of a situation because you are too worried about the details. • *My sister didn't see eye to eye with me about the arrangements* (= she didn't agree with me about the arrangements). • If you **see the light,** you understand something you didn't understand before: *It wasn't until I was in my thirties that I saw the light and started to work hard. •* They *couldn't see the point of further training* (= understand the reason for it).

see CONSIDER /siː/ *v* [I/T] *past simple* **saw** /sɔː/, *past part* **seen** /siːn/ to consider (someone or

something) in a particular way, or to imagine (someone) doing a particular activity • *Under the circumstances, I can't see her accepting the job* (= I don't think she will accept it). [T] ○ *I can't see my brother as a businessman.* [T] ○ *As I see it/the situation, we'll have to get extra help.* [T] ○ *"Do you think there'll be time to stop for lunch?" "We'll see* (= I will consider it).*"* [I] ○ *I'll see how I feel tomorrow.* [+ *wh*- word] • If you **see fit** to do something, you think it is good or necessary to do it: *You can leave it here or take it home with you, whichever you see fit.* • **Seeing that/as (how)** means considering that: *We might as well go, seeing as we've already paid for the tickets.*

see MEET /siː/ *v* [T] *past simple* **saw** /sɔː/, *past part* **seen** /siːn/ to meet, visit, or spend time with (someone) • *I saw Darlene last week.* ○ *Mom is seeing the doctor tomorrow.* ○ *They see each other on weekends* (= they are often together then). ○ *How long has she been seeing him* (= having a romantic relationship with him)? • **See you/See you later** are informal ways of saying goodbye.

see TRY TO DISCOVER /siː/ *v* [+ *wh*- word] *past simple* **saw** /sɔː/, *past part* **seen** /siːn/ to try to discover • *Will you see who is at the door?*

see MAKE CERTAIN /siː/ *v* [+ *that* clause] *past simple* **saw** /sɔː/, *past part* **seen** /siːn/ to make certain (that something happens) • *She said she'd see that her boss gets the message.*

see EXPERIENCE /siː/ *v* [T] *past simple* **saw** /sɔː/, *past part* **seen** /siːn/ to experience (something) • *This coat has seen a lot of wear.* ○ *She's seen a lot of changes in this office over the years.* • If a time or place has seen something, it happened or existed there or then: *This summer has seen unusually high temperatures.*

□ **see about** /'--,-/ *v prep* [T] to deal with (something), esp. by getting information • *I'll see about movie times and call you back.*

□ **see off** *obj,* **see** *obj* **off** /'-'-/ *v adv* [M] to go with (someone) to an airport or other place to watch them leave on a trip • *My parents saw me off at the airport.*

□ **see through** NOT BE DECEIVED /'-,-/ *v prep* [T] to understand the truth about (someone or something) and not allow yourself to be deceived • *She saw through his excuse as an effort to shift the blame to someone else.*

□ **see** *obj* **through** CONTINUE DOING /'-'-/ *v prep* [T] to continue until (something) is finished, or to support (someone) through a difficult time • *She saw the project through to the end.* ○ *He was a real friend to see me through my long illness.*

□ **see to** /'-,-/ *v prep* [T] to deal with (something that has to be done) • *"These letters have to be mailed." "I'll see to it later."* ○ *Please see to it that no one comes in without identification.*

seed PLANT /siːd/ *n* [C/U] a small, usually hard part of a plant from which a new plant can grow • *packaged seeds* [C] ○ *I'm going to have* *fix up my lawn, you know, spread some seed and fertilizer and stuff.* [U]

seed /siːd/ *v* [T] to plant seeds in (the ground) • *We seeded the lawn with a different grass this year.*

seeded /'siːd·dəd/, **seedless** /'siːd·ləs/ *adj* [not gradable] with the seeds removed • *seeded grapes*

seed BEGINNING /siːd/ *n* [C usually pl] the beginning or cause of something • *A good defense lawyer knows how to plant these little seeds of doubt in the minds of jurors.* • **Seed money** is money used to start a development or activity.

seed SPORTS /siːd/ *n* [C] any of the players or teams ranked among the best in a particular competition

seeded /'siːd·əd/ *adj* [not gradable] ranked as one of the better players or teams, in order to arrange that these do not compete early in a competition • *Michigan State University, seeded first in the Southeast, also plays today.*

seedy /'siːd·i/ *adj* [-er/-est only] in bad condition, esp. because not cared for and therefore unattractive • *We had quarters in a rather seedy hotel near the railroad tracks.*

seek SEARCH /siːk/ *v* [T] *past* **sought** /sɔːt/ to search for (something) or try to find or obtain (something) • *She is actively seeking work.* ○ *The government is seeking ways to reduce the cost of health care.* • If you seek advice/approval/help/permission, you ask for it: *They suggested she seek advice from the legal department.*

seek TRY /siːk/ *v* [+ *to* infinitive] *past* **sought** /sɔːt/ to try or attempt • *They sought to reassure people that their homes would be safe from the flood.*

seem /siːm/ *v* to appear to be • *You seem very quiet today.* [L] ○ *He's 16, but he seems younger.* [L] ○ *The news seemed too good to be true.* [L] ○ *She didn't seem (to be) particularly happy.* [L] ○ *They seemed like such a nice couple.* [I always + adv/prep] ○ *I can't seem to stay awake.* [+ *to* infinitive]

seeming /'siː·mɪŋ/ *adj* [not gradable] appearing true or obvious, although it might not be • *Their seeming reluctance to demand better treatment was puzzling.*

seemingly /'siː·mɪŋ·li/ *adv* [not gradable] • *He is seemingly untroubled by our recent problems.*

seen /siːn/ *past participle of* SEE

seep /siːp/ *v* [I always + adv/prep] (of liquids) to flow slowly through something • *The flood water seeped into the basement.*

seepage /'siː·pɪdʒ/ *n* [U]

seesaw /'siː·sɔː/, **teeter-totter** *n* [C] a device for children's play that consists of a board balanced at the center, with a place at each end for a child to sit on and push away from the ground with their feet, causing the other end to go down

seesaw /'siː·sɔː/ *v* [I] to change direction or

move backward and forward or up and down repeatedly • *The lead seesawed* (= first one side was winning, then the other) *throughout the game.*

seethe /siːð/ *v* [I] to feel very angry • *She was still seething, remembering how rudely she was treated.*

segment /'seg·mənt/ *n* [C] any of the parts into which something can be divided • *The news program contained a brief segment on white-collar crime.* • A segment is also one of several parts of an orange, lemon, or similarly divided fruits.

segregate /'seg·rə·ɡeɪt/ *v* [T] to keep separate (a group of people, esp. black people) from other people because of their race, or to separate (someone or something) from others • *Most people wouldn't remember that some ballparks were segregated* (= black people were kept apart) *in the early years.* ○ *The boys and girls were segregated into different classes.*

segregation /ˌseg·rəˈɡeɪ·ʃən/ *n* [U] • *racial segregation* ○ *Almost every community has laws prohibiting segregation in housing.*

seismic /'saɪz·mɪk/ *adj* [not gradable] *specialized* relating to, or caused by an **earthquake** (= sudden violent movement of the earth's surface)

seize /siːz/ *v* [T] to take (something) quickly and hold it • *He seized her arm to lead her through the crowd.* ○ (*fig.*) *While she was distracted, I seized the opportunity to take a cookie.* • Seize can also mean to take by force: *Rebel forces seized control of six towns.* • If police or other officials seize something, they take possession of it by legal authority: *Customs officers seized a shipment of cocaine.*

seizure /'siː·ʒər/ *n* [C/U] the act of taking hold or possession of something • *a seizure of illegal drugs* [C] ○ *Repressive actions included arbitrary arrests and seizure of property.* [U] • A seizure is also the sudden loss of control of your muscles and, often, the loss of consciousness, caused by certain medical conditions: *The cat suffered several seizures after eating some poison.* [C]

seldom /'sel·dəm/ *adv* almost never • *I seldom drive my car into the city.*

select CHOOSE /səˈlekt/ *v* [I/T] to choose (something), or to make a choice • *They have the option of selecting the school that they want their kids to go to.* [T] ○ *You can select from among the offerings shown on this screen.* [I]

selection /səˈlek·ʃən/ *n* [C/U] the act of choosing, or the person or thing chosen • *They performed a mix of old hits and selections from their new CD.* [C] • A selection can also be a range and variety of something from which to choose: *That bookstore has a wide selection of mystery novels.* [C] ○ *Shop early for the best selection.* [U]

selective /səˈlek·tɪv/ *adj* [not gradable] careful in choosing • *The school is very selective* *and accepts only those students who are extremely motivated.*

select BEST QUALITY /səˈlekt/ *adj* [not gradable] the best of its type or highest in quality • *select fruit/schools* ○ *a select group of people*

self /self/ *n* [C/U] *pl* **selves** /selvz/ who a person is, including the qualities such as personality and ability that make one person different from another • *Now I'm feeling better, and I'm back to my old self again.* [C] ○ *I still assert the validity of self over social convention.* [U]

selfish /ˈsel·fɪʃ/ *adj* caring only about what you want or need without any thought for the needs or wishes of other people • *Am I being selfish to want more?*

selfless /ˈsel·fləs/ *adj* caring more about other people's needs and interests than about your own • *She's a selfless person who is deeply concerned about social justice.*

self–absorbed /ˌsel·fəbˈsɔːrbd, -ˈzɔːrbd/ *adj* so involved with yourself that you do not think about anyone else; SELF-CENTERED • *Henry is so self-absorbed it's a miracle anyone bothers with him at all.*

self–addressed /ˌsel·fəˈdrest/ *adj* [not gradable] (of an envelope) having the name and address of the person who originally sent it on it • *a self-addressed, stamped envelope* • See also SASE.

self–appointed /ˌsel·fəˈpɔɪnt·əd/ *adj* [not gradable] behaving as if you had special knowledge or authority without actually having it • *Mrs. McElvey was the self-appointed spokeswoman for the group.*

self–assured /ˌsel·fəˈʃʊrd/ *adj* having confidence in yourself • *She moves with self-assured grace.*

self–assurance /ˌsel·fəˈʃʊr·əns/ *n* [U] • *His calm self-assurance had vanished.*

self–centered /selfˈsent·ərd/ *adj* caring only about yourself; SELF-ABSORBED • *Angela is a good kid who is also, at times, whiny and self-centered.*

self–confident /selfˈkɑn·fəd·ənt, -fə·dent/ *adj* certain that you can manage any situation by yourself • *She's one of the most self-confident young women I've ever met.*

self–confidence /selfˈkɑn·fəd·əns, -fə·dens/ *n* [U] • *the self-confidence of an experienced professional*

self–conscious /selfˈkɑn·ʃəs/ *adj* uncomfortable about yourself and worried about disapproval from other people • *She was self-conscious about her weight.*

self–consciously /selfˈkɑn·ʃə·sli/ *adv* • *She blushed self-consciously when I complimented her.*

self–contained /ˌself·kənˈteɪnd/ *adj* (of someone or something) having everything necessary to be independent or to work independently • *a self-contained environment* ○ *a self-contained, independent person*

self–control /ˌself·kənˈtroʊl/ *n* [U] control over your emotions and actions; SELF-RE-STRAINT • *They try to teach teamwork, self-control, and how to deal with adversity.*

self–defeating /ˌself·dɪˈfiːt̬·ɪŋ/ *adj* [not gradable] done in a way that keeps you from succeeding • *He raises the issue in a way that is self-defeating.*

self–defense /ˌself·dɪˈfens/ *n* [U] the protection of yourself • *She says she shot him in self-defense.*

self–denial /ˌself·dɪˈnɑɪ·əl/ *n* [U] a decision not to do or have something you want, esp. because it is good for you not to do or have it • *He felt he had wasted his youth in self-denial.*

self–destructive /ˌself·dɪˈstrʌk·tɪv/ *adj* (of behavior or actions) likely to harm or kill you • *Freedom is not an excuse to indulge in self-destructive behavior.*

self–destruction /ˌself·dɪˈstrʌk·ʃən/ *n* [U] • *Drugs and alcohol started her on the path of self-destruction.*

self–discipline /ˌselfˈdɪs·ə·plən/ *n* [U] the ability to make yourself do things when you should, even if you do not want to do them • *He lacked self-discipline and seemed unable to finish anything.*

self–employed /ˌsel·fɪmˈplɔɪd/ *adj* [not gradable] having your own business and working for yourself rather than for an employer

self–esteem /ˌsel·fəˈstiːm/ *n* [U] respect for yourself • *The program is intended to build students' self-esteem.* ○ *Does he suffer from low self-esteem?*

self–evident /selˈfev·əd·ənt, -ə,dent/ *adj* [not gradable] so clear or obvious that no proof or explanation is needed • *self-evident facts*

self–fulfilling /ˌself·fʊlˈfɪl·ɪŋ/ *adj* [not gradable] • **A self-fulfilling prophecy** describes a situation where something happens because you expected or said it would happen: *Sales predictions determine how a book is published, and a prediction of poor sales is often a self-fulfilling prophecy.*

self–help /ˈselfˈhelp/ *adj* [not gradable] providing ways to help you solve a problem, end a habit, learn a skill, etc. by yourself • *self-help books* ○ *a self-help organization*

self–image /ˈselfˈfɪm·ɪdʒ/ *n* [C] your opinion of yourself, esp. how you appear to other people • *Her self-image doesn't depend entirely on professional success.*

self–importance /ˌsel·fɪmˈpɔːrt·ᵊns/ *n* [U] the belief that you are more important or valuable than other people • *He strutted into the room, self-importance written all over his face.*

self–important /ˌsel·fɪmˈpɔːrt·ᵊnt/ *adj* • *You are a self-important little twerp.*

self–improvement /ˌsel·fɪmˈpruːv·mənt/ *n* [U] learning new things on your own that make you a more skilled or able person • *In the interest of self-improvement, I took a course in Spanish.*

self–indulgent /ˌsel·fɪnˈdʌl·dʒənt/ *adj* allowing yourself to have or do anything you want • *A lot of the poetry is just self-indulgent nonsense.*

self–indulgence /ˌsel·fɪnˈdʌl·dʒəns/ *n* [U] • *My parents' trip to Hawaii was an unusual self-indulgence for them.*

self–inflicted /ˌsel·fɪnˈflɪk·təd/ *adj* [not gradable] (of something bad) done to yourself • *a self-inflicted wound*

self–interest /selˈfɪn·trəst, -ˈfɪnt·ə·rəst/ *n* [U] consideration of advantages for yourself in making a decision, usually without worrying about its effect on others • *Each side was thinking only of their own self-interest.*

selfish /ˈsel·fɪʃ/ *adj* [not gradable] • See at SELF.

selfless /ˈsel·fləs/ *adj* [not gradable] • See at SELF.

self–made /ˈselfˈmeɪd/ *adj* [not gradable] successful as a result of your own effort • *a self-made man*

self–pity /ˈselfˈpɪt̬·i/ *n* [U] care and sadness about your own problems • *It's not easy to face serious illness without self-pity.*

self–portrait /ˈselfˈpɔːr·trət, -ˈpoʊr-/ *n* [C] a picture you make of yourself • *How accurate is his self-portrait?*

self–possession /ˌself·pəˈzeʃ·ən/ *n* [U] the quality of being calm and in control of your emotions • *She shows remarkable self-possession for a child.*

self–possessed /ˌself·pəˈzest/ *adj*

self–preservation /ˌselfˌprez·ərˈveɪ·ʃən/ *n* [U] the ability of an animal or person to protect themselves from danger or destruction • *an instinct for self-preservation*

self–proclaimed /ˌself·prəˈkleɪmd/ *adj* [not gradable] said or announced by yourself about yourself • *He is a self-proclaimed literary genius.*

self–reliance /ˌself·rɪˈlɑɪ·əns/ *n* [U] the ability to depend on yourself or your own abilities • *Learning self-reliance is a slow, hard process.*

self–reliant /ˌself·rɪˈlɑɪ·ənt/ *adj* • *She's cool, determined, and self-reliant.*

self–respect /ˌself·rɪˈspekt/ *n* [U] positive thoughts and feelings about yourself; SELF-ESTEEM • *His self-respect is based on solid achievement.*

self–respecting /ˌself·rɪˈspek·tɪŋ/ *adj* [not gradable] • *No self-respecting person would tolerate that.*

self–restraint /ˌself·rɪˈstreɪnt/ *n* [U] control over your emotions and actions; SELF-CONTROL. • *You need to exercise a little self-restraint.*

self–righteous /selˈfrɑɪ·tʃəs/ *adj* believing that you are better and more moral than other people, often expressed in an annoying or offensive way • *Spare us from your self-righteous nonsense.*

self–sacrifice /ˈselfˈsæk·rə·ˌfɑɪs/ *n* [U] a decision to give up something you want or need so that someone else can have what they want or need • *Heroism and self-sacrifice inspired the soldiers.*

self–satisfied /ˈselfˈsæt̬·əsˌfɑɪd/ *adj* too pleased with yourself and what you have achieved • *an annoyingly self-satisfied person*

self–service /ˈselfˈsɜr·vəs/ *adj* [not gradable] (of a business or machine) operated without employees to help you, so that you take items for yourself and then pay someone for whatever you have taken • *a self-service gas station/ cafeteria*

self–starter /ˈselfˈstɑrt̬·ər/ *n* [C] someone who can work well alone • *Applicants must be self-starters.*

self–sufficient /ˌself·səˈfɪʃ·ənt/ *adj* able to provide what is necessary without the help of others • *a self-sufficient economy/person*

self–sufficiency /ˌself·səˈfɪʃ·ən·si/ *n* [U] • *They showed their self-sufficiency by growing their own vegetables.*

self–supporting /ˌself·səˈpɔːrt̬·ɪŋ, -ˈpoʊrt̬-/ *adj* [not gradable] having enough money to take care of yourself • *Children eventually become self-supporting.*

self–taught /ˈselfˈtɔːt/ *adj* [not gradable] (of a skill or knowledge) learned or trained by yourself • *a self-taught artist/musician*

sell EXCHANGE FOR MONEY /sel/ *v* [I/T] *past* **sold** /soʊld/ to give (a thing) or perform (a service) in exchange for money • *The children sold lemonade.* [T] ○ *These baskets sell well* (= people buy a lot of them). [I] • If you **sell** someone **short**, you value them too little: *It's a mistake to sell your audience short.* • See also SALE SELL.

seller /ˈsel·ər/ *n* [C] • *The seller of the painting was kept secret.* • A seller is also something that is sold: *That CD is our best seller.*

sell PERSUADE /sel/ *v* [I/T] *past* **sold** /soʊld/ to persuade someone to accept (an idea or plan), or to cause something to be accepted • *That is a plan we can easily sell to the school board.* [T]

□ **sell off** /ˈ-ˈ-/ *v adv* [T] to exchange (all or a large part of something) for money • *The museum is selling off its less important European paintings.*

□ **sell out** *obj* EXCHANGE EVERYTHING , **sell** *obj* **out** /ˈ-ˈ-/ *v adv* [I/T] to get rid of (all of an item or control of a business) in exchange for money • *We sold out (of) the T-shirts in the first couple of hours.* [I/M]

sellout /ˈsel·ɑʊt/ *n* [C] • *Saturday's show was a sellout.*

□ **sell out** DO FOR MONEY /ˈ-ˈ-/ *v adv* [I/T] to give up (something) for money or selfish reasons • *Anyone who sells out their country should be locked up forever.* [T]

sellout /ˈsel·ɑʊt/ *n* [C] • *If the union backs down, it will be seen as a sellout to the government.*

seltzer /ˈselt·sər/ *n* [C/U] bubbly water

selves /selvz/ *pl of* SELF

semantic /səˈmænt·ɪk/ *adj* [not gradable] (of words and language) connected with meaning • *Words are semantic units that convey meaning.*

semantics /səˈmænt·ɪks/ *n* [U] the study of meaning in language

semblance /ˈsem·bləns/ *n* [U] a similarity to something, or the appearance of being or having something • *She's a single mother holding down a full-time job and trying to maintain some semblance of a personal life.*

semen /ˈsiː·mən/ *n* [U] a sticky, white liquid containing sperm which is produced by men and male animals

semester /səˈmes·tər/ *n* [C] either of the two periods into which a year is divided at a school or university • *fall/spring semester*

semi TRUCK (*pl* **semis**) /ˈsem·i, -ɑɪ/, **semitrailer** *n* [C] *infml* a large truck with a separate TRAILER (= vehicle without an engine) for carrying freight, or such a trailer itself • *The semi screeched to a halt.* • PIC TRACTOR-TRAILER

semi COMPETITION /ˈsem·i, -ɑɪ/ *n* [C] *pl* **semis** *short form of* SEMIFINAL

semi– HALF /ˌsem·i, -ɑɪ/ *combining form* half or partly • *semiretired* ○ *semiserious*

semiautomatic /ˌsem·iːˌɔːṭ·əˈmæṭ·ɪk, ˌsem·ɑɪ-/ *adj* [not gradable] (of a gun) having a bullet in position and ready for firing when the TRIGGER is pulled • *a semiautomatic pistol/rifle*

semicircle /ˈsem·iːˌsɜr·kəl/ *n* [C] half of a circle, or something in this shape • *Our tents were set in a semicircle.*

semicircular /ˌsem·iːˈsɜr·kjə·lər/ *adj* [not gradable] having the shape of half a circle • *a semicircular table*

semicolon /ˈsem·iˌkoʊ·lən/ *n* [C] a mark (;) used in writing for separating large or important independent parts of a sentence or items in a list

---

SEMICOLON [;]

A semicolon is used to join two parts of a sentence that could be two separate sentences but that the writer prefers to keep together.

Rachel's eyes began to close; Dan, too, was feeling tired. • *Seat belts make driving safer; furthermore, their use is legally required in most states.*

When two independent clauses are connected by *and, or,* or *but,* a semicolon is not normally used.

A semicolon is also used to separate groups of words in a series when at least one of the groups contains commas or is long.

Send this letter to McAllister, Dewey, and Schmidt; Baxter; and Hough. • *Canada has rich farmland; oil and ore deposits and abundant waterpower; and a growing, well-educated work force.*

---

semifinal /ˈsem·ɪˌfɑɪn·ᵊl/, *short form* **semi** *n* [C] the game or set of games before the final game in a competition • *France was eliminated in Saturday's semifinal.* • Compare FINAL COMPETITION.

seminal /ˈsem·ən·ᵊl/ *adj* containing important new ideas that influence later developments • *"The Adventures of Huckleberry Finn" is regarded as a seminal work of American literature.*

seminar /ˈsem·əˌnɑr/ *n* [C] a meeting of a group of people with a teacher or expert for training, discussion, or study on a particular subject • *Police officers attended a seminar on relieving rush-hour traffic jams.*

seminary /ˈsem·əˌner·i/ *n* [C] a college where people are trained to become priests, ministers, or rabbis

Semitic /səˈmɪṭ·ɪk/ *adj* [not gradable] being or having to do with the Arabs and Jews of the Middle East

semitrailer /ˈsem·ɪˌtreɪ·lər, ˈsem·ɑɪ-/ *n* [C] a SEMI TRUCK

senate /ˈsen·ət/ *n* [U] the group of politicians who have the most power to make laws in a government • *The US Senate has 100 members.* ○ *He served in the state senate.* • In Canada, members of the Senate advise about laws but do not make laws.

senator /ˈsen·ət·ər/ (*abbreviation* **Sen.**) *n* [C] a member of a senate, esp. of the US Senate • *Write to your senator about your concerns.*

senatorial /ˌsen·əˈtɔr·iː·əl, -ˈtoʊr-/ *adj* [not gradable] • *senatorial candidates* ○ *a Senatorial committee*

send HAVE DELIVERED /send/ *v* [T] *past* **sent** /sent/ to cause (something) to go or be taken somewhere without going yourself • *Send a letter to my office.* ○ *I like to send E-mail to my friends.* • *Maggie* **sends** *her* **love/regards** (= asked me to express her good feelings toward you).

send MAKE SOMEONE GO /send/ *v* [T] *past* **sent** /sent/ to cause or arrange for (someone) to leave or go • *The president was not eager to send troops.* ○ *My parents want to send me back to Argentina when I finish my studies.* ○ *Who can afford to send their kids to college these days?*

send MAKE SOMETHING MOVE /send/ *v* [T] *past* **sent** /sent/ to make (something) move quickly by force • *Wind sent clouds skittering across the sky.* ○ *One punch sent him flying.*

send CAUSE TO HAPPEN /send/ *v* [T] *past* **sent** /sent/ to cause (someone) to feel or behave in a particular way, or to cause (something) to happen • *Final exams always send me into a panic.* • If you **send a message/signal** by something you do or say, you are trying to influence someone else's attitudes or behavior: *We need to send a clear message that pollution will not be tolerated.*

□**send away for** /ˌ--ˈ--/ *v adv prep* [T] to

request (something) by mail • *Carson sent away for a magic kit.*

□ **send back** *obj*, **send** *obj* **back** /'-'-/ *v adv* [M] to return (something) to the place it came from • *Send your steak back if it's undercooked.*

□ **send for** /'--/ *v prep* [T] to request or demand that (someone or something) come • *Once he was settled in America, he sent for his wife.*

□ **send in** *obj* MAIL , **send** *obj* **in** /'-'-/ *v adv* [M] to mail (something) to a place • *I sent in my entry form, but I don't expect to win anything.*

□ **send in** *obj* CAUSE TO GO , **send** *obj* **in** /'-'-/ *v adv* [M] to cause (people, esp. soldiers) to go to a place • *Opposition forces are sending in more troops every day.*

□ **send off** *obj*, **send** *obj* **off** /'-'-/ *v adv* [M] to mail (something) • *She sent the manuscript off to her publisher.*

□ **send out** *obj* MAIL , **send** *obj* **out** /'-'-/ *v adv* [M] to mail (esp. a lot of things) • *Frank sends out about 400 Christmas cards every year.*

□ **send out** *obj* CAUSE TO GO , **send** *obj* **out** /'-'-/ *v adv* [M] to ask or demand that (someone) go somewhere • *Mom sent me out to weed the garden.* • If a signal is sent out, it is produced: *The laser sends out a long red beam of light.*

send–off /'sen·dɔːf/ *n* [C] an occasion at which people express good wishes to someone who is leaving • *Friends gave them a rousing send-off.*

senile /'siː·naɪl, 'sen·aɪl/ *adj* mentally confused as a result of old age • *Her children couldn't cope with her because she's somewhat senile.*

senility /sə'nɪl·ət·i/ *n* [U] • *Miller suffers from senility.*

senior MORE ADVANCED /'siːn·jər/ *adj* more advanced, or higher in rank • *Senior officials denied that a problem exists.* • Compare JUNIOR LESS ADVANCED .

seniority /siːn'jɔːr·ət·i, -'jɑr-/ *n* [U] higher rank or advantage obtained as a result of the length of job service • *Most of these workers have 20 to 30 years of seniority.*

senior SCHOOL /'siːn·jər/ *n* [C] a student in the fourth and final year of a program of study in a college, university, or HIGH SCHOOL (= a school for students 15 to 18 years old) • LP EDUCATION IN THE US

senior /'siːn·jər/ *adj* [not gradable] • *Alanna's in her senior year of high school.* • A **senior high school** is a HIGH SCHOOL.

senior OLDER /'siːn·jər/ *adj* older • *The senior Griffey played on the same baseball team as his son, Ken Griffey, Jr.* • A **senior citizen** (also **senior**) is an older person, usually over the age of 60 or 65, esp. one who has given up their job: *Senior citizens get a discount.*

senior /'siːn·jər/ *n* [U] • *She's dating a man almost 40 years her senior.*

sensation FEELING /sen'seɪ·ʃən, sən-/ *n* [C/U] a feeling in your body resulting from some-

thing that happens or is done to it, or the ability to feel as the result of touch • *He felt a sinking sensation in the pit of his stomach.* [C] ○ *This part of your body doesn't have a lot of sensation.* [U]

sensation EXCITEMENT /sen'seɪ·ʃən, sən-/ *n* [C] great excitement or interest, or someone or something that causes excitement • *His first recordings caused a sensation and became classics of rock.*

sensational /sen'seɪ·ʃən·əl, sən-/ *adj* very exciting, or extremely good • *She was absolutely sensational in that movie.* • (*disapproving*) Something or someone sensational purposely shocks people and attracts their interest: *Readers love sensational crime stories.*

sensationalism /sen'seɪ·ʃən·əl,ɪz·əm, sən-/ *n* [U] the use of shocking or exciting subjects, language, or style in order to interest the public • *Kids tend to watch news for its sensationalism.*

sense JUDGMENT /sens/ *n* the ability to make reasonable judgments • *If the boy had any sense he would be scared.* [U] ○ *You ought to have more sense than to get involved with him.* [U] ○ *Have you taken leave of your senses?* [pl]

sensible /'sen·sə·bəl/ *adj* having or using good judgment; reasonable • *She was sensible and easy to deal with.* ○ *The only sensible thing to do is recycle.* • If an object is sensible, it is practical but not exciting: *a sensible family car* ○ *sensible shoes*

sensibly /'sen·sə·bli/ *adv* • *You have to eat more sensibly.*

senseless /'sen·sləs/ *adj* lacking purpose or meaning • *a senseless killing* ○ *It was senseless to treat me like that.*

sense BODY POWER /sens/ *n* [C] any of the five physical abilities to see, hear, smell, taste, and feel • *Women have a better sense of smell than men.* • USAGE: The related adjective is SENSORY.

senseless /'sen·sləs/ *adj* unconscious • *They beat him senseless.*

sense AWARENESS /sens/ *n* [C usually sing] an awareness of something, or an ability to do or understand something • *I have a very bad sense of direction.* • A **sense of humor** is the ability to understand and enjoy jokes and amusing situations, or to make people laugh: *Matt has a great sense of humor.*

sense FEELING /sens/ *n* [C] a feeling about something • *They move with a sense of confidence.* ○ *Students need some sense of responsibility.*

sense /sens/ *v* [T] to feel or be aware of (something) • *Although she said nothing, I could sense her anger.* ○ *I sensed someone was approaching me from behind.*

sense MEANING /sens/ *n* [C] a meaning of a word or phrase • *This isn't a travel book in the usual sense of the word.*

sensibility /,sen·sə'bɪl·ət·i/ *n* the ability to

feel and react to something • *Racism is offensive to the modern sensibility.* [U] ○ *The issue has little to do with religious sensibilities.* [pl]

sensitive UNDERSTANDING /'sen·sət·ɪv/ *adj* having or showing awareness and understanding, esp. of other people's feelings and needs • *My experience made me very sensitive to the suffering of others.*

sensitively /'sen·sət·ɪv·li/ *adv* • *How can I say this sensitively?*

sensitivity /ˌsen·səˈtɪv·ət·i/ *n* [U] • *A good teacher has enthusiasm, intelligence, and sensitivity to students' needs.*

sensitive UPSET /'sen·sət·ɪv/ *adj* (of a person) easily upset • *Tom is extremely sensitive about his hair.* ○ *She's very sensitive to criticism.*

sensitivity /ˌsen·səˈtɪv·ət·i/ *n* the tendency to be upset • *The sensitivity of minority groups had increased over the years.* [U] ○ *He tried to avoid offending their sensitivities.* [pl]

sensitive REACTING EASILY /'sen·sət·ɪv/ *adj* easily influenced, changed, or damaged, esp. by a physical activity or effect • *an environmentally sensitive river* ○ *Their products include cleansers and moisturizers for sensitive skin.*

sensitivity /ˌsen·səˈtɪv·ət·i/, **sensitiveness** /'sen·sət·ɪv·nəs/ *n* [U] • *Many people have food sensitivities or allergies.*

sensitive NEEDING CAREFUL TREATMENT /'sen·sət·ɪv/ *adj* needing to be treated with care or secrecy • *Sex education and birth control are sensitive issues.*

sensitivity /ˌsen·səˈtɪv·ət·i/ *n* [U] • *This issue needs to be approached with special sensitivity.*

sensory /'sen·sə·ri/ *adj* [not gradable] of or related to the physical SENSES of touch, smell, taste, sight, and hearing • *Children in shopping malls often suffer from sensory overload.*

sensual /'sen·tʃə·wəl/ *adj* expressing or suggesting physical, esp. sexual, pleasure • *She smiled with pouty, sensual lips.* ○ *They shared the sensual satisfaction of French food.*

sensuality /ˌsen·tʃəˈwæl·ət·i/ *n* [U] • *He admired the sensuality of her movements.*

sensuous /'sen·tʃə·wəs/ *adj* pleasing to the physical SENSES • *Her flower garden is a totally sensuous environment.* • Sensuous can also mean SENSUAL: *She was a very sensuous woman, very much a flirt.*

sent /sent/ *past simple and past participle of* SEND

sentence GRAMMAR /'sent·ᵊns/ *n* [C] specialized (in grammar) a group of words, usually containing a subject and a verb, expressing a statement, question, instruction, or exclamation, and, when written, starting with a capital letter and ending with a PERIOD or other mark • *Your sentences are too long and complicated.* • LP CAPITAL LETTERS, PERIOD

sentence PUNISHMENT /'sent·ᵊns/ *n* [C] a punishment given by a law court to a person or organization that is guilty of a crime • *She served a three-year prison sentence.*

sentence /'sent·ᵊns/ *v* [T] • *He was sentenced to life imprisonment in the slaying of a store owner.*

sentiment GENERAL FEELING /'sent·ə·mənt/ *n* [C/U] a general feeling, attitude, or opinion about something • *Her book offends the religious sentiments of many Muslims.* [C] ○ *Boyd tried to turn community sentiment against the program.* [U]

sentiment EMOTION /'sent·ə·mənt/ *n* [U] often disapproving gentle emotions such as love, sympathy, or caring • *The film wallows in sentiment.* ○ *There was little room for compassion or sentiment in his world.*

sentimental /ˌsent·əˈment·ᵊl/ *adj* related to feelings rather than reason • *When you ask which team will win, my sentimental favorite would have to be Philadelphia.* • Sentimental also means expressing or causing gentle emotions: *He gets sentimental and starts crying when we talk about his mother.*

sentimentally /ˌsent·əˈment·ᵊl·i/ *adv* • *Children get sentimentally attached to their pets.*

sentimentality /ˌsent·ə·menˈtæl·ət·i, -mən-/ *n* [U] • *She had never liked that song's sentimentality.*

sentry /'sen·tri/ *n* [C] a soldier who guards a place and prevents those who are not allowed in from entering • *Sentries stood guard at the palace.*

separate /'sep·ə·rət, 'sep·rət/ *adj* existing or happening independently or in a different physical space • *The middle school and the high school are in two separate buildings.* ○ *I have my public life and my private life, and as far as possible I try to keep them separate.*

separate /'sep·əˌreɪt/ *v* [I/T] to cause (two or more people or things) to stop being with or near each other, or to be positioned between (two or more things) • *A six-foot high partition separates smokers from nonsmokers.* [T] ○ *Fighting broke out between two hockey players, and it took nearly five minutes to separate them.* [T] • If two married people separate, they stop living together as husband and wife, often as a part of a legal arrangement. [I]

separately /'sep·ə·rət·li, 'sep·rət-/ *adv* • *You have to wash dark clothes and white stuff separately.*

separation /ˌsep·əˈreɪ·ʃən/ *n* [C/U] • *The laws now require the separation of garbage that can be recycled, such as newspapers and glass bottles.* [U] • A separation is an often legal arrangement by which two married people stop living together as husband and wife. [C]

September /sepˈtem·bər, səp-/ (*abbreviation* **Sept.**) *n* [C/U] the ninth month of the year, after August and before October

sequel /'siː·kwəl/ *n* [C] a book, movie, or play that continues the story of a previous work • *Sequels to movies like "Jaws" and "Superman" have become big business in the film industry.*

sequence /'siː·kwəns, -ˌkwens/ *n* [C/U] a

series of related things or events, or the order in which things or events follow each other • *The first chapter describes the strange sequence of events that led to his death.* [C] ○ *The test papers were not in the correct alphabetical sequence.* [C]

sequester /sɪˈkwes·tər/ *v* [T] *law* to keep a JURY (= group of people deciding a legal case) separate from everyone else, even from their families, while deciding a case • *The judge refused to have the jury sequestered.*

sequin /ˈsiː·kwɑn/ *n* [C] a small, shiny metal or plastic disk sewn on clothes for decoration • *Her dress sparkled with sequins.*

sequoia /sɪˈkwɔɪ·ə/ *n* [C] an evergreen tree that can reach a height of more than 300 feet and grows in California and Oregon

serenade /ˌser·əˈneɪd/ *v* [T] to play music or sing for (someone) • *On Saturdays, shoppers at the mall are serenaded with live piano music.*

serenade /ˌser·əˈneɪd/ *n* [C] a piece of music or song performed for someone, esp. outside at night

serene /səˈriːn/ *adj* peaceful and calm, or (of a person) not worried or excited • *He approached the job with the serene confidence that he could succeed where others had failed.*

serenity /səˈren·ət̬·i/ *n* [U] • *He wrote of the beauty and serenity of the great river.*

sergeant /ˈsɑr·dʒənt/ *n* [C] a person in the military below the rank of a LIEUTENANT (= an officer of the lowest rank)

serial /ˈsɪr·i·əl/ *adj* [not gradable] happening one after another in time or order • *She's the librarian in charge of serial publications* (= magazines, newspapers, etc., that appear at regular periods). • A **serial killer** is a person who commits many murders, one after another, often over a long period of time. • A **serial number** is a particular number, different from all the others, printed on each item produced, such as a computer or televisions, in order to be able to recognize it.

serial /ˈsɪr·i·əl/ *n* [C] a story printed in a newspaper or magazine or broadcast on television or radio in several parts

series /ˈsɪr·iːz/ *n* [C] *pl* **series** a number of similar or related events or things, one following another • *A series of scandals over the past year has not helped public confidence in the administration.*

serious NOT JOKING /ˈsɪr·i·əs/ *adj* not joking; not intended to amuse • *You can never tell when he's serious.*

seriously /ˈsɪr·i·ə·sli/ *adv* • *Seriously* (= Without joking), *now, did he really say that?* ○ *You're not seriously* (= really) *thinking of quitting, are you?*

serious NEEDING ATTENTION /ˈsɪr·i·əs/ *adj* needing complete attention • *That's an interesting job offer—I'd give it serious consideration if I were you.*

seriously /ˈsɪr·i·ə·sli/ *adv* • *The police have to take any terrorist threat seriously.*

serious BAD /ˈsɪr·i·əs/ *adj* severe in effect; bad • *Fortunately, there were no serious injuries.*

seriously /ˈsɪr·i·ə·sli/ *adv* • *Uncooked shellfish can make you seriously ill.*

seriousness /ˈsɪr·i·ə·snəs/ *n* [U] • *I don't think he has any idea of the seriousness of the situation.*

serious DETERMINED /ˈsɪr·i·əs/ *adj* determined to follow a particular plan of action • *Is she serious about moving to Nevada?* ○ *You have to start getting serious about your studies.* • If two people who have a romantic relationship are serious about each other, they intend to stay together and possibly marry: *She's had a lot of boyfriends but he's the only one she's been serious about.*

sermon /ˈsɜr·mən/ *n* [C] a talk on a religious or moral subject, esp. one given by a religious leader during a religious ceremony

serpent /ˈsɜr·pənt/ *n* [C] *literary* a snake

serrated /səˈreɪt̬·əd, ˈser·ˌeɪt̬-/ *adj* having a row of sharp points along the edge • *You need a knife with a serrated edge for cutting bread.*

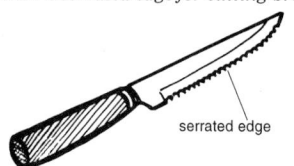

serrated edge

serum /ˈsɪr·əm/ *n* [C/U] the watery, colorless part of the blood, or this liquid taken from blood, used for medical purposes

servant /ˈsɜr·vənt/ *n* [C] a person who is employed to do work for another person, esp. to work in another person's home doing jobs such as cooking and cleaning • Servant is also used in combination to mean someone working for the public: *a civil/public servant*

serve HELP /sɜrv/ *v* [I/T] (esp. of a person working in a restaurant or store) to help (a customer) by getting what someone needs or by showing or selling goods, or to provide (food or drinks) to a customer or guest • *We've been in the restaurant for half an hour and we're still waiting to be served.* [T] ○ *Breakfast is served between seven and nine every morning.* [T] ○ *We'll be ready to serve (lunch) soon.* [I/T] • To serve is also to provide (an area or group of people) with something that is needed: *As long as I am your representative, I will continue to serve the needs of this community.* [T]

serving /ˈsɜr·vɪŋ/ *n* [C] the amount of one type of food given to one person • *This recipe makes enough for four servings.*

serve WORK FOR /sɜrv/ *v* [I/T] to work (for), esp. in doing your duty • *He served in the US Navy for twelve years.* [I] ○ *If memory serves me* *right* (= If I am remembering correctly), *I was 13 at the time.* [T] • (*infml*) If you say that something **serves** someone **right**, you mean that they deserve the punishment they have received: *"Alice hit me!" "It serves you right—you hit her first."*

serve SPEND TIME /sɜrv/ *v* [T] to spend (a period of time) in a job or activity • *He served four years in prison for robbery.*

serve HAVE A PURPOSE /sɜrv/ *v* [I/T] to have (something) as a purpose; result in (esp. something that is helpful or useful) • *Tougher prison sentences, he said, will serve to deter crime.* [+ *to* infinitive] ○ *The sofa can serve as* (= be used as) *a bed for a couple of nights.* [I]

serve HIT BALL /sɜrv/ *v* [I/T] (in tennis and other sports) to hit the ball to the other player or team as a way of starting play

serve /sɜrv/ *n* [C] • *He's got a powerful serve.*

server /'sɜr·vər/ *n* [C] a central computer from which other computers obtain information

service HELP /'sɜr·vəs/ *n* [U] the help provided to a customer by someone who works in esp. a restaurant or store • *The service in this restaurant is terrible—I've been waiting fifteen minutes.* • A **service charge** is an amount of money added to the basic price of something to pay for the cost of dealing with the customer: *There is a $4 service charge added to the price of each ticket if you order by phone.*

service WORK /'sɜr·vəs/ *n* work done or help provided, esp. for the public or for a person or an organization • *She was given the award for a lifetime of public service.* [U] ○ *The airplane had been in service* (= used) *for fifteen years.* [U] ○ *You should have the services of a lawyer.* [pl]

service SYSTEM /'sɜr·vəs/ *n* [C/U] a system, organization, or business that provides for a public need, or the operation of such a system • *the diplomatic/postal service* [C] ○ *medical/social services* [C] ○ *There is bus service to Newark Airport every twenty minutes.* [U] • A service is a business that provides something for people but does not produce goods: *My brother runs a car service* (= business that rents cars with drivers). [U] • The service is the armed forces: *He spent ten years in the service.* [U] • A **service station** is a place, usually near a road, where you can buy gas for your car and sometimes where you can get it repaired.

service RELIGIOUS CEREMONY /'sɜr·vəs/ *n* [C] a formal religious ceremony

service REPAIR /'sɜr·vəs/ *v* [T] to examine (a machine) and repair any faulty parts • *I'm taking the car in to have it serviced this afternoon.*

service EMPLOYMENT /'sɜr·vəs/ *n* [U] work done for others, such as cleaning or repairing, caring for a building, or making deliveries • *This building has five service employees including the super.* • A **service entrance** is an entrance to a building that is used for deliveries.

service BALL HIT /'sɜr·vəs/ *n* [U] the act of hitting a ball to put it in play in tennis and some other sports

serviceable /'sɜr·və·sə·bəl/ *adj* (of an object or activity) able to do the work intended • *If this fan is still serviceable, we could use it in the office.*

serviceman MILITARY PERSON (*pl* **-men**) /'sɜr·və,smæn, -smən/, **servicewoman** (*pl* **-women**) /'sɜr·və,swʊm·ən/ *n* [C] a member of the armed forces

serviceman REPAIR PERSON (*pl* **-men**) /'sɜr·və ,smæn, -smən/, **servicewoman** (*pl* **-women**) /'sɜr·və,swʊm·ən/ *n* [C] a person who repairs and takes care of equipment • *Did anyone call the serviceman about the broken copier?*

servile /'sɜr·vəl, -vaɪl/ *adj* eager to serve and please someone else in a way that shows a lack of respect for yourself • *As a waiter, you want to be pleasant to people without appearing servile.*

servitude /'sɜr·və,tuːd/ *n* [U] the state of being under the control of someone else and of having no freedom; the condition of a SLAVE

session FORMAL MEETING /'seʃ·ən/ *n* a formal meeting of an organization, esp. of a legislature or law court • *He wanted to introduce the bill before the present session of the state legislature adjourned.* [C] ○ *Congress is in session* (= continuing to have meetings) *until the end of the month.* [U]

session ACTIVITY /'seʃ·ən/ *n* [C] a period of time or a meeting arranged for a particular activity • *The musicians gathered in the studio, waiting for the start of the recording session.* • At a college or university, a session is any of the periods of time into which a teaching year is divided: *The first summer session starts June 3rd.*

set PUT /set/ *v* [T always + adv/prep] **setting**, *past* **set** to put (something) in a particular place or position • *Set the box on its end.* ○ *Our house is set back from the road.* • If you set something down, you put it on a surface: *She set down her teacup and leaned forward.* [M] • If you set a story in a particular place or time, the events happen then or there: *Banks's novel is set in the years before the Civil War.* • To **set foot** somewhere is to enter that place: *Can you believe she's never set foot in a McDonald's?* • When a boat or ship **sets sail**, it begins a trip.

setting /'set·ɪŋ/ *n* [C] the surroundings or place in which something is put • *The house has a beautiful setting overlooking the river.* ○ *The setting of the novel is Paris, in the 1920s.*

set CAUSE A CONDITION /set/ *v* **setting**, *past* **set** to cause (someone or something) to be in a particular condition, or to begin doing (something) • *He carelessly dropped a match and set the grass on fire.* [T] ○ *His remarks set me thinking.* [T] ○ *After years in prison, the men were finally set free.* [L] ○ *With the deadline only a few weeks away, I set to work right away.* [+ *to* infinitive] • If something is **set in motion**, it begins: *Newly discovered evidence set in motion a second investigation.* • If you **set** someone **straight** or **set the record straight**, you make the true facts known: *I had to set him straight about what really happened.* ○ *The article about the trial really set the record straight.* • If something **sets** your **teeth on edge**, it annoys you very much: *It seems like her only reason for being is to set my teeth on edge.*

set ARRANGE /set/ *v* [T] **setting**, *past* **set** to arrange or adjust (something) so it is ready to work or be used • *I've set the clock to daylight savings time.* ○ *To get rid of mice, set a trap—or get a cat.* ○ *My job is to set the table before dinner* (= arrange the plates, utensils, etc.).

set /set/ *adj* [not gradable] with everything arranged; ready • *Katy is set to go to college in September.* [+ *to* infinitive] ○ *Is everything all set for the party?*

setting /'seṭ·ɪŋ/ *n* [C] a position of the controls on a machine or instrument • *If the image is dark or fuzzy, adjust the settings.* • A setting (also **place setting**) is also the arrangement of dishes and utensils that a person uses when eating a meal at a table.

set ESTABLISH /set/ *v* [T] **setting**, *past* **set** to establish (a pattern or example) to follow • *Parents should try to set a good example.* ○ *The governor wants to set spending limits.* ○ *She set a new world record at the Wannamaker Games.*

set BECOME FIXED /set/ *v* [I/T] **setting**, *past* **set** to cause (something) to become fixed or firm • *Have they set a date for the wedding yet?* [T] ○ *Glue that sets quickly makes it easier to repair things.* [I] ○ *The old man's face was set in a continual scowl.* [T] • If you have your hair set, you have it arranged while it is wet so that it will stay in a particular style when it is dry. [T] • If a stone is set, it is fixed in a piece of jewelry: *The blue stone was set in a gold ring.* [T] • When a broken bone is set, it is kept in a fixed position so that it can heal. [T] • If something is **set in stone**, it is very difficult to change it: *The schedule isn't set in stone, but we'd like to stick to it pretty closely.* • If you **set** your **sights on** something or **set** your **mind to** something, you are determined to do it: *People can diet when they set their mind to it.*

set /set/ *adj* [not gradable] • *There wasn't a set time for us to get there.* • If people are described as **set in** their **ways**, they do not like change in their lives: *They're very set in their ways, and have to eat by 6 p.m.*

set /set/ *adj* • If you are set on something, you have firmly determined whether or not to do it: *HMOs are good if you aren't set on one specific doctor.*

set /set/ *n* [C/U] a position or an arrangement, esp. of the hair or body • *I could tell from the set of his jaw that he was angry.* [U] ○ *Could*

you give my hair a set like the one in the picture in this magazine? [C]

setting /'seṭ·ɪŋ/ *n* [C] the part of a piece of jewelry designed to hold a stone • *It was her grandmother's ring—a single diamond in a gold setting*

set PLAY BACKGROUND /set/ *n* [C] something built or put together to represent a place where the action happens in a play or movie • *The set looks just like a real subway car.*

set /set/ *v* • If you **set the stage** for a play, you put together what will be needed on the stage to perform the play: *Kei set the stage by lighting and wetting some large rocks.* • If you say that something has **set the stage**, you mean that events have reached a point which makes it likely that something else will happen: *The Supreme Court ruling against Tennessee set the stage for action against Virginia and other states.*

set MOVE DOWN /set/ *v* [I] **setting**, *past* **set** (esp. of the sun or moon) to sink in the sky until it cannot be seen • *The sun sets with a great show of color.* • USAGE: The opposite of set is RISE MOVE UP.

set GROUP /set/ *n* [C] a group of things that belong together or are used together • *a chess set* ○ *a number set* ○ *She has a strange set of symptoms.* • A set is also a group of people who have similar interests and spend time together: *the golf-playing set* • In tennis, a set is a group of games between the same competitors: *The match was over quickly, four sets to two.*

set TELEVISION /set/ *n* [C] a television • *I walked in the room and turned off the set.*

◻**set about** /'--,-/ *v prep* [T] to begin to do or deal with (something) • *After putting up the tent, she set about making a fire.*

◻**set** *obj* **against** *obj* COMPARE /'--,-/ *v prep* [T] to consider (one thing) in relation to (another) • *The film sets the horror of war against the innocence of childhood.*

◻**set** *obj* **against** *obj* OPPOSE /'--,-/ *v prep* [T] to cause (a person or group) to oppose (another) or to be opposed to (something) • *It's easy to learn, but most people just have their minds set against it.*

◻**set** *obj* **apart** /'--'-/ *v adv* [T] to show (someone or something) to be different or special • *Her original ideas set her apart from other students.*

◻**set aside** *obj* SAVE, **set** *obj* **aside** /'--'-/ *v adv* [M] to save for a particular purpose • *He sets aside some time every day to read to his children.* ○ *After melting the chocolate, set it aside and beat the eggs.*

◻**set aside** *obj* IGNORE, **set** *obj* **aside** /'--'-/ *v adv* [M] to decide not to deal with (something) • *We need to set aside our differences and begin to cooperate.* • To set aside a legal decision or a judgment is to state that it is no longer in effect: *The court of appeals set aside his conviction.*

◻**set back** *obj* DELAY, **set** *obj* **back** /'-'-/ *v adv*

[M] to delay or stop the progress of (someone or something) • *Then I needed a second operation, which really set me back.*

setback /'set,bæk/ *n* [C] • *Democrats suffered a serious setback in yesterday's election, losing all three contested seats.*

□ **set** *obj* **back** *(obj)* COST /'-'-/ *v adv* [T] *infml* to cost (someone) an amount of money • *Our vacation set us back over $3000.*

□ **set down** *obj*, **set** *obj* **down** /'-'-/ *v adv* [M] to write or print (words, ideas, information, etc.) • *It's often a lot of work to set your thoughts down on paper.*

□ **set forth** *obj*, **set** *obj* **forth** /'-'-/ *v adv* [M] *slightly fml* to explain (ideas), or make (rules or suggestions) • *She set forth her views in "The Art of Making Dance."* ○ *The board set forth the conditions for her release.*

□ **set in** /'-'-/ *v adv* [I] to begin • *If the wound is untreated, infection may set in.* ○ *In winter, darkness sets in so early!*

□ **set off** BEGIN TRIP /'-'-/ *v adv* [I] to start on a trip • *What time do we set off tomorrow?*

□ **set off** *obj* CAUSE, **set** *obj* **off** /'-'-/ *v adv* [M] to cause (an explosion or burst of activity) • *I accidentally set the alarm off.* ○ *Terrorists tried to set off a bomb.* ○ *Rumors set off a wave of selling on the stock exchange.*

□ **set** *obj* **on** *obj* /'-,-/ *v prep* [T] to cause (someone or something) to attack (someone) • *The security guards set their dogs on the intruders.*

□ **set out** START ACTION /'-'-/ *v adv* [I] to begin to carry out a plan of action • *So many young people set out to change the world.* [+ to infinitive]

□ **set out** *obj* GIVE DETAILS, **set** *obj* **out** /'-'-/ *v adv* [M] to give the details of or explain (something), esp. in writing • *Your contract sets out the terms and conditions of your employment.*

□ **set out** *obj* PUT IN ORDER, **set** *obj* **out** /'-'-/ *v adv* [M] to put (something) in a particular order, esp. for others to see or use • *The greenmarket was filled with fresh vegetables set out on tables.*

□ **set** *obj* **to** *obj* /'--/ *v adv* [T] • *If you set (a poem, story, etc.) to music, you write or provide music for it so that it can be performed.*

□ **set up** *obj* ESTABLISH, **set** *obj* **up** /'-'-/ *v adv* [M] to establish or create (something) • *I'd be willing to set up a seminar if I thought people would come.* ○ *We were so impressed that we set up a second interview for him with the company president.* • *If you set someone up, you establish them on a particular path through life esp. by paying for something or supplying money: His father set him up in the family business.* ○ *Their winnings set them up for life.* • *If you set up shop, you establish a business: Several chains have announced that they will set up shop in the new mall.*

setup /'set,ʌp/ *n* [C] • *He's in the sign business and has a nice setup with that.*

□ **set up** *obj* PREPARE, **set** *obj* **up** /'-'-/ *v adv* [M]

to prepare or arrange (something) for use • *We have a little area set up for serving food.*

□ **set up** *obj* DECEIVE, **set** *obj* **up** /'-'-/ *v adv* [M] to cause (someone) to seem to have done something they did not do, or to trick (someone) • *They said they weren't selling drugs but had been set up by the police.*

setup /'set,ʌp/ *n* [C] • *His family claims the trial was a setup from beginning to end.*

setter /'set,ər/ *n* [C] a type of dog with long hair, sometimes trained to help hunters find birds or animals

settle MAKE COMFORTABLE /'set,ᵊl/ *v* [always + adv/prep] to get or to become comfortable • *Campbell settled herself in front of a blazing fire.* [T] ○ *He settled back in his chair and lit a cigar.* [I]

settled /'set,ᵊld/ *adj* • *Although I lived there for over a year, I never really felt settled in that apartment.*

settle AGREE /'set,ᵊl/ *v* [I/T] to reach a decision or an agreement (about something), or to end (a disagreement) • *Rogers paid $2 million to settle the lawsuit.* [T] ○ *Americans turn to a dictionary to settle questions of language.* [T] ○ *Negotiators are hopeful the two sides will settle.* [I] • *If you settle out of court, you reach an agreement in a legal case without holding a trial in court.* • *If you settle a score, you do something to someone because they did something harmful or insulting to you in the past: After being embarrassed in front of the class, Midge was determined to settle the score.*

settlement /'set,ᵊl·mənt/ *n* [C] • *Both sides are working to negotiate a peace settlement.* • *A settlement is also an arrangement, often with payment of money, to end a legal disagreement without taking it to court.*

settle PAY /'set,ᵊl/ *v* [T] to pay (money owed) • *He sold his photographs to settle some old debts.*

settlement /'set,ᵊl·mənt/ *n* [C/U] • *We enclose a check in settlement* (= as payment) *of your claim.* [U]

settle LIVE /'set,ᵊl/ *v* [I/T] to live in a place or to go (somewhere) to live, esp. permanently • *After they got married, they settled in Virginia.* [I] ○ *Immigrants settled this island two hundred years ago.* [T] ○ *(fig.) After the recent riots, calm has finally settled on the city* (= the city has become calm). [I]

settled /'set,ᵊld/ *adj* • *After living in several countries, we're now enjoying a more settled life.*

settlement /'set,ᵊl·mənt/ *n* [C/U] • *Permanent European settlements were established here in the 1830s.* [C] ○ *Early settlement developed around a copper mine.* [U]

settler /'set,lər, 'set,ᵊl·ər/ *n* [C] • *The first settlers of this area were Germans.*

settle MOVE LOWER /'set,ᵊl/ *v* [I] to move to a lower level and stay there; drop • *Dust can settle into the wet paint and spoil the finish.* ○

Unused farm machinery settled in high weeds behind the house.

settle CALM /'set·ᵊl/ *v* • If you **settle** your **nerves/stomach**, you make them calmer: *After the accident, he had a drink to settle his nerves.*

▫**settle down** /ˌ--'-/ *v adv* [I] to become quieter • *OK, everybody, settle down.* • When someone settles down, they accept responsibilities and live a calmer life: *He settled down after he married Vicki.* • If you **settle down to** something, you give it all of your attention: *When the work was done, we settled down to a home-cooked meal.*

▫**settle for** /'---/ *v prep* [T] to agree to or accept (something), although it is not exactly what you want • *They were hoping to sell their car for $2000 but settled for $1500.*

▫**settle in** /ˌ--'-/ *v prep* [I] to arrange yourself and your belongings so you feel more comfortable in a new place • *Once we've settled in, you must come for dinner.*

▫**settle into** /ˌ--'--/ *v prep* [T] to become comfortable (somewhere) • *Students settled into their desks and took out their notebooks.*

▫**settle on** /'--ˌ-/ *v adv* [T] to make a final decision about (something), or to agree to accept (something) • *Have you settled on a name for the baby yet?* ○ *We wanted to buy a house, but at these prices we had to settle on an apartment.*

▫**settle up** /ˌ--'-/ *v adv* [I] to pay all of an amount you owe • *I've finished eating—just let me settle up and we can go.*

seven /'sev·ən/ *number* 7 • *I have seven sisters.* ○ *a seven-week course* • Seven can also mean seven o'clock. • LP NUMBERS

seventh /'sev·ənθ/ *adj, adv* [not gradable], *n* [C] • *Our team came in seventh.* ○ *It's the seventh of May today.* [C] • A seventh is one of seven equal parts of something. [C] • *Since they got married, they're* **in seventh heaven** (= extremely happy). • A **Seventh-Day Adventist** is a member of a Christian religious group that has Saturday as its day of worship.

seventeen /ˌsev·ən'tiːn/ *number* 17 • *It is seventeen days until my birthday.* ○ *a seventeen-story building* • LP NUMBERS

seventeenth /ˌsev·ən'tiːnθ/ *adj, adv* [not gradable], *n* [C] • *the seventeenth century* ○ *Her birthday is on the seventeenth.* [C] • A seventeenth is one of 17 equal parts of something. [C]

seventy /'sev·ən·ti, -di/ *number* 70 • *Grandpa turned seventy last week.* ○ *a seventy-room hotel* • LP NUMBERS

seventies, 70s, 70's /'sev·ən·tiz, -diz/ *pl n* the numbers 70 to 79 • *The temperature was in the seventies* (= between 70° and 79°). • The seventies are the years between 1970 and 1979. ○ *Ginny must be in her seventies* (= between 70 and 79 years old).

seventieth /'sev·ən·tiː·əθ, -diː-/ *adj, adv* [not gradable], *n* [C] • *Today is his seventieth birth-*

day. • A seventieth is one of 70 equal parts of something. [C]

sever /'sev·ər/ *v* [T] to separate (something), esp. by cutting, or to break away from (a connection or relationship) • *He severed a finger in the accident.* ○ *An explosion severed the plane's hydraulic systems.* ○ *The US severed diplomatic relations with Cuba in 1961.*

several /'sev·rəl, -ə·rəl/ *adj* [not gradable] (of an amount or number) more than two and fewer than many; some • *I've seen "Star Wars" several times.* • LP AMOUNTS

several /'sev·rəl, -ə·rəl/ *n* [U] • *Several in the building have complained about the fumes.*

severance /'sev·ə·rəns/ *n* [U] money paid by an employer to an employee ordered to give up a job • *a severance package* ○ *severance pay* ○ *The company offered severance to everyone who was let go.*

severe VERY SERIOUS /sə'vɪr/ *adj* causing great pain, difficulty, damage, etc.; very serious • *a severe earthquake* ○ *The family faced severe challenges when he lost his job.*

severely /sə'vɪr·li/ *adv* • *Several people were severely injured in the accident.* • LP VERY, COMPLETELY, AND OTHER INTENSIFIERS

severity /sə'ver·ət̬·i/ *n* [U] • *You can't imagine the severity of the heat here during the summer.*

severe NOT KIND /sə'vɪr/ *adj* not kind or sympathetic; HARSH • *severe criticism* ○ *Some crimes deserve the severest punishment.*

severely /sə'vɪr·li/ *adv* • *The teacher spoke severely to the noisy children.*

severity /sə'ver·ət̬·i/ *n* [U] • *The severity of her comments surprised everyone.*

sew /soʊ/ *v* [I/T] *past simple* **sewed**, *past part* **sewn** /soʊn/ or **sewed** to join together or attach (esp. pieces of cloth) by putting thread through it with a needle • *Do you like to sew?* [I] ○ *She sewed her outfit by hand.* [T] ○ *Would you sew on these buttons?* [M] ○ *I had to sew up* (= repair) *a hole in my jeans.* [M] • (*infml*) If you **sew up** an arrangement or event, you complete it successfully or control it completely: *The basketball team sewed up the championship this week with their ninth consecutive win.*

sewing /'soʊ·ɪŋ/ *n* [U] • *I have some sewing I need to finish.* • A **sewing circle** is a group, usually of women, that meets regularly to sew. • A **sewing machine** is a machine to which a needle and thread are attached and used to join together pieces of material.

sewer /'suː·ər, sʊr/ *n* [C] an artificial passage or pipe, usually underground, that carries waste and used water from sinks and toilets away from buildings to a place where they can be safely gotten rid of • *The county is putting in new sewers.*

sewage /'suː·ɪdʒ/ *n* [U] waste and liquid from toilets • *The storm caused raw sewage to flow into the bay.*

sex MALE OR FEMALE /seks/ *n* [C/U] the state of

being either male or female, or all males or all females considered as a group; GENDER • *List the name, age, and sex of each of your children.* [C] ○ *Employment discrimination on the basis of sex is illegal.* [U] • USAGE: The related adjective is SEXUAL.

sexism /ˈsekˌsɪz·əm/ *n* [U] actions based on a belief that particular jobs and activities are suitable only for women and others are suitable only for men • *Sexism continues to keep girls out of plumbing, electrical, and construction trades.*

sexist /ˈsek·səst/ *adj* • *sexist stereotypes* ○ *a sexist joke*

sexist /ˈsek·səst/ *n* [C] • *The girls said I was a sexist.*

sex ACTIVITY /seks/ *n* [U] the activity of sexual INTERCOURSE, or the activity of people kissing and touching each other's bodies to experience pleasurable feelings • *Many teens are having sex by their senior year in high school.* ○ *There's a lot of sex and violence in the film.* • *He's got real* **sex appeal** (= is sexually attractive). • **Sex education** is a school course about reproduction and sexual feelings • *Marilyn Monroe is one of the 20th century's most famous* **sex symbols** (= someone whom many people find sexually attractive or exciting).

sexy /ˈsek·si/ *adj* attractive in a sexual way • *She played a sexy detective in the movie.* • Sexy also means interesting and exciting: *a sexy job/car*

sexual CONNECTED WITH SEX ACTIVITY /ˈsek·ʃə·wəl/ *adj* connected with the activity of sex • *Their relationship isn't sexual.* • **Sexual harassment** is unwanted or offensive sexual attention, suggestions, or talk, esp. from an employer or other person in a higher position. • **Sexual intercourse** is INTERCOURSE (= the activity of a man putting his penis into a woman's vagina). • A person's **sexual preference** or **sexual orientation** is their desire for a romantic relationship with either members of the opposite sex or with members of the same sex.

sexually /ˈsek·ʃə·wə·li/ *adv* • *She was sexually involved with a teenager.* ○ *I find him sexually attractive.* ○ *The magazine is sexually explicit.* ○ *Three women in the neighborhood were sexually assaulted* (= attacked and forced to have sex). • A **sexually transmitted disease** (*abbreviation* STD) is one that infects people during sexual activity.

sexuality /ˌsek·ʃəˈwæl·ət̬·i/ *n* [U] attitudes and activities relating to sex • *human sexuality*

sexual BEING MALE OR FEMALE /ˈsek·ʃə·wəl/ *adj* connected with being male or female • *the sexual characteristics of butterflies* ○ *He's always believed in sexual equality.* • USAGE: The related noun is SEX MALE OR FEMALE.

sh /ʃ/ *exclamation* SHH

shabby BAD CONDITION /ˈʃæb·i/ *adj* looking old and in bad condition because of wear or lack

of care • *The man wore a long, shabby coat.* ○ *We parked near Bobby's shabby trailer.*

shabbily /ˈʃæb·ə·li/ *adv* • *A shabbily dressed man lay sleeping in the park.*

shabby NOT FAIR /ˈʃæb·i/ *adj* not honorable or fair; unacceptable • *Some blamed the Veterans Administration for the shabby treatment of disabled veterans.*

shabbily /ˈʃæb·ə·li/ *adv* • *We think the police treated us shabbily.*

shack /ʃæk/ *n* [C] a simple, small building • *The family lived in a one-room shack.*

shackle /ˈʃæk·əlz/ *n* [C usually pl] one of a pair of metal rings connected by a chain and fastened to a person's wrists or the bottoms of their legs to prevent them from escaping • *The prisoner was led away in shackles.*

shackle /ˈʃæk·əl/ *v* [T] • *The convicts were shackled and led onto the bus.* ○ (*fig.*) *She was no longer shackled by her memories* (= they did not prevent her from doing what she wanted to do).

shade DARKNESS /ʃeɪd/ *n* [C/U] darkness and coolness caused by something blocking the direct light from the sun • *The truck was parked in the shade.* [U] • A shade is a covering that is put over a light to make it less bright: *The lamps had matching shades.* [C] • A shade is also a cover, usually attached at the top of a window, that can be pulled over a window to block the light or to keep people from looking in. [C] • (*slang*) **Shades** are **sunglasses**. See at SUN.

shade /ʃeɪd/ *v* [T] • *She shaded her eyes with her hand.* ○ *The backyard is shaded by tall oaks.*

shady /ˈʃeɪd·i/ *adj* • *It's nice and shady in front of the house.* • See also SHADY.

shade DEGREE /ʃeɪd/ *n* [C] a degree of darkness of a color • *He painted the room a beautiful shade of red.* • **A shade** means slightly: *He weighs a shade under 300 pounds.* • A shade can also mean a type or variation: *Simple yes-or-no questions can't reveal all shades of opinion.*

shade /ʃeɪd/ *v* [I/T] • *Students shade* (= darken) *the ovals on multiple-choice tests.* [T] ○ *Use adjectives to shade in the mood of your sentences.* [I]

shadow DARKNESS /ˈʃæd·oʊ/ *n* [C/U] an area of darkness caused when light is blocked by something, usually in a shape similar to the object that is blocking the light • *Chloë kept jumping on Tyler's shadow.* [C] ○ *This corner of the room is always in shadow.* [U] ○ *He was standing in the shadows* (= a dark area). [C] • **Shadowboxing** is the exercise of boxing without a partner by hitting at the air with your hands as if another person were boxing with you.

shadowy /ˈʃæd·ə·wi/ *adj* causing or covered by shadows • *Orchids hung from shadowy trees.* • Shadowy can also mean mysterious: *A* *caller for the shadowy terror group claimed responsibility for the attack.*

shadow SMALL AMOUNT /ˈʃæd·oʊ/ *n* [C] a small amount • *He saw a shadow of malice in her dark eyes.* ○ *Are you convinced beyond a shadow of a doubt?* • If something or someone is **a shadow of itself** it is not as strong, powerful, or useful as it once was: *Since her accident, she's become a shadow of her former self.* • **The shadow of** someone or something important is the influence of that person or thing: *De-Marco plays a lawyer living in the shadow of a famous father.*

shadow FOLLOW /ˈʃæd·oʊ/ *v* [T] to follow (someone) closely • *Matsuoka was shadowed by a security officer.*

shady /ˈʃeɪd·i/ *adj* dishonest or illegal • *They'd been involved in shady real estate deals.* ○ *He has a shady reputation.* • See also **shady** at SHADE DARKNESS.

shaft POLE /ʃæft/ *n* [C] a long pole or rod • *Energy from the wheels turns the shafts and produces electricity.* ○ *The feathers at the end of the arrow's shaft help it travel in a straight line.* ○ *Sliced beef was curled around a scallion shaft, then fried.* • A shaft of light is a single beam.

shaft PASSAGE /ʃæft/ *n* [C] a long vertical or sloping passage through a building or through the ground • *a mine shaft* ○ *an elevator shaft* ○ *The window looks out on an air shaft.*

shaft UNFAIR TREATMENT /ʃæft/ *n* [U] *slang* bad or unfair treatment • *Corporations pay almost nothing while taxpayers get the shaft.*

shaggy /ˈʃæg·i/ *adj* having or covered with long, messy hair, or (of hair) long and messy • *a large, shaggy dog* ○ *His gray hair was shaggy.* • A **shaggy-dog story** is a long story that is intended to be amusing and has an intentionally silly or meaningless ending.

shake MOVE /ʃeɪk/ *v* [I/T] *past simple* **shook** /ʃʊk/, *past part* **shaken** /ˈʃeɪ·kən/ to move something backward and forward or up and down in quick, short movements • *Shake the can.* [T] ○ *She shook Dana gently.* [T] ○ *Cory shook some powdered sugar on her French toast.* [T] ○ *The explosion made the ground shake.* [I] ○ *Lily shook her long hair out* (= moved her hair to make it fall loosely around her shoulders). [M] ○ *She shook out the tablecloth* (= shook it so anything on it fell off). [M] • If you or part of your body shakes, you make quick, short movements, or you feel as if you are doing this, because you are cold, frightened, or upset: *She was soaking wet and shaking when she when she finally got home.* [I] ○ *Her hands shook as she opened the letter.* [I] • If someone's voice shakes, its sound frequently changes because of fear or other emotions. [I] • *Better shake a leg* (= move quickly), *we leave in ten minutes.* • If you **shake** your **fist**, you hold your hand up with your fingers and thumb closed and move it backward and forward to show you are angry: *They stood at the*

gate, shaking their fists and shouting obscenities. • If two people **shake hands**, they greet or say goodbye by briefly joining hands and moving them slightly up and down: *We shook hands and left.* • If you **shake** your **head**, you move it from side to side to show disagreement, sympathy, sadness, or that you do not believe something: *Frank shook his head in disbelief.*

shake /ʃeɪk/ *n* [C] • *Give the bottle a shake.* • *Maria answered no with a shake of her head.* • (*infml*) A shake is a **milk shake**. See at MILK • (*infml*) **The shakes** is a condition in which most or all of your body moves slightly from cold, fear, or illness: *Just thinking about the upcoming interview gave him the shakes.*

shaker /ˈʃeɪ·kər/ *n* [C] a container with holes in its lid from which spices and other powders can be shaken onto food • *a salt/pepper shaker* • A shaker is also a container with a tight-fitting lid in which liquids can be mixed together by moving the container quickly: *a cocktail shaker*

shaky /ˈʃeɪ·ki/ *adj* • *His hands were shaky.* • *She spoke in a shaky voice.*

shake UPSET /ʃeɪk/ *v* [T] *past simple* **shook** /ʃʊk/, *past part* **shaken** /ˈʃeɪ·kən/ to cause (someone) to feel upset and troubled • *Juanita was shaken and tried not to cry.* ○ *America was shaken by the bombing.*

shaky /ˈʃeɪ·ki/ *adj* • *This was my fourth time in a plane, but I still felt shaky.*

shake WEAKEN /ʃeɪk/ *v* [T] *past simple* **shook** /ʃʊk/, *past part* **shaken** /ˈʃeɪ·kən/ to make (someone's beliefs) less certain or strong; to weaken • *Nothing shook her conviction that there was no substitute for hard work.* ○ *The defense failed to shake Powell's testimony.*

shaky /ˈʃeɪ·ki/ *adj* • *It was a shaky marriage from the start.* ○ *The building's foundations are pretty shaky.* • Shaky also means uncertain: *The agreement is still shaky and hasn't been approved yet.* • If someone's performance is shaky, they are not performing well: *After a shaky start, the team started moving the ball and communicating.* • *Walter's argument is on* **shaky ground** (= not completely supported by facts).

shake GET RID OF /ʃeɪk/ *v* [T] *past simple* **shook** /ʃʊk/, *past part* **shaken** /ˈʃeɪ·kən/ to get rid of (something), or escape from (something) • *He couldn't shake the feeling that Tony had another motive.* ○ *I've had this cold all week and just can't seem to shake it.*

□ **shake down** *obj*, **shake** *obj* **down** /'-'-/ *v adv* [M] *infml* to get money from (someone) by using threats • *These punks tried to shake him down for five bucks.*

shakedown /ˈʃeɪk·daʊn/ *n* [C] *infml* • *Officers have been profiting from shakedowns since the military took power.*

□ **shake off** *obj*, **shake** *obj* **off** /'-'-/ *v adv* [M] to get rid of (something bad) • *Local leaders* *are trying to shake off the influence of drug smugglers.*

□ **shake up** *obj* CAUSE CHANGE , **shake** *obj* **up** /'-'-/ *v adv* [M] to cause changes to (something), esp. in order to make improvements • *He's running for senator as an outsider who will shake things up.*

shakeup /'ʃeɪ·kʌp/ *n* [C] • *CBS announced a shakeup of its Friday night TV schedule.*

□ **shake up** *obj* UPSET , **shake** *obj* **up** /'-'-/ *v adv* [M] to upset (someone) • *His mother's death really shook Gerry up.*

shaken /'ʃeɪ·kən/ *past participle of* SHAKE

shall /ʃæl, ʃəl/ *v aux slightly fml* used when referring to the future instead of "will," esp. in questions • *Shall we go?* ○ (*law*) *Nothing in this letter shall be construed as a license to use our property.* • USAGE: In the past, as taught in schools, the future tense in English was formed with "shall" in the first person ("I shall go," "we shall go") and "will" in the second and third persons ("you will go," "Mary will go," "they will go"). In modern American English, "will" is commonly used in speech and writing for all three persons ("I will go," etc.). "Shall" is used mainly in formal situations with the first person ("We shall be pleased to accept your invitation") and in legal documents. • LP AUXILIARY VERBS

shallow NOT DEEP /'ʃæl·oʊ/ *adj* [-er/-est only] having only a short distance from the top to the bottom • *shallow water* ○ *The body was found in a shallow grave in a wooded area.*

shallow NOT SERIOUS /'ʃæl·oʊ/ *adj* [-er/-est only] not thoughtful or serious; not showing real understanding • *Reviewers called the book lightweight, shallow, and simplistic.*

sham /ʃæm/ *n* [C usually sing] someone or something that is falsely represented, esp. as being important or powerful • *I thought the meeting was a total sham and a waste of time.*

sham /ʃæm/ *adj* [not gradable] pretended; not real • *a sham battle*

shambles /'ʃæm·bəlz/ *n* [U] a place or situation that is in a state of confusion or disorder • *The morning after the party, the house was a complete shambles.* ○ *The strike-shortened basketball season was a shambles.* • Shambles is also a messy or confused state: *The candidate claimed that the economy was in (a) shambles.*

shame GUILT /ʃeɪm/ *n* [U] an uncomfortable feeling of guilt or of being ashamed because of your own or someone else's bad behavior • *He pointed out that society needed to restore a sense of shame about certain things.* • If you say **shame on you** to someone, usually a child, you are saying that they should feel ashamed because of something they have done.

shame /ʃeɪm/ *v* [T] • *My aunt told us that in her day women who weren't married by the age of 25 were considered "old maids" and were so*

shamed by their families that they would do anything to get married.

shameful /'ʃeɪm·fəl/ *adj* causing you to feel guilty or ashamed, or being a cause for feeling ashamed • *It's shameful that his own country did not fully appreciate his talent until it was recognized abroad.* [+ *that* clause]

shameless /'ʃeɪm·ləs/ *adj* being something you should be ashamed of • *It was a shameless display of cowardice.* • Shameless also means done without worrying about whether your actions are right or wrong: *When the senator wanted something from a colleague, he first resorted to shameless flattery.* ○ *shameless manipulation of the press*

shamelessly /'ʃeɪm·lə·sli/ *adv*

shame MISFORTUNE /ʃeɪm/ *n* [U] an unlucky or regrettable situation • *What a shame that they left just before we arrived.* ○ *Have some more vegetables—it would be a shame to waste them.* [+ *to* infinitive]

shampoo /ʃæm'puː/ *n* [C/U] *pl* **shampoos** a liquid soap used for washing the hair, or the act of washing the hair with this liquid • *a bottle of shampoo* [U] ○ *The dog needs a shampoo.* [C] • A shampoo is also a liquid used to clean certain thick materials: *a rug shampoo* [C]

shampoo /ʃæm'puː/ *v* [T] he/she/it **shampoos**, **shampooing**, *past* **shampooed** • *He took a shower and shampooed his hair.*

shamrock /'ʃæm·rɑk/ *n* [C] a plant with three round leaves on each stem, known as the plant that represents Ireland

shanty /'ʃænt·i/ *n* [C] a small, badly built house, usually made from pieces of wood, metal, or cardboard, in which poor people live • *He lived in a little shanty in the desert, miles from anything else.* • A **shanty town** is an area in or near a city, in which poor people live in shanties.

shape APPEARANCE /ʃeɪp/ *n* [C/U] the particular way something looks as a whole • *Our table is oval in shape.* [U] ○ *The birthday cake for Luis was in the shape of a heart.* [C] ○ *These old sweatpants are all stretched out of shape* (= changed from their original form). [U] • A shape is also an arrangement that is formed by joining lines together in a particular way: *A triangle is a shape with three sides.* [C] • A shape is also a person or object that you cannot see clearly because it is too dark, or because the person or object is too far away. [C]

shape /ʃeɪp/ *v* [T] to make (something) look a particular way • *Shape the dough into balls.*

–shaped /ʃeɪpt/ *combining form* • *an L-shaped room* ○ *heart-shaped leaves*

shapeless /'ʃeɪp·ləs/ *adj disapproving* (of an object) not having an appearance that you consider clear, pleasing, or correct • *Summer and winter she wore the same array of faded gingham dresses and shapeless sweaters.*

shapely /'ʃeɪ·pli/ *adj approving* (esp. of a

woman or her body) having an attractive appearance • *shapely legs*

shape FORM /ʃeɪp/ *v* [T] to cause (something) to have a particular character or nature; form • *My generation's attitudes were shaped by the Vietnam War.* ○ *He had a major influence in shaping the government's economic policies.*

shape /ʃeɪp/ *n* [U] the way something is organized; the general character or nature of something • *The governor's new program is finally beginning to take shape* (= become better organized).

shape CONDITION /ʃeɪp/ *n* [U] (of a thing) condition, or (of a person) state of health • *The city's finances are in bad shape.* ○ *I keep myself in good shape by running five miles a day.* • Shape can also mean good physical condition: *He's in/out of shape* (= in good/not in good condition). ○ *I try to stay in shape.*

□**shape up** DEVELOP /'-'-/ *v adv* [I] to develop • *It's shaping up to be a fierce battle for the leadership of Congress.* [+ *to* infinitive]

□**shape up** IMPROVE /'-'-/ *v adv* [I] to improve (your behavior or performance) • *The coach told him to shape up and start practicing more.*

share PART /ʃer, ʃær/ *n* [C] one of the parts into which something has been divided • *The total bill comes to $200, so our share is $40.* ○ *She's not doing her fair share of the work.*

share /ʃer, ʃær/ *v* [I/T] to divide or use (something) with others • *Why don't we share the salad?* [T] ○ *All the employees in the company share (in) the profits.* [I/T] ○ *She shares an office with Anne.* [T] ○ *It's a long trip—why don't we share the driving* (= each do some of it)*?* [T] ○ *Our whole family shares an interest in hiking* (= We all like it). [T] ○ *I have an idea I'd like to share with you* (= tell you). [T]

share PART OWNERSHIP /ʃer, ʃær/ *n* [C] one of the equal parts into which the ownership of a company is divided • *She owns 2000 shares of General Electric.*

shark /ʃɑrk/ *n* [C] a type of large fish that has rows of sharp teeth • (*infml*) A shark is also a person who cheats other people, esp. if they seem trusting: *a card shark*

sharp ABLE TO CUT /ʃɑrp/ *adj* [*-er/-est* only] having a thin edge or point that can cut something • *a sharp blade/knife* ○ *She put a sharp point on the pencil.*

sharpen /'ʃɑr·pən/ *v* [T] • *We just had these knives/scissors sharpened.* ○ *He sharpened his pencil* (= made the end used for writing come to a point). • See also **sharpen** at SHARP CLEAR; SHARPEN.

sharpener /'ʃɑr·pə·nər/ *n* [C] a device or tool for making something sharper, esp. pencils or knives • *a pencil sharpener*

sharpness /'ʃɑrp·nəs/ *n* [U]

sharp SUDDEN /ʃɑrp/ *adj* [*-er/-est* only] sudden and immediately noticeable • *a sharp drop in temperature* ○ *a sharp increase in prices* ○ *There's a sharp curve in the road up ahead.*

sharply /'ʃɑr·pli/ *adv* • *Interest rates rose sharply last month.* • LP VERY, COMPLETELY, AND OTHER INTENSIFIERS

sharpness /'ʃɑrp·nəs/ *n* [U]

sharp STRONGLY FELT /ʃɑrp/ *adj* [*-er/-est* only] strongly felt • *As he leaned over, he felt a sudden, sharp pain in his lower back.* ○ *This sauce is pretty sharp* (= It has a strong taste).

sharply /'ʃɑr·pli/ *adv* • *She felt his loss sharply, and her grief was intense.*

sharp SEVERE /ʃɑrp/ *adj* [*-er/-est* only] intended to be strong enough to be felt as painful • *The candidate delivered a sharp attack on her opponent's voting record.* ○ *Leonard has a sharp tongue* (= often speaks in a severe and critical way).

sharply /'ʃɑr·pli/ *adv* • *The police were sharply criticized for their handling of the investigation.*

sharp CLEAR /ʃɑrp/ *adj* [*-er/-est* only] easy to see or understand; clear • *High-definition television produces a very sharp picture.* ○ *Sales this month were up, in sharp contrast to the dismal sales of the last few months.*

sharpen /'ʃɑr·pən/ *v* [T] to make (something) clearer • *Turn the knob to sharpen the focus of the slide projector.* • See also **sharpen** at SHARP ABLE TO CUT; SHARPEN.

sharply /'ʃɑr·pli/ *adv* • *We have sharply differing views on this issue.*

sharpness /'ʃɑrp·nəs/ *n* [U]

sharp QUICK /ʃɑrp/ *adj* [*-er/-est* only] able to understand or see quickly and easily • *She has a really sharp mind and a great sense of humor.*

sharp FASHIONABLE /ʃɑrp/ *adj* [*-er/-est* only] *infml* fashionable • *a sharp dresser*

sharp MUSIC /ʃɑrp/ *adj, adv* [*-er/-est* only] (in music) higher than a particular or the correct note • Compare FLAT MUSIC.

sharp EXACTLY /ʃɑrp/ *adv* [not gradable] exactly at the stated time • *The tour bus will leave at 8:30 a.m. sharp.*

sharpen /'ʃɑr·pən/ *v* [T] to make stronger or improve • *The dollar's decline in value sharpened fears of another recession.* ○ *I'm taking a course that should help me sharpen my computer skills.* • See also **sharpen** at SHARP ABLE TO CUT, SHARP CLEAR.

shatter /'ʃæt̬·ər/ *v* [I/T] to break suddenly or cause (something) to break suddenly into small pieces • *The earthquake shattered all the windows in the building.* [T] • (*fig.*) To shatter can also mean to end or damage: *The defeat shattered her confidence.* [T]

shave /ʃeɪv/ *v* [I/T] to remove hair from the face or body by cutting it close to the skin with a RAZOR (= a device with a blade) • *She shaved her legs.* [T] ○ *He carefully shaved around the cut on his cheek.* [I] ○ *I was amazed to see he had shaved off his beard.* [M] • If you shave an amount off or from an object or surface, you cut a thin layer from it: *She shaved about an*

shellfish

eighth of an inch off the door, and now it closes. [M]

shave /ʃeɪv/ *n* [C] • *After three days of camping, he needed a good shave.*

shaver /'ʃeɪ·vər/ *n* [C] a device, esp. an electric one, used to shave • Compare RAZOR.

shawl /ʃɔːl/ *n* [C] a large piece of cloth worn esp. by women or girls over their shoulders or head

she /ʃiː/ *pronoun female* the female being spoken about, who has already been mentioned • *I asked Barb if she'd lend me some money, but she said no.* ○ *She's such a cute dog!* • She is sometimes used instead of "it" to refer to something, such as a country, vehicle, or ship, that has already been mentioned: *Look at my new car—isn't she a beauty?*

she /ʃiː/ *n* [C] *female* • *The kitten is a she, not a he.*

sheaf /ʃiːf/ *n* [C] *pl* **sheaves** /ʃiːvz/ a number of things held or tied together • *A sheaf of papers lay on her desk.* ○ *Sheaves of dry corn stalks leaned against the fence.*

shear /ʃɪr/ *v* [T] *past simple* **sheared**, *past part* **sheared** or **shorn** /ʃɔːrn, ʃoʊrn/ to cut off (the hair of an animal or a person) • *The barber sheared Jim's hair, just like you'd shear a sheep.*

shears /ʃɪrz/ *pl n* large SCISSORS (= cutting tool), or a similar tool for cutting • *kitchen shears* ○ *pruning shears for the garden*

sheath /ʃiːθ/ *n* [C] a close-fitting, protective covering • *The cable is a copper wire with a heavy plastic sheath.* ○ *Hunting knives usually have leather sheaths.*

sheathe /ʃiːð/ *v* [T] • *She sheathed the knife* (= put it back inside its protective cover).

sheaves /ʃiːvz/ *pl of* SHEAF

shed BUILDING /ʃed/ *n* [C] a small building usually used for storage or shelter • *The lawn mower is kept in the shed.*

shed GET RID OF /ʃed/ *v* [T] **shedding**, *past* **shed** to get rid of (something) • *As the day warmed up, she shed her sweater.*

shed FALL OFF /ʃed/ *v* [I/T] to lose hair, leaves, or skin, or to cause (hair, skin, or leaves) to drop • *My cat shed all over the couch.* [I] ○ *By November, the trees had shed their leaves.* [T]

shed FLOW /ʃed/ *v* [T] to make (blood or tears) flow • *He didn't shed one tear when his old car was stolen.*

shed SPREAD /ʃed/ *v* [T] **shedding**, *past* **shed** to spread (light) • *A single bulb shed a harsh light on the table.* • If someone or something **sheds light on** a situation, they help to explain the situation or make it clear: *Experts hope the plane's flight recorders will shed light on the cause of the crash.*

she'd /ʃiːd/ *contraction of* **she had** or **she would** • *She'd already left.* ○ *I think she'd like to go to the dance with you.*

sheen /ʃiːn/ *n* [U] a smooth shine or bright-

ness • *The polished floor had a beautiful sheen to it.*

sheep /ʃiːp/ *n* [C] *pl* **sheep** a farm animal with thick curly hair that eats grass and is kept for its wool, skin, and meat • Compare LAMB; MUTTON; RAM.

sheepish /'ʃiː·pɪʃ/ *adj* embarrassed because you realize you have done something wrong or silly • *a sheepish grin*

sheepishly /'ʃiː·pɪʃ·li/ *adv* • *He sheepishly admitted he hadn't done his homework.*

sheer COMPLETE /ʃɪr/ *adj* [not gradable] not mixed with anything else; pure or complete • *Some of those books are sheer magic.*

sheer EXTREME /ʃɪr/ *adj* [not gradable] (of size or weight) very large • *The sheer size of the engine makes it difficult to transport.*

sheer STEEP /ʃɪr/ *adj* rising almost straight up or down; very steep • *She hauled herself up the sheer slope of the mountain.*

sheet /ʃiːt/ *n* [C] a large rectangular piece of cloth used to cover a bed, or a rectangular piece of any material, such as paper, glass, or metal • *She made up the bed with clean sheets.* ○ *Do you have a sheet of paper I could use?* ○ *She put the dough onto cookie sheets.* • A sheet is also a thin layer of something: *A sheet of ice formed on the puddles.*

sheik, sheikh /ʃiːk, ʃeɪk/ *n* [C] an Arab ruler or leader

shelf /ʃelf/ *n* [C] *pl* **shelves** /ʃelvz/ a long, flat board hung on a wall or supported by a frame or cabinet, used to hold objects • *Her shelves are filled with books and photographs.* • The **shelf life** of something, esp. a product, is the length of time it stays in good condition and can be used: *Because it is vacuum-packed, it has a much longer shelf life than regular beef.* • If something is **on the shelf**, it has been delayed or put off: *Plans to start a free film series have been put on the shelf.* • USAGE: The related verb is SHELVE.

shell COVERING /ʃel/ *n* [C/U] the hard outer covering of nuts, eggs, a few vegetables, and some animals • *Turtles, snails, and crabs all have shells to protect them.* [C]

shell /ʃel/ *v* [T] to remove the hard outer covering of (nuts and other foods) • *He sits in front of the TV, shelling peanuts.*

shell EXPLOSIVE /ʃel/ *n* [C] a tube filled with explosives that is fired from a large gun • Someone who is **shell-shocked** suffers from mental illness as a result of being in a war.

shell /ʃel/ *v* [T] to fire shells at (something) • *The guerillas shelled many government buildings, causing great damage.*

▫**shell out** /'-'-/ *v adv* [T] *infml* to pay (money) • *I hope we don't have to shell out a lot of money for tickets.* [M]

she'll /ʃiːl, ʃɪl/ *contraction of* **she will** or **she shall** • *She'll be there tomorrow, I'm sure.*

shellfish /'ʃel·fɪʃ/ *n* [C/U] *pl* **shellfish** an animal that lives in water and has a shell •

Lobsters, crabs, shrimp, mussels, and oysters are all shellfish commonly eaten as food. [C]

shelter /ˈʃel·tər/ *n* [C/U] something that gives protection, such as a building or tent, or the protection provided • *We took the stray dog to an animal shelter.* [C] ○ *The wall gave us some shelter from the wind.* [U] ○ *The program offers shelter to runaway teens.* [U]

shelter /ˈʃel·tər/ *v* [I/T] • *The city feeds, clothes, and shelters the orphans.* [T] ○ *We were caught in a thunderstorm and sheltered in a cave.* [I]

sheltered /ˈʃel·tərd/ *adj* • *We found a sheltered spot to have our picnic.* • If you have a sheltered life, you are protected from harmful, unpleasant, or frightening experiences: *I wonder how well she will do on her own after leading such a sheltered life.*

shelve PUT ON SHELF /ʃelv/ *v* [T] to put (something) on a shelf or shelves • *Would you shelve these books while I unpack the rest?*

shelve DELAY /ʃelv/ *v* [T] to delay action on (something) • *I shelved plans to buy a new car, because I can't afford it right now.*

shelves /ʃelvz/ *pl of* SHELF

shenanigans /ʃəˈnæn·ɪ·ɡənz/ *pl n* humorous or dishonest tricks • *I don't know how he puts up with their shenanigans.*

shepherd /ˈʃep·ərd/, *female* **shepherdess** /ˈʃep·ərd·əs/ *n* [C] a person who takes care of sheep

shepherd /ˈʃep·ərd/ *v* [T always + adv/prep] to move and care for (sheep), or to lead (people) somewhere • *Visitors are shepherded through the mansion by volunteers.* ○ *Roberti shepherded the legislation through Congress* (= made sure it was approved).

sherbet /ˈʃər·bət, ˈʃər·bərt/ *n* [U] a sweet, fruit-flavored ice, usually made with milk

sheriff /ˈʃer·əf/ *n* [C] an elected law officer in a COUNTY (= an area of local government)

sherry /ˈʃer·i/ *n* [C/U] a type of strong wine, usually brown in color, originally from Spain

she's /ʃiːz/ *contraction of* **she is** or **she has** • *She's about to have her baby.* ○ *I think she's already left the house.*

shh, **sh** /ʃ/ *exclamation* used to tell someone to be quiet; SHUSH • *Shh, you'll wake the baby.*

shield /ʃiːld/ *n* [C] a piece of metal or other material, carried to protect the front of the body when being attacked, or a person or thing that provides protection • *The police held up their riot shields.* ○ *The ozone layer is the earth's shield against radiation from the sun.*

shield /ʃiːld/ *v* [T always + adv/prep] • *When the lights came on, I shielded my eyes with my hands.* ○ *Mom tried to shield us from the bad news.*

shift MOVE OR CHANGE /ʃɪft/ *v* [I/T] to change direction or move from one person, position, or place to another • *The wind shifted to the east.* [I] ○ *She shifted her weight from one foot to the other.* [T] ○ *He tried to shift the blame on-*

to his sister. [T] • If you shift your emphasis or attitude, you change it: *Our attention has shifted from baseball to the election.* [T] • When you shift the gears of a vehicle, you move them into different positions to change the speed of the vehicle. [T] • If you or a story **shifts gears**, the character of what is being done or said changes: *The first half is a comedy, but then the movie shifts gears.*

shift /ʃɪft/ *n* [C] • *There's been a substantial shift in doctors' methods.*

shift PERIOD /ʃɪft/ *n* [C] the period that a person is scheduled to work, or a group of workers who work during the same period of time • *I'm working the day shift this month.* ○ *The night shift is finished at 7 a.m.*

shiftless /ˈʃɪft·ləs/ *adj* [not gradable] not having determination or purpose • *He says only the shiftless are unemployed.*

shifty /ˈʃɪf·ti/ *adj* [-er/-est only] *disapproving* intelligent and skilled in deceiving others • *Shifty parents can avoid making child-support payments.*

shimmer /ˈʃɪm·ər/ *v* [I] to shine with a soft light that changes strength • *The stars shimmered in the night sky.*

shimmer /ˈʃɪm·ər/ *n* [U] • *the shimmer of moonlight on the lake*

shin /ʃɪn/ *n* [C] the front part of your leg between your knee and your foot

shine SEND OUT LIGHT /ʃaɪn/ *v* [I/T] *past* **shone** /ʃoʊn/ *or* **shined** to send out or reflect light • *Cops shone their flashlights into the car window.* [T] ○ *The area shines like Times Square.* [I] ○ *(fig.) Her dark eyes shone with happiness* (= she looked very happy). [I]

shiny /ˈʃaɪ·ni/ *adj* • *Who owns the shiny new car?*

shine MAKE BRIGHT /ʃaɪn/ *v* [T] to make (something) smooth and bright by rubbing • *He used all my polish to shine his shoes!*

shine /ʃaɪn/ *n* [C usually sing] • *The stone was polished to a glossy shine.*

shine SHOW ABILITY /ʃaɪn/ *v* [I] to show great ability in an activity • *Shaw is an underrated actor who truly shines in this movie.*

shingle /ˈʃɪŋ·ɡəl/ *n* [C] a thin, flat piece of wood or other material, many of which are attached in rows to the outside of a roof or a wall • PIC OVERLAP

ship /ʃɪp/ *n* [C] a boat, esp. one that is large enough to travel on the sea • *a cruise/cargo ship* • A ship is also an aircraft or spacecraft.

ship /ʃɪp/ *v* [T] **-pp-** to transport (something or someone) by air, train, boat, or truck • *They shipped our furniture from Tennessee.* ○ *Parts for the space station are being shipped out there by spacecraft.* • If someone or something is **shipped off** to a place, they are sent there: *After it's put together, we'll ship it off to Florida.*

shipping /ˈʃɪp·ɪŋ/ *n* [U] ships as a group, or the business of transporting things • *Enemy forces attacked unprotected shipping.* • Ship-

ping or **shipping and handling** is the cost of sending something: *You'll be billed $15.95 plus shipping.*

shipment /'ʃɪp·mənt/ n [C/U] goods transported together, or the act of transporting them • *A shipment of raccoons arrived from Illinois.* [C] ○ *It was taken to the airport for shipment to Hawaii.* [U]

shipwreck /'ʃɪp·rek/, **wreck** n [C/U] the destruction or sinking of a ship at sea, or a ship destroyed this way • *Fog in the area caused many shipwrecks.* [C]

shipwreck /'ʃɪp·rek/ v [T] • *The crew was shipwrecked off the coast of Newfoundland.*

shirk /ʃɜrk/ v [I/T] to avoid (work or a duty) • *Town officials shirked their responsibilities by failing to follow up on residents' complaints.* [T]

shirt /ʃɜrt/ n [C] a piece of clothing worn on the upper part of the body, made of cloth and often having a collar and buttons at the front • *a short-sleeved/long-sleeved shirt* ○ *Her shirt was untucked.* • **Shirtsleeves** are the parts of a shirt that cover the arms: *Baker sat on the edge of his chair and rolled up his shirtsleeves.*

shish kebab, **shish kabob** /'ʃɪʃ·kə,bɑb/ n [C/U] small pieces of meat, esp. LAMB, and vegetables cooked on a stick or metal rod

shit WASTE MATTER /ʃɪt/ n [U] *taboo slang* solid waste that is excreted from the bowels • *dog shit* ○ *I need to take a shit* (= excrete solid waste). • When **the shit hits the fan**, a situation suddenly causes trouble, usually by making someone very angry: *When my father saw the dented car door, the shit really hit the fan.*

shit /ʃɪt/ v [I/T] **shitting**, *past* **shit** or **shitted** *taboo slang*

shit SOMETHING DISLIKED /ʃɪt/ n [C/U] *taboo slang* something or someone that is disliked or bad • *I almost forgot what a shit he was.* [C] • Shit is also insults, criticism, or unkind or unfair treatment: *Naomi gets a lot of shit from her parents about the way she dresses.* [U] • Shit also means anything: *You don't know shit!* [U] • Shit also means things: *Let's talk about all the serious shit.* [U]

shitty /'ʃɪt̬·i/ *adj* [-er/-est only] *taboo slang* • *It's been a shitty day.*

shit EXCLAMATION /ʃɪt/ *exclamation taboo slang* used to express annoyance, anger, disgust, or surprise • *Holy shit, I'm late!* ○ *"Shit," Bob muttered to his computer.*

shiver /'ʃɪv·ər/ v [I] (esp. of a person or animal) to shake slightly and quickly because of feeling cold, ill, or frightened • *Your creepy look makes me shiver.* ○ *Robbins shivered in the chill air.*

shiver /'ʃɪv·ər/ n [C] • *"The temperature is down to 12 degrees," she said with a shiver.* • *Hearing that song still sends shivers down my spine* (= excites me).

shoal LAND /ʃoʊl/ n [C] a raised bank of sand or rocks under the surface of the water

shoal FISH /ʃoʊl/ n [C] a large group of fish swimming together • *shoals of mackerel*

shock SURPRISE /ʃɑk/ n [C/U] a sudden, unexpected, and often unpleasant or offensive event, or the emotional or physical reaction to such an event • *It was kind of a shock to hear they wanted to throw it out.* [C] • Shock is also a medical condition caused by severe injury, pain, loss of blood, or fright that slows down the flow of blood around the body: *She was going into shock—her flesh was becoming chilled and her muscles were contracting.* [U] • A **shock wave** is a reaction to a sudden, upsetting piece of news: *The president's sudden illness sent shock waves around the world.*

shock /ʃɑk/ v [I/T] to make (someone) suddenly feel very upset or surprised • *Her painting might shock viewers.* [T] ○ *The ads were designed to shock.* [I]

shocked /ʃɑkt/ *adj* • *He was shocked to discover that gambling was going on in this hotel.* [+ to infinitive]

shocking /'ʃɑk·ɪŋ/ *adj* • *The book was considered shocking when it was first published.*

shock EFFECT FROM HITTING /ʃɑk/ n [U] the effect, often including damage or slight movement, of one object hitting another forcefully • *Running shoes lose their ability to absorb shock.* • **Shock absorbers** (also **shocks**) are devices attached to the wheels on a vehicle that reduce the effects of traveling over rough ground. • A **shock wave** is a sudden increase in pressure or temperature caused by an explosion or other violent movement or by an object moving faster than the speed of sound: *The bomb's shock wave tore the windshield off the truck.*

shock ELECTRIC CURRENT /ʃɑk/ n [C] a current of electricity going through the body • *If that cord is pulled loose, you'll get a shock from the plug.*

shoddy /'ʃɑd·i/ *adj* [-er/-est only] badly and carelessly made or done • *The furniture is shoddy and cheap.*

shoe /ʃuː/ n [C] one of a pair of covers for your feet, with an upper part made of a strong material such as leather and a base made usually of thick leather or rubber • *tennis shoes* ○ *high-heeled shoes* ○ *patent leather shoes* ○ *He said he couldn't afford a new pair of shoes.* • A shoe is also a **horseshoe**. See at HORSE. • If you are **in** someone else's **shoes**, you are in that person's condition or situation: *You don't know how they feel, you can't put yourself in their shoes or really understand them.* • A **shoelace** or **shoestring** is a thin cord of cloth or leather used to fasten shoes: *Your shoelace is untied.* • If you do something **on a shoestring**, you do it with a very small amount of money: *The theater company operates on a shoestring.*

shoe /ʃuː/ v [T] **shoeing**, *past* **shod** /ʃɑd/ or **shoed** to wear (shoes), or to put shoes on (someone) • *She was shod in loafers with soles as thin as paper.* • If you shoe a horse, you nail a curved piece of metal to its foot.

shoehorn /ˈʃuː·hɔːrn/ *n* [C] a smooth, curved piece of plastic or metal that is placed in the back of a shoe when putting it on in order to help the foot slide in more easily

shoehorn /ˈʃuː·hɔːrn/ *v* [T] to fit (something or someone) into a tight place • *We'd have to build another school to shoehorn all our students in.*

shone /ʃoʊn/ *past simple and past participle of* SHINE

shoo /ʃuː/ *exclamation infml* said to an animal or to a person to make them go away quickly • *"Shoo! Get out of here!"*

shoo /ʃuː/ *v* [T] he/she/it **shoos**, **shooing**, *past* **shooed** *infml* • *My husband shooed me out of the car.*

shoo-in /ˈʃuː·ɪn/ *n* [C] *infml* something that is certain to happen, or someone who is certain to win a competition • *If that election were held today, Kitzhaber would be a shoo-in.*

shook /ʃʊk/ *past simple of* SHAKE

shoot FIRE WEAPON /ʃuːt/ *v* [I/T] *past* **shot** /ʃɑt/ to fire a gun or other weapon, or to hit, injure, or kill (someone or something) by firing a gun or other weapon • *We'd take our rifles and shoot at sea gulls and rats.* [I] ○ *A long time ago I learned how to shoot a gun.* [T] ○ *An unidentified man was fatally shot yesterday afternoon in Southeast Washington.* [T] • (*infml*) If you say that someone or something should be shot, you are very annoyed by it: *This computer should be shot.* [T] • If you **shoot yourself in the foot**, you do something that spoils a situation for you: *We shot ourselves in the foot by letting the baby sleep all the way here—now she won't sleep at all tonight.*

shooting /ˈʃuːt·ɪŋ/ *n* [C/U] • *She heard shooting* (= guns being fired) *in the distance.* [U] • A shooting is also an occasion on which someone is injured or killed by a bullet fired from a gun: *a drive-by shooting* [C]

shoot SPORTS /ʃuːt/ *v* [I/T] *past* **shot** /ʃɑt/ to throw, hit, or kick (a ball or other object), esp. in order to score points • *Both teams shoot the ball well.* [T] ○ *When you shoot as poorly as we did, you can't expect to win.* [I] • (*slang*) If you **shoot baskets** or **shoot hoops** you play BASKETBALL. • (*slang*) If you **shoot pool** or **shoot craps** you play those games: *Pat and I were hanging out and shooting pool.*

shoot MOVE QUICKLY /ʃuːt/ *v* [I always + adv/prep] *past* **shot** /ʃɑt/ to move in a particular direction quickly and without unnecessary turns or stops • *The ambulance was shooting around the corner, its tires squealing.* ○ *Grace's eyebrows shot up when she heard his voice.* • A **shooting star** is a METEOR.

shoot PLANT /ʃuːt/ *n* [C] the first part of a plant to appear above the ground as it develops from a seed, or a new growth on an already

existing plant • *Little green shoots appeared in the spring.*

shoot FILM /ʃuːt/ *v* [I/T] *past* **shot** /ʃɑt/ to film or photograph (something) • *The movie will be shot in the fall.* [T]

shoot /ʃuːt/ *n* [C] • *I remember doing a shoot there.*

shoot DRUG /ʃuːt/ *v* [T] *past* **shot** /ʃɑt/ *slang* to take (an illegal drug) by INJECTING it (= putting it into your blood using a special needle) • *He was shooting heroin.*

shoot SPEAK /ʃuːt/ *exclamation infml* used to tell someone else they should speak • *"Dad, I need to talk to you." "Shoot."* • (*infml*) If you **shoot the breeze**, you talk with someone or a group of people about unimportant things for a long time: *We sat on the porch until late at night, just shooting the breeze.* • (*infml*) If you **shoot** your **mouth off**, you talk too much about things other people should not know: *It's just like Richard to go shooting his mouth off about other people's affairs.*

□ **shoot down** *obj*, **shoot** *obj* **down** /ˈ-ˈ-/ *v adv* [M] to destroy (an aircraft) or force it out of the sky by shooting it • *These weapons could be used by terrorists to shoot down commercial airliners.*

□ **shoot for** /ˈ--/ *v adv* [T] *infml* to try to achieve (something) • *Our football team will shoot for its first victory today.*

□ **shoot up** INCREASE /ˈ-ˈ-/ *v adv* [I] to increase very quickly in size or amount • *Mothers have always known babies can shoot up overnight.* ○ *Temperatures shot up into the 50s today.*

□ **shoot up** *obj* FIRE GUNS , **shoot** *obj* **up** /ˈ-ˈ-/ *v adv* [M] *infml* to fire guns in (a place), causing a lot of damage • *Sometimes they'd get drunk and shoot up a bar just for kicks.*

□ **shoot up** TAKE DRUGS /ˈ-ˈ-/ *v adv* [I] *slang* to take an illegal drug by INJECTING it (= putting it into your blood using a special needle) • *She saw a girl shooting up in the toilets.*

shop BUY THINGS /ʃɑp/ *v* [I] **-pp-** to look for and buy (things) • *We shop in malls because they're convenient.* • To **shop around** is to compare the price and quality of items in different stores before you decide which one to buy: *Did you shop around when you were looking for your car?*

shop /ʃɑp/ *n* [C] a place where you can buy goods or services; store • *a gift shop* ○ *a barber shop* ○ *a coffee shop*

shopper /ˈʃɑp·ər/ *n* [C] a person who is looking for things to buy • *Shoppers stroll through the stores.*

shopping /ˈʃɑp·ɪŋ/ *n* [U] the activity of looking for things to buy • *I was out shopping this afternoon.* ○ *My daughter and I go shopping together.* • A **shopping cart** is a large container made of metal rods that rests on a wheeled base and has an open top and a handle at the back that you push. • A **shopping center** is a group of stores with a common area for cars to park: *There's a little shopping center next door with a bank and a dry-cleaning place.* • A **shopping mall** is a very large building or buildings containing a lot of stores and restaurants, usually with space out-

shopping cart

side for parking: *A shopping mall is no longer just a place to go to buy something, it's a community and entertainment center.*

shop WORK AREA /ʃɑp/ *n* [C] a place where a particular type of thing is made or repaired • *a bicycle repair shop* ○ *I work in a machine shop making wire.*

shoplift /'ʃɑp·lɪft/ *v* [I/T] to take (goods) illegally from a store without paying for them • *He shoplifted a bottle of aspirin.* [T] ○ *The child hadn't meant to shoplift.* [I]

shoplifting /'ʃɑp·lɪf·tɪŋ/ *n* [U] • *He was charged with shoplifting.*

shoplifter /'ʃɑp·lɪf·tər/ *n* [C] • *Shoplifters will be arrested.*

shore /ʃɔːr, ʃoʊr/ *n* [C/U] the land along the edge of the sea, a lake, or a wide river • *We rode into the city along the shore of Lake Washington.* [U] ○ *Immigrants are often nervous when they show up on our shores* (= in this country). [pl] • *The shoreline is the edge of the sea, a lake, or a wide river: Most of the shoreline is swamp.*

shore up *obj*, **shore** *obj* **up** /'ʃɔːrˈʌp, 'ʃoʊr-/ *v adv* [M] to make (something) stronger by supporting it • *The plan will enable his company to shore up its financial position.* ○ *After the earthquake we had to shore up ceilings and walls.*

shorn /ʃɔːrn, ʃoʊrn/ *past participle of* SHEAR

short LENGTH /ʃɔːrt/ *adj* [-*er*/-*est* only] having little length, distance, or height • *Short skirts are back in style.* ○ *It's only a short walk to the store.* • A person might say **in short** at the beginning of a sentence to introduce a brief statement of something said at greater length before: *In short, we have to decide whether to continue losing money or change the way we do business.* • A word that is **short for** a related name or word is an abbreviated form of that name or word: *Their baby's name is Libby, short for Elizabeth.* • A **shortcut** is a route that is more direct than the usual route and is therefore quicker: *The kids take a shortcut through the parking lot to get to school.* • **Shortsighted** means showing a lack of thought for what might happen in the future: *It's shortsighted to spend all your money on having a good time.* • A **short story** is an invented story that is usually short enough to be read without stopping and that deals with a situation involving one set of characters. • A **shortwave** is a radio wave

that is smaller than that used in standard broadcasting.

short /ʃɔːrt/ *adv* [-*er*/-*est* only] • *She decided to cut her hair short.*

shorts /ʃɔːrts/ *pl n* pants that end above the knee or reach to the knee, or men's underwear worn below the waist • *She put on a pair of shorts and a T-shirt.* ○ *The doctor told him to strip to his shorts.*

shorten /'ʃɔːrt·ən/ *v* [T] • *I'd like to have this skirt shortened by about two inches.*

short TIME /ʃɔːrt/ *adj* [-*er*/-*est* only] of a small amount of time, or less than the average or usual amount of time • *Mary Lou was here a short while ago.* ○ *There will be a short delay in the flight while we load a few more bags.* • *This may save money* **in the short run** (= during the near future), *but it will eventually cost you more.* • To be **short with** someone is to be brief with them in a rude way: *You could tell Dad was worried about something because he was short with everyone.* • **Shorthand** is a system of fast writing, using lines, abbreviations, and symbols to represent letters, words, and phrases. • If a feeling or experience is **short-lived**, it lasts only for a brief time: *He was quick to anger but his anger was short-lived.* • If you are **short-tempered**, you are easily angered. • Something **short-term** happens, exists, or continues for only a little time: *Short-term interest rates are going down.*

short /ʃɔːrt/ *adv* [not gradable] • *I started to say something, but he cut me short* (= stopped me from continuing).

shorten /'ʃɔːrt·ən/ *v* [T] • *A high school knee injury probably shortened his football career.*

shortly /'ʃɔːrt·li/ *adv* [not gradable] soon • *Shortly after you left the office, your wife called.* ○ *We will be landing shortly.*

short LACKING /ʃɔːrt/ *adj* [not gradable] not reaching a desired amount or level; lacking • *The bill comes to $85, but we're $15 short.* • If something is **in short supply**, there is very little or not enough of it: *Money was in short supply.* • If you are **short of** something, you do not have enough of it: *I'm a bit short of cash right now, so I can't lend you anything.* ○ *She ran for the bus and then felt short of breath* (= she had to breathe very quickly to take in enough air). • A **shortcoming** is a fault of someone or something: *Whatever his shortcomings as a money-maker, he was a good father.* • A **shortfall** is an amount that is less than what was expected or needed: *The county had to close three of its four libraries because of a budget shortfall.* • **Short-handed** means not having the usual number of workers: *We've got two people out sick so we're short-handed today.*

shortage /'ʃɔːrt·ɪdʒ/ *n* [C] a lack of something needed • *There is a severe shortage of low-cost housing in the city.*

shortchange /'ʃɔːrtˈtʃeɪndʒ/ *v* [T] to give

(someone or something) less money, time, or attention than they deserve • *The report claimed that girls were being shortchanged in public education, particularly in math and science.*

short circuit /'ʃɔːrt'sɜr·kət/, *infml* **short** *n* [C] a faulty electrical connection that allows too much current to flow into a CIRCUIT (= a closed system of wires), causing a dangerous condition

shorten /'ʃɔːrt·ᵊn/ *v* • See at SHORT LENGTH, SHORT TIME.

shortening /'ʃɔːrt·nɪŋ/ *n* [U] butter or other fat used in cooking, esp. to make pastry

shortly /'ʃɔːrt·li/ *adv* • See at SHORT TIME.

shorts /ʃɔːrts/ *pl n* • See at SHORT LENGTH.

shortstop /'ʃɔːrt·stɑp/ *n* [C] (in baseball) the position of the player on the inner field between second and third BASE (= a position on a square that a player must touch), or the player at that position

shot SHOOT /ʃɑt/ *past simple and past participle of* SHOOT

shot WEAPON /ʃɑt/ *n* [C] the action of firing a gun or another weapon • *Several shots were fired.*

shot SPORTS /ʃɑt/ *n* [C] an attempt to score a point by throwing, hitting, or kicking a ball or other object • *Roberts sank two foul shots to win the game.*

shot FILM /ʃɑt/ *n* [C] a photograph, or a short piece in a movie in which there is a single action or a short series of actions • *I got some really good shots of the harbor at sunset.*

shot DRUG /ʃɑt/ *n* [C] an amount of a drug, whether medical or illegal, that is put into the body by a single INJECTION • *The doctor gave him a shot of morphine for pain.* • **A shot in the arm** is something that has a sudden and positive effect on something that has been in trouble: *Fresh investment would provide a welcome shot in the arm.*

shot METAL BALL /ʃɑt/ *n* [C/U] a heavy metal ball thrown in a sports competition, or small metal balls fired from a gun • **A shotgun** is a long gun that fires a large number of small metal bullets at one time, used esp. for hunting. • The **shot put** is a sports competition in which each competitor throws a heavy metal ball as far as possible.

shot ATTEMPT /ʃɑt/ *n* [U] *infml* an attempt to do or achieve something that is difficult, when success is uncertain • *I'm not sure they'll consider me for the job, but I'll give it a shot.*

shot DESTROYED /ʃɑt/ *adj* [not gradable] *infml* no longer working or effective • *The brakes are shot—you'd better take the car in to the garage.*

shot AMOUNT OF DRINK /ʃɑt/ *n* [C] a small amount of an alcoholic drink • *a shot of whiskey*

should DUTY /ʃʊd, ʃəd/ *v aux* used to express that it is necessary, desirable, advisable, or important to perform the action of the following verb • *He should have told me about the change in plans.* ○ *People like that should go to jail.* ○ *Where should we meet tonight?* • LP AUXILIARY VERBS

should PROBABLE /ʃʊd, ʃəd/ *v aux* used to express that the action of the main verb is probable • *She should be back at any minute.* ○ *If you follow these directions, you shouldn't have any trouble finding our house.* ○ *That should be enough food for five people.* • LP AUXILIARY VERBS

should OPINION /ʃʊd, ʃəd/ *v aux slightly fml* used to express a desire or opinion • *I should think he'd be happy just to have a job.* ○ *I shouldn't worry about that if I were you.* • LP AUXILIARY VERBS

should ASKING WHY /ʃʊd, ʃəd/ *v aux* used after a question word, such as "how" or "why," when asking a reason for something • *How should I know where you put the car keys?* • LP AUXILIARY VERBS

shoulder BODY PART /'ʃoʊl·dər/ *n* [C] one of the two rounded, bony parts of a person's body on either side of the neck where the top of the arm is joined • *She put her head on my shoulder.* • A shoulder of a road is an edge just beyond the part you drive along, where you can stop safely. • A **shoulder bag** is a type of HANDBAG carried by a strap over the shoulder. • A **shoulder blade** is one of the two large, flat bones on the upper part of the back. • PIC ARM

shoulder bag

shoulder /'ʃoʊl·dər/ *v* [T] • *Shouldering her pack* (= putting it on her shoulders to carry it), *she strode off up the road.*

shoulder ACCEPT RESPONSIBILITY /'ʃoʊl·dər/ *v* [T] to accept responsibility for (something) • *It is usually women who shoulder the responsibility for the care of elderly relatives.*

shouldn't /'ʃʊd·ᵊnt/ *contraction of* **should not** • *I shouldn't have said that.* ○ *Shouldn't we call and make a reservation first?*

shout /ʃaʊt/ *v* [I/T] to say (something) in a loud voice • *If anyone's up there," he shouted sternly, "come out now!"* [I]

shout /ʃaʊt/ *n* [C] a loud call • *When nominated for the presidency the entire audience came to its feet with a shout.*

shove /ʃʌv/ *v* [I/T] to push (someone or something) forcefully and with a lot of energy • *The police shoved him up against the wall and told him to put his hands over his head.* [T] • To shove is also to slide (something) along a surface by moving or pushing it: *She got into her coat and shoved her hands deep into her pockets.* [T] ○ *Jim shoved open the door* (= pushed the door to open it), *and invited his visitor in.* [M] • To **shove off** in a boat is to push the boat away from land into the water: *Ray released the last rope and shoved off from the dock with his foot.* • A **shoving match** is an angry disagreement in which two people push each other in the chest: *The discussion in the jury room got so heated that at one point two jurors got into a shoving match.*

shove /ʃʌv/ *n* [C] • *Someone in the crowd gave me a shove in the back, and I almost went sprawling.*

shovel /'ʃʌv·əl/ *n* [C] a tool consisting of a wide blade attached to a long handle, used for digging up or moving loose material, such as earth or snow

shovel /'ʃʌv·əl/ *v* [T] • *Sally is outside shoveling snow away from the driveway.*

show MAKE SEEN /ʃoʊ/ *v* [T] *past simple* **showed**, *past part* **shown** /ʃoʊn/ to cause or allow (something, esp. a condition) to be seen • *You should show that rash to your doctor.* ○ *These trees show the effects of acid rain.* ○ *He's starting to show his age.* • To **show** your **face** means to go somewhere where you are not expected or wanted, usually because you have done something offensive to someone else: *I don't know how he can show his face here after the way he spoke to my brother.* • **Show-and-tell** is a school activity in which a child brings an object to class and talks to the other children about it.

show /ʃoʊ/ *n* [C/U] • *Ray made a show of reaching for his wallet.* [C] ○ *Does this fireplace work or is it just for show?* [U] ○ *You don't pull out a gun just for show.* [U]

showy /'ʃoʊ·i/ *adj* attracting attention, sometimes by being extreme in color, design, or materials • *Her dress was too showy for such a solemn occasion.*

show MAKE KNOWN /ʃoʊ/ *v* [T] *past simple* **showed**, *past part* **shown** /ʃoʊn/ to make (something) known, esp. your opinion • *I do not know how to show my thanks for all your help.* ○ *He is a scrappy lawyer and shows no mercy to any opponent.*

show EXPLAIN /ʃoʊ/ *v* [T] *past simple* **showed**, *past part* **shown** /ʃoʊn/ to explain (something) to (someone) by helping them to do it or by giving instructions or examples to copy • *The diagram shows how to fit the pieces together.* [+ *wh-* word]

show PROVE /ʃoʊ/ *v* [T] *past simple* **showed**, *past part* **shown** /ʃoʊn/ to make (something) clear or prove (something) to be true • *Your writing shows you can be a good writer.* ○ *He has shown himself to be unreliable.*

show BE NOTICEABLE /ʃoʊ/ *v* [I/T] *past simple* **showed**, *past part* **shown** /ʃoʊn/ to be able to be seen or noticed, or to make (something) noticeable • *I've been working for hours, and I've got nothing to show for it.* [I]

show LEAD /ʃoʊ/ *v* [T] *past simple* **showed**, *past part* **shown** /ʃoʊn/ to lead (someone) somewhere or to point out (something) •

Could you show me the way to the post office? ○ *Show me which cake you want.* • If you **show** someone **the door**, you tell them or make it clear you want them to leave: *Your boss isn't going to show you the door just because you made a mistake.*

show EXPRESS /ʃoʊ/ *v* [T] *past simple* **showed**, *past part* **shown** /ʃoʊn/ to express (an amount or degree), as of temperature or time • *My barometer shows a change in the weather is coming.*

show ENTERTAINMENT /ʃoʊ/ *n* [C] a theatrical performance, a movie, or a television or radio program • *a stage/talk show* • **Show business** (*infml* **show biz**) is the entertainment industry. • A **showman** is someone who produces movies, stage shows, or other entertainment: *P.T. Barnum, a founder of the circus, was a great showman.* • A **showman** is also someone who is a skilled performer: *The President is a great showman and a clever politician.* ○ *His televised speeches demonstrate his* **showmanship** (= skillful performance).

show PUBLIC EVENT /ʃoʊ/ *n* [C] an event at which the public can view a particular collection of things • *a flower show* ○ *a fashion show*

show /ʃoʊ/ *v* [I/T] *past simple* **showed**, *past part* **shown** /ʃoʊn/ • *This gallery is a place where young artists can show their work.* [T] • To show a movie is to offer it for viewing in a movie theater or on television: *That channel often shows foreign films.* [T]

showing /'ʃoʊ·ɪŋ/ *n* [C] • *This is the first showing of his paintings in this country.* • See also SHOWING.

show ACTIVITY /ʃoʊ/ *n* [U] *infml* an activity, business, or organization, considered in relation to who is managing it • *Who will run the show when the boss retires?*

□ **show around** *obj*, **show** *obj* **around** /'-·'-/ *v adv* [M] to lead (someone) through a place • *Phil had never seen Chicago, so I offered to show him around.*

□ **show off** ATTRACT ATTENTION /'-'-/ *v adv* [I] to do something to attract attention to yourself • *I wrote my first poem because I wanted to show off how clever I was.*

show-off /'ʃoʊ·ɔːf/ *n* [C] • *David's a showoff in the kitchen—he loves having dinner guests.*

□ **show off** *obj* MAKE SEEN /'-'-/, **show** *obj* **off** *v adv* [M] to make it possible to see (something) in order to admire it • *She brought her new baby so she could show him off.* ○ *That shirt shows off the color of your eyes.*

□ **show up** ARRIVE /'-'-/, **show** *v adv* [I] to arrive for a gathering or event • *He showed up late for the meeting.*

□ **show up** APPEAR /'-'-/ *v adv* [I] to appear or be seen • *The virus does not show up in blood tests.*

□ **show up** *obj* EMBARRASS, **show** *obj* **up** /'-'-/ *v adv* [M] to do something that embarrasses (someone) or makes (someone) seem stupid •

She's always trying to show up her colleagues to make herself look smarter.

showcase CABINET /ˈʃoʊ·keɪs/ *n* [C] a cabinet, usually of glass, in which objects are kept that are valuable or easily broken • *a jeweler's showcase*

showcase OPPORTUNITY /ˈʃoʊ·keɪs/ *n* [C] a place or event where something, esp. something new or experimental, can be introduced • *The Sundance Film Festival is an especially sympathetic showcase for unusual films.*

showcase /ˈʃoʊ·keɪs/ *v* [T] • *In the opening set, he showcased his own songs.*

showdown /ˈʃoʊ·daʊn/ *n* [C] an event, such as a meeting or fight, that ends a disagreement or decides a winner • *a military showdown* ○ *Sunday's showdown will decide whether Mexico or Italy is the world soccer champion.*

shower RAIN /ˈʃaʊ·ər, ʃaʊr/ *n* [C] a brief rain, or a light fall of snow • *a snow shower* • A shower is also something that falls like rain: *a shower of sparks* ○ *a shower of confetti*

shower /ˈʃaʊ·ər, ʃaʊr/ *v* [I] • *It showered on and off all afternoon.*

shower GIVE /ˈʃaʊ·ər, ʃaʊr/ *v* [T always + adv/prep] to give a lot of (something) to someone • *His family showers him with love.*

shower /ˈʃaʊ·ər, ʃaʊr/ *n* [C] a party held to give presents to someone who will soon be married or will become a parent • *a bridal shower* ○ *a baby shower*

shower DEVICE /ˈʃaʊ·ər, ʃaʊr/ *n* [C] a device that sprays water on a person's body while they wash themselves, or an act of washing using such a device • *He stays in the shower until there is no more hot water!* ○ *Have I got time to take a shower before we go out?* • A **shower curtain** is a usually plastic curtain that you pull across an opening when you are having a shower to prevent the spray of water from getting out. • PIC) BATHROOM

shower /ˈʃaʊ·ər, ʃaʊr/ *v* [I] • *I usually shower in the morning.*

showing /ˈʃoʊ·ɪŋ/ *n* [C] a performance in a competitive activity • *He blames racism for his poor showing in the election.* • See also **showing** at SHOW PUBLIC EVENT

shown /ʃoʊn/ *past participle of* SHOW

showpiece /ˈʃoʊ·piːs/ *n* [C] an extremely good example of something that attracts attention or admiration • *This painting will be the showpiece of the exhibit.*

showroom /ˈʃoʊ·ruːm, -rʊm/ *n* [C] a room in which goods for sale are arranged • *a car dealer's showroom*

showy /ˈʃoʊ·i/ *adj* • See at SHOW MAKE SEEN.

shrank /ʃræŋk/ *past simple of* SHRINK

shrapnel /ˈʃræp·nəl/ *n* [U] small pieces of metal blown through the air when a bomb or other device explodes • *Most of the injuries were caused by flying shrapnel.*

shred CUT /ʃred/ *v* [T] **-dd-** to cut or tear (something) into small pieces • *Shred some let-*

tuce into the salad bowl. ○ *He shredded documents to get rid of them.*

shred /ʃred/ *n* [C usually pl] • *My silk blouse was ripped to shreds in the washing machine.*

shredder /ˈʃred·ər/ *n* [C] a machine used for cutting things into very small pieces

shred SMALL AMOUNT /ʃred/ *n* [C usually sing] a very small amount of something • *There isn't a shred of evidence to support her accusation.*

shrewd /ʃruːd/ *adj* [-er/-est only] able to judge a situation accurately and turn it to your own advantage • *He's a very shrewd businessman.* ○ *Barbara made some shrewd investments.*

shriek /ʃriːk/ *n* [C] a loud, high cry • *the shriek of sea gulls* ○ *She heard a high-pitched shriek.*

shriek /ʃriːk/ *v* [I/T] • *We shrieked with laughter.* [I]

shrill /ʃrɪl/ *adj* [-er/-est only] not pleasant to hear; loud and high • *a shrill voice*

shrilly /ˈʃrɪl·li/ *adv* • *The terrified woman shrilly ordered the goat out of her kitchen.*

shrimp ANIMAL /ʃrɪmp/ *n* [C/U] *pl* **shrimp** a small sea creature with a shell, ten legs, and a long tail, or its flesh eaten as food

shrimp PERSON /ʃrɪmp/ *n* [C] *infml* a short or small person • *It's hard to believe this sculpted athlete was once a shrimp.* • USAGE: This word can be offensive unless you are using it humorously with someone you know well.

shrine /ʃraɪn/ *n* [C] a place where people come to worship, usually because of a connection with a holy person or a mysterious religious event or object • A shrine can also be a place that is honored because of some connection with a famous person or event.

shrink BECOME SMALLER /ʃrɪŋk/ *v* [I/T] *past simple* **shrank** /ʃræŋk/ *or* **shrunk** /ʃrʌŋk/, *past part* **shrunk** /ʃrʌŋk/, *also* **shrunken** /ˈʃrʌŋ·kən/ to become smaller or cause (something) to become smaller • *The show's audience has shrunk in the last few months.* [I] ○ *I shrank my sweater by putting it in the dryer!* [T]

shrinkage /ˈʃrɪŋ·kɪdʒ/ *n* [U] • *Financial support for the university has undergone substantial shrinkage.*

shrink MOVE AWAY /ʃrɪŋk/ *v* [I always + adv/prep] *past simple* **shrank** /ʃræŋk/ *or* also **shrunk** /ʃrʌŋk/, *past part* **shrunk** /ʃrʌŋk/ *or* also **shrunken** /ˈʃrʌŋ·kən/ to move away from something unpleasant or frightening • *My first reaction was to shrink in disgust at the sight of it.* • If you shrink from something, you avoid it: *Kate's a good worker, but she seems to shrink from responsibility.*

shrink DOCTOR /ʃrɪŋk/ *n* [C] *slang* a PSYCHIATRIST, PSYCHOTHERAPIST, *or* PSYCHOANALYST

shrivel /ˈʃrɪv·əl/ *v* [I/T] **-l-** *or* **-ll-** to become dried out and smaller, appearing crushed or folded, or to make (something) do this • *The hot sun shriveled the flowers I put in the window.* [T]

shroud /ʃraʊd/ *n* [C] a cloth used to wrap a

dead body before it is buried • A shroud is also anything that covers: *He cleared the leafy shroud covering the sign.*

shroud /ʃraʊd/ *v* [T] to cover or hide (something) • *The mountains were shrouded in fog.* ○ *The fate of the explorer is shrouded in mystery.*

shrub /ʃrʌb/ *n* [C] a plant with a wooden stem and many small branches that usually does not grow very tall

shrubbery /'ʃrʌb·ə·ri/ *n* [U] low-growing plants considered as a group, or an arrangement of such plants in a garden

shrug /ʃrʌg/ *v* [I/T] **-gg-** to raise (your shoulders) to express that you do not know, do not care, or are not sure about something • *My brother just shrugged in reply, too lazy to answer in words.* [I] • If you **shrug** something **off**, you act as if it is unimportant or not a problem: *You can't just shrug off your responsibilities.*

shrug /ʃrʌg/ *n* [C] • *Bill's only explanation was a careless shrug of his shoulders.*

shrunk /ʃrʌŋk/ *past simple and past participle of* SHRINK

shrunken /'ʃrʌŋ·kən/ *past participle of* SHRINK

shucks /ʃʌks/ *exclamation dated* used to express slight disappointment or regret, or sometimes to show that something is not very important • *Shucks, I wish I could have been there.* ○ *Shucks, it wasn't that hard to do.*

shudder /'ʃʌd·ər/ *v* [I] to shake suddenly and briefly, esp. because of an unpleasant thought or feeling • *I shuddered, remembering the frightening stories I had heard.*

shudder /'ʃʌd·ər/ *n* [C] • *When the car flipped over, a shudder went through the crowd watching the race.* ○ *Just thinking about that film sends shudders down my spine.*

shuffle WALK /'ʃʌf·əl/ *v* [I/T] to walk by sliding your feet, rather than lifting them as you step • *Grandfather shuffled into the kitchen, leaning on his cane.* [I always + adv/prep] • If you **shuffle** your **feet**, you move your feet slightly to show that you are uncomfortable or embarrassed: *When I asked where he'd been, he just stared at the ground and shuffled his feet.* [T]

shuffle /'ʃʌf·əl/ *n* [U] • *the shuffle of shoes on city sidewalks*

shuffle MOVE AROUND /'ʃʌf·əl/ *v* [T] to arrange (things) into different positions again and again, esp. within a small space • *She shuffled papers on her desk as she waited for the phone to ring.* ○ *My mother could shuffle cards like a Las Vegas gambler.*

shuffle /'ʃʌf·əl/ *n* [C] • *She gave her papers a quick shuffle.* • A shuffle is also a change in the people in an organization, esp. those who manage it: *The top-level shuffle brought Groncki into the White House.*

shun /ʃʌn/ *v* [T] **-nn-** to avoid or refuse to accept (someone or something) • *She shunned publicity after she retired from the stage.*

shunt /ʃʌnt/ *v* [T always + adv/prep] to move (someone or something) to the side or away • *Seals can shunt blood away from their skin to maintain body temperature.* ○ *You can't just shunt your problems aside.*

shush /ʃʌʃ, ʃʊʃ/ *exclamation infml* used to tell someone to be quiet • *Shush! You're too loud.*

shush /ʃʌʃ, ʃʊʃ/ *v* [T] *infml* • *Marge put a finger to her lips to shush us.*

shut /ʃʌt/ *v* [I/T] **shutting**, *past* **shut** to close something, esp. by covering an opening • *Would you shut the door, please?* [T] ○ *I can't get this window shut.* [I] ○ *I shut the book* (= closed it) *and put it back on the shelf.* [T] • (*infml*) *He told me to* shut *my* mouth (= be quite).

shut /ʃʌt/ *adj* [not gradable] • *Her office door was shut all day.* ○ *Her eyes were shut, but she was still awake.*

☐ **shut down** (obj), **shut** (obj) **down** /'-'-/ *v adv* [I/M] to stop operating • *The company announced plans to shut down two factories.* [M] ○ *Our town's only grocery store shut down last year.* [I]

shutdown /'ʃʌt·daʊn/ *n* [C] • *The shutdown of the military base is scheduled for next summer.*

☐ **shut off** (obj) STOP, **shut** (obj) **off** /'-'-/ *v adv* [I/M] to stop the operation of (a machine or system) • *Did you shut off the light in the bedroom?* [M] ○ *Shut the engine off and take the keys.* [M] ○ *Lift your foot and the water shuts off.* [I]

☐ **shut off** obj SEPARATE /'-'-/, **shut** obj **off** *v adv* [M] to separate (something) from other parts, places, or people • *Railroad tracks shut the area off from the rest of the city.* ○ *On cooler evenings we shut the living room off and stay warm by the fireplace.* ○ *When her husband died she shut herself off from everyone.*

☐ **shut out** obj PREVENT ENTRANCE /'-'-/, **shut** obj **out** *v adv* [M] to prevent (someone or something) from entering a place • *The double-glazed windows shut most of the traffic noise out.* ○ (*fig.*) *She can't shut out the memory of the accident* (= stop remembering it).

☐ **shut out** obj PREVENT SCORING, **shut** obj **out** /'-'-/ *v adv* [M] to prevent (a competitor) from scoring any points • *The White Sox shut out the Orioles today at Comiskey Park.*

shutout /'ʃʌt·aʊt/ *n* [C] a competition in which an opponent fails to score any points • *He pitched a shutout.*

☐ **shut up** (obj) STOP TALKING, **shut** (obj) **up** /'-'-/ *v adv* [I/M] *infml* to stop talking or making a noise, or to make (someone) do this • *I wish you'd shut up and listen.* [I] ○ *Can you shut up that barking dog?* [M]

shut up /'-'-/ *exclamation* • *Shut up! I'm trying to think.*

☐ **shut up** obj KEEP LOCKED /'-'-/, **shut** obj **up** *v adv* [M] to keep (people or animals) in a locked place, or to completely close (a place) • *The zoo keepers shut the animals up in cages at the end* *of the day.* ○ *They shut up the country house for the winter.*

shuteye /'ʃʌt·ɑɪ/ *n* [U] *infml* sleep • *Try to get some shuteye.*

shutter CAMERA OPENING /'ʃʌt·ər/ *n* [C] the part of a camera that opens briefly to allow light to reach the film when a photograph is being taken

shutter WINDOW COVER /'ʃʌt·ər/ *n* [C] a wooden cover like a door on the outside of a window

shuttered /'ʃʌt·ərd/ *adj* [not gradable] • *In the midday heat, all the houses were shuttered* (= their shutters were closed). ○ *Most of the region's factories are shuttered* (= not operating).

shuttle /'ʃʌt·əl/ *n* [C] a vehicle or aircraft that travels regularly between two places, carrying people or things • *You can take the shuttle across town.* ○ *The New York to Boston shuttle is usually on time.* • A shuttle is also a **space shuttle**. See at SPACE BEYOND EARTH.

shuttle /'ʃʌt·əl/ *v* [always + adv/prep] • *A van shuttles between the hotel and the airport every ten minutes.* [I]

shuttlecock /'ʃʌt·əl,kɑk/, *infml* **birdie**, **shuttle** *n* [C] a small, light object with a rounded end to which real or artificial feathers are attached and which is hit over a net in the game of BADMINTON

shy NERVOUS WITH OTHERS /ʃɑɪ/ *adj* [-er/-est only] **shyer**, **shyest** uncomfortable with other people and unwilling to talk to them • *He was too shy to ask her to dance with him.*

shy /ʃɑɪ/ *v* [I] • If a horse shies, it moves back suddenly, esp. from fear or surprise. • If you **shy away from** something, you move away from or try to avoid it: *I've never shied away from hard work.*

shyly /'ʃɑɪ·li/ *adv* • *She smiled shyly.*

shyness /'ʃɑɪ·nəs/ *n* [U] • *They have no shyness about telling you what they think.*

shy LACKING /ʃɑɪ/ *adj* [not gradable] • If you are **shy of** something, you lack it: *The bill was four votes shy of a majority.*

shyster /'ʃɑɪ·stər/ *n* [C] *infml* a dishonest person, esp. a lawyer

sibling /'sɪb·lɪŋ/ *n* [C] a brother or sister • *I have four siblings.* • **Sibling rivalry** is competition among brothers and sisters.

sic /sɪk/ *adv* [not gradable] used in BRACKETS after a word or phrase copied from somewhere else to show the writer knows it appears to be wrong but this is intentional or exactly as in the original • *The sign said, "Closed on Wendsday" [sic].*

sic *(obj)* **on** *obj* /'--/ *v prep* [T] to order (esp. a dog) to attack (someone) • *The police will sic their dogs on you if they have to.*

sick ILL /sɪk/ *adj* [-er/-est only] physically or mentally ill; not well or healthy • *We've got a sick cat.* ○ *I feel sick.* ○ *Only a sick mind could think of such things.* ○ *He's out sick* (= absent because of illness). ○ *Samantha called in sick*

(= called to say she was ill and not coming to work). • A **sick day** is a day for which an employee receives pay while absent from work because of illness. • *Marcus is on* **sick leave** (= permitted absence because of illness).

sicken /'sɪk·ən/ *v* [I] • *The animals sickened and died.* • See also **sicken** at SICK UNPLEASANT.

sickly /'sɪk·li/ *adj* weak and unhealthy • *He was a sickly child.*

sickness /'sɪk·nəs/ *n* [C/U] the state or condition of being ill, or a disease • *No one escapes occasional sickness.* [U] ○ *Raymond has a rare sickness.* [C]

sick VOMITING /sɪk/ *adj* [-er/-est only] feeling as if you are going to vomit • *She was so nervous she got sick.* • *I feel* **sick to my stomach** (= likely to vomit).

sick UNPLEASANT /sɪk/ *adj* [-er/-est only] causing or experiencing unpleasant feelings • *Michelle is sick about not getting that job.* ○ *The way they treat prisoners here makes me sick.* • If you are **sick of** something or **sick and tired of** something, you have experienced it too much and want no more of it: *I'm sick of him whining about money.*

sicken /'sɪk·ən/ *v* [T] • *The violence in the film sickened me.* • See also **sicken** at SICK ILL.

sickening /'sɪk·ə·nɪŋ/ *adj* • *She slipped and fell with a sickening thud.*

sickle /'sɪk·əl/ *n* [C] a tool with a short handle and a curved blade, used for cutting grass and other plants

side SURFACE /sɑɪd/ *n* [C] a surface of something that is not the top or the bottom, or a surface of a flat object • *Label all four sides of the box.* ○ *I painted one side of the boat green to see if we like the color.* ○ *The trail leads up the side of the mountain.* ○ *Please write on only one side of the paper.* • A side is also a surface that is not the front or the back: *There's a scratch on the side of my new bookcase.*

side /sɑɪd/ *adj* [not gradable] at, on, of, or in the side of something • *a side view* ○ *Please use the side entrance.*

side EDGE /sɑɪd/ *n* [C] an edge or border of something • *A square has four sides.* ○ *We rested by the side of the river.* ○ *There are trees on both sides of the road.*

side NEXT POSITION /sɑɪd/ *n* [U] a place next to something • *I have a small table by the side of my bed.* • *I'll have* **a side of** *onion rings* (= a small serving of them in addition to the main dish). • *He drives a bus, but he's a tour guide* **on the side** (= in addition). ○ *I'll have the salad with the dressing* **on the side** (= separate from the salad). • *The children sat* **side by side** (= next to each other).

side LESS IMPORTANT /sɑɪd/ *adj* less important or smaller than the thing that is connected with • *a side issue* ○ *We parked on a side street.* • A **side dish** is a small serving of food, esp. vegetables, served in addition to the main dish. • *Does this drug have any* **side effects** (= effects other than those intended)? • A **side order** is a small serving of food sold at a restaurant to be eaten with other food or by itself. • A **side-show** is a small show in addition to the main one, esp. at a CIRCUS (= traveling entertainment).

side PART /saɪd/ n [C] a part of something, esp. in relation to a real or imagined central line • the right/left side ○ The swimming pool is on the other side of town. ○ I'm Irish on my mother's side (= her family is from Ireland). ○ Children came running from all sides (= from many directions).

side OPPOSING GROUP /saɪd/ n [C] one of two or more opposing groups or people • This is a war which neither side can win. ○ Which side are you on (= Whom do you support)? ○ (fig.) The other candidate had experience on his side (= as an advantage).

side /saɪd/ v [I always + adv/prep] • Peter always sides with you (= supports you).

side OPINION /saɪd/ n [C] an opinion held in an argument, or a way of considering something • There are two sides to every argument.

side PERSONAL QUALITY /saɪd/ n [C] a part of someone's character • He has a gentle side.

sideboard /'saɪd·bɔːrd, -bourd/ n [C] a piece of furniture with a flat top and enclosed shelves at the bottom, usually used for holding such things as glasses, plates, knives, and forks

sideburns /'saɪd·bɜrnz/ pl n areas of hair grown down the sides of a man's face in front of the ears

sidekick /'saɪd·kɪk/ n [C] infml a friend, or a person who works with someone more important • Police arrested the crook and his not-too-bright sidekick the next day.

sideline ACTIVITY /'saɪd·laɪn/ n [C] an activity that is less important than the main one • Jean teaches French in the evening as a sideline.

sideline MARK ON GROUND /'saɪd·laɪn/ n [C] (in some sports, esp. football) a line marking the side of the area of play • The ball fell just outside the sideline. ○ (fig.) I don't like dancing, I'd rather watch from the sidelines (= not to be directly involved).

sideline /'saɪd·laɪn/ v [T] to remove (a player) from a game • He was sidelined because of injuries.

sidelong /'saɪd·lɔːŋ/ adj, adv [not gradable] directed to or from the side • a sidelong glance

sidestep /'saɪd·step/ v [I/T] -pp- to avoid (something) • The developer tried to sidestep city building rules. [T] ○ She skillfully sidestepped questions about her past. [T] • If a person or animal sidesteps, they move quickly to the side. [I]

sideswipe /'saɪd·swaɪp/ v [T] to hit (a vehicle) on the side while passing in another vehicle • My car was sideswiped in the parking lot.

sidetrack /'saɪd·træk/ v [I] to direct (someone) away from an activity or subject toward another one that is often less important • Rhonda was looking for an envelope and got sidetracked reading some old letters.

sidewalk /'saɪd·wɔːk/ n [C] a path with a hard surface on which people walk along one or both sides of a road

sideways /'saɪd·weɪz/ adv, adj [not gradable] from one side to another, or with a side to the front • If you'd move sideways I could see better. ○ Turn the table sideways. • If you look at something sideways, you do not look at it directly.

siding /'saɪd·ɪŋ/ n [U] material that covers the outer walls of a building • vinyl/aluminum/wood siding

sidle /'saɪd·ᵊl/ v [I always + adv/prep] to move uncertainly or worriedly • Jordan sidled over to the girl and asked if she'd like to dance.

siege /siːdʒ, siːʒ/ n [C/U] the act of surrounding a place by an armed force in order to defeat those defending it • After a month-long siege, they gave themselves up to federal agents. [C] ○ The town was under siege. [U]

siesta /siː'es·tə/ n [C] a rest or sleep taken at the beginning of the afternoon, esp. in hot countries

sieve /sɪv/ n [C] a bowl-shaped tool with many very small holes in it, used to separate larger from smaller pieces or solids from a liquid

sift SEPARATE /sɪft/ v [T] to shake (a powdered substance) through a SIEVE, esp. in order to remove lumps • Sift some powdered sugar on top of the cake.

sift EXAMINE /sɪft/ v [I/T] to make a close examination of (something) • The police are carefully sifting the evidence. [T] ○ I had to sift through all my papers. [I]

sigh /saɪ/ v [I] to breathe out a deep breath that can be heard, esp. because you are tired, sad, pleased, or bored • Angelica sighed in relief. ○ She sighs again, looking bored. ○ (fig.) A soft breeze sighed through the trees.

sigh /saɪ/ n [C] • You could hear an occasional sigh from the crowd. • A **sigh of relief** is a feeling of comfort because something will happen: Business leaders are breathing a sigh of relief now that these issues are being addressed.

sight SEEING /saɪt/ n [U] the ability to see, or the act of seeing something • Machines don't have a sense of sight. ○ The sight of sick children disturbs her. • I know David **by sight** (= I know what he looks like). • The soldiers will shoot looters **on sight** (= as soon as they see them). • I never buy anything **sight unseen** (= without seeing it first). • If you can **sight-read**, you have the ability to play or sing written music the first time you see it.

sightless /'saɪt·ləs/ adj [not gradable] blind

sight VIEW /saɪt/ n [C/U] something that is in someone's view, or the view someone has • The finish line was a welcome sight for the runners. [C] ○ Don't let the children out of your *sight.* [C] ○ *Keep your bags in sight.* [U] • A sight is also an interesting place: *No sights in Moscow are more historic than the Kremlin.* [C] • (*infml*) *You're* **a sight for sore eyes** (= I am happy to see you). • **Sightseeing** is the act of visiting interesting places, esp. while on vacation: *Are you going to go sightseeing this afternoon?* ○ *All the others on line were* **sightseers** (= people visiting interesting places).

sight /saɪt/ *v* [T] • *After several days at sea, the sailors finally sighted land.*

sighting /'saɪt·ɪŋ/ *n* [C] • *This is the first sighting of an eastern bluebird in this part of the country.*

sight GUN PART /saɪt/ *n* [C] a device, esp. on a gun or TELESCOPE (= device for looking at distant objects), through which you look to help you aim at something • *Locate the target in your sight.*

sign MARK /saɪn/ *n* [C] a written or printed mark that has a standard meaning • *The symbol for subtraction is the minus sign.* • A **sign of the Zodiac** is any of the twelve divisions of the year in ASTROLOGY (= the study of the sun, moon, stars, and planets and the belief in their influence on life). • LP SYMBOLS, SIGNS, AND MARKS

sign PUBLIC INFORMATION /saɪn/ *n* [C] a device that gives information to people who see it • *a stop sign* ○ *A neon sign marked the entrance to the parking garage.* • A **signpost** is a pole with a sign on it, or (*fig.*) a clear signal of something: *The camp roads had signposts that read Sparks Street, Portage Avenue, Yonge Street, and the like.* ○ (*fig.*) *a signpost of progress*

sign BODY MOVEMENT /saɪn/ *n* [C] a movement of the hands or body that gives information or an instruction • *He kept giving me the cutthroat sign to end the speech.* • **Sign language** is a system of communication that uses hand and body movements, used esp. by people who cannot hear.

sign /saɪn/ *v* to communicate by using hand movements • *He signed that he'd be ready in five minutes.* [+ *that* clause]

sign SIGNAL /saɪn/ *n* [C] a signal that something exists or that shows what might happen in the future • *She was at least sharing her problems with me, and that was a sign of progress.* ○ *There was nobody in the place, and I thought that was a bad sign.* ○ *There are signs that he is thinking of running for president.*

sign WRITE /saɪn/ *v* [I/T] to write your name in the particular way you write it, esp. on a printed document to show that you have written it yourself • *to sign a letter/contract/check* [T] • If an organization signs someone, that person has officially become a member of the organization by agreeing to a contract: *The team signed four new players this week.* [T] ○ *Please sign for the package when it arrives* (= write your name on a form to show that you have received it). [I] • To **sign away** or **sign**

over something is to give up your rights to it or ownership of it by formally signing a document. • *Messengers are required to* **sign in** *and* **sign out** (= write their names on a form when entering and when leaving).

□ **sign off** /'-'-/ *v adv* [I] to end (a television or radio broadcast)

□ **sign up** /'-'-/ *v adv* [I] to join a group or organization • *Kathy signed up for the soccer team this year.*

signal ACTION /'sɪɡ·nəl/ *n* [C] an action, movement, or sound that gives information, a message, a warning, or an order • *I tried to call but kept getting a busy signal.* ○ *When the lieutenant gave the signal, five police officers charged into the apartment.* ○ *In retrospect, looking at how she was acting, we should have been able to recognize the danger signals.* • A signal is also a device, often with lights, that shows people or vehicles whether to stop, go, or move carefully.

signal /'sɪɡ·nəl/ *v* [I/T] • *When you learn to drive, you are told that you have to signal before you turn right or left.* [I] ○ *The police officer signaled us to stop.* [T]

signal WAVE /'sɪɡ·nəl/ *n* [C] a series of energy waves that carry a sound, picture, or other information • *a low-frequency radio signal*

signal IMPORTANT /'sɪɡ·nəl/ *adj fml* unusual and important • *You performed a signal service to our people, and we wish to express our gratitude.*

signatory /'sɪɡ·nə,tɔːr·i, -,toʊr·i/ *n* [C] a person, organization, or country that signs an agreement • *Canada was a signatory to the Geneva Convention.*

signature /'sɪɡ·nə·tʃər, -,tʃʊr/ *n* [C] your name written in the particular way you write it, esp. on a printed document to show that you have written it yourself • *I need your signature on the credit card receipt.* ○ *We collected hundreds of signatures on our petition.*

significant /sɪɡ'nɪf·ɪ·kənt/ *adj* important, large, or great, esp. in leading to a different result or to an important change • *This election reaffirms a significant shift of the center of power.* ○ *Marriage is a significant commitment.*

significance /sɪɡ'nɪf·ɪ·kəns/ *n* [U] • *The full significance of space exploration may not be understood for many years to come.*

significantly /sɪɡ'nɪf·ɪ·kənt·li/ *adv* by a noticeably large amount • *Our prison population has significantly increased in the last ten years.* ○ *Men are making significantly more money than women at the same professional level.*

signify MEAN /'sɪɡ·nə,faɪ/ *v* [T] to mean (something); be a sign of • *He wears a red ribbon to signify his concern about the AIDS epidemic and its victims.*

signify MAKE KNOWN /'sɪɡ·nə,faɪ/ *v* to make (something) known; to show • *All those in favor, please signify by raising your hands.* [I] ○

I need a letter from you signifying that this matter is closed. [+ *that* clause]

silence QUIET /'saɪ·ləns/ *n* [U] an absence of sound; complete quiet • *A profound silence spread itself through the sleeping house.*

silent /'saɪ·lənt/ *adj* • *Madeleine turned back down the empty, silent street.*

silently /'saɪ·lənt·li/ *adv* • *Silently, he crept up the stairs.*

silencer /'saɪ·lən·sər/ *n* [C] a part that can be attached to a gun to reduce the noise when it is fired

silence NO SPEAKING /'saɪ·ləns/ *n* [C/U] a state of not speaking or making noise • *The two men ate in silence and listened to traffic swishing past on the highway.* [U] ○ *Her question was*

followed by a long silence (= a long period of time in which no one spoke). [C]

silence /'saɪ·ləns/ *v* [T] to stop (someone) from speaking or from criticizing • *Successful action could silence the administration's critics.*

silent /'saɪ·lənt/ *adj* • *I have remained silent till now, Mike, but I have to tell you what I think.* • If a letter in a word is silent, it is not pronounced: *The "b" in doubt is silent.* • A **silent partner** is someone who owns part of a business but does not make decisions about how it operates.

silently /'saɪ·lənt·li/ *adv* without speaking, or only in the mind • *I silently cursed the stupidity of these arrangements.*

SILENT LETTERS

The following letters can be silent in the pronunciation of some words: **a, b, c, d, e, g, h, k, l, n, p, s, t, w**. In most cases, whether or not a letter is silent depends on its relationship to the letters that surround it and the position of the letters in the word.

Here are some examples, with rules where it is possible to give them:

a   *a* is usually silent in *-ically* at the end of a word: **practically, basically, specifically, physically, radically**

b   *b* is silent in the combination *mb* at the end of a word: **comb, climb, lamb, bomb, numb, limb, thumb, dumb, crumb, tomb;** and in the word **plumber**
b is also silent in *bt* at the end of a word: **debt, doubt;** and in the word **subtle**

c   *c* is silent in the combination *sc* before the letters *i, e,* and *y* at the beginning of a word: **scene, scenery, scent, science, scientist, scissors, scythe.**
c is usually silent in the combination *sc* in the middle of a word: **descend, discipline, fascinating, miscellaneous** (but not, for example, in *conscience, conscious, luscious, fascism.*)
c is also silent in *scle* at the end of a word: **muscle, corpuscle**

d   *d* is usually silent in these words: **handkerchief, handsome, Wednesday**

e   *e* is usually silent at the end of a word (but not, for example, in *maybe*). Notice that when it follows a single consonant in a word consisting of one syllable, as in **bite** or **smile** (or in a stressed syllable at the end of a word, as in **decide**), the final *e* often changes the sound of the vowel before the consonant.
e can also be silent in the middle of some words: **every, evening, vegetable, camera**

g   *g* is silent in *gn* at the beginning or end of a word: **gnome, gnaw, gnash, gnat, gnarled; sign, design, resign, assign, campaign, foreign, deign, reign;** and in the word **champagne**
g is also silent in *gm* at the end of a word: *diaphragm, paradigm, phlegm*

gh *gh* Both *g* and *h* are usually silent in the combination *gh* in the middle or at the end of a word: **night, light, might, fight, high, sigh, caught, taught, brought, bought, thought, thorough, although, dough, straight, weigh, eight, height, neighbor, throughout** (but not, for example, in *laugh, enough, cough, rough, tough*)

h   *h* is silent in *rh* at the beginning of a word: **rhyme, rhythm, rhinoceros, rheumatism, rhetoric**
h is also silent in *gh* at the beginning of a word: **ghost, ghetto, ghastly**
h is silent in these words, too: **exhibition, exhausted, heir, honest, honor, hour, herb, oh, scheme, school, scholarship**

k   *k* is silent in *kn* at the beginning of a word: **knee, knife, know, knowledge, knit, knock, knot**

l   *l* is usually silent in the combinations *alf, alk, olk, ould,* and *alm* at the end of a word: **half, calf, behalf; walk, talk, chalk, stalk; yolk, folk; should, could, would, calm, palm**
l is also silent in these words: **salmon, Lincoln**

n   *n* is silent in the combination *mn* at the end of a word: **autumn, column, damn, condemn, hymn, solemn**

p   *p* is silent in the combination *ps* at the beginning of a word: **psychology, psychiatrist, psychotic, psychic, psychopath, psalm, pseudonym**

CONTINUED

SILENT LETTERS (*continued*)

p is also silent in *pn* at the beginning of a word: **pneumatic, pneumonia**
p is silent in these words, too: **cupboard, raspberry, receipt, corps, coup**

s   *s* is silent in these words: **aisle, corps, island, debris, bourgeois, Illinois, Arkansas**

t   *t* is silent in words ending in *sten* and *stle*: **listen, fasten, moisten, hasten, glisten; castle, whistle, wrestle, thistle**
t is also silent in some words ending in *et* that are borrowed from French: **ballet, beret, bouquet, buffet, cabaret, chalet, crochet, croquet, filet, gourmet, ricochet, sorbet**
t is also silent in these words: **often, soften, Christmas, mortgage, debut, rapport, depot**

w   *w* is silent in *wr* at the beginning of a word: **write, wrong, wrist, wrap, wrinkle, wreck, wreath, wrench, wrestle, wring**
w is also silent in the combination *who* at the beginning of many words: **who, whole, whose, whom, wholly** (but not, for example, in *whopper* or *whoopee*)
w is also silent in these words: **answer, two, sword**

---

silhouette /ˌsɪl·ə'wet/ *n* [C/U] a dark shape seen against a light background • *An unidentified witness was shown on camera in silhouette.* [U]

silhouette

silhouette /ˌsɪl·ə'wet/ *v* [T] • *Kate was silhouetted in the pale light of the porch.*

silicon /'sɪl·ɪ·kən, -ə‚kɑn/ *n* [U] a common chemical element that is used in electronic devices, such as computers, and in making materials such as glass, concrete, and steel • **Silicon Valley** is an area in northern California where there are many companies that make or use computer materials and electronic devices.

silk /sɪlk/ *n* [U] a smooth, shiny cloth made from a thread produced by a type of CATERPILLAR (= small, tube-shaped insect), or the thread itself • *a silk shirt* • A **silkworm** is a type of small, tube-shaped insect that produces threads of silk.

silky /'sɪl·ki/, **silken** /'sɪl·kən/ *adj* made of silk, or soft and smooth like silk • *a silky nightgown* ○ *silky fabrics*

sill /sɪl/ *n* [C] a flat, horizontal piece, usually of wood, forming the base of the frame of a window • *She leaned on the sill and looked out through the open window.*

silly /'sɪl·i/ *adj* showing a lack of thought or judgment; not serious and not showing much intelligence • *a silly grin* ○ *I watched another silly movie last night.*

silliness /'sɪl·i·nəs/ *n* [U] • *It's time to stop the silliness and get serious.*

silo /'saɪ·loʊ/ *n* [C] *pl* **silos** a large structure, usually cylindrical, used for storing grain or winter food for farm animals • A silo is also an underground structure for storing and firing MISSILES (= flying weapons).

silt /sɪlt/ *n* [U] sand or earth that has been carried along by flowing water and then left esp. at a bend in a river or at a river's opening

silver METAL /'sɪl·vər/ *n* [U] a white metal that is highly valued and used esp. in utensils, jewelry, coins, and decorative objects • A **silver anniversary** is a celebration of the 25th year of esp. a marriage. • A **silver medal** is a disk-shaped prize made of or covered with silver, or silver in color, given to a person or team that is second in a competition. Compare **gold medal** at GOLD METAL; **bronze medal** at BRONZE. • **Silverware** are knives, forks, and spoons used for eating and serving food, which are sometimes made of silver or silver-covered metal, but often of STAINLESS steel.

silver /'sɪl·vər/ *adj* • *a silver tray*

silver COLOR /'sɪl·vər/ *adj* [not gradable], *n* [U] (of) a bright gray-white color • *silver hair* ○ *The book jacket was printed in silver and black.*

similar /'sɪm·ə·lər/ *adj* looking or being almost the same, although not exactly • *They both went to Ivy League schools and have similar backgrounds.* ○ *He used similar tactics to win the last election.*

similarity /ˌsɪm·ə'lær·ət·i/ *n* [C/U] the state of being almost the same, or a particular way in which something is almost the same • *Even though there are many similarities between men and women, there still remain many differences.* [C]

similarly /'sɪm·ə·lər·li/ *adv* • *The disease affects both sexes similarly.*

simile /'sɪm·ə·liː/ *n* [C/U] an expression including the words "like" or "as" to compare one thing with another • *They used metaphor, simile, and analogy to undermine reason and logic.* [U]

simmer /'sɪm·ər/ *v* [I/T] to cook (a liquid or something with liquid in it) at a temperature slightly below boiling • *Add broth and simmer for 15 minutes.* [I]

simmer /'sɪm·ər/ *n* [U] • *Bring the water to a simmer.*

simmering /'sɪm·ə·rɪŋ/ *adj* [not gradable] • *a pot of simmering water* • (*fig.*) Something that is simmering is controlled but may burst out at any time, often violently: *simmering passions* ○ *The simmering controversy now appears to be coming to an end.*

simple PLAIN /'sɪm·pəl/ *adj* [-*er*/-*est* only] without unnecessary or extra things or decorations; plain • *a simple black dress* ○ *It's a simple Boston lettuce salad.*

simplicity /sɪm'plɪs·əṭ·i/ *n* [U] • *What fascinated us was the simplicity and usefulness of the design.*

simply /'sɪm·pli/ *adv* • *He lived in a simply furnished apartment.* ○ *She lived simply, alone with her cat and her books.* • See also **simply** at SIMPLE EASY, SIMPLE CONSIDERED ALONE; SIMPLY.

simple EASY /'sɪm·pəl/ *adj* [-er/-est only] easy to understand or do; not difficult or complicated • *The recipe is very simple.* ○ *There's a simple solution if you don't like what's on TV—change the channel.*

simplicity /sɪm'plɪs·əṭ·i/ *n* [U] • *A flat tax has the virtue of simplicity, but I question how fair it would be.*

simplify /'sɪm·plə,fɑɪ/ *v* [T] • *We're looking for ways to simplify the process of applying for US citizenship.*

simplification /,sɪm·plə·fɪ'keɪ·ʃən/ *n* [C/U]

simply /'sɪm·pli/ *adv* • *To put it simply, we won't pay until we've received the goods we ordered.* • See also **simply** at SIMPLE PLAIN, SIMPLE CONSIDERED ALONE; SIMPLY.

simple CONSIDERED ALONE /'sɪm·pəl/ *adj* [not gradable] without considering or including anything else • *The simple fact is the fee is high because the rights are valuable.*

simply /'sɪm·pli/ *adv* [not gradable] • *Bowman said simply that "everything was OK."* • See also **simply** at SIMPLE PLAIN, SIMPLE EASY; SIMPLY.

simple COMMON /'sɪm·pəl/ *adj* [-er/-est only] common or ordinary • *I've got simple tastes, and I'm too old and cranky to change.*

simple FOOLISH /'sɪm·pəl/ *adj* [-er/-est only] *dated* foolish; easily deceived • *He's a very simple young man.* • Someone who is **simpleminded** cannot deal with complicated matters.

simplistic /sɪm'plɪs·tɪk/ *adj disapproving* simple but not effectively dealing with a real situation or problem, which is more complicated • *a simplistic idea/plan*

simply /'sɪm·pli/ *adv* [not gradable] just; only • *I simply don't trust him.* ○ *We simply go to camp, set it up, and spend the weekend.* ○ *They voted not simply for him and his party, but against Boris Yeltsin.* • Simply is sometimes used for emphasis: *That simply isn't so!* • See also **simply** at SIMPLE PLAIN, SIMPLE EASY, SIMPLE CONSIDERED ALONE.

simulate /'sɪm·jə,leɪt/ *v* [T] to create conditions or processes similar to (something that exists) • *Researchers are developing new techniques to simulate crashes.*

simulated /'sɪm·jə,leɪṭ·əd/ *adj* [not gradable] made to look like something else; artificial • *simulated leather*

simulation /,sɪm·jə'leɪ·ʃən/ *n* [C/U] a model of a real activity, created for training purposes

or to solve a problem • *Astronauts are trained using space flight simulation.* [U]

simultaneous /,sɑɪ·məl'teɪ·ni:·əs, ,sɪm·əl-/ *adj* [not gradable] happening or existing at exactly the same time • *The report will be broadcast in Russian with simultaneous English translation.*

simultaneously /,sɑɪ·məl'teɪ·ni:·ə·sli, ,sɪm·əl-/ *adv* [not gradable] • *To drive a car, you've got to learn to do several things simultaneously.*

sin /sɪn/ *n* [C/U] an act of breaking a religious law, or such acts considered together • *We were taught in Sunday school that Jesus died for our sins.* [C] • *A sin is also anything considered wrong: He leaked information, but that's hardly a sin in Washington, D.C.* [C]

sin /sɪn/ *v* [I] **-nn-** • *She didn't think that women sinned more than men.*

sinful /'sɪn·fəl/ *adj* • *He suggested that sex somehow had to be connected with something sinful or sensational.* • Sinful also means wrong: *It's sinful to waste food.*

sinner /'sɪn·ər/ *n* [C] a person who commits sins

SIN (number) /sɪn/ *n* [C] *Cdn abbreviation for* Social Insurance Number, see at SOCIAL OF HUMAN SOCIETY

since TIME /sɪns/ *adv* [not gradable] from a particular time in the past until now • *Alfredo left the house at six this morning, and we haven't seen him since.* ○ *I got my first job in 1973 and I've been working ever since* (= from then until now). • **Since when** is sometimes used to express anger and surprise at something and to refuse to accept it: *Since when do you have the right to tell me what to do?*

since /sɪns/ *prep* • *A lot has happened since 1980.*

since /sɪns/ *conjunction* • *It's been more than two years since we moved back to New York.*

since BECAUSE /sɪns/ *conjunction* because; as • *Since you've asked, I'll tell you what I really think.*

sincere /sɪn'sɪr/ *adj* (esp. of feelings, beliefs, opinions, or intentions) honest; not false or invented • *sincere modesty/belief/statement* ○ *More than sincere words of support, we need action.*

sincerely /sɪn'sɪr·li/ *adv* [not gradable] • *I sincerely hope she's happy with her decision.* • Sincerely or **Sincerely yours** is a common way to end a letter to someone who is not a friend or relative, before you sign your name.

sincerity /sɪn'ser·əṭ·i, -'sɪr-/ *n* [U] • *She spoke with such sincerity, you had to believe her.*

sinew /'sɪn·ju:/ *n* [C usually pl] a strong cord of muscle found in meat; a TENDON

sinewy /'sɪn·jə·wi/ *adj* • *lean, sinewy thighs*

sinful /'sɪn·fəl/ *adj* See at SIN.

sing /sɪŋ/ *v* [I/T] *past simple* **sang** /sæŋ/ or *dated* **sung** /sʌŋ/, *past part* **sung** /sʌŋ/ to make musical sounds with the voice • *She sings really terrible songs in the shower.* [T] ○ *At dawn,* *the birds began to sing.* [I] • If you **sing along**, you sing with someone or to music: *We sang along to the radio while driving.* • If you **sing** someone's **praises**, you show enthusiastic admiration for them: *Her paintings sing the praises of African women.* • If you **sing** someone **to sleep**, you sing to them until they feel sleepy: *She sang her baby to sleep.*

singer /ˈsɪŋ·ər/ *n* [C] a person who sings, esp. someone whose job is singing

singe /sɪndʒ/ *v* [T] **singeing** to burn (something) slightly, or to be burned slightly • *The candle singed his arm hairs.*

single ONE /ˈsɪŋ·gəl/ *adj* [not gradable] one only • *A single customer was left in the shop.* • A **single bed** is a bed for one person. • If you walk **single file**, you walk in a line with one person behind another: *The children walked single file down the hall.* PIC FILE • If something is done **single-handedly**, it is done without help: *She single-handedly supported the family after her husband's death.* • If you are **single-minded**, you only do things that relate to one activity or interest: *She is single-minded in her pursuit of her studies.* • Compare DOUBLE TWICE. LP WORDS WITH THE MEANING "ONE" at ONE SINGLE

singly /ˈsɪŋ·gli/ *adv* [not gradable] • *Students can work singly or in pairs.*

single /ˈsɪŋ·gəl/ *n* [C] • A single is a one-dollar bill. • A single is also a room for only one person.

singles /ˈsɪŋ·gəlz/ *n* [C] *pl* **singles** (esp. in tennis) a game played with one player on each side

single SEPARATE /ˈsɪŋ·gəl/ *adj* [not gradable] considered by itself or separate from other things • *Taxes are the single most important source of funds for the government.*

single NOT MARRIED /ˈsɪŋ·gəl/ *adj* [not gradable] not married • *He's been single for so long, I don't think he'll ever marry.*

single /ˈsɪŋ·gəl/ *n* [C] a person who is not married • *Singles pay more in income tax than married people do.*

□ **single out** *obj*, **single** *obj* **out** /ˈ--ˈ-/ *v adv* [M] to choose (someone or something) for special attention • *Rosa was singled out by the police because she filed a complaint.*

sing–song /ˈsɪŋ·sɔːŋ/ *adj* [not gradable] becoming higher and lower in a regular, boring way when speaking • *Her singsong reading of that report actually put me to sleep.*

singular GRAMMAR /ˈsɪŋ·gjə·lər/ *adj* [not gradable] *specialized* (in grammar) being the form of a word used to talk about only one thing • *a singular noun/verb* ○ *"Woman" is singular, but "women" is plural.* • Compare PLURAL.

singular /ˈsɪŋ·gjə·lər/ *n* [C/U] *specialized* • *The singular of "clouds" is "cloud."* [U]

singular NOTICEABLE /ˈsɪŋ·gjə·lər/ *adj* [not gradable] unusual and easily noticed; remarkable • *His campaign was singular because he*

talked about issues and did not attack his opponents' personal lives.

singularly /ˈsɪŋ·gjə·lər·li/ *adv* [not gradable] noticeably or particularly • *New England has some singularly beautiful towns.*

sinister /ˈsɪn·ə·stər/ *adj* [not gradable] evil, or suggesting that something evil is going to happen • *She has dark, sinister eyes that make you think of witches.*

sink GO BELOW WATER /sɪŋk/ *v* [I/T] *past simple* **sank** /sæŋk/ or **sunk** /sʌŋk/, *past part* **sunk** /sʌŋk/ to move below the surface of water • *The boat filled with water and began to sink.* [I] ○ *Enemy aircraft sank the ship.* [T] • If a situation is **sink or swim**, you will fail or succeed by your own efforts: *When we started the business, it was sink or swim.* • USAGE: The related adjective is SUNKEN.

sink FALL /sɪŋk/ *v* [I/T] *past simple* **sank** /sæŋk/ or **sunk** /sʌŋk/, *past part* **sunk** /sʌŋk/ to fall or move to a lower level • *The sun sank slowly below the horizon.* [I] ○ *Exhausted after the race, she sank to the ground.* [I] ○ *My feet sink into the sand with every step.* [I] ○ *Gasoline prices sank last year.* [I] ○ *Relations between the countries have sunk to a new low.* [I] • To sink a ball is to hit it into a hole, as in golf and POOL, or throw it through a HOOP (= ring with a net) in BASKETBALL. [T] • If a person or animal **sinks** their **teeth into** something, they bite hard: *I sank my teeth into the sandwich.* • If you **sink** your **teeth into** something, you become completely involved in it: *It was a story you could really sink your teeth into.*

sinking /ˈsɪŋ·kɪŋ/ *adj* • *He throws a sinking fastball* (= one that moves down). • A **sinking feeling** is a feeling that something bad is happening or will happen: *He had a sinking feeling that he would not make the team.*

sink DESTROY /sɪŋk/ *v* [T] *past simple* **sank** /sæŋk/ or **sunk** /sʌŋk/, *past part* **sunk** /sʌŋk/ to cause (something) to fail • *A price war sank the company.* ○ *I thought these issues would sink his career.*

sink CONTAINER /sɪŋk/ *n* [C] a container for water in a kitchen or bathroom used for washing and connected to pipes that bring and carry off water • PIC BATHROOM

□ **sink back** /ˈ-ˈ-/ *v adv* [I] to move into a comfortable position • *He sank back in his chair and closed his eyes.*

□ **sink in** /ˈ-ˈ-/ *v adv* [I] to become understood or known • *It took a while for the reality of my situation to sink in.*

□ **sink in/into** /ˈ-ˌ-, ˈ-ˌ-ˈ-/ *v adv* [T] (of liquid) to flow into and be absorbed • *Blot up the coffee you spilled before it sinks into the carpet.* • If you **sink money in/into** something, you give or invest it: *No developer is going to sink money into something he can't sell.*

□ **sink into** /ˈ-ˌ-ˈ-/ *v adv* [T] to change to (a worse state or condition) • *He sank into a coma.* ○

sit through

The play starts well, then sinks into melodrama.

sinus /ˈsaɪ·nəs/ *n* [C] any of the hollow spaces in the bones of the head that open into the nose

sip /sɪp/ *v* [T] **-pp-** to drink (a liquid) slowly by taking in small amounts at a time • *He sipped the hot coffee.*

sip /sɪp/ *n* [C] • *He took another sip of tea.*

siphon, syphon /ˈsaɪ·fən/ *n* [C] a tube for moving a liquid from one container to another or to a lower level, using the weight of air to keep the liquid flowing through the tube

siphon, syphon /ˈsaɪ·fən/ *v* [T always + adv/ prep] • *We had to siphon some gas into the tank before the car would start.* • If something, esp. money, is **siphoned off**, it is gradually stolen: *Over the years, she siphoned off hundreds of thousands of dollars from various accounts.*

sir MAN /sɜr/ *n* [C] a polite word used to address a man • *Excuse me, sir, do you know what time it is?* • Sir is used at the beginning of a formal letter to a man you do not know: *Dear Sir* • Compare MADAM WOMAN. LP TITLES AND FORMS OF ADDRESS

Sir TITLE /sɜr/ *n* [U] used as a title with the first or full name of a man given a rank of honor by a king or queen

sire MALE PARENT /saɪr/ *n* [C] the male parent of an animal with four feet

sire /saɪr/ *v* [T] to be the male parent of (an animal) • *The large bay colt was sired by Pleasant Colony.*

sire KING /saɪr/ *n* [C] *old use* used as a form of address to a king

siren DEVICE /ˈsaɪ·rən/ *n* [C] a device that makes a loud warning noise • *The terrible wail of sirens signaled a disaster.*

siren WOMAN /ˈsaɪ·rən/ *n* [C] (in ancient Greek literature) a creature who was half woman and half bird, whose singing attracted sailors into dangerous waters • The **siren call/song** of something is its very strong attraction: *I responded to the siren call of the road and went for lots of long drives.*

sirloin (steak) /ˈsɜr·lɔɪn (ˈsteɪk)/ *n* [C/U] the best meat from the lower back of cattle

sis /sɪs/ *n* [C] *short form of* SISTER

sissy /ˈsɪs·i/ *n* [C] *infml* a boy who seems to be easily frightened and not brave, or who is not interested in things boys usually like • *Dancing was for sissies when I was a kid.*

sister /ˈsɪs·tər/ *n* [C] a female who has the same parents as another person • *an older/ younger sister* • A sister is also a member of the same race, church, religious group, or organization: *a sorority sister* • Sister may be used as a form of address to a woman. • PIC FAMILY TREE

sisterhood /ˈsɪs·tərˌhʊd/ *n* [U] a feeling of shared interests and support among women

sister-in-law /ˈsɪs·tə·rənˌlɔː/ *n* [C] *pl* **sisters-in-law** /ˈsɪs·tər·zənˌlɔː/ the wife of someone's brother, or the sister of their husband or wife, or the wife of the brother of their husband or wife • PIC FAMILY TREE

sisterly /ˈsɪs·tər·li/ *adj* like or characteristic of a sister • *sisterly love*

sit REST /sɪt/ *v* [I/T] **sitting**, *past* **sat** /sæt/ to be in a position with your buttocks on a surface that supports your body, or to cause (someone) to be in this position • *Andrea was sitting on the couch, watching TV.* [I] ○ *Dad sat her on a chair and told her not to move.* [T] • If you **sit on** your **hands**, you do nothing: *She just sits on her hands all day, while I do the work.* • If you **sit on the fence**, you refuse to choose between two possibilities: *Todd's still sitting on the fence, trying to decide which school to attend.*

sitting /ˈsɪt·ɪŋ/ *n* [C] • *I read the book in one sitting.* ○ *It took several sittings for the artist to paint her portrait.* • A **sitting duck** is a person or thing in a situation that is easy to attack: *Without air support, we were sitting ducks for enemy guns.*

sit BE IN A POSITION /sɪt/ *v* [I] **sitting**, *past* **sat** /sæt/ to be or stay in a position or place • *That book is still sitting on my shelf unread.* ○ *The college sits on top of a hill.* • If you are **sitting pretty**, you are in a good situation: *Our apartment isn't expensive, so we're sitting pretty.*

sit MEET /sɪt/ *v* [I] **sitting**, *past* **sat** /sæt/ (of a legislature or court) to have an official meeting or series of meetings • *The Supreme Court sits from October to June.*

sit BE A MEMBER /sɪt/ *v* [I] **sitting**, *past* **sat** /sæt/ to be a member of an official group • *Our senator sat on the subcommittee for foreign relations.*

sit TAKE CARE /sɪt/ *v* [I/T] *short form of* BABY-SIT

sitter /ˈsɪt·ər/ *n* [C] *short form of* **baby-sitter**, see at BABY-SIT

□**sit around** (*obj*) /ˌ-ˈ-/ *v adv* [I/T] to sit (somewhere) and do nothing or do nothing in particular • *He just sits around the house watching TV.* [T]

□**sit back** /ˈ-ˈ-/ *v adv* [I] to rest in a comfortable position • *Sit back, relax, and enjoy the flight.* • To sit back is also to take no action: *You can't just sit back and let them close down the library.*

□**sit down** /ˈ-ˈ-/ *v adv* to move from a standing position to a sitting position • *They sat down on a park bench.* ○ *She slipped on the ice and sat down with a thump.*

□**sit in** BE PRESENT /ˈ-ˈ-/ *v adv* [I] to be present at an event without being involved • *Do you mind if I sit in on your class?*

□**sit in** ACT FOR SOMEONE /ˈ-ˈ-/ *v adv* [I] to fulfill a responsibility for another person • *The vice president will sit in for the president at today's meeting.* ○ *Jeanne needed a drummer and asked if I could sit in.*

□**sit still** /ˈ-ˈ-/ *v adv* to be quiet and not moving • *Sit still while I comb your hair!*

□**sit through** *obj* /ˈ-ˌ-/ *v adv* [T] to stay until

something is completed • *It's hard for little kids to sit through a whole baseball game.*

□ **sit tight** /-'-/ *v adv* to wait patiently and take no action • *You sit tight and I'll go get help.*

□ **sit up** STRAIGHTEN /-'-/ *v adv* [I] to straighten up or move into a sitting position • *She was finally strong enough to sit up in bed.* • If you **sit up and take notice**, you suddenly give attention to something: *The losses in the election have made many party leaders finally sit up and take notice.*

situp /'sɪt·ʌp/ *n* [C] • A **sit-up** is an exercise to strengthen your stomach muscles, in which you lie down and lift yourself into a sitting position without using your arms.

□ **sit up** STAY AWAKE /-'-/ *v adv* [I] to stay awake late, esp. past the time that you usually go to bed • *We sat up talking half the night.*

□ **sit well with** /-'--/ *v adv prep* [T] to be pleasing to (someone) • *Their long conversations didn't sit well with the boss.*

sitcom /'sɪt·kɑm/, **situation comedy** *n* [C] a television series in which the same characters are involved in amusing situations in each show

site /saɪt/ *n* [C] a place where something is, was, or will be • *The fort is now a historic site.* ○ *The fan club has its own Web site.*

sit–in /'sɪt·ɪn/ *n* [C] a public expression of dissatisfaction by a person or group that enters a place and refuses to leave until certain demands have been agreed to • *Students carried out a sit-in at the governor's office to protest higher tuition costs.*

situate /'sɪtʃ·ə,weɪt/ *v* [T always + adv/prep] to put (something) in a particular position • *The restaurant is situated near the Hudson River.*

situation /,sɪtʃ·ə'weɪ·ʃən/ *n* [C] a condition or combination of conditions that exist at a particular time • *I was in a situation where I didn't have cash handy.* • A **situation comedy** is a SITCOM.

six /sɪks/ *number* 6 • *My sister is six.* ○ *a six-sided figure* • Six can also mean six o'clock. • If you are **at sixes and sevens** you are in a state of confusion and disorder: *Ever since we moved, we've been at sixes and sevens.* • A **six-pack** is a set of six CANS or bottles of a drink sold together. • LP NUMBERS

sixth /sɪksθ/ *adj, adv* [not gradable], *n* [C] • *This skater is ranked sixth in the world.* ○ *We leave on the sixth of June.* [C] • A sixth is one of six equal parts of something. [C] • A **sixth sense** is an ability to know something without using the ordinary five SENSES of sight, hearing, smell, touch, and taste: *My sixth sense told me something awful was going to happen.*

sixteen /sɪk'stiːn/ *number* 16 • *Jamie just turned sixteen.* ○ *a sixteen-piece picnic set* • LP NUMBERS

sixteenth /sɪk'stiːnθ/ *adj, adv* [not gradable], *n* [C] • *On this list, my name is sixteenth.* ○ *This*

is the sixteenth of August. [C] • A sixteenth is one of sixteen equal parts of something. [C]

sixty /'sɪk·sti/ *number* 60 • *My uncle is sixty.* ○ *a sixty-foot boat* • LP NUMBERS

sixties, 60s, 60's /'sɪk·stiːz/ *pl n* the numbers 60 through 69 • *The temperature is expected to be in the sixties* (= between 60° and 69°). ○ *This building was a concert hall in the sixties* (= between 1960 and 1969). ○ *Uncle Buddy is in his sixties* (= between 60 and 69 years old).

sixtieth /'sɪk·stiː·əθ/ *adj, adv* [not gradable], *n* [C] • *He finished sixtieth in the marathon.* • A sixtieth is one of sixty equal parts of something. [C]

size DEGREE /saɪz/ *n* [C/U] the degree to which something or someone is large or small • *an average size* [C] ○ *to double in size* [U] ○ *Have you seen the size of their house?* [U] ○ *Skirts come in many colors and sizes.* [C] ○ *His cigar was the size of a small sausage.* [U]

sizable /'saɪ·zə·bəl/ *adj* large • *Emanuel already has a sizable amount of money saved up for college.*

–size /,saɪz/, **–sized** /,saɪzd/ *combining form* of a (particular) size • *The house is tiny, just three medium-size rooms and a kitchen.* ○ *We can give you special rental rates on full-size* (= larger) *and mid-size* (= neither the largest nor smallest) *cars.*

size MEASURE /saɪz/ *n* [C] one of the standard measures according to which goods are made or sold • *She generally wears a size 12.* ○ *What is your shoe size?* ○ *The boxes come in many sizes.*

size up *obj*, **size** *obj* **up** /-'-/ *v adv* [M] to examine (something) in order to make a judgment or form an opinion • *After sizing up the opposition, Abe suggested a strategy.*

sizzle /'sɪz·əl/ *v* [I] to make the sound of food frying • *Doughnuts sizzled in the hot fat.* ○ *(fig.) This movie sizzles with excitement.*

sizzle /'sɪz·əl/ *n* [U] • *(fig.) Their reporting lacks sizzle* (= excitement).

skate /skeɪt/ *n* [C] a special shoe or boot with wheels for moving quickly over a smooth surface, or an ICE SKATE (= shoe with a metal blade for sliding over ice) • *I caught my skates in a rut and fell.*

ice skate

in-line skate

skates

skate /skeɪt/ *v* [I] • *She skated over to me.*
skater /'skeɪṭ·ər/ *n* [C] • *Skaters glided across the ice.*

skating /'skeɪt̬·ɪŋ/ n [U] • *She loves to go skating.*

skateboard /'skeɪt̬·bɔːrd, -boʊrd/ n [C] a short, flat board with small wheels under each end which a person stands on and moves forward by pushing one foot on the ground
skateboard /'skeɪt̬·bɔːrd, -boʊrd/ v [I] • *He skateboards to school sometimes.*

skeletal /'skel·ət̬·ᵊl/ adj of or like a SKELETON (= frame of bones) • *skeletal injuries*

skeleton /'skel·ət̬·ᵊn/ n [C] the frame of bones supporting a human or animal body • *We found a deer skeleton.* • *Almost everybody has a skeleton in the closet* (= a secret that would cause embarrassment if it were known). • *On weekends the hospital has a skeleton crew/staff* (= the smallest number of people needed to keep it working).

skeptic /'skep·tɪk/ n [C] a person who doubts the truth or value of an idea or belief
skeptical /'skep·tɪ·kəl/ adj • *They're very skeptical of his motives.*
skepticism /'skep·tə·sɪz·əm/ n [U] • *He displays a healthy skepticism toward his own beliefs.*

sketch DRAWING /sketʃ/ n [C] a simple, quickly made drawing • *a pen and ink sketch*
sketch /sketʃ/ v [I/T] • *I like to sketch.* [I]

sketch HUMOROUS PERFORMANCE /sketʃ/ n [C] a short, humorous part of a stage, television, or radio show • *She helped write a sketch for a comedy show.*

sketch DESCRIPTION /sketʃ/ n [C] a short description that does not give many details • *a biographical sketch*
sketchy /'sketʃ·i/ adj not detailed or not complete • *Officials provided only sketchy details of the trip.*

□**sketch in/out** obj, **sketch** obj **in/out** /'-'-/ v adv [M] to give a few details about (something) • *Sketch out the situation for me.*

skew /skjuː/ v [T] to cause (information or results) to be changed • *Biased questions can skew the results.*
skewed /skjuːd/ adj • *Maybe your world view is a little skewed* (= not accurate). ○ *Her smile is slightly skewed* (= not straight).

skewer /'skjuː·ər, skjʊr/ n [C] a long, thin rod that is put through pieces of food, esp. meat, for cooking
skewer /'skjuː·ər, skjʊr/ v [T] • *He skewered the onion with a toothpick.*

ski /skiː/ n [C] either of a pair of long, narrow pieces of wood or other material which curve up at the front and are fastened to boots so the person wearing them can move quickly and easily over snow
ski /skiː/ v [I] he/she/it **skis, skiing**, past **skied** • *We skied a lot when we were younger.*
skier /'skiː·ər/ n [C] • *There are lots of skiers on the slopes today.*
skiing /'skiː·ɪŋ/ n [U] • *I'm going skiing.*

skid /skɪd/ v [I] **-dd-** (esp. of a vehicle) to slide

unintentionally on a surface • *His car skidded on a patch of ice.* ○ (*fig.*) *Stock prices skidded again today* (= they dropped suddenly).
skid /skɪd/ n [C] • *The roads were slick, and we went into a skid.* ○ (*fig.*) *They won three games, then went into a skid* (= begin to lose frequently). • *His personal life is on the skids* (= failing).

Skid Row /'skɪd'roʊ/ n [C usually sing] infml a street or part of a town that is poor and dirty, where many jobless, homeless, and drunk people live

skill /skɪl/ n [C/U] a special ability to do something • *Schools often do not provide students with marketable skills.* [C] ○ *He lacked skill as a painter.* [U]
skillful /'skɪl·fəl/ adj • *Kraft was a skillful composer.*
skillfully /'skɪl·fə·li/ adv • *Some students are unable to use dictionaries skillfully.*
skilled /skɪld/ adj • *Many companies depend on skilled labor.*

skillet /'skɪl·ət/ n [C] a **frying pan**, see at FRY
• PIC PANS

skim MOVE ABOVE /skɪm/ v [I/T] **-mm-** to move quickly just above or on a surface, or to cause (something) to move above or on a surface • *Skaters skim over the ice.* [I] ○ *I skimmed a pebble across the lake.* [T]

skim READ QUICKLY /skɪm/ v [I/T] **-mm-** to read or look at (something) quickly to understand the main points, without studying it in detail • *You can't just skim the tax forms.* [T] ○ *Skim through this report.* [I]

skim REMOVE /skɪm/ v [T] **-mm-** to remove (something solid) from the surface of a liquid • *Stew the chicken, then skim the fat.* • If someone **skims off** money, they steal it from a business or government in a way they hope no one will notice. [M] • **Skim milk** (also **skimmed milk**) is milk from which the fat has been removed.

skimp /skɪmp/ v [I] to use less of something than is necessary • *The district skimps on staff training.*
skimpy /'skɪm·pi/ adj [-er/-est only] • *skimpy knowledge* • Skimpy clothing is made with only a small amount of material: *skimpy swimsuits*

skin BODY COVER /skɪn/ n [C/U] the natural outer layer that covers a person or animal • *leopard skins* [C] ○ *He had dark, leathery skin.* [U] • *She escaped by the skin of her teeth* (= only just). • *That guy is just skin and bones* (= extremely thin). • *Her confidence was only skin-deep* (= not strongly felt). • *The speed skaters were wearing skin-tight outfits* (= clothes that fit very tightly).
skin /skɪn/ v [T] **-nn-** to remove skin from (an animal), or to rub skin off (a part of the body) • *Bridget fell off her bike and skinned her knee.*

skin FRUIT / VEGETABLE COVER /skɪn/ n [C] the

outer covering of some fruits and vegetables • *potato skins*

skin SURFACE /skɪn/ *n* [C/U] a thin, solid surface • *Those airplanes have titanium skins to survive the heat.* [C]

skinhead /'skɪn·hed/ *n* [C] *disapproving* a young person, esp. a man, who has very short hair or no hair, usually one who hates black people and Jews and may act violently toward them

skinny /'skɪn·i/ *adj* [-er/-est only] very thin • *She's shorter and skinnier than me.* ○ *My bike has skinny tires.*

skinny–dip /'skɪn·iː,dɪp/ *v* [I] *infml* to swim while naked

skinny–dipping /'skɪn·iː,dɪp·ɪŋ/ *n* [U] *infml* • *Grandma took her skinny-dipping in the lake.*

skip MOVE /skɪp/ *v* [I] *-pp-* to move lightly and quickly, esp. with small dancing or jumping steps • *He skipped off to school.* • If you **skip rope** (also **jump rope**), you jump over a rope that you hold and swing over your head and under your feet or which is swung by two other people: *The kids were skipping rope on the sidewalk.*

skip LEAVE /skɪp/ *v* [I/T] *-pp-* *infml* to leave (a place) quickly • *Mark took the money and then skipped town.* [T]

skip AVOID /skɪp/ *v* [T] to not do or have (something); avoid • *Martin skipped fifth grade.* ○ *I skipped lunch today.* • If you **skip over** something you avoid reading or looking at it: *I usually skip over the boring stuff.*

skipper /'skɪp·ər/ *n* [C] *infml* the person in charge of a ship or boat

skirmish /'skɜr·mɪʃ/ *n* [C] (in wars) a short fight that is usually not planned and happens away from the main area of fighting, or any short fight • *Government troops lost a minor skirmish.* ○ *The court skirmish over video rights to the movie continues.*

skirt CLOTHING /'skɜrt/ *n* [C] a piece of women's clothing that hangs from the waist and does not have material between the legs, or the part of a dress below the waist • *She looked good in a skirt and blouse.* • PIC PLEATED SKIRT

skirt GO AROUND /'skɜrt/ *v* [T] to go around or move along the edge of (something) • *We were skirting the highways and taking the back roads.*

skit /skɪt/ *n* [C] a short, amusing play • *I wrote a skit for my English class.*

skittish /'skɪṭ·ɪʃ/ *adj* (of people and animals) nervous and easily frightened • *The kitten was really skittish.*

skulk /skʌlk/ *v* [I] to hide or move around as if trying not to be seen, usually with bad intentions • *Dogs were skulking in the alleys.*

skull /skʌl/ *n* [C] the bones of the head that surround the brain, or (*infml*) someone's mind or head • *He fractured his skull in an automobile accident.* ○ (*infml*) *Cartoons will fill your skull full of mush.* • A **skullcap** is a

small, round hat that fits closely on the top of the head, worn esp. by some religious men.

skunk /skʌŋk/ *n* [C] a small, furry, black-and-white animal with a large tail, which makes a strong, unpleasant smell as a defense when it is attacked

sky /skaɪ/ *n* the area above the earth in which clouds, the sun, and the stars can be seen • *White clouds dotted the sky.* [U] ○ *They strolled beneath clear blue skies.* [pl] • *Our expectations of him were* **sky-high** (= very high). • *Houseboats can be inexpensive, but on prices for bigger boats* **the sky is the limit** (= there is no limit). • **Skydiving** is the sport of jumping from an aircraft and falling through the air before opening a PARACHUTE (= a circular cloth with ropes), which allows the jumper to land safely. • A **skylight** is a window built into a roof to let in light. • A **skyline** is the shape of buildings or mountains and trees against the sky: *a view of the Manhattan skyline* • *The restaurant is at the top of one of the big downtown* **skyscrapers** (= very tall buildings).

skyline

skyrocket /'skaɪ,rɑk·ət/ *v* [I] (esp. of amounts) to rise extremely quickly • *The value of their business skyrocketed last year.*

slab /slæb/ *n* [C] a thick, flat, usually square or rectangular piece of a solid substance • *a marble slab*

slack NOT TIGHT /slæk/ *adj* [-er/-est only] not tight; loose • *His jaw went slack, and he looked puzzled.*

slacken /'slæk·ən/ *v* [I/T] to loosen (something), or to become loose • *His muscles slackened under the steaming shower.* [I]

slack /slæk/ *n* [U] • *There was too much slack in the cable.*

slack NOT ACTIVE /slæk/ *adj* [-er/-est only] showing a lack of activity; not busy or happening in a positive way • *The teachers are kind of slack about enforcing rules.*

slack /slæk/ *n* • If you **pick up/take up the slack**, you improve a situation by doing something that someone else has not done or not completed: *With our best player injured, other players have to pick up the slack.*

slacken /'slæk·ən/ *v* [I/T] to become slower or less busy • *Let's slacken our pace a little.* [T]

slacker /'slæk·ər/ *n* [C] *infml disapproving* a person who does not work hard • *Dad says my boyfriend's a slacker.*

▫ **slack off** /slæk'ɔːf/ *v adv* [I] to work less hard or to be less than is usual or necessary • *Workers tend to slack off on Mondays and Fridays.*

slacks /slæks/ *pl n* a pair of pants • *They both wore gray slacks and white shirts.*

slag /slæg/ *n* [U] waste material produced when removing unwanted substances from metals

slain /sleɪn/ *past participle of* SLAY

slake /sleɪk/ *v* [T] to satisfy (a thirst or a desire) • *They slaked their thirst at a nearby bar.*

slam /slæm/ *v* [I/T] **-mm-** to move against a hard surface with force and usually a loud noise, or to cause (something) to move this way • *The truck slammed into an oncoming car.* [I] ○ *Ray slammed the door shut.* [T]

slam /slæm/ *n* [C usually sing] • *He closed the door with a slam.*

slammer /'slæm·ər/ *n* [U] *slang* prison • *He's doing ten years in the slammer.*

slander /'slæn·dər/ *n* [C/U] a false, spoken statement about someone which damages their reputation, or the making of such a statement • *Political campaigns are full of shameless slander.* [U] • Compare LIBEL.

slander /'slæn·dər/ *v* [T] • *The team name— Lady Reds—is not meant to slander women.*

slanderous /'slæn·də·rəs/ *adj* • *McCarthy unleashed slanderous accusations in every direction.*

slang /slæŋ/ *n* [U] very informal language that is used esp. in speech by particular groups of people and which sometimes includes words that are not polite • *computer/teenage slang*

slangy /'slæŋ·i/ *adj* • *a slangy style of writing*

slant LEAN /slænt/ *v* [I] to lean in a diagonal direction, or to cause (something) to slope • *Rays of sunlight slanted down on her.*

slant /slænt/ *n* [U] • *Most ocean beaches are on a slant.*

slant OPINION /slænt/ *n* [C] someone's opinion about a subject that is expressed by ignoring or hiding some information and emphasizing other information • *He put his own liberal slant on the general's writings.*

slant /slænt/ *v* [T] • *He was known to slant reports, writing what his boss wanted to hear.*

slap HIT /slæp/ *v* [T] **-pp-** to hit (someone) quickly with the flat part of the hand • *In the movie, he kisses her and she slaps his face.*

slap /slæp/ *n* [C] • *She testified that she had only given her child a slap and had not meant to hurt her.* • A **slap in the face** is an insult, esp. when it comes as a surprise: *Not even acknowledging our invitation was a slap in the face.* • A **slap on the wrist** is a small punishment, esp. when a more severe punishment is deserved: *They rob someone on the street and they get a slap on the wrist—thirty days in jail.*

slap PUT QUICKLY /slæp/ *v* [T always + adv/prep] to put or move (something) in a quick or careless manner • *Once I got to the counter, I slapped down my passport.*

slapdash /'slæp·dæʃ/ *adj* done or made hurriedly and carelessly

slapstick /'slæp·stɪk/ *n* [U] a type of acting intended to be amusing because of the timing of fast physical actions, typically of someone falling or being hit by something or someone

slash REDUCE /slæʃ/ *v* [T] to reduce (an amount) greatly • *Airfares have been slashed on most domestic routes.*

slash /slæʃ/ *n* [C] • *a slash in prices*

slash CUT /slæʃ/ *v* [I/T] to cut (someone or something) with a sharp blade in a quick, swinging action • *He threatened to slash his wrists with a knife.* [T]

slash SLOPING LINE /slæʃ/ *n* [C] a mark in the form of a sloping line (/), used in signs to mean not permitted, and to separate numbers or words • *The no-smoking sign had a red slash mark through a picture of a burning cigarette.* ○ *Fractions are often written with slashes, for example 2/3.*

SLASH [/]

The slash can be used to mean "or."

a doctor gets to know his/her patients very well. • *Payment by cash/credit card only.* • *Soup and/or salad comes with dinner.*

The slash is used to mean "and" or "combined with."

a TV writer/producer • *a toaster/oven* • *social/cultural changes*

A slash can show that two expressions have the same meaning.

Add 4 oz/115 g sugar, mix.

Slashes are often used to separate the numbers in a written date.

10/22/98

A slash can mean "for each" and is said as "per" or "a."

This car gets about 40 miles/gallon. • *The movers charge $20/hour or $100/day.*

Slashes separate lines of poetry when they are not written on different lines.

The soul selects her own society/Then shuts the door.

---

slat /slæt/ *n* [C] a thin, narrow piece of wood, plastic, or metal used to make such things as floors, furniture, or window coverings • *She closed the slats of the Venetian blinds.*

slate ROCK /sleɪt/ *n* [U] a dark gray rock that can be divided into wide, flat, thin pieces

slate SCHEDULE /sleɪt/ *v* [T] to schedule or expect to happen • *The festival is slated to run here January 28th to February 7th.*

slate POLITICS /sleɪt/ *n* [C] the people of a particular political party who are trying to be elected to offices in government in an election • *The Republicans are expected to announce their slate tomorrow.*

slaughter KILLING ANIMALS /'slɔːt̬·ər/ *n* [U] the killing of animals for their meat • A **slaughterhouse** is a place where animals are killed for their meat.

slaughter /ˈslɔːt̬·ər/ *v* [T] • *The cattle were slaughtered under federal inspection.*

slaughter KILLING PEOPLE /ˈslɔːt̬·ər/ *n* [U] the killing of large numbers of people, or the killing of large numbers of animals, intentionally or unintentionally, through cruelty or carelessness • *We must find ways of reducing the slaughter on the highways* (= deaths of many people in car accidents).

slaughter /ˈslɔːt̬·ər/ *v* [T] • *They slaughtered everyone in the village—men, women, and children.* • (*infml*) In sports and other competitions, to slaughter is to defeat easily: *The Red Sox slaughtered the Yankees in last night's baseball game, winning 12 to 0.*

slave /sleɪv/ *n* [C] a person who is legally owned by someone else and has no personal freedom • *Born a slave in 1760, he was sold as a child to a farmer in Delaware.*

slavery /ˈsleɪ·və·ri/ *n* [U] the condition of being legally owned by someone else, or the system in which some people are owned by others

slavish /ˈsleɪ·vɪʃ/ *adj* characterized by complete obedience • *He was criticized for his slavish devotion to rules and regulations.*

slaw /slɔː/ *n* [U] *short form of* COLESLAW

slay /sleɪ/ *v* [T] *past simple* **slew** /sluː/, *past part* **slain** /sleɪn/ to kill, esp. violently • *Four terrorists were slain in gun battles with police.*

sleazy /ˈsliː·zi/ *adj* morally bad and low in quality, but trying to attract people by a showy appearance or false manner • *It was a sleazy neighborhood with honky-tonk bars and neon-fronted strip joints.*

sled /sled/ *n* [C] a vehicle used for carrying people or goods over snow and ice, having narrow strips of wood or metal on the bottom instead of wheels • *The children are playing in the snow with their sleds.*

sled /sled/ *v* [I] **-dd-** to ride on a sled over snow or ice, esp. in play

sledgehammer /ˈsledʒ·hæm·ər/ *n* [C] a large, heavy hammer with a long handle, used for jobs like breaking stones or hitting posts into the ground

sleek /sliːk/ *adj* [-er/-est only] (esp. of hair or shapes) smooth, usually curved and shiny, and therefore looking healthy and attractive • *The two horses paused, their sleek sides heaving gently as they waited.*

sleep /sliːp/ *n* [U] the resting state in which the body is not active and the mind is unconscious • *I usually sit up in bed and watch the TV news before going to sleep.* • **Sleepwalking** is the activity of a person who gets out of bed and walks around while they are sleeping.

sleep /sliːp/ *v* [I/T] *past* **slept** /slept/ • *I was too excited to sleep much that night.* [I] ◦ *The boat sleeps four* (= has space for four people to sleep) *comfortably.* [T] • (*infml*) If someone **sleeps like a log**, noise or the activity of people near them will not wake them. • If you

sleep it off, you stop being drunk by sleeping for as long as it takes to feel not drunk. • When someone has an important decision to make, they sometimes say that they are going to **sleep on it**, meaning that want more time to think about it and will possibly decide the next day after a night's sleep: *Don't give me an answer now—sleep on it and tell me whenever you're ready.* • A **sleeping bag** is a large bag that you can sleep in when you are outside, and that has layers of material to keep you warm in cold weather. • A **sleeping pill** is a pill that you take to help you sleep better.

sleeper /ˈsliː·pər/ *n* [C] • If someone is a light sleeper, they wake easily, and if they are a heavy sleeper, they do not. • A sleeper is also a person or thing that is unexpectedly successful: *We almost gave up on this line of merchandise, but its a real sleeper—it keeps selling.*

sleepless /ˈsliː·pləs/ *adj* [not gradable] without sleeping, or without being able to sleep • *I've spent so many sleepless nights worrying about him.*

sleepy /ˈsliː·pi/ *adj* tired and needing sleep • A **sleepyhead** is a person, esp. a child, who is tired and looks as if they want to sleep: *Come on, sleepyhead, it's time for bed.*

sleepily /ˈsliː·pə·li/ *adv* [not gradable] • *She stumbled sleepily into the bathroom.*

□ **sleep around** /-ˈ--ˈ-/ *v adv* [I] *infml* to have sex with a lot of different people without having a close or long relationship with any of them

□ **sleep over** /-ˈ--ˈ/ *v adv* [I] to stay the night in someone else's home • *If you don't want to drive home this late, you're welcome to sleep over.*

sleepover /ˈsliː·poʊ·vər/ *n* [C] a child's visit to a friend's home in which the child spends the night • *We don't have to pick up Adam from school today because he's going home with Jonathan for a sleepover.*

□ **sleep together** /-ˈ--ˌ--/ *v adv* [I] (of two people who are not married) to have sex • *They started sleeping together a couple of weeks after they met.*

□ **sleep with** /-ˈ--/ *v prep* [T] to have sex with (a person you are not married to)

sleet /sliːt/ *n* [U] rain that is partly frozen • *The snow and sleet made driving hazardous.*

sleeve /sliːv/ *n* [C] the part of a piece of clothing that covers some or all of the arm • *I wore the black dress with the short sleeves.*

sleeveless /ˈsliːv·ləs/ *adj* [not gradable] (of clothing) without sleeves • *a sleeveless blouse/dress*

sleigh /sleɪ/ *n* [C] a large SLED (= vehicle for traveling over snow and ice) pulled by animals, esp. horses • *a sleigh ride*

sleight of hand /ˌslaɪt·əvˈhænd/ *n* [U] quickness and skill with the hands when performing tricks that seem to be magic

slender /ˈslen·dər/ *adj* thin and delicate, often

in a way that is attractive • *She had the slender figure of a dancer.*

slept KILL /slept/ *past simple and past participle of* sleep

sleuth /sluːθ/ *n* [C] *literary* someone who discovers information about crimes

slew KILL /sluː/ *past simple of* SLAY

slew LARGE AMOUNT /sluː/ *n* [C usually sing] *infml* a large amount or number • *There's a whole slew of new movies that I want to see.*

slice /slaɪs/ *n* [C] a flat, often thin piece of food that has been cut from a larger piece • *a slice of bread/cake/pizza* • (*fig.*) A slice is also any small part that has been separated from something larger: *She demanded a slice of the profits.* • If you describe a story as a **slice of** something, you mean that it shows believable, ordinary details of the lives of the people mentioned: *The drama is a slice of life about Puerto Ricans living in the Bronx.*

slice /slaɪs/ *v* [T] to cut (something) into thin pieces, or to cut one or more thin pieces from (something) • *Slice the onions and fry them in butter.* • **Any way/no matter how you slice it** means there is only one possible result: *No matter how you slice it, they just can't afford to go on spending as much as they are.* • PIC CUT

slick SKILLFUL /slɪk/ *adj* operating or performing skillfully and effectively and without seeming to try hard • *Maz was such a slick fielder, one of the best in baseball.* • Slick can sometimes mean skillful and effective but lacking in sincerity: *He was a slick politician with an answer for everything.*

slick SMOOTH /slɪk/ *adj* having a smooth, shiny surface so that you tend to slide when walking or riding on it • *roads slick with ice*

slick /slɪk/ *v* [T] to cause (hair) to be smooth and shiny • *His hair was slicked back.*

slicker /ˈslɪk.ər/ *n* [C] a waterproof coat used in wet weather

slide MOVE EASILY /slaɪd/ *v past* **slid** /slɪd/ to cause (something) to move easily over a surface, or to move in this way • *My mother slid into the car seat next to me.* [I] ○ *He slid his hand into his back pocket.* [T]

slide /slaɪd/ *n* [C] a structure used by children in their play that has a smooth, sloping side which lets them move down quickly from the top to the ground

slide GET WORSE /slaɪd/ *v* [I] *past* **slid** /slɪd/ to go into a worse state, often through lack of control or care • *The stock market crashed in October 1929 and the nation slid into a depression.*

slide /slaɪd/ *n* [C usually sing] • *He felt he was on a downward slide in which nothing was going right in his life.*

slide PHOTOGRAPHIC FILM /slaɪd/ *n* [C] a small piece of photographic film in a frame which, when light is passed through it, shows a larger image on a screen • *The art history professor showed us slides of the Parthenon today.* •

A **slide projector** *is a machine that shines a light through a slide and special glass and produces a larger image on a screen.* • (*specialized*) In scientific study, a slide is a small piece of glass on which you put something in order to look at it through a MICROSCOPE (= device that makes small objects look larger) and see its structure.

slight SMALL IN AMOUNT /slaɪt/ *adj* [-er/-est only] small in amount or degree • *He speaks with a slight French accent.* ○ *She had a slight cold, but wasn't feeling too bad.*

slightly /ˈslaɪt·li/ *adv* • *She's slightly taller than her sister.*

slight THIN /slaɪt/ *adj* [-er/-est only] (of people) thin and delicate • *He was a young man of slight build with sensitive eyes and expressive hands.*

slight INSULT /slaɪt/ *v* [T] to insult (someone) by not paying attention or by treating them as if they are not important • *He slighted his wife by neglecting to introduce her.*

slim /slɪm/ *adj* [-er/-est only] **-mm-** thin, or (esp. of people) attractively thin • *She's published several slim volumes of poetry.* • Slim also means only a little or not much: *Coaches told him his chances of making the team were slim at best.*

slim down /ˈ-ˈ-/ *v adv* [I] (of people) to become thinner or (of things) smaller • *Many firms have slimmed down, consolidating offices and closing some.*

slime /slaɪm/ *n* [U] a smooth, sticky, liquid substance usually considered unpleasant • *A greenish slime covered the surface of the water near the sewer pipe.*

slimy /ˈslaɪ·mi/ *adj* [-er/-est only] • *slimy seaweed* • If you describe a person as slimy, you mean that they appear to be friendly but cannot be trusted and are not sincere: *He was really a slimy character.*

sling THROW /slɪŋ/ *v* [T always + adv/prep] *past* **slung** /slʌŋ/ to throw or drop (something) with a quick, usually careless motion • *She came in and slung her coat over a chair.* • A **slingshot** is a Y-shaped stick with a piece of elastic fixed to the top parts, used esp. by children for shooting small stones.

sling SUPPORTING DEVICE /slɪŋ/ *n* [C] a device used to support, lift, or carry objects, often by ropes or straps • *The helicopter lowered a sling to the boat and rescued the sailor.* • (*medical*) A sling is a piece of material tied around the neck and providing support for a broken or damaged arm while it heals: *They put his arm in a sling.*

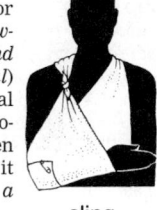
sling

slink /slɪŋk/ *v* [I always + adv/prep] *past* **slunk** /slʌŋk/ to walk or leave quietly, esp. because you do not want to be noticed or are ashamed of something • *I was so embarrassed that I tried to slink away.*

slinky /'slɪŋ·ki/ *adj* (of women's clothes) fitting the body closely in a way that is sexually attractive, or (of a woman) sexually attractive • *She wore a slinky black knit dress.*

slip SLIDE /slɪp/ *v* [I] **-pp-** to slide suddenly and without intending to • *He slipped on an icy sidewalk and broke his hip.* ○ *The blanket began to slip off my shoulders.*

slippery /'slɪp·ə·ri/ *adj* • *The sidewalks were slippery with ice.* • Slippery also means not certain: *Choosing the perfect juror can be a slippery matter.* • (*infml*) A person who is slippery is someone you feel you cannot trust: *He is a slippery fellow, full of schemes.*

slip MOVE EASILY /slɪp/ *v* [I/T] **-pp-** to move easily and quietly so you are not noticed, or to move (something) easily into position • *He was able to slip out of the room without disturbing anyone.* [I always + adv/prep] ○ *Ben slipped the credit card into the machine.* [T always + adv/prep] ○ (*fig.*) *While I napped in my chair, the hours slipped by.* [I always + adv/prep] • If you slip something to someone, you give it to them without attracting attention: *I slipped some money to the maitre d' to get a table.* [T always + adv/prep] ○ *She slipped her hand into his.* [T always + adv/prep]

slip GET WORSE /slɪp/ *v* [I] **-pp-** to change to a worse state or condition • *We've slipped even further behind schedule.* ○ *After slipping into a coma, he never woke up.*

slip PIECE OF PAPER /slɪp/ *n* [C] a small piece of paper • *You get a slip from the cash machine when you take out money.*

slip MISTAKE /slɪp/ *n* [C] a careless mistake • *She has made some slips lately that show she's thinking about other things.* • A **slip of the tongue** is a mistake made when what someone says is different from what they meant to say: *Just one slip of the tongue caused me big trouble.* • A **slip-up** is also a mistake: *That slip-up cost a lot of money.*

slip /slɪp/ *v* [I/T] **-pp-** • *They slipped up and ordered the wrong part for the car.* [I] ○ *My daughter let the news slip that she is going to get married.* [+ *that* clause]

slip UNDERWEAR /slɪp/ *n* [C] women's underwear that is shaped like a skirt or a dress

slip ESCAPE /slɪp/ *v* [I/T] **-pp-** to get away from or get free from (something) • *The dog slipped its leash and ran off.* [T] ○ *The ball slipped through my fingers.* [I always + adv/prep] • If something **slips** your **mind**, you forget it: *I was supposed to attend the meeting, but it completely slipped my mind.* • You can't let this opportunity **slip through** your **fingers** (= pass without being acted on)! • If something **slips through the cracks**, it is not noticed: *Little details often slip through the cracks.*

□**slip away** /'--'-/ *v adv* [I] to leave without being noticed • *Shortly before midnight, he*

slipped away to meet her. • If an opportunity slips away, it is no longer available.

□**slip into** /'-,--/ *v adv* [T] to put (clothing) on quickly and easily • *Nancy slipped into her pajamas.*

□**slip off** *obj*, **slip** *obj* **off** /'-'-/ *v adv* [M] to remove (clothing) quickly and easily • *She slipped off her gloves.*

□**slip on** *obj*, **slip** *obj* **on** /'-'-/ *v adv* [M] to put (clothing) on quickly and easily • *After breakfast, we slipped on our coats.*

□**slip out of** /'-'--/ *v adv* [T] to remove (clothing) quickly and easily • *Rose slipped out of her work clothes.*

slipcover /'slɪp,kʌv·ər/ *n* [C] a cover for a chair or SOFA (= seat for two or more people) that is easily removed

slipper /'slɪp·ər/ *n* [C] a soft, comfortable shoe worn inside the house

slippery /'slɪp·ə·ri/ *adj* • See at SLIP SLIDE.

slipshod /'slɪp·ʃɑd/ *adj* showing lack of effort and attention; careless • *slipshod repairs*

slit /slɪt/ *v* [T] **slitting**, *past* **slit** to make a straight, narrow cut in (something) • *I slit open the envelope with a knife.*

slit /slɪt/ *n* [C] • *Cut slits in the piecrust.* ○ *Her eyes are like little slits.*

slither /'slɪð·ər/ *v* [I always + adv/prep] to move by twisting or sliding • *A long snake slithered toward them.*

sliver /'slɪv·ər/ *n* [C] a thin, sharp piece, usually broken off something larger • *The glass smashed into slivers.* • A sliver is also any narrow or thin piece: *I just want a sliver of cake.*

slob /slɑb/ *n* [C] *infml* a person who is messy, unattractive, and rude • *Some guys are real slobs.* • A slob is also someone who is just an ordinary person: *a working slob*

slobber /'slɑb·ər/ *v* [I] to let SALIVA (= the liquid in the mouth) or other liquid run out of the mouth • *No one likes to have a dog slobber on them.*

slog /slɑg, slɔːg/ *v* [always + adv/prep] **-gg-** to walk heavily and with difficulty, or to work hard on something difficult • *I slogged through a mess of paperwork.* [I] ○ *We slogged our way through the mud.* [T]

slogan /'sloʊ·gən/ *n* [C] a short, easily remembered phrase used to characterize something, esp. a political idea or a product • *That old campaign slogan really means that there should be jobs and enough food for all citizens.*

slop /slɑp/ *v* [I/T] **-pp-** (of a liquid) to flow or fall over the edge of a container, or to cause (a liquid) to do this • *The wine slopped onto the tablecloth.* [I]

slope /sloʊp/ *n* [C] a surface that rises at an angle, esp. a hill or mountain, or the angle at which something rises • *Students learn to ski on gentle slopes in a straight line.* ○ *Snow had settled on some of the higher slopes.*

slope /sloʊp/ *v* [I] • *The path slopes down to the house.*

sloppy CARELESS /ˈslɑp·i/ *adj* messy or careless • *sloppy clothes* ○ *a sloppy administrator*

sloppily /ˈslɑp·ə·li/ *adv* • *We played sloppily and lost the game.*

sloppiness /ˈslɑp·i:·nəs/ *n* [U] • *Such remarkable sloppiness was the result of too much hurry.*

sloppy TOO WET /ˈslɑp·i/ *adj* very wet, esp. unpleasantly wet • *a sloppy kiss* ○ *sloppy weather*

slosh /slɑʃ, slɔːʃ/ *v* [always + adv/prep] (of a liquid) to hit against the inside of a container, or to cause (liquid) to move around in this way • *Water sloshed over the sides of the pool as the children jumped in.* [I] ○ *Jim sloshed wine on his jacket by pouring too fast.* [T]

sloshed /slɑʃt, slɔːʃt/ *adj slang* feeling the effects of drinking alcohol; drunk

slot HOLE /slɑt/ *n* [C] a narrow hole or opening • *Drop the letter in the mail slot.* • A **slot machine** is a machine on which you play a game of chance each time you put a coin in its slot: *Bob's mom likes to play the slot machines.*

slot POSITION /slɑt/ *n* [C] a place or position available to someone or something • *Perry will fill one of the open slots on the commission.* ○ *Shaap's program can be heard in the same time slot every morning.*

slot /slɑt/ *v* [T] **-tt-** to put (someone or something) in a particular position • *Weather reports are slotted between commercials.*

sloth /slɔːθ, sloʊθ/ *n* [C] an animal that moves very slowly and spends much of its time hanging upside down from trees

slouch /slaʊtʃ/ *v* [I] to stand, sit, or walk with the shoulders and head bent forward • *In a bad mood, the boy slouched off to the beach.*

slouch /slaʊtʃ/ *n* [C] • *He's developed a slouch from leaning over his books all day.*

slough off *obj*, **slough** *obj* **off** /ˈslʌfˈɔːf/ *v adv* [M] to get rid of (something, esp. a skin or shell) • If you slough something off, you treat it as unimportant or do not take it seriously: *Politicians sloughed off the issue.*

slovenly /ˈslʌv·ən·li/ *adj* messy, dirty, or careless • *slovenly work* ○ *a slovenly housekeeper*

slow /sloʊ/ *adj* [-er/-est only] lacking speed; not fast or quick • *He was far too slow to catch me.* ○ *We were slow to understand how we could use computers in our work.* • A clock or watch that is slow shows a time that is earlier than the correct time. • A person who is slow does not understand or learn things quickly: *a class for slower students* • **Slow motion** is action on film that is made to appear slower than it was when it happened: *a slow motion replay*

slow /sloʊ/ *v* [I/T] • *Traffic slowed to a crawl.* [I] ○ *Drinking slowed my development as a writer.* [T]

slow /sloʊ/ *adv* [-er/-est only] • *You're driving too slow.*

slowly /ˈsloʊ·li/ *adv* • *The medication took effect slowly.*

□ **slow down** (*obj*), **slow** (*obj*) **down** /ˈ-ˈ-/ *v adv* [I/M] to move slower, or to cause (someone or something) to move slower • *The car slowed down, then suddenly pulled away.* [I] ○ *We tried to slow the guy down.* [M]

slowdown /ˈsloʊ·daʊn/ *n* [C] a reduction in speed or activity • *Consumer buying has picked up again after a summer slowdown.*

sludge /slʌdʒ/ *n* [U] wet dirt, or any other thick, wet substance • *The dirty water left a layer of sludge in the bottom of the pail.*

slug CREATURE /slʌɡ/ *n* [C] a small animal with a soft body like a SNAIL without a shell • If you say that someone is a slug, you mean that they would rather do very little or nothing at all: *I suppose you think I'm a slug for not helping.* • PIC SNAIL

sluggish /ˈslʌɡ·ɪʃ/ *adj* moving, acting, or working with less than normal speed or energy • *a sluggish economy* ○ *a sluggish drain*

slug BULLET /slʌɡ/ *n* [C] *infml* a bullet

slug DRINK /slʌɡ/ *n* [C] *infml* a mouthful of a drink, esp. an alcoholic drink • *She took a long slug from her glass.*

slug HIT /slʌɡ/ *v* [T] **-gg-** *infml* to hit (someone) hard; PUNCH • *She didn't slug me for what I said.* • If you slug a baseball, you hit it very hard. • If you **slug** something **out**, you fight or argue fiercely until one person wins or agreement is reached: *We've been slugging this out for years.*

slug COIN /slʌɡ/ *n* [C] a piece of metal used instead of a coin in a machine • *The new toll machines will reject slugs.*

slum /slʌm/ *n* [C] a very poor and crowded area of a city • *Slums are a breeding ground for crime.*

slum /slʌm/ *v* [I] **-mm-** *infml* to visit a place where poor people are likely to be • *She and her friends liked to go slumming to get a small taste of poverty.*

slumber /ˈslʌm·bər/ *n* [C/U] *esp. literary* sleep • *She felt as if she had awakened from a long slumber.* [C] • A **slumber party** is a party in which a group of friends, esp. girls, sleep at one friend's home.

slumber /ˈslʌm·bər/ *v* [I] *esp. literary* • *The small town slumbered in the moonlight.*

slump FALL /slʌmp/ *v* [I always + adv/prep] to fall heavily and suddenly • *She slumped to the floor in a faint.*

slump BEND /slʌmp/ *v* [I always + adv/prep] to stand or sit bent over, with the head and shoulders forward; SLOUCH • *The old man slumped in his chair, asleep.* ○ *We both slumped against the wall.*

slump REDUCE SUDDENLY /slʌmp/ *v* [I] to fall suddenly in price, amount, or value • *Home computer sales slumped dramatically last year.*

slump /slʌmp/ *n* [C] • *a slump in the economy* ○ *The team is in a slump this year.*

slung /slʌŋ/ *past simple and past participle of* SLING

slunk /slʌŋk/ *past simple and past participle of* SLINK

slur PRONOUNCE BADLY /slɜr/ *v* [I/T] **-rr-** to pronounce (words) in a way that is not clear, esp. by combining syllables or words • *How can you possibly understand someone who slurs his speech?* [T]

slur /slɜr/ *n* [C] • *The drug made her speak with a slur.*

slur INSULT /slɜr/ *n* [C] words intended to insult someone or injure their reputation • *Racial slurs were scrawled on the wall.*

slurp /slɜrp/ *v* [I/T] to make sucking noises while eating or drinking • *I wanted to tell him not to slurp his soup.* [T]

slush /slʌʃ/ *n* [U] snow or ice that has started to melt • *The city's streets were covered with dirty, gray slush.*

slushy /'slʌʃ·i/ *adj* • *Slushy snow can be very slippery.*

slut /slʌt/ *n* [C] *disapproving rude slang* a woman who has sexual relationships with a lot of men, esp. for money

sly /slaɪ/ *adj* **slyer, slyest** secretive, by hiding true opinions or intentions, or dishonest • *She thought that by being sly, she could fool people.* ○ *A cat can be a very sly animal.*

sly /slaɪ/ *n* [U] • Something done **on the sly** is done secretly: *She's been seeing him on the sly.*

slyly /'slaɪ·li/ *adv* • *He winked slyly and lowered his voice, as if he had some secret to reveal.*

smack HIT FORCEFULLY /smæk/ *v* [I/T] to hit (someone or something) forcefully, usually making a loud noise • *She smacked him across the face.* [T] ○ *The car spun around and smacked into a tree.* [I] ○ *She smacked the ball over the fence.* [T] ○ *He smacked his hand down on the table to get our attention.* [M] • If you **smack** your **lips**, you make a noise to show that something is good by opening and closing your lips.

smack /smæk/ *n* [C] • *She got a bruise from that smack.*

smack DIRECTLY /smæk/ *adv* [not gradable] directly and with force • *He stopped the car so suddenly, the car behind ran smack into him.* • If something is **smack dab** in a place or time, it is exactly there: *You called smack dab in the middle of dinner.*

smack DRUG /smæk/ *n* [U] *slang* HEROIN (= a powerful illegal drug)

□ **smack of** /'--/ *v prep* [T] to show or seem to have (a characteristic or quality) • *Their behavior smacks of very bad judgment.*

small LESS /smɔːl/ *adj* [-er/-est only] not big; less in size or amount than is average • *a small business* ○ *small lunches* ○ *He's small for his age.* ○ *Those jackets come in small, medium, and large sizes.* • The **small of** your **back** is the back below the waist where it curves in slightly. • **Small claims court** is a court where legal action can be taken against a person who owes a small amount of money. • A

small fortune is an amount of money that seems to be a lot: *Getting the car fixed will cost a small fortune.* • *(disapproving)* Someone who is **small-minded** does not like different ideas or things that are not familiar. • If something is **small-scale**, it

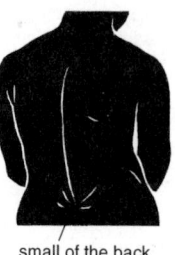
small of the back

is small, esp. when compared to other things like it: *The house is like a small-scale castle.* • The **small screen** is television: *His novel has been adapted for the small screen.*

small /smɔːl/ *adv* [-er/-est only] • *The ingredients are printed so small I can hardly read them.*

small YOUNG /smɔːl/ *adj* [-er/-est only] (of children) very young • *His mother died when he was small.*

small LACKING IMPORTANCE /smɔːl/ *adj* [-er/-est only] not having much importance or effect • *a small problem* ○ *a small part in a movie* • Coins of little value are called **small change**. • *(infml)* If someone or something is **small potatoes**, they seem unimportant: *Compared to her problems, mine seem like small potatoes.* • **Small talk** is social conversation about unimportant things, often between people who do not know each other well: *I hate conversation that is nothing but small talk.* • Someone or something that is **small-time** is not very important or successful: *a small-time gambler* • **Small-town** describes someone who has limited experience of the world or something that is simple: *a small-town girl* ○ *small-town politics*

small LETTER SIZE /smɔːl/ *adj* [not gradable] (of a letter of the alphabet) LOWERCASE • Compare CAPITAL (LETTER).

smallpox /'smɔːl·pɑks/ *n* [U] an extremely infectious and deadly viral disease that causes fever and spots on the skin • *smallpox vaccinations*

smart INTELLIGENT /smɑrt/ *adj* [-er/-est only] intelligent, or able to think and understand quickly in difficult situations • *Jed's smart enough to get A's in this class.* ○ *Her daughter is smarter than she is.* ○ *Ginny is a very smart kid.* ○ *Quitting that job was a smart move.* • Smart devices are ones that operate using computers: *smart bombs* ○ *a smart card* • *(infml)* A **smart-aleck** is an annoying person who thinks they are smarter then other people: *That kid's a real smart-aleck.* • **Smart money** is money invested by experienced people who know a lot about investing money.

smart STING /smɑrt/ *v* [I] to feel a stinging pain • *Abby's eyes smarted from the smoke.* ○ *(fig.) Sacramento is still smarting from the loss* (= is upset by it).

smart STYLISH /smɑrt/ *adj* [-er/-est only] *dated* having a clean, neat, stylish appearance • *She wore smart dresses and dashing hats.*

smartly /ˈsmɑrt·li/ *adv* • *Sid dresses very smartly.* • Smartly also means quickly: *Soldiers marched smartly up the avenue.*

smash BREAK /smæʃ/ *v* [I/T] to break into small pieces, esp. by hitting or throwing • *Some kids smashed her bedroom window.* [T] ◦ *Her cup fell and smashed to pieces on the stone floor.* [I] ◦ *Police had to smash the door down to get into the house.* [M] ◦ *The band reportedly smashed up their hotel room.* [M]

smash /smæʃ/ *n* [U] • *I heard a smash and glass breaking.*

smash HIT /smæʃ/ *v* [I/T] to hit or move with force against something hard, usually causing damage or injury • *She smashed her right knee in the accident.* [T] ◦ *His car flipped over and smashed into a tree.* [I]

smash /smæʃ/ *n* [C] a forcefully hit ball • *Robinson hit a smash to my left.*

smash DESTROY /smæʃ/ *v* [T] to defeat or destroy completely • *The government smashed the rebellion.*

smash (hit) /ˈsmæʃ (ˈhɪt)/ *n* [C] a popular and successful song, play, or movie • *a smash hit album* ◦ *His first movie was a box-office smash.*

smashed /smæʃt/ *adj slang* feeling the effects of drinking alcohol; drunk

smattering /ˈsmæt̬·ə·rɪŋ/ *n* [C usually sing] a slight knowledge of something, or a small amount • *I know a smattering of German.* ◦ *There was a smattering of boos when he was introduced.*

smear SPREAD /smɪr/ *v* [T always + adv/prep] to spread (something soft or wet) over a surface • *Mom smeared peanut butter and grape jelly on bagels for lunch.*

smear /smɪr/ *n* [C] • *He had a smear of paint on his shirt.*

smear ACCUSATION /smɪr/ *n* [C] an accusation made publicly with the intention of harming a person's reputation • *Throughout the election he had to contend with smears about his personal life.* ◦ *She was upset by the smear tactics used by her opponents.*

smear /smɪr/ *v* [T] • *He was smeared in the newspapers.*

smell ABILITY /smel/ *n* [U] the ability of the nose to discover the presence of a substance in the air • *Smell is one of the five senses.* ◦ *Dogs have a very good sense of smell.*

smell /smel/ *v* [I/T] • *I have a cold and I can't smell anything.* [T]

smell CHARACTERISTIC /smel/ *n* [C] the characteristic of something that can be recognized or noticed using the nose • *a sweet/strong/unpleasant smell* ◦ *the smell of flowers/perfume/coffee/paint* ◦ *I woke up to the smell of bacon and eggs.* ◦ *I wish we could get rid of that smell in the garage.*

smell /smel/ *v* • *My hands smell of onions.* [I]

◦ *It smells like you've been baking in here.* [I] ◦ *That soup smells good.* [L] ◦ *Your feet smell* (= have an unpleasant smell). [I] • If something **smells fishy**, it does not seem to be truthful or honest: *His excuses smell fishy to me.*

smelly /ˈsmel·i/ *adj* having an unpleasant smell • *smelly feet* ◦ *The basement is damp and smelly.*

smell DISCOVER /smel/ *v* [T] to become aware of or to discover (something) using the nose • *Just smell this perfume!* ◦ *She smelled something burning.* ◦ *(fig.) Brenda can smell trouble a mile off.* (= knows when there will be trouble.) • If you **smell a rat**, you believe something is wrong: *When I saw those strangers being shown around the plant last week, I smelled a rat.*

smell /smel/ *n* [U] • *Have a smell of this thyme.*

smelt /smelt/ *v* [T] to obtain (a metal) from rock by heating it to a very high temperature

smidgen /ˈsmɪdʒ·ən/ *n* [U] *infml* a very small amount • *I have a smidgen of hope that things will turn out all right.*

smile /smaɪl/ *n* [C] a facial expression in which the ends of the mouth curve up slightly, often with the lips moving apart so that the teeth can be seen, expressing esp. happiness, pleasure, amusement, or a friendly feeling • *a big/happy/pretty smile* ◦ *a smile of joy/satisfaction/amusement* ◦ *We exchanged smiles as we passed in the hallway.*

smile /smaɪl/ *v* [I/T] • *I couldn't help smiling.* [I] ◦ *When he smiled at me, I knew everything was OK.* [I] ◦ *She smiled to herself.* [I] ◦ *He smiled a happy smile.* [T]

smiley /ˈsmaɪ·li/ *adj infml* • *He's a very smiley, friendly baby.* • *(infml)* A **smiley face** is a drawing that represents a person smiling.

smirk /smɜrk/ *v* [I] to smile in a way that expresses satisfaction with yourself or pleasure about having done something or knowing something that is not known by someone else • *When she told him he was cool, he just smirked.*

smirk /smɜrk/ *n* [C] • *Her lips curled into a smirk.*

smithereens /ˌsmɪð·əˈriːnz/ *pl n* a lot of small, broken pieces • *The vase smashed to smithereens when it fell.*

smitten /ˈsmɪt̬·ən/ *adj* [not gradable] strongly influenced by someone or feeling the effects of something • *He's clearly smitten with publicity.* ◦ *Howard was smitten by her beauty.*

smock /smɑk/ *n* [C] a piece of clothing like a long shirt that is worn loosely over other clothing to protect it when working • *an artist's smock* ◦ *a painting/gardening smock*

smog /smɑg, smɔːg/ *n* [C/U] air pollution caused by smoke or chemicals mixing with fog • *We get a lot of smog downtown.* [U] ◦ *A poisonous smog killed 20 people.* [C]

smoggy /ˈsmɑg·i, ˈsmɔː·gi/ *adj* • *a smoggy city/day*

smoke CLOUDY AIR /smoʊk/ *n* [U] a cloudy gray or black mixture of air and very small pieces of carbon produced by something that is burning • *cigarette/tobacco smoke* ○ *The building filled with smoke.* ○ *Nobody died in the fire, but three people were treated for smoke inhalation.* • *They didn't have a* **smoke detector** (= a device that makes a loud noise when smoke is present). • A **smokestack** is a tall, vertical pipe through which smoke or steam leaves a building or engine.

smoke /smoʊk/ *v* [I] to produce or give off smoke • *The oil in the frying pan started smoking.* • If you **smoke out** an animal or person, you force them to leave a place where they are hiding: *He didn't just walk in and surrender, we had to smoke him out.*

smokeless /ˈsmoʊ·kləs/ *adj* • *smokeless candles*

smoky, **smokey** /ˈsmoʊ·ki/ *adj* • *The chicken has a nice smoky flavor.*

smoke BREATHE SMOKE /smoʊk/ *v* [I/T] to breathe smoke into the mouth or lungs from burning tobacco, such as cigarettes • *to smoke a pipe/cigar/cigarette* [T] ○ *Several of our friends smoke.* [I]

smoke /smoʊk/ *n* [C] an act of smoking • *I'm going outside to have a smoke.* ○ (*infml*) *Have you got any smokes* (= cigarettes)?

smokeless /ˈsmoʊ·kləs/ *adj* • Smokeless tobacco is tobacco that is chewed and not burned or smoked.

smoker /ˈsmoʊ·kər/ *n* [C] someone who smokes • *a cigarette/pipe/cigar smoker*

smoking /ˈsmoʊ·kɪŋ/ *n* [U] the action or activity of smoking • *Smoking is not permitted.*

smoky, **smokey** /ˈsmoʊ·ki/ *adj* • *This bar is too smoky.*

smoke PRESERVE /smoʊk/ *v* [T] to preserve and add a smoky flavor to (meat, fish, or cheese) using smoke from burning wood • *They smoke the fish over wood chips.*

smoke screen /ˈsmoʊk·skriːn/ *n* [C] something that hides the truth about a person's actions or intentions • *The story served as a useful smoke screen to conceal where he really got the money.*

smoking gun /ˌsmoʊ·kɪŋˈɡʌn/ *n* [C] information that proves who committed a crime • *The tapes provided prosecutors with the smoking gun they needed.*

smolder /ˈsmoʊl·dər/ *v* [I] to burn slowly with smoke but without flames • *The fire was still smoldering the next morning.* • If a strong emotion smolders, it continues to exist but is not expressed: *Their religious rivalry has smoldered for hundreds of years.*

smooch /smuːtʃ/ *v* [I] *infml* to kiss someone • *They were smooching by the swimming pool.*

smooch /smuːtʃ/ *n* [C usually sing] *infml* • *She gave him a smooch on the way out.*

smooth REGULAR /smuːð/ *adj* [-er/-est only] having a surface or substance that is perfect-

ly regular and has no holes or lumps or areas that rise or fall suddenly • *a smooth surface* ○ *Mix together the butter and sugar until smooth.* ○ *The baby's skin is so smooth!*

smooth /smuːð/ *v* [T] • *Use fine sandpaper to smooth the surface before varnishing.* ○ *She smoothed the wrinkles from her skirt.*

smoothness /ˈsmuːð·nəs/ *n* [U] • *I love the smoothness of silk.*

smooth NOT INTERRUPTED /smuːð/ *adj* [-er/-est only] happening without any sudden changes, interruption, inconvenience, or difficulty • *a smooth ride/flight* ○ *The bill had a smooth passage through both houses of Congress.*

smooth /smuːð/ *v* [T] • *We must do more to smooth the country's path to democratic reform.*

smoothly /ˈsmuːð·li/ *adv* • *Oil is used to make the parts of a machine move smoothly when they rub together.* ○ *It's nice to work in such a smoothly run office.*

smoothness /ˈsmuːð·nəs/ *n* [U] • *The car delivers power with the smoothness of a jet engine.*

smooth POLITE /smuːð/ *adj* [-er/-est only] polite, confident, and persuasive, esp. in a way that lacks sincerity • *I trust an honest face more than a smooth talker.*

▫ **smooth down** *obj*, **smooth** *obj* **down** /ˈ-ˈ-/ *v adv* [M] to make (something) flat • *He straightened his tie nervously and smoothed down his hair.*

▫ **smooth out** *obj*, **smooth** *obj* **out** /ˈ-ˈ-/ *v adv* [M] to reduce or remove differences or changes in (something) • *If you get too much paint in one spot, you can't smooth it out.*

▫ **smooth over** *obj*, **smooth** *obj* **over** /ˈ-ˈ--/ *v adv* [M] to make less serious or easier to solve • *Muslims and Jews are meeting to smooth over differences between them.*

smorgasbord /ˈsmɔːr·ɡəs·bɔːrd, -ˌboʊrd/ *n* [C] a mixture of many different hot and cold dishes that are arranged so that you can serve yourself as much as you want; a BUFFET • *We'll have a smorgasbord at the party.* ○ (*fig.*) *Candidates offered a smorgasbord of reforms* (= a large variety of them).

smother PREVENT BREATHING /ˈsmʌð·ər/ *v* [T] to prevent (a person or animal) from getting oxygen • *Several animals were smothered by smoke from the fire.* • To smother someone is to kill them by covering their face so that they cannot breathe: *She was smothered with a pillow.*

smother COVER /ˈsmʌð·ər/ *v* [T] to cover most or all of a surface • *The pasta was smothered with a creamy sauce.*

smother STOP FIRE /ˈsmʌð·ər/ *v* [T] to stop (a fire) from burning by covering it with something that prevents air from reaching it • *Firefighters smothered the blaze with chemical foam.*

smother GIVE LOVE /'smʌð·ər/ v [T] to give (someone you love) too much attention and make them feel that they have lost their independence • *He was cute and shy, and women ached to smother him.*

smudge /smʌdʒ/ n [C] a mark left on a surface, usually unintentionally, from having touched something wet or sticky • *Trev wiped a smudge of chocolate from the side of his mouth.*

smudge /smʌdʒ/ v [T] • *She was sweaty and her face was smudged with dirt.* • *If you smudge something that is neat, you make it messy: If I kiss you I'll smudge my lipstick.*

smug /smʌg/ adj [-er/-est only] -gg- *disapproving* very pleased and satisfied with yourself, and having no doubt about the value of what you know or have done • *His attitude showed a smug indifference to the hardships others faced.*

smuggle /'smʌg·əl/ v [T] to take (things or people) to or from a country or place illegally and secretly • *He was charged with trying to smuggle cocaine across the US-Canadian border.*

smuggler /'smʌg·lər/ n [C] • *drug smugglers*

smut /smʌt/ n [U] pictures, writing, or performances that deal with sex or show naked people in a way that is offensive to you • *The senator called the pictures of nudes smut and said the government should withdraw its funding for such art.*

smutty /'smʌt̬·i/ adj • *smutty jokes*

snack /snæk/ n [C] a small amount of food, esp. when eaten between meals • *A snack bar is a place where you can buy small amounts of food that are packaged or easy to prepare: The snack bar on the train is open now.*

snafu /snæ'fuː/ n [C] a situation in which nothing happens as planned and everything goes wrong • *The snowstorm created a terrible snafu at the airport, with hundreds of passengers waiting for flights to be rescheduled.*

snag PROBLEM /snæg/ n [C] a problem or difficulty that stops or slows the progress of something • *The team was close to signing him to a long-range contract, but talks have hit a snag.*

snag BECOME CAUGHT /snæg/ v [I/T] -gg- to cause (a material, esp. clothing) to catch on something sharp or rough, usually unintentionally, so that it cannot be moved without damaging it • *Be careful not to snag your sweater on the rose bushes.* [T]

snag /snæg/ n [C] a tear, hole, or loose fiber in a piece of clothing or cloth caused by a sharp or rough object • *a snag in a stocking*

snag OBTAIN /snæg/ v [T] -gg- *infml* to obtain or catch (something) by acting quickly • *I hoped to snag a good job.*

snail /sneɪl/ n [C] a small animal with a

snail

protective shell that moves very slowly • *The roads were jammed and we were moving* at a snail's pace (= extremely slowly). • Snail mail is mail that is sent through the post office, esp. in comparison with E-MAIL.

snake ANIMAL /sneɪk/ n [C] an animal with a long, cylindrical body and no legs • PIC RATTLESNAKE

snake TWIST /sneɪk/ v [I always + adv/prep] to move along a route that includes a lot of twists or bends • *People spent hours waiting in lines that snaked around the stadium to get tickets.*

snap BREAK /snæp/ v [I/T] -pp- to break (something) quickly with a cracking sound • *High winds caused some power lines to snap, and we lost our electricity.* [I] • (*fig.*) If a person snaps, they lose control of their behavior, esp. by becoming violent: *His lawyer said he just snapped.* [I]

snap /snæp/ n [C usually sing] the act of breaking something stiff, or the cracking sound made when it breaks • *The plastic handle broke with a loud snap.*

snap MOVE QUICKLY /snæp/ v -pp- to move (something) or change into a new position quickly • *The sudden stop of the car snapped his head back.* [M] • If you snap your fingers, you make a sudden, cracking noise by pushing a finger against the base of your thumb, usually in order to get someone's attention. [T] • If you **snap out of** a condition, you suddenly stop experiencing it: *He thinks he's in love with me, but he'll snap out of it.*

snap FASTEN / CLOSE /snæp/ v [I/T] -pp- to make a quick, cracking sound by suddenly bringing together the two parts of (something) • *She snapped her briefcase shut and marched out of the room.* [T] • If a dog snaps at you, it suddenly tries to bite you. [I]

snap /snæp/ n [C usually pl] • *The shirt fastens with snaps.*

snap SPEAK /snæp/ v [I/T] -pp- to speak or say (something) suddenly in anger • *Don't snap at your brother like that.* [I]

snap TAKE PHOTOGRAPHS /snæp/ v [T] -pp- to use a camera to take (a photograph) without spending a lot of time doing it • *Washington is full of tourists snapping pictures of each other.* • A snapshot is an informal photograph.

snap SOMETHING EASY /snæp/ n [C usually sing] *infml* something that can be done without any difficulty • *Thinking that the exam would be a snap, she didn't bother to study for it.*

snap SUDDEN /snæp/ adj done suddenly without allowing time for careful thought or preparation • *Don't make a snap decision—take some time to think it over.*

□**snap up** obj, **snap** obj **up** /'-'-/ v adv [M] to buy or obtain (something) quickly and enthusiastically • *Tickets for the concert were snapped up within three hours of going on sale.*

snapdragon /'snæp,dræg·ən/ n [C] a garden

plant with white, yellow, pink, or red flowers that open like a pair of lips when they are pressed

snapper /'snæp·ər/ n [C] an edible fish that lives in warm seas

snappy /'snæp·i/ adj immediately effective in getting people's attention or communicating an idea • The music video was full of snappy editing and atmospheric lighting. • Snappy also means stylish and attractive: a snappy dresser/outfit

snare /sner, snær/ n [C] a device for catching small animals, usually with a rope or wire that tightens around the animal • A snare is also a trick or situation that deceives you or involves you unexpectedly in a problem: The legal system is full of snares for the unwary.

snare /sner, snær/ v [T] to get or achieve (something that is difficult to get) • Arriving in Nashville, she had hopes of snaring a country-music record contract.

snarl [THREATEN] /snɑrl/ v [I/T] (esp. of dogs) to make a fierce sound while showing the teeth, usually to frighten you, or (of people) to speak or say (something) angrily and fiercely • "Drop dead," he snarled. [I]

snarl [STOP MOVEMENT] /snɑrl/ v [I/T] to make or become stuck, knotted, or blocked, and so unable to move easily • The collision snarled traffic for 10 miles on the Interstate. [T]

snatch /snætʃ/ v [T] to take hold of (something) suddenly and without warning • They snatched up their coats and hats and ran outside. [M] ○ A mugger knocked her down and snatched her purse. • To snatch something is to do it in the short amount of time available: We rushed in and snatched the best seats we could get.

snatch /snætʃ/ n [C] a brief part (of something) • I could hear snatches of conversation from the people in the booth next to ours.

snazzy /'snæz·i/ adj infml modern and stylish in a way that attracts attention • snazzy computer graphics

sneak /sniːk/ v [always + adv/prep] past **sneaked** or infml **snuck** /snʌk/ to go or do (something) secretly, or take (someone or something) somewhere secretly • He sneaked out of the house, going out through the back way. [I always + adv/prep] ○ I sneaked a look at my watch. [T] ○ He was arrested for trying to sneak a gun past security in boarding a flight. [T] ○ Jackie snuck out for a smoke. [I always + adv/prep]

sneaky /'sniː·ki/ adj secretive or dishonest • sneaky tricks ○ a sneaky way to raise taxes

sneaker /'sniː·kər/ n [C] a light shoe that has a top made of cloth and a bottom made of rubber, worn esp. for sports

sneaking /'sniː·kɪŋ/ adj [not gradable] (of feelings or thoughts) slowly becoming stronger • I have a sneaking suspicion that I need more memory in my computer.

sneer /snɪr/ v [I/T] to show in your facial expression or manner of speaking that someone or something is so foolish that it deserves to be ridiculed • You may sneer (at it), but a lot of people like this kind of music. [I]

sneer /snɪr/ n [C] • "Is that the best you can do?" he asked with a sneer.

sneeze /sniːz/ v [I] to send air out from the nose and mouth in an explosive way that you cannot control • I don't know why, but I couldn't stop sneezing.

snicker /'snɪk·ər/ v [I] infml to laugh quietly at someone or something that you think is silly or slightly ridiculous • The audience of sportswriters tried to keep from snickering, but failed miserably.

snicker /'snɪk·ər/ n [C]

snide /snɑɪd/ adj containing indirect and unkind criticism • snide remarks

sniff [SMELL] /snɪf/ v [I/T] to smell (something) by taking in air through the nose, or to take in (esp. air) through the nose, usually in the act of smelling • Jack crushed a bit of dried grass between his fingers and sniffed its scent. [T] • To sniff is also to take in breath through the nose, esp. with a noise. [I]

sniff [SHOW DISAPPROVAL] /snɪf/ v [I/T] to express a bad opinion of (something or someone); to show disapproval • The museum's front lawn does not need to be cluttered with silly pop art, sniffed a newspaper editorial. [I]

□**sniff out** obj, **sniff** obj **out** /'-'-/ v adv [M] to discover (something), usually only after a special effort • Professors are always trying to sniff out plagiarized term papers.

sniffle /'snɪf·əl/ v [I] to take in air through the nose repeatedly in a way that others can hear usually because you are crying or because you have a cold • I could hear her sniffling into her handkerchief.

sniffle /'snɪf·əl/ n [C] • The sniffles is a slight cold.

snip /snɪp/ v [T] **-pp-** to cut (something), usually with a few quick actions using SCISSORS (= cutting device with two blades) or a similar device • I asked the barber just to snip the ends of my hair.

snipe /snɑɪp/ v [I] to criticize, esp. in a mean way because you are annoyed or angry • Frustrated by the war, Republicans and southern Democrats contented themselves with sniping at the president.

sniper /'snɑɪ·pər/ n [C] someone who, while hidden, tries to shoot a person with a gun • A sniper's bullet killed her husband in Italy in World War II.

snippet /'snɪp·ət/ n [C] a small bit or part of something • I'll watch snippets of baseball games, but I just don't have that much time to sit and watch the whole thing.

snit /snɪt/ n [C] infml an angry mood • He's in a snit because his train was late.

snitch [TELL SECRETLY] /snɪtʃ/ v [I] infml to se

cretly tell someone in authority that someone else has done something bad, often in order to cause trouble • *If you keep snitching on your friends, you won't have many left.*

snitch /snɪtʃ/ *n* [C] *infml* • *Don't be a snitch.*

snitch STEAL /snɪtʃ/ *v* [T] *infml* to steal, or to take without permission • *I snitched a pencil from your desk—hope you don't mind.*

snob /snɑb/ *n* [C] a person who values people as important mainly because of their social position or wealth, and who considers their own social position or wealth as making them better than others • *A snob can also be a person who gives a very high value to any quality which they believe they have, and which makes them better than other people:* *intellectual snobs*

snobbish /'snɑb·ɪʃ/, **snobby** /'snɑb·i/ *adj* • *a snobbish remark*

snobbery /'snɑb·ə·ri/, **snobbishness** /'snɑb·ɪʃ·nəs/ *n* [U]

snoop /snuːp/ *v* [I] *infml* to look around a place secretly in order to discover things about it or the people connected with it • *You have no business snooping around my office.*

snoop /snuːp/ *n* [C] *infml*

snooty /'snuːṭ·i, 'snʊṭ·i/ *adj infml* seeming by your manner to think that you are better than everyone else • *Some snooty kid opened the door and told me to use the side entrance.*

snooze /snuːz/ *v* [I] *infml* to sleep lightly for a short time • *The dog was snoozing in front of the fire.*

snooze /snuːz/ *n* [C] *infml*

snore /snɔːr, snoʊr/ *v* [I] to make loud noises as you breathe while you are sleeping • *My husband snores so loudly it keeps me awake at night.*

snore /snɔːr, snoʊr/ *n* [C]

snorkel /'snɔːr·kəl/ *n* [C] a tube that a swimmer can use to breathe while under water, by keeping one end in the mouth while the other ends sticks up above the surface of the water

snorkeling /'snɔːr·kə·lɪŋ/ *n* [U] • *We went snorkeling off the coast of Key West.*

snorkeling

snort /snɔːrt/ *v* [I/T] to make an explosive sound by forcing air quickly through the nose • To snort an illegal drug is to take it in through the nose: *They are snorting cocaine in the bathroom.* [T] • To snort is also to express strong negative feelings, esp. by making a sound: *She snorted her disapproval and walked away.* [T]

snort /snɔːrt/ *n* [C] • *The teacher's explanation drew snorts of laughter from the students.*

snot /snɑt/ *n* [U] *rude slang* a green or yellow substance sometimes produced in the nose, esp. when a person has a cold

snotty /'snɑṭ·i/ *adj infml* rude and showing a lack of respect for others, esp. because you think you are better than they are • *He has three snotty teenage daughters.*

snot /snɑt/ *n* [C] *infml* a person who is disliked because they are rude and lack respect for others • *I remember this one little snot in my class who always talked back to the teacher.*

snout /snaʊt/ *n* [C] the nose and mouth that stick out from the face of some animals • *a pig's snout*

snow WEATHER /snoʊ/ *n* [C/U] water that falls from clouds as soft, white FLAKES (= thin pieces) of ice when it is cold, or an amount of these flakes • *Six inches of snow fell overnight.* [U] ○ *We have had several snows in the past week.* [C] • A **snowball** is snow pressed into a ball. See also SNOWBALL. • A **snowboard** is a board shaped like a wide SKI that you stand on to slide on the snow. • A **snowdrift** is a hill of snow piled up by the wind: *There were some snowdrifts as high as twenty feet.* • A **snowfall** is a period during which snow falls, or the amount of snow that falls during a period of time. • **Snowflakes** are single pieces of snow that fall from the sky. • A **snowplow** is a large blade attached to the front of a truck that pushes snow off roads. • A **snowstorm** is a storm that brings a lot of snow and usually strong winds. • A **snow tire** is a tire designed to prevent sliding on ice or snow.

snowboard

snow /snoʊ/ *v* [I] • *It snowed all weekend.* • If you are **snowed under**, you have too much to do: *I am totally snowed under by work.* • If you are **snowbound** or **snowed in**, you cannot go anywhere because the snow is too deep.

snowy /'snoʊ·i/ *adj* • *It was one of the snowiest winters on record.*

snow DECEIVE /snoʊ/ *v* [T] *infml* to deceive (someone) with charming, persuasive talk • *This guy is very smooth and can snow anybody.*

snowball /'snoʊ·bɔːl/ *v* [I] to grow quickly in size or importance • *Public support for*

military action has snowballed. • See also
snowball at SNOW WEATHER.

snowmobile /'snoʊ·moʊ,biːl/ n [C] a small
motor vehicle for traveling over snow

snowmobile

snub /snʌb/ v [T] **-bb-** to treat (someone) rudely, esp. by ignoring them • They're likely to
snub people who aren't just like them.
snub /snʌb/ n [C] • She was annoyed by their
snubs.

snuck /snʌk/ past simple and past participle of
SNEAK

snuff /snʌf/ n [U] tobacco in the form of a
powder that people breathe in through their
noses

snuff out obj, **snuff** obj **out** /'snʌf'aʊt/ v adv
[M] to stop (a flame) from burning, usually by
covering it • The child was allowed to snuff out
the candles. • To snuff out also means to end
something: Opposition was snuffed out by the
threat of imprisonment. ○ Another young life
has been snuffed out by gang violence.

snug WARM /snʌg/ adj [-er/-est only] **-gg-**
warm, comfortable, and protected • Are you
nice and snug in that sleeping bag?
snugly /'snʌg·li/ adv [not gradable] • The cat
curled up snugly in the armchair.

snug CLOSE FITTING /snʌg/ adj fitting closely or
tightly • She wore a snug black dress.
snugly /'snʌg·li/ adv [not gradable] • His vest
fitted snugly.

snuggle /'snʌg·əl/ v [I always + adv/prep] to
move close to someone for affection, warmth,
or comfort, or to arrange something around
yourself • They snuggled together on the
couch.

so TO SUCH A DEGREE /soʊ, sə/ adv [not grad-
able] to such a great degree; very • He's so stupid he'd believe anything you tell him. ○ Our
families live so far away. • If someone says
something in so many words, they say it directly: He didn't say he'd marry me in so many
words, but I think he's interested. • **So much**
means to a great degree or very much: She
wanted to go so much. • **So much as** means
even or really, and is used for emphasis: I did-
n't listen so much as survive the conversation.
• **So much so** also means to such a great degree: It was a great project, so much so that it
won first prize.

so SIMILARLY /soʊ/ adv [not gradable] (used usually before the verbs have, be, do, and other

auxiliary verbs) in the same way; similarly •
He was interested, and so were a lot of other
people.

so IN ORDER THAT /soʊ/ conjunction in order
that, or with the result that • They moved so
they could be closer to her family.

so THEREFORE /soʊ, sə/ conjunction and for that
reason; therefore • My knee started hurting, so
I stopped running. • (infml) So or **So what**
shows that you do not care about what was
mentioned or think it is not important: "We
are not supposed to be here." "So what?" •
(infml) **So there** emphasizes how something
you have said was proved correct: I said that
book would be a hit, and it was. So there!

so IT IS THE SITUATION /soʊ/ adj, adv [not grad-
able] (used instead of repeating something
that has just been mentioned) it is the situation • "I hope our paths cross again." "I hope
so too." • If you say **so be it**, you mean that
you accept the situation as it is: If she spends
all her money on clothes, so be it! • **So far** describes a situation at a particular time or up
to a particular point: So far, only two Democrats have entered the race for governor. • If you
say **so far, so good**, you mean the situation is
satisfactory up to this stage: "How's your new
job?" "So far, so good." • People say **so help me**
to emphasize that they mean something: So
help me, they were having so much fun they did-
n't hear me come in. • **So long** means goodbye •
So long, see you Thursday. • You say **so long
as** to mean that you will do one thing if something else is done or happens: I'll lend you the
money so long as you'll pay me back. • You say
so much for something when it does not happen in the way you hoped or expected: "It's
raining." "So much for our day at the beach."

so TRUE /soʊ/ adv [not gradable] true, or truly
• He thinks I'm out to get him, but that simply
isn't so.

so IN THIS WAY /soʊ/ adv [not gradable] more or
less like this or in this way • Grandpa could
be generous when he so desired. • So is also
used to suggest the approximate size of someone or something: The box is about so big. • **So
to speak** is a way of saying that something is
more or less true: I am a writer, so to speak.

So. SOUTH n [U], adj abbreviation for SOUTH or
SOUTHERN

soak MAKE WET /soʊk/ v [I/T] to make (something) very wet, or (of a liquid) to be absorbed
• The hikers got soaked in the downpour. [T] •
Water soaked through my shoes. [I] • To soak
something means to leave it in liquid for a period of time, esp. to clean or soften it: Let's just
soak the dishes. [T]
soaking /'soʊ·kɪŋ/, **soaking wet** /,soʊ·kɪŋ'wet/
adj • It's so humid that my shirt is soaking wet
before I leave the house.

soak CHARGE /soʊk/ v [T] slang to charge
(someone) too much money • I got soaked for
the cab ride.

□ **soak up** *obj*, **soak** *obj* **up** /'-'-/ *v adv* [M] to absorb or enjoy (something that exists around you) • *I just want to lie on the beach and soak up the sun.* ○ *She soaks up everything that's said in class.*

so–and–so /'soʊ·ən,soʊ/ *n* [C] *pl* **so-and-sos** *infml* (used instead of an actual name) a particular person or thing • *He asked if I knew where so-and-so lives.* • If you say that someone is a so-and-so, you do not have a good opinion of them: *You cannot trust that so-and-so.*

soap /soʊp/ *n* [U] a substance used with water for washing or cleaning, or a block of this substance • *liquid soap* • **Soapsuds** are bubbles that form when soap is mixed with water.

soap /soʊp/ *v* [I/T] to rub or cover (someone or something) with soap • *He soaped up and then rinsed off.* [I]

soapy /'soʊ·pi/ *adj* containing soap • *Wash your hands in soapy water.*

soap opera /'soʊp,ɑp·rə/, *infml* **soap** /soʊp/ *n* [C] a television program, usually broadcast five days a week, about the lives of a particular group of characters

soar INCREASE QUICKLY /sɔːr, soʊr/ *v* [I] to increase or go up quickly to a high level • *temperatures/prices soared* ○ *My spirits soared when I heard the good news.*

soar RISE IN AIR /sɔːr, soʊr/ *v* [I] (esp. of a bird or aircraft) to rise or fly high in the air • *Planes soared overhead.* • If you say that a mountain, building, or other object soars, you mean that it has great height: *The mountain soars 10,000 feet above the village.*

S.O.B. /,es,oʊ'biː/ *n* [C] *rude slang abbreviation for* SON OF A BITCH

sob /sɑb/ *v* [I/T] **-bb-** to cry in a noisy way, taking in sudden, short breaths

sob /sɑb/ *n* [C] • *I never heard such sobs.* • (*infml disapproving*) A **sob story** is a sad story, often used as an excuse or explanation, that is meant to make you feel sorry for someone.

sober NOT DRUNK /'soʊ·bər/ *adj* having had no alcohol; not drunk • USAGE: The related noun is SOBRIETY.

sober up (*obj*), **sober** (*obj*) **up** /,soʊ·bə'rʌp/ *v adv* [I/M] • *Burton sobered up and went to work.* [I]

sober SERIOUS /'soʊ·bər/ *adj* serious and calm or thoughtful • *The sober expression had not left Martin's face.*

soberly /'soʊ·bər·li/ *adv* • *The jury soberly considered the evidence.*

sobering /'soʊ·bə·rɪŋ/ *adj* • *Jail has had a sobering effect on Hicks.*

sobriety /sə'brɑɪ·ət̬·i/ *n* [U] the state or quality of being SOBER (= not drunk) • Sobriety also means the state of being serious, calm, or thoughtful: *This judge is known for his sobriety and fairness.*

so–called /'soʊ'kɔːld/ *adj* [not gradable] named or called in a particular way • *Married taxpayers are hit hard by the so-called mar-*

riage penalty. • Someone or something that is so-called may not fit their name: *These so-called experts don't know anything.*

soccer /'sɑk·ər/ *n* [U] a game in which two teams of eleven players try to send a ball into the goal of the opposing side without using their arms or hands

sociable /'soʊ·ʃə·bəl/ *adj* liking to be with people; friendly • *The new sales rep is savvy and sociable.*

social OF HUMAN SOCIETY /'soʊ·ʃəl/ *adj* [not gradable] related to the way people live together or to the rank a person has in a society • *social conditions/position* • (*disapproving*) A **social climber** is someone who tries to move into a higher social rank. • (*Cdn*) A **Social Insurance Number** (*abbreviation* **SIN**) is a number given to each citizen and used by the Canadian federal government to provide citizens with government services or to collect taxes. • **Social science** is the study of the customs and culture of a society. • The **social sciences** include such subjects as history, politics, economics, ANTHROPOLOGY, and SOCIOLOGY. • **Social Security** is a US government program that provides financial help and services for old people, people whose husbands or wives have died, and people who are unable to work because of illness. • **Social services** are services provided by governments or other organizations to people with particular needs. • **Social studies** is a course for younger students that includes many of the social sciences. • A **social worker** is a person who is specially trained to help people who need social services.

socially /'soʊ·ʃə·li/ *adv* • *Certain behavior is socially unacceptable.*

social OF MEETING PEOPLE /'soʊ·ʃəl/ *adj* [not gradable] related to meeting and spending time with other people for pleasure • *He had almost no social life.*

socially /'soʊ·ʃə·li/ *adv* [not gradable] • *We first met socially and later worked together.*

socialize /'soʊ·ʃə,lɑɪz/ *v* [I] • *Although he works a lot, Manny still finds time to socialize with friends.*

socialism /'soʊ·ʃə,lɪz·əm/ *n* [U] any economic or political system based on government ownership and control of important businesses and methods of production • Compare CAPITALISM; COMMUNISM.

socialist /'soʊ·ʃə·ləst/ *adj* [not gradable] • *Socialist ideas are not as radical as we once thought.*

socialist /'soʊ·ʃə·ləst/ *n* [C] • *He is a dedicated socialist.* • Compare **communist** at COMMUNISM.

socialized /'soʊ·ʃə,lɑɪzd/ *adj* [not gradable] • *Political leaders are opposed to socialized medicine* (= government control of medical care).

society PEOPLE /sə'sɑɪ·ət̬·i/ *n* [C/U] people considered as a group, or a group of people who live together in a particular social system • *Society does not permit murder.* [U] ○ *Societies change over the course of time.* [C] • Society also refers to that group of people who are rich, powerful, or fashionable: *He's a part of Boston society.* [U]

society [ORGANIZATION] /sə'saɪ·əṭ·i/ *n* [C] an organization for people who have special interests or who want to support particular activities • *Zoological societies protect and study wild animals.*

sociology /ˌsoʊ·siˈɑl·ə·dʒi/ *n* [U] the study of human societies

sociologist /ˌsoʊ·siˈɑl·ə·dʒəst/ *n* [C] • *He trained as a sociologist at the university.*

sock [FOOT COVERING] /sɑk/ *n* [C] *pl* **socks** or *infml* **sox** /sɑks/ a covering for your foot, worn inside a shoe and made of soft material

sock [HIT] /sɑk/ *v* [T] to hit (someone) • *He socked his brother in the eye.*

□**sock in** /'-'-/ *v prep* [T] to stop all travel or movement of vehicles in an area because of bad weather, esp. heavy, thick fog • *The entire coast was socked in all week.*

socket /'sɑk·ət/ *n* [C] a hollow or curved part into which something fits • *The bulb screwed easily into a socket.* ○ *Somehow the bone was pulled from its socket.*

sod /sɑd/ *n* [U] dirt with grass rooted in it • *Truckloads of sod were needed to make the new lawn.*

soda /'soʊd·ə/, *dated* **soda pop** /'soʊd·ə,pɑp/ *n* [C/U] *regional* a soft drink, see at SOFT [WEAK] • Soda or **soda water** is also plain water containing air bubbles.

sodden /'sɑd·ən/ *adj* [not gradable] extremely wet as a result of absorbing liquid • *The carpet was a sodden mess.*

sodium /'soʊd·iː·əm/ *n* [U] a soft, silver-white chemical element that is found only combined with other elements • *(specialized)* **Sodium chloride** is salt.

sodomy /'sɑd·ə·mi/ *n* [U] the sexual act of putting the penis into the ANUS or mouth of another person

sofa /'soʊ·fə/ *n* [C] a long, soft seat with a back and usually arms, large enough for two or more people to sit on; a COUCH • A **sofa bed** is a bed that folds out of a sofa.

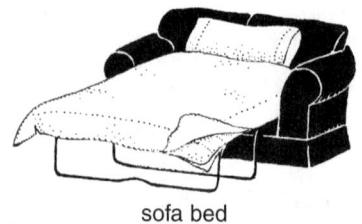

sofa bed

soft [NOT HARD] /sɔːft/ *adj* [-er/-est only] not hard or firm; changing its shape when pressed • *The crabs are plucked from the water before*

their soft shells have had a chance to harden. ○ *The baby's skin feels so soft* (= smooth and enjoyable to touch). • When an egg is **soft-boiled**, it has been boiled with its shell on and removed from the water while the yellow part is still not hard. Compare **hard-boiled** at HARD [SOLID].

soften /'sɔː·fən/ *v* [I/T] • *The butter will soften if you leave it out.* [I]

softness /'sɔːft·nəs/ *n* [U] • *I sank into the softness of my bed.*

soft [GENTLE] /sɔːft/ *adj* [-er/-est only] not forceful, loud, or easily noticed • *a soft voice* ○ *She likes soft pastel colors.* • Someone who is **softhearted** is kind and is willing to help other people. Compare **hardhearted** at HARD [SEVERE]. • If you **soft-pedal** something unpleasant, you treat it as less important than you know it is because you want to avoid angering or hurting people: *The movie soft-pedals the more sensational aspects of his life.* • Someone who is **soft-spoken** usually speaks in a quiet voice: *a soft-spoken, understated style* • If you have a **soft spot** for someone or something, you like them very much: *I'll always have a soft spot in my heart for Denver.*

soften /'sɔː·fən/ *v* [I/T] • *He made an effort to soften his tone.* [T]

softly /'sɔːf·tli/ *adv* • *She spoke so softly it was hard to hear her.*

softness /'sɔːft·nəs/ *n* [U] • *There was a softness in her voice.*

soft [WEAK] /sɔːft/ *adj* [-er/-est only] not strong; weak • *Car sales were soft last year.* • Supporters of the death penalty say he is **soft on crime** (= not forceful enough in punishing criminals). • A **soft drink** (*regional* **soda**, **pop**) is a sweet, flavored drink that does not contain alcohol.

soften /'sɔː·fən/ *v* [T] • *Congress will move to soften the law's impact.* • *A hug can soften the blows that life delivers* (= make them less unpleasant). • *The governor is trying to soften up the angry mood of the state's voters* (= weaken their anger).

softness /'sɔːft·nəs/ *n* [U] • *A lot of people think that kindness is a sign of softness.*

soft [EASY] /sɔːft/ *adj* [-er/-est only] not difficult; easier than other things of the same type • *She asked some soft questions.* • If someone is a **soft touch**, it is easy to make them do what you want, esp. give you money: *The chief, obviously a soft touch, gave him ten bucks.*

softball /'sɔːft·bɔːl/ *n* [C/U] a game similar to baseball but played with a larger, softer ball, or the ball used in this game

software /'sɔːf,twer, -,twær/ *n* [U] the instructions that control what a computer can do; computer programs • *educational software* • Compare HARDWARE [COMPUTER].

soggy /'sɑg·i, 'sɔː·gi/ *adj* (of a substance) very wet from having absorbed liquid • *They played on a wet, soggy field.*

soil EARTH /sɔɪl/ n [C/U] the material on the surface of the ground in which plants grow; earth • *Plant the seeds in potting soil.* [U] • Soil is sometimes a country: *American boys are fighting on foreign soil.* [U]

soil MAKE DIRTY /sɔɪl/ v [T] to make (something) dirty

soiled /sɔɪld/ adj • *soiled diapers*

sojourn /'soʊ·dʒɜrn/ n [C] a temporary stay at one place, esp. while traveling

sojourn /'soʊ·dʒɜrn, soʊ'dʒɜrn/ v [I always + adv/prep] • *They sojourned in Memphis to celebrate Elvis Presley's birthday.*

solace /'sɑl·əs/ n [U] help and comfort when you are feeling sad or worried • *She found solace in her memories of her grandmother.*

solar /'soʊ·lər/ adj [not gradable] of or from the sun, or using the energy from the sun to produce electric power • *solar energy* ○ *solar power* • The **solar system** is the sun and the group of planets that move around it.

sold /soʊld/ *past simple and past participle of* SELL

solder /'sɑd·ər/ n [U] a type of soft metal that is melted to join separate metal parts which are then permanently attached when the metal cools

solder /'sɑd·ər/ v [T] • *Wrap metal foil around the glass pieces and solder them together.*

soldier /'soʊl·dʒər/ n [C] a person who is in an army and wears its uniform, esp. someone who fights when there is a war • *American/ Italian/Chinese soldiers*

sole ONLY /soʊl/ adj [not gradable] being the only one; single • *She is the sole survivor of the accident.* • Sole also means belonging to one person or group: *The team moved into sole possession of first place.* • LP WORDS WITH THE MEANING "ONE" at ONE SINGLE

solely /'soʊl·li/ adv [not gradable] • *These industries aren't solely responsible for hazardous wastes.*

sole BOTTOM PART OF FOOT /soʊl/ n [C] the bottom part of a foot which touches the ground when you stand or walk, or the front part of the bottom of a shoe • *shoes with leather/rubber soles* • PIC FOOT

sole FISH /soʊl/ n [C/U] pl **sole** a flat, round fish that is eaten as food

solemn /'sɑl·əm/ adj having or showing serious purpose and determination • *He looked stern and solemn, and rarely spoke.* ○ *The memorial was a very solemn occasion.*

solemnly /'sɑl·əm·li/ adv • *Borden solemnly promised that he would take care of it.*

solemnity /sə'lem·nət·i/ n [U] • *There was an air of solemnity in the room.*

solicit /sə'lɪs·ət/ v [T] to ask for (something) in a persuasive and determined way • *He's soliciting funds to keep the library open.* ○ *He was charged by police with soliciting a prostitute* (= asking her to have sex with him in exchange for money).

solicitation /sə,lɪs·ə'teɪ·ʃən/ n [C/U] • *I get a lot of phone solicitations from banks.* [C]

solicitous /sə'lɪs·ət·əs/ adj slightly fml eager to help • *Carla becomes angry at her overly solicitous mother.*

solid FIRM / NOT LIQUID /'sɑl·əd/ adj having a fixed shape that cannot be changed easily • *After flying all night, he was glad to be on solid ground.* • Something that is solid is not liquid or gas: *solid food* ○ *The lake will be frozen solid when you wake up.* ○ *Our company recycles 45% of its solid waste.*

solid /'sɑl·əd/ n [C] specialized an object with three DIMENSIONS (= height, width, and length) • *A cube is a solid.* ○ *After the operation, Mrs. Groncki couldn't eat solids* (= food that is not liquid).

solidify /sə'lɪd·ə,faɪ/ v [I/T] to make (something) firm, or to become firm • *A chemical reaction solidifies the resin.* [T] ○ *Lava solidifies as it cools.* [I]

solidity /sə'lɪd·ət·i/ n [U] • *For solidity, glue the strip in place.*

solid DENSE /'sɑl·əd/ adj completely packed with material; not hollow • *solid rock* ○ *a solid oak table* • A solid metal or color is pure and does not have anything else mixed together with it: *solid gold* ○ *a solid blue background*

solid /'sɑl·əd/ adv [not gradable] with no openings; full • *He has 54 tin boxes, packed solid with baseball cards.*

solidly /'sɑl·əd·li/ adv • *The holes are solidly filled with concrete.*

solid STRONG /'sɑl·əd/ adj (of objects) made in a way that is strong, or (of a person) strong • *It's a solid house.* ○ *David has a solid, muscular body.*

solidly /'sɑl·əd·li/ adv • *The rocking chair is solidly built.*

solid CERTAIN /'sɑl·əd/ adj being of a good quality that can be trusted; certain or safe • *All the performers showed solid musicianship and technique.* ○ *Relations between them are based on a solid foundation of friendship and trust.*

solidly /'sɑl·əd·li/ adv completely; safely • *He appears to be solidly in control of the organization.*

solidify /sə'lɪd·ə,faɪ/ v [I/T] to make (something) complete, or to become more certain or safer • *The play solidified his reputation as a serious writer.* [T] ○ *Her voice strengthened and solidified as she sang.* [I]

solidarity /,sɑl·ə'dær·ət·i/ n [U] agreement between and support for the members of a group • *Wear this ribbon to show your solidarity with AIDS victims.*

soliloquy /sə'lɪl·ə·kwi/ n [C/U] a speech in a play which the character speaks to himself or herself or to the people watching rather than to the other characters • *Hamlet's soliloquy begins, "To be or not to be."* [C]

solitaire JEWEL /'sɑl·ə,ter, -,tær/ n [C] a single

jewel that is part of a piece of jewelry, esp. a ring, or the ring itself • *a diamond solitaire*

solitaire CARDS /'sɑl·ə,ter, -,tær/ *n* [U] a game played with cards by one person

solitary /'sɑl·ə,ter·i/ *adj* being the only one, or not being with other similar things, often by choice • *I live a solitary, monkish life.* ○ *He enjoys solitary walks in the wilderness.* • Someone who is in **solitary confinement** (*infml* **solitary**) is kept alone in a room in prison.

solitude /'sɑl·ə,tuːd/ *n* [U] the situation of being alone, often by choice • *He prefers the solitude of the country to the chaos of the city.*

solo /'soʊ·loʊ/ *adj, adv* [not gradable] alone; without other people • *She takes long, solo bike rides to relax after work.* ○ *He decided to go solo instead of touring with the band.*

solo /'soʊ·loʊ/ *n* [C] *pl* **solos** a musical performance done by one person or one instrument alone, or in which one person is featured • *a piano solo* ○ *a Miles Davis solo*

soloist /'soʊ·lə·wəst/ *n* [C] • *The cellist is a featured soloist at the recital.*

solstice /'sɑl·stəs, 'soːl-, 'soʊl-/ *n* [C] either of the two times during the year when the sun is farthest from the equator, about June 21st when the sun is farthest north of the equator and about December 22nd when it is farthest south • *The summer solstice has the longest days, and the winter solstice has the shortest.* • Compare EQUINOX.

solution ANSWER /sə'luː·ʃən/ *n* [C] an answer to a problem • *It seemed a reasonable solution to a difficult problem.* • USAGE: The related verb is SOLVE.

solution LIQUID /sə'luː·ʃən/ *n* [C/U] *specialized* a liquid in which other substances have been mixed and dissolved • *a saline solution* [C]

soluble /'sɑl·jə·bəl/ *adj* able to be dissolved when mixed with a liquid • *Sugar is soluble in water.*

solve /sɑlv, soːlv/ *v* [T] to find an answer to (a problem) • *The arrests have not solved the mystery of what happened to the stolen cash.* • USAGE: The related noun is SOLUTION ANSWER.

solvable /'sɑl·və·bəl, 'soːl-/, **soluble** /'sɑl·jə·bəl/ *adj* • *Hunger in this city is a solvable problem.*

solvent HAVING MONEY /'sɑl·vənt, 'soːl-/ *adj* (esp. of companies) having enough money to pay all your debts

solvency /'sɑl·vən·si, 'soːl-/ *n* [U] • *The government should certify the solvency of the companies it regulates.*

solvent LIQUID /'sɑl·vənt, 'soːl-/ *n* [C] *specialized* a liquid in which another substance can be dissolved • *a cleaning solvent*

somber /'sɑm·bər/ *adj* serious and sad in appearance or feeling • *Raji is in a somber mood today.* • Somber colors or clothes are dark and plain: *Koch wore his somber blue suit.*

sombrero /səm'brer·oʊ/ *n* [C] *pl* **sombreros** a large hat with a wide BRIM (= the bottom part that sticks out all around), worn esp. by men in Mexico and the southwestern US

sombrero

some UNKNOWN AMOUNT /sʌm, səm/ *adj* [not gradable] having an amount or number that is not known or not stated, or being a part of something • *Let's get some work done.* ○ *Some stories he wrote were made into movies.* • LP AMOUNTS, DETERMINERS

some /sʌm, səm/ *pronoun* • *If you want more spaghetti, please take some.* ○ *I like some of the people in my class.* • Some can also mean some people: *Some have compared him to President Kennedy.* • USAGE: In negative sentences, you use "any" or "no" instead of "some." In questions, you usually use "any" instead of "some."

some /sʌm/ *adv* [not gradable] *infml* • *I slept some in the car on the way home.*

some LARGE AMOUNT /sʌm/ *adj* [not gradable] being a large amount or number of something • *She was married to him for some years.* ○ *These things have been going on for some time.* • LP AMOUNTS, DETERMINERS

some PERSON OR THING /sʌm, səm/ *adj* [not gradable] used to refer to a person or thing when you cannot say exactly who or what it is • *Some jerk backed into my car in the parking lot.* ○ *There's got to be some way out of here.* • For **some** reason **or other**, these people have no place to go (= the exact reason is not known). • LP DETERMINERS

some UNUSUAL /sʌm/ *adj* [not gradable] *infml* used before a noun and spoken with emphasis to show that something is unusual • *Some party that turned out to be—nobody showed up.* ○ *Margo is really a terrific cook—that was some dinner!*

some APPROXIMATELY /sʌm, səm/ *adv* [not gradable] (used in front of a number) approximately; about • *Some 200 people applied for the job.*

somebody /'sʌm,bɑd·i, -bəd·i/ *pronoun* a person; someone • *I'd rather take care of my own kids than let somebody I don't know raise them.* ○ *You don't have the right to interfere in somebody else's life.*

someday /'sʌm·deɪ/ *adv* [not gradable] at some time in the future which is not yet known or not stated • *I keep thinking that maybe someday we'll move.*

somehow /'sʌm·haʊ/ *adv* [not gradable] in a way which is not known or not stated • *Money has been extremely tight, but we've managed somehow.* ○ *He felt that everything was somehow connected.*

someone /'sʌm·wən, -wʌn/ *pronoun* a person • *I'm not interested in someone else's experience.* ○ *I hate cutting the lawn, so I pay someone to do it.* • USAGE: "Anyone" is usually used instead of "someone" in negative sentences and questions.

someplace /'sʌm·pleɪs/ *adv* [not gradable] in, to, or at a place which is not known or not stated; somewhere • *The only time I've been to Florida I was on the way someplace else.*

somersault /'sʌm·ər,sɔːlt/ *n* [C] a rolling movement or jump, either forward or backward, in which you turn over completely, with your body above your head, and finish on your feet • *She turned somersaults on the lawn.*

somersault /'sʌm·ər,sɔːlt/ *v* [I] • *The bus plunged down the hill, somersaulted twice, and landed on its side.*

something /'sʌm·θɪŋ/ *pronoun* a thing which is not known or stated • *I was anxious to do something.* ○ *Can I read you something else?* ○ *I was sure something had happened to him.* • Something is a situation or an event you are thankful for, although it is not everything you had hoped for: *I exercise three times a week— it's not enough, but at least it's something.* • If you describe a person or thing as **something else**, you mean they are very unusual, esp. extremely good or extremely bad: *"He sang better than anyone I've ever heard." "Yeah, I know, he's something else."* • **Something like** means similar to but not exactly like: *The town's Algonquian name means something like "water over a white bottom."* • **Something like** also means approximately when used about an amount or a number: *She's on page 285 or something like that.* • **Something to do with** means in some way connected: *The ball and bat arrive at the same place at the same time, and the rest has something to do with the laws of physics.* • USAGE: "Anything" is usually used instead of "something" in negative sentences and questions.

sometime /'sʌm·taɪm/ *adv* [not gradable] at a time in the future or the past which is not known or stated • *I'm having lunch with an old friend sometime next week.*

sometimes /'sʌm·taɪmz/ *adv* [not gradable] on some occasions but not all the time • *Sometimes you think you can't really trust anybody.*

somewhat /'sʌm·hwʌt, -wʌt, -hwɑt, -wɑt/ *adv* [not gradable] to some degree • *Washington, D.C., is somewhat smaller than Baltimore.* ○ *I was somewhat disappointed.* • USAGE: Somewhat is usually not used in negative phrases or sentences.

somewhere PLACE /'sʌm·hwer, -wer, -hwær, -wær/ *adv* [not gradable] in, to, or at a place which is not known or not stated • *I want to live somewhere else.* ○ *Can we go somewhere and talk?* • USAGE: "Anywhere" is usually used instead of "somewhere" in negative sentences and questions.

somewhere APPROXIMATELY /'sʌm·hwer, -wer, -hwær, -wær/ *adv* [not gradable] (used esp. before a number) approximately; about • *CDs cost somewhere around $15 apiece.* • *He made a*

sound **somewhere** between *a gurgle and a cough* (= having some qualities of each).

son /sʌn/ *n* [C] a male child in relation to his parents • *I have two sons.* • PIC FAMILY TREE

son–in–law /'sʌn·ən,lɔː/ *n* [C] *pl* **sons-in-law** /'sʌn·zən,lɔː/ the husband of a person's daughter • PIC FAMILY TREE

sonata /sə'nɑt̬·ə/ *n* [C] a piece of music in three or four parts, either for a piano or for another instrument, such as a VIOLIN, sometimes also with a piano

song /sɔːŋ/ *n* [C/U] a usually short piece of music with words that are sung • *We bought a CD of Cole Porter songs.* [C] • Song is also the act of singing, or singing when considered generally: *He was so happy he wanted to burst into song* (= start singing). [U] • The song of a bird is the musical sound it makes. [C]

sonnet /'sɑn·ət/ *n* [C] a poem that has 14 lines and a particular pattern of RHYME and word arrangement

son of a bitch /ˌsʌn·ə·və'bɪtʃ/ (*abbreviation* **S.O.B.** /ˌes,oʊ'biː/) *n* [C] *pl* **sons of bitches** /ˌsʌn·zəv'bɪtʃ·əz/ *rude slang* a person, esp. a man, whom you do not like

soon /suːn/ *adv* [-*er*/-*est* only] in or within a short time; before long; quickly • *We'll soon be there.* ○ *How soon* (= When) *can we sign the contract?* ○ *"When would you like to meet?" "The sooner the better."* • Something that will happen **sooner or later** will certainly happen in the future, although it is not known exactly when: *Don't worry, sooner or later the cat will come home.*

soot /sʊt/ *n* [U] a black powder produced when coal, wood, etc., is burned

soothe /suːð/ *v* [T] to cause (someone) to be less upset or angry, or to cause (something) to hurt less • *I picked up the crying child and tried to soothe her.*

soothing /'suː·ðɪŋ/ *adj* • *a soothing ointment for sunburn*

sop /sɑp/ *n* [C] something unimportant or of little value that is offered to stop complaints or unhappiness • *He regarded third prize as just a sop.*

▫**sop up** *obj*, **sop** *obj* **up** /'sɑp'ʌp/ *v adv* [M] to absorb (a liquid) into a piece of solid matter • *She spilled some orange juice and sopped it up with paper towels.*

sophisticated /sə'fɪs·tə,keɪt̬·əd/ *adj* knowledgeable of the world and its ways, so that you are not easily fooled, and having an understanding of people and ideas without simplifying them • *Sophisticated readers understood the book's hidden meaning.* • If a way of thinking, a system, or a machine is sophisticated, it is complicated or made with great skill: *sophisticated military equipment*

sophomore /'sɑf,mɔːr, -,moʊr/ *n* [C] a student in the second year of a program of study in a college, university, or HIGH SCHOOL (= a school for students aged 14 to 18)

sophomoric /sɑf'mɔːr·ɪk, -'moʊr-/ *adj* (of an adult) childish and silly • *sophomoric behavior*

sopping /'sɑp·ɪŋ/ *adj* [not gradable] extremely wet • *You're sopping wet—go put some dry clothes on.*

soprano /sə'præn·oʊ, -'prɑn-/ *n* [C] *pl* **sopranos** a woman's or young boy's singing voice in the highest range, or a singer or musical instrument with this range

sorbet /sɔːr'beɪ/ *n* [C/U] a food made from frozen fruit juice and water • *(a) raspberry sorbet* [C/U]

sorcery /'sɔːr·sə·ri/ *n* [U] *esp. literary* a type of magic in which spirits, esp. evil ones, are used to make things happen

sordid MORALLY BAD /'sɔːrd·əd/ *adj* morally ugly, so that being involved makes you feel dirty • *In the movie, Bickle tries to rescue a child prostitute from her sordid profession.*

sordid DIRTY /'sɔːrd·əd/ *adj* dirty and in bad condition • *The sordid condition of many of the city school buildings was shocking.*

sore PAINFUL /sɔːr, soʊr/ *adj* painful and uncomfortable, esp. (of a body part) because of injury or infection or (of a muscle) from being used too much • *If you have a sore throat, take aspirin.* ○ *I went rowing yesterday for the first time in years, and my arms are sore today.*

sore /sɔːr, soʊr/ *n* [C] a painful area on the surface of a body, esp. an infected area

soreness /'sɔːr·nəs, 'soʊr-/ *n* [U]

sore ANGRY /sɔːr, soʊr/ *adj* [-er/-est only] *infml* angry, esp. because you feel you have been unfairly treated • *Chris wants to win, but he's not a sore loser.*

sorority /sə'rɔːr·ət̬·i, -'rɑr-/ *n* [C] a social organization for female students at a college or university • Compare FRATERNITY.

sorrow /'sɑr·oʊ, 'sɔːr-/ *n* [C/U] a feeling of great sadness or regret, or something that causes this feeling • *My mother still carried the sorrow and pain of my father's death twenty years ago.* [U]

sorry ASKING FORGIVENESS /'sɑr·i, 'sɔːr·i/ *adj* feeling bad because you have caused trouble or difficulty to someone else • *I'm really sorry (that) I forgot about our appointment yesterday.* [+ *(that)* clause] • Sorry is also used as a polite way to show your sympathy to someone because of a loss, disappointment, or trouble they have had: *We were sorry to learn about the death of your grandmother.* [+ *to* infinitive] • Sorry is also used as a polite way of asking someone to excuse you for having done something that might have annoyed them: *The train will be moving shortly—we are sorry for the inconvenience.*

sorry POLITE REFUSAL /'sɑr·i, 'sɔːr·i/ *adj* used as a polite way of expressing refusal or disagreement • *I'm sorry, but I think you've made a mistake in our check.* ○ *Sorry, you can't go in there.*

sorry BAD CONDITION /'sɑr·i, 'sɔːr·i/ *adj* [-er/-est only] *slightly dated* (of a situation or condition) so bad as to cause feelings of sympathy • *They were a sorry sight, dressed in rags and so weak they could hardly stand up.*

sort TYPE /sɔːrt/ *n* [C] a group of things that are of the same type or that share similar qualities • *What sort of equipment will she need?* ○ *He was squinting through the eyepiece of some sort of navigational device.* • Sort can sometimes refer to a person of a particular type: *What sort of person do you think I am?* • A person might say **a sort of/sort of** when they do not have a clear or exact knowledge of something and want to express their uncertainty about it: *He's a sort of agent for athletes, but not officially.* ○ *She's sort of running the company, I think, but her parents are still involved.* • **Sort of** also means in some way or to some degree: *It's sort of strange, but I felt I'd met her somewhere before.*

sort PUT IN ORDER /sɔːrt/ *v* [I/T] to put (things) in a particular order or separate them into groups according to a principle • *We have to sort the job applications into groups based on their qualifications.* [T] ○ *Paper, plastic, and cans are sorted for recycling.* [T] ○ *Sort out the clothes that you don't want, and we'll donate them to a charity.* [M] ○ *He spent hours, sorting through the photos* (= searching them to find one). [I always + adv/prep]

▫ **sort out** *obj*, **sort** *obj* **out** /'-'-/ *v adv* [M] to deal satisfactorily or successfully with (a problem or a situation) • *Her financial records are in a mess, but we'll sort them out.*

SOS /ˌes·oʊ'es/ *n* [C] (esp. from a boat or ship) an urgent request for help

so–so /'soʊ'soʊ/ *adj, adv* [not gradable] not very good but not very bad either • *"You had a bad time with the flu—how are you feeling?" "So-so, I'm still pretty weak."*

sought /sɔːt/ *past simple and past participle of* SEEK • If something is **sought-after**, it is wanted or desired: *He was one the most sought-after speakers at political rallies.*

soul SPIRIT /soʊl/ *n* [C] the part of a person that some people believe is spirit and that continues to exist in some form after their body has died, or the part of a person or thing that expresses the basic qualities that make it what it is • *May her soul rest in peace.* • If you say that someone is the soul of a quality, you mean they have that quality in a high degree: *He is the soul of honor, and would never intentionally try to deceive you.* • **Soul-searching** is deep and careful consideration of inner thoughts: *After much soul-searching, she decided not to run for reelection.*

soulful /'soʊl·fəl/ *adj* • *The dog looked at me with her big, soulful, brown eyes.*

soul BLACK CULTURE /soʊl/ *n* [U] a deep understanding of and pride in the culture of African Americans • **Soul food** is food that originated in the South and is esp. popular among

African Americans: *Corn bread, black-eyed peas, ham hocks, sweet potato pie, and southern fried chicken are all soul food.* • **Soul music** is a type of popular music with a strong beat and rhythm that developed from African-American GOSPEL MUSIC.

soul PERSON /soʊl/ *n* [C] a person of a stated type • *a happy soul* • Soul can also mean any person, and is usually used in negative statements: *There wasn't a soul around when we arrived at the beach.*

sound SOMETHING HEARD /saʊnd/ *n* [C/U] something heard or that may be heard • *They could hear the sound of an airplane overhead.* [C] • A **sound bite** is a short sentence or phrase said publicly esp. by a politician because it is likely to be repeated in newspapers or on television and radio. • In a radio or television program or a movie, the **sound effects** are the sounds other than speech or music that are added to make it seem more real. • A room or other inside space that is **soundproof** does not allow sound to go beyond it: *a soundproof television studio* • A **soundtrack** is a recording of the music from a movie or a play.

sound /saʊnd/ *v* [I/T] • *A bell sounds* (= makes a noise) *after fifty minutes to signal the end of the class period.* [I] ○ *Sound the alarm—a prisoner has escaped!* [T]

sound SEEM /saʊnd/ *v* to suggest a particular feeling, state, or thing by the way something is said or a noise is made • *He sounded rather discouraged when I called him yesterday.* [L] ○ *You sound as if you have a sore throat.* [I always + adv/prep] ○ *From what you told me, she sounds like* (= seems to be) *a nice person.* [I always + adv/prep] ○ *That sounds like fun* (= seems likely to be enjoyable). [I always + adv/prep] • A **sounding board** is a person or group you can use to test something, such as a new idea or suggestion, to see if they like it: *President Johnson said he used his wife as a sounding board for many of his ideas.*

sound HEALTHY /saʊnd/ *adj* [-er/-est only] in good condition; (of a person) healthy, or (of a thing) not broken or damaged • *a person of sound mind* ○ *Engineers had to close the bridge because it was not sound.* • If you say that someone is a sound sleeper, you mean they sleep easily and well, and are not easily waked up. ○ *She was sound asleep* (= completely in the sleeping state) *when the phone rang.*

WORDS THAT SOUND ALIKE

There are a number of words in English that are pronounced the same as another word but have a different spelling and meaning. For example, *son* and *sun* are both pronounced the same. Usually the meaning of words like this is clear from the sentences they are in.

My **son** *is a doctor.* • *The* **sun** *is really hot today.*

Here are some common words that most American and Canadian speakers pronounce alike:

air - heir	heal - heel	rap - wrap
aisle - I'll - isle	hear - here	read (past) - red
allowed - aloud	heard - herd	right - rite - write
ascent - assent	hi - high	road - rode
bare - bear	higher - hire	role - roll
base - bass	hole - whole	sail - sale
be - bee	knew - new	scene - seen
been - bin (US)/bean (Cdn)	knight - night	sea - see
berry - bury	knot - not	seam - seem
berth - birth	know - no	sew - so - sow
blew - blue	lead (= metal) - led	sole - soul
board - bored	leased - least	some - sum
brake - break	lessen - lesson	son - sun
bread - bred	loan - lone	stair - stare
buy - by - bye	made - maid	stake - steak
cell - sell	mail - male	stationary - stationery
cent - scent - sent	meat - meet	steal - steel
cereal - serial	medal - meddle	tail - tale
chord - cord	miner - minor	their - there - they're
coarse - course	morning - mourning	threw - through
dear - deer	none - nun	to - too - two
dew - do - due	one - won	toe - tow
die - dye	pain - pane	vain - vein
eye - I	pair - pare - pear	waist - waste
fair - fare	passed - past	wait - weight
fir - fur	peace - piece	war - wore
flew - flu - flue	plain - plane	wares - wears
flour - flower	pole - poll	warn - worn
foul - fowl	principal - principle	way - weigh
guessed - guest	rain - reign - rein	weak - week

sound GOOD /saʊnd/ *adj* [-*er*/-*est* only] good because based on good judgment or correct methods • *It was a sound approach to investing money.*

sound WATER PASSAGE /saʊnd/ *n* [C] a passage of sea connecting two larger areas of sea, or an area of sea mostly surrounded by land • *Puget Sound ○ Long Island Sound*

□**sound off** /-ˈ-, ˈ-,-/ *v adv* [I] *infml* to express opinions forcefully, esp. without being asked for them • *He's always sounding off about having to pay so much in taxes.*

□**sound out** *obj*, **sound** *obj* **out** /ˈ-ˈ-/ *v adv* [M] to discover the opinions or intentions of (a person) • *Why don't you sound her out before the meeting, to see which way she's going to vote?*

soundly /ˈsaʊn·dli/ *adv* completely • *She always sleeps soundly. ○ He was soundly defeated in his bid for reelection.*

soup /suːp/ *n* a liquid food made esp. by cooking vegetables and sometimes also meat or fish in water and usually served hot • *chicken/tomato/vegetable soup* [U] • A **soup kitchen** is a place where free soup and other food is given to people with no money or no homes.

□**soup up** *obj*, **soup** *obj* **up** /suːˈpʌp, ˈsuːˌpʌp/ *v adv* [M] to make mechanical changes to (something, esp. a car) to make it unusually powerful • *He souped it up so that it could go at speeds of over 100 mph.*

souped-up /ˈsuːpˈtʌp, -ˈdʌp/ *adj* • *a souped-up motorcycle*

sour TASTE /saʊr/ *adj* (esp. of food) having a sharp taste • *The four basic tastes are sweet, salty, bitter, and sour.* • **Sour cream** is cream that is made sour by adding special bacteria, and which is used in cooking.

sour /saʊr/ *v* [I] to become sour • *I'm afraid the milk has soured.*

sour UNPLEASANT /saʊr/ *adj* unfriendly or unpleasant in manner or attitude • *The relationship turned/went sour* (= became bad) *when David began to drink heavily.* • **Sour grapes** is said when someone cannot have something that they really want and so pretend that it is of no value to them: *After Claire failed to get into drama school, she said she never wanted to be an actress anyway, but we think that's just sour grapes.*

sour /saʊr/ *v* [I/T] to become bad or unpleasant, or cause (someone) to feel bad or unhappy • *The experience soured her toward men, and she never had another long-term relationship.* [T]

source /sɔːrs, soʊrs/ *n* [C] something or someone that causes or produces something, or is the origin of it • *a source of energy/light ○ Spinach is a good source of vitamins. ○ His wife was a constant source of inspiration to him.* • A source is also someone or something from which you obtain information: *The reporter refused to cite the names of her sources.*

south /saʊθ/ (*abbreviation* **S.**, **So.**) *n* [U] the direction opposite north, or the part of an area or country in this direction • *The points of the compass are north, south, east, and west.* • In the US, the South is the southeastern part of the country: *We moved to the South when I was a child.* • In the US Civil War, the South was the group of STATES that fought to become separate from the federal government. • **South of the border** means Mexico and the other countries south of the US border with Mexico.

south /saʊθ/ (*abbreviation* **S.**, **So.**) *adj*, *adv* [not gradable] • *The University is on the south side of town. ○ We drove south.* • The **South Pole** is the point on the earth's surface that is farthest south.

southerly /ˈsʌð·ər·li/ *adj* • *a southerly direction*

southern /ˈsʌð·ərn/ (*abbreviation* **S.**, **So.**) *adj* [not gradable] • *Louisiana is in the southern part of the US.*

southerner /ˈsʌð·ər·nər/ *n* [C] a person from the southern part of a country, or (in the US) a person from the South

southward /ˈsaʊθ·wərd/ *adj* [not gradable] toward the south • *a southward direction*

southward /ˈsaʊθ·wərd/, **southwards** /ˈsaʊθ·wərdz/ *adv* [not gradable] toward the south • *They drove southward toward the Mexican border.*

southeast /saʊˈθiːst/ (*abbreviation* **S.E.**) *n* [U] the direction between south and east, or the part of an area or country in this direction • *The house faces northwest, so southeast is behind us.*

southeast /saʊˈθiːst/ (*abbreviation* **S.E.**) *adj*, *adv* [not gradable] • *She lives on the southeast side of town. ○ They drove southeast.*

southeastern /saʊˈθiː·stərn/ (*abbreviation* **S.E.**) *adj* [not gradable] • *There will be rain in southeastern Massachusetts.*

southpaw /ˈsaʊθ·pɔː/ *n* [C] *infml* a left-handed person, esp. in sports and particularly a PITCHER (= person who throws the ball in baseball)

southwest /saʊθˈwest/ (*abbreviation* **S.W.**) *n* [U] the direction between south and west, or the part of an area or country that is in this direction • *He's currently living in the Southwest.*

southwest /saʊθˈwest/ (*abbreviation* **S.W.**) *adj*, *adv* [not gradable] • *The district is in the southwest corner of the state. ○ We drove southwest.*

southwestern /saʊθˈwes·tərn/ (*abbreviation* **S.W.**) *adj* [not gradable] • *She grew up in southwestern Ohio.*

souvenir /ˌsuː·vəˈnɪr/ *n* [C] something you keep or give as a remembrance of a special visit or event • *I'll keep this as a souvenir of my trip to New York.*

sovereign /ˈsɑv·rən/ *n* [C] a king or queen, or

a person having the power to govern a country

sovereign /'sɑv·rən/ *adj* [not gradable] • *Algeria was a colony but now is a sovereign nation.*

sovereignty /'sɑv·rən·ti/ *n* [U] the power or authority to rule

sow PLANT /soʊ/ *v* [I/T] *past simple* **sowed**, *past part* **sown** /soʊn/ *or* **sowed** to put (seeds) in the ground so that plants will grow • *Settlers sowed the seeds they had brought with them.* [T]

sow ANIMAL /sɑʊ/ *n* [C] an adult female pig

soybean /'sɔɪ·biːn/ *n* [C] a type of bean grown esp. in Asia and the US, used as a food for people and animals

soy sauce /'sɔɪ·sɔːs/ *n* [U] a salty, dark brown liquid made from SOYBEANS, used as a flavoring esp. in Chinese and Japanese cooking

spa /spɑ/ *n* [C] a place where people can stay to improve their appearance or health by eating well and exercising and sometimes also by drinking or bathing in water with natural substances in it

space EMPTY PLACE /speɪs/ *n* [C/U] an empty place • *a parking/storage space* [C] ○ *He was staring into space, seeing nothing.* [U] • Open space is land that has nothing built on it: *Out west there are lots of wide open spaces.* [C] • A **space bar** is a long key on a computer or TYPE-WRITER that you press to make an opening between words.

space /speɪs/ *v* [T] to arrange the distance between (things) • *Try to space the stitches evenly as you sew.*

spacing /'speɪ·sɪŋ/ *n* [U] • *Make sure there is equal spacing between you.*

spacious /'speɪ·ʃəs/ *adj* having a lot of space • *A spacious house is comfortable.*

space BEYOND EARTH /speɪs/ *n* [U] the area beyond the ATMOSPHERE (= air) of the earth • *space travel* ○ *The rocket blasted off to outer space.* • **Space-age** describes something that is very modern or esp. electronic: *space-age special effects* ○ *space-age machinery* • A **spacecraft** or a **spaceship** is a vehicle designed for travel in space: *an unmanned spacecraft* • A **space shuttle** is a vehicle to take people into space and back again. • A **space station** is a structure in space where people can live and work.

space TIME /speɪs/ *n* [U] an amount of time • *Within the space of three weeks, I felt much better.*

space /speɪs/ *v* [T] • *The moves are spaced about eight to ten seconds apart.*

spacing /'speɪ·sɪŋ/ *n* [U] • *Parents often plan the spacing of their children* (= the amount of time between them).

spaced out /speɪs'dɑʊt/, **spacey** /'speɪ·si/ *adj* *slang* not aware of or paying attention to what is happening around you • *I just got home from work and I'm kind of spaced out.*

spacious /'speɪ·ʃəs/ *adj* See at SPACE EMPTY PLACE.

spade /speɪd/ *n* [C] a tool with a blade for digging, esp. one with a long handle

spades /speɪdz/ *pl n* one of the four SUITS (= groups) of playing cards, the symbol for which is a black pointed leaf with a small stem • PIC SUITS

spaghetti /spə'ɡeṭ·i/ *n* [U] pasta made in long, thin, round strips

span /spæn/ *n* [C] the length of something • *A lifetime is a span of about seventy years.* ○ *The Rangers scored three goals in the span of five minutes.* • A span is also the distance between two points, esp. between the towers of a bridge: *In 1855, an 850-foot span was built to carry trains across the gorge.*

span /spæn/ *v* [T] **-nn-** • *An old bridge spans the river just outside the town.*

spangle /'spæŋ·ɡəl/ *n* [C] a small piece of shiny metal or plastic, used esp. to decorate clothes

spangled /'spæŋ·ɡəld/ *adj* • *She wore a spangled top and a short skirt.*

spaniel /'spæn·jəl/ *n* [C] a type of dog of small or medium size with soft hair and long ears that hang down

spank /spæŋk/ *v* [T] to hit (esp. a child) with the open hand on the buttocks, usually as a punishment

spanking /'spæŋ·kɪŋ/ *n* [C/U] • *My parents didn't believe in spanking.* [U]

spanner /'spæn·ər/ *n* [C] *Br for* WRENCH TOOL

spar /spɑr/ *v* [I] **-rr-** to practice the sport of boxing without hitting hard • *Dexter sparred with his partner for about an hour.* • To spar also means to argue: *State officials are still sparring over funding.*

spare SAVE /spær, sper/ *v* [T] to decide not to hurt or destroy (something or someone) • *Terrorists killed all the men but spared the women and children.*

spare AVOID /spær, sper/ *v* [T] to avoid (something) • *A quiet chat about this would spare everyone embarrassment.* • If you **spare no effort/expense** to do something, you have worked hard or spent as much money as necessary to achieve something: *She spared no expense in decorating her office.*

sparing /'spær·ɪŋ, 'sper-/ *adj* • *He certainly is sparing in his praise* (= avoids giving much of it).

sparingly /'spær·ɪŋ·li, 'sper-/ *adv* • *Apply the lotion sparingly.*

spare GIVE /spær, sper/ *v* [T] to give or lend (esp. time or money) • *Can you spare a dollar?* ○ *I'd love to come, but I'm afraid I can't spare the time.*

spare EXTRA /spær, sper/ *adj* [not gradable] not being used, or more than what is usually needed • *I keep my spare change in a jar.* • If you have an amount **to spare**, you have that much still available after using what you need:

I caught the plane with only five minutes to spare. • **Spare parts** are extra pieces that are used to replace pieces that break, esp. in a machine. • **Spare time** is time when you are not working or do not have anything you must do: *What do you like to do in your spare time?*

spare /ˈspær, sper/ *n* [C] • *In case I lose my key, I keep a spare in the garage.* • A spare or a **spare tire** is an extra tire for a car: *New cars come with good tires except for the spare.*

spare THIN /ˈspær, sper/ *adj* [-er/-est only] (of people) thin with no extra fat on the body • *He had the spare build of a runner.*

spareribs /ˈspær-rɪbz/, short form **ribs** *pl n* the RIBS (= chest bones) of a pig, with most of the meat removed • *Barbecued spareribs are a Texas specialty.*

spark /spɑrk/ *n* [C] a very small bit of something burning that flies out from a fire, or a flash of light seen when an electric current crosses an open space • *Flame, smoke, and sparks climbed into the dark sky.* ○ *Sparks from the old wiring started the fire.* ○ (*fig.*) *That one event was the spark for the riots* (= the small thing that started them). • A spark of something is a small amount of it: *When students show a spark of interest, I try to give them extra encouragement.* • When **sparks fly**, there is angry disagreement between people: *The sparks really fly when my mother and her sister get together.* • A **spark plug** (also **plug**) is a device in an engine that produces an electrical spark that burns the fuel.

spark /spɑrk/ *v* [T] • *Downed power lines sparked fires in several parts of town.* ○ *The killing sparked an outcry in the neighborhood.* ○ *We try to find stories that will spark our students' imaginations.*

sparkle /ˈspɑr-kəl/ *v* [I] to shine brightly • *The lake sparkled in the sunlight.* • (*fig.*) Someone or something that sparkles is energetic, interesting, and exciting: *His writings sparkle with intelligence.*

sparkle /ˈspɑr-kəl/ *n* [U] • *We could tell she was happy by the sparkle in her eyes.*

sparkling /ˈspɑr-kə-lɪŋ, ˈspɑr-klɪŋ/ *adj* • *His writing is known for its sparkling dialogue.* ○ *The whole house was sparkling clean.* • Sparkling wine or water has bubbles in it.

sparkler /ˈspɑr-klər/ *n* [C] a wire stick held in your hand and covered with a substance that produces SPARKS as it burns

sparrow /ˈspær-oʊ/ *n* [C] a common, small, gray-brown bird

sparse /spɑrs/ *adj* [-er/-est only] small in number or amount and not dense or close together • *plants with sparse foliage* ○ *sparse attendance* ○ *a sparse vocabulary*

sparsely /ˈspɑr-sli/ *adv* • *This area is very sparsely settled because there isn't much water.*

spartan /ˈspɑrt-ən/ *adj* simple and not particularly comfortable • *Our spartan way of life included hard beds, hard work, and no TV.*

spasm /ˈspæz-əm/ *n* [C] a sudden, uncontrollable tightening of a muscle, or a sudden, burst of activity or energy • *He left the game because of back spasms.* ○ *The rebels' spasm of resistance was short-lived.*

spat FORCE OUT /spæt/ *past simple and past participle of* SPIT FORCE OUT

spat ARGUMENT /spæt/ *n* [C] an argument about something not important • *This was a spat, not a serious fight.*

spate /speɪt/ *n* [U] an unusually large number of events that happen suddenly and at about the same time • *We have had a spate of burglaries recently.*

spatter /ˈspæt̬-ər/ *v* [I/T] to scatter (small drops or bits of liquid) on a surface, or (of liquid) to fall in small drops • *The taxi hit a puddle and spattered us with mud.* [T]

spatter /ˈspæt̬-ər/ *n* [C] • *You left paint spatters on the floor!*

spatula /ˈspætʃ-ə-lə/ *n* [C] a kitchen utensil with a wide flat blade, used esp. for lifting and spreading foods

spawn /spɔːn/ *n* [U] the eggs of fish

spawn /spɔːn/ *v* [I/T] (esp. of fish) to lay eggs • *Salmon swim up rivers and streams to spawn.* [I] ○ (*fig.*) *Generous loans have spawned hundreds of small businesses* (= caused them to be started). [T]

spay /speɪ/ *v* [T] to remove (the organs that produce eggs) from an animal

speak SAY WORDS /spiːk/ *v* [I/T] *past simple* **spoke** /spoʊk/, *past part* **spoken** /ˈspoʊ-kən/ to say (words), to use the voice, or to have a conversation with someone • *I heard someone speaking in the hallway.* [I] ○ *Please speak louder.* [I] ○ *"I'll never speak to you again," he said angrily.* [I] ○ *No one spoke a word* (= No one said anything). [T] ○ *She spoke in a whisper* (= very quietly). [I] • Speaking is used with adverbs ending in -ly to show that you are talking from a particular point of view: *Generally speaking, this is what happens when you see a nutritionist.* [I] • If you and another person are **on speaking terms**, you are friendly, or you are willing to talk to each other: *We had an argument, but we're back on speaking terms.* • **Speaking as** *a mother of four* (= with this experience), *I can tell you that children are exhausting.* [I] • *Casey is at a birthday party—* **speaking of** (= on the subject of) *birthdays, Abe's is Friday.* • If something **speaks for itself**, it is clear and needs no further explanation: *The senator's record speaks for itself.* • If you **speak too soon** you say something which is quickly shown not to be true: *It looks like Hanna will be late—I spoke too soon, here she comes now.* • *There was no snow* **to speak of** (= to mention) *this winter.* • USAGE: The related noun is SPEECH TALKING. • LP SAY, TELL, TALK, AND SPEAK at SAY SPEAK

speak KNOW A LANGUAGE /spiːk/ *v* [T] *past simple* **spoke** /spoʊk/, *past part* **spoken** /ˈspoʊ-kən/ to talk in (a language) • *How many languages do you speak?* ○ *He speaks fluent Italian.* ○ *When I arrived in Canada, I didn't speak a word of English* (= I did not know any English).

speaker /'spiː·kər/ *n* [C] someone who speaks a particular language • *a French/Chinese speaker* • See also **speaker** at SPEAK FORMAL TALK; SPEAKER.

speak FORMAL TALK /spiːk/ *v* [I] *past simple* **spoke** /spouk/, *past part* **spoken** /'spou·kən/ to give a formal talk • *Will you be speaking at the conference?* ○ *Ted will speak about careers in education.* • USAGE: The related noun is SPEECH FORMAL TALK.

speaker /'spiː·kər/ *n* [C] a person who gives a speech at a public event • *There will be three speakers at the graduation ceremony.* ○ *She's not a good public speaker.* • A speaker is also the person who controls the way in which business is done in an organization which makes laws, such as the US House of Representatives: *the Speaker of the House* • See also **speaker** at SPEAK KNOW A LANGUAGE; SPEAKER.

speaking /'spiː·kɪŋ/ *n* [U] • *She looks on public speaking as an opportunity to share information.* ○ *He has several speaking engagements* (= occasions when he will give a talk) *next month.*

speak SUGGEST /spiːk/ *v* [I/T] *past simple* **spoke** /spouk/, *past part* **spoken** /'spou·kən/ to show or express (something) without using words • *The incident spoke of shady financial dealings between the partners.* [I always + adv/prep] ○ *Her face spoke volumes* (= showed clearly what she thought). [T]

□ **speak for** /'--/ *v prep* [T] to express the opinions or wishes of (someone) • *I can't speak for the others.* • People say **speak for yourself** when they want to make it clear that they do not agree with what you said: *"None of us like the hotel." "Speak for yourself—I think it's OK."*

□ **speak out** /'-'-/ *v adv* [I] to say, esp. publicly, what you think about something such as a law or an official plan or action • *He spoke out against the school's admissions policy.*

□ **speak up** TALK LOUD /'-'-/ *v adv* [I] to speak louder • *Speak up! We can't hear you in the back.*

□ **speak up** EXPRESS OPINION /'-'-/ *v adv* [I] to express your opinion about something or someone • *If you disagree, please speak up.* ○ *He spoke up for me when I was in trouble.*

speaker /'spiː·kər/ *n* [C] a piece of electrical equipment through which recorded or broadcast sound can be heard • *We bought new speakers for our stereo system.* • See also **speaker** at SPEAK KNOW A LANGUAGE, SPEAK FORMAL TALK.

spear /spɪr/ *n* [C] a pole with a sharp point at

one end, used as a weapon that is either thrown or held in the hand

spear /spɪr/ *v* [T] • *They catch the fish by spearing them.* ○ *(fig.) She speared the steak with her fork and lifted it off the grill.*

spearhead /'spɪr·hed/ *v* [T] to lead (esp. a course of action or an attack) • *Joe will spearhead our new marketing campaign.*

spearmint /'spɪr·mɪnt/ *n* [U] a strong, sweet flavoring, or the plant from which this flavoring comes • *spearmint gum/toothpaste/tea*

spec CHANCE /spek/ *n* [U] *infml* • If something is done or made **on spec**, it is hoped, but not certain, that what is done will be paid for or sold: *These houses were built on spec.*

spec PLAN /spek/ *n* [C usually pl] *short form of* SPECIFICATION • *We're drawing up the specs for your new bathroom this week.*

special NOT USUAL /'speʃ·əl/ *adj* not ordinary or usual • *a special occasion* ○ *special attention/treatment* ○ *The car has a number of special safety features.* ○ *Is there anything special you'd like to do today?* ○ *The magazine published a special anniversary issue.* • Special can also mean unusually great or important: *You're very special to me.* • **Special effects** are artificial images, esp. in a film, that appear real but are created by artists and technical experts: *The movie won several awards for its special effects.*

special /'speʃ·əl/ *n* [C] • *There's a two-hour special* (= a television program that is not regularly shown) *on the Olympics tonight.* ○ *Our restaurant's specials today are pasta primavera, baked chicken with rice, and shrimp scampi* (= these foods are not always sold). • A special is also the sale of goods at a reduced price: *The store had a special on lawn furniture this week.*

specialty /'speʃ·əl·ti/, *Br* **speciality** /ˌspeʃ·iː'æl·ət·i/ *n* [C] a product that is unusually good in a particular place • *Oysters are a local specialty.* ○ *Paella is the specialty of the house at this restaurant.*

special PARTICULAR /'speʃ·əl/ *adj* [not gradable] having a particular purpose • *Kevin goes to a special school for the blind.* ○ *She's a special correspondent for the National Public Radio.* • **Special education/special ed** is education for children with physical or mental problems, who need to be taught in a different way.

specialist /'speʃ·ə·ləst/ *n* [C] someone who limits their studying or work to a particular area of knowledge, and who is an expert in that area • *She's a specialist in financial management.* • A specialist is also a doctor who works in and knows a lot about one particular area of medicine: *an eye/heart/joint specialist*

specialty /'speʃ·əl·ti/, *Br* **speciality** /ˌspeʃ·iː'æl·ət·i/ *n* [C] the subject of one's study or work, or a particular skill • *Her specialty is heart surgery.* ○ *The company's specialty is high-performance cars.*

specialize /'speʃ·ə,laɪz/ *v* [I] • *She's a lawyer who specializes in divorce cases.* ○ *The store specializes in Asian antiques.*

specialization /,speʃ·ə·lə'zeɪ·ʃən/ *n* [C/U] the limiting of one's study or work to one particular area, or a particular area of knowledge • *My main specialization was literature.* [C]

specialized /'speʃ·ə,laɪzd/ *adj* • *Her job is very specialized.*

specially /'speʃ·ə·li/ *adv* [not gradable] in a particular way or for a particular purpose • *Her wheelchair was specially designed for her.*

species /'spiː·ʃiːz, -siːz/ *n* [C] *pl* **species** a set of animals or plants, members of which have similar characteristics to each other and which can breed with each other • *an endangered/extinct/protected species* ○ *We found a rare species of orchid.*

specific /spɪ'sɪf·ɪk/ *adj* relating to one thing and not others; particular • *The virus attacks specific cells in the body.* ○ *The meeting is for the specific purpose of discussing the merger.*

specifically /spɪ'sɪf·ɪ·kli/ *adv* • *These jeans were designed specifically for women.* ○ *We went to New York specifically to visit the Metropolitan Museum.*

specification /,spes·ə·fə'keɪ·ʃən/, *short form* **spec** *n* [C usually pl] a clear, detailed plan or description of how something will be made • *Specifications have been drawn up for the new aircraft.* ○ *The house was built to the architect's specifications.*

specify (*obj*) /'spes·ə,faɪ/ *v* to state or describe (something) clearly and exactly • *The treaty specified terms for the withdrawal of troops.* [T] ○ *He didn't specify how much was spent on advertising.* [+ *wh-* word]

specific /spɪ'sɪf·ɪk/ *adj* clear and exact • *The report makes specific recommendations.* ○ *Can you be more specific?*

specifically /spɪ'sɪf·ɪ·kli/ *adv* • *I specifically asked you not to be late.* ○ *She mentioned you specifically.*

specifics /spɪ'sɪf·ɪks/ *pl n* exact details • *The proposal lacked specifics.* ○ *The specifics of the plan need to be worked out.*

specimen /'spes·ə·mən/ *n* [C] something shown or examined as an example; a typical example • *He has a collection of rare insect specimens.* • (*medical*) A specimen is a small amount of something, such as urine or blood, taken for testing.

specious /'spiː·ʃəs/ *adj slightly fml* seeming to be right or true, but really wrong or false • *a specious distinction* ○ *His whole argument is specious.*

speck /spek/ *n* [C] a very small mark, piece, or amount • *There are paint specks all over the floor.* ○ *These small islands are just specks on the map.* ○ *There's not a speck of dust in their house.*

speckled /'spek·əld/ *adj* having very small marks of a different color from the surface on

which they are found • *We saw some speckled goose eggs.*

spectacle UNUSUAL EVENT /'spek·tɪ·kəl/ *n* [C] an unusual or unexpected event or situation that attracts attention • *an amazing/terrible spectacle* ○ *The trial became a public spectacle.* ○ *She made a spectacle of herself* (= behaved in a way that attracted attention and made her look ridiculous).

spectacle PUBLIC SHOW /'spek·tɪ·kəl/ *n* [C] a large public event or show • *The fireworks were a magnificent spectacle.*

spectacles *dated* /'spek·tɪ·kəlz/, *infml short form* **specs** /speks/ *pl n* glasses • *You could just see his eyes behind the thick lenses of his spectacles.*

spectacular /spek'tæk·jə·lər/ *adj* exciting and interesting because of being large or extreme • *a spectacular sunset* ○ *The scenery is spectacular.* ○ *He scored a spectacular touchdown.* ○ *The raffle was a spectacular success.*

spectacularly /spek'tæk·jə·lər·li/ *adv* • *The city is spectacularly lit at night.* ○ *She is spectacularly well paid.*

spectacular /spek'tæk·jə·lər/ *n* [C] a large, exciting event, show, or performance • *a television spectacular*

spectator /'spek,teɪt·ər/ *n* [C] a person who watches an activity, esp. a public event, without taking part • *The stadium was packed with cheering spectators.* • A **spectator sport** is one which people go to watch: *Swimming is a popular form of recreation but not a popular spectator sport.*

specter, spectre /'spek·tər/ *n* [C] something that causes fear or worry • *The specter of violence surrounds the game.* ○ *Civil rights groups raised the specter of racial prejudice.* • A specter is also a GHOST (= the spirit of a dead person that can be seen).

spectrum RANGE /'spek·trəm/ *n* [C] a range of objects, ideas, or opinions • *There's agreement across the political spectrum.* ○ *A wide spectrum of opinion was represented at the meeting.*

spectrum LIGHT / BROADCASTING /'spek·trəm/ *n* [C] *pl* **spectra** /'spek·trə/ *or* **spectrums** the set of colors into which a beam of light can be separated, or a range of waves, such as light waves or radio waves • *the visible spectrum* ○ *Part of the radio spectrum is used by mobile phones.*

speculate GUESS /'spek·jə,leɪt/ *v* [I] to form opinions about something without having the necessary information or facts; to make guesses • *I'm just speculating about what happened.* ○ *Officials refused to speculate on the cause of the crash.*

speculation /,spek·jə'leɪ·ʃən/ *n* [C/U] • *The rumors were dismissed as mere speculation.* [U] ○ *There is widespread speculation that the company is about to collapse.* [U] ○ *Len kept his speculations to himself.* [C]

speculative /'spek·jə,lət·ɪv/ *adj* • *Our forecast for next year is speculative.*

speculate TRADE /'spek·jə,leɪt/ *v* [I] to buy and sell with the hope that the value of what you buy will increase and that it can then be sold at a higher price in order to make a profit • *He made his money speculating in the gold and silver markets.*

speculation /,spek·jə'leɪ·ʃən/ *n* [C/U] • *currency/land speculation* [U]

speculative /'spek·jə·lət̬·ɪv/ *adj* • *a speculative venture*

speculator /'spek·jə,leɪt̬·ər/ *n* [C] • *a real estate speculator*

sped /sped/ *past simple and past participle of* SPEED

speech TALKING /spiːtʃ/ *n* [U] the ability to talk, or the activity of talking • *People who suffer a stroke may experience a loss of speech.* • Your speech is also your way of talking: *His speech became slurred and indistinct.* • Speech can also mean the language used when talking: *Some expressions are used more in speech than in writing.* • USAGE: The related verb is SPEAK SAY WORDS.

speechless /'spiːtʃ·ləs/ *adj* [not gradable] temporarily unable to talk or to know what to say, esp. because of having strong feelings • *Her remark left me speechless.*

speech FORMAL TALK /spiːtʃ/ *n* [C] a formal talk given usually to a large number of people on a special occasion • *an acceptance speech* ◦ *I'm nervous about the speech I'm making tomorrow.* • A **speechwriter** is a person whose job is to write formal talks for someone else. • USAGE: The related verb is SPEAK FORMAL TALK.

speed /spiːd/ *n* [C/U] (a) rate at which something moves or happens • *a speed of 25 miles per hour* [C] ◦ *Both cars were traveling at high speed.* [U] ◦ *They came racing down the hill at*

top speed (= as fast as they could go). [U] ◦ *The processing speed of my new computer is much faster.* [U] ◦ *This electric drill has two speeds* (= rates at which it turns). [C] • A speed is also a GEAR (= part that controls the rate at which a vehicle moves): *I have a ten-speed bicycle.* [C] • A **speedboat** is a small boat that has a powerful engine and can travel very fast. • A **speed limit** is the fastest rate at which vehicles can legally travel on a particular road: *They raised the speed limit on the interstate to 65 miles per hour.*

speed /spiːd/ *v* [I/T] *past* **sped** /sped/ or **speeded** to move, go, or happen fast, or to cause (something) to happen fast • *The train sped along at over 120 miles per hour.* [I] ◦ *This year seems to be speeding by/past.* [I] ◦ *Ambulances sped the injured people* (= moved them quickly) *away from the scene.* [T]

speeding /'spiːd·ɪŋ/ *n* [U] the act of driving a vehicle faster than is legally allowed • *He was fined $75 for speeding.*

speedy /'spiːd·i/ *adj* very quick or fast • *They hope to bring a speedy end to the conflict.*

speedily /'spiːd·ə·li/ *adv* • *The error can be speedily corrected.*

□ **speed up** (*obj*), **speed** (*obj*) **up** /'-'-/ *v adv* [I/M] to go or happen faster, or to cause (something) to happen faster • *The car suddenly speeded up and went through a red light.* [I] ◦ *He developed a new system to help speed up the work.* [M]

speedometer /spɪ'dɑm·ət̬·ər/ *n* [C] a device in a vehicle that shows how fast the vehicle is moving

spell FORM WORDS /spel/ *v* [I/T] to form (a word or words) with the letters in the correct order • *As a child he never learned to spell, so now he*

WORDS THAT ARE SPELLED THE SAME

There are many words in English that are spelled the same as another word but that have a different meaning and origin. The pronunciation of these words is often the same.

We saw a polar **bear** *at the zoo.* • *I just can't* **bear** *the excitement.*

Some words that are spelled alike differ in their pronunciation.

Gold is heavier than **lead** • *You* **lead** *and I'll follow you.*

Here are some examples:

close	*v*	**Close** *your eyes and count to ten.*
	adj	*Please stay* **close**—*it's easy to get lost.*
live	*v*	*I* **live** *on a busy street.*
	adj	*The restaurant had a tank of* **live** *fish.*
minute	*n*	*Can I speak to you for a* **minute**?
	adj	*We have a* **minute** *apartment.*
tear	*n*	*She noticed a* **tear** *in the corner of his eye.*
	v	*To open,* **tear** *along the dotted line.*
used to	*phrasal auxiliary*	*There* **used to** *be a farm here, years ago.*
	v	*Explosives were* **used to** *enter the building.*
wind	*n*	**Wind** *speeds reached 80 miles an hour.*
	v	*You have to* **wind** *the handle to the left.*
wound	*v*	*He* **wound** *the rope around his arm.*
	n	*One man received a knife* **wound**.

CONTINUED

WORDS THAT ARE SPELLED THE SAME *(continued)*

Sometimes words that are spelled alike have different stress patterns. In these cases, nouns are usually stressed on the first syllable and verbs on the second syllable. Some common examples are:

contract	*n*	*The new export* **contract** *is worth $16 million.*
	v	*Your muscles will* **contract** *if you get cold.*
object	*n*	*This stone* **object** *is over 5000 years old.*
	v	*I strongly* **object** *to the spending cuts.*
project	*n*	*The housing* **project** *will create new homes.*
	v	*They* **project** *an increase in sales next year.*
record	*n*	*He set a new* **record** *for the mile run.*
	v	*The orchestra plans to* **record** *all of Mozart.*

---

looks everything up in the dictionary. [I] ○ *Send it to Dr. Mikolajczyk—I'll spell that name (out) for you* (= say the letters that form the word). [T/M] • If you **spell** something **out**, you explain it in detail: *The mayor has so far refused to spell out how he intends to raise the money.*

spelling /'spel·ɪŋ/ *n* [C/U] the forming of words with the letters in the correct order, or the way in which a word is formed • *I shouldn't be marked wrong just because I used British spellings rather than American.* [C] • A **spelling bee** is a competition in which people, often students, try to spell increasingly difficult words until all but one make a mistake.

spell RESULT /spel/ *v* [T] to have (usually something unpleasant) as a result • *This cold weather could spell trouble for gardeners.*

spell PERIOD /spel/ *n* [C] a period of time during which an activity or condition lasts • *a spell of wet weather* ○ *She lived in London for a short spell in the 1980s.*

spell MAGIC /spel/ *n* [C] magic produced by speaking a set of words or taking a specific set of actions • *The curse put him under a spell until the princess kissed him.*

spellbound /'spel·baʊnd/ *adj* having your attention completely held by something, so that you cannot think about anything else • *At the circus, the children are spellbound, watching the acrobats perform.*

spend MONEY /spend/ *v* [I/T] *past* **spent** /spent/ to give (money) as a payment for something • *We spent a lot of money on our vacation but we had a great time.* [T]

spending /'spen·dɪŋ/ *n* [U] the act of giving money for goods and services • *Government spending for scientific research will be increased in next year's budget.* ○ *We have to find ways to cut spending and keep down costs.*

spend TIME /spend/ *v* [T] *past* **spent** /spent/ to use (time), to allow (time) to go past • *It doesn't look as if you spent very long on your homework.* ○ *I've spent many years building up my collection.* ○ *You can spend the night here if you like* (= stay here for the night).

spend FORCE /spend/ *v* [T] *past* **spent** /spent/ to use (energy, effort, force, etc.), esp. until there is no more left • *For the past month he's been spending all his energy trying to find a job.*

spent /spent/ *adj* [not gradable] completely used to the point of no longer having any power or effectiveness • *Following the shooting, police searched for spent shells and other evidence.* • Spent also means having no energy left: *After doing her Christmas shopping, she was spent.*

spendthrift /'spend·θrɪft/ *n* [C] *disapproving* a person who spends money foolishly and wastes it, or spends more than is necessary • *I'm not a spendthrift and I really have to think about my purchases.*

sperm /spɜrm/ *n* [C/U] *pl* **sperm** a reproductive cell produced by a male animal • *In human reproduction, usually only one sperm fertilizes an egg.* [C] • Sperm is also SEMEN (= liquid containing the reproductive cells of male animals). [U]

spew /spjuː/ *v* [I/T] to flow or let out, esp. in large amounts • *The volcano spewed (out) a giant cloud of ash, dust, and gases into the air.* [I/T]

sphere AREA /sfɪr/ *n* [C] a range or area of activity • *In the foreign policy sphere, Li also indicated that China is ready to include human rights in its diplomacy.* ○ *When the children played they always remained within the sphere of their own little group.*

sphere ROUND OBJECT /sfɪr/ *n* [C] an object shaped like a round ball • *This changes the shape of the cornea from a spoonlike form to a sphere.*

spherical /'sfɪr·ɪ·kəl, 'sfer-/ *adj* • *The earth is not perfectly spherical.*

sphinx /sfɪŋks/ *n* [C] *pl* **sphinxes** an ancient, imaginary creature with a lion's body and a human head

spice /spaɪs/ *n* [C/U] a flavoring for food made from part of a plant, such as its fruit, seeds, or root, usually dried and often made into a powder • *Cinnamon, ginger, and cloves are all spices.* [C] ○ *This curry needs a little more spice.* [U] • Spice can also mean excitement or interest: *"Variety is the spice of life" is a common expression.* [U]

spice /spaɪs/ *v* [T] • *Low-calorie sauces can spice up bland chicken.* [M] • To spice something is to add excitement or interest to it: *In order to keep them interested, spice (up) their training with breaks in the routine.* [T/M]

spicy /ˈspaɪ·si/ *adj* flavored with spices that are hot to the taste • *spicy Mexican food*

spick–and–span /ˌspɪk·ənˈspæn/ *adj* [not gradable] very clean and neat

spider /ˈspaɪd·ər/ *n* [C] a small, insectlike creature with eight thin legs

spiel /spiːl, ʃpiːl/ *n* [C] a speech, esp. one that is long and spoken quickly and is intended to persuade the listener about something • *a sales/marketing spiel*

spiffy /ˈspɪf·i/ *adj* [-er/-est only] *infml* stylish, attractive, or pleasing • *She got a spiffy haircut.*

spigot /ˈspɪg·ət, ˈspɪk-/ *n* [C] a device used to control a flow of liquid, esp. from a container or pipe • *(fig.) Unless you turn the spigot off at the source, you'll continue to have more crime.*

spike POINT /spaɪk/ *n* [C] a long metal nail used to hold something in place, or a shape that is long and narrow and comes to a point at one end • *railroad spikes* • Spikes are also pointed pieces of metal fixed on the bottom of special shoes, used in some sports to catch in the ground and prevent falling or sliding, or the shoes themselves. • A spike is also a sudden increase, often shown on a GRAPH (= type of drawing) by a long, narrow shape that comes to a point at the top: *The upward spike in prices was attributed to bad weather in farm areas.*

spike MAKE STRONGER /spaɪk/ *v* [T] to make (esp. a drink) stronger by adding alcohol • *She claimed that someone had spiked her drink.*

spill /spɪl/ *v* [I/T] to cause (a liquid) to flow or fall over the edge of a container or beyond the limits of something, or (of a liquid) to flow or fall in this way • *I just spilled gravy on my shirt.* [T] ○ *He tried to fill the sugar bowl and managed to spill sugar all over the floor.* [T] ○ *Some milk spilled on the floor.* [I] • To **spill the beans** is to tell a secret or let a secret become known unintentionally: *We'll all be there at 6 for the surprise party—now don't spill the beans!*

spill /spɪl/ *n* [C] • *The tanker started to leak oil and officials worried about a major oil spill.* • A spill is also a fall: *Jockey Luis Ortega suffered a broken ankle in a spill at Hollywood Park yesterday.*

□**spill over** /ˈ-ˈ--/ *v adv* [I always + adv/prep] to reach or influence a larger area; spread • *The conflict threatens to spill over into neighboring regions.*

spillover /ˈspɪlˌoʊ·vər/ *n* [U] • *The TV series created spillover interest in the Civil War.*

spin TURN /spɪn/ *v* [I/T] **spinning**, past **spun** /spʌn/ to turn around and around, esp. quickly, or to cause (something or someone) to turn • *The earth spins on its axis.* [I] ○ *She heard footsteps behind her, and spun around to see who was there.* [I] ○ *The slight contact spun Joyce around.* [T] • If you **spin** your **wheels**, you use a lot of effort but don't get anything

done: *For almost an hour now he had been spinning his wheels, accomplishing nothing.*

spin /spɪn/ *n* [C/U] a fast turning movement • *I hit a patch of ice in the road, which sent the car into a spin.* [C]

spin WAY OF REPRESENTING /spɪn/ *n* [U] a particular way of representing an event or situation to the public so that it will be understood in a way that you want it to be understood • *They tried to put a positive/negative spin on the story* (= They tried to make it seem better or worse), *but nobody was fooled.* ○ *To understand spin, he said, is to understand that you get your story told without getting your fingerprints on it.* • **Spin control** is an effort to control the damage done by a bad situation: *Various spokespersons attempted a desperate exercise in spin control to deny that Reagan ever made such a promise.* • *(slang)* A **spin doctor** is a person who represents esp. a political situation in a way that is likely to help one side and hurt another: *News coverage of the campaign can be influenced to a candidate's advantage by spin doctors.*

spin MAKE THREAD /spɪn/ *v* [T] **spinning**, past **spun** /spʌn/ to make (thread) by twisting fibers, or to produce (something) using thread • *Cotton is spun into thread.* ○ *Spiders spin webs.*

spin TRIP /spɪn/ *n* [C] a short trip taken for pleasure, usually in a car • *We went for a spin in Bill's new car.*

□**spin off** *obj*, **spin** *obj* **off** /ˈ-ˈ-/ *v adv* [M] to produce (something additional), often something not originally planned • *The space program has spun off many new commercial technologies.* • To spin off something is also to form a separate company from parts of an existing company: *The corporation will spin its maintenance department off as an independent business.*

spinoff /ˈspɪn·ɔːf/ *n* [C] products produced in addition to the main products of a process • *The research has spinoffs in the development of medical equipment.* • A spinoff is also a separate company formed from parts of an existing company.

□**spin out** *obj*, **spin** *obj* **out** /ˈ-ˈ-/ *v adv* [M] to discuss in greater detail; give more information about • *Let me spin this out in a little bit more detail.*

spinach /ˈspɪn·ɪtʃ/ *n* [U] a vegetable that has wide, dark green leaves that are eaten cooked or raw • *a spinach salad*

spindly /ˈspɪn·dli/ *adj* long or tall and thin, and not appearing to be very solid or strong • *Carrie, almost six, was all spindly arms and legs.*

spine BONE /spaɪn/, **backbone**, **spinal column** *n* [C] the line of bones down the center of the back that provides support for the body

spinal /ˈspaɪn·əl/ *adj* [not gradable] • *He suffered a spinal injury from the fall.* • *The*

spinal cord is the set of nerves inside the spine that connect the brain to other nerves in the body.

spine POINT /spaɪn/ n [C] one of the pointy, needlelike objects that are part of the outer surface of some animals and plants • *Be careful of the cactus spines.*

spine BOOK PART /spaɪn/ n [C] the end of a book where the pages are attached and which usually shows the writer's name and title on its outer part

spineless /'spaɪn·ləs/ adj disapproving lacking determination and the willingness to take risks • *It upset me to realize how spineless I was.*

spine

spinster /'spɪn·stər/ n [C] dated a woman who is not married, esp. a woman who is no longer young and seems unlikely ever to marry • USAGE: This word is likely to be offensive except if it is used about people in the past.

spiral /'spaɪ·rəl/ n [C] a shape of a continuous, curving line that forms circles around a center point • *A corkscrew is made in a spiral.* ○ (fig.) *Roy was bitter about the downward spiral of his life* (= it was becoming continuously worse).

spiral /'spaɪ·rəl/ adj [not gradable] • *New playground equipment includes a large spiral slide.* • A **spiral notebook** is a book of paper for writing that is held together along one edge by a spiral wire.

spiral /'spaɪ·rəl/ v [I] **-l-** or **-ll-** • *The engine quit, and my beautiful model airplane spiraled downward.* ○ *High winds spiraled around the storm center.*

spire /spaɪr/ n [C] a structure that rises to a point, esp. a church tower • *The mountains' rocky spires surrounded us.*

spirit STATE OF MIND /'spɪr·ət/ n [U] a state of mind or attitude • *It's very important to play the game in the right spirit.* ○ *Rock music in the 1960s expressed the spirit of the times.*

spirits /'spɪr·əts/ pl n a mood • *I've been in low spirits all day.* • See also SPIRITS.

spirit INNER CHARACTER /'spɪr·ət/ n [C/U] the inner character of a person, thought of as different from the material person we can see and touch • *All her life she remained young in spirit, bubbling with ideas.* [U] ○ *It is a belief of many religions that your spirit lives on after your body dies.* [C] • A spirit is also something that can be felt to be present but cannot be seen, similar to a GHOST. *Evil spirits seemed to fill the empty rooms.* [C]

spiritual /'spɪr·ət·ʃ·ə·wəl/ adj • *Religion focuses on the spiritual side of life.* ○ *The Dalai Lama is the spiritual leader of Tibet.* • See also SPIRITUAL.

spiritually /'spɪr·ət·ʃ·ə·wə·li/ adv • *He seemed to be a rare person, both spiritually and physically.*

spirit ENTHUSIASM /'spɪr·ət/ n [U] enthusiasm and energy • *The orchestra performed the symphony with great spirit.*

spirited /'spɪr·ət·əd/ adj • *It was an unusually spirited performance of the play.*

spirit MOVE /'spɪr·ət/ v [T always + adv/prep] to move (someone or something) secretly • *Everyone wonders who spirited away the body.* [M]

spirits /'spɪr·əts/ pl n fml strong alcoholic drink; LIQUOR • *Sale of beer, wine, or spirits to anyone under 21 is illegal.* • See also **spirits** at SPIRIT STATE OF MIND.

spiritual /'spɪr·ət·ʃ·ə·wəl/ n [C] a kind of religious song, originally developed by African-Americans • See also **spiritual** at SPIRIT INNER CHARACTER.

spit FORCE OUT /spɪt/ v [I/T] **spitting**, past **spat** /spæt/ or **spit** to force out (liquid in the mouth), esp. SALIVA (= liquid produced in the mouth) • *She spat on the guard's shoes to show her contempt.* [I] ○ (fig.) *He angrily spat an insult out* (= said it quickly). [M] • (infml) If you say **spit it out** to someone, you are asking them to tell you something that they find it hard to say or seem unwilling to say. • If someone is **the spitting image** of someone else, they look just like that person.

spit /spɪt/ n [U] infml SALIVA (= liquid produced in the mouth) • *Spit dribbled down his chin.*

spit ROD /spɪt/ n [C] a long, thin rod put through meat to hold it while it cooks over a fire

spit LAND /spɪt/ n [C] a long, thin point of land that sticks out into water • *Our hotel was perched on a spit of land in the harbor.*

spite DESIRE TO HURT /spaɪt/ n [U] the desire to annoy, upset, or hurt someone • *He let the air out of your tires just for spite.*

spite /spaɪt/ v [T] • *I think he died without making a will just to spite his family.*

spiteful /'spaɪt·fəl/ adj • *They were just spiteful gossips spreading rumors.*

spite DESPITE /spaɪt/ n • **In spite of** means without considering or being prevented by: *In spite of his injury, Ricardo will play in Saturday's game.*

splash HIT WITH LIQUID /splæʃ/ v [I/T] to scatter (liquid) or to cause liquid to scatter through the air or onto something • *She splashed her face with cold water.* [T] ○ *Kids love to splash around in mud puddles.* [I]

splash /splæʃ/ n [C] an amount of liquid scattered, or the sound made by liquid being scattered • *I wiped up the splashes from the floor.* ○ *Jimmy jumped into the pool with a splash.*

splash AREA OF BRIGHTNESS /splæʃ/ n [C] a bright area of color or light • *a splash of sunlight* ○ *The child's red dress brought a splash of color to the picture.*

splashy /'splæʃ·i/ adj attracting attention,

particularly colorful or showy • *Her dress was made of a bright, splashy print.*

splat /splæt/ *n* [U] *infml* the sound of something wet hitting a surface • *The tomato hit the window with a splat.*

splatter /'splæt·ər/ *v* [I/T] (esp. of something wet) to hit and scatter onto (a surface) in small drops, or to cause this to happen • *The bike was splattered with mud.* [T]

splatter /'splæt·ər/ *n* [C] • *Splatters of paint covered the floor.*

splay /spleɪ/ *v* [I/T] to spread wide apart • *He lay on the floor, his legs splayed out beneath him.* [I]

splendid /'splen·dəd/ *adj* extremely good, large, or important • *Our splendid weather ended with a terrible storm.* ○ *The splendid old opera house was torn down.*

splendidly /'splen·dəd·li/ *adv* very well; admirably • *Although we were very different, we got along splendidly.*

splendor /'splen·dər/ *n* [C/U] great beauty, or something that causes admiration and attention • *It took several years to restore the building to its original splendor.* [U] ○ *We can only imagine the splendors of ancient Rome.* [C]

splice /splaɪs/ *v* [T] to join (the ends of something) so that they become one piece • *Scientists splice genes to produce the protein.*

splint /splɪnt/ *n* [C] a flat piece of material that does not bend, used to support a broken bone and to keep it in one position

splinter /'splɪnt·ər/ *n* [C] a small, sharp, piece of wood, glass, or similar material that has broken off a larger piece • *She tried to ignore the splinter in her foot.* • A **splinter group** is a group of people who have left a political party or other organization to form a new, separate organization.

splinter /'splɪnt·ər/ *v* [I] • *The old tree cracked and splintered as it fell.*

split /splɪt/ *v* [I/T] **splitting**, *past* **split** to divide into two or more parts, esp. along a particular line • *I suggest we split the profits between us.* [T] ○ *The teacher split the class into three groups.* [T] ○ *His pants split when he jumped the fence.* [I] • (*slang*) To split also means to leave a place: *The movie was boring, so I split.* [I] • If you **split the difference** with someone, you agree to take a position or pay an amount between what each of you originally wanted: *You want $50 for the bike and I say it's worth $30—let's split the difference and I'll pay you $40.* • If two people **split up**, their marriage or relationship ends.

split /splɪt/ *n* [C] a long, thin tear, or a division • *There's a split in this sheet.* ○ *Peace talks are threatened by a split among rebel leaders.* • A **split-level (house)** is a house in which some rooms are half a floor above or below others. • A **split second** is a very short period of time: *For a split second we thought the bus would crash.*

splitting /'splɪt̬·ɪŋ/ *adj* [not gradable] very strong, severe, or painful • *a splitting headache* ○ *an ear-splitting noise*

splotch /splɑtʃ/ *n* [C] a mark or spot with an irregular shape • *The rash showed as red splotches on her face.*

splurge /splɜrdʒ/ *v* [I/T] to spend (money) on something that is more expensive or luxurious than you usually buy • *We could save the money or splurge on a new car* [I]

splurge /splɜrdʒ/ *n* [C] • *We go to that restaurant for our big end-of-the-year splurge.*

spoil DESTROY /spɔɪl/ *v* [I/T] *past* **spoiled** or **spoilt** /spɔɪlt/ to destroy or damage (something), or to become destroyed or damaged • *The oil spill spoiled five miles of coastline.* [T] ○ *Don't tell me how it ends, you'll spoil the movie for me.* [T] ○ *Food spoils quickly in hot weather.* [I]

spoiled /spɔɪld/ *adj* [not gradable] • *spoiled meat*

spoil TREAT TOO WELL /spɔɪl/ *v* [T] *past* **spoiled** or **spoilt** /spɔɪlt/ to treat (someone) very well, esp. by being too generous • *My vacation spoiled me.* ○ *"We're spoiling you," he said, handing her another cookie.*

spoiled /spɔɪld/ *adj* [not gradable] • *You're acting like a spoiled brat.*

spoils /spɔɪlz/ *pl n* goods, advantages, or profits obtained by winning a war or being in a particular position or situation • *Only one competitor wins and gets the spoils of victory.*

spoke SPEAK /spoʊk/ *past simple of* SPEAK

spoke WHEEL PART /spoʊk/ *n* [C] any of the rods that join the edge of a wheel to its center to strengthen it • PIC BICYCLE

spoken /'spoʊ·kən/ *past participle of* SPEAK

spokesperson (*pl* **-people**) /'spoʊk,spɜr·sən/, **spokesman** (*pl* **-men**) /'spoʊk·smən/, **spokeswoman** (*pl* **-women**) /'spoʊk,swʊm·ən/ *n* [C] a person who makes official, public statements for a group or organization • *a government spokesperson*

sponge SUBSTANCE /spʌndʒ/ *n* [C/U] a substance that is full of holes, soft when wet, and able to absorb a lot of liquid, used for washing and cleaning • *He wiped off the table with a soapy sponge.* [C]

sponge /spʌndʒ/ *v* [T] to wash or clean, esp. by using a wet sponge or cloth • *Sponge the stain promptly with cold water.* ○ *She's always sponging off the kitchen counter.* [M]

spongy /'spʌn·dʒi/ *adj* • *The ground was damp and spongy* (= soft).

sponge GET MONEY /spʌndʒ/ *v* [I/T] to get (money, food, or other needs) from other people rather than by taking care of yourself, or to live by getting help from other people • *He's been sponging off her for years.*

sponge cake /'spʌndʒ (,keɪk/ *n* [C] a soft, light cake made with eggs, sugar, and flour but without fat

sponsor /'spɑn·sər/ *v* [T] to support (a person,

organization, or activity) by giving money, encouragement, or other help • *The Rotary Club sponsors Little League baseball in the summer.*

sponsor /'spɑn·sər/ *n* [C] • *Corporate sponsors support many public TV programs.*

sponsorship /'spɑn·sər‚ʃɪp/ *n* [C/U] • *corporate sponsorship of the arts* [U]

spontaneous /spɑn'teɪ·ni·əs/ *adj* happening naturally, without planning or encouragement • *a spontaneous performance* ∘ *spontaneous affection*

spontaneously /spɑn'teɪ·ni·ə·sli/ *adv* • *The children spontaneously gave us hugs and kisses.*

spontaneity /‚spɑnt·ᵊn'eɪ·ət·i, -'iː·ət·i/ *n* [U] • *There seemed to be no time for spontaneity—or even joy.*

spoof /spuːf/ *n* [C] an original work that copies the style of another work in a way meant to be ridiculous or humorous • *The book ends with a hilarious spoof of an academic conference.*

spoof /spuːf/ *v* [I/T] • *The funniest part of the show spoofed TV news.* [T]

spook FRIGHTEN /spuːk/ *v* [T] to frighten (a person or animal) • *That car wreck spooked me badly.*

spooky /'spuː·ki/ *adj infml* • *I think it's very spooky sleeping in a dark and creaky house.*

spook SPIRIT /spuːk/ *n* [C] *infml for* GHOST

spook PERSON /spuːk/ *n* [C] *slang* SPY PERSON

spool /spuːl/ *n* [C] a cylinder that is wider at each end, around which esp. thread, wire, or film is wrapped • *TV cables were unwound from huge spools.*

spoon /spuːn/ *n* [C] a utensil that is a flattened bowl with a handle, used for mixing, serving, and eating food • *a wooden cooking spoon* ∘ *a silver baby spoon*

spoon /spuːn/ *v* [T always + adv/prep] • *Spoon a little gravy over the meat.* • If you **spoon-feed** someone, esp. a baby, you feed them soft food with a spoon. • (*disapproving*) If you **spoon-feed** something to someone, you give it to them in a way that prevents them from acting or thinking independently: *I was being spoon-fed friendly audiences that wouldn't give me trouble.*

spoonful /'spuːn·fʊl/ *n* [C] *pl* **spoonfuls** or **spoonsful** /'spuːnz·fʊl/ the amount that a spoon will hold • *a spoonful of mustard*

sporadic /spə'ræd·ɪk/ *adj* not happening or appearing in a pattern; not continuous or regular • *She makes sporadic trips to Europe.* ∘ *Sporadic shooting continued throughout the night.*

sporadically /spə'ræd·ɪ·kli/ *adv* • *I've been working sporadically this year.*

sport GAME /spɔːrt, spoʊrt/ *n* [C/U] a game, competition, or similar activity, done for enjoyment or as a job, that takes physical effort and skill and is played or done by following particular rules • *Football, baseball, and bas-*

ketball are all team sports. [C] ∘ *Do you hunt for sport or in order to eat?* [U] • A **sport utility vehicle** (*abbreviation* SUV) is a very large car that looks like a small truck and can be driven where there are no roads.

sporting /'spɔːrt̬·ɪŋ, 'spoʊrt̬-/ *adj* connected with sports • *The Olympics is the biggest sporting event in the world.*

sports /spɔːrts, spoʊrts/ *adj* [not gradable] connected with sports • *He only reads the sports section of the newspaper.* • A **sports car** is a fast, low car, often big enough for only two people. • A **sportscaster** is someone who broadcasts descriptions of sporting events and news about sports.

sportsmanship /'spɔːrts·mən‚ʃɪp, 'spoʊrts-/ *n* [U] the quality of showing fairness, respect, and generosity toward the opposing team or player and for the sport itself when competing

sport PERSON /spɔːrt, spoʊrt/ *n* [C] *infml* a person who has a good attitude about playing a game or having to do something • *He was a very bad sport when he lost a game.* ∘ *Be a sport and take your little sister to the movies with you.*

sport WEAR /spɔːrt, spoʊrt/ *v* [T] to wear or be decorated with (something) • *Back in the 1960s he sported bellbottoms and long hair.*

sports jacket /'spɔːrts ‚dʒæk·ət, 'spoʊrts-/, **sport coat** /'spɔːrt ‚koʊt, 'spoʊrt-/ *n* [C] a man's jacket, which is worn with pants of a different color or cloth

sportswear /'spɔːrt·swer, -swær/ *n* [U] informal clothing designed for comfort • *Sportswear has become popular around the world.*

sporty /'spɔːrt̬·i, 'spoʊrt̬·i/ *adj* stylish and suitable for active people • *They drive a sporty red car.* ∘ *You're looking very sporty in your new jacket.*

spot MARK /spɑt/ *n* [C] a mark, usually round, that is different esp. in color from the area around it • *You got a spot on your new blouse.* • (*esp. Cdn and Br*) A spot is a PIMPLE.

spot SEE /spɑt/ *v* [T] **-tt-** to see or notice (someone or something) • *Darryl spotted a woodpecker high on the tree.*

spot PLACE /spɑt/ *n* [C] a particular place • *a vacation spot* ∘ *Our cat has a favorite spot where he loves to sleep.* • A spot is also a job in a particular organization or a position within a group, esp. in sports: *When Sain was injured, they asked me to fill his spot.* • **On the spot** means at that moment or place: *He was arrested on the spot.* • If someone is put **on the spot**, they are forced to do or say something they would rather not do or say: *I'm not trying to put you on the spot, but could you give us an example?* • A **spot check** is a surprise examination that is not part of a pattern or plan: *A spot check revealed that many students are out with flu.*

spot BROADCAST /spɑt/ *n* [C] a period of time

during which a broadcast takes place • *NBC put the show on in the 7 p.m. spot.* • A spot is also an advertisement: *a 30-second spot*

spotless /'spɑt·ləs/ *adj* extremely clean • *Her kitchen counters were spotless.* • If someone's behavior or reputation is spotless, it is extremely good: *a spotless career*

spotlight /'spɑt·lɑɪt/ *n* [C] a circle of strong light that comes from a LAMP whose beam can be directed • *Spotlights followed the two dancers around the stage.* ○ (*fig.*) *The incident brought toxic waste into the national spotlight* (= directed attention to it).

spotlight /'spɑt·lɑɪt/ *v* [T] • (*fig.*) *Special-interest groups are effective at spotlighting neglected issues* (= directing attention to them).

spotlight

spouse /spɑʊs, spɑʊz/ *n* [C] a person's husband or wife

spout FLOW /spɑʊt/ *v* [I/T] to send out (liquid or flames) quickly and with force, or (of liquid or flame) to flow quickly • *The volcano spouted flames and red-hot rocks.* [T]

spout OPENING /spɑʊt/ *n* [C] a tube-shaped opening that allows liquids to be poured out of a container • *a beer spout*

spout SPEAK /spɑʊt/ *v* [I/T] to say or repeat (something), often in a way that is annoying for other people • *The old man spouted Bible verse endlessly.* [T]

sprain /spreɪn/ *v* [T] to stretch or tear (the tissue that limits the movement of a joint in the body) • *My dad fell and sprained his knee.*

sprain /spreɪn/ *n* [C] • *He twisted his ankle and suffered a bad sprain.*

sprang /spræŋ/ *past simple of* SPRING

sprawl /sprɔːl/ *v* [I] to spread out esp. awkwardly over a large area • *Police found her body sprawled just inside the door.*

sprawling /'sprɔː·lɪŋ/ *adj* existing or reaching over a large area • *the sprawling city of Los Angeles*

sprawl /sprɔːl/ *n* [C usually sing] • *A massive sprawl of high-rise buildings fills the site.*

spray LIQUID /spreɪ/ *n* [C/U] a mass of very small drops of liquid forced through the air, or a container from which small drops of liquid are forced out • *As the waves crashed over the rocks, some of the ocean spray reached them*

where they stood. [U] ○ *When my nose is stuffy, I use a nasal spray.* [C]

spray /spreɪ/ *v* [I/T] • *Store employees offer to spray you with perfume.* [T] ○ (*fig.*) *The building was sprayed with gunfire.* [T]

spray FLOWERS /spreɪ/ *n* [C] a single, small branch or stem with leaves and flowers on it, or a small arrangement of cut flowers • *At the grave site was a spray of fresh flowers.*

spread COVER /spred/ *v* [I/T] *past* **spread** to cover or cause (something) to cover an object or an area • *Pianist Eubie Blake could spread his fingers over 20 keys.* [T] ○ *She spread out the tablecloth.* [M] ○ *I had toast spread with strawberry jam.* [I] ○ *A strange look spread over his face.* [I] • If something **spreads out**, it covers a larger area: *Soldiers spread out among the trees.* • If you **spread out** an event or **spread** it **over** a period of time, it happens during that time, often in stages: *The ceremonies are spread over four days.* • To **spread** your**self thin** is to try to do too many different things at the same time: *Be careful you don't spread yourself too thin.*

spread /spred/ *n* [C] • A spread is a cover for a bed. • A spread is also a soft food put on bread or other food: *a cheese spread* • A spread is also a meal, esp. one with a lot of different foods arranged on a table: *This is quite a spread.*

spread MOVE /spred/ *v* [I/T] to move from one place to another, or to cause (something) to move or be communicated • *The flames quickly spread to the next room.* [I] ○ *Youth-gang violence may be spreading.* [I] ○ *Doctors fear the cancer may spread to other organs.* [I] ○ *She's been spreading lies about him.* [T]

spread /spred/ *n* [U] • *Jazz records fostered the spread of American culture.* ○ *More should be done to stop the spread of AIDS.*

spree /spriː/ *n* [C] a short period of doing something in an extreme way without control • *a shopping/spending spree*

sprig /sprɪg/ *n* [C] a small branch of a plant with leaves on it • *a sprig of mint*

spring SEASON /sprɪŋ/ *n* [C/U] the season of the year between winter and summer, lasting from March to June north of the equator and from September to December south of the equator, when the weather becomes warmer and leaves and plants start to grow again • *last/this/next spring* [C] ○ *It was a beautiful spring day.* [U] • **Spring break** is a school vacation in the spring. • (*infml*) If you say someone is not a **spring chicken**, you mean they are not young: *I thought she was very attractive, considering she's no spring chicken.* • **Spring fever** is a feeling either that you do not want to work or that you can't stay still, which seems to be caused by the weather suddenly becoming warmer. • **Springtime** is the season of spring.

spring CURVED METAL /sprɪŋ/ *n* [C] a piece of

curved or bent metal that can be pressed into a smaller space but will return to its usual shape if released • *I could feel the springs of the lumpy mattress.*

spring MOVE QUICKLY /sprɪŋ/ *v past simple* **sprang** /spræŋ/ or **sprung** /sprʌŋ/, *past part* **sprung** /sprʌŋ/ to move quickly and suddenly toward a particular place or to a new condition • *She sprang out of bed and ran to the window.* [I always + adv/prep] ○ *A single kick made the door spring open.* [L] • *By nine o'-clock, the town had* **sprung to life** (= become active). • *Mention fashion and Kate's name immediately* **springs to mind** (= is quickly thought of).

spring APPEAR SUDDENLY /sprɪŋ/ *v* [always + adv/prep] *past simple* **sprang** /spræŋ/ or **sprung** /sprʌŋ/, *past part* **sprung** /sprʌŋ/ to appear or exist suddenly, or to cause (something) to happen suddenly • *Little patches of weeds seem to spring up everywhere in my backyard.* [I always + adv/prep] ○ *Mr. Pollack likes to spring quizzes on the class.* [T always + adv/prep]

spring WATER /sprɪŋ/ *n* [C] a place where water flows out from the ground • *The lake is fed by underground springs.*

springboard /'sprɪŋ·bɔːrd, -boʊrd/ *n* [C] a board that bends when you jump on the end of it, used to help you jump higher in some sports or physical exercises • A springboard is also something that provides an opportunity to achieve something: *Many young women hope modeling will be a springboard to stardom.*

sprinkle /'sprɪŋ·kəl/ *v* [I/T] to scatter (a few drops or small pieces of something) • *Sprinkle cheese on the pizza.* [T] • If someone says that it is sprinkling, they mean it is raining lightly. [I]

sprinkle /'sprɪŋ·kəl/, **sprinkling** /'sprɪŋ·klɪŋ/ *n* [C] • *We might get a sprinkle today* (= a light rain).

sprinkler /'sprɪŋ·klər/ *n* [C] a device used in gardens and areas of grass for scattering drops of water over the ground • A **sprinkler system** is a set of pipes and devices that carry water through a building in order to spray it on a fire.

sprint /sprɪnt/ *v* [I] to run very fast esp. for a short distance, either as a competitor in a sport or because you are in a hurry to get somewhere • *Clark sprinted past Smith and caught the ball in the end zone.* ○ *He sprinted off to meet his girlfriend.*

sprint /sprɪnt/ *n* [C] a short race run at full speed, or any short period of fast running

sprinter /'sprɪnt·ər/ *n* [C] • *Carl Lewis was a world-class sprinter for many years.*

sprout /spraʊt/ *v* [I/T] to begin to grow, or to produce (new growth) • *Our new seedlings have begun to sprout.* [I]

sprout /spraʊt/ *n* [C] a new growth of a plant • *a bean sprout*

spruce /spruːs/ *n* [C/U] an evergreen tree with needlelike leaves, or the wood of this tree

spruce up *obj*, **spruce** *obj* **up** /'spruːs'sʌp/ *adv* [M] to improve the appearance of (something) by making it neater or by adding decorations • *She'd spruce the place up with plastic flowers.*

sprung /sprʌŋ/ *past simple and past participle of* SPRING

spry /spraɪ/ *adj* (esp. of an old person) active and able to move quickly and energetically • *A spry elderly lady was pulling weeds in a large garden.*

spud /spʌd/ *n* [C] *infml* a potato

spun /spʌn/ *past simple and past participle of* SPIN

spunk /spʌŋk/ *n* [U] *approving* brave determination and confidence even in discouraging situations • *The kid showed lots of spunk to compete with her arm in a cast.*

spunky /'spʌŋ·ki/ *adj approving* • *a spunky nine-year-old*

spur ENCOURAGE /spɜr/ *v* [T] **-rr-** to encourage (an activity or development), or to cause something to develop faster • *The huge new factory spurred economic growth in the entire region.* • To **spur** someone **on** is to encourage them: *Ambition spurred him on.*

spur /spɜr/ *n* [C] • If something is done **on the spur of the moment**, it is done suddenly without any planning: *He tended to do things on the spur of the moment, without thinking about the consequences.*

spur SHARP OBJECT /spɜr/ *n* [C] a sharp metal object sticking out of a U-shaped device that is attached to the heel of a boot and used by a rider to encourage a horse to go faster

spurious /'spjʊr·i·əs/ *adj slightly fml* based on false reasoning or information that is not true, and therefore not to be trusted • *They made spurious claims of personal injury.*

spurn /spɜrn/ *v* [T] to refuse to accept (something) • *She spurned his attentions and refused to see him.*

spurt /spɜrt/ *v* [I/T] to flow out suddenly and with force • *Water spurted from the faucet into the sink.* [I]

spurt /spɜrt/ *n* [C] • *There was a sudden spurt of flame.* • A spurt is also a sudden and brief period of increased activity, effort, or speed: *a child's growth spurt* ○ *Penn State ended the game with a 10-4 spurt* (= period of scoring).

sputter /'spʌt̬·ər/ *v* [I/T] to make repeated explosive sounds, often (esp. of a machine) as a sign that something is not working well and may fail • *The plane's engine began to sputter.* [I] • To sputter is also to speak in a way that is not clear esp. because you are angry: *He sputtered and flapped his hands in response.* [I]

spy PERSON /spaɪ/, *slang* **spook** *n* [C] a person employed by a country or organization to secretly gather and report information about another country or organization

spy /spaɪ/ v [I] • *Bazoft confessed on television that he spied for Israel.*

spy SEE /spaɪ/ v [T] to see or notice (someone or something) • *He kept on their trail until he spied firelight from a camp nestled in the rocks.*

squabble /'skwɑb·əl/ n [C] a disagreement, often about an unimportant matter • *family squabbles with your brothers and sisters*

squabble /'skwɑb·əl/ v [I] • *They squabbled about how the money would be spent.*

squad /skwɑd/ n [C] a small group of people trained to work together as a unit • *The rescue squad managed to free the child.* • A **squad car** (also **patrol car**) is a car used by police officers that has radio equipment for communicating with other police officers.

squadron /'skwɑd·rən/ n [C] a unit of one of the armed forces • *a squadron of Navy jets*

squalid /'skwɑl·əd/ adj extremely dirty, poor, and unpleasant • *The squalid refugee camp became the birthplace of her first child.*

squalor /'skwɑl·ər/ n [U] • *He lived in dreadful squalor in a crowded slum, sharing his bed with two brothers.*

squall /skwɔːl/ n [C] a sudden, strong wind or brief storm, esp. over water • *Occasional rain squalls blow furiously across the sea.*

squander /'skwɑn·dər/ v [T] to waste (money), or to use (something valuable that you have a limited amount of) badly or foolishly • *Government should not squander the taxpayers' money.* ○ *Don't squander your opportunities when you are young.*

square SHAPE /skwer, skwær/ n [C] a flat shape with four sides of equal length and four angles of 90°, or an area or object having this shape • *I bought him a tie with dark blue squares against a gray background.* • A square is also a small area of open land in a city or town, often one in the shape of a square.

square /skwer, skwær/ adj [-er/-est only] • *They set up the square card tables for the bridge players.* • A square unit of measurement is an area that is a particular distance wide and the same distance long: *The box was three feet square.* • A **square meal** is a satisfying meal with enough to eat.

square EQUAL /skwer, skwær/ adj [-er/-est only] having all debts paid or other matters arranged fairly • *I paid last time, so if you pay now, we're square.* • A **square deal** is a fair agreement: *All I want is a square deal.*

square PERSON /skwer, skwær/ n [C] dated slang a person who is old-fashioned

square MULTIPLY /skwer, skwær/ v [T] to multiply (a number) by itself • *Ten squared equals a hundred.*

square /skwer, skwær/ n [C] the result of multiplying a number by itself • *The square of 7 is 49.*

□**square away** obj, **square** obj **away** /'--'-/ v adv [M] infml to make (esp. arrangements) ready, finished, or corrected • *I've got my tickets and hotel squared away.*

□**square off** /'skwer 'ɔːf, 'skwær-/ v adv [I] to oppose someone in a competition or prepare to fight them • *Bradley is expected to square off with Cook in the next election.*

□**square** (obj) **with** obj /'--/ v prep [T] to accept (an idea or understanding) as able to exist with (something else) • *It's hard to square his honest record in the past with these charges.*

square dance /'skwer·dæns, 'skwær-/ n [C] active, often fast-moving dance in which each of four pairs of dancers takes a position opposite another pair and at the same distance, forming a square

squarely /'skwer·li, 'skwær-/ adv [not gradable] directly and with no doubt • *We have to face these issues squarely and honestly.* ○ *The blame for Wade's death rests squarely on him.* • Squarely also means in a direct way and esp. with force: *Williams hit the ball squarely, sending it over the fence.*

squash VEGETABLE /skwɑʃ/ n [C/U] pl **squash** or **squashes** a vegetable with a hard skin and many seeds at its center

squash CRUSH /skwɑʃ/ v [T] to press down or crush (something) so that it becomes flat • *Kate squashed the paper cup and dropped it into the trash can.* • If you squash a plan or idea, you stop it completely and suddenly: *Republican leaders will probably try to squash the tax cut.*

squash PUSH /skwɑʃ/ v [I/T] to push (a person or thing) into a small space • *Four of us were squashed into the back seat of his car.* [T]

squash SPORT /skwɑʃ/ n [U] a game played in an enclosed playing area between two or four people who use RACKETS (= tightly fixed nets in frames attached to long handles) to hit a hard rubber ball against a wall

squat SIT /skwɑt/ v [I] -tt- to position yourself close to the ground by bending your legs under you and balancing on the front part of your feet • *He squatted down and picked up some pebbles.*

squat SHORT /skwɑt/ adj [-er/-est only] -tt- short and wide • *Mickey was a squat, dark man with a ragged beard.*

squatter /'skwɑt·ər/ n [C] a person who lives in an empty building or area of land without the permission of the owner

squawk /skwɔːk/ v [I] to make a loud, unpleasant cry • *Sea gulls squawked overhead.* • (infml) If someone squawks about something, they complain about it in a way that gets attention: *Employers have begun to squawk because of rising health insurance costs.*

squawk /skwɔːk/ n [C] • *The owl flew off with a squawk.*

squeak MAKE SOUND /skwiːk/ v [I/T] to make a short, very high sound or cry • *Her expensive shoes squeaked when she walked.* [I]

squeak /skwi:k/ *n* [C] • *Every time I stepped on the brakes I'd hear a little squeak.*

squeaky /ˈskwiː·ki/ *adj* • *The door swung open on its squeaky hinges.* • *The elderly get more government funding because they write more letters—as usual,* **the squeaky wheel gets the grease** (= the problems that receive attention are those that people complain most about). • (*infml*) *I like the kitchen to be* **squeaky-clean** (= extremely clean). • (*infml*) If someone is **squeaky-clean**, they are completely correct, esp. in their public behavior, and have never done anything immoral.

squeak JUST DO /skwi:k/ *v* [I always + adv/prep] to just manage to do something • *Our team squeaked out a victory in Sunday's game.*

squeal MAKE SOUND /skwi:l/ *v* [I/T] to make a long, very high sound or cry • *The tires squealed as I sped away.* [I] ○ *"This is awesome," Mary Lou squealed in her coach's ear.* [T]

squeal /skwi:l/ *n* [C] • *She collapsed into giggles and squeals when he tickled her.*

squeal GIVE INFORMATION /skwi:l/ *v* [I] *slang* to give the authorities information about people you know who have committed crimes or done something wrong • *He refused to squeal on his buddies.*

squeamish /ˈskwiː·mɪʃ/ *adj* easily upset or disgusted by things or actions you find unpleasant • *Dad was squeamish about killing roaches.*

squeeze PRESS TOGETHER /skwi:z/ *v* [T] to press (something) firmly, or to force (something, esp. a liquid) out by pressing • *Grandpa steadied the gun, shut one eye, and squeezed the trigger.* ○ *I squeezed her shoulder* (= pressed it with a hand, esp. to show affection).

squeeze /skwi:z/ *n* [C] • *I gave his shoulder a squeeze.* ○ (*fig.*) *State parks will feel the squeeze from budget cuts* (= the cuts will have a limiting effect).

squeeze FORCE INTO /skwi:z/ *v* [always + adv/prep] to force (someone or something) into a small space or a short period of time • *I'm just not able to squeeze into last year's swimsuit.* [I] ○ *She's asking me to squeeze a shopping trip into my day off.* [T] ○ *You can squeeze in six people at the table.* [M]

squeeze /skwi:z/ *n* [C usually sing] • *It'll be a tight squeeze with four other people in the car, but I'll give you a lift.*

□ **squeeze** *obj* **out of** /ˈ-ˈ-, ˈ-ˌ-/ *v adv prep* [T] to get or obtain (something) with difficulty, or to cause (something to happen) by a continuous and difficult effort • *He used various tricks to squeeze money out of his father in England.* ○ *Small businesses are being squeezed out of the neighborhood by developers.*

squelch /skweltʃ/ *v* [T] to stop (something) quickly and completely • *Arnold hoped to squelch rumors that he had been drunk.*

squid /skwɪd/ *n* [C/U] *pl* **squid** an edible sea creature that has a long body with eight arms and two TENTACLES (= arm-like parts) around the mouth • *deep-fried squid* [U]

squiggle /ˈskwɪɡ·əl/ *n* [C] a short line written or drawn in an irregular, curving way • *To my eye this picture just looks like squiggles.*

squiggly /ˈskwɪɡ·li/ *adj* • *squiggly lines*

squint /skwɪnt/ *v* [I] to look with your eyes partly closed • *He squinted into the morning sun.*

squire OWNER /skwaɪr/ *n* [C] *old use* (in the past in England) a man who owned most of the land around a village

squire TAKE /skwaɪr/ *v* [T always + adv/prep] *slightly fml* to take (someone) places; ESCORT • *Skinner uses the plane to squire around bureaucrats.*

squirm /skwɜrm/ *v* [I] to make twisting movements with the body, esp. because of embarrassment, pain, or excitement • *The kids squirmed in their chairs.*

squirrel /ˈskwɜr·əl, ˈskwʌ·rəl/ *n* [C] a small furry animal with a long tail which climbs trees and feeds on nuts and seeds

squirt /skwɜrt/ *v* [I/T] to quickly force (a liquid) out of something, or (of liquids) to flow through a narrow opening • *Squirt lemon juice on the clams and enjoy them.* [T] ○ (*fig.*) *The ball squirted free* (= moved quickly away) *and bounced out of bounds.* [I]

squirt /skwɜrt/ *n* [C] • *A squirt of glue should fix it.* • (*infml*) A **squirt** is also a small person you consider unimportant. This use is usually intended to be insulting.

squish /skwɪʃ/ *v* [I/T] to crush (something), or to make the sound you make when you walk through something soft and wet • *We squished through the mud.* [I always + adv/prep]

squishy /ˈskwɪʃ·i/ *adj* soft and easily crushed or shaped • *squishy white bread*

St. STREET /striːt/ *n abbreviation for* street, used in writing after the name or number of a street • *19 East 17th St.*

St. PERSON *n abbreviation for* SAINT • *St. Bartholomew's Church*

stab /stæb/ *v* [T] **-bb-** to injure (someone) using a sharp, pointed object • *A man was stabbed to death yesterday in a bar in Queens.* • If someone **stabs** you **in the back**, they harm you when you thought that you could trust them: *He's tried to work within the system, but he's been stabbed in the back one too many times.*

stab /stæb/ *n* [C] • *He's recovering from stab wounds.* • A **stab** is also a sudden feeling: *Cheri felt a sudden stab of guilt.* • A **stab** is also an attempt to do something that you may not be able to do: *I wouldn't even take a stab at estimating its cost.*

stabbing /ˈstæb·ɪŋ/ *n* [C] • *He was arrested after a fatal stabbing at a party.*

stable FIXED /ˈsteɪ·bəl/ *adj* firmly fixed or not likely to move or change • *Don't climb the lad-*

der until you're sure it's stable. ○ *She's in the hospital in stable condition.* ○ *Their relationship was stable until he started drinking again.*

stability /stə'bɪl·əṭ·i/ *n* [U] • *economic and political stability* ○ *I'm worried about his mental stability.*

stabilize /'steɪ·bə,laɪz/ *v* [I/T] to cause (something) to become fixed and stop changing, esp. in order to keep it from becoming worse, or to become fixed and stop changing • *These medicines stabilize your heart rate and lower blood pressure.* [T] ○ *Once your salary stabilizes you can start to save a little money.* [I]

stabilization /,steɪ·bə·lə'zeɪ·ʃən/ *n* [U] • *stabilization of the economy*

stable [BUILDING] /'steɪ·bəl/ *n* [C] a building in which horses or cattle are kept • *The horses in the stable have plenty of straw.*

staccato /stə'kɑṭ·oʊ/ *adj, adv* (of music) played as short, separate notes • If a noise is described as staccato, it consists of a series of short, quick sounds: *The sudden staccato burst of machine guns terrified us.*

stack /stæk/ *n* [C] a pile of things arranged one on top of another • *a stack of pancakes* ○ *stacks of newspapers* • In a LIBRARY (= a building with a collection of books and study materials), **the stacks** are the area where books are stored: *He happened upon the book in the library stacks.*

stack /stæk/ *v* [T] • *The cases were stacked neatly in the middle of the room.* • If you **stack the cards/deck/odds**, you arrange things so that the results are not fair: *Critics say that having so many businessmen on the panel stacks the deck against the environment.* • The way one thing **stacks up** against another is the way it compares with the other: *In my opinion, our team stacks up pretty well against Minneapolis.*

stadium /'steɪd·i:·əm/ *n* [C] a large structure consisting of many rows of seats surrounding an area of land on which sports are played and where sometimes other public events happen • *a football stadium* ○ *Yankee Stadium*

staff [PEOPLE] /stæf/ *n* [C] a group of people who work for an organization, often for a special purpose, or who work for a manager within an organization • *The coaching staff felt we needed more defense.* ○ *She joined the staff of the Smithsonian Institution in 1954.*

staff /stæf/ *v* [T] • *The after-school program is staffed entirely by volunteers.*

staff [MUSIC] /stæf/, **stave** /steɪv/ *n* [C] the five lines and four spaces between them on which musical notes are written

stag [ANIMAL] /stæg/ *n* [C] an adult male deer

stag [FOR MEN] /stæg/ *adj* [not gradable] for men only • *a stag evening* • A **stag party** is a party given for a man who will soon be married to which only men are invited.

stage [PART] /steɪdʒ/ *n* [C] a part of an activity, or a period of development • *The software is*

in the early stages of development. ○ *At that stage of my life, I was married but didn't have any children.* • If you do something **in stages**, you divide the activity into parts and complete each part separately: *We're repairing the house in stages—first the roof and chimney, then the windows.*

stage [THEATER] /steɪdʒ/ *n* [C/U] the area in a theater, often raised above ground level, on which actors or entertainers perform • *When you're sitting in the balcony, you see more of the ceiling than the stage.* [C] ○ *Berlin's most successful stage musical was "Annie Get Your Gun."* [U] ○ *She was a popular star of the musical stage* (= of this type of theater). [U] • A stage is also a particular area of public life: *His novel includes such actors on the world stage as Fidel Castro and the Pope.* [C] • As a child, he appeared **on stage** (= performing in theaters). • Actors or performers who have **stage fright** are nervous because they are about to perform.

stage /steɪdʒ/ *v* [T] to arrange the performance of (a play or other entertainment) • *Bejart was staging his own ballets.* • If you stage an event, you organize it: *Bus drivers are planning to stage a 24-hour strike.*

staging /'steɪ·dʒɪŋ/ *n* [C] • *The theater produced the first staging of any of Eugene O'Neill's works.* • A **staging area** is a place where people gather before doing something: *Bangalore is a comfortable staging area for several South India tours.*

stagecoach /'steɪdʒ·koʊtʃ/ *n* [C] (in the past) a covered vehicle pulled by horses that carried passengers and goods on regular routes • *The coming of the stagecoach was once a major event in remote American settlements.*

stagger [MOVE] /'stæg·ər/ *v* [I/T] to walk or move awkwardly, as if you have lost your balance, or to cause (someone) to move awkwardly or to lose their balance • *A blow to his head momentarily staggered him.* [T] ○ *Although badly hurt, she staggered to a phone.* [I]

stagger [ARRANGE] /'stæg·ər/ *v* [T] to arrange (esp. events) so that they happen at different times, or to arrange (objects) so that they are not regular

staggered /'stæg·ərd/ *adj* [not gradable] • *staggered payments* ○ *Cabinets can be hung at staggered heights.*

staggering /'stæg·ə·rɪŋ/ *adj* shocking because of being extremely large • *Nursing care costs a staggering $15,000 per week!*

staging /'steɪ·dʒɪŋ/ *n* [C] • See at STAGE [THEATER].

stagnant [NOT FLOWING] /'stæg·nənt/ *adj* (of liquids or air) not flowing or moving, and often smelling unpleasant • *Hot, stagnant air filled the subway.*

stagnant [NOT BUSY] /'stæg·nənt/ *adj* not growing or developing • *Jobs become scarce in a stagnant economy.*

stagnate /'stæg·neɪt/ v [I] • *The local economy stagnated when the factories closed.*

stagnation /stæg'neɪ·ʃən/ n [U] • *High costs have caused stagnation in the building industries.*

staid /steɪd/ adj not exciting or fashionable; serious • *She never adjusted to her husband's staid lifestyle.*

stain /steɪn/ v [I/T] to leave (a mark) on something that is difficult to remove, or to become colored or spoiled by a mark • *Strawberry juice stained my shirt.* [T] ○ *This carpet is practical because it doesn't stain easily.* [I] • If you stain wood, you put a substance on it that changes its color: *Instead of painting the woodwork, she stained it dark brown.* [T]

stain /steɪn/ n [C] • *The red wine left a stain on the tablecloth.* • A stain is also a thin, oily liquid used to change the color of wood.

stainless /'steɪn·ləs/ adj • **Stainless steel** is a type of steel which does not chemically react with air or water and does not change color.

stained glass /steɪnd 'glæs/ n [U] pieces of colored glass that have been joined to form a picture or pattern, used esp. in the windows of churches

staircase /'ster·keɪs, 'stær-/ n [C] a set of stairs inside a building, including the bars and posts that people to hold on to as they go up or down

stairs /sterz, stærz/ pl n a set of steps that lead from one level to another, esp. in a building • *Her office is at the top of the stairs.*

stair /ster, stær/ n [C] a step in a set of stairs • *The top stair creaked loudly as she stepped on it.*

stairway /'ster·weɪ, 'stær-/ n [C] a passage that contains a set of steps

stake SHARE /steɪk/ n [C] a share in something, esp. a financial share in a business, or an emotional investment in something • *He holds a 20% stake in the company.* ○ *Parents have a large stake in their children's education.* • In an activity or competition, the stakes are the share or reward that goes to the winner: *Global competition has raised the stakes of doing business.*

stake RISK /steɪk/ n [C] the amount of money that you risk on the result of a game or competition • *He loved to gamble and would double his stake if he lost.* • If something is at stake, it is in danger: *About 3000 jobs are at stake if the company closes down.*

stake /steɪk/ v [T] • *He has talent and ambition, and I'd stake my reputation on his success.*

stake POLE /steɪk/ n [C] a thick, strong, pointed wood or metal pole pushed into the ground and used to mark a spot or to support something • *Stakes in the ground marked the outline of the new building.*

□**stake out** obj, **stake** obj **out** /'-'-/ v prep [M] to claim ownership of or a particular interest in (something) • *All politicians will stake out*

lowering taxes as their very own idea. • If the police stake out someone or something, they watch it secretly: *The police staked out the hotel where the two terrorists were though to be staying.*

stakeout /'steɪ·kaʊt/ n [C] a watch on a place or a person that is done in secret • *The stakeout did not provide much help to investigators.*

stale /steɪl/ adj [-er/-est only] not fresh or new • *stale bread* ○ *Stale air smells very bad.* ○ *I used to like that sitcom, but it's getting kind of stale.*

stalemate /'steɪl·meɪt/ n [C/U] a situation in which nothing can change or no action can be taken • *Stalemate in Congress over education reform has made voters angry.* [U] ○ *The arrival of fresh troops broke the military stalemate.* [C]

stalk PLANT PART /stɔːk/ n [C] any stem on a plant, esp. the main stem • *Cynthia says those flowers have pretty tall stalks.*

stalk FOLLOW /stɔːk/ v [T] to follow (an animal or person) as closely as possible without being seen or heard • *He spent the weekend stalking deer to photograph them.* ○ *Celebrities are often stalked by photographers and reporters.*

stalker /'stɔː·kər/ n [C] someone who follows a person, usually intending to hurt them • *The idea of a stalker on the lose is quite frightening.*

stalking /'stɔː·kɪŋ/ n [U] • *People convicted of stalking would be denied gun permits.*

stalk WALK /stɔːk/ v [I always + adv/prep] to walk in an angry or proud way • *She didn't say anything but stalked furiously out of the room.*

stall DELAY /stɔːl/ v [I/T] to delay or put off action, esp. by trickery • *They're just stalling, trying to avoid making a decision.* [I] ○ *I can stall him for a few minutes.* [T]

stall STOP WORKING /stɔːl/ v [I/T] to cause (a vehicle or engine) to stop suddenly, or (of a vehicle or engine) to stop suddenly • *My car stalled at the traffic light.* [I]

stall AREA /stɔːl/ n [C] a separate area in which an animal is kept • A stall is also a small enclosed space used for a particular purpose: *The bathroom had a tiled shower stall.*

stallion /'stæl·jən/ n [C] an adult male horse, esp. one used for breeding • Compare MARE.

stalwart /'stɔːl·wərt/ adj very loyal to someone or something • *She has always been a stalwart supporter of the arts.*

stamina /'stæm·ə·nə/ n [U] the physical or mental strength to do something for a long time, esp. something difficult • *The triathlon is a great test of stamina.*

stammer /'stæm·ər/ v [I/T] to speak or say (something) with unusual pauses or repeated sounds; STUTTER • *He stammers when he is nervous.* [I]

stammer /'stæm·ər/ n [U] • *Robert has a slight stammer which was much worse when he was younger.*

stamp HIT WITH FOOT /stæmp, stɑmp/ v [I/T] to

hit the floor or ground hard with a foot, usually making a loud noise • *She stood by the road, stamping her feet to stay warm.* [T] ○ *I wish those people upstairs would stop stamping around.* [I] • If you **stamp** something **out**, you stop or destroy it: *Our first goal is to stamp out hunger.* • Compare STOMP.

stamp /stæmp, stɑmp/ *n* [C] • *With a stamp of her foot she hurried out.*

stamp MAIL /stæmp/, **postage stamp** *n* [C] a small piece of paper, usually with a colorful design, that is attached to a package or envelope to show that the charge for sending it through the mail has been paid • *The new stamps depict blues singers.* • PIC POSTMARK

stamped /stæmpt/ *adj* [not gradable] • *Send a stamped, self-addressed envelope.*

stamp MARK /stæmp/ *n* [C] a tool for printing or cutting a mark into an object, or the mark made by such a tool • *The guard examined the permit, then reached for his rubber stamp.* ○ *The stamp on the rim shows that Paul Revere made this mug.*

stamp /stæmp/ *v* [T] • *An immigration official stamped his passport.* ○ (*fig.*) *That scene will be stamped in my memory forever.*

stamp QUALITY /stæmp/ *n* [U] a particular quality or character • *This painting clearly bears the stamp of genius.*

stampede /stæm'piːd/ *n* [C] a situation where a large group of frightened animals, esp. horses or cattle, all run in the same direction • (*fig.*) *A stampede of fans tried to enter the stadium at once.*

stampede /stæm'piːd/ *v* [I/T] • *A loud clap of thunder stampeded the herd.* [T]

stance OPINION /stæns/ *n* [C] an opinion about something, esp. one that is publicly expressed • *The governor's stance on the issue of abortion is well known.*

stance WAY OF STANDING /stæns/ *n* [C] a way of standing • *He had the stance of a baseball player focusing on the ball.*

stanch /stɔːntʃ, stɑntʃ/ *v* [T] STAUNCH STOP

stand BE VERTICAL /stænd/ *v* [I/T] *past* **stood** /stʊd/ to be on your feet or get into a vertical position, or to put (someone or something) into a vertical position • *I stood motionless as the snake slithered by.* [I] ○ *Please stand back so the paramedics can get through.* [I] ○ *I stood the ironing board against the wall.* [T always + adv/prep] • If someone or something **stands** their **ground**, they refuse to change their opinion or give in to an argument. • If people **stand guard** over something, they guard it: *Soldiers stood guard over the prisoner.* • If someone **stands on** their **hands/head**, they hold themselves vertically upside down, with their feet in the air. • When a person **stands on** their **own two feet**, they take care of themselves: *Ever since college, Jim has stood on his own two feet.*

standing /'stæn·dɪŋ/ *adj* [not gradable] • *On-*

ly one building was left standing after the earthquake. • If a group of people give a performer or speaker a **standing ovation**, it means that they stand and clap to show their appreciation: *What began as applause turned into a long standing ovation.* • If you buy a ticket for **standing room**, you stand to see a performance: *He buys standing room for whatever is playing because the tickets are cheaper.* • If something is **standing room only**, it means that all seats are filled: *Last night, every bus was standing room only.* • See also STANDING.

stand BE IN SITUATION /stænd/ *v past* **stood** /stʊd/ to be or get into a particular state or situation • *As things stand right now, there's no telling who will win.* [I] ○ *Let the mixture stand for fifteen minutes.* [I] ○ *Some of these older houses have stood empty for years.* [L] ○ *He stands accused of murder.* [L] ○ *Even without her shoes, she stands over six feet tall.* [L] • To **stand a chance** is to have a chance of success: *He doesn't stand much of a chance against her.* • When a person says that they **stand corrected**, they admit that they were wrong about something: *I stand corrected—the company was founded in 1927, not 1926.* • If something **stands to reason**, it is obviously correct, according to the facts: *It stands to reason that with all his experience, he would not make such a foolish mistake.* • If a person **stands trial**, accusations against them are examined in a court of law.

stand BE IN PLACE /stænd/ *v* [I] *past* **stood** /stʊd/ to be in a particular place • *A desk stood in the middle of the room.* ○ *A taxi stood at the curb, waiting for a fare.* ○ (*fig.*) *If you want to apply for promotion, I won't stand in your way.*

stand ACCEPT /stænd/ *v* [T] *past* **stood** /stʊd/ to be able to accept or bear (esp. something unpleasant or difficult) • *Our tent won't stand another storm like the last one.* ○ *How can you stand all that pressure at work?*

stand OPINION /stænd/ *n* [C] an opinion, esp. one publicly expressed • *What's his stand on health care reform?* ○ *She'll no doubt take a strong stand against raising taxes.*

stand /stænd/ *v* [I always + adv/prep] *past* **stood** /stʊd/ • *On foreign policy, the president seems to stand to the left of his party.*

stand COURT /stænd/ *n* [C] *short form of* **witness stand**, see at WITNESS PERSON IN COURT

stand STRUCTURE /stænd/ *n* [C] a small structure where food, newspapers, candy, and other small items are sold • *Hot dog stands with colorful umbrellas always attract a crowd.*

stand GROUP /stænd/ *n* [C] a group of trees or tall plants • *Stands of spruce trees dotted the hills.*

stand FRAME /stænd/ *n* [C] a piece of furniture designed to hold something • *a coat stand* ○ *He mounts the baseballs on marble stands.*

▢**stand around** /'--'-/ *v adv* [I] to stay in one place doing little or nothing • *We stood around in the cold for an hour.*

▢**stand by** LET HAPPEN /'-'-, -'-/ *v adv* [I] to let something happen or to be unable to do anything to stop something from happening • *How could anyone simply stand by while the man was beaten?* ○ *We stood by helplessly while the fire destroyed our barn.*

▢**stand by** SUPPORT /'-,-, -'-/ *v prep* [T] to support or be loyal to (someone or something) • *The editors stand by the story.* ○ *The boy's friends stood by him, firmly convinced of his innocence.*

▢**stand by** BE PREPARED /'-'-/ *v adv* [I] to be prepared for something • *The general ordered his troops to stand by for a possible attack.*

standby /'stænd,baɪ/ *n* [C] *pl* **standbys** someone or something available for use when needed • *I have several meals I use as standbys for unexpected company.* • If you fly standby, you hold a ticket and are ready to travel when space becomes available on a flight. • When someone or something is **on standby**, they are ready to be used if necessary: *Hospitals are on standby to care for the casualties of the crash.*

▢**stand for** REPRESENT /'--/ *v prep* [T] to represent (something) • *She explained that DIN stands for "do it now."* ○ *Uncle Sam stands for the US.*

▢**stand for** SUPPORT /'--/ *v prep* [T] to support or accept (particular principles or values) • *I'm not sure what the Republican candidate stands for.* ○ *Maybe you think his behavior is OK, but I won't stand for it.*

▢**stand out** /'-'-/ *v adv* [I] to be easily seen or noticed • *The black lettering really stands out against that background.* ○ *The applicant we hired was so well qualified, she stood out from all the rest.*

standout /'stæn·daʊt/ *n* [C] • *Fleming and Berry were the standouts at this year's tournament.*

▢**stand over** /'-'--/ *v adv* [T] to watch (someone) closely • *When you stand over me all the time, it makes me nervous.*

▢**stand up** *obj* NOT MEET , **stand** *obj* **up** /'-'-/ *v adv* [M] *infml* to fail to meet (someone you had arranged to see) • *I didn't mean to stand you up last night, but I was caught in traffic.*

▢**stand up** PROVE TRUE /'-'-/ *v adv* [I] to prove to be true when closely examined • *The evidence is weak and will not stand up in court.* ○ *Good research will stand up under any criticism.* • To stand up also means to not be changed or damaged by something: *This fabric will stand up well even if it gets lots of wear.*

▢**stand up for** /-'--/ *v adv prep* [T] to defend or support (someone or something) • *Don't be bullied—stand up for yourself and your beliefs.*

▢**stand up to** /-'--/ *v adv prep* [T] to deal effectively with (a person or situation) • *She stood up to her boss when he accused her of arriving late and leaving work early.*

stand–alone /'stæn·də,loʊn/ *adj* [not gradable] single, complete by itself • *Stand-alone houses have become too expensive for many people.*

standard USUAL /'stæn·dərd/ *adj* usual or expected; not involving something special or extra • *a standard contract* ○ *I don't work a standard, 35-hour week.* ○ *The car came with an air conditioner and tape player as standard equipment.* ○ *This is a standard medical text* (= a commonly used medical book). • A standard unit of measurement is an accepted method of measuring things of a similar type. • **Standard time** is the time that is officially used in a region in the fall, winter, and spring. Compare **daylight saving time** at DAYLIGHT. • **Standard operating procedure** is the usual method followed in doing a particular thing: *Running a credit check before opening new accounts is standard operating procedure.*

standardize /'stæn·dərd,aɪz/ *v* [T] to make (one thing) the same as others of that type, or to compare (one thing) to something accepted as a model • *Governor Vizard wants to standardize school spending throughout the state.*

standardized /'stæn·dərd,aɪzd/ *adj* [not gradable] • *Standardized tests will be used to measure their progress.*

standardization /ˌstæn·dərd·ə'zeɪ·ʃən/ *n* [U] • *At first, they made no attempt at standardization.*

standard LEVEL OF QUALITY /'stæn·dərd/ *n* [C] something that others of a similar type are compared to or measured by, or the expected level of quality • *moral/ethical/community standards* ○ *That's not their usual standard of service.* ○ *The new standard will allow data to be sent over telephone wires at higher speeds.* • A **standard of living** is the level of wealth and comfort people have in a particular society: *Our country has a very high standard of living.*

standard SONG /'stæn·dərd/ *n* [C] a song or piece of music that has been popular for many years and that musicians often perform

standard FLAG /'stæn·dərd/ *n* [C] a flag used as the symbol of a person, group, or organization • *Pete carried the troop's standard in the parade.* • A **standard-bearer** is also a person who leads a group or a political party: *Is he qualified to be the UN's standard-bearer for democracy and freedom?*

standby /'stænd·baɪ/ *n* • See at STAND BY BE PREPARED .

stand–in /'stæn·dɪn/ *n* [C] a person who takes the place or does the job of another person • *Critics serve as a kind of stand-in for the average person.*

standing PERMANENT /'stæn·dɪŋ/ *adj* [not

gradable] permanent or always continuing to exist or happen • *African-Americans headed five standing committees in the House of Representatives.* • See also **standing** at STAND BE VERTICAL.

standing RANK /'stæn·dɪŋ/ *n* rank, position, or reputation in an area of activity, system, or organization • *Financial scandal will affect the institute's standing in the academic community.* [U] ○ *You must pay dues to remain a member in good standing.* [U] • Standings are ranked lists of people or things: *the league standings* [pl] • See also **standing** at STAND BE VERTICAL.

standoff /'stæn·dɔːf/ *n* [C] a situation in which neither side has won a competition or argument, or an occasion when someone prevents officials from acting, usually by threatening violence • *The battle of wills between teacher and student was a standoff.* ○ *After a four-hour standoff, police captured the gunman.*

standpoint /'stænd·pɔɪnt/ *n* [C] a set of beliefs and ideas from which opinions and decisions are formed • *He looks at things from a technological standpoint.* ○ *From a fundraising standpoint, he's been very successful.*

stands /stændz/ *pl n* the large area containing many seats arranged in rising rows from which people can watch sports or other events • *Gordon was sitting in the stands, eating hot dogs and watching the game.* • Compare GRANDSTAND.

standstill /'stænd·stɪl/ *n* [U] a condition in which all movement or activity has stopped • *Bad weather brought construction to a standstill.* ○ *The truck came to a standstill in the muddy field.*

stand-up /'stæn·dʌp/ *adj* [not gradable] related to a type of performance in which someone stands in front of a group of people and tells jokes • *stand-up comedy*

standup /'stæn·dʌp/ *n* [U] • *She doesn't do a lot of standup anymore.*

stank /stæŋk/ *past simple of* STINK

stanza /'stæn·zə/ *n* [C] a related group of lines in a poem or song; a VERSE

staple WIRE /'steɪ·pəl/ *n* [C] a short, thin, U-shaped piece of wire with ends that bend to fasten sheets of paper together • *Put a staple in the upper left-hand corner.* • A staple is also a small, thick, U-shaped piece of metal with sharp ends that is hammered into a surface to hold something in place. • A **staple gun** is a

tool used in place of a hammer to push staples into a surface such as wood.

staple /'steɪ·pəl/ *v* [T] • *Please staple the reports together.*

stapler /'steɪ·plər/ *n* [C] a device used to attach papers together with staples

staple BASIC ITEM /'steɪ·pəl/ *n* [C] a basic food, or a main product or material • *Because of the storm, most stores were low on staples such as bread and milk.* ○ *Scandals are a newspaper staple.*

staple /'steɪ·pəl/ *adj* [not gradable] • *staple foods*

star OBJECT IN SPACE /stɑr/ *n* [C] a large ball of burning gas in space that is usually seen from earth as a point of light in the sky at night • *Stars twinkled in the night sky.* • **Starlight** is the light produced by stars: *We ate on the terrace by starlight.* • *It was a clear, starlit night* (= in which the light came from stars). • USAGE: The related adjective is STELLAR.

starry /'stɑr·i/ *adj* • *a starry night/sky*

star SHAPE /stɑr/ *n* [C] a shape having four or more pointed parts coming out from a center at equal distances • *The children were cutting stars out of paper to make decorations.* • A star is sometimes used as a symbol of quality: *The Times gave this restaurant three stars.* • A star is also used as a symbol of rank or position: *a four-star general* • A star is also an ASTERISK (= the symbol *.) • The **Star of David** is a star with six points that symbolizes Judaism.

star PERFORMER /stɑr/ *n* [C] a famous and successful person, esp. a performer such as a musician, actor, or sports player • *a rock/movie/basketball star* • A star is also someone who is especially good at something: *Janet is our star math student.*

star /stɑr/ *v* [I/T] **-rr-** to be one of the most important performers in a show • *He has starred in several recent movies.* [I] ○ *The school play stars children in the seventh and eighth grades.* [T]

stardom /'stɑrd·əm/ *n* [U] • *He was destined for stardom* (= fame).

starboard /'stɑr·bərd/ *n* [U] *specialized* the right side of a ship or aircraft as you are facing forward • USAGE: The opposite of starboard is PORT LEFT.

starch FOOD /stɑrtʃ/ *n* [C/U] a substance that exists in large amounts in many vegetables • *There is a lot of starch in rice.* [U] • Starches are foods containing a large amount of starch, such as potatoes, rice, bread, pasta, and CEREAL. [C]

starchy /'stɑr·tʃi/ *adj* [*-er*/*-est* only] • *starchy foods*

starch CLOTH /stɑrtʃ/ *n* [U] a chemical that is used to make cloth stiff

starch /stɑrtʃ/ *v* [T] • *I starch all my dress shirts.*

stare /ster, stær/ *v* [I/T] to look directly at (someone or something) for a long time • *Don't*

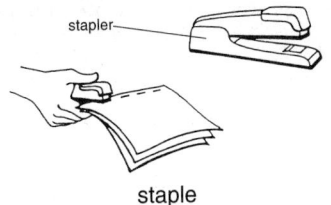

staple

stare at people. [I] ○ *The fighters tried to stare each other down* (= cause the other to turn away). [M] • If something **stares** you **in the face** it is obvious or easy to see: *The answer was staring us in the face.*

stare /ster, stær/ *n* [C] • *She tried to silence him with a hard stare.*

starfish /'stɑr·fɪʃ/ *n* [C] *pl* **starfish** a sea animal with five pointed parts growing out from around a circular body

stark /stɑrk/ *adj* [-er/-est only] empty or bare; without decoration • *stark white walls* • Stark also means completely clear: *The dim halls made a stark contrast with the bright, sun-drenched apartment.* • If someone is **stark na-ked**, they are not wearing any clothes.

starlet /'stɑr·lət/ *n* [C] a young actress who hopes to be or is thought likely to be famous in the future

starling /'stɑr·lɪŋ/ *n* [C] a common bird with dark-colored feathers that lives in large groups in many parts of the world

starry /'stɑr·i/ *adj* • See at STAR ⟨OBJECT IN SPACE⟩.

start ⟨BEGIN⟩ /stɑrt/ *v* [I/T] to begin to do (something) or go (somewhere), or to begin or happen • *When do you start your new job?* [T] ○ *We started with nothing when we got married.* [I] ○ *Classes start next month.* [I] ○ *Work starts at 9:00 a.m.* [I] ○ *Ticket prices start at $20* (= these are the cheapest prices). [I] ○ *I just started this book* (= began to read it). [T] ○ *We'll start out with Lucy* (= She will be the first). [I] • (*infml*) If you tell someone not to start, you are warn-ing them not to begin complaining or annoy-ing you: *Don't start—I said no!* [I] • *I knew al-most nothing when I started off in this business* (= began working). • *We decided to throw out the first draft of the report and start over* (= begin again).

start /stɑrt/ *n* [C/U] the time where some-thing begins, or the act of beginning • *We were worried from the start.* [U] ○ *They announced the start of the race.* [U] ○ *The play got off to a bad start.* [C]

starter /'stɑrt·ər/ *n* [C] a person, thing, or organization that is involved at the beginning of an activity, esp. a race • *Only four of the ten starters finished the race.*

start ⟨CAUSE⟩ /stɑrt/ *v* [T] to cause (something) to be or happen • *His mother started the craft market at the community center.* ○ *You've been starting trouble all morning.* • (*infml*) If you **start something** you cause trouble: *He really started something when he wrote that letter to the paper.*

start ⟨MOVE SUDDENLY⟩ /stɑrt/ *v* [I] to move your body suddenly because something has sur-prised you • *He started when the car backfired.*

start /stɑrt/ *n* [U] • *He woke with a start when the alarm sounded.*

start ⟨OPERATE⟩ /stɑrt/ *v* [I/T] to cause (some-thing) to operate, or to begin to work or oper-

ate • *Annie went outside to start (up) the car.* [T/M] ○ *I heard a lawnmower start.* [I]

startle /'stɑrt·əl/ *v* [T] to surprise (a person or animal) • *She startled him when she said hello.*

startling /'stɑrt·əl·ɪŋ/ *adj* • *We've made some startling discoveries.*

start–up /'stɑrt·ʌp/ *n* [C] a new business, or the activities involved in starting a new busi-ness • *Start-ups need to generate revenue quickly.*

start–up /'stɑrt·ʌp/ *adj* [not gradable] • *start-up costs*

starve /stɑrv/ *v* [I/T] to become weak or die because there is not enough food to eat • *Many people could starve because of the drought.* [I] • If someone says they are starving, they want to eat: *I'm starved because I missed lunch to-day.* [I]

starvation /stɑr'veɪ·ʃən/ *n* [U] • *The animals died of starvation.*

stash /stæʃ/ *v* [T] to store or hide (something) • *Extra blankets are stashed in the closet.*

stash /stæʃ/ *n* [C] • *He has a stash of old comic books in the attic.*

state ⟨WAY OF BEING⟩ /steɪt/ *n* [C] a condition or way of being • *The stable was preserved in its original state.* ○ *Your room is in a terrible state.* • A **state of emergency** is an extreme condi-tion caused by severe weather or war in which a government allows itself special powers: *The governor declared a state of emergency in two counties hit by the hurricane.* • We were worried about Leo's **state of mind** (= emotion-al health). • If something is **state-of-the-art**, it is the best and most modern of its type: *a state-of-the-art computer system*

state ⟨PLACE⟩ /steɪt/ *n* [C] one of the political units that some countries, such as the US, are divided into • *New York State* ○ *the State of Ar-izona* • A state is also a country or its gov-ernment: *the member states of the United Na-tions* • When will you be visiting **the States** (= the United States)?

state /steɪt/ *adj* [not gradable] • *a state legis-lature/law* ○ *state police* • State also refers to formal or official government activities: *a state dinner* • The **State Department** is the part of the US government that deals with oth-er nations.

statewide /'steɪt·wɑɪd/ *adj* [not gradable] in every part of a state • *statewide elections*

state ⟨EXPRESS⟩ /steɪt/ *v* [T] to express (informa-tion), esp. clearly and carefully • *His will states the property is to be sold.* ○ *Please state your preference.*

statement /'steɪt·mənt/ *n* [C] something that is said, esp. formally and officially • *The can-didate made a statement to the press.* • A state-ment is also an act or object that expresses an idea or opinion: *a fashion statement* ○ *They burned the flag as a political statement.* • A statement is also a piece of paper that lists financial details: *a bank/credit card statement*

stately /'steɪt·li/ *adj* formal in style and appearance • *a stately old hotel*

statesman (*pl* **-men**) /'steɪt·smən/, **stateswoman** (*pl* **-women**) /'steɪt·swʊm·ən/ *n* [C] a politician or government official who is respected and experienced

statesmanlike /'steɪts·mən,lɑɪk/ *adj* • *a statesmanlike speech*

static /'stæt̬·ɪk/ *adj* staying in one place without moving, or not changing for a long time • *Oil prices remained static worldwide.*

static (electricity) /'stæt̬·ɪk (ɪ,lek'trɪs·ət̬·i)/ *n* [U] an electrical charge that collects esp. on the surfaces of some objects • *There's a lot of static in here—I keep getting shocks when I touch things.* • Static is also noise that interrupts radio or television signals.

station [BUILDING] /'steɪ·ʃən/ *n* [C] a building or buildings and the surrounding area where a particular service or activity takes place • *a train/bus station* ○ *a gas station* ○ *a police/fire station* • A **station house** is a police or fire station.

station [BROADCAST ORGANIZATION] /'steɪ·ʃən/ *n* [C] a place or organization that sends out radio or television broadcasts, or the broadcasts sent out • *At our house in the mountains we only get two TV stations.* ○ *I can't tune in that radio station.*

station [POSITION] /'steɪ·ʃən/ *v* [T] to cause (esp. soldiers) to be in a particular place to do a job • *I hear your son's in the army—where's he stationed?*

station /'steɪ·ʃən/ *n* [C] • *The honor guard took their stations at the side of the road.*

stationary /'steɪ·ʃə,ner·i/ *adj* [not gradable] not moving, or not changing • *House prices have been stationary for months.*

stationery /'steɪ·ʃə,ner·i/ *n* [U] paper, esp. that used for writing letters, or writing materials such as pens, pencils, and books for writing in • *business/personal stationery* ○ *I got these folders at the stationery store.*

station wagon /'steɪ·ʃən ,wæg·ən/ *n* [C] a type of car with a large area behind the back seats for carrying things • [PIC] CAR

statistics /stə'tɪs·tɪks/, *infml* **stats** /stæts/ *pl n* a collection of NUMERICAL facts or measurements, as about people, business conditions, or weather • *The statistics show that, in general, women live longer than men.*

statistics /stə'tɪs·tɪks/ *n* [U] the science of using information discovered from collecting, organizing, and studying numbers

statistic /stə'tɪs·tɪk/ *n* [C] a single number in a range of STATISTICS • *The city's most shocking statistic is its infant mortality rate.*

statistical /stə'tɪs·tɪ·kəl/ *adj* • *There is little statistical evidence to support the idea that stocks do better in summer than in other seasons.*

statistically /stə'tɪs·tɪ·kli/ *adv*

statistician /,stæt̬·ə'stɪʃ·ən/ *n* [C] a person who studies or works with statistics

statue /'stætʃ·uː/ *n* [C] a large art object, often representing a person or an animal, that is made from a hard material, esp. stone or metal • The **Statue of Liberty** is an extremely large statue of a woman holding a lighted TORCH above her head: *The Statue of Liberty was given to the US by France and stands on Liberty Island in New York harbor.*

Statue of Liberty

statuette /,stætʃ·ə'wet/ *n* [C] a very small statue

stature [REPUTATION] /'stætʃ·ər/ *n* [U] reputation and importance based on admirable qualities or achievements • *He is a philosopher of great stature in the academic community.*

stature [HEIGHT] /'stætʃ·ər/ *n* [C usually sing] the height of a person or an animal • *Although short in stature, his voice and stage presence were remarkable.*

status [POSITION] /'steɪt̬·əs, 'stæt̬-/ *n* [U] position or rank, esp. in a social group or legal system • *The association works to promote the status of retired people as active and useful members of the community.* • Status can also mean state or condition at a particular time: *The type of treatment used will depend on the patient's health status.*

status [RESPECT] /'steɪt̬·əs, 'stæt̬-/ *n* [U] the position of respect and importance given to someone or something • *The leaders often seemed to be more concerned with status and privilege than with the problems of the people.* • A **status symbol** is something that people want to have or do because they think other people will respect or admire them for it: *The car phone has become the status symbol of the successful executive.*

status quo /,steɪt̬·ə'skwoʊ, ,stæt̬-/ *n* [U] present situation or condition • *Are you in favor of statehood, independence, or the status quo for Puerto Rico?*

statute /'stætʃ·uːt/ *n* [C/U] a law that has

been formally approved and written down • *The salaries of most federal workers are set by statute.* [U]

statutory /ˈstætʃ·ə‚tɔːr·i, -‚toʊr·i/ *adj* [not gradable] • (*law*) **Statutory rape** is the crime of having sex with a person younger than the age at which she or he can legally have sex.

staunch LOYAL /stɔːntʃ, stɑntʃ/ *adj* [-*er*/-*est* only] strongly loyal to a person, organization, or set of beliefs or opinions • *a staunch defender of free speech*

staunchly /ˈstɔːntʃ·li, ˈstɑntʃ-/ *adv* • *She staunchly supports the party's candidates.*

staunch STOP /stɔːntʃ, stɑntʃ/, **stanch** *v* [T] to stop (liquid, esp. blood), from flowing out • *Mike pressed hard on the wound and staunched the flow of blood.* • To staunch is also to keep (something) from continuing: *It was crucial to try to staunch the outflow of refugees.*

stave /steɪv/ *n* a STAFF MUSIC

stave off *obj*, **stave** *obj* **off** /ˈsteɪvˈɔːf/ *v adv* [M] to keep (something or someone) away or keep something from happening, esp. until a later time • *The Federal Reserve lowered interest rates to stimulate the economy and stave off a recession.*

stay NOT LEAVE /steɪ/ *v* [I] to not move away from or leave a place • *I have a meeting at three so I can't stay long.* ○ *They need an assistant who is willing to stay for six months.* ○ *Can you stay for dinner?* ○ *James had to stay after school to complete the assignment.* ○ *Because of the snow, he stayed home from school today.* ○ *She's come back home to stay* (= She will not move away again). • *Just stay put* (= don't move from here) *and I'll get the car.*

stay CONTINUE /steɪ/ *v* to continue to be in a particular state or position, or to continue doing something • *Stay away from the edge of the cliff.* [I always + adv/prep] ○ *His boss asked him to stay on as manager for another year.* [I always + adv/prep] ○ *Mom told me not to stay out/up too late.* [I always + adv/prep] ○ *I found it difficult to stay awake/calm/warm.* [L] ○ *The store stays open until 9 p.m.* [L] ○ *They stayed friends, even after their divorce.* [L] ○ *For further news of the hurricane, stay tuned* (= keep listening to this program). [L]

stay LIVE TEMPORARILY /steɪ/ *v* [I] to live in a place for a short time as a visitor, or just sleep there • *We stayed in San Francisco for a few days before flying to Hawaii.* ○ *I'll be staying overnight at my sister's house.*

stay /steɪ/ *n* [C] • *They plan a short stay at a motel while the house is being painted.*

STD *n* [C] *abbreviation for* **sexually transmitted disease**, see at SEXUAL CONNECTED WITH SEX ACTIVITY

steadfast /ˈsted·fæst/ *adj* staying the same for a long time; not changing or losing purpose • *steadfast beliefs* ○ *a steadfast friend*

steady GRADUAL /ˈsted·i/ *adj* happening or developing in a gradual, regular way over a period of time • *steady improvement* ○ *steady growth in profits* ○ *His recovery has been slow but steady.*

steadily /ˈsted·əl·i/ *adv* • *Prices have risen steadily.*

steady FIRM /ˈsted·i/ *adj* not moving or changing suddenly; continuing in the same condition • *a steady job/relationship* ○ *I'll hold the boat steady while you climb in.* ○ *We drove at a steady 65 mph for most of the trip.*

steady /ˈsted·i/ *v* [I/T] • *He wobbled a little on the bike and then steadied himself.* [T] ○ *The stock market has steadied after a sharp fall in prices.* [I]

steady CONTROLLED /ˈsted·i/ *adj* calm and under control • *Her voice was steady as she described the accident.*

steady /ˈsted·i/ *v* [T] • *He asked for a drink to steady his nerves.*

steak /steɪk/ *n* [C/U] a thick, flat slice of meat or fish that is cooked quickly

steal TAKE AWAY /stiːl/ *v* [I/T] *past simple* **stole** /stoʊl/, *past part* **stolen** /ˈstoʊ·lən/ to take (something) without the permission or knowledge of the owner and keep it or use it • *They broke into cars to steal the radios.* [T] ○ *He never paid me back, so basically he ended up stealing a hundred dollars from me.* [T] • To steal is also to do something quickly while trying not to be seen doing it: *to steal out of a room* [I always + adv/prep] ○ *She stole a glance at her watch.* [T]

steal CHEAP ITEM /stiːl/ *n* [C] *infml* something obtained at a much lower price than its true value • *At half the original price, that designer dress is a steal.*

stealth /stelθ/ *n* [U] movement that is quiet and careful in order to avoid notice, or secret or indirect action • The **stealth bomber/fighter** is an aircraft designed so that it cannot be seen on enemy RADAR (= equipment used for watching aircraft when they cannot be seen with the eyes).

stealthy /ˈstel·θi/ *adj* • *a stealthy burglar*

stealthily /ˈstel·θə·li/ *adv*

steam /stiːm/ *n* [U] the hot gas that is produced when water boils • Steam can be used to provide power: *a steam engine*

steam /stiːm/ *v* [I/T] • *The ship steamed* (= moved by steam power) *out of the harbor.* [I] • If food is steamed, it is cooked by steam. [T] • If a glass surface **steams up** or something **steams up**, it becomes covered with a thin layer of steam: *Going into the warm room steamed my glasses up.* • (*infml*) If a person is **steamed up**, they show their anger: *She got all steamed up about the dirty dishes in the sink.* • PIC COOKING METHODS

steamy /ˈstiː·mi/ *adj* • *By the time Hannah finished her shower, the bathroom was all steamy* • (*infml*) Steamy also means sexually exciting or including a lot of sexual activity: *a steamy love scene*

steamroller VEHICLE /'stiːm‚roʊ·lər/ *n* [C] a vehicle whose wheels are large, heavy cylinders that roll over a road surface to make it flat

steamroller FORCE /'stiːm‚roʊ·lər/, **steamroll** /'stiːm·roʊl/ *v* [T] to use great force to make (someone) do something or to make (something) happen • *He steamrollered the bill through Congress.*

steel METAL /stiːl/ *n* [U] a strong metal that is made by processing iron to remove some of the carbon • *steel doors/girders* ○ *the steel industry* • **Steel wool** is a mass of thin steel threads twisted together and used to clean a surface or rub it smooth.

steely /'stiː·li/ *adj* (of a person's behavior or character) hard and strong as steel • *Only their steely determination to survive kept them going.*

steel PREPARE /stiːl/ *v* [T] to prepare (yourself) to be able to do something unpleasant or difficult • *She steeled herself to face her accusers.*

steep NOT GRADUAL /stiːp/ *adj* [-er/-est] only] (of a slope) rising or falling at a sharp angle • *The train slowed as it went up a steep incline.* • A steep rise or fall is one that goes very quickly from low to high or from high to low: *Yesterday's steep decline in the value of the dollar was unexpected.*

steeply /'stiː·pli/ *adv* • *The beach slopes steeply down to the sea.*

steep TOO HIGH /stiːp/ *adj* [-er/-est] only] (esp. of prices) too high; more than is reasonable • *We enjoyed our stay at the hotel, but the charges were a bit steep.*

steep MAKE WET /stiːp/ *v* [I/T] to stay or cause to stay in a liquid, esp. in order to become soft or clean or to improve flavor • *This stain will come out if you steep the cloth in cold water.* [T] ○ *Let the tea steep for five minutes.* [I] • To be steeped in something is to be filled with it or knowledgeable about it: *The college is steeped in tradition.* [T]

steeple /'stiː·pəl/ *n* [C] a tower, esp. on a church, having a narrow, pointed part at the top

steer DIRECT /stɪr/ *v* [I/T] to control the direction of (a vehicle) • *It's not easy to steer the car through these narrow streets.* [T] ○ *(fig.) The speech steered clear of (= avoided) controversial issues.* [I] • To steer someone or something is to take them or cause them to go in a particular direction: *She steered her guests into the dining room.* [T] ○ *I'd like to steer the discussion back to our original topic.* [T] • A **steering wheel** in a vehicle is the wheel that the driver turns in order to make the vehicle go in a particular direction.

steer MALE COW /stɪr/ *n* [C] a young male of the cattle family that has had its sex organs removed and that is usually raised for meat

stellar OF OBJECTS IN SPACE /'stel·ər/ *adj* [not gradable] of a star or stars • *stellar light*

stellar HIGH IN QUALITY /'stel·ər/ *adj* [not gradable] (of people or their activities) extremely high in quality; excellent • *The cellist gave a stellar performance before an enthusiastic audience.*

stem CENTRAL PART /stem/ *n* [C] a central part of something from which other parts can develop or grow, or which forms a support • The stem of a plant is the straight part that grows above the ground and from which leaves and flowers grow. • The stem of a glass is the narrow, vertical part that supports the container into which you put liquid.

stem STOP /stem/ *v* [T] **-mm-** to stop (something unwanted) from spreading or increasing • *These measures are designed to stem the rise of violent crime in the country.*

□**stem from** /'--/ *v prep* [T] to develop or originate from • *These practices stem from traditional Chinese medicine.*

stench /stentʃ/ *n* [U] a strong, unpleasant smell • *the stench of rotting fish*

stencil /'sten·səl/ *n* [C] a piece of flat material in which shapes or letters have been cut out, so that when you paint or draw over it, images of the shapes or letters that have been cut out will be left on the surface below, or the patterns or letters made by this method

stencil /'sten·səl/ *v* [T] • *The back of the chair was painted solid black with designs stenciled in gold.*

stenographer /stə'nɑg·rə·fər/ *n* [C] a person who does **shorthand** (= system of fast writing) in an office or records speech using a special machine in a court

stenography /stə'nɑg·rə·fi/ *n* [U] a system for recording speech quickly by writing it down in **shorthand** or by using a special machine

step MOVE FOOT /step/ *v* [I always + adv/prep] **-pp-** to lift one foot and put it down in front of the other foot, as in walking or running • *He stepped to his left, picked up the ball, and threw.* ○ *We stepped carefully along the slippery path.* • If you tell someone to **step on it**, you want them to hurry or to speed up: *You'll have to step on it to catch that train.* • If you **step on** someone's **toes**, you have been rude and have upset or embarrassed someone: *It's a very competitive business—you can't afford to step on too many toes.*

step /step/ *n* [C] • *He took a couple of steps into the room.* • A step is the distance covered by one step: *I'd only gone about three steps before I fell.* • A step is also the sound of making such a movement: *I heard my father's step on the stairs.* • A step is also a particular movement that you make with your feet when you dance: *I've finally learned some dance steps.* • If you move **in step with** someone, you move your feet at the same time and in the same way: *Three angry women marched in step down the hall.* • If you are **in step with** someone or something, your ideas agree with theirs: *She is very much in step with the times.*

step STAGE /step/ *n* [C] a stage in a process • *The first step in fixing our house is to put on a new roof.* ◦ *Let's make these changes carefully, a step at a time.* • If you do something **step-by-step**, you do one thing at a time in a particular order: *She followed the instructions step-by-step.*

step ACTION /step/ *n* [C] one action in a series, taken for a particular purpose • *As a first step, both sides agreed to a cease-fire.*

step FLAT SURFACE /step/ *n* [C] a flat surface on which you put your foot when going up or down from one level to another • *Mom took a picture of us sitting on the front steps of the house.* • A **stepladder** is a piece of equipment for climbing up and down that can stand on its own or be folded for storage. • Compare STAIRS.

step MUSIC /step/, **tone** *n* [C] the largest difference in sound between two notes next to each other in a musical SCALE (= series of notes) • *Tones in a scale are arranged in steps and half steps.*

□ **step back** /'-'-/ *v adv* [I] to stop being involved in something • *We need to step back and look at all our options.*

□ **step down** /'-'-/, **step aside** /'--'-/ *v adv* [I] to give up a job or position • *She stepped down as captain of the team.*

□ **step in** /'-'-/ *v adv* [I] to become involved • *An outside buyer stepped in to save the company.*

□ **step out** /'-'-/ *v adv* [I] to leave a place, esp. for a short time • *Mr. Taylor just stepped out of the office to get the mail.*

□ **step up** *obj*, **step** *obj* **up** /'-'-/ *v adv* [M] to make (something) more effective, or to increase the size or speed of (something) • *Following the explosion, security at the airport was stepped up.*

stepchild /'step·tʃaɪld/ *n* [C] *pl* **stepchildren** /'step,tʃɪl·drən/ a child of a previous marriage of either a husband or a wife

stepdaughter /'step,dɔːt̬·ər/ *n* [C] a daughter of a previous marriage of either a husband or a wife

stepfather /'step,faθ·ər/ *n* [C] a man who is married to the mother of a child but is not the biological father

stepmother /'step,mʌð·ər/ *n* [C] a woman who is married to the father of a child but is not the biological mother

stepping stone /'step·ɪŋ,stoʊn/ *n* [C] something that helps someone advance or achieve something • *I hope this job will be a stepping stone to something better.* • A stepping stone is also a stone that you step on to cross a stream or wet area: *Flat stepping stones crossed the stream.*

stepson /'step·sʌn/ *n* [C] a son of a previous marriage of either a husband or a wife

stereo /'ster·iː,oʊ/ *n* [C/U] *pl* **stereos** a device

that plays recorded sound through two or more SPEAKERS, or sound produced in this way • *Music was blaring from her car stereo.* [C]

stereo /'ster·iː,oʊ/, **stereophonic** /,ster·iː·ə'fɑn·ɪk/ *adj* [not gradable] • *stereo sound* ◦ *stereo equipment*

stereotype /'ster·iː·ə,taɪp/ *n* [C] *disapproving* an idea that is used to characterize a particular type of person or thing, or a person or thing thought to represent such an idea • *He fits the stereotype of the cigar-smoking, rumpled politician.*

stereotype /'ster·iː·ə,taɪp/ *v* [T] *disapproving* • *That unfortunate statement stereotypes all men as wimps.*

stereotypical /,ster·iː·ə'tɪp·ɪ·kəl/ *adj disapproving* • *I'm not your stereotypical Texan.*

sterile UNABLE TO PRODUCE /'ster·əl/ *adj* [not gradable] (of a person or animal) unable to produce young, or (of land) unable to produce plants or crops • *It was a small oasis surrounded by sterile desert.*

sterility /stə'rɪl·ət̬·i/ *n* [U] • *Certain chemicals cause sterility in farm animals.*

sterilize /'ster·ə,laɪz/ *v* [T] • *The clinic will sterilize your cat for free.*

sterilization /,ster·ə·lə'zeɪ·ʃən/ *n* [U] • *Sterilization is a drastic way to control births.*

sterile WITHOUT BACTERIA /'ster·əl/ *adj* [not gradable] free from bacteria • *Medical equipment must be kept sterile.*

sterilize /'ster·ə,laɪz/ *v* [T] • *Dental instruments are routinely sterilized.*

sterilization /,ster·ə·lə'zeɪ·ʃən/ *n* [U] • *Sterilization of milk products kills dangerous bacteria.*

sterile LACKING /'ster·əl/ *adj* [not gradable] lacking in imagination, ideas, or enthusiasm • *Suburban housing developments are often sterile environments.*

sterling /'stɜr·lɪŋ/ *adj* [not gradable] of the highest quality • *McCoy had a sterling season last year.*

sterling (silver) /'stɜr·lɪŋ ('sɪl·vər)/ *adj* [not gradable] silver that is very pure • *The bracelet is made of sterling silver.*

stern SEVERE /'stɜrn/ *adj* [-er/-est only] severe • *Sterner punishment may produce better behavior, but I doubt it.*

sternly /'stɜrn·li/ *adv* • *He sternly reminded his son to drive carefully.*

stern SHIP PART /'stɜrn/ *n* [C] the back end of a ship • *A rope on the stern towed the little boat.* • Compare BOW SHIP PART.

steroid /'stɪr·ɔɪd, 'ster-/ *n* [C] any of a large group of chemical substances produced in the body, or an artificial form of these substances used to treat various medical conditions • Steroids are also illegally used to improve the performance of competitors in some sports

stethoscope /'steθ·ə,skoʊp/ *n* [C] a medical device that allows a doctor to listen to your heart, lungs, or other part of your body

stew [COOK] /stuː/ *v* [I/T] to cook (food) slowly in liquid or to cook slowly in liquid • *Stew the pears gently in red wine for a couple of hours.* [T]

stew /stuː/ *n* [C/U] a dish consisting usually of meat or fish and vegetables cooked slowly in a small amount of liquid

stew [BE ANXIOUS] /stuː/ *v* [I always + adv/prep] *infml* to be anxious or upset about something • *You're not still stewing over the election results, are you?*

stew /stuː/ *n* [C] • *She has been in a stew over plans for her wedding.*

steward /'stuː·ərd/ *n* [C] a person who is responsible for an event or for the management of a place • *a race steward* ○ *He has been a careful steward of our parks.* • A steward is also a person who is responsible for food or drink at a restaurant: *a wine steward* • On a ship, a steward (*female* **stewardess**) helps and serves passengers.

stewardship /'stuː·ərd,ʃɪp/ *n* [U] care or management • *The team has fallen to new lows under his stewardship.*

stick [THIN PIECE] /stɪk/ *n* [C] a thin piece of wood • *The campers collected sticks to start a fire.* • A stick is also a long, thin handle with a specially shaped end, used esp. to play HOCKEY and LACROSSE. • A stick can also be a long, thin piece of something: *sticks of dynamite* ○ *a stick of chewing gum* • A **stick figure** is a drawing of a person with the body made of straight lines. • A **stick shift** is a **gearshift**, or a car that has a stick shift. See at GEAR [MACHINE PART].

stick figure

stick [PUSH INTO] /stɪk/ *v* [always + adv/prep] *past* **stuck** /stʌk/ to push (something pointed) into or through something, or to be pushed into or through something • *I simply cannot watch when someone sticks a needle in my arm.* [T] ○ *He throws the knife, and the blade sticks in the wall.* [I]

stick [ATTACH] /stɪk/ *v* [I/T] *past* **stuck** /stʌk/ to attach or become attached • *Stick the tape to the back of the picture.* [T] ○ *It was so hot that my clothes stuck to me.* [I] • If a food **sticks to** your **ribs**, it makes you feel full: *Meat, potatoes, bread—those are the foods that stick to your ribs.*

sticky /'stɪk·i/ *adj* tending to stick, or covered with a substance that sticks • *You had better wash your sticky fingers.* • If the weather is sticky, it is hot and the air feels wet. • See also STICKY.

sticker /'stɪk·ər/ *n* [C] a small piece of paper with a picture or writing on one side and a sticky substance on the other • *Dana collects stickers of cartoon characters.*

stick [PUT] /stɪk/ *v* [T always + adv/prep] *past* **stuck** /stʌk/ *infml* to put (something) somewhere, usually temporarily • *Stick the packages under the table for now.*

stick [UNABLE TO MOVE] /stɪk/ *v* [I] *past* **stuck** /stʌk/ to be fixed in position and unable to move • *The window sticks, making it hard to shut it.* • A **sticking point** in a discussion is a point on which it is very difficult to reach agreement: *Dividing up the land is the main sticking point of the peace talks.* • If something **sticks in** your **mind**, you remember it: *Her angry remarks stuck in my mind for a long time.* • USAGE: The related adjective is STUCK [FIXED].

▫ **stick around** /ˌ--'-/ *v adv* [I] *infml* to stay somewhere and wait for someone or for something to happen • *You go ahead—I'll stick around until Candice shows up.*

▫ **stick by** /'-ˌ-/ *v prep* [T] to continue to support (someone), or to not change your mind about (something) • *He stuck by his earlier statements and never changed his story.*

▫ **stick out** *obj* [GO BEYOND] , **stick** *obj* **out** /'-'-/ *v adv* [I/M] to reach beyond (the surface or edge of something) • *They built the house on a little peninsula that sticks out into the lake.* [I] ○ *He stuck his arm out to hail a cab.* [M] • If you **stick** your **neck out**, you take a risk: *I'm really sticking my neck out by investing my money in this idea.* • If you **stick out** your **tongue**, you push your tongue out of your mouth, usually as an insult or to show your bad opinion of someone: *She stuck her tongue out at him and smiled.* This action is usually done by children.

▫ **stick** *obj* **out** [CONTINUE] /'-'-/ *v adv* [T] to continue to do (something) to its end • *I didn't really like the movie, but I stuck it out.*

▫ **stick out** [BE NOTICEABLE] /'-'-/ *v adv* [I] to be very noticeable because of being different • *Dye your hair orange and you'll really stick out in a small town like this.* ○ *My colorful clothes stuck out like a sore thumb.*

▫ **stick to** /'--/ *v prep* [T] to keep to (something) without changing it in some way • *Would you stick to the point, please?* • If you **stick to** your **guns**, you refuse to change your beliefs or actions, even when other people pressure you to change: *My parents don't want me to be an actor, but I'm sticking to my guns.*

▫ **stick together** /ˌ--'--/ *v adv* [I] to support each other • *If we all stick together, we can succeed.*

▫ **stick up** [GO ABOVE] /'-'-/ *v adv* [I] to reach above the surface of something • *A few green shoots were sticking up out of the ground.*

▫ **stick** *obj* **up** [STEAL] , **stick up** *obj* /'-'-/ *v adv* [M] *infml* to use a gun to steal something from (a person or place) • *Did you hear that someone stuck the post office up?*

stickup /'stɪk·ʌp/ *n* [C] *infml* • *The stickup at the bank was carried out in broad daylight.*

▫ **stick up for** /-'--/ *v adv prep* [T] *infml* to support or defend (something or someone) • *Her* *friends stuck up for her when other people said she was guilty.*

□**stick with** STAY CLOSE /'--/ *v prep* [T] *infml* to stay close to (someone), or to continue to do (something) • *Stick with me, and we'll do lots of interesting things.* ◦ *Once Stephen takes up a hobby, he sticks with it.*

□**stick** *obj* **with** *obj* FORCE TO HAVE /'--/ *v prep* [T] to force (someone) to have or do (something less desirable) • *Big power companies grab cheap supplies and stick everyone else with more expensive ones.*

sticker /'stɪk·ər/ *n* [C] See at STICK ATTACH.

stickler /'stɪk·lər/ *n* [C] someone who believes in closely following rules or in maintaining a high standard of behavior • *He was a stickler when it came to office manners.*

sticks /stɪks/ *pl n infml disapproving* • The sticks is a humorous way of referring to a place in the country: *My parents live out in the sticks.*

sticky /'stɪk·i/ *adj* difficult to deal with or solve • *a sticky situation* ◦ *a sticky issue* • See also **sticky** at STICK ATTACH.

stiff FIRM /stɪf/ *adj* [*-er/-est* only] firm or hard and not bending or moving easily • *He had stiff leather shoes on.* ◦ *If the dough is stiff, add more sour cream.* • If your body is stiff, you cannot move easily and your muscles hurt when moved: *He was unable to turn his head because of a stiff neck.*

stiffen /'stɪf·ən/ *v* [I/T] • *To paint on linen, you first have to stiffen the fabric with a glue mixture.* [T] ◦ *His back stiffened up after the game.* [I]

stiffly /'stɪf·li/ *adv* • *The gown is constructed so stiffly that it could stand up on its own.*

stiffness /'stɪf·nəs/ *n* [U] • *I had some muscle stiffness after the bike ride.*

stiff NOT RELAXED /stɪf/ *adj* [*-er/-est* only] not relaxed or friendly; formal • *The performance was stiff and rather predictable.* ◦ *You can't be stiff with a guy who takes you into his confidence.*

stiffen /'stɪf·ən/ *v* [I] to become nervous and less relaxed • *I stiffened when she tried to kiss me.*

stiffly /'stɪf·li/ *adv* • *"I don't think it has anything to do with you," he said stiffly.*

stiffness /'stɪf·nəs/ *n* [U] • *His early stiffness and formality evolved into friendliness.*

stiff SEVERE /stɪf/ *adj* [*-er/-est* only] severe; difficult to deal with or do • *The penalties for drug possession are stiff.* ◦ *Most of the team's losses have come against stiff competition.*

stiffen /'stɪf·ən/ *v* [I/T] • *The measure would stiffen the penalties for using a gun.* [T] ◦ *Competition will stiffen considerably if another store opens in town.* [I]

stiff STRONG /stɪf/ *adj* strong or powerful • *A stiff wind beat against the house.* • A stiff drink is a strong alcoholic drink.

stiff VERY MUCH /stɪf/ *adv* [not gradable] *infml*

very much; to a great degree • *I was scared stiff during the air raids.*

stiff PERSON /stɪf/ *n* [C] *slang* a person of the type described • *I'm just a working stiff.* ◦ *You lucky stiff!* • (*slang*) A stiff is also a dead person's body.

stiff CHEAT /stɪf/ *v* [T] to cheat (someone) out of money • *She stiffed the taxi driver.*

stifle /'staɪ·fəl/ *v* [T] to prevent (something) from happening, being expressed, or continuing • *It is the responsibility of schools to encourage learning, not to stifle it.*

stifling /'staɪ·flɪŋ/ *adj* extremely hot, with a lack of fresh air • *Summers in Virginia have always had stifling humidity.*

stigma /'stɪg·mə/ *n* [C/U] a strong lack of respect for someone or a bad opinion of them because they have done something society does not approve of • *There's a stigma associated with low-income food programs.* [C usually sing]

stigmatize /'stɪg·mə,taɪz/ *v* [T] to make (someone) feel that they are not respected • *She was stigmatized because of her race.*

still UNTIL NOW /stɪl/ *adv* [not gradable] continuing until now or until a particular time • *The universe is still expanding.* ◦ *Two years later she still had scars on her knees.*

still DESPITE /stɪl/ *adv* [not gradable] despite that • *He was diagnosed with cancer but still returned to work.* ◦ *I'm a mother of two and I still hold down a job.*

still EVEN GREATER /stɪl/ *adv* [not gradable] to an even greater degree or in an even greater amount • *Lulu's apartment is crammed with papers and boxes that hold still more papers.*

still NOT MOVING /stɪl/ *adj, adv* [*-er/-est* only] not moving; staying in the same position • *Just hold still—you've got a little cut on your head.* ◦ *Time seems almost to stand still here, doesn't it?* • A **still life** is a painting or drawing of an arrangement of objects that do not move, such as flowers or fruit.

still /stɪl/ *n* [U] *esp. literary* • *In the still* (= quiet) *of the night, nothing moved.*

still EQUIPMENT /stɪl/ *n* [C] a piece of equipment used for making alcohol

stillbirth /'stɪl·bɜrθ/ *n* [C] the birth of a baby who has already died inside the mother

stillborn /'stɪl·bɔːrn/ *adj* [not gradable] dead at the time of birth • *Her first child was stillborn.*

stilted /'stɪl·təd/ *adj* (of behavior, speech, or writing) too formal and not smooth or natural • *Legal language tends to be very stilted.*

stilts /stɪlts/ *pl n* long pieces of wood with supports for the feet on which someone can stand and walk, or long pieces of wood that support small buildings above the ground or above water

stimulate /'stɪm·jə,leɪt/ *v* [T] to encourage (something) to grow, develop, or become active • *Tax cuts will stimulate the economy.* ◦ *Read* books to stimulate your child's imagination. ○ *Some vegetables stimulate cells to manufacture a cancer-fighting enzyme.*

stimulant /'stɪm·jə·lənt/ *n* [C] a drug or chemical substance that encourages growth or increases activity • *The horse was found to have a powerful stimulant in his system.*

stimulating /'stɪm·jə‚leɪt·ɪŋ/ *adj* causing enthusiasm and interest • *The conversation was stimulating, witty, and learned.*

stimulation /‚stɪm·jə'leɪ·ʃən/ *n* [U] • *I need the intellectual stimulation of work.*

stimulus /'stɪm·jə·ləs/ *n* [C/U] *pl* **stimuli** /'stɪm·jə‚laɪ, -‚liː/ something that causes growth, activity, or reaction • *Scientists are studying the cell's response to stimuli.* [C] ○ *The aid package would provide very little fiscal stimulus.* [U]

sting HURT /stɪŋ/ *v* [I/T] *past* **stung** /stʌŋ/ (esp. of insects, plants, and animals) to produce a small but painful injury by making a very small hole in the skin • *Why do bees sting?* [I] • If something stings, it causes you to feel pain: *Cold air stung Jack's lungs.* [T] ○ *The soap made his eyes sting.* [I] • If someone's remarks sting you, they make you feel upset and annoyed: *Managers were stung by criticism from environmentalists.* [T]

sting /stɪŋ/ *n* [C] • *Bee stings covered his hands.*

stinger /'stɪŋ·ər/ *n* [C] the pointed part of an insect, plant, or animal that stings

sting POLICE ACTIVITY /stɪŋ/ *n* [C] an operation in which police officers or others pretend to be criminals so they can catch people committing crimes • *Officers set up a sting in which they sold him the gun, and when he drove off with it they arrested him.*

sting /stɪŋ/ *v* [T] *past* **stung** /stʌŋ/ *infml* • *Retailers were stung when the teens made illegal tobacco purchases.*

stingy /'stɪn·dʒi/ *adj* [*-er/-est*] only not generous, or unwilling to spend money • *Some bankers are stingy in lending to small businesses.*

stink SMELL /stɪŋk/ *v* [I] *past simple* **stank** /stæŋk/ *or* **stunk** /stʌŋk/, *past part* **stunk** /stʌŋk/ *infml* to smell very unpleasant • *Your feet stink.* [I]

stink /stɪŋk/ *n* [C] • *I can't stand the stink of rotten meat.*

stinking /'stɪŋ·kɪŋ/ *adj* [not gradable] • *Houses were built along stinking drainage ditches.*

stink BE BAD /stɪŋk/ *v* [I] *past simple* **stank** /stæŋk/ *or* **stunk** /stʌŋk/, *past part* **stunk** /stʌŋk/ *infml* to be extremely bad or unpleasant • *The music scene here stinks.*

stink /stɪŋk/ *n* [U] *infml* a negative reaction from a group of people or from the public • *City employees are raising a stink over drug testing.*

stinker /'stɪŋ·kər/ *n* [C] *infml* an unpleasant

person, thing, or situation • *Don was punished for calling his mother a stinker.*

stinking /'stɪŋ·kɪŋ/ *adj infml* • *I hate this stinking job!*

□ **stink up** *obj*, **stink** *obj* **up** /'-'-/ *v adv* [M] *infml* to make (a place) smell unpleasant • *That perfume stunk up the whole store.*

stint PERIOD /stɪnt/ *n* [C] a period of time spent doing a particular job or activity • *He took up boxing during his stint in the army.*

stint LIMIT /stɪnt/ *v* [I] to give, take, or use only a small amount of something • *She doesn't stint when it comes to buying new clothes.*

stipend /'staɪ·pend, -pənd/ *n* [C] a fixed, regular income that is usually not based on an amount of work done • *As a student advisor, she gets a monthly stipend from the college.*

stipulate /'stɪp·jə‚leɪt/ *v* [T] to state exactly (what must be done) • *State laws stipulate that public education be free.* [+ *that* clause]

stipulation /‚stɪp·jə'leɪ·ʃən/ *n* [C] • *There was a stipulation that the land be used as a park.*

stir MIX /stɜr/ *v* [I/T] *-rr-* to mix (liquids or other substances), or to move an object such as a spoon in a circular movement • *Chad stirred the thick paint in the buckets.* [T] ○ *Add tomatoes, stir, and bring to boil.* [I] ○ *Let the rice sit, and then stir it up.* [M]

stir /stɜr/ *n* [C] • *Give the onions a stir.*

stir MOVE /stɜr/ *v* [I/T] *-rr-* to move slightly, or to cause (something) to move • *A breeze stirred the palm trees.* [T] ○ *The old man stirred in his chair.* [I] ○ *Her boat went ahead of mine, so she'd stir up the fish and I'd catch them.* [M]

stir CAUSE /stɜr/ *v* [T] to cause (feelings or emotions) to be felt • *That music stirred some old emotions.* ○ *Hate-mongers like to stir up unrest.* [M]

stir /stɜr/ *n* [U] • *His promise to support the rights of homosexuals is creating a stir.*

stir–fry /'stɜr·fraɪ/ *v* [T] to cook (pieces of meat or vegetables) quickly in very hot oil, moving them around all the time • *She stir-fried the vegetables.*

stir–fry /'stɜr·fraɪ/ *n* [C] • *Tomatoes add color to a stir-fry.*

stirrup /'stɜr·əp, 'stɪr-/ *n* [C] one of a pair of metal pieces that hangs from the side of a horse's SADDLE (= seat), which you put your foot in when riding

stitch THREAD /stɪtʃ/ *n* [C] a piece of thread sewn in cloth, or the single movement of a needle and thread into and out of the cloth that produces this • *She sewed neat, firm stitches.* • A stitch is also a length of special thread used to join the edges of a deep cut in the flesh: *A cut on his left ankle required six stitches.*

stitch /stɪtʃ/ *v* [T] • *His name is stitched onto the back of his boxing trunks.* • If someone is stitched up, they have a deep cut closed with stitches: *The operation started at 8 a.m., and Bobby was stitched up by midafternoon.* [M]

stitching /'stɪtʃ·ɪŋ/ *n* [U] • *I sew it on so you can't see the stitching.*

stitch PAIN /stɪtʃ/ *n* [C] a sharp pain in the side of your stomach or chest • *I got a stitch while I was running.*

stitches /'stɪtʃ·əz/ *pl n* • If someone is **in stitches**, they are laughing in an uncontrolled way.

stock SUPPLY /stɑrk/ *n* [C/U] a supply of something for use or sale • *New regulations should preserve stocks of haddock and other fish.* [C] ○ *The company won't let you return unsold stock.* [U] • Stock is also the total amount of goods or the amount of a particular type of goods available in a store: *New Video has 4000 titles in stock.* [U] ○ *Those CDs are out of stock.* [U]

stock /stɑrk/ *v* [T] • *They stock all sorts of gifts for travelers.* • If you **stock up on** something, you buy a large amount of it: *I hadn't stocked up on food, so I wasn't ready to feed Kate and her friends.*

stock INVESTMENT /stɑk/ *n* [C/U] a part of the ownership of a company that people buy as an investment • *There is more risk with stocks than with bonds.* [C] ○ *Stock prices fell this week.* [U] • A **stockbroker** is a person or company that buys and sells stocks for other people. • A **stock exchange** or **stock market** is a place where stocks are bought and sold, or the organization of people whose job is to do this buying and selling: *The company's shares fell sharply on the London stock exchange.* • The **stock market** is also the value of stocks bought and sold: *Rumors about the president's illness caused the stock market to go down yesterday.* • A **stockholder** is a person or group that owns stock in a company.

stock USUAL /stɑk/ *adj* [not gradable] (of an idea, expression, or action) usual or typical • *a stock phrase/response* • A person's **stock-in-trade** is their typical way of behaving, or a job or skill that is usual for them: *I might as well make a fool of myself, it's my stock-in-trade.*

stock FLAVORED LIQUID /stɑk/ *n* [U] a liquid made by boiling vegetables or the bones from meat or fish in water which is used to add flavor to soups and other food • *vegetable/beef/chicken stock*

stock ANIMALS /stɑk/ *pl n* short form of LIVESTOCK (= animals, such as cows or sheep, kept on a farm) • A **stockyard** is a set of enclosed areas where farm animals are kept before being sold or killed.

stock ORIGIN /stɑk/ *n* [U] the family or group from which a person originates • *He's an American of Irish stock.*

stock GUN PART /stɑk/ *n* [C] the part of a RIFLE (= long gun) that rests against the shoulder

stockade /stɑ'keɪd/ *n* [C] a strong wooden fence built around an area to defend it against attack

stocking /'stɑk·ɪŋ/ *n* [C usually pl] one of a pair of tight-fitting, thin, cloth covers for the feet and legs worn esp. by women • *I wore a red velvet dress, black pumps, and sheer black stockings.* • A stocking is also a large sock in which presents are put at Christmas. • If someone is **in stocking feet** they are not wearing shoes: *She met me at the door in stocking feet.*

stockpile /'stɑk·paɪl/ *n* [C] a large amount of goods kept ready for future use • *a stockpile of weapons*

stockpile /'stɑk·paɪl/ *v* [T] • *She stockpiled chocolate bars in her car.*

stock–still /'stɑk'stɪl/ *adv* [not gradable] without moving; completely still • *He stood stock-still, waiting for them to pass.*

stocky /'stɑk·i/ *adj* (esp. of a man) wide and strong-looking • *He was shorter and stockier than I expected.*

stodgy /'stɑdʒ·i/ *adj* acting according to old, established methods and unwilling to change or consider new ideas • *one of the stodgiest and most private of the nation's banks*

stoic /'stoʊ·ɪk/, **stoical** /'stoʊ·ɪ·kəl/ *adj* not showing or not feeling any emotion, esp. in a situation in which the expression of emotion is expected • *He is somewhat stoic as he speaks of his Holocaust past.*

stoke /stoʊk/ *v* [T] to add fuel to (a large enclosed fire) and move the fuel around so that it burns well and produces a lot of heat • *Returning to the camp, he stoked the fire.* ○ *(fig.) Her execution stoked the flames of (= increased) the public's indignation.*

stole /stoʊl/ *past simple of* STEAL

stolen /'stoʊ·lən/ *past participle of* STEAL

stolid /'stɑl·əd/ *adj* showing little or no emotion or imagination • *Stolid and impassive, the customs inspector listened to her explanation.*

stomach /'stʌm·ək/ *n* [C] *pl* **stomachs** an organ in the body where food is digested, or the front part of your body near the waist • Stomach can also mean desire or an interest in doing something: *Most citizens quickly lost their stomach for a long war.* • A **stomachache** is a pain in the stomach.

stomach /'stʌm·ək/ *v* [T] to accept or be able to deal with (something that causes you difficulty) • *Vernon was simply too unreliable, and after awhile we couldn't stomach his behavior.*

stomp /stɑmp, stɔːmp/ *v* [I/T] to put (your foot) down so that it hits the ground with a lot of force, or to walk with heavy steps • *She had waited hours already and was about to stomp away furiously.* [I always + adv/prep]

stone HARD SUBSTANCE /stoʊn/ *n* [C/U] the hard, solid substance found in the ground that is often used as a building material, or a small piece of this substance • *The museum was made of stone.* [U] • A stone is also a jewel: *He wore a ring with a black stone on his little finger.* [C] • A stone is also a piece of hard material that can form in an organ in the body: *kid-*

ney stones [C] • A **stone's throw** is a short distance: *The lodge is within a stone's throw of the ski slopes.* • If a person is **stone-faced**, they do not show any emotion.

stone /stoʊn/ *v* [T] to throw rocks or other hard objects at (someone or something)

stone /stoʊn/ *adv* [not gradable] completely • *By the time he was 80, he was stone deaf.*

stony /ˈstoʊ·ni/ *adj* • *The ground was too stony to be used as a farm.* • Stony also means not showing any emotion, esp. sympathy, when you might expect it to be shown: *Though we begged him, he gave us a stony look and turned away.*

stone SEED /stoʊn/ *n* [C] a PIT SEED • *a cherry stone*

stoned /stoʊnd/ *adj slang* experiencing the effects of alcohol or an illegal drug

stonewall /ˈstoʊn·wɔːl/ *v* [I/T] to prevent (someone) from discovering information by not being helpful or by refusing to answer questions • *If you refuse to be interviewed, or stonewall and make it difficult for us to do our job, you might face punishment later.* [I]

stood /stʊd/ *past simple and past participle of* STAND

stool SEAT /stuːl/ *n* [C] a seat without any support for the back or arms • *a piano stool* ○ *Sarah sat on a kitchen stool.*

stool SOLID WASTE /stuːl/ *n* [C] *medical* a piece of excrement

stoop BEND /stuːp/ *v* [I] to bend the top half of the body forward and down • *The mother stooped to button up the coat of her little girl.* • If someone **stoops to** doing something, they lower their moral standards to do it: *The president shouldn't stoop to the level of exchanging insults.*

stoop /stuːp/ *n* [U] • *He walks with a stoop because of arthritis.*

stoop STEPS /stuːp/ *n* [C] a structure that is part of the front of a house consisting of a few steps leading up from ground level, often with a raised, flat area near the door

stoops

stop FINISH /stɑp/ *v* [I/T] **-pp-** to finish (doing something) or end, or to cause (someone or something) to finish • *When do you think the snow will stop?* [I] ○ *When will it stop snowing?* [T] ○ *Please stop pushing.* [T] ○ *Fortunately, police stopped the fight before anyone got hurt.* [T]

stop /stɑp/ *n* [C] • *Please wait until the plane comes to a complete stop before leaving your*

seat. • A **stopwatch** is a watch that you can start and stop to measure exactly how much time has passed, used esp. in sports events such as races.

stop PREVENT /stɑp/ *v* [T] **-pp-** to prevent (someone) from doing something • *Lifeguards stopped them from going into the water because sharks had been spotted in the area.*

stop PAUSE /stɑp/ *v* [I/T] **-pp-** to pause or stay in a place, or cause (someone) to pause • *We stopped for gas and had something to eat.* [I] ○ *We'd better stop at the next rest area to let the kids go to the bathroom.* [+ *to* infinitive] ○ *Naomi was stopped at the gate and asked to show identification.* [T] • If you stop by/in, you visit someone for a short time, esp. when you are on the way to somewhere else: *A group of friends stopped by to say hello.* [I] • If you stop off, you go to a place when you are on the way to another place: *I'll stop off on my way home and pick up some wine.* [I] • If you can **stop on a dime**, you can stop almost immediately: *He runs up the field and stops on a dime to catch the ball.*

stop /stɑp/ *n* [C] • *It was a five-hour drive including a 30-minute stop for lunch.* • A stop is a place where vehicles, esp. buses and trains, pause to allow passengers to get off and on: *I'm getting off at the next stop.* • A **stoplight** is a **traffic light**. See at TRAFFIC MOVING THINGS. • A **stop sign** is a red, eight-sided sign at the side of a road that signals drivers of vehicles to pause before continuing.

stoppage /ˈstɑp·ɪdʒ/ *n* [C] • *After a two-day work stoppage in early July, another strike started in September.*

▫**stop over** /-ˈ--/ *v adv* [I] to stay at a place for a short period of time on the way to somewhere else or before returning home • *Marj decided to stop over in Pittsburgh to see an old friend.*

stopover /ˈstɑpˌoʊ·vər/ *n* [C] a short stay at a place, esp. when planned in advance, while in the middle of a trip • *The tour included a stopover in Pisa on the way to Florence.*

stopgap /ˈstɑp·ɡæp/ *n* [C] something that can be used until something better or more permanent can be obtained • *Housing the homeless in shelters has to be seen as a stopgap measure.*

stopper /ˈstɑp·ər/ *n* [C] a round object that fits into or covers a hole, such as in a sink, to prevent liquids from escaping it • *a rubber sink stopper*

store PLACE TO BUY THINGS /stɔːr, stoʊr/ *n* [C] a place where you can buy goods or services • *a grocery/hardware/liquor/video store* ○ *convenience/department stores* • A **storefront** is the part of a store that faces the street, usually a glass front: *In the downtown area, there are dozens of boarded-up storefronts.* ○ *He was a preacher in a storefront church* (= church that uses the space of a store). • A **storekeeper** is a person who owns or operates a store.

store [KEEP] /stɔːr, stoʊr/ v [T] to put or keep (things) for use in the future • *We store the garden tools in a shed in the backyard.* ○ *All the information is stored on a hard disk.*

storage /'stɔːr·ɪdʒ, 'stoʊr-/ n [U] • *Fire broke out in a basement storage area.* ○ *Much of the art they've acquired is still in storage* (= being kept in a safe place and not yet in use).

store /stɔːr, stoʊr/ n [C] • *The captured terrorists had an extensive store* (= a large amount) *of dynamite and bomb-making material.* • *We have a big surprise* **in store for** *you* (= planned and ready for you). • A **storehouse** is a WAREHOUSE. • A **storeroom** is a room in which things that are not being used can be kept: *You can get a mop from the school's storeroom downstairs.*

stork /stɔːrk/ n [C] a large bird with long legs, a long neck, and a long beak that walks in water to find its food

storm [VIOLENT WEATHER] /stɔːrm/ n [C] an extreme weather condition with strong winds and heavy rain or snow • *The storm left over a foot of snow on the ground.*

stormy /'stɔːr·mi/ adj • *I remember one stormy afternoon when Marcelle and I were kept indoors by the weather.* ○ (fig.) *The new president's promise of dramatic change has already run into some stormy weather* (= difficult problems) *on Capitol Hill.*

storm [STRONG FEELING] /stɔːrm/ n [C] a strong expression of feeling, esp. in reaction to a statement or event • *The new rent regulations raised a storm of criticism from both renters and landlords.*

storm /stɔːrm/ v [I always + adv/prep] to move quickly and forcefully to show you are angry • *Henry stormed into Giffen's office waving a copy of the newspaper and yelling at the top of his lungs.*

stormy /'stɔːr·mi/ adj full of difficulties or fights • *He is best remembered for his stormy marriage to actress Bette Davis.*

storm [ATTACK] /stɔːrm/ v [T] to attack (a place or building) suddenly • *A group of about 40 youths armed with baseball bats and clubs stormed a recreation center last night.*

story [DESCRIPTION] /'stɔːr·i, 'stoʊr·i/ n [C] a description of events that actually happened or that are invented • *There was a news story on television about flooding on the west coast.* ○ *My daughter won't go to bed without hearing a bedtime story.* • A story can also be a lie: *Don't tell me any stories—I want to know what really happened.* • A **storybook** is a book containing stories, esp. stories for children. • A **storyteller** is a person who tells or reads stories to others.

story [LEVEL] /'stɔːr·i, 'stoʊr·i/ n [C] a level of a building • *She lived on the third floor of a seven-story building.*

stout [FAT] /staʊt/ adj [-er/-est only] (of people) fat and solid-looking, esp. around the waist, or (of things) thick and strong • *He was seen as a pleasant man—short, a bit stout and balding, with a radiant smile.* ○ *There is much to be said for having a stout fence to protect your flower beds.*

stout [DETERMINED] /staʊt/ adj [-er/-est only] determined and strong, esp. in opinion • *He became a stout defender of religious freedom.*

stove /stoʊv/ n [C] a piece of kitchen equipment having a top for cooking food in containers placed over gas flames or circles of metal heated electrically, and that usually has an OVEN below • *She got some eggs out and heated a pan on the stove.* • A stove is also a piece of equipment for heating a space inside a room, often using wood or a form of COAL as a fuel: *a potbellied stove*

stow /stoʊ/ v [T] to put (something) in a place where it can be kept safely • *Please stow your carry-on bags under the seat in front of you.*

stowaway /'stoʊ·ə,weɪ/ n [C] someone who hides on a ship or aircraft to travel without having to pay

straddle /'stræd·əl/ v [T] to have or put your legs on either side of (something) • *Grace straddled her chair.* • To straddle (something) is also to be unable to decide which of two opinions about something is better, and so to partly support both opinions: *The president has tried to straddle the issue of political fund-raising.*

straggle /'stræg·əl/ v [I] to move singly or in small groups slowly and usually separated in distance or time from those who went earlier • *Concentration camp survivors straggled back to Poland after being liberated.*

straggler /'stræg·lər/ n [C] • *I want all you children to stay together and hold hands when crossing a street—no stragglers!*

straight [NOT CURVING] /streɪt/ adj, adv [-er/-est only] not bending or curving • *Draw a straight line between the two dots.* • *Stand up straight.* ○ *The car seemed to be coming straight at me.* • If you follow **the straight and narrow (path)**, you follow a course of behavior that is correct and never do what you should not do: *Once you stop smoking, you have to stay on the straight and narrow.*

straighten /'streɪt·ən/ v [I/T] to make (something) so that it does not bend • *Her shoulders straightened, and she cleared her throat.* [I] ○ *First bend and then straighten your leg.* [T] ○ *You must straighten out the pipe.* [M] • If you **straighten** someone **out**, you improve their behavior or character: *I thought marriage would straighten him out.* • If you **straighten** something **out/up**, you arrange or organize it: *It took her a while to straighten out her father's accounts.* ○ *You need to straighten up your room.*

straight [LEVEL] /streɪt/ adj, adv [-er/-est only]

not leaning to either side; level • *Since the wall is crooked, how can the picture hang straight?*

straighten /'streɪt.ᵊn/ *v* [T] • *Please straighten the lampshade—it tilts to the right.*

straight IMMEDIATELY /streɪt/ *adv* [not gradable] without delay; immediately or directly • *I got to the hotel and went straight to bed.* • If you get straight to the point, you say immediately what is on your mind: *My boss simply said, "I'll get straight to the point. You're fired!"*

straight BASIC /streɪt/ *adj, adv* [-er/-est only] without anything added or changed; basic or true • *Things have gotten so bad, I think it's time for some straight talk.* ○ *She couldn't give a straight answer to any question.* ○ *It's important to tell the story straight, exactly as it happened.* • If an alcoholic drink is taken straight, it has no water, ice, or other liquid added to it: *I thought politicians shaved on Sunday and drank their whiskey straight.* • If you tell someone something **straight out**, you tell them immediately and without a long explanation or any excuses: *I walked in, and she told me straight out what had happened.* • If someone is a **straight arrow**, they are thought of as being completely honest and moral: *We wondered how this model student, this straight arrow, could end up in jail.* • If you keep a **straight face**, the expression on your face hides what you really think: *It's hard to argue that point of view with a straight face.*

straight DIRECTLY /streɪt/ *adv* [not gradable] clearly or directly • *This Valentine comes straight from my heart.*

straight CLEARLY /streɪt/ *adv* [not gradable] clearly; plainly • *I'm so tired I can't think straight anymore.*

straight FOLLOWING /streɪt/ *adj, adv* [not gradable] following one after another without an interruption; CONSECUTIVE • *The team had won four straight games before they lost this one.* ○ *Sometimes we work 16 hours straight.*

straight NOT HOMOSEXUAL /streɪt/ *adj* [not gradable] *infml* not homosexual; HETEROSEXUAL

straight NOT USING DRUGS /streɪt/ *adj* [-er/-est only] *infml* not using illegal drugs • *It has been six months since he was in rehab, and he's still straight.*

straightforward UNDERSTANDABLE /streɪt 'fɔːr·wərd/ *adj* easy to understand; clear • *The doctor explained the operation in straightforward English.*

straightforward HONEST /streɪt'fɔːr·wərd/ *adj* honest and without unnecessary politeness • *She's a straightforward, no-nonsense teacher.*

straightjacket /'streɪt,dʒæk·ət/ *n* [C] a STRAITJACKET

strain WORRY /streɪn/ *n* [C/U] something that causes anxiety, worry, or difficulty • *Loss of funding has put a lot of strain on the day-care*

center. [U] ○ *The benefits of keeping our daughter at home make the strains of having only one income worthwhile.* [C]

strain /streɪn/ *v* [T] to cause (anxiety or problems) • *This relationship has been strained almost to the breaking point.* ○ *These extra costs have strained our financial resources.*

strained /streɪnd/ *adj* • *She had a strained expression on her face.*

strain PRESSURE /streɪn/ *n* [U] physical pressure • *The bookcase collapsed under the strain.*

strain /streɪn/ *v* [I] to create pressure or use effort • *The dog strained at the leash, pulling his master along.* ○ *I had to strain to hear the audio.* [+ *to* infinitive]

strain INJURY /streɪn/ *n* [C] an injury caused by working the muscles too hard • *Running puts a strain on your heart.*

strain /streɪn/ *v* [T] • *I strained my back carrying those boxes.*

strained /streɪnd/ *adj* • *a strained knee*

strain SEPARATE /streɪn/ *v* [I/T] to separate (solid pieces) from a liquid by pouring it through a utensil with small holes at the bottom of it or through a cloth • *Strain the liquid and discard the vegetables.* [T]

strainer /'streɪ·nər/ *n* [C] • *Force the cooked fruit through a strainer*

strain DIFFERENT TYPE /streɪn/ *n* [C] an animal or plant that is only slightly different from other animals or plants of the same type • *A new strain of the AIDS virus has been found.* • A strain is also a quality that gives something a particular character: *There is a religious strain in American politics.* • A strain is also a particular sound: *Strains of piano music drifted across the room.*

strait /streɪt/ *n* [C] a narrow area of water that connects two larger areas of water • *The strait lies between the Atlantic Ocean and the Mediterranean Sea.*

straitjacket, **straightjacket** /'streɪt,dʒæk·ət/ *n* [C] a special item of clothing like a coat that ties the arms to the body and limits the movement of a violent or mentally ill person

strand /strænd/ *n* [C] a fiber or group of fibers twisted together that form one part of a length of rope, cord, thread, etc., or a single string, hair, or line of objects • *a strand of hair* ○ *She wore three strands of beads around her neck.* • (*fig.*) *There are many strands* (= types) *of pacifism.*

stranded /'stræn·dəd/ *adj* [not gradable] lacking what is necessary to leave a place or to get out of a situation • *During the storm, stranded passengers slept at the airport.*

strange UNUSUAL /streɪndʒ/ *adj* [-er/-est only] not familiar, or difficult to understand; different • *We kept hearing strange noises coming from the attic.* ○ *I had a strange feeling that we had met before.* ○ *That's strange—I thought I had locked this door when we left.*

strangely /'streɪndʒ·li/ *adv* • *It seemed to me*

that she was acting strangely. • **Strangely enough** means that something is unusual or hard to explain: *Strangely enough, most film-makers don't seem to have a strong point of view.*

strange NOT FAMILIAR /streɪndʒ/ *adj* [*-er/-est* only] not known or familiar • *I really don't like strange people coming to my door.*

stranger /ˈstreɪn·dʒər/ *n* [C] someone not known or not familiar • *After being away so long, my sister seemed like a stranger.* • A stranger in a particular place is someone who has never been there before: *Sorry, I can't direct you—I'm a stranger here myself.*

strangle /ˈstræŋ·gəl/ *v* [T] to kill (someone) by pressing their throat so that they cannot breathe

strangulation /ˌstræŋ·gjəˈleɪ·ʃən/ *n* [U] • *An autopsy showed that he had died of strangulation.*

strap /stræp/ *n* [C] a narrow piece of strong material, esp. leather, used for holding or fastening something • *Her bag hung from its shoulder strap.* ○ *I lost my watch when the strap broke.*

strap /stræp/ *v* [T always + adv/prep] **-pp-** • *I strapped on my helmet and rode off.* ○ *We had to strap the mattress to the top of our car.*

strapless /ˈstræp·ləs/ *adj* [not gradable] • *a strapless dress*

strapped /stræpt/ *adj* not having enough money • *In the early days, we were strapped.* • If you are **strapped for** something, you lack it: *Busy executives are strapped for time.*

strapping /ˈstræp·ɪŋ/ *adj* [not gradable] healthy, big, and strong • *The sickly child grew up to be a strapping six-footer.*

stratagem /ˈstræt·ə·dʒəm, -ˌdʒem/ *n* [C] a plan or trick to achieve something • *Barry devised several stratagems for escape.*

strategy /ˈstræt·ə·dʒi/ *n* [C/U] a long-range plan for achieving something or reaching a goal, or the skill of making such plans • *Chess is a game that requires strategy.* [U]

strategic /strəˈtiː·dʒɪk/ *adj* • *The hill was of strategic importance for control of the countryside.* • **Strategic weapons** are designed to attack an enemy.

strategist /ˈstræt·ə·dʒəst/ *n* [C] someone who is skilled in planning, esp. in military, political, or business matters • *Democratic/Republican strategists*

stratified /ˈstræt·əˌfɑɪd/ *adj* [not gradable] arranged in separate layers • *stratified rock* ○ *a stratified society*

stratosphere /ˈstræt·əˌsfɪr/ *n* [U] specialized the layer of gases that surrounds the earth from about seven to 30 miles above it

stratum /ˈstræt·əm, ˈstreɪt-/ *n* [C usually pl] *pl* **strata** /ˈstræt·ə, ˈstreɪt·ə/ *slightly fml or specialized* a single layer of something • *(specialized) the earth's strata* ○ *(slightly formal)* the upper strata of society

straw DRIED STEMS /strɔː/ *n* [U] the dried yellow stems of crops such as wheat, used for animals or for weaving • *straw hats/baskets* ○ *The horse had a warm bed of fresh straw.* • **The last/final straw** is the latest problem added to a series of problems, making a situation impossible to bear: *The last straw was when the company fired most of the managers.*

straw TUBE /strɔː/ *n* [C] a thin tube, usually made of plastic, used to suck a drink from a container

strawberry /ˈstrɔːˌber·i, -bə·ri/ *n* [C] a small, juicy, red fruit shaped like a cone with seeds on its surface, or the plant on which this fruit grows

stray MOVE AWAY /streɪ/ *v* [I] to move away from a place where you should be or from a direction in which you should go • *The children were told to stay together and not to stray.* ○ *The plane disappeared after straying several hundred miles off course.*

stray LOST /streɪ/ *adj* [not gradable] (of an animal) having no home, or lost • *Humane societies care for stray cats and dogs.* • Stray also means happening by chance and lacking direction: *It was just a stray thought I had while washing the dishes.*

stray /streɪ/ *n* [C] • *We have given a home to a number of strays.*

streak MARK /striːk/ *n* [C] a mark of a color that is different from what surrounds it, or a thin strip of light • *Streaks of gray and black colored the marble.* ○ *The comet appeared as a dazzling streak in the sky.*

streak /striːk/ *v* [T] • *Her cheeks were streaked with sweat and dirt.*

streak CHARACTERISTIC /striːk/ *n* [C] a noticeably different characteristic in a personality • *He seems to have a mean streak that I hadn't noticed before.*

streak PERIOD /striːk/ *n* [C] a period during which a series of things happens • *What will the team do after this memorable eight-game winning streak?*

streak MOVE FAST /striːk/ *v* [I always + adv/prep] to move quickly • *The space shuttle rose from its launching pad and streaked into the sky.*

stream SMALL RIVER /striːm/ *n* [C] a small river that flows on or below the surface of the ground • *Rivers are wider, deeper, and longer than streams.*

stream FLOW /striːm/ *n* [C] a continuous flow • *The faucet leaked in a steady stream.* ○ *An endless stream of traffic clogged the roads today.*

stream /striːm/ *v* [I] to move continuously • *Thousands of refugees are streaming into the city.* ○ *Tears streamed down her cheeks.* ○ *Sunlight was streaming through the window.*

streamline SHAPE /ˈstriːmˌlɑɪn/ *v* [T] to shape (something) so that it moves as easily as possible through air or water • *Designers stream-*

lined the boat, hoping to improve its perfor-mance.

streamlined /'striːm·laɪnd/ *adj* • *a stream-lined shape/appearance*

streamline IMPROVE /'striːm·laɪn/ *v* [T] to change (something) so that it works better, esp. by simplifying it • *The company stream-lined its operations and increased its profits.*
streamlined /'striːm·laɪnd/ *adj* • *a stream-lined system*

street /striːt/ *n* [C] a road in a city or town, usually with buildings along one or both sides • *Our daughter lives across the street from us.* ○ *Look both ways when you cross the street.* • A street sometimes means a road and the SIDE-WALKS (= paths) along it: *The streets were full of people.* ○ *I was walking down the street when I saw my friend Joe.* • A **streetcar** is a TROL-LEY. • A **streetlight** (also **streetlamp**) is a light, usually on a tall post, at the side of a road. • **Street people** are people who have no homes and live on the streets. • LP ADDRESSES

strength PHYSICAL POWER /streŋθ, streŋkθ/ *n* [U] the ability to do things that demand physical effort, or the degree to which something is strong or powerful • *After having surgery, it takes a while to get your strength back.* ○ *Mak-ing baskets requires skill more than physical strength.* ○ *The storm is gathering/gaining strength.* • The strength of a drug is its abili-ty to have an effect.

strengthen /'streŋ·θən, 'streŋk-/ *v* [I/T] to be-come more powerful or more difficult to break, or to make (something) stronger • *If something isn't done to strengthen the railroad bridge, it may collapse.* [T] ○ *The tone of her voice strengthened suddenly.* [I] ○ *Exercise will strengthen your legs.* [T]

strength BRAVERY /streŋθ, streŋkθ/ *n* [U] brav-ery in dealing with difficulties • *He showed re-al strength in refusing to change his vote in spite of the call from the president.*

strength GOOD FEATURE /streŋθ, streŋkθ/ *n* [C/U] a positive quality that makes you more ef-fective • *The plan had both strengths and weaknesses.* [C] ○ *Her drive to succeed was a re-al strength.* [C] • The strength of a company or economy is its ability to produce goods, profits, and jobs: *a period of continuing ec-onomic strength* [U] • *I invested in the company* **on the strength of** (= because of the positive features of) *my brother's advice.*

strengthen /'streŋ·θən, 'streŋk-/ *v* [I/T] • *Some-how his illness strengthened their marriage and brought them closer together.* [T] ○ *Parents can strengthen ties with their children.* [T]

strength NUMBER /streŋθ, streŋkθ/ *n* [U] the number of people in a group • *Estimates of en-emy troop strengths differed.*

strenuous /'stren·jə·wəs/ *adj* needing or us-ing a lot of effort or energy • *I think football is much more strenuous than baseball.*

strenuously /'stren·jə·wə·sli/ *adv* • *He strenu-ously denies that he is guilty.*

strep (throat) /'strep ('θroʊt)/ *n* [C] a bacte-rial infection of the throat

stress WORRY /stres/ *n* [C/U] worry caused by a difficult situation, or something that causes this condition • *Luis is under a lot of stress right now.* [U] ○ *It's hard to cope with the stresses of raising a family.* [C]
stressed /strest/, **stressed–out** /'strest'aʊt/ *adj* • *The kids are sick, I just lost my baby-sitter, and our toilet doesn't work—no wonder I feel stressed-out!*
stressful /'stres·fəl/ *adj* • *Working in the emer-gency room of a major hospital is highly stress-ful work.*

stress IMPORTANCE /stres/ *v* [T] to give special importance or emphasis to (something) • *I'd like to stress the differences between our opin-ions.*
stress /stres/ *n* [U] • *There's constant stress on status in this community.*

stress PRONOUNCE /stres/ *v* [T] to pronounce (a word or syllable) with greater force than oth-er words in the same sentence or other sylla-bles in the same word • *In the word "engine," you should stress the first syllable.*
stress /stres/ *n* [C/U] • *The main stress in the word "command" is on the second syllable.* [C]

stress FORCE /stres/ *n* [C/U] a force that tends to change the shape or strength of an object • *If a metal object experiences constant stress, it may bend or break.* [U] • A **stress fracture** is a crack in a bone, esp. in the leg or foot.

stretch BECOME LONGER /stretʃ/ *v* [I/T] to reach across a distance or become longer or wider, or to cause (something) to do this • *Rub-ber stretches when you pull it.* [I] ○ *The banner was stretched across the street.* [T] ○ *He removed his hat and stretched out his arms to embrace her.* [M] • If you stretch your body, your arms, or your legs, you straighten them so that they are as long as possible: *"I'm so tired," she said, yawning and stretching her arms.* [T] • If you stretch your legs, you stand or walk after sit-ting for a long time: *We drove there in five hours, including a couple of stops to stretch our legs.*
stretch /stretʃ/ *n* [C] • *Before jogging, you should always do some stretches* (= stretch parts of your body).

stretch BREAK LIMITS /stretʃ/ *v* [T] to go beyond, or almost beyond, the usual limit of (some-thing) • *Buying a new dishwasher will really stretch our budget.* ○ *We try to stretch our-selves in our reading group, picking books we wouldn't ordinarily read.*

stretch /stretʃ/ *n* [C usually sing] an unusual and sometimes difficult situation • *Playing two games in two days is a bit of a stretch for us, but I think we'll make it.* • **By no stretch/ Not by any stretch of the imagination** is used to describe things that you cannot believe: *By no stretch of the imagination could you think of her as a real artist.*

stretch SPREAD OVER AREA /stretʃ/ *v* [I always + adv/prep] to spread over a large area or distance • *A huge cloud of dense smoke stretched across the sky.*

stretch /stretʃ/ *n* [C usually sing] an area of land or water • *Traffic is at a standstill along a five-mile stretch of Route 17 just south of Bridgeport.*

stretch EXIST OVER TIME /stretʃ/ *v* [I always + adv/prep] to spread over a long period of time • *The dispute stretches back over many years.* [I] ○ *I'd like to stretch my mortgage payments out for 30 years.* [M]

stretch /stretʃ/ *n* [C usually sing] a continuous period of time • *We had a long stretch of days with sub-zero temperatures last month.* • If you do something **at a stretch**, you do it continuously: *Sometimes I work for ten hours at a stretch.*

stretcher /'stretʃ·ər/ *n* [C] a light bed made of cloth with poles for a frame, used for carrying people who are injured or dead

strew /struː/ *v* [T] *past simple* **strewed**, *past part* **strewn** /struːn/ or **strewed** to scatter (things) messily over (a surface) • *The park was strewn with litter after the concert.*

strict /strɪkt/ *adj* [-er/-est only] greatly limiting someone's freedom to behave as they wish • *The school is an old-fashioned institution with strict discipline.* ○ *Do you think stricter laws would help reduce automobile accidents?* • *He's not a vegetarian in the strictest sense* (= if you are exact about the word's meaning).

strictly /'strɪk·tli/ *adv* completely or entirely • *Photography is strictly forbidden.* ○ *Public assistance is strictly limited to those who are willing to work.* • **Strictly speaking** (= Being completely accurate), *they're still married, but they've been living apart for years.*

stride WALK /straɪd/ *v* [I always + adv/prep] *past* **strode** /stroʊd/ to walk somewhere quickly with long steps • *She strode across the room and demanded to speak to the manager.*

stride /straɪd/ *n* [C] a step, esp. a long step • *He reached me in one long stride.*

stride DEVELOPMENT /straɪd/ *n* [C usually pl] an important positive development • *They have already made great strides in improving service.*

strident /'straɪd·ənt/ *adj* forceful, or noticeably loud • *strident criticism* ○ *a strident voice*

strife /straɪf/ *n* [U] angry disagreement or violent actions • *civil/ethnic/political strife* ○ *He led the union through several violent years of labor strife.*

strike HIT /straɪk/ *v* [I/T] *past* **struck** /strʌk/ to hit or physically attack (someone or something) • *A car struck and killed 21-year-old man trying to cross a major highway.* [T] ○ *The victim was struck in the back of the head with a heavy object.* [T] • If you strike a match, you

cause it to burn by rubbing it against a rough surface. [T]

strike /straɪk/ *n* [C] a brief military attack • *The United Nations has authorized the use of air/military strikes against terrorist bases.*

strike CAUSE HARM /straɪk/ *v* [I/T] *past* **struck** /strʌk/, *past part also* **stricken** /'strɪk·ən/ to bring sudden harm, damage, or injury (to a person or thing) • *It was a disease that struck mainly young people.* [T] ○ *A serial rapist is obviously on the loose, and no one knows when he will strike again.* [I] ○ *He was stricken with polio at the age of 13 and lost the use of his legs.* [T]

stricken /'strɪk·ən/ *adj* suffering severely from the effects of something • *She grew up in a poverty-stricken area of the state.* ○ *The little boy got absolutely panic-stricken when his mother left the doctor's office.*

strike STOP WORK /straɪk/ *v* [I/T] *past* **struck** /strʌk/ (of workers or their **labor union** (= employees' organization that tries to win better working conditions for its members)) to refuse to continue working because they cannot come to an agreement with an employer over pay or other conditions of the job • *Flight attendants are threatening to strike to get more flexible schedules.* [I]

strike /straɪk/ *n* [C/U] • *If the teachers go on strike again and close the schools down, I don't know what I'll do with the kids.* [U]

striker /'straɪ·kər/ *n* [C] a person, esp. a member of a **labor union**, who refuses to work until a satisfactory agreement with their employer has been reached

strike CAUSE AN IDEA /straɪk/ *v* [T] *past* **struck** /strʌk/ to cause (someone) to have a feeling or idea about something • *From what you've said, it strikes me that you would be better off working for someone else.* ○ *I was struck by her sincerity.* • To strike also means to suddenly cause (someone) to think of something: *I was immediately struck by the similarities in their appearance.* • If something **strikes a chord**, it causes people to remember something: *Seeing that photograph of the old car struck a chord, reminding me of how much my mother had loved to drive.*

strike DISCOVER /straɪk/ *v* [T] *past* **struck** /strʌk/ to discover (esp. something valuable in the earth) • *to strike gold/oil* • If you **strike it rich**, you become suddenly and unexpectedly rich or successful.

strike AGREE /straɪk/ *v* [T] *past* **struck** /strʌk/ to agree to or achieve (a solution) • *My children and I have struck a deal—they can play any kind of music they want as long as I don't hear it.* • If you strike a balance between two things, you try to give an equal amount of attention or importance to each: *It's a question of striking the right balance between quality and productivity.*

strike SHOW THE TIME /straɪk/ *v* [I/T] *past*

struck /strʌk/ (esp. of a clock) to make a sound or a series of sounds that show (the time) • *The clock struck midnight.* [T]

□**strike down** /'-'-/ *v adv* [T] (of a court in the US) to decide that (a law or rule) is illegal and should not be obeyed • *The court struck down the law on the grounds that it was unconstitutional.*

□**strike out** BEGIN /'-'-, '-,-/ *v adv* [I] to begin a new and independent activity • *I needed to strike out on my own.* ○ *Next year I'm hoping to strike out and find a job where I could make some money.*

□**strike out** *(obj)* BASEBALL , **strike** *(obj)* **out** /'-'-/ *v adv* [I/M] (in baseball) to be called OUT (= lose your chance to hit) because you have failed three times to hit the ball or have not tried to hit it when you could have, or to throw the ball in a way that causes (someone) to do this • *The relief pitcher struck out the first two batters he faced.* [M] ○ *(fig.) "How did you do at the auction?" "We really struck out (= failed)— there wasn't anything worth getting."* [I]

strikeout /'straɪk,aʊt/ *n* [C] • *Nolan Ryan was a great pitcher, and usually led the league in strikeouts.*

□**strike up** START FRIENDSHIP /'-,-/ *v prep* [T] to create or establish (a relationship or conversation) with someone • *She struck up a relationship with an artist soon after she arrived in Paris.*

□**strike up** START MUSIC /'-,-/ *v adv* [I/T] to start to play (music) • *The band struck up a medley of Cole Porter tunes.* [T]

striking /'straɪ·kɪŋ/ *adj* obvious, interesting, and (esp. of a person) often attractive • *Perhaps the most striking feature of this computer is that it is so easy to use.* ○ *There was a striking physical resemblance between the two men.* ○ *He was a striking figure with full beard and flowing, collar-length hair.*

string CORD /strɪŋ/ *n* [C/U] a thin length of cord • *a piece of string* [U] • If there are **strings attached** to something, such as an agreement, there are special demands or limitations involved: *Most of these opportunities to win something for free come with strings attached.* • A **string tie** is a length of cord, worn with a shirt, that goes under the collar and down the front and is held by a decorative device at the neck.

string tie

string /strɪŋ/ *v* [T] *past* **strung** /strʌŋ/ to attach a length of (string or something similar) by the ends, so that the middle hangs • *They strung ribbons of bright paper around the room in preparation for the party.*

stringy /'strɪŋ·i/ *adj* [-er/-est only] having the

appearance of strings, or (of food) hard to chew • *stringy meat* ○ *His black hair was stringy and brushed his shoulders.*

string MUSIC /strɪŋ/ *n* [C] a thin wire or cord that is stretched across a musical instrument and produces musical notes when pulled or hit • *Guitar strings are made from steel or nylon.* • The strings in an ORCHESTRA is a group of instruments that produce sound with strings: *Violins, cellos, and double basses are all strings.* • A **string quartet** is a group of four people who play music together on instruments with strings.

string SET /strɪŋ/ *n* [C] a set of objects joined together in a row on a single cord or thread • *a string of pearls*

string /strɪŋ/ *v* [T] *past* **strung** /strʌŋ/ to put a thread or cord through (each of a set of things) • *The child sat on the floor, stringing wooden beads.* ○ *(fig.) I can just barely string together (= say) a couple of sentences in Japanese.*

string SERIES /strɪŋ/ *n* [C] a series of related things or events • *He told the committee a string of lies.* ○ *Her new novel is the latest in a string of successes.*

string beans /'strɪŋ'biːnz/ *pl n* **green beans**, see at GREEN COLOR

stringent /'strɪn·dʒənt/ *adj* extremely limiting or difficult; severe • *Members of the religious order have to be willing to abide by the stringent rules.* ○ *The city has stringent fire-safety standards.*

strip REMOVE COVERING /strɪp/ *v* [T] **-pp-** to remove, pull, or tear (the covering or outer layer) from something • *I have this cabinet that had about eight layers of paint on it, and I stripped it down to refinish it.* • If you strip someone of something, you remove it from them: *Canada wants to strip Luitjens, a retired University of British Columbia botany instructor, of his citizenship.*

strip REMOVE CLOTHING /strɪp/ *v* [I/T] **-pp-** to remove your clothes, or to remove the clothes from (someone else) • *It was so hot that we stripped off our shirts.* [M] • If you strip (down) to some clothing, you remove everything except that clothing: *The nurse told me to strip down to my underwear.* [I] ○ *We were told to strip to the waist (= remove our clothes above the waist).* [I]

strip /strɪp/ *n* [U] • A **strip search** is the act of searching someone in which they are forced to remove all their clothes: *Probert was arrested after a packet of cocaine fell out of his underwear during a strip search by US Customs agents.*

stripper /'strɪp·ər/ *n* [C] someone whose job is removing all their clothes, often in a sexually exciting way, to entertain other people

strip PIECE /strɪp/ *n* [C] a long, flat, narrow piece • *a strip of land* ○ *He didn't have a bandage, so he ripped up his shirt into thin strips.* ○

To prolong the working life of your credit card, keep the magnetic strip protected from scratches, heat, and moisture.

stripe /straɪp/ *n* [C] a line on a surface that is a different color from the rest of the surface • *a blue tie with gray stripes* • A stripe is also a particular type, esp. when there are many possible types: *Governments of every stripe* (= of all political opinions) *have a tendency to try to control the press.*

striped /straɪpt/ *adj* [not gradable] • *a striped red-and-white shirt*

striptease /ˈstrɪp·tiːz/ *n* [C/U] a performance in which someone, usually a woman, takes off their clothes in a sexually exciting way to entertain people watching, or this activity

strive /straɪv/ *v* [I] *past simple* **strove** /stroʊv/ or **strived**, *past part* **striven** /ˈstrɪv·ən/ or **strived** to try hard to do something or make something happen, esp. for a long time or against difficulties • *Neither Jefferson nor Madison was a pacifist, though both strove to keep America at peace.* [+ *to* infinitive]

strode /stroʊd/ *past simple and past participle of* STRIDE WALK

stroke TOUCH /stroʊk/ *v* [T] to move something, esp. your hand, gently over (something), usually repeatedly and for pleasure • *She lovingly stroked Chris's face with the tips of her fingers.*

stroke MARK /stroʊk/ *n* [C] a movement of a pen or pencil when writing, or by a brush when painting, or the line or mark made by such a movement • *With a stroke of his pen, the governor signed the bill into law.*

stroke ILLNESS /stroʊk/ *n* [C] a sudden change in the blood supply to a part of the brain, which can result in a loss of some mental or physical abilities, or death • *He suffered a stroke and died two days later.*

stroke SWIMMING ACTION /stroʊk/ *n* [C/U] a particular type of repeated movement used in a method of swimming • *He swims the breast stroke competitively, but for his ads he did the butterfly stroke.* [U]

stroke EVENT /stroʊk/ *n* [C] an unexpected but decisive event or experience • *The bid to take over the company was seen as a bold stroke.* ○ *To get a job in those years was an incredible stroke of luck.*

stroke TIME /stroʊk/ *n* [C] an exact time, or a sound or series of sounds that show this time • *The fireworks will start at the stroke of 10.*

stroll /stroʊl/ *v* [I] to walk in a slow, relaxed manner, esp. for pleasure • *We could stroll into town if you like.*

stroll /stroʊl/ *n* [C] • *Sometimes he would take a stroll before dinner.*

stroller /ˈstroʊ·lər/ *n* [C] a small chair having wheels, suitable for a small child to sit in and be pushed around

strong PHYSICALLY POWERFUL /strɔːŋ/ *adj* [*-er/ -est* only] physically powerful or energetic •

You must be strong to be able to lift all that weight. ○ *I feel a little stronger every day.* ○ *Strong winds blew down a number of trees.* ○ *The doctor prescribed a stronger pain-killer.* • USAGE: The related noun is STRENGTH PHYSICAL POWER.

strong DIFFICULT TO BREAK /strɔːŋ/ *adj* [*-er/ -est* only] not easily broken or damaged • *The swings are strong enough for any of the kids.* • USAGE: The related noun is STRENGTH PHYSICAL POWER.

strongly /ˈstrɔːŋ·li/ *adv* • *The castle walls were strongly constructed of stone.*

strong DETERMINED /strɔːŋ/ *adj* [*-er/ -est* only] having a forceful and determined personality • *He has a strong personality, but don't let him intimidate you.* • (*disapproving*) A **strong-arm** way of doing something involves forcing something to happen or getting people to do something, and sometimes includes the use of threats: *The curfew is just one more strong-arm policy of this city administration.* • A **strong-minded** person is sure that their opinions and beliefs are right and will try to force them on other people. • A person who is **strong-willed** is determined to do what seems right for them, no matter what other people think: *She's very strong-willed, and if she's decided to do something, nothing will change her mind.* • USAGE: The related noun is STRENGTH GOOD FEATURE.

strong IMPORTANT /strɔːŋ/ *adj* [*-er/ -est* only] having a lot of influence or importance • *My grandmother had a strong influence on me as a child.* ○ *He is a strong supporter of the arts in the city.*

strongly /ˈstrɔːŋ·li/ *adv* • *Beliefs are strongly tied to culture.*

strong PERSUASIVE /strɔːŋ/ *adj* [*-er/ -est* only] believed or expressed without any doubt; persuasive • *She has strong opinions about religion.* ○ *There are strong arguments to support both sides.*

strongly /ˈstrɔːŋ·li/ *adv* [not gradable] • *He is strongly opposed to capital punishment.* ○ *Voters strongly supported the candidate.*

strong OBVIOUS /strɔːŋ/ *adj* [*-er/ -est* only] easily noticed, felt, tasted, or smelled; obvious • *He bears a strong likeness to his brother.* ○ *This coffee is too strong!* ○ *There was a strong smell of gas.*

strong REALISTIC /strɔːŋ/ *adj* [*-er/ -est* only] likely or realistic • *There's a strong possibility that the naval base will close next year.*

stronghold /ˈstrɔːŋ·hoʊld/ *n* [C] a place that is well defended or is a center for particular beliefs or activities • *The airport remains the last stronghold of the rebel forces.* ○ *That county has always been a Democratic stronghold.*

strove /stroʊv/ *past simple of* STRIVE

struck /strʌk/ *past simple and past participle of* STRIKE

structure ARRANGEMENT /ˈstrʌk·tʃər/ *n* [C/U] the arrangement or organization of parts in a system • *Grammatical structure changes from language to language.* [U] ○ *When the United States broke away from England, the social structure did not change very much.* [C]

structure /'strʌk·tʃər/ *v* [T] • *Office hours are structured to accommodate individual workers' needs.*

structural /'strʌk·tʃə·rəl/ *adj* [not gradable] • *Private ownership of companies was the greatest structural change that occurred in the economy.*

structure [BUILDING] /'strʌk·tʃər/ *n* [C] something built, such as a building or a bridge • *The bridge is the longest steel structure in the world.*

structural /'strʌk·tʃə·rəl/ *adj* [not gradable] • *Many of the city's buildings suffered structural damage as a result of the earthquake.*

struggle [TRY HARD] /'strʌg·əl/ *v* [I] to work hard to do something • *We watched boys on skateboards struggle to keep their balance.* ○ [+ *to* infinitive]

struggle /'strʌg·əl/ *n* [C] • *The struggle everywhere against racism is not over.*

struggle [FIGHT] /'strʌg·əl/ *v* [I] to fight, esp. physically • *He struggled with the intruder and held him until the police arrived.*

struggle /'strʌg·əl/ *n* [C] • *Both men were arrested after their struggle in the bar.*

struggle [MOVE] /'strʌg·əl/ *v* [I] to move with difficulty • *She struggled out of her chair.*

strum /strʌm/ *v* [I/T] **-mm-** to play (a guitar or similar instrument) by moving the fingers lightly across all of the strings rather than playing them singly

strung /strʌŋ/ *past simple and past participle of* STRING

strung out /,strʌŋ'ɑut/ *adj* [not gradable] *slang* not functioning normally, esp. because of the strong effects of illegal drugs • *She must be strung out on something.* ○ *Bill seems a little emotionally strung out.*

strut [WALK] /strʌt/ *v* [I] **-tt-** to walk stiffly or proudly with your chest pushed forward and your shoulders back • *The boys strutted around like peacocks, showing off to some girls nearby.* • (*infml*) To **strut** your **stuff** is to show other people what you can do well: *Winnie loves to dance and has been strutting her stuff since she was very young.*

strut [SUPPORT] /strʌt/ *n* [C] a support for a structure such as an aircraft wing, roof, or bridge

stub [SHORT END] /stʌb/ *n* [C] the short end which is left after the main part of something has been used or removed, as of a cigarette or a pencil • *I put the ticket stubs in my pocket after we went into the theater.*

stubby /'stʌb·i/ *adj* • *A toddler's legs are short and stubby.*

stub [HURT] /stʌb/ *v* [T] **-bb-** to hit (your foot or toe) against a hard object • *I stubbed my toe on a rock.*

□ **stub out** *obj*, **stub** *obj* **out** /'-'-/ *v adv* [M] to stop (the burning end) of a cigarette or CIGAR by pressing it against something

stubble [HAIR] /'stʌb·əl/ *n* [U] the short hair that grows on a man's face if he has not recently SHAVED (= cut the hair)

stubble [STEMS] /'stʌb·əl/ *n* [U] the stems left in the ground after a crop has been cut

stubborn /'stʌb·ərn/ *adj* [not gradable] opposed to change or suggestion • *He's sick, but he's too stubborn to see a doctor.* • If something is stubborn, it is hard to fix or deal with: *stubborn stains* ○ *a stubborn problem*

stucco /'stʌk·oʊ/ *n* [U] a material used esp. for covering the outside walls of a building that is soft and wet when it is spread on a surface and is hard when it dries

stuck [STICK] /stʌk/ *past simple and past participle of* STICK

stuck [FIXED] /stʌk/ *adj* [not gradable] unable to move from a particular position or place, or unable to change a situation • *This door seems to be stuck.* ○ *I hate being stuck at a desk all day.* ○ *Ty got stuck with doing the laundry.* • (*infml*) If you are **stuck on** someone, you are strongly attracted to them: *Mark's been stuck on Andrea for ages.* • USAGE: The related verb is STICK [UNABLE TO MOVE].

stuck-up /'stʌk'ʌp/ *adj infml disapproving* too proud or satisfied with yourself

stud [MALE ANIMAL] /stʌd/ *n* [C] a male animal kept esp. for breeding

stud [MAN] /stʌd/ *n* [C] *slang* an attractive man who is sexually active with many women

stud [DECORATION] /stʌd/ *n* [C] a small, bright-colored nail, often specially shaped, that is fixed esp. to cloth or leather as decoration

studded /'stʌd·əd/ *adj* [not gradable] • *a studded jacket* • If an object or place is **studded with** something, it has a lot of that thing: *a hillside studded with trees*

stud [JEWELRY] /stʌd/ *n* [C] a small ball fixed to a metal post that fits through a hole made in the body, esp. in the ear

stud [POST] /stʌd/ *n* [C] any of the vertical wood or metal posts used to make the frame of a wall

student /'stuːd·ənt, *Southern also* -ənt/ *n* [C] a person who is studying at a school, college, or university • *He is a student at the University of California.* • If someone is a student of a particular subject, they are very interested in it: *As a nurse, you get to be a student of human nature.* • The **student body** of a school is all of the students in the school: *Chatsworth School's student body is 90% white.*

studied /'stʌd·iːd/ *adj* [not gradable] carefully prepared or considered, esp. to create an effect • *Settlers showed a studied disregard for native ways of life.*

studies /'stʌd·iːz/ *pl n* • See at STUDY [LEARN].

studio [ROOM] /'stuːd·iː,oʊ/ *n* [C] *pl* **studios** a room where an artist paints or a musician practices • *an artist's studio* • A **studio**

(apartment) is an apartment with one room, a bathroom, and a kitchen area.

studio RECORDING PLACE /'stu:d·i:,ου/ *n* [C] *pl* **studios** a specially equipped place where television or radio programs or music recordings are made

studio MOVIE PRODUCTION /'stu:d·i:,o:/ *n* [C] a place where movies are produced, or a company that produces movies • *Most of the big studios are in Hollywood.*

study LEARN /'stʌd·i/ *v* [I/T] to learn (a particular subject or subjects), esp. in a school or college or by reading books • *Next semester we'll be studying biology.* [T] ○ *I've got to study tonight.* [I]

study /'stʌd·i/ *n* [C/U] the activity of studying • *He began the study of violin when he was only three.* [U] • A study is a room used for reading and writing in a person's home. [C]

studies /'stʌd·i:z/ *pl n* the work a student does at school • *His studies will suffer if he has to stay home for too long.*

studious /'stu:d·i:·əs/ *adj* liking to study • *She was a studious child who spent hours reading.*

study EXAMINE /'stʌd·i/ *v* [T] to look at (something) carefully to learn about it • *She studied the embroidery to see how it was done.*

study /'stʌd·i/ *n* [C] • *Studies show that exercise is important to health.*

stuff SUBSTANCE /stʌf/ *n* [U] a substance or material • *What's the black stuff on the rug?* ○ *This stuff tastes good.*

stuff THINGS /stʌf/ *n* [U] a group of different things, activities, or matters • *We helped him move his stuff to the new apartment.* ○ *I've got a lot of stuff to do this weekend.* ○ *They'd heard all this stuff before.*

stuff FILL /stʌf/ *v* [T] to fill the inside of (something) • *I can't stuff another thing into this suitcase.* • To stuff a TURKEY, or other meat or vegetable, is to fill it with other food before cooking it. • If you stuff yourself, you eat a large amount of food: *The kids stuffed themselves with snacks.*

stuffed /stʌft/ *adj* [not gradable] filled with some material • *Children love stuffed animals.* • When someone is **stuffed-up**, it is hard for them to breathe, usually because of a cold.

stuffing /'stʌf·ɪŋ/ *n* [U] material that is used to fill something • *The stuffing was coming out of the mattress.* • Stuffing is also food, usually a mixture of bread, onions, and herbs, which is used as a filling for TURKEY or other meats or vegetables.

stuffy FORMAL /'stʌf·i/ *adj* formal, boring, and not modern • *a stuffy, arrogant man*

stuffy LACKING AIR /'stʌf·i/ *adj* lacking fresh air • *The office gets so stuffy in the afternoon.*

stumble FALL /'stʌm·bəl/ *v* [I] to hit your foot against something while walking and almost fall, or to walk awkwardly as if you might fall • *She stumbled over a toy.* ○ *He stumbled around in the dark.* • A **stumbling block** is a

difficulty that prevents progress, understanding, or agreement: *Several major stumbling blocks must be resolved.*

stumble MAKE A MISTAKE /'stʌm·bəl/ *v* [I] to make a mistake, or to pause unexpectedly when speaking • *He stumbled through several early career choices.* ○ *Several times the reader stumbled over lines in the poem.*

□ **stumble across/on** /'---,-; '--,-/ *v prep* [T] to discover or find (something or someone) by chance • *Look at what I stumbled across at the flea market!*

stump PART LEFT /stʌmp/ *n* [C] the part of a tree, arm, etc. that is left after another part has been removed

stump CONFUSE /stʌmp/ *v* [T] to confuse or cause (someone) to be unable to understand or explain something • *He seemed stumped by our questions.*

stump SPEAK /stʌmp/ *v* [I] to talk in support of a politician or idea • *Taylor stumped for him throughout the state.*

stun SHOCK /stʌn/ *v* [T] **-nn-** to shock (someone) so much that they do not know how to react • *She was stunned by his generous offer.*

stunning /'stʌn·ɪŋ/ *adj* • *a stunning victory*

stun MAKE UNCONSCIOUS /stʌn/ *v* [T] **-nn-** to make (a person or animal) unconscious or confused, esp. by hitting them hard • *He was stunned by the sudden blow to his head.*

stung /stʌŋ/ *past simple and past participle of* STING

stunk /stʌŋk/ *past simple and past participle of* STINK

stunning /'stʌn·ɪŋ/ *adj* [not gradable] extremely beautiful or attractive • *She was tall, blond, and absolutely stunning.*

stunt DANGEROUS ACT /stʌnt/ *n* [C] an exciting and often dangerous act, usually performed for use in a movie by someone specially trained • A **stunt man** is a person whose job is performing difficult stunts, esp. in a film.

stunt ACTIVITY /stʌnt/ *n* [C] something done mainly to attract attention • *This was not just some publicity stunt.*

stunt PREVENT GROWTH /stʌnt/ *v* [T] to slow or prevent (the growth or development of someone or something) • *Drought has stunted this year's corn crop.*

stupefy TIRE /'stu:·pə,faɪ/ *v* [T] to tire or bore (someone) so much that they cannot think or do anything • *His classes totally stupefied me.*

stupefy SURPRISE /'stu:·pə,faɪ/ *v* [T] to shock (someone); STUN • *He was stupefied to learn that he was fired.*

stupendous /stu:'pen·dəs/ *adj* very great in amount or size • *He ran up stupendous debts.*

stupid /'stu:·pəd/ *adj* lacking thought or intelligence • *I just made another stupid mistake.* • (*infml*) A person might say something is stupid because it annoys them: *Turn off that stupid program!*

stupidity /stuːˈpɪd·ət̬·i/ n [U] • *Can you believe my stupidity? I locked my keys in the car!*

stupor /ˈstuː·pər/ n [C usually sing] a state in which a person is almost unconscious • *a drunken stupor*

sturdy /ˈstɜrd·i/ adj strong or solid • *That ladder doesn't look sturdy enough to hold you.*

stutter /ˈstʌt̬·ər/ v [I/T] to speak or say something with difficulty, esp. to repeat the first part of a word or to pause before it • *He doesn't normally stutter when he speaks.* [I]

stutter /ˈstʌt̬·ər/ n [C] • *I type up tapes of people talking, all the stutters and everything.*

style WAY /staɪl/ n [C/U] a way of doing something, esp. one which is typical of a person, group of people, place, or period • *Puente fused Latin with other musical styles.* [C] ○ *The book is written in the style of an 18th-century novel.* [C] ○ *His portraits were awkward in style.* [U] • Style is also a special quality that makes a person or thing seem different and attractive: *I like this team—the players have style.* [U]

stylistic /staɪˈlɪs·tɪk/ adj • *The first major stylistic change in popular music after rock was punk.*

stylized /ˈstaɪlˌaɪzd/ adj represented in a way that simplifies details rather than trying to show naturalness or reality • *Curtis took stylized photographs of Native Americans.*

style DESIGN /staɪl/ v [T] to shape or design (something such as a person's hair or an object like a piece of clothing or furniture), esp. so that it looks attractive • *Most women style their hair.*

style /staɪl/ n [C] • *They had hundreds of styles* (= designs) *of light fixtures in stock.* • Style is also fashion, esp. in clothing: *I keep up with the latest styles.* [C] ○ *The classic black dress is always in style.* [U]

stylish /ˈstaɪ·lɪʃ/ adj • *stylish people* ○ *stylish clothing*

stymie /ˈstaɪ·mi/ v [T] **stymieing** /ˈstaɪ·miː·ɪŋ/ to prevent (someone) from achieving a goal or doing something they planned to do • *Students were stymied by the test.*

Styrofoam trademark /ˈstaɪ·rəˌfoʊm/ n [U] a light, usually white plastic used to make containers that prevent foods and liquids from changing temperature or to protect delicate objects inside containers • *a Styrofoam cup/cooler* ○ *Styrofoam packing materials*

suave /swɑv/ adj (esp. of men) having a pleasant and charming manner that may not be sincere • *He's a suave Texas-bred lawyer.*

sub REPLACEMENT /sʌb/ n [C] *short form of* **substitute (teacher)**, see at SUBSTITUTE

sub /sʌb/ v [I] **-bb-** • *She subs at three schools.*

sub SHIP /sʌb/ n [C] *short form of* SUBMARINE • *a nuclear sub*

sub FOOD /sʌb/ n [C] *short form of* SUBMARINE (SANDWICH)

subcommittee /ˈsʌb·kəˌmɪt̬·i/ n [C] a number of people chosen from a COMMITTEE (= a small group of people who represent a larger organization) to study or manage a particular subject

subcompact /sʌbˈkɑmˌpækt/ n [C] a very small car • *We're renting a subcompact.*

subconscious /sʌbˈkɑn·tʃəs/ adj [not gradable] relating to thoughts and feelings that exist in the mind and influence your behavior although you are not aware of them • *On some subconscious level he wants to make her miserable.*

subconscious /sʌbˈkɑn·tʃəs/ n [U] • *My subconscious works on things while I'm asleep.*

subconsciously /sʌbˈkɑn·tʃə·sli/ adv [not gradable] • *When people see these pictures, they subconsciously think of sex.*

subculture /ˈsʌbˌkʌl·tʃər/ n [C] the way of life, customs, and ideas of a particular group of people within a society, which are different from the rest of that society • *An entire subculture grew up around female bodybuilding.*

subdivide /ˈsʌb·dɪˌvaɪd/ v [T] to divide (something) into smaller parts

subdivision /ˈsʌb·dɪˌvɪʒ·ən/ n [C] • *The book's chapters have major subdivisions.* • A subdivision is also an area of land containing many homes built at about the same time: *We moved to a brand-new subdivision in 1965.*

subdue /səbˈduː/ v [T] to reduce the force of (someone or something) • *She'd be hard to subdue if she got mad.*

subdued /səbˈduːd/ adj (of color or light) not very bright, or (of sound) not very loud • *a subdued voice* ○ *a subdued chalk-stripe suit* • If a person is subdued, they are unusually quiet: *Most of the fans were subdued, quietly waiting for the race to start.*

subject AREA OF DISCUSSION /ˈsʌb·dʒɪkt, -dʒekt/ n [C] something that is being discussed or considered • *School officials broached the subject of extending the school year.* ○ *It seemed like a good idea to change the subject.* • *Critics were upset by the* **subject matter** (= subject) *of the book.*

subject SCHOOL COURSE /ˈsʌb·dʒɪkt, -dʒekt/ n [C] an area of knowledge that is studied in school or college • *My favorite subjects are history and geography.*

subject PERSON /ˈsʌb·dʒɪkt, -dʒekt/ n [C] a person who lives or who has the right to live in a particular country, esp. a country with a king or queen • *a British subject* • Compare CITIZEN.

subject GRAMMAR /ˈsʌb·dʒɪkt, -dʒekt/ n [C] *specialized* (in grammar) the person or thing that performs the action of a verb, or which is joined to a description by a verb • *"Bob" is the subject of the sentence, "Bob threw the ball."* • Compare OBJECT GRAMMAR.

subject obj **to** obj /səbˈdʒekt tə, ˈsʌbˌdʒekt tə/ v prep [T] to cause (someone or something) to experience (something, esp. something unpleasant) • *How do you feel about subjecting people to random drug testing?*

subject to /ˈsʌb·dʒɪkt tə, ˈsʌb,dʒekt tə/ *adj* • *The bay is subject to heavy fog in summer.* ○ *Drunk drivers are subject to heavy fines.*

subjective /səbˈdʒek·tɪv/ *adj* influenced by or based on personal beliefs or feelings, rather than based on facts • *Whether something is indecent is a subjective question.* • USAGE: The opposite of subjective is OBJECTIVE FAIR OR REAL.

subjugate /ˈsʌb·dʒə,ɡeɪt/ *v* [T] *slightly fml* to defeat (people or a country) and rule them in a way that allows them no freedom

subjugation /ˌsʌb·dʒəˈɡeɪ·ʃən/ *n* [U] *slightly fml* • *The subjugation of women is deeply rooted in their culture.*

subjunctive /səbˈdʒʌŋk·tɪv/ *n* [U], *adj* [not gradable] *specialized* (in grammar) the MOOD (= form) of a verb used to refer to actions that are possibilities rather than facts • *In the sentence "I wish I were rich," the verb "were" is in the subjunctive.*

sublet /ˈsʌbˈlet/ *v* [I/T] **subletting,** *past* **sublet** to rent (all or part of a rented apartment, house, or other building) to someone else

sublet /ˈsʌbˈlet/ *n* [C] • *a summer sublet*

sublime /səˈblaɪm/ *adj* extremely good, beautiful, or enjoyable, and therefore satisfying • *sublime food/scenery*

subliminal /səbˈlɪm·ən·ʔl/ *adj* not recognized or understood by the conscious mind, but still having an influence on it • *a subliminal message*

submarine /ˈsʌb·mə,riːn, ˌsʌb·məˈriːn/, *short form* **sub** *n* [C] a ship that can travel under water • *a nuclear submarine*

submarine

submarine (sandwich) /ˈsʌb·mə,riːn (ˈsæn·dwɪtʃ)/, *short form* **sub** *n* [C] *Cdn and US regional* a long, narrow sandwich filled with such things as meat, cheese, and vegetables; a HERO (SANDWICH)

submerge /səbˈmɜrdʒ/ *v* [I/T] to go below the surface of an area of water • *Take a normal breath and completely submerge yourself.* [T] ○ *Seals exhale so they can submerge more easily.* [I]

submit GIVE POWER /səbˈmɪt/ *v* [I/T] **-tt-** to give power or authority over a person or group to someone, or to accept (something) unwillingly • *He had never been able to submit himself to that sort of discipline.* [T] ○ *All newly hired employees must submit to a urine test.* [I]

submission /səbˈmɪʃ·ən/ *n* [U] • *We raised our arms in submission.*

submissive /səbˈmɪs·ɪv/ *adj* showing a willingness to be controlled by other people • *a submissive gesture*

submit OFFER FOR DECISION /səbˈmɪt/ *v* [T] **-tt-** to give or offer (something) for a decision to be made by others • *Companies are required to submit monthly financial statements to the board.*

submission /səbˈmɪʃ·ən/ *n* [C/U] • *The films were chosen from 350 submissions.* [C]

subordinate /səˈbɔːrd·ʔn·ət/ *adj* having a lower or less important position • *I'm happy in a subordinate role.* • (*specialized*) In grammar, a **subordinate clause** is a **dependent clause.** See at DEPEND ON/UPON.

subordinate /səˈbɔːrd·ʔn·ət/ *n* [C] • *You need to assign this job to a subordinate.*

subordinate /səˈbɔːrd·ʔn,eɪt/ *v* [T] to treat (someone or something) as less important than something else • *Japan has a tradition of subordinating individual desires to group goals.*

subpoena /səˈpiː·nə, -niː/ *v* [T] *law* to order (someone) to go to a court of law to answer questions, or to order (the appearance of documents) in a court of law • *to subpoena a witness*

subpoena /səˈpiː·nə, -niː/ *n* [C] *law* • *The judge issued a subpoena.*

subscribe /səbˈskraɪb/ *v* [I] to pay money to an organization in order to receive a product or use a service regularly • *She subscribes to a couple of magazines.*

subscriber /səbˈskraɪ·bər/ *n* [C] • *cable TV subscribers*

subscription /səbˈskrɪp·ʃən/ *n* [C] • *a magazine subscription*

□ **subscribe to** /-ˈ--/ *v prep* [T] to agree with or support (an opinion, belief, or theory) • *I subscribe to the notion of lying down when the urge to exercise strikes me.*

subsequent /ˈsʌb·sɪ·kwənt, -,kwent/ *adj* [not gradable] happening after something else • *Everything I do makes me better at each subsequent thing.*

subsequently /ˈsʌb·sɪ·kwənt·li, -,kwent·li/ *adv* [not gradable] • *He was made a partner, but he subsequently retired.*

subservient /səbˈsɜr·viː·ənt/ *adj disapproving* willing to do what other people want, or considering your wishes as less important than those of other people • *Traditionally, women were viewed as subservient to men.*

subservience /səbˈsɜr·viː·əns/ *n* [U] *disapproving* • *Your subservience to your boss disgusts me.*

subside BECOME WEAKER /səbˈsaɪd/ *v* [I] (of a condition) to become less strong, or (of an activity or disagreement) to become less violent • *When her pain didn't subside, Matt drove her to the hospital.* ○ *Friction between the groups subsided gradually.*

subside GO DOWN /səbˈsaɪd/ *v* [I] (of a building, area of land, or level of water) to go down to a lower level • *Forecasters predict the high tides will subside today.*

subsidiary /səb'sɪd·i:,er·i, -'sɪd·ə·ri/ *n* [C] a company that is owned by a larger company **subsidiary** /səb'sɪd·i:,er·i, -'sɪd·ə·ri/ *adj* • *All the major record companies had subsidiary labels under their control.*

subsidy /'sʌb·səd·i/ *n* [C] money given as part of the cost of something to help or encourage it to happen • *export subsidies* ○ *farm subsidies* **subsidize** /'sʌb·sə,dɑɪz/ *v* [T] to pay part of the cost of (something) • *Taxpayers shouldn't subsidize a golf course.* ○ *The tenants live in federally subsidized apartments.*

subsist /səb'sɪst/ *v* [I] to obtain enough food or money to stay alive • *These people subsist on rice, beans, fruits, and vegetables.*

subsistence /səb'sɪs·təns/ *n* [U] what a person needs in order to stay alive • *Art satisfies a need beyond mere subsistence.* ○ *Palau's economy is based on subsistence agriculture* (= producing enough food to feed themselves).

substance MATERIAL /'sʌb·stəns/ *n* [C] a material with particular physical characteristics • *The pesticide contains a substance that is toxic to insects.* • (*medical*) **Substance abuse** is the use of drugs for reasons that are not medical or the drinking of alcohol beyond reasonable levels. People who use drugs or alcohol in this way are **substance abusers**.

substance IMPORTANCE /'sʌb·stəns/ *n* [U] slightly *fml* importance, seriousness, or relationship to real facts • *Surprisingly, these filmmakers opted for substance over style.*

substandard /sʌb'stæn·dərd/ *adj* below a satisfactory standard • *There's plenty of substandard child care available.*

substantial /səb'stæn·tʃəl/ *adj* large in size, value, or importance • *He took a substantial amount of money.* ○ *They do a substantial portion of their business by phone.*

substantially /səb'stæn·tʃə·li/ *adv* to a large degree • *Serious crime is down substantially.*

substantiate /səb'stæn·tʃi:,eɪt/ *v* [T] slightly *fml* to show (something) to be true, or to support (a claim) with facts • *They have enough evidence to substantiate complaints of vandalism.*

substitute /'sʌb·stə,tu:t/ *v* [I/T] to use (someone or something) instead of another person or thing • *You can substitute oil for butter in this recipe.* [T] ○ *He was called on to substitute for the ailing star last night.* [I] **substitute** /'sʌb·stə,tu:t/ *n* [C] • *Talk is a poor substitute for action.* • A **substitute (teacher)** (*short form* **sub**) is a teacher who replaces other teachers when they are absent from work: *We had a substitute in math yesterday.*

substitution /,sʌb·stə'tu:·ʃən/ *n* [C/U] • *Substitution of less costly materials for bricks will hurt brick-makers.* [U] ○ *People who have difficulty digesting beans can make substitutions.* [C]

subterfuge /'sʌb·tər,fju:dʒ/ *n* [C/U] an action taken to hide something from someone • *His excuse sounded more like subterfuge than a real reason.* [U]

subterranean /,sʌb·tə'reɪ·ni:·ən/ *adj* [not gradable] under the ground • *a subterranean passage/river*

subtitle /'sʌb,tɑɪt·ᵊl/ *n* [C] a word, phrase, or sentence that is used as the second part of a book title and is printed under the main title at the front of the book, or the words shown at the bottom of a film or television picture to explain what is being said in another language **subtitle** /'sʌb,tɑɪt·ᵊl/ *v* [T] • *The novel is subtitled "A Fable."*

subtle /'sʌt·ᵊl/ *adj* not loud, bright, noticeable, or obvious • *subtle flavors* ○ *a subtle shade of pink* ○ *The subtle nuances of English pronunciation are hard to master.* • Subtle can also mean small but important: *There are subtle differences between the two.*

subtly /'sʌt·ᵊl·i, 'sʌt·li/ *adv* • *He subtly affects the lives of everyone he encounters.*

subtlety /'sʌt·ᵊl·ti/ *n* [C/U] • *Her acting was full of subtlety.* [U] ○ *He's baffled by the subtleties of modern life.* [C]

subtotal /'sʌb,toʊt·ᵊl/ *n* [C] the total of one set of numbers to which other numbers will be added • *Add the tax to the subtotal.*

subtract /səb'trækt/ *v* [T] to remove (something, esp. a number) • *Four subtracted from ten equals six.* • Compare ADD; DIVIDE; MULTIPLY.

subtraction /səb'træk·ʃən/ *n* [C/U] • *The test involves simple addition and subtraction.* [U]

suburb /'sʌb·ɜrb/ *n* [C] an area outside a city but near it and consisting mainly of homes, sometimes also having stores and small businesses • *Most of the people who live in the suburbs work in the city.* [pl]

suburban /sə'bɜr·bən/ *adj* • *He grew up in a wealthy suburban community near Chicago.*

suburbia /sə'bɜr·bi:·ə/ *n* [U] the suburbs of a city, or suburbs in general

subversive /səb'vɜr·sɪv, -zɪv/ *adj* tending to weaken or destroy an established political system, organization, or authority • *The FBI had the duty of obtaining evidence of subversive activity.*

subvert /səb'vɜrt/ *v* [T] *fml* • *The book describes the techniques that Hitler used to subvert democracy in the Weimar Republic.*

subway /'sʌb·weɪ/ *n* [C] an underground, electric railroad in a city • *Take the subway to Times Square.* • (*Br*) A subway is an underground passage that people who are walking can use to cross under a busy street.

succeed ACHIEVE SOMETHING /sək'si:d/ *v* [I] to achieve something that you have been aiming for, or (of a plan or piece of work) to have the desired results • *She's been trying to pass her driving test for years and she finally succeeded.* ○ *He succeeded in building the business into one the leaders in its field.*

succeed FOLLOW /sək'siːd/ *v* [T] *slightly fml* to come after (another person or thing) in time, taking their place • *Kamen was named company chairman, succeeding Robert Schwartz, who is retiring after 44 years.* [T]

succession /sək'seʃ·ən/ *n* [C/U] a series of things coming one after another • *In quick/ rapid succession he lost his job, his wife, and his health.* [U] ○ (*slightly fml*) At that time, the secretary of state followed the vice president in line of presidential succession (= the order of taking over a position of authority). [U]

successive /sək'ses·ɪv/ *adj* [not gradable] • *It was the team's third successive defeat.*

successor /sək'ses·ər/ *n* [C] a person who follows and esp. who takes the job that was held by another • *The company will announce the appointment of a successor to its retiring chairman at the next board meeting.*

success /sək'ses/ *n* [C/U] the achieving of desired results, or someone or something that achieves positive results • *We've tried to contact him, but so far without success.* [U] ○ *The dinner party was a great success.* [C] • A **success story** is something or someone who achieves an unusual degree of success: *My mother's sister, Karla, was a doctor and the success story in her family.*

successful /sək'ses·fəl/ *adj* achieving desired results, or achieving the result of making a lot of money • *a successful architect/doctor/lawyer* ○ *Fortunately, my second attempt at marriage was more successful than my first.*

successfully /sək'ses·fə·li/ *adv* • *A number of patients have been successfully treated with the new drug.*

succinct /sək'sɪŋkt, sə'sɪŋkt/ *adj* (of writing or speech) clear and short; expressing what needs to be said without unnecessary words • *Keep your letter succinct and to the point.*

succulent /'sʌk·jə·lənt/ *adj* (of food) pleasantly juicy • *The sirloin is a quality piece of meat, tender and succulent.*

succumb /sə'kʌm/ *v* [I] to lose the determination to oppose something, or to give up and accept something that you first opposed • *She succumbed to temptation and had a second helping of ice cream.* • If you succumb to an illness, you die from it.

such SO GREAT /sʌtʃ, sətʃ/ *adj* used before a noun or noun phrase to add emphasis • *I've never in my life had such delicious food.* ○ *It seems like such a long way to drive.* ○ *It was such a pity they missed the show.* ○ *It was such a large fire that over 100 firefighters were on the scene.* [+ *that* clause] • LP DETERMINERS

such OF THAT TYPE /sʌtʃ, sətʃ/ *adj, pronoun* of that or a similar type • *With such evidence, they should have no difficulty getting a conviction.* ○ *Small companies such as ours are having a hard time.* ○ *They'll pay our expenses, such as food and lodging.* ○ (*infml*) *We talked*

about the kids and the weather and such (= and that type of thing). • LP DETERMINERS

such and such /'sʌtʃ·ən,sʌtʃ/ *adj, pronoun* used to represent a specific person or thing when you cannot or do not want to give the actual information • *If they tell you to arrive at such and such a time, get there about ten minutes early.*

suck TAKE IN /sʌk/ *v* [I/T] to take in (esp. liquid) through your mouth without using your teeth, or to move the tongue and muscles of the mouth around (something inside your mouth), often in order to dissolve it • *The two-year-old sucked his thumb.* [T] ○ *Sometimes a nursing baby will hold the nipple in her mouth without really sucking.* [I] ○ *We were all sucking (on) lollipops.* [I/T] • Something that sucks something in a particular direction pulls it with great force: *The vacuum cleaner sucks dirt into a disposable bag.* [T] • To **be/get sucked into** something is to become involved in a situation when you do not want to be involved: *I got sucked into this thing because I was a friend of the family, but I really didn't know anything about their financial dealings at the time.*

suck BE BAD /sʌk/ *v* [I] *slang* to be bad or worthless • *We all thought the movie sucked.*

▫ **suck up to** /-'--/ *v adv prep* [T] *disapproving* to try to win the approval and good opinion of (someone in authority) • *She's always sucking up to the boss, telling him how wonderful he is.*

sucker FOOLISH PERSON /'sʌk·ər/ *n* [C] *infml* a person who believes everything they are told and is therefore easy to deceive • If you are a sucker for something, you like it so much that you cannot refuse it: *Josie's a sucker for burnt almond ice cream.*

sucker THING /'sʌk·ər/ *n* [C] *infml* used to refer to a thing that is remarkable or troublesome • *My car won't start again, and hopefully between the two of us we can figure out how to make that sucker work.*

sucker CANDY /'sʌk·ər/ *n* [C] a LOLLIPOP

suction /'sʌk·ʃən/ *n* [U] the process of reducing air pressure by removing air or liquid from an enclosed space, or the force created by this reduction that causes two surfaces to stick together • *Cylinder vacuum cleaners work entirely by suction.*

sudden /'sʌd·ən/ *adj* happening or done quickly or unexpectedly • *The cyclist lowered his head and put on a sudden burst of speed.* • **Sudden death** is a method of deciding the winner of a game with equal scores in which the first player or team to score wins: *The football game went into sudden death overtime, and Cleveland's field goal won the game.*

suddenly /'sʌd·ən·li/ *adv* • *Suddenly, from somewhere behind us, a loud voice spoke out.* ○ *Carpenter suddenly felt dizzy.*

suds /sʌdz/ *pl n* the mass of small bubbles that

forms on the surface of soapy water or other liquid

sue /suː/ v [I/T] to take legal action against (a person or organization), esp. by making a legal claim for money because of some harm that they have caused you • *She was hit by a city bus and is suing the city for $2 million.* [T]

suede /sweɪd/ n [U] leather whose surface has been slightly roughened to make it soft but not shiny • *She decided to wear her brown suede shoes.*

suffer ~~EXPERIENCE~~ /'sʌf·ər/ v [I/T] to experience or show the effects of (something bad) • *About 50,000 bicyclists suffer serious head injuries each year.* [T] ○ *Block's own farm has suffered large financial setbacks.* [T] ○ *If you and your husband have jobs in different cities, your marriage is likely to suffer.* [I]

suffer ~~FEEL PAIN~~ /'sʌf·ər/ v [I] to experience physical or mental pain • *She suffers in cold weather when her joints get stiff.* ○ *He suffers from migraine headaches.*

sufferer /'sʌf·ə·rər/ n [C] someone who experiences physical or mental pain of a type that is mentioned • *High pollen counts are bad news for allergy sufferers.*

suffering /'sʌf·ə·rɪŋ/ n [U] • *The prolonged drought and famine caused widespread suffering.*

sufficient /sə'fɪʃ·ənt/ adj [not gradable] enough for a particular purpose • *The company did not have sufficient funds to pay for the goods it had received.* [+ to infinitive]

sufficiently /sə'fɪʃ·ənt·li/ adv [not gradable] • *Kulkowski hopes to have recovered sufficiently from his knee injury to play in the semifinals next week.* [+ to infinitive]

suffice /sə'faɪs/ v [I] fml to be enough • *The problems were of global importance, and only an international effort would suffice to deal with them.*

suffix /'sʌf·ɪks/ n [C] specialized (in grammar) a letter or group of letters added at the end of a word to make a new word • *In the word "quickly," "-ly" is a suffix meaning "in the specified manner."* • Compare PREFIX. ~~LP~~ COMBINING FORMS

suffocate /'sʌf·ə,keɪt/ v [I/T] to die because of a lack of oxygen, or to kill (someone) by preventing them from breathing • *The government warned parents yesterday not to let infants sleep on small plastic pillows because the babies could suffocate.* [I]

suffrage /'sʌf·rɪdʒ/ n [U] fml the right to vote in an election • *She wrote a book about the women's suffrage movement in America.*

sugar /'ʃʊg·ər/ n [U] a sweet substance obtained esp. from particular plants and used to sweeten food and drinks • *Would you like some sugar for your coffee?*

suggest (obj) ~~MENTION~~ /səg'dʒest, sə-/ v to mention (an idea, possible plan, or action) for other people to consider • *They were won-*

dering where to hold the office party and I suggested the Italian restaurant on Main Street. [T] ○ *I suggest that we ask someone for directions, or we'll never find the place.* [+ that clause]

suggestion /səg'dʒes·tʃən, sə-/ n [C/U] • *She made some helpful suggestions on how to cut our costs.* [C] ○ *They didn't like my suggestion that we should all share the cost.* [C] ○ *We're open to suggestion* (= willing to listen to other people's ideas). [U]

suggest (obj) ~~SHOW~~ /səg'dʒest, sə-/ v to communicate or show (an idea or feeling) without stating it directly • *His manner suggested a lack of interest in what we were doing.* [T] ○ *She's applied for a lot of jobs recently, which suggests that she's not altogether happy with her position.* [+ that clause]

suggestive /səg'dʒes·tɪv, sə-/ adj causing you to think about sex • *He was accused of making suggestive sexual comments to his female employees.*

suggestion /səg'dʒes·tʃən, sə-/ n [C] something that shows the existence of something but is not obvious • *Police said there was no suggestion of foul play and that the death was the result of an accident.*

suicide /'suː·ə,saɪd/ n [C/U] the act of killing yourself intentionally • *She had often threatened to commit suicide.* [U] ○ *Three teenage suicides in the last year have shaken the entire community.* [C] • Suicide can also refer to any act that has the effect of causing defeat: *It would be political suicide for him to refuse to support his own party's platform.* [U]

suicidal /ˌsuː·ə'saɪd·əl/ adj having the tendency to want to kill yourself • *Prisoners deemed suicidal are closely observed.* • Suicidal also means likely to cause your own defeat: *The union leader argued that a strike now would be suicidal.*

suit ~~WORK WELL~~ /suːt/ v [T] to be convenient or work well for (someone or something) • *What time suits you best?* ○ *The job of a salesman seems to suit him.* • To suit also means to make (someone) look more attractive: *That new hairstyle really suits you—you look terrific.* • When you tell someone **suit yourself**, you mean that they can do whatever they want to do, and may express slight annoyance: *"I don't think I will be able to go with you after all." "Suit yourself."*

suitable /'suːt·ə·bəl/ adj being right or correct for a particular situation or person • *The book is suitable as a text for a course in beginning chemistry.* ○ *The movie is rated R and is not suitable for children.*

suitability /ˌsuːt·ə'bɪl·ət·i/ n [U]

suit ~~CLOTHES~~ /suːt/ n [C] a set of clothes made of the same material and usually consisting of a jacket and pants or skirt • A suit is also a set of clothes or a piece of clothing to be worn in a particular situation or for a particular activity: *a bathing suit* • A **suitcase** is a large, often box-shaped container with a handle for carrying clothes and possessions while traveling: *Have you packed your suitcase yet?* • (*slang*) A suit is also someone in business, esp. when compared with an artist or athlete: *The network suits don't care about the fans who show up at the ballpark.*

suit LEGAL CASE /suːt/ *n* [C] a **lawsuit**, see at LAW RULE • *She brought a suit against the HMO for medical malpractice.*

suit CARD TYPE /suːt/ *n* [C] any of the four types of cards in a set of playing cards, each having a different symbol printed on it • *The four suits in a deck of cards are hearts, spades, clubs, and diamonds.*

suits

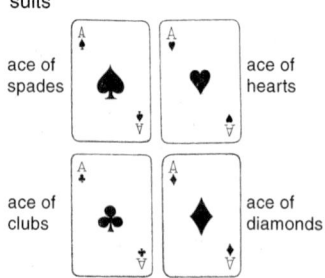

ace of spades

ace of hearts

ace of clubs

ace of diamonds

suite /swiːt/ *n* [C] a set of connected rooms, esp. in a hotel • *Guests were invited to the publisher's hospitality suite to meet the author.* • A suite is also a set of matching furniture for one room: *They bought a living room suite consisting of a sofa and two easy chairs.*

suitor /ˈsuːt̬·ər/ *n* [C] a man who wants a particular woman to agree to marry him • A suitor is also a person or company that wants to take control of another company.

sulfur, **sulphur** /ˈsʌl·fər/ *n* [U] a pale yellow chemical element with a strong smell that is found in various physical forms and burns with a blue flame

sulk /sʌlk/ *v* [I] to be silent and unpleasant because you are angry or annoyed • *She pouts and sulks, and she almost never smiles or laughs.*

sullen /ˈsʌl·ən/ *adj* silent and unpleasant • *They stared at him with an expression of sullen dislike.* ○ (*fig.*) *The skies looked very sullen* (= dark and unpleasant).

sulphur /ˈsʌl·fər/ *n* [U] SULFUR

sultan /ˈsʌlt·ən/ *n* [C] a ruler in some Muslim countries

sultry HOT /ˈsʌl·tri/ *adj* (of weather) very hot and HUMID (= with air that contains very small drops of water) • *It was a sultry night, and I was walking home.*

sultry SEXY /ˈsʌl·tri/ *adj* sexually attractive • *West plays Frank's sultry young wife.* ○ *The tango is a very sultry dance.*

sum AMOUNT OF MONEY /sʌm/ *n* [C] a particular amount of money • *The sum involved in the sale was not reported.*

sum TOTAL /sʌm/ *n* [U] a total found by the addition of two or more numbers • *The sum of seven and twelve is nineteen.* • **In sum** means **in summary**. See at SUMMARY. • The **sum total** of something is the whole amount: *That's the sum total of our knowledge about this.*

sum up (*obj*), **sum** (*obj*) **up** /ˈsʌm ˈʌp/ *v adv* [I/M] to express briefly (the important facts about something or the characteristics of someone) • *He's a small man with a big ego—that about sums him up.* [M]

summary /ˈsʌm·ə·ri/ *n* [C] a brief, clear statement giving the most important facts about something • *The assignment was to write a summary of the news.* • **In summary** is said before giving a final, brief statement: *In summary, Chen's book is a good introduction to the subject.*

summarize /ˈsʌm·əˌrɑɪz/ *v* [I/T] • *Before each episode, the narrator summarizes earlier events in the story.* [T]

summer /ˈsʌm·ər/ *n* [C/U] the season of the year between spring and fall, lasting from June to September north of the equator and from December to March south of the equator, when the weather is warmest • *We always spend our summers on the island.* [C] • **Summer school** is a variety of classes offered during the summer. • **Summertime** is the season of summer: *We get quite a few tourists here in the summertime.* • **Summer vacation** is a vacation during the summer, esp. a school vacation: *We took several short trips during summer vacation.*

summit TOP /ˈsʌm·ət/ *n* [C] the top or highest point, esp. of a mountain • *We climbed to the summit of Mount Rainier.*

summit MEETING /ˈsʌm·ət/ *n* [C] a meeting of government leaders from several countries • *The economic summit did not accomplish all that the President had hoped it would.*

summon /ˈsʌm·ən/ *v* [T] to demand that (someone) come to a particular place, or to officially order (someone) to be present • *The president summoned an emergency meeting of his advisers.* ○ *I have been summoned to appear in court.* • To summon (up) something, esp. a quality such as bravery or energy, is to use it to achieve something: *I had to summon all my courage to make that phone call.*

summons /ˈsʌm·ənz/ *n* [C] *pl* **summonses** a demand to appear in a particular place, esp. in a court of law • *I received a summons to appear in court on June 25th.*

sumptuous /ˈsʌm·tʃə·wəs/ *adj* luxurious and expensive • *I had never seen such a sumptuous apartment.*

sun /sʌn/ *n* [U] the star around which the earth moves and that provides light and heat for the earth • *The sun is the center of our solar system.* • Sun also means the light or heat that the earth receives from this star: *Sit in the sun where it's a lot warmer.* • If you get a **sunburn**, your skin will be sore and red because you spent too much time in the sun: *A long day at the beach gave him a bad sunburn.* • A **sundial** is a device that uses the light of the sun to show the time of day. • **Sunglasses** are dark glasses you wear to protect your eyes from the light of the sun: *Sunglasses are a must at the beach.* • **Sunlight** is the light that comes from the sun: *These flowers need bright sunlight.* • If something is **sunlit**, it receives light from the sun: *a sunlit room/meadow* • **Sunrise** (also **sunup**) is the time in the morning when you first see the sun: *In winter, I leave the house before sunrise.* • A **sun roof** is an opening like a window in the roof of your car. • **Sunrise** is also the appearance of the sky at that time: *a beautiful sunrise* • **Sunset** (also **sundown**) is the time in the evening when you last see the sun. • **Sunset** is also the appearance of the sky at that time: *a brilliant purple sunset* • **Sunscreen** (also **sunblock**) is a substance you put on your skin to prevent it from being burned by the sun. • **Sunshine** is the light and heat that come from the sun: *The towels dried quickly in the sunshine.* • If you have a **suntan** (also **tan**), your skin has turned darker because of having been in the sun.

sun /sʌn/ *v* [I/T] **-nn-** • *All morning, the cat sunned herself on the stone wall.* [T]

sunny /'sʌn·i/ *adj* • *Flowers filled a sunny corner of the garden.* • A person who is sunny is happy and pleasant.

sunbathe /'sʌn·beɪð/ *v* [I] to sit or lie in the sun

sundae /'sʌn·di, -deɪ/ *n* [C] ice cream with a topping of sweet sauce, nuts, and cream

Sunday /'sʌn·di, -deɪ/ (*abbreviation* **Sun.**) *n* [C/U] the day of the week after Saturday and before Monday • **Sunday school** is a religious school held on Sunday by many Christian religions esp. for children.

sundry /'sʌn·dri/ *adj* [not gradable] several and different types of; various • *Diaz is surrounded by sundry laboratory equipment.*

sunflower /'sʌn·flɑʊ·ər, -flɑʊr/ *n* [C] a tall plant having a large, round, flat, yellow flower whose seeds can be eaten or used to make cooking oil

sung /sʌŋ/ *past participle of* SING

sunk SINK /sʌŋk/ *past simple and past participle of* SINK

sunk IN TROUBLE /sʌŋk/ *adj* [not gradable] *infml* experiencing serious trouble, or unable to solve a problem • *If I had to pay off that debt, I'd be sunk.*

sunken /'sʌŋ·kən/ *adj* [not gradable] lying at the bottom of the sea or below a surrounding surface • *A few steps below the path lay a beautiful sunken garden.* • USAGE: The related verb is SINK GO BELOW WATER.

sunny /'sʌn·i/ *adj* [*-er/-est* only] See at SUN.

super EXCELLENT /'suː·pər/ *adj* [not gradable] *infml* excellent; extremely good • *She's done a super job and deserves to be promoted.* ○ *Your new haircut looks super.* • The **Super Bowl** is an important football game that is played once a year between the two American teams that are the best in their divisions.

super /'suː·pər/ *adv* [not gradable] *infml* very; extremely • *Todd's a super nice guy.*

super PERSON /'suː·pər/ *n* [C] *short form of* SUPERINTENDENT BUILDING MANAGER

superb /sʊ'pɜrb/ *adj* [not gradable] of the very best quality; excellent • *superb seafood* ○ *The cast is superb, especially Philip Bosco.*

superbly /sʊ'pɜr·bli/ *adv* • *a superbly illustrated book*

superficial NOT DEEP /ˌsuː·pər'fɪʃ·əl/ *adj* on the surface only; not deep • *a superficial wound* • If something written or said is superficial, it does not show any real understanding of the subject and does not include many details: *Her book on the history of racism in America was extremely superficial.* • If a person is described as superficial, they do not want to think seriously about anything, even important matters.

superficially /ˌsuː·pər'fɪʃ·ə·li/ *adv* • *Superficially, these books are very different.*

superficial NOT MUCH /ˌsuː·pər'fɪʃ·əl/ *adj* slight; not much • *The storm was not bad, and most property damage was superficial.*

superficially /ˌsuː·pər'fɪʃ·ə·li/ *adv* • *Half asleep, I was only superficially aware of what was going on.*

superfluous /sʊ'pɜr·flə·wəs/ *adj* more than is needed; extra and not necessary • *Our new mayor plans to eliminate superfluous programs.* ○ *Much of the school day is wasted on superfluous activities.*

superhighway /ˌsuː·pər'hɑɪˌweɪ/ *n* [C] a wide road with two or more LANES (= parallel divisions) in each direction, usually separated, and on which traffic travels at high speeds

superhuman /ˌsuː·pər'hjuː·mən, -'juː-/ *adj* [not gradable] having or requiring powers or abilities that are greater than those of most people • *Cops say he exhibited superhuman strength in resisting arrest.*

superimpose /ˌsuː·pər·ɪm'poʊz/ *v* [T] to position (an image) over another image so that both images can be seen together

superintendent PERSON IN CHARGE /ˌsuː·pə·rɪn'ten·dənt/ *n* [C] a person who is in charge of work done and who manages the employees in a particular office, department, or area • *She was appointed superintendent of schools in Tacoma, Washington.* • LP EDUCATION IN THE US

superintendent BUILDING MANAGER /ˌsuː·pə·rɪn'ten·dənt/, *short form* **super** *n* [C] a person in charge of keeping a building in good condition • *Ask the superintendent to check the boiler—we're not getting any hot water.*

superior BETTER /sʊ'pɪr·iː·ər/ *adj* [not gradable] better than average, or better than others of the same type • *They were clearly the superior team.* ○ *Some people think acoustic recordings are superior to digital ones.* • (*disapproving*) Someone who is superior or behaves in a superior way believes that they are better than other people: *I can't stand Bill's superior attitude.* • Compare INFERIOR.

superiority /sʊˌpɪr·iː'ɔːr·ət·i, -'ɑr·ət·i/ *n* [U] • *Advertisements are designed to show the superiority of one product over its competitors.*

superior HIGHER /sʊ'pɪr·iː·ər/ *adj* [not gradable] higher in rank or position than others • *When your superior officer gives you an order, you do it.*

superior /sʊ'pɪr·iː·ər/ *n* [C] • *We will need a letter of recommendation from one of your superiors.*

superlative GRAMMAR /sʊ'pɜr·lət·ɪv/ *n* [C] *specialized* (in grammar) the form of an adjective or adverb that shows the thing or action described has more of the quality than all others of the same type • *"Funniest" is the superlative of "funny." "Most" is the superlative of "more" and "many."* • Compare COMPARATIVE.
LP COMPARING

superlative /sʊ'pɜr·lət·ɪv/ *adj* [not gradable] • *The superlative form of "slow" is "slowest."*

superlative BEST /sʊ'pɜr·lət·ɪv/ *adj* [not gradable] of the highest quality; the best • *a superlative performance*

supermarket /'suː·pər,mɑr·kət/ *n* [C] a large store where many different foods and other goods used in the home are sold • *I have to stop at the supermarket on the way home.*

supernatural /ˌsuː·pər'nætʃ·ə·rəl/ *adj* (of something's cause or existence) not able to be explained by the laws of science • *From the center of the tree, a supernatural light began to glow.*

supernatural /ˌsuː·pər'nætʃ·ə·rəl/ *n* [U] forces or events that cannot be explained by science • *Remarkably, these are boom times for both religion and belief in the supernatural.*

superpower /'suː·pər,pɑʊ·ər, -,pɑʊr/ *n* [C] any of the few countries considered to be among the most powerful in the world • *a military/economic superpower*

supersede /ˌsuː·pər'siːd/ *v* [T] to take the place of (something), esp. because it is considered old or not good enough • *No sooner do you buy a computer than they bring out a new one that supersedes it.*

supersonic /ˌsuː·pər'san·ɪk/ *adj* [not gradable] faster than the speed of sound, or able to fly faster than sound travels • *a supersonic plane* ○ *supersonic speed*

superstar /'suː·pər,star/ *n* [C] a person who performs publicly, esp. in sports or entertainment, and is extremely famous and widely admired because they are considered one of the best at what they do • *She is definitely one of the superstars of country music.*

superstition /ˌsuː·pər'stɪʃ·ən/ *n* [C/U] a belief that is not based on reason or scientific thinking and that explains the causes for events in ways that are connected to magic • *Do you have any superstitions about cutting your hair?* [C]

superstitious /ˌsuː·pər'stɪʃ·əs/ *adj* • *Superstitious baseball players will wear the same shirt every days when they are on a hitting streak.*

superstructure /'suː·pər,strʌk·tʃər/ *n* [C] a structure built on top of something else, esp. the part of a building above the ground or the part of a ship above the main DECK (= floor)

supervise /'suː·pər,vaɪz/ *v* [T] to be responsible for the good performance of (an activity or job), or for the correct behavior or safety of (a person) • *The Red Cross supervised the distribution of food to refugees.* ○ *She supervises 75 employees in our order department.*

supervision /ˌsuː·pər'vɪʒ·ən/ *n* [U] • *City schools were placed under state supervision last week.*

supervisor /'suː·pər,vaɪ·zər/ *n* [C] • *a nursing/construction supervisor* ○ *I have to get off the phone—my supervisor just walked into the office.*

supervisory /ˌsuː·pər'vaɪ·zə·ri/ *adj* [not gradable] • *He applied for a supervisory position in the bank.*

supper /'sʌp·ər/ *n* [C/U] a meal eaten in the evening, esp. when eaten at home and usually the main meal of the day • *I usually heat a quick supper in the microwave when I get home from work.* [C] ○ *She has supper on the table* (= it is ready to eat). [U] • **Suppertime** is the evening: *I got home well past suppertime.* • Compare DINNER.

supplant /sə'plænt/ *v* [T] to take the place of (something or someone) • *Travel videos do not supplant guidebooks, but they can be useful when planning a trip.*

supple /'sʌp·əl/ *adj* bending or able to be bent easily; not stiff • *His supple fingers manipulated the needle with the utmost delicacy.* ○ (*fig.*) *Adams brings a supple* (= changeable) *voice to Mayfield's songs.*

supplement /'sʌp·lə·mənt/ *n* [C] something that is added to something else in order to improve it or complete it; something extra • *hormone/vitamin supplements* • A supplement is also an extra part of a magazine or newspaper: *an advertising supplement*

supplement /'sʌp·lə,ment/ *v* [T] to add to (something) • *She got a second job to supplement her income.*

supplementary /ˌsʌp·lə'ment·ə·ri, -'men·tri/, **supplemental** /ˌsʌp·lə'ment·ᵊl/ *adj* [not gradable] • *Teachers often create supplementary materials for their classes.* ○ *Some workers are eligible for supplemental unemployment benefits.*

supply /sə'plaɪ/ v [T] to provide (something that is needed or wanted), or to provide (someone) with what they need or want • *Authorities say he supplied alcoholic beverages to teenagers.* ○ *The dam supplies San Francisco with water and power.*

supply /sə'plaɪ/ n [C/U] an amount of something that is available for use • *In New York, demand for housing far outstrips supply.* [U] ○ *Medical supplies were desperately needed in the war zone.* [C] • **Supply and demand** is the balance between the amount of goods available and the amount that people want to buy: *Oil prices should be set by supply and demand, and not artificially regulated.*

supplies /sə'plaɪz/ pl n food and other ordinary goods needed by people every day • *On their fourth day out, the climbers began to run low on supplies.*

supplier /sə'plaɪ·ər/ n [C] a person, company, or country that provides goods of a particular kind • *They are the world's largest supplier of baby foods.*

support ENCOURAGE /sə'pɔːrt, -'poʊrt/ v [T] to give encouragement and approval to (someone or something) because you want them to succeed • *The president strongly supported Egypt's role in the negotiations.*

support /sə'pɔːrt, -'poʊrt/ n [U] • *The senator voiced his support for making health care available to all.*

supporter /sə'pɔːrt̬·ər, -'poʊrt̬·ər/ n [C] • *He is a strong supporter of states' rights.*

supportive /sə'pɔːrt̬·ɪv, -'poʊrt̬·ɪv/ adj • *They were supportive of immigration reform* (= They encouraged it).

support HELP /sə'pɔːrt, -'poʊrt/ v [T] to help (someone or something) emotionally or practically • *My family always supported me in whatever I wanted to do.* ○ *Many companies support public television very generously.*

support /sə'pɔːrt, -'poʊrt/ n [U] • *I got a lot of support from my friends and colleagues.* • A **support group** is a group of people who meet regularly to give and receive help for a problem by talking about it among themselves: *Alcoholics Anonymous is a support group for people with a drinking problem.*

supporter /sə'pɔːrt̬·ər, -'poʊrt̬·ər/ n [C] a person who actively helps someone • *Supporters of the rebel leader demanded his release.*

supportive /sə'pɔːrt̬·ɪv, -'poʊrt̬·ɪv/ adj giving help and encouragement, esp. to someone who needs it • *He was suspended from baseball for taking drugs, but fans were very supportive during his rehabilitation.*

support PROVIDE MONEY /sə'pɔːrt, -'poʊrt/ v [T] to provide (someone or something) with money or physical things that they need, esp. in order to continue to exist • *She has to work at two jobs to support her family.*

support /sə'pɔːrt, -'poʊrt/ n [U] • *The gov-*

ernment promised financial support to the areas affected by the flooding.

support SHOW TO BE TRUE /sə'pɔːrt, -'poʊrt/ v [T] to show or seem to show (something) to be true • *New research supports the theory.*

support /sə'pɔːrt, -'poʊrt/ n [U] • *He produced charts and graphs in support of his argument.*

support STOP FROM FALLING /sə'pɔːrt, -'poʊrt/ v [T] to hold (something) firmly or bear its weight, esp. from below, to stop it from falling • *The pole is supported by wires.*

support /sə'pɔːrt, -'poʊrt/ n [C/U] • *The floor is held up by wooden supports.* [C] ○ *You may have to use crutches for support while your ankle heals.* [U]

suppose THINK LIKELY /sə'poʊz/ v [I/T] to expect or believe • *"Will you be going with them?" "Yes, I suppose (so)."* [I] ○ *"You don't suppose (that) they forgot about meeting us, do you?"* [+ (that) clause] • Suppose can also show that you are guessing about something: *I suppose it's about six months since I last had the brakes checked.* [T]

suppose WHAT IF /sə'poʊz/, **supposing** /sə'poʊ·zɪŋ/ conjunction (used at the beginning of a sentence or clause) what would happen if • *Suppose we miss the train—what would we do then?* ○ *Supposing that you had that opportunity, Mrs. Gallagher, what would you say?*

supposed POSSIBLY TRUE /sə'poʊ·zəd, -'poʊzd/ adj [not gradable] believed by many people to be true, but not proven and often doubted by the person who is speaking or writing • *Nighttime experiments demonstrated that supposed eyewitnesses could not have seen anyone clearly enough to identify them at the distances described.* ○ *The cost of the plan far outweighs its supposed benefits.*

supposedly /sə'poʊ·zəd·li/ adv [not gradable] • *The tickets are supposedly in the mail.* ○ *I've been down to the south of England where supposedly King Arthur's castle was.*

supposition /ˌsʌp·ə'zɪʃ·ən/ n [C] slightly fml an idea that something may be true, although it is not certain • *The investment was based on the supposition that there was adequate demand for a new modern office building.* [+ that clause]

supposed RESPONSIBLE FOR /sə'poʊzd/ adj [not gradable] • If you are **supposed to** do something, you have a responsibility to do it: *The children are supposed to be at school by 8:45 a.m.* ○ *You're not supposed to park here* (= you are not allowed).

supposed INTENDED /sə'poʊzd/ adj • **Supposed to** means intended to: *These batteries are supposed to last for a year.*

supposed CONSIDERED /sə'poʊzd/ adj [not gradable] • If something is **supposed to** be good or of a particular quality, it is generally believed to be of that quality: *Her new book is supposed to be excellent.*

suppress END BY FORCE /sə'pres/ v [T] to end

(something) by force • *The governor called in the National Guard to help suppress prison riots.*

suppression /sə'preʃ·ən/ *n* [U]

suppress KEEP HIDDEN /sə'pres/ *v* [T] to prevent (something) from being expressed or known • *The police were accused of manufacturing confessions, suppressing evidence, and lying under oath.* ○ *They wanted to live in a country where religious freedom was not suppressed.* ○ *She could barely suppress a smile.*

suppression /sə'preʃ·ən/ *n* [U] • *the suppression of human rights* ○ *The police chief said there was no suppression of evidence.*

supreme /sə'priːm, su:-/ *adj* [not gradable] at the highest level • *The dictionary was called the supreme authority on all matters relating to the language.* • The **Supreme Being** is God. • The US **Supreme Court**, consisting of nine judges, is the country's highest court.

supremely /sə'priːm·li, su:-/ *adv* [not gradable] • *He was supremely self-confident.*

supremacy /sə'prem·ə·si, su:-/ *n* [U] the highest authority or greatest power • *He approved the supremacy of a strong federal government over the demands of states.* ○ *They worked for racial equality at a time when many of their neighbors believed in white supremacy* (= the belief that white people are better than people of other races).

surcharge /'sɜr·tʃɑrdʒ/ *n* [C] a charge in addition to the usual amount paid for something • *If you order the tickets by mail, there is a $5.00 surcharge.*

sure /ʃʊr, *Southern also* ʃɔʊr/ *adj* [-er/-est only] certain; without any doubt • *"No more dessert for me, thank you." "Are you sure?"* ○ *I'm sure (that) I left my keys on the table.* [+ *(that)* clause] ○ *I'm not sure where they live.* [+ *wh*-word] ○ *If there's anything you're not sure of/about, just ask.* ○ *He said that he wasn't completely sure of his facts* (= not certain that his information was correct). ○ *We arrived early, to be sure of getting a good seat.* ○ *She's sure to win.* [+ *to* infinitive] • If you are sure of yourself, you are confident: *She's much more sure of herself since she started work.* • A **sure thing** is something certain to win or succeed: *Your promotion is a sure thing—you're the best person for the job.*

sure /ʃʊr, *Southern also* ʃɔʊr/ *adv* [-er/-est only] • *"Do you want to come swimming with us?" "Sure* (= Yes, certainly).*"* ○ *I sure am hungry* (= I am very hungry). • *He said he left the book on the desk, and* **sure enough** (= as expected), *there it was.*

surely /'ʃʊr·li, *Southern also* 'ʃɔʊr·li/ *adv* [not gradable] • *She is slowly but surely getting her strength back.* • Surely can be used to express surprise, doubt, or disagreement: *Surely you're joking!* ○ *Surely they could have done better than that* (= I believe they could have done better).

surf WAVES /sɜrf/ *n* [U] the waves on the sea when they approach the coast or hit against rocks • A **surfboard** is a long, narrow board made of wood or plastic that you can stand or lie on to ride on waves as they come toward the beach.

surf /sɜrf/ *v* [I] to use a **surfboard** (= long, narrow board) to ride waves toward a beach • *They go surfing every weekend.*

surfer /'sɜr·fər/ *n* [C] • *When the waves are big, the surfers come out.*

surfing /'sɜr·fɪŋ/ *n* [U] • *Dale took up surfing after his family moved to Los Angeles.*

surf MOVE QUICKLY /sɜrf/ *v* [T] to move quickly from one place to another within (a system) to learn what each place is offering • *You can turn on your computer now and go surfing on the Web.* ○ *He spends a lot of time surfing TV channels.*

surface /'sɜr·fəs/ *n* [C] the outer or top part or layer of something • *the earth's surface* ○ *a rough/smooth surface* ○ *Try to find a level surface on the ground where you can spread out your sleeping bags.* ○ *There was very little wind, and the surface of the water was calm.* • The surface can also be what is obvious about a person or situation rather than truer or more important facts that are hidden or hard to see: *But the fear that lurks just below the surface emerges quickly in talks with villagers.* ○ *That may seem absurd on the surface, but in a few years it will seem like wisdom.*

surface /'sɜr·fəs/ *v* [I] • *The ducks would dive to the bottom of the lake and surface* (= appear at the surface) *a minute or two later yards away.* • If a feeling or information surfaces, it becomes known: *This story first surfaced about a week ago.*

surface /'sɜr·fəs/ *adj* [not gradable] • Surface means using the surface of the land or sea: *When you land in the airport, look for signs directing you to surface transportation to get a bus to the city.* ○ *If you send it overseas by surface mail it will take forever.*

surge /sɜrdʒ/ *n* [C] a sudden and great increase • *a surge in sales* ○ *a surge in the stock market* ○ *The young American's victory touched off a surge of interest in golf across the country.*

surge /sɜrdʒ/ *v* [I] (of a large group) to move suddenly forward • *The crowd surged onto the field after the game ended.*

surgeon /'sɜr·dʒən/ *n* [C] a doctor who performs medical operations • *a brain/heart surgeon*

surgery /'sɜr·dʒə·ri/ *n* [C/U] the treatment of injuries or diseases by cutting open the body and removing or repairing the damaged part, or an operation of this type • *He had undergone open heart surgery two years ago.* [U] *I'm recovering from back surgery, so it's going to be awhile before I can ride a horse again.* [U] ○ *She has undergone several surgeries and will* *require more.* [C] • (*Br*) The surgery is a doctor's office where you go to be examined. [C]

surgical /'sɜr·dʒɪ·kəl/ *adj* [not gradable] • *surgical equipment/procedures*

surly /'sɜr·li/ *adj* not wanting to please you or to be friendly • *The clerks in this post office are sullen, surly, and inefficient.*

surmise /sər'mɑɪz/ *v* [T] to decide that (something is true) without having complete information or proof • *Local police surmise (that) this is a murder-suicide, and it certainly looks that way.* [+ (*that*) clause]

surmount /sər'mɑʊnt/ *v* [T] to deal successfully with (a difficulty or problem) • *She had to surmount the difficulties of bringing up five children on her own.*

surname /'sɜr·neɪm/ *n* your **last name**, see at LAST FINAL

surpass /sər'pæs/ *v* [T] to do or be better or more than (something else) • *Our team's achievements surpass those of teams in earlier years.*

surplus /'sɜr·pləs, -plʌs/ *n* [C] an amount that is more than is needed • *The world is now producing large food surpluses.* ○ *The government is forecasting a budget surplus this year* (= all the money available to be spent will not be spent). • A surplus is also the amount of money you have left when you sell more than you buy: *a trade surplus*

surplus /'sɜr·pləs, -plʌs/ *adj* [not gradable] • *Farmers are feeding their surplus wheat to pigs.*

surprise /sər'prɑɪz, sə-/ *n* [C/U] an unexpected event, or the feeling caused when something unexpected happens • *Don't tell Ann we're having a party for her—I want it to be a surprise.* [C] ○ *Last night's heavy snow came as a complete surprise.* [C] ○ *To my great surprise, they gave us everything we asked for.* [U]

surprise /sər'prɑɪz, sə-/ *adj* [not gradable] • *Weapons experts made a surprise inspection.*

surprise /sər'prɑɪz, sə-/ *v* [T] (of an event you did not expect) to cause (you) to feel excitement over a sudden discovery • *She surprised a lot of tennis fans by winning the Canadian Open.* • If you say that you are not surprised or would not be surprised if something happened, you mean that you almost expect it: *I'm not surprised that their parents don't want them to get married.* ○ *I would not be surprised to see the economy slow down next year.* • To surprise someone is also to find them when they are not expecting it: *She surprised a burglar in her apartment and ran out into the hall, screaming.*

surprised /sər'prɑɪzd, sə-/ *adj* • *He seemed surprised by the question.* ○ *We were pleasantly surprised to find that the hotel was so comfortable.* [+ *to* infinitive] ○ *You'd be surprised how quickly the time passes.* [+ *wh-* word]

surprising /sər'prɑɪ·zɪŋ, sə-/ *adj* unexpected and causing surprise • *The election results were surprising for a number of reasons.* ○ *There was a surprising amount of talk about resignations.*

surprisingly /sər'prɑɪ·zɪŋ·li, sə-/ *adv* • *These chairs are surprisingly comfortable.* • LP VERY, COMPLETELY, AND OTHER INTENSIFIERS

surreal /sə'riːl/ *adj* strange, esp. because of combining items that are never found together in reality • *In a surreal moment, soldiers play catch with a human skull.*

surrealistic /sə,riː·ə'lɪs·tɪk/ *adj*

surrender ACCEPT DEFEAT /sə'ren·dər/ *v* [I] to stop fighting and accept defeat • *They would rather die than surrender.*

surrender /sə'ren·dər/ *n* [C/U] • *Robert E. Lee's surrender, which ended the Civil War, was one of the most important events in American history.* [C]

surrender GIVE /sə'ren·dər/ *v* [T] to give (something that is yours) to someone else, usually because you have been forced to do so • *U.S. Magistrate Celeste Bremer restricted Gruenwald's travel and ordered that he surrender his passport.*

surreptitious /,sɜr·əp'tɪʃ·əs/ *adj* done secretly, without anyone seeing or knowing • *a surreptitious glance*

surrogate /'sɜr·ə·gət, -,geɪt/ *n* [C] someone or something that replaces or is used instead of someone or something else; a SUBSTITUTE for another • *She seems to regard him as a surrogate for her father.* • A **surrogate mother** is a woman who become pregnant and has a baby for another woman.

surround /sə'rɑʊnd/ *v* [T] to be around (something) on all sides • *Snow-capped mountains surround the city.* ○ *The house was surrounded by dense woods.* • To surround something also means to have to do with it or to result from it: *I'm interested in the circumstances surrounding the accident.* ○ *The controversy that surrounded the police action led to a number of investigations.*

surrounding /sə'rɑʊn·dɪŋ/ *adj* [not gradable] • *Hundreds of people fled from the city and are now living in the surrounding countryside.*

surroundings /sə'rɑʊn·dɪŋz/ *pl n* the place where you live and the conditions in which you live • *For those of us living in safe, comfortable surroundings, the thought of being forced out of our homes and becoming refugees is almost unimaginable.*

surveillance /sər'veɪ·ləns/ *n* [U] the act of watching a person or a place, esp. a person believed to be involved with criminal activity or a place where criminals gather • *The police have kept the nightclub and its owner under surveillance.*

survey INFORMATION /'sɜr·veɪ/ *n* [C] a collection of information gathered by asking many people the same questions, usually to find out how they live or their opinions about different things, or the activity of collecting such information • *A recent survey found that working women want better child care and flexible hours.*

survey /sər'veɪ, 'sɜr·veɪ/ *v* [T] • *Researchers surveyed the political opinions of 2000 college students.*

survey LOOK AT /sər'veɪ, 'sɜr·veɪ/ *v* [T] to look at or examine (all of something) • *After we'd finished painting the kitchen, we stood back and surveyed our work.*

survey /'sɜr·veɪ/ *n* [C] • *His new book is a survey of contemporary Latin American architecture.*

survey MEASURE /sər'veɪ, 'sɜr·veɪ/ *v* [T] to measure and describe the details of (an area of land), esp. its size and position • *The property must be surveyed before you can buy it.*

survey /'sɜr·veɪ/ *n* [C] • *Geological surveys are an important tool used in locating oil reserves.*

surveyor /sər'veɪ·ər/ *n* [C] • *It took a team of surveyors about three months to lay out this part of the new highway.*

survive /sər'vaɪv/ *v* [I/T] to continue to live, esp. despite some dangerous or threatening event, or to exist after (something bad happens) • *The baby was born with a defective heart and survived for only a few hours.* [I] ○ *The building survived the earthquake with little damage.* [T] • If someone is survived by relatives, those relatives are still alive when that person dies: *He is survived by his wife and two children.* [T]

survival /sər'vaɪ·vəl/ *n* [U] • *Doctors told my wife I had a 50/50 chance of survival.* • **Survival of the fittest** means that only someone who is very energetic, has a strong desire to succeed, and is able to meet changing conditions will achieve success: *Survival of the fittest will determine which farms make it.*

survivor /sər'vaɪ·vər/ *n* [C] • *a Holocaust survivor* ○ *He was the sole survivor of the crash.* ○ *Business is bad, but she's a survivor, she'll deal with it.* • A survivor is also a person who continues to live after a close relative dies: *Her survivors include two children and five grandchildren.*

susceptible /sə'sep·tə·bəl/ *adj* easily influenced or likely to be hurt by something • *Some people are more susceptible to peer pressure than others.* ○ *He's very susceptible to colds.*

sushi /'suː·ʃi/ *n* [U] a type of food, originally from Japan, made from cold, boiled rice pressed into a ball or square with small pieces of raw fish or other food on top

suspect THINK LIKELY /sə'spekt/ *v* [T] to think or believe (something) is likely • *Medical investigators suspect the outbreak was caused by bacteria in the water supply.* • The related noun is SUSPICION FEELING OR BELIEF.

suspect THINK GUILTY /sə'spekt/ *v* [T] to think or believe that (someone) is guilty of something • *No one knows who killed her, but the*

police suspect her husband. • The related noun is SUSPICION BELIEF IN GUILT.

suspect /'sʌs·pekt/ *n* [C] • *After the robbery, the usual suspects were rounded up.*

suspect DOUBT /sə'spekt/ *v* [T] to doubt or not believe in (something) • *There is no reason to suspect their loyalty.* • The related noun is SUSPICION DOUBT.

suspect /'sʌs·pekt, sə'spekt/ *adj* • *I can't understand why my reasons seem suspect to a number of people.*

suspend STOP /sə'spend/ *v* [T] to stop doing (an activity) • *Relief agencies suspended aid yesterday.* • If a person is suspended from a job, school, or an activity, they are not allowed to be involved in it, usually to punish them: *Two students were suspended for damaging school property.*

suspension /sə'spen·tʃən/ *n* [C/U] • *Stevens will begin his three-day suspension Tuesday.* [C] ○ *Students who are warned twice may face suspension.* [U]

suspend HANG /sə'spend/ *v* [T always + adv/prep] to hang down from something • *The lights were suspended from long cords.*

suspenders /sə'spen·dərz/ *pl n* a pair of adjustable straps that hold up a pair of pants, which are attached to the waist of the pants and stretch over the shoulders

suspense /sə'spens/ *n* [U] a feeling of excitement or anxiety while waiting for something uncertain to happen • *The suspense of waiting for her answer nearly drove him crazy.*

suspension (system) /sə'spen·tʃən ('sɪs·təm)/ *n* [C] a system connected with the wheels in a vehicle that reduces the effects of traveling over an uneven surface • *The suspension can be raised for driving in snow.*

suspension bridge /sə'spen·tʃən ˌbrɪdʒ/ *n* [C] a bridge supported by strong steel ropes hung from a tower at each of its ends

suspension bridge

suspicion FEELING OR BELIEF /sə'spɪʃ·ən/ *n* [C] a feeling or belief that something is likely or true • *There are suspicions that he may not be able to play at all.* [+ *that* clause] • The related verb is SUSPECT THINK LIKELY.

suspiciously /sə'spɪʃ·ə·sli/ *adv* • *The bulge in his pocket looked suspiciously like a bottle* (= it probably was a bottle).

suspicion BELIEF IN GUILT /sə'spɪʃ·ən/ *n* [C/U]

the belief that someone is guilty of something • *His strange behavior raised suspicions among his co-workers.* [C] • The related verb is SUSPECT THINK GUILTY.

suspicious /sə'spɪʃ·əs/ *adj* • *Last night's fire at the bank is being treated as suspicious.* ○ *Neighbors were asked if they had noticed anything suspicious.*

suspicion DOUBT /sə'spɪʃ·ən/ *n* [U] lack of belief in someone or something; doubt • *Because he was a new arrival, other workers looked at him with suspicion.* • The related verb is SUSPECT DOUBT.

suspicious /sə'spɪʃ·əs/ *adj* • *Americans tend to be suspicious and wary of rules.*

suspiciously /sə'spɪʃ·ə·sli/ *adv* • *Our mayor won election by a suspiciously narrow margin.* ○ *Her eyes narrowed suspiciously* (= in a way that expresses doubt).

sustain MAINTAIN /sə'steɪn/ *v* [T] to keep (something) in operation; maintain • *It is hard to see what will sustain them when they have no income.*

sustained /sə'steɪnd/ *adj* continuing for a time • *sustained applause* ○ *We'll have to make a sustained effort to finish this job on time.*

sustain SUFFER /sə'steɪn/ *v* [T] *slightly fml* to suffer or experience (damage or loss) • *She sustained serious injuries in the accident.*

sustain SUPPORT /sə'steɪn/ *v* [T] to support (someone) emotionally • *Throughout his captivity, he was sustained by religious beliefs.*

SUV *n* [C] *abbreviation for* **sport utility vehicle**, see at SPORT GAME

S.W. *n* [C], *adj*, *adv* [not gradable] *abbreviation for* SOUTHWEST

swab /swɑb/ *n* [C] a small piece of soft material usually wound around a thin stick, used esp. for cleaning something or for putting on medicine • *a cotton swab*

swagger /'swæg·ər/ *v* [I] to walk, esp. with a swinging movement, in a way that shows that you are confident and think you are important • *He swaggered into the room just like any bully would.*

swagger /'swæg·ər/ *n* [C/U] • *He walked out of the room with a swagger that made me want to punch him.* [C]

swaggering /'swæg·ə·rɪŋ/ *adj* [not gradable] • *Such swaggering self-confidence irritates a lot of people.*

swallow MOVE FOOD /'swɑl·oʊ/ *v* [I/T] to force (food or liquid) in your mouth to move into your stomach by use of the muscles of your throat • *My throat is so sore that it really hurts when I swallow.* [I]

swallow /'swɑl·oʊ/ *n* [C] • *He said he only wanted one swallow of milk—but it was a big one!*

swallow ACCEPT /'swɑl·oʊ/ *v* [T] *infml* to accept (something) without question or without expressing disagreement • *Not surprisingly, this excuse was too much for them to swallow.*

swallow NOT EXPRESS /'swɑl·oʊ/ *v* [T] not to express or show (feelings or emotions) • *I swallowed my anger and tried to be friendly.*

swallow BIRD /'swɑl·oʊ/ *n* [C] any of various types of small bird with pointed wings and a tail shaped like a fork, which flies quickly, catching insects

▫**swallow up** *obj*, **swallow** *obj* **up** /'--'-/ *v adv* [M] to make (something) disappear by becoming part of something else and no longer separate • *The company was swallowed up by a competitor.*

swam /swæm/ *past simple of* SWIM

swamp WET LAND /swɑmp, swɔːmp/ *n* [C/U] an area of very wet, soft land • *Alligators live in these swamps.* [C]

swampy /'swɑm·pi, 'swɔːm-/ *adj* • *a low-lying, swampy region*

swamp COVER WITH WATER /swɑmp, swɔːmp/ *v* [T] to cover (a place or thing) with a large amount of water • *The boat was swamped by an enormous wave.*

swamp BE TOO MUCH /swɑmp, swɔːmp/ *v* [T] to have (too many of something), or to give (someone) too much to do • *Foreign cars have swamped the market.* ○ *We've been swamped with emergencies today.*

swan /swɑn/ *n* [C] any of various types of a large, usually white bird with a long neck that lives on rivers and lakes

swanky /'swæŋ·ki/, **swank** /swæŋk/ *adj* [-*er*/-*est* only] *infml* expensive and fashionable, and therefore admirable or desirable • *a swanky new restaurant*

swan

swap /swɑp/ *v* [I/T] **-pp-** *infml* to exchange one thing for another • *The two computers can easily swap data.* [T]

swap /swɑp/ *n* [C] • *They proposed a straight swap of guns for hostages.*

swarm /swɔːrm/ *n* [C] a large group of insects, esp. bees, or any large, busy group • *Swarms of reporters descended on the little town.*

swarm /swɔːrm/ *v* [I always + adv/prep] to move in a large group • *In summer, mosquitoes swarm around that pond.* ○ *The playground swarmed with little kids.*

swarthy /'swɔːr·ði, -θi/ *adj* [not gradable] having a dark or slightly dark skin • *His companion was skinny, with a swarthy complexion.*

swastika /'swɑs·tɪ·kə/ *n* [C] a symbol in the form of a cross with each of its arms bent in the middle at a 90° angle • *The swastika is mainly associated with the Nazis in Germany.*

swat /swɑt/ *v* [T] **-tt-** to hit (something) hard by suddenly swinging your hand or an object • *I swatted the fly with a folded newspaper.*

swat /swɑt/ *n* [C] • *A buddy took a swat at him* (= tried to hit him).

swath /swɑθ, swɔːθ/ *n* [C] a strip or belt, or a

long area of something • *The sheriff's department polices a wide swath of the county.*

sway MOVE /sweɪ/ *v* [I] to move slowly from side to side • *The trees sway in the wind.*

sway /sweɪ/ *n* [U] • *She walked with a sway to her hips.*

sway PERSUADE /sweɪ/ *v* [T] to persuade (someone) to believe or to do something • *Were you swayed by her arguments?*

sway /sweɪ/ *n* [U] the ability to persuade • *The growing sway of hate groups is frightening.* ○ *Large corporations hold sway with Congress.*

swear USE RUDE WORDS /swer, swær/ *v* [I] *past simple* **swore** /swɔːr, swoʊr/, *past part* **sworn** /swɔːrn, swoʊrn/ to use rude or offensive language for emphasis or as an insult • *He started swearing at his teacher.* • A **swear word** is a rude or offensive word.

swear PROMISE /swer, swær/ *v* [I/T] *past simple* **swore** /swɔːr, swoʊr/, *past part* **sworn** /swɔːrn, swoʊrn/ to state or promise that you are telling the truth or that you will do something or behave in a particular way • *I swear to God I'll take care of you.* [I] ○ *All the soldiers swore allegiance to the republic.* [T] ○ (*infml*) *I think she's upstairs, but I wouldn't swear to it* (= I am not completely sure). [I]

□**swear by** /'-,-/ *v prep* [T] to strongly believe in the effectiveness of (something) • *These people swear by their refrigerator.*

□**swear in** *obj*, **swear** *obj* **in** /'-'-/ *v prep* [M] to cause (someone) to make a formal promise to be honest or loyal, either because they are in a law court or because they are starting a new official job • *A ceremony to swear in the new government took place Wednesday.*

□**swear off** /'-'-/ *v prep* [T] to make a decision to stop using (something, esp. something harmful) • *He has sworn off drugs completely.*

sweat /swet/, *slightly fml* **perspire** *v* [I] *past simple* **sweat** or **sweated** to excrete a salty, colorless liquid through the skin, esp. when you are hot, sick, or frightened • *He was sweating profusely.* • If something sweats, it has drops of liquid on the outside: *The beer cans sweat in this humidity.* • Someone may say they sweat if they feel anxious: *We have to sweat about money because we don't have much of it.* • To **sweat** something **out** is to be very anxious while waiting for something to happen or come to an end: *Cleveland held on to win the game, but they made the coach sweat it out.*

sweat /swet/, *slightly fml* **perspiration** *n* [U] the salty, colorless liquid that you excrete through your skin • *beads of sweat* • Sweat is also effort or work: *They lived off the sweat and toil of others.* • *You have to learn the importance of creating things by the sweat of your brow* (= through hard work). • **Sweat-pants**, **sweatshirts**, and **sweat socks** are soft, informal clothing usually made of thick cotton and worn esp. for exercising. • **Sweats** are sweatpants, a sweatshirt, or both of these.

sweaty /'swet̬·i/ *adj* • *His face was sweaty* (= covered in sweat).

sweater /'swet̬·ər/ *n* [C] a warm piece of clothing with long sleeves, made of KNITTED wool or other material and worn on the upper part of the body • *a turtleneck sweater* • PIC TURTLENECK

sweatshop /'swet·ʃɑp/ *n* [C] a small factory where workers are paid very little and work many hours under bad conditions

sweep CLEAN /swiːp/ *v* [I/T] *past* **swept** /swept/ to clean (esp. a floor) by using a brush to collect the dirt into one place from which it can be removed • *She sweeps the street in front of her house.* [T] ○ *The classroom is filthy—could you sweep it out?* [M] ○ *I swept under every piece of furniture.* [I] • If you **sweep** something **under the rug** you hide something damaging or unpleasant and try to keep it secret: *This scandal can't be swept under the rug.*

sweep REMOVE /swiːp/ *v* [T always + adv/prep] *past* **swept** /swept/ to remove or take (something) in a particular direction, esp. suddenly and with force • *She paused, sweeping a hair from her brow.* ○ *Floodwaters were sweeping away gardens and driving residents to higher ground.* [M] • If you **sweep** someone **off** their **feet**, you cause them to have a sudden, strongly positive feeling about you: *He flew into New York on New Year's Eve and swept me off my feet.*

sweep MOVE /swiːp/ *v* [I/T] *past* **swept** /swept/ to move quickly and sometimes forcefully • *A stiff breeze swept across the parking lot.* [I always + adv/prep] ○ *He would sweep through the room shaking hands with everyone.* [I always + adv/prep] ○ *Our headlights were sweeping the trees ahead.* [T]

sweep /swiːp/ *n* [C] a large movement across an area • *the sweep of the clock's hour hand* ○ *Sixteen people were arrested in a police sweep of the area last year.* • The sweep of an idea or piece of writing is the range of its subject: *He is aware of the epic sweep of this project.*

sweeping /'swiː·pɪŋ/ *adj* having great effect or range • *The proposal calls for sweeping changes in public land use.*

sweep WIN /swiːp/ *v* [T] *past* **swept** /swept/ to win all the parts of (a competition) • *New York swept their series with Vancouver, 3-0.*

sweep /swiːp/ *n* [C] • *She prevented Republicans from making a clean sweep of the election by winning the race in District 27.*

sweepstakes /'swiːp·steɪks/ *pl n* a competition for a prize, esp. for money, in which one or more winners are chosen, usually by chance • *She won $5000 in a charity sweepstakes.*

sweet /swiːt/ *adj* [-er/-est only] (esp. of food or drink) having a taste similar to that of sugar or HONEY • *The four basic tastes are sweet, salty, bitter, and sour.* ○ *I like sweet cherries.* ○ *The desserts were not overly sweet.* • If a smell or sound is sweet, it is pleasant and enjoyable: *a* *sweet-smelling rose bush* ○ *These singers are famous for their sweet voices.* • Sweet can be used, esp. of something or someone small, to mean charming and attractive: *What a sweet baby!* • Sweet can also mean kind, generous, and likable: *He was very sweet to her.* • **Sweet-and-sour** food is flavored with a sauce usually containing sugar and vinegar: • A **sweet pepper** is a PEPPER [VEGETABLE] with a flavor that is not spicy. • A **sweet potato** (also **yam**) is a brown or orange-colored vegetable with yellow or orange flesh. • (*infml*) **Sweet talk** is pleasing speech intended to persuade someone to do or believe something: *I tried to sweet-talk my way out of going.* • A **sweet tooth** is a strong liking for sweet foods: *This pie satisfies my insatiable sweet tooth.*

sweets /swiːts/ *pl n* sweet food, such as candy or cake • *Rosie tries to avoid sweets.*

sweeten /ˈswiːt·ᵊn/ *v* [T] • *Sweeten the nut bread by adding dried fruit.* ○ (*infml*) *If they want to settle the strike, the owners still must sweeten their offer* (= make it more valuable and attractive).

sweetener /ˈswiːt·ᵊn·ər/ *n* [C/U] an artificial substance that tastes sweet • *Excessive use of any artificial sweetener is unwise.* [C]

sweetly /ˈswiːt·li/ *adv* • *The birds sang sweetly.*

sweetness /ˈswiːt·nəs/ *n* [U] • *Melons have more sweetness in the summer.*

sweetheart /ˈswiːt·hɑrt/, *infml* **sweetie** /ˈswiːt̬·i/ *n* [C] a person you love, esp. one with whom you have a romantic relationship • *Jeanne was my high school sweetheart.* ○ *Hi, sweetheart.* • A sweetheart is also a kind, generous person: *She's a sweetheart.*

swell [INCREASE] /swel/ *v* [I/T] *past simple* **swelled**, *past part* **swollen** /ˈswoʊ·lən/ *or* **swelled** to become larger and rounder • *It's spring, and the buds on the trees are beginning to swell.* [I] ○ *One of his eyes swelled shut.* [I] ○ *Immigrants swelled the city's population* (= increased it). [T] ○ (*fig.*) *His chest swelled with pride at being chosen* (= He felt extremely proud). [I]

swelling /ˈswel·ɪŋ/ *n* [C/U] • *We won't know how serious the injury is until the swelling subsides.* [U]

swell [WAVE MOVEMENT] /swel/ *n* [C] the slow up and down movement of a long, smooth wave or series of waves in the sea • *ocean swells*

swell [EXCELLENT] /swel/ *adj* [*-er/-est* only] *dated infml* excellent; very good • *The food was good and the service was swell.*

sweltering /ˈswel·tə·rɪŋ/ *adj* extremely and uncomfortably hot • *a sweltering summer day*

swept /swept/ *past simple and past participle of* SWEEP

swerve /swɜrv/ *v* [I/T] to turn suddenly to one side while moving forward • *The cab slowed down and swerved towards the curb.* [I]

swift /swɪft/ *adj* [*-er/-est* only] moving or able

to move at great speed, or happening within a very short time; fast or quick • *A swift current carried him downstream.* ○ *Public reaction has been swift and negative.*

swiftly /ˈswɪf·tli/ *adv* • *The sky was swiftly becoming dark.*

swig /swɪɡ/ *v* [I/T] **-gg-** *infml* to drink (something) in large swallows

swig /swɪɡ/ *n* [C] *infml* • *He took a swig of coffee.*

swill [DRINK] /swɪl/ *v* [T] *infml* to drink (esp. alcohol) in large amounts • *He was swilling beer all evening.*

swill [PIG FOOD] /swɪl/ *n* [U] waste food used for feeding pigs, or (*fig.*) bad or unpleasant food

swim /swɪm/ *v* [I/T] **swimming**, *past simple* **swam** /swæm/, *past part* **swum** /swʌm/ to move through water by moving parts of the body • *He jumped in the river and swam.* [I] ○ *Gertrude Ederle was the first woman to swim the English Channel.* [T] • If food is **swimming in** a liquid, it has too much of that liquid on it: *This salad is swimming in oil.*

swim /swɪm/ *n* [C] • *Let's go for a swim this afternoon.* • A **swimsuit** (also **bathing suit**) is a piece of clothing worn for swimming.

swimmer /ˈswɪm·ər/ *n* [C] • *Katy is a good swimmer.*

swimming /ˈswɪm·ɪŋ/ *n* [U] • *Swimming is excellent exercise.* • A **swimming pool** (also **pool**) is an artificial area of water for swimming.

swindle /ˈswɪn·dᵊl/ *v* [T] to obtain money or property from (someone) by deceiving or cheating them • *She tried to swindle him out of the tickets.*

swindle /ˈswɪn·dᵊl/ *n* [C] • *a stock swindle*

swindler /ˈswɪn·dlər/ *n* [C] • *a convicted swindler*

swine [PERSON] /swaɪn/ *n* [C] *pl* **swine** a person whom you consider to be extremely unpleasant and unkind • *Her ex-husband is a real swine.*

swine [ANIMAL] /swaɪn/ *n* [C usually pl] *pl* **swine** a pig, esp. when raised for food

swing [MOVE SIDEWAYS] /swɪŋ/ *v* [I/T] *past* **swung** /swʌŋ/ to move backward and forward

swing

or from one side to the other, esp. from a fixed point, or to cause (something) to move this way • *He hung upside down and swung back and forth.* [I] ○ *The heavy door swung open.* [I] ○ *Campanella knew how to swing a bat.* [T] ○ *He swung the car into the garage.* [T] • If you **swing around**, you turn quickly to face another direction: *Juan swung around to look at her.* • If you **swing at** someone, you try to hit them: *They were arguing, and then I saw him swing at Howie.* • If you **swing by/past** a place, you briefly go to it: *I told Paul we'd swing by his place around 7:30.*

swing /swɪŋ/ *n* [C] • *Scott took a big swing at the ball and missed.* • A swing can be an attempt to hit someone, esp. with your hand: *This guy took a swing at me.* • A swing is also a seat that moves backward and forward and hangs from ropes or chains. • A swing can also be a brief trip: *Ed took a 10-day swing through France.*

swing CHANGE /swɪŋ/ *v* [I] *past* **swung** /swʌŋ/ to change from one condition or attitude to another • *The company swung from record profits last year to huge losses this year.*

swing /swɪŋ/ *n* [C] • *He's very creative but prone to mood swings.*

swing BE EXCITING /swɪŋ/ *v* [I] *past* **swung** /swʌŋ/ *dated slang* to be exciting, enjoyable, and active

swinging /'swɪŋ·ɪŋ/ *adj dated slang* • *a swinging party/nightclub*

swing MUSIC /swɪŋ/ *n* [U] a form of jazz music that was popular esp. in the 1930s and 1940s

swing ARRANGE /swɪŋ/ *v* [T] *past* **swung** /swʌŋ/ *infml* to arrange to obtain or achieve (something) • *The kids need new clothes, and I don't see how I can swing it.*

swipe HIT /swaɪp/ *v* [I/T] to hit or try to hit (something), esp. with a sideways movement of the arm • *Ray swiped at a tear running down his cheek.* [I always + adv/prep]

swipe /swaɪp/ *n* [C] • *No one took a swipe at the ball or tried to knock it away from me.* ○ *(fig.) Thomas took a swipe at the competition* (= criticized them).

swipe STEAL /swaɪp/ *v* [T] *infml* to steal • *He was trying to swipe a sweatshirt.*

swirl /swɜrl/ *v* [always + adv/prep] to move quickly with a twisting circular movement, or to cause (something) to move this way • *Snowflakes swirled down from the sky.* [I] ○ *(fig.) Accusations continue to swirl around him.* [I] ○ *I swirled cocoa through the dough.* [T]

swirl /swɜrl/ *n* [C] • *We arrived in a swirl of jet fumes.*

swish /swɪʃ/ *v* [I/T] to move quickly through the air making a high, soft sound, or to cause (something) to move this way • *The elevator doors swished open.* [I] ○ *Vizard swished the ball through the hoop.* [T]

swish /swɪʃ/ *n* [C] • *the swish of tires on wet pavement*

switch DEVICE /swɪtʃ/ *n* [C] a device that controls an electric current and turns it on or off • *Flip a switch and the coffee makes itself.*

switch CHANGE /swɪtʃ/ *v* [I/T] to change suddenly or completely from one thing to another, or to exchange (one person or thing) with another • *Jeff decided to switch his major from engineering to medicine.* [T] ○ *I used to have tapes, but I switched to CDs.* [I] • If you **switch gears** you suddenly change esp. the way you think about a particular activity: *First they threatened us, then they switched gears and started acting nice.*

switch /swɪtʃ/ *n* [C] • *The team made a switch to a smaller, quicker lineup.*

switch STICK /swɪtʃ/ *n* [C] a thin stick that bends easily and is used for hitting animals or people

□ **switch on/off** *obj*, **switch** *obj* **on/off** /'-'-/ *v adv* [M] to start or stop (a device powered by electricity) • *She switched the light off.* ○ *Switch on the video camera, please.*

switchblade /'swɪtʃ·bleɪd/ *n* [C] a knife having a blade hidden inside its handle which springs out when a button is pressed

switchboard /'swɪtʃ·bɔrd, -boʊrd/ *n* [C] a piece of equipment that is used to direct all the telephone calls esp. in an office or hotel

swivel /'swɪv·əl/ *v* [I/T] **-l-** or **-ll-** to turn around from a fixed point in order to face in another direction, or to turn (something) in this way • *Kennedy swiveled around in his seat.* [I] ○ *He swiveled his face toward Jack.* [T]

swollen /'swoʊ·lən/ *adj*, *past participle of* SWELL INCREASE • *a swollen lip* ○ *swollen glands*

swoon /swuːn/ *v* [I] to have a feeling of extreme pleasure or happiness, or (*dated*) to FAINT (= lose consciousness) • *Sarah swooned when her baby was handed to her.*

swoop /swuːp/ *v* [I] to move quickly and smoothly, esp. through the air • *Swarms of birds swooped down from the sky.*

swoop /swuːp/ *n* [C] • *He lifted the baby up in one swoop.*

sword /sɔrd, soʊrd/ *n* [C] a weapon with a long, sharp, metal blade and a handle, used esp. in the past

swordfish /'sɔrd·fɪʃ, 'soʊrd-/ *n* [C/U] a large fish, often eaten as food, having a long, pointed part at the front of its head

swore /swɔr, swoʊr/ *past simple of* SWEAR

sworn /swɔrn, swoʊrn/ *adj*, *past participle of* SWEAR; formally or officially stated to be true • *He was asked to give a sworn statement* (= statement formally and officially stated as true) *for the trial.* • **Sworn enemies** are people who are completely opposed to each other

swum /swʌm/ *past participle of* SWIM

swung /swʌŋ/ *past simple and past participle of* SWING

sycamore /'sɪk·əˌmɔr, -ˌmoʊr/, **plane tree** *n* [C

a tree with divided leaves, spreading branches, and round fruit

syllable /ˈsɪl·ə·bəl/ n [C] a single unit of speech, in English usually containing a vowel, consisting of either a whole word or one of the parts into which a word is separated when it is spoken or printed • *There are two syllables in the word silver and three in appetite.*

syllabus /ˈsɪl·ə·bəs/ n [C] pl **syllabi** /ˈsɪl·ə‚baɪ/ or **syllabuses** a plan showing the subjects or books to be studied in a particular course

symbol /ˈsɪm·bəl/ n [C] anything used to represent something else, such as a sign or mark, a person, or an event • *The swastika, used as a symbol of Nazism, has become symbol of hate.* • Symbols are used in mathematics, music, and science and also have various practical uses: *The symbol on this label means that the shirt is washable.*

symbolic /sɪmˈbɑl·ɪk/ adj • *The Oval Office in the White House has come to be regarded as symbolic of the presidency.*

symbolism /ˈsɪm·bə‚lɪz·əm/ n [U] the use of symbols to represent ideas, or the meaning of something as a symbol • *religious symbolism*

symbolize /ˈsɪm·bə‚laɪz/ v [T] • *The lighting of the Olympic torch symbolizes (= represents) peace and friendship.*

symmetry /ˈsɪm·ə·tri/ n [U] the quality of having parts on either side or half that match, esp. in a way that is attractive, or similarity of shape

symmetrical /səˈme·trɪ·kəl/ adj • *The layout of the garden was perfectly symmetrical, with a wide path in the middle.*

sympathy UNDERSTANDING /ˈsɪm·pə·θi/ n [U] a feeling or expression of understanding and caring for someone else who is suffering or has problems that make them unhappy • *When Robert died, I sent a letter of sympathy to his wife.*

sympathetic /‚sɪm·pəˈθeţ·ɪk/ adj showing, esp. by what you say, that you understand and care about someone's problems or suffering • *He suffers from back trouble too, so he was sympathetic.* • A sympathetic character in a book or movie is one whose actions are understandable and who is therefore likable.

sympathize /ˈsɪm·pə‚θaɪz/ v [I] • If you sympathize with someone who has a problem, you listen to them and show them that you understand and you care: *I know what it's like to have migraine headaches, so I do sympathize with you.*

sympathy SUPPORT /ˈsɪm·pə·θi/ n [U] a feeling or expression of support and agreement • *She tends to be in sympathy with the left wing of the party.* ○ *On the subject of wilderness, her sympathies were clearly pro-environmental.* [pl]

sympathetic /‚sɪm·pəˈθeţ·ɪk/ adj • *We are sympathetic with that point of view and have the same goals.*

sympathize /ˈsɪm·pə‚θaɪz/ v [I] • *I sympathize*

SYMBOLS, SIGNS, AND MARKS

Punctuation marks

,	comma
.	period
:	colon
;	semicolon
( )	parentheses
[ ]	brackets
'	apostrophe
"…"	double quotation marks
'·'	single quotation marks
– or —	dash
-	hyphen
?	question mark
!	exclamation mark
…	dots
/	slash

The uses of these punctuation marks are explained in separate Language Portraits. Look in the dictionary at the name of the mark.

Other common marks and symbols

&	ampersand (say this as "and")
*	asterisk or star (*the* * [star] *key on the phone*)
"	ditto
©	copyright symbol
™	trademark symbol
®	registered trademark symbol
√	check mark
•	bullet
c/o	care of
'	prime mark or stress mark

Common signs and symbols used with numbers

+	plus or positive
–	minus or negative
×	multiplied by (3×2=6)
*	multiplied by (3*2=6)
·	multiplied by (3·2=6)
x	by (a 5 x 7 photo)
÷	divided by
=	equals
.	point (2.3, said as "two point three")
%	percent
@	at
'	feet or minutes
"	inches or seconds
°	degrees (temperature or angle)
#	number or pound
$	dollar
¢	cents

with your position that it would be irresponsible to lower taxes now.

symphony /ˈsɪm·fə·ni/ n [C] a long piece of music usually in four parts and played by an ORCHESTRA (= large group playing different instruments)

symptom /ˈsɪm·təm/ n [C] any feeling of illness or physical or mental change that is caused by a disease • *Muscle aches and fever are symptoms of the flu.* • A symptom is also a situation or problem that seems to represent a more serious and general problem: *Rising divorce rates are a symptom of a breakdown of family values, she said.*

synagogue /'sɪn·ə,gɑg/ *n* [C] a building in which Jewish people worship and study their religion

sync /sɪŋk/ *n* [U] *infml* • Two people or things that are **in sync** happen at the same time or in the same way, or are suited to each other: *The president and Senate majority leader are in sync on the big issues.* • Two people or things that are **out of sync** happen at different times or are not suited to each other: *She found that the job was out of sync with her principles, and she had to leave.*

synchronize /'sɪŋ·krə,naɪz/ *v* [T] to cause (something) to happen in a planned way at exact times • *The traffic lights were synchronized to allow cars to go at 30 mph and not have to stop for a red light.* • If you synchronize clocks or watches, you change them so that they all show the same time.

syndicate /'sɪn·dɪ·kət/ *n* [C] a group of people or companies that join together in order to share the cost of a business operation, such as the buying and publishing of newspaper stories, photographs, etc.

syndicated /'sɪn·də,keɪt·əd/ *adj* [not gradable] (of articles and photographs) sold to different newspapers and magazines for publishing, or (of television or radio programs) sold to different stations • *Her syndicated column appears in over 150 newspapers.*

syndrome /'sɪn·droʊm, -drəm/ *n* [C] a combination of medical problems that commonly go together and that show the existence of a disease • Syndrome is often used in the names of diseases: *acquired immune deficiency syndrome (AIDS)*

synonym /'sɪn·ə,nɪm/ *n* [C] a word or phrase that has the same or nearly the same meaning as another word or phrase • *Pleasant and agreeable are synonyms.* • Compare ANTONYM.

synonymous /sə'nɑn·ə·məs/ *adj* [not gradable] (of words) having the same or nearly the same meaning • If you say that one thing is synonymous with another, you mean that the two things are so closely connected in most people's minds that one suggests the other: *The name of Alfred Hitchcock is synonymous with movie thrillers.*

syntax /'sɪn·tæks/ *n* [U] *specialized* the grammatical arrangement of words in a sentence

synthesis /'sɪn·θə·səs/ *n* [C/U] *pl* **syntheses** /'sɪn·θə,siːz/ the act of combining different ideas or things to make a whole that is new and different from the items considered separately • *His latest album is a synthesis of African and Latin rhythms.* [C]

synthesize /'sɪn·θə,saɪz/ *v* [T] *specialized* • *Heroin was first synthesized in England in 1874 as a painkiller.*

synthesizer /'sɪn·θə,saɪ·zər/ *n* [C] an electronic instrument used to reproduce, combine, and vary sounds, esp. of musical instruments or voices

synthetic /sɪn'θeţ·ɪk/ *adj* of or relating to products made from artificial substances, often copying a natural product • *synthetic sweeteners* ○ *a synthetic fiber*

syphilis /'sɪf·ə·ləs/ *n* [U] a disease caught during sexual activity with an infected person

syphon /'saɪ·fən/ *n* [C] SIPHON

syringe /sə'rɪndʒ/ *n* [C] a tube for collecting blood or other liquids or for putting liquids into the body usually through a needle that can be put under the skin • *As a diabetic, she uses a syringe to inject herself with insulin.*

syringe

syrup /'sɜr·əp, 'sʌ·rəp, 'sɪr·əp/ *n* [U] a sweet, sometimes thick liquid made from dissolving sugar in water, to which flavoring is often added

system SET /'sɪs·təm/ *n* [C] a set of connected items or devices that operate together • *the system of interstate highways* ○ *We're having a new computer system installed.* • In the body, a system is a set of organs or structures that have a particular job to do: *the digestive system*

system METHOD /'sɪs·təm/ *n* [C] a way of doing things; a method • *My assistant will explain the system for filing a medical claim.* ○ *Under the US legal system, an accused person is innocent until proven guilty.* • A system is also a particular method of counting, measuring, or weighing things: *the metric system*

systematic /,sɪs·tə'mæţ·ɪk/ *adj* using an organized method that is often detailed • *In his typically systematic way, he laid out the pros and cons in nine numbered paragraphs.*

T, t

T, t /tiː/ *n* [C] *pl* **T's** or **Ts** or **t's** or **ts** the 20th letter of the English alphabet

tab SMALL PIECE /tæb/ *n* [C] a small piece of material on a box, can, or container that is pulled to open it • A tab is also a small piece of paper or plastic attached to a paper or file so it can be found easily.

tab AMOUNT CHARGED /tæb/ *n* [C] an amount charged for a service or for a meal in a restaurant • *He offered to pick up the tab for lunch* (= pay for it).

tabernacle /'tæb·ər,næk·əl/ *n* [C] a place of religious worship • *We stopped for a prayer meeting at a roadside tabernacle.*

table FURNITURE /'teɪ·bəl/ *n* [C] a piece of furniture that has a flat top supported by legs • *We ate our meals sitting around a large dining room table.* • The table also means all the people at a table: *The whole table had a very good time.* • If a subject is **on the table**, it has not been decided: *I'd like to throw another question on the table.* • A **tablecloth** is a piece of cloth or paper used to cover a table, esp. during a meal. • **Table tennis** (also *trademark* **Ping-Pong**) is a game played on a large table where players at each end use paddles to hit a small, light ball back and forth over a low net.

table INFORMATION /'teɪ·bəl/ *n* [C] an arrangement of facts and numbers, usually in rows on a page, that makes information easy to understand • A **table of contents** is a list of what is in a book.

tabulate /'tæb·jə,leɪt/ *v* [T] to arrange (facts, numbers, or other information) in the form of a table • *We plan to tabulate the findings of our survey.*

table NOT DISCUSS /'teɪ·bəl/ *v* [T] to leave (something) for discussion or consideration at a later time • *We'll have to table these last two items until our next meeting.*

tablespoon /'teɪ·bəl,spuːn/ (*abbreviation* **tbsp.**) *n* [C] a large spoon used for measuring or serving food, or the amount this spoon holds • *Add three tablespoons of butter.*

tablet MEDICINE /'tæb·lət/ *n* [C] a small, round, solid object made of medicine; a pill • *aspirin tablets*

tablet STONE /'tæb·lət/ *n* [C] a piece of stone or other hard material used for writing, esp. in ancient times • *Six tablets bear the names of those who died here.*

tablet PAPER /'tæb·lət/ *n* [C] sheets paper that have been fastened together at one edge, used for writing or drawing; a PAD • *His pen swept across his drawing tablet.*

tabloid /'tæb·lɔɪd/ *n* [C] a type of newspaper that has smaller pages, many pictures, and short reports • *The tabloids often attract readers with sensational headlines.*

taboo /tə'buː, tæ-/ *n* [C] *pl* **taboos** something that is avoided or forbidden for religious or social reasons • *There is a taboo in Navajo culture that a pregnant woman must not look at a dead animal.*

taboo /tə'buː, tæ-/ *adj* [not gradable] • *At one time, sex and money were taboo subjects in this culture.*

tacit /'tæs·ət/ *adj* [not gradable] understood without being expressed directly • *He gave tacit approval to the plan.*

taciturn /'tæs·ə,tɜrn/ *adj slightly fml* (of a person) usually speaking very little • *He was always quiet, reserved, and taciturn.*

tack NAIL /tæk/ *n* [C] a short, sharp nail with a wide, flat end, or a **thumbtack**, see at THUMB

tack (up) /tæk ('ʌp)/ *v* [T] • *We tacked up a few decorations for the party.*

tack WAY OF DEALING /tæk/ *n* [C] one of several possible ways of dealing with something • *When this tack didn't work, I tried another.*

▫ **tack on** *obj*, **tack** *obj* **on** /'-'-/ *v adv* [M] to add (something extra) • *They tacked an additional 18% on the bill as a service charge.*

tackle KNOCK DOWN /'tæk·əl/ *v* [T] to catch and knock down (someone who is running), esp. in the game of football • *Secret Service agents tackled the gunman before he could escape.*

tackle /'tæk·əl/ *n* [C] an act of knocking someone down, or a football player who is supposed to do this • *A flying tackle brought him down.* ○ *He's an offensive/defensive tackle.*

tackle ATTACK /'tæk·əl/ *v* [T] to attack or to deal with (something) • *There are many ways of tackling this problem.*

tackle EQUIPMENT /'tæk·əl/ *n* [U] the equipment used in fishing or to lift or raise things on a ship

tacky STICKY /'tæk·i/ *adj* [-er/-est only] (of a substance) sticky • *I left a fingerprint in the tacky paint.*

tacky CHEAP /'tæk·i/ *adj* [-er/-est only] *infml disapproving* cheap in quality or design • *She reads those tacky romance novels.*

taco /'tɑk·oʊ/ *n* [C] *pl* **tacos** /'tɑk·oʊz, -oʊs/ a folded TORTILLA (= thin, flat bread) filled with meat, cheese, or salad vegetables, that is fried and served with various sauces

tact /tækt/ *n* [U] the ability to say or do things in such a way that you do not make anyone unhappy or angry • *The editors of this book have shown tact and good sense in their selections.*

tactful /'tækt·fəl/ *adj* • *You were very tactful about the awful meal my mother fixed.*

tactfully /'tækt·fə·li/ *adv* • *I tried to say as tactfully as I could that she was totally wrong.*

tactic /'tæk·tɪk/ *n* [C usually pl] a specific action intended to get a particular result • *Oliver's clumsy tactics doomed the plan from* *the start.* • (*specialized*) Tactics is the science of planning the arrangement and use of military forces and equipment in war.

tactical /'tæk·tɪ·kəl/ *adj* [not gradable] • *He made a tactical error in agreeing to the debates.* • (*specialized*) Tactical military operations or weapons are used to achieve specific goals.

tad /tæd/ *n* [U] *infml* a little bit; a small amount • *Those French fries were a tad greasy.*

tadpole /'tæd·poʊl/ *n* [C] a newly born creature with a large head, long tail, and no arms or legs, which lives in water and develops into a FROG or TOAD

tag [SIGN] /tæg/ *n* [C] a small piece of paper, cloth, or metal attached to an item and containing information about it • *Did you check the price tag on that sweater?* • A **tag sale** is a **garage sale**. See at GARAGE.

tag /tæg/ *v* [T] **-gg-** • *The items are tagged and stacked on shelves.*

tag [GAME] /tæg/ *n* [U] a game for children in which one child chases the others and tries to touch one of them, who then is the one who chases the children

tag /tæg/ *v* [T] **-gg-** • *I tagged you, now you're it!*

□**tag along** /'tæg·ə'lɔːŋ/ *v adv* [I] *infml* to follow after a person or group of people, esp. when you have not been invited to • *James doesn't want his little brother to tag along.*

tail [BODY PART] /teɪl/ *n* [C] a part of the body of an animal attached to the base of the back, or something similar in shape or position • *The dog greeted us, wagging its tail.* ○ *The comet's tail glowed in the night sky.* • (*infml*) A tail can also be a person's buttocks: *The staff of the emergency room worked their tails off.* • The **tail end** of something is the final part of it: *the tail end of the evening* • **Tail lights** are the red lights on the back of a vehicle. [PIC] CAR • A **tail wind** is a wind blowing from behind: *Flights from America to Europe usually have the help of a strong tail wind.*

tail [FOLLOW] /teɪl/ *v* [T] *infml* to follow and watch the movements of (someone), esp. without their knowledge • *FBI agents tailed him for a month.*

tail /teɪl/ *n* [C] *infml* • *Police put a tail on the suspect as he left the airport.*

□**tail off** /'teɪl'ɔːf/ *v adv* [I] to become gradually less or smaller • *Profits tailed off in the last half of the year.*

tailgate [DRIVE CLOSE] /'teɪl·geɪt/ *v* [I/T] to follow very closely behind another vehicle

tailgate

this car is tailgating

tailgate [CAR DOOR] /'teɪl·geɪt/ *n* [C] a door at the back of a vehicle that opens down for loading

tailor [CLOTHES MAKER] /'teɪ·lər/ *n* [C] someone whose job is to make, repair, and adjust clothes

tailored /ˌteɪ·lərd/, **tailor–made** /ˌteɪ·lər'meɪd/ *adj* [not gradable] • *a tailored suit* ○ *Her clothes fit perfectly—they must be tailor-made.*

tailor [ADJUST] /'teɪ·lər/ *v* [T] to adjust (something) to suit a particular need or situation • *Their services are tailored to clients' needs.*

tailpipe /'teɪl·paɪp/ *n* [C] the pipe at the back end of a vehicle that carries gases away from the engine

tails /teɪlz/ *pl n* the side of a coin that does not have an image of a head on it • USAGE: The opposite of tails is HEADS.

tailspin /'teɪl·spɪn/ *n* [C] a sudden fall that cannot be controlled • *The plane went into a tailspin and crashed.* ○ *Events in Asia sent the stock market into a tailspin.*

taint /teɪnt/ *v* [T] to damage the quality, taste, or value of (something) • *Bacteria had tainted the meat.* ○ *His reputation was permanently tainted by the scandal.*

taint /teɪnt/ *n* [U] • *The taint of scandal followed him for years.*

tainted /'teɪnt·əd/ *adj* • *tainted seafood* ○ *tainted election results*

take [MOVE] /teɪk/ *v* [T] *past simple* **took** /tʊk/, *past part* **taken** /'teɪ·kən/ to move (something or someone) from one place to another • *Please, take me with you!* ○ *It may rain, so take your umbrella.* ○ *The suitcases were taken to Madrid by mistake.* ○ *I thought I'd take her some chocolates.* ○ *I take home about $200 a week.*

take [REMOVE] /teɪk/ *v* [T] *past simple* **took** /tʊk/, *past part* **taken** /'teɪ·kən/ to remove (something) • *Here's your pen—I took it by mistake.* ○ *A radio was taken from the car.* • To **take** someone's **life** is to kill them: *The fire took her life.* ○ *He tried to take his own life.* • If you **take the wraps off** something, you let people know about it: *Today the company takes the wraps off their newest product, a drug that they have spent millions of dollars developing.*

take [ACCEPT] /teɪk/ *v* [T] *past simple* **took** /tʊk/, *past part* **taken** /'teɪ·kən/ to accept (something), or to receive (something) willingly • *I tried to phone him, but he refused to take my call.* ○ *Does this restaurant take credit cards?* ○ *Take this medicine three times a day.* ○ *I can take three more people in my car.* ○ *It's a girls' school that has now started taking boys.* ○ *Bob took a lot of criticism for his decision.* ○ *I refuse to take responsibility for what's happened.* • People say **take care** instead of saying goodbye. • To **take care of** someone or something is to be responsible for them or do whatever needs to be done: *She took care of her little sister all afternoon.* ○ *I was hoping this would take care of the problem.* • If you **take charge**

of something, you accept responsibility for it or have control over it: *She took charge of the project and made sure it was finished on time.* • To **take** something **with a grain of salt** means to believe that it is not really important or completely true: *I've seen the article, which I take with a grain of salt.* • If you **take heart**, you feel encouraged. • When someone can't **take a joke**, they are not amused by jokes or tricks directed at them. • If someone offers something and says **take it or leave it**, they mean that you must either accept it without any change or refuse it. • If you **take** something **lying down**, you accept it without complaint: *I can't take that criticism lying down.* • If you **take pains** to do something, you are very careful doing it: *He took great pains to dress appropriately.* • If you **take** something **in stride**, you do not let it influence your attitude or keep you from getting things done: *Somehow they took all the confusion in stride.* • If something **takes its toll**, it causes a lot of harm or suffering: *Divorce takes its toll on the children involved.* • *If she says she's sick, you have to* **take** *her* **word for it** (= believe her).

take [THINK OF] /teɪk/ *v* [T] *past simple* **took** /tʊk/, *past part* **taken** /'teɪ·kən/ to think of (someone) or understand (something) in a particular way; PERCEIVE • *I took him to be more honest than he really was.* [+ *to* infinitive] ○ *The police are taking the bomb threats very seriously.* ○ *In the dim light I could have taken them for brothers.* ○ *I'm not going to forge his signature! What do you take me for?* • Take is sometimes used to introduce an example of what you mean: *It's been really busy. Take last week—we had meetings every day.* • If you **take** something **into account** or **take account of** something, you consider or remember something when judging a situation: *The report fails to take into account the problems of illegal immigrants.* • If you **take** something **for granted**, you do not even think about it because you believe it will always be available or exactly the same: *I took it for granted that I would find the perfect job.* ○ *It's easy to take your kids for granted.* • To **take a hint** is to understand something suggested or communicated indirectly: *I've tried to get him to leave, but he can't take a hint.* • If you **take notice** or **take note** of something, you give it your attention: *Voters are beginning to take notice of him as a serious candidate.* • To **take stock** of something is to think carefully about it: *It is time for us to take stock of our attitudes and ideals.*

take /teɪk/ *n* [C] • *What's your take on the new proposals for new health care?*

take [HOLD] /teɪk/ *v* [T] *past simple* **took** /tʊk/, *past part* **taken** /'teɪ·kən/ to hold (something) • *He took my arm and led me to my seat.* ○ *Can you take this bag while I open the door?* • To **take hold** or **take root** means to become

established: *The economic recovery is just beginning to take hold now.* ○ *Fascism has never taken root in the United States.* • If you **take the bull by the horns**, you deal with a difficult situation in a very direct way: *I took the bull by the horns and confronted him about his drinking.*

take [CATCH] /teɪk/ *v* [T] *past simple* **took** /tʊk/, *past part* **taken** /'teɪ·kən/ to catch, win, or get possession of (something) • *Rebels ambushed the train and took several prisoners.* ○ *My roses took first prize at the flower show.* • If you **take advantage of** something or someone, you use an opportunity to achieve results, sometimes in an unfair way: *Let's take advantage of the good weather and go on a picnic.* ○ *You shouldn't take advantage of Carol's generosity like that.* • (*infml*) Something that **takes the cake** is either wonderful or very bad: *I've had some pretty bad injuries, but this one takes the cake.*

take [NEED] /teɪk/ *v* [T] *past simple* **took** /tʊk/, *past part* **taken** /'teɪ·kən/ to have as a necessary condition; need • *Parachuting takes a lot of nerve.* ○ *I take a size 9 shoe.* ○ *Transitive verbs take a direct object.* ○ *It didn't take much persuasion to get her to go with us.* ○ *How long does this paint take to dry?* ○ *Broken bones always take time to mend.* • If something **takes forever**, it happens very slowly: *In rush-hour traffic, it takes forever to get home.* • Someone who **takes the time to** do something thinks it is important and worth the effort or time to do it: *She didn't even take the time to say goodbye.* • If you **take your time to** do something, it means that you spend as much time as you need to do it right: *He took his time before answering the question.*

take [ACT] /teɪk/ *v* [T] *past simple* **took** /tʊk/, *past part* **taken** /'teɪ·kən/ to do (something) • *I've started taking piano lessons.* ○ *The government urged both sides to take steps to end the strike.* • Take is used with many nouns to make a verb phrase: *We can't delay any longer—we have to take action* (= to act). ○ *In the evening I like to take a walk* (= to walk). ○ *If you're tired, you need to take a nap* (= to sleep). • If you **take a deep breath**, you pause, esp. because you have something difficult to do: *She took a deep breath and walked into the courtroom.* • If someone tells you to **take it easy**, they are advising you to rest or to relax: *You'd better take it easy until you feel better.* ○ *Take it easy—don't get mad.* • To **take effect** means to start working: *The medicine should take effect quite quickly.* • If you **take a fancy to** someone, you like them or think they are attractive: *He took a fancy to her right away.* • (*infml*) If someone tells you to **take a hike**, they are telling you rudely to leave. • To **take the initiative** is to use an opportunity to do something before someone else does, esp. to solve a problem. • (*rude slang*) If you **take a**

leak, you urinate. • To **take** your **pick** means to choose what you want: *You can take your pick of any dessert on the cart.* • To **take part in** something means to do it with other people: *All the children took part in the Thanksgiving play.* • To **take place** is to happen at a stated time or place: *The story takes place in the 18th century.* ○ *What took place here last night?* • If you **take the plunge**, you decide to do something, esp. something risky: *They took the plunge and got married last month.* • *There's help available for those who take the trouble to ask for it* (= make an effort to do this). • If a person or a situation **takes a turn for the better** or **the worse**, their condition becomes better or worse: *I'm afraid that our discussions have taken a turn for the worse.* • If you **take turns**, you and other people do the same thing, one after the other: *The mothers in our group take turns driving the children to school.* • ⓛⓟ DO: VERBS MEANING "PERFORM"

take MEASURE /teɪk/ *v* [T] *past simple* **took** /tʊk/, *past part* **taken** /'teɪ·kən/ to measure (something) • *Better take the baby's temperature—she may have a fever.*

take REACT /teɪk/ *v* [T] *past simple* **took** /tʊk/, *past part* **taken** /'teɪ·kən/ to have or cause to have (a particular feeling or opinion) • *He takes little interest in current events.* ○ *She takes offense too easily.* • To **take a dim view of** something means to disapprove of it: *Most bosses take a dim view of long lunches.* • (*infml*) If you **take a shine to** someone, you get to like them very much. • If you **take a** place or people **by storm**, you are suddenly extremely successful in that place or popular with those people: *As everyone knows, the Beatles took the US by storm.* • To **take** someone **by surprise** means to surprise them completely: *His sudden proposal took her totally by surprise.* • If you **take issue with** someone, you disagree strongly: *I take issue with parents who push their children too hard.* • To **take sides** means to support one person or opinion over another: *My mother never took sides when my brother and I argued.*

take CHEAT /teɪk/ *v* [T] *past simple* **took** /tʊk/, *past part* **taken** /'teɪ·kən/ *infml* to cheat (someone) • *You paid $500 for that thing? I think you got taken.*

take WRITE /teɪk/ *v* [T] *past simple* **took** /tʊk/, *past part* **taken** /'teɪ·kən/ to write (information provided by someone or something) • *Take notes as you read.* ○ *Journalists took down every word he said during the interview.*

take PHOTOGRAPH /teɪk/ *v* [T] *past simple* **took** /tʊk/, *past part* **taken** /'teɪ·kən/ to make (a photograph) of someone or something • *We took lots of pictures of the new baby.*

take TRAVEL ON /teɪk/ *v* [T] *past simple* **took** /tʊk/, *past part* **taken** /'teɪ·kən/ to travel on (something) to get from one place to another •

I always take the train. ○ *Take the road on the left to get to my house.*

take FILM /teɪk/ *n* [C] the filming of a small part of a movie • *That scene needed ten takes before they got it right.*

take MONEY /teɪk/ *n* [U] the amount of money received from an activity • *The box office take has been huge for the new show.*

☐ **take after** /-'--/ *v prep* [T] to be like or to look like (a family member or group) • *Most of my children take after my husband.*

☐ **take apart** *obj*, **take** *obj* **apart** /'-'-/ *v adv* [M] to separate the parts of (something) so that they are not together • *I like to take things apart to see how they work.*

☐ **take away** *obj*, **take** *obj* **away** /'-'-/ *v adv* [M] to remove or subtract (one thing) from (a place or amount) • *Take these chairs away—we don't need them.* ○ *Twelve take away four equals eight.*

☐ **take back** *obj*, **take** *obj* **back** /'-'-/ *v adv* [M] to receive or accept (something that you previously sold, offered, or gave away) • *If you're not satisfied with your purchase, we'll take it back and refund your money.* • If you **take back** something you have said, you admit that it was wrong: *I said she was lying, but I take it back.* • Something that **takes** you **back** makes you remember: *That song takes me back to my miserable adolescence.*

☐ **take down** *obj*, **take** *obj* **down** /'-'-/ *v adv* [M] to remove (something, esp. decorations) • *It must be time to take down the Christmas lights.*

☐ **take in** *obj* UNDERSTAND , **take** *obj* **in** /'-'-/ *v adv* [M] to completely understand (the meaning or importance of something) • *I had to read the letter twice before I could take it all in.*

☐ **take in** *obj* SHELTER , **take** *obj* **in** /'-'-/ *v adv* [M] to provide a place for (someone) to live or stay • *His aunt took him in when his mother died.*

☐ **take in** SEE /'-'-/ *v adv* [T] to go to see (something of interest) • *to take in a movie* ○ *We drove around the island and took in all the sights.*

☐ **take in** *obj* DECEIVE , **take** *obj* **in** /'-'-/ *v adv* [M] to deceive or trick (someone) • *Do you think the teacher was taken in by your excuse?* ○ *That sales pitch totally took us in.*

☐ **take in** *obj* MAKE SMALLER , **take** *obj* **in** /'-'-/ *v adv* [M] to make (clothes) smaller • *These pants fit much better since I had them taken in.* • USAGE: The opposite of take in is LET OUT WIDEN.

☐ **take in** *obj* RECEIVE , **take** *obj* **in** /'-'-/ *v adv* [M] to receive (money) from sales • *The show took in $100,000.*

☐ **take off** LEAVE /-'-/ *v adv* [I] (of an aircraft) to leave the ground and fly, or (of a person) to leave suddenly • *The plane took off on time.* ○ (*infml*) *When he saw me coming, he took off in the other direction.*

takeoff /'teɪ·kɔːf/ *n* [C] • *Night takeoffs and*

landings are banned at this airport. • See also TAKEOFF.

□**take off** *obj* **off** REMOVE , **take off** *obj* /'-'-/ *v adv* [M] to remove or get rid of (something) • *He took off his clothes and jumped in the lake.* ○ *After the poisoning scare, the product was taken off the market.*

□**take off** *obj* BE ABSENT , **take** *obj* **off** /'-'-/ *v adv* [M] to use (a period of time) for a purpose that is different from what a person usually does • *I've decided to take next semester off and travel and write.*

□**take off** BECOME POPULAR /'-'-/ *v adv* [I] to suddenly become popular or successful • *The new product really took off among teens.*

□**take on** *obj* BEGIN , **take** *obj* **on** /'-'-/ *v adv* [M] to begin to have, use, or do (something) • *A chameleon takes on the color of its surroundings.* ○ *Her voice took on a troubled tone.*

□**take on** *obj* FIGHT , **take** *obj* **on** /'-'-/ *v adv* [M] to fight or compete against (someone or something) • *I'll take you on in a game of chess.* ○ *You have to be brave to take on a big corporation in court.*

□**take out** *obj* GET , **take** *obj* **out** /'-'-/ *v adv* [M] to arrange to obtain (something) from a company, bank, etc. • *I'm going to take out a life insurance policy.* ○ *He had to take out a loan to pay his taxes.*

□**take out** *obj* BRING , **take** *obj* **out** /'-'-/ *v adv* [M] to bring (someone) to a public place where they can eat with you or be entertained, and usually pay for them and yourself • *Our boss took us out for dinner.*

□**take out** *obj* RID , **take** *obj* **out** /'-'-/ *v adv* [M] to get rid of • *Take out the seeds before you slice the papaya.* [M]

□**take** *obj* **out on** *obj* /'-'-,-/ *v adv prep* [T] to make (someone else) suffer or be responsible for your own mistakes, anger, disappointment, etc. • *Don't take it out on me—I'm not your boss!*

□**take over** *(obj)*, **take** *(obj)* **over** /'-'--/ *v adv* [I/M] to get control of something, or to do something instead of someone else • *He's taken over the spare bedroom for his model railroad.* [M] ○ *She took over management of this department last winter.* [M] ○ *They made changes the minute they took over.* [I]

takeover /'teɪˌkoʊ·vər/ *n* [C] • *This is the year for huge corporate takeovers.*

□**take to** LIKE /'--/ *v prep* [T] to like (something or someone) • *We took to our new neighbors very quickly.* ○ *Americans don't take kindly to being told what to say.* ○ *The children have really taken to tennis.*

□**take to** START A HABIT /'--/ *v prep* [T] to start to use or do (something) as a habit • *She's taken to walking along the beach after work.*

□**take to** ESCAPE /'--/ *v prep* [T] to go to or escape to (a place) • *The refugees took to the hills for safety.*

□**take up** *obj* BEGIN , **take** *obj* **up** /'-'-/ *v adv*

[M] to begin to do (something) • *I'm not very good at golf—I only took it up recently.*

□**take up** *obj* DISCUSS , **take** *obj* **up** /'-'-/ *v adv* [M] to discuss or deal with (something) • *The school plans to take the matter up with the parents.*

□**take up** *obj* FILL , **take** *obj* **up** /'-'-/ *v adv* [M] to fill (space or time) • *This desk takes up too much room.* ○ *My day is completely taken up with meetings.*

□**take up** *obj* SHORTEN , **take** *obj* **up** /'-'-/ *v adv* [M] to shorten (clothes) • *This skirt is too long—I'll have to take it up.*

□**take** *obj* **up on** *obj* /'-'-,-/ *v adv prep* [T] to accept (an offer or invitation) from someone • *I think I'll take him up on his offer of a free ticket.*

□**take** *obj* **upon** *obj* /'--,-/ *v prep* [T] • If you **take** something **upon** yourself, you take full responsibility for it: *He took it upon himself to personally thank each of the guests.*

□**take up with** BECOME FRIENDLY /'-'-,-/ *v adv prep* [T] to become friendly with or spend time with (someone) • *She's recently taken up with a strange group of people.*

□**take up with** *obj* DISCUSS , **take up** *obj* **with** *obj* /'-'-,-/ *v adv prep* [M] to begin discussing (a subject) with (someone) • *You'll have to take this up with the head of the department.*

taken /'teɪ·kən/ *past participle of* TAKE

takeoff /'teɪ·kɔːf/ *n* [C] a humorous copy of the speech, manner, or style of someone, esp. someone famous • *He does a great takeoff of Kermit the Frog.* • See also **takeoff** at TAKE OFF LEAVE .

takeout /'teɪ·kaʊt/, **carryout** *n* [C/U] a meal bought at a store or restaurant and taken somewhere else to be eaten • *Let's have Chinese takeout for dinner tonight.* [U]

talcum powder /'tæl·kəm,paʊd·ər/, **talc** /tælk/ *n* [U] a powder for the skin that makes it feel smooth or keeps it dry

tale /teɪl/ *n* [C] a story or report, esp. one that is invented or difficult to believe • *a fairy tale* ○ *His life story makes a pretty remarkable tale.*

talent /'tæl·ənt/ *n* [C/U] a special natural ability to do something well, or people who have this ability • *His talents are being wasted in that job.* [C] ○ *The baseball scouts are looking for new talent.* [U]

talented /'tæl·ənt·əd/ *adj* • *A very young and talented violinist was the guest soloist.*

talk /tɔːk/ *v* [I/T] to say words aloud, usually to give or exchange information; to speak • *I talked with Carol on the phone yesterday.* [I] ○ *We talked about books.* [I] ○ *The candidates want to talk taxes* (= discuss this subject). [T] • **Talk about** is used to add emphasis to a statement you are making: *Talk about hot—it's 97 today.* • If someone **talks dirty**, they describe sexual activity, or they swear. • If you **talk tough**, you try to sound strong or powerful: *The president talks tough but then backs down.* • If you **talk shop**, you talk about your job when not at work. • LP SAY, TELL, TALK, AND SPEAK at SAY SPEAK

talk /tɔːk/ *n* [C/U] • *Talk won't get us anywhere.* [U] ○ *I had a talk with my boss.* [C] ○ *Sarah gave a talk* (= a speech before a group of people) *on skyscrapers.* [C] ○ *I've heard talk of a layoff* (= unofficial information about it). • Talks are official discussions between organizations or countries: *Contract talks between the airline and the union began today.* [C] • **Talk radio** is a type of radio program on which events and people in the news are discussed and listeners call to talk. • A **talk show** is a television or radio program on which guests are asked questions, esp. about themselves.

talker /'tɔː·kər/ *n* [C] • *I'm not much of a talker* (= a person who is comfortable speaking).

□ **talk back** /'-'-/ *v adv* [I] to answer someone in a rude way • *Don't talk back to your teacher.*

□ **talk down to** /'-'--/ *v adv prep* [T] to speak to (someone) in a simple way, as if they cannot understand things as well as you can • *Our history teacher never talks down to us.*

□ **talk** obj **into** obj /'-,--/ *v prep* [T] to persuade (someone) to do (something) • *I tried to talk her into ordering ice cream.*

□ **talk out** obj, **talk** obj **out** /'-'-/ *v adv* [M] to discuss (the details of something) • *They've been talking out their problems.*

□ **talk** obj **out of** obj /-'--/ *v adv prep* [T] to persuade (someone) not to do (something) • *I talked him out of running on his sore ankle.*

□ **talk over** obj, **talk** obj **over** /'-'--/ *v adv* [M] to discuss (something) • *We should get together and talk this over.*

talkative /'tɔː·kəṭ·ɪv/ *adj* talking a lot • *Cynthia is lively and talkative.*

tall VERY HIGH /tɔːl/ *adj* [-er/-est only] of more than average height • *She's tall and slim.* ○ *The Sears Tower is taller than the World Trade Center.* • A **tall order** is a request that is difficult to fulfill: *Asking me to be charming at 7 a.m. is a pretty tall order.* • A **tall tale** is a story that may or may not be true, but that contains details that are hard to believe. • USAGE: The opposite of tall is SHORT LENGTH.

tall THIS HIGH /tɔːl/ *adj* [-er/-est only] of a particular height • *Four of her friends are six feet or taller.*

tally COUNT /'tæl·i/ *n* [C usually sing] a record or count of a number of items • *The final tally was 21 for and 16 against.*

tally /'tæl·i/ *v* [I/T] • *The judges are tallying the scores.* [T] ○ *Zolga tallied* (= scored) *16 points.* [T] ○ *She tallies up our expenses each month.* [M]

tally AGREE /'tæl·i/ *v* [I/T] to match or agree • *I need to finish tallying the receipts.* [T] ○ *His statement doesn't tally with the other witnesses'.* [I]

Talmud /'tɑl·mʊd, 'tæl·məd/ *n* [U] the collection of Jewish laws and traditions relating to religious and social matters

talon /'tæl·ən/ *n* [C usually pl] a sharp nail on the foot of a bird that it uses esp. when hunting animals

tambourine /ˌtæm·bə'riːn/ *n* [C] a small drum with metal disks around its frame that make a ringing sound, and which is played by holding it in one hand and hitting it with the other or by shaking it

tame /teɪm/ *adj* (esp. of animals) not wild or fierce, either naturally or because of training or long involvement with humans • *Their goats seem very tame.* • If an entertainment is tame, it is not very exciting.

tame /teɪm/ *v* [T] • *He tames wild horses.*

tamper /'tæm·pər/ *v* [I] to touch or change something without permission or without enough knowledge of how it works • *Don't tamper with the boiler.*

tampon /'tæm·pɑn/ *n* [C] a small cylinder of cotton or other material which a woman puts in her vagina to absorb her MENSTRUAL blood

tan COLOR /tæn/ *adj* [-er/-est only], *n* [U] **-nn-** (of) a light brown or yellow-brown color • *a tan jacket*

tan SKIN /tæn/, **suntan** *n* [C usually sing] the darker skin that white people often get from being in the sun • *Ann's sundress shows off her tan.*

tan /tæn/, **tanned** *adj* **-nn-** • *a tanned face*

tan /tæn/ *v* [I] **-nn-** • *Judy tans easily.*

tan CHANGE INTO LEATHER /tæn/ *v* [T] **-nn-** to change (an animal skin) into leather by wetting it with special chemicals

tandem /'tæn·dəm/ *n* [C] two people or pieces of equipment that work together to achieve a result, or a team of two people or animals • *Several races were held, including one for father-and-son tandems.* • A tandem is also a bicycle built for two people. • If something is done **in tandem**, two people develop or work on it together or during the same period of time: *This director and composer have worked in tandem on several films.*

tang /tæŋ/ *n* [U] a pleasantly strong taste or smell • *the tang of sea air*

tangy /'tæŋ·i/ *adj* • *the tangy taste of garlic*

tangent /'tæn·dʒənt/ *n* [C] a subject or activity that is different than the one you are talking about or doing • *We were talking about exercise and got off on a tangent.*

tangential /tæn'dʒen·tʃəl/ *adj* • *a tangential issue*

tangerine /ˌtæn·dʒə'riːn/ *n* [C] a type of orange that is small and has a thin skin

tangible /'tæn·dʒə·bəl/ *adj* real and able to be shown or touched • *Drivers will see tangible improvements on major roadways.*

tangle /'tæŋ·gəl/ *n* [C] a messy mass of things • *She pulled the tangle of wires out of the box.* ○ *Her hair was in a tangle.*

taps

tangle /'tæŋ·gəl/ *v* [I/T] • *I tangled the cables and don't know which is which.* [T] ○ *Her hair tangles easily.* [I] ○ *Who tangled these wires up?* [M]

tangled /'tæŋ·gəld/ *adj* • *She ran a hand through her tangled hair.* ○ *The whole issue is getting too tangled* (= confused). • If someone is **tangled up** in something, they are involved in it: *I was not about to get* **tangled up** *in drugs.*

□**tangle with** /'---/ *v adv* [T] to disagree or fight with (someone) • *She's not afraid to tangle with her father.*

tango /'tæŋ·goʊ/ *n* [C] *pl* **tangos** a dance of Latin American origin for two people, or the music for this dance

tangy /'tæŋ·i/ *adj* • See at TANG.

tank CONTAINER /tæŋk/ *n* [C] a container that holds liquid or gas • *a water tank* ○ *fuel/gas/ oxygen tanks* ○ *a fish tank*

tanker /'tæŋ·kər/ *n* [C] a ship, aircraft, or truck built to carry liquids or gases • *an oil tanker* ○ *We watched a tanker coming into the harbor.*

tank up *(obj)*, **tank** *(obj)* **up** /'-'-/ *v prep* [I/M] *infml* to fill the fuel container of a car • *Dad asked me to tank the car up.* [M]

tank VEHICLE /tæŋk/ *n* [C] an enclosed military vehicle that travels on metal belts turned by wheels and is armed with large guns

tankard /'tæŋ·kərd/ *n* [C] a large drinking cup with a handle and usually a lid, mainly used for drinking beer

tanked /tæŋkt/ *adj* [not gradable] *slang* having had too much alcohol; drunk • *Randy was really tanked after that dinner party.*

tank top /'tæŋk'tɑp/ *n* [C] a type of shirt that covers the upper part of the body but not the arms and is pulled on over the head

tantalize /'tænt·əl,aɪz/ *v* [T] to excite or attract (someone) by offering or suggesting something that is unlikely to be provided or is not enough • *Her paintings tantalize the eye.*

tantalizing /'tænt·əl,aɪ·zɪŋ/ *adj* • *a tantalizing woman* ○ *a tantalizing question*

tantamount /'tænt·ə,maʊnt/ *adj* • If something is **tantamount to** something else, it is the same as or equal to it: *Her silence was tantamount to an admission of guilt.*

tantrum /'tæn·trəm/ *n* [C] a sudden period of extreme anger • *My mom would throw a tantrum if I wouldn't eat.*

tap HIT /tæp/ *v* [I/T] **-pp-** to hit (something) lightly and quickly, or to make a sound by doing this • *She tapped the back of his hand.* [T] ○ *Casey is tapping away at his computer.* [I] • To tap is also to TAP-DANCE.

tap /tæp/ *n* [C] • *She gave him a tap on the shoulder.* ○ *There was a tap at the door.*

tap DEVICE /tæp/ *n* [C] a device that controls the flow of liquid, esp. water; a FAUCET • *Please turn off the tap.* • Beer that is **on tap** is served from a BARREL (= large container) through a

tap. • *There are several new movies* **on tap** (= available) *this weekend.* • **Tap water** is the water that comes from the main supply of the local water system.

tap OBTAIN /tæp/ *v* [I/T] **-pp-** to obtain or make use of (something) • *Their try to tap the students' natural abilities.* [T] ○ *I can tap into computers all over the world.* [I]

tap LISTEN SECRETLY /tæp/ *v* [T] **-pp-** to secretly listen to (someone's communications with other people, esp. on a telephone) • *The FBI tapped her phone.*

tap /tæp/ *n* [C] • *They monitor my mail and use a telephone tap.*

tap–dance /'tæp·dæns/ *v* [I] to dance wearing shoes with metal pieces attached to the bottoms to make a rhythmic sound

tap dance /'tæp·dæns/ *n* [C] • *She does a tap dance with no music.*

tap dancing /'tæp,dæn·sɪŋ/ *n* [U] • *I took tap dancing when I was little.*

tape RECORDING MATERIAL /teɪp/ *n* [C/U] a magnetic strip made of thin plastic or metal used to record and play sound or sound and pictures; a CASSETTE or VIDEOTAPE • *Did you make a tape of Tyler's concert?* [C] ○ *Is that movie available on tape yet?* [U] • A **tape deck** is a machine that plays, and sometimes also records, sound, esp. music, on tape. • A **tape recorder** is a machine that is used for playing and recording sound.

tape /teɪp/ *v* [T] • *This song was taped* (= recorded) *live in concert.*

tape STICKY MATERIAL /teɪp/ *n* [U] a thin strip of material, usually sticky on one side, that is used to join things together • *masking/adhesive tape* ○ *packing/electrical tape* ○ (*trademark*) *Scotch tape* • A **tape measure** is a strip of cloth, plastic, or thin metal that can bend, that is marked in units and is used for measuring. Compare RULER.

tape /teɪp/ *v* [T] • *I taped a note on her door.* ○ *He taped the pages back together.*

taper /'teɪ·pər/ *v* [I/T] to become gradually narrower • *The drill bit is tapered on one end.* [T]

□**taper off** /'---'/ *v adv* [I] to become smaller in size or less in degree • *Mortgage rates may taper off in the spring.* ○ *The rain will taper off by morning.*

tapestry /'tæp·ə·stri/ *n* [C/U] a strong cloth with colored threads woven into it to create a picture or design, usually hung on a wall or used to cover furniture • *Mitchell creates tapestries that depict river landscapes.* [C]

tapeworm /'teɪp·wɜrm/ *n* [C] a PARASITE (= animal that lives in another organism and feeds from it) that sometimes lives inside the bowels of humans and other animals

taps /tæps/ *pl n* a musical signal played at military funerals and in the evening to tell soldiers that lights are to go off • *We heard the bugle playing taps.*

tar /tɑr/ n [U] a black substance, sticky when hot, used esp. for making roads • *The wooden buildings were covered with* **tar paper** (= heavy, tar-covered paper). • Tar is also one of the solids present in tobacco smoke.

tar /tɑr/ v [T] **-rr-** • *They'll be tarring our street this week.*

tarantula /təˈræn·tʃə·lə/ n [C] a type of large, hairy SPIDER (= insectlike creatures with eight legs), some of which have a painful bite

tardy /ˈtɑrd·i/ adj late in happening or arriving • *a tardy payment/delivery* ○ *You were tardy for school twice in the last week.*

target OBJECT AIMED AT /ˈtɑr·gət/ n [C] an object aimed and fired at during shooting practice, often a circle with a pattern of rings, or any object or place at which arrows, bullets, bombs, and other MISSILES are aimed • *I missed the target.* ○ *The plane passed over the target.* • A target is also a person or group attacked in some way: *The clinic has been a target of anti-abortion groups.* • **Target practice** is the act of shooting at targets in order to improve your skill.

target /ˈtɑr·gət/ v [T] • *Stores selling fur were targeted by animal-rights activists* (= chosen as places to aim disapproval at).

target INTENDED RESULT /ˈtɑr·gət/ n [C] a result or situation that you intend to achieve • *We met our sales target for the year.* • *Your calculations were* **on target** (= accurate).

target /ˈtɑr·gət/ v [T] to intend to achieve (an effect or purpose), or to direct toward (a particular person or group) • *The candidate's ads target conservative, middle-class voters.*

tariff /ˈtær·əf/ n [C] a government charge on goods entering or leaving a country • *import tariffs*

tarmac /ˈtɑr·mæk/ n [U] an area of ground covered with a hard surface, esp. the areas of an airport where aircraft park, land, and take off • *The plane was damaged on landing when it slid off the tarmac.*

tarnish /ˈtɑr·nɪʃ/ v [I/T] (of metal surfaces) to become less bright or a different color, esp. because of being in the air • *Silver tarnishes easily.* [I] • If something tarnishes your opinion of someone or something, you no longer believe they are as good as you had thought: *The scandal has tarnished the agency's reputation.* [T]

tarot /ˈtær·oʊ/ n [U] a set of cards with pictures on them that represent different parts of life and that are believed to show what will happen in the future

tarp /tɑrp/, **tarpaulin** /tɑrˈpɔː·lən, ˈtɑr·pə-/ n [C] a large piece of waterproof cloth or plastic that is used as a cover • *We hung a tarp above the picnic table to keep it dry if it rains.* ○ *A tarp was draped over the boxes.*

tarry /ˈtær·i/ v [I] literary to stay somewhere longer than you should • *The boy tarried awhile.*

tart SOUR /tɑrt/ adj tasting sour • *I like tart, firm apples, like Grannie Smiths.*

tart FOOD /tɑrt/ n [C] a small pastry with a usually sweet filling and no top • *fruit tarts* ○ *I ordered the blueberry tart.*

tartan /ˈtɑrt·ən/ n [C] a cloth woven in a pattern of different colored straight strips crossing each other at 90° angles, or the pattern itself; PLAID • *a tartan kilt*

tartar /ˈtɑrt·ər/ n [U] a hard yellow or brown substance that forms on the teeth • *I use a toothpaste that removes tartar.*

tartar sauce /ˈtɑrt·ər·sɔːs/ n [U] MAYONNAISE (= a cold, thick, creamy sauce) containing small pieces of herbs and vegetables, usually eaten with fish

task /tæsk/ n [C] a piece of work to be done, esp. one done regularly, unwillingly, or with difficulty • *Our first task after we moved was to find a doctor.* ○ *Making these pastries is no easy task.* ○ *They face the daunting task of rebuilding their economy.* • A **task force** is a group of people working together to do a particular job. • A **taskmaster** is someone who gives others a lot of work to do and expects them to work hard: *Our new teacher is a tough taskmaster.*

tassel /ˈtæs·əl/ n [C] a group of short strings or cords held together at one end and used as a hanging decoration esp. on hats, curtains, and furniture

taste FLAVOR /teɪst/ n [C/U] a feeling produced by a substance, esp. food or drink, when it is in your mouth, which tells you what it is and lets you appreciate it, or the ability to have this feeling • *Sugar has a sweet taste and lemons have a sour taste.* [U] ○ *I've lost my taste for* (= stopped enjoying the taste of) *spicy foods.* [U] • A taste of food is a small amount of it: *Have a taste of this sauce and tell me if it's too salty.* [C usually sing] ○ (fig.) *I had a taste of* (= I briefly experienced) *factory work last summer, and I didn't like it at all.* [C usually sing] • **Taste buds** are a group of cells, found esp. on the tongue, that allow different tastes to be recognized.

taste /teɪst/ v • *Coffee always tastes good in the morning.* [L] ○ *This tastes as if/as though/like it has pepper in it.* [I always + adv/prep] ○ *I hope you can taste the garlic.* [T] ○ *Taste* (= try a little of) *this and tell me if you like it.* [T]

tasteless /ˈteɪs·tləs/ adj (of food) not producing any feeling in the mouth that tells you what is being eaten • *The soup was watery and tasteless.*

tasty /ˈteɪ·sti/ adj (of food) producing a pleasant feeling in the mouth when eaten • *a tasty meal/dessert*

taste JUDGMENT /teɪst/ n [C/U] a person's ability to judge and appreciate what is good and suitable, esp. in art, beauty, style, and manners • *Barbara has good/poor taste in clothes.* [U] •

Taste is also a person's liking for or appreciation of something: *My son and I have very different tastes in music.* [C]

tasteful /'teɪst·fəl/ *adj* showing good judgment, esp. in style • *a tasteful Oriental rug*

tastefully /'teɪst·fə·li/ *adv*

tasteless /'teɪs·tləs/ *adj* showing such bad judgment as to be offensive • *They received more than 30 complaints from women who said the ads were sexist and tasteless.*

tatters /'tæt̬·ərz/ *pl n* • If something is **in tatters**, it is torn apart or destroyed: *His clothes were in tatters.*

tattered /'tæt̬·ərd/ *adj* (of cloth) damaged by continuous use or age, esp. torn in strips • *old tattered flags*

tattoo /tæ'tuː/ *n* [C] *pl* **tattoos** a permanent picture, pattern, or word on the surface of skin, created by using needles to put colors under the skin

tattoo /tæ'tuː/ *v* [T] **tattooing**, *past* **tattooed** • *An eagle was tattooed on his chest.*

taught /tɔːt/ *past simple and past participle of* TEACH

taunt /tɔːnt, tɑnt/ *v* [T] to try to make (someone) angry or upset, esp. by referring in a cruel way to something they may feel worried about or that makes them unusual • *The movie is about a serial killer who taunts the police with phone calls.*

taunt /tɔːnt, tɑnt/ *n* [C] • *At school, he had received jeers and taunts because of his mixed racial heritage.*

Taurus /'tɔːr·əs/ *n* [C/U] the second sign of the ZODIAC, covering the period April 20 to May 20 and represented by a BULL, or a person born during this period

taut /tɔːt/ *adj* stretched tightly; tight • *She tightened the strings of the guitar to make them taut.* ○ *(fig.) The story is a taut* (= exciting, with fast action) *psychological drama.*

tavern /'tæv·ərn/ *n* [C] a place where alcoholic drinks are sold and drunk

tawdry /'tɔː·dri, 'tɑ·dri/ *adj* showy, cheap, and of poor quality • *tawdry jewelry/furnishings*

tawny /'tɔː·ni, 'tɑn·i/ *adj* [-er/-est only] of a light yellow-brown color, like that of a lion • *tawny fur*

tax MONEY /tæks/ *n* [C/U] (an amount of) money paid to the government, usually a percentage of personal income or of the cost of goods or services bought • *income/sales/Social Security tax* [C] ○ *a cigarette/gasoline tax* [C] ○ *The senator proposed a tax increase/cut.* [U] • A **tax break** is a change in law that results in the opportunity to pay less in taxes: *With this change, high-income people will get a tax break.* • Income or expenses that are **tax-deductible** can be subtracted from your total income before you calculate the money that you have to pay to the government. • If something is **tax-exempt**, you do not have to pay any money to the government because of having

it or because of earning money from it: *tax-exempt municipal bonds* • A **taxpayer** is a person who pays taxes: *$130 million of taxpayers' money will be needed to build the new stadium.* • A **tax refund** is money returned to you from the government because you have paid more than you needed to for a particular year. • **Tax returns** are documents on which you report your income each year, showing how much money you owe the government or the government owes you. • A **tax shelter** is a financial arrangement by which a person can avoid paying the government the usual percentage of money earned from investments or income.

tax /tæks/ *v* [T] • *He maintained that corporations were not being taxed enough.*

taxable /'tæk·sə·bəl/ *adj* [not gradable] (of income) that must be included in calculating the percentage you have to pay the government

taxation /tæk'seɪ·ʃən/ *n* [U] the process by which the government of a country obtains money from its people in order to pay for its expenses

tax NEED EFFORT /tæks/ *v* [T] to be difficult for (someone) or use too much of (something) • *All he has to do is wash a few dishes—that shouldn't tax him too much.* ○ *Round-the-clock nursing care severely taxed her resources.*

taxing /'tæk·sɪŋ/ *adj* needing too much effort • *After the surgery, I couldn't do anything too taxing for a while.*

taxi VEHICLE /'tæk·si/, **taxicab** /'tæk·siː,kæb/, **cab** *n* [C] a car with a driver whom you pay to take you where you want to go • *The buses weren't running, so we took a taxi.*

taxi MOVE /'tæk·si/ *v* [I] **taxis**, **taxiing**, *past* **taxied** (of an aircraft) to move slowly on the ground • *After a half-hour delay, our plane taxied to the runway for takeoff.*

TB *n* [U] *abbreviation for* TUBERCULOSIS

tbsp. *n* [C] *pl* **tbsp.** *abbreviation for* TABLESPOON • *Add 1 tbsp. sugar.*

tea /tiː/ *n* [C/U] the dried and cut leaves of esp. the tea plant, or a drink made by pouring hot water onto these • *I'd love a nice cup of hot tea.* [U] ○ *We have a variety of herbal teas.* [C] • (*Br*) Tea is also a light meal eaten in the late afternoon or early evening. [U] • A **tea bag** is a small bag filled with tea leaves. • A **teapot** is a container with a handle and a SPOUT (= tube-shaped opening) in which you make tea and from which tea is served.

teach /tiːtʃ/ *v* [I/T] *past* **taught** /tɔːt/ to instruct or train (someone) or give someone knowledge of (something) • *I taught for a few years before becoming a lawyer.* [I] ○ *He taught his children English/taught English to his children.* [T] • To **teach school** is to be employed to instruct children in a school. • *I sat in the sun all day at the beach and got a terrible sunburn—it really taught me a lesson* (= showed me what not to do in the future).

teacher /'tiː·tʃər/ *n* [C] a person who instructs

or trains others, esp. in a school • *an English/ math/kindergarten teacher*

teaching /'tiː·tʃɪŋ/ *n* [C/U] • *I enjoy teaching, but it can be exhausting.*

teachings /'tiː·tʃɪŋz/ *pl n* an accepted set of beliefs, esp. religious beliefs • *the teachings of the Buddha/Koran/Catholic Church*

teak /tiːk/ *n* [U] the wood of a tree that grows in hot areas of the world, often used in furniture • *a teak table*

team /tiːm/ *n* [C] a number of people who act together as a group, either in a sport or in order to achieve something • *a baseball/basketball/football team* ○ *My favorite team is the New York Giants.* • A team is also two or more horses or other animals working together to pull a load: *a team of oxen* • A **teammate** is a player on your own team. • A **team player** is a member of a group who tries to do what is good for the group rather than what is good for just himself or herself. • **Team spirit** is a feeling of loyalty that the members of a group have toward others in the group. • **Teamwork** is the combined actions of a group of people working together effectively to achieve a goal.

team up /'tiːm'ʌp/ *v adv* [I] (of a person or group) to join another person or group, esp. in order to work together to do something • *She's an excellent cook and her friend is good at organizing parties, so they've teamed up to start a catering business.*

teamster /'tiːm·stər/ *n* [C] someone who drives a TRUCK as a job

tear EYE LIQUID /tɪr/ *n* [C usually pl] a drop of salty liquid that flows from the eye when it is hurt or as a result of strong emotion, esp. unhappiness or pain • *By the end of the movie I had tears in my eyes* (= I was ready to cry). • *The child had lost his money and was almost in tears* (= crying). • **Tear gas** is a gas that hurts the eyes and produces tears, and is used sometimes by police to control crowds. • (*infml*) A **tearjerker** is a book, movie, or other story that makes people cry or sad.

tearful /'tɪr·fəl/ *adj* with tears of sadness • *The school year ended with tearful farewells to favorite teachers and best friends.*

tear PULL APART /ter, tær/ *v* [I/T] *past simple* **tore** /tɔːr, toʊr/, *past part* **torn** /tɔːrn, toʊrn/ to pull or be pulled apart or away from something else, or to cause this to happen to (something) • *I caught my shirt on a nail and tore the sleeve.* [T] ○ *I tore a hole in my sleeve.* [T] ○ *Several pages had been torn out of the book.* [T] ○ *She tore off a strip of bandage and wrapped it around the wound.* [M] ○ *He angrily tore the letter up* (= into small pieces). [M] ○ *They tore down* (= destroyed) *the old building.* [M] ○ (*fig.*) *The political situation threatened to tear the country apart.* [M]

tear /ter, tær/ *n* [C] • *There's a tear in the lining of my coat.*

tear HURRY /ter, tær/ *v* [I always + adv/prep]

past simple **tore** /tɔːr, toʊr/, *past part* **torn** /tɔːrn, toʊrn/ *infml* to move hurriedly; to RUSH • *She was late and went tearing around the house looking for her car keys.*

□**tear apart** *obj*, **tear** *obj* **apart** /'--'-/ *v adv* [M] to criticize severely • *The critics tore apart his first novel, but he never gave up.*

□**tear** *obj* **away** /'--'-/ *v adv* [T] to persuade (someone) to leave with difficulty • *We were having such a good time that I had trouble tearing myself away from the party.*

□**tear into** /'-ˌ--/ *v prep* [T] to attack with strong words in order to show that (something or someone) is wrong or false • *He tore into the witnesses and exposed inconsistencies.*

□**tear off** *obj*, **tear** *obj* **off** /'-'-/ *v adv* [M] to quickly remove (clothes) • *She tore off her apron and ran into the living room.* [M]

tease /tiːz/ *v* [I/T] to intentionally annoy (a person or animal) by laughing at them or pretending to do something, often in a playful way • *Don't tease the dog by showing her the treat if you're not going to give it to her.* [T] ○ *I was only teasing* (= joking), *I didn't mean anything by it.* [I]

tease /tiːz/ *n* [C] a person who likes to annoy other people by laughing at them or pretending to do something

teaspoon /'tiːˌspuːn/ *n* (*abbreviation* **tsp.**) *n* [C] a small spoon used to put sugar in coffee or tea and for eating or measuring food, or the amount this spoon holds

teat /tiːt, tɪt/ *n* [C] the raised part of the female breast of a mammal through which an animal takes its mother's milk; a NIPPLE

technical /'tek·nɪ·kəl/ *adj* involving or needing special skills or knowledge, esp. in science or ENGINEERING (= the design and building of machines, equipment, and structures) • *The computer company ran into some last-minute technical problems with its new disk drives.*

technician /tek'nɪʃ·ən/ *n* [C] a worker trained with special skills or knowledge, esp. in how to operate machines or equipment used in science • *an X-ray technician* ○ *a laboratory technician*

technically /'tek·nɪ·kli/ *adv* according to rules or to the law • *Technically, we were still married, though we hadn't lived together for years.*

technicality /ˌtek·nɪ'kæl·əţ·i/ *n* [C] a decision based only on a specific rule or rules and not on any other consideration • *The case was dismissed on a technicality and will be retried at a later date.*

Technicolor *trademark* /'tek·nɪˌkʌl·ər/ *n* [U] a method of making movies in color, or the colors typically produced by this method

technique /tek'niːk/ *n* [C/U] a way of performing a skillful activity, or the skill needed to do it • *New surgical techniques are constantly being developed.* [C] ○ *The violinist's technique was flawless.* [U] • A technique is also a way of doing anything that involves planning: *She devised numerous techniques for annoying her father.* [C]

technology /tek'nɑl·ə·dʒi/ *n* [C/U] the methods for using scientific discoveries for practical purposes, esp. in industry • *computer/ medical/space technology* [U] • Technology is also a particular method by which science is used for practical purposes: *Dairy producers are experimenting with new technologies to reduce the cholesterol in milk.* [C]

technological /,tek·nə'lɑdʒ·ɪ·kəl/ *adj* • *We live in an era of rapid technological change.*

teddy bear /'ted·i·,ber, -,bær/ *n* [C] a soft toy bear

tedious /'ti:d·i·əs/ *adj* boring and tiring, esp. because long or repetitious • *tedious work/ tasks* ○ *Learning a new computer program can be a tedious process.*

tee /ti:/ *n* [C] in golf, the place where you begin to hit the ball at each HOLE (= area of play), or the small stick that holds the ball up so that you can hit it easily

tee *obj* **off** /'ti:'ɔːf/ *v adv* [T] *slang* to make (someone) very angry • *It really tees me off when she won't listen to me.*

teem /ti:m/ *v* [I] to rain heavily • *You can't go out without an umbrella—it's teeming out there.*

□**teem with** /'--/ *v prep* [T] to contain large numbers of (esp. animals or humans) • *a river teeming with trout* ○ *streets teeming with children/shoppers/traffic*

teeming /'ti:·mɪŋ/ *adj* [not gradable] filled with the activity of many people or things • *He was enchanted by the teeming streets and outdoor markets in the village.*

teenager /'ti:,neɪ·dʒər/, *short form* **teen** /ti:n/ *n* [C] a person who is 13 through 19 years old

teenage /'ti:·neɪdʒ/, **teenaged** /'ti:·neɪdʒd/, *short form* **teen** /ti:n/ *adj* [not gradable] • *They have two teenage sons.* ○ *Tomorrow's show will discuss teenage pregnancies.*

teens /ti:nz/ *pl n* • *If you are* **in** *your* **teens**, you are a teenager: *Both my daughters are in their teens.*

teeny /'ti:·ni/ *adj* [*-er/-est* only] *infml* small or

little • *a teeny baby* ○ *I can't help thinking you're a teeny bit jealous.*

teepee /'ti:·pi:/ *n* [C] a TEPEE

tee shirt /'ti:·ʃɜrt/ *n* [C] a T-SHIRT

teeter /'ti:t·ər/ *v* [I always + adv/prep] to appear to be about to fall while moving or standing • *They teetered around the room like a pair of drunks, helpless with laughter.* ○ *(fig.) The city is teetering on the brink/edge of* (= dangerously close to) *a financial calamity.*

teeter–totter /'ti:t·ə,tɑt·ər/ *n* [C] a SEESAW

teeth TOOTH /ti:θ/ *pl of* TOOTH

teeth POWER /ti:θ/ *pl n* effective force or power • *This committee can make recommendations but it has no real teeth to enforce them.*

teethe /ti:ð/ *v* [I] (of a baby or small child) to grow teeth • *The baby was often cranky because she was teething.*

Teflon /'tef·lɑn/ *n* [U] *trademark* a chemically-produced substance that is put on the inside of cooking pans to keep food from sticking

telecommunications /,tel·ə·kə,mju:·nə'keɪ·ʃənz/ *pl n* the sending and receiving of messages by computer, telephone, radio, and television, or the business of doing this

telecommuting /'tel·ə·kə,mju:ṭ·ɪŋ/ *n* [U] the activity of working for a company but staying at home and communicating with an office by computer and telephone

telecommuter /'tel·ə·kə,mju:ṭ·ər/ *n* [C] • *There are now millions of telecommuters with virtual offices.*

telegram /'tel·ə,græm/, **wire** *n* [C] a message sent by TELEGRAPH

telegraph /'tel·ə,græf/ *n* [U] a method of sending and receiving messages by electric signals that was used in the past, or the equipment used to do this

telegraph /'tel·ə,græf/, **wire** *v* [T] • *Reporters telegraphed details of the trial to their editors.*

telemarketing /'tel·ə,mɑr·kəṭ·ɪŋ/ *n* [U] the selling of goods or services by telephone

telepathy /tə'lep·ə·θi/ *n* [U] communication with another person by thinking rather than by using words or other signals

telephone /'tel·ə,foʊn/, **phone** *n* [C/U] a device for speaking to someone in another place

---

TELEPHONE

A **pay phone** (= public telephone) may be **coin operated** or used with a **phone card** that you buy in advance. You can also use a **calling card** with an identification number that allows you to pay for the call later. A **collect call** is paid for by the person who receives it.

To use a pay phone, **pick up** the **receiver/handset**. **Insert** (= put in) coins or a phone card into the slot. **Dial** the number by pressing the buttons.

If the phone you are calling is in use, you will hear a **busy signal**. If the phone is free, it will **ring**.

Telephone numbers

area code	phone number	extension
212	924-3900	Ext. 101

The numbers are usually pronounced separately: "area code seven one eight, eight three seven, nine o nine two." If the last four numbers of a phone number end in 000, they are usually said as thousand; for example, 825-4000 ("eight two five, four thousand"). If the last four numbers end

CONTINUED▷

TELEPHONE (*continued*)

in 00, they are usually said as hundred; for example, 924-3900 ("nine two four, thirty-nine hundred").

If you don't know a phone number, you can look it up in the **phone book/telephone directory**, or call **directory assistance**.

For help with a call, you can dial 0 to speak to the **operator**.

Making a telephone call

Telephone is not commonly used as a verb. Common phrases meaning "to telephone" include:

She said she'd **call/phone** *you next week.*
I'll **give** *you* **a call/ring** *tomorrow.*
I need to **make a call/phone ca** il).
Were there any **calls** *while I was out?*
Why don't you **call** *your grandmother* **up** *and see how she's doing?*
"Mr. Richards isn't in right now." "Could you ask him to **call** *me* **back**? *My number is 379-2194."*

At home, many people answer the phone by just saying Hello.

"Hello." "Hi, Kate. This is Jeff."

At work, people often answer by saying their own name or the name of the organization or department.

"Sales, Richard Moore." "Could I speak to/with Janet Rodriguez, please?"

Some people have an **answering machine** that plays a recorded message if they do not answer the telephone. This message usually ends with a "beep" sound: *Leave a message after the beep, and I'll* **get back to** *you as soon as I can.*

Businesses often have **voice mail** for leaving messages for people not at their desks.

---

by means of electrical signals • *Your telephone is ringing.* [C] ○ *I tried to reach her by telephone.* [U] • A **telephone book** is a **phone book**. See at PHONE. • A **telephone number** is a **phone number**. See at PHONE.

telephone /ˈtel·əˌfoʊn/ *v* [I/T] • *Palmer telephoned her attorney.*

telescope DEVICE /ˈtel·əˌskoʊp/ *n* [C] a cylindrical device that you look through to make objects that are far away look nearer and bigger

telescopic /ˌtel·əˈskɑp·ɪk/ *adj* [not gradable] • *My camera's telescopic lens lets me take great close-ups.*

telescope SHORTEN /ˈtel·əˌskoʊp/ *v* [T] to shorten (something) • *Redford telescoped decades of history into a two-hour TV show.*

telethon /ˈtel·əˌθɑn/ *n* [C] a long television show broadcast to collect money for a CHARITY (= an organization that helps people)

televise /ˈtel·əˌvaɪz/ *v* [T] to broadcast (an event or show) on television • *The game will be televised live from Cincinnati.*

televised /ˈtel·əˌvaɪzd/ *adj* [not gradable] • *a televised speech*

television /ˈtel·əˌvɪʒ·ən/ (*abbreviation* **TV**) *n* [C/U] a large box with a viewing screen which receives electrical signals and changes them into moving pictures and sound • *Is there anything interesting on television tonight?* [U] ○ *Most homes have televisions.* [C] • Television is also the programs that you watch, or the business of broadcasting them: *Your problem is that you watch too much television.* [U]

tell SAY /tel/ *v* [I/T] *past* **told** /toʊld/ to say (something) to (someone), esp. to give instructions or information; report • *Can you tell me*

how to get to the bus station? [T] ○ *She told about her travels overseas.* [I] • If you **tell the truth**, you speak honestly. • People sometimes say to **tell the truth** when they are about to admit something: *To tell the truth, I couldn't hear a word he said.* • People say **tell you what** to introduce an offer: *I tell you what, we'll pay your airfare.* • People say **I'll tell you**, **I'm telling you**, or **let me tell you** to emphasize a statement: *We've been waiting a long time for this, I'll tell you.* • LP SAY, TELL, TALK, AND SPEAK at SAY SPEAK

tell SHOW /tel/ *v* [T] *past* **told** /toʊld/ to show or give information in ways other than talking • *This light tells you when the battery is low.*

tell ORDER /tel/ *v* [T] *past* **told** /toʊld/ to order (someone) to do something • *I told you to be home by eleven.*

tell KNOW /tel/ *v* [I/T] *past* **told** /toʊld/ to know or recognize • *It's hard to tell which is better.* [I] ○ *It's easy to tell a robin by its red breast.* [T] ○ *I could tell that you were unhappy.* [+ (that) clause] ○ *This one is supposed to be better, but how can you tell the difference?* • To **tell time** is to read the time from a clock: *Has Adam learned to tell time yet?*

□ **tell off** *obj*, **tell** *obj* **off** /ˈ-ˈ-/ *v adv* [M] to criticize (someone) angrily • *Rob told off his boss, then quit.*

□ **tell on** /ˈ-ˌ-/ *v adv* [T] *infml* to give information, esp. about bad behavior, to someone in authority • *If you don't stop hitting, I'm going to tell on you.*

teller /ˈtel·ər/ *n* [C] a person in a bank who receives and pays out money to customers

telltale /ˈtel·teɪl/ *adj* important because of

showing information • *There are many telltale signs of drug abuse.*

temp /temp/ *n* [C] *infml* a person employed to work temporarily for a business

temp /temp/ *v* [I] *infml* • *I temped for a long time.*

temper STATE /'tem·pər/ *n* [C/U] the state of your mind or feelings • *John has a bad temper.* [C] • Temper is also strong emotion, esp. anger: *a fit of temper* [U] ○ *You need to learn to control your temper.* [C] • A **temper tantrum** is a sudden show of great anger.

temper LESSEN /'tem·pər/ *v* [T] to lessen the force or effect of (something) • *Perhaps you should temper your language.*

temperament /'tem·prə·mənt/ *n* [C/U] the emotional character or state of mind of a person or animal, as shown in their behavior • *Their temperaments are very different.* [C] ○ *Trudy has the nicest temperament of all our dogs.* [U]

temperamental /ˌtem·prə'ment·ᵊl/ *adj* [not gradable] expressive of your emotional character • *a temperamental young man* • If a machine is temperamental, it sometimes works and sometimes does not: *Our VCR can be temperamental.*

temperate /'tem·pə·rət/ *adj* [not gradable] not extreme; within a middle range • *The climate here is pretty temperate.*

temperature /'tem·pə·rə·tʃər, -ˌtʃʊr/ *n* [C/U] the measured amount of heat in a place or in the body • *Temperatures should reach the 50s today.* [C] ○ *An increase in temperature is normal.* [U] • A temperature is also a fever: *You have a temperature.* [C]

tempest /'tem·pəst/ *n* [C] *literary* a violent storm • A **tempest in a teapot** is something of no importance that causes a great deal of excitement: *It seemed like an innocent remark, but it set off a tempest in a teapot.*

tempestuous /tem'pes·tʃə·wəs/ *adj* violently emotional • *They finally divorced, ending their tempestuous marriage.*

template /'tem·plət/ *n* [C] a shape made of metal, plastic, or paper which is used to make copies or to guide someone in cutting something • *The use of templates is crucial to stone carving.*

temple BUILDING /'tem·pəl/ *n* [C] a building used for religious worship

temple PART OF HEAD /'tem·pəl/ *n* [C] the flat area at each side of the upper part of the face

tempo /'tem·poʊ/ *n* [C/U] *pl* **tempos** the speed of a movement or activity, or the speed at which a piece of music is played • *Tracy likes the tempo of city life.* [U] ○ *It sounded like they were playing at different tempos.* [C]

temporary /'tem·pəˌrer·i/ *adj* [not gradable] not lasting or PERMANENT • *a temporary condition* ○ *a temporary contract*

temporarily /ˌtem·pə'rer·ə·li/ *adv* [not grad-

able] • *The player was temporarily suspended from the tournament.*

tempt /tempt/ *v* [T] to encourage (someone) to want to do something, esp. something they should not or usually would not do • *I'm trying to diet—don't tempt me with that cake!* • If you **tempt fate**, you take a foolish risk because you depend too much on luck: *Leaving your door unlocked is just tempting fate.*

temptation /temp'teɪ·ʃən/ *n* [C/U] • *It's not easy to resist temptation.* [U] ○ *Ice cream is always a real temptation for me.* [C]

tempting /'temp·tɪŋ/ *adj* [not gradable] • *Any free offer is always tempting.*

ten /ten/ *number* 10 • *The twins are ten.* ○ *a ten-seat minivan* • Ten can also mean ten o'clock.
• LP NUMBERS

tenth /tenθ/ *adj, adv* [not gradable], *n* [C] • *My sister spoke tenth, right after me.* ○ *It was the tenth of May.* [C] • A tenth is one of ten equal parts of something. [C]

tenacious /tə'neɪ·ʃəs/ *adj* [not gradable] unwilling to accept defeat or stop doing or having something • *Seles is a tenacious opponent—she never gives in.*

tenacity /tə'næs·əṭ·i/ *n* [U] • *They cling with admirable tenacity to their traditions.*

tenant /'ten·ənt/ *n* [C] a person who rents a room, a building, or land • *For years, they were tenants on my father's property.*

tend BE LIKELY /tend/ *v* [I] to be likely to happen or to have a particular characteristic or effect • *We tend to eat at home.* ○ *Children tend to be like their parents.*

tendency /'ten·dən·si/ *n* [C] • *She has a tendency to work late.* ○ *There's a growing tendency to try kids as adults.*

tend CARE /tend/ *v* [T] to care for (something or someone) • *He carefully tends his garden all summer.*

tender GENTLE /'ten·dər/ *adj* gentle, caring, or sympathetic • *He gave her a tender kiss.* • A **tenderhearted** person is gentle and caring: *He was extremely tenderhearted with little children.*

tender PAINFUL /'ten·dər/ *adj* easily hurt; painful • *My arm was very tender after the injection.*

tender SOFT /'ten·dər/ *adj* (of food) easily cut or chewed • *My steak was juicy and tender.*

tenderize /'ten·dəˌraɪz/ *v* [T] • *Certain ingredients and cooking methods tenderize tough foods.*

tender YOUNG /'ten·dər/ *adj* [not gradable] *literary* young and not experienced • *At the tender age of 17, he joined the army.*

tender OFFER /'ten·dər/ *v* [T] to offer something, usually in writing, or to make (an offer in writing to do something) • *The Secretary wants to leave but has not yet tendered his resignation.* ○ *This is the richest contract ever tendered to a baseball player.*

tender /'ten·dər/ n [C] a formal offer, esp. to buy something

tendon /'ten·dən/ n [C] a strong cord that connects a muscle to a bone and allows movement, esp. of the arms, legs, and head

tendril /'ten·drəl/ n [C] a thin stem of a plant that twists and curls, or anything similar, such as a curl of hair

tenement /'ten·ə·mənt/ n [C] a type of apartment building, esp. one with many small apartments that is in a poor area

tenet /'ten·ət/ n [C] a principle that is an accepted belief of a particular group • *A major tenet of the women's movement has been that society needs their talents.*

tennis /'ten·əs/ n [U] a game played on a specially marked playing area in which two or four people use RACKETS to hit a small ball across a center net • *A* **tennis shoe** *is a* SNEAKER, esp. one designed especially for playing tennis.

tenor VOICE /'ten·ər/ n [C] a man's singing voice in the highest range, or a singer or musical instrument with this range

tenor CHARACTER /'ten·ər/ n [U] the character or usual pattern of something • *Suddenly the tenor of the meeting changed, and people started insulting each other.*

tense STIFF /tens/ adj tight and stiff • *Relax! Why are you so tense?*

tense /tens/ v [I/T] • *He tensed his body just before diving from the high board.* [T] ∘ *She tensed up as the car went faster and faster.* [I]
tension /'ten·tʃən/ n [U] • *We need more tension in the wires, so pull them tighter.*

tense NERVOUS /tens/ adj nervous, anxious, unable to relax, or causing anxiety • *She was very tense as she waited for the interview.* ∘ *The family was faced with a tense financial situation.*
tension /'ten·tʃən/ n [U] • *The tension was unbearable as we waited for our exam results.*

tense VERB FORM /tens/ n [C] specialized (in grammar) any of the forms of a verb which show the time at which an action happened • *"I sing" is in the present tense and shows action happening now, and "I will sing" is in the future tense, showing action that will happen later.*

tent /tent/ n [C] a movable shelter, usually made of a strong cloth supported by poles and held in position by ropes fixed to the ground • *We pitched our tents near the stream.* • PIC CAMP, PEGS

tentacle /'tent·ɪ·kəl/ n [C] a long, thin, arm-like part of some sea animals, such as the OCTOPUS and JELLYFISH • PIC OCTOPUS

tentative /'tent·ət·ɪv/ adj not certain or confident • *We have tentative plans to go to Hawaii in February.*
tentatively /'tent·ət·ɪv·li/ adv • *We have tentatively agreed to buy that house.*

tenth /tenθ/ adj, adv, n See at TEN.

tenuous /'ten·jə·wəs/ adj weak, unimportant, or doubtful • *The aging dictator's hold on power is tenuous.*

tenure /'ten·jər/ n [U] the period of time when someone holds a job, esp. an official position, or the right to keep a job permanently • *During his tenure as mayor, relations with the police department worsened.* ∘ *Michelle has tenure in her new teaching position.*

tepee, teepee, tipi /'tiː·piː/ n [C] a type of round tent made from animal skins and supported by a frame of poles, used by some American Indians

tepid /'tep·əd/ adj [not gradable] (of liquid) not very warm, or (of feelings or actions) not very strong • *There is only tepid support in Congress for the proposal.*

tequila /tə'kiː·lə/ n [C/U] a strong alcoholic drink originally from Mexico

term TIME /tɜrm/ n [C] a period of time during which something lasts • *Watson's term as chairman expired last month.* ∘ *He served a prison term for manslaughter.* ∘ *This budget plan is good for the long term but it hurts in the short term.* • A term can be one of the periods into which a year is divided at a school or college: *I'm taking computer programming during the fall term.* • A **term paper** is the main report written by a student for a particular class or subject during a school term.

term WORD /tɜrm/ n [C] a word or expression used in relation to a particular subject • *Erikson is said to have coined the term "identity crisis."* • See also TERMS.

term /tɜrm/ v [T] • *None of the problems was termed serious.*

terminal COMPUTER /'tɜr·mən·əl/ n [C] a piece of equipment used for communicating with a computer processor, esp. a keyboard and screen • *a computer terminal* ∘ *Terminals at checkout counters let shoppers use credit cards.*

terminal DEADLY /'tɜr·mən·əl/ adj [not gradable] (of a disease or illness) leading to death • *His mom has a terminal illness.*
terminally /'tɜr·mən·əl·i/ adv [not gradable] • *terminally ill cancer patients*

terminal BUILDING /'tɜr·mən·əl/ n [C] the place where a train, bus, aircraft, or ship begins or ends a trip, or the building used by passengers who are arriving or leaving • *Your flight leaves from Terminal 3.*

terminal ELECTRICITY /'tɜr·mən·əl/ n [C] a point at which a connection can be made to an electrical CIRCUIT (= system through which electricity flows)

terminate /'tɜr·mə,neɪt/ v [I/T] slightly fml to end or stop, or to cause (something) to end or stop • *Trains that used to terminate in Hoboken now run into New York.* [I] ∘ *It sounded like she was trying to terminate the conversation.* [T] • If an employee is terminated, they no longer have their job: *Employees can be terminated if they test positive for drugs.* [T]

TENSES

Present simple

Used to express events with no particular time, for example, general truths, complete events, and unchanging situations in present time.

Water boils at 212°F (100°C).	Expressing general or scientific truth.
Her sister works in Chicago.	A situation that does not change.
We visit my parents every Christmas.	Something that happens regularly.
I agree. • I think you're right	Conditions, beliefs, and feelings.
The flight to Miami leaves at 2 o'clock.	Information about arrangements.
As soon as I get there, I'll call you.	Future time, after the conjunctions: *after, before, as soon as, until, when.*
Earthquake kills 500 • So then he says, "I'm getting out of here."	Describing past events, for example, in newspaper headlines.

Continuous (or progressive) form

Used to express actions or events that are, were, or will be happening at a particular point in time or that have reached a stage somewhere between their beginning and their end. When the continuous form is used with verbs referring to very brief events, it shows that the event is repeated.

Your bag is hitting my leg. Can you move it?

Verbs such as *seem, know, own,* or *wish,* which refer to conditions rather than to events that happen, are rarely used in a continuous form.

Present continuous

Used to express actions or events happening now or developing.

He's watching TV. • It's raining hard.	Action or event happening now.
The weather's getting colder.	Event or change now developing.

Present continuous + time phrase

I'm flying to Paris tomorrow. • The latest Spielberg film is opening soon.	Future plans; fixed events for which arrangements have been made.
They're staying with me for a few days.	Temporary situation.

Present continuous with *always*

The children are always arguing.	Events that tend to happen often.
Puppies are always growing.	Events that do not stop.

<u>being</u> + adjective describing behavior or character

You're not being very helpful.	Temporary behavior or quality.

Past simple

Used to express completed actions and events in past time.

They built the bridge ten years ago.	Reporting completed events in the past.
I lived in Toronto when I was a child.	Completed periods in the past.
She recorded six songs before she made her first hit single in 1990.	Completed events or actions following each other in past time.
I wanted to see the manager. Is she free?	Polite expressions of desires.

Past continuous

Used to express incomplete or interrupted past actions or events.

"What were you doing at 6 p.m.?" "I think we were walking home."	Event incomplete at a point in the past.
The plane was approaching the airport when an engine failed. • While I was crossing the street I noticed a crowd.	Past action or event with another one that interrupts it or occurs during it.

Present perfect

Used to express connections between completed or unchanging actions or events of the past and the present. This tense is not generally used when a reference is given to a particular point or period in the past (*last week, in January, at 3 a.m.*).

She's been all over the world. • Sorry, I don't know you. Have we met? • He's visited Japan twice since 1995.	Completed actions or events at some time before now (no particular time given).

(CONTINUED)

TENSES (*continued*)

That's twice I've made that mistake today! • *"Have you* **ever** *flown?" "No, I've* **never** *even been on a ship."*	Actions or events in periods of time not yet finished. Used with *ever, never,* or *yet* to refer to any time up to now.
"How long have you lived here?" "I've been here **(for)** *a year now."*	Unchanging situations in period of time up to now.
He's won!	Achievements.
We won't leave until I've checked that all the doors are locked.	Future time. Used after some conjunctions: *after, before, as soon as, until, when.*

Present perfect continuous

Used to express connections between incomplete actions or events in the past and the present.

Who's been drinking my coffee? It's nearly all gone!	Effects of past action that are noticeable now.
They've been fixing that house for ages.	Events over periods of time up to now.
He's been getting to work late recently.	Situation up to now, seen as temporary.

Past perfect

Used to express complete actions or events that happened before another point in the past.

When Paul returned to the parking lot his car had been stolen.	Connects a point in the past to a still earlier event (no particular time given).
Pat had reported to work at seven that night.	Action or event at a particular time before the main time the writer is referring to.
He had been with the company for 25 years when he retired.	Period of time up to a point in the past.

Past perfect continuous

Used to express actions or events happening before a point in the past.

It was sunny, but we could see that it had been raining earlier.	Effects of a still earlier event or action noticeable at a point in the past.
He had been playing tennis for an hour when he started to feel dizzy.	Something that was happening up to a point in the past.

Expressing the idea of the future

Future with <u>will</u>

Used to suggest certainty and to state what you know will happen.

It will rain tomorrow.	Predicting a complete future event.
I'll write and complain!	Stating a decision.
It will be raining in the morning.	Predicting a continuing future event.
I'll be standing under the station clock when you arrive.	States a future event that will happen when another event occurs.

Future with <u>going to</u>

Used to connect the present with the future.

Look at those black clouds—it's going to rain soon.	There is a reason now to believe that an event will happen in the future.
My sister's going to have a baby.	The process has now started.

Future with <u>be</u> + *to*-infinitive

Used to describe future fixed arrangements. Implies that the arrangements were made by someone else.

He's to have surgery tomorrow. • *You're to collect the keys at 9:30.*

Present continuous + time phrase (see examples above at PRESENT CONTINUOUS

Present simple + time phrase (see examples above at PRESENT SIMPLE)

Future Perfect

Used to say that something will already have happened before a certain time in the future.

I'm late. The meeting will have started by the time I get to the office.

LP **Auxiliary Verbs**

termination /ˌtɜr·məˈneɪ·ʃən/ n [C/U] • The contract provides for termination after two years. [U]

terminology /ˌtɜr·məˈnɑl·ə·dʒi/ n [U] special words or expressions used in relation to a particular subject or activity • religious terminology ○ scientific terminology

termite /ˈtɜr·mɑɪt/ n [C] a small, pale insect that eats wood

terms /tɜrmz/ pl n the conditions that are part of an agreement or arrangement, or the features of an activity or idea • He violated the terms of the agreement. ○ She considers results in purely economic terms. ○ I want to leave this job on my own terms. • If two people are on good/bad/friendly terms, they have a good/bad/friendly relationship with one another: He was on good terms with important people in Brazil. • She organized the classification of stars **in terms of** (= according to) their surface temperature. • See also TERM WORD.

terrace /ˈter·əs/ n [C] a flat area outside a building, often with a stone floor, or a narrow, flat strip of land on the slope of a hill that is used for growing crops

terra cotta /ˌter·əˈkɑt̬·ə/ n [U] hard, baked, red-brown clay • terra-cotta tiles

terra firma /ˌter·əˈfɜr·mə/ n [U] dry or solid land, when compared with the sea or air • He stepped off the ladder onto terra firma.

terrain /təˈreɪn/ n [U] an area of land, esp. when considering its natural features • rugged mountain terrain

terrestrial /təˈres·tri:·əl/ adj [not gradable] slightly fml relating to the planet earth, or living or existing on the land rather than in the sea or air • Newton investigated terrestrial and celestial motion. ○ marine and terrestrial environments

terrible /ˈter·ə·bəl/ adj very unpleasant or serious or bad • I saw terrible things happen. ○ My mother was a terrible cook.

terribly /ˈter·ə·bli/ adv (usually about something bad or unpleasant) very much • I'm terribly disappointed I couldn't be there. • Sometimes terribly is used to emphasize something good: I'm terribly excited about tonight's show. • LP VERY, COMPLETELY, AND OTHER INTENSIFIERS

terrier /ˈter·iː·ər/ n [C] any of several types of small, active dogs

terrific VERY GOOD /təˈrɪf·ɪk/ adj very good or enjoyable • Kate looks absolutely terrific tonight.

terrific VERY GREAT /təˈrɪf·ɪk/ adj used to emphasize the great amount or degree of something • This book has had a terrific influence on me.

terrifically /təˈrɪf·ɪ·kli/ adv • That's not a terrifically good idea.

terrify /ˈter·ə·fɑɪ/ v [T] to frighten (someone) severely • His looks are enough to terrify anyone.

terrified /ˈter·ə·fɑɪd/ adj • She's always been terrified of spiders.

terrifying /ˈter·ə·fɑɪ·ɪŋ/ adj • a terrifying experience

territory /ˈter·ə·tɔːr·i, -ˌtoʊr·i/ n [C/U] an area of land, sea, or space, esp. when it belongs to or is connected with a particular country, person, or animal • Maryland gave up territory to form Washington, DC. [U] ○ The UN is sending aid to the occupied territories. [C] • If something **comes/goes with the territory** it is part of a particular activity: Criticism goes with the territory in politics.

territorial /ˌter·əˈtɔːr·iː·əl, -ˈtoʊr-/ adj [not gradable] • He served as territorial governor. ○ Some animals are territorial (= they defend particular areas against other animals).

terror /ˈter·ər/ n [C/U] extreme fear, or violent action that causes fear • She was screaming in terror as the flames got closer. [U] ○ You can't hide from the terrors of the world. [C] • A terror is also a child who behaves badly and is difficult to control: My brother is a little terror. [C]

terrorize /ˈter·əˌrɑɪz/ v [T] • Criminal gangs terrorized the neighborhood.

terrorism /ˈter·əˌrɪz·əm/ n [U] violent action for political purposes • We're fighting both domestic and international terrorism.

terrorist /ˈter·ə·rəst/ n [C] • A terrorist with a truckload of explosives attacked the military base.

terse /tɜrs/ adj using few words • He was shouting terse orders for vehicles to pull over.

tersely /ˈtɜr·sli/ adv • "Storm coming," he said tersely.

TESL /ˈtes·əl/ n [U] abbreviation for teaching English as a second language

TESOL /ˈtiː·sɑl, -sɔːl/ n [U] abbreviation for teaching English to speakers of other languages

test /test/ n [C] a set of questions or practical activities that show what someone knows or what someone or something can do or is like • a spelling test • A test is also a medical examination of part of your body or of something from your body: an eye test ○ All players have to take a drug test. • A test is also an act of using something to find out whether it is working correctly or how effective it is: a safety test • The **test of time** is how well something continues to work over time: The US Constitution has withstood the test of time. • A **test ban** is an agreement between countries to stop testing the effectiveness of nuclear weapons. • A **test case** is a case in a court that establishes principles which are considered in other similar cases in the future. • A **test pilot** is someone whose job is to fly new aircraft in order to make sure that they work correctly. • A **test tube** is a small, glass tube with one closed end which is used in some scientific experiments.

test /test/ v [T] • Multiple-choice questions

tested the students' knowledge. ○ We test every component we make. • To test someone or something can also be to present them with a situation which shows how good they are at dealing with difficulties: His generation was tested by a world war. • To **test the water(s)** is to find out whether something is likely to be successful before you do or try it: Candidates like to test the waters before running for office.

testing /'tes·tɪŋ/ n [U] • Statewide testing begins this fall.

testament /'tes·tə·mənt/ n [C/U] proof of something • He is a walking testament to the value of hard work. [C usually sing] • A testament is also a WILL DEATH PLAN. [C]

test–drive /'tes·draɪv/ v [T] past simple **test-drove** /'tes·droʊv/, past part **test-driven** /'tes ‚drɪv·ən/ to drive (a car that you are considering buying) in order to see if you like it

test drive /'tes·draɪv/ n [C] • We went for a test drive in the new Toyota.

testicle /'tes·tɪ·kəl/ n [C] pl **testicles** or medical **testes** /'tes·tiːz/ either of the two round male sex organs that produce sperm and are enclosed in the SCROTUM (= bag of skin) behind and below the penis

testify /'tes·tə‚fɑɪ/ v to speak seriously about something, esp. to tell what you know about a case in a court of law after you have officially promised to tell the truth • Elizabeth testified before a grand jury. [I] ○ One witness testified that she saw the soldier shoot. [+ that clause]

testimony /'tes·tə‚moʊ·ni/ n [C/U] a spoken or written statement that something is true, esp. one given in a court of law, or the act of giving such a statement • The value of their testimony is questionable. [U]

testosterone /tes'tɑs·tə‚roʊn/ n [U] a male HORMONE (= chemical substance produced in the body) that causes growth and change in older boys and makes men able to make a woman pregnant

testy /'tes·ti/ adj lacking patience and feeling upset • My wife gets testy if we don't have dessert.

tetanus /'tet·ən·əs/ n [U] an infectious disease that causes the muscles esp. around the mouth to stiffen

tête–à–tête /‚tet·ə'tet, ‚teɪt·ə'teɪt/ n [C] a private conversation between two people • a romantic tête-à-tête

tether /'teð·ər/ n [C] a rope, chain, or other device used to attach a person or animal to a fixed object

tether /'teð·ər/ v [T] • Asthma kept him tethered to an oxygen tank.

Tex–Mex /'tek'smeks/ adj [not gradable] referring to the Mexican-American culture existing in Texas and the southwestern US • In Texas the food is all Tex-Mex cooking and barbecue.

text /tekst/ n [C/U] written or printed material • The text is based on Irish legends. [U] •

A text or **textbook** is a school book: Several of his texts were classics. [C usually pl] ○ medical textbooks

textual /'teks·tʃə·wəl/ adj [not gradable] relating to written or printed material • textual errors/analysis

textbook /'teks·bʊk/ adj [not gradable] (of an example) usual or typical • President Johnson has been called a textbook example of a politician without morals.

textile /'tek·stɑɪl, 'teks·təl/ n [C] a cloth, esp. one that is woven • Imports of textiles rose last year.

texture /'teks·tʃər/ n [C/U] the quality of something that can be known by touch, or the degree to which something is rough or smooth or soft or hard • Wall hangings add texture to a room. [U] ○ She uses unique colors and textures in her paintings. [C]

textured /'teks·tʃərd/ adj • textured fabrics ○ (fig.) The book is a richly textured re-creation of life in the early 1900s (= it has a lot of detail).

than /ðæn, ðən/ prep, conjunction used to join two parts of a comparison • My brother's older than you. ○ You're earlier than usual. • Than is used with more or less to compare numbers or amounts: He wrote more than 20 books. ○ He spent less than a year there.

thank /θæŋk/ v [T] to express appreciation to (someone) for something they have done • Don't thank me, thank my father—he paid for it. • (usually disapproving) If you thank someone for something bad, you mean that they are responsible for it: You can thank John for this disaster. • You can say **thank God/goodness/ heaven(s)** to express happiness that something bad has been avoided or has finished: Spring is coming at last, thank goodness.

thankful /'θæŋk·fəl/ adj pleased or grateful • I was thankful that school was over. [+ that clause]

thankfully /'θæŋk·fə·li/ adv • It's been hard work, but thankfully it's finished.

thankless /'θæŋ·kləs/ adj (of a job or piece of work) unlikely to be appreciated • a thankless task

thanks /θæŋks/ pl n appreciation and pleasure because of something that has been done for you • I want to offer a word of thanks to all those who helped. • **Thanks to** means because of: Thanks to Sandy, I found this great apartment.

Thanksgiving /θæŋks'gɪv·ɪŋ/, **Thanksgiving Day** n [C/U] a national holiday on the fourth Thursday in November in the US and on the second Monday in October in Canada, when families get together for a big meal and express their appreciation for life, health, etc.

thank you /'θæŋ·kjuː/, infml **thanks** /θæŋks/ exclamation used to express appreciation to someone for offering or giving you something, for helping you, or for asking how you are feeling • *Thank you for calling.* ○ *Thanks for cleaning up.* ○ *"How are you?" "Fine, thank you."*

thank you /ˈθæŋ·kjuː/ *n* [C] something you say or do to express your appreciation for something • *You deserve a big thank you.* ○ *He wrote a thank you note to his grandmother for the birthday present.*

that SOMETHING NOT HERE /ðæt, ðət/ *adj* [not gradable], *pronoun pl* **those** /ðoʊz/ used to refer to a person, object, event, etc., separated from the speaker by distance or time, or to something that has been referred to before, or to point to a particular thing • *This peach isn't ripe—can I have that one* (= the one farther away) *on the table?* ○ *Put that box* (= the particular box referred to) *down before you drop it.* ○ *Where's that pen* (= the one I was using earlier)*?* ○ *If she could play like that* (= the way she is now playing) *every day, she'd be a star.* • That is also used to make a connection with an earlier statement: *My usual train was canceled. That's why I'm late.* ○ *I didn't know she'd been so ill. That's terrible.* • *She called him an imbecile, and* **at that** (= immediately after that) *he stormed out of the room.* • You say **that is** when you want to give further details or be more exact about something: *I should be there by seven, that is, unless there's a lot of traffic.* • (*infml*) **That's it** means something has ended: *It's been nice talking to you, but that's it for now—I've got to go back to work.* • **That's life** means you have to accept what happens, even if it is not exactly what you wanted: *She's had some good jobs and some not so good, but that's life.* • **That's that** means something has ended and will not continue: ○ *I won't agree to it and that's that* (= I will not discuss it any longer). • Compare THIS THING REFERRED TO. • LP DETERMINERS

that INTRODUCING A CLAUSE /ðæt, ðət/ *conjunction* used to introduce a clause reporting something or giving further information, although it can often be omitted • *She said (that) she'd pick up Michael after work.* ○ *It's possible (that) there'll be a job opening in a few weeks.* ○ *It was so dark (that) I couldn't see anything.*

that USED TO REFER /ðæt, ðət/ *pronoun* used to show what particular thing is being referred to • *Have you been to the new restaurant that just opened?* ○ *That's the guy I was talking about.*

that AS MUCH /ðæt, ðət/ *adv* [not gradable] as much as suggested • *It cost at least that much, if not more.* ○ *The movie really wasn't that good* (= was not very good).

thaw /θɔː/ *v* to cause (something frozen and hard) to become warmer and often softer or liquid, or to rid of (frozen material) by warming • *Remove the meat from the freezer and let it thaw.* [I] ○ *It may take a couple of hours to thaw (it) out.* [I/M]

thaw /θɔː/ *n* [C usually sing] a period of warmer weather when snow and ice begin to melt • *With the spring thaw, the rivers and lakes swelled.* • A thaw is also a change to a friendlier attitude esp. between people or countries that were enemies: *It was hoped that the agreement to exchange athletes would lead to a thaw in relations between the two countries.*

the PARTICULAR /ðiː, ðə/ *definite article* used before a noun to refer to something that a listener or reader will understand as a particular thing because it is clear which one is intended • *I just bought a new shirt and tie. The shirt was expensive, but the tie wasn't.* ○ *There's someone at the front door.* ○ *I'll pick you up at the airport at 6 o'clock.* • "The" is used before some nouns to refer to a type of activity or thing intended: *Let's go to the movies.* • "The" is used to refer to things or people when only one exists at any one time: *the Statue of Liberty* • "The" is also used before superlatives and other words, such as first or only or numbers: *What's the highest mountain in North America?* ○ *She's leaving on the 24th of May.* • "The" can mean each or every: *My car gets 30 miles to the gallon.* • When used before some adjectives, "the" changes the adjective into a noun to refer to all of what is described: *the homeless/poor/rich* • You can use "the" before a singular noun to refer to all the things or people represented by that noun: *Nicole is learning to play the piano.* • You use "the" before numbers that refer to periods of 10 years: *the 1930s* • LP ARTICLES, DETERMINERS

the YOUR /ðiː, ðə/ *definite article* used instead of your, my, his, her, etc. • *He tapped me on the* (= my) *shoulder.* ○ *How are Grace and the* (= her) *kids?* • LP ARTICLES, DETERMINERS

the ENOUGH /ðiː, ðə/ *definite article* enough • *He hasn't got the experience for this kind of work.* • LP ARTICLES, DETERMINERS

theater BUILDING , **theatre** /ˈθiː·ət̬·ər, θiːˈet̬·ər/ *n* [C] a building, room, or outside structure with rows of seats, each row usually higher than the one in front, from which people can watch a performance, a movie, or another activity • *Lincoln Plaza Cinema has five movie theaters.*

theater PERFORMING ARTS , **theatre** /ˈθiː·ət̬·ər, θiːˈet̬·ər/ *n* [U] the art or activity of writing and performing plays, or the public performance of plays • *We have tickets to the theater tonight* (= to watch a performance).

theatrical /θiːˈæ·trɪ·kəl/ *adj* • *theatrical performances* • Theatrical also means intended to attract attention, as if acting in a play: *He threw out both arms to greet me in a theatrical gesture.*

theft /θeft/ *n* [C/U] the act of taking something that belongs to someone else and keeping it; stealing • *car theft* [U]

their /ðer, ðær, ðər/ *pronoun* [pl] belonging to or connected with them; the possessive form of they, used before a noun • *It was their money, and they could spend it as they liked.* •

Their is also used to refer to a person whose sex is not known: *Someone forgot to take their umbrella.* • LP DETERMINERS

theirs /ðerz, ðærz/ *pronoun* [pl] belonging to them, or that which belongs to them • *Here's my car. Where's theirs?*

them /ðem, ðəm/ *pronoun* [pl] the things or people being spoken about, who have already been mentioned; the objective form of they • *I lost my keys and I can't find them anywhere.* • Them is also used to refer to a person whose sex is not known: *As each person arrives, we ask them to fill out a form.*

themselves /ðem'selvz, ðəm-/ *pronoun* [pl] the people being spoken about, the reflexive form of they • *The girls made themselves sandwiches for lunch.* • Themselves is sometimes used to emphasize the subject or object of a sentence: *The police themselves apologized for overreacting.* • *They were left* **by themselves** (= alone). • If people do something **by themselves**, they do it alone or without help from anyone: *The children set up the tent (all) by themselves.* • If people have something **to themselves**, they have it for their own use only: *When their youngest child went off to college, they had the whole house to themselves.* •
LP REFLEXIVE PRONOUNS

theme SUBJECT /θiːm/ *n* [C] the main subject or idea of a talk, book, movie, etc. • *The theme of the conference was the changing role of women in modern society.* • A **theme park** is a large, permanent area for public entertainment, with amusements, restaurants, etc., all connected with a single subject.

theme TUNE /θiːm/ *n* [C] a short, simple tune on which a piece of music is based • A **theme song** or **theme music** is a piece of music played at the beginning of a television or radio show or several times in a movie and which is therefore remembered as belonging to that show or movie.

then TIME /ðen/ *adv, adj* [not gradable] at that time (in the past or in the future) • *She was then sixteen years old.* ○ *Soon the sun will go down, and then it will be time to go.* • *She walked in and I decided to tell her* **then and there** (= immediately).

then NEXT /ðen/ *adv* [not gradable] next or after that • *He smiled, then turned to me and nodded.*

then IN ADDITION /ðen/ *adv* [not gradable] in addition • *We both want to go, and then there's Carmen, so we need three tickets.* • *It would be fun to see them*—**then again** (= but after thinking about it), *I don't really have the time.*

then AS A RESULT /ðen/ *adv* [not gradable] as a result; in that case; also used as a way of joining a statement to an earlier piece of conversation • *Why don't you call them to tell them we'll be late? Then they won't worry.* ○ *If I don't hear from you by Friday, then I'll assume you're not coming.*

theology /θiːˈɑl·ə·dʒi/ *n* the study of religion and religious belief, or a set of beliefs about a particular religion

theologian /ˌθiː·ə·ˈloʊ·dʒən/ *n* [C] a person who studies or is a specialist in religion • *a Catholic/Protestant theologian*

theological /ˌθiː·ə·ˈlɑdʒ·ɪ·kəl/ *adj* • *The minister had attended the Princeton Theological Seminary.*

theorem /ˈθɪr·əm/ *n* [C] *specialized* (in mathematics) a statement that can be shown to be true

theory /ˈθɪr·i, ˈθiː·ə·ri/ *n* [C/U] something suggested as a reasonable explanation for facts, a condition, or an event, esp. a systematic or scientific explanation • *Adele took a course in modern political theory.* [U] ○ *I have a theory* (= an opinion) *about why everybody in the city is in such a hurry.* [C] • *They could,* **in theory** (= possibly), *have been paid twice if someone hadn't caught the error.*

theoretical /ˌθiː·ə·ˈreṭ·ɪ·kəl/ *adj* based on theory or on possibilities • *The president does not want to answer any theoretical questions.*

theorize /ˈθiː·ə·ˌrɑɪz/ *v* [I] to suggest an explanation for something • *Investigators theorized that ice had built up on the wings of the plane, causing it to stall soon after takeoff.*

therapeutic /ˌθer·ə·ˈpjuːṭ·ɪk/ *adj* having a healing effect; tending to make a person healthier • *For arthritis sufferers, moderate exercise is therapeutic.*

therapy /ˈθer·ə·pi/ *n* [C/U] treatment to help a person get better from the effects of a disease or injury • *With physical therapy, you should eventually be able to walk again.* [U]

therapist /ˈθer·ə·pəst/ *n* [C] • *a physical/ speech therapist*

there PLACE /ðer, ðær/ *adv* [not gradable] in, at, or to that place • *Put the chair there.* ○ *The museum was closed today, so we'll go there tomorrow.*

there INTRODUCING A SENTENCE /ðer, ðær/ *pronoun* used to introduce sentences, esp. before the verbs be, seem, and appear • *There's someone on the phone for you.* ○ *There will be plenty of time to pack tomorrow.*

thereafter /ðerˈæf·tər, ðær-/ *adv* [not gradable] continuing on from a particular point in time, esp. after something else has stopped happening • *For the first month you'll be working here, and thereafter in Chicago.*

thereby /ðerˈbɑɪ, ðær-/ *adv* [not gradable] because of this; as a result of this action • *They had failed to agree to a settlement, thereby throwing 250 people out of work.*

therefore /ˈðer·fɔːr, ˈðær-, -foʊr/ *adv* [not gradable] as a result; because of that; for that reason • *We were unable to get funding and therefore had to abandon the project.*

therein /ðerˈɪn, ðær-/ *adv fml* in or into a particular place, thing, or condition • *Therein lies the risk* (= Here is the risk).

THERE

There is often used to introduce a sentence rather than to refer to a place.

Uses with *be*

There is often used to refer to something for the first time. It is possible to say *A cat is in the kitchen* but it is much more common to use a sentence introduced by **there**:

	rather than
There's *a cat in the kitchen*	*A cat is in the kitchen*
There *are lots of people outside.*	*Lots of people are outside.*
There *was ice all over the road.*	*Ice was all over the road.*

In the sentences with **there**, the verb agrees with the noun that follows. In conversation, however, people often use **there's** even if a plural noun follows.

There's *some cookies on the table.*

There is not usually followed by *the*, although in some cases this is possible.

Come look—**there's** *the most beautiful rainbow outside.*

There can be followed by words stating a number or amount. (⬡ **Amounts**)

There are **no** *seats left.* • *I think there's* **someone** *at the door.* • *Is there* **anything** *I can do?* • *There were* **three** *phone calls for you.* • *There was* **a pint of** *water in the bottle.*

But **it** is used with distances.

It's two miles to the station.

There can be followed by a noun and a present participle, past participle (with passive meaning), *to-* infinitive, or *that* clause:

There was a man drawing pictures on the sidewalk. • *There were two cars stolen from the lot.* • *There are some letters to write* (= that should be written). • *There's no doubt* (**that**) *he's lying.*

There can be followed by an adjective such as *sure, certain, likely,* or *unlikely.*

There is **likely to be** *disagreement.* • *There are* **expected to be** *hundreds of applicants for the position.*

Uses with other intransitive verbs

There can describe states or locations.

There **seems** *to be something wrong with this computer.* • *Fortunately, there* **happened** *to be a drugstore around the corner.*

There can be used with modal auxiliary verbs.

There **must** *be an answer.* • *There* **should** *be more support for local businesses.*

⬡ **Verbs: Transitive and Intransitive Grammar Patterns**

---

thereof /ðer'ʌv, ðær-/ *adv fml* from that cause, or of that • *The fund pays for tuition and books, or a portion thereof.*

thermal /'θɜr·məl/ *adj* of, connected with, or preserving heat • **Thermal underwear** is underwear that has been specially designed to keep you warm.

thermometer /θər'mɑm·ət·ər, θə'mɑm-/ *n* [C] a device used for measuring temperature, esp. of the air or in a person's body

Thermos (bottle) /'θɜr·məs ('bɑt̬·ˀl)/ *n* [C] *trademark* a **vacuum bottle**, see at VACUUM

thermostat /'θɜr·mə‚stæt/ *n* [C] a device that controls the temperature of a system by automatically switching the supply of heat or cool air on and off when the temperature becomes too cool or too hot

thesaurus /θə'sɔr·əs/ *n* [C] *pl* **thesauri** /θə'sɔr‚ɑɪ, -'sɔr‚iː/, **thesauruses** a book or electronic text that helps you find words with similar meanings esp. by listing them together

these /ðiːz/ *pl of* THIS ⎡THING REFERRED TO⎤ • **These days** (= Now), *we hardly speak to each other.* • ⬡ DETERMINERS

thesis /'θiː·səs/ *n* [C] *pl* **theses** /'θiː·siːz/ a piece of writing involving original study of a subject, esp. for a college or university degree • *a master's thesis* • A thesis is also the main idea, opinion, or theory of a person or group: *His thesis was that World War I could have been avoided.*

they /ðeɪ/ *pronoun* [pl] the things or people being spoken about, who have already been mentioned • *Where are my glasses? They were on the table a minute ago.* ○ *They* (= People who know) *say we're going to get some rain.* • They is also used to refer to a person whose sex is not known: *"There is someone on the phone for you." "What do they want?"*

they'd /ðeɪd/ *contraction of* **they had** or **they would** • *They'd* (= They would) *come if you asked them to.* ○ *They'd* (= They had) *better be here on time.*

they'll /ðeɪl, ðel/ *contraction of* **they will** or **they shall** • *They'll be in Baltimore for the next few days.*

they're /ðer, ðər/ *contraction of* **they are**

they've /ðeɪv, ðəv/ *contraction of* **they have** • *They've always paid their bills promptly in the past.*

thick DEEP /θɪk/ *adj* [*-er/-est* only] having a large distance from one side of something to the opposite side • *a thick book/steak* ○ *The walls are a foot thick.* • Someone who is **thick-skinned** is not easily hurt by criticism.

thickly /'θɪk·li/ *adv* • *thickly carpeted floors*

thickness /'θɪk·nəs/ *n* [C/U]

thick CLOSE TOGETHER /θɪk/ *adj* [*-er/-est* only] (of particular things) close together with little space between them • *a thick fog* ○ *She had wonderful, thick, brown hair.*

thick NOT FLOWING /θɪk/ *adj* [*-er/-est* only] (of a liquid) not flowing easily • *thick gravy/soup* • (*fig.*) If your voice is thick, it is lower than usual and not as even, usually because you are feeling a strong emotion: *Tony could hardly speak, and when he did his voice was thick with emotion.*

thicken /'θɪk·ən/ *v* [T] • *Thicken the gravy with a little flour.*

thicket /'θɪk·ət/ *n* [C] an area of trees and bushes growing closely together

thief /θiːf/ *n* [C] *pl* **thieves** /θiːvz/ a person who steals • *The thieves stole $10,000 and several pieces of jewelry.*

thigh /θɑɪ/ *n* [C] the part of a person's leg below the hip and above the knee

thimble /'θɪm·bəl/ *n* [C] a small, hard cover, shaped like a cup, that fits over the end of a finger to help you push a needle through material when sewing

thin NOT DEEP /θɪn/ *adj* [*-er/-est* only] **-nn-** having a small distance from the top to the other side • *thin summer clothing* ○ *The statue is coated with a thin layer of gold.* • Someone who is **thin-skinned** is easily hurt by criticism.

thinly /'θɪn·li/, **thin** /θɪn/ *adv* • *Thinly sliced cheese is good for sandwiches.*

thin NOT FAT /θɪn/ *adj* [*-er/-est* only] **-nn-** having little extra flesh on the body • *thin arms/legs* ○ *a thin face* ○ *Models must be tall and thin.*

thin FEW /θɪn/ *adj* [*-er/-est* only] **-nn-** having only a few of something covering an area; not dense • *His hair is thin on top.* ○ *Where there is little rain, grass and trees get thinner.*

thin /θɪn/ *v* [I/T] **-nn-** • *Traffic thins out after seven o'clock.* [I] ○ *An improving economy helped thin unemployment lines.* [T]

thin FLOWING EASILY /θɪn/ *adj* [*-er/-est* only] **-nn-** (of a liquid) flowing easily • *We began dinner with a thin but tasty soup.*

thinner /'θɪn·ər/ *n* [C] a substance that makes a liquid flow more easily • *Paint thinner comes*

in gallon cans. ○ *Aspirin is an effective blood thinner.*

thin WEAK /θɪn/ *adj* [*-er/-est* only] **-nn-** lacking force or substance; weak • *a thin, metallic tone* ○ *I thought the plot was a bit thin.* ○ *We slept poorly that night in the thin mountain air.* • To **disappear/vanish into thin air** is to disappear suddenly and completely: *The ship simply vanished into thin air.*

thinly /'θɪn·li/ *adv* • *It was a thinly disguised attempt to gain control.*

thing OBJECT /θɪŋ/ *n* [C] a device, product, or part of nature that is not specifically named • *There's a new thing that seals plastic bags.* ○ *There are some nice things in the stores on sale right now.* • Your things are your small personal possessions, esp. clothes: *Get your things together and we'll leave.*

thing ANY POSSIBILITY /θɪŋ/ *n* [C] an event, thought, subject of discussion, or possibility • *A strange thing happened on my way to work today.* ○ *I have a few things to bring up at the next meeting.* ○ *Don't worry about a thing—it's all under control.* • Things can refer to a situation in general: *Things have been going really well for us this year.* • When someone says **the thing is**, they want to talk about some subject, problem, or question: *The thing is, my car is being repaired, so how can I drive?*

thing PERSON / ANIMAL /θɪŋ/ *n* [C] a person or animal • *When did you eat last, you poor thing?* • USAGE: This is used to refer to a person or animal affectionately or sympathetically.

thingamajig /'θɪŋ·ə·mə,dʒɪg/, **thingy** /'θɪŋ·i/ *n* [C] *infml* (esp. in spoken English) a thing, the name of which has been forgotten • *He stood there holding this thingamajig.*

think HAVE OPINION /θɪŋk/ *v* [I/T] *past* **thought** /θɔːt/ to have or to form an opinion or idea about something • *"Do you think this is the right address?" "I don't think so."* [T] ○ *It doesn't make much sense when you think about it.* [I] ○ *Cloning animals has happened sooner than anyone thought (it would).* [I/T] ○ *I always thought he was a bit weird.* [T] ○ *What do you think of my new hat?* [I] ○ *I'll always think of him as someone I can rely on.* [I] ○ *I think (that) I'd better go now.* [+ (that) clause] • If you **think better of** something, you decide it is not a good idea: *He considered quitting college but thought better of it.* • If you **think for yourself**, you form opinions and solve problems without depending on other people's ideas: *She's intelligent and can think for herself.* • If you **don't think much of** someone or something, you have a low opinion of them: *I don't think much of this techno music.* • *I still think of myself as* (= believe I am) *her friend.* • If you **think well of**, **think highly of**, or **think the world of** someone or something, you have a lot of respect or affection for them. • To **think nothing of** something means it is easy or simple to do: *When I was younger, I thought nothing of running 20 miles a week.*

thinking /'θɪŋ·kɪŋ/ *n* [U] the process of forming an opinion or idea about something, or the opinions or ideas formed by this process • *I feel that his thinking is outdated in some ways.* ○ *Several new books have changed my thinking about terrorism.*

think USE REASON /θɪŋk/ *v* [I] *past* **thought** /θɔːt/ to use your mind to understand matters, make judgments, and solve problems • *I'll have to think about this.* ○ *She was thinking about running for the Senate.* ○ *I can't think of anything to say right now.* • To **think long and hard** or **think twice** about something means to take the time needed to understand something before making a decision about it: *You really should think long and hard before quitting your job.* • If you can **think on** your **feet**, you have answers ready and can express them quickly and clearly: *When you're called on in class, you have to be able to think on your feet.* • To **think** something **over**, **think** something **through**, or **think** something **out** is to consider something carefully: *They've made me a good offer, but I'll have to think it over.* ○ *We can't make a decision until we've thought through the different possibilities.* • If you **think** something **up**, you invent a plan or solution: *Just give him five minutes and he'll think up an excuse.*

thinker /'θɪŋ·kər/ *n* [C] • *He's a creative thinker and a good administrator.*

thinking /'θɪŋ·kɪŋ/ *n* [U] • *I've done some serious thinking about our relationship.* ○ *Thinking, for me, is hard work!*

think REMEMBER /θɪŋk/ *v* [I always + adv/prep] *past* **thought** /θɔːt/ to remember or imagine • *I can't stop thinking about her.* ○ *I can picture her, I just can't think of her name.* ○ *Think back to the early days of the Civil War.*

think tank /'θɪŋk·tæŋk/ *n* [C] an organization consisting of people from various specialties whose work is to study specific problems and suggest solutions, often with a particular political view

third /θɜrd/ *adj, adv, n* [C] (a person or thing) coming immediately after the second and before all others • *My horse finished third in the race.* ○ *They were married on the third of November.* [C] • A third is one of three equal parts of something. [C] • In baseball, third or **third base** is the third place a player has to touch in order to score, or the position played by a member of the team in the field. • **Third class** or **third rate** means of low quality: *The company is earning third-rate profits.* • To give someone the **third degree** is to question them carefully and completely to find out as much as you can: *We gave the babysitter the third degree before we hired her.* • A **third-degree burn** is the most serious type of burn. • (*specialized*) In grammar, the **third person** is the

form of pronouns and verbs people use when speaking or writing about other people: *"He," "him," and "his" are third person singular pronouns, and "they," "them," and "their" are third person plural pronouns.* ○ *Novels are usually written in the third person.* ○ Compare **first person** at FIRST; **second person** at SECOND POSITION. • A **third rail** is a metal bar, running parallel with train tracks, that supplies electricity to some types of trains. • The **Third World** is a name for a group of countries whose economies are less developed. • USAGE: The related number is THREE. • LP NUMBERS

thirst /θɜrst/ *n* [U] the need or desire to drink something, esp. water • *He took a long drink of water to quench his thirst.* • A thirst is also a strong desire for something: *She slaked her thirst for knowledge by reading everything she could.*

thirsty /'θɜr·sti/ *adj* • *She was very thirsty but took only a few sips of water.* ○ (*fig.*) *Always thirsty for power, he would do anything to get it.*

thirteen /θɜrt'tiːn/ *number* 13 • *The bus has thirteen seats for passengers.* ○ *a thirteen-story building* • LP NUMBERS

thirteenth /θɜrt'tiːnθ/ *adj, adv, n* [C] • *He came in thirteenth in the marathon.* ○ *The baby was born on the thirteenth of May.* [C] • A thirteenth is one of thirteen equal parts of something. [C]

thirty /'θɜrt·i/ *number* 30 • *There are thirty students taking this course.* ○ *a thirty-mile journey* • LP NUMBERS

thirties, 30s, 30's /'θɜrt·iz/ *pl n* the numbers 30 through 39 • *My sisters are in their thirties* (= between 30 and 39 years old). ○ *The temperature is expected to be in the thirties* (= between 30 and 39 degrees) *tomorrow.* ○ *These dresses were fashionable in the thirties* (= between 1930 and 1939).

thirtieth /'θɜrt·i·əθ/ *adj, adv, n* [C] • *Ashley's having a party to celebrate her thirtieth birthday.* ○ *Today is the thirtieth of September.* [C] • A thirtieth is one of thirty equal parts of something. [C]

this THING REFERRED TO /ðɪs/ *pronoun, adj pl* **these** /ðiːz/ used for a person, object, or thing to show which one is referred to or has been referred to before • *This book is mine—yours is over there.* ○ *Try on these sunglasses to see how you look in them.* ○ *If you wear the scarf like this, it will look better.* ○ (*infml*) *So I said to this guy, "Do I know you?"* • This also refers to something that is nearest to the speaker in time and sometimes in space: *I've got to see the doctor again this Thursday.* ○ *By this time tomorrow, I'll be in Paris.* ○ *How do the police handle such disputes* **in this day and age** (= now)? • People say **this is** to introduce someone: *Harry, this is Joan.* • (*infml*) **This side of** somewhere means between here and the place mentioned: *This is the best pizza I've tasted this side of Chicago.* • **This minute** means now: *It doesn't have to be done this minute, but it should be done before lunch.* • Compare THAT SOMETHING NOT HERE. • LP DETERMINERS

this AS MUCH /ðɪs/ *adv* [not gradable] as much as shown, or to a particular degree • *Can you jump this high?* ○ *She's never been this late before.*

thistle /ˈθɪs·əl/ *n* [C] a wild plant with sharp, pointed leaves and, typically, purple flowers

thong /θɔːŋ, θɑŋ/ *n* [C] a light shoe, often made of rubber, consisting of a flat bottom attached to the foot by a narrow strap that fits between the big toe and the toe next to it • A thong is also a narrow strip of material used to fasten something or worn for swimming or as underwear.

thong

thorn /θɔːrn/ *n* [C] a small, sharp, pointed growth on the stem of a plant • *Rose bushes have thorns.* • A **thorn in** your **side** is someone or something that continually annoys or hurts you.

thorny /ˈθɔːr·ni/ *adj* [-er/-est only] • *Roses are thorny shrubs.* • A thorny problem is one that is full of difficulties: *The thorny issue of illegal immigration remains unresolved.*

thorough COMPLETE /ˈθɜr·oʊ, ˈθʌ·roʊ/ *adj* with nothing left out or omitted; complete • *The district attorney's office conducted a thorough investigation.* ○ *The doctor gave him a thorough medical examination.*

thoroughly /ˈθɜr·ə·li, ˈθʌ·rə-/ *adv* • *The drug was thoroughly tested before being put on the market.*

thoroughness /ˈθɜr·ə·nəs, ˈθʌ·rə-/ *n* [U] • *You can rely on the thoroughness of his research.*

thorough VERY GREAT /ˈθɜr·oʊ, ˈθʌ·roʊ/ *adj* [not gradable] (used for emphasis) very great • *The meeting was a thorough waste of time.*

thoroughly /ˈθɜr·ə·li, ˈθʌ·rə-/ *adv* • *The movie left me thoroughly confused about its real meaning.* ○ *We thoroughly enjoyed the movie.* • LP VERY, COMPLETELY, AND OTHER INTENSIFIERS

thoroughbred /ˈθɜr·ə,bred, ˈθʌ·rə-/ *n* [C] a horse with good qualities typical of a particular breed and with parents that are officially recognized as being the same breed

thoroughfare /ˈθɜr·ə,fer, ˈθʌ·rə-, -,fær/ *n* [C] a road that connects to other roads • *I live right on the main thoroughfare.*

those /ðoʊz/ *pl of* THAT SOMETHING NOT HERE • *Those of you who would like to come with us should sign up now.* ○ *Those houses are huge.* • If you say **those were the days**, you are remembering a period in the past affectionately. • LP DETERMINERS

though /ðoʊ/ *conjunction* despite the fact that; although • *There's a chance he'll recover, though the doctors can't say for certain.* ○ *Even*

though I was very young, I remember a little about the war.

though /ðoʊ/ *adv* despite this • *He felt a little guilty about being overpaid, though he wasn't about to give it back.*

thought THINK /θɔːt/ *past simple and past participle of* THINK

thought THINKING /θɔːt/ *n* [C/U] the act of thinking about something to form ideas and opinions, or an idea or opinion produced by thinking • *I have given this matter considerable thought.* [U] ○ *Do you have any thoughts on what we should do now?* [C] ○ *That fact never entered my thoughts.* [C] ○ *His early religious training helped to shape his thought.* [U] ○ *It's just a thought, but since it's such a beautiful day, why don't we go for a drive?* [C] ○ *The very thought of standing up in front of an audience scares me to death.* [U]

thoughtful /ˈθɔːt·fəl/ *adj* tending to think seriously about things • *You're looking very thoughtful—what's on your mind?* • Thoughtful also means showing care and consideration in how you treat other people: *"Oh, how thoughtful of you," Dina said, opening the gift.*

thoughtfully /ˈθɔːt·fə·li/ *adv* • *He answers questions thoughtfully* (= after thinking seriously).

thoughtfulness /ˈθɔːt·fəl·nəs/ *n* [U] • *She was surprised by the thoughtfulness* (= kindness) *of people who wanted to help her.*

thoughtless /ˈθɔːt·ləs/ *adj* not showing care for others • *I'm sorry I was late—it was thoughtless of me not to call.*

thoughtlessly /ˈθɔːt·lə·sli/ *adv* • *He thoughtlessly made an unkind remark about her mother.*

thousand /ˈθaʊ·zənd/ *number* 1000 • *A thousand people came to the game.* ○ *a thousand-dollar ring* • LP NUMBERS

thousandth /ˈθaʊ·zənθ/ *adj, adv* [not gradable], *n* [C] • *You are our one thousandth customer.* • A thousandth is one of a thousand equal parts of something. [C]

thrash /θræʃ/ *v* [I/T] to make a series of wild, violent movements • *The startled animal thrashed around in the stall.* [I] • To thrash (a person or animal) means to hit them hard and repeatedly: *He hit me once, and if you hadn't come along, he would have thrashed me.* [T] • (*fig.*) To thrash also means to defeat badly: *Atlanta thrashed New York, 119-87.* [T]

▫**thrash out** *obj*, **thrash** *obj* **out** /-ˈ-/ *v adv* [M] to discuss (a problem) completely in order to come to a solution about it • *These issues will be thrashed out in court.*

thread FIBER /θred/ *n* [C/U] a very thin twisted string of esp. cotton or silk, used mostly for sewing • *It takes practice to use a needle and thread well.* [U] ○ *There's a loose thread on your dress.* [C] • A thread is also something continuous that connects different ideas or thoughts together: *A common thread runs* *through their various experiences.* [C] ∘ *A ringing phone interrupted the thread of her story.* [U]

thread /θred/ *v* [T] to put thread through the hole in (a needle), or to put (something narrow) through a small opening • *to thread a needle* ∘ *He threaded a thin strip of tape through the machine.* ∘ (*fig.*) *She threaded her way through the crowd* (= moved along a narrow path to go around people in her way).

thread TWISTING CUT /θred/ *n* [C] a continuous cut that twists around the outside of a screw or around an opening, as on a pipe • *The threads are worn, and I can't tighten the screw.*

threadbare /'θred·ber, -bær/ *adj* (of material) looking worn and thin from much use • *Her clothes were faded and threadbare.*

threat PROMISE TO HURT /θret/ *n* [C] a statement that someone will be hurt or harmed, esp. if they do not do something in particular • *She was arrested after making threats to a judge.*

threaten /'θret·ᵊn/ *v* [I/T] • *The gang threatened to kill him if he didn't pay them.* [I] ∘ *Don't threaten me!* [T]

threatening /'θret·ᵊn·ɪŋ/ *adj* • *She received several threatening phone calls after her appearance on television.*

threat UNWANTED POSSIBILITY /θret/ *n* [C/U] the possibility that something unwanted will happen, or a person or thing that is likely to cause something unwanted to happen • *A threat of rain is in today's forecast.* [U] ∘ *The boundary dispute raised the threat of war.* [U]

threaten /'θret·ᵊn/ *v* [T] to warn of (something unpleasant or unwanted) • *She threatened legal action against the newspaper.* ∘ *Because of continuing drought, millions are threatened with starvation.*

threatening /'θret·ᵊn·ɪŋ/ *adj* • *Threatening skies meant a storm was coming.*

three /θriː/ *number* 3 • *Ann-Marie has three children.* ∘ *a three-bedroom house* • *Three can also mean three o'clock.* • *If an object if* **three-dimensional** (*abbreviation* **3-D**), it has or appears to have height, length, and width: *a three-dimensional carving* • USAGE: The related adjective is THIRD. • LP NUMBERS

threesome /'θriː·səm/ *n* [C] *infml* three people as a group • *These guys do as good a job as any threesome in broadcasting.*

thresh /θreʃ/ *v* [T] to remove the seeds of (crop plants) by hitting, using either a machine or a hand tool

threshold STARTING POINT /'θreʃ·hoʊld/ *n* [C/U] a point at which something starts • *a low threshold for pain* [C] ∘ *His behavior is below the threshold of criminal activity.* [U] ∘ *We are on the threshold of a new era.* [U]

threshold ENTRANCE /'θreʃ·hoʊld/ *n* [C] the part of a floor at the entrance to a building or room • *It's traditional for a man to carry his bride over the threshold.*

threw /θruː/ *past simple of* THROW

thrift /θrɪft/ *n* [C/U] *dated* the careful use of money, esp. by avoiding waste • *Trina learned thrift from her mother.* [U] • A thrift is also a type of bank. [C] • A **thrift shop/store** is a store that sells used things such as clothes, books, and furniture.

thrifty /'θrɪf·ti/ *adj* • *They have plenty of money now, but they're still thrifty.*

thrill /θrɪl/ *n* [C] a feeling of great excitement and pleasure • *It gave me a thrill to see her again after so many years.*

thrill /θrɪl/ *v* [I/T] • *Just standing next to him thrilled her.* [T]

thrilled /θrɪld/ *adj* extremely pleased • *My parents weren't too thrilled when they found out.*

thriller /'θrɪl·ər/ *n* [C] a book, play, or movie that has an exciting and frightening story

thrilling /'θrɪl·ɪŋ/ *adj* very exciting • *a thrilling adventure*

thrive /θraɪv/ *v* [I] to grow, develop, or be successful • *She seems to thrive on hard work.*

thriving /'θraɪ·vɪŋ/ *adj* very healthy or successful • *The dog is thriving in its new home.*

throat /θroʊt/ *n* [C] the front of the neck, or the space inside the neck down which food and air can go • *A cop grabbed him around the throat.* ∘ *I have a sore throat.* ∘ *He cleared his throat and started speaking.*

throaty /'θroʊt̬·i/ *adj* having a low sound • *a throaty voice/laugh*

throb /θrɑb/ *v* [I] **-bb-** to produce a regular, forceful beat • *His head throbbed with pain.*

throb /θrɑb/ *n* [C/U] • *We could feel the throb of the music from the party upstairs.* [U]

throes /θroʊz/ *n* • If you are **in the throes of** something, you are doing something difficult, unpleasant, or painful: *While she was in the throes of childbirth, her doctor got sick.*

throne /θroʊn/ *n* [C] a special chair used by a king or queen, or the condition of being such a ruler • *He is heir to the throne.*

throng /θrɔːŋ/ *n* [C] a large group of people • *A huge throng had gathered around the speaker.*

throng /θrɔːŋ/ *v* [I/T] • *The narrow streets were thronged with tourists.* [T] ∘ *Reporters thronged around her.* [I always + adv/prep]

throttle CONTROL /'θrɑt̬·ᵊl/ *n* [C] a device that controls how much fuel goes into an engine

throttle PRESS THROAT /'θrɑt̬·ᵊl/ *v* [T] to try to kill (someone) by pressing their throat so that they cannot breathe • *I'm so mad I could throttle him.*

through ACROSS /θruː/ *prep, adv* [not gradable] from one side or end to the other, from one part to another, or from the beginning to the end • *We drove through the tunnel* ∘ *We took a shortcut through the woods.* ∘ *Have you read the report all the way through?* • If you drive through a red light or stop sign, you do not stop at it. • *My mother is Italian* **through and through** (= completely).

through FINISHED /θruː/ *adj, adv* [not gradable] finished or completed • *Are you through with that book?* ○ *My girlfriend says we're through* (= our relationship is over).

through DURING /θruː/ *prep, adv* [not gradable] during a period of time, esp. from the beginning to the end • *We sat through two lectures and then left.* ○ *She had just enough energy to get through the day.* ○ *I work Tuesdays through Saturdays* (= each day during this period). • *My brother has stuck with me* **through thick and thin** (= in good and bad times).

through AS A RESULT /θruː/ *prep* as a result of • *Bob learned of the contract through a story in the newspaper.*

through USING /θruː/ *prep* by; using • *Schools are financed through lottery receipts.*

throughout /θruːˈaʊt/ *prep, adv* [not gradable] in every part, or during the whole period of • *Grass grows throughout the world.* ○ *She was calm throughout her visit to the dentist.*

throughway /ˈθruːˌweɪ/ *n* [C] a THRUWAY

throw SEND THROUGH AIR /θroʊ/ *v* [I/T] *past simple* **threw** /θruː/, *past part* **thrown** /θroʊn/ to send (something) through the air, esp. by a sudden movement of the arm • *Throw me the ball./Throw the ball to me.* [T] ○ *I didn't throw as well as I expected to.* [I] ○ *He was thrown from his motorcycle.* [T] • *The judge was not lenient—he* **threw the book at** *him* (= punished him as severely as possible). • *The cops* **threw** *him* **in jail** (= put him in prison). • When someone **throws in the towel**, they admit defeat. • If you **throw yourself into** something, you do it actively and enthusiastically: *She's thrown herself into this new job.* • *His teammates didn't appreciate how he* **threw his weight around** (= acted as if he had authority).

throw /θroʊ/ *n* [C] • *She timed her throw so the ball reached the base when he did.*

throw MOVE QUICKLY /θroʊ/ *v* [T] *past simple* **threw** /θruː/, *past part* **thrown** /θroʊn/ to move (something) quickly or carelessly, or to cause (someone or something) to move quickly • *He threw the switch and the lights came on.* ○ *Cops grabbed him and threw him to the ground.* ○ *They threw up their hands to protect their heads.* [M] ○ *He threw his head back and laughed.* [M] ○ *Throw a few peppers in the pot.* [M] • If you **throw money around**, you spend it carelessly: *He doesn't earn much, but still seems to have plenty to throw around.* • If someone **throws money at** something, they spend it without careful planning: *Problems aren't solved just by throwing money at them.*

throw CONFUSE /θroʊ/ *v* [T] *past simple* **threw** /θruː/, *past part* **thrown** /θroʊn/ *infml* to confuse (someone) • *That question really threw me*

at first. • If something **throws** you **for a loop**, it surprises you greatly.

throw ENTERTAIN /θroʊ/ *v* *past simple* **threw** /θruː/, *past part* **thrown** /θroʊn/ • To **throw a party** is to have a party: *Janelle threw a party for Dick's 18th birthday.*

throw SHOW ANGER /θroʊ/ *v* [T] *past simple* **threw** /θruː/, *past part* **thrown** /θroʊn/ • If you **throw a fit**, you express great anger: *My mother threw a fit when she saw the mess.*

▢ **throw away** *obj*, **throw** *obj* **away** /ˈ--ˈ-/ *v adv* [M] to get rid of (something) by treating it as garbage • *When are you going to throw away those old magazines?*

throwaway /ˈθroʊ-əˌweɪ/ *adj* [not gradable] • *throwaway cups/gloves* • A **throwaway line/remark** is something said in a way that suggests the speaker considers it unimportant.

▢ **throw in** *obj*, **throw** *obj* **in** /ˈ-ˈ-/ *v adv* [M] *infml* to include (something extra) when selling something • *I bought a new sofa and they threw in a chair.*

▢ **throw on** *obj*, **throw** *obj* **on** /ˈ-ˈ-/ *v adv* [M] *infml* to quickly put (clothes) on • *She threw on her jacket.*

▢ **throw off** *obj*, **throw** *obj* **off** /ˈ-ˈ-/ *v adv* [M] *infml* to quickly remove (clothes) • *He threw off his shirt.*

▢ **throw out** *obj* GET RID OF , **throw** *obj* **out** /ˈ-ˈ-/ *v adv* [M] to get rid of (something) by treating it as garbage • *Throw it out!* ○ *I threw out everything we didn't eat.*

▢ **throw out** *obj* FORCE TO LEAVE , **throw** *obj* **out** /ˈ-ˈ-/ *v adv* [M] to force (someone) to leave a place • *I threw him out of my house.*

▢ **throw together** *obj*, **throw** *obj* **together** /ˈ--ˈ-/ *v adv* [M] to suddenly put (people or things) in one place without much planning • *We were thrown together at a conference.* ○ *I just threw the cake together at the last minute* (= made it quickly).

▢ **throw up** *(obj)*, **throw** *(obj)* **up** /ˈ-ˈ-/ *v adv* [I/M] to vomit • *He threw up all over his shoes.* [I] ○ *I fed the baby some fruit, but she threw it up.* [M]

throwback /ˈθroʊˌbæk/ *n* [C] something that is like a thing from an earlier time • *This year's styles are throwbacks to the fashions of the 1940s.*

thrown /θroʊn/ *past participle of* THROW

thrush /θrʌʃ/ *n* [C] any of a large family of singing birds that includes the ROBIN

thrust /θrʌst/ *v* [always + adv/prep] *past* **thrust** to push suddenly and strongly • *She thrust the money into his hand.* [T] ○ *He thrust at me with a knife.* [I]

thrust /θrʌst/ *n* [C/U] • *a sword thrust* [C] ○ (fig.) *The thrust* (= main point) *of her argument was the schools need improvement.* [C] • (specialized) Thrust is also the force produced by an engine that pushes in one direction. [U]

thruway, **throughway** /ˈθruːˌweɪ/ *n* [C] a wide road for fast-moving traffic, with a lim-

tide

thud /θʌd/ n [C] a sound made when something heavy hits a hard surface • *the thud of boots on the stairs*

thud /θʌd/ v [I always + adv/prep] **-dd-** • *Her bag thudded to the floor.*

thug /θʌg/ n [C] a man who acts violently, esp. a criminal • *Some thugs smashed his windows.*

thumb /θʌm/ n [C] the short finger that is at an angle to the other fingers • *How did you cut your thumb?* • **Thumbs down** is a sign of disapproval, and **thumbs up** is a sign of approval: *Legislators gave the thumbs up to new tax credits.* • A **thumbnail** is the nail on the thumb. • A **thumbnail sketch** is a short description: *He gave a thumbnail sketch of life in Moscow in the 1960s.* • A **thumbtack** is a short, sharp pin with a flat, round top that can be pushed into soft wood or other material to hold esp. papers to it. • [PIC] HAND

thumb /θʌm/ v infml • If you **thumb a ride**, you HITCHHIKE. • To **thumb** your **nose at** someone or something is to show a lack of respect toward them: *Pedestrians thumbed their noses at jaywalking laws.* • You **thumb through** a book or some papers by turning the pages quickly and reading only small parts.

thump /θʌmp/ v [I/T] to hit (something), making a soft, heavy noise • *He thumped his chest.* [T]

thump /θʌmp/ n [C] • *I heard a thump upstairs.*

thunder /ˈθʌn·dər/ n [U] the sudden, loud noise that comes after a flash of lightning • *a clap of thunder* • A **thunderbolt** is a flash of lightning, esp. with the sound of thunder. • A **thunderclap** is a single, loud sound of thunder. • A **thundercloud** (also **thunderhead**) is a large, dark cloud. • A **thunderstorm** is a rain storm with thunder and lightning.

thunder /ˈθʌn·dər/ v [I] • *The sky grew dark and it started to thunder.* ○ *The horses thundered past* (= moved making a lot of noise), *shaking the house.*

thunderous /ˈθʌn·də·rəs/ adj very loud • *thunderous applause*

Thursday /ˈθɜrz·di, -deɪ/ (abbreviation **Thur.**, **Thurs.**) n [C/U] the day of the week after Wednesday and before Friday

thus /ðʌs/ adv [not gradable] fml in this way, or with this result • *This plan will reduce waste, and thus cut costs.* • **Thus far** means until now: *We haven't had any problems thus far.*

thwart /θwɔrt/ v [T] to stop (something) from happening or (someone) from doing something • *The city council thwarted his reform efforts.*

thyme /taɪm/ n [U] an herb with sweet-smelling leaves that is used to flavor foods in cooking

thyroid (gland) /ˈθaɪ·rɔɪd (ˌglænd)/ n [C] a GLAND (= organ) in the front of the neck that helps to control growth and chemical processes in the body

tiara /tiːˈær·ə, -ˈer·ə, -ˈɑr·ə/ n [C] a piece of jewelry worn on the head by a woman at very formal social occasions

tic /tɪk/ n [C] a sudden, small, uncontrolled movement, esp. of the face • *He developed a tic when he was nervous.*

tick [MAKE SOUND] /tɪk/ v [I] to make a quiet, short, regularly repeated sound like that made by a clock • *That clock ticks too loudly.*

tick /tɪk/ n [C] • *I could hear the ticks of the passing seconds.*

ticking /ˈtɪk·ɪŋ/ n [U] • *the ticking of a clock*

tick [ANIMAL] /tɪk/ n [C] any of several types of very small animals that suck the blood of other animals

□ **tick off** obj [LIST] , **tick** obj **off** /ˈ-ˈ-/ v adv [M] to name (items in a list) • *She ticked off six reasons for saying no.*

□ **tick off** obj [MAKE ANGRY] , **tick** obj **off** /ˈ-ˈ-/ v adv [M] infml to make (someone) angry • *Bad service in a restaurant ticks him off.*

ticket [PROOF OF PAYMENT] /ˈtɪk·ət/ n [C] a small card that shows its holder has paid for an activity • *a train/movie ticket* ○ *an airline ticket* ○ *a lottery ticket* ○ *Have you bought your ticket yet?*

ticket [LEGAL NOTICE] /ˈtɪk·ət/ n [C] an official piece of paper that tells someone that they have broken a traffic law • *a speeding/parking ticket* ○ *Carla got a ticket for making a U-turn on a bridge.*

ticket /ˈtɪk·ət/ v [T] • *Charles was ticketed for speeding.*

ticket [POLITICAL GROUP] /ˈtɪk·ət/ n [C] a group of people from one political party who are trying to get elected at one time • *She's running on the Democratic and Independent tickets.*

tickle /ˈtɪk·əl/ v [T] to touch (someone) in a way that causes a slightly uncomfortable physical feeling which makes you laugh • *She tickled his feet.* • If you are **tickled pink** or **tickled to death**, you are very pleased: *I was tickled pink to be invited.*

tickle /ˈtɪk·əl/ n [C] • A tickle in your throat is an unpleasant feeling that might make you cough.

ticklish /ˈtɪk·ə·lɪʃ/ adj • *Are you ticklish* (= Do you laugh if someone tickles you)*?* • A ticklish situation is one that needs to be dealt with carefully.

tick–tack–toe, **tic–tac–toe** /ˌtɪk,tæk'toʊ/ n [U] a game in which two players take turns putting O's or X's in a pattern of nine squares, trying to get three O's or X's in a straight line

tidbit /ˈtɪd·bɪt/ n [C] a small piece of interesting information, or a small item of food • *We learned all sorts of historical tidbits.* ○ *She feeds her dog tidbits from the dinner table.*

tide /taɪd/ n [C] the rise and fall of the sea that

happens twice every day • *high/low tide* • A tide is also any large change in something, esp. an increase in the amount of something: *There's a growing tide of violence against children.*

tidal /'taɪd·ᵊl/ *adj* connected with, or influenced or powered by, the rise and fall of the sea • *a tidal river* • A **tidal wave** is an extremely large wave caused by violent movement of the earth under the sea.

□ **tide** *obj* **over** /'-'--/ *v adv* [T] to supply (someone) with something they lack for a short period • *Can you lend me some money to tide me over till next month?*

tidy [NEAT] /'taɪd·i/ *adj* (of appearance or behavior) neat • *a tidy house*

tidy [LARGE] /'taɪd·i/ *adj* (of amounts of money) large • *He made a tidy sum/profit.*

tie [FASTEN] /taɪ/ *v* [I/T] **tying,** *past* **tied** to fasten together (two pieces of string or other long, thin material), or to hold together with string, rope, etc. • *This dress ties at the back.* [I] ○ *She tied the ribbon in a bow/knot.* [T] • *So when are you two going to* **tie the knot** (= get married)? • [PIC] BOW TIE

tie /taɪ/, **necktie** *n* [C] a long, thin piece of material worn esp. by men which fits under a shirt collar, is tied in a knot, and hangs down the front of the shirt • *a silk tie* • A tie is also any piece of string, plastic, etc., used to hold together something: *Can you find the ties for the garbage bags?* • [PIC] BOW TIE, STRING TIE

tie [FINISH EQUAL] /taɪ/ *v* [I] **tying,** *past* **tied** to finish at the same time or score the same number of points as someone or something else in a competition • *Jane and I tied for first place.* ○ *The score is tied (up) at 3 to 3.*

tie /taɪ/ *n* [C] • *It's a tie for first place.* • A **tiebreaker** is an additional competition to decide the winner among competitors who have finished with equal scores.

□ **tie down** *obj* [HOLD IN PLACE] , **tie** *obj* **down** /'-'-/ *v adv* [M] to hold (someone or something) in place with ropes • *Tie down anything that might blow away in the storm.*

□ **tie down** *obj* [LIMIT] , **tie** *obj* **down** /'-'-/ *v adv* [M] to limit (someone's freedom) • *Family obligations tied him down.*

□ **tie** *obj* **in with** *obj* /'-,--/ *v adv prep* [T] to show that (something) is connected to (something else) • *Our dance teacher showed us the turn, then tied it in with the basic step.*

□ **tie** *obj* **to** *obj* [CONNECT] /'--/ *v prep* [T] to show how (one thing) is connected to (another) • *Researchers have tied the increase in asthma to certain types of pollution.*

□ **tie** *obj* **to** *obj* [UNABLE TO LEAVE] /'--/ *v prep* [T] to force (someone) to stay in (a place) • *Her work ties her to the east coast.*

□ **tie up** *obj* [HOLD] , **tie** *obj* **up** /'-'-/ *v adv* [M] to hold (something) with string or rope • *Tie your newspapers up with string.* ○ *Thieves tied up the night watchman.*

□ **tie up** *obj* [LIMIT MOVEMENT] , **tie** *obj* **up** /'-'-/ *v adv* [M] to limit (someone's or something's movement or use) • *It's a good investment, but your money will be tied up for a long time.* ○ *Sorry I'm late—I got tied up in traffic.* ○ *Try not to tie up the phone—I'm expecting a call.*

tie-up /'taɪ·ʌp/ *n* [C] a stop caused by having too many things come or happen together • *An overturned truck caused a huge traffic tie-up.*

tier /tɪr/ *n* [C] one of several layers or levels • *We sat in one of the upper tiers of the stadium.*

tiff /tɪf/ *n* [C] *infml* a slight argument • *We had a little tiff over whose turn it was to walk the dog.*

tiger /'taɪ·gər/, *female* **tigress** /'taɪ·grəs/ *n* [C] a large, wild cat that has yellow-orange fur with thick lines of black fur

tight [FIRMLY TOGETHER] /taɪt/ *adj, adv* [-er/-est only] (held or kept together) firmly or closely • *You have to wrap the bandage tight enough so that it really supports your ankle.* ○ *Make sure the door is shut tight* (= completely closed) *before you leave.* • Clothes that are tight fit the body closely, sometimes so closely that they are uncomfortable: *She wore a tight black skirt.* ○ *These shoes feel a bit tight.* • If you say about two people that they are tight, you mean they are close friends. • If someone is **tight-lipped,** they refuse to say much about something: *He remained tight-lipped about whether the union would declare a strike.*

tightly /'taɪt·li/ *adv* • *Dorothy held her dog tightly so he wouldn't run after them.*

tighten /'taɪt·ᵊn/ *v* [I/T] • *You've got to tighten the laces of your ice skates.* [T] ○ *His arms tightened around her.* [I] • *If you* **tighten** *your* **belt,** you spend less money.

tight [LIMITED] /taɪt/ *adj* [-er/-est only] (esp. of time or money) limited in availability • *Arnold has a very tight schedule today and I don't know if he can see you.* ○ *We're on a tight budget and can't afford to eat out much.* ○ *Parking is very tight on weekdays around here.* • (*infml*) Someone who is tight with money, or **tightfisted,** is unwilling to spend it.

tighten /'taɪt·ᵊn/ *v* [T] to make (something) less easily available • *The government plans to tighten credit and slow the growth of the money supply.*

tight [CONTROLLED] /taɪt/ *adj* strongly controlled • *Security was tight at the meeting between the two leaders.*

tighten /'taɪt·ᵊn/ *v* [T] • *Security was tightened at US embassies around the world.* ○ *The government moved to tighten the rules on toxic substances in the air.* ○ *Our team will have to tighten up its defense if we want to win.* [M]

tightly /'taɪt·li/ *adv* • *Her decision to run for office was a tightly held secret.*

tight [DIFFICULT] /taɪt/ *adj* (of situations) difficult or hard to deal with • *We were in a tight financial situation.* ○ *I was in a tight spot* (= difficult situation) *and wasn't sure what I should* *do.* • In a competition, **tight** means close, with the competitors almost even: *He was involved in a very tight race for governor.*

tightrope /'taɪt·roʊp/ *n* [C] a stretched wire or rope fixed above the ground that skilled people walk across, esp. in a CIRCUS performance

tights /taɪts/ *pl n* a piece of clothing made of a material that stretches to cover the body below the waist, including the legs, worn esp. by dancers and people doing physical exercises • *Ballet students should wear a leotard and tights.* • (*Br*) Tights are also PANTYHOSE.

tightwad /'taɪt·wɑd/ *n* [C] *disapproving* a person who is not willing to spend money

tile /taɪl/ *n* [C] a flat, thin, usually square piece of baked clay, plastic, or other material used for covering floors, walls, or roofs • *a tile floor* ○ *ceiling tiles*

tile /taɪl/ *v* [T] • *We're going to tile the bathroom ourselves.*

till UNTIL /tɪl, təl, t^əl/ *prep, conjunction* up to (the time that); until • *Tell him to take it easy till we get there.*

till PREPARE LAND /tɪl/ *v* [T] to prepare and use (land) for growing crops • *to till the soil*

till MONEY DRAWER /tɪl/ *n* [C] a drawer where money is kept in a store • (*fig.*) *We suspected him of dipping into the till* (= stealing money from the store).

tilt /tɪlt/ *v* [I/T] to cause (something) to move into a sloping or uneven position, or to be in this position • *He tilted his chair back and put his feet up on the desk.* [T] ○ *The woman tilted her head back, laughing at something Pascal had just said.* [T] • (*fig.*) Something that tilts toward/away from something increases or lessens its support for it: *UN spending has tilted away from development toward relief,* O'Reilly says. [I]

tilt /tɪlt/ *n* [C usually sing] • *The house was on a tilt* (= not horizontal).

timber /'tɪm·bər/ *n* [C/U] wood from trees that is used for building, or trees grown for this use • *The houses were constructed of timber and whitewashed clay.* [U]

time MEASURE OF EXISTENCE /taɪm/ *n* [U] the seconds, minutes, hours, days, weeks, months, years, etc., in which existence is measured, or the past, present, and future considered as a whole • *I really don't have time to call her today.* ○ *The children spent most of their time outdoors.* ○ *We'd save time* (= It would be quicker) *if we didn't have to pick up Bobby on the way.* • If you **waste time**, you do not make good use of the amount of time available to you. • **Time flies** means that minutes, hours, or days have gone past surprisingly quickly. • **Time will tell** (= We will discover in the future) *whether we made the right decision.* • If something is **time-honored**, it is considered important because it has existed for many years: *Family*

Thanksgiving dinners are a time-honored tradition. • LP TIME

time PARTICULAR PERIOD /taɪm/ *n* [C/U] a particular period of seconds, minutes, hours, days, weeks, months, years, etc., during which something has been happening or is needed or available • *The kids are well-behaved most of the time.* [U] ○ *She was very lonely at that time.* [C] ○ *They talked for a long time.* [C] ○ *She spent most of her free time listening to music.* [U] ○ *It's unusual to get snow at this time of year.* [C] ○ *Those kids are over here all the time* (= often or continuously). [U] • If you pass time, you do something while waiting for something else to happen: *While he was waiting, Joe passed the time looking through magazines.* [U] • Your time in a race is the number of seconds, minutes, and hours you take to complete it: *The track was soft, and the times were slow.* [C] • *I can only do one thing* **at a time** (= during any one time or moment). • To **do/serve time** is to spend a period of weeks, months, or years in prison. • *Now that she was retired, Mary found that she had a lot of* **time on** *her* **hands** (= she had nothing to do). • (*infml*) *OK, everyone,* **time's up** (= there are no more minutes available)*—hand in your tests.* • If you are paid **time and a half** for a job, you are paid one and a half times what you are usually paid. • A **timeout** is a short pause during a game in some sports when the players rest and plan what to do next.

time /taɪm/ *v* [T] to measure the seconds, minutes, and hours for (something to happen) or (someone to do something) • *We ran two miles and were timed at 12 minutes and 30 seconds.* ○ *You've got to time the roast or it will get overdone.*

time MEASUREMENT ON A CLOCK /taɪm/ *n* [C/U] a particular moment in the day, as expressed in hours and minutes and shown on a clock, or a particular point in the day, week, month, or year • *What time is it?* [U] ○ *What time do you finish work?* [U] ○ *He's teaching his daughter to tell time* (= to recognize what particular point in the day it is by looking at a clock). [U] ○ *I catch the train at the same time every day.* [C] ○ *Parking is not allowed here at any time* (= ever). [U] • Time is also used to refer to the system of recording hours used in different parts of the world: *Mountain Standard Time* [U] ○ *daylight saving time* [U] • A **time bomb** is a bomb attached to a device that will make it explode at a particular moment in the day. • A **time clock** is a clock that employees use to record the particular moment in the day at which they arrive at and leave work. • A **time zone** is one of 24 parts into which the world is divided in order to express the hour of the day. • LP COLON

time /taɪm/ *v* [T] to arrange for (something to happen) at a specific moment • *We timed our*

TIME

Telling time

Common ways of giving the time

a.m. = before noon	7:00	seven o'clock/seven
	8:05	five after eight/five past eight/five minutes after eight/five minutes past eight/eight o five
	9:17	nine seventeen/seventeen past nine/seventeen minutes after nine
	10:30	ten thirty/half past ten
	11:40	eleven forty/twenty to twelve/twenty of twelve/twenty minutes to twelve
noon	12:00	twelve o'clock/twelve/noon/twelve noon
p.m. = after noon	2:01	two o one/one minute after two/one minute past two/ a minute after two/a minute past two
	3:15	a quarter after three/three fifteen/a quarter past three
	8:45	a quarter to nine/a quarter of nine/eight forty-five
	9:57	nine fifty-seven/three minutes to ten
midnight	12:00	twelve o'clock/midnight/twelve midnight

When giving the time, the word *minutes* is often not used. The word *hour* may also not be used.

It's ten after.

A phrase describing the part of the day can be used.

four o'clock **in the morning** · *two thirty* **in the afternoon** · *six* **in the evening** · *11:30* **at night**

The abbreviations *a.m.* and *p.m.* can be used after the time. When they are used, you say the letters *a m* or *p m* after the number, but you do not say "o'clock."

7 a.m. · *10:30 p.m.*

Giving approximate times

almost four
nearly four
just before four
shortly before four

around four
about four

just after four
shortly after four

Periods of time

Time periods during the day

in the morning · *this evening* · *yesterday afternoon* · *tomorrow night* · *early afternoon* · *mid-morning* · *late morning*

at night · *tonight* · *last night* · *tomorrow night*
in/during the daytime · *in/during the nighttime*
at breakfast · *at lunchtime* · *at dinnertime* · *at bedtime*

Exact lengths of time

There are only a small number of words referring to exact periods of time.

millenium (1000 years)	**hour** (60 minutes)
week (7 days)	**year** (365 days)
century (100 years)	**minute** (60 seconds)
day (24 hours)	**month** (28-31 days)
decade (10 years)	**second**

Centuries, years, and hours are often divided into halves or quarters.

Approximate lengths of time

Some of the words for exact lengths of time can also be used to talk about approximate lengths of time, or to emphasize how long or short a period is.

He's been doing the same job for **years**. · *At this rate, it'll take* **weeks** *to get it done.* · *I've been waiting for* **hours**. · *I'll be ready in just a* **second**.

Other words are also used for approximate lengths of time.

I've been waiting **forever**. · *That meeting took* **an eternity**. · *We haven't been there in* **ages**. · *She's had that coat for* **quite a while**. · *Can you wait a* **moment**? · *He'll be with you* **shortly/momentarily**.

A **generation** is about 25 years.

It will take a **generation** *for the new trees to grow.*

arrivals at the airport so that we could meet and share a taxi to the city.

timer /'taɪ·mər/ *n* [C] a device that starts or stops something at a set time or that makes a sound after a particular amount of time has passed • *He set the timer on the VCR to start recording at 11:30.*

time SUITABLE POINT /taɪm/ *n* [C/U] a point of the day, week, month, or year that is suitable for a particular activity, or at which something is expected to happen • *We had enjoyed our visit, but now it was time to go home.* [U] ○ *Put away your toys, Leni, it's time for bed.* [U] ○ *The times for meals are listed on the schedule.* [C] ○ *This is no time* (= not a suitable moment) *to change your mind.* [U] • To be **in time** for something is to arrive at the right moment for an event, before it has started: *We arrived just in time for the show.* • *The plane is expected to arrive* **on time** (= when scheduled).

timely /'taɪm·li/ *adj* given or made available at a suitable moment, esp. now • *timely advice*

timing /'taɪ·mɪŋ/ *n* [U] the ability to choose the right moment to do or say something, or the time when something happens • *The difference between a joke told well and a joke told badly is the timing.* ○ *The timing of the airline strike was bad for our vacation plans.*

time OCCASION /taɪm/ *n* [C] an occasion or period, or the experience connected with it • *This is a time to be serious.* ○ *There were times when he almost gave up, but somehow he managed to survive.* ○ *We visit my mother a few times a year.* ○ *She takes the medicine three times a day.* ○ *He was holding down three jobs at the same time.* ○ *We had a good time at the party.* • **Time after time** (= Again and again) *she gets involved with men who abuse her.* • *I've told you* **time and (time) again** (= very often) *to lock both doors before you leave.*

time HISTORICAL PERIOD /taɪm/ *n* [C], **times** *pl n* a period in history • *Indians since ancient times have ground their corn by hand.* • If something or someone is before your time, they happened or existed before you were born or were old enough to remember them: *The Beatles were way before my time.* • *My dad doesn't seem to understand that* **times have changed** *since he was a kid* (= what was not acceptable then is acceptable now).

timeless /'taɪm·ləs/ *adj* lasting forever; never showing the effects of aging • *That song stands out as a timeless classic.*

timely /'taɪm·li/ *adj* • See at TIME SUITABLE POINT.

timer /'taɪ·mər/ *n* • See at TIME MEASUREMENT ON A CLOCK.

times MULTIPLIED BY /taɪmz/, *symbol* × *prep* multiplied by • *Two times two equals four.*

times AMOUNT /taɪmz/ *prep* used to show the difference in amount of two things, by multiplying one of them by the stated number • *She earns five times as much as I do.*

timetable /'taɪm,teɪ·bəl/ *n* [C] a list of the times when particular activities or events will happen; schedule • *An election is expected in one or two years, although no timetable has been announced.*

timid /'tɪm·əd/ *adj* easily frightened; not brave or confident • *She was timid about swimming in deep water.* • USAGE: The opposite of timid is BOLD.

timidly /'tɪm·əd·li/ *adv* • *She sang timidly but sweetly.*

timidity /tə'mɪd·ət̬·i/ *n* [U] • *A shaky voice revealed his timidity.*

timing /'taɪ·mɪŋ/ *n* [U] • See at TIME SUITABLE POINT.

tin /tɪn/ *n* [C/U] a soft, silver metal that is often combined with other metals or used as a protective layer on various metals • A **tin can** (*Br* **tin**) is a CAN CONTAINER. • **Tinfoil** is FOIL METAL SHEET.

tinder /'tɪn·dər/ *n* [U] a substance that burns easily, such as paper or thin sticks of wood, used to light fires • A **tinderbox** is a situation or place where sudden violence is likely to happen: *The press seems to encourage violence in an area that is already a tinderbox.*

tinge /tɪndʒ/ *v* [T] to add a slight amount of color or a quality to something • *The sunset tinged the sky red.*

tinge /tɪndʒ/ *n* [C] • *The flowers are purple with tinges of pink.*

tingle /'tɪŋ·gəl/ *v* [I] to have a slight stinging feeling • *Her skin tingled after swimming in the cold, salty water.*

tingle /'tɪŋ·gəl/ *n* [C/U] • *I often get a tingle in my toes when they're cold.* [C usually sing]

tinker /'tɪŋ·kər/ *v* [I always + adv/prep] to make small changes in something, because you hope to improve or fix it • *Chuck tinkers with the car's engine all the time.*

tinkle /'tɪŋ·kəl/ *v* [I] to make light, ringing sounds • *The wind chimes tinkled in the breeze.* • Tinkle is also a child's word for urinate.

tinkle /'tɪŋ·kəl/ *n* [C usually sing] • *We heard the tinkle of ice in a whiskey glass.*

tinny /'tɪn·i/ *adj* (of sound) weak or metallic; lacking a full sound • *The music sounded good even on the TV's tinny speakers.*

tinsel /'tɪn·səl, -zəl/ *n* [U] thin strips of a shiny material used as decoration, esp. on Christmas trees

tint /tɪnt/ *v* [T] to color (something) slightly • *Do you think he tints his hair?*

tint /tɪnt/ *n* [C] a variety of a color, or a pale color • *Here, the ocean is gray with a blue tint.* • A tint is also a substance used to change slightly the color of something, esp. hair or paint.

tiny /'taɪ·ni/ *adj* [-er/-est only] extremely small • *Just trim a tiny bit off my hair, please.*

tip END /tɪp/ *n* [C] the pointed end of something • *The tip of the cat's tail is white.* ○ *She has a house on the western tip of the island.* •

The tip of the iceberg is a small and known part of something large and unknown: *As with many injuries, the damage we can see is only the tip of the iceberg.* • If a name or word is **on the tip of** your **tongue**, you know it, but cannot remember it at that moment.

tip INFORMATION /tɪp/ *n* [C] a useful piece of information or advice, esp. something secret or not generally known • *She gave me some helpful gardening tips.* ∘ *Acting on a tip, the police arrested most of the drug ring.*

tip LEAN /tɪp/ *v* [I/T] **-pp-** to lean to one side, or to cause (something) to lean to one side • *She tipped the umbrella to keep the sun off the picnic table.* [T] • If something **tips the scales**, it changes the balance between things: *Introducing new fish to the lake tipped the scales against the trout that were already living there.*

tip FALL OVER /tɪp/ *v* [I/T] to fall or turn over, or to cause (something) to fall or turn over • *If everyone sits on one side of the boat, it will tip (over).* [I]

tip PAY /tɪp/ *v* [I/T] **-pp-** to give money to (someone) for service which is in addition to the amount being charged • *He tipped the porter generously.* [T]

tip /tɪp/ *n* [C] • *"That guy didn't bother to leave a tip," the waitress said disgustedly.*

▫**tip off** *obj*, **tip** *obj* **off** /'-'-/ *v adv* [M] to give secret information to (someone) • *Apparently the mob leaders were tipped off that police were watching them.*

tip–off /'tɪp-ɔːf/ *n* [C] *infml* • *He began cutting classes—a tip-off that he was in trouble.*

tipi /'tiː-piː/ *n* [C] a TEPEE

tipsy /'tɪp-si/ *adj infml* slightly drunk • *He seemed a bit tipsy, so I drove him home.*

tiptoe /'tɪp-toʊ/ *v* [I always + adv/prep] to walk with your heels raised off the ground • *She tiptoed out of the room so she wouldn't wake him.*

tiptoe /'tɪp-toʊ/ *n* [C] • *He had to stand on his tiptoes to reach the shelf.*

tiptop /'tɪp-tɑp/ *adj* [not gradable] *infml* excellent; perfect • *He swam a mile every day and kept himself in tiptop shape.*

tirade /'taɪ-reɪd, 'taɪ-reɪd/ *n* [C] an angry speech, often lasting a long time, that expresses strong disapproval • *My father's tirades against politicians were famous.*

tire LOSE ENERGY /taɪr/ *v* [I/T] to cause (someone) to lose energy, or to be without energy • *Weakened by the infection, he tires easily.* [I] ∘ *Running tired her.* [T] ∘ *Going up all those stairs tires me out.* [M] • To **tire of** something is to become bored with it: *Viewers never tire of nature programs.*

tired /taɪrd/ *adj* [not gradable] • *I had been up all night with the baby and was really tired.* • If you are **tired of** something, you are bored or annoyed by it: *I'm tired of cleaning up after you.*

tireless /'taɪr-ləs/ *adj* [not gradable] not stopping or taking a rest from something • *a tireless woman*

tirelessly /'taɪr-lə-sli/ *adv* • *He worked tirelessly to improve the local schools.*

tiring /'taɪ-rɪŋ/ *adj* [not gradable] causing you to feel you have no energy • *Dad had a tiring day at work.*

tire WHEEL /taɪr/ *n* [C] a rubber ring, usually filled with air, that fits around the wheel of a car, bicycle, or other vehicle • *Most cars now have radial tires.* • PIC CAR

tiresome /'taɪr-səm/ *adj* [not gradable] tiring, annoying, or boring • *It's getting a little tiresome, listening to you complain.*

tissue PAPER /'tɪʃ-uː/ *n* [C] a piece of soft, thin paper which absorbs liquids • *He wiped his nose with a tissue.* • **Tissue paper** (also **tissue**) is light, thin paper used for wrapping things.

tissue CELLS /'tɪʃ-uː/ *n* [U] *specialized* a group of related cells that forms larger parts of animals and plants • *They examined bits of lung tissue under a microscope, looking for damage.*

tit /tɪt/ *n* [C usually pl] *rude slang* a woman's breast • USAGE: This word is often considered offensive.

tit for tat /'tɪt-fər'tæt/ *n* [U] something, esp. something annoying or unpleasant, done to someone because they have done the same thing to you • *She would not continue to fight, and rejected returning tit for tat.*

titillate /'tɪt̬-ᵊl,eɪt/ *v* [I/T] to cause (someone) to feel pleasantly excited, often about something sexual • *The public was titillated by the gossip about the president's alleged affair.* [T]

titillating /'tɪt̬-ᵊl,eɪt̬-ɪŋ/ *adj* • *The tabloids are filled with titillating sex stories.*

title NAME /'taɪt̬-ᵊl/ *n* [C] the name of a book, movie, play, song, or work of art • *The book is an index to song titles.* • A **title page** is a page at the front of a book giving the name of the book and its writer and publisher. • A **title role** is the main character in a play or similar work whose name is in its title: *Brando played the title role in "The Godfather."* • A **title track** is the piece of music on a recording that has the same name as the recording itself. • LP CAPITAL LETTERS, ITALICS

title /'taɪt̬-ᵊl/ *v* [T] • *He titled his autobiography "Beneath the Underdog."*

title RANK /'taɪt̬-ᵊl/ *n* [C] a word or phrase that shows a person's rank or job • *Her job title is director of human resources.*

title SPORTS PRIZE /'taɪt̬-ᵊl/ *n* [C] a prize or public statement showing that someone is the best in a particular sport or competition • *She won her third straight title in speed skating.*

title LEGAL RIGHT /'taɪt̬-ᵊl/ *n* [U] *specialized* the legal right to own something, esp. a piece of land or a building • *That little paper is your title to the car, so don't lose it.*

titter /'tɪt̬-ər/ *v* [I] to laugh in a nervous and

TITLES AND FORMS OF ADDRESS

English has a number of titles and ways of addressing people.

When you don't know the person's name

Titles and other forms of address are generally not used in most situations when talking to people you do not know. When you want to attract their attention or show you are talking to them, you use phrases like *excuse me*. LP **Greetings**

Excuse me, can you tell me how to get to Canyon Road?

In particular situations you might hear the following forms of address used.

sir	*Can I get you the menu, sir?*	Polite; used typically with older people.
ma'am/madam	*Excuse me, ma'am, can you help me?* (in a letter) *Dear Sir or Madam:*	*Sir* and *Madam* are also used in the opening greeting of a letter to address someone you do not know.
miss	*You can leave your car here, miss. Excuse me, miss, is this your scarf?*	Polite; used typically with younger women.
folks	*See you later, folks.*	(*informal*) Used to a group of people.
everybody	*Hi, everybody!*	
guys	*Where are you guys going?* • *Bye, guys!*	(*informal*) Used with a group of men, or of men and women.
Ladies and Gentlemen	*Ladies and Gentlemen, it is a great honor to be speaking to you today.*	(*formal*) Used to a group, esp. at the beginning of a speech.

When you know the person's name

It is common to use the first name with the family name to refer to a person, especially when the family name is needed to clarify who is meant.

Do you know Jonathan Brent?

It is not common to address a person this way.

Informal situations

In general, you use somebody's first name, even at work.

See you tomorrow, Jane. • *Daniel, have you sent that payment yet?* • *I'm having dinner with Maggie tonight.*

Formal situations

To address a person to whom you want to show respect, you can put a title before the family name. Less commonly, the title may be put before the full name when referring to a person. Note that **Ms.**, **Mr.**, and **Mrs.** are not used on their own without a name to address someone.

Ms.	*Please come in, Ms. Johnson. I'm looking for Ms. Pamela Hillman.*	Used for women, both married and unmarried. Many women prefer this title to *Miss* or *Mrs.*
Mr.	*Can I speak to Mr. Grant, please?*	Used for men.
Mrs.	*Do you have a moment, Mrs. Park? This week's winner is Mrs. Sue Burton*	Used for married women. The family name is that of the husband.
Miss	*Miss Lubofsky is in a meeting right now.* *the famous actress, Miss Elizabeth Taylor*(becoming dated)	Used for women who are not married and occasionally for a married woman who has kept her original name.
Dr.	*Dr. Forster can see you this morning at ten.* *Can I speak to you after class, Dr. Lake?*	doctors and dentists, and also for people who have a Ph.D. degree.

Sometimes people are referred to by their family name on its own. This is especially common when talking about well-known people, for example in politics, sports, literature, art, and music. It is also common in news reports when referring to a person repeatedly. In the US and Canada, it is not common to address a person this way.

They played Mozart's symphony. • *I prefer Hemingway's short stories to his novels.* • *When did Lincoln become president?* • *Contreras didn't play because of his injured arm.* • (used between students or between teachers) *Is Warner teaching that course?*

(CONTINUED)

TITLES AND FORMS OF ADDRESS (*continued*)

Names of jobs are not often used alone as forms of address, except sometimes for doctors, nurses, the police, and members of the military.

Excuse me, Officer. • *Nurse, can you help me?* • *Dismiss the men, Sergeant.*

Some titles are used with a name, usually a family name, to address or refer to a person.

Professor Bhatia • *President Clinton* • *Governor Barnes* • *Sergeant Kuhn* • *Father Shea* • *Rabbi Gordon*

Talking to your family

Mom, Mommy	*Mommy, read me a story.*	*Mother* is more formal than the others.
Mother	*Can I go, too, Mom?*	*Mommy* and *Mama* are use mostly by
Mama, Ma		young children. *Ma* is informal.
Dad, Daddy	*Maybe Dad can fix it.*	*Father* is more formal than the others.
Father	*Are you all right, Father?*	*Daddy* is used mostly by young children.
Papa, Pa, Pop		*Papa* is slightly dated. *Pa* and *Pop* are informal.
Grandma,	*Grandma and Grandpa are*	*Granny* is less common than the others
Granny	*coming to visit.*	to address a grandmother.
Grandpa		
Aunt	*It's a present from Aunt Molly.*	Used with a first name.
Uncle	*Is this yours, Uncle Fred?*	Used with a first name.

Other names for family members are not generally used to address a person.

---

quiet way • *Some kids tittered at the boys who were making faces in class.*

titter /'tɪt̮·ər/ *n* [C] • *There were titters from the audience but no big laughs.*

tizzy /'tɪz·i/ *n* [C usually sing] *infml* a state of excitement or confusion • *She's in a tizzy because she locked her keys in the car.*

TNT /ˌtiː·ɛnˈtiː/ *n* [U] a powerful explosive

to INFINITIVE /tuː, tʊ, tə/ *prep* used before a verb showing that it is in the infinitive • *She agreed to help.* ○ *I asked her to finish by Friday.* ○ *I need to eat something.* ○ *I'd love to visit New York.* ○ *I want to go now.* • "To" followed by an infinitive is used after adjectives: *It's not likely to happen.* ○ *I was afraid to tell her.* • "To" followed by an infinitive is used after nouns: *He has the ability to do two things at once.* • "To" followed by an infinitive can begin a clause: *To be honest* (= Speaking honestly), *I prefer the gray skirt.* • "To" followed by an infinitive can be used to express requests or orders: *Is it possible to have tea instead?* ○ *You're not to go there by yourself.* • "To" followed by an infinitive is used after "how," "what," "when," "where," "whether," "which," "who," "whom," or "whose": *I don't know what to do.* ○ *Can you tell me how to get there?* • "To" followed by an infinitive is used after "enough": *I was close enough to touch him.*

to INSTEAD OF VERB /tuː, tʊ, tə/ *prep* used instead of a verb clause when answering questions • *"Would you like to go to the movies tonight?" "Yes, I'd love to."*

to FOR /tuː, tʊ, tə/ *prep* for the purpose of doing something • *I asked Helen out to dinner.*

to SHOWING DIRECTION /tuː, tʊ, tə/ *prep* in the direction of or as far as • *We went to Montreal last year.* ○ *I'm going to the bank.* ○ *We were in*

mud up to our ankles. • "To" can be used to show the position of something or someone in relation to something or someone else: *We came face to face in the elevator.* ○ *The Rocky Mountains are to the west of the Great Plains.* • "To" can show something is on or around something: *Can you tie the dog's leash to the fence?*

to BETWEEN /tuː, tʊ, tə/ *prep* used in phrases that show a range of things or a distance between places • *There must have been 30 to 35 people there.* ○ *We got two to three inches of snow at home.* ○ *Read pages 10 to 25.* ○ *It's two to three hundred miles from Boston to Washington.* • LP DASH

to RECEIVING /tuː, tʊ, tə/ *prep* used for showing who receives something or who experiences an action • *I told that story to Glen.* ○ *Who's the letter addressed to?*

to IN CONNECTION WITH /tuː, tʊ, tə/ *prep* in connection with • *They exercise to music.* ○ *What was their response to that news?*

to COMPARED WITH /tuː, tʊ, tə/ *prep* compared with • *Paul beat me three games to two.* ○ *I scored 80 to Talia's 90.*

to UNTIL /tuː, tʊ, tə/ *prep* until a particular time, state, or condition is reached • *It's only two weeks to your birthday.* ○ *We're open daily from 2 to 6 p.m.* ○ *My shirt was torn to shreds.* • "To" is used, when giving the time, to mean minutes before the stated hour: *It's twenty to six.*

to CAUSING /tuː, tʊ, tə/ *prep* causing a particular feeling or effect in someone • *To my great relief, she decided against going.*

to CONSIDERED BY /tuː, tʊ, tə/ *prep* considered by • *Does this make any sense to you?* ○ *Fifty dollars is very little to him.*

to MATCHING /tuː, tʊ, tə/ *prep* matching or belonging to • *the top to a bottle* ○ *the keys to my apartment* ○ *There is a funny side to everything.*

to FOR EACH /tu:, tʊ, tə/ *prep* for each of; PER • *This car gets about 30 miles to the gallon.*

toad /toʊd/ *n* [C] a small animal, similar to a FROG, that has dry, brown skin and lives mostly on land

toadstool /ˈtoʊd·stuːl/ *n* [C] a MUSHROOM (= plant), esp. a poisonous one

to and fro /ˌtuː·ənˈfroʊ/ *adv* [not gradable] in one direction and then in the opposite direction • *Outside my door I could hear people walking to and fro.*

toast BREAD /toʊst/ *n* [U] sliced bread that has been browned by being put near a high heat • *buttered toast*

toast /toʊst/ *v* [T] • *Would you like me to toast your bagel?*

toaster /ˈtoʊ·stər/ *n* [C] an electric device for making toast

toast DRINK /toʊst/ *n* [C] a short speech in honor of someone or in celebration of something, followed by everyone present taking a drink of wine or other liquid • *Ted raised his glass and proposed a toast "to absent friends."*

toast /toʊst/ *v* [T] • *At midnight, we toasted the New Year.*

toasty /ˈtoʊ·sti/ *adj* warm and comfortable • *You must feel nice and toasty sitting in front of the fire.*

tobacco /təˈbæk·oʊ/ *n* [U] a type of plant, or the dried leaves of this plant which are prepared and smoked in cigarettes, pipes, or CIGARS, or sometimes chewed • *tobacco smoke* • PIC PIPES

toboggan /təˈbɑg·ən/ *n* [C] a piece of equipment used for sliding over snow and ice which consists of long, thin boards fixed together that curve up at the front

today /təˈdeɪ/ *adv* [not gradable] on this day • *What's the date today?* ○ *We could go today or tomorrow.* • Today can also be used more generally to mean now rather than in the past: *People are more worried today than ever before.*

today /təˈdeɪ/ *n* [U] • *Today is even hotter than yesterday!*

toddle /ˈtɑd·əl/ *v* [I] (esp. of a young child) to walk awkwardly with short steps • *Our two-year-old toddled after his puppy.*

toddler /ˈtɑd·lər/ *n* [C] a young child, esp. one just learning to walk • *Are these toys suitable for toddlers?*

toe BODY PART /toʊ/ *n* [C] any of the five long, thin parts at the end of the foot, similar to the fingers of the hand • *I broke a toe when I caught my foot in a door.* • Toe also refers to the end of a shoe or sock: *That sock has a hole in the toe.* • If you are on your toes, you are prepared and noticing what is happening: *Teaching four different subjects keeps you on your toes.* • If two people or things go toe-to-toe, they oppose each other in direct competition or disagreement: *We don't have to go toe-to-toe*

with our competitors in every market. • A toenail is the hard, flat covering on the end of a toe. • PIC FOOT

toe OBEY /toʊ/ *v* [T] • To toe the line is to do what you are expected to do: *If you want to get ahead, you'd better learn to toe the line.*

TOEFL /ˈtoʊ·fəl/ *n* [U] *abbreviation for* Test of English as a Foreign Language (= a standardized test for people learning English)

toehold /ˈtoʊ·hoʊld/ *n* [C] a starting point in a job or other opportunity from which you can advance • *The young person who gets a toehold in that business will do well.*

tofu /ˈtoʊ·fuː/, **bean curd** *n* [U] a soft, pale food with little flavor, but high in PROTEIN, that is made from SOYBEANS

together WITH THE OTHER /təˈɡeð·ər/ *adv* [not gradable] (of two people or things) each with the other, or (of more than two) as a group • *We've worked together before.* ○ *Sara and I were at college together.* ○ *Add these figures together.* ○ *We should all get together for lunch.* ○ *Jim and Mary live together.*

togetherness /təˈɡeð·ər·nəs/ *n* [U] the feeling of being friendly and close with other people • *The project encourages family pride and togetherness.*

together AT THE SAME TIME /təˈɡeð·ər/ *adv* [not gradable] at the same time • *All the guests arrived together.*

together COMBINED /təˈɡeð·ər/ *adv* [not gradable] in a combined condition • *Together, they must earn over $80,000 a year.* ○ *I'll get my things together so we can leave.* ○ *You mix the eggs and sugar together before adding milk.* • If things go together, they are attractive when combined: *Do purple and pink go together?* ○ *Those pants and jacket go well together.* • To-gether with means in addition to: *The cost of food together with drinks and prizes made it an expensive party.*

together ORGANIZED /təˈɡeð·ər/ *adj* [not gradable] *infml approving* organized, confident, and able to do whatever you decide to do • *I just feel like the men have it more together than the women here do.*

toil /tɔɪl/ *n* [U] *literary* hard and tiring work • *He rested from the backbreaking toil of putting in fences.*

toil /tɔɪl/ *v* [I] • *Walter toiled in obscurity while his boss took the credit.*

toilet /ˈtɔɪ·lət/ *n* [C] a device into which people excrete waste, esp. a bowl-shaped device with a seat that has a hole in it, or a BATHROOM • *I need to go to the toilet.* • Toilet paper/tissue is soft, absorbent paper that people use to clean themselves after using the toilet. • A child who is toilet-trained has learned how to use a toilet and no longer needs to wear a DIAPER. • PIC BATHROOM

toiletries /ˈtɔɪ·lə·triːz/ *pl n* soaps, SHAMPOOS, **toothpaste**, and other items used to keep yourself clean

token SYMBOL /'toʊ·kən/ n [C] something you give to someone or do for someone to express your feelings or intentions • *It isn't a big present—it's just a token of thanks for your help.*

token /'toʊ·kən/ adj [not gradable] small or limited but having a symbolic importance • *a token fee* ○ *a token gesture of goodwill*

token DISK /'toʊ·kən/ n [C] a round, metal or plastic disk which is used instead of money in some machines • *subway tokens*

told /toʊld/ past simple and past participle of TELL • If someone says they **told you (so)**, they are emphasizing that they had earlier said your actions would have a bad result: *"I should never have joined the swim club." "I told you so."*

tolerable /'tɑl·ə·rə·bəl/ adj of a quality that is acceptable but not wonderful • *A job in a theme park is tolerable only if you're young.*

tolerably /'tɑl·ə·rə·bli/ adv to a limited or reasonable degree • *I was tolerably good at sports.*

tolerance ACCEPTANCE /'tɑl·ə·rəns/, **toleration** /ˌtɑl·ə·'reɪ·ʃən/ n [U] willingness to accept behavior and beliefs that are different from your own, even if you disagree with or disapprove of them • *religious/racial/sexual tolerance* ○ *There is zero tolerance of guns at this school—if you're caught with one, you'll be expelled.*

tolerant /'tɑl·ə·rənt/ adj • *Working with young people helps me be a little more tolerant.*

tolerate /'tɑl·ə,reɪt/ v [T] • *They don't have the best service, but I tolerate it because I love their food.*

tolerance ABILITY TO BEAR /'tɑl·ə·rəns/ n [U] the ability to bear something unpleasant or annoying, or to keep going despite difficulties • *I don't have much tolerance for hot, humid weather.*

tolerant /'tɑl·ə·rənt/ adj • *Some grasses are very tolerant of drought.*

tolerate /'tɑl·ə,reɪt/ v [T] • *Athletes often have to tolerate a lot of pain.*

toll MONEY /toʊl/ n [C] an amount of money that you have to pay to travel along some main roads, to cross bridges, etc., or to make telephone calls over long distances • *They're raising the bridge toll to $5.00.* ○ *The number you dialed is a toll call—please deposit an additional fifty cents.* • A **tollbooth** is a small, enclosed room on a road, bridge, etc., where a person collects money from drivers as they enter or leave. • A telephone call that is **toll-free** is free for the person making the call.

toll SUFFERING /toʊl/ n [U] a high degree of suffering or damage • *In addition to the physical destruction caused by the flooding, the emotional toll on its victims was immense.*

toll RING /toʊl/ v [I/T] (of a large bell) to ring slowly and repeatedly, or to cause (a large bell) to ring in this way • *The church bells tolled, calling worshipers to the Sunday service.* [I]

tomahawk /'tɑm·ə,hɔːk/ n [C] a small fighting AX (= tool with a blade) used by American Indians

tomato /tə'meɪt̬·oʊ, *New Eng and eastern Virginia also* -'mɑːt̬-/ n [C] pl **tomatoes** a juicy, red fruit eaten raw, esp. in salads, or cooked as a vegetable • *tomato sauce/soup*

tomb /tuːm/ n [C] a structure or underground room where someone, esp. an important person, is buried • A **tombstone** (also **gravestone** or **headstone**) is a stone with a flat surface that marks where a person is buried under ground and that usually has their name and the years of their birth and death written on it.

tomboy /'tɑm·bɔɪ/ n [C] a girl who dresses and acts like a boy, esp. in playing physical games that boys usually play

tomcat /'tɑm·kæt/ n [C] a male cat

tome /toʊm/ n [C] a large, heavy book

tomfoolery /tɑm'fuː·lə·ri/ n [U] foolish, often playful, behavior

tomorrow /tə'mɑr·oʊ, -'mɔːr-/ adv [not gradable] on the day after today • *He said he'll call tomorrow after work.*

tomorrow /tə'mɑr·oʊ, -'mɔːr-/ n [C/U] • *Tomorrow's meeting has been postponed.* [U] • If you say you will see someone tomorrow night/evening/etc., you mean you will see them on the night/evening/etc. of the next day: *I've arranged to see Rachel tomorrow morning/afternoon.* [U] • Tomorrow can also mean the future: *Today's problem child may be tomorrow's criminal.* [U]

ton /tʌn/ n [C] a unit of measurement of weight equal to 2000 pounds or about 907 kilograms • (*infml*)A ton or tons of something is a very large amount: *I've got a ton of homework to do tonight.*

tone VOICE EXPRESSION /toʊn/ n [U] a quality in the voice, esp. one that expresses the speaker's feelings, often toward the person being addressed • *His tone was apologetic.*

tone MOOD /toʊn/ n [U] a mood or general feeling that characterizes something, esp. a situation or a piece of writing • *The tone of his remarks was confident and reassuring.*

tone SOUND /toʊn/ n [C usually sing] a musical, mechanical, or voice sound on one note • *If you wish to leave a message, please wait until after the tone.* • Someone who is **tone-deaf** is not able to recognize different notes or sing tunes accurately. • A tone is also a STEP MUSIC.

tone MUSICAL QUALITY /toʊn/ n [C/U] the quality of sound of a musical instrument or singing voice

tone FIRMNESS OF BODY /toʊn/ n [U] the healthy firmness of the body, esp. the muscles • *Swimming helps to develop good muscle tone.*

tone down, **tone** obj **down** /'toʊn'daʊn/ v adv [M] to make (something) less forceful or offensive • *The foul language in the original play has been toned down for television.*

tongs /tɔːŋz/ *pl n* a device, often U-shaped, having long sides for picking up objects without touching them, used by pressing or moving the sides together until the free ends hold the object • *She moved the smoldering logs around in the fireplace with a set of tongs.*

tongue MOUTH PART /tʌŋ/ *n* the movable, fleshy part in the mouth that is used in tasting and swallowing food and, in people, in producing speech • If you say something **tongue in cheek** or **with** your **tongue in** your **cheek**, you intend it to be understood as a joke, although you might appear to be serious. • If you give someone a **tongue-lashing**, you criticize them, often angrily and using strong language, for something they have done: *The mayor's public tongue-lashing of a member of his own party was unprecedented.* • If you are **tongue-tied**, you find it difficult to speak, usually because you are nervous: *I was practically tongue-tied.* • A **tongue twister** is a name or set of words that are difficult to pronounce.

tongue LANGUAGE /tʌŋ/ *n* [C] a language • *McAdam could speak the Eskimo tongue, too.*

tonic /'tɑn·ɪk/ *n* [C] a liquid medicine intended to make you feel better generally rather than treating a particular health problem • A tonic is also anything that makes you feel better: *Seeing his grandchildren was the perfect tonic for him.*

tonic (water) /'tɑn·ɪk ('wɔːʈ·ər, 'wɑʈ-)/ *n* [C/ U] flavored, bubbly water usually added to alcoholic drinks • *a gin and tonic* [C]

tonight /tə'nɑɪt/ *adv* [not gradable], *n* [U] (during) the night of the present day • *The game will be shown on TV beginning at 8 o'clock tonight.*

tonsils /'tɑn·səlz/ *pl n* the two small, soft organs at the back of the mouth

Tony /'toʊ·ni/ *n* [C] one of a set of prizes given each year to the best plays and for special achievements in the theater

too MORE /tuː/ *adv* [not gradable] more than is needed or wanted; more than is suitable or enough • *The sofa is too big for this room.* ○ *The apartment was nice but it was just too expensive.* ○ *This dress is too large for me—I'll need a smaller size.* • If you say that it's **too bad** that something happened or that a situation exists, you are sorry but feel that it might have been avoided: *It's too bad parents don't read these studies.* • If something is **too good to be true**, it is so good that you find it difficult to believe: *Her new job sounds too good to be true.* • (*slang*) If someone or something is **too much**, they are admired very much or are considered very surprising or amusing: *Sally is just too much—she'll do anything to attract attention.*

too VERY /tuː/ *adv* [not gradable] very, or completely • *I'm not too sure I want to go out tonight.*

too ALSO /tuː/ *adv* [not gradable] (esp. at the end of a sentence) in addition; also • *Bring your tennis racket, and your bathing suit, too.*

took /tʊk/ *past simple of* TAKE

tool /tuːl/ *n* [C] a piece of equipment that you use to help you do a job, esp. something that you use with your hands to make or repair something • *The only tools you need for this job are a hammer and a screwdriver.* • A tool is also anything that helps you to do something you want to do: *We believe the new law will be an effective tool in curbing organized crime.*

toonie /'tuː·ni/ *n* [C] *Cdn infml* a Canadian coin worth two dollars

tooth /tuːθ/ *n* [C] *pl* **teeth** /tiːθ/ any of the hard, white, bonelike objects in the mouth, which are used for biting and chewing food • A **toothache** is a pain caused by something being wrong with one of your teeth. • A **toothbrush** is a small brush with a long handle which you use to clean your teeth. ○ PIC BRUSH • **Toothpaste** is a thick, creamy substance that you put on a **toothbrush** to clean your teeth. • A **toothpick** is a small pointed piece of wood or plastic used to get bits of food out from between the teeth, esp. after meals.

toothy /'tuː·θi/ *adj* showing a lot of your teeth • *a toothy grin/smile*

top HIGHEST PART /tɑp/ *n* [C] the highest point, place, or part • *We set out for the top of the mountain at daybreak.* • *She shouted his name* **at the top of** *her* **lungs/voice** (= very loudly). • *She came out* **on top** (= in first place) *in every race.* • *The stock market has been unpredictable, and you really have to stay* **on top of** *things* (= be aware of changes and in control). • **On top of** is also used to mean in addition to (esp. something unpleasant): *We missed the bus, and on top of that it started raining.* • *She was feeling* **on top of the world** (= very happy). • USAGE: The opposite of top is BOTTOM LOWEST PART.

top /tɑp/ *adj* [not gradable] • *The pages are numbered on the top, right-hand corner.* • *We couldn't reach the apples on the* **topmost** (= highest) *branches.*

top /tɑp/ *v* [T] **-pp-** to be more than • *The school building fund now tops $180,000.* • To **top off** something is to make it complete, esp. in a satisfactory way: *A marvelous cherry pie topped off the meal.* [M] • *We have enough gas to get there, but we ought to* **top** *it* **off** (= fill it completely) *so we won't have to bother tanking up tomorrow.*

topping /'tɑp·ɪŋ/ *n* [C] a food substance put on top of other food to give extra flavor or as a decoration • *You can get pizza with six different choices of toppings.* [C]

top UPPER /tɑp/ *adj* [not gradable] in the highest or upper part • *She tripped over the top step and nearly fell.* ○ *The book was on (the) top of the table* (= on the upper surface of the table). • If something is **top-heavy**, it has more weight in the higher part than in the lower part and tends to fall easily: *A canoe is so light that if you stand up in it, you make it top-heavy, and it can turn over easily.* ○ *(fig.) The organization was top-heavy with vice presidents.*

top /tɑp/ *n* [C] a piece of clothing worn esp. by women on the part of the body above the waist • *I'm looking for a matching top to go with this skirt.*

topless /'tɑp·ləs/ *adj, adv* [not gradable] (of women's clothing) not covering the breasts, or (of a woman) appearing with the breasts bare • *a topless dancer*

top [BEST] /tɑp/ *adj, adv* [not gradable] (in the position of being) at the highest level of importance, achievement, or success; best • *It was rated among the ten top universities in the nation.* ○ *She's one of the top executives in the fashion industry.* ○ *As a chess player, he's among the top 10% in the country.* • Top is used with many different words to mean best: *top-ranked athletes* ○ *top-rated bonds* ○ *top-seeded tennis players* • If someone is **at the top of** an activity or condition, they are performing at the highest level: *He was at the top of his game, and won in straight sets.* • If something is **top drawer**, it is of very high quality: *She brought together a team of top-drawer designers and engineers.* • *He's one of our* **top-flight** (= best) *engineers.* • *His level of fitness will have to be* **top-notch** (= excellent) *for him to play professional basketball.* • Something **top secret** is very secret and must not be told or shown to anyone apart from a special group of people.

top /tɑp/ *n* [U] • *At forty he was at the top of* (= one of the leaders of) *his profession.*

top /tɑp/ *v* [T] **-pp-** to make (something) more or better • *"They've offered me $1000." "I'm afraid we can't top* (= offer more than) *that."* • **To top/topping it (all) off** is to add something else unusually good or bad to a situation that is already unusual: *Topping it all off, they found themselves locked out of their own house.*

tops /tɑps/ *adj* [not gradable] • *She is tops* (= excellent) *in her field.*

top [LID] /tɑp/ *n* [C] a cover or lid used to close a container • *a bottle top* • [PIC] LID

top [TOY] /tɑp/ *n* [C] a toy with rounded sides that you can spin on a point at its bottom

topic /'tɑp·ɪk/ *n* [C] any subject of study or discussion • *We must pick topics for our research papers by next week.*

topical /'tɑp·ɪ·kəl/ *adj* relating to matters of importance at the present time • *It was an interesting discussion of topical issues in medicine.*

topless /'tɑp·ləs/ *adj, adv* • See at TOP [UPPER]

topmost /'tɑp·moʊst/ *adj* highest • *We sat on the topmost step and waited.*

topography /tə'pɑg·rə·fi/ *n* [U] the natural features of land, esp. the shape of its surface, or the science of mapping those features •

Volcanoes have sculpted the topography of the island.

topographical /ˌtɑp·ə'græf·ɪ·kəl/ *adj* [not gradable] • *Borden drew the first topographical map of Texas.*

topographer /tə'pɑg·rə·fər/ *n* [C] a person who maps the surface features of land

topple /'tɑp·əl/ *v* [I/T] to lean forward and fall • *A large tree was toppled by the wind.* [T] • If a government topples, it is forced from power: *Rebels tried to topple the government.* [T]

topsoil /'tɑp·sɔɪl/ *n* [U] the layer of earth in which plants grow • *rich topsoil*

topsy–turvy /ˌtɑp·si·'tɜr·vi/ *adj infml* confused, or lacking organization; UPSIDE DOWN • *Things are so topsy-turvy at work these days.*

Torah /'tɔːr·ə, 'toʊr·ə, 'tɔɪ·rə/ *n* [U] the holy writings of the Jewish religion, esp. the first five books of the Old Testament

torch /tɔːrtʃ/ *n* [C] a stick that burns at one end and is held at the other end and is used esp. as a light • *Which athlete will carry the Olympic torch into the stadium?* • *(fig.)* The torch is the basic responsibilities and characteristics of a group, organization, or society, esp. when someone new takes control: *After he died, the torch passed to his wife, who now runs the organization.* • A torch is also a BLOW-TORCH.

torch /tɔːrtʃ/ *v* [T] *infml* to burn (something) intentionally and usually illegally • *They torched the warehouse and ran.*

torch song /'tɔːrtʃ sɔːŋ/ *n* [C] a song about love or lovers

tore /tɔːr, toʊr/ *past simple of* TEAR

torment /'tɔːr·ment/ *n* [C/U] great mental or physical suffering, or something that causes such pain • *After three days of torment, she went to a dentist.* [U] ○ *That child acts like it's a torment to see me.* [C]

torment /tɔːr'ment, 'tɔːr·ment/ *v* [T] • *The cows were tormented by flies.*

torn /tɔːrn, toʊrn/ *past participle of* TEAR • If you are **torn between** two possibilities, you find it very difficult to choose between them: *She's torn between her loyalty and her desire to tell the truth.*

tornado /tɔːr'neɪd·oʊ/, *infml* **twister** *n* [C] *pl* **tornadoes** or **tornados** a dangerous storm which is a spinning cone of wind that destroys

tornado

anything in its path as it moves across the ground

torpedo /tɔːrˈpiːd·oʊ/ *n* [C] *pl* **torpedoes** a bomb designed to travel under water which explodes when it hits something • *No one on the ship saw the torpedo coming, not even the men on watch.*

torpedo /tɔːrˈpiːd·oʊ/ *v* [T] he/she/it **torpedoes, torpedoing,** *past* **torpedoed** • *The ship was torpedoed by a submarine.* ◦ *(fig.) In fact, both sides torpedoed the ceasefire* (= destroyed its chances for success).

torrent /ˈtɔːr·ənt, ˈtɑr-/ *n* [C] a large stream of water that moves very fast • *Heavy storms turned the river into a raging torrent.* ◦ *(fig.) The TV station received torrents of angry letters* (= many of them).

torrential /təˈren·tʃəl/ *adj* [not gradable] • *The torrential rains caused mud slides.*

torrid HOT /ˈtɔːr·əd, ˈtɑr-/ *adj* [not gradable] (of weather) extremely hot • *Summers in the tropics are torrid.*

torrid POWERFUL /ˈtɔːr·əd, ˈtɑr-/ *adj* [not gradable] involving very powerful emotions • *A torrid love affair is just a bit hotter than a passionate one.*

torrid PERFORMING WELL /ˈtɔːr·əd, ˈtɑr-/ *adj* [not gradable] performing or doing something extremely well • *He kept up his torrid hitting pace with a sixth homer in eight days.* ◦ *After a couple of months of torrid sales, business began to settle down.*

torso /ˈtɔːr·soʊ/ *n* [C] *pl* **torsos** the main part of the human body without the head, arms, or legs

tortilla /tɔːrˈtiː·ə/ *n* [C] a thin, flat, round bread made of corn or wheat flour and baked on top of a stove • *I could eat tortillas filled with cheese every day.* • **Tortilla chips** are small fried pieces of a tortilla, usually eaten with a spicy sauce.

tortoise /ˈtɔːrt̬·əs/ *n* [C] a TURTLE, esp. one that lives only on land

tortoiseshell /ˈtɔːrt̬·əsˌʃel/ *n* [U] the hard shell of a TURTLE that has attractive brown and yellow markings, which was used in the past to make devices to hold hair in place, frames for eyeglasses, and other items, or plastic made to look like this shell • *a tortoiseshell barrette*

tortuous /ˈtɔːr·tʃə·wəs/ *adj* full of twists and turns; not straight or direct • *His so-called shortcut turned out to be tortuous and slow.*

torture /ˈtɔːr·tʃər/ *n* [C/U] an injury or severe mental pain • *All drivers suffer the tortures of traffic and bad weather.* [C] • Torture is also the act of injuring someone or making them suffer in an effort to force them to do or say what you want them to: *The museum has many examples of instruments of torture.* [U]

torture /ˈtɔːr·tʃər/ *v* [T] • *She was tortured by the memory of their last argument.*

toss /tɔːs/ *v* [T] to throw (esp. something light)

carelessly or easily • *He tossed his dirty clothes on the floor.* ◦ *Matthew tossed the ball to his brother.* • If you toss something, or **toss** it **out**, you get rid of it by treating it as garbage: *She tossed out my old chair.* • When you toss food,

tossing the salad

you mix it by gently lifting and turning it, esp. with a DRESSING or sauce: *I tossed the salad.* • If you toss your hair or your head, you move it suddenly: *The girl tossed her hair out of her eyes.* • If you **toss (a coin)**, you choose between two possibilities by throwing a coin into the air and letting each side represent one of the possibilities, then accepting the possibility represented by the side that lands facing up: *We tossed to see who would go first.* • To **toss (and turn)** is to move about restlessly: *I was tossing and turning all night.* • If you **toss around** an idea, you think about it: *Some of us have been tossing around suggestions for improving the show.* • If you **toss** something **off**, you do it quickly, easily, and almost carelessly: *Mercer tosses off songs that others would labor over.*

toss /tɔːs/ *n* [C] • *"I don't care," she replied with a toss of her head.* • A **toss-up** is a situation in which two possibilities are equally likely: *It was a toss-up who would win, right to the end of the game.*

tot /tɑt/ *n* [C] a small child • *The tiny tot was trying so hard to keep up with his brother.*

total AMOUNT /ˈtoʊt̬·əl/ *n* [C] the whole amount • *Add these up and give me the total.* ◦ *We paid a total of $473.* • **In total** means including everything added together: *Last week 45 people in total came to the senior center.*

total /ˈtoʊt̬·əl/ *adj* [not gradable] • *Total wine exports have increased.*

total /ˈtoʊt̬·əl/ *v* [T] **-l-** or **-ll-** • *This history series totals twelve volumes in all.*

total COMPLETE /ˈtoʊt̬·əl/ *adj* [not gradable] complete or extreme • *Negotiations had to be held in total secrecy.*

totally /ˈtoʊt̬·əl·i/ *adv* • *This book is totally different from her last one.* • LP VERY, COMPLETELY, AND OTHER INTENSIFIERS

total DESTROY /ˈtoʊt̬·əl/ *v* [T] to destroy (something) completely • *She didn't total the car, but she did a lot of damage.*

totalitarian /toʊˌtæl·əˈter·iː·ən/ *adj* [not gradable] of or relating to a government that has almost complete control over the lives of its citizens and does not permit political opposition

tote /toʊt/ *v* [T] *infml* to carry (something) with you • *Tommy always totes around his cell phone.* [M] • A **tote bag** is a bag with handles and an open top, used for carrying things.

totem /'toʊṭ·əm/ *n* [C] an object that is a symbol for a group of people • *They thought of him as a good-luck totem.* • A **totem pole** is a wooden pole with symbols cut or painted on it which is connected esp. with American Indians of the northwest.

totem pole

totter /'tɑṭ·ər/ *v* [I] to move or walk in a shaky way, as if about to fall • *She tottered down the stairs.*

touch [USE FINGERS] /tʌtʃ/ *v* [I/T] to put the fingers or hand lightly on or against (something) • *That paint is wet, so don't touch.* [I] • (*infml*) If you cannot touch something, you are not allowed to have or use it: *She can't touch the money from her father until she's 21.* [T] • (*infml*) If you say you do not touch something, you mean that you do not drink or eat it: *I never touch candy.* [T] • If someone will **not touch** something **with a ten-foot pole**, they will not be involved with it in any way. • A situation that is **touch-and-go** is uncertain: *At one point, the operation was touch-and-go.*

touch /tʌtʃ/ *n* [C/U] the ability to know what something is like by putting your hand or fingers on it • *This cloth is soft to the touch.* [U] • A touch is an act of putting your hand or fingers briefly on something to operate it: *At a touch of the button, the door opened.* [C]

touch [BE CLOSE] /tʌtʃ/ *v* [I/T] to be so close together that there is no space between • *Don't let the back of the chair touch the wall.* [T] ○ *Push the bookcases together until they touch.* [I] • If one thing does not touch something similar, it is not as good as the other thing: *Her cooking can't touch her sister's.* [T]

touch /tʌtʃ/ *n* [U] • If you are **in touch** with someone, you see them or communicate with them regularly: *We haven't kept in touch.* ○ *We stay in close touch with the New York office.* ○ Compare **lose touch** at LOSE [NOT MAINTAIN]. • If you are **in touch** with a subject, activity, or situation, your knowledge of it is recent: *I stay in touch with the modern music scene.*

touch [CAUSE FEELINGS] /tʌtʃ/ *v* [T] to cause (someone) to feel sympathetic or grateful • *Your kindness has touched my family.*

touched /tʌtʃt/ *adj* • *She was touched by the letters and cards sent by people she didn't even know.*

touching /'tʌtʃ·ɪŋ/ *adj* • *Many find stories about cats more touching than any human stories.*

touch [SKILL] /tʌtʃ/ *n* [U] a skill or special quality • *He seems to be losing his touch at poker.* ○ *The flowers were a nice touch.*

touch [SMALL AMOUNT] /tʌtʃ/ *n* [C] a small amount • *There was a touch of regret in her voice.* ○ *I had a touch of flu yesterday.*

□**touch down** /'-'-/ *v adv* [I] to land at an airport • *The flight touched down on time.*

touchdown /'tʌtʃ·daʊn/ *n* [C] • *High winds delayed the space shuttle's touchdown.* • See also TOUCHDOWN.

□**touch off** *obj*, **touch** *obj* **off** /'-'-/ *v adv* [M] to start (a fight or violent activity), or to cause (a fire or explosion) • *Plans for a new airport touched off a storm of protest.* ○ *Brown's raid touched off the Civil War.* ○ *Wind-blown wires touched off the blaze.*

□**touch on** /'--/ *v adv* [T] to speak briefly about (something) • *Of course, we only touched on how much I would be paid.*

□**touch up** *obj*, **touch** *obj* **up** /'-'-/ *v adv* [M] to improve (something) with small changes • *I had to touch up the paint job on my car.*

touchdown /'tʌtʃ·daʊn/ *n* [C] (in football) the act of scoring six points by carrying or catching the ball behind the other team's goal line • *He scored three touchdowns early in the game.* • See also **touchdown** at TOUCH DOWN.

touching /'tʌtʃ·ɪŋ/ *adj* • See at TOUCH [CAUSE FEELINGS].

touchstone /'tʌtʃ·stoʊn/ *n* [C] a basic principle for judging quality • *Perfect service is the touchstone of a fine restaurant.*

touchy /'tʌtʃ·i/ *adj* [-er/-est only] easily angered or made unhappy • *She's touchy about people borrowing her books.* • A touchy subject or situation is one that must be dealt with carefully: *Immigration is a very touchy subject among some people.*

tough [STRONG] /tʌf/ *adj* [-er/-est only] not easily broken, weakened, or defeated; strong • *These toys are made of tough plastic.* ○ *You have to be tough to be successful in politics.* • Results or actions that are tough are severe and determined: *Tough new safety standards for cars are being introduced this week.* ○ *The police are getting tougher on drunk drivers.*

toughen /'tʌf·ən/ *v* [T] • *They're going to toughen existing drug laws.* • *The army certainly toughened these men up* (= made them stronger).

toughness /'tʌf·nəs/ *n* [U] • *He lacks the inner toughness needed in a leader.*

tough [DIFFICULT] /tʌf/ *adj* [-er/-est only] difficult to do or deal with • *They will be a tough team to beat.* ○ *We've had to make some very tough decisions.* ○ *It's going to be a tough win-*

ter. • Food that is tough is difficult to cut or eat: *a tough steak* • (*infml*) If you say that someone or something is **a tough act to follow**, you mean that it will be difficult for anyone coming after them to do as well. • A **tough row to hoe** is a difficult task to accomplish.

tough VIOLENT /tʌf/ *adj* [*-er/-est* only] likely to be violent or to contain violence • *a tough guy* ○ *a tough neighborhood*

tough NO SYMPATHY /tʌf/ *exclamation infml* • If you say something is **tough (luck)**, you are showing that you do not have any sympathy for someone's problems: *Anyone who misses three classes will fail, and if you don't like it, tough.*

tough out *obj*, **tough** *obj* **out** /'-'-'/ *v adv* [M] *infml* to be strong during (a difficult situation) • *Should we tough it out, or should we quit now and cut our losses?*

toupée /tuːˈpeɪ/ *n* [C] a specially shaped piece of artificial hair that can be worn by a man to cover an area of his head that has no hair

tour /tʊr/ *n* [C] a visit to a place or area, esp. one during which you look around the place or area and learn about it • *a walking tour* ○ *a sightseeing tour* • A tour is also a planned visit to several places to give performances: *The band is currently on tour in Australia.*

tour /tʊr/ *v* [I/T] • *We spent a month touring France.* [T] ○ *Alanis is touring to promote her new album.* [I]

tourist /'tʊr·əst/ *n* [C] a person who travels and visits places for pleasure and interest • *Millions of tourists visit Rome every year.*

tourism /'tʊr·ɪz·əm/ *n* [U] the business of providing services, such as transportation, places to stay, or entertainment, for tourists

tournament /'tʊr·nə·mənt, 'tɜr-, 'tɔːr-/, **tourney** /'tʊr·ni, 'tɜr-, 'tɔːr-/ *n* [C] a competition in which many persons compete in a series of games and the winner of one part continues to play in the next until only one winner is left • *a chess/golf tournament*

tourniquet /'tʊr·nɪ·kət, 'tɜr-/ *n* [C] a strip of cloth that is tied tightly around an injured arm or leg to stop the flow of blood

tousled /'taʊ·zəld, -səld/ *adj* (esp. of hair) looking messy • *She ran her fingers through her tousled hair.*

tout /taʊt/ *v* [T] to advertise or praise (something or someone) repeatedly, esp. as a way of encouraging their sale or popularity • *Critics are touting him as the next big superstar.*

tow /toʊ/ *v* [T] to pull (esp. a vehicle) along, using a rope or a chain • *The town tows abandoned cars and then fines their owners.* • A **tow truck** is a truck that has special equipment for pulling vehicles that cannot be driven.

tow /toʊ/ *n* [C] • *My car broke down and Bob gave me a tow.* • If someone is **in tow**, they are with someone else: *She arrived with her three children in tow.*

toward MOVEMENT /twɔːrd, twoʊrd, təˈwɔːrd/,

towards /twɔːrdz, twoʊrdz, təˈwɔːrdz/ *prep* in the direction of; closer to • *She stood up and walked toward him.* ○ *The hurricane is heading toward Florida.*

toward RELATION /twɔːrd, twoʊrd, təˈwɔːrd/, **towards** /twɔːrdz, twoʊrdz, təˈwɔːrdz/ *prep* in relation to • *Their attitudes toward women have changed.*

toward POSITION /twɔːrd, twoʊrd, təˈwɔːrd/, **towards** /twɔːrdz, twoʊrdz, təˈwɔːrdz/ *prep* near to; just before or around • *Our seats were toward the back of the theater.* ○ *Harry's book will be published toward the end of the year.*

toward PURPOSE /twɔːrd, twoʊrd, təˈwɔːrd/, **towards** /twɔːrdz, twoʊrdz, təˈwɔːrdz/ *prep* for the purpose of (buying or achieving something) • *I'm saving up to buy a car, and Dad gave me some money toward it.* ○ *Government should be working toward a cleaner environment.* ○ *How much does this exam count toward our final grade?*

towel /taʊ·əl, taʊl/ *n* [C] a usually rectangular piece of cloth or paper used for drying something • *a bath towel* ○ *paper towels*

towel /'taʊ·əl, taʊl/ *v* [T] **-l-** or *also* **-ll-** • *She toweled her hair dry.* • If you **towel off/down**, you dry yourself with a towel.

tower /'taʊ·ər, taʊr/ *n* [C] a tall, narrow structure that either forms part of a building or stands alone • *a clock tower* • A tower is also a tall, usually metal structure used for broadcasting: *a television tower*

tower /'taʊ·ər, taʊr/ *v* [I always + adv/prep] to appear very tall or large, or to be much taller than something else • *As we drove on, the Rocky Mountains towered before us.* ○ *Although he's only 14, David towers over his mother.*

towering /'taʊ·ə·rɪŋ, 'taʊ·rɪŋ/ *adj* • *Fielder hit a towering* (= very high) *home run.* ○ *Bresson's towering* (= great) *masterpiece explores the nature of freedom.*

town /taʊn/ *n* [C/U] a place where there are a lot of houses, stores, and other buildings which is smaller than a city • *He was born in the small town of Elnora, Indiana.* [C] ○ *We stayed at the best hotel in town.* [U] • Town can also mean the place where you live or work: *Barbara is out of town this week.* [U] • Town is also the part of a town where the main stores are: *I'm going into/to town to do some shopping.* [U] • Town can also refer to the people who live in the town: *The whole town is hoping our team will win.* [C] • **On the town** means enjoying yourself by going to places of entertainment in a town or city: *I was out on the town last night.* • A **town hall** is a building in which local government officials and employees work and have meetings. • A **townhouse** is one of a series of similar houses that are usually joined by a shared wall.

township /'taʊn·ʃɪp/ *n* [C] (in parts of the US

and Canada) a unit of local government consisting of a town and the area surrounding it

townspeople /ˈtaʊnzˌpiːpəl/, **townsfolk** /ˈtaʊnzˌfoʊk/ *pl n* the people who live in a particular town, considered as a group

toxic /ˈtɑk·sɪk/ *adj* poisonous, or relating to poisonous substances • *toxic waste*

toxicity /tɑkˈsɪs·ət·i/ *n* [U] the quality of being poisonous, or the degree to which something is poisonous • *The toxicity of the drug severely limits its use.*

toxin /ˈtɑk·sən/ *n* [C] a poisonous substance, esp. one that is produced by bacteria and causes disease

toy PLAY OBJECT /tɔɪ/ *n* [C] an object that children play with • *a stuffed toy ○ a toy train/soldier*

toy SMALL DOG /tɔɪ/ *adj* [not gradable] (of a breed of dog) very small and kept as a pet • *a toy poodle*

toy with /ˈtɔɪ wɪθ, wɪð/ *v prep* [T] to consider or think about (something) in a not very serious way, and without making a decision • *We're toying with the idea of going to Peru next year.*

trace FIND /treɪs/ *v* [T] to find (someone or something) by searching carefully and methodically • *Police are trying to trace the mother of the abandoned baby. ○ The phone company was unable to trace the call* (= find where it came from). • To trace something is also to discover its cause or origin: *The outbreak of food poisoning was traced to contaminated shellfish. ○ They trace their family back to the early settlers.* • To trace something is also to describe the way it developed: *The movie traces the events leading up to the Russian Revolution.*

trace /treɪs/ *n* [C] a mark or sign that something happened or existed • *They found traces of a lost civilization in the jungle. ○ He vanished without a trace.*

trace DRAW /treɪs/ *v* [T] to copy (a drawing, pattern, etc.) by drawing its lines on a thin piece of paper that is placed over it

trace SLIGHT AMOUNT /treɪs/ *n* [C] a very slight amount or degree • *There was a trace of a smile on his face, ○ She speaks English without the slightest trace of an accent.*

track PATH /træk/ *n* [C] a path that is narrower than a road, often with an uneven surface • *We walked along a muddy track at the side of the field.* • A track is also one or a pair of parallel metal bars on which trains travel. • If something is **on track**, it is developing as expected: *We were behind schedule on this job, but we're back on track now.*

track MARKS /træk/ *n* [C usually pl] a mark or line of marks left on a surface, esp. the ground, by a moving animal, person, or vehicle, that shows the direction of travel • *deer tracks in the snow* • **In** your **tracks** means in the exact place where you are standing: *I stopped dead*

in my tracks at a window display of Irish cookbooks. • If you are **on the right/wrong track**, you are dealing with a situation or problem in a way that is likely or not likely to succeed: *If you suspect my son was involved, you are on the wrong track.*

track /træk/ *v* [T] to follow (something that moves or changes) by noticing marks or signs that it has left behind • *The study tracked the careers of 1226 doctors who trained at Harvard Medical School.* • If you track something messy or dirty, you leave messy or dirty marks when walking because you had something on your shoes or feet: *The kids are always tracking mud in the kitchen.*

track SPORTS /træk/ *n* [C/U] the sport of competitive running, or a wide, circular path that is made for this sport • *Fall sports include football, hockey, and track.* [U] • A track is also a specially prepared surface for any kind of racing: *a dog/thoroughbred track* [C] • **Track and field** is a sport that tests a person's ability to run faster, jump farther or higher, or throw an object farther, when competing against others. • A **track event** is a running race over a fixed distance. Compare **field event** at FIELD SPORTS. • A **track meet** is a sporting competition between two or more teams, involving running races as well as jumping and throwing competitions. • Your **track record** is all your achievements or failures in the past: *We invest in large companies with an impressive track record of introducing new technology.*

track MUSIC /træk/ *n* [C] one of several songs or pieces of music on a musical recording

□**track down** *obj*, **track** *obj* **down** /ˈ-ˈ-/ *v adv* [M] to search for (someone or something), often when it is difficult to find them • *I'm trying to track down one of my old classmates from college.*

tract LAND /trækt/ *n* [C] a large area of land, or a measured area of land • *The house is surrounded by vast tracts of woodland. ○ A new hospital will be built on the 60-acre tract.*

tract BODY SYSTEM /trækt/ *n* [C] a system of tubes and organs in the body that are connected and have a particular purpose • *the digestive/urinary tract*

tract WRITING /trækt/ *n* [C] *fml* a short piece of writing, esp. on a religious or political subject, that is intended to influence people's opinions

traction HOLDING /ˈtræk·ʃən/ *n* [U] the ability of a wheel or tire to hold the ground without sliding • *I reduce the air pressure in all four tires during winter for better traction on slick, icy roads.*

traction PULLING /ˈtræk·ʃən/ *n* [U] the pulling of a heavy load over a surface, or the power used to do this • (*medical*) Traction is also a state in which an injured part of the body is gently pulled with special equipment: *His broken leg was put in a cast and was in traction.*

tractor /'træk·tər/ *n* [C] a motor vehicle with large back wheels and thick tires that is used on farms for pulling heavy loads and machinery

tractor–trailer /ˌtræk·tər'treɪ·lər/ *n* [C] a powerful vehicle for moving heavy loads, esp. over long distances, consisting of a separate part at the front for the driver attached to a large boxlike container on wheels

trailer   semi

tractor-trailer

trade BUYING AND SELLING /treɪd/ *n* [C/U] the activity of buying and selling goods and services esp. between countries • *foreign trade* [U] ○ *a trade agreement* [U] • A trade is the act of exchanging one thing for another. [C]

trade /treɪd/ *v* [I/T] to buy, sell, or exchange goods • *For centuries, Native Americans traded with European settlers.* [I] • To trade is also to exchange something: *The children traded comics.* [T] ○ *The two players traded insults and nearly came to blows.* [T] • If you trade something in, such as a car, you give it as part of the payment for something new: *He recently traded in his Jeep for a red Mercedes.* [M] • If you **trade places** with someone, you go to where they are and they come to where you are: *We traded places so he could sit near the window.*

trader /'treɪd·ər/ *n* [C] someone who buys and sells goods or services

trade JOB /treɪd/ *n* [C/U] a job, esp. one that needs special skill and that involves working with your hands, or the type of work in which such skills are needed • *the building trades* [C] ○ *He's an auto mechanic/electrician by trade.* [U] • A trade is also any business: *the book/tourist trade* [C] • A **trade secret** is a piece of information about a product that is known only to the company that makes it. • A **trade union** is a **labor union**, see at LABOR WORK.

□**trade on/upon** /'-ˌ-; '--ˌ-/ *v prep* [T] to use (something) for your own advantage, esp. unfairly • *He ran the kind of political campaign that trades on people's fear of crime.*

trademark /'treɪd·mɑrk/, *symbol* ™ *n* [C] a name or a symbol on a product that shows it is made by a particular company

tradeoff, **trade–off** /'treɪd·ɔːf/ *n* [C] a balancing of two opposing situations or qualities, both of which are desired • *The tradeoff in a*

democracy is between individual liberty and an orderly society.* • A tradeoff is also a situation in which the achieving of something you want involves the loss of something else which is also desirable, but less so: *They both had successful careers, but the tradeoff was they seldom saw each other.*

tradition /trə'dɪʃ·ən/ *n* [C/U] a way of behaving or a belief that has been established for a long time, or the practice of following behavior and beliefs that have been so established • *It is a western tradition for brides to wear white.* [C] ○ *The Dinka people are cattle-farmers by tradition.* [U]

traditional /trə'dɪʃ·ən·ᵊl/ *adj* • *the traditional two-parent family* ○ *traditional Southern cooking* ○ *the traditional politeness of Japanese culture*

traditionally /trə'dɪʃ·ən·ᵊl·i/ *adv* • *Quaker meetings are traditionally held in silence.*

traffic MOVING THINGS /'træf·ɪk/ *n* [U] the movement of vehicles or people along roads, or the movement of aircraft, trains, or ships along a route • *heavy/rush-hour traffic* ○ *Air traffic has increased 30% in the last decade.* • A **traffic circle** (also **rotary**) is a place where roads come together into a circle around which traffic moves in only one direction. • A **traffic jam** is a situation on a road in which there are too many cars, trucks, etc., and therefore they can move only very slowly or not at all. ○ PIC BUMPER-TO-BUMPER TRAFFIC • A **traffic light** (also **light**, **stoplight**) is a set of red, yellow, and green lights that control the movement of vehicles at a point where two or more streets meet. ○ PIC INTERSECTION

traffic TRADE /'træf·ɪk/ *n* [U] illegal trade • *They're trying to cut down on the traffic in drugs crossing the border.*

traffic /'træf·ɪk/ *v* [I] **trafficking**, *past* **trafficked** • *He was charged with trafficking in cocaine.*

tragedy /'trædʒ·ə·di/ *n* [C/U] a very sad event or situation, esp. one involving death or suffering • *Drinking and driving so often lead to tragedy.* [U] • A tragedy is also a regrettable situation or result: *It's a tragedy (that) so many children are unable to get a decent education.* [C] • In the theater, a tragedy is a serious play that ends with the death or suffering of the main character: *Shakespeare's tragedies* [C]

tragic /'trædʒ·ɪk/ *adj* very sad because connected with death and suffering • *Two men lost their lives in a tragic accident.* • In the theater, tragic means having to do with a TRAGEDY (= type of play having a sad ending): *a tragic actor*

tragically /'trædʒ·ɪ·kli/ *adv* • *Tragically, the side effects of the drug were not discovered until many people had been seriously hurt by it.*

trail PATH /treɪl/ *n* [C] a path through the countryside, often made or used for a particular purpose • *a bike/mountain/nature trail* ○

(fig.) Presidential candidates were on the campaign trail in Mississippi yesterday. • A trail is also a series of marks left by a person, animal, or thing as it moves along: *A trail of bloody footprints led to the victim.* • A **trailblazer** is a person who is the first to do something, and whose actions show other people like them that they can do it too: *She was a trailblazer as the only woman in the US Senate.*

trail FOLLOW /treɪl/ *v* [I/T] to follow or come behind • *Ray trailed Kate up to the porch.* [T] ○ *A string of police cars led the president's limousine and others trailed behind.* [I always + adv/prep] • In a competition, to trail is to be losing to someone: *Dallas trailed 34-21 with less than seven minutes to play in the football game.* [I] ○ *Bush trailed the governor by only 4 percentage points.* [T] ○ *Though trailing in the polls, she predicted victory.* [I]

▫**trail off** /'-'-/ *v adv* [I] to become less in amount or loudness • *His voice trailed off weakly and we could not hear the rest.*

trailer VEHICLE /'treɪ·lər/ *n* [C] a vehicle without an engine, often in the form of a flat frame or a container, that can be pulled by another vehicle • A trailer is also a long, narrow house on wheels: *We bought a trailer for camping trips.* • PIC TRACTOR-TRAILER

trailer ADVERTISEMENT /'treɪ·lər/ *n* [C] an advertisement for a movie, often showing a few, brief parts of it

train VEHICLE /treɪn/ *n* [C] a railroad engine and the connected, wheeled containers it pulls along the tracks in carrying goods or people • *a freight/passenger train* ○ *a commuter train*

train PREPARE /treɪn/ *v* [I/T] to prepare (someone) or be prepared for a job, activity, or sport by learning skills or by mental or physical exercise • *She trained as a pilot.* [I] ○ *He trains teachers to use new technology.* [T] ○ *She trained hard for the race, sometimes running as much as 60 miles a week.* [I]

trainee /treɪˈniː/ *n* [C] a person who is learning and practicing new skills, esp. ones connected with a job • *We have three new trainees in the accounting department.*

trainer /'treɪ·nər/ *n* [C] a person who teaches skills to people or animals to prepare them for a job, activity, or sport • *They showed pictures of the winning horse and its trainer.*

training /'treɪ·nɪŋ/ *n* [U] • *We got two weeks of on-the-job training on how to conduct interviews.* • When you are in training for a competition, you exercise in a way that prepares you for it.

train SERIES /treɪn/ *n* [C] a line of animals, people, or things moving along together, or a series of connected thoughts or events • *a mule/wagon train* ○ *Now I've lost my train of thought and forgot what I was going to say.*

train PART OF DRESS /treɪn/ *n* [C] the part of a long dress that spreads out onto the floor behind

trainer /'treɪ·nər/ *n* [C usually pl] *Br for* SNEAKER

trait /treɪt/ *n* [C] a characteristic, esp. of a personality • *Patience is one of his best traits.*

traitor /'treɪt·ər/ *n* [C] a person who gives away or sells secrets of their country, or someone who is not loyal to their beliefs or friends • *Benedict Arnold was a traitor during the American Revolution.* ○ *Opponents called the mayor "a traitor to the cause."*

trajectory /trəˈdʒek·tə·ri/ *n* [C] the curved path an object follows after it is thrown or shot into the air • *The missile came in on a very low trajectory.*

tram /træm/ *n* [C] an electric vehicle that is similar to a bus but travels on tracks laid along roads • *I hopped off the tram near the park.* • A tram is also a car that travels on a heavy wire up mountains or across rivers.

tramp WALK /træmp, trɑmp/, **tromp** /trɑmp, trɔmp/ *v* [I/T] to walk with heavy steps • *I've been tramping through museums all day.* [I]

tramp /træmp/ *n* [U] • *We listened to the rhythmical tramp of soldiers' feet.*

tramp POOR PERSON /træmp/ *n* [C] dated a person who travels around, asking for temporary work, food, or money from other people • *Tramps knew the houses where you got good food.*

trample /'træm·pəl/ *v* [I/T] to step heavily on or crush (someone or something) • *The commuter in a hurry tramples anyone who gets in the way.* [T] ○ *(fig.) An employer cannot trample on the rights of employees* (= damage or destroy them). [I]

trampoline /ˌtræm·pəˈliːn/ *n* [C] a piece of equipment that is a sheet of strong material attached by springs to a frame, on which people jump

trance /træns/ *n* [C] a mental state between sleeping and waking in which a person does not move but can hear and understand what is being said • *The priest went into a trance and began to chant.*

tranquil /'træŋ·kwəl/ *adj* calm, quiet, and peaceful • *I lay on the dock under a tranquil blue sky.*

tranquility, tranquillity /træŋˈkwɪl·ət̬·i/ *n* [U] • *The tranquility of the forest helps me relax.*

tranquilize /'træŋ·kwəˌlaɪz/ *v* [T] • *Vets had to tranquilize the coyote before moving her.*

tranquilizer /'træŋ·kwəˌlaɪ·zər/ *n* [C] a drug that makes people or animals calm • *You take a tranquilizer to calm down and then drink coffee to stay awake!*

transact /trænˈzækt/ *v* [T] *slightly fml* to do (business), to buy or sell things • *Now you can transact business electronically.*

transaction /trænˈzæk·ʃən/ *n* [C] • *It was the biggest real estate transaction in the city's history.*

transatlantic /ˌtræn·zətˈlænt̬·ɪk/ *adj* [not gradable] crossing the Atlantic Ocean • *New-*

foundland was once an important stop for transatlantic flights.

transcend /træn'send/ *v* [T] to go beyond or rise above (a limit), or be greater than (something ordinary) • *She said that society must transcend its racial and ethnic divisions.*

transcontinental /ˌtræn͵skɑnt·ᵊn'ent·ᵊl/ *adj* [not gradable] crossing a continent • *Kennedy Airport handles primarily overseas and transcontinental flights.*

transcribe /træn'skraɪb/ *v* [T] to make a complete written record of (spoken or written words) • *Only an expert could transcribe my notes so well.*

transcript /'træn·skrɪpt/ *n* [C] a complete written copy of spoken or written words • *I had them send me a transcript of the program.*
transcription /træn'skrɪp·ʃən/ *n* [U] • *The language of the characters in the novel is like a transcription of real criminals' talk.*

transfer /træns'fɜr, 'træns·fɜr/ *v* [I/T] **-rr-** to move from one place, person, or position to another, or to cause (someone or something) to move • *She studied for two years at Smith College, then transferred to the University of Chicago.* [I] ○ *Transfer your weight to your front foot as you swing.* [T] • When property is transferred to someone, legal ownership is changed from one person to another: *Franklin transferred the car to his brother.* [T]
transfer /'træns·fɜr/ *n* [C/U] • *I got my money through an electronic transfer into my account.* [C]

transfixed /træns'fɪkst/ *adj* (of a person or animal) unable to move, usually because of great fear or interest in something • *The entire nation will sit transfixed in front of TV sets.*

transform /træns'fɔːrm/ *v* [T] to change completely (the appearance or character) of something or someone • *Computers have transformed the way work is done.* ○ *Salinas dramatically transformed the country's economy.*
transformation /ˌtræns·fər'meɪ·ʃən/ *n* [C/U] • *This plan means a complete transformation of our organization.* [C]
transformer /træns'fɔːr·mər/ *n* [C] specialized a device that changes the characteristics of an electrical current

transfusion /træns'fjuː·ʒən/ *n* [C/U] the activity or process of putting new blood into a person's or animal's body, or an amount of blood received this way • *He needs regular blood transfusions and a lot of medication.* [C] ○ (*fig.*) *The new prime minister brought a transfusion* (= fresh supply) *of young ideas into the government.* [C]

transgression /trænz'greʃ·ən/ *n* [C/U] *slightly fml* an action that breaks a law or rule • *It is hard to keep the transgressions of famous people out of the news.* [C] ○ *Murder is the ultimate social transgression.* [U]
transgress /trænz'gres/ *v* [T] *slightly fml* • *He transgressed the military code of honor and paid a heavy penalty.*

transient /'træn·ʃənt, -dʒənt, -ziː·ənt/ *adj* [not gradable] lasting for only a short time; TEMPORARY • *The weakness was transient, and soon I was feeling strong again.* • Transient also means staying for only a short time: *Transient workers come to pick apples and then head south to harvest other crops.*
transient /'træn·ʃənt, -dʒənt, -ziː·ənt/ *n* [C] • *Even transients just staying a day or two pay sales taxes.*

transistor /træn'zɪs·tər/ *n* [C] a small electronic device that controls electric current in televisions, radios, and other equipment

transit /'træn·zət, -sət/ *n* [U] the process of moving, or the movement of goods or people from one place to another • *Our boxes are in transit and should arrive tomorrow.*

transition /træn'zɪʃ·ən/ *n* [C/U] the process of changing, or a change from one form or condition to another • *It was a neighborhood in transition from Jewish to Italian with a sprinkling of Irish.* [U] ○ *Retirement is a big transition.* [C]
transitional /træn'zɪʃ·ən·ᵊl/ *adj* [not gradable] • *We're in a transitional period right now, and no one knows what to expect.*

transitive /'træn·zət·ɪv, -sət·ɪv/ *adj* [not gradable] *specialized* (in grammar) (of a verb) having or needing an object • *In the sentence "The*

VERBS: TRANSITIVE AND INTRANSITIVE GRAMMAR PATTERNS

The **subject** of a sentence is the thing or person that is being discussed.

Nora packed her bags. • *My friend laughed.* • *The roads are quiet.* • *You should come.*

Transitive verbs have an **object**. What the subject does has a direct effect on someone or something—the object.

*Nora packed **her bags**.*

Intransitive verbs refer to an action that does not directly affect anything, and so they do not have an object.

My friend laughed.

There are other types of verbs that have no object and do not refer to an action: **linking verbs** (*The roads **are** quiet*), **auxiliary verbs** (***Do** you like it?* and *You **should** come*).

LP Linking verbs and Auxiliary verbs

CONTINUED

VERBS: TRANSITIVE AND INTRANSITIVE GRAMMAR PATTERNS (*continued*)

Many verbs can be followed by a clause or by another verb.

She demanded **that** *he return the books.* [+ *that* clause] • *Do you know* **wh**ere *these birds go in the winter?* [+ *wh*- word] • *Do you want* **to** *leave?* [+ *to* infinitive]

Sometimes all uses of a verb follow a particular grammar pattern. In these cases the grammar code is given before the definition. Often a verb has additional grammar patterns that are found only in some uses. These are shown in example sentences followed by the grammar code.

Transitive verb patterns

carry	*I'll carry the baby*	[T]	A verb that always has an object has [T] im-
	mediately before its definition.		
put	*Put your bags* **down**.	[T always	The object must be followed by an adverb or
	Put your bags **in** *the corner.*	+ adv/prep]	by a phrase beginning with a preposition. The verb cannot be used with the object on its own. For example, you cannot say sim ply "Put your bags" but must say something like *Put your bags* **on** *the table* (adding a phrase that begins with a preposition).

Intransitive verb patterns

exist	*Only two copies of the book exist.*	[I]	A verb that never has an object has [I] immediately before its definition.
live	*She lives* **upstairs**.	[I always	The verb cannot be used alone but must be
	She lives **on** *the first floor.*	+ adv/prep]	followed by an adverb or by a phrase begin ning with a preposition.

Verbs that have both transitive and intransitive uses

A verb that can be used either with or without an object has [I/T] before the definition, and examples showing transitive and intransitive uses are marked [T] or [I].

eat [I/T]	*He ate two cheeseburgers.*	[T]	Transitive use.
	Should we eat soon?	[I]	Intransitive use.
	We were eating (dinner).	[I/T]	This example shows both a transitive and an intransitive use.

LP **Phrasal verbs**

---

car hit a tree," "hit" is a transitive verb and "tree" is the object. • Compare INTRANSITIVE.

transitory /ˈtræn·zəˌtɔːr·i, -ˌtoʊr·i/ *adj* [not gradable] *slightly fml* not permanent; TEMPO-RARY • *the transitory nature of life*

translate /trænˈsleɪt, ˈtrænˌsleɪt/ *v* [I/T] to change (writing or speech) from one language into another • *Poetry does not translate easily.* [I] • If you translate an activity, you change it into a new form or condition: *The ability to talk clearly does not automatically translate in-to the ability to write clearly.* [I]

translation /trænˈsleɪ·ʃən/ *n* [C/U] • *I do translations at international meetings.* [C]

translator /trænˈsleɪt·ər, ˈtrænˌsleɪt·ər/ *n* [C] • *He is a translator at the UN.*

translucent /trænzˈluː·sənt/ *adj* (of a sub-stance) allowing some light to pass through • *The vase was made from translucent, milky glass.* • Compare OPAQUE; TRANSPARENT.

transmit /trænzˈmɪt/ *v* [I/T] **-tt-** to send or give something • *Germs transmit disease.* [T] ○ *To avoid delay, transmit by fax.* [I]

transmission /trænzˈmɪʃ·ən/ *n* [C/U] • *You can stop the transmission of some diseases by washing your hands often.* [U] • The transmis-sion in a vehicle is the machinery that moves power from to the engine to the wheels. [C]

transmitter /trænzˈmɪt·ər, ˈtrænzˌmɪt·ər/ *n* [C] • *A television transmitter sends the signals that reach your TV.* ○ *She wants to do original work, not just be a transmitter of others' ideas.*

transparent /trænˈspær·ənt, -ˈsper-/ *adj* (of a substance) allowing light through so that ob-jects can be clearly seen through it • *Those transparent plastic boxes are called jewel box-es.* • Transparent also means obvious: *The re-al reason for her leaving was so transparent, no one believed it.* • Compare OPAQUE; TRANSLU-CENT.

transparency /trænˈspær·ən·si, -ˈsper-/ *n* [C/U] • *This plastic has the transparency of glass.* [U] • A transparency is a picture you can show on a screen: *They used transparencies to show pages of the new book.* [C]

transpire /trænˈspaɪr/ *v* [I] *slightly fml* to hap-pen • *A lot has transpired since we last spoke.*

transplant CHANGE ENVIRONMENT /trænˈsplænt/ *v* [I/T] to move (someone or something), or to be moved from one place to another • *I trans-planted those bushes to the back of the house.* [T]

transplant /ˈtrænˌsplænt/ *n* [C] • *I'm a trans-plant from California.*

transplant MOVE ORGAN /trænˈsplænt/ *v* [T] to

move (tissue or an organ) from one person's body to another's

transplant /'træn·splænt/ n [C] • *He survived a kidney transplant.*

transport /træn'spɔːrt, -'spoʊrt/ v [T] to take (goods or people) from one place to another • *The movers will transport thousands of pictures, charts, and recordings to the library.*

transport /'træn·spɔːrt, -spoʊrt/ n [C/U] something that takes things, esp. soldiers or military supplies, from one place to another • *I had to arrange for transport to get to my new assignment.* [U]

transportation /ˌtræn·spər'teɪ·ʃən/ n [U] • *In many cities, people depend on public transportation to get around.*

transpose /træn'spoʊz/ v [T] to change (the order of something) • *The total was wrong because I had transposed two numbers.*

transsexual /træn'sek·ʃə·wəl/ n [C] a person who has had a medical operation to change their sex

transvestite /trænz'ves,taɪt/ n [C] a person who wears the clothes of the opposite sex

trap DEVICE FOR CATCHING /træp/ n [C] a device or hole for catching and holding things • *A bear was caught in the trap.* • A trap is also a bad situation from which it is difficult or impossible to escape: *Simply by answering the letter, Robin had fallen into a trap.* • A **trap door** is a door in a floor or ceiling that covers an opening to a room or building: *In the middle of the living room was a trap door to the cellar.*

trap /træp/ v [T] **-pp-** • *Morrison was trapped by the fire.*

trapper /'træp·ər/ n [C] someone who catches wild animals, esp. to sell their fur

trap MOUTH /træp/ n [C] *slang* a mouth • *Oh, shut your trap!*

trapeze /træ'piːz/ n [C] a short horizontal bar hanging from two ropes, on which ACROBATS perform • *I held my breath as I watched the performers on the trapeze.*

trappings /'træp·ɪŋz/ pl n the possessions that are typical or symbolic of a position or situation • *He enjoyed all the trappings of wealth.*

trash /træʃ/ n [U] anything that is worthless and of low quality; waste • *We filled three cans with trash from the garage.* • A **trash bag** is a large plastic bag that holds waste. • A **trash bin** is a large container for holding waste: *There were several trash bins behind the store.* • A **trash compactor** is a device that crushes waste so that it fits into less space.

trash /træʃ/ v [T] *infml* • *I simply trash (= destroy) that kind of mail.* ○ *Some people seem to enjoy trashing their neighbors (= severely criticizing them).*

trashy /'træʃ·i/ adj *infml disapproving* worthless, or of low quality • *trashy romance novels*

trauma /'trɔː·mə, 'traʊ-/ n [C/U] severe shock caused by an injury • *She never recovered from*

the trauma of her mother's death. [U] ○ *The surgeon specialized in trauma (= sudden, severe injury), especially from gunshots.* [U]

traumatic /trɔː'mæt̬·ɪk, traʊ-/ adj • *The death of someone we love is a traumatic event.*

traumatize /'trɔː·mə,taɪz, 'traʊ-/ v [T] • *Children can be traumatized by violence in their homes.*

travel /'træv·əl/ v [I/T] **-l-** or **-ll-** to go from one place to another, esp. over a long distance in an aircraft, car, train, bus, etc. • *The train was traveling (at) about 100 miles an hour.* [I] ○ *I travel long distances as part of my job, so on vacations I like to stay close to home.* [T] ○ *(infml) We were doing 70 miles an hour, so the guy who whizzed past us must have really been traveling (= going very fast).* [I] • If you **travel light**, you bring very few things with you when you go somewhere.

travel /'træv·əl/ n • *A lot of my travel is business related.* [U] ○ *I've met some pretty interesting people in my travels (= trips).* [pl] • A **travel agent** is a person or company (also **travel agency**) that can give you information about prices and schedules for a trip and arrange for your tickets and hotel rooms.

traveler, traveller /'træv·ə·lər/ n [C] • *Travelers in a hurry like these self-service machines.* • A **traveler's check** is a piece of paper bought from a bank or other company and that can be used as money or exchanged for the local money of a country.

traverse /trə'vɜrs, træ-/ v [T] to move or travel through (an area) • *Moving sidewalks traverse the airport.*

travesty /'træv·ə·sti/ n [C] something that completely fails to do what it is intended or expected to do, and therefore seems ridiculous • *The police chief called the judge's ruling a travesty of justice.*

trawl /trɔːl/ v [I/T] to pull a large net through the sea behind a boat in order to catch fish

trawler /'trɔː·lər/ n [C] a boat that pulls a large net behind it in order to catch fish

tray /treɪ/ n [C] a flat container, usually with slightly raised edges, for carrying food and drinks • *She set the tray down between them.*

treacherous DANGEROUS /'tretʃ·ə·rəs/ adj (of the ground or the sea) extremely dangerous, esp. because of bad weather conditions • *Freezing rain made driving treacherous.*

treacherous NOT LOYAL /'tretʃ·ə·rəs/ adj (of a person) guilty of deceiving someone who trusts you • *He was treacherous, or at least sneaky.*

treachery /'tretʃ·ə·ri/ n [U] • *a play about treachery and betrayal*

tread STEP /tred/ v [I/T] *past simple* **trod** /trɑd/, *past part* **trodden** /'trɑd·ᵊn/ or **trod** /trɑd/ to put the foot down while stepping, or to step on (something) • *(fig.) I hope I haven't trod on other people's toes by saying this.* [I]

tread /tred/ n [C] the sound that someone's

feet make in walking • *I heard the heavy tread of my father overhead.* • A tread is also the horizontal surface on which you put your foot on a step.

tread FLOAT /tred/ *v* • To **tread water** is to float with your head above the water's surface and your feet below you by moving your legs and arms up and down. • To **tread water** is also to be active but without making progress or falling further behind: *Stock prices continued to tread water this week.*

tread PATTERN /tred/ *n* [C/U] the raised pattern on a tire that holds the vehicle to the road as it moves • *fat tires with knobby tread* [U]

treadmill /'tred·mɪl/ *n* [C] a machine for exercising on which you run or walk on a strip that moves back, so that you must move at the same speed as the strip • *She works out on a treadmill.* • A treadmill is also a boring, repetitive activity or experience: *My life has been a treadmill lately.*

treason /'triː·zən/ *n* [U] the crime of helping your country's enemies or attempting to illegally remove its government • *He was convicted of treason and sentenced to death.*

treasure /'treʒ·ər/ *n* [C/U] great wealth, esp. in the form of a store of gold, silver, precious stones, or money • *Pirates are said to have buried treasure there.* [U] • A treasure is also anything of great value: *Jazz is America's national treasure.* [C] • A **treasure hunt** is a game in which the players are given a series of CLUES (= pieces of information) to direct them to a hidden prize. • A **treasure trove** is a great store of valuable objects: *The book was a treasure trove of information.*

treasure /'treʒ·ər/ *v* [T] • If you treasure something you take good care of it because you value it highly: *I treasure these old snapshots of my grandparents.*

treasurer /'treʒ·ə·rər/ *n* [C] an officer who is responsible for the money in a company, government, or other organization

treasury /'treʒ·ə·ri/ *n* [U] the government department responsible for financial matters such as spending and taxes

treat DEAL WITH /triːt/ *v* [T always + adv/prep] to behave toward (someone) or deal with (something) in a particular way • *He treated his children badly.* ○ *She always tried to treat her students as/like adults.* • If someone **treats** you **like dirt/like a dog**, they have behaved very badly toward you: *Those people treat foreigners like dirt.* • If you **treat** someone **with kid gloves**, you treat them with special care and consideration.

treatment /'triːt·mənt/ *n* [U] • *He accused the governor of giving rich people special treatment.*

treat GIVE MEDICAL CARE /triːt/ *v* [T] to do something to improve the condition of (a sick or injured person), or to try to cure (a disease) • *The hospital treats hundreds of patients a day.*

○ *The new drug may allow us to treat diabetes more effectively.*

treatment /'triːt·mənt/ *n* [C/U] • *Chronic back pain may not respond to treatment.* [U]

treat PUT IN NEW CONDITION /triːt/ *v* [T] to change the condition of (a substance) by adding something to it or putting it through a special process • *The sewage is treated with chemicals before being dumped.*

treatment /'triːt·mənt/ *n* [C/U] • *The city is exploring other methods of water treatment.* [U]

treat SPECIAL EXPERIENCE /triːt/ *n* [C] a special and enjoyable occasion or experience • *It was a real treat seeing my old friends last weekend.*

treat PAY FOR /triːt/ *v* [I/T] to buy or pay for something for (someone) • *I'm going to treat myself to a new pair of sunglasses.* [T]

treat /triːt/ *n* [U] • *You paid for the taxi, so lunch is my treat* (= I will pay).

treatise /'triːt·əs/ *n* [C] a formal piece of writing that deals with a particular subject • *a medical treatise*

treaty /'triːt̬·i/ *n* [C] a written agreement between two or more countries that is formally approved and signed by their leaders • *Under the treaty* (= according to the agreement), *inspections are required to see if any country is secretly developing nuclear arms.*

treble THREE TIMES /'treb·əl/ *v* [I/T] *slightly fml* to become three times greater; TRIPLE • *My property taxes have almost trebled in the last ten years.* [I]

treble MUSIC /'treb·əl/ *n* [U] the higher musical notes • *The music was too loud, the treble rattling my eardrums.*

tree /triː/ *n* [C] a tall plant that has a wooden trunk and branches growing from its upper part • *a pine tree* • A **tree house** is a small structure among the branches of a tree: *My dad built us a tree house when we were little.* • PIC TRUNKS

trek /trek/ *v* [I always + adv/prep] **-kk-** to walk a long way or with some difficulty • *Many people trekked for miles to reach safety.*

trek /trek/ *n* [C] • *It's a long trek from the railroad station to the stadium.*

trellis /'trel·əs/ *n* [C] a frame of crossed bars that supports plants as they grow, sometimes against the side of a house • *Roses climbed the trellises.*

tremble /'trem·bəl/ *v* [I] (of your body or a part of it) to shake without your intending to, usually because you are frightened, ill, tired, or upset • *Grant was trembling with excitement.* ○ *Her hand trembled as she lifted her cup.*

tremble /'trem·bəl/ *n* [U] • *There was a slight tremble in her voice as she recalled her husband.*

tremendous /trɪ'men·dəs/ *adj* great in amount, size, or degree; extremely large • *She is under tremendous pressure at work.* • (*infml*) Someone or something that is tremendous is extremely good: *a tremendous book/concert/ athlete*

tremendously /trɪˈmen·də·sli/ *adv* • *a tremendously expensive house* ◦ *I enjoyed your show tremendously.* • LP VERY, COMPLETELY, AND OTHER INTENSIFIERS

tremor BODY MOVEMENT /ˈtrem·ər/ *n* [C] a shaking movement in a person's body, usually because of fright, excitement, or illness • *I felt a tremor of anxiety as the plane lifted off the ground.*

tremor EARTH MOVEMENT /ˈtrem·ər/ *n* [C] a slight **earthquake** (= sudden, violent movement of the earth's surface) • *The tremor was centered just south of San Francisco.*

trench /trentʃ/ *n* [C] a narrow channel dug into the ground • *I dug a trench around the tent to keep rain water from getting in.*

trenchant /ˈtren·tʃənt/ *adj* (of something said or written) forcefully and effectively expressed, and often in few words • *I enjoy reading Murray's trenchant comments on the relationship between sports and society.*

trench coat /ˈtrentʃ·koʊt/ *n* [C] a long, loose coat with a belt, usually made from waterproof material and similar in style to a military coat

trend /trend/ *n* [C] the general direction of changes or developments • *fashion trends* ◦ *The trend is toward working longer hours for less money.*

trendy /ˈtren·di/ *adj* influenced by or expressing the most recent fashions or ideas; modern in style • *New York City is full of trendy shops and restaurants.*

trepidation /ˌtrep·əˈdeɪ·ʃən/ *n* [U] worry or anxiety about something that is going to happen • *With some trepidation, I set out to find my first job.*

trespass /ˈtres·pæs, -pəs/ *v* [I] to enter someone's property without permission • *I didn't realize I was trespassing on their land.*

trespasser /ˈtres·pæs·ər, -pə·sər/ *n* [C] • *They have several dogs to keep trespassers out.*

trestle /ˈtres·əl/ *n* [C] a set of sloping supports holding a horizontal structure, used esp. for railroad bridges, or a bridge supported in this way • *The train was crossing a trestle above a river near Baltimore.*

trial LEGAL PROCESS /traɪl/ *n* [C/U] the examination in a court of law of the facts of a case to decide whether a person is guilty of a crime or responsible for an injury to another person • *a criminal/civil trial* [C] ◦ *The case will soon go to trial* (= begin). [U] ◦ *She must still stand trial* (= be judged in a court of law). [U] • If someone is **on trial**, the case in which their guilt is being judged has begun: *He was on trial for aggravated assault and robbery.* • USAGE: The related verb is TRY EXAMINE IN COURT.

trial TEST /traɪl/ *n* [C/U] a test, usually over a limited period of time, to discover how effec-

tive or suitable something or someone is • *The agency plans to conduct clinical trials of the drug.* [C] ◦ *We have the videotapes on a trial basis for one week—if we don't like them, we can send them back.* [U] • **Trial and error** is a way of achieving an aim or solving a problem by trying a different methods and learning from the mistakes that you make: *In a language lab, students learn by trial and error.*

trial PROBLEM /traɪl/ *n* [C] something or someone that causes anxiety or problems • *the trials of adolescence*

triangle /ˈtraɪˌæŋ·gəl/ *n* [C] a flat shape with three straight sides • *Her earrings were in the shape of triangles.* • A triangle is also a musical instrument consisting of a thin metal bar having three sides, which makes a high sound when held up in the air and hit with a metal bar.

triangular /traɪˈæŋ·gjə·lər/ *adj* having the shape of a triangle • *triangular flags*

triathlon /traɪˈæθˌlɑn/ *n* [C] a race in which the competitors swim, ride a bicycle, and run without stopping between events • *He has won Hawaii's Ironman Triathlon four times.*

tribe /traɪb/ *n* [C] a group of people, often of related families, who live in the same area and share the same language, culture, and history • *She has studied Native American tribes from Mexico to Maine.*

tribal /ˈtraɪ·bəl/ *adj* [not gradable] • *tribal culture* ◦ *tribal land* ◦ *Tribal leaders support the proposed casino.*

tribunal /traɪˈbjuːn·əl/ *n* [C] a special court chosen, esp. by a government or governments, to examine a particular problem • *An international tribunal of judges was established to investigate alleged war crimes.*

tributary /ˈtrɪb·jəˌter·i/ *n* [C] a river or stream that flows into a larger river or lake • *The Misssouri River is a tributary of the Mississipi River*

tribute SHOW OF RESPECT /ˈtrɪb·juːt/ *n* [C/U] respect or admiration for someone, or a formal event at which respect and admiration are expressed • *The memorial pays tribute to Africans brought here as slaves.* [U] ◦ *There was a special tribute to Arthur Ashe by leading tennis players.* [C]

tribute GOOD EFFECT /ˈtrɪb·juːt/ *n* [C usually sing] something showing the benefit or positive effect of something else • *His ability to cook and manage a household is a tribute to the training he received from his mother.*

trick ACT OF DECEIVING /trɪk/ *n* [C] an action intended to deceive, either as a way of cheating someone or as a joke or form of entertainment • *He showed us some card tricks.* • **Trick or treat** is what children say on HALLOWEEN, when they dress to look frightening or amusing and visit people's homes to ask for candy: *Are your kids too old for trick or treating* (= visiting people's homes to ask for candy)?

trick /trɪk/ *v* [T] to make (someone) believe something that is not true, or to persuade (someone) to do something based on their false understanding of the facts • *She tricked me into telling her what I was up to.*

trickery /'trɪk·ə·ri/ *n* [U] • *The agency used trickery, fraud, and deceit to obtain the computer software.*

tricky /'trɪk·i/ *adj* • *He's a tricky fellow—you can't always trust him.* • See also TRICKY.

trick [METHOD] /trɪk/ *n* [C] a quick or effective way of doing something • *What's the trick to pulling out this sofa bed?*

trick [WEAK] /trɪk/ *adj* [not gradable] (of a part of the body, esp. a joint) sometimes feeling weak suddenly and unexpectedly • *I've had a trick knee ever since I played football.*

trickle /'trɪk·əl/ *v* [I] (of liquid) to flow slowly and without force • *Blood trickled from a cut in his forehead.* • To trickle is also to happen gradually and in small numbers: *After the hurricane, all the telephones were out, and it was some time before reports of damage began to trickle in.*

trickle /'trɪk·əl/ *n* [C] • *A trickle* (= small flow) *of sweat ran down his chest.* ○ *Only a trickle* (= small amount) *of goods reached the village.*

tricky /'trɪk·i/ *adj* (of a piece of work or a problem) difficult to deal with and needing careful attention or skill • *Removing scar tissue can be a very tricky operation.* • See also **tricky** at TRICK [ACT OF DECEIVING].

tricycle /'traɪ·sɪk·əl/ *n* [C] a vehicle with two wheels at the back and one in front, having a seat for a rider whose feet push PEDALS around in circles to make the wheels turn • *Our three-year-old loves her red tricycle.*

tricycle

tried /traɪd/ *past simple and past participle of* TRY • Something that is **tried-and-true** has been used many times in the past and proven to work well: *A cup of warm milk is my tried-and-true remedy for insomnia.*

trifle /'traɪ·fəl/ *n* [C] a matter or item of little value or importance • *A trifle* means slightly or to a small degree: *He admits to being a trifle nervous before every show.*

trifling /'traɪ·flɪŋ/ *adj* • *It was such a trifling sum of money to argue about.*

trigger [GUN PART] /'trɪg·ər/ *n* [C] a part of a gun that causes the gun to fire when pressed • *to pull the trigger* • A person who is **trigger-happy** is too willing to use a gun to shoot someone. • A **trigger man** is a man who shoots someone during a crime.

trigger [START] /'trɪg·ər/ *v* [T] to cause (something) to start • *The attacks triggered a war in*

the Middle East. ○ *Eating chocolate can trigger a migraine headache in some people.*

trigonometry /ˌtrɪg·ə'nɑm·ə·tri/, *short form* **trig** /trɪg/ *n* [U] a type of mathematics that deals with the relationship between the angles and sides of triangles

trill /trɪl/ *n* [C] a series of quickly repeated high notes such as those sung by a bird

trillion /'trɪl·jən/ *number* 1,000,000,000,000 • *Distances in space can be measured in trillions of miles.* • [LP] NUMBERS

trilogy /'trɪl·ə·dʒi/ *n* [C] a set of three books, plays, or movies dealing with the same characters or the same subject

trim [CUT] /trɪm/ *v* [T] **-mm-** to make (something) neater or more even by cutting a small amount off • *He had a neatly trimmed beard.* • To trim is also to reduce: *We have to trim costs by not making any unnecessary trips.*

trim [DECORATE] /trɪm/ *v* [T] **-mm-** to decorate (something), esp. around the edges • *The robe was trimmed with fur.*

trim /trɪm/ *n* [U] • *The team's new uniforms are blue with black trim.*

trimmings /'trɪm·ɪŋz/ *pl n* • *I want a plain black jumper with no fancy trimmings.* • Trimmings are also other foods that are usually served with the main dish of a meal: *For Thanksgiving, we always have turkey with all the trimmings.*

trim [THIN] /trɪm/ *adj* [-er/-est only] **-mm-** thin and appearing to be in good physical condition • *He was a short, trim, wiry man.*

trimester /traɪ'mes·tər/ *n* [C] • A trimester is any of the three, three-month periods that a human pregnancy is divided into. • A trimester is also any of the three periods into which the school or college year is sometimes divided.

trinket /'trɪŋ·kət/ *n* [C] a small, decorative object or item of jewelry of little value

trio /'tri·oʊ/ *n* [C] *pl* **trios** three people who sing or play musical instruments together, or a piece of music written for three people • Compare DUET, QUARTET, QUINTET.

trip [TRAVEL] /trɪp/ *n* [C] an occasion on which someone goes to a place and returns from it, or the act of traveling from one place to another • *a camping/shopping trip* ○ *We plan to take a trip out west later this year.* ○ *They went on a three-week trip to Europe.* ○ *Alejandro had to make a number of business trips to New York.*

trip [LOSE BALANCE] /trɪp/ *v* [I/T] **-pp-** to lose your balance because your foot hits against something when you are walking or running, or to cause (someone) to lose their balance • *He injured his ankle when he tripped over a water sprinkler while jogging.* [I] ○ *She nearly tripped on the rug.* [I]

trip [EXPERIENCE] /trɪp/ *n* [C] *slang* a strongly felt experience, esp. one caused by taking illegal drugs

▫**trip** *obj* **up** /'-'-/ *v adv* [T] to cause (someone)

to make a mistake • *I did OK on the exam except for the last question, when I got tripped up by a word I didn't understand.*

triple /'trɪp·əl/ *adj* [not gradable] consisting of three parts, or three times (in number or amount) • *If he loses the case, the defendant can be required to pay triple damages.*

triple /'trɪp·əl/ *v* [I/T] • *We've tripled our output over the past two years.* [T]

triplet /'trɪp·lət/ *n* [C] one of three children born to the same mother at the same time

triplicate /'trɪp·lɪ·kət/ *n* • If something is **in triplicate**, it consists of an original and two exact copies.

tripod /'traɪ·pɑd/ *n* [C] a support with three adjustable legs for a piece of equipment such as a camera • *Photographers set up their tripods.*

trite /traɪt/ *adj* done or expressed too often to be of any interest • *Even good acting couldn't make up for the trite story.*

triumph /'traɪ·əmf/ *n* a complete victory or success achieved esp. after great difficulties, making the result particularly satisfying • *The elimination of smallpox was one of medicine's greatest triumphs.* [C]

triumph /'traɪ·əmf/ *v* [I] • *We visited Yorktown Battlefield on the York River, where in 1781 George Washington's forces triumphed over the English army.*

triumphant /traɪ'ʌm·fənt/ *adj* • *He made a triumphant return to the stage after several years working in television.*

trivia /'trɪv·i·ə/ *pl n* unimportant or little-known details or information • *This is a game for trivia buffs* (= people interested in knowing little-known facts).

trivial /'trɪv·i·əl/ *adj* having little value or importance • *Sexual harassment in the workplace is no trivial matter.*

trivialize /'trɪv·i·ə,laɪz/ *v* [T] to make (something unusual) seem ordinary or unimportant • *The casual way violence is shown in movies tends to trivialize it.*

trod /trɑd/ *past simple and past participle of* TREAD

trodden /'trɑd·ən/ *past participle of* TREAD

troll /troʊl/ *v* [I] to fish from a boat that is moving slowly in the water and pulling a fishing LINE (= length of string with something attached that attracts fish) behind it • *Many of his friends had large boats, and they frequently traveled together trolling for mackerel.*

trolley /'trɑl·i/, **trolley car** /'trɑl·i:,kɑr/, **streetcar** *n* [C] an electric vehicle that transports people, usually in cities, and goes along metal tracks in the road

trombone /trɑm'boʊn/ *n* [C/U] a long, BRASS musical instrument with a U-shaped piece that is slid in and out of the main part of the instrument to vary the notes and played by

trombone

blowing into it, or this type of instrument generally; a HORN

tromp /trɑmp, trɔːmp/ *v* to TRAMP WALK

troop GROUP /truːp/ *n* [C] a group of soldiers or police, esp. one equipped with horses • A troop is also an organized group of young people who are **Boy Scouts** or **Girl Scouts**. See at BOY; girl.

trooper /'truː·pər/ *n* [C] a police officer belonging to a US state police force

troops /truːps/ *pl n* soldiers on duty in a large group • *More and more troops were sent to Vietnam during the war years.*

troop WALK /truːp/ *v* [I always + adv/prep] to walk or go somewhere as a group • *Hundreds of thousands of visitors troop through the museum every year.*

trophy /'troʊ·fi/ *n* [C] a prize, such as a large silver cup or bowl, given to the winner of a competition or race • A trophy is also something used as a symbol of success from hunting or war: *Under the long high-beamed ceiling, affixed to stone walls, were the trophies—heads of a rhinoceros and an African buffalo with huge horns.*

tropics /'trɑp·ɪks/ *pl n* the hottest area of the earth, the area on either side of the equator reaching to 23.5 degrees to the north and south

tropical /'trɑp·ɪ·kəl/ *adj* [not gradable] of or characteristic of the tropics • *a tropical climate* ○ *a tropical storm*

trot /trɑt/ *v* [I always + adv/prep] (of a horse or other animal with four legs) to move in a way that is slightly faster than walking • If a person trots, they run slowly: *She trotted along behind them, determined to keep up.*

trot /trɑt/ *n* [C usually sing] • *The horse was moving at a slow trot.*

□**trot out** *obj*, **trot** *obj* **out** /'-'-/ *v adv* [M] to cause (someone or something) to be shown in order to get attention • *The military trotted out all their experts to testify for the new weapons system.*

trouble DIFFICULTIES /'trʌb·əl/ *n* [C/U] a problem, or difficulties • *Trouble began when he came to live with us.* [U] ○ *She thought her troubles would be over when she got divorced.* [C] ○ *The patient is having trouble breathing.* [U] • Trouble can also be a characteristic that is a problem or disadvantage: *His trouble is that he's too impatient.* [C] • Sometimes trouble is a problem or difficulty caused when a machine or system does not work as it should: *I'm* having trouble with my new computer. [U] • Trouble can be a cause of arguments or fights: *Our brother is the source of trouble between my sister and me.* [U] • If someone is **in trouble**, they are in a situation that is a problem or difficulty, esp. with the law: *He would have been in real trouble if he had been caught.* • **The trouble with** *this place is they don't care about the people who work here* (= this characteristic is not as it should be). • A **troublemaker** is someone who causes problems for other people.

trouble /'trʌb·əl/ *v* [T] to cause (someone) to have problems or difficulties • *He has been troubled by a knee injury for most of the season.*

troubled /'trʌb·əld/ *adj* • *This troubled region has suffered more than its share of bombings and killings.*

troublesome /'trʌb·əl·səm/ *adj* causing problems or difficulties • *His back has been troublesome for quite a while.*

trouble INCONVENIENCE /'trʌb·əl/ *n* [U] inconvenience or effort • *"I'd love some coffee, if it isn't too much trouble." "Oh, it's no trouble at all."* ○ *The sweater is a bit large, but I'm keeping it because it's too much trouble to return it.*

trouble /'trʌb·əl/ *v* [T] • *Could I trouble you to open that window?* ○ *You don't need to trouble yourself with all the details.*

trouble WORRY /'trʌb·əl/ *v* [T] to cause (someone) worry or anxiety • *What's troubling you? You seem upset.* ○ *It troubles me that she didn't tell me this sooner.*

troubled /'trʌb·əld/ *adj* • *The children were not troubled when the dinosaurs in the movie ate up some unlucky humans.*

troubling /'trʌb·ə·lɪŋ/ *adj* • *Perhaps most troubling is the information that some reporters have simply made up stories.*

troubleshooting /'trʌb·əl,ʃuːt·ɪŋ/ *n* [U] the process of solving problems, esp. complicated problems in a system • *He's very good at troubleshooting because he knows these computers as well as anybody.*

troubleshooter /'trʌb·əl,ʃuːt·ər/ *n* [C] • *An experienced politician was hired as a troubleshooter for the election campaign.*

troublesome /'trʌb·əl·səm/ *adj* causing worry or anxiety • *The troublesome fact is that we haven't gotten much done.*

trough CONTAINER /trɔːf/ *n* [C] a narrow, open box to hold water or food for animals

trough LOW POINT /trɔːf/ *n* [C] a low point between two high points, as on a GRAPH or record of activity • *Investors have to live through stock market troughs.*

trounce /traʊns/ *v* [T] to defeat (a competitor) decisively • *The Red Sox trounced the Yankees 12 to 1 in the first game.*

troupe /truːp/ *n* [C] a group of performers, such as actors, singers, or dancers, who perform and travel together

trousers /'traʊ·zərz/ *pl n* a piece of clothing covering the lower part of the body from the waist to the foot and including separate sections for each leg; pants • *He had a rip in his trousers.*

trout /traʊt/ *n* [C] *pl* **trout** a fish found in both rivers and the sea that is a very popular food • *Fish farmers raise trout in refrigerated tanks.*

trowel /'traʊ·əl, traʊl/ *n* [C] a small tool that has a flat, metal blade and a handle, used to spread building materials such as PLASTER or CEMENT, or a similar tool with a curved, pointed blade used to garden

truant /'truː·ənt/ *n* [C] someone who is absent from school without permission

truancy /'truː·ən·si/ *n* [U] • *Truancy is a serious problem in many schools.*

truce /truːs/ *n* [C] a temporary agreement to stop fighting or arguing, or a brief interruption in a disagreement • *We seemed to be arguing so much, we have declared a truce in my family.*

truck /trʌk/ *n* [C] a large vehicle with an open or covered space in the back to hold a load of goods • A **truck farm** is a farm where fruits and vegetables are grown to be sold locally. • A **truckload** is the amount a truck can carry: *(fig.) In this case, lawyers filed court papers by the truckload* (= in large amounts). • A **truck stop** is an area near a main road that usually offers fuel, food, and repair services, used esp. by truck drivers. • PIC TRACTOR-TRAILER

truck /trʌk/ *v* [T always + adv/prep] • *Most supplies are trucked into the city, although some come by rail or plane.*

trucker /'trʌk·ər/ *n* [C] • *Truckers spend long periods away from home.*

trucking /'trʌk·ɪŋ/ *n* [U] • *Railroads have lost business to trucking companies.*

truculent /'trʌk·jə·lənt/ *adj* having a bad state of mind, or behaving in a threatening manner • *He was a truculent bully.*

trudge /trʌdʒ/ *v* [I always + adv/prep] to walk slowly with a lot of effort, esp. on an uneven surface or while carrying something heavy • *We had to trudge through deep snow to get to school.*

trudge /trʌdʒ/ *n* [C] • *Twelve miles over rocks and hills is a long trudge for a hiker.*

true CORRECT /truː/ *adj* [-er/-est only] agreeing with fact; not false or wrong • *The story is actually true.* ○ *It is true that the risk of breaking your hip increases with age.* [+ *that* clause] • If you say that a statement or idea is **true enough**, you mean that while it is correct or accurate, it does not completely explain something: *Critics complain about his racial stereotypes, and true enough, they are easy to find, but there are sympathetic portraits within them.* • USAGE: The related noun is TRUTH FACT.

truism /'truː,ɪz·əm/ *n* [C] a statement that is so obvious or said so often that its truth is not questioned • *It's a truism that preventing disease is much better than curing it.*

truly /'truː·li/ *adv* • *Can it be truly said that he represents all the people of his country?*

true REAL /truː/ *adj* [-er/-est only] based on what is real, or actual, not imaginary • *His staff tried to keep the true nature of his illness a secret.* • If you discover someone's **true colors**, you have found out what kind of person they really are. • A **true love** is someone you like more than all others or something you like more than anything else: *When you meet her, you'll know it's true love.* ○ *Her true love is music.* • If something is **true-life** or **true-to-life**, it is realistic or based on real life: *true-life adventures* ○ *Some of her stories are very true to life.*

truly /'truː·li/ *adv* • *The area is truly beautiful.*

true SINCERE /truː/ *adj* [-er/-est only] sincere and loyal • *I am lucky to have true friends.* ○ *She is one politician who remains true to her principles.* • Someone who does something **true to form** behaves the way other people expect them to, based on previous experience: *True to form, he tried to get out of his share of the work.* • If someone is **true to** their **word**, they make a sincere promise and keep it: *True to his word, he paid back the money I loaned him.* • If you are **true to** yourself, you behave according to your beliefs and do what you think is right. • Someone who is **true-blue** is completely loyal to a person or belief.

truly /'truː·li/ *adv* sincerely • *I'm truly sorry about the accident.* • Truly is sometimes used at the end of a letter instead of sincerely: *Yours truly, Anne* ○ *Very truly yours, Joseph Logan*

true HAVING NECESSARY QUALITIES /truː/ *adj* [-er/-est only] having all the characteristics necessary to be an example of a particular thing • *Only true deer have antlers.* ○ *This portrait is supposed to be a true likeness of Washington.*

truly /'truː·li/ *adv* • *Tomatoes aren't truly vegetables—they're fruit.*

trump card /'trʌmp·kɑrd/ *n* [C] something that gives you an advantage over others • *The ultimate trump card for the space program is that it is a very exciting thing.*

trumped–up /'trʌmp'tʌp/ *adj* not true; invented • *He was sent to prison on a trumped-up charge of armed robbery.*

trumpet INSTRUMENT /'trʌm·pət/ *n* [C/U] a BRASS musical instrument that plays high notes, with keys that are pressed to vary the notes and played by blowing into it, or this type of instrument generally; a HORN

trumpet

trumpet ANIMAL CALL /'trʌm·pət/ *v* [I] (of an animal, esp. an ELEPHANT) to produce a loud call • *We heard the elephants trumpeting in the distance.*

trumpet MAKE KNOWN /'trʌm·pət/ *v* [T] to make people aware of (something important) • *He's been trumpeting political reform for years.* ○ *The boys were not shy about trumpeting their successes.*

truncated /'trʌŋ,keɪt·əd/ *adj* [not gradable] made briefer or shorter, usually by removing a part • *The truncated article fit into the space allowed but made little sense.*

trundle /'trʌn·dəl/ *v* [always + adv/prep] to push something on wheels, or to cause (something) to roll along • *She trundled the wheelbarrow down the road.* [T]

trundle bed /'trʌn·dəl'bed/ *n* [C] a low bed on wheels that is stored under an ordinary bed and pulled out when it is needed • *We bought a trundle bed for unexpected guests.*

trunk MAIN PART /trʌŋk/ *n* [C] the thick main stem of a tree, from which the branches grow • A person's trunk is the main part of their body, not including the head, legs, or arms.

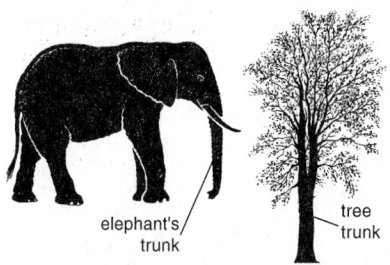

elephant's trunk

tree trunk

trunk NOSE /trʌŋk/ *n* [C] an ELEPHANT's nose, which is like a long tube that bends easily

trunk STORAGE SPACE /trʌŋk/ *n* [C] a closed space at the back of a car where things can be stored • A trunk is also a large, strong case used to store or transport clothes and other possessions. • PIC CAR

trunks /trʌŋks/ *pl n* [C] very short pants, esp. worn by men for swimming • *He spent the summer in swim trunks and Hawaiian shirts.*

truss /trʌs/ *n* [C] *specialized* a support for a building or bridge, made of wood or steel • *No one knows if the fire damaged the building's trusses and support beams.*

trust BELIEVE /trʌst/ *v* [I/T] to have confidence in (something), or to believe in (someone) • *Trust me—I would never lie to you.* [T] ○ *I was tested, but I'm not sure I trust the results.* [T] ○ *The priest said I should trust in God.* [I]

trust /trʌst/ *n* [U] • *Their relationship is based on trust and understanding.* ○ *We were obviously wrong to put our trust in her.*

trusted /'trʌs·təd/ *adj* • *She was an old and trusted friend.*

trusting /'trʌs·tɪŋ/, **trustful** /'trʌst·fəl/ *adj* •

You shouldn't be so trusting—people will take advantage of you.

trusty /'trʌs·ti/ *adj* [*-er/-est* only] deserving confidence; RELIABLE • *So far, our trusty old car has gone 150,000 miles.*

trust ARRANGEMENT /trʌst/ *n* [C/U] a legal arrangement in which a person or organization controls property or money for the benefit of another person or organization • *The money is being held in trust for her until she turns 21.* [U] • A trust is also a group of people or organizations that controls property or money for their own benefit, or the property or money controlled by them: *The danger of trusts is that they can become very powerful.* [C]

trustee /trʌs'ti:/ *n* [C] a person, often one of a group, who controls property or money for the benefit of another person or an organization • *He was a member of the museum's board of trustees.*

trust HOPE /trʌst/ *v* [I/T] to hope and expect that (something is true) • *I trust (that) you slept well?* [T]

trustworthy /'trʌst,wɜr·ði/ *adj* deserving of trust, or able to be trusted • *Not even a newspaper always gives trustworthy information.*

trustworthiness /'trʌst,wɜr·ði:·nəs/ *n* [U] • *He has a well-earned reputation for absolute trustworthiness.*

trusty /'trʌs·ti/ *adj* • See at TRUST BELIEVE.

truth FACT /truθ/ *n* [U] the actual fact or facts about a matter • *Tell the truth, now, how did the chair get broken?* ○ *We may never know the truth about what happened.* • **Truth is stranger than fiction** means that strange things often happen in real life. • USAGE: The related adjective is TRUE CORRECT.

truth QUALITY /truθ/ *n* [U] the quality of being true • *I can see some truth in what she said.* • *We kept climbing but,* **in truth** (= actually), *we knew we could not reach the summit.*

truthful /'truθ·fəl/ *adj* • *Are you being completely truthful?*

truth PRINCIPLE /truθ/ *n* [C] *pl* **truths** /truːðz, truːθs/ a statement or principle that is generally considered to be true • *a scientific truth* ○ *Our system of belief is based on a few simple truths.*

try ATTEMPT /traɪ/ *v* [I/T] to make an effort to do (something) • *Try to open this jar for me.* [I] ○ *You'll have to try harder.* [I] ○ *I'm trying my best.* [T] ○ *Maybe you should try getting up earlier* (= should wake earlier). [I] • *Mike decided to* **try** *his* **hand at** *tennis* (= attempt it for the first time).

try /traɪ/ *n* [C] • *This will be her third try at an Olympic medal.* ○ *I decided to give skiing a try.*

try TEST /traɪ/ *v* [T] to test (something) to see if it is suitable, useful, or workable • *Have you tried that new recipe yet?* ○ *I want to try scuba diving.* ○ *Try the back door* (= see if it is open). • If something **tries** your **patience**, it makes

you less patient: *Little kids get into everything, and it really tries your patience.*

try EXAMINE IN COURT /traɪ/ *v* [T] *law* to examine (a person accused of committing a crime) in a court of law to decide if they are guilty • *He was tried for murder.* • See also TRIAL LEGAL PROCESS.

□ **try on** *obj*, **try** *obj* **on** /'-'-/ *v adv* [M] to put on (clothes) to see how they look or if they fit • *Try on those shoes.*

□ **try out** COMPETE /'-'-/ *v adv* [I] to compete for a position on the team or a part in the play • *Jim tried out for the school play.*

tryout /'traɪ·aʊt/ *n* [C] • *Tryouts for the team will be held next week.*

□ **try out** *obj* USE, **try** *obj* **out** /'-'-/ *v adv* [M] to use (something) to see if it works well • *Lanny is trying out her new bicycle.* • *I like the idea, but you should* **try** *it* **out on** *Abby* (= find out what she thinks of it).

tryout /'traɪ·aʊt/ *n* [C] • *After a tryout in Boston, the play opens on Broadway.*

trying /'traɪ·ɪŋ/ *adj* annoying; IRRITATING • *Most people find him very trying.* ○ *Julie's having a trying time at work lately.*

tsar /zɑr, tsɑr/ *n* [C] CZAR

T-shirt, **tee shirt** /'tiː·ʃɜrt/ *n* [C] a type of shirt that covers the upper part of the body, has short sleeves and no collar, and is pulled on over the head • *He wore a T-shirt and jeans.*

tsp. *n* [C] *pl* **tsp.** abbreviation for TEASPOON • *Add 1 tsp. baking powder.*

tub BATH /tʌb/ *n* [C] short form of **bathtub**, see at BATH

tub CONTAINER /tʌb/ *n* [C] a container, esp. one used for storing food • *a tub of potato salad* ○ *Plant lilies in three-gallon plastic tub.*

tuba /'tuː·bə/ *n* [C/U] a large BRASS musical instrument that plays low notes which is played by blowing into it and has keys that are pressed to vary the notes, or this type of instrument generally

tube PIPE /tuːb/ *n* [C] a long, hollow cylinder of plastic, metal, rubber, or glass, used for moving or containing liquids or gases • *a copper tube* ○ *She lay in the hospital, tubes going in and out of her.* • A tube is also one of the body's hollow cylindrical structures that carries air or liquid: *bronchial tubes*

tube CONTAINER /tuːb/ *n* [C] a cylindrical container made of soft metal or plastic which is closed at one end and has a small opening at the other, usually with a cover, and is used for holding thick liquids • *a tube of toothpaste/ointment*

tube TELEVISION /tuːb/ *n* [U] *infml* television • *What's on the tube tonight?*

tuberculosis /tʊˌbɜr·kjə'loʊ·səs/ (*abbreviation* **TB**) *n* [U] an infectious disease that can attack many parts of the body, esp. the lungs

tuck MAKE NEAT /tʌk/ *v* [T always + adv/prep] to push the ends or edges of (usually clothing or material) tightly into a particular place or position, esp. to make something neat or comfortable • *He tucked the sheet under the mattress.* ○ *Richard needs to tuck in his shirt.* [M] • If you tuck part of your body, you hold it in a particular position: *She sat with her legs tucked under her.* ○ *Tuck your tummy in.* [M]

tuck STORE SAFELY /tʌk/ *v* [T always + adv/ prep] to put (something) into a safe or convenient place • *She tucked her doll under her arm.* ○ *I found the pictures tucked away in a box.* • If something is **tucked away**, it is hidden or difficult to find: *Van's house is tucked away at the end of the road.*

□ **tuck** *in obj*, **tuck** *obj* **in** /-'-/ *v adv* [M] to cover (a child) comfortably in their bed • *I tucked the children in.*

Tuesday /'tuːz·di, -deɪ/ (*abbreviation* **Tue.**, **Tues.**) *n* [C/U] the day of the week after Monday and before Wednesday

tuft /tʌft/ *n* [C] a number of short pieces of something, such as hair or grass, that grow close together or are held together at the base • *He had only a few tufts of hair on his chin.*

tug /tʌg/ *v* [I/T] **-gg-** to pull (something) quickly with force or effort • *We tugged the sled up the hill.* [T] ○ *He had to tug hard.* [I]

tug /tʌg/ *n* [C] • *She felt a tug at her sleeve.* • A **tug of war** is a competition in which two teams pull at opposite ends of a rope, each trying to pull the other team over a line between them, or (*fig.*) a fight between two people or groups.

tugboat /'tʌg·boʊt/, *short form* **tug** /tʌg/ *n* [C] a boat with a powerful engine which can change direction easily and is used to pull large ships into and out of port

tuition /tʊ'ɪʃ·ən/ *n* [U] the money paid for being taught, esp. at a college or university

tulip /'tuː·ləp/ *n* [C] a plant that grows from a BULB and has a large, brightly colored, bell-shaped flower on a stem, or the flower itself

tumble /'tʌm·bəl/ *v* [I] to fall or roll quickly and without control • *Rocks tumbled down the hill.* ○ *She lost her balance and tumbled into the mud.* ○ (*fig.*) *Stock prices tumbled* (= quickly lost a lot of value).

tumble /'tʌm·bəl/ *n* [C] • *I took a tumble and hurt my knee.*

tumbledown /'tʌm·bəl,daʊn/ *adj* (of a building) in a bad condition, esp. in a state of decay • *They lived in a tumbledown cottage near the railroad tracks.*

tummy /'tʌm·i/ *n* [C] *a child's word for* a stomach • *My tummy hurts.*

tumor /'tuː·mər/ *n* [C] a mass of cells in the body that grow faster than usual and can cause illness • *a malignant/benign tumor*

tumult /'tuː·mʌlt/ *n* [C/U] noise and excitement, or a state of confusion, change, or uncertainty • *mental tumult* [U] ○ *a tumult of emotion* [C usually sing] ○ *The garden sits amid the tumult of downtown Vancouver.* [U]

tumultuous /tʊ'mʌl·tʃə·wəs/ *adj* • *The honoree received tumultuous applause.*

tuna /'tuː·nə/ *n* [C/U] *pl* **tuna** a large fish that lives in warm seas, or its flesh eaten as food • *a can of tuna* [U] ○ *tuna salad* [U]

tundra /'tʌn·drə/ *n* [U] any of the very large, flat areas of land in northern parts of Asia, North America, and Europe where, because it is cold, trees do not grow and the earth below the surface is permanently frozen

tune MUSICAL NOTES /tuːn/ *n* [C] a series of musical notes, esp. one that is pleasant and easy to remember; a MELODY • *That's a very pretty tune.* • **To the tune of** means to the stated amount of: *We're in debt to the tune of $50,000.*

tune ADJUST INSTRUMENT /tuːn/ *v* [I/T] to adjust (a musical instrument) so the sounds produced are the correct PITCH (= degree to which the sound is high or low) • *Tune your guitar before you practice.* [T] ○ *The orchestra tuned up.* [I] ○ *She tuned up her violin.* [M]

tune /tuːn/ *n* [U] • *This piano is out of tune* (= the notes are too high or low). ○ *Paul just can't sing in tune* (= with correctly produced notes). • *Younger consumers are* **in tune with** *computers* (= understand and value them).

tune ADJUST SIGNAL /tuːn/ *v* [T] to move the controls on (a radio or television set) so that it receives programs broadcast from a particular station • *Tune your radio to 88.3 FM.*

tuner /'tuː·nər/ *n* [C] the part of a radio or television that allows you to choose the stations you want to listen to or watch

tune ADJUST ENGINE /tuːn/ *v* [T] to change the setting of particular parts of (an engine), esp. slightly, so that it works as well as possible • *The engine needs tuning.*

□ **tune in** (*obj*), **tune** (*obj*) **in** /-'-/ *v adv* [I/M] to turn on (a radio or television) • *Millions of viewers tuned in to learn more about the princess's death.* [I] • If someone is **tuned in** to something, they are aware of it: *She's tuned in to all the latest fashions.*

□ **tune out** (*obj*), **tune** (*obj*) **out** /-'-/ *v adv* [I/ M] *infml* to stop paying attention • *Beverly always tunes out in the middle of her music lesson.* [I] ○ *She tends to tune out her parents' advice and make her own decisions.* [M]

□ **tune up** *obj*, **tune** *obj* **up** /-'-/ *v adv* [M] to adjust (esp. an engine) so it works as effectively as possible • *I haven't tuned my car up in two years.*

tuneup /'tuː·nʌp/ *n* [C] • *The engine needs a tune-up.*

tunic /'tuː·nɪk/ *n* [C] a piece of clothing that fits loosely over a person's body, reaching to the hips or knees and often worn with a belt

tunnel /'tʌn·əl/ *n* [C] a long passage under or through the earth, esp. one made for vehicles • *The train entered the tunnel.*

tunnel /'tʌn·əl/ *v* [I/T] **-l-** or **-ll-** • *Earthworms digest organic matter as they tunnel.* [I] ○ *The* people trapped in the collapsed building had to tunnel their way out. [T]

turban /ˈtɜr·bən/ n [C] a head covering made from a long piece of cloth that is wrapped around the head

turbine /ˈtɜr·bən, -ˌbaɪn/ n [C] a type of machine through which liquid or gas flows and turns a special wheel with blades in order to produce power • a steam turbine

turbulence CONFUSION /ˈtɜr·bjə·ləns/ n [U] a state of confusion and lack of order • political turbulence ○ His songs reflect the turbulence of his marriage.

turbulent /ˈtɜr·bjə·lənt/ adj • His book discusses the turbulent years of the civil rights struggle.

turbulence CURRENTS /ˈtɜr·bjə·ləns/ n [U] strong, uneven currents in air or water • The plane ran into some turbulence over the Atlantic.

turbulent /ˈtɜr·bjə·lənt/ adj • Turbulent seas kept us from sailing.

turd /tɜrd/ n [C] rude slang a piece of solid excrement

turf GRASS /tɜrf/ n [U] a surface layer of land consisting of grass and the earth in which its roots grow • Lush turf lined the river's banks. • Turf is also ground cover that looks like grass: artificial turf

turf AREA /tɜrf/ n [U] infml the area that a person or group considers its own • Judges feel that the courtroom is their private turf. ○ Rival gangs have started a turf war.

turgid TOO SERIOUS /ˈtɜr·dʒəd/ adj (of speech or writing) too serious and very boring • turgid prose

turgid SWOLLEN /ˈtɜr·dʒəd/ adj swollen • turgid rain clouds

turkey /ˈtɜr·ki/ n [C/U] a large North American bird grown for food, or the flesh of this bird • wild turkeys [C] ○ roast turkey [U]

turmoil /ˈtɜr·mɔɪl/ n [U] a state of extreme confusion, uncertainty, or lack of order • Her mind was in turmoil. ○ She grew up in the turmoil of the 1960s.

turkey

turn GO AROUND /tɜrn/ v [I/T] to move or cause (something) to move in a circle around a central point or line • The earth turns on its axis once every 24 hours. [I] ○ She turned the doorknob and opened the door. [T]

turn /tɜrn/ n [C] • This little wheel will shut off the water if you give it several turns.

turn CHANGE DIRECTION /tɜrn/ v [I/T] to change the direction in which you are facing or moving, or to cause (someone or something) to face or move in a different direction • They told us to turn right at the first traffic light. [I] ○ Turn your head this way so that you're looking right at the camera. [T] ○ I turned to the person next to me and asked her what time it was. [I] ○ The car turned (= went around) the corner. [T] ○ (fig.) He felt desperate and didn't know where to turn for help. [I] • If you turn over, you move your body so that the side that was facing up is now facing down. [I] • If you turn something (over), you place the surface that was on top on the bottom: She turned the baby over onto his stomach. [M] ○ He turned the pages of a magazine. [T] • To **turn a profit** is to begin to earn a profit: He's been in business five years but has yet to turn a profit. • If you **turn** your **back on** someone or something, you ignore it: He said the nation had turned its back on the poor for many years. • If you **turn back the clock**, you change something so that it behaves or exists as it did in the past: They oppose efforts to turn the clock back on civil rights. • If you **turn** your **nose up at** something, you feel that it is not good enough for you and refuse to accept it: She turned up her nose at the job because she didn't think it had enough status. • Your father would **turn over in** his **grave** (= he would strongly disapprove) if he could hear the way you are talking to me now. • If you **turn the other cheek**, you decide not to do anything to hurt someone who has hurt you. • To **turn over a new leaf** is to change your behavior in a positive way: She turned over a new leaf and began getting to work on time. • When you **turn the tables** on someone, you change from being in a weaker position to being in a stronger one: The plaintiff's lawyer turned the tables this morning by producing some startling new evidence. • A **turning point** is the time when a situation starts to change in an important, esp. positive, way: Having the baby was a turning point in their lives. • A **turn signal** is one of the lights on a vehicle that flashes to show in which direction the driver is intending to turn.

turn /tɜrn/ n [C] • Make a left turn at the next traffic light. • A **turn of events** is a new development or change in a situation: Salazar was not pleased with this turn of events but accepted his new assignment. • The **turn of the century** is the time when a particular century ends and another begins.

turn BECOME /tɜrn/ v to become or cause to become, change, or come to be • The weather suddenly turned colder, and it started to rain. [L] ○ By mid-September, the leaves are starting to turn (= change color). [I] • If a person turns a particular color, their face changes in color because they are feeling a strong emotion or are feeling ill: He turned red with embarrassment. [L] • Turn is used with times and ages to show that a particular point has been reached or passed: My little girl just turned six in February. [L] • To **turn** something **loose** is to let it go or allow it to do what it wants: He turned the horse loose in the field.

turn [SWITCH] /tɜrn/ v [always + adv/prep] to use a control to switch (a piece of equipment) on or off, or to adjust it to change the amount of what it is producing • *Please turn off/out the lights when you leave.* [M] ○ *Who turned my computer on/off?* [M] ○ *Turn the TV down (=* make the sound quieter)—*it's too loud.* [M] ○ *Turn up the volume—I can't hear what they're saying.* [M]

turn [OPPORTUNITY] /tɜrn/ n [C] an opportunity or a duty to do something at a particular time or in a particular order, before or after other people • *It's your turn to do the grocery shopping.* [+ to infinitive] • *She spoke to each of the guests* **in turn** (= one after the other.)

turn [TWIST] /tɜrn/ v [T] to damage the muscles in (the foot) by suddenly bending it too strongly • *to turn your ankle*

turn [MAKE ILL] /tɜrn/ v [I/T] to feel sick, esp. that you are going to vomit, or to cause (your stomach) to feel this way • *The stench made my stomach turn/turned my stomach.* [I/T]

□ **turn against** /ˌ--'-/ v prep [T] to change from supporting to opposing (someone) • *A lot of his supporters turned against him.*

□ **turn** obj **around** /'--'-/ v adv [T] to cause (a situation or organization) to change in a positive direction • *They were losing badly but they turned things around in the second half of the game.*

turnaround /'tɜr·nə,raʊnd/ n [C usually sing] a positive change; improvement • *Business was up over 40% in a dramatic turnaround from last year.*

□ **turn down** obj, **turn** obj **down** /'-'-/ v adv [M] to refuse to accept or agree to • *The bank turned down her request for a loan.*

□ **turn in** obj [GIVE], **turn** obj **in** /'-'-/ v adv [M] to give or return (something) to someone in authority • *to turn in a report* ○ *He learned that the police were looking for him and turned himself in* (= made himself available to them).

□ **turn in** [SLEEP] /'-'-/ v adv [I] to go to your bed in order to sleep • *I'm getting sleepy—I think I'll turn in.*

□ **turn** obj **off** /'-'-/ v adv [T] infml to cause (someone) to lose interest • *Her offensive remarks really turned me off.*

turnoff /'tɜr·nɔːf/ n [C] • *Younger readers find the newspaper's traditional format a turnoff.* • See also TURNOFF.

□ **turn on** (obj) [DEPEND ON] /'-,-/ v prep to depend on (something) in an important way • *The success of the talks turns on whether both sides are willing to compromise.*

□ **turn on** [ATTACK] /'-,-/ v prep [T] to attack or criticize (someone) suddenly • *He suddenly turned on me and accused me of not supporting him when he needed it.*

□ **turn** obj **on** [EXCITE] /'-'-/ v adv [T] infml to cause (someone) to feel excited and very interested • *What turns the kids on these days?*

□ **turn out** [RESULT] /'-'-/ v adv to happen or be-

come known to happen in a particular way • *She assured him that everything would turn out all right.* [L] ○ *It turns out (that) Ray had borrowed the money from one of his students.* [+ (that) clause]

□ **turn out** obj [PRODUCE], **turn** obj **out** /'-,-/ v adv [M] to produce or make • *Our factory is turning the dolls out as fast as we can make them.*

□ **turn out** [COME] /'-'-/ v adv [I] to come, appear, or be present • *A lot of actors turned out for the audition.*

turnout /'tɜr·naʊt/ n [C usually sing] the number of people who are present for an event or the number of people who vote in an election • *Considering the rain, there was a good turnout.*

□ **turn out** obj [REMOVE], **turn** obj **out** /'-'-/ v adv [M] to force to leave • *They turned him out of the shelter when they found he was hiding drugs.*

□ **turn over** obj, **turn** obj **over** /'-'--/ v adv [M] to give into the possession of or put under the power of another • *Eventually he turned over control of the company to his son.* • See also TURNOVER.

□ **turn to** [GET HELP] /'--/ v prep [T] to get help from (someone) • *You can always turn to me for help if you need it.*

□ **turn to** [CONSIDER] /'--/ v prep [T] to think about or begin to consider (something) • *I think we've spent enough time on this issue— let's turn to the new business now.*

□ **turn to** [FIND PAGE] /'--/ v prep [T] to open a book to a particular page • *Turn to page 27.*

□ **turn up** /'-'-/ v adv [I/T] to appear or come to your attention, or to cause (something) to become known • *She said she'd let me know if anything new turned up.* [I]

turnabout /'tɜr·nə,baʊt/ n [C] a complete change from one situation or condition to its opposite • *In a complete turnabout, the mayor has decided not to run for reelection.*

turnaround /'tɜr·nə,raʊnd/ n [C] • See at TURN AROUND.

turncoat /'tɜrn·koʊt/ n [C] a person whose support changes from one side to an opposite side in a way that shows a lack of loyalty; a TRAITOR

turnip /'tɜr·nəp/ n [C] a round, white root that is cooked and eaten as a vegetable, or the plant that produces it

turnoff /'tɜr·nɔːf/ n [C] a short road that leads from a large road onto a smaller one • *If you miss the turnoff, you'll have to go 20 miles to the next exit.* • See also **turnoff** at TURN OFF.

turnout /'tɜr·naʊt/ n [C] • See at TURN OUT [COME].

turnover [EMPLOYEE CHANGES] /'tɜr,noʊ·vər/ n [U] the rate at which employees leave a company and are replaced • *The high turnover among daycare workers is an ongoing problem.* • See also TURN OVER.

turnover PASTRY /'tɜr‚noʊ·vər/ n [C] a piece of pastry that is folded to contain fruit within it • *an apple turnover*

turnpike /'tɜrn·paɪk/ n [C] a main road intended for fast travel, which you usually have to pay to use • *the New Jersey Turnpike*

turnstile /'tɜrn·staɪl/ n [C] a device with waist-high horizontal bars that one person at a time can push around to enter a place, esp. a place that you pay to use • *More than 18 million visitors have poured through Disneyland's turnstiles.*

turntable /'tɜrn‚teɪ·bəl/ n [C] a piece of equipment used in **record players** and having a flat, round surface that turns the record around while it is being played

turpentine /'tɜr·pən‚taɪn/ n [U] a strong-smelling, colorless liquid used to thin paint

turquoise /'tɜr·kwɔɪz/ n [C/U] a blue-green precious stone often used in jewelry • Turquoise is also a blue-green color. [U]

turret /'tɜr·ət, 'tʌr·ət/ n [C] a circular tower that is part of a CASTLE or other large building

turtle /'tɜrt̬·əl/ n [C] an animal that lives in or near water, having a thick, outer shell that covers and protects its body

turtleneck /'tɜrt̬·əl‚nek/ n [C] a high, round collar that folds over on itself and covers the neck, or a piece of clothing with a collar of this type

turtleneck

tush /tʊʃ/ n [C] *slang* BOTTOM BODY PART

tusk /tʌsk/ n [C] either of the two, long, curved teeth that stick out from the mouth of some animals, esp. ELEPHANTS and WALRUSES

tussle /'tʌs·əl/ n [C] a physical argument involving pushing and holding, usually between two people • *(fig.) He had numerous tussles with the law during his career as a nightclub owner.*

tutor /'tuː·t̬ər/ n [C] a teacher paid to work privately with one student or a small group

tutor /'tuː·t̬ər/ v [T] to teach by working with one student or a small group, esp. because they need special help • *Volunteers from the college tutor elementary school children in reading, mathematics, and science.*

tuxedo /tʌk'siː·doʊ/, *infml* **tux** /tʌks/ n [C] *pl* **tuxedos** a type of black jacket, or jacket and pants, worn by men on formal occasions, usually with a **bow tie**

TV n [C] *abbreviation for* TELEVISION

twang /twæŋ/ n [C usually sing] a ringing sound that begins suddenly and continues, gradually getting less strong, like the sound made when the string of a musical instrument is pulled and quickly released • A twang is also a quality of voice heard in some speakers that is related to the passing of air through the nose as they speak.

'twas *literary* /twʌz, twɑz, twəz/ *contraction of* **it was** • *'Twas the night before Christmas*

tweak ADJUST /twiːk/ v [T] to change slightly, esp. in order to make something more effective or correct • *Writers and producers kept tweaking the script even as the movie was being shot.*

tweak PULL /twiːk/ v [T] to pull and twist (something) • *He jumped when she tweaked his ear.*

tweed /twiːd/ n [U] a thick, rough material woven from wool and used in clothing, esp. suits and coats • *a gray tweed jacket*

tweezers /'twiː·zərz/, **tweezer** /'twiː·zər/ *pl n* a small device having two narrow, metal sides joined at one end and open at the other, used to hold or pull a small thing, such as a hair, by pressing the two sides until the open ends come together on the thing to be held • *He tried to get the splinter out with tweezers.*

twelfth /twelfθ/ adj, adv [not gradable], n [C] (a person or thing) coming immediately after the eleventh and before all others • *She finished twelfth in her age group.* ○ *We will arrive on the twelfth of December.* [C] • *A twelfth is one of twelve equal parts of something.* [C] • USAGE: The related number is TWELVE. • LP NUMBERS

twelve /twelv/ *number* 12 • *Casey is twelve.* ○ *a twelve-volume set* • Twelve can also mean twelve o'clock. • USAGE: The related adjective is TWELFTH. • LP NUMBERS

twenty /'twent̬·i/ *number* 20 • *She's twenty years old.* ○ *a twenty-story building* • LP NUMBERS

twenties, 20s, 20's /'twent̬·iːz/ *pl n* the numbers 20 through 29 • *Temperatures were in the twenties* (= between 20° and 29°). • The twenties are the years between 1920 and 1929. ○ *Both of our children are now in their twenties* (= between 20 and 29 years old).

twentieth /'twent̬·i·əθ/ adj, adv [not gradable], n [C] • *This is our twentieth wedding anniversary.* ○ *The meeting is on the twentieth of November.* [C] • A twentieth is one of twenty equal parts of something. [C]

twice /twaɪs/ adv [not gradable] two times • *Take the medicine twice a day.* ○ *I've already asked him twice.* • LP DETERMINERS

twiddle /'twɪd·əl/ v [T] to move (something) repeatedly between your fingers, esp. because you are nervous or bored • *She kept twiddling her necklace.* • If you **twiddle** your **thumbs**, you do nothing, usually while you are waiting for something to happen: *She put me on hold and left me to twiddle my thumbs for ten minutes until she got back to me.*

twig /twɪg/ n [C] a small, thin branch of a tree or bush, esp. one removed from the tree or bush and without any leaves • *We gathered some dry twigs to start the fire.*

twilight /'twaɪ·laɪt/ n [U] the low level of light when it is late in the day, just before the darkness of night, or this period of the day • (*fig.*) Twilight is also any late period, when the end of something is near: *The book presents a compelling portrait of the singer in the twilight of her career.*

twill /twɪl/ *n* [U] a strong cotton cloth that has raised diagonal lines on the surface

twin /twɪn/ *n* [C] either of two children born to the same mother on the same occasion

twin /twɪn/ *adj* [not gradable] • *a twin brother/sister* • Twin is used of two things that are the same or similar: *twin engines/towers* • A **twin bed** is one of a set of two beds, each of which is suitable for one person.

twine /twaɪn/ *n* [U] strong string made by twisting together two or more lengths of string

twinge /twɪndʒ/ *n* [C] a sudden, brief feeling of pain • *When she saw her old boyfriend, she felt a twinge of sadness.*

twinkle /'twɪŋ·kəl/ *v* [I] (of light) to shine brightly then weakly, as if quickly flashing on and off • *Stars twinkled in the clear night sky.* • If someone's eyes twinkle, they have a bright, intelligent expression: *His eyes twinkled with mischief.*

twinkle /'twɪŋ·kəl/ *n* [C] • *We could see the twinkle of lights across the bay* ○ *I know that twinkle in your eye means trouble!* • **In a twinkle** or **in the twinkling of an eye** means in a moment: *The job was done in a twinkle.* ○ *Microprocessors do calculations in the twinkling of an eye.*

twinkling /'twɪŋ·klɪŋ/ *adj* [not gradable] • *a mass of twinkling stars* ○ *twinkling eyes*

twirl /twɜrl/ *v* [I/T] to turn in a circle, or to cause (something) to do this • *Skaters leapt and twirled on the ice.* [I always + adv/prep]

twirl /'twɜrl/ *n* [C] • *She does a twirl to show off her pretty dress.*

twist TURN /twɪst/ *v* [I/T] to turn repeatedly, or to combine (thin lengths of a material) by turning or wrapping • *A river twists through the valley.* [I] ○ *Vines twisted around the trunk of the old tree.* [I] • If you twist a part of your body, you hurt it by turning it awkwardly: *He twisted his knee in the game on Saturday.* [T] • If you **twist** someone's **arm**, you get them to do what you want by making it very difficult for them to refuse: *I didn't want to go to the exhibition, but Linda twisted my arm.*

twist /twɪst/ *n* [C] • *The path wound its way down the hill in a series of twists.* ○ *One more twist should tighten the cover.* • A twist can also be something that has been twisted: *She added a twist of lemon to her drink.*

twisted /'twɪs·təd/ *adj* [not gradable] • *He missed the first game of the season because of a twisted ankle.*

twisting /'twɪs·tɪŋ/ *adj* • *a twisting country road*

twist CHANGE /twɪst/ *v* [T] to change the meaning of (facts or a statement); DISTORT • *You're*

twisting my words—that's not what I meant at all. ○ *During the trial, lawyers twisted the truth to gain the jury's sympathy.*

twist /twɪst/ *n* [C] an unexpected change • *The incident was the latest twist in the story of the robbery.* ○ *Walnuts give a new twist to regular banana bread.*

twisted /'twɪs·təd/ *adj* [not gradable] unusual and strange; PERVERSE • *The letter was clearly written by someone with a twisted mind.*

twister /'twɪs·tər/ *n* [C] a dangerous wind storm; a TORNADO • PIC TORNADO

twit /twɪt/ *n* [C] a person you think is stupid or foolish

twitch /twɪtʃ/ *v* [I/T] to make a short and sudden movement, or to cause (part of your body) to move suddenly • *She saw his mouth twitch into a little smile that disappeared almost at once.* [I]

twitch /twɪtʃ/ *n* [C] • *She signalled with a twitch of her finger.*

two /tu/ *number pl* **twos** 2 • *Josh'll be two in February.* ○ *a two-time winner* • Two can also mean two o'clock. • Your **two cents/two cents' worth** is your opinion about something, esp. when it was not asked for or wanted: *If it's going to affect me, then I want to put my two cents in.* • If you are **of two minds**, you have more than one opinion about something: *Congress is always of two minds.* • If things are described as **two sides of the same coin**, they are opposite expressions of the same emotion, idea, or principle: *Freedom from restrictive taxes and freedom from restrictive laws are really two sides of the same coin.* • A **two-by-four** (usually written 2x4) is a standard size of finished wood used for building, that is about two inches thick and four inches wide. • **Two-dimensional** means flat, having width and length but not depth: *Painting is a two-dimensional art that tries to give the illusion of three dimensions.* • (*disapproving*) Someone who is **two-faced** is someone you cannot trust: *He's a dirty, two-faced cheater.* • Clothing that is **two-piece** is made in two matching parts: *She looked wonderful in her brief, two-piece bathing suit.* • (*infml*) If you **two-time** someone, you have a secret, second relationship with another person. • Something that is **two-tone** or **two-toned** has two different colors. • **Two-way** means permitting movement or communication in two directions: *There are only a few two-way streets left in town.* ○ *This should be a two-way relationship.* ○ *a two-way radio* • USAGE: The related adjective is SECOND. • LP NUMBERS

two–bit /'tu·bɪt/ *adj* [not gradable] unimportant • *He's just a two-bit crook.*

twosome /'tu·səm/ *n* [C] two people thought of as a pair • *We were a twosome, best friends, and almost never played with other kids.*

tycoon /taɪ'kun/ *n* [C] a person who has

achieved great success in business and is very wealthy and powerful

tying /'taɪ·ɪŋ/ *present participle of* TIE

tyke, **tike** /taɪk/ *n* [C] *infml* a small child

type CHARACTERISTICS /taɪp/ *n* [C] the characteristics of a group of people or things that set them apart from other people or things, or a person, thing, or group that share particular characteristics • *I'm more comfortable in jeans and T-shirts, and that type of thing.* ○ *We have makeup for all different types of skin.* ○ *Grant's my type of guy—strong and cool—but Willie's not my type at all.*

typical /'tɪp·ɪ·kəl/ *adj* showing the characteristics of a particular kind of person or thing • *He looked like the typical tourist with his camera and baseball cap.* ○ *This dish is typical of Southern cooking.* • (*disapproving*) Typical also means behaving as you would expect: *"He called to say he wasn't coming." "Typical! You can't rely on Michael for anything!"*

typically /'tɪp·ɪ·kli/ *adv* • *It's a typically American town.* ○ *I typically go running at lunchtime.*

typify /'tɪp·ə,faɪ/ *v* [T] to be an example of (a particular thing or kind of thing) • *This trial typifies the problems juries face all the time.*

type WRITE /taɪp/ *v* [I/T] to write using a **keyboard**, esp. for a computer • *I never learned how to type.* [I] ○ *He typed the report yesterday.* [T]

typing /'taɪ·pɪŋ/ *n* [U] • *Her typing is very accurate most of the time.*

typist /'taɪ·pəst/ *n* [C] • *Typists don't use typewriters any more, they use keyboards.*

type PRINTED LETTERS /taɪp/ *n* [U] printed letters and symbols, or small pieces of metal with the shapes of letters and symbols on them that were used in the past in printing • *In big bold type, the headline announced the first nuclear bomb.* • A **typeface** is a FONT LETTERS.

□ **type in** *obj*, **type** *obj* **in** /'-'-/ *v adv* [M] to use a **keyboard** to put information into a computer or onto a piece of paper • *How can I type in my password if I can't remember it?*

□ **type out/up** *obj*, **type** *obj* **out/up** /'-'-/ *v adv* [M] to use a **keyboard**, esp. on a TYPEWRITER, to make a copy of something in writing • *Did you type up the minutes of yesterday's meeting?*

typewriter /'taɪp,raɪt̬·ər/ *n* [C] a machine for putting print on a page, operated with keys

typewritten /'taɪp,rɪt̬·ᵊn/ *adj* [not gradable] • *We found several old typewritten manuscripts in the attic.*

typhoid (fever) /'taɪ·fɔɪd/ *n* [U] an infectious disease spread by bacteria, esp. in water and food, causing fever and severe pain in the bowels

typhoon /taɪ'fuːn/ *n* [C] a type of violent storm with strong circular winds that happens esp. in the Pacific Ocean

typhus /'taɪ·fəs/ *n* [U] an infectious disease caused by organisms carried by LICE and causing fever, severe pain in the head, and dark red spots on the body

typical /'tɪp·ɪ·kəl/ *adj* • See at TYPE CHARACTERISTICS.

typically /'tɪp·ɪ·kli/ *adv* • See at TYPE CHARACTERISTICS.

typify /'tɪp·ə,faɪ/ *v* [T] • See at TYPE CHARACTERISTICS.

typing /'taɪ·pɪŋ/ *n* [U] • See at TYPE WRITE.

typist /'taɪ·pəst/ *n* [C] • See at TYPE WRITE.

typo /'taɪ·poʊ/ *n* [C] *pl* **typos** a mistake made in printed material produced by a computer or a TYPEWRITER

tyranny /'tɪr·ə·ni/ *n* [C/U] unlimited authority or use of power, or a government which exercises such power without any control or limits

tyrannical /tɪ'ræn·ɪ·kəl/ *adj* • *American revolutionaries believed the British government was tyrannical.*

tyrannize /'tɪr·ə,naɪz/ *v* [T] • *In school, he was the big bully who tyrannized the whole playground.*

tyrant /'taɪ·rənt/ *n* [C] • *Their father was a tyrant, feared by all his children.*

tyre /taɪr/ *n* [C] *Br for* TIRE WHEEL

U, u

U, u /juː/ *n* [C] *pl* **U's** or **u's** the 21st letter of the English alphabet • A **U-turn** is a turn like a U, made by a vehicle to go back in the direction from which it came: *My car was hit while making a U-turn.* • A **U-turn** is also a complete change from one opinion or plan to an opposite one.

udder /ˈʌd·ər/ *n* [C] the baglike part of a cow, goat, or other animal that hangs between the back legs and produces milk

UFO /ˌjuː·efˈoʊ/ *n* [C] *pl* **UFOs** abbreviation for an unidentified flying object (= an object seen in the sky that some people believe is a spacecraft from another planet)

ugh /ʌg/ *exclamation* the written form of the sound people sometimes use to express a strong feeling of disgust at something very unpleasant • *Ugh, that smells really bad!*

ugly VERY UNATTRACTIVE /ˈʌg·li/ *adj* [-er/-est only] extremely unattractive in appearance • *He's a really ugly dog.*
ugliness /ˈʌg·liː·nəs/ *n* [U] • *The city's ugliness struck me.*

ugly UNPLEASANT /ˈʌg·li/ *adj* [-er/-est only] unpleasant and threatening or violent • *This policy could have some ugly consequences.*
ugliness /ˈʌg·liː·nəs/ *n* [U] • *He has ugliness in his heart.*

uh /ʌ, ə/, **um** /ʌm, ᵊm/ *exclamation* the written form of the sound people sometimes make when they pause in speaking, thinking of what to say next or how to say it • *I try not to, uh, rely on my parents.*

uh–huh /ˈʌ̃·hə̃, ˈᵊm·hᵊm/ *exclamation infml* said to express agreement to what has just been said, or to mean yes • *"Did you hear what I said?" "Uh-huh."*

uh–oh /ˈʌ·oʊ/ *exclamation infml* the written form of the sound that people sometimes make when they have made a mistake or when something bad has happened • *Uh-oh, I think I just locked my keys in the car.*

uh–uh /ˈʌ̃·ə̃, ˈᵊm·ᵊm/ *exclamation infml* the written form of the sound that people sometimes make to say no • *"Did you do the shopping?" "Uh-uh."*

ulcer /ˈʌl·sər/ *n* [C] a sore on the skin or inside the body that will not heal without treatment • *a stomach ulcer*

ulterior /ʌlˈtɪr·iː·ər/ *adj* [not gradable] (of a reason) hidden or secret • *She had no ulterior motive for helping them out—she just wanted to do it.*

ultimate /ˈʌl·tə·mət/ *adj* [not gradable] most important, highest, last, or final • *Your ultimate goal is to play the game as well as you can.* • Ultimate also means the best, most, or greatest of its kind: *Some people believe that he is the ultimate painter of this century.*

ultimate /ˈʌl·tə·mət/ *n* [U] • *Winning was the ultimate, because our team had never won before.*

ultimately /ˈʌl·tə·mət·li/ *adv* [not gradable] finally; in the end • *Our plans ultimately depend on the weather.*

ultimatum /ˌʌl·təˈmeɪt̬·əm/ *n* [C] a demand that a person or group do something to avoid something unpleasant • *The workers got an ultimatum—go back to work or face dismissal.*

ultra– /ˌʌl·trə/ *combining form* extreme or extremely • *ultraconservative* ○ *ultramodern*

ultrasonic /ˌʌl·trəˈsɑn·ɪk/ *adj* [not gradable] (of sound waves) too high for people to hear

ultrasound /ˈʌl·trəˌsaʊnd/ *n* [U] sound waves that are higher than people can hear, esp. ones used to examine and treat medical problems • *An ultrasound scan revealed tissue damage.*

ultraviolet /ˌʌl·trəˈvɑɪ·ə·lət/ *adj* [not gradable] (of light) at the purple end of the SPECTRUM (= set of colors into which light is separated), which cannot be seen by human beings

um /ˈʌm, ᵊm/ *exclamation* UH

umbilical cord /ʌmˈbɪl·ɪ·kəl/ *n* [C] the tubelike cord that connects a baby to its mother and carries oxygen and food to it before birth

umbrella /ʌmˈbrel·ə/ *n* [C] a cover that protects from rain or sun, esp. waterproof material fitted on a folding frame with a handle at one end • *A figure carrying an open umbrella walked slowly through the rain.* • An umbrella is also something that includes a number of similar things: *an umbrella term* ○ *an umbrella organization*

umpire /ˈʌm·paɪr/, *short form* **ump** /ʌmp/ *n* [C] (in some sports) a person who controls a game and makes sure that the rules are followed
umpire /ˈʌm·paɪr/ *v* [I/T] • *Who's going to umpire the game tonight?* [T]

un– /ʌn/ *combining form* used to add the meaning "not," "lacking," or "the opposite of" to adjectives, adverbs, verbs, and nouns • *unrealistic* ○ *unhappily* ○ *unfasten* ○ *unfairness*

UN /juːˈen/ *n* [U] abbreviation for the United Nations (= an international organization that was established in 1945 to maintain world peace)

unabashed /ˌʌn·əˈbæʃt/ *adj* not worried about being criticized or embarrassed • *an unabashed critic of Congress* ○ *an unabashed supporter of the team*

unabated /ˌʌn·əˈbeɪt̬·əd/ *adj* without weakening in strength or force • *Their arguments continue unabated.*

unable /ʌnˈeɪ·bəl/ *adj* [not gradable] not ABLE HAVING WHAT IS NEEDED • *I was unable to find a pay phone.*

unacceptable /ˌʌn·ɪkˈsep·tə·bəl/ *adj* too bad to be accepted, approved of, or allowed to continue • *These mistakes are unacceptable.* ○ *The proposal is unacceptable to theater owners.*

unaccompanied /ˌʌn·ə'kʌm·pə·niːd/ *adj* [not gradable] without anyone with you, or (of the voice or an instrument) sung or played without other musical instruments • *Unaccompanied teens were banned from the mall.* ○ *The kids sang an unaccompanied version of "Skylark."*

unaccountable /ˌʌn·ə'kɑʊnt·ə·bəl/ *adj* [not gradable] not able to be explained or understood • *For some unaccountable reason, he forgot his car keys.* • If someone is unaccountable, they do not have to explain their actions to anyone in authority.

unaccustomed /ˌʌn·ə'kʌs·təmd/ *adj* [not gradable] (of a person) not familiar with or experienced at something • *She was unaccustomed to driving in heavy traffic.* • Unaccustomed can also mean unusual or unexpected: *His unaccustomed nervousness made us all anxious.*

unadulterated /ˌʌn·ə'dʌl·tə,reɪt̬·əd/ *adj* not spoiled or made weaker by the addition of other things • *She sings pure, unadulterated gospel.*

unaffected NOT CHANGED /ˌʌn·ə'fek·təd/ *adj* [not gradable] not influenced or changed in any way • *Internet access will be unaffected by the upgrade.*

unaffected SINCERE /ˌʌn·ə'fek·təd/ *adj* [not gradable] natural and sincere • *Her writing is very unaffected and easy to read.*

unambiguous /ˌʌn·æm'bɪɡ·jə·wəs/ *adj* expressed in a way which makes it completely clear what is meant • *an unambiguous answer*

un-American /ˌʌn·ə'mer·ɪ·kən, -'mær-/ *adj* showing opposition or a lack of loyalty to the US and its political system • *It seems un-American to tell me how to run my business.*

unanimous /jʊ'næn·ə·məs/ *adj* [not gradable] in complete agreement or showing complete agreement • *Americans are unanimous in their support for the hostages.* ○ *The jury reached a unanimous verdict.*

unanimously /jʊ'næn·ə·mə·sli/ *adv* [not gradable] • *Sportswriters unanimously picked him for the award.*

unanimity /ˌjuː·nə'nɪm·ət̬·i/ *n* [U] • *Unanimity allows us to get things done quickly.*

unannounced /ˌʌn·ə'nɑʊnst/ *adj, adv* [not gradable] sudden and unexpected • *Several unannounced acts made this concert special.* ○ *The President appeared unannounced.*

unanswered /ʌn'æn·sərd/ *adj, adv* [not gradable] (esp. of a letter, question, or telephone call) not reacted to or explained • *She wondered why her calls went unanswered.*

unarmed /ʌn'ɑrmd/ *adj* [not gradable] not carrying or having a weapon • *How could an unarmed man be so frightening?*

unassuming /ˌʌn·ə'suː·mɪŋ/ *adj* not attracting attention; quiet, modest • *a shy and*

unassuming person ○ *an unassuming little restaurant*

unattached NOT MARRIED /ˌʌn·ə'tætʃt/ *adj* [not gradable] *infml* not married or involved with anyone • *an unattached woman*

unattached NOT CONNECTED /ˌʌn·ə'tætʃt/ *adj* [not gradable] not joined or connected; independent

unattended /ˌʌn·ə'ten·dəd/ *adj* [not gradable] not being watched or taken care of • *unattended boxes and packages* ○ *unattended children*

unattractive /ˌʌn·ə'træk·tɪv/ *adj* ugly in appearance, or unpleasant in character • *an unattractive room* ○ *an unattractive personality*

unauthorized /ʌn'ɔː·θə,rɑɪzd/ *adj* [not gradable] without official permission • *an unauthorized biography* ○ *An unauthorized version of the software is being sold abroad.*

unavailable /ˌʌn·ə'veɪ·lə·bəl/ *adj* [not gradable] (of things) not able to be used or obtained, or (of people) not willing or able to be met • *Fresh fruit and vegetables had been unavailable for some time.* ○ *I'm sorry, the colonel is unavailable now.*

unavoidable /ˌʌn·ə'vɔɪd·ə·bəl/ *adj* [not gradable] unable to be prevented or stayed away from • *War is now unavoidable.*

unaware /ˌʌn·ə'wer, -'wær/ *adj* not knowing that something exists, or not having knowledge or experience of something • *I was unaware of the risks involved.* ○ *Bowman was unaware that the car was gone.* [+ *that* clause]

unawares /ˌʌn·ə'werz, -'wærz/ *adv* suddenly and unexpectedly; without warning • *We were caught unawares by the fierce storm.*

unbalanced /ʌn'bæl·ənst/ *adj* emphasizing one thing or one side over another • *an unbalanced diet* ○ *unbalanced reporting* • A person who is unbalanced is mentally ill.

unbearable /ʌn'ber·ə·bəl, -'bær-/ *adj* [not gradable] so unpleasant or painful that you find it hard to accept • *We had an unbearable summer here.* ○ *Prison conditions are unbearable.*

unbearably /ʌn'ber·ə·bli, -'bær-/ *adv* • *an unbearably hot day* ○ *unbearably painful memories*

unbeatable /ʌn'biːt̬·ə·bəl/ *adj* [not gradable] unable to be defeated, or better than any other • *an unbeatable team* ○ *unbeatable pizza*

unbeaten /ʌn'biːt·ən/ *adj* [not gradable] not defeated • *The Royals remain unbeaten after 12 games.*

unbecoming /ʌn·bɪ'kʌm·ɪŋ/ *adj* not suitable or acceptable • *Such conduct is unbecoming to an official.*

unbelievable SURPRISING /ˌʌn·bɪ'liː·və·bəl/ *adj* [not gradable] extremely surprising • *That little dog eats an unbelievable amount of food.*

unbelievably /ˌʌn·bɪ'liː·və·bli/ *adv* [not grad-

able] • *It was unbelievably stupid of you to go.*
• LP VERY, COMPLETELY, AND OTHER INTENSIFIERS

unbelievable UNLIKELY /ˌʌn·bɪˈliː·və·bəl/ *adj* not able to be believed because unlikely • *an unbelievable story/excuse* ○ *unbelievable luck*

unborn /ʌnˈbɔːrn/ *adj* [not gradable] not yet born; in the mother's uterus • *an unborn child/calf*

unbounded /ʌnˈbɑʊn·dəd/ *adj* [not gradable] very great; seeming to have no limits • *an unbounded commitment to excellence*

unbridled /ʌnˈbraɪd·ᵊld/ *adj* [not gradable] not controlled or limited • *unbridled passion/joy/fury/greed/authority*

uncalled–for /ʌnˈkɔːld‚fɔːr/ *adj* [not gradable] not suitable and therefore unnecessary • *uncalled-for violence*

uncanny /ʌnˈkæn·i/ *adj* strange or mysterious; difficult or impossible to explain • *He has an uncanny ability to pick a winner.* ○ *Barb's uncanny resemblance to Tia is scary.*

uncertain /ʌnˈsɜrt·ᵊn/ *adj* [not gradable] unclear, or not sure • *She faces an uncertain future.* ○ *We're uncertain of the cause of death.*

uncertainly /ʌnˈsɜrt·ᵊn·li/ *adv* [not gradable] not confidently or surely • *She looked at John uncertainly.*

uncertainty /ʌnˈsɜrt·ᵊn·ti/ *n* [C/U] • *They live in uncertainty and confusion.* [U]

uncharted /ʌnˈtʃɑrt·əd/ *adj* [not gradable] (of a place) never before described, or (of a situation) completely new • *New drugs lead doctors into uncharted territory.*

unchecked /ʌnˈtʃekt/ *adj* [not gradable] not stopped or ended • *These problems will worsen if current trends continue unchecked.*

uncivilized /ʌnˈsɪv·ə‚lɑɪzd/ *adj* [not gradable] (of a society or country) without what is thought to be a highly developed culture and way of life, or (of a person) rude and thoughtless • *uncivilized behavior*

uncle /ˈʌŋ·kəl/ *n* [C] the brother of someone's mother or father, or the husband of someone's aunt • *My aunt and uncle moved to Arizona when they retired.* • PIC FAMILY TREE • LP TITLES AND FORMS OF ADDRESS

unclean PHYSICAL /ʌnˈkliːn/ *adj* not clean or not pure and therefore likely to cause disease • *unclean water* ○ *unclean kitchens*

unclean MORAL *fml* /ʌnˈkliːn/ *adj* not acceptable or usable according to religious or moral standards • *unclean thoughts/practices*

unclear /ʌnˈklɪr/ *adj* not obvious or easy to see or know • *It's unclear what actually happened that night.* [+ *wh-* word] • If a person is unclear about something, they are not sure about it: *I'm unclear about a couple of things he said on the phone.*

unclearly /ʌnˈklɪr·li/ *adv*

Uncle Sam /ˌʌŋ·kəlˈsæm/ *n* [U] a name that symbolizes the US or its government, pictured esp. in political drawings as a tall, thin man

with white facial hair and a tall hat wearing clothes colored like the American flag

Uncle Tom /ˌʌŋ·kəlˈtɑm/ *n* [C] *disapproving* a black person who is considered to be too eager to be friendly to white people and not willing to complain of unfair treatment by them

uncomfortable /ʌnˈkʌm·fərṭ·ə·bəl, -ˈkʌmf·tər·bəl/ *adj* [not gradable] not COMFORTABLE or relaxed, or feeling anxiety • *an uncomfortable chair* ○ *She feels uncomfortable in a room full of strangers.*

uncomfortably /ʌnˈkʌm·fərṭ·ə·bli, -ˈkʌmf·tər·bli/ *adv* • *an uncomfortably warm day*

uncommon NOT FREQUENT /ʌnˈkɑm·ən/ *adj* [not gradable] not seen, happening, or experienced often • *It's not uncommon for someone to change jobs several times.*

uncommonly /ʌnˈkɑm·ən·li/ *adv* • *an uncommonly gifted singer*

uncommon UNUSUALLY LARGE /ʌnˈkɑm·ən/ *adj* (esp. of a human quality) unusually large in amount or degree • *She's a woman of uncommon kindness.*

uncompromising /ʌnˈkɑm·prə‚mɑɪ·zɪŋ/ *adj* (of a person or their opinions) fixed and not easily changed • *People are intimidated by her uncompromising ways.*

unconcerned /ˌʌn·kənˈsɜrnd/ *adj* not worried or anxious • *How can you be unconcerned about racism?*

unconditional /ˌʌn·kənˈdɪʃ·ən·ᵊl/ *adj* [not gradable] complete and not limited in any way • *unconditional love* ○ *He got an unconditional release from prison.*

unconfirmed /ˌʌn·kənˈfɜrmd/ *adj* [not gradable] (of information) not proven to be true or false • *an unconfirmed report*

unconscionable /ʌnˈkɑn·tʃə·nə·bəl/ *adj* unacceptable because of being too extreme • *It is unconscionable to say that some kids don't deserve an education.*

unconscious /ʌnˈkɑn·tʃəs/ *adj* [not gradable] not CONSCIOUS AWAKE • *The fall from his horse knocked him unconscious for several minutes.* • Unconscious feelings or actions are ones you are not fully aware of: *unconscious anxiety* ○ *There's an unconscious classification within the group.*

unconscious /ʌnˈkɑn·tʃəs/ *n* [U] *specialized* (in PSYCHOANALYSIS) the part of the mind you are not aware of but which influences behavior

unconsciously /ʌnˈkɑn·tʃə·sli/ *adv* • *He unconsciously assumes that everyone agrees with him.*

unconstitutional /ˌʌn‚kɑn·stəˈtuː·ʃən·ᵊl/ *adj* [not gradable] not allowed by the CONSTITUTION (= set of political principles) of a country or organization

uncontrollable /ˌʌn·kənˈtroʊ·lə·bəl/ *adj* [not gradable] too strong or violent to be controlled • *an uncontrollable temper* ○ *I felt an uncontrollable desire to sit down.*

uncontrollably 946

uncontrollably /ˌʌn·kən'troʊ·lə·bli/ *adv* • *He was laughing uncontrollably.*

uncontrolled /ˌʌn·kən'troʊld/ *adj* • *uncontrolled shivering* ○ *the uncontrolled spread of guns*

unconventional /ˌʌn·kən'ven·tʃən·ᵊl/ *adj* different from what is usual or from the way most people do things • *He has an unconventional attitude toward work.*

uncountable noun /ʌn'kaʊnt·ə·bəl/ *n* [C] *specialized* (in grammar) a noun that has one form with no plural and names something that there can be more or less of but that cannot be counted • *"Heat" is an uncountable noun.* • USAGE: Uncountable nouns are marked [U] in this dictionary. • Compare COUNTABLE NOUN. • ⓛⓟ PLURALS OF NOUNS

uncouth /ʌn'kuːθ/ *adj* (of a person or their behavior) rude and unpleasant

uncover /ʌn'kʌv·ər/ *v* [T] to remove (what is covering something), or to discover (what was hidden) • *uncover the pot* ○ *It's the press's responsibility to uncover the truth.*

uncut /ʌn'kʌt/ *adj* [not gradable] not made smaller or shorter, or not changed in any way • *an uncut book/film/play* ○ *uncut diamonds*

undated /ʌn'deɪt̬·əd/ *adj* [not gradable] (of something written) without the day, month, and year on it • *an undated letter*

undaunted /ʌn'dɔːnt·əd, -'dɑnt-/ *adj* [not gradable] not frightened or discouraged, despite problems or lack of success • *Undaunted by the cold and the rain, we continued our hike.*

undecided /ˌʌn·dɪ'saɪd·əd/ *adj* [not gradable] not having made a decision or judgment about something • *Are you still undecided about that job in San Francisco?*

undeniable /ˌʌn·dɪ'naɪ·ə·bəl/ *adj* [not gradable] so obviously true that it cannot be doubted • *It is an undeniable fact that ice is cold.*

undeniably /ˌʌn·dɪ'naɪ·ə·bli/ *adv* [not gradable] • *She is undeniably brilliant.*

under ⃞LOWER POSITION /ˌʌn·dər/ *prep* in or to a position below or lower than (something else), often so that one thing covers the other • *Our dog hides under the bed whenever we have a lightning storm.* ○ *She was holding the umbrella under her arm* (= between her upper arm and the side of her chest). • To have something **under** your **belt** is to have learned or succeeded in something that you needed to do: *Now that you've got the required courses under your belt, you can take some electives.* • *"Let's go," she muttered under her breath* (= quietly so that other people could not hear). • If something is **under** someone's **nose**, it is where they should have seen it easily: *I've been looking for my keys and they were right here under my nose all the time.* • *I've tried everything under the sun* (= everything possible) *to fix this lock, but I just can't get it to work.*

• If something is done **under the table**, it is done secretly: *If you want to get a good apartment, you may have to give the manager some money under the table.* • If someone is **under the weather**, they do not feel completely well. • If you keep something **under wraps**, you keep it secret.

under /'ʌn·dər/ *adv* [not gradable] • *Several lifeguards tried desperately to reach him before he went under* (= sank below the surface of the water).

under ⃞LESS THAN /ˌʌn·dər/ *prep* less than • *The price is still under a dollar.* ○ *No one under 21 can legally be served alcohol in this state.*

under /'ʌn·dər/ *adv* [not gradable] • *There is no admission charge for children six and under.*

under– /ˌʌn·dər/ *combining form* not enough • *The potatoes were undercooked.* ○ *Classes were too large because the school was understaffed.*

under ⃞EXPERIENCING /ˌʌn·dər/ *prep* in the process of, influenced or controlled by, or according to • *Construction had to be done under difficult conditions.* ○ *Under current law, stores in this town can't do business on Sunday.* ○ *We liked working under her because she made us feel appreciated.* ○ *"Where can I find books on swimming?" "Look under sports"* (= within the subject of sports). ○ *We seemed to be under attack* (= in the process of being attacked) *by a swarm of bees.* ○ *Your request for a transfer to our Denver office is under consideration* (= being considered). ○ *I was under the impression* (= I believed) *that she was married. I find it difficult to work under pressure* (= with this influence). • If you are **under fire**, you are being shot at with bullets or other explosives: *The troops were under fire for weeks.* ○ *(fig.) The president has come under fire* (= is being criticized) *for vetoing the bill to cut taxes.* • If someone is **under guard**, they are being protected or are being prevented from escaping: *The suspected drug dealer was placed under armed guard.* • **Under no circumstances** means that there is no condition that could make something possible: *He publicly said that under no circumstances was he returning to Phoenix.* • If a person is **under oath**, they have legally promised to tell the truth: *He was accused of lying under oath.* • **Under the circumstances** means because of the present conditions: *He feels that under the circumstances he shouldn't be here.* ○ *I don't feel happy about flying under the best of circumstances.* • *He was arrested for driving **under the influence*** (= while legally drunk). • An event or process that is **under way** (also **underway**), is beginning to exist or is happening now: *Economic recovery is already under way.* ○ *Plans are underway to build a new bridge over this part of the river.* ○ *It's time to get this project underway* (= started).

underachiever /ˌʌn·də·rə'tʃiː·vər/ *n* [C] a

person whose performance is lower than you would expect, based on their ability

underage /ˌʌn·də'reɪdʒ/ *adj* [not gradable] younger than the age at which a particular activity is legally allowed • *The police closed the bar for serving alcohol to underage students.*

underarm /ˈʌn·də,rɑrm/ *adj* [not gradable] of or for use in the **armpit** (= the hollow place under your arm where your arm joins your body) • *underarm deodorants*

underbrush /ˈʌn·dər,brʌʃ/, **undergrowth** /ˈʌn·dər,groʊθ/ *n* [U] a mass of bushes, small trees, and plants growing under the trees in woods or a forest

underclass /ˈʌn·dər,klæs/ *n* [C] the lowest economic and social class in society, consisting of people who are considered to have few opportunities to improve themselves

underclothes /ˈʌn·dər,kloʊðz/ *pl n* UNDERWEAR

undercover /ˌʌn·dər,kʌv·ər/ *adj* [not gradable] working secretly to obtain information, esp. for the police • *an undercover cop*

undercurrent /ˈʌn·dər,kɜr·ənt, -,kʌ·rənt/ *n* [C] a hidden emotion or belief that is usually negative or harmful and has an indirect effect • *There is an undercurrent of suspicion and even hostility in the military for their new commander-in-chief.*

undercut /ˌʌn·dər'kʌt/ *v* [T] **undercutting**, *past* **undercut** to weaken, damage, or cause the failure of (something); UNDERMINE • *The compromise undercuts a UN directive not to give the Serbs fuel under any circumstances.* • To undercut is also to charge less than a competitor: *Large supermarkets can undercut their smaller rivals.*

underdog /ˈʌn·dər,dɔːg/ *n* [C] the weaker of two competitors, or anyone not expected to win a competition • *He began the race for governor as the underdog.*

underestimate /ˌʌn·də'res·tə,meɪt/ *v* [T] to think that (something) is less or lower than it really is, or that (someone) is less strong or less effective than they are • *Homeowners often underestimate the cost of repairing a roof.*

underfoot /ˌʌn·dər'fʊt/ *adv* [not gradable] under your feet as you walk • *The grass felt pleasant and cool underfoot.* ○ *The cat keeps getting underfoot* (= in the way).

undergo /ˌʌn·dər'goʊ/ *v* [T] he/she/it **undergoes**, **undergoing**, *past simple* **underwent** /ˌʌn·dər'went/, *past part* **undergone** /ˌʌn·dər'gɔːn, -'gɑn/ to experience (something that is unpleasant or has a strong effect) • *He recently underwent heart bypass surgery.*

undergraduate /ˌʌn·dər'grædʒ·ə·wət/ *n* [C] a student at a college or university who has not yet received a BACHELOR'S DEGREE (= the first degree given) • [LP] EDUCATION IN THE US

underground /ˌʌn·dər'graʊnd/ *adj, adv* [not gradable] below the surface of the earth; be-

low ground • *an underground garage* • Something that is done underground is secret or hidden, usually because it is not traditional or is shocking or illegal : *an underground newspaper* ○ *Officials believe the sighting of the suspect may have forced him (to go) underground* (= to become secret).

underground /ˈʌn·dər,graʊnd/ *n* [U] • The underground is an organization that secretly works against those in power: *He was a member of the French underground in World War II.*

undergrowth /ˈʌn·dər,groʊθ/ *n* [U] UNDERBRUSH

underhand /ˈʌn·dər,hænd/ *adj, adv* [not gradable] (done) by moving the arm from back to front with the hand below shoulder level and with the inner part of the hand facing forward • *an underhand toss*

underhanded /ˌʌn·dər'hæn·dəd/, **underhand** /ˈʌn·dər,hænd/ *adj* done secretly, and sometimes dishonestly, in order to achieve an advantage • *Shareholders sued the company, alleging an underhanded attempt to deprive them of their rights.*

underline /ˈʌn·dər,laɪn/ *v* [T] to draw a line under (a word), esp. in order to show its importance • *to underline significant parts of a text* • To underline is also to emphasize: *The announcement underlines IBM's newfound willingness to employ technologies developed by other companies.*

underlying /ˌʌn·dər,laɪ·ɪŋ/ *adj* [not gradable] real but not immediately obvious • *The investigation focused on the underlying causes of the fire.*

underlie /ˌʌn·dər'laɪ/ *v* [T] **underlying**, *past simple* **underlay** /ˌʌn·dər'leɪ/, *past part* **underlain** /ˌʌn·dər'leɪn/ *slightly fml* to be an esp. hidden cause of or strong influence on (something) • *More fundamental economic problems may underlie last week's stock market slide.*

undermine /ˌʌn·dər'maɪn/ *v* [T] to gradually weaken or destroy (someone or something), esp. in a way that is not obvious • *The incompetence and arrogance of the city's administration have undermined public confidence in government.*

underneath /ˌʌn·dər'niːθ/ *prep, adv* [not gradable] directly under and usually hidden by (something else) • *The Lincoln Tunnel passes underneath the Hudson River that separates New York from New Jersey.* ○ *When the painting was restored, an older painting was discovered underneath.*

undernourished /ˌʌn·dər'nɜr·əʃt, -'nʌ·rəʃt/ *adj* not eating enough food to maintain good health

underpaid /ˌʌn·dər'peɪd/ *adj* paid too little money for the work you do

underpants /ˈʌn·dər,pænts/ *pl n* a piece of underwear covering the area between the waist and the top of the legs • *a pair of under-pants*

underpass /'ʌn·dər,pæs/ *n* [C] a passage that goes under something such as a busy road, allowing people or vehicles to go from one side to the other

underprivileged /,ʌn·dər'prɪv·lɪdʒd/ *adj* lacking the money and the basic social advantages that most people have; poor • *a summer camp for underprivileged children*

underrate /,ʌn·də'reɪt/ *v* [T] to fail to recognize the importance, value, skill, power, etc., of (someone or something) • *Never underrate your opponent in a political contest.*

underrated /,ʌn·də'reɪt̬·əd/ *adj* • *He is one of Hollywood's most underrated actors* (= He is much better than people think).

undershirt /'ʌn·dər,ʃɜrt/ *n* [C] a type of underwear that covers the upper part of the body and is worn under a shirt

underside /'ʌn·dər,saɪd/ *n* [C] the lower or bottom side of something • *Mites feed on the underside of leaves.*

undersigned /'ʌn·dər,saɪnd/ *pl n* the people whose signatures appear below, usually at the end of a formal letter • *We, the undersigned, wish to protest the planned closing of the local library.*

understaffed /'ʌn·dər'stæft/ *adj* not having enough employees • *The facility is chronically understaffed and short of supplies.*

understand (*obj*) KNOW /,ʌn·dər'stænd/ *v past* **understood** /,ʌn·dər'stʊd/ to know the meaning of (something), or to know how (a person) feels and why they behave in a particular way • *I don't understand what he means.* [+ *wh*- word] ∘ *Is there anyone here who understands English?* [T] ∘ *It was so noisy I couldn't understand* (= recognize) *a word he was saying.* [T] ∘ *If you choose not to come, I'll understand.* [I] ∘ *He claimed that no one ever understood him* (= had any sympathy for him or knew what he was feeling). [T] ∘ *I understand how she feels about the loss of her dog.* [+ *wh*-word]

understandable /,ʌn·dər'stæn·də·bəl/ *adj* • *You've got to tell a story to three-year-olds in a way that's understandable to them.* • If you say that something a person does is understandable, you feel that it is the way most people would behave in that situation: *Her actions are understandable when you consider how badly she was treated.*

understandably /,ʌn·dər'stæn·də·bli/ *adv* • If you say that someone is understandably feeling a particular emotion, you mean that most people would feel the same way in that situation: *She was understandably upset when no one returned her call.*

understanding /,ʌn·dər'stæn·dɪŋ/ *n* [U] knowledge of a particular thing • *He doesn't have any real understanding of mathematics.* • Understanding is also a feeling of kindness and caring based on knowledge, esp. of the causes of behavior: *The values he had in mind were simply family love and understanding.*

understanding /,ʌn·dər'stæn·dɪŋ/ *adj* sympathetic and caring • *an understanding friend*

understand (*obj*) BELIEVE /,ʌn·dər'stænd/ *v past* **understood** /,ʌn·dər'stʊd/ to believe (something) is true because you have been told something that causes you to think it • *I understand (that) the show will go on, but with a different cast.* [+ (*that*) clause] ∘ *I understood him to say* (= I believed that he said) *that the trip had been canceled.* [T] • **It is understood that** (= Everyone knows and accepts that) *you don't bring food or drinks into the library.* • Understand is also used, sometimes in a threatening way, to make certain that someone knows what you want: *I do not want you hanging around the shopping mall late at night. Understand?/Do you understand?/Is that understood?* [I/T]

understanding /,ʌn·dər'stæn·dɪŋ/ *n* [C usually sing] something that you have reason to believe • *Ours was a generation brought up with the understanding* (= belief) *that science meant progress.* [+ *that* clause] • An understanding is also an informal agreement between people: *The two sides have come to/reached an understanding about the sale of the house.* • If you do something **on the understanding that** something else will happen, you do it because someone has promised that it will: *We purchased the computer on the understanding that it could be returned within ten days.*

understate /,ʌn·dər'steɪt/ *v* [T] to say that (the amount or importance of something) is less than it really is • *The company was accused of understating potential side effects of the drug.*

understated /,ʌn·dər'steɪt̬·əd/ *adj* not intended to be obvious • *The apartment was luxurious but furnished in a tastefully understated way.*

understatement /,ʌn·dər'steɪt·mənt/ *n* [C/U] • *To say I was confused is an understatement—I hadn't the slightest idea what to do.* [C]

understudy /'ʌn·dər,stʌd·i/ *n* [C] an actor or other performer who learns the parts of others in a play, opera, etc., so that he or she can replace them if necessary

undertake (*obj*) /,ʌn·dər'teɪk/ *v past simple* **undertook** /,ʌn·dər'tʊk/, *past part* **undertaken** /,ʌn·dər'teɪ·kən/ to take responsibility for and begin doing (something) • *The president directed the Department of Justice to undertake an investigation of the allegations.* [T] ∘ *I undertook to help him learn English.* [+ *to* infinitive]

undertaking /'ʌn·dər,teɪ·kɪŋ/ *n* [C usually sing] an effort to do something, esp. to do a large or difficult job, or the job that is done •

Preparing for the US national census every ten years is a massive undertaking.

undertaker /'ʌn·dərˌteɪ·kər/, **mortician** n [C] a person whose business is to have the dead prepared to be buried or CREMATED (= burned) and to organize funerals

undertone [CHARACTERISTIC] /'ʌn·dərˌtoʊn/ n [C] a quality of something that you realize exists although it is not expressed directly • *When two people meet at a bar, their conversation often has a sexual undertone.*

undertone [LOW VOICE] /'ʌn·dərˌtoʊn/ n [C] a low voice • *José muttered something to me in an undertone.*

undertow /'ʌn·dərˌtoʊ/ n [C] a strong current that flows under water away from a beach at the same time as waves on the surface move toward the beach

underwater /ˌʌn·dərˈwɔːt̬·ər, -'wɑt̬-/ adj, adv [not gradable] under the surface of water, esp. under the surface of the sea • *an underwater camera* ○ *Some ducks can stay underwater for nearly two minutes.*

underway /ˌʌn·dərˈweɪ/ adj, adv **under way**, see at UNDER [EXPERIENCING]

underwear /'ʌn·dərˌwer, -ˌwær/ n [U], **underclothes** pl n clothes worn next to the skin, under other clothes

underweight /ˌʌn·dərˈweɪt/ adj weighing less than usual • *The children were found to be malnourished and underweight.*

underwent /ˌʌn·dərˈwent/ past simple of UNDERGO

underworld /'ʌn·dərˌwɜrld/ n [U] the criminal organizations and activities that exist within society

underwrite /'ʌn·dəˌraɪt/ v [T] past simple **underwrote** /'ʌn·dəˌroʊt/, past part **underwritten** /'ʌn·dəˌrɪt·ən/ to support (something that costs money) by promising to pay for it, or by promising to pay if necessary to protect others who are risking their money • *The museum show was largely underwritten by a grant from the government of Sweden.*

undesirable /ˌʌn·dɪˈzaɪ·rə·bəl/ adj not wanted or welcomed; disliked • *undesirable body fat*

undeveloped /ˌʌn·dɪˈvel·əpt/ adj (of a place or land) not built on or used for farming

undisclosed /ˌʌn·dɪˈskloʊzd/ adj [not gradable] not announced; kept private • *The Rembrandt painting was sold at auction for an undisclosed amount.*

undisguised /ˌʌn·dɪsˈɡaɪzd/ adj [not gradable] (of feelings) clearly shown or expressed • *On the way home from the party, she said, with undisguised relief, "Well, I'm glad that's over."*

undisputed /ˌʌn·dɪˈspjuːt̬·əd/ adj about which there is no disagreement • *It's an Oundisputed fact that women on average live longer than men.*

undivided /ˌʌn·dɪˈvaɪd·əd/ adj existing as a whole, not in separate parts • *an undivided Germany* • If you give someone, or if someone has, your undivided attention, you stop whatever else you are doing and listen to them: *Just as soon as I've finished this letter, I'll give you my undivided attention.*

undo [UNFASTEN] /ʌnˈduː/ v [T] **undoing**, past simple **undid** /ʌnˈdɪd/, past part **undone** /ʌnˈdʌn/ to unfasten (something that is closed or tied) • *He undid the top button of his shirt and loosened his tie.*

undone /ʌnˈdʌn/ adj [not gradable] • *Her long hair had come undone* (= become loose).

undo [REMOVE EFFECTS] /ʌnˈduː/ v [T] **undoing**, past simple **undid** /ʌnˈdɪd/, past part **undone** /ʌnˈdʌn/ to remove the effects of (something that happened earlier) • *It's difficult to undo the damage caused by a father who abandons his child.*

undoing /ʌnˈduː·ɪŋ/ n [U] the cause of a person's failure or loss of power or wealth • *His failure to delegate authority and his arrogance led to his undoing.*

undoubtedly /ʌnˈdaʊt̬·əd·li/ adv [not gradable] very likely; almost certainly • *It is undoubtedly one of the best movies of the year.* ○ *The highlight of the evening was undoubtedly* (= without a doubt) *the speech by the guest of honor.*

undreamed of /ʌnˈdriːmˌdʌv/, **undreamt of** /ʌnˈdremˌtɒv/ adj [not gradable] better or greater than anyone would think possible • *Through the Internet, we have access to information that was undreamed of 30 years ago.*

undress /ʌnˈdres/ v [I/T] to remove your clothes or remove the clothes from (someone else) • *She undressed quickly and took a shower.* [I]

undressed /ʌnˈdrest/ adj [not gradable] • *The nurse said to get undressed.*

undue /ʌnˈduː/ adj [not gradable] more than is necessary, acceptable, or reasonable • *The court said the state law placed an undue burden on working mothers.*

unduly /ʌnˈduː·li/ adv [not gradable] • *He does not seem unduly concerned about the state of the economy.*

undying /ʌnˈdaɪ·ɪŋ/ adj [not gradable] literary (of a feeling or a belief) permanent; without end • *undying love*

unearth [DIG EARTH] /ʌnˈɜrθ/ v [T] to find (something) by digging in the ground • *Searchers have unearthed a mass grave in the forest.*

unearth [DISCOVER] /ʌnˈɜrθ/ v [T] to discover (proof or other information), often after careful searching • *Reporters unearthed documents indicating that the government had known about the shipment of arms.*

unearthly /ʌnˈɜrθ·li/ adj strange and mysterious, and sometimes frightening • *The streetlights cast an unearthly glow in the thick fog.* • *(infml)* If something happens at an unearthly hour, it happens at an unusual and unreasonable time: *I was awakened at some unearthly hour by a telephone call from Australia.*

uneasy /ʌnˈiːˑzi/ *adj* uncomfortable or anxious • *Polls indicate that most Americans are increasingly uneasy about violence on TV.*

uneasily /ʌnˈiːˑzəˑli/ *adv* • *He stirred uneasily in his chair as she stared at him.*

uneducated /ʌnˈedʒˑəˌkeɪtˑəd/ *adj* having received little education

unemployed /ˌʌnˑɪmˈplɔɪd/ *adj* [not gradable] not having a job that provides money • *an unemployed actor*

unemployed /ˌʌnˑɪmˈplɔɪd/ *pl n* • *At that time, the unemployed numbered over two million people.*

unemployment /ˌʌnˑɪmˈplɔɪˑmənt/ *n* [U] the situation of not having a job that provides money, or the number of people in this situation at any time • *high/low unemployment* ○ *The unemployment rate was 4 percent in October.* • **Unemployment benefits** are a series of payments made by a government to a person who has lost a job.

unending /ʌnˈenˑdɪŋ/ *adj* [not gradable] without limit or end • *He seemed to have an unending supply of stories.*

unequal [NOT THE SAME] /ʌnˈiːˑkwəl/ *adj* not the same • *The unequal status of parent and child is recognized in law.*

unequal [UNFAIR] /ʌnˈiːˑkwəl/ *adj* not treating everyone the same; unfair • *In 1954, the Supreme Court declared that racial segregation in the public schools was inherently unequal.*

unequivocal /ˌʌnˑɪˈkwɪvˑəˑkəl/ *adj* clear and firm • *The US surgeon general has taken an unequivocal stand against smoking.*

unerring /ʌnˈerˑɪŋ, -ˈɜr-/ *adj* [not gradable] always right; never wrong • *She brings an unerring sense of timing to the role.*

unethical /ʌnˈeθˑɪˑkəl/ *adj* not morally acceptable • *unethical business practices*

uneven [NOT EQUAL] /ʌnˈiːˑvən/ *adj* not EVEN [EQUAL] • *The contest was uneven because one team was much stronger than the other.*

uneven [NOT FLAT] /ʌnˈiːˑvən/ *adj* not EVEN [FLAT] • *an uneven surface*

uneven [NOT GOOD] /ʌnˈiːˑvən/ *adj* varying in quality; not always good • *It's an uneven movie, but some of the scenes are hilariously funny.*

uneventful /ˌʌnˑɪˈventˑfəl/ *adj* without any unusual events • *The flight to Europe was uneventful.*

unexpected /ˌʌnˑɪkˈspekˑtəd/ *adj* not expected; surprising • *What an unexpected treat to meet you here!*

unexpectedly /ˌʌnˑɪkˈspekˑtədˑli/ *adv* • *Her ex-husband would sometimes show up unexpectedly at her front door.*

unfailing /ʌnˈfeɪˑlɪŋ/ *adj* [not gradable] (of a positive quality of someone's character) showing itself at all times • *She was known for her unfailing good humor.*

unfair /ʌnˈfer, -ˈfær/ *adj* not FAIR [RIGHT] • *It seems unfair to tax you both where you work and where you live.*

unfairly /ʌnˈferˑli, -ˈfær-/ *adv* • *The company unfairly denied her medical benefits.*

unfairness /ʌnˈferˑnəs, -ˈfær-/ *n* [U]

unfaithful /ʌnˈfeɪθˑfəl/ *adj* having a sexual relationship with a person who is not your husband, wife, or usual sexual partner

unfamiliar /ˌʌnˑfəˈmɪlˑjər/ *adj* not previously experienced or known • *I'm unfamiliar with that word—what does it mean?*

unfasten /ʌnˈfæsˑən/ *v* [I/T] to loosen or take apart (something that fastens or is fastened) • *Cal loosened his tie and unfastened his collar.* [T]

unfavorable [CRITICIZING] /ʌnˈfeɪˑvəˑrəˑbəl/ *adj* having or showing a negative opinion • *The play received generally unfavorable reviews.*

unfavorable [NOT HELPFUL] /ʌnˈfeɪˑvəˑrəˑbəl/ *adj* not tending to help; not likely to lead to a positive result • *Unfavorable weather conditions this morning caused a postponement of the launch of the space shuttle.*

unfeeling /ʌnˈfiːˑlɪŋ/ *adj* not feeling sympathy for other people's suffering • *an unfeeling man*

unfit /ʌnˈfɪt/ *adj* **-tt-** lacking the qualities needed or expected for something; not suitable • *The court ruled that she was an unfit mother and ordered that the child be placed in a foster home.*

unfold [DEVELOP] /ʌnˈfoʊld/ *v* [I] (of a situation or story) to develop or become clear • *Events unfolded in a way that no one could have predicted.*

unfold [OPEN] /ʌnˈfoʊld/ *v* [T] to open or spread out (something that has been folded) • *She took the old wedding dress out and carefully unfolded it.*

unforeseen /ˌʌnˑfərˈsiːn, -fɔːr-/ *adj* unexpected and often unwanted • *Due to unforeseen circumstances, tonight's performance has been canceled.*

unforgettable /ˌʌnˑfərˈgetˑəˑbəl/ *adj* (of an experience) having such a strong effect or influence on you that you cannot forget it • *One unforgettable morning, we were among the elephants, perfectly situated to watch their descent to the river.*

unfortunate [UNLUCKY] /ʌnˈfɔːrˑtʃəˑnət/ *adj* unlucky or having bad effects • *What happened to Monica was just a freak accident—it was very unfortunate.*

unfortunately /ʌnˈfɔːrˑtʃəˑnətˑli/ *adv* • *Unfortunately, by the time we got there the party was almost over.*

unfortunate [UNSUITABLE] /ʌnˈfɔːrˑtʃəˑnət/ *adj* (of remarks or behavior) unsuitable in a way that could cause offense • *It was an unfortunate remark that he later regretted.*

unfounded /ʌnˈfaʊnˑdəd/ *adj* (of a claim or

piece of news) not based on fact; UNTRUE • *un-founded rumors*

unfriendly /ʌnˈfren·dli/ *adj* having an attitude or acting in a way that shows you do not like people and do not care if they like you • *an unfriendly person*

  unfriendliness /ʌnˈfren·dli·nəs/ *n* [U]

unfurl /ʌnˈfɜrl/ *v* [I/T] (of a flag, sail, etc.) to become open from a rolled position, or to cause (something) to become open from a rolled position

ungainly /ʌnˈɡeɪn·li/ *adj* awkward in movement

ungrateful /ʌnˈɡreɪt·fəl/ *adj* not showing or expressing thanks, esp. when it is expected or deserved

unhappy NOT PLEASED /ʌnˈhæp·i/ *adj* not HAPPY PLEASED • *It was an unhappy time of her life.* ○ *They were unhappy about their hotel room* (= did not like it) *and asked to be moved.*

  unhappiness /ʌnˈhæp·i·nəs/ *n* [U]

unhappy NOT LUCKY /ʌnˈhæp·i/ *adj* (of a condition or situation) not HAPPY LUCKY • *We found ourselves in the unhappy situation of having had our bags, passports, and money stolen.*

unhealthy ILL /ʌnˈhel·θi/ *adj* ill or appearing to be ill

unhealthy HARMFUL /ʌnˈhel·θi/ *adj* harmful to your health • *It's unhealthy to eat fatty foods all the time.*

unheard-of /ʌnˈhɜrd,ʌv, -,ɑv/ *adj* surprising or shocking because not known about or previously experienced • *In the 1950s it was almost unheard-of for an unmarried couple to live together.*

unicorn /ˈjuː·nɪˌkɔːrn/ *n* [C] an imaginary, horselike creature with a single horn growing from the front of its head

unidentified /ˌʌn·aɪˈdent·əˌfaɪd/ *adj* [not gradable] (of a person or image of a person) whose name is not known • *The photo shows the two leaders shaking hands, with an unidentified woman behind them.*

unification /ˌjuː·nə·fəˈkeɪ·ʃən/ *n* [U] the formation of a single thing by bringing together separate parts • *He worked toward the unification of the Protestant churches.*

uniform CLOTHES /ˈjuː·nəˌfɔːrm/ *n* [C/U] a special set of clothes worn by people belonging to an organization to show others that they are members of it • *soldiers in uniform* [U]

  uniformed /ˈjuː·nəˌfɔːrmd/ *adj* [not gradable] • *Only uniformed personnel are permitted to enter this building.*

uniform SAME /ˈjuː·nəˌfɔːrm/ *adj* the same; not varying or different in any way • *The laws for adopting a child are not uniform among the states.*

  uniformly /ˈjuː·nəˌfɔːrm·li/ *adv* • *Critics were uniformly enthusiastic.*

  uniformity /ˌjuː·nəˈfɔːr·məṭ·i/ *n* [U]

unify /ˈjuː·nəˌfaɪ/ *v* [T] to bring (separate parts of something) together so that they are one • *With his speech, the president sought to unify the country.*

unilateral /ˌjuː·nˈəlˈæṭ·ə·rəl/ *adj* [not gradable] done independently by one group or country • *a unilateral action*

unimportant /ˌʌn·ɪmˈpɔːrt·ənt/ *adj* not important • *The money we lost is relatively unimportant, but the emotional stress of being robbed is hard to get over.*

unintelligible /ˌʌn·ɪnˈtel·ə·dʒə·bəl/ *adj* (of speech or writing) not clear enough to be understood

unintentional /ˌʌn·ɪnˈten·tʃən·əl/ *adj* not planned or intended

  unintentionally /ˌʌn·ɪnˈten·tʃən·əl·i/ *adv* [not gradable]

uninterested /ʌnˈɪn·trə·stəd, -ˈɪnt·ə,res·təd/ *adj* not excited or not wanting to become involved • *He's completely uninterested in sports.*

union /ˈjuːn·jən/ *n* [C/U] the act or the state of being joined together • *The union of two people refers to marriage.* [U] • *A union is a* **labor union.** See at LABOR WORK. [C]

unionize /ˈjuːn·jəˌnaɪz/ *v* [T] to organize (workers) into **labor unions** • *We're launching a campaign to unionize workers at all major discount stores in the area.*

unique /juˈniːk/ *adj* being the only existing one of its type or, more generally, unusual or special in some way • *Each person's DNA is unique.*

unisex /ˈjuː·nəˌseks/ *adj* intended for use by both males and females • *a unisex toilet*

unison /ˈjuː·nə·sən/ *n* • When people do something **in unison,** they do it at the same time: *The audience rose to its feet in unison, applauding and cheering.*

unit SEPARATE PART /ˈjuː·nət/ *n* [C] a single item or a separate part of something larger • *The first year of the course is divided into four units.* ○ *This apartment building has 60 units* (= separate apartments). • *A unit is also a small machine or part of a machine that has a particular purpose: the central processing unit of a computer* • *A unit is also a piece of furniture or equipment used as part of a set of similar or matching pieces: a unit of a bookcase*

unit PEOPLE /ˈjuː·nət/ *n* [C] a group of people living or working together, esp. for a particular purpose • *a military unit* ○ *He's the surgeon in charge of the burn unit at the hospital.*

unit MEASUREMENT /ˈjuː·nət/ *n* [C] a standard measure used to express amounts • *An inch is a unit of length.* ○ *The dollar is the standard unit of currency in the US.*

unite /juˈnaɪt/ *v* [I/T] to bring (different groups or things) together to become one, or to join together to become one • *The thirteen American colonies united to form a new nation.* [I]

united /juˈnaɪṭ·əd/ *adj* • (Cdn) The **United**

Church **(of Canada)** is a large Christian church that combined several Christian churches. • The **United Nations** (*abbreviation* **UN**) is an international organization that was established in 1945 to maintain world peace. • The **United States** (*abbreviation* **US**) is the United States of America, a nation consisting of 50 states, all but one (Hawaii) in North America.

unity /ˈjuː·nət̬·i/ *n* [U] the state of being joined together or in agreement

universal /ˌjuː·nəˈvɜr·səl/ *adj* [not gradable] existing everywhere or involving everyone • *Congress rejected the proposal for universal health insurance.*

universe /ˈjuː·nə,vɜrs/ *n* [U] everything that exists, esp. all physical matter, including all the stars and planets in space

university /ˌjuː·nəˈvɜr·sət̬·i/ *n* [C/U] a place of higher education usually for people who have finished twelve years of schooling and where they can obtain more specialized knowledge and skills, and get a degree to recognize this • *a university campus/professor* [U] ○ *She applied to six universities and was accepted by three.* [C] • ⓛⓟ EDUCATION IN THE US

unjust /ʌnˈdʒʌst/ *adj* not morally right; not fair • *Opposition to unjust laws is part of the American tradition.*

unjustified /ʌnˈdʒʌs·tə,faɪd/ *adj* not able to be explained in a reasonable way; not deserved • *Many believed that the war in Vietnam was unjustified.*

unkempt /ʌnˈkemt/ *adj* not neat or cared for; messy • *He needed a shave and his hair was unkempt.*

unkind /ʌnˈkaɪnd/ *adj* not KIND GOOD • *He made an unkind remark about his ex-wife.*

unknowingly /ʌnˈnoʊ·ɪŋ·li/ *adv* without intending or realizing something • *Parents may unknowingly make their child feel inadequate or pressured by expecting too much of them.*

unknown /ʌnˈnoʊn/ *adj* not known, or not known to many people • *His whereabouts are still unknown.*

unknown /ʌnˈnoʊn/ *n* [C] a person who is not known to many people • *A year ago she was a virtual unknown on the figure-skating scene.*

unlawful /ʌnˈlɔː·fəl/ *adj* not according to or acceptable to the law • *In this state, selling alcohol to a person under 18 is unlawful.*

unleaded /ʌnˈled·əd/ *adj* [not gradable] (of GASOLINE (= a fuel)) not containing LEAD (= a metallic element) • *Most cars today use unleaded gas.*

unleash /ʌnˈliːʃ/ *v* [T] to let happen or begin (something powerful) that, once begun, cannot be controlled • *The vice president unleashed a furious attack on leading Democratic representatives in Congress.*

unless /ənˌles, ᵊnˈ-/ *conjunction* used to say what will or will not happen if something else does not happen or is not true; except if • *She*

won't go unless you go (= If you do not go, she will not go either, but if you go, she will go). ○ *You can't get a job unless you've got the experience* (= You can only get a job if you have experience).

unlike DIFFERENT FROM /ʌnˈlaɪk/ *prep* different from • *Unlike you, I'm not a great dancer.*

unlike NOT TYPICAL /ʌnˈlaɪk/ *prep* not typical or characteristic of • *It's unlike Debbie to be so late.*

unlikely /ʌnˈlaɪ·kli/ *adj* not expected to happen; not LIKELY • *It's unlikely (that) we will ever learn what happened.* [+ (*that*) clause]

unlimited /ʌnˈlɪm·ət̬·əd/ *adj* not having a limit or highest possible amount, number, or level • *If you rent the car for the week, you get unlimited mileage* (= the amount you pay is not related to how many miles you drive).

unlisted /ʌnˈlɪs·təd/ *adj* [not gradable] (of a telephone number) not included in a printed list of telephone numbers available to the public

unload /ʌnˈloʊd/ *v* [I/T] to remove the contents of (something), esp. a load of goods from a vehicle, the bullets from a gun, or the film from a camera • *She unloaded her grocery bags from the back of the minivan.* [T] • (*infml*) If you unload (something that you no longer want), you get rid of it: *Monaghan has said he is ready to unload his pizza business and retire to Florida.* [T]

unlock /ʌnˈlɑk/ *v* [T] to open (a lock) using a key, an electronic device, or a series of numbers or letters • *Could you unlock the door for me?*

unlucky /ʌnˈlʌk·i/ *adj* having or bringing bad luck • *It was an unlucky day when the police came to the door.*

unmarked /ʌnˈmɑrkt/ *adj* [not gradable] having no signs or symbols on the outside • *Border agents kept watch in unmarked cars.*

unmarried /ʌnˈmær·iːd, -ˈmer-/ *adj* [not gradable] having no husband or wife • *Their youngest son is still unmarried.*

unmask /ʌnˈmæsk/ *v* [T] to show the previously hidden truth about (someone or something) • *Lopes was unmasked as a fugitive last week.*

unmistakable /ˌʌn·məˈsteɪ·kə·bəl/ *adj* not likely to be confused with something else; clearly recognizable • *There was an unmistakable smell of chocolate.*

unmitigated /ʌnˈmɪt̬·ə, geɪt̬·əd/ *adj* (esp. of something unpleasant or unsuccessful) complete • *Her new business proved to be an unmitigated disaster.*

unmoved /ʌnˈmuːvd/ *adj* not feeling any emotion • *McCain was unmoved by the antiwar demonstrators.*

unnatural /ʌnˈnætʃ·ə·rəl/ *adj* not found in nature; artificial • *Nothing unnatural or polluting can be used.* ○ *The recordings have an unnatural sound.* • Behavior or feelings that are described as unnatural are not usual or acceptable: *The church considers homosexuality unnatural.*

unnecessary /ʌn'nes·ə,ser·i/ *adj* not needed or wanted, or more than is needed or wanted • *unnecessary expenses* ○ *There's a lot of unnecessary violence in that movie.*

unnecessarily /ʌn,nes·ə'ser·ə·li/ *adv* • *I thought his explanation was unnecessarily complex.*

unnerve /ʌn'nɜrv/ *v* [T] to make (someone) feel less confident and slightly frightened • *The long silence unnerved him.*

unnerving /ʌn'nɜr·vɪŋ/ *adj* • *It's the way that he stares that I find so unnerving.*

unnoticed /ʌn'noʊţ·əst/ *adj* [not gradable] not seen, or not attracting any attention • *She saw flaws that normally would have gone unnoticed.*

unobtrusive /,ʌn·əb'truː·sɪv, -zɪv/ *adj* not noticeable; seeming to belong • *A good waiter is efficient and unobtrusive.*

unoccupied /ʌn'ɑk·jə,paɪd/ *adj* [not gradable] without anyone in it, or not busy • *Are there any unoccupied seats in that row?*

unofficial /,ʌn·ə'fɪʃ·əl/ *adj* [not gradable] not connected with or coming from a recognized office or authority • *We think of him as the unofficial town historian.*

unofficially /,ʌn·ə'fɪʃ·ə·li/ *adv* • *Unemployment has been unofficially estimated at 70%.*

unorthodox /ʌn'ɔːr·θə,dɑks/ *adj* (of behavior, ideas, or methods) different from what is usual or expected • *He has an unorthodox teaching style.*

unpack /ʌn'pæk/ *v* [I/T] to remove (things) from (a container) • *I haven't even unpacked my bags yet.* [T]

unpaid /ʌn'peɪd/ *adj* [not gradable] owed, or without receiving payment • *unpaid bills* ○ *an unpaid leave of absence*

unparalleled /ʌn'pær·ə,leld/ *adj* having no equal; better or greater than any other • *We have an unparalleled record of solid growth.*

unpleasant /ʌn'plez·ənt/ *adj* not attractive or enjoyable or easy to like • *an unpleasant surprise* ○ *unpleasant memories* ○ *an unpleasant young man*

unpleasantly /ʌn'plez·ənt·li/ *adv* • *Rob chuckled unpleasantly.*

unplug /ʌn'plʌg/ *v* [T] **-gg-** to remove a plug for an electrical device from a SOCKET • *I unplugged the TV.*

unpopular /ʌn'pɑp·jə·lər/ *adj* not liked or enjoyed by many people • *I'm not surprised the mayor is unpopular.*

unprecedented /ʌn'pres·ə,dent·əd/ *adj* never having happened or existed in the past • *We've entered an age of unprecedented prosperity.*

unpredictable /,ʌn·prɪ'dɪk·tə·bəl/ *adj* tending to change suddenly and seemingly without reason, and therefore not able to be de-

pended on • *unpredictable weather* ○ *The world is pretty unpredictable.*

unprepared /,ʌn·prɪ'perd, -'pærd/ *adj* not ready • *He was completely/totally unprepared for what he saw.*

unprincipled /ʌn'prɪn·sə·pəld/ *adj* having or showing no moral rules or standards of good behavior • *an unprincipled politician*

unproductive /,ʌn·prə'dʌk·tɪv/ *adj* not useful, or not creating anything • *We wasted three days in unproductive discussions.*

unprofessional /,ʌn·prə'feʃ·ən·əl/ *adj* not showing the standard of behavior or skills that are expected of a person in a skilled job • *Dressing like that was very unprofessional of him.*

unprofitable /ʌn'prɑf·əţ·ə·bəl/ *adj* not resulting in profit • *unprofitable investments/ businesses*

unprotected /,ʌn·prə'tek·təd/ *adj* not safe from injury, damage, or loss • *Many of our forests remain unprotected by environmental laws.* • Unprotected sex is sexual activity without using any device to prevent diseases or pregnancy.

unprovoked /,ən·prə'voʊkt/ *adj* (esp. of an unpleasant action or remark) not caused by anything and therefore unfair • *Witnesses said the attack was unprovoked.*

unqualified WITHOUT SKILLS /ʌn'kwɑl·ə,faɪd/ *adj* lacking the skills and experience needed for a particular job • *I liked her, but she was unqualified for the job.*

unqualified TOTAL /ʌn'kwɑl·ə,faɪd/ *adj* [not gradable] not limited in any way • *My first attempt was an unqualified success.*

unquestionable /ʌn'kwes·tʃə·nə·bəl/ *adj* [not gradable] not open to question or doubt; INDISPUTABLE • *Her achievements are unquestionable.*

unquestionably /ʌn'kwes·tʃə·nə·bli/ *adv* [not gradable] • *Sakow is unquestionably the most remarkable woman writing today.*

unquestioned /ʌn'kwes·tʃənd/ *adj* not doubted • *unquestioned loyalty*

unravel SEPARATE /ʌn'ræv·əl/ *v* [I/T] **-l-** or also **-ll-** (of woven cloth) to separate into threads, or to separate the fibers of (a thread, rope, or cloth) • *My sweater is unraveling.* [I] ○ *(fig.) The movie unraveled at the end* (= was not complete and satisfying). [I]

unravel SOLVE /ʌn'ræv·əl/ *v* [T] **-l-** or **-ll-** to solve (a crime) or explain (a mystery) • *He liked to help authorities unravel crimes.*

unreal IMAGINARY /ʌn'riːl/ *adj* as if imagined; strange and dreamlike • *His face was an eerie, unreal color.*

unreal SURPRISING /ʌn'riːl/ *adj* slang surprising, unusual, and hard to believe • *We just ate and ate, and I was so full it was unreal.*

unrealistic /,ʌn,riː·ə'lɪs·tɪk/ *adj* not reasonable, or not likely to be achieved • *We're placing unrealistic demands on our schools.*

unreasonable /ʌn'riː·zə·nə·bəl/ *adj* not based on or using good judgment; not fair • *It's unreasonable to expect him to work every weekend.*

unreasonably /ʌn'riː·zə·nə·bli/ *adv* • *He thinks the cops acted unreasonably.*

unrelated /ˌʌn·rɪ'leɪt̬·əd/ *adj* not having a connection • *His answer was completely unrelated to my question.* • If a person is unrelated to you, they are not part of your family.

unrelenting /ˌʌn·rɪ'lent̬·ɪŋ/ *adj* extremely determined; never weakening or ending • *unrelenting toughness/opposition* ○ *unrelenting neglect/pollution*

unreliable /ˌʌn·rɪ'lɑɪ·ə·bəl/ *adj* not to be trusted or depended on • *Their carpenter was totally unreliable—he never finished the job.*

unrequited /ˌʌn·rɪ'kwɑɪt̬·əd/ *adj* [not gradable] (of love) felt toward someone who does not feel the same way toward you

unresolved /ˌʌn·rɪ'zɑlvd, -'zɔːlvd/ *adj* [not gradable] (esp. of a problem or difficulty) not solved or ended • *The unresolved tension in the area makes another war likely.*

unresponsive /ˌʌn·rɪ'spɑn·sɪv/ *adj* not reacting or answering, or not reacting or answering satisfactorily • *The company has been unresponsive to US pressure.*

unrest /ʌn'rest/ *n* [U] disagreements or fighting between groups of people • *civil/social/labor unrest* ○ *More than 200 people died in the unrest.*

unrestrained /ˌʌn·rɪ'streɪnd/ *adj* [not gradable] not limited in any way • *unrestrained fury* ○ *unrestrained capitalism*

unrivaled /ʌn'rɑɪ·vəld/ *adj* having no equal; better than any others • *unrivaled beauty*

unroll /ʌn'roʊl/ *v* [I/T] to open and become flat from a rolled position, or to cause (something) to do this • *She unrolled a bolt of silk for us to look at.* [T]

unruly /ʌn'ruː·li/ *adj* difficult to control or manage • *Her unruly behavior caused chaos in class.*

unsafe /ʌn'seɪf/ *adj* dangerous, or at risk • *The bridge is closed because it's unsafe.* ○ *Carol feels unsafe in planes.*

unsaid /ʌn'sed/ *adj* [not gradable] not spoken, although thought of or felt • *Some things are better left unsaid.*

unsanitary /ʌn'sæn·ə,ter·i/ *adj* dirty, esp. in a way that is dangerous to health • *unsanitary conditions*

unsatisfactory /ˌʌn,sæt̬·əs'fæk·tə·ri/ *adj* not good, or not good enough • *Jacob's answers were unsatisfactory.*

unsavory /ʌn'seɪ·və·ri/ *adj* unpleasant or morally offensive • *Attorneys have an unsavory reputation.*

unscathed /ʌn'skeɪðd/ *adj* without injuries or damage being caused • *Her husband died in the accident, but she escaped unscathed.*

unscrew /ʌn'skruː/ *v* [T] to remove (the lid or top) from something by twisting it, or to remove (screws) from something • *Unscrew the gas cap.*

unscrupulous /ʌn'skruː·pjə·ləs/ *adj* willing to lie or cheat to succeed, or characterized by lying or cheating • *an unscrupulous salesman*

unseasonable /ʌn'siː·zə·nə·bəl/ *adj* (of weather) not usual for the time of year • *We had an unseasonable warm spell in January.*

unseat /ʌn'siːt/ *v* [T] to remove (someone) from a powerful job, esp. a job to which a person is elected • *She has a good chance to unseat the governor.*

unseemly /ʌn'siːm·li/ *adj* not suitable or polite • *unseemly language* ○ *unseemly haste* ○ *unseemly behavior*

unseen /ʌn'siːn/ *adj, adv* not seen or not able to be seen • *She found the door open and slipped into the house unseen.*

unselfish /ʌn'sel·fɪʃ/ *adj* caring about or generous toward others • *He's an unselfish player who puts team goals first.*

unsettled CHANGEABLE /ʌn'set̬·ᵊld/ *adj* tending to change suddenly; not having a regular pattern • *Things are unsettled in the state's political arena.* ○ *The forecast is for unsettled weather, with more snow to come.*

unsettling /ʌn'set·lɪŋ, -'set̬·ᵊl·ɪŋ/ *adj* • *A rise in unemployment has an unsettling effect on the stock market.*

unsettled ANXIOUS /ʌn'set̬·ᵊld/ *adj* anxious and worried; unable to relax • *She was feeling unsettled the entire morning before her interview.*

unsettling /ʌn'set·lɪŋ, -'set̬·ᵊl·ɪŋ/ *adj* • *I received the unsettling news that I may lose my job next month.*

unsightly /ʌn'sɑɪt·li/ *adj* not pleasing to see; UNATTRACTIVE • *The garden was full of unsightly weeds.*

unskilled /ʌn'skɪld/ *adj* (of people) without any particular work skills, or (of work) not needing any particular skills • *Unskilled workers may lose their jobs.*

unsophisticated /ˌʌn·sə'fɪs·tə,keɪt̬·əd/ *adj* not complicated, not educated, or without a good understanding of culture • *He's an unsophisticated man, but he has been very successful in business.*

unsound NOT ACCEPTABLE /ʌn'sɑʊnd/ *adj* (esp. of activities) not suitable or acceptable • *He was involved in unsound banking practices.*

unsound WEAK /ʌn'sɑʊnd/ *adj* (esp. of a building) in bad condition and likely to fall down or fail • *The bridge is structurally unsound.*

unspeakable /ʌn'spiː·kə·bəl/ *adj* too bad or shocking to be described or expressed • *unspeakable crimes*

unspecified /ʌn'spes·ə,fɑɪd/ *adj* [not gradable] not stated or described in detail • *The company was sold for an unspecified amount.*

unspoken /ʌn'spoʊ·kən/ *adj* [not gradable] not stated, although thought, understood, or felt • *We have an unspoken agreement to share the housework.*

unstable /ʌnˈsteɪ·bəl/ *adj* not firm and therefore not strong, safe, or likely to last • *It is a poor and politically unstable country.* • An unstable person suffers from sudden and extreme changes of mental state: *He's emotionally unstable—you never know how he'll react.*

unsteady /ʌnˈsted·i/ *adj* moving or changing, or not firm • *She's been sick, and she's still a bit unsteady on her feet.*

unstoppable /ʌnˈstɑp·ə·bəl/ *adj* continuous, or unable to be stopped • *The band was enjoying what seemed to be an unstoppable rise in popularity.*

unsuccessful /ˌʌn·sək'ses·fəl/ *adj* not ending in success, or not achieving success • *After writing three unsuccessful plays, Miller finally had a hit.*

unsuccessfully /ˌʌn·sək'ses·fə·li/ *adv* • *Howard's been unsuccessfully looking for an affordable apartment.*

unsuitable /ʌnˈsuːt·ə·bəl/ *adj* not right for a particular person, situation, or occasion • *Parts of this movie may be unsuitable for children.*

unsung /ʌnˈsʌŋ/ *adj* [not gradable] not noticed or praised for hard work, bravery, or achievements • *A teacher is often the unsung hero of a great writer's success.*

unsure /ʌnˈʃʊr/ *adj* in doubt, or not certain • *Officials were unsure who was in control of the city.* [+ *wh-* word] • If you are unsure of yourself, you are not confident: *He has been unsure of himself ever since he failed to get that job.*

unsuspecting /ˌʌn·sə'spek·tɪŋ/ *adj* trusting; not aware of any danger or harm • *The crooks prey on unsuspecting tourists.*

unswerving /ʌnˈswɜr·vɪŋ/ *adj* (esp. of trust or a belief) always strong; never weakening • *unswerving support*

untangle /ʌnˈtæŋ·gəl/ *v* [T] to remove the knots from (a mass of string, wire, hair, etc.) and separate the different threads • *I spent ages trying to untangle Rosie's hair.* ○ (*fig.*) *It took years to untangle the facts of the case* (= make them clear and understandable).

untapped /ʌnˈtæpt/ *adj* [not gradable] (of a supply of something valuable) not yet used or taken advantage of • *The country's forests are largely untapped resources.*

untenable /ʌnˈten·ə·bəl/ *adj* not able to be supported or defended against criticism, or no longer able to continue • *The position of the players' union has become untenable.*

unthinkable /ʌnˈθɪŋ·kə·bəl/ *adj* too shocking or unlikely to be imagined as possible • *Nowadays wines are being produced in areas that would have been unthinkable even ten years ago.* • *The president's car did* **the unthinkable**—*it stopped at a red light.*

untidy /ʌnˈtaɪd·i/ *adj* not neat or well-arranged • *an untidy yard*

untie /ʌnˈtaɪ/ *v* [T] **untying**, *past* **untied** to unfasten (a knot or something tied) • *I had to help her untie her shoelaces.*

until TIME /ən,tɪl, ʌn-, ᵊn-/, **till** *prep, conjunction* up to the stated time • *I was up until 3 a.m.* • **Not until** means not before a particular time or event: *Don't move until I tell you.*

until DISTANCE /ən,tɪl, ʌn-, ᵊn-/, **till** *prep, conjunction* as far as • *Stay on the bus until 57th Street and then walk one block west.*

untimely /ʌnˈtaɪm·li/ *adj* (of something bad) happening unexpectedly early or at a time which is not suitable • *A love of fast cars led to his untimely death at the age of 34.*

untiring /ʌnˈtaɪ·rɪŋ/ *adj* (esp. of qualities such as energy, interest, and enthusiasm) never weakening • *Without Tony's untiring enthusiasm, this campaign would not have succeeded.*

untold /ʌnˈtoʊld/ *adj* [not gradable] so great in amount or level that it can not be measured or expressed in words • *The software saves the company untold thousands in paper and labor.*

untouchable /ʌnˈtʌtʃ·ə·bəl/ *adj* [not gradable] not able to be punished, criticized, or changed in any way • *His home run record remained untouchable.*

untouched /ʌnˈtʌtʃt/ *adj* [not gradable] not changed or spoiled in any way • *These prewar apartment buildings have been virtually untouched since they were built.* • If food is untouched, it has not been eaten: *She left her dinner untouched.*

untoward /ʌnˈtwɔrd, -ˈtwoʊrd, -tə'wɔrd/ *adj* [not gradable] unexpected, inconvenient, or unsuitable • *I was nervous about what he might do, but nothing untoward happened.*

untrue /ʌnˈtruː/ *adj* [not gradable] not true; false • *Her remarks were irresponsible and untrue.*

unused /ʌnˈjuːzd/ *adj* [not gradable] not being used at present, or never having been used • *The stationary exercise bike sits unused in the basement.*

unused to /ʌnˈjuːs·tə, -,tuː/ *adj* [not gradable] not familiar with (a particular habit or experience) • *If you're unused to exercise you'll find your joints ache the next day.*

unusual /ʌnˈjuː·ʒə·wəl/ *adj* different from what is usual or expected • *I was actually on time, which is unusual for me.*

unusually /ʌnˈjuː·ʒə·wə·li/ *adv* [not gradable] in a way or to a degree that is different from what is usual or expected • *We had unusually warm weather in December.* ○ *There is no evidence of unusually high rates of disease.*

unveil /ʌnˈveɪl/ *v* [T] to make (something secret) known • *The president's new drug policy was unveiled at the press conference.*

unwanted /ʌnˈwɔːnt·əd, -'wɑnt-, -'wʌnt-/ *adj* [not gradable] not desired or needed • *He was charged with making unwanted sexual advances toward two female employees.*

unwarranted /ʌn'wɑr·ənt·əd, -'wɔːr-/ *adj* [not gradable] lacking a good reason; unnecessary • *They denounced the investigation as an unwarranted interference with their business.*

unwelcome /ʌn'wel·kəm/ *adj* not wanted or desirable • *Dogs stand watch for unwelcome visitors to the estate.*

unwieldy DIFFICULT TO MOVE /ʌn'wiːl·di/ *adj* [not gradable] (of an object) difficult to move or handle because it is heavy, large, or strangely shaped

unwieldy NOT EFFECTIVE /ʌn'wiːl·di/ *adj* [not gradable] (of a system) difficult to manage, usually because it is too big or badly organized • *an unwieldy bureaucracy*

unwilling /ʌn'wɪl·ɪŋ/ *adj* not wanting to do something • *The bank was unwilling to lend her money.* [+ *to* infinitive]

unwillingly /ʌn'wɪl·ɪŋ·li/ *adv* [not gradable]
unwillingness /ʌn'wɪl·ɪŋ·nəs/ *n* [U]

unwind UNFASTEN /ʌn'wɑɪnd/ *v* [T] *past* **unwound** /ʌn'wɑʊnd/ to unfasten (something) that is wrapped around an object • *to unwind string*

unwind RELAX /ʌn'wɑɪnd/, **wind down** *v* [I] *past* **unwound** /ʌn'wɑʊnd/ to relax after a period of work or anxiety • *I'm just going to watch some TV and unwind.*

unwise /ʌn'wɑɪz/ *adj* not showing good judgment or understanding of a situation • *We made several unwise investments and lost quite a bit of money.*

unwisely /ʌn'wɑɪz·li/ *adv* [not gradable]

unwitting /ʌn'wɪt̬·ɪŋ/ *adj* [not gradable] without knowing or planning • *The harmful radiation tests were performed long ago on unwitting subjects.*

unwittingly /ʌn'wɪt̬·ɪŋ·li/ *adv* [not gradable]

unworkable /ʌn'wɜr·kə·bəl/ *adj* (of a plan or a system) not practical or able to operate effectively • *The budget was considered unworkable and had to be revised.*

unwritten /ʌn'rɪt·ᵊn/ *adj* [not gradable] not written • An unwritten law/rule is one that does not exist officially, but which people generally accept and obey: *There's an unwritten rule at work that you don't wear jeans.*

unyielding /ʌn'yiːl·dɪŋ/ *adj* [not gradable] not giving up control or responsibility for (something) as a result of influence or persuasion • *The economist showed an unyielding commitment to tough financial stability.*

unzip /ʌn'zɪp/ *v* [T] **-pp-** to open the ZIPPER (= a fastener consisting of two rows of metal or plastic teeth) on something

up HIGHER /ʌp/ *adv* [not gradable] toward a higher position, or toward a higher value, number, or level • *Pick up your clothes and put them away.* ○ *We need to push sales figures up higher next quarter.* ○ *The kids were jumping up and down on the bed.* • A person or thing that is **up-and-coming** is likely to achieve success in the near future: *Tatiana is an up-and-*

coming young actress. • **Up in arms** means angry or upset: *The union is up in arms over the reduction in health benefits.* • **Up till**, **up to**, and **up until** mean until: *Up to yesterday, we had no idea where the child was.* • If someone or something, such as a decision, is **up in the air**, it is uncertain: *The whole future of the project is still up in the air.* • **Uphill** means leading to a higher place on a slope, or (*fig.*) needing a large amount of effort: (*fig.*) *It will be an uphill battle for her, but she's come a long way.* • **Upstairs** means toward or on the highest floor or floors of a building.

up /ʌp/ *prep* • *We followed the others up the stairs.*

up /ʌp/ *adj* [not gradable] • *Take the up escalator to the housewares department.* ○ *Gas prices are up* (= have increased).

up /ʌp/ *n infml* Someone who is **on the up and up** is honest and can be trusted.

up /ʌp/ *v* [T] **-pp-** *infml* to increase the amount or level of something • *We won't be able to make a profit unless we up our prices.*

up VERTICAL /ʌp/ *adv* [not gradable] in or into a vertical position • *She jumped up to answer the phone.* ○ *They put up* (= built) *the house in a matter of weeks.*

up TOP /ʌp/ *adv* [not gradable] in a high position; at the top • *They moved to a house up in the hills.*

up /ʌp/ *prep* at the top of • *His house is up the hill.*

up ALONG /ʌp/ *prep* (farther) along • *There's a coffee shop just up the street.* • (*infml*) *If any more people quit, we'll really be* **up the creek** (= in trouble). • *The dog was running* **up and down** *the path* (= in one direction and then in the opposite direction, esp. repeatedly).

up INCREASINGLY /ʌp/ *adv* [not gradable] to a greater degree; in order to increase • *The afternoon sun really heats up this room* (= increases the heat in this room). ○ *Please speak up* (= louder)—*I can't hear you.*

up OUT OF BED /ʌp/ *adj, adv* [not gradable] out of bed • *What time did you get up?* • (*infml*) If someone is **up and about/around**, they are feeling well enough after a period of illness to get out of bed and move around.

up INTO EXISTENCE /ʌp/ *adv* [not gradable] into existence, view, or consideration • *I didn't hesitate to bring up the salary issue.* ○ *Something came up at the office and I had to work late.* • **Up for grabs** means available: *The job was still up for grabs.*

up /ʌp/ *adj* [not gradable] • *What's up* (= What is happening or what is wrong)?

up EQUAL /ʌp/ *adv* [not gradable] so as to be equal in quality or achievement • *It's impossible to keep up with all the new computer developments.* • If you are **up to par**, you are feeling or performing as good as usual, and nothing is wrong: *Jenny had not been up to par physically and did not come close to winning a* *medal.* • Something that is **up to scratch** is as good as the usual standard: *The last few episodes of the TV program haven't been quite up to scratch.*

up NEAR /ʌp/ *adv* [not gradable] very near • *He walked right up to me and introduced himself.* ○ *The cop pushed me up against the wall.*

up TOGETHER /ʌp/ *adv* [not gradable] in a state of being together with other similar things • *Gather up your things—it's time to go.* ○ *She added up the numbers in her head.*

up TIGHTLY /ʌp/ *adv* [not gradable] tightly or firmly in order to keep something safe or in position • *Tie the boat up at the dock.* ○ *You'd better bundle up* (= wear warm clothes)—*it's cold outside.*

up IN OPERATION /ʌp/ *adj* [not gradable] (of a system or machine, esp. a computer) operating, esp. in its usual way • *The new inventory system should be up and running by the end of the month.*

up SMALLER /ʌp/ *adv* [not gradable] made smaller in area or amount, esp. by cutting or dividing • *Cut the cheese up into bite-size pieces.* ○ *They broke the company up into three separate units.* ○ *He folded up the newspaper and put it in his briefcase.*

up AGE /ʌp/ *adv* [not gradable] to a greater age • *She wants to be a singer when she grows up.*

up INTENDED /ʌp/ *adj* [not gradable] intended, suggested, or being considered • *The house at the end of our street is up for sale.* ○ *Ray's up for promotion.*

up /ʌp/ *adv* [not gradable] • *They put the building up for sale* (= offered it for sale).

up INTO IMPROVED POSITION /ʌp/ *adv* [not gradable] into an improved position or state • *By the third lap, Simms had moved up into second position.* • If something or someone is **up to speed**, they are performing at a desirable level: *It took me awhile to get up to speed after the flu.*

up /ʌp/ *n* • If someone or something experiences **ups and downs**, good and bad things happen to them.

up ENDED /ʌp/ *adj, adv* [not gradable] finished, or to an end, finish, or state of completion • *Finish up your breakfast—it's almost time for school.* ○ *My time is almost up on the parking meter.*

up TOWARD NORTH /ʌp/ *adv* [not gradable] toward the north • *She comes up from Washington about once a month.*

up ACT SUDDENLY /ʌp/ *v* **-pp-** *infml* • If you **up and** do something, you do something that is unexpected or different: *After 20 years of marriage, she up and left him.*

upbeat /ʌpˈbiːt/ *adj* full of hope, happiness, and good feelings • *The mood is upbeat at Shaw's campaign headquarters tonight.*

upbringing /ˈʌpˌbrɪŋ·ɪŋ/ *n* [C usually sing] the way in which someone is treated and

trained when they are young • *a Catholic upbringing*

upcoming /ˈʌpˈkʌm·ɪŋ/ *adj* [not gradable] happening soon • *Party officials met to nominate candidates for the upcoming election.*

update /ʌpˈdeɪt/ *v* [T] to make (something) more accurate and suitable for use now by showing new facts or conditions • *The school's budget is updated annually.* ○ *When you move, don't forget to update your mailing address.* • To update is also to make (something) more modern: *The old procedures need to be updated and streamlined.*

update /ˈʌp·deɪt/ *n* [C] new or more accurate information based on new facts or conditions • *You can get hourly news updates on the Internet.*

upfront CLEAR /ʌpˈfrʌnt/ *adj* [not gradable] speaking or behaving in a way that makes your intentions and beliefs clear • *She's very upfront about her faith.*

upfront IN ADVANCE /ʌpˈfrʌnt/ *adj, adv* [not gradable] paid or obtained in advance • *The roofer wants 20% of the money upfront.*

upgrade /ʌpˈɡreɪd/ *v* [T] to improve the quality or usefulness of (something), or to raise (something or someone) to a higher position or rank • *If you want to raise rents, you have to upgrade the housing first.* ○ *They're spending more than $4 million next year to upgrade computer systems.* ○ *In 1992 the college was upgraded to a university.* ○ *We were upgraded from tourist to business class on our flight to London.*

upheaval /ʌpˈhiː·vəl/ *n* [C/U] (a) great change, causing or involving difficulty or trouble • *The long garbage strike in 1970 caused much political upheaval.* [U]

uphold /ʌpˈhoʊld/ *v* [T] *past* **upheld** /ʌpˈheld/ to defend or maintain (a principle or law), or to state that (a decision that has already been made, esp. a legal one) is correct • *The Supreme Court upheld California's term limit measure.*

upholster /əˈpoʊl·stər/ *v* [T] to fill (a seat, chair, or SOFA) with a suitable material and cover it with cloth

upholstery /əˈpoʊl·stə·ri/ *n* [U] the cloth and other materials used in upholstering furniture, or the process of using them

upkeep /ˈʌp·kiːp/ *n* [U] the process or cost of keeping something, such as a building, in good and usable condition • *It costs the landlord about $2000 a month just for upkeep.*

uplifting /ʌpˈlɪf·tɪŋ/ *adj* [not gradable] positive in a way that encourages the improvement of a person's mood or spirit • *The sermon was about the uplifting effect of prayer.*

upon /əˈpɑn, əˈpɔːn/ *prep* on • *That depends upon the circumstances.* ○ *She insisted upon knowing the truth.* • Upon can be used to show that something happens soon after, and often because of, something else: *Upon hearing the good news, we all congratulated Murphy.*

upper /'ʌp·ər/ *adj* [not gradable] at a higher position or level (than something else), or being the top part of something • *Our company occupied the three upper floors of the building.* • The **upper class** is the group of people who have the highest position and the most influence socially and economically in a society. • Something that is **uppermost** is in the highest position or is most important: *Her health is uppermost in my mind* (= the most important thing to consider).

upper /'ʌp·ər/ *n* [C] the top part of a shoe

uppercase /ˌʌp·ər'keɪs/ *n* [U] the large form of letters when they are printed or written; capital letters • Compare LOWERCASE.

uppercase /ˌʌp·ər'keɪs/ *adj* [not gradable]

uppity /'ʌp·ət·i/ *adj disapproving* acting in a way that is too confident for someone in your social class or for your young age • *I was just an uppity kid.*

upright STRAIGHT /'ʌp·rɑɪt/ *adj, adv* [not gradable] (standing or being) vertical and as straight as possible • *He stood upright.*

upright MORAL /'ʌp·rɑɪt/ *adj* honest, responsible, and moral • *an upright young man*

uprising /'ʌp·rɑɪ·zɪŋ/ *n* [C] an act of opposition by many people, sometimes using violence, against those who are in power

uproar /'ʌp·rɔːr, -ˌrour/ *n* [C/U] loud complaints esp. by angry people, or a noisy state of confusion • *There was an uproar over the proposed rent increases.* [C]

uproot PULL /ʌp'ruːt/ *v* [T] to pull (a plant including its roots) out of the ground

uproot REMOVE /ʌp'ruːt/ *v* [T] to remove (a person) from their home or usual surroundings • *More than a million people were uprooted by the war in Angola.*

upscale /'ʌp·skeɪl/ *adj* characteristic of or suitable for the wealthy • *an upscale residential neighborhood* ○ *an upscale restaurant*

upset WORRY /ʌp'set/ *v* [T] **upsetting**, *past* **upset** to make (someone) worried, unhappy, or angry • *The governor's veto upset a lot of people.*

upset /ʌp'set/ *adj* • *Mom gets really upset if we don't call and tell her where we are.* ○ *She was very upset about losing her wallet.*

upsetting /ʌp'set·ɪŋ/ *adj* • *an upsetting remark*

upset CHANGE /ʌp'set/ *v* [T] **upsetting**, *past* **upset** to change the usual or expected state or order of (something) in a way that stops it from happening or working • *The airline strike could upset our vacation plans.*

upset /'ʌp·set/ *n* [C] (in sports) a surprising victory by a person or team that was expected to lose

upset FEEL SICK /ʌp'set/ *v* [T] **upsetting**, *past* **upset** • If something **upsets** your **stomach**, it makes you feel sick.

upshot /'ʌp·ʃɑt/ *n* [C usually sing] something that happens as a result of other actions, events, or decisions • *The upshot of the discussions was that no one will be laid off.*

upside /'ʌp·sɑɪd/ *n* [U] the positive part of a situation • *It's too bad we can't go until Thursday, but the upside is that we get to stay through the weekend.* • Compare DOWNSIDE.

upside down /ˌʌp·sɑɪd'dɑʊn/ *adj, adv* [not gradable] having the part that is usually at the top turned to be at the bottom • *He put the pots upside down on a dish towel to let them dry.*

upstage /ʌp'steɪdʒ/ *v* [T] to take people's attention away from (someone) and make them listen to or look at you instead • *The mayor doesn't like to be upstaged by his subordinates—he likes to make all the public announcements.*

upstanding /ʌp'stæn·dɪŋ/ *adj approving* behaving in a moral way • *She is an upstanding member of the community.*

upstart /'ʌp·stɑrt/ *adj* [not gradable] new and not experienced • *Upstart airlines like Southwest are competing today with the established carriers like Delta.*

upstream /ʌp'striːm/ *adj, adv* [not gradable] against the current toward the starting point of a river • *Rowing upstream was hard going.* • Compare DOWNSTREAM.

upsurge /'ʌp·sɜrdʒ/ *n* [C] a sudden or large increase • *Department stores report a recent upsurge in credit-card fraud.*

upswing /'ʌp·swɪŋ/ *n* [C] an increase or improvement • *Many analysts are predicting an upswing in the economy.*

uptight /'ʌp'tɑɪt/ *adj infml* nervous, anxious, or worried • *I was really uptight about the interview, but it went fine.*

up to ALMOST EQUAL /'ʌp·tə/ *adv* less than or equal to, but not more than, a stated value, number, level, or time • *Research suggests that up to half of those who were prescribed the drug suffered side effects.* ○ *You have up to ten minutes.* • If something is **up to snuff**, it is good enough: *Her work isn't up to snuff.* • **Up-to-date** means having the most recent information: *We go to a lot of trouble to keep our database up-to-date.* • **Up-to-the-minute** means containing the very latest information: *up-to-the-minute news reports*

up to RESPONSIBILITY /ˌʌp·tə/ *prep* being the responsibility of (someone) • *The decision is up to you.* ○ *If it were up to me, I'd do it.*

up to DOING /ˌʌp·tə/ *prep* doing (something that might be bad or illegal), often secretly • *When it's so quiet, I think the kids are up to something.*

uptown /ʌp'tɑʊn/ *adj, adv* [not gradable] in or toward the northern part of a city or town • *We could walk uptown or we could take the train.*

upward /'ʌp·wərd/, **upwards** /'ʌp·wərdz/ *adv* [not gradable] from a lower to a higher position, level, or value • *Tachi glanced upward to the stars.* ○ *The stock market charged upward yesterday.*

upward /ˈʌp·wərd/ *adj* [not gradable] • *It was an upward climb to the campsite.*

upwind /ʌpˈwɪnd/ *adj, adv* in the direction from which the wind is blowing • *Stay upwind of the fumes if you can.* • USAGE: The opposite of upwind is DOWNWIND.

uranium /jʊˈreɪ·niː·əm/ *n* [U] a heavy metallic element that is RADIOACTIVE, used in the production of nuclear power and nuclear weapons

Uranus /ˈjʊr·ə·nəs, jʊˈreɪ·nəs/ *n* [U] the planet seventh in order of distance from the sun, after Saturn and before Neptune

urban /ˈɜr·bən/ *adj* of or in a city or town • *Many Americans were leaving the farm for the promise of urban life.* ○ *Over 82% of Texans live in urban areas.* • **Urban renewal** is the replacement of buildings in a city, esp. of whole neighborhoods of housing. • **Urban sprawl** is the spread of a city into the area surrounding it, often without planning: *Huge tourist attractions have produced choking urban sprawl.* • Compare RURAL.

urbane /ɜrˈbeɪn/ *adj* knowledgeable about the world and showing experience and confidence • *urbane conversation/pleasures* ○ *His urbane manners impressed me.*

urchin /ˈɜr·tʃən/ *n* [C] *dated* a small child who is badly dressed and dirty • *Little urchins begged for money.*

urethra /jʊˈriː·θrə/ *n* [C] *medical* a tube in mammals that carries urine out of the body, and also carries sperm in males

urge ADVISE /ɜrdʒ/ *v* [T] to strongly advise (someone) to do something or to ask that (something) be done • *Party leaders urged her to run for Congress.* • To **urge** someone **on** is to encourage them: *His parents urge him on to greater and greater accomplishments.*

urge DESIRE /ɜrdʒ/ *n* [C] a strong desire or need • *The sexual urge is common to all species.* ○ *Sometimes I get an urge to go swimming at lunchtime.*

urgent /ˈɜr·dʒənt/ *adj* needing immediate attention • *The plumbing in this building is in urgent need of repair.*

urgency /ˈɜr·dʒən·si/ *n* [U] • *There was a sense of urgency in her voice.*

urgently /ˈɜr·dʒənt·li/ *adv* • *Flood victims urgently need medical care.*

urine /ˈjʊr·ən/ *n* [U] liquid waste excreted by people and animals

urinate /ˈjʊr·əˌneɪt/ *v* [I] to excrete urine

urinal /ˈjʊr·ən·ºl/ *n* [C] a device to urinate in, used by men and boys and usually attached to a wall

urn /ɜrn/ *n* [C] a large, round container from which coffee or tea is served, or a decorative container, esp. one that holds the ASHES of a body after it has been CREMATED (= burned)

US COUNTRY /juˈes/ *n* [U] *abbreviation for* the United States • *a US citizen*

us ME AND OTHERS /ʌs, əs/ *pronoun* [pl] the person speaking with other people included; the form of "we" that follows the verb • *Thanks for giving us a lift to the airport.*

USA /ˌju·ˌesˈeɪ/ *n* [U] *abbreviation for* the United States of America

usage USE OF WORDS /ˈjuː·sɪdʒ, -zɪdʒ/ *n* [C/U] the way in which words are used by the people who speak and write a particular language, or an example of such use • *We use African-American, which is the current preferred usage.* [C]

usage USE OF THINGS /ˈjuː·sɪdʒ, -zɪdʒ/ *n* [U] the use of something, the way in which it is used, or how much it has been used • *The study tracks credit card usage over the last ten years.*

use PUT INTO SERVICE /juːz/ *v* [T] to put (something) into your service for a purpose • *Do you know how to use a rifle?* ○ *We could use your help.* ○ *She uses so many big words, it's hard to understand her.*

use /juːs/ *n* [C/U] • *There are so many uses for computers in the classroom.* [C] ○ *Players are regularly tested for drug use.* [U] ○ *Do you have any use for these old magazines?* [U] ○ *After her stroke, she lost the use of her left arm.* [U] • If someone or something is of no use, it cannot be of help: *There's no use paying for a permit if you won't need it.* [U] ○ *He was of no use to us because he couldn't work every day.* [U] • If something is **in use**, it is being used: *Is the washing machine in use right now?*

usable /ˈjuː·zə·bəl/ *adj* • *The house needs a lot of work to make it usable.*

useful /ˈjuːs·fəl/ *adj* helping you to do or obtain something • *Your advice was very useful, saving me a lot of time.*

usefully /ˈjuːs·fə·li/ *adv* • *I was usefully occupied packing dishes all morning.*

usefulness /ˈjuːs·fəl·nəs/ *n* [U] • *There is no question of the usefulness of aspirin.*

useless /ˈjuː·sləs/ *adj* of no value; worthless • *With dead batteries, the flashlight was useless.*

user /ˈjuː·zər/ *n* [C] • *a drug/library/computer user* ○ *The number of cell phone users has grown tremendously.* • If something is **user-friendly** it is easy to make it work: *This software is very user-friendly.*

use MAKE IT LESS /juːz/ *v* [T] to reduce (the amount of something) • *We have used all the funds in that account.* ○ *Have we used up all of the paper towels?* [M]

use ACT SELFISH /juːz/ *v* [T] to be friendly toward (someone) for your own advantage or purposes • *She used him to help her get into movies and then discarded him.*

used NOT NEW /juːzd/ *adj* [not gradable] already owned or put to a purpose by someone else; not new • *We're looking for a used car in good condition.*

used FAMILIAR /juːzd/ *adj* [not gradable] • If

you are **used to** something or someone, you are familiar with them: *We were used to a cold climate, so the weather didn't bother us.* ○ *She's used to working hard.*

used to /'juːs·tə, -tʊ, -,tuː/ *phrasal auxiliary* done or experienced in the past, but no longer done or experienced • *I used to eat meat, but now I'm a vegetarian.* ○ *We don't go to the movies now as often as we used to.*

usher /'ʌʃ·ər/ *v* [T always + adv/prep] to show (someone) where to go or to sit, esp. for some formal or official event • *The guard ushered the jury members into the courtroom.* [T] • To **usher** someone or something **in** is to welcome them or be at the beginning of something: *The party was an elegant way to usher in the new year.*
usher /'ʌʃ·ər/ *n* [C] • *The ushers handed out the church bulletin.*

usual /'juː·ʒə·wəl/ *adj* [not gradable] happening or done most of the time; ordinary • *I'll put the keys in the usual place.* ○ *If you can believe it, the food was worse than usual.*
usually /'juː·ʒə·wə·li/ *adv* [not gradable] • *He usually gets home from work at about six.*

usurp /jʊ'sɜrp, -'zɜrp/ *v* [T] *fml* to take (power or control of something) by force or without the right to do so • *Some senators fear the organization will usurp congressional power.*

utensil /jʊ'ten·səl/ *n* [C] a device or tool having a particular use, esp. in a kitchen • *We packed plates, cups, napkins, and eating utensils for the picnic.*

uterine /'juːt·ə·rən, -,rɑɪn/ *adj* [not gradable] medical of or relating to the uterus • *uterine cancer*

uterus /'juːt·ə·rəs/ *n* [C] the organ in the body of a woman or other female mammal in which a baby develops before birth; WOMB

utility PUBLIC SERVICE /juː'tɪl·ət̬·i/ *n* [C] a supply of gas, electricity, water, or telephone service to homes and businesses, or a business that supplies such services • *a utility bill* ○ *After I call the movers, I'll call to have the utilities turned on.* • A **utility pole** is a tall pole to which telephone or electrical wires are attached.

utility USEFULNESS /juː'tɪl·ət̬·i/ *n* [U] *slightly fml* ability to satisfy a particular need; usefulness • *Its basic utility lies in being able to drive where other vehicles can't go.*

utilize /'juːt̬·əl,ɑɪz/ *v* [T] to make use of (something) • *The library's great collection allowed me to utilize many rare sources.*

utmost /'ʌt·moʊst/ *adj* [not gradable] greatest or most or farthest • *Speed was of the utmost importance.*
utmost /'ʌt·moʊst/ *n* [U] the most or best that is possible • *He's doing his utmost to disrupt the proceedings.*

utopia /jʊ'toʊ·piː·ə/ *n* [C/U] a perfect society in which everyone is happy • *She was not expecting to find utopia in Cuba.* [U] ○ *The monastery provided a utopia of sorts.* [C]
utopian /jʊ'toʊ·piː·ən/ *adj* • *a utopian vision* ○ *utopian communities*

utter COMPLETE /'ʌt̬·ər/ *adj* [not gradable] complete or extreme • *What an utter fool I was!*
utterly /'ʌt̬·ər·li/ *adv* • *She felt isolated and utterly alone.* • LP VERY, COMPLETELY, AND OTHER INTENSIFIERS

utter SAY /'ʌt̬·ər/ *v* [T] to say (something) or make (a sound) with your voice • *She sat through the entire meeting and didn't utter a word.*

utterance /'ʌt̬·ə·rəns/ *n* [C] *fml* • *We hope their utterances will be matched by their actions.*

V, v

V ~~LETTER~~ , **v** /viː/ *n* [C] *pl* **V's** or **Vs** or **v's** or **vs** the 22nd letter of the English alphabet • A **V-neck** (also **V-necked**) piece of clothing is one with a neck opening in the shape of a V at the front: *She wore a blue, V-neck sweater.*

V ~~NUMBER~~ , **v** /viː, faɪv/ *number* the ROMAN NUMERAL for the number 5

vacant ~~EMPTY~~ /'veɪ·kənt/ *adj* [not gradable] (of a place) not being lived in or used, or (of a job or office) available for someone to do • *We have three vacant apartments in our building.*

vacancy /'veɪ·kən·si/ *n* [C] a place or position that is available • *The motel was full—we saw the "No Vacancy" sign.* ○ *These companies have a lot of vacancies* (= jobs) *to fill, and they pay well.*

vacant ~~NOT AWARE~~ /'veɪ·kənt/ *adj* not showing much awareness or interest in the world around you • *There was a sad, vacant look in his eyes.*

vacate /'veɪ·keɪt, veɪ'keɪt/ *v* [T] to leave (a place or position) empty, esp. in order to make available for other people • *When he left the university, he had to vacate his university-provided housing.*

vacation /veɪ'keɪ·ʃən, və-/ *n* [C/U] a period of time to relax or travel for pleasure instead of doing your usual work or school activities • *The family had just left for a vacation in the Bahamas.* [C] ○ *We always went on vacation in August.* [U]

vacation /veɪ'keɪ·ʃən, və-/ *v* [I always + adv/prep] • *He was vacationing in San Francisco.*

vacationer /veɪ'keɪ·ʃə·nər, və-/ *n* [C] • *Tourists and winter vacationers are now key to the economy.*

vaccine /'væk·siːn, væk'siːn/ *n* [C] a special substance that a person takes into their body to prevent them from getting a disease, and that contains a weakened or dead form of the disease-causing organism

vaccinate /ˌvæk·sə,neɪt/ *v* [T] • *Our children have been vaccinated for measles and other childhood diseases.*

vaccination /ˌvæk·sə'neɪ·ʃən/ *n* [C] • *Most states require all children to receive the vaccination before beginning elementary school.*

vacillate /'væs·ə,leɪt/ *v* [I] to be unable to decide something and esp. to continue to change opinions • *The president continues to vacillate over foreign policy.*

vacuous /'væk·jə·wəs/ *adj* not showing purpose, meaning, or intelligence; empty • *The religious leader denounced America's vacuous, consumer-oriented culture and called for a return to religious values.*

vacuum /'væk·juːm, -juˑəm/ *n* [C] a space without any gas or other matter in it, or a space from which most of the air or gas has

been removed • *Edison knew that he had to create a vacuum inside the lightbulb.* ○ *(fig.) No marriage exists in a vacuum* (= in a situation where nothing else has any influence). • A **vacuum bottle** is a specially made container for keeping hot liquids hot or cold liquids cold. • A **vacuum (cleaner)** is a piece of electrical equipment that sucks dirt from floors and other surfaces.

vacuum /'væk·juːm, -juˑəm/ *v* [I/T] to clean (something) by using a **vacuum cleaner** • *Then I vacuumed the carpet.* [T]

vagina /və'dʒaɪ·nə/ *n* [C] a tubelike organ of female mammals that connects the womb to an opening between the legs and is used for sex

vaginal /'vædʒ·ən·əl/ *adj* [not gradable] • *This is used to treat chronic vaginal infections.*

vagrant /'veɪ·grənt/ *n* [C] a person who has no home or job and who moves from place to place

vague /veɪg/ *adj* [-er/-est only] not clearly stated, described, or explained, or not clearly seen or felt • *She had a vague feeling that something had gone terribly wrong.* ○ *I have only a vague memory of the house where I lived as a child.* • If a person is vague, they are not able or do not wish to state, describe, or explain something clearly: *Officials were vague about the ship's location.*

vaguely /'veɪ·gli/ *adv* • *She stood in silence for several minutes, only vaguely aware of the people around her.*

vain ~~UNSUCCESSFUL~~ /veɪn/ *adj* [-er/-est only] unsuccessful or useless; failing to achieve a purpose • *a vain attempt to avoid responsibility* ○ *Employers clearly hoped that the workers would stay longer, but their efforts were largely in vain* (= unsuccessful).

vain ~~SELFISH~~ /veɪn/ *adj* [-er/-est only] too proud of yourself, esp. in your appearance or achievements • USAGE: The related noun is VANITY.

valedictorian /ˌvæl·ə,dɪk'tɔːr·iˑən, -'tour-/ *n* [C] a student, usually the one who has the best school record in a group of students, and who makes a speech at the group's GRADUATION ceremony (= ceremony to recognize the successful completion of their studies)

valentine /'væl·ən,taɪn/ *n* [C] someone you love or admire affectionately • A **valentine (card)** is a decorative card given on **Valentine's Day** (February 14th) to someone you admire or love: *Schoolteachers get lots of valentine cards from their first-graders on Valentine's Day.*

valet /væ'leɪ, 'væl·eɪ/ *n* [C] (esp. in the past) the personal male servant of a wealthy man, or (in the present) an employee of a restaurant or hotel, who puts your car in a parking space for you • *Valet parking is available for our customers.*

valiant /ˈvæl·jənt/ *adj* brave or determined, esp. when conditions are difficult or dangerous • *The team made a valiant effort to take the lead in the third quarter, but they were too far behind.*

valid /ˈvæl·əd/ *adj* based on truth or reason; able to be accepted • *The money was gone, and the only valid conclusion was that someone had stolen it.* • A valid document is legally acceptable, usually because it has been done according to official rules: *You must have a valid driver's license to drive a car.*

validate /ˈvæl·əˌdeɪt/ *v* [T] to make (something) officially acceptable or approved • *Janie drove to Richmond to have her winning lottery ticket validated.*

validity /vəˈlɪd·ət·i/ *n* [U] • *Some experts questioned the validity of the president's ideas.*

valley /ˈvæl·i/ *n* [C] an area of low land between hills or mountains, often with a river or stream running through it

valor /ˈvæl·ər/ *n* [U] *fml* great bravery • *The former pilot received a medal for valor in the Vietnam War.*

value IMPORTANCE /ˈvæl·juː/ *n* [U] importance, worth, or benefit • *They discussed the value of having cameras in the courtroom.* ○ *The value of the thing* (= its worth in money) *was probably only a few dollars but it had great sentimental value.* • A **value judgment** is a personal opinion about whether something is good or bad.

value /ˈvæl·juː/ *v* [T] to consider (something) as important and worth having • *I value his friendship more than I can ever say.*

valuable /ˈvæl·jə·wə·bəl, -jə·bəl/ *adj* important, useful, or beneficial • *Niekro was named the most valuable player in baseball.* ○ *They perform valuable services for poor, rural women.*

value MONEY /ˈvæl·juː/ *n* [C/U] the amount of money that can be received for something; the worth of something in money • *a decline in property values* [C] ○ *The value of the dollar fell against the mark and the yen yesterday.* [U] • LP PRICE

value /ˈvæl·juː/ *v* [T] to state the worth of (something) • *The painting was valued at $450,000.*

valuable /ˈvæl·jə·wə·bəl, -jə·bəl/ *adj* worth a lot of money • *ABC's valuable radio and TV licenses are up for renewal.*

valuables /ˈvæl·jə·wə·bəlz, -jə·bəlz/ *pl n* small objects, esp. jewelry, that can be sold for a lot of money • *You may store your valuables in the hotel safe while you are here.*

values /ˈvæl·juːz/ *pl n* the principles that help you to decide what is right and wrong, and how to act in various situations • *The political*

platform is based on traditional values associated with the rural South.

valve /vælv/ *n* [C] a device that controls the flow of air or liquid from one place to another • *a heart valve* ○ *The explosion apparently was caused by a faulty gas valve.* • PIC PIPES

vampire /ˈvæm·paɪr/ *n* [C] an imaginary humanlike creature, said to be a dead person returned to life, who sucks blood from people at night

van /væn/ *n* [C] a box-shaped road vehicle of medium size • *a delivery van*

vandal /ˈvæn·dəl/ *n* [C usually pl] a person, often in a group, who intentionally damages public or private property

vandalism /ˈvæn·dəlˌɪz·əm/ *n* [U] • *The mayor promised to crack down on vandalism.*

vandalize /ˈvæn·dəlˌaɪz/ *v* [T] • *The teenager was accused of vandalizing cars.*

vanguard /ˈvæn·gɑrd/ *n* [U] the front part of a group of people who are moving forward, esp. an army, or (*fig.*) people who are making changes or new developments • *These families were only the vanguard of what turned into a flood of refugees.*

vanilla /vəˈnɪl·ə, -ˈnel·ə/ *n* [U] a substance made from the seeds of a plant, used to give flavor to sweet foods • *vanilla yogurt*

vanish /ˈvæn·ɪʃ/ *v* [I] to disappear or stop existing, esp. suddenly • *Her smile vanished.*

vanity /ˈvæn·ət·i/ *n* [U] the personal characteristic of being too proud of and interested in yourself, esp. in your appearance or achievements • USAGE: The related adjective is VAIN SELFISH.

vanquish /ˈvæŋ·kwɪʃ, væn-/ *v* [T] to defeat completely • *Smallpox, a once deadly disease, has now been vanquished.*

vantage point /ˈvænt·ɪdʒˌpɔɪnt/ *n* [C] a place that provides a good view • *From our vantage point atop the mountain, we could see the whole city below.* • A vantage point is also a way of thinking or a set of opinions based on your particular situation: *The movie shows the effects of divorce from the vantage point of the children.*

vapor /ˈveɪ·pər/ *n* [C/U] a gas that escapes from a liquid or solid, esp. as a result of heating • *Warm air is able to hold more water vapor than cold air.* [U]

vaporize /ˈveɪ·pəˌraɪz/ *v* [I/T] to turn from a solid or liquid into a gas, or to cause this to happen • *When water boils, it vaporizes.* [I]

variable /ˈver·iː·ə·bəl, ˈvær-/ *adj* likely to change, or showing change or difference as a characteristic • *Our weather is very variable in the spring.*

variable /ˈver·iː·ə·bəl, ˈvær-/ *n* [C] something that can change, esp. in a way that cannot be known in advance • *Among the variables that could prevent us from finishing the building by June are the weather and the availability of materials.*

variance /'ver·i:·əns, 'vær-/ *n* [C] • See at VARY.

variant /'ver·i:·ənt, 'vær-/ *n* [C] • See at VARY.

variation /ˌver·i:'eɪ·ʃən, ˌvær-/ *n* [C/U] • See at VARY.

varicose veins /'vær·əˌkoʊs'veɪnz/ *pl n* a condition in which the tubes that carry blood, esp. those in the legs, are swollen and can be seen on the skin • *Pregnant women often get varicose veins.*

varied /'ver·i:d, 'vær-/ *adj* • See at VARY.

variety DIFFERENCE /və'rɑɪ·ət·i/ *n* [U] the characteristic of frequently changing, or of including many different types or things • *The YWCA offers a variety of religious, educational, and recreational activities for young single females.* ○ *You can get foods there that have a little bit more variety.*

variety TYPE /və'rɑɪ·ət·i/ *n* [C] a type, esp. one among a group of things that share general features and differ in some details • *Several different varieties of sparrows live around here.*

various /'ver·i:·əs, 'vær-/ *adj* • See at VARY.

variously /'ver·i:·ə·sli, 'vær-/ *adv* • See at VARY.

varnish /'vɑr·nɪʃ/ *n* [C/U] a clear liquid that you can put on a wooden surface, to protect it and give it a shiny, attractive appearance after drying • *The wood can be stained any color and then sealed with a coat of varnish.* [U]

varsity /'vɑr·sət·i/ *n* [C usually sing] one of the main sports teams at a university, college, or school • *He was hoping to make the varsity next year.*

varsity /'vɑr·sət·i/ *adj* [not gradable] • *Eight varsity players will return to the football team next season.*

vary /'ver·i, 'vær·i/ *v* [I/T] to change or be different, esp. from one occasion to another or from one item to another within a group, or to cause this to happen • *The value of stocks will vary from month to month.* [I] ○ *My husband varies the vegetables he plants each year.* [T]

varying /'ver·i:·ɪŋ, 'vær-/ *adj* [not gradable] • *He tried a number of different businesses with varying degrees of success.*

varied /'ver·i:d, 'vær-/ *adj* having or showing many different types, or changing often • *The varied symptoms included severe muscle pain, headaches, and dizziness.*

various /'ver·i:·əs, 'vær-/ *adj* [not gradable] several and different • *He underwent various treatments for the disease, none of them successful.* ○ *We enjoy eating in various types of restaurants.* ○ *After holding various jobs in different states, he settled in Oregon and opened a law office in Portland.*

variously /'ver·i:·ə·sli, 'vær-/ *adv* [not gradable] in several different ways or at several different times • *Studies variously put the US homeless population today at a high of 2 million and a low of 230,000.*

variance /'ver·i:·əns, 'vær-/ *n* [C] permission to do something differently from the official or usual way • *He requested a variance to build an addition to his house.* • To be **at variance** is to be different: *The official census count was at variance with the count we had made.*

variant /'ver·i:·ənt, 'vær-/ *n* [C] something that differs slightly from other similar things • *There are four variants of malaria, all transmitted to humans by mosquitoes.*

variation /ˌver·i:'eɪ·ʃən, ˌvær-/ *n* [C/U] change in quality, amount, or level • *The variation in the price during the past month is startling.* [U] • A variation also is a difference, or a thing that differs slightly from another of its type: *Her movies are all variations on the same theme.* [C]

vase /veɪs, veɪz, vɑz/ *n* [C] a container for holding flowers or for decoration • *Please put this vase of flowers on the table.*

vasectomy /və'sek·tə·mi, veɪ'zek-/ *n* [C/U] the medical operation of cutting the tubes through which a man's SEMEN (= liquid containing sperm) move, in order to make him unable to make a woman pregnant

vast /væst/ *adj* [*-er/-est* only] extremely large • *The vast majority of our students—nearly 90 percent—graduate within four years.*

vastly /'væs·tli/ *adv* • *I think the original movie was vastly superior to the remake.*

vat /væt/ *n* [C] a large container for mixing or storing liquids, esp. as used in industry • *The grapes are crushed in deep wooden vats.*

vault ARCH /vɔːlt/ *n* [C] a type of arch that supports a roof or ceiling, esp. in a church or public building, or a ceiling or roof supported by several of these arches

vault ROOM /vɔːlt/ *n* [C] a room, esp. in or under the ground floor of a large building, that is used to store things safely • *The museum keeps many of its treasures in temperature-controlled storage vaults.* • In a bank, a vault is where money, jewelry, important documents, etc., are locked for protection.

vault JUMP /vɔːlt/ *v* [I/T] to jump over (something) • *He vaulted (over) the gate.* [I/T] • To vault is also to move someone suddenly to a much higher or more important position: *The speech vaulted him into the national spotlight.* [T]

vaunted /'vɔːnt·əd, 'vɑnt-/ *adj* [not gradable] praised too frequently • *His much vaunted new plan has serious weaknesses.*

VCR /ˌviː·siː'ɑr/, **videocassette recorder** *n* [C] a machine that can record pictures and sounds from a television onto **magnetic tape**, and on which tapes of that type can be played • *They have a sale on VCRs and CD players.*

VD *n* [U] *abbreviation for* VENEREAL DISEASE

veal /viːl/ *n* [U] meat from very young cattle

veep /viːp/ *n* [C] *infml* a **vice president**, esp. the vice president of the US, see at VICE TITLE

veer /vɪr/ *v* [I] to suddenly change direction •

The officer saw the car veer off the side of the road.

vegetable /'vedʒ·tə·bəl, 'vedʒ·ət·ə-/ *n* [C] a plant that is used as food, or the part of a plant, such as a root, stem, or flower, that is used as food • *For vegetables, we eat a lot of broccoli, spinach, and corn.* • A person may be called a vegetable if they are completely unable to move and to react, usually because of brain damage.

vegetarian /ˌvedʒ·ə'ter·i·ən/ *n* [C] a person who does not eat meat for health or for religious or moral reasons • *Some vegetarians avoid eggs and dairy products as well as meat.*

vegetarian /ˌvedʒ·ə'ter·i·ən/ *adj* [not gradable] • *a vegetarian diet*

vegetarianism /ˌvedʒ·ə'ter·i·ə,nɪz·əm/ *n* [U]

vegetate /'vedʒ·ə,teɪt/, *slang* **veg (out)** /'vedʒ 'ɑʊt/ *v* [I] to live or spend time in a way that lacks physical and mental activity and effort • *The children just vegetate in front of the TV all morning.*

vegetation /ˌvedʒ·ə'teɪ·ʃən/ *n* [U] plants in general, or the plants that are found in a particular area • *The park rangers cleared vegetation from the hiking trails.*

vehement /'viː·ə·mənt/ *adj* expressing very strong feelings, or characterized by great energy or force • *They are killing some of the birds, to the vehement protests of animal-rights groups.*

vehemently /'viː·ə·mənt·li/ *adv* • *The defense counsel vehemently objected.*

vehicle MACHINE /'viː·hɪk·əl, 'viː·ɪ·kəl/ *n* [C] a machine used for transporting people or goods on land or roads, esp. one with wheels and an engine such as a car or bus • *A truck driver was badly hurt when his vehicle overturned.* ○ *The number of motor vehicles on the roads rises every year.*

vehicular /viːˈhɪk·jə·lər/ *adj* [not gradable] • *Pedestrian and vehicular traffic in the neighborhood have both increased.*

vehicle WAY /'viː·hɪk·əl, 'viː·ɪ·kəl/ *n* [C usually sing] a way of achieving something • *The conference on AIDS prevention will be an ideal vehicle for increasing awareness of the problem.* ○ *She used her celebrity status as a vehicle to run for political office.*

veil /veɪl/ *n* [C] a piece of thin material worn to protect or hide the face or head • *The bride wore a veil made of French lace.* ○ *(fig.) A veil of secrecy surrounded the appointment of the new college president.*

veil /veɪl/ *v* [T] • *In that country, women are veiled when they go out in public.*

veiled /veɪld/ *adj* (of statements, opinions, or intentions) not direct or clearly expressed • *He took the comment as a veiled threat.*

vein TUBE /veɪn/ *n* [C] a tube that carries blood to the heart from the other parts of the body • Compare ARTERY TUBE.

vein LAYER /veɪn/ *n* [C] a layer of a substance in a crack in rocks or earth • *a vein of iron ore*

vein MOOD /veɪn/ *n* [U] a style or a temporary mood • *She published many novels and stories in the romantic vein then popular.*

Velcro /'vel·kroʊ/ *n* [U] *trademark* special cloth material having two rough surfaces that stick together when pressed, used for fastening clothing and other objects

velocity /və'lɑs·ət·i/ *n* [C] the speed at which something is traveling • *The wind velocity recorded at the airport was 78 miles per hour at 4 p.m.*

velour /və'lʊr/ *n* [U] a cloth similar to VELVET with a soft surface

velvet /'vel·vət/ *n* [U] a cloth with a soft, furry surface

velvety /'vel·vət·i/ *adj* soft, like velvet • *She patted the dog's velvety ears.*

vendetta /ven'det·ə/ *n* [C] a strong desire to harm a person or group, often because of political reasons or feelings of hate • *They accused the special prosecutor of carrying on a vendetta against the White House.*

vending machine /'ven·dɪŋ·mə,ʃiːn/ *n* [C] a machine you put money into to buy small items such as packages of food, candy, and drinks

vendor /'ven·dər/ *n* [C] a person or company that sells goods or services • *Our company deals with many vendors of women's clothing.* • A vendor is also a person who sells food or goods on the street: *a hot dog vendor* ○ *a street vendor*

veneer /və'nɪr/ *n* [C/U] a thin layer of decorative wood or other material used to cover a cheaper or less attractive material • *It's a pine table with a mahogany veneer.* [C] • A veneer is also something that hides something unpleasant or unwanted: *He had a veneer of sophistication but was really just a bully.* [U]

venerate /'ven·ə,reɪt/ *v* [T] to honor or greatly respect (a person or thing) • *The American writer Mark Twain has been venerated for almost a century.*

venerable /'ven·ə·rə·bəl/ *adj* respected, esp. because of long experience or age • *The venerable American jeweler, Tiffany & Company, appointed a new president.*

venereal disease /və'nɪr·iː·əl/ (*abbreviation* **VD**) *n* [C/U] a disease caused or spread by sexual activity with another person • *Venereal diseases such as syphilis are now usually called sexually transmitted diseases.* [C]

venetian blind /və,niː·ʃən'blɑɪnd/ *n* [C] a set of narrow, horizontal pieces of wood, plastic, or metal that can be raised or lowered to cover a window and set at different angles to block light from the outside or let it in

vengeance /'ven·dʒəns/ *n* [U] a hurtful or violent action against someone to punish them for having hurt you • *She cried out for vengeance.*

vengeful /'vendʒ·fəl/ *adj fml* desiring to hurt someone, often violently, in order to punish them for having hurt you • *God is not vengeful, he said, but just.*

venison /'ven·ə·sən/ *n* [U] the flesh of a deer used as meat

venom /'ven·əm/ *n* [U] a poisonous liquid produced by some snakes, insects, and SPIDERS when they bite • *(fig.) His diary was full of venom and hate for everyone in authority.*

venomous /'ven·ə·məs/ *adj* • *a venomous snake/spider*

vent OPENING /vent/ *n* [C] an opening that allows air, smoke, or gas to escape or enter an enclosed space • *The residents of the basement apartment ran outside after smelling smoke coming through a vent.*

vent EXPRESS FEELINGS /vent/ *v* [T] to express (a negative emotion) forcefully • *Walking relieves a lot of tension and it's a good way to vent frustration.*

ventilate /'vent·ᵊl,eɪt/ *v* [T] to cause fresh air to enter and move around (an enclosed space) • *There's a designated smoking area, but it's not ventilated properly.*

ventilation /,vent·ᵊl'eɪ·ʃən/ *n* [U]

venture /'ven·tʃər/ *n* [C] an activity or plan of action, often in business, that involves risk or uncertainty • *His most recent business venture ended in bankruptcy.*

venture /'ven·tʃər/ *v* [I/T] to risk going somewhere or doing something that might be dangerous or unpleasant • *Ever since she was attacked and robbed, she has been too frightened to venture out of the house alone.* [I always + adv/prep] • *(fml)* To venture something is to attempt it when you are likely to be wrong or to be criticized: *I wouldn't venture an opinion about that.* [T]

venue /'ven·juː/ *n* [C] the place where a public event or meeting happens • *They changed the venue at the last minute because they realized the meeting room would have been much too small.*

Venus /'viː·nəs/ *n* [U] the planet second in order of distance from the sun, after Mercury and before the earth

veranda, **verandah** /və'ræn·də/ *n* [C] a raised, open area, often covered, attached to the front or side of a house, esp. common in the southern US • *I went up the walk onto the big veranda and knocked on the door.*

verb /vɜrb/ *n* [C] *specialized* (in grammar) a word or phrase that describes an action, condition, or experience • *"Run," "keep," and "feel" are all verbs.* • LP CONTRACTIONS OF VERBS, PHRASAL VERBS, TRANSITIVE AND INTRANSITIVE VERBS

verbal SPOKEN /'vɜr·bəl/ *adj* [not gradable] spoken rather than written • *Our apartment lease is really just a verbal agreement.*

verbal RELATING TO WORDS /'vɜr·bəl/ *adj* [not gradable] having to do with or using words •

The children were tested for their physical coordination and verbal skills.

verbatim /vər'beɪt·əm/ *adj, adv* [not gradable] using exactly the same words that were originally used • *He could quote long passages verbatim from the King James version of the Bible.*

verdict /'vɜr·dɪkt/ *n* [C] a decision by a JURY as to whether someone is guilty after having heard the facts given at a trial • *The jury reached/returned a verdict of not guilty after six hours of deliberation.* • A verdict is also any judgment or opinion given after considering the facts of a situation: *City planners think it's a good idea to ban traffic from downtown streets, but the public's verdict is that it's a stupid idea.*

verge /vɜrdʒ/ *n* [C] the edge, border, or limit of something • If someone or something is **on the verge of** an experience or event, they are very near to doing or experiencing it: *He was on the verge of saying something but stopped and shook his head.*

verge on /vɜrdʒ/ *v prep* [T] to come close to being or becoming • *Some parts of the biography verge on the trivial, and the book would be better if it were shorter.*

verify *(obj)* /'ver·ə,faɪ/ *v* to make certain of or prove the truth or accuracy of (something) • *The complaint of police brutality could not be verified.* [T] ○ *Tests verified (that) Beck had torn a shoulder muscle.* [+ (that) clause]

veritable /'ver·ət·ə·bəl/ *adj* [not gradable] (used to emphasize how great or unusual something is by comparing it to something else) • *If current projections hold, Montgomery County will experience a veritable explosion in its school-age population* (= it will have many more students).

vermin /'vɜr·mən/ *pl n* small animals and insects that are harmful or annoying and are often difficult to control • *She reported an infestation of vermin, including rats, in the basement of the apartment house.*

vernacular /vər'næk·jə·lər, və'næk-/ *n* [C/U] the form of a language commonly spoken by the people of a particular region or by a particular group, esp. when it is different from the standard language • *He was, in the Yiddish vernacular of his immigrant grandparents, a "mensch."* [U]

vernacular /vər'næk·jə·lər, və'næk-/ *adj* • *a vernacular expression*

versatile /'vɜr·sət·ᵊl/ *adj* (of people) able to do many different things or to adjust to new conditions, or (of things) able to be used for many different purposes • *He was a versatile guitarist, and recorded with many leading rock bands.* ○ *It is an especially versatile insecticide known to control a range of insects.*

verse /vɜrs/ *n* [C/U] writing that is arranged in a rhythmic pattern; poems • *She has a talent for writing humorous verse.* [U] • *A verse* is also one of the parts into which a poem or song is divided: *We'll sing only the first and last verses.* [C] • A verse is also one of the short parts into which the Bible is divided. [C]

versed /vɜrst/ *adj* prepared by having knowledge or experience of something • *He was well versed in all branches of the field and published extensively.*

version /'vɜr·ʒən/ *n* [C] a particular form of something that varies from other forms of the same thing • *They're producing several versions of the TV commercial to see which one works best.* • A version can also be a TRANSLATION: *Originally published in German, it was published in New York in an English-language version.* • Someone's version of an event is their description of it: *Her version of the accident was completely different from that given by the driver of the other car.*

versus /'vɜr·səs/ (*abbreviation* **vs.**) *prep* (used to show the names of two teams or sides) against • *The next soccer match is Mexico versus the United States.* ○ (*fig.*) *It was a question of artistic integrity versus love of money, and money won.*

vertebra /'vɜrt̬·ə·brə/ *n* [C] *pl* **vertebrae** /'vɜrt̬·ə,breɪ, -bri, -brə/ *medical* one of the small bones that form the SPINE (= the line of bones down the middle of the back)

vertical /'vɜrt̬·ɪ·kəl/ *adj* standing or pointing straight up or at an angle of 90° to a horizontal surface or line • *Water that had leaked from above formed a vertical line down one wall.* • Compare HORIZONTAL.

vertigo /'vɜrt̬·ɪ,goʊ/ *n* [U] *medical* a feeling that everything is spinning around, causing you to be unable to balance and therefore to fall

verve /vɜrv/ *n* [U] a lot of energy and enthusiasm • *She expressed herself with verve and wit.*

very EXTREMELY /'ver·i/ *adv* [not gradable] (used to add emphasis to an adjective or adverb) to a great degree, or extremely • *I was working very hard, but I enjoyed it.* ○ *It's very easy to find our house.* ○ *She was a very good teacher.* ○ *People didn't like him very much.* • If something could or could not **very well** happen, it is likely or unlikely to happen: *Stress could very well have triggered the attack.*

very EXACT /'ver·i/ *adj* [not gradable] (used to add emphasis to a noun) exact or particular • *I'd heard stories about him and now here he was, the very person I now accompanied.* ○ *This very moment was what he had been waiting for.* ○ *He found the missing paper at the very bottom of the pile.*

vessel SHIP /'ves·əl/ *n* [C] a large boat or ship • *A scattering of vessels anchored in the harbor.*

vessel CONTAINER /'ves·əl/ *n* [C] a container used to hold liquids • *We used bowls, pots, bottles, pitchers—any vessels we could find.*

vessel TUBE /'ves·əl/ *n* [C] a tube that carries liquid, esp. blood, through the body • *Blood clots clogged the vessels.*

vest CLOTHING /vest/ *n* [C] a piece of clothing like a coat without sleeves that reaches to the waist • *My grandfather always wore his vest buttoned up.* ○ *The police use bulletproof vests for protection.* • (*Br*) A vest is an UNDERSHIRT.

vest GIVE POWER TO /vest/ *v* [T] *slightly fml* to give (someone or something) control over something or the power to do something • *Political power is now vested in an elected parliament.* • Someone with a **vested interest** in something has a special interest in it and often benefits from it: *She doesn't have a vested interest in one particular idea.*

vestibule /'ves·tə,bjuːl/ *n* [C] a room just inside a house or building, through which you enter the building • *In the school's vestibule is a sign reading, "Enter here and find a friend."* ○ *You can hang your coat in the vestibule.*

vestige /'ves·tɪdʒ/ *n* [C] a small part left from something larger and more important, esp. one that is no longer used • *Vestiges of ancient settlements can be seen in the caves.*

vet MILITARY PERSON /vet/ *n* [C] *short form of* VETERAN (= a person who was in the military)

vet ANIMAL DOCTOR /vet/ *n* [C] *short form of* VETERINARIAN

vet EXAMINE /vet/ *v* [T] **-tt-** to study (something), or to examine (a person's record) to see that it is acceptable or accurate • *All agencies must carefully vet new workers.* ○ *Before we signed this contract, our lawyer vetted it.*

veteran EXPERIENCED PERSON /'vet̬·ə·rən, 've·trən/ *n* [C] a person who has had a lot of experience in a particular activity or job • *Ms. Beasly is one of our veterans—she has been teaching here for over 20 years.*

veteran MILITARY PERSON /'vet̬·ə·rən, 've·trən/, *short form* **vet** *n* [C] a person who was once a member of the armed forces • *The American Legion is an organization of veterans of the US armed forces.* • In the US, **Veterans Day** is a legal holiday on November 11 in honor of members of the armed forces who fought for the US in wars.

veterinarian /,vet̬·ə·rə'ner·i·ən, ,ve·trə'ner-/, *short form* **vet** *n* [C] a person trained in the medical treatment of animals • *He is the chief veterinarian for the zoo and deals with all kinds and sizes of animals.*

veterinary /'vet̬·ə·rə,ner·i, 've·trə,ner·i/ *adj* [not gradable] • *The practice of veterinary medicine has become very sophisticated.*

veto /'viːt̬·oʊ/ *n* [C/U] *pl* **vetoes** the power to refuse to allow something to be done, or such a refusal • *The president has promised a veto if Congress passes that bill.* [C] ○ *NATO did not give Russia any veto over its decisions.* [U]

veto /'viːt̬·oʊ/ *v* [T] he/she/it **vetoes**, **vetoing**, *past* **vetoed** to refuse to allow (something) to be done • *The governor said she*

VERY, COMPLETELY, **AND OTHER INTENSIFIERS**

Intensifiers are adverbs or adjectives that increase the strength of other words. They can be used with most parts of speech.

With adjectives

Certain adverbs can be used before adjectives and past participles to give them a more powerful meaning. Often an adverb is used especially with particular adjectives. For example, someone can be **extraordinarily** *happy* or **deeply** *depressed*. I might be **totally** *unprepared* for some bad news, but **absolutely** *delighted* by a surprise. Words that are connected like this are sometimes called word partners.

Adverbs meaning "very"

In addition to making the meaning of the adjective stronger, some intensifiers add a comment or description.

bitterly disappointed/opposed/cold
incredibly/unbelievably beautiful/hot/boring/stupid/smart/difficult
surprisingly easy/well/inexpensive/ignorant
wildly successful/popular/different/funny/inaccurate/exaggerated
wonderfully refreshing/funny/well

Much, considerably, and **far** may be used when making comparisons.

Our new house is **much** *bigger.* • *She was* **considerably** *older than her husband.* • *It's* **far** *more difficult than I expected.*

Very, really, extremely, and *exceptionally* are used with most adjectives. Other intensifying adverbs commonly connect with positive and negative adjectives as follows:

WITH POSITIVE ADJECTIVES	•	WITH NEGATIVE ADJECTIVES
awfully		
awfully (esp informal) glad/nice/good	•	sorry/hard/slow/late/long/hot/tired
deeply		
deeply grateful/concerned/involved/ affected/committed/religious	•	hurt/depressed/disturbed/suspicious/ offended/divided/unpopular
enormously		
popular/impressed/beneficial/important	•	complex
especially		
important/true/useful/strong/valuable/ pleased/nice	•	difficult
extraordinarily		
lucky/happy/amusing/generous/powerful	•	difficult/complex
heavily		
involved/favored/discounted	•	dependent/armed/used/damaged/ polluted/loaded/indebted
highly		
successful/intelligent/reliable/qualified/ skilled/educated/ respected/desirable/ probable/amused	•	critical/competitive/unlikely/undesirable
hugely		
popular/successful/talented/enjoyable/ entertaining	•	expensive
immensely		
popular/rich/valuable/powerful/satisfying	•	difficult
intensely		
personal/dramatic/moving/political	•	competitive/irritated
seriously		
interested/(humorous) rich	•	injured/ill/weakened/damaged/hurt/ wrong/disturbed
severely		
	•	disabled/damaged/restricted/limited/ depressed/disturbed
terribly		
important/excited/funny	•	wrong/sad/upset/hard/sorry
tremendously		
exciting/successful/popular/enjoyable/ powerful/useful	•	difficult

(CONTINUED)

VERY, COMPLETELY, AND OTHER INTENSIFIERS (*continued*)
Adverbs meaning "completely"

WITH POSITIVE ADJECTIVES	•	WITH NEGATIVE ADJECTIVES
absolutely		
wonderful/right/clear/sure/necessary/ certain/essential	•	awful/ridiculous/impossible/appalling/ crazy
completely		
satisfied/different/innocent	•	false/dependent/lost/impossible/useless/ unaware/unrealistic/unprepared
entirely		
predictable/devoted/separate/due to/ clear/natural/free/different	•	mistaken/selfish/wrong/dependent
fully		
aware/recovered/justified/appreciated	•	
perfectly		
normal/natural/acceptable/reasonable/ clear/good	•	ridiculous
quite		
sure/capable/right/happy/different	•	wrong/absurd
thoroughly		
modern/professional/satisfactory/ entertaining/modern	•	unpleasant/spoiled
totally		
different/new/separate/satisfying/devoted/ secure/free/(*informal*) awesome	•	opposed/unacceptable/confused/lacking/ useless/unprepared/absurd
utterly		
persuasive/charming/delightful	•	wrong/evil/mistaken/false/absurd
wholly		
convincing	•	unexpected/unacceptable/inadequate

With verbs

The adverb can go before or after the verb, although some adverbs occur in only one of these positions. The adverb cannot be placed immediately before the object of the verb.

Our political views differ **greatly**. • *Working conditions in the factory have* **greatly** *improved*. • *Her death affected him* **deeply**. (after the verb and object) • *I* **really** *admire what you're doing*. (before the verb)

Strong intensifiers are often used with verbs that have a powerful meaning:

It's **absolutely** *pouring* (= raining very hard). • *I* **utterly** *despise them* (= very much dislike them).

Really and *very much* can be used with a wide variety of verbs. Other common intensifiers used with verbs include the following.

absolutely refuse/agree/love/adore/hate
badly need/want/miss/hurt/injure/wound
completely understand/agree/disagree/change/forget/destroy
vary/strengthen **considerably** (after the verb)
affect/sleep/love **deeply** (after the verb)
help/vary/enjoy/benefit **enormously** (after the verb)
entirely depend on/rely on/consist of/agree
greatly improve/increase/reduce/help/benefit/change/appreciate/admire/exaggerate/enjoy
rely/rain/drink/favor/count on/advertise/invest **heavily**
enjoy/improve/grow **immensely**
contrast/fall/rise/improve/differ/increase/drop **sharply** (usually after the verb)
strongly encourage/oppose/criticize/object/support/feel/believe/deny
totally disagree/agree/oppose/forget/destroy

With nouns

The following adjectives are commonly used as intensifiers before nouns.

absolute certainty/minimum/nonsense/disgrace
big fan/eater/spender/bully/success/surprise/relief
complete disaster/confidence/failure/idiot/contrast/mess
deep trouble/mistrust/concern/regret/depression/sleep
great difficulty/success/surprise/skill/care/danger/joy/sadness/importance/pity
heavy rain/losses/traffic/responsibility/smoker/drinker
perfect happiness/harmony/timing/example/opportunity/conditions

pure chance/coincidence/invention/speculation/guesswork/conjecture/bliss/delight
real problem/bargain/nuisance/pleasure/sweetheart/gentleman/jerk/idiot/mess
total stranger/failure/chaos/disaster/confidence/idiot
tremendous amount/pressure/opportunity/achievement/excitement/speed
utter confusion/nonsense/lack of/despair/disbelief/amazement/chaos/misery

With adverbs and pronouns

Some adverbs can be given a stronger meaning by putting another adverb in front:

She worked **really hard** *on the project.*
You know **perfectly well** *what I mean.*
Quite clearly *you don't understand.*
His plan went **horribly wrong.**

Very, really, and **extremely** are often used in this way.

---

would veto the bill unless certain parts were changed. ○ *Cory wanted to pierce her nose, but her mom vetoed it.*

vex /veks/ *v* [T] to cause (someone) to feel annoyance or trouble • *The question that vexes Ben the most is, "Why me?"*

vexed /vekst/ *adj* troubling and difficult • *a vexed question*

vexing /'vek·sɪŋ/ *adj* • *Drug use among young people is a particularly vexing problem.*

via /'vaɪ·ə, 'viː·ə/ *prep* by way of, or by use of • *I sent the application papers via fax.*

viaduct /'vaɪ·ə,dʌkt/ *n* [C] a high bridge that carries a road or railroad over an area that is difficult to cross, such as a deep valley, very wet land, or the steep side of a hill • *An ancient Roman viaduct crosses the valley.*

vial /'vaɪ·əl, vaɪl/ *n* [C] a small bottle used to hold a liquid • *The store gave away vials of their new perfume.*

vibes /vaɪbz/ *pl n slang* the feeling you get from being in a particular place or situation or from being with a particular person • *I'm afraid to go there—that place has bad vibes.*

vibrant /'vaɪ·brənt/ *adj* energetic, bright, and full of life or excitement • *The city is youthful, vibrant—an exciting place.* ○ *Flowers of vibrant colors were on each table.*

vibrate /'vaɪ·breɪt/ *v* [I/T] to move quickly backward and forward, or to cause (something) to shake • *Musical sounds are produced when the strings of the piano vibrate.* [I] ○ *A thundering boom made the windows vibrate.* [I]

vibration /vaɪ'breɪ·ʃən/ *n* [C/U] • *We felt the earthquake's vibrations 120 miles away!* [C]

vicarious /vaɪ'ker·iː·əs, -'kær-/ *adj* experienced by reading or watching someone else do something • *This disaster movie will provide you with plenty of vicarious thrills.*

vice MORAL FAULT /vaɪs/ *n* [C] a moral fault or weakness in a person's character • *His only vice is smoking a cigar once in a while.* • Vice is also immoral behavior: *Gambling is a vice that is becoming more acceptable these days.* • Compare VIRTUE GOODNESS.

vice TITLE /vaɪs/ *combining form* used as part of a title to show the rank of an officer or of-

ficial of a company or organization, immediately below a president or CHAIRMAN • *a vice principal* ○ *Vice Premier Zhu Rongji* ○ *He served as vice chairman of the federal reserve.* ○ *There are three vice presidents in that company.* • The **vice president** of the US (*abbreviation* **VP**) is the elected official immediately below the president and is elected with the president every four years.

vice versa /ˌvaɪs'vɜr·sə, ˌvaɪ·sə'vɜr-/ *adv* (of an opposite) being also true • *With this software, descriptions can replace names and vice versa.*

vicinity /vɪ'sɪn·ət̬·i/ *n* [U] the area immediately surrounding something • *There are many stores in the vicinity where she can shop.* ○ *A truck was stolen from the vicinity of the prison on the night the prisoners escaped.* • Something **in the vicinity of** an amount is approximately that amount: *The price for a house here is in the vicinity of $150,000.*

vicious /'vɪʃ·əs/ *adj* (of an act) intending to hurt badly, or (of a person or animal) likely to be violent • *I don't believe he is a vicious dog.* ○ *A gang armed with sticks and clubs was responsible for the vicious attacks on old people.* • A **vicious circle** or **vicious cycle** is a situation in which one problem causes another one, making the original problem impossible to solve: *In a kind of vicious circle, girls did not study science because other girls didn't study science, even though they were good at it.*

victim /'vɪk·təm/ *n* [C] a person who has suffered the effects of violence or illness or bad luck • *an accident victim* ○ *a rape victim* ○ *She's just a victim of circumstances beyond her control.*

victimize /'vɪk·tə,maɪz/ *v* [T] • *A gang victimized many old people in that neighborhood, stealing from them and frightening them.*

victimization /ˌvɪk·tə·mə'zeɪ·ʃən/ *n* [U] • *National reports of victimization show a decline in certain kinds of assault.*

victimless /'vɪk·təm·ləs/ *adj* [not gradable] (of a crime) lacking a victim, or thought not to involve a victim • *Some people believe gambling and prostitution are victimless crimes.*

victor /'vɪk·tər/ *n* [C] the winner of a competition, election, war, etc. • *The victor in the 1996 presidential election was Bill Clinton.*

victory /'vɪk·tə·ri, -tri/ *n* [C/U] the act or an example of winning a competition or war • *A goal in the last half minute assured victory and the World Cup for the Mexicans.* [U]

victorious /vɪk'tɔːr·iː·əs, -'toʊr-/ *adj* [not gradable] • *The city honored the victorious general with a huge parade.*

video /'vɪd·iː,oʊ/ *n* [C/U] *pl* **videos** a series of images recorded on a **magnetic strip** which is used in television broadcasting or viewed on a television screen with a VCR • *We can send audio and video over the Internet.* [U] • A video is also a VIDEOTAPE: *We watched two videos—both new films.* [C] • A **video camera** records moving pictures and often sound on a VIDEO-TAPE: *Video cameras are used as security devices for ATMs.* • A **videocassette** (also **video**) is a VIDEOTAPE. • A **videocassette recorder** is a VCR. • A **video game** is a game in which the player controls moving pictures on a television screen by pressing buttons or moving a short handle: *The best video games let you blow guys up and shoot them.*

video /'vɪd·iː,oʊ/ *adj* [not gradable] • *The CD-ROM includes video clips.* • Compare AUDIO.

videotape /'vɪd·iː·oʊ,teɪp/, *short form* **video**, **tape** *n* [C] a long, narrow, magnetic strip inside a rectangular plastic container which records sounds and moving images that can be heard and seen on a television, or a recording of images and sounds • *I bought the videotape of "Jurassic Park" for the kids.* ○ *He watches videotapes of his performances so he can see what needs work.*

videotape /'vɪd·iː·oʊ,teɪp/, *short form* **tape** *v* [T] • *Why don't you videotape the ballgame so you can watch it later?*

vie /vaɪ/ *v* [I] **vying**, *past* **vied** to compete • *Several companies are vying for the contract to build the new hospital.*

view SIGHT /vjuː/ *n* [C/U] what you can see from a particular place, or the ability to see from a particular place • *She turned a corner and disappeared from view.* [U] ○ *Our room had spectacular views of the mountains.* [C] • If something is **on view**, it is placed where the public can see it: *Plans for the new design of the park are on view in the library this week.*

view /vjuː/ *v* [T] • *The President viewed the hurricane damage from a helicopter.*

viewer /'vjuː·ər/ *n* [C] • *Millions of viewers watch the Super Bowl on TV every year.*

view OPINION /vjuː/ *n* [C] *slightly fml* a way of looking at something; an opinion • *It's our view that it's time we did something and stopped just talking!* ○ *He takes a pessimistic view of our chances of success.* ○ *The meeting was an opportunity for the two leaders to exchange views.* • **In view of** means because of, or considering: *In view of the late hour, we'll have to put off that discussion until our next*

meeting. • A **viewpoint** is a **point of view**. See at POINT TIME OR PLACE.

view /vjuː/ *v* [T] *slightly fml* to look at or consider (something) • *How do you view your chances of getting that job?*

vigil /'vɪdʒ·əl/ *n* [C] a period of staying awake to be with someone who is sick or to call public attention to something • *The boy's parents kept a long vigil in his hospital room.* ○ *A candlelight vigil on the steps of the courthouse was held to protest the verdict in this trial.*

vigilant /'vɪdʒ·ə·lənt/ *adj* being very careful to notice things, esp. signs of danger • *Security personnel need to be more vigilant in checking bags and packages.*

vigilance /'vɪdʒ·ə·ləns/ *n* [U] • *The vigilance of a mother fox protects her young from danger.*

vigilante /,vɪdʒ·ə'lænt·i/ *n* [C] a person who forces obedience to the law without legal authority to do so, or a member of a group that decides to force obedience to the law without official authority • *Support for vigilantes will grow if people lose confidence in the police.*

vigor /'vɪg·ər/ *n* [U] strength, energy, or enthusiasm • *After vacation, she returned to work with renewed vigor.*

vigorous /'vɪg·ə·rəs/ *adj* • *a vigorous debate/campaign* ○ *He still walks with vigorous steps.*

vigorously /'vɪg·ə·rə·sli/ *adv* • *Don't exercise too vigorously at first.*

vile /vaɪl/ *adj* evil or disgusting • *He responded with the vilest language imaginable.* • Vile also means very bad or unpleasant: *a vile mood/temper*

vilify /'vɪl·ə,faɪ/ *v* [T] *slightly fml* to say or write unpleasant things about (someone or something), in order to cause other people to have a bad opinion of them • *He was vilified by civil rights leaders.*

villa /'vɪl·ə/ *n* [C] a large house, usually in a rural area or near the sea

village /'vɪl·ɪdʒ/ *n* [C] a group of houses, stores, and other buildings which is smaller than a town • *We live just outside the village of Larchmont.* • A village is also the people who live in a village: *The whole village came out for the parade.*

villain /'vɪl·ən/ *n* [C] a bad person who harms other people or breaks the law, or a cruel or evil character in a book, play, or film • *In her version of the story, Hoover emerges as the villain.*

vinaigrette /,vɪn·ə'gret/ *n* [U] a sauce made from oil and vinegar, and sometimes other flavorings, that is used esp. on salad

vindicate /'vɪn·də,keɪt/ *v* [T] to show (something) to have been right or true, or to show (someone) to be free from guilt or blame • *The decision to include Morris on the team was vindicated when he scored three touchdowns.*

vindication /,vɪn·də'keɪ·ʃən/ *n* [C/U] • *They are hoping for vindication in court.* [U]

vindictive /vɪn'dɪk·tɪv/ *adj* having or showing a desire to harm someone because you think that they have harmed you; unwilling to forgive • *She was immature, spiteful, even vindictive at times.*

vine /vaɪn/ *n* [C] a type of plant that climbs or grows along the ground and has a twisting stem • *a grape vine* ○ *pea vines*

vinegar /ˈvɪn·ɪ·gər/ *n* [U] a strong-tasting liquid, made esp. from sour wine or apple juice, that is used for flavoring or preserving food • *Would you like oil and vinegar on your salad?*

vineyard /ˈvɪn·jərd/ *n* [C] a piece of land on which vines that produce grapes are grown

vintage WINE /ˈvɪnt·ɪdʒ/ *n* [C] the wine made in a particular year, or a particular year in which wine was made • *The 1983 vintage was one of the best.*

vintage /ˈvɪnt·ɪdʒ/ *adj* [not gradable] (of wine) of high quality that was made in a particular year, and that can be kept for several years in order to improve it • *vintage champagne*

vintage HIGH QUALITY /ˈvɪnt·ɪdʒ/ *adj* [not gradable] (esp. of something old) of high quality and lasting value, or showing the best characteristics typical of its creator • *a vintage pistol/airplane/car* ○ *"Sophisticated Lady" is vintage Duke Ellington.*

vinyl /ˈvaɪn·əl/ *n* [U] strong plastic that can be bent and that is used to make floors, furniture, clothing, etc. • *vinyl flooring/upholstery* ○ *a vinyl raincoat*

viola /viːˈoʊ·lə/ *n* [C/U] a wooden musical instrument with four strings, slightly larger than a VIOLIN, which a player holds against their neck and plays with a BOW (= stick with hairs fixed to it), or this type of instrument generally

violate /ˈvaɪ·əˌleɪt/ *v* [T] to break or act against (esp. a law, agreement, or principle), or to not respect (something that should be treated with respect) • *The planes appear to have deliberately violated the cease-fire agreement.* ○ *Some of the gravestones in the cemetery had been overturned and violated.* • If someone violates a place or situation, they go where they are not wanted or do something they should not do: *Questions of this kind violate my privacy.* • Violate can also be used to avoid saying RAPE.

violation /ˌvaɪ·əˈleɪ·ʃən/ *n* [C/U] • *a traffic violation* [C] ○ *The invasion constitutes a violation of international law.* [C] ○ *They had not acted in violation of the rules.* [U]

violator /ˈvaɪ·əˌleɪt·ər/ *n* [C] • *Violators can be fined up to $500.*

violence /ˈvaɪ·ə·ləns/ *n* [U] extremely forceful actions that are intended to hurt people or are likely to cause damage • *racial/ethnic/domestic violence* ○ *She was concerned about the amount of sex and violence on television.* ○ *The storm turned out to be one of unexpected violence.*

violent /ˈvaɪ·ə·lənt/ *adj* using or involving force to hurt or attack • *violent crime* ○ *A violent clash/confrontation between demonstrators and police left six people hospitalized.* • A violent death is one that is caused suddenly and unexpectedly by the use of physical force, esp. murder. • Violent can mean very strong: *a violent explosion* • A violent person or attitude is one that expresses great anger.

violently /ˈvaɪ·ə·lənt·li/ *adv* in a forceful way that causes people to be hurt • *He was violently assaulted/beaten on his way home last night.* • Violently can mean strongly or extremely: *They are violently opposed to the plans.*

violet COLOR /ˈvaɪ·ə·lət/ *adj* [not gradable], *n* [U] (of) a color that is between blue and purple • *violet ink* ○ *Violet is too dark for the walls of this room.* [U]

violet PLANT /ˈvaɪ·ə·lət/ *n* [C] a small plant with pleasant-smelling purple, blue, or white flowers

violin /ˌvaɪ·əˈlɪn/ *n* [C/U] a small, wooden musical instrument with four strings that a player holds against their neck and plays with a BOW (= stick with hairs fixed to it), or this type of instrument generally • PIC BOW, BRIDGE

VIP /ˌviː·aɪˈpiː/ *n* [C] *abbreviation for* very important person (= a person who is treated better than ordinary people because they are famous or influential in some way) • *We were given the full VIP treatment.*

viper /ˈvaɪ·pər/ *n* [C] a small, poisonous snake • *The vipers slithered and hissed.*

viral /ˈvaɪ·rəl/ *adj* [not gradable] • See at VIRUS SMALL ORGANISM.

virgin /ˈvɜr·dʒən/ *n* [C] someone who has never had sex • *They were both still virgins when they married.*

virgin /ˈvɜr·dʒən/ *adj* [not gradable] • *a virgin bride* • Virgin can be used of forests and areas of land that have not yet been cultivated or used by people: *a virgin forest* ○ *Antarctica is virgin territory.*

virginity /vərˈdʒɪn·ət·i/ *n* [U] • *She lost her virginity at the age of seventeen.*

Virgo /ˈvɜr·goʊ, ˈvɪr-/ *n* [C/U] *pl* **Virgos** the sixth sign of the ZODIAC, covering the period August 23 to September 22 and represented by a young woman, or a person born during this period

virile /ˈvɪr·əl, -aɪl/ *adj* full of strength, power, and energy in a way that is manly and sexually attractive • *The ads show virile young men playing on the beach.*

virtual /ˈvɜr·tʃə·wəl/ *adj* [not gradable] almost, but not exactly or in every way • *She was a virtual unknown before this movie.* ○ *Snow brought Minneapolis to a virtual standstill yesterday.* • **Virtual reality** is a set of images and sounds produced by a computer that seem to represent a real place or situation.

virtually /ˈvɜr·tʃə·wə·li/ *adv* [not gradable] •

Unemployment in this part of the country is virtually nonexistent.

virtue GOODNESS /'vɜr·tʃuː/ *n* [C/U] a good moral quality in a person, or the general quality of goodness in a person • *Patience is a virtue.* [C] • Compare VICE MORAL FAULT.

virtuous /'vɜr·tʃə·wəs/ *adj* possessing good moral qualities • *I've been up working since six o'clock this morning so I'm feeling very virtuous.*

virtue ADVANTAGE /'vɜr·tʃuː/ *n* [C/U] an advantage or benefit • *Most people seem convinced of the virtues of capitalism.* [C] • **By virtue of** mean as a result of: *They were excluded from voting by virtue of being women.*

virtuoso /ˌvɜr·tʃə'woʊ·soʊ, -zoʊ/ *n* [C] *pl* **virtuosos** a person who is extremely skilled at something, especially at playing an instrument or performing • *Famous mainly for his wonderful voice, Cole was also a virtuoso on the piano.*

virtuoso /ˌvɜr·tʃə'woʊ·soʊ, -zoʊ/ *adj* [not gradable] • *The world's greatest tenor treated us to a virtuoso display of his abundant talent.*

virulent ACTING QUICKLY /'vɪr·jə·lənt/ *adj* (of a disease) dangerous and spreading quickly, or (of poison) having an effect very quickly • *a virulent strain of flu*

virulent FULL OF HATE /'vɪr·jə·lənt/ *adj* fierce and full of hate • *virulent racism* ○ *Several newspapers mounted virulent attacks.*

virus SMALL ORGANISM /'vaɪ·rəs/ *n* [C] a very small organism that causes disease in humans, animals, and plants • *a chickenpox/flu/ herpes/mumps virus* • A virus is also a disease caused by a virus: *She's had a virus for several days.*

viral /'vaɪ·rəl/ *adj* [not gradable] • *a viral infection*

virus COMPUTER PROBLEM /'vaɪ·rəs/ *n* [C] a hidden set of instructions in a computer program that is intended to introduce faults into a computer system or cause it to perform actions that were not planned

visa /'viː·zə, -sə/ *n* [C] an official document or mark made in a PASSPORT that allows you to enter or leave a particular country • *an entry/ exit visa*

vis–a–vis /ˌviː·zə'viː, -sə-/ *prep* in relation to, or in comparison with • *Later I asked him more directly about government's role vis-a-vis the environment.*

visceral /'vɪs·ə·rəl/ *adj* based on emotional reactions rather than on reason or thought • *He has a visceral feel for our problems.*

viscous /'vɪs·kəs/ *adj* (of a liquid) thick and sticky; not flowing easily • *viscous oil*

vise /vaɪs/ *n* [C] a tool having two flat sides that can be moved closer together to hold something firmly while it is being worked on • *After gluing both surfaces of the wood, clamp it in a vise to dry.* • Something that is **viselike** is very tight: *a viselike handshake*

visible /'vɪz·ə·bəl/ *adj* able to be seen • *There are few visible signs of her recent illness.* ○ *The comet is visible to the naked eye as a fuzzy ball in the western sky.* • Visible also means able or tending to attract public attention: *In a very short time, she became a highly visible environmental spokesperson.*

visibly /'vɪz·ə·bli/ *adv* noticeably or obviously • *Earl became visibly upset.*

visibility /ˌvɪz·ə'bɪl·ət·i/ *n* [U] the degree to which distant objects can be seen outside, as influenced by weather conditions • *There will be reduced visibility because of the fog.*

vision SIGHT /'vɪʒ·ən/ *n* [U] the ability to see • *good/impaired/blurred vision*

vision MENTAL IMAGE /'vɪʒ·ən/ *n* [C] an imagined mental image of something • *We lack a vision of what love really is.* • A vision can be an experience or understanding of something that is the result of a religious experience, mental illness, or taking drugs: *She'd seen Jesus in a vision during childbirth.*

vision VIEW OF THE FUTURE /'vɪʒ·ən/ *n* [U] the ability to imagine how a country, society, industry, etc., will develop in the future and to plan in a suitable way • *The theater's director is a woman of great artistic vision.*

visionary /'vɪʒ·ə,ner·i/ *n* [C] • *She was a social reformer, a true visionary.*

visit /'vɪz·ət/ *v* [I/T] to go to a place in order to experience it, or to go to a person in order to spend time with them • *We visited a few galleries while we were in New York.* [T] ○ *When are we going to visit Grandma?* [T] ○ *She's not staying here—she's just visiting for the afternoon.* [I] • **Visiting hours** are the time periods when you can visit someone esp. in a hospital or prison.

visit /'vɪz·ət/ *n* [C] • *I think I'll pay a visit to the barbershop while I'm in town.* ○ *We had a visit from the fire inspector last week.*

visitation /ˌvɪz·ə'teɪ·ʃən/ *n* [C/U] the act of visiting, or a visit • *The hospital has strict rules about visitation.* [U] • (*law*) Visitation is the act of a DIVORCED parent spending time with a child he or she no longer lives with at agreed times and according to agreed conditions. [C/U]

visitor /'vɪz·ət·ər/ *n* [C] • *Every summer, this tiny fishing village receives thousands of visitors.*

visor /'vaɪ·zər/ *n* [C] a curved piece of stiff material that is worn above the eyes to give protection from the sun • A visor is also a movable part of a HELMET (= hard protective head cover) that can be lowered to cover the face. • PIC BASEBALL CAP

vista /'vɪs·tə/ *n* [C] a view from a high position • *After a hard climb, we were rewarded by a vista of rolling hills.*

visual /'vɪʒ·ə·wəl/ *adj* relating to seeing • *These animals have excellent visual ability/*

acuity. • The **visual arts** are the arts of drawing, painting, SCULPTURE, photography, etc.

visually /'vɪʒ·ə·wə·li/ *adv* • *a visually stunning production* ○ *Guide dogs improve the lives of the visually impaired.*

visualize /'vɪʒ·ə·wə,lɑɪz/ *v* [T] to imagine or remember (someone or something) by forming a picture in your mind • *I was so surprised when I saw him—I'd visualized someone much older.*

vital /'vɑɪt̬·ᵊl/ *adj* necessary or extremely important for the success or continued existence of something • *The existence of a strong opposition is vital to a healthy democracy.* ○ *The kidneys play a vital role/part in removing waste from the blood.* ○ *It's vital that you respond at once.* [+ *that* clause] • (*medical*) A person's **vital signs** include their body temperature and the rate at which they are breathing and their heart is beating. • **Vital statistics** are a group of official facts that include the number of births, deaths, and marriages in a particular place, or the ages and races of the people that live there.

vitally /'vɑɪt̬·ᵊl·i/ *adv* • *It's vitally important that we get there by tomorrow.*

vitality /vɑɪ'tæl·ət̬·i/ *n* [U] energy and strength • *youthful vitality* ○ *The new factory should improve the economic vitality of the region.*

vitamin /'vɑɪt̬·ə·mən/ *n* [C] any of a group of natural substances that are necessary in small amounts for growth and good health and that are obtained from food • *a vitamin pill* ○ *Vitamin C is found in citrus fruits.*

vitriolic /,vɪ·tri:'ɑl·ɪk/ *adj* intentionally unkind or hurtful • *He launched a vitriolic attack on the senator, accusing him of shielding corrupt friends.*

vivacious /və'veɪ·ʃəs, vɑɪ-/ *adj* (esp. of a woman or girl) full of energy and enthusiasm • *Judy Garland was bright and vivacious, with a vibrant singing voice.*

vivid /'vɪv·əd/ *adj* brightly colored or (of descriptions or memories) producing clear, powerful, and detailed images in the mind • *vivid colors* ○ *vivid memories*

vividly /'vɪv·əd·li/ *adv* • *The novel vividly depicts the horrors of modern warfare.*

vivisection /,vɪv·ə'sek·ʃən/ *n* [U] the cutting into or other use of living animals in tests for the purpose of increasing knowledge of human diseases and the effects of using particular drugs

vocabulary /vou'kæb·jə,ler·i/ *n* [C/U] all the words used by a particular person, or all the words that exist in a particular language or subject • *Reading helps to improve your vocabulary.* [C]

vocal OF THE VOICE /'vou·kəl/ *adj* [not gradable] relating to or produced by the voice, either in singing or speaking • *vocal music* • The **vocal cords** are a pair of folds at the upper end of the throat that produce sound when air from the lungs moves over them.

vocal /'vou·kəl/ *n* [C usually pl] the singing in a piece of popular music • *At times his vocals were drowned out by the audience singing along.*

vocally /'vou·kə·li/ *adv* [not gradable]

vocalist /'vou·kə·ləst/ *n* [C] a person who sings, esp. with a group that plays popular music

vocalize /'vou·kə,lɑɪz/ *v* [I/T] to sing, speak, or make sounds • *She studied how often infants vocalized.* [I]

vocal OFTEN HEARD /'vou·kəl/ *adj* often expressing opinions and complaints in speech • *He is emerging as his party's most vocal critic of the president.*

vocation /vou'keɪ·ʃən/ *n* [C] a type of work that you feel you are suited to doing and to which you give much of your time and energy • *It wasn't until "The North American Review" published his story that he embraced writing as a vocation.*

vocational /vou'keɪ·ʃən·ᵊl/ *adj* [not gradable] providing skills and education that prepare you for a job • *vocational education/training* ○ *The school offers vocational programs in welding, electrical work, and building maintenance.*

vociferous /vou'sɪf·ə·rəs/ *adj* repeatedly and loudly expressing your opinions and complaints, or (of demands, complaints, etc.) expressed in this way • *a vociferous opponent of gay rights* ○ *vociferous objections*

vociferously /vou'sɪf·ə·rə·sli/ *adv* • *He protested vociferously, but to no avail.*

vodka /'vɑd·kə/ *n* [C/U] a colorless, alcoholic drink made from any of various grains or potatoes

vogue /voug/ *n* [C/U] the state of being popular and widely practiced, or a period during which an activity or style is popular and widely used • *I remember when jogging first came into vogue.* [U]

voice SOUNDS /vɔɪs/ *n* [C/U] the sound made when people speak or sing, or the ability to make such a sound • *She spoke in a low, soft voice, and I had to ask her to speak louder.* [C] ○ *I heard the murmur of voices.* [C] ○ *I've been talking so much that my voice is getting hoarse.* [C] ○ *I've got a cold and I'm losing my voice* (= becoming unable to speak). [U] • **Voice mail** is a telephone system that lets you record a message for people calling you and lets them leave a recorded message for you. LP TELEPHONE

voice OPINION /vɔɪs/ *n* [C/U] an expression of opinion, or the right to express an opinion • *The senator added his voice to the protest.* [C] ○ *The kids want to have a voice in where we go on our vacation.* [U]

voice /vɔɪs/ *v* [T] to express (esp. an opinion or feeling) • *Conservative groups voiced strong objections to the TV film about nuclear war.*

void EMPTY SPACE /vɔɪd/ *n* [C] a space with nothing in it • *Some parents use television to fill the void they have created by not spending enough time with their kids, he said.*

void UNACCEPTABLE /vɔɪd/ *adj* [not gradable] having no legal authority and therefore unacceptable • *The original version of her will was declared void.*

void /vɔɪd/ *v* [T] to remove the legal force from (an agreement or contract) • *I'll just void the check and pay you in cash.*

volatile /'vɑl·ət̬·ʔl/ *adj* likely to change suddenly and unexpectedly, or suddenly violent or angry • *It was a volatile situation, and the police handled it well.* ○ *The stock market was highly volatile in the early part of the year.* • (*specialized*) If a substance, esp. a liquid, is volatile, it will change easily into a gas: *volatile chemicals*

volcano /vɑl'keɪ·noʊ, vɔːl-/ *n* [C] *pl* **volcanoes** or **volcanos** a mountain made from burned materials that may throw out hot rocks and LAVA (= hot liquid rock) from a hole in its top

volcanic /vɑl'kæn·ɪk, vɔːl-/ *adj* [not gradable] • *volcanic ash/rock*

volition /və'lɪʃ·ən, voʊ-/ *n* [U] *fml* the power to make your own decisions • *It was announced that he resigned of his own volition* (= because he chose to), *but I believe he was forced out.*

volley WEAPONS FIRE /'vɑl·i/ *n* [C] a large number of bullets or arrows fired at the same time • *The settlers threw rocks, and the soldiers responded with volleys of gunfire.* • (*fig.*) A volley is also a lot of things done or said at the same time: *a volley of questions*

volley SPORTS SHOT /'vɑl·i/ *n* [C] (in tennis and other sports) a hit to return a ball before it touches the ground • *I was ahead in the first game, but then hit a bad volley and a bad forehand.*

volleyball /'vɑl·i,bɔːl/ *n* [U] a game in which two teams use their hands to hit a large ball from one side of a high net to the other, without allowing the ball to touch the ground

volt /voʊlt/ *n* [C] the standard unit used to measure how strongly an electrical current is sent around an electrical system • *Many household appliances run on a current of 120 volts.*

voltage /'voʊl·tɪdʒ/ *n* [C] • *high/low voltage*

volume SPACE /'vɑl·jəm, -juːm/ *n* [C/U] an amount of space having length, height, and width • *You need a big air conditioner to cool a large volume of space.* [C] ○ *About 8 percent of the total volume of garbage is plastic packaging.* [U]

volume AMOUNT /'vɑl·jəm, -juːm/ *n* [C usually sing] the number or amount of something having a lot of units or parts • *The main difficulty with teaching is the sheer volume of work.* ○ *The system could not handle the volume of*

electronic mail. ○ *We are looking for a high volume of sales.*

volume SOUND LEVEL /'vɑl·jəm, -juːm/ *n* [U] the level of sound produced by a television, radio, etc., or the switch or other device controlling this • *Could you turn the volume down, please—I'm trying to sleep.*

volume BOOK /'vɑl·jəm, -juːm/ *n* [C] a book, esp. one book in a set of related books • *a slim volume of poetry* ○ *I'm missing the last volume of the set.*

voluntary /'vɑl·ən,ter·i/ *adj* [not gradable] done, made, or given willingly, without being forced or paid to do it • *Employees can make voluntary contributions to the savings plan of up to 25% of their earnings.* ○ *He said that he had always supported voluntary prayer in the schools.*

voluntarily /,vɑl·ən'ter·ə·li/ *adv* • *She voluntarily gave up her lunch break to supervise the lab.*

volunteer /,vɑl·ən'tɪr/ *n* [C] a person who does something, esp. for other people or for an organization, willingly and without being forced or paid to do it • *The church relies on volunteers to run the office and answer the phones.*

volunteer /,vɑl·ən'tɪr/ *adj* [not gradable] • *a volunteer fireman* ○ *I do volunteer work for the American Lung Association.*

volunteer /,vɑl·ən'tɪr/ *v* [I/T] • *During the emergency a lot of people volunteered to work through the night.* [+ *to* infinitive] ○ *Three physicians volunteered their services.* [T]

voluptuous /və'lʌp·tʃə·wəs/ *adj* (esp. of women or their bodies) sexually attractive, esp. because of the full, curving shapes of their breasts or hips • *The Renoir drawing features two voluptuous women.*

vomit /'vɑm·ət/ *v* [I/T] to empty the contents of the stomach through the mouth, usually in explosive bursts • *Frequently the sights I saw made me feel like vomiting.* [I]

vomit /'vɑm·ət/ *n* [U] food or other matter that has come up from the stomach through the mouth • *He remembered the awful trip on the overcrowded boat, the smell of vomit lingering everywhere.*

vomiting /'vɑm·ət̬·ɪŋ/ *n* [U] • *It causes a range of ailments, including vomiting and diarrhea.*

voodoo /'vuː·duː/ *n* [U] a religion involving magic and the worship of spirits, originating in Africa and developed in Haiti

voracious /və'reɪ·ʃəs, vɔː-/ *adj* needing a lot of something to be satisfied • *Wolves are voracious eaters.* ○ *As a child, I had a voracious appetite for books.*

vortex /'vɔːr·teks/ *n* [C] *pl* **vortices** /'vɔːr·t̬ə,siːz/ *specialized* a mass of air or water that spins around very fast and pulls objects into its empty center

vote /voʊt/ *v* [I/T] to express your choice or opinion as one member of a group in order to decide an issue of importance to the whole group or to elect someone to an office • *I voted early this morning just after the polls opened.* [I] ○ *In a democracy, all adult citizens have the right to vote.* [I] ○ *Local residents have twice voted against raising property taxes.* [I] ○ *Who did you vote for in the last election?* [I] ○ *A majority of workers voted to accept the offer of an 8% pay raise.* [+ to infinitive] ○ *She was voted best director at the Cannes Film Festival.* [T]

vote /voʊt/ *n* [C/U] • *She won a majority of the votes, 15 to 13, and was declared the winner.* [C] ○ *Polls showed that the Catholic vote was split evenly between the two candidates.* [U] ○ *She cast her vote* (= voted) *for Gillespie.* [C] ○ *We called a meeting in order to take a vote on the issue.* [C] ○ *In some countries women still don't have the vote* (= are not allowed to vote in elections). [U] • A **vote of confidence** is a vote to show support esp. for a government: *(fig.) Richardson said that foreign investment amounts to a vote of confidence in the basic soundness of the U.S. economy.*

voter /ˈvoʊt̬·ər/ *n* [C] a person who votes, or a person who has the legal right to vote • *Voters are interested in issues that affect their pocketbooks, he said.*

vouch for /ˈvaʊtʃ·fər, -fɔːr/ *v prep* [T] to support the truth of something or the good character of someone based on your knowledge or experience • *Our accountant will vouch for the accuracy of the financial report.* ○ *I've known him for years and can vouch for his honesty.*

voucher /ˈvaʊ·tʃər/ *n* [C] a piece of paper that is a record of money paid or one that can be used to pay for particular goods or services • *Just present your travel voucher to the airline ticket agent, and she will give you the tickets.*

vow /vaʊ/ *v* to make a firm promise or decision to do something • *They vowed (that) they would never forget her kindness.* [+ (that) clause] ○ *After my illness I vowed to exercise every day.* [+ to infinitive]

vow /vaʊ/ *n* [C] • *They exchanged marriage vows in a Manhattan courthouse.*

vowel /ˈvaʊ·əl, vaʊl/ *n* [C] a speech sound produced by human beings when the breath flows out through the mouth without being blocked by the teeth, tongue, or lips • A vowel is also a letter that represents a sound produced in this way: *The vowels in English are a, e, i, o, u, and sometimes y.* • Compare CONSONANT.

voyage /ˈvɔɪ·ɪdʒ, ˈvɔː·ɪdʒ/ *n* [C] a long trip, esp. by ship • *Christopher Columbus brought cattle on his second voyage to America in 1493.*

voyeur /vwɑˈjɜr, vɔɪˈɜr/ *n* [C] a person who gets sexual pleasure esp. from secretly watching other people in sexual situations

voyeuristic /ˌvwɑ·jəˈrɪs·tɪk, ˌvɔɪ·ə-/ *adj*

VP *n* [C] *abbreviation for* **vice president**, see at VICE TITLE

vs. *prep abbreviation for* VERSUS

vulgar NOT SUITABLE /ˈvʌl·gər/ *adj* not polite or socially acceptable; not suitable or acceptable in style • *His speech was coarse and vulgar, filled with cursing and racial slurs.*

vulgar RUDE /ˈvʌl·gər/ *adj* rude or offensive, esp. because referring to sex • *The movie is rated PG and has a few mildly vulgar jokes.*

vulgarity /vʌlˈɡær·ət̬·i/ *n* [C/U] • *The movie contains sex, nudity, profanity, vulgarity, and violence.* [U]

vulnerable /ˈvʌl·nə·rə·bəl/ *adj* able to be easily hurt, influenced, or attacked • *The UN's 24,000 peacekeepers would then be completely vulnerable to attack.* ○ *His parents divorced when he was at the vulnerable age of 13.*

vulnerability /ˌvʌl·nə·rəˈbɪl·ət̬·i/ *n* [U]

vulture /ˈvʌl·tʃər/ *n* [C] a large bird that eats the flesh of dead animals • A vulture is also someone who is eager to get some advantage from other people's difficulties or weaknesses.

vying /ˈvaɪ·ɪŋ/ *present participle of* VIE

W, w

W LETTER , **w** /'dʌb·əl·juː/ n [C] pl **W's** or **Ws** or **w's** or **ws** the 23rd letter of the English alphabet

W. WEST n [U], adj abbreviation for WEST or WESTERN

w ELECTRICITY n [C] abbreviation for WATT

wacko /'wæk·oʊ/ n [C] pl **wackos** slang a person whose behavior is strange

wacky /'wæk·i/ adj slang strange in a pleasing and exciting or silly way • *The film has a wacky originality that is appealing.*

wad /wɑd/ n [C] a number of thin pieces of something pressed together, or something pressed into a lump • *a wad of bills/cash* ○ *a wad of chewing gum*

wad /wɑd/ v [T] **-dd-** to fold or press together (something) to form a mass • *He wadded his towel into a ball.*

waddle /'wɑd·ᵊl/ v [I] to walk with short steps, swinging the body from one side to the other, like a duck

wade (obj) /weɪd/ v [I always + adv/prep] to walk into or through (an area of water) that is not very deep • *We waded across the stream.* ○ *They come to the creek and waded in to drink.* • A **wading pool** is an artificial pool only a few inches deep that small children can play in.

□ **wade in** /'-'-/ v adv [I] to start to do something in a forceful and determined way • *If there's a problem, she'll wade in without hesitation and try to solve it.*

□ **wade through** /'-,-/ v prep [T] to spend a lot of time and effort doing (something boring or difficult) • *Some readers will not want to wade through the details of how the data were gathered and analyzed.*

wafer /'weɪ·fər/ n [C] a very thin, dry cookie that is often sweet and flavored • *chocolate wafers*

waffle CAKE /'wɑf·əl/ n [C] a thin, light cake, the surface of which is formed into a pattern of raised squares, often eaten for breakfast

waffle NOT DECIDE /'wɑf·əl/ v [I] to keep changing your decisions about something so that no clear decision is made • *This administration has a tendency to waffle on important questions.*

waft /wɑft, wæft/ v [I/T] to move gently through the air, or to cause this to happen • *I could smell cigarette smoke wafting down the hallway.* [I always + adv/prep]

wag /wæg/ v [I/T] **-gg-** (esp. of a tail or finger) to move from side to side or up and down, esp. quickly and repeatedly, or to cause this to happen • *When she came in, the dog sprang to its feet and wagged its tail.* [T]

wage MONEY /weɪdʒ/ n [U] an amount of money that is paid to an employee, esp. for each hour worked • *an hourly wage* • A **wage earner** is a person who works at a job for money, esp. at an hourly rate.

wages /'weɪ·dʒəz/ pl n the money earned by an employee, esp. when paid for the hours worked • *He was notorious for being anti-union and for paying low wages.*

wage FIGHT /weɪdʒ/ v [T] to fight (a war) • *The President vowed to wage a war on terrorism.*

wager /'weɪ·dʒər/ n [C] slightly fml an agreement to risk money on the unknown result of an event in the hope of winning more money than you have risked, or the amount of money risked; a BET

wager (obj) /'weɪ·dʒər/ v slightly fml • *Over $2 million was wagered at the track this month.* [T] • To wager is also to suggest as a likely idea: *I would wager that not one person in ten could tell an expensive wine from a cheaper one.* [+ that clause]

wagon /'wæg·ən/ n [C] a vehicle with four wheels, which must be pulled or pushed • *European settlers journeyed across America in covered wagons.* • If you are **on the wagon**, you have given up drinking alcohol: *I've been on the wagon for ten years, and hope to stay sober for the rest of my life.* • PIC COVERED WAGON

waif /weɪf/ n [C] literary a child or animal without a home or enough care • *a poor little waif*

wail /weɪl/ v to make a long, high cry, usually because of pain or sadness, or to make a sound like this • *Teenagers and elderly women wailed over the death.* [I] ○ *Air-raid sirens wailed.* [I] ○ (fig.) *Investors wailed* (= complained) *that interest rates were skyrocketing.* [+ that clause]

wail /weɪl/ n [C] • *The wail of the siren woke me up.*

waist /weɪst/ n [C] the part of the body above and slightly narrower than the hips • *These jeans are too tight around my waist.* • The waist or **waistline** of a piece of clothing is the part that covers this area of the body. • A **waistline** is also the length of your waist, often used to show if a person weighs too much: *When he quit smoking, his waistline started to grow.*

wait /weɪt/ v [I/T] to allow time to go by, esp. without doing much, until something happens or can happen • *I waited in the car.* [I] ○ *Wait here for me—I'll be back in a minute.* [I] ○ *The dentist kept me waiting for ages.* [I] ○ *Several people are waiting to use the phone.* [+ to infinitive] ○ *Please get in line and wait your turn like everyone else.* [T] • If something waits, it is being delayed or is ready: *The meeting will have to wait until tomorrow.* [I] ○ *An envelope was waiting for me when I got home.* [I] • You say **wait a minute/a second** in order to interrupt someone or to get their attention, or when you suddenly think of something important: *Wait a second—I know what we can do.* • *No decision will be made until next year, so you'll just have to* **wait and see** (= be patient until then). • To **wait on** someone is to serve them: *She waited on customers all day at the department store.* • To **wait (on) tables** is to serve meals to people in a restaurant. • *We'd better* **wait out** *the storm* (= wait until the end of it) *before we start out on our trip.* • A **waiting list** is a list of people who asked for something that is not immediately available but that they might be able to receive in the future: *The flight is full, but I can put you on the waiting list in case someone cancels.* • A **waiting room** is a room where people can sit while waiting, as in a railroad station or a doctor's office.

wait /weɪt/ *n* [U] • *We had a three-hour wait at the airport.*

waiter *male* /'weɪt̬·ər/, *female* **waitress** /'weɪ·trəs/ *n* [C] a person whose job is to serve meals to people in a restaurant • *A waiter came to the table to take our order.*

waive /weɪv/ *v* [T] to not demand (something you have a right to) or not cause (a rule) to be obeyed • *The bank waived the charge, because the mistake was their fault.*

wake [STOP SLEEPING] /weɪk/ *v* [I/T] *past simple* **woke** /woʊk/ or **waked**, *past part* **woken** /'woʊ·kən/ or **waked** to become awake and conscious after sleeping, or to cause (someone) to stop sleeping and become awake • *Did you wake (up) at all during the night?* [I] ○ *The noise of the storm woke the kids (up).* [T/M] • A person who is not patient may say **wake up** to get someone's attention: *Hey, wake up! The light changed to green—let's get going!* [I] • If you **wake up** to something, you become aware of it: *I wish Dad would wake up to the fact that I'm no longer a kid.* • A **wake-up call** is a telephone call or signal to wake you in the morning, typically in a hotel. • (*fig.*) A **wake-up call** is also a shocking event that changes the way many people think: *The Oklahoma City bombing was seen as a wake-up call that the US was not immune to terrorism.*

waken /'weɪ·kən/ *v* [I/T] • *He tried to waken her, but she didn't stir.* [T]

wake [WATER] /weɪk/ *n* [C] an area of water whose movement has been changed by a boat or ship moving through it • (*fig.*) *The storm left a massive amount of destruction in its wake.*

wake [GATHERING] /weɪk/ *n* [C] a gathering held before a dead person is buried, at which their family and friends talk about the person's life

walk /wɔːk/ *v* [I/T] to move along by putting one foot in front of the other, or to move (a distance) in this way • *I walked home.* [I] ○ *We just walked past a famous actress.* [I] ○ *They walked all around Chinatown.* [I] ○ *I walk to work every morning.* [I] ○ *It's not that far—you can*

walk it in half an hour. [T] ○ *We must have walked miles today.* [T] • To walk someone to a particular place is to walk with them until they have reached it: *He offered to walk her home.* [T] • To walk an animal, esp. a dog, is to take it along with you outside while you walk. [T] • A **walk-in** storage space is one that is large enough for a person to enter and walk around in: *a walk-in closet* • A **walk-up** is a building with usually four or more floors and no ELEVATOR (= device for taking people from one floor to another), or an apartment on an upper floor in such a building.

walk /wɔːk/ *n* [C] • *He went for/took a walk around the block.* • When people talk about **walks of life**, they are referring to different levels of social position or achievement: *In my work I see people from all walks of life.*

walker /'wɔː·kər/ *n* [C] • *She's a very fast walker.* • A walker is also a metal frame to help people who have difficulty walking, by using it to support them as they move it in front of them.

□ **walk all over** /ˌ-ˌ-ˈ--/ *v adv prep* [T] to treat (someone) badly and without respect • *You shouldn't let him walk all over you like that.*

□ **walk away/off with** /ˌ-ˈ--ˌ ˈ-ˈ-/ *v adv prep* [T] to win (something) easily • *The German soccer team is once again favored to walk away with the championship.*

□ **walk off with** /ˈ-ˈ--/ *v adv prep* [T] to take (something) without asking • *Who walked off with my drink?*

□ **walk out** /ˈ-ˈ-/ *v adv* [I] to leave an event before it is finished because you are not enjoying it or because you do not agree with it, or to go on STRIKE (= stop working at your job in order to express a complaint) • *It was such a bad movie that I felt like walking out in the first fifteen minutes.* ○ *Airline pilots are threatening to walk out* (= go on strike) *next week.*

walkout /'wɔː·kɑʊt/ *n* [C] • *Some people who were unhappy with the changes staged a walkout during the meeting.* ○ *The mayor met with union officials in an effort to avert a walkout* (= refusal to work) *of sanitationmen who are demanding a better wage increase.*

□ **walk out on** /ˈ-ˈ-ˌ-/ *v adv prep* [T] to end your relationship or involvement with (someone) suddenly • *She walked out on her husband and two children after 12 years of marriage.*

□ **walk** *obj* **through** *obj* /ˈ-ˈ-/ *v adv* [T] to show (someone) how to do (something) from beginning to end • *They can walk you through the process one more time, to give you some practice and confidence.*

walkie–talkie /ˌwɔː·kiːˈtɔː·ki/ *n* [C] a small radio held in the hand and used for both sending and receiving messages

Walkman /'wɔːk·mən, -ˌmæn/ *n* [C] *pl* **Walkmans** or **Walkmen** /'wɔːk·mən, -ˌmen/ *trademark* a small machine that plays magnetic sound recordings, sometimes with a radio, using **headphones** (= device placed over a person's ears) to make the sound so that it can be heard privately

wall /wɔːl/ n [C] a vertical structure that divides or encloses something • *The walls of the fortress were more than eighteen inches thick.* ○ *We'd like the walls painted white.* • A wall of people or things is a mass of them formed in such a way that you cannot get through or past them: *The police formed a solid wall so that no one could get past.* • **Wall-to-wall** means covering the whole floor: *a wall-to-wall carpet*

wallboard /'wɔːl·bɔːrd, -bourd/ n [U] a large, thin, rectangular piece of building material used to make the walls inside some buildings

wallet /'wɑl·ət/ n [C] a small, folding case for paper money, **credit cards** (= plastic cards you use to buy things), and other cards that you want to carry with you • *a leather wallet*

wallop /'wɑl·əp/ v [T] *infml* to hit (someone) hard with the hand or with something held in the hand • *She walloped him across the back of the head.*

wallow /'wɑl·oʊ/ v [I] (esp. of animals) to lie or roll about slowly in deep, wet earth, sand, or water • *The pig wallowed in the mud.* • (*fig.*) To wallow in an emotion or situation is to stay in that state without trying to change: *I wallowed in self-pity after the divorce.*

wallpaper /'wɔːl·peɪ·pər/ n [C/U] a type of decorative paper sometimes used to cover the walls of a room instead of painting them • *We found some beautiful wallpaper with an orange floral pattern.* [U]

wallpaper /'wɔːl·peɪ·pər/ v [T] • *We decided to wallpaper Annie's bedroom.*

Wall Street /'wɔːl·striːt/ n [U] a street in New York City that represents the financial center of the US • *On Wall Street today, stocks closed higher.*

walnut /'wɔːl·nət, -nʌt/ n [C/U] a nut with a hard shell, the tree that produces these nuts, or the wood from the tree

walrus /'wɔːl·rəs/ n [C] a sea mammal, similar to a SEAL (= a large, fish-eating animal) but larger and with two very long teeth that stick out from the mouth

waltz DANCE /wɔːlts/ n [C/U] a type of dance that includes a repeating movement of three steps, or a piece of music written for this style of dancing

waltz /wɔːlts/ v [I] • *Several couples were waltzing around the floor.*

waltz WALK /wɔːlts/ v [I always + adv/prep] *infml* to walk somewhere quickly and confidently • *Glen waltzed in an hour late as though nothing were wrong.*

wan /wɑn/ adj (of a person's face or expression) pale, tired, or weak • *a wan smile*

wand /wɑnd/ n [C] a thin stick waved by a person who is performing magic • *a magic wand*

wander /'wɑn·dər/ v [I/T] to walk around slowly in a relaxed way or without any clear

purpose or direction • *The lost child wandered the streets for hours.* [T] ○ *We spent the morning wandering around the old part of the city.* [I] • If your mind or your thoughts wander, you stop thinking about what you should be giving your attention to and start thinking about other matters: *As he droned on, my mind began to wander.* [I]

wane /weɪn/ v [I] to weaken in strength or influence • *By the late 70s, the band's popularity was beginning to wane.*

wangle /'wæŋ·gəl/ v [T] to succeed in obtaining or doing (something) by persuading someone or getting them to do it by not being completely honest • *I still wangled an expense-account trip to New York.*

wanna /'wɑn·ə, 'wʌn·ə, 'wɔː·nə/ v [T] *not standard* (spelled the way it is often spoken) want to • *I wanna be a rock star.*

wannabe /'wɑn·ə·bi, 'wʌn·ə-, 'wɔː·nə-/ n [C] *infml* a person who wants to be like someone else, esp. someone famous, or who wants to be thought of as famous • *She's a pop singer wannabe.*

want DESIRE /wɑnt, wʌnt, wɔːnt/ v [I/T] to feel that you would like to have (something) or would like (something to happen) • *Who wants ice cream?* [T] ○ *I want the cold weather to end.* [T] ○ *She wanted to get new shoes.* [I] ○ *I don't want him talking about me.* [T] ○ *I've been wanting to thank you for helping me.* [I] • If you are wanted, someone wishes to see or talk with you: *Harry! You're wanted on the phone.* [T] • A **want ad** is a CLASSIFIED AD.

wanted /'wɑnt·əd, 'wʌnt-, 'wɔːnt-/ adj being searched for by the police • *He was one of the ten most wanted criminals in America.*

want NEED /wɑnt, wʌnt, wɔːnt/ v [I/T] to need (something) • *You want to be careful to stay out of the sun.* [I] • If you **want for** something, you lack it: *We didn't have much, but we never wanted for food.*

want /wɑnt, wʌnt, wɔːnt/ n [C/U] • *A cat's wants are few—food and companionship.* [C]

wanting /'wɑnt·ɪŋ, 'wʌnt-, 'wɔːnt-/ adj • *It was a perfect party—nothing was wanting* (= missing).

wanton /'wɑnt·ən, 'wɔːnt-/ adj acting thoughtlessly or causing harm, often intentionally • *Some people stereotype black kids as wanton thugs.*

war /wɔːr/ n [C/U] armed fighting between two or more countries or groups, or a particular example of such fighting • *Can the US fight two wars at the same time?* [C] ○ *War is something to avoid.* [U] ○ *Several nations were at war.* [U] • A war can also be any situation in which there is strong competition between opposing sides or a joint effort against something harmful: *Airlines engage in fare wars to attract new customers.* [C] ○ *It seems impossible to win the war on drugs.* [U] • (*infml*) A **war chest** is money that has been collected or saved to pay for something, esp. a long fight for something or to help someone trying to get elected to a political office. • A **war crime** is an act that breaks the rules of war, such as those dealing with treatment of people who are not fighting or prisoners of war. • **War games** are practices held by armed forces to test new equipment and test plans for fighting. • A **warplane** is an armed military aircraft: *Fifty new warplanes were delivered to the army.* • A **warship** is a boat equipped with guns and other weapons of war. • **Wartime** is a period of armed fighting between two countries: *During wartime, everyone's life changes a lot.*

warring /'wɔːr·ɪŋ/ *adj* [not gradable] fighting a war or as if fighting a war • *Warring groups roamed the countryside, making travel very dangerous.* ○ *Warring factions inside the Democratic party weaken it.*

warlike /'wɔːr·laɪk/ *adj* suited to or liking war, or threatening, as if going to fight • *a warlike mood* ○ *a warlike speech*

warble /'wɔːr·bəl/ *v* [I] to sing as a bird does with a sound that rises and falls • *This morning it seemed as if every bird began to warble at once.*

ward HOSPITAL ROOM /wɔːrd/ *n* [C] a large room in a hospital which is used for treating people with similar illnesses or conditions • *the pediatric/maternity ward*

ward PERSON /wɔːrd/ *n* [C] *law* a person, esp. a child, who is legally under the protection or care of another person or of a court or government • *The agency serves youths who are wards of the state.*

ward AREA /wɔːrd/ *n* [C] a political division within a city • *the fifth ward*

ward off *obj*, **ward** *obj* **off** /'wɔːrd'ɔːf/ *v adv* [M] to keep (something) away or prevent it from happening or harming you • *He used his umbrella to ward off his attacker.*

warden /'wɔːrd·ən/ *n* [C] a person who is in charge of a prison

wardrobe /'wɔːr·droʊb/ *n* [C] the clothes that a person owns, or a particular type of clothes that a person owns • *She has a different wardrobe for every occasion.* • A wardrobe is also a piece of furniture where clothes are kept.

warehouse /'wer·haʊs, 'wær-/ *n* [C] *pl* **warehouses** /'wer,haʊ·zəz, -səz/ a large building used for storing goods • *Textbooks are sent right from the warehouse to the schools.* • A warehouse is also a type of large store where goods are sold at a reduced price.

warehousing /'wer,haʊ·zɪŋ, 'wær-/ *n* [U] • *She opposes the warehousing of the mentally ill* (= the act of keeping them somewhere without treating them).

wares /werz, wærz/ *pl n* items offered for sale, or a company's goods • *More than 40 dealers in furniture, art, and silver will display their wares.*

warfare /'wɔːr·fer, -fær/ *n* [U] the activity of

fighting a war or strongly competing, esp. with reference to the type of weapons used or to the way the fighting is done • *psychological/ nuclear warfare* ○ *economic warfare*

warhead /'wɔːr·hed/ *n* [C] the end of a bomb or MISSILE that contains explosives

warily /'wer·ə·li, 'wær-/ *adv* See at WARY.

warlike /'wɔːr·laɪk/ *adj* • See at WAR.

warlord /'wɔːr·lɔːrd/ *n* [C] a military leader who controls a country or, more frequently, an area within a country, esp. when the central government is not in control

warm HIGH TEMPERATURE /wɔːrm/ *adj* [-er/-est only] having a comparatively high temperature, but not hot • *Warm bread always tastes better.* ○ *Just let me sit in the sun so I can get warm.* • Warm clothes or covers keep out the cold and make you feel comfortable: *a warm winter coat* ○ *a warm woolen hat and mittens* • **Warm-blooded** animals, such as mammals and birds, have a body temperature that stays the same and does not change with the temperature of their surroundings. Compare **cold-blooded** at COLD LOW TEMPERATURE.

warm /wɔːrm/ *v* [I/T] to rise to a higher temperature, or to cause (something) to rise to a higher temperature • *He rubbed his hands together to warm them.* [T] ○ *The water in the kettle warms quickly.* [I]

warmly /'wɔːrm·li/ *adv* • *He was warmly dressed in a heavy overcoat and a fur hat.*

warmth /wɔːrmθ/ *n* [U] • *She laid down on the sand and enjoyed the warmth of the sun.* ○ *The dogs huddled together for warmth.*

warm FRIENDLY /wɔːrm/ *adj* [-er/-est only] friendly and affectionate • *Grace is a warm, caring woman.* • A **warm-hearted** person is kind and affectionate: *He was a warm-hearted man who helped me when I needed a job.*

warmly /'wɔːrm·li/ *adv* • *He shook my hand warmly.*

warmth /wɔːrmθ/ *n* [U] • *He brought warmth and wisdom to his work with children.*

▫ **warm up** *obj* HEAT , **warm** *obj* **up** /'-'-/ *v adv* [M] to make (something) hotter • *I can warm up the leftover soup for lunch.* ○ *We warmed the rolls up in the oven.*

▫ **warm up** *(obj)* PRACTICE , **warm** *(obj)* **up** /'-'-/ *v adv* [I/M] to exercise or practice in order to prepare for something that takes a lot of effort • *Ballet dancers have to warm up before performing.* [I] ○ *A new pitcher is warming up in the bullpen.* [I] ○ *She warms up her voice by singing scales.* [M] • *If you warm up a car, you let the engine get warm enough to work well.* [M]

warmup /'wɔːr·mʌp/ *n* [C] • *He injured his knee during pregame warmups.* ○ *I bought an exercise video, but I never got further than the warmup exercises.*

▫ **warm up to** /-'--/ *v adv prep* [T] to begin to like or enjoy (someone or something) • *She was not a person who was easy to warm up to.*

warn /wɔːrn/ v [I/T] to make (someone) aware of a possible danger or problem so that it can be avoided • *I warned her not to waste her money on that movie.* [T] ○ *We'd been warned that we should lock our cars in the parking lot.* [T] ○ *The radio warned all day of the bad weather coming.* [I]

warning /'wɔːr·nɪŋ/ n [C/U] notice of a possible danger or problem, so that it can be prevented or avoided • *Flood warnings were issued by the National Weather Service.* [C] ○ *The earthquake struck without warning while the city was asleep.* [U] • A **warning sign** is an early signal that something bad or dangerous might happen: *You should know the warning signs of a stroke.*

warp BEND /wɔːrp/ v [I/T] (esp. of wood) to bend or twist, or to cause (esp. wood) to become bent or twisted • *The shelves of the bookcase warped when water soaked them.* [I] ○ *Dampness warped all of the boards in the shed.* [T]

warped /wɔːrpt/ adj • *Those old floorboards were warped and uneven.*

warp MAKE WRONG /wɔːrp/ v [T] to cause (something or someone) to no longer do what is usual or right • *Kim's judgment was warped by his worshipful followers.*

warped /wɔːrpt/ adj • *a warped vision of the future* ○ *a warped character*

warpath /'wɔːr·pæθ/ n usually humorous • If someone is **on the warpath**, it means that they are angry and ready to argue or fight: *I told my friends to watch out because my mother was on the warpath.*

warrant MAKE NECESSARY /'war·ənt, 'wɔːr-/ v [T] slightly fml to make (a particular action) necessary or correct, or to be a reason to do (something) • *Not every murder warrants the death penalty.* ○ *I can see circumstances in which drug testing would be warranted.*

warrant DOCUMENT /'war·ənt, 'wɔːr-/ n [C] an official document approved by an authority, esp. a judge, which gives the police permission to do certain things • *a search warrant* ○ *an arrest warrant*

warranty /ˌwar·ən'tiː, ˌwɔːr-/ n [C/U] a written promise by a company to repair or replace a product that breaks within a fixed period of time or do again a piece of work that is not satisfactory • *a five-year warranty* [C] ○ *I've had problems with the car, but it's still under warranty.* [U]

warring /'wɔːr·ɪŋ/ adj See at WAR.

warrior /'wɔːr·jər/ n [C] a person who has experience and skill in fighting, esp. as a soldier • *The Apache chief Geronimo had a reputation as a fearless warrior.*

wart /wɔːrt/ n [C] a small, hard lump that grows on the skin and is caused by a virus • **Warts and all** means with faults or unpleasant facts included: *She's anxious to tell her story, warts and all.*

wary /'wer·i, 'wær·i/ adj careful because you do not completely trust someone or something or are not certain about what you should do • *Teachers are often wary of standardized tests.*

warily /'wer·ə·li, 'wær-/ adv • *Ted warily eyed the stranger.*

was /wʌz, waz, wəz/ past simple of BE

wash CLEAN /waʃ, wɔːʃ/ v [I/T] to make (something or yourself) clean, or to become clean, using water and usually soap • *Alex washed his face and combed his hair.* [T] ○ *I hate washing dishes.* [T] • If you say you are going to **wash** your **hands of** something, you mean that you are not going to have anything more to do with it: *You can't start a fight and then just wash your hands of it.* • If you say that something **won't/doesn't wash**, you mean it is unacceptable: *Don't think you can get credit without doing the work—that doesn't wash around here.* • A **washcloth** is a small cloth used with soap and water to clean your face and body. • A **washroom** is a bathroom.

wash /waʃ, wɔːʃ/ n [C/U] an act of washing, or clothing, sheets, and other cloth items being cleaned together • *I went days without a wash or a change of clothes.* [C usually sing] ○ *She did a load of wash and hung it up to dry.* [U]

washable /'waʃ·ə·bəl, 'wɔː·ʃə-/ adj [not gradable] able to be cleaned in water without damaging the material • *Are these pants washable?* • If a type of material or a piece of clothing is machine-washable, it can be cleaned in a **washing machine**.

washer /'waʃ·ər, 'wɔː·ʃər/ n [C] a **washing machine** • A **washer-dryer** is a unit that contains two machines, one for cleaning clothes, sheets, etc., and another for drying them. • See also WASHER.

washing /'waʃ·ɪŋ, 'wɔː·ʃɪŋ/ n [U] the act of cleaning clothes, or cloth items being washed together • *He does his own washing and ironing.* • A **washing machine** is a machine for washing clothes, sheets, and other cloth items.

wash FLOW /waʃ, wɔːʃ/ v [I/T] (esp. of water) to flow or to cause to flow, often carrying something along • *Waves washed against the boat.* [I] ○ *Heavy rains always wash the sand down the hill.* [T] • If something is washed away, it is carried off by heavy rain or a flood: *Even trees and cars were washed away in this flood.* [M] • If something washes up or washes ashore, water has moved it there: *That storm washed a lot of crabs up on the shore.* [M]

wash NO CHANGE /waʃ, wɔːʃ/ n [C usually sing] an event or situation in which positive and negative things balance each other • *I sold my car for about what it cost me, so it was a wash.*

□ **wash down** obj, **wash** obj **down** /'-'-/ v adv [M] to clean (something) by causing water to flow over it • *I took the hose and washed down the front porch.* • (infml) If you wash down food, you drink something after eating it: *She* *was eating bread and cheese and washing it down with iced tea.*

□ **wash off** *(obj)*, **wash** *(obj)* **off** /'-'-/ *v adv* [I/M] (of dirt and marks) to be removed by washing • *She could hardly wait to wash the dirt off.* [M] ○ *I don't know if ketchup will wash off.* [I]

□ **wash out** *(obj)* BE REMOVED , **wash** *(obj)* **out** /'-'-/ *v adv* [I/M] (of dirt and marks) to be removed from cloth by washing • *I hope this stain will wash out.* [I]

washed–out /ˈwɑʃˈaʊt, ˈwɔːʃt-/ *adj* • Something that looks washed-out has lost color or looks old as a result of being washed over and over again: *a pair of washed-out jeans* • If you say that someone looks washed-out, they look pale and tired.

□ **wash out** *obj* BE DESTROYED , **wash** *obj* **out** /'-'-/ *v adv* [M] (esp. of bad or violent weather) to cause (something) to fail or be destroyed • *Rain washed tonight's game out.* ○ *The storm washed out roads and bridges.*

washout /ˈwɑʃˈaʊt, ˈwɔːˈʃaʊt/ *n* [C usually sing] *infml* a complete failure • *The dance was a washout—only three people showed up.*

□ **wash up** /-'-/ *v adv* [I] to clean your hands, esp. before a meal • *She told the children to wash up for dinner.*

washed–up /ˈwɑʃtˈʌp, ˈwɔːʃt-/ *adj* [not gradable] *infml* • *Lunch is ready—are you washed up?* • If someone is washed up, they are no longer fit or able to do what they did in the past: *a washed-up comic*

washable /ˈwɑʃ·ə·bəl, ˈwɔːˈʃə-/ *adj* • See at WASH CLEAN.

washer /ˈwɑʃ·ər, ˈwɔːˈʃər/ *n* [C] a flat ring of metal, rubber, or plastic that is used to make a tighter connection between two pieces or parts of something • See also **washer** at WASH CLEAN.

washing /ˈwɑʃ·ɪŋ, ˈwɔːˈʃɪŋ/ *n* [U] • See at WASH CLEAN.

wasn't /ˈwʌz·ənt, ˈwɑz-/ *v contraction of* was not • *I wasn't hungry so I didn't eat.*

wasp /wɑsp, wɔːsp/ *n* [C] a flying insect that is able to sting repeatedly

WASP PERSON /wɑsp, wɔːsp/ *n* [C] *abbreviation for* White Anglo-Saxon Protestant (= a white American who is Protestant and who is thought of as being part of an important social group) • *He wanted entrance into the WASP world of yachts and cocktail parties.*

waste BAD USE /weɪst/ *n* [U] a bad use of something valuable that you have only a limited amount of • *a waste of time/money* ○ *a waste of talent/ability* ○ *I felt like being there was just a waste.*

waste /weɪst/ *v* [T] to use (something) without care or thought • *Why should I waste my time on her?* ○ *You're just wasting your money buying that stuff.* • If you **waste** your **breath**, you are saying something that will be ignored: *Don't waste your breath arguing with him.* • If you **waste no time**, you do something right

away: *Caroline wasted no time in tackling her new responsibilities.* • If you say that something is **wasted on** someone, you mean that they cannot appreciate what you have to offer: *Your excellent wine will be wasted on them.*

wasteful /ˈweɪst·fəl/ *adj* • *wasteful spending* ○ *a wasteful use of resources*

waste UNWANTED MATTER /weɪst/ *n* unwanted matter or material of any type, esp. what is left after use • *hazardous/toxic wastes* [C] ○ *Most people don't recycle kitchen waste.* [U] • Human waste is excrement. [U] • **Waste disposal** is the process or system for getting rid of unwanted material by burying it, burning it, or dropping it in the sea. • A **wastebasket** is a container to hold paper or other small things you want to get rid of.

□ **waste away** /'--'-/ *v adv* [I] (of a person) to gradually get thinner and weaker, esp. from disease or lack of food • *It was hard to watch her waste away.*

wasteland /ˈweɪst·lænd/ *n* [C] a large area of land that has not been developed, usually because it cannot be easily used • *Rain forests are being transformed into barren wasteland.* • A wasteland can also be anything that seems to lack positive qualities: *Television is a vast wasteland.*

watch SMALL CLOCK /wɑtʃ, wɔːtʃ/ *n* [C] a small clock usually worn on a strap around the wrist, or sometimes carried in a pocket • *She looked at her watch and said, "It's a quarter to five."*

watch LOOK AT /wɑtʃ, wɔːtʃ/ *v* to look at (something) for a period of time • *He spent the evening watching an old movie on TV.* [T] ○ *The police were watching to see who left the house.* [+ *to* infinitive] ○ *Do you want me to watch the kids* (= notice what they are doing and care for them) *when you go out?* [T] • LP SEE, LOOK, AND WATCH at SEE USE EYES

watch /wɑtʃ, wɔːtʃ/ *n* [C/U] • *The prison guards kept a close watch on him.* [U] • Watch is also a period during which someone is responsible for guarding or looking around to be sure that property or people are safe, or the person who is responsible: *The soldiers on the night watch had to be careful not to fall asleep.* [C]

watchful /ˈwɑtʃ·fəl, ˈwɔːtʃ-/ *adj* giving careful attention so as to notice what is happening and be prepared for something that might happen • *If you invest heavily in the stock market, you have to stay watchful and be ready to move your money quickly.*

watch BE CAREFUL /wɑtʃ, wɔːtʃ/ *v* [T] to be careful of (something) • *We have to watch our bank account to make sure there's enough money in it to pay our credit card bills.* ○ *I've got to start watching my weight* (= be careful not to become fat). ○ *The sign says "Watch for* (= be careful of) *falling rocks."* • To **watch** your **step** is to be careful about how you behave:

He'll have to watch his step if he wants to keep his job. • Someone might say **watch out** to warn you of danger or an accident that seems likely to happen: *Watch out for that last step— it's a lot steeper than the others.*

▫**watch over** /'-,--/ *v prep* [T] to protect (someone) and make certain that they are safe • *She had to watch over four young children and take care of a sick husband.*

watchdog ORGANIZATION /'wɑtʃ·dɔːg, 'wɔːtʃ-/ *n* [C] a person or organization responsible for making certain that companies or other organizations maintain standards and do not act illegally • *a watchdog agency/organization*

watchdog DOG /'wɑtʃ·dɔːg, 'wɔːtʃ-/ *n* [C] a dog trained to protect a place

water /'wɔːt̬·ər, 'wɑt̬-/ *n* [U] a clear, colorless liquid that falls from the sky as rain and is necessary for animal and plant life • *a drink/ glass of water* ○ *bottled/tap water* ○ *cold/hot water* ○ *I'm boiling water to make some more coffee.* • The water often refers to an area of water, such as the sea or a lake: *The water's much warmer today—are you coming for a swim?* • Waters is an area of natural water, such as a part of the sea: *coastal waters* [pl] • If someone refers to problems that they had in the past as **water under the bridge**, they mean that they do not worry about them because they happened a long time ago and cannot now be changed: *Yes, we did have our disagreements, but that's water under the bridge.* • A **waterbed** is a bed in which the MATTRESS (= the part you lie on) is a container filled with water. • A **waterfall** is water esp. from a river falling over an edge of rock from a high level to a much lower level. • A **water fountain** is a device that maintains a supply of water for drinking. • **Waterfowl** (also **water birds**) are the types of birds that live on or near rivers, lakes, or the sea. • A **waterfront** is a part of a town next to an area of water such as a lake or the sea. • A **water main** is a large underground pipe in a system of pipes supplying water to an area. • **Water polo** is a game played in water in which two teams of swimmers try to get the ball into the other team's goal. • A piece of clothing that is **water-repellent** (also **water-resistant**) tends to keep rain from being absorbed. **Waterskiing** is a sport in which you are pulled along the surface of the water by a boat, while balancing on a pair of SKIS fastened to your feet. • A **water supply** is the water that is provided and treated for a particular area: *When we don't get enough rainfall, we have to worry about our water supply.* • A **waterway** is a regularly used route across water. • A **waterworks** is a system of buildings and pipes in which a public supply of water is stored and treated and from which it is sent out.

water /'wɔːt̬·ər, 'wɑt̬-/ *v* [I/T] to provide water to (a plant or animal) • *I've asked my neighbor*

to water the plants while I'm away. [T] • When your eyes water, they produce tears but not because you are unhappy: *The icy wind made his eyes water.* [I] • If your mouth waters, it produces a lot of SALIVA, usually because you can see or smell food that you would like to eat: *The smell of that bread is making my mouth water.* [I] • If something is **watered down**, it is made weaker: *After complaints from city officials, the governor watered down her opposition to funding mass transit* (= she became less strongly opposed to it).

watery /'wɔːt̬·ə·ri, 'wɑt̬-/ *adj* having a lot of or too much water • *The soup was thin and watery.*

watercolor /'wɔːt̬·ər,kʌl·ər, 'wɑt̬-/ *n* [C] paint that is mixed with water to create pictures, or a picture made with this paint • *The art gallery is having a show of early 20th-century American watercolors.*

watermelon /'wɔːt̬·ər,mel·ən, 'wɑt̬-/ *n* [C/U] a large, round or oval-shaped fruit with dark green skin, sweet, watery, pink or yellow flesh, and a lot of black seeds

waterproof /'wɔːt̬·ər,pruːf, 'wɑt̬-/ *adj* not allowing water to go through • *waterproof boots*

watershed BIG CHANGE /'wɔːt̬·ər,ʃed, 'wɑt̬-/ *n* [U] an event or period that is important because it represents a big change and the start of new developments • *The acceptance of Jackie Robinson as the first African-American major league baseball player was a watershed in the history of race relations in America.*

watershed AREA /'wɔːt̬·ər,ʃed, 'wɑt̬-/ *n* [C] a high area of land where rain collects, some of it flowing down to supply rivers, lakes, etc., at lower levels

watertight /'wɔːt̬·ər,tɑɪt, 'wɑt̬-/ *adj* having no openings to allow the passage of water • *They're doing some repairs on the church to make the roof watertight.*

watery /'wɔːt̬·ə·ri, 'wɑt̬-/ *adj* • See at WATER.

watt /wɑt/ (*abbreviation* **w**) *n* [C] the standard measure of electrical power • *a 60-watt bulb*

wave MOVE /weɪv/ *v* [I/T] to move (the hand or arm), usually in a raised position, as a sign of greeting or a way of getting attention or giving information • *She leaned out the window and waved (good-bye).* [I] ○ *As soon as we showed our papers as journalists, the policeman waved us in* (= moved his hand to allow us to go in). [M] • If you wave something or something waves, you move it from side to side while holding it in the hand, or something else moves it in this way: *He was very excited and rushed into the room waving a piece of paper.* [T] ○ *Flags waved in the breeze.* [I]

wave /weɪv/ *n* [C] • *She looked at him for a long time, and then, with a wave of her hand, she was off.*

wave WATER MOVEMENT /weɪv/ *n* [C] a raised movement of water rolling across the surface esp. of the sea • *We were so close we could hear* *the waves breaking on the beach.* • A wave is also a sudden increase in an activity or in the strength of a condition or feeling: *A wave of emotion swept through her as she visited her home town.*

wave ENERGY FORM /weɪv/ *n* [C] the steady, repeating pattern in which some types of energy, such as sound, light, and heat, are spread or carried • *radio/sound waves* • **Wavelength** is the distance between two waves of energy, or the length of the radio wave used by a particular radio station for broadcasting. • (*fig.*) Wavelength is also someone's particular way of understanding or communicating about things: *We just don't seem to be on the same wavelength—I can't figure him out.*

waver /'weɪ·vər/ *v* [I] to begin to doubt or lose your determination to do something • *He never wavered as the leading voice of African-Americans' call for freedom and equality.* • If you waver between two possibilities, you have difficulty deciding between them: *She wavered between believing him and thinking that he was lying.*

wavy /'weɪ·vi/ *adj* curving in shape, or having a series of curves • *Jasmine's got wavy blond hair.*

wax SUBSTANCE /wæks/ *n* [U] a solid, fatty substance that softens and melts at a low temperature • *Candle wax dripped on the tablecloth.* • **Wax paper** (also **waxed paper**) is a type of paper that has a thin layer of wax on it and is used for wrapping food.

wax /wæks/ *v* [T] to put a thin layer of wax on the surface of (something) • *I just waxed the floor, so don't go in there yet.*

waxy /'wæk·si/ *adj* having the appearance of or feeling like wax • *He had a waxy complexion and looked ill.*

wax APPEAR LARGER /wæks/ *v* [I] (of the moon) to gradually appear larger and increasingly round • (*fig.*) *Such controversies have waxed and waned* (= become stronger and weaker) *but continue to this day.*

wax BECOME /wæks/ *v* [L] *fml* to become • *Brad waxed eloquent on the subject of free enterprise.*

way ROUTE /weɪ/ *n* [C] a route or path to follow in order to get to a place • *Do you know the way to the train station?* • If you don't know your way, can't find your way, or have lost your way, you are not sure or do not know how to get where you want to go: *I don't really know my way around town yet.* • Way also means street: *Our office is at 17 Harbor Way.* • Way can mean the direction, position, or order of something: *The numbers should be the other way around—71, not 17.* • Someone's way is also the progress of their life: *After Frank's death, June seemed to lose her way and had trouble working.* ○ *He made his way through the sales department to head of sales.* • If you say **by the way**, you are introducing a statement or subject that may not be directly on the subject being discussed: *By the way, I heard that Phyllis may be moving to Dallas.* • If someone or something is **in the way**, it prevents something from happening or someone from moving: *Work often gets in the way of my social life.* ○ *It's a small street, and he parked right in the way.* • If someone or something is **on** its **way**, it will happen or arrive soon: *They have three kids, and another on the way.* ○ *My school is well on its way to a championship.* ○ *We're on our way from Logan, and should be there soon.* • **On** your **way** also means leaving: *Give me a kiss and I'll be on my way.*

way DISTANCE /weɪ/, **ways** /weɪz/ *n* [U] distance, or a period of time • *We walked just a short way before he got tired.* ○ *When Mom called us for supper, we were still a ways from being finished.*

way MANNER /weɪ/ *n* [C] a particular manner, characteristic, or fashion • *I like the way your hair is fixed.* ○ *Jack and Beth feel the same way about animals.* ○ *There is no way I can leave her.* ○ *They don't write songs the way they used to.* • Your way is also the ability to do things in the manner you want: *My little sister gets furious if she doesn't get her way.* • **In a way** (= To some degree), *I hope he doesn't win.* • **The way things are/stand** means the situation as it is now: *The way things stand, I cannot continue to work.* • A person's **way of life** is how they live: *Sleeping in hotels three or four nights a week is not an ideal way of life.*

way FAR /weɪ/ *adv* [always + adv/prep; not gradable] *infml* (used for emphasis) far or long • *That skirt's way too much money.* ○ *Come on now, Alexander, it's way past your bedtime.* • (*slang*) Way can also mean very: *That car is way cool!*

wayward /'weɪ·wərd/ *adj* not behaving or moving as expected • *He was a wayward kid.* ○ *A wayward ball bounced into the yard.*

we PEOPLE /wiː, wɪ/ *pronoun* [pl] the person speaking and one or more others • *If you don't hurry up we won't be on time.* • We can be used by a speaker or a writer to refer to the listener or reader and the person speaking or writing: *We have to get started now if we're going to finish this afternoon.* • We can also mean you: *Now everyone, we don't want to be late, do we?*

we ALL PEOPLE /wiː, wɪ/ *pronoun* [pl] all people; everyone • *We live on planet earth.*

weak NOT STRONG /wiːk/ *adj* [-er/-est only] lacking strength or energy, or likely to stop working or break • *After having been so sick, it's not surprising you still feel weak.* ○ *That old chair is very weak and needs gluing.* • A drink that is weak lacks flavor: *The coffee was weak and tasteless.* • A **weak link** is the part of something that is most likely to break: *This year, the team's only weak link is that third baseman.*

weaken /'wiː·kən/ v [I/T] • *The country's economy continues to weaken.* [I] ∘ *Long exposure to vibration can weaken aircraft parts.* [T]

weakly /'wiː·kli/ adv • *"I'm feeling a little better now," he said weakly.*

weakness /'wiːk·nəs/ n [C/U] • *The building's collapse was caused by weakness in several beams.* [U] • Weakness is also a fault in someone's character: *Is crying always a sign of weakness?* [U] • A weakness is also a strong liking for something: *She admitted to a weakness for desserts.* [C]

weak BELOW STANDARD /wiːk/ adj [-er/-est only] below standard; not good enough • *He was always weak in languages but strong in science.*

weakling /'wiː·klɪŋ/ n [C] someone who is weak, either physically or in character • *Exercise can turn a weakling into a big, tough guy.*

wealth MONEY /welθ/ n [U] a large amount of money and other valuable possessions • *His wealth is so great that money doesn't mean much to him.*

wealthy /'wel·θi/ adj • *Natural resources and a well-trained workforce make a country wealthy.*

wealth LARGE AMOUNT /welθ/ n [U] a large amount • *Jim has a wealth of teaching experience.*

wean /wiːn/ v [T] to cause (a baby or young animal) to stop feeding on its mother's milk and to eat other foods • *She started to wean her baby at six months.*

weapon /'wep·ən/ n [C] an object used in fighting or war, such as a gun or a bomb, or something used against someone • *A knife like that was the murder weapon.* ∘ *Even laughter can be used as a weapon.*

wear COVER THE BODY /wer, wær/ v [T] *past simple* **wore** /wɔːr, woʊr/, *past part* **worn** /wɔːrn, woʊrn/ to have (clothing or jewelry) on your body • *He wears glasses for reading.* ∘ (*fig.*) *The prisoner wore a confident smile throughout the trial.* • To wear your hair in a particular style is to have it arranged in a certain way: *She wears her hair in a ponytail.* • In a relationship, the person who **wears the pants** is the person who makes decisions for both people: *Lisa certainly wears the pants in that family.*

–wear /wer, wær/ *combining form* clothes designed for a particular use or of a particular type • *She designed sportswear and very elegant evening wear.*

wear WEAKEN /wer, wær/ v [I/T] *past simple* **wore** /wɔːr, woʊr/, *past part* **worn** /wɔːrn, woʊrn/ to make (something) become weaker, damaged, or thinner because of continuous use • *My favorite shirt wore at the collar.* [I] ∘ *I wore a hole in my favorite sweater.* [T] ∘ *Wind and water slowly wore away the mountain's jagged peak, making it round.* [M] • If you **wear** something **out**, you use it until it is no longer useful or you destroy it: *I wore out my old boots walking through the mountains last summer.* ∘ *Moving parts in a machine finally wear out.* • If something **wears** someone **out**, it makes them very tired: *Taking care of the kids wears me out.*

wear /wer, wær/ n [U] • *I've gotten a lot of wear out of this coat.* • **Wear and tear** means the damage that comes from ordinary use: *A shovel must be able to take a lot of wear and tear.*

wearisome /'wɪr·iː·səm/ adj [not gradable] causing a person to be tired; boring • *A long project becomes wearisome and loses its excitement for me.*

weary /'wɪr·i/ adj very tired, esp. from hard work • *Even my brain is weary tonight!*

wearily /'wɪr·ə·li/ adv • *I dragged myself wearily out of bed.*

weariness /'wɪr·iː·nəs/ n [U] • *My weariness was so great, I couldn't even answer the telephone.*

weasel /'wiː·zəl/ n [C] a small mammal with reddish brown fur and a long body, which feeds on small animals such as mice and birds

weasel out /'wiː·zəl'aʊt/ v adv [I] *infml* to escape responsibility for something • *My roommate always tries to weasel out of doing the dishes.* [I]

weather AIR CONDITIONS /'weð·ər/ n [U] the conditions in the air at a particular time, such as wind, rain, or temperature • *I always wear gloves in cold weather.* ∘ *Expect some nasty weather tomorrow, possibly even a thunderstorm.* • If something is **weather-beaten**, it has not been protected from sun, wind, or rain and has been marked or damaged by them: *The fisherman had a weather-beaten face.* • A **weather forecaster** (also **weatherperson**; *male* **weatherman**) on a television or radio program is someone who reports what the weather will be like for the next few days.

weather /'weð·ər/ v [I/T] to change in color or form over a period of time because of the effects of sun, wind, rain, or other conditions in the air • *The yellow paint will weather to a grayish white.* [I]

weathered /'weð·ərd/ adj • *The wall was made from rounded, weathered stones.*

weather LIVE THROUGH /'weð·ər/ v [T] to live through (a difficult situation or a problem) • *At 34, she's weathered a lot—broken marriage, nervous breakdown, and no money.* • If someone or something **weathers the storm**, they continue what they are doing despite serious problems: *Will the ambassador be able to weather the storm caused by his remarks?*

weave MAKE CLOTH /wiːv/ v [I/T] *past simple* **wove** /woʊv/ or **weaved**, *past part* **woven** /'woʊ·vən/ or **weaved** to make cloth by repeatedly passing a single thread in and out through long threads on a LOOM (= special frame) • *How long does it take to weave three yards of cloth?* [T] • You can also weave dried grass, leaves, and thin branches into hats, containers, and other items.

weave /wiːv/ n [C] the way in which cloth has been woven • *The blanket has a loose weave.*

weave MOVE /wiːv/ v [always + adv/prep] *past* **weaved** to frequently change direction while moving forward, esp. to avoid things that could stop you • *The taxi weaved through traffic to get us to the airport.* [I]

web NET /web/ n [C] *short form of* COBWEB • *A spider's web hung in a corner of the window.* • See also COBWEB.

web SKIN /web/ n [C] the skin connecting the toes of some water birds and animals which helps them to swim

webbed /webd/ adj • *Ducks, gulls, and frogs all have webbed toes.*

Web COMPUTER /web/ n [U] *short form of* World Wide Web, see at WORLD THE EARTH • *Can you log onto the Web?* • A **website** is a screen or series of screens that give information about someone or something to anyone who can use the INTERNET.

wed MARRY /wed/ v [I/T] *past* **wedded** or **wed** to marry (someone) • *They are planning to wed in June.* [I]

wedded /'wed·əd/ adj [not gradable] • *a wedded couple* • If someone is **wedded to** something, they strongly believe in it or it is an important part of them: *He's really wedded to the notion of an all-in-one computer system.* ○ *San Diego's economy is wedded to the military.*

wedding /'wed·ɪŋ/ n [C] • *Rosie's wedding is in July.* ○ *She had an elegant wedding dress.*

Wed. DAY OF THE WEEK n *abbreviation for* WEDNESDAY

we'd /wiːd/ *contraction of* we had or we would • *By then, we'd heard the same story six times.*

wedge /wedʒ/ n [C] a piece of wood, metal, or other material with a pointed edge at one end and a wide edge at the other, used to keep two things apart or, when forced between two things, to break them apart • *A wedge under the door kept it open.*

wedge /wedʒ/ v [T] • *He wedged the window open with a screwdriver.*

wedlock /'wed·lɑk/ n [U] the state of being married • If a child is born out of wedlock, the parents are not married to each other.

Wednesday /'wenz·di, -deɪ/ (*abbreviation* **Wed.**) n [C/U] the day of the week after Tuesday and before Thursday

weed /wiːd/ n [C] any wild plant that grows in a garden or field where it is not wanted • *My garden is overrun with weeds.* • (*dated slang*) Weed also means MARIJUANA.

weed /wiːd/ v [I/T] to remove wild, unwanted plants • *I weeded all afternoon.* [I]

▫**weed out** *obj*, **weed** *obj* **out** /'-'-/ v *adv* [M] to get rid of (someone or something not wanted) • *The administration plans to weed out failed programs.*

week /wiːk/ n [C] a period of seven days, either from the beginning of Sunday to the end of Saturday or from the beginning of Monday to the end of Sunday • *next/last week* ○ *We go to the movies about once a week.* • A week (also **work week**) can also be Monday through Friday or the days or hours a person spends working during a week: *Many offices operate on a thirty-five hour week.* • **A week from** a particular day means one week following that day: *The first performance of the play is a week from tomorrow.* • **A week ago (this)** day means one week before this particular day: *The problem with the TV started a week ago Monday.* • **Week after week** and **week in, week out** both mean for many weeks, for a long time, or usually: *I get up very early, week in, week out.* • A **weekday** is any day of the week except Saturday or Sunday: *The bank is open from 9 a.m. to 4 p.m. on weekdays.* • The **weekend** is Saturday and Sunday, when most people do not work: *Do you have anything planned for the weekend?* • A **weeknight** is the night of any day of the week except Saturday and Sunday.

weekly /'wiː·kli/ adj, adv [not gradable] happening or appearing every week • *a weekly magazine* ○ *We go to the city weekly.*

weekly /'wiː·kli/ n [C] • *I subscribe to several weeklies* (= magazines or newspapers that are published once a week).

weep /wiːp/ v [I/T] *past* **wept** /wept/ to cry (tears) • *At the king's funeral, there were dramatic scenes of thousands of people weeping.* [I]

weigh SHOW WEIGHT /weɪ/ v to be pulled toward the earth with (a particular force that can be measured), or to measure this force in an object; to show (an amount of weight) • *The baby weighed six pounds, ten ounces at birth.* [L] ○ *This table weighs a lot.* [L] ○ *She weighs herself every morning.* [T] • *This suitcase weighs a ton* (= is very heavy). • To **weigh down** someone is to cause difficulty for them by giving them a lot of heavy things to carry: *She checked her bags because she didn't want to be weighed down.* ○ (*fig.*) *She was weighed down* (= made anxious and tired) *by the pains and aches of old age.*

weight /weɪt/ n [C/U] a quality of an object that is a measure of the force by which the earth attracts it, or an object considered as having this quality • *The maximum weight the bridge can support is 15 tons.* [U] ○ *You've lost some weight since the last time I saw you.* [U] ○ *I don't want to put on weight* (= become heavier). [U] ○ *When lifting a heavy weight, keep your back straight and bend your knees.* [C] • A weight is also a piece of metal whose force toward earth has been measured, and by which you can measure other objects: *a one-pound weight* [C] • A weight is also sports equipment, esp. a piece of metal attached to each end of a bar or to a special machine which you move or lift to strengthen your muscles: *He lifts weights.* [C] • If something is a **weight off** your **mind**, a worry that you had about something is now gone, and you can relax: *It was a weight off my mind, knowing she arrived home safe.* • **Weightlifting** is the activity of lifting bars with round pieces of metal attached to each end in order to strengthen the muscles, either for exercise or in a competition. A **weightlifter** is someone who competes in weightlifting.

weightless /'weɪt·ləs/ *adj* being in a state in which GRAVITY (= the force by which the earth attracts objects) does not cause movement of objects • *The astronauts are weightless in space.*

weightlessness /'weɪt·lə·snəs/ *n* [U]

weigh INFLUENCE /weɪ/ *v* [I always + adv/prep] to have an influence • *The factor that weighed most heavily in her favor was her record of success as a lawyer.*

weight /weɪt/ *n* [U] • *Her word carried weight with her neighbors.*

weighty /'weɪt̬·i/ *adj* important and serious • *They discussed weighty topics like arms control, the Middle East, and the federal budget deficit.*

weigh CONSIDER /weɪ/ *v* [T] to consider (something) carefully, esp. by comparing facts or possibilities in order to make a decision • *The judge told the jury to weigh the facts and the evidence.* ○ *You have to weigh the advantage of early graduation against the disadvantage of being younger than everyone else.*

□ **weigh in** GIVE OPINION /'-'-/ *v adv* [I] to give an opinion or enter a discussion or argument • *When our readers feel the paper has gone too far in one direction, they're not afraid to weigh in.* ○ *The senator weighed in with a blistering attack on welfare cheats.*

□ **weigh in** MEASURE /'-'-/ *v adv* [I] to measure someone's weight, esp. before a competition • *The boxers both weighed in at 162 pounds.*

□ **weigh on** /'-,-/ *v prep* [T] to make (someone) feel anxious or worried • *Problems at work are weighing on him.*

weird /wɪrd/ *adj* [-er/-est only] strangely different from anything natural or ordinary • *She is a little weird in the way she dresses, I have to admit.*

weirdo /'wɪrd·oʊ/ *n* [C] *pl* **weirdos** *slang* a person who you think is strange and who makes you uncomfortable • *That guy is a real weirdo.*

welcome MEET /'wel·kəm/ *v* [T] to meet or speak to (someone) in a friendly way when they come to the place where you are • *We went next door to welcome our new neighbors.* ○ *The prime minister of Canada welcomed the president warmly.*

welcome /'wel·kəm/ *exclamation* • *Welcome! Come on in.* ○ *Welcome home!* • LP GREETINGS

welcome /'wel·kəm/ *n* [C] • *We were given a warm welcome.*

welcome /'wel·kəm/ *adj* • If you tell someone they are welcome, you are telling them that you will be happy to have them visit you: *You'll always be welcome here.*

welcome SUPPORT /'wel·kəm/ *v* [T] to be pleased about or support (something) • *Baseball fans welcomed the end of the players' strike.* ○ *She welcomed the opportunity to explain herself.*

welcome /'wel·kəm/ *adj* • *The cool weather was a welcome change.* ○ *You're welcome to the pie* (= you can have it). • "You're welcome" is a polite answer when someone thanks you: *"Thanks for taking care of our cat." "You're welcome."*

weld /weld/ *v* [I/T] to join (pieces of metal) together permanently by melting the parts that touch, or to join (one piece of metal) to another in this way • *Iron spikes were welded to the railing around the embassy.* [T]

weld /weld/ *n* [C] • *A weld on the base of the chair had broken.*

welder /'wel·dər/ *n* [C] • *He works as a welder.*

welfare HEALTH AND HAPPINESS /'wel·fer, -fær/ *n* [U] physical and mental health and happiness • *We were concerned for our parents' welfare when we heard about the storm in Florida.*

welfare HELP /'wel·fer, -fær/ *n* [U] help given, esp. money, by a government to people who are poor and who do not have jobs • *welfare benefits* ○ *The family had to go on welfare.* • A **welfare state** is a nation that pays for the health care, unemployment pay, and other social benefits for its citizens.

well HEALTHY /wel/ *adj* **better**, **best** healthy • *I don't feel well.* ○ *I feel better now.*

wellness /'wel·nəs/ *n* [U] the condition of being healthy • *The book promotes wellness through diet and exercise.*

well EXCLAMATION /wel, wəl/ *exclamation* used to introduce something you are about to say, or to connect one statement with the next, or to show doubt or disagreement, annoyance, surprise, or understanding • *Well, what happened next?* ○ *He started yelling at me, and well, I was scared at first.* ○ *Well, what are you going to do now that you've lost your job?* ○ *Oh well, there's not much we can do about it now.*

well IN A GOOD WAY /wel/ *adv* **better** /'bet̬·ər/, **best** /best/ in a good way; to a high or satisfactory standard • *The car was well designed.* ○ *She manages people very well.* ○ *I can't sing as well as Jessica* (= She sings better). ○ *His point about reducing waste is well taken* (= accepted as a fair criticism). ○ *The two hours of discussion was time well spent* (= it was a useful discussion). ○ *I want to congratulate you on a job well done.* • You say **well done** to praise someone: *"I passed the test for my driver's license." "Well done!"* See also **well-done** at

WELL [TO A GREAT DEGREE]. • If someone is **well-advised**, they are showing good judgment: *You would be well-advised to reserve a room in advance.* • **Well-balanced** means containing a good range of foods that a person needs in order to stay healthy: *a well-balanced diet* • If someone is described as **well-behaved**, they are behaving or usually behave in a way that is considered correct: *a well-behaved boy* • **Well-being** is the state of feeling healthy and happy: *Seeing her grandchildren gave her a sense of well-being.* • *He was tall and* **well-built** (= had an attractive, strong body). • If a person is **well-dressed**, they are wearing or usually wear attractive and stylish clothes. • A person who is **well-educated** has had a good education. • *Her fears were* **well-founded** (= based on facts). • *He was* **well-groomed** (= had a neat, clean appearance). • *Marilyn is* **well-informed** (= has a lot of knowledge) *about the stock market.* • If someone is **well-mannered**, they are behaving or usually behave in a pleasant and polite way: *The other visitors were so well-mannered to complain, but I said the service was terrible.* • *The offer was* **well-meant** (= meant to help). • Someone who is **well-thought-of** is considered by most other people to be a good person or is admired for their ability: *He was well thought of as a foreign-policy expert.* • Something that is **well-timed** happens or is made to happen at a particularly suitable time: *Her appearance was well-timed to coincide with the arrival of the president.* • A **well-wisher** is a person who encourages or supports you: *Hundreds of well-wishers surrounded the team.*

well [TO A GREAT DEGREE] /wel/ *adv* **better** /'beṭ·ər/, **best** /best/ to a great degree; much or completely • *I know her well.* ○ *Put in two eggs and stir well.* ○ *He sent away for tickets well in advance* (= very early). ○ *I knew perfectly well what time it was.* ○ *I knew her pretty well when I lived in Iowa City.* • Well is used with some prepositions and adverbs for emphasis: *Keep the children well away from the edge of the pool.* ○ *It costs well over $100.* • Well is used with a few adjectives for emphasis: *The museum is well worth a visit.* • If someone is **well-heeled**, they are rich. • Meat that is **well-done** is cooked all the way through: *a well-done steak* See also **well done** at WELL [IN A GOOD WAY]. • *His decision to resign was a* **well-kept** *secret* (= was kept hidden from everyone). • Someone or something **well-known** is known or recognized by many people: *The book is by a well-known historian.* • *Myers is generally* **well-liked** (= liked by many people). • *Once you get behind, it is* **well-nigh** (= almost) *impossible to catch up.* • *She is quite* **well-off** (= wealthy). • *She was extremely* **well-read** (= had read many books). • Someone who is **well-rounded** has had experience or has knowledge in a number of different ar-

eas, not just a few. • *He was* **well-versed** *in* (= knew a lot about) *the history of slavery.*

well [REASONABLY] /wel/ *adv* [not gradable] with good reason • *I couldn't very well say no.*

well [HOLE] /wel/ *n* [C] a deep hole in the ground from which water, oil, or gas can be obtained • *an oil well* ○ *well water*

well [COME TO SURFACE] /wel/ *v* [I] (of a liquid) to come to the surface or into view • *As she read the letter, tears welled in her eyes.* ○ *(fig.) He could feel the anger well up inside him.*

we'll /wiːl, wɪl/ *contraction of* **we shall** or **we will** • *We'll be there tomorrow.*

wellness /'wel·nəs/ *n* • See at WELL [HEALTHY].

well–to–do /ˌwel·tə'duː/ *adj* showing signs of being successful; rich • *It was a well-to-do neighborhood of large, single-family homes with big backyards.*

welt /welt/ *n* [C] a raised, red area of skin usually caused by being hit

welter /'wel·tər/ *n* [U] a large number of things in a confusing or disorderly condition • *The report was issued amid a welter of conflicting evidence.*

went /went/ *past simple of* GO

wept /wept/ *past simple and past participle of* WEEP

were /wɜr, wər/ *past simple of* BE

we're /wɪr, wər, wiːr/ *contraction of* **we are** • *We're ready now.*

weren't /wɜrnt, wərnt/ *contraction of* **were not** • *They weren't outside.*

werewolf /'wɪr·wʊlf, 'wer-, 'wɜr-/ *n* [C] *pl* **werewolves** /'wɪr·wʊlvz, 'wer-, 'wɜr-/ an imaginary creature in stories that is a person who changes into a WOLF (= wild animal) when the moon is a complete circle

west /west/ (*abbreviation* **W.**) *n* [U] the direction where the sun goes down in the evening that is opposite east, or the part of an area or country which is in this direction • *The points of the compass are north, south, east, and west.* ○ *The sun sets in the west.* • In the US, **the West** is the part of the country west of the Mississippi River. • **The West** is also North America and the countries in the western part of Europe.

west /west/ (*abbreviation* **W.**) *adj, adv* [not gradable] • *the west coast* ○ *The town is west of here.* • In the US, the **west coast** is the part of the country near the Pacific Ocean.

westerly /'wes·tər·li/ *adj* toward or near the west • *a westerly wind*

western /'wes·tərn/ (*abbreviation* **W.**) *adj* [not gradable] • *Grand Rapids is in the western part of Michigan.*

western /'wes·tərn/ *n* [C] a movie based on stories about life in the part of the US west of the Mississippi River when white people began going there to live in the 19th century

westerner /'wes·tər·nər, -tə·nər/ *n* [C] a person from the western part of a country, or (in the US) a person from the part of the country west of the Mississippi River

westward /'wes·twərd/ *adj* [not gradable] toward the west • *a westward route*

westward /'wes·twərd/, **westwards** /'wes·twərdz/ *adv* [not gradable] toward the west • *The clouds drifted westward.*

wet /wet/ *adj* [-*er*/-*est* only] **-tt-** with liquid in, on, or around (something); not dry • *I stepped in a puddle of water and got my shoes wet.* • If paint, ink, etc., is wet, it has not had time to dry. • Wet weather is weather with rain.

wet /wet/ *v* [T] **wetting**, *past* **wet** or **wetted** • *Wet a sponge and wipe off the table.* • If esp. a child wets something, they cause it to become wet by urinating: *He still sometimes wets his bed.*

wetness /'wet·nəs/ *n* [U] • *A lot of the wetness will evaporate before the rain reaches the plant's roots.*

wetback /'wet·bæk/ *n* [C] *taboo slang* a Mexican worker who illegally crosses the border to get work in the US • USAGE: This is an offensive word.

wetlands /'wet·ləndz, -lændz/, **wetland** /'wet·lənd, -lænd/ *pl n* an area of land that is naturally wet • *Thousands of acres of wetlands are destroyed every year by development.* [U]

we've /wiːv/ *contraction of* we have

whack /hwæk, wæk/ *v* [T] to give (someone or something) a hard, noisy hit • *He whacked his dog with the rolled-up newspaper.*

whack /hwæk, wæk/ *n* [C] • *She gave him a whack on the behind.*

whale /hweɪl, weɪl/ *n* [C] a very large sea mammal • **A whale of a** means a great amount of (something) or a very good (thing): *Perry's done a whale of a job for us.* ○ *A whale of a lot of other people were there, too.*

wham /hwæm, wæm/ *exclamation infml* used to suggest the sound of a sudden hit, or to signal that something sudden and unexpected happened • *All of a sudden, wham, I couldn't leave my house, except to go to school.*

wharf /hwɔːrf, wɔːrf/ *n* [C] *pl* **wharves** /hwɔːrvz, wɔːrvz/ *or also* **wharfs** a raised, level structure built beside the edge of the sea or a river, where ships can be tied and goods unloaded

what QUESTION /hwʌt, wʌt, hwɑt, wɑt, hwət, wət/ *adj* [not gradable], *pronoun, exclamation* used to introduce general questions • *What did the teacher say?* ○ *What is the capital of Nevada?* • As an adjective, what can refer to people or things: *What time is it?* ○ *I don't know what children she was talking about.* • What may be used to show that you did not hear something and to ask that it be repeated: *"Humphrey Jones called." "What (was that)?" "I said Humphrey Jones called."* • **What about** asks for your opinion: *What about Laurie—should we invite her?* • (*infml*) **What do you say** (= I suggest that) *we sell the car?* •

What for questions the purpose of or need for an action or plan: *"We really need a bigger car." "What for? The one we have seems big enough to me."* • **What if** asks about the result of something that might happen: *What if our plane is delayed and we can't make the connection?* • People say **what on earth** to show they are very surprised: *What on earth is going on in there?* • (*infml*) If you ask **what's eating** someone, you are asking what is making them anxious or annoyed: *What's eating Bobby? He hasn't said anything all night.* • Someone might say **what the devil/heck/hell** to show they are angry or surprised: *What the hell are you doing to my car?* • People ask **what's the matter** to find out if there is a problem: *You look worried—what's the matter?* • (*infml*) **What's up** means how are you or tell me about your activities: *"Hi, Chuck, what's up?" "Nothing much."* • LP DETERMINERS

what THAT WHICH /hwʌt, wʌt, hwɑt, wɑt, hwət, wət/ *pronoun* the thing which; that which • *I really didn't know what to say.* ○ *What annoyed me was her attitude.* ○ *I hope you like the sweater—it's what you asked for.* • *I've never been able to understand* **what makes** *him* **tick** (= why he acts as he does). • **What's more** means the next thing is more important: *The decorations were beautiful and, what's more, the kids made them themselves.* • If you say **what** someone **says goes**, you mean that they must be obeyed: *I don't agree with the boss either, but what he says goes.*

what OPINION /hwʌt, wʌt, hwɑt, wɑt, hwət, wət/ *pronoun* used to introduce your opinion • *"She can't come." "What a pity* (= I am sorry to hear that)*!"*

whatchamacallit /'hwʌtʃ·ə·mə,kɔː·lət, 'wʌtʃ-, 'hwɑtʃ-, 'wɑtʃ-/ *n* [C] (used when you cannot remember or do not know the name of something) an object • *My whatchamacallit is broken—the thing that controls the oven temperature.*

whatever SOMETHING UNKNOWN /hwʌt'ev·ər, wʌt-, hwɑt-, wɑt-/ *pronoun* something whose particular nature or type you do not know • *Whatever happens, you'll be all right.* ○ *You seem to criticize me whatever I do.*

whatever ANYTHING /hwʌt'ev·ər, wʌt-, hwɑt-, wɑt-/ *pronoun* anything or everything • *Give him whatever he wants.* • If you say **whatever** someone **says goes**, you mean that they must be obeyed: *Whatever Mom says goes.* • LP DETERMINERS

whatever NOT IMPORTANT WHAT /hwʌt'ev·ər, wʌt-, hwɑt-, wɑt-/ *adv* [not gradable] used to say that something is not important or makes no difference • *"Can I dress casually or do I have to dress up?" "Whatever."*

whatsoever /,hwʌt·soʊ'ev·ər, ,wʌt-, ,hwɑt-, ,wɑt-/, **whatever** *adv* [not gradable] used after a negative phrase to add emphasis to the idea that is being expressed • *He has no respect for authority whatsoever.*

wheat /hwi:t, wi:t/ *n* [U] a plant whose yellow-brown grain is used for making flour, or the grain itself

wheedle /'hwi:d·əl, 'wi:d-/ *v* [I/T] to try to persuade (someone) to do something or to give you (something) by using your charm and by repeatedly asking in a way that would make refusal embarrassing • *He wasn't going to tell me but I wheedled it out of him.* [T always + adv/prep]

wheel ROUND OBJECT /hwi:l, wi:l/ *n* [C] a circular object, connected at the center to a bar, that is used for making vehicles or parts of machines move • *the wheel of a bicycle* • The wheel refers to a **steering wheel** (= wheel in a vehicle that you turn to make the vehicle go left or right): *I never feel safe with Richard behind the wheel* (= driving). ○ *Would you mind taking the wheel* (= driving) *for a couple of hours?* • PIC BICYCLE

wheel /hwi:l, wi:l/ *v* [T always + adv/prep] to push or pull (an object with wheels under it) • *She was wheeling a stroller in the park.*

wheel CHANGE DIRECTION /hwi:l, wi:l/ *v* [I always + adv/prep] to turn around quickly • *She wheeled around and slapped his face.* • **Wheeling and dealing** is the attempt to make a deal or get an advantage by using complicated and sometimes dishonest or unfair methods.

wheelbarrow /'hwi:l,bær·oʊ, 'wi:l-/ *n* [C] a movable container with a wheel at the front and two handles at the back, used esp. for moving building materials and in gardening

wheelchair /'hwi:l·tʃer, 'wi:l-, -tʃær/ *n* [C] a chair on wheels that people who are unable to walk use for moving around

wheelchair

wheeze /hwi:z, wi:z/ *v* [I] to make a noise while breathing because of some breathing difficulty • *Since I stopped smoking, I no longer wheeze when I run for a train.*

when AT WHAT TIME /hwen, wen, hwən, wən/ *adv* [not gradable], *conjunction* at what time; at the time at which • *When is supper going to be ready?* ○ *When did the American Civil War begin?* ○ *I was just getting into the shower when the phone rang.*

when CONSIDERING THAT /hwen, wen, hwən, wən/ *conjunction* considering the fact that • *I can't really call myself a vegetarian when I eat fish.*

when ALTHOUGH /hwen, wen, hwən, wən/ *conjunction* despite the fact that • *He says he hasn't got any money when the truth is he's got plenty.*

whenever EVERY TIME /hwen'ev·ər, wen-, hwən-, wən-/ *adv* [not gradable], *conjunction* every or any time • *I'm embarrassed whenever I think about it.* ○ *I try to let the kids out to play whenever possible.*

whenever NOT IMPORTANT WHEN /hwen'ev·ər, wen-, hwən-, wən-/ *adv* [not gradable] used to say that the time something is done is not important or makes no difference • *"Will it be okay if we meet tomorrow instead of today?" "Sure, whenever."*

where /hwer, wer, hwær, wær/ *adv* [not gradable], *conjunction* to, at, or in what place • *Where did she got to college?* ○ *I forget where I put the car keys.* ○ *I read it somewhere—I don't know where* (= the exact place). • Where can be used to mean at what stage: *You reach a point where you just want to get the thing finished.* • **Where** someone is **coming from** means the feelings someone has that cause them to have a particular opinion: *I don't agree with you entirely, but I understand where you're coming from.* • If you do not know **where to turn**, you do not know what to do or how to find help: *She had no money and didn't know where to turn for help.*

whereabouts /'hwer·ə,baʊts, 'wer-, 'hwær-, 'wær-/ *pl n* the place where a person or thing is • *Moreno's whereabouts are unknown, but some people think he is in Panama.*

whereabouts /'hwer·ə,baʊts, 'wer-, 'hwær-, 'wær-/ *adv* [not gradable] in what place; where • *Whereabouts is your office?*

whereas /hwer'æz, wer-, hwær-, wær-/ *conjunction* compared with the fact that; but • *Girls were more likely than boys to want a home computer, whereas boys were more likely to have a home computer that they rarely used.*

whereby /hwer'baɪ, wer-, hwær-, wær-/ *conjunction* by which way or method • *They've set up a plan whereby you can spread the cost over several months.*

wherein /hwer'ɪn, wer-, hwær-, wær-/ *conjunction* in which, or in which part • *The industry will have a situation wherein many companies will be unable to afford to stay in business.*

whereupon /'hwer·ə,pan, 'wer-, 'hwær-, 'wær-, -ə,pɔːn/ *conjunction* immediately after which • *We went home for coffee, whereupon Viv became violently ill.*

wherever /hwer'ev·ər, wer-, hwær-, wær-/ *adv* [not gradable], *conjunction* to or in any or every place • *We can go wherever you like.* • Wherever can also mean in all types of situations *We try to save money wherever possible,* *for instance by using coupons when we buy groceries.*

wherewithal /ˈhwer·wɪˌðɔːl, ˈwer-, ˈhwær-, ˈwær-, -ˌθɔːl/ *n* [U] the money necessary for a particular purpose • *Most people don't have the wherewithal to hire the best lawyers.*

whet /hwet, wet/ *v* **-tt-** • If something **whets** your **appetite**, it makes you hungry or increases your interest in and desire for something: *I read a short story he wrote, and it whetted my appetite for more.*

whether /ˈhweð·ər, ˈweð-/ *conjunction* (used to refer to one or more possibilities or to express uncertainty) if • *I didn't know whether he was too busy or (whether) he just didn't want to see me.* ○ *I wasn't sure whether (or not) you'd like it.* • **Whether or not** can also be used to introduce a statement and means that it is not important which of two possibilities is true: *Whether or not you like it/Whether you like it or not, I'm going out tonight.*

whew, phew /hjuː, fjuː/ *exclamation* an expression that shows you are surprised, tired, or RELIEVED (= happy that something worrying you is not going to happen)

which QUESTION /hwɪtʃ, wɪtʃ/ *adj* [not gradable], *pronoun* (used in questions and statements having a limited number of possibilities) what one or ones • *Which train do you want to take—the one in the morning or the one in the afternoon?* ○ *She had trouble deciding which of her dresses to wear to the party.* ○ *She speaks Spanish or Portuguese, but I've forgotten which.* • *The twins look so much alike I'm surprised anyone can tell* **which is which** (= can recognize each one separately). • *When both her parents died, she didn't know* **which way to turn** (= what to do or whom to ask for help). • LP DETERMINERS

which USED TO REFER /hwɪtʃ, wɪtʃ/ *pronoun* used to show what particular thing (not usually people) is being referred to • *It was a subject which he had never thought much about.* ○ *The club to which he belonged had just become too expensive.*

which ADDS INFORMATION /hwɪtʃ, wɪtʃ/ *pronoun* used to add extra information about something mentioned earlier, in writing following a comma • *She said it would be done by March, which I doubt.* ○ *The training, for which you will be paid, takes four weeks.*

whichever /hwɪtʃˈev·ər, wɪtʃ-/ *adj* [not gradable], *pronoun* used to say that among various possibilities, there is no important difference or that you are free to choose the one you like • *We can go either Thursday or Friday, whichever is best for you.* ○ *Taxpayers could take their choice between the standard deduction and itemizing, and use whichever produced a better result.* ○ *It's going to be expensive whichever way you do it.* • LP DETERMINERS

whiff /hwɪf, wɪf/ *n* [C] a smell that you notice

briefly • *I got a whiff of perfume as she walked by.* ○ *(fig.) A whiff of scandal was in the air.*

while LENGTH OF TIME /hwaɪl, waɪl/ *n* [U] a length of time • *He only had to wait a short while.* ○ *It was a while before any waiter took their order.* ○ *That happened a while ago* (= did not happen recently). ○ *I haven't seen him for a while* (= a long time). ○ *She's getting dressed, and she'll be ready in just a little while* (= soon).

while DURING /hwaɪl, waɪl/ *conjunction* during the time that, or at the same time as • *I read it while you were drying your hair.* ○ *"I'm going to the post office." "While you're there can you get me some stamps?"*

while ALTHOUGH /hwaɪl, waɪl/ *conjunction* despite the fact that; although • *While I know he's not perfect, I do like him.*

while BUT /hwaɪl, waɪl/ *conjunction* compared with the fact that; but • *Tom is very outgoing, while Ken's shy and quiet.*

while away *obj*, **while** *obj* **away** /ˈhwaɪ·lə ˌweɪ, ˈwaɪ-/ *v adv* [M] to spend (time) in a relaxed way, sometimes when waiting for something else to happen • *I used to knit a lot when I was pregnant just to while away the time.*

whim /hwɪm, wɪm/ *n* [C] a sudden desire or idea • *The whims of rock stars can be hard to satisfy.*

whimper /ˈhwɪm·pər, ˈwɪm-/ *v* [I] to cry, making small, weak sounds • *She whimpered pathetically.*

whimper /ˈhwɪm·pər, ˈwɪm-/ *n* [C] • *There wasn't a whimper of complaint from anyone.*

whimsical /ˈhwɪm·zɪ·kəl, ˈwɪm-/ *adj* unusual and very imaginative • *The songs have a whimsical charm.* • Whimsical also describes actions that change suddenly and for no obvious reason: *Unfortunately, his decisions are often whimsical.*

whimsy /ˈhwɪm·zi, ˈwɪm-/ *n* [C/U] something imaginatively playful and amusing • *The second book is as full of happy whimsy as the first.* [U]

whine /hwaɪn, waɪn/ *v* [I] to make a high, complaining sound, or to complain continually • *If you don't stop whining, we won't go at all!*

whine /hwaɪn, waɪn/ *n* [C usually sing] • *(fig.) The whine of Tracey's hair dryer wakes me every morning.*

whinny /ˈhwɪn·i, ˈwɪn·i/ *v* [I] (of a horse) to make a soft sound, like a gentle NEIGH

whip STRAP /hwɪp, wɪp/ *n* [C] a piece of leather or rope fastened to a stick, used to train and control animals or, esp. in the past, to hit people • *The trainer cracked his whip, and the lions sat in a circle.*

whip /hwɪp, wɪp/ *v* [T] **-pp-** • *Some guards brutally whipped the prisoners.* ○ *(fig.) Dallas whipped Buffalo 52 to 17* (= beat them by this score).

whipping /ˈhwɪp·ɪŋ, ˈwɪp-/ *n* [C] a beating, esp. with a whip • A **whipping boy** is someone who is blamed or punished for the faults and mistakes of others.

whip MOVE QUICKLY /hwɪp, wɪp/ v [always + adv/prep] **-pp-** to bring or take (something) quickly, or to move quickly • *They whipped my plate away before I'd even finished.* [M] ∘ *Bill whipped out his harmonica.* [M] ∘ *The wind whipped around the corner of the building.* [I] • If you **whip up** someone or something or **whip** someone or something **into** a particular emotional state, you cause or encourage them to feel that way: *He whipped the crowd into a frenzy.* ∘ *I couldn't whip up any enthusiasm for the assignment.* • If you **whip** something **up**, you make it very quickly: *He whipped up a really good dinner.*

whip BEAT FOOD /hwɪp, wɪp/ v [T] **-pp-** to beat (food, esp. cream or an egg) with a special utensil in order to make it thick and firm • *Whip the egg whites until stiff.*

whip POLITICS /hwɪp, wɪp/ n [C] an elected representative of a political party in a LEGISLATURE whose job is to gather support from other legislators for particular legislation and to encourage them to vote the way their party wants them to

whiplash /'hwɪp·læʃ, 'wɪp-/ n [U] a neck injury caused by a sudden movement forward and back of the head, as in a car accident

whir /hwɜr, wɜr/, **whirr** v [I] **-rr-** (esp. of machines) to make a soft, continuous sound like a wheel turning very quickly • *I could hear the dishwasher whirring in the kitchen.*

whir /hwɜr, wɜr/ n [C usually sing] • *There was a whir of wings as the ducks rose up into the air.*

whirl /hwɜrl, wɜrl/ v [I/T] to cause (something) to spin • *The wind came up and the snow began to whirl around us.* [I]

whirl /hwɜrl, wɜrl/ n [C] • *The dance was an exciting, dizzy whirl.* • A **whirlpool** is water that moves in a powerful, circular current, sucking into its center anything that floats near it. • A **whirlpool** is also a **bathtub** with currents of water flowing through it: *Some health clubs have whirlpools and steam rooms.* • A **whirlwind** is a storm with strong winds that move in a circle. • A **whirlwind** event happens quickly: *a whirlwind tour* • A **whirlwind of** something is a large amount of it that happens quickly: *a whirlwind of activity*

whisk REMOVE /hwɪsk, wɪsk/ v [T always + adv/prep] to take away or remove (something or someone) quickly • *A limo whisked us off to dinner.* ∘ *The horse whisked flies from its back with its tail.*

whisk BEAT FOOD /hwɪsk, wɪsk/ v [T] to beat (eggs, cream, or other liquid) with a

whisk

utensil that adds air to the food, making it light • *Whisk the vanilla into the batter.*

whisk /hwɪsk, wɪsk/ n [C] a wire kitchen utensil that you use for beating a mixture

whisker /'hwɪs·kər, 'wɪs-/ n [C] one of the long, stiff hairs that grow near the mouth of a cat, mouse, or other mammal • *The cat carefully cleaned the milk off its whiskers.*

whiskers /'hwɪs·kərz, 'wɪs-/ pl n the hair that grows on a man's face; BEARD

whiskey, **whisky** /'hwɪs·ki, 'wɪs-/ n [C/U] a strong, pale brown, alcoholic drink made from grain • *whisky and soda* [U]

whisper /'hwɪs·pər, 'wɪs-/ v [I/T] to say (something) very softly, using the breath but not the voice • *What are you girls whispering about?* [I]

whisper /'hwɪs·pər, 'wɪs-/ n [C] • *They spoke in whispers, not wanting anyone to hear them.*

whistle /'hwɪs·əl, 'wɪs-/ v [I/T] to make a musical sound by forcing the breath through a small passage between the lips or through a special device • *I whistled to my dog and she came running back.* [I] ∘ *(fig.)The wind whistled through the trees.* [I]

whistle /'hwɪs·əl, 'wɪs-/ n [C] • *I lay in bed and listened to the whistles of trains across the river.* • A whistle is also a device that makes a loud, high sound when you blow into it. • A **whistle-blower** is a person who tells someone in authority about something illegal that is happening, esp. in a business or government.

white COLOR /hwaɪt, waɪt/ adj [-er/-est only], n [C/U] (of) a color like that of snow, milk, or bone • *white hair* ∘ *a white shirt* ∘ *We used a bright white on the ceilings.* [C] • The white of an egg is the part of an egg that becomes white when cooked. [C/U] • **Whitecaps** are waves that are white at their tops. • A **white-collar** person works in an office: *These days, few white-collar workers actually wear white shirts.* ∘ Compare **blue-collar** at BLUE COLOR. • A **white flag** symbolizes an acceptance of defeat or giving up on something. • The **White House** is the official home and offices of the president of the US: *The White House has scheduled a news conference.* • A **white lie** is a lie that is told either to be polite or to keep someone from being upset by the truth. • **White meat** is the lightest flesh, usually the breast, of a cooked bird. • The **White Pages** is a book that lists the names, addresses, and telephone numbers of the people and businesses in a city or area. Compare **yellow pages** at YELLOW COLOR. • **White water** is water in a river that flows quickly and has a lot of bubbles: *white-water rafting*

whiten /'hwaɪt·ən, 'waɪt-/ v [I/T] to make (something) whiter, or to become whiter • *This toothpaste is supposed to whiten your teeth.* [T]

white PALE SKIN /hwaɪt, waɪt/ adj [-er/-est only] belonging to a race whose skin is pale in color; CAUCASIAN • *It's a predominantly white neighborhood.* • (*rude slang*) **White trash** means poor, badly educated white people.

white /hwaɪt, waɪt/ *n* [C] • *For a long time, whites controlled nearly everything here.*

whitewash /'hwaɪt·wɑʃ, 'waɪt-, -wɔːʃ/ *n* [C/U] paint made from water and white powder which is used esp. on walls and ceilings • A whitewash is something that hides a wrong or illegal action: *He called the report a whitewash.* [C]

whitewash /'hwaɪt·wɑʃ, 'waɪt-, -wɔːʃ/ *v* [T] • *whitewashed houses* ○ *He's whitewashing the fence.*

whittle /'hwɪt̬·ᵊl, 'wɪt̬-/ *v* [I/T] to slice thin pieces from a piece of wood, or to form (something) from wood by slicing pieces off it • *He likes to whittle.* [I] • To **whittle away (at)** something or **whittle** something **down** is to make it gradually smaller or less important: *We've whittled away at our debts.* ○ *By halftime their lead had been whittled down to two points.*

whiz EXPERT /hwɪz, wɪz/ *n* [C] *infml* a person with a very high level of skill or knowledge in a particular area • *Everyone knows at least one computer whiz.* ○ *Jo was one of those whiz kids who are millionaires by the time they're 25.*

whiz MOVE FAST /hwɪz, wɪz/ *v* [I always + adv/prep] to move very fast • *He whizzed through the job but made lots of mistakes.*

who ASKING /huː/ *pronoun* used esp. in questions to ask which person or people, or to ask someone's name • *Who did this?* ○ *Who's she?* • People say **who cares** to show they are not interested in something: *"Are they getting divorced?" "Who cares?"* • People say **who needs** something to show they do not want something: *Men! Who needs them?* • People ask **who would have thought** when they are surprised by information: *She's written two novels since graduating? Who'd have thought?* • USAGE: In formal speech or writing, whom is the form of who used when it is the object of a verb or preposition.

who ADDING INFORMATION /huː/ *pronoun* used as the subject or object of a verb when referring to a particular person or when adding information about a person just mentioned • *The other people who live in the house are really friendly.* ○ *This is Frank, who I told you about.* • USAGE: In formal speech or writing, whom is the form of who used when it is the object of a verb or preposition.

whoa /hwoʊ, woʊ/ *exclamation* used to tell a person or a horse to stop or slow down, or to express surprise • *Whoa! Not so fast.*

who'd /huːd/ *contraction* of **who would** or **who had** • *Who'd have thought we'd be married for this long?* ○ *It's about a boy who'd been around the world.*

whodunit /huː'dʌn·ət/ *n* [C] *infml* a story, book, or movie about a mystery and its solution

whoever PERSON /huː'ev·ər/ *pronoun* the person who • *Whoever broke the window will have to pay for it.* • USAGE: In formal speech or writing, whomever is the form of whoever used when it is the object of a verb or preposition.

whoever ANYONE /huː'ev·ər/ *pronoun* any person who • *The picketers were shouting at whoever entered the building.* ○ *Whoever they are, I don't want to see them!* • USAGE: In formal speech or writing, whomever is the form of whoever used when it is the object of a verb or preposition.

whoever WHAT PERSON /huː'ev·ər/ *pronoun* (used in place of who for emphasis in questions) what person or persons • *Whoever would believe such a ridiculous story?*

whole /hoʊl/ *adj* [not gradable] all of something; the full amount • *They partied the whole night.* ○ *He cooked a meal for the whole school.* • Whole can also mean in one piece: *You can eat the fruit whole or cut it up.* • (*infml*) Whole can also be used to emphasize something: *I've got a whole lot to do this afternoon.* • **The whole bit, the whole shebang,** or **the whole thing** means everything related to an activity or idea: *He's got a fancy stove, gourmet cookware, the whole shebang.* ○ *I fell asleep and missed the whole thing.* • **Wholehearted** means completely enthusiastic: *I'd like to thank all of you for your wholehearted support of this event.* • A **whole number** is a number, such as 1, 17, or 3126, that has no FRACTIONS and does not contain a **decimal point.** • **Whole wheat** is flour made from whole grains of wheat: *whole wheat bread*

whole /hoʊl/ *n* [C/U] all of the parts of something considered together as one thing, or all of something • *Two halves make a whole.* [C] ○ *She'll be away the whole of next month.* [U] • **On the whole** means generally: *On the whole, I prefer classical music.*

wholly /'hoʊl·li/ *adv* completely • *I didn't think her explanation was wholly truthful.* LP VERY, COMPLETELY, AND OTHER INTENSIFIERS

wholesale SELLING /'hoʊl·seɪl/ *n* [U] the activity of selling goods, usually in large amounts, to businesses which then sell them to the public • Compare RETAIL.

wholesale /'hoʊl·seɪl/ *adj, adv* [not gradable] • *wholesale prices* ○ *Do you sell wholesale?*

wholesaler /'hoʊl·seɪ·lər/ *n* [C] • *a bike/food wholesaler*

wholesale COMPLETE /'hoʊl·seɪl/ *adj* involving everyone or everything; complete • *What the system needs is wholesale reform.*

wholesome /'hoʊl·səm/ *adj* good for you, and likely to benefit you physically, morally, or emotionally • *Wholesome food helps keep you healthy.* ○ *This movie is good wholesome family entertainment.*

who'll /huːl/ *contraction of* **who will** • *Who'll be at your party?*

whom ADDING INFORMATION /huːm/ *pronoun* used as the object of a verb or after a preposition when referring to a particular person or when adding information about a person just mentioned • *The Kenyans have three runners in the race, any of whom could win.* ○ *He took out a photo of his son, whom he adores.* • USAGE: In informal speech and writing, who is more often used. Whom is more often used immediately after prepositions than in other positions.

whom ASKING /huːm/ *pronoun* used esp. in questions as the object of a verb or after a preposition, when asking which person or people, or when asking what someone's name is • *Of whom can it truly be said that they have never been dishonest?* • USAGE: In informal speech and writing, who is more often used. Whom is more often used immediately after prepositions than in other positions.

whomever /huːˈmev·ər/ *pronoun* WHOEVER PERSON or WHOEVER ANYONE • *Give it to whomever you please.* • USAGE: In informal speech and writing, whoever is more often used. Whomever is more often used immediately after prepositions than in other positions.

whoop /huːp, hʊp, hwuːp, hwʊp/ *v* [I/T] to shout loudly or excitedly, esp. because of happiness or enjoyment • *I was so happy it was hard not to whoop out loud.* [I] • To **whoop it up** is to enjoy yourself in a noisy and enthusiastic way.

whoop /huːp, hʊp, hwuːp, hwʊp/ *n* [C] • *Jake let out a whoop of triumph.*

whoops /hwʊps, wʊps, wuːps/ *exclamation* OOPS

whopper /ˈhwɑp·ər, ˈwɑp-/ *n* [C] *infml* something that is much bigger than the usual size • *Your monthly payment is a whopper.* • A whopper is also a big lie: *Fishermen are supposed to tell the biggest whoppers.*

whopping /ˈhwɑp·ɪŋ, ˈwɑp-/ *adj* [not gradable] *infml* • *The mayor was elected by a whopping majority.*

whore /hɔːr, hoʊr, hʊr/ *n* [C] a PROSTITUTE (= someone who is paid for sex), or a person, esp. a woman, who is considered immoral • A **whorehouse** is a place where usually men go and pay to have sex with PROSTITUTES.

who're /huː·ər, hʊr/ *contraction of* **who are** • *The film begins with a young couple, who're just about to get married.*

who's /huːz/ *contraction of* **who is** or **who has** • *Who's coming over tonight?* ○ *This is Bob, who's kept our software running.*

whose /huːz/ *pronoun* used to ask which person owns or is responsible for something, or to say who is responsible for something • *Whose bag is this?* ○ *I don't care whose fault it is.* • Sometimes whose refers to a thing, not a

person: *That's the house whose kitchen is painted purple.* • LP DETERMINERS

who've /huːv/ *contraction of* **who have** • *I know people who've found homes on the Internet.*

why /hwaɪ, waɪ/ *adv* [not gradable], *conjunction* for what reason • *Why do you like living in Paris?* ○ *She'll ask why you don't have your homework.* • **Why not** can be used to make a suggestion or to express agreement: *If you're so unhappy, why not leave?* ○ *"Do you want Italian food tonight?" "Sure, why not."*

wick /wɪk/ *n* [C] a piece of string in the center of a candle, or a similar part of a light, which supplies fuel to a flame

wicked /ˈwɪk·əd/ *adj* morally wrong and bad • *He was a wicked, ruthless, and dishonest man.* • Wicked can also mean slightly bad, but in an attractive way: *She has a wicked sense of humor.* • (*slang*) Wicked also means extreme: *The demands of fund-raising are wicked.*

wicker /ˈwɪk·ər/ *adj* [not gradable] made of very thin pieces of wood twisted together • *a wicker basket*

wide DISTANT FROM SIDE TO SIDE /waɪd/ *adj* [-er/-est only] distant from one side to the other, esp. in comparison with length from top to bottom, or being a particular distance across • *a wide window* ○ *a wide yard* ○ *The bay is 15 miles wide here.* • USAGE: The related noun is WIDTH.

widen /ˈwaɪd·ən/ *v* [I/T] • *After it passes through town, the road widens.* [I]

wide MANY OR MUCH /waɪd/ *adj* [-er/-est only] covering a large area, or including many types of things • *They sell a wide range of skin-care products.* ○ *The candidate has wide support (= the support of many people).* • **Widespread** means existing or happening in many places or among many people: *Minnesota has experienced widespread flooding.*

widely /ˈwaɪd·li/ *adv* by many • *French was widely spoken there.*

widen /ˈwaɪd·ən/ *v* [I/T] • *Let's widen the discussion by listening to people with other points of view.* [T]

wide COMPLETELY /waɪd/ *adv* [-er/-est only] to the greatest degree possible; completely • *I was wide awake.* ○ *The dentist said, "Open wide."* • If someone is **wide open to/for** something, they are likely to be influenced by it: *I'm wide open to suggestions.* • **Wide open spaces** are land with no buildings on it.

widow /ˈwɪd·oʊ/ *n* [C] a woman whose husband has died and who has not married again

widower /ˈwɪd·ə·wər/ *n* [C] a man whose wife has died and who has not married again

widowed /ˈwɪd·oʊd/ *adj* [not gradable] having lost a husband or wife through death • *My widowed uncle lives upstairs.*

width /wɪtθ, wɪdθ/ *n* [C/U] the distance across something from one side to the other • *The shoes are available in three widths.* [C] • USAGE:

The related adjective is WIDE DISTANT FROM SIDE TO SIDE. • Compare LENGTH DISTANCE.

wield /wiːld/ *v* [T] to have or use (power, authority, or influence), or to hold and use (a weapon) • *He thinks women are uncomfortable wielding power.*

wife /waɪf/ *n* [C] *pl* **wives** /waɪvz/ the woman to whom a man is married; a married woman • Compare HUSBAND.

wig /wɪg/ *n* [C] a covering of hair that can be removed and is worn on the head to hide a lack of hair or to cover your own hair • *a blond wig* • Compare TOUPÉE.

wiggle /'wɪg·əl/ *v* [I/T] to move up and down or from side to side with small, quick movements, or to cause this to happen • *He wiggled the handle but nothing happened.* [T]

wiggle /'wɪg·əl/ *n* [C] • *He gave his hips a wiggle.*

wigwam /'wɪg·wɑm/ *n* [C] a cone-shaped tent made and lived in, esp. in the past, by American Indians in the eastern US

wild NATURAL /waɪld/ *adj, adv* [-er/-est only] living or growing independently of people, in natural conditions, and with natural characteristics • *wild turkeys* ∘ *These herbs grow wild.* • **Wildflowers** are flowers that grow without having been planted by people. • **Wildlife** is animals that live independently of people, usually in natural conditions: *Wildlife in the area includes deer, bears, and raccoons.*

wild /waɪld/ *n* [U] places that have few towns or roads, are difficult to get to, and lack conveniences • *In Kenya we saw elephants and lions in the wild.*

wild NOT CONTROLLED /waɪld/ *adj* [-er/-est only] extreme or violent and not controlled • *He led a wild life.* ∘ *When I told him what I'd done, he went wild* (= became angry). ∘ *I'll make a wild guess* (= one not based on careful thought). • (*slang*) Wild also means excellent, special, or unusual: *The music they play is just wild.* • (*infml*) If you are **wild about** something, you like it a lot: *I'm not wild about apples.* • In some card games, a **wild card** is a card that can be used instead of any other: (*fig.*) *Undecided voters are this election's wild card.* • In sports, a **wild card** is an extra opportunity to qualify for a **championship** competition. • Your **wildest dreams** are your hopes or thoughts about the best things that could happen in your future: *Never in my wildest dreams did I think I'd win.* • A **wildfire** is a powerful fire that burns out of control across a large area: *Wildfires destroyed thousands of acres across Oregon.*

wildly /'waɪld·li/ *adv* • *He danced wildly for hours.* • LP VERY, COMPLETELY, AND OTHER INTENSIFIERS

wild /waɪld/ *adv* [-er/-est only] • *The teacher left the room, and the kids ran wild* (= were not controlled).

wilderness /'wɪl·dər·nəs/ *n* [C usually sing] an area of land that has not been cultivated or had towns and roads built on it, esp. because it is difficult to live in as a result of its extremely cold or hot weather or bad earth • *Large parts of Canada are still wilderness.*

wiles /waɪlz/ *pl n* skill at getting what you want, usually by tricking others or (esp. of women) by acting sexy • *She uses her feminine wiles to get to the top.* • USAGE: The related adjective is WILY.

will FUTURE /wɪl, wəl/ *v aux* **will** used only with the base forms of verbs when referring to the future • *Claire will be five years old next month.* • **Will have** is used to refer to the past from a point in the future: *By the time we get there, Jim will have left.* • USAGE: The negative contraction is WON'T. See also SHALL. • LP AUXILIARY VERBS

will INTENTION /wɪl, wəl/ *v aux* he/she/it **will**, *past simple* **would** /wʊd, wəd/ used to express your intentions • *This time I will learn from my mistakes.* • USAGE: The negative contraction is WON'T. • LP AUXILIARY VERBS

will REQUEST /wɪl, wəl/ *v aux* he/she/it **will**, *past simple* **would** /wʊd, wəd/ used to ask or tell someone to do something • *Will you give me her address, please?* ∘ *You will do it because I said so!* • Will can be used as a polite way of inviting someone to do something, or of offering someone something: *Will you come in?* • USAGE: The negative contraction is WON'T. • LP AUXILIARY VERBS

will CAN /wɪl, wəl/ *v aux* he/she/it **will**, *past simple* **would** /wʊd, wəd/ used to refer to what is possible; to be able to do something • *This car will seat six people comfortably.* • USAGE: The negative contraction is WON'T. • LP AUXILIARY VERBS

will ACCEPTANCE /wɪl, wəl/ *v aux* he/she/it **will**, *past simple* **would** /wʊd, wəd/ used to say that behavior which usually happens is acceptable because it is expected • *Boys will be boys.* • LP AUXILIARY VERBS

will MENTAL POWER /wɪl/ *n* [C/U] the mental power used to control and direct your thoughts and actions, or a determination to do something, despite any difficulties or opposition • *He'll need an iron will to stick to that diet.* [C] ∘ *After six months in the hospital, she lost the will to live* (= the desire and determination to stay alive). [U] • Someone's will is also what they want to happen: *I went there against my will.* [U] ∘ *I guess the hurricane was God's will.* [U] • *Some actors can cry* **at will** (= when they want to). • **Willpower** is the ability to control your own thoughts and the way in which you behave: *Staying on a diet takes a lot of willpower.* • .

will /wɪl/ *v* [T] to try to make (something) happen by using your thoughts • *She willed herself to remain optimistic.*

will DEATH PLAN /wɪl/ *n* [C] your official statement of what should be done with your money and property after you die • *Your will isn't valid until you sign it.*

will /wɪl/ *v* [T] to officially arrange for someone to receive part or all of your money or property after your death • *She willed the house to her brother.*

willful /ˈwɪl·fəl/ *adj* (of something bad) done intentionally, or (of a person) determined to do exactly as you want, even if you know it is wrong • *The children suffered from their mother's willful neglect.*

willing /ˈwɪl·ɪŋ/ *adj* not opposed to doing something; ready or eager to do something • *If you're willing to fly on Thursday you can get a cheaper ticket.*

willingly /ˈwɪl·ɪŋ·li/ *adv* readily and enthusiastically • *I willingly babysit for my granddaughter.*

willingness /ˈwɪl·ɪŋ·nəs/ *n* [U] • *She shows a willingness to work hard.*

willow (tree) /ˈwɪl·oʊ (ˈtriː)/ *n* [C] a tree that usually grows near water and has long, thin branches that hang down

willowy /ˈwɪl·ə·wi/ *adj* (esp. of a woman) graceful and thin, with long arms and legs • *a willowy figure*

willy–nilly /ˌwɪl·iˈnɪl·i/ *adv* [not gradable] suddenly and without planning or order • *Her words tumbled out all willy-nilly.*

wilt /wɪlt/ *v* [I] (of a plant) to become weak and begin to bend toward the ground, or (of a person) to become weaker, tired, or less confident • *Put the flowers in water before they wilt.*

wily /ˈwɑɪ·li/ *adj* quick to think of things, having a very good understanding of situations and possibilities, and often willing to use tricks to achieve an aim • *a wily hunter* • USAGE: The related noun is WILES.

wimp /wɪmp/ *n* [C] *infml disapproving* a person who is not strong, brave, or confident • *I always thought he was a wimp.*

win /wɪn/ *v* [I/T] **winning**, *past won* /wʌn/ to defeat a competitor, or to achieve first position or get a prize in a competition • *Did they win last night?* [I] ○ *Our team won the game!* [T] • If something **wins out** over something else, it gets a controlling position over it: *Greed won out over principles.* • If you **win** someone **over**, you succeed in getting their support or agreement, esp. when they were previously opposed to you: *He had some good ideas, but failed to win over Congress.* • A **win-win** situation is one in which an agreement is reached that is beneficial to both sides.

win /wɪn/ *n* [C] • *It was the team's sixth win this season.*

winner /ˈwɪn·ər/ *n* [C] • *The winner of this game will play Gigante in the semifinals.* • (*infml*) In sports, a winner is also a goal or point that allows a person or a side to win a game: *Eaves scored the winner in the final seconds of the game.* • (*infml*) A winner is also something that is extremely successful and

popular: *That chocolate cake was a winner.* • In a **winner-takes-all** competition, a prize or money is given only to the person who wins, and the other competitors get nothing.

winning /ˈwɪn·ɪŋ/ *adj* • *It's nice to be on the winning side for a change!* • If someone has a winning smile or way of behaving, it is friendly and tends to make people like them: *I'm sure Anna, with her winning ways, can persuade him.*

wince /wɪns/ *v* [I] to tighten the muscles of the face briefly and suddenly in a show of pain, worry, or embarrassment • *She cut her finger, but didn't even wince.*

wince /wɪns/ *n* [C usually sing] • *"These pictures are disgusting," Jones said with a wince.*

winch /wɪntʃ/ *n* [C] a machine that lifts heavy objects by turning a chain or rope around a tube-shaped device

winch /wɪntʃ/ *v* [T] • *He winched the crate off the truck.*

wind MOVEMENT OF AIR /wɪnd/ *n* [C/U] the movement of air outside, esp. when strong enough to be felt • *The wind is so strong that it's hard to keep an umbrella up.* [U] ○ *We expect light winds from the west today.* [C] • **Windchill** is the effect that wind has on how cold the air feels: *It's 15 degrees outside, but with the windchill factor it feels like minus five.* • A **wind instrument** is a musical instrument whose sound is produced by blowing: *Saxophones, clarinets, and flutes are wind instruments.* • A **windmill** is a building or structure with large blades on the outside which, when turned by the force of the wind, provide the power for getting water out of the ground, crushing grain, or making electricity.

windmill

windy /ˈwɪn·di/ *adj* • *It will be wet and windy for most of the week.*

wind BREATH /wɪnd/ *n* [U] breath or the ability to breathe • *She ran so hard that it took her a few seconds to get her wind (back) before she could speak.*

winded /ˈwɪn·dəd/ *adj* having difficulty breathing, usually because you have just done some physical activity that caused you to breathe too quickly • *He was overweight and out of shape, and he got winded easily.*

wind TWIST /waɪnd/ *v* [I/T] *past* **wound** /waʊnd/ to twist (something) around something else or turn (something) in a circle, or become twisted or turned in such a way • *She wound the string around the spool.* [T] • To wind (up) a timing device is to cause it to work by turning a key or handle: *to wind a clock* [T/M]

wind TURN /waɪnd/ *v* [I always + adv/prep] *past* **wound** /waʊnd/ (of a road, path, or river) to follow a route that turns repeatedly in different directions • *The river winds through the valley.*

winding /'waɪn·dɪŋ/ *adj* • *a winding road*

□ **wind down** *(obj)*, **wind** *(obj)* **down** /'waɪn 'daʊn/ *v adv* to end gradually or in stages, or to cause (something) to end in this way • *The storm finally began to wind down after four hours of heavy rain.* [I]

□ **wind up** *(obj)* FINISH , **wind** *(obj)* **up** /'waɪn 'dʌp/ *v adv* to end (something) • *We should be able to wind (things) up by 10 o'clock.* [I/M]

□ **wind up** BECOME /'waɪn'dʌp/ *v adv* to come to be in a particular situation or condition, esp. a bad one • *If he goes on like this he's going to wind up in jail.* [I always + adv/prep] ○ *You could wind up dead before you're 40 if you don't change your life style.* [L]

windfall /'wɪnd·fɔːl/ *n* [C] an amount of money that you receive unexpectedly • *The Belridge School, after receiving a financial windfall, purchased computers for all students and teachers.*

window OPENING /'wɪn·doʊ, -də/ *n* [C] an opening in the wall of a building or vehicle, usually covered with glass, to let light and air in and to allow people inside to see out • *to open/close a window* ○ *From her bedroom window she could see a lovely garden.* • In a store, a window is the large glass-covered front behind which goods for sale are usually shown: *We walked along Fifth Avenue, looking in the shop windows.* • A window is also a period when there is an unusual opportunity to do something: *If a window of opportunity presents itself, I'd be a fool not to take advantage of it.* • **Window dressing** is a person or thing whose name is used in connection with an activity to make the activity appear important or attractive, when in reality they have little to do with it, or the act of arranging this. • A **windowpane** is a single piece of glass in the window of a building. • A **window shade** is a cover that can be pulled over a window to block the light or to keep people from looking in. • If you go **window-shopping**, or you **window-shop**, you spend time looking at the goods on sale in store windows without buying them. • A **windowsill** is a shelf formed by the bottom part of the frame of a window.

window COMPUTER /'wɪn·doʊ, -də/ *n* [C] an

area of a computer screen that shows a particular type of information

windpipe /'wɪnd·paɪp/ *n* [C] the tube in the body that carries air that has been breathed in from the upper end of the throat to the lungs

windshield /'wɪnd·ʃiːld/ *n* [C] the window at the front of a car or other four-wheeled vehicle • A **windshield wiper** is a blade, often one of a pair, having a rubber edge that moves repeatedly against the outer surface of a windshield, cleaning it of rain or snow. • PIC CAR

windsurfing /'wɪnd,sɜr·fɪŋ/ *n* [U] the activity of sailing over water while standing on a narrow board and holding onto a sail

windswept /'wɪnd·swept/ *adj* (of places) open to and not protected from strong winds • *We drove along the windswept coast of Big Sur in Southern California.*

windy /'wɪn·di/ *adj* • See at WIND MOVEMENT OF AIR.

wine /waɪn/ *n* an alcoholic drink made from GRAPES, or less commonly an alcoholic drink made in a similar way but from other fruits • *a glass of red/white wine* [U] ○ *I usually buy California wines.* [C] • A **wine cooler** is a drink of wine, fruit juice, and bubbly water.

wine /waɪn/ *v* • To **wine and dine** someone is to treat them very well by giving them food and drink: *His business could potentially bring in lots of new jobs, so he was wined and dined by government officials and the social elite.*

wing STRUCTURE FOR FLYING /wɪŋ/ *n* [C] one of the movable, usually long and flat, parts on either side of the body of a bird, insect, or BAT that it uses for flying, or one of the long, flat, horizontal structures that stick out on either side of an aircraft • *The duck flapped its wings and took off.* • A **wingspan** is the distance between the ends of the wings of a bird or aircraft: *Some eagles have a wingspan of over seven feet.*

wing POLITICAL GROUP /wɪŋ/ *n* [C] a group within a political party or organization whose beliefs are in some way different from those of the main group • *She's in the conservative wing of the party.*

wing PART OF BUILDING /wɪŋ/ *n* [C] a section of a large building that connects to a side of the main part • *His office is in the west wing of the White House.*

wings /wɪŋz/ *pl n* the sides of a stage which cannot be seen by the people watching the play

wink /wɪŋk/ *v* [I] to close one eye briefly as a way of greeting someone or of showing that you are not serious about something you have said • *He winked when he said it.*

winnings /'wɪn·ɪŋz/ *pl n* an amount of money won • *What are you going to spend your winnings on?*

winnow /'wɪn·oʊ/ *v* [T] to reduce (a large number of people or things) to a much smaller number by judging their quality • *The six ar-*

chitects chosen to compete for the commission were winnowed from an original list of 27.

wino /'waɪ·noʊ/ *n* [C] *pl* **winos** *slang* a person who drinks a lot of wine or other alcoholic drink and is often drunk, and who lives on the streets

winsome /'wɪn·səm/ *adj* charming and attractive in a simple, childlike way • *Just then Nancy opened her eyes and gave Cherry a winsome smile.*

winter /'wɪnt·ər/ *n* [C/U] the season when the weather is coldest between fall and spring, lasting from November to March north of the equator and from May to September south of the equator • *last/next/this winter* [C] ○ *My grandparents often vacation in Florida for part of the winter.* [C] • **Wintertime** is the season of winter: *This lake becomes a skating rink in (the) wintertime.*

wintry /'wɪn·tri/ *adj* typical of winter's cold, windy, and snowy weather • *You'll definitely need snow tires on your car for the wintry weather around here.*

wipe /waɪp/ *v* [T] to slide (something) over the surface of (something else), in order to remove (dirt, food, or liquid) • *Please wipe your feet before you come into the house.* ○ *She gently wiped the blood away and cleaned the wound.* ○ *Just take the sponge in the sink and wipe the table off.* [M]

wiper /'waɪ·pər/ *n* [C] a **windshield wiper**, see at WINDSHIELD • *One of our wipers is stuck.*

□ **wipe out** *obj*, **wipe** *obj* **out** /'-'-/ *v adv* [M] to destroy (something) completely or cause (something) to be completely lost • *Poor investments wiped out most of his earnings.*

wire METAL THREAD /waɪr/ *n* [C/U] thin metal that can be bent, used in a stiff form in fences and in a form more easily shaped for fastening things or for carrying electric currents • *telephone wires* [C] ○ *There was a six-foot high wire fence around the playground.* [U]

wire /waɪr/ *v* [T] connected or fastened by wire • *Our building is wired for cable TV.* • A person or place that is wired is secretly equipped with an electric device that records sounds such as conversations: *Wired by the FBI, he began recording meetings with Chicago officials.*

wiring /'waɪr·ɪŋ/ *n* [U] the system of wires in a building that carry electricity • *Faulty electrical wiring could cause a fire.*

wiry /'waɪr·i/ *adj* • If hair or fur is wiry, it is stiff and not soft. • See also WIRY.

wire SEND MESSAGE /waɪr/ *v* [T] to send (a message or money) using an electrical communication system • *My father wired me $300.* • (*dated*) To wire is also to TELEGRAPH.

wire /waɪr/ *n* [C] *dated* a TELEGRAM

wiretap /'waɪr·tæp/ *v* [I/T] to secretly listen to (people) by connecting a listening device to their telephone, or to attach a listening device to (a telephone) for this purpose • *The court*

gave permission to have his phone wiretapped to gather evidence. [T]

wiretap /'waɪr·tæp/ *n* [C] • *The government put a wiretap on his phone.*

wiry /'waɪr·i/ *adj* (of a person) thin but strong • *He was a wiry man 5 feet 10 inches tall and weighing 145 pounds.* • See also **wiry** at WIRE METAL THREAD.

wisdom /'wɪz·dəm/ *n* [U] the ability to make good judgments based on what you have learned from your experience, or the knowledge and understanding that gives you this ability • Wisdom also means the quality of being a good judgment: *I question the wisdom of separating a child from his brothers and sisters whatever the circumstances.* • The **wisdom teeth** are the four teeth at the back of the JAW that are the last to develop.

wise /waɪz/ *adj* [-*er*/-*est* only] having or showing good judgment, or the ability to make good judgments, based on what you have learned from your experience • *a wise man/woman* ○ *They decided that it was wiser to wait until they were making a little more money before having a child.* [+ *to* infinitive] • (*infml*) If you are or are getting **wise to** a dishonest situation or way of doing something, you are aware of it: *He calls in sick almost every Monday with some phony story—I'm wise to him.* • A **wisecrack** is a remark that criticizes someone or something in a humorous way.

wise up /'waɪ'zʌp/ *v adv* [I] *infml* to begin to understand the truth about an unpleasant situation or a fact, although it is difficult or unpleasant to accept • *It's about time that Congress wised up to the fact that most citizens do not trust politicians to tell the truth.*

wisely /'waɪz·li/ *adv* • *Spend your money wisely.*

–wise /ˌwaɪz/ *combining form* relating to • *Moneywise, of course, I'm much better off than I used to be.*

wish DESIRE DIFFERENT SITUATION /wɪʃ/ *v* [+ (*that*) clause] to desire some situation that is different from the one that exists • *I wish (that) I didn't have to go to work today.* ○ *She wished she could afford a new car.* ○ *I wish I hadn't eaten so much.*

wish EXPRESS DESIRE /wɪʃ/ *v* [I/T] to hope that you will get something or that something will happen • *I was wishing for summer so hard I could almost make it happen at that moment.* [I] • *Having the flu was awful—I* **wouldn't wish** *it* **on anyone/on** *my* **worst enemy** (= would not want anyone to suffer in that way).

wish /wɪʃ/ *n* [C] • *It was his greatest wish that one of his children would become a scientist.* [+ *that* clause] ○ *Close your eyes and make a wish.*

wish WANT SOMETHING /wɪʃ/ *v slightly fml* to want (something) or want to do something • *If you wish to volunteer to work in the museum, please indicate what department you are interested in.* [+ *to* infinitive]

wish /wɪʃ/ *n* [C] • *It was my mother's wish to be buried next to my father.* [+ *to* infinitive]

wish EXPRESS KIND FEELINGS /wɪʃ/ *v* [T] to express kind feelings for (someone) on a particular occasion • *Don't forget to wish her a happy birthday.* ○ *I'm off for the interview now—wish me luck.* ○ *His old teammates wished him well* (= hoped that he did well).

wishes /'wɪʃ·əz/ *pl n* • *When you see Joyce, please give her my best wishes.*

wishful thinking /'wɪʃ·fəl'θɪŋ·kɪŋ/ *n* [U] the imagining of an unlikely future event or situation that you wish were possible • *We talked about buying a house someday, but right now it's just wishful thinking.*

wishy–washy /'wɪʃ·iː,waʃ·i, -,wɔː·ʃi/ *adj* lacking in firm ideas, principles, or the ability to make a decision • *He's got TV ads accusing Dole of being wishy-washy on the issues.*

wisp /wɪsp/ *n* [C] a delicate, thin, and sometimes twisting piece or line of something • *Rita brushed back the stray coppery wisps of hair escaping her braid.* ○ *Blue wisps of cigarette smoke curled in the air.*

wistful /'wɪst·fəl/ *adj* sad and thinking about something that is impossible or past • *She cast a wistful glance at the bridal gowns in the window.*

wistfully /'wɪst·fə·li/ *adv* • *She spoke wistfully of their early years together.*

wit /wɪt/ *n* [C/U] the ability to use words in an amusing and intelligent way, or a person who has this ability • *The warmth and wit of her literary style bring the subject to life.* [U]

witty /'wɪt̬·i/ *adj* using words in an amusing and intelligent way; full of wit • *a witty remark* ○ *I think she's one of the wittiest comics on television.* • USAGE: A witty remark is a WITTICISM.

witch /wɪtʃ/ *n* [C] a woman who is believed to have magical powers, esp. one who uses her powers to do evil • **Witchcraft** is the activity of using magic to make things happen, esp. in order to help or harm other people. • A **witch doctor** is a person in some societies who is said to cure people by using traditional magic. • (*disapproving*) A **witch hunt** is an attempt to find and punish people whose opinions are unpopular and who are said by some to be a danger to society. • Compare WIZARD.

with IN THE PRESENCE OF /wɪð, wɪθ/ *prep* in the presence of (a person or thing) or doing something together • *She's in the kitchen with Dad.* ○ *He's an impossible person to work with.* ○ *I think I'll have some ice cream with my pie.* ○ *I'll be with you* (= I will give you my attention) *in a moment.* ○ *She's been with the magazine* (= working for it) *for two years.* • To be **with it** means to be aware of popular ideas and fashions: ○ *She reads all the style magazines and thinks she's really with it.*

with USING /wɪð, wɪθ/ *prep* using (something) or by means of (something) • *He was shot with*

a rifle. ○ *I bought it with my gift certificate.* ○ *The label on the box says, "Handle with care."* ○ *He caught the crabs with a large net.* • *I love you* **with all my heart** (= completely). • If you do something **with a vengeance**, you use great force or energy or do a lot of it: *She works out every day with a vengeance.* • If you can do something **with** your **eyes closed**, you can do it very easily: *I can find your house with my eyes closed.* • If you greet someone **with open arms**, you greet them in a very friendly way. • If you can see something **with the naked eye**, you can see it without using any special device for making images larger: *We live miles away, but on a clear night, you can see the city skyscrapers with the naked eye.*

with HAVING /wɪð, wɪθ/ *prep* having or possessing (someone or something) • *I'd like a room with an ocean view.* ○ *He's married with three children.* ○ *The doctor spoke with a German accent.* ○ *We're a multinational company with offices in London, Paris, and New York.* ○ *With a little luck, we should be back in time for dinner.* ○ *Both their children graduated with degrees in economics.* • With can also mean including: *With your contribution, we have a total of $450.* • **With all due respect** is used to express polite disagreement: *I've been thinking about what you said and, with all due respect, I think you're mistaken.* • (*fml*) If a woman is **with child**, she is pregnant. • If you do something **with flying colors**, you do it easily: *She passed the exam with flying colors.*

with RELATING TO /wɪð, wɪθ/ *prep* relating to or in the case of (a person or thing) • *How are things with you?* ○ *That has nothing to do with the subject.* ○ *Her books are popular with teenage girls.* ○ *He's very careless with his money.* ○ *The trouble with this skirt is that it wrinkles too easily.* ○ *What's the matter with her?*

with CAUSED BY /wɪð, wɪθ/ *prep* because of or caused by (something) • *He was trembling with fear.* ○ *She's at home with a bad cold.* ○ *His confidence was bolstered with the support of a lot of friends and relatives.* ○ *With all the excitement and confusion, I forgot to say goodbye to her.*

with AGAINST /wɪð, wɪθ/ *prep* against (something) • *She has fought a battle with depression throughout her career.* ○ *I always end up arguing with him about politics.*

with SUPPORTING /wɪð, wɪθ/ *prep* supporting (someone or something) • *If you want to go for a promotion, I'll be with you all the way.* ○ *Where do you stand on this issue—are you with us or against us?*

with DESPITE /wɪð, wɪθ/ *prep* despite (something) • *With all her faults, she's still one of the best teachers we've ever had.*

with AND /wɪð, wɪθ/ *prep* and; followed by • *I'd like a hamburger and French fries with a small salad.* ○ *Two hundred dollars is payable immediately, with a further $100 payable on delivery.*

withdraw /wɪð'drɔː, wɪθ-/ v [I/T] past simple **withdrew** /wɪð'druː, wɪθ-/, past part **withdrawn** /wɪð'drɔːn, wɪθ-/ to take (something) back, or to remove (something) • Israel agreed to withdraw (its troops) from occupied territories. [I/T] ○ He asked that his name be withdrawn from nomination for a Golden Globe Award. [T] ○ Democrats threatened to withdraw (= stop giving) their support of the tax bill. [T] ○ I have to withdraw (= take out) some money from an ATM machine. [T]

withdrawal /wɪð'drɔː·əl, wɪθ-/ n [C/U] • a troop withdrawal [C] ○ He had made several large withdrawals from his bank account (= He had taken out a lot of money). [C] ○ Her sudden withdrawal from the competition surprised everyone. [C] • Withdrawal also means the physical and mental effects that a person experiences when they stop using a drug: Research has confirmed that nicotine withdrawal impairs mental performance. [U]

withdrawn /wɪð'drɔːn, wɪθ-/ adj (of a person) preferring to be alone and taking little interest in other people • She became depressed and withdrawn after her husband's death.

wither /'wɪð·ər/ v [I/T] to become, or cause (something) to become, weak, dry, and smaller • Hot, dry weather withered the peanut crop in the southeast. [T] ○ (fig.) Public interest in the sex scandal will not wither away any time soon. [I]

withering /'wɪð·ə·rɪŋ/ adj expressing strong criticism • She delivered a withering attack on the book and its authors.

withhold /wɪθ'hoʊld, wɪð-/ v [T] past **withheld** /wɪθ'held, wɪð-/ to refuse to give (something), or to keep back (something) • Has the government been withholding crucial information? ○ The governor said he would withhold judgment until he receives the committee's report. • **Withholding tax** is money taken from a person's income and paid directly to the government by their employer.

within /wɪð'ɪn, wɪθ-/ prep, adv [not gradable] inside or not beyond (a particular area, limit, or period of time) • Most Californians live within 20 miles of the coast. ○ The tickets should reach you within a week. ○ The company has always acted within the law (= legally). • She came **within an inch of** losing her life (= She almost died). • We can wear what we like to work, **within limits** (= following certain rules). • You can say whatever you like, **within reason** (= using good judgment).

without /wɪð'aʊt, wɪθ-/ prep, adv [not gradable] not having or doing (something), or not having the use or help of (someone or something) • He came out without a coat. ○ He looks younger without the moustache. ○ Thanks for your help—I couldn't have done it without you. ○ You shouldn't drive for more than three hours without taking a break. ○ That was without (a) doubt/without question (= certainly) the best

vacation I've ever had. ○ When you have no money, you just have to learn to do without. • **Without fail** means in every case, or for certain: She takes a walk every morning without fail. • And now, **without further ado** (= with no more talking about it), here is our special guest speaker.

withstand /wɪθ'stænd, wɪð-/ v [T] past **withstood** /wɪθ'stʊd, wɪð-/ to receive without being changed or damaged by (something powerful); bear • The building has to be strong enough to withstand severe winds and storms. ○ Coaches have to be tough to withstand the constant pressure to win.

witness [PERSON WHO SEES] /'wɪt·nəs/ n [C/U] a person who sees an event happening, esp. a crime or an accident • According to witnesses, the car used in the robbery was a green van with Pennsylvania license plates. [C] • If someone is witness to something, they see it: She was witness to the tragic event. [U] • A witness is also someone who is asked to be present at a particular event and sign their name in order to prove that things have been done correctly: The will has to be signed by two witnesses. [C] • If something **is/bears witness to** something, it shows or proves it: The latest sales figures are witness to the success of our advertising campaign.

witness /'wɪt·nəs/ v [T] • We were there at the time of the riots and witnessed a lot of looting. ○ The university has witnessed (= experienced) quite a few changes over the years. • Witness also means to show or give proof of something: The program aroused strong feelings, as witnessed by the number of letters the station received. ○ Rock music is becoming a health problem—witness the loss of hearing (= for proof, look at the loss of hearing) in some of our youth. • If you are asked to witness an event, you are asked to be present at it and sign your name to prove that things have been done correctly.

witness [PERSON IN COURT] /'wɪt·nəs/ n [C] a person in a law court who promises to tell the truth and answers questions about what they saw or know • defense/prosecution witnesses ○ Five witnesses are expected to testify at the trial today. • A **witness stand** is a raised place usually near the judge where a witness sits when being questioned.

wits /wɪts/ pl n practical intelligence or understanding • She's learned to survive on her wits. • If you are **at** your **wits' end**, you are so worried, confused, or annoyed that you do not know what to do next: She was at her wits' end trying to figure out how to control her 14-year-old son. • If you **have/keep** your **wits about** you, you are able to think and react quickly when something dangerous or difficult happens unexpectedly: She managed to keep her wits about her and escaped unharmed. • If something or someone frightens you **out**

of your **wits**, they frighten you very badly: *That strange noise during the night scared me out of my wits.*

witticism /'wɪt·ə,sɪz·əm/ *n* [C] a remark that is WITTY (= both intelligent and amusing)

witty /'wɪt̬·i/ *adj* • See at WIT.

wives /waɪvz/ *pl of* WIFE

wizard /'wɪz·ərd/ *n* [C] a man who is believed to have magical powers and who uses them to help or harm other people • (*approving*) You might call someone a wizard (also *infml* **wiz**) who has great skill or who manages to do something that is extremely difficult: *a financial wizard* ○ (*infml*) *Adele is a wiz at fixing computer problems.* • Compare WITCH.

wizened /'wɪz·ənd/ *adj* having dry skin showing many lines, esp. because of old age • *a wizened old man*

wobble /'wɑb·əl/ *v* [I/T] to shake or move from side to side in a way that shows a lack of balance, or to cause (something) to do this • *The table wobbles because its legs are uneven.* [I]

wobbly /'wɑb·li, -ə·li/ *adj* • *a wobbly ladder* ○ *I was still weak, and my legs felt a little wobbly.*

woe /woʊ/ *n* [U] *fml* bad troubles causing much suffering • *She poured out her tale of woe.* • Woes are great problems or troubles: *The country has been beset by economic woes for the past few years.*

woefully /'woʊ·fə·li/ *adv* (of a bad situation) extremely; very • *Medical resources were woefully inadequate during the emergency.* ○ *The staff was woefully underpaid and thoroughly demoralized.*

woeful /'woʊ·fəl/ *adj* very bad, or (of something bad) very great or extreme • *They displayed a woeful ignorance of the safety rules.*

wok /wɑk/ *n* [C] a large, bowl-shaped pan used for frying food quickly in hot oil

woke /woʊk/ *past simple of* WAKE STOP SLEEPING

woken /'woʊ·kən/ *past participle of* WAKE STOP SLEEPING

wolf ANIMAL /wʊlf/ *n* [C] *pl* **wolves** /wʊlvz/ a wild animal of the dog family • **A wolf in sheep's clothing** is someone or something that seems to be good but is actually not good at all: *My grandfather was a wolf in sheep's clothing—he looked like a sweet old man, but he was really mean.*

wolf EAT /wʊlf/ *v* [T] *infml* to eat (a large amount of food) very quickly • *He wolfed down lunch in five minutes.*

woman /'wʊm·ən, *Southern also* 'wʌm-/ *n* [C] *pl* **women** /'wɪm·ən/ an adult female human being • *The driver of the other car was a woman.* ○ *He showed no sensitivity to women's concerns.*

womanhood /'wʊm·ən,hʊd/ *n* [U] the state of being a woman • *The girl had matured into womanhood.*

womanly /'wʊm·ən·li/ *adj* typical of a woman • *Mrs. Willis listens with womanly sympathy.*

womanizer /'wʊm·ə,naɪ·zər/ *n* [C] *disapproving* a man known for having many temporary, informal sexual relationships with women • *He's a liar and a womanizer.*

womankind /'wʊm·ən,kaɪnd/ *n* [U] the female part of the human race • *We're talking about womankind, not about men!*

womb /wuːm/ *n* [C] the organ of a woman or other female mammal in which a baby develops before birth; uterus • *She must stay healthy for the sake of the baby in her womb.*

women /'wɪm·ən/ *pl of* WOMAN • A **women's room** (also **ladies' room**) is a public bathroom for women and girls. Compare **men's room** at MEN.

won /wʌn/ *past simple and past participle of* WIN

wonder QUESTION /'wʌn·dər/ *v* to think about things in a questioning and sometimes doubting way • *I often wonder about those kids.* [I] ○ *I wonder what he is doing here.* [+ *wh-* word] ○ *Don't you ever wonder if she's happy?* [I]

wonder SURPRISE /'wʌn·dər/ *n* [C/U] a feeling of great surprise and admiration, or someone or something that causes such feelings • *People simply stared at her in wonder.* [U] ○ *She's a wonder!* [C] ○ *If you didn't study, no wonder you failed the test.* [U] ○ *Among the wonders of medicine is anesthetic.* [C] • If you say **it is a wonder** something happens, you are surprised by it: *After having so many problems with the house, it's a wonder they stayed.* • (*infml*) A **wonder drug** is an extremely effective medicine: *Doctors hope for a wonder drug to fight AIDS.*

wonderful /'wʌn·dər·fəl/ *adj* extremely good • *Becoming a father was the most wonderful experience of my life.*

wonderfully /'wʌn·dər·fə·li/ *adv* • *I took a vacation and feel wonderfully rested.* • LP VERY, COMPLETELY, AND OTHER INTENSIFIERS

wonk /wɔːŋk, wɑŋk/ *n* [C] *slang* a person who likes to think about or study something and spends a great amount of time doing it • *He's a policy wonk and will talk for hours about solutions to problems.*

won't /woʊnt/ *contraction of* **will not** • *You won't believe this, but that cactus is a member of the lily family.* • Won't can be used as a more formal way of inviting someone to do something, or of offering someone something: *Won't you come in?*

wont /wɔnt, woʊnt/ *n* [U] (used after a possessive) habit or custom • *Mr. Rivers, as is his wont, has asked some difficult questions.*

wont /wɔnt, woʊnt/ *adj* [+ *to* infinitive] • *They were wont to use the word inspiration too much* (= this was their habit).

woo /wuː/ *v* [T] he/she/it **woos**, **wooing**, *past* **wooed** to try to persuade (someone) to support you • *A candidate must woo voters by mak-*

ing them feel important. • (*dated*) If a man woos a woman, he tries to persuade her to marry him: *He wooed her with romantic dinners, the theater, gifts.*

wood HARD MATERIAL /wʊd/ *n* [C/U] the hard substance that forms the inside part of the branches and trunk of a tree, used to make things or as a fuel • *He makes tables and other things from different kinds of wood.* [C] • A **woodshed** is a small building where wood used as fuel is stored. • A **wood stove** or **wood-burning stove** is a stove for heating or cooking that uses wood for fuel. • **Woodwork** is anything made of wood inside a building, esp. the wood around the edges of doors, windows, and floors. • **Woodworking** is the activity of making objects, esp. furniture, from wood.

wooden /'wʊd·ᵊn/ *adj* [not gradable] • *They ate at a long wooden table.*

wood GROUP OF TREES /wʊdz/ *n* [C] WOODS • *Beyond them lay a dense wood.* • A **woodland** is an area of land on which many trees grow.

woodchuck /'wʊd·tʃʌk/, **groundhog** *n* [C] a small North American mammal with short legs and rough red-brown fur

woodcut /'wʊd·kʌt/ *n* [C] a picture printed from a pattern cut into the surface of a block of wood • *Long ago, woodcuts were used by printers for illustrations.*

wooded /'wʊd·əd/ *adj* • See at WOODS.

wooden WOOD /'wʊd·ᵊn/ *adj* [not gradable] • See at WOOD HARD MATERIAL.

wooden AWKWARD /'wʊd·ᵊn/ *adj* stiff and awkward, or lacking expression • *She's a wooden speaker.*

woodpecker /'wʊd·pek·ər/ *n* [C] a bird with a strong beak that it hammers into tree trunks to find insects to eat

woods /wʊdz/ *pl n*, **wood** /wʊd/ *n* [C] an area of land covered with a thick growth of trees • *Shaded from the sun, the woods were cool and quiet.*

wooded /'wʊd·əd/ *adj* • *The house stood on a wooded hillside.*

woodwind /'wʊd·wɪnd/ *n* [C/U] a type of musical instrument that is played by blowing over a REED • *The recording has some nice woodwind parts.* [U] ○ *She uses keyboards and woodwinds.* [C]

woof /wʊf/ *n* [C] the noise that a dog makes when it BARKS

wool /wʊl/ *n* [U] the soft, curly hair from sheep, or thread or cloth made from this • *I bought some fine wool to knit a baby sweater.*

woolen /'wʊl·ən/, **wool** /wʊl/ *adj* [not gradable] • *She lay under a red woolen blanket.*

woolens /'wʊl·ənz/ *pl n* clothes made from wool • *I wear woolens a lot.*

woozy /'wuː·zi/ *adj infml* slightly sick, confused, and likely to fall • *This medicine may make you woozy.*

word LANGUAGE UNIT /wɜrd/ *n* [C] a single unit of language that has meaning and can be spoken or written • *The word "environment" means different things to different people.* ○ *She spoke so fast I couldn't understand a word* (= anything she said). • If someone says you should **not breathe/say a word** about something, they do not want you to tell other people about it: *Don't breathe a word of this to anyone.* • If something is **word for word**, it uses exactly the same words as something else: *She copied it word for word from the encyclopedia.* • **Word processing** is the act of putting documents, letters, and other texts in electronic form on a computer. • A **word processor** is a computer program used for preparing documents and letters.

word /wɜrd/ *v* [T always + adv/prep] to choose the words with which to express (something) • *His description was carefully worded to cover various possibilities.*

–word /ˌwɜrd/ *combining form* used after the first letter of another word to avoid saying that word • *Ten years ago, you rarely heard the F-word in a movie.*

worded /'wɜrd·əd/ *adj* [not gradable] • *a strongly worded letter*

wording /'wɜrd·ɪŋ/ *n* [U] the exact choice of words • *The wording of the agreement was too vague.*

wordy /'wɜrd·i/ *adj* containing too many words • *Your memo is too wordy—make it short and to the point.*

word BRIEF STATEMENT /wɜrd/ *n* [C usually sing] a brief discussion or statement • *Could I have a word with you?* ○ *Let me give you a word of advice.*

word NEWS /wɜrd/ *n* [U] news or a message • *We were excited when word of the discovery reached us.* • **The word is** (= It has been reported but is not certain) *that the boss is retiring soon.* • If you learn about something by **word of mouth**, someone tells you about it: *Students discovered the center by word of mouth.*

word PROMISE /wɜrd/ *n* [U] a promise • *You have my word—I won't tell a soul.* • A **man of his word/woman of her word** is someone who does what they say they will do.

word ORDER /wɜrd/ *n* [C usually sing] an order or request • *If you want me to leave, just say/give the word.*

wore /wɔr, wour/ *past simple of* WEAR

work DO A JOB /wɜrk/ *v* [I/T] to use effort in doing something, esp. a job, or to use effort for (a period of time), for which you are paid • *She works long hours.* [T] ○ *Richie worked the night shift.* [T] ○ *Designers worked with the director.* [I] ○ *Mike works for a computer company.* [I] ○ *Medics were working on him for an hour.* [I] ○ *She worked on the project with Luce.* [I] ○ *Anna works well with others.* [I] ○ *I have to work on Saturday.* [I] • If you **work like a dog** or

work your **ass off**, you work very hard. • If you **work the land/soil**, you grow crops.

work /wɜrk/ n [U] the use of effort to do or make something that has value, and for which you are usually paid • outdoor/office/manual work ○ Steve's out of work again (= not employed). • If someone is **at work**, they are doing a job: Bob's at work on that software. • A **workday** is a day on which most people do a job for money, or the amount of time each day a person spends doing their job. • The **work ethic** (also **Protestant ethic**) is the belief that work is valuable as an activity and is morally good. • A **work force** is the people available to work or actually employed in a particular area, industry, or company. • A **workload** is an amount of work that a person is expected to do. • A **workman** is a man who uses physical skill and especially his hands in doing his job. • **Workmanlike** means done with skill: a workmanlike job/performance • **Workmanship** is the skill with which something was made or done: good/poor workmanship • A **workweek** is the amount of time in days or hours a person spends doing their job: a 40-hour workweek

worker /'wɜr·kər/ n [C] a person who is paid for using effort to do something • clerical/factory/farm workers ○ skilled/unskilled workers

working /'wɜr·kɪŋ/ adj [not gradable] • Employees are unhappy with working conditions. • A working person is employed: working mothers • The **working class** is the group of people in society who use physical skills in their jobs and are usually paid by the hour: a working-class neighborhood/family

work PLACE /wɜrk/ n [U] the place where a person regularly goes to do their job • I had to leave work early. ○ Does it take long to commute to work? • A **workbench** is a strong, solid table on which machines or objects are cut, built, combined, or separated. • A **workplace** is a place where people do their jobs. • A **workshop** is a space in a building equipped with tools and often machines for making or repairing things. See also WORKSHOP. • A **workstation** is an area in a place of business where one person works, esp. at a computer.

work PERFORM AS INTENDED /wɜrk/ v [I/T] to perform as intended or desired, or to cause (something) to do what it was intended to do • The medicine ought to work right away. [I] ○ Our plan worked perfectly. [I] ○ I don't know how to work this computer. [T] ○ He knows how to work the system (= get what he wants from it). [T] • Something that **works wonders** is very effective: A little flattery can work wonders.

workable /'wɜr·kə·bəl/ adj likely to do or achieve what is intended • a workable plan/solution

working /'wɜr·kɪŋ/ adj [not gradable] • The mechanic finally got the car back in working order. • If you have a **working knowledge** of

something, you have enough practical experience to be able to use it or do it: a working knowledge of English

workings /'wɜr·kɪŋz/ pl n the way something, such as an organization or machine, does what it is intended to do • Photographs showed the inner workings of the bomb.

works /wɜrks/ pl n the parts of a machine, esp. the parts that move • Something that is **in the works** is being done: Salary increases are already in the works. • See also WORKS.

work OBJECT /wɜrk/ n [C] an object produced as a result of effort, esp. something intended to be art • The museum is showing works by 20th-century artists. • A **work of art** is an object made by an artist, esp. a picture or statue.

work /wɜrk/ v [T] to shape (something) with your hands • She carefully works the clay.

work HAVE EFFECT /wɜrk/ v [I always + adv/prep] (of a condition or fact) to have an effect, esp. one that either helps or causes difficulties • Time was working against us. ○ Jimmie has a lot working in his favor.

□ **work out** obj AGREE TO , **work** obj **out** /'-'-/ v adv [M] to agree to or arrange (something), esp. after discussion • Committee members met today to work out a compromise.

□ **work out** obj DISCOVER , **work** obj **out** /'-'-/ v adv [M] to discover (an answer), develop (an idea), or calculate (an amount) • You can use a calculator to work out the solution. ○ She works out each scene on paper.

□ **work out** HAPPEN /'-'-/ v adv [I] (of a situation) to happen or develop in a particular, esp. a satisfactory, way, or (of a person) to be suitable for a particular situation • Nothing was working out right. ○ Is your new assistant working out OK?

□ **work out** EXERCISE /'-'-/ v adv [I] to exercise in order to improve fitness, strength, or physical appearance, or to improve your skill in a sport • I work out on my stationary bike.

workout /'wɜr·kaʊt/ n [C] • After a one-hour workout, Sam felt good.

□ **work up** BRING INTO BEING /'-'-/ v prep [T] to bring (something) into existence, esp. gradually or in stages • I can't work up any enthusiasm for this plan. ○ You went running and barely worked up a sweat. • If someone **works their way up** in an organization, they achieve a better job there: She quickly worked her way up to vice president.

□ **work** obj **up** MAKE UPSET /'-'-/ v adv [T] to make (yourself or another person) excited or upset • You've worked yourself up over nothing.

worked up /wɜrk't ʌp/ adj • He gets worked up over silly things.

workaholic /ˌwɜr·kə'hɔː·lɪk, -'hɑl·ɪk/ n [C] a person who works a lot of the time and finds it difficult not to work

workfare /'wɜrk·fer, -fær/ n [U] a government program under which people who receive WEL-

FARE (= money from the government) and are able to work must work

workout /'wɜr·kɑut/ n [C] • See at WORK OUT EXERCISE.

works /wɜrks/ pl n infml all the extra things that may be offered with something • *This camera came with a carrying case, zoom lens, tripod—the works.* • See also **works** at WORK PERFORM AS INTENDED.

workshop /'wɜrk·ʃɑp/ n [C] a meeting in which people discuss and often show in a practical way how they do a job or perform an activity, so that experiences can be shared and skills can be improved • *a teacher-training workshop* • See also **workshop** at WORK PLACE.

world THE EARTH /wɜrld/ n [U] the planet on which human life has developed, esp. including all people and their ways of life • *People from all over the world will be attending the conference.* ○ *The rapid growth of computers has changed the world.* • The world can also mean the whole physical universe: *The world contains many solar systems, not just ours.* • A **man/woman of the world** has a lot of experience of life and can deal with most situations. • You can use **in the world** to emphasize a question or a statement: *What in the world are you doing in the closet?* • If a person or thing is **world-class**, they are among the best of their type: *a world-class athlete* • A person or thing that is **world-famous** is famous in many parts of the world: *a world-famous actress* • A **world power** is a country that has enough economic, military, and political strength to influence events in many other countries. • The **World Series** is a set of baseball games played each year between the two best teams in the US and Canada. • The **World Wide Web** (also the **Web**) is an information network of text, pictures, and sound that people have access to when they use the INTERNET (= system in which many computers are connected around the world).

world WHOLE AREA /wɜrld/ n [C] all of a particular group or type of thing, such as countries or animals, or a whole area of human activity or understanding • *the animal/plant world* ○ *the business world* ○ *the world of entertainment* ○ *In the world of politics, the president's voice is still the most powerful in the nation.* • If a person is in a **world of** their **own**, they consider their own ideas and do not give much attention to what is happening around them.

world LARGE DEGREE /wɜrld/ n [U] a large degree; a lot • *There's a world of difference between the two hotels.*

worlds /'wɜrldz/ pl n • *The two men are worlds apart* (= completely opposed) *in their political views.*

worldly PHYSICAL /'wɜrl·dli/ adj having to do with physical things and ordinary life • *world-*

ly *success* ○ *She lost all her worldly possessions in the fire.*

worldly EXPERIENCED /'wɜrl·dli/ adj experienced in the ways of the world • *He's older and more worldly than the other students in his class.*

worldwide /'wɜrld'dwɑɪd/ adj, adv [not gradable] existing or happening in all parts of the world • *a worldwide recession* ○ *Their worldwide sales were growing by 20% a year.* ○ *The rock group has sold six million copies of the album worldwide.*

worm ANIMAL /wɜrm/ n [C] a small animal with a long, narrow, soft body without legs or bones • PIC EARTHWORM

worm MOVE SLOWLY /wɜrm/ v [T always + adv/prep] to move slowly or carefully, esp. because of difficulties • *He wormed his way through the crowd as quickly as he could.* ○ (fig.) *He was a spy who wormed his way into friendship with the German high command.*

worn /wɔːrn, woʊrn/ past participle of WEAR • A **worn-out** object is no longer usable because it has been used too much: *The city is looking for a place to dump its worn-out equipment.* • If a person or an animal is **worn out**, they are extremely tired: *They were worn out after their long walk.*

worrisome /'wɜr·iː·səm, 'wʌ·riː-/ adj causing worry • *Alcohol and tobacco use by young people is especially worrisome.*

worry /'wɜr·i, 'wʌ·ri/ v [I/T] to think about unpleasant things that might happen or about problems, esp. in a way that makes you unhappy, or to cause (someone) to think that way • *If you buy a train ticket for the whole month, you won't have to worry about getting a ticket every day.* [I] ○ *My mother always worries about me when I don't come home by midnight.* [I] ○ *"Will you be all right walking home?" "Don't worry—I'll be fine."* [I] ○ *She worried that she might not be able to find another job.* [+ that clause] ○ *A lot of things worried him about his roommate.* [T]

worry /'wɜr·i, 'wʌ·ri/ n [C/U] • *Fortunately, right now we don't have any worries about money.* [C]

worried /'wɜr·iːd, 'wʌ·riːd/ adj • *We were very worried when he did not answer his phone.* ○ *She had a worried look on her face.*

worse /wɜrs/ adj [not gradable], *comparative of* BAD; more unpleasant, difficult, or severe than before or than something else • *Annette may be bad at math, but Bill is even worse.* ○ *If this sore throat gets any worse, I'll have to see a doctor.*

worse /wɜrs/ adv [not gradable], *comparative of* BADLY • *The storm grew worse.* ○ *Walking only made the cough worse.* • To be **worse off** is to be in a less satisfactory or less successful situation than you were before: *If you keep borrowing money to pay off your debts, you'll be even worse off than you are now.*

worse /wɜrs/ n [U] • *"How was the movie?" "I've seen worse."*

worsen /'wɜr·sən/ v [I/T] • *The next day his fever went up and his condition worsened.* [I]

worship PRAY /'wɜr·ʃəp/ v [I/T] **-p-** or **-pp-** to pray to (God or a god) • *They went on a pilgrimage to India to worship at the holy Buddhist shrines there.* [I] • To worship is also to go regularly to a place for religious ceremonies: *They work for the same company, socialize together, and worship at the same church.* [I]

worship /'wɜr·ʃəp/ n [U] • *Native Americans took part in Christian worship in growing numbers.* • A **house/place of worship** is a building for religious ceremonies and prayer.

worshiper, worshipper /'wɜr·ʃə·pər/ n [C] • *By noon, worshipers had begun streaming out of the cathedral.*

worship ADMIRE /'wɜr·ʃəp/ v [T] to love and admire (someone or something) greatly • *As kids, we worshiped our Aunt Martha, who let us sleep late and took us to great places.*

worshiper, worshipper /'wɜr·ʃə·pər/ n [C] • (*fig.*) *Sun worshipers were at the beach all day long.*

worst /wɜrst/ adj [not gradable], *superlative of* BAD; of the lowest quality, or the most unpleasant, difficult, or severe • *That was the worst meal I've ever eaten.* • If you are planning something, a **worst-case** is the worst result of all the possibilities: *Military planners have told us to prepare for a worst-case scenario involving many casualties.*

worst /wɜrst/ n [U] • *None of my brothers were very good in sports, but I was easily the worst.* • **At worst** means in the worst possible case: *There's no harm in applying for the job—at worst, they'll turn you down.*

worsted /'wɜr·stəd, 'wʊs·təd/ n [U] a type of woolen cloth used to make clothes

worth MONEY /wɜrθ/ n [U] the amount of money that something can be sold for • *The estimated worth of her jewels alone is about $30 million.* • A particular amount of money's worth of something is the amount of money that it costs: *$20 worth of gasoline* • LP PRICE

worth /wɜrθ/ adj [not gradable] having a value in money of • *They're asking $10,000 for the car, but I don't think it's worth that much.* ○ *It is an expensive restaurant, but for special occasions it's worth it* (= the value of what you get is equal to the money spent). • If a person is worth a particular amount of money, they have that amount or own things that would cost that amount: *She must be worth at least half a million.*

worthless /'wɜrθ·ləs/ adj having no value in money • *Now that the company has gone bankrupt, your contract is worthless.*

worthlessness /'wɜrθ·lə·snəs/ n [U]

worth IMPORTANCE /wɜrθ/ n [U] the importance or usefulness of something or someone • *a sense of personal worth* ○ *As a teacher, I find*

it's extremely difficult to convince the younger generation that history has worth.

worth /wɜrθ/ adj [not gradable] • If something is worth having or doing, it is important or useful enough to have or do: *There are only two things worth reading in this newspaper—the TV listings and the sports page.* ○ *I don't think it's worth talking about any more.* • If something for which you have to make an effort is **worth it**, it is enjoyable or beneficial despite the effort needed: *It was a long climb to the top of the hill, but the view from the top was worth it.* • If an activity is **worth your while**, you will benefit from doing it: *It would be worth your while to see if you can still get tickets to the show.*

worthless /'wɜrθ·ləs/ adj unimportant or useless • *When I felt worthless, I found that my religious values were a help.*

worthlessness /'wɜrθ·lə·snəs/ n [U] • *Feelings of worthlessness overwhelmed him.*

worth AMOUNT /wɜrθ/ n [U] an amount of something that will last a stated period of time or that takes a stated amount of time to do • *We got a week's worth of diapers at the supermarket.* ○ *When the computer crashed, we lost six month's worth of work.*

worthwhile /wɜrθ'hwaɪl, -'waɪl/ adj useful, important, or beneficial enough to be a suitable reward for the money or time spent or the effort made • *She considers teaching a worthwhile career.*

worthy DESERVING RESPECT /'wɜr·ði/ adj deserving respect, admiration, or support • *a worthy goal/project* ○ *It was a worthy cause, and we were glad to make a contribution.* ○ *She soon proved herself worthy of the trust we placed in her.*

worthy DESERVING /'wɜr·ði/ adj deserving or suitable for • *Each of the ten chapters is worthy of a separate book.* ○ *After viewing the damage, the president decided that the area was worthy of federal disaster relief.*

would FUTURE /wʊd, wəd/ v aux used to refer to future time after a verb in the past tense • *He said he would see his brother tomorrow.* ○ *They hoped they would go to France for their next vacation.* • LP AUXILIARY VERBS

would INTENTION /wʊd, wəd/ v aux used to express an intention or plan after a verb in a past tense • *He said he would love her forever.* ○ *They promised that tomorrow they would help.* • **Would-be** means wanting or trying to be: *a would-be artist/politician* • LP AUXILIARY VERBS

would REQUEST /wʊd, wəd/ v aux used as a form of will in requests and offers • *"Would you like some cake?" "Yes, I would."* ○ *Would you pick up a newspaper on your way home?* • LP AUXILIARY VERBS

would WILL /wʊd, wəd/ *past simple of* WILL CAN • *The car wouldn't start this morning.*

would POSSIBLE /wʊd, wəd/ v aux used to refer to a possibility or probability • *I would* *hate to miss the show.* • Would is used with if in sentences that show what will happen if something else happens: *What would you do if you lost your job?* • LP AUXILIARY VERBS

would ALWAYS /wʊd, wəd/ *v aux* used to suggest that in the past something happened often or always • *In summer my dad would sit on the back porch after supper and read the newspaper.* • LP AUXILIARY VERBS

wouldn't /'wʊd·ənt/ *contraction of* **would not** • *He wouldn't say yes and he wouldn't say no.*

wound WIND /waʊnd/ *past simple and past participle of* WIND

wound INJURY /wuːnd/ *n* [C] a hurt or injury to the body, such as a cut or tear in the skin or flesh • *a gunshot/stab wound* ○ *He had a deep wound in his arm and had lost a lot of blood.*

wound /wuːnd/ *v* [T] • *Several people were wounded in the attack.*

wound HURT FEELINGS /wuːnd/ *v* [T] to hurt the feelings of (someone); upset • *He totally ignored her, and she was deeply wounded.*

wove /woʊv/ *past simple of* WEAVE MAKE CLOTH

woven /'woʊ·vən/ *past participle of* WEAVE MAKE CLOTH, WEAVE TWIST

wow /waʊ/ *exclamation infml* used to show surprise or pleasure • *Wow! Did you hear that noise?*

wrangle /'ræŋ·ɡəl/ *v* [I] to argue, often in a noisy or angry way • *We have been wrangling with the management for weeks over parking spaces for employees.*

wrap /ræp/ *v* [T] **-pp-** to cover or enclose (something or someone) with paper, cloth, or other material • *She wrapped (up) the present and tied it with ribbon.* [T/M] ○ *Wrap the chicken in foil and cook it for two hours.* ○ *If you wrap yourself in this blanket, you will stay warm.* • If a person wraps their fingers or arms around something, they hold it tightly: *She sat back in her chair and wrapped her arms around her knees.* • If you can **wrap** someone **around** your **little finger**, you can easily persuade them to do what you want: *She could wrap her father around her little finger.*

wrap /ræp/ *n* [C/U] • A wrap is a piece of clothing that a person, esp. a woman, wears around the shoulders to keep warm or as a stylish addition to a suit, coat, etc.: *a silk/woolen wrap* [C] • Wrap is material that is used to cover or protect something, such as food: *Put some plastic wrap around the leftover meat.* [U] • **Wrapping paper** is decorated paper that is used to cover presents.

wrapper /'ræp·ər/ *n* [C] • A wrapper is a piece of paper or plastic that has been used to cover something: *a candy wrapper*

▫ **wrap up** *obj*, **wrap** *obj* **up** /'-'-/ *v adv* [M] to complete or finish (something) • *It's getting late—let's wrap it up.* ○ *She wrapped up a deal just before she left on vacation.*

wraparound /'ræp·ə‚raʊnd/ *adj* [not gradable] (of clothing) made so that it can be tied around the body • *She wore a blue wraparound skirt.* • Wraparound also means curving around in one continuous piece: *wraparound sunglasses* ○ *a wraparound windshield*

wrath /ræθ/ *n* [U] *fml* extreme anger • *He left home to escape his father's wrath.*

wreak /riːk, rek/ *v* [T] *past* **wreaked** or **wrought** /rɔːt/ to cause (something) to happen in a violent way • *Her death is the latest reminder of the violence wrought by gangs.* ○ *Changes in the climate have wreaked/wrought havoc with the region's usual weather pattern.*

wreath /riːθ/ *n* [C] *pl* **wreaths** /riːðz, riːθs/ a ring made of flowers and leaves or evergreens • *The bride wore a wreath of flowers on her head.*

wreck /rek/ *v* [T] to destroy or badly damage (something) • *The explosion wrecked one house and shattered nearby windows.* ○ *A prison record would wreck his chances of becoming a lawyer.*

wreck /rek/ *n* [C] • A wreck is a vehicle or ship that has been destroyed or badly damaged. • A wreck can also be something that is badly in need of repair: *We bought this old wreck of a house and fixed it up.* • If a person is described as a wreck, they are in bad physical or mental condition: *Coping with three kids and a mother in the hospital, she's a nervous wreck.*

wreckage /'rek·ɪdʒ/ *n* [U] what is left of something badly damaged • *Safely experts were studying the wreckage to find out what caused the crash.*

wren /ren/ *n* [C] a very small brown bird

wrench TWIST /rentʃ/ *v* [T] to pull and twist (something) suddenly or violently away from a fixed position • *The ball was wrenched from his hands by another player.* • If you wrench part of your body, such as your arm or knee, you twist it badly and injure it: *He wrenched his back while digging in the garden.*

wrenching /'ren·tʃɪŋ/ *adj* extremely stressful • *He arrived as part of a second assault wave on the beach to find a wrenching scene of slaughter and bewildered, hiding survivors.*

wrench TOOL /rentʃ/ *n* [C] a tool for holding and turning objects • *an adjustable wrench*

wrest /rest/ *v* [T] *fml* to obtain (something) with difficulty, effort, or violence • *Shareholders will try to wrest control of the company from the current management.*

wrestle /'res·əl/ *v* [I/T] to fight with (someone) by holding them and trying to throw them to the ground, or to do this as a sport • *He wrestled for Iowa State University.* [I]

wrestler /'res·lər/ *n* [C] • *professional wrestlers*

wrestling /'res·lɪŋ/ *n* [U] a sport in which you use your arms and legs, or sometimes the arms only, to try to force the other competitor to the ground and hold them there for a short time

□**wrestle with** /'---/ *v prep* [T] to try to solve (a difficult problem) or make (a difficult decision) • *He wrestled with the problem for several weeks, not sure what to do.*

wretch /retʃ/ *n* [C] *literary* someone who has suffered a lot and deserves sympathy • *The poor wretches had no chance to survive.*

wretched /'retʃ·əd/ *adj* unhappy or extremely sad • *He looked so ill and wretched as he spoke that he made me feel wretched myself.* • Something described as wretched is very bad or of poor quality: *Workers lived in wretched, overcrowded shacks.*

wriggle /'rɪg·əl/ *v* [I/T] to make small quick movements with the body, turning from side to side • *Somehow he twisted himself about and wriggled free of Farkas's grip and danced away.* [I]

wring /rɪŋ/ *v* [T] *past* **wrung** /rʌŋ/ to twist (esp. a piece of wet material) held tightly in the hands by pressing your hands together and turning them in opposite directions to push the liquid out • *She wrung out the shirt and hung it up to dry.* [M] • If someone wrings the neck of animal, such as a chicken, they kill it by twisting and breaking its neck. • If you **wring** something **from/out of** someone, you force or persuade them to give or tell it to you: *Congress is seeking to wring concessions from a weakened President.* • To **wring** your **hands** is to show that you are anxious and worried: *We should do something to help rather than just wringing our hands about it.* • If you say you will **wring** someone's **neck**, you are very angry with them: *I could wring her neck for getting me in such a state.* • **Wringing wet** means extremely wet: *By the time we got home we were both wringing wet.*

wrinkle /'rɪŋ·kəl/ *n* [C] a small line in the skin, or a small fold in cloth • *You need to iron out the wrinkles in your skirt.* ○ *(fig.) We still need to iron out a few wrinkles* (= slight problems) *in our agreement.*

wrinkle /'rɪŋ·kəl/ *v* [I/T] • *If you don't pack the dress carefully, it will wrinkle.* [I] • If you **wrinkle** your **nose**, you show surprise, uncertainty, or disgust at something: *"Oooh, yuck!" 7-year-old Pamela says, wrinkling her nose as she wipes gooey paste from her fingers onto her sweat pants.*

wrist /rɪst/ *n* [C] the narrow part of the arm above the hand that can bend to move the hand in different directions • *He developed strong wrists playing baseball.* • A **wristwatch** is a watch that is worn on the wrist. • PIC⃝ ARM

writ /rɪt/ *n* [C] *law* a legal document from a court of law which orders someone to do something or not to do something

write /raɪt/ *v* [I/T] *past simple* **wrote** /roʊt/, *past part* **written** /'rɪt·ən/ to create something for other people to read or use, such as a book, poem, or piece of music • *to write a poem/a story/a textbook* [T] ○ *They wrote some of the*

best songs of the 70s. [T] ○ *They have written computer software to handle our sales records.* [T] ○ *Hammond wrote a letter to his mother/ wrote his mother a letter.* [T] ○ *He writes well and is always a pleasure to read.* [I] • To write is also to make marks that represent letters, words, or numbers on a surface, esp. with a pen or pencil: *Please write your name on the dotted line.* [T] • If someone's job is to write, they create articles, stories, or books to be published: *She writes for the New York Times.* [I] • To write also means to express an idea or opinion in an article, book, etc.: *He writes that our highways are getting safer.* [+ *that* clause]

writer /'raɪt·ər/ *n* [C] • A writer is a person who writes articles, books, etc., to be published: *a sports writer* ○ *a well-known writer of children's books*

writing /'raɪt·ɪŋ/ *n* [U] • Writing is a person's style of forming letters and words with a pen or pencil, or something written: *Do you recognize the writing on the envelope?* ○ *There was writing in the margins of many pages in the book.* • Writing is also articles, books, etc., esp. of a particular type or on a particular subject: *fiction/nonfiction writing* ○ *travel writing* • Writing is also the activity of creating stories, poems, or articles: *He talked about the experience of teaching writing through interactive television.* • **In writing** means in the form of a document, printed or written on paper: *We need to have your offer in writing before we can respond to it.*

writings /'raɪt·ɪŋz/ *pl n* • Writings are the written works of a person: *the writings of Abraham Lincoln*

□**write down** *obj*, **write** *obj* **down** /'-'-/ *v* [M] to record information on paper • *If I don't write it down, I'll forget it.*

□**write in** *obj* VOTE , **write** *obj* **in** /'-'-/ *v adv* [M] (when voting in an election) to give (the name of someone who is not officially listed) as your choice

write-in /'raɪt·ɪn/ *adj* [not gradable] • *He got 32 write-in votes to Mr. Rose's 16.* ○ *They were running a last-minute write-in campaign.*

□**write in** MAKE A REQUEST /'-'-/ *v adv* [I] to send a letter or an E-MAIL message to make a request or a statement, esp. to an organization or business • *A lot of consumers write in and get nothing in response.*

□**write off** *obj* LOSE MONEY , **write** *obj* **off** /'-'-/ *v adv* [M] to accept that (a debt) will not be paid • *Last year the bank wrote off $17 million in bad debts.*

□**write off** *obj* CONSIDER UNIMPORTANT , **write** *obj* **off** /'-'-/ *v adv* [M] to decide that (someone or something) is not suitable or good enough to be successful • *When he lost the election for governor, some observers wrote him off as a future candidate, but they were proven wrong.*

□**write out** *obj*, **write** *obj* **out** /'-'-/ *v* [M] to write (something on paper) with all the necessary details • *Write the check out to me.*

▫ **write up** *obj*, **write** *obj* **up** /'-'-/ *v adv* [M] to record (something) completely on paper or on a computer, often using notes that you have made • *We have to write up the lab report for chemistry.* • To write up something or someone is also to write an article or report about them to be published: *My sister was written up in the school newspaper.*

write–up /'raɪt‧ʌp/ *n* [C] • A write-up is a report or article that makes a judgment about something, such as a play or movie: *I liked the show and gave it a good write-up in the college magazine.*

writhe /raɪð/ *v* [I] to make twisting movements with the body, esp. because you are feeling strong emotion • *He writhed in agony at the thought.*

written /'rɪt‧ᵊn/ *past participle of* WRITE

wrong NOT CORRECT /rɔːŋ/ *adj* not correct or not accurate • *Three of your answers were wrong.* ○ *That clock is wrong—it's 12:30, not 12:15.* ○ *I dialed the wrong number.* • USAGE: The opposite of wrong is RIGHT CORRECT.

wrong /rɔːŋ/ *adv* [not gradable] • *It doesn't work—what am I doing wrong?*

wrongly /'rɔːŋ‧li/ *adv* [not gradable] • *He was wrongly accused of the crime.*

wrong /rɔːŋ/ *n* • If someone is **in the wrong**, they are at fault: *We had a green light, so she was clearly in the wrong when she hit us.*

wrong NOT SUITABLE /rɔːŋ/ *adj* not suitable or desirable, or not as it should be • *It was the wrong time to ask for a raise.* ○ *She was just the wrong person for the job.* • If you are in the **wrong place at the wrong time**, something happens to you that should not have happened to you: *Cops say the kid who got shot was just in the wrong place at the wrong time.* • Someone who is **wrongheaded** continues to have an unsuitable idea or follow an unsuitable

course of action and often makes bad judgments: *It seems wrongheaded to me to spend public money on private schools.* • USAGE: The opposite of wrong is RIGHT SUITABLE.

wrong IMMORAL /rɔːŋ/ *adj* [not gradable] not morally acceptable • *He believes that capital punishment is wrong.* • USAGE: The opposite of wrong is RIGHT MORAL RULE.

wrong /rɔːŋ/ *n* [C/U] behavior or an act that is morally unacceptable; evil or an evil act • *She has a keen sense of right and wrong.* [U] ○ *It's impossible to exaggerate the wrongs inflicted by slavery.* [C] • **Wrongdoing** is a bad or illegal act, or bad or illegal behavior: *Investigators found no evidence of wrongdoing.*

wrong TREAT UNFAIRLY /rɔːŋ/ *v* [T] to treat (someone) in an unfair or unacceptable way • *He felt he had been wronged, but everyone else blamed him for what happened.* • To wrong someone is also to judge them unfairly and express uncertainty about their character: *That reporter wronged her, saying she was an unfit mother.*

wrongful /'rɔːŋ‧fəl/ *adj* [not gradable] unfair or illegal • *He has suffered terribly, after 15 years of wrongful imprisonment.*

wrong NOT WORKING /rɔːŋ/ *adj* [not gradable] not working correctly • *Something's wrong with the dishwasher—it's leaking again.*

wrote /roʊt/ *past simple of* WRITE

wrought CAUSED /rɔːt/ *past simple and past participle of* WREAK

wrought MADE /rɔːt/ *adj* [not gradable] *slightly formal* brought into being; made • *She's modest about what she has wrought.*

wrought iron /rɔːtˈaɪ‧ərn/ *n* [U] a type of iron that can be shaped • *a wrought-iron gate*

wrung /rʌŋ/ *past simple and past participle of* WRING

wry /raɪ/ *adj* [*-er/-est* only] showing that you find a bad or difficult situation slightly amusing • *a wry smile* ○ *a wry sense of humor*

X, x

X LETTER , **x** /eks/ n [C] pl **X's** or **Xs** or **x's** or **xs**
the 24th letter of the English alphabet

X NUMBER , **x** /ten, eks/ number the ROMAN NU-
MERAL for the number 10

X SEXUAL /eks/ adj [not gradable] (of movies,
electronic images, etc.) used to show that the
images or subject is strongly sexual • A movie or show that is **X-rated** contains strongly
sexual parts: an X-rated Web site • Compare G
MOVIE; NC-17; PG; R MOVIE.

x AMOUNT NOT STATED /eks/, **X** n [U] used to represent a number, or the name of person or
thing, that is not known or stated • If 2x = 8,
then x = 4.

Xerox /'zɪr·ɑks/ n [C] trademark a copy of a
document or other piece of paper with writing or printing on it made by a machine that
uses a photographic process, or the machine
itself • I can give you a Xerox of the letter if
you like.

Xerox /'zɪr·ɑks/ v [T] • Would you Xerox six
copies of the report, please?

Xmas /'krɪs·məs, 'ek·sməs/ n [U] abbreviation
for CHRISTMAS

X–ray /'eks·reɪ/ n [C] a type of RADIATION (= energy in movement) that can go through many
solid substances, allowing hidden objects
such as bones in the body to be photographed
• An X-ray is also a photograph of a part of the
body made by using X-rays: Fortunately the X-
rays showed no broken bones.

X–ray /'eks·reɪ/ v [T] • All luggage has to be X-
rayed before you can board the plane.

xylophone /'zaɪ·lə,foʊn/ n [C/U] a musical instrument of flat, wooden bars of different
lengths that produce notes when hit with sticks

Y, y

Y, y /waɪ/ *n* [C] *pl* **Y's** or **Ys** or **y's** or **ys** the 25th letter of the English alphabet

ya /jə/ *pronoun not standard* (spelled the way it is often spoken) you • *He greeted me with "How ya doin'?"*

yacht /jɑt/ *n* [C] a large and usually expensive boat, used for racing or for traveling around for pleasure • *Now he's had to sell his yacht, his place in the Bahamas, his wife's diamonds.* • A **yacht club** is a private organization for people owning yachts or other boats: *the New York Yacht Club*

yak ANIMAL /jæk/ *n* [C] a type of cattle with long hair and long horns, found mainly in Tibet

yak TALK /jæk/ *v* [I] **-kk-** *infml* to talk for a long time about unimportant matters or without achieving anything

y'all /jɔːl, jə'ɔːl/ *pronoun regional* YOU-ALL

yam /jæm/ *n* [C] a **sweet potato**, see at SWEET

yank /jæŋk/ *v* [T] to pull (something) forcefully with a quick movement • *They yanked open the screen door to run into the kitchen for cookies.*

yank /jæŋk/ *n* [C] • *She gave a yank to the reins and the horse stopped.*

Yankee /'jæŋ·ki/ *n* [C] *regional* (used mainly in the South) an American who comes from the northern US

yap /jæp/ *v* [I] **-pp-** (of a small dog) to make short, high sounds • (*disapproving slang*) (of a person) To yap is to talk: *If you weren't so busy yapping you wouldn't have missed our exit.*

yard MEASUREMENT /jɑrd/ (*abbreviation* **yd.**) *n* [C] a unit of measurement of length equal to 3 feet or approximately 0.914 meter

yard LAND AROUND HOUSE /jɑrd/ *n* [C] a piece of land surrounding a house, usually grassy land with trees and other plants • *The kids are playing in the yard out back.* • A **yard sale** (also **garage sale** or **tag sale**) is an occasion when people living in a house sell their clothes, toys, books, furniture, and other things that they do not want.

yard LAND NEXT TO BUILDING /jɑrd/ *n* [C] an area of ground next to a building that is used for a particular, usually business, purpose • *a boat yard* ○ *a prison yard*

yardstick /'jɑrd·stɪk/ *n* [C] a way of measuring how good, accurate, or effective something is • *A high salary isn't the only yardstick for success.* ○ *The only valid yardstick for measuring traffic safety is deaths per miles driven.*

yarmulke /'jɑm·ə·kə, 'jɑr·məl·kə/ *n* [C] a small, circular cover for the head worn by some Jewish men, esp. at religious ceremonies

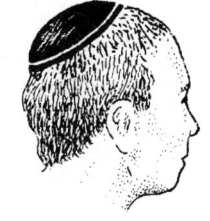
yarmulke

yarn THREAD /jɑrn/ *n* [U] thick thread used for making cloth or for making a piece of clothing esp. by KNITTING

yarn STORY /jɑrn/ *n* [C] a story, usually a long one with a lot of excitement or interest • *a boys' adventure yarn*

yawn /jɔːn/ *v* [I] to open the mouth wide and take in and let out a deep breath without conscious effort, usually when you are tired or bored • *She yawned, covering her mouth with her hand.*

yawn /jɔːn/ *n* [C] • *It had been an especially long day, she thought, barely stifling a yawn.*

yd. *n* [C] *pl* **yd.** abbreviation for YARD MEASUREMENT

yeah /jeə, jæə/ *adv* [not gradable] *infml* (spelled the way it is often spoken) yes • *"Will you drive?" "Yeah, sure."*

year /jɪr/ *n* [C] any period of twelve months, or a particular period of twelve months beginning with January 1 • *last/next year* ○ *She brought along her eight-year-old daughter.* ○ *My parents have been married for 30 years.* ○ *Richard earned his degree in the year 1995.* ○ *You can get cheaper fares now, so it's a good time of year to travel abroad.* • *We haven't seen Marie in years* (= for a very long time). • In a school, a year refers to the part of the year during which courses are taught: *September is the start of the new academic year.* • If something happens or is true **year in and year out** or **year in, year out**, it is the same for many years: *Year in and year out, he has been one of the best players in baseball.* • A **yearbook** is a book published every year by a school or other organization that gives facts about the events and achievements of the previous year.

yearly /'jɪr·li/ *adj, adv* [not gradable] • *A yearly subscription costs $25.* ○ *Members receive a newsletter twice yearly* (= two times each year).

yearn /jɜrn/ *v* [I] to desire something strongly, esp. something difficult or impossible to obtain • *Joy yearns to earn enough money from her job as a doctor's assistant for her to become independent.* [+ *to* infinitive]

yeast /jiːst/ *n* [U] a type of FUNGUS (= simple organism) that is used in making alcoholic drinks such as beer and wine, and in making bread swell and become soft

yell /jel/ *v* [I/T] to shout (words) or make a loud noise, often when you want to get someone's attention or because you are angry, excited, or in pain • *"Come back," they yelled.* ○ *Snyder heard a woman yell for help.* [I]

yell /jel/ *n* [C] • *We all let out a yell of satisfaction.*

yellow /ˈjel·oʊ/ *adj, n* [C/U] (of) a color like that of a lemon • *yellow roses* ○ *sweet yellow corn* • A **yellow jacket** is a black and yellow flying insect that stings. • The **yellow pages** is a telephone book or part of one printed on yellow paper and containing telephone numbers, addresses, and often advertisements for businesses, arranged by subject, so that people can find the particular type of business they need.

yelp /jelp/ *v* [I] to make a sudden, short, high sound, usually when in pain • *He screwed up his face and yelped in pain.*

yelp /jelp/ *n* [C] • *She let out a yelp of fear.*

yen /jen/ *n* [C usually sing] *infml* a strong but often sudden and temporary desire • *That day she had a yen for pizza.*

yep /jep, jʌp/ *adv infml* (spelled the way it is often spoken) yes • *"Should we leave?" "Yep."*

yes /jes, jeə, jæə/ *adv* [not gradable] used to express acceptance, willingness, or agreement • *"Would you like a glass of wine?" "Yes, please."* ○ *"Is Chambers Street in this direction?" "Yes, just keep going and you'll come to it."* ○ *If you would say yes* (= agree), *you'd save us all a lot of trouble.* • Yes can be used to show that you are ready to listen to someone or to answer their request for information: *"Daddy." "Yes, what do you want, honey?"* • People say **yes, sir** to show strong agreement: *He asked if he could talk to me, and I said, "Yes, sir."*

yes /jes/ *n* [C] • *The answer is yes.*

yesterday /ˈjes·tər·di, -deɪ/ *adv* [not gradable] on the day before this day • *We got back from our vacation yesterday.* ○ *Yesterday I started exercising seriously.*

yesterday /ˈjes·tər·di, -deɪ/ *n* [U] • *"Is that today's paper?" "No, it's yesterday's."*

yet NOW / THEN /jet/ *adv* [not gradable] (used in negative statements and questions) at this time or at that time; now or then • *"Is dinner ready?" "Not yet."* ○ *Has Janet finished her homework yet?* ○ *He had not yet decided what to do.*

yet IN THE FUTURE /jet/ *adv* [not gradable] in the future; still • *The best was yet to come.*

yet DESPITE THAT /jet/ *adv* [not gradable], *conjunction* despite that • *Melissa was not doing well in her physics course, yet overall she had a B average.*

yet IN ADDITION /jet/ *adv* [not gradable] (used esp. when describing a long process or an event in a series) in addition; once more • *The governor commissioned yet another study.* ○ *She didn't want to explain yet again why she was disappointed.*

yet EVEN NOW /jet/ *adv* [not gradable] even at this stage or time • *We may yet succeed—you never know.*

yield PRODUCE /jiːld/ *v* [T] to supply or produce (something positive such as a profit, an amount of food, or information) • *Some mutual funds are currently yielding 15% on new money invested.*

yield /jiːld/ *n* [C usually pl] a profit or an amount (esp. of a crop) produced • *Over the past 50 years, crop yields have risen steadily in the US.*

yield GIVE UP /jiːld/ *v* [I/T] to give up the control of or responsibility for (something), often because you have been forced to • *The Indians had not yielded their lands without a struggle.* [T] • If you yield to something, you accept that you have been defeated by it: *It's easy to yield to the temptation to borrow a lot of money.* • To yield to traffic coming from another direction is to wait and allow it to go first. [I]

y'know /jəˈnoʊ/ *contraction of* **you know**, see at YOU PERSON/PEOPLE

yodel /ˈjoʊd·ᵊl/ *v* [I] to sing by making a series of fast changes between the natural voice and a much higher voice

yodel /ˈjoʊd·ᵊl/ *n* [C]

yoga /ˈjoʊ·gə/ *n* [U] a set of physical and mental exercises that are intended to give control over the body and mind

yogurt, yoghurt /ˈjoʊ·gərt/ *n* [U] a thick, liquid food made from milk with bacteria added to it, that is slightly sour but is sometimes sweetened and flavored with fruit

yoke /joʊk/ *n* [C] (esp. in the past) a wooden bar fastened over the necks of two animals, esp. cattle, and connected to a vehicle or load that they are pulling • (*fig.*) Yoke can also refer to something that unfairly limits freedom: *the yoke of slavery*

yokel /ˈjoʊ·kəl/ *n* [C] a person who lives in an area far from cities, is not familiar with city ways, and is therefore considered slightly stupid • This word is offensive.

yolk /joʊk/ *n* [C/U] the yellow, middle part of an egg • *an egg yolk* [C]

Yom Kippur /ˌjoʊm·kəˈpʊr, ˌjɔːm-; jəmˈkɪp·ər/, **Day of Atonement** *n* [U] a Jewish holy day in September or October

yonder /ˈjɑn·dər/ *adj, adv* [not gradable] *dated* in the place or direction shown; over there • *She lives in that town yonder.*

you PERSON / PEOPLE /juː, jə/ *pronoun* the person or people spoken to • *You look nice.* ○ *I love you.* ○ *Are you two ready?* • *You will pick up Alice tonight, won't you?* **You bet** (= That is right, I certainly will). • **You can say that again!** means I completely agree with you. • *To get to the church, go to the next traffic light and make a left—you can't miss it* (= it is very easy to find). • (*infml*) **You know** (also **y'know**) is used when people pause while speaking, when they are thinking of what to say next or how to say it: *She was cleaning the house, you know, when the phone rang.* • (*infml*) **You know** (also **y'know**) is also used at the end of a statement to make sure the person you are talking to understands: *It didn't have to happen that way, you know?* • (*infml*)

You know something and **You know what** are used before an opinion or a piece of information: *You know what? I think it's time to go home.* • When people say **you mean** as part of a question, they are not sure of the facts or are expressing surprise: *"They all showed up." "You mean the entire family?"* • *Coke, ginger ale, root beer—***you name it** (= whatever you choose), *I've got it.* • **You're telling me** means I strongly agree with what you just said: *"Stephen's in a really bad mood today." "You're telling me!"* • **You're welcome** is usually said to be polite when someone thanks you for doing something: *"Thanks for returning the video." "You're welcome!"* • *It was stupid of me to lend him that money.* **You said it** (= I did not want to say that, but I agree with you)*!* • *You have to hold the bar down while you lock it—***(do) you see what I mean** (= do you understand what I am trying to explain to you)*?*

you PEOPLE GENERALLY /juː, jə/ *pronoun* people in general; anyone • *How do you get this thing to start?* • *I was sorry to hear that someone else got the job.* *"Oh well,* **you can't win them all/you win some, you lose some** (= no person can always succeed)*."* • **You never can tell** or **you never know** means there is no way of knowing or being certain, esp. about the future: *It sounds like a nice place to live, but you never can tell—we may end up hating it.*

you–all, y'all /juːˈɔːl, jəˈɔːl, jɔːl/ *pronoun regional* you • *Do you-all want some coffee before you leave?* • USAGE: You-all is a normal part of polite speech in the southeast of the US, and usually refers to more than one person.

you'd /juːd, jʊd, jəd/ *contraction of* **you had** or **you would** • *You'd* (= You would) *be warmer in your black jacket.* ○ *It happened just after you'd* (= you had) *left the room.*

you'll /juːl, jʊl, jəl/ *contraction of* **you will** or **you shall** • *I don't know if you'll like it.*

young /jʌŋ/ *adj* [*-er/-est* only] (esp. of something living) at an early stage of development or existence; not old • *Young children should not be left alone at home.* ○ *I work with wonderful young people mostly in their late teens.* ○ *The new law creates a new driver's license for those as young as 14.*

young /jʌŋ/ *pl n* • *In my opinion, miniskirts are strictly for the young.* • Young are the babies of an animal: *The bird flew back to the nest to feed her young.*

youngster /ˈjʌŋ·stər/ *n* [C] a young person • *The program was designed to find summer jobs for city youngsters ages 14 to 21.*

your BELONGING TO YOU /jʊr, joʊr, jɔːr, jər/ *pronoun* belonging to or connected with the person or people being spoken to; the possessive form of you • *Is this your umbrella?* ○ *Let's take your car because it has more room than mine.* • (*slang*) **In your face** means behaving or done in a direct, often rude way that is annoying and cannot be ignored: *If you don't tell them to get lost, they'll be back in your face faster than you know it.* • LP DETERMINERS

yours /jʊrz, joʊrz, jɔːrz, jərz/ *pronoun* belonging to you, or that which belongs to you • *Our apartment isn't as large as yours, but it suits us.* ○ *I've got something of yours* (= that belongs to you). • **Yours (truly)** is a polite way of ending a traditional letter, before you sign your name. • (*humorous*) **Yours truly** can also refer to yourself: *The plan was not made to please teachers, but to please yours truly* (= myself).

yourself /jərˈself/ *pronoun pl* **yourselves** /jərˈselvz/ the person or people being spoken to; the reflexive form of you • *Be careful with that knife or you'll cut yourself.* • Yourself is sometimes used to emphasize the subject of the sentence: *Did you girls actually raise this money yourselves?* • If you do something **by yourself**, you do it alone or without help from anyone: *You're old enough to take the bus by yourself, aren't you, Joyce?* • *Now that Neil and Sam are away, you've got the whole house* **to yourself** (= for use by you only). • LP REFLEXIVE PRONOUNS

your OF PEOPLE GENERALLY /jʊr, joʊr, jɔːr, jər/ *pronoun* belonging to or connected with any person or people generally • *Exercise is good for your health.* • LP DETERMINERS

you're /ˈjuː·ər, jər, jʊr, joʊr, jɔːr/ *contraction of* **you are**

youth /juːθ/ *n* [C/U] the period of your life when you are young, or the state of being young • *I was a good football player in my youth.* [U] • Youth also refers to young people in general: *It's quite a job, training the youth of the country to be mature, responsible citizens.* [U] • A youth is a boy or a young man: *Three of the youths were arrested for cocaine possession.* [C]

youthful /ˈjuːθ·fəl/ *adj* characteristic of young people, or relating to the period of life when you are young • *youthful enthusiasm* ○ *The sad, sometimes tragic effects of youthful drinking reach to every corner of campus life and beyond.*

youthfulness /ˈjuːθ·fəl·nəs/ *n* [U]

you've /juːv, jəv/ *contraction of* **you have** • *You've told me that story at least twice before.*

yo–yo /ˈjoʊ·joʊ/ *n* [C] *pl* **yo-yos** a toy consisting of a circular object that can be made to roll down and up a string that is tied to your hand if you spin the object and move your hand quickly at the same time

yo–yo /ˈjoʊ·joʊ/ *adj* [not gradable] *fig.* characterized by large and sudden changes from one condition to another • *Research on yo-yo dieting indicates that going on and off diets repeatedly will make weight control difficult in the long run.*

yucca /ˈjʌk·ə/ *n* [C] a plant with long, stiff

leaves on a thick stem and sometimes with white, bell-shaped flowers

yuck /jʌk/ *exclamation* an expression of disgust • *"Do you want to hold the snake?" "Yuck, no thanks."*

yucky /ˈjʌk·i/ *adj infml* disgusting or unpleasant • *My daughter says broccoli is yucky and refuses to eat it.*

yule /juːl/ *n* [U] *literary* Christmas

yummy /ˈjʌm·i/ *adj infml* (of food) tasting extremely good • *The chocolate cake was yummy.*

yuppie /ˈjʌp·i/ *n* [C] *esp. disapproving* a young, educated person who lives in a city and is successful in business, and who has a life style that involves spending a lot of money • *Once the yuppies started moving in, rents went way up.*

Z, z

Z, z /ziː, *Cdn often* zed/ *n* [C] *pl* **Z's** or **Zs** or **z's** or **zs** the 26th and last letter of the English alphabet

zany /'zeɪ·ni/ *adj* surprisingly different and a little strange, and therefore amusing and interesting • *He was responsible for the zany Sesame Street puppet characters loved by children worldwide.*

zap /zæp/ *v* [T] **-pp-** *infml* to destroy or attack (something) suddenly, esp. with electricity, RADIATION, or another form of energy • *Doctors can use a laser to zap skin blemishes.* • To zap something is also to cook or heat it in a MICROWAVE OVEN: *Do you want that meatloaf cold, or should I zap it?*

zeal /ziːl/ *n* [U] great enthusiasm or eagerness • *religious zeal* ○ *In his zeal to get his work finished on time, he made a lot of mistakes.* [+ *to* infinitive]

zealous /'zel·əs/ *adj* enthusiastic and eager • *His zealous campaign against the tobacco industry included three books about cancer and smoking.*

zebra /'ziː·brə, *Cdn often* 'zeb·rə/ *n* [C] an African wild animal that looks like a horse but has black and white or brown and white lines on its body

zed /zed/ *n* [C] *Br and Cdn* the last letter of the English alphabet; z

Zen /zen/ *n* [U] a religion that is a form of Buddhism developed in Japan

zenith /'ziː·nəθ, *Cdn often* 'zen·əθ/ *n* [C] the best, highest, or most successful point or time • *Their popularity reached its zenith in the mid-1990s.*

zero NUMBER /'zɪr·oʊ, 'ziː·roʊ/ *number pl* **zeros** or **zeroes** 0

ZERO

The number 0 is usually said as "zero" in American English.

Five, four, three, two, one, zero! • *The temperature was ten below zero.*

It is often said as "o" in telephone numbers, addresses, bank account numbers, zip codes, and other numbers that do not show an amount.

The class meets in room 602 ("six o two"). • *The zip code is 01060* ("o one o six o").

In giving sports scores, *nothing* is often used.

The Chicago Cubs beat the Cincinnati Reds, 5-0 ("five nothing"/"five to nothing").

---

zero NOTHING /'zɪr·oʊ, 'ziː·roʊ/ *n* [U] nothing; not anything • *Visibility in the fog was just about zero.* • A **zero-sum** game or situation is one in which the amount of success for one side is matched by an equal loss for the other side.

zero /'zɪr·oʊ, 'ziː·roʊ/ *adj* [not gradable] not any or no • *The economy showed zero growth in the first quarter of this year.*

zero in /'zɪr·oʊ, 'ziː·roʊ/ *v adv* [I] to direct all your attention to one object • *Really listening requires so totally zeroing in on what we want to hear that nothing can distract us from it.* • If you zero in a weapon, you aim it directly at something you want to hit: *Computers help the pilots to zero in on their targets.*

zest /zest/ *n* [U] enthusiasm, eagerness, and energy • *She's over 80, but she still has an amazing zest for life.*

zigzag /'zɪg·zæg/ *v* [I] **-gg-** to move by going first in one direction and then in a different direction, and continuing in this way • *We zigzagged through the crowds of tourists in the Vatican Museums.*

zilch /zɪltʃ/ *n* [U] *infml* nothing • *Tom knew zilch about sports.*

zillion /'zɪl·jən/ *n* [C] *infml* an extremely large number or amount • *There were zillions of people to help you, all the time.*

zinc /zɪŋk/ *n* [U] a blue-white metal used esp. in combination with other metals or for covering other metals to protect them

zinfandel /'zɪn·fən,del/ *n* [C/U] a dry, red wine made in California, or the GRAPES that it comes from

zip FASTEN /zɪp/ *v* [T] **-pp-** to fasten (a bag, clothing, etc.) with a ZIPPER • *I've got so much stuff in this bag, I can't zip it shut.* [T] ○ *You have to help the kids zip their coats up.* [M]

zip MOVE FAST /zɪp/ *v* [I always + adv/prep] **-pp-** to travel very fast • *Messengers on bicycles zipped fearlessly through the capital's traffic.*

zip /zɪp/ *n* [U] *infml* something that creates a feeling of energy or excitement • *Add pepper to give a little zip to the sauce.* • A **zip code** is a series of numbers that forms part of an address in the US and is used to help organize mail so that it can be delivered more quickly.

zipper /'zɪp·ər/ *n* [C] a device for fastening together an opening in clothes, bags, etc., and

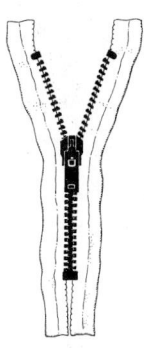

zipper

consisting of two rows of little metal or plastic parts that can be locked together by sliding another part over them

zodiac /ˈzoʊd·iːˌæk/ *n* [C/U] an area of the sky in which the positions of the sun, moon, stars, and planets are believed in ASTROLOGY to influence human behavior, and which is divided into twelve equal sections

zombie /ˈzɑm·bi/ *n* [C] someone who moves around as if they are unconscious and being controlled by someone else • *I was so tired, I walked around like a zombie.* • (in stories, movies, etc.) A zombie is a dead person brought back to life, esp. to frighten people.

zone /zoʊn/ *n* [C] an area, esp. one that has different characteristics from the ones around it or is used for different purposes • *a combat/ war zone* ◦ *He was charged with driving 75 mph in a 55 mph zone.*

zone /zoʊn/ *v* [T] to set rules for the use of (land) or for the types of structures that can be built on it • *The land is now zoned for single-family homes on two-acre plots.* ◦ *This area was originally zoned commercial.*

zoning /ˈzoʊ·nɪŋ/ *n* [U] the act of setting rules for the use of land and the types of structures that can be built on it • *The town's new zoning establishes a height limit of eight stories on any new building.* ◦ *San Francisco has strict zoning laws to preserve neighborhoods.*

zoo /zuː/ *n* [C] *pl* **zoos** an area in which animals, esp. wild animals, are kept so that people can go and look at them • *The children love to visit the elephants at the zoo.*

zoology /zoʊˈɑl·ə·dʒi, zəˈwɑl-/ *n* [U] the scientific study of animals

zoological /ˌzoʊ·əˈlɑdʒ·ɪ·kəl/ *adj* [not gradable] • *zoological research*

zoom MOVE QUICKLY /zuːm/ *v* [I] *infml* to move very quickly • *Cars and trucks zoom past.* • If costs, sales, etc., zoom, they increase quickly: *In two months the magazine's circulation zoomed to 26,000.*

zoom CAMERA /zuːm/ *v* [I] • (of a camera) To **zoom in/out** is to cause the person or thing being photographed to appear closer or farther away: *At the beginning of the movie, the camera zooms in to show two people sitting by the side of a river.*

zucchini /zʊˈkiː·ni/ *n* [C/U] *pl* **zucchini** or **zucchinis** a long, thin vegetable with a green or yellow skin that is usually cooked before being eaten

Idioms Index

A

from **A** to Z FROM RANGE
can't **abide** ABIDE
about time ABOUT APPROXIMATELY
crazy **about** CRAZY
forget (**about**) it FORGET
forget **about** *something* FORGET
have *your* wits **about** *you* WITS
how **about** HOW
is **about** it ABOUT APPROXIMATELY
keep quiet **about** *something* KEEP STAY
keep *your* wits **about** *you* WITS
know what *someone* is talking **about**
  KNOW HAVE INFORMATION
make no bones **about** MAKE CAUSE TO BE
no buts **about** it NO NOT ANY
no two ways **about** it NO NOT ANY
not any buts **about** it NO NOT ANY
not know the first thing **about** KNOW
  HAVE INFORMATION
talk **about** TALK
up and **about** UP OUT OF BED
was **about** it ABOUT APPROXIMATELY
what **about** WHAT QUESTION
wild **about** WILD NOT CONTROLLED
above all ABOVE
head and shoulders **above** HEAD BODY PART
keep *your* head **above** water KEEP STAY
rise **above** RISE INCREASE
conspicuous by *your* **absence**
  CONSPICUOUS
by **accident** ACCIDENT EVENT NOT PLANNED
in **accordance** with ACCORD AGREEMENT
on **account** of ACCOUNT REASON
on *someone's* **account** ACCOUNT REASON
take **account** of TAKE THINK OF
take *something* into **account** TAKE THINK OF
make *your* **acquaintance** MAKE PERFORM
acquired taste ACQUIRE
a tough **act** to follow TOUGH DIFFICULT
act on ACT DO SOMETHING
act *your* age ACT DO SOMETHING
get in on the **act** GET MOVE
get *your* **act** together GET TOGETHER
a piece of the **action** PIECE PART
actions speak louder than words ACTION
  SOMETHING DONE
acts out ACT PERFORM
acts up ACT DO SOMETHING
add fuel to the fire ADD
add insult to injury ADD
add up ADD
add up to ADD
without further **ado** WITHOUT

in **advance** ADVANCE HAPPENING EARLY
take **advantage** of TAKE CATCH
to *someone's* **advantage** ADVANTAGE
sad state of **affairs** SAD UNPLEASANT
run **afoul** of RUN BE/CONTINUE
after all AFTER DESPITE
day **after** day DAY
hour **after** hour HOUR
life **after** death LIFE TIME BEING ALIVE
name *someone* **after** NAME
night **after** night NIGHT
one **after** another ONE NUMBER
one **after** the other ONE NUMBER
time **after** time TIME OCCASION
week **after** week WEEK
again and **again** AGAIN
every now and **again** EVERY REPEATED
(every) now and **again** NOW AT PRESENT
once **again** ONCE AT ONE TIME
over and **over** (again) OVER AGAIN
then **again** THEN IN ADDITION
time and (**time**) again TIME OCCASION
you can say that **again** YOU PERSON/PEOPLE
against *your* better judgment AGAINST
  IN OPPOSITION
dead set **against** DEAD COMPLETE
guard **against** GUARD
the cards are stacked **against** *someone*
  CARD GAME
against *your* will AGAINST IN OPPOSITION
act *your* **age** ACT DO SOMETHING
come of **age** COME CHANGE
in this day and **age** THIS THING REFERRED TO
a week **ago** (this) WEEK
couldn't **agree** less COULDN'T
couldn't **agree** more COULDN'T
ahead of time AHEAD IN THE FUTURE
lie **ahead** LIE POSITION
press **ahead** PRESS PUSH
get **ahold** of AHOLD
clear the **air** CLEAR SEEING THROUGH
disappear into thin **air** THIN WEAK
floating on **air** FLOAT MOVE ON LIQUID
hot **air** HOT VERY WARM
nip in the **air** NIP COLD
out of thin **air** OUT OF ORIGINATING FROM
up in the **air** UP HIGHER
vanish into thin **air** THIN WEAK
rolling in the **aisles** ROLL MOVE
alive and kicking ALIVE
alive and well ALIVE
above **all** ABOVE
after **all** AFTER DESPITE
all along ALL COMPLETELY
all at once ALL COMPLETELY

turn back the **clock** TURN CHANGE DIRECTION
like **clockwork** LIKE SIMILAR TO
close call CLOSE NEAR
close shave CLOSE NEAR
behind **closed** doors BEHIND IN BACK OF
with *your* eyes **closed** WITH USING
a skeleton in the **closet** SKELETON
out of the **closet** OUT OF NOT IN A STATE OF
a wolf in sheep's **clothing** WOLF ANIMAL
cloud over CLOUD
cloud up CLOUD
join the **club** JOIN BECOME A MEMBER
don't have a **clue** HAVE POSSESS
coast to **coast** COAST LAND
the **coast** is clear COAST LAND
cog in a machine COG
toss (a **coin**) TOSS
two sides of the same **coin** TWO
cold turkey COLD LOW TEMPERATURE
get **cold** feet COLD LOW TEMPERATURE
give *someone* the **cold** shoulder GIVE OFFER
have **cold** feet COLD LOW TEMPERATURE
in **cold** blood COLD UNFRIENDLY
leave out (in the **cold**) LEAVE CAUSE TO STAY
leave *you* **cold** LEAVE CAUSE TO STAY
call *someone* **collect** CALL TELEPHONE
on a **collision** course COLLIDE
true **colors** TRUE REAL
with flying **colors** WITH HAVING
in **combination** COMBINE
come a long way COME ARRIVE
come before COME ORDER
come down in the world COME DOWN
come forward COME APPROACH
come in COME ARRIVE
come in handy COME ARRIVE
come of age COME CHANGE
come off it COME OFF COMPLETE
come on strong COME ON
MAKE INTEREST KNOWN
come out of *your* shell COME OUT
BECOME KNOWN
come to a head COME CHANGE
come to an end COME HAPPEN
come to light COME TO REACH
come to rest COME TO REACH
come to terms with COME TO REACH
come to *your* attention COME APPROACH
come to *your* rescue COME ARRIVE
come to *your* senses COME TO REACH
come true COME HAPPEN
come up in the world COME CHANGE
come with the territory TERRITORY
dream **come** true DREAM HOPE
easy **come** easy go EASY COMFORTABLE
first **come** first served FIRST
how **come** HOW
if worse **comes** to worst IF IN THAT SITUATION
if worst **comes** to worst IF IN THAT SITUATION

push **comes** to shove PUSH
USE FORCE AGAINST
get what's **coming** to *you* GET PUNISH
have another think **coming** HAVE POSSESS
have it **coming** HAVE RECEIVE
where *someone is* **coming** from WHERE
out of **commission** OUT OF
NOT IN A STATE OF
commit suicide COMMIT CRIME
common denominator COMMON SHARED
common ground COMMON SHARED
common knowledge COMMON USUAL
in **common** COMMON SHARED
keep *someone* **company** KEEP STAY
misery loves **company** MISERY
compare notes COMPARE
EXAMINE DIFFERENCES
pale by **comparison** with PALE
pale in **comparison** with PALE
fish for **compliments** FISH SEARCH
as far as *someone* is **concerned** AS
COMPARISON
in **conclusion** CONCLUDE END
jump to **conclusions** JUMP OMIT STAGES
condescend to CONDESCEND
mint **condition** MINT COIN FACTORY
out of **condition** OUT OF NOT IN A STATE OF
in **connection** with CONNECT RELATE
pros and **cons** PRO ADVANTAGE
conspicuous by *your* absence
CONSPICUOUS
bone of **contention** BONE
on the **contrary** CONTRARY OPPOSITE
to the **contrary** CONTRARY OPPOSITE
out of **control** OUT OF NOT IN A STATE OF
preach to the **converted** PREACH PERSUADE
goose *is* **cooked** GOOSE BIRD
cool it COOL CALM
lose *your* **cool** LOSE NOT MAINTAIN
around the **corner** AROUND
IN THIS DIRECTION
corner the market CORNER
out of the **corner** of *your* eye OUT OF
ORIGINATING FROM
cut **corners** CUT CROSS
stand **corrected** STAND BE IN SITUATION
at any **cost** COST SOMETHING GIVEN
at **cost** COST MONEY
cost a small fortune COST MONEY
cost an arm and a leg COST MONEY
at all **costs** COST SOMETHING GIVEN
could care less COULD BE POSSIBLE
could count on one hand COUNT CALCULATE
could do with COULD SUGGEST
could hardly believe *your* ears COULD
BE POSSIBLE
could hardly believe *your* eyes COULD
BE POSSIBLE
could have died COULD BE POSSIBLE

a raw **deal** RAW `UNFAIR`
big **deal** BIG `IMPORTANT`
no big **deal** BIG `IMPORTANT`
wheeling and **dealing** WHEEL
  `CHANGE DIRECTION`
dear to *someone's* heart DEAR `LOVED`
for **dear** life FOR `IN RELATION TO`
a fate worse than **death** FATE
a matter of life and **death** MATTER
  `SITUATION`
bored to **death** BORE `FAIL TO INTEREST`
kiss of **death** KISS
life after **death** LIFE `TIME BEING ALIVE`
scare *someone* to **death** SCARE
tickled to **death** TICKLE
to **death** DEATH
on *their* **deathbed** DEATH
in *someone's* **debt** DEBT
hit the **deck** HIT `ARRIVE AT`
stack the **deck** STACK
deep down DEEP `STRONGLY FELT`
deep pockets DEEP `DOWN`
in **deep** (trouble) DEEP `DOWN`
take a **deep** breath TAKE `ACT`
on the **defensive** DEFENSE `PROTECTION`
by **definition** DEFINITION `EXPLANATION`
common **denominator** COMMON `SHARED`
make a **dent** in DENT
put a **dent** in DENT
it **depends** DEPEND
that **depends** DEPEND
in **depth** DEPTH `SERIOUSNESS`
in the **depths** DEPTH `DISTANCE BACKWARD`
in the **depths** of DEPTH `STRENGTH`
by **design** DESIGN `INTEND`
leave a lot to be **desired** LEAVE
  `CAUSE TO STAY`
in **detail** DETAIL `INFORMATION`
in minute **detail** MINUTE `SMALL`
gory **details** GORE `BLOOD`
bound and **determined** BOUND `CERTAIN`
leave *someone* to *their* own **devices** LEAVE
  `GIVE RESPONSIBILITY`
what the **devil** WHAT `QUESTION`
devoid of DEVOID
have **dibs** on HAVE `POSSESS`
could have **died** COULD `BE POSSIBLE`
difference of opinion DIFFERENT
do not make any **difference** MAKE
  `CAUSE TO BE`
make a **difference** MAKE `CAUSE TO BE`
make all the **difference** MAKE `CAUSE TO BE`
make no **difference** MAKE `CAUSE TO BE`
same **difference** SAME `EXACTLY LIKE`
split the **difference** SPLIT
dig a hole for *yourself* DIG `MOVE EARTH`
dig *yourself* into a hole DIG `MOVE EARTH`
take a **dim** view of *something* TAKE `REACT`
a **dime** a dozen DIME

nickel and **dime** NICKEL `COIN`
stop on a **dime** STOP `PAUSE`
wine and **dine** WINE
by **dint** of DINT
dip into DIP `PUT INTO LIQUID`
dirt cheap DIRT `EARTH`
treat *someone* like **dirt** TREAT `DEAL WITH`
quick and **dirty** QUICK
talk **dirty** TALK
at a **disadvantage** DISADVANTAGE
disappear into thin air THIN `WEAK`
blessing in **disguise** BLESS
dish it out but *you* can't take it DISH OUT
at *your* **disposal** DISPOSE
in **dispute** DISPUTE
dissolve in DISSOLVE `BE ABSORBED`
dissolve into DISSOLVE `BE ABSORBED`
at a **distance** DISTANCE
from a **distance** DISTANCE
in the **distance** DISTANCE
could **do** with COULD `SUGGEST`
damned if *you* **do** and damned if *you*
  don't DAMN `BLAME`
do justice to DO `CAUSE TO HAPPEN`
do more harm than good DO
  `CAUSE TO HAPPEN`
do not make any difference MAKE
  `CAUSE TO BE`
do not think much of *someone or*
  something THINK `HAVE OPINION`
do *someone* credit DO `CAUSE TO HAPPEN`
do *someone* justice DO `CAUSE TO HAPPEN`
do the job DO `CAUSE TO HAPPEN`
do the trick DO `CAUSE TO HAPPEN`
do time TIME `PARTICULAR PERIOD`
do wonders for DO `CAUSE TO HAPPEN`
(**do**) you see what I mean YOU
  `PERSON/PEOPLE`
do *your* damnedest DAMN `VERY`
do *your* level best BEST `EXCELLENCE`
do *your* very best BEST `EXCELLENCE`
have to **do** with HAVE `CONTAIN`
how **do** you do HOW
make **do** MAKE `CAUSE`
nothing to **do** with NOTHING
something to **do** with SOMETHING
the least *someone* could **do** LEAST
what **do** you say WHAT `QUESTION`
easy **does** it EASY `COMFORTABLE`
doesn't wash WASH `CLEAN`
it **doesn't** take a rocket scientist ROCKET
treat *someone* like a **dog** TREAT `DEAL WITH`
work like a **dog** WORK `DO A JOB`
dog-eat-dog DOG `ANIMAL`
in the **doghouse** DOG `ANIMAL`
go to the **dogs** GO `BECOME`
rain cats and **dogs** RAIN
know what *someone* is **doing** KNOW
  `HAVE INFORMATION`

E

go from one **extreme** to the other GO CHANGE

a bird's **eye** view BIRD

a gleam in *your* **eye** GLEAM

an **eye** for an **eye** EYE

catch *someone's* **eye** CATCH TAKE HOLD

have an **eye** for HAVE POSSESS

have *your* **eye** on HAVE POSSESS

in the twinkling of an **eye** TWINKLE

in *your* mind's **eye** MIND THINKING

keep *your* **eye** on KEEP STAY

look *someone* in the **eye** LOOK SEE

not bat an **eye** *or* eyelid BAT MOVE EYE

out of the corner of *your* **eye** OUT OF ORIGINATING FROM

see **eye** to **eye** with SEE UNDERSTAND

with the naked **eye** WITH USING

not bat an eye *or* **eyelid** BAT MOVE EYE

a sight for sore **eyes** SIGHT VIEW

bags under *the* **eyes** BAG SIMPLE CONTAINER

could hardly believe *your* **eyes** COULD BE POSSIBLE

feast *your* **eyes** on FEAST

keep *your* **eyes** off EYE

keep *your* **eyes** open KEEP STAY

keep *your* **eyes** out KEEP STAY

keep *your* **eyes** peeled KEEP STAY

open *someone's* **eyes** OPEN POSITIONED FOR ACCESS

pull the wool over *someone's* **eyes** PULL BE DISHONEST

roll *your* **eyes** ROLL MOVE

take *your* **eyes** off EYE

with *your* **eyes** closed WITH USING

give *your* **eyeteeth** GIVE OFFER

F

at **face** value FACE FRONT

cut off *your* nose to spite *your* **face** CUT DIVIDE

egg on *someone's* **face** EGG FOOD

in *someone's* **face** FACE HEAD

in the **face** of FACE HEAD

in your **face** YOUR BELONGING TO YOU

let's **face** it LET SUGGEST

look *someone* in the **face** LOOK SEE

lose **face** LOSE BE DEFEATED

make a **face** MAKE CAUSE TO BE

make a **face** at MAKE CAUSE TO BE

on the **face** of it FACE FRONT

save **face** SAVE MAKE SAFE

show *your* **face** SHOW MAKE SEEN

slap in the **face** SLAP HIT

stare *someone* in the **face** STARE

to *someone's* **face** FACE HEAD

face-to-**face** FACE HEAD

make **faces** at MAKE CAUSE TO BE

as a matter of **fact** AS BEING

fact of life FACT

in **fact** FACT

facts of life FACT

without **fail** WITHOUT

if all else **fails** IF IN THAT SITUATION

leap of **faith** LEAP

fall by the wayside FALL BE DEFEATED

fall flat FALL BE DEFEATED

fall in love FALL CHANGE STATE

fall into place FALL INTO

fall into the wrong hands FALL INTO

fall short FALL BE DEFEATED

fall victim to FALL CHANGE STATE

falls go pieces PIECE PART

claim to **fame** CLAIM SAY

run in *someone's* **family** RUN BE/CONTINUE

fan out FAN DEVICE

the shit hits the **fan** SHIT WASTE MATTER

catches *your* **fancy** FANCY LIKE

strikes *your* **fancy** FANCY LIKE

take a **fancy** to TAKE ACT

tickles *your* **fancy** FANCY LIKE

as **far** as FAR DISTANCE

as **far** as *someone* is concerned AS COMPARISON

by **far** FAR AMOUNT

far from FAR DISTANCE

far from it FAR DISTANCE

few and **far** between FEW

from **far** and wide FROM PLACE

go **far** GO TRAVEL

so **far** SO IT IS THE SITUATION

so **far** as FAR DISTANCE

so **far** so good SO IT IS THE SITUATION

thus **far** THUS

fast asleep FAST ATTACHED

get nowhere (**fast**) NOWHERE

go nowhere (**fast**) NOWHERE

in the **fast** lane FAST QUICK

pull a **fast** one PULL BE DISHONEST

chew the **fat** CHEW

fat chance FAT FLESHY

a **fate** worse than death FATE

tempt **fate** TEMPT

the **father** of FATHER PARENT

at **fault** FAULT RESPONSIBILITY

to a **fault** FAULT SOMETHING WRONG

in **favor** of FAVOR SUPPORT

in *someone's* **favor** FAVOR SUPPORT

fear the worst FEAR

feast *your* eyes on FEAST

(as) light as a **feather** LIGHT NOT HEAVY

feather in *your* cap FEATHER

feather *your* (own) nest FEATHER

knock *someone* over with a **feather** KNOCK OVER

ruffle **feathers** RUFFLE MAKE UPSET

feel bad FEEL EXPERIENCE

in on the ground **floor** GROUND LAND
ebb and **flow** EBB
flunk out FLUNK
fly by the seat of *your* pants FLY
TRAVEL THROUGH AIR
fly in the ointment FLY INSECT
fly into a rage FLY MOVE QUICKLY
fly off the handle FLY MOVE QUICKLY
sparks **fly** SPARK
with **flying** colors WITH HAVING
fogged in FOG
a tough act to **follow** TOUGH DIFFICULT
follow in *someone's* footsteps FOLLOW
MOVE AFTER
follow suit FOLLOW MOVE AFTER
follow *your* nose FOLLOW MOVE AFTER
as **follows** AS THE SAME WAY
food for thought FOOD
fool around FOOL
fool around FOOL
fool with FOOL
no **fool** NO NOT ANY
foot the bill FOOT PAY
on **foot** FOOT BODY PART
on the right **foot** RIGHT SUITABLE
put *your* **foot** down PUT MOVE
put *your* **foot** in *your* mouth PUT MOVE
set **foot** SET PUT
shoot *your*self in the **foot** SHOOT
FIRE WEAPON
follow in *someone's* **footsteps** FOLLOW
MOVE AFTER
God **forbid** FORBID
heaven **forbid** FORBID
a **force** to be reckoned with FORCE
INFLUENCE
by **force** of habit FORCE DO UNWILLINGLY
in **force** FORCE OPERATION
to the **fore** FORE
first and **foremost** FIRST
can't see the **forest** for the trees SEE
UNDERSTAND
take **forever** TAKE NEED
forget (about) it FORGET
forget about *something* FORGET
true to **form** TRUE SINCERE
hold the **fort** HOLD CONTROL
and so **forth** AND ALSO
back and **forth** BACK FARTHER AWAY
cost a small **fortune** COST MONEY
come **forward** COME APPROACH
nowhere to be **found** NOWHERE
on all **fours** ALL EVERY ONE
frame of mind FRAME EXPRESS
feel **free** FEEL EXPERIENCE
for **free** FOR PAYMENT
free and clear FREE NO CHARGE
free and easy FREE NOT LIMITED
free lunch FREE NO CHARGE

free of charge FREE WITHOUT
free ride FREE NO CHARGE
home **free** HOME ORIGIN
freeze over FREEZE
hell **freezes** over HELL EXPRESSION
fresh from FRESH RECENT
fresh out FRESH RECENT
fresh out of FRESH RECENT
fresh start FRESH DIFFERENT
freshen up FRESH CLEAN
man's best **friend** MAN PERSON
friends in high places FRIEND
make **friends** MAKE BE OR BECOME
the **fright** of *someone's* life FRIGHT
a **frog** in *someone's* throat FROG
front burner FRONT PLACE
in **front** FRONT PLACE
in **front** of FRONT PLACE
frown on FROWN
bear **fruit** BEAR PRODUCE
out of the **frying** pan into the fire OUT OF
OUTSIDE
add **fuel** to the fire ADD
at **full** throttle FULL GREATEST POSSIBLE
full blast FULL GREATEST POSSIBLE
full circle FULL WHOLE
full of crap FULL CONTAINING A LOT
full of it FULL CONTAINING A LOT
full of shit FULL CONTAINING A LOT
full of *your*self FULL CONTAINING A LOT
full well FULL WHOLE
have (got) *your* hands **full** HAVE EXPERIENCE
in **full** swing FULL CONTAINING A LOT
on a **full** stomach FULL ATE ENOUGH
in the **fullness** of time FULL WHOLE
fun and games FUN
in **fun** FUN
make **fun** of MAKE CAUSE TO BE
poke **fun** at POKE PUSH
functions as FUNCTION PURPOSE
further from the truth FURTHER MORE
without **further** ado WITHOUT
the **furthest** thing from FURTHEST AMOUNT
in the **future** FUTURE TIME

G

gales of laughter GALE
the name of the **game** NAME
fun and **games** FUN
run the **gamut** RUN TRAVEL/GO
like **gangbusters** LIKE SIMILAR TO
gather dust GATHER COLLECT
in high **gear** HIGH ABOVE AVERAGE
shift **gears** SHIFT MOVE OR CHANGE
switch **gears** SWITCH CHANGE
as a (**general**) rule AS BEING
in **general** GENERAL COMMON

in on the **ground** floor GROUND [LAND]
on shaky **ground** SHAKE [WEAKEN]
stand *someone's* **ground** STAND [BE VERTICAL]
grow up GROW UP
catch *someone* off **guard** CATCH [TAKE HOLD]
guard against GUARD
on (*your*) **guard** GUARD
stand **guard** STAND [BE VERTICAL]
under **guard** UNDER [EXPERIENCING]
anybody's **guess** GUESS
anyone's **guess** GUESS
your **guess** is as good as mine GUESS
keep *someone* **guessing** KEEP
  [CONTINUE DOING]
be my **guest** MY
gum up the works GUM [STICKY SUBSTANCE]
jump the **gun** JUMP [MOVE QUICKLY]
at **gunpoint** GUNPOINT
stick to *your* **guns** STICK TO
hate *someone's* **guts** HATE

H

by force of **habit** FORCE [DO UNWILLINGLY]
kick a **habit** KICK [HIT]
kick the **habit** KICK [HIT]
make a **habit** of MAKE [CAUSE TO BE]
hack it HACK [MANAGE]
be **had** HAD [TRICKED]
had better HAD [HAVE]
have **had** enough HAVE [PERFECT TENSE]
have **had** it HAVE [PERFECT TENSE]
have **had** it HAVE [PERFECT TENSE]
if it **hadn't** been for IF [IN THAT SITUATION]
get in *your* **hair** GET [ANNOY]
let *your* **hair** down LET [ALLOW]
hair-raising HAIR
hale and hearty HALE
half the battle HALF
meet *someone* **halfway** MEET
  [COME TOGETHER]
call a **halt** to *something* CALL [ASK FOR]
grind to a **halt** GRIND [ACTIVITY]
ham it up HAM [ACTOR]
at **hand** HAND [BODY PART]
at second **hand** SECOND [POSITION]
by **hand** HAND [BODY PART]
can count on one **hand** COUNT [CALCULATE]
could count on one **hand** COUNT [CALCULATE]
eating out of the palm of *your* **hand** EAT
  [HAVE FOOD]
hand in **hand** HAND [BODY PART]
have (got) a **hand** in HAVE [CAUSE]
have (got) to **hand** it to HAVE TO
in **hand** HAND [BODY PART]
in the palm of *your* **hand** PALM
lay a **hand** on *someone* LAY [PUT DOWN]
lend a **hand** LEND

on **hand** HAND [BODY PART]
on the one **hand** *but* on the other **hand**
  ONE [PARTICULAR THING/PERSON]
on the other **hand** OTHER [DIFFERENT]
try *your* **hand** at TRY [ATTEMPT]
fly off the **handle** FLY [MOVE QUICKLY]
at the **hands** of HAND [BODY PART]
change **hands** CHANGE [BECOME DIFFERENT]
fall into the wrong **hands** FALL INTO
hands down HAND [BODY PART]
hands off HAND [BODY PART]
have (got) *your* **hands** full HAVE [EXPERIENCE]
hold **hands** HOLD [TAKE FIRMLY]
in *someone's* **hands** HAND [BODY PART]
into *someone's* **hands** HAND [BODY PART]
join **hands** JOIN [FASTEN]
shake **hands** SHAKE [MOVE]
sit on *your* **hands** SIT [REST]
stand on *your* **hands** STAND [BE VERTICAL]
time on *your* **hands** TIME [PARTICULAR PERIOD]
wash *your* **hands** of WASH [CLEAN]
wring *your* **hands** WRING
come in **handy** COME [ARRIVE]
get the **hang** of *something* GET [UNDERSTAND]
hang in the balance HANG [ATTACH AT TOP]
hang in there HANG [ATTACH AT TOP]
hang over *your* head HANG [STAY]
hang up on HANG UP [TELEPHONE]
hang *your* head HANG [ATTACH AT TOP]
leave *someone* **hanging** LEAVE
  [CAUSE TO STAY]
not a **happy** camper HAPPY [PLEASED]
(as) **hard** as nails HARD [SEVERE]
drive a **hard** bargain DRIVE [FORCE]
hard feelings HARD [SEVERE]
hard to swallow HARD [DIFFICULT]
hard to take HARD [DIFFICULT]
hard up HARD [DIFFICULT]
learn *something* the **hard** way LEARN
no **hard** feelings NO [NOT ANY]
the school of **hard** knocks SCHOOL
  [EDUCATION]
think long and **hard** THINK [USE REASON]
hard-and-fast HARD [SOLID]
play **hardball** PLAY [COMPETE]
could **hardly** believe *your* ears COULD
  [BE POSSIBLE]
could **hardly** believe *your* eyes COULD
  [BE POSSIBLE]
hark back HARK
do more **harm** than good DO
  [CAUSE TO HAPPEN]
in **haste** HASTE
at the drop of a **hat** DROP [FALL]
pass the **hat** PASS [GIVE]
don't count your chickens before they
  hatch COUNT [CALCULATE]
bury the **hatchet** BURY
hate *someone's* guts HATE

haul ass HAUL MOVE
haul off HAUL MOVE
haul *someone* in HAUL MOVE
the long **haul** LONG TIME
could **have** died COULD BE POSSIBLE
don't **have** a clue HAVE POSSESS
have a go at *something* HAVE DO
have a good day HAVE EXPERIENCE
have a (good) head for HAVE POSSESS
have a good one HAVE EXPERIENCE
have a heart HAVE POSSESS
have a nice day HAVE EXPERIENCE
have a screw loose HAVE POSSESS
have an axe to grind HAVE POSSESS
have an eye for HAVE POSSESS
have another think coming HAVE POSSESS
have both feet on the ground HAVE DO
have cold feet COLD LOW TEMPERATURE
have dibs on HAVE POSSESS
have (got) a hand in HAVE CAUSE
have (got) only *your*self to blame HAVE
 CAUSE
have (got) to be HAVE TO
have got to be joking JOKE AMUSING
have got to be kidding KID JOKE
have (got) to hand it to HAVE TO
have (got) *your* hands full HAVE EXPERIENCE
have (got) *your* heart set on HAVE CAUSE
have had enough HAVE PERFECT TENSE
have had it HAVE PERFECT TENSE
have had it HAVE PERFECT TENSE
have heard of HAVE PERFECT TENSE
have it coming HAVE RECEIVE
have it in HAVE POSSESS
have it in for HAVE POSSESS
have it made HAVE POSSESS
have more than *your* share of HAVE
 EXPERIENCE
have nothing to lose HAVE POSSESS
have priority over PRIORITY
have seen better days HAVE PERFECT TENSE
have the final word on HAVE POSSESS
have the heart HAVE POSSESS
have the hots for HAVE POSSESS
have the last word on HAVE POSSESS
have the time HAVE POSSESS
have time HAVE POSSESS
have to be seen to be believed HAVE TO
have to do with HAVE CONTAIN
have what it takes HAVE POSSESS
have *your* cake and eat it too HAVE
 POSSESS
have *your* eye on HAVE POSSESS
have *your* feet on the ground HAVE DO
have *your* fill of HAVE EXPERIENCE
have *your* share of HAVE EXPERIENCE
have *your* wits about *you* WITS
have *your* work cut out for *you* HAVE
 POSSESS

let *someone* **have** it LET CAUSE
not **have** a leg to stand on HAVE POSSESS
times **have** changed TIME HISTORICAL PERIOD
who would **have** thought WHO ASKING
will **have** WILL FUTURE
you don't **have** to be a rocket scientist
 ROCKET
play **havoc** with PLAY COMPETE
hem and **haw** HEM SOUND
hit the **hay** HIT ARRIVE AT
a needle in a **haystack** NEEDLE TOOL
go **haywire** GO BECOME
a roof over *your* **head** ROOF
bite *someone's* **head** off BITE USE TEETH
come to a **head** COME CHANGE
from **head** to toe FROM DISTANCE
get it through *your* thick **head** GET
 THROUGH BE UNDERSTOOD
go to *your* **head** GO TRAVEL
hang over *your* **head** HANG STAY
hang *your* **head** HANG ATTACH AT TOP
have a (good) **head** for HAVE POSSESS
head and shoulders above HEAD BODY PART
head off HEAD BODY PART
head off *someone* HEAD GO
head over heels HEAD BODY PART
head over heels in love HEAD BODY PART
head *someone* off HEAD GO
hit the nail on the **head** HIT TOUCH
keep *your* **head** above water KEEP STAY
lose *your* **head** LOSE NOT MAINTAIN
over *your* **head** OVER ABOVE
rear its (ugly) **head** REAR RISE
scratching *someone's* **head** SCRATCH CUT
shake *your* **head** SHAKE MOVE
stand on *your* **head** STAND BE VERTICAL
head-on HEAD BODY PART
head-to-head HEAD BODY PART
make **heads** or tails of MAKE OF
make **headway** MAKE CAUSE
a **heap** of *something* HEAP
heaps of *something* HEAP
hear from HEAR BE TOLD
hear *someone* out HEAR LISTEN
hear the end of it HEAR BE TOLD
have **heard** of HAVE PERFECT TENSE
a **heart** of gold HEART EMOTIONS
at **heart** HEART EMOTIONS
bless *your* **heart** BLESS
break *someone's* **heart** BREAK DAMAGE
by **heart** HEART EMOTIONS
dear to *someone's* **heart** DEAR LOVED
from the bottom of *your* **heart** FROM
 ORIGIN
from the **heart** FROM ORIGIN
have a **heart** HAVE POSSESS
have (got) *your* **heart** set on HAVE CAUSE
have the **heart** HAVE POSSESS
heart goes out to HEART EMOTIONS

hold *your* own HOLD CONTINUE
hold *your* tongue HOLD DELAY
on **hold** HOLD DELAY
take **hold** TAKE HOLD
dig a **hole** for *yourself* DIG MOVE EARTH
dig *yourself* into a **hole** DIG MOVE EARTH
in the **hole** HOLE DIFFICULTY
hole-in-the-wall HOLE SPACE
the **Holocaust** HOLOCAUST
holy cow HOLY EMPHASIS
holy mackerel HOLY EMPHASIS
holy shit HOLY EMPHASIS
holy smoke HOLY EMPHASIS
at **home** HOME ORIGIN
hit **home** HIT ARRIVE AT
home free HOME ORIGIN
her **honor** HONOR RESPECT
his **honor** HONOR RESPECT
in **honor** of HONOR RESPECT
your **honor** HONOR RESPECT
with **honors** HONOR REWARD
by **hook** or by crook HOOK
hook line and sinker HOOK
off the **hook** OFF REMOVED
play **hookey** PLAY ENJOY
play **hooky** PLAY ENJOY
jump through **hoops** JUMP
  RAISE UP SUDDENLY
shoot **hoops** SHOOT SPORTS
give a **hoot** GIVE PRODUCE
take the bull by the **horns** TAKE HOLD
eat like a **horse** EAT HAVE FOOD
(straight) from the **horse's** mouth FROM
  ORIGIN
on **horseback** HORSE
hot air HOT VERY WARM
hot potato HOT VERY WARM
in **hot** pursuit HOT CLOSE
in **hot** water HOT VERY WARM
into **hot** water HOT VERY WARM
like **hot** cakes LIKE SIMILAR TO
hotfoot it HOTFOOT
have the **hots** for HAVE POSSESS
by the **hour** HOUR
hour after **hour** HOUR
hour upon **hour** HOUR
on the **hour** HOUR
hours (and **hours**) HOUR
on the **house** HOUSE BUSINESS
household name HOUSEHOLD
household word HOUSEHOLD
how about HOW
how are things? HOW
how are you HOW
how come HOW
how dare you HOW
how do you do HOW
no matter **how** you slice it SLICE
seeing as (**how**) SEE CONSIDER

how's everything? HOW
how's it going? HOW
in a **huff** HUFF ANGER
a **hundred** percent HUNDRED
one **hundred** percent HUNDRED
hunt *someone* down HUNT SEARCH
hurry it up HURRY
hurry up HURRY
in a **hurry** HURRY
in no **hurry** HURRY
not in any **hurry** HURRY
hurt *your* feelings HURT
won't **hurt** *you* to HURT
wouldn't **hurt** *you* to HURT
hustle and bustle HUSTLE ACT QUICKLY

I

aren't **I** AREN'T
(do) you see what **I** mean YOU
  PERSON/PEOPLE
(**I**) beg your pardon BEG
I wouldn't bet on it BET
if **I** were you IF IN THAT SITUATION
need **I** say more NEED MUST DO
I'll tell you TELL SAY
(**I'm**) pleased to meet you PLEASE
  MAKE HAPPY
I'm telling you TELL SAY
dot the **i's** and cross the t's DOT
break the **ice** BREAK DAMAGE
the tip of the **iceberg** TIP END
icing on the cake ICING
identified with IDENTIFY
identify with IDENTIFY
idle away IDLE
as **if** AS THE SAME WAY
as **if** AS THE SAME WAY
damned **if** *you* do and damned **if** *you* don't
  DAMN BLAME
even **if** EVEN EMPHASIS
if I were you IF IN THAT SITUATION
if all else fails IF IN THAT SITUATION
if and when IF IN THAT SITUATION
if it hadn't been for IF IN THAT SITUATION
if it weren't for IF IN THAT SITUATION
if need be IF IN THAT SITUATION
if only IF IN THAT SITUATION
if the shoe fits IF IN THAT SITUATION
if worse comes to worst IF IN THAT SITUATION
if worst comes to worst IF IN THAT SITUATION
if you will IF IN THAT SITUATION
what **if** WHAT QUESTION
no **ifs** ands or buts NO NOT ANY
ill at ease ILL BADLY
project an **image** PROJECT MAKE AN IMAGE
the spitting **image** of SPIT FORCE OUT

lord it over LORD TITLE
have nothing to **lose** HAVE POSSESS
lose count COUNT CALCULATE
lose count of LOSE NOT BE ABLE TO FIND
lose face LOSE BE DEFEATED
lose heart LOSE NO LONGER POSSESS
lose it LOSE NOT MAINTAIN
lose out LOSE BE DEFEATED
lose sight of LOSE NOT BE ABLE TO FIND
lose sleep over LOSE HAVE LESS OF
lose touch LOSE NOT MAINTAIN
lose track LOSE NOT BE ABLE TO FIND
lose *your* cool LOSE NOT MAINTAIN
lose *your* head LOSE NOT MAINTAIN
lose *your* mind LOSE NOT MAINTAIN
lose *your* temper LOSE NOT MAINTAIN
you win some **you** lose some YOU
   PEOPLE GENERALLY
at a **loss** LOSS NOT CONTROLLING
get **lost** GET BECOME
make up for **lost** time MAKE UP FOR
a **lot** LOT LARGE AMOUNT
a **lot** of LOT LARGE AMOUNT
an awful **lot** AWFUL VERY GREAT
give a **lot** GIVE OFFER
leave a **lot** to be desired LEAVE
   CAUSE TO STAY
say a **lot** for SAY EXPRESS
lots of LOT LARGE AMOUNT
for crying out **loud** FOR OCCASION
loud and clear LOUD NOISY
out **loud** OUT ALOUD
actions speak **louder** than words ACTION
   SOMETHING DONE
fall in **love** FALL CHANGE STATE
head over heels in **love** HEAD BODY PART
in **love** LOVE LIKE SOMEONE
make **love** MAKE PERFORM
send *someone's* **love** SEND HAVE DELIVERED
true **love** TRUE REAL
misery **loves** company MISERY
lie **low** LIE POSITION
lower *yourself* LOW NOT KIND
better **luck** next time BETTER
   HIGHER STANDARD
in **luck** LUCK
out of **luck** LUCK
tough (**luck**) TOUGH NO SYMPATHY
a **lump** in *your* throat LUMP
free **lunch** FREE NO CHARGE
out to **lunch** OUT NOT AWARE
at the top of *your* **lungs** TOP HIGHEST PART
leave *someone* in the **lurch** LEAVE
   CAUSE TO STAY
take *something* **lying** down TAKE ACCEPT

M

cog in a **machine** COG
holy **mackerel** HOLY EMPHASIS
like **mad** LIKE SIMILAR TO
have it **made** HAVE POSSESS
made for each other MADE
made of money MADE
do not **make** any difference MAKE
   CAUSE TO BE
make a beeline for MAKE PERFORM
make a dent in DENT
make a difference MAKE CAUSE TO BE
make a face MAKE CAUSE TO BE
make a face at MAKE CAUSE TO BE
make a habit of MAKE CAUSE TO BE
make a mountain out of a molehill MAKE
   CAUSE TO BE
make a pass at MAKE PERFORM
make a point of MAKE PERFORM
make all the difference MAKE CAUSE TO BE
make allowances for MAKE CAUSE TO BE
make an appearance APPEAR BE PRESENT
make believe MAKE CAUSE TO BE
make do MAKE CAUSE
make ends meet MAKE CAUSE
make faces at MAKE CAUSE TO BE
make friends MAKE BE OR BECOME
make fun of MAKE CAUSE TO BE
make good MAKE BE OR BECOME
make good time MAKE ARRIVE
make heads or tails of MAKE OF
make headway MAKE CAUSE
make it (big) MAKE BE OR BECOME
make light of MAKE CAUSE TO BE
make love MAKE PERFORM
make much of MAKE OF
make no apologies MAKE CAUSE TO BE
make no bones about MAKE CAUSE TO BE
make no difference MAKE CAUSE TO BE
make or break MAKE CAUSE TO BE
make sense MAKE CAUSE TO BE
make short work of MAKE CAUSE TO BE
make *someone's* blood boil MAKE CAUSE
make sure MAKE CAUSE TO BE
make that MAKE CAUSE TO BE
make the grade MAKE BE OR BECOME
make the most of MAKE CAUSE TO BE
make time MAKE CAUSE TO BE
make up for lost time MAKE UP FOR
make (up) the bed MAKE PERFORM
make up *your* mind MAKE UP FORM
make waves MAKE CAUSE
make way MAKE CAUSE
make *your* acquaintance MAKE PERFORM
on the **make** MAKE BE OR BECOME
what **makes** *someone* tick WHAT THAT WHICH
man and wife MAN MALE
man in the street MAN PERSON

N

spread *something* **over** SPREAD [COVER]
start **over** START [BEGIN]
take priority **over** PRIORITY
think *something* **over** THINK [USE REASON]
turn **over** a new leaf TURN
[CHANGE DIRECTION]
turn **over** in *someone's* grave TURN
[CHANGE DIRECTION]
win *someone* **over** WIN
go **overboard** GO [BECOME]
owe it to *your*self OWE [HAVE A DEBT]
night **owl** NIGHT
feather *your* (**own**) nest FEATHER
hold *your* **own** HOLD [CONTINUE]
in *your* **own** right RIGHT [LEGAL OPPORTUNITY]
in *your* **own** words OWN
leave *someone* to *their* **own** devices LEAVE
[GIVE RESPONSIBILITY]
mind *your* **own** business MIND [CARE FOR]
my **own** MY
on its (**own**) merits MERIT
on *your* **own** OWN
stand on *someone's* **own** two feet STAND
[BE VERTICAL]
world of *their* **own** WORLD [WHOLE AREA]

P

at a snail's **pace** SNAIL
put *someone or something* through *their*
 paces PUT THROUGH [CAUSE TO EXPERIENCE]
pack it in PACK [FILL]
a **pain** PAIN
a **pain** in the ass PAIN
a **pain** in the neck PAIN
take **pains** TAKE [ACCEPT]
paint a picture PAINT
pair off PAIR
pale by comparison with PALE
pale in comparison with PALE
eating out of the **palm** of *your* hand EAT
[HAVE FOOD]
in the **palm** of *your* hand PALM
flash in the **pan** FLASH [HAPPEN QUICKLY]
out of the frying **pan** into the fire OUT OF
[OUTSIDE]
(as) flat as a **pancake** FLAT [LEVEL]
hit the **panic** button PANIC
press the **panic** button PANIC
push the **panic** button PANIC
by the seat of *your* **pants** SEAT [FURNITURE]
fly by the seat of *your* **pants** FLY
[TRAVEL THROUGH AIR]
kick in the **pants** KICK [HIT]
wear the **pants** WEAR [COVER THE BODY]
on **paper** PAPER
on a **par** with PAR [EQUAL]

par for the course PAR [STANDARD]
up to **par** UP [EQUAL]
(I) beg your **pardon** BEG
pardon me PARDON
take **part** in TAKE [ACT]
the better **part** of BETTER [HIGHER STANDARD]
parting of the ways PART [SEPARATE]
throw a **party** THROW [ENTERTAIN]
make a **pass** at MAKE [PERFORM]
pass judgment on PASS [GIVE OPINION]
pass the buck PASS [GIVE]
pass the hat PASS [GIVE]
pass the time PASS [TIME]
rite of **passage** RITE
in **passing** PASS [GO PAST]
swing **past** SWING [MOVE SIDEWAYS]
wouldn't put it **past** *someone* PUT [MOVE]
a **pat** on the back PAT [TOUCH]
patch *something* up PATCH
[PIECE OF MATERIAL]
off the beaten **path** OFF [AWAY FROM]
the straight and narrow (**path**) STRAIGHT
[NOT CURVING]
try *someone's* **patience** TRY [TEST]
pave the way PAVE
pay lip service to LIP [BODY PART]
pay *someone* a visit PAY [PROVIDE]
pay through the nose PAY [GIVE MONEY FOR]
pay *your* dues PAY [GIVE MONEY FOR]
at **peace** PEACE [NO VIOLENCE]
peace of mind PEACE [CALM]
rest in **peace** REST [RELAX]
peck at PECK
on a **pedestal** PEDESTAL
keep *your* eyes **peeled** KEEP [STAY]
pencil *something* in PENCIL
pinch **pennies** PINCH [PRESS]
a **penny** for your thoughts PENNY
of all **people** ALL [EVERY ONE]
a hundred **percent** HUNDRED
one hundred **percent** HUNDRED
in **perpetuity** PERPETUITY
in **person** PERSON
in **perspective** PERSPECTIVE [VIEW]
for **Pete's** sake FOR [CONSIDERING]
phase *something* in PHASE
phase *something* out PHASE
pick a fight PICK [CHOOSE]
pick and choose PICK [CHOOSE]
pick *someone's* brain PICK [REMOVE]
pick *someone's* pocket PICK [REMOVE]
pick *someone's* way PICK [CHOOSE]
pick up steam PICK UP [IMPROVE/INCREASE]
pick up the bill PICK UP [OBTAIN]
pick up the slack SLACK [NOT ACTIVE]
pick up the tab PICK UP [OBTAIN]
take *your* **pick** TAKE [ACT]
the **pick** of PICK [CHOOSE]
paint a **picture** PAINT

skip **rope** SKIP MOVE
on the **ropes** ROPE
the **ropes** ROPE
bed of **roses** BED AREA OF GROUND
rough it ROUGH DIFFICULT
ride **roughshod** over ROUGHSHOD
run **roughshod** over ROUGHSHOD
round and **round** ROUND MOVE AROUND
round of applause ROUND SINGLE EVENT
round of drinks ROUND SINGLE EVENT
round the clock ROUND MOVE AROUND
in a **row** ROW LINE
tough **row** to hoe TOUGH DIFFICULT
rub elbows with RUB
rub it in RUB
rub *someone* the wrong way RUB
rue the day RUE
ruffle feathers RUFFLE MAKE UPSET
pull the **rug** out (from under *you*) PULL
    REMOVE FROM SOMEWHERE
sweep *something* under the **rug** SWEEP
    CLEAN
in **ruins** RUIN
as a (general) **rule** AS BEING
rule of thumb RULE INSTRUCTION
bend the **rules** BEND
give *someone* a **run** for *their* money GIVE
    PRODUCE
in the long **run** LONG TIME
in the short **run** SHORT TIME
on the **run** RUN GO QUICKLY
run a fever RUN OPERATE
run a temperature RUN OPERATE
run afoul of RUN BE/CONTINUE
run amok RUN BE/CONTINUE
run an errand RUN GO QUICKLY
run in *someone's* family RUN BE/CONTINUE
run roughshod over ROUGHSHOD
run the gamut RUN TRAVEL/GO
run the risk of RUN OPERATE
run with it RUN GO QUICKLY
hit the ground **running** HIT TOUCH
in the **running** RUN POLITICS
out of the **running** OUT OF
    NOT IN A STATE OF
in a **rush** RUSH
in a **rut** RUT

S

line *your* pocket(**s**) LINE COVER
test the water(**s**) TEST
thank heaven(**s**) THANK
hit the **sack** HIT ARRIVE AT
sad state of affairs SAD UNPLEASANT
sad to say SAD UNPLEASANT
in the **saddle** SADDLE

better **safe** than sorry BETTER
    HIGHER STANDARD
play it **safe** PLAY ACT
safe and sound SAFE FREE FROM DANGER
to be on the **safe** side SAFE
    FREE FROM DANGER
easier **said** than done EASY NOT DIFFICULT
like *someone* **said** LIKE SIMILAR TO
no sooner **said** than done NO NOT
you **said** it YOU PERSON/PEOPLE
sail through SAIL
set **sail** SET PUT
for Pete's **sake** FOR CONSIDERING
for goodness **sake** FOR CONSIDERING
for heaven's **sake** FOR CONSIDERING
for old times' **sake** FOR BECAUSE OF
for pity's **sake** FOR CONSIDERING
for **sale** FOR PURPOSE
on **sale** SALE LOWER PRICE
take *something* with a grain of **salt** TAKE
    ACCEPT
all the **same** to *you* ALL COMPLETELY
along the **same** lines ALONG BESIDE
at the **same** time SAME NOT ANOTHER
by the **same** token SAME EXACTLY LIKE
in the **same** boat SAME NOT ANOTHER
same difference SAME EXACTLY LIKE
same here SAME EXACTLY LIKE
the **same** old **same** old SAME NOT ANOTHER
the **same** old thing SAME NOT ANOTHER
two sides of the **same** coin TWO
heart **sank** HEART EMOTIONS
save face SAVE MAKE SAFE
save *your* breath SAVE NOT WASTE
need I **say** more NEED MUST DO
needless to **say** NEED MUST DO
not **say** a word WORD LANGUAGE UNIT
sad to **say** SAD UNPLEASANT
say a lot for SAY EXPRESS
say *something* to *your*self SAY EXPRESS
say what you will SAY EXPRESS
say when SAY EXPRESS
to **say** the least SAY EXPRESS
what do you **say** WHAT QUESTION
you can **say** that again YOU PERSON/PEOPLE
go without **saying** GO BE TRUE
no **saying** NO NOT ANY
says who SAY EXPRESS
what *someone* **says** goes WHAT THAT WHICH
whatever *someone* **says** goes WHATEVER
    ANYTHING
tip the **scales** TIP LEAN
scare *someone* to death SCARE
scare the daylights out of SCARE
scare the hell out of SCARE
in the **scheme** of things SCHEME
teach **school** TEACH
the **school** of hard knocks SCHOOL
    EDUCATION

take charge TAKE `ACCEPT`
take effect TAKE `ACT`
take forever TAKE `NEED`
take heart TAKE `ACCEPT`
take hold TAKE `HOLD`
take issue with TAKE `REACT`
take it easy TAKE `ACT`
take it or leave it TAKE `ACCEPT`
take its toll TAKE `ACCEPT`
take note TAKE `THINK OF`
take notice TAKE `THINK OF`
take pains TAKE `ACCEPT`
take part in TAKE `ACT`
take place TAKE `ACT`
take priority over PRIORITY
take root TAKE `HOLD`
take sides TAKE `REACT`
take *someone* back TAKE BACK
take *someone* by surprise TAKE `REACT`
take *someone's* life TAKE `REMOVE`
take *someone's* word for it TAKE `ACCEPT`
take *something* for granted TAKE `THINK OF`
take *something* in stride TAKE `ACCEPT`
take *something* into account TAKE `THINK OF`
take *something* lying down TAKE `ACCEPT`
take *something* upon *your*self TAKE UPON
take *something* with a grain of salt TAKE `ACCEPT`
take stock TAKE `THINK OF`
take the bull by the horns TAKE `HOLD`
take the cake TAKE `CATCH`
take the initiative TAKE `ACT`
take the plunge TAKE `ACT`
take the time to TAKE `NEED`
take the trouble to TAKE `ACT`
take the wraps off *something* TAKE `REMOVE`
take turns TAKE `ACT`
take up the slack SLACK `NOT ACTIVE`
take *your* eyes off EYE
take *your* pick TAKE `ACT`
take *your* time TAKE `NEED`
have what it **takes** HAVE `POSSESS`
nature **takes** its course NATURE `LIFE`
talk about TALK
talk dirty TALK
talk shop TALK
talk tough TALK
know what *someone* is **talking** about KNOW `HAVE INFORMATION`
money **talks** MONEY
in **tandem** TANDEM
tangled up TANGLE
tantamount to TANTAMOUNT
on **tap** TAP `DEVICE`
red **tape** RED
on **target** TARGET `INTENDED RESULT`
acquired **taste** ACQUIRE
leave a bad **taste** (in *your* mouth) LEAVE `CAUSE TO STAY`

in **tatters** TATTERS
cup of **tea** CUP
teach school TEACH
teach *someone* a lesson TEACH
tempest in a **teapot** TEMPEST
bored to **tears** BORE `FAIL TO INTEREST`
in **tears** TEAR `EYE LIQUID`
in *your* **teens** TEENAGER
by the skin of *someone's* **teeth** SKIN `BODY COVER`
gnash *your* **teeth** GNASH
grit *your* **teeth** GRIT `PRESS`
set *your* **teeth** on edge SET `CAUSE A CONDITION`
sink *your* **teeth** into SINK `FALL`
sink *your* **teeth** into SINK `FALL`
I'll **tell** you TELL `SAY`
let me **tell** you TELL `SAY`
tell the truth TELL `SAY`
tell time TELL `KNOW`
tell you what TELL `SAY`
time will **tell** TIME `MEASURE OF EXISTENCE`
to **tell** the truth TELL `SAY`
you never can **tell** YOU `PEOPLE GENERALLY`
I'm **telling** you TELL `SAY`
no **telling** NO `NOT ANY`
you're **telling** me YOU `PERSON/PEOPLE`
keep *your* **temper** KEEP `STAY`
lose *your* **temper** LOSE `NOT MAINTAIN`
run a **temperature** RUN `OPERATE`
tempest in a teapot TEMPEST
tempt fate TEMPT
not touch *something* with a **ten-foot** pole TOUCH `USE FINGERS`
come to **terms** with COME TO `REACH`
in **terms** of TERMS
on speaking **terms** SPEAK `SAY WORDS`
come with the **territory** TERRITORY
go with the **territory** TERRITORY
put *something* to the **test** PUT `CONDITION`
test the water(s) TEST
the **test** of time TEST
at the end of *your* **tether** END `LAST PART`
thank God THANK
thank goodness THANK
thank heaven(s) THANK
thanks to THANK
at **that** THAT `SOMETHING NOT HERE`
Cut **that** out CUT `STOP`
in the event **that** EVENT
it is understood **that** UNDERSTAND `BELIEVE`
leave it at **that** LEAVE `GO AWAY`
make **that** MAKE `CAUSE TO BE`
not **that** NOT
on the understanding **that** UNDERSTANDING
plenty more where **that** came from PLENTY
seeing **that** SEE `CONSIDER`

Idioms Index

wasted on WASTE BAD USE
watch out WATCH BE CAREFUL
watch *your* step WATCH BE CAREFUL
a fish out of water FISH ANIMAL
hold water HOLD CONTAIN/SUPPORT
in hot water HOT VERY WARM
into hot water HOT VERY WARM
keep *your* head above water KEEP STAY
like oil and water LIKE SIMILAR TO
test the water(s) TEST
tread water TREAD FLOAT
water under the bridge WATER
watered down WATER
muddy the waters MUD
ride a wave of *something* RIDE
make waves MAKE CAUSE
a long way to go LONG TIME
along the way ALONG BESIDE
any way you slice it SLICE
by the way WAY ROUTE
clear the way CLEAR GET RID OF
come a long way COME ARRIVE
feel *your* way FEEL TOUCH
get out of the way GET OUT OF STOP
give way GIVE PRODUCE
go a long way GO TRAVEL
go out of *your* way GO TRAVEL
in a way WAY MANNER
in the way WAY ROUTE
know *your* way around KNOW
    BE FAMILIAR WITH
learn *something* the hard way LEARN
make way MAKE CAUSE
no way NO NOT
on *its* way WAY ROUTE
one way or another ONE
    PARTICULAR THING/PERSON
out of the way OUT OF OUTSIDE
pave the way PAVE
pick *someone's* way PICK CHOOSE
point the way POINT SHOW
rub *someone* the wrong way RUB
the way things are WAY MANNER
the way things stand WAY MANNER
under way UNDER EXPERIENCING
way of life WAY MANNER
which way to turn WHICH QUESTION
work *your* way up WORK UP
    BRING INTO BEING
cut both ways CUT DIVIDE
mend *someone's* ways MEND REPAIR
no two ways about it NO NOT ANY
parting of the ways PART SEPARATE
set in *your* ways SET BECOME FIXED
fall by the wayside FALL BE DEFEATED
wear *someone* out WEAR WEAKEN
wear *something* out WEAR WEAKEN
wear the pants WEAR COVER THE BODY
under the weather UNDER LOWER POSITION

weather the storm WEATHER LIVE THROUGH
wedded to WED MARRY
a week ago (this) WEEK
a week from WEEK
week after week WEEK
week in week out WEEK
weigh a ton WEIGH SHOW WEIGHT
weigh down WEIGH SHOW WEIGHT
carry weight CARRY HAVE
pull *your* weight PULL BRING BEHIND YOU
throw *your* weight around THROW
    SEND THROUGH AIR
weight off *your* mind WEIGH SHOW WEIGHT
you're welcome YOU PERSON/PEOPLE
alive and well ALIVE
as well AS COMPARISON
as well as AS COMPARISON
full well FULL WHOLE
leave well enough alone LEAVE
    CAUSE TO STAY
may as well MAY SUGGESTION
mean well MEAN INTEND
think well of THINK HAVE OPINION
very well VERY EXTREMELY
well done WELL IN A GOOD WAY
well-heeled WELL TO A GREAT DEGREE
if it weren't for IF IN THAT SITUATION
the West WEST
get *your* feet wet GET CAUSE
a whale of a WHALE
(do) you see what I mean YOU
    PERSON/PEOPLE
for what it's worth FOR IN RELATION TO
have what it takes HAVE POSSESS
know what it is (like) to KNOW
    HAVE UNDERSTANDING
know what *someone* is doing KNOW
    HAVE INFORMATION
know what *someone* is talking about
    KNOW HAVE INFORMATION
know what's what KNOW HAVE INFORMATION
not know what hit *you* KNOW
    HAVE INFORMATION
practice what *you* preach PRACTICE
    REGULAR ACTIVITY
say what you will SAY EXPRESS
so what SO THEREFORE
tell you what TELL SAY
what about WHAT QUESTION
what became of BECOME OF
what do you say WHAT QUESTION
what for WHAT QUESTION
what if WHAT QUESTION
what makes *someone* tick WHAT THAT WHICH
what on earth WHAT QUESTION
what *someone* says goes WHAT THAT WHICH
what the devil WHAT QUESTION
what the heck WHAT QUESTION
what the hell WHAT QUESTION

think the **world** of THINK [HAVE OPINION]
woman of the **world** WORLD [THE EARTH]
world of *their* own WORLD [WHOLE AREA]
the early bird catches the **worm** EARLY
the early bird gets the **worm** EARLY
a fate **worse** than death FATE
bark is **worse** than *someone's* bite BARK
  [DOG]
for the **worse** FOR [TOWARD]
go from bad to **worse** GO [BECOME]
if **worse** comes to worst IF [IN THAT SITUATION]
none the **worse** NONE
take a turn for the better *or* the **worse**
  TAKE [ACT]
worse off WORSE
at **worst** WORST
fear the **worst** FEAR
if worse comes to **worst** IF [IN THAT SITUATION]
if **worst** comes to worst IF
  [IN THAT SITUATION]
wouldn't wish *something* on *someone's*
  worst enemy WISH [EXPRESS DESIRE]
for what it's **worth** FOR [IN RELATION TO]
get *your* money's **worth** GET [OBTAIN]
two cents' **worth** TWO
worth it WORTH [IMPORTANCE]
worth *your* while WORTH [IMPORTANCE]
who **would** have thought WHO [ASKING]
I **wouldn't** bet on it BET
wouldn't be caught dead CATCH [DISCOVER]
wouldn't hurt *you* to HURT
wouldn't last five minutes LAST [CONTINUE]
wouldn't last long LAST [CONTINUE]
wouldn't put it past *someone* PUT [MOVE]
wouldn't wish *something* on anyone WISH
  [EXPRESS DESIRE]
wouldn't wish *something* on *someone's*
  worst enemy WISH [EXPRESS DESIRE]
lick *your* **wounds** LICK [MOVE TONGUE]
wrap *someone* around *your* little finger
  WRAP
take the **wraps** off *something* TAKE [REMOVE]
under **wraps** UNDER [LOWER POSITION]
wring *someone's* neck WRING
wring *something* from WRING
wring *something* out of WRING
wring *your* hands WRING
wrinkle *your* nose WRINKLE
slap on the **wrist** SLAP [HIT]
in **writing** WRITE
barking up the **wrong** tree BARK [DOG]
fall into the **wrong** hands FALL INTO
get *someone* **wrong** GET [UNDERSTAND]
get up on the **wrong** side of the bed GET
  UP [RISE]
go **wrong** GO [BECOME]
in the **wrong** WRONG [NOT CORRECT]
in the **wrong** place at the **wrong** time
  WRONG [NOT SUITABLE]

on the **wrong** track TRACK [MARKS]
rub *someone* the **wrong** way RUB

Y

year in and **year** out YEAR
year in **year** out YEAR
in **years** YEAR
yes sir YES
any way **you** slice it SLICE
between **you** and me BETWEEN [AMONG]
bless **you** BLESS
(do) **you** see what I mean YOU
  [PERSON/PEOPLE]
don't **you** dare DON'T
(God) bless **you** BLESS
God bless (**you**) GOD [CREATOR]
here **you** are HERE
here **you** go HERE
how are **you** HOW
how dare **you** HOW
how do **you** do HOW
I'll tell **you** TELL [SAY]
(I'm) pleased to meet **you** PLEASE
  [MAKE HAPPY]
I'm telling **you** TELL [SAY]
if I were **you** IF [IN THAT SITUATION]
if **you** will IF [IN THAT SITUATION]
let me tell **you** TELL [SAY]
no matter how **you** slice it SLICE
say what **you** will SAY [EXPRESS]
screw **you** SCREW [HAVE SEX]
see **you** SEE [MEET]
see **you** later SEE [MEET]
shame on **you** SHAME [GUILT]
tell **you** what TELL [SAY]
told **you** (so) TOLD
what do **you** say WHAT [QUESTION]
you bet YOU [PERSON/PEOPLE]
you can say that again YOU [PERSON/PEOPLE]
you can't miss it YOU [PERSON/PEOPLE]
you can't win them all YOU
  [PEOPLE GENERALLY]
you don't have to be a rocket scientist
  ROCKET
you know YOU [PERSON/PEOPLE]
you know something YOU [PERSON/PEOPLE]
you know what YOU [PERSON/PEOPLE]
you mean YOU [PERSON/PEOPLE]
you name it YOU [PERSON/PEOPLE]
you never can tell YOU [PEOPLE GENERALLY]
you never know YOU [PEOPLE GENERALLY]
you said it YOU [PERSON/PEOPLE]
you win some **you** lose some YOU
  [PEOPLE GENERALLY]
you're telling me YOU [PERSON/PEOPLE]
you're welcome YOU [PERSON/PEOPLE]
a penny for **your** thoughts PENNY

Frommer's

P9-AGU-263

Peru
day BY day

1st Edition

by Neil Edward Schlecht

WILEY

John Wiley and Sons, Inc.

Contents

PAGE 113

PAGE 146

PAGE 181

PAGE 194

PAGE 246

PAGE 325

PAGE 361

PAGE 385

PAGE 429

PAGE 443

PAGE 450

PAGE 458

PUBLISHED BY

John Wiley & Sons, Inc.

111 River St., Hoboken, NJ 07030-5774

ISBN 978-0-470-89071-4

Frommer's®

Editorial by Frommer's

EDITOR
Anuja Madar

PHOTO EDITOR
Cherie Cincilla

CARTOGRAPHER
Guy Ruggiero

CAPTIONS
Neil Edward Schlecht

COVER PHOTO EDITOR
Richard Fox

COVER DESIGN
Paul Dinovo

Produced by Sideshow Media

PUBLISHER
Dan Tucker

MANAGING EDITOR
Megan McFarland

PROJECT EDITOR
Pamela Nelson

PHOTO EDITOR
John Martin

PHOTO RESEARCHERS
Tessa Perliss and Julia Rydholm

DESIGN
Kevin Smith, And Smith LLC

SPOTLIGHT FEATURE DESIGN
Em Dash Design LLC

For information on our other products and services or to obtain technical support, please contact our Customer Care Department within the U.S. at 800/762-2974, outside the U.S. at 317/572-3993 or fax 317/572-4002.

Wiley also publishes its books in a variety of electronic formats. Some content that appears in print may not be available in electronic formats.

MANUFACTURED IN CHINA

5 4 3 2 1

How to Use This Guide

The Day by Day guides present a series of itineraries that take you from place to place. The itineraries are organized by time (The Sacred Valley in 3 Days), by region (The Colca Valley), by town (San Blas), and by special interest (Gourmet Lima). You can follow these itineraries to the letter, or customize your own based on the information we provide. Within the tours, we suggest cafes, bars, or restaurants where you can take a break. Each of these stops is marked with a coffee-cup icon ☕. In each chapter, we provide detailed hotel and restaurant reviews so you can select the places that are right for you.

The hotels, restaurants, and attractions listed in this guide have been ranked for quality, value, service, amenities, and special features using a star-rating system. Hotels, restaurants, attractions, shopping, and nightlife are rated on a scale of zero stars (recommended) to three stars (exceptional). In addition to the star-rating system, we also use a kids icon **kids** to point out the best bets for families.

The following **abbreviations** are used for credit cards:

AE American Express	**MC** MasterCard
DC Diners Club	**V** Visa
DISC Discover	

A Note on Prices

Frommer's lists exact prices in local currency, but because many establishments in Peru accept/prefer U.S. dollars ($), you will also find prices listed in $ throughout the book. Currency conversions fluctuate, so before departing consult a currency exchange website such as **www.oanda.com/currency/converter** to check up-to-the-minute conversion rates.

How to Contact Us

In researching this book, we discovered many wonderful places—hotels, restaurants, shops, and more. We're sure you'll find others. Please tell us about them, so we can share the information with your fellow travelers in upcoming editions. If you were disappointed with a recommendation, we'd love to know that, too. Please email us at frommersfeedback@wiley.com or write to:

Frommer's Peru Day by Day, 1st Edition
John Wiley & Sons, Inc.
111 River Street
Hoboken, NJ 07030-5774

Travel Resources at Frommers.com

Frommer's travel resources don't end with this guide. **Frommers.com** has travel information on more than 4,000 destinations. We update features regularly, giving you access to the most current trip-planning information and the best airfare, lodging, and car-rental bargains. You can also listen to podcasts, connect with other Frommers.com members through our active reader forums, share your travel photos, read blogs from guidebook editors and fellow travelers, and much more.

An Additional Note

Travel information can change quickly and unexpectedly, and we strongly advise you to confirm important details locally before traveling, including information on visas, health and safety, traffic and transport, accommodation, shopping and eating out. We also encourage you to stay alert while traveling and to remain aware of your surroundings. Avoid civil disturbances, and keep a close eye on cameras, purses, wallets, and other valuables.

While we have endeavored to ensure that the information contained within this guide is accurate and up-to-date at the time of publication, we make no representations or warranties with respect to the accuracy or completeness of the contents of this work and specifically disclaim all warranties, including without limitation warranties of fitness for a particular purpose. We accept no responsibility or liability for any inaccuracy or errors or omissions, or for any inconvenience, loss, damage, costs or expenses of any nature whatsoever incurred or suffered by anyone as a result of any advice or information contained in this guide.

The inclusion of a company, organization or Website in this guide as a service provider and/or potential source of further information does not mean that we endorse them or the information they provide. Be aware that information provided through some Websites may be unreliable and can change without notice. Neither the publisher or author shall be liable for any damages arising herefrom.

About the Author

Neil Edward Schlecht realized a lifelong dream by trekking to Machu Picchu during a junior year abroad spent in Quito, Ecuador, and he has continued making frequent pilgrimages to Peru ever since. He is the author of several other travel guides, including *Frommer's Peru, Buenos Aires Day by Day, Barcelona Day by Day,* and *Mallorca & Menorca Day by Day.* After long stints in Brazil and Spain, he resides in rural Litchfield County, Connecticut.

About the Photographers

Thornton Cohen is a Central America–based photographer who has spent the last 25 years in perpetual motion and has used this as an opportunity to observe and capture the human experience. He has worked on international guidebooks, including several Frommer's guides, and for international media outlets. You can see more of his work at www.thorntoncohen.com.

Italian photographer **Axel Fassio** has spent the last decade living, working, and shooting in Europe, Africa, Asia, and North and South America, and he speaks five languages fluently. His photography reflects a distinct vision and style, and his photos narrate stories, illustrate concepts, and revel in the sheer beauty of one moment.

Pilar Olivares is a Peruvian photographer based in Lima. She has worked for Reuters since 1999, covering breaking news around the South American continent, and treasures the opportunity to be close to different cultures and lifestyles. Through her work on this guidebook, she has grown closer to her own people and learned a lot about her home country.

Dado Galdieri is a Brazilian-Italian, multilingual photographer, photo editor, and travel enthusiast based in Rio de Janeiro, Brazil. His visual exploration is focused on five different yet interconnected areas of the human experience: man and the environment; drugs and obsessive-compulsive behavior; religion as a social control device; land and the limits of our growth; and Native peoples and their ways of living. You can see more of his work at www.dadogaldieri.org.

Ernesto Benavides is a member of the Supayfotos photography collective and works as a stringer photographer at the Agence France-Presse news agency. His independent work has appeared in publications including *Private, El País, Le Monde, 6Mois, Zmala, Gatopardo,* and *Somos.*

1
The Best of Peru

Favorite Peru Moments

Doing a gourmet tour of Lima. Peruvian cuisine is wonderfully diverse, creative, and accomplished, and ceviche is only the beginning of great things to try in Lima, the best dining city in South America. From cool, open-air restaurants and celebrity chefs to *huariques* (neighborhood holes-in-the-wall), dining in Lima is reason enough to travel to Peru. See p. 64.

Puzzling over the Nasca Lines. From the window of a small plane, these enigmatic lines, etched into the desert folds between 300 B.C. and A.D. 700, make no sense at all. Observers have called them agricultural and astronomical calendars, signs from the gods, and even extraterrestrial airports. Mysterious figures such as the "Astronaut" will have you wondering the same. See p. 103, ❹.

Discovering Santa Catalina at night. One of Peru's most magnificent colonial structures, this white-stone convent in the southern city of Arequipa is a world unto itself. It literally shines at night, when candles light the cells and niches, and a roaring fire illuminates the kitchen. The experience is enough to transport you to the 16th century. See p. 136, ❶.

Marveling at Andean condors. Colca Canyon, the world's second-deepest canyon, is the best spot in South America to witness the majesty of giant Andean condors soaring just overhead. With wingspans of up to 3.5m (11½ ft.), they slowly circle and gain altitude and then silently glide downriver, high above the canyon walls. See p. 145, ❽.

Hopping an Andean train. There aren't many trains in Peru, but a few lines are among the most thrilling rides in the world. The train to Machu Picchu from Cusco is a spectacular journey through the sacred Urubamba Valley, while the train south to Lake Titicaca is a wonder of stunning scenery, with a giant payoff at the end. For true thrill-seekers, however, there's nothing like the "Tren Macho," the world's highest train, from Lima to Huancayo. See p. 54.

Floating on Lake Titicaca. The world's highest navigable body of water at more than 3,600m (11,810 ft.) above sea level, Lake Titicaca is a sacred place to Andean natives. Among the highlights of life on the lake are the ancient cultures of two inhabited natural islands, Amantaní and Taquile. There's nothing like canoeing or kayaking across the lake's placid, deep-blue expanse. Climb a hilltop on the private Isla Suasi, and you'll feel like you're on top of the world. See p. 170.

Stargazing in the Sacred Valley. Almost no artificial light mars the immense Andean sky, making it clear why the Incas worshipped the natural world. The carpet of stars above—and, for those of us in the Northern Hemisphere, the sight of the Southern Cross—is breathtaking. To the Incas, the moon was a deity; if your visit coincides with a full moon, you'll also be a believer. See p. 242.

> PREVIOUS PAGE *Legendary Machu Picchu, delicately placed by the Incas among the Andes mountaintops.* THIS PAGE *An* apacheta, *stones piled to petition the gods, on Isla Suasi overlooks Lake Titicaca.*

Watching the sun rise over Machu Picchu. Machu Picchu lives up to the hype. Cloaked in clouds and tucked amid the imposing Andes, it's a thrilling sight, especially at sunrise, when dramatic rays of light creep over the mountaintops and slowly illuminate each successive row of the ruins. I've seen it produce gasps of delight in jaded travelers. See p. 260.

Triumphing over a 4-day Andes trek. Hiking the Inca Trail to Machu Picchu is still one of the greatest eco-adventures on the planet, but it's gotten a little well trodden for true adventurers. Trekkers in search of more solitude and authenticity should head instead to the ruins of Choquequirao and other sites in the southern highlands, where the Incas once roamed but few tourists do. See p. 272.

Spotting wildlife in the jungle. Peru's massive tracts of Amazon-basin rainforest hold untold

secrets. It's a thrill to see a family of giant river otters on an oxbow lake in Tambopata National Reserve; catch a glimpse of a pink river dolphin emerging from an Amazon tributary; watch a cock-of-the-rock hold court in a cloud forest; or stare in wonder at thousands of brilliantly colored macaws and parrots feeding at a clay lick. See p. 294.

Singing protest songs in the wee hours. A musical highlight of a trip to Peru is visiting an authentic *peña*, a small, informal club featuring musicians and patrons singing the songs of *música criolla* (Peruvian music with African, Spanish, and Andean influences) or *música folclórica* (folk music). The best are generally in Lima, but one of my favorites is Peña Usha Usha, in the northern town of Cajamarca, where you may find yourself joining in on a Spanish chorus long after bedtime. See p. 407.

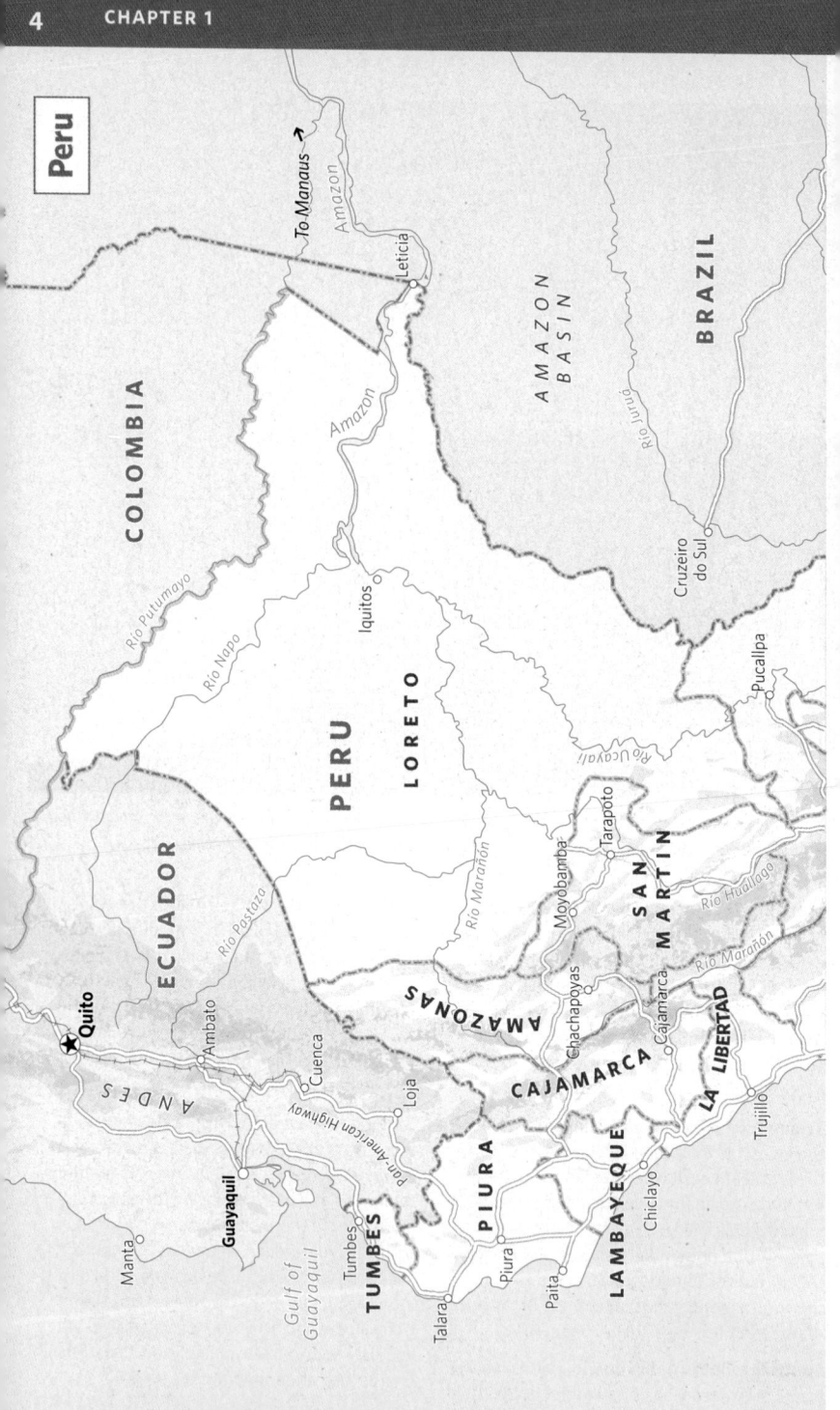

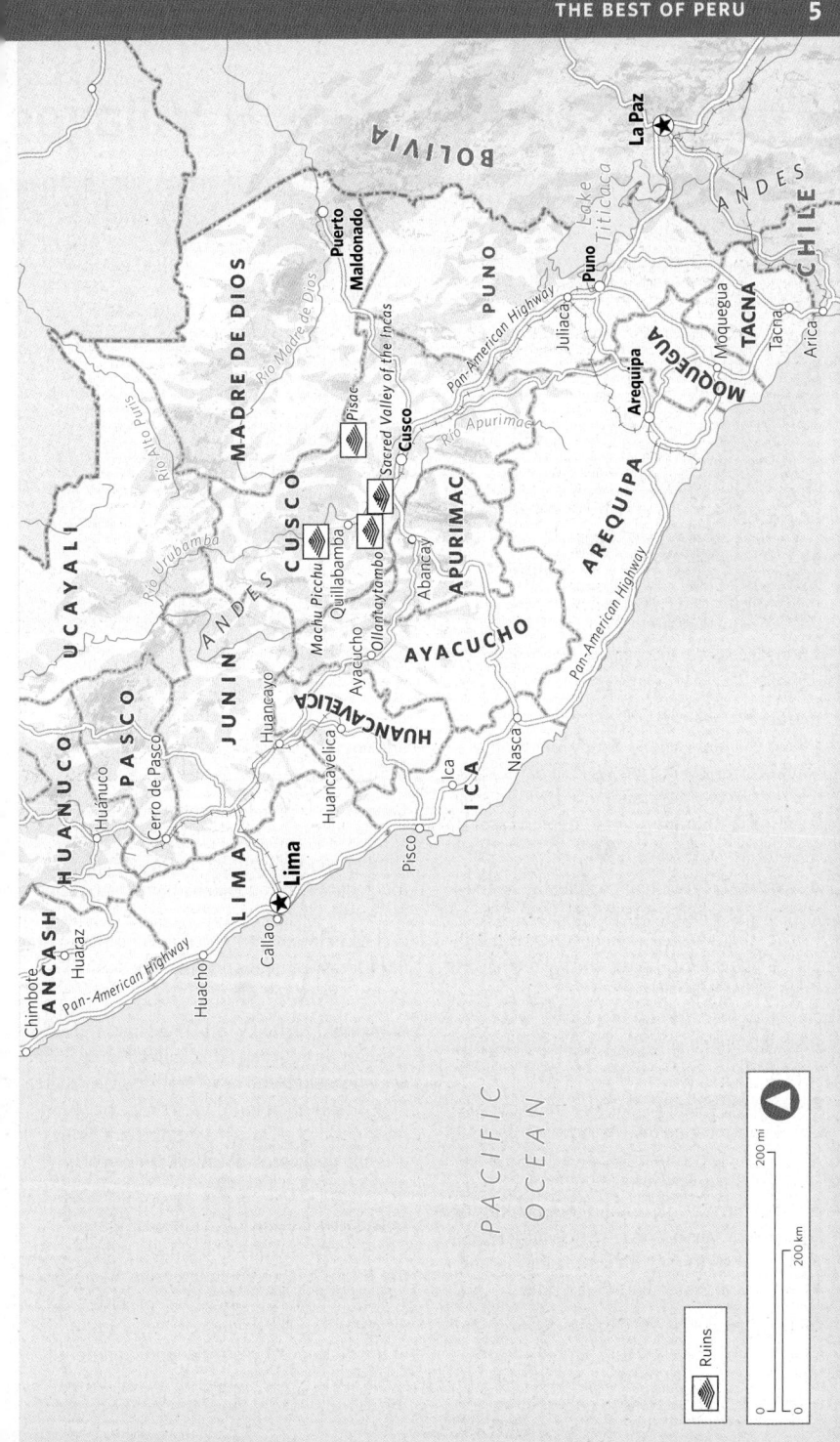

The Best Small Towns & Villages

> *More than 5 centuries ago, the Incas engineered an immaculate grid of cobblestone streets in Ollantaytambo.*

Barranco. Now a suburb of Lima, this seaside village still feels wholly removed from the capital. Overlooking the sea, the barrio has a relaxed, artsy vibe, great old mansions, cool bars and restaurants, and a couple of great places to stay. See p. 54, ❹.

Ayacucho. This colonial gem nestled in the central highlands was, until recently, prisoner to a homegrown guerrilla movement. Thankfully, that's the dirty past, and we're now free to relish its collection of stunning colonial-era churches, its extraordinary Easter and Carnaval celebrations, and Peru's best handicrafts. See p. 110.

Colca Valley villages. Across the Colca Valley are 14 charming colonial villages dating to the 16th century, each marked by a centerpiece church and an adherence to tradition. Descendants of the pre-Inca ethnic communities Collaguas and Cabanas maintain a vibrant style of traditional dress, with fantastically embroidered and sequined hats. See p. 142.

Ollantaytambo. Lovely Ollanta (as locals call it) is home to a formidable temple-fortress and an old town, built by the Incas, that's a perfect grid of streets (the only such layout remaining in Peru). The cobblestone streets are lined with canals carrying rushing water from the mountains. See p. 252, ❹.

Caraz. A peaceful village in the Callejón de Huaylas valley, Caraz is the base for mountain climbers and adventure fanatics. It was spared much of the earthquake damage that leveled its neighboring towns and is a pretty spot to rest up before or after your adventures among Peru's highest peaks and most beautiful lagoons. See p. 385, ❻.

Máncora. This funky little town has long been popular with surfing addicts and hippie travelers who visited and never left. Today, it's winning a reputation for more than its waves and bars; new hotels and restaurants are luring a whole new breed of traveler to Peru's best beaches. See p. 356, ❺.

Cajamarca. Delightful Cajamarca, a mini-Cusco in the northern highlands, is framed by the Andes and green countryside. Its historic core of colonial buildings occupies the spot where an important Inca city once stood, site of the invasion of Pizarro and the murder of the emperor Atahualpa, which precipitated the downfall of the Inca Empire. See p. 386.

The Best Ruins & Archaeological Sites

Huaca Pucllana, Lima. Surveying Lima's high-rise apartments from the top of this adobe pyramid, built in the 5th century, is one of the more breathtaking sights in Peru. The 15-hectare (37-acre) site is still undergoing daily excavation. See p. 57, **③**.

Sacsayhuamán, Cusco. The monumental stonework at Sacsayhuamán forms massive zigzagged defensive walls of three tiers. Some granite blocks, which fit together seamlessly without mortar, weigh as much as 300 tons. It's a fitting stage for the main pageant of the splendid Inti Raymi festival in June. See p. 212, **①**.

Fortress ruins, Ollantaytambo. Though unfinished, this magnificent fortress and temple for worship and astronomical observation is one of the greatest examples of the Incas' unparalleled engineering and craftsmanship, with rows of incredibly steep stone terraces carved into the hillside. See p. 253, **⑥**.

Machu Picchu, Sacred Valley. One of the world's most spectacular ruins, this is environmental architecture that continues to fill visitors with awe, crowds be damned. See p. 260.

Chan Chan, Libertad. The capital of the Chimú Empire, begun around A.D. 1300, is the largest adobe complex of pre-Columbian America. Among its nine royal palaces, the partially restored Nik-An Palace contains unusual friezes, enough to conjure the sophistication of the Chimú kingdom. See p. 349, **④**.

Túcume. This complex of 26 eroded adobe pyramids—spread across the valley north of Chiclayo in northern Peru—was constructed around A.D. 1000 and was the region's most important elite urban center. Huaca Larga is the largest adobe brick structure in South America. See p. 345, **⑤**.

Choquequirao & Kuélap, Sacred Valley/Cajamarca. Choquequirao, a massive Inca construction that's only one-third uncovered,

> *Water still flows down from the mountains to a fountain at Ollantaytambo's fortress ruins.*

boasts incredible terracing high above the Apurímac River, well worth the 4 days on foot it takes to get there. Remote Kuélap, more than 800 years old, is one of the man-made wonders of Peru; the complex of 400 round buildings, surrounded by a massive defensive wall, rewards adventurous amateur archaeologists. See p. 272 and 391.

Cumbe Mayo, Cajamarca. Amid peculiar rock formations that look like a stone forest, this pre-Inca aqueduct (constructed c. 1000 B.C.) is an 8km (5-mile) canal carved from volcanic stone. It collects and redirects water on its way to the Pacific Ocean, even employing right angles to slow the water's flow. See p. 390, **⑩**.

The Best of Natural Peru

> The ancient agricultural terraces in Colca Valley turn emerald green in spring.

Reserva Nacional de Paracas. Paracas National Reserve is one of the world's richest and most peculiar habitats of marine life and seabirds. This subtropical coastal desert zone is considered the "Peruvian Galápagos," home to an amazing roster of protected species, including huge colonies of sea lions, endangered turtles, Humboldt penguins, red boobies, pelicans, turkey vultures, and red-footed cormorants. See p. 96, **4**.

Colca Valley. Nobel Prize winner Mario Vargas Llosa called Colca the "Valley of Wonders," an apt moniker for an extraordinarily scenic place of snowcapped volcanoes, patchwork valleys of green, narrow gorges, and beautiful desert landscapes. Colca Canyon is twice as deep as the Grand Canyon and is the best place in the world to see the flight of giant Andean condors. See p. 142.

Sacred Valley. Although renowned for its villages, markets, and Inca ruins, the Sacred Valley is also a place where you can embark on multiday treks into the Cusco highlands, go white-water rafting and mountain biking, or take gentle day hikes amid some of the most beautiful mountain and valley scenery Peru has to offer. See p. 242.

The Amazon basin. The southern Peruvian Amazon basin includes two immense protected tracts that teem with wildlife: Tambopata National Reserve and remote Manu National Park. Tambopata has more species of birds (nearly 600) and butterflies (1,200) than any place of similar size on earth; a dozen different types of forest and gorgeous oxbow lakes; and at least 13 endangered animal species. Manu, the second-largest protected area in Peru, has the highest bird, mammal, and plant diversity of any park on the planet. In the northern Amazon near Iquitos, Pacaya Samiria National Reserve is the largest protected area in Peru and the largest protected flooded forest in the Amazon. See p. 294.

Parque Nacional Huascarán. A UNESCO Biosphere Reserve, Huascarán contains nearly the whole of the Cordillera Blanca, the longest tropical mountain range in the world and home to Peru's highest peaks. For trekkers and climbers, there are few greater places on earth: 50 soaring peaks, nearly 300 alpine lakes (including the famous turquoise-colored Lagunas Llanganuco), and 600 glaciers. See p. 375.

Favorite Outdoor Adventures

> *The northern coast near Máncora is one of the world's best-kept surfing secrets.*

Surfing big sand. The southern desert is an odd and unrelenting landscape, but it has the highest sand dunes in South America. An extreme sport fast gaining popularity is sandboarding. The biggest dunes are near Nasca, at Cerro Blanco, but the prettiest spot is Huacachina Lagoon outside of Ica. See p. 117.

Trekking to Inca ruins. The most famous trek in Peru is the Inca Trail, 4 days of strenuous hiking with a superlative payoff: a sunset arrival at Machu Picchu. Other, much less crowded treks share the same extraordinary scenery and feature Inca ruins, including Choquequirao and Salcantay. See p. 266 and 272.

Running big-time white water. River rafting, from Class II to super-technical Class VI, can be done in the Urubamba Valley, on the Apurímac and Tambopata rivers in the Amazon jungle, near Colca Canyon, and on Río Santa in Callejón de Huaylas. See p. 444.

Hiking down Colca Canyon. The Cusco region and Callejón de Huaylas in northern Peru may draw the lion's share of adventurers, but for scenic beauty and independent hikes, Colca rivals both. One of the greatest hikes is the descent into the canyon itself, from the Cruz del Cóndor lookout. If that's not enough adventure for you, there are even longer and more demanding treks, including to remote Cotahuasi Canyon, even deeper than Colca. See p. 148.

Climbing in the Cordillera Blanca. The Cordillera Blanca, the highest tropical mountain chain in the world, offers plenty for trekkers and mountaineers: snowcapped peaks, glaciers, lakes, and rivers. There are myriad trekking and climbing opportunities for expert mountaineers and the rest of us, including the classic 4-day Santa Cruz trek. See p. 375.

Mountain biking in the Callejón de Huaylas. The best single-track spot is this valley, where hundreds of horse trails lace lush fields and push past picturesque Andean villages and alpine lakes. Bikers can test their lung capacity climbing to 5,000m (16,400-ft.) mountain passes. See p. 393.

Surfing the waves of Peru's Pacific coast. Surf connoisseurs know that Peru's Pacific coastline is home to an incredible variety of left and right reef breaks, point breaks, and monster waves. Northern Peru is the top choice. See p. 354.

The Best Luxury Hotels

> *The colonial-style bar at Casa Andina Private Collection Arequipa, the city's top luxury hotel.*

Country Club Lima Hotel. An elegant 1920s hacienda, this grand estate—a surprisingly good value—is replete with antiques but is still a relaxed place for families. It's a luxurious retreat from the stress of modern Lima. See p. 82.

Hotel Paracas, Paracas National Reserve. Few makeovers are as successful as the one given to this hotel overlooking Paracas Bay. A spectacular new infinity pool leads to a modern lounge and restaurant, a dose of contemporary style never before seen in the southern Peruvian desert. See p. 126.

Casa Andina Private Collection Arequipa. Brilliantly carved out of a stately colonial building—once Arequipa's Mint House—this incredible property in the historic quarter has the feel of a chic boutique hotel and the services of an upscale business hotel. See p. 158.

Aranwa Cusco Boutique Hotel. Converting historic *casonas* (colonial noble houses) in Cusco is all the rage, but few *casonas* are as well done as this one. The hotel reeks of luxury, with technological innovation and Cusqueña School art and antiques at every turn. A smart system pumps hyper-oxygenated air throughout, helping guests acclimate to Cusco's brutal altitude. See p. 232.

Hotel Monasterio, Cusco. The granddaddy of Peru's luxury hotels, this spectacular place is carved out of a 16th-century monastery. It's still the most dignified and historic place to stay in Peru. Rooms are gracefully decorated with colonial touches, particularly the rooms off the serene first courtyard. See p. 235.

La Casona, Cusco. This boutique hotel has just 11 rooms, but more luxury and space than pretty much any other hotel in Peru. Come here to be pampered in a beautiful colonial house, teeming with art and antiques, on a pretty plaza. See p. 235.

Inkaterra Machu Picchu Pueblo Hotel, Aguas Calientes. An ecostyled but upscale, this compound of bungalows is enveloped in lush tropical gardens and cloud forest, making it a perfect retreat for naturalists. It blows everything else in Aguas Calientes out of the water. Junior suites, with fireplaces and small terraces, are the place to crash after a visit to Machu Picchu. See p. 288.

Favorite Inns & Boutique Hotels

> *You can hear the waves crash from the airy, modern rooms at DCO Suites, Lounge & Spa in Máncora.*

Second Home Peru, Lima. Inhabiting the home of one of Peru's best-known artists, Victor Delfín, this very personal inn hugs the coastline in bohemian Barranco. Rooms are elegant, and the entire house is a museum of Delfín's work. See p. 84.

3B: Barranco's Bed & Breakfast, Lima. Combining contemporary style and friendly service at a value price, this small hotel has terrific all-around appeal. It's close to great restaurants and bars in Barranco, and removed from some of Lima's less savory aspects. See p. 84.

La Casa de Melgar Hostal, Arequipa. In a pretty colonial house constructed of *sillar* (white volcanic stone), this charming small inn has thick walls, multiple interior courtyards, gardens, and ground-floor rooms with spectacular vaulted brick ceilings. It's a huge step up from other inexpensive hotels. See p. 160.

Niños Hotel, Cusco. This unique Dutch-owned hotel dedicates its profits to helping and housing Cusco's street children, and it's also one of the best inexpensive and laid-back places to stay in Peru. Occupying a restored colonial house, it has unexpected modern style. See p. 235.

Fallen Angel: The Guest House, Cusco. A tiny boutique hotel with huge, art-filled rooms that border on hallucinatory, this wild place, the brainchild of a very creative Cusqueño, is a den of bold decorating that's not for conservative tastes. See p. 234.

El Albergue, Ollantaytambo. This cool inn anticipated Ollanta's surge in popularity. Owned by an American artist who's a longtime resident in town, it has relaxing gardens, a terrific restaurant next to the railroad tracks, and rooms that are surprisingly stylish in a modern, minimalist way. See p. 284.

Hotel Posada del Puruay, Cajamarca. In a restored 1830 farmhouse, this small hotel takes full advantage of its site in the countryside just outside Cajamarca. The elegant grounds, with gardens and horses, are as much of a draw as the large, antique-filled rooms. See p. 406.

DCO Suites, Lounge & Spa, Máncora. Setting new standards in a scrappy surfers' hangout, this incredibly chic little hotel, which looks like an architect's townhouse right on top of the surf, has style to burn, with sleek rooms, a great restaurant, infinity pool, and open-air rooftop spa. See p. 366.

The Best Eco-Lodges

> *Casa Andina is a secluded, luxurious eco-lodge on Isla Suasi, a private island in Lake Titicaca.*

Casa Andina Private Collection Suasi, Isla Suasi. Hidden on the only private island in the middle of Lake Titicaca, this unique lodging is a world unto itself, with mesmerizing views of the lake and the kind of solitude and serenity that are nearly impossible to come by. The solar-powered eco-lodge is much more luxe than you might expect in so remote a location. See p. 182.

Colca Lodge, Colca Valley. Hugging the banks of the Colca River, this rustic, handsome hotel has real style and something no one else in Colca can claim: fantastic stone hot springs overlooking the river. It's the perfect place to recover after a long canyon trek. See p. 161.

Explorer's Inn, Tambopata. One of the most respected eco-lodges in the Peruvian Amazon, this pioneering lodge plays host to both ecotourists and scientists, and is excellent for viewing otters, monkeys, and jungle birds. See p. 307.

Reserva Amazónica Lodge, Tambopata. If you need a little bit of pampering to go along with your excursion into the Amazon, this is your place. You won't miss out on the jungle experience, but you certainly won't be roughing it, either: There are cocktails and dinner in the stylish main house, plush African-style bungalows, and a swanky spa overlooking the river. See p. 306.

Amazon Yarapa River Lodge, northern Amazon. This award-winning conservationist lodge operates a Cornell University field lab, but it also makes a perfect retreat for ecotourists. It is situated on a reserve with access to Pacaya Samiria National Park, one of the top spots for wildlife viewing and the largest of Peru's protected areas (part of which is managed by the lodge), and is unexpectedly comfortable with huge private bungalows, a lounge, and a hammock house overlooking the river. See p. 326.

Tahuayo Lodge, northern Amazon. The only lodge with access to the Tamshiyacu-Tahuayo Reserve, this superb eco-lodge, associated with the Rainforest Conservation Fund and about 4 hours from Iquitos, is remote and small, but it features excellent jungle programs, including zip-line canopy ropes for treetop nature viewing. See p. 327.

The Best Dining Experiences

> *Celebrated chef Gastón Acurio's restaurant Chicha is a great spot to sample regional Arequipeña cuisine.*

Astrid y Gastón, Lima. Gastón Acurio, TV restaurant star in several countries, made his reputation at this iconic Miraflores restaurant. It has inspired countless Peruvian chefs to dream big, and is still one of the most sophisticated restaurants in the country. It's a must-visit to see what really jump-started the buzz. See p. 73.

El Mercado, Lima. Rafael Osterling's great-looking new restaurant is eminently cool and *the* place to be at lunchtime. Hipper and less precious than the famed chef's other places, it serves amazing ceviches and grilled fish and meats. See p. 76.

Sophie Bistró, Lima. A great addition to Lima is this surprisingly stylish Miraflores neighborhood restaurant, a great place for Spanish tapas and classics from across Peru. See p. 80.

Toshiro's, Lima. There's an Asian flair to much of great Limeño cooking, and one of the best places to see the ways influences meld is the Japanese chef Toshiro Konishi's restaurant, which is heaven for sushi lovers. See p. 80.

Chicha, Arequipa. Gastón Acurio, who's taken his Midas touch up and down the continent, promotes Arequipeña cuisine through this emblematic colonial manor house in the heart of historic Arequipa. His take on one of the finest regional cuisines in Peru is inspired. See p. 154.

Cicciolina, Cusco. Seemingly everyone's favorite restaurant in the Inca capital, this warm upstairs spot serves not just great *novo Andino* cuisine, but unusual spiced dishes and tapas, too. The hopping bar looks lifted from Tuscany. See p. 227.

Limo, Cusco. With spectacular views overlooking the Plaza de Armas, this sleek restaurant doesn't need to be as good as it is. Chic but relaxed, it brings great sushi and *tiraditos* (a raw fish dish) to Cusco, and it's a bargain given the stylish surroundings, splendid cocktails, and the city's best views. See p. 229.

Fiesta Restaurant Gourmet, Chiclayo. Few outsiders know Chiclayo for its dining, but cognoscenti are well aware that its Lambayeque cooking from the north of Peru is one of the country's top regional cuisines. Fiesta is its top ambassador. See p. 360.

Favorite Andean Experiences

> *Handcrafted textiles are a principal attraction of village crafts markets throughout the Peruvian Andes.*

Savoring a pisco sour. Peru's classic cocktail is a delicious concoction based on pisco, a white-grape brandy. In the last few years, sours made with all sorts of exotic tropical fruit juices, or with pisco macerated with coca leaves, have become all the rage. See p. 118.

Easter Week, Ayacucho. The stately but modest Andean town of Ayacucho erupts with the most inspired ceremonial celebration of Easter Week, which features nightly candlelit processions and culminates in the parading of an enormous throne made entirely of white wax. See p. 116.

Virgen de la Candelaria, Puno. Known as the epicenter for Peruvian folklore, Puno, during any of its major festivals, is Peru's biggest party scene. This 2-week celebration is one of the greatest folk religious festivals in South America. The music, dance, costumes, and masks are intoxicating; the participants intoxicated. See p. 184.

Shopping for native textiles, Titicaca/Sacred Valley. Picking up handmade alpaca *chullos* (caps) and blankets from the very artisans who've crafted them is a quintessential Andean experience. My favorite spots are Isla Taquile, on Lake Titicaca, and the market in Chinchero. See p. 172, **2**, and 254, **1**.

Inti Raymi, Cusco. The Festival of the Sun, one of the greatest pageants in South America, celebrates the winter solstice and honors the Inca sun god with a bounty of colorful Andean parades, music, and dance. The festival transforms the Sacsayhuamán ruins overlooking the city into a grand stage. See p. 206.

Virgen del Carmen, Paucartambo. Interest in the remote Andean colonial village of Paucartambo grows out of proportion to its tiny size once a year, when it hosts Peru's most surreal festival: 3 days of wild dancing, drinking, and freakish masks. See p. 216.

Carnaval, Cajamarca. Laid-back Cajamarca blows its pre-Lenten lid with parties that soak participants with water, paint, and more. It's the best and most fun Carnaval celebration in Peru. See p. 386.

Jungle cuisine, Amazon. The cuisine of Peru's vast Amazon offers plenty of exotica, even if you rightly avoid sea-turtle soup or caiman. Opt instead for *paiche,* an Amazon-size local white fish, and *chonta,* a hearts of palm salad. Outside the jungle, another way to go native is to eat *cuy* (guinea pig), but my taste buds recommend this less enthusiastically. See "Jungle Food Exotica," p. 318.

The Best Architecture & Museums

Lima Centro. Lima today is chaotic, but its colonial core makes its rich past very evident. Starting with the elegant Plaza de Armas and fanning out, there's a surfeit of gorgeous colonial churches and *casonas* (mansions). See p. 60.

Museo Arqueológico Rafael Larco Herrera, Lima. More than 45,000 pieces of magnificent ceramics from the Moche dynasty are on view in the world's largest private collection of pre-Columbian art. The X-rated Sala Erótica is for mature audiences only. See p. 52, **2**.

Convento de Santa Catalina, Arequipa. This convent is a village unto itself, with Spanish-style cobblestone passageways, plazas, and cloisters where elite sequestered nuns once lived. Like most of Arequipa's handsome historic quarter, it's carved from *sillar* (white volcanic stone). See p. 136, **1**.

Qoricancha (Templo del Sol), Cusco. The best place to see Inca and Spanish cultures collide is the Temple of the Sun. The Incas' masterful masonry is on view there, as well as on Cusco's streets, which are lined with giant, delicately carved granite blocks. See p. 194, **5**.

Rubber-boom mansions, Iquitos. The rubber barons who made fortunes in the 19th century erected mansions swathed in colorful Portuguese glazed tiles along the riverfront *malecón* (promenade). A few blocks away is an iron house designed by Gustave Eiffel and shipped from Paris to Peru. See p. 312, **1**, and 314, **2**.

Museo Tumbas Reales de Sipán, Lambayeque. This striking museum is a suitable home for one of Peru's finest archaeological finds: the spectacular tomb of the Lord of Sipán. The Moche royal figure, Peru's "King Tut," was buried 1,700 years ago with a wealth of ceremonial ornaments and treasures. See p. 350, **7**.

Casas antiguas (old houses), Trujillo. Colorful pastel facades and elegant iron window grilles ring Trujillo's Plaza de Armas. The colonial- and republican-era houses have spectacular

> *Arequipa's Santa Catalina convent is a secret village unto itself behind thick* sillar *walls.*

interior courtyards and *mudéjar*-style (Moorish-Christian) details. See p. 336.

Conjunto Monumental de Belén, Cajamarca. A complex of carved volcanic stone, Belén is both a notable architectural site and a museum, comprising a beautiful colonial church and two former hospitals housing medical and archaeological exhibits, including textiles and ceramics dating from 1500 B.C. See p. 388, **7**.

2
Strategies for Seeing Peru

Strategies for Seeing Peru

Machu Picchu is such a part of global folklore that it's tempting to equate Peru with the great Inca retreat in the clouds. However, Peru is a wonderfully diverse country, much more than its Inca legacies, with an astounding amount to explore. Whether you're a first-time visitor or someone who's returned to see more of Peru than the greatest hits, the following tips and suggestions will help you maximize your time, increase your appreciation and enjoyment of this incredible country, and focus on the best ways to discover what Peru has to offer.

> PREVIOUS PAGE On Lake Titicaca's Isla Suasi, hike to the hilltop for mesmerizing sunset views.
> THIS PAGE Surfing is a way of life along the Peruvian coast, such as here at Punta Hermosa beach.

Tip #1: Get outdoors. Peruvians are fond of describing their country as having three components: *costa* (coast), *sierra* (highlands), and *selva* (jungle). That makeup translates into a basic imperative for travelers: To see the best of Peru, you've got to get outdoors. Sure, you can go ice climbing or on an 11-day high-altitude trek through the Andes, but Peru's not just for hard-core adventure travelers. Go on a boat trip around Paracas; take a gentle walk in the Sacred Valley; paddle a canoe through the Amazon basin; or, heck, just hang out on a beach. (Though it's primarily identified by its majestic mountains and dense rainforest, Peru does have 2,500km/1,550 miles of coastline.)

Tip #2: Seek out other pre-Columbian civilizations. The Incas, who built a continent-long empire and left behind the grandest of South American ruins, Machu Picchu, rightly get the lion's share of attention from travelers. But Peru's history is a glorious ramble of sophisticated civilizations that preceded not only the Spaniards but the Incas, too. The Chavín, Moche, Chimú, Nasca, Huari, Paracas, and others left behind tantalizing and enigmatic examples of their cultures, from splendid ceramics and textiles to earthen mounds that once constituted enormous cities. Along the southern desert coast, and north around Trujillo and Chiclayo, there's ample opportunity to venture way beyond the Incas.

Tip #3: Test yourself. Peru provides opportunities to try something new. If you're going on a hike, don't just opt for a 2-hour walk. Plan a multiday trek; even though Peru's altitude and mountain climbs are forbidding, you might be surprised by what you can accomplish, and not all treks surmount "Dead Woman's Pass," as the Inca Trail does. Or, do something you never thought you'd attempt: Take a canopy walk or zip line among the treetops in the Amazon; go surfing in Peru's great waves near Máncora; hop on a mountain bike at 4,877m (16,000 ft.) outside Colca Canyon; or kayak out on Lake Titicaca, the world's highest navigable lake.

Tip #4: Get off the beaten path. Peru may already seem pretty exotic, but it definitely has a well-worn "gringo trail" that encompasses the south and its great attractions. I'm not saying you should skip Cusco, the Sacred Valley of the Incas, Machu Picchu, and Titicaca (there's a reason everyone goes to these parts), but it's also rewarding to go places where you're unlikely to run into your neighbor. In Peru, that might mean the jungle, inland, or the untrodden north, which gets undeservedly passed over. Head to Cajamarca or Ayacucho, and you won't believe there aren't more tourists around.

Tip #5: Go local. Peru is one of those countries where you get the most by doing as the locals do. If you fly above the fray in chartered cars

> Combis *are the cheapest and most colorful way to get around Peru.*

to the Sacred Valley and fancy trains with white-gloved service to Machu Picchu, you'll miss how the great majority of Peruvians live. Take *motocarros* (motorcycle rickshaws) and *combis* and *colectivos* (privately owned vans that stop and pick up passengers along the road for less than a dollar). If you're bigger than most Peruvians, you may have to squeeze in, and it won't be the most comfortable ride of your life, but you may have a baby goat sitting across from you, and you'll hear locals speaking in Quechua on their cellphones (incredibly, they get better reception in the Andes than I do an hour outside New York City). And small hotels may have Peruvian touches you won't find at big hotels accustomed to hosting groups of gringos, where everyone speaks perfect English. Cheap doesn't always mean authentic and better, but in Peru, it often does.

Tip #6: Eat local. This isn't a locavore concern, exactly, but a note that Peru is one of the finest eating countries on the planet, and up and down the coast and into the mountains, you'll find opportunities to eat your way through your vacation. That means not only delectable

> *Kayaking on the placid waters of Lake Titicaca, the world's highest navigable body of water.*

ceviche, but *tiradito* (the Peruvian version of sashimi), peculiar jungle dishes (such as *paiche* and piranha direct from the Amazon River), *pachamanca* (barbecue cooked underground), *chifa* (Chinese-Peruvian fusion), mouth-watering *ajíes* (hot peppers), regional cuisine such as Arequipeña, and, yes, even *cuy* (guinea pig), an inexplicable local delicacy that has more teeth and bones than meat. Have a few pisco sours, but go one better and try one made with *maracuyá* (passion fruit), pisco macerated in coca leaves, or any number of tropical fruit juices, such as *lúcuma*.

Tip #7: Prepare for the altitude. If you're headed to the highlands, and most people are, you've got to be aware of *soroche* (acute mountain sickness). It doesn't affect everyone, but it's debilitating for some. When you hit Cusco (3,353m/11,000 ft. above sea level), Titicaca (3,810m/12,500 ft.), or Colca (as high as 4,877m/16,000 ft.), you need to acclimate. That involves at least a couple of days of taking it easy, drinking lots of water and *mate de coca* (coca-leaf tea), avoiding alcohol, and maybe even having oxygen pumped into your

hotel room. There are also *soroche* pills, which are pretty effective in dealing with nausea and headaches. If you're doing a high-altitude trek in the Andes, proper acclimatization is serious business, and skimping on the time your body needs just won't cut it.

Tip #8: Deal with the jungle. One-third of Peru is jungle, a wondrous subtropical zone with incredible flora and fauna. But beware: The Amazon region is extremely hot and humid, sticky and wet, and full of mosquitoes and other pests. It's hell to some, but with the right attitude, a trip to an eco-lodge in Tambopata, Manu, or the northern Amazon basin can be spectacular. If you think you can cope, be sure to bring suitable clothes, mosquito repellent, and patience. Good camera equipment and a pair of binoculars (so you don't have to depend on the one being passed around the boat) are also advisable.

Tip #9: Slow down. Be courteous. This is Latin America, and things don't always move on a European or North American schedule. Tours may leave late or wait for stragglers.

Restaurant service may seem inattentive or haphazard. If you accept delays as part of the rhythm of life below the Equator, you'll better enjoy your time here. Also, manners and formality are very important in Latin America. Even if you don't speak Spanish, making the effort to greet people and bid adieu with *"buenos dias"* and *"hasta luego"* when entering and leaving an establishment goes a long way.

Tip #10: Choose your season. It's not as simple as knowing the seasons of the Southern Hemisphere. Peru is more a matter of rainy and dry seasons. During the rainy season (Nov–Mar), traveling in the highlands and the Amazon can be not only difficult but in some cases impossible. There are mudslides in the Andes every year, and several times the train tracks to Machu Picchu—to use Peru's best-known site as an example—have been wiped out by heavy rains and flooding, leaving travelers stranded. In those regions, the dry season (June–Aug) is best weather-wise, but that's also when the crush of tourism is at its worst. I prefer to visit during the shoulder seasons, April to May and September to October. The coast is another matter entirely. January to March are by far the best months to hit Peru's long coastline, and probably the only times all year in Lima that you'll see the sun break out of the thick, gray *garúa* (misty fog) that dominates the sky.

Tip #11: Come to terms with privilege and poverty. I know this statement may, on the surface, sound cruel or cynical, and I surely don't mean to sound indifferent to the grinding poverty of a good many Peruvians. But to understand and enjoy Peru, or any developing nation for that matter, you've got to face inequality. In many places, especially in Cusco, you'll find yourself continually confronted by small children asking for *propinas* (tips, which is essentially panhandling) or selling chocolates and postcards, sometimes alarmingly late at night; or by girls and women demanding money for photos with llamas. Although it can be overwhelming, the best response is to be polite and calmly reply *"no, gracias"* (this quickly becomes a refrain). Consider doing something other than dispensing coins and bills: Give gifts of pens, notepads, or other items of interest to schoolchildren; or, if you have a meaningful conversation with someone, buy

> *Informal juice stands offer all kinds of fresh fruit juices at markets across Peru.*

him or her a sandwich or ice-cream cone. Even better, look into some of the great volunteer programs available in Peru (p. 447).

Tip #12: Use this book as a reference, not a blueprint. The suggestions and tours throughout this book are geared to help you maximize your time and experience the best sights, attractions, and activities across Peru. But even though they are envisioned as day-by-day numbered tours, don't take that too rigidly. It's impossible to plan for all travelers' interests and stamina, so if it seems that some of the tours and itineraries in this guide are too long and exhausting, or give a sense of rushing about the country, feel free to pick and choose the destinations and activities most important to you.

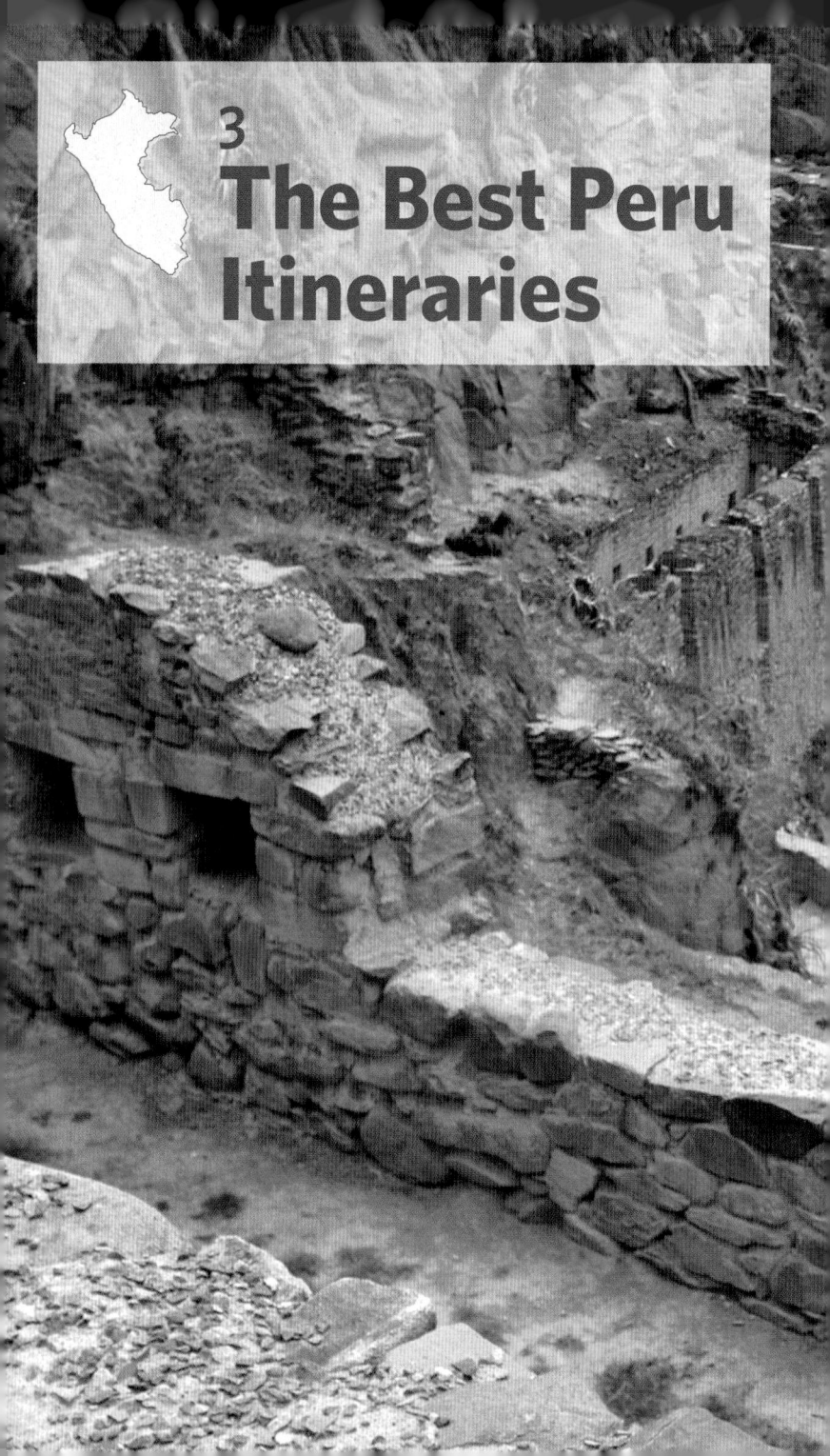

3 The Best Peru Itineraries

The Cusco Highlands in 1 Week

With only a week, most people don't have time to experience the full range of Peru's variety. Still, you can manage to pack an awful lot into a week. Machu Picchu is on every first-timer's list, and with 1 week, there's just enough time to see the best of Cusco and Incan Peru (without jumping all over the country). This itinerary essentially covers the Incas' greatest hits: the ancient capital, the Urubamba Valley that the Incas held sacred, and the alluring ruins of the imperial retreat hidden in the clouds.

> *PREVIOUS PAGE It's easy to see why the Incas thought of the beautiful Urubamba Valley as sacred.*
  THIS PAGE Pisac's Sunday crafts market is the most famous in Peru.

START Take an overnight flight to Lima that allows you to catch an early-morning flight to Cusco (1 hr.).

❶ Cusco. Transfer from the capital city of Cusco to your Sacred Valley lodging (in Pisac, Ollantaytambo, or Machu Picchu; see p. 284 and 288), and spend the day becoming acclimated to the region's high altitude. ⏱ 1 day.

Take a *combi* or taxi to Pisac.

❷ Pisac. If possible, schedule your trip so that Day 2 is one of Pisac's market days (Tues, Thurs, or, best of all, Sun). Check out the lively **crafts market** (p. 248, ❶) in the main square. After lunch, visit the great **Pisac ruins** (p. 250, ❸) looming above the town; either hike up to them (although the high altitude can make this

1 Cusco
2 Pisac
3 Ollantaytambo
4 Machu Picchu
5 Cusco
6 Lima

Ruins

150 mi
150 km

very challenging for those who've just arrived) or take a taxi. ☺ 1 day.

Wake up early on Day 3 and take a *combi* **or taxi to Ollantaytambo.**

❸ **Ollantaytambo.** Arrive early to explore the spectacular **fortress ruins** (p. 253, ❻) before the busloads arrive. After lunch, wander the Inca **old town** (p. 252, ❹), nicknamed "Ollanta" by locals. Energetic travelers can climb the path to old Inca granaries for great views of the town and the valley. Or, take a taxi back toward Urubamba and hike along the river to **Salineras de Maras** (p. 258, ❻), the ancient salt mines, or catch a *combi* and then taxi to

> The 17th-century Iglesia y Convento de San Francisco is one of Cusco's largest churches.

> *Climb to the mirador in San Blas for a private moment and contemplative view of Cusco's red-tiled rooftops.*

Moray (p. 256, ❷), an enigmatic Inca agricultural site. ☉ 1 day.

Catch an early-morning train from Ollantaytambo to Aguas Calientes (90 min.). From there, take a bus up the mountain to Machu Picchu.

❹ **Machu Picchu.** Spend the day exploring the ruins (p. 260); if you're in shape, hike up to the **Huayna Picchu** peak (p. 265, ⓭) for panoramic views. Have lunch next to the ruins at the Machu Picchu Sanctuary Lodge (p. 290), and linger until late afternoon, after the tour groups have left. Spend the night back down in Aguas Calientes (p. 259, ❽), relaxing at the restaurants and bars near the railroad tracks. ☉ 1 day.

Take an early-morning train to Cusco.

❺ **Cusco.** Stroll around the delightful **Plaza de Armas** (p. 192, ❶), pop into a few alpaca and silver jewelry shops, and visit **La Catedral** (p. 192, ❷). After lunch, go to **Convento de Santa Catalina** (p. 196, ❶) and the stunning **Qoricancha** temple (p. 194, ❺). Take a walk along **Loreto** and **Hatunrumiyoc** streets (p. 204, ❶, and 207 ❾) to see some more magnificent Inca stonework. At day's end, have a pisco sour at one of the lively cafes or bars near the Plaza de Armas. The next day, visit the beautiful **Museo de Arte Precolombino** (p. 195, ❼). Stroll around **San Blas** (p. 208), site of artisans' shops and art galleries. After lunch, catch a cab (or walk) up to **Sacsayhuamán** (p. 199, ❺), the splendid ruins overlooking the city. In the evening, get a taste of Cusco's hopping nightlife at one of the pubs or nightclubs around the Plaza de Armas. ☉ 2 days.

On the morning of Day 7, fly back to Lima.

❻ **Lima.** Make the most of a day in Lima with lunch at a *cevichería* and a short tour of colonial **Lima Centro** in the late afternoon. ☉ 1 day. See "Lima in 1 Day," p. 48.

> Vertiginous steps lead to the top of
Ollantaytambo's fortress ruins.

Southern Peru in 2 Weeks

This itinerary takes in southern Peru's historic colonial cities and natural wonders, from Cusco and the Amazon jungle to Lake Titicaca and scenic Colca Valley. This is largely the time-honored "gringo trail," but there's good reason southern Peru is so popular with travelers: It's got the best infrastructure and some of the indisputable highlights of South America. If your primary interest is the outdoors, you might want to build this itinerary around hiking the Inca Trail or a longer visit to the Amazon.

> It feels as if you can almost touch the clouds on Lake Titicaca, 3,800m (12,467 ft.) above sea level.

START Lima.

❶ Lima. Peru's capital is chaotic, but it has a superb colonial core and the country's best restaurants and museums. Spend the morning touring the colonial quarter of **Lima Centro.** After lunch at a great *cevichería* or a cutting-edge *novo Andino* restaurant, visit **Museo Arqueológico Rafael Larco Herrera** (p. 52, **❷**), home of the country's premier collection of pre-Columbian ceramics. ⏱ 1 day. See "Lima in 1 Day," p. 48.

Take an early-morning flight to Cusco (1 hr.).

❷ Cusco. Use your first day in Cusco to acclimate to the city's daunting altitude (3,400m/11,000 ft.). Take in the **Plaza de Armas** and **Cathedral,** touring the old Inca capital's **Centro Histórico** at a relaxed pace. The next day, steel yourself for the hilly climb to the artsy **San Blas** district, and visit **Sacsayhuamán,** the great Inca ruins above the city. Cusco is one of the best places in Peru to shop, eat, and party, so make sure to save some energy and squeeze those activities in with your sightseeing. ⏱ 2 days. See "Cusco in 2 Days," p. 196.

Take an early-morning train from Cusco to Aguas Calientes (90 min.).

❸ Machu Picchu. Spend most of Day 4 exploring the famous Machu Picchu ruins (p. 260), returning to Cusco on the latest afternoon train. ⏱ 1 day.

Take an early-morning flight from Cusco to Puerto Maldonado (30 min.).

4 Southern Amazon. The most accessible part of the southern Amazon is **Reserva Nacional de Tambopata** (p. 302). Board a boat for a 2-day, 1-night trip to one of the jungle lodges along the Río Madre de Dios (just enough time to get a taste of the Amazon). Head back to Puerto Maldonado and catch a return flight to Cusco, where you'll spend the night. ⏲ **2 days.**

On Day 7, take the scenic train ride from Cusco to Puno (10 hr.).

5 Lake Titicaca. Spend the night in Puno, and the next day take a boat trip out on the lake.

The best way to experience life on Titicaca is with an overnight trip that first visits the **Uros Floating Islands** and then allows you to spend a night with a family on **Isla Taquile** or **Amantaní.** ⏲ **3 days. See p. 170.**

Return to Puno to spend the night, and on Day 10 catch an early-morning flight from Juliaca (the nearest airport, an hour from Puno) to Arequipa (45 min.).

6 Arequipa. In "La Ciudad Blanca," explore the colonial quarter's grand *sillar* (white volcanic stone) buildings. Hang out on the **Plaza de Armas** (p. 138, **2**), and spend the late afternoon and early evening at the **Convento de**

> *Quiet corners and beautiful niches abound at Convento de Santa Catalina in Arequipa.*

Santa Catalina (p. 136, ❶), one of the finest examples of colonial religious architecture in the Americas. ⏱ 1 day.

Early on the morning of Day 11, set off on a 2-day, 1-night trip to Colca Valley.

Be Creative

There are numerous ways to expand upon outdoor activities here. In Colca Canyon, go on an extended volcano-climbing trek and add on a river-rafting expedition (p. 148). Or, deviate from the itinerary and go to Lake Titicaca after Colca for a once-in-a-lifetime opportunity to kayak on the placid surface of the world's highest navigable lake, 3,810m (12,500 ft.) above sea level (p. 172). For surfers, several of the best spots to catch a wave on the whole continent are here, too. The options are endless, so focus on your favorite outdoor sport. You'll find more information on adventure options in the various regional destination chapters and in chapter 14.

❼ **Colca Valley.** Colca Valley is home to **Colca Canyon,** one of the deepest canyons in the world. While in the valley, explore several of the ancient **colonial villages,** relax in riverside thermal baths (or visit the public hot springs at La Calera), and spend the night at a rustic hotel. The next morning, set out for **Cruz del Cóndor** (p. 145, ❽) to see the magnificent Andean condors soar overhead. Return to Arequipa late on Day 12 for dinner. The next day, visit **Museo Santuarios Andinos** (p. 138, ❸) to see the remains of Juanita, the Inca princess, take in some of the fine colonial mansions and churches of the historic quarter, and shop for some of Peru's finest alpaca goods. ⏱ 3 days. For information on Colca Valley, see p. 142.

Fly back to Lima on the morning of Day 14.

❽ **Lima.** If you have a night flight out of Lima, head to seaside **Barranco** (p. 54, ❹), the city's most serene and bohemian neighborhood, ideal for a relaxed lunch, a little handicrafts shopping, and a day's-end cocktail overlooking the Pacific Ocean. ⏱ 1 day.

> Hikers to the top of Huayna
Picchu are rewarded with a
bird's-eye view of Machu Picchu.

The Best Outdoor Adventures in 2 Weeks

Few places rival Peru for outdoor bounty and natural beauty. This itinerary is designed for the high-octane thrill-seeker who's looking for unusual ways to tackle the outdoors (and isn't averse to some bus travel). The tour opts for variety and omits some obvious outdoor choices, including the great Amazon basin and the great Andes peaks and valleys near Huaraz in the north (either could be the focal point of a 2-week adventure trip to Peru). Instead, its thrills include incredible Andean treks, white-water rafting, mountain biking at insane altitudes, and even sandsurfing on towering dunes. With travel time, this full itinerary stretches to 15 days.

> Relax after a day of outdoor adventure at the La Calera hot springs in Colca Valley.

START From Lima's airport, catch a bus down the southern coast to Nasca (7 hr. and most of Day 1).

❶ Nasca. To get a look at the famous **Nasca Lines** (p. 103, ❹) etched in the desert floor, and also an incredible view of the craggy,

Legend:
1 Nasca
2 Colca Valley
3 Cusco
4 Choquequirao
5 Sacred Valley
6 Lima

interminable desert, catch a mid-morning overflight at the Nasca airport. In the afternoon, try one of the newest extreme sports in Peru, **sandboarding** (p. 117). Cerro Blanco, just 8km (5 miles) from Nasca, has the highest sand dunes in the Americas and is the destination of choice for sandboarders. The next day head out on an all-day **dune-buggy** adventure to San Fernando (p. 117), a secret desert coastal oasis where you'll see sea lions, penguins, and maybe even guanacos and condors (Casa Andina Classic Nasca, p. 128, can arrange a trip). ⏱ **2 days.**

On the morning of Day 4, catch a bus from Nasca down the coast to Arequipa (9 hr.).

2 Colca Valley. Spend the late afternoon wandering around the historic quarter of Arequipa (p. 136), which is ringed by three volcanoes, and check out the **Convento de Santa Catalina** (p. 136, **1**), open for spectacular night visits. The next morning, take a bus to Colca Valley (3 hr.), where you'll spend the next 3 days. Check into one of the country lodges and go for an afternoon **horseback ride** (p. 148). Cap off the day lounging in stone **hot springs** overlooking the river at Colca Lodge (p. 161). The next morning, get an early start to witness the goosebump-inducing flight of giant Andean condors at **Cruz del Cóndor** (p. 145, **8**). In the afternoon, go **mountain biking;** a great ride

> *Buggy rides over sand dunes are one of the unexpected thrills of the southern desert coast.*

starts from Patapampa, at 4,877m (16,000 ft.), and rockets down single-track paths used by local llama herders to Chivay (p. 148). The next day, hike down 1,000m (3,280 ft.) into the canyon to the Sangalle oasis (minimum 7 hr.). ⏱ **4 days.**

Return to Arequipa early on the morning of Day 8, and fly back to Lima's airport (90 min.), where you'll catch a flight to Cusco (1 hr.).

❸ **Cusco.** On Day 9, which is essentially a rest day, there's time for a little urban adventure. The walk up to the hilly San Blas neighborhood leaves most visitors huffing and puffing, but outdoors types will relish the strenuous climb to the spectacular **Sacsayhuamán** ruins (p. 199, ❺), some of the Incas' most magnificent. ⏱ **1 day.**

Have all your gear in order, as you'll be picked up very early from your Cusco hotel to begin this multiday trek.

One-Stop Adrenaline Shopping

Rather than travel around the country, hardcore adventurers can focus all their time on a variety of activities in just one area. Huaraz, the great Cordillera Blanca, and Callejón de Huaylas (see chapter 12) have limitless outdoors possibilities, including lengthy and arduous multiday treks through some of the planet's most astounding scenery, with views of Peru's highest peaks and emerald lagoons. You could also throw in ice climbing, mountain biking, river rafting, and rock climbing and easily come up with 2 weeks or more of concentrated adrenaline without ever leaving the region, one of the most spectacular outdoor areas on the planet. A great 5-day trek such as the Santa Cruz trail (p. 384) might be only the beginning of your adventures.

> *In the Sacred Valley, a trek up to the ruins of Pisac affords magnificent views of the town below.*

4 Choquequirao. An alternative to the more famous Inca Trail (p. 266), this 4-day trek (p. 272, **2**) goes to spectacular and untrammeled Inca ruins high above the Apurímac River. The route descends to a campsite next to the river, only to climb vertically 1,219m (4,000 ft.) the next day. (Choquequirao is just one of several stunning multiday treks in the Cusco highlands; if you've never been to Peru before, you may want to start with the grand-daddy of them all, the Inca Trail, which takes you right to the foot of Machu Picchu. White-water fanatics might prefer to use this 4-day period for a 3-day rafting trip and a day hike in the Sacred Valley, stop **5**). ⏱ **4 days.**

5 Sacred Valley. After your trek down from Choquequirao, come back to earth on Day 14 in the serene Sacred Valley of the Incas. Here you can relax at one of the Valley's country inns (several have great spas) or, if you've still got energy to burn, do a white-water rafting day trip on the Urubamba River (p. 277). If you prefer to keep your hiking boots on, take a day hike (3 hr.) from the Inca site of Moray to the **Salineras salt mines** (p. 258, **6**), a downhill route that's also fun to do on a mountain bike. ⏱ **1 day.**

Head back to Cusco the next morning and catch a return flight to Lima.

6 Lima. If you're waiting for a night flight and are lucky, you'll have a chance for one last adventure: catching a thermal current in a **paraglider** to soar over the cliffs of Miraflores and the Costa Verde. There's more to adventure in the Peruvian capital than surviving murderous traffic and the chaotic downtown.

Undiscovered Peru

Cusco and Machu Picchu are at the forefront of Peru's tried-and-true "gringo trail" through the southern Andes. If you have an aversion to going where everybody else does, try venturing inland to pristine highland colonial cities; northward to ancient archaeological sites that—due to erosion, less reconstruction, and fewer tourists—remain more mysterious than more popular sites in the south; and to the country's finest beaches and surf spots. And, if you have 2 weeks to discover the undiscovered, you could even make it to the extremely remote, rewarding ruins of Kuélap, which give Machu Picchu a run for its money.

> Peru has more than 2,400km (some 1,500 miles) of coastline; it's not uncommon to find northern beaches virtually deserted.

START Fly from Lima to Ayacucho (1 hr.). **TRIP LENGTH** 11 days.

1 Ayacucho. For many years, this long-suffering city was held by terrorists and cut off from the rest of Peru. Newly welcoming, it's a feast of **colonial churches** (p. 113, **9**) and *casonas* (manor houses; p. 112, **2**) cradled in the Andes. The city also throws the most spectacular Easter festivities in the country.

Just beyond Ayacucho are the massive, 1,400-year-old ruins of the Huari culture at the **Complejo Arqueológico de Huari** (p. 114, **14**) and the town of **Quinua** (p. 116, **15**), famous as the site of the epic battle for Peruvian independence and for its homegrown artisans, the finest in Peru. ☺ 2 days.

Fly back to Lima's airport and transfer to a flight (1 hr.) north to Trujillo.

> The curious rock formations of
> Cumbe Mayo near Cajamarca,
> where a still-functioning aqueduct
> was crafted circa 1000 B.C.

2 Trujillo. Spend a half-day touring the handsome colonial core of Trujillo (p. 336, **1**–**9**), one of the most elegant in Peru. In the afternoon, visit the **Huacas de Moche** (p. 348, **3**), enormous adobe pyramids dating to A.D. 500. The next morning, explore the various sites of **Chan Chan** (p. 349, **4**), the huge Chimú complex on the outskirts of Trujillo. In the afternoon, relax in the tranquil fishing village and summer/weekend resort **Huanchaco** (p. 349, **5**), hardly undiscovered but charming nonetheless, and have ceviche in an open-air restaurant overlooking the ocean. ☺ 2 days.

On Day 5, travel by bus to Chiclayo (3 hr.).

3 Chiclayo. Although this busy city is aesthetically unimpressive, it, along with Trujillo, is at the epicenter of northern Peru's archaeology circuit. Visit Chiclayo's fascinating street market, **Mercado Modelo** (p. 350, **6**). Then, head to the countryside to the **Museo Tumbas Reales de Sipán** (p. 350, **7**), which contains the spectacular funereal chamber and treasures of the Lord of Sipán, and the **Museo Nacional Sicán** (p. 351, **8**). The next day, explore the "Valley of the Pyramids" at **Túcume** (p. 345, **5**), a mystifying complex of 26 pre-Columbian adobe pyramids. ☺ 2 days.

On Day 7, fly from Chiclayo to Piura (1 hr.), and either catch a *colectivo* or rent a car to travel north to Máncora (3 hr.).

4 Máncora. The northern coast is home to Peru's prettiest beaches and greatest surfing breaks and swells. Although the desert coast around Máncora was previously known only to hippies and *surfistas,* it's recently been "discovered" by the cognoscenti and is growing in popularity. Outside of summer vacation, though, it still feels pretty cutting-edge and is a great place to eat and drink well and relax by the beach (if you're not on your board). ☺ 3 days. See p. 356, **5**.

On Day 10, return by car or *colectivo* to Piura, and then fly to Chiclayo (1 hr.), where you'll catch a bus to Cajamarca (5 hr.).

5 Cajamarca. Cajamarca is often called the "Cusco of the North." This alluring highlands town shares characteristics with the Inca capital but not the crowds. When you arrive in town, explore Cajamarca's market and colonial

> *The squat cathedral in Cajamarca's elegant Plaza de Armas was carved from volcanic stone.*

core, including **Conjunto Monumental de Belén** (p. 388, **7**). The next day, head out to the evocative rock formations of **Cumbe Mayo** (p. 390, **10**) before catching a flight back to Lima. ☺ 2 days.

Kuélap

For those with a few extra days to discover Peru, these magnificent, remote ruins are more than 300 years older than Machu Picchu and in some ways nearly equal for the dramatic setting and evocative stonework. The site, still undergoing excavation, is certainly much less visited; if you make it here, you may have the fortress ruins of some 400 buildings all to yourself. Spend the night at the site or in a nearby lodge. Kuélap can be reached from Chiclayo or Cajamarca; the least time-consuming route is from Chiclayo. No phone. Admission S/15. Daily 8:30am–5pm.

Peru with Kids

Traveling in Peru with children is an adventure.

Transportation difficulties, foreign food, and the country's rugged nature may prove overtly challenging to some families. But, Peru can be a rewarding learning experience about South American history, ecology, Peruvian culture, and the developing world. Older kids and teens, especially those with a taste for adventure, will enjoy the outdoor settings of Inca ruins, Lake Titicaca's island culture, and the flora and fauna of the Amazon jungle. Families for whom this trip may involve too much travel can pass on either Lake Titicaca or the Amazon and try to stick to the "gringo trail," where there's better infrastructure.

> *Hardworking llamas are seen throughout the Peruvian highlands, and children are often their shepherds.*

START Fly into Lima and make a connection to Cusco (1 hr.), followed by a transfer (1 hr.) by taxi or *combi* to a hotel in the Sacred Valley of the Incas. **TRIP LENGTH** 11 days.

❶ Sacred Valley. Instead of beginning your tour of the highlands in its capital, Cusco, head straight to the peaceful Sacred Valley, where the altitude is lower and things are less congested. Stay at a country hotel (which can

arrange a transfer from the Cusco airport), where the kids can go horseback riding or swimming; teenagers could even go white-water rafting or mountain biking in the Valley. Climbing the Inca ruins of **Pisac** (p. 250, ❸) or **Ollantaytambo** (p. 253, ❻) is also fun, educational, and a great way to burn off energy. ⏱ 2 days. See "The Sacred Valley in 3 Days" (p. 248); for hotels in the area, see p. 284.

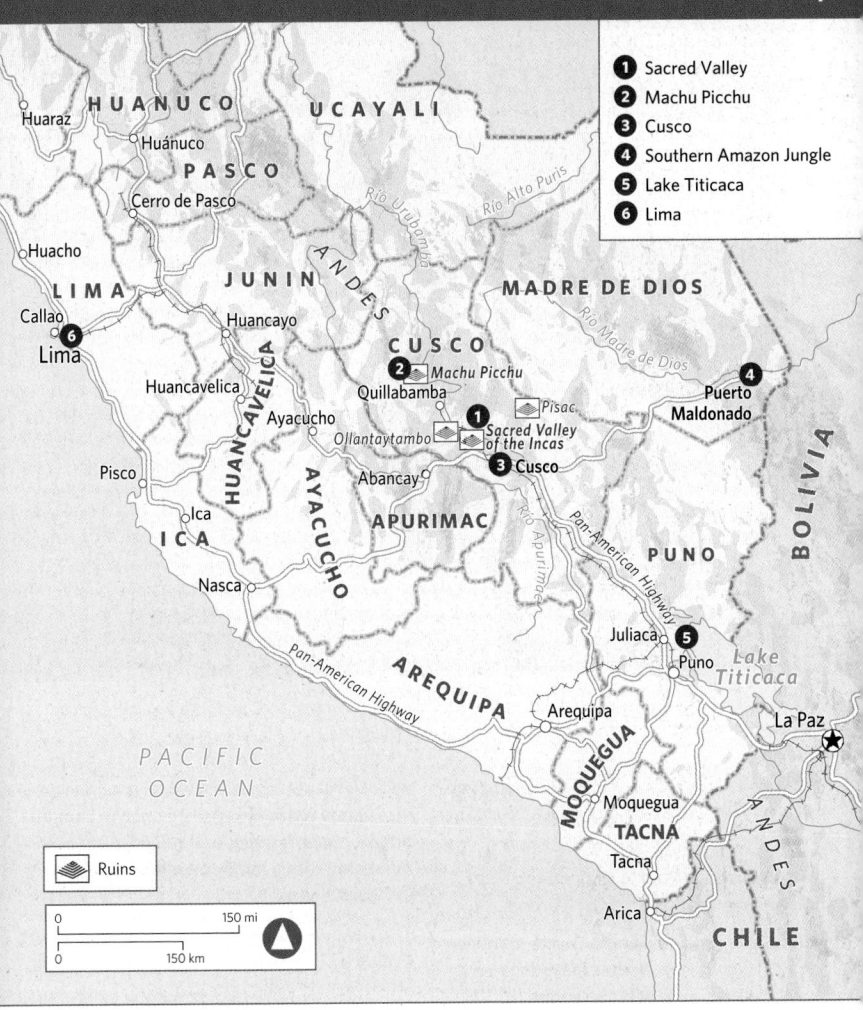

Take a taxi or *combi* to Ollantaytambo and then the early-morning train (90 min.) to Aguas Calientes, followed by a short bus ride up to the ruins.

2 Machu Picchu. The train to Machu Picchu is a delightful, scenic adventure that appeals to all ages. Spend the day exploring the ruins. Older and athletic children will love the hike up to **Huayna Picchu** for sensational panoramic views. This day involves a lot of climbing and stamina, so plan to stay overnight in Aguas Calientes. ⏱ 1 day. See p. 260.

On the morning of Day 4, take the train to Cusco.

3 Cusco. Cusco is full of visual inputs, such as colorfully attired llamas on the streets. Kids can check out the masonry of a 500-year-old Inca palace with giant stones that fit together like a jigsaw puzzle; have them locate the **12-Angled Stone** on Calle Hatunrumiyoc and the stones that form the shape of a puma in the **Inca Roca** alleyway. At the ruins of **Sacsayhuamán,** there are mammoth rocks with slick grooves that make great slides for kids of all ages. Cusco has a number of informal restaurants, such as the pizzeria Chez Maggy

> *While walking among the cobblestones of Cusco's Calle Hatunrumiyoc, look for the famous 12-Angled Stone in the ancient foundation of the palace of an Inca emperor.*

(p. 225) and Jack's Café Bar (p. 228), that will appeal to young ones. ⏱ 2 days. See "Cusco in 2 Days," p. 196.

Fly from Cusco to Puerto Maldonado (30 min.) and transfer to a lodge riverboat.

❹ **Southern Amazon Jungle.** Two eco-lodges that don't require too much exhausting river travel time are **Sandoval Lake Lodge** (p. 307), for those who don't mind roughing it, on an oxbow lake where a family of giant river otters lives; and **Reserva Amazónica Lodge** (p. 306), for a bit of pampering, which has a private tree-top canopy walk and boats that take guests out at night to look for caimans on the river. ⏱ 3 days.

Late on Day 8, fly back to Cusco; spend the night here before taking the train to Puno the next day (10 hr.).

❺ **Lake Titicaca.** The train ride to Lake Titicaca is long, but it's one of the most scenic in South America. Once here, stay at a hotel overlooking the lake, and head out on a boat tour of Titicaca (either a day trip or with an overnight stay). Kids open to new experiences will marvel at the natives who live on the floating islands **(Islas Uros)** or the native communities on **Isla Taquile,** and will enjoy an overnight stay with a family on **Isla Amantaní.** ⏱ 2 days. See p. 170.

The next day, fly from Puno (from the airport in nearby Juliaca) to Lima (2½ hr., including land travel to Juliaca).

❻ **Lima.** Although challenging for families, Lima has the country's best museums. Parents can either seek out—or avoid at all costs, depending on their attitudes—the excellent **Museo Arqueológico Rafael Larco Herrera** (p. 52, ❷), which has a collection of eye-popping (i.e., X-rated) ceramics of ancient Peruvian civilizations. If that's too much, head south to **Barranco** (p. 54, ❹), a seaside district with ocean views that's about as easy-going as Lima gets, or to the city's newest attraction, the colored water fountains of the **Circuito Mágico del Agua** (p. 51, ⓫). ⏱ 1 day.

> The massive granite blocks of the
Sacsayhuamán ruins above Cusco
weigh as much as 300 tons each.

4
Lima

Favorite Lima Moments

Founded by Francisco Pizarro in 1535, Lima—then La Ciudad de los Reyes (City of Kings)—became the richest and most beautiful colonial settlement in the Americas. Today's cosmopolitan capital is sprawling, frenetic, and, on first view, grimy and unlovely. But, with one-third of Peru's population and as the seat of the national government and the headquarters of most industry, Lima dominates Peru's political, commercial, and cultural life. For visitors, the city is home to the country's finest museums, restaurants, and nightlife, as well as, unexpectedly, some pre-Inca archaeological sites. And you'll find that the gorgeous colonial core is still intact, a reminder of Lima's glorious past.

> PREVIOUS PAGE Lima was once the wealthiest colonial city in the Americas. THIS PAGE The seaside district of Barranco offers a welcome respite from Lima's hustle and bustle.

❶ **Slurping ceviche.** Peru's signature dish is a tantalizing plate of raw fish and shellfish marinated in lime or lemon juice and *ajíes* (chili peppers). A heaping plate of tangy ceviche served at an informal neighborhood restaurant—a *huarique* to locals—is an unforgettable Limeño experience. Canta Rana in Barranco is one of my favorite barrio joints. See p. 74.

❷ **Strolling colonial Lima.** Lima Centro is home to some of Peru's finest colonial- and Republican-era palaces and mansions, baroque and Renaissance churches, and the continent's first university. A stroll through the historic quarter is a powerful reminder of the city's extraordinary early importance. See p. 60.

❸ **Plunging into the pre-Columbian past.** The country's finest museums are in Lima, and they are the best introduction to Peru's complex labyrinth of ancient cultures, from the Moche to the Chimú. At museums both big and small, you'll find a wealth of intricate textiles, glittering burial treasures, and extraordinary ceramics (including brazenly erotic examples at **Museo Arqueológico Rafael Larco Herrera,** p. 52, ❷). A curious tie to the past are the massive and ancient adobe pyramids (such as **Huaca Pucllana,** p. 57, ❸) plunked down in the midst of the modern city.

❹ **Imbibing Barranco.** Though just a short taxi or bus ride from the grime and congestion of downtown, this tranquil former seaside village with colorfully painted old houses is worlds removed from the big city. In recent years it's become equally famous for its nightlife.

> *Calle Cajamarca in Barranco is filled with colorful houses.*

It's the place to escape the capital when you're feeling overwhelmed. See p. 54, ④.

⑤ **Gorging on Peru's gourmet scene.** Prized by food fanatics as the most extraordinary dining city in South America, Lima is an explosion of gastronomic fusions: *criollo* (coastal Peruvian with European and African influences), Japanese, and Chinese. The combination of innovative young chefs and a local population of adventurous eaters has transformed the capital. Gastón Acurio's Astrid y Gastón is recognized as the restaurant that jump-started the movement. See p. 64.

⑥ **Stocking up on *artesanía popular*.** Lima is Peru's shopping mecca, with a superb selection of fine regional handicrafts ranging from excellent handmade textiles and colonial-style artwork to altarpieces from Ayacucho. Most visitors head straight to the massive markets in Miraflores, but I prefer small boutiques and galleries run by collectors and connoisseurs; my favorite stop in Barranco is Las Pallas. See p. 69.

⑦ **Pumping up the *peña*.** Lima's renowned *criollo* music culture is on rousing display at any number of *peñas*, lively music clubs where folkloric and Afro-Peruvian music and dance, with a heavy emphasis on percussion and audience participation, continue deep into the night. *Peñas* are the quintessential Lima nighttime destination. Brisas del Titicaca in Lima Centro is a revered cultural institution. See p. 87.

① Slurping ceviche
② Strolling colonial Lima
③ Plunging into the pre-Columbian past
④ Imbibing Barranco
⑤ Gorging on Peru's gourmet scene
⑥ Stocking up on *artesanía popular*
⑦ Pumping up the *peña*

Lima in 1 Day

With 1 day in the capital, concentrate on Lima Centro, with its handsome (if somewhat dilapidated) core of colonial- and Republican-era churches, palaces, and mansions. The city's finest period architecture is a powerful reminder of Lima's early wealth and importance. Lima Centro is a relatively compact area and easily covered by foot. The district is fairly well patrolled by police officers, but by day it is very congested, so be careful with your belongings. And while in the evening some of the buildings are beautifully illuminated, it's frankly not the safest time to visit.

> The Palacio Episcopal's ornate facade is one of the highlights of colonial Lima Centro.

START Take a taxi to Plaza Mayor or the Metropolitano Bus to Jr. Unión.

❶ ★★ **Plaza Mayor.** Lima's grand main square (also called the Plaza de Armas) marks the spot where Francisco Pizarro founded La Ciudad de los Reyes (The City of Kings) in 1535. It's largely a modern reconstruction, though, since a 1746 earthquake leveled most of the 16th- and 17th-century buildings in the old center. The 1651 bronze fountain is the oldest surviving part of the square, which over the centuries has been the site of bullfights as well as Inquisition-related executions. The north side of the plaza is occupied by the early-20th-century **Palacio del Gobierno** (Presidential Palace; ☎ 01/311-3930; guided visits Mon–Fri 9:30am–noon), where a changing of the guard takes place daily at noon. The **Palacio Episcopal** (Archbishop's Palace), on the east side, features an extraordinary wooden balcony (not open to the public). ⏱ 20 min. Jr. Junín (btw. Jr. Unión and Carabaya).

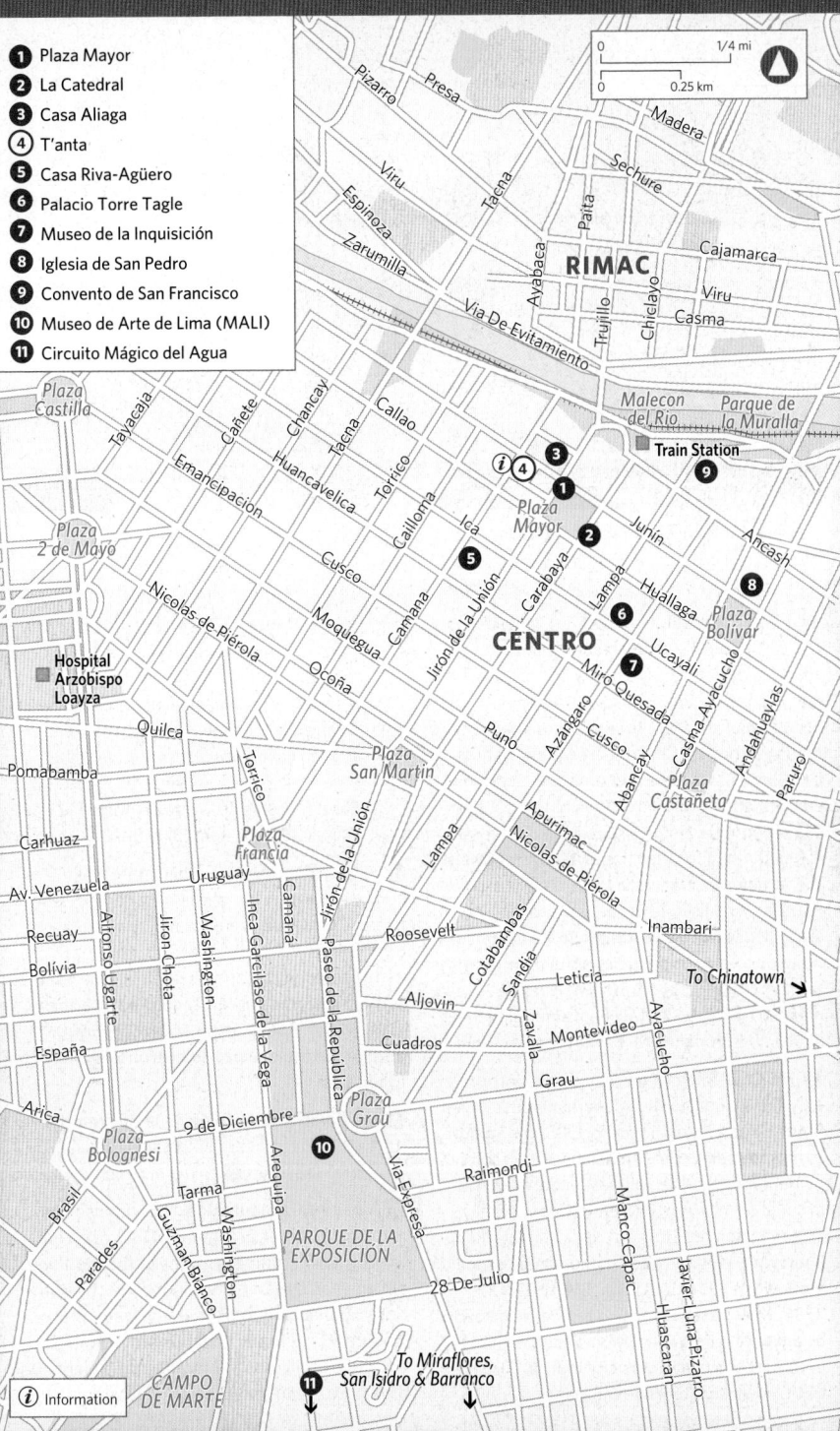

1 Plaza Mayor
2 La Catedral
3 Casa Aliaga
4 T'anta
5 Casa Riva-Agüero
6 Palacio Torre Tagle
7 Museo de la Inquisición
8 Iglesia de San Pedro
9 Convento de San Francisco
10 Museo de Arte de Lima (MALI)
11 Circuito Mágico del Agua

Information

> Alfajores *are among the delicious* postres *(desserts) at T'anta.*

② ★★ **La Catedral.** The baroque cathedral, with an elaborate stone facade and twin towers, was damaged repeatedly by earthquakes and is an 18th- and 19th-century reconstruction of the 1622 original. The interior is distinguished by Churrigueresque (Spanish baroque) altars and splendidly carved 17th-century choir stalls (the work of the Catalan artist Pedro de Noguera). But the cathedral is best known for the chapel and tomb where the remains of Francisco Pizarro (killed in the Plaza de Armas in 1541) are said to lie. The small **Museo de Arte Religioso** (Museum of Religious Art) contains beautiful painted-glass mirrors from Cusco. ⏱ 30 min. Plaza de Armas. ☎ 01/427-9647. Museum admission S/10 adults, S/5 students. Mon–Sat 10am–4:30pm.

③ ★★ **Casa Aliaga.** Not only is this purportedly the oldest surviving colonial house in South America, dating from 1535, the year of Lima's founding, but the palace is, incredibly, owned and occupied by descendants of the original family (now 17 generations strong). The mansion features an extraordinary inner courtyard, elegant salons, and some original stonework. ⏱ 1 hr. Jr. Unión 224. ☎ 01/427-7736. www.casadealiaga.com. Admission S/30, by advance reservation. Mon–Sat 9am–5pm, or as part of a Lima Tours city tour (☎ 01/619-6900; www.limatours.com.pe).

④ 🍽 ★★ **T'anta.** This smart, modern cafe, part of the ever-expanding empire of famed Lima chef Gastón Acurio, offers a great range of casual eats, including fresh salads, panini, Peruvian sandwiches called *sánguches,* and excellent desserts, as well as prepared foods to go. Pasaje Nicolás de Rivera del Viejo 142–148. ☎ 01/428-3115. Items S/8–S/20.

⑤ ★ **Casa Riva-Agüero.** This impressive 18th-century mansion has a stunning carved-stone facade, as well as a green-and-red courtyard, original furniture, and a folk-art museum with interesting rotating exhibits in the handsomely restored, vibrantly colored interior. ⏱ 30 min. Jr. Camaná 459. ☎ 01/626-6600. http://ira.pucp.edu.pe. Admission S/2. Mon–Fri 10am–5pm.

⑥ ★★ **Palacio Torre Tagle.** One of Lima Centro's most magnificent colonial mansions. ⏱ 15 min. See p. 62, ⑨.

⑦ **Museo de la Inquisición.** This handsomely restored 16th-century mansion, across from the House of Congress, dates to the founding of Lima and became the tribunal for the notorious Spanish Inquisition, which lasted from 1570 to 1820. Today, the museum soberly addresses religious intolerance (and elements of torture) from the Middle Ages through colonial times; Peru's role in the Inquisition is plainly evident in the grim catacombs, which served as prison cells. ⏱ 1 hr. Junín 548 (Plaza Bolívar). ☎ 01/311-7801. www.congreso.gob.pe/museo.htm. Free admission. Daily 10am–6pm.

8 ★ **Iglesia de San Pedro.** Precious few pieces of early colonial religious architecture remain in Lima; this 1638 Jesuit church is perhaps the best-preserved example. Although the exterior is somewhat austere, the interior explodes with gilded altars and balconies. The main altar is a magnificent showpiece of columns, balconies, and sculpted figures, and there are also some beautiful 17th- and 18th-century baroque *retablos* (altars) of carved wood and gold leaf. ⏱ 20 min. Jr. Azángaro at Ucayali. ☎ 01/428-3017. Free admission. Mon–Sat 7am–12:30pm and 5–8pm.

9 ★★★ **Convento de San Francisco.** This impressively restored 17th-century complex survived the massive earthquake in 1746 and is Lima's most spectacular colonial-era church. It's also a favorite with thousands of pigeons, who mark the ribbed yellow-and-white towers like black ink spots. Cloisters and interiors are lined with beautiful *azulejos* (glazed ceramic tiles) from Seville, with carved *mudéjar* (Moorish-style) ceilings overhead. The fine museum of religious art contains beautifully carved saints and a series of portraits of the apostles by the studio of Spanish master Francisco Zurbarán; the library overflows with 25,000 books, some of which date to the first years after Lima's foundation. By far the coolest part of a tour here is descending to the catacombs, begun in 1546 as a burial ground for priests, servants, and others. (Some 75,000 bodies were interred here before the construction of the city's main cemetery in 1821.) File past vast piles of bones to a round well lined with perfectly laid skulls and femurs. ⏱ 1 hr. Plazuela San Francisco (Jr. Ancash at Lampa). ☎ 01/426-7377. www.museocatacumbas.com. Admission S/7 adults, S/3.50 students. Daily 9:30am–5:30pm.

10 ★ **Museo de Arte de Lima (MALI).** South of the colonial core and Plaza San Agustín, in Parque de Lima, this newly refurbished museum in the handsome 19th-century Palacio de Exposiciones is well worth a visit. It holds the country's finest collection of contemporary Peruvian art, fine colonial and

> *San Francisco is the namesake saint of Lima's most extraordinary colonial church.*

Republican-era art and furnishings, and pre-Columbian textiles and ceramics. ⏱ 1 hr. Paseo Colón 125. ☎ 01/204-0000. www.mali.pe. Admission S/12 adults, S/4 students and seniors. Tues–Fri and Sun 10am–8pm; Sat 10am–5pm.

11 ★ **kids** **Circuito Mágico del Agua.** The best time to visit this water park is at night, when its 13 fountains shoot into the sky, and a spectacle of colorful effects and dancing waters are set to music. On a hot afternoon, it's also a great place for kids to cool off. The centerpiece, the **Magic Fountain,** propels a stream 76m (250 ft.) into the air, a Guinness World Record. ⏱ 1 hr. Parque de la Reserva (Av. Petit Thouars at Jr. Madre de Dios), Santa Beatriz. ☎ 01/427-1993. www.munlima.gob.pe/contenidos/recrea_circuitomagico.aspx. Admission S/4, free for children 3 and under. Wed–Sun 4am–11pm.

Lima in 2 Days

Having seen the highlights of colonial Lima on Day 1, follow up with a visit to the city's two finest museums, which offer a primer on Peru's fascinatingly complex history. The art and artifacts from a web of pre-Columbian civilizations, some of the oldest and most advanced on earth, are spectacular. Then head south along the coast to the relaxed, artsy district of Barranco, the perfect place to get away from the capital's congestion.

> One of Peru's finest Chavín relics, the Tello Obelisk, at the Museo Nacional de Arqueología, Antropología e Historia.

START Take a taxi to Plaza Bolívar in Pueblo Libre; or, take a "Todo Brasil" *colectivo* to Av. Vivanco, and walk 15 minutes to the museum.

1 ★ kids **Museo Nacional de Arqueología, Antropología e Historia.** This all-encompassing museum, less dry than it sounds, covers Peruvian civilization from prehistoric times to the colonial and Republican periods. In a 19th-century mansion (once occupied by South American independence heroes San Martín and Bolívar), there are ceramics, carved stone figures and obelisks, metalwork and jewelry, and lovely textiles. Of special note are the early ceramics (c. 2800 B.C.) from the central Andes; the great granite Tello Obelisk from the Chavín period; burial tombs; and mummies in the fetal position wrapped in burial blankets. Individual rooms are dedicated to the Nasca, Paracas, Moche, and Chimú cultures. Kids like the large-scale model of Machu Picchu. ☉ 1 hr. Plaza Bolívar s/n, Pueblo Libre. ☎ 01/463-5070. http://museonacional. perucultural.org.pe. Admission S/12 adults, S/3.50 seniors and students. Tues–Sat 9am–5pm; Sun 10am–4pm.

Take a taxi or walk along the path (about 1.5km/1 mile) connecting the two museums, indicated with a painted blue line.

2 ★★★ kids **Museo Arqueológico Rafael Larco Herrera.** The world's largest private collection of pre-Columbian art, founded in 1926 in an 18th-century colonial building, concentrates on the Moche dynasty, especially its refined ceramics. The collection of some 45,000 pieces also includes superb textiles, jewelry, and stonework from several other ancient cultures. The Moche (A.D. 200–700) are credited with achieving one of the greatest artistic expressions of ancient Peru; their ceramics offer fascinating insights into such aspects

1 Museo Nacional de Arqueología, Antropología e Historia

2 Museo Arqueológico Rafael Larco Herrera

3 Café del Museo

4 Barranco

of their society as diseases, curing practices, architecture, transportation, dance, agriculture, music, and religion. The Moche are also celebrated for their erotic ceramics, and the explicit Sala Erótica here—separate from the general collection, like the porn section in a video store—is not for prudes (or giggle-prone kids): Get ready for some kinky positions and a host of mighty phalluses. ⏲ 2 hr. Av. Bolívar 1515, Pueblo Libre. ☎ 01/461-1312. www.museo larco.org. Admission S/30 adults, S/25 seniors, S/15 students. Daily 9am–6pm.

③ 🍽 ★★ **Café del Museo.** Museum cafes can be hit or miss, but this terrific on-site restaurant, under the auspices of famed chef Gastón Acurio, is definitely the former. Grab a table outside on the terrace overlooking the garden, and nibble on ceviche or an empanada and sip a terrific pisco cocktail. Or, sit down for a more substantial lunch of creative Peruvian specialties. Av. Bolívar 1515, Pueblo Libre. ☎ 01/462-4757. www.museolarco.org/ cafedelmuseo. Items S/12–S/25.

> *Moche ceramics are the highlight of the stunning Museo Arqueológico Rafael Larco Herrera, the world's largest private collection of pre-Columbian art.*

Take a taxi to Calle Cajamarca (at Av. Miguel Grau) or the Metropolitano Bus to Bulevar.

SITE GUIDE PAGE 55

❹ ★★ kids Barranco. One of Lima's most treasured escape valves is this easygoing residential neighborhood, originally a seaside village founded in the 18th century. Its serenity and artiness is a welcome, even necessary, contrast to the untidy and seedy character of much of the rest of the city. The tranquil side streets, lined with brightly colored bungalows and elegant colonial- and Republican-era mansions, have long been favored by artists, writers, and musicians, and are home to some great options for lodging and dining. At night, the area is transformed into Lima's hedonistic hot spot, with locals and visitors flocking to the discos and watering holes.

The World's Highest Train

One of South America's most spectacular rail journeys is the nerve-rackingly high trip linking the Peruvian capital to the central highlands. The **Ferrocarril Central Andino Railroad** (☎ 01/226-6363; www. ferrocarrilcentral.com.pe) from Lima to Huancayo, completed in 1908, is the highest railway in the world, reaching a height of 4,781m (15,686 ft.). The incredible 12-hour passenger train crosses 58 bridges and passes through 69 tunnels, and while the destination—the commercial highlands city of Huancayo—may not be among Peru's highlights, the trip is worth considering for railroad aficionados and travelers who love amazingly scenic journeys. The rail line has a problematic history, which in the past has been enough to discourage most reasonable travelers from planning their trips to Peru around it. The so-called "Tren Macho" was shut down for most of the 1980s and 1990s when it was a homegrown terrorist target; after more recent periods of inactivity (unrelated to terrorism), it is again operating. At press time, the train was running twice a month between July and November (S/226–S/324 round-trip). Trains depart Lima from the **Estación Central de Desam-parados,** Jr. Ancash 201, just behind the Palacio del Gobierno. Check for updates before you arrive in Peru and schedule a trip around this rail journey.

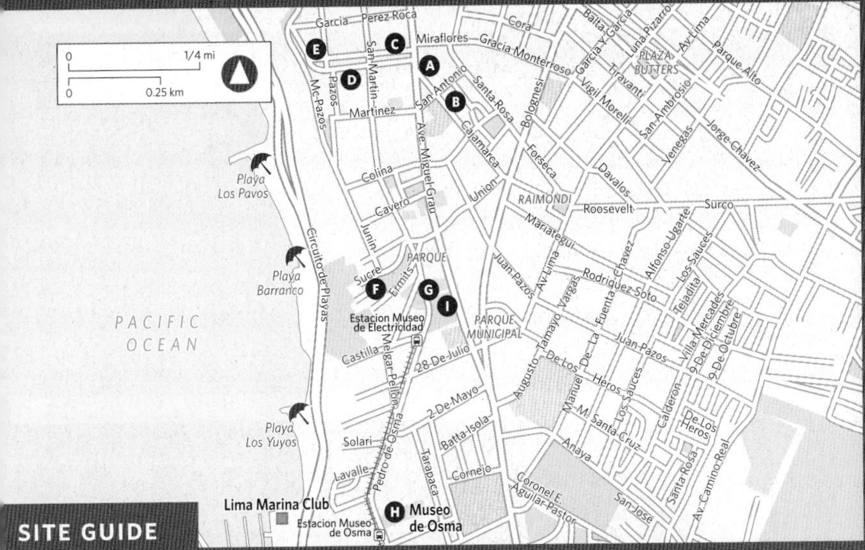

SITE GUIDE

4 Barranco

One of Barranco's most colorful streets is **A** **Calle Cajamarca,** full of brightly painted 19th-century houses. **B** ★★ **Las Pallas,** no. 212, is home to a superb selection of folk art from across Peru, assembled by a British woman who has been collecting it for 3 decades. The modern art gallery **C** ★ **Lucía de la Puente,** Sáenz Peña 206, in a beautiful old Barranco home, exhibits well-known contemporary Peruvian painters, sculptors, and photographers. Nearby, **D** ★ **Dédalo,** Sáenz Peña 295, has multiple rooms of excellent Peruvian handicrafts and home furnishings, as well as a little cafe in the garden. At the end of Alameda Sáenz Peña is a **E** *mirador* (viewpoint; see above) with great sea views. Take a right on Av. San Martín, which brings you past a church and grassy knoll to the neighborhood's most famous feature, the poetically named wooden footbridge **F** **Puente de los Suspiros** (Bridge of Sighs), which rises above a gentle passageway, **La Bajada de Baños,** lined with squat single-family houses and tall trees. This area has some of the coolest watering holes in Lima, such as Santos, Jr. Zepita 203; and La Posada del Mirador, Pasaje La Ermita 104. Across the bridge and up a flight of stairs is the heart of Barranco, **G** **Plaza de Barranco.** A few blocks down leafy Av. Pedro de Osma,

past the old electric train that once connected the village with Miraflores, is Barranco's main cultural attraction, housed in an ornate Barranco mansion: **H** ★★ **Museo de Arte Colonial Pedro de Osma,** Av. Pedro de Osma 421 (☎ 01/467-0141; www.museopedrodeosma.org; S/10 adults, S/5 students; Tues–Sun 10am–1:30pm and 2:30–6pm), is a private museum showcasing exceptional colonial religious art. Finally, back near the plaza, a good spot to wind up is **I** ★ **Bodega Juanito,** Av. Miguel Grau 274, a former apothecary and now a watering hole for chain-smoking intellectuals and locals, who knock back pitchers of beer and locally famous ham sandwiches in retro-styled environs that seem almost pre-perestroika Soviet Union. Beware the peculiar rule that men not accompanied by women have to retreat to the back room. ☉ At least 2 hr.

Lima in 3 Days

On your third day in Lima, visit a few more of the city's better-known museums and get to know the upscale residential and business district of Miraflores, which hugs the coastline just south of Lima Centro and is home to the city's most fashionable restaurants, hotels, and boutiques. Miraflores's high-rises are built around a historical oddity: the ancient ruins of an adobe pyramid, reminding citizens and visitors that no matter how modern Lima might be, in Peru you're never far from the past.

> *Restaurant Huaca Pucllana overlooks 5th-century adobe ruins right in the middle of busy Miraflores.*

START Take a taxi to Av. Javier Prado Este 2465 (in San Borja, east of Centro Lima); or, take the Metropolitano Bus to Javier Prado, and then a taxi to the museum.

1 ★ Museo de la Nación. The best thing about the massive National Museum is that it presents Peru's complicated ancient history in chronological order. Peru's pre-Columbian civilizations were among the most sophisticated of their times; when Egypt was building pyramids, cultures in Peru were constructing great cities. The exhibits give a sense of the overlapping and conquering cultures and their achievements, tracing the art and history of the earliest inhabitants to the Inca Empire. There are scale models of most major ruins in Peru and a fascinating facsimile of the Lord of Sipán discovery from the archaeology-rich north—one of the most important finds in the world in recent years (p. 350, **7**). ⏱ 2 hr. Av. Javier Prado Este 2465 (San Borja). ☎ 01/476-9878. Admission S/9 adults, S/3 seniors, S/1 students. Tues–Sun 9am–6pm.

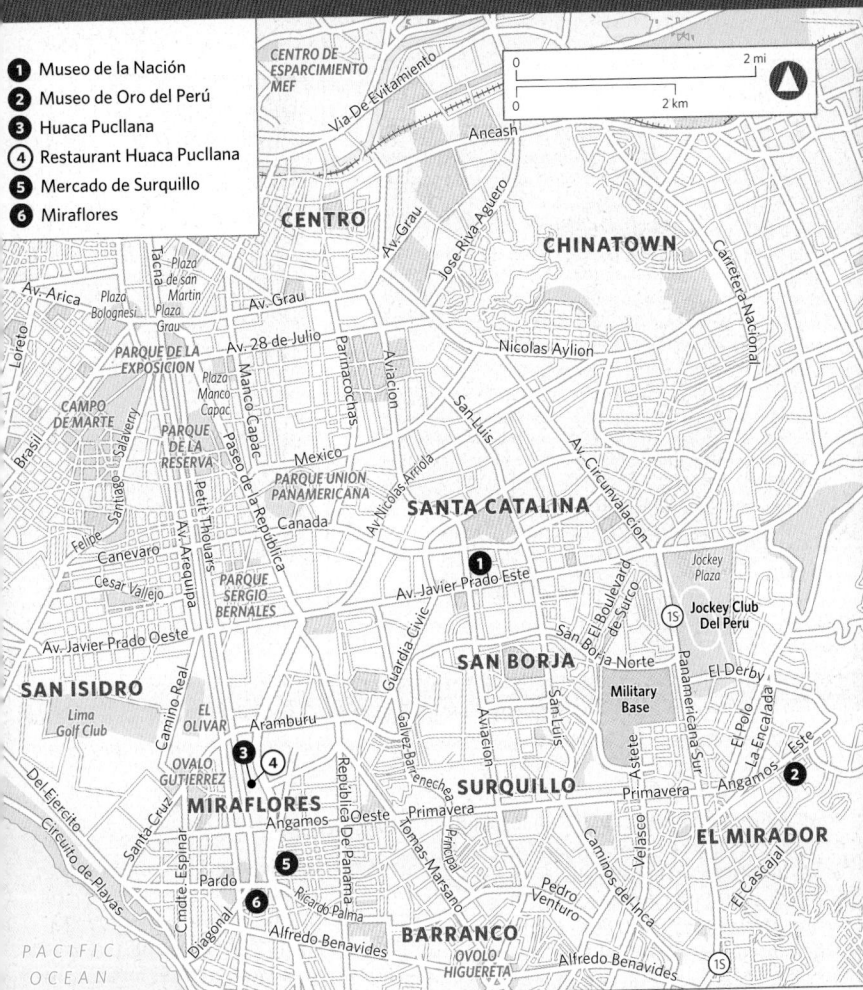

1. Museo de la Nación
2. Museo de Oro del Perú
3. Huaca Pucllana
4. Restaurant Huaca Pucllana
5. Mercado de Surquillo
6. Miraflores

Catch a taxi to Monterrico.

② Museo de Oro del Perú. For years, Lima's Gold Museum was far and away the most visited museum in Peru. Then in 2001, the National Institute of Culture and the Tourism Protection Bureau declared pretty much everything in it—as many as 7,000 pieces—elaborate fakes. Miguel Mujica Gallo, who died just days before the investigation was launched, single-handedly assembled the collection, most of it reputed to be pre-Columbian gold. Whether he had unknowingly purchased fakes or his family had sneakily replaced the authentic pieces is impossible to know. What is now on display, however, is authentic, and while the museum remains cluttered and poorly organized, there are thousands of fabulous, glittering ceremonial objects and masks, as well as tapestries, mummies, and military weaponry from medieval Europe to ancient Japan to the Nazis. It's enough to make your head spin, real or not. ⏲ 2 hr. Av. Alonso de Molina 1100 (Monterrico). ☎ 01/345-1292. www.museoroperu.com.pe. Admission S/33 adults, S/16 students. Daily 11:30am–7pm.

③ ★ kids Huaca Pucllana. Surrounded by modern Miraflores apartment buildings, this sacred pyramid, built by the Lima culture in the 5th century (A.D. 200–700), looks like an immense and dusty clay mound plunked

> *Among the treasures at Museo de la Nación is colonial artwork from the Escuela Cusqueña (Cusco School).*

down in the midst of the city. Still undergoing daily excavation, the 15-hectare (37-acre) site leaves a bit to the imagination but features an informative museum with reconstructed tombs, ceramics, and textiles. From the pyramid's top, you can see across the roofs of this busy residential and business district. ⏱ 1 hr. General Borgoño cuadra 8 s/n (at Tarapacá, near Av. Arequipa). ☎ 01/445-8695. http://pucllana.perucultural.org.pe. Admission S/7 adults, S/3 students. Guided visits Wed–Mon 9am–4:30pm.

---

④ 🍴 ★★★ **Restaurant Huaca Pucllana.** A great stop for a leisurely lunch is this distinguished restaurant—called "La Huaca" by local patrons—right across from the pyramidal ruins of the same name. It serves creative and fusion takes on classic Peruvian dishes. General Borgoño cdra. 8 s/n (at Tarapacá). ☎ 01/445-4402. www.resthuacapucllana.com. Items S/24–S/48.

Take the Metropolitano Bus to Angamos.

❺ ★★ **Mercado de Surquillo.** If you want to see where Lima's top chefs and local families go for fresh produce, seafood, meats, and a wide array of cooking implements, this market at the edge of Miraflores makes for a fascinating food-shopping and cultural experience. ⏱ 45 min. Av. Paseo de la República (at Ricardo Palma). Daily 6:30am–5pm.

SITE GUIDE
PAGE 59

❻ kids **Miraflores.** One of the most desirable residential districts in Lima, bustling Miraflores is also ground zero for most visitors, home to the lion's share of stylish restaurants, clubs, shopping boutiques (from antiques to high fashion), and hotels, many within easy walking distance. Green space within the capital is in short supply, and Miraflores's parks, which hug the Pacific coast from high above a bluff, make it a popular weekend spot with residents of greater Lima.

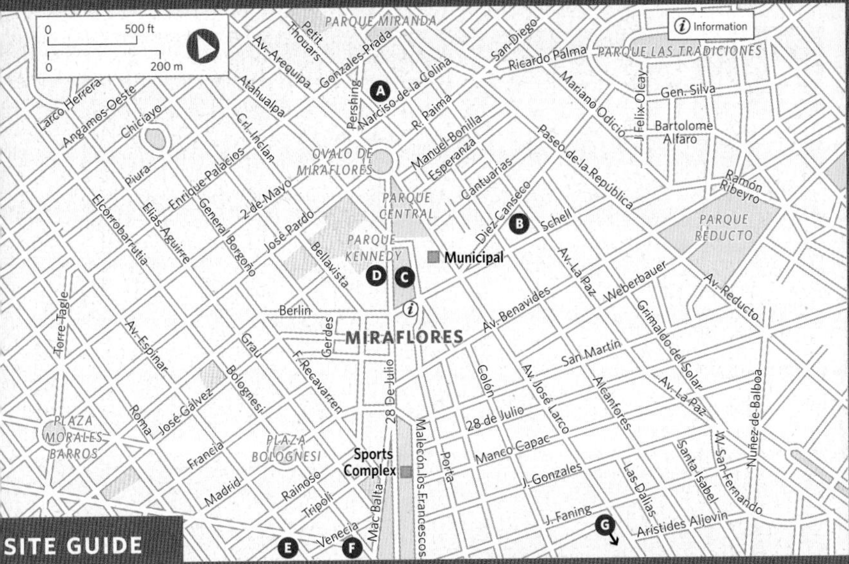

⑥ Miraflores

Ⓐ Mercado Indio (at right), the so-called "Indian Market," is a sprawling *artesanía* (handicrafts) zone with dozens of stalls featuring Peruvian handicrafts from across the country. For one-stop souvenir shopping, it's hard to beat, even if everything quickly begins to look the same. Antiques hounds head to **Ⓑ ★ Avenida La Paz**—particularly the pedestrian-only passageway at Av. La Paz 646—which is lined with small, independent shops featuring everything from furnishings and jewelry to Cusqueña School religious art. Triangle-shaped **Ⓒ ★ Parque Kennedy** (also called Parque Central), the green hub of Miraflores, is one of Limeños' favorite places to stroll, get their shoes shined, and survey outdoor crafts markets; the park is frequently host to outdoor music concerts and other festivities. A good stop for a coffee (or pisco sour) and people-watching is the terrace at the **Ⓓ ★ Café Haiti** (Diagonal 160). A few blocks away, along the ocean at the edge of Miraflores, **Ⓔ Parque del Amor** is also a popular hangout, especially for young couples who sprawl on the benches of broken-tile mosaics. The giant, almost grotesque statue of a couple making out seems to set the example. The benches are inscribed with sentimental murmurs of love. Nearby along the Malecón (at El Parque Raimondi) is where **Ⓕ paragliders** take flight over the coastline. If there's any wind at all, you're likely to see a few up in the sky, and tandem lessons are available for visitors. Finally, frenzied **Ⓖ Centro Comercial Larcomar,** a Western-style, multilevel shopping mall overlooking the ocean, is almost like a theme park for consumption-minded Limeños on weekends. ⊙ At least 2 hr.

Colonial Lima

If you have time to see more than just the highlights of Lima Centro (see "Lima in 1 Day," p. 48), set out on this walking tour of Colonial Lima's other worthy sights, including lesser-known convents, churches, and colonial mansions. Although police presence is more noticeable and the center is more orderly and clean than in past years, it remains very congested and a place that demands you keep your eyes open and on your belongings. Allow a full morning or afternoon to explore, and even longer if you plan to take time out for meals.

> Lima's baroque cathedral dominates the Plaza Mayor, the heart of Lima Centro.

START Take a taxi to Plaza Mayor (Lima Centro) or the Metropolitano Bus to Jr. Unión.

1 ★★ **Plaza Mayor.** The heart of Lima Centro, where Francisco Pizarro founded the city in 1535, is home to the **Palacio del Gobierno,** the **Palacio Episcopal,** and **La Catedral.** ⏱ 30 min. See p. 48, **1**, and 50, **2**.

2 **Casa Aliaga.** Lima's oldest colonial house (said to be the oldest surviving private house in the Americas), this extraordinary 1535 manor house is still owned by descendants of the original family. It was formerly open only to tour groups, but now individuals can enjoy its ornate salons and gorgeous interior courtyard. ⏱ 1 hr. See p. 50, **3**.

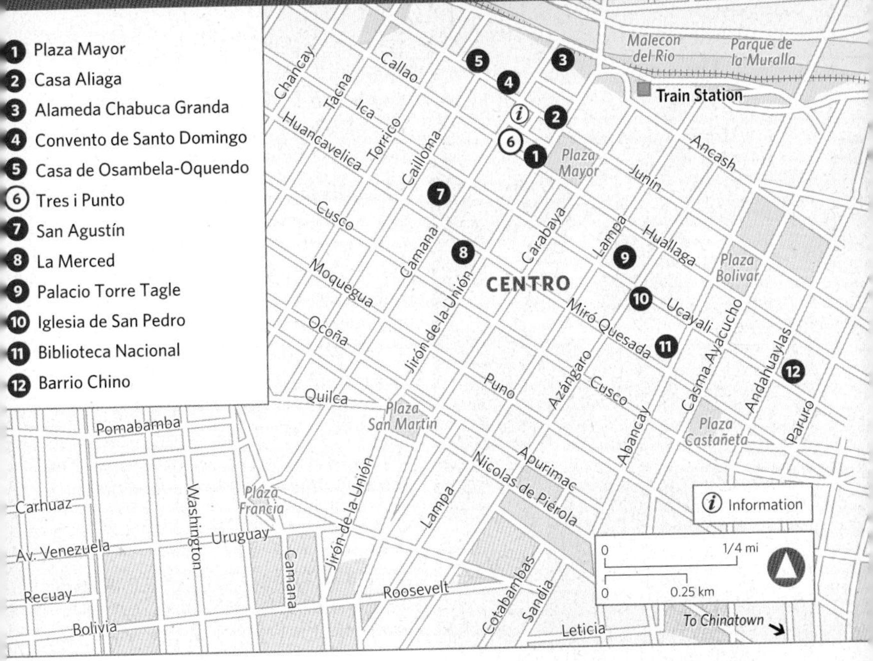

1 Plaza Mayor
2 Casa Aliaga
3 Alameda Chabuca Granda
4 Convento de Santo Domingo
5 Casa de Osambela-Oquendo
6 Tres i Punto
7 San Agustín
8 La Merced
9 Palacio Torre Tagle
10 Iglesia de San Pedro
11 Biblioteca Nacional
12 Barrio Chino

3 **Alameda Chabuca Granda.** Named for one of Peru's greatest Afro-Peruvian singers, this pedestrian-only street is given over to public sculpture, artists, musicians, and strolling Limeños. ⏱ 20 min. Jr. Unión at Malecón Rímac.

4 **Convento de Santo Domingo.** This convent draws many faithful Peruvians to visit the tombs of two Dominican saints, Santa Rosa de Lima and San Martín de Porras. Although perhaps of less interest to foreign visitors, the convent—the site of the first university in the Americas, San Marcos—has a beautiful main cloister. ⏱ 20 min. Conde de Superunda at Camaná. ☎ 01/427-6793. Admission S/3. Mon–Sat 9am–12:30pm and 3–6pm.

5 ★ **Casa de Osambela-Oquendo.** The tallest house in colonial Lima, which today operates a cultural center with occasional exhibits, is also one of the city's prettiest, with five different mahogany balconies on the baby-blue exterior. The caretaker occasionally takes visitors up four levels to the rooftop for views over the city (the original owner built the house so he could see all the way to the port). The house contains a spectacular patio, 40 bedrooms,

> Lima's oldest surviving house, the elegant mansion Casa Aliaga, dates to 1535.

> *Visitors can only walk by and imagine the grandeur within at Palacio Torre Tagle.*

facade, one of the finest of its kind in Peru, dating to the early 18th century. ⏱ 30 min. Corner of Jr. Ica and Jr. Camaná. ☎ 01/427-7548. Free admission. Daily 8–11am and 4:30–7pm, though it's frequently closed.

⑧ La Merced. Originally constructed on the site of Lima's first Mass (just prior to the city's founding), this 1754 church—with a striking facade and a superb sacristy embellished with Moorish tiles—welcomes the followers of Padre Urraca (a 16th-century, Spanish-born monk), who come daily in droves to pay their respects, praying and touching the large silver cross dedicated to the priest and leaving many mementos of their veneration. ⏱ 20 min. Jr. Unión at Miró Quesada. ☎ 01/427-8199. Free admission. Mon–Sat 8am–noon and 4–8pm.

⑨ ★★ Palacio Torre Tagle. This is one of the most exquisite private palaces in Peru, built in the early 18th century by a marquis and treasurer of the Royal Spanish fleet. Today it belongs to the Peruvian Ministry of Foreign Affairs and is not open to visitors. The exterior, however, with a gorgeous baroque stone doorway and intricately carved mahogany balconies, is very much worth a look. Jr. Ucayali 363.

⑩ ★★ Iglesia de San Pedro. ⏱ 20 min. See p. 51, **⑧**.

⑪ ★ Biblioteca Nacional. Peru's National Library, the largest and grandest in the country, was founded by José de San Martín (the general donated his personal collection of books) in 1821. The building takes up a city block and is featured on the Peruvian 100 soles bank note. ⏱ 30 min. Av. Abancay cdra. 4 s/n (at Miró Quesada). ☎ 01/513-6900. www.bnp.gob. pe. Free admission. Mon–Sat 8am–5pm.

⑫ ★ Barrio Chino. Lima's Chinatown is the largest Chinese community in South America, with a population of more than 200,000. Thousands of Chinese arrived in Peru in the late 19th century to work on railroads, and many more fled here from China in the 1930s and 1940s. The neighborhood *chifas* are the best restaurants for a taste of the Peruvian twist on traditional Chinese cooking. The official entrance to Chinatown is the large, ornate gate on Jr. Ucayali. ⏱ 45 min. Jr. Ucayali at Andahuaylas.

and eight wooden balconies—a sure sign of the original owner's great wealth. ⏱ 30 min. Jr. Conde de Superunda 298. ☎ 01/428-7919. Free admission (tips accepted). Daily 9am–5pm.

⑥ 🍽 Tres i Punto. This little bistro, with a sidewalk terrace overlooking a pedestrian-only alleyway, makes a great stop, whether for homemade desserts and coffee or a quick lunch of sandwiches and salads. It's also a good breakfast spot. Pasaje Nicolás de Rivera El Viejo 125. ☎ 01/427-0592. Items S/8–S/20.

⑦ ★ San Agustín. Practically destroyed during an 1895 revolution, this church is distinguished by a spectacular Churrigueresque

> *Peru's version of Westminster Abbey: The changing of the guards at the Presidential Palace takes place daily at noon.*

Gourmet Lima

The last decade has seen an explosion of worldwide interest in Peruvian cuisine, and Lima is now recognized as the gastronomic capital of South America. The city is suddenly a foodie destination, with travelers planning trips here just to eat. Limeño cuisine is all about the fusion of different cultures and amazing ingredients: seafood from rich fishing grounds in the Pacific; spicy Creole dishes, both European- and Afro-influenced; Nikkei, or 2nd-generation Japanese; and Chinese-Peruvian fusion, served at ubiquitous *chifa* restaurants. This tour is designed to do in a very full (pun intended) day or perhaps 2, depending on your appetite and willingness to hop cabs and skip around the city a bit.

> *The relentlessly curious chef Gastón Acurio has become the face of creative Peruvian cuisine.*

START Take a taxi to the restaurant; or, take the Metropolitano Bus to Angamos, and then take a taxi.

❶ ★★★ kids Mercado de Surquillo. This famed, scruffy food market at the edge of the tony Miraflores district is the place to see Peru's incredible food bounty. You may even run into a famous chef haggling next to the local housewives and cooks. You'll find colorful, spicy *ajíes* (chili peppers); dark purple corn; exotic Amazonian tropical fruits; countless varieties and colors of *papas* (potatoes); giant-kernel yellow *choclo* (maize); and, of course, amazing fresh seafood, meats, and other produce. See p. 58, **❺**.

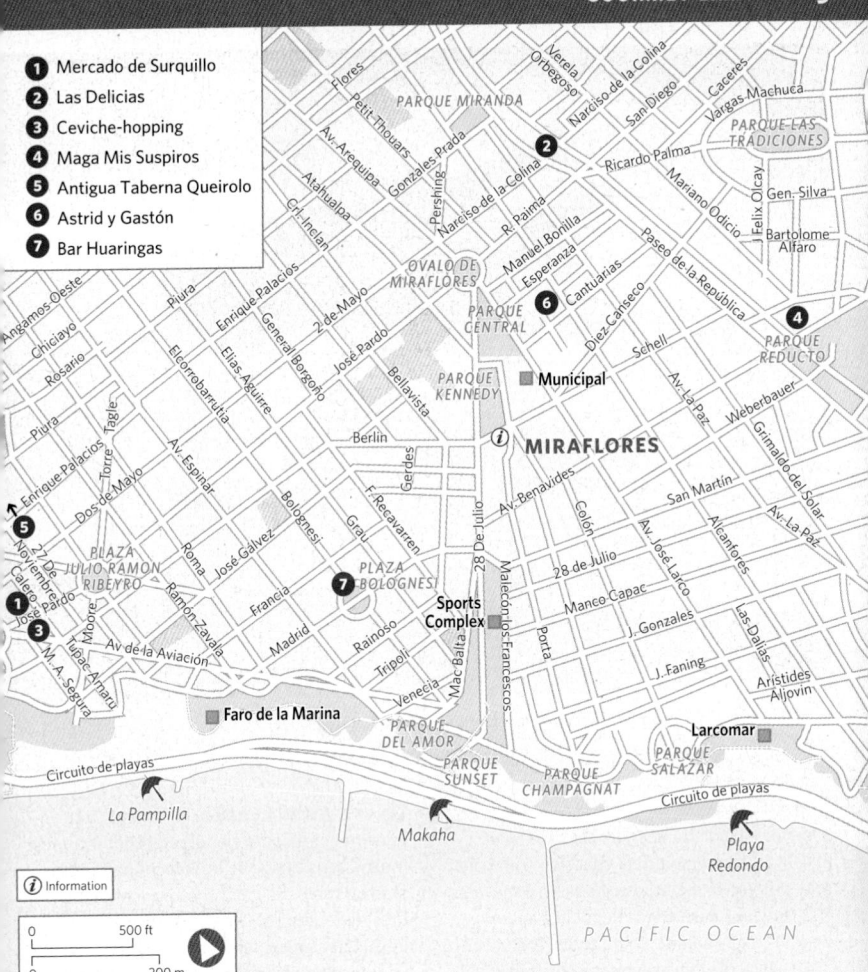

1. Mercado de Surquillo
2. Las Delicias
3. Ceviche-hopping
4. Maga Mis Suspiros
5. Antigua Taberna Queirolo
6. Astrid y Gastón
7. Bar Huaringas

Information

2 ★ **Las Delicias.** Limeños aren't really that big on breakfast, but one place they do love early in the morning is a good *juguería* (juice bar). This standout serves the best tropical fruit juices (nearly 100 varieties) in the city, as well as pastries and baked goods. Try a mixed fruit juice such as passion fruit with cactus fruit or mandarin orange. Jr. Ignacio Merino 505, Miraflores. ☎ 01/422-8798. Items S/7– S/15. No credit cards. Sun–Thurs 8am–10pm; Fri 8am–6pm; Sat 6am–10pm.

3 ★★★ **Ceviche-hopping.** Lima's signature dish is ceviche, which Limeños eat only at midday (because of the high acidity). So why not do a bit of ceviche-hopping for lunch? You can also mix in *tiraditos* (thinly sliced, raw, marinated fish) and other seafood specialties. If you're going to hit two or three joints in Miraflores, start right at noon or even a bit earlier. La Red is a local favorite for its large portions and low prices. For a taste of the most innovative and fashionable takes on ceviche, drop into trendsetting La Mar Cebichería or buzzed-about El Mercado, where you can get newfangled interpretations of seafood dishes in cool modern surroundings. See p. 76.

4 ★★ **Maga Mis Suspiros.** Peruvians are famous for their sweet tooth, and this terrific, tiny place in a former garage is all about homemade desserts. Its *arroz con leche* (rice

> *No visit to Lima is complete without a lunch of tangy, tantalizing ceviche.*

with milk), *crocante de lúcuma* (fruit ice cream), *alfajores* (filled cookies), *tres leches* (three milk) cake, and *maracuyá* (passion fruit) pie may put you in sugar overload. **Av. Benavides 1113 (btw. Av. Paseo de la República and Av. República de Panamá), Miraflores. ☎ 01/243-3140. www.magamissuspiros.com. Items S/3–S/8. MC, V. Daily 10am–8pm.**

❺ ★ Antigua Taberna Queirolo. This atmospheric pisco bar and winery is one of the oldest in Peru, now into its second century. Sit at the long, marble-topped bar and taste one of the piscos while imbibing the genuine 19th-century ambience. There are good *piqueos* (snacks) and more substantial Peruvian specialties such as *rocoto relleno* (stuffed hot pepper) if you need something to go with your pisco cocktail. **Av. San Martín 1090 (at Av. Vivanco), Pueblo Libre. ☎ 01/460-0441. www.antiguatabernaqueirolo.com. Items S/9–S/24. No credit cards. Mon–Wed 9:30am–11pm; Thurs–Sat 9:30am–midnight; Sun 9:30am–4pm.**

❻ ★★★ Astrid y Gastón. For dinner, your gourmet choices are endless, but it probably makes sense to go to the place that jump-started the Lima gastronomic scene: the first restaurant of Gastón Acurio, the face of Peruvian cuisine, who has gone on to star in cooking shows and found an international restaurant empire (others in Peru include La Mar Cebichería, p. 76; Panchita; and Chicha, p. 154). Acurio's take on Limeño classics remains the standard-bearer, and although some say this warmly stylish place has slipped a notch, it remains one of the top restaurants in Peru. See p. 73.

❼ ★★ Bar Huaringas. For a nightcap and the most celebrated pisco sour in the city, make a stop at this elegant bar, upstairs from the restaurant Brujas de Cachique. The list of piscos is impressive, and the mixologists pour perfect variations of a pisco sour, beginning with a coca or *maracuyá* sour. See p. 73.

> *Shaking one of the city's best pisco sours at Bar Huaringas.*

Peruvian Dishes

Ají de gallina Spicy/creamy chicken

Anticuchos Beef-heart brochettes

Causa Mashed potatoes with avocado, stuffed with chicken or tuna

Ceviche Marinated raw fish

Chaufa Chinese fried rice

Chicha Fermented maize beer

Chicha morada Blue-corn nonalcoholic beverage

Chifa Peruvian-Chinese food

Chupe Soup or chowder (*chupe de camarones*, prawn chowder, is the most common)

Choclo Maize (large-kernel corn)

Cuy Guinea pig

Flan Caramel custard

Lomo saltado Strips of beef with fried potatoes, onions, and tomatoes over rice

Manjar blanco Sweetened condensed milk

Pachamanca Roast meat and potatoes, prepared underground

Paiche Amazon river fish

Palta Avocado

Palta rellena (or palta a la Reina) Stuffed avocado (with chicken or tuna salad)

Panqueque Crepe

Papa a la huancaina Boiled potatoes in a creamy and spicy cheese sauce

Papa rellena Stuffed and fried potato

Quinua Andean grain (quinoa), often in soup (*sopa de quinua*)

Rocoto relleno Stuffed hot pepper

Sopa a la criolla Creole soup (noodles or grain, often quinoa, vegetables, and meat)

Tamal Ground corn cooked and stuffed with chicken or pork, wrapped in banana leaves or corn husks, and then steamed

Tiradito Ceviche-like strips of raw fish, marinated with *ají* peppers and lime but without sweet potatoes or onions, akin to Peruvian sashimi or carpaccio

Lima Shopping Best Bets

Best Alpaca Designs
★★ **Kuna by Alpaca 111** Av. Larco 671, Miraflores (p. 69)

Best People-Watching & Diversions
★★ **Centro Comercial Larcomar** Malecón de la Reserva, Miraflores (p. 70)

★★ **Mercado de Surquillo** Av. Paseo de la República, Surquillo (p. 70)

Best Mini-Mall for Antiques & Jewelry
Pedestrian-only passageway Av. La Paz 646, Miraflores (see La Línea del Tiempo, p. 69)

Best Places to Load Up on Peruvian Handicrafts
★★★ **Dédalo** Sáenz Peña 295, Barranco (p. 69)

★ **Mercado Indio** Av. Petit Thouars 5245, Miraflores (p. 70)

Best Food Market
★★ **Mercado de Surquillo** Av. Paseo de la República, Surquillo (p. 70)

Best Galleries of Unique Artesanía
★★ **Kuntur Wasi** Ocharan 182, Miraflores (p. 70)

★★★ **Las Pallas** Cajamarca 212, Barranco (p. 70)

Best Spots for Non-Shoppers
★ **Dédalo** Sáenz Peña 295, Barranco (p. 69)

★★ **Centro Comercial Larcomar** Malecón de la Reserva, Miraflores (p. 70)

Best Jewelry Designs
★ **Ester Ventura** Almirante Grau 1157, Chorrillos (p. 70)

★★ **Ilaria** Dos de Mayo 308, San Isidro (p. 70)

Best Religious Antiques
★★ **La Casa Azul** Alfonso Ugarte 150, Miraflores (p. 69)

★★ **La Línea del Tiempo** Av. La Paz 646, Miraflores (p. 69)

> *Well-chosen handicrafts such as this retablo, or altarpiece, are available at Las Pallas in Barranco.*

Lima Shopping A to Z

Alpaca Goods & Fashions

★ Alpaca Mon Repos SAN ISIDRO

An upscale boutique with nice designs on shawls, scarves, and sweaters, with many feminine and light pieces. **Centro Comercial Camino Real.** ☎ 01/221-5331. AE, DC, MC, V.

★★ Kuna by Alpaca 111 MIRAFLORES

One of the most original and highest-quality purveyors of all things alpaca, this chain, with locations throughout Peru, has excellent contemporary designs for men and women. Other locations in Lima include Larcomar mall (p. 70) and the Museo Arqueológico Rafael Larco Herrera (p. 52, ❷). **Av. Larco 671.** ☎ 01/447-1623. AE, MC, DC, V.

Antiques & Art

★★ La Casa Azul MIRAFLORES

This well-stocked shop specializes in colonial furniture, religious art, and other terrific decorative pieces. The friendly owners can help arrange shipping and assist with getting export approval for especially valuable pieces. **Alfonso Ugarte 150.** ☎ 01/446-6380. MC, V.

★★ La Línea del Tiempo MIRAFLORES

Just off one of Miraflores's main shopping avenues, Av. La Paz, which is lined with silver jewelry and antiques shops, is a small pedestrian-only passageway of several small antiques dealers, ideal for browsing. This little shop features some great antique religious art and jewelry. **Av. La Paz 646.** ☎ 01/241-5461. MC, V.

Handicrafts (Artesanía)

★★★ Dédalo BARRANCO

One of the nicest upscale purveyors of Peruvian crafts and well-chosen home furnishings, this attractive, multiroom shop in an old Barranco house has an amazingly wide variety of goods. There is a little cafe in the back garden. **Sáenz Peña 295.** ☎ 01/652-5400. AE, DC, MC, V.

★ Indigo SAN ISIDRO

One of Lima's top handicrafts and gift stores, with thoughtfully selected original designs from most regions of Peru. You'll find items here that you won't find in the big, multibooth markets. **Av. El Bosque 260.** ☎ 01/440-3099. www.galeriaindigo.com.pe. AE, DC, MC, V.

> *Survey fresh produce and seafood at Mercado de Surquillo, a market that's a favorite among local chefs.*

> *Mercado Indio comprises dozens of shops, selling all manner of* artesanía *from across Peru.*

★ Killari MIRAFLORES
An interesting shop with unique artisanal items from Ayacucho and the breadth of Peru. Alcanfores 699. ☎ 01/447-8684. MC, V.

★★ Kuntur Wasi MIRAFLORES
This beautiful shop is run by the owners, who are seasoned collectors, and is brimming with some of the highest-quality *arte popular* from around Peru. Ocharan 182. ☎ 01/9809-2056. MC, V.

★★★ Las Pallas BARRANCO
The doyenne of Peruvian folk art is Mari Solari, a British woman who's been collecting Peruvian folk art for 3 decades. Her shop, occupying several rooms of her fine Barranco house, is more art gallery than handicrafts shop. Cajamarca 212. ☎ 01/477-4629. No credit cards.

★ Museo-Galería Popular de Ayacucho BARRANCO
The best place if you're looking to get your hands on fine *retablos* and artisanship typical of Ayacucho (the central highlands region that produces some of Peru's most notable pieces). Av. Pedro de Osma 116. ☎ 01/247-0599. MC, V.

★★ Peru Artcrafts MIRAFLORES
One of the largest shops in town dealing in a huge range of Peruvian handicrafts from all over the country, this nicely designed storefront in the upscale Larcomar shopping mall is considerably more expensive than other shops (prices are in dollars), but for last-minute and one-stop shopping it's tough to beat. Malecón de la Reserva 610. ☎ 01/446-5429. AE, DC, MC, V.

Jewelry

★ Ester Ventura CHORILLOS
This studio, on the boardwalk in Chorrillos, south along the coast from Barranco, showcases the work of the boutique's namesake local designer. Her fine silver jewelry is based on pre-Incan and original designs. Malecón Almirante Grau 1157. ☎ 01/467-1180. www.esterventura.com. MC, V.

★★ Ilaria SAN ISIDRO
The granddaddy of Peruvian jewelry stores, with 24 shops across the country, this is simply the finest in terms of design in elegant silver art objects, jewelry, and decorative items. Many designs are based on traditional, antique Peruvian designs. There are other locations across the city, including major luxury hotels and Centro Comerical Larcomar. Dos de Mayo 308. ☎ 01/444-2347. www.ilariainternational.com. AE, DC, MC, V.

Malls & Markets

★★ Centro Comercial Larcomar MIRAFLORES
The most popular mall in Lima, with a slew of restaurants, movie theaters, and upscale shops overlooking the ocean. Equal parts entertainment complex and shopping mall, it's a favorite weekend destination for many Limeños. Malecón de la Reserva. ☎ 01/445-7776. www.larcomar.com. AE, DC, MC, V.

★ Jockey Plaza Shopping Center SURCO
A modern, upscale American-style shopping mall, Jockey has department stores, restaurants, movie theaters, a supermarket, and 200 exclusive shops. Javier Prado Este (at Av. Panamericana Sur). ☎ 01/437-4100. AE, DC, MC, V.

★★ Mercado de Surquillo SURQUILLO
Visiting this diverse market is a fascinating food-shopping experience. It's where Limeños as well as many of the top chefs in town go to get fresh produce, seafood, meats, and a wide array of kitchen implements. Av. Paseo de la República (at Ricardo Palma). No credit cards.

★ Mercado Indio MIRAFLORES
For most visitors to Lima, this is one-stop shopping for Peruvian handicrafts, arts, gifts, and souvenirs from around the country. In fact, almost all of Av. Petit Thouars, from Ricardo Palma to Vidal, is lined with similarly well-stocked handicrafts shops. Av. Petit Thouars 5245 (at General Vidal). MC, V.

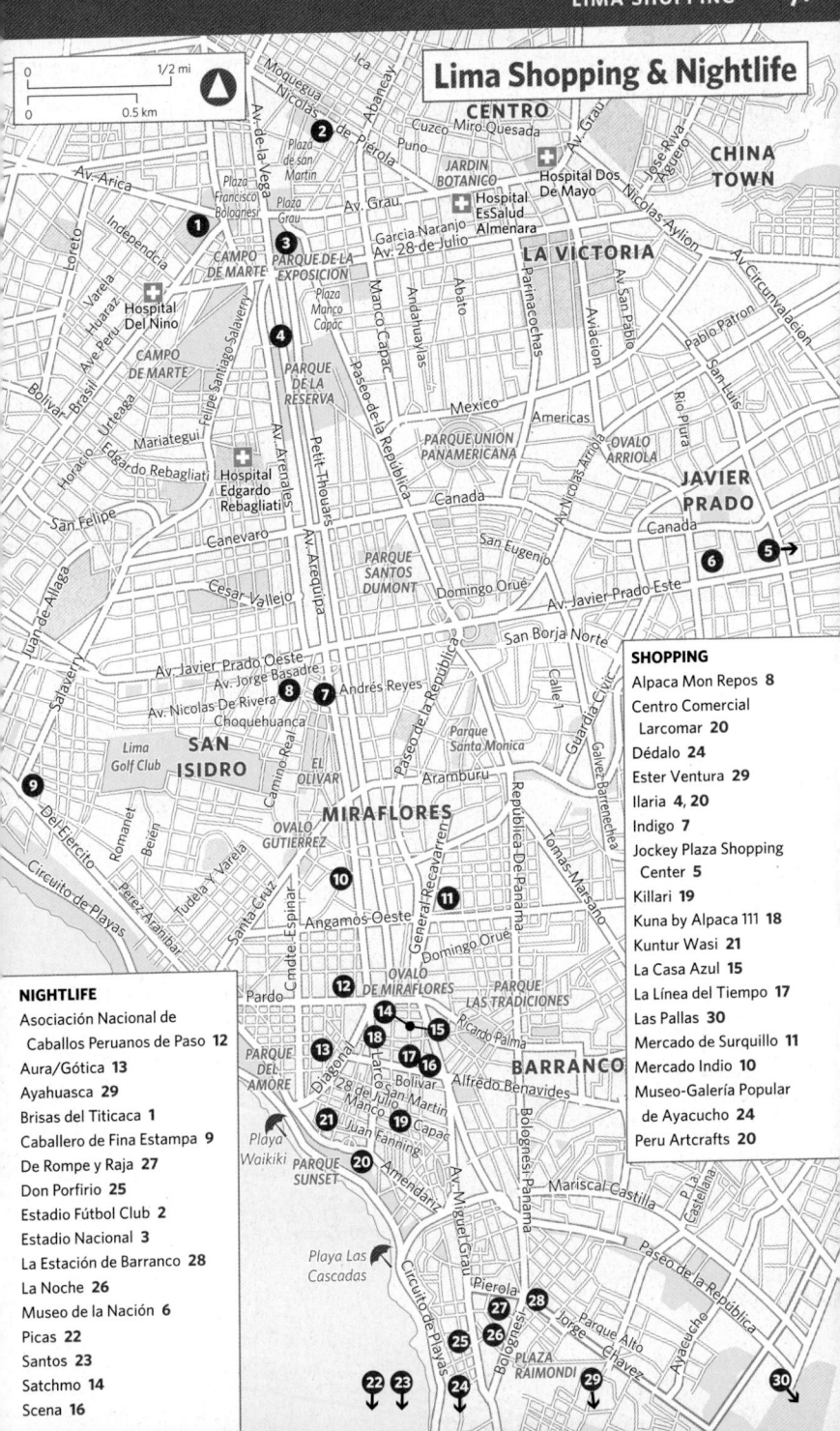

Lima Shopping & Nightlife

SHOPPING

Alpaca Mon Repos **8**
Centro Comercial
   Larcomar **20**
Dédalo **24**
Ester Ventura **29**
Ilaria **4, 20**
Indigo **7**
Jockey Plaza Shopping
   Center **5**
Killari **19**
Kuna by Alpaca 111 **18**
Kuntur Wasi **21**
La Casa Azul **15**
La Línea del Tiempo **17**
Las Pallas **30**
Mercado de Surquillo **11**
Mercado Indio **10**
Museo-Galería Popular
   de Ayacucho **24**
Peru Artcrafts **20**

NIGHTLIFE

Asociación Nacional de
   Caballos Peruanos de Paso **12**
Aura/Gótica **13**
Ayahuasca **29**
Brisas del Titicaca **1**
Caballero de Fina Estampa **9**
De Rompe y Raja **27**
Don Porfirio **25**
Estadio Fútbol Club **2**
Estadio Nacional **3**
La Estación de Barranco **28**
La Noche **26**
Museo de la Nación **6**
Picas **22**
Santos **23**
Satchmo **14**
Scena **16**

Lima Restaurant Best Bets

Best Homage to Ancient Peru
★ **Brujas de Cachiche** Jr. Bolognesi 460, Miraflores (p. 73)

★★ **Restaurant Huaca Pucllana** General Borgoño cdra. 8, Miraflores (p. 80)

Best Deli & Desserts
★★ **T'anta** Av. 28 de Julio 888, Miraflores (p. 80)

Best for Date Night
★★ **Restaurant Huaca Pucllana** General Borgoño cdra. 8, Miraflores (p. 80)

★ **Chala** Bajada de Baños 343, Barranco (p. 74)

Best Japanese-Peruvian
★★★ **Toshiro's** Av. Conquistadores 450, San Isidro (p. 80)

Best Northern Peruvian
★★ **Fiesta Restaurant Gourmet** Av. Reducto 1278, Miraflores (p. 76)

Best Views
★★ **Restaurant Huaca Pucllana** General Borgoño cdra. 8, Miraflores (p. 80)

Best Neighborhood Gourmet
★ **LA 73** Av. El Sol 175, Barranco (p. 76)

★★ **Sophie Bistró** Cl. Juan Moore 176, Miraflores (p. 80)

Best *Huariques*
★ **Canta Rana** Génova 101, Barranco (p. 74)

★ **El 550** Jr. Cañete 550, Lima Centro (p. 74)

Best Old-School Creole Cooking
★ **El Rincón Que No Conoces** Bernardo Alcedo 363, Lince (p. 76)

Best for Ceviche & Beautiful People
★★ **Amor a Mar** García y García 175, Barranco (p. 73)

★★★ **El Mercado** Hipólito Unánue 203, Miraflores (p. 76)

Best *Chifa*
★ **Salón Capón** Jr. Paruro 819, Chinatown (p. 80)

> Follow an elegant dinner at Restaurant Huaca Pucllana with a night tour of the illuminated ruins of the same name.

Lima Restaurants A to Z

★★ kids **Amor a Mar** BARRANCO *SEAFOOD/ CRIOLLO* Fashionable and deserving of the hype, this open-air spot in the backyard of a Barranco mansion looks something like an upscale Scandinavian take on a *biergarten.* The classic coastal seafood dishes, some with creative twists, are the big draw. García y García 175. ☎ 01/651-1111. www.amoramar.com. Entrees S/27–S/59. AE, DC, MC, V. Lunch and dinner Mon–Sat; lunch Sun. Map p. 75.

★ kids **Antica Trattoria** BARRANCO *ITALIAN* At this rustic Italian restaurant, the house specialty is pizza from the wood-fired ovens, but you may be tempted by homemade pastas and osso buco. San Martín 201. ☎ 01/247-5752. Entrees S/19–S/42. AE, DC, MC, V. Lunch and dinner daily. Map p. 75.

★★★ **Astrid y Gastón** MIRAFLORES *PERUVIAN/ INTERNATIONAL* Gastón Acurio, Peru's top celebrity chef, has a TV show and an empire of restaurants in Peru and the Americas. The buzz started here, though some contend that it's riding on its laurels. The menu might be called *criollo*-Mediterranean: Peruvian with a light touch. Cantuarias 175. ☎ 01/242-4422. www.astridygaston.com. Entrees S/38–S/79. AE, DC, MC, V. Lunch and dinner Mon–Sat. Map p. 77.

★ **Brujas de Cachiche** MIRAFLORES *CRIOLLO* Celebrating the indigenous cuisines of pre-Columbian Peru, the menu at this sleek restaurant includes classic Peruvian dishes, but concentrates on fresh fish and fine cuts of meat with unusual accompaniments. Bar Huaringas upstairs is the top spot in Lima for pisco cocktails. Jr. Bolognesi 460. ☎ 01/447-1883. www.brujasdecachiche.com.pe. Entrees S/32–S/65. AE, DC, MC, V. Lunch and dinner Mon–Sat; lunch Sun. Map p. 77.

Café Tostado BARRANCO *PERUVIAN/HOME COOKING* More like a little country eating club in the Argentine pampas than a big-city restaurant, this cozy place is popular with Limeños of all stripes, who sit at communal tables and eat the daily dish from the cook, Pepe, who's found deep in pots and pans at the open

> *There's no menu, but there's a busy open kitchen at no-frills Café Tostado in Barranco.*

> *Open-air Pescados Capitales has become one of the trendiest ceviche joints in Miraflores.*

kitchen in back. Odd and not for everyone. Nicolás de Pierola 232. ☎ 01/247-7133. Entrees S/10–S/25. No credit cards. Lunch and very early dinner daily. Map p. 75.

★ **kids** **Canta Rana** BARRANCO *CEVICHE/SEA-FOOD* The very definition of a neighborhood *cevichería*. The menu lists 15 types of sea bass, as well as infinite varieties of ceviche. The shack-like interior is decorated with simple wood tables, and the walls are festooned with *fútbol* paraphernalia. Génova 101. ☎ 01/247-7274. Entrees S/18–S/40. AE, MC, V. Lunch and dinner Tues–Sat; lunch Sun–Mon. Map p. 75.

★ **Chala** BARRANCO *PERUVIAN/FUSION* This sleek restaurant and lounge down by the "Bridge of Sighs" serves imaginative fare it calls "*costa* fusion": adaptations of Peruvian coastal and Limeño dishes with Mediterranean influences. The long deck, under tall trees and squawking birds, has a great tropical feel. Bajada de Baños 343. ☎ 01/252-8515. Reservations recommended. Entrees S/28–S/55. AE, DC, MC, V. Lunch and dinner Tues–Sat; lunch Sun. Map p. 75.

★★ **Dánica** SAN ISIDRO *ITALIAN/MEDITERRANEAN/PERUVIAN* A San Isidro favorite helmed by an up-and-coming young female chef, this good-value gourmet eatery looks casual, but it turns out pretty ambitious Italian and elaborate fusion dishes. The signature dish is the stir-fried beef risotto. Av. Emilio Cavenecia 170. ☎ 01/421-1891. Entrees S/22–S/35. AE, DC, MC, V. Lunch and dinner daily. Map p. 75.

★ **El Fayke Piurano** LIMA CENTRO *CEVICHE* A local favorite for ceviche, *tiradito,* and *arroz con mariscos* (seafood with rice), this simple but colorful place with vibrant paintings on the walls is probably the best *cevichería* in Lima Centro. Jr. Huancavelica 165. ☎ 01/428-6697. www.cevicheria-faykepiurano.com. Entrees S/20–S/39. AE, DC, MC, V. Lunch Tues–Sun. Map p. 75.

★ **El 550** LIMA CENTRO *PERUVIAN* This chef-driven outpost is a find for good eats when checking out the colonial center. The chef studied in Barcelona and puts out an affordable menu of excellent Peruvian dishes in this homey but good-looking place. His new

Lima Restaurants & Hotels

0   1/2 mi
0   0.5 km

HOTELS

Casa Bella B&B **10**

Country Club Lima Hotel **11**

Hotel España **4**

La Posada del Parque Hostal **8**

Second Home Peru **16**

Sonesta Hotel El Olívar Lima **3**

3B: Barranco's Bed & Breakfast **15**

RESTAURANTS

Amor a Mar **18**

Antica Trattoria **17**

Café Tostado **5**

Canta Rana **17**

Chala **17**

Dánica **14**

El Fayke Piurano **2**

El 550 **1**

El Rincón Que No Conoces **9**

LA 73 **19**

Salón Capón **6**

Segundo Muelle **12**

Toshiro's **13**

Wa Lok **7**

> Canta Rana is what is known in Lima as a **huarique** (neighborhood hole-in-the-wall).

restaurant in Miraflores (550 Kriollo Gurmet, on Av. 2 de Mayo 385) is a more elaborate take on Peruvian standards. Jr. Cañete 550. ☎ 01/425-0706. Entrees S/22–S/30. AE, DC, MC, V. Lunch daily; dinner Thurs–Sat. Map p. 75.

★★★ **El Mercado** MIRAFLORES SEAFOOD/ CRIOLLO Perhaps the hottest new restaurant in town, this cool seafood lunch spot by famed chef Rafael Osterling has an indoor-outdoor industrial aesthetic and a long bar backed up by a grill. It throbs with energy and delightful preparations from superb ceviches to designer sandwiches. Hipólito Unánue 203. ☎ 01/221-1322. www.rafaelosterling.com. Entrees S/22–S/47. AE, DC, MC, V. Lunch daily. Map p. 77.

★ **El Rincón Que No Conoces** LINCE PERUVIAN/ CREOLE This authentic, amiable, old-school Peruvian restaurant, helmed by Doña Teresa,

a 70-something chef, is worth the trek. In nearly 4 decades, her cozy neighborhood eatery hasn't deviated from its mission: classic Creole cooking, such as *tacu-tacu* (rice and beans) with *asado a la tira* (short ribs). Bernardo Alcedo 363 (near cdra. 20 de Av. Petit Thouars). ☎ 01/471-2171. Entrees S/20–S/32. No credit cards. Lunch Tues–Sun. Map p. 75.

★★ **Fiesta Restaurant Gourmet** MIRAFLORES NORTHERN PERUVIAN The little-known but superb, hearty cuisine of Chiclayo, a city in northern Peru, is the raison d'être at this unfussy gourmet restaurant. Try the charcoal-grilled ceviche or the Chiclayana specialties baby goat and *arroz con pato* (rice with duck). Av. Reducto 1278. ☎ 01/242-9009. Entrees S/39–S/59. AE, DC, MC, V. Lunch and dinner daily. Map p. 77.

★★★ **La Mar Cebichería** MIRAFLORES CEVICHE/ SEAFOOD Gastón Acurio's trendy, hip restaurant has had Limeños lining up to get in for years now—and it's easy to see why. La Mar is stylishly designed, and it represents the best of traditional Limeño cooking, but with an edge. The cool cocktail bar serves great pisco-based drinks. Av. La Mar 770. ☎ 01/421-3365. www.lamarcebicheria.com. Entrees S/19–S/49. AE, DC, MC, V. Lunch daily. Map p. 77.

★ **La Red** MIRAFLORES CEVICHE/SEAFOOD La Red may be less slick and self-conscious than Pescados Capitales and La Mar, but this more modest place is pretty much their equal for fresh fish and seafood, such as the tuna filet with *tacu tacu*. Av. La Mar 391. ☎ 01/441-1026. www.lared.com.pe. Entrees S/17–S/35. MC, V. Lunch daily. Map p. 77.

★ kids **LA 73** BARRANCO PERUVIAN FUSION A gourmet neighborhood restaurant that's surprisingly hip, this place is a favorite of visitors as well as barrio regulars for after-work cocktails, lunches on the outdoor patio, and home-cooked favorites for dinner. Av. El Sol 175. ☎ 01/247-0780. www.restaurantela73. com. Entrees S/24–S/40. AE, DC, MC, V. Lunch and dinner Tues–Sat; lunch Sun–Mon. Map p. 75.

★★ **Pescados Capitales** MIRAFLORES CEVICHE/ SEAFOOD A hip, upscale ceviche and seafood restaurant with a large open-air terrace and some of the vibe of La Mar Cebichería, this place is hugely popular with Lima's *gente bella*

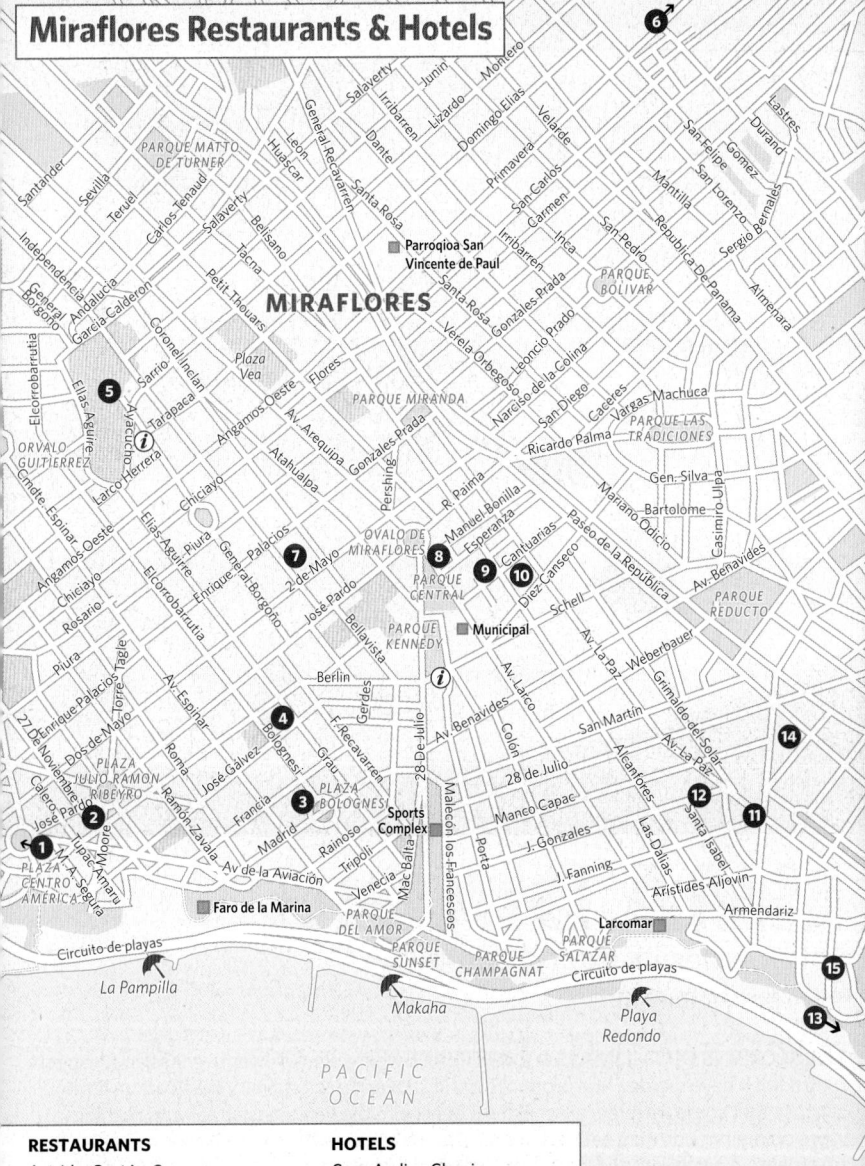

Miraflores Restaurants & Hotels

RESTAURANTS

Astrid y Gastón **9**

Brujas de Cachiche **3**

El Mercado **1**

Fiesta Restaurant Gourmet **14**

La Mar Cebichería **1**

La Red **1**

Pescados Capitales **1**

Restaurant Huaca Pucllana **5**

Sophie Bistró **2**

T'anta **6**

HOTELS

Casa Andina Classic
 Miraflores San Antonio **13**

Casa Andina Private
 Collection Miraflores **11**

Hostal El Patio Miraflores **10**

Hotel Antigua Miraflores **4**

Hotel Señorial **12**

Inka Lodge **7**

Miraflores Park Hotel **15**

Pariwana Hostel Lima **8**

(i) Information

0 — 500 ft
0 — 200 m

LIMA DINING
South America's Food Capital

BY NEIL EDWARD SCHLECHT

THE SECRET IS OUT—LIMA IS A RARE PLACE where playful inventiveness and respect for tradition have melded and produced a truly adventurous culinary destination. It's no surprise that some travelers are making a beeline to the Peruvian capital with nothing more on their minds than eating. Lima's restaurants range from ramshackle *huariques* (inexpensive neighborhood joints) and informal *cevicherías* to industrial-chic, chef-driven restaurants in the hippest *barrios.*

"Fusion" has long been the key word in Limeño cooking, which has emerged from a miscegenation of ethnic cooking, with Spanish, native *criollo,* African, Chinese, and Japanese influences. In the last decade or so, a group of young, inventive chefs—many who've trained at cooking schools and restaurants abroad and returned to Peru to explore and adapt traditional Peruvian cooking—have led the way with their *novo Andino,* or nouvelle Andean, cuisine, merging Peruvian and Andean culinary traditions and ingredients with international techniques and presentation.

The ABCs of Limeño Cuisine

AJÍ AMARILLO
The predominantly yellow (though it can also be orange) chile pepper used in Limeño cooking.

CAUSA
A cold chicken or shell-fish mashed-potato pie with tomato and *ají* and stuffed with tuna, chicken, avocado, shrimp, or crab.

CEVICHE
Fresh raw fish and seafood mixed with purple onions, lemon juice, and salt and marinated in lime juice, purple onions, and *ají*

or *rocoto* pepper (all "cooked" by the acids in the lime).

CHIFA
A Peruvian take on Chinese cooking, created by Peru's Chinese immigrant community, one of the largest in the world. Classic dishes are *chaufa* (fried rice) and *chi*

jau kay (chicken with vegetables in a salty brown sauce).

NIKKEI
Japanese immigrant cuisine, often using Peruvian ingredients and sauces in dishes such as *tiradito*, freshly caught, raw marinated fish that's thinly sliced and served with an *ají* pepper or *rocoto* chile sauce.

TACU-TACU
A classic *criollo* dish of seasoned (tradition-ally day-old) rice and

beans that are fried and served with purple on-ions and a fried banana.

Peru's Culinary Stars

GASTÓN ACURIO
No chef is more famous or has done more for popularizing Peruvian cuisine. Acurio's restau-rant Astrid y Gastón is the standard bearer for elegant Limeño dining (and a new entrant into the World's 50 Best Restaurants, at no. 42); La Mar is his hip take on a traditional *cevichería;* Panchita focuses on street food; and two Chicha restaurants in Arequipa and Cusco offer the chef's interpretations of those regional cuisines. Acurio now has restaurants across South America and in Madrid and San Francisco (and is due to open a La Mar in New York City soon).

TOSHIRO KONISHI
The chef behind Toshiro's, thought by many to be Lima's finest Japanese restaurant, arrived in Peru from Japan more than 3 decades ago. He has artfully taken the best of Peruvian ingredients and traditions and melded them with Japanese haute cuisine, or Kaiseki.

PEDRO MIGUEL SCHIAFFINO
Trained at the Culinary Institute of America and restaurants in Italy, Schiaffino was the chef at Lima's Huaca Pucllana before opening his own place, Malabar, in San Isidro. Fond of under-appreciated exotic Amazonian ingredi-ents and dishes (such as monster Amazonian snails), Schiaffino blends Andean and Amazon elements with classical European techniques.

RAFAEL OSTERLING
This esteemed chef studied at Le Cordon Bleu in Paris and worked in London before taking over the kitchen at famed Lima res-taurant La Gloria. His decade-old restaurant Rafael was named Peru's finest restaurant by the prestigious Summum awards, and his newest venture, lunch-only El Mercado, is the hottest restaurant in Lima. Osterling, whose cooking is perhaps more cosmo-politan than most of his peers, also has two restaurants in Bogotá and will soon be inaugurating one in Buenos Aires.

> *Suspiro Limeño can make locals, known to have a sweet tooth, sigh.*

(beautiful people), and its name riffs on the phrase for "original sin" *(pecado original)*. Av. La Mar 1370. ☎ 01/421-8808. Entrees S/28–S/48. AE, DC, MC, V. Lunch and dinner daily. Map p. 77.

★★ **Restaurant Huaca Pucllana** MIRAFLORES *NOUVEAU PERUVIAN* Directly across from a 1,500-year-old adobe pyramid, this superb restaurant is one of the city's greatest dining surprises. The archaeological site is illuminated at night, and diners can take a tour after dinner. The menu is creative Peruvian, with Asian fusion touches. General Borgoño cdra. 8. ☎ 01/445-4042. Entrees S/32–S/60. AE, DC, MC, V. Lunch and dinner Mon–Sat; lunch Sun. Map p. 77.

★ **Salón Capón** CHINATOWN (LIMA CENTRO) *CHIFA* Noted for its dim sum, this two-story spot, similar to the better-known Wa Lok, remains very popular with Chinese Peruvians. Though it's not much to look at, it's a great spot for authentic *chifa*. Jr. Paruro 819. ☎ 01/426-9286. Entrees S/18–S/35. MC, V. Lunch and dinner daily. Map p. 75.

kids **Segundo Muelle** SAN ISIDRO *CEVICHE/SEAFOOD* A dependable *cevichería* that's a longtime Limeño favorite. Kids' plates are available for S/15. Av. Carnaval y Moreyra 605. ☎ 01/241-5040. www.segundomuelle.com. Entrees S/18–S/40. MC, V. Lunch daily. Map p. 75.

★★ **Sophie Bistró** MIRAFLORES *PERUVIAN/TAPAS* A neighborhood joint with real flair, this casually elegant corner spot has banquettes, chandeliers, and a handsome, long bar. The prices on fresh fish, a long menu of tapas, and iconic dishes from both northern and southern Peru are just as attractive. Cl. Juan Moore 176. ☎ 01/628-1229. www.sophiebistro.com. Entrees S/16–S/34. AE, DC, MC, V. Lunch and dinner daily. Map p. 77.

★ kids **T'anta** MIRAFLORES *PERUVIAN/CAFE/DESSERTS* This modern deli/bistro has prepared foods to go and a complete menu, with a full range of creative snack foods and small meals, from fresh salads and panini to *sángu-ches* (Peruvian sandwiches) and pastas. The desserts, especially, are terrific. Av. 28 de Julio 888. ☎ 01/421-9708. Entrees S/19–S/42. AE, DC, MC, V. Breakfast, lunch, and dinner daily. Map p. 77.

★★★ **Toshiro's** SAN ISIDRO *JAPANESE-PERU-VIAN* Chef Toshiro Konishi's restaurant looks like a traditional sushi bar and is probably the finest place in Lima to sample authentic Japanese fusion cuisine. Toshiro came to Peru 3 decades ago and let the interest in Japanese and Peruvian cooking catch up to him. Av. Conquistadores 450. ☎ 01/221-7243. Entrees S/28–S/60. AE, MC, V. Lunch and dinner Mon–Sat. Map p. 75.

★ **Wa Lok** CHINATOWN (LIMA CENTRO) *CHIFA* One of Lima's best-known *chifas* serving a wide variety of well-prepared Chinese-Peruvian dishes, such as steamed shrimp with garlic cream and salted chicken with lychee. A second location in Miraflores is at Av. Angamos Oeste 700 (☎ 01/447-1329). Jr. Paruro 864. ☎ 01/427-2750. www.walok.com.pe. Entrees S/15–S/36. MC, V. Lunch and dinner daily. Map p. 75.

Lima Hotel Best Bets

Best Art-Filled Home as Inn
★★★ **Second Home Peru** Domeyer 366, Barranco (p. 84)

Best Indoor Pool
★★ **Casa Andina Private Collection Miraflores** Av. La Paz 463, Miraflores (p. 82)

Best Luxury Hotels
★★★ **Country Club Lima Hotel** Los Eucaliptos 590, San Isidro (p. 82)

★★★ **Miraflores Park Hotel** Av. Malecón de la Reserva 1035, Miraflores (p. 84)

Best *Hostales*
★ **Casa Bella B&B** Las Flores 459, San Isidro (p. 82)

★ **Inka Lodge** Elias Aguirre 278, Miraflores (p. 83)

Best-Value Boutique Hotel
★★★ **3B: Barranco's Bed & Breakfast** Jr. Centenario 130, Barranco (p. 84)

Best Place to Meet Fellow Backpackers
★ **Hotel España** Jr. Azángaro 105, Lima Centro (p. 83)

Best Business Hotels
★★ **Casa Andina Private Collection Miraflores** Av. La Paz 463, Miraflores (p. 82)

★★★ **Miraflores Park Hotel** Av. Malecón de la Reserva 1035, Miraflores (p. 84)

Best Views
★★★ **Miraflores Park Hotel** Av. Malecón de la Reserva 1035, Miraflores (p. 84)

★★★ **Second Home Peru** Domeyer 366, Barranco (p. 84)

Most Personal Service
★ **La Posada del Parque Hostal** Parque Hernán Velarde 60, Lima Centro (p. 83)

★★★ **3B: Barranco's Bed & Breakfast** Jr. Centenario 130, Barranco (p. 84)

Best In-House Restaurants
★★ **Casa Andina Private Collection Miraflores** Av. La Paz 463, Miraflores (p. 82)

★★★ **Miraflores Park Hotel** Av. Malecón de la Reserva 1035, Miraflores (p. 84)

> *Go for a night swim at the indoor pool at Casa Andina Private Collection Miraflores.*

> *Country Club Lima Hotel, a hacienda-like retreat in San Isidro, is one of the city's most sophisticated hotels.*

Lima Hotels A to Z

★ **Casa Andina Classic Miraflores San Antonio**
MIRAFLORES A well-run midsize hotel with ample and cheerfully decorated rooms, large marble bathrooms, and a great breakfast buffet. Ideal for travelers looking for comfort and no unpleasant surprises at a good price. Av. 28 de Julio 1088. ☎ 866/220-4434 in U.S., or 01/213-9739 in Peru. www.casa-andina.com. 49 units. $98–$131 double. Rates include breakfast. AE, DC, MC, V. Map p. 77.

★★ **kids** **Casa Andina Private Collection Miraflores** MIRAFLORES Lima's first five-star hotel, later abandoned, has become Casa Andina's flagship. The high-rise is a favorite of business travelers, as it offers all the amenities and services of the city's top luxury business hotels but without the exorbitant prices of many of its competitors. The sleek, modern restaurant is very good, and the spa and heated swimming pool are excellent bonuses. La Paz 463. ☎ 866/220-4434 in U.S., or 01/213-9739 in Peru. www.casa-andina.com. 148 units.

$190–$317 double; $350 and up suite. Rates include breakfast. AE, DC, MC, V. Map p. 77.

★ **Casa Bella B&B** SAN ISIDRO
A midrange choice that is safe, modern, quiet, and exceptionally clean. It's a tad larger than the typical B&B, but this nicely furnished, contemporary home still gives travelers a nice impression of staying at a friend's home. Several rooms have backyard garden views. Las Flores 459. ☎ 720/470-7237 in the U.S., or 01/421-7354 in Peru. www.casabellaperu.net. 12 units. $65–$75 double; $85–$175 suite. Rates include breakfast. MC, V. Map p. 75.

★★★ **kids** **Country Club Lima Hotel** SAN ISIDRO
Grand and sprawling, this hacienda-style hotel, built in the 1920s, is the most elegant hotel in Lima. Rooms are very spacious and refined, with antiques and old-world appeal. Public rooms seem straight out of a local nobleman's estate, and the hotel is actually fairly priced for its level of luxury and service. Los Eucaliptos 590. ☎ 800/745-8883 in the

U.S. and Canada, or 01/611-9000 in Peru. www.
hotelcountry.com. 75 units. $345–$455 double;
$490–$1,650 suite. AE, DC, MC, V. Map p. 75.

★ Hostal El Patio Miraflores MIRAFLORES
Set back from the street and built around a
flower-filled Andalusian-style patio, this good-
value inn has personality. Rooms in the rambling colonial mansion are very comfortable
and decently outfitted. Ernesto Diez Canseco
341. ☎ 01/444-2107. www.hostalelpatio.net.
25 units. S/150–S/180 double; S/195–S/225
suite. Rates include breakfast. AE, DC, MC, V.
Map p. 77.

★ Hotel Antigua Miraflores MIRAFLORES
This North American–owned hotel is housed
in a charming and colorful early-20th-century
mansion built around a leafy courtyard and
features colonial Peruvian art. Rooms range
from huge suites with large Jacuzzis and
kitchenettes to comfortable doubles with
handcrafted furniture and good-quality beds.
Av. Grau 350. ☎ 01/241-6116. http://peru-
hotels-inns.com. 35 units. $94–$109 double;
$129 suite. Rates include breakfast. AE, DC, MC,
V. Map p. 77.

★ Hotel España LIMA CENTRO
Just 4 blocks from the Plaza de Armas, this
funky and popular budget *hostal* has a communal atmosphere. The rambling colonial
building—teeming with art, faux Roman busts,
plants, and the occasional skull—has a maze
of rooms. The rooms are spare and most have
shared bathrooms. The leafy rooftop garden
terrace, with views of San Francisco, is a good
place to hang out and trade travel tales. Azángaro 105. ☎ 01/428-5546. www.hotelespanaperu.
com. 30 units. $11 double w/o bathroom, $15 w/
bathroom. No credit cards. Map p. 75.

★ Hotel Señorial MIRAFLORES
Just 3 blocks from Larcomar mall, this conveniently located and relaxed midsize hotel is
built around an attractive garden courtyard
and offers a host of amenities, including a
solarium with Jacuzzi, restaurant, and bar
(where it serves its very own pisco); Wi-
Fi; and a substantial breakfast. Rooms are
very clean and quite nice for the price. José
Gonzáles 567. ☎ 01/444-5755. www.senorial.
com. 75 units. $72 double. Rate includes break-
fast. AE, DC, MC, V. Map p. 77.

> *The rooftop terrace of Hotel España is a place to
sunbathe and meet fellow backpackers.*

★ Inka Lodge MIRAFLORES
A favorite among newer budget inns, this
modern and well-run small *hostal* has excellent
facilities, such as a roof terrace and kitchen
use. While rooms aren't large, they're tastefully decorated for the price, and the location
is safe and convenient. Thoughtful touches
include free bottled water and coffee round-
the-clock. Elias Aguirre 278. ☎ 01/242-6989.
www.inkalodge.com. 7 units. $28 double w/
shared bathroom; $14 per person in shared dorm
room. Rates include breakfast. MC, V. Map p. 77.

★ La Posada del Parque Hostal SANTA BEATRIZ
(LIMA CENTRO) This safe and good-value
guesthouse, which occupies a lovely 1920s
casona (manor house) on a peaceful cul-de-
sac lined with stately homes, has plenty of
personal touches. It offers unusual amenities,
including satellite TV and even homemade

> *Folk art enlivens the homey La Posada del Parque Hostal.*

pizzas and beer upon request. The owner, Monica, is exceedingly helpful. **Parque Hernán Velarde 60.** ☎ 01/433-2412. www.incacountry.com. 9 units. $45–$48 double. MC, V. Map p. 75.

★★★ Miraflores Park Hotel MIRAFLORES

One of the most elegant business and luxury hotels in Lima, this sophisticated retreat along the *malecón* (promenade) and overlooking the coastline welcomes travelers with a cozy, library-like lobby and handsome restaurant. Rooms are plush, with marble-and-granite bathrooms, king-size beds, and sitting areas; many have ocean views. **Av. Malecón de la Reserva 1035.** ☎ 01/610-4000. www.mira-park.com. 81 units. $655–$680 deluxe double; $795 and up suite. AE, DC, MC, V. Map p. 77.

Pariwana Hostel Lima MIRAFLORES

Although not as terrific as its sister property in Cusco (p. 236), this cheerful hostel has a convenient location facing Parque Kennedy, making it a good choice for students and backpackers (and single women, for whom there are sex-segregated dorm rooms) looking more for inexpensive digs and bonhomie than anything else. There are lots of group activities, as well as a bar/restaurant, games, breakfast 'til 1pm, and more. **Av. Larco 189.** ☎ 01/242-4350. www.pariwana-hostel.com. 60 units. S/90 double; S/27–S/36 per person in dorm room w/ shared bath. Rates include breakfast. No credit cards. Map p. 77.

★★★ Second Home Peru BARRANCO

One of Peru's most unique inns is the extraordinary home of the celebrated Peruvian painter and sculptor Victor Delfín (now run by his daughter, Lilian). The place, upstairs from the artist's studio and living quarters, is a rambling, two-story 1913 house full of art and bohemian flavor, perched on a cliff above the Lima coastline. Rooms are extremely spacious and elegant, but this inn is for folks who like whimsy and personal touches. It's one of the coolest and best-value places to stay in all of Peru. If you're headed to Cusco, check out Lilian's brother's place, Second Home Cusco (p. 236). **Domeyer 366.** ☎ 01/477-5021. www.secondhomeperu.com. 5 units. $95–$100 double; $120 suite. Rates include breakfast. AE, DC, MC, V. Map p. 75.

★★ [kids] Sonesta Hotel El Olívar Lima SAN ISIDRO

Sonesta's flagship property, aimed squarely at business travelers, is a seven-story hotel in a peaceful section of San Isidro. Accommodations are a step up from the more rustic decor in the chain's Posadas del Inca and are quite large, with boldly colored fabrics and beige marble bathrooms. The revamped restaurant is an excellent spot for lunch or dinner. **Pancho Fierro 194.** ☎ 800/SONESTA in the U.S., or 01/712-6000 in Peru. www.sonesta.com/lima. 134 units. $170–$200 double; $220–$400 suite. Rates include breakfast buffet. Kids 7 and under stay free in parent's room. AE, DC, MC, V. Map p. 75.

★★★ 3B: Barranco's Bed & Breakfast BARRANCO

A smart and terrific-value boutique hotel, with chic and immaculate contemporary rooms and public spaces (including a kitchen and airy lounge, with plans for a rooftop terrace as well as additional third-floor accommodations to come). This new inn is a real winner and welcome upgrade from Lima's middle-of-the-road midprice options, with plenty of unexpected amenities, exceptional and friendly service, and a good location in Barranco. **Jr. Centenario 130 (btw. cdras. 9 and 10 Av. Miguel Grau).** ☎ 01/247-6915. www.3bhostal.com. 16 units. $55 double. Rate includes breakfast. AE, DC, MC, V. Map p. 75.

Lima Nightlife Best Bets

Best Trendy Bars
★★ **Ayahuasca** Prolongación San Martín 130, Barranco (p. 86)

★★ **Santos** Jr. Zepita 203, Barranco (p. 86)

Best Live Music
★ **La Estación de Barranco** Pedro de Osma 112, Barranco (p. 87)

★★ **La Noche** Jr. Bolognesi 307, Barranco (p. 87)

Best Peruvian Spectator Sport
★★ **Asociación Nacional de Caballos Peruanos de Paso** Bellavista 549, Miraflores (p. 87)

Best Peñas
★★★ **Brisas del Titicaca** Jr. Héroes de Tarapaca 168, Lima Centro (p. 87)

★★ **Don Porfirio** Manuel Segura 115, Barranco (p. 87)

Best Lounge/DJs
★ **Scena** Francisca de Paula 280, Miraflores (p. 86)

Best Disco Scene
★★ **Aura/Gótica** Malecón de la Reserva 610, Miraflores (p. 87)

Best Jazz Club
★ **Satchmo** Av. La Paz 538, Miraflores (p. 87)

Best Places to Meet Beautiful People
★★ **Aura/Gótica** Malecón de la Reserva 610, Miraflores (p. 87)

★ **Picas** Bajada de Baños 340, Barranco (p. 86)

Best Sports Bar
Estadio Fútbol Club Av. Nicolás de Piérola 926, Lima Centro (p. 86)

> *La Noche is one of the most happening nightspots in Barranco, with a varied roster of live music.*

Lima Nightlife A to Z

Bars & Pubs

★★ Ayahuasca BARRANCO

One of the hottest—and biggest—nightspots of the moment is this stylish bar in a stately colonial mansion with swank furnishings, art exhibits, and great cocktails, including an impressive array of pisco sours. **Prolongación San Martín 130.** ☎ 9810-44745. Map p. 71.

Estadio Fútbol Club LIMA CENTRO

A spot strictly for *fútbol* (soccer) fans, with a three-level bar (and disco on weekends) that amounts to a museum of soccer and dozens of big-screen TVs. It can get pretty rowdy when a big Peruvian or international game is on. **Av. Nicolás de Piérola 926.** ☎ 01/428-8866. Map p. 71.

★ Picas BARRANCO

Beneath Barranco's "Bridge of Sighs," this fashionable upscale bar and restaurant serves great (if pricey) cocktails to a chic crowd. **Bajada de Baños 340.** ☎ 01/252-8095. www. picas.com.pe. Map p. 71.

★★ Santos BARRANCO

Laid-back but hip, this joint is popular with a young crowd and is the quintessential Barranco watering hole. It has an inventive decor, easygoing vibe, and slender balcony with views that peek out to the ocean. Generally packed on weekend nights. **Jr. Zepita 203.** ☎ 01/247-4609. Map p. 71.

★ Scena MIRAFLORES

This sleek and colorful restaurant-lounge, tucked away on a side street in Miraflores, has a good wine selection and lively bar scene. DJs spin tunes in the evenings. **Francisca de Paula 280.** ☎ 01/445-9688. www.scena.com.pe. Map p. 71.

> *The popular watering hole Santos, near the Puente de Suspiros in Barranco.*

Discos

★★ Aura/Gótica MIRAFLORES

These twin discotheques, the hottest on the scene, face each other in the Larcomar shopping center and feature interconnected open-air terraces, great sea views, and dance music ranging from electronica to the Latin specialty, *pachanga*. Malecón de la Reserva 610. Aura: ☎ 01/242-5516. www.aura.com.pe. Gótica: ☎ 01/445-6343. www.gotica.com.pe. Cover S/25. Map p. 71.

Live Music Clubs

★ La Estación de Barranco BARRANCO

Housed in an old train station, this amiable club features live music, often *criollo*, Tuesday through Saturday; it's popular with a slightly more mature crowd of both locals and tourists. Pedro de Osma 112. ☎ 01/247-0344. Cover S/10–S/20. Map p. 71.

★★ La Noche BARRANCO

Lima's best live-music club for pop, rock, and Latin is a sprawling multilevel club, with a great stage, sound system, and good nightly bands that run the gamut of styles. The crowd is a mix of Limeños and international folks. There's also a La Noche outpost in Lima Centro, at the corner of Jr. Camaná and Jr. Quilca. Bolognesi 307. ☎ 01/477-1012. Cover S/5–S/30. Map p. 71.

★ Satchmo MIRAFLORES

This sophisticated joint hosts a varied roster of live bands, mostly jazz combos—as the name would indicate. It's a good date spot. Av. La Paz 538. ☎ 01/444-4957. Cover S/20–S/60. Map p. 71.

Peñas

★★★ Brisas del Titicaca LIMA CENTRO

Of the city's *peñas*, this comes closest to being a cultural institution. It features *noches folclóricas*—indigenous music-and-dance shows—that are some of the finest in Lima. Shows are Tuesday to Saturday. There are even occasional afternoon dance shows on Friday and Saturday. Jr. Héroes de Tarapaca 168 (cdra. 1 of Av. Brasil, near Plaza Bolognesi). ☎ 01/332-1901. www.brisasdeltiticaca.com. Cover S/30–S/70. Map p. 71.

★ Caballero de Fina Estampa MIRAFLORES

Named for one of the most famous Peruvian songs of all time, this is one of the city's chicest *peñas*, with a large colonial salon and balconies. Av. del Ejército 800. ☎ 01/441-0552. Cover S/50. Map p. 71.

★ De Rompe y Raja BARRANCO

A favorite of Limeños (open Thurs–Sat), this homey place often hosts the popular Matices Negros, an Afro-Peruvian dance trio. Manuel Segura 127. ☎ 01/247-3271. www.derompeyraja.net. Cover S/35. Map p. 71.

★★ Don Porfirio BARRANCO

A bit more downscale than most *peñas* and preferred by locals, this amiable, hidden spot invites participation in its good-quality music-and-dance shows. Manuel Segura 115. ☎ 01/477-3119. Cover S/20. Map p. 71.

Performing Arts

Museo de la Nación LIMA CENTRO

This theater is now home to the National Symphony Orchestra and the National Ballet Company, since Lima's stunning Teatro Municipal—once the pride of the local performing-arts scene and the primary locale for theater, ballet, opera, and symphony performances—burned to the ground in 1998. Av. Javier Prado Este. ☎ 01/476-9875. Tickets S/10–S/65. Map p. 71.

Spectator Sports

★★ Asociación Nacional de Caballos Peruanos de Paso MIRAFLORES

Caballos de paso (Peruvian Paso horses), among the showiest of all horse breeds, are known for their unique four-beat lateral gait and are considered by many to be the world's smoothest riding horse. Seeing them prance on their home turf is thrilling. There are *concursos* (show events) scheduled at different times of the year, with an especially big one in April. Bellavista 549. ☎ 01/444-6920 or 01/447-6331. Free admission. Map p. 71.

★ Estadio Nacional LIMA CENTRO

Important league and national *fútbol* matches are held at the venerable 50-year-old stadium just 5 minutes from the city center. Popular teams include Alianza Lima, Alianza Atlético, Universitario (known as "La U"), and Sporting Cristal. Av. Paseo de la República cdras. 7–9. ☎ 01/242-2823. Tickets S/10–S/75. Map p. 71.

Lima Fast Facts

Arriving

BY PLANE All flights from North America and Europe arrive at Lima's **Aeropuerto Internacional Jorge Chávez** (☎ 01/511-6055), located 16km (10 miles) west of the city center. To get downtown or to suburbs such as Miraflores, San Isidro, and Barranco, take a taxi or private bus. Taxis cost around S/45 to Miraflores (a 30-min. to 1-hr. ride) and S/35 to downtown Lima—though drivers will almost certainly begin by asking for more. **Super Shuttle** (☎ 01/221-7611; www.supershuttleairport.com) delivers passengers to the doors of their hotels (to downtown, S/45; to Miraflores and San Isidro, S/90). Private limousine taxis (*taxis ejecutivos,* or *remises*) also have desks in the airport; their fares are about S/135 one-way. One to try is **Mitsoo Remisse** (☎ 01/261-7788; www.mitsoo.net).

ATMs/Cashpoints

ATMs are plentiful throughout Lima Centro, especially in the outer neighborhoods such as Miraflores, San Isidro, and Barranco.

Currency Exchange

In addition to Peruvian and international banks with currency-exchange bureaus, you will often find independent money-changers, usually wearing colored smocks (sometimes with obvious "$" insignias), who patrol the main streets off Parque Kennedy in Miraflores and central Lima with calculators and dollars in hand. Principal banks include **Banco Central,** Jr. Antonio Miró Quesada 441 (☎ 01/427-6250); **Banco de Comercio,** Jr. Lampa 560 (☎ 01/428-9400); and **Citibank,** Miguel Dasso 121, San Isidro (☎ 01/442-5146).

Dentists & Doctors

U.S. and British embassies (p. 470) provide lists of English-speaking doctors and dentists in Lima. **Doctor Más** (☎ 01/444-9377) sends English-speaking doctors to hotels for emergencies and prescriptions. For dentists, contact the **International Academy of Integrated Dentistry,** Centauro 177, Urbanización Los Granados, Monterrico, Surco (☎ 01/435-2153).

Try the following hospitals and clinics for English-speaking medical personnel and 24-hour emergency services: **Clínica Anglo-Americana,** Alfredo Salazar, cdra. 3, San Isidro (☎ 01/712-3000); **Maison de Sante,** Miguel Adgouin 208–222, Lima Centro (☎ 01/428-3000, emergency 01/427-2941); and **Clínica Ricardo Palma,** Av. Javier Prado Este 1066, San Isidro (☎ 01/224-2224).

Emergencies

Call the **24-hour traveler's hot line** (☎ 01/574-8000) or the **tourist police** (POLTUR; ☎ 01/460-1060 or 01/460-0965 in Lima). The INDECOPI 24-hour hotline can also assist in contacting police to **report a crime** (☎ 01/224-7888 in Lima, 01/224-8600, or toll-free 0800/42579 from any private phone). The general **police** emergency number is ☎ 105; for **fire,** dial ☎ 116.

Internet Access

Internet *cabinas* (booths) are everywhere in Lima. Rates are about S/3 per hour, and most are open daily from 9am to 10pm or later. Try **Telnet,** Jr. Camaná 315; **Internet Pardo,** Av. José Pardo 620; **Cybersandeg,** Jr. Unión 853, office 112; **Wamnet,** corner of Diez Canseco and Alcanfores, mezzanine, Miraflores; or **C@bin@s de Internet,** Diez Canseco 380, Miraflores.

Pharmacies

Two huge, multiservice pharmacies (*farmacias*) open 24 hours a day are **Farmacia Deza,** Av. Conquistadores 1140, San Isidro (☎ 01/440-3798), and **Pharmax,** Av. Salaverry 3100, San Isidro, in the Centro Comercio El Polo (☎ 01/264-2282). A chain throughout Lima is **Superfarma,** Av. Benavides 2849 (☎ 01/222-1575) and Av. Armendariz, Miraflores (☎ 01/446-3333).

Police

The **Policía Nacional de Turismo** (National Tourism Police) has staff members that speak English and are specifically trained to handle the needs of foreign visitors. The main office in Lima is at Av. Javier Prado Este 2465, fifth floor, San Borja (next to the Museo de la Nación); the **24-hour tourist police line** is ☎ 01/574-8000.

Post Office & Mail

Lima's **main post office** (Central de Correos) is on the Plaza de Armas at Camaná 195 (☎ 01/427-0370) in central Lima. The **Miraflores branch** is at Av. Petit Thouars 5201 (☎ 01/445-0697). A **DHL/Western Union** office is at Nicolás de Piérola 808 (☎ 01/424-5820).

Public Transportation

The modern, clean, and very efficient **Metropolitano Bus** (☎ 01/203-9000; www.metropolitano.com.pe) travels along the Vía Expresa and Paseo de la República, connecting Lima Centro to Miraflores, Barranco, and as far south along the coast as Chorrillos. It's convenient, but the single, straight line of stops will still leave you a long walk or short taxi ride from many destinations (six new routes are planned for the future). Fares are S/1.50, deducted from a minimum fare card of S/5. The buses run daily from 6am to 9:50pm. The major stops are Tacna and Jr. Unión in Lima Centro; Javier Prado, Canaval y Moreyra, and Aramburú in San Isidro; Angamos, Ricardo Palma, Benavides, and 28 de Julio in Miraflores; and Balta and Bulevar in Barranco.

Micros, colectivos, and *combis* (varying sizes of buses that make both regular and unscheduled stops) are very inexpensive but slow, confusing, and not recommended. Routes are identified by signs with street names placed in the windshield. Most *micros* and *combis* cost S/3, and slightly more after midnight and on Sundays and holidays. When you want to get off, shout *"baja!"* ("getting off!") or *"esquina!"* ("at the corner!").

Safety

In downtown Lima and the city's residential and hotel areas, the risk of street crime remains high. Armed attacks at ATMs have also occurred. Use ATMs during the day, with other people present. Most thefts occur on public transportation, such as buses and *combis.* There have been several reports of thieves who've boarded buses in and out of Lima, relieving passengers at gunpoint of their valuables. Be very careful with your belongings; leave your passport and other valuables in the hotel safe, and use a money belt. Public street markets are also frequented by thieves, as are parks (especially at night) and the beaches in and around Lima.

Taxis

Taxis hailed on the street are a reasonable and relatively quick way to get around in Lima. However, they are wholly unregulated by the government. If you're not fluent in Spanish or have an obviously non-Peruvian appearance, be prepared to negotiate fares. Limeños tell enough stories of theft and even the occasional violent crime in unregistered cabs to make hailing one on the street inadvisable. If you hail a taxi on the street, try to pick out older drivers; young punks are almost wholly responsible for taxi crime. Best, especially at night, is to call a registered company from your hotel or restaurant, even though the fare can be twice as much. Registered, reputable taxi companies include **Taxi Amigo** (☎ 01/349-0177), **Taxi Móvil** (☎ 01/422-6890), **Taxi Line** (☎ 01/330-2795), and **Taxi Seguro** (☎ 01/275-2020). Whether you call or hail a taxi, you'll need to establish a price beforehand—be prepared to bargain. Most fares range from S/8 to S/15. From Miraflores to downtown, expect to pay S/10; from Miraflores to San Isidro or from San Isidro to downtown, about S/8; and from Miraflores to Barranco, S/10.

Telephone

Lima's area code is 01. It need not be dialed when making local calls within Lima, but it must be dialed when calling Lima from another city. Telephone booths are found throughout the city; the principal **Telefónica del Perú** office, where you can make long-distance and international calls, is on Plaza San Martín (Carabaya 937) in Lima Centro (☎ 01/224-9355); open Monday to Saturday 8am to 6pm, Sunday 8am to 1pm.

Visitor Information

A 24-hour tourist information booth, **iPerú** (☎ 01/574-8000), operates in the international terminal at the Jorge Chávez International Airport. The most helpful iPerú office is in Miraflores, at the Larcomar shopping mall, Módulo 10, Av. Malecón de la Reserva 610 (☎ 01/445-9400), open Monday to Friday 11am to 1pm and 2 to 8pm. Another office is in San Isidro at Jorge Basadre 610 (☎ 01/421-1627), open Monday through Friday from 8:30am to 6:30pm. The **Oficina de Información Turística** in Lima Centro is at Pasaje Los Escribanos 145, just off the Plaza de Armas, in Lima Centro (☎ 01/427-6080); open Monday to Saturday 9am to 6pm.

5
Southern Desert Coast & Central Highlands

Favorite Moments

Peru's southern desert coast is among the most arid places on earth, best known for earthquakes and a mysterious phenomenon, the Nasca Lines: inscrutable pre-Columbian drawings in the sunbaked sand that can only be appreciated from the air. But there are oases, too: the Reserva Nacional de Paracas and Islas Ballestas, renowned for their unique bird and marine life; wineries that produce Peru's distinctive white-grape brandy, pisco; and palm-tree-lined Huacachina Lagoon. In the central highlands, stately Ayacucho—once a terrorist stronghold that endured decades of isolation from the rest of Peru—is home to the country's finest collection of colonial-era churches and most celebrated folk art.

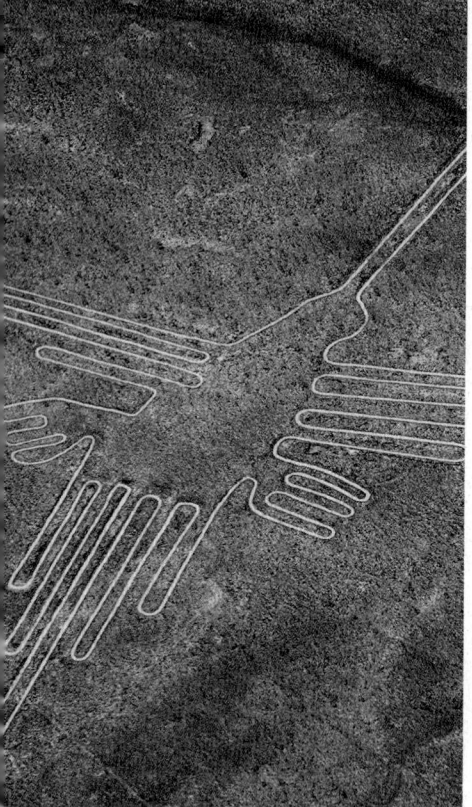

> PREVIOUS PAGE Peru's southern desert coast is one of the most arid places on earth. THIS PAGE "The hummingbird" of the Nasca Lines.

❶ Surfing the dunes. A relatively new extreme sport, sandboarding—a cross between downhill skiing and snowboarding, but on grainy sand rather than white powder—is all the rage on the towering dunes along the southern desert coast. The sport is hot and dusty and involves trudging up sand dunes (or paying for the expense of a dune buggy), but you can really build up speed, and accomplished boarders can maneuver almost as they would on the slopes. Cerro Blanco, the highest sand dune in South America, and Laguna de Huacachina are the two best sandboarding spots. See p. 117.

❷ Marveling at the Nasca Lines. You've heard about the crazy desert lines etched into the dry pampas, and the oddball "Chariots of the Gods" theories proposed to explain them, but until you're flying over them in a light-craft airplane, clearly identifying figures such as a giant hummingbird and the Astronaut, it's hard to imagine just how remarkable and thought-provoking these 1,000-year-old desert drawings are. See p. 103, ❹, and 108.

❸ Savoring pisco. Peru's national cocktail is the pisco sour, based on the white-grape brandy Peru bodegas have been producing since the time of the Spanish viceroyalty in the 16th century. In the countryside around Ica, you can tour both large and small homespun family bodegas and taste pure quebranta, aged and aromatic piscos. For me, a trip to Peru hasn't started until I've downed a shot of

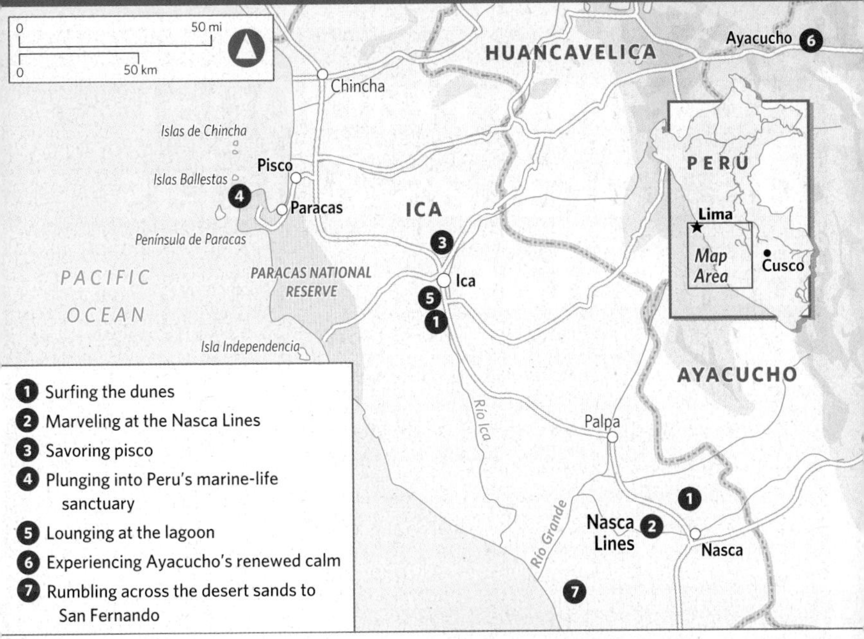

Map showing the Ica and Nasca region of Peru, with the Pacific Ocean, Paracas National Reserve, and locations including Chincha, Pisco, Paracas, Ica, Palpa, Nasca, and Ayacucho.

1. Surfing the dunes
2. Marveling at the Nasca Lines
3. Savoring pisco
4. Plunging into Peru's marine-life sanctuary
5. Lounging at the lagoon
6. Experiencing Ayacucho's renewed calm
7. Rumbling across the desert sands to San Fernando

quebranta or a coca sour, made from pisco macerated with coca leaves. See p. 118.

❹ Plunging into Peru's marine-life sanctuary. The Islas Ballestas and Reserva Nacional de Paracas hold one of the densest populations of marine life and seabirds on the planet, including sea lions, Humboldt penguins, endangered turtles, and red boobies. See them during a boat trip around the islands and at several spots on the Paracas Peninsula. It's not quite the Galápagos, but it's close. See p. 94.

❺ Lounging at the lagoon. An oasis in the desert, palm-tree-lined Laguna de Huacachina is an elite resort that dates to the 1940s, when it was first prized for the curative powers of its mud and waters. It's so welcome amid the unrelenting sand dunes and dry pampas that you may think you've stumbled upon a mirage. Its laid-back charms are hard to resist. See p. 101, ❻.

❻ Experiencing Ayacucho's renewed calm. After a couple of decades of being held siege by terrorists, this colonial highland gem is again a safe and serene place to visit. Home to 33 colonial churches and Peru's finest crafters of folk art, it's modest and quiet—except during Carnaval and Easter, two of Peru's greatest festivals. See p. 110.

> A Humboldt penguin dives from the rocks of the Islas Ballestas.

❼ Rumbling across the desert sands to San Fernando. Hop aboard an *arenero* (dune buggy) and bound across the waves of desert sands toward a little-known coastal oasis, San Fernando, site of a pretty beach and colonies of sea lions, seals, penguins, and maybe even some Andean condors circling overhead. You'll get hot and dirty on this all-day dunes excursion, but it's a thrill ride devoid of tourists. See p. 117.

Reserva Nacional de Paracas & Islas Ballestas

The maritime sanctuary Reserva Nacional de Paracas, established in 1975, comprises Peru's largest section of protected coastline. The wind-blasted and sun-baked area is one of fascinating desert landscapes, odd rock formations, and unusual fauna, including thousands of sea lions and endangered Humboldt penguins. The reserve and Ballestas Islands—which Peruvians compare to Ecuador's more famous Galápagos—are in the Humboldt Current, which flows 3,200km (2,000 miles) from Antarctica along the Pacific coastline, a natural phenomenon that stimulates an ecological food chain in the warm, shallow waters along the Peruvian coast and attracts one of the largest concentrations of birds on the planet. The most convenient way to see the Reserva Nacional de Paracas and the Islas Ballestas is to take a 1-day organized tour (see "Practical Matters").

> The Reserva Nacional de Paracas, the foremost marine conservation area in Peru, is about two-thirds water.

START Pisco is a 3-hour bus ride from Lima. From Pisco, take a taxi (30 min.) south to El Chaco waterfront in Paracas (22km/14 miles).

1 Playa El Chaco. The Bahía de Paracas waterfront, called El Chaco or El Balneario, is populated by seafood restaurants and boats waiting to depart for the Islas Ballestas. Most organized boat excursions begin here, and it's a cute enough place to kill time waiting for your boat trip to Ballestas. ⏱ 30 min. *Combis for the Islas Ballestas and Reserva Nacional de Paracas (marked EL CHACO-PARACAS) depart from*

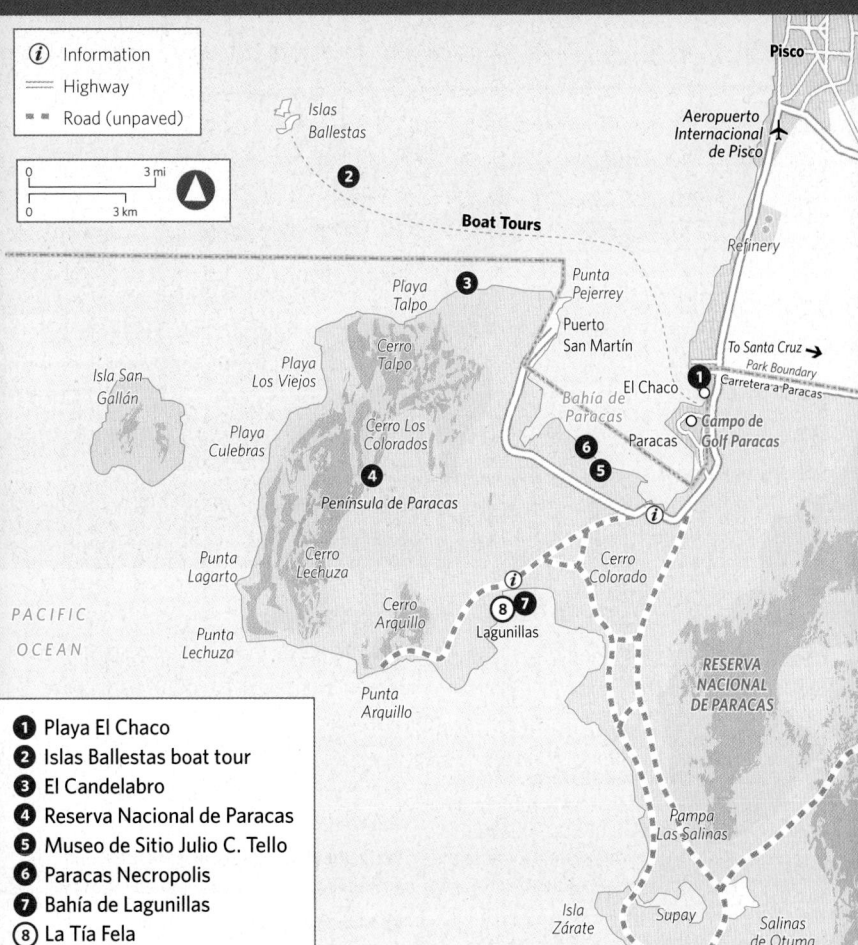

Legend:
- ① Playa El Chaco
- ② Islas Ballestas boat tour
- ③ El Candelabro
- ④ Reserva Nacional de Paracas
- ⑤ Museo de Sitio Julio C. Tello
- ⑥ Paracas Necropolis
- ⑦ Bahía de Lagunillas
- ⑧ La Tía Fela

the Pisco market on Fermín Tangus every 30 min. (S/2). Taxis charge about S/15 from Pisco.

② ★★ kids Islas Ballestas boat tour. The islands themselves are off-limits to visitors, so the only way to get up close to the habitat's rich roster of protected species—including huge colonies of barking sea lions, endangered turtles, Humboldt penguins, red boobies, pelicans, turkey vultures, and red-footed cormorants—is by boat (and for almost all visitors, that means by organized tour). The steep, cantilevered islands are literally covered with birds; some 200 migratory and seabird species have been documented, and the bay is a stopover point in the Alaska-Patagonia migration route. During the summer months (Jan–Mar),

the community becomes even noisier when the baby sea lions are born. Packs of dolphins are occasionally seen knifing through the water; somewhat rarer are glimpses of humpback whales, or massive Andean condors overhead. ⊕ At least 2 hr. See "Practical Matters," p. 97, for information on tours.

③ El Candelabro. En route to the islands, boats pass the famous Candelabro, a giant candelabra-like drawing etched into a cliff overlooking the bay. Similar to the Nasca Lines (p. 102), the huge design, which measures 126m tall and 72m wide (413 x 236 ft.), is just as inscrutable. While some contend it was a ritualistic symbol of the ancient Paracas or Nasca cultures, most archaeologists claim

> *Fishing boats bob in Paracas Bay.*

it dates only to the 18th or 19th century and that it served as a protective symbol and navigational guide for fishermen and sailors (or perhaps pirates).

❹ ★★ **Reserva Nacional de Paracas.** Paracas is the primary marine conservation center in Peru. The 14,504-sq.-km (5,600-sq.-mile) reserve is about two-thirds ocean. Explore the land portions of the reserve either by arranged tour or independently (in-shape walkers can cover the dry, hot terrain by foot). A paved road goes out toward Punta Pejerrey, near El Candelabro. The dirt roads that crisscross the Paracas Peninsula are in poor condition but more interesting, reaching minuscule

fishing villages, beaches, and a cliff-top lookout point. Sadly, the 2007 earthquake destroyed **La Catedral,** a famous rock and cave formation that for decades was one of the reserve's great attractions. ⏱ At least 2 hr. See "Practical Matters," at right, for information on tours.

Walk about 2km (1¼ miles) just beyond the entrance of the Paracas National Reserve.

❺ **Museo de Sitio Julio C. Tello.** This small museum, named for the Peruvian archaeologist credited with uncovering many of the mysteries of the ancient Paracas culture, was severely damaged in the 2007 earthquake and has yet to be rebuilt (call ahead to make sure it's open). The museum depicts the evolution of the Paracas culture through ceramics, textiles, and mummies. The Paracas were experts at mummifying their dead (the mummies show evidence of cranial deformation and trepanation, or brain surgery), and they also were big fans of trophy heads—warriors often attached the heads of defeated foes to their armor to intimidate their opponents. ⏱ 1 hr. Ctra. Pisco–Puerto San Martín Km 27, Paracas. ☎ 056/620-436. Admission S/10 adults, S/5 students and seniors, S/3 kids 9 and under. Daily 9am–5pm.

Excrement Islands

The Islas Ballestas are referred to by locals as "Las Islas Guaneras" because they're covered in bird droppings. (*Guano* is the Quechua word for excrement.) The nitrogen-rich guano is harvested every 10 years and made into fertilizer. There's even a guano factory on the first island. No humans other than the guano collector—no doubt a contender for the world's dirtiest job—are allowed on the islands, as all the species in the reserve are protected by law.

Practical Matters: Reserva Nacional de Paracas & Islas Ballestas

The most convenient way to see the Reserva Nacional de Paracas and the Islas Ballestas is to take a 1-day organized tour. Tour boats for the Ballestas depart from Playa El Chaco. You can also independently contract an island boat tour here ($15–$25 per person; guides, transportation, and entrance fees included) from one of the dozen operators on the main street. Most tours start early in the morning, around 7 or 8am. Visitors are not allowed to set foot on the Islas Ballestas, but boats get close enough for good viewing. Sweaters and windbreakers, hats, and sunscreen are essential. Those who visit the reserve on their own pay an entrance fee (S/5 adults and students 14 and older, free for kids 13 and under). The main agencies covering Paracas and Ballestas are: **Zarcillo Connections,** Jr. Callao 137, Pisco (☎ 056/536-636; www.zarcilloconnections.com); **Huacachina Tours,** Av. La Angostura 355, L-47, Ica (☎ 056/256-582; www.huacachinatours.com); and **Ballestas Travel Service,** San Francisco 249, Pisco (☎ 056/ 533-095).

> Loud, barking sea lions are one of the principal marine-life populations of the Islas Ballestas.

⑥ Paracas Necropolis. Near the Julio C. Tello Museum is the oldest discovered site in the region (100 B.C.–A.D. 300), comprising the archaeological sites of Cabezas Largas and Cerro Colorado. Beginning in the 1920s, Tello discovered Paracas burial sites with outstanding funerary cloths, skulls, and other artifacts, and these became key elements in his groundbreaking studies of the Paracas culture. Today, there's not a whole lot to see at the sites, though there is a viewing tower near the bay that allows visitors to view the dozens (or hundreds) of pink flamingos often gathered on the beach (usually July–Nov). ⊕ 20 min. No phone. Free admission.

Head 5km (3 miles) from the Museo Tello across the neck of the peninsula.

⑦ Bahía de Lagunillas. This quaint fishing village on an exceedingly flat part of the peninsula is home to several seafood restaurants popular with visitors to the reserve. About 2km (1¼ miles) farther along the coastal road is a clifftop *mirador* with superb views of the coastline and the Pacific Ocean. The beach of **La Mina,** also within walking distance of Lagunillas (20 min.), is one of the most beautiful on the peninsula, and very popular in summer. Stout walkers who wish to brave the heat after a late lunch or before an early dinner can walk another 5km (3 miles) southwest of Lagunillas to Punta Arquillo and its **Mirador de Los Lobos,** overlooking a large and famous colony of sea lions that are usually basking in the sun.

---

⑧ 🍴 **La Tía Fela.** In the fishing village of Lagunillas there are several simple seafood restaurants, especially popular on weekends. La Tía Fela is by far the best choice for ceviche and fresh grilled fish. Playa de Lagunillas s/n. No phone. Entrees S/7–S/18. No credit cards.

Ica & Huacachina

Though it's been devastated by earthquakes over the years, most recently in 2007 (from which it is still struggling to recover), Ica, surrounded by sand dunes, is a bustling colonial town that was settled as early as 10,000 years ago. It's known primarily for its *bodegas*, wineries that produce a range of wines and pisco, the classic Peruvian white-grape brandy. Just beyond the city is the desert oasis of Laguna de Huacachina, which almost appears as a mirage amid an unending landscape of sand. Note that this tour is 1 (rather long) day in and around Ica, followed by a morning at Laguna de Huacachina.

> *Sandboarding on the steep dunes of the southern desert coast.*

START Ica is 75km (47 miles) southeast of Pisco via *colectivo* (1 hr.); once in Ica, walk or take a taxi a few blocks west to the Plaza de Armas.

① ★ **Colonial Ica.** A bustling desert town, where Peru's independence from Spain was declared in 1820, Ica boasts a number of colonial churches and mansions of note, most within just a few blocks of the Plaza de Armas. Sadly, the city's most beautiful and important church, **Templo del Santuario de Luren,** was destroyed in the massive 2007 earthquake that struck the region. **Iglesia de La Merced** (also called La Catedral), on the southwest corner of the Plaza de Armas, is a late-19th-century colonial church with a handsomely carved altar,

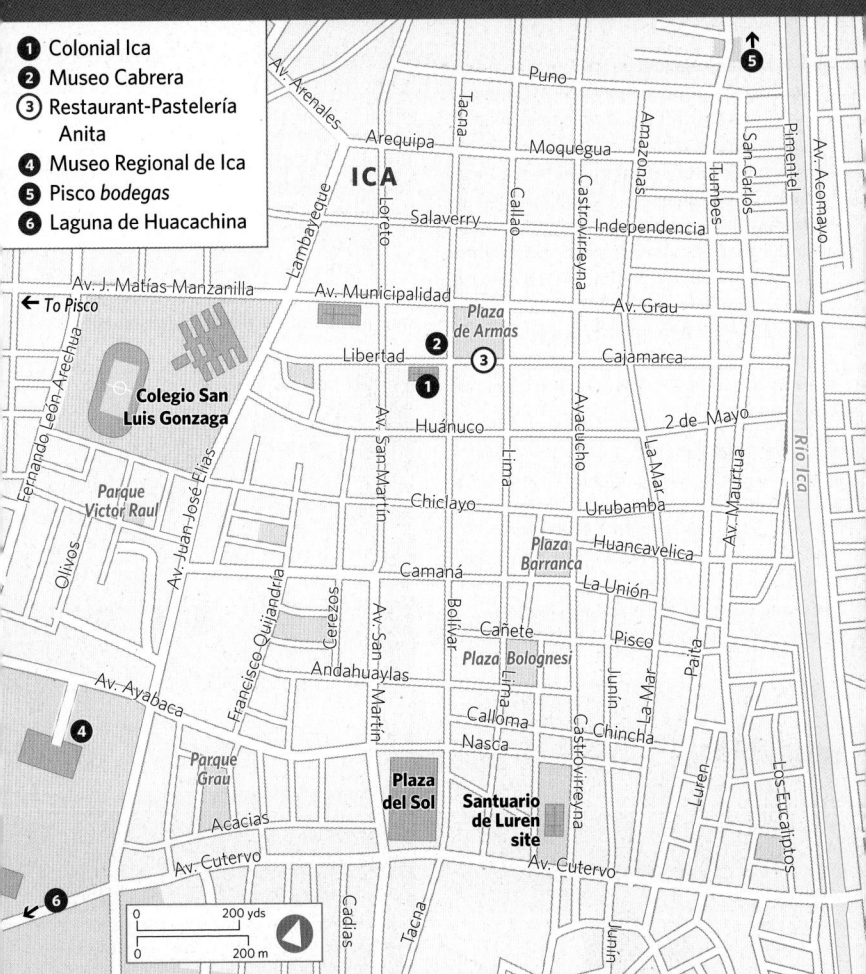

1 Colonial Ica
2 Museo Cabrera
3 Restaurant-Pastelería
   Anita
4 Museo Regional de Ica
5 Pisco *bodegas*
6 Laguna de Huacachina

while **Iglesia de San Jerónimo,** Cajamarca 262, is primarily of interest for its altar mural. Although **Iglesia de San Francisco,** Av. Municipalidad at San Martín, dates just to 1950, it features remarkable stained glass. Among the most architecturally interesting Ica *casonas* (colonial mansions) to view from the street are **Casona del Marqués de Torre** (today Banco Continental), Libertad cdra. 1 s/n; **Casona Alvarado,** Cajamarca 178; and **Casona Colonial El Portón,** Loreto 223. ⏱ At least 90 min. Plaza de Armas.

2 kids **Museo Cabrera.** An altogether different museum experience, this idiosyncratic private collection specializes in some 10,000 stones.

The museum's founder claimed the stones date to an unprecedented advanced Stone Age culture that flourished in Peru long before the reign of the Inca Empire; in truth, they were almost surely engraved by talented artisans. ⏱ 30 min. Bolívar 170 (Plaza de Armas). ☎ 056/231-933. Admission S/18. Mon–Sat 9am–1pm and 4–8pm.

3 🍴 **Restaurant-Pastelería Anita.** For a set-menu lunch or a snack of sandwiches, pastries, or sweets, check out this popular cafe on the Plaza de Armas, open daily from very early to very late. **Libertad 133.** ☎ 056/218-582. Items S/6–S/15.

4 ★★ Museo Regional de Ica. Considered one of the best small museums in Peru, this excellent collection of intricate Paracas textiles; Nasca ceramics, mummies, deformed skulls, and *quipus* (knotted strings used by the Incas to maintain calculations, records, and historical notes); and colonial- and Republican-era art provides a primer on the region's rich history and archaeology. ⏱ 1 hr. Jr. Ayabaca cdra. 8 s/n (1.5km/1 mile south of Plaza de Armas). ☎ 056/234-383. Admission S/6 adults, S/3 students. Mon–Sat 8am–7pm; Sun 9am–1pm. Walk 20 min. from Ica's Plaza de Armas, or take bus 17 from the plaza.

5 ★ Pisco *bodegas.* Dotting the countryside on the outskirts of Ica are some 85 traditional artisanal wineries that produce pisco, the white-grape brandy that is the essential ingredient in Peru's national drink, the pisco sour. Drop in on a couple of the *bodegas* that welcome visits for a fascinating (if often homespun) tour, and to get out of the desert sun. Several *bodegas* also make Peruvian table wines (which can't yet compete with Argentina's or Chile's, but are up-and-coming). The best way to visit more than one of the *bodegas* is to take either a taxi or an organized tour (check with a travel agency in Ica). Don't expect much English except at the largest *bodegas*. Harvest time, from late February to April, is the best time to visit. ⏱ At least 3 hr. Admission and hours vary. See *"Bodegas"* for information on individual establishments.

Tambo Colorado

If you find yourself with additional time on the southern desert coast (you'll need about a half-day), consider checking out Tambo Colorado, 45km (28 miles) northeast of Pisco and 5km (3 miles) outside Humay (admission S/5; about S/120 for a round-trip taxi, S/75 for an organized tour; daily 9am–5pm), the best-preserved ancient architectural complex on the central coast. The outpost served as an administration checkpoint in the Inca Empire and a rest stop for the Inca chieftain on travels between Cusco and coastal settlements. The name of the complex, *colorado,* refers to the red color of the walls; at least some of the original red, white, and yellow colors are still preserved. The complex contains a central plaza, storehouses, living quarters, and military installations. While the site can't compare to Inca ruins in the Andes, it does make for a rewarding visit for archaeology fans and Inca completists.

> A visit to Peru's traditional bodegas *offers a glimpse into the production of the country's famed* pisco.

> *Human remains dating back as far as 7000 B.C. have been identified in the Paracas region.*

On Day 2, take a taxi or *colectivo* 5km (3 miles) southwest of Ica to Laguna de Huacachina.

6 ★★ kids **Laguna de Huacachina.** On the outskirts of Ica, in the midst of unrelenting desert and sand dunes, this gentle oasis surrounded by palm trees looks like a mirage. Huacachina (Wah-kah-*chee*-nah) Lagoon is a great place to relax and swim, though the water can be a tad murky. According to locals, the sulfur-rich waters of the lagoon have curative medicinal properties. A boardwalk rings the lagoon, and there's a small resort village with a few hotels and restaurants. Several outlets rent boards for sandboarding on the dunes (p. 117), and you can also paddleboat across the lagoon. ⏱ At least 1 hr.

If you want to continue on with a tour of the Nasca Lines, Nasca is 130km (81 miles) south of Huacachina.

Bodegas

Bodegas Vista Alegre, Camino a La Tinguiña, Km 2 (☎ 056/232-919; www.vistaalegre.com.pe; free admission; Mon–Fri 9am–2pm), in the La Tinguiña district just 3km (2 miles) north of Ica, is one of the oldest and largest wineries in Peru. A Jesuit hacienda until the late 18th century, the winery was established in 1857 by the Picasso brothers (unrelated to the great Spanish artist). An interesting old-time winery, **Bodega Catador,** Fondo Tres Esquinas 102/Ctra. Panamericana Sur Km 296, Subtanjalla, 7km (4⅓ miles) northeast of Ica (☎ 056/403-295 or 056/403-427; free admission; daily 8am–6pm), has a small wine museum, as well as a restaurant/tavern that often has live music. A small Centro Turístico displays photographs and videos of the production process and offers free tours and tastings. Occupying a 16th-century colonial hacienda, ★★ **Hacienda Tacama Bodega,** Camino a La Tinguiña s/n, 10km (6¼ miles) northeast of Ica (☎ 056/228-395; www.tacama.com; free admission; daily 9am–3pm), is one of the largest producers in the region. Known internationally, it exports its pisco and red and white table wines—probably the best in Peru—to several countries. The Olaechea family has owned the winery since 1889, and though it's one of the oldest in the valley, the *bodega* uses modern technology (though the vineyard is still irrigated, incredibly, by the amazing Achirana irrigation canal built by the Incas). Also of interest, but considerably more removed from Ica and requiring a full morning or afternoon to visit, the traditional winery ★ **Bodega Ocucaje,** Av. Principal s/n, 35km (22 miles) south of Ica (☎ 056/408-001 or 056/837-049; www.ocucaje.com; S/10 per person; Mon–Fri 9am–noon and 2–5pm; Sat 9am–noon), dates to the 16th century and occupies a colonial hacienda; the winery and its on-site resort suffered significant damages in the 2007 earthquake and it is still moving slowly to reopen winery tours to the public.

Nasca & the Nasca Lines

The famous Nasca Lines are one of the most remarkable sights in Peru: massive, mysterious drawings carved into the impossibly dry pampas more than a millennium ago. The purpose of this vast tapestry of "geoglyphs" has baffled observers for decades and given rise to wild conjecture about Peru's ancient past. Most of the etchings, on flat sand canvasses amid the desert's unending expanse of brown, craggy, origami-like folds, are so large they can only be properly appreciated from the air. The town of Nasca plays second fiddle to its famous attraction, although a couple of good museums and archaeological sites are clues to the sophistication of the pre-Columbian Nasca culture.

> *El Candelabro, a giant candelabra-like etching on a cliff overlooking the Bay of Paracas.*

START Nasca is 443km (275 miles) south of Lima (a 6-hr. bus ride). **TRIP LENGTH** 2 days.

❶ Jr. Bolognesi. Were it not for the presence of those strange desert etchings, Nasca would be just a dusty little town with a frontier feel, and one that has been repeatedly damaged by earthquakes. This popular pedestrian-only boulevard, leading from the Plaza de Armas to Plaza Bolognesi, is the town's recent attempt to make itself more presentable for visitors. ⏱ 30 min. Btw. Bolívar and Plaza de Armas.

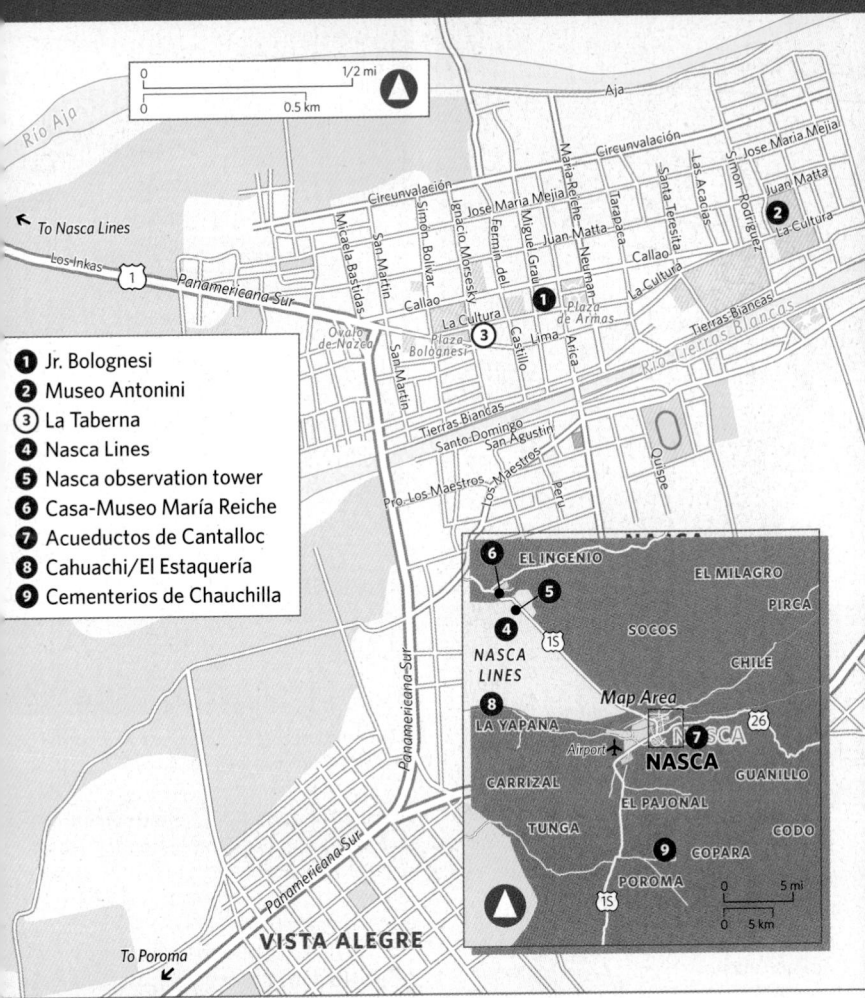

1 Jr. Bolognesi
2 Museo Antonini
3 La Taberna
4 Nasca Lines
5 Nasca observation tower
6 Casa-Museo María Reiche
7 Acueductos de Cantalloc
8 Cahuachi/El Estaquería
9 Cementerios de Chauchilla

2 ★★ kids **Museo Antonini.** A visit to this unexpectedly terrific private archaeology museum, funded by an Italian foundation, is essential to get a handle on the sophisticated Nasca culture and archaeological excavations. On view are fine ceramics, trophy heads worn by warriors after beheadings (to inspire fear among enemies), musical instruments, and a few well-preserved mummies. In the garden out back is the Bisambra aqueduct, an ancient Nasca stone irrigation canal. ⏱ 1 hr. Av. de la Cultura 600, Bisambra (a 10-min. walk from the Plaza de Armas). ☎ 056/523-444. Admission S/15. Daily 9am–7pm.

③ 🍴 **La Taberna.** For lunch, drop into this amiable little restaurant adorned with the graffiti of hundreds of visitors. It can be touristy, but it's a comfy place with a varied international menu and some dependable Peruvian specialties. Jr. Lima 321. ☎ 056/806-783. Items S/9–S/18.

4 ★★★ **Nasca Lines.** One of the world's great enigmas, these etchings of giant plant and animal figures and mysterious geometric lines are carved into the barren surface of the Pampa de San José desert. Throughout the Nasca Valley, an area of nearly 1,000 sq. km (390 sq. miles), there are at least 10,000

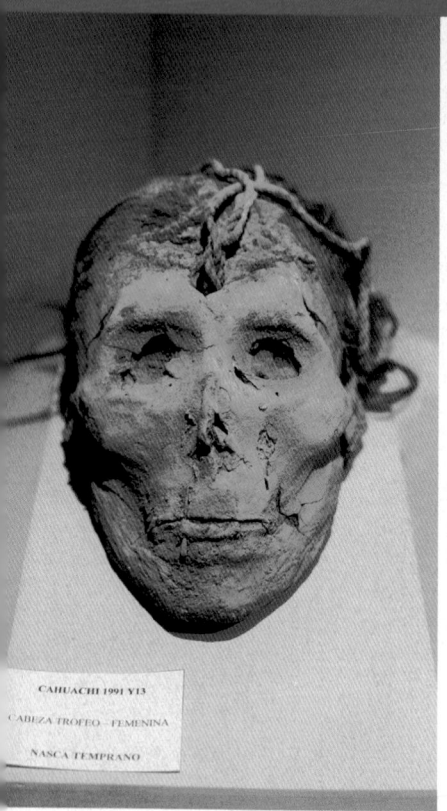

> *The Nasca culture lives on at the Museo Antonini, a private archaeological museum.*

> *The Acueductos de Cantalloc are part of a masterful subterranean irrigation system.*

lines and 300 different figures. Most are found alongside a 48km (30-mile) stretch of the Pan-American Highway. The lines were discovered in the 1920s when commercial airlines began flights over the Peruvian desert. Most experts believe they were constructed by the Nasca (pre-Inca) culture between 300 B.C. and A.D. 700, although predecessor and successor cultures—the Paracas and Huari—also may have contributed to the desert canvas. The peculiar figures are easy to identify from the air: You'll spot the outlines of a parrot, hummingbird, spider, condor, dog, whale, monkey with its tail wound like a top, giant spirals, huge trapezoids, and, perhaps oddest of all, a cartoonish anthropomorphic figure with its hand raised to the sky that has come to be known as "the Astronaut." Some figures are as long as 300m (1,000 ft.), and some

lines are 30m (100 ft.) wide and stretch more than 9.5km (6 miles). Travel agencies and air carriers organize overflights (see "Practical Matters," p. 107). For the best visibility, try to go in midafternoon (2–5pm) or early in the morning, but be prepared for conditions that frequently delay flights and occasionally make them impossible. ⏱ 1 hr.

Take a taxi or any northbound *colectivo* **from Nasca along the Ctra. Panamericana Sur and and ask to get off at** *la torre* **(19km/12 miles).**

❺ **Nasca observation tower.** While the only way to see the Nasca Lines in their entirety is from above, this *mirador* (lookout) beside the Pan-American Highway permits a vague and partial view of three figures: hands, lizard, and tree. It can't compare to a bird's-eye view, but it's the best you'll be able to do if you can't take the stomach-turning dips and dives of the light-craft flights. ⏱ 30 min. Ctra. Panamericana Sur. Admission S/3 adults, S/2 students. Daily 9am–7pm.

Continue by taxi or *colectivo* northward along the Ctra. Panamericana Sur.

6 Casa-Museo María Reiche. A German mathematician, María Reiche, became the world's foremost expert on the Nasca Lines in the latter half of the 20th century. The "Dame of the Desert" dedicated her life to studying and publicizing them, assiduously debunking the crazier theories about their purpose. The Spartan adobe house where Reiche worked and lived (she died in 1998 at the age of 95) is now a small museum about her life and the Lines, complete with maps, models, plans, and photos. ⊕ 45 min. Caserío la Pascana, Ctra. Panamericana Sur Km. 420, San Pablo (27km/17 miles north of Nasca). ☎ 056/234-383. Admission S/5. Mon–Fri 9am–7pm; Sat 8:30am–6:30pm; Sun 9am–1pm. By taxi S/50 round-trip.

On Day 2, head 4km (2½ miles) southeast of Nasca along Ctra. Puquio–Cusco.

7 ★ Acueductos de Cantalloc. These well-preserved stone aqueducts were part of a sophisticated subterranean system constructed by the Nasca to irrigate the bone-dry fields in the pampas. Three dozen beautifully engineered pre-Columbian *puquios* (aqueducts), many S-shaped to slow the flow of water, still

Getting Around

Several of the sights beyond Nasca are remote and difficult to get to on your own. Without a rental car, the only real options for reaching them are by taxi (most often, the best idea is to hire one round-trip from Nasca and have it wait for you during your visit) or organized tour (by far the cheapest and most convenient option). Private (2-person minimum) and group tours are easy to arrange at any of the major Nasca travel agencies listed in "Practical Matters" (p. 107).

function and are used by local farmers. ⊕ 45 min. Ctra. Puquio–Cusco. No phone. Admission S/12; organized tour S/45–S/110 per person. Daily 8am–5pm. By taxi S/25 round-trip.

Take an organized tour to Cahuachi, 30km (19 miles) west of Nasca.

8 ★ Cahuachi/ El Estaquería. An ancient adobe complex, Cahuachi was the Nascas' most important ceremonial and administrative center. The ruins are in poor condition, largely buried under sand, and are still undergoing excavation, but they are said to be twice as

> *The vast Pan-American Highway, the region's principal artery, slices through the southern desert.*

Nasca Lines

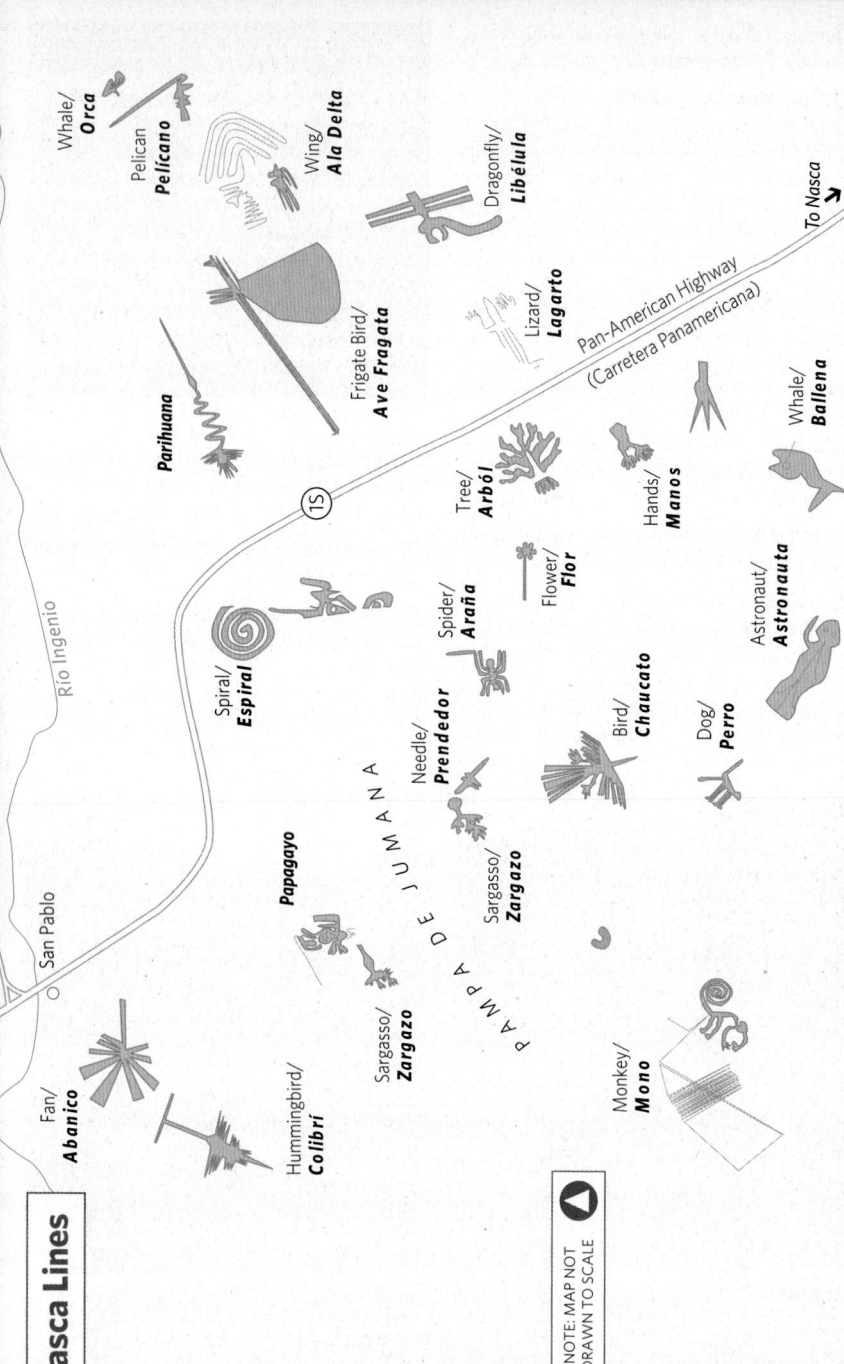

Whale/ *Orca*

Pelican/ *Pelicano*

Wing/ *Ala Delta*

Dragonfly/ *Libélula*

Frigate Bird/ *Ave Fragata*

Lizard/ *Lagarto*

Pan-American Highway
(Carretera Panamericana)

To Nasca

Parihuana

Whale/ *Ballena*

Tree/ *Arból*

Hands/ *Manos*

Astronaut/ *Astronauta*

Río Ingenio

1S

Spider/ *Araña*

Flower/ *Flor*

Spiral/ *Espiral*

Needle/ *Prendedor*

Bird/ *Chaucato*

Dog/ *Perro*

San Pablo

Papagayo

P A M P A   D E   J U M A N A

Sargasso/ *Zargazo*

Fan/ *Abanico*

Hummingbird/ *Colibri*

Sargasso/ *Zargazo*

Monkey/ *Mono*

NOTE: MAP NOT
DRAWN TO SCALE

Practical Matters: Nasca Lines & Greater Nasca

A half-dozen small charter airlines offer flights over the Lines from the small airport in Nasca. Flights (35–45 min.) cost $65 to $95. The small aircrafts seat between three and five passengers. In high season, make advance reservations. Companies operating Nasca Lines overflights from Nasca's Aeródromo de Nasca, Ctra. Panamericana Sur, Km 447 (☎ 056/523-665), include **Aerodina** (☎ 01/444-3075; www.aerodiana.com.pe); **AeroCondor** (☎ 01/421-3105); **AeroIca** (☎ 01/445-0859; www.aeroica.net/icahomeing.html); and **Aeroparacas** (☎ 01/265-8073; www.aeroparacas.com). Agencies offering organized tours to the major attractions in and around Nasca, including the Nasca Lines, include **Alegría Tours,** Jr. Lima 168 (☎ 056/523-431; www.alegriatoursperu.com); **Nanasca Tours,** Jr. Lima 160 (☎ 034/522-917); **Nasca Travel,** Lima 438 (☎ 056/522-085); and **Nasca Trails,** Jr. Bolognesi 299 (☎ 056/522-858; nascatrails@terra.com.pe). **Mystery Peru,** Av. Ignacio Morsesky 126 (☎ 056/522-379; www.mysteryperu.com), goes beyond standard Nasca Lines tours and offers 1-hour ($190) helicopter flights over the Nasca Lines and Palpa, and packages from Lima.

> *The Nasca culture's massive complex Cahuachi is still being excavated.*

large as Chan Chan (p. 349, **4**), the massive Chimú city along Peru's northern coast. Many of the finest examples of Nasca ceramics in existence were discovered at Cahuachi. Only a handful of temples and pyramids may be visited, and only by guided tour. Nearby is **El Estaquería,** rows of *huarango* trees that probably marked important grave sites. ☉ At least 2 hr. No phone. Free admission. Daily 8am–5pm. Travel agencies in Nasca usually offer the site as part of a tour for around S/75–S/105 per person.

Take a taxi or organized tour to this ancient cemetery 30km (19 miles) south of Nasca.

❾ ★ Cementerios de Chauchilla. No mere cemetery, this valley of tombs from the Inca-Chincha period (A.D. 1000–1400) is a vast necropolis consisting of thousands of graves. There are a dozen underground tombs exposed for visitors, and even though they were discovered by *huaqueros* (grave robbers) and many stripped of their possessions, they present a rich picture of the ancient culture of the desert valley. One tomb holds only children; others are populated with the remains of adults with thick, Rasta-like dreadlocks. The desert's very dry conditions helped preserve the mummies over the centuries. ☉ At least 4 hr. Admission S/5; organized tour S/60 per person. Daily 8am–5pm. By taxi S/75–S/100 round-trip, including wait time.

THE NASCA LINES

Riddle in the Sand

BY NEIL EDWARD SCHLECHT

THE NASCA LINES, AN ANCIENT SERIES OF ETCHINGS and geoglyphs in the desert sands 402km (250 miles) south of Lima, cover nearly 581km (361 sq. miles). Carved into the arid surface sometime between 500 B.C. and A.D. 500, they were discovered in the late 1920s, when planes began to fly over the region. They were designated a UNESCO World Heritage Site in 1994. The biggest question about the Lines, even more than *how* pre-Columbian cultures created these long-lasting earth drawings, is *why*, since for the most part they can only be appreciated in their entirety from the air and were created at a time when there was no known means of human aviation.

Theories

RELIGIOUS

Signs to deities in the sky, tied to the Nasca worship of *apus* (mountain spirits) and water sources. Essentially offerings to the gods for rainfall or symbols related to ancestor, water, fertility, and mountain cults.

CEREMONIAL

An offbeat theory claiming pre-Columbian cultures constructed primitive hot-air balloons, and that they would fly over the pampas to take in the drawings.

TEXTILE PRODUCTION

An oversized loom for the sophisticated textile weaving of the Nascas.

ASTRONOMICAL

A calendar marking the solar phases tied to winter and summer solstices. A sort of astronomical observatory, depicting reflections of constellations in the heavens and pointing to positions of the sun, moon, and stars.

EXTRATERRESTRIAL AIRFIELDS

Engineered by aliens from other galaxies, who used them as landing strips (and presumably made contact with the Nasca people).

MAPS

A surface map of either subterranean canals, used in irrigation systems of the desert, or fault lines in this seismically active area.

María Reiche, Dame of the Desert

María Reiche (1903–1998), a German-born mathematician who devoted 5 decades of her life to the study and protection of the Nasca Lines, was recognized in her lifetime as the world's foremost Lines expert. Known as "Dame of the Desert" or "Angel of the Plains," Reiche (who was not trained as an archaeologist) not only studied the Lines but led efforts to promote and protect them. Reiche, who first visited the area in 1941, tirelessly walked, cleaned, measured, and mapped the Lines, and she persuaded the Peruvian Air Force to take aerial photographs of the region. She concluded that they formed a vast astronomical calendar and were fundamental in calculating planting and harvest schedules. She worked and lived alone and is buried in the Nasca desert. Her Spartan home, full of drawings and models, serves as a small museum.

Who, When, What & How

The Nasca culture (200 B.C.–A.D. 500) probably wasn't the only civilization responsible for the Lines, which were most likely created in three chronological phases, with the Chavín (500–300 B.C.) and Paracas (400–200 B.C.) peoples also

having a hand in their execution. However, the third phase, during the time of the Nasca, is when most of the great geoglyphs were created.

About 70 geoglyphs (the largest being about 274m/900 ft. long) depict natural forms, including plants, trees, and animal figures. Similar figures are found in Nasca and Paracas ceramics and textiles. The most puzzling figure, which no doubt propelled some of the wilder theories about the Lines, is the Astronaut, an anthropomorphic figure appearing to wave to the heavens. In addition to the geoglyphs, there are many kilometers' worth of straight and crisscrossing lines and geometric shapes.

Archaeologists believe that over many generations, the Nasca people used simple tools and surveying instruments to remove hard, reddish-brown stones (turned dark by the sun) and "drew" the surprisingly superficial lines in the lighter-colored sand beneath. They have been preserved by the bone-dry desert, one of the most arid spots on the planet, where it rains an average of only 50cm (20 in.) a year.

Ayacucho in 3 Days

One of Peru's most dignified colonial towns, Ayacucho remained in virtual hiding for decades, firmly in the grip of the Shining Path guerrilla movement. But this central highlands gem, home to the country's finest collection of colonial-era churches and Peru's most celebrated folk artists, is begging to be discovered. Despite a name that means "City of Blood" and a history of violent clashes dating back to the Huari culture, Ayacucho is an uncommonly graceful and serene city. Nestled in the Andes, it comes alive during spectacular Easter and Carnaval celebrations. Ayacucho and two sights northeast of the city, the archaeological complex of Huari and the handicrafts center Quinua, can be visited in as little as 2 days, but allow 3 for a more relaxed visit.

> *Life in newly tranquil Ayacucho revolves around its seductive Plaza Mayor.*

START Ayacucho is 585km (364 miles) southeast of Lima (a 1-hr. flight).

❶ ★★ Plaza Mayor. The main square (also called Plaza de Armas), the heart of the city, is lined by grand 16th- to 18th-century homes with stone arches and red-tile roofs. It's one of the finest examples of colonial architecture in Peru and the epitome of a highlands town square.

Eight walkways radiate out from the center in the form of a star, leading to lovely gardens and soaring views of the cathedral and surrounding mountains. On the south side of the plaza is **La Catedral** (stop ❽, below); come back for evening Mass to see its spacious, gilded interior. ⏰ 45 min. Bordered by Jr. 9 de Diciembre, Jr. Callao, Jr. Lima, and Jr. Asamblea.

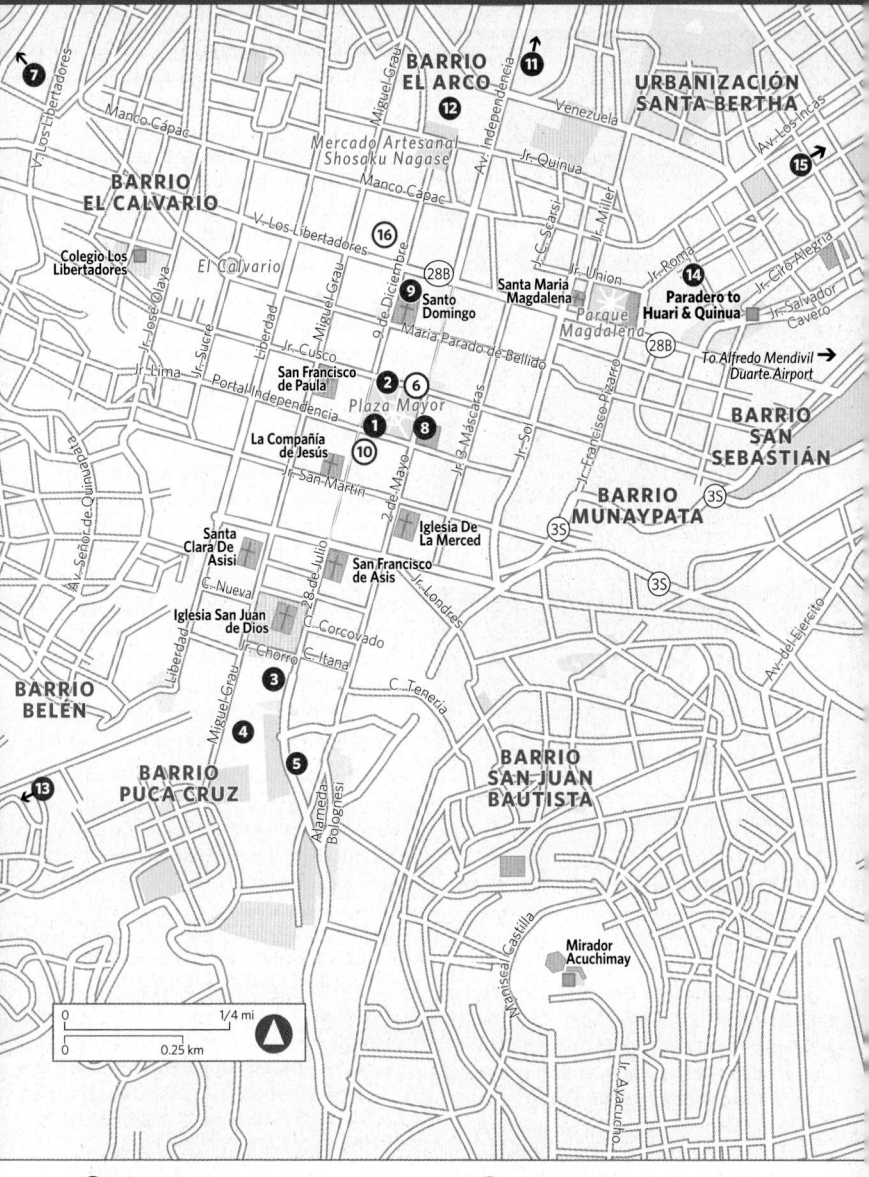

1 Plaza Mayor
2 Colonial *casonas*
3 Mercado 12 de Abril
4 Templo de Santa Teresa
5 Templo de San Cristóbal
6 La Miel
7 Museo de la Memoria
8 Catedral de Ayacucho
9 Colonial churches
10 Sandra
11 Museo Arqueológico Hipólito
   Unanue
12 Templo del Arco
13 Barrio Santa Ana
14 Complejo Arqueológico de Huari
15 Quinua
16 La Magia Negra

> *The handsome Catedral de Ayacucho is one of 33 churches in the highland city.*

2 ★★ **Colonial *casonas*.** In the 16th and 17th centuries, the wealthiest and most powerful citizens of Ayacucho built their stately colonial homes around the Plaza Mayor, and several can be visited: **Casona Castilla y Zamora,** Portal Municipal 50 (Mon–Fri 8am–4pm), with a handsome courtyard and now part of the Universidad Nacional de Huamanga, founded in 1677; **Casona Boza y Solís,** Portal Constitución 15 (Mon–Fri 8am–noon and 2–6pm), one of the oldest in Peru, with a gorgeous garden patio and stone arcades; and **Casona Ruiz**

Going to Church

Ayacucho's 33 colonial-era churches are for the most part open only early in the morning. Since most visitors likely will be arriving early by air from Lima, a roundup of church visits makes sense to save for Day 2. See stop **9** on this tour.

de Ochoa (Casa Jáuregui), Jr. 2 de Mayo 210 (Mon–Fri 8am–5pm), a block west of the main square and distinguished by its massive portal with carved eagles and beautiful courtyard. Now owned by banks and not officially open to visitors are two other handsome 16th-century colonial residences: **Casona Chacón,** Portal Unión 28, and **Casona Olano,** Jr. 28 de Julio 175. ⏱ 1 hr. Free admission to all *casonas*.

3 **Mercado 12 de Abril.** Ayacucho's popular food market is bustling with all manner of food and juice kiosks and produce and meat vendors. ⏱ 45 min. Jr. 28 de Julio (btw. Chorro and San Juan de Dios). ☎ 066/836-166. Free admission. Daily 7am–4pm.

4 ★ **Templo de Santa Teresa.** On a pretty, relaxed plaza, this 1703 convent is home to 20 cloistered Carmelite nuns. The main altar is a fabulously chunky example of gold-leaf carving. Although only officially open for Mass daily at 6:30am, often visitors are allowed in at other times if they knock (to the right of the church's main door) and ask permission (the nuns sell sweets and other items through a closed window). ⏱ 20 min. Jr. 28 de Julio cdra. 6. ☎ 066/312-355. Free admission.

5 **Templo de San Cristóbal.** Constructed in 1540, this tiny church is one of the oldest in South America, but little except for an exterior wall and original bell tower remains. It's not open to the public. ⏱ 10 min. Jr. 28 de Julio at Jr. 2 de Mayo.

6 🍽 ★ **La Miel.** This cafe and soda fountain on the main square has delicious empanadas, fruit juices, salads, milk shakes, and, above all, desserts, including *maracuyá* (passion fruit) pie; there are more than 3 dozen *tortas* (cakes) and pastries. Portal Constitución 11–12. ☎ 066/317-183. Items S/4–S/8.

7 ★★ **Museo de la Memoria.** This area's recent history includes a disastrous period of conflict and dirty war: 2 decades (1980–2000) of Sendero Luminoso (Shining Path) terrorism, and overzealous armed forces attempting to eradicate their presence. Ayacucho and the surrounding countryside were at the epicenter of these clashes and held in virtual lockdown by the Shining Path. The conflict resulted in the disappearance and murder of about 70,000 people, most of them peasants and about half of them from the Ayacucho area. This small but affecting museum chronicles that time and is dedicated to the victims. There are photographs of those who disappeared, clothing articles from those taken prisoner, and a facsimile of a torture chamber. The exterior of the museum is swathed in a mural proclaiming "Never again," and the Parque de Memoria in front contains a sculpture depicting the wounds of violence. ⏱ 1 hr. Prolongación Libertad 1229. ☎ 066/317-170. Admission S/3. www.anfasep.org. Mon–Fri 9am–1pm and 3–6pm.

8 ★★★ **Catedral de Ayacucho.** Completed in 1672, the dignified cathedral has an ornate stone facade, an elaborately carved pulpit, some of Peru's most beautiful baroque gold-leaf altars (nine total, including the main altar), intricately carved wood confessionals, and a collection of colonial-era religious paintings. ⏱ 30 min. Plaza de Armas s/n. ☎ 066/312-590. Free admission. Mon–Sat 5:30pm–7pm; Sun 10am–11am.

Very early on Day 2, visit several of the city's colonial churches. Begin your tour 1 block north of the Plaza Mayor, at Jr. 9 de Diciembre and Jr. Maria Parado de Bellido.

9 ★★★ **Colonial churches.** One of the few Peruvian cities to retain a significant colonial architectural core, Ayacucho overflows with 33 churches—as Ayacuchanos are fond of saying, one for each year Jesus lived—in a compact area walking distance from the Plaza Mayor. If you're a fan of colonial religious architecture, you'll be in heaven in Ayacucho. Get a very early start, as many of the churches are open only briefly (from about 6:30am or 7am to 8:30am during the week for Mass); a few also open for short periods in the late afternoon, so if you can't get to all you'd like before breakfast, try back later.

SITE GUIDE
PAGE 115

10 🥤 **Sandra.** This unadorned little cafe and *juguería* (juice bar) on newly pedestrianized Jr. 28 de Julio is ideal for a *café con leche*, a jug of fresh fruit juice, and a breakfast of tamales or sandwiches. Jr. 28 de Julio 183. No phone. Items S/4–S/12.

> *Ayacucho is famed for its handicrafts, including this sophisticated hand-woven textile, on view at Galería Wari.*

11 ★ **Museo Arqueológico Hipólito Unanue.** This well-executed museum focuses on the ancient cultures of the Ayacucho area, including the Huari and Chancas. There are some excellent ceramics, a trio of tiny mummies, and a room full of a half-dozen, massive stone sculptures taken from the Huari site outside Ayacucho. In front of the museum is an unexpected treat, a botanical garden of varied species of cacti. ⏱ 1 hr. Av. Independencia 502 (Centro Cultural Simón Bolívar). ☎ 066/312-056. Admission S/3. Tues–Sun 9am–5pm.

12 **Templo del Arco.** This small, snow-white, 17th-century church (officially called Templo del Pilar de Zaragoza) sits on a leafy square, a popular hangout with students. While it's rarely open, you can admire the exterior, the postcard-perfect definition of a simple South

> *The tiny village of Quinua is home to dozens of artisans who produce Ayacucho's renowned ceramics.*

American village colonial church. ⏱ 15 min. Plazoleta Maria Parado de Bellido (5 blocks north of Plaza Mayor).

Take a 5-minute taxi ride or walk 10 blocks (25 min.) southwest of the Plaza Mayor.

⑬ **Barrio Santa Ana.** This cobblestone residential neighborhood is the heart of local Quechua culture and *artesanía* (handicrafts), especially weaving. Several family-run galleries ring the main square, although the zone seems considerably less active and vital than in recent years (and sometimes the neighborhood can seem distressingly forlorn). To see some fine and highly valued rugs and textiles, visit Alejandro Gallardo's **Galería Latina,** Plazuela de Santa Ana 105 (☎ 066/528-315); **Alfonso Sulca Chávez,** Plazuela de Santa Ana 83 (☎ 066/312-990); and **Galería Arte Popular de Fortunato Fernández,** Plazuela de Santa Ana 63–64 (☎ 066/313-192). **Galería Wari,** Mariscal Cáceres 302 (☎ 066/312-529), is the studio and home of Gregorio Sulca, a renowned textile and plastics artist

who has exhibited his sophisticated rugs and paintings abroad. ⏱ At least 1 hr. Free admission. Most galleries daily 11am–6pm.

On Day 3, take a bus to Huari, 22km (14 miles) northeast of Ayacucho. *Colectivos* (40 min; S/3) headed to Quinua depart from the corner of Jr. Salvador Cavero and Jr. Ciro Alegría in eastern Ayacucho (Urbanización Santa Bertha); tell the driver you're getting off at Huari.

⑭ ★★ 🧒 **Complejo Arqueológico de Huari.** This Huari (also written Wari) site dates to

Tours of Huari & Quinua

To visit Huari and Quinua with a more convenient, organized tour rather than on your own, try **Wari Tours,** Jr. Lima 138 (☎ 066/311-415; http://waritoursayacucho. blogspot.com), or **Urpillay Tours,** Portal Constitución 4 (☎ 066/315-074; http:// ayacuchoviajes.blogspot.com). Group and private tours range from S/35 to S/150.

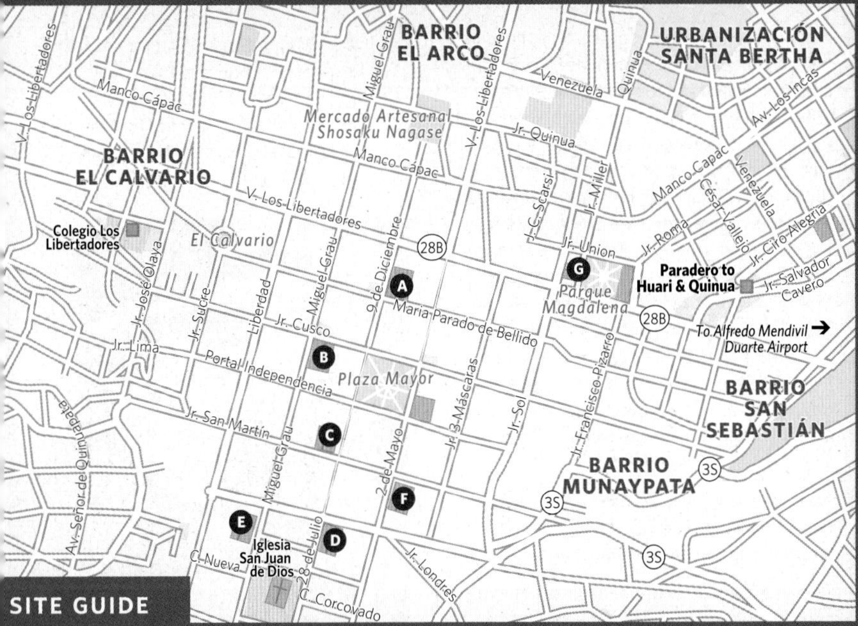

9 Colonial Churches

The most visually impressive of Ayacucho's churches, the finely sculpted but oddball **A Templo de Santo Domingo** (at right), Jr. 9 de Diciembre at Jr. Maria Parado de Bellido (Mon–Sat 7–8am, Sun 10–11am), is the city's second convent, dating to 1548. Its exterior is marked by rustic, earth-colored bricks; twin towers framing what looks like a row of spikes; and three Romanesque arches. Inside is a magnificent carved–gold leaf main altar that holds la Virgen del Rosario. **B San Francisco de Paula,** Jr. Callao cdra. 1 (Mon–Sat 7–8am, Sun 7–10am and 7–8pm), founded in 1716, is unique for its dark-wood carved altars (most are gold leaf). The baroque **C Templo de la Compañia de Jesús,** Jr. 28 de Julio cdra. 1 (Mon–Sat 7–7:30am and noon–12:30pm, Sun 6:30–7:30am and noon–1pm), was founded in 1605 as a Jesuit school and church. **D San Francisco de Asís,** Jr. 28 de Julio at Jr. Vivanco (Mon–Sat 7–7:30am and 6–6:30pm, Sun 7–10am and 6–7pm), from 1552, is the only church besides the cathedral (**8**) to have three naves. The first monastery in Ayacucho (the second in Peru), **E Santa Clara de Asís,** Jr. Miguel Grau at Nazareno (Mon–Sat

6:30–7:15am and 6–6:30pm, Sun 7–10am and 6–7pm), from 1568, features excellent examples of Gothic-*mudéjar* (Moorish-style) woodcarving. **F Templo de La Merced,** Jr. 2 de Mayo at Jr. San Martín (Sun 7:30–8:30am and noon–1pm), was begun in 1540, the year of the Spanish founding of the city. The baroque **G Templo de Santa María Magdalena,** Jr. Sol at Av. Mariscal Cáceres/Parque Magdalena (Mon–Sat 7–7:30am and 6–6:30pm, Sun 7–10am and 7–8pm), founded by the Dominican order in 1588, has thrice been a victim of fire; not for nothing does its image of the Lord of Agony participate in Easter Week processions. ☉ At least 2 hr. Admission free to all churches.

A.D. 600, making it one of the oldest urban walled centers in the Americas. The Huari Empire, considered the first centrally governed "nation" in the Andes, stretched north to Cajamarca and south to Cusco. Archaeologists believe the Huari's urban planning and religious, political, and military organization served as models for the empire-building Incas. The large (300-hectare/750-acre) ruins site, though badly deteriorated, contains thick, 10m-high (33-ft.) stone walls, houses, tunnels, and flat ceremonial areas. The gorgeous desert-like High Andes setting is covered in bright green cacti, and the serene views of the mountains are breathtaking. ⏱ At least 1 hr. Ctra. Ayacucho-Quinua. No phone. Admission S/3. Tues–Sun 9am–5pm.

Take the same *colectivo* **15km (9 miles) northeast from Huari to Quinua (a wait for another bus can be painfully long).**

⑮ ★★ **Quinua.** This appealingly quiet Quechua village—with cobblestone streets and red-tile roofs crowned by small clay churches (roof-bound protectors against evil spirits)—is home to artisans who produce many of the finest clay churches and *retablos* (altarpieces) seen in galleries and shops across Peru. Here, you're likely to purchase directly from the artisan who crafted the work rather than from a mere salesperson. For the best shopping, venture up the stairs from the main plaza to the heart of the village and the peaceful back streets behind the quiet Plazuela de Armas. Most of the art galleries line Jr. Sucre and Jr. San Martín, including ★ **Galería Familia Sánchez,** Jr. San Martín 151 (☎ 066/810-212), the studio and gallery of the son of Mamerto Sánchez, one of the most famous artisans from Quinua; and **Galería Ayllu,** Jr. San Martín s/n (no phone). Quinua is embedded in most Peruvians' memories as the site of the battle for independence from Spain; **La Pampa,** an expansive plain with stunning panoramic views of the surrounding mountains (especially in the sweet light of late afternoon), is crowned by a large white obelisk commemorating the 1824 Battle of Ayacucho. The walk up from town takes about 30 minutes. ⏱ At least 3 hr.

Return by *combi* **(the bus stop is across the road from the main entrance and stairway to Quinua) to Ayacucho to spend the night.**

⑯ **La Magia Negra.** After a day in the countryside, pop into this cool little tavern with local art for a cocktail or beer and a slice of pizza. 9 de Diciembre 293 (at Mariscal Cáceres). ☎ 066/328-289. Items S/8–S/15.

Ayacucho, Festival City

Two of Peru's most celebrated popular festivals take place in otherwise modest and unassuming Ayacucho. The stunning weeklong Easter celebration, **Semana Santa** (above), features nightly candlelit processions and daily fairs, and culminates in a spectacular and emotional procession on Easter Sunday; a massive (15x8m/49x26-ft.) throne made entirely of white wax and carried by 200 people makes its way around the Plaza Mayor. Hotels and *hostales* in Ayacucho are booked months in advance (at triple the normal rate) for Easter week, although you might find lodging offered in private homes. **Carnaval Ayacuchano** is a resolutely Quechua carnival celebration and one of the most colorful in Peru. For 3 days (in late Feb or early Mar), exuberant dancing and hedonism, with political songs and elaborate masks, take over the colonial streets of Ayacucho, including the official proclamation of the *Ño Carnavalon,* a giant papier-mâché figure of the Rey Momo. For more information on festivals in Ayacucho, visit the city calendar at www.peru.travel.

Outdoor Adventures A to Z

Boating. Most boating opportunities along the coast are standard 2- to 4-hour wildlife tours of the Islas Ballestas (p. 95, ❷). These are handled by all the major tour operators in Pisco and independent guides and boats on the El Chaco waterfront and range from $20 to $35 per person. See "Practical Matters," p. 97.

Dune Buggies & 4x4 Safaris. Adrenaline-fueled adventure trips across the sands in dune buggies, *areneros,* are available through local tour operators. In Paracas, try the **Hotel Paracas** (p. 126). The Nasca agencies **Mystery Peru** (p. 107) and **Alegría Tours** (p. 107) both offer buggy and sandboarding trips to Laguna de Huacachina. At Huacachina, the *hostales* **El Huacachinero** (p. 124) and **Hostería Suiza** (p. 126) offer their own buggy trips. **Hotel Cantayo Spa & Resort** (p. 128), through its in-house agency Picopaco Travel, offers 4x4 off-road excursions through the desert and to isolated beaches. **Casa Andina Classic Nasca** (p. 128) organizes intense, 7-hour 4x4 journeys across the desert to San Fernando, a little-visited coastal oasis, in addition to more standard dunes excursions. Prices range from $25 per person for organized buggy and sandboarding to Huacachina to $300 for full-day excursions for a group of four.

Hiking & Trekking. Though it can be forbiddingly hot and dusty, independent outdoor types who are prepared with plenty of sun protection and water can hike around the Paracas Peninsula (about 21km/13 miles round-trip to the lookout point). An easier trek is 5km (3 miles) from the Tello Museum near the entrance of Reserva Nacional de Paracas to Lagunillas; begin at a turnoff left of the paved road just beyond the museum. Note that there are few facilities of any kind on the peninsula, but you are allowed to camp on the beaches, often unpopulated save for wildlife. Maps of the Paracas National Reserve are available at the gift shop in the Museo Julio C. Tello or at the visitor center next door. For hardcore organized desert treks, contact **Wasipunko Nasca** (☎ 056/523-212; www.nascawasipunko.com). Treks to Cerro Blanco,

> *Bounding over sand dunes in a dune buggy is the hottest sport along the southern desert coast.*

the Nasca Lines *mirador,* and more range from 6 to 12 hours.

Sandboarding. Surfing the sand dunes on boards is steadily gaining in popularity. The largest sand dunes in South America—Cerro Blanco (2,080m/6,824 ft.)—are just 8km (5 miles) from Nasca, and there are also high dunes (210m/689 ft.) around the Huacachina Lagoon outside of Ica. It can be extremely hot, though, and tough going, because there aren't lifts to transport you back up the dune (unless you've contracted a group with a dune buggy). Also, accidents can occur, so it's best to get some instruction from a local or from the outfit renting the boards. At Huacachina, sandboards can be rented (for about S/3 an hour) at several restaurants and cafes, and at **Hostal Rocha** (☎ 056/222-256). The Nasca agencies **Mystery Peru** (p. 107) and **Alegría Tours** (p. 107) offer combo buggy and sandboarding trips to Laguna de Huacachina.

A TOAST TO PISCO

Peru's National Drink BY NEIL EDWARD SCHLECHT

PISCO, THE GRAPE BRANDY DISTILLED IN *BODEGAS* largely in and around Ica, along the southern desert coast, is the principal ingredient in the frothy national cocktail, the pisco sour. Pisco dates to the colonial era, brought to Peru by Spanish settlers in the 16th century. Peruvians are intensely proud of their pisco (Chile also claims to have invented pisco) and have made it and the pisco sour their own.

At its most basic, pisco is a clear, white spirit distilled from grapes in single-batch copper stills. Peruvian law dictates that nothing else (including water) may be added to reach the desired 80 proof (40% ABV). Pisco comes in many styles and can range from elegant and smooth to fiery and rough-edged. While purists insist on sipping it neat, many drinkers mix it with fruit juices.

Pisco in Literature

Pisco made frequent appearances in more than a half dozen novels by Mario Vargas Llosa, the Peruvian Nobel Prize winner. *Death in the Andes* includes this bit of wisdom: "'Don't gulp down beer and cane liquor, boys. Learn how to drink!' he preached to the miners. 'Just taste this fine grape pisco from Ica, it makes you forget your troubles, it brings out the happy man you have inside.'" The Chilean poet Pablo Neruda (also a Nobel winner) was likewise a friend of pisco. He called it "a million years of sun, in just one drop."

Making Your Own

Its exact origins are unknown, but some say the pisco sour was invented in the 1920s by a North American bartender, "Gringo Morris," at the Morris Bar in Lima.

Ingredients:
3 oz. pisco
1 oz. simple syrup
1 oz. key lime juice
½ raw egg white
ice
dash Angostura bitters

Place all ingredients save the Angostura bitters in a cocktail shaker. Shake vigorously until the drink becomes frothy. Strain and pour into a chilled 8-oz. cocktail glass. Garnish with 3 drops of Angostura bitters.

Mixology 101

Athough the pisco sour is Peru's undisputed classic cocktail, bartenders have adapted it for a new generation of drinkers. Many use local tropical fruits; look for drinks based on *sauco, tumbo,* and *tuna* (a desert fruit).

LÚCUMA SOUR
A variation using the sweet Andean fruit *lúcuma* (sometimes called "Peruvian eggfruit"), commonly found in desserts such as the *Suspiro de Lúcuma.*

AGUAYMANTO SOUR
Made with fresh *aguaymanto* (tomatillo or gooseberry), a tasty Andean fruit that looks like a yellow cherry.

MARACUYÁ SOUR
Made with fresh passion-fruit juice; just the right mix of sweet and sour.

COCA SOUR
Coca leaves are macerated in pisco for several days, imparting a subtle but delectable taste of coca leaves.

Glossary

PISCO *PURO*
Pure pisco, made from a single, non-aromatic grape (Quebranta, Mollar, or Common Black) that results in a pisco less fruity and floral than others, but complex in taste.

PISCO *ACHOLADO*
"Half-breed" pisco, a blend of several grapes, such as Quebranta, Italia, and Torontel. Generally sweeter and more aromatic than pure Quebranta and most often used in pisco sours.

PISCO *AROMÁTICO*
Made from aromatic varietals, such as Muscatel and Italia.

PISCO *MOSTO VERDE*
"Green must" pisco, distilled after being only partially fermented (and thus retaining more residual sugar). Best drunk straight.

Where to Sample a Sour

BAR HUARINGAS, LIMA
Bolognesi 472, Miraflores

CAPITÁN MELÉNDEZ, LIMA
Alcanfores 199, Miraflores

LA CALESA, LIMA
Manuel Bañón 255, San Isidro

▲ **THE ENGLISH BAR AT COUNTRY CLUB HOTEL, LIMA**
Los Eucaliptos 590, San Isidro

PICAS, LIMA
Bajada de Baños 340, Barranco

LIMO, CUSCO
Portal de Carnes 236, Cusco

Southern Desert Coast & Central Highlands Restaurants

Ica & Paracas

Don Manuel PISCO PERVUIAN
This is about as upmarket as restaurants in Pisco get (which isn't saying a whole lot). It serves a variety of inexpensive meals, including *churrasco* (grilled meats) and good fresh fish. Jr. Comercio 179. ☎ 056/532-035. Entrees S/12–S/24. MC, V. Lunch and dinner daily. Map p. 121.

★ **El Chorito** EL CHACO CEVICHE/SEAFOOD
Set back a block from the waterfront, this contemporary-looking restaurant is nonetheless the best of the seafood places in El Chaco. Perfect for a lunch of ceviche and grilled fish. Av. Paracas s/n. ☎ 056/545-054. Entrees

S/7–S/28. AE, MC, V. Breakfast, lunch, and dinner daily. Map p. 121.

★ **kids El Otro Peñoncito** ICA PERUVIAN
The nicest place in the city center, this long-time family-owned, art-filled restaurant offers a hugely varied menu of *criollo* (creole) specialties (including the house chicken dish, stuffed *pollo a la Iqueña*); basic chicken, meat, and fish dishes; and some vegetarian plates. Bolívar 422. ☎ 056/233-920. Entrees S/12–S/26. No credit cards. Breakfast, lunch, and dinner daily. Map p. 121.

La Villa de Ica ICA BARBECUE
Specialties here include grilled meats, rotisserie chicken, and barbecue, as well as regional dishes, served to a mixed crowd of families and young people. Jr. Lima 139 (Plaza de Armas). ☎ 056/213-108. Entrees S/9–S/24. MC, V. Lunch and dinner daily. Map p. 121.

Dining Tip

The best dining bets for many guests in the Pisco/Paracas/Ica area are their hotels; several, including the Doubletree, Hotel Paracas, Hostal Villa Manuelita, and Hostal Posada Hispana, have quite nice restaurants (open to nonguests as well).

> *Thousands of travelers have left their graffiti scrawls on the walls of La Taberna in Nasca.*

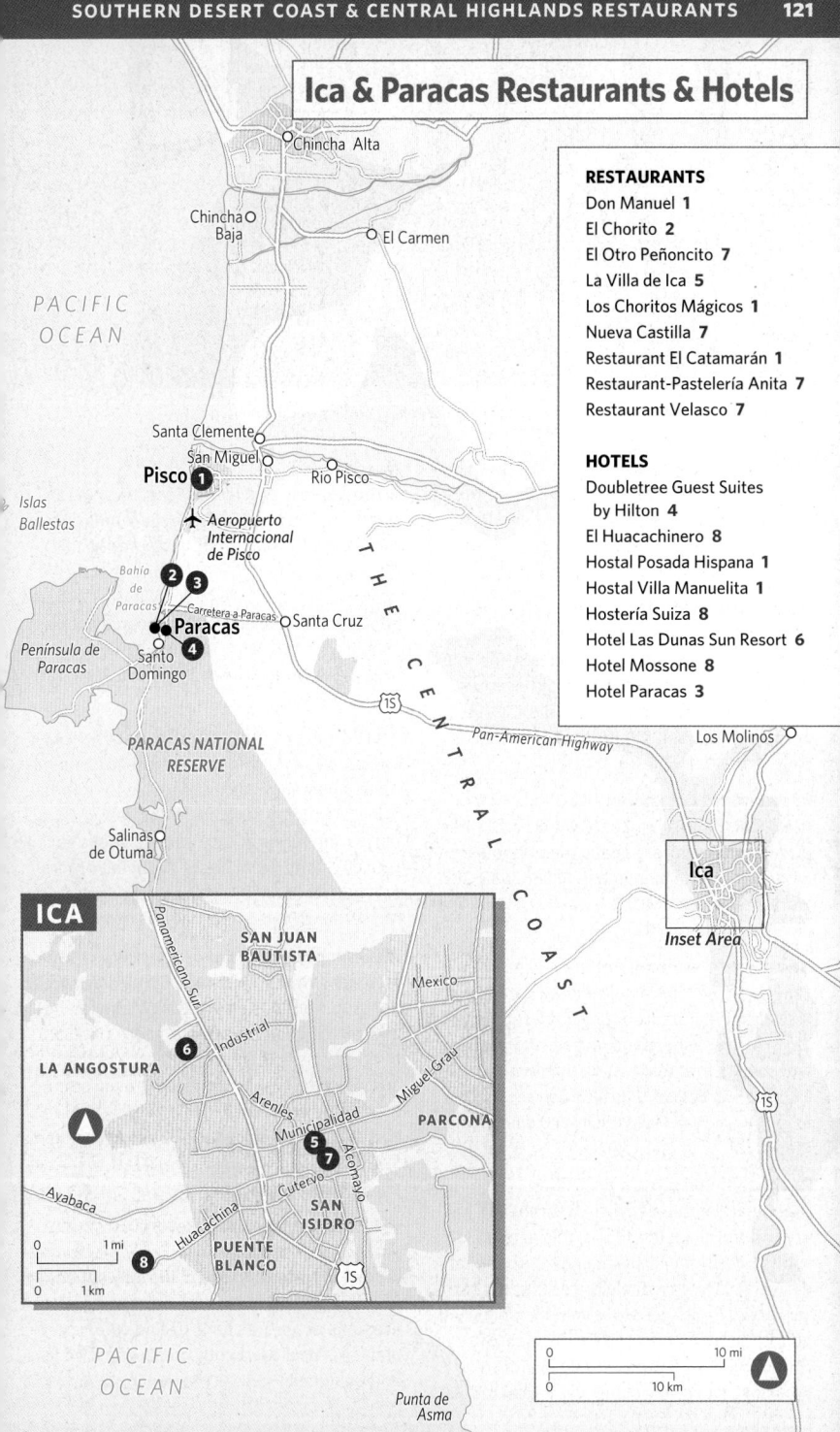

Ica & Paracas Restaurants & Hotels

RESTAURANTS
Don Manuel **1**
El Chorito **2**
El Otro Peñoncito **7**
La Villa de Ica **5**
Los Choritos Mágicos **1**
Nueva Castilla **7**
Restaurant El Catamarán **1**
Restaurant-Pastelería Anita **7**
Restaurant Velasco **7**

HOTELS
Doubletree Guest Suites
  by Hilton **4**
El Huacachinero **8**
Hostal Posada Hispana **1**
Hostal Villa Manuelita **1**
Hostería Suiza **8**
Hotel Las Dunas Sun Resort **6**
Hotel Mossone **8**
Hotel Paracas **3**

> *Ayacucho specialties such as* puca picante *are the calling card of La Casona.*

Los Choritos Mágicos PISCO *CEVICHE/SEA-FOOD* A *cevichería* serving inexpensive mussels and, of course, ceviche. Jr. 28 de Julio 116. ☎ 056/534-158. Entrees S/8–S/21. No credit cards. Lunch daily 11am–4pm. Map p. 121.

Nueva Castilla ICA *PERUVIAN*
This attractive restaurant serves basic Peruvian fare. After dinner on weekends, the music is pumped up and the restaurant becomes a disco of sorts. Libertad 252. ☎ 056/213-140. Entrees S/12–S/24. MC, V. Lunch and dinner daily 11am–10pm. Map p. 121.

Restaurant El Catamarán PISCO *PIZZA/PERUVIAN* This simple joint serves the town's best pizzas and has a very cheap menu popular with locals. Jr. Comercio 166. ☎ 056/680-327. Entrees S/8–S/21. MC, V. Breakfast, lunch, and dinner daily. Map p. 121.

Restaurant-Pastelería Anita ICA *PERUVIAN*
Fairly upscale for Ica, this longtime cafe and restaurant features a pretty good set menu for lunch, a long list of sandwiches, and pastries and sweets for breakfast or a pick-me-up. Libertad 133. ☎ 056/218-582. Entrees S/10–S/27. MC, V. Breakfast, lunch, and dinner daily. Map p. 121.

Restaurant Velasco ICA *PERUVIAN*
A popular cafeteria-style restaurant and bakery, around since the 1930s, this agreeable spot serves both Peruvian and international dishes at very affordable prices, but it's better known for its generous selection of baked goods, desserts, and coffee. Libertad 137. ☎ 056/218-182. Entrees S/9–S/24. MC, V. Breakfast, lunch, and dinner daily. Map p. 121.

Nasca

★ **Don Hono** DOWNTOWN *PERUVIAN/INTERNATIONAL* Just off the Plaza de Armas, where there are several touristy restaurants, this agreeable, simple, and inexpensive little joint is a local favorite serving tasty Peruvian home cooking and international standards such as lasagna. Jr. Arica 254. ☎ 056/523-066. Entrees S/11–S/22. MC, V. Lunch and dinner Mon–Sat; lunch Sun. Map p. 125.

★ **El Portón** DOWNTOWN *PERUVIAN/INTERNATIONAL* With its colonial-style decor, this traditional restaurant is dependable for international standards such as pastas, lasagna, and pizzas, as well as *criollo* (creole) dishes such as *seco de cabrito* (goat stew). Av. Ignacio Morseski 460. ☎ 056/523-490. Entrees S/14–S/25. MC, V. Lunch and dinner daily. Map p. 125.

kids **Grumpy's Snack Bar** DOWNTOWN *INTERNATIONAL/SNACKS* This simple little place with bamboo walls has a surprisingly long menu and serves good breakfasts, snacks, salads, burgers, and fruit juices perfect for a light lunch—because you don't want a full stomach before your small-plane overflight of the Nasca Lines. Jr. Bolognesi 182. No phone. Items S/4–S/18. No credit cards. Breakfast, lunch, and dinner daily. Map p. 125.

★★ **Hotel Cantayo Spa & Resort** OUTSKIRTS *PERUVIAN/INTERNATIONAL* Easily the best restaurant in Nasca and one of the only options for fine dining along the southern desert coast, this elegant place serves hard-to-find organic vegetables and salads, lightly prepared grilled fish, and an Andean specialty for lunch: *pachamanca,* a barbecue of potatoes, meat, and vegetables roasted in an underground pit. If you're pining for a good bottle of wine or imported cheeses, this is your place to splurge. Ctra. Puquio–Cusco (4km/2½ miles southwest of Nasca). ☎ 056/522-264. Entrees S/21–S/55. AE, DC, MC, V. Lunch and dinner daily. Map p. 125.

La Encantada DOWNTOWN *PERUVIAN*
This agreeable restaurant is pretty dependable for *criollo* standards such as roasted chicken and pizzas. Callao 592. ☎ 056/522-930. Entrees S/17–S/26. MC, V. Breakfast, lunch, and dinner daily. Map p. 125.

Las Cañas DOWNTOWN *PERUVIAN/INTERNA-TIONAL* Restaurant by day and early evening, noisy bar by night, this place serves a large menu of Peruvian and international dishes, including ceviche, pastas, salads, and hamburgers; it's quite a hangout on weekend nights. Jr. Bolognesi 279. ☎ 056/806-891. Entrees S/12–S/26. MC, V. Lunch and dinner daily. Map p. 125.

Las Líneas DOWNTOWN *PERUVIAN*
Part of the hotel of the same name, Las Líneas looks rather like a Chinese restaurant, but it serves Peruvian fare such as ceviche, *papas a la huancaina* (boiled potatoes in a spicy cream sauce), and garlic chicken. Jr. Arica 299-A. ☎ 056/522-066. Entrees S/8–S/25. MC, V. Breakfast, lunch, and dinner Mon–Sat; breakfast and lunch Sun. Map p. 125.

★ kids **La Taberna** DOWNTOWN *INTERNATIONAL*
The graffiti scrawlings on the walls are by hundreds of international visitors, testament to this restaurant's popularity among travelers. It serves a wide variety of dishes, including Peruvian specialties such as *lomo saltado* (stir-fry) and ceviche; salads and pastas; and *fideua* (noodle paella). There's usually live music in the evenings. Jr. Lima 321. ☎ 056/806-783. Entrees S/14–S/25. MC, V. Lunch and dinner daily. Map p. 125.

★ **Restaurante El Huarango** DOWNTOWN *PE-RUVIAN* One of the best restaurants in Nasca, this charming place has a rooftop garden terrace with an energetic vibe. Dishes are largely coastal Peruvian favorites such as *ají de gallina* (spicy creamed chicken). Jr. Arica 602. ☎ 056/521-287. Entrees S/14–S/28. MC, V. Lunch and dinner Mon–Sat. Map p. 125.

Ayacucho

★ **Antonino** DOWNTOWN *PIZZA/ITALIAN*
A local favorite for its long roster of pizzas and pastas, both pretty authentic, with good cocktails to boot. In the front room is a pizza oven and chef kicking out homemade pastas; the dining room tucked away in back is where locals on dates tend to go. Jr. Cusco 144. ☎ 066/315-738. Entrees S/6–S/15. MC, V. Dinner daily. Map p. 127.

Café Bar New York DOWNTOWN *SNACK BAR*
In the courtyard of the Centro Cultural, there are several cafes for light meals, snacks, coffee, and desserts; this is the best of them, with seats outdoors overlooking the patio. Jr. 28 de Julio 178. ☎ 066/313-079. Entrees S/6–S/15. MC, V. Lunch and dinner daily. Map p. 127.

El Monasterio DOWNTOWN *PERUVIAN*
With a relaxing colonial courtyard location and tables under umbrellas, this dependable place does a good-value lunch menu as well as the usual Andean suspects, such as *lomo saltado* (strips of beef with fried potatoes, onions, and tomatoes over rice). Jr. 28 de Julio 178 (in Centro Cultural). ☎ 066/313-905. Entrees S/9–S/20. No credit cards. Lunch and dinner daily. Map p. 127.

★★ **La Casona** DOWNTOWN *PERUVIAN*
Brightly lit and built around a plant-filled courtyard, this is a great place to sample a good-value menu of Andean *criollo* cooking, grilled meats, and a host of *platos típicos* (regional specialties), such as *chancho al horno con qapchi* (oven-baked pork) and *puca picante* (beets, peanuts, pork, potatoes, rice, and spicy peppers). Jr. Maria Parado de Bellido 463. ☎ 066/312-733. Entrees S/10–S/25. MC, V. Breakfast, lunch, and dinner daily. Map p. 127.

★★ **Wallpa Sua** DOWNTOWN *PERUVIAN*
This bustling restaurant with multiple dining rooms and a massive grill and rotisserie is hugely popular with Ayacuchanos, who flood the place for its delectable spit-roasted chicken and grilled meats. The chicken is as good as advertised by locals; the quarter bird with fries and salad is a steal at S/10. Garcilaso de la Vega 240. ☎ 066/313-905. Entrees S/10–S/28. No credit cards. Lunch and dinner daily. Map p. 127.

Southern Desert Coast & Central Highlands Hotels

Ica & Paracas

★★★ kids Doubletree Guest Suites by Hilton

BAHÍA DE PARACAS A new contemporary hotel and waterfront resort on Santo Domingo beach next to the entrance to the reserve. Large rooms have crisp, modern furnishings and great bay views; the huge pool and plenty of outdoor activities, including a kid's club and nautical sports, make it ideal for families. Urbanización Santo Domingo, Reserva Nacional de Paracas. ☎ 01/617-1000 in Lima. www. starwoodhotels.com. 120 units. $179–$259 double. AE, DC, MC, V. Map p. 121.

★ El Huacachinero LAGUNA DE HUACACHINA

This friendly inn, very popular with young travelers, is the best choice for staying right on the lagoon. Well-maintained and comfortable rooms are built around an outdoor pool with a sun terrace and bar. The hotel focuses on dune experiences, operating its own "green buggy" services and sandboarding trips. Av. Perotti,

Balneario de Huacachina. ☎ 056/217-435. www. elhuacachinero.com. 21 units. S/110 double. No credit cards. Map p. 121.

★ Hostal Posada Hispana PISCO

Small and charming, this popular and good-value colonial-style hotel is managed by a Spanish-Peruvian couple. The inn is clean and nicely decorated for the price; rooms have loft spaces and bathrooms, and the hotel has a backyard garden and a nice little restaurant that serves paella, pizzas, and Peruvian dishes. Bolognesi 222. ☎ 056/536-363. www. posadahispana.com. 24 units. $30 double. No credit cards. Map p. 121.

★★ Hostal Villa Manuelita PISCO

A colorful and nicely restored 100-year-old colonial house, this small, good-value hotel is a half-block from the main square and offers spacious rooms and a Spanish-style central courtyard with a fountain—real style for modest Pisco. There's a decent pizzeria/bar on the

> *The spectacular pool at Doubletree Guest Suites by Hilton provides relief from the desert heat.*

Nasca Restaurants & Hotels

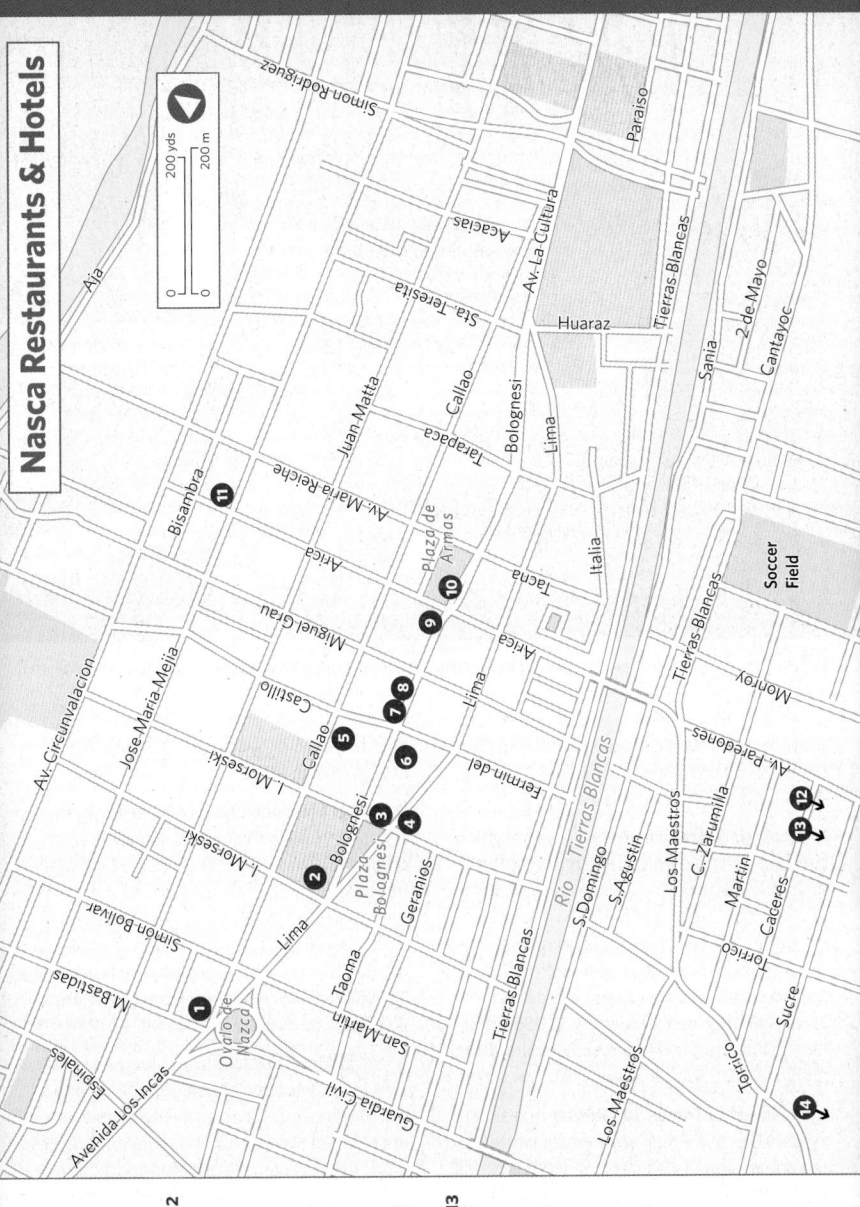

RESTAURANTS

Don Hono **10**
El Portón **3**
Grumpy's Snack Bar **6**
Hotel Cantayo Spa & Resort **12**
La Encantada **5**
Las Cañas **7**
Las Líneas **9**
La Taberna **4**
Restaurante El Huarango **11**

HOTELS

Casa Andina Classic Nasca **8**
Hotel Alegría **1**
Hotel Cantayo Spa & Resort **13**
Hotel Majoro **14**
Hotel Nazca Lines **2**

> *The relaxing pool and bar area at El Huacachinero, a favorite of young travelers in Laguna de Huacachina.*

premises, too. San Francisco 227. ☎ 056/535-218. www.villamanuelitahostal.com. 16 units. $30 double. No credit cards. Map p. 121.

kids **Hostería Suiza** LAGUNA DE HUACACHINA This homey and comfortable *hostal* at the edge of the lagoon is a good value. Rooms are a bit Spartan but clean, and some overlook the water. The outdoor pool and flower-filled gardens are a nice bonus at this price. The inn operates its own desert sand buggy excursions. Balneario de Huacachina. ☎ 056/238-762. hostesuiza@terra.com.pe. 22 units. $45 double. AE, DC, MC, V. Map p. 121.

★ **kids** **Hotel Las Dunas Sun Resort** OUTSKIRTS OF ICA This sprawling complex of white Mediterranean-style villas has nicely landscaped grounds, three swimming pools, and plenty of sports opportunities, including horseback riding, golf, tennis, and sandboarding. Rooms are large and nicely furnished; most have garden views. There's even a planetarium with a Nasca Lines show. Av. La Angostura 400. ☎ 056/256-224, or 01/241-8000 for reservations. www.lasdunashotel.com. 106 units. S/366–S/458 double Sun-Thurs, S/449–S/561

double weekend; S/760–S/890 suite. AE, DC, MC, V. Map p. 121.

kids **Hotel Mossone** LAGUNA DE HUACACHINA A century-old mansion and former luxury resort, this was once *the* place in Huacachina, but today it feels a little uncared for. Rooms are in need of updating, but the restaurant, with a relaxing deck overlooking the oasis, is a great place to relax. Balneario de Huacachina. ☎ 056/236-136. reservas@derramajae.org.pe. 43 units. $86 double. AE, DC, MC, V. Map p. 121.

★★★ **kids** **Hotel Paracas** BAHÍA DE PARACAS This large, Mediterranean-style hotel on the bay was given a recent makeover as an upscale Starwood property. Airy and beachy, it has great views of the water and a glamorous infinity pool, lounge bar and deck, and spa. The upgraded rooms have either bay or garden views and small terraces. Family options include a children's playground, kayaks, and paddleboats. Av. Paracas s/n, Reserva Nacional de Paracas. ☎ 056/581-333. www.starwoodhotels.com. 120 units. $225–$465 double; $625 suite. AE, DC, MC, V. Map p. 121.

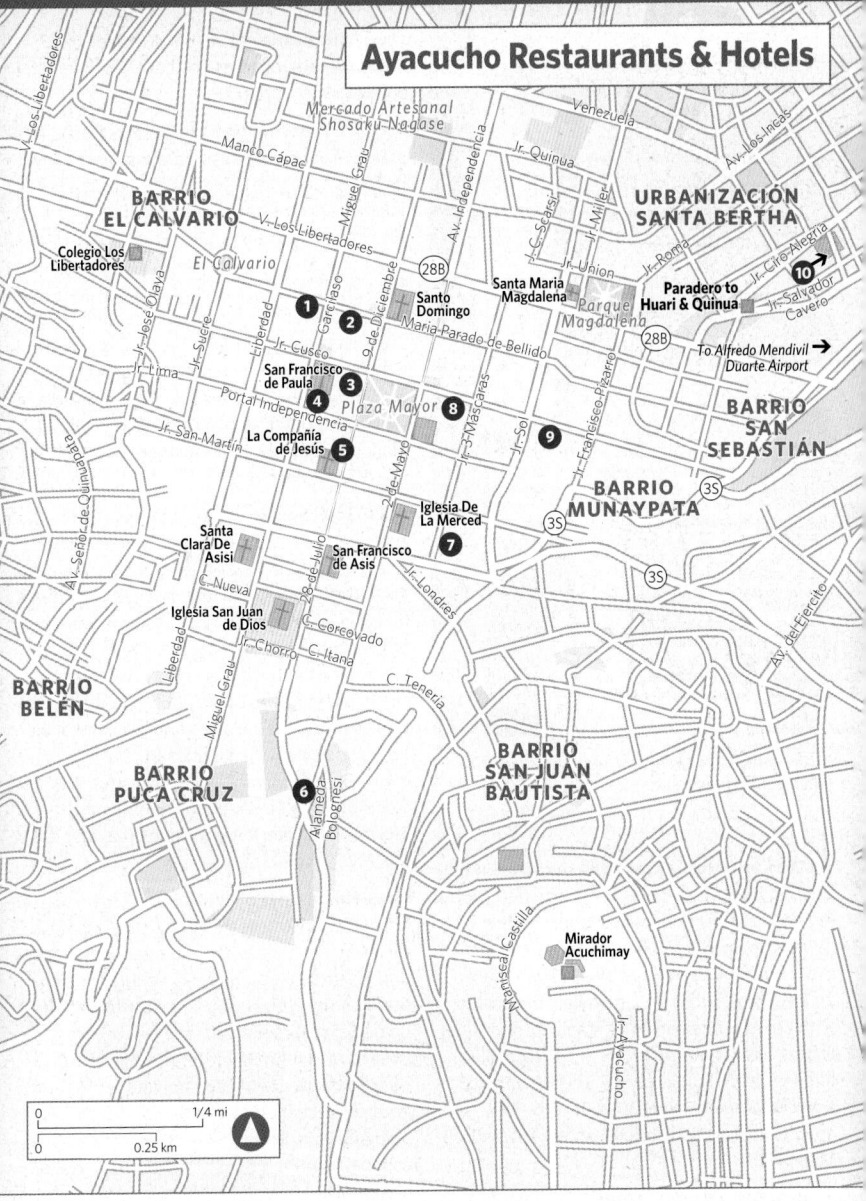

Ayacucho Restaurants & Hotels

RESTAURANTS

Antonino **8**

Café Bar New York **5**

El Monasterio **5**

La Casona **2**

Wallpa Sua **1**

HOTELS

Hostal El Marqués de Valdelirios **6**

Hostal La Florida **9**

Hostal Las Américas **10**

Hotel Santa Rosa **4**

Hotel Tres Máscaras **7**

Via Via Ayacucho **3**

> *The whitewashed villas of Hotel Las Dunas Sun Resort, just outside Ica.*

Nasca

★★ **kids Casa Andina Classic Nasca** DOWNTOWN
Though the largest hotel in Nasca, this charming and very dependable property on the pedestrian mall feels like a small inn and is great for families. Rooms overlook an open-air interior corridor and are nicely decorated, with colorful interiors. The small outdoor pool is next to the restaurant and a bougainvillea-filled patio. Jr. Bolognesi 367. ☎ 056/523-563. www.casa-andina.com. 60 units. $69–$99 double. Rates include breakfast. AE, DC, MC, V. Map p. 125.

★ **Hotel Alegría** DOWNTOWN
The most popular inexpensive hotel in town and a mainstay of backpackers. Rooms are a little Spartan, but bonuses include a leafy patio garden, small pool, travel agency, and loads of facilities and services, including free Internet access for guests, bus-station pickup, and luggage storage. Lima 168. ☎ 056/522-497.

www.hotelalegria.net. 43 units. $60 double. Rate includes breakfast and bus station transfer. DC, MC, V. Map p. 125.

★★★ **kids Hotel Cantayo Spa & Resort** OUTSKIRTS This grand, mission-style former hacienda is now a serene and sprawling spa hotel. Spacious rooms have Asian touches, and the grounds have mountain views, a huge swimming pool, extensive gardens, and a jogging track. Activities include tai chi, yoga, and Japanese meditation, as well as horseback riding. The restaurant is tops in Nasca. Ctra. Puquio-Cusco (4km/2½ miles southwest of Nasca). ☎ 056/522-264, or 056/522-283 for reservations. www.hotelcantayo.com. 40 units. $190 double; $272 suite. Rates include breakfast. AE, DC, MC, V. Map p. 125.

★ **kids Hotel Majoro** MAJORO (NEAR AIRPORT)
A revived, rustic old hacienda along a dusty road beyond the airport, this country inn has a great deal of charm, with large gardens full of bougainvillea and spacious accommodations built around courtyards. Families and those suffering from the desert heat will appreciate the two large, gardenlike pools. Online promotions sometimes include good package deals for Nasca Lines overflights and other excursions. Ctra. Panamericana Sur Km 452. ☎ 056/522-481. www.hotelmajoro.com. 39 units. $95–$140 double. Rates include breakfast. AE, DC, MC, V. Map p. 125.

Hotel Nazca Lines DOWNTOWN
Once the most upscale hotel in town, today this is merely a decent option, but it does have unusual amenities: old tennis courts and a planetarium with Nasca Lines presentations named for María Reiche (see p. 109), who lived here in room no. 130 for many years. There's also a good-size pool and rooms with good air-conditioning but dated furnishings. Jr. Bolognesi s/n. ☎ 056/522-293. nazca@invertur.com.pe. 34 units. $85–$101 double. DC, MC, V. Map p. 125.

Ayacucho

★ **Hostal El Marqués de Valdelirios** SOUTH OF DOWNTOWN Though a 10-minute walk from the Plaza Mayor, this handsome colonial house has real character. Rooms, all on the interior, don't quite live up to the promise of the exterior, but for the bargain price, they're

> *Rooms at the well-run Casa Andina Classic Nasca overlook a leafy central courtyard.*

more than comfortable. Breakfast is served on the sunny terrace. **Alameda Valdelirios 720.** ☎ 066/318-944. 14 units. S/75 double. Rate includes breakfast. MC, V. Map p. 127.

★ Hostal La Florida DOWNTOWN

This small, family-run *hostal* is relaxed and friendly, and just three blocks from the main square. It's secure, quiet, and clean; rooms on the top floor across the small, leafy courtyard have good views of the surrounding rooftops and mountains. **Jr. Cusco 310.** ☎ 066/812-565. 12 units. S/60 double. No credit cards. Map p. 127.

Hostal Las Américas QUINUA

In the tiny village of Quinua, this small *hostal* has four comfortable rooms above the house of one of the best-known local artisans. **Jr. San Martín s/n (above Artesanía Anclla).** ☎ 066/965-7721. S/30 double. MC, V. Map p. 127.

★ Hotel Santa Rosa DOWNTOWN

While all of the colonial character is in the magnificent arcaded courtyards and exterior—the rooms could use a serious update in style, starting with the bedspreads—this is still a recommended place to stay. It's got Wi-Fi and a great central location, and the courtyard is a splendid place for breakfast on a sunny morning. **Jr. Lima 166.** ☎ 066/312-083. www.hotel-santarosa.com. 38 units. S/130 double. Rate includes breakfast. No credit cards. Map p. 127.

★★ Hotel Tres Máscaras DOWNTOWN

One of the best deals in town is this exceedingly friendly *hostal* built around a plant-filled courtyard with soothing distant views of the mountains. Rooms are *muy* comfortable and clean, making this fresh-air retreat a true bargain for budget travelers. **Jr. Tres Máscaras 194.** ☎ 066/312-921. 14 units. S/50 double. No credit cards. Map p. 127.

★★ Via Via Ayacucho DOWNTOWN

This Belgian/Dutch traveler's *hostal* in reality is a pretty stylish boutique hotel right on the gorgeous main square, with stunning views and nicely equipped rooms named for regions of the world. There's a good restaurant and a rooftop sun terrace. **Portal Constitución 4.** ☎ 066/312-834. www.viaviacafe.com. 10 units. S/110–S/120 double; S/150 suite. No credit cards. Map p. 127.

Southern Desert Coast & Central Highlands Fast Facts

Arriving

To get to the southern desert coast, the only option is land travel (bus). **Ormeño** (☎ 01/472-5000; www.grupo-ormeno.com.pe) and **Cruz del Sur** (☎ 01/311-5050; www.cruzdelsur.com.pe) travel from Lima to Pisco, Ica, and Nasca. **Transportes Soyuz** (☎ 01/265-0501; www.soyuz.com.pe) travels between Pisco and Ica (as well as Lima) and is the fastest and best service (with the most frequent departures) from either city. Frequent colectivos travel to Ica from Pisco.

To get to Ayacucho, the best means is to fly from Lima on **Star Peru** (☎ 01/705-9000; www.starperu.com) or **LC Busre** (☎ 01/619-1313; www.lcbusre.com.pe); both offer daily, 1-hour flights. **Ormeño** and **Cruz del Sur** (see above) operate executive service buses from Lima via Pisco or Ica, which take 9 hours on a demanding road through the mountains.

ATMs/Cashpoints

ATMs aren't as common along the southern coast as in big cities, but major banks around the Plazas de Armas are all equipped with ATMs.

Currency Exchange

There are often cambistas, or money exchangers, hovering around the main squares. **Banco de Crédito** is the major bank that exchanges money. In Pisco, Pérez Figuerola 162 (☎ 056/532-954); in Ica, Av. Grau 109 (☎ 056/233-711); in Nasca, Av. Miguel Grau at Jr. Lima (☎ 056/522-445); in Ayacucho, Unión 27 (Plaza Mayor) (☎ 066/522-445).

Doctors

PISCO EsSalud, San Francisco 322 (☎ 056/532-784), and Hospital San Juan de Dios, Av. San Juan de Dios 350 (☎ 056/532-332). ICA Hospital Félix Torrealba Gutiérrez, Bolívar 1065 (☎ 056/234-798), and Hospital de Apoyo, Camino a Huacachina s/n (☎ 056/235-231). NASCA EsSalud, María Reiche 308 (☎ 056/522-438), and Hospital de Apoyo, Callao s/n at Av. Ignacio Morsesky (☎ 056/

522-586). AYACUCHO Hospital Regional de Ayacucho (Central), Av. Independencia 355 (☎ 066/312-180).

Emergencies

The general police emergency number is ☎ **105;** for fire, dial ☎ **116.** See also police telephone numbers below for individual towns. Call the national **24-hour traveler's hotline** (☎ 01/574-8000). The **INDECOPI** 24-hour hotline can also assist in contacting police to report a crime (☎ 0800/42579 toll-free).

Internet Access

Cafes internet (cybercafes) are widely available in the main towns, particularly around the Plazas de Armas, and larger hotels are equipped with Wi-Fi. Perhaps best equipped for travelers is the one at Hotel Alegría in Nasca (p. 128).

Pharmacies

PISCO InkaFarma and Botica Fasa pharmacies are on Beatita de Humay, nos. 519 and 521. ICA InkaFarma and Botica Fasa pharmacies are on Av. Municipalidad, nos. 244 and 249. NASCA InkaFarma is at Jr. Lima 596. AYACUCHO InkaFarma is at Jr. 28 de Julio 250, and Farmacia del Pino is at Jr. 28 de Julio 123.

Police

PISCO San Francisco, Plaza de Armas (☎ 056/532-165). ICA Lambayeque, block 1 (☎ 056/224-553). NASCA Av. Los Incas, block 1, next to the roundabout on Lima and Panamericana Sur (☎ 056/522-442). AYACUCHO Jr. 2 de Mayo 100 at Jr. Arequipa (☎ 066/312-055) and Jr. 28 de Julio 325 (☎ 066/312-332).

Post Office & Mail

PISCO Av. Bolognesi 173 (☎ 056/220-208). ICA San Martín 156 (☎ 056/234-549). NASCA Fermín de Castillo 379. AYACUCHO Jr. Asamblea 295 (☎ 066/312-224).

Safety

Near Pisco, Playa El Chaco, where boats depart for Islas Ballestas, is known for pickpockets after dark. Some Ica streets beyond the

> *The fortress of Tambo Colorado was key to the Incas' transportation network connecting the coast to Cusco.*

colonial center can be dangerous and should be avoided by solo travelers (if doing a winery tour, it's better to go by taxi than attempt to walk to those closest to Ica). Ayacucho, despite its many years of being under siege by the Sendero Luminoso (Shining Path) terrorist group, is now completely safe.

Telephone

The local area codes are: Pisco, 056; Ica, 056; Nasca, 056; Ayacucho, 066. There are Telefónica del Perú offices in Pisco at Bolognesi 298; in Ica at Jr. Huanuco 289; and in Nasca at Lima 545.

Visitor Information

PISCO Plaza de Armas (☎ 056/532-525). ICA Grau 150 (☎ 056/227-287). NASCA Callao 783, Plaza de Armas (☎ 056/522-418). AYACUCHO tourist counter in the airport and iPerú office, Portal Municipal 48, Plaza Mayor (☎ 066/818-305).

Along the southern desert coast, the best source of visitor information is most often the many local travel agencies in each town (even though they're primarily concerned with selling tours).

6
Arequipa &
Colca Valley

Favorite Arequipa & Colca Valley Moments

The southern city of Arequipa is Peru's most elegant. Founded in 1540, it retains a historic center built almost entirely of *sillar* (porous, white volcanic stone), which gives the city its distinctive look and the nickname La Ciudad Blanca (White City). Colonial churches and mansions, a spectacular Plaza de Armas, and one of the country's true treasures, the 16th-century Santa Catalina convent, gleam beneath palm trees and year-round sun. Within easy reach of Arequipa are volcanoes; deep canyons; and valleys that hold tiny, ancient villages, tradition-bound peoples, and endless opportunities to explore the outdoors and view magnificent Andean condors, which soar above Colca Canyon.

> PREVIOUS PAGE *Agricultural terraces of the Colca Valley.* THIS PAGE *An Andean condor.*

❶ Coming under the spell of Santa Catalina. Peru's greatest religious monument, this 16th-century convent of cloistered nuns is an architectural feast. During the day, the interplay of sunlight and shadows, brilliant bursts of color, and splendid isolation from the city beyond make for an incredible aesthetic experience. A visit at night, with candles and fires burning in cells, is even more magical. See p. 136, ❶.

❷ Dining Arequipeño-style. Arequipa's indigenous, often spicy cuisine is among the most distinguished and delicious in Peru. While there are several standout traditional restaurants on the outskirts of Arequipa, my favorite place is Chicha, famed chef Gastón Acurio's new venture, a delightful restaurant occupying a sprawling *sillar* colonial mansion. See p. 154.

❸ Seeing giant Andean condors soar overhead. There's no better place in the world to see giant Andean condors, magnificent birds with wingspans of up to 3.5m (11½ ft.). At Cruz del Cóndor in Colca Canyon, the spectacle of these creatures circling on thermal currents as they gain altitude and head down the river is mesmerizing. See p. 145, ❽.

❹ Strolling Arequipa's historic quarter. Arequipa is called the White City because nearly its entire historic quarter is carved out of *sillar*, porous white stone from the nearby volcanoes. The collection of elegant churches and *casonas* (mansions) provides a lesson in colonial architecture. See p. 139, ❼.

❺ Pondering the fate of Juanita. The famous discovery of a remarkably preserved Inca maiden, sacrificed more than 5 centuries ago and found buried in ice high on Mount

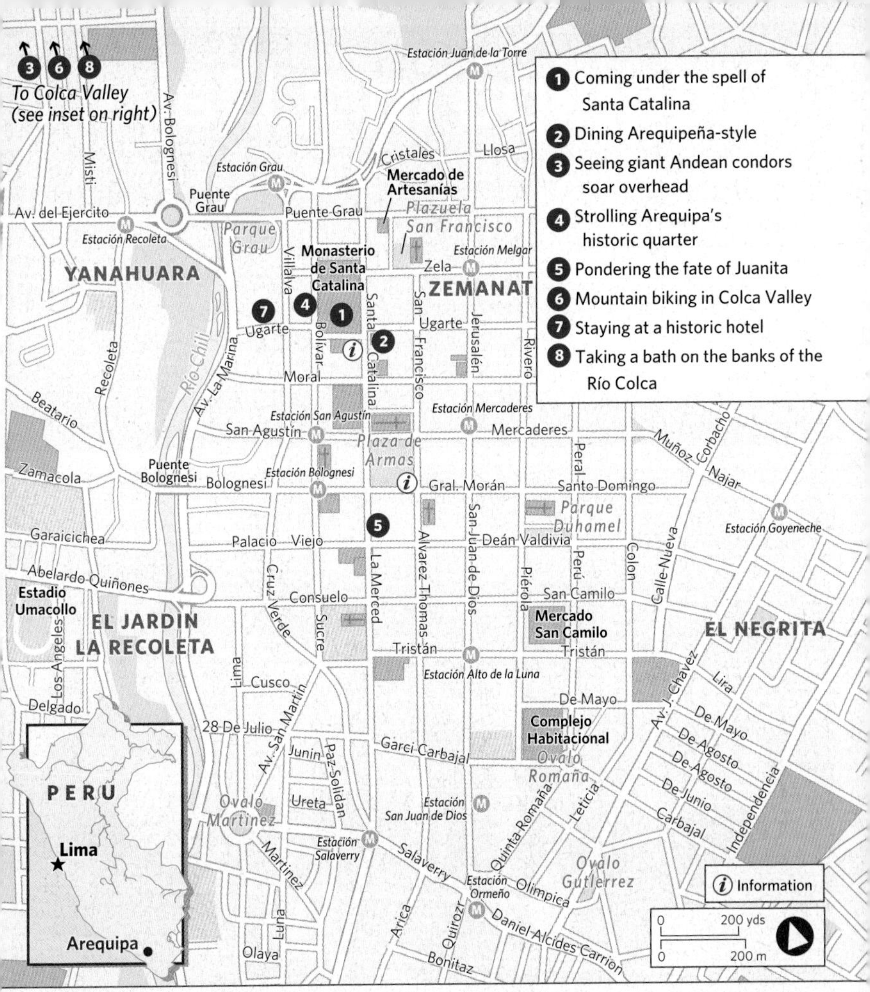
3 6 8
To Colca Valley (see inset on right)
Estación Juan de la Torre
1 Coming under the spell of Santa Catalina
2 Dining Arequipeña-style
3 Seeing giant Andean condors soar overhead
4 Strolling Arequipa's historic quarter
5 Pondering the fate of Juanita
6 Mountain biking in Colca Valley
7 Staying at a historic hotel
8 Taking a bath on the banks of the Río Colca
Av. Bolognesi
Misti
Estación Grau
Puente Grau
Av. del Ejercito
Estación Recoleta
Cristales
Llosa
Mercado de Artesanías
Puente Grau
Plazuela San Francisco
Parque Grau
Monasterio de Santa Catalina
Estación Melgar
Zela
YANAHUARA
Villalva
ZEMANAT
Ugarte
Santa Catalina
San Francisco
Ugarte
Jerusalén
Rivero
Bolívar
Recoleta
Río Chili
Av. La Marina
Moral
Beatario
Estación San Agustín
Estación Mercaderes
San Agustín
Mercaderes
Plaza de Armas
Muñoz
Corbacho
Najar
Zamacola
Puente Bolognesi
Bolognesi
Estación Bolognesi
Gral. Morán
Santo Domingo
Peral
Parque Duhamel
Estación Goyeneche
Garaicichea
Palacio Viejo
San Juan de Dios
Deán Valdivia
Colon
Calle Nueva
Abelardo Quiñones
Cruz Verde
La Merced
Alvarez Thomas
Piérola
Perú
Estadio Umacollo
Consuelo
San Camilo
EL JARDIN
LA RECOLETA
Sucre
Mercado San Camilo
EL NEGRITA
Los Angeles
Tristán
Tristán
Lima
Cusco
Estación Alto de la Luna
Av. J. Chavez
Lira
Delgado
De Mayo
De Mayo
28 De Julio
Av. San Martin
Complejo Habitacional
De Agosto
De Agosto
Junin
Paz Solidan
Garci Carbajal
Ovalo Romaña
De Junio
PERU
Ovalo Martinez
Ureta
Estación San Juan de Dios
Quinta Romaña
Leticia
Carbajal
Independencia
Lima
Estación Salaverry
Salaverry
Martinez
Ovalo Gutlerrez
Information
Estación Ormeño
Olimpica
Arica
Quiroz
Luna
0 200 yds
0 200 m
Daniel Alcides Carrion
Arequipa
Olaya
Bonitaz

Ampato, is an incredible window onto Inca culture. Juanita graced the pages of *National Geographic* and can now be seen at the Museo Santuarios Andinos. See p. 138, 3.

6 Mountain biking in Colca Valley. Extreme sports fans are drawn to Colca's volcanoes and deep canyons for mountain climbing, white-water rafting, and hardcore trekking. But I'm partial to racing down on single track—normally populated by llamas—on mountain bike, starting at Patapampa, an elevation of more than 4,877m (16,000 ft.). See p. 148.

7 Staying at a historic hotel. Arequipa's historic quarter is beautiful to stroll, but a real treat is to stay in a historic mansion made of *sillar.* At the top end is one of Peru's finest hotels, Casa Andina Private Collection; more accessible but no less charming is La Casa de Melgar Hostal. See p. 158 and 160.

8 Taking a bath on the banks of the Río Colca. The stone pools of Colca Lodge's thermal hot springs—perched right on the banks of the river—are far and away the best place to take a load off after a canyon hike or mountain biking expedition in Colca Valley. See p. 161.

Arequipa in 3 Days

Citizens of Arequipa have, justly or unjustly, earned a reputation for thinking themselves different or more sophisticated than their compatriots to the north in Lima. Certainly their city's historic center, constructed almost entirely of white volcanic stone, looks distinct from the rest of Peru, and Arequipa's splendid cuisine is also unique. Ringing the city, in full view, are three towering, delightfully named volcanoes: El Misti, Chachani, and Pichu Pichu. And suiting its reputation as an outdoor paradise, Arequipa enjoys perfect weather: more than 300 days a year of sunshine, huge blue skies, and low humidity. In 3 relaxed days, you can see the best of Peru's White City.

> The main altar of Arequipa's Catedral, the centerpiece of the Plaza de Armas.

START **Arequipa is 766km (476 miles; a 1-hr. flight) from Lima; begin in Centro Histórico, on Santa Catalina 301.**

❶ ★★★ kids **Convento de Santa Catalina.** One of Peru's most glorious sights, this historic monastery transports visitors to another time and nearly another place. Behind the thick *sillar* walls you'll feel as though you're in southern Spain. The convent was founded in 1579 under the Dominican order, and it remained a mysterious world unto itself until 1972. A cross between a village and military fortress, it's a labyrinth of narrow cobblestone streets, plant-lined passageways, plazas, fountains, chapels, and secret niches and quiet corners. Walls painted sunburned orange, cobalt blue, and brick red hide dozens of

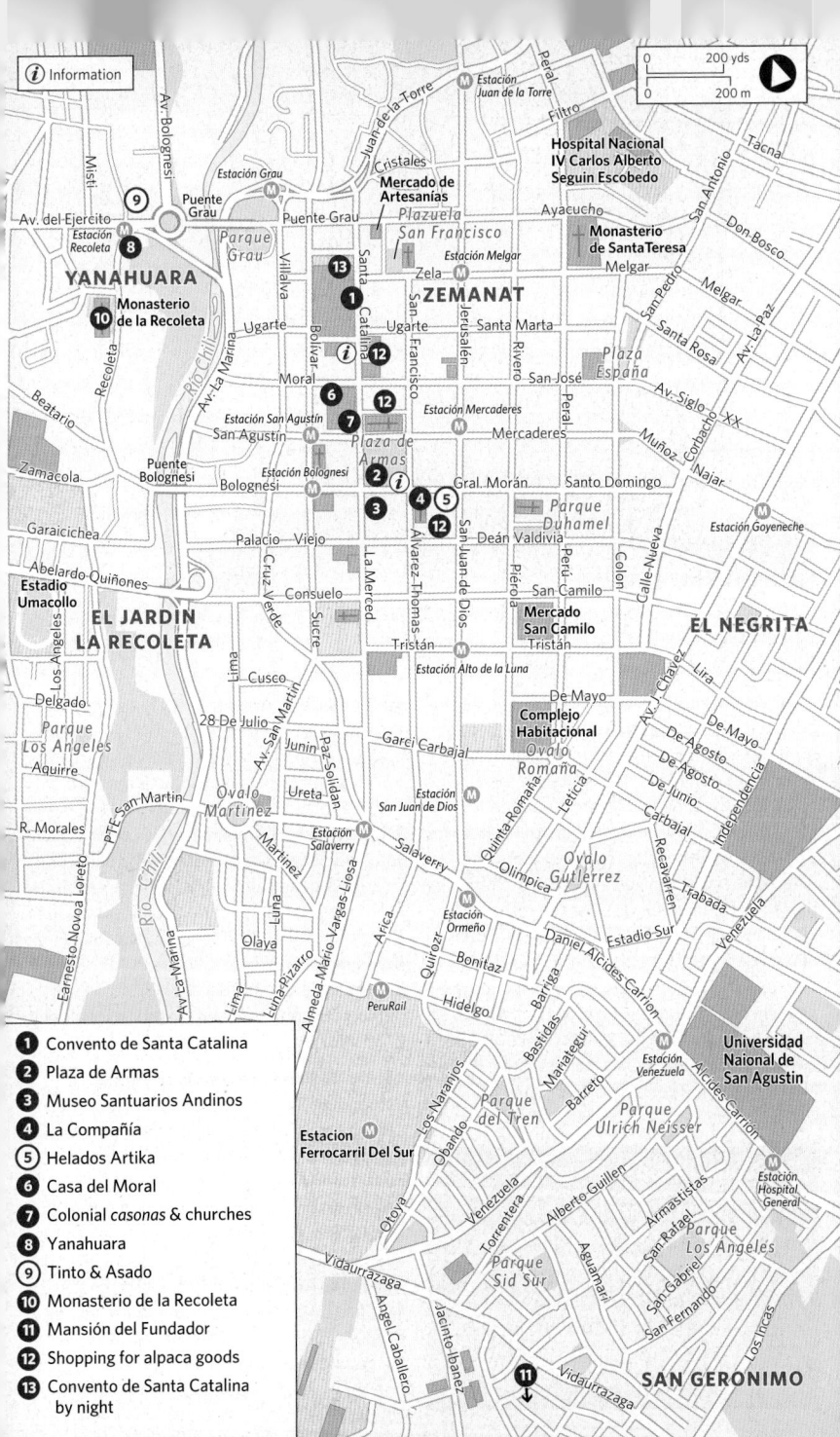

Information ⓘ

0 ────── 200 yds
0 ────── 200 m

Av. Bolognesi
Estación Grau
Puente Grau
Av. del Ejercito
⑨
Ⓜ
Estación Recoleta
⑧
Parque Grau
Puente Grau
Puente Grau
Cristales
Juan de la Torre
Estación Juan de la Torre
Peral
Filtro

YANAHUARA

Monasterio de la Recoleta
⑩

Recoleta
Rio Chili
Av. La Marina
Beatario
Zamacola
Garaicichea
Abelardo Quiñones
Estadio Umacollo

EL JARDIN LA RECOLETA

Los Angeles
Delgado
Av. San Martin
Parque Los Angeles
Aquirre
R. Morales
PTE San Martin
Rio Chili
Ernesto Novoa Loreto
Av. La Marina

Puente Bolognesi
Villalva
Ugarte
Moral
San Agustín
Estación San Agustín
Bolognési
Estación Bolognesi
Palacio
Viejo
Consuelo
Cruz Verde
Sucre
Lima
Cusco
28 De Julio
Junin
Ovalo Martinez
Ureta
Martinez
Estación Salaverry
Ⓜ
Luna Pizarro
Luna
Olaya
Alameda Mario Vargas Llosa
Paz Soldan

Santa Catalina
Bolívar
San Francisco
ⓘ ⑫
⑥
⑦ ⑫
Estación Mercaderes
San Agustín
⑬ ①
ZEMANAT
Ugarte
Santa Marta
Jerusalén
Rivera
San José
Mercaderes
Mercaderes
Santo Domingo
Plaza de Armas
② ⓘ
③ ④ ⑤
Gral. Morán
⑫
Alvarez Thomas
San Juan de Dios
La Merced
Tristán
Estación Alto de la Luna
Garci Carbajal
Estación San Juan de Dios
Ⓜ
Salaverry
Arica
Quiroz
Bonitaz
Estación Ormeño
Olimpica
Hidelgo
PeruRail
Ⓜ

Mercado de Artesanías
Plazuela San Francisco
Estación Melgar
Zela
Melgar

Peral
Deán Valdivia
Perú
San Camilo
Mercado San Camilo
Tristán
De Mayo
Complejo Habitacional
Ovalo Romaña
Quinta Romaña
Letica
Daniel Alcides Carrion
Estadio Sur

Ayacucho
Melgar
Monasterio de SantaTeresa
Hospital Nacional IV Carlos Alberto Seguin Escobedo

Tacna
Don Bosco
San Antonio
San Pedro
Santa Rosa
Av. La Paz
Av. Siglo XX
Muñoz
Najar
Corbacho
Plaza España
Parque Duhamel
Estación Goyeneche
Colon
Calle Nueva

EL NEGRITA

Lira
Av. J. Chavez
De Mayo
De Agosto
De Junio
Carbajal
Ovalo Gutiérrez
Recavarren
Trabada
Venezuela
Independencia

Parque del Tren
Los Naranjos
Mariategui
Barreto
Bastidas
Estación Venezuela
Ⓜ
Alcides Carrion

Universidad Naional de San Agustin

Estacion Ferrocarril Del Sur
Ⓜ

Parque Ulrich Neisser
Alberto Guillen
Obando
Otoya
Venezuela
Torrentera
Aguamari
Vidaurrazaga
Angel Caballero
Jacinto Ibañez
Parque Sid Sur
Armastistas
San Rafael
San Gabriel
San Fernando
Parque Los Angeles
Estación Hospital General
Ⓜ
Los Iricas

⑪
↓

SAN GERONIMO

① Convento de Santa Catalina
② Plaza de Armas
③ Museo Santuarios Andinos
④ La Compañía
⑤ Helados Artika
⑥ Casa del Moral
⑦ Colonial *casonas* & churches
⑧ Yanahuara
⑨ Tinto & Asado
⑩ Monasterio de la Recoleta
⑪ Mansión del Fundador
⑫ Shopping for alpaca goods
⑬ Convento de Santa Catalina by night

> *As many as 200 cloistered nuns, having taken vows of poverty, once lived in the cells of the Convento de Santa Catalina.*

small cells where more than 200 sequestered nuns once lived. (Today only 19 cloistered nuns ages 20–90 remain, mostly out of sight.) Among the convent's highlights are the Orange Tree Cloister, with murals painted over the arches; Calle Toledo, a long boulevard with a communal *lavandería* (laundry) at its end, where the sisters once washed their clothes in halved earthenware jugs; and the 17th-century kitchen with charred walls. Take an informative guided tour (for a tip of about S/20), or wander idly around discovering its niches, especially before or after the crowds arrive. ⏱ At least 2 hr. Santa Catalina 301. ☎ 054/608-282. www.santacatalina.org.pe. Admission S/30. Fri–Mon 9am–5pm; Tues–Thurs 8am–8pm.

The Nuns' Relative Poverty

Although in the early days Santa Catalina's nuns, all from wealthy Spanish families, entered the convent having taken vows of poverty, they lived in relative luxury, paying a dowry to live the monastic life along with servants (who outnumbered the nuns at Santa Catalina), full kitchens, and art collections.

② ★★ **Plaza de Armas.** Arequipa's grand Plaza de Armas is one of Peru's prettiest. Gardens and a central fountain are framed by arcaded buildings on three sides and the massive, 17th-century neoclassical **Catedral** (no phone; Mon–Sat 7–11:30am and 5–7:30pm, Sun 7am–1pm and 5–7pm) on the other. The cathedral interior is peach and white, with carved arches and a massive pipe organ. On the east side of the plaza (Portal de Flores 136), **Casona Flores del Campo** is the oldest house in Arequipa, begun in the late 1500s; sadly, today it's in deplorable condition and closed to the public. ⏱ 30 min.

③ ★★ kids **Museo Santuarios Andinos.** An astounding local discovery—a perfectly preserved Inca teenage maiden sacrificed on the summit of a volcano more than 500 years ago—is the highlight of this small museum. The museum features other mummies and artifacts from the Inca Empire but is dominated by that one tiny girl: Juanita, the so-called Ice Maiden of Ampato, the victim of a ritualistic sacrifice by Inca priests, found buried in ice at 6,380m (20,930 ft.). Discovered in impeccable condition in September 1995 by an expedition led by Johan Rhinehard, Juanita had been buried for more than 5 centuries (the eruption of a nearby volcano temporarily melted ice on the peak and facilitated the discovery). She was just 13 when she died from a violent blow to the head. Her remarkable preservation has allowed researchers to analyze her DNA and gain great insights into Inca culture. Guided visits begin with a *National Geographic* film on the discovery. ⏱ At least 1 hr. La Merced 110. ☎ 054/200-345. Admission S/15 adults, S/5 children, free for seniors. Mon–Sat 9am–6pm; Sun 9am–3pm.

④ ★ La Compañía. This late-17th-century Jesuit church is distinguished by an elaborate plateresque facade carved of *sillar* stone that includes a magnificent portal, one of the finest in Peru. Inside, you'll find a carved-cedar main altar bathed in gold leaf and two impressive chapels: the Capilla de San Ignacio, which has a remarkable painted cupola, and the Capilla Real, or Royal Chapel. ⏱ 30 min. General Morán at Álvarez Thomas. No phone. Free admission. Mon–Sat 9–11am and 3–6pm.

⑤ 🍴 **Helados Artika.** Arequipeños love their ice cream. Dip into this old-school ice-cream parlor next to the La Compañía church for a taste of the local *queso helado* (cheese ice cream made from sweet milk with a touch of cinnamon and coconut) or an exotic fruit flavor. General Morán 120. ☎ 054/284-915. Items S/2–S/5.

Start Day 2 by heading 2 blocks northwest of the Plaza de Armas.

⑥ ★★ Casa del Moral. The largest of Arequipa's colonial residences, this handsome baroque mansion, built in 1733 by a Spanish knight, is a great window onto colonial times. Named for the ancient mulberry tree in the courtyard, the home has a magnificent stone portal with heraldic emblems carved in *sillar* and a collection of attractive furnishings, carved wooden doors, and Cusco School oil paintings decorating large salons. The roof has a great view of Arequipa and the surrounding volcanoes. ⏱ 45 min. Moral 318 (at Bolívar). ☎ 054/210-084. Admission (guided tour) S/5 adults, S/3 students. Mon–Sat 9am–5pm; Sun 9am–1pm.

> The carved stone facade of Parroquia de Yanahuara, across the river from Arequipa.

SITE GUIDE PAGE 141

⑦ ★★ Colonial *casonas* & churches. In addition to Casa del Moral and La Compañía, the historic quarter of Arequipa is filled with fine colonial mansions and churches, most within easy walking distance of the Plaza de Armas.

Take a taxi or 30-minute walk from downtown Arequipa across Puente Grau and Río Chili, and up Av. del Ejército.

⑧ ★ 🧒 Yanahuara. One of the best views in Arequipa is from the elevated *mirador* in the tranquil suburb of Yanahuara. Next to the delightful **Plaza de Yanahuara**—its tall palm trees and lovely gardens making it a pleasant place to duck out of Arequipa's intense sun—are *sillar* stone arches that beautifully frame the volcanic peaks of El Misti and Chachani. Across from the *mirador* is the **Parroquia de Yanahuara,** Plaza de Yanahuara (no phone; daily 8am–4pm), a 1730 church also built of *sillar* and featuring a splendid baroque carved facade and bell tower with a long, single nave and vaulted ceiling. ⏱ At least 2 hr. (including walk).

Facing the church, head across the square.

⑨ 🍴 **Tinto & Asado.** This amiable bar-restaurant has a relaxing terrace with terrific views of El Misti, as well as happy-hour drinks. Cuesta del Olivo 318. ☎ 054/272-380. Items S/9–S/15.

adults, S/3 students, free for seniors. Mon–Sat 9am–noon and 3–5pm.

Take a 20-minute taxi ride to the outskirts of Huasacache.

⑪ ★★ Mansión del Fundador. In the peaceful countryside district of Huasacache is one of the most important colonial estates in Arequipa, said to have been constructed by the founder of Arequipa, Manuel de Carbajal, for his son. The *sillar* mansion features terrific vaulted ceilings and a large interior patio. ⏱ At least 2 hr. (including transportation). 9km (5½ miles) south of Arequipa. ☎ 054/442-460. Admission S/10. Daily 9am–5pm.

⑫ ★ Shopping for alpaca goods. Arequipa is perhaps the number-one spot in Peru—better even than Cusco and Lima—to shop for top-quality vicuña-fleece and woolen goods. My favorite spots are the **La Compañía cloisters,** General Morán (climb to the top for great views of the city's rooftops and distant volcanoes); **Pasaje Catedral,** the pedestrian mall just behind the cathedral; and **Casona de Santa Catalina,** Santa Catalina 210 (☎ 054/281-334), a colonial patio with several nice shops. ⏱ At least 1 hr.

⑬ ★★★ kids Convento de Santa Catalina by night. I can't get enough of Santa Catalina, no matter how many times I visit. For an especially transfixing experience, visit at night, when wood fires and flickering candles illuminate the convent cells and huge kitchen (better yet, come in the early evening as the sun sets). If you are enthralled during the day, trust me, it's special and unique to visit at night and wander about the place in total silence, discovering new niches you may have missed. See p. 136, ❶.

> The colonial home Mansión del Fundador, near Arequipa, once belonged to the city's founder.

Start Day 3 with a 10-minute walk from the Plaza de Armas across Puente Bolognesi and Río Chili.

⑩ ★ kids Monasterio de la Recoleta. Founded in 1648 and rebuilt after earthquakes, this Franciscan convent, distinguished by a tall, white-and-brick-red steeple, contains impressive cloisters with *sillar* columns and gardens. The museum holds pre-Inca culture artifacts, mummies, a series of paintings of the 12 Inca emperors, and curious items collected by Franciscan missionaries in the Amazon basin—souvenirs that pose an interesting contrast to the Dominicans' fine library containing some 20,000 volumes, including rare published texts from the 15th century. ⏱ 1 hr. Recoleta 117. ☎ 054/270-966. Admission S/5

Earthquake City

Despite its ageless beauty, Arequipa has a history of natural disaster. The most recent devastating earthquake, which registered 8.1 on the Richter scale, struck the city and other points farther south in 2001. Although international reports at the time painted a picture of a city that had caved in on itself, thankfully that wasn't the case. The colonial, largely *sillar* core of the city survived intact, as elegant as ever.

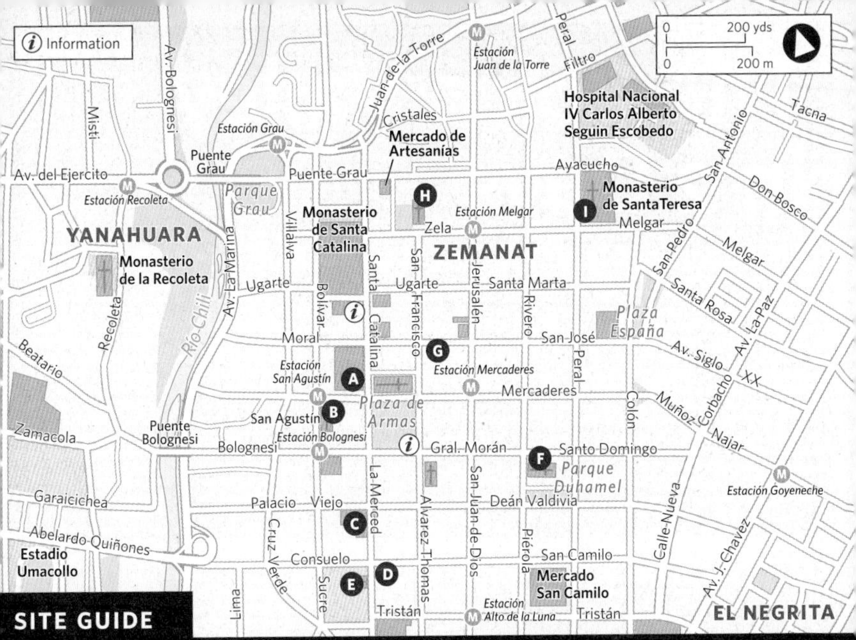

Map labels:

- Av.-Bolognesi
- Misti
- Estación Juan de la Torre
- Juan de la Torre
- Peral
- Filtro
- 0 — 200 yds
- 0 — 200 m
- Estación Grau
- Cristales
- Hospital Nacional IV Carlos Alberto Seguin Escobedo
- Tacna
- San Antonio
- Puente Grau
- Mercado de Artesanías
- Ayacucho
- Av. del Ejército
- Estación Recoleta
- Puente Grau
- Parque Grau
- Monasterio de Santa Catalina
- **H**
- Estación Melgar
- Zela
- Don Bosco
- Monasterio de Santa Teresa
- Melgar
- **I**
- YANAHUARA
- Villalva
- ZEMANAT
- San Pedro
- Melgar
- Monasterio de la Recoleta
- Santa Catalina
- San Francisco
- Ugarte
- Jerusalén
- Santa Marta
- Rivero
- Santa Rosa
- La Paz
- Recoleta
- Av. La Marina
- Ugarte
- ⓘ
- Moral
- Bolívar
- San José
- Plaza España
- Av. Siglo XX
- Río Chili
- Estación San Agustín
- **A**
- Estación Mercaderes
- Peral
- Av. Siglo XX
- Beaterio
- **B**
- Plaza de Armas
- Mercaderes
- Colón
- Muñoz Najar
- Zamacola
- San Agustín
- Estación Bolognesi
- ⓘ
- Gral. Morán
- **F** Santo Domingo
- Corbacho
- Puente Bolognesi
- Bolognesi
- San Juan de Dios
- Parque Duhamel
- Estación Goyeneche
- Garaicichea
- Palacio
- Viejo
- Deán Valdivia
- Calle Nueva
- Abelardo Quiñones
- **C**
- Cruz Verde
- Consuelo
- Piérola
- San Camilo
- Av. y. Chávez
- Estadio Umacollo
- **E**
- **D**
- Mercado San Camilo
- Lima
- Sucre
- Estación Alto de la Luna
- Tristán
- Tristán
- EL NEGRITA

SITE GUIDE

7 Colonial *Casonas* & Churches

Opposite the cathedral, the late-18th-century **A Casa Arróspide** (also called Casa Iriberry; at right), Santa Catalina 101 (at San Agustín), is one of the most distinguished *sillar* mansions in the city. Today, it's the cultural center of San Agustín University (☎ 054/204-482) and hosts exhibits of contemporary art and photography. It also houses an art shop and cafe with great views over the top of the cathedral. Though rebuilt in 1898 after earthquake damage and again restored, with an unfortunate new bell tower, in 2005, **B Iglesia de San Agustín,** San Agustín and Sucre, remains an excellent example of 16th- and 17th-century mestizo architecture, with a superbly stylized baroque facade. Handsome **C Casa Goyeneche,** La Merced 201, today houses the offices of Banco de Reserva. **D Casa Arango,** Consuelo and La Merced, is a squat and eclectic 17th-century home, while across the street, **E Iglesia de La Merced,** La Merced 303, built in 1607, boasts a lovely carved *sillar* facade and an impressive colonial library. **F Iglesia de Santo Domingo,** Santo Domingo at Piérola, is recognized for its handsome 1734 cloisters. Just off the main

square, at San Francisco 108, the former seminary **G Casa Ricketts** (also called Casa Tristán del Pozo) is today the offices of Banco Continental. Built in the 1730s, it features a beautiful portal with delicate representations of the life of Jesus. Inside are two large courtyards with gargoyle drainage pipes. A couple blocks north, **H Iglesia de San Francisco,** Zela 103, built of *sillar* and brick in the 16th century, is renowned for its impressive all-silver altar and a beautiful vaulted ceiling. And finally, the newly restored **I Monasterio de Santa Teresa,** Melgar at Peral, of brilliant *sillar*, has a small museum and lovely outdoor terrace. ⊙ At least 2 hr.

The Colca Valley in 2 Days

Described by Mario Vargas Llosa, the Peruvian Nobel Prize-winning novelist, as the "Valley of Wonders," Colca is one of the most scenic regions in Peru: a land of imposing volcanoes, narrow gorges, stunning agricultural terraces that predate the Incas, and remote traditional villages. The biggest draw remains the spectacle of giant Andean condors soaring over Colca Canyon, which at 3,400m (11,160 ft.) is twice as deep as the Grand Canyon. Colonial-era villages on the left and right banks of the canyon are home to descendants of pre-Inca ethnic communities that have lived in the region for 2,000 years.

> Crowds gather daily at the Cruz del Cóndor mirador for sightings of Andean condors taking flight above the canyon.

START From Arequipa, take a bus, taxi, or car 160km (99 miles; 3–4 hr.) north along Ctra. 34A toward Chivay, the valley's main town, making two brief stops (**1** and **2**) on the way.

1 ★ **Reserva Nacional Salinas y Aguada Blanca.** On the road to Chivay (45km/28 miles outside of Arequipa), you'll pass through this national reserve of high-altitude grasslands, populated only by a dispersed collection of grazing alpacas and vicuñas, as well as geese, flamingos, and other wildlife. The road used to be torturous, but the section of unpaved and very bumpy travel is down from 120km (75 miles) to just 23km (14 miles). The reserve's visitor center (daily 8am–5pm) has maps of the region; informational exhibits on the region's ecology, flora, and fauna; and bathrooms.

Continue along Ctra. 34A for about 90km (56 miles) to a lookout point, where there are always groups of women selling sweaters, gloves, and other artisan crafts.

1. Reserva Nacional Salinas y Aguada Blanca
2. Mirador de los Andes
3. Chivay
4. Coporaque
5. Mirador de Ocolle
6. Lari

7. La Calera hot springs
8. Cruz del Cóndor
9. Cabanaconde
10. Choquetico stone
11. Maca
12. Yanque

To Cusco

0   5 mi

0   5 km

CORDILLERA DE CHILA

▲ Mismi
5,825

Sibayo

Tuti

Callalli

Canocota

Tapay

Río Colca

Madrigal

8 Cruz del Cóndor

Cabanaconde

To Majes Valley

Pinchollo

Lari

10 Choquetico

Maca

Ichupampa

Achoma

5 Mirador de Ocolle

Coporaque

Yanque

La Calera

Chivay

Pulpera

2 Patapampa
4,910

Salinas y
Aguada Blanca
National Reserve

1

▲ Hualca Hualca
6,025

▲ Sabancaya
5,976

▲ Ampato
6,288

To Arequipa

Ruins

Mismi
5,825 ▲ Peak (elevation in meters)

2 Mirador de los Andes. This spot, also called Patapampa, is the highest point (4,910m/16,110 ft.) before "descending" to the valley. If you hop off the bus here, you may have to catch your breath; the air's pretty thin. Ringed by eight snowcapped volcanoes, a small army of *apachetas* (tiny towers of piled stones) marks the spot locals considered closest to mountain *apus* (gods). Most if not all of these offerings, however, have been left behind by travelers. ⏱ 20 min.

Continue north on 34A for 27km (17 miles).

3 Chivay. Colca Valley's main hub, surrounded by extraordinary scenery, is a market town with the region's concentration of tourist services, including most restaurants and affordable hotels. There's an artisan's market and the attractive Plaza de Armas, the town's focal point. ⏱ 1 hr. Admission $12, collected at the entrance to town; you'll get a *boleto turístico* (tourist ticket) that serves as admission to a half-dozen sights in the region, including churches and the Cruz del Cóndor.

Travel to the right bank (north side) of Río Colca, 8km (5 miles) west of Chivay.

4 ★ Coporaque. Just across the river from Chivay, this sleepy village has the oldest church in the valley, the delightful **Templo de Coporaque,** with twin bell towers, built in 1569. ⏱ 30 min.

> *The restored 19th-century Templo de la Purísima Concepción, in the village of Lari.*

⑤ ★★ Mirador de Ocolle. Just outside Corporaque, on the way to Colca Lodge (p. 161), this stunning natural "amphitheater" is formed by agricultural terraces of varying shades of green. Especially in spring, it's a remarkable sight. ⏱ 20 min.

Exploring the Valley

Most travelers choose to visit Colca Valley on inexpensive and convenient 2- or 3-day organized tours (which travel with guides in minivans and smaller *combis*). For information on tour operators, see p. 163. Independent travel (by bus to Chivay, rental car, or with a hired car and driver) is considerably more challenging because you have to arrange transportation to places spread across the valley on bumpy, unpaved, or poorly paved roads. This 2-day tour includes the major sites that all the tours visit, but posits an independent schedule that travelers with their own transportation (bus, rental car, hired car and driver) could undertake (though in reality the order of your tour will depend largely on where you're staying).

⑥ ★ Lari. The primary attraction is Lari's splendidly simple 1886 church, **Templo de la Purísima Concepción de Lari.** Stark white with red trim, an orange-and-green portal, and double bell towers, it looks something like a rural Mexican church. The interior is full of colorful murals and paintings, while the entire altar is adorned with brilliant baroque murals and painted columns. If the church is locked, the shop next door has a key. ⏱ 30 min.

Walk 4km (2½ miles) northeast from Chivay, or take a *colectivo*.

⑦ ★ kids La Calera hot springs. The soothing and clean thermal baths just outside Chivay are a great way to end the day. Evening visits to the hot springs—large and occasionally crowded pools—allow visitors to bathe beneath a huge, star-filled sky. (The best hot-springs pools, though, are along the river at Colca Lodge; see p. 161). ⏱ 1 hr. No phone. Admission S/10. Daily 8am–8pm.

Start out early (via taxi, *colectivo*, or group tour) on Day 2 on the left bank (south side) of Río Colca in order to get to Cruz del Cóndor, 50km (31 miles) west of Chivay, by at least 8:30am.

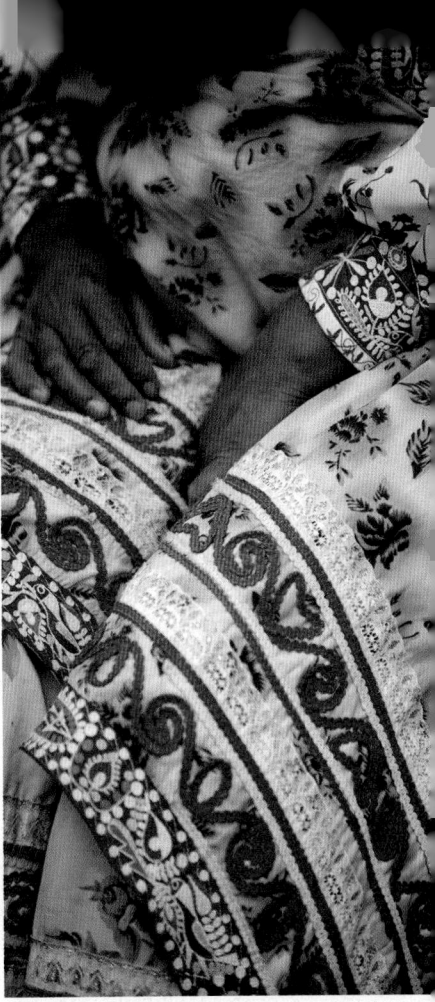

> The elaborate dress of Cabanas women features intricately embroidered skirts and sequined hats.

8 ★★★ kids **Cruz del Cóndor.** At a spot 1,200m (3,937 ft.) above the canyon river, large crowds gather every morning, zoom lenses poised, to witness a stunning wildlife spectacle. Beginning around 9am, graceful Andean condors (*Vultur gryphus*)—one of the largest species of birds in the world, with awesome wingspans of up to 3.5m (11½ ft.)—suddenly begin to appear, theatrically circling far below in the gorge and gradually gaining altitude with each pass, until they soar silently above the heads of awe-struck admirers before heading out along the river in search of prey. Condors are such immense and heavy creatures that they cannot simply lift off from the ground; instead, they take flight from cliff perches. Despite the lookout point's popularity, the sight is mesmerizing; no wonder the Incas believed the birds to be sacred creatures. The dry months of June through September are when you're likely to see the largest group of condors in flight. ⏱ At least 1 hr. By *colectivo* from the plaza in Chivay, or by taxi (S/50–S/60).

Head 18km (11 miles) west of Cruz del Cóndor.

9 ★ **Cabanaconde.** The last town in the Colca Valley, this remote, reserved village is gaining popularity among independent travelers, hikers, and backpackers as an alternative to Chivay. Some trekkers base themselves here and walk 15km (9⅓ miles) to Cruz del Cóndor (or it's 20 min. by bus); the village is also well positioned for other hikes in the canyon and throughout the valley. The views of the canyon are tremendous, and short walks take you to excellent vantage points overlooking some of the most brilliant agricultural terracing in the area. The locals are descendants of the Cabanas people, and they maintain traditional dress and customs; women wear hats embroidered with flowers and wide skirts. Ask at the tourist information office on the plaza for information about hikes and guides. ⏱ 45 min.

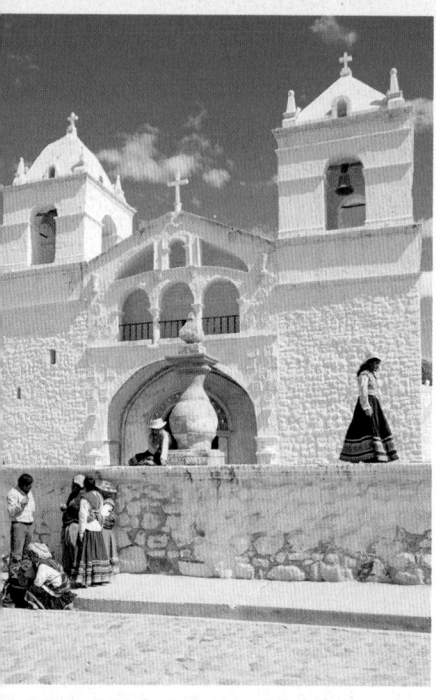

> *The pristine Santa Ana church, in Maca.*

Return (east) by *colectivo* or taxi along the main road from Cabanaconde to Chivay, stopping at a point beyond Cruz del Cóndor and Pinchollo and just before Maca.

⑩ Choquetico stone. Perched overlooking the river, this carved-stone scale model of the mountains across the canyon dates to pre-Inca peoples. You'll also see ancient Inca tombs carved out of the cliff face. ⏱ 15 min.

Continue east on the main road to just beyond Choquetico (24km/15 miles), west of Chivay.

⑪ ★ Maca. This small, unassuming village, nearly destroyed by a 1979 earthquake, is home to Santa Ana, a restored, brilliant white church with a surprising gilded interior. ⏱ 30 min.

Continue 14km (8¾ miles) on the main road to the last major town before Chivay.

⑫ Yanque. A modest town with a baroque 18th-century church, Imaculada Concepción. There's also a small museum about the region and a path just outside of town that leads to a picturesque, ancient stone bridge over the Río Colca. ⏱ 30 min.

Practical Information: Colca Valley

The Valle del Colca is generally thought of in terms of left (south) and right (north) banks of the canyon, with villages and hotels of interest on either side. Villages aren't separated by many kilometers, but the roads on both sides are unpaved and meandering, making for arduous and time-consuming driving. The left bank, which leads to Cruz del Cóndor, sees many more tourists.

The great majority of visitors to the Colca Valley and the canyon come on 2-day, 1-night guided tours, arranged in Arequipa. Conventional travel agencies offer day trips from Arequipa to Cruz del Cóndor, usually leaving at 3 or 4am, with a brief stop at Chivay before returning to Arequipa—such trips are an awful lot to pack into a single day, especially at a high altitude, and they leave no time to enjoy what makes the region unique (though you do arrive in time to see the condors at 8 or 9am). Expect to pay about $30 per person. Two-day "pool" (grouped) tours are much more enjoyably paced and cost $50 to $130, depending on hotel arrangements (they include transportation, a guide, hotel accommodations, and breakfast; other meals are extra).

Local buses travel from Arequipa to Cabanaconde (6 hr.), near Cruz del Cóndor, with a stop in Chivay (4 hr.). Two companies that make these runs are **La Reyna,** Terminal Terrestre, Arequipa (☎ 054/426-549), and **Cristo Rey,** San Juan de Dios 510, Arequipa (☎ 054/213-094). The ride costs S/15. Unless you have plenty of time and patience, or a real need to be on your own, your best bet for getting to Colca is to go with an organized group. Local *combis* also travel the main route, from Chivay to Cabanaconde, for example, but they are infrequent and time consuming. You can also hire a taxi in Chivay (best to hire for the day). See also "Arequipa & Colca Valley Fast Facts," p. 162.

Day Trips from Arequipa

The countryside just beyond Arequipa, known locally as ★ *la campiña,* is stunningly beautiful farmland in the shadow of towering volcanoes. Most visitors explore the countryside on a convenient, organized, 3-hour tour. Among the sights are **Paucarpata,** 7km (4⅓ miles) southeast of Arequipa, a pretty little town surrounded by Inca-terraced farmlands and, in the distance, El Misti volcano. Just down the road, the peaceful village of **Sabandía** is where many Arequipeños go on weekends to dine at country-style restaurants. For out-of-town visitors, the highlight of the village is a large, early-17th-century stone *molino,* a water-powered mill; the *molino* is on the same road as the **El Lago Resort,** Camino al Molino s/n, Sabandía (054/448-383), which is a good spot for lunch. There are several nice colonial estates in the surrounding countryside. The most famous is ★ **La Mansión del Fundador,** Huasache s/n, vía Paisajista Hunter (054/442-460, or 054/213-423 in Arequipa; www.lamansiondelfundador.com; S/10; daily 9am–5pm), a beautiful mansion in the suburb of Huasacache, 10km (6¼ miles) southeast of Arequipa. The house, once the property of Arequipa's founder, Don García Manuel de Carbajal, is handsomely outfitted with original antique paintings and furnishings. It's simplest to visit the mansion on an organized tour (p. 163), but if you choose to go on your own, catch a Sabandía *colectivo* from San Juan de Dios or Independencia, a few blocks from Arequipa's Plaza de Armas, or, much easier, take a taxi for S/15.

★ **Toro Muerto** (above), Ctra. Arequipa-Lima (desvío hacia Corire), Uraca district (S/5; hours vary)—about 3 hours (164km/102 miles) northwest from Arequipa and about 7km (4 miles) from the town of Corire—claims to be the world's largest field of petroglyphs. Carved on hundreds of volcanic boulders, the glyphs—of somewhat crude animal, human, and geometric representations—lie scattered in an area at least a couple of kilometers long. Most historians believe they were created by the Huari culture more than 1,000 years ago (and perhaps added to by subsequent peoples, including the Incas). The enormous scale and beautiful desert setting are most impressive, even more so than the individual drawings. There are an estimated 6,000 engraved stones at Toro Muerto, but many more stones are not carved, and searching for engraved ones requires considerable effort. The site draws few tourists given its distance from Arequipa and the difficulty getting there. General-service tour agencies in Arequipa arrange group trips to Toro Muerto for $85 to $95 per person, including transportation; see p. 163 for information. You can also hire a taxi from Arequipa at a cost of about $75 each way.

Colca Outdoor Adventures A to Z

Hiking & Trekking
The walks between the villages skirt the edge of the canyon and are gentle and beautiful. From **Chivay** to **Yanque** along the main road is about 7km (4.3 miles). You can continue from Yanque to the villages of **Achoma** (another 7km/4.3 miles), **Maca** (12km/7.5 miles), and **Pinchollo** (10km/6.2 miles). From there, on the way to Cabanaconde, it's about an hour to the **Colca Geyser** (Hatun Infiernillo).

Among the best adventurous hikes is a 2- to 3-hour, 1,300m (4,265-ft.) **descent into Colca Canyon** from the Cruz del Cóndor lookout. Because of the arduous, 6-hour climb back out, most travelers who do this hike end up camping at sites down below near the San-galle oasis, where there are palm trees and water suitable for swimming. Hikers to the canyon floor should be in very good physical condition and prepared with plenty of water, food, sunscreen, etc. Going with a guide is highly recommended.

Horseback Riding
A good alternative to trekking is to get a horse to do the hard work. Several hotels in the region, including Casa Andina Classic Colca (p. 161), Colca Lodge (p. 161), and Las Casitas del Colca (p. 161), organize easy-paced horse-back jaunts around the valley. It's also easy to organize one independently in Cabanaconde; ask at the tourism information office on the plaza.

Mountain Biking
One of the best rides is to start at the high point of Patapampa and descend on llama trails to Chivay. Casa Andina Classic Colca (p. 161) can arrange mountain bikes and guides.

Mountain & Volcano Climbing
The best months for climbing are July to September, although some peaks can be climbed year-round. Climbers should be sufficiently acclimatized before making any ascents. The most popular climb among both locals and visitors, **El Misti** (a nearly 6,000m/19,685-ft.

> *Horseback riding is one of the rewarding ways to get around the steep Colca Valley.*

> *Snowcapped volcanoes at more than 6,000m (19,685 ft.), such as Chachani and El Misti, are beacons for experienced mountain climbers.*

volcano), is a demanding 2- or 3-day trek with few technical challenges, suitable for inexperienced climbers accompanied by professional guides. Most climbers stay the first night at the base camp Nido de Aguilas (Eagle's Nest)

and reach the summit after about 7 hours of climbing on the second day. Arequipa's other major volcano, **Chachani** (6,075m/19,931 ft.), also presents an excellent and technically straightforward climb, a good opportunity for inexperienced climbers to brag about reaching a 6,000m (19,685-ft.) summit.

The Colca Valley has a number of peaks that draw serious climbers; these include the **Ampato** volcano (6,288m/20,630 ft.), a 3- or 4-day climb; the **Hualca Hualca** glacier (6,025m/19,767 ft.); and **Coropuna** (6,425m/ 21,079 ft.), perhaps the most stunning mountain in the Cotahuasi Valley, which requires a couple of days of travel from Arequipa.

River Rafting

The best months for rafting are May to September, when water levels are low. (In the rainy season, when water levels are high, canyon rivers can be extremely dangerous.) The most accessible rafting, suitable for first-timers (Class III and IV runs on a half-day trip), is on the **Río Chili,** just 15 minutes from downtown Arequipa. Year-round runs of similarly moderate difficulty and scenic beauty can be arranged on day trips to the **Río Majes** (the Río Colca beyond the gorge). Rafting in Cotahuasi and Colca canyons is serious stuff for confident rafters (from 3- to 12-day trips). **Río Colca** (Class IV–V) is extremely technical, although some upriver sections are less dangerous and difficult. **Río Cotahuasi** has 120km (75 miles) of Class IV and V rapids (and some Class VI).

Arequipa Shopping

Alpaca Goods

★ Alpaca 111 CENTRO HISTÓRICO
This shop, part of an all-Peru chain, has some of the country's most consistent designs in sweaters, scarves, and shawls. Zela 212.
☎ 054/223-238. AE, DC, MC, V.

★ Incalpaca CENTRO HISTÓRICO & TAHUAYCANI
These factory outlets are good spots to get last season's items at discounted prices. One is in town, within the cloisters courtyard of La Compañía. The other, about 10 minutes outside of town in the Tahuaycani district, even has a small zoo of camelids to entertain the kids while parents shop for alpaca as well as rare and expensive vicuña items. La Compañía: General Morán at Álvarez Thomas. ☎ 054/205-931. Tahuaycani: Juan Bustamante s/n.
☎ 054/251-025. AE, DC, MC, V.

★★ Kuna CENTRO HISTÓRICO
A somewhat hipper line from Alpaca 111, this fashionable shop with two branches has more contemporary designs for men and women.

> *Many of Peru's finest manufacturers of alpaca goods are based in Arequipa.*

Santa Catalina 210. ☎ 054/282-485; Calle Mercaderes 141 ☎ 054/225-550. AE, DC, MC, V.

Millma's Baby Alpaca CENTRO HISTÓRICO
This friendly little shop has more homespun designs than places such as Kuna, but it's a good place for jackets, coats, and sweaters for both sexes. Pasaje Catedral 177. ☎ 054/205-134. MC, V.

Antiques

★ Álvaro Valdivia Montoya CENTRO HISTÓRICO
This longtime antiques dealer has two

Arequipa's Top Shopping Areas

Newly pedestrian-only **Calle Mercaderes** has become the city's top shopping avenue, but you should also check out the **cloisters** next to La Compañía church, where there are a number of alpaca boutiques and outlets; **Pasaje Catedral,** the pedestrian mall just behind the cathedral; and **Santa Catalina,** where you'll find dozens of shops lining the street and the colonial patio **Casona de Santa Catalina,** a mini-mall of sorts.

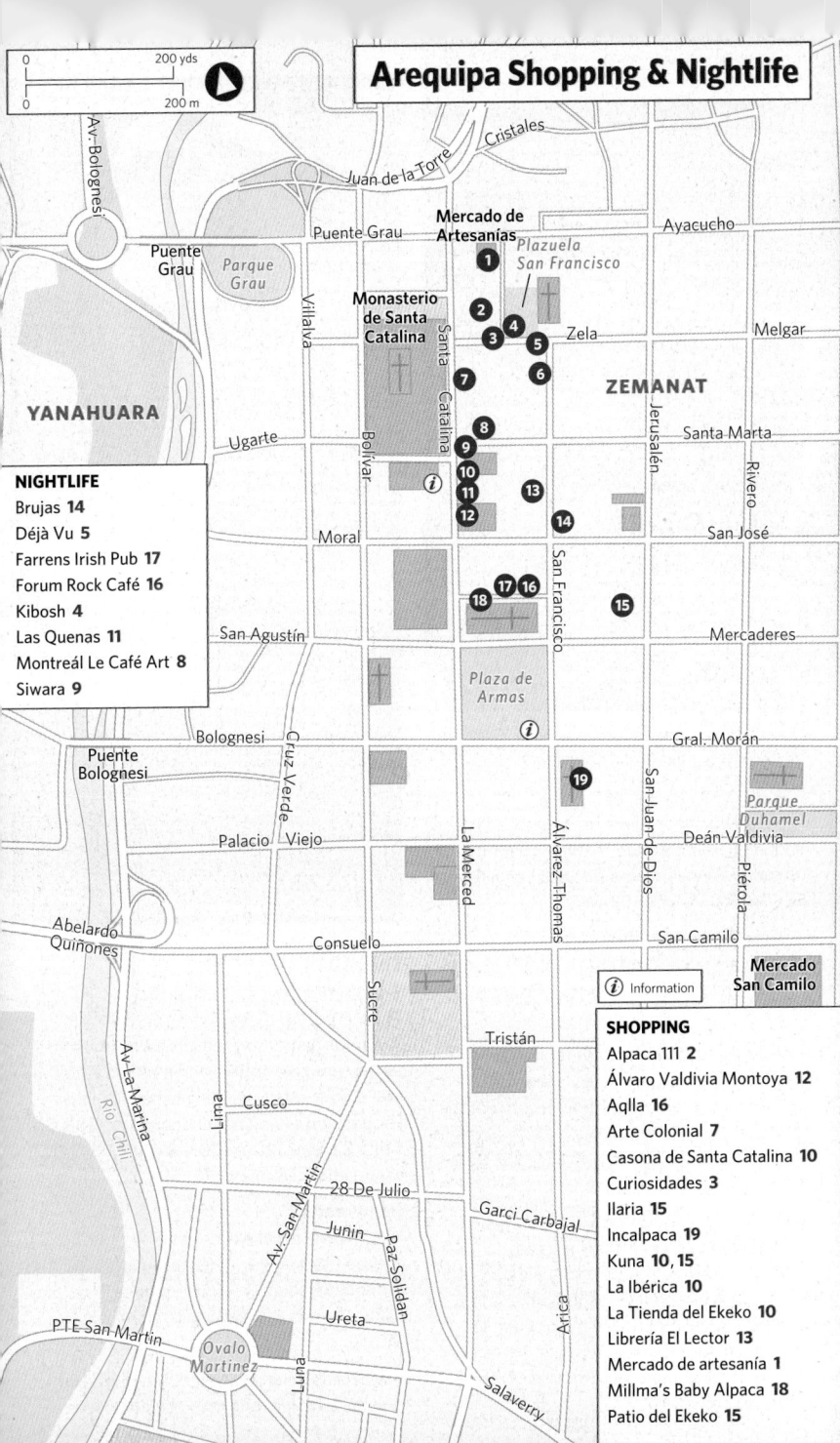

Arequipa Shopping & Nightlife

NIGHTLIFE

Brujas **14**
Déjà Vu **5**
Farrens Irish Pub **17**
Forum Rock Café **16**
Kibosh **4**
Las Quenas **11**
Montreál Le Café Art **8**
Siwara **9**

SHOPPING

Alpaca 111 **2**
Álvaro Valdivia Montoya **12**
Aqlla **16**
Arte Colonial **7**
Casona de Santa Catalina **10**
Curiosidades **3**
Ilaria **15**
Incalpaca **19**
Kuna **10**, **15**
La Ibérica **10**
La Tienda del Ekeko **10**
Librería El Lector **13**
Mercado de artesanía **1**
Millma's Baby Alpaca **18**
Patio del Ekeko **15**

> *The* sillar *courtyard of Casona de Santa Catalina houses fine boutiques and restaurants.*

Collaguas & Cabanas

These two ancient peoples, descendants of pre-Inca inhabitants of the region, speak different languages. They can be distinguished by their hats: Aymara-speaking Collagua women wear tall straw hats with colored ribbons, while Quechua-speaking Cabanas sport elaborately embroidered and sequined, flat and round felt headgear. (The men once wore distinctive dress as well, but today are decidedly less colorful.) Colca villages are also celebrated for their vibrant festivals, which remain as authentic as any in Peru, throughout the year. The valley's meticulous agricultural terracing, even more extraordinary and extensive than the Inca terraces seen in the Sacred Valley near Cusco, were first cultivated more than 1,000 years ago.

well-stocked shops just a few blocks apart. You'll find art, ceramics, textiles, furniture, and more. Santa Catalina 204 and Santa Catalina 406. ☎ 054/229-103. MC, V.

★★ **Arte Colonial** CENTRO HISTÓRICO
A cool, warrenlike shop chock full of colonial-era and replica antiques. Santa Catalina 312. ☎ 054/214-887. MC, V.

Curiosidades CENTRO HISTÓRICO
The name means "curiosities," and you're apt to find several here, although some of the textiles might not be quite as old as you might be told to believe. Zela 207. ☎ 054/952-986. No credit cards.

Books
★ **Librería El Lector** CENTRO HISTÓRICO
A superb and friendly bookstore with art books, English-language paperbacks, and a good selection on Peruvian history and culture, including cooking and travel. There's a book exchange, too. San Francisco 221. ☎ 054/288-677. MC, V.

Chocolates
★ **La Ibérica** CENTRO HISTÓRICO
This century-old chocolate purveyor and Arequipa institution sells its own chocolates, *turrón* (nougat), toffee, and marzipan at several storefronts (including Lima). The first shop began selling hot chocolate in 1909. Santa Catalina 210, no. 103. ☎ 054/218-842. www.laiberica.com.pe. AE, DC, MC, V.

Handicrafts
★ **La Tienda del Ekeko** CENTRO HISTÓRICO
A shop brimming with Peruvian *artesanía* from around the country, from ceramics to textiles. Santa Catalina 210. ☎ 054/281-334. AE, DC, MC, V.

★ **Mercado de artesanía** CENTRO HISTÓRICO
A general handicrafts market with dozens of

Arequipa Nightlife

Bars & Pubs

★ **Brujas** A cozy little watering hole, popular with young locals and serving up good happy-hour drink specials. San Francisco 300. No phone.

Farrens Irish Pub In the alleyway behind the cathedral, this cool two-level joint has a pool table, rock and pop soundtrack, and good drink specials—making it very popular with visiting gringos. Pasaje Catedral 107. ☎ 054/238-465.

★ **Montreál Le Café Art** A cafe-pub that features an eclectic variety of live music Wednesday through Saturday and has extended nightly happy hours. Ugarte 210. ☎ 054/931-2796.

★ **Siwara** A great-looking beer tavern across from the Santa Catalina monastery that spills into two patios. Santa Catalina 210. ☎ 054/626-218.

Nightclubs

★ **Déjà Vu** Part bar and part nightclub, this spot is very popular with a mix of locals and gringos. It has a lively dance floor and English-language movies on a big screen every night. It is also known for its spectacular rooftop terrace, which is a good spot for drinks, dinner, or even breakfast after a long night of partying. San Francisco 319. ☎ 054/221-904.

★★ **Forum Rock Café** Equal parts restaurant, bar, disco, and concert hall, this huge place sports a rainforest theme, with jungle vegetation and "canopy walkways" everywhere. Live bands (rock or *rock en español*) take the stage Thursday through Saturday. San Francisco 317. ☎ 054/202-697.

Kibosh A chic, upscale pub with four bars, a wood pizza oven, dance floor, and live music Wednesday through Saturday (music ranges from Latin to hard rock). Zela 205. ☎ 054/626-218.

Peñas

★ **Las Quenas** This folkloric bar and restaurant features live Andean music Monday through Saturday, and special dance performances on Friday and Saturday nights. It's a cozy place that serves pretty good Peruvian dishes; many patrons treat it like a supper club. Santa Catalina 302. ☎ 054/281-115.

---

stalls located in the old town jail. It's a good spot to pick up inexpensive *chullos* (Peruvian-style woolen or alpaca-fleece caps with ear flaps) and scarves. Plazuela San Francisco (btw. Zela and Puente Grau). No phone. No credit cards.

Jewelry

★ **Aqlla** CENTRO HISTÓRICO
Cool artisanal designs in silver jewelry, at more accessible prices than the top shops such as Ilaria. There are also nice scarves and other gift items. Pasaje Catedral 112. No phone. MC, V.

★★ **Ilaria** CENTRO HISTÓRICO
Peru's top silver and gold jewelry dealer has a shop in the Patio del Ekeko. For exquisite quality and stylish designs, this is always a dependable stop. Mercaderes 141. ☎ 054/287-749. www.ilariainternational.com. AE, DC, MC, V.

Malls & Markets

★★ **Casona de Santa Catalina** CENTRO HISTÓRICO A handsome former colonial mansion, this chic "mall" contains several upscale boutiques with alpaca goods, handicrafts, and chocolates, built around a colonial courtyard. The excellent Chicha restaurant is also here, a perfect place for a lunch stop. Santa Catalina 210. ☎ 054/281-334. www.santacatalina-sa.com.pe. AE, DC, MC, V.

★ **Patio del Ekeko** CENTRO HISTÓRICO
A three-story indoor shopping mall on Arequipa's main pedestrian-only shopping boulevard that's the place for one-stop shopping. It's glitzy but has good upscale shops with reasonable prices on alpaca goods, handicrafts, jewelry, straw hats, and liquor. There are also food shops, a cafeteria, and a bar. Calle Mercaderes 141. ☎ 054/215-861. www.patiodelekeko.com.

Arequipa & Colca Valley Restaurants

Arequipa

★ **Arte y Comida** CENTRO HISTÓRICO *MEDITERRANEAN/TURKISH* Middle Eastern specialties are the calling card here, a long space carved out of *sillar* and opening onto a relaxing courtyard. In addition to vegetarian dishes, Turkish grilled meats, *sis kebaps,* and Mediterranean salads, you'll find Arequipeño dishes. San Francisco 315. ☎ 054/215-729. Entrees S/15–S/38. MC, V. Breakfast, lunch, and dinner daily. Map p. 155.

★ **Ary Quepay** CENTRO HISTÓRICO *AREQUIPEÑO* With a dining room under a bamboo roof and skylights, this down-to-earth restaurant specializes in traditional Peruvian cooking. Main courses are classic: *rocoto relleno* (minced-meat-stuffed spicy red peppers) and *adobo* (pork stew with *ají,* or spicy pepper). There's often live folkloric music. Jerusalén 502. ☎ 054/672-922. Entrees S/16–S/30. DC, MC, V. Breakfast, lunch, and dinner daily. Map p. 155.

★★★ **Chicha** CENTRO HISTÓRICO *AREQUIPEÑO* This stylish new restaurant in a colonial home is famed chef Gastón Acurio's take on Arequipeño cooking, its emphasis on local-accented fare labeled *"la tradición,"* such as *rocoto relleno* (stuffed spicy pepper). Chicha is quite reasonable for creative cooking with indigenous ingredients. Santa Catalina 210 (courtyard). ☎ 054/287-360. Entrees S/18–S/39. AE, DC, MC, V. Lunch and dinner Mon–Sat; lunch only Sun. Map p. 155.

★ **Crepisimo** CENTRO HISTÓRICO *CREPES* This little restaurant looks more like a bar or cafe but is a great spot for lunch, especially if you nab one of the tables on the interior courtyard and opt for the superb-value *menú*. Or, go à la carte and pick any of more than 100 varieties of sweet and savory crepes. Santa Catalina 208. ☎ 054/206-620. www.crepisimo.com. Entrees S/12–S/22. AE, DC, MC, V. Lunch and dinner daily. Map p. 155.

> *There are more than 100 varieties of crepes, both savory and sweet, on the menu at Crepisimo.*

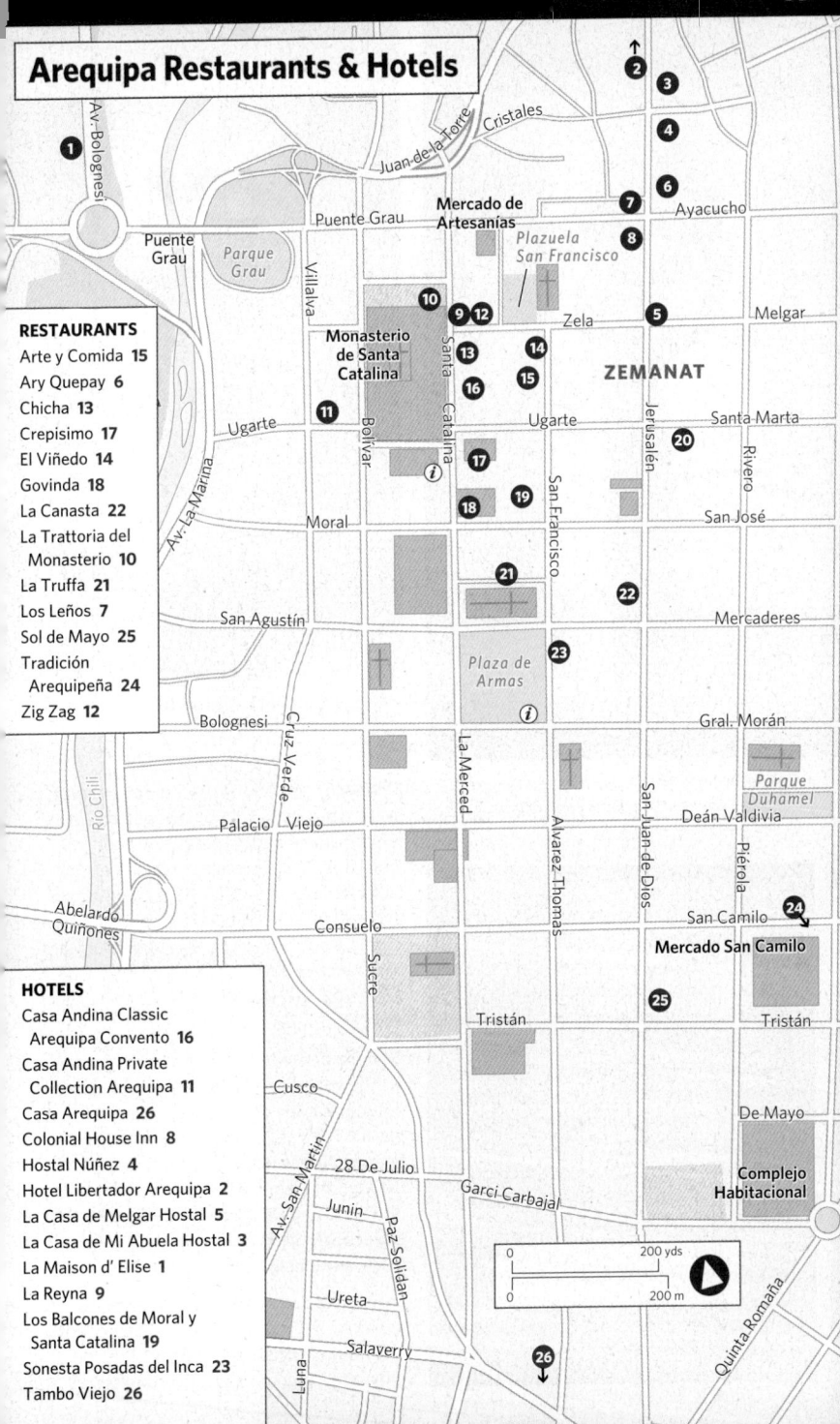

Arequipa Restaurants & Hotels

Mercado de Artesanías

Plazuela San Francisco

Monasterio de Santa Catalina

ZEMANAT

Plaza de Armas

Parque Duhamel

Mercado San Camilo

Complejo Habitacional

RESTAURANTS

Arte y Comida **15**
Ary Quepay **6**
Chicha **13**
Crepisimo **17**
El Viñedo **14**
Govinda **18**
La Canasta **22**
La Trattoria del Monasterio **10**
La Truffa **21**
Los Leños **7**
Sol de Mayo **25**
Tradición Arequipeña **24**
Zig Zag **12**

HOTELS

Casa Andina Classic Arequipa Convento **16**
Casa Andina Private Collection Arequipa **11**
Casa Arequipa **26**
Colonial House Inn **8**
Hostal Núñez **4**
Hotel Libertador Arequipa **2**
La Casa de Melgar Hostal **5**
La Casa de Mi Abuela Hostal **3**
La Maison d' Elise **1**
La Reyna **9**
Los Balcones de Moral y Santa Catalina **19**
Sonesta Posadas del Inca **23**
Tambo Viejo **26**

0   200 yds
0   200 m

> Chicha, by famed chef Gastón Acurio, is one of Arequipa's most sophisticated restaurants.

Chivay Dining

Although most visitors eat all meals at their hotels, several restaurants, mostly in Chivay, play host to lunchtime tourist groups that come through town. **Witite,** Calle Siglo XX 328 (☎ 054/531-036), has a respectable Andean menu. **Solar Rosario,** Calle Arequipa 504 (☎ 054/531-133), is a nice-looking spot that offers a buffet lunch, and **Casablanca,** Plaza de Armas 705 (☎ 054/521-019), serves a good-value *menú* (prix-fixe meal) and a handful of vegetarian dishes. For a little dinner theater, *peña*-style, check out **El Encanto del Colca,** Calle Mariscal Castilla 500 (no phone), down a little side street in Chivay. Good folkloric *peña* music and alpaca dinners can also be found at **El Nido,** Zarumilla 216 (☎ 054/531-010), around the corner from El Encanto.

> The pizza oven at homey Los Leños, a favorite of young travelers and families.

El Viñedo CENTRO HISTÓRICO *ARGENTINE/ GRILL* This rustic yet refined spot is heaven for carnivores and does a pretty good job with its *parrilladas* (mixed grills). There's a free salad bar as well as "Argentine" pizzas and pastas. In addition to the candlelit dining rooms, there's a nice little garden courtyard. San Francisco 319-A. ☎ 054/205-053. Entrees S/10–S/33. AE, DC, MC, V. Lunch and dinner daily. Map p. 155.

Govinda CENTRO HISTÓRICO *VEGETARIAN* A little vegetarian restaurant with a pleasant outdoor garden dining area and good-value *menús*. The vegetarian Italian, Asian, and Peruvian items make it a nice change for travelers tired of chicken and pork. Breakfast is great. Santa Catalina 120. ☎ 054/285-540. Entrees S/6–S/20. No credit cards. Breakfast, lunch, and dinner daily. Map p. 155.

La Canasta CENTRO HISTÓRICO *BAKERY/ BREAKFAST* This neat little lunch and break-fast nook is not a place to linger, but you can get pizzas, empanadas (stuffed pastries), and hamburgers, as well as excellent breakfast items. Jerusalén 115. ☎ 054/287-138. Entrees S/5–S/9. No credit cards. Breakfast, lunch, and dinner daily. Map p. 155.

★★ **La Trattoria del Monasterio** CENTRO HISTÓRICO *ITALIAN* A chic place carved out of a thick *sillar* wall of the Santa Catalina convent, this is an excellent spot to linger over a dinner of Italian favorites such as risotto, lasagna, ravioli, and *osso buco.* You'll also find a good selection of wines, great desserts, and attentive service. Santa Catalina 309. ☎ 054/204-062. Entrees S/22–S/32. AE, DC, MC, V. Lunch and dinner Mon–Sat; lunch only Sun. Map p. 155.

La Truffa CENTRO HISTÓRICO *ITALIAN* Tucked behind the cathedral on a small alleyway, this homey restaurant focuses on homemade pastas and good pizzas, but also serves well-prepared fish dishes. The rooftop tables are the most sought-after during nice weather. Pasaje Catedral 111. ☎ 054/242-010. Entrees S/12–S/30. DC, MC, V. Lunch and dinner Mon–Sat. Map p. 155.

kids **Los Leños** CENTRO HISTÓRICO *PIZZERIA* A little pizza cave with long wooden tables, this joint feels like a college tavern, with the graffiti of travelers covering the stone walls. The house specialty is pizza from the wood-fired oven. Also choose among 20 different "American breakfasts." Jerusalén 407. ☎ 054/289-179. Entrees S/8–S/18. No credit cards. Breakfast, lunch, and dinner daily. Map p. 155.

★★ **Sol de Mayo** YANAHUARA *PERUVIAN/ AREQUIPEÑO* The standard-bearer for Arequipeño cooking, this longtime favorite has a delightful setting with a courtyard and elegant dining rooms inside the *sillar* building. Great for a leisurely lunch of authentic Arequipeño specialties, such as *chicharrón de chancho* (fried pork) and ostrich. Jerusalén 207 (Yanahuara is a 5-min. taxi from downtown). ☎ 054/254-148. Entrees S/15–S/48. AE, DC, MC, V. Lunch and dinner daily. Map p. 155.

★★ **Tradición Arequipeña** PAUCARPATA *AREQUIPEÑO* A classic open-air restaurant with gardens and views of the El Misti volcano from the upper deck, this lunch-only spot serves large portions of Peruvian and Arequipeño dishes, such as *cuy* (guinea pig), *adobo,* and ceviche. Prices are quite reasonable. Av. Dolores 111 (Paucarpata is a 10-min. taxi ride from downtown). ☎ 054/426-467. Entrees S/15–S/39. AE, DC, MC, V. Lunch daily. Map p. 155.

★★ **Zig Zag** CENTRO HISTÓRICO *SWISS/GRILL* "Alpandino" grilled meats and fondues are the calling card of this stylish restaurant in a two-level, *sillar*-walled space. The stone-grilled meats include ostrich and alpaca, both healthy alternatives to beef. Zela 210. ☎ 054/206-020. www.zigzagrestaurant.com. Entrees S/25–S/48. AE, DC, MC, V. Dinner daily. Map p. 155.

Evening at the Convent

A great plan for an evening in Arequipa is to visit Santa Catalina (p. 136, ❶) by night. Illuminated by candles and fires in the monastic cells and medieval kitchen, the convent takes on a mysterious air, and you'll often have the small niches and passageways almost to yourself (something virtually impossible during the day). Then continue your tour of the *sillar* walls by dining at La Trattoria del Monasterio, which is carved right into the thick outer ramparts of Santa Catalina.

> *Arequipeño regional specialties are the calling card of Sol de Mayo in Yanahuara.*

Arequipa & Colca Valley Hotels

Arequipa

★★ Casa Andina Classic Arequipa Convento

CENTRO HISTÓRICO In an 18th-century manor house that once belonged to Santa Catalina's nuns, this terrific midrange choice has vaulted *sillar* ceilings in common rooms, a pretty central patio, and a nice outdoor pool with sundeck. Rooms have been very nicely refurbished. Santa Catalina 300. ☎ 866/220-4434 toll-free in the U.S., or 054/226-907 in Peru. www.casa-andina.com. 47 units. $79–$119 double; $149 suite. Rates include breakfast. AE, DC, MC, V. Map p. 155.

★★★ Casa Andina Private Collection Arequipa

CENTRO HISTÓRICO In one of Arequipa's emblematic colonial buildings, the Mint House (a national historic monument), this is one of Peru's finest hotels. It has a boutique feel but all the services of a larger luxury hotel. It features *sillar* walls, lovely interior courtyards, and an elegant gourmet restaurant. Accommodations in the modern wing are understated and spacious, while the sprawling suites in the historic main house are sumptuous. Ugarte 403. ☎ 866/220-4434 toll-free in the U.S., or 054/226-907 in Peru. www.casa-andina.com. 41 units. $124–$208 double; $263–$494 suite. Rates include breakfast. AE, DC, MC, V. Map p. 155.

★ Casa Arequipa VALLECITO

This unusual boutique inn provides luxury at a bargain price. In a pink 1950s mansion in a quiet residential district, a short walk or cab ride from the Plaza de Armas, it has elegant guest rooms, comfortable beds, and swank linens. Av. Lima in Vallecito. ☎ 202/518-9672 in the U.S., or 054/284-219 in Peru. www.arequipacasa.com. 10 units. $65–$99 double. AE, DC, MC, V. Map p. 155.

Colonial House Inn CENTRO HISTÓRICO

A rambling 200-year-old house, this eclectic inn is perfect for budget travelers in search of

> *Casa Andina Private Collection Arequipa occupies an elegant* sillar *mansion that was once the Mint House.*

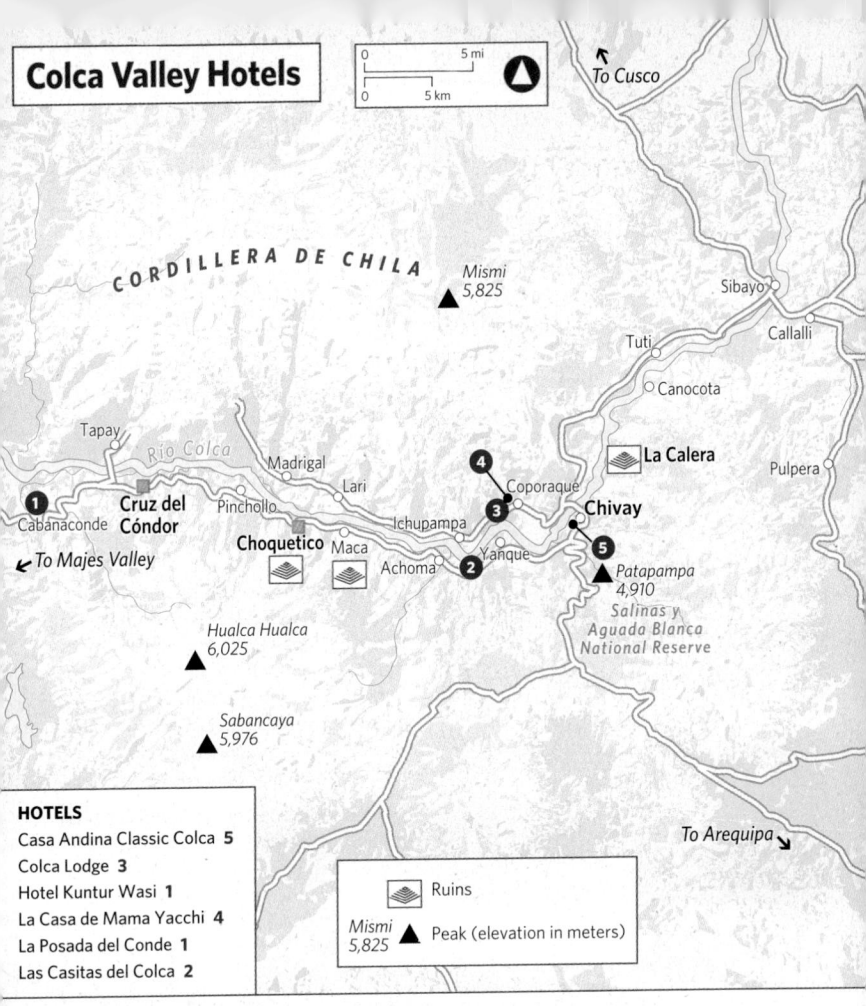

Colca Valley Hotels

HOTELS

Casa Andina Classic Colca **5**
Colca Lodge **3**
Hotel Kuntur Wasi **1**
La Casa de Mama Yacchi **4**
La Posada del Conde **1**
Las Casitas del Colca **2**

Ruins

Mismi 5,825 ▲ Peak (elevation in meters)

local flavor. It has a great rooftop terrace, large rooms, and good breakfasts in a little cafe area. Puente Grau 114. ☎ 054/223-533. www.colonialhouseinn-arequipa.com. 7 units. $18 double. No credit cards. Map p. 155.

Hostal Núñez CENTRO HISTÓRICO
Affordable and popular with budget travelers, this friendly *hostal* has colorful accommodations and congenial, plant-filled public rooms. A rooftop terrace has excellent views of the city. Single rooms are tiny. Jerusalén 528. ☎/fax 054/218-648. www.hotel-nunez.de. 7 units. $30 double. Rates include breakfast. No credit cards. Map p. 155.

★ kids **Hotel Libertador Arequipa** SELVA ALEGRE
No longer the city's most luxurious accommodations, this sprawling 1940s colonial-style hotel nevertheless is removed from the old-quarter hubbub and has soaring ceilings and older-style dark-wood period furnishings in huge, elegantly appointed rooms. Families will appreciate the pool and outdoor recreation and game area for kids. Plaza Bolívar, in Selva Alegre. ☎ 054/215-110. www.libertador.com.pe. 88 units. $125–$160 deluxe double; $185 suite. Rates include breakfast. AE, DC, MC, V. Map p. 155.

> *The planetarium at Casa Andina Classic Colca, in Chivay.*

★★ La Casa de Melgar Hostal CENTRO
HISTÓRICO This former residence of the bishop of Arequipa is the perfect place to stay if you're a fan of colonial architecture. The charming small hotel is set in a restored 18th-century colonial mansion and a terrific value. The best rooms are those on the ground floor that have high, vaulted brick ceilings. Melgar 108. ☎ 054/222-459, or 01/446-8343 for reservations. www.lacasademelgar.com. 30 units. $45 double. Rates include breakfast. V. Map p. 155.

★ La Casa de Mi Abuela Hostal CENTRO
HISTÓRICO This quirky place has grown from a tiny B&B operation into a popular hotel and self-contained tourism complex and miniresort, with a live-music *peña* bar and travel agency. Some of the simple rooms have roof terraces; others have balconies. Jerusalén 606. ☎ 054/241-206. www.lacasademiabuela. com. 50 units. $54 double; $66 suite. DC, MC, V. Map p. 155.

★ La Maison d' Elise YANAHUARA
Like a small Mediterranean village, with villas clustered around courtyards, this quirky hotel has large double rooms, matrimonial suites, and apartments with private terraces. Av. Bolognesi 104 (Yanahuara is a 5-min. taxi ride from downtown). ☎ 054/256-185. http:// aqplink.com/hotel/maison. 88 units. $70 double; $78–$96 suite. AE, DC, MC, V. Map p. 155.

La Reyna CENTRO HISTÓRICO
Popular with backpackers, this small hotel has rooms that feed off a labyrinth of narrow staircases climbing three floors to a roof terrace. There are dormitory rooms with rock-bottom prices for zero-budget travelers and a couple of rooftop casitas with their own terraces, offering great views of Santa Catalina convent below. No. 20 is the best of the lot. Zela 209. ☎ 054/286-578. 20 units. $10 double w/o bathroom, $12 double w/ bathroom; $6 single. No credit cards. Map p. 155.

★ Los Balcones de Moral y Santa Catalina
CENTRO HISTÓRICO An inviting small hotel that's a step up from budget hostels for not too much more money. Half the house is colonial (first floor); the other is Republican-era (1800s). Many rooms have hardwood floors and large balconies with views toward the cathedral; others are carpeted and less desirable (though quieter). Moral 217. ☎ 054/201-291. www.balconeshotel.com. 17 units. S/135 double. MC, V. Map p. 155.

★ Sonesta Posadas del Inca CENTRO
HISTÓRICO This chain hotel's location on the Plaza de Armas is its best feature. Rooms have a retro feel to them; executive rooms on upper floors have terraces under the porticoes with plaza views. There's also a nice little rooftop pool. Portal de Flores 116 (Plaza de Armas). ☎ 054/215-530. www.sonesta.com/arequipa. 58 units. $125 double; $140 deluxe double; $155 suite. Rates include breakfast. AE, DC, MC, V. Map p. 155.

Tambo Viejo MODERN AREQUIPA
This budget *hostal* occupies an old colonial family home that's a 15-minute walk south of the Plaza de Armas. Backpackers are drawn by word of mouth to the garden with sun terraces, cafe serving veggie breakfasts, book exchange, and TV lounge. Av. Malecón Socabaya 107. ☎ 054/288-195. www.tamboviejo. com. 20 units. S/55–S/92 double. Rates include breakfast and bus station pickup (with 2-night stay). DC, MC, V. Map p. 155.

Colca Valley

★★ kids **Casa Andina Classic Colca** CHIVAY
Chivay's nicest hotel, this easygoing, well-managed place has comfortable rooms with stone walls, thatched roofs, and cozy furnishings with thick wool blankets. Newer bungalow-style rooms are slightly larger. The restaurant features folk music and dance shows as well as a cool planetarium and telescope. Huayna Cápac s/n. ☎ 866/220-4434 toll-free in the U.S., or 054/531-020 in Peru. www.casa-andina.com. 52 units. $87 double. Rates include breakfast. AE, DC, MC, V. Map p. 159.

★★★ **Colca Lodge** YANQUE (RIGHT BANK)
This rustic but upscale eco-style property, on a beautiful bend in the river, has one feature no other lodge can match: its own private thermal baths, carved in stone right on the river bank. Continually expanding, the lodge features adobe, stone, and thatched-roof architecture, solar power, and a swank new spa. The views of the valley are excellent from nearly everywhere. Nonguests can experience the thermal pools for $10. Across the river from Yanque (about 10km/6¼ miles west of Chivay). ☎ 054/531-191. www.colca-lodge.com. 29 units. $181 double; from $284 suite. Rates include breakfast. AE, DC, MC, V. Map p. 159.

Colca Valley

Rustic upscale and more modest lodges beyond Chivay are dispersed through the valley, either on the right bank (north side) or left bank (south side) of the Río Colca. The other town with a number of *hostales* is Cabanaconde, the last town in the valley past Cruz del Cóndor. Outside of Chivay, the main town in the valley, most guests eat all their meals at their hotels.

★ **Hotel Kuntur Wasi** CABANACONDE (LEFT BANK) Quiet Cabanaconde is emerging as a Colca base for hikers and travelers who prefer not to be in Chivay or one of the fancy lodges. The top spot, on a hill above the village, this rambling small hotel has nicely decorated rooms with high ceilings, faux stone bathrooms, and plant-lined walkways. With a good restaurant and bar, it's a nice place to relax after a long hike. La Ladera 360. ☎ 054/812-166 or 054/812-166. www.kunturwassi.com. 25 units. $55 double; $70–$100 suite. MC, V. Map p. 159.

★★ **La Casa de Mama Yacchi** COPORAQUE (RIGHT BANK) Giardino Tours (p. 163) books its guests at this country inn. It has very comfortable rooms with exposed beams, great views, a fireplace lounge, and an attractive rustic restaurant featuring good local preparations. It's owned by the same folks who run La Casa de Mi Abuela Hostal in Arequipa. ☎ 054/241-206. www.lacasademamayacchi. com. 50 units. $70 double. Rates include breakfast. AE, DC, MC, V. Map p. 159.

La Posada del Conde CABANACONDE (LEFT BANK) Among the *hostales* in Cabanaconde, this is a pretty good low-end choice. Rooms are clean and have private bathrooms. San Pedro at Bolognesi. ☎ 054/440-197. 10 units. $25 double. AE, DC, MC, V. Map p. 159.

★★★ **Las Casitas del Colca** YANQUE (LEFT BANK) Part of the Orient Express chain and easily the most exclusive inn in the valley, this formerly low-key eco-lodge has gone upscale with a stunning transformation. Perched on the lip of the canyon, its extraordinary *casitas* (individual thatched-roof bungalows), the height of country luxury, are elegant and nestled about the property, with private terraces and plunge pools. They're joined by a spectacular spa and free-form swimming pool, solar energy and electricity, horseback riding, and a breakfast terrace with gorgeous valley views of extensive gardens, terraced fields, and the river. Parque Curiña s/n (outskirts of Yanque). ☎ 01/610-8300 or 054/959-672-480. www.lascasitasdelcolca.com. 20 units. $1,000 double. Rates include all meals and activities. AE, DC, MC, V. Map p. 159.

Arequipa & Colca Valley Fast Facts

Arriving

BY PLANE There are daily flights to Arequipa from Lima and Juliaca (near Puno) on **LAN** (☎ 01/213-8200; www.lanperu.com) and from Lima on the much cheaper **Peruvian Airlines** (☎ 01/716-6000; www.peruvian airlines.pe). Flights from Lima and Cusco start at about $109 one-way on LAN; Peruvian Airlines originated its service with offers as low as $59 one-way from Lima. **Aeropuerto Rodríguez Ballón,** Av. Aviación s/n, Zamácola, Cerro Colorado (☎ 054/443-464), is about 7km (4⅓ miles) northwest of the city. From the airport to downtown hotels, transportation is by taxi (S/15) or *colectivo* (about S/5 per person).

BY BUS The main **Terminal Terrestre,** Av. Andrés Avelino Cáceres at Av. Arturo Ibáñez s/n (☎ 054/427-798), is about 4km (2½ miles) south of downtown Arequipa. Nearby is a newer station, **Nuevo Terrapuerto,** Av. Arturo Ibáñez s/n (☎ 054/348-810). A huge number of bus companies travel in and out of Peru's second city from across the country, so ask if your bus departs from Terminal or Terrapuerto. Taxis are usually present at both stations. From Lima (16 hr.), recommended companies include **Ormeño** (☎ 01/472-5000; www.grupo-ormeno.com.pe), **Cruz del Sur** (☎ 01/311-5050; www.cruzdelsur.com.pe), **Civa** (☎ 01/418-1111; www.civa.com.pe), and **Oltursa** (☎ 01/708-5000; www.oltursa.com. pe). For service from Puno (5 hr.) and Juliaca, contact **Cruz del Sur** or **Civa. Ormeño** travels to Arequipa from Puno as well as Cusco. Other options from Cusco (10–12 hr.) are **Civa** and **Cruz del Sur. Reyna** (☎ 054/426-549) and **Cristo Rey** (☎ 054/213-094) handle service to Chivay/Colca Canyon (3–4 hr.).

ATMs/Cashpoints

You'll find ATMs in Arequipa in the courtyards of the historic Casa Ricketts at San Francisco 108, now the offices of **Banco Continental.** Other banks in the historic center include **Banco Latino,** at San Juan de Dios 112, and **Banco de Crédito,** at General Morán 101. There are Global Net ATMs in several shops around the Plaza de Armas; one is **Arequipa Inversiones,** Jerusalén 109.

Currency Exchange

Money-changers can generally be found waving calculators and stacks of dollars on Arequipa's Plaza de Armas and major streets leading off the main square. There are several *casas de cambio* (currency exchanges) around the Plaza de Armas.

Dentists & Doctors

If you need medical attention, go to **Clínica Arequipa,** Av. Bolognesi at Puente Grau (☎ 054/253-416), which has good service and English-speaking doctors. You can also try **Hospital General,** Peral s/n (☎ 054/231-818), or **Hospital Regional,** Av. Daniel Alcides Carrión s/n (☎ 054/231-818). For dental help, try **Clínica Dental,** Av. Ejército 208 (2do piso; ☎ 054/251-001).

Emergencies

The general emergency number in Arequipa is ☎ **105.** For fire emergencies, call ☎ **116.**

Internet Access

Arequipa has plenty of Internet *cabinas*. Most are open daily from 8am to 10pm, charge S/2 per hour, and have programs that allow very cheap Web-based international phone calls. Two of the cheapest and fastest *cabinas* are **La Red,** Jerusalén 306B (☎ 054/286-700), and **TravelNet,** Jerusalén 218 (☎ 054/205-548). Another good spot is **Catedral Internet,** in the small passageway behind the cathedral. An only slightly more expensive option that's open a bit later is **Catedral Internet,** Pasaje Catedral 101 (☎ 054/282-074), on the pedestrian mall just behind the cathedral.

Pharmacies

In Arequipa, **InkaFarma** pharmacies are at Calle Mercaderes 214, Av. Santo Domingo 113, and Puente Bolognesi 108; **Botica Fasa** pharmacies are at Calle Mercaderes 145 and Portal de la Municipalidad 122.

Police

The **Policía Nacional** (national police) are at ☎ 054/254-020; **Policía de Turismo** (tourist police) are in Arequipa at Jerusalén 315 (corner of Ugarte), ☎ 054/201-258.

Post Office & Mail

The main **Serpost** (post office) is located at Moral 118 (☎ 054/215-247). A **DHL** office is located at Santa Catalina 115 (☎ 054/220-045).

Safety

Arequipa's bus stations—and the buses themselves—are notorious for attracting thieves. Travelers are advised to pay very close attention to their belongings, even going so far as to lock them to luggage racks. The route between Arequipa and Puno, especially, has earned a bad reputation. Arequipa—which on the surface seems to be one of Peru's most placid, easygoing cities—is rife with pickpocketing. Late at night you should be especially cautious when exiting bars and restaurants in the historic center; as always, leave your daypack and other unnecessary belongings in your hotel. Some taxi drivers in Arequipa warn about colleagues who set up tourists for ambushes. They suggest either calling for a cab or getting into taxis with older drivers because most of the crimes have been perpetrated by younger drivers.

Taxis

Taxis are inexpensive and plentiful, easily hailed on the street, and best when traveling at night (but see "Safety," above). Most trips in town cost no more than S/4. To call a taxi at night, try **Taxi Seguro** (☎ 054/450-250), **Taxi Sur** (☎ 054/465-656), **Master Taxi** (☎ 054/220-505), or **Ideal Taxi** (☎ 054/288-888). An excellent private driver for trips to Colca and elsewhere is Manuel Pino Torres of **Privatour** (☎ 054/952-6495).

Telephone

Arequipa's area code is 054, which must be dialed when calling from another city. The

Telefónica del Perú office is at Álvarez Thomas 209 (☎ 054/281-112).

Tours

The best all-purpose agencies in Arequipa offer city tours, organized excursions to La Campiña and Toro Muerto, tours of Colca, and hard-core adventure. Try ★ **Giardino Tours,** Jerusalén 604-A (☎ 054/241-206; www.giardinotours.com); **Colonial Tours,** Santa Catalina 106 (☎ 054/286-868;); **Illary Tours,** Santa Catalina 205 (☎ 054/220-844; www.illarytour.com); **Ideal Tours,** Urbanización San Isidro F-2, Vallecito (☎ 01/9883-5617; idealperu@terra.com.pe); **Peru Adventure Tours,** Jerusalen 410 (☎ 054/221-658; www.peruadventurestours.com); and **Santa Catalina Tours,** Santa Catalina 219 (☎ 054/216-994; santacatalina@star.com.pe). All of these agencies are also equipped to organize private transportation and hotel packages to Colca, which range from $95 per person for 1-day trips to $400 per person with accommodations at one of the top lodges in the region, such as Colca Lodge or the Las Casitas del Colca. For information on specialist adventure tour operators in Arequipa and Colca, see p. 149.

Visitor Information

AREQUIPA There's a **tourist information booth** at the Aeropuerto Rodríquez Ballón (☎ 054/444-564), open Monday through Friday from 9am to 4pm. The best information office in town is in **Casona de Santa Catalina,** Santa Catalina 210, across from the convent (☎ 054/221-227); it's open daily from 9am to 9pm. There's also an office on the Plaza de Armas across from the cathedral at Portal de la Municipalidad 112 (☎ 054/223-265); it's open daily from 8am to 6pm. You can also get information and free maps from the **tourist police,** Jerusalén 315, at the corner of Ugarte (☎ 054/201-258). COLCA A **Centro de Visitantes** is located within Aguada Blanca National Reserve, 45km (28 miles) outside of Arequipa. It has maps and a small exhibit on the region and is open daily from 8am to 5pm.

7
Lake Titicaca
& the Altiplano

Favorite Titicaca & Altiplano Moments

Straddling the border of Peru and Bolivia, fabled Lake Titicaca, South America's largest lake and the world's highest navigable body of water (3,800m/12,467 ft.), is a magnificent and placid expanse of deep blue, seemingly more ocean than lake. Of mystical importance to Peruvians, Titicaca is home to unique island-dwelling peoples of ancient traditions and finely crafted textiles. The scruffy city of Puno is the gateway to the lake and the surrounding windswept Altiplano (high mountain plains), as well as the host of several of Peru's greatest and wildest popular festivals.

> PREVIOUS PAGE The sweeping vista of stunning Lake Titicaca. THIS PAGE Puno's raucous celebrations are among the most colorful in Peru.

1 Living festival madness. Puno is known as the folklore capital of Peru; its festivals include Candlemas (La Candelaria) and Puno Week, both spectacular expressions of local culture, with wild masks, fervent dancing, and usually wild orgies of intoxication. They have to be experienced to be believed. See p. 184.

2 Taking in Taquile. In the midst of massive Lake Titicaca, this gentle agricultural island is home to a reserved people and some of South America's finest weavers. On an organized visit to the island, you'll get a chance to meet with a community and see up close their stunningly accomplished textiles and colorful dances. See p. 172, **2**.

3 Hitting the town in Puno. Although Puno's no great shakes, there's a certain scruffy, backpacker charm to the town on a cold evening. Gringos donning newly purchased alpaca hats and sweaters stroll along pedestrian-only Pasaje Lima, duck into Pizzeria Buho's for a wood-fired pizza, and follow up with potent cocktails at a nightspot such as Kamizaraky Rock Pub. See p. 168.

4 Hiking to the Suasi hilltop. Spot rare vicuñas on your way up a path to this tiny private island's hilltop, where sunset can be a surreal thing of beauty. At 3,962m (13,000 ft.) above sea level, the colors are incredible—and you'll understand why ancient peoples left small stone offerings, or apachetas, to mountain-dwelling gods. You'll wish the sun would never fully set. See p. 173, **4**.

5 Kayaking Titicaca. The world's highest navigable lake may already seem more like an ocean, but never more so than when you're paddling its placid waters under the immense, dreamlike horizon. Greater serenity is hard to imagine. If that's more than you're willing to take on, enjoy a gentle canoe trip around the tiny island of Suasi. See p. 172.

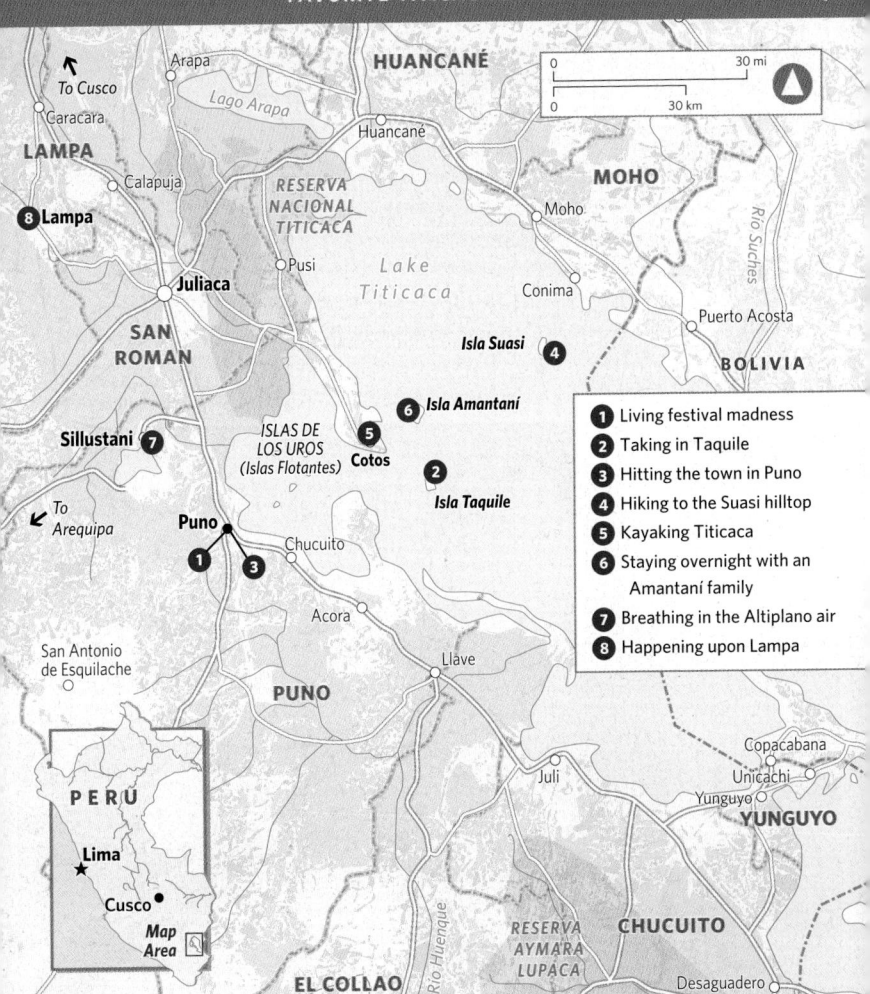

1 Living festival madness
2 Taking in Taquile
3 Hitting the town in Puno
4 Hiking to the Suasi hilltop
5 Kayaking Titicaca
6 Staying overnight with an Amantaní family
7 Breathing in the Altiplano air
8 Happening upon Lampa

6 Staying overnight with an Amantaní family. If a visit to the floating Uros Islands seems depressingly commercialized and touristy, sleeping at a family's home on rustic Isla Amantaní, within view of two peaks (named for Father Earth and Mother Earth) and the immensity of Lake Titicaca, may be the perfect alternative. See p. 173, 3.

7 Breathing in the Altiplano air. Most people don't often find themselves at altitudes of 3,500m (11,500 ft.) and above. Although the high plateau of southern Peru can be forbiddingly stark, windy, and chilly, there's something amazing about the wide-open skies,

especially at night, and the clean air as you head out beyond Puno. You'll need to catch your breath and dress in warm clothes at sites such as Sillustani. See p. 176.

8 Happening upon Lampa. The windswept Altiplano beyond Puno and Lake Titicaca can be forbidding, but the sweet little colonial town of Lampa is an unexpected gem. With its peaceful town squares, pastel-colored houses, and stone cathedral, crowned by green glazed tiles and sitting atop miles of catacombs and tunnels, it has been bypassed by time and progress. See p. 179, 4.

Puno in 1 Day

Founded in the late 17th century following the discovery of nearby silver mines, Puno has one thing going for it that no other city can claim: It hugs the shores of mesmerizing Lake Titicaca. And that's enough for this ramshackle town to draw numbers of visitors wholly disproportionate to its own attractions. Cold, dry, and rather plain, with little aesthetic appeal, Puno nonetheless reigns as the capital of Peruvian folklore, with traditional, vibrant, and uninhibited *fiestas* that are true blasts of *cultura popular*.

> The panoramic view of Puno and Lake Titicaca from Huajsapata Park.

START Puno is 297km (185 miles) from Arequipa, 388km (241 miles) from Cusco, and 1,011km (628 miles) from Lima. Take a bus (5 hr.) from Arequipa; a bus (7 hr.), train (10 hr.), or plane (2 hr.) from Cusco; or a plane (1 hr.) from Lima. If flying, see p. 186 for information on getting from the airport in Juliaca to Puno.

1 Catedral. This 18th-century baroque cathedral on the main square is a focal point of downtown Puno, more notable for its size and elaborate exterior than its Spartan interior.
⏱ 30 min. Plaza de Armas. No phone. Free admission. Daily 8am–7pm.

2 Museo Municipal Carlos Dryer. Puno's small museum is not essential but features a decent selection of pre-Inca ceramics and textiles, as well as mummies with cranial deformations.
⏱ 30 min. Conde de Lemos 289. No phone. Admission S/5. Mon–Fri 7:30am–3:30pm.

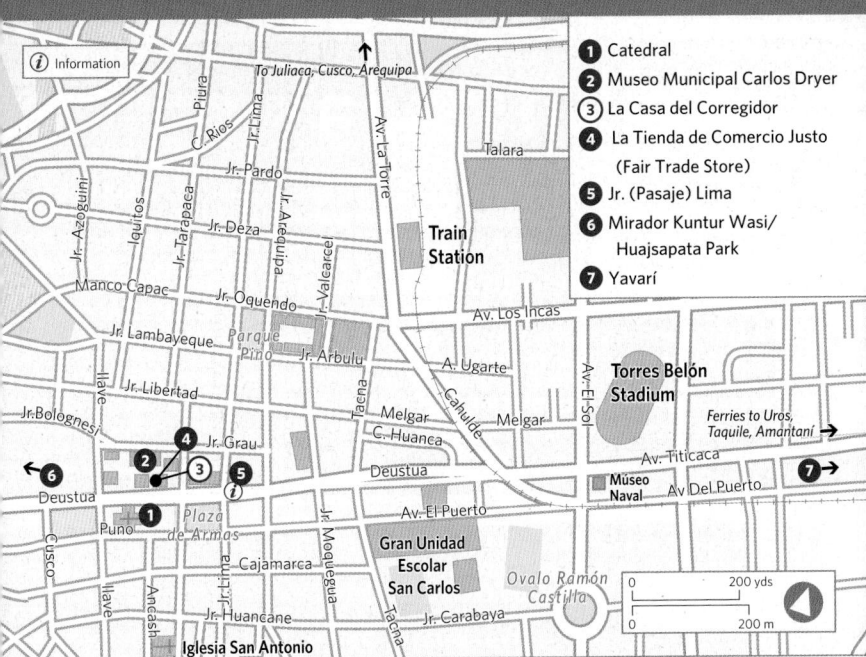

1 Catedral
2 Museo Municipal Carlos Dryer
3 La Casa del Corregidor
4 La Tienda de Comercio Justo
   (Fair Trade Store)
5 Jr. (Pasaje) Lima
6 Mirador Kuntur Wasi/
   Huajsapata Park
7 Yavarí

③ ☕ ★ **La Casa del Corregidor.** Puno's oldest structure, this 17th-century manor house boasts an impressive Spanish balcony. Of greatest interest to most travelers is the cool little "cultural cafe" house within, the best spot in town to take a coffee break. **Deustua 576. ☎ 051/351-921. Items S/6–S/15.**

4 ★ **La Tienda de Comercio Justo (Fair Trade Store).** This nonprofit shop ensures that a full 50% of the purchase price goes directly to the vastly underpaid artisans in rural communities. ⏱ 30 min. **Jr. Deustua 576 (patio of La Casa del Corregidor). ☎ 051/365-603. No credit cards.**

Head north along the pedestrian-only street from Plaza de Armas (at Jr. Puno).

5 ★ **Jr. (Pasaje) Lima.** This pedestrian-only mall lined with shops, restaurants, cafes, and bars is Puno's true heart—though that may speak more to Puno's limited attractions than the boulevard's innate charms. ⏱ 45 min. **Btw. Giraldo (Parque Pino) and Plaza de Armas (Deustua).**

Walk 10 minutes southwest of Plaza de Armas to the vantage point overlooking downtown. The easiest route is to climb Deustua, then take a right on Llave and then another left on Bolognesi until you come to a series of steps leading to the hilltop.

6 ★ **Mirador Kuntur Wasi/Huajsapata Park.** This vantage point will remind you why you're here, for it affords a superb view of Lake Titicaca. From this perspective, Puno looks considerably more attractive than it does up close. The park is crowned by a blindingly white statue of Manco Cápac, the legendary first Inca, said to have emerged from the lake to found the Inca Empire. ⏱ 1 hr. Free admission.

Take a taxi or walk to the shore of Lake Titicaca, near Sonesta Posadas del Inca hotel, 3km (2 miles) from downtown Puno.

7 ★ **Yavarí.** This restored steamship, built in 1862 in Birmingham, England, sailed Lake Titicaca for a century. Today it has been converted into a small museum and bar. The steamship was originally shipped as a kit from England to Arica, Chile, and then transported by mule, a total journey of 6 years, to Titicaca. ⏱ 1 hr. ☎ 051/369-329. www.yavari.org. Free admission. Daily 8am–5pm.

Lake Titicaca

According to Andean legend, Lake Titicaca—which straddles the modern border between Peru and Bolivia—is the birthplace of civilization. Manco Cápac, the original Inca chieftain believed to be a direct descendant of the sun, is said to have emerged from the lake's waters to found the Inca Empire. Lake Titicaca exerts a mystical hold on many visitors, too. It's a dazzling sight, with deep azure waters that seem to extend forever. The greatest way to experience Titicaca is by boat tour out to its islands, home to Quechua and Aymara communities; staying overnight on one of the islands is one of the most unique experiences you can have in Peru. Most visitors travel to the Uros Islands, as well as Amantaní and Taquile, as part of inexpensive organized tours.

> The only permanent residents of Isla Suasi, a private island in the midst of Titicaca, are a few alpacas and rarely seen vicuñas.

START Your tour operator will pick you up at your hotel; or, take a taxi from downtown Puno to the port (15 min.).

1 ★ **kids Islas Uros (Islas Flotantes).** As improbable as it sounds, the Uros Indians live on floating, shifting "islands" made from *totora* reeds that grow in the shallow waters of the Bay of Puno. The islands first came into contact with the modern world in the mid-'60s; now their inhabitants live mostly off

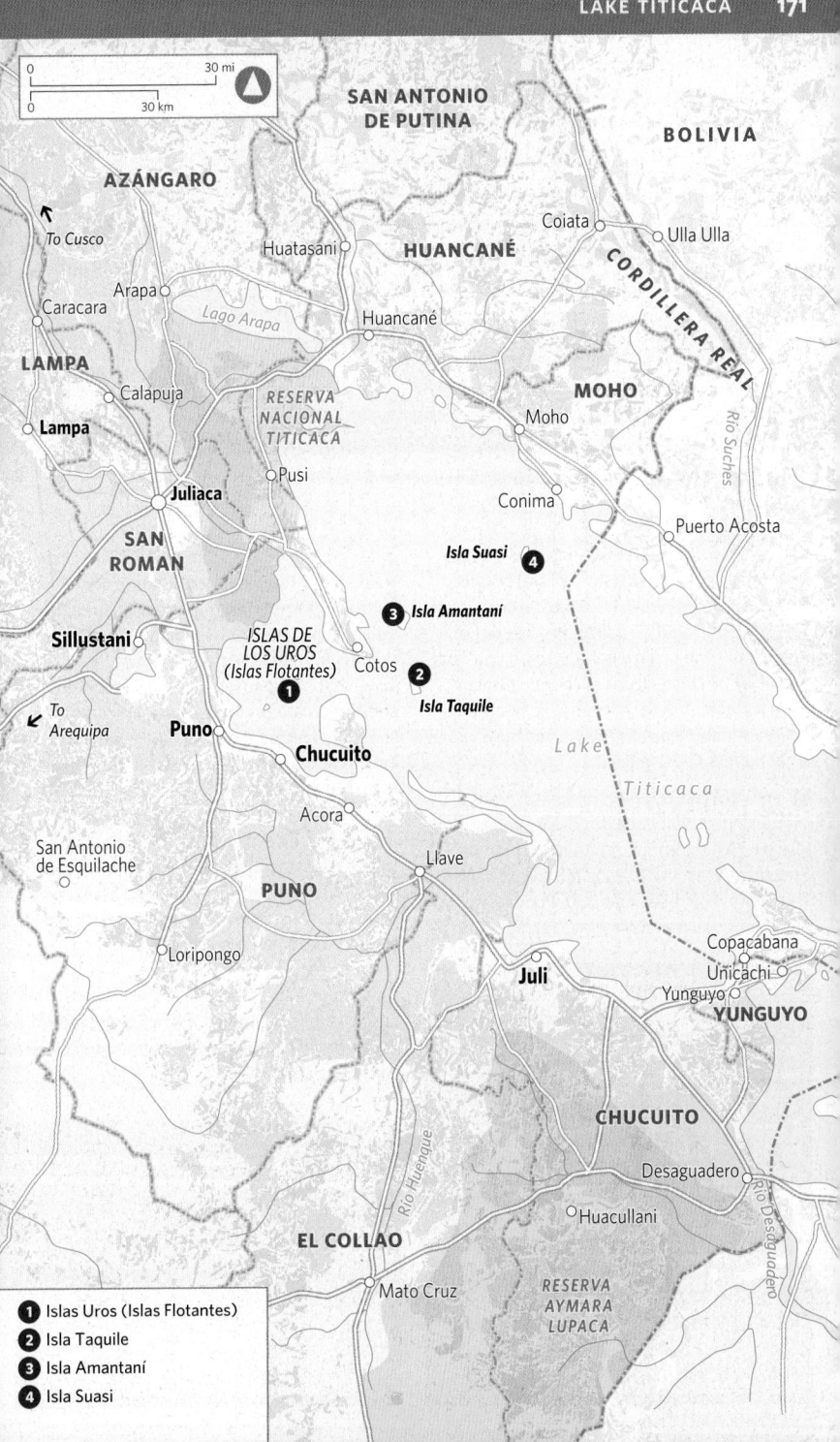

0 | 30 mi
0 | 30 km

To Cusco

SAN ANTONIO
DE PUTINA

BOLIVIA

AZÁNGARO

Coiata
Ulla Ulla

Huatasaní

HUANCANÉ

CORDILLERA REAL

Arapa

Caracara

Lago Arapa

Huancané

LAMPA

MOHO

Calapuja

Moho

Río Suches

Lampa

RESERVA
NACIONAL
TITICACA

Pusi

Conima

Puerto Acosta

Juliaca

SAN
ROMAN

Isla Suasi ❹

Sillustani

ISLAS DE
LOS UROS
(Islas Flotantes)
❶

❸ Isla Amantaní

*To
Arequipa*

Cotos

❷

Puno

Isla Taquile

Lake

Chucuito

Titicaca

Acora

San Antonio
de Esquilache

Llave

PUNO

Copacabana

Loripongo

Unicachi

Juli

Yunguyo

YUNGUYO

CHUCUITO

Desaguadero

Río Huenque

Río Desaguadero

Huacullani

EL COLLAO

Mato Cruz

RESERVA
AYMARA
LUPACA

❶ Islas Uros (Islas Flotantes)
❷ Isla Taquile
❸ Isla Amantaní
❹ Isla Suasi

> *The floating Islas Uros are manmade from indigenous* totora *reeds.*

tourism, a somewhat unseemly dependency and forced commercialism. Several hundred Titicaca natives live year-round on the islands. The largest island, Huacavacani, has not only homes, but the bizarre juxtaposition of a floating Seventh-Day Adventist church. Others have schools, a post office, public telephone, and huts outfitted with televisions powered by solar panels. ⏲ 30 min.

② ★★★ **kids** **Isla Taquile.** Life on the natural islands of Lake Titicaca is more authentic and less overtly dependent on tourism than on the Uros. A fascinating and stunning island, Taquile (a 4-hr. boat ride from Puno) has steep hillsides marked by Inca terraces and other pre-Columbian stone ruins. The expert weavers on Taquile produce some of the finest textiles in Peru—and that's saying something. The insular, Quechua-speaking islanders are famous for their spectacular dress. Men wear *fajas* (embroidered, woven red waistbands) and *chullos* (embroidered wool stocking caps, so tightly knitted they can hold water) that indicate their marital status: red for married men, red and white for bachelors. Women wear multilayered skirts and black shawls over their heads. The island has been inhabited for 10,000 years, and life remains starkly traditional, with no electricity or vehicles. Some Taquile natives allow tourists to stay at private houses, and there are a couple of simple restaurants serving visitors. (If you go to Taquile with a tour, you'll visit one of the communities on the island; buying your lunch there is a good way to contribute to a community.) ⏲ At least 2 hr.

Kayaking Titicaca

Paddling Lake Titicaca in a sea kayak is a unique way to grasp the immensity and incredible serenity of the lake and to explore quiet niches around Taquile, Amantaní, and Ticonata islands. Contact **Andean Kayak** (☎ 084/232-520, or 206/734-4625 in the U.S.; www.titicacakayakadventure.com) or one of Puno's two top travel agencies (p. 178). Kayaking trips range from a few hours to single- or multiday packages, all departing from Llachón on the Capachica peninsula, about a 1½-hour drive south of the city. Prices range from $45 for a 3-hour trip to $205 for multiday tours (all equipment and transfers included).

Titi & Caca

Titicaca, which covers some 8,288 sq. km (3,200 sq. miles), is South America's largest lake, and is more or less evenly shared by Peru and Bolivia (it is, in fact, more like a 60/40 breakdown). Yet Peruvians are fond of claiming it as their own, and there are maps that conspicuously label the lake with "Titi," covering the Peruvian half, and "caca," designating the Bolivian half.

Take a 2-hour boat ride from Taquile to Amantaní.

❸ ★★ 🧒 Isla Amantaní. Unspoiled Amantaní is beautiful but barren and rocky, with a handful of tiny villages clinging to the island's two peaks, Pachatata (Father Earth) and Pachamama (Mother Earth). There's great hiking and terrific views of Titicaca. Ancient stone walls mark the fields and terraces of agricultural fields and communities. The islanders here are more approachable than natives of Taquile, and the highlight of a visit is an overnight stay with a local family. The family prepares meals, and guests are invited to a dance in the village meeting place. Amantaní islanders make lovely hand-woven textiles, particularly the show-stopping black shawls embroidered with seven colors. ⊕ At least 2 hr.

From Puno, take a boat ride to Suasi (about 4 hr.).

❹ ★★★ Isla Suasi. Titicaca's only private island, miniscule Suasi is isolated and extraordinarily beautiful. It makes for a unique

> A woman's shawl showcases the embroidery work of Isla Amantaní's skilled artisans.

Practical Matters: Titicaca

You can go on your own to the Islas Uros (also known as the Islas Flotantes, or Float-ing Islands) by catching a *lancha* (small boat) at the port; the cost is usually about S/25. However, the only practical and con-venient way to visit the other islands and explore Lake Titicaca is with an inexpen-sive, small-group guided tour, arranged by a Puno travel agency (half-day tour of the Floating Islands, $12 per person; full-day tour that includes Taquile Island, $25 per person). A 2- or 3-day visit ($30–$35), with time to spend the night on either Taquile or Amantaní, is preferable. Amantaní is best visited this way, and it's a good idea to bring small gifts for your host family, such as pens, pencils, and batteries. Those with the luxury of time and money can explore the singular experience of staying on private Isla Suasi, contracted through the lodge's operator, Casa Andina (p. 182). Most single-day tours of the Uros and Taquile islands depart early in the morning and stop at the Uros Islands en route.

getaway, even if it's a long (and expensive) way to go for relaxation. There are no cars, TVs, or electricity, and no full-time inhabitants other than a dozen alpacas and eight free-ranging vicuñas. The island's owner is the sociologist Martha Giraldo; she has allowed the Casa Andina hotel chain to administer the solar-powered refuge she started (and transform it into a sensitive but upscale eco-lodge). The goal is simple: Enjoy high-altitude sunsets, panoramic views of Titicaca, and total peace and quiet. Activities are limited to reading in hammocks, canoeing around the island, trekking up to the *cerro* (hilltop) for sunset, and stargazing. The return to Puno is either by boat or a very scenic but extremely rough ride in a car or van. ⊕ At least 2 days/1 night.

CAMELIDS
Peru's Fine-Haired Beasts

BY NEIL EDWARD SCHLECHT

WITH THEIR BANANA-SHAPED EARS; POINTY MOUTHS; AND THICK, fuzzy fleece, llamas are the quintessential Andean beast, at home in the thin air of mountain ranges and the cold, bleak Altiplano. But llamas are just one of four main types of camelids indigenous to the Andes that include alpacas, guanacos, and vicuñas. Herbivores and members of the biological family Camelidae, camelids have a history of cultural and economic importance in Peru. Their images are found on pre-Inca pottery and textiles, and their remains have been uncovered at the burial sites of ancient high priests. Andean peoples have employed llamas and alpacas as pack animals, sources of food, and for clothing.

South American Camelids

LLAMA
Domesticated thousands of years ago, this iconic beast of burden is found in the Andes and actively bred today. Because the llama has a coarse-fibered coat, it has long been used primarily as a pack animal. Like alpacas, llamas have soft-padded hooves that don't beat up trails, and they are thus celebrated for their low environmental impact.

GUANACO
Large but rarely sighted, this camelid has a light brown or cinnamon-colored coat (often with a white underbelly) and roams freely throughout the Andes and, unusually, near the desert coast, too. Its thin coat is very fine and soft, though less so than that of a vicuña. Today protected by international law, its South American population is more than a half million.

ALPACA
Generally smaller than llamas, the alpaca produces the longest and some of the most lustrous fibers of the camelids. Alpaca meat, much leaner than beef, was considered a delicacy by pre-Columbian cultures, and today it is popular in Peruvian restaurants. There are two main alpaca varieties: the ubiquitous Huacaya, with a thick, spongy coat of more than 50 classified colors; and the smaller, less common Suri, with a coat of long silky fibers that look like dreadlocks.

VICUÑA
The vicuña is the national animal of Peru and appears on the coat of arms. The smallest (100 lb./45kg or less), most delicate, and rarest of the camelids, the vicuña's coat has spectacularly fine fibers, and the Incas considered it more valuable than gold (only nobility were permitted to wear garments made from it). On the brink of extinction 3 decades ago, the vicuña is a protected species in Peru, and its numbers have increased substantially. Vicuñas tend to move in small packs and are notoriously reclusive. One place to spot them is on Lake Titicaca's Isla Suasi.

Fibers & Textiles

The fibers of South American camelids, particularly those of alpacas, are of enormous importance to Peru's textile industry. Alpaca is finer and warmer than sheep's wool, stronger and softer than cashmere, and resistant to pilling. It is also hypoallergenic. Because individual strands are hollow, alpaca fibers have exceptional thermal and breathable characteristics. The finest, most lustrous alpaca is used to make elegant garments, including shawls, gloves, and jackets. Alpacas are sheared like sheep (usually every 2 years). The thick coat of the vicuña can be sheared only about every 3 years, producing very small quantities of incredibly silky fibers. A vicuña cape can cost thousands of dollars. Downy guanaco fibers are second in value and fineness to those of the vicuña, while coarse llama wool is used primarily for rugs and rope.

Baby alpaca (an industry term connoting the fineness of the fiber, not the age of the animal) and the highest grade royal baby alpaca, make the finest garments (beyond rare and precious vicuña fibers).

In boutiques in Lima, Arequipa, and Cusco, items are specified as such on the label. Beware when buying in markets and on the street: Many inexpensive alpaca garments may be laced with fiberglass and other manmade fibers, making them shiny in appearance and itchy.

The Altiplano Beyond Puno

The Altiplano (Spanish for "high plains") of southern Peru is almost perversely impressive. It's a place of singular landscapes and massive skies, but at more than 3,500m (11,500 ft.), it's also harsh, chilly, and windswept, perhaps better suited to camelids than most humans. Still, the region is home to megalithic pre-Columbian ruins, a bizarre fertility temple, and colonial churches and towns that hint at its former importance. Most travelers join organized tours to see the region's highlights; most typical are tours to Sillustani and Chucuito. Other more distant sites, such as Juli and undervalued Lampa, are infrequently visited but worthwhile for visitors with an extra day or two.

> *Cylindrical funeral towers, or* chullpas, *are the attraction at Sillustani, on the windswept plains outside Puno.*

START Your tour operator will pick you up from your hotel.

1 ★ **Sillustani.** These pre-Inca ruins, on a windy peninsula overlooking Lake Umayo, might appear to be granaries but they are in fact *chullpas*, or funeral towers, perfectly

constructed cylindrical tombs, some rising 12m (39 ft.). The Collas—an ancient, Aymara-speaking warrior tribe and the dominant people of the region prior to their conquest by the Incas in the early 15th century—typically buried their elite in these towers, sealing them

1 Sillustani
2 Chucuito & Inca Uyo
3 Juli
4 Lampa

inside along with food, jewels, and other possessions. The stonemasonry of the towers, which widen at the top, is particularly incredible (many historians find them superior even to masterful Inca engineering). ⏱ At least 3 hr. 35km (22 miles) northwest of Puno. No phone. Admission S/15. Daily 7am–6pm.

From Puno, take a bus 20km (12 miles) south to Chucuito. *Colectivos* bound for Acora depart Puno from Av. El Sol; tell the driver you want to get off at Chucuito, halfway between Chimú and Acora (S/3; 20 min.).

❷ **Chucuito & Inca Uyo.** Chucuito, a tiny Aymara town on a promontory on Lake Titicaca's southern shore, was the primary Inca settlement in the region and capital of the province during colonial times. The town has a pretty main square and colonial church—Nuestra Senora de La Asuncion, built in 1601—but its notoriety comes from Inca Uyo, dozens of large, mushroom-shaped phallic stones, most several feet high. Locals claim the stones comprise an ancient fertility temple. Some of the anatomically correct stones take aim at the sun god, Inti, while others are inserted into the ground, directed at Pachamama (Mother Earth). Holding court over them all, at the center of the ring, is the king phallus. Local guides tell (surely dubious) tales of rituals during which virgins purportedly sat for hours atop the phalluses to increase their shot at getting pregnant. While it's possible that the stones do indeed predate the Incas, most observers believe their display at least to be a tourist-oriented hoax. (Since Spanish missionaries were committed to destroying pagan symbols and structures, it seems unlikely that they would have constructed two churches in the vicinity of such a temple.) ⏱ At least 3 hr.

On Top of the World

Unless you're coming to Puno after some days in Cusco, Arequipa, or other high-altitude spot, you'll need to take it easy in Puno. The city's (and Lake Titicaca's) extreme elevation of 3,830m (12,566 ft.) is higher even than Cusco, and the very thin, cold, windy air takes some getting used to. See "On Thin Air" (p. 198) for information on how to combat altitude sickness.

The trip to Juli, 84km (52 miles) southeast of Puno, must be arranged with a travel agency (see "Practical Matters," below).

❸ **Juli.** This small town was the epicenter of Jesuit missionary activities throughout South America (indeed, it was called "Little Rome," reflecting the Catholic Church's investment). Today the town's former religious importance is obvious, with four Spanish churches from

Practical Matters: Altiplano

Sillustani and Chucuito are both popular stops on convenient and inexpensive organized tours (usually 3 hrs. long; $12–$15 per person). It is also possible, although complicated, to reach these sites on your own. To get to **Sillustani,** catch a Juliaca-bound *colectivo* (S/3; 20 min.) from downtown Puno and tell the driver to let you off at the fork in the road that leads to Sillustani (look for the sign, DESVÍO PARA SILLUSTANI); from there, catch another *colectivo*, 15km (9 miles) and a half-hour farther, to Sillustani, but keep in mind they don't run frequently. To return to Puno, you're best off trying to hitch a ride. To reach **Chucuito,** catch a *colectivo* (S/3; 20 min.) bound for Acora from Puno's Av. El Sol; tell the driver to let you off at Chucuito, which is about halfway between Chimú and Acora. Taxis from Puno to Sillustani and Chucuito are also available, and charge S/25 to S/30.

Most travel agencies in Puno handle conventional tours of Lake Titicaca and Sillustani, along with a handful of other ruins. The two best, offering a better and more interesting range of programs, are **All Ways Travel,** Jr. Deustua 576, in the courtyard of La Casa del Corregidor (☎ 051/ 353-979; www.titicacaperu.com), with good guides and several carefully planned, progressive cultural trips; and **Edgar Adventures,** Jr. Lima 328 (☎ 051/353-444; www.edgaradventures.com). Few of the Puno agencies offer organized tours to Juli and Lampa, so taxis might be your best bet (though you can check with the two tour operators above to see if transport can be arranged). *Colectivos* travel to Lampa from Av. 2 de Mayo in Juliaca (S/3).

> The 17th-century church Inmaculada Concepción in Lampa is one of the region's most spectacular, although least known, sights.

the 16th and 17th centuries, in varying states of disrepair and restoration, nearly all within touching distance of one another: the Plateresque San Pedro Mártir, brick-and-adobe San Juan Bautista, Santa Cruz de Jerusalén, and Nuestra Señora de la Asunción. ⊕ At least 4 hr.

Take a taxi to Lampa, 80km (50 miles) north of Puno.

❹ ★ **Lampa.** Little-known Lampa, a colonial gem near best-overlooked Juliaca (site of the regional airport but little else; in fact, the seedy place is big into contraband and corruption), isn't on most tours but is well worth a visit to see a once-important town seemingly preserved in aspic. Lampa is a place of faded-pink colonial homes, relaxed plazas, and the spectacular 17th-century Inmaculada Concepción church, Plaza Mayor s/n (Mon–Sat 8am–4pm), the centerpiece of town. Beyond its honey-colored stone exterior and unique roof of green glazed ceramic tiles is a labyrinth of catacombs (including tunnels, now sealed, said to stretch all the way to Puno, Arequipa, and even Cusco) and, peculiarly, an exact copy of the Vatican's *Pietà*. ⊕ At least 4 hr.

Puno Shopping

> A vendor at Puno's Mercado de Artesanía.

★ **Alpaca 111**
If you're in the market for better-quality alpaca fashions than you'll find on the street in Puno, visit this Peruvian chain. It will cost you more, but the designs and workmanship are worth it. Jr. Lima 343. ☎ 051/366-050. MC, V. Map p. 183.

★ **La Tienda de Comercio Justo (Fair Trade Store)** This nonprofit shop in the patio of La Casa del Corregidor is a welcome find in Puno. Fifty percent of the purchase price of alpaca and wool scarves, ponchos, and other goods goes directly to the artisans (who are identified by name on the garments) in rural communities. Jr. Deustua 576. ☎ 051/365-603. No credit cards. Map p. 183.

Mercado Central
The city's seedy central market, 2 blocks east of Jr. Lima, spills across several streets. It isn't remotely photogenic or all that pleasant, but it's a realistic look at Peruvian trade at its most basic. Jr. Tacna at Jr. Oquendo. No credit cards. Daily 8am–8pm. Map p. 183.

Mercado de artesanía
This open-air craft market beyond the railroad tracks has a few dozen stalls that attract tourists looking for inexpensive alpaca and woven woolen goods, as well as cheapo Titicaca souvenirs. Quality ranges from good to mediocre. Try on sweaters before purchasing. Btw. Jr. Melgar and Av. Titicaca. No credit cards. Daily 8am–7pm. Map p. 183.

On to Bolivia

Many travelers who make it to Puno and Lake Titicaca continue on to Bolivia, which shares not only a border with Peru but half of Lake Titicaca. Several travel agencies (see "Practical Matters," p. 178) in Puno sell packages and "through" bus tickets to Bolivia. The most common and scenic route is to travel from Puno to La Paz via **Yunguyo** (Peru) and **Copacabana** (Bolivia). You will be dropped off at the Peruvian border, where you'll pick up a *colectivo* or taxi shuttle to go through customs and passport control. The trip to La Paz takes 7 or 8 hours by bus. Buses also go to La Paz via **Desaguadero.** Another option is to go by a combination of overland travel and hydrofoil or catamaran, a unique but time-consuming journey (13 hr.). However you go, at the Bolivian border, visitors get an exit stamp from Peru and a tourist visa (30 days) to enter Bolivia. Foreigners have been hit up for phony departure and entry fees, so resist blatant attempts at corruption. The **Bolivian consulate** is located at Jr. Arequipa 120 (☎ 051/351-251). Americans, Canadians, Europeans, New Zealanders, and Australians do not need a visa to enter Bolivia, but the border was closed as recently as 2005, when widespread strikes paralyzed parts of Bolivia, so it's wise to check on the status of the crossing before traveling. For more information about Bolivia, pick up a copy of *Frommer's South America*.

Puno Restaurants

★ **Incabar** *PERUVIAN/INTERNATIONAL*
Stylish and almost funky (as well as relatively expensive) for rough-around-the-edges Puno, this lounge bar/restaurant features a more creative and flavorful menu than other places in town (even if dishes don't always succeed), with artful presentations, interesting sauces for lake fish and alpaca steak, curries, and stir-fries. Also check out the owners' other restaurant down the street, **Colors Lounge,** Jr. Lima 342. Jr. Lima 348. ☎ 051/368-031. Entrees S/22–S/35. AE, DC, MC, V. Breakfast, lunch, and dinner daily. Map p. 183.

★ **La Casona** *PERUVIAN/INTERNATIONAL*
With traditional, old-school Spanish charm in three dining rooms filled with antiques and religious art, this is about as formal as Puno gets. It's known for Titicaca lake fish, such as trout and *pejerrey* (kingfish). Service can be slow. Jr. Lima 517. ☎ 051/351-108. Entrees S/15–S/36. DC, MC, V. Breakfast, lunch, and dinner daily. Map p. 183.

★★ **Mojsa** *PERUVIAN/INTERNATIONAL*
The prospects for dining in Puno aren't Peru's greatest, so this little place just off the Plaza de Armas comes as a nice surprise. It's got real charm, good thin-crust pizza, Peruvian specialties such as trout *causa* (a Creole casserole), steaks, and desserts (such as lemon pie). Service can be a little haphazard, but that's pretty much true for anywhere in Puno. Jr. Lima 635, 2nd floor. ☎ 051/363-182. Entrees S/15–S/26. MC, V. Lunch and dinner daily. Map p. 183.

Pizzería El Buho *PIZZA*
Popular, cozy, and known for some of Puno's best pizzas from its wood-burning oven, though the menu also lists a good number of pastas and a handful of soups. Jr. Lima 371. ☎ 051/363-955. Entrees S/10–S/25. DC, V. Dinner daily. Map p. 183.

Restaurant Don Piero *PERUVIAN*
Though this longtime traditional restaurant seems a little stale, you can still get a pretty decent *palta rellena* (avocado stuffed with chicken salad) or *lomo saltado* (beef strips with

> The wood-fired pizzas at El Buho are one way to deal with Puno's cold winds.

french fries, onions, and peppers). Jr. Lima 348–364. ☎ 051/351-766. Entrees S/15–S/34. DC, V. Lunch and dinner daily. Map p. 183.

Rico's Pan *CAFE/BAKERY*
For inexpensive sandwiches, pastries, and cakes, this little cafe doesn't disappoint. It also serves good coffee and is a good spot for breakfast or for stockpiling goodies for boat trips on Titicaca. Jr. Lima 420, Puno. ☎ 051/354-179. Entrees S/6–S/12. No credit cards. Breakfast, lunch, and dinner daily. Map p. 183.

Ukuku's *PIZZA/PERUVIAN*
Overlooking the main drag, this large pizzeria focuses on its wood-burning oven but also offers a full menu of Peruvian specialties, such as alpaca steak cooked in red wine and ceviche; pastas; and even *chifa* (Peruvian-Chinese). Jr. Grau 172 (at Jr. Lima), 2nd floor. ☎ 051/367-373. Entrees S/12–S/27. MC, V. Lunch and dinner daily. Map p. 183.

Puno & Titicaca Hotels

> Intiqa Hotel is one of Puno's newest and best-value places to stay.

★ Casa Andina Classic Tikarani DOWNTOWN PUNO

One of two comfortable midsize hotels from a proliferating Peruvian chain of mid-range and luxury hotels, this branch, 5 blocks from the Plaza de Armas, is the quieter of the two. (The other, Casa Andina Classic Puno Plaza, on Jr. Grau 270, is a short block from the square and off the main pedestrian drag.) Rooms are clean and well equipped, if predictably decorated. For quiet, ask for an interior room on the second floor. Jr. Independencia 185. ☎ 866/220-4434 toll-free in the U.S., or 051/367-803 in Peru. www.casa-andina.com. 53 units. $87 double. Rates include breakfast. AE, DC, MC, V. Map p. 183.

★★ Casa Andina Private Collection Puno

TITICACA SHORE Perched over Titicaca, with phenomenal lake views from its deck and dining room, this handsomely rustic upscale hotel is an excellent step up from most Puno hotels. About half the rooms, which are decorated in a warm, Andean style, have lake views and are worth the small supplement in price. The hotel has its own lake pier and a private train stop. Av. Sesquicentenario 1970-72, Sector Huaje. ☎ 866/220-4434 toll-free in the U.S., or 051/363-992 in Peru. www.casa-andina.com. 46 units. $91-$186 double; $318 pressurized oxygen suite. Rates include breakfast. AE, DC, MC, V. Map p. 183.

★★★ Casa Andina Private Collection Suasi

ISLA SUASI What started out as a basic, solar-powered eco-lodge has morphed into a luxurious but sensitively designed inn on a private island. It's a feast of fantastic Titicaca views and total serenity. Isla Suasi. ☎ 01/213-9739. www.casa-andina.com. 24 units. $249-$369 per person, all-inclusive. AE, DC, MC, V. Reached by fast *lancha* (motorized boat) in under 3 hr., though most boats take 5-6 hr. (round-trip transportation extra; contact Casa Andina for details).

Hostal Los Uros DOWNTOWN PUNO

One of the most popular Puno *hostales* targeting backpackers, this is a decent value at the low end, with very basic and clean rooms. About half the rooms have private bathrooms. Jr. Teodoro Valcarcel 135. ☎ 051/352-141. www.losuros.com. 24 units. S/50 double w/ private bathroom, S/40 w/ shared bathroom. No credit cards. Map p. 183

★ Hotel Colón Inn DOWNTOWN PUNO

This Belgian-owned hotel, in a 19th-century Republican-era building, is built around a colonial-style lobby and has three floors of comfortably appointed, carpeted rooms. Jr. Tacna 290. ☎ 051/351-432. www.coloninn.com. 21 units. $60 double; $95 suite. Rates include breakfast. AE, DC, MC, V. Map p. 183.

★ Hotel Libertador Lake Titicaca TITICACA SHORE

A white-block 1970s building, this large luxury hotel hardly blends in with the grandeur of the lake, but it does enjoy great peace and isolation—and spectacular views. Rooms are spacious if a little bland, and about half have panoramic views of the lake. Isla Esteves s/n. ☎ 877/778-2281 toll-free in the U.S. and Canada, or 051/367-780 in Peru. www.libertador.com.pe.

Lake Mysticism

The people who live near Lake Titicaca consider themselves descendants of Mama Qota (the Sacred Mother), and they believe that powerful spirits live in the lake's depths. Viracocha, the creator deity, lightened a dark world by having the sun, moon, and stars rise from the lake to occupy their places in the sky.

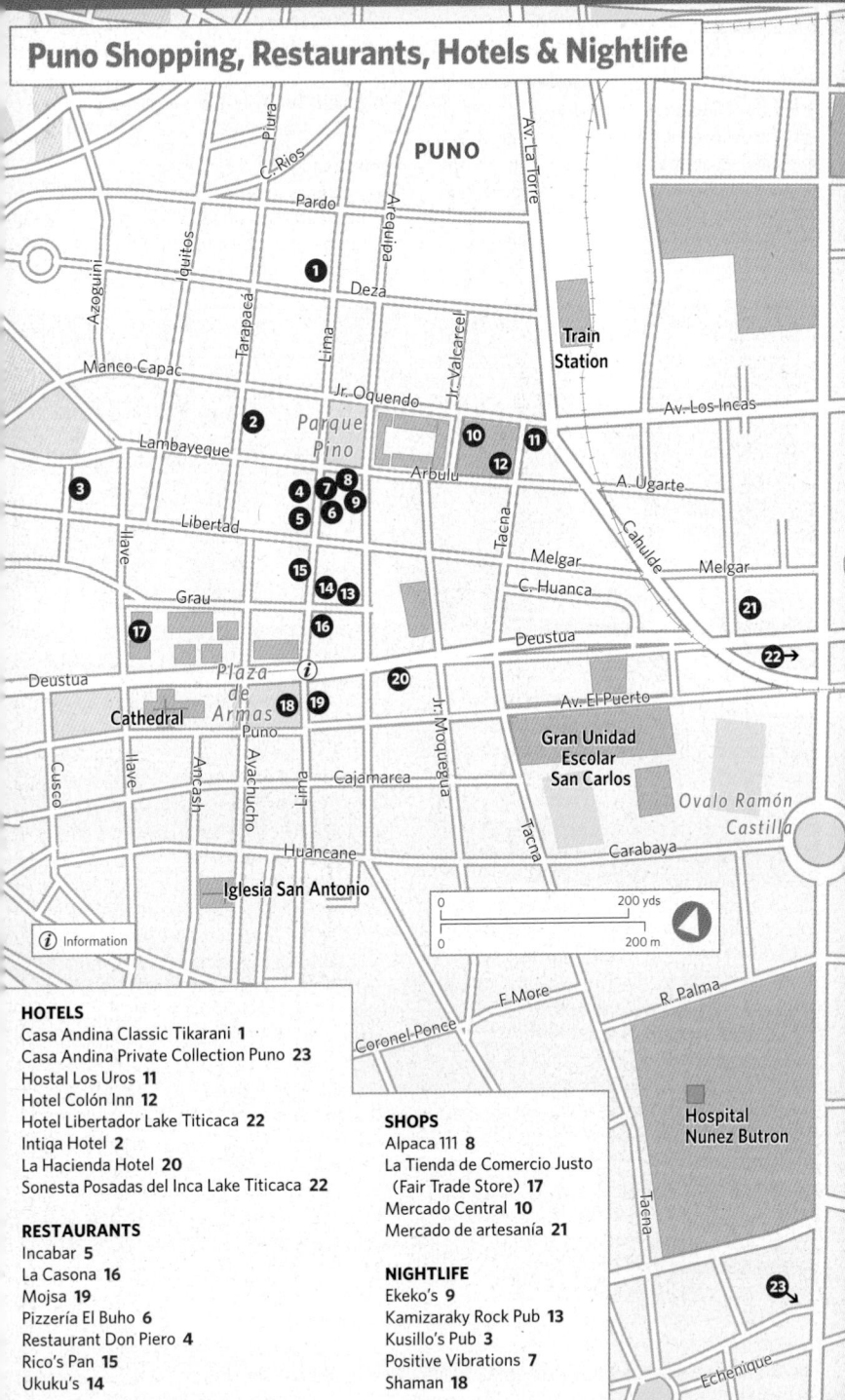

Puno Shopping, Restaurants, Hotels & Nightlife

HOTELS
Casa Andina Classic Tikarani 1
Casa Andina Private Collection Puno 23
Hostal Los Uros 11
Hotel Colón Inn 12
Hotel Libertador Lake Titicaca 22
Intiqa Hotel 2
La Hacienda Hotel 20
Sonesta Posadas del Inca Lake Titicaca 22

RESTAURANTS
Incabar 5
La Casona 16
Mojsa 19
Pizzería El Buho 6
Restaurant Don Piero 4
Rico's Pan 15
Ukuku's 14

SHOPS
Alpaca 111 8
La Tienda de Comercio Justo
  (Fair Trade Store) 17
Mercado Central 10
Mercado de artesanía 21

NIGHTLIFE
Ekeko's 9
Kamizaraky Rock Pub 13
Kusillo's Pub 3
Positive Vibrations 7
Shaman 18

123 units. $170–$195 double; $220–$260 suite. Rates include breakfast. AE, DC, MC, V. Map p. 183.

★★ Intiqa Hotel DOWNTOWN PUNO

A particularly good midrange value, this well-managed small hotel is a nice alternative to the upscale hotels along Titicaca's shores. Rooms are large and stylishly contemporary, with high-quality bedding and linens, double-paned windows, and thermal floors (hot-water bottles warm beds in cold months). Jr. Tarapacá 272. ☎ 051/366-900. www.intiqahotel.com. 24 units. $70 double; $80 suite. Rates include buffet breakfast. MC, V. Map p. 183.

Kantuta Lodge ISLA AMANTANÍ

Many visitors to Amantaní stay with local families, but if you prefer the privacy of a small inn, this is a nice place to spend the night and appreciate the utter quiet and remoteness

Puno, Festival City

Puno is far and away the folkloric capital of Peru. Its multitudinous festivals, celebrated with explosions of pre-Columbian dances and costumes, take color to the level of wild all-night and all-week partying. Lake Titicaca is said to be the birthplace of Inca civilization, and the ancestral traditions and cultural expressions of this region are assiduously guarded. Festivals are renowned for their variety, unique choreography, and lilting Altiplano music. The National Institute of Culture has registered more than 360 indigenous dances from the Titicaca region.

The **Festival de la Virgen de la Candelaria (Candlemas),** held during the first 2 weeks of February, is one of the most famous expressions of popular culture in Peru. The feast of Puno's patron saint brings bands and more than 200 groups of dancers from villages and towns all over the region. Festivities, based on ancient rituals linked to agricultural cycles and harvests, blend traits associated with the dominant native local groups: the sober Quechua people and the animated Aymara. The most famous Candlemas dance is the *diablada*, or devil dance. Dancers decked out in wild costumes and grotesque masks play panpipes and make offerings to Pachamama, or Mother Earth. On the final weekend, there are pre-Columbian dances on Saturday and the post-Columbian exercises on Sunday. The final Monday is a grand 12-hour parade through Puno. Street dancing is observed every day of the festival, so even if you miss the first couple of days, you're sure to get a healthy dose of the Virgen de la Candelaria.

Puno Week (above), celebrated the first week of November, honors Manco Cápac, who, according to legend, emerged from the waters of Lake Titicaca and founded the Inca Empire. A major procession leads from the shores of the lake to Puno's stadium. Street dances and music take over the city, as do alcohol-fueled losses of inhibition. Puno is also well known for its pre-Lenten **Carnaval** celebrations (late Feb to early Mar), celebrated primarily with native dances, lots of drinking, and water bombs. Other lively festivals in and around Puno and Lake Titicaca include **San Juan de Dios** (Mar 7–8); **Fiesta de las Cruces Alasitas** (May 8); **San Juan, San Pedro,** and **San Pablo** (June 24–29); and **Apóstol Santiago** (July 25), which is the most enthusiastically celebrated day on Isla Taquile.

of the island after the day-trippers depart. Run by the family of Segundino Cari near the port of Comunidad Pueblo, the lodge features clean and brightly decorated rooms with local textiles. Isla Amantaní. ☎ 051/812-664. www.punored.com/titicaca/amantani/img/lodge.html. 6 units. $20 per person; meals $5. No credit cards.

La Hacienda Hotel DOWNTOWN PUNO

A remodeled midsize hotel, this pleasant impersonation of a hacienda-style inn has large rooms built around two courtyards. Half the hotel's rooms were newly constructed just a few years ago, and the hotel is brighter and more welcoming than in the past. Jr. Deustua 297. ☎ 051/356-109. www.lahaciendapuno.com. 40 units. $70 double; $90–$120 suite. Rates include breakfast. MC. Map p. 183.

★ kids Las Cabañas CHUCUITO

Near the Inka Uyo fertility temple (p. 178, ❷), this smart, comfortable, and well-priced inn has pretty gardens, an attractive setting by the lake, and a cute restaurant. In addition to regular rooms (some of which have fireplaces), there are cool bungalows, which sleep six and have fireplaces and balconies. Jr. Tarapacá 538. ☎ 051/368-494. www.chucuito.com. 12 units. S/96 double; S/168 duplex bungalow. MC, V.

★★ kids Sonesta Posadas del Inca Lake Titicaca

TITICACA SHORE   Hugging the shores of Titicaca, this easygoing luxury hotel is imaginatively designed and fits nicely into its surroundings. The restaurant and many rooms look over the lake; other rooms have views of the mountains. Kids will enjoy the mini-version of a floating lake community on the grounds by the lake. Av. Sesquicentenario 610, Sector Huaje. ☎ 800/SONESTA (766-3782) in the U.S. and Canada, or 051/364-111 in Peru. www.sonesta.com/laketiticaca. 62 units. $99–$125 double. Rates include breakfast. Kids 8 and under stay free in parent's room. AE, DC, MC, V. Map p. 183.

Puno Nightlife

Ekeko's

This agreeable nightspot often has live bands to go with its small dance floor and big-screen TV showing soccer matches and videos. Jr. Lima 355, 2nd floor. ☎ 051/365-986. Map p. 183.

★ Kamizaraky Rock Pub

My favorite watering hole in Puno is this cozy and cool hangout with a loft space; it looks like a graffiti-filled mountain cabin, plays loud rock and reggae music (with occasional live bands), and serves strong cocktails to a young, rowdy clientele. Pasaje Grau 148. No phone. Map p. 183.

Kusillo's Pub

A nightly happy hour and reggae, jazz, and blues, as well as occasional folklore shows. Libertad 259. ☎ 051/351-301. Map p. 183.

Positive Vibrations

This pub, with the look of a jungle lodge, is the place in town to get your reggae fix. Jr. Lima 378. No phone. Map p. 183.

> *Kamizaraky Rock Pub is a reliable spot for some good tunes and late-night drinks.*

Shaman

A simple, second-floor bar that has pizzas, drinks, and free Internet access. Jr. Puno 505 (Plaza de Armas), 2nd floor. No phone. Map p. 183.

Titicaca & Altiplano Fast Facts

> *The Cusco-to-Puno train route is one of the most scenic in Peru.*

Arriving

BY PLANE The nearest airport, **Aeropuerto Manco Cápac** (☎ 051/322-905), is in Juliaca, 45km (28 miles) north of Puno. **LAN** (☎ 01/213-8300; www.lanperu.com) flies daily from Lima and Arequipa to Juliaca; flights start at about $139 one-way from Lima. Tourist buses run from the Juliaca airport to Puno (1 hr.), depositing travelers on Jr. Tacna for S/15. **Rossy Tours** (☎ 051/366-709) runs inexpensive *combis* to the airport in Juliaca (picking passengers up at their hotels) for S/20 per person. Most better hotels in Puno can arrange pickup. **BY BUS** Puno's modern bus station is **Terminal Terrestre** (☎ 051/364-733), Av. Primero de Mayo 703, Barrio Magistral. From Cusco, the bus is faster and cheaper than the train; executive-, imperial-, or royal-class buses make the trip in about 7 hours and cost about $50 (though some services, such

as Inka Express, make stop-offs at Inca ruins en route, extending the trip by a couple of hours, which is highly recommended if you have the time. **Imexso** (☎ 084/240-801; www.perucuzco.com/imexsotours), **Inka Express** (☎ 084/247-887; www.inkaexpress.com), **Cruz del Sur** (☎ 01/311-5050; www.cruzdelsur.com.pe), and **Ormeño** (☎ 01/472-5000; www.grupo-ormeno.com.pe) operate buses with videos and English-speaking tour guides. The trip from Arequipa is 5 hours, and **Cruz del Sur** and **Ormeño** make the trip for around S/45. **BY TRAIN** The Titicaca Route from Cusco to Puno is one of the most scenic in Peru, reaching an altitude of 3,500m (11,500 ft.). Though slower (10 hr. and prone to late arrivals) and more expensive, the experience and views make it preferable to taking the bus for some visitors. Peru Rail's Andean Explorer trains (www.perurail.com)

depart from **Cusco's Estación Huanchaq** (☎ 084/238-722) at 6am and arrive in Puno at 6pm; departures are April to October Monday, Wednesday, Friday, and Saturday; and November to March Monday, Wednesday, and Saturday. Fare is $220 one-way in luxurious coaches and includes lunch in dining cars; tickets can be reserved. The **Puno train station** (☎ 051/351-041) is at Av. La Torre 224, a few blocks north of downtown; Casa Andina Private Collection, along the banks of Lake Titicaca, has its own train stop.

ATMs/Cashpoints
In Puno there are numerous banks and ATMs along Jr. Lima (Pasaje Lima). There's also an ATM at Hotel Casa Andina, Jr. Independencia 185.

Currency Exchange
Peruvian Banks include **Banco Continental,** at Jr. Lima 400, and **Banco de Crédito,** on the corner of Jr. Lima and Jr. Grau. Moneychangers are generally found along Jr. Tacna, where most bus stations are located, and at the market near the railway and Av. de los Incas.

Doctors
For a medical emergency, go to **Clínica Puno,** Jr. Ramón Castilla 178–180 (☎ 051/368-835), or **Hospital Nacional,** Av. El Sol 1022 (☎ 051/369-696).

Emergencies
The general police emergency number is ☎ **105;** for fire, dial ☎ **116.**

Internet Access
Internet *cabinas* are found across Puno. There are several Internet cafes along Jr. Lima. A nice, quiet spot for surfing the Web is behind the cafe at **La Casa del Corregidor,** Deustua 576 (☎ 051/351-921).

Pharmacies
You'll find a couple of pharmacies along the main pedestrian-only thoroughfare, Jr. Lima. Look for **InkaFarma,** part of a large Peruvian chain, at Jr. Lima 364.

Police
The tourist police are located at Jr. Deustua 538 (☎ 051/352-720).

Post Office & Mail
Puno's main post office (☎ 051/351-141) is at Moquegua 269.

Safety
Travelers should exercise extreme caution on the train from Cusco and at the train and bus stations, where thieves are known to target tourists. In Puno, also be careful with belongings at the market near the railroad track and along busy Jr. Lima, on the walk Mirador Kuntur Wasi (which you shouldn't do alone). Although Puno's famed folkloric festivals are a time of celebration, general inebriation might impair people's judgment and lead to altercations, so watch not only your belongings, but also your intake.

Taxis
Taxis are inexpensive and plentiful in Puno, easily hailed on the street, and good to use at night and to get back and forth from the hotels on the banks of Lake Titicaca. Most trips in town cost no more than S/3. You can also hire a taxi for round-trips to nearby ruins or for half- or full days. Call **Taxi Milenium** (☎ 051/363-134) or **Taxi Tour Puno** (☎ 051/369-900).

Telephone
Puno's area code is 051, which must be dialed when calling Puno from another city. The Telefónica del Perú office is on the corner of Moquegua and Arequipa.

Visitor Information
An **iPerú** tourist information office with maps and some basic information is located on the pedestrian-only main drag of Puno, Jr. Lima 549 (☎ 051/365-088). Better are the travel agencies that organize Lake Titicaca–area trips, such as **All Ways Travel** or **Edgar Adventures** (see p. 178).

8
Cusco

Favorite Cusco Moments

Historic and scenic Cusco, the former capital of the Inca Empire and gateway to Machu Picchu, is one of South America's highlights. Spectacularly cradled by the Andes, Cusco sits at a daunting altitude of 3,400m (11,000 ft.), its Inca presence found in stone streets and building foundations laid 5 centuries ago. And while Cusco—with its fascinating blend of pre-Columbian and colonial history and vibrant contemporary expressions of Amerindian and mestizo culture—looks and feels like an Andean capital, it's also a dynamic travelers' mecca, with an engaging vibe that makes people want to linger.

1 Hanging out on the Plaza de Armas at dusk. The centerpiece of Cusco is never more alluring than in the early evening, as lights cascading up the hills twinkle, and street lanterns glow amber against a blue-black sky and the silhouettes of the imposing Andes. The arcaded plaza retains its colonial, Andean feel and is an essential hub of social activity. See p. 205, **2**.

2 Catching a spontaneous display of *cultural popular*. Thousands of visitors plan their trips to Cusco around the Inti Raymi festival, one of Peru's greatest expressions of Andean culture, but the city's Amerindian roots are on display throughout the year, and you're almost guaranteed to stumble across a parade or an homage to them if you spend a few days here. See p. 206

3 Barhopping across old Cusco. The historic quarter of Cusco is littered with bars and cafes, great places to meet up with both locals and foreigners from all over and trade travel war stories, get advice on treks, and make new travel plans. See p. 238.

> PREVIOUS PAGE *As day turns to night, Cusco's Plaza de Armas becomes a magical place.* THIS PAGE *The popular bar at Cicciolina is a lively spot for a cocktail and some tapas.*

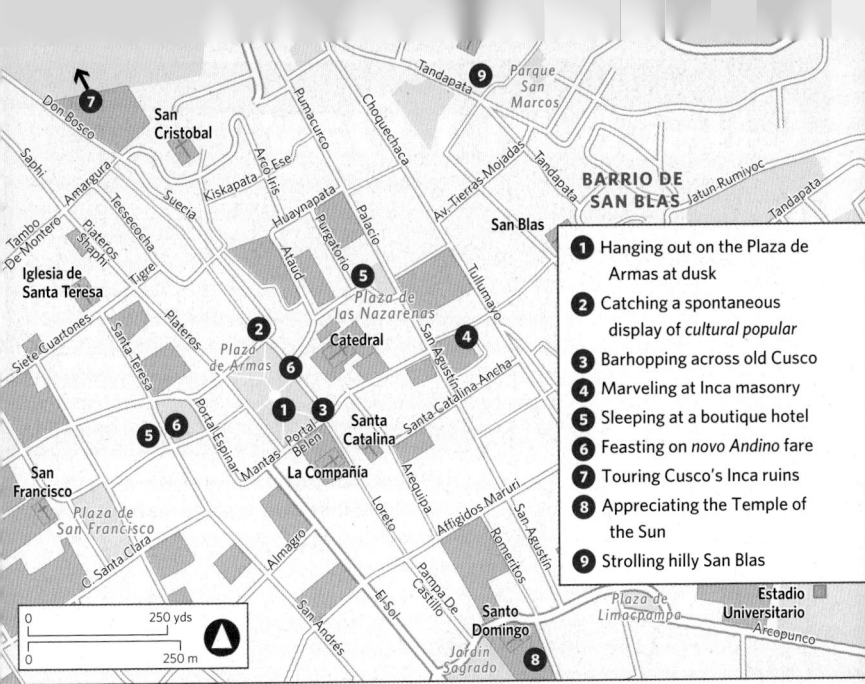

4 **Marveling at Inca masonry.** The streets of Cusco are a living history lesson. The conquistadors astutely recognized the brilliance of the Incas' engineering, so while they raided and razed almost everything else in the Inca capital, in many cases they constructed mansions and churches right atop the ancient stone foundations. See p. 204.

5 **Sleeping at a boutique hotel.** A number of Peru's finest boutique hotels, with palpable historic and artistic flavor, are in the historic center of Cusco, with several inhabiting gorgeously restored colonial mansions. My favorites: Aranwa Cusco Boutique Hotel and Fallen Angel: The Guest House, the latter an unexpected avant-garde art-project inn. See p. 232.

6 **Feasting on *novo Andino* fare.** Cusco wasn't always a dining capital, but with the advent of New Andean cooking, things have changed. My favorite places are Chicha, the brainchild of Peruvian culinary darling Gastón Acurio (his creative take on Cusqueña cooking), and Limo, which serves sushi and *tiraditos,* the fresh seafood and Peruvian coastal fusion most associated with Lima. See p. 227 and 229.

7 **Touring Cusco's Inca ruins.** On the outskirts of Cusco is a series of fine Inca ruins, beginning with one of the greatest, Sacsayhuamán, magnificently perched on a hill overlooking the city. The ruins circuit, which hardy trekkers can do on foot, is a terrific primer before heading on to the famous Inca sites in the Sacred Valley. See p. 212.

8 **Appreciating the Temple of the Sun.** From the sumptuously curved wall on the exterior to the perfect alignment of niches and doorjambs inside, one can almost imagine when Qoricancha, the Incas' Temple of the Sun, was lined in gold and home to Inca high priests. During the summer solstice, the sun still magically illuminates a niche where the Inca chieftain held court. See p. 194, 5.

9 **Strolling hilly San Blas.** Atmospheric San Blas, where the Inca elite once lived, rises into the hills above Cusco. The city's most bohemian district, it's full of art galleries, bars and pubs, and squat, whitewashed colonial buildings with red-tile roofs. It's ideal for strolling, as long as you can manage the steep inclines. See p. 208.

Cusco in 1 Day

With a single day in Cusco, you likely won't have adjusted to the altitude, so concentrate on the highlights of the historic center, where you won't have to climb many hills and everything is within easy walking distance. This will give you a feel for the city's Andean character and its vibrancy, as well as its fundamental clash of cultures: Inca and Spanish colonial. Take it all in, but take it easy, as the air is very thin, and make lots of stops for water or *mate de coca* (coca-leaf tea). Admission for several sights is included on the Cusco *boleto turístico* (tourist ticket; p. 202).

> The fountain in front of the cathedral in the Plaza de Armas is a gathering spot for young and old.

START **Cusco is 1,165km (724 miles; a 1-hr. flight) from Lima; begin on the Plaza de Armas.**

❶ ★★ **Plaza de Armas.** It's easy to see why the Incas chose Cusco as their capital when you stand on the city's elegant and lively central square, framed on all sides by the Andes Mountains. The plaza, which was twice its present size in Inca days, is the site of Cusco's most prominent churches, as well as, on its northwest side, the remains of original Inca walls thought to be the foundation of the Inca Pachacútec's palace. The city's colonial character endures in graceful stone arches and carved wooden balconies. A great people-watching spot, the square is at its best in the early evening, when yellowish lanterns are illuminated against the night sky and lights twinkle in the surrounding foothills. ⏱ 30 min.

❷ ★★★ **La Catedral.** Built on the site of the palace of the Inca Viracocha, Cusco's magnificent Renaissance cathedral, completed in 1669, dominates the Plaza de Armas. Inside are 400 canvasses of the Escuela Cusqueña (Cusco School), painted from the 16th to 18th centuries; splendidly carved cedar choir stalls; and a main altar fashioned from silver mined in Potosí, Bolivia. To the right of the altar is a Peruvian take on the Last Supper, a painting in which the apostles are drinking *chicha* (fermented maize beer) and eating *cuy*. A chapel off the principal nave features El Señor de los Temblores (Lord of the Earthquakes), considered the patron saint of Cusco. In the connected **Capilla del Triunfo** (the first Christian church in Cusco; ☎ 084/246-222-799; www.cuscovirreinal.com) is an evocative painting

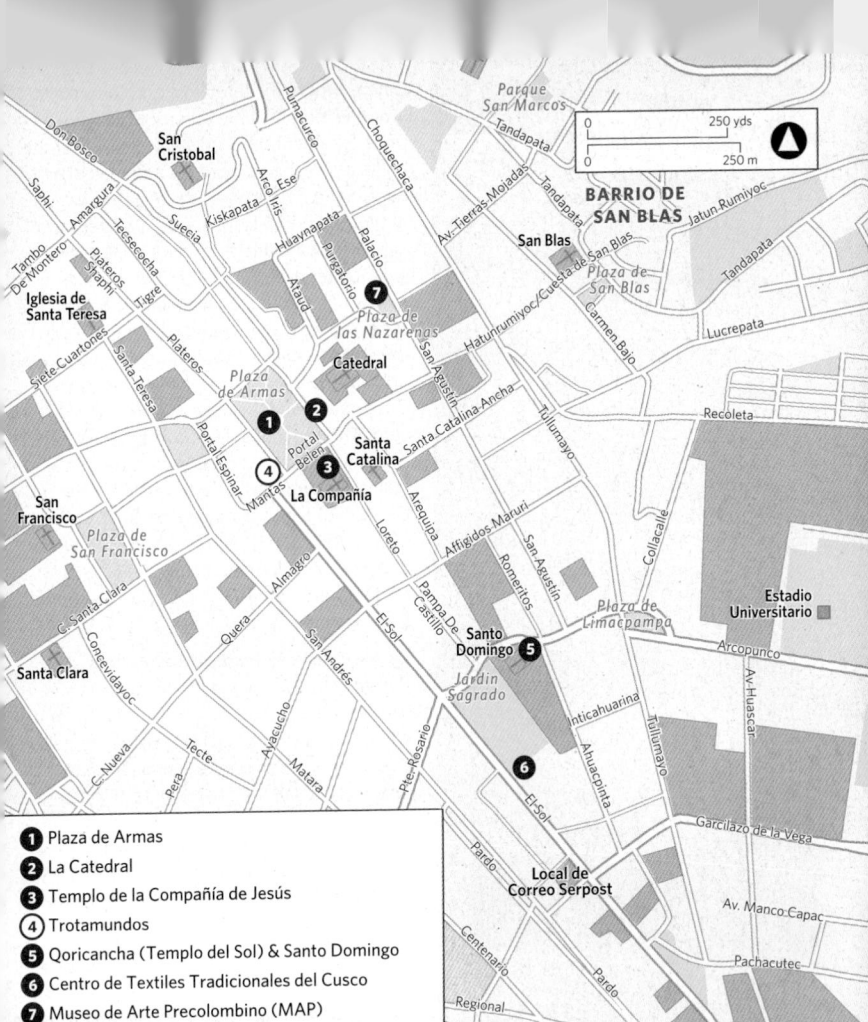

1. Plaza de Armas
2. La Catedral
3. Templo de la Compañía de Jesús
4. Trotamundos
5. Qoricancha (Templo del Sol) & Santo Domingo
6. Centro de Textiles Tradicionales del Cusco
7. Museo de Arte Precolombino (MAP)

by Alonso Cortés de Monroy that depicts the devastating earthquake of 1650. ⏱ 1 hr. Plaza de Armas (north side). No phone. Admission S/25 adults, S/13 students. Mon–Sat 10am–6pm; Sun 2–6pm.

❸ ★★ **Templo de la Compañía de Jesús.** Rivaling La Catedral for grandeur, this late-16th-century Jesuit church, almost destroyed by the 1650 earthquake, was built on the site of the sumptuous palace of the Inca Huayna Cápac. The church is dark inside, but its gilded altar is stunning. Important works of art here include a depiction of St. Ignatius de Loyola, by the local painter Marcos Zapata. Also of note are the paintings to either side of the entrance depicting the marriages of Saint Ignatius's nephews; one is a symbol of Peru's mestizo character, as the granddaughter of Manco Inca weds the man who captured the last Inca, the rebellious leader Tupac Amaru. ⏱ 30 min. Plaza de Armas (southeast side). ☎ 084/246-799. www.cuscovirreinal.com. Admission S/10 adults, S/5 students. Mon–Sat 9am–5:30pm.

④ ★ **Trotamundos.** With a coveted balcony and great views of the Plaza de Armas and cathedral, this longtime cafe

> The interior of La Catedral features a wealth of Cusco School art works and gold-leaf altars.

is here, where the temple of one culture sits atop the temple of the other. Qoricancha (The Temple of the Sun), where 4,000 of the highest-ranking Inca priests and their attendants were housed, was dedicated to worship of the sun and was apparently a glittering palace, with gold panels lining its walls, life-size gold figures, solid-gold altars, and a huge gold sun disc that reflected the sun and bathed the temple in light. During the summer solstice, the sun still shines directly into a niche where only the Inca chieftain was permitted to sit. Qoricancha was the main astronomical observatory for the Incas. The Spaniards ransacked the temple but used its exquisite polished stone walls for the foundations of the baroque Convent of Santo Domingo, constructed in the 17th century. ⏱ 1 hr. Plazoleta Santo Domingo. ☎ 084/222-071. Admission S/10 adults, S/5 students and kids. Mon–Sat 8:30am–6:30pm; Sun 2–5pm.

⑥ ★★ Centro de Textiles Tradicionales del Cusco. Before shopping for handicrafts and textiles at any of the innumerable shops and stalls across Cusco, have a look here to get an idea of what the highest-quality Andean textiles look like. Dedicated to fair-trade practices, the store ensures that 70% of the sale price goes directly to highland communities and individual artisans. You'll also find a weaving demonstration and a small but informative textiles museum. ⏱ 30 min. Av. El Sol 603. ☎ 084/228-117. www.textilescusco.org. Free admission. Daily 10am–6pm.

is a hangout for young Peruvians and international globetrotters. Grab a coffee and pastry, check email, and, if it's cold, warm up by the fireplace. Portal de Comercio 177, 2nd floor. ☎ 084/239-590. Items S/3–S/12.

⑤ ★★★ kids Qoricancha (Templo del Sol) & Santo Domingo. The best illustration of how the colonizing Spanish collided with the Incas

El Negrito

A famous local figure is "El Negrito" (also called El Señor de los Temblores, or Lord of the Earthquakes), a brown-skinned figure of Christ on the cross who's known as the protector of Cusco. Today housed in a chapel in La Catedral (stop ②), the figure was paraded around the city by frightened residents during the 1650 earthquake. When the earthquake finally ceased, locals attributed it to a miracle and transformed El Negrito into an object of devotion. Locals still deliver fresh flowers in his honor daily, and on Easter Monday the figure is paraded through Cusco in an evening procession that terminates at La Catedral.

> *The Santo Domingo church was built on the foundation of an Inca temple and today holds a large collection of Cusco's colonial art.*

⑦ ★★ Museo de Arte Precolombino (MAP).
This sophisticated archaeological museum features a superb selection of the vast collection of pre-Columbian works belonging to Lima's Museo Arqeológico Rafael Larco Herrera (p. 52, ②). The space—once an Inca ceremonial court, then the Santa Clara convent, and later colonial mansion (Casa Cabrera) of the Conquistador Alonso Díaz—holds 450 pieces dating from 1250 B.C. to A.D. 1532, including gold and silver handicrafts, jewelry, ceramics, and other artifacts depicting the rich traditions from the Nasca, Moche, Huari, Chimú, Chancay, and Inca cultures. The museum is especially worthwhile for anyone unable to visit the major museums in Lima or any of the top archaeological sites in northern Peru. ⏱ 1 hr. Casa Cabrera, Plaza de las Nazarenas s/n. ☎ 084/237-380. www.map.org.pe. Admission S/22 adults, S/11 students and kids. Daily 10am–10pm.

> *The Santo Domingo church holds a large collection of Cusco's colonial art.*

Cusco in 2 Days

After seeing the highlights of the historic quarter on Day 1, take in some of the other important sights in the *centro*, but save some energy to wander up the hilly streets to the atmospheric San Blas neighborhood, and finish the day with a visit to the spectacular Inca ruins, Sacsayhuamán, high above the city. Get an early start, because you could easily spend an entire afternoon at the ruins; if you want to walk there, you'll need to be in good shape and at least somewhat acclimated to Cusco's high altitude.

> The most celebrated street in Cusco is Calle Hatunrumiyoc, where you'll find the famous "12-Angled Stone."

START **Santa Catalina Angosta, just south of the Plaza de Armas.**

❶ ★★ Convento y Museo de Santa Catalina. Built in 1610 on the foundations of the Acclla-huasi, the palace where the Inca emperor sequestered his chosen maidens, the Virgins of the Sun, this small convent contains a museum of colonial and religious art, with superb Escuela Cusqueña paintings. The collection also includes four paintings of the Lord of the Earthquakes (see "El Negrito," p. 194) painted by Amerindians. Look also for the curious trunk that, when opened, displays the life of Christ in 3-D figurines (employed by the Catholic Church's "traveling salesmen" who converted natives in far-flung regions of Peru). The lovely interior of the monastery has an

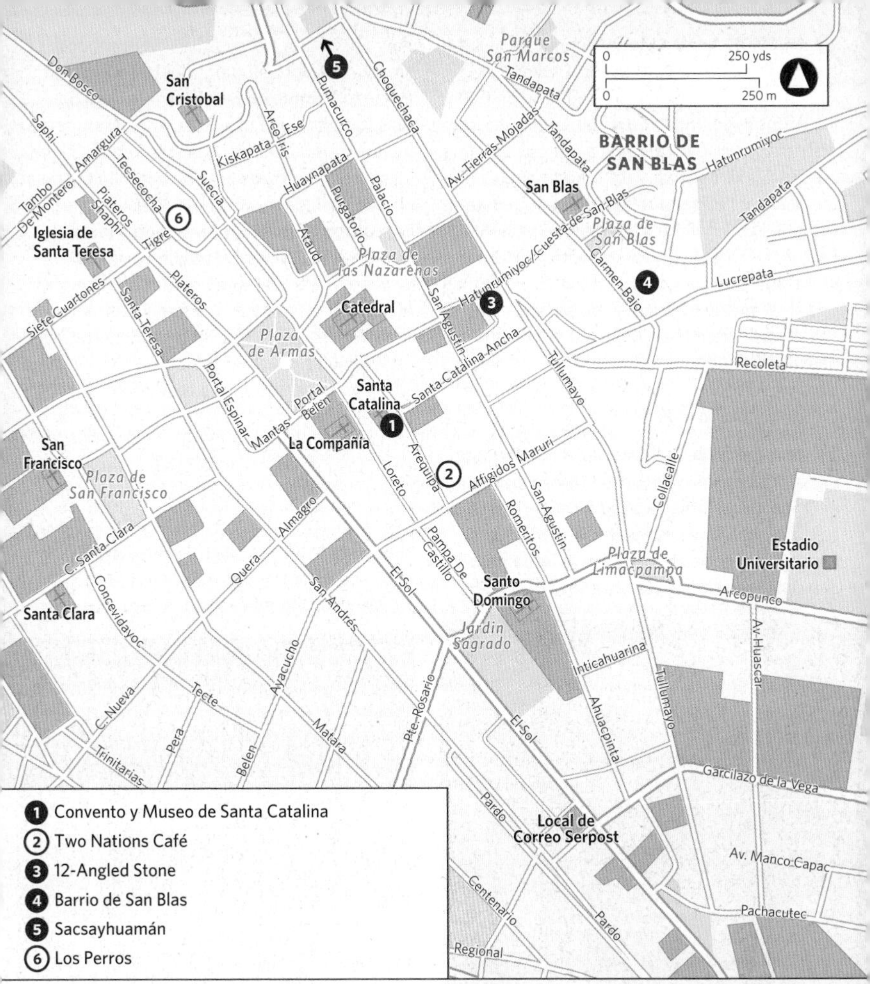

Map legend:

1. Convento y Museo de Santa Catalina
2. Two Nations Café
3. 12-Angled Stone
4. Barrio de San Blas
5. Sacsayhuamán
6. Los Perros

interesting chapel with baroque frescoes of Inca vegetation. ⏱ 1 hr. Santa Catalina Angosta s/n. ☎ 084/226-032. Admission S/8 adults, S/5 students. Daily 8am–5:30pm.

② 🍺 ★★ **Two Nations Café.** Just down the street from Santa Catalina, this relaxing restaurant/beer garden, with tables on a colonial courtyard, is a great retreat from the bustle of Cusco. Have a coffee or snack, or even an early, fortifying micro-brew (the restaurant makes its own, Inca Gold and Outback Amber). Arequipa 159. ☎ 084/634-000. Items S/6–S/34.

> Stop in for a beer, coffee, or snack at Two Nations Café.

③ ★★ kids **12-Angled Stone.** Remnants of spectacular Inca masonry are scattered across Cusco, but the most famous is found on Calle Hatunrumiyoc, which leads up to the San Blas district. The street contains a famous building block, ingeniously cut with 12 right angles fitted without mortar into a massive foundation (originally part of the palace of the Inca Roca). For kids, it makes a great game to pick out the stone and count its angles. Around the corner, on the alleyway Inca Roca, is a series of stones said to represent the shape of a puma—the basis for the original layout of Cusco (there's usually someone pointing out the formation). ⏱ 15 min. Triunfo at Palacio.

④ ★★★ **Barrio de San Blas.** Full of artists' studios and artisans' workshops, this picturesque neighborhood is also a base for plenty of backpacker sorts, since many of the coolest bars and an overload of hostels are located here. San Blas is a great area to wander during the day. The centerpiece of the neighborhood is a small plaza at the top of Cuesta de San Blas, home to **Templo de San Blas,** Plaza de San Blas (no phone; S/15 adults, S/7.50 students, includes audio guide; Mon–Sat 9am–5:30pm), said to be the oldest parish church in Cusco (1562). Inside the simple adobe exterior is a baroque gold-leaf main altar and a fantastic Churrigueresque cedar pulpit, carved from a single tree trunk. Most contend that it was created by a famous Quechua woodcarver, Juan Tomas Tuyrutupa, from Ayacucho. Another legend says that the artisan was a leper who created the pulpit to honor San Blas (St. Blaise) after he was miraculously cured, and it's supposedly the sculptor's skull resting for eternity at the feet of San Pablo at the very top. It's too bad someone doesn't get definitive credit, because the creative detail is stunning. ⏱ At least 1 hr. Plaza de San Blas. ☎ 084/246-799. www.cuscovirreinal.com. See p. 208 for a walking tour of San Blas.

On Thin Air

The air is noticeably thinner in Cusco, at an altitude of just over 3,353m (11,000 ft.), than in almost any city in South America. Cusco is best explored on foot, but this demands hiking up steep stone steps—leaving even the fittest of travelers gasping for breath and saddled with headaches and nausea. Some travelers are afflicted with severe nausea (others may barely feel the effects of the altitude except when walking up Cusco's steep hills). Take it easy for the first few hours or even days. Drink lots of water, avoid heavy meals, and do as the locals do: Drink *mate de coca,* or coca-leaf tea. (Don't worry, you won't get high or arrested, but you will adjust a little more smoothly to the thin air.) If that doesn't cure you, ask whether your hotel has an oxygen tank you can use for a few moments of assisted breathing. If you're really suffering, look for an over-the-counter medication in the pharmacy called *soroche* (altitude-sickness) pills. And if all that doesn't do the trick, it may be time to seek medical assistance. Those prone to altitude sickness should consider staying the first couple of nights in the lower Sacred Valley (p. 284).

> Baroque frescoes and artwork from the Escuela Cusqueña, in the Convento de Santa Catalina.

> The 1562 Templo de San Blas, the oldest parish church in Cusco, is steeped in legend.

> The stunning ruins of Sacsayhuamán above Cusco, home to the annual Inti Raymi festival.

Take a taxi from Plaza de San Blas to the ruins. Or, if you're up for a steep 30- to 45-minute walk, take Tandapata as it bends around and a right on Pumacurco until you come to a curve and the old Inca road. Past the San Cristóbal church at the top, beyond a small plaza, is the main entrance to the ruins.

5 ★★★ kids Sacsayhuamán. The fortress-like ruins looming above Cusco are some of the finest ruins in the region, with some of the Incas' most monumental stonework and architecture. Begun by the Inca emperor Pachacútec in the mid-15th century, the site took a century and many thousands of men to complete. What one sees today is perhaps only one-quarter of the original complex, which could house more than 10,000 men. Assumed to be a fortress for its imposing walls, in all likelihood it was a religious temple (though with some military component). What survive are impressive outer walls, constructed in a zigzag formation of three tiers, with 22 distinct zigzags. (In the puma-shape layout of the Inca capital, Sacsayhuamán was said to form the animal's head, and the zigzag of its defense walls the teeth.) Many of the base stones employed are almost unimaginably massive; some are 3.5m (11½ ft.) tall, and one is said to weigh 300 tons. They were brought from as far as 32km (20 miles) away. Like all Inca constructions, the stones fit together perfectly without aid of mortar. It's easy to see how hard it would have been to attack these ramparts; the design would automatically expose the flanks of an opponent. Above the walls are the circular foundations of three towers that once stood here; they were used for storage of provisions and water. At least 2 hr. Circunvalación s/n (2 km/1¼ miles north of Plaza de Armas). Admission included in *boleto turístico* (see p. 202). Daily 9am–6pm. For more on Sacsayhuamán, see p. 212, **1**.

⑥ 🍺 ★★ **Los Perros.** After all that hiking around San Blas and up to Sacsayhuamán, take a load off at this cool lounge cafe with comfy couches, a great, laid-back spot for cocktails, beer, sandwiches, or full meals. See p. 238.

Cusco in 3 Days

Having already seen a good amount of the old quarter, as well as San Blas and Sacsayhuamán, your third day is a good time to see parts of Cusco that many visitors overlook. Of course, if you've had your fill of the historic center and its incessant tourist trade, it might also be a good time to see other Inca ruins just outside the city (p. 212), do some shopping, or just relax and take in the genial vibe of the city in its cafes and plazas.

> Just behind the Plaza de Armas are the arches of Plaza Regocijo, originally part of the Incas' grand central square in the capital.

START Santa Clara at Cascaparo.

① ★★ Mercado de San Pedro. The fascinating, frenzied Cusco central market is an amazing place to tap into the city at its most quotidian and traditional, a place where tourists are no more than an afterthought. The range of produce, meats, juice bars, household items, and oddities (such as medicinal plants from the rainforest) is daunting; for most, it's an experience not to be missed. However, exercise caution because pickpockets targeting tourists are known to frequent the market. ⊕ At least 1 hr. Santa Clara s/n. No phone. Free admission. Daily 7am–4pm.

② ★ Iglesia y Convento de San Francisco. One of Cusco's largest churches, on the second-largest plaza in Cusco, this imposing and austere 17th-century Franciscan convent church occupies an entire square. It's best known for its collection of colonial artworks, including a massive canvas depicting the genealogy of San Francisco de Asís (nearly 700 family members). You'll also find handsome ceiling frescoes, a carved-wood choir, and displays of skulls and bones—reminders of man's mortality. ⊕ 45 min. Plaza de San Francisco s/n. ☎ 084/221-361. Admission S/5 adults, S/3 students. Mon–Sat 9am–4pm.

③ 🍴 ★ Varayoc Café. In a sweet new location in the courtyard of a colonial mansion, this cool

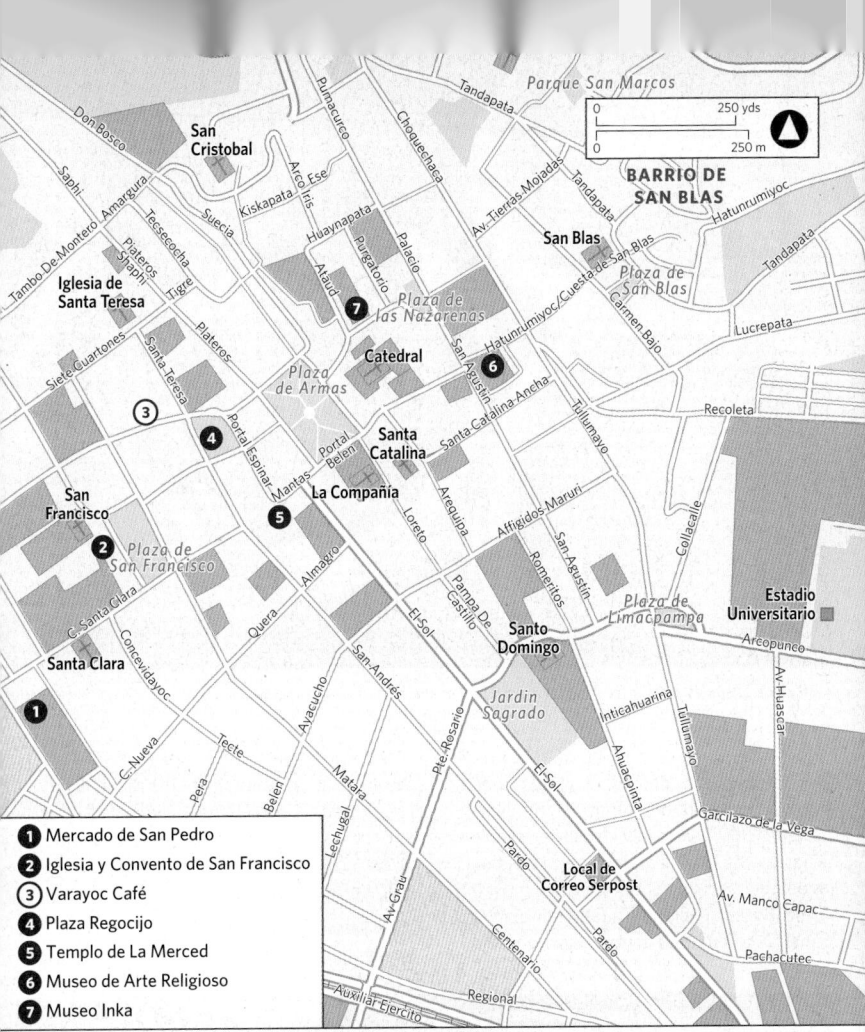

1 Mercado de San Pedro
2 Iglesia y Convento de San Francisco
3 Varayoc Café
4 Plaza Regocijo
5 Templo de La Merced
6 Museo de Arte Religioso
7 Museo Inka

little cafe has great coffee, fruit juices, sandwiches, salads, and, the house specialty, fondues. Aficionados come for the *ponche de leche* (a milky beverage, often served with a shot of pisco). San Juan de Dios 250 (courtyard). ☎084/232-404. Items S/8–S/17.

4 ★ **Plaza Regocijo.** During Inca times, this pleasant, leafy square formed part of the main plaza, along with today's Plaza de Armas. Today it's full of shops, restaurants, and notable historic mansions, and it's slightly less feverish than the main square. There is a pair

of oft-overlooked museums here, too. The **Museo Histórico Regional** is a regional history museum with archaeological finds and colonial artifacts, including furnishings and Escuela Cusqueña art; the museum is housed in the mansion where Garcilaso de la Vega, an important Peruvian writer and chronicler of Inca history and culture (and himself a descendant of the Incas), once lived. The small **Museo de Arte Contemporáneo,** within the Palacio Municipal, features contemporary works of local artists. ⏰ At least 1 hr. Garcilaso at Heladeros. Admission to both museums by *boleto turístico* (p. 202); daily 9am–5pm.

> *All kinds of spices and native foods can be found at the bustling Mercado de San Pedro.*

5 ★ **Templo de La Merced.** Originally built in 1536 but reconstructed after the great earthquake of 1650, this lovely church is notable for its handsome facade and beautiful cloisters. Inside, the sacristy contains a small museum of religious art, including a fantastic solid-gold monstrance swathed in precious stones. In the vaults of the church are the remains of two famous conquistadors, Diego de Almagro and Gonzalo Pizarro. ⏱ 30 min. Mantas s/n. ☎ 084/231-831. Admission S/5. Mon–Sat 8:30am–noon and 2–5pm.

6 ★ **Museo de Arte Religioso.** In a superb colonial palace now belonging to the Archbishop

Cusco's *Boleto Turístico*

The city's *boleto turístico* (tourist ticket) includes admission to 16 places of interest in and around Cusco and the Sacred Valley. Though it's no longer much of a bargain, the *boleto* is the only way you can get into a number of churches, museums, and ruins (not all of these attractions are indispensable). The full ticket costs S/130 for adults and S/70 for students with ID and kids; is valid for 10 days; and is available at the **Oficina de Información Turística,** Mantas 117-A (☎ 084/263-176), open Monday to Friday 8am to 6:30pm and Saturday 8am to 2pm. In addition to the main tourist office, the *boleto* can be purchased at **Galerías Turísticas,** Av. El Sol 103, office 101 (☎ 084/227-037), Monday to Saturday 8am to 6pm, and at **Casa Garcilaso,** Garcilaso and Heladeros s/n (☎ 084/226-919), Monday to Friday 8am to 5pm and Saturday 8am to 4pm. You can also buy a partial ticket for S/70 that covers either attractions in the city or ruins outside of Cusco, but not both. Make sure you carry the ticket with you when you're planning to make visits (especially on day trips outside the city), as guards will ask to see it so they can punch a hole alongside the corresponding picture. Guards also often ask students to show their International Student Identification Card (ISIC). For additional information, visit www.cosituc.gob.pe.

> *The Spanish mansion that houses the Museo de Arte Religioso was built upon Inca foundations.*

> *Talented textile weavers quietly toil in the courtyard of the Museo Inka.*

of Cusco (previously it was the home of a Spanish marquis and before that the site of the palace of Inca Roca) is the Museum of Religious Art. It displays a collection of colonial religious paintings with impressive historical detail, but the paintings compete for attention with the mansion's architectural features: a stunning portal, stained-glass windows, and Moorish-style doors, balconies, and carved-cedar ceilings, all of which effectively double the museum's value as a colonial artifact. ⏱ 1 hr. Corner of Hatunrumiyoc and Palacio. ☎ 084/225-211. www.cuscovirreinal.com. Admission S/15 adults, S/7.50 students. Mon–Fri 8am–12:30pm and 3–6pm.

7 ★ kids **Museo Inka.** This museum examines pre-Inca civilizations and Inca culture, as well as the impact of the Spanish Conquest and colonial times on native cultures. Perhaps fittingly, the museum is housed in a colonial mansion built on top of an Inca palace at the beginning of the 17th century. The collection includes ceramics, textiles, jewelry, mummies, architectural models, and an interesting collection—reputed to be the world's largest—of *qeros,* Inca drinking vessels carved out of wood, many meticulously painted. The palace's ornate portal is one clue to the original owner's importance and wealth. ⏱ 1 hr. Cuesta del Almirante 103 (corner of Ataúd and Tucumán). ☎ 084/237-380. Admission S/10 adults, S/5 students. Mon–Sat 9am–6pm.

Cusco's Inca Foundations

Dominating the ancient streets of Cusco are dramatic Inca
walls constructed of mammoth granite blocks so exquisitely carved they fit
together without mortar, like puzzle pieces, and have proven to be resistant to
earthquakes. The Spaniards razed many Inca constructions and built churches
and mansions right on top of some original foundations. In many cases, their
colonial architecture has not stood up nearly as well as the Incas' terrific
masonry and engineering. This walking tour takes in streets that still have
evocative Quechua-language names that date to Inca times, such as Saqracalle
("where the demons dwell") and Pumaphaqcha ("puma's tail").

> The solid Inca stonework on Calle Loreto, where blocks were fitted together without mortar and designed to withstand earthquakes.

START Calle Loreto, at Maruri.

1 ★★ Calle Loreto. This principal Inca thoroughfare, originally called Intikkijllu, is famously distinguished by a massive, magnificent stone wall. The oldest surviving Inca wall in Cusco, it's composed of meticulously cut rectangular stones that once formed part of the Accllahuasi, or "house of the chosen maidens" (the maidens being the Inca emperor's Virgins of the Sun).

Walk the length of Loreto, which terminates in the Plaza de Armas.

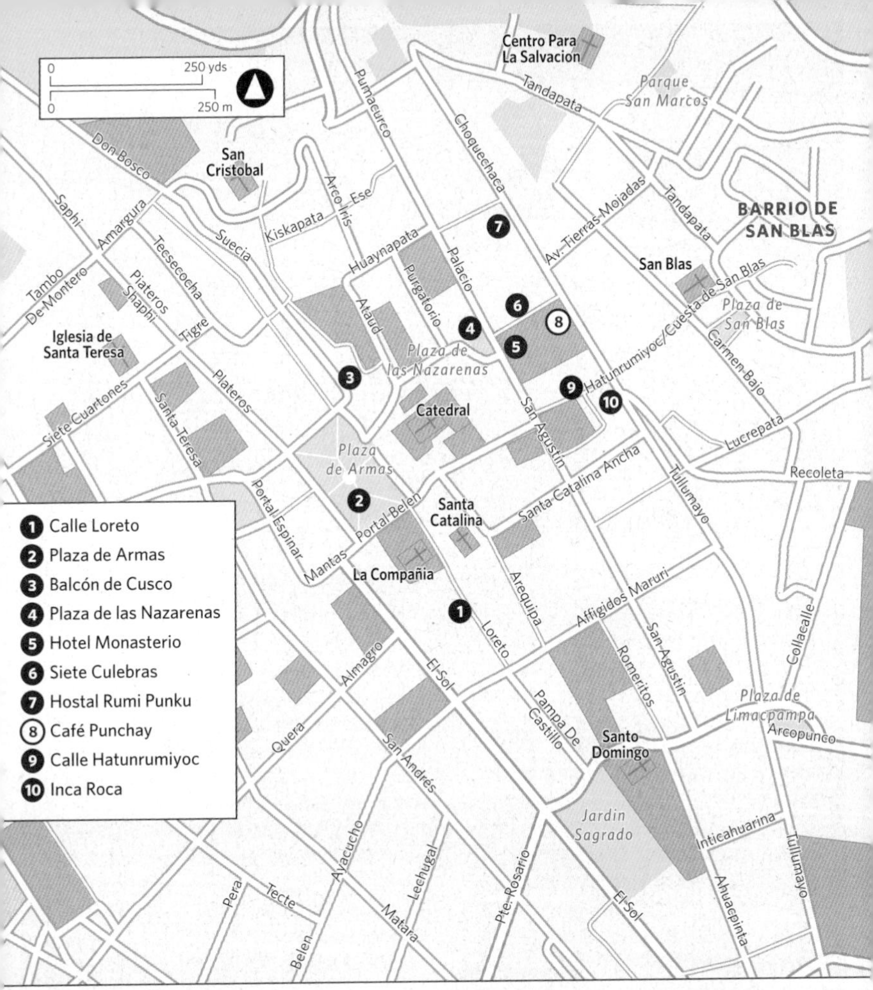

Map Legend

1. Calle Loreto
2. Plaza de Armas
3. Balcón de Cusco
4. Plaza de las Nazarenas
5. Hotel Monasterio
6. Siete Culebras
7. Hostal Rumi Punku
8. Café Punchay
9. Calle Hatunrumiyoc
10. Inca Roca

2 ★★★ **Plaza de Armas.** Refashioned by the Spanish, this centerpiece of the Inca Empire was originally known as Huacaypata (Weeping Square). It was built by the Inca Pachacútec, the Empire's great builder, and was the site of military demonstrations and parades.

Walk to the left of the Cathedral, where Tucumán (also called Almirante) climbs in the direction of San Blas.

3 ★ kids **Balcón de Cusco.** In front of Colegio Real Francisco de Borja (founded 1621), this elevated platform offers spectacular panoramic views over the Plaza de Armas, Cathedral, and

> Street signs in the San Blas neighborhood are still in the original, and complicated, Quechua language.

Cusco Festivals

Cusco festivals are a joyous celebration of both the city's Amerindian roots and its Christian influences. It's a terrific, albeit crowded, time to visit if you can find accommodations.

Inti Raymi (above), the Festival of the Sun, is one of the greatest pageants in South America, celebrating the winter solstice (in June here, below the Equator) and honoring the Inca sun god with a bounty of colorful Andean parades, music, and dance. The festival takes over Cusco and transforms the Sacsayhuamán ruins overlooking the city into a majestic stage, with an eruption of Inca folk dances, exuberant costumes, and grand pageants and parades, including a faithful reenactment of the traditional Inca Festival of the Sun. It culminates in high priests sacrificing two llamas, one black and one white, to predict the fortunes of the coming year.

Semana Santa, or Easter Week (late Mar or Apr), is an exciting traditional expression of religious faith, with stately processions through the streets of Cusco, including a great procession led by El Señor de los Temblores (Lord of the Earthquakes) on Easter Monday. On Good Friday, booths selling traditional Easter dishes are set up on the streets.

In early May, the **Fiesta de las Cruces** (Festival of the Crosses), a celebration popular throughout the highlands, is marked by communities decorating large crosses and delivering them to churches. Crucifix vigils are held on all hilltops that are crowned by crosses. Festivities, as always accompanied by lively dancing, give thanks for bountiful harvests.

Early June's **Corpus Christi** festival is another momentous occasion, with colorful religious parades featuring 15 effigies of saints through the city and events at the Plaza de Armas and the cathedral (where the effigies are displayed for a week).

On December 24 Cusco celebrates the **Santuranticuy Festival,** one of the largest arts-and-crafts fairs in Peru. Hundreds of artisans lay out blankets in the Plaza de Armas and sell carved Nativity figures and saints' images, in addition to ceramics and *retablos* (altars). The tradition was begun by the Bethlehemite Order and Franciscan Friars.

During the festival of **Virgen del Carmen,** the tiny, remote, Andean colonial village of Paucartambo is transformed by one of Peru's wildest parties, 3 days of dance, revelry, drinking, and outlandish costumes. Revelers camp all over town (there's almost nowhere to stay) and wind up at the cemetery.

red-tiled rooftops of Cusco, and of the Andes framing the city.

④ ★ Plaza de las Nazarenas. At the end of Tucumán, this delightful small plaza is home to the elegant Museo de Arte Precolombino (p. 195, **⑦**), once the site of an Inca ceremonial court; a handful of chic shops and restaurants; and a couple of the city's finest hotels.

⑤ Hotel Monasterio. Long Cusco's most distinguished place to stay, the former 16th-century San Antonio Abad monastery (itself constructed on the foundations of an Inca palace) has several lovely interior courtyards and its own chapel. Generally, though, you

> *Hostal Rumi Punku retains an original Inca wall and portal.*

need to be a guest of the hotel or restaurant to take a look around. See p. 235.

Follow the alley to the left of Hotel Monasterio.

⑥ Siete Culebras. The Inca alleyway connecting Plaza de las Nazarenas to Calle Choquechaca, poetically named "seven snakes," contains original Inca stones that were incorporated into the foundation of the chapel that is now part of Hotel Monasterio.

Turn left on Choquechaca.

⑦ ★ Hostal Rumi Punku. One of Cusco's few remaining genuine Inca portals can be found at the entrance to this inn, whose name translates as "stone door." See p. 234.

Retrace your steps along Choquechaca.

⑧ 🍽 ★★ kids **Café Punchay.** This German-owned *kaffeehaus* has a cute covered garden terrace on a second level, with good street views and a colorful interior. It's a good place to duck out of the sun and grab a coffee or beer. Choquechaca 229. No phone. Items S/4–S/10.

Turn right on Hatunrumiyoc.

⑨ ★★★ kids Calle Hatunrumiyoc. The name of this pedestrian-only cobblestone alleyway, lined with thick polygonal stones, means "great stone way" in Quechua. See p. 198, **③**.

From Hatunrumiyoc, backtrack and make a right down the first pedestrian alleyway.

⑩ ★★ kids Inca Roca. A small passageway also noted for its Inca foundations and the stones that form a puma.

Inca Emperors

The Inca Empire had 12 dynastic rulers from the late 12th century to the mid-16th century. The emperors were themselves called Incas; the legendary founder of the dynasty was Manco Cápac. The foundations of the palaces of the sixth and eighth leaders, Inca Roca and Viracocha Roca, respectively, are still visible in Cusco. Pachacútec was a mighty military figure and unparalleled urban planner, responsible for creating the empire. He made Cusco the capital of his kingdom, and under his reign the Incas built Qoricancha, the fortresses at Pisac and Ollantaytambo, and Machu Picchu. Huayna Cápac, who ruled in the early 16th century, was the last Inca to oversee a united empire. He divided the Inca territory, which by that time stretched north to Ecuador and south to Bolivia and Chile, between his sons Huáscar and Atahualpa, which resulted in a civil war. Atahualpa eventually defeated his brother but was captured by Francisco Pizarro in Cajamarca and killed by the Spaniards in 1533, which led to the ultimate downfall of the Incas. The 12 Inca emperors, in order:

1. Manco Cápac
2. Sinchi Roca
3. Lloque Yupanqui
4. Mayta Cápac
5. Cápac Yupanqui
6. Inca Roca
7. Yahuar Huácac
8. Viracocha Inca
9. Pachacútec
10. Tupac Inca
11. Huayna Cápac
12. Atahualpa

San Blas

Hilly San Blas, a picturesque district that's home to some of Cusco's finest artisans, art galleries, and crafts shops, is a great place to wander, although the hills are forbidding, especially if you haven't yet acclimated to the altitude. The narrow cobblestone streets in this walking tour feature some of Cusco's most traditional colonial architecture: squat white-adobe houses with red-tile roofs, stone-framed windows, and sky-blue doorways and balconies. Young travelers tend to hang out in San Blas, which has some of the city's most attractive small hotels, *hostales,* and cool bars. It certainly has some of the finest views over the tile rooftops.

> *Barrio de San Blas is known for its artisans and art galleries.*

START Cuesta de San Blas, at Choquechaca.

❶ Cuesta de San Blas. Ascend to the San Blas district along this very steep, narrow street, which leaves most people huffing and puffing.

At the top of Cuesta de San Blas, turn right at Carmen Alto.

❷ ★★★ Templo de San Blas. The oldest parish church in Cusco holds one of the artistic wonders of the New World. See p. 198, ❹.

❸ kids Plaza de San Blas. To the right of the church is a large, open square with gardens, fountains, and a high wall at the rear, a popular hangout on weekends.

❹ ★ *Talleres de Artesanía.* Lining Plaza de San Blas are workshop-galleries, run by artisan families who have been creating folk art for generations. The best known are **Artesanías Mendivil,** Plaza de San Blas 619 and 634, known for its unique, long-necked saint figures; **Artesanías Olave,** Plaza de San Blas 100

VILLA SAN BLAS

BARRIO DE SAN BLAS

① Cuesta de San Blas
② Templo de San Blas
③ Plaza de San Blas
④ *Talleres de Artesanía*
⑤ Calle Tandapata
⑥ Museo de la Coca
⑦ Mirador de San Blas
⑧ Colonial stone portals of Carmen Alto
⑨ El Buen Pastor Panadería

and 651; and **Juan Garboza,** Tandapata 676, which features pre-Inca-style ceramics.

Take the stairs past the fountain at the rear of Plaza de San Blas, and turn left at the top.

⑤ **Calle Tandapata.** This atmospheric, winding street is lined with bars, restaurants, and *hostales.* The hilly part of San Blas used to be agricultural terraces in the days when the district was known as T'oqocachi. The street climbs and wends its way through a residential section of the neighborhood.

Turn right on Suyt'uquhatu.

⑥ **Museo de la Coca.** This small museum tells the story of the "sacred leaf of the Incas," coca, and how it's been used throughout history in the Andes (including its more polemical role today). ⏱ 30 min. Suyt'uqhatu 705. ☎ 084/974-772-505. Admission S/10 adults, S/5 students, free for kids. Daily 9am–8pm.

Continue on Tandapata. Notice the Quecha street names, such as P'asñapakana ("where the young women are hidden"). The adobe walls are lined with cacti on one side and stones on the other. Take a right on Siete Angelitos ("seven little angels") for a taste

of the lung-burning climbs in San Blas. Take a right on Siete Diablitos ("seven little devils").

⑦ ★ **Mirador de San Blas.** The clearing on the right, a somewhat forlorn little plaza, has spectacular views over the tiled roofs of San Blas and all of Cusco.

Backtrack on Siete Diablitos and pass Siete Angelitos; on the right, the tall wall with cascading pink flowers and green gate belongs to a *colegio* (high school). Take a left on Atoqsayk'uchi and then another left on Carmen Alto.

⑧ ★ **Colonial stone portals of Carmen Alto.** Some of San Blas's finest colonial doorways are found on this street; pause for a look at no. 288 (Hostal El Arcano); the one next door, dated 9 September 1660; and no. 162, Colegio de Arquitectos Regional Cusco.

Turn right on Cuesta de San Blas.

⑨ 🍴 **El Buen Pastor Panadería.** Relax with a coffee or pastry at this cool little bakery; there are seats upstairs. Cuesta de San Blas 579. ☎ 084/248-586. Items S/3–S/6.

THE INCAS

Genius Builders

BY NEIL EDWARD SCHLECHT

THE INCAS KNEW NOTHING OF THE WHEEL OR IRON TOOLS, yet they were masterful stonemasons and engineers, and they left behind a mesmerizing architectural legacy. Machu Picchu and other temples, palaces, and fortresses are more than archaeological sites—they're works of art. Though minimalist in design, they were grandiose in scale: the Incas built their capital city, Cusco, in the form of a puma (with the head formed by the fortress of Sacsayhuamán).

Somehow the Incas succeeded in moving massive stones, weighing more than 100 tons, from quarries to sites many miles away. Using local limestone and granite, they built walls of perfectly cut and smooth stones, many the size of immense boulders, that fit together seamlessly without the use of mortar; in many joins, the stones are so tight a razor blade won't fit between them.

Building Theories

TOOLS & SHAPING OF STONES
Lacking iron tools, the Incas cut stones with other stones and bronze or copper tools, splitting them along natural fracture lines. They wedged in pieces of wood, adding water to make the wood expand and fissure, and then shaped and polished the stones with sand and stone. Another theory is that they perforated the stones with metal tools, making them easier to split.

RAMPS, ROLLERS & LEVERS
Laborers rolled stones up wood beams over earthen ramps; perhaps 2,000 men were needed to drag the largest blocks across inclined planes, using ropes and perhaps levers or ladders functioning as sleds.

MASSIVE LABOR FORCE
The Incas' strict hierarchical organization allowed them to dedicate extraordinary manpower to labor-intensive projects.

Architectural Highlights

OLLANTAYTAMBO FORTRESS
Though unfinished, with *piedras cansadas* ("tired stones") abandoned en route from a quarry across the Urubamba River, this is one of the Incas' finest achievements in stonemasonry, with exquisite double doorjambs.

MACHU PICCHU
Stunningly sited and with superb individual architectural features, such as the Temple of the Sun, this is the Incas' greatest example of landscape art.

SACSAYHUAMÁN
The foremost example of "cyclopean polygonal masonry," with mind-bogglingly large granite blocks (weighing 100–150 tons or more) forming the famous zigzag walls of this fortress.

QUORICANCHA
Cusco's Temple of the Sun, the holiest of buildings for the Incas, contains perfectly aligned niches and outstanding doors inside, and smooth and curved sculptural walls outside.

Design Elements

TRAPEZOIDS & DOORJAMBS
Trapezoidal doorways, windows, and wall niches, with sides tapering inward toward a lintel at top, preceded the arch. The finest palaces and temples feature double-jamb doorways, the wide recessed lip inside the outer trapezoid indicating the doorway opened to a site of high status.

NETWORK OF ROADS
The Inca empire extended nearly from one end of the continent to the other, connected by an incredible system of roads, many paved in stone and crossing long valleys and mountains. The Inca Royal Road is more than 3,000 miles (4,830km) long, exceeding the longest Roman road.

CANALS & FOUNTAINS
A gravity-driven system of hydraulic engineering produced canals and fountains that were not just a practical consideration, but an aesthetic one. Some fountains likely served as liturgical baths.

AGRICULTURAL TERRACES
The Incas farmed on steep mountainsides

by creating *andenes*, terraces formed by stone-retaining walls to prevent erosion.

STEPPING STONES & STAIRWAYS
Agricultural terraces were connected by stepping stones built into terrace walls. Pathways to temples, fortresses, and Inca roads were marked by precise stone stairways, flights either of continuous,

elongated flat stones; a series of stones fitted together on each step; or steps carved directly out of the bedrock.

Cusco Ruins Circuit

Before moving on to Machu Picchu and the Sacred Valley (chapter 9), get a primer on Inca history by visiting the series of ruins on the outskirts of Cusco, beginning with the most famous, Sacsayhuamán. Many visitors take in all four of the ruins on easy-to-arrange and inexpensive tours available through virtually any travel agency in the city. The four sets of ruins are described below in order as they fan out from Cusco on the main road to Pisac. Hearty travelers may want to do the tour in reverse, taking a taxi out to the farthest ruin, Tambomachay, and then walking back, to end at Sacsayhuamán (total walking distance: 8km/5 miles); this makes for a full day, and a tiring one for all but the most athletic.

> *The giant granite blocks of Sacsayhuamán will have you puzzling over the Incas' incredible engineering feats.*

START Take a taxi (10 min.) or walk (30 min.) uphill to Sacsayhuamán from the Plaza de Armas or San Blas.

1 ★★★ **kids** **Sacsayhuamán.** These stunning ruins just above Cusco are one of the city's most spectacular sights. While the primary function of Sacsayhuamán continues to be

Visiting the Ruins

Admission to the sites in this tour is included in the *boleto turístico* (p. 202). Sites are open from 8am to 6pm, with the exception of Sacsayhuamán, which opens at 9am.

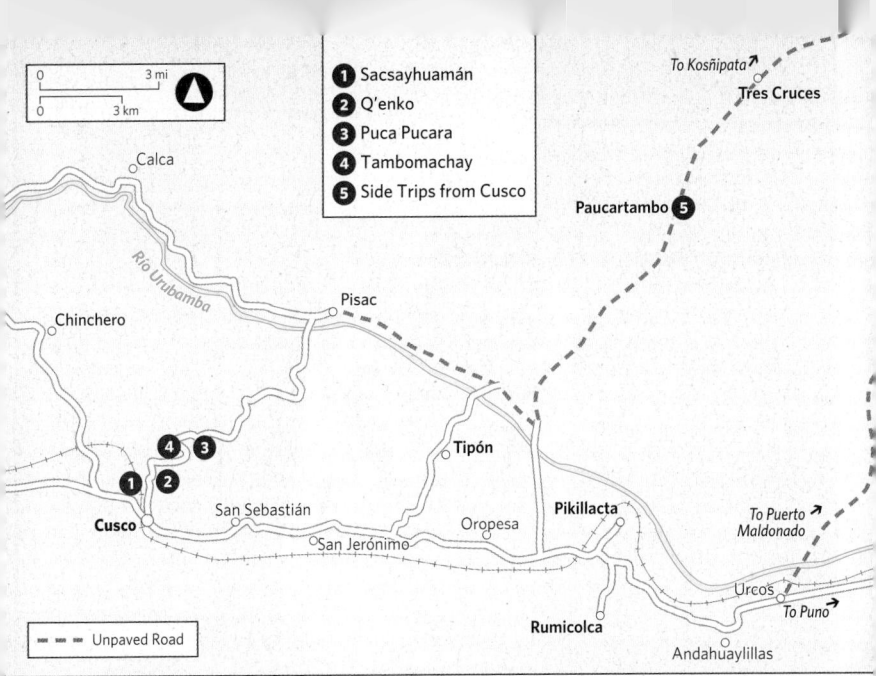

❶	Sacsayhuamán
❷	Q'enko
❸	Puca Pucara
❹	Tambomachay
❺	Side Trips from Cusco

- - - Unpaved Road

debated, what is certain is that it was the site of one of the bloodiest battles between the Spaniards and native Cusqueños. More than 2 years after the Spaniards initially marched on Cusco and installed a puppet government, the anointed Inca (Manco Inca) led a seditious campaign that took back Sacsayhuamán and nearly defeated the Spaniards. Juan Pizarro and his vastly outnumbered but superior armed forces stormed Sacsayhuamán in a horrific battle in 1536 that left thousands dead. After the defeat of the Inca troops and the definitive Spanish occupation of Cusco, the Spaniards used the more manageably sized stone blocks from Sacsayhuamán to build houses and other structures in the city below. The famed Inti Raymi festival (see "Cusco Festivals," p. 206), one of the finest expressions of popular culture in the Americas, is celebrated here annually. It's a spectacular demonstration of Inca pageantry and ritual. ⏱ At least 2 hr. Circunvalación s/n. No phone. Daily 9am–6pm. For more on Sacsayhuamán, see p. 199, ❺.

Follow the main road from Sacsayhuamán for about 1km (⅗ mile).

❷ ★ **Q'enko.** The temple and amphitheater of Q'enko (*kehn-koh*) is a great limestone outcrop hollowed out by the Incas; in the void, they constructed a cave-like altar. (Some have claimed that the smooth stone table inside was used for animal sacrifices.) Visitors can duck into the caves and tunnels beneath the rock. You can also climb on the rock and see the many channels cut into it, where it is thought that either *chicha* (fermented maize beer) or, perhaps, sacrificial blood coursed during ceremonies. (Q'enko might have been a site of ritual ceremonies performed in fertility rites and solstice and equinox celebrations.) ⏱ 30 min. Ctra Cusco-Pisac s/n. No phone.

Puca Pucara is a 90-minute walk from Q'enko along the main road (or 10 min. by taxi or *colectivo*).

❸ **Puca Pucara.** This small fortress (the name means "red fort") may have functioned as a storage facility or lodge, or perhaps as a guard post on the road from Cusco to the villages of the Sacred Valley. It is probably the least impressive of the area sites, although there are good views from here of the surrounding countryside. ⏱ 30 min. Ctra Cusco-Pisac s/n. No phone.

> *There are caves and tunnels at Q'enko, where some claim the Incas held animal sacrifices.*

Take a short walk beyond Puca Pucara.

4 ★★ **Tambomachay.** This site is also known as Los Baños del Inca (Inca Baths). Located near a spring, the ruins consist of three tiers of stone platforms. Water still flows across a sophisticated system of aqueducts and canals in the small complex of terraces and a pool, but these were not baths as we know them. Most likely this was instead a place of water ceremonies and worship. The exquisite stonework is an indicator that the *baños* were reserved for high priests and nobility. ⊙ 45 min. Ctra Cusco-Pisac s/n. No phone.

5 **Side Trips from Cusco.** In addition to the Cusco ruins circuit described in this tour, there are other rewarding excursions, both day trips and overnight visits, from Cusco. Destinations include beautiful colonial mountain towns, scenic views, and elaborate Inca ruins.

SITE GUIDE
PAGE 216

Cusco Shopping Best Bets

Best Alpaca Designs for Women
★★★ **Montse Aucells** Palacio 116 (p. 221)

Best "Fair Trade" Textiles
★★★ **Centro de Textiles Tradicionales del Cusco** Av. El Sol 603 (p. 220)

Best Outdoor Gear
★★ **Tatoo Adventure Gear** Calle del Medio 130 (p. 223)

Best Antique Ponchos & Blankets
★★ **Tienda-Museo de Josefina Olivera** Portal Comercio 173 (Plaza de Armas) (p. 221)

Best Religious Folk Art
★★ **Artesanías Mendivil** Plaza de San Blas 619 (p. 220)

Best Food Market
★ **Mercado de San Pedro** Santa Clara s/n (p. 222)

Best Young & Trendy Clothing
★ **Peru Moderno** Choquechaca 162 (p. 222)

Best Classic Jewelry Designs
★★★ **Ilaria** Portal Carrizos 258 (Plaza de Armas) (p. 223)

Best Alpaca Fashions (Men & Women)
★★ **Kuna** Plaza Recocijo 202 (p. 219)

Best Handmade Baroque Frames
★ **Taller Miguel Angel León Sierra** Córdoba del Tucumán 372 (p. 223)

Best Antiques
★ **Galería de Arte Cusqueño Antigüedades** Plaza de San Blas 114 (p. 219)

Best Funky Women's Designs
★★★ **Hilo** Carmen Alto 260 (p. 221)

Best *Artsesanía* Gifts
★ **Indigo Arte y Artesanía,** San Agustín 403–407 (p. 221)

> At the Centro de Textiles Tradicionales del Cusco, profits go to highland weavers.

5 Side Trips from Cusco

Machu Picchu and the villages and markets of the Sacred Valley (see chapter 9), both accessible from Cusco, are two of the primary reasons the great majority of visitors come to Peru. And, in addition to the Cusco Ruins Circuit described in this tour, there are several other rewarding destinations from Cusco. Paucartambo requires an overnight stay. The ruins of Tipón, Pikillacta, and Rumicolca can all be visited on a single trek southeast of Cusco (by taxi or *combi*). Admission to all the ruins is by *boleto turístico* (p. 202).

Remote **A** ★★ **Paucartambo,** 110km (68 miles) northeast of Cusco, is a beautiful and peaceful colonial town with fame disproportionate to its size. Its annual **Fiesta de la Virgen del Carmen** is one of Peru's wildest festivals. The mid-July party lasts several days, and revelers don elaborate and surreal masks and drink with abandonment. The processions and traditional dances, in honor of Mamacha Carmen, the patron saint of the mestizo population, are stunning. Most visitors have little choice but to camp out, since accommodations are at a premium. At other times, Paucartambo is a quiet mountain village, a former mining colony with cobblestone streets and a pretty Plaza de Armas with blue balconies that makes a rewarding off-the-beaten-track stop during the dry season (May–Oct; during the rainy season travel to the village is difficult and unpleasant). Adventurers traveling by land to the Manu Biosphere Reserve often stop here en route. Beyond Paucartambo (45km/28 miles) is another famous sight: **B** ★★ **Tres Cruces,** a spot on a mountain ridge at the edge of the Andes (at nearly 4,000m/13,100 ft.) that was sacred to the Incas and remains legendary for its mystical sunrises (sunrises during the winter months of May–July are best). The sunrise over the Amazon cloud forest is wildly colorful, with unusual optical effects. It's a hypnotic sight. Gallinas de Rocas minibuses leave daily for Paucartambo from Av. Huáscar in Cusco (near Garcilaso) and take 4 to 6 hours. To attend the Virgen del Carmen festival, it's most convenient to sign up with a local agency; several around Cusco organize

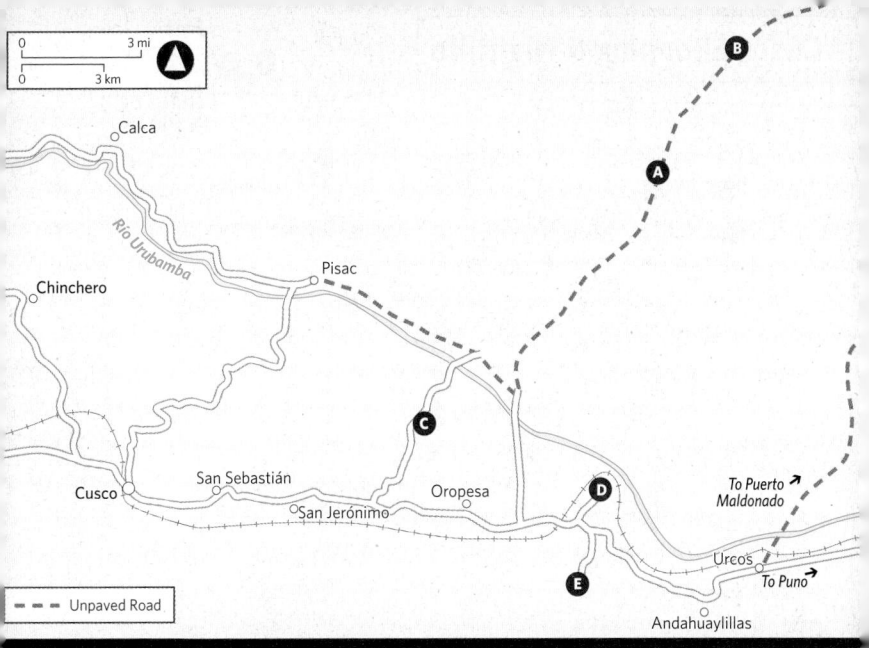

--- Unpaved Road

2- and 3-day visits, with transportation, food, and camping gear (or arrangements for use of a villager's bed or floor) included; look for posters in town the week before the festival. Cusco travel agencies also arrange trips to Tres Cruces; otherwise, you have to hitchhike from Paucartambo (catching a ride is often possible by asking around in town). Make sure you leave in the middle of the night to arrive in time for sunrise.

The extensive complex of **C** ★★ **Tipón** (daily 7am–5:30pm), 23km (14 miles) northeast of Cusco, is nearly the equal of more celebrated Inca ruins in the Sacred Valley. Its agricultural terracing, typical of the Incas, is especially elaborate. There are also handsomely constructed baths, a temple complex, irrigation canals, and aqueducts. Tipón can usually be visited only during the dry season (May–Oct). Either take a taxi from Cusco or an URCOS *combi* that leaves from Av. Huáscar in Cusco; ask the driver to drop you off near Tipón (btw. the villages of Saylla and Oropesa); the site is a healthy walk 4km (2½

miles) from the highway via a steep path that is about an hour's climb. Occasionally there are taxis near the bus drop-off; they can reach the ruins along a dirt road.

The Cusco region may be synonymous with the Incas, but other more ancient cultures, including the Huari, preceded them. **D** **Pikillacta** (daily 7am–5:30pm), 38km (24 miles) east of Cusco, is a huge ceremonial center built by the Huari between A.D. 700 and 900. This is the only pre-Inca site of importance near Cusco, although the two-story adobe buildings, surrounded by a defensive wall, aren't in great shape. The Museo Inka in Cusco (p. 203, **7**) exhibits small turquoise idols discovered at Pikillacta. **E** **Rumicolca,** an Inca gateway to the Sacred Valley that was constructed on the foundations of an ancient Huari aqueduct, lies across the main road, about a mile from Pikillacta. The site was a travel checkpoint controlling entry to the Cusco Valley under the Incas. URCOS *combis* leave from Av. Huáscar in Cusco and drop passengers for Pikillacta near the entrance.

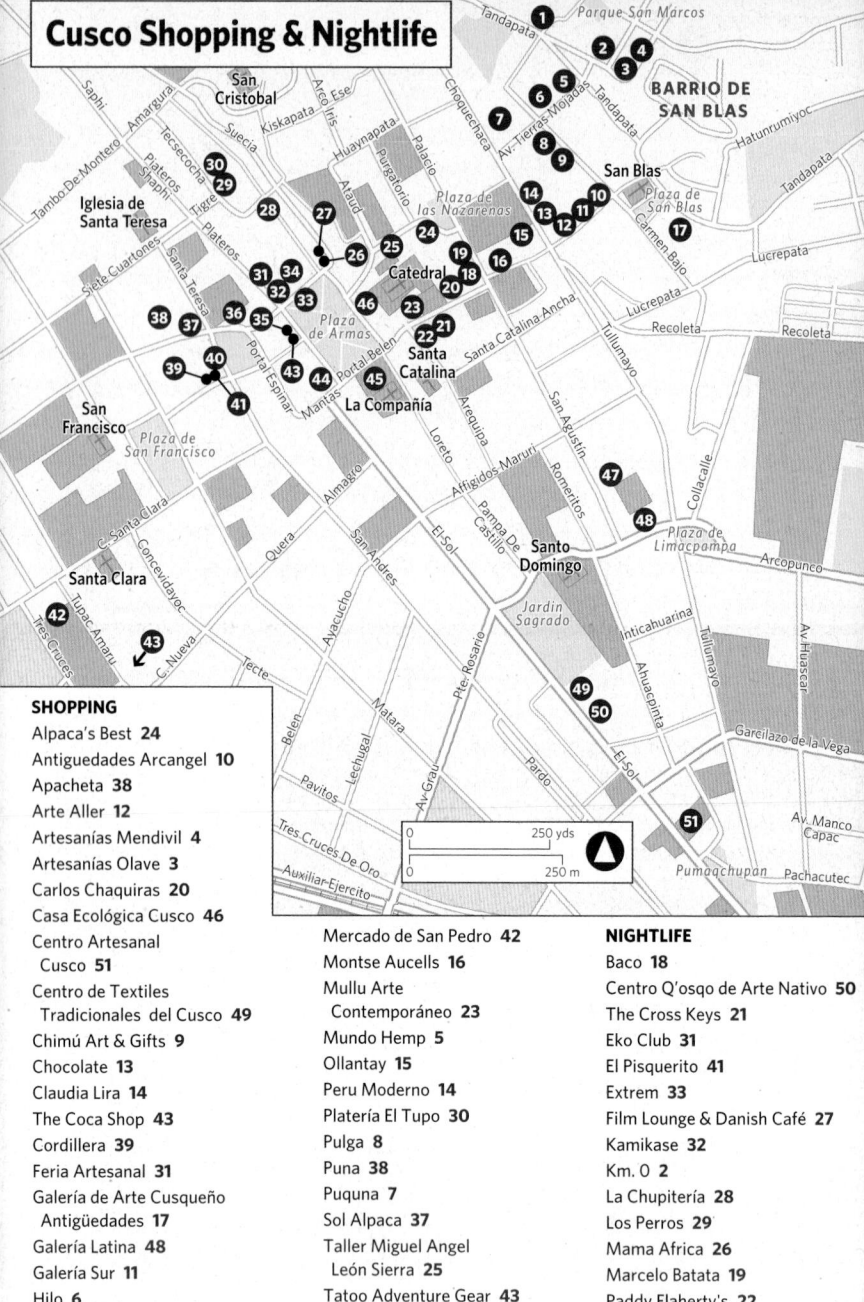

Cusco Shopping & Nightlife

Cusco Shopping A to Z

Alpaca & Andean Fashions

★ Alpaca's Best CENTRO HISTÓRICO
A wide range of very nice and colorful alpaca sweaters, scarves, and hats, including good gift items, although some designs are a bit dated. Plaza de las Nazarenas 197–199. ☎ 084/245-331. AE, DC, MC, V.

★★ Kuna CENTRO HISTÓRICO
Some of the finest and most stylish contemporary alpaca and wool fashions for men and women, including great shawls and modern overcoats. There's another branch on the Plaza de Armas, at Portal de Panes 127. Plaza Recocijo 202. ☎ 084/243-233. AE, DC, V, MC.

Mullu Arte Contemporáneo CENTRO HISTÓRICO
This little shop is all about T-shirts with hip Andean motifs. Triunfo 120. ☎ 084/229-831. No credit cards.

Mundo Hemp SAN BLAS
A different take on Peruvian fashions, sure to appeal to stylish backpackers, this place stocks 100% natural hemp clothes and housewares, and has a little on-site cafe. Qanchipata 596. ☎ 084/258-411. No credit cards.

★★ Sol Alpaca CENTRO HISTÓRICO
One of Cusco's most stylish and contemporary alpaca goods shops, with great sweaters and shawls, and the bonus of an excellent Indigo Arte y Artesanía shop inside. Santa Teresa 317. ☎ 084/232-687. AE, DC, MC, V.

Antiques

Antiguedades Arcangel SAN BLAS
A mix of religious and other antiques from the Cusco region and across Peru, including some accessibly priced gift items. Cuesta de San Blas 591. ☎ 084/633-754. No credit cards.

★ Galería de Arte Cusqueño Antigüedades SAN BLAS You'll find a huge array of antiques here, ranging from textiles to art and furniture. Plaza de San Blas 114. ☎ 084/237-857. MC, V.

> *Not for nothing does the family of Josefina Olivera call her textile boutique on Plaza de Armas a "shop/museum."*

> The clothing shop Pulga sports a young, hipster mentality.

Art & Handicrafts (*Artesanía*)

★ Apacheta CENTRO HISTÓRICO
Half contemporary art gallery and half shop dedicated to nicely selected, handmade *artesanía* and jewelry. San Juan de Dios 250 (interior). ☎ 084/238-210. MC, V.

★ Arte Aller SAN BLAS
A crowded little shop that features great folk and religious art, including handmade Christmas ornaments. Cuesta de San Blas 580. ☎ 084/241-171. No credit cards.

★★ Artesanías Mendivil SAN BLAS
Known internationally for its singular saint figures with elongated necks, this family of artisans also creates a nice selection of mirrors, carved wood frames, Escuela Cusqueña reproduction paintings, and ceramics. Other nearby locations are at Hatunrumíyoc 486 (☎ 084/233-234) and Plaza de San Blas 634 (☎ 084/240-527). Plaza de San Blas 619. ☎ 084/233-247. MC, V.

★★ Artesanías Olave SAN BLAS
This high-quality crafts shop does big business with tourists. Other locations are at Triunfo 342 (☎ 084/252-935) and Plaza de San Blas 651 (☎ 084/231-835). Plaza de San Blas 100. ☎ 084/246-300. MC, V.

★ Casa Ecológica Cusco CENTRO HISTÓRICO
Tucked away in a courtyard off the Plaza de Armas, this interesting shop stocks a good selection of high-quality, handmade textiles from highland communities in the Cusco region, in addition to natural medicines and organic food products. Portal de Carnes 236 (interior). ☎ 084/255-427. MC, V.

Centro Artesanal Cusco AV. EL SOL
At the end of Av. El Sol, across from the large painted waterfall fountain, is Cusco's largest indoor market of handicraft stalls. There's a huge selection of similar-looking goods, many of which are slightly cheaper here than they are closer to the plaza, so if you're looking for a bunch of *chullpas* (Peruvian caps) or scarves, this place is a good bet. Av. El Sol s/n. No phone. No credit cards.

★★★ Centro de Textiles Tradicionales del Cusco
AV. EL SOL This boutique shop and museum is run by an organization dedicated to "fair trade" practices, ensuring that 70% of each purchase of very fine textiles goes directly to the six communities and individual artisans it works with. On-site there is an ongoing demonstration of weaving and a very good textiles museum. Prices are higher than what you may find in generic shops around town, though the textiles are also higher quality, and much more of your money goes to the women who work for days on individual pieces. There's also a small outlet of the Centro in the courtyard at the Museo de Arte Precolombino (MAP), Plaza de las Nazarenas 231. Av. El Sol 603. ☎ 084/228-117. www.textilescusco.org. MC, V.

★ Feria Artesanal CENTRO HISTÓRICO
For antique textiles, there's a very good little stall at the end of the corridor (on the right side) within this small market. Stalls aren't numbered, and you might have to ask the owner to pull his older, more valuable pieces from a trunk he keeps them in, but he has some of the finest quality ceremonial textiles in Cusco. Plateros 334. No phone. No credit cards.

Galería Latina CENTRO HISTÓRICO
For a general selection of *artesanía*, this large, cozy shop has a wide range of top-end antique blankets, rugs, alpaca-fleece clothing, ceramics, jewelry, and handicrafts from the Amazon jungle. Zetas 309. ☎ 084/236-703. MC, V.

> *The Catalan Montse Aucells, a longtime resident of Cusco, designs and sells elegant alpaca clothing and accessories for women.*

★ **Galería Sur** SAN BLAS
Unique in Cusco, this gallery exclusively features very fine, distinctive tapestries from Ayacucho, which are internationally prized. Hatunrumiyoc 487-B. ☎ 084/238-371. MC, V.

★ **Indigo Arte y Artesanía** CENTRO HISTÓRICO
If you're in search of good gift items, this shop is loaded with well-chosen items from across Peru. San Agustín 403–407. ☎ 084/240-145. AE, DC, MC, V.

★★ **La Casa de la Llama** CENTRO HISTÓRICO
Featuring very nice quality and distinctive alpaca designs and leather goods, including embroidered reversible belts and baby-alpaca stoles. Palacio 121. ☎ 084/240-813. AE, DC, MC, V.

Puquna SAN BLAS
A small and stylish shop that features original design and popular art objects, including photography, textiles, and jewelry. Choquechaca 408. ☎ 084/255-257. MC, V.

★★ **Tienda-Museo de Josefina Olivera** CENTRO HISTÓRICO For a massive selection of antique Andean textiles, this shop on the Plaza de Armas stocks some fantastic vintage alpaca ponchos and blankets, many 25 to 100 years old. The shop, which from the street appears to have no name, is much more than meets the eye: downstairs is a large basement that's stuffed wall-to-wall with antique textiles. Portal Comercio 173 (Plaza de Armas). ☎ 084/233-484. No credit cards.

Design & Fashion

★★★ **Hilo** SAN BLAS
The most unique designer in Cusco is a transplant from Northern Ireland. Eibhlin Cassidy makes and sells extremely original clothing designs for women, including beautiful tops and jackets. Her unique patterns and sometimes startling use of fabrics, color, and adornments translate into whimsical and wearable art. Carmen Alto 260. ☎ 084/254-536. MC, V.

★★★ **Montse Aucells** CENTRO HISTÓRICO
This friendly Catalan designer, a longtime resident of Cusco, has a little shop near Hotel Monasterio that features very fashionable, sleek, and original alpaca designs and knitwear for women. Palacio 116. ☎ 084/226-330. MC, V.

★ **Ollantay** SAN BLAS
Although handbags and hats are also made at this artisan's shop, it's best known for its brightly colored suede boots, with swatches of antique Andean fabrics. My wife came home

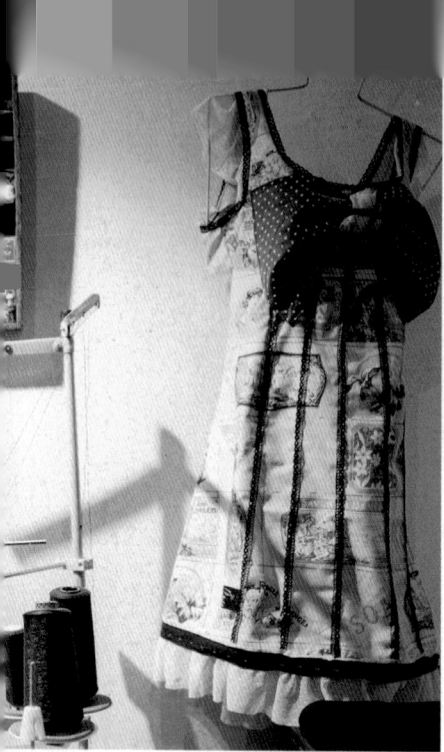

> *Hilo is the funky dress shop of a woman from Northern Ireland, who makes her designs by hand.*

> *Tradition reigns at Mercado de San Pedro.*

with three pairs to strut around New York City. Choquechaca 211. ☎ 984/616-844. No credit cards.

★ Peru Moderno SAN BLAS
A contemporary shop with an emphasis on wildly colorful and hip (and often neon) clothing, bags, and accessories. Choquechaca 162. ☎ 084/244-135. www.perumoderno.com. MC, V.

Pulga SAN BLAS
A good spot for young and trendy types, this small shop focuses exclusively on the funky designs (clothing, bags, and accessories for both men and women) of young Peruvian designers from Lima and across Peru. Carmen Alto 237. ☎ 084/9844-93537. www.pulgalatienda.com. MC, V.

★ Puna CENTRO HISTÓRICO
A sleek, contemporary gallery with art prints, hip design items, graphic T-shirts, and fun accessories such as colorful bags, pillows, gloves, and acrylic items. San Juan de Dios 250 (interior). ☎ 084/225-590. www.puna.com.pe. MC, V.

Foodstuffs

★ Chocolate SAN BLAS
Truth in advertising: this small shop is the place to get your chocolate fix, with a great selection of homemade chocolates, including hot chocolate. Choquechaca 162. ☎ 084/229-001. No credit cards.

The Coca Shop SAN BLAS
Coca leaves have myriad uses beyond the most obvious and are a very traditional component of highland culture. Here you'll find a variety of items derived from coca leaves, including chocolates infused with coca and *lúcuma* (tropical fruit), ice cream, and teas. Carmen Alto 115. ☎ 084/260-774. www.thecocashop.com. No credit cards.

★★ Mercado de San Pedro SAN PEDRO
Join Cusco citizens on their daily run to the city's Central Market, a frenetic place near the San Pedro train station that has everything from a slew of juice bars and produce to meats and household items, as well as lots of curious things you won't find outside Peru. Adventurous eaters can pull up to street stalls

for a ridiculously cheap lunch. You're probably wise to leave valuables and your camera at the hotel. Santa Clara s/n. No phone. No credit cards. Daily 8am–4pm.

Mundo Hemp SAN BLAS
All things hemp, including sweets and soups in the cafe, as well as the expected hemp T-shirts and home-design accessories. Qanchispata 596. ☎ 084/258-411. www.mundohemp.com. No credit cards.

Jewelry & Silver

Carlos Chaquiras CENTRO HISTÓRICO
This contemporary jewelry designer is an excellent craftsman; many of his pieces feature pre-Columbian designs. Triunfo 375. ☎ 084/227-470. MC, V.

★ **Chimú Art & Gifts** SAN BLAS
A tiny boutique featuring cool contemporary designs in silver, many based on interpretations of Chimú culture. Carmen Alto 187-B. ☎ 084/801-968. No credit cards.

★ **Claudia Lira** SAN BLAS
This Lima designer's elegant and unique gold and silver pieces are featured within the colorful clothing and design shop Peru Moderno. Choquechaca 162. ☎ 084/244-135. www.claudialira.com. MC, V.

★★★ **Ilaria** CENTRO HISTÓRICO
One of Peru's top jewelry stores deals in fine silver and unique Andean-style pieces. Many items, although not inexpensive, are an excellent value for handmade silver. There are branches in several Cusco hotels, too: Hotel Monasterio, Palacio 136 (☎ 084/221-192); Casa Andina Private Collection, Plazoleta de Limacpampa Chico 473 (p. 233); and Hotel Libertador, Plazoleta Santo Domingo 259 (☎ 084/223-192). Portal Carrizos 258 (Plaza de Armas). ☎ 084/246-253. AE, DC, MC, V.

Platería El Tupo CENTRO HISTÓRICO
A nice shop with a wide selection of silver items. Portal de Harinas 181 (Plaza de Armas). ☎ 084/229-809. AE, DC, MC, V.

Outdoor Goods & Apparel

Cordillera CENTRO HISTÓRICO
Very similar to Tatoo, perhaps without that shop's range of goods, but a good place to pick up a last-minute parka or hiking boots. Garcilaso 210. ☎ 084/244-133. AE, DC, MC, V.

★ **Tatoo Adventure Gear** CENTRO HISTÓRICO
On the alleyway leading just off Plaza de Armas, this well-stocked place has probably the best selection of camping, trekking, and mountain climbing shoes, backpacks, and equipment. Calle del Medio 130. ☎ 084/224-797. AE, DC, MC, V.

Woodworking

★ **Taller Miguel Angel León Sierra** CENTRO HISTÓRICO In this small studio, Sr. León and his children and grandchildren make splendid handmade cedar frames to order (the kind one sees around most art from the Escuela Cusqueña originals and imitations). Córdoba del Tucumán 372 (just off Plaza de las Nazarenas). ☎ 084/236-271. No credit cards.

> *Claudia Lira's jewelry designs fuse the traditional and modern, Peruvian and international.*

Cusco Restaurant Best Bets

Best Sushi & Seafood
★★★ **Limo** Portal de Carnes 236, 2nd floor (p. 229)

Best Tapas
★★★ **Cicciolina** Triunfo 393, 2nd floor (p. 227)

Best Wine List
★★ **Baco** Ruinas 465 (p. 225)

Best Auteur's Take on Cusqueña Cuisine
★★★ **Chicha** Plaza Regocijo 261, 2nd floor (p. 227)

Best Lunch Spot
★★ **Jack's Café Bar** Choquechaca 509 (p. 228)

Best Farm-to-Table
★ **Granja Heidi** Cuesta de San Blas 525, 2nd floor (p. 227)

Best Organic Dining
★★ **Greens** Santa Catalina Angosta 135, 2nd floor (p. 227)

Best Chic Dining Experience
★★ **MAP Café** Plaza de las Nazarenas 231 (p. 229)

★★★ **Cicciolina** Triunfo 393, 2nd floor (p. 227)

Best Surreal Dining Experience
★★ **Fallen Angel** Plaza de las Nazarenas 221 (p. 227)

Best Courtyard Dining
★ **Two Nations Café** Arequipa 159 (p. 229)

Best Pizza & Family Dining
Chez Maggy Procuradores 348 (p. 225)

★ **Incanto** Santa Catalina Angosta 135 (p. 227)

Best Views
★★★ **Limo** Portal de Carnes 236, 2nd floor (p. 229)

Best Breakfasts
★★ **Jack's Café Bar** Choquechaca 509 (p. 228)

★ **La Tertulia** Procuradores 44, 2nd floor (p. 228)

> *Two Nations Café can be quiet for lunch and a party scene at night.*

Cusco Restaurants A to Z

Al Grano CENTRO HISTÓRICO *ASIAN*
A corner cafe featuring exposed Inca stonework, this informal place unexpectedly serves largely mild fare from Indonesia, India, Pakistan, and Sri Lanka, including chutneys, vegetarian curries, and lamb in spices and yogurt. Santa Catalina Ancha 398 (at San Agustín). ☎ 084/228-032. Entrees S/7–S/24. No credit cards. Lunch and dinner Mon–Sat.

★ **A Mi Manera** CENTRO HISTÓRICO *ANDEAN*
This relaxed upstairs spot serves creative Andean dishes with vegetarian options. Traditionalists should check out the *rocoto relleno* (stuffed pepper with meat, peanuts, and raisins) or *adobo* (chicken made with *chichi* fermented maize and yuca); the house specialty is the traditional oven-baked *cuy* (guinea pig). Triunfo 393, 2nd floor. ☎ 084/243-629. http://amimaneraperu.com. Entrees S/20–S/50. AE, DC, MC, V. Breakfast, lunch, and dinner daily.

★★ **Baco** CENTRO HISTÓRICO *WINE BAR/PIZZA/NOVO ANDINO* Owned by the team behind one of Cusco's best restaurants, Cicciolina, this is both a sleek wine bar and chic restaurant. It serves excellent gourmet pizzas and sophisticated *novo Andino* (nouvelle Andean) and international fare. Ruinas 465. ☎ 084/242-808. www.cicciolinacuzco.com. Entrees S/17–S/48. AE, DC, MC, V. Dinner Mon–Sat.

kids **Chez Maggy** CENTRO HISTÓRICO *PIZZERIA/PERUVIAN* A longtime cheapie favorite on "Gringo Alley," this joint's big draw is freshly baked pizzas made in a traditional wood-burning brick oven. If that's not your thing, the wide-ranging menu includes trout, alpaca, homemade pastas, and Mexican food. Procuradores 348. ☎ 084/234-861. www.pizzeriachezmaggy.com. Entrees S/12–S/30. MC, V. Dinner daily.

> *Cicciolina is named for an Italian porn star, and its menu offers a wide range of items.*

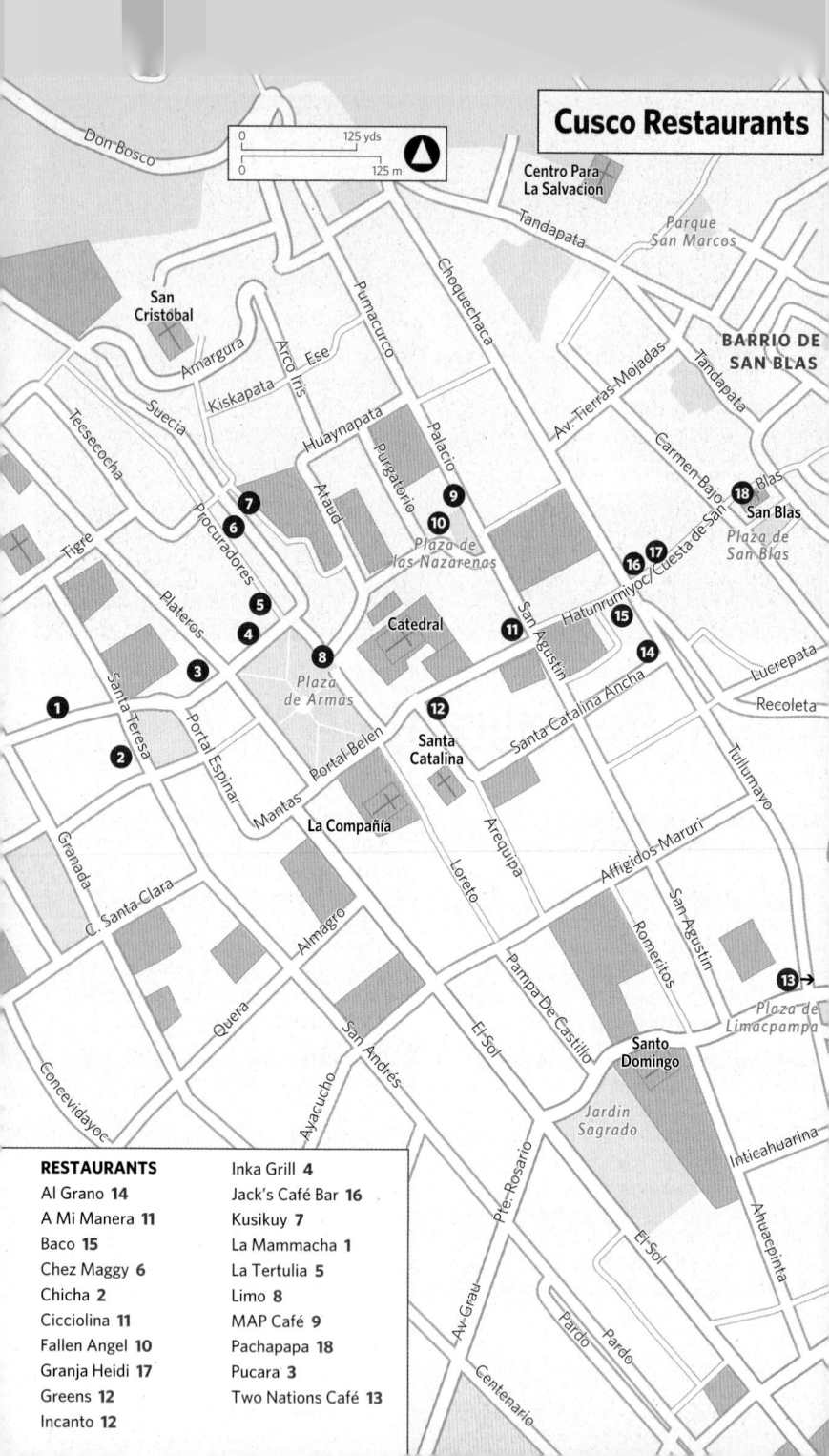

Cusco Restaurants

RESTAURANTS

Al Grano **14**
A Mi Manera **11**
Baco **15**
Chez Maggy **6**
Chicha **2**
Cicciolina **11**
Fallen Angel **10**
Granja Heidi **17**
Greens **12**
Incanto **12**
Inka Grill **4**
Jack's Café Bar **16**
Kusikuy **7**
La Mammacha **1**
La Tertulia **5**
Limo **8**
MAP Café **9**
Pachapapa **18**
Pucara **3**
Two Nations Café **13**

★★★ **Chicha** CENTRO HISTÓRICO *NOVO AN-DINO/PERUVIAN* Peru's celebrity chef Gastón Acurio's take on highland cuisine, in a warm and chic, nearly hidden second-story space. Acurio uses local ingredients such as quinoa for his tabbouleh and offers an upscale version of *pachamanca* (a traditional countryside barbecue of meat and potatoes cooked in an underground pit). Plaza Regocijo 261, 2nd floor. ☎ 084/240-520. Entrees S/26–S/49. AE, DC, MC, V. Lunch and dinner Mon–Sat; lunch Sun.

★★★ **Cicciolina** CENTRO HISTÓRICO *MEDITERRANEAN/NOVO ANDINO* A delightfully chic upstairs restaurant that takes its cue from Tuscany. The long bar is perfect for cocktails or dinner itself, especially the creative tapas that aren't served in the more formal dining room. Main courses include large, superb salads, excellent homemade pastas, and alpaca filet. At lunchtime, there's usually a great pasta special. Triunfo 393, 2nd floor. ☎ 084/239-510. www.cicciolinacuzco.com. Entrees S/23–S/48. AE, DC, MC, V. Breakfast, lunch, and dinner daily.

★★ **Fallen Angel** CENTRO HISTÓRICO *NOVO ANDINO/STEAK* This eccentric funhouse looks more nightclub than restaurant, and while plenty come to gawk at the baroque decor, the menu is pretty simple: essentially beef tenderloin, with a choice of 15 different salsas, some with Asian and exotic combinations. Vegetarians can opt for the pastas and ceviche, but the best bet here is the steaks. Plaza de las Nazarenas 221. ☎ 084/258-184. www.fallenangelincusco.com. Entrees S/45. MC, V. Dinner Mon–Fri; lunch and dinner Sat–Sun.

★ **Granja Heidi** SAN BLAS *HEALTH FOOD/VEGETARIAN* Run by a German woman with a farm outside Cusco, this hard-to-find restaurant features fresh ingredients and products that taste farm-fresh. The menu offers surprising meat dishes, including ostrich steak, and typical Peruvian dishes. There's a great-value daily lunch menu. Cuesta de San Blas 525, 2nd floor. ☎ 084/238-383. Entrees S/9–S/25. No credit cards. Breakfast, lunch, and dinner daily.

★★ **Greens** CENTRO HISTÓRICO *HEALTH FOOD/NOVO ANDINO* One of Cusco's most stylish and intimate restaurants, this cool, colorful place features an organic menu of

> *Chicha is Lima chef Gastón Acurio's interpretation of the highland fare of Cusco.*

vegetarian options, including delicious salads, as well as alpaca tenderloin, whole-wheat pastas, and tropical chicken curry. Santa Catalina Angosta 135, 2nd floor. ☎ 084/243-579. www.cuscorestaurants.com. Entrees S/19–S/25. No credit cards. Lunch and dinner daily.

★ **Incanto** CENTRO HISTÓRICO *PERUVIAN/NOVO ANDINO* Focusing on homemade pastas and pizzas from a wood-burning oven, this large, agreeable restaurant just off the Plaza de Armas, with an interior Inca stone wall, is a crowd-pleaser. Santa Catalina Angosta 135. ☎ 084/254-753. www.cuscorestaurants.com. Entrees S/20–S/42. AE, DC, MC, V. Lunch and dinner Mon–Sat.

★ **Inka Grill** CENTRO HISTÓRICO *PERUVIAN/NOVO ANDINO* One of Cusco's first upscale restaurants is still a dependable dining experience. The best dishes are the Peruvian standards such as sautéed alpaca tenderloin served over quinoa and *ají de gallina* (shredded

> *Jack's Café Bar is one of the most dependable and popular breakfast and lunch joints in town.*

> *Get your fill of fresh seafood, such as ceviche and tiraditos—a rarity away from the coast—at Limo.*

chicken with nuts, cheese, and chile peppers). Portal de Panes 115. ☎ 084/262-992. www. cuscorestaurants.com. Entrees S/23–S/55. AE, DC, MC, V. Breakfast, lunch, and dinner Mon–Sat.

★★ kids **Jack's Café Bar** SAN BLAS *CAFE/INTERNATIONAL* Don't overlook this joint just because it's a gringo hangout. Crowds come throughout the day for a wide variety of fresh, generously portioned meals. Breakfast pancakes are winners, as are the towering salads and gourmet sandwiches. There are plenty of items for vegetarians. Choquechaca 509 (corner of Cuesta de San Blas). ☎ 084/806-960. Entrees S/12–S/22. No credit cards. Breakfast, lunch, and dinner daily.

Kusikuy CENTRO HISTÓRICO *ANDEAN/INTERNATIONAL* This cozy restaurant's name in Quechua means "happy little guinea pig,"

so *cuy al horno* (oven-baked guinea pig) is, of course, the house dish. The menu focuses on typical Peruvian dishes and adds stuff for gringos, such as pastas and chicken and meat dishes. It serves a good-value lunch. Suecia 339. ☎ 084/262-870. Entrees S/14–S/38. MC, V. Breakfast, lunch, and dinner Mon–Sat.

★ **La Mammacha** CENTRO HISTÓRICO *PERUVIAN/ITALIAN* A good-looking, modern, and open space with several tables overlooking the beautiful courtyard of this old house that's been converted into a dining, shopping, and nightlife destination. This new restaurant calls itself a "trattoria Peruana" and serves what it calls Peruvian fusion—largely pastas with Peruvian accents. San Juan de Dios 250, 2nd floor. ☎ 084/242-493. Entrees S/23–S/34. AE, DC, MC, V. Lunch and dinner Mon–Sat; lunch Sun.

kids **La Tertulia** CENTRO HISTÓRICO *BREAKFAST/CAFE FARE* Travelers come here to read newspapers and foreign magazines and exchange advice on treks. Fuel up before your adventures with the superb breakfast buffet.

Procuradores 44, 2nd floor. ☎ 084/241-422. Entrees S/8–S/24. MC, V. Breakfast, lunch, and dinner daily.

★★★ **Limo** CENTRO HISTÓRICO *SUSHI/PERUVIAN* A sleek and chic place with amazing views of the Plaza de Armas, great cocktails, and the best sushi and ceviche in Cusco. Lima-style seafood is the main draw, but there are also traditional highland entrees such as pork shoulder and *adobo de cerdo* (marinated pork). Everything is carefully executed and a very good value. Portal de Carnes 236, 2nd floor. ☎ 084/240-668. www.cuscorestaurants.com. Entrees S/26–S/50. AE, DC, MC, V. Lunch and dinner daily.

★★ **MAP Café** CENTRO HISTÓRICO *NOVO ANDINO/INTERNATIONAL* In a modern, minimalist glass-and-steel box with views of the colonial patio belonging to historic Casa Cabera, this restaurant is definitely something different. The artistically presented food (at dinner a prix-fixe menu only) is a bit pricey, but if you're looking for a sophisticated night out and creative Andean cuisine, this is a good date spot. Plaza de las Nazarenas 231 (within Museo de Arte Precolombino). ☎ 084/242-476. www.cuscorestaurants.com. Entrees S/24–S/50; pre-fixe dinner $50. AE, DC, MC, V. Lunch and dinner daily.

★ **Pachapapa** SAN BLAS *PERUVIAN* A popular *quinta,* or open-air, traditional-style highland restaurant, this leafy courtyard is a delightful place for authentic Andean dishes. You'll also find soups and salads, as well as *cuy* served with Huacatay mint, trout, and even a spicy ham and cheese calzone—all from the wood-fired oven. Plaza de San Blas 120. ☎ 084/241-318. www.cuscorestaurants.com. Entrees S/18–S/34. MC, V. Lunch and dinner daily.

Pucara CENTRO HISTÓRICO *PERUVIAN/INTERNATIONAL* Intimate and dimly lit, this restaurant represents one of the better values in the historic center and is often packed. It features dependable traditional Peruvian and international dishes, including a tasty *lomo saltado* (strips of beef with fried potatoes, onions, and tomatoes) and several different soups daily. Plateros 309. ☎ 084/222-027. Entrees S/14–S/32. No credit cards. Lunch and dinner Mon–Sat.

> *Alfresco dining at Pachapapa, one of the city's traditional open-air* quinta *restaurants.*

★★ **Two Nations Café** CENTRO HISTÓRICO *ANDEAN/INTERNATIONAL* The newest location of this laid-back place, in a colonial house with an attractive beer garden courtyard, is a winner. The Australian chef-owner serves satisfying comfort food with a twist, and there are items such as an Aussie burger with fried egg and beetroot, and the Two Nations burger with alpaca tenderloin and caramelized onions. It's also a great place for a coffee, microbrew, or cocktail any time of day or night. The older location at Huaynapata 410 (☎ 084/240-198) is scruffier but charming as well. Arequipa 159. ☎ 084/634-000. Entrees S/15–S/34. AE, DC, MC, V. Breakfast, lunch, and dinner daily.

Cusco Hotel Best Bets

Best Erstwhile Monastery/Historic Luxury Hotel
★★★ **Hotel Monasterio** Palacio 136 (p. 235)

Best Luxury Boutique Hotel
★★★ **Aranwa Cusco Boutique Hotel** San Juan de Dios 255 (p. 232)

★★★ **La Casona** Plaza de las Nazarenas 167 (p. 235)

Best *Hostal*
★ **Amaru Hostal** Cuesta de San Blas 541 (p. 232)

Best-Value Boutique Hotel
★★ **Second Home Cusco** Atocsaycuchi 616 (p. 236)

Best Dreamlike Hotel
★★★ **Fallen Angel: The Guest House** Plaza de las Nazarenas 221 (p. 234)

Best Place to Meet Fellow Backpackers
★ **Pariwana Hostel Cusco** Mesón de la Estrella 136 (p. 236)

Best Views
★ **Casa Andina Classic San Blas** Chihuampata 278 (p. 232)

★ **Los Apus Hotel & Mirador** Atocsaycuchi 515 (p. 235)

Best Breakfast Buffet
★ **Torre Dorada** Calle los Cipreses (p. 236)

Best Colonial Feel
★★★ **Hotel Monasterio** Palacio 136 (p. 235)

★ **El Andariego Hostal** San Andrés 270 (p. 233)

Best Inca Legacy
★ **Hostal Rumi Punku** Choquechaca 339 (p. 234)

★★ **Libertador Palacio del Inka** San Agustín 400 (p. 235)

Best Service
★★★ **La Casona** Plaza de las Nazarenas 167 (p. 235)

Best Oxygen Service
★★★ **Aranwa Cusco Boutique Hotel** San Juan de Dios 255 (p. 232)

★★★ **Hotel Monasterio** Palacio 136 (p. 235)

Best Altruistic/Feel-Good Hotel
★★★ **Niños Hotel** Meloq 442 (p. 235)

Best for Families
★ **Casa Andina Classic San Blas** Chihuampata 278 (p. 232)

★★★ **Niños Hotel** Meloq 442 (p. 235)

> *The stately courtyard at Casa Andina Classic San Blas.*

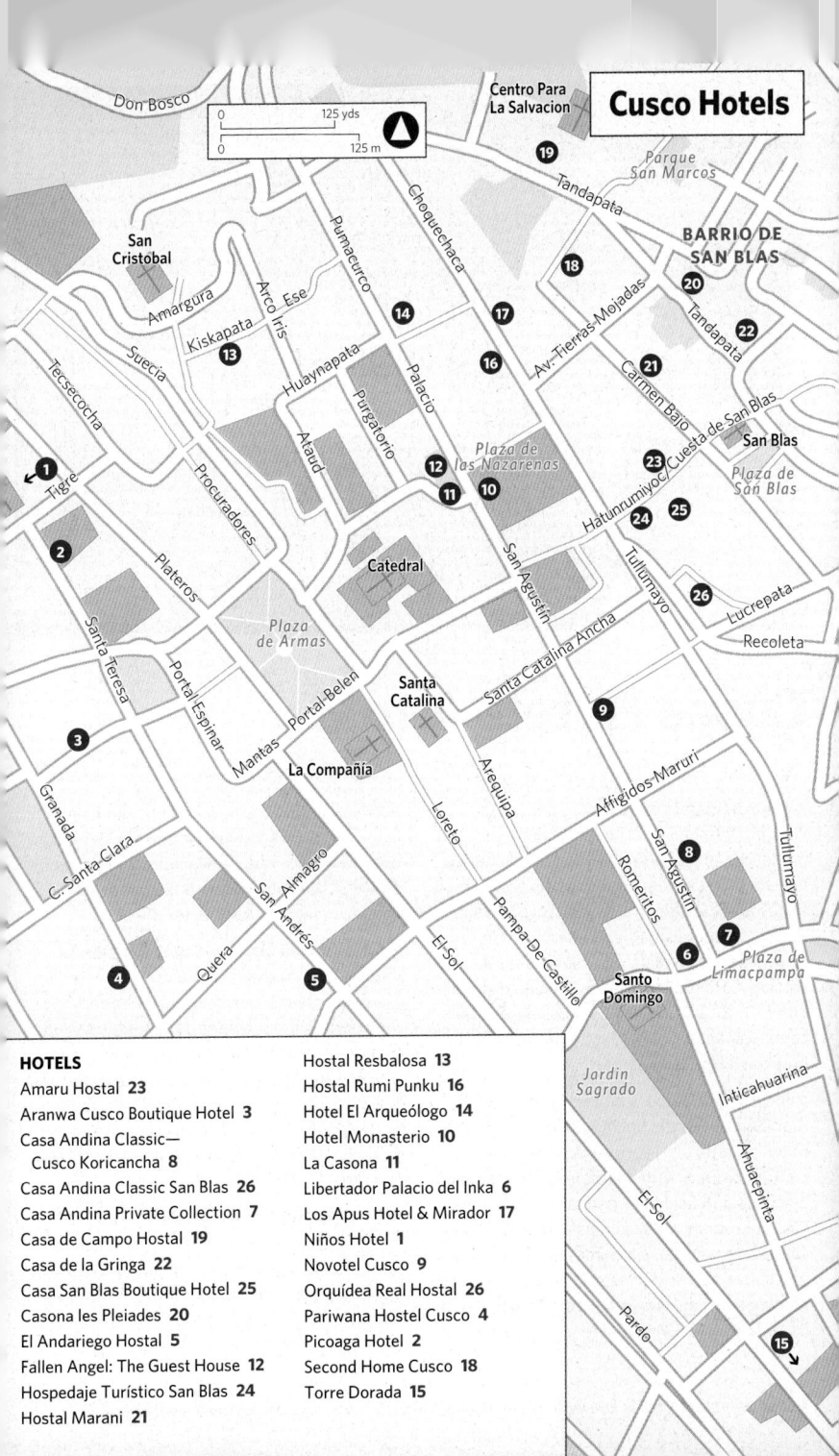

Cusco Hotels

HOTELS

Amaru Hostal **23**
Aranwa Cusco Boutique Hotel **3**
Casa Andina Classic—
  Cusco Koricancha **8**
Casa Andina Classic San Blas **26**
Casa Andina Private Collection **7**
Casa de Campo Hostal **19**
Casa de la Gringa **22**
Casa San Blas Boutique Hotel **25**
Casona les Pleiades **20**
El Andariego Hostal **5**
Fallen Angel: The Guest House **12**
Hospedaje Turístico San Blas **24**
Hostal Marani **21**

Hostal Resbalosa **13**
Hostal Rumi Punku **16**
Hotel El Arqueólogo **14**
Hotel Monasterio **10**
La Casona **11**
Libertador Palacio del Inka **6**
Los Apus Hotel & Mirador **17**
Niños Hotel **1**
Novotel Cusco **9**
Orquídea Real Hostal **26**
Pariwana Hostel Cusco **4**
Picoaga Hotel **2**
Second Home Cusco **18**
Torre Dorada **15**

Cusco Hotels A to Z

★ Amaru Hostal SAN BLAS

Popular with legions of backpackers, this hostel in a pretty colonial-Republican house has a relaxed garden area. Rooms are comfortable, nicely decorated, and a good value (some are quite small). Its nearby sister property, Amaru Hostal II, on Chihmpata 642 (☎ 084/223-521), is similar. Cuesta de San Blas 541. ☎ 084/225-933. www.amaruhostal.com. 16 units. $23–$48 double. Rates include breakfast. No credit cards.

★★★ Aranwa Cusco Boutique Hotel CENTRO

HISTÓRICO Stately and luxurious, this new hotel inhabits a brilliantly converted 16th-century *casona*, with an impressive display of antiques and Escuela Cusqueña art. Rooms have incredibly high ceilings and are as elegant as any in Cusco. In fact, only La Casona and suites at the Monasterio come close. But its biggest competitive advantage may be its "intelligent oxygen system" that pumps purified air into the entire hotel. San Juan de Dios 255. ☎ 084/604-444, or 01/434-1452 for reservations. www.aranwahotels.com. 43 units. $280–$310 double; $320–$350 suite. Rates include breakfast. AE, DC, MC, V.

★ Casa Andina Classic—Cusco Koricancha

CENTRO HISTÓRICO Built around a restful colonial courtyard, this very professionally run, mid-price hotel provides dependable service and clean, colorfully decorated rooms, just 3 blocks from the main square. San Agustín 371. ☎ 084/252-633, ☎ 866/220-4434 in the U.S., or 01/213-9739 in Lima. www.casa-andina.com. 57 units. $99–$130 double. Rates include breakfast. AE, DC, MC, V.

★ Casa Andina Classic San Blas SAN BLAS

Most inns in San Blas are small, simple *hostales;* this is one of the nicest hotels, with a full complement of services and wonderful views over the city. The courtyard and fireplace bar are great places to relax after walking Cusco's

> *Design freaks will fall in love with Fallen Angel: The Guest House, an over-the-top boutique hotel.*

hilly streets. Chihuampata 278. ☎ 866/220-4434 in the U.S., or 01/213-9739 in Lima. www.casa-andina.com. 57 units. $99–$145 double. Rates include breakfast. AE, DC, MC, V.

★★ **Casa Andina Private Collection** CENTRO HISTÓRICO In a beautiful 18th-century co-lonial mansion with rooms built around four interior patios, this is like a budget version of the elegant and expensive Hotel Monasterio. It's one of the best-value luxury options in town. There's a gorgeous sitting room with a massive fireplace and a gourmet restaurant. Plazoleta de Limacpampa, Chico 473. ☎ 084/232-610, 866/220-4434 in the U.S., or 01/213-9739 in Lima. www.casa-andina.com. 100 units. $124–$207 double; $279 suite. Rates include breakfast. AE, DC, MC, V.

Casa de Campo Hostal SAN BLAS
The chalet-style rooms at this friendly inn are rather small, but they have good, firm beds and are rustically decorated; the reward for the steep climb to the top of San Blas is nice gardens and terraces with sweeping views of the city. However, most visitors will find the inn too far removed from the action and too much of an effort to get to over the course of a few days. The owners also operate the Am-auta Spanish-language school. Tandapata 296. ☎ 084/244-404. www.hotelcasadecampo.com. 25 units. $55 double; $75 suite. Rates include breakfast and airport pickup. AE, MC, V.

★ **Casa de la Gringa** SAN BLAS
This tranquil South African–owned *hostal* is a find and favorite of those who come to Cusco on spiritual and mystical journeys. Its rooms are decorated with bohemian flair and lively, colorful art. It features a lounge and an annexed cottage with a patio with glass-enclosed roof for star-gazing. Pasnapacana 148. ☎ 084/241-168. www.casadelagringa.com. 7 units. $30 double. No credit cards.

Casa San Blas Boutique Hotel SAN BLAS
Tucked down a small alleyway, this modern boutique hotel has a great location and good services; best are the two-level junior suites with kitchenettes and spectacular views of Cusco from upstairs. The panoramic-view terrace is an excellent spot to relax and take in the views. Tocuyeros 566. ☎ 888/569-1769 in the U.S. and Canada, or 084/237-900 in Peru.

> On a cold Cusco night, have a drink at the fireplace bar at Casa Andina Private Collection.

www.casasanblas.com. 18 units. $110 double; $156–$192 suite. Rates include breakfast and airport pickup. AE, DC, MC, V.

★ **Casona les Pleiades** SAN BLAS
A three-story house, this French-owned bou-tique hotel has a treasured sunny terrace and rooms that are ample and colorfully decorated with down comforters. Tandapata 116. ☎ 084/506-430. www.casona-pleiades.com. 7 units. $50 double. Rate includes breakfast. AE, MC, V.

★ **El Andariego Hostal** CENTRO HISTÓRICO
Family-owned, cozy, and well hidden, this quiet *hostal* retains a great deal of the flavor of a 19th-century Cusco colonial house. Room nos. 101 and 103, both of which have function-ing wood-burning fireplaces and exposed stone walls, are tops: large and comfortable with hardwood floors and a smattering of an-tiques. San Andrés 270. ☎ 084/225-593. www.andariegocusco.com. 14 units. $50–$55 double. Rates include breakfast. MC, V.

> *La Casona's swank bathrooms are bigger than most hotel rooms in town.*

★★★ Fallen Angel: The Guest House CENTRO HISTÓRICO
Perhaps Peru's most unique hotel, this fantasy-like guest house has just four theatrically decorated—but luxurious and huge—rooms. All guests need is an open mind. Plaza de las Nazarenas 221. ☎ 084/258-184. www.fallenangelincusco.com. 4 units. $280–$330 suite. Rates include breakfast, airport transfer, and massage. MC, V.

Hospedaje Turístico San Blas SAN BLAS
One of San Blas's most attractive inexpensive inns, this is a nice step up from run-of-the-mill budget options in Cusco and a good place to meet up with fellow travelers. Rooms are pretty spacious, and the airy colonial house has a glassed-in courtyard and a sun terrace with good views. Cuesta de San Blas 526. ☎ 084/244-481. www.sanblashostal.com. 20 units. S/110 double. Rate includes breakfast and airport pickup. No credit cards.

★ kids Hostal Marani SAN BLAS
Following the concept of the more stylish Niños Hotel (p. 225), this Dutch-owned boutique hotel is active in social programs to benefit disadvantaged Peruvian children. Occupying a colonial-era house, it features spacious and light rooms located around a Spanish-style courtyard. Carmen Alto 194. ☎ 084/249-462. www.hostalmarani.com. 17 units. $51 double. Rate includes breakfast and airport or bus station pickup. No credit cards.

Hostal Resbalosa CENTRO HISTÓRICO
A longtime favorite of backpackers, this inn has good-size rooms with hardwood floors, large windows, and immaculate bathrooms. Try to get a room with a view, or enjoy the large rooftop terrace with 180-degree views. Resbalosa 494. ☎ 084/224-839. www.hostalresbalosa.com. 20 units. $15–$22 double. No credit cards.

★ kids Hostal Rumi Punku SAN BLAS
Behind an original Inca portal is a charming colonial courtyard, chapel, and gardens. Clean bedrooms are ample, with hardwood floors and Norwegian thermal blankets. The top-floor dining room has panoramic views of Cusco's rooftops, and there's also a sauna and Jacuzzi. Choquechaca 339. ☎ 084/221-102. www.rumipunku.com. 30 units. $90–$120 double. Rates include breakfast. MC, V.

★ kids Hotel El Arqueólogo CENTRO HISTÓRICO
The unprepossessing facade of a late-19th-century house hides an interior courtyard and sunny garden, where kids can unwind. Rooms are cozy, warm, and even romantic, with nice hardwood floors and quality bedding and linens; some feature peaked ceilings. Pumacurco 408. ☎ 084/232-522. www.hotelarqueologo.com. 20 units. $99–$120 double; $180 suite. Rates include breakfast. MC, V.

★★★ Hotel Monasterio CENTRO HISTÓRICO

Cusco's most emblematic hotel, this Orient-Express luxury property is a 16th-century monastery built on the foundations of an Inca palace. Rooms are impeccably decorated in both colonial and modern styles, with large Escuela Cusqueña paintings; the accommodations off the first courtyard are more traditionally designed. If you're suffering from altitude sickness, you can even get oxygen piped directly into your room through the ventilation. Palacio 136. ☎ 084/241-777. www.monasteriohotel.com. 122 units. $399–$499 double; $580–$1,089 suite. Rates include breakfast. AE, DC, MC, V.

★★★ La Casona CENTRO HISTÓRICO

One of the newest ultra-luxe boutique hotels in Cusco, this sophisticated Relais & Châteaux property feels like an elegant mansion. There's no front desk, though there's plenty of luxury and attentive service (personal concierges take care of guests' every whim). Accommodations are enormous, with stunning marble-and-stone bathrooms. Plaza de las Nazarenas 167. ☎ 800/442-5042 in U.S. and Canada, 01/610-0400 for reservations, or 084/245-314 in Peru. www.inkaterra.com/en/cusco. 11 units. $720–$1,128 double. Rates include breakfast. AE, DC, MC, V.

★★ Libertador Palacio del Inka CENTRO HISTÓRICO

Elegant and traditional, filled with art and antiques, this has long been one of Cusco's finest luxury hotels. There are exposed Inca walls in the lobby, while guest rooms are spacious and refined; furnishings have rustic colonial touches. Many rooms have small terraces. Service is extremely attentive and professional, making this perhaps the best option for travelers who want top-of-the-line amenities and the anonymity of a larger, urban hotel. San Agustín 400. ☎ 084/231-961. www.summithotels.com. 254 units. $305 double; $345 suite. AE, DC, MC, V.

★ Los Apus Hotel & Mirador CENTRO HISTÓRICO

On a hilly street, this homey, Swiss-managed small hotel has a bit of a chalet feel. There is an attractive rooftop terrace with excellent views of Cusco. Rooms don't quite equal the hotel's public spaces, but those on the third and fourth floors with private balconies have the

> *Rooms at Niños Hotel in Cusco overlook a sunny courtyard.*

best views. Atocsaycuchi 515. ☎ 084/264-243. www.losapushotel.com. 20 units. $109 double. Rate includes breakfast. AE, DC, MC, V.

★★★ kids Niños Hotel CENTRO HISTÓRICO

The Dutch-owned "Children's Hotel" is part of an extraordinary foundation that puts all its profits toward care for homeless and needy children. But it's also an immaculate, great-value boutique inn. Rooms are minimalist chic, with white-painted hardwood floors, and they ring a lovely sunny courtyard. Niños runs a second hotel and four apartments for longer stays, ideal for small families. Make reservations far in advance. If you're planning

> To meet up with other travelers for treks in the region, head for the bar at Pariwana Hostel Cusco.

on an extended stay in Cusco, there's no better choice. Meloq 442. ☎ 084/231-424. www.ninoshotel.com. 20 units. $40–$44 double; $32 per person per day or $350 per month apartment. No credit cards.

Novotel Cusco CENTRO HISTÓRICO
The guts of this hotel are a 16th-century colonial building with a lovely central courtyard, even though most rooms are in newly built additions. Well equipped and brightly colored, the rooms are otherwise standard accommodations. San Agustín 239. ☎ 084/881-030. www.novotel.com. 99 units. $109–$170 double. Rates include breakfast. AE, DC, MC, V.

Orquídea Real Hostal SAN BLAS
An unassuming inn with surprises that include some of the top views in Cusco and working fireplaces in each room. The colonial building has original Inca walls and exposed wood beams, and the rustic accommodations are

decorated in a cozy mountain lodge aesthetic. Alabado 520. ☎ 877/260-2423 in the U.S., or 084/221-662 in Peru. www.cusco-hotel.net. 11 units. $44 double; $55 suite. Rates include breakfast and airport pickup. AE, MC, V.

★ Pariwana Hostel Cusco CENTRO HISTÓRICO
This fantastic, low-priced hostel option for students and young backpackers is in fact an elegant 16th-century colonial manor house built around a beautiful courtyard. Rooms are clean, safe, and well thought out, and there are even dorm rooms for women only. The bar/lounge buzzes. Mesón de la Estrella 136. ☎ 084/233-751. www.pariwana-hostel.com. 60 units. S/90 double. Rate includes breakfast. No credit cards.

★ Picoaga Hotel CENTRO HISTÓRICO
A reasonably priced alternative to Cusco's top luxury hotels, this serviceable hotel occupies a 17th-century colonial mansion and is a good option for small groups. Rooms in the front section overlooking the patio are the most desirable. Santa Teresa 344. ☎ 084/252-330. www.picoagahotel.com. 70 units. $160–$180 double; $220–$250 suite. Rates include breakfast. AE, DC, MC, V.

★★ Second Home Cusco SAN BLAS
A tiny guest house with just three rooms, this personable and great-value find has the comfort of much more expensive and larger hotels. Rooms have a modern sensibility, along with top-quality bedding and linens. The owner is the brother of the woman who runs Second Home Peru in Lima (p. 84). Atocsaycuchi 616. ☎ 084/235-873. www.secondhomecusco.com. 3 units. $95 double; $120 suite. Rates include breakfast. MC, V.

★ Torre Dorada MODERN CUSCO
A personalized boutique hotel in a quiet residential neighborhood, this friendly inn offers services and attention to detail that are nearly the equal of five-star hotels, including a spectacular breakfast buffet. The staff goes out of its way to look out for guests: the hotel generously ferries its guests back and forth to downtown Cusco for free. Calle los Cipreses (Residencial Huancaro). ☎ 084/241-698. www.torredorada.com.pe. 21 units. $85 double. Rate includes breakfast and airport pickup. AE, DC, MC, V.

Cusco Nightlife Best Bets

Best Beer Pub
Paddy Flaherty's Triunfo 124 (p. 238)

Best Dance Clubs
★ **Eko Club** Plateros 334, 2nd floor (p. 239)

★★ **Ukuku's** Plateros 316, 2nd floor (p. 239)

Best Live Music
★★ **Ukuku's** Plateros 316, 2nd floor (p. 239)

Best Andean Folklore
★ **Centro Q'osqo de Arte Nativo** Av. El Sol 684 (p. 239)

Best Cocktail Lounge
★★ **Los Perros** Tecsecocha 436 (p. 238)

Best Places to Meet Locals
★★ **Pepe Zeta** Tecsecocha 415 (p. 238)

★★ **Ukuku's** Plateros 316, 2nd floor (p. 239)

Best Wine Bar
★ **Baco** Ruinas 465 (p. 238)

Best Hangout for Cinephiles
Film Lounge & Danish Café Procuradores 389, 2nd floor (p. 239)

Best Places to Get Your Drink On
La Chupitería Tecsecocha 400 (p. 238)

★ **7 Angelitos** Siete Angelitos 638 (p. 239)

Best Pisco Bar & Pisco Sour
★★ **El Pisquerito** San Juan de Dios 250 (p. 238)

Best Televised Football Matches & Expat Bonding
★ **The Cross Keys** Triunfo 350 (p. 238)

Best Restaurant Cocktail Bars
★★★ **Cicciolina** Triunfo 393, 2nd floor (p. 227)

★★★ **Limo** Portal de Carnes 236, 2nd floor (p. 229)

> El Pisquerito is the best bar in Cusco to try a variety of perfectly mixed pisco cocktails.

Cusco Nightlife A to Z

Bars, Pubs & Lounges

★★ Baco CENTRO HISTÓRICO
Although primarily a (very good) restaurant, this elegant and sophisticated place is also excellent for an early- or late-evening glass of wine from its list, one of the best in the city, or a cocktail. Ruinas 465. ☎ 084/242-808. www.cicciolinacuzco.com. Map p. 218.

★ The Cross Keys CENTRO HISTÓRICO
Around longer than virtually any other bar in town, this pub is extremely popular with dart-playing Brits catching up on European soccer and knocking back pints of ale. Often very crowded near closing time. Triunfo 350 (Plaza de Armas). ☎ 084/229-227. Map p. 218.

★★★ El Pisquerito CENTRO HISTÓRICO
In a new, cozy location with a fireplace, this terrific cocktail bar specializes in Peruvian piscos and offers a great variety of well-prepared pisco sours. More a haunt of locals than gringos. San Juan de Dios 250 (interior). ☎ 084/235-223. www.elpisquerito.com. Map p. 218.

La Chupitería CENTRO HISTÓRICO
A rock-n-roll sort of place to knock back shots or one of the very suggestively named drink combos off the big board. Tecsecocha 400. ☎ 084/984-725-241. Map p. 218.

★★ Los Perros CENTRO HISTÓRICO
A laid-back lounge bar with comfy sofas, good cocktails (including hot wine), and a hip soundtrack, including live jazz on Sunday and Monday nights. It's also got a good food menu. Tecsecocha 436. ☎ 084/241-447. Map p. 218.

★ Marcelo Batata CENTRO HISTÓRICO
More restaurant than bar, this sleek place has something no other place does: an incredible little rooftop terrace with views of the back side of the cathedral. Palacio 121. ☎ 084/224-424. Map p. 218.

★ Paddy Flaherty's CENTRO HISTÓRICO
A cozy and crowded Irish pub that does its job by serving Guinness on draft. Often filled with expats catching up on football (soccer) and rugby. Triunfo 124 (Plaza de Armas). ☎ 084/247-719. Map p. 218.

★★ Pepe Zeta CENTRO HISTÓRICO
Gringos are outnumbered by locals at this rustic, very popular bar that features live Peruvian rock music on weekends. A great place to meet young Peruvians. Tecsecocha 415. ☎ 084/223-082. Map p. 218.

> *A nice mix of international and Peruvian music and patrons goes late at Mama Africa.*

★ 7 Angelitos SAN BLAS

A rowdy reveler's bar that tends to go later and drunker than most other places in town. There's live music most nights, and a crowd of folks working on hangovers. Siete Angelitos 638. ☎ 084/806-070. Map p. 218.

Dance/Nightclubs
★ Eko Club CENTRO HISTÓRICO

One of Cusco's hottest dance clubs, this hopping spot has a large dance floor that often goes until the wee hours with a variety of techno, trance, and rock. There's a chill-out lounge out back for a breather. Plateros 334, 2nd floor. No phone. Map p. 218.

Extrem CENTRO HISTÓRICO

One of Cusco's youngest crowds gathers here for happy hour and free drinks (from cards given out by young girls on the plaza). If you want a break from the two bars, there's a fireplace, movie screen, and pizzeria. Portal de Carnes 298 (Plaza de Armas). ☎ 084/240-901. Map p. 218.

Mama Africa CENTRO HISTÓRICO

A dark and sweaty club with DJs spinning an international dance mix of Latin, reggae, rock, and techno for a young crowd of backpackers and Peruvians. Portal de Panes 108 (Plaza de Armas), 2nd floor. ☎ 084/246-544. www. mamaafricaclub.com. Map p. 218.

Film
Film Lounge & Danish Café CENTRO HISTÓRICO

The best selection of international films, from classic to art house and even children's flicks, are shown at three daily screenings. This spot also serves food and drinks at an attractive bar. Procuradores 389, 2nd floor. ☎ 084/123-236. Map p. 218.

Live Music Clubs
★ Centro Q'osqo de Arte Nativo AV. EL SOL

A long-running cultural center featuring good Peruvian music and folkloric dance performances. Check with the tourist information office for a current schedule of events. Av. El Sol 684. ☎ 084/227-901. Map p. 218.

★ Kamikase CENTRO HISTÓRICO

This well-worn place, an old favorite up steep stairs with a two-level bar and a live music area, hosts everything from *rock en Español* to reggae, with plenty of locals on hand. Plaza Regocijo 274, 2nd floor. ☎ 084/233-865. Map p. 218.

> The lounge bar Los Perros is a great international spot to kick back with a cocktail or a light meal.

★ Km. 0 SAN BLAS

A Spanish-owned joint with a rocker's heart, this tiny ramshackle place has live rock, Latin, and blues music nightly; "happy hours all night"; and a variety of tapas. Tandapata 100. ☎ 084/254-240. Map p. 218.

Tunupa CENTRO HISTÓRICO

Offering a traditional, tourist-targeted folklore music-and-dance show with panpipes and costumes, with the bonus of a panoramic view of the Plaza de Armas. Other restaurants with similar shows include **El Truco,** Plaza Regocijo 261 (☎ 084/232-441), and **La Retama,** Portal de Panes 123, 2nd floor (☎ 084/226-372). Portal Confiturías 233 (Plaza de Armas), 2nd floor. ☎ 084/252-936. Map p. 218.

★★ Ukuku's CENTRO HISTÓRICO

For at least a decade, this has been Cusco's hippest live-music venue, with music ranging from bar rock to Afro-Peruvian and *rock en Español*. The crowd is usually about half foreigner and half Peruvian, adding up to a full dance floor. There's also Internet access, a pizza bar, and daily afternoon movies. Plateros 316, 2nd floor. ☎ 084/227-867. www.ukukusbar.com. Map p. 218.

Cusco Fast Facts

Arriving

BY PLANE Flights arrive from Lima (1 hr.) as well as Arequipa; Puerto Maldonado; and La Paz, Bolivia, at **Aeropuerto Internacional Velasco Astete** (☎ 084/222-611), 5km (3 miles) southeast of the historic center of Cusco. All major Peruvian airlines fly into Cusco, including **LAN** (☎ 01/213-8200; www.lan.com), **Taca** (☎ 01/511-8222; www.taca.com), and **Peruvian Airlines** (☎ 01/716-6000; www.peruvianairlines.pe), which recently began offering flights from Lima to Cusco. Flights to Cusco are very popular, so make reservations as far in advance as possible.

Transportation from the airport to downtown Cusco (20 min.) is by taxi or private hotel car. Most hotels and even *hostales* prearrange airport pickup. Taxi fare is officially S/10 from the airport to the center; many drivers will initially try to get S/15 or even S/20. **BY BUS** Buses to Cusco arrive from Lima (26 hr.), Arequipa (12 hr.), Puno/Juliaca (10 hr.), and Puerto Maldonado. Most buses arrive at **Terminal Terrestre,** Av. Vellejos Santoni, cdra. 2, Santiago (☎ 084/224-471), outside the city center on the way to the airport. From Lima, contact **Ormeño** (☎ 01/472-5000; www.grupo-ormeno.com.pe), **Cruz del Sur** (☎ 01/311-5050; www.cruzdelsur.com.pe), **Oltursa** (☎ 01/708-5000; www.oltursa.com.pe), and **Civa** (☎ 01/418-1111; www.civa.com.pe). From Puno, **Cruz del Sur** (see above), **Inka Express** (☎ 084/247-887; www.inkaexpress.com), and **Imexso** (☎ 084/240-801; www.perucuzco.com/imexsotours) offer daily service to Cusco. **BY TRAIN** Trains from Puno arrive at **Estación de Huanchaq** (also spelled Wanchaq), Av. Pachacútec s/n (☎ 084/581-414; www.perurail.com), at the southeast end of Av. El Sol. Trains from Ollantaytambo and Machu Picchu arrive at **Estación Poroy** (☎ 084/581-414) on the outskirts of Cusco.

ATMs/Cashpoints

Most banks with ATMs are located along Av. El Sol. Banks include **Banco Santander Central Hispano,** Av. El Sol 459; **Banco de Crédito,** Av. El Sol 189; and **Banco Continental,** Av. El Sol 366. The external ATMs nearest the Plaza de Armas are at **Banco de Crédito, Banco del Sur,** Av. El Sol 457; and **Banco Latino,** Av. El Sol 395. A few ATMs are also located at the entrances to stores and restaurants on the Plaza de Armas and at the Huanchaq train station.

Currency Exchange

Money-changers in colored smocks patrol the main streets off the Plaza de Armas and Av. El Sol. The banks listed in "ATMs/Cashpoints" all have ATMs and currency-exchange bureaus. Several small *casas de cambio* operate out of travel agencies and shops on Plaza de Armas and Av. El Sol.

Dentists & Doctors

In an emergency, contact **Tourist Medical Assistance** (TMA), Heladeros 157 (☎ 084/260-101), for 24-hour emergency medical services and health information. English-speaking personnel are available at **Hospital EsSalud,** Av. Anselmo Álvarez s/n (☎ 084/237-341); **Clínica Pardo,** Av. de la Cultura 710 (☎ 084/624-186); **Hospital Antonio Loren,** Plazoleta Belén 1358 (☎ 084/226-511); **Hospital Regional,** Av. de la Cultura s/n (☎ 084/223-691); and **Clínica Paredes,** Lechugal 405 (☎ 084/225-265). For those headed to the Southern Amazon, **yellow-fever vaccinations** (which should be given 10 days prior to a visit to the jungle) can be arranged at Hospital Antonio Loren on Tuesday or Hospital Regional on Saturday from 9am to 1pm.

For dental assistance, contact **Centro Odontológico Americano Cusco,** Av. Pardo 605 (D-2) (☎ 084/248-124).

Embassies & Consulates

The **U.S. consulate** is located at Av. Pardo 845 (☎ 084/231-474; CoresES@state.gov). The honorary **U.K. consulate** is at Manu Expeditions, Urbanización Magisterial, G-5 Segunda Etap (☎ 084/239-974; bwalker@terra.com.pe).

Emergencies

For general emergencies and police, call ☎ **105.** For tourist police, call ☎ **084/**

249-654. For fire, call ☎ **103.** In a medical emergency, go to **Hospital EsSalud,** Av. Anselmo Álvarez s/n (☎ 084/223-030), or contact **Tourist Medical Assistance** (☎ 084/260-101).

Internet Access
Internet *cabinas* are everywhere in the old section of Cusco, and many permit cheap overseas Internet-based calls for as little as S/1 per minute. Among the *cabinas:* **Explora,** Arequipa 251, and **Speed X,** Procuradores 50 and Tecsecocha 400.

Pharmacies
Find **InkaFarma** locations at Av. El Sol 210 and Ayacucho 175; **Botica Fasa** locations at Ayacucho 220 and Av. El Sol 130.

Police
The **Policía Nacional de Turismo,** Saphy 510 (☎ 084/249-654), has an English-speaking staff trained to handle the needs of foreign visitors. Or, contact **iPerú/INDECOPI** (Servicio de Protección al Turista, or Tourist Protection Bureau), Portal Carrizos 250, Plaza de Armas (☎ 084/252-974).

Post Office & Mail
Cusco's main post office, **Serpost,** is at Av. El Sol 800 (☎ 084/224-212). A **DHL/Western Union** office is at Av. El Sol 627-A (☎ 084/244-167).

Public Transportation
Informal buses (*colectivos, micros,* and *combis*) in and around Cusco cost S/1.50. *Combis* (more like vans) are most frequently used to travel to the Sacred Valley; those depart from small terminals on Puputi cdra. 2 s/n (via Pisac) and Av. Grau cdra. 1 s/n (via Chinchero). Advance tickets are not necessary; travelers merely wait for the next departure.

Safety
Cusco has earned a reputation for being somewhat unsafe for foreign visitors, especially at night, with isolated reports of attempted rapes and other sexual assaults, as well as violent muggings (some using the "chokehold" method) on empty streets. Most visitors have never had problems, but it's advisable to take precautions and remain vigilant at all times. Incidents of drink-spiking have been reported; be aware of your drinking companions in bars, and don't allow strangers to buy you drinks. Don't walk alone late at night (young women should travel in groups larger than two); have restaurants and bars call registered taxis to transfer you to your hotel. Be at your most vigilant in San Blas, side streets off the Plaza de Armas, near the Central Market, and at bus and train hubs; robberies and attacks have also occurred at the ruins at Sacsayhuamán and on hiking trails.

Taxis
Taxis charge standard rates but are not metered (S/3 for any trip within the historic core during the day, S/4–S/5 at night) and are a good way to get around, especially at night. It's wise to call a registered taxi when traveling from your hotel to train or bus stations or the airport, and when returning to your hotel late at night. Licensed taxi companies include **Okarina** (☎ 084/247-080) and **Aló Cusco** (☎ 084/222-222). To the airport, taxis charge S/10 from the city center; to the distant Terminal Terrestre (bus station), they charge S/8.

Telephone
Cusco's area code is 084. The principal Telefónica del Perú office, where you can make long-distance and international calls, is at Av. El Sol 382-6 (☎ 084/241-114; Mon–Sat 8am–10pm).

Visitor Information
The principal **Oficina de Información Turística** is located on Mantas 117-A, a block from the Plaza de Armas (☎ 084/222-032; Mon–Sat 7am–7pm, Sun 7am–noon). It sells the *boleto turístico* (tourist ticket; see p. 202). The **iPerú office,** Av. El Sol 103, ste. 102 (☎ 084/252-974; daily 8:30am–7:30pm), is more helpful. Another information office is in the **Terminal Terrestre de Huanchaq** train station, Av. Pachacútec s/n (☎ 084/238-722; Mon–Sat 8am–6:30pm). **South American Explorers** has a club at Choquechaca 188, no. 4 (☎ 084/245-484; www.saexplorers. org), with lists of trail reports for members and a library for trekking and mountaineering. For up-to-date information on cultural happenings, bars, and restaurants, check out **www.agendacusco.com.**

9
Machu Picchu & the Sacred Valley

Favorite Sacred Valley Moments

The Incas held the Urubamba Valley sacred, and it's easy to see why. The extraordinary stretch of ancient villages and fertile agricultural fields alongside the Urubamba River is framed by a backdrop of magnificent Andes peaks and a massive sky. Stunning Inca ruins—from Pisac to Ollantaytambo and, of course, Machu Picchu—dot the landscape. Whether you get to Machu Picchu by train or make the 4-day trek along the Inca Trail, nearly everyone who comes to Peru makes it here, one of the most mystical places on earth. The Valley is about 300m (1,000 ft.) lower than Cusco, making it a better and more relaxing base for visitors prone to altitude-related health problems.

> PREVIOUS PAGE *Machu Picchu, cradled high in the Andes, was never discovered by marauding Spaniards.* THIS PAGE *The Sacred Valley is a relaxed base for visitors to the region.*

❶ Reliving history in Ollantaytambo. An unexpected example of the Incas' incredible engineering is the old town's perfect grid of 15th-century *canchas*, or city blocks, part of a masterful urban plan. Each has a single entrance opening onto a main courtyard, and canals that line the stone streets to this day carry water rushing down from the mountains. See p. 252, ❹ .

❷ Reveling in sunrise at Machu Picchu. Virtually every angle, vista, and detail is extraordinary, but there's nothing quite like the thrill of being there at sunrise, when rays of light creep over the mountaintops and shine a dramatic and slowly expanding spotlight on successive rows of ruins. See p. 260.

1. Reliving history in Ollantaytambo
2. Reveling in sunrise at Machu Picchu
3. Checking out Chinchero's market
4. Strolling to the Salineras salt mines
5. Conquering Choquequirao
6. Relaxing at a country lodge
7. Ascending Pisac's ruins
8. Scaling Huayna Picchu
9. Surviving Dead Woman's Pass

> *The Sacred Valley comprises a series of small towns between Cusco and Machu Picchu.*

> *Highland traditions, such as the native Quechua language and dress, remain strong throughout the Urubamba Valley.*

❸ Checking out Chinchero's market. Pisac's crafts market gets the lion's share of attention and tourists, but the smaller market at high-altitude Chinchero rates higher in terms of authenticity and textile quality. The air's thin at this small village, so don't rush here as soon as you land in the Andes, but do come if you're in the market for superb Andean ponchos, shawls, and blankets, often sold by the very artisans who craft the items in their highland villages. See p. 254, ❶.

❹ Strolling to the Salineras salt mines. The pretty countryside of the Urubamba Valley is splendid for gentle walks. My favorite is the gorgeous route from the Inca site Moray to the Salineras salt mines, where thousands of ancient salt pans cascade down a ravine, forming a mosaic of crystallized salt, with workers wading knee-high in the resource that's been their family's livelihood for generations. See p. 258, ❻.

❺ Conquering Choquequirao. As the Inca Trail has gotten more popular and highly regulated, independent travelers have sought out alternative treks off the beaten track. Among the greatest routes, with dramatic gorge views over the Apurímac River and the payoff of magnificent Inca ruins at the end, is the 4- or 5-day route to Choquequirao. The ruins are still only one-third excavated and devoid of large groups, so arrive early, and you can have them all to yourself. See p. 272, ❷.

❻ **Relaxing at a country lodge.** The Sacred Valley has become a destination unto itself rather than a mere add-on to trips to Cusco and Machu Picchu. The Valley has some of the finest country luxury hotels in all of Peru. It seems like every year the ante is raised. The current king of swank and serenity is Aranwa Sacred Valley. If that's too fancy or pricey, try an affordable alternative such as The Green House. See p. 284.

❼ **Ascending Pisac's ruins.** Leave the artisans' market behind and set out on an athletic hike up the mountainside to Pisac's Inca ruins.

> *The snowcapped Andes mountains tower above the Sacred Valley at every turn.*

Along the way are some of the finest views in the Sacred Valley: spectacular Inca agricultural terracing, gorgeous mountain vistas, and Pisac laid out beneath your feet. See p. 250, ❸.

❽ **Scaling Huayna Picchu.** As much as I love the classic postcard view of Machu Picchu from the Sun Gate, it's the panoramic bird's-eye view from the top of the peak Huayna Picchu that sends chills up my spine. And best of all, you've got to work for it by climbing a steep path to the summit (it takes most mortals an hour or so, but the record is about 15 min.). See p. 265, ❸.

❾ **Surviving Dead Woman's Pass.** Hiking the mythic, 4-day Inca Trail to Machu Picchu is one of the planet's great ecoadventures, though it may have gotten too popular for its own good and that of the environment. In high season it's no longer a solitary trek, but that takes nothing away from the achievement of making it over poetically named Dead Woman's Pass—the highest point on the trail, a 4,200m (13,780-ft.) pass in thin Andean air—on grueling Day 2. See p. 266, ❷.

Endangered Machu Picchu

As Machu Picchu's popularity grows, so do the threats to its infrastructure and the fragile surrounding ecosystem. The Peruvian government has limited the numbers of visitors to the site and along the Inca Trail to protect the landmark ruins. World Monuments Fund, which included Machu Picchu on the 2010 World Monuments Watch and details the 100 Most Endangered Sites in the World, has noted, "little has been done to address the impacts of tourism on the site or the resulting environmental degradation of the area." Planned projects, which include a bridge across the Vilcanota River, are representative of "uncontrolled development and environmental mismanagement in Aguas Calientes." While the Peruvian government has limited visitors to Machu Picchu and along the Inca Trail, annual visitors have increased from 9,000 in 1992 to nearly 1 million today. One unconventional, positive measure was a debt-swap initiative, in which the government of Finland traded 25% of Peru's outstanding debt (more than $6 million) for conservation programs targeting Machu Picchu. However, most observers agree that more needs to be done to protect these singular ruins.

The Sacred Valley in 3 Days

For years travelers seemed to treat the Sacred Valley as an afterthought, visiting it on blitzkrieg-like bus tours and bouncing from one market and set of ruins to the next. Today, the region is its own destination, both as an alternative, lower-altitude stay to Cusco and for its historic and outdoor offerings. In 3 easy-paced days, you can see the main highlights of the Valley: the famed artisanal markets and the ruins, including Machu Picchu. To get the most out of your time here, stay at least 1 or 2 nights in a country hotel in the Valley and perhaps another in Aguas Calientes at the base of Machu Picchu.

> Pisac's colorful market on Tuesdays, Thursdays, and Sundays is a big deal for villagers and tourists alike.

START Fly from Lima (1 hr.; 1,165km/724 miles) to Cusco, and then take a bus (45 min.; 32km/20 miles) to Pisac.

1 ★★ kids **Pisac.** At the eastern end of the valley, this traditional Andean town is known for its hugely popular **crafts market** (Sun, with somewhat smaller versions on Tues and Thurs). In high season, the market draws crowds of shoppers on Sunday morning and makes for a very lively experience, with hundreds of stalls taking over the main square. Sellers come from villages throughout the highlands to hawk sweaters, hats, ponchos, tapestries, musical instruments, and ceramics. Though the affair can feel a bit touristy,

> *The Inca ruins in Pisac rise above the Sacred Valley. The best way to get there is the strenuous hike up the hill behind town.*

it's pretty much an obligatory Sacred Valley experience. Village elders lead processions after the Quechua Mass on Sunday. ⏱ At least 1 hr. Plaza de Armas (Plaza Constitución). Free admission. Tues, Thurs, and Sun 8am–3pm.

② **Horno Colonial Santa Lucía.** An old-school bakery turning out terrific empanadas (meat- and cheese-filled turnovers) from traditional adobe, wood-fired ovens, this is a great place to duck in for a bit of sustenance on the run. The empanadas are often gone by 2pm on market days. SW corner of the Plaza de Armas (next to Hotel Pisaq). No phone. Items S/3–S/20.

❸ ★★★ kids **Pisac ruins.** The Inca ruins at Pisac may not be as well known as those of Ollantaytambo, and that's unfortunate. The largest fortress complex ever built by the Incas is perched high on a cliff with ravishing views across the Valley. The ruins are in good shape, but scholars argue about the site's purpose, which appears to have been equal parts ceremonial center, religious temple, military complex, and perhaps royal estate of the Inca emperor Pachacútec. The best way to experience the ruins is to climb the hillside, following a path used by locals coming down to the Pisac market. The trek up is about 5km (3 miles) and takes at least an hour for fit travelers. Start at the back (north side) of Pisac's main square, to the left of the church; the path climbs through agricultural terraces, arriving at very steep stairs and a semicircular terrace and fortified section at the top, the

Cusco Tourist Pass

The Cusco *boleto turístico* (tourist ticket; see p. 202) is essential for visiting the Sacred Valley, in particular the ruins of Pisac and Ollantaytambo, as well as the market and town of Chinchero. You can purchase it at any of those places if you haven't already bought it in Cusco before traveling to the Valley. If you aren't planning to make use of the full ticket in Cusco, purchase the half-price partial ticket that covers just the Sacred Valley sites.

Where to Shop in the Sacred Valley

For information on the famous handicrafts markets in **Pisac** and **Chinchero,** see p. 248, ❶, and 254, ❶. There is also a smaller artisans' market at the entrance to the fortress ruins in **Ollantaytambo** (p. 253, ❻). No credit cards.

★★ **Awamaki** OLLANTAYTAMBO
The retail outlet of an NGO that runs a weaving project and ensures that profits go to women artisans. Great gifts include textiles, bracelets, and hats. The NGO arranges trips to Patacancha communities for visits with local Quechua families and weaving retreats. Chaupi s/n. ☎ 084/792-529. www. awamaki.org. No credit cards.

★★ **Lanandina** URUBAMBA
It requires some resourcefulness to find this little artisanal operation, which features stylish and funky felt slippers, handbags, and hats, all made by hand by an Austrian woman, Christa Quiroz. Call for directions. Los Girasoles s/n (past Torrechayoc church). ☎ 084/201-390. No credit cards.

★★ **Pablo Seminario** URUBAMBA
A renowned ceramist. See p. 258, ❺.

★ **Wasi Alpaca** URUBAMBA
This little shop across from Pablo Seminario has a nice selection of alpaca capes, scarves, sweaters, and handcrafted boiled-wool items. Av. Berriozabal. ☎ 084/201-394. No credit cards.

> *Climb the steep path to Pinculluna hilltop for superb views of Ollantaytambo old town.*

Qorihuayrachina. On the upper section of the ruins, the Templo del Sol (Temple of the Sun), an astronomical observatory, was the complex's most important component and one of the Incas' most impressive examples of stonemasonry. The Intihuatana, or "hitching post of the sun," resembles a sundial but was actually an instrument that helped the Incas predict the arrival of important growing seasons. To the west is a temple thought to be the Templo de la Luna (Temple of the Moon) and beyond that a bathing complex fed by water canals. Paths lead from here to defensive ramparts and down to where taxis wait to take passengers back to Pisac. The entire site is quite large; one could easily spend a half-day exploring it. ⊕ At least 3 hr. Above Pisac. No phone. Admission by Cusco's *boleto turístico* (p. 202). Daily 7am–5:30pm. Taxis (best arranged on market days) leave from the road near the bridge in Pisac and charge around S/15 to the ruins (10km/6 miles).

On Day 2, take a taxi (45 min.) or *combi* (90 min.) from Pisac west to Ollantaytambo (60km/37 miles).

❹ ★★★ kids Ollantaytambo old town. In the shadow of fortress ruins towering above, the old town of "Ollanta" is a remarkably well-preserved grid of Inca streets dating to the 15th century, a superb example of Inca urban planning. The stone passageways are lined by canals constructed by the Incas that still deliver rushing water from the mountains. The tight alleyways of adobe brick walls and bougainvillea hide simple homes and courtyards. Though the number of visitors escalates each year, the town remains a traditional Andean village with locals in colorful native dress. It's a great place to wander. ⊕ 1 hr. Behind (northeast of) the main square (bordered by Calle Principal and Río Patacancha).

⑤   ★★ Café Mayu. Opening onto the platform of the train station near the river, Ollanta's coolest and best restaurant is perfect for a lunch of homemade pastas and organic salads, or just dessert and coffee. Estación de Tren Ollantay-tambo s/n. ☎ 084/204-014. Items S/6–S/20.

6 ★★★ kids **Ollantaytambo fortress ruins.**
The steep terraced ruins of this enormous
temple-fortress, built by the Inca Pachacútec,
are one of the Inca Empire's most formidable
feats of architecture. The Incas successfully defended the site against the Spanish in
1537, protecting the rebel Manco Inca after
his retreat here from defeat at Sacsayhuamán (see p. 212, **1**). A climb of 200 steps
leads to several examples of the Incas' most
superlative stonework, including an elegant
doorjamb, the Temple of Ten Niches, and,
above, massive pink granite blocks, part of the
unfinished Temple of the Sun. The views over
the Urubamba Valley toward the snowcapped
peak of Verónica are dazzling. The Baños de la
Ñusta (Princess Baths), a place of ceremonial
bathing, sit at the bottom of the terraces, next
to the Patacancha River. ⏱ **At least 2 hr. Plaza
Araccama. No phone. Admission by Cusco's**
boleto turístico **(p. 202). Daily 7am–5:30pm.**

On Day 3, take the train from Ollantaytambo
to Machu Picchu (30km/19 miles; 90 min.).

> *Perfectly cut stone doorjambs at the Ollantaytambo
> ruins, an example of the Incas' fine masonry.*

Crowds at Ollanta

On Sunday afternoons, the most popular
market day, the Inca fortress ruins at Ollantaytambo are frequently overrun with
tourists on bus tours of the Sacred Valley.
The ruins are normally enjoyably serene
other days of the week and early on Sunday
morning before the buses arrive, so plan to
visit then, if at all possible.

7 ★★★ kids **Machu Picchu.** These are the
greatest ruins in South America, and, despi[
being a popular tourist spot, they live up to th[
celebrated image of mystery, enchantment,
and spectacular natural beauty. For decades
thought to be the fabled "lost city of the Incas,"
Machu Picchu, stunningly sited amid the Andes Mountains, remained hidden from the conquering Spaniards. ⏱ **At least 4 hr. See p. 260.**

> *The switchback road from Aguas Calientes up to
> Machu Picchu is carved into a steep mountainside.*

The Sacred Valley in 5 Days

With a more relaxed pace in the Sacred Valley, this tour expands upon the highlights in the 3-day itinerary, giving you more time to better appreciate the area's serenity, dramatic beauty, and sights bypassed by the bus tours. Of course, if you want to add on some outdoor activities (whitewater rafting, trekking, mountain biking, or horseback riding), which the valley is becoming known for, or if you're planning to do a long trek in the Valley, whether the Inca Trail or an alternative trek, you'll need quite a bit more than 5 days. For your first day, follow Day 1 (**❶**–**❸**) of "The Sacred Valley in 3 Days" tour (p. 248). Day 2 is a long day, especially if you wish to cover some of the territory by *colectivo* or on foot (rather than by taxi), in which case you should budget extra time (or perhaps save Urubamba for Day 4).

> *The sleepy village of Chinchero sits at an elevation of 3,800m (12,470 ft.), higher even than Cusco.*

START On Day 2, catch a bus from Terminal Terrestre in Urubamba to Chinchero (50 min.).

❶ ★ **Chinchero.** More prized than Pisac among in-the-know shoppers for its bustling **artisanal Sunday market** (Sun, with smaller versions on Tues and Thurs, 8am–3pm), Chinchero is a sleepy village with hardscrabble Andean character. The town is gorgeously sited, with views of the snowy peak of Salcantay and the distant Vilcabamba and Urubamba

> *Pablo Seminario is a local artisan renowned for his creative ceramics.*

mountain ranges. At 3,800m (12,470 ft.), it is even higher than Cusco, and those prone to altitude sickness should take it easy here. The market is the top place in the Valley for quality Andean textiles. Those selling the goods are usually also the artisans, dressed in traditional garb. Besides the market, Chinchero's main points of interest are the wide main square; the handsome, early-17th-century **adobe church** (Mon–Sat 9am–5pm, Sun 9am–6pm), with frescoes under the porticoes and murals covering the entire ceiling and built on Inca foundations; and a smattering of Inca ruins. In the main plaza, look for the famous Inca wall, composed of huge stones and 10 trapezoidal niches, once belonging to the palace of the late-15th-century Inca Tupac Yupanqui. A small, spare **Museo de Sitio** (Municipal Museum; Tues–Sun 8am–5pm) contains a handful of Inca ceramics and instruments. ⏱ At least 3 hr. (including transportation time). Plaza de Armas. No phone. Admission to museums by Cusco's *boleto turístico* (p. 202).

Walking from Moray to Salineras de Maras

From Moray, it's possible to walk (3 hr.; 14km/8.7 miles) along a trail down to the salt pans at Salineras de Maras (**6** on this tour). The path is ill defined at points; near Maras (a distance of 9km/5.6 miles) you may have to ask farmers or follow workers from the salt mines, who walk the distance back and forth daily.

Take a taxi (25km/16 miles; 20 min.; at least S/130) from Chinchero to Moray; the driver will have to wait for you because there's nothing nearby. Or, take a *colectivo* from Chinchero to Urubamba, and get off halfway, at the road to Maras (ask the driver for the "desvío a Maras," or "detour to Maras"). There are usually taxis waiting there to take visitors to Moray (negotiate a round-trip price).

2 ★★ **Moray.** One of the most enigmatic sites in Peru, the concentric ring terraces of Moray are unlike anything else left behind by the Incas. The three main sets of rings are carved deep into the earth, forming sculpted terraces thought to have served as an agricultural laboratory, where the Incas tested experimental crops and conditions. The site isn't thought to have been a temple, although many visitors find it to transmit a very strong energy or spiritual presence. To some, it may look like a large-scale environmental art installation. Some scholars have observed that the depressions in the earth produce unique microclimates, with remarkable differences in temperature from top to bottom. The site is most photogenic after the end of the rainy season, when it's a brilliant green. ⏱ At least 3 hr. (including transportation time). 9km (5¾ miles) northwest of Maras. No phone. Free admission. Daily dawn–dusk.

Take a *colectivo* or taxi from Maras to Urubamba (15km/9 miles; 20–45 min.).

3 🍴 ★★★ **El Huacatay.** My favorite restaurant in the Valley, this chic but relaxed place may seem out of place in Urubamba, but it's great for a leisurely lunch or dinner of creative Andean specialties using local ingredients. See p. 280.

4 **Urubamba.** The main hub of the Sacred Valley is centrally located Urubamba. The town's best features are an attractive **Plaza de Armas,** marked by a twin-towered colonial church and tall pisonay trees; one of the area's best restaurants (**3**, above); and a couple of shopping destinations. But Urubamba is mainly of interest because it's within easy reach of the Valley's finest country lodges and hotels and connects by bus, taxi, and *mototaxi* to the villages and sights of the region. ⏱ 30 min.

5 ★ kids **Pablo Seminario.** The home workshop, or *taller,* of this internationally known

> The 6,000 individual salt pans at Salineras de Maras, ringed by crystallized salt, have been mined since pre-Columbian days.

> *A twin-towered colonial church and tall pisonay trees rise in Urubamba's Plaza de Armas.*

ceramicist, whose whimsical designs feature pre-Columbian motifs, is not your typical *taller*. On the grounds is a minizoo, with llamas, parrots, nocturnal monkeys, falcons, and rabbits. Seminario also has shops in the Sonesta Posada del Inca hotel in Yucay as well as Cusco. ⏱ 30 min. Berriozábal 111. ☎ 084/201-002. www.ceramicaseminario.com. Free admission. Mon–Sat 10am–6pm.

On Day 3, head for Salineras de Maras (see "Getting to Salineras de Maras").

❻ ★★ **Salineras de Maras.** An ancient site of thousands of individual salt pans that form cascading terraces in a hillside makes for a surreal-looking sight, especially when workers are teetering on the edges as they do the backbreaking task of extracting salt from the small pools. Coated with crystallized salt, the mines have been here since the time of the Incas, and family ownership of the 6,000 individual pans has passed down for generations. From a distance the mines look like a patchwork quilt spread over a ravine. ⏱ At

least 3 hr. (including walking time). Near village of Tarabamba, 6km (3¾ miles) down the main road toward Ollantaytambo from Urubamba. No phone. Admission S/5. Daily dawn–dusk.

In the afternoon, follow stops ❹ to ❻ of "The Sacred Valley in 3 Days" (p. 248). Early on Day 4, take a taxi or *colectivo* to Ollantaytambo to catch one of the early-morning trains (90 min.) to Aguas Calientes/Machu Picchu.

Getting to Salineras de Maras

Take a taxi (S/10) from Urubamba to a point near the restaurant Tunupa, and then follow a footpath 4km (2.5 miles; 1 hr.) across and alongside the river. There are no signs; as you begin the gentle climb up the hillside, stay on the right path to avoid the narrow, cliff-hugging trail that forks to the left. If you're fit and would prefer to walk to Salineras from Moray (❷ on this tour) or the town of Maras, you should switch Salineras and Urubamba (❹ and ❻ on this tour).

7 ★★★ **kids** **Machu Picchu.** The empire-raiding Spaniards never found Machu Picchu, which the Incas had tucked away on a mountaintop, where it's not visible from below. But today, Machu Picchu has certainly been discovered. You can get there by high-speed train from Cusco or via the old-fashioned way—today a very popular ecotourism route—by trekking the 4-day Inca Trail (p. 266). However you go, it's advisable to spend as much time as possible at the ruins, which is why this tour envisions an overnight stay next to or below the ruins in Aguas Calientes. This allows you to stay later than most day-trippers, and perhaps return for a second day or the sunrise. ⊙ At least 4 hr. See p. 260.

If you're going back to Machu Picchu, get up early to catch the sunrise and avoid the crowds. Otherwise, sleep in before starting Day 5 in Aguas Calientes.

8 **Aguas Calientes.** The humid frontier-like town at the base of Machu Picchu is a touristy gringo outpost of *mochileros* (backpackers) and folks celebrating their good fortune for having made it to Machu Picchu. The scrappy place is a bit like an Andean Katmandu, with trekkers hanging out, sharing beers and tales of the trail, and scoring alpaca trophy wear. For most, that's the highlight of the town. The outdoor **baños termales** (hot springs), Av. Pachacútec s/n (no phone; S/10; no credit cards; daily 5am–9pm), a 10-minute climb from the train station, aren't the most appealing except for those who've spent days walking over mountain passes to get here. The iron smell is a bit much. ⊙ At least 1 hr.

Head across the river from Machu Picchu and access the trail on the right side of the railroad just outside of Aguas Calientes; the signpost reads KM 111.

9 ★★ **Putukusi.** This peak, held sacred by the Incas, provides commanding views of the ruins. First, veer to the right up stone steps; then it's an athletic climb up vertical ladders (several in need of repair) until reaching a clearing and stone-carved switchbacks. From here, Machu Picchu looks like an architectural model between its two famous peaks. The trek up takes an hour to 90 minutes, while the descent takes 45 minutes. For those not quite

> *Aguas Calientes is the humid, ramshackle town just below the ruins of Machu Picchu.*

fit enough to climb Putukusi, a nice alternative, especially for bird-watchers, is the short trail to the waterfall at Mandor Ravine. From the railroad tracks, walk downstream (past the old train station) to the ravine, a total of about 3km (2 miles). A short climb takes you to the waterfall. ⊙ At least 3 hr.

10 🍺 **Blues Bar Café.** The bars of Aguas Calientes are popular spots to hang out in the evening after a day at the ruins. This amiable joint, an airy, two-story place next to the park on the main drag, is great for live music and drinks. It has excellent views of Putukusi, the mountain across from Machu Picchu. Av. Pachacútec s/n. ☎ 084/211-125. Items S/8–S/15.

Machu Picchu

Unknown to the outside world for 4 centuries and infused with mystery, Machu Picchu is one of the world's most magnificent sights. The Incas' legendary ruins are cradled by the Andes Mountains, swathed in clouds, and hidden from the valley below—which effectively saved them from marauding Spaniards—and they leave most visitors awe-struck. The sensitive placement, like a work of landscape art, speaks to the Incas' reverence of the natural world. A visit takes at least 3 hours, and most people visit on a day trip. But if you can arrive the night before and begin your visit at sunrise, stay late in the afternoon, or even come back a second day, your appreciation of this spectacular site will be greatly enhanced.

> *Machu Picchu was a royal retreat, with very distinct agricultural, residential, and elite sectors.*

START If you're coming by train from Cusco (3 hr.) or Ollantaytambo (90 min.), catch an early departure. Once you're in Aguas Calientes, catch a shuttle bus at the stop next to the railroad tracks to take you up the mountain (10km/6¼ miles).

1 ★ **Caretaker's Hut/Funerary Rock.** Just past the entrance, the path to the left climbs to the spot above the ruins for a classic postcard overview of Machu Picchu, with the whole of the ruins laid out before you. This is a grand view, especially at sunrise.

2 **Moat.** This dry moat separating the agricultural and urban sectors is a vantage point from which one can appreciate the layout of Machu Picchu. It's thought that at its apex, the complex was home to a population of 1,000.

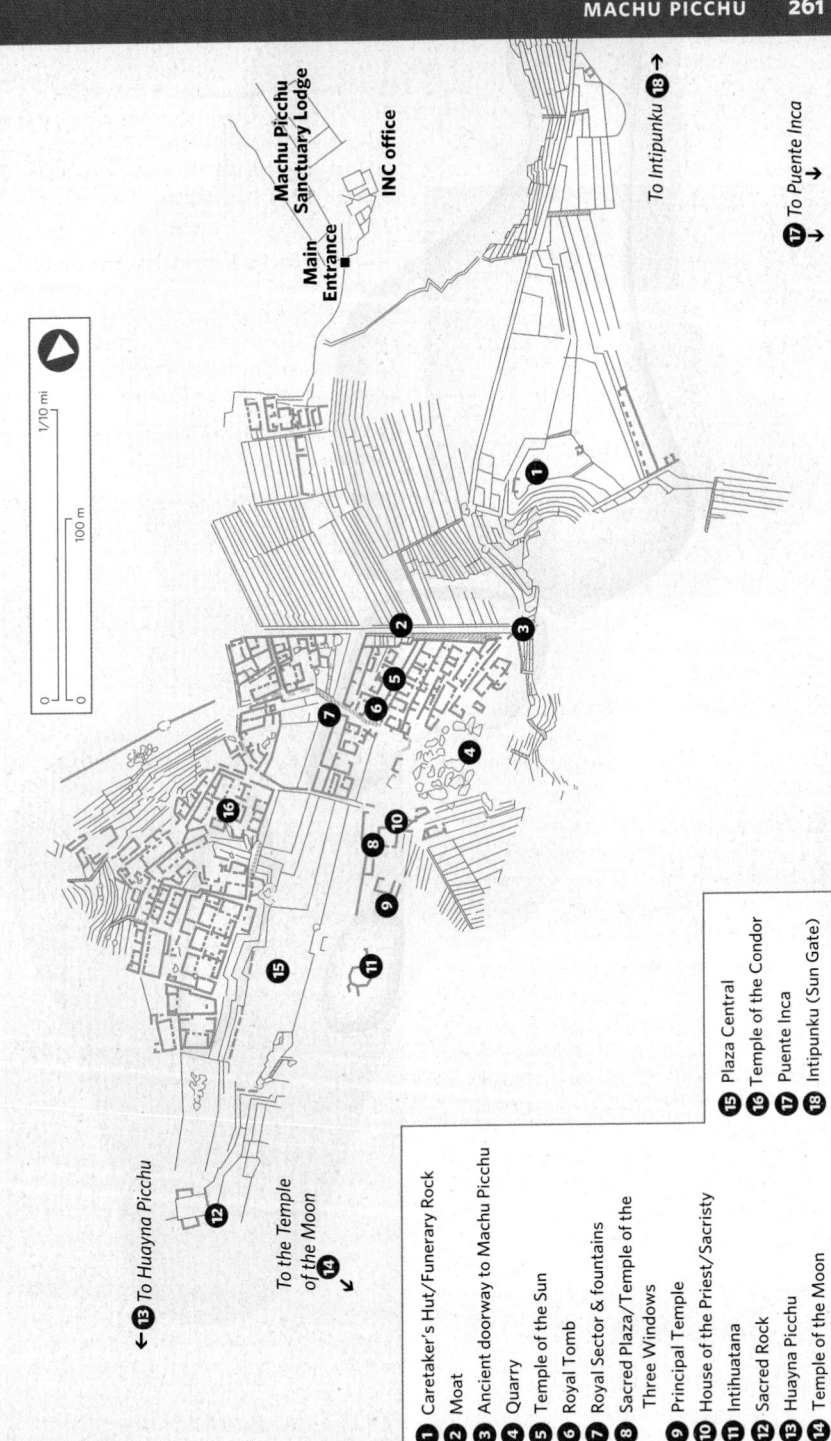

1/10 mi
100 m

To Intipunku 18 →

17 To Puente Inca →

Machu Picchu Sanctuary Lodge
INC office
Main Entrance

1

2
3
5
6
7
4
10
8
9
16
11
15
12

← 13 To Huayna Picchu

To the Temple of the Moon
14 ↓

1 Caretaker's Hut/Funerary Rock
2 Moat
3 Ancient doorway to Machu Picchu
4 Quarry
5 Temple of the Sun
6 Royal Tomb
7 Royal Sector & fountains
8 Sacred Plaza/Temple of the Three Windows
9 Principal Temple
10 House of the Priest/Sacristy
11 Intihuatana
12 Sacred Rock
13 Huayna Picchu
14 Temple of the Moon
15 Plaza Central
16 Temple of the Condor
17 Puente Inca
18 Intipunku (Sun Gate)

> *Perfectly aligned structures, such as the Temple of Three Windows, show the Incas' appreciation for aesthetics.*

❸ Ancient doorway to Machu Picchu. This is the entrance to the main section of the ruins, leading past a series of burial grounds and dwellings.

❹ Quarry. Above a clearing with views of the Cordillera Vilcabamba's snowcapped peaks, this assortment of large stones was most likely a quarry supplying Machu Picchu's stonemasons.

❺ ★★★ Temple of the Sun. Down a steep series of stairs, this tapered tower is famous among Inca constructions. The only rounded structure in the complex, its stonework is the finest in Machu Picchu. Above the temple is a ledge from which visitors can appreciate a trapezoidal window cut into the stone, perfectly aligned for the winter solstice (in June)—when the sun's rays come streaming through at dawn and illuminate the altar stone at the center of the temple.

Tip

Stops ⑬, ⑭, ⑰, and ⑱ should be considered extras, meant for those with the stamina and time to explore additional areas of the site.

❻ ★ Royal Tomb. Just below the temple is a cave carved from the rock, with a carved altar and series of niches and steps. Despite the fact that no human remains were ever found here, the cave has traditionally been referred to as a tomb.

❼ ★ Royal Sector & fountains. Immediately north of the Royal Tomb are stairs dividing this section of dwellings from the Royal Sector, a still-functioning water canal, and 16 large, interconnected fountains (likely ceremonial baths) with splendid stonework.

❽ ★★★ Sacred Plaza/Temple of the Three Windows. North of the quarry, back up the

Más Machu Picchu

Though much of its architecture is in remarkably good condition (and much has been reconstructed), the exact nature of Machu Picchu remains a matter of debate. Astoundingly, this complex of fine architecture and stonemasonry was constructed, inhabited, and abandoned all in less than a century, yet most people consider it the crowning achievement of 4,000 years of history of Andean Peru. Most historians now believe that the ninth Inca emperor, Pachacútec, the founder of the Inca Empire and the civilization's great builder, ordered the complex constructed in the mid-1400s as a royal retreat. Whether it served as a citadel, agricultural site, astronomical observatory, or ceremonial city and sacred retreat for the Inca emperor—or a combination of all of these—has not been conclusively proved. Machu Picchu may have been abandoned well before the arrival of the Spanish, a result of civil war or drought.

Reputed to be the legendary "lost city of the Incas," Machu Picchu was never mentioned in the Spanish chronicles and remained essentially hidden for 4 centuries. Some locals knew of its presence, but the site was effectively rediscovered for the world in 1911 by the Yale archaeologist and historian Hiram Bingham. Bingham erroneously believed he had found the lost city of Vilcabamba, the last refuge of the Inca Manco Cápac, a site that is in fact deeper in the jungle at Espíritu Pampa.

> For 4 days over tough mountain passes, hikers on the Camino del Inca dream about their arrival at Machu Picchu.

stairs to the high section of the ruins, is the main ceremonial area. One of Machu Picchu's most famous features is a series of three windows, each trapezoid magnificently cut to frame views of the mountains across the Urubamba gorge.

⑨ ★ Principal Temple. Left of the Temple of the Three Windows is this three-walled temple, which features excellent stonework, including a carved rock in the shape of a kite that may have been a representation of the Southern Cross.

⑩ ★ House of the Priest/Sacristy. A small cell opposite the Principal Temple, called the Sacristy, is celebrated for its masterful masonry. To the left of the doorjamb is a magnificent stone with 32 distinct angles, cut and fit to other blocks by talented Inca stonemasons.

⑪ ★ Intihuatana. Climb a small flight of stairs to another of Machu Picchu's most distinctive elements, a ritualistic carved rock or sundial that's commonly called the Hitching Post of the Sun. It's likely that the Incas used the stone as an astronomical and agricultural calendar, judging constellations and solar events to gauge the seasons. The Spaniards destroyed similar monuments at other Inca sites, thinking them to be instruments of pagan worship.

⑫ ★ Sacred Rock. Follow a trail through agricultural terraces and past a small plaza to a small clearing with covered stone benches on either side, home to a huge, sculpted stone. The stone's form echoes the shape of the sacred peak Putukusi, directly across the Valley. While the plaza is thought to have been merely a communal area for meetings and performances, many locals and visitors claim the Sacred Rock possesses a very real force of energy, and you'll see folks placing their palms flat on its surface in an effort to tap that energy.

Practical Information: Machu Picchu

Travelers reach Machu Picchu from Cusco or Ollantaytambo by train and bus, or by hiking the Inca Trail (p 266). At the train station in Aguas Calientes, buses up the hillside to the site begin running at 5:30am and return all day, the last one descending at 6pm (cost is $14 round-trip; buy your ticket at the booth in front of the lineup of buses, at the bottom of the market stalls). Note that during peak afternoon hours, lines for buses can be long. You may also purchase a one-way ticket ($7) up and later walk down (a steep but easily managed path, which cuts off the curves of the road; 45 min.) to Aguas Calientes. The ruins are open daily from 6am to 6pm. Tickets (S/126 adults; S/63 students with an ISIC card; free for children 7 and under) must be purchased in advance (take your passport) at the **Machu Picchu Cultural Center** in Aguas Calientes, Av. Pachacútec s/n (☎ 084/211-196), near the main plaza. Tickets are also sold at the **Instituto Nacional de Cultural (INC)** offices in Cusco, on San Bernardo s/n (☎ 084/246-074). Tickets are valid for 3 days from date of purchase, but good for a single day's entrance only. English-speaking guides can be independently arranged on-site—most charge around $30 for a private 2-hour tour; it is also sometimes possible to hook up with an established group for about $5 per person. No food, drink, or backpacks are allowed within the ruins (though most people smuggle in some snacks and a bottle of water, which you will need). There's a snack bar outside the entrance, and the buffet lunch at Machu Picchu Sanctuary Lodge, open to the public, is excellent if pricey (p. 290).

The site is large enough to escape most tour-group bottlenecks, although people fearful of the crush should plan to arrive as early as possible in the morning, hopefully early enough to see the sunrise, and/or stay past 3pm. The worst times to visit are from July 28 to August 10, when Peruvian national holidays bring huge groups of schoolchildren and families, and solstice days (June 21 and Dec 21), when masses hope for a glimpse of the dazzling effects of the sun's rays. During the rainy season (Nov–Mar), you're very likely to get rain for (often) brief periods during the day.

> *Visitors place their hands on the Intihuatana, or "Hitching Post of the Sun"; many travelers attest to a palpable spiritual presence at Machu Picchu.*

⑬ ★★★ **Huayna Picchu.** This famous peak is the dramatic backdrop to Machu Picchu seen in countless photographs. What many visitors don't realize is that a (quite demanding) trail leads to the summit, a huge outcrop that affords spectacular birds-eye views of the ruins and a 360-degree panorama of the mountains all around. Only 400 people per day are permitted to make the climb, and hikers must register with the guards. (The trail is open 7am–1pm, and the first group of 200 must exit by 10am; young children are not allowed.) The climb up Huayna Picchu is strenuous, but anyone in relatively good shape can do it; most people take about an hour to ascend to the summit. Reached via a path to the left of the Sacred Rock, the trail is steep and very narrow in sections, with stone steps that can be treacherous in wet weather. At what would appear to be the summit is a platform overlooking the ruins. However, if you're not claustrophobic, you can continue up through a tight tunnel carved out of the stone, which leads to a final rocky perch with the most glorious views of all.

⑭ ★ **Temple of the Moon.** Off the path to Huayna Picchu is a trail around the mountain's back side and through cloud forest to this little-visited, mysterious temple (the round-trip walk takes at least 90 min.). Despite the name, this site of caverns and portals, with carved stonework, was probably a temple used to worship the Huayna Picchu mountain spirit rather than any sort of lunar observatory.

⑮ **Plaza Central.** Returning to the main Machu Picchu complex, a massive plaza separates the lower, residential, and industrial section of the ruins from the spiritually oriented upper section.

⑯ ★ **Temple of the Condor.** The lower section's most interesting feature is this carving, said to be that of a giant condor (the dark rock above symbolizing the wings, the pale rock below the head). If you're not claustrophobic, you can crawl through the cave at the base of the rock and emerge on the other side.

⑰ **Puente Inca.** Removed from the main complex, this Inca drawbridge overlooks a sheer, 610m (2,000-ft.) drop. It's about a half-hour walk to the bridge along a narrow, marked trail.

⑱ ★★ **Intipunku (Sun Gate).** Hikers on the Inca Trail (p. 266) arrive at Machu Picchu, as the Incas once did, through the Sun Gate. You can reach Intipunku in an hour or less by climbing a path that begins just below the Caretaker's Hut. The views from the gateway are stunning. The two stone gates figure into the winter and summer solstices, when the sun directly illuminates the gates like no other days of the year.

The Inca Trail

Followed by ecotourists and modern-day pilgrims, the Camino del Inca (Inca Trail) to Machu Picchu is one of the world's most spectacular treks. The Incas conceived of Machu Picchu and the royal route leading to it in grand artistic and spiritual terms, and hiking the *camino* makes clear their architectural sophistication and regard for nature. The 4-day, 43km (27-mile) route passes three formidable mountain passes and traverses the Machu Picchu Historical Sanctuary, full of incredible Inca ruins, cloud-forest vegetation, and stunning mountain vistas. The trail's enormous popularity has become its enemy, though, threatening the environment and trail itself and necessitating strict regulations.

> *The elaborate ruins of Sayacmarca on the Inca Trail, a warm-up for Machu Picchu.*

START Take a *colectivo* from Cusco to just outside Ollantaytambo (2 hr.; there is no train service that terminates in Ollantaytambo).

❶ Day 1. From Km 88, cross Río Urubamba; the first gentle ascent is to Inca ruins at **Llaqtapata.** The path then crosses the Río Cusicacha and follows the river before climbing to the small village of **Huayllabamba,** a 2- to 3-hour hike. Most groups spend their first night at campsites here. **Total distance 10km (6.2 miles).**

❷ Day 2. The second day covers the most difficult section of the Inca Trail. From Huayllabamba, it is an hour's climb to ruins at **Llullucharoc** (3,800m/12,470 ft.), and the trail then continues to **Llulluchapampa,** a difficult 2-hour climb through cloud forest. The reward: extraordinary valley views. Continue to one of the trail's highlights, Abra de Huarmihuañusqa, or **Dead Woman's Pass,** the highest point on the trail—a brutal climb in thin air over a 4,200m (13,780-ft.) pass. After a rest at the summit, descend sharply

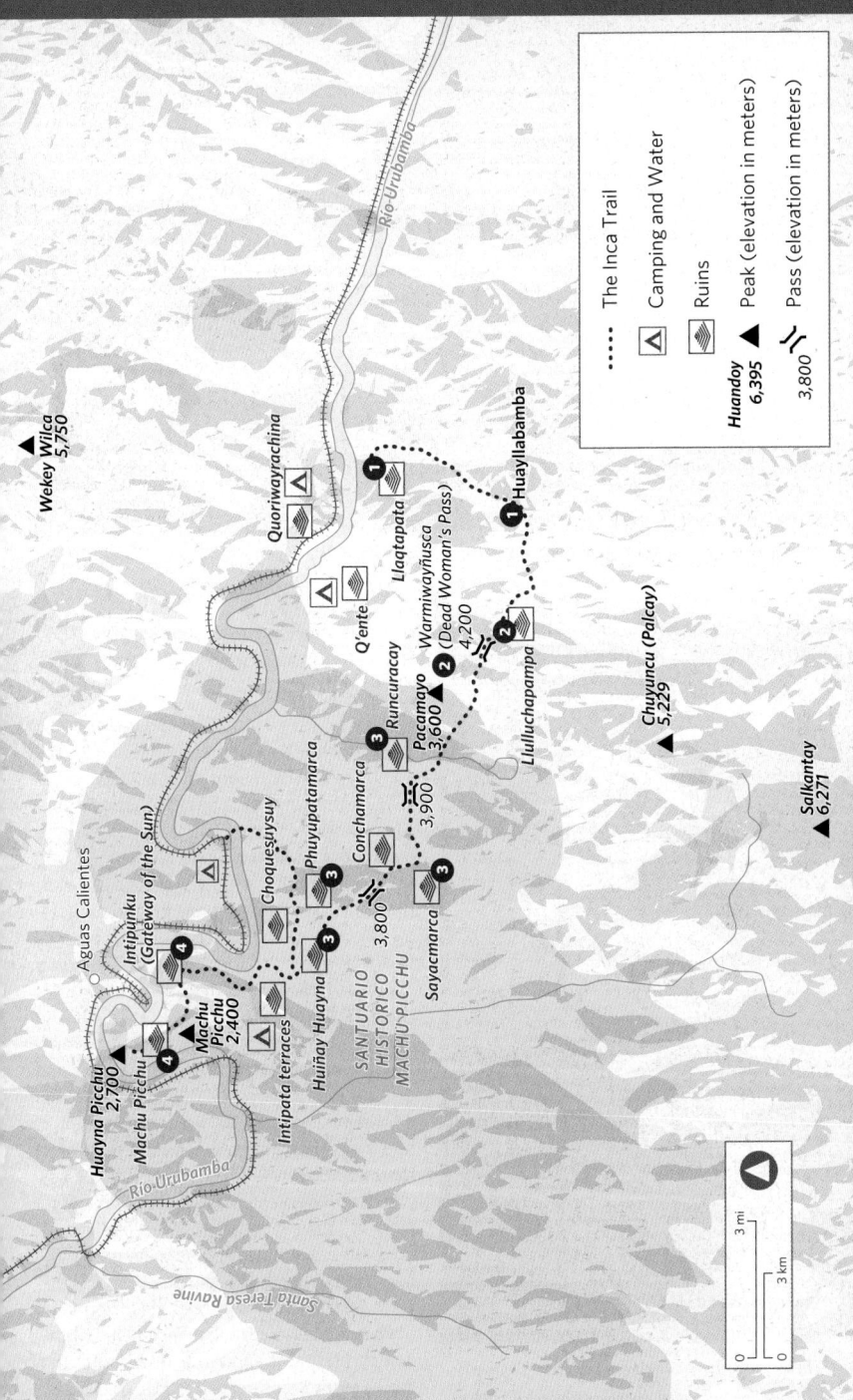

Legend:

- ⋯⋯ The Inca Trail
- △ Camping and Water
- ▨ Ruins
- ▲ Peak (elevation in meters)
  Huandoy 6,395
- 〉〈 Pass (elevation in meters)
  3,800

Wekey Wilca 5,750 ▲

Quoriwayrachina

Rio Urubamba

Huayllabamba

Chuyuncu (Palcay) 5,229 ▲

Salkantay 6,271 ▲

Q'ente

Llaqtapata

Warmiwayñusca (Dead Woman's Pass) 4,200

Pacamayo 3,600 ▲

Runcuracay

Llulluchapampa

Phuyupatamarca

Conchamarca

3,900

Sayacmarca

3,800

Choquesuysuy

Intipunku (Gateway of the Sun)

Aguas Calientes

Huiñay Huayna

Intipata terraces

Huayna Picchu 2,700 ▲

Machu Picchu 2,400 ▲

Rio Urubamba

Santa Teresa Ravine

SANTUARIO HISTORICO MACHU-PICCHU

3 mi
3 km

> *The highest point on the Inca Trail, "Dead Woman's Pass," is a severe test, but the views are heavenly.*

> *The Huiñay Huayna ruins are perhaps the most extraordinary of those found along the Camino del Inca.*

on stone steps to **Pacamayo** (3,600m/11,810 ft.), where groups camp for the night. **Total distance 11km (6.8 miles).**

❸ **Day 3.** After a brutal second day, the third day is the trek's most memorable. A 1-hour climb to the next mountain pass leads to the ruins of **Runcuracay,** a unique circular structure. Another 1-hour climb leads to a second pass, **Abra de Runcuracay** (3,900m/12,800 ft.), where there's an official campsite just past the Runcuracay summit and great views of the Vilcabamba mountain range. From here, the trail passes a lake and ascends a remarkable staircase to **Sayacmarca** (3,500m/11,480 ft.), ritual baths, and a terrace overlooking the Aobamba Valley. The trail then backtracks on the way to **Conchamarca,** another rest stop, and drops into thick jungle. After passing through an Inca tunnel, the trail climbs steadily for 2 hours toward a third major pass, **Phuyupata-marca** (3,800m/12,470 ft.), a gentler ascent than its predecessors. Several of the region's highest snowcapped peaks are clearly visible from here. Below lies Aguas Calientes, and the back side of Machu Picchu peak comes into view. Continue to the handsome Inca ruins of Phuyupatamarca, an ancient village with ceremonial baths and terraces. A staircase of 2,250 stone steps descends 1,000m (3,281 ft.) through cloud forest (90 min.), and the trail forks. To the right are the magnificent ruins of **Huiñay Huayna,** a 10-minute detour from the trail and a somewhat rowdy, gringo hangout (there are showers and a restaurant serving beer). Incredibly, the Huiñay Huayna ruins weren't discovered until 1941. Around the site are dozens of stone agricultural terraces and 10 ritual baths, which still have running water. **Total distance 15km (9.3 miles).**

❹ **Day 4.** The goal is finally in sight: **Intipunku** (the Sun Gate) and the descent to Machu Picchu for sunrise over the ruins. Most groups depart their Night 3 camp at 4am or earlier to arrive at the pass at Machu Picchu—a trek along narrow stone paths and a final vertical climb—in time for daybreak. The final descent from Intipunku to Machu Picchu takes about 45 minutes. **Total distance 7km (4.3 miles).**

> Arriving at the Sun Gate at sunrise is the goal of trekkers on the Inca Trail.

Practical Information: Inca Trail

There are two principal ways to walk to Machu Picchu: the traditional, arduous 4-day/3-night trek with three serious mountain passes; or a 2-day/1-night trail that might be called "Camino Lite," which begins 14km/8.7 miles from Machu Picchu, at Km 104 (but misses some of the finest ruins and scenery). For both trails, trekkers must go as part of an organized group arranged by an officially sanctioned tour agency (at last count, 160 agencies, both in Cusco and beyond, were allowed to sell Inca Trail packages). The Peruvian government has capped the number of trekkers on the Inca Trail (200 trekkers or 500 total, including trek staff, per day). Standard-class 4-day treks, the most common and economical service, start at about $450 per person, including trail fees ($88 adults, $44 students) and return by tourist-class rail. The cost includes a bus to Km 88 to begin the trek, an English-speaking guide, tents, mattresses, three daily meals, and porters who carry all common equipment. Tips for porters or guides are extra. Groups tend to be between 12 and 16 people, with guaranteed daily departures. Premium-class, smaller groups range from $750 per person to as high as $1,000. For the 2-day "Camino Sagrado," the shorter trek along the Inca Trail, basic pooled service (maximum 16 trekkers) costs about $150 per person (including the entrance fee).

Never purchase Inca Trail packages from anyone other than officially licensed agencies, and avoid the rock-bottom, cost-cutting agencies. Reservations can be made as much as a year in advance. To guarantee a spot (the agency must request a trek permit for each trekker), make a reservation and pay for your entrance fee a minimum of 15 days in advance (in practice, however, it's usually necessary to reserve at least 3–6 months in advance if you plan to go during peak months of May–Oct). Changing dates once you have a reservation is complicated. If spots remain on agency rosters, they are offered on a first-come, first-served basis.

The trail is closed for maintenance the month of February. The best time to go weatherwise is during the dry season (June–Oct), but this is also the most crowded time on the trail. Shoulder seasons can be good, even with the threat of a bit of rain; May is perhaps best, with usually good weather and low numbers of trekkers. December through March is too wet for all but the hardest-core trail vets.

DESCENDANTS OF THE SUN

Inca Cosmology BY NEIL EDWARD SCHLECHT

THE POLYTHEISTIC INCAS HAD A PROFOUND RESPECT for the natural world. Their belief system was based on elements of animism, or the belief that spiritual forces underlie all natural phenomena. In their view, there was no sharp division between the physical and spiritual worlds, and indeed, the Incas worshipped everything from animals to inanimate objects, including stones and mountains. An agrarian society, the Incas believed that many different deities ruled over the natural world, controlling weather, changes of seasons, and fertility. If appeased, the gods would bring good fortune; if angered, they would wreak disease, drought, and natural disaster. The Incas (and their Andean descendants today) made ritualistic offerings to Pacha Mama, or Mother Earth. In the society's strictly hierarchical structure, a priestly class served as intermediaries between gods and humans.

Guide to the Gods

VIRACOCHA
The creator god, source of all life and creator of the sun, moon, and stars. Viracocha could move freely among the three realms of the universe.

INTI
The Incas called themselves Children of the Sun, and all Inca emperors were said to descend from Inti, the Sun God. Represented by a golden sun disc, Inti was considered the mythological father of the royal Inca family.

ILLAPA
The god of thunder and lightning, worshipped for rainfall in the growing season.

MAMA QUILLA
The moon goddess, wife of Inti and daughter of Viracocha, protector of women and marriage and keeper of the heavenly calendar.

PACHA MAMA
Mother Earth and personification of fertility, venerated by crop growers.

RÍO VILCANOTA (WILCAMAYU)
Not a god, but a section of the Urubamba River considered sacred, as it reflected the constellations of the celestial river, the Milky Way.

The Chakana

The distinctive Inca cross (found at many Inca temples and monuments) reflects the Incas' concept of the world. The three-stepped symmetrical cross has 12 points and a hole in its center. Each of the three steps represents one realm of the Inca universe. The void in the center is thought to represent Cusco, the capital city or *q'osco* ("navel") of the Inca Empire, as well as the space through which a shaman can access the other levels—a metaphorical uniting of heaven and earth. The word *chakana* is derived from the Quechua word *chakay*, which means "to cross" or "bridge." Some have posited that the 12 points of the cross represent the 12 months of the year, while the four arms represent the points of a compass.

Condor, Puma, Snake

The Incas conceived of the world as composed of three realms or levels of existence: Hanan Pacha, the celestial world of stars, heavenly beings, and gods; Kay Pacha, the present, human world, or middle earth; and Uku Pacha, the interior or underworld inhabited by spirits of the dead, ancestors, and deities in close contact with Kay Pacha. Each realm was represented by a revered animal: the condor (upper world), puma (middle earth), and snake (underworld). The Incas did not conceive of a linear past, present, and future; in their conception, humans were able to access all three dimensions.

The Incas believed strongly in an afterlife, and ancestor worship was central to their belief system. Death was viewed as a rite of passage to either the upper or lower realm

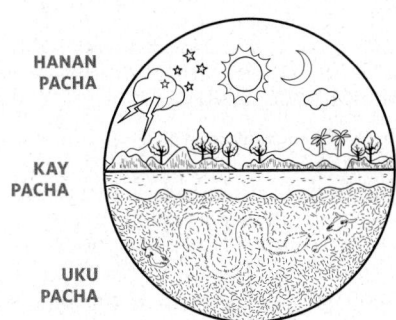

(Hanan Pacha or Uku Pacha). Ancestors were considered protective spirits, actively engaged in the well-being of the living, and bodies and tombs of the dead were considered sacred.

Alternatives to the Inca Trail

> A view of Ausangate peak, one of the mesmerizing highlights of an alternative Inca Trail trek.

❶ ★★★ **Ausangate.** One of the most beautiful but toughest (and coldest) treks in the region, this is only an option for trekkers in good shape who've acclimated to the high altitude. Much of the trek of the Ausangate circuit, through the stunning Cordillera Vilcanota, is at or above 4,500m (14,760 ft.), including campsites. The trail covers two passes higher than 5,000m (16,400 ft.), and it circumvents several peaks that are 6,000m (19,690 ft.) or higher (Ausangate itself is 6,384m/20,945 ft.). The scenery of snowcapped peaks, lakes, glaciers, hot springs, and highland villages is stunning. **6–7 days of trekking.**

❷ ★★★ **Choquequirao.** A spectacular trek to only recently discovered (early 1980s) ruins that are estimated to be perhaps eight times larger than Machu Picchu and still only 30 percent excavated. The trek descends sharply to the Apurímac River and then climbs 1,220m (4,000 vertical ft.). There are a couple of campsites with showers and toilet facilities along the way; the final campsite is just below the ruins, at a spot 1,750m (5,741 ft.) above the river canyon. The ruins boast stunning agricultural terracing, some with unusual decorative motifs not seen at other Inca sites. Choquequirao was an important 15th-century Inca citadel and likely royal retreat for the Inca Tupac Yupanqui, son of the Inca who built Machu Picchu. Peruvian tourism officials have their eyes on developing (or, some would say, exploiting) this route. A longer route (7 days) continues on to Machu Picchu. **4–5 days of trekking, including a day exploring the ruins.**

❸ ★★ **Salcantay.** A true Inca Trail alternative, this trek begins at the same spot in the Urubamba Valley and passes through similar areas of the Cordillera Vilcabamba. While it passes fewer Inca ruins, it's more peaceful and there's more opportunity for interaction with local communities. Most Salcantay treks begin in Mollepata and terminate in Aguas Calientes (or Santa Teresa), and some even join the Inca Trail at Huayllabamba on Day 5, before continuing on to Machu Picchu. At 6,271m (20,574 ft.), Salcantay is the second-highest mountain in southern Peru; these treks approach the dramatic Salcantay Pass, at 4,700m (15,420 ft.). One "soft adventure"

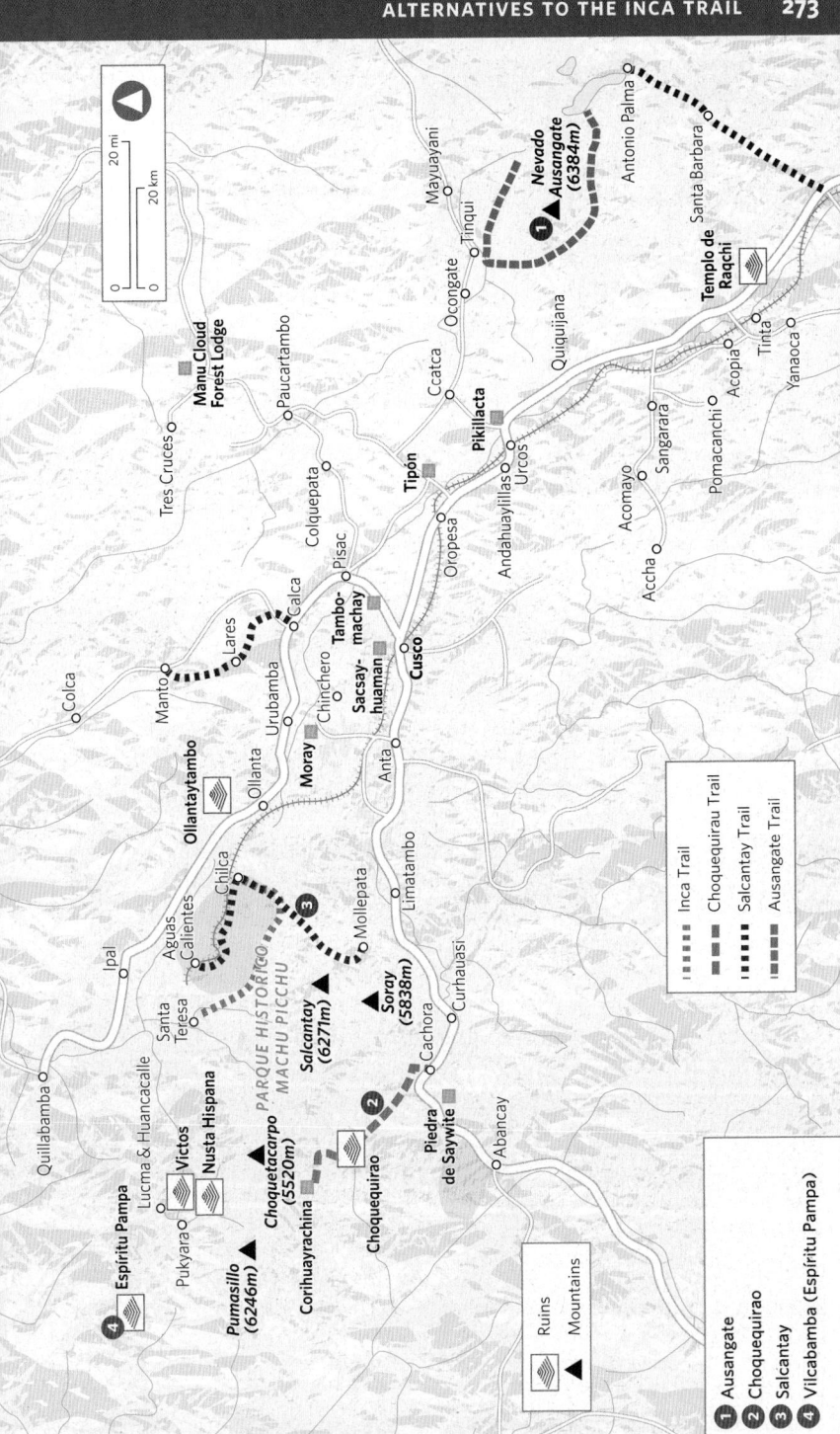

> *Horses make the 1,220m (4,000-ft.) climb to Choquequirao's spectacular ruins, estimated to be eight times larger than Machu Picchu.*

option is to stay in beautifully designed eco-lodges (see "Mountain Lodges of Peru," below) while walking this route. **5–7 days of trekking.**

❹ ★ **Vilcabamba (Espíritu Pampa).** This is among the most remote and adventurous of alternative treks. Although Hiram Bingham was convinced he'd found the last, and lost, Inca stronghold of Vilcabamba at Machu Picchu (see "Más Machu Picchu," p. 262), the magnificent, remote ruins of Espíritu Pampa, deep in the jungle and discovered in 1964 by the American explorer Gene Savoy, are believed by most experts to be the real deal. Getting there requires a fully prepared expedition, since there are no services of any kind along the route. **7–10 days trekking.**

Alternative Trail Outfitters

★ **Adventure Life.** Among its alternatives is an 11-day Ausangate trip. ☎ 800/344-6118. www.adventurelife.com.

★ **Andean Lodges.** A joint initiative between the Peruvian tour group Auqui Mountain Spirit and local Quechua shepherding communities, operating four simple, eco-friendly mountain lodges along the Camino del Apu Ausangate (in the Vilcanota range), which they claim are the highest-altitude lodges in the world (3,962–4,572m/13,000–15,000 ft.). Starting at $845 per person. ☎ 084/224-613. www.andeanlodges.com.

★★ **Andean Treks.** Four-day Moonstone to Sun Temple trek, as well as others to Choquequirao and Ausangate. ☎ 800/683-8148. www.andeantreks.com.

★★★ **Mountain Lodges of Peru.** A pioneer Peruvian adventure travel company that has constructed four stunning lodges on private lands in the Vilcabamba mountain range for Salcantay treks. The inns boast amazing high-altitude locations and sophisticated architecture and amenities (including whirlpools, hot showers, fireplaces, and sleek dining rooms). Seven-day treks ($2,650 per person) culminate in a visit to Machu Picchu. The company also contracts with

international outfitters, including **Backroads** (☎ 800/462-2848; www.backroads.com) and **Wilderness Travel** and **Mountain Travel Sobek** (see below), which book the lodges for their own 9-day (5 days trekking) Machu Picchu Lodge to Lodge or Inn to Inn packages. Prices for full trips, including stays in Cusco, run up to $4,995 per person. ☎ 01/421-7777, or 510/525-8846 in the U.S. and Canada. www.mountainlodgesofperu.com.

★★ **Mountain Travel Sobek.** This company offers alternatives to the Inca Trail, including a 10-day trek to Choquequirao, a 7-day "Inn to Inn Machu Picchu Express Trek," an Ausangate "Inn to Inn" trek, and a 12-day (7 days hiking) "Other Inca Trail" that does 4 days of "hidden trails" before joining up with the Inca Trail on Day 8. Treks start at $2,650. ☎ 888/831-7526. www.mtsobek.com.

★★ **Peru for Less.** Recently launched economical, small-group alternative treks to Choquequirao, Ausangate, and Espíritu Pampa. ☎ 877/2609-0309. www.peruforless.com.

★★ **Wilderness Travel.** A 17-day (13 days hiking) Choquequirao to Machu Picchu "Hidden Inca Trail" tour. Treks range from about $600 to $4,000 per person. ☎ 800/368-2794. www.wildernesstravel.com.

Sacred Valley Outdoor Adventures A to Z

Bungee Jumping & Zip-Lining

Action Valley Cusco Adventure Park, Plazoleta Regocijo (☎ 084/240-835; Cusco office at Santa Teresa 325; www.actionvalley.com), is 11km (7 miles) from Cusco and was the first establishment in Peru to offer bungee jumping (from a platform) as well as other suspended-line activities and paintball. **Cola de Mono Canopy,** village of Santa Teresa (15 km/9 miles from Machu Picchu; ☎ 084/792-413; www.canopyperu.com), claims to have the highest zip line in South America; try high-wire zipping of up to 48kmph (30mph) through the treetops.

Day Hikes

Km 82 of Inca Trail. The classic Inca Trail begins at Km 88. The section preceding it is much gentler than other parts of the trail; along the railroad side of the Río Urubamba, past ruins sites, including Salapunku and Pinchanuyoq, before reaching the Inca bridge at Km 88 and the site of the Qoriwayrachina ruins, with stone sculptures and altars. Beginning: just beyond Ollantaytambo.

Maras to Salineras. A pretty valley walk is from the village of Maras to the salt pans of Salineras (p. 258, **6**), about 9km (5.6 miles), or 1 hour, along the path taken by some of the salt-mine workers. More extreme is the 14km (8.7-mile) 3-hour walk to the salt mines from the Inca ruins at Moray. You'll pass blue-green cacti, purple-flowering potatoes, and small children and their flocks of sheep, and take in dazzling views of distant snowcapped mountains.

Pinkuylluna. Climb the mountain overlooking the old town of Ollantaytambo for great views of the town, valley, and ruins. The trail is steep at first, but then becomes gentler, and the payoff—the Inca terracing and granaries carved out of the hillside—are worth the effort. Take the stairs off Calle Lares K'ikllu, just northeast of Ollantaytambo's Plaza de Armas. A handmade sign points to Pinkuylluna.

Pumamarca Ruins. These well-preserved Inca ruins are reached by a walk from Ollantaytambo along the banks of the Río Patacancha. The walk takes about 5 hours round-trip. Take

> *The Sacred Valley has developed into a beacon for outdoors enthusiasts.*

> *Horseback riding is a great way to take in the gentle Sacred Valley.*

the road that leads north out of town along the river. After crossing the river, the road becomes a footpath and passes the village of Munaypata. Veer left toward the valley and then turn sharply to the right (northeast) toward the agricultural terraces straight ahead.

Horseback Riding

Perol Chico, Ctra. Urubamba-Ollantaytambo Km 77 (☎ 01/994-147-267 or 084/984-624-475; www.perolchico.com), operates one of the best horseback-riding agencies in Peru, with 1- and 2-day rides, full riding vacations, Peruvian Paso horses, and ranch stays in rustic cottages.

Hot-Air Ballooning

Globos de los Andes, Av. de la Cultura 220, of. 36, Cusco (☎ 084/232-352; www.globosperu.com), is the only regional outfit offering hot-air balloon excursions. While this veteran company, run by American Jeff Hall, can't fly over Machu Picchu, you will get aerial panoramas of the Sacred Valley, Inca ruins, and Andes peaks.

Mountain Biking

Omar Zarzar's **Eco Montana** (www.ecomontana.com) is a professional local outfit with good equipment and guides, handling mountain bike rentals and both short and long *ciclotourism* routes around Urubamba. A popular trip is the ride from Moray to Salineras de Maras. **Peru Discovery,** Santa Maria F-3, San

> *Mountain biking in the Valley has taken off; there are even pro races.*

Sebastian (☎ 054/274-541; www.perudiscovery.com), is one of the top mountain-biking specialists, with a half-dozen bike trips in the region, including hard-core excursions. **Amazonas Explorer, Apumayo Expediciones, Eric Adventures, Instinct Travel** (see "White-Water Rafting," below), and **Manu Ecological Adventures,** Plateros 356, Cusco (☎ 213/283-6987 in the U.S. or Canada, or 084/261-640 in Peru; www.manuadventures.com), all offer 1- to 5-day organized mountain-biking excursions for all skill levels.

Multiday Trekking

Highland trekking is big business in Cusco and the Sacred Valley, and many dozens of agencies handle innumerable treks. See the groups listed in "Inca Trail Agencies A to Z" (p. 278) as well as the following: **Andina Travel,** Plazoleta Santa Catalina 219 (☎ 084/251-892; www.andinatravel.com); **Apuandino Expediciones,** Tupac Katari, San Sebastian (☎ 084/274-789; www.apuandino-expeditions.com); **Aventours,** Saphi 456

> *White-water rafting ranges from Class II to Class V on the Urubamba and Apurímac rivers.*

(☎ 084/224-050; www.aventours.com); **Enigma,** Jr. Clorinda Matto de Turner, 100 Urbanización Magisterial (☎ 084/221-155; www.enigmaperu.com); **Manu Expeditions,** Clorinda Matto de Turner 330, Urbanización Magisterial (☎ 084/225-990; www.manuexpeditions.com); **Mayuc,** Portal Confiturías 211, Plaza de Armas (☎ 084/242-824; www.mayuc.com); and U.S.-based ★★ **Andean Treks** (☎ 800/683-8148 or 617/924-1974; www.andeantreks.com). **Peru Discovery** (see "Mountain Biking," above) also organizes excellent trekking expeditions, as does Chalo, the Chilean-born owner of the eco-styled lodge **Las Chullpas** in Urubamba (p. 287).

A good 2-day hike is from Yucay to the small village of **Huayoccari.** You'll pass lovely scenery, including Inca terraces along the San Juan River ravine and ancient rock paintings overlooking caves. After camping overnight, trekkers continue to the Tuqsana pass (4,000m/13,120 ft.) and descend to Yanacocha Lake before arriving at Huayoccari.

White-Water Rafting

In the rivers of the Sacred Valley there are some fantastic river runs, ranging from mild Class II to world-class advanced runs (Class IV and V). Choose from 1-day Urubamba River trips (Huambutío–Pisac and Ollantaytambo–Chillca) and multiday trips on the more challenging Apurímac. Recommended agencies in Cusco include **Amazonas Explorer,** Av. Collasuyo 910, Urbanización Miravalle (☎ 084/252-846; www.amazonas-explorer.com); **Apumayo Expediciones,** Jr. Ricardo Palma N-5, Santa Mónica, Wanchaq (☎ 084/246-018; www.apumayo.com); **Eric Adventures,** Urbanización Velasco Astete B-8-B (☎ 084/234-764; www.ericadventures.com); **Instinct Travel,** Av. de la Cultura 1318 (☎ 084/233-451; www.instinct-travel.com); **Loreto Tours,** Calle del Medio 111 (☎ 084/228-264; www.loretotours.com); **Mayuc,** Portal Confiturías 211, Plaza de Armas (☎ 084/242-824; www.mayuc.com); and ★ **Swissraft-Perú,** Heraderos 129 (☎ 084/264-124; www.swissraft-peru.com).

Inca Trail Agencies A to Z

★★ **Andean Treks.** A longtime, respected outdoors operator based in Watertown, MA (USA), running Inca Trail treks and numerous other programs in Latin America. Av. Pardo 705, Cusco. ☎ 800/683-8148 in the U.S. and Canada, or 084/225-701 in Cusco. www.andeantreks.com.

Andina Travel. An upstart, progressive company interested in sustainable development, owned by a Cusco native and his North American business partner. Plazoleta Santa Catalina 219, Cusco. ☎ 084/251-892. www.andinatravel.com.

Big Foot Tours. A popular budget agency. Triunfo 392, 2nd floor, Cusco. ☎ 084/991-3851. www.bigfootcusco.com.

★ **Enigma.** An operator with a good reputation and specialized and alternative hiking and trekking options. Good for small-group treks. Jr. Clorinda Matto de Turner, 100 Urbanización Magisterial, Cusco. ☎ 084/221-155. www.enigmaperu.com.

★★ **Explorandes.** One of the top high-end agencies and the most experienced in treks and mountaineering across Peru. Especially good for small private groups. Garcilaso 316-A, Cusco. ☎ 084/238-380. www.explorandes.com.

★★ **Inca Explorers.** A top all-purpose agency, with midrange, small-group Inca Trail treks. Porters carry hikers' packs. Ruinas 427, Cusco. ☎ 084/241-070. www.incaexplorers.com.

★ **Mayuc.** Good for pampered, small-group Inca Trail expeditions. Portal de Confiturías 211 (Plaza de Armas), Cusco. ☎ 866/777-9213 in the U.S. and Canada, or 084/242-824 in Cusco. www.mayuc.com.

★ **Q'Ente.** Praised by budget trekkers and competitively priced, with good guides. Garcilaso 210, Cusco. ☎ 084/222-535. www.qente.com.

★ **SAS Adventure Travel.** A large, long-established agency serving budget-oriented trekkers. Popular, responsible, and well organized. Garcilaso 270, Plaza de San Francisco, Cusco. ☎ 084/249-194. www.sastravelperu.com.

★ **United Mice.** A top midrange agency with affordable treks started by one of the trail's most respected guides. Plateros 351, Cusco. ☎ 084/221-139. www.unitedmice.com.

Tip

In addition to cost, hikers should ask about group size (12 or fewer is best; 16 is the most allowed); guides and their English-speaking abilities; and quality of food, porters, and equipment. Make sure the agency guarantees daily departures.

A Note on Safety

Bargain hunting in this category isn't a great idea: Quality equipment and professional, English-speaking guides are important for safety.

> *The number of hikers permitted on the Inca Trail is strictly regulated by the Peruvian government to guard against environmental concerns.*

Sacred Valley & Aguas Calientes Restaurants

Sacred Valley

★ **Alhambra** URUBAMBA *PERUVIAN*
Somewhat less tour-bus-oriented than its highway neighbors, this hacienda-style restaurant has small dining rooms and outdoor tables, with lunch buffets on market days and a good three-course *menú turístico*. Ctra. Urubamba-Ollantaytambo s/n (near Hotel Sol y Luna). ☎ 084/201-200. Entrees S/18–S/28. MC, V. Lunch daily. Map p. 281.

Ayahuasca PISAC *PERUVIAN*
An appealing little cafe a few blocks off the Plaza, serving cheap classic Peruvian highlander dishes such as *lomo saltado* (stir-fry). Jr. Bolognesi s/n. ☎ 084/797-625. Entrees S/10–S/18. No credit cards. Lunch and dinner daily. Map p. 281.

★ **Blue Puppy Lounge & Restaurant** OLLANTAYTAMBO *INTERNATIONAL/VEGETARIAN*
An upstairs joint just off the main square, this is as much a bar as it is a restaurant, but if you're in need of uncomplicated comfort food, it does the trick, with quesadillas, burritos, pizzas, salads, and chicken and steaks with a wide variety

of sauces. There's a full menu of veggie items, too. Horno s/n (Plaza de Armas). ☎ 084/630-464. Entrees S/17–S/30. No credit cards. Breakfast, lunch, and dinner daily. Map p. 281.

★★ kids **Café Mayu** OLLANTAYTAMBO *PERUVIAN/INTERNATIONAL*   Though it's located on the train platform, it's much more than just a place to grab something for the ride. The handsome cafe, part of El Albergue (p. 284), has excellent homemade pastas, sandwiches, and quinoa salad. Don't miss the brownie with vanilla ice cream. Trekkers can score a nice boxed lunch for their daypacks. Estación de Tren Ollantaytambo. ☎ 084/204-014. www.elalbergue.com. Entrees S/13–S/38. No credit cards. Lunch and dinner daily. Map p. 281.

★★ **El Bar del Huerto** URUBAMBA ENVIRONS
About as stylish a spot as you'll find in the Sacred Valley, this upscale lounge in Hotel Rio Sagrado has views of the Urubamba River and a well-heeled rustic look. There are garden tables, too. Ctra. Urubamba-Ollantaytambo s/n. ☎ 084/201-620. AE, MC, V. Lunch and dinner daily. Map p. 281.

> *Café Mayu, right along the railroad tracks in Ollantaytambo, is the town's best restaurant.*

> *A refreshing glass of chicha morada awaits at El Huacatay, one of the best restaurants in the Valley.*

dinners. Plaza de Armas s/n. ☎ 084/204-078. Entrees S/6–S/22. No credit cards. Breakfast, lunch, and dinner daily. Map p. 281.

★★★ Huayoccari Hacienda Restaurant

HUAYOCCARI *CLASSIC PERUVIAN* This special restaurant, in an elegant, antiques-filled farm-house high in the foothills, isn't a place you can just drop in on. You have to make arrange-ments through a tour agency for a lunch of classic Peruvian fine dining in what feels like a private club. The cash-only *prix-fixe* menu is simple but features well-prepared local veg-etables, soups, and fresh river trout or meats. Ctra. Cusco-Urubamba Km 64. ☎ 084/962-2224, or 084/226-241 in Cusco. *Prix-fixe* lunch $35. No credit cards. Lunch daily. Map p. 281.

★★ Killa Wasi URUBAMBA ENVIRONS *NOVO ANDINO*

Enjoy Andean specialties with a cre-ative twist at this elegant, rustic restaurant, part of the chic Sol y Luna Lodge (p. 287). Its nouveau Andean specialties, fresh pastas, and rice dishes are very good, if a tad pricey for the zone. Ctra. Urubamba-Ollantaytambo s/n. ☎ 084/201-620. www.hotelsolyluna.com. Entrees S/25–S/45. AE, DC, MC, V. Breakfast, lunch, and dinner daily. Map p. 281.

Kusicoyllor OLLANTAYTAMBO *PERUVIAN*

Looking out at Ollanta's ruins, this cafe-restau-rant serves standard Peruvian and Italian dishes and pretty good breakfasts. Plaza Araccama s/n. ☎ 084/204-114. Entrees S/12–S/28. MC, V. Breakfast, lunch, and dinner daily. Map p. 281.

★★★ El Huacatay URUBAMBA *NOVO ANDINO*

The best all-purpose restaurant in the Valley, this relaxed but stylish gourmet place, with a warm and intimate dining room, colorful bar, and garden area, draws both foreigners and wealthier Peruvians. The creative menu is by a Peruvian chef (he owns the restaurant with his German wife), who offers his takes on Andean specialties, including alpaca lasagna and coca-infused gnocchi. Jr. Arica 620. ☎ 084/201-790. www.elhuacatay.com. Entrees S/18–S/42. V. Lunch and dinner Mon–Sat. Map p. 281.

★ kids Hearts Café OLLANTAYTAMBO *BISTRO/ CAFE*

An agreeable if unadorned little joint right on Ollanta's main square, this feel-good restaurant is owned by a British woman who donates all profits to an NGO (www. livingheartperu.org) working with highland community women and children. It makes for a relaxed spot for breakfast (served all day), sandwiches, empanadas, and good-value

The Acquired Taste of *Chicha*

Dotting the valley, in villages and outside nondescript homes on the side of the main road, are long poles displaying red flags (or red balloons). These aren't political meeting houses or brothels, but places where you can score a home-brewed jug of *chicha*, fermented maize beer. Enter to find a usually barren room and a handful of taciturn locals quietly knocking back giant tumblers of room-temperature, pale yellow liquid. *Chicha* may be the peoples' brew, but it's not for everyone (most gringos find it distinctly unappealing). If you do want to partake, you might want to bring a water bottle to be filled rather than drink out of unwashed plastic glasses.

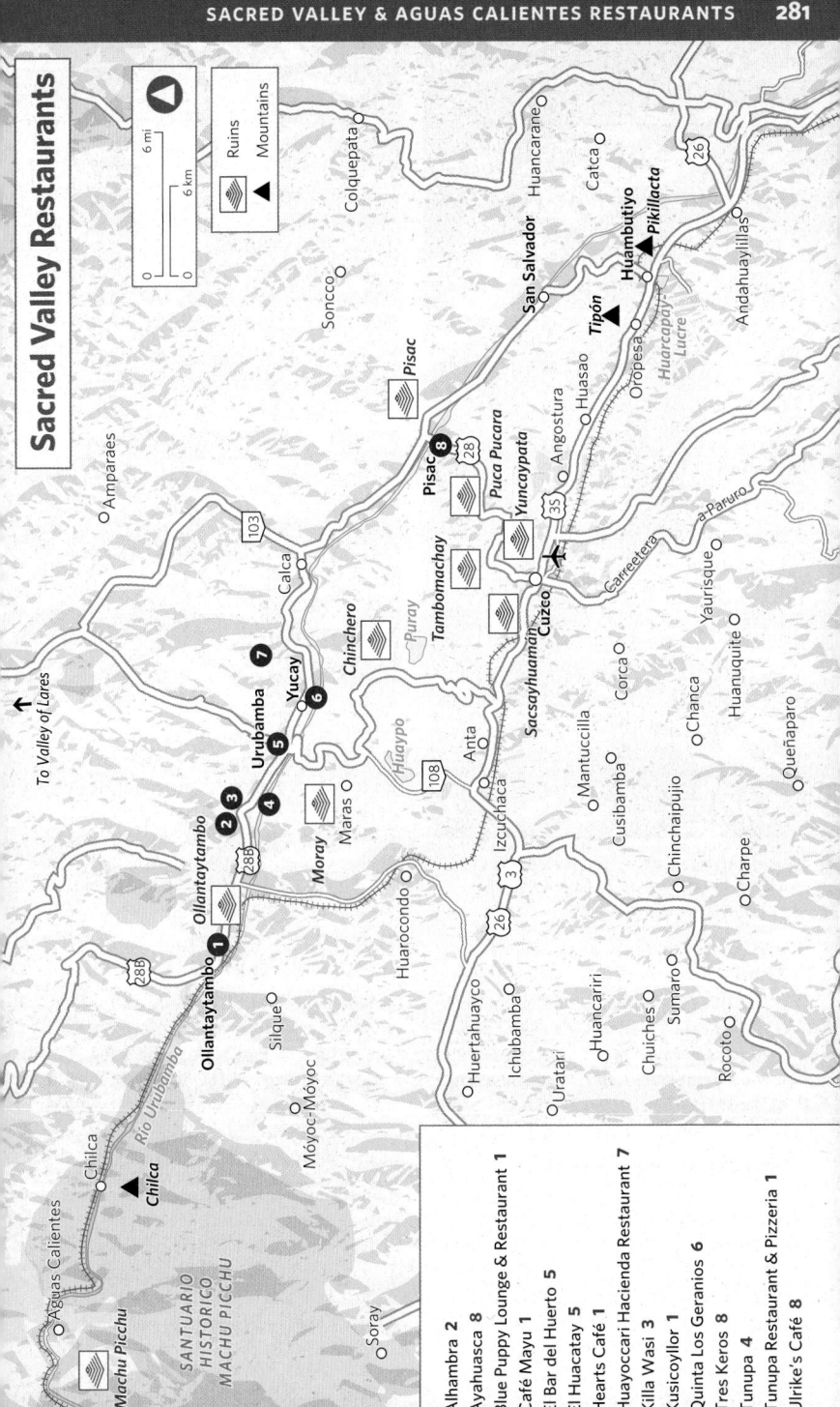

Sacred Valley Restaurants

6 mi
6 km

Ruins
Mountains

To Valley of Lares

Amparaes

Colquepata

Soncco

Huancarane

Catca

26

Andahuaylillas

San Salvador

Huambutiyo

Pikillacta

Tipón

Huasao

Oropesa

Huarcapay-
Lucre

a-Paruro

Pisac

Puca Pucara

Yuncaypata

Angostura

35

Carreetera

Yaurisque

Machu Picchu

SANTUARIO
HISTORICO
MACHU PICCHU

Aguas Calientes

Chilca

Río Urubamba

Silque

Móyoc-Móyoc

Soray

Ollantaytambo

28B

28B

Moray

Maras

108

Huarocondo

Huertahuayco

Ichubamba

Uratari

Huancariri

Chuiches

Sumaro

Rocoto

26

3

Izcuchaca

Anta

Huaypo

Cusibamba

Chinchaipujio

Charpe

Mantuccilla

Corca

Chanca

Huanuquite

Queñaparo

Huambutiyo

Sacsayhuamán

Cuzco

Tambomachay

Chinchero

Puray

Calca

Yucay

Urubamba

Pisac

28

103

Colquepata

Alhambra 2
Ayahuasca 8
Blue Puppy Lounge & Restaurant 1
Café Mayu 1
El Bar del Huerto 5
El Huacatay 5
Hearts Café 1
Huayoccari Hacienda Restaurant 7
Killa Wasi 3
Kusicoyllor 1
Quinta Los Geranios 6
Tres Keros 8
Tunupa 4
Tunupa Restaurant & Pizzeria 1
Ulrike's Café 8

> *Colorful Ulrike's Café in Pisac, owned by a longtime German resident, is a good stop for lunch or a homemade dessert.*

Sacred Valley Nightlife

★ **Blue Puppy Lounge & Restaurant**
OLLANTAYTAMBO Both restaurant and lounge-bar, this laidback upstairs place serves up some good cocktails, as well as fruit juices and milkshakes. Tables at one end have views of the main square. Horno s/n (Plaza de Armas). ☎ 084/630-464. Entrees S/17–S/30. No credit cards.

★ **Blues Bar Café** OLLANTAYTAMBO
A laid-back rock-n-roll joint, this is a good spot if you're staying in town and need a fix of tunes, munchies, and beer and cocktails. There's a nightly 2-for-1 happy hour. Set back from Calle Chaupi (btw. ruins and main square). ☎ 984/322-911.

★ **Chichi Wasi** URUBAMBA ENVIRONS
A cozy lounge at the upscale country hotel Sol y Luna, this is a good place to mingle and have an well-prepared pisco sour or other cocktail with exotic fruits. Ctra. Urubamba-Ollantaytambo s/n. ☎ 084/201-620. MC, V.

Quinta Los Geranios YUCAY PERUVIAN
Targeting the tour-bus trade just outside of Yucay, this open-air restaurant prepares dependable versions of Peruvian standards such as *rocoto relleno* (stuffed hot pepper) and indigenous soups. Av. Cabo Conchatupa s/n. ☎ 084/201-093. Entrees S/12–S/30. No credit cards. Lunch and dinner daily. Map p. 281.

★ **Tres Keros** PISAC NOVO ANDINO
The hands-on chef and owner, Ricardo Behar, from Lima, prepares surprisingly creative Peruvian cuisine, with great local ingredients and fish that comes in from the capital, at this small and cozy spot. The *lomo saltado* and alpaca steak are both quite good. Av. Sr. Torrechayoc s/n (off main road Urubamba-Ollantaytambo). ☎ 084/201-701. Entrees S/18–S/35. V. Lunch and dinner Mon–Sat. Map p. 281.

Tunupa URUBAMBA PERUVIAN
One of the big restaurants between Urubamba and Ollantaytambo, this large hacienda has a cavernous dining hall overlooking the Urubamba River serving buffet lunches to daytrippers. It's a decent deal, but you'll definitely feel like you're part of a tour, whether you are or not. Ctra. Pisac-Ollantaytambo, Km 77 (left side of the road on way to Ollantaytambo). ☎ 084/963-0206. Entrees S/15–S/28. DC, MC, V. Lunch daily. Map p. 281.

Tunupa Restaurant & Pizzeria URUBAMBA ENVIRONS CHIFA/INTERNATIONAL This family-run restaurant offers everything from pancakes to pizza and *chifa* (Peruvian-Chinese dishes). Av. Beneterio s/n. ☎ 084/204-077. Entrees S/9–S/22. No credit cards. Breakfast, lunch and dinner daily. Map p. 281.

★ **Kids Ulrike's Café** PISAC INTERNATIONAL
This welcoming place on the plaza is owned by a German expat and serves perfect home-cooked meals ranging from good-value, set-menu lunches to vegetarian dishes, lasagna, salads, and desserts (a variety of cheesecakes). Plaza de Armas 828. ☎ 084/203-195. Entrees S/10–S/24. No credit cards. Breakfast, lunch, and dinner daily. Map p. 281.

> *The Tree House in Aguas Calientes offers unexpectedly fine dining, as well as cooking classes.*

Aguas Calientes

kids Chez Maggy *PERUVIAN/PIZZA*
A relaxed longtime favorite, this branch of Chez Maggy has good wood-fired pizzas, pisco sours, and cold beers, as well as standard Peruvian fare and Mexican dishes, but pizza's the thing. Av. Pachacútec 156. ☎ 084/211-006. Entrees S/12–S/33. MC, V. Lunch and dinner daily. Map p. 289.

★★ Indio Feliz *PERUVIAN/FRENCH*
About as chichi as this ramshackle town gets, this is the best restaurant in town, with a very good fixed-price menu and nicely prepared entrees such as garlic trout and ginger chicken. Lloque Yupanqui 4–12 (down an alley to the left off Av. Pachacútec). ☎ 084/211-090. Entrees S/26–S/40. MC, V. Lunch and dinner daily. Map p. 289.

kids Pueblo Viejo *PERUVIAN*
A large, animated, and cozy standby on restaurant row, Pueblo Viejo feels like a good place to revel in a trip to Machu Picchu, with live Andean music, a roaring fire, and grilled meats and trout. Av. Pachacútec 108. ☎ 084/211-193. Entrees S/24–S/38. MC, V. Lunch and dinner daily. Map p. 289.

★ Toto's House *PERUVIAN/PIZZA*
Overlooking the river and with great mountain views, this high-ceilinged restaurant is dominated by a barbecue pit. You can get a mixed grill as well as the traveler's standby, wood-fired pizza. Av. Imperio de los Incas s/n. ☎ 084/211-020. Entrees S/25–S/40. MC, V. Lunch and dinner daily. Map p. 289.

★★ The Tree House *NOVO ANDINO*
More creative and upscale than most in town, the house restaurant of the Rupa Wasi lodge feels like its namesake and has a good deal of rustic charm. The menu focuses on *novo Andino* dishes with local ingredients from the inn's garden. There are multicourse tasting menus and some dishes with real flair, plus well-regarded cooking lessons during the day. Jr. Huanacaure 180. ☎ 084/211-101. www. rupawasitreehouse.com. Entrees S/32–S/45. AE, MC, V. Lunch and dinner daily. Map p. 289.

Sacred Valley Hotels

★★ 🅺🆁 **Aranwa Sacred Valley** HUAYLLA-BAMBA This sprawling, upscale country retreat is not for those looking for rustic and understated. It encompasses a 17th-century hacienda and features elegant colonial manor-house rooms; modern rooms and suites; a movie theater; and a huge, swank spa. It's a statement of luxury the rustic Sacred Valley hadn't previously seen, and a bit of an Andean fantasyland, with a man-made lake and reproduction chapel. Antigua Hacienda Yaravilca. ☎ 01/434-1452 for reservations, or 084/205-080. www.aranwahotels.com. 115 units. $225–$250 double; from $400 suite. Rates include breakfast. AE, DC, MC, V.

★★ 🅺🆁 **Casa Andina Private Collection** YA-NAHUARA Styled like a mountain chalet and with a lovely setting and mountain views, this welcoming, professionally run hotel is great for individuals or groups. Bonuses include a fantastic spa, planetarium and observatory for stargazing, and all kinds of outdoor activities. Quinto paradero (sector Pucará). ☎ 084/984-765-501. www.casa-andina.com. 85 units. $125–$185 double; $295 suite. Rates include breakfast. AE, DC, MC, V.

★★ **El Albergue** OLLANTAYTAMBO Owned by a longtime American resident of Ollantaytambo, this rustic, very comfortable *hostal* is next to the train station. It's a traveler's favorite, with handsomely furnished, minimalist but warm rooms; good beds; gardens; and an excellent restaurant (Café Mayu; p. 279). Av. Estación s/n (next to railway station platform). ☎ 084/204-014. www.elalbergue.com. 6 units. $58–$74 double. Rates include breakfast. No credit cards.

★ 🅺🆁 **The Green House** CALCA A tiny, personal B&B, tucked away near Calca, is run by an Englishman and his Argentinean partner. It has pretty gardens and lovely mountain views, as well as a soaring, fireplace-equipped living area. Rooms are comfortable if not luxurious, and the owners prepare very nice home-cooked meals for guests. Ctra. Pisac-Ollantaytambo Km 60. ☎ 084/984-770-130. www.thegreenhouseperu.com. 4 units. S/150 double. Rate includes breakfast. No credit cards.

★ **Hostal Casa de Campo Urubamba** PALCCA-RAQUI The sister hotel of Casa de Campo in San Blas (Cusco), this inviting, relaxed place

> *Aranwa Sacred Valley offers a level of sophistication and comfort unknown to the region a few years ago.*

Aranwa Sacred Valley **13**
Casa Andina Private Collection **3**
El Albergue **1**
The Green House **12**
Hostal Casa de Campo Urubamba **9**
Hostal El Tambo **1**
Hostal Iskay **1**
Hostal La Ñusta **1**
Hostal Las Orquideas **1**
Hostal Paz y Luz **14**
Hostal Sauce **1**
Hotel Pakaritampu **1**
Hotel Pisaq **15**
Hotel Río Sagrado **7**
Inkallpa Valle Sagrado Lodge & Spa **2**
KB Tambo Hotel **1**
K'uychi Rumi **4**
Las Chullpas **7**
Posada Las Tres Marías **8**
Sol y Luna Lodge & Spa **5**
Sonesta Posadas del Inca Sacred Valley **10**
Ticllabamba Maison d'Hôtes **11**

> The laid-back Hotel Pisaq, owned by a Peruvian-American couple, sits right on the square.

has a garden setting, a cool rustic flavor, and a peaked-ceilinged, light-filled dining room. The rooms are attractive, homey, and a fair deal. Palccaraqui, 3km (2 miles) west from Urubamba. ☎ 084/244-404. www.hotelcasadecampourubamba.com. 20 units. $55 double; $90 suite. Rates include breakfast. AE, DC, MC, V.

★ Hostal Iskay OLLANTAYTAMBO

This new, comfortable *hostal* has something no one else can claim: incredible views of the Ollantaytambo ruins. If that weren't enough to recommend it, it's also a friendly and cool place, run by a Catalan guy with dreadlocks, with very clean and nicely decorated, simple rooms that are a bargain. Ask for a room that opens onto the terrace with killer views. Patacalle s/n. ☎ 084/204-004. www.hostaliskay.com. 5 units. $38 double; $45–$50 mini-suite/family room. Rates include breakfast. MC, V.

★ Hostal Paz y Luz PISAC

A country B&B and healing center run by an American woman, this friendly spot features Andean healing workshops, meditation, and sacred-plant ceremonies. It's a nice hike from Pisac, and is restful or spiritual, depending on your bent. Ctra. Pisac Ruinas s/n. ☎ 084/203-204. www.pazyluzperu.com. 14 units. S/160 double; S/220 suite. Rates include breakfast. AE, DC, MC, V.

Hostal Sauce OLLANTAYTAMBO

Connecting the old town to Ollanta's ruins, this modern, small hotel has clean rooms, some with good ruins views, and a small restaurant. Ventidero 248. ☎ 084/204-044. www.hostalsauce.com.pe. 8 units. S/274 double. Rate includes breakfast. V.

★ Hotel Pakaritampu OLLANTAYTAMBO

With lovely grounds behind a tall wall, this large, rather upscale hotel is tasteful and well done, though some might feel it lacks personality. Av. Ferrocarril s/n. ☎ 084/204-020. Fax 084/205-105. www.pakaritampu.com. 39 units. S/396 double. Rate includes breakfast. AE, DC, MC, V.

★ Hotel Pisaq PISAC

A pleasant traveler's hangout right on the main plaza in Pisac, where all the action takes place on market days, this engaging inn (owned by a Peruvian-American couple) has nice rooms with Andean textiles and hand-painted murals. The hotel restaurant serves pizza made in a wood-burning oven. Plaza Constitución 333. ☎ 084/203-062. www.hotelpisaq.com. 11 units. $50–$65 double w/ private bathroom, $40–$45 w/ shared bathroom. No credit cards.

★★ kids Hotel Río Sagrado URUBAMBA ENVIRONS

Nestled next to the Urubamba River, this stylish boutique hotel may be just a touch below other Orient-Express hotels, known for their no-holds-barred luxury, but it's definitely one of the nicest properties in the Valley, and certainly the closest to the river. There's a nice spa and colorfully decorated, contemporary rooms. Check online for packages and deals. Ctra. Cusco-Urubamba Km 75.8. ☎ 01/610-8300 for reservations, or 084/201-631. www.riosagrado.com. 115 units. $355–$405 double. Rates include breakfast. AE, DC, MC, V.

★ Inkallpa Valle Sagrado Lodge & Spa YANAHUARA

With the look of a small village, this hotel's stucco buildings and gardens cater to those looking for a peaceful retreat. The views are great, even though the location is quite a bit removed from the main road from Urubamba to Ollantaytambo. Quinto paradero (sector Pucará). ☎ 084/201-408. 16 units. $130 double. Rate includes breakfast. AE, DC, MC, V.

★ kids **K'uychi Rumi** URUBAMBA ENVIRONS
Less a hotel than a community of adobe condos, this architect-owned property offers plenty of space, privacy, and tranquility, with kitchens and fireplaces, making it a good spot to retreat and bundle up. Ctra. Urubamba-Ollantaytambo s/n. ☎ 084/201-169. www.urubamba.com. 6 units. S/430 double; S/720 family bungalow (4 people). AE, DC, MC, V.

★ **Las Chullpas** URUBAMBA ENVIRONS
A cool young Chilean guy runs this funky, secluded "ecological guesthouse" with rooms that are comfortable, connected huts. Chalo, who also leads treks to local mountain ranges, prepares organic and vegetarian meals in the fireplace-warmed dining room. Gonzalo Múnoz s/n. ☎ 084/201-568. www.chullpas.uhupi.com. 9 units. $50 double; $70 suite. Rates include breakfast. No credit cards.

Posada Las Tres Marías URUBAMBA
If you're looking for a simple, inexpensive spot right in Urubamba, this small modern house in the center of town with gardens and large rooms might serve the purpose. Jr. Zavala 307. ☎ 084/201-006 or 984/650-225. www.posadatresmarias.com. $50 double. MC, V.

★ kids **Sol y Luna Lodge & Spa** HUICHO-URUBAMBA ENVIRONS One of the first upscale country hotels in the valley, this French- and Swiss-owned place has great gardens and a cluster of circular, rustically elegant bungalow-style rooms. The restaurant offers fancy tasting menus, and there's a very nice spa and horse stables. The pricey new *casitas de lujo* are indeed luxurious. Ctra. Urubamba-Ollantaytambo s/n. ☎ 084/201-620. www.hotelsolyluna.com. 33 units. $235 double; $381 family bungalow; $528–$880 casitas de lujo. Rates include breakfast. AE, DC, MC, V.

★ kids **Sonesta Posadas del Inca Sacred Valley** YUCAY Once a 17th-century monastery, this ranch-style hotel is a village-like complex with a colonial chapel, gardens, and a small Peruvian ceramics and textiles museum. The spa offers yoga, and there are mountain bikes for guests' use, as well as horseback riding. Plaza Manco II de Yucay 123. ☎ 084/201-107, or 1-800-SONESTA (766-3782) for reservations in the U.S. and Canada, or 01/222-4777 in Peru. www.sonesta.com. 84 units. $109–$180 double; $150–$250 suite. Rates includes breakfast. AE, DC, MC, V.

★★★ **Ticllabamba Maison d'Hôtes** YUCAY
With just two luxury rooms hidden in the mountains above Yucay, this gorgeous country "home-stay" with great style was converted from a colonial farm by a one-time Peruvian model, Suzy Dyson. Arranged only through Aracari Travel (p. 446), it's an exclusive place for those who want something special in the Sacred Valley. Bonus features near old Inca terraces are a cold plunge pool, Jacuzzi, and Andean steam sauna. Camino a Vinopata. ☎ 01/999-352-664. www.aracari.com/hotels/ticllabamba-maison-dhotes-cuzco-cuzco-area.html. 4 units. $280 double. Rate includes breakfast and light dinner. AE, MC, V.

Budget *Hostales* in Ollantaytambo

Alluring Ollantaytambo gets more popular every year, and travelers who can't or don't want to spend the money at bigger, luxurious country lodges pack the modest, inexpensive inns and tend to linger. Here is a selection of good alternative lodgings:

Hostal El Tambo. Secluded on a quiet street in the old town, this simple and comfortable backpackers' inn is built around a verdant courtyard. Horno s/n. ☎ 084/204-003. $15 double. No credit cards.

Hostal La Ñusta. A clean and friendly place with good views from the balcony but small and plain rooms. Ctra. Ocobamba. ☎ 084/204-035. $20 double. No credit cards.

Hostal Las Orquídeas. Clean and simple rooms with a shared bathroom around a courtyard. Av. Ferrocarril s/n. ☎ 084/204-032. $20 double. No credit cards.

KB Tambo Hotel. Owned by a mountain-biking American, with nice rooms constructed in the last few years. Ventidero s/n. ☎ 084/204-091. http://kbperu.com. $15 to $29 per person. No credit cards.

Aguas Calientes Hotels

★★ El MaPi

Filling a huge niche in the center of town is this new, modern, and surprisingly hip midsize hotel (owned by Inkaterra, who operate a much more upscale hotel in town). Rooms are plainer than public spaces, but the beds are excellent, and there's a hot springs pond, computer room, sleek cafeteria, and lively bar. **Av. Pachacútec 109.** ☎ 084/211-011 or 084/244-598. www.elmapihotel.com. 48 units. $200–$250 double. Rates include breakfast. AE, DC, MC, V.

★ Gringo Bill's Hostal

This backpacker's institution from the early days of Machu Picchu, begun by an American expat, has upgraded and is now a plant-filled *hostal*. Rooms are very nice, and there's a lounge bar with a fireplace and a pretty good restaurant. While backpackers may find it too pricey for budget travel, there's still a cool traveler's vibe. **Colla Raymi 104, Plaza de Armas.** ☎ 084/211-046, or 084/241-545 for reservations. www.gringobills.com. 86 units. $75 double; $105–$135 suite. Rates include breakfast. AE, MC, V.

Hostal Machu Picchu

Well positioned for barhopping, and with a balcony overlooking the Vilcanota River, this midsize hotel is a decent inexpensive option. Rooms are clean and airy; some sport vibrant colors. **Av. Imperio de los Incas s/n.** ☎ 084/211-065 or 084/244-598. www.hostalmachupicchu.com. 24 units. $65 double. Rate includes breakfast. MC, V.

★★★ kids Inkaterra Machu Picchu Pueblo Hotel

A rustic but sophisticated and stylish place, this captures the feel of the area with lush grounds—surrounded by several acres of cloud forest—featuring magnificent bird- and plant-life. Naturalists will enjoy orchid tours, bird-watching, and guided ecological hikes, while sybarites will appreciate the charming colonial, tile-roofed *casitas* (bungalows), junior suites with fireplaces, and spring-water pool. **Av. Imperio de los Incas (Línea Férrea Cusco Km 10, Quillabamba).** ☎ 800/442-5042 in the U.S. and Canada; 084/211-122 in Peru, or 084/245-314 for reservations. www.inkaterra.com.pe. 86 units. $459–$516 double; $569–$960 suite. Rates include breakfast. AE, DC, MC, V.

> *Inkaterra Machu Picchu Pueblo Hotel is nestled in cloud-forest vegetation, and many rooms have fireplaces.*

Aguas Calientes Restaurants & Hotels

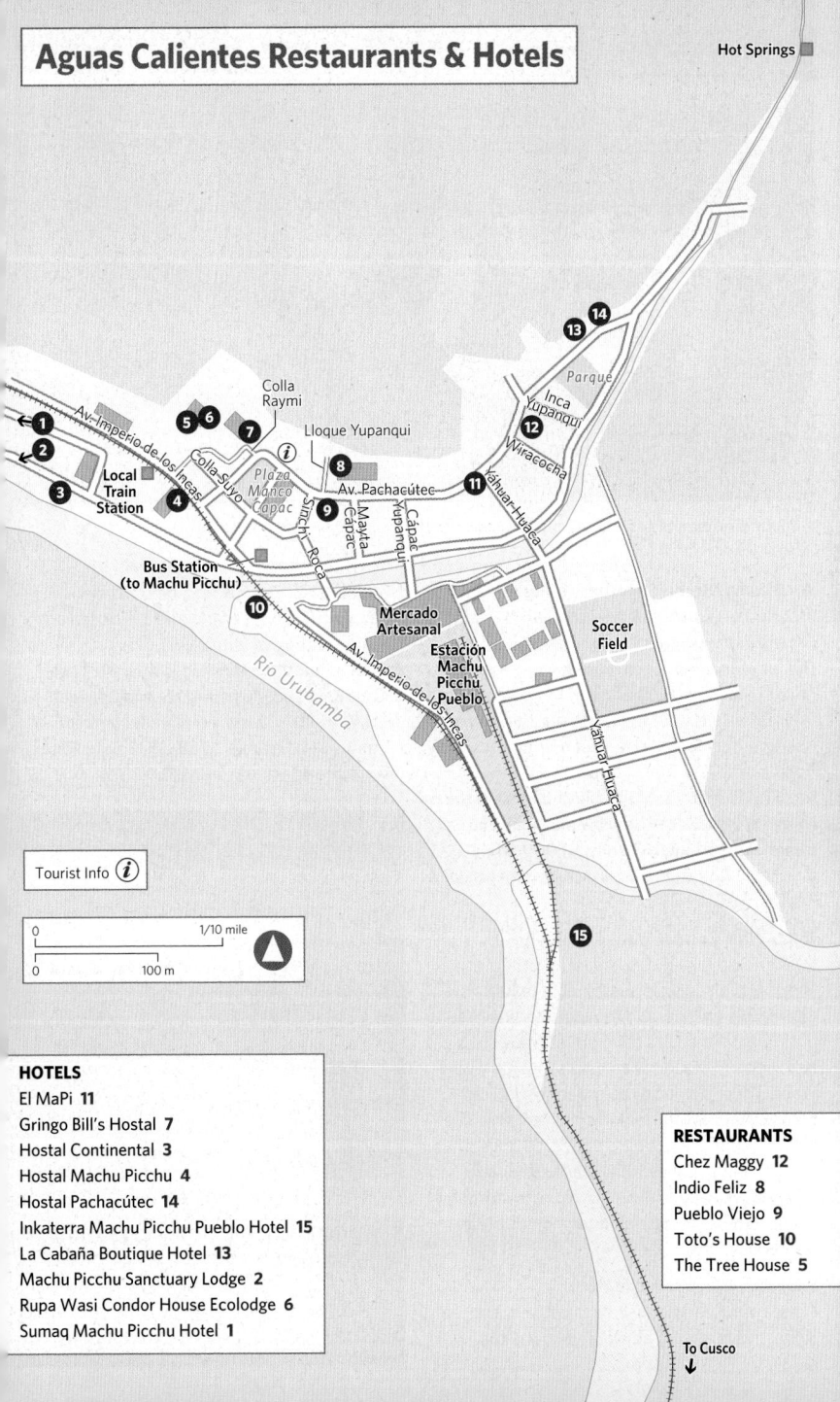

Hot Springs

Parque

Colla Raymi

Lloque Yupanqui

Inca Yupanqui

Wiracocha

Yahuar Huaca

Av. Imperio de los Incas

Colla Suyo

Plaza Manco Capac

Local Train Station

Sinchi Roca

Mayta Capac

Capac Yupanqui

Av. Pachacútec

Bus Station (to Machu Picchu)

Mercado Artesanal

Estación Machu Picchu Pueblo

Soccer Field

Río Urubamba

Av. Imperio de los Incas

Yahuar Huaca

Tourist Info (i)

0 — 1/10 mile
0 — 100 m

HOTELS

El MaPi 11
Gringo Bill's Hostal 7
Hostal Continental 3
Hostal Machu Picchu 4
Hostal Pachacútec 14
Inkaterra Machu Picchu Pueblo Hotel 15
La Cabaña Boutique Hotel 13
Machu Picchu Sanctuary Lodge 2
Rupa Wasi Condor House Ecolodge 6
Sumaq Machu Picchu Hotel 1

RESTAURANTS

Chez Maggy 12
Indio Feliz 8
Pueblo Viejo 9
Toto's House 10
The Tree House 5

To Cusco
↓

> *Informal restaurants and gringo-oriented bars line the main drag in Aguas Calientes.*

★★ Machu Picchu Sanctuary Lodge MACHU

PICCHU For a pretty penny, you can stay at this Orient-Express luxury lodge virtually on top of the famous ruins. Rooms are swank, and most have small terraces that open to gardens with impressive views of the ruins and the Andes. Reservations far in advance are required. The hotel's excellent buffet lunch ($35) is open to all ruins visitors. Machu Picchu (next to the ruins). ☎ 084/246-419. www.machupicchu. orient-express.com. 33 units. $1,009–$1,420 double; $1,584 suite. Rates include 3 meals daily. AE, DC, MC, V.

Rupa Wasi Condor House Ecolodge

A treehouse-like lodge isolated from town, this funky place uses sustainable materials, alternative energy, and biodegradable products. Upstairs suites have private balconies and views of the Andean peaks, but very thin walls. There's a good restaurant (The Tree House) and terrific cooking classes. If you've just hiked the Inca Trail, you should know that it's up a flight of about 80 stairs. Jr. Huanacaure 180. ☎ 084/211-101. www.rupawasi.net. 5 units. $69–$99 double. Rates include breakfast. MC, V.

★ Sumaq Machu Picchu Hotel

A sprawling, large, upscale hotel near the ruins, this is a good alternative to the top two hotels in town, though its rates have skyrocketed. Bonuses include a nice spa and restaurant terrace with views of the surrounding mountains. Av. Hermanos Ayar Mz 1 Lote 3. ☎ 866/682-0645 in the U.S. and Canada, or 01/447-0579. www.sumaqhotelperu.com. 60 units. $603 double; $738–$932 suite. Rates include breakfast. AE, DC, MC, V.

More Lodgings in Aguas Calientes

While this tourist town exists entirely because of Machu Picchu, in high season the two main streets crammed with hostels, restaurants, and bars can get quite crowded. If you've arrived without reservations, check out these clean, small hotels (ranging from $20 per person to $110 for a double):

Hostal Continental. Av. Imperio de los Incas 177. ☎ 084/211-065. presidente@terra.com.pe.

Hostal Pachacútec. Av. Pachacútec s/n. ☎ 084/211-061. pachacuteq@hotmail.com.

La Cabaña Boutique Hotel. With a makeover, this is now a nice little midrange hotel with 20 handsomely decorated rooms. Av. Pachacútec 20. ☎ 084/211-048. www.lacabanamachupicchu.com.

> *Rupa Wasi Condor House is a treehouse-like, sustainably built eco-lodge.*

Machu Picchu & Sacred Valley Fast Facts

Arriving

BY BUS To Pisac: *Combis* depart from Cusco on Puputi s/n, cdra. 2 (no phone); the trip takes about 45 minutes and costs S/5. *Combis* drop passengers a 3-block walk from the main square (and market). Buses depart from the same spot in Pisac for other parts of the valley: Urubamba (30 min.) and Ollantaytambo (1 hr.). **To Urubamba:** From Cusco (90 min.), buses (S/5) depart from Av. Grau s/n, cdra. 1 and arrive at the bus terminal in Urubamba, Terminal Terrestre (no phone), 1km (½ mile) past town on the main road to Ollantaytambo. To continue from Urubamba **to Ollantaytambo** (there are no direct buses from Cusco), catch a *combi* at the terminal (S/3; 30 min.) or a taxi on the main road (S/15).

BY TAXI A taxi from Cusco to Pisac is about S/35; it's usually possible to go by private *auto* (private car functioning as a taxi) for S/10 per person; vehicles congregate near the bus terminal and depart when they have four passengers. Shared private cars to Urubamba leave from Pavitos 567, with four passengers per car (50 min.). A taxi from Cusco to Urubamba runs about S/70; to Ollantaytambo, S/90–S/100. If you're headed directly to the Sacred Valley upon arrival in Cusco, have your hotel arrange for airport pickup.

BY TRAIN Only one rail service, PeruRail, travels from Cusco to Aguas Calientes (with a brief stop in Ollantaytambo, the midpoint, to pick up passengers). Competing services, on either Inca Rail or Andean Railways, originate in Ollantaytambo.

PeruRail (☎ 01/612-6700 in Lima, or 084/581-414 in Cusco; www.perurail.com) trains depart Cusco from Estación Poroy, a 15-minute taxi ride from Cusco. Direct from Cusco to Machu Picchu, PeruRail operates three trains from Cusco, all arriving in under 4 hours: Expedition ($48 one-way); Vistadome, the faster first-class service ($71); and the luxury Hiram Bingham ($294 one-way, including 2 meals, cocktails, and a guided

tour at the ruins). Make reservations as far in advance as possible. Tickets can be purchased on PeruRails' website by credit card; in person (for tickets reserved in advance) at the PeruRail office in Cusco, Portal de Carnes 214 (Plaza de Armas); at Lima's Jorge Chavez International Airport (domestic terminal, 2nd floor btw. gates 13 and 14); and in Cusco's **Estación Huanchaq,** on Av. Pachacútec (in cash, dollars, or *soles;* Mon–Fri 7am–5pm, Sat–Sun 7am–12pm); or by telephone (☎ 084/581-414).

For travelers already based in the Sacred Valley, there are now three train options to Machu Picchu. You can travel aboard PeruRail (which has alternated between offering service from Ollantaytambo and not) or one of its new competitors. On **Inca Rail,** Av. El Sol 611, Cusco (☎ 084/233-030; www.incarail. com), first-class travel from Ollantaytambo to Machu Picchu is $110 one-way adults and $50 kids 12 and under; Executive Class is $60 one-way adults and $50 kids 12 and under. On **Andean Railways,** Av. El Sol 576, Cusco (☎ 084/221-199; www.machupicchutrain. com), the one-way fare from Ollantaytambo to Machu Picchu is $59. Note that train schedules and rates change frequently; check websites for the latest information. Tickets for Inca Rail and Andean Railways can be purchased by telephone or at their offices in Cusco, and, perhaps soon, online. Inca Rail currently allows online reservations.

Tip: For the best views on the way to Machu Picchu, sit on the left side of the train.

ATMs/Cashpoints

In Pisac and Urubamba, there are ATMs on the main squares; you'll also find ATMs on either side of the main road to Yucay near the gas station at the edge of Urubamba. In Aguas Calientes, there's a Banco de Crédito ATM on Av. Imperio de los Incas near the railroad tracks.

Currency Exchange

In general, it's best to exchange a sum of money before leaving Cusco (especially when going to the Pisac or Chinchero market). In Aguas Calientes, you can exchange cash or traveler's checks at Gringo Bill's Hostal (Colla Raymi 104). Shops and restaurants along the two main streets, Av. Imperio de los Incas and Av. Pachacútec, buy dollars from travelers at standard exchange rates.

Dentists & Doctors

URUBAMBA **Centro de Salud,** Av. Cabo Conchatupa s/n (☎ 084/201-334), or Hospital del Instituto Peruano de Seguridad Social, Av. 9 de Noviembre s/n (☎ 084/201-032). OLLANTAYTAMBO **Centro de Salud,** Principal (☎ 084/204-090). AGUAS CALIENTES There's a 24-hour **EsSalud** clinic near the railroad tracks (☎ 084/ 211-037).

Emergencies

For general emergencies and police, call ☎ **105.** For fire, call ☎ **103.**

Internet Access

Larger hotels are your best bet; the better ones in the region are equipped with Wi-Fi. Urubamba is the best spot for Internet cabinas, with a good supply of machines and fast connections all around town. In Pisac, there are several cabinas around the Plaza de Armas. In Urubamba, Academia Internet Urubamba (no phone) is 2 blocks northeast of the Plaza de Armas, on the corner of Jr. Belén and Jr. Grau. In Ollantaytambo, there's an upstairs cabina in the block next to the ruins entrance (by the restaurant Kusikoyllor). In Aguas Calientes, try Café Internet (no phone) on Av. Imperio de los Incas, a block from the main square. Gringo Bill's Hostal (☎ 084/211-046), on Colla Raymi 104, also has Internet access.

Pharmacies

PISAC There are several along Av. Bolognesi. URUBAMBA Among many central locations, one is at Bolívar 469. OLLANTAYTAMBO There's one on the Plaza. AGUAS CALIENTES There's a pharmacy just off the main square, on Puputi s/n.

Police

URUBAMBA Palacio s/n (☎ 084/201-012). AGUAS CALIENTES Av. Imperio de los Incas s/n, near the railway station (☎ 084/211-178).

Post Office & Mail

PISAC The post office is on the corner of Comercio and Intihuatana (on the plaza). URUBAMBA & OLLANTAYTAMBO The post office is on the Plazas de Armas. AGUAS CALIENTES The post office is on the corner of Manco Cápac and Av. Imperio de los Incas.

Public Transportation

Local buses (usually small combis or colectivos) are the easiest and cheapest (S/1.50) way to get around the Sacred Valley. Buses depart the Urubamba terminal for Cusco, Chinchero (both 1 hr.), and Ollantaytambo (30 min.).

Taxis

Taxis and mototaxis operate out of Urubamba, traveling to Pisac, Chinchero, and Ollantaytambo. For taxi or minivan trips around the Valley, try **Roberto Angles Ochoa** (☎ 084/ 984-752-565). Or, have your hotel arrange a taxi if you wish to travel to Maras, Moray, or Salineras.

Telephone

The area code of towns in the Sacred Valley is 084. In Aguas Calientes, the Telefónica del Perú office is at Av. Imperio de los Incas 132.

Tours

Virtually all Cusco travel agencies offer 1-day Sacred Valley tours (as little as $25 per person for a full-day guided tour); tours tend to coincide with market days (Tues, Thurs, and Sun) and generally include Pisac, Ollantaytambo, and Chinchero. You will travel comfortably by air-conditioned bus, but you'll have precious little time in each place: only long enough for a quick look around and a visit to ruins or the market.

Visitor Information

You're probably best off getting information on the Sacred Valley at the tourist information offices in **Cusco** (p. 241). Cusco's South American Explorers Club (p. 241) is an excellent source of information on the Inca Trail and alternative treks, mountaineering, and whitewater rafting in the valley. **Aguas Calientes** has an iPerú office, Av. Pachacútec cdra. 1 s/n (☎ 084/211-104), with maps and basic hotel and Machu Picchu information.

10
The Amazon

Favorite Amazon Moments

Two-thirds of Peru—about the size of California—is Amazon rainforest, and many naturalists and biologists believe it holds the greatest biodiversity in the world. The vast region stands in stunning contrast to the country's pre-Columbian civilizations, Andean peaks, and arid coasts, and is now more accessible than ever—a double-edged sword. The southern Amazon includes the Tambopata National Reserve and Manu National Park; the northern Amazon reaches all the way to Peru's borders with Colombia and Brazil.

> PREVIOUS PAGE *A canopy walk affords a unique perspective on the dense vegetation of the Amazon jungle.* THIS PAGE *In the Belén district of Iquitos on the Amazon River, transportation is often by canoe.*

❶ **Marveling at a macaw clay lick.** There is no spectacle so awe-inspiring in the Amazon as watching hundreds of *guacamayos* (macaws) feeding at a clay lick. Parrots generally start off the show before the stars—the brilliantly colored squawking macaws—swoop in.

❷ **Descending through cloud forest.** The road from Cusco to Parque Nacional Manu (p. 303) is harrowing and unforgettable. From the steep Andes Mountains, it plummets 4,000m (13,120 ft.) to the dense tropical forests of the Amazon basin, passing through habitats with as many as 1,000 species of birds.

❸ **Tangling with the treetops.** Get some perspective on the dense Amazon rainforest by traveling through treetops on a canopy walkway or zip line. There are superb canopy walks high above the forest floor at Reserva Amazónica

Lodge and ExplorNapo, and a great zip line at Tahuayo Lodge. See p. 306, 326, and 327.

❹ **Spotting giant river otters and pink dolphins.** Among the most prized of sightings in the Amazon are endangered giant river otters and freshwater pink river dolphins. Unlike your chances of seeing jaguars or other big game, the likelihood of spotting giant otters, particularly on Sandoval Lake, or pink dolphins while out on a boat on the rivers and tributaries of the northern Amazon, is actually pretty good. See p. 324.

❺ **Luxuriating at a swank lodge.** Venturing into the sweltering rainforest normally means roughing it, but you don't have to. There are several surprisingly luxe eco-lodges; my favorite is Reserva Amazónica, with swank rooms, a thatched-roof cocktail lounge, and a spa overlooking the river. See p. 306.

1. Marveling at a macaw clay lick
2. Descending through cloud forest
3. Tangling with the treetops
4. Spotting giant river otters and pink dolphins
5. Luxuriating at a swank lodge
6. Wading into Belén
7. Seeing butterflies and orphaned exotic animals
8. Rolling on an Amazon riverboat
9. Trippin' on *ayahuasca*

6 Wading into Belén. This fascinating Iquitos shantytown, a (very) poor man's Venice, is an extraordinary scene of houses on stilts and others that float on the river during the rainy season. To really get a feel for it, get out on a boat, and don't miss the Belén market. See p. 314, 6.

7 Seeing butterflies and orphaned exotic animals. Pilpintuwasi, a nonprofit butterfly farm and an orphanage for exotic Amazon animals that would have served as trophies or otherwise been killed, makes for a rewarding day trip from Iquitos. See p. 315, 9.

8 Rolling on an Amazon riverboat. Getting out on the mighty Amazon is what a trip to the northern jungle is all about. Although there are some romantic rubber-boom-era riverboats trawling the rivers, it would be hard to beat the sleekly modern MV *Aqua* of Aqua Expeditions, where'll you'll eat and cruise the river in true style. See p. 327.

9 Trippin' on *ayahuasca*. *Ayahuasca*, literally "spirit vine" in Quechua, is a psychoactive brew of ingredients made from Amazon vines and plants. I can't really claim this as a favorite moment, since I don't have much tolerance for the requisite vomiting, but some travelers with a thirst for the wild gravitate toward *ayahuasca* ceremonies, with the natural hallucinogens administered by a jungle shaman.

Puerto Maldonado in 1 Day

The once-prosperous rubber town Puerto Maldonado is a scruffy and humid place that's seen its share of boom and bust. Today its primary industries are still based on exploiting the surrounding rainforest: gold prospecting, Brazil-nut harvesting, and ecotourism. For most, Puerto Maldonado is little more than the nearest town to the jungle, and groups booked on Tambopata tours barely blink on their way to waiting riverboats. Good jungle experiences, with opportunities for fauna sightings and walks in primary and secondary forest, are within easy reach of Puerto Maldonado. If you plan to do this tour in 1 day, start very early, as you'll need the entire afternoon to visit Sandoval Lake.

> At the Mercado Modelo in Puerto Maldonado, you'll find a host of exotic Amazon fruits.

START Puerto Maldonado is 1,068km (664 miles) southeast of Cusco (a 30-min. flight); begin in the Plaza de Armas.

❶ Plaza de Armas. The main square is marked by tall palm trees and an oddball, blue-and-yellow clock tower-cum-gazebo at its center. Puerto Maldonado is the kind of place where streets just off the main square are still unpaved and full of potholes, but there are some colorful tin-roofed houses that speak to the town's frontier ethos. The town's main drag, Jr. León de Velarde, is lined with shops and restaurants and is perpetually buzzing with activity and *mototaxis*. ⏱ 15 min. Bounded by Jr. Carrión, Jr. León de Velarde, Loreto, and Arequipa.

❷ Mercado Modelo. The main market, 8 blocks southeast of the Plaza de Armas,

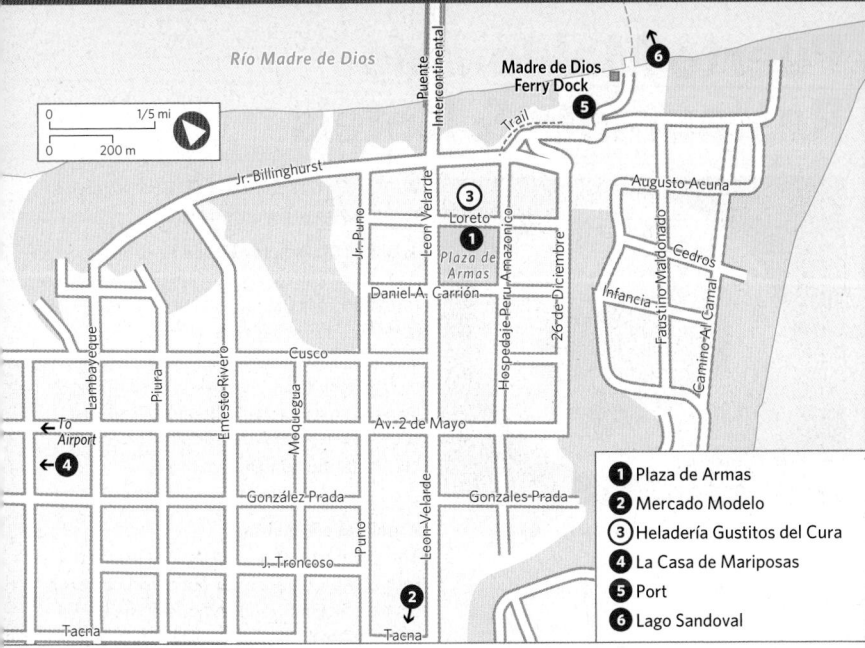

throbs with noisy *chiringuitos* (little storefronts serving food and fruit juices), Brazil nuts and other jungle produce, and natural rainforest remedies. ⏱ 30 min. Av. Fitzcarrald (at Ernesto Rivero). Daily 7am–3pm.

③ 🍦 ★ kids **Heladería Gustitos del Cura.** A little ice cream parlor and dessert shop that donates its profits to a local charity and where you can taste *sorbetes* (sorbets) and *helados* (ice creams) made from exotic fruits. Loreto 258 (Plaza de Armas). No phone. Items S/2–S/8.

Take a *mototaxi* to the airport road (10 min.).

❹ ★ kids **La Casa de Mariposas.** This conservation and learning center run by Inkaterra (which runs the Reserva Amazónica Lodge, p. 306) has several hundred species of butterflies (of the 3,800 that exist in Peru). ⏱ 1 hr. Av. Circunvalación s/n. ☎ 01/610-0400. www.inkaterra.com/en/reserva-amazonica/ butterfly-house. $25; free for guests of Inkaterra Reserva Lodge, and many lodge tours include admission. Daily 8am–5pm.

❺ **Port.** Puerto Maldonado sits on the banks of the Río Madre de Dios, and the port is where most visitors head to catch a motorized

canoe to Sandoval Lake or one of the lodges. The view of the muddy river, especially at dusk, is rather fetching. There's a viewing platform over the river at Plaza Grau, on Jr. Billinghurst at Arequipa, and steep steps down to the river. ⏱ 30 min.

Take a boat from the port to Lago Sandoval 5km (3 miles; 1 hr.) away.

❻ ★★ kids **Lago Sandoval.** This pretty and serene oxbow lake, ringed by palm trees, makes an excellent day trip downriver from Puerto Maldonado. It boasts a surprising diversity of wildlife, including macaws, parrots, herons, caimans, turtles, and even a family of giant river otters. Catch a canoe or motorboat at the port. You'll then have to walk a couple kilometers along a path through the jungle, but it's a beautiful hour-long trek. Of course, the best way to visit the lake, and have the best chance of seeing the river otters, is to stay at the lodge here (p. 307). Most other nearby jungle lodges offer excursions to Lago Sandoval, though they tend to arrive in the heat of the day, when wildlife activity is least observable (birds, monkeys, caimans, and resident river otters are much more active in the early morning and early evening hours). ⏱ At least 4 hr.

Puerto Maldonado Restaurants & Hotels

> Simple comfort food is perfect after a day of jungle exploration.

Restaurants

El Califa CEVICHERIA/PERUVIAN
A cevichería and open-air joint on a small side street, this place looks the part of a small-town tropical eatery, with bright-green paneling, ceiling fans, a tin roof, and a garden. It serves local jungle cuisine and good Peruvian meals. Jr. Piura 266. ☎ 082/571-119. Entrees S/8–S/15. No credit cards. Lunch and dinner daily.

kids La Casa Nostra CAFE/SNACKS
A good cafe stop for hamburgers, tamales, typical Peruvian dishes such as papas rellenas (potatoes stuffed with ground beef), and a host of desserts and cakes, as well as tropical fruit juices. Av. León de Velarde 515. ☎ 082/573-833. Entrees S/4–S/12. No credit cards. Lunch and dinner daily.

kids Pizzería Trattoria El Hornito PIZZA
This convivial pizza joint and pub serves pretty good wood-fired pies and is open daily until midnight. Just down the street is a large sister restaurant, Leña y Carbón El Hornito, where the house specialty is grilled meats and chicken. Jr. Carrión 271 (Plaza de Armas). ☎ 082/572-082. Entrees S/9–S/18. MC, V. Lunch and dinner daily.

Pollos a la Brasa La Estrella ROTISSERIE CHICKEN A local favorite and good standby in Puerto Maldonado is charcoal-grilled chicken and fries. Av. León de Velarde 474.

☎ 082/573-107. Entrees S/7–S/17. No credit cards. Lunch and dinner daily.

★ **Wasaí Maldonado Lodge** PERUVIAN/INTERNATIONAL The nicest hotel in town has a restaurant that is the best place to dine. Serving good Andean standards with jungle accents and international fish and chicken dishes, it's in a gazebo that sits above the riverbank, with good river views. Jr. Guillermo Billinghurst. ☎ 01/436-8792. Entrees S/12–S/22. MC, V. Lunch and dinner daily.

Hotels

Hotel Cabañaquinta
This comfortable if plain inn has pretty decent rooms with private bathrooms, a nice garden, a small outdoor pool, and one of the better restaurants in town. Jr. Cusco 535. ☎ 082/571-045. www.hotelcabanaquinta.com.pe. 50 units. S/130–S/170 double. MC, V.

Hotel Don Carlos Puerto Maldonado
Above the banks of the Tambopata River, about 5 blocks south of the center of town, this hotel is more rustic than the chain's other hotels, but it has plenty of services and amenities, including a restaurant, outdoor swimming pool, and air-conditioning. Rooms are nice enough, but hardly a steal. Jr. Velarde 1271. ☎ 082/571-029. www.hotelesdoncarlos.com. 31 units. $60 double. MC, V.

★ **Wasaí Maldonado Lodge**
Easily the best place in town, this charming hotel, though just a block from the Plaza de Armas, resembles a mini jungle lodge. Several of the bungalows are perched on stilts and have river views. The location is lovely, overlooking the Madre de Dios River. The hotel arranges jungle expeditions with stays at the **Wasaí Tambopata Lodge & Research Center,** 120km (75 miles)—about 6 hours—upriver on the Tambopata River (4 days/3 nights, $395), as well as visits to Sandoval Lake and other jungle junkets. Jr. Guillermo Billinghurst. ☎ 01/436-8792. www.wasai.com. 18 units. $52 double. AE, DC, V.

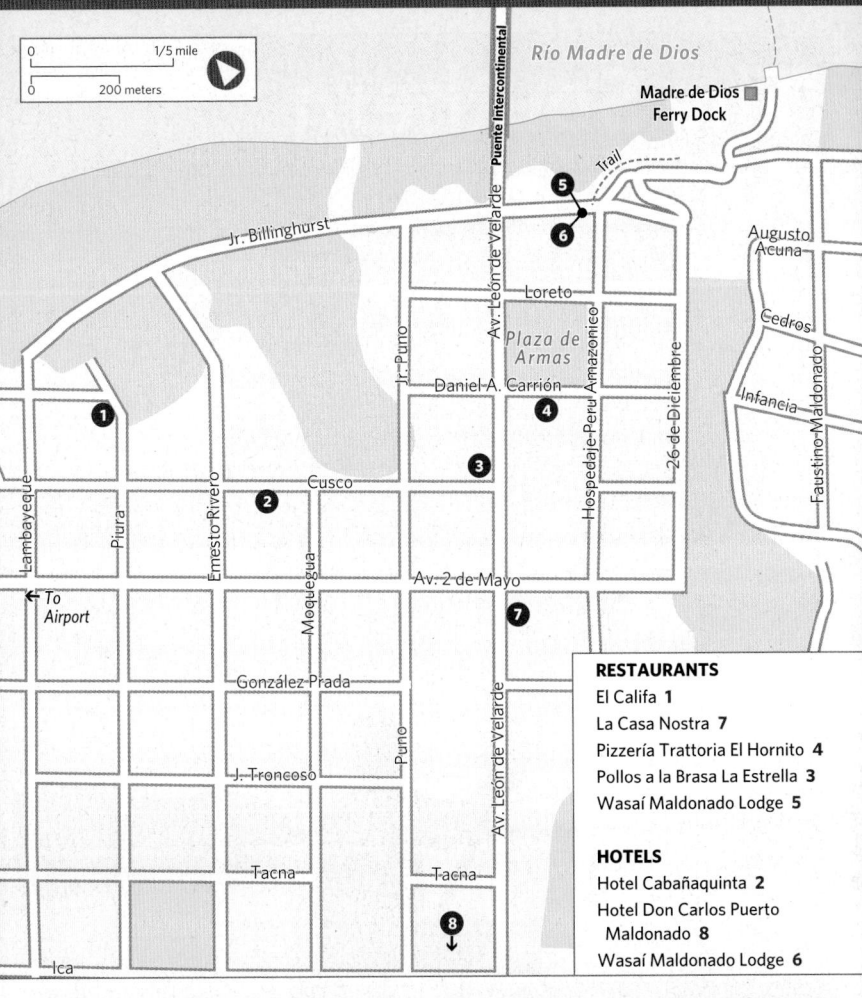

RESTAURANTS

El Califa **1**
La Casa Nostra **7**
Pizzería Trattoria El Hornito **4**
Pollos a la Brasa La Estrella **3**
Wasaí Maldonado Lodge **5**

HOTELS

Hotel Cabañaquinta **2**
Hotel Don Carlos Puerto
 Maldonado **8**
Wasaí Maldonado Lodge **6**

When to Go

The best time to visit the Amazon is during the dry season, May through the end of October. During the rainy season, parts of the southern Amazon are flooded and impassable. The northern jungle does not have a pronounced rainy season, per se, and travel there is less restricted during the winter; however, water levels can rise from 7.5m (25 ft.) to more than 15m (50 ft.) from December to May, and some villages become flooded. That said, many naturalists find high-water months best for wildlife observation.

The Amazon's Oxbow Lakes

An oxbow lake is a uniquely crescent-shaped lake (like an old-fashioned, U-shaped oxen yoke) formed by the natural shifting of riverbanks. Oxbow lakes are essentially designed to become extinct. After forming, they have life expectancies of perhaps 400 years: They first expand; then become shallower as river flooding and runoff deposits sediment, sand, and leaves; and eventually dry up as grasses and trees take root. These lakes can be very large and are often superb spots for wildlife viewing.

The Southern Amazon

The southern Amazon region extends to the Bolivian and Brazilian borders. Concentrated in the southeast department (province) of Madre de Dios, it's the least populated area in Peru and home to two of the country's top three jungle zones—among the finest in South America. The region's two principal protected areas, Reserva Nacional de Tambopata and Parque Nacional Manu, are both excellent for jungle expeditions, although they differ in terms of remoteness and facilities. The southern jungle boasts some of Peru's finest and least spoiled Amazon rainforest; it remained largely unexplored until expeditions in the 1950s.

> *Serene Lake Sandoval, just downriver from Puerto Maldonado, is an oxbow lake.*

Reserva Nacional de Tambopata. This massive tract of subtropical rainforest covers 275,000 hectares (nearly 680,000 acres), while the entire zone, including the contiguous Bahuaja-Sonene National Park, encompasses 1.5 million hectares (3.7 million acres) of jungle. Peru prohibited hunting and logging in the area in 1977 and created the reserve (then the Tambopata-Candamo Reserve Zone) in 1990. The area is one of superb environmental diversity, with a dozen different types of forest and several gorgeous oxbow lakes. Tambopata has more species of birds (595) and butterflies (more than 1,200) than any place of similar size on earth. According to environmentalists, Tambopata's great diversity of wildlife is due to its location at the confluence of lowland Amazon forest with three other ecosystems. At least 13 endangered species are found here, including the jaguar, ocelot, giant armadillo, harpy eagle, and giant river otter. The Tambopata *collpa de guacamayos* (macaw clay lick), where thousands of brilliantly colored macaws and parrots arrive daily to feed on mineral salts, is one of the largest natural clay licks in Peru. 527km (327 miles) from Cusco. For lodges in the reserve, see p. 306.

Parque Nacional Manu. A UNESCO World Biosphere Reserve and World Heritage Site, Manu—declared a national park in 1973—is one of the largest protected natural areas in the Americas and one of the most pristine jungle regions in the world. The national park comprises three zones: the **Core Zone,** an area of dedicated conservation reserved for scientific study (the largest zone, at 3.7 million hectares/9.1 million acres, or about three-fourths of the entire reserve); the **Reserve Zone,** up the Manu River northwest of Boca Manu, accessible by permit and authorized guide only for ecotourism activities; and the Multi-Use or **Cultural Zone,** home to traditional nomadic groups and open to all visitors. First penetrated by rubber barons and loggers in the late 1800s, it contains the least explored jungle of primary and secondary forest in Peru. About half the size of Switzerland, at just less than 2 million hectares (nearly 5 million acres), its surface area of varied habitats includes Andes highlands, cloud forests, and lowland tropical rainforests; it climbs from an altitude near sea level to elevations of 3,500m (11,480 ft.). Manu has the highest bird, mammal, and plant diversity of any park on the planet: nearly 1,000 species of birds, 1,200 species of butterflies, 20,000 species of plants, 200 species of mammals, and 13 species of primates. Endangered species found here include the spectacled bear, giant armadillo, and cock-of-the-rock. Its bird population accounts for 10% of the world's total. Scientists estimate that perhaps 15,000 animal species have yet to be identified. Manu is also home to dozens of native Amerindian tribes, a few of which remain secluded. 200km (124 miles) from Cusco. For tour operators in the park, see p. 309.

> *Spotting fauna, like this heron on Lake Sandoval, is a highlight of visiting the Southern Amazon.*

Jungle Health Precautions

Yellow fever vaccinations are a wise idea before visiting the jungles of southeastern Peru. Even though the only reported outbreaks of yellow fever in the last couple of years have been in the northern Amazon around Iquitos, local authorities in Puerto Maldonado make sure that visitors who want to be protected are. At the airport arrival terminal, Health Ministry nurses administer yellow fever shots. Vaccinations for hepatitis A and typhoid are also worth considering, and malaria pills are a good idea, especially if you're planning to venture deep into the jungle. You should carry your vaccination records with you while traveling in Peru. For more information on health issues, see p. 470; also speak to your doctor or consult the World Health Organization or Centers for Disease Control websites.

Southern Amazon

PARQUE NACIONAL MANU

Río Manu

Cocha Salvador

Cocha Otorongo

ANDES

MADRE

Boca Manú

Boca Manu Airport

Tambo Blanquillo Macaw Lick

Fitzcarrald Island

Río Madre de Dios

Río Colorado

Shintuya

Atalaya

Río Paucartambo

Tres Cruces Viewpoint

Machu Picchu

Río Urubamba

Cordillera Urubamba

Cordillera Vilcanota

CUSCO

Paucartambo

Cusco

0   50 mi
0   50 km

MANU NATIONAL PARK
Cock-of-the-Rock Lodge **1**
Erika Lodge **4**
Manu Cloud Forest Lodge **2**
Manu Lodge **6**
Manu Wildlife Center **7**
Orquídeas de San Pedro Lodge **3**
Pantiacolla Lodge **5**

RÍO TAMBOPATA LODGES
Explorer's Inn **11**
Posada Amazonas **12**
Refugio Amazonas **9**
Tambopata EcoLodge **10**
Tambopata Research Center **8**

RÍO MADRE DE DIOS LODGES
EcoAmazonia Lodge 14
Reserva Amazónica Lodge 15
Sandoval Lake Lodge 13

Reserva Nacional de Tambopata Lodges

> *Tambopata Research Center Ecolodge is right by the jungle's most famous macaw clay lick.*

Río Madre de Dios

EcoAmazonia Lodge. About an hour by boat from Puerto Maldonado, this large lodge features long rows of basic bungalows and trails leading to a canopy-viewing platform. Its approach is essentially "jungle light," making it a comfortable place that primarily caters to large groups, and it offers *ayahuasca* ceremonies. Prices range from $160 for a 2-day, 1-night stay to $280 for 4 days and 3 nights. Calle Garcilazo 210, ste. 206, Cusco. ☎ 084/236-159. www.ecoamazonia.com.pe. AE, DC, MC, V. Map p. 304.

★★ Reserva Amazónica Lodge. This completely upgraded lodge, operated by a small hotel group with some magnificent properties in Peru, is just 15km (9 miles), or 1 hour, down the Río Madre de Dios from Puerto Maldonado. It's one of the plushest in the rainforest. The large main house is stylishly designed like an Indian roundhouse, and it features a dining room and upstairs cocktail lounge. Strewn about the riverside property, the 43 thatched-roof bungalows, with private bathrooms and terraces with hammocks, are a significant step up from most accommodations in the jungle. Kerosene lamps left at the door add to the romance of the place. The quality of the food is excellent, and eco-outfitted guides are very professional. Although the surrounding forest doesn't teem with wildlife, there's a good system of trails nearby, as well as an island that's home to a dozen or so rescued monkeys and a terrific canopy walk. An unusual, luxurious bonus is the spa, overlooking the river, offering a full slate of massage services. Rates range from $337 per night in a standard *cabaña* to $573 for 3 nights in an Amazonia suite. Plaza de las Nazarenas 211, Cusco. ☎ 800/442-5042 in the U.S. and Canada, 800/458-7506 in the U.K., 084/245-314 in Cusco, or 01/610-0400 in Lima. www.inkaterra.com. AE, DC, MC, V. Map p. 304.

★★ **Sandoval Lake Lodge.** Run by the respected outfit InkaNatura along with Tropical Nature Travel, this pioneering lodge overlooks Sandoval Lake (p. 299, ⑥) and is the best option close to Puerto Maldonado if you're more into wildlife than plush accommodations. It's surrounded by palm trees and thick forest, and is one of just three lodges in the Amazon in a nationally protected zone; its greatest advantage is its unique location on one of the jungle's prettiest oxbow lakes. The journey to the lodge is part of the experience; after a 45-minute boat ride, you walk a couple of kilometers (another 45 min.) through secondary forest, then hop in a wooden canoe and paddle along a canal and across the lake. Most visitors not only see a wealth of aquatic and jungle birds, including macaws, but several species of monkeys, caimans, and the highly prized community of giant river otters. Prices range from $178 to $438 for 2- to 4-day stays. InkaNatura operates another, more remote lodge, the **Heath River Wildlife Center** (another 3 hr. downriver near the Bolivian border), that's near a large macaw clay lick and owned and staffed by the indigenous Ese'Eja Sonene people. One option is to combine a couple of nights at either lodge. Heath River prices range from $575 for 4 days to $855 for 6 days. InkaNatura is the Peruvian partner of the American environmental organization Tropical Nature. Ricardo Palma N J1, Urbanización Santa Monica, Cusco. ☎ 01/440-2022, or 877/870-7378 in the U.S. and Canada. www.inkanatura. com. Outside Peru, organize trips through Tropical Nature Travel, P.O. Box 5276, Gainesville, FL 32627-5276. ☎ 877/827-8350 toll-free in the U.S. and Canada. www.tropicalnaturetravel.com. AE, DC, MC, V. Map p. 304.

Staying Near Reserva Nacional de Tambopata

Upstream from Puerto Maldonado, jungle lodges in and around the Tambopata National Reserve are located along the Río Madre de Dios (east of the city) or the Río Tambopata (which extends south of Puerto Maldonado). Packages begin with 2-day/1-night arrangements, but 3-day/2-night packages are preferable. The area around the Río Tambopata, with greater primary forest, is generally considered better for wildlife viewing. Lodges in Tambopata are easier to get to and cheaper than those in Manu (see p. 309), although a couple require up to 12 hours of boat travel from Puerto Maldonado. Travelers interested in the least time-consuming and least expensive way to see the Peruvian jungle can visit one of the lodges on the Río Madre de Dios or Lago Sandoval, the latter an oxbow lake within a couple of hours of Puerto Maldonado. Because they are located in secondary jungle and are not nearly as remote, they best serve as introductory visits to the Amazon. The forest along the Madre de Dios is generally not as pristine as that along the Tambopata. *Note:* Package prices are per person for a double room and include transportation from Puerto Maldonado.

Río Tambopata

★★★ **Explorer's Inn.** The only lodge located within the Tambopata National Reserve, this well-regarded and comfortable lodge has hosted eco-tourists and scientists for more than 3 decades. About 3 hours upriver from Puerto Maldonado along the Tambopata River, it's excellent for viewing fauna, including otters, monkeys, and particularly jungle birds— this is perhaps the top spot in Tambopata for birding. On the grounds are 7 rustic, thatched-roof bungalows and 30 rooms with private bathrooms. The lodge has an excellent network of trails, including to nearby oxbow lakes. Guides are biologists. The organization **Amazonia Tours** arranges travels; prices range from $198 for 2 nights to $530 for a 4-night Macaw Clay Lick program. Alcanfores 459, Miraflores, Lima. ☎ 01/447-8888. www. explorersinn.com or www.peruviansafaris.com. AE, DC, MC, V. Map p. 304.

★★ **Posada Amazonas/Tambopata Research Center/Refugio Amazonas.** About 2 hours up the Tambopata from Puerto Maldonado, **Posada Amazonas lodge** is owned jointly with the Infierno indigenous community and is quite good for inexpensive, introductory nature tours. It has an eagle nest site and a canopy observation tower, and two parrot clay licks are located within a kilometer of the lodge. The rustic lodge, featuring 30 rooms

> Ayahuasca *is a tradition-bound ritual deep in the Amazon jungle, and it shouldn't be taken lightly.*

and a wall open to the forest, is operated by the award-winning **Rainforest Expeditions.** This veteran ecotourism company promotes tourism with environmental education, research, and conservation, and operates two Tambopata lodges. Prices range from $295 to $565 for 3- to 5-day trips. Extras include canopy walks, sea kayaking, and biking to Puerto Maldonado. The excellent 18-room **Tambopata Research Center** is more remote (8 hr. upriver from Puerto Maldonado), just 500m (1,640 ft.) from the jungle's largest and most famous macaw clay lick. Just one of three Peruvian lodges in a protected national nature reserve, it's the best lodge in Tambopata for in-depth tours and viewing wildlife, including several species of monkeys. It's certainly *the* place to see flocks of colorful macaws and parrots. Trips usually entail an overnight at Posada Amazonas before continuing on to the Research Center. Prices are $745 to $945 for 5- to 7-day trips. The newest lodge run by the group is the 32-room **Refugio Amazonas,** adjacent to the Tambopata National Reserve and about 4 hours by boat upriver from Puerto Maldonado. Portal de Carnes 236, Cusco. ☎ 877/870-0578 in the U.S. and Canada, or 01/719-6422. Jr. Arequipa 401, Puerto Maldonado. ☎ 082/571-056. www.perunature.com. AE, DC, MC, V. Map p. 304.

Tambopata EcoLodge. This 2-decade-old lodge is about 3 hours upstream from Puerto Maldonado along the Río Tambopata. The lodge, with an attractive dining room and bar, is slightly more luxurious than most, with more of a jungle hotel feel than others; newer bungalows are constructed of cement rather than wood. The lodge has plenty of trails nearby, including routes to lake systems on the opposite bank of the Tambopata, in about 100 hectares (247 acres) of secondary forest, and offers overnight trips to the macaw clay lick. Prices range from $338 for 3 days to $937 for 5 nights including a visit to the macaw clay lick. Nueva Baja 432, Cusco. ☎ 084/245-695. www.tambopatalodge.com. AE, DC, MC, V. Map p. 304.

Parque Nacional Manu Operators

> *Many eco-lodges in the southern Amazon, like Cock-of-the-Rock Lodge, are surprisingly comfortable.*

★★★ InkaNatura. Perhaps the most serious and sophisticated outfit operating ecotourism trips in the Peruvian Amazon, InkaNatura, associated with the Peruvian conservation group PerúVerde and the American organization Tropical Nature, organizes stays at the famed **Manu Wildlife Center.** The 15-year-old lodge is located near the world's largest tapir clay lick, and also the Blanquillo macaw clay lick, and it features 48km (30 miles) of nature trails and two canopy-viewing platforms. Accommodations are in 22 spacious, private bungalows with tiled bathrooms. Packages at the Manu Wildlife Center range from $1,285 for 4 days/3 nights to $1,475 for 5 days/4 nights. InkaNatura also operates shorter trips to the **Cock-of-the-Rock Lodge** ($595 for 3 days/2 nights, in the Selva Sur Nature Reserve at an elevation of 1,600m/5,250 ft., excellent for birders) and **Manu tented camps** at Manu National Park ($1,380 for 5 days/4 nights). Calle Ricardo Palma N J1, Urbanización Santa Monica, Cusco. ☎ 01/440-2022, or 877/870-7378 in the U.S. and Canada. www.inkanatura. com. AE, DC, MC, V.

★ Manu Ecological Adventures. This 10-year-old agency offers some of the most affordable trips to Manu, ranging from 5 days/4 nights (in and out by plane, $724 not including flights) to 8 days/7 nights (overland, $550), with 2 nights in open-air lodges (the cloud-forest **Orquídeas de San Pedro** or **Erika Lodge,** where there's a zip line) and the rest in campsites. A 4-day visit to the Cultural Zone is $300 (overland). Plateros 356, Cusco. ☎ 213/283-6987 in the U.S. and Canada, or 084/261-640. www.manuadventures.com. AE, DC, MC, V.

> At Manu Wildlife Center, nature—and mosquito nets—is within arm's length.

★★★ Manu Expeditions. Run by an ornithologist who is also the British Consul in Cusco, this ecotourism pioneer has been organizing rainforest tours for more than 2 decades. Tours include stays at the **Manu Wildlife Center,** near the famed macaw clay lick (and considered the best lodge in Peru for birding), and a safari camp facility deep at Cocha Salvador within the Manu Biosphere Reserve. Longer tours include initial stays at the **Cock-of-the-Rock Lodge** in cloud forest. Four-, six-, and nine-day fixed-departure tours range from $1,450 to $2,275 per person. Calle Clorinda Matto de Turner 330, Urbanización Magisterial, Cusco. ☎ 084/225-990. www.manuexpeditions.com. AE, DC, MC, V.

★★ Manu Nature Tours. One of the first groups to send expeditions to the reserve, this highly professional outfit operates the well-known **Manu Lodge,** next to a pristine oxbow lake (great for viewing giant river otters) and the only full-service lodge within Manu National Park itself ($1,029–$1,500 for 5-day/4-night trips); and the excellent **Manu Cloud Forest Lodge,** overlooking a waterfall ($849 for 3-day/2-night trips). Add-on options include mountain biking, rafting, and tree canopy climbs. Av. Pardo 1046, Cusco. ☎ 084/252-721. www.manuperu.com. AE, DC, MC, V.

★ Pantiacolla. The collaboration of a Dutch biologist and Boca Manu–born conservationist, this agency operates the small **Pantiacolla Lodge,** with double rooms in bungalows on bluffs overlooking the Río Madre de Dios at the edge of Manu. The organization also operates a community-based ecotourism project with the Yine Indians of the Manu rainforest. Pantiacolla offers camping and lodge trips ranging from $990 for 5 days to $1,064 for 7 days. Saphy 554, Cusco. ☎ 084/238-323. www.pantiacolla.com. AE, DC, MC, V.

Visiting Parque Nacional Manu

Manu is complicated and expensive to visit. Most expeditions are a week or more and involve both significant overland and air (not to mention extensive river) travel. Access from Cusco involves either a spectacular 2-day journey through 4,000m (13,120-ft.) mountains and cloud forest before descending into lowland rainforest or a 30-minute flight, followed by a couple of days by boat. Because Manu is so isolated and access is so restricted, reserve visits are beyond the scope of many budget travelers (generally costing $700 to more than $2,500 per person for a 5- to 8-day trip). Only a small number of tour companies are permitted to run organized expeditions to Manu, and the number of travelers they can take there each week is strictly limited. The best outfitters are closely involved with conservation efforts and local development programs. Most companies operate with fixed departure dates only in the dry season, from May to November. *Note:* Prices listed do not include air transportation from Cusco.

Camping-Based Trips for Budget Travelers

Expediciones Vilca. Vilca has been organizing Manu expeditions for a decade, with trips that split time between lodges and campsites. It has earned a sturdy reputation among budget-minded travelers. Plateros 359, Cusco. ☎ 084/253-773. www.cbc.org.pe/manuvilca.

Mayuc. A traditional tour operator with good budget-camping programs to Manu. Portal de Confiturías 211 (Plaza de Armas), Cusco. ☎ 084/242-824. www.mayuc.com.

SAS Travel. This well-run and popular all-purpose agency offers varied programs to both Manu and Tambopata, with stays at various lodges. Garcilaso 270 (Plaza de San Francisco), Cusco. ☎ 084/249-194. www.sastravelperu.com.

> Brilliantly colored macaws are one of the biggest draws in the Amazon.

Iquitos in 2 Days

Iquitos is essentially an island city, defined by water—not just the mighty Amazon, which borders it to the west, but also a complex network of smaller rivers and streams, and a series of lakes just outside the city. Peru's largest jungle town is the gateway to the most accessible reaches of the Peruvian Amazon basin. Founded in 1754 by Jesuit missionaries, Iquitos became rich in the 1860s, when pioneering merchants built a booming rubber trade and mansions along the river, but the city soon went from boom to bust. Today, this bustling place of nearly half a million can be noisy and chaotic, but it exudes a sultry charm.

> *Inexpensive* mototaxis *are the preferred mode of transportation in Iquitos.*

START Iquitos is 1,013km (630 miles; a 2-hr. flight) from Lima; begin at the Plaza de Armas.

❶ ★ **Plaza de Armas.** The main square is marked by the neo-Gothic, early-20th-century **Iglesia Matríz** (parish church); its tower was a later addition. Across the square is the **Casa de Fierro** (Iron House), designed by Gustave Eiffel for the 1889 Paris Exhibition. Said to be the first prefabricated house in the Americas, it was shipped unassembled from Europe and built on-site. The walls, ceiling, and balcony are plastered in rectangular sheets of iron. Just off the main square, at Napo 200 (corner of Raymondi), is **Casa Fitzcarrald,** popularly known as the **Casa de Barro,** a wood-and-mud house employed as a warehouse in the

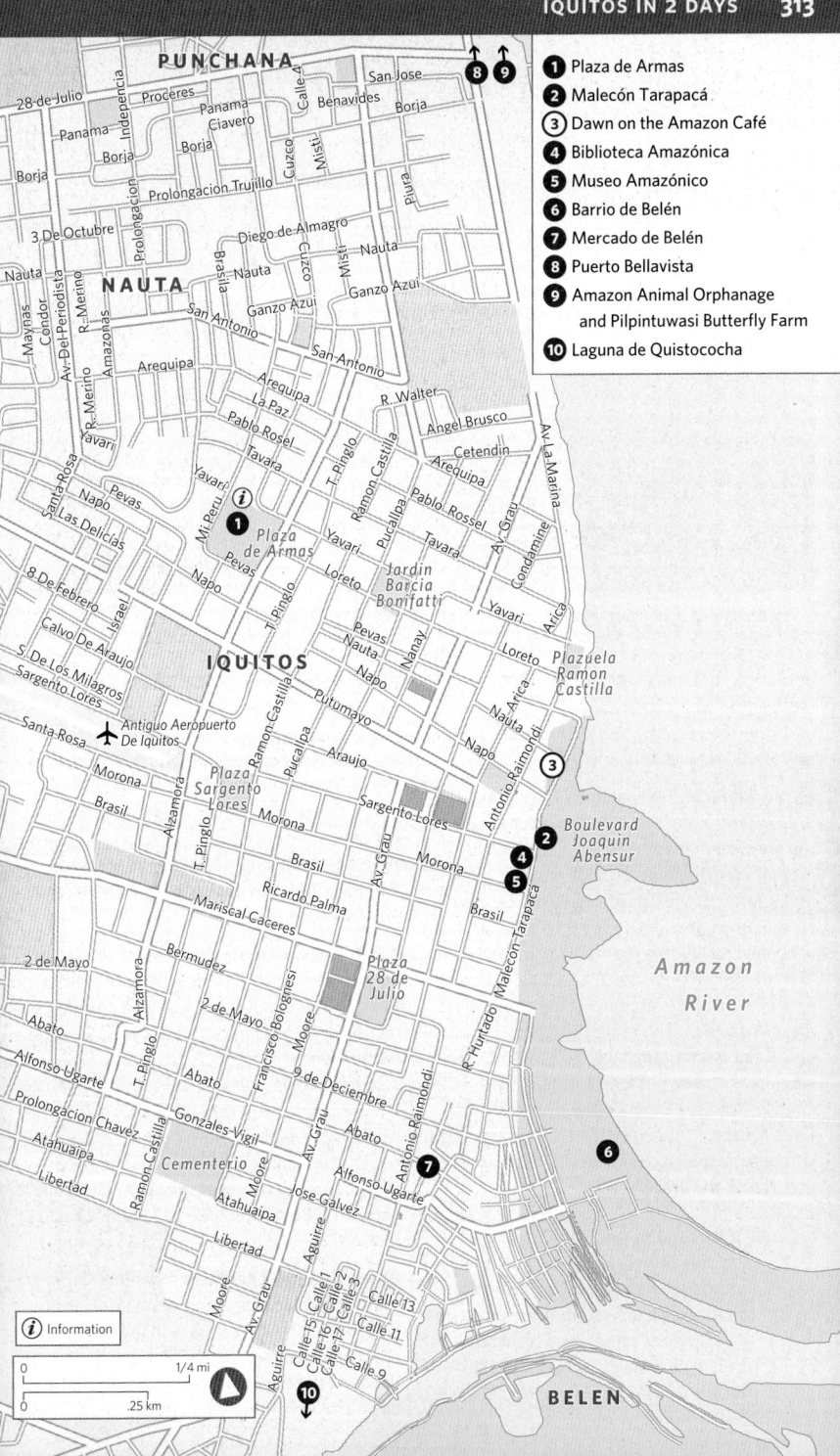

1. Plaza de Armas
2. Malecón Tarapacá
3. Dawn on the Amazon Café
4. Biblioteca Amazónica
5. Museo Amazónico
6. Barrio de Belén
7. Mercado de Belén
8. Puerto Bellavista
9. Amazon Animal Orphanage and Pilpintuwasi Butterfly Farm
10. Laguna de Quistococha

PUNCHANA

NAUTA

IQUITOS

Amazon River

BELEN

Information

0   1/4 mi
0   .25 km

> *Textiles from native Amazon communities can be found at the Mercado de Belén.*

operations of famed rubber baron Fitzcarrald (subject of Werner Herzog's film *Fitzcarraldo*). ⏱ 45 min. Bounded by Napo, Fitzcarrald, Putumayo, and Antonio Raimondi.

❷ ★★ Malecón Tarapacá. The riverfront promenade along the Amazon reaches all the way from downtown to the shabby but picturesque Belén district. It's been enlarged and improved with fountains, benches, and street lamps, making it the focus of Iquitos urban life. Lining the promenade are exquisite 19th-century mansions, relics from Iquitos' rubber heyday, covered in Portuguese glazed tiles, or *azulejos*. The most spectacular is probably **Casa Hernández,** nos. 302 to 308. Other elegant, if somewhat faded, mansions worth checking out are **Casa Cohen,** Próspero 401; **Casa Morey,** Próspero 502 at Brasil; and **Logia Unión Amazónica,** Nauta 262. ⏱ At least 1 hr. Btw. Nauta and Brasil.

③ 🍴 Dawn on the Amazon Café. This amiable little cafe overlooking the promenade and river has outdoor seating and serves great breakfasts, sandwiches, salads, and tropical fruit juices. Malecón Tarapacá 185. ☎ 065/223-730. Items S/9–S/22.

❹ Biblioteca Amazónica. The Iquitos municipal library is a handsome public space in an old rubber baron's mansion, overlooking the *malecón* (promenade) and Río Amazonas. The reading room features carved wood and colorful tiles and has old maps and the largest collection of historical documents on the Amazon basin in Peru. ⏱ 30 min. Malecón Tarapacá 354, 2nd floor. ☎ 065/242-353. Mon-Fri 9am–noon.

❺ Museo Amazónico. This small museum, in a period mansion, features exhibits of Amazon folklore and tribal art, as well as a curious collection of 76 Indian statues made of fiberglass but fashioned as if they were bronze. The story goes that when some mothers saw their children, who were serving as models for the works, covered in plaster for the molds, they became very unsettled, thinking the children were being buried alive. ⏱ 45 min. Malecón Tarapacá 386. ☎ 065/231-072. Admission S/5. Mon-Fri 8am–1pm and 3–7pm; Sat 9am–1pm.

❻ ★★ Barrio de Belén. Iquitos's most unusual quarter, this poor and endlessly fascinating waterfront shantytown is a squalid but photogenic pile of ramshackle wooden houses on the banks of the river. Some are propped up by stilts, while others float, tethered to poles, when the river rises 6m (20 ft.) or more. When the river is high, transportation here is by canoe. Visitors are free to walk about in dry season (or, for much of the year, take a locally arranged canoe trip, the best way to see the district) and see the houses, but for safety's sake, go in a group and only during the day. You'll see scrappy kids playing with pet monkeys and a few houses proudly outfitted with cable TV and other modern conveniences. If you have a hard time dealing with poverty (and stench), this is not the place for you. ⏲ At least 1 hr.

7 ★ Mercado de Belén. Belén is known for its animated and odiferous open-air market, which stretches over several blocks and is full of Amazon fish, fauna, and fruits, and all sorts of exotic items for sale, including potions used by faith healers. If you venture into the Belén market, be prepared for such exotic foodstuffs as monkey and lizard meat. ⏲ 45 min. 9 de Diciembre at Próspero. Daily 8am–5pm.

On Day 2, take a *colectivo* marked BELLAVISTA/NANAY, which leaves from points along Próspero, north to Puerto Bellavista (3km/1¾ miles).

8 Puerto Bellavista. This port on the Río Nanay has a pretty white-sand beach (Playa Nanay) that's a favorite of locals and safe for swimming during summer. There are casual bars under thatched roofs here. It's also a good spot from which to hire a motorboat or canoe and cruise down to the confluence of the Amazon and Nanay rivers, where you can appreciate the difference in water colors (muddy brown and black); you'll pass beaches and a handful of local communities (including the Boras and Yaguas) at San Andrés along the way. ⏲ At least 1 hr.

From Bellavista-Nanay, take a 20-minute boat ride upriver, and then walk 15 minutes along the jungle trail from the landing.

9 ★★ kids Amazon Animal Orphanage and Pilpintuwasi Butterfly Farm. This very special nonprofit garden refuge and learning center, started by an Austrian woman, Gudrun Sperrer, is home to more than 40 species of colorful butterflies, as well as orphaned and rescued exotic animals, including a spider

> *Puerto Belén is a fascinating, if poor, riverfront district of houses on stilts and residents getting about on canoe.*

monkey, jaguar, anteater, tapir, ocelot, parrots, and turtles. It's a great learning experience and adventure for families. Sperrer receives no assistance from the Peruvian government, so she runs the place entirely on admission fees and donations from visitors. ⏲ 1 hr. Across the river from the village of Padre Cocha. ☎ 063/232-665. www.amazonanimalorphanage. org. Admission $5 adults, $3 kids. Tues–Sun 9am–4pm.

Return to Iquitos and take a 20-minute *mototaxi* or *colectivo* (marked QUISTOCOCHA) from the corner of Moore and Bermúdez to a point 13km (8 miles) southwest of Iquitos.

10 kids Laguna de Quistococha. A resort complex with a nice beach and swimming area, this spot draws local families on weekends with paddleboats, an aquarium, a walking path around the lagoon, a zoo with exotic jungle animals, and a fish hatchery that's populated by giant *paiche* fish. ⏲ At least 1 hr.

THE COCA CURE

Sacred Leaf of the Incas

BY NEIL EDWARD SCHLECHT

COCA MAY BE THE BASE PLANT FOR THE CULTIVATION OF COCAINE, but drinking coca tea or chewing coca leaves is a far cry from doing drugs. The coca plant, native to the Andes, is an indelible part of Andean society, identity, and heritage, with a long tradition of cultural, economic, religious, and medicinal importance stretching back to the Incas and beyond. Today, visitors to Cusco sip coca tea to combat the effects of the city's altitude (about 3,353m/11,000 ft. above sea level), and *campesinos* in the mountains chew on coca leaves, which promotes stamina and suppresses hunger.

Early Use

Coca was integral to nearly all pre-Columbian societies in Peru; along the northern coast, there's evidence of its use dating to c. 2500–1800 B.C. Folk medicine remedies have long incorporated the leaves, and people carried small pouches with them to offer as gifts or in rituals paying homage to Mother Earth. Coca was also used to subdue and stimulate peasant labor populations, although the Incas considered it a sacred plant and restricted its use as a natural stimulant to nobles. In the 19th and 20th centuries, coca was used to persuade laborers to descend into mines.

Today, coca remains important in social and cultural rituals in the high Andes, among the Quechua and Aymara descendants of the Incas.

Take Note

> Chewing coca leaves won't get you high, though it is a mild stimulant

> It's not illegal to buy, sell, or possess coca leaves in Peru

> Cocaine is illegal in Peru

> You can't legally bring coca leaves or even *mate de coca* teabags back to the U.S.

Partaking in the Plant

In chewing coca leaves, the absorption of alkaloids is rapid and can stimulate respiration, eliminate fatigue, and produce a sense of euphoria or have an antidepressant effect. Habitual chewers of coca, such as miners and farmers, may chew the leaf two or three times a day. Although the chewing of coca leaves in Peru today is primarily associated with rural and working-class populations, coca-leaf tea, or *mate de coca*, cuts across economic and cultural divisions. In hotels in high-altitude locations, you'll find teabags or mounds of coca leaves; simply steep them in boiling water and add sugar. *Mate de coca*, which tastes like a bitter green tea, is extremely effective in combating headaches and nausea associated with altitude sickness, or *soroche*.

Cocaine

Coca was an ingredient in wine in the 19th century and in the original Coca-Cola recipe, and Sigmund Freud administered cocaine to patients, but its narcotic and profit-generating potential were soon exploited. Most of Peru's harvested coca leaves are still shipped to Bolivia and Colombia for further refinement into cocaine, though Peru threatens to displace Colombia as its top exporter. Since the 1980s, the U.S. has partnered with (some might say led) the Peruvian government in attempts to identify growers and eradicate crops. Though coca cultivation provides much-needed income in rural communities, there are environmental and political implications that range from rampant deforestation (from the slash-and-burn methods of farmers growing coca) to the involvement of Peruvian guerrilla organizations such as MRTA (Tupac Amaru Revolutionary Movement) and Sendero Luminoso. It remains an important cash crop for many peasant farmers deep in the Andes and jungle valleys, and despite U.S. and Peruvian government attempts to eradicate coca crop production in the name of the war on drugs, production in Peru has increased as much as 45% over the past decade.

Iquitos Restaurants

> *The elegant La Gran Maloca serves platos de la selva, typical Amazon jungle dishes.*

and discos. Próspero 127 (at Napo). No phone. Entrees S/5–S/18. MC, V. Breakfast, lunch, and dinner daily.

★ **Dawn on the Amazon Café** *PERUVIAN/IN-TERNATIONAL* This friendly, American-owned sidewalk cafe, a new addition to the Iquitos dining scene, aims high and is already an ex-pat favorite. There are excellent tropical fruit juices and salads (all items are triple-washed), good smoothies, and a mix of casual international and Peruvian dishes. Malecón Tarapacá 185. ☎ 065/223-730. Entrees S/9–S/22. MC, V. Breakfast, lunch, and dinner daily.

El Nuevo Mesón *PERUVIAN*
Right on the *malecón,* this lively restaurant with sidewalk tables is a good place for an

Jungle Food Exotica

Amazon jungle delicacies include *paiche* (Amazon river fish), hearts of palm salad, and *juanes* (rice tamales made with minced chicken, pork, or fish; prepared with black olives and egg; and wrapped in *bijao* leaves). Other local dishes worth a try are *patarashca,* a steamed river fish wrapped in banana leaves; *timbuche,* a thick soup made with local fish; and *tacacho,* or bananas cooked over coals and served with fried pork and chopped onions. *Mazato* is a local beverage of fermented yucca, bananas, and milk. Although protected species are not supposed to appear on menus, they often do. You might want to think twice before ordering *motelo* (turtle-meat soup served in its shell), caiman, and *muchangue* (turtle eggs with steamed bananas), which only encourages restaurateurs.

★★ **Antica Pizzeria** *PIZZA/ITALIAN*
The sister restaurant to popular pizzerias in Lima, this stylish, modern Italian place serves very good thin-crust pizzas from the wood-burning stove and straightforward pastas. There's also a fusion menu with more sophisticated fare, such as tuna tartare, octopus salad, and porcini mushroom risotto. Jr. Napo 159. ☎ 065/241-988. Entrees S/15–S/35. AE, MC, V. Lunch and dinner daily.

Ari's Burger *AMERICAN*
A local hangout, this brightly lit fast-food joint opens to the street and Plaza de Armas on two sides, making it great for people-watching. The American-style menu is nothing new, but you can pick up a serviceable burger and fries, fruit salad, ice cream, or milkshake. Open late, it draws crowds after rounds at the bars

Iquitos Restaurants & Hotels

RESTAURANTS

Antica Pizzeria **6**
Ari's Burger **5**
Dawn on the Amazon Café **9**
El Nuevo Mesón **8**
La Gran Maloca **11**
Restaurant Fitzcarraldo **10**

HOTELS

Casa Hospedaje La Pascana **7**
Hobo Hideout Travelers Hotel **1**
Hotel El Dorado Plaza **2**
Hotel La Casona **3**
La Casa Fitzcarraldo **4**
La Casa Morey **13**
Victoria Regia **12**

---

introduction to regional specialties. Although service can be lacking, most dishes, such as the regional favorite *pescado a la loretana* (fish filet with yucca, fried bananas, and hearts of palm salad), steaks, and fish, are pretty well prepared. Malecón Tarapacá 153. ☎ 065/231-837. Entrees S/18–S/33. MC, V. Lunch and dinner daily.

La Gran Maloca *PERUVIAN/AMAZONIAN*
In a grand 19th-century house, this longtime restaurant serves both *platos de la selva* (jungle dishes) and standard Peruvian cooking. In addition to tenderloin with mushroom risotto, you can try Amazon-style venison (with cilantro, coconut, and yucca). The place is oddly

formal for a jungle-town restaurant, perhaps reflective of delusions of grandeur. Sargento Lores 170. ☎ 065/233-126. Entrees S/18–S/36. AE, DC, MC, V. Lunch and dinner daily.

★ **Restaurant Fitzcarraldo** *INTERNATIONAL*
A popular hangout on the *malecón,* this easy-going place has a diverse menu that includes good fresh salads, pizzas, sandwiches, and hamburgers, plus more exotic jungle fare. The open-air house once belonged to a British rubber company and features updated colonial touches, views of the Amazon, and sidewalk tables. Napo 100 (at Malecón Tarapacá). ☎ 065/243-434. Entrees S/13–S/40. MC, V. Lunch and dinner daily.

Iquitos Hotels

> *Hotel El Dorado Plaza is the only five-star hotel in Iquitos.*

Casa Hospedaje La Pascana

A good basic budget inn, just a 2-minute walk from the *malecón* and the Plaza de Armas, this friendly, small place has rooms built around a plant-lined, open-air courtyard. Rooms are plain, but not uncomfortable; they have fans rather than air-conditioning. Pevas 133. ☎ 065/231-418. www.pascana.com/hospedaje.htm. 18 units. S/50 double. Rate includes breakfast. MC, V. Map p. 319.

Hobo Hideout Travelers Hotel

This quirky budget *hostal*, built with native materials, including palm leaves and native woods, has a jungle feel in the city (there are parrots and macaws, and the decor involves snakeskins and animal hides). It's good for backpackers and outdoors types who don't mind sleeping without air-conditioning. Jr. Putumayo 437. ☎ 065/234-099. 10 units. $11–$15 double; $8 per person dorm room. Rates include breakfast. No credit cards. Map p. 319.

★ Hotel El Dorado Plaza

Occupying a privileged place on the Plaza de Armas, this is the only bona fide high-end hotel in town. In a modern high-rise building, it has a soaring lobby, good restaurant, and excellent pool. Rooms are large and nicely outfitted, although they fall short of big-city luxury. The website often offers good deals. Napo 258 (Plaza de Armas). ☎ 065/222-555. 65 units. $242–$297 double; $385–$660 suite. Rates include breakfast. AE, DC, MC, V. Map p. 319.

★★ Hotel La Casona

Outstanding for its bargain prices, this family-owned small hotel just off the Plaza de Armas is safe and well equipped. Rooms are simply decorated but spacious and very clean, with either fans or air-conditioning. Add to that a communal kitchen, leafy little patio, and terrific service. Calle Fitzcarraldo 147. ☎ 065/234-394. www.hotellacasonaiquitos.com. 23 units. S/65–S/90 double. MC, V. Map p. 319.

★★ La Casa Fitzcarraldo

Occupying the house where the filmmaker Werner Herzog lived while making *Fitzcarraldo,* this small boutique inn exudes tropical flavor. It's a lovely retreat from Iquitos's bustle: There's a gorgeous pool, lush gardens full of flowers and tropical plantings, a nice outdoor restaurant, and even a soaring treehouse. Rooms are colorful, spacious (except for the aptly named Small Room), and well outfitted. Film buffs might want to stay in the bungalow, out back by the pool; it was Herzog's preferred spot. Av. La Marina 2153. ☎ 065/601-138. http://sites.google.com/site/lacasafitzcarraldo. 4 units. $40–$80 double. MC, V. Map p. 319.

★★★ La Casa Morey.
The renaissance of this historic property along the riverfront—a magnificently restored rubber-boom mansion that

goes a long way toward reviving the sense of opulence of that storied period—is the biggest news in Iquitos. Reasonably priced accommodations are huge, with high ceilings, and some have views of the Amazon River. There's an elegant pool, antiques, Victorian artifacts, and an extensive library of books about Iquitos and the Amazon. Virtually every other hotel in town now takes a back seat to this boutique hotel. Loreto 200 (Plaza Ramón Castilla). ☎ 065/231-913. www.lacasamorey.com. 14 units. $90 double. Rate includes breakfast. MC, V. Map p. 319.

★ Victoria Regia

This midsize, modern block hotel on a busy residential street a few blocks from the main square is a good middle-of-the-road choice. The colorful and well-equipped rooms with good air-conditioning are built around an attractive indoor pool. Also good is the sister hotel, Acosta (closer to the Plaza de Armas, at Huallaga 254). Av. Ricardo Palma 252. ☎ 01/442-4515 for reservations, or 065/231-983. www.victoriaregiahotel.com. 25 units. S/297 double; S/429–S/495 suite. Rates include breakfast. AE, DC, MC, V. Map p. 319.

Ayahuasca: Going *Way Out* into the Jungle

Especially in the northern Amazon, a host of would-be guides and lodges with lesser reputations offer *ayahuasca* ceremonies. *Ayahuasca* involves taking an herbal drug made from diverse Amazonian plants and roots in a serious, and seriously hallucinogenic, ritual that can last 6 hours or more (and involve intense vomiting). It is designed to cleanse the mind, body, and soul. The ritual is culturally important among indigenous communities, but its attraction to foreigners is the chance to trip on a natural hallucinogen as administered by a (perhaps authentic) local shaman. The real thing can be a mind-bending experience, but for that you'd almost certainly have to have a good contact deep in the jungle and really immerse yourself in the jungle. As sold to tourists, it's more often like a spring-break party, Amazon-style: Not the way *ayahuasca* should be experienced.

The Northern Amazon

The northern Amazon reaches all the way to Peru's borders with Colombia and Brazil. The Amazon River (the second-longest river in the world) reaches widths of about 4km (2½ miles) beyond Iquitos, and the river basin contains 2,000 species of fish (among them, piranhas); 4,000 species of birds (including 120 hummingbirds); native mammals such as anteaters, tapirs, marmosets, and pink river dolphins; and 60 species of reptiles, including caimans and anacondas. The northern Amazon basin within reach of Iquitos has been explored and exploited far longer than the more remote southern jungle areas of Manu and Tambopata.

> *Reserva Nacional Pacaya-Samiria, one of the densest and most pristine areas of the Amazon, is the largest protected nature reserve in Peru and home to the Cocamas community.*

Iquitos. Iquitos lies nearly 3,220km (1,988 miles) from the mouth of the Río Amazonas; other than an arduous journey by boat, the only way to get to Iquitos is by air. The gateway to the northern Amazon, at the confluence of the Nanay and Itaya rivers, Iquitos has the humid, intoxicating feel of a jungle frontier town. Ecotourism is the primary draw for visitors, and beyond the city along the giant Amazon river system are rustic jungle lodges, canopy walks, and opportunities for bird-watching, piranha fishing, visits to Indian villages, and wildlife spotting (as well as less-standard activities, such as shaman

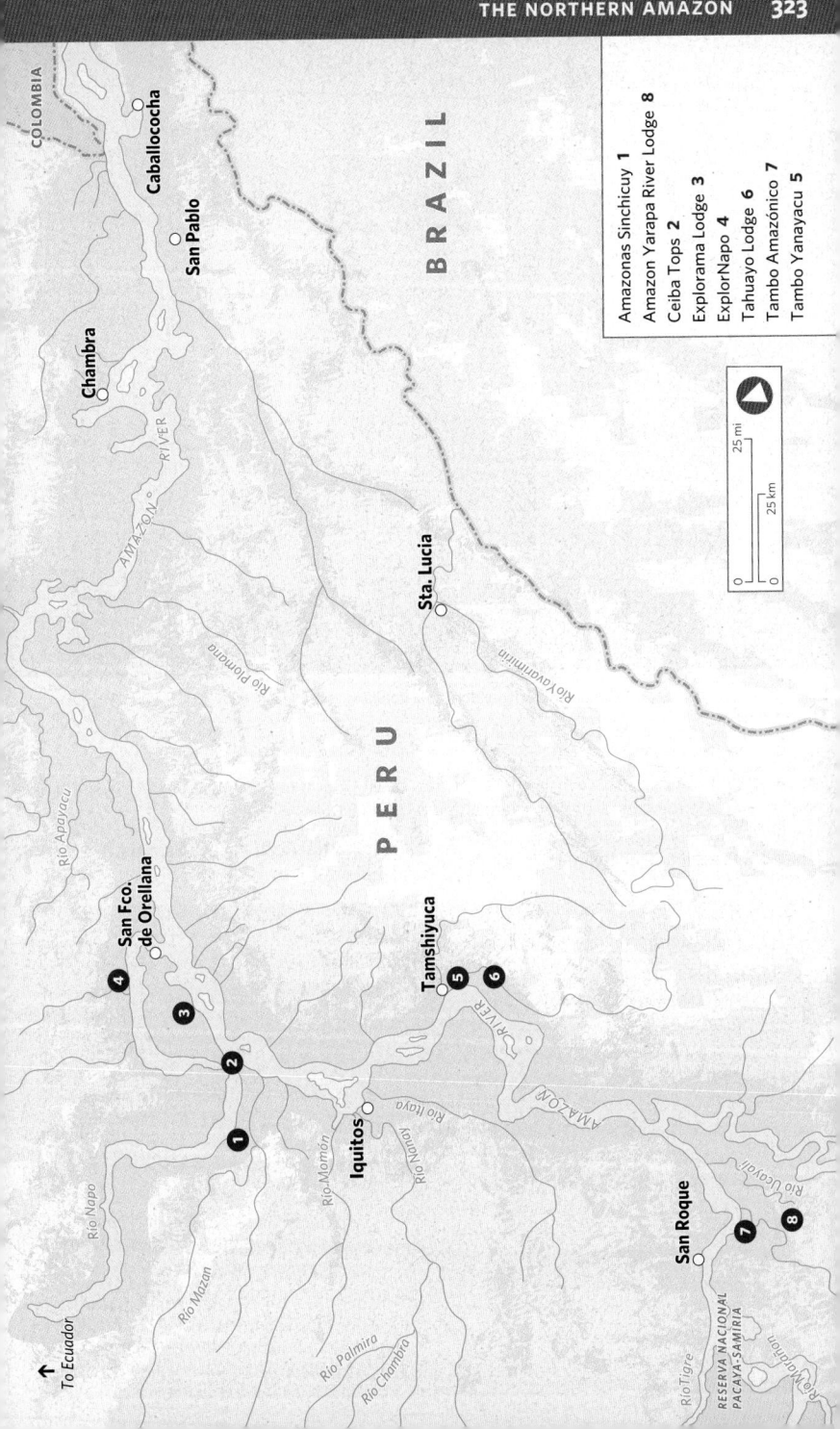

Amazonas Sinchicuy **1**
Amazon Yarapa River Lodge **8**
Ceiba Tops **2**
Explorama Lodge **3**
ExplorNapo **4**
Tahuayo Lodge **6**
Tambo Amazónico **7**
Tambo Yanayacu **5**

> *Spotting wildlife, from piranhas to the legendary pink dolphins, is made easier by canoe along tributaries of the Amazon.*

consultations and *ayahuasca* drug ceremonies). Iquitos is the capital of Peru's largest department, Loreto, which occupies nearly a third of the national territory and is nearly the size of Germany. For more on Iquitos, see "Iquitos in 2 Days," p. 312.

Reserva Nacional Pacaya Samiria. This remote reserve, the largest protected area

Exploring the Reserve

It's difficult to get to and doesn't have the roster of eco-lodges found elsewhere in the northern Amazon, but Pacaya Samiria National Reserve's opportunities for sighting spectacular wildlife and experiencing how locals truly live are greater than in most areas where jungle lodges are located. Eco-tourists with time and an appetite for roughing it can go to Pacaya Samiria with a guide and camp or stay at a native lodge. An easier alternative is to travel with one of several midrange and luxury cruise operators that organize riverboat cruises to the zone.

Guides typically take visitors by dugout canoe from Lagunas (upstream from Iquitos) through the reserve. Villages worth visiting on the outskirts of the reserve are San Martín de Timpishia and Puerto Miguel. To enter the reserve, you need permission from **INRENA,** the Peruvian parks authority; the entrance fee is $33. Contact INRENA's office in Iquitos, Pevas 350 (☎ 065/231-230), or in Lima, Los Petirrojos 355, Urbanización El Palomar (☎ 01/224-3298), or at the Iquitos **Reserva Nacional Pacaya Samiria office,** Ricardo Palma 113 (☎ 065/233-980). You can also visit **www.pacayasamiria.com. pe** for additional information. You'll need a minimum of 5 days to do the trip from Iquitos. **Aqua Expeditions, Dawn on the Amazon, GreenTracks Amazon Cruises,** and **Jungle Expeditions** (p. 327 and 328) all organize Pacaya Samiria National Reserve river cruises, while **Paseos Amazónicos** (p. 327) does camping trips.

Exploring the Jungle

Most visitors head for lodges of varying degrees of rusticity and distance from Iquitos both up- and downriver. Other options for rainforest excursions include river cruises, and, for the adventurous, independent guided camping treks. Immersing yourself in anything resembling pristine jungle in the northern Amazon basin is both costly and time-consuming. Because the region is the most trafficked and developed of the Peruvian Amazon, costs for most jungle excursions are lower than they are in the more exclusive Parque Nacional Manu in southeastern Peru (p. 303). To lay eyes on exotic wildlife, such as pink dolphins, caimans, and macaws, you have to get far away from Iquitos, at least 80km (50 miles) out and onto secondary waterways.

> The ExplorNapo Lodge has one of the longest canopy walks in the Amazon region.

in Peru and one of the most pristine in the world, lies 180km (112 miles) southwest of Iquitos and is accessible only by river (7–15 hr. by boat). Sandwiched between the Marañon and Ucayali rivers, Pacaya Samiria, established in 1982, contains 2,080,000 hectares (5,139,800 acres) of dense, nearly untouched rainforest and wetlands. It accounts for 1.5% of Peru's total surface area and is the largest

protected tract of flooded forest in the Amazon. Riddled with rivers (its black rivers are famous for their mirror-like surface) and 85 lakes, it's huge and daunting and should be explored only with an experienced guide. Some of the Amazon's finest and most abundant wildlife resides in the reserve, including pink dolphins, macaws, black caimans, spider monkeys, and giant river turtles. The reserve's wildlife statistics are staggering: It's home to more than 1,000 species of fauna (more than a quarter of all vertebrates in Peru), including some 500 species of birds, more than 100 species of mammals, 269 kinds of fish, 69 species of reptiles, and 58 species of amphibians, as well as some 1,200 species of wild and cultivated plants (including 22 orchids). It's also home to a population of more than 90,000 people from 94 indigenous communities, many from the Cocama-Cocamilla ethnic group. See "Exploring the Reserve," p. 324.

Northern Amazon Lodges & Cruises

> *Tahuayo Lodge is near the Tamshiyacu-Tahuayo Reserve, noted for its wildlife.*

Jungle Lodges

★★ **Amazon Explorama Lodges.** This American-owned jungle-tour company, the longest-established in Iquitos (now deep into its 5th decade), operates three lodges and a campsite, ranging from 160km (100 miles) to 40km (25 miles) downriver from Iquitos. The company has a good reputation; fine guides, facilities, and food; and a range of activities. The company's first lodge, **Explorama Lodge** (80km/50 miles from Iquitos), is large and attractive, with two long wings and a restaurant/bar and communal area. The luxury lodge **Ceiba Tops** (40km/25 miles from Iquitos) is a jungle resort hotel with air-conditioning, a great pool, and a Jacuzzi. There are trails nearby, and boats take you out onto the river for dolphin-spotting and fishing, but Ceiba Tops is much more about relaxing in style surrounded by jungle. Near **ExplorNapo**

(deepest in the jungle; 160km/100 miles from Iquitos), there's a fantastic canopy walkway at a height of 36m (118 ft.) and a rambling length of 500m (1,640 ft.). It's possible to mix and match lodges. Prices range from $280 for a 2-day/1-night trip to Ceiba Tops to $950 for a 5-day/4-night trip to ExplorNapo. Av. La Marina 340, Iquitos. ☎ 065/252-530, or 800/707-5275 in the U.S. and Canada. www.explorama. com. AE, DC, MC, V.

★★★ **Amazon Yarapa River Lodge.** This award-winning and conservation-minded lodge associated with Cornell University (which built a tropical biology field lab for students and faculty here), is 177km (110 miles) upriver on the Yarapa River, an Amazon tributary, near the Pacaya Samiria Reserve. Surrounded by pristine jungle and oxbow lakes teeming with wildlife, the beautiful lodge features full solar power, composting, and flush toilets with a waste-management system. Lodge facilities and guides are first-rate and among the finest in the Peruvian Amazon. A 4-day/3-night trip runs $840 to $920 per person; a 7-day/6-night trip is $1,260 to $1,470 per person. Travelers can opt for an overnight in the remote Pacaya Samiria National Reserve (4 hr. by boat). ☎ 065/993-1172, or 315/952-6771 in the U.S. and Canada. www.yarapa.com. AE, DC, MC, V.

★ **Paseos Amazónicos.** This company operates three well-run lodges. The farthest, **Tambo Amazónico,** is 180km (112 miles) upriver from Iquitos on the Yarapa River; the other two are much closer and focus on quick in-and-out tours: **Amazonas Sinchicuy** (30km/19 miles from Iquitos) is one of the oldest established lodges in the zone; **Tambo Yanayacu** is 60km (37 miles) from the city. The company offers good budget- to mid-range standard tours in rustic lodges (offered by several Peruvian and international travel agents and tour operators). There are also camping trips to the Pacaya Samiria National Reserve ($759), which provide one of the best opportunities to "rough it" and catch glimpses of Amazonian wildlife. A 4-day/3-night trip to the Sinchicuy and Yanayacu lodges starts at $296, while 2-night trips to the nearer lodges start at $259. Pevas 246, Iquitos. ☎ 065/231-618, or 01/417-576 in Lima. www.paseosamazonicos.com. AE, DC, MC, V.

★★★ **Tahuayo Lodge.** One of the most outstanding Amazon eco-lodges in Peru, this low-impact eco-property, associated with the Rainforest Conservation Fund, lies on the shores of the River Tahuayo, about 4 hours (145km/90 miles) from Iquitos. *Outside* magazine has touted it as one of the top 10 travel finds in the world. It's the only lodge with access to the Tamshiyacu-Tahuayo Reserve, a prime area for primate and other wildlife viewing. Because of its remoteness, visits of at least a week are recommended, and programs are individually tailored. The lodge offers an excellent schedule of excursions ranging from rugged (jungle survival training) to relaxed, including the longest canopy zip line in the Amazon. An 8-day/7-night trip is $1,295 per person (additional days $100), although trips as short as 3 days/2 nights are possible.

Amazonia Expeditions, 10305 Riverburn Dr., Tampa, FL 33647. ☎ 800/262-9669. www.perujungle.com. AE, DC, MC, V.

Riverboat Cruises

★★★ **Aqua Expeditions.** This company's luxury river cruises aboard the sleek, modern, 130-foot MV *Aqua* have blown the old concept of creaky, uncomfortable Amazon cruises out of the water. With a menu overseen by

Choosing a Lodge

Lodges vary in terms of rusticity and proximity to prime subtropical forest habitats. For a quick, simple experience, you can stay at a lodge an hour or 2 by boat from Iquitos (within a 50km/31-mile radius), in secondary jungle. To see more fauna and have a more authentic experience in primary rainforest, you'll have to travel beyond a radius of 80km (50 miles; 4 hr. by boat). Short trips (2–3 days) are unlikely to produce much in the way of wildlife. A foray into virgin jungle requires at least a week of camping and trekking. Cruises on rivers and tributaries aboard historic riverboats, where the objective is the romance of river travel, don't allow you to see much in the way of fauna or pristine jungle, though you'll likely spot lots of birds and perhaps black caimans and river dolphins. Many cruises stop off at reserves for jungle walks and visits to local villages. Some of the best cruises are those to the remote Pacaya Samiria National Reserve.

Prices for lodges and tours vary tremendously. For conventional, easy-to-reach lodges contracted in Iquitos, tours average around $50 to $65; tours are $175 or more per person per day for lodges farthest from the city. Some budget lodges offer bargain rates, but in most cases, you get what you pay for. Costs are proportional to distance from Iquitos—the farther they are, the more expensive they are—and include transportation, lodging, buffet-style meals, and guided activities (beverages cost extra). Note that Iquitos throbs with hustlers and con artists, and you need to exercise great caution before paying for a promised itinerary.

> *Amazon Yarapa River Lodge is associated with Cornell University, which established a field lab for academic research at the lodge.*

distinguished Lima chef Miguel Schiaffino, and stylishly contemporary sleeping quarters and lounge spaces, this is no ordinary riverboat cruise. The 12 air-conditioned rooms have high-quality bedding and large, panoramic windows that make it look like you're watching a big-screen movie of the Amazon. Cruises depart from Iquitos and go through the Pacaya Samiria National Reserve. Prices range from $2,400 to $5,600 per person for 3-, 4-, and 7-day cruises. Calle Huallaga 215, Iquitos. ☎ 866/603-3687 in the U.S. and Canada, or 065/601-053 in Peru. www.aquaexpeditions.com. AE, DC, MC, V.

★ **Dawn on the Amazon.** Run by Captain Bill Grimes, an enthusiastic onetime Indiana farmer who relocated to Iquitos and built a couple of handsome hardwood riverboats, this custom-oriented cruise company gets high marks for its service, honesty, and flexibility. There are both day trips and multiday excursions (but not set departures), which are charged per person, per day (ranging from $173–$310). Malecón Maldonado 185, Iquitos. ☎ 065/22-3730. www.dawnontheamazon.com. AE, DC, MC, V.

GreenTracks Amazon Cruises. This American-owned company has been active in the northern Amazon for more than 4 decades. Its midlevel cruises are aboard air-conditioned fleets. A 4-night riverboat cruise on the *Delfin II* is $1,989 per person in a double room; a 7-night cruise on a historic (rubber-boom-era) riverboat to the Pacaya Samiria National Reserve is $2,500 per person. Requena 336, Iquitos. ☎ 800/892-1035 or 970/884-6107 in the U.S. and Canada. www.amazontours.net. AE, DC, MC, V.

★ **Jungle Expeditions.** This upscale company offers luxury river cruises on a fleet of six classic, 19th-century-style boats on jaunts upriver along the Río Ucayali. Prices are about $2,700 for 7-day expeditions to $3,298 for 10 days. The company accepts passengers through their Lima booking office or through International Expeditions (☎ 800/234-9620; www.ietravel.com) in the United States. Av. Quiñones 1980, Iquitos. ☎ 01/241-3232 in Lima for reservations, or 065/262-340. www.junglex.com. AE, DC, MC, V.

> The Amazon River basin is home to 4,000 bird species and a number of native mammals, including the margay, shown here.

Amazon Fast Facts

Arriving

**BY PLANE—TO PUERTO MALDONADO &
THE SOUTHERN AMAZON** The **Aeropuerto
Internacional Padre Aldamiz Puerto
Maldonado** (☎ 082/571-531) is 8km (5 miles)
outside of Puerto Maldonado. Flights arrive
daily from Cusco and Lima on **LAN** (☎ 01/
213-8200; www.lan.com) and **Star Perú**
(☎ 01/705-9000; www.starperu.com)
starting at $135 one-way. Health Ministry
nurses are on hand at the airport to vaccinate
visitors against *fiebra amarilla* (yellow
fever). The best bet into town is a *motocarro*
(motorcycle rickshaw; S/7). **TO IQUITOS**
Aeropuerto Francisco Secada Vigneta, Av.
Abelardo Quiñones Km 6 (☎ 065/260-147),
receives flights on **LAN** (☎ 01/213-8200;
www.lan.com), **StarPerú** (☎ 01/705-9000;
www.starperu.com), and the newest carrier,
Peruvian Airlines (☎ 01/716-6000; www.
peruvianairlines.pe), which fly daily from Lima
(as well as Pucallpa and Tarapoto). Flights from
Lima start at $109 one-way. The airport is
usually chaotic when flights arrive, with dozens
of tour operator reps and countless touts and
con men competing for your attention. Do not
let anyone take your bags, and don't let anyone
you don't know hop in a cab with you. Definitely
wait before even discussing Amazon lodge
packages. To downtown Iquitos, an automobile
taxi costs about S/10; a *motocarro* S/7. **BY BOAT**
Traveling to Iquitos by boat is an option only for
those with ample time and patience. It takes
about a week when the river is high and 3 to 4
days in the dry season to reach Iquitos upriver
along the Amazon from Pucallpa or Yurimaguas.
To travel to Colombia or Brazil (Manaus,
Santarém, and Belém) by boat, your best bet is
by river cruise. The Iquitos port, Puerto Masusa,
is about 3km (2 miles) north of the Plaza de
Armas. **BY TRUCK** Adventurous budget travelers
with patience and capacity for suffering can
travel to Puerto Maldonado from Cusco by
truck. The journey takes 3 days in the dry
season and up to 10 days in wetter conditions,
and the route traverses more than 500km (310
miles); it's certainly one of the worst (if not *the*
worst) roads in Peru connecting two points of

obvious interest. It costs about $15. Trucks leave
from Plaza Tupac Amaru in Cusco and arrive in
Puerto Maldonado at the Mercado Modelo on
Calle Ernesto Rivero.

ATMs/Cashpoints/Currency Exchange

PUERTO MALDONADO Banks on the Plaza de
Armas include Banco de la Nación, Jr. Car-
rión 233 (☎ 082/571-064), and Banco de
Crédito, Arequipa 334 (☎ 082/571-001). Only
Banco de Crédito changes traveler's checks.
There are also *casas de cambio* along Jr. Puno.
Credit cards are not widely accepted in Puerto
Maldonado, so you should plan on bringing
cash for incidentals if you've already booked
a lodge or tour program. **IQUITOS** ATMs and
banks are located along Putumayo and Próspero, on the south side of the Plaza de Armas.
Banco de Crédito, Putumayo 201 at Próspero,
and Banco Continental, Sargento Lores 171,
exchange traveler's checks and cash. Money-
changers can usually be found hanging around
the Plaza de Armas and along Putumayo and
Próspero, but calculate the exchange beforehand, and count your money carefully.

Consulates & Immigration

PUERTO MALDONADO For required exit stamps
to travel to Bolivia via Puerto Heath (a trip of
3–4 days by boat), visit the Peruvian Immigration Office, 26 de Diciembre 356, a block
from the Plaza de Armas (Mon–Fri 9am–1pm).
IQUITOS To cross into Brazil or Colombia from
Iquitos, the Brazilian Consulate is located at
Sargento Lores 363 (☎ 065/232-081), and the
Colombian Consulate is at Callao 200
(☎ 065/231-461). However, it's wise to make
contact with the embassies in Lima or even at
home before traveling to Peru for travel into
either country to see if you require a visa. For
questions about border-crossing formalities,
visit the Migraciones office at Malecón Tarapacá 382 (☎ 065/235-371). The U.S. Consulate is at Av. 28 de Julio s/n (☎ 065/252-122).

Dentists & Doctors

PUERTO MALDONADO For medical attention, go
to Hospital Santa Rosa, Jr. Cajamarca 171 (at
Velarde; ☎ 082/571-019), or EsSalud, Dos de
Mayo s/n (☎ 082/571-230). **IQUITOS** Clínica

Ana Stahl, Av. La Marina 285 (☎ 065/252-535); EsSalud, Av. La Marina 2054 (☎ 065/250-333); or Hospital Regional de Loreto, Av. 28 de Julio s/n (☎ 065/252-004).

Emergencies

For general emergencies and police, call ☎ **105.** For fire, call ☎ **103.** In Iquitos, you can also call **Cruz Roja (Red Cross)** at ☎ 065/241-072 for medical emergencies.

Internet Access

PUERTO MALDONADO Internet cafes are located on the Plaza de Armas and along Jr. León de Velarde. IQUITOS There are several Internet *cabinas* along Fitzcarrald, on and near the Plaza de Armas. One to try is Estación Internet, Fitzcarrald 120 (☎ 065/223-608). Several other *cabinas* are located on Próspero and Putumayo.

Pharmacies

PUERTO MALDONADO There are several pharmacies along Jr. León de Velarde. IQUITOS There is an InkaPharma location at Jr. Próspero 397 and several others at the corner of Próspero and Morona.

Police

The police station in Puerto Maldonado is at Jr. Carrión 410 (☎ 082/571-022). The tourist police office in Iquitos is located at Sargento Lores 834 (☎ 065/242-081).

Post Office & Mail

The post office in Puerto Maldonado is on Av. León Velarde 675 (☎ 082/571-088). The post office in Iquitos is at Arica 402 (corner of Morona; ☎ 065/223-812).

Public Transportation

In Iquitos, *combis* and *omnibuses* (buses) travel principal routes but are much less comfortable and not much less expensive than more convenient *motocarros*. Most *combis* leave from the corner of Jr. Próspero and Jr. José Gálvez.

Rental *Motos*

In Iquitos, if you want to travel around town as locals do, rent a small *moto,* or motorcycle, at **Visión Motos,** Nauta 309 (☎ 065/234-759). Rates are about $30 per day or $5 per hour.

Safety

In Iquitos, the poor Belén district should be visited with some caution, especially if you're traveling with expensive camera equipment. Most other safety concerns relate to the contracting of guides and dealing with hucksters on the street hawking jungle lodges and tours. Do not entertain these solicitors.

Taxis

PUERTO MALDONADO Cheap *motocarros* are everywhere; most rides in town cost S/2. Ferries cross the Ríos Madre de Dios and Tambopata daily. If you just want to cruise across the river you'll have to negotiate the price (generally S/20 per person). IQUITOS *Motocarros* are everywhere in Iquitos; in-town fares are S/2. Regular car taxis are only slightly less ubiquitous; most trips in town cost S/3.

Telephone

The area code in Puerto Maldonado is 082; there's a Telefónica del Perú office at Jr. Puno 670 (☎ 082/571-600). In Iquitos, the area code is 065 and the Telefónica del Perú office is at Arica 276.

Visitor Information

PUERTO MALDONADO There's a small booth at the airport with limited information on the city and jungle lodges. Most visitors leave for the southern jungle from Cusco, so if you spend a few days there first, it's worthwhile to pick up more complete information on Puerto Maldonado and the rest of the jungle at the main Tourist Information Office at Mantas 117-A, a block from the Plaza de Armas (☎ 082/263-176). Anyone traveling to Manu or Tambopata with an organized expedition should be able to get all the necessary information from the tour organizer. IQUITOS A municipal tourism information booth (☎ 065/260-251) is at the arrivals terminal baggage claim at the airport; it has a chart of hotels and costs. A helpful tourism information office is on the north side of the Plaza de Armas at Napo 232 (☎ 065/236-144; Mon–Sat 8am–8pm). The English-speaking staff has free maps and lists of all recommended hotels and tour operators (including photo albums of lodges).

11

Trujillo & the Northern Coast

Favorite Northern Coast Moments

Many visitors to Peru overlook the northern coast, but from Trujillo to Máncora, you'll find a fascinating blend of desert landscapes and some of the country's most inscrutable archaeological treasures and finest beaches. Among the highlights are Chan Chan, the massive adobe city; 1,500-year-old Moche temples; the royal tomb of the Lord of Sipán, Peru's very own King Tut; and Máncora, the epicenter of the country's best beaches and the coast's hot new party and surf destination.

> PREVIOUS PAGE Fishermen in Huanchaco head to sea in primitive totora-reed boats. THIS PAGE Reliefs carved in adobe at Chan Chan, the capital of the Chimú Empire.

❶ Wandering Chan Chan. One of the largest adobe sites in the Americas, this 14th-century capital of the Chimú Empire covers more than 25 sq. km (10 sq. miles) just north of Trujillo. The friezes of the royal palace Nik-An are an indication of its grandeur. See p. 349, ❹.

❷ Surfing big waves. The growing swell of interest in surfing along the northern coast makes it obvious that the talk about Peru's great waves—which used to be a well-guarded secret—isn't just hype. See p. 357.

❸ Marveling at Peru's King Tut. The royal tomb of the Lord of Sipán is one of the Americas' great recent archaeological discoveries, and the exhibition of its spectacularly conserved treasures at the modern Museo Tumbas Reales de Sipán in Lambayeque, near Chiclayo, depicts how momentous a find this was. The Moche royal figure, buried more than 1,700 years ago, really deserves to be thought of as Peru's King Tut. See p. 350, ❼.

❹ Devouring sashimi and ceviche. The waters of the Pacific Ocean produce a bounty of fresh fish along the north coast, where you can dive into fresh tuna sashimi and yummy ceviche— at backpacker prices.

❺ Staying at a boutique beach hotel. Formerly the haunt of budget backpackers, Máncora and its surrounding beaches are increasingly home to chic boutique hotels. One of the most stylish small hotels in all of Peru is DCO Suites, Lounge & Spa, overlooking the surf in Las Pocitas. See p. 366.

❻ Taking in colonial Trujillo. The northern city of Trujillo was one of Peru's most important colonial settlements, evident in the magnificent, pastel-colored colonial *casonas*, or mansions, that ring the Plaza de Armas. Unique to

1. Wandering Chan Chan
2. Surfing big waves
3. Marveling at Peru's King Tut
4. Devouring sashimi and ceviche
5. Staying at a boutique beach hotel
6. Taking in colonial Trujillo
7. Checking out Huanchaco's ancient fishing boats
8. Getting a beachside massage
9. Picking up *bruja* potions

Trujillo are the homes' elegant white window grilles. See p. 346, **1**.

7 Checking out Huanchaco's ancient fishing boats. The low-key fishing village and beach resort near Trujillo is one of the few places in Peru to preserve the ancient handmade boats used by fishermen in these parts for a millennium. The *caballitos del mar* ("seahorses"), made of bound totora reeds, are propped up on the beach when they're not out to sea in search of the day's fresh catch. See p. 349, **5**.

8 Getting a beachside massage. Having an outdoor massage close enough to the beach to hear the waves crashing is just what the doctor ordered. Two great spas are on Vichayito and Las Pocitas beaches south of Máncora: Orígenes, which also has a great pool, and the small but swanky rooftop spa at DCO Suites, Lounge & Spa. See p. 356 and 366.

9 Picking up *bruja* potions. You can find virtually anything at Chiclayo's street market Mercado Modelo, including odd goodies used by shamans, witch doctors, and faith healers. There are exotic herbs and spices, and peculiar items invested with healing or hex-like properties, such as tiny dried crocodiles, snakeskins, and bottles of hooves and claws. It's cool and a little creepy. See p. 350, **6**.

Trujillo in 3 Days

Founded in 1534, Trujillo is the third-largest city in Peru,

but it retains the feel of a small town—if you can silence the taxis. The *centro* is a grid of streets lined with magnificent colonial *casonas* (mansions). The importance of the region, though, greatly predates the Spanish settlement, as seen in a remarkable collection of pre-Columbian archaeological sites just outside the city, including Moche temples from A.D. 500 and Chan Chan, a monumental adobe complex of royal palaces. A stone's throw from Trujillo is Huanchaco, an easygoing fishing village and beach resort that attracts weekenders and young surfers. In 3 days, you can take in the best of colonial, pre-Columbian, and modern Trujillo.

> *Trujillo's graceful Plaza de Armas, the heart of one of Peru's most magnificent colonial quarters.*

START Trujillo is 560km (348 miles) from Lima (a 1-hr. flight or an 8-hr. bus ride); begin at the Plaza de Armas.

1 Plaza de Armas. This grandly laid-out, graceful main square—one of Peru's loveliest—with a Libertad monument at its center is the heart of the *centro histórico*. On one side is the sober, 17th-century **Catedral** (which contains a **Museo Catedrático; ☎** 044/235-083; S/5; Mon–Fri 9am–1pm and 4–7pm, Sat 9am–1pm) with silver and gold chalices and bishops' vestments. Trujillo's main sights are all nearby on the major streets leading off the square. ⏲ 30 min.

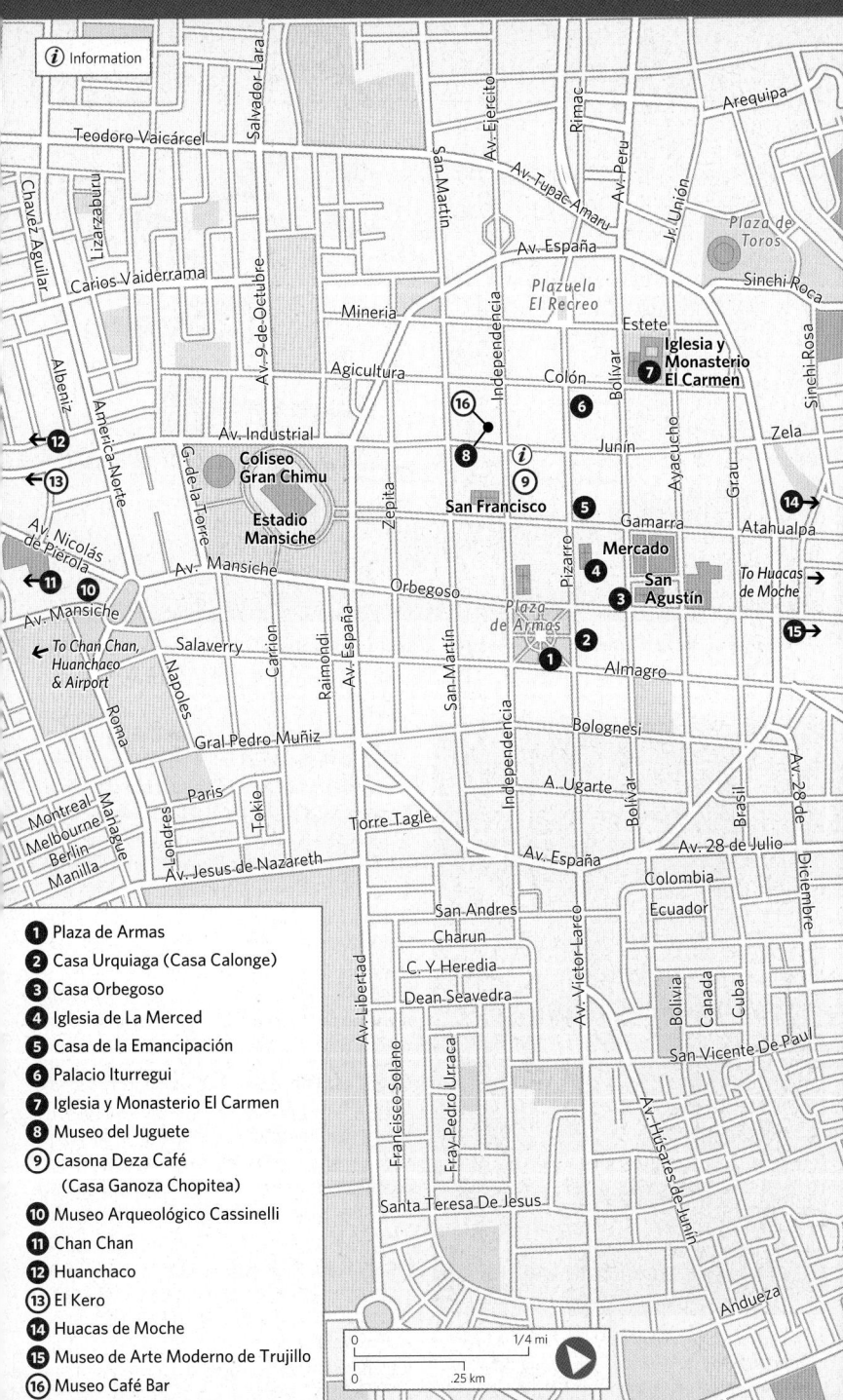

1 Plaza de Armas
2 Casa Urquiaga (Casa Calonge)
3 Casa Orbegoso
4 Iglesia de La Merced
5 Casa de la Emancipación
6 Palacio Iturregui
7 Iglesia y Monasterio El Carmen
8 Museo del Juguete
9 Casona Deza Café
   (Casa Ganoza Chopitea)
10 Museo Arqueológico Cassinelli
11 Chan Chan
12 Huanchaco
13 El Kero
14 Huacas de Moche
15 Museo de Arte Moderno de Trujillo
16 Museo Café Bar

> *The Carmelite museum inside Trujillo's Monasterio El Carmen houses the city's top colonial art collection.*

> *Simón Bolívar, the renowned* Libertador, *lived in Casa Urquiaga for a period after declaring Peru's independence from Spain.*

❷ ★★★ **Casa Urquiaga (Casa Calonge).** One of Trujillo's most notable and historic colonial homes is this large and handsome structure on the east side of the Plaza de Armas. The house conserves the 18th-century desk and gifts donated by Simón Bolívar, who lived here for several months after proclaiming Peru's independence in 1824. The home also hosted the first viceroy of Peru in 1604 and was the headquarters of the first bank in Trujillo. ⏱ 45 min. Jr. Pizarro 446. No phone. Free admission, but passport or other identification required. Mon–Fri 9am–3pm; Sat–Sun 10am–1pm.

❸ ★ **Casa Orbegoso.** A massive yellow-and-brown mid-18th-century mansion on its own plaza, this was once the property of former president Luis José de Orbegoso (who fought alongside Bolívar in the War of Independence and is buried in a mausoleum in the house). The *mudéjar* (Moorish-Christian) mural paintings in the entrance were uncovered beneath successive baroque, rococo, and finally neoclassical murals. Inside, original furnishings and mural paintings can be seen around the lower sections of some rooms. The front part

> *Totora-reed fishing boats are lined up on Huanchaco's beach after bringing in the day's catch.*

of the house still belongs to descendants of the original owners. ⏱ 30 min. Orbegoso 553. ☎ 044/234-950. Free admission. Daily 9:30am–7pm.

4 ★ **Iglesia de La Merced.** Set back from the pedestrian-only street on a small square, this baroque church is one of Trujillo's most impressive. It dates to 1634 (the original, built in 1536, was destroyed by an earthquake) and is notable for the colorful carved figures in relief around the cupola, including alternating series of perhaps 100 angels and cherubs supporting the top section. ⏱ 20 min. Jr. Pizarro 550. No phone. Free admission. Daily 8am–noon and 4–6pm.

5 **Casa de la Emancipación.** Independence from Spain was proclaimed on December 29, 1820, from this *casona,* which now belongs to Banco Continental and has a small museum of antiques, books, and documents inside. It also served as the governing palace of president Riva Agüero. ⏱ 30 min. Jr. Pizarro 610.

No phone. Free admission. Daily 9am–1pm and 4–8pm.

6 ★ **Palacio Iturregui.** A bright yellow mansion and excellent example of 19th-century neoclassical civil architecture, this is home to Club Central, Trujillo's traditional social club. Although the club is members-only, visitors are welcome to take a look around the two-story mansion, with its Italian marble statues and large central courtyard. Upstairs is a small museum containing Moche ceramics. Elegantly dressed club members still drop by the club for lunch or dinner, followed by a game of cards. ⏱ 20 min. Jr. Pizarro 688. ☎ 044/234-212. Admission (guided tour) S/5. Mon–Sat 11am–6pm.

7 ★ **Iglesia y Monasterio El Carmen.** This handsome church and monastery, founded in 1724 and occupying an entire city block, contains the most important collection of colonial art in Trujillo, including baroque and rococo paintings from the 17th and 18th centuries,

> *See contemporary works by Latin American masters at Trujillo's Museo de Arte Moderno.*

as well as paintings of the Quito Art School. The church's main *retablo* (altar) was created by Master Fernando Collado de la Cruz, a free black Peruvian. The monastery, home to two cloisters and fewer than a dozen cloistered nuns, cannot be visited. ⏱ 20 min. Jr. Bolívar (at Colón). ☎ 044/233-091. Admission S/3 adults, S/1 children. Mon–Sat 9am–1pm.

8 kids **Museo del Juguete.** A small and sweet museum, upstairs from the best watering hole in Trujillo, this collection of antique toys assembled by the artist Gerardo Chávez includes examples dating from the pre-Columbian era all the way to the 1950s. ⏱ 30 min. Jr. Independencia 705 (at Junín). ☎ 044/208-181. Admission S/6. Mon–Sat 10am–6pm; Sun 10am–2pm.

9 ☕ ★★★ **Casona Deza Café (Casa Ganoza Chopitea).** Both cafe stop and tourist sight, this splendid 17th-century *casona*, better known as La Casa de los Leones (House of the Lions) because of the carved stone lions crowning the main door, is one of Trujillo's most magnificent colonial buildings. It originally belonged to the first tax collector in Trujillo, and the entrance is loaded with baroque details, including river stone walkways and a *concha venera*, or welcoming shell, above the door. The front room

of the house and courtyard are now home to a decidedly cool, old Europe-style cafe (soon to be joined by a lounge-bar and, potentially, a boutique hotel). Jr. Independencia 630. ☎ 044/474-756. Items S/6–S/12.

Take a taxi or walk 10 minutes from the Plaza de Armas to the intersection of Huanchaco and Ctra. Panamericana.

10 ★ kids **Museo Arqueológico Cassinelli.** From the outside, this private archaeological museum—tucked beneath a Mobil gas station—doesn't look too promising, yet it houses one of Peru's largest private collections of ancient ceramics. Incredibly, over 5 decades Señor Casinelli, the owner of a gas station and car wash, assembled a superb collection of Moche, Nasca, Chavín, Huari, Recua, and Chimú cultures that includes some 4,000 pieces and spans more than 2,500 years. Discretely displayed behind a wall are the famed erotic ceramics of the Moche. ⏱ 1 hr. Av. Nicolás de Piérola 607. ☎ 044/246-110. Admission S/7. Mon–Sat 9am–1pm and 3–7pm.

On Day 2, take a *colectivo* or taxi from Trujillo northwest to Chan Chan (5km/3 miles; 20 min.).

11 ★★★ **Chan Chan.** This is the largest adobe city in the Americas, capital of the Chimú Empire. ⏱ At least 3 hr. See p. 349, **4**.

Continue northwest from Chan Chan via taxi or *colectivo* (8km/5 miles).

⑫ ★ Huanchaco. Part fishing village, part beach resort. ⏱ At least 1 hr. See p. 349, ➎.

⑬ 🍽 **El Kero.** Fronting the beach, this restaurant has a cool bar upstairs and a terrace lounge on the third floor, with a bamboo ceiling and white leather sofas and chairs. It's a good spot for an early-evening cocktail while watching the sun set over the ocean. Av. La Ribera 612. ☎ 044/461-184. Items S/12–S/21.

On Day 3, take a taxi from Trujillo east to Huacas de Moche (4km/2½ miles).

⑭ ★ Huacas de Moche. Massive, ancient pyramids of the Moche civilization, built around A.D. 500. ⏱ At least 2 hr. See p. 348, ➌.

Take a taxi from the Huacas de Moche back west toward Trujillo, to the El Bosque district just northeast of downtown.

⑮ ★ Museo de Arte Moderno de Trujillo. The small Museum of Modern Art, a relatively new addition to Trujillo and unusual in a city that celebrates its colonial past, houses the private collection of the Trujillano painter and sculptor Gerardo Chávez. You'll see several of Chávez's own pieces, as well as the contemporary works of renowned international artists such as Alberto Giacometti, Paul Klee, and the celebrated Latin American painters Roberto Sebastián Matta, Wifredo Lam, Joaquín Torres-García, Oswaldo Guayasamín, and Rufino Tamayo. ⏱ 45 min. Ctra. Industrial s/n (via Laredo, at Av. Federico Villarreal), El Bosque. ☎ 044/215-668. www.mamtrujillo.blogspot. com. Admission S/10. Mon–Sat 9:30am–5:30pm.

⑯ 🍽 ★★★ **Museo Café Bar.** One of the coolest spots in Trujillo, this old-world cafe, which has a gorgeous antique bar, is my definition of the perfect cocktail bar, at least in Peru. If you're not a drinker, it also has great fresh-fruit juices and a good menu of snacks. Jr. Independencia 713. ☎ 044/297-200. Items S/8–S/15.

La Cultura Moche

The Moche, who inhabited the northern coastal desert of Peru from A.D. 100 to 700, left detailed information about their entire civilization in finely detailed ceramics, some of the finest produced in pre-Columbian Peru (including their notoriously erotic ceramics). The Moche, along with the Nasca civilization from the desert coast south of Lima, are the best-documented culture of the Classical period. The apogee of Moche society was A.D. 500 to 600. Although they possessed no written language, their superior painted pottery presents evidence of nearly all elements of their society, from disease, dance, and architecture to transportation, agriculture,

music, and religion. The Moche (sometimes referred to as "Mochica") were a strictly hierarchical, elite-dominated society that developed into a theocracy. They also constituted one of the first true urban cultures in Peru. *Huacas* (religious temples or pyramids) were restricted to nobles, warriors, and priests; common citizens lived in areas removed from the temples. The finest selection of Moche ceramics in the country is found at the Museo Arqueológico Rafael Larco Herrera (p. 52, ➋) in Lima, the largest private collection of pre-Columbian art in the world. The founder of the museum is the author of the classic study *Los Mochicas.*

Chiclayo & Lambayeque in 2 Days

Chiclayo, Peru's fourth-largest city, is known for what's *outside* its borders: the archaeological sites Sipán and Túcume, two of the most important related to the Moche and Lambayeque cultures, and the spectacular Museo Tumbas Reales de Sipán, which houses one of the country's most remarkable finds of the past several decades, the tomb of the Lord of Sipán. Modern Chiclayo is a sprawling, bustling place of only passing interest for most visitors, but if you're an archaeology or history buff, there's plenty to explore. And the regional cuisine is heralded, at least within Peru, as one of the country's best.

> The Sipán culture was the first to discover bronze in northern Peru.

START Chiclayo is 200km (124 miles) north of Trujillo (3 hr. by bus) and 770km (478 miles) northwest of Lima (90 min. by plane); begin at Parque Principal.

❶ Downtown Chiclayo. The most interesting part of this bustling city is its **Mercado Modelo.** See p. 350, **❻**.

Travel northwest from Chiclayo to Lambayeque (12km/7½ miles; 30 min.). *Colectivos* depart from Av. Angamos at Vicente de la Vega and pass right in front of the museum.

❷ ★★★ Museo Tumbas Reales de Sipán. A stunning museum dedicated to a Moche royal figure who might be described as Peru's King Tut. ⏱ At least 2 hr. See p. 351, **❼**.

❸ Museo Arqueológico Nacional Brüning. No longer home to the Lord of Sipán treasures, which are now displayed in the Tumbas Reales Museum (stop **❷**, above), this archaeology museum has slipped in importance, but it still retains some important finds, including Sicán masks from Batán Grande, excellent Moche ceramics, and an assortment of artifacts found at Túcume. The collection includes pieces from the Lambayeque, Moche, Chavín, Vicus, and Inca civilizations; some date back 10,000 years. ⏱ 45 min. Av. Huamachuco cdra. 7, Lambayeque. ☎ 074/282-110. www.museobruning.com. Admission S/8 adults, S/3 students. Daily 9am–5:30pm.

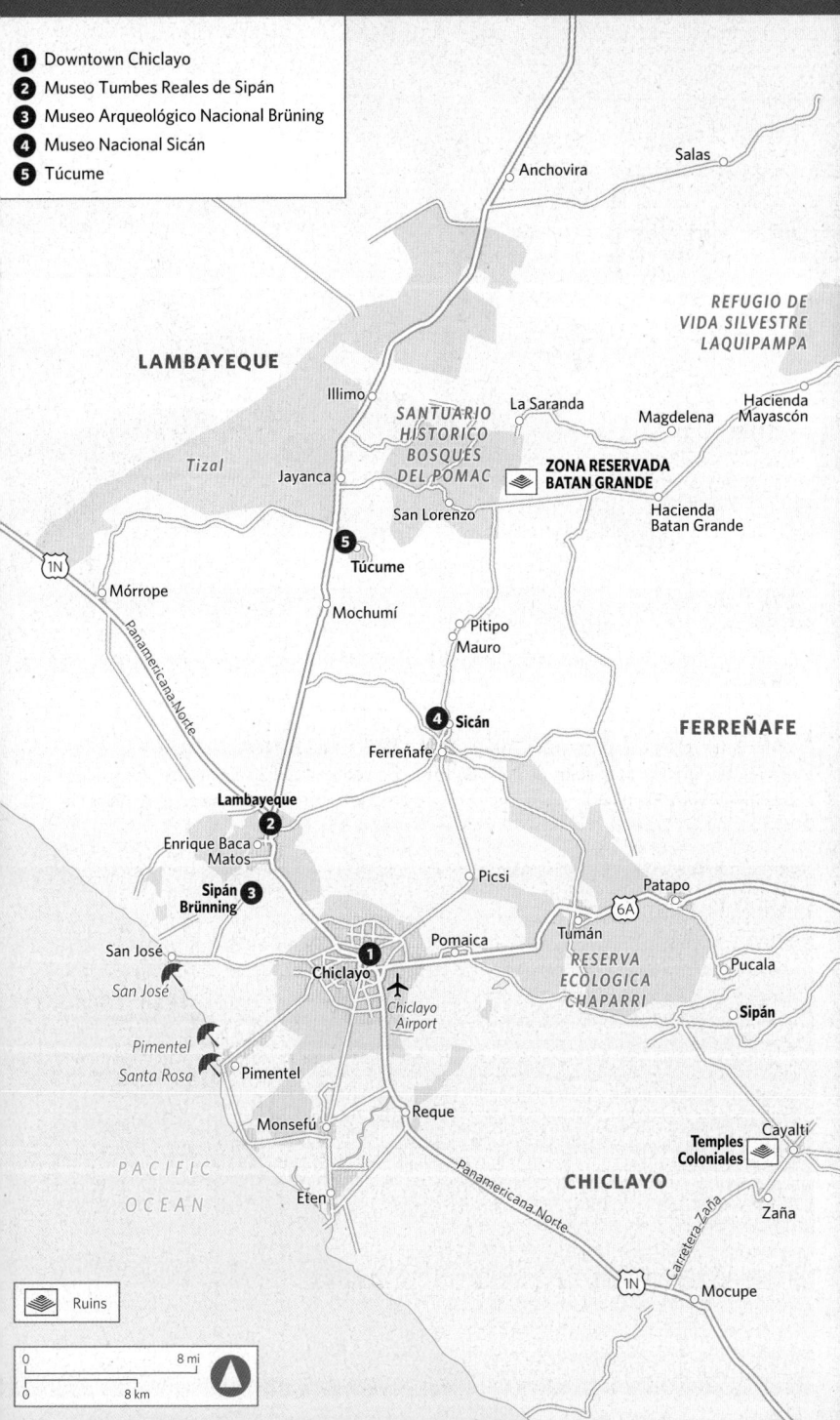

1 Downtown Chiclayo
2 Museo Tumbes Reales de Sipán
3 Museo Arqueológico Nacional Brüning
4 Museo Nacional Sicán
5 Túcume

> *In addition to meat and produce stalls, Chiclayo's Mercado Modelo has a section featuring witchcraft items and elixirs.*

On Day 2, travel by *colectivo* (from Terminal de Epsel, Av. Oriente at Nicolás de Piérola) to Ferreñafe (20km/12 miles).

④ ★★ **Museo Nacional Sicán.** A terrific museum of the Sicán culture, known for its masks with "winged eyes." ⏱ At least 1 hr. See p. 351, ⑧.

Other Archaeological Sites Near Chiclayo

For those interested in exploring other archaeological sites in the region, it's most convenient to go by organized tour, as the sites are spread out and complicated to reach unless you hire a taxi to take you around. Contact **Sipán Tours** (☎ 074/229-053; www.sipantours.com). The major sites are:

Batán Grande: A set of Sicán culture ruins of 50 adobe pyramids and tombs. 57km (35 miles) southeast of Chiclayo, 5km (3 miles) northeast of Túcume. ☎ 074/201-470. Daily 7am–4pm. Admission S/10 adults, S/4 students.

Templo de Sipán: A Moche burial ground where the Lord of Sipán was discovered in 1987. Although it's interesting to see where the tombs were found, and the views from the top of the large pyramid across from the Sipán excavation site are excellent, the ruins pale in comparison to the spectacular exhibit of jewels and ornaments housed at the Museo Tumbas Reales. Complejo Arqueológico de Huaca Rajada, Sicán. 35km (22 miles) southeast from Chiclayo. Daily 8am–6pm. ☎ 074/800-048. Admission S/5.

Zaña: An altogether different set of ruins, this once-wealthy colonial 16th-century outpost was decimated by a massive flood in 1720 and became a ghost town. Today it's a peculiar sight of ornate columns, church arches, and the remains of the once-grand, Gothic Convento de San Agustín; cool if you're into such things (some may find it desolate). 46km (29 miles) southeast of Chiclayo, via Panamericana Norte south and Ctra Zaña-Oyotún east. No set hours.

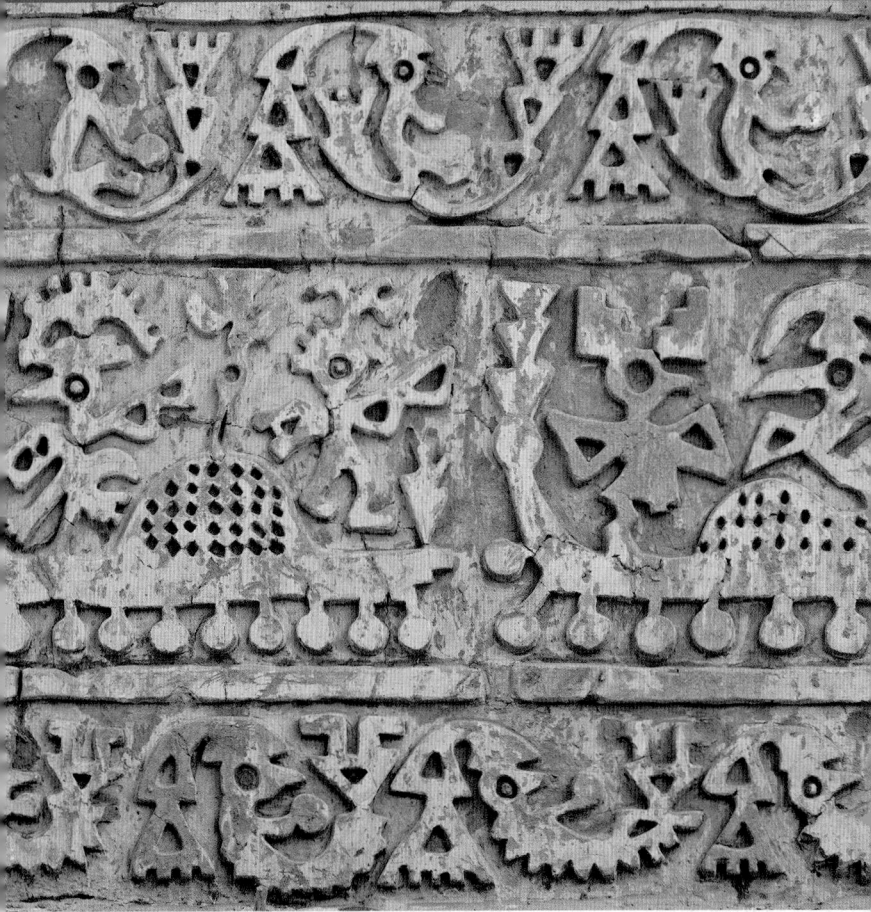

> *Reliefs at Huaca Larga, one of Túcume's 26 pyramids, thought to be the biggest adobe structure in South America.*

Travel by *colectivo* or taxi north to the district of Túcume (33km/20 miles). *Colectivos* depart from Av. Angamos in Chiclayo but leave passengers about 2km (1¼ mile) from the entrance to Túcume.

⑤ ★★ Túcume. Known as the "Valley of Pyramids," this sprawling complex of 26 adobe pyramids was constructed by the Sicán civilization around A.D. 1000 and developed over a period of nearly 500 years. Túcume was the most important elite urban center of the region and is considered the last great capital of the Lambayeque culture (later inhabited by the Chimú and Incas). Spread out over nearly 80 acres, the site is impressive, if enigmatic.

Many of the *huacas* (pyramids) are badly eroded and still under excavation, but Huaca Las Balsas, a long walk from the entrance, displays intricate reliefs and human burial chambers. Huaca Larga is reputed to be the largest adobe brick structure in South America: it's 700m (2,297 ft.) long, 280m (919 ft.) wide, and 30m (98 ft.) high. Clamber to the top of a massive platform for great views of the entire complex. ⊕ At least 90 min. Complejo Arqueológico Túcume, Caserío La Raya. ☎ 074/422-027, or 074/800-052 site museum. www.museodesitiotucume.com. Admission S/12 adults, S/4 students; guides available for negotiated price/tip. Daily 8am–4:30pm.

The Northern Coast in 1 Week

The northern coast has a lot of ground to cover, but 1 week will give you time to explore what makes this region different from the well-trodden south: one of Peru's finest colonial historic centers in Trujillo; a handful of the most important archaeological sites in the country; a pair of its finest archaeological museums, with one of the greatest finds of the last century on dramatic display; and the very best beaches Peru has to offer, beacons for surfers, families, and partying Peruvians and backpackers.

> *Huanchaco, just northwest of Trujillo, is a traditional fishing village that has developed into a weekend and summer resort.*

START Trujillo is 832km (517 miles) from Lima, a 1-hour flight or 8-hour bus ride; begin at the Plaza de Armas.

① ★★ **Colonial Trujillo.** Trujillo's collection of elegant *casas antiguas* (colonial- and Republican-era houses and baroque churches) is

one of the finest in Peru. The enormous but graceful **Plaza de Armas,** with polished stone as slippery as marble, is the focal point of the city. The square is ringed by colorful colonial mansions painted lemon yellow, brick red, and bright blue and distinguished by their

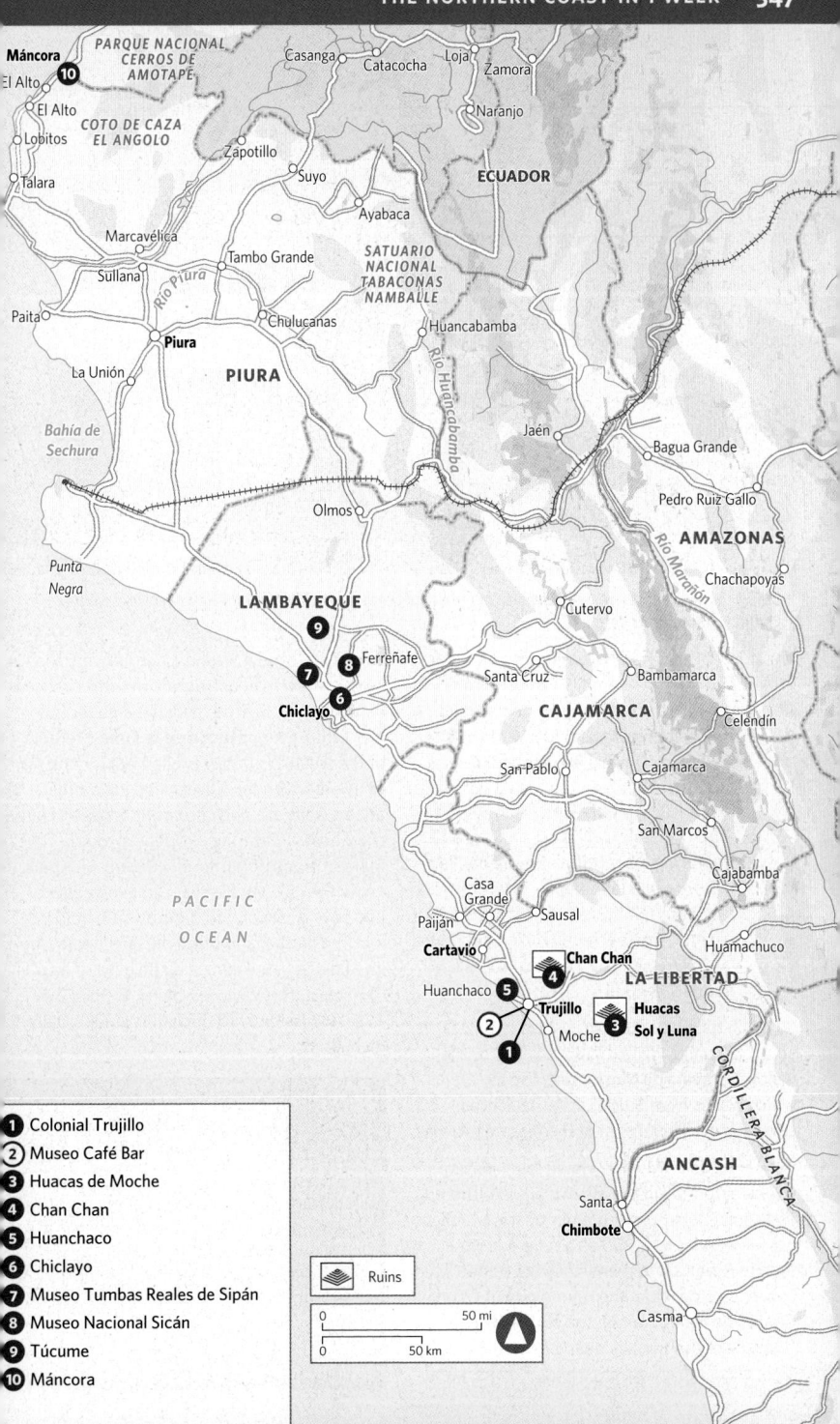

1 Colonial Trujillo
2 Museo Café Bar
3 Huacas de Moche
4 Chan Chan
5 Huanchaco
6 Chiclayo
7 Museo Tumbas Reales de Sipán
8 Museo Nacional Sicán
9 Túcume
10 Máncora

Ruins

0   50 mi
0   50 km

> *Trujillo is one of northern Peru's busiest commercial centers, but it has a small-town feel and elegant colonial homes at its core.*

unusually ornamental wrought-iron window grilles, and the 17th-century **Catedral** (p. 336, ❶). Perhaps the finest colonial home open to visits is **Casa Urquiaga** (p. 338, ❷). ⏱ At least 2 hr. For more on Trujillo, see p. 336

---

② 🍺 ★★★ **Museo Café Bar.** This elegant and cool cafe, full of art posters and featuring a beautiful antique bar, is my favorite place in Trujillo to while away the hours. It has good fruit juices, snacks, and perfectly mixed cocktails. Jr. Independencia 713. ☎ 044/297-200. Items S/8–S/15.

To reach the pyramids, travel 8km (5 miles) south of Trujillo via taxi (about S/20) or the yellow Campiña de Moche *colectivo* (S/2), which leaves from Suárez at Av. Los Incas, several blocks northeast of the Plaza de Armas.

❸ ★ **Huacas de Moche.** These two *huacas*, adobe pyramids in the desert, are weathered and significantly eroded. Built by the Moche people around A.D. 500 as a religious center and urban settlement, they are about 7 centuries older than the ruined city of Chan Chan. The first pyramid, the **Huaca del Sol** (Temple of the Sun), is nearly 20m (66 ft.) high, although it was once bigger by perhaps two-thirds, and it was in all probability the largest man-made structure in the Americas in its day. Across the field, the smaller but more interesting **Huaca de la Luna** (Temple of the Moon) is better preserved. It consists of five independent levels, and inside the adobe walls are polychromatic friezes of large rhomboids, featuring a repeated motif of the fearsome anthropomorphic figure Ai-Apaek, known as "El Degollador" ("the decapitator"), and several secondary figures. The bold yellow, red, white, and black designs depict the god having hair of the sea and eyes of an owl. ⏱ At least 2 hr. Valle de Moche. ☎ 044/291-894. Admission S/10 (including guide). Daily 9am–4pm.

Surf Pilgrims

Although the coast around Máncora is known as surf central, Puerto Chicama (also known as Malabrigo), about 80km (50 miles) up the coast from Trujillo, is legendary among hard-core surfers. Waves there can be ridden up to a half-mile, and it's the site of the longest left break in the world. There's little else of note in the ramshackle town; this is strictly a place for wave hunters.

> *The massive complex of Chan Chan contains no doors, arches, or stairs—only ramps.*

On Day 2, take a taxi or bus (Huanchaco bus from Av. España) to Chan Chan, 5km (3 miles) north of Trujillo.

❹ ★★★ Chan Chan. An enormous adobe city begun around 1300, the one-time capital of the Chimú Empire, which stretched nearly 1,000km (620 miles) along the northern coast of Peru from Lima to the current Ecuadoran border, is the largest complex of its kind from pre-Columbian America. Covering more than 25 sq. km (10 sq. miles), it's one of the most important archaeological sites in Peru. The Chimú, an urban people, preceded the Incas. The city once contained a dozen citadels and a maze of living quarters, thick defensive walls, plazas, gardens, warehouses, narrow streets, a huge reservoir, a royal cemetery, pyramidal temples, and nine palaces belonging to Chimú chieftains. There are four main sites at Chan Chan, spread over a large area that requires a couple of taxi rides. The principal complex, the **Palacio Nik-An,** is a royal palace that was home to a noble population of 500 to 1,000 and whose foundations and ceremonial courtyard decorated with aquatic-themed friezes have been meticulously restored. The other sites, including Huaca Arco Iris, Huaca Esmeralda, and a site museum, are less impressive, so if you're pressed for time, you could make do with a visit only to Nik-An. ☺ At least 2 hr. Valle de Moche. Huaca Arco Iris: Jr. Pedro Murillo 1681, La Esperanza, Trujillo, off Panamericana Norte. ☎ 044/284-744. Admission S/11 (ticket good for 48 hr. and all four sites of the complex). Daily 9am–4:30pm (site museum closed Mon). To visit all Chan Chan sites, it's best to contract a taxi to wait for you (S/75).

Catch a taxi (some occasionally wait at the turnoff to Chan Chan) or a Huanchaco-bound bus on the main road northwest to Huanchaco (8km/5 miles).

❺ ★ Huanchaco. This traditional fishing village does double duty as a burgeoning beach resort, springing to life on summer weekends with Trujillanos, vacationing Peruvians, and, increasingly, foreign visitors. With its roster of resort hotels and seafood restaurants, and nice stretches of beach, Huanchaco makes an excellent alternative to Trujillo as a base for exploring the archaeological sites of the

> *The wide and serene sands of Vichayito, one of northern Peru's most beautiful beaches.*

Chimú and Moche. The town is famous for its handcrafted boats made of bound totora reeds, called *caballitos del mar* ("seahorses"), or *caballitos de totora*—small boats used by fishermen on the coast for more than 1,000 years, since the reign of the Moche. Huanchaco is one of the few places in Peru where this ancient sea vessel has not disappeared from use. ⊙ At least 1 hr.

On Day 3, travel by bus from Trujillo north to Chiclayo (200km/124 miles).

❻ Chiclayo. This large city's proximity to prominent archaeological museums and ruins is what puts it on an itinerary. The attractive **Parque Principal,** dominated by the twin-domed, neoclassical, 19th-century **Catedral,** is the focal point of life in the city. Ten blocks south of the plaza, the **Paseo de las Musas** is an attractive park area oddly lined with neo-classical statuary of mythological figures. The most fascinating feature of Chiclayo is **Mercado Modelo,** 5 blocks north of Parque Principal (daily dawn–dusk), an open street market

that is one of Peru's most raucous and a good impression of markets in India or Morocco. It throbs with any- and everything, from luggage and natural Viagra substitutes to guitars, machetes, and calves' brains, plus dozens of beauty salons and shoe and electronics repair headquarters. But it's famed for the *mercadillo de brujas* (witches' market) near Calle Arica, a section of stalls bursting with the elixirs and potions of shamans and faith healers. Redolent with exotic spices and herbs, its visual chaos includes hanging shells, small altarpieces, and bottles filled with hooves and claws, snakeskins, miniature desiccated crocs, claws, skunks, and fish eggs. ⊙ 1 day.

On Day 4, take a *colectivo* northwest from Chiclayo to Lambayeque (12km/7½ miles; 30 min.). *Colectivos* depart from Av. Angamos and Vicente de la Vega and pass right in front of the museum.

❼ ★★★ 🅺🅸🅳🆂 Museo Tumbas Reales de Sipán. The tomb of the Lord of Sipán (considered Peru's King Tut) is one of the most important archaeological discoveries in the Americas of the past century. Unearthed in 1987, this funeral tomb of a Moche royal figure was buried more than 1,700 years ago, and its undisturbed layers and ceremonial ornaments and treasures provide key clues to Moche culture. Buried with the king, a sort of living deity, were companions joining him on his journey to the afterlife: a Moche warrior, a priest, three female concubines, a dog, two llamas, a child, food and beverage vessels, and a guard with a copper shield, gold helmet, and amputated feet—symbolic of his everlasting protection over the king's tomb. This modern museum certainly stands out in northern Peru, land of dusty archaeological pyramids and colonial towns, and the space dedicated to the Lord of Sipán is a revelation compared to archaeological sites in the area that are difficult-to-decipher, colossal piles of clay. On display from the main funerary chamber—amazingly, never looted—headdresses, garments, and breastplates of gold, silver, and precious stones tell an intricate story of power and rank.

🕐 At least 2 hr. Juan Pablo Vizcardo y Guzman s/n, Lambayeque. ☎ 074/283-977. www.museotumbasrealessipan.pe. Admission S/10 adults, S/4 seniors, S/1.50 students. Tues–Sun 9am–5pm.

To reach Ferreñafe, take a taxi, or return to Chiclayo and catch a *colectivo* (at Terminal de Epsel, Av. Oriente at Nicolás de Piérola; 20km/12 miles).

❽ ★★ Museo Nacional Sicán. Less well known than the Museo Tumbas Reales (if only because it doesn't possess a blockbuster like the Lord of Sipán), this excellent museum focuses on the Sicán (also called Lambayeque) culture that succeeded the Moche and thrived in northern Peru until the 14th century. The Sicán were the first in the region to discover bronze, and they surrounded their dead, buried in unique vertical rooms, with large collections of objects made from gold and other valuable metals. Sicán masks with *ojos alados* ("winged eyes") are prized among institutions and collectors; some excellent examples are on view here. 🕐 At least 1 hr. Av. Batán Grande cdra. 9, (Ctra. a Pítipo), Ferreñafe. ☎ 074/286-469. sican.perucultural.org.pe. Admission S/10, seniors S/4, students S/1.50. Tues–Sun 9am–5pm.

Return to Chiclayo and travel by *colectivo* or taxi north to the district of Túcume (33km/20 miles). *Colectivos* depart from Av. Angamos in Chiclayo but leave passengers about 2km (1¼ miles) from the entrance to Túcume.

❾ Túcume. An entire valley of enigmatic pyramids. 🕐 At least 2 hr. See p. 345, **❺**.

On Day 5, fly from Chiclayo to Piura, and then travel the remaining 204km (127 miles) north to Máncora by *colectivo*, taxi, or rental car. Or, travel by bus from Chiclayo to Máncora (7 hr.).

❿ ★★ Máncora. Despite Peru's nearly 2,500km (1,500 miles) of coastline, the country hasn't really been celebrated for its beaches. Limeños, surfers, and leftover hippies, though, have long staked out a northern section of some of the prettiest coastline in and around the desert sands near Máncora, and in the last few years the area has become highly touted as a hot destination. Even though Máncora is gaining in popularity with a newer, more moneyed crowd, it retains its low-key charm. The surfer shacks are still here, as are the rowdy bars along the main drag, but so too are chic boutique hotels and a handful of nice restaurants. Two of the most attractive stretches of beach are just a few kilometers south of Máncora: **Las Pocitas** and **Vichayito**, both undergoing rapid development. 🕐 3 days. See "Máncora & Northern Beaches," p. 354.

The Peruvian Hairless Dog

Especially in the deserts of northern Peru, you may spot a curiously smooth, black-skinned creature, often strewn with blotches, that only vaguely resembles a canine. The less-than-blessed creature is the *biringo*, or Peruvian hairless dog, a breed domesticated by pre-Inca cultures of the region. You'll find *biringos* hanging about the Chan Chan site museum, on the main drag in Máncora, and elsewhere. While beloved by Peruvians, to those unfamiliar with the breed they may seem prehistoric and, well, downright ugly. They are hot to the touch, and it is said that ancient nobles kept them as portable heaters (the Lambayeque and Chimú also made them part of their diets).

LAND OF FESTIVALS & FOLKLORE

Peru's Biggest Parties **BY NEIL EDWARD SCHLECHT**

PERU CELEBRATES SOME OF THE MOST VIBRANT and impressive folkloric traditions and festivals on the planet. Many, or perhaps most, of the country's 3,000 popular festivals are expressions of traditional pre-Columbian religious and cultural roots (or a blend of indigenous and Catholic rituals). While many are very serious and hold great meaning for participants, many are also a seriously good time, opportunities for locals (and visitors) to lose themselves in wild dancing, intense music, and celebratory inebriation. Peruvian festivals are spectacles of movement and color, with glorious costumes, surreal masks, and dramatic candle-light processions. Puno and Cusco are the granddaddies of folkloric expression, but Ayacucho, Cajamarca, and Isla Taquile, among others, also have their own unique celebrations. From the capital of Lima to the smallest Andean villages, you'll find multiple expressions of what makes Peru such a rich destination.

Popular Parties

FESTIVAL OF VIRGEN DE LA CANDELARIA
The 2 frenetic weeks of this festival, celebrating religious faith and pre-Columbian planting and harvest traditions, transform Puno into the country's folklore capital. Some 200 groups of singers and dancers perform in elaborate costumes and masks. Musicians play *zampona* pan-pipes and dancers give life to *la diablada*, the spectacular dance of the demons.

INTI RAYMI
The most famous festival in Peru celebrates the sun, a pivotal god in the Inca cosmos, and winter solstice. Re-creating the Inca Festival of the Sun at the dramatic ruins of Sacsayhuamán in Cusco, it's a grand and colorful pageant of elaborately dressed participants; folk dances and music; and detailed rituals.

SEMANA SANTA
Ayacucho's Easter celebrations are the most magnificent Catholic festival in Peru. After historical reenactments on Holy Friday, Christ is paraded through darkened streets carpeted with fresh flowers and illuminated by thousands of white candles. Christ's resurrection is represented by an enormous pyramid of white candles, supported by 200 people.

LA VIRGEN DEL CARMEN
In a quiet colonial village on the way to the cloud forest from Cusco, this spectacular festival honors the local patron saint, known as Mamacha Carmen. In one of the most colorful events in Peru, wildly costumed singers, dancers, and musicians take over the main square, and dancers dressed as devils ascend to rooftops for acrobatic maneuvers.

Celebrated Dances

UKUKU
This dancing, mythological trickster speaks in a high-pitched voice and plays pranks, but also maintains order. The half-human offspring of a woman and a bear, the *ukuku* is said to possess supernatural strength.

LA DIABLADA
Devil characters engage in a battle of good versus evil, overseen by St. Michael the Archangel.

SCISSOR DANCERS
The traditional *danza de las tijeras*, performed mostly in the central highlands, is a dance of incredible flexibility and acrobatic stunts, performed to harp and violin and with scissors in hand. The dancers, or *danzaq*, walk on fire, have their skin pierced by knives, lie on beds of glass shards, swallow swords, and even eat live frogs, rats, or snakes.

Máncora & Northern Beaches

The extremely dry northern desert coast is graced by Peru's finest long, sandy beaches, but for decades their inaccessibility kept them poorly developed and the secret of pioneering locals, land travelers on their way down from Ecuador, and surfers drawn to the Pacific Ocean's extraordinary swells and breaks. Only in the last few years has the region begun to take off with a more diverse crowd. It's still complicated to get to; access is via a long drive or bus from either Piura or Tumbes. Máncora is the fashionable destination of choice, with the most facilities, but there are quieter beaches and even more amazing surfing waves both south and north (beaches are listed below from south to north).

> The wide and serene sands of Vichayito, one of northern Peru's most beautiful beaches.

START Cabo Blanco is 150km (93 miles; a 2-hr. drive) north of Piura; take Ctra. 1N and 1A to Talara and pick up the Panamericana Norte north to Máncora.

1 Cabo Blanco. This modest, even desolate fisherman's village is famous in Peru as the inspiration for Ernest Hemingway's *The Old Man and the Sea* (while Hemingway did spend time in the area and at the famous Fishing Club in 1956,

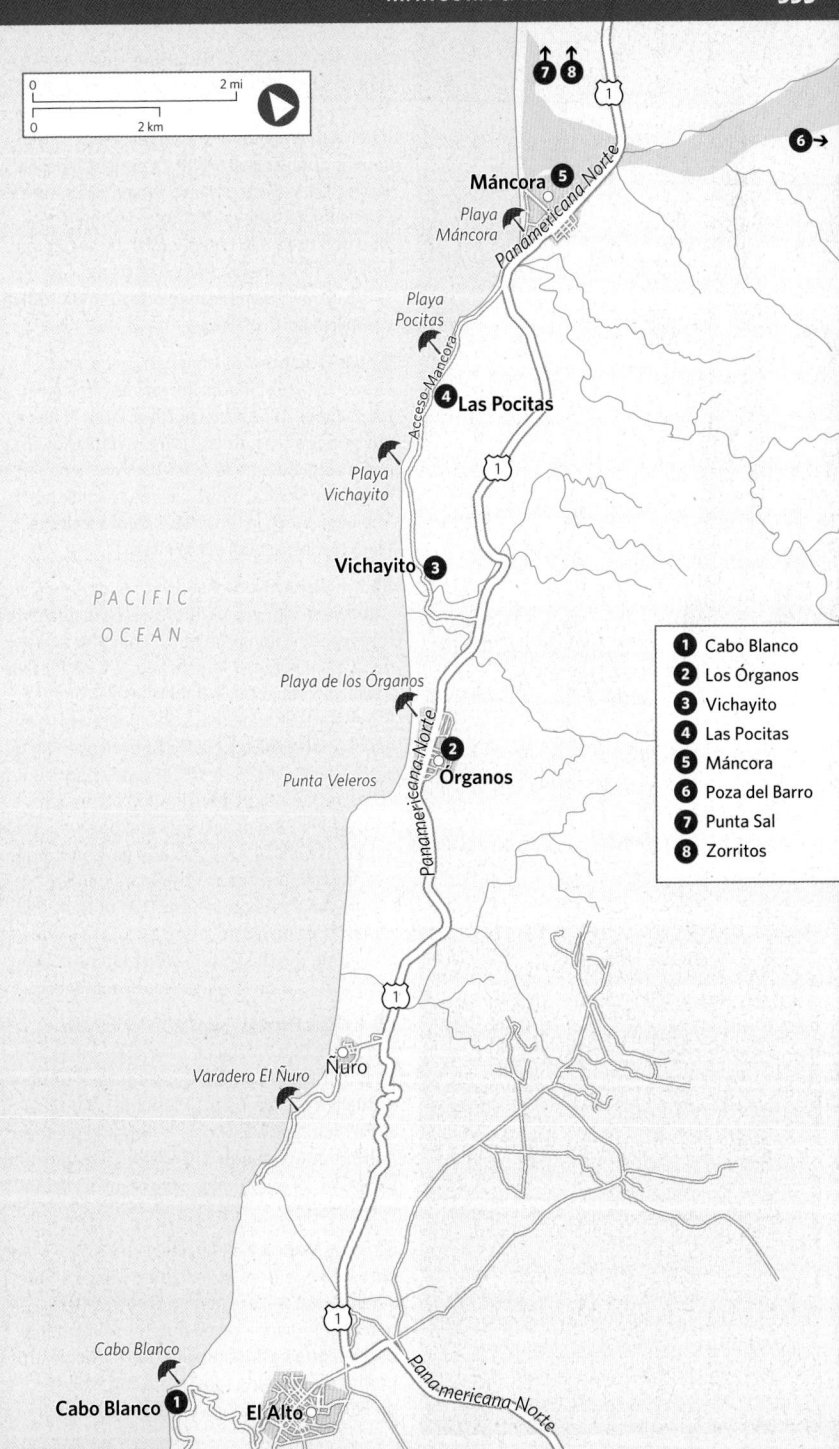

PACIFIC
OCEAN

Máncora
Playa
Máncora

Playa
Pocitas

Las Pocitas

Playa
Vichayito

Vichayito

Playa de los Órganos

Órganos

Punta Veleros

Ñuro

Varadero El Ñuro

Cabo Blanco

Cabo Blanco

El Alto

Panamericana Norte

Acceso Máncora

1. Cabo Blanco
2. Los Órganos
3. Vichayito
4. Las Pocitas
5. Máncora
6. Poza del Barro
7. Punta Sal
8. Zorritos

0   2 mi
0   2 km

> *Rent a board from Soledad Surf Shop in Máncora and hit the waves.*

Getting Around

Covering much distance along the northern coast pretty much requires a rental car, which you will drive along Ctra. Panamericana Norte, making stops as you please. But if you just want to stick to Máncora and the nearest beaches, such as Vichayito and Las Pocitas (and are mostly interested in a relaxing resort, good beaches, and nightlife), you could easily make do with a bus to Máncora or a flight to Piura. You can take a *colectivo* from the airport, and then depend on local *mototaxis* to get around. Máncora is 185km (115 miles) north of Piura and 102km (63 miles) south of Tumbes (less recommended for flights due to flight schedules). Beaches (and resorts) in this section are listed from south to north.

deep-sea fishing and carousing, most literary scholars believe Cuba was the real inspiration). The area is renowned for sportfishing, however; it holds the record for the largest black marlin caught off the coast. With its perfect pipeline waves, Cabo Blanco is also a magnet for surfers (Panic Point is the much buzzed-about spot), who don't seem to care much that the natural beauty of the area is marred by oil rigs just offshore. **Ctra. Panamericana Norte Km 1137, 150km (93 miles) north of Piura.**

❷ **Los Órganos.** Laid-back Órganos, as it's known to locals, marks the real beginning of the tourist zone of beaches north of Piura. It has a few good *cevicherías* and is more family-oriented and a bigger destination for the Peruvian middle class than several of the beaches farther north. The best beach in this area is **Punta Veleros. 13km (8 miles) south of Máncora.**

❸ ★★ **Vichayito.** Blessed with wide sands and calm waters, this beautiful stretch is one of the top beaches along the north coast for swimming, sunning, and kitesurfing. It's perfect for a relaxing vacation, but still close enough to the restaurants and bars of Máncora for easy access. **Orígenes,** Ctra. Panamericana Norte Km 1155 (☎ 073/694-460; www.spaorigenes. com), is a fantastic spa right on the beach, with a full menu of services and open-air massages, as well as a hot tub and gorgeous pool overlooking the ocean. There are two entrances to Vichayito: at Km 1150 of the Ctra. Panamericana Norte, just past Los Órganos; and along the dusty, unpaved road back from Las Pocitas. **7km (4 miles) south of Máncora.**

❹ ★★ **Las Pocitas.** Similar to Vichayito, though with a narrower, palm tree–lined beach, this upscale zone just south of (and virtually contiguous to) Máncora is home to a growing number of chic hotels and weekend and summer houses. The waters are calm and excellent for swimming. **3km (2 miles) south of Máncora.**

❺ ★★★ **Máncora.** Only a few years ago, Máncora was a remote little fishing village where a handful of surfers and budget travelers had alighted and stayed put. It has suddenly become the hottest destination in the north, both among young foreigners and well-to-do Peruvians, although outside of summer season and other busy holiday periods, it still seems pretty easygoing and charmingly rough around the edges. Máncora is essentially one main drag, lined end-to-end with open-air bars and restaurants, with the impenetrable desert to one side and the open sea on the other. Check out the **artisans' market,** on Av. Piura, or the chic little shop **Sirena,** Av. Piura 336 (☎ 073/258-445), featuring stylish bikinis, sundresses, *pareos* (beach wraps), sandals, and other beach apparel and accessories designed by an Argentine woman and made in Máncora. **The Birdhouse,** a gringobuilt warren of breezy shops, restaurants, and bars between the main street and the beach (Pasaje Piura), is hangout central. **Soledad Surf Shop,** Av. Piura 316 (☎ 01/9983-0425), is the go-to place for hard-core *surfistas* or for beachy types who just want to look the part. For those into the burgeoning sport of kitesurfing, **Máncora Kite Club** and **Máncora Kite Surf** (www.mancorakitesurf.com) arrange lessons, gear, and trips.

⑥ **Poza del Barro.** These rustic thermal and mineral-rich mud baths (where the temperature reaches about 40°C/104°F), said to have healing properties, are surrounded by *algarrobo* trees and make for a relaxing alternative to the beach. Some people choose to hike, bike, or ride horses to get here, but the easiest way is to hop a *mototaxi* (30 min). ⏱ **2 hr. 30km (19 miles) northeast of Máncora. No phone. Admission S/3. Daily 8am–6pm.**

⑦ ★ **Punta Sal.** Home to a beautiful, long, white-sand beach (which some contend is the loveliest in Peru) and calm waters, this relaxed resort has a couple of large hotels frequented mostly by Peruvian (largely Limeña) families. **23km (14 miles) north of Máncora.**

⑧ ★ **Zorritos.** This mellow, often empty beach destination south of Tumbes, the capital of the department (province) just 30km (19 miles) from the Ecuadoran border, marks the northern end of the region's stretch of beaches. With a pretty beach with a tropical feel; good waves; and a smattering of rustic, thatchedroof *cabaña* accommodations, it is developing into a young people's alternative to Máncora (an alternative to the alternative, as it were); access is much simpler from Tumbes than Piura. **27km (17 miles) south of Tumbes.**

> *The only practical way to get around Máncora is by mototaxi.*

Surfing Safari

The dry desert of the north is enlivened by great beaches and an oceanic phenomenon that produces ideal conditions for surfing. Two currents, the cold Humboldt from the south and Ecuatorial from the north, meet just south of Cabo Blanco, creating vastly different water temperatures (the north being considerably warmer year-round). For surfing fanatics, this section of the Pacific is renowned for its excellent swells, long waves, perfect barrels, superb point breaks, and awesome lefts. Top spots for surfing, some of which are for advanced boarders only, include Cabo Blanco, Punta Ballenas, Órganos, Panic Point, Lobitos, and El Golf. Long, sandy beaches in Máncora extend about 25km (15 miles) north and south. The water is warm; the sun shines virtually all year (as opposed to farther south, in and around Lima, where it seems rarely to peek through the gray haze); and, to put it in the local parlance, the seafood and ceviche are killer and the waves rad.

Trujillo & Northern Coast Restaurants

> Ceviche goes down easy at Huanchaco's Big Ben restaurant, high above the Pacific Ocean.

Trujillo & Huanchaco

★ **Big Ben** HUANCHACO *SEAFOOD*
It's hard to miss this white, three-level restaurant on a curve in the beach. This is a favorite upscale destination for vacationing Peruvians, who like the fresh seafood and commanding views from the open-air, top-floor dining room. The ceviche and fresh fish dishes are excellent. Av. Larco 1182, Urbanización El Boquerón. ☎ 044/461-378. www.bigbenhuanchaco.com. Entrees S/18–S/42. AE, DC, MC, V. Lunch and dinner daily. Map p. 359.

★★★ **Club Colonial** HUANCHACO *BELGIAN/FRENCH* This refined restaurant's new incarnation, right on the beachfront, is more inviting than ever. Decorated with antiques and colorful contemporary art, it has an elegant outdoor, candlelit terrace that looks out to the promenade and sea. The menu is an interesting mix of Peruvian and Franco-Belgian items, including *cordon bleu* and nicely prepared fish dishes, such as sole en papillote with herbs and artichoke sauce. Av. La Rivera 541. ☎ 044/461-639. Entrees S/20–S/34. AE, DC, MC, V. Breakfast, lunch, and dinner daily. Map p. 359.

★ **El Mochica** TRUJILLO *PERUVIAN*
Consistently recommended by Trujillanos for authentic northern Peruvian cooking, this place is both sophisticated (it's housed in a lovely colonial building) and informal (the dining room has white plastic chairs and a large TV). The kitchen produces well-prepared and good-value *criollo* cooking and classic dishes such as roasted guinea pig and *parrilladas* (mixed grilled meats), in addition to fresh fish. Bolívar 462. ☎ 044/293-441. Entrees S/12–S/34. AE, DC, MC, V. Lunch and dinner daily. Map p. 359.

El Peñón HUANCHACO *SEAFOOD*
A casual place with a small terrace overlooking the surf, this family-run restaurant is a favorite of locals for ceviche, seafood omelets, *arroz con mariscos* (rice with shellfish), and fresh seafood. Av. Víctor Larco 549 (at Raymondi) ☎ 044/461-549. Entrees S/10–S/30. DC, MC, V. Lunch and dinner daily. Map p. 359.

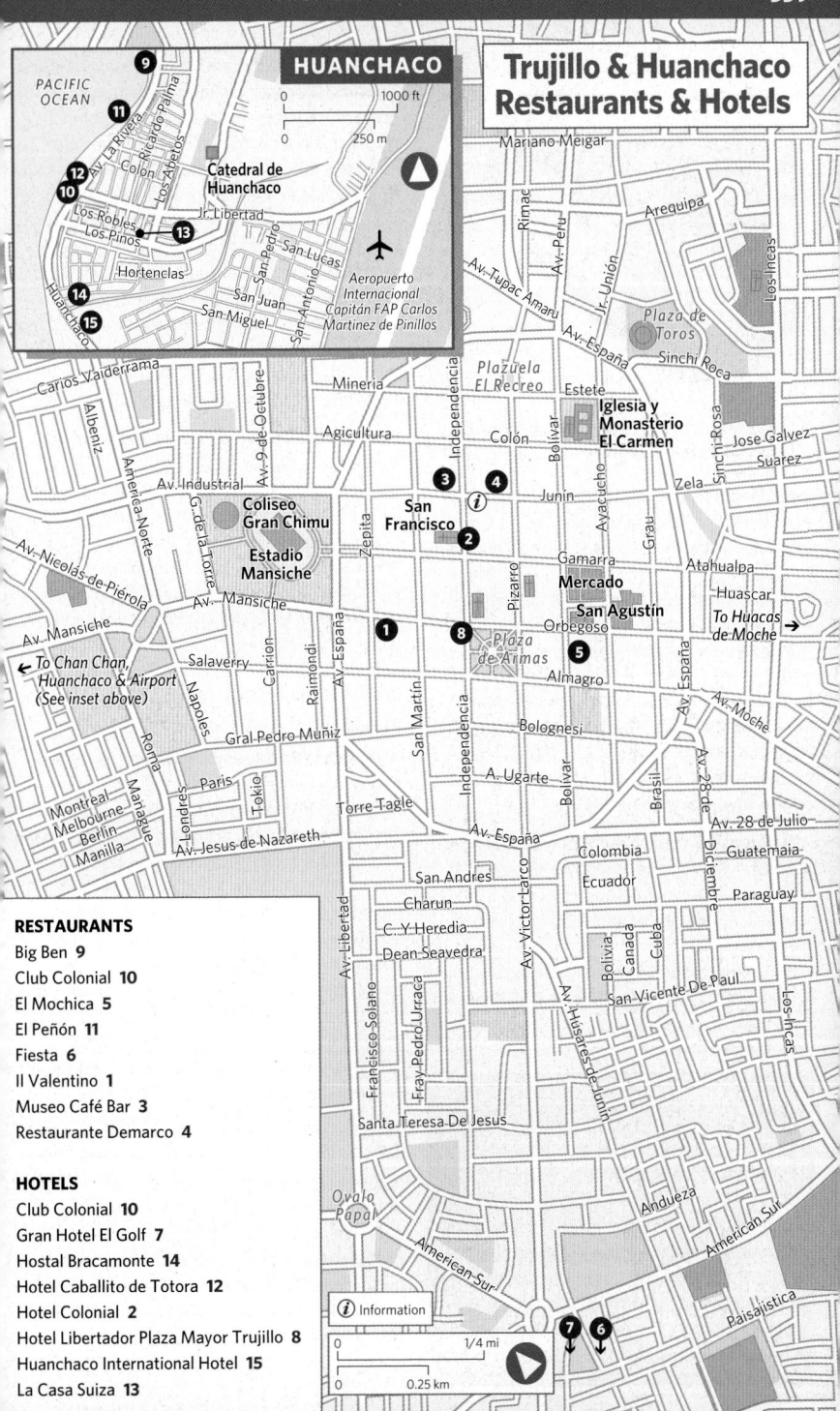

Trujillo & Huanchaco Restaurants & Hotels

HUANCHACO

PACIFIC OCEAN

Catedral de Huanchaco

Aeropuerto Internacional Capitán FAP Carlos Martínez de Pinillos

Plazuela EL Recreo

Iglesia y Monasterio El Carmen

Coliseo Gran Chimu

San Francisco

Estadio Mansiche

Mercado San Agustín

To Huacas de Moche →

← To Chan Chan, Huanchaco & Airport (See inset above)

Plaza de Armas

Plaza de Toros

RESTAURANTS
Big Ben **9**
Club Colonial **10**
El Mochica **5**
El Peñón **11**
Fiesta **6**
Il Valentino **1**
Museo Café Bar **3**
Restaurante Demarco **4**

HOTELS
Club Colonial **10**
Gran Hotel El Golf **7**
Hostal Bracamonte **14**
Hotel Caballito de Totora **12**
Hotel Colonial **2**
Hotel Libertador Plaza Mayor Trujillo **8**
Huanchaco International Hotel **15**
La Casa Suiza **13**

ⓘ Information

0 — 1/4 mi
0 — 0.25 km

> *La Sirena d' Juan adds a touch of sophistication to Máncora's restaurant row.*

★★★ Fiesta TRUJILLO SUBURBS *NORTHERN PERUVIAN* Few foreigners know about Chiclayana cuisine, but it's one of Peru's most sophisticated. Trujillo's best and most elegant restaurant is located outside of the *centro*, but it's worth the cab fare to indulge in hearty northern cooking, including roasted baby goat and the restaurant's unusual grilled ceviche, one of the house specialties. Portions are large and filling, and the cocktails are superb. Av. Larco 854 (Vista Alegre). ☎ 044/421-572. Entrees S/21–S/45. AE, DC, MC, V. Lunch and dinner Tues–Sun. Map p. 359.

★ Il Valentino TRUJILLO *PIZZA/ITALIAN* Vaguely Mediterranean in style, this sophisticated-looking restaurant across from Trujillo's most popular movie theater serves well-prepared pizzas and pastas, as well as steaks. Orbegoso 224. ☎ 044/221-328. Entrees S/15–S/35. AE, DC, MC, V. Lunch and dinner Tues–Sun. Map p. 359.

Don't-Miss Dining

Keep a lookout for a coming branch of Gastón Acurio's excellent **Chicha,** which the celebrity Lima chef has already inaugurated with success in Cusco (p. 227) and Arequipa (p. 154); if plans to open one in Trujillo pan out, it will surely be the city's top restaurant. One hotel restaurant that's worth a visit even for nonguests, especially for weekend brunch, is **Las Bóvedas** at the Hotel Libertador (p. 363).

★★ Museo Café Bar TRUJILLO *BAR/CAFE* This isn't a proper restaurant, though it's a great place to pop in for a snack, light lunch, or especially a cocktail. This fantastic cafe-bar looks like a turn-of-the-20th-century Buenos Aires cafe. It's got a stunning wood and marble-topped bar, cozy booths, and a nice little menu of sandwiches and *piqueos* (snacks), as well as a whole roster of breakfasts. It's the kind of place you may want to camp out in, or return to several times. I do both. Jr. Independencia 713 (at Junín). ☎ 044/297-200. Entrees S/8–S/15. AE, DC, MC, V. Breakfast, lunch, and dinner daily. Map p. 359.

Restaurante Demarco TRUJILLO *PERUVIAN/INTERNATIONAL* An old-school, good-value, cafe-style restaurant that's been around forever, this place serves a bit of everything for everybody, even though it mostly resembles an ice-cream parlor. Locals and visitors to Trujillo hit it up for sandwiches, pastas, *criollo* specialties, and excellent cakes and ice creams. Jr. Pizarro 725. ☎ 044/234-251. Entrees S/12–S/30. AE, DC, MC, V. Breakfast, lunch, and dinner daily. Map p. 359.

Chiclayo

★★★ Fiesta Restaurant Gourmet *NORTHERN PERUVIAN* One of the finest restaurants in northern Peru, this friendly, elegant place specializes in the local cuisine, that of Chiclayo and Lambayeque, prized by Peruvians but known to few others. The rich, hearty fare includes *mero causa* (grouper with mashed potatoes), a dish that in Chiclayo is typically eaten only on Sundays (but here is served daily), and succulent barbecued goat ribs. Bar Sipán is a cozy spot for an impeccably mixed pre-dinner cocktail. Salaverry 1820. ☎ 074/201-970. Entrees S/22–S/46. AE, DC, MC, V. Lunch and dinner daily. Map p. 365.

Jhon SEAFOOD/CEVICHE

A tiny, informal neighborhood *cevichería*, this is a low-key, dependable spot for any number of types of ceviche, as well as rice dishes with fish or shellfish. There are also several preparations of fish, such as *mero* and a nice *picante de camarones* (spicy shrimp). Colón 276 (at Tacna). ☎ 074/208-593. Entrees S/12–S/30. No credit cards. Lunch daily. Map p. 365.

★ kids **La Parra** *GRILL*
Carnivores will take note of the open grill at the entrance and be assured of what awaits them: grilled meats, served with fries and a salad, which is all that's on the menu. There are choices, of course: *lomo fino* (sirloin), shish kabob, sausage, and chicken. Very popular with local families on weekends. Manuel María Izaga 752. ☎ 074/227-471. Entrees S/15–S/32. AE, DC, MC, V. Lunch and dinner daily. Map p. 365.

Máncora & the Northern Beaches
Angela's Place *MÁNCORA VEGETARIAN*
This little Austrian-owned vegetarian spot offers great hummus, salads, whole-grain bread, veggie main-course options, and a fixed-price meal deal. Av. Piura 396. ☎ 073/258-603. www.vivamancora.com/deangela. Entrees

> *The hot spot Praia Bar, on the main drag in Máncora, does a mean mojito.*

S/18–S/34. No credit cards. Lunch and dinner daily. Map p. 367.

★★ **Donde Teresa** *LAS POCITAS PERUVIAN/ SEAFOOD* Named for the mother of one of the owners of this boutique hotel (Teresa Ocampo, a celebrity chef in Peru who had the country's first TV cooking show), this open-air restaurant serves excellent local seafood and specialties such as *chancho al barril* (wood-fired, slow-cooked pork). Las Pocitas s/n (1km/½ mile south of Máncora). ☎ 073/258-702. www.hotelier.pe. Entrees S/20–S/36. MC, V. Lunch and dinner daily. Map p. 367.

★ **La Sirena d' Juan** *MÁNCORA SEAFOOD* A warm and intimate little place with hip music and terrace seating, this is a good option for date night. It serves excellent seared tuna with ginger and passion-fruit salsa and creative *novo Andino* dishes. Av. Piura 316. ☎ 073/258-173. Entrees S/15–S/32. MC, V. Dinner Mon–Sat. Map p. 367.

★★ **Praia Bar** *MÁNCORA PERUVIAN/INTER-NATIONAL* Máncora's most stylish bar, an all-white cocktail lounge, doubles as a very nice little restaurant. There's fantastically fresh tuna sashimi, generous *lomo saltado* (strips of beef mixed with onions, tomatoes, peppers, and fried potatoes, served over rice), and a large, messy cheeseburger. Not to mention great nightly drink specials. Av. Piura 336. ☎ 073/258-571. Entrees S/18–S/34. MC, V. Dinner Mon–Sat. Map p. 367.

Máncora Nightlife

Máncora has a rowdy bar scene in season, with lots of young Peruvians, international travelers, and surfing fans hitting the rustic bars along the main drag, Av. Piura, and the clubs in hotels and *hostales* on the beach.

Iguana's Place. A fun, rustic bar (restaurant and outdoors travel agency by day) for beers and cocktails. Av. Piura 245. ☎ 01/9853-5099.

★ **Poto Blanco (White Ass Bar).** This two-story bar at the party-hardy Point Máncora Beach hostel (p. 366) has great open-air views of the beach. It's a place to meet other young travelers and down innumerable tropical-themed drinks. On summer weekends, the hostel generally sponsors raucous parties. Playa del Amor s/n. ☎ 073/706-320.

★★ **Praia Bar.** A sleek bar and restaurant behind a pull-down metal garage door, this spot is more upscale than the rowdier bars along the main drag, but it has terrific nightly drink specials. Av. Piura 336. ☎ 073/258-571.

Runa Wasi. Within the large Sol y Mar *hostal*, this is the town's most happening disco, with a mix of Latin and international rock and pop, popular with both Peruvian and international young folks. Av. Piura s/n. ☎ 073-258-106.

Trujillo & Huanchaco Hotels

> The upscale Gran Hotel El Golf enjoys a residential setting away from Trujillo's hustle and bustle.

★ Club Colonial HUANCHACO

Sequestered above the terrific, Belgian-owned restaurant of the same name are five pretty, chic rooms, nicely decorated with artwork and antiques. Several rooms have fantastic sea views and a couple even have balconies overlooking the promenade. With the best restaurant in town just downstairs, this is a smart choice. Av. La Rivera 541. ☎ 044/461-015. ccolonial@hotmail.com. 5 units. S/90–S/230 double. Rates include breakfast. AE, MC, V. Map p. 359.

kids Gran Hotel El Golf TRUJILLO OUTSKIRTS

A large, modern resort hotel in an upscale residential district and close to a golf country club, this is a good choice for families turned off by the bustle and taxis of Trujillo. Rooms are spacious and built around a large swimming pool and gardens. Additional distractions include tennis courts, a spa, and children's games. Los Cocoteros 505, Urbanización El Golf. ☎ 044/484-150. www.granhotelgolftrujillo.com. 120 units. $110–$123 double; $200–$275 suite. Rates include breakfast. AE, V. Map p. 359.

kids Hostal Bracamonte HUANCHACO

A mini-resort with the feel of a motel, this place is a couple of blocks from the beach and has a playground and gardens for kids to run around, as well as a large pool, barbecue grill area, and game room. Rooms are beachy, with tile floors but comfortable beds, while bungalows can sleep four. Jr. Los Olivos 503. ☎ 044/461-162. www.hotelbracamonte.com. pe. 28 units. S/117–S/185 double; S/190–S/285 suite. AE, DC, MC, V. Map p. 359.

★★ Hotel Caballito de Totora HUANCHACO

This formerly simple *hostal* facing the beach has undergone a dramatic transformation and is suddenly a chic and contemporary boutique-style hotel, Huanchaco's top choice. Rooms are very stylish and comfortable, and many have excellent sea views. Out back is a great garden area and pool. Av. La Rivera 348. ☎ 044/462-636. http://hotelcaballitodetotora. blogspot.com. 21 units. S/190–S/220 double; S/360–S/450 suite. AE, DC, MC, V. Map p. 359.

★ Hotel Colonial TRUJILLO

This midsize hotel in a handsome colonial house has been intent on upgrading its status in recent years, and it's now a very solid mid-range choice. Just a block from the Plaza de Armas, it has comfortable rooms overlooking the lovely interior patio, though the best ones open up to a great balcony with views of the Plaza. Jr. Independencia 618. ☎ 044/258-261. www.hostalcolonial.com.pe. 40 units. S/85 double. Rate includes breakfast. No credit cards. Map p. 359.

> *True to its name, Hotel Colonial in Trujillo exudes colonial flavor.*

★★ Hotel Libertador Plaza Mayor Trujillo TRU-JILLO Trujillo's top hotel has a privileged location—right on the Plaza de Armas—and great historic bones. Occupying an extraordinary colonial mansion with a courtyard patio and a great pool amid gardens, it's both convenient and relaxed. There's colonial flavor in public areas, and accommodations are large, if not flat-out luxurious. Those on the interior are quieter and have views of the pool. The hotel restaurant, Las Bóvedas, has an excellent brunch. Jr. Independencia 48, Plaza de Armas. ☎ 044/232-741, or 877/778-2281 in the U.S. and Canada. www.libertador.com.pe. 78 units. $125 double; $165–$1,950 suite. Rates include breakfast. AE, DC, MC, V. Map p. 359.

kids Huanchaco International Hotel HUANCHACO Right on the beach but a bit out of town and removed from Huanchaco's restaurants and bars, this modern beach resort hotel is nonetheless a good place for families. It has a huge pool; yellow-and-white house-like bungalows; and gardens with sea views. Autopista a Huanchaco Km 13.5, Playa Azul. ☎ 044/461-754. www.huanchacointernational.com. 40 units. $49 double; $69–$89 bungalow. Rates include breakfast. AE, DC, MC, V. Map p. 359.

★ La Casa Suiza HUANCHACO This longtime backpackers' favorite is a welcoming and friendly inn. It's a warren of plain rooms of all shapes and sizes scattered across three floors, but there's a great rooftop terrace, cable TV room, Wi-Fi, good restaurant, and surfing gear. It's hard to beat for the bargain prices. Los Pinos 451. ☎ 044/461-285. www.lacasasuiza.com. 16 units. S/50–S/75 double with private bathroom; S/20–S/25 per person shared room. No credit cards. Map p. 359.

Chiclayo Hotels

> The contemporary Costa del Sol is one of the best lodging options in downtown Chiclayo.

★ Casa Andina Select CHICLAYO

Formerly the Gran Hotel Chiclayo, this hotel, the city's largest, was undergoing renovations at press time. The existing modern block offers the kind of spacious and well-equipped rooms that appeal to business travelers, as well as an attractive pool for leisure visitors, and the renovation will likely bring a higher standard to the hotel's existing quality. Av. Federico Villarreal 115. ☎ 01/213-9739. www. granhotelchiclayo.com.pe. 129 units. $98 double; $158 suite. Rates include breakfast and airport transfer. AE, DC, MC, V.

★ Costa del Sol CHICLAYO

This midsize hotel offers a good mix of amenities, with remodeled, stylish rooms. Unexpected features include a rooftop pool and Jacuzzi with dry sauna. Av. José Balta 399. ☎ 074/227-272. www.costadelsolperu.com. 40 units. S/329 double; S/503 suite. Rates include breakfast. AE, DC, MC, V.

Hostal Royal CHICLAYO

Although a bit run-down, this large, rambling old colonial hotel right on the Parque Principal manages to have a great bit of character, with a formerly grand, winding central staircase and large, Spartan rooms (some with balconies overlooking the plaza). Jr. San José 787. ☎ 074/233-421. 30 units. S/45 double. No credit cards.

★★ Hostería San Roque LAMBAYEQUE

One of the best options for anyone primarily interested in the great museums in and near Lambayeque is this cheerful boutique hotel in a handsomely renovated, 19th-century colonial manor house. The colorful and simply furnished rooms are built around three interior patios and a large, inviting outdoor pool. 2 de Mayo 437. ☎ 074/282-860. www. hosteriasanroque.com. 12 units. S/160 double. Rate includes breakfast. MC, V.

★ Hotel Embajador CHICLAYO

This smart new hotel, with a gleaming mirrored exterior, has cheerfully colored, clean rooms and friendly, attentive service, as well as Wi-Fi and a nice little coffee shop and cafeteria. 7 de Enero 1368. ☎ 074/204-729. http:// hotelembajadorchiclayo.com. 20 units. S/100–S/120 double; S/150 suite. MC, V.

★★ Los Horcones de Túcume TÚCUME

The best place to stay in the entire Chiclayo area is quite removed. In the shadows of the Túcume pyramids, this relaxing and well-designed inn, constructed of adobe and local *algarrobo*-wood beams and designed by the architect-owner, makes for a peaceful retreat. Rooms are enormous and colorfully decorated, with sun terraces and luxurious bathrooms. Antigua Ctra. Panamericana Norte Lambayeque-Túcume (30km/19 miles north of Chiclayo). ☎ 01/242-1866 in Lima. www. loshorconesdetucume.com. 12 units. $40 double. Rate includes breakfast. MC, V.

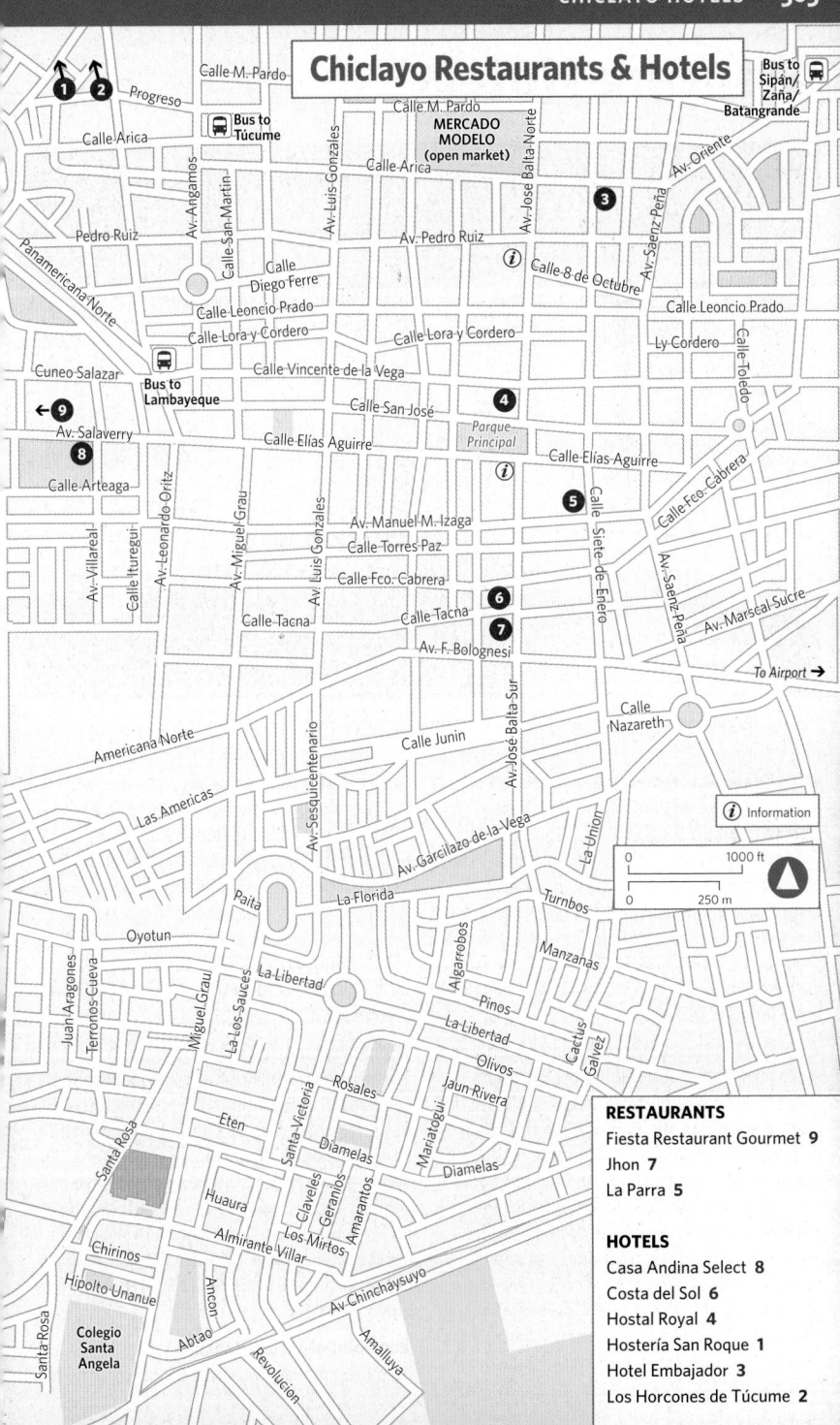

Chiclayo Restaurants & Hotels

RESTAURANTS

Fiesta Restaurant Gourmet 9

Jhon 7

La Parra 5

HOTELS

Casa Andina Select 8

Costa del Sol 6

Hostal Royal 4

Hostería San Roque 1

Hotel Embajador 3

Los Horcones de Túcume 2

Máncora Hotels

> *Rustic elegance right on the beach at Vichayito Carpas & Bungalows.*

★ kids **Costa Azul Hotel & Spa** ZORRITOS
The most upscale of offerings on low-key Zorritos, this comfortable spa-hotel is built around a pair of lush pools and has clean and cute rooms, an attractive beachside restaurant, and the only spa in the area, making it an oasis way up north. **Antigua Ctra. Panamericana Norte Km 1229. ☎ 98/105-6361. www. costaazulperu.com. S/255 double. Rate includes breakfast. AE, DC, MC, V.**

★★★ **DCO Suites, Lounge & Spa** LAS POCITAS
A portent of the future along the northern coast, this stunningly stylish and sophisticated boutique hotel is perched right on the beach. Airy and contemporary, the multilevel hotel is like an architect's townhouse, blending local stone and wood with retro accents. Rooms are chic, and there's an infinity pool; lounge terrace; open-air, top-floor spa; and swank restaurant. **Las Pocita s/n (3km/2 miles south of Máncora). ☎ 01/242-3961 for reservations, or 073/258-171. www.hoteldco.com. 7 units. $180 double; $280 master suite. Rates include breakfast. AE, DC, MC, V.**

★★ **Hotelier Arte y Cocina** LAS POCITAS
A small and unpretentious three-story place with friendly and knowledgeable young owners, this little hotel has a cool vibe, excellent beachside restaurant, and stunning sea views. Rooms are minimalist and modern, with a beachy feel. **Las Pocitas s/n (1km/½ mile south of Máncora). ☎ 073/258-702. www.hotelier. pe. 9 units. S/120–S/360 double. Rates include breakfast. MC, V.**

Pink Parrot MÁNCORA
This airy beachside place, previously called Del Wawa, is one of the better inexpensive options in Máncora. It's got a funky, relaxed style (perhaps too relaxed: management can be lax), and some of the new rooms have high ceilings and loft spaces. On weekends, the bar is hopping, and loud. **Av. Piura s/n (facing El Point coastline). ☎ 073/258-427. www. delwawa.com. 10 units. S/65–S/90 double. No credit cards.**

The Point Máncora Beach MÁNCORA
If you've come north strictly for the party, this

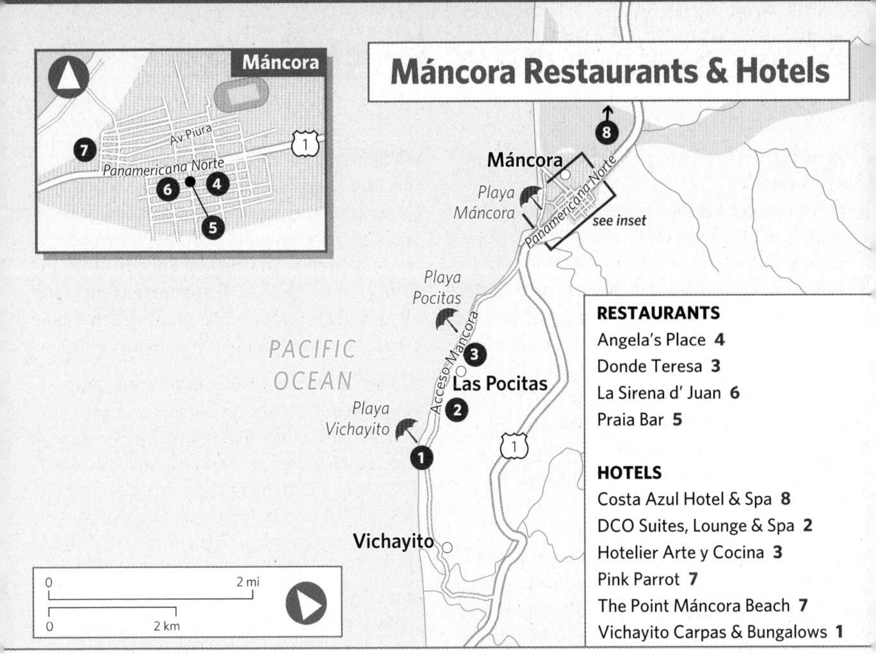
Máncora Restaurants & Hotels
Máncora
Av Piura
Panamericana Norte
Playa Máncora
see inset
Playa Pocitas
PACIFIC OCEAN
Acceso Máncora
Las Pocitas
Playa Vichayito
Vichayito
0 2 mi
0 2 km
RESTAURANTS
Angela's Place 4
Donde Teresa 3
La Sirena d' Juan 6
Praia Bar 5
HOTELS
Costa Azul Hotel & Spa 8
DCO Suites, Lounge & Spa 2
Hotelier Arte y Cocina 3
Pink Parrot 7
The Point Máncora Beach 7
Vichayito Carpas & Bungalows 1

backpacker's resort on the beach should do the trick. It's got a large pool and a rocking bar, as well as a mix of two-story beachfront bungalows and shared hostel rooms, though sleep seems to be the last thing on anyone's mind. **Playa del Amor s/n. ☎ 073/706-320. www.thepointhostels.com. 30 units. S/68 private cabin; S/20–S/30 per person shared dorm room. No credit cards.**

★★ kids **Vichayito Carpas & Bungalows**
VICHAYITO Formerly a low-key eco-lodge, this sprawling property on one of the prettiest stretches of sandy beach in the region has been given a top-to-bottom makeover. Joining the thatched-roof bungalows are newly added *carpas* (luxury tents) with first-class furnishings and amenities housed within a tough French canvas. A brand-new spa has been added to the pool, restaurant, game room, and outdoor hot tub. **Antigua Ctra. Panamericana Norte Km 1211. ☎ 01/436-4173 or 01/434-1452. www.vichayito.com. 34 units. $85–$150 bungalow; $120–$160 *carpa*. Rates include breakfast. AE, DC, MC, V.**

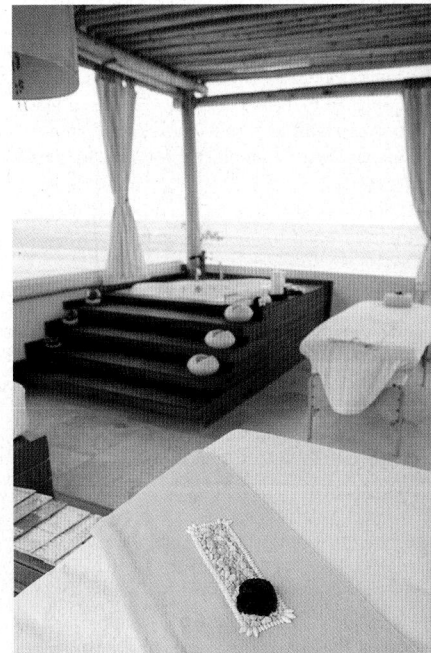

> *Hear waves crash below while getting a massage on the rooftop of DCO Suites, Lounge & Spa.*

Northern Coast Fast Facts

Arriving

BY PLANE

TO TRUJILLO **LAN** (☎ 01/213-8200; www.lan.com) and **Star Peru** (☎ 01/705-9000; www.starperu.com) fly daily to Trujillo from Lima (1 hr.); flights arrive at the **Aeropuerto Carlos Martínez de Pinillos** in the Huanchaco district (☎ 044/464-013), about 20 minutes northwest of downtown (a taxi costs about S/20).

TO CHICLAYO **Star Peru** and **LAN** also fly daily from Lima to Chiclayo (90 min. if direct; 2 hr. with stopover in Trujillo); flights arrive at **Aeropuerto José Quiñones González,** Av. Bolognesi s/n (☎ 074/233-192), 2km (1¼ miles) east of downtown (a taxi costs S/5).

TO MÁNCORA **LAN** flies daily to Piura or Tumbes from Lima. **Taca** (☎ 01/511-8222; www.taca.com) recently announced daily direct flights from Chiclayo to Piura. The drive to Máncora from Piura is longer (2½ hr.) than from Tumbes, but flights arrive throughout the day, giving you daylight hours to make it to your destination. Flights to Tumbes, about an hour north of Máncora, depart daily only at 7:15pm, arriving at 9pm. From the airports, private taxis to Máncora run about $80 from Piura and $50 from Tumbes; buses make the trip for S/18. **Máncora Travel** (☎ 073/258-571; www.mancoratravel.com.pe) arranges shared and private minivans from Piura and Tumbes ($50–$150).

BY BUS

TO TRUJILLO The major companies making the 9-hour trip from Lima are **Ormeño** (☎ 01/472-5000; www.grupo-ormeno.com.pe), **Cruz del Sur** (☎ 01/311-5050; www.cruzdelsur.com.pe), and **Oltursa** (☎ 01/708-5000; www.oltursa.com.pe). **Transportes Línea** (☎ 044/286-538 in Trujillo, 076/823-956 in Cajamarca, or 074/233-497 in Chiclayo; www.transporteslinea.com.pe) makes the 6-hour trip from Cajamarca and 3-hour journey from Chiclayo. **ITTSA** (☎ 044/222-541; www.ittsabus.com) goes to Trujillo from Lima, Chiclayo, and Piura. TO CHICLAYO The major carriers making the 8-hour trip from Lima are **Ormeño, CIVA** (☎ 01/418-1111; www.civa.com.pe), **Cruz del Sur,** and **Oltursa. Transportes Línea** and **ITTSA** make the 3-hour trip from Trujillo to Chiclayo. Transportes Línea is also the major carrier from Cajamarca. TO MÁNCORA The bus from Lima is about 16 hours (overnight recommended) on **Cruz del Sur, Oltursa,** and **CIVA.** From Chiclayo, **Transportes Chiclayo** (☎ 074/223-632; www.transporteschiclayo.com) travels to Máncora (just under 7 hr.).

ATMs/Cashpoints/Currency Exchange

TRUJILLO Banks that exchange traveler's checks and cash and that have ATMs are Banco de Crédito, Jr. Gamarra 562 (☎ 044/242-360), and Banco Latino, Jr. Gamarra 572 (☎ 044/243-461); Interbanc, located at Pizarro and Gamarra, has a Cirrus/PLUS ATM. Money-changers can usually be found hanging about the Plaza de Armas or along Gamarra. CHICLAYO Most banks (and money-changers) are clustered around the Parque Principal, including Banco de Crédito, José Balta 630, and Interbanc, Elías Aguirre 680. MÁNCORA There are ATMs on Av. Piura.

Dentists & Doctors

TRUJILLO Clínica Peruana-Americana, Av. Mansiche 702 (☎ 044/231-261); Hospital Regional Docente de Trujillo, Av. Mansiche 795 (☎ 044/231-581); and Hospital Belén, Bolívar 350 (☎ 044/245-281). HUANCHACO A *posta médica* (clinic) is at Atahualpa 437 (☎ 044/461-547). CHICLAYO Hospital Las Mercedes, González 635 (☎ 074/237-021); Clínica Lambayeque, Vicente de la Vega 415 (☎ 074/237-961); and Clínica Santa Cecilia, González 668 (☎ 074/237-154). LAMBAYEQUE Hospital Belén de Lambayeque, Ramón Castilla 597 (☎ 074/281-190).

Emergencies

For general emergencies, call ☎ **105.** For fire, call ☎ **103.**

Internet Access

TRUJILLO Cibercafé Internet, Manuel María Izaga 716 (☎ 044/228-729), and Deltanet, Orbegoso 641 (☎ 044/294-327). CHICLAYO Sic@n Internet, Vicente de la Vega 204 (☎ 074/227-668), and Efenet, Elías Aguirre 181 (no phone). There are also Internet *cabinas* clustered around the Parque Principal and on

Manuel María Izaga near Av. Balta. **MÁNCORA** Your best bet is hotels with Wi-Fi, although there are a couple unnamed Internet *cabinas* on Av. Piura.

Pharmacies

TRUJILLO There are InkaPharma locations at Jr. Pizarro 525 and Jr. Bolívar 623; Botica Fasa at Jr. Pizarro 525 and Jr. Bolívar 393. **CHICLAYO** There are InkaPharma outlets at Av. Balta 1095, and Botica Fasa at Av. Balta 390 and 999. **MÁNCORA** There's a Botica San José at Av. Piura 525.

Police

TRUJILLO The tourist police are located at Independencia 630 (☎ 044/291-705). For complaints, you can also call the Tourist Protection Service at ☎ 044/204-146. **CHICLAYO** The tourist police are located at Sáenz Peña 830 (☎ 074/236-700). **MÁNCORA** The national police are on Av. Piura s/n.

Post Office & Mail

TRUJILLO The post office is at Independencia 286 (☎ 044/245-941); a DHL/Western Union branch is at Almagro 579 (☎ 044/203-686). **CHICLAYO** The post office is at Elías Aguirre 140 (☎ 074/237-031).

Public Transportation

TRUJILLO *Combis* cost S/1; buses travel from just outside the *centro histórico* in Trujillo to Huanchaco (S/3). **CHICLAYO** *Combis* and omnibuses are most useful for getting to Lambayeque and several archaeological sites outside Chiclayo (S/2).

Rental Cars

TRUJILLO To travel to Chan Chan and other sites, or around the northern region: Global Car Rental, Ecuador 122, of. 201, Urbanización El Recreo (☎ 044/295-548). **CHICLAYO** A rental car might be useful to travel to Lambayeque, Sipán, Túcume, and other sites; Chiclayo Rent a Car in the Casa Andina Select, Av. Federico Villarreal 115 (☎ 074/237-512), rents four-wheel-drive vehicles. **MÁNCORA** Most car-rental agencies are located in Piura. Rent a Car San José (☎ 073/303-240) has good cars ($40–$50 per day) in Piura and meets travelers at the airport.

Safety

Up and down the coast, night buses especially have a reputation for being unsafe. Trujillo and Chiclayo are like any other city, in which caution

should be exercised at night and walking alone. In Máncora, travelers should be careful not to buy drugs from strangers and *mototaxistas* (*mototaxi* drivers) or change dollars on the street.

Taxis

TRUJILLO Taxis are plentiful in Trujillo. Most in-town fares, inside the Av. España ring, are about S/3. A taxi ride to Chan Chan or Huanchaco costs about S/15. You can hire taxis by the hour (S/20) or by the day (S/100–S/125) to tour archaeological sites in the environs. **CHICLAYO** Inexpensive *mototaxis* buzz about downtown, as do regular taxis. You can hire the latter by the hour (S/25) or by the day (S/120–S/150) to tour archaeological sites or to visit Lambayeque. A round-trip taxi ride to Túcume from Chiclayo costs about S/70. **MÁNCORA** Unless you have a rental car, getting around the region is almost entirely by *mototaxi* (S/2 for a basic journey).

Telephone

Trujillo's area code is 044; the Telefónica del Perú office is at Pizarro 561. Chiclayo's area code is 074; the Telefónica del Perú office is Elías Aguirre 631. Máncora's area code is 073.

Tours

TRUJILLO Agencies offering standard city and archaeological tours include Guía Tours, Jr. Independencia 580 (☎ 044/245-170); Chacón Tours, Av. España 106 (☎ 044/255-212); Consorcio Turístico del Norte, Jr. Pizarro 478 (☎ 044/205-645); and Trujillo Tours, Diego de Almagro 301 (☎ 044/233-091). Most standard tours cost S/45 to S/60 per person. Tours to El Brujo are generally S/90 to S/120. **CHICLAYO** Sipán Tours, 7 de Enero 772 (☎ 074/229-053), is one of the most reputable agencies in town offering city and archaeological tours.

Visitor Information

TRUJILLO iPerú offices are located at the airport (☎ 044/464-226) and downtown at Jr. Diego de Almagro 420 (Plaza Mayor; ☎ 044/294-561; Mon–Fri 9am–1pm and 2–5pm). **CHICLAYO** The iPerú office is located at Av. Sáenz Peña 838 (☎ 074/205-703). **MÁNCORA** Your best source of information is www.vivamancora.com, a good site for information including distances; details on the best surf spots, breaks, equipment, and lessons; and fishing and diving.

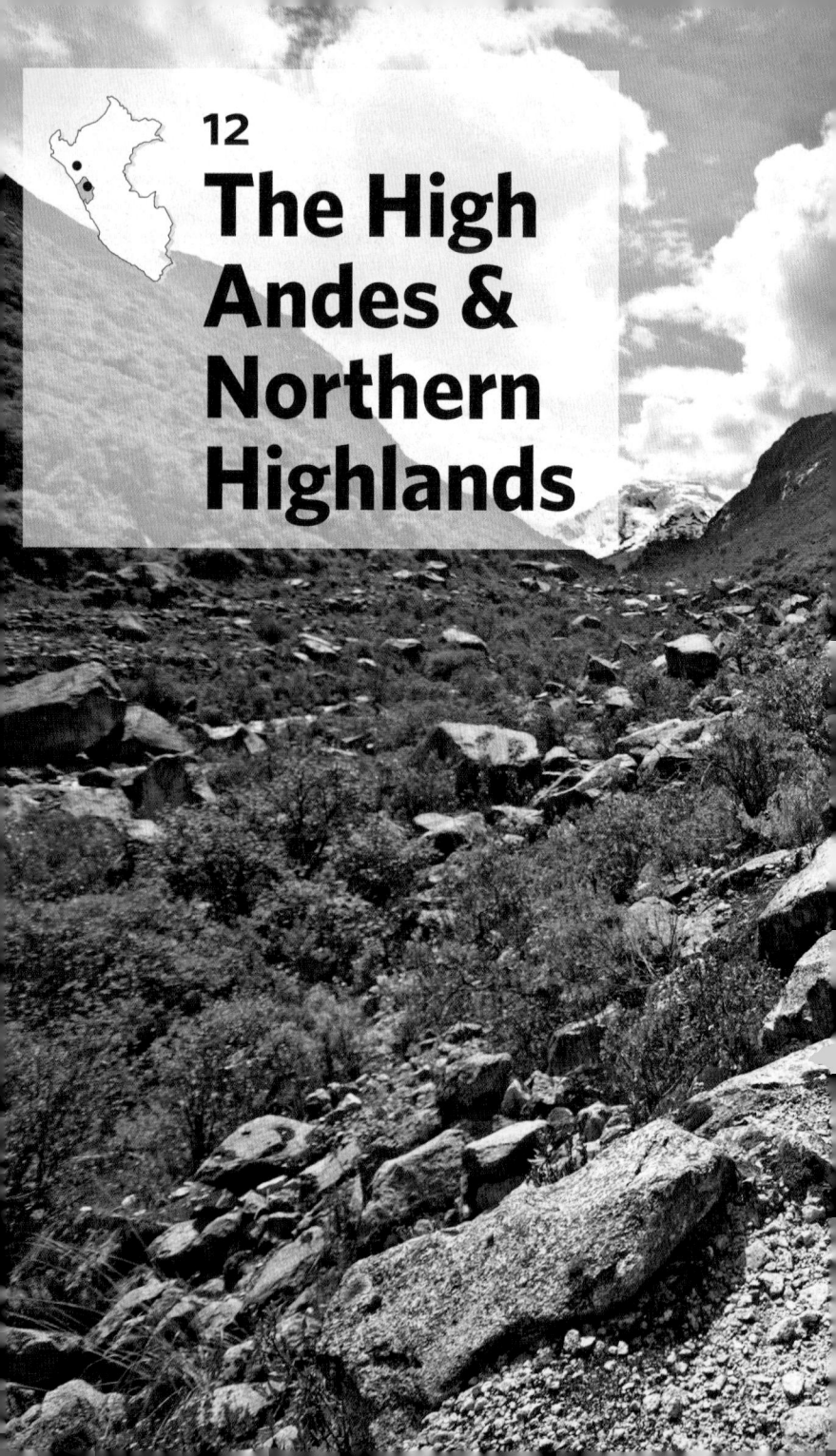

Favorite High Andes & Northern Highlands Moments

The Cordillera Blanca is the base for outdoor adventurers in Peru. The spectacular mountain range and Callejón de Huaylas, the valley it skirts, are the country's premier spots for mountain climbing and trekking. But the area is not just for experienced outdoors fanatics: There are also gentle hikes, 3,000-year-old ruins, and stunning mountain scenery. In the northern highlands, Cajamarca is an Andean gem, often called "the Cusco of the north," and while it has much of that city's colonial character, it's not burdened by Cusco's unrelenting tourist industry. Blessed with great weather and surrounded by verdant countryside and mysterious ruins, Cajamarca begs to be discovered.

> PREVIOUS PAGE *The Cordillera Blanca, the world's highest tropical mountain range, is a beacon for climbers and trekkers.* THIS PAGE *Cajamarca has great colonial architecture and a lovely highland setting, but few of Cusco's crowds.*

1 Marveling at Lagunas de Llanganuco. Whether you arrive on a day trip or as part of a multiday trek, this pair of brilliant turquoise, high-altitude lakes are a sight to behold. At 3,850m (12,631 ft.) above sea level and framed by Peru's highest and most beautiful peaks, they are one of the most stunning sights in the country. See p. 381, **8**.

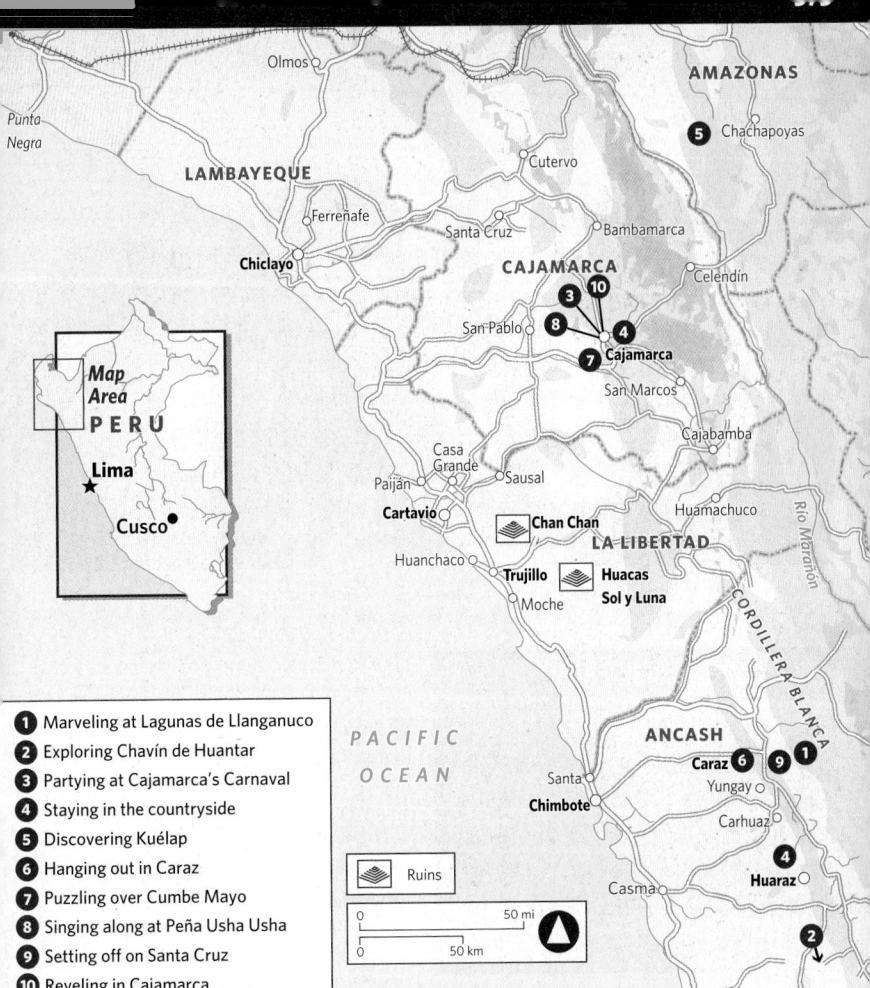

1 Marveling at Lagunas de Llanganuco
2 Exploring Chavín de Huantar
3 Partying at Cajamarca's Carnaval
4 Staying in the countryside
5 Discovering Kuélap
6 Hanging out in Caraz
7 Puzzling over Cumbe Mayo
8 Singing along at Peña Usha Usha
9 Setting off on Santa Cruz
10 Reveling in Cajamarca

Ruins

0   50 mi
0   50 km

2 Exploring Chavín de Huantar. These 3,000-year-old ruins south of Huaraz, a legacy of the Chavín culture, may not be as aesthetically appealing as stone constructions left behind by the Incas, but their importance is undeniable. In subterranean chambers, the 4.6m-tall (15-ft.) dagger-like Lanzón, emblazoned with animal figures of cult worship, is unique in the Peruvian archaeology canon. See p. 380, **7**.

3 Partying at Cajamarca's Carnaval. Normally a reserved, traditional Andean highland city, Cajamarca lets loose once a year during Carnaval, when its pre-Lenten festivities are the wildest in Peru. Full of music and dance, it also

takes on aspects of a high-school locker room. Paint, water, and even bodily fluids are flung around with abandon. See p. 462.

4 Staying in the countryside. The spectacular vistas of the high Andes and northern highlands are what draw people here, and staying at a relaxed country lodge with great views is one of the best ways to enjoy the region. My favorites are Lazy Dog Inn (outside Huaraz), Hotel Posada del Puruay (on the outskirts of Cajamarca), and Llanganuco Lodge (in the Callejón de Huaylas). See p. 404.

5 Discovering Kuélap. While at Machu Picchu you might run into your neighbor, these

> There's a touch of revolutionary spirit at Peña Usha Usha in Cajamarca.

> The 3,000-year-old ruins Chavín de Huantar, a fortress-temple of the oldest major pre-Columbian culture in Peru.

800-year-old Chachapoyas ruins are another story, the kind of place sought out by modern-day adventurers and would-be explorers. Crowning a mountain ridge, this massive fortress complex of round buildings, surrounded by a monumental defensive wall, is still being discovered. See p. 391.

6 Hanging out in Caraz. Popularly known as Caraz Dulzura (Sweet Caraz), this charming and relaxed mountain town, which escaped devastating earthquake damage, is known for its dairy products and honeyed sweets. With its year-round springlike climate, it makes a perfect base to chill before and after strenuous treks and mountain expeditions. See p. 385, **6**.

7 Puzzling over Cumbe Mayo. Outside Cajamarca, this enigmatic set of rock formations hold petroglyph-laced caves and grottoes, and an ancient pre-Inca aqueduct perfectly carved out of volcanic stone (which dates to c. 1000 B.C.). See p. 390, **10**.

8 Singing along at Peña Usha Usha. Regulars crowd the tables late at night at this tiny, graffiti-filled *peña* bar and plunge right in, singing Andean standards and protest songs until the wee hours. It's a rollicking good time. See p. 407.

9 Setting off on Santa Cruz. One of the most spectacular trekking routes in Peru, the Santa Cruz loop is a gorgeous 4- or 5-day hike through the Callejón de Huaylas, a feast of pristine lakes, rivers, and meadows, in the shadows of Peru's most imposing Andean peaks. It's popular for a reason. See p. 384.

10 Reveling in Cajamarca. Cajamarca is marked by one of the most violent episodes in Peruvian history—Pizarro's assassination of the Inca Atahualpa—but the city today has the charming feel of a laid-back colonial town, where locals stroll the delightful plaza eating artisanal ice cream. See p. 386.

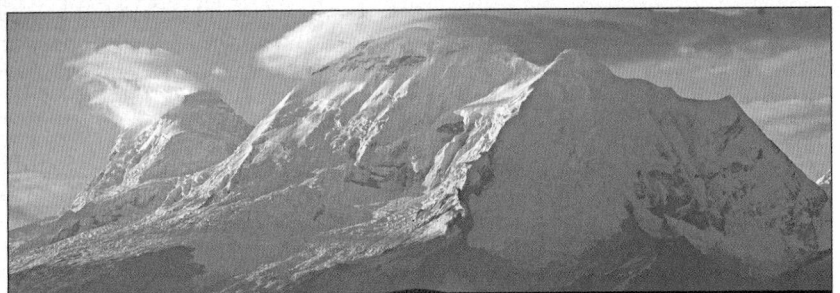

Parque Nacional Huascarán

The highest tropical mountain chain in the world, **Cordillera Blanca** possesses imposing peaks that stretch 180km (112 miles) through the heart of Peru. Fifty summits soar between 4,800 and 6,662m (15,748–21,857 ft.) high. Although the most challenging peaks are beacons to some of the most experienced mountaineers in the world, there are plenty of trekking and climbing activities for those who haven't quite perfected their ascent techniques. Access to the trailheads is fairly straightforward, reached by public transportation in just a few hours from Huaraz.

Nearly the entire Cordillera Blanca range forms part of **Parque Nacional Huascarán,** a 340,000-hectare (839,800-acre) national park, created in 1975, and a UNESCO World Heritage Site. Within the park are the towns Recuay, Huaraz, Carhuaz, Yungay, Huaylas, Bolognesi, Huari, Asunción, Piscobamba, and Pomabamba, several of which serve as bases for explorers. The park counts 32 peaks higher than 6,000m (19,685 ft.), which includes Huascarán, Peru's highest summit (6,768m/22,205 ft.) and the highest tropical mountain in the world, and Alpamayo, whose legendary fourth face is considered by many mountaineers to be the most beautiful in the world. There are also 269 lakes, 41 rivers, and indigenous flora and fauna that include among its spectacular roster of natural blessings 800 varieties of blossoming flowers (*Puya raimondi* and ancient *queñual* and cacti forests), Andean condors, vicuñas, pumas, and 100 species of birds.

In recent years, both trekkers and agencies have voiced concern about the deteriorating state of the Parque Nacional Huascarán, complaining that it is not well maintained. Some of the most popular trails are littered with refuse, and bribes have supplanted some group payment of entry fees (the single source of revenue for the seriously underfunded park). Neglecting this national treasure will greatly impact not only the local environment but also the local economy, as many individuals and communities depend upon the income produced by adventure travelers who come to enjoy the remote beauty of the Peruvian Andes.

The best time for trekking and climbing is during the dry season, between May and October, with July and August perhaps the top months. (The traditional dry season has shifted a bit in recent years, with rains often lasting until the end of May but often not beginning until late November.) Huaraz serves as the base for most adventure-tour operators; its roster of restaurants, bars, and hotels are where most travelers get acclimated to the altitude and organize forays into the mountains. Many expeditions to the scenic Llanganuco lakes in the Huascarán National Park begin at Yungay, while Caraz, a pretty and pleasant small mountain town known for its agreeable climate, is a quieter alternative to Huaraz, with similar services for ascents and other adventure activities.

The fee to enter Huascarán National Park is S/5 for a single-day visit and S/65 for visits of 2 days or more (valid up to 1 month). The entrance ticket to Huascarán National Park can be purchased at the Llanganuco and other entrances. Keep a copy of your passport ready when entering and leaving the park. For more information, visit www.areasprotegidasperu.com/pnh or whc.unesco.org/en/list/333.

Huaraz in 3 Days

At an elevation of 3,100m (10,170 ft.), Huaraz enjoys a spectacular setting but requires at least a day of acclimatization. The town is ringed by 20 snowcapped peaks, all of them higher than 6,000m (19,680 ft.). It's hardly a perfect alpine village, however; a major 1970 earthquake leveled nearly the entire city. Today the city thrives on the business of mountain adventure tourism. Adventurers will need at least a week (or longer if planning on doing a multiday trek or mountain expedition) to explore the great outdoors of the Huaraz area and the Cordillera Blanca. But in a short visit, one can get the flavor of this rugged if ramshackle Andean town and get a glimpse of the region's spectacular scenery.

> *The ramshackle Andean town of Huaraz is a gateway for trekkers and climbers.*

START Huaraz is 420km (261 miles) north of Lima (a 1-hr. flight).

❶ **kids** **Museo de Miniaturas del Perú.** This offbeat museum of miniatures, in the gardens of the Gran Hotel Huascarán east of town, isn't a major site and plenty of visitors would be just as well to skip it and jump to the next stop, but it does display dolls in traditional Peruvian dress as well as scale models of the ruins at Chavín de Huántar, pre-earthquake Huaraz, and the city of Yungay. ⏱ 30 min. Jr. Lúcar y Torre 46. ☎ 043/421-466. Admission S/3. Mon–Fri 8am–1pm and 3–6pm.

❷ ★ **Museo Arqueológico de Ancash.** Good clues to the long and complex history—dating back more than 12,000 years—of the high Andes around Huaraz are on view in this small but interesting and well-organized archaeology museum. It's chock-full of mummies, bizarrely adulterated crania (heads hammered in the interest of aesthetics and primitive medicine), and fantastic, finely carved monoliths from the Chavín, Recuay, and Huari cultures, as well as Moche and Chimú textiles, ceramics, and other pieces. ⏱ 45 min. Av. Luzuriaga 762. ☎ 043/421-551. Admission S/10 (good for same-day entrance to the Wilcahuaín ruins). Mon–Sat 9am–5pm; Sun 9am–2pm.

1 Museo de Miniaturas
   del Perú

2 Museo Arqueológico
   de Ancash

3 California Café

4 Mirador de Rataquenua

5 Monumento Arqueológico
   de Wilcahuaín

6 Baños Termales de Monterrey

7 Chavín de Huantar

8 Lagunas de Llanganuco

> *The Huari culture thrived in the region north of Huaraz, near the present-day Monumento Arqueológico de Wilcahuaín, around A.D. 1000.*

> *Ceramics of several pre-Columbian cultures are found at the Museo Arqueológico de Ancash.*

③ 🍺 ★★ **California Café.** This comfortable hangout has a relaxed lounge area and is popular with gringos and outdoor adventure types either preparing for or just back from a trekking or mountaineering excursion. It has fresh-roasted coffee, snacks, great breakfasts, Wi-Fi, and a book exchange. Av. 28 de Julio 562. ☎ 043/428-354. Items S/4–S/12.

Walk about an hour south to the mirador, following Av. Luzuriaga to Villón, then the road at the end, just beyond the cemetery; or take a taxi.

④ ★ **Mirador de Rataquenua.** For a taste of what draws people to Huaraz—the incredible mountain scenery—climb up to this lookout spot, a 3,650m (12,000-ft.) mountain pass with stupendous panoramic views. The trail (about 1 hr. each way) is steep, but there's also a less-demanding dirt road of switchbacks. Locals advise visitors to walk only during the day and with a group because the area has experienced a spate of crime in recent years. A round-trip taxi (S/25) is by far the safest way to go. ⏱1 hr.

Glaciar Pastoruri & *Puya Raimondi*

A good day trip from Huaraz is **Glaciar Pastoruri** (70km/43 miles south of Huaraz). This relatively flat glacier makes a worthwhile outing for those without the time, equipment, conditioning, or inclination to attempt one of the longer treks in the region. It requires acclimatization to the altitude, but the trek up the glacier (5,240m/17,192 ft.) isn't difficult—just 45 minutes one-way—and can be done without specialized equipment (though it does get cold, so parkas and good boots are required). Most organized trips to Pastoruri include a visit to the valley of Pachacoto, 57km (35 miles) south of Huaraz, where the Callejón de Huaylas's famous and ancient *Puya raimondi* plants (above) grow (found only in a few isolated, high-altitude parts of the Andes). The enormous, odd-looking and spiky plants aren't cacti but the largest members of the bromeliad family (which also includes the pineapple). The plants can reach a height of 12m (39 ft.) and live 100 years, but they flower just once and die immediately afterward. Their tragically brief but beautiful blooms usually occur in May and make for a stunning visual against the backdrop of snowcapped mountains. Organized Pastoruri/*Puya raymondi* visits begin at about S/30 per person. See p. 381 for tour groups.

> *Travelers returning from mountain treks often hit the mineral-rich, rejuvenating waters at the Baños Termales de Monterrey.*

Take a taxi or *combi* marked WILCAHUAÍN from the Río Quillcay bridge near Av. 13 de Diciembre north of Huaraz to Wilcahuaín (8km/5 miles; 30 min. with stops).

❺ ★ **Monumento Arqueológico de Wilcahuaín.** The Huari culture, an empire-building people, inhabited this region around A.D. 600 to 1000. These intact ruins, which encompass two sites named for their size, Grande and Chico, were burial grounds and storage centers. The major temple was built around 1100. Return *combis* to Huaraz leave from near Grande. ⏱ 1 hr. Ctra. Wilcahuaín s/n. No phone. Admission S/5 adults, S/2 students. Daily 8am–6pm.

Walk 6km (3¾ miles) from Wilcahuaín along the road to Caraz; or, from Huaraz take a *colectivo* from Av. Luzuriaga.

❻ kids **Baños Termales de Monterrey.** If you have time at the end of the day, visit these mineral-rich thermal baths in Monterrey, frequented by trekkers after area excursions and locals on weekends. Although the iron

> *Stone carvings found at Chavín de Huantar depict deities and creatures worshipped by the Chavín culture.*

and other minerals make the two large pools an unappealing brown, they do the job. ⊕ 1 hr. Monterrey. ☎ 043/427-690. Admission S/5. Daily 7am–6pm.

On Day 2, go on an organized tour to Chavín de Huantar, 110km (68 miles) east of Huaraz.

7 ★ ★ kids **Chavín de Huantar.** The best-preserved ruins of the Chavín culture are found at this nearly 3,000-year-old site, which features a U-shaped fortress-temple with excellent stonework constructed over several centuries. One of the oldest and most sophisticated cultures in the Americas, the Chavín reigned from 1200 to 200 B.C., and their influence stretched from Ecuador to southern Peru—making them perhaps more important than any other culture in Peru until the arrival of the dynasty-building Incas 2,000 years later. Although a UNESCO World Heritage Site, these ruins don't have the immediate aesthetic attributes of some Inca constructions, but they are unique among Peruvian ruins for their underground chambers. The

Castillo, or "castle," a large pyramid, is the main structure on the premises, built over canals. A large, sunken central plaza was a ceremonial gathering place. There are a dozen or more underground galleries, some of which were buried by a landslide in the 1940s. The undisputed highlight of the site, in an underground passage behind the original temple, is the **Lanzón,** a mammoth (4.5m-tall/15-ft.) and unusual cultist monolith carved out of white granite and shaped like a dagger. It depicts three figures worshipped by the Chavín culture: the serpent, the bird, and the feline, the latter the culture's principal deity. Other important artifacts, including the famous Tello Obelisk and Raymondi Stela, were long ago transferred to the Museo de la Nación in Lima. ⊕ 1 day. Monumento Arqueológico (Chavín de Huántar). ☎ 044/754-042. Admission S/11. Daily 8am–4pm. The easiest way to visit Chavín is by organized tour from Huaraz with Huaraz Chavín Tours or Pablo Tours (see "Practical Matters: Tour Agencies"). Most tours cost about S/50 per person (plus the ruins

> *The scenery along the Llanganuco–Santa Cruz trek makes it one of the most rewarding in South America.*

entrance fee); they leave Huaraz around 9am and return around 8pm. Chavín Express, Mariscal Cáceres 338 (☎ 043/424-652), also operates a couple of buses daily to Chavín from Huaraz.

Stay the night either in Yungay or Huaraz. On Day 3, go by organized tour or take a *colectivo* to the Llanganuco lakes, 26km (16 miles) northeast of Yungay and 56km (35 miles) north of Huaraz.

⑧ ★★★ ᴋⁱᵈˢ Lagunas de Llanganuco. One of the undisputed highlights of Parque Nacional Huascarán is the stunning sight of these two turquoise, glacier-fed alpine lakes. They lie at 3,850m (12,631 ft.) above sea level, framed by the Cordillera Blanca's highest snowcapped summits: Chopicalqui (6,354m/20,846 ft.), Huandoy (6,395m/20,981 ft.), and Huascarán (6,768m/22,205 ft.). The lakes are at their finest on clear mornings, when the sun makes them shimmer and their colors change. Take a rowboat (available for rent) out on the first of the two lakes, **China Cocha,** for a spectacular experience. Many visitors incorporate the lakes into multiday hikes, including one of the most celebrated in Peru, the Santa Cruz trek (p. 384). The most efficient way to see them

on a short trip is to take an organized tour from Huaraz (about S/35 per person; see below); many of these tours also stop in Yungay to see the Campo Santo (p. 384). ⏱ At least 3 hr. From Huaraz, take a Caraz-bound *colectivo* to Yungay, and in Yungay board a *combi* from Av. 28 de Julio.

Practical Matters: Tour Agencies

Virtually every agency in Huaraz runs the basic and most popular no- or little-difficulty programs to Lagunas de Llanganuco, Glaciar Pastoruri, and Chavín de Huántar for S/30 to S/45 per person. Agencies often pool travelers when they can't round up enough on their own. **Huaraz Chavín Tours,** Av. Luzuriaga 502 (☎ 043/421-578 or 01/447-0024; www.chavintours.com.pe), is a good company offering standard tours, including trips to Chavín de Huántar, Pastoruri Glacier, and Llanganuco lakes. **Pablo Tours,** Av. Luzuriaga 501 (☎ 043/421-145; www.pablotours.com), is a standard tour company, similar to Huaraz Chavín Tours but offering a few more options, including good group treks.

The Cordillera Blanca in 6 Days

With a week, you can take in Huaraz and the best of the Callejón de Huaylas, the valley that runs right down the middle of Peru. The spectacular Cordillera Blanca range, a string of dramatic snowcapped 5,000m (16,400-ft.) peaks east of the valley, is a magnet for thousands of mountaineers and adventure-sports travelers. Nearly the entire chain is contained within the protected Parque Nacional Huascarán (see p. 375), a UNESCO Biosphere Reserve and World Heritage Site. While the region appeals primarily to outdoor adventurers, those with less time and less interest in testing their physical mettle will appreciate the extraordinary alpine lakes, mountain towns, and busy markets.

> *Campo Santo is all that remains of the village Yungay, destroyed by a 1970 earthquake and landslide.*

START On Days 1 and 2, follow stops ❶ through ❽ in "Huaraz in 3 Days" (p. 376). On Day 3, take a *colectivo* from Huaraz north to Carhuaz (30km/19 miles; 30 min.).

❶ **Carhuaz.** One of the principal towns in the Callejón de Huaylas, this laid-back Andean village (2,650m/8,694 ft.) is becoming an alternative base for mountain-adventure travel. It has a pretty, palm tree–lined Plaza de Armas

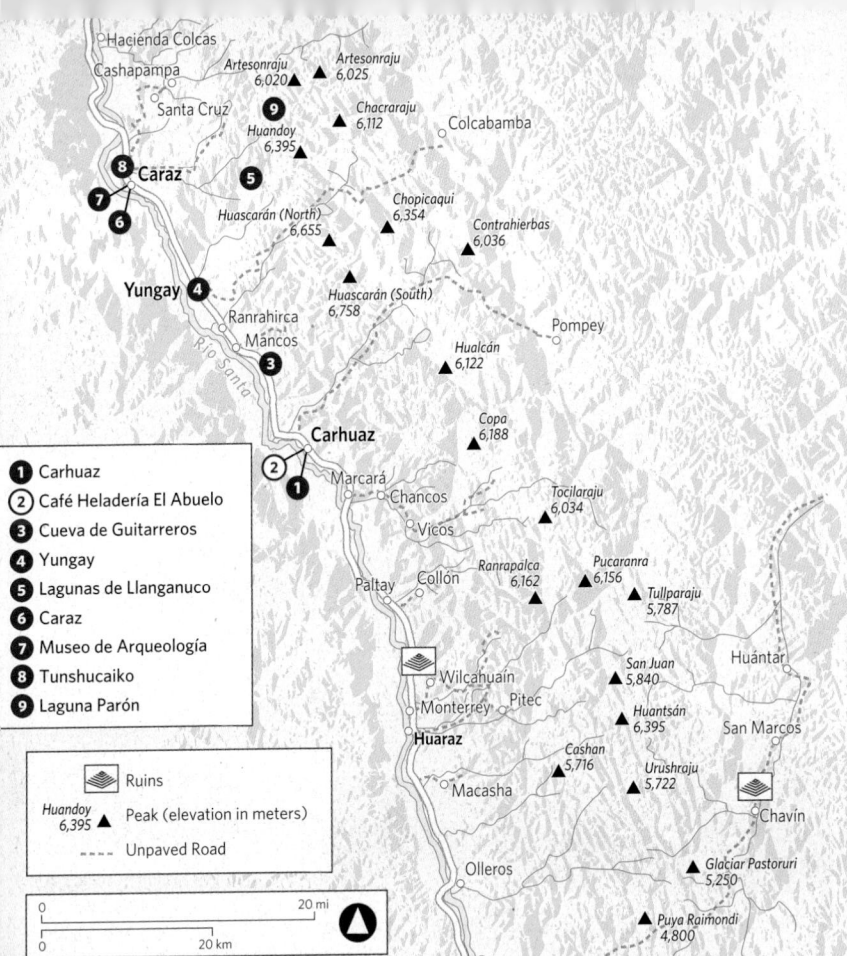

1 Carhuaz
2 Café Heladería El Abuelo
3 Cueva de Guitarreros
4 Yungay
5 Lagunas de Llanganuco
6 Caraz
7 Museo de Arqueología
8 Tunshucaiko
9 Laguna Parón

	Ruins
Huandoy 6,395 ▲	Peak (elevation in meters)
- - - -	Unpaved Road

0 ——————————— 20 mi
0 ——————————— 20 km

and is much quieter than Huaraz—except during its renowned Virgen de las Mercedes festival, which takes place for 10 days in mid-September and is perhaps the most raucous festival in the valley. The rest of the year, there are few sights other than the bustling Sunday market. ☺ At least 1 hr.

② ♨ ★ **Café Heladería El Abuelo.** Most people pop in for the famous homemade ice cream in unexpected flavors (including pisco sour and beer), but you can also get a nice lunch of Peruvian standards, sandwiches, and salads. La Merced 727. ☎ 043/394-149. Items S/8–S/18.

Take a 30-minute *combi* from Carhuaz, or walk 30 minutes south from Mancos across the river.

❸ Cueva de Guitarreros. This ancient cave, which may be 12,000 years old, contains primitive rock paintings. There are excellent views of the majestic Huascarán peak. ☺ 2 hr. Free admission. Daily dawn–dusk.

Travel via *combi* 20km (12½ miles) north from Carhuaz to Yungay.

❹ Yungay. This small Andean mountain town made headlines when it was essentially wiped off the map by a crushing landslide in 1970. A massive earthquake, which measured 7.8 on the Richter scale, sent tons of granite and ice from Huascarán's north peak raining down on the town, burying it in minutes and killing nearly 20,000 people—almost the entire population. The only survivors were a handful of children and others who scrambled to safety in the local cemetery. Only the facade of the village church remains from the original settlement. **Campo Santo** (Sacred Ground), the mound of rubble, has been preserved as a monument to the dead and is a macabre tourist attraction. The rebuilt town is a half-mile from the old Plaza de Armas. Built quickly and with few resources, the town is, as expected, ramshackle, though its magnificent alpine location remains. Today Yungay functions as

Llanganuco–Santa Cruz Trek

The Santa Cruz trek (4–5 days or more) is the classic route in the Cordillera Blanca, one of the most scenic on the continent and probably second in terms of popularity in Peru after the Inca Trail (p. 266). Touted as one of the top five treks in the world by several outdoor magazines, and manageable and relatively short by Cordillera Blanca standards, its beauty is extraordinary, taking in towering snowcapped peaks, brilliant lakes, glacier-fed rivers, waterfalls, and pretty meadows. The route across the Santa Cruz gorge usually begins in the village of Cashapampa. Most groups cap the trek with a visit to emerald-green Lagunas de Llanganuco, although not all include it as part of the actual trek; some go the final 2 hours by arranged car or *combi*. Although the 45km (28-mile) trail takes in some formidable elevations, ranging from 2,900 to 4,750m (9,514–15,584 ft.), it's rated moderate to difficult, and anyone in good physical shape who has allowed for time to acclimatize in Huaraz can do it. In peak season (July–Aug), the trail can be quite crowded and the campsites and pit toilets along the route become taxed. Trekkers can begin the trail either at Cashapampa (2 hr. by bus from Caraz) or Vaquería (2½ hr. by bus from Carhuaz). Some independent travelers prefer to start the trail at Vaquería because the daily bus from Huaraz allows time to make it to the campsite on the first day and get a good jump on the high pass the following day. All-inclusive treks from Santa Cruz to Llanganuco in a "pooled" service start at about $175 per person.

a transportation hub for those looking to approach the Lagunas de Llanganuco (stop ❺ on this tour). 🕐 At least 1 hr. Campo Santo: Admission S/2. Daily 8am–6pm.

On Day 4, take a *combi* from Yungay east to the lakes (26km/16 miles).

❺ ★★★ kids **Lagunas de Llanganuco.** These turquoise alpine lakes are one of the region's most spectacular sights. 🕐 At least 5 hr. See p. 381, ❽.

Start Day 5 by journeying 12km (7 miles) by taxi or *combi* north from Yungay.

❻ ★★ **Caraz.** Thoroughly charming and more attractive than highland neighbors that suffered much greater natural disaster, as well as nearly 1,000m (3,280 ft.) lower than Huaraz, Caraz makes an excellent, low-key base for trekking and climbing in the Cordillera Blanca. The town has a lovely, colonial-style Plaza de Armas and a growing infrastructure to serve trekkers and mountaineers. Many trekkers end up (and rest up) in Caraz after tackling the popular Santa Cruz route, although a good number embark from here to more remote treks into the northern Cordillera Blanca. 🕐 At least 2 hr.

❼ **Museo de Arqueología.** This small archaeology museum contains some deformed skulls and artifacts uncovered at the Cueva de Guitarreros (stop ❸ on this tour). 🕐 30 min. 1 de Mayo and Manuel Cáceres. ☎ 043/791-029. Admission S/3. Tues–Sun 9am–1pm and 2–5pm.

Walk about 2km (1¼ miles) north from the center of Caraz across the Río Llullán, near the turnoff to Laguna Parón.

❽ **Tunshucaiko.** This set of ruins, a collection of stone walls that's one of the largest in the Callejón de Huaylas and possibly built by the Chavín culture, dates to about 1800 B.C. 🕐 1 hr. Av. Noe Bazán Peralta s/n. ☎ 043/791-004. Admission S/3. Daily 9am–noon and 3–5pm.

On Day 6, travel 30km (19 miles) east of Caraz. *Colectivos* run from Santa Rosa in Caraz to Parón (90 min.), but they don't go all the way to the lake, requiring a lengthy hike. A taxi from Caraz (S/75 round trip) is a better if much more expensive option.

> *The brilliant turquoise waters of Laguna Parón, an alpine lake at 4,000m (13,120 ft.) above sea level.*

❾ ★★ **Laguna Parón.** At an elevation of more than 4,000m (13,120 ft.), this remote, ridiculously gorgeous and crystalline turquoise lake is surrounded by towering snowcapped peaks. At the head of the lake is the dramatic summit of Pirámide (5,885m/19,300 ft.). The rough but spectacular road getting here (making this an all-day trip) slices through a canyon with granite walls 1,000m (3,280 ft.) high and passes a number of rural villages; the last one before reaching the ravine and lake is Parón, marked by a tiny white colonial church. There's a gentle hiking trail along the edge of the lake, as well as a campsite/refuge. 🕐 At least 7 hr. www.huaraz.com/paron.

Cajamarca in 3 Days

A traditional highlands town with colonial beauty to spare, Cajamarca is surrounded by the Andes and fertile countryside. Just beyond the city are ancient archaeological sites and graceful hacienda estates. The Incas conquered the Caxamarca culture in the 15th century and transformed the settlement into a major link in the transcontinental Andes highway—until Francisco Pizarro arrived, marking the beginning of the end of the Inca Empire and the advent of colonial Peru. Famous for its dairy products, Cajamarca is filled with bakeries, cafes, and ice-cream shops, and this sedate city takes a wild turn during Carnaval celebrations, when revelers are doused with water and paint.

> The sculpted volcanic stone of Iglesia de San Francisco, on Cajamarca's Plaza de Armas.

START Cajamarca is 855km (531 miles) northeast of Lima, a 2-hr. plane ride or 12-hr. bus ride; or a 6-hr. bus ride from Trujillo or Chiclayo; begin at the market, on Jr. Amazonas (at Batán).

❶ ★★ Mercado Central. Cajamarca's colorful central market sprawls over several downtown streets. Besides dairy products and produce of all kinds, there are *alforjas* (saddlebags), ceramics, and Cajarmarquiña mirrors with decorative

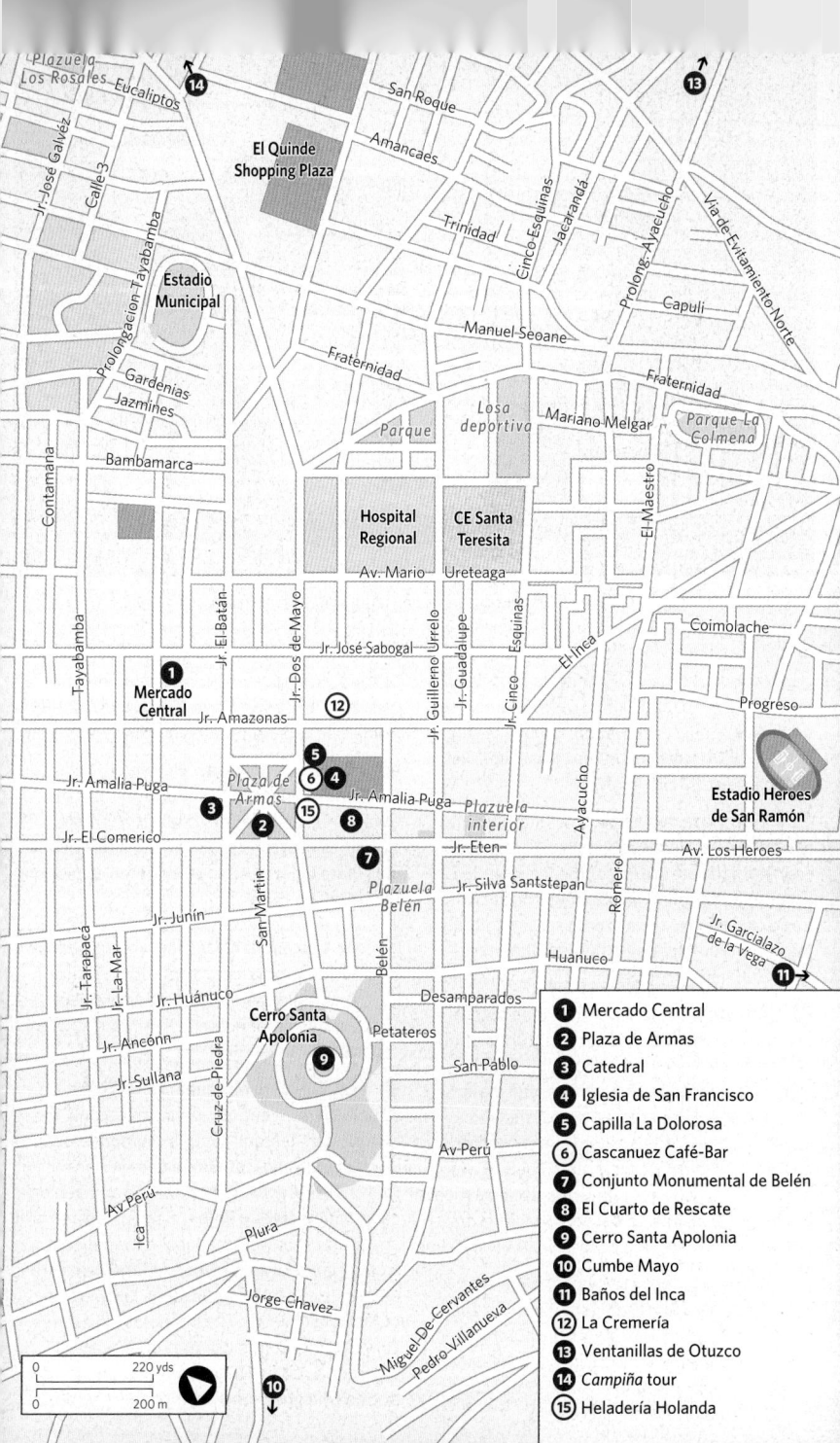

1. Mercado Central
2. Plaza de Armas
3. Catedral
4. Iglesia de San Francisco
5. Capilla La Dolorosa
6. Cascanuez Café-Bar
7. Conjunto Monumental de Belén
8. El Cuarto de Rescate
9. Cerro Santa Apolonia
10. Cumbe Mayo
11. Baños del Inca
12. La Cremería
13. Ventanillas de Otuzco
14. *Campiña* tour
15. Heladería Holanda

> *Cajamarca's Mercado Central covers several blocks and is an indispensable feature of city life.*

glass frames. But my favorite items for sale are the finely woven (and expensive), incredibly tall *sombreros de paja* (straw hats), famous throughout Peru. ⏱ At least 1 hr. Jr. Amazonas (btw. Batán and Apurímac). Daily 7am–5pm.

❷ ★★ kids **Plaza de Armas.** One of the finest plazas in Peru, it was originally a triangular courtyard during the era of the Incas. In 1532 Pizarro's small band of invading troops captured the square; they later assassinated the Inca Emperor Atahualpa here after a mock trial. ⏱ 30 min. Jr. del Batán (at Jr. Amalia Puga).

❸ ★ **Catedral.** Cajamarca's baroque cathedral, built in the 17th and 18th centuries upon original Inca stonework, is ornately carved from volcanic stone. A boldly carved main altar and a pulpit of carved wood and gold leaf enliven the rather gloomy interior. The cathedral's belfry was left unfinished to avoid paying a Spanish tax on finished ecclesiastical buildings. ⏱ 20 min. Jr. del Batán s/n (Plaza de Armas). No phone. Free admission. Daily 8–11am and 7–9pm.

❹ ★ **Iglesia de San Francisco.** Grander than the cathedral, this 18th-century church is a feast of stone sculpting. Inside is the Museo de Arte Religioso Colonial and its collection of colonial art, including icons and paintings. ⏱ 45 min. Jr. Dos de Mayo 435. ☎ 076/322-994. Admission S/3. Mon–Sat 9am–noon and 3–6pm.

❺ ★ **Capilla La Dolorosa.** This small, beautiful chapel is named for the patron saint of Cajamarca. Its facade is one of the greatest examples of stone carving in the city. ⏱ 20 min. Plaza de Armas. No phone. Free admission. Mon–Fri 9am–5pm.

❻ 🍴 **Cascanuez Café-Bar.** This congenial little spot is terrific for a quick snack or meal, such as *humitas* (made of sweet maize), or for dessert. Jr. Amalia Puga 554. ☎ 076/366-089. Items S/6–S/15.

❼ ★★★ **Conjunto Monumental de Belén.** Constructed almost entirely of volcanic stone, this historic architectural complex comprises a colonial church and women's and men's hospitals (now housing ancient medical and archaeological exhibits). **Iglesia Belén,** a church on a small and pretty square, is the most extraordinary work of colonial architecture in Cajamarca; its delicately carved baroque stone facade is one of the finest in Peru. The interior is full of large, carved polychromatic figures of angels and warriors, and the richly decorative cupola, supported by eight almost cartoon-like cherubs,

> *The extraordinary colonial architecture at Hospital de Hombres, a Franciscan hospital dating to 1630.*

> *Spanish conquistadors led by Francisco Pizarro invaded Cajamarca and executed the Inca emperor Atahualpa in 1533.*

was painted by highland natives. The **Hospital de Hombres** is an austere Franciscan hospital, which began receiving patients in 1630. To the right of the entrance is a gallery of vibrant paintings, several of them portraits of highlands *campesinos*, by Andrés Zevallos. Across the street is the **Hospital de Mujeres;** its facade is marked by a woman with child above the portal and, on either side of it, female figures with four breasts, symbols of the valley's fertility. Inside is the fascinating **Museo de Arqueología y Etnografía,** a museum with a collection of textiles and ceramics dating from as far back as 1500 B.C., replicas of Moche vessels, and local artisanship, dress (including Carnaval costumes), and silver *milagros* (prayer fetishes). ⊙ 2 hr. Jr. Belén s/n (at Junín). ☎ 076/322-601. Admission S/7.50 adults, S/4 students; ticket also admits visitors to El Cuarto de Rescate (below). Mon and Wed–Fri 9am–1pm and 3–6pm; Sat–Sun 9am–1pm.

❽ ⋆ **El Cuarto de Rescate.** This small room was the site of a tragic episode that changed the course of Peruvian history. In 1532, Francisco Pizarro and his troops took the Inca Emperor Atahualpa prisoner and held him in this small cell, in the back of a colonial courtyard, once part of Atahualpa's palace. Bargaining for his life, Atahualpa promised to fill the cell with gold and silver many times over (which is why the cell is now famously called the Ransom Room). The last intact example of Inca architecture in the city, it features a red line drawn across one wall, ostensibly the very line Atahualpa drew to demonstrate how high his men would fill the cell with treasures. Pizarro's men didn't wait for the promised riches, however, and executed Atahualpa here. ⊙ 30 min. Jr. Amalia Puga 750. ☎ 076/322-601. Admission S/7.50 adults, S/4 students; ticket also admits visitors to the Conjunto Monumental de Belén (above). Mon and Wed–Fri 9am–1pm and 3–6pm; Sat–Sun 9am–1pm.

Head to the southeast end of Jr. Dos de Mayo, 2 blocks from Plaza de Armas.

❾ **Cerro Santa Apolonia.** For good views of Cajamarca, climb the steep stairs to Santa Apolonia hill. Partway up is a small 19th-century chapel, the Virgen de Fátima. Rocks carved with petroglyphs are believed to date to the Chavín civilization (1000–500 B.C.). To the right of the white cross is a stone altar nicknamed the Inca's Throne, said to be the spot from which the Inca chief gazed down on Cajamarca and his troops. According to legend, a tunnel here went all the way to Cusco. ⊙ 1 hr. Admission S/1. Daily 8am–6pm.

> *Niches carved into the hillside at Ventanillas de Otuzco served as tombs for Caxamarca elite.*

On Day 2, join an organized tour to Cumbe Mayo (S/30), 20km (12 miles) southwest of Cajamarca; or, catch a *colectivo* leaving from behind Cerro Santo Apolonia.

⑩ ★★★ Cumbe Mayo. Tucked into rolling green hills, at an elevation of 3,400m (11,155 ft.), this enigmatic site of massive rock formations is peculiar enough on its own. But the evidence of human intervention—caves etched with petroglyphs and a pre-Inca aqueduct—lends it even more mystery. Carved out of volcanic stone in perfect, smooth lines, the canal, a marvel of hydraulic engineering, collected and redirected water from various sources on its way to the Pacific Ocean. At certain points, right angles ingeniously slow the flow of water and lessen the effects of erosion. Built around 1000 B.C. by the Caxamarca culture, the aqueduct stretches some 9km (5½ miles). Stairs carved in stone lead to sacrificial altars (for llamas, not humans) and platforms. The so-called Stone Forest contains rock formations that have over time come to be known as a group of monks, phalluses, breasts, a pirate's head, and mushrooms. ⏱ At least 4 hr. Daily 8am–5pm.

Return to Cajamarca and catch a taxi or *colectivo* **labeled** BAÑOS DEL INCA **at Jr. Amazonas, and head 6km (3¾ miles) east of town.**

⑪ ★ kids Baños del Inca. Cajamarca is famed for its thermal waters, and these relaxing pools have been in use since the time of the Incas (according to legend, Atahualpa was roused from his bath when Pizarro and his troops entered the city). Choose between a private indoor bath or a communal outdoor pool. ⏱ At least 1 hr. Av. Manco Cápac s/n. ☎ 076/821-563. Admission S/5 for individual bathing cabins; S/3 for communal pool. Daily 5am–7pm.

⑫ ☕ ★★ La Cremería. Cajamarca is famous for its dairy products and ice cream. This is one of the best shops in town and has great fruit flavors. Amazonas 741. ☎ 076/362-235. Items S/3–S/8.

On Day 3, take an organized tour to Ventanillas de Otuzco, 7km (4⅓ miles) northwest of Cajamarca; the tour (S/30) generally includes stops at a rural hacienda. You can also go via *colectivo;* catch one along Batán, a few blocks from the Plaza de Armas.

⑬ ★ Ventanillas de Otuzco. The Caxamarca culture created this large necropolis, with gravesites marked by small, square window niches carved out of a hillside, around 500 B.C. The niches served as funereal tombs for the society's elites. ⏱ 2 hr. Admission S/3. Daily 8am–5pm.

In the afternoon, take an organized tour into the countryside 30km (19 miles) north of Cajamarca.

⑭ ★ Campiña tour. The *campiña* (countryside) just beyond Cajamarca is a beautiful and fertile expanse of rolling hills, meadows, and eucalyptus trees. Agencies in town organize standard day trips (about S/25 per person) to rural haciendas, the best of which is **Granja Porcón** (☎ 076/365-631), a huge cooperative farm and agrotourism experiment that runs entirely on hydroelectric power. ⏱ At least 2 hr.

⑮ ☕ ★★ Heladería Holanda. One of Cajamarca's celebrated ice-cream shops, this Dutch-owned place is frequented by locals and is right on the Plaza de Armas. Jr. Amalia Puga 657 (Plaza de Armas). ☎ 076/340-113. Items S/3–S/8.

Kuélap: An Adventurous Side Trip from Cajamarca

Unknown to most of the hordes on their way to Machu Picchu, the citadel of Kuélap is one of the archaeological wonders of Peru. Like that tourist magnet, Kuélap is a formerly lost citadel tucked in highland cloud forest on top of an Andean mountain ridge. Yet Kuélap predates the Incas by at least 3 centuries. Because getting to the ruins—far northeast of Cajamarca, near the small town of Chachapoyas—is complicated, Kuélap for now remains primarily a destination for independent adventure travelers. The fortress complex, still being excavated, comprises some 400 buildings, most of them round, surrounded by a massive perimeter defensive wall (30m/98 ft. high). It must once have been nearly impregnable. The site is said to have employed more stone during its 200-year construction than even the Great Pyramids of Egypt. At its height, from around A.D. 1000 to 1300, Kuélap was home to 2,000 people—but not much more is known about its builders and inhabitants. They were most likely the Chachapoya, a group later absorbed by the Incas in their efforts to consolidate the highlands.

The ruins are open daily from 8:30am to 5pm; admission is S/12. Getting to Kuélap remains time-consuming and difficult, involving long buses to Chachapoyas, capital of the Amazonas department, or Tingo, plus a 3-hour *combi* ride to the site. (From Cajamarca to Chachapoyas, it's a scenic but wearying 16- to 20-hr. bus ride, or it's a less exciting 10-hr. journey from Chiclayo.) Organized visits might not suit modern-day explorers, but they are the most convenient way to get to what remains a remote outpost. Group trips from Cajamarca begin at $250 per person. Agencies handling Kuélap trips include **Cumbe Mayo Tours** and **Inca Baths Tours** (p. 409), both in Cajamarca. But much better is **Chachapoyas Tours,** Jr. Grau 534, Chachapoyas (☎ 041/478-078 or 866/396-9582 in the U.S.; www.chachapoyastours.com), an American/Peruvian-owned agency that specializes in tours of Kuélap and the region departing from Chachapoyas. Smaller tour groups in Chachapoyas run day trips to Kuélap for as little as $10 per person. There is a small Institute of National Culture *albergue* (lodge) at the site, which sleeps 8 in dorm rooms, and Chachapoyas Tours runs two comfortable lodges in Choctamel and Levanto (☎ 866/396-9582 in U.S, or 041/478-838; www.kuelap.org).

High Andes & Northern Highlands Outdoor Adventures A to Z

Hang Gliding

Pan de Azúcar (Sugar Loaf Mountain) near Yungay is the most common spot for hang gliding. For information, contact **Monttrek** (☎ 043/421-124; www.monttrek.pe).

Hiking & Trekking

Trekkers from around the globe are drawn to the Cordillera Blanca, which contains some of the greatest trails and most spectacular scenery in South America: gorgeous valleys and mountain passes nearly 5,000m (16,400 ft.) high, brilliant lakes, waterfalls, and rivers, enlivened by indigenous flora and fauna. There are campsites throughout the valley and

excellent guides, porters, and mules for expeditions. However, some caution is advised: Even the more accessible hikes in the region should be undertaken only by individuals in good physical shape; tackling a daunting mountain pass at nearly 5,000m (16,400 ft.) loaded with gear and food is not easy for those unaccustomed to high altitudes.

There are at least 3 dozen well-established and popular treks in the Cordillera Blanca (and many dozens more that you may have to yourself). Of the many treks possible from Huaraz, the classic **Llanganuco–Santa Cruz** route (see the box on p. 384) is one of the most ·

> For bragging rights, how about mountain biking at 4,878m (16,000 ft.) in the Andes?

beautiful on the continent and understandably the most popular. The 45km (28-mile) route across the Santa Cruz gorge usually begins in the village of Cashapampa and makes its way to the emerald-green lakes at the Llanganuco ravine in 4 or 5 days. Other popular circuits include **Alpamayo,** a beautiful trek among snowcapped summits (about 12 days); **Cedros Gorge,** which takes in mountains in the northern sector of the Huascarán National Park (4 days); and **Llanganuco** and **Portachuelo,** a less demanding trek through the Quillcayhuanca ravine (1–2 days). Other well-known routes are: **Cojup Valley** (Huaraz to Laguna Palcacucha), 20km (12 miles) and 2 days (moderate); **Laguna Churup,** 25km (16 miles) and 1 to 2 days (difficult); **Olleros to Chavín,** a pre-Columbian trail that ends at Chavín de Huántar, 40km (25 miles) and 3 days (moderate); and **Quebrada Quillcayhuanca to Cayesh,** 25km (16 miles) and 2 to 3 days (easy to moderate).

The Casa de Guías (see p. 394) in Huaraz has detailed information about these and other treks, and South American Explorers (www.saexplorers.org) produces a good map of various treks in the region. Another good resource is *Peru & Bolivia: Backpacking and Trekking* (Bradt Publications, 2002), by Hilary Bradt, which gives descriptions of a number of treks in the Cordillera Blanca. See also www.huaraz.com/routes.html and www.casadeguias.com.pe. There is also good information on day and multiday hikes at www.llanganucolodge.com/day-treks.htm and www.llanganucolodge.com/multi-day-hiking.htm.

While plenty of independent and self-reliant trekkers simply arm themselves with a trail map, hire an *arriero* (muleteer), and set off without a proper guide, others will definitely wish to go with an organized group. ★★★ **Explorandes Peru,** Av. Centenario 489, Huaraz (☎ 01/715-2323; www.explorandes.com), is an environmentally sensitive and serious agency, with fixed-departure treks in the Cordillera Blanca. Explorandes offers both hardcore- and soft-adventure programs, and will custom-tailor a trip for small groups. The agencies listed under "Mountain Climbing," on p. 394, are also well versed in organized treks of varying lengths.

Ice Climbing

The Cordillera Blanca—particularly the mountains Pisco, Ishinca, Huascarán, Alpamayo, Chopicalqui, and Artesonraju—is excellent for ice climbing. Contact **Pony Expeditions** (☎ 043/391-642; www.ponyexpeditions. com) or **Monttrek** (☎ 043/421-124; www. monttrek.pe) for more information.

Mountain Biking

The Callejón de Huaylas is one of Peru's top destinations for mountain biking, a sport still on the rise in Peru, with hundreds of mountain and valley horse trails cutting across fields, bridges, and creeks, and past traditional Andean villages. For experienced cyclists, there's the high-altitude thrill of climbing up to 5,000m (16,400 ft.) on mountain passes. Mountain bikes are available for rent in Huaraz by the hour, day, or week. ★★ **Mountain Bike Adventures,** Jr. Lúcar y Torre 530, Huaraz (☎ 043/424-259; www.chakinaniperu. com), run by Julio Olaza, is the top company for single-track riding in the Cordilleras Blanca and Negra. He has Trek front-suspension bikes for rent (including helmets) and offers several 4- to 7-day itineraries, as well as day trips. The company also runs a small and enjoyable guesthouse. Two of Peru's other top mountain-bike agencies are **Mountain Bike Adventures** in Huaraz (☎ 043/424-259; www. chakinaniperu.com) and **Pony Expeditions** in Caraz (☎ 043/391-642; www.ponyexpeditions. com). Both provide equipment rental and biking itineraries.

Getting Out

The previous general-interest tours don't budget time for day hikes, multiday treks, or other hard-core outdoor pursuits, which, let's face it, are the primary reason many travelers venture to the Huaraz region. Most visitors to the Cordillera Blanca mountain range, which has become one of the world's mountaineering meccas, want to view the stunning scenery of snowcapped peaks, glaciers, lakes, and rivers from up close. If you have additional time, or a specific interest in, say, trekking, mountaineering, or mountain biking, I suggest you focus instead on that activity and plan a trip around it.

Mountain Climbing

Climbing in the Cordillera Blanca ranges from rigorous but nontechnical climbs to highly technical ascents that should be attempted only with specialized gear and experienced guides. Several climbs are not only arduous, but also extremely dangerous. The optimal climbing season is May through September. Huaraz is the principal hub for contracting qualified guides and tour operators and for renting gear; Caraz, which provides similar infrastructure but on a smaller scale, is preferred by many outdoor folks for its calmer environment. The **Casa de Guías** in Huaraz, Parque Ginebra 28-G (☎ 043/421-811; www. casadeguias.com.pe), is the best pre-climb resource, with a list of registered and experienced guides.

For experienced climbers up to the challenge, the Cordillera Blanca is in a league with the Himalayas and Alps. The range includes 50 permanently snowcapped mountain peaks of more than 5,610m (18,400 ft.), packed into an area just 177km (110 miles) long and 19km (12 miles) wide. Tested mountaineers can bag several 6,000m (19,685-ft.) summits in a 2- or 3-week trip. Less experienced climbers can choose among several easier and more popular climbs. For all climbs, acclimatization is a prerequisite: Allow between 3 days and 1 week before attempting a serious ascent.

The peaks of **Ishinca** (5,534m/18,156 ft.) and **Pisco** (5,752m/18,871 ft.)—3-day climbs—require appropriate gear, conditioning, and guides, but can be undertaken by inexperienced climbers. One of the world's most beautiful mountains, **Alpamayo** (5,957m/19,544 ft.), is great for climbers with some experience. **Huascarán** (6,768m/22,205 ft.), the highest mountain in the Peruvian Andes and the tallest tropical mountain in the world, takes between 6 and 9 days and is an extremely challenging climb, suitable only for experienced climbers with technical knowledge.

The best mountain-climbing agencies are: **JM Expeditions,** Av. Luzuriaga 465, no. 4, Huaraz (☎ 043/428-017 or 01/426-0599; www. jmexpeditions.com), with good mountain-climbing equipment and guides; ★ **Montañero Aventura y Turismo,** Parque Ginebra 30B, Huaraz (☎ 043/726-386), operated by the founder of the Casa de Guías; ★★★ **Monttrek,**

Gear Checklist

Appropriate technical gear is required for nearly all treks and climbs in the Cordillera Blanca. If you're going with an organized group, you can rent anything that's not provided. Independent trekkers and climbers can also rent almost anything they need in Huaraz. Invariably, some equipment is dated and in less than optimal condition, so experienced mountain climbers pursuing technical climbs will want to bring their own. At a minimum, you'll need cold-weather and water-repellent clothing; heavy-duty, waterproof hiking or climbing boots; tent, sleeping bag, camping stove, and cookware; filter and/or water-purification tablets; compass; and topographical maps of trails.

Av. Luzuriaga 646, 2nd floor, Huaraz (☎ 043/421-124; www.monttrek.pe), a climbing and trekking pioneer, organizing hard-core ascents and expeditions, including ice and rock climbing, as well as programs for budget-conscious trekkers, with equipment rental, guides, and mountain- and ice-climbing classes (the owner,

> *If the technical ascents of Parque Nacional Huascarán aren't enough for you, try rock climbing.*

Pocho, has technical drawings of nearly every peak in the region); ★★ **Pony Expeditions,** Jr. Sucre 1266, Plaza de Armas, Caraz (☎ 043/391-642; www.ponyexpeditions.com), a professional outfitter run by a respected guide, Alberto Cafferata, with an extensive program of trekking and climbing itineraries, mountain biking, and rock and ice climbing; and **Pyramid Adventures,** Luzuriaga 530, Huaraz (☎ 043/421-864; www.pyramidadventures.net), a knowledgeable climbing agency run by a family of brothers.

For mountain-climbing gear, equipment rentals, and guides, visit **Galaxia Mountain Shop,** Leoniza y Lescano 603, Huaraz (☎ 043/422-792), offering good budget treks, and **MountClimb,** Mariscal Cáceres 421, Huaraz (☎ 043/426-060).

For more information about mountaineering and climbs in the region, see www.huaraz.com/climbs.html and www.casadeguias.com.pe.

River Rafting

The Río Santa, which runs the length of the Callejón de Huaylas from Laguna Conococha (near Carhuaz), is the site of river rafting, with sections that vary from easy (Classes II and III) to technical (Class V). The section most often rafted runs between Jangas and Caraz. Rafting season is May through September, when water levels are low. **Monttrek** (☎ 043/421-124; www.monttrek.pe) and a few other tour operators in Huaraz offer rafting.

Rock Climbing

Several agencies in Huaraz offer full-day rock-climbing tours in Caraz and Yungay, ranging from easy to moderate. Monterrey's Rocódromo and Uquia are the most popular spots. For more information, contact **Monttrek** (☎ 043/421-124; www.monttrek.pe); the agency even has an interior climbing wall at its headquarters in Huaraz.

High Andes & Northern Highlands Shopping

> *Finely woven, tall straw hats, or* sombreros de paja, *are ubiquitous in Cajamarca.*

Huaraz

★ Andean Expressions

Specializes in handprinted T-shirts with cool Andean designs; its products are sold in several shops in town and at its factory site in the Soledad district. **Jr. Julio Arguedas 1246.** ☎ **043/422-529. www.andeanexpressions.com. No credit cards. Map p. 399.**

★★ Artesanos Don Bosco

Just north of Huaraz, this incredible cooperative of woodworkers and furniture makers was begun 4 decades ago by an Italian Catholic priest who taught locals with few opportunities to become skilled craftsmen. The studio is open to the public; visitors should arrange a visit and get directions beforehand. The co-op now has a shop in Baltimore, MD (and a Facebook page). **Jr. Lima s/n, Jangas (near Marcará).** ☎ **043/83-7105. www.artesanosdonbosco.com. Map p. 399.**

Market Ortiz

This well-stocked supermarket has cheese and *manjar blanco* (the local, caramel-like sweet), good stuff to take along on an expedition. **Av. Luzuriaga 401.** ☎ **043/421-653. MC, V. Map p. 399.**

Mercados de Artesanía

There are daily open-air handicrafts markets along Pasaje Cáceres (the covered walkway off Av. Luzuriaga) and along the streets Juan de la Cruz Romero, Av. Raymondi, and Av. Tarapacá. A street market takes place Monday and Thursday on Av. Bolognesi and Confraternidad Oeste. **No credit cards. Map p. 399.**

Mercado de Huaraz (Mercado Modelo)

If you're stocking up on provisions for a trekking excursion, check out the main market, which has canned foods, nuts, and fresh fruits and vegetables. **Jr. Cruz Romero s/n (just south of Raymondi). No phone. No credit cards. Map p. 399.**

Cajamarca

★ Colors & Creations

An artisans' cooperative selling good-quality crafts, including ceramics, jewelry, and textiles. **Belén 628.** ☎ **076/343-875. No credit cards. Map p. 402.**

El Quinde Shopping Plaza

Cajamarca's major, modern shopping mall east of downtown has everything from shoe and clothing stores, a supermarket and a bookshop to ice-cream shops and a movie theater. **Av. Hoyos Rubio s/n (at Jr. Sor Manuela Gil).** ☎ **076/344-099. Map p. 402.**

★★ Mercado Central

The focus of shopping in Cajamarca, for locals as well as visitors, is the colorful, sprawling central market. It's a great place to absorb the flavor of Cajamarca and a genuine Andean town market. Items to look for include *alforjas* (saddlebags), decorative glass-and-silkscreen mirrors, and dairy products, but it's also the place to nab one of those finely crafted, very tall straw hats that all *campesinos* wear. They're so well made that they're famous in Peru and, incredibly, the very best ones can cost as much as $400. **Calle Amazonas s/n. No phone. Daily 7am–5pm. No credit cards. Map p. 402.**

High Andes & Northern Highlands Restaurants

> *The gringo hangout California Café is a good stop for freshly brewed coffee and a Wi-Fi fix.*

Huaraz

Alpes Andes *PIZZA/INTERNATIONAL*
An informal cafe next door to the Casa de Guías, this place is in business to give sustenance to guides, trekkers, and adventurers. Breakfasts are good, as are staples such as pizza and pastas. Av. Julián de Morales 753 (Parque Ginebra). ☎ 043/421-811. Entrees S/10–S/24. No credit cards. Breakfast, lunch, and dinner daily. Map p. 399.

★ **Bistro de Los Andes** *INTERNATIONAL/PERUVIAN* One of the city's nicer restaurants is this longtime, relatively upscale (for Huaraz) spot, serving a mix of French and Peruvian entrees. Good options include the vegetarian stir-fries, pastas, and grilled trout. Jr. Julián de Morales 823. ☎ 043/426-249. Entrees S/10–S/29. DC, V. Breakfast, lunch, and dinner Mon–Sat. Map p. 399.

★ **Café Andino** *CAFE/SNACKS*
An American-owned popular hangout that serves good coffees (including cappuccinos and lattes), sandwiches, salads, and breakfasts. It has a book exchange, board games, Wi-Fi, good tunes, and plenty of trekking and trail information. Jr. Lucar y Torre 530, 3rd floor. ☎ 043/421-203. Entrees S/5–S/15. No credit cards. Breakfast, lunch, and dinner daily. Map p. 399.

★ **California Café** *CAFE/SNACKS*
This small, gringo-flavored coffee house is the place to get fresh-roasted coffee (on the premises) and American-style breakfast all day, including Belgian waffles. You can also get light lunches, check out a book, and suck off the Wi-Fi. Av. 28 de Julio 562. ☎ 043/428-354. Entrees S/4–S/16. No credit cards. Breakfast and lunch daily. Map p. 399.

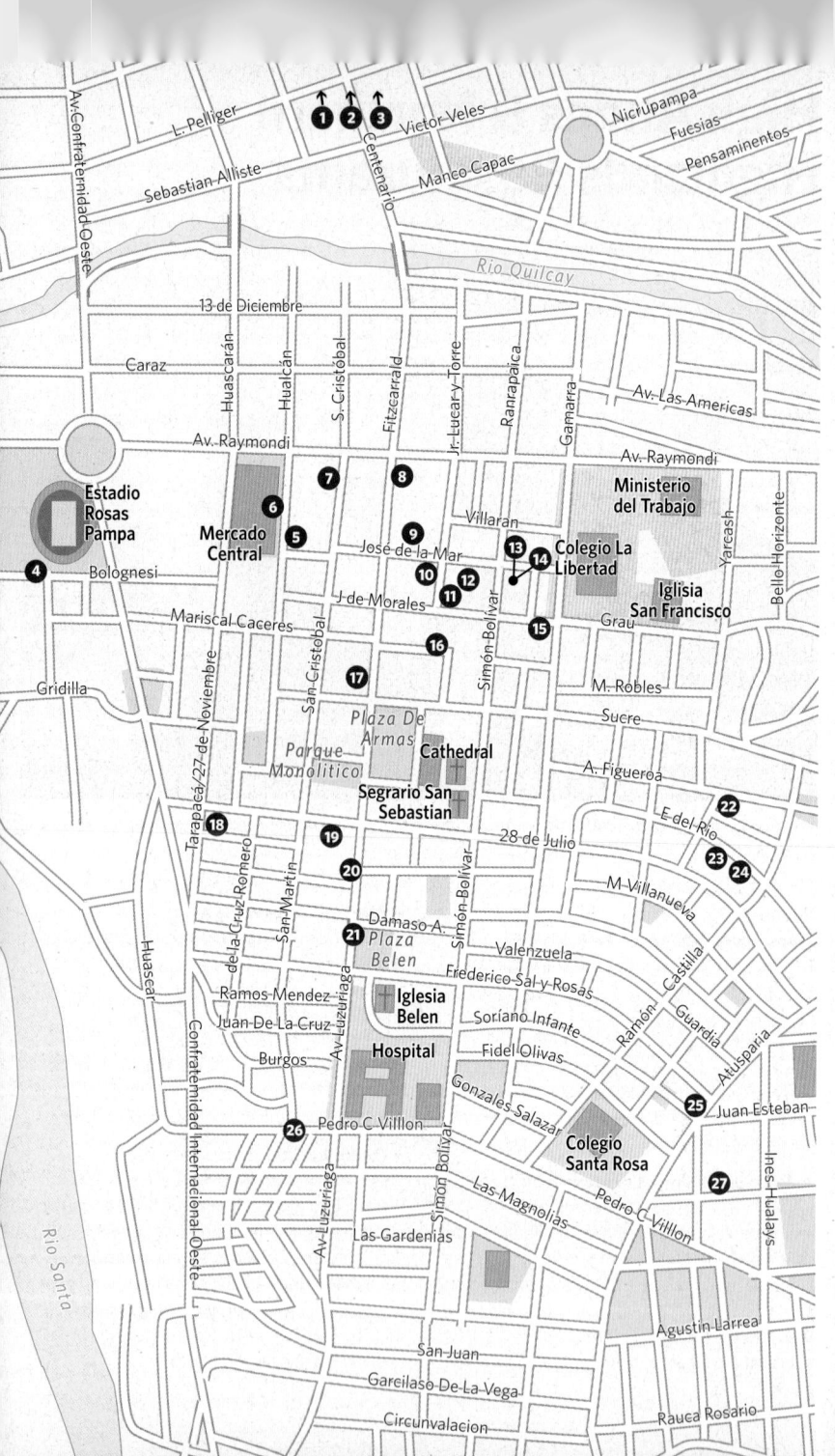

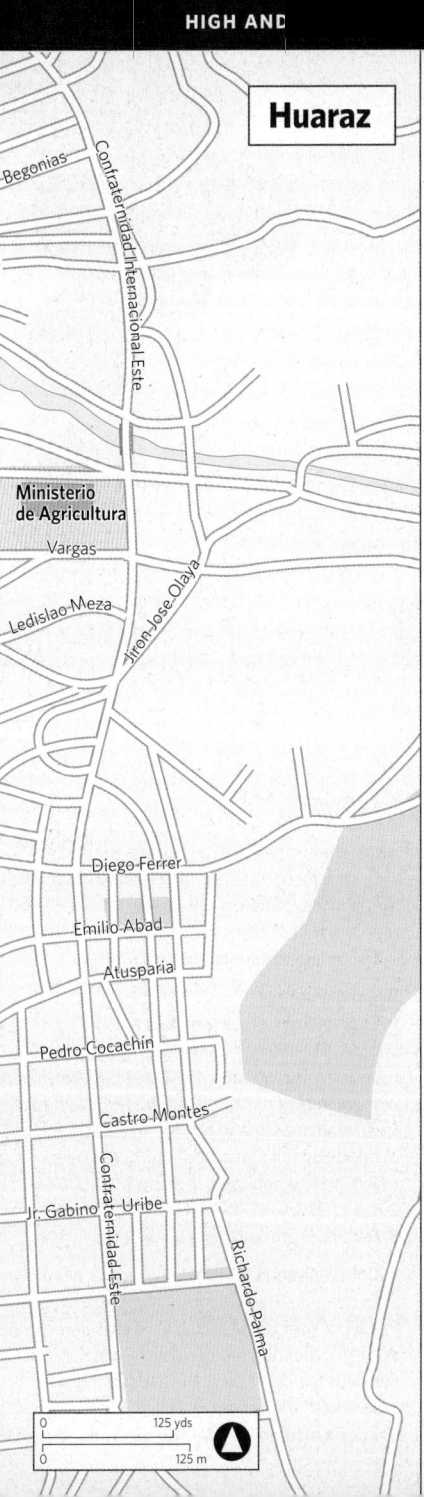

Huaraz

RESTAURANTS
Alpes Andes **16**
Bistro de Los Andes **13**
Café Andino **10**
California Café **19**
Chalet Suisse **26**
Inka Pub Monte Rosa **9**
Pizza Bruno **20**
Siam de Los Andes **15**

HOTELS
Albergue Churup **22**
Alpes Andes **16**
Andino Club Hotel **26**
Edward's Inn **4**
Hostal El Patio de Monterrey **1**
Hotel Santa Cruz **27**
Lazy Dog Inn **2**
Olaza's Bed & Breakfast **24**
Steel Guest House **25**

SHOPS
Andean Expressions **23**
Artesanos Don Bosco **3**
Market Ortiz **8**
Mercados de Artesanía **5**, **7**, **18**
Mercado de Huaraz (Mercado Modelo) **6**

NIGHTLIFE
Taberna El Tambo **12**
Makondo's **14**
Monttrek Pub **17**
X-Treme **21**
Vagamundo Travelbar & Maps **11**

> *Unwind after a mountain excursion at Café de Rat in Caraz.*

Chalet Suisse PEDREGAL DISTRICT *SWISS/ FONDUE* Connected to the city's fanciest hotel, this sophisticated but relaxed chalet-style restaurant serves hearty fare such as steaks and Swiss fondues, mostly to hotel guests. Pedro Cochachín 357. ☎ 043/421-949. Entrees S/21–S/38. AE, DC, MC, V. Lunch and dinner daily. Map p. 399.

★ **Inka Pub Monte Rosa** *PERUVIAN/INTERNATIONAL* With the inviting look of a mountain lodge, this popular restaurant features an extensive and varied menu ranging from traditional *criollo* cooking and *chifa* to pizza and good beer. Jr. José de la Mar 661. ☎ 043/421-447. Entrees S/10–S/35. MC, V. Lunch and dinner Tues-Sun. Map p. 399.

Pizza Bruno *PIZZA/INTERNATIONAL* The focus is on thin-crust pizzas and pastas at this mostly Italian and Mediterranean restaurant, although you can also try more elevated entrees such as beef sirloin flambéed with whiskey. Av. Luzuriaga 834. ☎ 043/425-689. Entrees S/14–S/35. AE, MC, V. Lunch and dinner daily. Map p. 399.

★ **Siam de Los Andes** *THAI* An oddity in Huaraz, this Thai restaurant (started by a native Thai) with a fireplace is a nice change of pace, serving excellent stir-fries and curries. Gamarra 419 (at Av. Julián de Morales). ☎ 043/428-006. Entrees S/12–S/33. DC, V. Lunch and dinner daily. Map p. 399.

Beyond Huaraz

★ **Café de Rat** CARAZ *INTERNATIONAL* On the Plaza de Armas above the outdoors outfitter Pony Expeditions, this place with simple wooden tables has good pizzas, pastas, crepes, vegetarian meals, and beer. It also has a balcony overlooking the plaza, and Internet access, maps, and guidebooks. Jr. Sucre 1286. ☎ 043/291-642. Entrees S/8–S/20. No credit cards. Breakfast, lunch, and dinner daily. Map p. 401.

★ **Café Heladería El Abuelo** CARHUAZ *PERUVIAN* This congenial, airy spot on the plaza serves Peruvian specialties (such as *lomo saltado* and stuffed avocado), sandwiches and salads. For dessert, don't miss the artisanal ice cream with funky flavors (such as pisco sour). La Merced 727. ☎ 043/394-149. www.

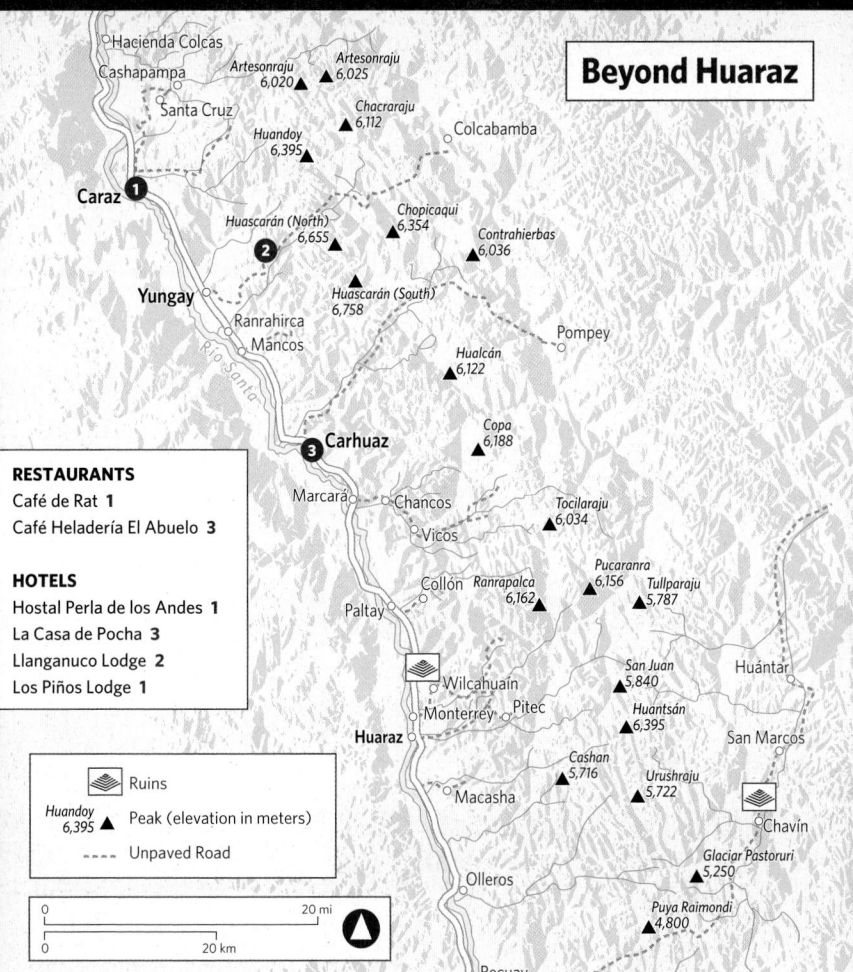

Beyond Huaraz

RESTAURANTS
Café de Rat **1**
Café Heladería El Abuelo **3**

HOTELS
Hostal Perla de los Andes **1**
La Casa de Pocha **3**
Llanganuco Lodge **2**
Los Piños Lodge **1**

Ruins

Huandoy
6,395 ▲ Peak (elevation in meters)

- - - - Unpaved Road

0   20 mi
0   20 km

elabuelohostal.com/cafe_el_abuelo/index_en.
html. Entrees S/8–S/18. No credit cards.
Breakfast, lunch, and dinner daily. Map p. 401.

Cajamarca

★ **El Batán** DOWNTOWN *PERUVIAN*
A longtime standard of Cajamarca dining, with
an art gallery upstairs, this fairly sophisticated
place is in a 18th-century colonial house, with
dining in the covered courtyard or art-filled
interior. It offers a series of meat-heavy, fixed-
price menus. On weekends, there's *peña* music. Jr. del Batán 369. ☎ 076/366-025. Entrees
S/12–S/25. AE, DC, MC, V. Lunch and dinner
daily. Map p. 402.

★ **El Querubino** DOWNTOWN *PERUVIAN*
Just off the Plaza de Armas, this cheery and
colorful restaurant is popular with well-heeled
locals and serves house specialties such as
mollejas al ajillo (sweetbreads in garlic), mushroom ceviche, and mustard chicken. Jr. Amalia
Puga 589. ☎ 076/340-900. Entrees S/15–S/32.
AE, DC, MC, V. Breakfast, lunch, and dinner
daily. Map p. 402.

La Casa de la Abuela DOWNTOWN *INTERNA-
TIONAL/DESSERT* A cute place that takes
its cues from a country kitchen, with wood
beams, dried flowers, and little tables with
blue-and-white-checked tablecloths. It's big

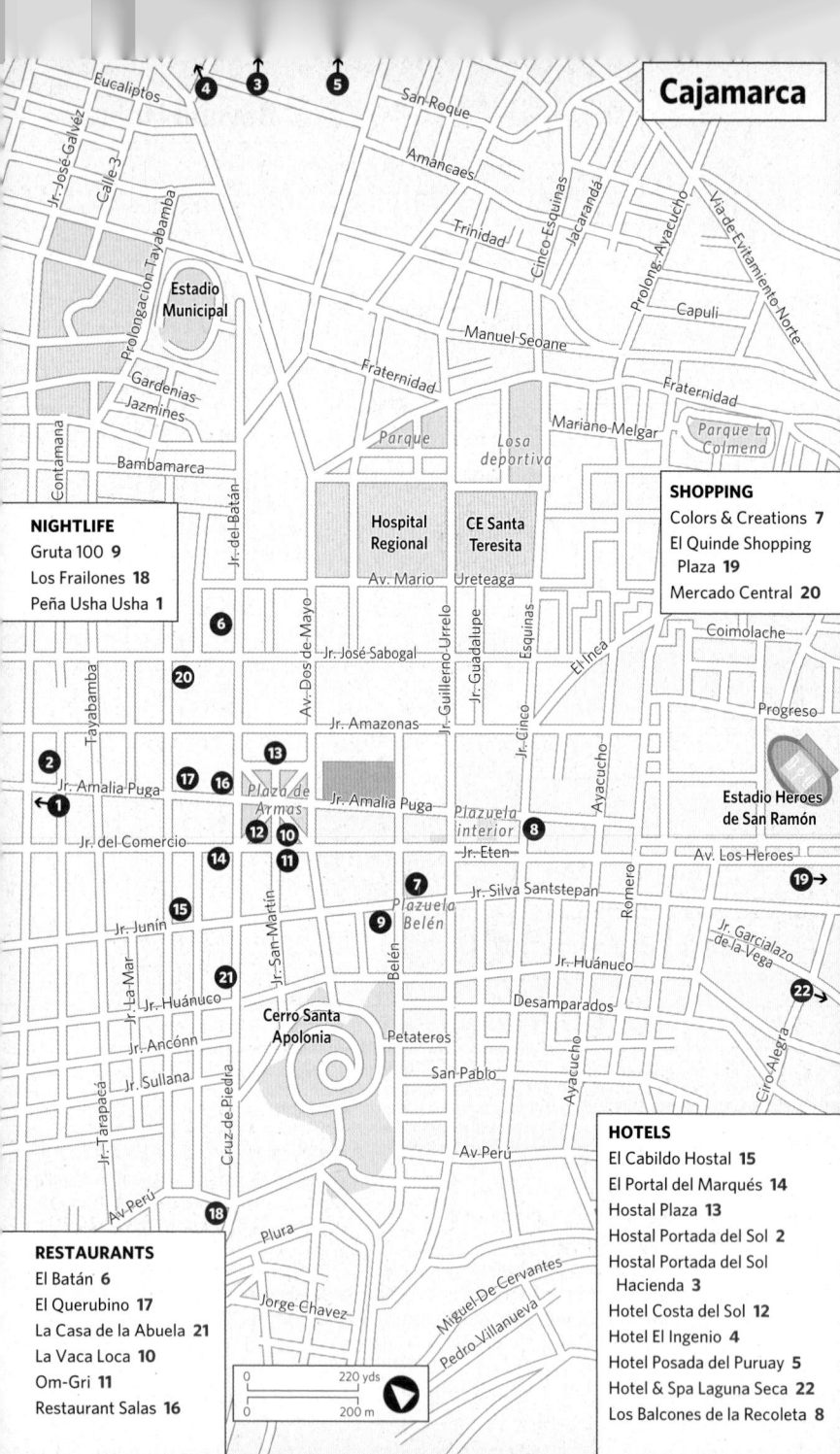

Cajamarca

NIGHTLIFE
Gruta 100 **9**
Los Frailones **18**
Peña Usha Usha **1**

SHOPPING
Colors & Creations **7**
El Quinde Shopping Plaza **19**
Mercado Central **20**

RESTAURANTS
El Batán **6**
El Querubino **17**
La Casa de la Abuela **21**
La Vaca Loca **10**
Om-Gri **11**
Restaurant Salas **16**

HOTELS
El Cabildo Hostal **15**
El Portal del Marqués **14**
Hostal Plaza **13**
Hostal Portada del Sol **2**
Hostal Portada del Sol Hacienda **3**
Hotel Costa del Sol **12**
Hotel El Ingenio **4**
Hotel Posada del Puruay **5**
Hotel & Spa Laguna Seca **22**
Los Balcones de la Recoleta **8**

> *Dining in the colonial courtyard at the restaurant El Batán in Cajamarca.*

on desserts, including ice cream, cheesecakes, and other cakes, but also serves a variety of items for breakfast, lunch, and dinner such as sandwiches, hamburgers, pizzas, and pastas. Jr. Cruz de Piedra 671. ☎ 076/362-027. Entrees S/10–S/27. MC. Breakfast, lunch, and dinner daily. Map p. 402.

★ **La Vaca Loca** DOWNTOWN *PIZZA/ITALIAN*
For a pizza fix, this fun little place (whose name means "the crazy cow") is brightly colored and stuffed with cows in all sorts of incarnations, from paintings to figurines to cartoons; seats and booths are black-and-white faux cowhide. It serves 19 different types of pizzas, plus salads and pastas. Jr. San Martín 320. ☎ 076/828-230. Entrees S/8–S/18. No credit cards. Lunch and dinner daily. Map p. 402.

★ **Om-Gri** DOWNTOWN *ITALIAN*
A tiny place that features Tito Carrera Montes preparing his homemade pastas at a tiny stove tucked behind a bar, right in front of five tables. Choose the pasta (fettuccine, spaghetti, lasagna) and the sauce; Tito fetches sauces from the freezer and proceeds to whip up your dish. Jr. San Martín 360. ☎ 076/367-619. Entrees S/10–S/25. No credit cards. Lunch and dinner Mon–Sat; dinner Sun. Map p. 402.

Restaurant Salas DOWNTOWN *PERUVIAN*
Locals line up to chow down at this traditional restaurant, which has occupied the same

> *Dependable pizzas and pastas are the draw of La Vaca Loca.*

spot on the Plaza de Armas since 1947 and serves huge portions of its *platos del día* (daily specials). It's basically a large eating hall with high ceilings and white-coated waiters. There are standard Peruvian dishes and roasted and barbecued meats. Jr. Amalia Puga 637. ☎ 076/362-867. Entrees S/8–S/27. V. Breakfast, lunch, and dinner daily. Map p. 402.

High Andes & Northern Highlands Hotels

> The comfortable lounge at family-run Albergue Churup in Huaraz.

Huaraz

★ Albergue Churup

A friendly and low-key family-run budget *hostal* in a quiet residential area 5 blocks from the Plaza de Armas. Rooms are clean, and the relaxing backyard, lounge, and kitchen are nice bonuses. Jr. Amadeo Figueroa 1257 (near Iglesia Soledad). ☎ 043/422-584. www.churup.com. 12 units. S/70–S/120 double; S/20–25 per person dorm room w/ shared bathroom. MC, V. Map p. 399.

Alpes Andes

Part of the Casa de Guías (guide headquarters), the city's official youth hostel is well-run, clean, and safe, with kitchen and laundry facilities. It's where independent trekkers and mountaineers come together to form groups. Parque Ginebra 28G. ☎ 043/421-811. casa_de_guias@hotmail.com. S/25 per person dorm room. No credit cards. Map p. 399.

★★ Andino Club Hotel

Huaraz's most upscale hotel, this Swiss-owned alpine lodge plays host to European climbing and trekking groups. It features a good Swiss restaurant, spacious rooms (some with fireplaces and private balconies with panoramic views), and equipment rental and horseback riding. Pedro Cochachín 357. ☎ 043/421-662, or 01/241-5927 for reservations. www.hotelandino.com. 60 units. S/339–S/388 double; S/470 suite. Rates include breakfast. AE, DC, MC, V. Map p. 399.

Edward's Inn

A long-running, laid-back inn, Edward's is removed from town (a 15-min. walk from the Plaza de Armas) but popular with trekkers who congregate on the rooftop patio. Rooms are good-sized, though facilities are pretty basic. The owner is an experienced trekker and mountaineer and rents gear. Av. Bolognesi 121. ☎ 043/422-692. www.edwardsinn.com. 14 units. $35 double. DC, MC, V. Map p. 399.

★ Hostal El Patio de Monterrey MONTERREY

Although not inexpensive for the area, this hacienda-style rustic hotel just 6km (3¾ miles) beyond Huaraz, near the thermal baths of Monterrey, is an agreeable place, with red tile-roofed stucco buildings built around a stone patio and pleasant gardens. Ctra. Huaraz-Caras Km 206. ☎ 043/424-965. www.elpatio.com.pe. 25 units. $77 double. Rate includes breakfast. AE, MC, V. Map p. 399.

Hotel Santa Cruz

This modern, three-story hotel has great mountain views and is a good midrange choice. Rooms are cozy, with a nod to Scandinavian simplicity. Public spaces include a nice terrace and fireplace lounge. Jr. Gabino Uribe 255. ☎ 043/396-096. www.santacruzperu.com.

12 units. $50 double. Rate includes breakfast. AE, MC, V. Map p. 399.

★★★ Lazy Dog Inn ENVIRONS

This Canadian-run, eco-styled inn features an adobe lodge with three cozy, colorful, and stylish rooms and two large private cabins (perfect for families) with fireplaces and bathtubs. Bonuses include an outdoor sauna, fire pit, and horseback riding. Ctra Huaraz-Wilcahuaín, Km 12. ☎ 043/94378-9330. www.thelazydoginn.com. 5 units. $40–$90 double. Rates include breakfast and dinner. No credit cards. Map p. 399.

★ Olaza's Bed & Breakfast LA SOLEDAD DISTRICT

Run by one of the ubiquitous Olaza brothers, this small and friendly inn is a great value: quiet and safe, as well as very comfortable for the price. The top floor terrace and lounge are great places to hang out. Julio Arguedas 1242. ☎ 043/422-529. www.olazas.com. 9 units. S/70–S/90 double. Rates include breakfast. AE, V. Map p. 399.

★ Steel Guest House PEDREGAL DISTRICT

Near the fancier Andino Club Hotel, this five-story hotel has a welcoming feel, with a kitchen, sauna, DVD lounge, pool table, and terrace with good views. Rooms are spacious and colorfully decorated. Alejandro Maguina 1467. ☎ 043/429-709. www.steelguest.com. 15 units. $45 double. Rate includes breakfast. AE, MC, V. Map p. 399.

Beyond Huaraz
Hostal Perla de los Andes CARAZ

Next door to the cathedral and overlooking the Plaza de Armas, this simple hotel has clean and basic rooms. Ask for a room with a view of the plaza. Daniel Villar 179. ☎ 043/392-007. www.huaraz.com/perladelosandes. $18 double. MC, V. Map p. 401.

★★ La Casa de Pocha CARHUAZ

An eco-style rustic ranch about a mile outside of town, this amiable place positions itself as a retreat focusing on alternative living and health, social wellbeing, and harmony with nature. The adobe guesthouse has cozy rooms and excellent views of Hualcán peak, while the organic farm provides produce for meals. There are good hikes in the nearby forest, a wood sauna, and yoga studio. 1.5km (1 mile) east of Carhuaz. ☎ 043/943-613-058.

www.socialwellbeing.org/lacasadepocha.htm. 8 units. $80 double. Rate includes all meals. No credit cards. Map p. 401.

★★★ Llanganuco Lodge YUNGAY ENVIRONS

At 3,500m (11,483 ft.), on the edge of Huascarán National Park and adjacent to Keushu Lake, this outdoorsman's lodge, founded and run by Charlie, an expat Brit, has a singular location and some of the finest views a hotel could have in the Peruvian Andes—of the three highest peaks of the Cordillera Blanca. Within walking distance of Llanganuco gorge, it has excellent, well-equipped, and spacious rooms, and a very nice restaurant. It's complicated to get to, but for day treks or to recover after days in the mountains, it's ideal. Ctra. Carhuaz-Llanganuco, Km 16.6, 30 min. taxi from Yungay. ☎ 043/943-688-791. www.llanganucolodge.com. 10 units. S/118–S/236 double; S/153–S/306 suite. MC, V. Map p. 401.

★ Los Piños Lodge CARAZ

This attractive, colonial-looking hotel has a well-worn, old-school feel, as well as lovely gardens with good views, a nice cafe, and relaxing lounge. The founder, Luís, is happy to share travel tips. Parque San Martín 103. ☎ 043/391-130. www.lospinoslodge.com. 12 units. $20 double. No credit cards. Map p. 401.

Cajamarca
kids El Cabildo Hostal

Solid and well-located 1 block from the Plaza de Armas, this small hotel with a lovely colonial courtyard has cozy rooms, including four loft-style accommodations that would suit families. It's a little worn around the edges, however. Jr. Junín 1062. ☎ 076/367-025. 22 units. S/100–S/147 double. Rates include breakfast. DC, MC, V. Map p. 402.

★ El Portal del Marqués

A good midrange option, this nicely furnished colonial *casona* has character and is comfortable and friendly, with clean rooms around the brightly painted central courtyard and garden. The bar and restaurant are welcoming spots, with a daily happy hour. Jr. del Comercio 644. ☎ 076/368-464, or 01/9880-5440 for reservations. www.portaldelmarques.com. 30 units. S/110 double; S/225 family suite. Rates include breakfast. V. Map p. 402.

> *In the countryside outside Cajamarca, Hotel Posada del Puruay features enormous rooms in a lovely old hacienda.*

Hostal Plaza

In a rambling, wooden colonial house, this place right on the Plaza de Armas is a favorite of bargain-hunting backpackers. Although rooms are simple and dorm-like, the place has character (in its rickety wooden floors) and is cheap. **Plaza de Armas s/n.** ☎ 076/362-058. 22 units. S/25–S/50 double. No credit cards. Map p. 402.

★ Hostal Portada del Sol

Occupying a handsome colonial house, this affordable, family-style inn has older-style furnishings and small bathrooms, but the central courtyard is attractive and there's a charming restaurant onsite. **Jr. Pisagua 731.** ☎ 076/365-395, or 01/225-4306 for reservations. portasol@amet.com.pe. 20 units. $35 double. MC, V. Map p. 402.

★ kids Hostal Portada del Sol Hacienda

Just outside town (about 6km/3¾ miles), this easygoing country hacienda inhabits a pretty house. It has nice gardens and nicely decorated but simple rooms. It also offers tennis courts, football fields, children's games, horseback riding, and trails for walking. **Camino al Cumbe Mayo Km 6.** ☎ 076/365-395, or 01/225-4306 for reservations. portasol@amet.com.pe. 15 units. $35 double. MC, V. Map p. 402.

★★ Hotel Costa del Sol DOWNTOWN

With a coveted location next to the cathedral on the Plaza de Armas, this is the only upscale hotel right in town. With ample and nicely decorated rooms, a pool, spa, casino, and attractive, glass-enclosed restaurant, it's the top choice of visiting business travelers. **Jr. del Comercio 773.** ☎ 076/343-434. www.costadelsolperu.com. 71 units. S/268–329 double; S/384–S/534 suite. Rates include breakfast. V. Map p. 402.

★ Hotel El Ingenio OUTSKIRTS

This engaging hotel, about a 20-minute walk to downtown, feels like a small village within the city. The colonial-hacienda-style buildings are built around pretty courtyards and gardens; rooms are quite large, if a tad dark. **Vía de Evitamiento 1611-1709.** ☎ 076/368-733. www.elingenio.com. 15 units. $55–$70 double. MC, V. Map p. 402.

★★★ kids Hotel Posada del Puruay

In an elegant 1830 hacienda, this handsome country hotel on a ranch-like swath of land just 7km (4⅓ miles) from downtown Cajamarca is pure relaxation, with landscaped gardens and great mountain views. The rooms, built around a pretty courtyard, are massive and outfitted with antiques and large, luxurious bathrooms. **Ctra. Porcón-Hualgayoc Km 4.5.** ☎ 076/367-928, or 01/336-7869 for reservations. www.posadapuruay.com.pe. 14 units. S/191 double; S/207–S/280 suite. Rates include breakfast. AE, DC, MC, V. Map p. 402.

★★ kids Hotel & Spa Laguna Seca

This country-style spa hotel, next to the Baños del Inca, qualifies as luxurious for low-key Cajamarca. It has unusual amenities: thermal pools, Turkish baths, horseback riding, and in-room thermal baths. Rooms are large and nicely outfitted, although most visitors will find that they fall a bit shy of luxury. **Av. Manco Cápac 1098.** ☎ 076/584-300. www.lagunaseca.com.pe. 40 units. $120–$135 double; $144–$170 suite. Rates include breakfast. AE, DC, MC, V. Map p. 402.

Los Balcones de la Recoleta

The attractive colonial balconies and verdant central courtyard are the best features of this small inn in a 19th-century house. Rooms have hardwood floors and ceiling beams, but are a little dark. **Jr. Amalia Puga 1050.** ☎ 076/363-302. 12 units. S/90 double. Rate includes breakfast. DC, MC, V. Map p. 402.

High Andes & Northern Highlands Nightlife

Huaraz

★ **Taberna El Tambo.** This pub-disco is the most happening place in town, with drinking, dancing, and smoking until the wee hours. The music is international Top 40 and Latin, and there's a good mix of locals and travelers. Nightly live folkloric music sets the stage. Jr. José de la Mar 776. ☎ 043/423-417. www.huaraz.com/tambo. Cover S/10. Map p. 399.

Makondo's. A full-throttle nightclub and disco with loud salsa and Latin pop. Upstairs, the bar **Los 13 Bujos** is a quieter spot for a beer, perhaps a place to start the evening. Jr. José de la Mar 812. ☎ 043/428-424. Map p. 399.

Monttrek Pub. A laid-back pub that's a good place to relax over a few beers. Av. Luzuriaga 646. ☎ 043/421-121. Map p. 399.

★ **X-Treme.** This fun cocktail lounge has a lively atmosphere and dance floor, good drinks, and tunes ranging from classic to *rock en Español.* Av. Luzuriaga 1044. ☎ 043/682-115. www.huaraz.info/xtreme/index.html. Map p. 399.

★ **Vagamundo Travelbar & Maps.** Maps decorating the walls welcome a consistent crowd of international travelers to good rock, funk, and blues tunes, a lounge-y bar with couches, and frequent bonfires out on the patio. Av. Julián de Morales 753. ☎ 043/614-374. www.huaraz.info. Map p. 399.

Cajamarca

★★ **Gruta 100.** This lively two-level bar near the Plazuela de Belén has good, unique cocktails (including one with a monastic moniker, El Frailón) and live music and dance (including *peña* on weekends). Av. Silva Sant Estéban 100 (next to stairs to Santa Apolonia hill, on Jr. Junín). No phone. Map p. 402.

Los Frailones. The most chic disco in town, which isn't saying that much, but it's a favorite of locals. Av. Perú 701 (at Cruz de la Piedra, at the base of Santa Apolonia hill). ☎ 076/364-113. Cover S/10–S/15. Map p. 402.

> Regulars at Peña Usha Usha delight in joining the owner Jamie Valera Bazán in folk and protest song sing-alongs.

★★★ **Peña Usha Usha.** One of my favorite nightspots in northern Peru, this funky *peña* bar has just a handful of tables and benches, as well as kerosene lamps, a small altar, and graffiti covering the walls. The proprietor and main performer, Jamie Valera Bazán, has been singing politically motivated songs here, along with a few friends, for years. Locals crowd the bar on weekends; it opens at 9pm and usually goes nearly until sunrise. Jr. Amalia Puga 142. ☎ 076/997-4514. Cover S/10. Map p. 402.

Tip

Most bars and nightclubs in downtown Cajamarca are clustered along José Galvez between Jr. Amalia Puga and Amazonas; among those popular with locals are **Orni, Bambolé,** and **Indio Bar.**

High Andes & Northern Highlands Fast Facts

Arriving

BY PLANE

TO HUARAZ There are now daily afternoon flights (80 min.) from Lima on **LC Busre** (☎ 01/619-1313; www.lcbusre.com.pe). Flights start at $119 one-way. Check the website for updates, as in recent years no Peruvian airline has consistently flown into Huaraz. Flights arrive at Aeropuerto de Anta, 23km (14 miles) north of Huaraz. **TO CAJAMARCA** There are daily 2-hour flights from Lima on **LAN** (☎ 01/213-8200; www.lan.com) and **LC Busre.** Flights start at $115 one-way. The Armando Revoredo Aeropuerto de Cajamarca (☎ 076/362-523) is 3km (2 miles) east of downtown.

BY BUS

TO HUARAZ For the 7- to 8-hour journey to Huaraz from Lima, major companies offering daily service include **CIVA** (☎ 01/418-1111; www.civa.com.pe), **Cruz del Sur** (☎ 01/311-5050; www.cruzdelsur.com.pe), and **Móvil Tours** (☎ 01/433-9000; www.moviltours.com.pe). Móvil Tours and **Transportes Línea** (☎ 01/424-836 or 044/297-000; www.transporteslinea.com.pe) are the principal carriers to and from Trujillo (8 hr.). **TO CAJAMARCA Cruz del Sur** and **Expreso Cia** (☎ 01/428-5218) make the 12-hour trip from Lima. **Transportes Línea** (☎ 076/222-221 or 044/297-000; www.transporteslinea.com.pe) travels from Lima, Trujillo (6–7 hr.), and Chiclayo (5–6 hr.).

ATMs/Cashpoints

In Huaraz, there are ATMs around the Plaza de Armas and along Av. Luzuriaga, while in Cajamarca there are ATMs on the Plaza de Armas and Jr. del Comercio.

Currency Exchange

HUARAZ Most banks are found around the Plaza de Armas and along Av. Luzuriaga. Among those that exchange traveler's checks and cash are Banco de Crédito, Av. Luzuriaga 669 (☎ 043/421-170); Interbank, Sucre 913 (☎ 044/423-015); and Banco Wiese, Sucre 766 (☎ 043/421-500). Money-changers can usually be found hanging around the Plaza de Armas. **CAJAMARCA** Two banks are Interbank, 2 de Mayo on the Plaza de Armas (☎ 076/362-4600), and Banco de Crédito, Jr. del Comercio 679 (☎ 076/362-742), but neither exchanges traveler's checks. There are generally money-changers on the Plaza de Armas and Jr. del Batán; there are also several small *casas de cambio* in the same area.

Dentists & Doctors

HUARAZ Hospital de Apoyo Víctor Ramos Guardia, Av. Luzuriaga s/n (☎ 043/421-290), or Hospital Regional de Huaraz, Av. Luzuriaga s/n (☎ 043/421-321). **CAJAMARCA** Hospital Regional, Mario Urteaga 500 (☎ 076/362-156); Clínica San Francisco, Av. Grau (☎ 076/362-050); or Clínica Limatambo, Puno 265 (☎ 076/364-241).

Emergencies

For general **emergencies,** call ☎ 105. For **fire,** call ☎ 103. In Huaraz, for **climbing accidents and assistance,** including evacuations, contact Unidad de Salvamento de Alta Montaña (High Altitude Rescue), Av. Arias Grazziani s/n, Yungay (☎ 043/493-333 or 043/493-327), or Casa de Guías, Parque Ginebra 28 (☎ 043/421-811). In Cajamarca, the **police** are located at Jr. Amalia Puga 807 (☎ 076/362-832).

Internet Access

HUARAZ There are many Internet *cabinas* across the downtown area. Try Avance, Av. Luzuriaga 672, 2nd floor (☎ 043/426-736), open late. **CAJAMARCA** Efenet, Jr. Dos de Mayo; CyberNet, Comercio 924; or Atajo, Jr. del Comercio 716 (☎ 076/362-245), which is open until 1am and offers cheap international Internet calls.

Pharmacies

HUARAZ There are InkaPharma locations at Av. Luzuriaga 435 and 488, and a Botica Fasa at Av. Luzuriaga 591. **CAJAMARCA** There are InkaPharma outlets at Amazonas 580 and Av. Sor Manuela Gil 151, and a Botica Fasa at Jr. del Batán 137.

Police

HUARAZ The tourist police have an office just off the Plaza de Armas, at Av. Luzuriaga 734 (☎ 043/421-341); the national police are at Larrea y Loredo 720 (☎ 043/421-461). **CAJAMARCA** The police are located at Jr. Amalia Puga 807 (☎ 076/362-832).

Post Office & Mail

In Huaraz, the post office is at Av. Luzuriaga 702 (☎ 043/421-030). The Cajamarca post office is at Jr. Amalia Puga 778 (☎ 076/364-065), and there's a DHL/Western Union office at Dos de Mayo 323 (☎ 076/364-674), within the Cajamarca Tours office.

Public Transportation

In Huaraz, *combis* service the main towns in the Callejón de Huaylas, including Chavín (4 hr.), Caraz (90 min.), and Yungay (90 min.). Most depart from the Quillcay Bridge on Alameda Fitzcarrald; others leave from Calle Caraz, a half-block east of Fitzcarrald. In Cajamarca, *colectivos* run out to Cumbe Mayo, but service is very spotty; tours or taxis are a better bet.

Safety

Night bus trips departing Huaraz for Trujillo, Chiclayo, and other cities in northern Peru have earned reputations for theft, with occasional stories of armed thieves boarding long-distance buses. Perhaps for this reason, the better "executive-level" services don't stop between Lima and their final destination. Be very careful with your belongings on board, even if it means threading your arms through the straps of your carry-on, if you plan to sleep. The only cause for concern in Cajamarca is the Mercado Central, where the commotion demands that visitors keep a close eye on cameras and other valuables.

Taxis

HUARAZ Taxis cruise Av. Luzuriaga day and night. Rides in town cost S/2, and cabs can be safely and easily hailed on the street. One operator to call is Radio Taxi (☎ 043/721-482). **CAJAMARCA** Taxis are easy to come by in the center of Cajamarca around the Plaza de Armas and streets leading off it. Most in-town fares are about S/3. To call a cab, try Taxi Seguro (☎ 076/365-103) or Taxis Unidos (☎ 076/368-888).

Telephone

The area code of towns in Huaraz and the Callejón de Huyalas is 043; in Cajamarca, 076. In Huaraz, the Telefónica del Perú office is at Bolívar and Sucre, just east of the Plaza de Armas; in Cajamarca, at Dos de Mayo 460 on the Plaza de Armas (☎ 076/364-008).

Tours

For Huaraz, see the section on outdoor adventures (p. 392) for mountaineering, trekking, and other organizations. In Cajamarca, reliable tour agencies include **Inca Baths Tours,** Jr. Amalia Puga 653 (☎ 076/362-938); **Cumbe Mayo Tours,** Jr. Amalia Puga 635 (☎ 076/822-938); and **Cajamarca Travel,** Jr. Dos de Mayo 570 (☎ 076/365-651). These companies offer city tours and inexpensive, pooled half- and full-day tours to sights in the countryside around Cajamarca (including Cumbe Mayo, Otuzco, and Inca Baths). Most standard tours cost S/25 to S/35.

Visitor Information

HUARAZ The iPerú tourist office is at Av. Luzuriaga 734, Pasaje Atusparía, of. 1, across from the Plaza de Armas (☎ 043/428-812; Mon–Fri 8am–1pm and 4–7pm). For mountaineering and trekking information, the best source is Casa de Guías, Parque Ginebra 28 (☎ 043/421-811; Mon–Fri 9am–6pm, Sat 9am–1pm). They have up-to-date information on trails, maps, lists of certified guides, and message-board postings for those looking to form trekking and climbing groups. Basic information on visiting the Huascarán National Park can be obtained from the Parque Nacional Huascarán office, in the Ministerio de Agricultura building on Av. Raymondi s/n (☎ 043/422-086). A good website for Huaraz and environs is www.huaraz.info/turismo.html. **CAJAMARCA** There's a branch of the regional tourism office within Conjunto Monumental de Belén complex, Jr. Belén 600 (☎ 076/362-997; Mon–Fri 8:30am–1pm and 2:30–6:30pm). There's a small Oficina de Información Turística, associated with the university, at Batán 289 (☎ 076/361-546; Mon–Fri 8:30am–1pm), which is helpful and gives out free city maps.

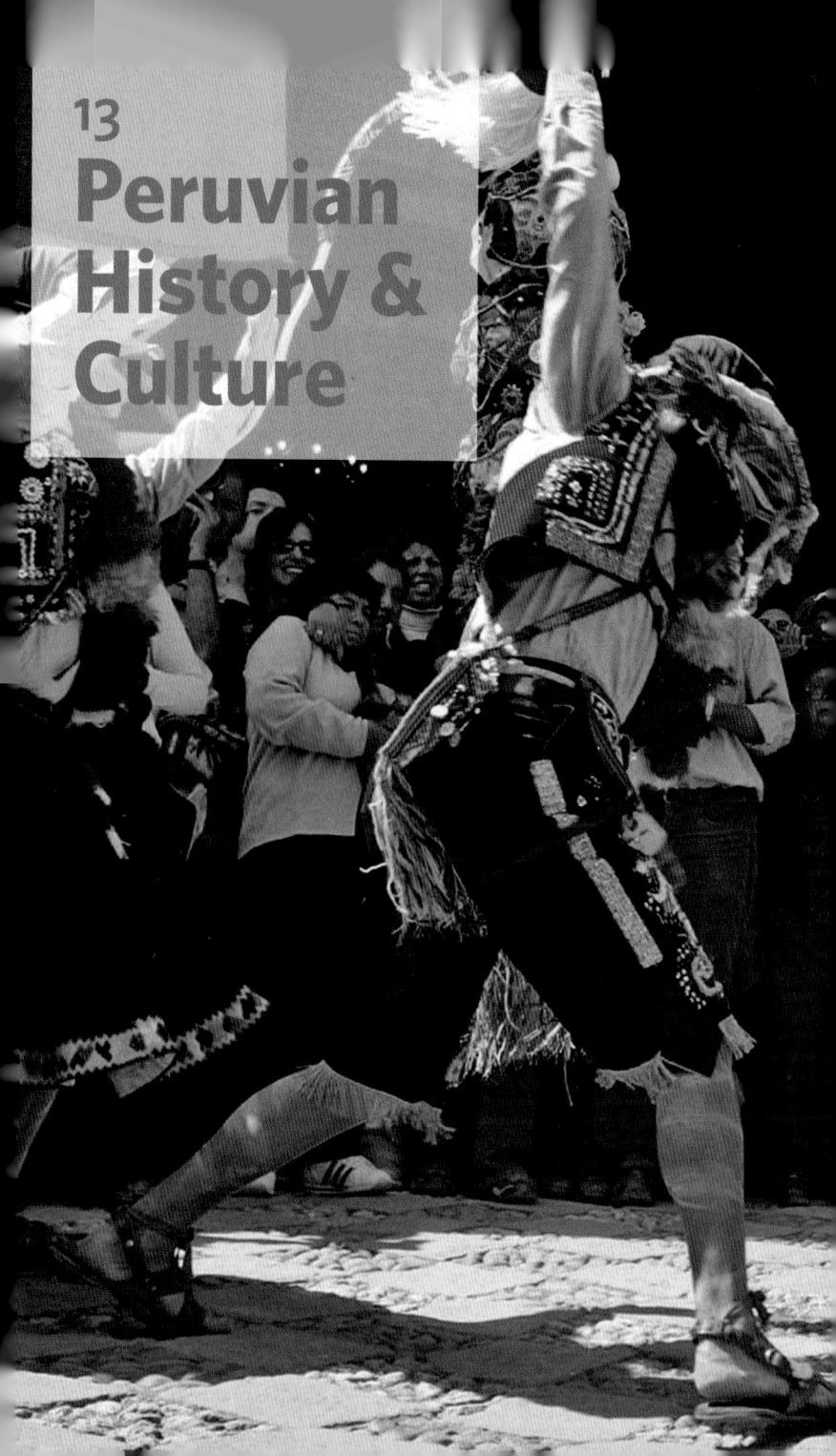

13
Peruvian
History &
Culture

Peru: A Brief History

> **PREVIOUS PAGE** *Tiny Paucartambo explodes during its Fiesta de la Virgen del Carmen, one of Peru's wildest parties.* **THIS PAGE** *The Chavín were the earliest civilization in Peru's rich history of pre-Columbian cultures.*

Most historians believe the first inhabitants of Peru crossed the Bering Strait in Asia during the last ice age, traveled across the Americas, and settled the region around 20,000 B.C. (although some scholars dispute this migratory pattern). The Pikimachay cave, which dates to 12,000 B.C., is the oldest site in Peru. The earliest human remains, discovered near Huánaco in highland Peru, are from around 7000 B.C. Early Peruvians were responsible for cave paintings at Toquepala (province of Tacna, 7000 B.C.) and houses in Chillca (province of Lima,

5000 B.C.). Experts say that recent analysis of findings at the coastal site Caral, in the Supe Valley, demonstrates the existence of the earliest complex civilization in the Americas. The city may have been inhabited as many as 4,700 years ago, 1,000 years earlier than once believed.

Peru has been home to several of the most ancient and sophisticated pre-Columbian civilizations in the Americas. The Chavín, Paracas, Nasca, Huari, Moche, and Incas, among others, form a long line of occasionally overlapping and frequently warring

cultures that stretch back to 2000 B.C. The best known of these cultures is the Incas, but before them, two other civilizations, the Chavín and the Huari-Tiahuanaco, achieved pan-Andean empires. Most of what is known about pre-Columbian cultures, which were located mainly in the coastal areas and highlands, is based on the unearthing of temples and tombs because none possessed a written language. As one culture succeeded a previous one, it imposed its values and social structure on the vanquished but also assimilated features useful to it, complicating distinctions among some early cultures. Civilizations fell victim to warfare, cyclical floods, drought, and earthquakes. The archaeological evidence of pivotal pre-Columbian cultures—ruined temples; spectacular collections of ceramics, masks, and jewelry; and tombs found with well-preserved mummies—is ubiquitous in Peru, and many sites continue to be excavated and combed for clues.

Pre-Inca Cultures

Over the course of nearly 15 centuries, pre-Inca cultures settled principally along the Peruvian coast and highlands. Around 6000 B.C., the Chinchero people along the southern desert coast mummified their dead, long before the ancient Egyptians had thought of the process. By the 1st century B.C., during what is known as the Formative, or Initial, period, Andean society had designed sophisticated irrigation canals and produced the first textiles and decorative ceramics. Another important advance was the specialization of labor, aided in large part by the development of a hierarchical society.

The earliest known Peruvian civilization was the **Chavín** culture (1200–400 B.C.), a theocracy that worshipped a feline, jaguar-like god and settled in present-day Huántar, Ancash (central Peru). The Chavín, who never developed into a military or mercantilistic empire, unified groups of peoples across Peru. The most spectacular

remnant of this culture, known for its advances in stone carving, pottery, weaving, and metallurgy, is the Chavín de Huantar temple (p. 380, ❼), 40km (25 miles) east of Huaraz. This ceremonial center, a place of pilgrimage, at one time contained wondrous authentic examples of religious carving, such as the Tello Obelisk, and demonstrates evidence of sophisticated engineering.

A subsequent society, the **Paracas** culture (700 B.C.–A.D. 200), which took root along the southern coast, is renowned for its superior weaving; perhaps the finest examples of pre-Columbian textiles in the Americas have been found in Paracas sites. The Paracas peoples practiced trepanation, a form of brain surgery that involved drilling holes in the skull to cure various ailments and to correct cranial deformation.

The Classical period (A.D. 200–1100) was one of significant social and technological development. The Moche and Nasca cultures, likely descendants of the Paracas, are among the best studied in pre-Columbian Peru. The **Moche** (or Mochica) civilization (A.D. 200–700), a highly organized hierarchical civilization and one of the first true urban societies, dominated the valleys of the north coast near Trujillo and conquered a number of smaller groups while building their widespread empire. The Moche's extraordinary achievements include adobe

platform complexes—such as the Temples of the Sun and Moon near Trujillo (p. 348, ❸), the former the largest man-made structure of its day in the Americas—and the burial site of Sipán (p. 344), southeast of Chiclayo, where the remains and riches of the famous Lord of Sipán, a religious and military authority, were unearthed in remarkably preserved royal tombs. Moche pottery, produced from molds, contains vital clues to this culture's way of life, down to very explicit sexual representations. Its frank depictions of phalluses, labia, and nontraditional bedroom practices might strike some visitors as pre-Columbian pornography.

> The Huacas de Moche in northern Peru were constructed 7 centuries before Chan Chan, in around A.D. 500.

> *The Chimú kingdom, which built their capital Chan Chan around A.D. 1300, was the last great state in Peru prior to Inca domination.*

The **Nasca** culture (A.D. 300–800) established itself along the coastal desert south of Lima. Nasca engineers created outstanding underground aqueducts, which permitted agriculture in one of the most arid regions on earth, and its artisans introduced polychrome techniques in pottery. But the civilization is internationally known for the enigmatic **Nasca Lines** (p. 102), geometric and animal symbols etched indelibly into the desert, elements of an agricultural and astronomical calendar that are so vast they can only really be appreciated from the window of an airplane.

The **Huari** (also spelled **Wari**) culture (A.D. 600–1100), an urban society that was the first in Peru to pursue explicitly expansionist goals through military conquest, settled the south-central sierra near Ayacucho. Along with the **Tiahuanaco** people (20,000 B.C.–A.D. 1200), with whom they shared a central god figure, they came to dominate the Andes, with an empire spreading all the way to Chile and Bolivia. Both

cultures achieved superior agricultural technology in the form of canal irrigation and terraces.

Separate regional cultures, the best known of which is the **Chimú** culture (A.D. 700), developed and thrived over the next 4 centuries. The Chimú, adroit metallurgists and architects, built the citadel of Chan Chan (p. 349, ❹), a compound of royal palaces and the largest adobe city in the world. The Chimú were the dominant culture in Peru before the arrival and expansion of the Incas, and they initially represented a great northern and coastal rivalry to the Incas. Other cultures that thrived during the same period were the **Chachapoyas,** who constructed the impressive Kuélap fortress in the northern highlands; the **Ica** (or **Chincha**) south of Lima; and the Altiplano (high plains) groups, who built the finely crafted *chullpa* towers (p. 176, ❶) near Puno and Lake Titicaca. The **Sicán** (or **Lambayeque**) culture, which built great temple sites and buried its dead with

extraordinary riches, fell to the Chimú near the end of the 14th century. The Chimú themselves were, in turn, conquered by the Incas.

The Inca Empire

Though Peru has become synonymous with the Incas, they were merely the last in a long line of pre-Columbian cultures. The relatively short-lived Inca Empire (1200–1532) is the best documented of all Peruvian civilizations. (Even so, calling the entire culture "the Incas" is a bit of a historical misnomer, as technically the Inca was the society's religious and military leader, or emperor. Today, most historians refer to both the ruler and the civilization as Inca.) The height of the culture's power lasted only about a century, but the empire extended all the way from present-day Colombia down to Chile, a stretch of more than 5,635km (3,500 miles). At its apex, the Inca Empire's geographic reach was greater even than that of the Romans.

The Incas were a naturalistic and ritualistic people who worshiped the sun god Inti and the earth goddess Pachamama, as well as the moon, thunder, lightning, and the rainbow, all regarded as deities. Inca emperors were believed to be direct descendants of the sun god. The Andes Mountains were considered dwelling places of respected spirits, which is why towering peaks were the sites of human sacrifices. The Incas founded Q'osco (Cusco, p. 188) as the sacred city and capital of the empire (which they called Tahuantinsuyo, or

Land of Four Quarters). The society's ruling sovereign was properly called the Inca, but today the term refers to the people as well as the empire.

The Incas achieved Andean dominance through formidable organization, a highly developed economic system, political alliances, and military conquests. Though they imposed their social structure, the Incas also assimilated some practices of and granted administrative positions to defeated nobles of the Chimú and other cultures, a useful practice for achieving political and religious unification across most of their domain. The Incas never developed a system of writing, but they kept extraordinary records with an accounting system of knots on strings, called *quipus*. They laid a vast network of roadways, nearly 32,200km (20,000 miles) total across the difficult terrain of the Andes, connecting cities, farming communities, and religious sites. A network of runners, called *chasquis*, operated on these roads, relaying messages and even transporting foodstuffs from the coast to the Andes. *Tambos*, or way stations, dotted the highways, serving as inspection points and shelters for the relay runners. The Inca Trail was a sacred highway, connecting the settlements in the Urubamba Valley to the ceremonial center, Machu Picchu (p. 242).

The Incas' agricultural techniques were exceedingly skilled and efficient, with advanced irrigation systems and soil conservation. The Incas also were extraordinary

> *The relatively short-lived Inca Empire stretched from present-day Quito all the way south to the deserts of northern Chile.*

architects and unparalleled stonemasons. Inca ruins reveal splendid landscaping and graceful construction of perfectly cut stones and terraces on inaccessible sites with extraordinary views of valleys and mountains.

A rigid hierarchy and division of labor ruled Inca society. At the top, just below the Inca sovereign (who was also the chief military and religious figure and considered a descendant of the sun), were the ruling elite, nobles, and priests. Tens of thousands of manual laborers provided the massive manpower necessary to construct temples and palaces throughout the empire. The Inca kept *acllas*—chosen maidens, or so-called Virgins of the Sun—who serviced him and the nobles.

Extraordinarily tight community organization was replicated across the empire. At the heart of the structure was the Inca's clan, the *panaca*, composed of relatives and descendants. Spanish conquistadors chronicled a dynasty that extended to 12 rulers, from **Manco Cápac,** the empire's

founder in 1200 who was said to have risen out of Lake Titicaca, to **Atahualpa,** whose murder in Cajamarca by Spanish conquerors spelled the end of the dynasty. **Pachacútec,** who ruled from 1438 to 1463, is considered the great builder of Inca civilization. Under his rule, Cusco was rebuilt, and some of the most brilliant examples of Inca architecture were erected, including Cusco's Qoricancha (Temple of the Sun), the Ollantaytambo and Sacsayhuamán fortresses, and Machu Picchu. Pachacútec initiated the empire's expansion, but it was his successor, **Tupac Yupanqui** (1463–93), who defeated his Chimú rivals in northern Peru and achieved dominance from Ecuador to Chile.

After the death of the **Huayna Cápac** in 1525, civil war ensued, brought on by the division of the empire between his two sons, Atahualpa and Huáscar. The Spaniards arrived in northern Peru in 1532 and found a severely weakened empire, facilitating the small band of invading Spaniards' swift

> *A murderous encounter between Francisco Pizarro and Atahualpa in 1533 precipitated the end of the Inca empire.*

defeat of the Incas. Although vastly outnumbered, the Spaniards possessed superior military technology, pitting cannons and cavalry against the Incas' slings and battle-axes. Still, the Spaniards were so outnumbered that their conquest of the Incas remains puzzling to many scholars.

In 1911 the Yale historian Hiram Bingham happened upon the ruins of the imperial city Machu Picchu—a discovery that would begin to unravel some of the mystery of the Incas and further demonstrate their greatness.

Spanish Conquest & Colonialism

Cristóbal Colón (Columbus) and his cohorts landed in the Americas in 1492, and by the 1520s, Spanish conquistadors had reached South America. Francisco Pizarro led an expedition along Peru's coast in 1528. Impressed with the riches of the Inca Empire, he returned to Spain to raise money and recruit men for anotherexpedition. In 1532, Pizarro returned to Peru overland from Ecuador. After founding the first Spanish city in Peru, San Miguel de Piura, near the Ecuadorean border, he advanced upon the northern highland city of Cajamarca, an Inca stronghold. There, a small number of Spanish troops—about 180 men and 30 horses—cunningly captured the Inca emperor Atahualpa. The emperor promised to pay a king's ransom of gold and silver for his release, offering to fill his cell several times over. But in 1533, having received warning of an advancing Inca army, Pizarro executed Atahualpa. It was a catastrophic blow to an already weakened empire.

Pizarro and his men massacred the Inca army, estimated at between 5,000 and 6,000 warriors. The Spaniards installed a puppet Inca, Tupac Huallpa (the brother of Huáscar, who had died during Atahualpa's detainment), and marched on Cusco. They captured the capital city on November 15, 1533, and emptied the Sun Temple of its vast golden treasures. A new puppet, Manco Inca, was appointed. Pizarro founded the coastal city of Lima 2 years later; it became the capital of the new colony, the viceroyalty of Peru. The Spanish crown appointed Spanish-born viceroys the rulers of Peru, but Spaniards battled among themselves for control of Peru's riches, and the remaining Incas continued to battle the conquistadors. A great siege was laid to Cusco in 1536, with Manco Inca and his brothers directing the rebellion from Sacsayhuamán. Pizarro was assassinated in 1541, and the indigenous insurrection ended with the beheading of Manco Inca, who had escaped to Vilcabamba, deep in the jungle, in 1544. Inca Túpac Amaru led a failed rebellion in 1572 but was killed.

Over the next 2 centuries, Lima gained in power and prestige at the expense of the old Inca capital and became the preeminnent colonial city of the Andean nations. The Peruvian viceroyalty stretched from Panama to Tierra del Fuego. Cusco, meanwhile, retained its cultural importance if not its central political role, becoming the epicenter of the Escuela Cusqueña (Cusco School) of painting, which incorporated indigenous elements into Spanish styles, in the 16th and 17th centuries.

Independence

By the 19th century, anger over high taxes and Spanish controls grew in Peru, as it did in most colonies in the Americas. After liberating Chile and Argentina, José de San Martín set his sights northward on Lima in 1821 and declared it an independent nation the same year. Simón Bolívar, the other hero of independence on the continent, arrived from the other direction. His successful campaigns in Venezuela and Colombia led him southward to Ecuador and finally Peru. Peru won its independence from Spain after crucial battles in late 1824. Though Peru mounted its first civilian government, defeat by Chile in the War of the Pacific (1879–83) left the country in a dire economic position.

Several military regimes ensued, and Peru finally returned to civilian rule in 1895. Land-owning elites dominated this new "Aristocratic Republic."

In response to growing international demand for rubber for car tires and other products, the harvesting of latex from Amazonian trees in Peru's northern Amazon produced a rubber boom beginning in the late 19th century. The local boom attracted large groups of European immigrants and produced concentrated wealth in Iquitos among bankers and rubber merchants, many of whom built the famed rubber baron mansions lining the river in the port city. It also led to new inroads into virgin Amazon forest and colonization of sorts in the region.

20th-Century & Contemporary Peru

Peru's modern political history has been largely a turbulent mix of military dictatorships, coups d'état, and disastrous civilian governments, engendering a near-continual cycle of instability. The country launched a war with Ecuador over a border dispute in 1941, and though the 1942 Treaty of Río de Janeiro granted the area north of the Marañon River to Peru, Ecuador would continue to claim the territory until the end of the 20th century. Particularly in the 1980s and 1990s, Peru became notorious for government corruption at the highest levels—leading to the exile of two recent presidents—and widespread domestic terrorism fears.

Peru shook off 2 decades of dictatorship in 1945 after the free election (the first in many decades) of José Luis Bustamante y Rivero. Bustamante served for just 3 years; in 1948 General Manuel A. Odría led a coup and installed a military regime. The country returned to civilian rule, with Fernando Belaúnde Terry as president from 1963 until 1968, when the armed forces overthrew Belaúnde and again took control. Contrary to other right-leaning dictatorships in Latin America, this new military regime expanded the role of the state, nationalized a number of industries, and instituted agrarian reform. The land-reform initiatives failed miserably, and Belaúnde was reelected

> The independence hero General José de San Martín, known as the "Protector of Peru," established the Republican government in 1821.

> *Alejandro Toledo, a former shoeshine boy, rose to become Peru's first president of native Amerindian descent in 2001.*

in 1980. He and his successor, Alan García (1985–90), were faced with hyperinflation, nationwide strikes, and two homegrown guerrilla movements—the Maoist Sendero Luminoso (Shining Path) and the Tupac Amaru Revolutionary Movement (MRTA)—that destabilized Peru with violent terror campaigns throughout the late 1980s and early 1990s. They were largely unsuccessful in dealing with Peru's problems. Peruvians fled the capital and the countryside, fearful of attack; few travelers were brave enough to plan vacations in the troubled nation. Meanwhile, Peru's role on the production end of the international cocaine trade grew exponentially. García (who refused to pay Peru's external debt, prompting both the IMF and the World Bank to cut off support) was charged with

embezzling millions and fled into exile.

With the economy in ruins and the government in chaos, Alberto Fujimori, the son of Japanese immigrants, defeated the Peruvian novelist Mario Vargas Llosa and became president in 1990. In 1992 Fujimori's government arrested key members of both the MRTA and the Shining Path, catapulting the president to unprecedented popularity. His administration turned authoritarian, however, shutting down Congress in 1992, suspending the constitution, and decreeing an emergency government that Fujimori effectively ruled as dictator. His austerity measures got Peru on the right track economically, with reforms leading to widespread privatizations, growth of 7%, and a drop in inflation from more than 10,000% annually

to about 20%, so many Peruvians reluctantly accepted his overturn of democracy. Having pushed to get the constitution amended so that he could run for successive terms, Fujimori was reelected in 1995.

Fujimori resigned the presidency and escaped into exile in Japan in late 2000, after a corruption scandal that involved his shadowy intelligence chief, Vladimiro Montesinos. Videotape of Montesinos bribing a congressman and subsequent investigations (including a daily barrage of secret videotapes broadcast on national television) revealed a government so thoroughly corrupt that it was itself involved in the narcotics trade it was ostensibly stamping out. Fujimori had funneled at least $12 million to private offshore accounts. Montesinos escaped to Venezuela, where the government protected him until he was found and returned to Peru for imprisonment.

Alejandro Toledo, a political newcomer from a poor Indian family, won the 2001 election and became Peru's first president of the 21st century. The U.S. State Department Human Rights Report named Peru among the success stories of the year, praising the country for meeting international standards for free elections and addressing past abuses and corruption under the Fujimori administration. Toledo had labeled himself an "Indian rebel with a cause," alluding to his intent to support the nation's native Andean populations, or *cholos*. A shoeshine boy and son of peasants who went to Harvard and Stanford, became a World Bank economist, and ultimately wrestled the top office from a corrupt leader was the very embodiment of the dream of social mobility—in a country where there is little upward movement by non-whites. Toledo offered an encouraging symbol of hope to both Peruvians and the international community. Yet like previous governments, Toledo's administration was plagued by instability, abuse of power, and poor management.

Fujimori was arrested in Chile in 2005 while attempting to return to Peru in a surprise bid to run for president. Extradited to Peru and jailed in 2006, Fujimori stood trial on charges of ordering the murders of suspected Shining Path guerrillas and their collaborators by death squad. (He remains in a jail in Lima, sentenced to 25 years for his role in ordering death squads, as

> *Ex-president Alberto Fujimori resigned in disgrace, fled to exile in Japan, and is now imprisoned in Lima.*

well as three other concurrent sentences for abuse of power, bribery, and illegal wiretapping of phones.) The trial marked the first time in Peru's history that a former president had been tried for crimes committed during his administration.

Another exiled former president, Alan García—who had fled the country after a disastrous term in the 1980s—returned to Peru and, improbably, captured the 2006 presidential election. García, a one-time populist, positioned himself as a centrist, seeking to put a clamp on inflation and pursuing free-market policies. Most notably, he pushed aggressively for a free trade agreement with the United States, a treaty that was ratified by the U.S. Congress in December 2007 and which entered into force in February 2009. (Peru is seeking similar agreements with Mexico and Canada.) The Peruvian economy recorded a robust growth rate of 9.2% in 2008, a 15-year high and one of the most impressive in the world, and to date the García

presidency has been largely stable and peaceful. The pace of growth dropped by half in 2009, however, and the divide between rich and poor, coastal elites and indigenous highlanders, and modern and traditional continues to loom large. Half the population lives at or below the poverty line.

The horrendous violence of 2 decades ago has now almost completely abated, and besides places deep in the jungle, there are no areas where visitors should not feel welcome to travel. Indeed, rumors of a Shining Path revival have not been borne out, even though at least two major attacks in the last decade, including a bombing near the U.S. embassy in Lima, have been attributed to the group.

In proof that past sins are easily forgotten in Peru, one of the leading contenders for the presidential election in 2011 is Keiko Fujimori, the daughter of the jailed former president and a right-wing lawmaker whose candidacy is apparently largely based on her desire to free her father from incarceration.

A Timeline of Peruvian History

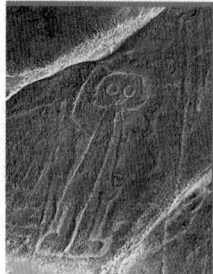

PRE-INCA

20,000–10,000 B.C. The earliest settlers, most likely migrants from Asia, arrive.

1000 B.C.–900 B.C. The Chavín Empire establishes Chavín de Huántar.

700 B.C. The Paracas culture thrives in the southern desert.

300 B.C.–A.D. 700 The Nasca Lines (left) are created.

A.D. 200 The Moche culture consolidates its dynasty in northern Peru.

C. 300 The Lord of Sipán is buried.

1150 Construction of Chan Chan begins.

INCA EMPIRE

1200 Manco Cápac becomes the first Inca (emperor) and founds the Inca Empire.

1438 During Inca Pachacútec's reign, Sacsayhuamán and Machu Picchu (left) are built.

1460–1465 The Incas conquer the southern desert coast; the empire extends to Ecuador.

1527 Inca civil war begins.

1532 The Inca Atahualpa defeats his brother, Huáscar, and gains control of the Inca Empire. Spanish military leader Francisco Pizarro captures Atahualpa.

SPANISH CONQUEST & COLONIALISM

1533 The Spaniards assassinate Atahualpa and sack and burn Cusco.

1535 Francisco Pizarro (left) establishes Lima and names it the capital of the viceroyalty of Peru.

1541 Pizarro is killed in Lima.

1572 Tupac Amaru, the last Inca emperor, is captured and executed.

1780 Tupac Amaru II leads a failed revolt against the Spaniards.

1821 General José de San Martín captures Lima and proclaims Peru's independence.

1824 Peru defeats Spain and becomes the last colony in Latin America to gain its independence.

INDEPENDENT PERU

1849–74 Chinese workers (100,000) arrive in Peru as menial laborers.

1911 Yale researcher Hiram Bingham "discovers" Machu Picchu.

1968 The civilian government is ousted in a coup led by General Juan Velasco Alvarado (left).

1969 Velasco initiates large-scale land reform and nationalization programs.

CRISIS

1975 Velasco is ousted in a coup.

1980 Peru returns to civilian rule. Sendero Luminoso (Shining Path) and Tupac Amaru (MRTA) launch armed guerrilla struggle.

1982 Debt crisis, deaths, and "disappearances" escalate following a military crackdown on guerrillas and drug traffickers.

1985 Alan García, constitutionally elected successor since 1945, wins the presidency and promises to rid Peru of military and police "old guard."

1990 Both insurgent and government actors commit as many as 10,000 political murders. Alberto Fujimori (left), son of Japanese immigrants, is elected president.

1992 Fujimori suspends the constitution and imposes censorship. Shining Path leader Abimael Guzmán is arrested and sentenced to life in prison.

CONTEMPORARY PERU

1996 Tupac Amaru guerrillas seize 490 hostages at the Japanese ambassador's residence. American Lori Berenson is convicted of treason and sentenced to life in prison for plotting with terrorists.

2000 Fujimori is re-elected but his chief of intelligence is caught bribing a politician; Fujimori resigns and goes into exile in Japan.

2001 Alejandro Toledo becomes Peru's first president of native Indian origin.

2007 A 7.9 earthquake devastates the southern desert coast (left).

2010 Mudslides kill 5 tourists at Machu Picchu. Mario Vargas Llosa is awarded the Nobel Prize for Literature. Lori Berenson is released from prison after 15 years.

2011 Ollanta Humala, a former army officer turned left-leaning populist, is sworn in as president. Afro-Peruvian singer Susana Baca is named Minister of Culture.

The Lay of the Land

> The Cordillera Blanca boasts a dozen peaks higher than 5,000m (16,400 ft).

Ecosytems

Peru consists of three distinct geological components: coast, sierra (highlands), and *selva* (jungle). Although the largest cities are situated along the coast, it's the Amazon rainforest and the Andes, South America's longest mountain range, that dominate the country. The Pacific coastal region is a narrow strip that runs from one end of the country to the other (a distance of some 2,200km/1,400 miles) and is almost entirely desert. The mountain ranges in the center of Peru, north of Lima, are among the highest in Peru. Within Huascarán National Park (p. 375), the Cordillera Blanca stretches 200km (124 miles) and contains a dozen peaks higher than 5,000m (16,400 ft.); the highest is Huascarán, at 6,768m (22,205 ft.). In extreme southern Peru, near Puno and Lake Titicaca, the Andes yield to the Altiplano, the arid high plains, with altitudes of 3,300m (10,830 ft.). The jungle ranges from cloud forest in the south to low-lying flatlands in the north. Although 60% of Peru is Amazon rainforest, only about 5% of the country's human inhabitants reside there. Lake Titicaca (p. 170), shared with Bolivia, is the largest lake in South America and the world's highest navigable body of water (at 3,830m/12,566 ft.).

Flora & Fauna

Nearly two-thirds of Peru is jungle, and many naturalists and biologists believe that Peru's Amazon rainforest holds the greatest diversity in the world. It teems with a staggering roster of wildlife: more than 400 species of mammals, 2,000 species of fish, 300 reptiles, 1,800 birds, and more than 50,000 plants. Among its remarkable statistics, Peru counts 87 of the planet's 103 existing ecosystems and 28 of the 32 climates. Recent studies have shown that a region just south of Iquitos has the highest concentration of mammals anywhere in the world. Peru's significant fauna include the great Andean

> *The extraordinary marine wildlife in the protected Islas Ballestas has earned them the nickname "The Peruvian Galápagos."*

> *Peru is two-thirds jungle, but deforestation remains a major threat to the country's Amazon basin.*

condors, found principally in Colca Canyon, near Arequipa; and the rich marine life of the Paracas National Reserve and Islas Ballestas (p. 94; Peru's version of the Galápagos Islands), including communities of endangered Humboldt penguins and sea turtles, sea lions, red boobies, and flamingos. Coastal Peru south of Lima is also home to one of the greatest population densities of dolphins in the world, with one-third of the world's species identified.

The Environment

Peru has 72 million hectares (178 million acres) of natural-growth forests—70% in the Amazon jungle region—that comprise nearly 60% of the national territory. However, the country is losing nearly 300,000 hectares (740,000 acres) of rainforest annually. The primary threat to Peru's tropical forests is deforestation, caused by agricultural expansion, cattle ranching, logging, oil extraction and spills, mining, illegal coca farming, and colonization initiatives.

Deforestation has shrunk territories belonging to indigenous peoples and contributed to wiping out more than 90% of the population. The Peruvian Amazon holds a phenomenal wealth of flora and fauna but a dwindling human presence. Indigenous Amazonian tribes have been greatly reduced by centuries of disease, deforestation, and assimilation. There were once some six million people, 2,000 tribes and/or ethnic groups, and innumerable languages in the Amazon basin; today the indigenous population is less than two million. Still, many traditions and languages have yet to be extinguished, especially deep in the jungle—though most visitors are unlikely to come into contact with groups of unadulterated, non-Spanish-speaking native peoples.

Peru has done a slightly better job of setting aside tracts of rainforest as national park reserves and of regulating industry than have some other Latin American and Asian countries. Manu National Park (p. 303), Tambopata National Reserve (p. 302) , and the Pacaya Samiria National Reserve (p. 324) are three of the largest protected rainforest areas in the world, and the government regulates entry of tour groups. Peru augmented the Bahuaja-Sonene National Park by 809,000 hectares (nearly 2 million acres) in 2001. INRENA, Peru's Institute for Natural Resource Management, enforces logging regulations and reseeds Peru's Amazon forests, and in 2008, President García created the country's first Ministry of the Environment. A handful of Peruvian and international environmental and conservation groups, such as ProNaturaleza and Conservation International, are active in Peru, working on reforestation and sustainable forestry projects.

Jungle ecotourism has exploded in Peru, and rainforest regions are now much more accessible than they once were, with more lodges and eco-options than ever. Many of these are taking leading roles in sustainable tourism even as they introduce protected regions to more travelers.

People & Culture

Peru's 28 million people are predominantly mestizo (of mixed Spanish and indigenous heritage) and Andean Indian, but the population is a true melting pot of ethnic groups. Significant minority groups include Afro-Peruvians (descendants of African slaves, living mainly in the coastal area south of Lima); immigrant Japanese and Chinese populations that are among the largest in South America; and smaller groups of European immigrants, including Italians and Germans. In the early days of the colony,

Peruvian-born offspring of Spaniards were called *criollos*, though that term today refers mainly to coastal residents and coastal Peruvian cuisine.

After Bolivia and Guatemala, Peru has the largest population by percentage of Amerindians in Latin America. Perhaps half the country lives in the sierra, or highlands, and most of these people, commonly called *campesinos* (peasants), live in either small villages or rural areas. Descendants of Peru's many Andean indigenous groups in remote rural areas continue to speak the native languages Quechua (made an official language in 1975) and Aymara or other Amerindian tongues, and for the most part, they adhere to traditional regional dress. However, massive peasant migration to cities from rural highland villages has contributed to a dramatic weakening of indigenous traditions and culture across Peru.

Peruvians are a predominantly Roman Catholic people (more than 90% claim to be Catholic), although Protestant evangelical churches have been winning converts, a fact that is worrisome to the Catholic Church. Animistic religious practices (worship of deities representing nature) inherited from the Incas and others and incorporated into the daily lives of many Peruvians can be seen in festivals and small individual rituals such as offerings of food and beverage to Pachamama, or Mother Earth.

> *Traditional language and culture have been preserved in the remote, high Andes mountains.*

Peru in Popular Culture

> Mario Vargas Llosa, Peru's preeminent novelist, became the country's first recipient of the Nobel Prize for Literature in 2010.

Books

FICTION

More than ever, the towering figure in contemporary Peruvian fiction is **Mario Vargas Llosa,** the 2010 winner of the Nobel Prize for Literature. Vargas Llosa's distinguished oeuvre includes *Aunt Julia and the Scriptwriter* (Farrar, Straus and Giroux, 1998), one of his most popular works; *The Real Life of Alejandro Mayta* (Picador, 2007), a dense meditation on Peruvian and South American revolutionary politics that blurs the lines between truth and fiction; *Death in the Andes* (Picador, 2007), a deep penetration into the contemporary psyche and politics of Peru; *In Praise of the Stepmother* (Picador, 2002), a surprisingly erotic and beautifully illustrated book; and *The Feast of the Goat* (Farrar, Straus and Giroux, 2001),

about the Dominican dictator Rafael Trujillo, which made the year-end best list of many critics in 2001. Vargas Llosa is an erudite and even a difficult or "heavy" writer, but he is an unusually engaging one.

Alonso Cueto is one of the next generation's most ballyhooed novelists; he won several international awards for *La Hora Azul* (*The Blue Hour;* Editorial Anagrama, 2005). *El Susurro de la Mujer Ballena* (*The Whisper of the Whale Woman;* Planeta, 2007) is his latest work. Another young Peruvian novelist garnering prizes and a lot of attention is **Santiago Roncagliolo,** whose novels include *Pudor* (Punto de Lectura, 2007) and *Red April* (Vintage International, 2010), a page-turning political thriller about Sendero Luminoso.

César Vallejo, born in Peru in 1892, is one of the great poets of Latin America and the Spanish language. *César Vallejo: Complete Posthumous Poetry* (University of California Press, 1980), in translation; *The Complete Poetry: César Vallejo* (University of California Press, 1980); and *Trilce* (Wesleyan University Press, 2000), a bilingual publication, are the best places to start with this great poet. While in prison, Vallejo wrote some of the poems in *Trilce,* a wildly creative and innovative avant-garde work that is considered a masterpiece of modernism. Vallejo later fled to Europe and immersed himself in the Spanish Civil War.

HISTORICAL WORKS

The classic work on Inca history and the Spanish conquistadors is John Hemming's *The Conquest of the Incas* (Mariner Books, 2003), a very readable narrative of the fall of a short-lived but uniquely accomplished empire. *Lost City of the Incas* (Phoenix Press, 2003) is the travelogue and still-amazing story of Hiram Bingham, the Yale academic who brought the "Lost City" to the world's attention in 1911. Bingham's book makes for a very interesting read, especially after so many years of speculation and theory about the site. Also available by Bingham is *Inca Land: Explorations in the Highlands of Peru* (General Books, 2009), detailing four expeditions into the Peruvian Andes, originally published in 1922.

The Last Days of the Incas, by Kim MacQuarrie (Simon & Schuster, 2008), is an ambitious and vivid account of the struggle between a small band of Spaniards and a sophisticated continental empire, a conflict and mystery that continue to hold the attention of scholars and fire the imaginations of archaeologists seeking to understand the origins of modern-day Peru. *The Incas and their Ancestors* (Thames and Hudson, 2001), by Michael Moseley, is a good account of the Inca Empire and, importantly, its lesser-known predecessors. For most readers, it serves as a good introduction to Peru's

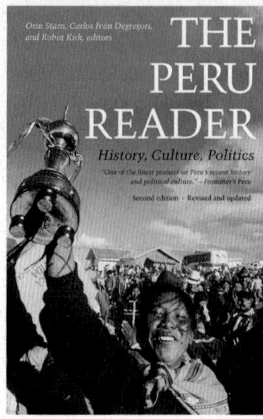

Orin Starn, Carlos Iván Degregori, and Robin Kirk, editors

THE PERU READER

History, Culture, Politics

"One of the finest primers on Peru's recent history and political culture." —*Frommer's Peru*

Second edition · Revised and updated

> Brush up on the country's recent history and politics with **The Peru Reader.**

archaeology and the sites they will visit, although some people find that it reads too much like a textbook. Illustrations include black-and-white photographs of Inca drawings and a few color photos.

A terrific story of a recent archaeological find is *Discovering the Inca Ice Maiden: My Adventures on Ampato* (National Geographic Society, 1998), by Johan Reinhard. Reinhard's account of his discovery of a mummified Inca princess sacrificed 500 years ago on a volcano summit in southern Peru details the team's search and its race to save what is considered one of the most important archaeological finds in recent decades. The book contains excellent color photographs of the maiden, who can be viewed in Arequipa (p. 138, ❸). Reinhard's *The Ice Maiden: Inca Mummies, Mountain Gods, and Sacred Sites in the Andes* (National Geographic, 2005) is a memoir of archaeological adventures and the impact of his

discovery (on both him personally and the interpretation of Peruvian history).

The Peru Reader: History, Culture, Politics (Duke University Press, 2005), edited by Orin Starn, is one of the finest primers on Peru's recent history and political culture. It includes essays by several distinguished voices, including Mario Vargas Llosa.

The Madness of Things Peruvian: Democracy Under Siege, by Álvaro Vargas Llosa (Transaction Publishers, 1994), isn't easy to find, and it only chronicles up to the mid-'90s, but it's a well-rendered analysis of the failings of Peruvian democracy. Robin Kirk's *The Monkey's Paw: New Chronicles from Peru* (University of Massachusetts Press, 1997) is a story of the impact of social and economic upheaval in Peru on marginalized peoples, with the homegrown guerrilla movements taking center stage.

GUIDEBOOKS

Naturalists and birders might want to pick up the very complete *Birds of Peru (Princeton Field Guides): Revised and Updated Edition* (Princeton University Press, 2010), by Thomas S. Schulenberg. It's the field guide to Peru that birders have long been waiting for. *A Field Guide to the Birds of Peru* (Ibis Pub Co., 2001), by James F. Clements, is another, though less comprehensive, guide. Also of interest is *A Parrot Without a Name: The Search for the Last Unknown Birds on Earth* (University of Texas Press, 1991), by Don Stap, an account of John O'Neill and Louisiana State University scientists

documenting new species in the jungles of Peru.

Travellers' Wildlife Guides Peru (Interlink Books, 2008), by David L. Pearson, Les Beletsky, Priscilla Barrett, David Beadle, et al, is a 500-page handbook survey of Peruvian flora and fauna, including information about conservation, habitats, national parks, and reserves. It's an excellent introduction for readers ready to explore the Peruvian outdoors, from the Andes to the Amazon and other repositories of Peru's magnificent animal and plant life.

Peter Frost's *Exploring Cusco* (Nuevas Imágenes, 1999) is one of the best-detailed local guides, with excellent historical information and frank commentary by the author, a longtime Cusco resident, on the ancient Inca capital, the Sacred Valley, and, of course, Machu Picchu. *Peru and Bolivia: The Bradt Trekking Guide* (Bradt Publications, 2002), by Hilary Bradt, is a trusty guide of classic treks in Peru and Bolivia. Although it's in its eighth edition, with several new walks and treks added, some readers find it outdated. Still, it's a good all-around guide for trekkers and walkers.

The Cloud Forest: A Chronicle of the South American Wilderness (Random House, 2003) is a travelogue by Peter Matthiessen, who trekked some 10,000 miles through South America, including the Amazon and Machu Picchu. Matthiessen found larger-than-life characters and ancient trails deep in the jungle, experiences that led to the author's novel, *At Play in*

> *The film* The Motorcycle Diaries *depicts Che Guevara's two-wheeled travels across South America, which took him to Peru in 1952.*

the Fields of the Lord (Vintage Books, 1991). Set in the unnamed Peruvian jungle, it's a thriller about the travails of the missionary Martin Quarrier and an outsider, Lewis Moon, a mercenary who takes a much different tack while immersing himself in a foreign culture. Both are displaced outsiders whose lives have an irreversible impact on native Amerindian communities deep in the Amazon. Another good travelogue on Peru is *The White Rock* (Overlook, 2003) by Hugh Thomson, an absorbing account of Thomson's 20 years traveling throughout the Andes of Peru, Bolivia, and Ecuador in search of lost Inca cities.

Film

Peru's film industry trails far behind those of its neighbors Argentina and Brazil, though a recent Oscar nomination may begin to change that. In a historic achievement for Peruvian film, *La Teta Asustada (The Milk of Sorrow),* by Claudia Llosa, was nominated for an Academy Award for Best Foreign Language Film in 2010 (it also received the

Golden Bear award at the Berlin International Film Festival in 2009). Less exalted perhaps but also recently reaching an international audience was *Máncora* (2008), a sexy Peruvian road movie set largely among surfing sites along the northern coast.

The best-known films about or featuring Peru are still foreign. Peter Matthiessen's 1965 novel *At Play in the Fields of the Lord* was made by Hector Babenco into a silly but occasionally pretty 1991 movie starring John Lithgow, Daryl Hannah, and Tom Berenger with a bowl-cut and face paint, and relocated from the Amazon basin of Peru to Brazil.

Two recent documentaries try to untangle the lasting impact of disgraced former president Alberto Fujimori. *The Fall of Fujimori: When Democracy and Terrorism Collide* (Stardust Productions, 2005) is a portrait of the eccentric ex-President and his controversial war against guerrilla movements in Peru. *State of Fear* (Skylight Pictures, 2006), based on the

findings of the Peruvian Truth Commission, chronicles the 2-decade-long reign of terror by Shining Path. It doesn't shy away from documenting the abuses of the government in fighting terrorism. *Touching the Void* (IFC Films, 2004) is the harrowing dramatic reenactment (based on the book by Joe Simpson) of a climber's disastrous and near-fatal accident climbing in the Andes mountains near Huaraz. It's gripping, but may derail any mountaineering plans you had.

The Dancer Upstairs (Fox Searchlight, 2002), a drama directed by John Malkovich and starring Javier Bardem, is a political thriller loosely based on the hunt for Abimael Guzmán, the Shining Path leader, and the complicated story of the American Lori Berenson, implicated and imprisoned as a terrorist collaborator in Peru (though the movie is set in an unnamed South American nation). *The Motorcycle Diaries,* an excellent 2004 film by Walter Salles about the young Che Guevara, is in large part a travelogue of Argentina, Chile, Colombia, and Venezuela, but Machu Picchu plays a scene-stealing role. The latest installment in the Raiders of the Lost Ark series, *Indiana Jones and the Kingdom of the Crystal Skull* (Paramount Home Entertainment, 2008), takes place in part in Peru, including the Nasca Lines and the Peruvian jungle (although the jungle scenes were actually filmed in Hawaii).

Music

There is evidence of music in Peru dating back 10,000

> The quena (pan flute) of Andean music reverberates throughout the Peruvian highlands.

years, and musical historians have identified more than 1,000 genres of music in the country. Traditional instruments include **pututos** (trumpets made from seashells) and many other wind instruments crafted from cane, bone, horns, and precious metals, as well as a wide range of percussion instruments. Exposure to Western cultures has introduced new instruments such as the harp, violin, and guitar to Peruvian music, but Peruvian music can still be identified by its distinctive instruments.

The **cajón** is a classic percussion instrument, typically heard in Peru's indigenous coastal rhythms, such as *música criolla* and *música negra*, as well as *marinera*. A simple wooden box with a sound hole in the back, the *cajón* is played by a musician who sits on top and pounds the front like a bongo. The *cajón* has been introduced into flamenco music by none other than the legendary flamenco guitarist Paco de

Lucía. Another popular instrument is the **zampoña,** which belongs to the panpipe family and varies greatly in size. The *zampoña* is never absent at festivals in southern Peru, particularly Puno.

Most travelers are at least superficially familiar with the dominant strains of Peruvian music. Anyone who has traveled in Europe, South America, or even Asia is likely to have seen and heard roving bands of street musicians in highlander garb playing the *música folclórica* (folk music) that emanates from high in the Andes mountains. The distinctive sounds of this Peruvian music—characterized by the **quena** (pan flute), played like a recorder; **charango** (from the lute family); and mandolin—are similar to those heard in other Andean countries, such as Bolivia and Ecuador. They are widely sampled in the Simon and Garfunkel song "El Cóndor Pasa," which is based on a melody by a Peruvian composer, Daniel Alomía Robles, who himself had appropriated a traditional Quechua *huayno* folk melody.

Adventurous ears with an interest in ethnomusicology might gravitate toward a handful of Andean *música folclórica* recordings released by the Smithsonian Folkways Series. *Mountain Music of Peru*, a two-volume series released in the early 1990s, includes recordings, celebratory and religious in nature, made in mountain villages in the 1960s. As such, they are raw and lack studio polish. Smithsonian also issues other volumes covering the

traditional regional music of Peru, from *Cajamarca and the Colca Valley* (vol. 3) to *The Ayacucho Region* (vol. 6). Though its song selections aren't specifically Peruvian, listeners may also enjoy the *Rough Guide to the Music of the Andes* compilation.

Just as there is a notable divide in Peruvian cuisine, with radically different takes in the sierra and *costa* (coast), so, too, is Peruvian music divided along these lines. In coastal areas, principally Lima and communities just south, such as El Carmen, the most distinctive music comes from the Afro-Peruvian population, who are descendants of slaves. Black Peruvians created a unique mix of African rhythms and Spanish and other European influences called *música criolla*. Percussion is fundamental, in addition to strings and vocals, but the music is frequently more bluesy than its jazz-inflected Afro counterparts that developed in Brazil and Cuba. A great place to start exploring is the compilation, selected by David Byrne and released on his Luaka Bop label, *Afro-Peruvian Classics: The Soul of Black Peru,* featuring the influential singers and groups Eva Ayllón, Susana Baca, Perú Negro, Chabuca Granda, Nicomedes Santa Cruz, and others. Those same stars (but no repeat songs) are also featured on *The Rough Guide to Afro Peru*.

Susan Baca, with her recordings on the Luaka Bop label, has reached an audience of American and international ears. Look for her eponymous album or *Ecos de Sombra*. In

Peru, **Eva Ayllón** is even more of a megastar. A good recording available worldwide is *Eva! Leyenda Peruana.* Another longtime female Afro-Peruvian performer is **Chabuca Granda;** a greatest hits collection of her work is called *Latinoamericana.* **Perú Negro**'s albums *Sangre de un Don* and *Jolgorio,* recorded after the death of the group's founder Ronaldo Campos in 2001, are both widely available.

A taste of Peruvian music serves either as great preparation for a trip to Peru or as a fond souvenir after the fact. But nothing equals grooving to live Peruvian coastal *música criolla* in a nightclub, at a stylish Lima jazz bar, or *peña*—a one-time social club now frequented by locals and tourists for live music—or hearing highlands *música folclórica* during an Andean festival or stumbling upon it in a town square. The renaissance of Peru's indigenous musical forms is a hugely welcome development in this culturally rich country.

Chicha is a relatively new addition to the list of musical genres. A hybrid of sorts of the *huayno* and Colombian *cumbia, chicha* is an extremely popular urban dance, especially among the working class. It has spread rapidly across Peru and throughout Latin America.

Artisanry

Woven textiles have to be considered among the great traditional arts of Peru. Peru has one of the richest and most ancient weaving traditions in the world; for more than 5,000 years, Peruvian artisans have used fine natural fibers for hand weaving, and the wool produced by alpacas, llamas, and vicuñas is some of the finest in the world, rarer even than cashmere. The most ancient textiles that have been found in Peru come from the Huaca Prieta temple in Chicama and are more than 4,000 years old. In pre-Columbian times, hand-woven textiles, which required extraordinary patience and skill, were prized and extremely valuable; distinctive textiles were indicators of social status and power. They were traded as commodities. Paracas, Huari, and Inca weavings are among the most sophisticated and artful ever produced in Peru. The Paracas designs were stunningly intricate, with detailed animals, human figures, and deities against dark backgrounds. Huari weaving features abstract figures and bold graphics. The Incas favored more minimalist designs, without embroidery. The finest Inca textiles were typically part of ritualistic ceremonies—many were burned as offerings to spirits.

Pre-Columbian civilizations

> *Peru's mesmerizing popular culture is a mix of indigenous, Afro, and European cultures.*

in Peru had no written language, but their textiles were loaded with symbolic images, and these serve as indelible clues to the cultures and beliefs of the artists. Worship of nature and spiritual clues are frequently represented by motifs in textiles. Many of the finest textiles unearthed were sacred and elaborately embroidered blankets that enveloped mummies in burial sites. Found in tombs in the arid coastal desert, one of the world's driest climates, the textiles often are remarkably preserved.

Contemporary Peruvian artisans continue the traditions, sophisticated designs, and techniques of intricate weaving inherited from pre-Columbian civilizations, often employing the very same instruments used hundreds of years ago and still favoring natural dyes. The drop spindle (weaving done with a stick and spinning wooden wheel), for example, is still used in many regions, and it's not uncommon to see women and young girls spinning the wheel as they tend to animals in the fields. Excellent-quality woven items, the best of which are much more than mere souvenirs, include typical Andean *chullos* (wool or alpaca hats with earflaps), ponchos, scarves, sweaters, and blankets.

Dance

Although there are a bewildering number of indigenous dances in Peru, especially along the coast, two dances have become synonymous with Peru: the *huayno* and the *marinera*. The **huayno** is the essential dance in the Andes,

> *Local Collagua girls dance in the square at Yanque, in the Colca Valley.*

with pre-Columbian origins fused with Western influences. Couples dancing the *huayno* perform sharp turns, hops, and tap-like *zapateos* to keep time. *Huayno* music is played on *quena, charango,* harp, and violin. The **marinera,** a sleek, sexy, dance of highly coordinated choreography, is derivative of other folkloric dances in Peru, dating back to the 19th century. There are regional variations of the dance, which differs most from the south coast to the northern highlands. Dancers keep time with a handkerchief in one hand. *Marinera* music in Lima is performed by guitar and *cajón,* while a marching band is de rigueur in the north. *Marinera* festivals are held across Peru, but the most celebrated one is in Trujillo in January.

One of the most attention-getting dances in Peru, though, is performed by **scissors dancers,** whose *danza de las tijeras* is an exercise in athleticism and balance. Dancers perform gymnastic leaps and daring stunts to the sounds of harp, violin, and—the main instrument to accompany the dance—a pair of scissors, made from two independent sheets of metal around 25cm (10 in.) long. The best places to see scissors dancers are Ayacucho, Arequipa, and Lima.

Dances associated with Afro-Peruvian music include lively and sensual **festejo** dances, in which participants respond to the striking of the *cajón,* one of the Afro-Peruvian music's essential instruments. The **alcatraz** is an extremely erotic dance: Females enter the dance floor with tissue on their posteriors, and the men, meanwhile, dance with lit candles; the not-so-subtle goal on the dance floor is for the man to light the woman's fire (and thus become her partner).

Eating & Drinking in Peru

> *Peru's rich bounty of produce and mix of European, Asian, and African elements have created one of the world's great cuisines.*

Dining

Until recently a rather well-guarded secret, Peruvian cuisine is among the most accomplished and diverse cuisines found anywhere. As knowledge of Peruvian food spreads, more travelers are even making focused gastronomic pilgrimages to Peru, and for a certain type of visitor, dining out will rank among the highlights of a trip to Peru.

Peruvian cooking differs significantly by region, and subcategories closely mirror the country's geographical divides: coastal, highlands, and jungle/tropical. The common denominator among regional cooking is a blend of indigenous and Spanish (or broader European) influences, which has evolved over the past 4 centuries. Traditional Peruvian coastal cooking, with European and African influences, is often referred to as *comida criolla,* and it's found across Peru. The other main type of cuisine is *andino* (highlands), and a creative or haute variant, *novo Andino.* Several celebrity chefs, including Gastón Acurio and Pedro Miguel Schiaffino, have led the charge of contemporary Peruvian cuisine on television and in restaurants across Peru and abroad, often offering their creative takes on traditional dishes.

As a dining city, the cosmopolitan capital Lima is on par with some of the finest eating cities in the world. But it's far from the only place one can expect to eat very well. Arequipa has its own, very distinguished cuisine, with liberal and creative use of *ajíes,* or hot peppers. Cusco used to be somewhat bland

Tip

For additional information on Peruvian cooking, check out **www.yanuq.com,** which features a history of Peruvian cuisine, a glossary, recipes, and a guide to restaurants in Peru. A good food blog dedicated to Peruvian restaurants and cooking is **perufood.blogspot.com.**

> *Unique sauces made from ají amarillo (yellow peppers) enliven seafood dishes along the coast.*

in its offerings, but no more; today it, too, thrives with innovative restaurants. And northern coastal cooking, particularly that of Chiclayo and Lambayeque, is quickly earning its own adherents.

Coastal preparations concentrate on seafood and shellfish. The star dish, and the most exported example of Peruvian cuisine, is ceviche (also spelled *cebiche*), a classic preparation of raw fish and shellfish marinated (not cooked) in lime or lemon juice and hot chile peppers, served with raw onion, sweet potato, and toasted corn. Ceviche has been around since the time of some of Peru's earliest civilizations, although a traditional Andean argument over whether Peruvians or Ecuadorians should be credited with creating it persists. *Cevicherías*, traditionally open only for lunch, usually serve several types of ceviche as well as a roster of other seafood. *Tiradito* is finely sliced fish marinated with lime juice and *ají* peppers, essentially Peruvian sashimi or carpaccio. Other coastal favorites include *escabeche* (a tasty fish concoction served with peppers, eggs, olives, onions, and prawns), *conchitas* (scallops), and *corvina* (sea bass). Land-based favorites are *cabrito* (roast kid) and *ají de gallina* (a tangy creamed chicken and chile dish).

Highlanders tend to favor a more substantial style of cooking. Corn and potatoes were staples of the Incas and other mountain civilizations before them. Meat, served with rice and potatoes, is a mainstay of the diet, as is *trucha* (trout). *Lomo saltado*, strips of beef mixed with onions, tomatoes, peppers, and french-fried potatoes and served with rice, seems to be on every menu. *Rocoto relleno*, a hot bell pepper stuffed with vegetables and meat, and *papa rellena*, a potato stuffed with veggies and then fried, are just as common (but are occasionally extremely spicy). Soups are generally excellent. In the countryside, you might see people in the fields digging small cooking holes in the ground; they are preparing *pachamanca*, a roast cooked underground—the Peruvian version of a picnic barbecue. *Cuy* (guinea pig) is considered a delicacy in many parts of Peru, including the sierra, although its elevated status is lost on many visitors. It comes roasted or fried, with head and feet upturned on the plate.

In the Amazon jungle regions, most people fish for their food, and diets consist almost entirely of fish such as river trout and *paiche* (a huge white river fish). Restaurants feature both of these, with accompaniments including yucca, *palmitos* (palm hearts) and *chonta* (palm-heart salad), bananas and plantains, and rice tamales known as *juanes*. Common menu items such as chicken and game are complemented by exotic fare (and occasionally endangered species) such as caiman, wild boar, turtle, monkey, and piranha fish.

Visitors will also find plenty of international cuisine, including Japanese and Chinese restaurants. A particularly Peruvian variation, *chifas*, are restaurants serving Peruvian-influenced Chinese food, developed by the large immigrant Chinese population and a mainstay among many non-Chinese Peruvians. *Chifas* are nearly as common as restaurants serving *pollo a la brasa* (spit-roasted chicken), which are ubiquitous.

Drinking
With one exception, drinking is less of an event in Peru than eating. Peru makes still wines in the coastal desert south, and while they're rapidly improving, they don't quite yet compare with more

celebrated wines from Chile and Argentina. Those two countries, along with Spain, tend to dominate wine lists in better restaurants. The one area where Peru really stands out is in its production of pisco, a powerful white-grape brandy. The pisco sour (a cocktail mixed with pisco, egg whites, lemon juice, sugar, and bitters) is the national drink and something equivalent to Peru's margarita: tasty, refreshing, and omnipresent. New takes on the pisco sour have sprung up at sophisticated mixology bars: *maracuyá* (passion fruit) sours, coca sours (made with macerated coca leaves), and other sours highlighting indigenous tropical fruits, such as *lúcuma*. Pisco is also drunk straight.

Highlanders, especially, drink *chicha*, a tangy, fermented brew made from maize and inherited from the Incas and other pre-Columbian cultures. Often served tepid in huge vessels, it is unlikely to please the palates of most foreign visitors, although it's certainly worth a try if you come upon a small, informal place with the red *chicha* flag flying in a rural village (a signal that there's fresh *chicha* available). *Chicha morada*, on the other hand, is nothing to be afraid of. It's a delicious nonalcoholic beverage, deep purple in color, prepared with blue corn and served chilled, the perfect accompaniment to ceviche. *Masato* is a beer made from yucca, typical of the Amazon region. Among soft drinks, the native Inca Kola, a neon-yellow beverage that looks nuclear and tastes a little like

> *Pisco, Peru's distinctive white-grape brandy, is the basis for this cocktail at Bar Huaringas in Lima.*

bubble gum, is the drink of choice for many Peruvians.

Meals & Dining Customs

Among Peru's more interesting dining customs—beyond the consumption of guinea pig—is the poetic offering, before a meal, of a sip of beer or *chicha* to Pachamama (Mother Earth). Many Peruvians still ritualistically thank the earth for its bounty, and they show their appreciation by spilling just a bit before raising the drink to their mouths. Set three-course meals, usually served at lunch, are referred to by a variety of terms: *menú del día, menú económico, menú ejecutivo, menú de la casa,* and *menú turístico.* They are all essentially the same thing and can sometimes be had for as little as S/7. Informal eateries serving Peruvian cooking are frequently called *picanterías* and *chicherías.*

Most restaurants include taxes and services in their menu prices. Others (including some upscale restaurants), however, separate taxes and services, and the bill can get pretty byzantine, especially when it comes to imported wine. You might see a subtotal, followed by a 10% service charge, a 20% wine tax, and a 19% IGV (general sales tax). Fortunately, the restaurants that do this are rare.

Dining hours don't differ much from typical mealtimes in cities in North America or the U.K., except that dinner (*cena*) is generally eaten after 8pm in restaurants. Peruvians do not eat nearly as late as Spaniards. Although lunch (*almuerzo* or *comida*) is the main meal of the day, for most visitors it generally isn't the grand midday affair it is in Spain.

Note: If you invite a Peruvian to have a drink or to dine with you, it is expected that you will pay (the Spanish verb *invitar* literally connotes this as an invitation). It's not advised to ask a Peruvian acquaintance join you in what will certainly be an expensive restaurant or cafe for him or her, and then pony up only half the tab.

14
The Best Special Interest Trips

Organized Adventure Trips

Organized ecotourism or adventure travel packages, arranged by tour operators abroad or in Peru, are a good option for those with limited time and resources looking to combine cultural and outdoor activities. Traveling with a group has several advantages over traveling independently. Your accommodations and transportation are arranged and included in the cost of a package. If your tour operator has a reasonable amount of experience and a decent track record, you should proceed to each of your destinations quickly without the snags and long delays you might face when traveling on your own. Some group trekking trips include *porteros* or *arrieros* (porters or muleteers) who carry extra equipment.

In the best packages, group size is kept small (10–20 people), and tours are escorted by knowledgeable guides who are either naturalists or biologists. If you're booking a tour that includes outdoor activities such as trekking, mountaineering, or surfing, be sure to ask about the level of difficulty involved. Most companies offer "soft adventure" packages that those who are in reasonable shape can handle; others focus on hard-core activities, geared toward only adventure travelers and seasoned athletes.

In addition to the companies listed below, many extremely well-regarded environmental organizations offer organized trips to Peru. The **Nature Conservancy** (☎ 800/628-6860; www.nature.org/aboutus/travel/travel) offers eco-trips with members; the trips change from year to year, but past trips to Peru have included a riverboat Amazon voyage that visits the Nature Conservancy project in the Pacaya Samiria National Reserve. ★★ **Smithsonian Journeys** (☎ 877/338-8687; www.smithsonianjourneys.org), offered by the Smithsonian Institution, are study tours for members, which have included a river cruise of the northern Amazon and a long (and expensive) trip down the Amazon from Belém, Brazil, to Pevas, Peru. Trips with **Audubon Nature Odysseys** (☎ 800/967-7425; travel.audubon.org), a division of the National Audubon Society, focus on birding and natural history arranged through carefully selected travel partners.

Peru-Based Tour Operators

Class Adventure Travel (☎ 877/240-4770 in the U.S. and Canada, 0207/0906-1259 in the U.K.; www.cat-travel.com) is a fine all-purpose agency with offices in Lima and Cusco (it also has offices in Bolivia, Chile, and Argentina). In addition to professionally organizing virtually any kind of travel detail in Peru, its adventure offerings include rafting, trekking, and jungle tours.

Explorandes Peru (☎ 01/715-2323; www.explorandes.com) has been doing trekking and river expeditions in Peru for nearly 3 decades, and has regional offices in Lima, Cusco, Huaraz, and Puno. One of the top high-end agencies for treks and mountaineering in Peru, it's reasonably priced and especially good for forming very small private groups. It offers a number of soft-adventure trips (with stays in hotels and full- and half-day river trips) and an even more impressive lineup of real adventure, including cool trips such as llama trekking to Chavín, a festival trek, rafting on the Apurímac River, treks on southern peaks around Cusco, and hard-core trekking in the Cordillera Blanca and Huayhuash. Amazon extensions are available.

Mountain Lodges of Peru (☎ 01/421-7777; www.mountainlodgesofperu.com), a Peruvian trekking company, has built a series of small, spectacular lodges on private lands in the Vilcabamba mountain range west of the Sacred Valley. The sleek inns have whirlpools, fireplaces, and nice dining rooms. The company offers its own 6-day treks to Machu Picchu and also contracts with a handful of international adventure tour operators, including Backroads, Mountain Travel Sobek, and Wilderness Travel (see below).

Peru Expeditions Overland (☎ 01/447-2057; www.peru-expeditions.com) is a Lima-based company run by Rafael Belmonte, an amiable fellow and dedicated cyclist. His company runs all kinds of cool trips across Peru, including treks, four-wheel-drive vehicle tours, and mountain biking, as well as Andean festivities tours, and more standard tours to destinations such as Arequipa, Cusco, and Colca Canyon.

Peru for Less (☎ 877/269-0309, or 203/002-0571 in the U.K.; www.peruforless.com), originally based in Texas and now headquartered in Lima, lives up to its plainspoken name. It has a great roster of affordable Peru tour packages, such as Historical Peru, which visits Lima, Paracas, Nasca, Arequipa, Cusco, and Machu Picchu, and very competent teams on the ground. It has recently branched out with alternative trekking tours in the Cusco region, including small-group treks to Choquequirao, Vilcabamba, and a dozen more. Tours include guides, hotels, all visits and transfers, plus daily breakfast.

SAS Travel Peru (☎ 084/249-194; www.sastravelperu.com), based in Cusco, is one of the most popular agencies organizing outdoor travel for backpackers and budget-minded travelers. Its roster includes the Inca Trail, a number of short treks in the Cusco area and a couple of longer, more challenging mountain treks lasting up to a week. Jungle treks are to Manu and Tambopata. SAS also offers whitewater rafting, paragliding, climbing, mountain biking, and horseback riding.

International Adventure-Tour Operators

★★ **Abercrombie & Kent** (☎ 800/554-7016; www.abercrombiekent.com) calls itself the "original luxury travel company." It runs an extensive lineup of high-end luxury trips, all of which are well managed and pampered, with stays in many of the finest hotels available. The tours aren't cheap, but if you want to go in style, A&K is the way to go. Group size is generally limited to 16 people. About a dozen Peru itineraries are available (such as the 9-day Wonders of Peru, a family adventure, and combo trips with Bolivia and the Galápagos); check the website for occasional discounts on selected tours and dates.

Adventure Life (☎ 800/344-6118; www.adventure-life.com), based in Missoula, Montana, and specializing in Central and South America, has an interesting roster of rugged Peru trips, frequently with a community focus, including a 12-day multisport tour (mountain biking, hiking, rafting, jungle tour, and Machu Picchu), rainforest eco-lodge tours, and the 10-day Cachiccata Trek: The Inca Trail Less Traveled, as well as plenty of tour extensions. One Peru trip is specifically designed to raise money (40% of trip cost) for the organization's nonprofit fund, which aims to give back to local communities.

Adventure Specialists (☎ 719/783-2086; www.adventurespecialists.org) travels only to the Copper Canyon (Mexico), Colorado, and Peru. In Peru, it specializes in treks, horseback trips, and archaeology expeditions, as well as wildlife and birding adventures by dugout canoe in the Manu Biosphere Reserve. The founder is one of the archaeologists credited with the November 2003 rediscovery of Llactapata, a "lost" Inca city.

Amazonia Expeditions (☎ 800/262-9669; www.perujungle.com or www.peruandes.com) has offered good-value, personalized, and flexible ecotourism trips to the Peruvian jungle and the Andes since 1981. Trips of up to 7 days are all-inclusive (even laundry and tips are included). Jungle trips are to the Tahauyo Lodge (4 hr. from Iquitos) and the Tamshiyacu-Tahuayo Reserve (they are the only licensed tour operator to the latter). The two websites focus on the group's jungle adventures and Inca ruins/Andes treks, respectively.

Andean Treks (☎ 800/683-8148; www.andeantreks.com) is a personalized, high-quality Latin American adventure-tour operator that focuses on trekking in the Andes and exploring the jungle throughout Peru. The Massachusetts-based group's roster of reasonably priced trips for all levels includes cloud-forest treks, llama trekking, trips to Manu and Tambopata, and highlands treks that combine white-water rafting or Amazon lodge stays. Trips range from easy to hard-core.

Backroads (☎ 800/462-2848; www.backroads.com) is a luxury tour company that offers upscale, light-adventure trips around the globe, and it has several tours of Peru on its menu. It specializes in walking, hiking, and biking tours from Cusco to Machu Picchu, some of which incorporate stays at the Mountain Lodges of Peru (p. 274). Service is personalized and the guides are top-notch.

Butterfield & Robinson (☎ 866/551-9090 or 800/6781-1477 in Europe; www.butterfield.com) is a top upscale tour company that promotes biking and walking trips. You'll stay at some of the country's finest hotels and will get full van support for any light adventure trips. To Peru, it offers an 8-day Peru Walking tour. Trips are top of the line (with commensurate pricing).

★★ **Gap Adventures** (☎ 888/800-4100 440-4677; www.gapadventures.com), the "great adventure people," offers a wide variety of trips, including adventure-travel, comfort-oriented, and value-priced journeys to Peru's greatest destinations. Trips aren't necessarily innovative, but they are very professionally run and include "Peru on a Shoestring," starting at $1,399, and "Inca Heartland," which ends in La Paz (Bolivia).

GorpTravel (☎ 877/440-GORP 440-4677; www.adventurefinder.com), a self-styled "guide to outdoor travel," is a wholesaler with a vast range of options for adventure- and more general travel throughout Peru and the world offered by outfitters across the globe. It recently offered more than 150 outdoor-oriented vacations to Peru (including a Peru Top-20 list). A few are basic highlights trips, while others are cultural and language vacations or specialist tours for very active and adventurous sorts.

International Expeditions (☎ 800/633-4734; www.ietravel.com) features Amazon cruises and jungle-lodge tours (including luxurious river cruises run by Jungle Expeditions). The main tours to Peru are Amazon Explorer Jungles of Peru and a 9-day Amazon Voyage. Visitors help with reforestation projects and participate in conservation programs and tree planting with local naturalists. Extensions to Cusco, Machu Picchu, Lima, and the Nasca Lines are available.

Journeys International (☎ 800/255-8735; www.journeys.travel), based in Ann Arbor, Michigan, offers small-group (4–12 people) natural history tours guided by naturalists. Trips include the 9-day Amazon & Andes Odyssey, which includes the Tambopata National Reserve along with Cusco, Machu Picchu, and the Sacred Valley, and special Amazon and Inca trips for families.

Mountain Travel Sobek (☎ 888/831-7526 or 0808/234-2243 in the U.K.; www.mtsobek.com) offers seven itineraries to Peru, including the 8-day Andean Explorer, with day hikes and rafting. Options for mountaineers and committed trekkers include 13 days of strenuous trekking in Cordillera Blanca (mostly camping); a 5-day (but still hard-core) trekking option in the same area; and a challenging 15-day rafting trip along the Tambopata River (half camping, half inns). A unique trip is the off-the-beaten path Other Inca Trail—the company also arranges luxury treks to Machu Picchu with stays at the cool inns owned and operated by **Mountain Lodges of Peru** (p. 274). Trips are rated for difficulty.

Overseas Adventure Travel (☎ 800/493-6824; www.oattravel.com) offers natural history and "soft adventure" itineraries, with optional add-on excursions. Tours are limited to 16 people and are guided by naturalists. All accommodations are in small hotels, lodges, or tent camps. The 11-day Real Affordable Peru includes rafting on the Urubamba and a *curandero* healing ceremony. The 16-day Machu Picchu & Galápagos tour features a good bit of walking. Amazon River cruises and rainforest trips are also featured.

★ **Southwind Adventures** (☎ 800/377-9463; www.southwindadventures.com) plans distinctive and high-end adventure trips in South America with a cultural emphasis. Among them are 16 Peruvian trips, from mountain biking to specialty tours such as the Urubamba Weaver's Trek. Custom trips include a 21-day Grand Andean Traverse trekking expedition, with possibilities for bird-watching, rafting, and family adventure.

Tropical Nature Travel (☎ 877/827-8350; www.tropicalnaturetravel.com) is known as one of the most sophisticated conservation groups organizing travel to jungle wildlife lodges in Manu and Tambopata. In tandem with its local conservation partner, InkaNatura, it operates four lodges, including Manu Wildlife Center, Cock of the Rock Lodge, Sandoval Lake Lodge, and the new Heath River Wildlife Center; and its Amazon jungle trips can't be beat. The outfit has expanded its itineraries to include trekking, rafting, and archaeology culture trips to places such as Chachapoyas and Colca Canyon.

Wilderness Travel (☎ 800/368-2794; www.wildernesstravel.com) is a Berkeley-based outfitter specializing in cultural, wildlife, and hiking group tours that are arranged with tiered pricing (the cost of the trip varies according to group size). There are 13 different tours to Peru, including a 17-day trek in the Cordillera Huayhuash Blanca, the Choquequirao trail to Machu Picchu, as well as a unique Peru Festivals trek. Wilderness Travel also offers soft-luxury treks to Machu Picchu with stays at the cool inns owned and operated by **Mountain Lodges of Peru** (p. 274). Trips are helpfully graded according to difficulty.

Wildland Adventures (☎ 800/345-4453; www.wildland.com), based in Seattle, is one of the top international outdoor-tour companies with operations in Peru. It offers excellent special-interest trekking and rainforest expedition

> *Bird-watchers are drawn to Manu National Park and its 1,000 species of birds.*

programs, with customizing options. There are lodge-based programs, primarily in the jungle; trekking expeditions, such as the Machu Picchu mountain lodges trek; and special adventures focusing on photographing Peru's Ancient Lands and Native Spirits. Wildland's programs are well designed, guides are very professional, and the organization is focused on authentic travel experiences.

Outdoor Activities A to Z

Bird-Watching

Peru is easily one of the greatest places on earth for birders. The bird population in Peru is, incredibly, about 10% of the world's total. With nearly 2,000 species of resident and migrant birds identified throughout Peru, great bird-watching sites abound.

Manu National Park, believed to have the highest concentration of bird life on the planet and more than 1,000 species of birds, is legendary among birders. Cocks-of-the-rock, quetzals, toucanets, tanagers, and seven species of colorful macaws await patient birders. Some visitors have spotted as many as 500 species in relatively short visits to Manu. For specialists, the **Manu Wildlife Center** (p. 310)

> *Explore Colca Canyon by horseback.*

has the best reputation among birders, although **Pantiacolla Lodge** (p. 310) is highly recommended, too. Tambopata National Reserve is also extraordinary for birding and more accessible than Manu. The reserve, about a third the size of Costa Rica, claims more species of birds (around 600) and butterflies (more than 1,200) than any place of similar size. Both Tambopata and Manu are famous for their *collpas,* or clay licks, where hundreds of macaws, parrots, and other birds appear daily to feed. Nearer to Puerto Maldonado, good birding areas include the Sandoval and Valencia lakes, but they cannot compare to either of the major reserves. **Explorer's Inn** (p. 307) is renowned as one of the top birding lodges in South America. In the northern Amazon, the Pacaya Samiria National Reserve is home to more than 500 species of birds. The northern Amazon doesn't have quite the reputation that the varied cloud forests leading to Manu and the rest of the southeastern jungle do, although there is excellent birding in and around the protected Machu Picchu Sanctuary.

A handful of jungle lodges and river-cruise operators offer specialized birding options, but none are as complete as the trips offered by the specialist tour operators below. Birding sites worth visiting are **Ornifolks** (www.ornifolks.org), a network of birding enthusiasts, and **WorldTwitch** (www.worldtwitch.com), which has links to birding lodges, tour operators, and organizations throughout Peru, as well as the Americas and the Caribbean. A portal with good information on birding in Peru is **Peru Birding Routes** (www.perubirdingroutes.com), with articles on birding, multimedia and photo guides, conservation information, and birding forums. In addition to the outfitters below, **Inkaterra Machu Picchu Pueblo Hotel** (p. 288) organizes birding tours and has more than 100 species of birds on its property in Aguas Calientes.

Birding Peru (www.birdingperu.com) is a Peru-based tour operator that links to birding trips offered by major outfitters to all regions of the country, including the highlands, coasts, and rainforest, and provides good general information on birding throughout Peru.

Field Guides (☎ 800/728-4953; www.fieldguides.com) is a specialty bird-watching travel operator based in Austin, Texas, that offers trips worldwide. It features six birding trips to Peru, including Manu, Tambopata, Machu Picchu and the eastern slope of the Andes, the Amazon, and a 24-day tour of the endemic-rich region of northern Peru. Group size is limited to 14 participants.

Kolibri Expeditions (☎ 01/273-7246; www.kolibriexpeditions.com), based in Lima, offers birding tours across Peru and South America, including condor-watching trips. Most are no-frills, budget camping trips, but the outfit now also offers a few pampered, high-end trips (such as the Marvelous Spatuletail Tours).

Tanager Tours (☎ 01/9858-36609; www.tanagertours.com) is a Dutch-owned specialist bird-watching tour operator based in Trujillo. It organizes birding trips to Manu, Puerto Maldonado, and many other spots in Peru.

Wings (☎ 888/293-6443; wingsbirds.com) is a specialty bird-watching travel operator with 3 decades of experience in the field. It promotes three trips to Peru, including an 18-day trip to Machu Picchu and the Manu Biosphere Reserve, and one to the north and Andes in search of the long-whiskered owlet. Group size is usually between 6 and 18 people.

Horseback Riding

Lovers of horseback riding will find several areas in Peru to pursue their interest, as well as hotels and operators that can arrange everything from a few hours in a saddle to a 2-week trip. The best areas for treks on horseback are the Colca Canyon, near Arequipa, and the Callejón de Huaylas valley, near the peaks of the Cordillera Blanca; a couple of local and international tour operators offer horse trekking in those areas. Otherwise, your options are mostly limited to a few country hotels in Cajamarca, the Sacred Valley, and Colca Valley.

In the area around Pisco, horseback riding is available in Ica at **Hotel Las Dunas** (p. 126). For riding on the outskirts of Cusco, the **Casa Andina** hotel group (www.casa-andina.com) arranges excellent day-long trips, available for walking between the ruins (Sacsayhuamán, Q'enko, Puca Pucara, and Tambomachay) just beyond Cusco and in the countryside. In the Sacred Valley, check out **Sonesta Posadas del Inca** (p. 287) and **Sol y Luna Lodge & Spa** (p. 287); in Ollantaytambo, you can usually arrange horseback riding along valley trails by asking around the main square. **Las Casitas del Colca** (p. 161) has horses for treks in the Colca Valley and Canyon; local agencies in Arequipa that arrange horseback treks through the Colca Canyon include **Colca Trek** (☎ 054/202-461; www.colcatrek.com) and **Peru Trekking** (☎ 054/223-404). In Huaraz, try **Andino Club Hotel** (p. 404) or **Monttrek** (☎ 043/421-124), which arranges good horseback mountain and valley treks. A number of country hotels just outside Cajamarca have horses for riding, including **Hotel & Spa Laguna Seca, Hotel Posada del Puruay,** and **Hostal Portada del Sol Hacienda;** see chapter 12 for details. Finally, although most people go to the jungle for bird-watching or canoe trips, **Manu Expeditions** (☎ 084/226-671; www.manuexpeditions.com) organizes horseback riding from Manu Wildlife Center.

Adventure Specialists (☎ 719/630-2086; www.adventurespecialists.org) organizes horse-supported Machu Picchu treks, including the 8-day Machu Picchu Pony Express.

Monttrek (☎ 043/421-124), based in Huaraz, offers horseback riding and other adventure sports in the area around the Cordillera Blanca.

Perol Chico (☎ 084/9846-24475; www.perolchico.com), in Urubamba, operates a ranch and is one of the top horseback-riding agencies in Peru, offering full riding vacations with Peruvian Paso horses and stays at the ranch, as well as 1- and 2-day rides (and up to 12-day horseback adventures in the Sacred Valley).

Southwind Adventures (☎ 800/377-9463; www.southwindadventures.com) offers horse-packing among its roster of adventure trips in Peru.

Sol y Luna Lodge & Spa (p. 287) in Urubamba also organizes horseback-riding programs that range from a half-day to 14-days in the Sacred Valley on Peruvian Paso horses.

Hot-Air Ballooning

In the mid-'70s, two foreigners constructed a balloon out of cotton and reed in an effort to prove that ancient cultures could have used balloons to design the mysterious Nasca Lines drawings in the southern desert sands. Although that didn't seem to instigate a serious interest in ballooning and hang gliding in Peru, the U.S.-owned company **Globos de los Andes,** Av. de la Cultura 220, of. 36, Cusco (☎ 084/232-352; www.globosperu.com), offers flights mainly in the Urubamba Valley. If you're interested, contact the company before your trip to Peru (and have backup plans, as flights have been somewhat inconsistent over the years). Flights are generally May through August only.

Jungle Lodges & River Cruises

Nearly two-thirds of Peru is rainforest, and options for exploring it are myriad, from jungle lodges and independently guided treks to river cruises. You can opt for an add-on including a trip to Cusco, a full-scale jungle trek, or a cruise lasting a couple weeks. The most important issue is choosing which major jungle destination fits best with your interests, time, and budget. Nearly all the international and Peruvian tour operators that do outdoor and adventure travel—for that matter, almost all agencies that handle travel to Peru—have some sort of jungle package available. Specialists that focus on Amazon nature travel are more immersion-oriented than general tour operators. See chapter 10, as well as the adventure-tour operators listed above.

> *With its scenic beauty and ancient paths that become single-track, the Sacred Valley is increasingly popular with mountain bikers.*

Mountain Biking

Mountain biking may still be in its infancy in Peru, and less practiced than trekking, mountaineering, and jungle tours, but fat-tire options and popularity are growing fast. Colca Valley and Canyon, Huaraz and the Callejón de Huaylas, and the Sacred Valley are the major areas for off-road cycling. The Manu jungle is also good for hard-core biking. Several tour companies in those places rent bikes, and the quality of the equipment is continually being upgraded. If you're a committed mountain biker and plan to do a lot of biking, you might want to consider bringing your own bike, though it would severely limit your ability to travel Peru when not on two wheels.

My favorite mountain-biking spots are horse and mountain trails in the Callejón de Huaylas, which provide the kind of amazing climbing found in the Rockies of the western United States and mountain views that are second to none. Mountain bikers, along with other adventure-sports fans, descend on Huaraz and the valley every June for its celebrated Semana del Andinismo. The Colca Valley is also an outstanding region for hardcore mountain biking, though there are fewer tour outfitters targeting the area. For gentler but also incredibly scenic trail riding (as well as more technical single track), the Sacred Valley is excellent.

In Huaraz and the Callejón de Huaylas, the top two agencies for mountain biking are ★★ **Mountain Bike Adventures** (☎ 043/424-259; www.chakinaniperu.com), run by Julio Olaza, and **Pony Expeditions** (☎ 043/391-642; www.ponyexpeditions.com), run by Alberto Cafferata.

Peru Bike (☎ 01/260-8225; www.perubike.com), based in Lima, has a great schedule of Andes mountain-biking trips across Peru, including Huascarán and Lake Titicaca loops, and cool day trips on GT bikes. **Monttrek** (☎ 043/421-124) also offers organized mountain-biking tours. ★ **Peru Expeditions Overland** (☎ 01/447-2057; www.peru-expeditions.

com), based in Lima, is run by a former top cyclist and runs mountain-biking trips in the Sacred Valley to Machu Picchu.

In Cusco, **Peru Discovery,** Triunfo (Sunturwasi) 392, of. 113 (☎ 054/274-541; www.perudiscovery.com/en), is the top specialist, with a half-dozen bike trips that include hard-core excursions. The local outfitters **Amazonas Explorer** (☎ 084/252-846; www.amazonas-explorer.com), **Apumayo Expediciones** (☎ 084/ 9847-66732; www.apumayo.com), **Eric Adventures** (☎ 084/234-764; www.ericadventures.com), and **Instinct Travel** (☎ 084/233-451; www.instinct-travel.com) offer 1- to 5-day organized mountain-biking excursions for novices and experienced single-trackers. In the Sacred Valley, **Eco Montana** (no phone; www.ecomontana.com), run by the mountain biker Omar Zarzar, rents good mountain bikes and organizes extended as well as shorter *ciclo*-tourism rides around Urubamba, with top equipment.

Manu Adventures (☎ 084/261-640; www.manuadventures.com) and **Manu Nature Tours** (☎ 084/252-721; www.manuperu.com) offer mountain-biking add-ons to lodge stays and jungle treks.

In Arequipa, **Colca Trek** (☎ 054/202-461; www.colcatrek.com) and **Peru Trekking** (☎ 054/223-404) feature mountain biking in the Colca Canyon.

Surfing

Surfing in Peru for now is still the domain of surf freaks and specialists, remaining somewhat under the general public's radar. Yet interest is surging, and Peru has become one of the world's top surfing destinations among surfing aficionados. It has 2,500km (1,550 miles) of Pacific coastline and huge possibilities for left and right reef breaks, point breaks, and massive waves. Boarders can hit the surf year-round, especially in the north. Northern beaches, especially Puerto Chicama north of Trujillo and Cabo Blanco and other spots near Máncora, even farther north, draw surfers to some of the gnarliest waves in South America. There are also good surfing beaches south of Lima, though they aren't as spectacular as in the north, where the waters are also much warmer. The north is better from October to March, while the surfing in the south is good April through December

> *The top surfing destination within easy reach of Lima is Punta Hermosa beach, south of the capital.*

and tops in May. The best surfing site, with webcams and reports on water conditions and the best beaches up and down Peru, is **www.peruazul.com**. Check out **www.wannasurf.com/spot/South_America/Peru** for basic surfing information and maps, as well as **Wave Hunters** (see below) for good information and surf tours to Peru.

Pure Vacations (☎ 44/0845-229-0045; www.purevacations.com/south-america/peru), based in the U.K., has organized surf travel since 1999 and combines northern Peru with Ecuador for 14-day surf trips.

Wave Hunters (☎ 760/494-7392; www.wavehunters.com/peru-surfing/peru.asp), a California-based organization, offers a surfeit of good information on Peru's coastline and celebrated waves, as well as different, inexpensive small-group surfing tours in central and northern Peru, including stays at Pico Alto International Surf Camp in Punta Hermosa. They work with a group called **Octopus Surf Tours** (☎ 01/99-400-5518; www.octopussurftours.com) in northern Peru.

> *Whitewater rafters can test their skills across Peru: in Colca Canyon, the Urubamba Valley, and the Callejón de Huaylas.*

Trekking & Mountain Climbing

In terms of adventure tourism, trekking and climbing rank with expeditions into the Amazon jungle as Peru's biggest outdoor draws. Peru is one of the world's great trekking and mountain-climbing destinations; its mountains and resplendent valleys are ideal for everything from hard-core ascents of 6,000m (19,700-ft.) peaks to gentle walks. Experienced mountaineers, ice climbers, trekkers, and regular travelers with a hankering to get outdoors can find in Peru the grandeur of the great Cordillera Blanca, the volcanoes and canyons around Arequipa, and, of course, the Andes mountains in and around Cusco.

Trekking circuits of varying degrees of difficulty lace the valleys and mountain ridges of Peru's sierra, yet only a few have become popular commercial trekking routes. Independent trekkers who like to blaze their own trail (metaphorically speaking—you should always stick to existing trails) have a surfeit of options in Peru for uncrowded treks. The most celebrated trek, of course, is the Inca Trail to Machu Picchu—one of the world's most rewarding treks, provided that the crowds and need to be accompanied by an organized group don't spoil your fun. For guided treks to Machu Picchu and alternatives to the Inca Trail, see chapter 9 for additional information on recommended tour operators.

Scores of outfitters, both international and local, organize a full gamut of mountain-climbing and trekking package tours. If you do outdoor travel in Peru, you should include some easy hikes, at a minimum. Independent travelers can hook up with local agencies for tailored experiences. For more details on trekking, see destination chapters in this book, especially chapters 6, 8, 9, and 11.

White-Water Rafting

Home to the origin of the mighty Amazon and great canyon rivers, Peru offers some excellent opportunities for white-water rafting. Whether you're a total novice or a world-class river runner, Peru has white water suited to your abilities. The rivers flowing through the Colca and Cotahuasi canyons, other rivers nearer to Arequipa, and the Andean rivers of the Urubamba Valley stand out. A good adventurous experience is rafting in the Amazon jungle on the Tambopata River. There's also good white water on the Río Santa in the Callejón de Huaylas. If you're just experimenting with river rafting, stick to Class II and III rivers. If you already know your way around a raft and a paddle, there are plenty of Class IV

> *Take a class in Lima, and learn to cook with Peru's native* ajíes *(hot peppers) and exotic fruits and vegetables.*

and V sections to run. Hard-core river runners come to Peru for multiday rafting trips to Class V and even Class VI rivers in remote canyons. The best months for rafting are May through September, when water levels are low. (During the rainy season, canyon rivers can be extremely dangerous.)

A half-dozen or more agencies in Arequipa, Cusco, and the Sacred Valley organize a range of local white-water opportunities. Specialists include **Amazonas Explorer** (☎ 084/252-846; www.amazonas-explorer.com), which offers white-water rafting tours that can be combined with Inca Trail treks. Trips, which feature small groups, can be booked from abroad. Among its Peru trips are rafting on the Río Apurímac, inflatable canoeing on the source of the Amazon (combined with trekking the Inca Trail), rainforest rafting, and extreme Class IV to VI in Cotahuasi, the world's deepest canyon. **SwissRaft Peru,** Plateros 369 (☎ 084/264-124; www.swissraft-peru.com), based in Cusco, organizes 1-day rafting trips year-round on the Apurímac, Cusipata, and Chuquicahuana, as well as 4-day trips on the Apurímac.

Learning Trips & Language Classes

Particularly well suited to Peru's pre-Columbian archaeological sites and vast jungle, the programs of **Earthwatch Institute** (☎ 800/776-0188; www.earthwatch.org) send travelers out to work in the field alongside scientists involved in archaeology and environmental conservation. There are three Peru research and education trips: join a 13-day excavation of a pre-Inca site, assist with researching Peruvian macaws, or document the biology of Andean rivers. The trips are a unique way to see a fascinating slice of the country from an academic or conservationist perspective.

Most people intent on learning something in Peru have language in mind. **Study Abroad International** (☎ 602/765-1205; www.studyabroadinternational.com/file/schools_Peru.html) lists a number of Spanish-study programs in Cusco. **GorpTravel** (☎ 877/440-GORP 440-4677; gorptravel.com) occasionally lists Spanish-study programs of short duration in Peru and other South American

> *Cusco's Amigos Spanish School offers short- and long-term immersion language programs.*

countries; follow the "Learning Vacations" link on the website for options.

One standout school in Cusco is the **Amigos Spanish School,** Zaguan del Cielo B-23 (☎ 084/242-292; www.spanishcusco.com); it's a nonprofit school that assists disadvantaged children through its Amigos Foundation. In Lima, **El Sol Escuela de Español,** Grimaldo de Solar 469, Miraflores (☎ 800/381-1806; elsol.idiomasperu.com), marries language classes to cooking workshops, dance classes, and other activities. Other schools to try in Lima are the **Instituto Cultural Peruano Norteamericano,** Angamos Oeste 160, Miraflores (☎ 01/241-1940; www.icpna.edu.pe), and **Instituto de Idiomas,** Camino Real 1037, San Isidro (☎ 01/442-8761). In Arequipa, classes are offered via **Centro de Intercambio Cultural,** Cercado Urbanización Universitaria (☎ 054/221-165; www.ceica-peru.com); **Centro de Idiomas UNSA,** San Agustín 106 (☎ 054/247-524); and **Centro Cultural Peruano Norteamericano,** Melgar 209 (☎ 054/801-022).

Peru's sophisticated, diverse cuisine is getting a lot of attention from travelers. Three companies (at last count) offer food-centric vacations. **A Taste of Peru** (☎ 01/247-5208; www.atasteofperu.com) is run by two young Peruvian sisters with resumes in the culinary world that include stints in the U.S., Europe, Peru, and Asia. They offer half- and full-day culinary experiences, as well as 8-day foodie trips to Lima, Cusco, and Machu Picchu. Their upscale gourmet trips take in food markets and restaurants in Lima and Cusco, and participants attend pisco tastings and ceviche demonstrations. **Pica Peru Culinary Vacations** (☎ 866/440-2561; www.peruculinaryvacations.com), based in Denver, Colorado, is run by a food and travel writer. Her company offers culinary tours that include cooking classes, beginning in Lima restaurants and then traveling to Cusco, the Sacred Valley, and Machu Picchu, or instead venture to the north coast and the surfing capital Máncora. Trips last 9 to 10 days, with a maximum of 8 travelers, and include four cooking classes. **Aracari** (☎ 312/239-8726 in the U.S., or and 020/3287-5262 in the U.K.; www.aracari.com) is an upscale Peruvian agency that designs excellent custom tours; it offers a Peru for Art Lovers and Foodies trip and creates personalized culinary tours with exclusive visits to private houses and haciendas for luncheons and cocktails, as well as cooking classes, visits to food markets, and dining at some of the finest restaurants in Peru.

> *Volunteer programs assist local communities with building projects, disaster relief, and crafts marketing.*

Volunteer Trips

Peru is a country with a great many needs, and thus there are opportunities to volunteer with programs that build schools and work on disaster relief, conservation, and more.

Cross-Cultural Solutions (☎ 800/380-4777; www.crossculturalsolutions.org), with offices in New Rochelle, New York, and Brighton, U.K., offers weeklong volunteer programs in Peru (in Lima's Villa El Salvador shantytown and Ayacucho, formerly a stronghold of the guerilla organization the Shining Path). Its "Volunteering Abroad" section lists a number of opportunities for volunteering in Peru, including teaching and environmental research.

Projects Abroad (☎ 888/839-3535; www.projects-abroad.org), with headquarters in New York and a local field office in Urubamba (in the Sacred Valley), organizes several volunteer and internship opportunities in Peru, including Inca restoration projects (such as the Sacsayhuamán ruins on the outskirts of Cusco), rainforest conservation, teaching, and nursing.

★ **Pro World** (☎ 877/429-6753 in the U.S. and Canada, or 0870/750-7202 in the U.K.; www.myproworld.org), headquartered in Bellingham, Washington, offers work, study, and internship programs in Peru in the fields of health, conservation, and social and economic development. The organization has built schools, irrigation systems, and fish farms.

World Leadership School (☎ 888/831-8109; www.worldleadershipschool.com) is a Colorado-based organization that operates 3- to 4-week programs, concentrating on infrastructure and natural disaster prevention in El Carmen on the desert coast; cultural preservation in Ollantaytambo, in the Sacred Valley; and climate change and ecosystem preservation in Puerto Maldonado, the gateway to the southern Amazon jungle.

Other volunteer programs include ★★★ **Habitat for Humanity** (Comité Nacional Hábitat para la Humanidad Perú; ☎ 800/422-4828, or 054/422-724 in Peru; www.habitat.org), with a base in Arequipa, and **Volunteers for Peace** (☎ 802/259-2759; www.vfp.org), based in Vermont.

15
Guide to Peru's Flora & Fauna

Helpful Hints for Finding Wildlife

Unless you have lots of experience in the tropics, your best hope for getting the most out of a walk through the jungle lies in employing a trained and knowledgeable guide. Most animals of the forest are nocturnal (active at night), and those that are diurnal (active by day) are usually elusive and on the watch for predators. Birds are easier to spot in clearings or secondary forests than they are in primary forests, since primary forests are darker, with denser foliage and a higher canopy.

Here are a few helpful hints for scoring wildlife sightings:

Listen. Pay attention to rustling in the leaves; whether it's a monkey in the treetops or a tapir on the ground, you'll likely hear an animal before you see it.

Keep quiet. Noise will scare off animals and prevent you from hearing their movements and calls.

Don't try too hard. Relax, soften your focus, and let your peripheral vision take over, allowing you to catch glimpses of motion and then focus in on the area.

Bring binoculars. It's also a good idea to practice and get the hang of them prior to your trip. It would be a shame to be fiddling around and staring at empty sky while everyone else in your group *oohs* and *aahs* over a magnificent giant river otter.

Dress appropriately. You'll have a hard time focusing your binoculars if you're busy swatting mosquitoes. Light-colored long pants and long-sleeved shirts are your best bet. Comfortable, waterproof hiking boots are a real boon, except where heavy rubber boots are necessary. Avoid loud colors; the better you blend in with your surroundings, the better your chances of spotting wildlife.

Be patient. The jungle isn't on your vacation schedule. Timing is everything, along with some luck. Your best shots at seeing forest fauna are during the very early morning and late afternoon.

> *OPPOSITE PAGE Installing an artificial macaw nest high in Tambopata's tree canopy is complicated work. THIS PAGE Alpacas and other Andean camelids are quintessential work animals in the Peruvian highlands and Altiplano.*

Peru is extraordinarily rich in biodiversity. Its Amazon rainforest—which occupies nearly two-thirds of the country—is believed by many naturalists and biologists to hold the greatest biodiversity in the world. Peru is home to more than 400 species of mammals (of which about 70 are endemic and about 100 are threatened or endangered), 2,000 species of fish, 1,800 birds, and more than 50,000 plants (including 3,000 species of orchids). Incredibly, Peru boasts 87 of the world's existing 103 ecosystems and 28 of 32 total climates.

Actual wildlife viewing differs greatly, of course, from perusing rosters of species. Most casual visitors and even many dedicated naturalists may never see a rare jungle cat such as the jaguar. However, anyone on a dedicated lodge tour or river cruise in the Amazon with a good guide or visiting other parts of Peru celebrated for their wildlife (such as Paracas National Reserve or Colca Canyon) will be exposed to an impressive display of nature. Whether you go to Peru to check 100 species off your lifetime bird list, or just to get a taste of what ecotourism is all about, you'll be surrounded by a rich and varied collection of flora and fauna. The information in this chapter is only a limited introduction to the incredible wealth found in Peru's rainforests, highlands, and coastal regions.

Fauna
The Sierra & Desert Coast

In the Andes mountains and Altiplano region, the most emblematic creatures are the four species of camelids, both domesticated and wild, that roam at high elevations. Highland birds (see p. 455) are led by the Andean condor, with its magnificent wingspan. The Humboldt current brings cold Pacific waters to the Peruvian coast, facilitating a rich habitat for marine life, especially seabirds and marine mammals (33 species). At Paracas National Reserve alone, there are 200-plus species of birds, including vast high-density colonies.

Alpaca

SCIENTIFIC NAME *Vicugna pacos*

WORTH NOTING This species of camelid has been domesticated for thousands of years. It's smaller than the llama and was bred for its fibers rather than as a beast of burden. Alpacas come in two varieties: Wakayo and Suri. The Wakayo has dense and spongy fiber that grows over most of its body. The Suri has long, dreadlock-like fibers. The finest alpaca fiber is extremely soft and fine baby alpaca, used in the finest garments. In Peru, 52 colors of alpaca have been classified. Alpaca meat is extremely lean and served throughout Peru.

PRIME VIEWING Throughout the Andes highlands.

Guanaco

SCIENTIFIC NAME *Lama guanicoe*

WORTH NOTING Rare guanacos are almost all similarly colored, with dense, short fur of light reddish-brown tones with white accents underneath. Considered the wildest of the Andean camelids, the guanaco is one of the largest wild mammal species found in South America. Its soft fiber is valued second only to that of the vicuña. Once threatened, today its population status is stable.

PRIME VIEWING Rarely sighted; principal range is southern Andes and Patagonia regions of Chile and Argentina. Occasionally viewed on Peru's southern desert coast.

Llama

SCIENTIFIC NAME *Lama glama*

WORTH NOTING The domesticated llama is the largest, strongest, and most common of the four camelids found in Peru. Able to carry as much as one-third of its body weight for long distances (40kg/88 lb. a day on long trips and up to 60kg/132 lb. on shorter journeys), it is used as a pack animal. Llamas come in two varieties, Q'ara (with sparse fiber on the body) and Ch'aku (woolly); their fiber is less dense than that of alpacas.

PRIME VIEWING Throughout the Andes highlands.

South American sea lion

SCIENTIFIC NAME *Otaria flavescens*

WORTH NOTING Known in Peru as *lobo marino* (sea wolf), this species gathers on beaches. Males can be three times the size of females, weighing up to 350kg (772 lb.). Groups generally comprise multiple females and one or a couple of males (bulls), which defend the territory and loudly threaten intruders. This species' population in Peru has fluctuated in accordance with the El Niño phenomenon.

PRIME VIEWING Shorelines and beaches of the southern Pacific coast, particularly Paracas National Reserve and Ballestas Islands. Best months for observation are between November and March, when they reproduce.

Spectacled bear

SCIENTIFIC NAME *Tremarctos ornatus*

WORTH NOTING This bear is known in Peru as the Andean bear and as *oso de anteojos* (eyeglasses bear), for the light rings around its eyes that resemble eyeglasses. It's the only species of native bear in South America and is listed as vulnerable, with its population decreasing. It is an omnivore but prefers vegetation (only about 5% of its diet is meat). The popular figure of children's literature, Paddington Bear, came from "deepest darkest Peru" and thus would have been a spectacled bear.

PRIME VIEWING All three Andean ranges of Peru, including a portion of the Pacific coastal desert; rarely sighted.

Vicuña

SCIENTIFIC NAME *Vicugna vicugna*

WORTH NOTING The smallest of the Andean camelids, the wild vicuña is valued for its incredibly fine fibers (classified as the world's finest). The vicuña is light brown on its back and white on its chest and inside of the legs. Now protected by the Peruvian State in national parks, the vicuña was recently in danger of extinction; poaching remains a problem. Peru has the largest vicuña population in the entire Andean region, with approximately 120,000 of 170,000 total.

PRIME VIEWING Throughout the Andes at altitudes of 3,800m (12,470 ft.) and higher. Pampa Galeras National Reserve has the largest concentration in Peru, but the best place to glimpse them up close is Isla Suasi in Lake Titicaca.

Vizcacha

SCIENTIFIC NAME *Lagidium peruanum*

WORTH NOTING This rabbit-like rodent, similar to a chinchilla, is gray or brown and has a long, bushy tail and long, furry ears. It lives in individual family units of large colonies.

PRIME VIEWING Central and southern Peruvian Andes, at elevations between 4,000 and 5,000m (13,000–16,000 ft.).

The Amazon Basin

The tropical rainforest east of the Andes, which occupies more than 60% of Peru, is one of the world's richest habitats, with tremendous plant and animal life. The jungle is home to 32 species of primates; several types of great jungle cats; rare large mammals such as giant otters and pink river dolphins; an array of reptiles, amphibians, and fish; and more than 1,000 species of birds (see p. 455). Macaw clay licks, where thousands of parrots and macaws gather to feed off the minerals, are one of the world's great nature sights.

Black Caiman

SCIENTIFIC NAME *Melanosuchus niger*

WORTH NOTING The largest predator in the Amazon, the black caiman can grow to more than 6m (20 ft.) in length. It has distinctive markings that include gray or brown banding on the lower jaw, and white or yellowish bands on the sides of the body. Its diet consists largely of fish, including piranhas, though it also preys on some larger animals such as capybara, turtles, and deer. It hunts mostly in the water, but also hunts on land, usually at night.

PRIME VIEWING Throughout much of the Amazon Basin; there are locally strong populations in Peru in isolated, hard-to-reach areas of swampland.

Capybara

SCIENTIFIC NAME *Hydrochaeris hydrochaeris*

WORTH NOTING Endemic to South America and known as *ronsoco* in Peru, this is the largest rodent in the world, weighing up to 66kg (146 lb.). The capybara is semi-aquatic and an excellent swimmer (it can survive underwater for up to 5 min.). Its feet are partially webbed, which along with the location of the eyes, ears, and nostrils on top of the head, make it well-suited to semi-aquatic life. It's an herbivore, grazing mainly on grasses and aquatic plants.

PRIME VIEWING Flooded grasslands and lowland forests.

Giant otter

SCIENTIFIC NAME *Pteronura brasiliensis*

WORTH NOTING The largest of the 13 known otter species, the giant otter is endemic to the rainforests and wetlands of South America. Family groups of five to eight individuals, composed of a breeding pair and their offspring, rest, play, sleep, travel, and fish together. Diurnal and semi-aquatic, the giant otter is known to travel large distances. Its diet consists almost exclusively of fish, though it may also eat caimans, anacondas, and other snakes. Classified as endangered, due to habitat loss and exploitation.

PRIME VIEWING Tropical lowland rainforests; large slow-moving rivers, streams, and lakes; swamps; and oxbow lakes.

Jaguar

SCIENTIFIC NAME *Panthera onca*

WORTH NOTING This large, powerful cat measures 1 to 1.8m (3–6 ft.) and is distinguished by its tan-yellow, black-spotted fur. The third-largest feline after the tiger and the lion, and the largest cat in the Americas, the jaguar is considered nocturnal, although it's most active in the periods around dawn and dusk. It's considered "near threatened" (mainly due to deforestation and habitat fragmentation) and is very difficult to find in the wild.

PRIME VIEWING Major tracts of primary forest in Peru, as well as seasonally flooded swamp areas.

Jaguarundi

SCIENTIFIC NAME *Puma yagouaroundi*

WORTH NOTING This small to midsize cat has a solid black, brown, or reddish coat and an oval-shaped face and long tail that are often compared to that of an otter. The jaguarundi is a diurnal hunter and eats an array of small animals; it can occasionally be spotted in a clearing or climbing a tree.

PRIME VIEWING Often spotted in middle-elevation, moist forests.

Leafcutter ant

SCIENTIFIC NAME *Atta cephalotes*

WORTH NOTING You can't miss the miniature rainforest highways formed by industrious little red leafcutter ants carrying their freshly cut payload. The ant does not actually eat the leaves, but instead feeds off a fungus that grows on the decomposing leaves stored in its massive underground nest.

PRIME VIEWING Most forests throughout Peru.

Ocelot

SCIENTIFIC NAME *Leopardus pardalis*

WORTH NOTING The ocelot, with black spots and a striped torso, is known as an *ocelote* or *gato onza* in Peru. The tail of this small, wild cat is longer than its slender rear legs, which makes for easy identification. The ocelot is mostly nocturnal, sleeping in trees by day. Listed as vulnerable as recently as 1996, but now rated of "least concern" according to the 2008 IUCN Red List.

PRIME VIEWING Mountains of northern Peru and forests throughout the Amazon Basin

Paca

SCIENTIFIC NAME *Agouti paca*

WORTH NOTING The paca is a small, stocky nocturnal rodent that feeds on fallen fruit, leaves, and tubers. Its dark brown or black back fur has ribbons of white spots.

PRIME VIEWING Near water in many forested habitats, from river valleys to swamps to dense tropical forests.

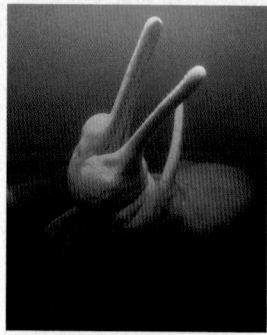

Pink river dolphin

SCIENTIFIC NAME *Inia geoffrensis*

WORTH NOTING Also called *boto* or Amazon river dolphin, this species is the largest of the river dolphins. Males are generally pinker than females. Typically solitary, the pink dolphin is rarely seen in groups of more than three. A slower swimmer than other dolphins, it's equally playful and curious. It swims into flooded forests in the high-water season and hunts fish among the roots and trunks of partially submerged trees.

PRIME VIEWING Throughout the northern Amazon river basin, including in main rivers, tributaries, small channels, mouths of rivers, lakes, and just below waterfalls and rapids.

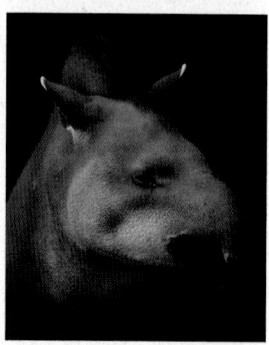

Tapir

SCIENTIFIC NAME *Tapirus terrestris*

WORTH NOTING The Brazilian tapir is one of the largest forest mammals in Peru (reaching a length of more than 2m/6½ ft.). It has a short, stumpy tail and hind feet with three hoofed toes. Its unique proboscis is long, flexible, and prehensile. Nocturnal, the tapir emerges to feed in grassland or scrubland. Its pronounced vocalizations include a shrill call, click, and snort.

PRIME VIEWING Lowland humid and swamp forests, dry and moist shrub lands and grasslands, and a wide variety of wetlands. Highest density in Amazonian forests that contain salt licks and palm swamps.

White-faced capuchin monkey

SCIENTIFIC NAME *Cebus capucinus*

WORTH NOTING Known as *mono capuchin* in Peru, the white-faced capuchin is a midsize, diurnal monkey, about 46cm (18 in.) in length, with distinctive white fur around its face, head, and forearms. Known as the "organ grinder" monkey, it travels in large troops or family groups of 6 to 40 members.

PRIME VIEWING Humid forests throughout eastern Peru.

Get a Good Guide

If you've got more than a passing interest in the flora and fauna you may encounter on a trip to Peru, it's a great idea to get a specialized field guide with much more information than I can hope to provide here. One of the best general guides is *Travellers' Wildlife Guides Peru,* by David L. Pearson, Les Beletsky, Priscilla Barrett, David Beadle, et al. Dedicated birders will want to pick up the very complete, though hardly portable, *Birds of Peru (Princeton Field Guides),* by Thomas S. Schulenberg; and perhaps *Field Guide to the Birds of Peru,* by James F. Clements and Naom Shany.

Birds

Peru counts more than 1,800 species of birds within its borders, the second highest number of any country. Dedicated birders find Manu National Park and Tambopata National Reserve among the world's greatest birding destinations. The following section highlights only a handful of the most notable species found in Peru.

Andean cock-of-the-rock

SCIENTIFIC NAME *Rupicola peruvianus*

WORTH NOTING Considered the national bird of Peru, this medium-size bird belonging to the Cotinga family is native to Andean cloud forests in South America. The male has a large, disk-like crest and scarlet orange plumage, which it displays when competing for females (while hopping and initiating calls); the female is darker and browner. It tends to nest in rock walls.

PRIME VIEWING Cloud forests of the Andes, largely in ravines and forested streams at elevations of 500 to 2,400m (1,640–7,870 ft.).

Andean condor

SCIENTIFIC NAME *Vultur gryphus*

WORTH NOTING The only living species of its genus, *Vultur*, the Andean condor has the largest wingspan (up to 3.5m/11½ ft.) of any bird and was held sacred by pre-Columbian civilizations, who associated it with the sun deity. Mostly black, with a ruff of white feathers along the base of the neck, it's one of the world's longest-living birds (up to 50 years) and mates for life. It nests at elevations of up to 5,000m (16,000 ft.), frequently on inaccessible rock ledges, from which it launches flight with little wing-flapping. Listed as "near threatened" on the IUCN Red List.

PRIME VIEWING Over open grassland, in the Andes mountains, and in lowland desert regions.

Guanay cormorant

SCIENTIFIC NAME *Phalacrocorax bougainvillii*

WORTH NOTING A member of the cormorant family classified as "near threatened," this species is now protected in Peru. Its population has declined by 30%. The guanay cormorant builds its nest on mountains of guano, or bird droppings, in high-density colonies.

PRIME VIEWING Shallow seawater and rocky shores of Peru's Pacific coast; particularly Paracas National Reserve and Ballestas Islands.

Hoatzin

SCIENTIFIC NAME *Opisthocomus hoazin*

WORTH NOTING The hoatzin is an unusual, noisy tropical bird with a blue face, red eyes, and spiky crest. The young are born without feathers but develop a layer of black down after birth. The species is also known as stinkbird (its manure-like smell is a function of its eating leaves and the bacterial fermentation that takes place in its digestive system, in some ways similar to ruminants such as cows).

PRIME VIEWING Throughout the Amazon basin; swamps, fresh water marshes, forests, and the banks of rivers, lakes, and streams.

Humboldt penguin

SCIENTIFIC NAME *Spheniscus humboldti*

WORTH NOTING Named after its cold-water habitat, this South American penguin is found in coastal Peru and Chile. It has a black head with a white border from behind the eye and under the chin. It's capable of diving to 150m (492 ft.), although in practice it rarely dives a third of that depth. The penguin is currently classified as threatened due to over-fishing, climate change, and habitat destruction and has been granted protection under the U.S. Endangered Species Act.

PRIME VIEWING Southern Pacific coast, particularly Paracas National Reserve and Ballestas Islands.

Scarlet macaw

SCIENTIFIC NAME *Ara macao*

WORTH NOTING This long-tailed member of the parrot family has a loud squawk and rainbow-colored feathers. Capable of living 75 years in captivity, in the wild it usually lives 40 to 50 years. Although scarlet macaws gather in flocks to sleep, the species is monogamous and mates for life and is usually nesting or flying in pairs.

PRIME VIEWING High in the canopy of rainforest habitats below 1,000m (3,280 ft.) and macaw clay licks in Manu and Tambopata.

Torrent duck

SCIENTIFIC NAME *Merganetta armata*

WORTH NOTING A bird, often seen in pairs or family groups, with a singular talent: It's the only bird in the world with the ability to dive and swim up fast-moving white waters of rivers such as the Urubamba and Colca.

PRIME VIEWING Machu Picchu Historical Sanctuary and Colca Canyon.

Flora

If you venture into Peru's vast Amazon region and think you can't see the trees for the forest, well, that might be because the density of the rainforest, and its number and diversity of species of trees and plants, is staggering. And while there's no region in Peru or pretty much on the planet that can come close to the Amazon, the barren coastal desert and highlands are also home to some very unique flora.

Algarrobo

SCIENTIFIC NAME *Prosopis pallida*

WORTH NOTING A New World native, this shrub-like tree, a species of mesquite tree, thrives in dry, harsh climates near the coast. Similar in shape to the acacia, the tree has spines, greenish-yellow flowers, and long pods filled with brown seeds. It is extremely efficient at extracting moisture from soil and can kill nearby plants by depriving them of water. From its pods comes a sticky pulp both sweet and tangy, used in creating algarrobina syrup that's a fundamental ingredient of a classic Peruvian cocktail, the *coctél de algarrobina,* which is creamy and rather similar to a brandy Alexander.

PRIME VIEWING Coastal desert.

Ayahuasca

SCIENTIFIC NAME *Banisteriopsis caapi*

WORTH NOTING The famed plant used by shamans in Amerindian communities of the Amazon, this so-called "vine of the soul" (from the Quechua) is capable of producing psychedelic reactions when taken in a brew that combines several elements of the plant (which contains the alkaloid DMT) and causes often violent purging. For natives *ayahuasca* constitutes part of a spiritual ceremony; for some visitors, it is seen more as a drug trip.

PRIME VIEWING Northwestern Amazon region.

Brazil nut tree

SCIENTIFIC NAME *Bertholletia excelsa*

WORTH NOTING One of the giants of the Amazon forest, a Brazil nut tree, known as *castaño* in Peru, can grow to a height of nearly 61m (200 ft.). The tree's fruit is much more valuable than its timber; Brazil nuts are a global business of at least $50 million annually and are considered a sustainable Amazonian enterprise. A single tree can produce as much as 115kg (250 lb.) of buttery Brazil nuts—found in large (up to 2.25kg/5-lb.) fruit pods that drop from great heights—each year. They are also used as organic hair, skin, and lip oils.

PRIME VIEWING Endemic to the Amazon basin, most common in the Madre de Dios department.

Ceiba

SCIENTIFIC NAME *Ceiba pentandra*

WORTH NOTING The ceiba tree's large umbrella-shape crown emerges above the forest canopy, reaching as high as 60m (197 ft.). Among the tallest trees of Peru's tropical forest, it has a thick trunk, often with large buttresses. The ceiba's seedpod produces a light, buoyant, and insulating fiber traditionally used for bedding and as stuffing for pillows, clothing, and even life jackets. The ceiba flowers infrequently, sometimes only once every 5 years, especially in wetter forests.

PRIME VIEWING Tropical forests throughout Peru.

Coca

SCIENTIFIC NAME *Erythroxylum coca*

WORTH NOTING Native to South America, coca is of great import to traditional Andean culture; several pre-Columbian civilizations grew and chewed coca leaves for the mildly stimulant effect and to suppress hunger, fatigue, and the effects of high altitude. It is used to make *mate de coca* (coca-leaf tea), with the same effects. The plant's pharmacologically active ingredient is the alkaloid cocaine, found in a very small amount of fresh leaves. Chewing coca leaves is not nearly the equal of taking purified forms of cocaine and does not produce the same euphoric effects.

PRIME VIEWING Throughout the highlands.

Heliconia

SCIENTIFIC NAME *Heliconia*

WORTH NOTING More than 70 species of heliconia are found in Peru. The visually striking plants have banana tree–like leaves and large, orange-red and yellow flowers shaped like lobster claws. The flowers are pollinated by hummingbirds.

PRIME VIEWING Tropical forests near streams and gardens throughout Peru.

Manioc

SCIENTIFIC NAME *Socratea exorrhiza*

WORTH NOTING The manioc, or cassava, plant is a tall, woody, perennial shrub known as *yuca* in Peru. Its edible tuberous roots, usually roasted, are an important subsistence staple of the local diet, being rich in carbohydrates and enzymes, and are the basis for tapioca. Manioc is one of the world's most important tropical food crops and was cultivated 4,000 years ago in Peru.

PRIME VIEWING Lowland tropical forests in the Amazon basin.

Palo Santo

SCIENTIFIC NAME *Bursera graveolens*

WORTH NOTING The wood of Palo Santo (which translates as "holy wood") was used by the Incas and other pre-Columbian cultures as a spiritual remedy for purifying and cleansing. Reputed to eliminate negative energies, it is used in folk remedies as a tea for stomach aches, rheumatism, and other maladies. It is also added to perfumes, natural incenses, and skin oils (to treat acne and infections and as insect repellent). It belongs to the same family (Burseraceae) as frankincense and myrrh. In Peru Palo Santo is a protected species, endangered through overharvesting.

PRIME VIEWING Dry, low-elevation forests and coastal areas.

Puya raimondii

SCIENTIFIC NAME *Puya raimondii*

WORTH NOTING This rare and spectacular terrestrial plant, the largest of more than 3,000 species of bromeliads in the world, is known as Queen of the Andes. Endemic to altitudes of 3,200 to 4,800m (10,500–15,750 ft.) in Peru and Bolivia, it can reach as high as 9m (30 ft.) tall. Like most bromeliads, it dies soon after flowering (which generally happens after 80–100 years). An adult plant can have more than 3,000 flowers and six million seeds. Considered endangered.

PRIME VIEWING Meadows of the high Andes, particularly the Ancash department and Cordilleras Blanca and Negra near Huaraz and Chavín de Huantar.

Strangler fig

SCIENTIFIC NAME *Ficus crassiuscula*

WORTH NOTING This parasitic tree gets its name from the curious fact that it envelops and eventually strangles its host tree. Also known as *matapalo,* the strangler fig begins as an epiphyte, its seeds deposited high in a host tree's canopy by bats, birds, or monkeys. The young strangler then sends long roots down to the ground. The sap of this tree is used to relieve burns.

PRIME VIEWING Primary and secondary forests in Peru.

Walking palm

SCIENTIFIC NAME *Socratea exorrhiza*

WORTH NOTING A palm tree with a unique adaptation that gives the impression of being nomadic, this tree forms stilt-like roots and can seemingly "walk" up to 1m (3.3 in.) a year to get more sunlight. It allows roots on one side to rot and grows new ones in the direction it seeks. A walking palm can grow to 25m (82 ft.) in height.

PRIME VIEWING Throughout the Amazon forest in Peru.

16
The Savvy Traveler

156

> A train pulls into Puno station, near Lake Titicaca.

Before You Go

Government Tourist Offices

Peru doesn't maintain national tourism offices abroad, so your best official source of information before you go is the website of **Prom Perú** (Commission for the Promotion of Peru; www.peru.info). Other helpful trip-planning websites include **www.peruvianembassy.us,** the Peruvian embassy in Washington, D.C.; and **South American Explorers** (☎ 800/274-0568 or 607/277-0488 in the U.S.; www.saexplorers.org), with clubhouses in Lima and Cusco and an excellent source of information, particularly on trekking and mountaineering in Peru.

Best Times to Go

Peak travel season for foreigners is in great part determined by weather. Peru experiences two very distinct seasons, wet and dry—terms that are much more relevant than "summer" and "winter." Peru's high season for travel (to the highlands, in particular) coincides with the driest months: May through October, with by far the greatest number of visitors in July and August. May and September are particularly fine months to visit much of the country. Airlines and hotels also consider the period from mid-December through mid-January as peak season. From June to September (winter in the Southern Hemisphere) in the highlands, days are clear and often spectacularly sunny, with chilly or downright cold nights, especially at high elevations. For trekking in the mountains, including the Inca Trail, these are by far the best months. This is also the best time of the year to visit the Amazon basin: Mosquitoes are fewer, and many fauna stay close to the rivers (although some people prefer to travel in the jungle during the wet season, when higher water levels allow for more river penetration). Note that Peruvians travel in huge numbers around July 28, the national holiday, and finding accommodations in popular destinations around this time can be difficult.

Festivals & Special Events

For a month-by-month schedule of cultural events and festivals (there are more than 3,000 annually) in Peru, check www.peru.travel.

JANUARY

At Cusco's **Entrega de Varas** (Jan 1), *yayas* (community elders) designate the highest authorities of their villages in this pre-Columbian festival, which is celebrated with *chicha* (fermented maize beer) and *llonque* (sugarcane alcohol); elders give the mayor the *vara* (a staff, or scepter) as a symbol of his position of authority. In Lake Titicaca, the main **Fiesta de la Santa Tierra** (3rd Thurs in Jan) on Isla Amantaní sees the population split in two—half at the Temple of Pachamama (Mother Earth) and the other half at the Temple of Pachatata (Father Earth), symbolizing the islanders' ancient dualistic belief system. Trujillo's **Marinera Dance Festival** (Jan 20–30) celebrates one of the stateliest dances in Peru. The flirtatious *marinera* involves a couple, each partner with a handkerchief in his or her right hand. The man wears a wide-brimmed hat and poncho, and the woman wears a lace Moche dress. For 10 days, the festival, which draws couples from all over the country, is held in the Gran Chimú soccer stadium. There are also float processions throughout the city and dancing in the Plaza de Armas.

FEBRUARY

Puno lives up to its billing as Folk Capital of the Americas with the **Fiesta de la Virgen de la Candelaria,** or Candlemas (Feb 1–14), which gathers more than 200 musicians and dance troupes. On the festival's main day, February 2, the Virgen is carried through the city in a colorful procession of priests and pagans carefully maintaining the hierarchy. Especially thrilling is the dance of the demons, or *la diablada*. Dancers in wild costumes and masks blow panpipes and make offerings to Pachamama. **Carnaval**'s lively pre-Lenten festivities take place the weekend before Ash Wednesday. Cajamarca is reputed to have the best and wildest parties; Puno and Cusco are also good. Look out for balloons filled with water—or worse.

MARCH

Ica's **Festival Internacional de la Vendimia** (Wine Festival; 2nd week of March) is a celebration of the grape harvest and the region's wine and pisco brandy, with fairs, beauty contests, floats, and musical festivals, including Afro-Peruvian dance. Near Cajamarca,

PERU'S AVERAGE DAILY HIGH/LOW TEMPERATURE & RAIN DAYS

LIMA	JAN	FEB	MAR	APR	MAY	JUNE	JULY	AUG	SEPT	OCT	NOV	DEC
TEMP °F	77/66	79/68	79/66	75/65	70/61	66/59	63/57	63/56	63/56	66/57	68/61	73/63
TEMP °C	25/19	26/20	26/19	24/18	21/16	19/15	17/14	17/13	17/13	19/14	20/16	23/17
RAIN DAYS	1	0	0	0	1	1	1	2	1	0	0	0

CUSCO	JAN	FEB	MAR	APR	MAY	JUNE	JULY	AUG	SEPT	OCT	NOV	DEC
TEMP °F	66/44	66/44	67/44	68/41	68/37	67/34	67/34	68/34	68/39	70/42	69/43	68/43
TEMP °C	19/7	19/7	19/7	20/5	20/3	19/1	19/1	20/1	20/4	21/6	21/6	20/6
RAIN DAYS	12	11	10	6	4	3	4	3	2	2	1	5

a dawn procession of massive decorated wooden crosses through the valley of Porcón re-creates the entry of Christ into Jerusalem. The main day of **Las Cruces de Porcón,** Palm Sunday (mid-March to 1st week of Apr), presents four separate ceremonies. Ultimately, the crosses are decorated with mirrors (symbolizing the souls of the dead), and locals hang metal bells to announce the arrival of the crosses to the community. During **Semana Santa** (late March/early Apr), handsome and spectacularly reverent processions mark Easter Week. The finest are in Cusco and Ayacucho. On Easter Monday, the image of the El Señor de los Temblores (Lord of the Earthquakes), representing a 17th-century painting of Christ on the cross that is said to have saved the city from a devastating earthquake, is carried through the streets of Cusco in a reverential procession, much like the Incas once paraded the mummies of their chieftains and high priests.

APRIL

The Peruvian Paso horse, one of the world's most beautiful breeds, is celebrated at the **Peruvian Paso Horse Festival** (Apr 15–20) with the most important annual national competition at the Mamacona stables near Pachacámac, 30km (19 miles) south of Lima.

MAY

Fiesta de la Cruz (Festival of the Cross; May 2–3) features folk music and dance, including "scissors dancers" (p. 353), and processions in which communities decorate crosses and prepare them for the procession to neighboring churches. The *danzantes de tijeras* (scissors dancers) re-create old times, when they performed on top of church bell towers. Today the objective is still to outdo one another with daring feats. Celebrations are especially lively in Lima, Cusco, and Ica. A massive indigenous pilgrimage in Quispicanchis, near Cusco, marks **Qoyllur Rit'i** (1st week of May), which is tied to the fertility of the land and the worship of Apus, the spirit of the mountains. It forms part of the greatest festival of native Indian nations in the hemisphere. The main ceremony is held at the foot of Mount Ausangate, with 10,000 pilgrims climbing to the snowline along with dancers in full costume representing mythical characters. Others head to the summit, in search of the Snow Star, and take huge blocks of ice back down on their backs—holy water for irrigation purposes. Also known as El Señor de la Soledad, **Fiesta de Mayo** (May 2–10) is celebrated with traditional dances, ski races, and a lantern procession in Huaraz.

JUNE

During **Corpus Christi** (early June) in Cusco, a procession of saints and virgins arrives at the Catedral to "greet" the body of Christ. Members of nearby churches also take their patron saints in a procession. An overnight vigil is followed by a new procession around the Plaza de Armas, with images of five virgins clad in embroidered tunics and the images of four saints: Sebastian, Blas, Joseph, and the Apostle Santiago (St. James). In Paucartambo, a remote highland village 4 hours from Cusco, thousands come to honor the **Virgen del Carmen,** or Mamacha Carmen, patron saint of the mestizo population, with 4 days (June 15–18) of splendidly festive music and dance, as well as some of the wildest costumes in Peru. Dancers even perform daring moves on rooftops. The festival ends in the cemetery in a show of respect for the souls of the dead. Pisac also celebrates the Virgen del Carmen festival, almost as colorfully. **Semana del Andinismo** (mid- to late June), in Huaraz and Callejón de Huaylas, celebrates outdoor adventure with opportunities to partake in trekking, skiing, mountain biking, rafting, rock climbing, and hang gliding—and plenty of parties to accompany them. **Inti Raymi** (Inca Festival of the Sun)—the mother of all pre-Columbian festivals—celebrates the winter solstice and honors the sun god with traditional pageantry, parades, and dances. One of the most vibrant and exciting of all Andean festivals, it draws thousands of visitors who fill Cusco's hotels. The principal event takes place on June 24 at the Sacsayhuamán ruins and includes the sacrifice of a pair of llamas. General celebrations last several days. The **feast day of St. John the Baptist** (June 24 in Cusco, June 25 in Iquitos), a symbol of fertility and sensuality, is the most important date on the festival calendar in the entire Peruvian jungle. John the Baptist has taken on a major symbolic significance because of the importance of water as a vital element in the entire Amazon region. Events include fiestas with lots of music and regional cuisine. In Iquitos, don't miss the aphrodisiac potions with suggestive names. Near fishing villages in Lima and Chiclayo, the patron saints of fishermen and farmers, Saint Peter and Saint Paul, are honored at **Fiesta de San Pedro y San Pablo** on June 29; figures of the saints are carried with incense, prayers, and hymns down to the sea and are taken by launch around the bay to bless the waters.

JULY

Fiesta de Santiago (July 25, Aug 1–2) in Isla Taquile, celebrates St. James with a festive and very traditional pageant of color, exuberant dances, and women in layered, multicolored skirts. A series of *fiestas patrias* (patriotic parties; July 28–29), mark Peru's independence from Spain in 1821. Official parades and functions are augmented by cockfighting, bullfighting, and Peruvian Paso horse exhibitions in other towns. The best celebrations are in Cusco, Puno, Isla Taquile, and Lima.

AUGUST

During **Fiesta de Santa Rosa de Lima** (Aug 30), major devotional processions honor the patron saint of Lima.

SEPTEMBER

Trujillo's **International Spring Festival** (last week of Sept) celebrates the season with *marinera* dance, decorated streets and houses, floats, and schoolchildren dancing in the streets —led, of course, by the pageant beauty queen.

OCTOBER

The festival of **El Señor de los Milagros** (Lord of Miracles; Oct 18) is the largest procession in South America and dates from colonial times. Lasting nearly 24 hours and involving tens of thousands of purple-clad participants, it celebrates a Christ image (painted by an Angolan slave) that survived the 1746 earthquake and has since become the most venerated image in Lima.

NOVEMBER

Peruvians salute the dead during **Todos Santos** and **Día de los Muertos** (Nov 1–2) by visiting cemeteries with flowers and food. Families hold candlelight vigils in the cemetery until dawn. The holiday is most vibrantly celebrated in the highlands. During **Puno Week** (1st week of Nov), a major procession from the shores of the lake to the town stadium celebrates Manco Cápac, who, according to legend, rose from the waters of Lake Titicaca to establish the Inca Empire. Dances and music take over Puno, with events often taking a turn for the inebriated. Spectacular Day of the Dead celebrations coincide with Puno Week.

DECEMBER

One of the largest arts-and-crafts fairs in Peru, **Santuranticuy Fair,** literally "saints for sale" (Dec 24), is held in Cusco's Plaza de Armas. Artisans lay out blankets around the square, as in traditional Andean markets, and sell figurines and Nativity scenes as well as ceramics, carvings, pottery, and *retablos* (altars). Vendors sell hot rum punch called *ponche.*

Weather

Generally, May through October is the dry season; November through April is the rainy season, with the wettest months January through April. Peru's climate, though, is markedly different among its three regions. The coast is predominantly arid and mild, the Andean region is temperate to cold, and the eastern lowlands are tropically warm and humid.

On the desert coast, summer (Dec–Apr) is hot and dry, with temperatures reaching 77°F to 95°F (25°C–35°C) or higher along the north coast. In winter (May–Oct), temperatures are much milder, though with high humidity. Much of the coast, including Lima, is shrouded in a gray mist called *garúa*. Only extreme northern beaches are warm enough for swimming.

In the highlands from May to October, rain is scarce. Daytime temperatures reach a warm 68°F to 77°F (20°C–25°C), and nights are often quite cold (near freezing), especially in June and July. Rainfall is very abundant from December to March, when temperatures are slightly milder—64°F to 68°F (18°C–20°C) dropping only to 59°F (15°C) at night. The wettest months are January and February. Most mornings are dry, but clouds move in during the afternoon and produce heavy downpours. In mountain areas, roads and trek paths can become impassable.

Although the Amazon jungle is consistently humid and tropical, with significant rainfall year-round, it, too, experiences two clearly different seasons. During the dry season (May–Oct), temperatures reach 86°F to 100°F (30°C–38°C) during the day. From November to April, there are frequent rain showers (which last only a few hours at a time), causing the rivers to swell; temperatures are similarly steamy.

Cellphones (Mobiles)

World phones—or GSM (Global System for Mobiles)—work in Peru (and most of the world). If your cellphone is on a GSM system, and you have a world-capable multiband phone, you can make and receive calls from Peru. Just call your wireless operator and ask for "international roaming" to be activated. Unfortunately, per-minute charges can be high.

For many, renting a phone is a better idea. **Peru Rent-a-Cell** (☎ 01/517-1856; www.proturismo.com.pe) has representatives and a booth awaiting arriving flights in baggage claim at the Lima and Cusco airports and rents small Nokia cellphones for just $10 per month. Incoming calls are free. If you use your phone only to receive incoming calls, either from within Peru or from any other country, you only pay that one-time activation fee.

Otherwise, domestic calls cost 70¢ per minute, and calls placed to other countries cost $1.50 per minute. Anyone headed to more remote parts of Peru might consider renting a satellite phone ("satphone"). It's different from a cellphone in that it connects to satellites and works where there's no cellular signal or ground-based tower. Per-minute call charges can be even cheaper than roaming charges with a regular cellphone, but the phone itself is more expensive.

Getting There

By Plane

All overseas flights from North America and Europe arrive at Lima's **Jorge Chávez International Airport** (☎ 01/517-3502, or 01/575-1712 for flight information; www.lap.com.pe; airport code LIM). Major international airlines from North and South America, Europe, and Asia all fly to Lima. In Peru, it's important to reconfirm airline tickets in advance. For local flights, reconfirm 48 hours in advance; for international flights, reconfirm 72 hours before traveling (and be sure to arrive at the airport a minimum of 2 hr. in advance). The airport tax on domestic flights is about $6, and on international flights $31. The tax must be paid—in cash only (either in U.S. dollars or Peruvian *soles*)—before boarding.

By Bus

You can travel overland to Peru through Ecuador, Bolivia, or Chile. If traveling from Quito or Guayaquil, you'll pass through the major northern coastal cities on the way to Lima. From Bolivia, there is frequent service from La Paz and Copacabana to Puno and then on to Cusco. From Chile, most buses travel from Arica to Tacna, making connections to either Arequipa or Lima. The most common overland trip to Peru from a neighboring country is from La Paz, Bolivia, to Puno, on the banks of Lake Titicaca (which is partly in Peru and partly in Bolivia). The trip is about a 5-hour direct ride. **Ormeño** (☎ 01/472-5000; www.grupo-ormeno.com.pe) travels to La Paz as well as Venezuela, Colombia, Ecuador, Chile, and Argentina.

Getting Around

Because of its size and natural barriers, including difficult mountain terrain, long stretches of desert coast, and extensive rainforest, Peru is complicated to navigate. Train service is limited, covering only a few principal tourist routes, and many trips take several days by land. Visitors with limited time tend to fly everywhere they can. Travel overland, though inexpensive, can be extremely time-consuming and uncomfortable. For certain routes, however, intercity buses are your only real option.

By Plane

Flying to major destinations within Peru is the only practical way around the country if you want to see several places in a couple weeks or less. Flying to major destinations such as Lima, Cusco, Arequipa, Puerto Maldonado, and Iquitos is simple and relatively inexpensive. One-way flights to most destinations are between $89 and $219. Prices fluctuate according to the season. Peru's carriers, some of which are small airlines with limited flight schedules, include **LAN** (☎ 866/435-9526 in the U.S., 305/670-9999, or 01/213-8200 in Lima; www.lan.com), **LC Busre** (☎ 01/619-1313; www.lcbusre.com.pe), **StarPerú** (☎ 01/705-9000; www.starperu.com); **Taca Peru** (☎ 800/400-TACA in the U.S., or 01/511-8222; www.taca.com); and **Peruvian Airlines** (☎ 01/716-6000; www.peruvianairlines.pe).

All airlines fly in and out of Lima. LAN is the only domestic airline that flies to most major destinations in Peru, but it is considerably more expensive for foreigners than other carriers. Connections through Lima are often necessary, although many destinations are accessible directly from Arequipa and Cusco, and some routes might be limited to only several days a week, or one flight per day. Flight schedules and fares are apt to change frequently and without notice. Flights should be booked several days in advance, especially in high season, and you should also make sure that you get to the airport at least 45 minutes before your flight to avoid being bumped. LAN has a complicated and inconvenient air pass program for those who fly to Peru on its airline; passengers may purchase a minimum of three flight coupons (purchase must be made prior to landing in Peru).

By Train

The four tourist or passenger train routes operated by PeruRail (a private company owned by Orient-Express) are all very popular and scenic journeys. Because luggage theft has long been a problem on Peruvian trains, you should (if possible) purchase a premium-class ticket that limits access to ticketed passengers. By far the most popular train routes in Peru connect Cusco, the Sacred Valley, and Machu Picchu. The train to Machu Picchu from Cusco is a truly spectacular journey. Two new tourist train companies, Inca Rail and Andean Railways, now travel from the Sacred Valley (Ollantaytambo) to Machu Picchu. For the prices and schedules of these and all Cusco and Sacred Valley trains, see chapters 8 and 9. PeruRail's journey from Cusco to Puno/Lake Titicaca is one of the most scenic and popular in Peru, although it is rather slow and pricey.

There are no PeruRail train passes. For additional information, contact **PeruRail** (☎ 01/612-6700 in Lima, or 084/581-414 in Cusco; www.perurail.com); **Inca Rail** (☎ 084/233-030; www.incarail.com); or **Andean Railways** (☎ 084/221-199; www.machupicchutrain.com).

The **Ferrocarril Central Andino** (☎ 01/226-6363; www.ferrocarrilcentral.com.pe), the spectacular high-altitude journey from Lima to Huancayo in the central highlands—the world's highest passenger line—is again in service for passenger travel, though its notoriously problematic history makes it very difficult to plan a trip around riding the train. It runs once a month between July and November. For additional information, check the website for updates before you arrive in Peru.

By Bus

Buses (*autobuses* or *omnibuses*) are the cheapest and most popular form of transportation in Peru—for many Peruvians, they are the only means of getting around—and they have by far the greatest reach. A complex network of private bus companies crisscrosses Peru, with many competing lines covering the most popular routes. Many companies operate their own bus stations, and their locations, dispersed across many cities, can be endlessly frustrating to travelers. Luggage theft is an issue on many buses; passengers should keep a watchful eye on carry-on items and pay close attention when bags are unloaded. Only a few long-distance companies have luxury buses comparable in comforts to European models (bathrooms, reclining seats, and movies). These premium-class ("Royal" or "Imperial" class) buses cost up to twice as much as regular-service buses, although for many travelers, the additional comfort and services are worth the difference in cost (which remains inexpensive).

The major long-distance carriers are: **Ormeño** (☎ 01/472-5000; www.grupo-ormeno.com.pe); **Cruz del Sur** (☎ 01/311-5050; www.cruzdelsur.com.pe); **Oltursa** (☎ 01/708-5000; www.oltursa.com.pe); and **Civa** (☎ 01/418-1111; www.civa.com.pe).

For many short distances (such as Cusco to Pisac), *colectivos, combis,* and *micros* (smaller buses or vans without assigned seats) are the fastest and cheapest options.

By Car

Getting around Peru by means of a rental car isn't the best option for the great majority of travelers. It is also far from the cheapest. Distances are long, the terrain is either difficult or unrelentingly boring for long stretches along the desert coast, roads are often not in very good condition, Peruvian drivers are aggressive, and accident rates are very high. The U.S. State Department warns against driving in Peru, particularly at night or alone on rural roads at any time of day. A four-wheel-drive vehicle is the best option in many places, but trucks and jeeps are exceedingly expensive. However, if you want maximum flexibility and independence for travels in a particular region (say, to get around the Sacred Valley outside of Cusco, visit Colca Canyon beyond Arequipa, or explore the northern beaches around Máncora) and can share the cost, a rental car could be a decent option. Do not plan to rent a car in Lima and head off for the major sights across the country; you'll spend all your time in the car.

Tips on Accommodations

The Basics

A wide range of accommodations—including world-class luxury hotels in modern high-rise buildings and 16th-century monasteries; affordable small hotels in colonial houses; rustic ecolodges; and inexpensive budget inns—can be found in Peru. Midrange options have expanded in recent years, but the large majority of accommodations still court budget travelers and backpackers (outside Lima's hosting of international business travelers). Note that pricing in this guide is given according to the way each property itself lists its tariffs; some, predominantly at the mid- and upper level, list prices in U.S. dollars ($); others in Peruvian *nuevos soles* (S/).

Types of Accommodations

Accommodations go by many names in Peru. Hotel generally refers only to comfortable hotels with a range of services, but *hostal* (or *hostales,* plural) is used for a wide variety of smaller hotels, inns, and pensions. (*Hostal* is distinct from the English-language term "hostel" and connotes a variety of inexpensive but often quite comfortable inns). At the lower end are *hospedajes, pensiones,* and *residenciales.* However, these terms are often poor indicators of an establishment's quality or services. Required signs outside the properties reflect these categories: H (hotel), HS (*hostal*), HR (*hotel residencial*), and P (*pensión*). The government's hotel-rating system means that establishments are awarded stars for the presence of certain criteria—a pool, restaurant, elevator, and so on—more than

Addresses

"Jr." doesn't mean "junior"; it is a designation meaning *jirón* (street), just as "Av." (sometimes "Avda.") is an abbreviation for *avenida* (avenue). "Ctra." is the abbreviation for *carretera,* or highway; cdra. means *cuadra,* or block; and "of." is used to designate an *oficina* (office) number. Perhaps the most confusing element in Peruvian street addresses is *s/n,* which frequently appears in place of a number after the name of the street; *s/n* means *sin número,* or no number. The house or building with such an address simply is unnumbered. At other times, a building number may appear hyphenated, such as "102-105," meaning that the building in question simply contains both address numbers (though usually only one main entrance).

for standards of luxury. Luxury hotels are rare outside larger cities; budget accommodations are plentiful across the country, and many of them are quite good for the price. Some represent amazing values at less than $50 a night for a double—with a dose of local character and breakfast, to boot.

The great majority of hotels in Peru are small and midsize independent inns; few international hotel chains operate in Peru. By and large, the chains you'll come into contact with are Peruvian chains. The most prominent, although they have only a handful of hotels each, are Casa Andina, Sonesta, and Libertador.

In-room air-conditioning isn't as common, especially in lower-priced and moderately priced inns and hotels, as it is in many countries. In highland towns, such as Cusco and Puno, that's not usually a problem, as even in warmer months it gets pretty cool at night. In coastal and jungle towns (and at jungle lodges), it gets considerably warmer, though most hotels that don't offer air-conditioning units have ceiling or other fans. If you're concerned about having air-conditioning in your room in a warmer destination, it may be necessary to bump up to a more expensive hotel.

Advance reservations are strongly recommended during high season (June–Oct) and during national holidays and important festivals. This is especially true for hotels in the middle and upper categories in popular places such as Cusco and Machu Picchu. Many hotels quote their rates in U.S. dollars (they're listed in this guide according to how they list their rates). At many budget and midrange hotels, credit cards are not accepted. Most published rates can be negotiated and travelers can often get greatly reduced rates outside of peak season simply by asking. This is especially true of jungle lodges, where published international prices differ greatly from the rate one might obtain on-site.

Hotel taxes and service charges are an issue that has caused some confusion in recent years. Most upper-level hotels add a 19% general sales tax (IGV) and a 10% service charge to the bill. However, foreigners who can demonstrate they live outside of Peru are not charged the 19% tax (though they are responsible for the 10% service charge). In practice, hotels sometimes either mistakenly or purposely include the IGV on everyone's bill; presentation of a passport is sufficient to have the tax deducted from your tab. Many hotels—usually those at the midlevel and lower ranges—simplify matters by including the tax in their rates; at these establishments, you cannot expect to have the tax removed from your charges. At high-end hotels, be sure to review your bill and ask for an explanation of additional taxes and charges. Prices in this book do not include taxes and service charges unless otherwise noted.

Fast Facts

ATMs/Cashpoints

Automated teller machines (ATMs) are the best way of getting cash in Peru; they're found in most towns and cities, although not on every street corner, and in all but the most remote locations. ATMs allow customers to withdraw money in either Peruvian *soles* or U.S. dollars. Screen instructions are in English as well as Spanish. Some bank ATMs dispense money only to those who hold accounts there. Most ATMs in Peru accept only one type of credit/debit card and international money network, either Cirrus (☎ 800/424-7787; www.mastercard.com) or PLUS (☎ 800/843-7587; www.visa.com). Visa and MasterCard ATM cards are the most widely accepted; Visa/PLUS is the most common. Be sure you know your personal identification number (PIN) and daily withdrawal limit before you depart. At some ATMs, your personal identification number (PIN) must contain four digits.

Note: Remember that many banks impose a fee every time you use a card at another bank's ATM, and that fee can be higher for international transactions (up to $5 or more) than for domestic ones. In addition, the bank from which you withdraw cash may charge its own fee. Check with your bank for their policy on international withdrawal fees. Also, note that many credit and debit cards now assess a 1% to 3% "transaction fee" on all charges you incur abroad (whether you're using the local currency or your native currency). It's a good idea to advise your bank/credit card carrier of your impending travel plans, since some companies are prone to reject charges from unfamiliar destinations as a security measure.

Business Hours

Most stores are open from 9 or 10am to 12:30pm, and from 3 to 5 or 8pm. Banks are generally open Monday through Friday from 9:30am to 4pm, although some stay open until 6pm. In major cities, most banks are also open Saturday from 9:30am to 12:30pm. Offices are open from 8:30am to 12:30pm and 3 to 6pm, although many operate continuously from 9am to 5pm. Government offices are open Monday through Friday from 9:30am to 12:30pm and 3 to 5pm. Nightclubs in large cities often don't get going until after midnight, and many stay open until dawn.

Car Rentals

The major international rental agencies are found in Lima, and a handful of international and local companies operate in other cities, such as Cusco and Arequipa. Costs average about $40 to $70 a day, plus 18% insurance, for an economy-size vehicle. To rent a car, you need to be at least 25 years old and have a valid driver's license and passport. Deposit by credit card is usually required. Driving under the influence of alcohol or drugs is a criminal offense. For mechanical assistance, contact the **Touring Automóvil Club del Perú** (Touring Club of Peru; ☎ 01/221-3225 in Lima, or 084/224-561 in Cusco).

Customs

Exports of protected plant and endangered animal species—live or dead—are strictly prohibited by Peruvian law and should not be purchased. This includes headpieces and necklaces made with macaw feathers, and even common "rain sticks," unless authorized by the Natural Resources Institute (INRENA). Vendors in jungle cities and airports sell live animals and birds, as well as handicrafts made from insects, feathers, or other natural products. Travelers have been detained and arrested by the Ecology Police for carrying such items. It is also illegal to take pre-Columbian archaeological items and antiques, including ceramics and textiles, and colonial-era art out of Peru. Reproductions of many such items are available, but even their export could cause difficulties at Customs or with overly cautious international courier services if you attempt to send them home. To be safe, look for the word "reproducion" or an artist's name stamped on reproduction ceramics, and keep business cards and receipts from shops where you have purchased them. Particularly fine items might require documentation from Peru's National Institute of Culture (INC) verifying that the object is a reproduction and may be exported. You might be able to obtain a certificate of authorization from the INC kiosk at Lima's Jorge Chávez International Airport or the **INC office** at the National Museum Building, Av. Javier Prado Este 2465, 6th floor, San Borja (☎ 01/476-9900).

Drug & Liquor Laws

Until recently, Peru was the world's largest producer of coca leaves, the base product that is mostly shipped to Colombia for processing into cocaine. Cocaine and other illegal substances are perhaps not as ubiquitous in Peru as some might think, although in Lima and Cusco, they are commonly offered to foreigners. (This is especially dangerous; many would-be dealers also operate as police informants, and some are said to be undercover narcotics officers themselves.) Penalties for the possession and use of or trafficking in illegal drugs in Peru are strict; convicted offenders can expect long jail sentences and substantial fines. Peruvian police routinely detain drug smugglers at Lima's international airport and land-border crossings. Since 1995, more than 40 U.S. citizens have been convicted of narcotics trafficking in Peru. If you are arrested on drug charges, you will face protracted pretrial detention in poor prison conditions. Coca leaves, either chewed or brewed for tea, are not illegal in Peru, where they're not considered a narcotic. The use of coca leaves is an ancient tradition dating back to pre-Columbian civilizations in Peru. You might very well find that *mate de coca* (coca-leaf tea) is very helpful in battling altitude sickness. However, if you attempt to take coca leaves back to your home country from Peru, you should expect them to be confiscated, and you could even find yourself prosecuted. The hallucinogenic plants consumed in *ayahuasca* ceremonies are legal in Peru.

A legal drinking age is not strictly enforced in Peru. Anyone over the age of 16 is unlikely to have any problems ordering liquor in any bar or other establishment. Wine, beer, and alcohol are widely available—sold daily at grocery stores, liquor stores, and in all cafes, bars, and restaurants—and consumed widely, especially in public during festivals. There is very little taboo associated with public inebriation at festivals.

Electricity

All outlets are 220 volts, 60 cycles AC (except in Arequipa, which operates on 50 cycles), with two-prong outlets that accept both flat and round prongs. Some large hotels also have 110-volt outlets.

Embassies & Consulates

The following are all in Lima: **United States,** Av. La Encalada, cdra. 17, Surco (☎ 01/434-3000); **Australia,** Victor A. Belaúnde 147/Vía Principal 155, building 3, of. 1301, San Isidro (☎ 01/222-8281); **Canada,** Calle Bolognesi 228, Miraflores (☎ 01/319-3200); **United Kingdom and New Zealand,** Av. Jose Larco 1301, 22nd floor, Miraflores (☎ 01/617-3000).

Emergencies

In case of an emergency, call ☎ **105.** You may also call the 24-hour traveler's hotline at ☎ **01/574-8000,** or POLTUR, the tourist police (☎ **01/460-1060** in Lima, or 01/460-0965). The Tourist Protection Service can also assist in contacting police to report a crime; call ☎ **01/224-7888** in Lima, or 0800/4-2579 toll-free from any private phone (the toll-free number cannot be dialed from a public pay phone).

Gay & Lesbian Travelers

Although the Inca nation flag looks remarkably similar to the rainbow flag, Peru, a predominantly Catholic and socially conservative country, is not considered among the world's most progressive in terms of societal freedoms for gays and lesbians. It remains a male-dominated, macho society where homosexuality is considered deviant. Across Peru, there is still considerable prejudice exhibited toward gays and lesbians who are out, or men—be they straight or gay—who are thought to be effeminate. The word *maricón* is, sadly, a commonly used derogatory term for homosexuals. In the larger cities, especially Lima and Cusco, there are a number of establishments—bars, discos, inns, and restaurants—that are either gay-friendly or predominantly gay. Outside those areas, and in the small towns and villages of rural Peru, openly gay behavior is unlikely to be tolerated by the general population.

There are a number of helpful websites for gay and lesbian travelers to Peru. **Gay Peru** (www.gayperu.com) includes gay-oriented package tours, news items, and nightclubs and hotels (with versions in both English and Spanish). **Purple Roofs** (www.purpleroofs.com/southamerica/peru.html) has a decent listing of gay and lesbian lodgings, restaurants, and nightclubs throughout Peru. **Gay Lima** (lima.queercity.info) covers Lima and other parts of Peru, with English-language information on nightclubs and gay-friendly establishments and activities. If you can read Spanish, www.deambiente.com also has detailed listings and articles about gay life in Peru. **GlobalGayz** (www.globalgayz.com) includes a very interesting article on gay life in Peru.

Health

No vaccinations are officially required of travelers to Peru, but you are wise to take certain precautions, especially if you are planning to travel to jungle regions. A yellow-fever vaccine is strongly recommended for trips to the Amazon. Peruvian authorities confirmed an outbreak of yellow fever in the northeastern Department of Amazonas in December 2005. The Pan American Health Organization reported an outbreak and 52 total cases of yellow fever in Peru during the first 6 months of 2004, with slightly more than half of those resulting in death. (However, just two of those occurred in areas covered in this book, Loreto and Madre de Dios.) The Centers for Disease Control and Prevention (☎ **800/311-3435;** www.cdc.gov) warns that there is a risk of malaria and yellow fever in all areas except Arequipa, Moquegua, Puno, and Tacna; Lima and the highland tourist areas (Cusco, Machu Picchu, and Lake Titicaca) are not at risk.

The Centers for Disease Control and Prevention also recommend taking antimalarial drugs at least 1 week before arriving in the jungle, during your stay there, and for at least 4 weeks afterward. In addition, the CDC recommends vaccines for hepatitis A and B and typhoid, as well as booster doses for tetanus, diphtheria, and measles, although you might want to weigh your potential exposure before getting all these shots. For additional information on travel to tropical South America, including World Health Organization news of disease outbreaks in particular areas, see the CDC website at **www.cdc.gov/travel/ tropsam.htm.** Also of interest is the WHO's informational page on Peru, www.who.int/ countries/per/en.

Remember to carry your vaccination records with you if you are traveling to the jungle. It's wise to get all vaccinations and obtain malarial pills before arriving in Peru, but if you decide at the last minute to go to the jungle and need to get a vaccine in the country, you can go to the following Oficinas de Vacunación in Lima: Av. del Ejército 1756, San Isidro (☎ **01/264-6889**); Jorge Chávez International Airport, 2nd floor; and the International Vaccination Center, Dos de Mayo National Hospital, Av. Miguel Grau, cdra. 13. In the airport at Puerto Maldonado, in the southern jungle, public nurses are also frequently on hand to administer yellow-fever shots to travelers who have not received the vaccination.

Visitors should drink only bottled water, which is widely available. Do not drink tap water, even in major hotels. Try to avoid drinks with ice. *Agua con gas* is carbonated; *agua sin gas* is still.

As a tropical South American country, Peru presents certain health risks and issues, but major concerns are limited to those traveling outside urban areas and to the Amazon jungle. The most common ailments for visitors to Peru are common traveler's diarrhea and altitude sickness, or acute mountain sickness (AMS; altitude sickness), called *soroche* locally; sun exposure; and dietary distress.

Holidays
National public holidays in Peru include New Year's Day (Jan 1), Three Kings Day (Jan 6), Maundy Thursday and Good Friday (Easter Week, March or Apr), Labor Day (May 1), Fiestas Patrias (July 28–29), Battle of Angamos (Oct 8), All Saints' Day (Nov 1), Feast of the Immaculate Conception (Dec 8), and Christmas (Dec 24–25).

Insurance
For information on traveler's, trip cancellation, and medical insurance while traveling, go to **www.frommers.com/tips**.

Internet Access
Internet access is plentiful, both in *cafés Internet* or *cabinas* (cybercafes) and frequently in hotels, several of which now offer Wi-Fi.

More and more hotels, airports, cafes, and retailers are offering free Wi-Fi. To find public Wi-Fi hotspots in Peru and throughout South America, go to www.jiwire.com.

Language
Spanish is the official language of Peru. The Amerindian languages Quechua (recently given official status) and Aymara are spoken primarily in the highlands. (Aymara is mostly limited to the area around Lake Titicaca.) English is not widely spoken but is understood by those affiliated with the tourist industry in major cities and tourist destinations. Most people you meet on the street will have only a very rudimentary understanding of English, if that. Learning a few key phrases of Spanish will help immensely. Check the glossary at the end of this chapter, and consider picking up a copy of *Frommer's Spanish PhraseFinder & Dictionary.*

Legal Aid
If you need legal assistance, your best bets are your embassy (which, depending on the situation, might not be able to help you much) and the **Tourist Protection Service** (☎ 0800/ 4-2579 toll-free, or 01/574-8000 24-hr.), which might be able to direct you to an English-speaking attorney or legal assistance organization. Note that bribing a police officer or public official is illegal in Peru, even if it is a relatively constant feature of traffic stops and the like. If a police officer claims to be an undercover cop, do not automatically assume that he is telling the truth. Do not get in any vehicle with such a person. Demand the assistance of your embassy or consulate, or of the Tourist Protection Service.

Lost Property
If your passport is lost or stolen, contact your country's embassy immediately. Call credit card companies the minute you discover your wallet has been lost or stolen, and file a report at the nearest police precinct. Your credit card company or insurer may require a police report number or record. **Visa**'s U.S. emergency number is ☎ 800/847-2911, or 800-890-0623 in Peru. **American Express** cardholders and traveler's check holders should call ☎ 800/869-3016 in the U.S., or 905/474-0870 (international; collect). **MasterCard** holders should call ☎ 800/627-8372 in the U.S., or 800-307-7309 in Peru.

Mail & Postage

Peru's postal service is reasonably efficient, especially now that it's managed by a private company (Serpost S.A.). *Correos* (post offices) are open Monday through Saturday from 8am to 8pm; some are also open Sunday from 9am to 1pm. Major cities have a main post office and often several smaller branch offices. Letters and postcards to North America take between 10 days and 2 weeks, and cost S/5.50 for postcards, S/7.20 for letters; to Europe either runs S/7.80. If you are purchasing large quantities of textiles and other handicrafts, you can send packages home from post offices, but it's not cheap—more than $100 for 10kg (22 lb.), similar to what it costs to use DHL, where you're likely to have an easier time communicating. UPS is found in several cities, but for inexplicable reasons, its courier services cost nearly three times as much as those of DHL.

Money

Peru's official currency is the *nuevo sol* (S/), divided into 100 *centavos*. Coins are issued in denominations of 5, 10, 20, and 50 *centavos*, and bank notes in denominations of 10, 20, 50, 100, and 200 *soles*. The U.S. dollar is the second currency; many hotels post their rates in dollars, and plenty of shops, taxi drivers, restaurants, and hotels across Peru accept U.S. dollars for payment. For up-to-the minute exchange rates, check the currency converter website www.xe.com/ucc.

Passports

Always keep a photocopy of your passport with you while traveling. And, always keep your passport in a secure place, such as your hotel safe. Citizens of the United States, Canada, Great Britain, South Africa, New Zealand, and Australia do not require visas to enter Peru as tourists—only valid passports. Citizens of any of these countries conducting business or enrolled in formal educational programs in Peru do require visas. Tourist (or landing) cards, distributed on arriving international flights or at border crossings, are good for stays of up to 90 days. Keep a copy of the tourist card for presentation upon departure from Peru. (If you lose it, you'll have to pay a small fine.) A maximum of three extensions of 30 days each, for a total of 180 days, are allowed.

Pharmacies

Prescriptions can be filled at *farmacias* and *boticas;* it's best to know the generic name of your drug. For most health matters that are not serious, a pharmacist will be able to help and prescribe something. In the case of more serious health issues, contact your hotel, the tourist information office, or, in the most extreme case, your consulate or embassy for a doctor referral. Hospitals with English-speaking doctors are listed in individual destination chapters.

Police

For police emergencies, call ☎ **105.** Peru has special tourist police forces (Policía Nacional de Turismo) with offices and personnel in all major tourist destinations, including Lima, Cusco, Arequipa, and Puno. Tourist police officers are distinguished by their white shirts. The Tourist Protection Service (Servicio de Protección al Turista), which handles complaints and questions about consumer rights, operates a **24-hour traveler's assistance line** at ☎ 0800/42-579, or 01/224-7888 in Lima.

Safety

Peru has not earned a great reputation for safety among some travelers, although the situation is no longer as dangerous as during the violent crime wave and terrorist threats of the late 1980s and early 1990s. Personal safety is an issue to be taken seriously in most large Peruvian cities, especially Lima, Cusco, Arequipa, and Huaraz. Simple theft and pickpocketing are fairly common; most thieves look for moments when travelers, laden with bags and struggling with maps, are distracted. Assaults and robberies are rare, but have been reported in some cities. In most heavily touristed places in Peru, a heightened police presence is noticeable. In downtown Lima and the city's residential and hotel areas, the risk of street crime, including theft and muggings, remains high. Carjackings, assaults, and armed robberies are not unheard of in Lima. Occasional armed attacks at ATMs occur. Be especially vigilant at Lima's international airport, where a number of robberies and attacks have been reported. Street crime is prevalent in Cusco, Arequipa, and Puno, and pickpockets are known to patrol public markets. In Cusco, "strangle" muggings (in which victims are choked unconscious and then relieved of all belongings) were reported in recent years, particularly on the streets leading off the Plaza de Armas, in the San Blas neighborhood, and near the train station. You should still not walk alone late at night on deserted streets. There were at least three reports of rape in Cusco in the last decade, one by a gang. In rural areas outside Cusco, trekkers should travel in groups. But while hiking with others is essential, it doesn't guarantee one's safety; indeed, in recent years, a couple of groups of hikers along the Inca Trail were attacked and robbed.

In major cities, taxis hailed on the street can lead to assaults—I highly recommend using telephone-dispatched radio taxis, especially at night. Ask your hotel or restaurant to call a cab, or call one yourself from the list of recommended taxi companies in the individual city chapters. Travelers should exercise extreme caution on public city transportation, where pickpockets are rife, and on long-distance buses and trains (especially at night), where thieves employ any number of strategies to relieve passengers of their bags. You need to be supremely vigilant, even to the extreme of locking your backpack and suitcases to luggage racks. Be extremely careful in all train and bus stations, too. Several provincial and intercity buses and *combis* traveling from cities to villages have been attacked and passengers robbed.

In general, do not wear expensive jewelry, keep expensive camera equipment out of view as much as possible, and use a money belt inside your pants or shirt to safeguard your cash, credit cards, and passport. Wear your daypack on your chest rather than your back when walking in crowded areas. The time to be most careful is when you have most of your belongings on your person—for example, when going from the airport or train or bus station to your hotel. Safety is occasionally an issue at hotels, especially at the lower end, and extreme care should be taken with regard to personal belongings left in the hotel. Leaving valuables lying around is asking for trouble. Except for hotels at the lowest levels, most have safety deposit boxes or room safes.

Report any criminal activity to the nearest police station or tourism police office; contact information is listed in the "Fast Facts" sections of individual destination chapters.

Women traveling alone in Peru may attract unwanted attention and harassment from local men, who may be very insistent and persistent. Their advances can usually warded off with a forceful "No!", simple *"Déjame en paz"* ("Leave me alone"), or a claim that one is married and traveling with her husband (*"Estoy casada. Ya viene mi marido."*). Though one hopes the stereotype is dying out, some Peruvian men may still assume that foreign women are more sexually permissive than local women. Gays and travelers of color may also be subjected to discrimination and very unwelcoming behavior, either on the street or occasionally at bars and nightclubs.

Senior Travelers

Discounts for seniors are not automatic across Peru, though many attractions do offer a senior rate. Mention the fact that you're a senior (and carry ID with your birthdate) when you make travel reservations; many hotels still offer lower rates for seniors.

Smoking

Smoking is common in Peru, and it is rare to find a hotel, restaurant, or bar with nonsmoking rooms. However, there are now a few hotels (usually high-end) and restaurants with designated nonsmoking rooms, and the trend is growing, albeit slowly. There are nonsmoking cars on trains, and most long-distance buses are also nonsmoking.

Taxes

A general sales tax (IGV) is added automatically to most consumer bills (19%). In some upmarket hotels or restaurants, service charges of 10% are added. At all airports, passengers must pay a departure tax: $31 for international flights, and $6 for domestic flights, payable in cash only (either U.S. dollars or Peruvian *nuevos soles*).

Telephones

Your best bet for making international calls from Peru is to head to any Internet cafe with an international calling option. These cafes have connections to Skype, Net2Phone, or some other VoIP service. International calls made this way can range anywhere from 5¢ to $1 per minute—much cheaper than making direct international calls or using a phone card.

If you have your own Skype or similar account, you just need to find an Internet cafe that provides a computer with a headset. The easiest way to make a long-distance call within the country is to purchase a phone card (maximum S/30). Many of these cards, purchased at newspaper kiosks and street vendors who sell nothing else, are called Tarjeta 147. To use such a card, rub off the secret number, dial the numbers 1-4-7, and then dial the 12-digit number on your card. A voice recording will tell you (in Spanish) the value remaining on the card and instruct you to dial the desired telephone number. It will then tell you how many minutes you can expect to talk with the amount remaining. You can also make international calls from Telefónica offices and hotels, although surcharges levied at the latter can be extraordinarily expensive. Toll-free numbers beginning with 0800 within Peru are toll-free when called from a private phone (not from a public pay phone).

The area codes for the regions covered in this book are: Lima, 01; Ica, Nasca, and Pisco, 056; Cusco and the Sacred Valley, 084; Puerto Maldonado, 082; Puno/Lake Titicaca, 051; Arequipa, 054; Huaraz, 043; Trujillo, 044; Cajamarca, 076; Chiclayo, 074; and Iquitos, 065.

Time Zone
Peru is 5 hours behind GMT (Greenwich Mean Time) and does not observe daylight saving time.

Tipping
Most people leave about a 10% tip for the waitstaff in restaurants. Taxi drivers are not usually tipped unless they provide additional service. Bilingual tour guides on group tours should be tipped ($1–$2 per person for a short visit, and $5 or more per person for a full day). If you have a private guide, tip about $10 to $20.

Toilets
Baños públicos (public lavatories) are rarely available except in railway stations, restaurants, and theaters. Some Peruvian men choose to urinate in public, against a wall in full view, especially late at night; it's not recommended that you emulate them. Use the bathroom of a bar, cafe, or restaurant; if it feels uncomfortable to dart in and out, have a coffee at the bar. Public restrooms are labeled wc (water closet), DAMAS (ladies), and CABALLEROS or HOMBRES (men). Toilet paper is not always provided, and when it is, most establishments request that patrons throw it in the wastebasket rather than the toilet, to avoid clogging.

Travelers with Disabilities
Peru is considerably less equipped for accessible travel than most parts of North America and Europe. Comparatively few hotels are outfitted for travelers with disabilities, and only a few restaurants, museums, and means of public transportation make special accommodations for such patrons. There are few ramps, very few wheelchair-accessible bathrooms, and almost no telephones for the hearing-impaired. Though it continues to lag behind Europe and North America, Peru has been a perhaps unlikely leader in South America in terms of seeking to make its tourist infrastructure more accessible to people with disabilities.

Request a copy of the report *Tourism for People with Disabilities: The First Evaluation of Accessibility to Peru's Tourist Infrastructure,* available from the Peruvian embassy in your home country, before your visit to Peru; it features evaluations of hotels, restaurants, museums, attractions, airports, and other services in Lima, Cusco, Aguas Calientes, Iquitos, and Trujillo.

A helpful website for accessible travel in Peru is **Access-Able Travel Source** (www.access-able.com), which offers detailed destination articles on accessible travel in Peru and a wealth of specific information about Aguas Calientes, Chiclayo, Cusco, Huanchaco, Iquitos, Lima, the Chicama and Moche valleys, Pisac, Trujillo, and Yucay. Within individual reviews, you'll find information on ramps, door sizes, room sizes, bathrooms, and wheelchair availability. Many travel agencies offer customized tours and itineraries for travelers with disabilities. **Apumayo Expediciones** (☎ 054/246-018; www.apumayo.com) is way out in front in Peru, offering tours specifically designed for travelers with physical disabilities. **Accessible Journeys** (☎ 800/846-4537 or 610/521-0339; www.disabilitytravel.com) caters specifically to slow walkers and wheelchair travelers and their families and friends; the organization offers a 10-day Peru Explorer trip to Lima, Paracas, Cusco, the Sacred Valley, and Machu Picchu. **InkaNatura Travel**

(☎ 888-870-7378 toll-free in U.S./Canada, or 01/ 203-5000 in Lima; www.inkanatura.com) is also particularly well equipped to deal with travelers with disabilities: Beyond the website's specifics on Peru, it's an excellent resource with all kinds of general information and answers to frequently asked questions about traveling with disabilities.

Useful Websites

www.peru.info: The most comprehensive official Peru site, from PromPerú. It has detailed sections on Peruvian history, festivals, trip-planning, and outdoor "adrenaline rushes," all with extensive pull-down menus, as well as a stock of photo and video images and audio files.

www.saexplorers.org: The website of the rightly famous South American Explorers (based in Ithaca, New York, with clubhouses in Lima, Cusco, and Quito, Ecuador) has vital information such as travel advisories and links to websites on specific Peruvian destinations. You can also order the club's information packet of fact sheets and member tips.

www.livinginperu.com: An English-language site directed toward foreign residents of Peru, this is the best place to get the latest news on Peru, including transportation issues, political info, and other practical matters that affect not only residents but also visitors. It also contains up-to-date cultural and event information.

Visitor Information

Within Peru, there's a 24-hour tourist information line, **iPerú** (☎ 01/574-8000). Peru doesn't maintain national tourism offices abroad, so your best official source of information before you go is the website of **PromPerú** (Commission for the Promotion of Peru; www.peru.travel). The **Tourist Protection Bureau** (Servicio de Protección al Turista), La Prosa 138, San Borja, Lima (☎ 0800/42-579 toll-free from cities other than Lima, or 01/224-7888 in Lima), which handles complaints and questions about consumer rights, operates a 24-hour traveler's assistance line. For local branch locations and telephone numbers of the Tourist Protection Bureau, see "Fast Facts" in individual destination chapters.

Useful Phrases & Menu Terms

Phrases

ENGLISH	SPANISH	PRONUNCIATION
Good day	Buenos días	*bweh*-nohs *dee*-ahs
Hi/hello	Hola	*oh*-lah
Pleasure to meet you	Mucho gusto/Un placer	*Moo*-choh *goos*-toh/Oon plah-*sehr*
How are you?	¿Cómo está?	*Koh*-moh es-*tah*
Very well	Muy bien	Mwee byehn
Thank you	Gracias	*Grah*-syahs
How's it going?	¿Qué tal?	Keh tahl
You're welcome	De nada	Deh *nah*-dah
Goodbye	Adiós	Ah-*dyohs*
Please	Por favor	Pohr fah-*bohr*
Yes	Sí	See
No	No	Noh
Excuse me (to get by someone)	Perdóneme/Con permiso	Pehr-*doh*-neh-meh/Kohn pehr-*mee*-soh
Excuse me (to begin a question)	Disculpe	Dees-*kool*-peh
Give me	Déme	*Deh*-meh
What time is it?	¿Qué hora es?	Keh *ohr*-ah ehs
Where is... ?	¿Dónde está... ?	*Dohn*-deh eh-*stah*
the station	la estación	lah eh-stah-*syohn*
(bus/train)	estación de ómnibus/tren	eh-stah-*syohn* deh *ohm*-nee-boos/trehn
a hotel	un hotel	oon oh-*tel*
a gas station	una estación de servicio	*oo*-nah eh-stah-*syohn* deh sehr-*bee*-syoh
a restaurant	un restaurante	oon res-tow-*rahn*-teh
the toilet	el baño (or servicios)	el *bah*-nyoh (sehr-*bee*-syohs)
a good doctor	un buen médico	oon bwehn *meh*-dee-coh
the road to...	el camino a/hacia...	el cah-*mee*-noh ah/*ah*-syah
To the right	A la derecha	Ah lah deh-*reh*-chah
To the left	A la izquierda	Ah lah ee-*skyehr*-dah
Straight ahead	Derecho	Deh-*reh*-choh
Is it far?	¿Está lejos?	Eh-*stah leh*-hohs

Phrases

ENGLISH	SPANISH	PRONUNCIATION
It is close?	¿Está cerca?	Eh-*stah sehr*-kah
Open	Abierto	Ah-*byehr*-toh
Closed	Cerrado	Seh-*rah*-doh
North	Norte	*Nohr*-teh
South	Sur	Soor
East	Este	*Eh*-steh
West	Oeste	Oh-*eh*-steh
Expensive	Caro	*Cah*-roh
Cheap	Barato	Bah-*rah*-toh
I would like	Quisiera	Kee-*syeh*-rah
I want	Quiero	*Kyeh*-roh
to eat	comer	koh-*mehr*
a room	una habitación	oo-nah ah-bee-tah-*syohn*
Do you have... ?	¿Tiene usted... ?	*Tyeh*-neh oo-*stehd*
a book	un libro	oon *lee*-broh
a dictionary	un diccionario	oon deek-syoh-*na*-ryoh
change	cambio	*kahm*-byoh
How much is it?	¿Cuánto cuesta?	*Kwahn*-toh *kwes*-tah
When?	¿Cuándo?	*Kwahn*-doh
What?	¿Qué?	Keh
There is (Is/Are there... ?)	(¿)Hay (... ?)	eye
What is there?	¿Qué hay?	Keh eye
Yesterday	Ayer	Ah-*yehr*
Today	Hoy	Oy
Tomorrow	Mañana	Mah-*nyah*-nah
Good	Bueno	*Bweh*-noh
Bad	Malo	*Mah*-loh
Better (best)	(Lo) Mejor	(Loh) Meh-*hohr*
More	Más	Mahs
Less	Menos	*Meh*-nohs

Phrases

ENGLISH	SPANISH	PRONUNCIATION
No smoking	Se prohibe fumar	Seh proh-*ee*-beh foo-*mahr*
Postcard	Tarjeta postal	Tahr-*heh*-tah pohs-*tahl*
Insect repellent	Repelente contra insectos	Reh-peh-*lehn*-teh *cohn*-trah een-*sehk*-tohs
Now	Ahora	Ah-*ohr*-ah
Right now	Ahora mismo (ahorita)	Ah-*ohr*-ah *mees*-moh (ah-ohr-ee-tah)
Later	Más tarde	Mahs *tahr*-deh
Never	Nunca	*Noon*-kah
Guide	Guía	*Ghee*-ah
Heat	Calor	Kah-*lohr*
It's hot!	¡Qué calor!	Keh kah-*lohr*
Cold	Frío	*Free*-oh
Rain	Lluvia	*Yoo*-byah
It's cold!	¡Qué frío!	Keh *free*-oh
Wind	Viento	*Byehn*-toh
It's windy!	¡Cuánto viento!	*Kwahn*-toh *byehn*-toh
Money-changer	Cambista	Kahm-*bee*-stah
Bank	Banco	*Bahn*-koh
Money	Dinero	Dee-*neh*-roh
Small (correct) change	Sencillo	Sehn-*see*-yoh
Credit card	Tarjeta de crédito	Tahr-*heh*-tah deh *creh*-dee-toh
ATM	Cajero automático	Kah-*heh*-roh ow-toh-*mah*-tee-koh
Tourist information office	Oficina de información turística	Oh-fee-*see*-nah deh een-for-mah-*syohn* too-*ree*-stee-kah

Numbers

ENGLISH	SPANISH	PRONUNCIATION
1	uno	*oo*-noh
2	dos	dohss
3	tres	trehss
4	cuatro	*kwah*-troh
5	cinco	*seen*-koh
6	seis	sayss
7	siete	*syeh*-teh
8	ocho	*oh*-choh
9	nueve	*nweh*-beh
10	diez	dyehs
11	once	*ohn*-seh
12	doce	*doh*-seh
13	trece	*treh*-seh
14	catorce	kah-*tohr*-seh
15	quince	*keen*-seh
16	dieciséis	dyeh-see-*sayss*
17	diecisiete	dyeh-see-*syeh*-teh
18	dieciocho	dyeh-*syoh*-choh
19	diecinueve	dyeh-see-*nweh*-beh
20	veinte	*bayn*-teh
30	treinta	*trayn*-tah
40	cuarenta	kwah-*ren*-tah
50	cincuenta	seen-*kwen*-tah
60	sesenta	seh-*sehn*-tah
70	setenta	seh-*tehn*-tah
80	ochenta	oh-*chen*-tah
90	noventa	noh-*ben*-tah
100	cien	syehn
200	doscientos	do-*syehn*-tohs
500	quinientos	kee-*nyehn*-tohs
1,000	mil	meel

Days of the Week

ENGLISH	SPANISH	PRONUNCIATION
Monday	Lunes	*loo*-nehss
Tuesday	Martes	*mahr*-tehss
Wednesday	Miércoles	*myehr*-koh-lehs
Thursday	Jueves	*wheh*-behss
Friday	Viernes	*byehr*-nehss
Saturday	Sabado	*sah*-bah-doh
Sunday	Domingo	doh-*meen*-goh

Restaurant & Menu Term

ENGLISH	SPANISH	PRONUNCIATION
beef/steak	lomo	*loh*-moh
bread	pan	*pahn*
chicken	pollo	*poh*-yo
dessert	postre	*poh*-stray
eggs	huevos	*way*-vohs
fish	pescado	pays-*kah*-doh
fruit	fruta	*froo*-tah
lamb	cordero	cor-*der*-o
meat	carne	*kahr*-nay
pork	cerdo/puerco	*sayr*-doh/*pwair*-koh
potatoes	papas	*pah*-pahs
french fries	papas fritas	*pah*-pahs *free*-tas
rice	arroz	ah-*ros*
roast	asado	ah-*sah*-doh
salad	ensalada	ehn-sah-*lah*-dah
seafood	mariscos	mah-*rees*-kohs
shrimp	camarones	ka-ma-*rohn*-es
soup	sopa/chupe	*soh*-pah/*choo*-pay
vegetables	verduras	vair-*door*-ahs

Drinks

ENGLISH	SPANISH	PRONUNCIATION
beer	cerveza	ser-*vay*-sah
mixed fruit juice	refresco	reh-*frehs*-koh
juice	jugo	*hoo*-go
milk	leche	*leh*-cheh
soft drink	gaseosa	*gah*-see-oh-sa
water	agua	*ah*-gwah
carbonated water	agua con gas	*ah*-gwah kohn gahs
still water	agua sin gas	*ah*-gwah sin gahs
wine	vino	*vee*-noh

Common Quechua Menu Items

Adobo Meat dish in a spicy chile sauce

Alpaca Alpaca steak

Anticuchos Shish kebab

Cabrito Goat

Carne de res Beef

Chicharrones Fried pork skins

Conejo Rabbit

Cordero Lamb

Corvina Sea bass

Empanada Pastry turnover filled with meat, vegetables, fruit, *manjar blanco,* or sometimes nothing at all

Estofado Stew

Langosta Lobster

Lomo asado Roast beef

Langostinos Prawns

Lenguado Sole

Mero Mediterranean grouper

Paiche Large Amazon fish

Parrillada Grilled meats

Pato Duck

Pollo a la brasa Spit-roasted chicken

Tollo Spotted dogfish

Venado Venison

Common Quechua Terms

ENGLISH	QUECHUA	PRONUNCIATION
Yes	Riki	*Ree*-kee
No	Mana	*Mah*-nah
Madam	Mama	*Mah*-mah
Sir	Tayta	*Tahy*-tah
Thank you	Añay	Ah-*nyahy*

Altiplano Plateau/high plains

Apu Sacred summit/mountain spirit

Campesino Rural worker/peasant

Chacra Plot of land

Cocha Lake

Huayno Andean musical style

Inca Inca ruler/emperor

Inti Sun

Intiwatana "Hitching post of the sun" (stone pillar at Inca ceremonial sites)

Mestizo Person of mixed European and Amerindian lineage

Nuna Spirit or soul

Pachamama Mother Earth

Pucara Fortress

Runasimi Quechua language

Soroche Altitude sickness (hypoxia)

Tambo In-transit checkpoint on Inca highway

Tawantinsuyu Inca Empire

Tumi Andean knife

Viracocha Inca deity (creator god)

Index

Photo Credits

Note: l= left; r= right; t= top; b= bottom; c= center